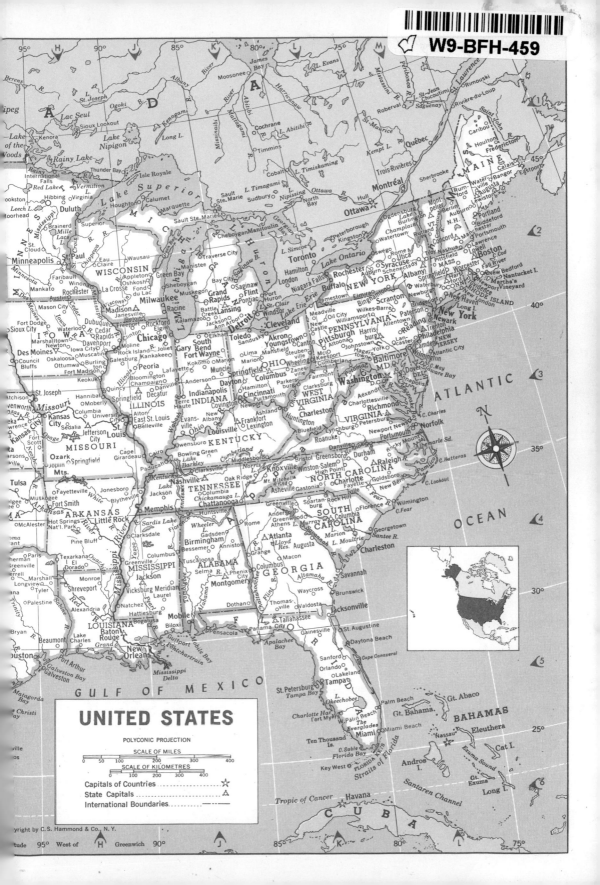

UNITED STATES

POLYCONIC PROJECTION

SCALE OF MILES

0   50   100   200   300   400

SCALE OF KILOMETRES

0   100   200   300   400

Capitals of Countries .... ☆
State Capitals .... △
International Boundaries ....

Copyright by C.S. Hammond & Co., N.Y.

MODERN DESK EDITION

WEBSTER'S NEW WORLD DICTIONARY

OF THE
AMERICAN LANGUAGE

MODERN DESK EDITION

WEBSTER'S NEW WORLD DICTIONARY

OF THE
AMERICAN LANGUAGE

David B. Guralnik, *Editor in Chief*

COLLINS PUBLISHERS

Published by
William Collins Publishers, Inc.
2080 West 117th Street
Cleveland, Ohio 44111
Webster's New World Dictionary, Modern Desk Edition
Copyright © 1979 by

William Collins Publishers, Inc.
Copyright © 1976 by

William Collins+World Publishing Co., Inc.
Copyright under the Universal Copyright Convention;
the International Copyright Union;
Pan-American Conventions of Montevideo, Mexico,
Rio de Janeiro, Buenos Aires and Havana

Previous edition Copyright © 1963,
1968, 1971 by
The World Publishing Company

Webster's New World Dictionary, Modern Desk Edition
is based upon and includes material from
Webster's New World Dictionary, Second College Edition
Copyright © 1978 and 1974, 1976 by
William Collins+World Publishing Co., Inc. and
Copyright © 1972 and 1970 by
The World Publishing Company

Library of Congress Catalog Card Number: 79-52089
ISBN 0-529-05333-0

The type for this dictionary was created on the Fototronic CRT Typesetter, controlled by a Univac 1108 computer at Chi Corporation in Cleveland, Ohio. The typefaces used were 7 point Century Schoolbook and 8 point Univers 65. The database for the dictionary was created and maintained by the publisher's staff in his own office using a video editing terminal connected via phone line to the Univac computer.

PRINTED IN THE UNITED STATES OF AMERICA

FOREWORD

This *Modern Desk Edition* of WEBSTER'S NEW WORLD DICTIONARY is an abridgment of the popular *Second College Edition* of WNWD. It replaces the earlier *Modern Desk Edition,* which was in turn based upon the original *College Edition* of WEBSTER'S NEW WORLD DICTIONARY. Through a judicious selection of vocabulary and a careful compression of the definitions and other lexical material, the editors have managed to bring together the answers to most of the questions that people generally ask about the words they read and use.

There are more than 72,000 vocabulary entries in this *Modern Desk Edition,* including all the commonly used terms that make up the basic vocabulary of English. In addition, a selection of the specialized terms used in the sciences and arts, in business, law, medicine, and the like, will be found here, depending upon the frequency with which they are encountered in present–day general writings. Also included in the single alphabetical listing of the dictionary text are those biographical, geographical, Biblical, and literary names, as well as abbreviations, that users of a dictionary of this scope are likely to seek.

Illustrations, both pictorial and verbal, have been included where they will help to shed additional light upon the definitions. The user of this dictionary will also receive guidance to appropriate usage through the labels and notes that accompany the definitions when necessary. A considerable number of those idiomatic phrases that are so characteristic of English will be found; the phrases have been added to the entry for the key word of each phrase. Unusual in a dictionary of limited scope are the brief etymologies to be found here, little histories of the origin and development of words, that often help one to a clearer understanding of the current meanings.

Following the dictionary text are tables of weights and measures and lists of common given names with their etymologies, or original meanings.

A careful reading of the *Guide to the Use of the Dictionary* on the following pages will make clear the many kinds of information available in this reference book and increase its usefulness to the reader.

David B. Guralnik

EDITORIAL STAFF

Editor in Chief	David B. Guralnik
Managing Editor	Samuel Solomon
Editors	Clark C. Livensparger, Thomas Layman, Andrew N. Sparks, Christopher T. Hoolihan, Paul B. Murry, Ruth Kimball Kent, Jonathan L. Goldman, Roslyn Block
Assistants	Virginia C. Becker, Cynthia Sadonick, Angie West, Gertrude Tullar
Chief Proofreader	Shirley M. Miller
Illustrator	Anita S. Rogoff

GUIDE TO THE USE OF
THE DICTIONARY

I. THE MAIN ENTRY WORD

Arrangement of Entries — All main entries, including single words, hyphenated and unhyphenated compounds, proper names, prefixes, suffixes, and abbreviations, are listed in strict alphabetical order.

a·kin (ə kin′) *adj.* . . .
Ak·ron (ak′rən) . . .
-al . . .
Al *Chem.* aluminum
à la, a la (ä′lə) . . .
Al·a·bam·a (al′ə bam′ə) . . .
al·a·bas·ter (al′ə bas′tər) *n.* . . .
a·la·carte (ä′lə kärt′) . . .

Variant Spellings — When variant spellings of a word are some distance apart alphabetically, the definition appears at the spelling most frequently used, the other or others being cross-referred to this. If the variant spellings would appear close to each other in alphabetical order and are used with nearly equal frequency, they are placed together at the head of the entry.
cav·i·ar, cav·i·are . . . *n.* . . . .

If a variant spelling is close in alphabetical order to a main-entry spelling but is used less often, it is placed at the end of the entry block or pertinent definition.
a·lign . . . *vt.* . . . -*vi.* . . . . Also sp. **aline** . . .

Cross-references — In an entry or sense consisting simply of a cross-reference to another entry with the same meaning, the entry cross-referred to is shown in small capitals.
gay·e·ty . . . *n.* . . . *same as* GAIETY
aer′o·plane′ . . . *n. Brit. sp. of* AIRPLANE

Homographs — Main entries that are spelled alike but are different in meaning and origin, as **bat** (a club), **bat** (the animal), and **bat** (to wink), are entered in separate blocks, with small numerals just after the boldface spellings.
bat¹ . . . *n.* . . . .
bat² . . . *n.* . . . .
bat³ . . . *vt.* . . . .

Cross-references to such entries show these numerals for identification.

Biographical Entries — In biographical entries, the given names are not pronounced if they are common ones. For their pronunciations and etymologies see the supplement, **COMMON GIVEN NAMES.**

Foreign Terms — Foreign words and phrases that appear fairly often in English speech and writing but are not yet felt to be fully a part of the English vocabulary are marked with a double dagger (‡).
‡bon jour . . . [Fr.] . . .

Prefixes, Suffixes, & Combining Forms — Prefixes and initial combining forms are indicated by a hyphen placed after the entry form.
re- . . . *a prefix meaning:* **1.** back [*repay*] **2.** again, aı. [*reappear*] . . .

Suffixes and combining forms used at the end of words are indicated by a hyphen placed before the entry form.
-hood . . . *a suffix meaning:* **1.** state or quality [*childhood*] **2.** the whole group of [*priesthood*]

Many such forms are entered in this dictionary, making it possible for the reader to determine the meaning of countless words not entered.

Syllabification — Center dots in the entry words show where the words can be divided if they need to be broken at the end of a line.
fun·da·men·tal . . .

All the syllables of a word are marked for the sake of consistency (e.g., **might·y, a·ban·don**). It is not, however, customary in writing or printing to break a word after the first syllable or before the last if that syllable consists of only a single letter, or, in the case of a long word, of only two.

Idiomatic Phrases — Idiomatic phrases are run in on the entry block for the key word in the phrase, in alphabetical order after the definition or definitions of the main-entry word. Each phrase is set in small boldface with a dash preceding it.
a·part . . . *adv.* . . . . —**apart from** . . . —**take apart** . . . —**tell apart** . . .

Run-in Derived Entries — It is possible in English to form a great many derived forms simply by adding certain suffixes or combining forms to the base word. This dictionary includes as run-in entries in small boldface type a number of common derived words, but only when their meaning can be readily understood from the meanings of the base word and the affix. Thus, **greatness** and **sadness** are run in at the end of the entries for **great** and **sad**, the suffix **-ness** being found as a separate entry in this dictionary, meaning "state, quality, or instance of being." Many words formed with common suffixes such as **-able, -er, -less, -like, -ly, -tion,** etc. are similarly treated as run-in entries with the base word from which they are derived. All such entries are syllabified and either accented to show stress in pronunciation or, where necessary, pronounced in full or in part.
par·tial (pär′shəl) *adj.* . . . . —**par′ti·al′i·ty** (-shē al′ə tē) *n.* —**par′tial·ly** *adv.*

When a derived word has a meaning or meanings different from those which can be deduced from the sum of its parts, it has been entered in a block of its own and fully defined (for example, **folder**).

II. PRONUNCIATION

Introduction — The pronunciations recorded are for the most part those heard in the normal, relaxed conversation of educated speakers. Occasionally, pronunciations that are dialectal, British, etc. are also given.

The symbols in the key below can be easily understood from the key words in which they are shown, and a speaker of any dialect of American English can readily read his own pronunciation into any symbol shown here.

Key to Pronunciation — A shortened form of this key appears on every right-hand page of the vocabulary.

Symbol	Key Words	Symbol	Key Words
a	fat, parrot	b	bed, dub
ā	ape, date	d	dip, had
ä	car, father	f	fall, off
		g	get, dog
e	ten, berry	h	he, ahead
ē	even, meet	j	joy, badge
		k	kill, bake
i	hit, mirror	l	let, ball
ī	bite, high	m	met, trim
		n	not, ton
ō	tone, go	p	put, tap
ô	all, horn	r	red, dear
o͞o	ooze, tool	s	sell, pass
oo	look, pull	t	top, hat
yo͞o	use, cute	v	vat, have
yoo	united, cure	w	will, always
oi	oil, toy	y	yet, yard
ou	out, crowd	z	zebra, haze
u	up, cut	ch	chin, arch
ur	urn, fur	sh	she, dash
		th	thin, truth
ə	a in ago	th	then, lathe
	e in agent	zh	azure, leisure
	i in sanity	ŋ	ring, drink
	o in comply	'	[see explanatory
	u in focus		note below]
		[See *Foreign Sounds*
ər	perhaps, murder	below]

A few explanatory notes on some of these symbols follow.

ä   This symbol represents the vowel of *car*. Some words shown with ä, such as *alms* (ämz) and *hot* (hät), are sometimes heard with the sound ô.

e   This symbol represents the vowel of *ten*. It is also used, followed by r, to represent the vowel sound of *care* (ker); for this sound, vowels ranging from ā (kār or kā′ər) to a (kar) are sometimes heard.

ē   This symbol represents the vowel of *meet* and is also used for the vowel in the unstressed syllables of such words as *lucky* (luk′ē) and *pretty* (prit′ē).

i   This symbol represents the vowel of *hit* and is also used for the vowel in the unstressed syllables of such words as *garbage* (gär′bij) and *deny* (di nī′). In such unstressed syllables, the schwa (ə) is often heard: (gär′bəj), (də nī′). This symbol is also used, followed by r, to represent the vowel sound of *dear* (dir); for this sound, vowels ranging to ē (dēr or dē′ər) are sometimes heard.

ô   This symbol represents the vowel of *all*. When followed by r, as in *more* (môr), vowels ranging to ō (mōr or mō′ər) are often heard. In certain words shown with ô, such as *lawn* (lôn), vowel sounds ranging all the way to ä (län) are heard.

ur, ər   These symbols represent, respectively, the stressed and unstressed r-colored vowels heard in the two syllables of *murder* (mur′dər). Where these symbols are shown, some Southern and Eastern speakers will "drop their r's" in pronouncing them.

ə   This symbol, called the schwa, represents the neutral vowel heard in the unstressed syllables of *ago, agent, focus*, etc. In some contexts, this vowel is also heard as i.

ŋ   This symbol represents the nasal sound of the *-ng* in *sing* and of n before k and g, as in *drink* (driŋk) and *finger* (fiŋ′gər).

'   The apostrophe occurring before l, m, and n indicates that the consonant has formed a syllable with little or no vowel sound, as in *apple* (ap′'l) or *happen* (hap′'n). Some people pronounce such words with the vowel sound of schwa (ə), as in *happen* (hap′ən).

Foreign Sounds — In recording the pronunciation of foreign words it has been necessary to use the following symbols in addition to those above.

ë   This symbol represents the sound made by rounding the lips as for (ô) and pronouncing (e).

ö   This symbol represents the sound made by rounding the lips as for (ō) and pronouncing (ä).

ü   This symbol represents the sound made by rounding the lips as for (o͞o) and pronouncing (ē).

kh   This symbol represents the sound made by arranging the speech organs as for (k) but allowing the breath to escape in a stream, as in pronouncing (h).

n   This symbol indicates that the vowel immediately preceding it should be sounded with the nasal passage left open so that the breath passes through both the mouth and nose.

r   This symbol represents any of various non-English sounds for the consonant r, produced by a rapid vibration of the tongue or uvula.

General Styling of Pronunciation — Pronunciations are given inside parentheses, immediately following the boldface entry. Syllables are separated by a space or stress mark. A primary, or strong, stress is shown by a heavy stroke (′) immediately following the syllable so stressed. A secondary, or weak, stress is shown by a lighter stroke (′) following the syllable so stressed. Some compound entries formed of words that are separately entered and pronounced in the dictionary are syllabified and stressed and pronounced only in part or not at all.

hard·ly (härd′lē) . . .
hard′-nosed′ (-nōzd′) . . .
hard palate . . .
hard′pan′ . . .

Variant pronunciations are shortened, wherever possible, with only the syllable or syllables in which change occurs shown. A hyphen after the shortened variant shows that it is the beginning of the word; a hyphen before the variant, that it is the end; and hyphens before and after the variant, that it is within the word.

ei·ther (ē′thər, ī′-) . . .
rec·ti·tude (rek′tə to͞od′, -tyo͞od′) . . .
fu·tu·ri·ty (fyo͞o toor′ə tē, -tyoor′) . . .

Shortened pronunciations are given for a series of words having the same first part, after the pronunciation of the first part has been established.

le·git·i·mate (lə jit′ə mit) . . .
le·git′i·ma·tize′ (-mə tīz′) . . .
le·git′i·mize′ (-mīz′) . . .

Variants — Where two or more pronunciations for a single word are given, the order in which they are entered does not necessarily mean that the first is "better" or preferred. Usually the form given first is the one more frequent in general cultivated use.

Variant pronunciations involving different parts of speech in the same entry block usually appear as follows:
con·duct (kän′dukt′; *for v.* kən dukt′) *n.* . . . .

In some cases, however, the variant pronunciation is entered directly with the part of speech to which it refers.

III. PART-OF-SPEECH LABELS

Part-of-speech labels are given for main entries that are solid or hyphenated forms, except for prefixes, suffixes, and abbreviations, and for the names of persons, places, etc. The labels appear in boldface italic type following the pronunciations.

When an entry word is used as more than one part of speech, long dashes introduce the label for each different part of speech in the entry block.

round . . . *adj.* . . . . —*n.* . . . . —*vt.* . . . . —*vi.* . . . . —*adv.* . . . . — *prep.* . . . .

Two or more part-of-speech labels are given jointly for an entry when the definition or definitions, or the cross-reference, will suffice for both or all.
link′ . . . *vt., vi.* to join; connect
des·patch . . . *vt., n. same as* DISPATCH

IV. INFLECTED FORMS

Inflected forms regarded as irregular or offering difficulty in spelling are entered in small boldface immediately following the part-of-speech labels. They are truncated where possible, and syllabified and pronounced where necessary.

hap·py ... *adj.* -pi·er, -pi·est ...
cit·y ... *n., pl.* -ies
a·moe·ba ... *n., pl.* -bas, -bae (-bē) ...
al·le·vi·ate ... *vt.* -at'ed, -at'ing ...

Forms regarded as regular inflections, and hence not normally entered, include:

a) plurals formed by adding -*s* to the singular (or -*es* after *s, x, z, ch,* and *sh*), as *bats, boxes;*
b) present tenses formed by adding -*s* to the infinitive (or -*es* after *s, x, z, ch,* or *sh*), as *waits, marches;*
c) past tenses and past participles formed by simply adding -*ed* to the infinitive with no other change in the verb form, as *waited, marched;*
d) present participles formed by simply adding -*ing* to the infinitive with no other change in the verb form, as *waiting, marching;*
e) comparatives and superlatives formed by simply adding -*er* and -*est* to the adjective or adverb with no other change in the positive form, as *taller, tallest* or *sooner, soonest.*

Where two inflected forms are given for a verb, the first is the form for the past tense and the past participle, and the second is the form for the present participle.

make ... *vt.* made, mak'ing

Where three forms are given, the first is the past tense, the second the past participle, and the third the present participle.

give ... *vt.* gave, giv'en, giv'ing ·

Where there are alternative forms for any of the principal parts, they are indicated as follows:

trav·el ... *vi.* -eled or -el·ling, -el·ing or -el·ling ...
drink ... *vt.* drank or archaic drunk, drunk or now colloq. drank or archaic drunk'en, drink'ing ...

V. ETYMOLOGY

The etymology, or word derivation, will be found inside heavy boldface brackets immediately before the definitions proper. The symbols, as < for "derived from," and the abbreviations of language labels, etc. used in the etymologies are dealt with in full in the list following this Guide.

ex·ca·vate (eks'kə vāt') *vt.* -vat'ed, -vat'ing [< L. *ex-*, out + *cavus*, hollow] 1. to make a hole ...

For some words etymologies are shown by means of cross-references (in small capitals) to the elements of which they are formed.

hy·dro·ther·a·py ... *n.* [HYDRO- + THERAPY]

VI. THE DEFINITIONS

Order of Senses — The standard, general senses of a word are given first. Senses that are colloquial, slang, archaic, obsolete, or the like come next, followed by specialized senses, whose field labels are arranged in alphabetical order.

Numbering & Grouping of Senses — Senses are numbered consecutively within any given part of speech in boldface numerals. Where a primary sense of a word can easily be subdivided into several closely related meanings, such meanings are indicated by italicized letters.

time ... *n.* ... 1. every ... 2. a system ... 14. *Music a)* rhythm ... *b)* tempo ... —*interj.* ... —*vt.* ... 1. to arrange ... 2. to adjust ... —*adj.* 1. having to ... 2. set to ... —in time 1. eventually ... 2. before ...

Capitalization — If a word is capitalized in all its meanings, the entry word itself is printed with a capital letter. If it is capitalized in its primary sense, a lower-case let-

ter in brackets, sometimes with a qualifying *often, usually,* etc., appears after the numeral or part of speech of any sense not capitalized.

Pur·i·tan ... *n.* ... 1. ... 2. [p-] ...

Conversely, capital letters are shown, where pertinent, with lower-case main entries.

north ... *n.* ... 1. ... 2. ... 3. [*often* N-] ...

Plural Forms — The designation [*pl.*] (or [*often pl.*], [*usually pl.*], etc.) before a definition indicates that it is the plural form of the entry word (or often or usually the plural form) that has the meaning given in the definition.

look ... *vi.* ... —*n.* 1. ... 2. ... 3. [Colloq.] *a)* [*usually pl.*] appearance *b)* [*pl.*] personal appearance ...

If a plural noun entry or sense is construed as singular, the designation "[*with sing. v.*]" is added.

phys·ics ... *n.pl.* ... [*with sing. v.*] ...

Verbs Followed by Prepositions or Objects — Where certain verbs are, in usage, always or usually followed by a specific preposition or prepositions, this has been indicated in either of the following ways: the preposition, italicized and enclosed in parentheses, has been worked into the definition, or a note has been added in parentheses.

strike ... —*vi.* ... 8. to come suddenly (*on* or *upon*) ...
read' ... *vt.* ... —*vi.* 1. ... 2. ... to learn by reading (with *about* or *of*)

In definitions of transitive verbs, the specific or generalized objects of the verb, where given, are enclosed in parentheses, since such objects are not part of the definition.

ob·serve ... *vt.* ... 1. to adhere to (a law, custom, etc.) 2. to celebrate (a holiday) ...

Illustrative Examples of Entry Words — Examples of a word in use have been given where such examples help to clarify the meaning. Such examples of usage are enclosed in slanted brackets, and the word being illustrated is set in italics.

spir·it ... *n.* ... 7. enthusiastic loyalty [school *spirit*] 8. true intention [the *spirit* of the law] ...

VII. USAGE LABELS

Although the conventional usage labels have been employed because of widespread familiarity with them, it is important that the reader keep their meaning clearly in mind. The labels, and what they are intended to indicate, are given below.

Colloquial: The term or sense is generally characteristic of conversation and informal writing. It is not to be regarded as substandard or illiterate.
Slang: The term or sense is not generally regarded as conventional or standard usage but is used, even by the best speakers, in highly informal contexts.
Obsolete: The term or sense is no longer used.
Archaic: The term or sense is rarely used today except in certain restricted contexts, as in church ritual.
Poetic: The term or sense is used chiefly in poetry, especially in earlier poetry.
Dialect: The term or sense is used regularly only in some geographical areas or in a certain designated area (*South, West,* etc.) of the United States.
British (or *Canadian, Scottish,* etc.): The term or sense is characteristic of British (or Canadian, etc.) English rather than American English.

If the label (which is placed in brackets and in some cases abbreviated) occurs directly after a part-of-speech label or after a boldface entry term, it applies to all senses given for that part of speech or term. If it occurs after a numeral, it applies only to the sense so numbered.

VIII. FIELD LABELS

Labels for specialized fields of knowledge and activity appear in italics (in abbreviated form where practical) immediately before the sense involved.

base' ... *n.* ... 8. *Chem.* ... 9. *Geom.* ...

ABBREVIATIONS USED IN THIS DICTIONARY

abbrev. abbreviated; abbreviation
acc. accusative
A.D. Anno Domini
adj. adjective
adv. adverb
Aeron. Aeronautics
Afr. African
Afrik. Afrikaans
Alb. Albanian
alt. altered; alternative
Am. American
AmInd. American Indian
AmSp. American Spanish
Anat. Anatomy
Anglo-Fr. Anglo-French
Anglo-Ind. Anglo-Indian
Anglo-L. Anglo-Latin
Ar. Arabic
Aram. Aramaic
Archit. Architecture
Arith. Arithmetic
Arm. Armenian
art. article
Assyr. Assyrian
Astron. Astronomy
at. no. atomic number
at. wt. atomic weight
Bab. Babylonian
B.C. before Christ
Biol. Biology
Bot. Botany
Braz. Brazilian
Bret. Breton
Brit. British
Bulg. Bulgarian
C Celsius; Central
c. century; circa
Canad. Canadian
CanadFr. Canadian French
cap. capital
Celt. Celtic
cent. century; centuries
cf. compare
Ch. Church
Chem. Chemistry
Chin. Chinese
Colloq. colloquial
comp. compound; compounds
compar. comparative
conj. conjunction
contr. contracted; contraction
cu. cubic
Dan. Danish
deriv. derivative
Dial., dial. dialectal
dim. diminutive
Du. Dutch
DuFl. Dutch Flemish
E East; eastern
E. East; English
EC east central
Ec. Ecclesiastic
Eccles. Ecclesiastical
Ecol. Ecology
Econ. Economics
Educ. Education
e.g. for example
Egypt. Egyptian
Elec. Electricity
Eng. English
Esk. Eskimo
esp. especially
etym. etymology

Ex. example
F Fahrenheit
fem. feminine
ff. following
fig. figurative; figuratively
Finn. Finnish
Fl. Flemish
fl. flourished
Frank. Frankish
freq. frequentative; frequently
Fris. Frisian
ft. feet
fut. future
G. German
Gael. Gaelic
gal. gallon; gallons
Gaul. Gaulish
gen. genitive
Geol. Geology
Geom. Geometry
Ger. German
Gmc. Germanic
Goth. Gothic
Gr. Greek
Gram. Grammar
Gym. Gymnastics
Haw. Hawaiian
Heb. Hebrew
Hung. Hungarian
hyp. hypothetical
Ice. Icelandic
i.e. that is
in. inch; inches
Ind. Indian
indic. indicative
inf. infinitive
infl. influenced
intens. intensive
interj. interjection
Ir. Irish
Iran. Iranian
IrGael. Irish Gaelic
It. Italian
Jap. Japanese
Jav. Javanese
Jpn. Japanese
Kor. Korean
L Late
L. Latin
lb. pound
LGr. Late Greek
Linguis. Linguistics
lit. literally
Lith. Lithuanian
LL. Late Latin
LME. Late Middle English
LowG. Low German
M Medieval; Middle
masc. masculine
Math. Mathematics
MDu. Middle Dutch
ME. Middle English
Mech. Mechanics
Med. Medicine
met. metropolitan
Meteorol. Meteorology
Mex. Mexican
MexInd. Mexican Indian
MexSp. Mexican Spanish
MDu. Middle Dutch
MFl. Middle Flemish
MFr. Middle French
MGr. Medieval Greek

ix

Abbreviations

MHG. Middle High German
mi. mile; miles
Mil. Military
ML. Medieval Latin
MLowG. Middle Low German
Mod, Mod. Modern
ModDu. Modern Dutch
ModE. Modern English
ModL. Modern Latin
Mongol. Mongolic
Myth. Mythology
N North; northern
N. North
n. noun
Naut., naut. nautical
NC north central
NE northeastern
neut. neuter
n.fem. noun feminine
n.masc. noun masculine
nom. nominative
Norm, Norm. Norman
Norw. Norwegian
n.pl. noun plural
NW northwestern
O Old
obj. objective
Obs., obs. obsolete
occas. occasionally
ODu. Old Dutch
OE. Old English
OFr. Old French
OFrank. Old Frankish
OHG. Old High German
OIr. Old Irish
ON. Old Norse
ONormFr. Old Norman French
orig. origin; originally
OPer. Old Persian
OPr. Old Provençal
OS. Old Saxon
OSp. Old Spanish
OW. Old Welsh
oz. ounce
p. page
pass. passive
Per. Persian
perf. perfect
pers. person
Peruv. Peruvian
Philos. Philosophy
Phoen. Phoenician
Phonet. Phonetics
Photog. Photography
phr. phrase
Physiol. Physiology
PidE. Pidgin English
pl. plural
Poet. Poetic
Pol. Polish
pop. population
Port. Portuguese
poss. possessive
pp. past participle
Pr. Provençal
prec. preceding
prep. preposition

pres. present
prob. probably
pron. pronoun
pronun. pronunciation
Prov. Provincial
prp. present participle
pseud. pseudonym
Psychol. Psychology
pt. past tense
R.C.Ch. Roman Catholic Church
redupl. reduplication
refl. reflexive
Rom. Roman
Russ. Russian
S South; southern
S. South
SAmInd. South American Indian
Sans. Sanskrit
SC south central
Scand. Scandinavian
Scot. Scottish
ScotGael. Scottish Gaelic
SE southeastern
Sem. Semitic
Serb. Serbian
sing. singular
Sinh. Sinhalese
Slav. Slavic
Sp. Spanish
sp. spelled; spelling
specif. specifically
sq. square
subj. subjunctive
superl. superlative
SW southwestern
Sw., Swed. Swedish
Syr. Syrian
Tag. Tagalog
Tat. Tatar
Theol. Theology
Tibet. Tibetan
transl. translation
Turk. Turkish
TV television
ult. ultimately
unc. uncertain
U.S. United States
U.S.S.R. Union of Soviet Socialist Republics
v. verb
var. variant
v.aux. auxiliary verb
vi. intransitive verb
VL. Vulgar Latin
vt. transitive verb
W West; western
W. Welsh; West
WAfr. West African
WC west central
WInd. West Indian
Yid. Yiddish
Zool. Zoology

‡ foreign word or phrase
+ plus
< derived from
? uncertain; possibly; perhaps
& and

A

A, a (ā) *n., pl.* **A's, a's** the first letter of the English alphabet —*adj.* first in a sequence or group
A (ā) *n.* **1.** a grade indicating excellence **2.** *Music* the sixth tone in the ascending scale of C major —*adj.* first-class; superior; A 1
a (ə; *stressed* ā) *adj., indefinite article* [< *an*] **1.** one; one sort of [to plant *a* tree] **2.** each; any one [*a* gun is dangerous] **3.** per [once *a* day] *A* is used before words beginning with a consonant sound [*a* child, *a* union, *a* history]
a- *a prefix meaning:* **1.** [< OE.] *a)* in, into, on, at, to [aboard] *b)* the act or state of [asleep] *c)* up, out [arise] *d)* off, of [akin] **2.** [< Gr.] not [agnostic]
A. angstrom
a. **1.** about **2.** acre(s) **3.** adjective **4.** answer
Aa·chen (ä′kən; *G.* ä′khən) city in W West Germany: pop. 176,000
aard·vark (ärd′värk′) *n.* [< D. *aarde*, earth + *vark*, pig] a burrowing African mammal that feeds on ants and termites
Aar·on (er′ən) *Bible* the older brother of Moses and first high priest of the Hebrews
Ab *Chem.* alabamine
ab- [L.] *a prefix meaning* away, from, off, down [abdicate]
A.B. Bachelor of Arts
A.B., a.b. able-bodied (seaman)
a·ba·cá (ab′ə kə, äb′-) *n.* [Tag.] **1.** *same as* MANILA HEMP **2.** a Philippine plant yielding Manila hemp
a·back (ə bak′) *adv.* **1.** [Archaic] backward **2.** *Naut.* backward against the mast, as the sails in a wind from straight ahead —**taken aback** startled and confused; surprised
ab·a·cus (ab′ə kəs) *n., pl.* **-cus·es, -ci′** (-sī′) [< Gr. *abax*] **1.** a frame with sliding beads, for doing arithmetic **2.** *Archit.* a slab forming the top of the capital of a column
a·baft (ə baft′) *adv.* [< OE. *on*, on + *be*, by + *æftan*, aft] aft — *prep. Naut.* behind
ab·a·lo·ne (ab′ə lō′nē) *n.* [AmSp. < Calif. Ind. *aulun*] a marine mollusk with a spiral shell lined with mother-of-pearl
a·ban·don (ə ban′dən) *vt.* [< OFr. *mettre a bandon*, to put under (another's) ban] **1.** to give up completely **2.** to desert; forsake **3.** to yield (oneself) completely, as to a feeling —*n.* surrender to one's impulses —**a·ban′don·ment** *n.*

ABACUS

a·ban′doned *adj.* **1.** forsaken; deserted **2.** wicked; immoral **3.** unrestrained
a·base (ə bās′) *vt.* **a·based′, a·bas′ing** [< ML. *abassare*, to lower] to humble or humiliate —**a·base′ment** *n.*
a·bash (ə bash′) *vt.* [< L. *ex* + *bah* (interj.)] to make ashamed and ill-at-ease; disconcert —**a·bash′ed·ly** (-id lē) *adv.* —**a·bash′ment** *n.*
a·bate (ə bāt′) *vt., vi.* **a·bat′ed, a·bat′ing** [< OFr. *abattre*, to beat down] **1.** to make or become less **2.** *Law* to end; terminate —**a·bate′ment** *n.*
ab·at·toir (ab′ə twär′) *n.* [Fr.: see ABATE] a slaughterhouse
ab·ba·cy (ab′ə sē) *n., pl.* **-cies** an abbot's position, jurisdiction, or term of office
ab·bé (ä bā′) *n.* [Fr.: see ABBOT] a French title of respect for a priest
ab·bess (ab′əs) *n.* [see ABBOT] a woman who is head of an abbey of nuns

ab·bey (ab′ē) *n.* **1.** a monastery or nunnery **2.** a church belonging to an abbey
ab·bot (ab′ət) *n.* [< Aram. *abbā*, father] a man who is head of an abbey of monks
abbr., abbrev. **1.** abbreviated **2.** abbreviation
ab·bre·vi·ate (ə brē′vē āt′) *vt.* **-at′ed, -at′ing** [< L. *ad-*, to + *brevis*, short] to make shorter; esp., to shorten (a word) by leaving out letters —**ab·bre′vi·a′tor** *n.*
ab·bre′vi·a′tion (-ā′shən) *n.* **1.** a making shorter **2.** the fact or state of being made shorter **3.** a shortened form of a word or phrase, as *Mr.* for *Mister*, *N.Y.* for *New York*
A B C (ā′bē′sē′) *n., pl.* **A B C's 1.** [*usually pl.*] the alphabet **2.** the basic elements (of a subject)
ab·di·cate (ab′də kāt′) *vt., vi.* **-cat′ed, -cat′ing** [< L. *ab-*, off + *dicare*, to proclaim] **1.** to give up formally (a throne, etc.) **2.** to surrender (a right, etc.) —**ab′di·ca′tion** *n.*
ab·do·men (ab′də mən, ab dō′-) *n.* [L.] **1.** the part of the body between the diaphragm and the pelvis, containing the intestines, etc.; belly **2.** in insects and crustaceans, the hind part of the body —**ab·dom′i·nal** (-dä′mə n'l) *adj.*
ab·duct (ab dukt′) *vt.* [< L. *ab-*, away + *ducere*, to lead] to kidnap —**ab·duc′tion** *n.* —**ab·duc′tor** *n.*
a·beam (ə bēm′) *adv., adj.* at right angles to a ship's length or keel
a·bed (ə bed′) *adv., adj.* in bed
A·bel (ā′b'l) *Bible* the second son of Adam and Eve, killed by his brother Cain
Ab·é·lard (ä bā lär′), **Pierre** 1079–1142; Fr. philosopher & teacher: Eng. name Peter **Ab·e·lard** (ab′ə lärd′)
Ab·er·deen (ab′ər dēn′) a city in Scotland, on the North Sea: pop. 184,000
ab·er·ra·tion (ab′ər ā′shən) *n.* [< L. *ab-*, from + *errare*, to wander] **1.** a deviation from what is right, true, normal, etc. **2.** mental derangement **3.** *Optics* the failure of light rays from one point to converge to a single focus
a·bet (ə bet′) *vt.* **a·bet′ted, a·bet′ting** [< OFr. *a-*, to + *beter*, to bait] to incite or help, esp. in crime —**a·bet′ment** *n.* —**a·bet′tor, a·bet′ter** *n.*
a·bey·ance (ə bā′əns) *n.* [< OFr. *a-*, at + *bayer*, to gape] temporary suspension, as of an activity or ruling
ab·hor (ab hôr′) *vt.* **-horred′, -hor′ring** [< L. *ab-*, from + *horrere*, to shudder] to shrink from in disgust or hatred —**ab·hor′rence** *n.*
ab·hor′rent (-ənt) *adj.* causing disgust, hate, etc.; detestable —**ab·hor′rent·ly** *adv.*
a·bide (ə bīd′) *vi.* **a·bode′** or **a·bid′ed, a·bid′ing** [OE. *abidan*] **1.** to remain **2.** [Archaic] to reside —*vt.* **1.** to await **2.** to endure —**abide by 1.** to live up to (a promise, etc.) **2.** to submit to and carry out
a·bid′ing *adj.* enduring; lasting
a·bil·i·ty (ə bil′ə tē) *n., pl.* **-ties 1.** a being able; power to do **2.** skill or talent
ab·ject (ab′jekt, ab jekt′) *adj.* [< L. *ab-*, from + *jacere*, to throw] **1.** miserable; wretched **2.** degraded; contemptible —**ab′ject·ly** *adv.* —**ab′ject·ness** *n.*
ab·jure (ab joor′) *vt.* **-jured′, -jur′ing** [< L. *ab-*, away + *jurare*, to swear] to give up (rights, allegiance, etc.) on oath; renounce —**ab·ju·ra·tion** (ab′jə rā′shən) *n.* —**ab·jur′er** *n.*
ab·la·tive (ab′lə tiv) *n.* [< L. *ab-*, away + *ferre*, to carry] the grammatical case in Latin, etc. expressing removal, direction from, cause, agency, etc. —*adj.* of or in the ablative
ab·laut (äb′lout, ab′-) *n.* [G. < *ab-*, off + *laut*, sound] change of vowels in related words to show changes in tense, etc. (Ex.: drink, drank, drunk)
a·blaze (ə blāz′) *adj.* **1.** flaming **2.** very excited

---

a·ble (ā′b'l) *adj.* **a′bler, a′blest** [< L. *habere*, have] **1.** having enough power, skill, etc. (*to* do something) **2.** skilled; talented —**a′bly** *adv.*

-able [< L.] *a suffix meaning:* **1.** able to [*durable*] **2.** capable of being [*drinkable*] **3.** worthy of being [*lovable*] **4.** having qualities of [*comfortable*] **5.** tending to [*peaceable*]

a′ble-bod′ied *adj.* healthy and strong

able-bodied seaman a trained seaman, more highly skilled than an ordinary seaman

ab·lu·tion (ab lōō′shən) *n.* [< L. *ab-*, off + *luere*, to wash] **1.** a washing of the body, esp. as a religious ceremony **2.** the liquid used for this

-ably *an adv.-forming suffix corresponding to* -ABLE

ABM anti-ballistic missile

ab·ne·gate (ab′nə gāt′) *vt.* **-gat′ed, -gat′ing** [< L. *ab-*, from + *negare*, deny] to deny and refuse; renounce —**ab′ne·ga′tion** *n.*

ab·nor·mal (ab nôr′m'l) *adj.* not normal, average, or typical; irregular —**ab·nor′mal·ly** *adv.*

ab·nor·mal·i·ty (ab′nôr mal′ə tē) *n.* **1.** an abnormal condition **2.** *pl.* **-ties** an abnormal thing

a·board (ə bôrd′) *adv., prep.* **1.** on or in (a ship, airplane, etc.) **2.** alongside

a·bode (ə bōd′) *pt. and pp. of* ABIDE —*n.* a home; residence

a·bol·ish (ə bäl′ish) *vt.* [< L. *abolere*, destroy] to do away with; put an end to —**a·bol′ish·ment** *n.*

ab·o·li·tion (ab′ə lish′ən) *n.* **1.** an abolishing or being abolished **2.** [*occas.* **A-**] the abolishing of slavery in the U.S. —**ab′o·li′tion·ist** *n.*

A-bomb (ā′bäm) *n. same as* ATOMIC BOMB

a·bom·i·na·ble (ə bäm′ə nə b'l) *adj.* **1.** disgusting; vile **2.** very bad —**a·bom′i·na·bly** *adv.*

a·bom·i·nate (ə bäm′ə nāt′) *vt.* **-nat′ed, -nat′ing** [< L. *abominari*, regard as an ill omen] **1.** to hate; loathe **2.** to dislike greatly —**a·bom′i·na′tion** *n.*

ab·o·rig·i·nal (ab′ə rij′ə n'l) *adj.* **1.** existing (in a place) from the beginning; first **2.** of aborigines —*n.* an aboriginal animal or plant

ab′o·rig′i·ne′ (-ə nē′) *n., pl.* **-nes′** [L. < *ab-*, from + *origine*, the beginning] any of the first-known inhabitants of a region

a·born·ing (ə bôr′niŋ) *adv.* while being born

a·bort (ə bôrt′) *vi.* [< L. *aboriri*, miscarry] **1.** to have a miscarriage **2.** to fail to be completed —*vt.* **1.** to cause to have an abortion **2.** to cut short

a·bor·tion (ə bôr′shən) *n.* **1.** expulsion of a fetus from the womb before it is developed enough to survive **2.** anything immature and incomplete —**a·bor′tion·ist** *n.*

a·bor′tive *adj.* **1.** unsuccessful; fruitless **2.** *Biol.* rudimentary **3.** *Med.* causing abortion

a·bound (ə bound′) *vi.* [< L. *ab-*, away + *undare*, rise in waves] to be plentiful (often with *in* or *with*)

a·bout (ə bout′) *adv.* [OE. *onbutan*, around] **1.** all around **2.** here and there **3.** near **4.** in the opposite direction **5.** in succession or rotation [play fair — turn and turn *about*] **6.** nearly —*adj.* astir [he is up and *about*] —*prep.* **1.** on all sides of **2.** here and there in **3.** near to **4.** with; on (one's person) **5.** attending to [go *about* your business] **6.** intending; on the point of [*about* to speak] **7.** concerning

a·bout-face (ə bout′fās′, -fās′; *for v.* ə bout′fās′) *n.* a reversal of position or opinion —*vi.* **-faced′, -fac′ing** to turn in the opposite direction

a·bove (ə buv′) *adv.* [OE. *abufan*] **1.** in a higher place; up **2.** earlier (in a piece of writing) **3.** higher in rank, etc. —*prep.* **1.** over; on top of **2.** better or more than [*above* average] **3.** too honorable to engage in —*adj.* mentioned earlier —*n.* something that is above —**above all** most of all; mainly

a·bove′board′ *adv., adj.* without dishonesty

ab·ra·ca·dab·ra (ab′rə kə dab′rə) *n.* [LL.] **1.** a word supposed to have magic powers, used in incantations, etc. **2.** meaningless talk

ab·rade (ə brād′) *vt.* **-rad′ed, -rad′ing** [< L. *ab-*, away + *radere*, scrape] to rub off; wear away by scraping

A·bra·ham (ā′brə ham′) *Bible* the first patriarch of the Hebrews

ab·ra·sion (ə brā′zhən) *n.* **1.** an abrading **2.** an abraded spot

ab·ra′sive (-siv) *adj.* causing abrasion —*n.* a substance used for grinding, polishing, etc.

a·breast (ə brest′) *adv., adj.* **1.** side by side **2.** informed (*of*) or familiar (*with*) recent developments

a·bridge (ə brij′) *vt.* **a·bridged′, a·bridg′ing** [< L. *ad-*, to + *brevis*, short] **1.** to shorten, lessen, or curtail **2.** to shorten (a book, talk, etc.) by using fewer words —**a·bridg′ment, a·bridge′ment** *n.*

a·broad (ə brôd′) *adv.* **1.** far and wide **2.** current [rumors are *abroad*] **3.** outdoors [to stroll *abroad*] **4.** to or in foreign countries —**from abroad** from a foreign land

ab·ro·gate (ab′rə gāt′) *vt.* **-gat′ed, -gat′ing** [< L. *ab-*, away + *rogare*, propose] to cancel or repeal; annul —**ab′ro·ga′tion** *n.* —**ab′ro·ga′tor** *n.*

a·brupt (ə brupt′) *adj.* [< L. *ab-*, off + *rumpere*, to break] **1.** sudden; unexpected **2.** brusque **3.** very steep **4.** jerky and disconnected —**a·brupt′ly** *adv.* —**a·brupt′ness** *n.*

Ab·sa·lom (ab′sə ləm) *Bible* David's favorite son, who rebelled against him

ab·scess (ab′ses) *n.* [< L. *ab(s)-*, from + *cedere*, go] an inflamed area in body tissues, containing pus —*vi.* to form an abscess —**ab′scessed** *adj.*

ab·scis·sa (ab sis′ə) *n., pl.* **-sas, -sae** (-ē) [< L. *ab-*, off + *scindere*, to cut] in a coordinate system, the distance of a point from the vertical axis as measured along a line parallel to the horizontal axis: cf. ORDINATE

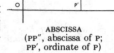

ABSCISSA
(PP″, abscissa of P;
PP′, ordinate of P)

ab·scond (ab skänd′) *vi.* [< L. *ab(s)-*, from + *condere*, to hide] to leave hastily and secretly to escape the law —**ab·scond′er** *n.*

ab·sence (ab′s'ns) *n.* **1.** a being absent **2.** the time of this **3.** a lack [in the *absence* of proof]

ab·sent (ab′s'nt) *adj.* [< L. *ab-*, away + *esse*, to be] **1.** not present; away **2.** not existing; lacking **3.** not attentive —*vt.* (ab sent′) to keep (oneself) away —**ab′sent·ly** *adv.*

ab·sen·tee (ab′s'n tē′) *n.* one who is absent, as from work —*adj.* designating or of a landlord who lives some distance away from the property that he owns —**ab′sen·tee′ism** *n.*

ab′sent-mind′ed *adj.* **1.** not attentive; preoccupied **2.** habitually forgetful —**ab′sent-mind′ed·ly** *adv.* —**ab′sent-mind′ed·ness** *n.*

ab·sinthe, ab·sinth (ab′sinth) *n.* [< Gr. *apsinthion*] **1.** wormwood **2.** a green, bitter liqueur with the flavor of wormwood and anise

ab·so·lute (ab′sə lōōt′) *adj.* [see ABSOLVE] **1.** perfect; complete **2.** not mixed; pure **3.** unrestricted [*absolute* rule] **4.** positive; definite **5.** actual; real [an *absolute* truth] **6.** not conforming to the usual relations of syntax [in the sentence "The weather being good, they went," *the weather being good* is an *absolute* construction] **7.** with no expressed object: said of a verb usually transitive —*n.* something that is absolute —**the Absolute** *Philos.* that which is thought of as existing completely in and by itself —**ab′so·lute′ly** *adv.* —**ab′so·lute′ness** *n.*

absolute pitch the ability to identify or sing any tone without hearing an identified tone first

absolute zero the hypothetical point at which matter would have neither molecular motion nor heat: theoretically equal to −273.15°C or −459.67°F

ab·so·lu·tion (ab′sə lōō′shən) *n.* **1.** a formal freeing (*from* guilt); forgiveness **2.** remission (*of* sin or its penalty)

ab·so·lut·ism (ab′sə lōō′tiz'm) *n.* government in which the ruler has unlimited powers; despotism —**ab′so·lut′ist** *n., adj.*

ab·solve (əb zälv′, -zälv′; -sälv′) *vt.* **-solved′, -solv′ing** [< L. *ab-*, from + *solvere*, to loose] **1.** to free from guilt, a duty, etc. **2.** to give religious absolution to

ab·sorb (əb zôrb′, -zôrb′; -sôrb′) *vt.* [< L. *ab-*, from + *sorbere*, drink in] **1.** to suck up; take in **2.** to interest greatly **3.** to assume the burden of (costs, etc.) **4.** to take in and not reflect or give back —**ab·sorbed′** *adj.* —**ab·sorb′ing** *adj.*

ab·sorb′ent *adj.* capable of absorbing moisture, etc. —*n.* a thing that absorbs —**ab·sorb′en·cy** *n.*

ab·sorp·tion (əb zôrp′shən, ab-; -sôrp′-) *n.* **1.** an absorbing **2.** great interest **3.** the passing of nutriment into the bloodstream or lymph —**ab·sorp′tive** *adj.*

ab·stain (əb stān′) *vi.* [< L. *ab(s)-*, from + *tenere*, to hold] to do without voluntarily; refrain (*from*) —**ab·stain′er** *n.* —**ab·sten′tion** (-sten′shən) *n.*

ab·ste·mi·ous (əb stē′mē əs) *adj.* [< L. *ab(s)-*, from + *temetum*, strong drink] eating and drinking sparingly —**ab·ste′mi·ous·ly** *adv.* —**ab·ste′mi·ous·ness** *n.*

ab·sti·nence (ab′stə nəns) *n.* an abstaining from some or all food, liquor, etc. —**ab′sti·nent** *adj.*

ab·stract (ab strakt′, ab′strakt) *adj.* [< L. *ab(s)-*, from + *trahere*, to draw] **1.** thought of apart from material objects **2.** expressing a quality so thought of **3.** theoretical

4. *Art* characterized by nonrealistic designs or forms —*n.* (ab'strakt) a summary —*vt.* **1.** (ab strakt') to take away **2.** (ab'strakt) to summarize —**in the abstract** in theory as apart from practice —**ab·stract'ly** *adv.* —**ab·stract'ness** *n.*

ab·stract'ed *adj.* withdrawn in mind; preoccupied

abstract expressionism a nonrepresentational style of painting popular after World War II, characterized by a free, self-expressive application of paint

ab·strac'tion *n.* **1.** an abstracting **2.** an abstract idea **3.** an unrealistic notion **4.** mental withdrawal **5.** an abstract painting, sculpture, etc.

ab·struse (ab strōōs') *adj.* [< L. *ab*(s)-, away + *trudere*, to thrust] hard to understand —**ab·struse'ly** *adv.* —**ab·struse'ness** *n.*

ab·surd (əb surd') *adj.* [< Fr. < L. *absurdus*, not to be heard of] so unreasonable as to be ridiculous —**ab·surd'ly** *adv.* —**ab·surd'ness** *n.*

ab·surd'i·ty *n.* **1.** a being absurd **2.** *pl.* **-ties** an absurd idea or thing

a·bun·dance (ə bun'dəns) *n.* [see ABOUND] a great supply; more than enough —**a·bun'dant** *adj.* —**a·bun'dant·ly** *adv.*

a·buse (ə byōōz') *vt.* **a·bused', a·bus'ing** [< L. *ab*-, away + *uti*, to use] **1.** to use wrongly **2.** to mistreat **3.** to insult; revile —*n.* (ə byōōs') **1.** wrong use **2.** mistreatment **3.** a corrupt practice **4.** insulting language —**a·bu'sive** (-byōōs'iv) *adj.* —**a·bu'sive·ly** *adv.*

a·but (ə but') *vi.* **a·but'ted, a·but'ting** [< OFr. *a*-, to + *bout*, end] to border (*on*) —*vt.* to border on

a·but'ment *n.* **1.** an abutting **2.** a part supporting an arch, bridge, etc.

a·bys·mal (ə biz'm'l) *adj.* **1.** of or like an abyss; bottomless **2.** very bad —**a·bys'mal·ly** *adv.*

a·byss (ə bis') *n.* [< Gr. *a*-, without + *byssos*, bottom] **1.** a bottomless gulf **2.** anything too deep for measurement *[an abyss of shame]*

Ab·ys·sin·i·a (ab'ə sin'ē ə) *same as* ETHIOPIA —**Ab'ys·sin'i·an** *adj., n.*

-ac [< Fr. < Gr.] *a suffix meaning:* **1.** relating to *[cardiac]* **2.** affected by *[maniac]*

Ac *Chem.* actinium

AC, A.C., a.c. alternating current

A/C, a/c *Bookkeeping* account

a·ca·cia (ə kā'shə) *n.* [< Gr. *akakia*, thorny tree] **1.** a tree or shrub with yellow or white flower clusters: some types yield dyes **2.** the locust tree

ac·a·dem·ic (ak'ə dem'ik) *adj.* **1.** of academies or colleges **2.** having to do with liberal arts rather than technical education **3.** formal **4.** merely theoretical —**ac'a·dem'i·cal·ly** *adv.*

academic freedom freedom of a teacher or student to express views without arbitrary interference

a·cad·e·mi·cian (ə kad'ə mish'ən, ak'ə də-) *n.* a member of an academy (sense 3)

a·cad·e·my (ə kad'ə mē) *n., pl.* **-mies** [< Gr. *akadēmeia*, place where Plato taught] **1.** a private secondary school **2.** a school offering training in a special field **3.** an association of scholars, writers, etc. for advancing an art or science

a·can·thus (ə kan'thəs) *n., pl.* **-thus·es, -thi** (-thī) [< Gr. *akē*, a point] **1.** a plant with lobed, often spiny leaves **2.** *Archit.* a representation of these leaves

a cap·pel·la (ä' kə pel'ə) [It., in chapel style] unaccompanied: said of choral singing

acc. **1.** accompanied **2.** account **3.** accusative

ac·cede (ak sēd') *vi.* **-ced'ed, -ced'ing** [< L. *ad*-, to + *cedere*, to yield] **1.** to enter upon the duties (of an office) **2.** to assent; agree (*to*)

ac·cel·er·an·do (ak sel'ə ran'dō, -rän'-) *adv., adj.* [It.] *Music* with gradually quickening tempo

ac·cel·er·ate (ək sel'ə rāt', ak-) *vt.* **-at'ed, -at'ing** [< L. *ad*-, to + *celerare*, hasten] **1.** to increase the speed of **2.** to cause to happen sooner —*vi.* to go faster —**ac·cel'er·a'tion** *n.*

ac·cel'er·a'tor *n.* **1.** a person or thing, as the foot throttle of an automobile, that accelerates something **2.** *Chem.* a substance that speeds up a reaction

ac·cent (ak'sent) *n.* [Fr. < L. *ad*-, to + *canere*, sing] **1.** the emphasis given a spoken syllable or word **2.** a mark showing such emphasis or indicating pronunciation **3.** a distinguishing manner of pronouncing *[an Irish accent]* **4.** special emphasis **5.** *Music & Verse* rhythmic stress —*vt.* (*also* ak sent') **1.** to emphasize; stress **2.** to mark with an accent

ac·cen·tu·ate (ak sen'chōō wāt') *vt.* **-at'ed, -at'ing** to accent; esp., to emphasize —**ac·cen'tu·a'tion** *n.*

ac·cept (ək sept') *vt.* [< L. *ad*-, to + *capere*, take] **1.** to receive willingly **2.** to approve **3.** to agree to **4.** to believe in **5.** to say "yes" to *[to accept an invitation]* **6.** to agree to pay —**ac·cept'er** *n.*

ac·cept'a·ble *adj.* satisfactory —**ac·cept'a·bil'i·ty** *n.* —**ac·cept'a·bly** *adv.*

ac·cept'ance *n.* **1.** an accepting or being accepted **2.** approval **3.** assent **4.** a promise to pay

ac·cep·ta·tion (ak'sep tā'shən) *n.* the generally accepted meaning (of a word or expression)

ac·cept·ed (ak sep'tid) *adj.* generally regarded as true, proper, etc.; conventional; approved

ac·cess (ak'ses) *n.* [see ACCEDE] **1.** approach or means of approach **2.** the right to enter, use, etc. **3.** an outburst *[an access of anger]*

ac·ces·sa·ry (ək ses'ər ē, ak-) *adj., n., pl.* **-ries** *same as* ACCESSORY

ac·ces'si·ble *adj.* **1.** that can be approached or entered, esp. easily **2.** obtainable **3.** open to the influence of (with *to*) *[not accessible to pity]* —**ac·ces'si·bil'i·ty** *n.* —**ac·ces'si·bly** *adv.*

ac·ces·sion (ak sesh'ən) *n.* **1.** an attaining (a throne, power, etc.) **2.** assent **3.** *a*) increase by addition *b*) an item added, as to a library

ac·ces·so·ry (ək ses'ər ē, ak-) *adj.* [see ACCEDE] **1.** extra; additional **2.** helping in an unlawful act —*n., pl.* **-ries 1.** something extra or complementary **2.** one who, though absent, helps another to break the law —**accessory before** (or **after**) **the fact** one who aids another before (or after) the commission of a felony —**ac·ces·so·ri·al** (ak'sə sôr'ē əl) *adj.*

ac·ci·dent (ak'sə dənt) *n.* [< L. *ad*-, to + *cadere*, to fall] **1.** an unintended happening **2.** an unintended happening that results in injury, loss, etc. **3.** chance *[to meet by accident]*

ac'ci·den'tal (-den't'l) *adj.* happening by chance —*n.* **1.** a nonessential quality **2.** *a*) a sign placed before a musical note to show a change in its pitch *b*) the tone of such a note —**ac'ci·den'tal·ly** *adv.*

ac·claim (ə klām') *vt.* [< L. *ad*-, to + *clamare*, to cry out] to greet or announce with loud applause or strong approval; hail —*n.* loud applause or strong approval

ac·cla·ma·tion (ak'lə mā'shən) *n.* **1.** an acclaiming or being acclaimed **2.** loud applause or strong approval **3.** an approving vote by voice without an actual count

ac·cli·mate (ak'lə māt', ə kli'mət) *vt., vi.* **-mat'ed, -mat'ing** [see AD- & CLIMATE] to accustom or become accustomed to a different climate or environment: also **ac·cli·ma·tize** (ə kli'mə tīz') **-tized', -tiz'ing** —**ac'cli·ma'tion** *n.*

ac·cliv·i·ty (ə kliv'ə tē) *n., pl.* **-ties** [< L. *ad*-, up + *clivus*, hill] an upward slope

ac·co·lade (ak'ə lād') *n.* [Fr. < It. *accollare*, to embrace] anything done or given as a sign of great respect, appreciation, etc.

ac·com·mo·date (ə käm'ə dāt') *vt.* **-dat'ed, -dat'ing** [< L. *ad*-, to + *com*-, with + *modus*, a measure] **1.** to adjust; adapt **2.** to help by supplying (*with* something) **3.** to do a favor for **4.** to have room for —*vi.* to become adjusted, as the lens of the eye in focusing

ac·com'mo·dat'ing *adj.* ready to help; obliging —**ac·com'mo·dat'ing·ly** *adv.*

ac·com'mo·da'tion *n.* **1.** adjustment **2.** willingness to do favors **3.** a help or convenience **4.** [*pl.*] lodgings or space, as in a hotel, on a ship, etc.

ac·com·pa·ni·ment (ə kump'ni mənt) *n.* **1.** anything that accompanies something else **2.** an instrumental part supporting a solo voice, etc.

ac·com·pa·nist (ə kum'pə nist) *n.* one who plays an accompaniment

ac·com·pa·ny (ə kum'pə nē, ə kump'nē) *vt.* **-nied, -ny·ing** [see AD- & COMPANION] **1.** to go with; attend **2.** to add to; supplement **3.** to play an accompaniment for or to

ac·com·plice (ə käm'plis) *n.* [< *a* (the article) + LL. *complex*, accomplice: see COMPLEX] one who knowingly helps another break a law

ac·com·plish (ə käm'plish) *vt.* [< L. *ad*-, intens. + *complere*, fill up] to succeed in doing; complete

ac·com'plished *adj.* **1.** done; completed **2.** skilled; expert

ac·com'plish·ment *n.* **1.** completion **2.** work completed; achievement **3.** a social art or skill

ac·cord (ə kôrd') *vt.* [< L. *ad*-, to + *cor*, heart] to grant

—vi. to agree or harmonize (*with*) **—n.** mutual agreement; harmony **—of one's own accord** willingly **—with one accord** all agreeing

ac·cord'ance *n.* agreement; conformity **—ac·cord'ant** *adj.*

ac·cord'ing *adj.* in harmony **—according as** to the degree that **—according to 1.** in agreement with **2.** as stated by

ac·cord'ing·ly *adv.* **1.** in a way that is fitting and proper **2.** therefore

ac·cor·di·on (ə kôr'dē ən) *n.* [< G., prob. < It. *accordare*, be in tune] a keyed musical instrument with a bellows which is pressed to force air through reeds **—ac·cor'di·on·ist** *n.*

ac·cost (ə kôst') *vt.* [< Fr. < L. *ad-*, to + *costa*, side] to approach and speak to, esp. boldly

ac·count (ə kount') *vt.* [< L. *computare*: see COMPUTE] to consider to be **—vi. 1.** to give a financial reckoning **2.** to make amends (*for*) **3.** to give reasons (*for*) **—n. 1.** a record of financial transactions **2.** *same as: a)* BANK ACCOUNT *b)* CHARGE ACCOUNT **3.** a credit customer **4.** worth; importance **5.** an explanation **6.** a report **—call to account 1.** to demand an explanation of **2.** to reprimand **—give a good account of oneself** to acquit oneself well **—on account** as partial payment **—on account of** because of **—on no account** under no circumstances **—take account of 1.** to allow for **2.** to take notice of **—take into account** to consider **—turn to account** to get use from

ACCORDION

ac·count'a·ble *adj.* **1.** responsible; liable **2.** explainable **—ac·count'a·bil'i·ty** *n.* **—ac·count'a·bly** *adv.*

ac·count'ant (-'nt) *n.* one whose work is accounting **—ac·count'an·cy** *n.*

ac·count'ing *n.* the setting up and auditing of financial accounts

ac·cou·ter (ə kōōt'ər) *vt.* [Fr., prob. < L. *con-*, together + *suere*, sew] to equip or attire: also **ac·cou'tre** -tred, -tring

ac·cou·ter·ments, ac·cou·tre·ments (ə kōōt'ər mənts, -kōō'trə-) *n.pl.* **1.** clothes; dress **2.** equipment; furnishings

Ac·cra (ə krä') capital of Ghana: pop. 491,000

ac·cred·it (ə kred'it) *vt.* [< Fr.: see CREDIT] **1.** to authorize; certify **2.** to believe in **3.** to attribute **—ac·cred'it·a'·tion** (-ə tā'shən) *n.*

ac·cre·tion (ə krē'shən) *n.* [< L. *ad-*, to + *crescere*, to grow] **1.** growth in size, esp. by addition **2.** accumulated matter **3.** a growing together of parts

ac·crue (ə krōō') *vi.* -crued', -cru'ing [see ACCRETION] to come as a natural growth or periodic increase, as interest on money **—ac·cru'al** *n.*

acct. account

ac·cul·tu·rate (ə kul'chə rāt') *vi., vt.* -rat'ed, -rat'ing to undergo, or alter by, acculturation

ac·cul'tu·ra'tion *n.* a conditioning or becoming adapted to a new or different culture

ac·cu·mu·late (ə kyōōm'yə lāt') *vt., vi.* -lat'ed, -lat'ing [< L. *ad-*, to + *cumulare*, to heap] to pile up or collect **—ac·cu'mu·la'tive** *adj.*

ac·cu'mu·la'tion *n.* **1.** an accumulating **2.** collected material; heap

ac·cu·ra·cy (ak'yər ə sē) *n.* the state of being accurate; precision

ac·cu·rate (ak'yər it) *adj.* [< L. *ad-*, to + *cura*, care] **1.** careful and exact **2.** free from errors **—ac'cu·rate·ly** *adv.* **—ac'cu·rate·ness** *n.*

ac·curs·ed (ə kur'sid, -kurst') *adj.* **1.** under a curse **2.** deserving to be cursed Also **ac·curst'** (-kurst')

ac·cu·sa·tion (ak'yə zā'shən) *n.* **1.** an accusing or being accused **2.** what one is accused of

ac·cu·sa·tive (ə kyōō'zə tiv) *adj.* [see ACCUSE] designating or in the case, as in Latin, of an object of a verb or preposition **—n. 1.** the accusative case **2.** a word in this case

ac·cu'sa·to'ry (-tôr'ē) *adj.* making or containing an accusation; accusing

ac·cuse (ə kyōōz') *vt.* -cused', -cus'ing [< L. *ad-*, to + *causa*, a lawsuit] **1.** to blame **2.** to bring charges against (*of* breaking the law) **—the accused** *Law* the person charged with committing a crime **—ac·cus'er** *n.*

ac·cus·tom (ə kus'təm) *vt.* to make familiar by custom, habit, or use; habituate (*to*)

ac·cus'tomed *adj.* **1.** customary; usual **2.** used (*to*); in the habit of

ace (ās) *n.* [< L. *as*, unit] **1.** a playing card, domino, etc. with one spot **2.** a serve, as in tennis, that one's opponent fails to return **3.** an expert, esp. an expert combat pilot **4.** *Golf* a hole in one **—adj.** [Colloq.] first-rate; expert **— within an ace of** on the verge of

ace in the hole [Slang] any advantage held in reserve

a·cerb (ə surb') *adj.* [< Fr. < L. *acerbus*, bitter] **1.** sour in taste **2.** sharp or bitter in temper, language, etc.: now usually **a·cer·bic** (ə sur'bik) **—a·cer'bi·ty** (-bə tē) *n.*

ac·e·tate (as'ə tāt') *n.* a salt or ester of acetic acid

a·ce·tic (ə sēt'ik) *adj.* [< L. *acetum*, vinegar] of, like, containing, or producing acetic acid or vinegar

acetic acid a sharp, sour, colorless liquid, $C_2H_4O_2$, found in vinegar

a·cet·i·fy (ə set'ə fī', -sēt'-) *vt., vi.* -fied', -fy'ing to change into vinegar or acetic acid

ac·e·tone (as'ə tōn') *n.* [< ACETIC] a colorless liquid used as a solvent for certain oils, etc.

a·cet·y·lene (ə set''l ēn') *n.* [< ACETIC + -YL + -ENE] a colorless gas, C_2H_2, used for lighting and, with oxygen, in blowtorches, etc.

ac·e·tyl·sal·i·cyl·ic acid (ə set''l sal'ə sil'ik) aspirin

ace·y·deuc·y (ā'sē dōō'sē) *n.* [< ACE + DEUCE] a variation of backgammon

ache (āk) *vi.* ached, ach'ing [OE. *acan*] **1.** to have or give dull, steady pain **2.** [Colloq.] to yearn **—n.** a dull, continuous pain

a·chene (ā kēn') *n.* [< Gr. *a-*, not + *chainein*, to gape] any small, dry, one-seeded fruit that ripens without bursting

Ach·er·on (ak'ə rän') *Gr. & Rom. Myth.* the river in Hades across which the dead were ferried

a·chieve (ə chēv') *vt.* a·chieved', a·chiev'ing [< L. *ad-*, to + *caput*, head] **1.** to succeed in doing; accomplish **2.** to get by effort; attain; gain **—a·chiev'a·ble** *adj.* **— a·chiev'er** *n.*

a·chieve'ment *n.* **1.** an achieving **2.** a thing achieved, esp. by skill, work, etc.; feat

A·chil·les (ə kil'ēz) *Gr. Myth.* Greek hero in the Trojan War, killed by an arrow that struck his vulnerable heel

Achilles' heel (one's) vulnerable spot

Achilles' tendon the tendon connecting the heel to the muscles of the calf of the leg

ach·ro·mat·ic (ak'rə mat'ik) *adj.* [< Gr. *a-*, without + *chrōma*, color] refracting white light without breaking it up into its component colors

ach·y (ā'kē) *adj.* -i·er, -i·est having an ache

ac·id (as'id) *adj.* [< L. *acidus*, sour] **1.** sour; sharp; tart **2.** sharp or sarcastic in speech, etc. **3.** of an acid **4.** having too much acid **—n. 1.** a sour substance **2.** [Slang] *same as* LSD **3.** *Chem.* any compound that reacts with a base to form a salt **—ac'id·ly** *adv.*

a·cid·ic (ə sid'ik) *adj.* **1.** forming acid **2.** acid

a·cid'i·fy' (-ə fī') *vt., vi.* -fied', -fy'ing **1.** to make or become sour or acid **2.** to change into an acid **—a·cid'i·fi·ca'tion** *n.*

a·cid'i·ty (-tē) *n., pl.* -ties **1.** acid quality or condition; sourness **2.** the degree of this

ac·i·do·sis (as'ə dō'sis) *n.* a condition in which the body's alkali reserve is below normal

acid test a crucial, final test, as of quality

a·cid·u·late (ə sij'oo lāt') *vt.* -lat'ed, -lat'ing to make somewhat acid or sour

a·cid'u·lous (-ləs) *adj.* **1.** somewhat acid or sour **2.** somewhat sarcastic **—a·cid'u·lous·ly** *adv.*

-acious [< L.] *a suffix meaning* inclined to, full of [*tenacious*]

-acity *a n.-forming suffix corresponding to* -ACIOUS [*tenacity*]

ack-ack (ak'ak') *n.* [echoic] [Slang] an antiaircraft gun or its fire

ac·knowl·edge (ək näl'ij) *vt.* -edged, -edg·ing [see KNOWLEDGE] **1.** to admit to be true **2.** to recognize the authority or claims of **3.** to respond to (a greeting, etc.) **4.** to express thanks for **5.** to state that one has received (a letter, etc.) **—ac·knowl'edg·ment, ac·knowl'edge·ment** *n.*

ACLU, A.C.L.U. American Civil Liberties Union

ac·me (ak'mē) *n.* [< Gr. *akmē*, a point, top] the highest point

ac·ne (ak'nē) *n.* [? < Gr. *akmē*: see prec.] a skin disease characterized by inflammation of the sebaceous glands, usually causing pimples on the face, etc.

ac·o·lyte (ak'ə līt') *n.* [< Gr. *akolouthos*, follower] **1.** *R.C.Ch.* a member of the highest of the four minor orders, who serves at Mass **2.** *same as* ALTAR BOY **3.** an attendant; helper

ac·o·nite (ak'ə nīt') *n.* [< Gr.] **1.** a poisonous plant with hoodlike flowers **2.** a drug made from its roots, formerly used in medicine

a·corn (ā'kôrn') *n.* [< OE. *æcern*, nut] the nut of the oak tree

acorn squash a kind of squash, acorn-shaped with a dark-green, ridged skin

a·cous·tic (ə kōōs'tik) *adj.* [< Fr. < Gr. *akouein*, to hear] **1.** having to do with hearing or acoustics **2.** designating a musical instrument whose tones are not electronically altered Also **a·cous'ti·cal** —**a·cous'ti·cal·ly** *adv.*

a·cous'tics (-tiks) *n.pl.* **1.** the qualities of a room, etc. that have to do with how clearly sounds can be heard in it **2.** [*with sing. v.*] the branch of physics dealing with sound

ac·quaint (ə kwānt') *vt.* [< L. *ad*, to + *cognoscere*, know] **1.** to inform **2.** to make familiar (*with*)

ac·quaint'ance *n.* **1.** knowledge got from personal experience **2.** a person whom one knows slightly —**ac·quaint'ance·ship'** *n.*

ac·qui·esce (ak'wē es') *vi.* **-esced'**, **-esc'ing** [< Fr. < L. *ad-*, to + *quiescere*, be at rest] to consent quietly without protest —**ac'qui·es'cence** *n.* —**ac'qui·es'cent** *adj.* —**ac'qui·es'cent·ly** *adv.*

ac·quire (ə kwīr') *vt.* **-quired'**, **-quir'ing** [< L. *ad-*, to + *quaerere*, seek] **1.** to gain by one's own efforts **2.** to get as one's own —**ac·quire'ment** *n.*

acquired character *Biol.* a modification of structure or function caused by environmental factors: now generally regarded as not inheritable: also **acquired characteristic**

ac·qui·si·tion (ak'wə zish'ən) *n.* **1.** an acquiring or being acquired **2.** something acquired

ac·quis·i·tive (ə kwiz'ə tiv) *adj.* eager to acquire money, etc.; grasping —**ac·quis'i·tive·ly** *adv.* —**ac·quis'i·tive·ness** *n.*

ac·quit (ə kwit') *vt.* **-quit'ted**, **-quit'ting** [< L. *ad*, to + *quietare*, to quiet] **1.** to release from a duty, etc. **2.** to declare not guilty of a charge **3.** to conduct (oneself); behave —**ac·quit'tal** *n.*

ac·quit'tance *n.* **1.** a settlement of, or release from, debt or liability **2.** a record of this

a·cre (ā'kər) *n.* [OE. *æcer*, field] **1.** a measure of land, 43,560 sq. ft. **2.** [*pl.*] lands; estate

a·cre·age (ā'kər ij, ā'krij) *n.* acres collectively

ac·rid (ak'rid) *adj.* [< L. *acris*, sharp] **1.** sharp or bitter to the taste or smell **2.** sharp or sarcastic in speech, etc. — **a·crid·i·ty** (a krid'ə tē) *n.* —**ac'rid·ly** *adv.*

ac·ri·mo·ny (ak'rə mō'nē) *n., pl.* **-nies** [< L. *acer*, sharp] bitterness or harshness of manner or speech —**ac'ri·mo'ni·ous** *adj.*

acro- [< Gr. *akros*, at the end or top] *a combining form meaning* highest, at the extremities

ac·ro·bat (ak'rə bat') *n.* [< Fr. < Gr. *akrobatos*, walking on tiptoe] a skilled gymnast, tumbler, etc. —**ac'ro·bat'ic** *adj.* —**ac'ro·bat'i·cal·ly** *adv.*

ac'ro·bat'ics (-iks) *n.pl.* [*also with sing. v.*] **1.** an acrobat's tricks **2.** any tricks requiring great skill

ac·ro·meg·a·ly (ak'rō meg'ə lē) *n.* [< Fr. < Gr. *akros* (see ACRO-) + *megas*, large] abnormal enlargement of the head, hands, and feet, caused by abnormal pituitary activity

ac·ro·nym (ak'rə nim) *n.* [< ACRO- + Gr. *onyma*, name] a word formed from the first (or first few) letters of several words, as *radar*

ac·ro·pho·bi·a (ak'rə fō'bē ə) *n.* [ACRO- + PHOBIA] an abnormal fear of high places

a·crop·o·lis (ə kräp''l is) *n.* [< Gr. *akros*, at the top + *polis*, city] the fortified hill of an ancient Greek city, esp. [A-] that of Athens, on which the Parthenon was built

a·cross (ə krôs') *adv.* **1.** crosswise **2.** from one side to the other —*prep.* **1.** from one side to the other of **2.** on the other side of **3.** into contact with by chance [he came *across* an old friend]

a·cros·tic (ə krôs'tik) *n.* [< Gr. *akros*, at the end + *stichos*, line of verse] a poem or other arrangement of words in which certain letters in each line, as the first or last, spell out a word, motto, etc.

a·cryl·ic fiber (ə kril'ik) [< ACR(ID) + -YL + -IC] any of a group of synthetic fibers derived from a compound of hydrogen cyanide and acetylene, and made into fabrics

act (akt) *n.* [< Fr. < L. *agere*, to do] **1.** a thing done **2.** a doing **3.** a decision (of a court, legislature, etc.) **4.** a main division of a drama or opera **5.** a short performance on a variety program **6.** something done merely for show —*vt.* **1.** to play the part of **2.** to perform in (a play) —*vi.* **1.** to

perform on the stage **2.** to behave as though playing a role **3.** to behave **4.** to function **5.** to serve as a spokesman (*for*) **6.** to have an effect (*on*) **7.** to appear to be — **act up** [Colloq.] to misbehave

ACTH [*a*(dreno)*c*(ortico)*t*(rophic) *h*(ormone)] a pituitary hormone that stimulates the hormone production of the adrenal cortex

act·ing (ak'tiŋ) *adj.* **1.** functioning **2.** temporarily doing the duties of another —*n.* the art of an actor

ac·tin·ic (ak tin'ik) *adj.* having to do with actinism — **actinic rays** violet or ultraviolet rays that produce chemical changes —**ac·tin'i·cal·ly** *adv.*

ac·ti·nide series (ak'tə nīd') a group of radioactive chemical elements from element 89 (actinium) through element 103 (lawrencium)

ac·tin·ism (ak'tən iz'm) *n.* [see ACTINIUM] that property of ultraviolet light, X-rays, etc. by which chemical changes are produced

ac·tin·i·um (ak tin'ē əm) *n.* [< Gr. *aktis*, ray] a radioactive chemical element found in pitchblende: symbol, Ac; at. wt., 227(?); at. no., 89

ac·ti·noid (ak'tə noid') *adj.* star-shaped

ac·tion (ak'shən) *n.* **1.** the doing of something **2.** a thing done **3.** [*pl.*] behavior **4.** an effect, as of a drug **5.** the way of working, as of a machine **6.** the moving parts, as of a gun **7.** the happenings, as in a story **8.** a lawsuit **9.** military combat **10.** [Slang] activity or excitement —**bring** (or **take**) **action** to start a lawsuit

ac'tion·a·ble (-ə b'l) *adj. Law* that gives cause for a lawsuit

ac·ti·vate (ak'tə vāt') *vt.* **-vat'ed**, **-vat'ing 1.** to make active **2.** to put (an inactive military unit) on an active status **3.** to make radioactive **4.** to aerate (sewage) so as to purify it —**ac'ti·va'tion** *n.* —**ac'ti·va'tor** *n.*

activated carbon a highly porous carbon that can adsorb gases, vapors, and colloidal particles

ac·tive (ak'tiv) *adj.* **1.** acting, working, etc. **2.** causing motion or change **3.** lively, quick, etc. **4.** requiring action [*active* sports] **5.** *Gram.* indicating the voice of a verb whose subject performs the action —*n. Gram.* the active voice —**ac'tive·ly** *adv.*

ac·tiv·ism (ak'tə viz'm) *n.* the doctrine or policy of taking direct action, esp. for political or social ends —**ac'tiv·ist** *adj., n.*

ac·tiv·i·ty (ak tiv'ə tē) *n., pl.* **-ties 1.** a being active **2.** liveliness **3.** a specific action [outside *activities*]

ac·tor (ak'tər) *n.* **1.** one who does something **2.** one who acts in plays, movies, etc. —**ac'tress** *n.fem.*

Acts (akts) the fifth book of the New Testament: full title, **The Acts of the Apostles**

ac·tu·al (ak'chōō wəl) *adj.* [< L. *agere*, to do] **1.** existing in reality; real **2.** existing at the time

ac'tu·al'i·ty (-wal'ə tē) *n.* **1.** reality **2.** *pl.* **-ties** an actual thing; fact

ac'tu·al·ize (-wə līz') *vt.* **-ized'**, **-iz'ing** to make actual or real —**ac'tu·al·i·za'tion** *n.*

ac'tu·al·ly *adv.* really

ac·tu·ar·y (ak'chōō wer'ē) *n., pl.* **-ies** [< L. *actuarius*, a clerk] one who calculates insurance risks, premiums, etc. —**ac'tu·ar'i·al** *adj.*

ac·tu·ate (ak'chōō wāt') *vt.* **-at'ed**, **-at'ing 1.** to put into action **2.** to cause to take action —**ac'tu·a'tion** *n.* —**ac'tu·a'tor** *n.*

a·cu·i·ty (ə kyōō'ə tē) *n.* [< Fr. < L. *acus*, a needle] keenness, as of thought or vision

a·cu·men (ə kyōō'mən, ak'yoo-) *n.* [< L. *acuere*, sharpen] keenness of mind; shrewdness

a·cute (ə kyōōt') *adj.* [< L. *acuere*, sharpen] **1.** sharp-pointed **2.** keen of mind; shrewd **3.** sensitive [*acute* hearing] **4.** severe or sharp, as pain **5.** severe but not chronic [an *acute* disease] **6.** very serious **7.** less than 90° [*acute* angles] —**a·cute'ly** *adv.* —**a·cute'ness** *n.*

acute accent a mark (´) showing the quality of a vowel, stress, etc.

-acy [ult. < Gr.] *a suffix meaning* quality, condition, etc. [*celibacy*]

ad (ad) *n.* [Colloq.] an advertisement

ad- [L.] *a prefix meaning* motion toward, addition to, nearness to: also spelled a-, ac-, af-, ag-, al-, an-, etc. before certain consonants

A.D. [L. *Anno Domini*, in the year of the Lord] of the Christian era: used with dates

ad·age (ad'ij) *n.* [Fr. < L. *ad-*, to + *aio*, I say] an old saying that most people regard as true

---

fat, āpe, cär; ten, ēven; is, bīte; gō, hôrn, tōōl, look; oil, out; up, fur; thin, *then*; zh, leisure; ŋ, ring; ə for *a* in *ago*; ' as in *able* (ā'b'l); ë, Fr. coeur; ö, Fr. feu; Fr. mon; ü, Fr. duc; r, Fr. cri; kh, G. doch, ich. ‡ foreign; < derived from

a·da·gio (ə dä′jō, -zhō) *adv.* [It. *ad agio*, at ease] *Music* slowly —*adj.* slow —*n., pl.* **-gios 1.** a slow movement in music **2.** a slow ballet dance

Ad·am (ad′əm) [Heb. < *ādām*, human being] *Bible* the first man

ad·a·mant (ad′ə mənt, -mant′) *n.* [< Gr. *a-*, not + *daman*, subdue] a very hard substance —*adj.* **1.** too hard to be broken **2.** inflexible; unyielding —**ad′a·man′tine** (-man′tēn, -tīn, -tin) *adj.*

Ad·ams (ad′əmz) **1. Henry,** 1838–1918; U.S. historian & writer **2. John,** 1735–1826; 2d president of the U.S. (1797–1801) **3. John Quin·cy** (kwin′sē), 1767–1848; 6th president of the U.S. (1825–29): son of *prec.*

Adam's apple the projection of cartilage in the front of the throat, esp. of a man

a·dapt (ə dapt′) *vt.* [< Fr. < L. *ad-*, to + *aptare*, to fit] **1.** to make suitable by changing **2.** to adjust (oneself) to new circumstances —*vi.* to adjust oneself —**a·dapt′a·bil′-i·ty** *n.* —**a·dapt′a·ble** *adj.* —**a·dapt′er, a·dapt′or** *n.*

ad·ap·ta·tion (ad′əp tā′shən) *n.* **1.** an adapting **2.** a thing or change resulting from adapting

a·dap·tive (ə dap′tiv) *adj.* **1.** showing adaptation **2.** able to adapt —**a·dap′tive·ly** *adv.*

A.D.C., ADC 1. aide-de-camp **2.** Aid to Dependent Children

add (ad) *vt.* [< L. *ad-*, to + *dare*, give] **1.** to join (*to*) so as to increase **2.** to state further **3.** to combine (numbers) into a sum —*vi.* **1.** to cause an increase (*to*) **2.** to find a sum —**add up** to seem reasonable —**add up to** to mean; signify

ad·dax (ad′aks) *n.* [L. < native Afr. word] a large antelope of N Africa, with long, twisted horns

ad·dend (ad′end, ə dend′) *n.* [< ADDENDUM] a number or quantity to be added to another

ad·den·dum (ə den′dəm) *n., pl.* **-da** (-də) [L.] a thing added, as an appendix to a book

ad·der (ad′ər) *n.* [< OE. *nædre*] **1.** a small poisonous snake of Europe; viper **2.** any of various other snakes

ad·der's-tongue (ad′ərz tuŋ′) *n.* **1.** *same as* DOGTOOTH VIOLET **2.** a fern with a narrow spike

ad·dict (ə dikt′; *for n.* ad′ikt) *vt.* [< L. *addicere*, give assent] **1.** to give (oneself) up (*to* some strong habit): usually in the passive **2.** to make an addict of —*n.* one addicted —**ad·dic′tion** *n.* —**ad·dic′tive** *adj.*

Ad·dis A·ba·ba (ä′dis ä′bə bə) capital of Ethiopia: pop. 644,000

Ad·di·son (ad′ə s′n), **Joseph** 1672–1719; Eng. essayist & poet —**Ad′di·so′ni·an** (-sō′nē ən) *adj.*

ad·di·tion (ə dish′ən) *n.* **1.** an adding to get a sum **2.** a joining of one thing to another **3.** a thing added on to another **4.** a room or rooms added on —**in addition (to)** besides; as well (as) —**ad·di′tion·al** *adj.* —**ad·di′tion·al·ly** *adv.*

ad·di·tive (ad′ə tiv) *adj.* **1.** of addition **2.** to be added —*n.* something added, as a preservative

ad·dle (ad′′l) *adj.* [< OE. *adela*, dirt] **1.** rotten: said of an egg **2.** muddled; confused —*vt., vi.* **-dled, -dling** to make or become rotten or confused

ad′dle·brained′ (-brānd′) *adj.* mentally muddled: also **ad′dle·head′ed, ad′dle·pat′ed** (-pāt′id)

ad·dress (ə dres′; *for n., esp. 2, 3, & 4, also* ad′res) *vt.* [< L. *dirigere*, to direct] **1.** to direct (words *to*) **2.** to speak or write to **3.** to write the destination on (a letter or parcel) **4.** to apply or direct, as oneself —*n.* **1.** a speech **2.** the place where one lives or gets mail **3.** the destination indicated as on mail **4.** the location in a computer's storage compartment of an item of information **5.** social skill and tact **6.** conversational manner

ad·dress·ee (ad′res ē′, ə dres′ē′) *n.* one to whom a letter, package, etc. is addressed

ad·duce (ə dōōs′, -dyōōs′) *vt.* **-duced′, -duc′ing** [< L. *adducere*, lead to] to give as a reason or proof; cite —**ad·duc′i·ble, ad·duce′a·ble** *adj.*

-ade [ult. < L.] *a suffix meaning:* **1.** the act of [*blockade*] **2.** participant(s) [*brigade*] **3.** drink made from [*lemonade*]

Ad·e·laide (ad′′l ād′) city in S Australia: pop. 727,000

A·den (äd′′n, ād′-) **1.** former Brit. colony in SW Arabia: now part of YEMEN (sense 2) **2.** seaport there: pop. 250,000 **3. Gulf of,** arm of the Arabian Sea, between S Arabia and E Africa

ad·e·nine (ad′′n ēn′) *n.* [< Gr. *adēn*, gland + -INE[3]] a crystalline base derived from an acid formed in the pancreas, spleen, etc.

ad·e·noid (ad′′n oid′) *adj.* [< Gr. *adēn*, gland + -OID] **1.** glandular **2.** of or like lymphoid tissue

ad′e·noi′dal *adj.* **1.** adenoid **2.** nasal or stertorous because of enlarged adenoids

ad·e·noids (ad′′n oidz′) *n.pl.* lymphoid growths, sometimes enlarged, in the throat, behind the nose

ad·e·no·ma (ad′′n ō′mə) *n.* [< Gr. *adēn*, gland + -*ōma*, tumor] a benign glandular tumor

a·den·o·sine (ə den′ə s′n, -sēn′) *n.* [< ADENINE + RIBOSE] a white, powdery, crystalline glucoside of adenine and ribose: see also ADP

ad·ept (ə dept′; *for n.* ad′ept) *adj.* [< L. *ad-*, to + *apisci*, attain] highly skilled; expert —*n.* an expert —**ad·ept′ly** *adv.* —**ad·ept′ness** *n.*

ad·e·quate (ad′ə kwət) *adj.* [< L. *ad-*, to + *aequare*, make equal] meeting requirements; sufficient or suitable —**ad′e·qua·cy** *n.* —**ad′e·quate·ly** *adv.*

ad·here (əd hir′, ad-) *vi.* **-hered′, -her′ing** [< L. *ad-*, to + *haerere*, to stick] **1.** to stick fast; stay attached **2.** to stay firm in supporting or approving —**ad·her′ence** *n.* —**ad·her′ent** *adj., n.*

ad·he·sion (-hē′zhən) *n.* **1.** a sticking or being stuck together **2.** devoted attachment **3.** *Physics* the force holding together the molecules of unlike substances in surface contact

ad·he·sive (-siv, -ziv) *adj.* **1.** sticking **2.** gummed; sticky —*n.* an adhesive substance, as glue —**ad·he′sive·ly** *adv.* —**ad·he′sive·ness** *n.*

adhesive tape tape with a sticky substance on one side, used as for holding bandages in place

ad hoc (ad′ häk′) [L., to this] for this case only

a·dieu (ə dyōō′, -dōō′; *Fr.* ä dyö′) *interj., n., pl.* **a·dieus′;** *Fr.* **a·dieux′** (-dyö′) [Fr.] goodbye

ad in·fi·ni·tum (ad in′fə nīt′əm) [L., to infinity] endlessly; forever; without limit

ad in·ter·im (ad in′tər im) [L.] **1.** in the meantime **2.** temporary

a·di·os (a′dē ōs′, ä′-; *Sp.* ä dyôs′) *interj.* [Sp.] goodbye; farewell

ad·i·pose (ad′ə pōs′) *adj.* [< L. *adeps*, fat] of or like animal fat; fatty —*n.* animal fat —**ad′i·pos′i·ty** (-päs′ə tē) *n.*

Ad·i·ron·dack Mountains (ad′ə rän′dak) mountain range in NE N.Y.: also **Ad′i·ron′dacks**

adj. 1. adjective **2.** adjutant

ad·ja·cent (ə jā′s′nt) *adj.* [< L. *ad-*, to + *jacere*, to lie] near or close (*to*); adjoining —**ad·ja′cen·cy** *n.* —**ad·ja′-cent·ly** *adv.*

ad·jec·tive (aj′ik tiv) *n.* [< L. *adjicere*, add to] a word, as *big*, qualifying a noun or other substantive —*adj.* of or like an adjective —**ad′jec·ti′val** (-tī′v′l) *adj.* —**ad′jec·ti′-val·ly** *adv.*

ad·join (ə join′) *vt., vi.* [< L. *ad-*, to + *jungere*, join] to be next to (another) —**ad·join′ing** *adj.*

ad·journ (ə jurn′) *vt.* [< L. *ad-*, to + *diurnus*, daily] to put off or suspend until a future time —*vi.* **1.** to close a session or meeting for a time **2.** [Colloq.] to go (*to* another place) [*let's adjourn to the patio*] —**ad·journ′ment** *n.*

ad·judge (ə juj′) *vt.* **-judged′, -judg′ing** [< L. *ad-*, to + *judicare*, to judge] **1.** to decide by law **2.** to order or declare by law **3.** to sentence by law

ad·ju·di·cate (ə jōō′də kāt′) *vt.* **-cat′ed, -cat′ing** [see prec.] *Law* to hear and decide (a case); adjudge —*vi.* to act as a judge (*in* or *on*) —**ad·ju′di·ca′tion** *n.* —**ad·ju′di·ca′tive** *adj.* —**ad·ju′di·ca′tor** *n.*

ad·junct (aj′uŋkt) *n.* [see ADJOIN] **1.** an added, secondary thing **2.** a subordinate associate **3.** *Gram.* a modifier —**ad·junc·tive** (ə juŋk′tiv) *adj.*

ad·jure (ə joor′) *vt.* **-jured′, -jur′ing** [< L. *ad-*, to + *jurare*, swear] **1.** to charge solemnly as under oath **2.** to beseech —**ad′ju·ra′tion** *n.*

ad·just (ə just′) *vt.* [< L. *ad*, to + *juxta*, near] **1.** to change so as to make fit, suitable, etc. **2.** to regulate, as a watch **3.** to settle rightly **4.** to decide the amount of, as an insurance claim —*vi.* to adapt oneself —**ad·just′er, ad·jus′tor** *n.* —**ad·just′ment** *n.*

ad·ju·tant (aj′ə tənt) *n.* [< L. *ad-*, to + *juvare*, to help] **1.** an assistant **2.** *Mil.* a staff officer who is an administrative assistant to the commanding officer **3.** a large stork of India and Africa

Adjutant General the U.S. Army general in charge of records, correspondence, etc.

ad-lib (ad′lib′) *vt., vi.* **-libbed′, -lib′bing** [< L. *ad libitum*, at pleasure] [Colloq.] to improvise (as words or gestures not in a script) —*n.* [Colloq.] something ad-libbed: also **ad lib** —*adj.* ad-libbed —*adv.* [Colloq.] in a free or ad-libbed way: also **ad lib**

Adm. 1. Admiral **2.** Admiralty

ad·man (ad'man') *n.*, *pl.* **-men'** (-men') a man whose work or business is advertising: also **ad man**

ad·min·is·ter (əd min'ə stər, ad-) *vt.* [< L. *ad-*, to + *ministrare*, serve] **1.** to manage or direct **2.** to dispense, give out, apply, etc., as justice or medicine **3.** to tender, as an oath or pledge **4.** *Law* to act as executor or administrator of (an estate) Also **ad·min'is·trate'** (-strāt'), **-trat'ed, -trat'ing** —*vi.* **1.** to act as administrator **2.** to provide help or service (*to*) —**ad·min'is·trant** *adj.*, *n.*

ad·min'is·tra'tion (-strā'shən) *n.* **1.** an administering or being administered **2.** [*often* A-] executive officials, as of a government, and their policies **3.** their term of office —**ad·min'is·tra'tive** *adj.*

ad·min'is·tra'tor (-tər) *n.* **1.** one who administers **2.** *Law* one appointed to settle an estate

ad·mi·ra·ble (ad'mər ə b'l) *adj.* deserving admiration; excellent —**ad'mi·ra·bly** *adv.*

ad·mi·ral (ad'mər əl) *n.* [< Ar. *amîr a'āli*, high leader] **1.** the commanding officer of a navy or fleet **2.** any of several high-ranking naval officers

ad'mi·ral·ty (-tē) *n.*, *pl.* **-ties 1.** the rank or authority of an admiral **2.** [*often* A-] a governmental department in charge of naval affairs **3.** maritime law or court

ad·mi·ra·tion (ad'mə rā'shən) *n.* **1.** an admiring **2.** a thing or person inspiring this

ad·mire (əd mīr', ad-) *vt.* **-mired', -mir'ing** [< L. *ad-*, at + *mirari*, to wonder] **1.** to regard with wonder, delight, and approval **2.** to have high regard for —**ad·mir'er** *n.* —**ad·mir'ing·ly** *adv.*

ad·mis·si·ble (əd mis'ə b'l, ad-) *adj.* that can or should be admitted, as evidence —**ad·mis'si·bil'i·ty** *n.* —**ad·mis'si·bly** *adv.*

ad·mis'sion (-mish'ən) *n.* **1.** an admitting or being admitted **2.** right of entry **3.** an entrance fee **4.** a thing conceded, confessed, etc.

ad·mit (əd mit', ad-) *vt.* **-mit'ted, -mit'ting** [< L. *ad-*, to + *mittere*, send] **1.** to permit or entitle to enter or use **2.** to allow; leave room for **3.** to have room for; hold **4.** to concede; grant **5.** to acknowledge; confess **6.** to permit to practice, as a profession —*vi.* **1.** to give entrance (*to*) **2.** to allow or warrant (with *of*) —**ad·mit'tance** *n.*

ad·mit'ted·ly *adv.* by admission or agreement

ad·mix (ad miks') *vt.*, *vi.* [ult. < L. *ad-*, to + *miscere*, to mix] to mix (a thing) in

ad·mix'ture (-chər) *n.* **1.** an admixing; mixture **2.** a thing or ingredient mixed in

ad·mon·ish (əd män'ish, ad-) *vt.* [< L. *ad-*, to + *monere*, warn] **1.** to warn; caution **2.** to reprove mildly **3.** to exhort —**ad·mo·ni·tion** (ad'mə nish'ən) *n.*

ad nau·se·am (ad' nô'zē əm, -shē-, -sē-) [L.] to the point of disgust

a·do (ə dōō') *n.* [ME. < dial. *at do*, to do] fuss

a·do·be (ə dō'bē) *n.* [Sp. < Coptic *tōbe*, brick] **1.** unburnt, sun-dried brick **2.** clay used for this **3.** a building of adobe

ad·o·les·cence (ad'l es''ns) *n.* the time of life between puberty and maturity; adolescent state

ad'o·les'cent *adj.* [< L. *ad-*, to + *alescere*, grow up] of, typical of, or in adolescence —*n.* an adolescent person; teen-ager

A·don·is (ə dän'is, -dō'nis) *Gr. Myth.* a young man loved by Aphrodite —*n.* a very handsome young man

a·dopt (ə däpt') *vt.* [< L. *ad-*, to + *optare*, choose] **1.** to take legally into one's own family and raise as one's own child **2.** to take as one's own **3.** to choose or accept —**a·dop'tion** *n.*

a·dop·tive (ə däp'tiv) *adj.* **1.** of adoption **2.** being such through adoption [*adoptive* parents]

a·dor·a·ble (ə dôr'ə b'l) *adj.* **1.** [Now Rare] worthy of adoration **2.** [Colloq.] delightful; charming —**a·dor'a·bly** *adv.*

ad·o·ra·tion (ad'ə rā'shən) *n.* **1.** an adoring **2.** great love or devotion

a·dore (ə dôr') *vt.* **a·dored', a·dor'ing** [< L. *ad-*, to + *orare*, speak] **1.** to worship as divine **2.** to love or honor greatly **3.** [Colloq.] to like very much —**a·dor'er** *n.* —**a·dor'ing·ly** *adv.*

a·dorn (ə dôrn') *vt.* [< L. *ad-*, to + *ornare*, to ornament] **1.** to add beauty or distinction to **2.** to ornament; decorate —**a·dorn'ment** *n.*

a·down (ə doun') *adv.*, *prep.* [Poet.] down

ADP [A(DENOSINE) *d*(*i*)*p*(*hosphate*)] a substance, $C_{10}H_{15}N_5O_{10}P_2$, of all living cells, essential to the energy processes of life

ad·re·nal (ə drē'n'l) *adj.* [AD- + RENAL] **1.** near the kidneys **2.** of the adrenal glands —*n. same as* ADRENAL GLAND

adrenal gland either of a pair of endocrine organs just above the kidneys: they produce various hormones

Ad·ren·al·in (ə dren''l in) *a trademark for* EPINEPHRINE —*n.* [a-] epinephrine: also **ad·ren'al·ine** (-in)

A·dri·at·ic (Sea) (ā'drē at'ik) arm of the Mediterranean between Italy and Yugoslavia

a·drift (ə drift') *adv.*, *adj.* **1.** drifting **2.** devoid of aim or purpose

a·droit (ə droit') *adj.* [Fr. < L. *ad-*, to + *dirigere*, to direct] skillful —**a·droit'ly** *adv.*

ad·sorb (ad sôrb', -zôrb') *vt.* [< L. *ad-*, to + *sorbere*, drink in] to collect, as a gas or liquid, in condensed form on a surface —**ad·sor'bent** *adj.*, *n.* —**ad·sorp'tion** (-sôrp'shən, -zôrp'-) *n.*

ad·u·late (aj'ə lāt') *vt.* **-lat'ed, -lat'ing** [< L. *adulari*, fawn upon] to flatter servilely —**ad'u·la'tion** *n.* —**ad'u·la'tor** *n.*

a·dult (ə dult', ad'ult) *adj.* [see ADOLESCENT] **1.** grown-up; mature **2.** of or for adults —*n.* an adult individual —**a·dult'hood** *n.*

a·dul·ter·ant (ə dul'tər ənt) *n.* an adulterating substance —*adj.* that adulterates

a·dul'ter·ate' (-tə rāt') *vt.* **-at'ed, -at'ing** [< L. *ad-*, to + *alter*, other] to make inferior, impure, etc. by adding a harmful, inferior, or unnecessary substance —**a·dul'ter·a'tion** *n.*

a·dul·ter·y (ə dul'tər ē) *n.*, *pl.* **-ies** [see ADULTERATE] voluntary sexual intercourse between a married person and another not the spouse —**a·dul'ter·er** *n.* —**a·dul'ter·ess** *n.fem.* —**a·dul'ter·ous** *adj.*

ad·um·brate (ad um'brāt, ad'əm brāt') *vt.* **-brat·ed,' -brat·ing** [< L. *ad-*, to + *umbra*, shade] **1.** to outline vaguely **2.** to foreshadow vaguely **3.** to obscure; overshadow —**ad'um·bra'tion** *n.*

adv. 1. adverb **2.** advertisement

ad va·lo·rem (ad' və lôr'əm) [L.] in proportion to the value: said of duties levied on imports according to their invoiced value: abbrev. **ad val.**

ad·vance (əd vans') *vt.* **-vanced', -vanc'ing** [< L. *ab-*, from + *ante*, before] **1.** to bring forward **2.** to raise, as in rank **3.** to help; further **4.** to put forward; propose **5.** to raise the rate of **6.** to pay (money) before due **7.** to lend —*vi.* **1.** to go forward **2.** to improve; progress **3.** to rise, as in rank —*n.* **1.** a moving forward **2.** an improvement; progress **3.** a rise, as in value **4.** [*pl.*] approaches to get favor, become acquainted, etc. **5.** a payment before due **6.** a loan —*adj.* **1.** in front [*advance* guard] **2.** beforehand [*advance* information] —**in advance 1.** in front **2.** ahead of time —**ad·vance'ment** *n.*

ad·vanced' *adj.* **1.** in front **2.** old **3.** being ahead or beyond **4.** higher than usual, as prices

ad·van·tage (əd van'tij) *n.* **1.** a better position or chance **2.** a favorable circumstance, event, etc. **3.** gain; benefit **4.** *Tennis* the first point scored after deuce —**take advantage of 1.** to use for one's own benefit **2.** to impose upon —**to advantage** so as to result in a good effect —**ad·van·ta·geous** (ad'vən tā'jəs) *adj.*

Ad·vent (ad'vent) *n.* [< L. *ad-*, to + *venire*, come] **1.** the period including the four Sundays just before Christmas **2.** *Theol. a)* Christ's birth *b) same as* SECOND COMING **3.** [a-] a coming or arrival

Ad·vent·ist (ad'vən tist) *n.* a member of any of various Christian sects holding that the Second Coming will soon occur —*adj.* of Adventists

ad·ven·ti·tious (ad'vən tish'əs) *adj.* [see ADVENT] not inherent; accidental —**ad'ven·ti'tious·ly** *adv.*

ad·ven·ture (əd ven'chər) *n.* [see ADVENT] **1.** an exciting or dangerous encounter, experience, or venture **2.** a stimulating or gratifying experience, often a romantic one **3.** a business venture or speculation **4.** a taste for excitement, danger, etc. —*vt.* **-tured, -tur·ing** to risk; venture —*vi.* **1.** to engage in adventure **2.** to take a risk —**ad·ven'tur·ous, ad·ven'ture·some** *adj.*

ad·ven'tur·er *n.* **1.** one having or liking adventures **2.** *same as* SOLDIER OF FORTUNE **3.** a financial speculator **4.** one trying to get ahead by questionable schemes —**ad·ven'tur·ess** *n.fem.*

ad·verb (ad'vurb) *n.* [< L. *ad-*, to + *verbum*, word] a word used to modify a verb, adjective, or another adverb and expressing time, place, degree, etc. —**ad·ver'bi·al** *adj.*, *n.* —**ad·ver'bi·al·ly** *adv.*

fat, āpe, cär; ten, ēven; is, bīte; gō, hôrn, tōōl, look; oil, out; up, fur; thin, then; zh, leisure; ŋ, ring; ə for *a* in *ago*; ' as in *able* (ā'b'l); ë, Fr. coeur; ö, Fr. feu; ü, Fr. mon; ü, Fr. duc; r, Fr. cri; kh, G. doch, ich. ‡ foreign; < derived from

ad·ver·sar·y (ad'vər ser'ē) *n., pl.* **-ies** [see ADVERT] an opponent; enemy

ad·verse (ad vurs', əd-; ad'vərs) *adj.* [see ADVERT] **1.** opposed **2.** unfavorable **3.** opposite in position

ad·ver·si·ty (ad vur'sə tē, əd-) *n., pl.* **-ties** affliction, misfortune, difficulty, trouble, etc.

ad·vert (ad vurt', əd-) *vi.* [< L. *ad-*, to + *vertere*, to turn] **1.** to turn one's attention (*to*) **2.** to allude

ad·vert'ent *adj.* attentive —**ad·vert'ence** *n.*

ad·ver·tise (ad'vər tīz') *vt.* **-tised'**, **-tis'ing** [see ADVERT] **1.** to tell about or praise (a product, service, etc.) as in a newspaper or on television, so as to sell **2.** to make known —*vi.* **1.** to advertise something **2.** to ask (*for*) by public notice —**ad'ver·tis'er** *n.* —**ad'ver·tis'ing** *n.*

ad·ver·tise·ment (ad'vər tīz'mənt, ad vur'tiz mənt) *n.* **1.** the act of advertising **2.** a public notice, usually paid for, as of things for sale, needs, etc.

ad·ver·tize (ad'vər tīz') *vt., vi.* **-tized'**, **-tiz'ing** *alt. sp. of* ADVERTISE —**ad'ver·tize'ment** *n.*

ad·vice (əd vīs') *n.* [< L. *ad-*, to + *videre*, to look] **1.** opinion given as to what to do **2.** [*usually pl.*] information or report

ad·vis·a·ble (əd vī'zə b'l) *adj.* to be advised; prudent —**ad·vis'a·bil'i·ty** *n.* —**ad·vis'a·bly** *adv.*

ad·vise (əd vīz') *vt.* **-vised'**, **-vis'ing** **1.** to give advice to; counsel **2.** to offer as advice; recommend **3.** to notify —*vi.* **1.** to discuss or consult (*with*) **2.** to give advice —**ad·vis'er, ad·vi'sor** *n.*

ad·vised' *adj.* showing or resulting from thought or advice: now chiefly in WELL-ADVISED, ILL-ADVISED

ad·vis·ed·ly (əd vī'zid lē) *adv.* with due consideration; deliberately

ad·vise'ment (-vīz'mənt) *n.* careful consideration —**take under advisement** to consider carefully

ad·vi·so·ry (əd vī'zər ē) *adj.* **1.** advising or empowered to advise **2.** of advice —*n., pl.* **-ries** a warning, esp. from the National Weather Service about weather conditions

ad·vo·cate (ad'və kit, -kāt'; *for v.* -kāt') *n.* [< L. *ad-*, to + *vocare*, to call] one pleading for or supporting something —*vt.* **-cat'ed, -cat'ing** to act as an advocate of —**ad'vo·ca·cy** (-kə sē) *n.* —**ad'vo·ca'tor** *n.*

advt. *pl.* **advts.** advertisement

adz, adze (adz) *n.* [OE. *adesa*] an axlike tool for trimming and smoothing wood

AEC, A.E.C. Atomic Energy Commission

a·e·des (ā ē'dēz) *n., pl.* **a·e'des** [Gr. *a-*, not + *hēdys*, sweet] the mosquito that carries the virus of yellow fever

Ae·ge·an (Sea) (ē jē'ən) sea between Greece and Turkey: an arm of the Mediterranean

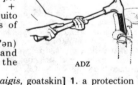

ADZ

ae·gis (ē'jis) *n.* [< Gr. *aigis*, goatskin] **1.** a protection **2.** sponsorship; auspices

Ae·ne·as (i nē'əs) *Gr. & Rom. Myth.* a Trojan warrior who escaped from ruined Troy, wandering many years

Ae·ne·id (i nē'id) *n.* a Latin epic poem by Virgil, about Aeneas and his adventures

ae·o·li·an harp (ē ō'lē ən) a boxlike instrument with strings vibrated musically by the wind

ae·on (ē'ən, ē'än) *n. alt. sp. of* EON

aer·ate (er'āt', ā'ər-) *vt.* **-at'ed, -at'ing** [AER(O)- + -ATE[1]] **1.** to make air go over or through **2.** to supply oxygen to (the blood) by respiration **3.** to charge (liquid) with gas, as in making soda water —**aer·a'tion** *n.* —**aer·a'tor** *n.*

aer·i·al (er'ē əl) *adj.* [< L. *aer*, air + -AL] **1.** of or like air **2.** unreal **3.** high up **4.** of aircraft or flying —*n.* an antenna for radio or television

aer·i·al·ist (-ist) *n.* an acrobat who performs on a trapeze, tightrope, etc.

aer·ie (er'ē, ir'ē) *n.* [< ML. *aeria*, area, but infl. by L. *aer*, air & ME. *ei*, egg] the high nest of an eagle or other such bird of prey

aer·o (er'ō) *adj.* of or for aeronautics or aircraft

aer·o- [< Gr. *aēr*, air] *a combining form meaning:* **1.** air **2.** aircraft or flying **3.** gas

aer·o·bic (er ō'bik) *adj.* [< Gr. *aēr* + *bios*, life] able to live, grow, or take place only where free oxygen is present

aer·o·dy·nam·ics (er'ō dī nam'iks) *n.pl.* [*with sing. v.*] aeromechanics dealing with forces exerted by air or other gas in motion —**aer'o·dy·nam'ic** *adj.*

aer'o·me·chan'ics (-mə kan'iks) *n.pl.* [*with sing. v.*] the branch of mechanics dealing with air or other gas in motion or in equilibrium

aer·o·nau·tics (er'ə nôt'iks) *n.pl.* [*with sing. v.*] [AERO- + Gr. *nautēs*, sailor + -ICS] the science of aircraft design or operation —**aer'o·nau'ti·cal, aer'o·nau'tic** *adj.* —**aer'o·nau'ti·cal·ly** *adv.*

aer'o·plane' (-plān') *n. Brit. var. of* AIRPLANE

aer'o·sol' (-sôl', -säl', -sōl') *n.* [AERO- + SOL(UTION)] a suspension of colloidal particles in a gas —*adj.* of or from a container that aerates and ejects liquid as a spray or foam

aer'o·space (er'ō spās') *n.* the earth's atmosphere and the space outside it

aer'o·stat' (-stat') *n.* [< Gr. *aēr*, air + *stasis*, a standing] a dirigible, balloon, or similar vehicle lifted and kept aloft by the buoyant effect of a contained gas that is lighter than air

Aes·chy·lus (es'kə ləs) 525?-456 B.C.; Gr. writer of tragedies

Aes·cu·la·pi·us (es'kyoo lā'pē əs) *Rom. Myth.* the god of medicine and healing

Ae·sop (ē'säp, -səp) real or legendary Gr. author of fables: supposed to have lived 6th cent. B.C.

aes·thete (es'thēt') *n.* [Gr. *aisthētēs*, one who perceives] **1.** one highly sensitive to art and beauty **2.** one artificially cultivating artistic sensitivity or making a cult of art and beauty —**aes·thet'i·cism** (-thet'ə siz'm) *n.*

aes·thet'ic (-thet'ik) *adj.* **1.** of aesthetics **2.** of or sensitive to art and beauty Also **aes·thet'i·cal** —*n.* the aesthetic principle —**aes·thet'i·cal·ly** *adv.*

aes·thet'ics (-iks) *n.pl.* [*with sing. v.*] the study or philosophy of art and beauty

Aet·na (et'nə) *same as* ETNA

a.f., A.F. audio-frequency

a·far (ə fär') *adv.* [Poet. or Archaic] at or to a distance —**from afar** from a distance

AFB Air Force Base

A.F.C., AFC automatic frequency control

AFDC, A.F.D.C. Aid to Families with Dependent Children

af·fa·ble (af'ə b'l) *adj.* [< L. *ad-*, to + *fari*, speak] **1.** easy to get along with; friendly **2.** gentle and kindly —**af'fa·bil'i·ty** *n.* —**af'fa·bly** *adv.*

af·fair (ə fer') *n.* [< L. *ad-*, to + *facere*, do] **1.** a thing to do **2.** [*pl.*] matters of business or concern **3.** any matter, occurrence, or thing **4.** a matter of public controversy **5.** a social gathering **6.** a sexual relationship outside of marriage

af·fect' (ə fekt') *vt.* [< L. *ad-*, to + *facere*, do] **1.** to have an effect on; influence **2.** to move or stir the emotions of —*n.* (af'ekt) Psychol. emotion or emotional response

af·fect² (ə fekt') *vt.* [< L. *affectare*, strive after] **1.** to like to have, use, etc. [she *affects* plaid coats] **2.** to pretend to have, feel, like, etc. [he *affects* lack of interest]

af·fec·ta·tion (af'ek tā'shən) *n.* **1.** mere show or appearance; pretense **2.** artificial behavior meant to impress others; also, a mannerism of this kind

af·fect·ed' *adj.* **1.** diseased **2.** influenced **3.** emotionally moved or stirred

af·fect·ed² *adj.* **1.** assumed for effect; artificial **2.** behaving in an artificial way so as to impress others —**af·fect'ed·ly** *adv.* —**af·fect'ed·ness** *n.*

af·fect'ing *adj.* emotionally moving; touching

af·fec·tion (ə fek'shən) *n.* **1.** fond or tender feeling **2.** a disease **3.** an affecting or being affected

af·fec'tion·ate *adj.* having or showing affection; fond; loving —**af·fec'tion·ate·ly** *adv.*

af·fec'tive *adj.* of affects, or feelings; emotional

af·fer·ent (af'ər ənt) *adj.* [< L. *ad-*, to + *ferre*, to bear] *Physiol.* bringing inward; specif., designating nerves transmitting impulses to a nerve center: opposed to EFFERENT

af·fi·ance (ə fī'əns) *vt.* **-anced, -anc·ing** [< L. *ad-*, to + *fidare*, to trust] to pledge, esp. in marriage; betroth

af·fi·da·vit (af'ə dā'vit) *n.* [ML., he has made oath] a written statement made on oath before a notary public or other authorized person

af·fil·i·ate (ə fil'ē āt') *vt.* **-at'ed, -at'ing** [< L. *ad-*, to + *filius*, son] **1.** to take in as a member **2.** to associate (oneself) —*vi.* to associate oneself; join —*n.* (-it) one affiliated; member —**af·fil'i·a'tion** *n.*

af·fin·i·ty (ə fin'ə tē) *n., pl.* **-ties** [< L. *ad-*, to + *finis*, the end] **1.** relationship by marriage **2.** relationship; connection **3.** a likeness implying common origin **4.** a natural liking; also, mutual attraction **5.** the attractive force between atoms

af·firm (ə furm') *vt.* [< L. *ad-*, to + *firmare*, make firm] **1.** to declare positively; state to be true **2.** to confirm; ratify —*vi.* to declare solemnly but not under oath —**af·firm'a·ble** *adj.* —**af·fir·ma·tion** (af'ər mā'shən) *n.*

af·firm·a·tive (ə fur'mə tiv) *adj.* saying or indicating "yes"; expressive of agreement or acceptance; not negative —*n.* an affirmative word, statement, etc. —**in the affirmative** in assent or agreement; in an affirmative way — **the affirmative** the side upholding the proposition being debated —**af·firm'a·tive·ly** *adv.*

af·fix (ə fiks') *vt.* [< L. *ad-*, to + *figere*, to fix] **1.** to fasten; attach **2.** to add at the end —*n.* (af'iks) **1.** a thing affixed **2.** a prefix or suffix

af·fla·tus (ə flāt'əs) *n.* [< L. *ad-*, to + *flare*, to blow] inspiration, as of an artist

af·flict (ə flikt') *vt.* [< L. *ad-*, to + *fligere*, to strike] to pain or make suffer; distress

af·flic·tion (ə flik'shən) *n.* **1.** pain; suffering; distress **2.** the cause or source of this

af·flu·ence (af'loo wəns) *n.* [< L. *ad-*, to + *fluere*, to flow] **1.** abundance **2.** wealth

af'flu·ent (-wənt) *adj.* **1.** abundant **2.** wealthy —*n.* a stream flowing into a river; tributary

af·ford (ə fôrd') *vt.* [OE. *geforthian*, to advance] **1.** to bear the cost of, as in money or time: usually with *can* or *be able* **2.** to undertake (*to* do something) because fit or equipped to do so: usually with *can* [I can *afford* to speak frankly] **3.** to make available; provide; furnish [to *afford* pleasure]

af·fray (ə frā') *n.* [ME. *affrai* < OFr.] a noisy quarrel or fight in public; brawl; fray

af·front (ə frunt') *vt.* [< L. *ad-*, to + *frons*, forehead] **1.** to insult openly or on purpose **2.** to confront defiantly — *n.* an open or intentional insult

Af·ghan (af'gan, -gən) *n.* **1.** a native of Afghanistan **2.** a hunting dog with silky hair and a long, narrow head **3.** [a-] a soft blanket or shawl, crocheted or knitted —*adj.* of Afghanistan

Af·ghan·i·stan (af gan'ə stan') country in SW Asia, between Iran and Pakistan: 250,000 sq. mi.; pop. 15,516,000; cap. Kabul

a·fi·cio·na·do (ə fish'ə nä'dō, -fis'ē ə-) *n., pl.* -dos [Sp. < L. *affectio*, warm liking] a devoted follower of some sport, art, etc.; devotee

a·field (ə fēld') *adv.* **1.** in, on, or to the field **2.** away (from home) **3.** off the right path; astray

a·fire (ə fīr') *adv., adj.* on fire

a·flame (ə flām') *adv., adj* afire

AFL-CIO American Federation of Labor and Congress of Industrial Organizations

a·float (ə flōt') *adv., adj.* **1.** floating freely **2.** at sea **3.** flooded **4.** drifting about **5.** in circulation, as a rumor **6.** out of difficulty

a·flut·ter (ə flut'ər) *adv., adj.* in a flutter

a·foot (ə foot') *adv.* **1.** on foot **2.** astir

a·fore (ə fôr') *adv., prep., conj.* [Archaic or Dial. except in compounds and in nautical use] before

a·fore'men'tioned (-men'shənd) *adj.* mentioned before or previously

a·fore'said' (-sed') *adj.* spoken of before; mentioned previously

a·fore'thought' (-thôt') *adj.* thought out beforehand; premeditated

a for·ti·o·ri (ā fôr'tē ôr'ē, -shē ôr'ī) [L.] with greater reason: used, in arguing, to introduce a point still stronger than one already accepted

a·foul (ə foul') *adv., adj.* in a collision or tangle —**run** (or **fall**) **afoul of** to get into trouble with

Afr. 1. Africa **2.** African

a·fraid (ə frād') *adj.* [ME. *affraied*] **1.** fearful; frightened **2.** [Colloq.] feeling regretful

a·fresh (ə fresh') *adv.* again; anew

Af·ri·ca (af'ri kə) second largest continent, in the Eastern Hemisphere, south of Europe: 11,500,000 sq. mi.; pop. 345,000,000

Af'ri·can (-kən) *adj.* of Africa, its peoples, etc. —*n.* a native of Africa

African violet any of several tropical African plants with hairy, dark-green leaves

Af·ri·kaans (af'ri känz') *n.* [Afrik.] an official language of South Africa, developed from 17th-cent. Dutch

Af·ri·ka·ner (af'ri kän'ər) *n.* [Du.] a South African of European, esp. Dutch, ancestry

Af·ro (af'rō) *adj.* [< inf.] designating or of a bouffant hair style, as worn by some Negroes

Afro- *a combining form meaning* Africa(n)

Af·ro-A·mer·i·can (af'rō ə mer'ə kən) *adj.* of Negro Americans —*n.* a Negro American

aft (aft) *adv.* [< OE. *afta*, behind] at, near, or toward the stern or back part of any ship

af·ter (af'tər) *adv.* [OE. *æfter*] behind in place or time; later or next —*prep.* **1.** behind in place or time **2.** in search of **3.** as a result of **4.** in spite of **5.** in the manner of **6.** for; in honor of **7.** concerning —*conj.* following the time when —*adj.* **1.** next; later **2.** rearward

af'ter·birth' *n.* the placenta and fetal membranes expelled from the uterus after a birth

af'ter·burn'er *n.* a device attached to some engines for burning or utilizing exhaust gases

af'ter·damp' *n.* an asphyxiating gas left in a mine after an explosion of firedamp

af'ter·ef·fect' *n.* a later or secondary effect

af'ter·glow' *n.* a glow remaining, as after sunset

af'ter·im'age *n.* a visual image continuing or returning after the external stimulus is withdrawn

af'ter·math' (-math') *n.* [AFTER + OE. *mæth*, cutting of grass] a result or consequence, esp. an unpleasant one

af'ter·most' *adj.* **1.** hindmost **2.** nearest the stern

af'ter·noon' *n.* the time from noon to evening —*adj.* in the afternoon

af'ter·taste' *n.* a taste lingering on

af'ter·thought' *n.* an added or later idea

af'ter·ward (-wərd) *adv.* later; subsequently: also **af'ter·wards**

Ag [L. *argentum*] *Chem.* silver

Ag. August

a·gain (ə gen'; *chiefly Brit.* -gān') *adv.* [< OE. *on-*, toward + *gegn*, direct] **1.** back to a former condition **2.** once more **3.** besides; further **4.** on the other hand —**again and again** repeatedly —**as much again** twice as much

a·gainst (ə genst'; *chiefly Brit.* -gānst') *prep.* [see prec.] **1.** in opposition to **2.** toward so as to strike **3.** in contrast with **4.** next to **5.** in preparation for **6.** as a charge on — **over against 1.** opposite to **2.** as compared with

Ag·a·mem·non (ag'ə mem'nän) *Gr. Myth.* commander in chief of the Greek army in the Trojan War

a·gape (ə gāp') *adv., adj.* [A- + GAPE] **1.** with the mouth wide open, as in wonder **2.** wide open

ag·ate (ag'ət) *n.* [< Gr. *achatēs*] **1.** a hard, semiprecious stone, a variety of chalcedony, with striped or clouded coloring **2.** a little ball of this or of glass, used in playing marbles

a·ga·ve (ə gä'vē) *n.* [< Gr. *agauos*, illustrious] a desert plant with tall flower stalks and thick, fleshy leaves

agcy. agency

age (āj) *n.* [< L. *aetas*] **1.** the length of time a person or thing has existed **2.** a particular period of life **3.** advanced years; oldness **4.** a generation **5.** a period in history, prehistory, or geological time **6.** [*often pl.*] [Colloq.] a long time —*vi., vt.* aged, ag'ing or age'ing to become or make old, older, or mature —**of age** of the age at which one has full legal rights

-age [< LL. *-aticum*] *a suffix meaning:* **1.** act, condition, or result [*usage*] **2.** amount or number [*acreage*] **3.** cost [*postage*] **4.** place [*steerage*] **5.** collection [*peerage*] **6.** home [*hermitage*]

a·ged (ā'jid *for 1 & 2*; ājd *for 3 & 4*) *adj.* **1.** grown old **2.** of old age **3.** properly matured **4.** of the age of —**the aged** (ā'jid) old people

age'less *adj.* **1.** not growing old **2.** eternal

age'long' *adj.* lasting a very long time

a·gen·cy (ā'jən sē) *n., pl.* -cies [see AGENT] **1.** action; power **2.** means **3.** the business or office of one authorized to act for another **4.** an administrative office of government

a·gen·da (ə jen'də) *n., pl.* -das [< L. *agere*, do] a program or list of things to be done or dealt with: also **a·gen'dum** (-dəm), *pl.* -da (-də), -dums

a·gent (ā'jənt) *n.* [< L. *agere*, do] **1.** one performing or effecting something or capable of doing so; specif., one acting for or representing another **2.** an active force or substance producing an effect

age-old (āj'ōld') *adj.* ages old; ancient

ag·er·a·tum (aj'ə rāt'əm) *n.* [< Gr. *a-*, not + *gēras*, old age] a plant belonging to the composite family and having small, thick heads of usually bluish flowers

ag·glom·er·ate (ə gläm'ə rāt') *vt., vi.* -at'ed, -at'ing [< L. *ad-*, to + *glomerare*, form into ball] to gather into a mass or ball —*adj.* (-ər it) so gathered —*n.* (-ər it) a jumbled heap, mass, etc. —**ag·glom'er·a'tion** *n.* —**ag·glom'er·a'tive** *adj.*

ag·glu·ti·nate (ə gloot''n it) *adj.* [< L. *ad-*, to + *gluten*, glue] stuck or clumped together —*vt., vi.* (-āt′) -nat′ed, -nat′ing to stick or clump together —ag·glu′ti·na′tion *n.* —ag·glu′ti·na′tive *adj.*

ag·gran·dize (ə gran′dīz′, ag′rən-) *vt.* -dized′, -diz′ing [< L. *ad-*, to + *grandis*, great] 1. to make greater, stronger, richer, etc. 2. to make seem greater —ag·gran′dize·ment (-diz mənt) *n.* —ag·gran′diz′er *n.*

ag·gra·vate (ag′rə vāt′) *vt.* -vat′ed, -vat′ing [< L. *ad-*, to + *gravis*, heavy] 1. to make worse 2. [Colloq.] to exasperate; annoy —ag′gra·va′tion *n.*

ag·gre·gate (ag′rə gət) *adj.* [< L. *ad-*, to + *grex*, a herd] total —*n.* a mass of distinct things gathered together; total —*vt.* (-gāt′) -gat′ed, -gat′ing 1. to gather into a mass 2. to amount to; total —in the aggregate taken all together —ag′gre·ga′tion *n.*

ag·gres·sion (ə gresh′ən) *n.* [< L. *ad-*, to + *gradi*, to step] 1. an unprovoked attack or warlike act 2. a being aggressive —ag·gres′sor *n.*

ag·gres·sive (ə gres′iv) *adj.* 1. ready to fight; quarrelsome 2. ready to undertake direct action; militant 3. bold and active; enterprising —ag·gres′sive·ly *adv.* —ag·gres′sive·ness *n.*

ag·grieve (ə grēv′) *vt.* -grieved′, -griev′ing [see AGGRAVATE] 1. to grieve, distress, or offend 2. to injure in one's legal rights

a·ghast (ə gast′) *adj.* [< OE. *a-*, intensive + *gast*, ghost] utterly horrified or dismayed

ag·ile (aj′'l; *chiefly Brit.* -īl) *adj.* [< L. *agere*, do] moving or thinking quickly and deftly; nimble —ag′ile·ly *adv.* — a·gil·i·ty (ə jil′ə tē) *n.*

ag·i·tate (aj′ə tāt′) *vt.* -tat′ed, -tat′ing [< L. *agere*, do] 1. to stir up; shake up 2. to excite; fluster 3. to keep discussing —*vi.* to keep talking and writing so as to change things —ag′i·tat′ed·ly *adv.* —ag′i·ta′tion *n.* —ag′i·ta′tor *n.*

a·glit·ter (ə glit′ər) *adv., adj.* glittering

a·glow (ə glō′) *adv., adj.* in a glow

ag·nos·tic (ag näs′tik) *n.* [< Gr. *a-*, not + base of *gignōskein*, know] one holding that it is impossible to know whether God or anything else beyond material phenomena exists —*adj.* of or characteristic of an agnostic —ag·nos′ti·cal·ly *adv.* —ag·nos′ti·cism (-tə siz′m) *n.*

a·go (ə gō′) *adj.* [< OE. *agan*, pass away] gone by; past [years *ago*] —*adv.* in the past [long *ago*]

a·gog (ə gäg′) *adv., adj.* [< OFr. < *a-*, to + *gogue*, joyfulness] with eager interest or excitement

ag·o·nize (ag′ə nīz′) *vi.* -nized′, -niz′ing 1. to make convulsive efforts; struggle 2. to be in agony —*vt.* to torture —ag′o·niz′ing adj.

ag·o·ny (ag′ə nē) *n., pl.* -nies [< Gr. *agōn*, a contest] 1. great mental or physical pain 2. death pangs 3. a convulsive struggle 4. a sudden, strong outburst (*of* emotion)

a·gou·ti, a·gou·ty (ə gōō′tē) *n., pl.* -tis, -ties [< SAmInd.] a rodent of tropical America, related to the guinea pig

a·grar·i·an (ə grer′ē ən) *adj.* [< L. *ager*, field] 1. of land or its ownership 2. of agriculture —*n.* one favoring equitable land division

a·gree (ə grē′) *vi.* -greed′, -gree′ing [< L. *ad-*, to + *gratus*, pleasing] 1. to consent 2. to be in harmony 3. to be of the same opinion 4. to arrive at an understanding 5. to be suitable, healthful, etc. (followed by *with*) [the climate *agrees* with him] 6. *Gram.* to correspond as in number —*vt.* to grant [I *agree* that it is so]

a·gree·a·ble *adj.* 1. pleasing 2. willing 3. conformable — a·gree′a·bil′i·ty *n.* —a·gree′a·bly *adv.*

a·gree′ment *n.* 1. an agreeing 2. a contract

ag·ri·busi·ness (ag′rə biz′nis) *n.* [AGRI(CULTURE) + BUSINESS] farming and the businesses and industries associated with farming

ag·ri·cul·ture (ag′ri kul′chər) *n.* [< L. *ager*, field + *cultura*, cultivation] the work of raising crops and livestock —ag′ri·cul′tur·al *adj.* —ag′ri·cul′tur·ist, ag′ri·cul′tur·al·ist *n.*

a·gron·o·my (ə grän′ə mē) *n.* [< Gr. *agros*, field + *nemein*, manage] the science and economics of raising crops —a·gron′o·mist *n.*

a·ground (ə ground′) *adv., adj.* on or onto the shore, a reef, etc. [the ship ran *aground*]

a·gue (ā′gyōō) *n.* [< ML. (*febris*) *acuta*, violent (fever)] 1. a fever, usually malarial, with regularly recurring chills 2. a fit of shivering

ah (ä) *interj.* an exclamation of pain, joy, etc.

a·ha (ä hä′) *interj.* an exclamation as of triumph

a·head (ə hed′) *adv., adj.* 1. in or to the front 2. onward 3. in advance 4. in a winning or leading position 5. in a profitable or advantageous position —get ahead to ad-

vance socially, financially, etc. —get ahead of to outdo or excel

a·hem (ə hem′) *interj.* a coughlike sound made to get attention, fill a pause, etc.

a·hoy (ə hoi′) *interj. Naut.* a call used in hailing

a·i (ä′ē) *n., pl.* a′is (-ēz) [< the animal's cry] a S. American sloth with three toes

aid (ād) *vt., vi.* [< L. *ad-*, to + *juvare*, to help] to give help (to); assist —*n.* 1. help; assistance 2. a helper 3. an aide; aide-de-camp

aide (ād) *n.* [Fr.] 1. a helper 2. an aide-de-camp

aide-de-camp (ād′də kamp′) *n., pl.* aides′-de-camp′ [Fr., lit., camp assistant] an officer, as in the army, serving as assistant to a superior

aid′man′ *n., pl.* -men′ an enlisted man in a medical corps in a combat area

ai·grette, ai·gret (ā′gret, ā gret′) *n.* 1. one or more of an egret's plumes used ornamentally, esp. formerly, as on a woman's hat 2. any ornamentation suggestive of this

ail (āl) *vt.* [< OE. < *egle*, harmful] to pain, distress, or trouble —*vi.* to be ill

ai·lan·thus (ā lan′thəs) *n., pl.* -thus·es [< native name in Malacca] a tree with pointed leaflets and with clusters of small, bad-smelling flowers

ai·le·ron (ā′lə rän′) *n.* [< L. *ala*, wing] a hinged section of an airplane wing, for control

ail′ing *adj.* in poor health; sickly

ail′ment (-mənt) *n.* an illness, esp. a mild one

aim (ām) *vi., vt.* [< L. *ad-*, to + *aestimare*, to estimate] 1. to point (a weapon) or direct (a blow, remark, etc.) 2. to direct (one's efforts) 3. to try or intend (*to* do or be something) —*n.* 1. an aiming 2. direction, as of a blow 3. intention or purpose —take aim to aim something

aim′less *adj.* having no aim or purpose; lacking direction —aim′less·ly *adv.* —aim′less·ness *n.*

ain't (ānt) [< *amn't*, contr. of *am not*] [Colloq.] am not: also a dialectal or substandard contraction for *is not*, *are not*, *has not*, and *have not*

air (er) *n.* [< Gr. *aēr*] 1. the invisible mixture of gases (chiefly nitrogen and oxygen, with some carbon dioxide, argon, etc.) surrounding the earth; atmosphere 2. space above the earth; sky 3. a movement of air 4. an outward appearance [an *air* of dignity] 5. a person's manner or bearing 6. [*pl.*] affected, superior manners 7. public expression [give *air* to his views] 8. transportation by aircraft 9. a song or melody —*adj.* of aircraft, air forces, etc. —*vt.* 1. to let air into, through, or onto 2. to publicize — *vi.* to become aired, dried, etc. —in the air 1. prevalent 2. not decided: also up in the air —on (or off) the air *Radio & TV* that is (or is not) broadcasting or being broadcast

air bag a large bag, as of nylon, installed in an automobile and, in a collision, inflating automatically to cushion and check a rider thrown forward

air base a base of operations for military aircraft

air bladder a sac with air or gas in it, found in most fishes, some other animals, and some plants

air′borne′ *adj.* 1. carried by air 2. flying; aloft

air brake 1. a brake operated by the action of compressed air on a piston 2. an airplane flap for reducing flight speed

air′brush′ *n.* a compressed-air atomizer to spray paint: also air brush —air′brush′ *vt.*

air′bus′ *n.* [AIR(PLANE) + BUS] an airplane designed for mass transportation of passengers; esp., such a plane scheduled for relatively short flights

air chamber a cavity or compartment full of air, esp. one used in hydraulics

air command the largest organizational unit of the U.S. Air Force

air′-con·di′tion *vt.* to provide with air conditioning — air′-con·di′tioned *adj.*

air conditioner a device for air conditioning

air conditioning mechanical control of the purity, humidity, and temperature of air within a building, room, car, etc.; esp., such control directed toward the dehumidifying and cooling of air

air′craft′ *n., pl.* -craft′ any machine or other device designed to fly, either heavier or lighter than air, as an airplane, glider, or passenger balloon

aircraft carrier an aircraft-carrying warship with a large, flat deck for the takeoff and landing of the aircraft

air·drome (er′drōm′) *n.* [< *air* + Gr. *dromos*, course] an area or place designed for the takeoff and landing of aircraft

air′drop′ *n.* the delivery of supplies or troops by parachute from an aircraft —*vt.* -dropped′, -drop′ping to deliver by parachute from an aircraft

Aire·dale (er'dāl') *n.* [< *Airedale,* valley in England] a large terrier with a wiry, tan coat

air'field' *n.* a field where aircraft take off and land; specif., the landing field of an airport

air·foil (er'foil') *n.* an aircraft wing, rudder, etc. interacting with the air through which it moves and so controlling lift, direction, etc.

air force 1. the aviation branch of armed forces **2.** in the U.S. Air Force, a unit lower than an air command

AIREDALE
(23 in. high
at shoulder)

air gun 1. a gun operated by compressed air **2.** a spraying device using compressed air

air hole 1. a hole letting air through **2.** an opening in the frozen surface of a pond, lake, etc.

air·i·ly (er'ə lē) *adv.* lightly; jauntily

air'i·ness *n.* **1.** the quality or state of being airy, or full of fresh air **2.** lack of heaviness; lightness, delicacy, etc. **3.** jauntiness

air'ing *n.* **1.** exposure to air, as for drying or freshening **2.** a walk or ride outdoors

air lane a prescribed route for travel by air

air'less *adj.* lacking air, esp. fresh air or any movement of air *[a hot, airless room]*

air'lift' *n.* a system of transporting troops, supplies, etc. by aircraft —*vt.* to transport by airlift

air'line' *n.* a system or company for moving passengers and freight by aircraft —*adj.* of, on, or by an airline

air'lin'er *n.* a large aircraft for many passengers

air lock an airtight compartment, with adjustable air pressure, between places of unequal pressure

air'mail' *n.* **1.** mail transportation by aircraft **2.** mail so transported —*vt.* to send by airmail

air'man (-mən) *n., pl.* **-men 1.** an aviator **2.** an enlisted person in the U.S. Air Force

air mass *Meteorol.* a large body of air maintaining virtually uniform conditions of temperature and moisture in a horizontal cross section as it moves

air·plane (er'plān') *n.* a power-driven winged aircraft that is lifted, supported, and maneuvered by the forces of air upon its airfoils

air pocket an atmospheric condition causing an airplane to make a sudden, short drop

air'port' *n.* a place where aircraft take off and land and where there are usually hangars, accommodations for passengers, etc.

air rifle a compressed-air rifle shooting BB's, etc.

air shaft 1. a passage through which fresh air can enter a tunnel, mine, etc. **2.** *same as* AIR WELL

air'ship' *n.* a steerable, self-propelled aircraft that is lighter than air

air'sick' *adj.* nauseated from traveling in an aircraft — **air'sick'ness** *n.*

air'space' *n.* **1.** space for maneuvering an aircraft **2.** space extending upward from a given land area

air'speed' *n.* the speed of an aircraft relative to the air rather than to the ground

air'strip' *n.* a temporary airplane runway

air taxi a small commercial airplane flying to places not regularly served by scheduled airlines

air'tight' *adj.* **1.** too tight for air to enter or escape **2.** unassailable *[an airtight alibi]*

air'waves' *n.pl.* the medium through which radio signals are transmitted

air'way' *n.* **1.** *same as:* a) AIR SHAFT (sense 1) b) AIR LANE c) [pl.] AIRWAVES **2.** *Med.* a respiratory passageway

air well an open shaft passing through the floors of a building so as to ventilate the building

air'y *adj.* **-i·er, -i·est 1.** of air **2.** open to the air; breezy **3.** unsubstantial as air; visionary **4.** light as air; graceful **5.** lighthearted; gay **6.** flippant **7.** [Colloq.] putting on airs; affected —**air'i·ly** *adv.* —**air'i·ness** *n.*

aisle (īl) *n.* [< L. *ala,* wing] **1.** a part of a church cut off by a row of columns or piers **2.** a passageway, as between rows of seats —**aisled** (īld) *adj.*

A·jac·cio (ä yät'chô) chief city of Corsica: birthplace of Napoleon: pop. 41,000

a·jar' (ə jär') *adv., adj.* [< OE. *cier,* a turn] slightly open, as a door

a·jar' (ə jär') *adv., adj.* [A-, on + JAR¹] not in harmony

A·jax (ā'jaks) *Gr. Myth.* a Greek hero in the Trojan War

AK Alaska

a·kim·bo (ə kim'bō) *adv., adj.* [ON. < *keng,* bent + *bogi,* a bow] with hands on hips and elbows bent outward [with arms *akimbo*]

a·kin (ə kin') *adj.* **1.** of one kin; related **2.** having similar qualities; similar

Ak·ron (ak'rən) city in N Ohio: pop. 275,000 (met. area 679,000)

-al [L.] *a suffix meaning:* **1.** of, like, or suitable for [*comical*] **2.** the act or process of [*denial*] **3.** [AL(DEHYDE)] *Chem.* a) an aldehyde [*chloral*] b) a barbiturate [*phenobarbital*]

Al *Chem.* aluminum

à la, a la (ä'lə) [Fr.] in the style of

Al·a·bam·a (al'ə bam'ə) Southern State of the SE U.S.: 51,609 sq. mi.; pop. 3,444,000; cap. Montgomery: abbrev. **Ala., AL** —**Al'a·bam'i·an** (-ē ən) *adj., n.*

al·a·bas·ter (al'ə bas'tər) *n.* [prob. < Egypt. name for "vessel of (the goddess) Bast"] **1.** a translucent, whitish variety of gypsum **2.** a streaked or mottled variety of calcite

a la carte (ä'lə kärt') [Fr., by the bill of fare] with a separate price for each item on the menu: opposed to TABLE D'HÔTE

a·lack (ə lak') *interj.* [A(H) + LACK] [Archaic] an exclamation of regret, surprise, dismay, etc.: also **a·lack'a·day'** (-ə dā')

a·lac·ri·ty (ə lak'rə tē) *n.* [< L. *alacer,* lively] eager willingness or readiness, often shown by quick, lively action —**a·lac'ri·tous** *adj.*

A·lad·din (ə lad'′n) a boy in *The Arabian Nights* who found a magic lamp and a magic ring

à la king (ä'lə kiŋ') [lit., in kingly style] diced and served in a sauce containing mushrooms, pimentos, and green peppers

Al·a·mo (al'ə mō') a mission at San Antonio, Tex.: scene of a massacre of Texans by Mexican troops (1836)

a la mode (al'ə mōd', ä'lə) [Fr.] **1.** in fashion **2.** made or served in a certain style, as (pie) with ice cream Also **à la mode, alamode**

a·lar (ā'lər) *adj.* [< L. *ala,* a wing] **1.** of or like a wing **2.** having wings

Al·a·ric (al'ə rik) 370–410 A.D.; king of the Visigoths (395?–410); captured Rome (410)

a·larm (ə lärm') *n.* [It. *all'arme,* to arms] **1.** [Archaic] a sudden call to arms **2.** a signal, sound, etc. to warn of danger **3.** a mechanism that warns of danger, arouses from sleep, etc. **4.** fear caused by danger —*vt.* **1.** to warn of danger **2.** to frighten

alarm clock a clock that can be set to ring, buzz, or flash a light at a desired time, as to awaken a person

a·larm'ing *adj.* frightening —**a·larm'ing·ly** *adv.*

a·larm'ist *n.* **1.** one who habitually spreads alarming rumors **2.** one who anticipates the worst —*adj.* of or like an alarmist

a·lar·um (ə ler'əm, -lär'-) *n.* [Archaic] alarm

a·las (ə las') *interj.* [< L. *lassus,* weary] an exclamation of sorrow, pity, regret, etc.

A·las·ka (ə las'kə) State of the U.S. in NW N. America: 586,400 sq. mi.; pop. 302,000: abbrev. **Alas., AK** —**A·las'kan** *adj., n.*

alb (alb) *n.* [< L. *albus,* white] a long, white linen robe worn by a priest at Mass

al·ba·core (al'bə kôr') *n.* [< Ar. *al,* the + *bakūrah,* albacore] any of various related saltwater fishes, as the tuna or bonito

Al·ba·ni·a (al bā'nē ə, -bān'yə) country in the W Balkans: 11,099 sq. mi.; pop. 2,019,000; cap. Tirana —**Al·ba'ni·an** *adj., n.*

Al·ba·ny (ôl'bə nē) capital of N.Y.: pop. 115,000

al·ba·tross (al'bə trôs') *n.* [< Ar. *al qādūs,* water container] any of several large, web-footed sea birds related to the petrel

ALB

al·be·it (ôl bē'it, al-) *conj.* [ME. *al be it,* al(though) it be] although; even though

Al·bert, Prince (al'bərt) 1819–61; husband of Queen Victoria of England

Al·ber·ta (al bʉr'tə) province of SW Canada: 255,285 sq. mi.; pop. 1,463,000; cap. Edmonton: abbrev. **Alta.**

al·bi·no (al bī'nō) *n., pl.* **-nos** [< L. *albus,* white] a person, animal, or plant lacking normal coloration: human albinos have white skin, whitish hair, and pink eyes —**al·bi·nism** (al'bə niz'm) *n.*

Al·bi·on (al'bē ən) [Poet.] England

al·bum (al′bəm) *n*. [< L. *albus*, white] **1**. a book with blank pages for mounting pictures, stamps, etc. **2**. *a*) a booklike holder for phonograph records *b*) a single long-playing record, not part of a set

al·bu·men (al byōō′mən) *n*. **1**. the white of an egg **2**. *same as* ALBUMIN

al·bu·min (al byōō′mən) *n*. [< L. *albus*, white] any of a class of water-soluble proteins found in milk, egg, muscle, blood, and in many plants —**al·bu′mi·nous** (-mə nəs) *adj*.

Al·bu·quer·que (al′bə kur′kē) city in C N.Mex.: pop. 244,000

Al·ca·traz (al′kə traz′) small island in San Francisco Bay

al·che·my (al′kə mē) *n*. [< Ar. < ? Gr. *cheein*, to pour] the chemistry of the Middle Ages, the chief aim of which was to change the baser metals into gold —**al·chem·ic** (al kem′ik), **al·chem′i·cal** *adj*. —**al·chem·ist** *n*.

al·co·hol (al′kə hôl′, -häl′) *n*. **1**. a colorless, volatile, pungent liquid, C_2H_5OH: it can be burned as fuel, is used in industry and medicine, and is the intoxicating element in whiskey, wine, beer, etc. **2**. any intoxicating liquor with this liquid in it **3**. any of a series of similarly constructed organic compounds with a hydroxyl group, as methyl (or wood) alcohol

al·co·hol·ic *adj*. **1**. of, containing, or caused by alcohol **2**. suffering from alcoholism —*n*. one who has chronic alcoholism

al·co·hol·ism *n*. the habitual drinking of alcoholic liquor to excess, or a diseased condition caused by this

Al·cott (ôl′kət), **Louisa May** 1832–88; U.S. novelist

al·cove (al′kōv) *n*. [< Ar. *al*, the + *qubba*, an arch] **1**. a recessed section of a room **2**. a summerhouse

al·de·hyde (al′də hīd′) *n*. [< AL(COHOL) + L. *de*, without + HYD(ROGEN)] a colorless fluid, CH_3CHO, obtained from alcohol by oxidation

Al·den (ôl′d′n), **John** 1599?-1687; Pilgrim settler in Plymouth Colony

al·der (ôl′dər) *n*. [< OE. *alor*] any of a group of trees and shrubs of the birch family, having durable wood and growing in cool, moist regions

al·der·man (ôl′dər mən) *n*., *pl*. **-men** [< OE. < *eald*, old + *man*] **1**. in some U.S. cities, a municipal officer representing a certain district or ward **2**. in England and Ireland, a senior member of a county or borough council —**al′der·man′ic** (-man′ik) *adj*.

Al·der·ney (ôl′dər nē) *n*., *pl*. **-neys** any of a breed of small dairy cattle originally from Alderney, one of the Channel Islands

ale (āl) *n*. [< OE. *ealu*] a fermented drink made from malt and hops, like beer, but produced by rapid fermentation at a relatively high temperature

a·lee (ə lē′) *adv*., *adj*. *Naut*. on or toward the lee

a·lem·bic (ə lem′bik) *n*. [< Ar. < *al*, the + *anbiq*, a still < Gr. *ambix*, a cup] **1**. an apparatus of glass or metal, formerly used for distilling **2**. anything that refines or purifies

A·lep·po (ə lep′ō) city in NW Syria: pop. 563,000

a·lert (ə lurt′) *adj*. [< L. *erigere*, to ERECT] **1**. watchful; vigilantly ready **2**. active; nimble —*n*. an alarm; warning signal —*vt*. to warn to be ready or watchful [the troops were *alerted*] —**on the alert** watchful; vigilant —**a·lert′ly** *adv*. —**a·lert′ness** *n*.

A·leu·tian Islands (ə lōō′shən) chain of islands of Alaska, extending c.1,200 mi. from the SW coast —**A·leu′tian** *adj*., *n*.

Al·ex·an·der the Great (al′ig zan′dər) 356–323 B.C.; king of Macedonia (336–323); military conqueror

Al·ex·an·dri·a (al′ig zan′drē ə) **1**. seaport in Egypt, on the Mediterranean: pop. 1,513,000 **2**. city in NE Va., near Washington, D.C.: pop. 111,000

al·ex·an·drine (al′ig zan′drin, -drēn) *n*. [*occas*. A-] *Prosody* an iambic line having six feet; iambic hexameter —*adj*. of an alexandrine or alexandrines

al·fal·fa (al fal′fə) *n*. [< Ar. *al-fasfasah*, the best fodder] a leguminous plant, much used for fodder, pasture, and as a cover crop

Al·fred the Great (al′frid) 849–900? A.D.; king of England (871–900?)

al·gae (al′jē) *n.pl.*, *sing*. **al′ga** (-gə) [L.] a group of plants, variously one-celled or colonial, containing chlorophyll and other pigments, found in water or damp places and including seaweeds —**al′gal** (-gəl) *adj*.

al·ge·bra (al′jə brə) *n*. [< Ar. *al*, the + *jabara*, to reunite] a mathematical system used to generalize certain arithmetical operations by use of letters or other symbols to stand for numbers: it is used esp. in the solution of polynomial equations —**al′ge·bra′ic** (-brā′ik) *adj*. —**al′ge·bra′i·cal·ly** *adv*.

Al·ger (al′jər), **Horatio** 1832–99; U.S. writer of boys' stories

Al·ge·ri·a (al jir′ē ə) country in N Africa: c.919,000 sq. mi.; pop. 13,547,000; cap. Algiers —**Al·ge′ri·an** *adj*., *n*.

-algia [< Gr. *algos*, pain] a suffix meaning pain [*neuralgia*]

Al·giers (al jirz′) capital of Algeria; seaport on the Mediterranean: pop. 943,000

Al·gon·qui·an (al gän′kē ən, -kwē-) *adj*. designating or of a widespread family of N. American Indian languages —*n*. **1**. this family of languages **2**. a member of any tribe using one of these languages

Al·gon·quin (al gän′kwin, -kin) *n*. **1**. a member of a tribe of Algonquian Indians of the Ottawa River area in Canada **2**. their Algonquian language

al·go·rithm (al′gər ith′m) *n*. [< *algorism*, Arabic system of numerals] *Math*. any special method of solving a certain kind of problem

Al·ham·bra (al ham′brə) a palace of the Moorish kings near Granada, Spain

a·li·as (ā′lē əs, āl′yəs) *n*., *pl*. **a′li·as·es** [< L., other] an assumed name —*adv*. otherwise named [Bell *alias* Jones]

A·li Ba·ba (ä′lē bä′bə, al′ē bab′ə) in *The Arabian Nights*, a poor woodcutter who finds the treasure of forty thieves in a cave

al·i·bi (al′ə bī′) *n*., *pl*. **-bis′** [L. < *alius ibi*, elsewhere] **1**. *Law* the plea that an accused person was elsewhere than at the scene of the crime **2**. [Colloq.] an excuse —*vi*. **-bied′**, **-bi′ing** [Colloq.] to offer an excuse

al·ien (āl′yən, -ē ən) *adj*. [< L. *alius*, other] **1**. foreign **2**. strange **3**. repugnant (*to*) **4**. of aliens —*n*. **1**. a foreigner **2**. a foreign-born resident who is not a naturalized citizen

al′ien·ate′ (-āt′) *vt*. **-at′ed**, **-at′ing 1**. to transfer the ownership of (property) to another **2**. to make unfriendly; estrange **3**. to cause a transference of (affection) —**al′ien·a·ble** *adj*. —**al′ien·a′tion** *n*. —**al′ien·a′tor** *n*.

al′ien·ee′ (-ē′) *n*. a person to whom property is transferred or conveyed

al′ien·ist *n*. a psychiatrist: term used in law

al′ien·or′ (-ôr′, -ər) *n*. a person from whom property is transferred or conveyed

a·light¹ (ə līt′) *vi*. **a·light′ed** or **a·lit′**, **a·light′ing** [ME. < *a-*, off + *lihtan*, to dismount] **1**. to get down or off; dismount **2**. to come down after flight

a·light² (ə līt′) *adj*. lighted up; glowing

a·lign (ə līn′) *vt*. [< Fr. < *a*, to + *ligne*, line] **1**. to bring into a straight line **2**. to bring (parts, as the wheels of a car) into proper coordination **3**. to bring into agreement, etc. —*vi*. to line up Also sp. **aline** —**a·lign′ment**, **a·line′ment** *n*.

a·like (ə līk′) *adj*. [< OE. *gelic*] like one another; similar —*adv*. **1**. similarly **2**. equally

al·i·ment (al′ə mənt) *n*. [< L. *alere*, to nourish] nourishment; food

al′i·men′ta·ry (-men′tər ē) *adj*. **1**. of food or nutrition **2**. nourishing

alimentary canal (or **tract**) the passage in the body (from mouth to anus) that food goes through

al·i·mo·ny (al′ə mō′nē) *n*. [< L. *alere*, to nourish] an allowance paid, esp. to a woman, by the spouse or former spouse after a legal separation or divorce

al·i·quant (al′ə kwənt) *adj*. [< L. *alius*, other + *quantus*, how much] *Math*. that does not divide a number evenly [8 is an *aliquant* part of 25]

al·i·quot (al′ə kwət) *adj*. [L. *alius*, other + *quot*, how many] *Math*. that divides a number evenly [8 is an *aliquot* part of 24]

a·lit (ə lit′) *alt. pt. & pp. of* ALIGHT¹

a·live (ə līv′) *adj*. [< OE. *on*, in + *life*, life] **1**. having life; living **2**. in existence, operation, etc. **3**. lively; alert —**alive to** fully aware of —**alive with** teeming with

al·ka·li (al′kə lī′) *n*., *pl*. **-lies′**, **-lis′** [< Ar. *al*, the + *qili*, ashes of a certain plant] **1**. any base, as soda, that is soluble in water and can neutralize acids **2**. any mineral salt that can neutralize acids

al′ka·line (-lin, -līn′) *adj*. of, like, or containing an alkali; basic —**al′ka·lin′i·ty** (-lin′ə tē) *n*.

al′ka·lize′ (-līz′) *vt*. **-lized′**, **-liz′ing** to make alkaline —**al′ka·li·za′tion** *n*.

al′ka·loid′ (-loid′) *n*. any of a number of basic organic substances, as caffeine, morphine, quinine, etc., found in certain plants

all (ôl) *adj*. [OE. *eall*] **1**. the whole quantity or extent of **2**. every one of [*all* men] **3**. the greatest possible [in *all* sincerity] **4**. any [beyond *all* doubt] **5**. alone; only [*all* work and no play] —*pron*. **1**. [with pl. v.] everyone [*all* are present] **2**. everything **3**. every part —*n*. **1**. everything one has [give your *all*] **2.** a totality; whole —*adv.* **1.** wholly; quite [*all* worn out] **2.** apiece [a score of two *all*] —**after all** nevertheless —**all but 1.** all except **2.** almost —**all in** [Colloq.] very tired —**all in all 1.** as a whole **2.** considering everything —**at all 1.** in the least **2.** in any way **3.** under any considerations —**for all** in spite of —**in all** altogether

all- *a combining form meaning:* **1.** wholly; entirely [*all-absorbing*] **2.** for every [*all-purpose*] **3.** of every part [*all-inclusive*]

Al·lah (al′ə, ä′lə, ä lä′) *the Muslim name for* GOD

all′-A·mer′i·can *adj.* chosen as the best in the U.S. —*n.* **1.** a hypothetical football (or other) team of college players chosen best of the year in the U.S. **2.** a player chosen for such a team

all′-a·round′ *adj.* having many abilities, talents, or uses; versatile

al·lay (ə lā′) *vt.* -**layed′**, -**lay′ing** [< OE. *a*-, down + *lecgan*, to lay] **1.** to put (fears, etc.) to rest; calm **2.** to lessen or relieve (pain, etc.)

all-clear (ôl′klir′) *n.* a signal that an air raid is over

al·le·ga·tion (al′ə gā′shən) *n.* **1.** an alleging **2.** an assertion **3.** an assertion without proof

al·lege (ə lej′) *vt.* -**leged′**, -**leg′ing** [< L. *ex*-, out of + *litigare*, to dispute] **1.** to declare or assert **2.** to assert without proof **3.** to give as a plea, excuse, etc.

al·leg′ed·ly (-id lē) *adv.* according to allegation

Al·le·ghe·ny (al′ə gā′nē) river in W Pa., joining the Monongahela to form the Ohio: 325 mi.

Allegheny Mountains mountain range of the Appalachians, in central Pa., Md., Va., and W.Va.: also **Al′le·ghe′nies**

al·le·giance (ə lē′jəns) *n.* [< OFr. *a*-, to + *ligeance* < L. *ligare*, to bind] **1.** the obligation of support and loyalty to one's ruler, government, or country **2.** loyalty; devotion, as to a cause

al·le·go·rize (al′ə gə rīz′) *vt.* -**rized′**, -**riz′ing** to treat as an allegory —*vi.* to use allegories

al·le·go·ry (al′ə gôr′ē) *n., pl.* -**ries** [< Gr. < *allos*, other + *agoreuein*, to speak] a story in which people, things, and happenings have another meaning, often instructive, as in a fable —**al′le·gor′i·cal** *adj.* —**al′le·gor′i·cal·ly** *adv.*

al·le·gret·to (al′ə gret′ō) *adj., adv.* [It., dim. of ALLEGRO] *Music* moderately fast

al·le·gro (ə leg′rō, -lā′grō) *adj., adv.* [It.] *Music* fast

al·le·lu·ia (al′ə loo̅′yə) *interj., n. same as* HALLELUJAH

Al·len·town (al′ən toun′) city in E Pa.: pop. 110,000

al·ler·gen (al′ər jən) *n.* [G. < *allergie*, ALLERGY + -*gen*, -GEN] a substance inducing an allergic state or reaction —**al′ler·gen′ic** (-jen′ik) *adj.*

al·ler·gic (ə lur′jik) *adj.* of, caused by, or having an allergy

al·ler·gist (al′ər jist) *n.* a doctor who specializes in treating allergies

al·ler·gy (al′ər jē) *n., pl.* -**gies** [< Gr. *allos*, other + *energēs*, active] an abnormal sensitivity to a specific substance (such as a food, pollen, dust, etc.) or condition (as heat or cold)

al·le·vi·ate (ə lē′vē āt′) *vt.* -**at′ed**, -**at′ing** [< L. *ad*-, to + *levis*, light] **1.** to lessen or relieve (pain, etc.) **2.** to reduce or decrease [to *alleviate* poverty] —**al·le′vi·a′tion** *n.* —**al·le′vi·a′tive** *adj.* —**al·le′vi·a′tor** *n.*

al·ley (al′ē) *n., pl.* -**leys** [< OFr. *aler*, go] **1.** a narrow street **2.** a long, narrow, wooden lane for bowling

al′ley·way′ *n.* an alley between buildings

All Fools′ Day *same as* APRIL FOOLS′ DAY

All-hal·lows (ôl′hal′ōz) *n.* [< OE. *ealle halgan* < *eall*, all + *halig*, holy] *same as* ALL SAINTS′ DAY

al·li·ance (ə lī′əns) *n.* **1.** an allying or being allied **2.** a close association, as of nations for a common objective or of families by marriage **3.** the countries, persons, etc. in such association

al·lied (ə līd′, al′īd) *adj.* **1.** united by kinship, treaty, etc. **2.** closely related **3.** [A-] of the Allies

Al·lies (al′īz′, ə līz′) *n.pl.* **1.** in World War I, the nations allied against the Central Powers **2.** in World War II, the nations allied against the Axis: esp., Great Britain, the U.S.S.R., and the U.S.

al·li·ga·tor (al′ə gāt′ər) *n.* [< Sp. *el lagarto* < L. *lacertus*, lizard] a large lizard of the U.S., similar to the crocodile but having a short, blunt snout

alligator pear *same as* AVOCADO

al·lit·er·ate (ə lit′ə rāt′) *vi.* -**at′ed**, -**at′ing 1.** to show alliteration **2.** to use alliteration

al·lit·er·a·tion (ə lit′ə rā′shən) *n.* [< L. *ad*-, to + *littera*, LETTER] repetition of an initial sound in two or more words of a phrase, etc. —**al·lit′er·a′tive** *adj.*

al·lo·cate (al′ə kāt′) *vt.* -**cat′ed**, -**cat′ing** [< L. *ad*-, to + *locus*, a place] **1.** to set apart for a specific purpose **2.** to distribute; allot —**al′lo·ca′tion** *n.*

al·lop·a·thy (ə läp′ə thē) *n.* [< Gr. *allos*, other + -*pathy*] treatment of disease by remedies that produce effects different from those produced by the disease: opposed to HOMEOPATHY —**al·lo·path·ic** (al′ə path′ik) *adj.*

al·lot (ə lät′) *vt.* -**lot′ted**, -**lot′ting** [OFr. *a*-, to + *lot*, lot] **1.** to distribute in shares; apportion **2.** to assign (a share) [each speaker is *allotted* ten minutes] —**al·lot′ment** *n.*

al·lo·trope (al′ə trōp′) *n.* an allotropic form

al·lot·ro·py (ə lät′rə pē) *n.* [< Gr. *allos*, other + *tropos*, manner] the property that certain chemical elements have of existing in two or more different forms, as carbon in charcoal, diamonds, etc.: also **al·lot′ro·pism** —**al·lo·trop·ic** (al′ə träp′ik) *adj.*

all′-out′ *adj.* complete or wholehearted [an *all-out* effort]

al·low (ə lou′) *vt.* [< L. *ad*-, to + *locus*, a place] **1.** to permit; let [I'm not *allowed* to go] **2.** to let have [*allowed* no sweets] **3.** to acknowledge as valid **4.** to provide (an extra quantity) as for shrinkage, waste, etc. —**allow for** to keep in mind —**allow of** to be subject to —**al·low′a·ble** *adj.* —**al·low′a·bly** *adv.*

al·low′ance (-əns) *n.* **1.** an allowing **2.** something allowed **3.** an amount given regularly, as money to a child or food to a soldier **4.** a reduction in price, as for a trade-in —*vt.* -**anced**, -**anc·ing 1.** to put on an allowance **2.** to apportion economically —**make allowance(s) for** to excuse because of mitigating factors

al·loy (al′oi) *n.* [< L. *ad*-, to + *ligare*, bind] **1.** a metal that is a mixture of two or more metals **2.** formerly, a less valuable metal mixed with a more valuable one **3.** a debasing addition —*vt.* (ə loi′) **1.** to make into an alloy **2.** to debase with an inferior addition

all right 1. satisfactory **2.** unhurt **3.** correct **4.** yes; very well **5.** [Colloq.] certainly

all′-round′ *adj. same as* ALL-AROUND

All Saints′ Day a church festival (November 1) in honor of all the saints

all·spice (ôl′spīs′) *n.* a spice, combining the tastes of several spices, made from the berry of a West Indian tree of the myrtle family

all′-star′ *adj.* made up entirely of outstanding or star performers

al·lude (ə lood′) *vi.* -**lud′ed**, -**lud′ing** [< L. *ad*-, to + *ludere*, to play] to refer indirectly (*to*)

al·lure (ə loor′) *vt., vi.* -**lured′**, -**lur′ing** [< OFr. *a*-, to + *lurer*, to LURE] to tempt with something desirable; attract —*n.* fascination; charm —**al·lure′ment** *n.* —**al·lur′ing** *adj.*

al·lu·sion (ə loo′zhən) *n.* **1.** an alluding **2.** an indirect or casual reference —**al·lu′sive** *adj.* —**al·lu′sive·ly** *adv.*

al·lu·vi·um (ə loo′vē əm) *n., pl.* -**vi·ums**, -**vi·a** (-vē ə) [< L. *ad*-, to + *luere*, wash] sand, clay, etc. deposited by flowing water —**al·lu′vi·al** *adj.*

al·ly (ə lī′) *vt.* -**lied′**, -**ly′ing** [< L. *ad*-, to + *ligare*, bind] **1.** to unite or join (*to* or *with*) for a specific purpose **2.** to relate by similarity of structure, etc. —*vi.* to become allied —*n.* (al′ī, ə lī′), *pl.* -**lies 1.** a country or person joined with another for a common purpose **2.** an associate

al·ma ma·ter (al′mə mät′ər, mät′ər) [L., fostering mother] **1.** the college or school that one attended **2.** its anthem

al·ma·nac (ôl′mə nak′) *n.* [< LGr. *almenichiaka*, calendar] **1.** a calendar with astronomical data, weather forecasts, etc. **2.** a book published annually, with varied information, records, etc.

al·might·y (ôl mīt′ē) *adj.* all-powerful —**the Almighty** God —**al·might′i·ly** *adv.* —**al·might′i·ness** *n.*

al·mond (ä′mənd, am′ənd, al′mənd) *n.* [< Gr. *amygdalē*] **1.** the edible, nutlike seed of a fruit like the peach **2.** the tree bearing this fruit —**al′mond·like′** *adj.*

al·mon·er (al′mən ər, ä′mən-) *n.* one who distributes alms, as for a church, etc.

al·most (ôl′mōst, ôl′mōst′) *adv.* very nearly; all but

alms (ämz) *n., pl.* **alms** [< Gr. *eleos*, pity] money, food, etc. given to poor people

alms′house′ *n.* a poorhouse

al·oe (al′ō) *n., pl.* -**oes** [< Gr. *aloē*] **1.** a South African plant related to the lily, with fleshy, spiny leaves **2.** [*pl., with sing. v.*] a laxative drug made from the juice of certain aloe leaves

---

fat, āpe, cär; ten, ēven; is, bīte; gō, hôrn, to̅o̅l, look; oil, out; up, fur; thin, *then*; zh, leisure; ŋ, ring; ə for *a* in *ago*; ′ as in *able* (ā′b'l); ë, Fr. coeur; ö, Fr. feu; Fr. mon; ü, Fr. duc; r, Fr. cri; kh, G. doch, ich. ‡ foreign; < derived from

a·loft (ə lôft′) *adv.* [< *a-*, on + *loft*] **1.** high up **2.** high above the deck of a ship

a·lo·ha (ə lō′ə, ä lō′hä) *n., interj.* [Haw., lit., love] a word used as a greeting or farewell

a·lone (ə lōn′) *adj., adv.* [< *all* + *one*] **1.** apart from anything or anyone else **2.** without any other person **3.** only —**let alone 1.** to refrain from bothering or interfering with **2.** not to speak of [we hadn't a dime, *let alone* a dollar]

a·long (ə lôŋ′) *prep.* [< OE. *and-*, over against + *-lang*, long] **1.** on or beside the length of **2.** in conformity with —*adv.* **1.** in a line; lengthwise **2.** progressively onward [he walked *along* slowly] **3.** as a companion **4.** with one [take your book *along*] —**all along** from the beginning —**get along 1.** to go forward **2.** to contrive **3.** to succeed **4.** to agree **5.** [Colloq.] to go away

a·long′side′ *adv.* at or by the side; side by side —*prep.* side by side with; beside

a·loof (ə lōōf′) *adv.* [< *a-*, on + Du. *loef*, to windward] at a distance but in view; apart —*adj.* cool and reserved [an *aloof* manner] —**a·loof′ly** *adv.* —**a·loof′ness** *n.*

a·loud (ə loud′) *adv.* **1.** loudly **2.** in an audible voice [read the letter *aloud*]

alp (alp) *n.* [< Alps] a high mountain

al·pac·a (al pak′ə) *n.* [Sp. < SAmInd. *allpaca*] **1.** a S. American mammal related to the llama **2.** its long, fleecy wool **3.** a cloth woven from this wool **4.** a glossy cloth of cotton and wool

al·pen·stock (al′pən stäk′) *n.* [G., Alpine staff] an iron-pointed staff used by mountain climbers

al·pha (al′fə) *n.* **1.** the first letter of the Greek alphabet (A, α) **2.** the beginning of anything

al·pha·bet (al′fə bet′) *n.* [< Gr. *alpha* + *beta*] the letters used in writing a language, arranged in a traditional order —**al′pha·bet′i·cal** *adj.* —**al′pha·bet′i·cal·ly** *adv.*

ALPACA (3 ft. high at shoulder)

al·pha·bet·ize (al′fə bə tīz′) *vt.* **-ized′, -iz′ing** to arrange in the usual order of the alphabet —**al′pha·bet′i·za′tion** (-bet′i zā′shən) *n.*

alpha particle a positively charged particle given off by certain radioactive substances: it consists of two protons and two neutrons

alpha ray a stream of alpha particles

Al·pine (al′pīn, -pin) *adj.* **1.** of the Alps **2.** [a-] of or like high mountains

Alps (alps) mountain system of SC Europe

al·read·y (ôl red′ē) *adv.* **1.** by or before the given or implied time **2.** even now or even then

al·right (ôl rīt′) *adv. var.* of ALL RIGHT: a disputed sp., but in common use

Al·sace (al säs′, al′sas) former province of NE France — **Al·sa′tian** (-sā′shən) *adj., n.*

Al·sace-Lor·raine (-lô rān′) region in NE France consisting of the former provinces of Alsace and Lorraine

al·so (ôl′sō) *adv.* [< OE. *eal*, all + *swa*, so] in addition; too: sometimes used in place of *and*

al′so-ran′ (-ran′) *n.* [Colloq.] any loser in a race, competition, election, etc.

alt. 1. alternate **2.** altitude **3.** alto

Alta. Alberta (Canada)

al·tar (ôl′tər) *n.* [< L. *altus*, high] **1.** a platform where sacrifices are made to a god, etc. **2.** a table, stand, etc. used for sacred purposes in a place of worship, as for Communion in Christian churches —**lead to the altar** to marry

altar boy a boy or man who helps a priest, vicar, etc. at religious services, esp. at Mass

al′tar·piece′ (-pēs′) *n.* an ornamental carving, painting, etc. above and behind an altar

al·ter (ôl′tər) *vt., vi.* [< L. *alter*, other] to change; make or become different —**al′ter·a·ble** *adj.*

al′ter·a′tion *n.* **1.** an altering **2.** the result of this

al·ter·cate (ôl′tər kāt′) *vi.* **-cat′ed, -cat′ing** [< L. *altercari*, to dispute] to quarrel

al′ter·ca′tion *n.* an angry or heated argument

al·ter e·go (ôl′tər ē′gō, eg′ō) [L., lit., other I] **1.** another aspect of oneself **2.** a very close friend

al·ter·nate (ôl′tər nit, al′-) *adj.* [< L. *alternus*, one after the other] **1.** succeeding each other **2.** every other —*n.* a substitute —*vt.* (-nāt′) **-nat′ed, -nat′ing** to do or use by turns —*vi.* **1.** to act, happen, etc. by turns **2.** to take turns regularly —**al′ter·nate·ly** *adv.* —**al′ter·na′tion** *n.*

alternating current an electric current that reverses its direction periodically

al·ter·na·tive (ôl tur′nə tiv, al-) *adj.* providing a choice between two (or, loosely, more than two) things —*n.* **1.** a choice between two or more things **2.** any of the things to be chosen —**al·ter′na·tive·ly** *adv.*

al·ter·na·tor (ôl′tər nāt′ər) *n.* an electric generator or dynamo producing alternating current

al·the·a, al·thae·a (al thē′ə) *n.* [< Gr. *althaia*, wild mallows] *same as* ROSE OF SHARON

alt·horn (alt′hôrn′) *n.* a brass-wind instrument, the alto saxhorn: also **alto horn**

al·though (ôl thō′) *conj.* in spite of the fact that; though: now sometimes sp. **altho**

al·tim·e·ter (al tim′ə tər, al′tə mēt′ər) *n.* an instrument for measuring altitude, as an aneroid barometer

al·ti·tude (al′tə tōōd′, -tyōōd′) *n.* [< L. *altus*, high] **1.** the height of a thing, esp. above sea level or the earth's surface **2.** a high place

al·to (al′tō) *n., pl.* **-tos** [It. < L. *altus*, high] **1.** the range of the lowest female or, esp. formerly, the highest male voice **2.** a singer with this range **3.** an instrument with a similar range —*adj.* of, in, for, or having this range

al·to·geth·er (ôl′tə geth′ər) *adv.* **1.** wholly; completely **2.** on the whole —**in the altogether** [Colloq.] nude

al·tru·ism (al′trōō iz′m) *n.* [< L. *alter*, other] unselfish concern for the welfare of others —**al′tru·ist** *n.* —**al′tru·is′tic** (-is′tik) *adj.* —**al′tru·is′ti·cal·ly** *adv.*

al·um (al′əm) *n.* [< L. *alumen*] a double sulfate of a trivalent metal and a univalent metal; esp., a double sulfate of potassium and aluminum, used in medicine and in making dyes, paper, etc.

al·u·min·ium (al′yoo min′yəm, -ē əm) *n. Brit. var.* of ALUMINUM

a·lu·mi·nize (ə lōō′mə nīz′) *vt.* **-nized′, -niz′ing** to cover, or treat, with aluminum

a·lu′mi·nous (-nəs) *adj.* of or containing alum or aluminum

a·lu·mi·num (ə lōō′mə nəm) *n.* [< L. *alumen*, alum] a silvery, lightweight, easily worked metallic chemical element: symbol, Al; at. wt., 26.9815; at. no., 13

a·lum·nus (ə lum′nəs) *n., pl.* **-ni** (-nī) [L., foster son] a boy or man who has attended or is a graduate of a particular school, college, etc. —**a·lum′na** (-nə) *n.fem., pl.* **-nae** (-nē)

al·way (ôl′wā) *adv.* [Archaic] always

al·ways (ôl′wiz, -wāz) *adv.* [see ALL & WAY] **1.** at all times **2.** all the time; forever

a·lys·sum (ə lis′əm) *n.* [< Gr. *alyssos*, curing madness] **1.** any of a number of garden plants, bearing white or yellow flowers **2.** *same as* SWEET ALYSSUM

am (am, əm) [OE. *eom*] *1st pers. sing., pres. indic.,* of BE

Am *Chem.* americium

AM amplitude modulation

A.M., AM [L. *Artium Magister*] master of arts

A.M., a.m., AM [L. *ante meridiem*] before noon: used to designate the time from midnight to noon

a·main (ə mān′) *adv.* [A-, on + MAIN, strength] [Archaic] **1.** forcefully **2.** at or with great speed

a·mal·gam (ə mal′gəm) *n.* [< Gr. *malagma*, an emollient] **1.** any alloy of mercury with another metal [silver *amalgam* is used as a dental filling] **2.** any mixture or blend

a·mal′ga·mate′ (-gə māt′) *vt., vi.* **-mat′ed, -mat′ing** to unite; mix; combine —**a·mal′ga·ma′tion** *n.*

a·man·u·en·sis (ə man′yoo wen′sis) *n., pl.* **-ses** (-sēz) [L. < *a-*, from + *manus*, a hand + *-ensis*, relating to] a secretary, stenographer, copyist, etc.

am·a·ranth (am′ə ranth′) *n.* [< Gr. *amarantos*, unfading] **1.** any of a family of plants, usually with colorful leaves **2.** [Poetic] an imaginary flower that never dies **3.** a dark purplish red —**am′a·ran′thine** (-ran′thin) *adj.*

Am·a·ril·lo (am′ə ril′ō) city in NW Texas: pop. 127,000

am·a·ryl·lis (am′ə ril′əs) *n.* [< Gr. name for a shepherdess] a bulb plant with white to red lilylike flowers

a·mass (ə mas′) *vt.* [< Fr. < L. *a-*, to + *massare*, to pile up] **1.** to pile up **2.** to accumulate (esp. wealth)

am·a·teur (am′ə choor, -toor, -tyoor) *n.* [< Fr. < L. *amare*, to love] **1.** one who engages in some art, sport, etc. for fun rather than for pay **2.** one who does something unskillfully —*adj.* of, done by, or being an amateur or amateurs —**am′a·teur′ish** *adj.* —**am′a·teur′ish·ly** *adv.* —**am′a·teur′ish·ness** *n.* —**am′a·teur·ism** *n.*

am·a·to·ry (am′ə tôr′ē) *adj.* [< L. *amare*, to love] of or showing love, esp. sexual love

a·maze (ə māz′) *vt.* **a·mazed′, a·maz′ing** [see MAZE] to fill with great surprise or wonder; astonish —**a·maz′ed·ly** (-id lē) *adv.* —**a·maz′ing·ly** *adv.*

a·maze′ment *n.* great surprise or wonder; astonishment

Am·a·zon (am′ə zän′) river in S. America: 3,300 mi. —n. 1. *Gr. Myth.* any of a race of female warriors 2. [a-] a large, strong, masculine woman —**Am′a·zo′ni·an** (-zō′nē ən) *adj.*

am·bas·sa·dor (am bas′ə dər) *n.* [< Pr. *ambaissador*] 1. the highest-ranking diplomatic representative of one country to another 2. an official messenger with a special mission —**am·bas′sa·do′ri·al** (-dôr′ē əl) *adj.* —**am·bas′sa·dor·ship′** *n.*

am·ber (am′bər) *n.* [< Ar. *'anbar,* ambergris] 1. a brownish-yellow fossil resin used in jewelry, etc. 2. its color —*adj.* amberlike or amber-colored

am′ber·gris (-grēs′, -gris′) *n.* [< Fr. *ambre gris,* gray amber] a grayish substance secreted by certain whales, used in making some perfumes

am′ber·jack′ (-jak′) *n.* a game fish of warm seas

am·bi- [< L. *ambo*] *a combining form meaning* both

am·bi·ance (am′bē əns) *n.* [Fr.: see AMBIENT] an environment or milieu: also **am′bi·ence**

am·bi·dex·trous (am′bə dek′strəs) *adj.* [see AMBI- & DEXTEROUS] able to use both hands with equal ease —**am′bi·dex·ter′i·ty** (-dek ster′ə tē) *n.*

am·bi·ent (am′bē ənt) *adj.* [< L. *ambire,* to go around] surrounding; on all sides

am·bi·gu·i·ty (am′bə gyoo′ə tē) *n.* 1. a being ambiguous 2. *pl.* **-ties** an ambiguous expression

am·big′u·ous (-yoo wəs) *adj.* [< L. *ambigere,* to wander around] 1. having two or more possible meanings 2. not clear; vague —**am·big′u·ous·ly** *adv.* —**am·big′u·ous·ness** *n.*

am·bi·tion (am bish′ən) *n.* [< L. *ambitio,* a going around (to solicit votes)] 1. a strong desire for fame, power, wealth, etc. 2. the thing so desired

am·bi′tious (-əs) *adj.* 1. full of or showing ambition 2. demanding great effort, skill, etc. —**am·bi′tious·ly** *adv.* —**am·bi′tious·ness** *n.*

am·biv·a·lence (am biv′ə ləns) *n.* [AMBI- + VALENCE] simultaneous conflicting feelings toward a person or thing —**am·biv′a·lent** *adj.*

am·ble (am′b'l) *vi.* **-bled, -bling** [< L. *ambulare,* to walk] 1. to move at an easy gait, raising first both legs on one side, then both on the other: said of a horse, etc. 2. to walk in a leisurely manner —*n.* 1. a horse's ambling gait 2. a leisurely walking pace —**am′bler** *n.*

am·bro·sia (am brō′zhə) *n.* [< Gr. *a-,* not + *brotos,* mortal] 1. *Gr. & Rom. Myth.* the food of the gods 2. anything that tastes or smells delicious —**am·bro′sial, am·bro′sian** *adj.*

am·bu·lance (am′byə ləns) *n.* [< L. *ambulare,* to walk] a vehicle equipped for carrying the sick or wounded

am′bu·lance-chas′er (-chās′ər) *n.* [Slang] a lawyer who encourages victims of accidents to sue for damages as his clients

am′bu·late′ (-lāt′) *vi.* **-lat′ed, -lat′ing** to move about; walk —**am′bu·lant** (-lənt) *adj.* —**am′bu·la′tion** *n.*

am′bu·la·to′ry (-lə tôr′ē) *adj.* 1. of or for walking 2. able to walk —*n., pl.* **-ries** any sheltered place for walking, as in a cloister

am·bus·cade (am′bəs kād′, am′bəs kād′) *n., vt., vi.* **-cad′ed, -cad′ing** same as AMBUSH

am·bush (am′boosh) *n.* [< ML. *in-,* in + *boscus,* woods] 1. an arrangement of persons in hiding to make a surprise attack 2. their hiding place —*vt., vi.* to attack from hiding

a·me·ba (ə mē′bə) *n., pl.* **-bas, -bae** (-bē) same as AMOEBA —**a·me′bic, a·me′ban** *adj.* —**a·me′boid** *adj.*

a·mel·io·rate (ə mēl′yə rāt′) *vt., vi.* **-rat′ed, -rat′ing** [< Fr. < L. *melior,* better] to make or become better; improve —**a·mel′io·ra·ble** *adj.* —**a·mel′io·ra′tion** *n.* —**a·mel′io·ra′tive** *adj.*

A·men (ā′mən) same as AMON

a·men (ā′men′, ä′-) *interj.* [< Heb. *āmēn,* truly] may it be so!: used after a prayer or to express approval

a·me·na·ble (ə mē′nə b'l, -men′ə-) *adj.* [< OFr. < L. *minare,* to drive (animals)] 1. responsible; answerable 2. responsive; submissive —**a·me′na·bil′i·ty** *n.* —**a·me′na·bly** *adv.*

a·mend (ə mend′) *vt.* [< L. *emendare,* to correct] 1. to correct; emend 2. to improve 3. to change or revise, as a law —*vi.* to improve one's conduct —**a·mend′a·ble** *adj.* —**a·mend′a·to′ry** *adj.*

a·mend′ment *n.* 1. a correction of errors, faults, etc. 2. an improvement 3. a revision or change proposed or made in a bill, law, etc.

a·mends (ə mendz′) *n.pl.* [*sometimes with sing. v.*] something given or done to make up for injury, loss, etc. that one has caused

a·men·i·ty (ə men′ə tē, -mē′nə-) *n., pl.* **-ties** [< L. *amoenus,* pleasant] 1. pleasantness 2. *a)* an attractive feature, as of a place *b)* a convenience 3. [*pl.*] the courtesies of polite behavior

am·ent (am′ənt, ā′mənt) *n.* [< L. *amentum,* thong] same as CATKIN

a·merce (ə murs′) *vt.* **a·merced′, a·merc′ing** [< OFr. *a merci,* at the mercy of] to punish, esp. by imposing a fine —**a·merce′ment** *n.*

A·mer·i·ca (ə mer′ə kə) [associated with *Amerigo* VESPUCCI] 1. North America and South America considered together 2. either North America or South America 3. the United States —**the Americas** America (sense 1)

A·mer·i·can (ə mer′ə kən) *adj.* 1. of or in America 2. of the U.S., its people, etc. —*n.* 1. a native or inhabitant of America; specif., *a)* an American Indian *b)* a citizen of the U.S. 2. the English language as used in the U.S.

A·mer·i·ca·na (ə mer′ə kan′ə, -kä′nə) *n.pl.* books, papers, objects, etc. having to do with America, its people, and its history

American cheese a kind of fairly hard, mild Cheddar cheese, popular in the U.S.

American Indian same as INDIAN (*n.* 2)

A·mer·i·can·ism (ə mer′ə kən iz′m) *n.* 1. a custom or belief of or originating in the U.S. 2. a word or idiom peculiar to American English 3. devotion or loyalty to the U.S., or to its traditions, customs, etc.

A·mer′i·can·ize′ (-īz′) *vt., vi.* **-ized′, -iz′ing** to make or become American in character, manners, etc. —**A·mer′i·can·i·za′tion** *n.*

American plan a system of hotel operation in which the charge to guests covers room, service, and meals

American Revolution the Revolutionary War (1775–1783), fought by the American colonies for independence from England, often including the series of events leading up to this, from 1763 to 1775

am·er·ic·i·um (am′ə rish′ē əm, -ris′-) *n.* [< AMERICA] a chemical element, one of the transuranic elements produced from plutonium: symbol, Am; at. wt., 243.13; at. no., 95

Am·er·ind (am′ə rind′) *n.* [AMER(ICAN) + IND(IAN)] an American Indian or Eskimo —**Am′er·in′di·an** *adj., n.*

am·e·thyst (am′ə thist) *n.* [< Gr. *amethystos,* not drunken (from the notion that it prevented intoxication)] 1. a purple variety of quartz or of corundum, used in jewelry 2. purple or violet

a·mi·a·ble (ā′mē ə b'l) *adj.* [< L. *amicus,* friend] good-natured; friendly —**a′mi·a·bil′i·ty** *n.* —**a′mi·a·bly** *adv.*

am·i·ca·ble (am′i kə b'l) *adj.* [see AMIABLE] friendly in feeling; peaceable —**am′i·ca·bil′i·ty** *n.* —**am′i·ca·bly** *adv.*

a·mid (ə mid′) *prep.* among; in the middle of

am·ide (am′īd, -id) *n.* [AM(MONIA) + -IDE] any of a group of organic compounds containing the CO·NH₂ radical or an acid radical in place of one hydrogen atom of an ammonia molecule

a·mid′ships′ *adv., adj.* in or toward the middle of a ship: also **a·mid′ship′**

a·midst (ə midst′) *prep.* same as AMID

a·mi·go (ə mē′gō) *n., pl.* **-gos** (-gōz) [Sp.] a friend

a·mine (ə mēn′, am′in) *n.* [AM(MONIA) + -INE³] a derivative of ammonia in which hydrogen atoms have been replaced by radicals containing hydrogen and carbon atoms —**a·mi·no** (ə mē′nō) *adj.*

amino acids a group of organic compounds that contain the amino radical and are structural units of proteins

Am·ish (ä′mish, am′ish) *n.pl.* [< Jacob *Ammann* (or *Amen),* the founder] Mennonites of a sect founded in the 17th cent. —*adj.* of this sect

a·miss (ə mis′) *adv.* [see A- & MISS¹] 1. astray 2. wrongly, faultily, etc. —*adj.* wrong, faulty, improper, etc.

am·i·ty (am′ə tē) *n., pl.* **-ties** [< L. *amicus,* friend] friendly, peaceful relations

Am·man (äm′än) capital of Jordan: pop. 330,000

am·me·ter (am′mēt′ər) *n.* [AM(PERE) + -METER] an instrument for measuring an electric current in amperes

am·mo (am′ō) *n.* [Slang] ammunition

am·mo·nia (ə mōn′yə) *n.* [ult. from a substance found near Libyan shrine of Jupiter *Ammon,* Roman-Egyptian god] 1. a colorless, pungent gas, NH₃, used in cleaning fluids, etc. 2. a water solution of this gas: also **ammonia water**

fat, āpe, cär; ten, ēven; is, bīte; gō, hôrn, tōōl, look; oil, out; up, fur; thin, *then*; zh, leisure; ŋ, ring; ə for *a* in *ago*; ′ as in *able* (ā′b'l); ë, Fr. coeur; ö, Fr. feu; Fr. mon; ü, Fr. duc; r, Fr. cri; kh, G. doch, ich. ‡ foreign; < derived from

am·mo·ni·um (ə mō′nē əm) *n.* the radical NH₄, present in salts produced by the reaction of ammonia with an acid

am·mu·ni·tion (am′yə nish′ən) *n.* [< L. *munire*, to fortify] **1.** anything hurled by a weapon or exploded as a weapon, as bullets, shells, bombs, grenades, etc. **2.** any means of attack or defense

am·ne·sia (am nē′zhə, -zhē ə) *n.* [< Gr. *a-*, not + *mnasthai*, to remember] partial or total loss of memory —**am·ne′si·ac′** (-zē ak′), **am·ne′sic** *adj., n.*

am·nes·ty (am′nəs tē) *n., pl.* **-ties** [< Gr. *amnēstia*, a forgetting] a general pardon, esp. for political offenses — *vt.* **-tied, -ty·ing** to grant amnesty to; pardon

am·ni·on (am′nē ən, -än′) *n., pl.* **-ni·ons, -ni·a** (-ə) [< Gr. *amnos*, lamb] the innermost membrane of the sac enclosing the embryo of a mammal, reptile, or bird —**am′ni·ot′ic** (-ät′ik) *adj.*

a·moe·ba (ə mē′bə) *n., pl.* **-bas, -bae** (-bē) [< Gr. *ameibein*, to change] a microscopic, one-celled animal multiplying by fission —**a·moe′bic, a·moe′ban** *adj.*

a·moe·boid (ə mē′boid) *adj.* like an amoeba, as in constantly changing shape

a·mok (ə muk′) *adj., adv.* [Malay *amoq*] **1.** in a frenzy to kill **2.** in a violent rage

A·mon (ä′mən) an ancient Egyptian deity, later identified with the sun god, **A′mon-Re′** (-rä′)

a·mong (ə muŋ′) *prep.* [< OE. *on*, in + *gemang*, a crowd] **1.** surrounded by [*among* friends] **2.** in the group of [best *among* books] **3.** with a share for each of [divided *among* us] **4.** by the joint action of

a·mongst (ə muŋst′) *prep. same as* AMONG

a·mon·til·la·do (ə män′tə lä′dō) *n.* [< Sp. < *Montilla*, a town in Spain] a pale, rather dry sherry

a·mor·al (ā môr′əl, -mär′-) *adj.* **1.** not to be judged by moral standards; neither moral nor immoral **2.** without moral principles —**a·mor·al·i·ty** (ā′mə ral′ə tē) *n.* — **a·mor′al·ly** *adv.*

am·o·rous (am′ər əs) *adj.* [< L. *amor*, love] **1.** fond of making love **2.** full of love **3.** of sexual love or lovemaking —**am′o·rous·ly** *adv.* —**am′o·rous·ness** *n.*

a·mor·phous (ə môr′fəs) *adj.* [< Gr. *a-*, without + *morphē*, form] **1.** shapeless **2.** of no definite type **3.** *Biol.* without specialized structure **4.** *Chem., Mineralogy* not crystalline —**a·mor′phism** *n.* —**a·mor′phous·ly** *adv.*

am·or·tize (am′ər tīz′, ə môr′-) *vt.* **-tized′, -tiz′ing** [< L. *ad*, to + *mors*, death] **1.** to put money aside at intervals for gradual payment of (a debt, etc.) **2.** *Accounting* to write off (expenditures) by prorating over a fixed period Brit. sp. **am′or·tise′, -tised′, -tis′ing** —**am′or·ti·za′tion** *n.*

A·mos (ā′məs) **1.** a Hebrew prophet of the 8th cent. B.C. **2.** a book of the Bible containing prophecies attributed to him

a·mount (ə mount′) *vi.* [< L. *ad*, to + *mons*, mountain] **1.** to add up (*to* a sum) **2.** to be equal in meaning, value, or effect —*n.* **1.** the sum of two or more quantities; total **2.** a principal sum plus its interest **3.** a quantity

a·mour (ə moor′) *n.* [Fr. < L. *amor*, love] a love affair, esp. an illicit one

amp. **1.** amperage **2.** ampere(s)

am·per·age (am′pər ij, am pir′-) *n.* the strength of an electric current in amperes

am·pere (am′pir) *n.* [after A. M. *Ampère* (1775–1836), Fr. physicist] the standard unit for measuring the strength of an electric current; rate of flow of charge of one coulomb per second

am·per·sand (am′pər sand′) *n.* [< *and per se and*, lit., (the sign) & by itself (is) *and*] a sign (&), meaning *and*

am·phet·a·mine (am fet′ə mēn′, -min) *n.* a colorless liquid, C₉H₁₃N, used as a drug to overcome depression, fatigue, etc. and to lessen the appetite

am·phib·i·an (am fib′ē ən) *n.* [see ff.] **1.** any of a class of vertebrates, including frogs, toads, salamanders, etc., that usually begin life in the water as tadpoles with gills, and later develop lungs **2.** any amphibious animal or plant **3.** an aircraft that can take off from or come down on either land or water **4.** a vehicle that can travel on either land or water —*adj. same as* AMPHIBIOUS

am·phib′i·ous (-əs) *adj.* [< Gr. *amphi-*, on both sides + *bios*, life] **1.** that can live both on land and in water **2.** that can operate on both land and water **3.** of or for a military operation involving the landing of troops from boats —**am·phib′i·ous·ly** *adv.*

am·phi·the·a·ter, am·phi·the·a·tre (am′fə thē′ə tər) *n.* [< Gr. *amphi-*, around + *theatron*, theater] a round or oval building with an open space (arena) surrounded by rising rows of seats

am·pho·ra (am′fər ə) *n., pl.* **-rae** (-ē), **-ras** [< Gr. *amphi-*,

on both sides + *pherein*, to bear] a tall jar with a narrow neck and base and two handles, used by the ancient Greeks and Romans

am·ple (am′p'l) *adj.* **-pler, -plest** [< L. *amplus*] **1.** large in size, extent, etc. **2.** more than enough; abundant **3.** adequate —**am′ply** *adv.*

am·pli·fi·er (am′plə fī′ər) *n.* **1.** a person or thing that amplifies **2.** an electronic device used to increase electrical signal strength

am·pli·fy (am′plə fī′) *vt.* **-fied′, -fy′ing** [< L. *amplus*, ample + *facere*, to make] **1.** to make stronger; esp., to strengthen (an electrical signal) **2.** to expand —*vi.* to expatiate —**am′pli·fi·ca′tion** *n.*

am·pli·tude (am′plə tōōd′) *n.* [see AMPLE] **1.** extent; largeness **2.** abundance **3.** scope or breadth **4.** the extreme range of a fluctuating quantity, from the average or mean to the extreme

amplitude modulation the changing of the amplitude of the transmitting radio wave in accordance with the signal being broadcast: distinguished from FREQUENCY MODULATION

am·pul (am′pool) *n.* [< Fr. < L. *ampulla*, bottle] a small glass container for one dose of a hypodermic medicine: also **am′pule** (-pyool), **am′pule** (-pōōl)

am·pu·tate (am′pyə tāt′) *vt.* **-tat′ed, -tat′ing** [< L. *am-*, for AMBI- + *putare*, to prune] to cut off (an arm, leg, etc.), esp. by surgery —**am′pu·ta′tion** *n.*

am·pu·tee (am′pyə tē′) *n.* a person who has had a limb or limbs amputated

Am·ster·dam (am′stər dam′) constitutional capital of the Netherlands: pop. 868,000

amt. amount

Am·trak (am′trak′) *n.* [*Am*(*erican*) *tr*(*avel*) (*tr*)*a*(*c*)*k*] a nationwide system of passenger railroad service

a·muck (ə muk′) *adj., adv. same as* AMOK

am·u·let (am′yə lit) *n.* [< L.] something worn on the body as a charm against evil

a·muse (ə myōōz′) *vt.* **a·mused′, a·mus′ing** [< Fr. *à*, at + OFr. *muser*, to stare fixedly] **1.** to keep pleasantly occupied; entertain **2.** to make laugh, smile, etc. —**a·mus′a·ble** *adj.* —**a·mus′er** *n.*

a·muse′ment (-mənt) *n.* **1.** a being amused **2.** something that amuses

amusement park an outdoor place with devices for entertainment, as a merry-go-round, etc.

am·yl·ase (am′ə lās′) *n.* [< Gr. *amylon*, starch] an enzyme that helps change starch into sugar, found in saliva, etc.

an (ən; *stressed* an) *adj., indefinite article* [< OE. *an*, one] **1.** one; one sort of **2.** each; any one **3.** per [two *an* hour] *An* is used before words beginning with a vowel sound [*an* eye, *an* honor, *an* ultimatum]

an, an′ (an) *conj.* [< *and*] **1.** [Dial.] and **2.** [Archaic] if

-an [< L. *-anus*] *an adj.-forming and n.-forming suffix meaning:* **1.** (one) belonging to [*diocesan*] **2.** (one) born in or living in [*American*] **3.** (one) believing in [*Mohammedan*]

a·nab·o·lism (ə nab′ə liz′m) *n.* [< Gr. *anabolē*, a rising up + -ISM] the biological process by which food is changed into living tissue

a·nach·ro·nism (ə nak′rə niz′m) *n.* [< Gr. *ana-*, against + *chronos*, time] **1.** anything out of its proper time in history **2.** the representation of this —**a·nach′ro·nis′tic** *adj.* —**a·nach′ro·nis′ti·cal·ly** *adv.*

an·a·con·da (an′ə kän′də) *n.* [< ?] **1.** a large S. American snake of the boa family **2.** any similar snake that crushes its victim in its coils

a·nae·mi·a (ə nē′mē ə) *n. same as* ANEMIA

an·aer·obe (an er′ōb, an′ə rōb′) *n.* [< Gr. *an-*, without + *aero-*, AERO- + *bios*, life] a microorganism that can live where there is no free oxygen —**an·aer·o·bic** (an′er ō′bik, -ə rō′-) *adj.*

an·aes·the·sia (an′əs thē′zhə) *n. same as* ANESTHESIA — **an′aes·thet′ic** *adj., n.* —**an·aes′the·tist** *n.* —**an·aes′the·tize′** *vt.* **-tized′, -tiz′ing**

an·a·gram (an′ə gram′) *n.* [< Gr. *anagrammatizein*, transpose letters] **1.** a word or phrase made from another by rearranging its letters (Ex.: *now—won*) **2.** [*pl., with sing. v.*] a game of forming words by arranging letters drawn randomly from a stock

An·a·heim (an′ə hīm′) city in SW Calif.: pop. 167,000

a·nal (ā′n'l) *adj.* of or near the anus

an·al·ge·si·a (an′'l jē′zē ə, -sē ə) *n.* [< Gr. *an-*, without + *algēsia*, pain] a state of not feeling pain although fully conscious

an′al·ge′sic (-zik, -sik) *adj.* of or causing analgesia —*n.* a drug producing analgesia

analog computer a computer that uses voltages to represent the numerical data of physical quantities

a·nal·o·gize (ə nal'ə jīz') vi., vt. -gized', -giz'ing to use, or explain by, analogy —a·nal'o·gist n.

a·nal'o·gous (-gəs) adj. [see ANALOGY] 1. similar or comparable in certain respects 2. Biol. similar in function but not in origin and structure —a·nal'o·gous·ly adv.

an·a·logue, an·a·log (an'ə lôg') n. a thing or part that is analogous —adj. of or by means of an analog computer: usually **analog**

a·nal·o·gy (ə nal'ə jē) n., pl. -gies [< Gr. ana-, according to + logos, ratio] 1. similarity in some respects 2. a comparing of something point by point with something similar 3. Biol. similarity in function but not in origin and structure

an·a·lyse (an'ə līz') vt. -lysed', -lys'ing chiefly Brit. sp. of ANALYZE

a·nal·y·sis (ə nal'ə sis) n., pl. -ses' (-sēz') [Gr. < ana-, up + lysis, a loosing] 1. a breaking up of a whole into its parts to find out their nature, etc. 2. a statement of these findings 3. same as PSYCHOANALYSIS 4. Chem. the separation of compounds and mixtures into their constituents to determine their nature or proportion —an·a·lyt·i·cal (an'ə lit'i k'l), an'a·lyt'ic adj. —an·a·lyt'i·cal·ly adv.

an·a·lyst (an'ə list) n. 1. a person who analyzes 2. same as PSYCHOANALYST

an'a·lyze (-līz') vt. -lyzed', -lyz'ing 1. to separate into parts so as to find out their nature, etc. 2. to examine carefully so as to determine the nature of 3. to psychoanalyze —an·a·lyz'a·ble adj. —an·a·lyz'er n.

an·a·pest, an·a·paest (an'ə pest') n. [< Gr. ana-, back + paiein, to strike] a metrical foot of three syllables, the first two unaccented and the third accented —an'a·pes'tic, an'a·paes'tic adj.

an·ar·chism (an'ər kiz'm) n. 1. the theory that all forms of government should be replaced by voluntary cooperation 2. resistance, sometimes by terrorism, to government

an'ar·chist (-kist) n. 1. a person who believes in anarchism 2. a promoter of anarchy —an·ar·chis'tic adj.

an'ar·chy (-kē) n. [< Gr. an-, without + archos, leader] 1. the complete absence of government 2. political disorder and violence 3. disorder; confusion —an·ar'chic (-är'kik), an·ar'chi·cal adj.

anat. 1. anatomical 2. anatomist 3. anatomy

a·nath·e·ma (ə nath'ə mə) n., pl. -mas [< Gr., thing devoted to evil] 1. a thing or person accursed 2. a thing or person greatly detested 3. a formal curse, as in excommunicating a person 4. any strong curse

a·nath'e·ma·tize' (-tīz') vt., vi. -tized', -tiz'ing to utter an anathema (against); curse

a·nat·o·mize (ə nat'ə mīz') vt., vi. -mized', -miz'ing 1. to dissect (an animal or plant) in order to study the structure 2. to analyze in detail —a·nat'o·mist n.

a·nat'o·my (-mē) n., pl. -mies [< Gr. ana-, up + temnein, to cut] 1. the dissecting of an organism in order to study its structure 2. the science of the structure of animals or plants 3. the structure of an organism 4. a detailed analysis —an·a·tom·i·cal (an'ə täm'i k'l), an'a·tom'ic adj. —an·a·tom'i·cal·ly adv.

-ance [< L.] a suffix meaning: 1. the act of [utterance] 2. a being [vigilance] 3. a thing that [conveyance] 4. a thing that is [dissonance, inheritance]

an·ces·tor (an'ses'tər) n. [< L. ante-, before + cedere, go] 1. a person from whom one is descended; forebear 2. an early type of animal from which later kinds have evolved 3. a predecessor —an'ces'tress (-trəs) n.fem.

an·ces·tral (an ses'trəl) adj. of or inherited from ancestors —an·ces'tral·ly adv.

an·ces·try (an'ses'trē) n., pl. -tries 1. family descent or lineage 2. ancestors collectively

an·chor (aŋ'kər) n. [< Gr. ankyra, a hook] 1. a heavy object, as an iron weight with flukes, lowered into the water by cable to keep a ship from drifting 2. anything giving security or stability —vt. to hold secure as by an anchor —vi. 1. to lower the anchor 2. to become fixed —at anchor anchored

an'chor·age (-ij) n. 1. money charged for the right to anchor 2. an anchoring or being anchored 3. a place to anchor

an·cho·rite (aŋ'kə rīt') n. [< Gr. ana-, back + chōrein, retire] a religious recluse; hermit: also **an'cho·ret** (-rit) —an'cho·ress n.fem.

ANCHOR

anchor man Radio & TV that member of a team of newscasters who coordinates various reports

an·cho·vy (an'chō'vē, -chə-; an'chō'vē) n., pl. -vies, -vy [< Port. anchova] a very small, herringlike fish

an·cient (ān'shənt) adj. [< L. ante, before] 1. of times long past 2. very old —n. an aged person —the ancients the people who lived in ancient times

an'cient·ly adv. in ancient times

an·cil·lar·y (an'sə ler'ē) adj. [< L. ancilla, maidservant] 1. subordinate (to) 2. auxiliary

and (and, ən, 'n; stressed and) conj. [OE.] 1. also; in addition 2. plus 3. as a result 4. [Colloq.] to [try and get it]

An·da·lu·sia (an'də lōō'zhə, -shə) n. region of S Spain — **An'da·lu'sian** adj., n.

an·dan·te (än dän'tā, an dan'tē) adj., adv. [< It. andare, to walk] Music moderate in tempo

An·der·sen (an'dər s'n), **Hans Christian** 1805–75; Dan. writer of fairy tales

An·des (Mountains) (an'dēz) mountain system along the length of W S. America —**An·de·an** (an dē'ən, an'dē-) adj.

and·i·ron (and'dī'ərn) n. [< OFr. andier] either of a pair of metal supports for holding wood in a fireplace

and/or either and or or, according to what is meant [personal and/or real property]

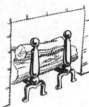

ANDIRONS

An·dor·ra (an dôr'ə) republic in the E Pyrenees, between Spain and France: 180 sq. mi.; pop. 19,000 — **An·dor'ran** adj., n.

An·drew (an'drōō) Bible one of the twelve apostles

an·dro·gen (an'drə jən) n. [< Gr. andros, man + -GEN] a male sex hormone that can give rise to masculine characteristics —an'dro·gen'ic (-jen'ik) adj.

An·drom·e·da (an dräm'ə də) 1. Gr. Myth. an Ethiopian princess whom Perseus rescued and then married 2. a northern constellation

an·ec·dote (an'ik dōt') n. [< Gr. anekdotos, unpublished] a short, entertaining account of some event —an'ec·dot'al (-dōt'l) adj.

a·ne·mi·a (ə nē'mē ə) n. [< Gr. a-, without + haima, blood] 1. a condition in which there is a reduction in the number of red blood corpuscles in the bloodstream 2. lifelessness —a·ne'mic (-mik) adj. —a·ne'mi·cal·ly adv.

an·e·mom·e·ter (an'ə mäm'ə tər) n. [< Gr. anemos, the wind + -METER] a gauge for determining the force or speed of the wind —an'e·mom'e·try n.

a·nem·o·ne (ə nem'ə nē') n. [< Gr., infl. by anemos, the wind] 1. a plant with cup-shaped flowers, usually white, purple, or red 2. same as SEA ANEMONE

a·nent (ə nent') prep. [< OE. on efen, lit., on even (with)] as regards; concerning

an·er·oid (an'ər oid') adj. [< Gr. a-, without + nēros, liquid + -OID] not using liquid —n. same as ANEROID BAROMETER

aneroid barometer a barometer in which a change in atmospheric pressure causes the elastic top of a box containing a partial vacuum to bend in or out, thus moving a pointer

an·es·the·sia (an'əs thē'zhə) n. [< Gr. an-, without + aisthēsis, feeling] a partial or total loss of the sense of pain, touch, etc., produced by disease or certain drugs

an'es·thet'ic (-thet'ik) adj. 1. of or with anesthesia 2. producing anesthesia —n. a drug, gas, etc. used to produce anesthesia —an'es·thet'i·cal·ly adv.

an·es·the·tist (ə nes'thə tist) n. a person trained to administer anesthetics

an·es'the·tize' (-tīz') vt. -tized', -tiz'ing to cause anesthesia in as by giving an anesthetic —an·es'the·ti·za'tion n.

an·eu·rysm, an·eu·rism (an'yər iz'm) n. [< Gr. ana-, up + eurys, broad] a sac formed by enlargement of an artery wall, caused by disease or injury

a·new (ə nōō') adv. again

an·gel (ān'j'l) n. [< Gr. angelos, messenger] 1. a) a messenger of God b) a supernatural being 2. a conventional image of a human figure with wings and a halo 3. a person regarded as beautiful, good, etc. 4. [Colloq.] a supporter who provides money, as for producing a play —an·gel·ic (an jel'ik), an·gel'i·cal adj. —an·gel'i·cal·ly adv.

---

fat, āpe, cär; ten, ēven; is, bīte; gō, hôrn, tōōl, lŏŏk; oil, out; up, fur; thin, then; zh, leisure; ŋ, ring; ə for a in ago; ' as in able (ā'b'l); ë, Fr. coeur; ö, Fr. feu; Fr. mon; ü, Fr. duc; r, Fr. cri; kh, G. doch, ich. ‡ foreign; < derived from

an·gel·fish (ān'j'l fish') *n., pl.:* see FISH a bright-colored tropical fish with spiny fins

angel food cake a light, spongy, white cake made with egg whites and no shortening: also **angel cake**

An·ge·lus (an'jə ləs) *n.* [L.: see ANGEL] [*also* a-] *R.C.Ch.* 1. a prayer said at morning, noon, and evening in commemoration of the Incarnation 2. a bell rung to announce the time for this

an·ger (aŋ'gər) *n.* [< ON. *angr,* distress] a feeling of displeasure and hostility resulting from injury, mistreatment, opposition, etc. —*vt.* to make angry —*vi.* to become angry

an·gi·na (an jī'nə) *n.* [< Gr. *anchein,* to squeeze] 1. any inflammatory disease of the throat, esp. one producing suffocation 2. *same as* ANGINA PECTORIS

angina pec·to·ris (pek'tər is) [L., angina of the breast] a condition marked by recurrent pain in the chest and left arm, caused by a sudden decrease of blood supply to the heart

an·gle[1] (aŋ'g'l) *n.* [< Gr. *ankylos,* bent] 1. the shape or space formed by two straight lines or plane surfaces that meet 2. the degrees of difference in direction between them 3. a sharp corner 4. a point of view 5. [Colloq.] a selfish motive or tricky plan —*vt., vi.* -gled, -gling 1. to move or bend at an angle 2. [Colloq.] to give a specific point of view to (a story, etc.)

an·gle[2] (aŋ'g'l) *vi.* -gled, -gling [OE. *angul,* fishhook] 1. to fish with a hook and line 2. to use tricks to get something [*angling* for attention] —*an'gler n.*

angle iron an angled piece of iron or steel used for joining or reinforcing two beams, etc.

An·gles (aŋ'g'lz) *n.pl.* a Germanic people that settled in E England in the 5th cent. A.D. —**An'gli·an** (-glē ən) *adj., n.*

an'gle·worm' *n.* an earthworm: so called because used as fishing bait

An·gli·can (aŋ'gli kən) *adj.* [< ML. *Anglicus,* of the Angles] 1. of England; English 2. of the Church of England or any related church with the same faith and forms —*n.* a member of an Anglican church

An·gli·cism (aŋ'glə siz'm) *n.* a word, idiom, trait, etc. peculiar to the English

An'gli·cize' (-sīz') *vt., vi.* -cized', -ciz'ing [*also* a-] to change to English idiom, pronunciation, customs, etc. —**An'gli·ci·za'tion** *n.*

an·gling (aŋ'gliŋ) *n.* the act or skill of fishing with hook and line

Anglo- *a combining form meaning* English [*Anglo-Norman*]

An·glo-Nor·man (aŋ'glō nôr'mən) *adj.* English and Norman —*n.* 1. a Norman settler in England after the Norman Conquest 2. the dialect of such settlers

An'glo-Sax'on (-sak's'n) *n.* 1. a member of the Germanic peoples living in England at the time of the Norman Conquest 2. *same as* OLD ENGLISH 3. a person of English nationality or descent —*adj.* of the Anglo-Saxons or their language

An·go·la (aŋ gō'lə) country on the W coast of Africa: 481,351 sq. mi.; pop. 5,362,000

An·go·ra (aŋ gôr'ə) *n.* [former name of ANKARA] 1. a kind of cat with long, silky fur 2. *a)* a kind of goat raised for its long, silky hair *b)* a cloth made from this hair; mohair: also **angora**

an·gos·tu·ra (bark) (an'gəs toor'ə) a bitter bark used as a tonic and as a flavoring in bitters

an·gry (aŋ'grē) *adj.* -gri·er, -gri·est 1. feeling or showing anger 2. wild and stormy —**an'gri·ly** *adv.*

ang·strom (aŋ'strəm) *n.* [after A. J. Ångström, 19th-c. Swed. physicist] one hundred-millionth of a centimeter, a unit used in measuring the length of light waves: also **angstrom unit**

an·guish (aŋ'gwish) *n.* [< L. *angustus,* narrow] great suffering, as from grief or pain; agony —*vt., vi.* to feel or make feel anguish —**an'guished** *adj.*

an·gu·lar (aŋ'gyə lər) *adj.* 1. having or forming an angle or angles; sharp-cornered 2. lean; gaunt 3. without ease or grace; awkward —**an'gu·lar'i·ty** (-ler'ə tē) *n., pl.* -ties —**an'gu·lar·ly** *adv.*

an·hy·drous (an hī'drəs) *adj.* [< Gr. *an-,* without + *hydōr,* water] 1. without water 2. *Chem.* having no water of crystallization

an·i·line (an''l in, -ēn') *n.* [< Ar. *al,* the + *nīl,* blue + -INE[3]] a colorless, oily liquid derivative of benzene, used in making dyes, etc.

an·i·mad·ver·sion (an'ə mad vur'zhən) *n.* a critical, esp. unfavorable, comment (*on* or *upon* something)

an'i·mad·vert' (-vurt') *vi.* [< L. *animus,* mind + *ad-,* to + *vertere,* to turn] to comment (*on* or *upon*), esp. with disapproval; criticize adversely

an·i·mal (an'ə m'l) *n.* [< L. *anima,* breath, soul] 1. any living organism except a plant or bacterium: most animals can move about 2. any such organism other than a human being 3. a brutish or inhuman person —*adj.* 1. of or like an animal 2. gross, bestial, etc. —**an'i·mal'i·ty** *n.*

an·i·mal·cule (an'ə mal'kyool) *n.* [< ModL. dim. of prec.] a very small or microscopic animal

an·i·mal·ism (an'ə m'l iz'm) *n.* 1. the activity, appetites, nature, etc. of animals 2. the doctrine that man is a mere animal with no soul —**an'i·mal·ist** *n.* —**an'i·mal·is'tic** *adj.*

an·i·mal·ize (an'ə mə līz') *vt.* -ized', -iz'ing to make (a person) resemble a beast; brutalize

an·i·mate (an'ə māt') *vt.* -mat'ed, -mat'ing [see ANIMAL] 1. to give life or motion to 2. to make gay or spirited 3. to inspire —*adj.* (-mit) 1. living 2. lively; spirited —**an'i·mat'ed** *adj.* —**an'i·ma'tor, an'i·mat'er** *n.*

animated cartoon a motion picture made by filming a series of drawings, each slightly changed from the one before, so that the figures in them seem to move when the film is projected

an'i·ma'tion *n.* 1. an animating or being animated 2. life 3. vivacity 4. *same as* ANIMATED CARTOON

an·i·mism (an'ə miz'm) *n.* [see ANIMAL & -ISM] 1. the doctrine that all life is produced by a spiritual force 2. the belief that all natural objects have souls —**an'i·mist** *n.* —**an'i·mis'tic** *adj.*

an·i·mos·i·ty (an'ə mäs'ə tē) *n., pl.* -ties [see ANIMUS] ill will; hostility

an·i·mus (an'ə məs) *n.* [L., passion] 1. an animating force 2. a feeling of ill will; animosity

an·i·on (an'ī'ən) *n.* [< Gr. *ana-,* up + *ienai,* to go] a negatively charged ion: in electrolysis, anions move toward the anode —**an'i·on'ic** (-än'ik) *adj.*

an·ise (an'is) *n.* [< Gr. *anēson*] 1. a plant related to parsley 2. its fragrant seed, used for flavoring: also **an·i·seed** (an'ə sēd')

An·ka·ra (aŋ'kə rə) capital of Turkey: pop. 906,000

an·kle (aŋ'k'l) *n.* [OE. *ancleow*] 1. the joint that connects the foot and the leg 2. the part of the leg between the foot and calf

an'kle·bone' *n.* the bone of the ankle

an·klet (aŋ'klit) *n.* 1. an ornament, etc. worn around the ankle 2. a short sock

an·nals (an''lz) *n.pl.* [< L. *annus,* year] 1. a written account of events year by year 2. historical records; history 3. any journal containing reports of a society, etc. —**an'nal·ist** *n.* —**an'nal·is'tic** *adj.*

An·nam (an am', an'am) region in EC Indochina, divided between North Vietnam and South Vietnam —**An'na·mese'** (-ə mēz') *adj., n., pl.* -mese'

An·nap·o·lis (ə nap'ə lis) capital of Md.: pop. 30,000

Ann Ar·bor (an är'bər) city in SE Mich.: pop. 100,000

an·neal (ə nēl') *vt.* [< OE. *an-,* on + *æl,* fire] 1. to heat (glass, metals, etc.) and then cool slowly to prevent brittleness 2. to temper (the mind, will, etc.) —**an·neal'er** *n.*

an·ne·lid (an''l id) *n.* [< Fr. < L. *anulus,* a ring] a worm with a body made of joined segments, as the earthworm

an·nex (ə neks') *vt.* [< L. *ad-,* to + *nectere,* to tie] 1. to attach, esp. to something larger 2. to add as a condition, etc. 3. to incorporate into a state, etc. the territory of (another state, etc.) —*n.* (an'eks) something added on; esp., an addition to a building —**an·nex'a·ble** *adj.* —**an'nex·a'tion** *n.*

an·ni·hi·late (ə nī'ə lāt') *vt.* -lat'ed, -lat'ing [< L. *ad-,* to + *nihil,* nothing] 1. to destroy completely; demolish 2. to kill —**an·ni'hi·la'tion** *n.* —**an·ni'hi·la'tor** *n.*

an·ni·ver·sa·ry (an'ə vur'sər ē) *n., pl.* -ries [< L. *annus,* year + *vertere,* to turn] 1. the date on which some event occurred in an earlier year 2. its celebration —*adj.* of, being, or connected with an anniversary

an·no Do·mi·ni (än'ō dō'mə nē) [L., lit., in the year of the Lord] in the (given) year since the beginning of the Christian Era

an·no·tate (an'ə tāt') *vt., vi.* -tat'ed, -tat'ing [< L. *ad-,* to + *nota,* a sign] to provide explanatory notes for (a literary work, etc.) —**an'no·ta'tion** *n.* —**an'no·ta'tive** *adj.* —**an'no·ta'tor** *n.*

an·nounce (ə nouns') *vt.* -nounced', -nounc'ing [< L. *ad-,* to + *nuntiare,* to report] 1. to declare publicly; proclaim 2. to say 3. to make known the arrival, etc. of 4. to be an announcer for —*vi.* to act as an announcer —**an·nounce'ment** *n.*

an·nounc'er *n.* 1. one who announces 2. one who introduces radio or television programs, identifies the station, etc.

an·noy (ə noi′) *vt.* [< L. *in odio habere,* to have in hate] **1.** to irritate, bother, or make somewhat angry **2.** to harm; harass —*vi.* to be annoying —**an·noy′er** *n.* —**an·noy′ing** *adj.* —**an·noy′ing·ly** *adv.*

an·noy′ance (-əns) *n.* **1.** an annoying or being annoyed **2.** that which annoys

an·nu·al (an′yoo wəl) *adj.* [< L. *annus,* year] **1.** of or measured by a year **2.** yearly **3.** for a year's time, work, etc. [an *annual* wage] **4.** living only one year or season — *n.* **1.** a yearly publication **2.** a plant that lives only one year or season —**an′nu·al·ly** *adv.*

an·nu·i·ty (ə noo′ə tē) *n., pl.* **-ties** [see prec.] **1.** a payment of a fixed sum of money at regular intervals, esp. yearly **2.** an investment yielding such payments

an·nul (ə nul′) *vt.* -nulled′, -nul′ling [< LL. *annullare,* to bring to nothing] **1.** to do away with **2.** to invalidate; cancel —**an·nul′la·ble** *adj.* —**an·nul′ment** *n.*

an·nu·lar (an′yoo lər) *adj.* [< L. *anulus,* a ring] of, like, or forming a ring

annular eclipse an eclipse in which a ring of sunlight can be seen around the disk of the moon

an·nun·ci·a·tion (ə nun′sē ā′shən) *n.* **1.** an announcing **2.** [A-] *a)* the angel Gabriel's announcement to Mary that she was to give birth to Jesus *b)* the church festival (March 25) commemorating this

an·ode (an′ōd) *n.* [< Gr. *ana-,* up + *hodos,* way] **1.** a positively charged electrode, as in an electrolytic cell, electron tube, etc. **2.** the negative electrode in a battery supplying current

an·o·dyne (an′ə dīn′) *adj.* [< Gr. *an-,* without + *odynē,* pain] relieving or lessening pain —*n.* anything that relieves pain or soothes

a·noint (ə noint′) *vt.* [< L. *in-,* on + *ungere,* to smear] to put oil on, as in consecrating —**a·noint′ment** *n.*

Anointing of the Sick *R.C.Ch.* the sacrament in which a priest prays for and anoints with oil a person dying or in danger of death

a·nom·a·lous (ə näm′ə ləs) *adj.* [< Gr. *an-,* not + *homos,* the same] **1.** deviating from the general rule; abnormal **2.** being or seeming inconsistent

a·nom′a·ly (-lē) *n., pl.* **-lies** **1.** departure from the usual; abnormality **2.** anything anomalous

a·non (ə nan′) *adv.* [OE. *on an,* in one] soon; shortly; at another time: now nearly archaic —**ever and anon** now and then

a·non·y·mous (ə nän′ə məs) *adj.* [< Gr. *an-,* without + *onyma,* name] **1.** with no name known or acknowledged **2.** given, written, etc. by one whose name is withheld or unknown **3.** lacking individuality —**an·o·nym·i·ty** (an′ə nim′ə tē) *n.* —**a·non′y·mous·ly** *adv.*

a·noph·e·les (ə näf′ə lēz′) *n.* [< Gr. *anophelēs,* harmful] the mosquito that can transmit malaria

an·oth·er (ə nuth′ər) *adj.* **1.** one more; an additional **2.** a different —*pron.* **1.** one additional **2.** a different one **3.** one of the same kind

ans. answer

an·swer (an′sər) *n.* [< OE. *and-,* against + *swerian,* swear] **1.** a reply to a question, letter, etc. **2.** any retaliation **3.** a solution to a problem —*vi.* **1.** to reply **2.** to respond (*to*) [he *answers* to the name of Dick] **3.** to be sufficient **4.** to be responsible (*to* a person *for*) **5.** to correspond (*to*) —*vt.* **1.** to reply to in some way **2.** to respond to the signal of **3.** to comply with; serve **4.** to refute (an accusation, etc.) **5.** to suit [he *answers* the description] — **answer back** [Colloq.] to reply insolently —**an′swer·a·ble** *adj.*

ant (ant) *n.* [OE. *æmete*] any of a group of insects, generally wingless, that live in colonies with a complex division of labor

-ant [ult. < L.] *a suffix meaning:* **1.** that has, shows, or does [*defiant*] **2.** a person or thing that [*occupant*]

ant·ac·id (ant′as′id) *adj.* counteracting acidity —*n.* an antacid substance

an·tag·o·nism (an tag′ə niz′m) *n.* **1.** a being opposed or hostile **2.** an opposing force, principle, etc.

an·tag′o·nist *n.* an adversary; opponent

an·tag′o·nis′tic *adj.* showing antagonism; acting in opposition —**an·tag′o·nis′ti·cal·ly** *adv.*

an·tag·o·nize (an tag′ə nīz′) *vt.* -nized′, -niz′ing [< Gr. *anti-,* against + *agōn,* a contest] **1.** to oppose or counteract **2.** to incur the dislike of; make an enemy of

ant·arc·tic (ant ärk′tik, -är′-) *adj.* [see ANTI- & ARCTIC] of or near the South Pole or the region around it —**the Antarctic** *same as* ANTARCTICA

Ant·arc′ti·ca (-ti kə) land area about the South Pole, covered by ice: c.5,000,000 sq. mi.

Antarctic Circle [also a- c-] an imaginary circle parallel to the equator, 66°33′ south of it

Antarctic Ocean the parts of the Atlantic, Pacific, and Indian oceans surrounding Antarctica

An·tar·es (an ter′ēz) the brightest star in the constellation Scorpio

ant bear a large anteater of tropical S. America

an·te (an′tē) *n.* [L., before] **1.** *Poker* the stake that each player must put into the pot before receiving cards **2.** [Colloq.] the amount one must pay as his share —*vt., vi.* -ted or -teed, -te·ing **1.** *Poker* to put in (one's stake) **2.** [Colloq.] to pay (one's share) —**ante up** to ante one's stake or share

ante- [< L. *ante,* before] *a prefix meaning* before [*antecedent, anteroom*]

ant·eat·er (ant′ēt′ər) *n.* any of several mammals with a long snout and a long, sticky tongue, that feed mainly on ants

an·te·bel·lum (an′ti bel′əm) *adj.* [L.] before the war; specif., before the American Civil War

an·te·ced·ent (an′tə sēd′′nt) *adj.* [< L. *ante,* before + *cedere,* go] prior; previous —*n.* **1.** any thing prior to another **2.** [*pl.*] one's ancestry, past life, etc. **3.** *Gram.* the word or phrase to which a pronoun refers —**an′te·ced′-ence** *n.* —**an′te·ced′ent·ly** *adv.*

an·te·cham·ber (an′ti chām′bər) *n.* a smaller room leading into a larger or main room

an·te·date (an′ti dāt′) *vt.* -dat′ed, -dat′ing **1.** to put a date on that is earlier than the actual date **2.** to come before —*n.* a date fixed for an event, etc. that is earlier than the actual one

an·te·di·lu·vi·an (an′ti də loo′vē ən) *adj.* [< ANTE- + L. *diluvium,* a flood + -AN] **1.** of the time before the Biblical Flood **2.** very old or old-fashioned —*n.* an antediluvian person or thing

an·te·lope (an′tə lōp′) *n.* [< MGr. *antholops,* deer] **1.** a swift, cud-chewing, hollow-horned, deerlike animal related to oxen and goats **2.** leather made from an antelope's hide

an·te me·ri·di·em (an′tē mə rid′ē əm) [L.] before noon: abbrev. **A.M.,** **a.m., AM**

an·ten·na (an ten′ə) *n.* [< L. *antemna,* sail yard] **1.** *pl.* -nae (-ē), -nas **1.** either of a pair of feelers on the head of an insect, crab, etc. **2.** *pl.* -nas *Radio & TV* an arrangement of wires, rods, etc. used in sending and receiving electromagnetic waves

ANTELOPE
(to 70 in. high at shoulder)

an·te·pe·nult (an′ti pē′nəlt) *n.* the second syllable from the last in a word, as *-lu-* in an·te·di·lu·vi·an

an·te·ri·or (an tir′ē ər) *adj.* [L., compar. of *ante,* before] **1.** at or toward the front: opposed to POSTERIOR **2.** previous; earlier —**an·te′ri·or·ly** *adv.*

an·te·room (an′ti room′) *n.* a room leading to a larger one; waiting room

ant·hel·min·tic (ant′hel min′tik, an′thel-) *adj.* [< Gr. *anti,* against + *helminus,* worm + -IC] killing or ejecting intestinal worms —*n.* an anthelmintic medicine

an·them (an′thəm) *n.* [< Gr. *anti-,* over against + *phōnē,* voice] **1.** a religious choral song usually based on words from the Bible **2.** a song of praise or devotion, as to a nation, college, etc.

an·ther (an′thər) *n.* [< Gr. *anthos,* a flower] the part of a stamen that contains the pollen

ant·hill (ant′hil′) *n.* the soil heaped up by ants around their nest opening

an·thol·o·gize (an thäl′ə jīz′) *vt., vi.* -gized′, -giz′ing to put into or make anthologies —**an·thol′o·gist** *n.*

an·thol·o·gy (-jē) *n., pl.* -gies [< Gr. *anthos,* flower + *legein,* to gather] a collection of poems, stories, etc. —**an·tho·log·i·cal** (an′thə läj′i k'l) *adj.*

An·tho·ny (an′thə nē) **1.** *Mark, see* ANTONY **2.** Susan **B(rownell),** 1820–1906; U.S. leader in the women's suffrage movement

an·thra·cene (an′thrə sēn′) *n.* [see ANTHRAX & -ENE] a crystalline hydrocarbon, $C_{14}H_{10}$, obtained from coal tar and used in making dyes, etc.

an·thra·cite' (-sīt') *n.* [< Gr. *anthrax*, coal] hard coal, which gives much heat but little flame and smoke —**an'-thra·cit'ic** (-sit'ik) *adj.*

an·thrax (an'thraks) *n.* [< Gr., (burning) coal, carbuncle] **1.** an infectious disease of cattle, sheep, etc., which can be transmitted to man: it is characterized by black pustules **2.** any such pustule

anthropo- [< Gr. *anthrōpos*, man] *a combining form meaning* man, human *[anthropology]*

an·thro·po·cen·tric (an'thrə pə sen'trik) *adj.* [prec. + CENTRIC] centering one's view of everything around man

an·thro·poid (an'thrə poid') *adj.* [ANTHROP(O)- + -OID] **1.** manlike; esp., designating or of any of the most highly developed apes, as the chimpanzee and gorilla **2.** apelike —*n.* any anthropoid ape —**an'thro·poi'dal** *adj.*

an·thro·pol·o·gy (an'thrə päl'ə jē) *n.* [ANTHROPO- + -LOGY] the study of the variety, distribution, characteristics, cultures, etc. of mankind —**an'thro·po·log'i·cal** (-pə läj'i k'l), **an'thro·po·log'ic** *adj.* —**an'thro·po·log'i·cal·ly** *adv.* —**an'thro·pol'o·gist** *n.*

an·thro·pom'e·try (-päm'ə trē) *n.* [ANTHROPO- + -METRY] the science dealing with measurement of the human body in comparing individual and group differences —**an'thro·po·met'ric** (-pə met'rik), **an'thro·po·met'ri·cal** *adj.* —**an'thro·po·met'ri·cal·ly** *adv.*

an'thro·po·mor'phism (-pə môr'fiz'm) *n.* [< ANTHROPO- + Gr. *morphē*, form + -ISM] the attributing of human shape to a god, animal, or inanimate thing —**an'thro·po·mor'phic** *adj.* —**an'thro·po·mor'phi·cal·ly** *adv.*

an·ti (an'tī, -tē) *n., pl.* **-tis** [< ANTI-] [Colloq.] a person opposed to some policy, proposal, etc. —*prep.* [Colloq.] opposed to; against

anti- [< Gr. *anti*, against] *a prefix meaning:* **1.** against; hostile to **2.** that operates against **3.** that prevents, cures, or neutralizes **4.** opposite; reverse **5.** rivaling

an·ti·air·craft (an'tē er'kraft) *adj.* used for defense against hostile aircraft

an·ti·bac·te·ri·al (an'ti bak tir'ē əl) *adj.* that checks the growth or effect of bacteria

an'ti·bi·ot'ic (-bī ät'ik) *adj.* [< ANTI- + Gr. *biōsis*, way of life] destroying, or stopping the growth of, bacteria and other microorganisms —*n.* an antibiotic substance

an·ti·bod·y (an'ti bäd'ē) *n., pl.* **-ies** a protein produced in the body in response to contact of the body with an antigen, serving to neutralize the antigen, thus creating immunity

an·tic (an'tik) *adj.* [< L.: see ANTIQUE] odd and funny — *n.* a playful or silly act, trick, etc.; caper —*vi.* **-ticked, -tick·ing** to perform antics

an·ti·christ (an'ti krist') *n.* an opponent of Christ —[A-] *Bible* the great antagonist of Christ: I John 2:18

an·tic·i·pate (an tis'ə pāt') *vt.* **-pat'ed, -pat'ing** [< L. *ante-*, before + *capere*, to take] **1.** to look forward to; expect **2.** to forestall **3.** to foresee and take care of in advance **4.** to use or enjoy in advance **5.** to be ahead of in doing something —**an·tic'i·pa'tion** *n.* —**an·tic'i·pa'tive** *adj.* —**an·tic'i·pa·to'ry** (-pə tôr'ē) *adj.*

an·ti·cler·i·cal (an'ti kler'ə k'l) *adj.* opposed to the influence of the clergy or church in public affairs —**an'ti·cler'i·cal·ism** *n.*

an'ti·cli'max (-klī'maks) *n.* **1.** a sudden drop from the dignified or important to the commonplace or trivial **2.** a final event which is in disappointing contrast to those coming before —**an'ti·cli·mac'tic** (-mak'tik) *adj.*

an·ti·cline (an'ti klīn') *n.* [< ANTI- + Gr. *klinein*, to incline] a fold of stratified rock in which the strata slope downward in opposite directions from the central axis — **an'ti·cli'nal** *adj.*

an·ti·co·ag·u·lant (an'ti kō ag'yə lənt) *n.* a drug or substance that delays or prevents the clotting of blood

an'ti·cy'clone (-sī'klōn) *n.* an atmospheric condition in which the winds at the edge blow outward —**an'ti·cy·clon'ic** (-klän'ik) *adj.*

an'ti·de·pres'sant (-di pres'ənt) *adj.* lessening emotional depression —*n.* an antidepressant drug

an·ti·dote (an'tə dōt') *n.* [< Gr. *anti-*, against + *dotos*, given] **1.** a remedy to counteract a poison **2.** anything that works against an evil or unwanted condition —**an'ti·dot'al** *adj.*

an·ti·freeze (an'ti frēz') *n.* a liquid substance of low freezing point added esp. to the water in automobile radiators to prevent freezing

an·ti·gen (an'tə jən) *n.* [ANTI- + -GEN] an enzyme, toxin, etc. to which the body reacts by producing antibodies — **an'ti·gen'ic** (-jen'ik) *adj.*

An·ti·gua (an tē'gə, -gwə) self-governing island under Brit. protection in the West Indies

an·ti·he·ro (an'ti hir'ō) *n., pl.* **-roes** the protagonist of a novel, play, etc. who lacks the virtues of a traditional hero

an·ti·his·ta·mine (an'ti his'tə mēn', -mən) *n.* any drug used to minimize the action of histamine in such allergic conditions as hay fever and hives

an·ti·knock (an'ti näk') *n.* a substance added to the fuel of internal-combustion engines to do away with noise caused by too rapid combustion

An·til·les (an til'ēz) main island group of the West Indies, including Cuba, Jamaica, etc. (**Greater Antilles**) and the Leeward Islands and Windward Islands (**Lesser Antilles**)

an·ti·log·a·rithm (an'ti lôg'ə rith'm) *n.* the number corresponding to a given logarithm *[the antilogarithm of 1 is 10]*

an'ti·ma·cas'sar (-mə kas'ər) *n.* [ANTI- + *macassar* (oil), a former hair oil] a small cover to protect the back or arms of a chair, etc. from soiling

an'ti·mag·net'ic (-mag net'ik) *adj.* made of metals that resist magnetism

an·ti·mat·ter (an'ti mat'ər) *n.* a form of matter in which the electrical charge or other property of each constituent particle is the reverse of that in the usual matter of our universe

an'ti·mis'sile (-mis''l) *adj.* designed as a defense against ballistic missiles

an·ti·mo·ny (an'tə mō'nē) *n.* [< ML.] a silvery-white, brittle, metallic chemical element, found only in combination: used to harden alloys, etc.: symbol, Sb; at. wt., 121.75; at. no., 51

An·ti·och (an'tē äk') capital of ancient Syria: now a city in S Turkey: pop. 46,000

an·ti·par·ti·cle (an'ti pär'tə k'l) *n.* any particle of antimatter

an·ti·pas·to (an'ti pas'tō, -päs'-) *n.* [It. < *anti-*, before + *pasto*, food] a dish of salted fish, meat, olives, etc. served as an appetizer

an·tip·a·thy (an tip'ə thē) *n., pl.* **-thies** [< Gr. *anti-*, against + *pathein*, to feel] **1.** a strong dislike; aversion **2.** the object of such dislike —**an·ti·pa·thet·ic** (an'ti pə thet'ik), **an'ti·pa·thet'i·cal** *adj.*

an·ti·per·son·nel (an'ti pur'sə nel') *adj.* for destroying people rather than objects *[antipersonnel mines]*

an'ti·per'spir·ant (-pur'spər ənt) *n.* a substance applied to the skin to reduce perspiration

an'ti·phlo·gis'tic (-flə jis'tik) *adj.* [< ANTI- + Gr. *phlegein*, to burn] counteracting inflammation —*n.* an antiphlogistic substance

an·ti·phon (an'tə fän') *n.* [see ANTHEM] a hymn, psalm, etc. chanted or sung in responsive, alternating parts —**an·tiph'o·nal** (-tif'ə n'l), **an'ti·phon'ic** *adj.* —**an·tiph'o·nal·ly** *adv.*

an·ti·pode (an'tə pōd') *n.* [< ff.] an exact opposite

an·tip·o·des (an tip'ə dēz') *n.pl.* [< Gr. *anti-*, opposite + *pous*, foot] **1.** any two places directly opposite each other on the earth **2.** [*with pl. or sing. v.*] a place on the opposite side of the earth: in British usage, New Zealand and Australia **3.** two opposite or contrary things —**an·tip'o·dal** *adj.* —**an·tip'o·de'an** (-dē'ən) *adj., n.*

an·ti·pope (an'ti pōp') *n.* a pope set up against the one chosen by church laws, as in a schism

an·ti·py·ret·ic (an'ti pī ret'ik) *adj.* [< ANTI- + Gr. *pyr*, a fire] reducing fever —*n.* anything that reduces fever

an·ti·quar·i·an (an'tə kwer'ē ən) *adj.* **1.** of antiques or antiquities **2.** of antiquaries **3.** of, or dealing in, rare old books —*n.* an antiquary

an·ti·quar·y (an'tə kwer'ē) *n., pl.* **-ies** a collector or student of relics and ancient art

an'ti·quate' (-kwāt') *vt.* **-quat'ed, -quat'ing** [see ANTIQUE] to make old, obsolete, or out-of-date —**an'ti·quat'ed** *adj.* —**an'ti·qua'tion** *n.*

an·tique (an tēk') *adj.* [< L. *antiquus*, ancient] **1.** of ancient times **2.** out-of-date; old-fashioned **3.** of, or in the style of, a former period **4.** dealing in antiques —*n.* **1.** an ancient relic **2.** a piece of furniture, etc. of a former period —*vt.* **-tiqued', -tiqu'ing** to make look antique —**an·tique'ness** *n.*

an·tiq·ui·ty (an tik'wə tē) *n., pl.* **-ties** **1.** the early period of history, esp. before the Middle Ages **2.** great age; oldness **3.** [*pl.*] relics, monuments, etc. of the distant past

an·ti·scor·bu·tic (an'ti skôr byoo'tik) *adj.* that cures or prevents scurvy —*n.* a remedy for scurvy

an'ti·Se·mit'ic (-sə mit'ik) *adj.* **1.** having or showing prejudice against Jews **2.** discriminating against or persecuting Jews —**an'ti·Sem'ite** (-sem'īt) *n.* —**an'ti·Sem'itism** (-ə tiz'm) *n.*

an·ti·sep·sis (an'tə sep'sis) *n.* [ANTI- + SEPSIS] **1.** a being antiseptic **2.** the use of antiseptics

an'ti·sep'tic (-sep'tik) *adj.* **1.** preventing infection, decay, etc.; effective against bacteria **2.** using antiseptics **3.** sterile —*n.* any antiseptic substance —**an'ti·sep'ti·cal·ly** *adv.*

an·ti·slav·er·y (an'ti slā'vər ē) *adj.* against slavery

an'ti·so'cial (-sō'shəl) *adj.* **1.** not sociable **2.** harmful to the welfare of people

an'ti·spas·mod'ic (-spaz mäd'ik) *adj.* relieving spasms — *n.* an antispasmodic drug

an·ti·tank (an'ti taŋk') *adj.* for use against tanks in war

an·tith·e·sis (an tith'ə sis) *n., pl.* **-ses'** (-sēz') [< Gr. *anti-*, against + *tithenai*, to place] **1.** a contrast or opposition, as of ideas **2.** the exact opposite —**an·ti·thet·i·cal** (an'tə thet'i k'l) *adj.*

an·ti·tox·in (an'ti täk'sin) *n.* **1.** an antibody formed by the body to act against a specific toxin **2.** a serum containing an antitoxin, injected into a person to prevent a disease —**an'ti·tox'ic** *adj.*

an'ti·trust' (-trust') *adj.* opposed to or regulating trusts, or business monopolies

an'ti·viv'i·sec'tion·ist (-viv'ə sek'shən ist) *n.* one opposing vivisection

ant·ler (ant'lər) *n.* [< L. *ante-*, before + *ocularis*, of the eyes] the branched, deciduous horn of any animal of the deer family —**ant'lered** *adj.*

ant lion an insect whose larva digs a pit in which to trap and eat ants, etc.

An·toi·nette (an'twə net'), **Marie** *see* MARIE ANTOINETTE

An·to·ny (an'tə nē), **Mark** *or* **Marc** (*Marcus Antonius*) 83?–30 B.C.; Rom. general & statesman

an·to·nym (an'tə nim') *n.* [< Gr. *anti-*, opposite + *onyma*, name] a word meaning the opposite of another word ["sad" is an *antonym* of "happy"]

an·trum (an'trəm) *n., pl.* **-tra** (-trə), **-trums** [< Gr. *antron*, cave] *Anat.* a cavity; esp., a sinus of the upper jaw

Ant·werp (an'twərp) seaport in N Belgium: pop. 240,000

a·nus (ā'nəs) *n., pl.* **a'nus·es**, **a'ni** (-nī) [L.] the opening at the lower end of the alimentary canal

an·vil (an'vəl) *n.* [OE. *anfilt*] **1.** an iron or steel block on which metal objects are hammered into shape **2.** a bone in the ear

ANVIL

anx·i·e·ty (aŋ zī'ə tē) *n., pl.* **-ties** **1.** worry or uneasiness about what may happen **2.** an eager desire [*anxiety* to do well]

anx·ious (aŋk'shəs) *adj.* [< L. *angere*, choke] **1.** uneasy in mind; worried **2.** causing anxiety **3.** eagerly wishing —**anx'ious·ly** *adv.* —**anx'ious·ness** *n.*

an·y (en'ē) *adj.* [OE. *ænig*] **1.** one, no matter which, of more than two [*any* pupil may answer] **2.** some, no matter what amount or kind [he hasn't *any* food] **3.** without limit [enter *any* number of times] **4.** every [*any* child can do it] —*pron. sing. & pl.* any one or ones —*adv.* to any degree or extent [is he *any* better?]

an'y·bod'y (-bud'ē, -bäd'ē) *pron.* **1.** any person **2.** an important person

an'y·how' *adv. same as* ANYWAY

an'y·more' *adv.* now; nowadays

an'y·one' *pron.* any person; anybody

any one any single (person or thing)

an'y·place' *adv.* [Colloq.] *same as* ANYWHERE (sense 1)

an'y·thing' *pron.* any object, event, fact, etc. —*n.* a thing, no matter of what kind —*adv.* in any way —**anything but** not at all

an'y·way' *adv.* **1.** in any manner **2.** in any case **3.** haphazardly; carelessly

an'y·where' *adv.* **1.** in, at, or to any place **2.** [Colloq.] at all; to any extent —**get anywhere** [Colloq.] to have any success

an'y·wise' *adv.* in any manner; at all

A/O, a/o account of

A one (ā' wun') [Colloq.] first-class; first-rate; superior: also **A 1, A number 1**

a·or·ta (ā ôr'tə) *n., pl.* **-tas**, **-tae** (-tē) [< Gr. *aeirein*, to raise] the main artery of the body, carrying blood from the left ventricle of the heart to arteries in all parts

a·ou·dad (ä'oo dad') *n.* [Fr. < Moorish *audad*] a wild North African sheep with large, curved horns

a·pace (ə pās') *adv.* at a fast pace; with speed; swiftly

A·pach·e (ə pach'ē) *n., pl.* **-es**, **-e** [prob. < Zuñi *ápachu*, enemy] a member of a tribe of SW U.S. Indians

a·pache (ə pash', -päsh') *n., pl.* **a·pach'es** (-iz) [Fr., Apache] a gangster of Paris —*adj.* designating a dance which represents an apache handling his girl brutally

a·part (ə pärt') *adv.* [< L. *ad*, to + *pars*, part] **1.** to one side; aside **2.** away in place or time **3.** separately in use, etc. [viewed *apart*] **4.** in or to pieces **5.** notwithstanding [all joking *apart*] —*adj.* separated —**apart from** other than; besides —**take apart** to reduce (a whole) to its parts —**tell apart** to distinguish one from another

a·part·heid (ə pärt'hāt, -hīt) *n.* [Afrik., apartness] in South Africa, the policy of strict racial segregation imposed on Negroes and other colored peoples

a·part·ment (ə pärt'mənt) *n.* [< Fr. < It. *parte*, part] a room or suite of rooms to live in

apartment house a building divided into a number of apartments: also **apartment building**

ap·a·thet·ic (ap'ə thet'ik) *adj.* [< *apathy*] **1.** feeling no emotion; unmoved **2.** not interested; indifferent —**ap'a·thet'i·cal·ly** *adv.*

ap·a·thy (ap'ə thē) *n., pl.* **-thies** [< Fr. < Gr. *a-*, without + *pathos*, emotion] **1.** lack of emotion **2.** indifference

ape (āp) *n.* [OE. *apa*] **1.** a chimpanzee, gorilla, orangutan, or gibbon **2.** any monkey **3.** a mimic **4.** a coarse, uncouth person —*vt.* **aped, ap'ing** to imitate —**ape'like'** *adj.*

Ap·en·nines (ap'ə nīnz') mountain range in C Italy: highest peak, 9560 ft.

a·pe·ri·ent (ə pir'ē ənt) *adj., n.* [see APERTURE] *same as* LAXATIVE

a·pe·ri·tif (ä'pā rə tēf') *n.* [Fr.] an alcoholic drink, esp. a wine, taken before meals

ap·er·ture (ap'ər chər) *n.* [< L. *aperire*, to open] an opening; hole; gap

a·pet·a·lous (ā pet'l əs) *adj. Bot.* without petals

a·pex (ā'peks) *n., pl.* **-pex·es**, **ap·i·ces** (ap'ə sēz', ā'pə-) [L.] **1.** the highest point; peak **2.** the pointed end; tip **3.** a climax

a·pha·sia (ə fā'zhə) *n.* [Gr. < *a-*, not + *phanai*, speak] a total or partial loss of the power to use or understand words —**a·pha'sic** (-zik) *adj., n.*

a·phe·li·on (ə fē'lē ən) *n., pl.* **-li·ons, -li·a** (-ə) [< Gr. *apo*, from + *hēlios*, sun] the point farthest from the sun in the orbit around it of a planet, comet, or man-made satellite: cf. PERIHELION

a·phid (ā'fid, af'id) *n.* [< Gr. *apheidēs*, lavish] a small insect that sucks the juice from plants: also **a·phis** (ā'fis, af'is), *pl.* **aph·i·des** (af'ə dēz')

aph·o·rism (af'ə riz'm) *n.* [< Gr. *apo-*, from + *horizein*, to bound] **1.** a concise statement of a principle **2.** a maxim or adage —**aph'o·ris'tic** *adj.*

aph·ro·dis·i·ac (af'rə diz'ē ak') *adj.* [< Gr. *Aphroditē*] arousing sexual desire —*n.* an aphrodisiac drug or other agent

Aph·ro·di·te (af'rə dīt'ē) the Greek goddess of love and beauty: identified with the Roman Venus

a·pi·ar·y (ā'pē er'ē) *n., pl.* **-ar'ies** [< L. *apis*, bee] a place where bees are kept —**a'pi·a·rist** (-ə rist, -er'ist) *n.*

ap·i·cal (ap'i k'l, ā'pi-) *adj.* of, at, or being the apex — **ap'i·cal·ly** *adv.*

a·pi·cul·ture (ā'pə kul'chər) *n.* [< L. *apis*, bee + CULTURE] the raising and care of bees; beekeeping —**a'pi·cul'tur·al** *adj.* —**a'pi·cul'tur·ist** *n.*

a·piece (ə pēs') *adv.* [see A & PIECE] for each one

ap·ish (āp'ish) *adj.* **1.** like an ape **2.** foolishly imitative **3.** silly, affected, etc. —**ap'ish·ness** *n.*

a·plen·ty (ə plen'tē) *adj., adv.* [Colloq.] in abundance

a·plomb (ə pläm', -plum') *n.* [< Fr.: see PLUMB] self-possession; poise

APO Army Post Office

a·poc·a·lypse (ə päk'ə lips') *n.* [< Gr. *apokalyptein*, disclose] a religious writing depicting symbolically the end of evil; specif., **[A-]** the last book of the New Testament; book of Revelation —**a·poc'a·lyp'tic** (-lip'tik), **a·poc'a·lyp'ti·cal** *adj.*

a·poc·o·pe (ə päk'ə pē') *n.* [< Gr. *apo-*, from + *koptein*, to cut off] the dropping of a sound or sounds at the end of a word

a·poc·ry·pha (ə päk'rə fə) *n.pl.* [< Gr. *apo-*, away + *kryptein*, to hide] **1.** any writings, anecdotes, etc. of doubtful authenticity or authorship **2.** **[A-]** fourteen books of the Septuagint rejected in Protestantism and Judaism: eleven are accepted in the Roman Catholic Biblical canon

a·poc′ry·phal adj. **1.** of doubtful authenticity **2.** not genuine; false; counterfeit **3.** [A-] of or like the Apocrypha

ap·o·gee (ap′ə jē′) n. [< Gr. apo-, from + gē, earth] **1.** the point farthest from the earth, the moon, or another planet, in the orbit of a satellite or spacecraft around it **2.** an apex

A·pol·lo (ə päl′ō) the Greek and Roman god of music, poetry, prophecy, and medicine —n., pl. **-los** a handsome young man

a·pol·o·get·ic (ə päl′ə jet′ik) adj. making apology; esp., expressing regret, as for a fault: also **a·pol′o·get′i·cal** — **a·pol′o·get′i·cal·ly** adv.

a·pol′o·get′ics n.pl. [with sing. v.] [see APOLOGY] the branch of theology dealing with the defense of Christianity

a·pol·o·gist (ə päl′ə jist) n. one who defends or attempts to justify a doctrine, faith, action, etc.

a·pol·o·gize′ (-jīz′) vi. -gized′, -giz′ing to make an apology; esp., to express regret, as for a fault

ap·o·logue (ap′ə lôg′, -läg′) n. [Fr. < Gr.] a short allegorical story with a moral; fable

a·pol·o·gy (ə päl′ə jē) n., pl. **-gies** [< Gr. apo-, from + logos, word] **1.** a formal defense of some idea, doctrine, etc. **2.** an expression of regret for a fault, wrong, etc. **3.** an inferior substitute [it is a sad apology for a meal]

ap·o·plec·tic (ap′ə plek′tik) adj. **1.** of, like, causing, or having apoplexy **2.** seemingly about to have apoplexy [apoplectic with rage] Also **ap′o·plec′ti·cal** —n. a person having or likely to have apoplexy

ap·o·plex·y (ap′ə plek′sē) n. [< Gr. apo-, down + plēssein, to strike] sudden paralysis with loss of consciousness and feeling, caused when a blood vessel in the brain breaks or becomes clogged; stroke

a·port (ə pôrt′) adv. Naut. on or to the left, or port, side

a·pos·ta·sy (ə päs′tə sē) n., pl. **-sies** [< Gr. apo-, away + stasis, standing] an abandoning of something that one once believed in, as a faith

a·pos′tate (-tāt′, -tit) n. a person guilty of apostasy; renegade —adj. guilty of apostasy

a pos·te·ri·o·ri (ā′ päs tir′ē ôr′ī, -ôr′ē) [ML.] **1.** from effect to cause or from particular instances to a generalization **2.** based on observation or experience

A·pos·tle (ə päs′'l) n. [< Gr. apo-, from + stellein, send] **1.** [occas. a-] any of the disciples of Jesus, esp. the original twelve **2.** [a-] the leader of a new reform movement

Apostles′ Creed an early statement of belief in the basic Christian doctrines

ap·os·tol·ic (ap′əs täl′ik) adj. **1.** of the Apostles, their teachings, work, etc. **2.** [often A-] of the Pope; papal Also **ap′os·tol′i·cal**

Apostolic See the Pope's see at Rome

a·pos·tro·phe′ (ə päs′trə fē) n. [< Gr. apo-, from + strephein, to turn] words addressed to a person or thing, whether absent or present

a·pos·tro·phe² (ə päs′trə fē) n. [Fr.: see prec.] the mark (′) indicating: **1.** the omission of a letter or letters from a word (Ex.: it's for it is) **2.** the possessive case (Ex.: Mary's dress) **3.** certain plural forms (Ex.: 6's, t's)

a·pos′tro·phize′ (-fīz′) vt., vi. -phized′, -phiz′ing to speak or write an apostrophe (to)

apothecaries′ measure a system of units used in measuring liquids in pharmacy: in the U.S., 60 minims = 1 fluid dram; 8 fluid drams = 1 fluid ounce; 16 fluid ounces = 1 pint; 8 pints = 1 gallon

apothecaries′ weight a system of weights used in pharmacy: 20 grains = 1 scruple; 3 scruples = 1 dram; 8 drams = 1 ounce; 12 ounces = 1 pound

a·poth·e·car·y (ə päth′ə ker′ē) n., pl. **-car′ies** [< Gr. apothēkē, storehouse] a pharmacist, or druggist

ap·o·thegm (ap′ə them′) n. [< Gr. apo-, from + phthengesthai, to utter] a short, pithy saying

a·poth·e·o·sis (ə päth′ē ō′sis, ap′ə thē′ə-) n., pl. **-ses′** (-sēz′) [< Gr. apo-, from + theos, god] **1.** the deifying of a person **2.** the glorification of a person or thing **3.** an ideal or exact type

a·poth·e·o·size (ə päth′ē ə sīz′, ap′ə thē′-) vt. -sized′, -siz′ing **1.** to deify **2.** to glorify; idealize

Ap·pa·la·chi·a (ap′ə lā′chə, -chē ə) the highland region of the E U.S.: characterized generally by economic depression and poverty

Ap′pa·la′chi·an Mountains mountain system extending from S Quebec to N Ala.: highest peak, 6,684 ft.: also **Ap′pa·la′chi·ans**

ap·pall, ap·pal (ə pôl′) vt. -palled′, -pal′ling [< L. pallidus, pale] to fill with horror or dismay; shock —**ap·pal′·ling** adj. —**ap·pal′ling·ly** adv.

ap·pa·loo·sa (ap′ə loo′sə) n. [< Palouse Indians of NW U.S.] a breed of Western saddle horse with black or white spots on the rump and loins

ap·pa·nage (ap′ə nij) n. [< Fr. < L. ad, to + panis, bread] **1.** money, land, etc. granted by a monarch to his younger children **2.** a benefit that is a perquisite or adjunct

ap·pa·ra·tus (ap′ə rat′əs, -rät′-) n., pl. **-tus**, **-tus·es** [< L. ad-, to + parare, prepare] **1.** the instruments, tools, etc. for a specific use **2.** any complex device or system **3.** Physiol. a set of organs having a specific function [the digestive apparatus]

ap·par·el (ə per′əl, -par′-) n. [< L. apparare: see prec.] clothing; attire —vt. -eled or -elled, -el·ing or -el·ling **1.** to clothe; dress **2.** to adorn; bedeck

ap·par·ent (ə per′ənt, -par′-) adj. [see APPEAR] **1.** readily seen; visible **2.** evident; obvious **3.** appearing to be real or true; seeming See also HEIR APPARENT —**ap·par′ent·ly** adv.

ap·pa·ri·tion (ap′ə rish′ən) n. [see APPEAR] **1.** anything that appears unexpectedly or remarkably **2.** a ghost; phantom **3.** an appearing —**ap′pa·ri′tion·al** adj.

ap·peal (ə pēl′) vt. [< L. ad-, to + pellere, drive] to make a request to a higher court for the rehearing of (a case) — vi. **1.** to appeal a law case **2.** to make an urgent request (for a decision, help, etc.) **3.** to resort (to) for decision, etc. **4.** to be attractive or interesting —n. **1.** a call upon some authority for a decision, etc. **2.** a request for help, etc. **3.** interest; attraction **4.** Law a request for the transference of a case to a higher court for rehearing —**ap·peal′ing** adj.

ap·pear (ə pir′) vi. [< L. ad-, to + parere, come forth] **1.** to come into sight or being **2.** to become understood [it appears I lost] **3.** to seem; look **4.** to present oneself formally, as in court **5.** to come before the public [he will appear in Hamlet]

ap·pear′ance n. **1.** an appearing **2.** the outward aspect of anything **3.** an outward show; pretense **4.** [pl.] the way things seem to be —**keep up appearances** to try to give the impression of being proper, etc. —**put in an appearance** to be present for a short time, as at a party

ap·pease (ə pēz′) vt. -peased′, -peas′ing [< L. pax, peace] **1.** to make peaceful or quiet, esp. by giving in to the demands of **2.** to satisfy or relieve [water appeases thirst] —**ap·peas′a·ble** adj. —**ap·pease′ment** n.

ap·pel·lant (ə pel′ənt) adj. Law appealing —n. one who appeals, esp. to a higher court

ap·pel·late (-it) adj. Law relating to, or having jurisdiction to review, appeals

ap·pel·la·tion (ap′ə lā′shən) n. [see APPEAL] **1.** the act of naming **2.** a name or title

ap·pel·la·tive (ə pel′ə tiv) adj. of appellation; naming — n. a name or title

ap·pend (ə pend′) vt. [< L. ad-, to + pendere, suspend] to attach or affix; add as an appendix

ap·pend′age n. **1.** anything appended; adjunct **2.** an external organ or part, as a tail

ap·pen·dec·to·my (ap′ən dek′tə mē) n., pl. **-mies** [see -ECTOMY] the surgical removal of the vermiform appendix

ap·pen·di·ci·tis (ə pen′də sīt′əs) n. [see -ITIS] inflammation of the vermiform appendix

ap·pen·dix (ə pen′diks) n., pl. **-dix·es**, **-di·ces′** (-də sēz′) [see APPEND] **1.** additional material at the end of a book **2.** Anat. an outgrowth of an organ; esp., a small sac (vermiform appendix) extending from the large intestine

ap·per·tain (ap′ər tān′) vi. [< L. ad-, to + pertinere, to reach] to belong properly as a function, part, etc.; pertain

ap·pe·tite (ap′ə tīt′) n. [< L. ad-, to + petere, seek] a desire or craving, esp. for food

ap′pe·tiz′er (-tī′zər) n. a tasty food that stimulates the appetite, served before a meal

ap′pe·tiz′ing adj. stimulating the appetite; savory; tasty —**ap′pe·tiz′ing·ly** adv.

ap·plaud (ə plôd′) vt., vi. [< L. ad-, to + plaudere, clap hands] **1.** to show approval (of) by clapping hands, etc. **2.** to praise; approve

ap·plause (ə plôz′) n. approval or praise, esp. as shown by clapping hands, cheering, etc.

ap·ple (ap′'l) n. [OE. æppel] **1.** a round, firm, fleshy, edible fruit with a red, yellow, or green skin **2.** the tree it grows on

ap′ple·jack′ (-jak′) n. brandy distilled from apple cider

apple polisher [Slang] a person who seeks favor by gifts, flattery, etc.

ap′ple·sauce′ (-sôs′) n. **1.** apples cooked to a pulp in water **2.** [Slang] nonsense

ap·pli·ance (ə plī′əns) n. a device or machine for a specific task

ap·pli·ca·ble (ap'li kə b'l) *adj.* that can be applied; appropriate —ap'pli·ca·bil'i·ty *n.* —ap'pli·ca·bly *adv.*

ap·pli·cant (ap'li kənt) *n.* a person who applies, as for employment, help, etc.

ap·pli·ca·tion (ap'lə kā'shən) *n.* 1. the act or a way of applying or being applied 2. anything applied, as a remedy 3. a request, or the form filled out in making a request [an employment *application*] 4. continued effort 5. relevance or practicality

ap'pli·ca'tor *n.* any device for applying medicine or paint, polish, etc.

ap·plied (ə plīd') *adj.* used in actual practice [applied science]

ap·pli·qué (ap'lə kā') *n.* [Fr. < L.: see APPLY] a decoration made of one material attached by sewing, etc. to another —*vt.* -quéd', -qué'ing to decorate with appliqué

ap·ply (ə plī') *vt.* -plied', -ply'ing [< L. *ad-*, to + *plicare*, to fold] 1. to put on [apply glue] 2. to use practically [apply your knowledge] 3. to employ (oneself) diligently — *vi.* 1. to make a formal request 2. to be suitable or relevant [this rule always *applies*] —ap·pli'er *n.*

ap·point (ə point') *vt.* [< L. *ad-*, to + *punctum*, a point] 1. to set (a date, place, etc.); decree 2. to name for an office, etc. [to *appoint* a chairman] 3. to furnish [well-appointed] —ap·point'ee' *n.*

ap·point'ive (-iv) *adj.* to which one is appointed, not elected [an *appointive* office]

ap·point'ment (-mənt) *n.* 1. an appointing or being appointed 2. a person appointed to an office, etc. 3. an office held in this way 4. an engagement to meet a person 5. [pl.] furnishings

Ap·po·mat·tox (Court House) (ap'ə mat'əks) former village in C Va., where Lee surrendered to Grant (April 9, 1865)

ap·por·tion (ə pôr'shən) *vt.* [see AD- & PORTION] to divide and distribute in shares according to a plan —ap·por'tion·ment *n.*

ap·pose (ə pōz') *vt.* -posed', -pos'ing [< L. *ad-*, near + *ponere*, put] to put side by side, next, or near —ap·pos'a·ble *adj.*

ap·po·site (ap'ə zit) *adj.* [see prec.] appropriate; apt —ap'po·site·ly *adv.* —ap'po·site·ness *n.*

ap·po·si·tion (ap'ə zish'ən) *n.* 1. an apposing or the position resulting from this 2. the placing of a word or phrase beside another so that the second explains and has the same grammatical construction as the first (Ex.: *Jim, my son*, is here) —ap·po·si'tion·al *adj.*

ap·pos·i·tive (ə päz'ə tiv) *adj.* of or in apposition —*n.* a word, phrase, or clause in apposition

ap·prais·al (ə prā'z'l) *n.* 1. an appraising 2. an appraised value Also **ap·praise'ment**

ap·praise (ə prāz') *vt.* -praised', -prais'ing [< L. *ad*, to + *pretium*, price] 1. to set a price for, esp. officially 2. to estimate the quantity or quality of —ap·prais'ing·ly *adv.*

ap·pre·ci·a·ble (ə prē'shə b'l, -shē ə-) *adj.* enough to be perceived; noticeable —ap·pre'ci·a·bly *adv.*

ap·pre·ci·ate (ə prē'shē āt') *vt.* -at'ed, -at'ing [see APPRAISE] 1. to think well of; enjoy 2. to recognize gratefully 3. to estimate the quality or worth of 4. to be fully or sensitively aware of 5. to raise the price of —*vi.* to rise in value —ap·pre'ci·a'tor *n.*

ap·pre·ci·a'tion *n.* 1. grateful recognition, as of a favor 2. sensitive awareness, as of art 3. a rise in value or price

ap·pre·ci·a·tive (ə prē'shə tiv, -shē ə-) *adj.* feeling or showing appreciation —ap·pre'ci·a·tive·ness *n.*

ap·pre·hend (ap'rə hend') *vt.* [< L. *ad-*, to + *prehendere*, seize] 1. to arrest (a suspect, etc.) 2. to perceive or understand 3. to fear; dread

ap'pre·hen'sion (-hen'shən) *n.* 1. capture or arrest 2. understanding 3. anxiety or dread

ap'pre·hen'sive (-siv) *adj.* uneasy or fearful about the future —ap'pre·hen'sive·ly *adv.* —ap'pre·hen'sive·ness *n.*

ap·pren·tice (ə pren'tis) *n.* [see APPREHEND] 1. a person working under a skilled craftsman to learn a trade 2. any beginner —*vt.* -ticed, -tic·ing to place or accept as an apprentice —ap·pren'tice·ship' *n.*

ap·prise', ap·prize' (ə prīz') *vt.* -prised' or -prized', -pris'ing or -priz'ing [see APPREHEND] to inform or notify

ap·prize², ap·prise² (ə prīz') *vt.* -prized' or -prised', -priz'ing or -pris'ing *same as* APPRAISE

ap·proach (ə prōch') *vi.* [< L. *ad*, to + *prope*, near] to come closer or draw nearer —*vt.* 1. to come near or nearer to 2. to be similar to; approximate 3. to bring near (to something) 4. to make a proposal or request to 5. to begin dealing with —*n.* 1. a coming closer 2. an approximation 3. an advance or overture (*to* someone): *often used in pl.* 4. a way of getting to a person, place, or thing; access 5. *Golf* a stroke from the fairway to the putting green —ap·proach'a·bil'i·ty *n.* —ap·proach'a·ble *adj.*

ap·pro·ba·tion (ap'rə bā'shən) *n.* [see APPROVE] official approval, permission, or praise

ap·pro·pri·ate (ə prō'prē āt') *vt.* -at'ed, -at'ing [< L. *ad-*, to + *proprius*, one's own] 1. to take for one's own use 2. to take improperly, as without permission 3. to set aside for a specific use [to *appropriate* funds for schools] —*adj.* (-it) suitable —ap·pro'pri·ate·ly (-it lē) *adv.* —ap·pro'pri·ate·ness *n.* —ap·pro'pri·a'tive (-āt'iv) *adj.*

ap·pro'pri·a'tion *n.* 1. an appropriating or being appropriated 2. money, etc. set aside for a specific use

ap·prov·al (ə prōō'v'l) *n.* 1. an approving 2. favorable opinion 3. consent —**on approval** for the customer to examine and decide whether to buy or return

ap·prove (ə prōōv') *vt.* -proved', -prov'ing [< L. *ad-*, to + *probus*, good] 1. to give one's consent to 2. to judge to be good, satisfactory, etc. —*vi.* to have a favorable opinion (*of*) —ap·prov'ing·ly *adv.*

approx. 1. approximate 2. approximately

ap·prox·i·mate (ə präk'sə mit) *adj.* [< L. *ad-*, to + *prope*, near] 1. near in position 2. much like 3. not exact, but almost so —*vt.* (-māt') -mat'ed, -mat'ing to come near to; be almost the same as [to *approximate* reality] — *vi.* to be almost the same —ap·prox'i·mate·ly *adv.*

ap·prox'i·ma'tion (-mā'shən) *n.* 1. an approximating 2. a fairly close estimate, etc.

ap·pur·te·nance (ə pur't'n əns) *n.* [see APPERTAIN] 1. something added to a more important thing 2. [pl.] accessories 3. *Law* an additional, subordinate right or privilege —ap·pur'te·nant *adj., n.*

a·pri·cot (ap'rə kät', ā'prə-) *n.* [< L. *praecoquus*, early matured (fruit)] 1. a small, yellowish-orange, peachlike fruit 2. the tree it grows on

A·pril (ā'prəl) *n.* [< L.] the fourth month of the year, having 30 days: abbrev. **Apr.**

April fool a victim of jokes on April Fools' Day

April Fools' Day April 1, All Fools' Day

a pri·o·ri (ā'prē ôr'ē, ā'prī ôr'ī) [L.] 1. from cause to effect or from a generalization to particular instances 2. based on theory instead of experience or experiment

a·pron (ā'prən, -pərn) *n.* [< L. *mappa*, napkin] 1. a garment worn over the front part of the body to protect one's clothes 2. anything like this, as the part of a stage in front of the curtain —*vt.* to put an apron on

apron string a string for tying an apron on —**tied to one's mother's** (or **wife's**, etc.) **apron strings** dominated by one's mother (or wife, etc.)

ap·ro·pos (ap'rə pō') *adv.* [Fr. *à propos*, to the purpose] at the right time; opportunely —*adj.* relevant; apt —**apropos of** with regard to

apse (aps) *n.* [< Gr. *haptein*, fasten] a semicircular or polygonal projection of a building, esp. one at the east end of a church, with a domed or vaulted roof

apt (apt) *adj.* [< L. *apere*, fasten] 1. appropriate; fitting 2. tending or inclined; likely 3. quick to learn —**apt'ly** *adv.* —**apt'ness** *n.*

apt. *pl.* **apts.** apartment

ap·ter·ous (ap'tər əs) *adj.* [< Gr. *a-*, without + *pteron*, a wing] *Biol.* having no wings; wingless

ap·ter·yx (ap'tər iks) *n.* [< Gr. *a-*, without + *pteryx*, wing] *same as* KIWI

ap·ti·tude (ap'tə tōōd', -tyōōd') *n.* [see APT] 1. suitability; fitness 2. a natural tendency, inclination, or ability 3. quickness to learn

aq·ua (ak'wə, äk'-) *n., pl.* **-uas, -uae** (-wē) [L.] water — *adj.* [< AQUAMARINE] bluish-green

Aq·ua·lung (ak'wə luŋ', äk'-) [AQUA + LUNG] a trademark for a kind of self-contained underwater breathing apparatus —*n.* such an apparatus: usually **aq'ua·lung'**

aq·ua·ma·rine (ak'wə mə rēn', äk'-) *n.* [L. *aqua marina*, sea water] 1. a transparent, pale bluish-green beryl 2. its color —*adj.* bluish-green

aq·ua·naut (ak'wə nôt', äk'-) *n.* [AQUA + (ASTRO)NAUT] one trained to use a watertight underwater chamber as a base for undersea experiments

AQUALUNG

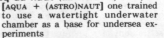

fat, āpe, cär; ten, ēven; is, bīte; gō, hôrn, tōōl, look; oil, out; up, fur; thin, then; zh, leisure; ŋ, ring; ə for *a* in *ago*; ' as in *able* (ā'b'l); ë, Fr. coeur; ö, Fr. feu; Fr. mon; ü, Fr. duc; r, Fr. cri; kh, G. doch, ich. ‡ foreign; < derived from

aq·ua·plane (ak'wə plān', äk'-) *n.* [AQUA + PLANE⁴] a board on which one rides standing up as it is pulled over water by a motorboat —*vi.* **-planed'**, **-plan'ing** to ride on such a board as a sport

a·quar·ist (ə kwer'ist) *n.* the keeper of an aquarium

a·quar·i·um (ə kwer'ē əm) *n., pl.* **-i·ums**, **-i·a** (-ē ə) [< L. *aquarius*, of water] 1. a tank, etc. for keeping live water animals and plants 2. a place where such collections are exhibited

A·quar·i·us (ə kwer'ē əs) [L., the water carrier] 1. a large S constellation 2. the eleventh sign of the zodiac: see ZO-DIAC, illus.

a·quat·ic (ə kwät'ik, -kwat'-) *adj.* 1. growing or living in water 2. done in or upon the water [*aquatic* sports] — **a·quat'i·cal·ly** *adv.*

aq·ua·tint (ak'wə tint') *n.* 1. a process by which spaces rather than lines are etched, producing an etching like a water color 2. such an etching

aqua vi·tae (vīt'ē) [L., water of life] 1. *Alchemy* alcohol 2. brandy or other strong liquor

aq·ue·duct (ak'wə dukt') *n.* [< L. *aqua*, water + *ducere*, to lead] 1. a large pipe or conduit for bringing water from a distant source 2. a bridgelike structure supporting this

a·que·ous (ā'kwē əs, ak'wē-) *adj.* of, like, or formed by water; watery

aqueous humor a watery fluid in the space between the cornea and the lens of the eye

aq·ui·line (ak'wə līn', -lən) *adj.* [< L. *aquila*, eagle] 1. of or like an eagle 2. curved like an eagle's beak [an *aquiline* nose]

A·qui·nas (ə kwī'nəs), Saint **Thomas** 1225?-74; It. theologian & philosopher

-ar [< L.] 1. *a suffix meaning* of, relating to, like [*polar*] 2. *a suffix denoting* agency [*vicar*]

Ar *Chem.* argon

AR Arkansas

Ar. 1. Arabic 2. Aramaic

Ar·ab (ar'əb) *n.* 1. a native of Arabia 2. any of a Semitic people originating in Arabia; commonly, a Bedouin —*adj. same as* ARABIAN

ar·a·besque (ar'ə besk') *n.* [< Ar. *'arab*] an elaborate design of intertwined flowers, foliage, etc.

A·ra·bi·a (ə rā'bē ə) peninsula in SW Asia: also **Arabian Peninsula**

A·ra'bi·an (-ən) *adj.* of Arabia or the Arabs —*n. same as* ARAB (sense 1)

Arabian Nights, The a collection of ancient tales from Arabia, India, Persia, etc.

Arabian Sea part of the Indian Ocean, between India and Arabia

Ar·a·bic (ar'ə bik) *adj.* 1. of Arabia 2. of the Arabs —*n.* the Semitic language of the Arabs, spoken from Iraq to N Africa

Arabic numerals the figures 1, 2, 3, 4, 5, 6, 7, 8, 9, and the 0 (zero)

ar·a·ble (ar'ə b'l) *adj.* [Fr. < L. *arare*, to plow] suitable for plowing and producing crops

Ar·a·by (ar'ə bē) [Archaic or Poet.] Arabia

a·rach·nid (ə rak'nid) *n.* [< Gr. *arachnē*, spider] any of a group of arthropods, including spiders, scorpions, and mites, with eight legs —**a·rach'ni·dan** (-ni dən) *adj., n.*

Ar·al Sea (ar'əl) inland body of salt water in SW Asiatic U.S.S.R.: also **Lake Aral**

Ar·a·ma·ic (ar'ə mā'ik) *n.* a group of Semitic languages spoken in Biblical times

A·rap·a·ho (ə rap'ə hō') *n., pl.* **-hos'**, **-ho'** [< ? Crow., lit., enemy] any member of a tribe of Indians orig. living in the central U.S.

Ar·a·rat (ar'ə rat') mountain in E Turkey: supposed landing place of Noah's Ark

ar·ba·lest, ar·ba·list (är'bə list) *n.* [< L. *arcus*, a bow + *ballista* < Gr. *ballein*, to throw] a medieval crossbow with a steel bow

ar·bi·ter (är'bə tər) *n.* [L., a witness] arbitrator; judge; umpire

ar·bit·ra·ment (är bit'rə mənt) *n.* 1. arbitration 2. an arbitrator's verdict or award

ar·bi·trar·y (är'bə trer'ē) *adj.* [see ARBITER] 1. left to one's own choice 2. based on one's whim or notion 3. absolute; despotic —**ar'bi·trar'i·ly** *adv.* —**ar'bi·trar'i·ness** *n.*

ar·bi·trate (är'bə trāt') *vt., vi.* **-trat'ed**, **-trat'ing** [see ARBITER] 1. to submit (a dispute) to arbitration 2. to decide (a dispute) as an arbitrator

ar'bi·tra'tion *n.* settlement of a dispute by someone chosen to hear both sides and come to a decision —**ar'bi·tra'tion·al** *adj.*

ar'bi·tra'tor *n.* one chosen to judge a dispute

ar·bor¹ (är'bər) *n.* [< L. *herba*, herb] a place shaded by trees, shrubs, or vines

ar·bor² (är'bər) *n., pl.* **-bo·res'** (-bə rēz') [L.] *Bot.* a tree — **Arbor Day** a tree-planting day observed in most States, usually in April

ar·bor³ (är'bər) *n.* [< Fr. < L. *arbor*, tree] 1. a shaft; beam; axle 2. a bar to hold cutting tools

ar·bo·re·al (är bôr'ē əl) *adj.* 1. of or like a tree 2. living in trees

ar·bo·res·cent (är'bə res''nt) *adj.* treelike

ar·bo·re·tum (är'bə rēt'əm) *n., pl.* **-tums**, **-ta** (-ə) [L.] a place where many kinds of trees and shrubs are grown for study or display

ar·bor·vi·tae (är'bər vīt'ē) *n.* [L., tree of life] any of several evergreen trees related to the cypress, with flattened sprays of scalelike leaves

ar·bu·tus (är byōōt'əs) *n.* [L.] 1. a tree or shrub with dark-green leaves and berries like strawberries 2. a related trailing plant with clusters of white or pink flowers

arc (ärk) *n.* [< L. *arcus*, a bow, arch] 1. a bowlike curved line or object 2. the band of incandescent light formed when an electric discharge is conducted between two electrodes 3. a part of a curve, esp. of a circle —*vi.* 'arced or arcked, arc'ing or arck'ing 1. to move in a curved course 2. to form an arc

ARC, A.R.C. American Red Cross

ar·cade (är kād') *n.* [Fr. < L. *arcus*, arch] 1. a covered passageway, esp. one lined with shops 2. a line of arches and their supporting columns

ar·cane (är kān') *adj.* [< L. *arcere*, shut up] 1. hidden or secret 2. esoteric

arch¹ (ärch) *n.* [< L. *arcus*, a bow, arch] 1. a curved structure that supports the weight of material over an open space, as in a doorway 2. the form of an arch 3. anything shaped like an arch —*vt., vi.* 1. to span with or as an arch 2. to form (into) an arch

arch² (ärch) *adj.* [< *arch-*] 1. main; chief 2. gaily mischievous; pert — **arch'ly** *adv.* —**arch'ness** *n.*

arch- [< Gr. *archos*, ruler] *a prefix meaning* main, chief [*archbishop*]

-arch [see ARCH-] *a suffix meaning* ruler [*matriarch*]

arch. 1. archaic 2. architecture

ar·chae·ol·o·gy (är'kē äl'ə jē) *n.* [< Gr. *arche*, the beginning + -LOGY] the study of the life of ancient peoples, as by excavation of ancient cities: also sp. **archeology** —**ar'chae·o·log'i·cal** (-ə läj'i k'l) *adj.* —**ar'·chae·ol'o·gist** *n.*

ar·cha·ic (är kā'ik) *adj.* [< Gr. *archaios*, ancient] 1. ancient 2. old-fashioned 3. seldom used except in poetry, the Bible, etc., as the word *thou* —**ar·cha'i·cal·ly** *adv.*

ar·cha·ism (är'kē iz'm, -kā-) *n.* 1. the use of archaic words, methods, etc. 2. an archaic word, etc.

arch·an·gel (ärk'ān'j'l) *n.* a chief angel

Arch·an·gel (ärk'ān'j'l) seaport in the U.S.S.R., on the White Sea: pop. 313,000

arch·bish·op (ärch'bish'əp) *n.* a chief bishop

arch'bish'op·ric (-ə prik') *n.* the office, rank, term, or church district of an archbishop

arch'dea'con (-dē'k'n) *n.* a church official ranking just below a bishop, as in the Anglican Church —**arch'dea'-con·ry** *n., pl.* **-ries**

arch'di'o·cese (-dī'ə sis, -sēs') *n.* the diocese of an archbishop

arch'duch'ess (-duch'is) *n.* the wife or widow of an archduke

arch'duch'y (-duch'ē) *n., pl.* **-ies** the territory of an archduke or archduchess

arch'duke' (-dōōk', -dyōōk') *n.* a chief duke

ar·che·go·ni·um (är'kə gō'nē əm) *n., pl.* **-ni·a** (-nē ə) [< Gr. *archos*, first + *gonos*, offspring] the female reproductive organ in mosses, ferns, etc. —**ar'che·go'ni·al** *adj.*

arch·en·e·my (ärch'en'ə mē) *n., pl.* **-mies** a chief enemy —the archenemy Satan

arch·er (ärch'ər) *n.* [< L. *arcus*, a bow] one who shoots with bow and arrow —[A-] the constellation Sagittarius

arch'er·y *n.* 1. the practice, art, or sport of shooting with bow and arrow 2. an archer's equipment 3. archers collectively

ar·che·type (är'kə tīp') *n.* [< Gr. *archos*, first + *typos*, a model] 1. an original pattern or model; prototype 2. a perfect example —**ar'che·typ'al**, **ar'che·typ'i·cal** (-tip'i k'l) *adj.*

ARCHES
(A, semicircular; B, horseshoe; C, pointed)

arch·fiend (ärch'fēnd') *n.* a chief fiend —**the archfiend** Satan

ar·chi·di·ac·o·nal (är'kə dī ak'ə n'l) *adj.* of an archdeacon or archdeaconry —**ar'chi·di·ac'o·nate** (-nit) *n.*

ar·chi·e·pis·co·pal (är'kē ə pis'kə p'l) *adj.* of an archbishop or archbishopric —**ar'chi·e·pis'co·pate** (-pət, -pāt') *n.*

Ar·chi·me·des (är'kə mē'dēz) 287?–212 B.C.; Gr. mathematician & inventor —**Ar'chi·me'de·an** (-mē'dē ən, -mi dē'ən) *adj.*

ar·chi·pel·a·go (är'kə pel'ə gō') *n., pl.* **-goes'**, **-gos'** [< Gr. *archi-*, chief + *pelagos*, sea] **1.** a sea with many islands **2.** such a group of islands

ar·chi·tect (är'kə tekt') *n.* [< Gr. *archi-*, chief + *tektōn*, carpenter] **1.** a person who designs buildings, bridges, etc. and administers their construction **2.** any builder or creator

ar·chi·tec·ton·ics (är'kə tek tän'iks) *n.pl.* [*with sing. v.*] **1.** the science of architecture **2.** structural design, as of a symphony —**ar'chi·tec·ton'ic** *adj.*

ar·chi·tec·ture (är'kə tek'chər) *n.* **1.** the science or profession of designing and constructing buildings, etc. **2.** a style of construction **3.** design and construction —**ar'chi·tec'tur·al** *adj.* —**ar'chi·tec'tur·al·ly** *adv.*

ar·chi·trave (är'kə trāv') *n.* [Fr. < L. *archi-*, first + *trabs*, a beam] *Archit.* **1.** the lowest part of an entablature, a beam resting directly on the tops of the columns **2.** the molding around a doorway, window, etc.

ar·chives (är'kīvz) *n.pl.* [Fr. < Gr. *archē*, the beginning] **1.** a place where public records are kept **2.** the records kept there —**ar'chi'val** *adj.*

ar·chi·vist (är'kə vist, är'kī'vist) *n.* a person having charge of archives

ar·chon (är'kän') *n.* [< Gr. *archein*, to rule] one of the nine chief magistrates of ancient Athens

arch·priest (ärch'prēst') *n.* a chief priest

arch·way (ärch'wā') *n.* a passage under an arch

-archy [< Gr. *archein*, to rule] *a suffix meaning* a ruling, or that which is ruled *[monarchy]*

arc lamp a lamp in which the light is produced by an arc between electrodes: also **arc light**

arc·tic (ärk'tik, är'-) *adj.* [< Gr. *arktikos*, northern] **1.** of or near the North Pole **2.** very cold —**the Arctic** the region around the North Pole

Arctic Circle [*also* a- c-] an imaginary circle parallel to the equator 66°33' north of it

Arctic Ocean ocean surrounding the North Pole, north of the Arctic Circle

arc'tics *n.pl.* [< ARCTIC] high, warm, waterproof overshoes, usually with buckles

Arc·tu·rus (ärk toor'əs, -tyoor'-) [< Gr. *arktos*, a bear + *ouros*, a guard] a giant red star, the brightest in the constellation Boötes

-ard [< MHG. *hart*, bold] *a suffix meaning* one who carries an action to excess *[sluggard]*

ar·dent (är'd'nt) *adj.* [< L. *ardere*, to burn] **1.** passionate **2.** zealous **3.** glowing; radiant **4.** burning; aflame —**ar'den·cy** (-d'n sē) *n.* —**ar'dent·ly** *adv.*

ar·dor (är'dər) *n.* [< L. *ardere*, to burn] **1.** emotional warmth; passion **2.** zeal **3.** intense heat

ar·dour (är'dər) *n. Brit. sp. of* ARDOR

ar·du·ous (är'joo wəs) *adj.* [L. *arduus*, steep] **1.** difficult to do; laborious **2.** using much energy; strenuous —**ar'du·ous·ly** *adv.* —**ar'du·ous·ness** *n.*

are¹ (är) [OE. *aron*] *pl. & 2d pers. sing., pres. indic.,* of BE

are² (er, är) *n.* [Fr. < L. *area:* see AREA] a unit of area equal to 100 square meters (119.6 sq. yd.)

ar·e·a (er'ē ə) *n.* [L., vacant place] **1.** a part of the earth's surface; region **2.** the size of a surface, in square units **3.** a yard of a building **4.** a particular part of a house, city, etc. **5.** scope or extent —**ar'e·al** *adj.*

ar'e·a·way' (-wā') *n.* **1.** a sunken yard leading into a cellar **2.** a passage between buildings

a·re·na (ə rē'nə) *n.* [L., sandy place] **1.** the center of an ancient Roman amphitheater, for gladiatorial contests **2.** any place like this **3.** any sphere of struggle

arena theater a theater having a central stage surrounded by seats

aren't (ärnt) are not

Ar·es (er'ēz) *Gr. Myth.* the god of war: identified with the Roman god Mars

ar·gent (är'jənt) *n.* [Fr. < L. *argentum*, silver] [Archaic or Poet.] silver —*adj.* [Poet.] of silver: also **ar·gen'tal** (-jen't'l)

Ar·gen·ti·na (är'jən tē'nə) country in S S. America: 1,084,120 sq. mi.; pop. 23,983,000; cap. Buenos Aires — **Ar'gen·tine'** (-tēn', -tīn'), **Ar'gen·tin'e·an** (-tin'ē ən) *adj.,* *n.*

Ar·go (är'gō) *Gr. Myth.* the ship on which Jason sailed to find the Golden Fleece

ar·gon (är'gän) *n.* [Gr., inert] a chemical element, a colorless, odorless gas found in the atmosphere and used in radio tubes, etc.: symbol, Ar; at. wt., 39,948; at. no., 18

Ar·go·naut (är'gə nôt') *n.* [< Gr. *Argō,* ARGO + *nautēs,* sailor] *Gr. Myth.* any of the men who sailed with Jason to search for the Golden Fleece

ar·go·sy (är'gə sē) *n., pl.* **-sies** [< It. *Ragusea,* ship of Ragusa, ancient Adriatic port] [Poet.] a large ship or a fleet of such ships

ar·got (är'gō, -gət) *n.* [Fr.] the specialized vocabulary of a particular group, as the secret jargon of criminals

ar·gue (är'gyōō) *vi.* **-gued**, **-gu·ing** [L. *arguere,* prove] **1.** to give reasons (*for* or *against*) **2.** to have a disagreement; quarrel —*vt.* **1.** to give reasons for and against; debate **2.** to maintain; contend **3.** to give evidence of; indicate **4.** to persuade by giving reasons

ar'gu·ment (-gyə mənt) *n.* **1.** an arguing; debate **2.** a reason or reasons offered in arguing **3.** a dispute **4.** a summary

ar'gu·men·ta'tion (-men tā'shən) *n.* the process of arguing; debate

ar'gu·men'ta·tive (-tə tiv) *adj.* **1.** controversial **2.** apt to argue Also **ar'gu·men'tive** —**ar'gu·men'ta·tive·ness** *n.*

Ar·gus (är'gəs) [< Gr. *argos,* bright] *Gr. Myth.* a giant with a hundred eyes —*n.* an alert watchman

ar·gyle (är'gīl) *adj.* [< *Argyll,* Scotland] knitted or woven in a diamond-shaped pattern, as socks

a·ri·a (ä'rē ə, er'-) *n.* [It. < L. *aer,* air] a melody in an opera, etc., esp. for solo voice

Ar·i·an (er'ē ən, ar'-) *adj.* of Arius or Arianism —*n.* a believer in Arianism

-arian [< L.] *a suffix denoting* age, sect, social belief, occupation *[octogenarian]*

Ar·i·an·ism (er'ē ə niz'm, ar'-) *n.* the doctrines of Arius, who taught that Jesus was not of the same substance as God

ar·id (ar'id, er'-) *adj.* [< L. *arere,* be dry] **1.** dry and barren **2.** not interesting; dull —**a·rid·i·ty** (ə rid'ə tē), **ar'id·ness** *n.* —**ar'id·ly** *adv.*

Ar·i·es (er'ēz, ar'-; -i ēz') [L., the Ram] **1.** a N constellation **2.** the first sign of the zodiac: see ZODIAC, illus.

a·right (ə rīt') *adv.* correctly

ar·il (ar'il, er'-) *n.* [< ML. *arillus,* dried grape] an additional covering that forms on certain seeds after fertilization —**ar'il·late'** (-ə lāt') *adj.*

a·rise (ə rīz') *vi.* **a·rose'**, **a·ris'en** (-riz''n), **a·ris'ing** [OE. < *a-,* out + *risan,* to rise] **1.** to get up **2.** to move upward; ascend **3.** to come into being **4.** to result (*from* something)

ar·is·toc·ra·cy (ar'ə stäk'rə sē) *n., pl.* **-cies** [< Gr. *aristos,* best + *kratein,* to rule] **1.** government by a privileged minority, usually of inherited wealth **2.** a country with such government **3.** a privileged ruling class; nobility **4.** those considered the best in some way

a·ris·to·crat (ə ris'tə krat', ar'is-) *n.* **1.** a member of the aristocracy **2.** one with the manners, beliefs, etc. of the upper class —**a·ris'to·crat'ic** *adj.* —**a·ris'to·crat'i·cal·ly** *adv.*

Ar·is·toph·a·nes (ar'ə stäf'ə nēz') 448?–380? B.C.; Gr. writer of satirical comedies

Ar·is·tot·le (ar'ə stät''l) 384–322 B.C.; Gr. philosopher — **Ar·is·to·te·li·an** (ar'is tə tēl'yən) *adj., n.* —**Ar'is·to·te'li·an·ism** *n.*

a·rith·me·tic (ə rith'mə tik) *n.* [< Gr. *arithmos,* number] the science of computing by positive real numbers —*adj.* (ar'ith met'ik) of or using arithmetic: also **ar'ith·met'i·cal** —**a'rith·me·ti'cian** *n.*

A·ri·us (ə rī'əs, er'ē əs) 256?–336 A.D.; Christian theologian of Alexandria: see ARIANISM

Ar·i·zo·na (ar'ə zō'nə) State of the SW U.S., one of the Mountain States: 113,909 sq. mi.; pop. 1,772,000; cap. Phoenix: abbrev. Ariz., AZ —**Ar'i·zo'nan, Ar'i·zo'ni·an** *adj., n.*

ark (ärk) *n.* [< L. *arcere,* enclose] **1.** *Bible* the boat in which Noah, his family, and two of every kind of creature survived the Flood **2.** *same as* ARK OF THE COVENANT

Ar·kan·sas (är'k'n sô') **1.** State of the SC U.S.: 53,104 sq. mi.; pop. 1,923,000; cap. Little Rock: abbrev. Ark., AR **2.**

(*also* är kan′zəs) river flowing from Colorado into the Mississippi: 1,450 mi. —**Ar·kan′san** (-kan′z′n) *adj., n.*

ark of the covenant *Bible* the chest containing the stone tablets inscribed with the Ten Commandments

Ar·ling·ton National Cemetery (är′liŋ tən) a national cemetery in Va., near Washington, D.C.

arm[1] (ärm) *n.* [OE. *earm*] **1.** *a)* an upper limb of the human body *b)* anything commonly in contact with this, as a sleeve, the support for the arm on a chair, etc. **2.** anything like an arm in structure, function, position, etc. —**at arm's length** at a distance —**with open arms** cordially —**arm′less** *adj.* —**arm′like′** *adj.*

arm[2] (ärm) *n.* [< L. *arma*, weapons] **1.** any weapon: *usually used in pl.* **2.** [*pl.*] warfare; fighting **3.** [*pl.*] heraldic insignia **4.** any branch of the military forces —*vt.* **1.** to provide with weapons, etc. **2.** to prepare for or against attack —*vi.* to prepare for war —**take up arms 1.** to begin a war or rebellion **2.** to enter a dispute —**to arms!** get ready to fight —**up in arms 1.** prepared to fight **2.** indignant —**armed** *adj.*

ar·ma·da (är mä′də) *n.* [Sp. < L. *arma*, weapons] **1.** *a)* a fleet of warships *b)* [**A-**] such a fleet sent against England by Spain in 1588 **2.** a fleet of military aircraft

ar·ma·dil·lo (är′mə dil′ō) *n., pl.* **-los** [Sp.: see prec.] a burrowing mammal of Texas and Central and South America, covered with bony plates

Ar·ma·ged·don (är′mə ged′′n) *Bible* the place described as the scene of the last, deciding battle between good and evil

ar·ma·ment (är′mə mənt) *n.* **1.** [*often pl.*] all the military forces and equipment of a nation **2.** all the military equipment of a warship, fortification, etc. **3.** an arming or being armed for war **4.** anything that protects or defends

ar·ma·ture (är′mə chər) *n.* [see ARMADA] **1.** any protective covering **2.** a soft iron bar placed across the poles of a magnet **3.** the iron core wound with wire, usually a revolving part, in a generator or motor **4.** *Sculpture* a framework for supporting the clay, etc.

arm′chair′ *n.* a chair with supports at the sides for one's arms

armed forces all the military, naval, and air forces of a country

Ar·me·ni·a (är mē′nē ə, -mēn′yə) **1.** former kingdom of SW Asia **2.** republic of the U.S.S.R., including most of this region: in full, **Armenian Soviet Socialist Republic** —**Ar·me′ni·an** *adj., n.*

arm·ful (ärm′fool′) *n., pl.* **-fuls** as much as the arms or one arm can hold

arm′hole′ (-hōl′) *n.* an opening for the arm in a garment

ar·mi·stice (är′mə stis) *n.* [Fr. < L. *arma*, arms + *sistere*, cause to stand] a temporary stopping of warfare by mutual agreement

Armistice Day *see* VETERANS DAY

arm·let (ärm′lit) *n.* an ornamental band worn around the upper arm

ar·mor (är′mər) *n.* [< L.: see ARMATURE] **1.** covering worn to protect the body against weapons **2.** any defensive or protective covering **3.** a quality serving as a defense difficult to penetrate —*vt., vi.* to put armor on —**ar′mored** (-mərd) *adj.*

ar·mor·er (är′mər ər) *n.* **1.** formerly, one who made or repaired armor **2.** a maker of firearms

ar·mo·ri·al (är môr′ē əl) *adj.* of coats of arms; heraldic

ar·mor·y (är′mər ē) *n., pl.* **-ies** [see ARM²] **1.** an arsenal **2.** a building housing the drill hall and offices of a National Guard unit **3.** a place where firearms are made

ar·mour (är′mər) *n., vi., vt.* Brit. sp. of ARMOR

arm′pit′ *n.* the hollow under the arm at the shoulder

ar·my (är′mē) *n., pl.* **-mies** [< L. *armata*: see ARMADA] **1.** a large, organized body of soldiers for waging war **2.** any large number of persons, animals, etc.

army worm any of the larvae of certain moths that travel in large groups, ruining crops

ar·ni·ca (är′ni kə) *n.* [ModL.] a preparation made from certain plants of the composite family, formerly used for treating bruises, sprains, etc.

Ar·nold (är′nəld) **1. Benedict,** 1741–1801; Am. Revolutionary general who became a traitor **2. Matthew,** 1822–88; Eng. poet, essayist, & critic

a·ro·ma (ə rō′mə) *n.* [< Gr. *arōma*, spice] a pleasant odor; fragrance

ar·o·mat·ic (ar′ə mat′ik) *adj.* of or having an aroma —*n.* an aromatic plant, substance, or chemical —**ar′o·mat′i·cal·ly** *adv.*

a·rose (ə rōz′) *pt.* of ARISE

a·round (ə round′) *adv.* **1.** in a circle **2.** in every direction **3.** to the opposite direction, belief, etc. **4.** [Colloq.] nearby

[*stay around*] —*prep.* **1.** so as to encircle or envelop **2.** on the border of **3.** in various places in or on **4.** [Colloq.] about [*around* 1890]

a·rouse (ə rouz′) *vt.* **a·roused′, a·rous′ing 1.** to awaken **2.** to stir, as to action —**a·rous′al** *n.*

ar·peg·gio (är pej′ō, -pej′ē ō) *n., pl.* **-gios** [< It. *arpa*, a harp] the playing of the notes of a chord in quick succession

arr. 1. arranged **2.** arrival

ar·raign (ə rān′) *vt.* [< L. *ad*, to + *ratio*, reason] **1.** to bring before a law court to answer charges **2.** to call to account; accuse —**ar·raign′ment** *n.*

ar·range (ə rānj′) *vt.* **-ranged′, -rang′ing** [< OFr. *a-*, to + *renc*, rank] **1.** to put in the correct or suitable order **2.** to classify **3.** to prepare or plan **4.** to settle or adjust (matters) **5.** *Music* to adapt (a composition) to particular instruments or voices —**ar·rang′er** *n.*

ar·range′ment *n.* **1.** an arranging **2.** a result or manner of arranging **3.** [*usually pl.*] a plan **4.** a settlement **5.** *Music* an adaptation of a composition for particular instruments, voices, etc.

ar·rant (ar′ənt) *adj.* [var. of ERRANT] that is plainly such; out-and-out [*an arrant fool*]

ar·ras (ar′əs) *n.* [< *Arras*, Fr. city] **1.** an elaborate kind of tapestry **2.** a wall hanging of tapestry

ar·ray (ə rā′) *vt.* [ult. < L. *ad-*, to + Gmc. base *raid-*, order] **1.** to put in proper order; marshal (troops, etc.) **2.** to dress in finery —*n.* **1.** an orderly grouping, esp. of troops **2.** an impressive display **3.** fine clothes —**ar·ray′al** *n.*

ar·rears (ə rirz′) *n.pl.* [< L. *ad*, to + *retro*, behind] overdue debts —**in arrears** (or **arrear**) behind in paying a debt, in one's work, etc.

ar·rest (ə rest′) *vt.* [< L. *ad-*, to + *restare*, to stop] **1.** to stop or check **2.** to seize by authority of the law **3.** to catch and keep (one's attention, etc.) —*n.* an arresting or being arrested —**under arrest** in legal custody —**ar·rest′er, ar·res′tor** *n.*

ar·rest′ing *adj.* attracting attention; interesting; striking —**ar·rest′ing·ly** *adv.*

ar·riv·al (ə rī′v′l) *n.* **1.** the act of arriving **2.** a person or thing that arrives or has arrived

ar·rive (ə rīv′) *vi.* **-rived′, -riv′ing** [< L. *ad*, to + *ripa*, shore] **1.** to reach one's destination **2.** to come [*the time has arrived*] **3.** to attain fame, etc. —**arrive at** to reach by thinking, work, etc.

ar·ri·ve·der·ci (ä rē′ve der′chē) *interj.* [It.] until we meet again; goodbye

ar·ro·gance (ar′ə gəns) *n.* overbearing pride or self-importance: also **ar′ro·gan·cy**

ar′ro·gant *adj.* [see ff.] full of or due to arrogance; haughty —**ar′ro·gant·ly** *adv.*

ar′ro·gate′ (-gāt′) *vt.* **-gat′ed, -gat′ing** [< L. *ad-*, for + *rogare*, ask] **1.** to claim or seize without right **2.** to ascribe without reason —**ar′ro·ga′tion** *n.*

ar·row (ar′ō) *n.* [OE. *arwe*] **1.** a slender shaft, usually pointed at one end and feathered at the other, for shooting from a bow **2.** anything like an arrow in form, etc. **3.** a sign (←) used to indicate direction

ar′row·head′ (-hed′) *n.* **1.** the pointed tip of an arrow **2.** a plant with arrow-shaped leaves

ar′row·root′ *n.* [< use as antidote for poisoned arrows] **1.** a tropical American plant with starchy roots **2.** the edible starch made from its roots

ar·roy·o (ə roi′ō) *n., pl.* **-os** [Sp. < L. *arrugia*, mine shaft] [Southwest] **1.** a dry gully **2.** a rivulet

ar·se·nal (är′s′n əl) *n.* [< Ar. *dār* (eṣ) *ṣinā'a*, workshop] **1.** a place for making and storing weapons and other munitions **2.** a store or collection [*an arsenal of facts*]

ar·se·nic (är′s′n ik; *for adj.* är sen′ik) *n.* [ult. < Per. *zar*, gold] **1.** a silvery-white, brittle, very poisonous chemical element, compounds of which are used in insecticides, medicines, etc.: symbol, As; at. wt., 74.9216; at. no., 33 **2.** loosely, arsenic trioxide, a poisonous, tasteless, white powder —*adj.* of or containing arsenic

ar·son (är′s′n) *n.* [< L. *ardere*, to burn] the crime of purposely setting fire to a building —**ar′son·ist** *n.*

art[1] (ärt) *n.* [< L. *ars*] **1.** human creativity **2.** skill **3.** any specific skill or its application **4.** any craft or its principles **5.** a making of things that have form or beauty **6.** any branch of this, as painting, sculpture, etc. **7.** drawings, paintings, statues, etc. **8.** a branch of learning; specif., [*pl.*] *same as* LIBERAL ARTS **9.** cunning **10.** sly trick; wile: *usually used in pl.*

art[2] (ärt) *archaic 2d pers. sing., pres. indic.,* of BE: *used with* thou

art. 1. article **2.** artificial

Ar·te·mis (är′tə mis) *Gr. Myth.* the goddess of the moon, wild animals, and hunting: identified with the Roman goddess Diana

ar·te·ri·al (är tir′ē əl) *adj.* **1.** of or like an artery or arteries **2.** designating or of the bright-red, oxygenated blood in the arteries **3.** of or being a main road with many branches

ar·te·ri·o·scle·ro·sis (är tir′ē ō sklə rō′sis) *n.* [see ff. & SCLEROSIS] a thickening, and loss of elasticity, of the walls of the arteries, as in old age —**ar·te′ri·o·scle·rot′ic** (-rät′ik) *adj.*

ar·ter·y (är′tər ē) *n., pl.* **-ies** [prob. < Gr. *aeirein*, to raise] **1.** any of the tubes carrying blood from the heart **2.** a main road or channel

ar·te·sian well (är tē′zhən) [< Fr. *Artois*, former Fr. province] a deep well in which water is forced up by pressure of underground water draining from higher ground

art·ful (ärt′fəl) *adj.* **1.** skillful or clever **2.** cunning; crafty **3.** artificial; imitative —**art′ful·ly** *adv.* —**art′ful·ness** *n.*

ar·thri·tis (är thrīt′is) *n.* [< Gr. *arthron*, a joint + -ITIS] inflammation of a joint or joints —**ar·thrit′ic** (-thrit′ik) *adj.* —**ar·thrit′i·cal·ly** *adv.*

ar·thro·pod (är′thrə päd′) *n.* [< Gr. *arthron*, a joint + -POD] any of a large group of invertebrate animals with jointed legs and a segmented body, as insects, crustaceans, arachnids, etc.

Ar·thur (är′thər) **1.** legendary 6th-cent. king of Britain who led the knights of the Round Table **2. Chester A.,** 1830–86; 21st president of the U.S. (1881–85) —**Ar·thu′ri·an** (-thoor′ē ən) *adj.*

ar·ti·choke (är′tə chōk′) *n.* [ult. < Ar. *al-harshūf*] **1.** a thistlelike plant **2.** its flower head, cooked as a vegetable

ar·ti·cle (är′ti k'l) *n.* [< L. *artus*, joint] **1.** one of the sections of a document **2.** a complete piece of writing, as in a newspaper, magazine, etc. **3.** a separate item [an *article* of luggage] **4.** a commodity **5.** *Gram.* any one of the words *a, an,* or *the,* used as adjectives —*vt.* **-cled, -cling** to bind by the articles of an agreement

ar·tic·u·lar (är tik′yə lər) *adj.* [< L. *artus,* a joint] of the joints [*articular* inflammation]

ARTICHOKE

ar·tic·u·late (är tik′yə lit; *for v.* -lāt′) *adj.* [< L. *artus,* a joint] **1.** jointed: usually **ar·tic′u·lat′ed 2.** spoken distinctly **3.** able to speak **4.** expressing oneself clearly —*vt.* **-lat′ed, -lat′ing 1.** to put together by joints **2.** to put together in a connected way **3.** to utter distinctly **4.** to express clearly —*vi.* **1.** to speak distinctly **2.** to be jointed —**ar·tic′u·late·ly** *adv.* —**ar·tic′u·late·ness** *n.*

ar·tic·u·la·tion (är tik′yə lā′shən) *n.* **1.** a jointing or being jointed **2.** enunciation **3.** a spoken sound **4.** a joint between bones or similar parts **5.** *Bot.* a node or space between two nodes

ar·ti·fact (är′tə fakt′) *n.* [see ff.] any object made by human work; esp., a primitive tool, etc.

ar·ti·fice (är′tə fis) *n.* [< L. *ars,* art + *facere,* to make] **1.** skill or ingenuity **2.** trickery **3.** a sly trick

ar·tif·i·cer (är tif′ə sər) *n.* **1.** a skilled craftsman **2.** an inventor

ar·ti·fi·cial (är′tə fish′əl) *adj.* [see ARTIFICE] **1.** made by human work or art; not natural **2.** simulated [*artificial* teeth] **3.** affected [an *artificial* smile] —**ar′ti·fi′ci·al′i·ty** (-fish′ē al′ə tē) *n., pl.* **-ties** —**ar′ti·fi′cial·ly** *adv.*

artificial insemination the impregnation of a female without sexual intercourse

artificial respiration an artificial maintenance of breathing, as by forcing breath into the mouth

ar·til·ler·y (är til′ər ē) *n.* [< Pr. *artilla,* fortification] **1.** mounted guns, as cannon or missile launchers **2.** the science of guns; gunnery —**the artillery** the military branch specializing in the use of artillery —**ar·til′ler·y·man** (-mən) *n., pl.* **-men**

ar·ti·san (är′tə z′n) *n.* [ult. < L. *ars,* art] a skilled workman; craftsman

art·ist (är′tist) *n.* **1.** one who is skilled in any of the fine arts, esp. in painting, sculpture, etc. **2.** one who does anything very well **3.** *same as* ARTISTE

ar·tiste (är tēst′) *n.* [Fr.] a professional in any of the performing arts

ar·tis·tic (är tis′tik) *adj.* **1.** of art or artists **2.** done skillfully **3.** sensitive to beauty —**ar·tis′ti·cal·ly** *adv.*

art·ist·ry (är′tis trē) *n.* artistic work or skill

art·less (ärt′lis) *adj.* **1.** lacking skill or art **2.** simple; natural **3.** without guile or deceit; ingenuous **4.** uncultured; ignorant —**art′less·ly** *adv.* —**art′less·ness** *n.*

art·sy-craft·sy (ärt′sē kraft′sē) *adj.* [Colloq.] of arts and crafts: usually a disparaging term connoting faddishness, amateurishness, etc.

art·y (ärt′ē) *adj.* **-i·er, -i·est** [Colloq.] affectedly artistic —**art′i·ness** *n.*

ar·um (er′əm) *n.* [< Gr. *aron*] any of a family of plants bearing small flowers enclosed by a hoodlike leaf

-ary [< L.] *a suffix meaning:* **1.** related to; connected with [*auxiliary*] **2.** a place for [*granary*]

Ar·y·an (er′ē ən, ar′-) *n.* [< Sans. *ārya,* noble] **1.** formerly, the hypothetical parent language of the Indo-European family **2.** a person supposed to be a descendant of the prehistoric peoples who spoke this language **3.** loosely, as in Nazi usage, a non-Jewish Caucasoid, a Nordic, etc.

as¹ (az; *unstressed* əz) *adv.* [< ALSO] **1.** to the same amount or degree; equally [he's just *as* happy at home] **2.** for instance [a card game, *as* bridge] **3.** when related in a specified way [this view *as* contrasted with that] — *conj.* **1.** to the same amount or degree that [straight *as* an arrow] **2.** in the same manner that [do *as* he does] **3.** while [she wept *as* she spoke] **4.** because [as you object, we won't go] **5.** that the consequence is [so clear *as* to be obvious] **6.** though [full *as* he was, he kept eating] —*pron.* **1.** a fact that [he is tired, *as* you can see] **2.** that (preceded by *such* or *the same*) [the same color *as* yours (is)] —*prep.* in the role or function of [he poses *as* a friend] —**as for** (or **to**) concerning —**as if** (or **though**) **1.** as it (or one) would if **2.** that [it seems *as if* she's never home] —**as is** [Colloq.] just as it is —**as it were** as if it were so

as² (as) *n., pl.* **as′ses** [L.] an ancient Roman coin of copper alloy

As *Chem.* arsenic

AS., A.S., A-S. Anglo-Saxon

as·a·fet·i·da, as·a·foet·i·da (as′ə fet′ə də) *n.* [< Per. *āzā,* gum + L. *f(o)etida,* fetid] a bad-smelling resin obtained from various Asiatic plants and formerly used in medicine

as·bes·tos, as·bes·tus (as bes′təs, az-) *n.* [< Gr. *a-,* not + *sbennynai,* to extinguish] a fire-resistant and heat-resistant, fibrous mineral used in fireproofing, roofing, insulation, etc.

as·cend (ə send′) *vi., vt.* [< L. *ad-,* to + *scandere,* to climb] **1.** to go up; mount **2.** to succeed to (a throne) — **as·cend′a·ble, as·cend′i·ble** *adj.* —**as·cend′er** *n.*

as·cend·an·cy, as·cend′en·cy (-ən sē) *n.* a position of control or power; domination: also **as·cend′ance, as·cend′ence**

as·cend′ant, as·cend′ent (-ənt) *adj.* **1.** ascending **2.** in control; dominant —*n.* a dominating position; ascendancy —**in the ascendant** at or nearing the height of power, fame, etc.

as·cen·sion (ə sen′shən) *n.* **1.** an ascending **2.** [A-] the fortieth day after Easter, celebrating the Ascension: also **Ascension Day** —**the Ascension** *Bible* the bodily ascent of Jesus into heaven

as·cent (ə sent′) *n.* **1.** an ascending or rising **2.** an upward slope

as·cer·tain (as′ər tān′) *vt.* [see AD- & CERTAIN] to find out with certainty —**as′cer·tain′a·ble** *adj.* —**as′cer·tain′·ment** *n.*

as·cet·ic (ə set′ik) *adj.* [< Gr. *askein,* to train the body] of or characteristic of ascetics or their way of life; self-denying —*n.* one who leads a life of contemplation and rigorous self-denial, esp. for religious purposes —**as·cet′i·cal·ly** *adv.* —**as·cet′i·cism** *n.*

as·cid·i·an (ə sid′ē ən) *n.* [< Gr. *askos,* a bag] any of a group of sea animals that are sac-shaped and have a tough outer covering

as·cid′i·um (-əm) *n., pl.* **-i·a** (-ə) [see prec.] a pitcherlike leaf or structure, as of the pitcher plant

as·co·my·cete (as′kə mī sēt′) *n.* [< Gr. *askos,* bladder + *mykēs,* fungus] any of a class of spore-reproducing fungi, including mildews and yeasts

a·scor·bic acid (ə skôr′bik) [A- (sense 2) + SCORB(UTIC) + -IC] a water-soluble vitamin occurring in citrus fruits, tomatoes, etc.; vitamin C: it prevents and cures scurvy

as·cot (as'kət) *n.* a necktie with very broad ends hanging from the knot

as·cribe (ə skrīb') *vt.* -cribed', -crib'ing [< L. *ad-*, to + *scribere*, to write] 1. to assign (*to* a supposed cause); attribute 2. to regard as belonging (*to*) or coming from someone —as·crib'a·ble *adj.* —as·crip·tion (ə skrip'shən) *n.*

ASCOT

a·sep·sis (ā sep'sis, ə-) *n.* 1. the condition of being aseptic 2. aseptic treatment or technique

a·sep'tic (-tik) *adj.* not septic; free from disease-producing germs — **a·sep'ti·cal·ly** *adv.*

a·sex·u·al (ā sek'shoo wəl) *adj.* 1. having no sex; sexless 2. of reproduction without the union of male and female germ cells —a·sex'u·al·ly *adv.*

ash¹ (ash) *n.* [OE. *æsce*] 1. the grayish powder left after something has burned 2. the gray color of wood ash 3. fine, volcanic lava See also ASHES

ash² (ash) *n.* [OE. *æsc*] 1. a shade tree of the olive family, having tough, elastic, straight-grained wood 2. the wood

a·shamed (ə shāmd') *adj.* 1. feeling shame because something wrong was done 2. reluctant because fearing shame beforehand —a·sham·ed·ly (ə shā'mid lē) *adv.*

ash·can (ash'kan') *n.* a can for ashes and trash

ash·en (ash'ən) *adj.* 1. of ashes 2. like ashes, esp. in color; pale; pallid

ash·es (ash'iz) *n.pl.* 1. the unburned particles and grayish powder left after a thing has burned 2. human remains, esp. after cremation

ash·lar, ash·ler (ash'lər) *n.* [< L. *assis*, board] 1. either of two kinds of square, cut stone used in building 2. masonry made of either of these

a·shore (ə shôr') *adv., adj.* 1. to or on the shore 2. to or on land

Ash·to·reth (ash'tə reth') Astarte

ash·tray (ash'trā') *n.* a container for tobacco ashes

Ash Wednesday the first day of Lent: from the putting of ashes on the forehead in penitence

ash·y (ash'ē) *adj.* -i·er, -i·est 1. of, like, or covered with ashes 2. of ash color; pale

A·sia (ā'zhə, -shə) largest continent, situated in the Eastern Hemisphere and separated from N Europe by the Ural Mountains: 16,900,000 sq. mi.; pop. 2,035,000,000 — A'sian, A·si·at·ic (ā'zhē at'ik) *adj., n.*

Asia Minor large peninsula in W Asia, between the Black Sea and the Mediterranean

a·side (ə sīd') *adv.* 1. on or to one side 2. away; in reserve [put this *aside* for me] 3. out of one's thoughts, etc. 4. apart; notwithstanding [joking *aside*] —*n.* words spoken by an actor and supposedly heard only by the audience —aside from 1. with the exception of 2. apart from

as·i·nine (as'ə nīn') *adj.* [< L. *asinus*, ass] like an ass; esp., having qualities thought of as asslike; stupid, silly, obstinate, etc. —as'i·nine'ly *adv.* —as'i·nin'i·ty (-nin'ə tē) *n., pl.* -ties

ask (ask) *vt.* [OE. *ascian*] 1. to use words in seeking the answer to (a question) 2. to put a question to (a person) 3. to request or demand 4. to require (a thing) 5. to invite —*vi.* 1. to make a request (*for*) 2. to inquire (*about*) —ask'er *n.* —ask'ing *n.*

a·skance (ə skans') *adv.* [< ME. *a-*, on + *skwyn*, sidewise] 1. with a sidewise glance 2. with suspicion, disapproval, etc.

a·skew (ə skyoo') *adv.* to one side; awry —*adj.* on one side; awry

a·slant (ə slant') *adv.* on a slant —*prep.* on a slant across —*adj.* slanting

a·sleep (ə slēp') *adj.* 1. sleeping 2. inactive; dull 3. numb [my arm is *asleep*] 4. dead —*adv.* into a sleeping or inactive condition

a·so·cial (ā sō'shəl) *adj.* 1. not social; characterized by withdrawal from others 2. selfish

asp (asp) *n.* [< Gr. *aspis*] any of several small, poisonous snakes of Africa and Europe

as·par·a·gus (ə spar'ə gəs) *n.* [< Gr. *asparagos*, a sprout] 1. a plant with small, scalelike leaves and edible shoots 2. these shoots

a·spar·kle (ə spär'k'l) *adj.* sparkling

A.S.P.C.A. American Society for the Prevention of Cruelty to Animals

as·pect (as'pekt) *n.* [< L. *ad-*, to + *specere*, to look] 1. the way one appears or looks 2. the appearance of a thing or idea from a specific viewpoint 3. a side facing in a given direction [the eastern *aspect* of the house]

as·pen (as'pən) *n.* [OE. *æspe*] a poplar tree whose leaves flutter in the least breeze —*adj.* trembling

as·per·i·ty (as per'ə tē) *n., pl.* -ties [< L. *asper*, rough] 1. roughness or harshness, as of surface, sound, etc. 2. sharpness of temper

as·perse (ə spurs') *vt.* -persed', -pers'ing [< L. *ad-*, to + *spargere*, to sprinkle] to slander

as·per·sion (ə spur'zhən) *n.* 1. a defaming 2. a damaging remark; slander

as·phalt (as'fôlt) *n.* [< Gr.] 1. a brown or black tarlike variety of bitumen 2. a mixture of this with sand or gravel, for paving, roofing, etc. —*vt.* to pave, roof, etc. with asphalt —as·phal'tic *adj.*

as·pho·del (as'fə del') *n.* [< Gr *asphodelos*] a plant with fleshy roots and white or yellow flowers

as·phyx·i·a (as fik'sē ə) *n.* [Gr. < *a-*, not + *sphyzein*, to throb] loss of consciousness from too little oxygen and too much carbon dioxide in the blood: suffocation causes asphyxia —as·phyx'i·ant *adj., n.*

as·phyx'i·ate' (-āt') *vt.* -at'ed, -at'ing 1. to cause asphyxia in 2. to suffocate —as·phyx'i·a'tion *n.* —as·phyx'i·a'tor *n.*

as·pic (as'pik) *n.* [< OFr. *aspe*] a jelly of meat juice, tomato juice, etc. used as a relish, etc.

as·pir·ant (as'pər ənt, ə spīr'ənt) *adj.* aspiring —*n.* a person who aspires, as after honors, etc.

as·pi·rate (as'pə rāt'; *for n. & adj.* -pər it) *vt.* -rat'ed, -rat'ing [< L.: see ASPIRE] 1. to begin (a word or syllable) with the sound of English *h* 2. to follow (a consonant) with an audible puff of breath —*n.* an aspirated sound —*adj.* aspirated

as'pi·ra'tion *n.* 1. *a*) a strong desire or ambition *b*) the thing so desired 2. an aspirating 3. an aspirate

as'pi·ra'tor *n.* a suction apparatus for removing air, fluids, etc. as from a body cavity

as·pire (ə spīr') *vi.* -pired', -pir'ing [< L. *ad-*, to + *spirare*, breathe] to be ambitious (*to* get or do something lofty); seek —as·pir'ing·ly *adv.*

as·pi·rin (as'pər in) *n.* [G.] a white, crystalline powder, acetylsalicylic acid, $C_9H_8O_4$, used for reducing fever, relieving headaches, etc.

ass (as) *n.* [< L. *asinus*] 1. an animal related to the horse but with longer ears 2. a silly person

as·sa·gai (as'ə gī') *n.* [< Ar. *az-zaghāyah*, the spear] a slender spear used by some African tribes

as·sail (ə sāl') *vt.* [< L. *ad*, to + *salire*, to leap] 1. to attack physically and violently 2. to attack with arguments, doubts, etc. —as·sail'a·ble *adj.*

as·sail'ant (-ənt) *n.* an attacker: also as·sail'er

as·sas·sin (ə sas''n) *n.* [Fr. < Ar. *ḥashshāshīn*, hashish users] a murderer who strikes suddenly; esp., the killer of a politically important person

as·sas'si·nate' (-āt') *vt.* -nat'ed, -nat'ing 1. to murder (esp. a politically important person) 2. to ruin (a reputation, etc.), as by slander —as·sas'si·na'tion *n.*

as·sault (ə sôlt') *n.* [< L. *ad*, to + *saltare*, to leap] 1. a violent physical or verbal attack; sometimes, specif., rape 2. *Law* a threat or attempt to harm another physically —*vt., vi.* to make an assault (upon) —as·sault'ive *adj.*

assault and battery *Law* the carrying out of threatened physical harm or violence

as·say (as'ā, a sā') *n.* [< L. *ex-*, out + *agere*, to act] 1. a testing 2. the analysis of an ore, metal, etc. to find out the nature and proportion of the ingredients 3. a report of such analysis —*vt.* (a sā', ə-) to make an assay of; test; analyze —as·say'er *n.*

as·sem·blage (ə sem'blij) *n.* 1. an assembling or being assembled 2. a group of persons or things gathered together; assembly

as·sem·ble (ə sem'b'l) *vt., vi.* -bled, -bling [< L. *ad-*, to + *simul*, together] 1. to gather into a group; collect 2. to fit or put together the parts of —as·sem'bler *n.*

as·sem·bly (-blē) *n., pl.* -blies 1. an assembling or being assembled 2. a group of persons gathered together 3. [A.] a legislative body 4. *a*) a fitting together of parts to form a unit *b*) such parts

assembly line an arrangement by which workers in succession perform single operations on the work as it moves along, often on a belt or track

as·sem·bly·man (-mən) *n., pl.* -men a member of a legislative assembly

as·sent (ə sent') *vi.* [< L. *ad-*, to + *sentire*, to feel] to agree (*to*); concur —*n.* consent or agreement

as·sert (ə surt') *vt.* [< L. *ad-*, to + *serere*, to join] 1. to declare; affirm 2. to maintain or defend (one's rights, etc.) —assert oneself to insist on one's rights, or on being recognized —as·sert'er, as·ser'tor *n.*

as·ser·tion (ə sur′shən) *n*. **1**. an asserting **2**. a positive statement; declaration

as·ser′tive (-tiv) *adj*. positive or confident in a persistent way —**as·ser′tive·ly** *adv*. —**as·ser′tive·ness** *n*.

as·sess (ə ses′) *vt*. [< L. *ad-*, to + *sedere*, sit] **1**. to set an estimated value on (property, etc.) for taxation **2**. to set the amount of (damages, a fine, etc.) **3**. to impose a fine, tax, etc. on

as·sess′ment (-mənt) *n*. **1**. an assessing **2**. an amount assessed

as·sess′or (-ər) *n*. one who assesses property, etc. for taxation

as·set (as′et) *n*. [< L. *ad*, to + *satis*, enough] **1**. anything owned that has value **2**. a desirable thing /charm is her chief *asset]* **3**. [*pl.*] all the property, accounts receivable, cash, etc. of a person or business **4**. [*pl.*] *Law* property, as of a bankrupt

as·sev·er·ate (ə sev′ə rāt′) *vt*. -**at′ed**, -**at′ing** [< L. *ad-*, to + *severus*, earnest] to state seriously or positively —**as·sev′er·a′tion** *n*.

as·si·du·i·ty (as′ə dyōō′ə tē) *n., pl.* -**ties** **1**. a being assiduous; diligence **2**. [*pl.*] constant personal attention

as·sid·u·ous (ə sij′ōō wəs) *adj*. [< L. *ad-*, to + *sedere*, sit] diligent; persevering; careful —**as·sid′u·ous·ly** *adv*. —**as·sid′u·ous·ness** *n*.

as·sign (ə sīn′) *vt*. [< L. *ad-*, to + *signare*, to sign] **1**. to set apart or mark for a specific purpose; designate **2**. to place at some task or duty **3**. to give out as a task; allot **4**. to ascribe (a motive, reason, etc.) **5**. *Law* to transfer (a claim, property, etc.) to another —*n*. [*usually pl.*] an assignee —**as·sign′a·ble** *adj*. —**as·sign′er**, *Law* **as·sign′or** (-ər, -ôr′) *n*.

as·sig·na·tion (as′ig nā′shən) *n*. **1**. an assigning **2**. anything assigned **3**. an appointment to meet, esp. one made secretly by lovers

as·sign·ee (ə sī′nē′) *n*. *Law* a person to whom a claim, property, etc. is transferred

as·sign·ment (ə sīn′mənt) *n*. **1**. an assigning or being assigned **2**. anything assigned, as a lesson, task, etc. **3**. *Law* *a)* a transfer of a claim, property, etc. *b)* a paper, as a deed, authorizing this

as·sim·i·late (ə sim′ə lāt′) *vt*. -**lat′ed**, -**lat′ing** [< L. *ad-*, to + *similis*, like] **1**. to absorb (food) into the body **2**. to absorb and incorporate into one's thinking **3**. to absorb (groups of different cultures) into the main culture **4**. to make like or alike (with *to*) —*vi*. to become assimilated —**as·sim′i·la·ble** *adj*.

as·sim·i·la·tion (ə sim′ə lā′shən) *n*. an assimilating or being assimilated; specif., *a)* the absorption of a minority group into the main culture *b) Physiol.* the change of digested or absorbed food into living tissue —**as·sim′i·la′tive** *adj*.

as·sist (ə sist′) *vt., vi*. [< L. *ad-*, to + *stare*, to stand] to help; aid —*n*. **1**. an act or instance of helping **2**. *Baseball* a defensive play by a fielder enabling a teammate to make a putout —**assist** at to be present at

as·sist′ance (-əns) *n*. help; aid

as·sist′ant (-ənt) *adj*. assisting; helping —*n*. one who assists; helper; aid

as·siz·es (ə sīz′iz) *n.pl.* [see ASSESS] **1**. court sessions held periodically in each county of England **2**. the time or place of these

assn. association

assoc. **1**. associate **2**. associated **3**. association

as·so·ci·ate (ə sō′shē āt′; *for n. & adj. usually* -it) *vt*. -**at′ed**, -**at′ing** [< L. *ad-*, to + *socius*, companion] **1**. to connect; combine; join **2**. to bring into relationship as partner, friend, etc. **3**. to connect in the mind —*vi*. **1**. to join (*with*) as a partner, friend, etc. **2**. to unite —*n*. **1**. a partner, colleague, friend, etc. **2**. a member of less than full status, as of a society **3**. anything joined with another **4**. a degree granted by a junior college at the end of a two-year course —*adj*. **1**. joined with others, as in some work **2**. of less than full status

as·so·ci·a·tion (-ā′shən) *n*. **1**. the act of associating **2**. fellowship; partnership **3**. an organization of persons having common interests, purposes, etc.; society **4**. a connection between ideas, feelings, etc. —**as·so′ci·a′tive** (-ā′tiv, -shə tiv) *adj*.

association football soccer

as·so·nance (as′ə nəns) *n*. [Fr. < L. *ad-*, to + *sonare*, to sound] **1**. likeness of sound **2**. a partial rhyme in which the stressed vowel sounds are alike, as in *late* and *make* —**as′so·nant** *adj., n*.

as·sort (ə sôrt′) *vt*. [< L. *ad-*, to + *sors*, lot] to separate into classes according to kinds; classify —*vi*. **1**. to match (*with*) **2**. to associate (*with*)

as·sort′ed *adj*. **1**. various; miscellaneous **2**. classified **3**. matched

as·sort′ment *n*. **1**. an assorting or being assorted **2**. a miscellaneous group; variety

ASSR, A.S.S.R. Autonomous Soviet Socialist Republic

asst. assistant

as·suage (ə swāj′) *vt*. -**suaged′**, -**suag′ing** [< L. *ad*, to + *suavis*, sweet] **1**. to lessen (pain, distress, etc.) **2**. to calm (passion, anger, etc.) **3**. to satisfy or slake (thirst, etc.) —**as·suage′ment** *n*.

as·sume (ə sōōm′, -syōōm′) *vt*. -**sumed′**, -**sum′ing** [< L. *ad-*, to + *sumere*, take] **1**. to take on (the appearance, role, etc. of) **2**. to seize; usurp /to *assume* control] **3**. to undertake **4**. to take for granted; suppose **5**. to pretend to have; feign —**as·sum′ed·ly** *adv*. —**as·sum′er** *n*.

as·sum′ing *adj*. presumptuous

as·sump·tion (ə sump′shən) *n*. **1**. the act of assuming **2**. a supposition **3**. presumption **4**. [**A-**] *R.C.Ch. a)* the taking up of the body and soul of the Virgin Mary into heaven after her death *b)* a church festival on August 15 celebrating this

as·sur·ance (ə shoor′əns) *n*. **1**. the act of assuring **2**. a being assured; sureness; confidence **3**. something that inspires confidence, as a promise; guarantee **4**. self-confidence **5**. impudent forwardness **6**. [Chiefly Brit.] insurance

as·sure (ə shoor′) *vt*. -**sured′**, -**sur′ing** [< L. *ad*, to +, *securus*, secure] **1**. to make (a person) sure of something; convince **2**. to give confidence to **3**. to promise confidently **4**. to guarantee **5**. [Brit.] to insure against loss —**as·sur′er** *n*.

as·sured′ *adj*. **1**. made sure; certain **2**. confident **3**. insured —**as·sur·ed·ly** (ə shoor′id lē) *adv*.

As·syr·i·a (ə sir′ē ə) ancient empire in SW Asia —**As·syr′i·an** *adj., n*.

As·tar·te (as tär′tē) a Semitic goddess of fertility and sexual love

as·ta·tine (as′tə tēn′) *n*. [< Gr. *astatos*, unstable + -INE³] a radioactive chemical element· symbol, At; at. wt., 210(?); at. no., 85

as·ter (as′tər) *n*. [< Gr. *astēr*, a star] any of a group of plants with variously colored daisylike flowers

as·ter·isk (as′tər isk) *n*. [< Gr. dim. of *astēr*, a star] a starlike sign (*) used in printing to indicate footnotes, omissions, etc.

a·stern (ə sturn′) *adv*. **1**. behind a ship or aircraft **2**. at or toward the rear of a ship or aircraft **3**. backward

as·ter·oid (as′tə roid′) *n*. [< Gr. *astēr*, star + -OID] **1**. any of the small planets between Mars and Jupiter **2**. a starfish

asth·ma (az′mə) *n*. [Gr.] a chronic disorder characterized by coughing, difficult breathing, etc. —**asth·mat′ic** (-mat′ik) *adj., n*.

NEW ENGLAND ASTER

a·stig·ma·tism (ə stig′mə tiz′m) *n*. [< Gr. *a-*, without + *stigma*, a mark + -ISM] **1**. an irregularity in the curvature of a lens, esp. of the eye, so that rays do not meet in a single focal point and images are distorted **2**. a distorted view or judgment —**as·tig·mat·ic** (as′tig mat′ik) *adj*.

a·stir (ə stur′) *adv., adj*. **1**. in motion **2**. out of bed

as·ton·ish (ə stän′ish) *vt*. [< L. *ex-*, out + *tonare*, to thunder] to fill with sudden wonder or great surprise; amaze —**as·ton′ish·ing** *adj*. —**as·ton′ish·ing·ly** *adv*. —**as·ton′ish·ment** *n*.

as·tound (ə stound′) *vt*. [see prec.] to astonish greatly —**as·tound′ing** *adj*. —**as·tound′ing·ly** *adv*.

a·strad·dle (ə strad′'l) *adv*. astride

As·tra·khan (as′trə kən) seaport in S European R.S.F.S.R.: pop. 376,000

as·tra·khan (as′trə kən) *n*. **1**. a loosely curled fur from the pelt of very young lambs orig. bred near Astrakhan **2**. a wool fabric made to look like this Also sp. **as′tra·chan**

as·tral (as′trəl) *adj*. [< Gr. *astron*, star] of, from, or like the stars

a·stray (ə strā′) *adv*. off the right path or way

a·stride (ə strīd′) *adv*. **1**. with a leg on either side **2**. with legs far apart —*prep.* **1.** with a leg on either side of (a horse, etc.) **2.** extending over or across

as·trin·gent (ə strin′jənt) *adj.* [< L. *ad-*, to + *stringere*, to draw] **1.** that contracts body tissues and checks secretions, capillary bleeding, etc. **2.** harsh; severe —*n.* an astringent substance —**as·trin′gen·cy** *n.* —**as·trin′gent·ly** *adv.*

astro- [< Gr. *astron*, a star] *a combining form meaning* of a star or stars [*astrophysics*]

as·tro·dome (as′trə dōm′) *n.* a transparent dome on top of an aircraft fuselage for the navigator

astrol. **1.** astrologer **2.** astrology

as·tro·labe (as′trə lāb′) *n.* [< Gr. *astron*, star + *lambanein*, take] an instrument once used to find the altitude of stars, etc.

as·trol·o·gy (ə sträl′ə jē) *n.* [< Gr. *astron*, star + -LOGY] a pseudoscience claiming to foretell the future by the supposed influence of the stars, planets, etc. on human affairs —**as·trol′o·ger** *n.* —**as·tro·log·i·cal** (as′trə läj′i k′l) *adj.*

astron. **1.** astronomer **2.** astronomy

as·tro·naut (as′trə nôt′) *n.* [< Fr.: see ff.] a person trained to make rocket flights in outer space

as·tro·nau·tics (as′trə nôt′iks) *n.pl.* [*with sing. v.*] [< Fr.: ult. < Gr. *astron*, star + *nautēs*, sailor] the science that deals with spacecraft and travel in outer space —**as′tro·nau′ti·cal** *adj.*

as·tro·nom·i·cal (as′trə näm′i k′l) *adj.* **1.** of astronomy **2.** very large, as the numbers used in astronomy Also **as′tro·nom′ic** —**as′tro·nom′i·cal·ly** *adv.*

as·tron·o·my (ə strän′ə mē) *n.* [< Gr. *astron*, star + *nemein*, arrange] the science of the stars and other heavenly bodies, dealing with their composition, motion, size, etc. —**as·tron′o·mer** *n.*

as·tro·phys·ics (as′trō fiz′iks) *n.pl.* [*with sing. v.*] the science of the physical properties and phenomena of the stars, planets, etc. —**as′tro·phys′i·cal** *adj.* —**as′tro·phys′i·cist** (-ə sist) *n.*

as·tute (ə stōōt′, -styōōt′) *adj.* [< L. *astus*, craft] shrewd; keen —**as·tute′ly** *adv.* —**as·tute′ness** *n.*

A·sun·ción (ä sōōn syôn′) capital of Paraguay: pop. 305,000

a·sun·der (ə sun′dər) *adv.* [OE. *on sundran*] **1.** in or into pieces **2.** apart or separate

a·sy·lum (ə sī′ləm) *n.* [< Gr. *a-*, without + *sylē*, right of seizure] **1.** a place of safety; refuge **2.** *an old name for* a place for the care of the mentally ill, or of the aged, poor, etc.

a·sym·me·try (ā sim′ə trē) *n.* lack of symmetry —**a·sym·met·ri·cal** (ā′sə met′ri k′l), **a′sym·met′ric** *adj.* —**a′sym·met′ri·cal·ly** *adv.*

at (at, ət) *prep.* [OE. *æt*] **1.** on; in; near; by [*at the office*] **2.** to or toward [*look at her*] **3.** from [*visible at one mile*] **4.** attending [*at the party*] **5.** busy with [*at work*] **6.** in the state or manner of [*at war, at a trot*] **7.** because of [*sad at his death*] **8.** with reference to [*good at tennis*] **9.** in the amount, etc. of [*at five cents each*] **10.** on or near the age or time of [*at noon*]

At *Chem.* astatine

At·a·brine (at′ə brin, -brēn′) [G. *atebrin*] *a trademark for* a synthetic drug used in treating malaria, etc. —*n.* [a-] this drug

at·a·rac·tic (at′ə rak′tik) *n.* [< Gr. *a-*, not + *tarassein*, to disturb] a tranquilizing drug —*adj.* of tranquilizing drugs or their effects Also **at′a·rax′ic** (-rak′sik)

at·a·vism (at′ə viz′m) *n.* [< Fr. < L. *atavus*, ancestor] resemblance or reversion to remote ancestral characteristics —**at′a·vis′tic** *adj.*

a·tax·i·a (ə tak′sē ə) *n.* [< Gr. *a-*, not + *tassein*, arrange] inability to coordinate voluntary muscular movements —**a·tax′ic** *adj., n.*

ate (āt; *Brit., or U.S. dial.*, et) *pt. of* EAT

-ate [< L. *-atus*, pp. ending] *a suffix meaning:* **1.** to become, cause to become, form, provide with [*maturate*, *vaccinate*] **2.** of or characteristic of, characterized by, having [*passionate*]

-ate [< L. *-atus*, a noun ending] *a suffix denoting* a function, agent, or official [*potentate*]

at·el·ier (at′'l yā′) *n.* [Fr.] a studio; workshop

a·the·ism (ā′thē iz′m) *n.* [< Gr. *a-*, without + *theos*, god] the belief that there is no God —**a′the·ist** *n.* —**a′the·is′tic**, **a′the·is′ti·cal** *adj.*

A·the·na (ə thē′nə) *Gr. Myth.* the goddess of wisdom, skills, and warfare, identified with the Roman Minerva: also **A·the′ne** (-nē)

ath·e·nae·um, ath·e·ne·um (ath′ə nē′əm) **1.** a literary or scientific club **2.** a library; reading room

Ath·ens (ath′'nz) capital of Greece, in the SE part: pop. 2,530,000 —**A·the·ni·an** (ə thē′nē ən) *adj., n.*

ath·er·o·scle·ro·sis (ath′ər ō sklə rō′sis) *n.* [< Gr. *athērōma*, grainy tumor + SCLEROSIS] formation of fatty nodules on hardening artery walls

a·thirst (ə thurst′) *adj.* **1.** [Archaic] thirsty **2.** eager; longing [*athirst* for knowledge]

ath·lete (ath′lēt′) *n.* [< Gr. *athlon*, a prize] a person trained in exercises, games, or contests requiring physical strength, skill, speed, etc.

athlete's foot a common fungous infection of the skin of the feet; ringworm of the feet

ath·let·ic (ath let′ik) *adj.* **1.** of, like, or proper to athletes or athletics **2.** physically strong, skillful, muscular, etc. —**ath·let′i·cal·ly** *adv.*

ath·let′ics (-iks) *n.pl.* [*sometimes with sing. v.*] athletic sports, games, exercises, etc.

at-home (ət hōm′) *n.* an informal reception at one's home, usually in the afternoon

a·thwart (ə thwôrt′) *prep.* **1.** from one side to the other of; across **2.** against **3.** *Naut.* across the course or length of —*adv.* crosswise

-atic [Gr.] *a suffix meaning* of, of the kind of [*dramatic*]

a·tilt (ə tilt′) *adj., adv.* tilted

a·tin·gle (ə tin′g′l) *adj.* tingling; excited

-ation [< Fr. or L.] *a suffix meaning:* **1.** the act of [*alteration*] **2.** the condition of being [*gratification*] **3.** the result of [*compilation*]

-ative [< Fr. or L.] *a suffix meaning* of or relating to, serving to, tending to [*demonstrative*]

At·lan·ta (ət lan′tə, at-) capital of Ga.: pop. 497,000 (met. area 1,390,000)

At·lan·tic (ət lan′tik, at-) ocean touching the American continents to the west and Europe and Africa to the east: area 31,830,000 sq. mi. —*adj.* of, in, on, or near this ocean

Atlantic City city in SE N.J., on the Atlantic: an ocean resort: pop. 60,000

At·lan·tis (ət lan′tis) legendary sunken continent in the Atlantic west of Gibraltar

At·las (at′ləs) *Gr. Myth.* a Titan forced to hold the heavens on his shoulders —*n.* [a-] a book of maps

Atlas Mountains mountain system in NW Africa, extending across Morocco, Algeria, and Tunisia

atm. **1.** atmosphere **2.** atmospheric

at·mos·phere (at′məs fir′) *n.* [< Gr. *atmos*, vapor + *sphaira*, sphere] **1.** all the air surrounding the earth **2.** the gaseous mass surrounding any star, planet, etc. **3.** the general mood or tone **4.** a unit of pressure equal to 14.69 lb. per sq. in. —**at′mos·pher′ic** (-fer′ik), **at′mos·pher′i·cal** *adj.* —**at′mos·pher′i·cal·ly** *adv.*

at. no. atomic number

at·oll (a′tôl, ä′-) *n.* [< Maldive Is. term] a ring-shaped coral island nearly or completely surrounding a lagoon

at·om (at′əm) *n.* [< Gr. *atomos*, uncut] **1.** a tiny particle; jot **2.** *Chem. & Physics* any of the smallest particles of an element that form compounds with similar particles of other elements: atoms consist of electrons revolving around a positively charged nucleus —**the atom** atomic energy

ATOLL

a·tom·ic (ə täm′ik) *adj.* **1.** of an atom or atoms **2.** of or using atomic energy or atomic bombs **3.** very small —**a·tom′i·cal·ly** *adv.*

atomic bomb, atom bomb a very destructive bomb, whose immense power derives from the energy released by a chain reaction of nuclear fission

atomic energy the energy released from an atom in nuclear fission or fusion

atomic number *Chem.* a number representing the relative position of an element in the periodic table; number representing the number of protons in an atomic nucleus

atomic theory the theory that all material objects and substances are composed of atoms

atomic weight *Chem.* a number representing the weight of one atom of an element as compared to one atom of another element taken as the standard (now usually carbon at 12)

at·om·ize (at′ə mīz′) *vt.* **-ized′, -iz′ing 1.** to separate into atoms **2.** to reduce (a liquid) to a fine spray

at′om·iz′er (-mī′zər) *n.* a device used to shoot out a fine spray, as of medicine or perfume

a·ton·al (ā tōn′l) *adj.* having atonality —**a·ton′al·ism** *n.* —**a·ton′al·is′tic** *adj.* —**a·ton′al·ly** *adv.*

a·to·nal·i·ty (ā'tō nal'ə tē) *n. Music* lack of tonality through intentional disregard of key

a·tone (ə tōn') *vi.* **a·toned', a·ton'ing** [< ME. *at one*, in accord] to make amends (for wrongdoing, etc.) —**a·ton'er** *n.*

a·tone'ment *n.* **1.** an atoning **2.** amends; expiation **3.** [A-] *Theol.* the reconciliation of God with man through Jesus' sufferings and death

a·top (ə täp') *adv.* on or at the top —*prep.* on the top of

-atory [L.] *a suffix meaning* of, characterized by, or produced by *[exclamatory]*

a·tri·um (ā'trē əm) *n., pl.* **a'tri·a** (-ə), **a'tri·ums** [L.] **1.** the main room of an ancient Roman house **2.** an entrance hall **3.** *Anat.* a chamber or cavity, esp. either of the upper chambers of the heart

a·tro·cious (ə trō'shəs) *adj.* [< L. *atrox*, fierce] **1.** very cruel, evil, etc. **2.** appalling or dismaying **3.** [Colloq.] offensive —**a·tro'cious·ly** *adv.* —**a·tro'cious·ness** *n.*

a·troc·i·ty (ə träs'ə tē) *n., pl.* **-ties 1.** atrocious behavior **2.** an atrocious act **3.** [Colloq.] a very offensive thing

at·ro·phy (at'rə fē) *n.* [< Fr. < Gr. *a-*, not + *trephein*, nourish] a wasting away, or the failure to grow, of an organ, tissue, etc. —*vi.* **-phied, -phy·ing** to waste away or fail to develop —*vt.* to cause atrophy in

at·ro·pine (at'rə pēn', -pin) *n.* [< Gr. *Atropos*, one of the Fates + -INE³] a poisonous alkaloid obtained from belladonna, used to dilate the pupil of the eye and to relieve spasms: also **at'ro·pin** (-pin)

att. 1. attention **2.** attorney

at·tach (ə tach') *vt.* [< OFr. *estache*, a post] **1.** to fasten by tying, etc. **2.** to join (often used reflexively) *[he attached himself to us]* **3.** to connect by ties of affection **4.** to affix (a signature, etc.) **5.** to ascribe **6.** *Law* to take (property, etc.) by writ **7.** *Mil.* to join (troops, etc.) temporarily to another unit —*vi.* to be joined; belong —**at·tach'a·ble** *adj.*

at·ta·ché (at'ə shā'; *chiefly Brit.* ə tash'ā) *n.* [Fr.: see *prec.*] a person with special duties on the staff of an ambassador, etc.

attaché case a flat, rectangular case for carrying documents, papers, etc.

at·tach'ment *n.* **1.** the act of attaching something **2.** anything that attaches; fastening **3.** devotion **4.** anything attached **5.** an accessory for an electrical appliance, etc. **6.** *Law* a taking of a person, property, etc. into custody

at·tack (ə tak') *vt.* [< OFr.: see ATTACH] **1.** to use force against in order to harm **2.** to speak or write against **3.** to undertake vigorously **4.** to begin acting upon harmfully —*vi.* to make an assault —*n.* **1.** an attacking **2.** an onset of a disease **3.** a beginning of a task —**at·tack'er** *n.*

at·tain (ə tān') *vt.* [< L. *ad-*, to + *tangere*, to touch] **1.** to gain; accomplish; achieve **2.** to arrive at —*vi.* to succeed in reaching or coming (*to* a goal) —**at·tain'a·bil'i·ty** *n.* —**at·tain'a·ble** *adj.*

at·tain·der (ə tān'dər) *n.* [OFr. *ataindre*, to attain] loss of a person's civil rights and property because he has been sentenced to death or outlawed

at·tain'ment *n.* **1.** an attaining or being attained **2.** anything attained, as a skill

at·taint (ə tānt') *vt.* to punish by attainder —*n.* an attainder

at·tar (at'ər) *n.* [< Ar. *'itr*, perfume] a perfume made from flower petals, esp. of damask roses

at·tempt (ə tempt') *vt.* [< L. *ad-*, to + *temptare*, to try] to try to do, get, etc.; endeavor —*n.* **1.** a try; endeavor **2.** an attack, as on a person's life

at·tend (ə tend') *vt.* [< L. *ad-*, to + *tendere*, to stretch] **1.** [Now Rare] to take care of **2.** to go with **3.** to accompany as a result **4.** to be present at —*vi.* **1.** to pay attention **2.** to wait (*on* or *upon*) **3.** to devote oneself (*to*) **4.** to give care (*to*)

at·tend'ance *n.* **1.** an attending **2.** the number of persons attending

at·tend'ant *adj.* **1.** attending or serving **2.** being present **3.** accompanying *[attendant difficulties]* —*n.* one who attends or serves

at·ten·tion (ə ten'shən) *n.* **1.** mental concentration or readiness for this **2.** notice or observation **3.** care or consideration **4.** an act of courtesy: *usually used in pl.* **5.** the erect posture of soldiers ready for a command

at·ten'tive (-tiv) *adj.* **1.** paying attention **2.** courteous, devoted, etc. —**at·ten'tive·ly** *adv.* —**at·ten'tive·ness** *n.*

at·ten·u·ate (ə ten'yoo wāt') *vt.* **-at'ed, -at'ing** [< L. *ad-*, to + *tenuis*, thin] **1.** to make thin or slender **2.** to dilute

3. to lessen or weaken —*vi.* to become thin, weak, etc. — **at·ten'u·a·ble** *adj.* —**at·ten'u·a'tion** *n.*

at·test (ə test') *vt.* [< L. *ad-*, to + *testari*, bear witness] **1.** to declare to be true or genuine **2.** to certify, as by oath **3.** to serve as proof of —*vi.* to testify (*to*) —**at·tes·ta·tion** (at'es tā'shən) *n.* —**at·test'er, at·tes'tor** *n.*

At·tic (at'ik) *adj.* **1.** Athenian **2.** classical in a simple, restrained way *[an Attic style]*

at·tic (at'ik) *n.* [< Gr. *Attikos*, of Attica (ancient Gr. region): with reference to architectural style] the room or space just below the roof; garret

At·ti·la (at'ʼl ə, ə til'ə) 406(?)-453 A.D.; king of the Huns (433(?)-453)

at·tire (ə tīr') *vt.* **-tired', -tir'ing** [< OFr. *a*, to + *tire*, order] to clothe; dress up —*n.* clothes; finery

at·ti·tude (at'ə tōōd', -tyōōd') *n.* [ult. < L. *aptus*, apt] **1.** the posture of the body in connection with an action, mood, etc. **2.** a way of acting, thinking, or feeling; one's disposition **3.** the position of an aircraft or spacecraft in relation to a given line or plane

at·ti·tu·di·nize (at'ə tōōd'ʼn īz', -tyōōd'-) *vi.* **-nized', -niz'ing** to pose for effect

at·tor·ney (ə tur'nē) *n., pl.* **-neys** [< OFr. *a-*, to + *torner*, to turn] any person having the legal power to act for another; esp., a lawyer

attorney at law a lawyer

attorney general *pl.* **attorneys general, attorney generals** the chief law officer of a government

at·tract (ə trakt') *vt.* [< L. *ad-*, to + *trahere*, to draw] **1.** to draw to itself or oneself *[a magnet attracts iron]* **2.** to get the admiration, attention, etc. of; allure —*vi.* to be attractive —**at·tract'a·ble** *adj.*

at·trac·tion (ə trak'shən) *n.* **1.** an attracting or the power of attracting; esp., charm or fascination **2.** anything that attracts **3.** *Physics* the mutual action by which bodies, particles, etc. tend to cohere

at·trac'tive (-tiv) *adj.* that attracts or has the power to attract; esp., charming, pretty, etc. —**at·trac'tive·ly** *adv.* —**at·trac'tive·ness** *n.*

at·trib·ute (ə trib'yoot) *vt.* **-ut·ed, -ut·ing** [< L. *ad-*, to + *tribuere*, assign] to think of as belonging to; assign or ascribe (*to*) —*n.* (a'trə byōot') **1.** a characteristic or quality of a person or thing **2.** a word or phrase used as an adjective —**at·trib'ut·a·ble** *adj.* —**at'tri·bu'tion** *n.*

at·trib'u·tive (-yoo tiv) *adj.* **1.** attributing **2.** preceding the noun it modifies: said of an adjective —*n.* an attributive adjective —**at·trib'u·tive·ly** *adv.*

at·tri·tion (ə trish'ən) *n.* [< L. *ad-*, to + *terere*, to rub] **1.** a wearing away by or as by friction **2.** loss of personnel in the normal course of events

at·tune (ə tōōn') *vt.* **-tuned', -tun'ing 1.** to tune **2.** to bring into harmony

atty. attorney

at. wt. atomic weight

a·typ·i·cal (ā tip'i k'l) *adj.* not typical; abnormal

Au [L. *aurum*] *Chem.* gold

au·burn (ô'bərn) *adj., n.* [< L. *albus*, white; infl. by ME *brun*, brown] reddish brown

Auck·land (ôk'lənd) seaport in New Zealand: pop. 152,000 (met. area 577,000)

auc·tion (ôk'shən) *n.* [< L. *augere*, to increase] a public sale where items are sold to the highest bidders —*vt.* to sell at auction

auction bridge a variety of the game of bridge in which the players bid for the right to say what suit shall be trump or to declare no-trump

auc·tion·eer (ôk'shə nir') *n.* one whose work is selling things at auction —*vt.* to auction

au·da·cious (ô dā'shəs) *adj.* [< L. *audere*, to dare] **1.** bold or daring; fearless **2.** rudely bold; insolent —**au·da'·cious·ly** *adv.* —**au·da'cious·ness** *n.*

au·dac·i·ty (ô das'ə tē) *n.* **1.** bold courage; daring **2.** brazen boldness; insolence **3.** *pl.* **-ties** an audacious act or remark

au·di·ble (ô'də b'l) *adj.* [< L. *audire*, to hear] loud enough to be heard —**au'di·bil'i·ty** *n.* —**au'di·bly** *adv.*

au·di·ence (ô'dē əns) *n.* [< L. *audire*, to hear] **1.** a group assembled to see and hear a play, concert, etc. **2.** all those reached by a radio or TV program, book, etc. **3.** the act of hearing **4.** a chance to be heard **5.** a formal interview

au·di·o (ô'dē ō) *adj.* [< L. *audire*, hear] **1.** of frequencies corresponding to normally audible sound waves **2.** of the sound phase of television

au'di·o-fre'quen·cy (-frē'kwən sē) *adj.* of the band of audible sound frequencies or corresponding electric current frequencies

au·di·ol·o·gy (ô'dē äl'ə jē) *n.* the science of hearing; esp., evaluation and rehabilitation of persons with hearing defects —**au'di·ol'o·gist** *n.*

au·di·om·e·ter (ô'dē äm'ə tər) *n.* an instrument for measuring hearing

au·di·o·phile (ô'dē ə fīl') *n.* a devotee of high-fidelity sound reproduction

au'di·o·vis'u·al (-vizh'oo wəl) *adj.* 1. involving both hearing and sight 2. designating such teaching aids as filmstrips, radio, etc.

au·dit (ô'dit) *n.* [< L. *audire,* to hear] an examination and adjustment of financial accounts —*vt., vi.* 1. to examine and check (accounts, etc.) 2. to attend (a college course) as a listener receiving no credits

au·di·tion (ô dish'ən) *n.* 1. the act or sense of hearing 2. a hearing to try out an actor, singer, etc. —*vt., vi.* to try out in an audition

au·di·tor (ô'də tər) *n.* 1. a hearer or listener 2. one who audits accounts 3. one who audits classes

au·di·to·ri·um (ô'də tôr'ē əm) *n.* 1. a room where an audience sits 2. a building or hall for concerts, speeches, etc.

au·di·to·ry (ô'də tôr'ē) *adj.* of hearing or the sense of hearing

Au·du·bon (ô'də bän'), **John James** 1785–1851; U.S. ornithologist, naturalist, & painter

‡**auf Wie·der·se·hen** (ouf vē'dər zā'ən) [G.] till we see each other again; goodbye

au·ger (ô'gər) *n.* [< OE. *nafogar* < *nafu,* hub (of a wheel) + *gar,* spear] a tool for boring holes in wood

aught (ôt) *n.* [< OE. *a,* one + *wiht,* creature] 1. anything whatever 2. [< (N)AUGHT] a zero —*adv.* [Archaic] to any degree

aug·ment (ôg ment') *vt., vi.* [< L. *augere,* to increase] to make or become greater; increase —**aug·ment'a·ble** *adj.* —**aug'men·ta'tion** *n.* —**aug·ment'er** *n.*

aug·ment·a·tive (ôg men'tə tiv) *adj.* augmenting —*n.* an intensifying word or affix

au gra·tin (ô grät'n) [Fr.] with a lightly browned crust of bread crumbs and grated cheese

Augs·burg (ôgz'bərg) city in Bavaria, S West Germany: pop. 211,000

au·gur (ô'gər) *n.* [L.; prob. < *augere,* to increase] a fortuneteller; soothsayer —*vt., vi.* 1. to foretell or prophesy 2. to be an omen (of) —**augur ill** (or **well**) to be a bad (or good) omen

au·gu·ry (ô'gyər ē) *n., pl.* **-ries** 1. the practice of divination 2. an omen; indication

Au·gust (ô'gəst) *n.* [< AUGUSTUS] the eighth month of the year, having 31 days: abbrev. **Aug.**

au·gust (ô gust') *adj.* [L. *augustus*] inspiring awe; imposing —**au·gust'ly** *adv.* —**au·gust'ness** *n.*

Au·gus·ta (ô gus'tə) capital of Me.: pop. 22,000

Au·gus·tan (ô gus'tən) *adj.* 1. of or like Augustus Caesar or his times 2. of or like any similar age; classical; elegant —*n.* a writer of the Augustan age

Au·gus·tine (ô'gəs tēn', ô gus't'n), **Saint** 1. 354–430 A.D.; Christian church father 2. ?–604? A.D.; Roman missionary among the English —**Au'gus·tin'i·an** (-tin'ē ən) *adj., n.*

Au·gus·tus (ô gus'təs) 63 B.C.–14 A.D.; 1st Roman emperor (27 B.C.–14 A.D.)

au jus (ō zhōō', ō jōōs') [Fr.] served in its natural juices: said of meat

auk (ôk) *n.* [< ON. *alka*] a diving bird of the northern seas, with webbed feet and short wings used as paddles

auld (ôld) *adj.* [Dial. & Scot.] old

auld lang syne (ôld' laŋ' zīn'; sīn') [Scot., old long since] the good old days

aunt (ant) *n.* [< L. *amita*] 1. a sister of one's mother or father 2. the wife of one's uncle

aunt·ie, aunt·y (an'tē) *n.* aunt

au·ra (ôr'ə) *n., pl.* **-ras, -rae** (-ē) [< Gr., akin to *aēr,* air] 1. an invisible emanation 2. a particular quality that seems to surround a person or thing

au·ral (ôr'əl) *adj.* [< L. *auris,* ear] of or received through the ear or the sense of hearing —**au'ral·ly** *adv.*

au·re·ate (ôr'ē it) *adj.* [< L. *aurum,* gold] 1. golden; gilded 2. splendid or brilliant, often affectedly so

Au·re·li·us (ô rē'lē əs), **Marcus** (*Marcus Aurelius Antoninus*) 121–180 A.D.; Roman emperor (161–180) & Stoic philosopher

GREAT AUK
(to 30 in. high)

au·re·ole (ôr'ē ōl') *n.* [< L. *aurum,* gold] 1. a halo 2. the sun's corona Also **au·re·o·la** (ô rē'ə lə)

Au·re·o·my·cin (ôr'ē ō mīs''n) [< L. *aureus,* golden + Gr. *mykēs,* fungus] *a trademark for* an antibiotic

au re·voir (ō'rə vwär') [Fr.] until we meet again; goodbye

au·ri·cle (ôr'ə k'l) *n.* 1. the external part of the ear 2. loosely, an atrium of the heart 3. an earlike part

au·ric·u·lar (ô rik'yoo lər) *adj.* 1. of the ear or the sense of hearing 2. said into the ear 3. ear-shaped 4. of an auricle —**au·ric'u·lar·ly** *adv.*

au·rif·er·ous (ô rif'ər əs) *adj.* [< L. *aurum,* gold + *ferre,* to BEAR¹ + -OUS] bearing or yielding gold

au·rochs (ô'räks) *n., pl.* **au'rochs** [G. *auerochs*] 1. the wild ox of Europe, now extinct 2. the nearly extinct European bison

Au·ro·ra (ô rôr'ə) the Rom. goddess of dawn —*n.* [a-] *pl.* **-ras, -rae** (-ē) the dawn

aurora aus·tra·lis (ô strä'lis) [L. < *auster,* south wind] luminous bands sometimes seen in the night sky of the Southern Hemisphere

aurora bo·re·a·lis (bôr'ē al'is) [L. < Gr. *Boreas,* north wind] luminous bands sometimes seen in the night sky of the Northern Hemisphere

aus·cul·ta·tion (ôs'kəl tā'shən) *n.* [< L. *auscultare,* to listen] a listening to sounds in the chest, abdomen, etc., as in diagnosis —**aus'cul·tate'** *vt., vi.* **-tat'ed, -tat'ing** —**aus'cul·ta'tor** *n.*

aus·pice (ôs'pis) *n., pl.* **-pi·ces'** (-pə sēz') [< L. *auspicium*] 1. an omen, esp. a favorable one 2. [*pl.*] guiding sponsorship; patronage

aus·pi·cious (ôs pish'əs) *adj.* 1. favorable; propitious 2. successful —**aus·pi'cious·ly** *adv.* —**aus·pi'cious·ness** *n.*

Aus·sie (ôs'ē) *adj., n.* [Slang] Australian

Aus·ten (ôs'tən), **Jane** 1775–1817; Eng. novelist

aus·tere (ô stir') *adj.* [< Gr. *austēros,* dry] 1. stern; harsh 2. showing strict self-discipline 3. very plain —**aus·tere'ly** *adv.* —**aus·tere'ness** *n.*

aus·ter·i·ty (ô ster'ə tē) *n., pl.* **-ties** 1. an austere quality, act, or practice 2. tightened economy, as from shortages of goods

Aus·tin (ôs'tən) capital of Tex.: pop. 252,000

aus·tral (ôs'trəl) *adj.* [< L. *auster,* the south] 1. southern; southerly 2. [A-] Australian

Aus·tral·a·sia (ôs'trə lā'zhə, -shə) the islands of the SW Pacific; specif., *a)* Australia, New Zealand, and adjacent islands *b)* Australia, New Zealand, the Malay Archipelago, and Oceania —**Aus'tral·a'sian** *adj., n.*

Aus·tral·ia (ô strāl'yə) 1. island continent between the S Pacific and Indian oceans 2. country comprising this continent and Tasmania: 2,971,081 sq. mi.; pop. 12,446,000; cap. Canberra —**Aus·tral'ian** *adj., n.*

Aus·tri·a (ôs'trē ə) country in C Europe: 32,375 sq. mi.; pop. 7,371,000; cap. Vienna —**Aus'tri·an** *adj., n.*

Aus'tri·a-Hun'ga·ry (huŋ'gər ē) former monarchy in C Europe (1867–1918)

au·tar·chy (ô'tär kē) *n., pl.* **-chies** [< Gr. *autos,* self + *archos,* ruler] 1. absolute rule; autocracy 2. a country under such rule 3. *same as* AUTARKY —**au·tar'chic, au·tar'chi·cal** *adj.*

au·tar·ky (ô'tär kē) *n.* [< Gr. *autos,* self + *arkein,* to suffice] economic self-sufficiency as a national policy —**au·tar'kic, au·tar'ki·cal** *adj.*

au·then·tic (ô then'tik) *adj.* [< Gr. *authentikos,* genuine] 1. that can be believed; reliable 2. genuine; real —**au·then'ti·cal·ly** *adv.* —**au·then·tic·i·ty** (ô'thən tis'ə tē) *n.*

au·then'ti·cate' (-tə kāt') *vt.* **-cat'ed, -cat'ing** to establish as authentic, or true, valid, genuine, etc. —**au·then'ti·ca'tion** *n.* —**au·then'ti·ca'tor** *n.*

au·thor (ô'thər) *n.* [< L. *augere,* to increase] 1. one who makes or creates something 2. the writer (*of* a book, etc.) —*vt.* to be the author of

au·thor·i·tar·i·an (ə thôr'ə ter'ē ən) *adj.* believing in or characterized by absolute obedience to authority —*n.* an advocate or enforcer of such obedience —**au·thor'i·tar'i·an·ism** *n.*

au·thor'i·ta'tive (-tāt'iv) *adj.* 1. having authority; official 2. based on competent authority; reliable 3. asserting authority; dictatorial —**au·thor'i·ta'tive·ly** *adv.* —**au·thor'i·ta'tive·ness** *n.*

au·thor·i·ty (ə thôr'ə tē) *n., pl.* **-ties** [see AUTHOR] 1. the power or right to give commands, take action, etc.; jurisdiction 2. [*pl.*] officials with this power 3. influence resulting from knowledge, prestige, etc. 4. a person, writing, etc. cited to support an opinion 5. an expert 6. self-assurance based on expertness

au·thor·ize (ô'thə rīz') *vt.* **-ized', -iz'ing** 1. to give official approval to 2. to give power or authority to; empower;

commission 3. to justify —au′thor·i·za′tion n. —au′thor-iz′er n.

Authorized Version the revised English translation of the Bible, published in 1611, authorized by King James

au·thor·ship (ô′thər ship′) n. 1. the profession of a writer 2. the origin (of a book, idea, etc.) [a story of unknown authorship]

au·tism (ô′tiz′m) n. [AUT(O)- + -ISM] Psychol. a mental state marked by fantasy, disregard of external reality, etc. —au·tis′tic adj.

au·to (ô′tō) n., pl. -tos an automobile

auto- [Gr. autos, self] a combining form meaning: 1. self 2. by oneself or itself

au·to·bi·og·ra·phy (ôt′ə bī äg′rə fē) n., pl. -phies the story of one's own life written or dictated by oneself — au′to·bi·og′ra·pher n. —au′to·bi′o·graph′i·cal (-bī′ə graf′i k'l), au′to·bi′o·graph′ic adj.

au·to·clave (ôt′ə klāv′) n. [Fr. < auto-, AUTO- + L. clavis, a key] a container for sterilizing, cooking, etc. by superheated steam under pressure

au·toc·ra·cy (ô täk′rə sē) n., pl. -cies [see AUTOCRAT] 1. a government in which one person has supreme power; dictatorship 2. unlimited power or authority of one person over others

au·to·crat (ôt′ə krat′) n. [< Gr. autos, self + kratos, power] 1. a ruler with absolute power; dictator 2. any domineering person —au′to·crat′ic, au′to·crat′i·cal adj. — au′to·crat′i·cal·ly adv.

au·to·da·fé (ôt′ō də fā′) n., pl. au′tos-da-fé′ [Port., lit., act of the faith] 1. the public ceremony in which the Inquisition judged and sentenced those tried as heretics 2. the execution of the sentence

au·to·gi·ro, au·to·gy·ro (ôt′ə jī′rō) n., pl. -ros [orig. a trademark < AUTO- + Gr. gyros, a circle] an earlier kind of aircraft having both a propeller and a large horizontal rotor

au·to·graph (ôt′ə graf′) n. [< Gr. autos, self + graphein, write] a person's own signature or handwriting —vt. to write one's signature on or in

au·to·hyp·no·sis (ôt′ō hip nō′sis) n. a hypnotizing of oneself or the state of being so hypnotized

au′to·in·tox′i·ca′tion (-in täk′sə kā′shən) n. poisoning by toxic substances (autotoxins) formed within the body

au·to·mat (ôt′ə mat′) n. [see AUTOMATIC] a restaurant in which patrons get food from small compartments opened by putting coins into slots

au·to·mate (ôt′ə māt′) vt. -mat′ed, -mat′ing [< AUTOMATION] to convert to or use automation in

au′to·mat′ic (-mat′ik) adj. [Gr. automatos, self-moving] 1. done without conscious thought or volition 2. involuntary or reflex 3. moving, operating, etc. by itself 4. done with automatic equipment 5. Firearms using the force of the explosion of a shell to eject, reload, and fire again, so that shots continue in rapid succession —n. an automatic rifle, pistol, etc. —au′to·mat′i·cal·ly adv.

au′to·ma′tion (-mā′shən) n. a manufacturing system in which many or all of the processes are automatically performed or controlled, as by electronic devices

au·tom·a·tism (ô täm′ə tiz′m) n. automatic quality, condition, or action

au·tom′a·ton′ (-tän′) n., pl. -tons′, -ta (-tə) [see AUTOMATIC] 1. anything that can move or act of itself 2. an automatic device, esp. a robot 3. a person acting in a mechanical way

au·to·mo·bile (ôt′ə mə bēl′, -mō′bēl) n. [see AUTO- & MOBILE] a passenger car propelled by an engine and used for traveling on streets or roads

au·to·mo·tive (ôt′ə mōt′iv) adj. [AUTO- + -MOTIVE] 1. self-moving 2. having to do with motor vehicles

au′to·nom′ic (-näm′ik) adj. of or controlled by the divisions of the nervous system (autonomic nervous system) that control the motor functions of the heart, lungs, glands, etc.

au·ton·o·mous (ô tän′ə məs) adj. [< Gr. autos, self + nomos, law] 1. having self-government 2. functioning independently —au·ton′o·mous·ly adv.

au·ton′o·my (-mē) n. 1. self-government 2. pl. -mies any state that governs itself

au·top·sy (ô′täp′sē) n., -sies [< Gr. autos, self + opsis, a sight] an examination of a dead body to discover the cause of death, etc.

au·tumn (ôt′əm) n. [< L. autumnus] the season between summer and winter; fall —au·tum·nal (ô tum′n'l) adj.

aux. auxiliary

aux·il·ia·ry (ôg zil′yər ē) adj. [< L. augere, to increase] 1. helping; assisting 2. subsidiary 3. additional; supplementary —n., pl. -ries 1. an auxiliary person, group, thing, etc. 2. [pl.] foreign troops aiding a country at war

auxiliary verb a verb that helps form tenses, moods, or voices of other verbs, as have or be

av. 1. average 2. avoirdupois

A.V. Authorized Version (of the Bible)

a.v., a/v, A/V ad valorem

a·vail (ə vāl′) vi., vt. [< L. ad, to + valere, be strong] to be of use, help, worth, or advantage (to), as in accomplishing an end —n. effective use or help [of no avail] — **avail oneself of** to take advantage of (an opportunity, etc.); utilize

a·vail·a·ble (ə vā′lə b'l) adj. 1. that can be used 2. that can be got or had; accessible —a·vail′a·bil′i·ty n. — a·vail′a·bly adv.

av·a·lanche (av′ə lanch′) n. [Fr. < L. labi, to slip] 1. a large mass of loosened snow, earth, etc. sliding down a mountain 2. an overwhelming amount that comes suddenly —vi., vt. -lanched′, -lanch′ing to come down (on) like an avalanche

a·vant-garde (ä vänt′gärd′) n. [Fr.] the leaders in new movements, esp. in the arts; vanguard —adj. of such movements

av·a·rice (av′ər is) n. [< L. avere, to desire] too great a desire to have wealth; greed; cupidity —av·a·ri·cious (av′ə rish′əs) adj. —av′a·ri′cious·ly adv. —av′a·ri′cious-ness n.

a·vast (ə vast′) interj. [< Du. houd vast, hold fast] Naut. stop! cease! halt!

av·a·tar (av′ə tär′) n. [Sans. avatāra, descent] 1. Hinduism a god's coming down in bodily form to the earth 2. any embodiment

a·vaunt (ə vônt′) interj. [< L. ab, from + ante, before] [Archaic] begone! go away!

avdp. avoirdupois

a·ve (ä′vā, ä′vē) interj. [L., be well] 1. hail! 2. farewell! — n. 1. the salutation ave 2. [A-] the prayer AVE MARIA

Ave., ave. avenue

A·ve Ma·ri·a (ä′vä mə rē′ə, -vē) [L.] 1. "Hail, Mary," the first words of a prayer to the Virgin Mary used in the Roman Catholic Church 2. this prayer

a·venge (ə venj′) vt., vi. a·venged′, a·veng′ing [< L. ad, to + vindicare, to claim] 1. to get revenge for (an injury, etc.) 2. to take vengeance on behalf of, as for a wrong — a·veng′er n.

av·e·nue (av′ə nōō′, -nyōō′) n. [< L. ad-, to + venire, come] 1. a road, path, or drive, often bordered with trees 2. a way of approach 3. a street, esp. a wide, principal one

a·ver (ə vur′) vt. a·verred′, a·ver′ring [< L. ad, to + verus, true] 1. to declare to be true; affirm 2. Law to state or declare formally; assert

av·er·age (av′rij, -ər ij) n. [< Fr. avarie, damage to ship: sense development from equal sharing of the loss among owners] 1. the result of dividing the sum of two or more quantities by the number of quantities 2. the usual or normal kind, amount, etc. —adj. 1. being a numerical average 2. usual; normal; ordinary —vi. -aged, -ag·ing to be or amount to on the average —vt. 1. to calculate the average of 2. to do, take, etc. on the average 3. to divide proportionately among more than two —average out to arrive at an average eventually —on the (or an) average as an average quantity, rate, etc.

a·verse (ə vurs′) adj. [see AVERT] unwilling; opposed (to) —a·verse′ly adv. —a·verse′ness n.

a·ver·sion (ə vur′zhən) n. 1. a strong or definite dislike; antipathy 2. the object disliked

a·vert (ə vurt′) vt. [< L. ab-, from + vertere, to turn] 1. to turn (the eyes, etc.) away 2. to ward off; prevent — a·vert′i·ble adj.

A·ves·ta (ə ves′tə) n. [< Per.] the sacred writings of Zoroastrianism —A·ves′tan adj., n.

avg. average

a·vi·an (ā′vē ən) adj. [< L. avis, bird + -AN] of or having to do with birds

a′vi·ar′y (-er′ē) n., pl. -ar′ies [< L. avis, bird] a large cage or building for keeping many birds

a·vi·a·tion (ā′vē ā′shən) n. [see AVIARY] 1. the science of flying airplanes 2. the field of airplane design, construction, etc.

a′vi·a·tor n. an airplane pilot —a′vi·a′trix (-ā′triks) n.fem.

---

av·id (av'id) *adj.* [< L. *avere,* to desire] very eager or greedy —**a·vid·i·ty** (ə vid'ə tē) *n.* —**av'id·ly** *adv.*

A·vi·gnon (ä vē nyôn') city in SE France: seat of the papacy (1309–77): pop. 73,000

a·vi·on·ics (ā'vē än'iks; *occas.* av'ē-) *n.pl.* [AVI(ATION) + (ELECTR)ONICS] [*with sing. v.*] electronics as applied in aviation and astronautics —**a'vi·on'ic** *adj.*

av·o·ca·do (av'ə kä'dō) *n., pl.* **-dos** [< MexInd. *ahuacatl*] 1. a thick-skinned, pear-shaped tropical fruit with yellow, buttery flesh, used in salads; alligator pear 2. the tree that it grows on

av·o·ca·tion (av'ə kā'shən) *n.* [< L. *ab-,* away + *vocare,* to call] something done in addition to regular work; hobby —**av'o·ca'tion·al** *adj.*

AVOCADO

a·void (ə void') *vt.* [< ME. < OFr. *esvuidier,* to empty] 1. to keep away from; shun 2. *Law* to make void; annul —**a·void'a·ble** *adj.* —**a·void'a·bly** *adv.* —**a·void'ance** *n.*

av·oir·du·pois (av'ər də poiz') *n.* [< OFr. *àveir de peis,* goods having weight] 1. an English and American system of weights in which 16 oz. = 1 lb.: also **avoirdupois weight** 2. [Colloq.] weight, esp. of a person

a·vouch (ə vouch') *vt.* [see ADVOCATE] 1. to vouch for; guarantee 2. to declare the truth of; affirm 3. to acknowledge openly; avow —**a·vouch'ment** *n.*

a·vow (ə vou') *vt.* [see ADVOCATE] to declare openly; acknowledge —**a·vow'al** *n.* —**a·vowed'** *adj.* —**a·vow·ed·ly** (ə vou'id lē) *adv.* —**a·vow'er** *n.*

a·vun·cu·lar (ə vuŋ'kyə lər) *adj.* [< L. *avunculus,* maternal uncle] of, like, or in the relationship of, an uncle

aw (ô, ä) *interj.* an exclamation of protest, dislike, disgust, sympathy, etc.

a·wait (ə wāt') *vt.* [< ONormFr. *a-,* to + *waitier,* wait] 1. to wait for 2. to be in store for —*vi.* to wait

a·wake (ə wāk') *vt., vi.* **a·woke'** or **a·waked', a·wak'ing** [< OE.] 1. to rouse from sleep; wake 2. to rouse from inactivity —*adj.* 1. not asleep 2. active or alert

a·wak·en (ə wāk''n) *vt., vi.* to awake; wake up; rouse —**a·wak'en·er** *n.*

a·wak'en·ing *n., adj.* 1. (a) waking up 2. (an) arousing, as of impulses, interest, etc.

a·ward (ə wôrd') *vt.* [< ME. < ONormFr. *eswarder*] 1. to give, as by legal decision 2. to give as the result of judging; grant (a prize, etc.) —*n.* 1. a decision, as by a judge 2. a prize

a·ware (ə wer') *adj.* [< OE. *wær,* cautious] knowing or realizing; conscious; informed —**a·ware'ness** *n.*

a·wash (ə wôsh') *adv., adj.* 1. at a level where the water washes over the surface 2. flooded 3. afloat

a·way (ə wā') *adv.* [< OE. *on,* on + *weg,* way] 1. from any given place [run *away*] 2. in another place or direction [*away* from here] 3. far [*away* behind] 4. off; aside [turn *away*] 5. from one's possession [give it *away*] 6. out of existence [fade *away*] 7. at once [fire *away*] 8. continuously [kept working *away*] —*adj.* 1. absent; gone 2. at a distance [a mile *away*] —*interj.* begone! —**away with** go, come, or take away —**do away with** 1. to get rid of 2. to kill

awe (ô) *n.* [ON. *agi*] a mixed feeling of reverence, fear, and wonder, caused by something sublime, etc. —*vt.* **awed, aw'ing** to inspire awe in; fill with awe —**stand** (or **be) in awe of** to respect and fear

a·weigh (ə wā') *adj. Naut.* just clear of the bottom: said of an anchor being weighed, or hoisted

awe·some (ô'səm) *adj.* inspiring or showing awe —**awe'-some·ly** *adv.* —**awe'some·ness** *n.*

awe-struck (ô'struk') *adj.* filled with awe: also **awe'-strick'en** (-strik'ən)

aw·ful (ô'fəl) *adj.* [see AWE & -FUL] 1. inspiring awe 2. causing fear; terrifying 3. [Colloq.] *a)* very bad, unpleasant, etc. [an *awful* joke] *b)* great [an *awful* bore] —*adv.* [Colloq.] very; extremely [*awful* happy] —**aw'ful·ness** *n.*

aw·ful·ly (ô'fə lē, -flē) *adv.* 1. in a way to inspire awe 2. [Colloq.] badly or offensively [to behave *awfully*] 3. [Colloq.] very; extremely

a·while (ə wīl', -hwīl') *adv.* for a short time

awk·ward (ôk'wərd) *adj.* [< ON. *ǫfugr,* turned backward + OE. *-weard,* -WARD] 1. clumsy; bungling 2. unwieldy 3. uncomfortable [an *awkward* position] 4. embarrassed

or embarrassing [an *awkward* remark] 5. not easy to deal with; delicate [an *awkward* situation] —**awk'ward·ly** *adv.* —**awk'ward·ness** *n.*

awl (ôl) *n.* [< OE. *æl, awel*] a small, pointed tool for making holes in wood, leather, etc.

awn (ôn) *n.* [ON. *ǫgn,* chaff] the bristly fibers on a head of barley, oats, etc. —**awned** *adj.*

awn·ing (ô'niŋ) *n.* [< ? MFr. *auvent,* window shade] a structure, as of canvas, extended before a window, etc. as a protection from sun or rain

a·woke (ə wōk') *pt. & occas. Brit. pp.* of AWAKE

A·WOL, a·wol (ā'wôl') *adj.* [*a(bsent) w(ith)o(ut) l(eave)*] absent without leave, but without intention of deserting —*n.* one who is AWOL

a·wry (ə rī') *adv., adj.* [see A- (sense 1) & WRY] 1. with a twist to a side; askew 2. wrong; amiss [our plans went *awry*]

ax, axe (aks) *n., pl.* **ax'es** [OE. *æx*] a tool with a long handle and a bladed head, for chopping wood, etc. —*vt.* **axed, ax'ing** to trim, split, etc. with an ax —**get the ax** [Colloq.] to be discharged from one's job —**have an ax to grind** [Colloq.] to have an object of one's own to gain or promote

ax·i·al (ak'sē əl) *adj.* 1. of, like, or forming an axis 2. around or along an axis —**ax'i·al·ly** *adv.*

ax·il (ak'sil) *n.* [< L. *axilla:* see AXILLA] the upper angle between a leaf, twig, etc. and the stem from which it grows

ax·il·la (ak sil'ə) *n., pl.* **-lae** (-ē), **-las** [L., armpit] 1. the armpit 2. an axil

ax·il·la·ry (ak'sə ler'ē) *adj.* 1. of or near the axilla 2. of, in, or growing from an axil

ax·i·om (ak'sē əm) *n.* [< Gr. *axios,* worthy] 1. a statement universally accepted as true; maxim 2. an established principle or law of science, art, etc. 3. a statement or proposition which is accepted as true without proof

ax'i·o·mat'ic (-ə mat'ik) *adj.* 1. of or like an axiom; self-evident 2. full of axioms; aphoristic —**ax'i·o·mat'i·cal·ly** *adv.*

ax·is (ak'sis) *n., pl.* **ax'es** (-sēz) [L.] 1. a real or imaginary straight line on which an object rotates 2. a central line or lengthwise structure around which the parts of a thing, system, etc. are evenly arranged —**the Axis** Germany, Italy, and Japan as allies in World War II

ax·le (ak's'l) *n.* [< ON. *ǫxull*] 1. a rod on or with which a wheel turns 2. *a)* a bar connecting two opposite wheels, as of an automobile *b)* the spindle at either end of such a bar

ax'le·tree' (-trē') *n.* [< prec. + ON. *tre,* beam] a bar connecting two opposite wheels of a wagon, etc.

Ax·min·ster (aks'min stər) *n.* [< *Axminster,* town in England] a varicolored, patterned carpet with a cut pile

aye[1] (ā) *adv.* [ON. *ei*] [Poet.] always; ever: also **ay**

aye[2] (ī) *adv.* [< ? prec.] yes; yea —*n.* an affirmative vote or voter Also **ay**

AZ Arizona

a·zal·ea (ə zāl'yə) *n.* [< Gr. *azaleos,* dry] 1. a shrub related to the heath with flowers of various colors 2. the flower of this plant

Az·er·bai·jan Soviet Socialist Republic (äz'ər bī jän', az'-) a republic of the U.S.S.R. in SW Asia: also **Azerbaijan**

az·i·muth (az'ə məth) *n.* [< Ar. *al,* the + *samt,* way, path] *Astron.,* etc. distance in angular degrees in a clockwise direction from the north point or, in the Southern Hemisphere, south point

A·zores (ā'zôrz, ə zôrz') group of Portuguese islands in the N Atlantic, west of Portugal

A·zov (ā'zôf), **Sea of** northern arm of the Black Sea, in S European U.S.S.R.: 14,000 sq. mi.

Az·tec (az'tek) *n.* 1. *pl.* **-tecs, -tec** a member of a people who had an advanced civilization in Mexico before the Spanish conquest in 1519 2. their language —*adj.* of the Aztecs, their language, culture, etc.: also **Az'tec·an**

az·ure (azh'ər) *adj.* [< Per. *lāzhuward,* lapis lazuli] of or like the color of a clear sky; sky-blue —*n.* 1. sky blue 2. [Poet.] the blue sky

az·u·rite (azh'ə rīt') *n.* [AZUR(E) + -ITE] 1. a brilliantly blue mineral, an ore of copper 2. a semiprecious gem cut from it

AWN

B

B, b (bē) *n., pl.* **B's, b's** the second letter of the English alphabet —*adj.* second in a sequence or group
B¹ (bē) *n.* **1.** a grade indicating above-average but not outstanding work **2.** *Chem.* boron **3.** *Music* the seventh tone in the scale of C major —*adj.* inferior to the best [a class B motion picture]
B² *Chess* bishop
B. 1. Bible **2.** British
B., b. 1. bachelor **2.** *Baseball a)* base *b)* baseman **3.** *Music* bass **4.** bay **5.** born
Ba *Chem.* barium
B.A. Bachelor of Arts
baa (bä) *n., vi.* [echoic] bleat
Ba·al (bā'əl, bāl) *n., pl.* **Ba'al·im** (-im), **Ba'als 1.** an ancient Semitic fertility god **2.** a false god; idol
bab·bitt, Bab·bitt (bab'it) *n.* [< the novel by Sinclair Lewis] a smugly conventional person interested chiefly in business and social success and indifferent to cultural values —**bab'bitt·ry, Bab'bitt·ry** *n.*
Babbitt metal [< I. *Babbitt* (1799–1862), U.S. inventor] a soft alloy of tin, copper, and antimony, used to reduce friction in bearings, etc.
bab·ble (bab''l) *vi.* **-bled, -bling** [echoic] **1.** to make incoherent sounds, as a baby does **2.** to talk foolishly or too much **3.** to make a low, bubbling sound, as a brook —*vt.* to say incoherently or foolishly —*n.* **1.** confused, incoherent vocal sounds **2.** foolish or meaningless talk **3.** a low, bubbling sound —**bab'bler** *n.*
babe (bāb) *n.* **1.** a baby **2.** a naive or helpless person: also **babe in the woods 3.** [Slang] a girl or young woman
Ba·bel (bā'b'l, bab''l) *Bible* a city where people tried to build a tower to the sky and were stopped by God, who caused them suddenly to speak in different languages —*n.* [*also* b-] **1.** a confusion of voices, languages, etc.; tumult **2.** a place of such confusion
bab·i·ru·sa, bab·i·rous·sa, bab·i·rus·sa (bab'ə rōōs'ə, bä'bə-) *n.* [Malay *bābī,* hog + *rūsa,* deer] a wild hog of the East Indies, with backward curving tusks
ba·boon (ba bōōn') *n.* [< OFr. *babuin,* ape, fool] a large and fierce, short-tailed monkey of Africa and Arabia, having a doglike snout and cheek pouches
ba·bush·ka (bə bōōsh'ka) *n.* [Russ., grandmother] a woman's scarf worn on the head
ba·by (bā'bē) *n., pl.* **-bies** [ME. *babi*] **1.** a very young child; infant **2.** one who behaves like an infant **3.** a very young animal **4.** the youngest or smallest in a group **5.** [Slang] *a)* a girl or young woman *b)* any person or thing —*adj.* **1.** of or for an infant **2.** very young **3.** small of its kind **4.** childish —*vt.* **-bied, -by·ing 1.** to pamper; coddle **2.** [Colloq.] to handle with great care —**ba'by·hood'** *n.* — **ba'by·ish** *adj.* —**ba'by·like'** *adj.*
baby carriage a light carriage for wheeling a baby about: also **baby buggy**
baby grand a small grand piano
Bab·y·lon (bab'ə lən, -län') capital of Babylonia, famous for wealth, luxury, and wickedness
Bab·y·lo·ni·a (bab'ə lō'nē ə) ancient empire in SW Asia —**Bab'y·lo'ni·an** *adj., n.*
ba·by's breath (bā'bēz breth') a plant having small, delicate, white or pink flowers
ba·by-sit (bā'bē sit') *vi., vt.* **-sat', -sit'ting** to act as a baby sitter (to)
baby sitter a person hired to care for children, as when the parents are away for the evening
bac·ca·lau·re·ate (bak'ə lôr'ē it) *n.* [see BACHELOR] **1.** the degree of Bachelor of Arts (or Science, etc.) **2.** a speech to a graduating class at commencement: also **baccalaureate address (or sermon)**
bac·ca·rat, bac·ca·ra (bak'ə rä') *n.* [Fr.] a gambling game played with cards
bac·cha·nal (bak'ə nəl, -nal') *n.* **1.** a worshiper of Bacchus **2.** a drunken carouser **3.** a drunken orgy

Bac·cha·na·li·a (bak'ə näl'yə, -nä'lē ə) *n.pl.* **1.** an ancient Roman festival honoring Bacchus **2.** [b-] a drunken party —**bac'cha·na'li·an** *adj., n.*
bac·chant (bak'ənt) *n., pl.* **-chants, -chan'tes** (-kan'tēz) **1.** a priest or worshiper of Bacchus **2.** a drunken carouser —**bac·chan·te** (bə kan'tē, -kant') *n.fem.* —**bac·chan'tic** *adj.*
Bac·chus (bak'əs) an ancient Greek and Roman god of wine and revelry —**Bac'chic, bac'chic** *adj.*
bach (bach) *vi.* [< BACHELOR] [Slang] to live alone or keep house for oneself, as a bachelor: usually in phr. **bach it** — *n.* [Slang] a bachelor
Bach (bäkh; *E. also* bäk), **Jo·hann Sebastian** (yō'hän), (1685–1750); Ger. organist & composer
bach·e·lor (bach''l ər, bach'lər) *n.* [< ML. *baccalaris,* squire (*n.* 1))] **1.** a man who has not married **2.** a person who is a BACHELOR OF ARTS (or SCIENCE, etc.) —*adj.* of or for a bachelor —**bach'e·lor·hood'** *n.*
Bachelor of Arts (or **Science,** etc.) **1.** a degree given by a college or university to one who has completed a four-year course in the humanities (or in science, etc.) **2.** one who has this degree
bachelor's button any of several plants having flowers shaped somewhat like buttons
ba·cil·lus (bə sil'əs) *n., pl.* **-cil'li** (-ī) [< L. *bacillum,* little stick] **1.** any of the rod-shaped bacteria **2.** [*usually pl.*] loosely, any bacterium
back (bak) *n.* [< OE. *bæk*] **1.** the rear part of the body from the nape of the neck to the end of the spine **2.** the backbone **3.** a part that supports or fits the back **4.** the rear part or reverse of anything **5.** *Sports* a player or position behind the front line —*adj.* **1.** at the rear **2.** distant **3.** of or for a time in the past [*back pay*] **4.** backward — *adv.* **1.** at, to, or toward the rear **2.** to or toward a former condition, time, etc. **3.** in reserve or concealment **4.** in return [*to pay one back*] —*vt.* **1.** to move backward **2.** to support **3.** to bet on **4.** to provide or be a back for —*vi.* **1.** to go backward **2.** to have the back facing —**back and forth** to and fro —**back down** to withdraw from a position, etc. —**back off** (or **away,** etc.) to move back (or away, etc.) —**back out** (**of**) **1.** to withdraw from an enterprise **2.** to evade keeping a promise, etc. —**back up 1.** to support **2.** to move backward **3.** to accumulate because of restricted movement [*traffic backed up*] —**get** (or **put**) **one's back up** to make or be obstinate —**go back on** [Colloq.] **1.** to betray **2.** to fail to keep (a promise, etc.) —**turn one's back on 1.** to turn away from, as in contempt **2.** to abandon
back·bite (bak'bīt') *vt., vi.* **-bit', -bit'ten** or **-bit', -bit'ing** to slander (someone absent) —**back'bit'er** *n.*
back'board' (-bôrd') *n. Basketball* a board or flat surface just behind the basket
back'bone' (-bōn') *n.* **1.** the spine **2.** a main support **3.** willpower, courage, etc.
back'break'ing (-brāk'in) *adj.* very tiring
back'drop' (-dräp') *n.* **1.** a curtain hung at the back of a stage **2.** background or setting
back'er *n.* **1.** a patron; supporter **2.** one who bets on a contestant
back'field' (-fēld') *n. Football* the players stationed behind the line; esp., the offensive unit
back'fire' (-fīr') *n.* **1.** the burning out of a small area, as in a forest, to check the spread of a big fire **2.** a premature explosion in a cylinder of an internal-combustion engine **3.** reverse explosion in a gun —*vi.* **-fired', -fir'ing 1.** to explode as a backfire **2.** to go wrong or boomerang, as a plan
back'gam'mon (-gam'ən) *n.* [BACK + ME. *gammen,* game] a game for two, with pieces moved according to the throw of dice
back'ground' (-ground') *n.* **1.** the part of a scene toward the back **2.** surroundings, sounds, data, etc. behind or

---

subordinate to something **3.** one's training and experience **4.** events leading up to something

back'hand' (-hand') *n.* **1.** handwriting that slants backward, up to the left **2.** a backhand catch, stroke, etc. — *adj.* **1.** done with the back of the hand turned inward, as for a baseball catch, or forward, as for a tennis stroke, and with the arm across the body **2.** written in backhand —*adv.* in a backhand way —*vt.* to hit, catch, swing, etc. backhand

back'hand'ed (-han'did) *adj.* **1.** *same as* BACKHAND **2.** indirect or sarcastic; equivocal —*adv.* in a backhanded way

back'ing (-iŋ) *n.* **1.** something forming a back for support **2.** support given to a person or cause **3.** supporters; backers

back'lash' (-lash') *n.* a sharp reaction; recoil

back'log' (-lôg') *n.* an accumulation or reserve —*vi., vt.* -logged', -log'ging to accumulate as a backlog

back order an order to be filled when stock is renewed

back'pack' (-pak') *n.* a kind of knapsack, often attached to a lightweight frame, worn as by hikers —*vi.* to hike wearing a backpack —**back'pack'er** *n.*

back'ped'al (-ped''l) *vi.* -ped'aled or -ped'alled, -ped'aling or -ped'al·ling **1.** to pedal backward as in braking a bicycle **2.** to move backward **3.** to retreat from an opinion

back'rest' *n.* a support for the back

back·sheesh, back·shish (bak'shēsh') *n. same as* BAKSHEESH

back'side' *n.* **1.** the back part **2.** the rump; buttocks

back'slap'per (-slap'ər) *n.* [Colloq.] an effusively friendly person

back'slide' (-slīd') *vi.* -slid', -slid' or -slid'den, -slid'ing to slide backward in morals, religion, etc. —**back'slid'er** *n.*

back'space' *vi.* -spaced', -spac'ing to move a typewriter carriage one or more spaces back along the line

back'spin' *n.* backward spin in a ball, etc., making it bound backward upon hitting the ground

back'stage' *adv., adj.* behind and off the stage, as in the wings or dressing rooms

back'stairs' (-sterz') *adj.* involving intrigue or scandal; secret: also **back'stair'**

back'stay' *n.* a rope extending aft from a masthead to the side or stern of the ship

back'stop' *n.* a screen, etc., as behind a baseball catcher, to stop balls from going too far

back'stretch' (-strech') *n.* the part of a race track farthest from the grandstand

back'stroke' *n.* a stroke made by a swimmer lying face upward —*vi.* -stroked', -strok'ing to perform a backstroke

back talk [Colloq.] saucy or insolent retorts

back'-to-back' *adj.* [Colloq.] one right after another

back'-track' *vi.* **1.** to return by the same path **2.** to withdraw from a position, etc.

back'up', back'-up' *adj.* **1.** standing by as an alternate or auxiliary **2.** supporting —*n.* a backing up; specif., *a*) an accumulation *b*) a support; help

back'ward (-ward) *adv.* **1.** toward the back **2.** with the back foremost **3.** in reverse order **4.** in a way contrary to normal **5.** into the past Also **back'wards** —*adj.* **1.** turned toward the rear or in the opposite way **2.** hesitant or shy **3.** slow or retarded —**back'ward·ly** *adv.* —**back'ward·ness** *n.*

back'wash' *n.* **1.** water or air moved backward by a ship, propeller, etc. **2.** a reaction caused by some event

back'woods' (-woodz') *n.pl.* [*occas. with sing. v.*] **1.** heavily wooded, remote areas **2.** any remote, thinly populated place —*adj.* of or like the backwoods: also **back'wood'** —**back'woods'man** *n., pl.* -men

ba·con (bāk'n) *n.* [< OS. *baco*, side of bacon] salted and smoked meat from the back or sides of a hog —**bring home the bacon** [Colloq.] **1.** to earn a living **2.** to succeed

Ba·con (bāk'n), **1.** Francis 1561–1626, Eng. philosopher & statesman **2.** Roger, 1214?–94; Eng. philosopher & scientist

bac·te·ri·a (bak tir'ē ə) *n.pl., sing.* -ri·um (-əm) [< Gr. dim. of *baktron*, a staff] microorganisms which have no chlorophyll and multiply by simple division: some bacteria cause diseases, but others are necessary for fermentation, etc. —**bac·te'ri·al** *adj.*

bac·te'ri·cide' (-ə sīd') *n.* an agent that destroys bacteria —**bac·te'ri·ci'dal** *adj.*

bac·te'ri·ol'o·gy (-ē äl'ə jē) *n.* the science that deals with bacteria —**bac·te'ri·o·log'ic** (-ē ə läj'ik), **bac·te'ri·o·log'i·cal** *adj.* —**bac·te'ri·ol'o·gist** *n.*

Bac·tri·an camel (bak'trē ən) [< *Bactria*, ancient country in W Asia] a camel with two humps, native to C Asia

bad' (bad) *adj.* **worse, worst** [ME.] **1.** not good; not as it should be **2.** inadequate or unfit **3.** unfavorable [*bad news*] **4.** rotten or spoiled **5.** incorrect or faulty **6.** *a*) wicked; immoral *b*) mischievous **7.** harmful **8.** severe [*a bad storm*] **9.** ill **10.** sorry; distressed [*he feels bad* about it] **11.** offensive **12.** [Slang] very good, etc. —*adv.* [Colloq.] badly —*n.* anything bad —**in bad** [Colloq.] in trouble or disfavor —**not (so or half) bad** [Colloq.] good; fairly good —**bad'ness** *n.*

bad' (bad) *archaic pt. of* BID

bad blood a feeling of (mutual) enmity

bade (bad; *occas.* bād) *pt. of* BID

bad egg [Slang] a mean or dishonest person: also **bad actor, bad apple, bad hat, bad lot,** etc.

badge (baj) *n.* [ME. *bage*] **1.** an emblem worn to show rank, membership, etc. **2.** any distinguishing sign, etc. — *vt.* **badged, badg'ing** to mark with a badge

badg·er (baj'ər) *n.* [< ?] **1.** a burrowing animal with a broad back and thick, short legs **2.** its fur —*vt.* to nag at; torment

bad·i·nage (bad'ə näzh', bad''n ij) *n.* [Fr. < ML. *badare*, to gape] playful, teasing talk; banter —*vt.* -naged', -nag'ing to tease with playful talk

bad·lands (bad'landz') *n.pl.* **1.** an area of barren land with dry soil and soft rocks eroded into odd shapes **2.** [B-] any area like this in the W U.S.: also **Bad Lands**

bad·ly (bad'lē) *adv.* **1.** in a bad manner **2.** [Colloq.] very much; greatly

bad'man' *n., pl.* -men' a cattle thief or desperado of the Old West

bad·min·ton (bad'min t'n) *n.* [< *Badminton*, Eng. estate] a game in which a shuttlecock is batted back and forth with rackets across a net

bad-mouth (bad'mouth') *vt., vi.* [Slang] to find fault (with); criticize or disparage

bad'-tem'pered (-tem'pərd) *adj.* having a bad temper or cranky disposition; irritable

Bae·de·ker (bā'də kər) *n.* **1.** any of a series of guidebooks to foreign countries first published in Germany by Karl Baedeker (1801–59) **2.** loosely, any guidebook

baf·fle (baf''l) *vt.* -fled, -fling [< ?] **1.** to confuse completely; confound **2.** to hinder; impede —*n.* a screen to deflect liquid, gases, etc., or to check sound waves —**baf'fle·ment** *n.* —**baf'fler** *n.* —**baf'fling** *adj.*

bag (bag) *n.* [ON. *baggi*] **1.** a nonrigid container of paper, plastic, etc. with a top opening that can be closed **2.** a satchel, suitcase, etc. **3.** a purse **4.** game taken in hunting **5.** a baglike shape or part **6.** [Slang] one's special interest **7.** [Slang] an unattractive woman **8.** *Baseball* a base —*vt.* **bagged, bag'ging 1.** to make bulge **2.** to capture **3.** to kill in hunting **4.** [Slang] to get —*vi.* **1.** to swell **2.** to hang loosely —**be left holding the bag** [Colloq.] to be left to suffer the bad consequences —**in the bag** [Slang] certain; assured

bag·a·telle (bag'ə tel') *n.* [Fr. < L. *baca*, berry] a trifle

ba·gel (bā'g'l) *n.* [Yid.] a hard, doughnut-shaped bread roll simmered in water, then baked

bag·gage (bag'ij) *n.* [< ML. *baga*, chest, bag] **1.** the bags, etc. of a traveler; luggage **2.** the supplies and gear of an army

bag·gy (bag'ē) *adj.* -gi·er, -gi·est **1.** puffed in a baglike way **2.** hanging loosely —**bag'gi·ly** *adv.* —**bag'gi·ness** *n.*

Bagh·dad (bag'dad) capital of Iraq: pop. 1,000,000: also sp. **Bagdad**

bag·pipe (bag'pīp') *n.* [*often pl.*] a shrill-toned musical instrument with a double-reed, fingered pipe and drone pipes, all sounded by air forced from a leather bag: now chiefly Scottish —**bag'pip'er** *n.*

ba·guette, ba·guet (ba get') *n.* [< Fr. < L. *baculum*, a staff] a gem, etc. cut in the shape of a narrow oblong

bah (bä) *interj.* an exclamation of contempt, scorn, or disgust

Ba·ha·mas (bə hä'məz, -hā'-) country on a group of islands (**Bahama Islands**) in the West Indies: 4,404 sq. mi.; pop. 185,000; cap. Nassau —**Ba·ha'mi·an** *adj.*

BAGPIPE

Bah·rain, Bah·rein (bä rān') independent Arab shiekdom consisting of a group of islands in the Persian Gulf: 231 sq. mi.; pop. 200,000

Bai·kal (bī käl'), **Lake** large lake in SE Siberia: 12,000 sq. mi.

bail' (bāl) *n.* [< L. *bajulare*, bear a burden] **1.** money deposited with the court to get an arrested person temporarily released until his trial **2.** such a release **3.** the person giving bail —**vt. 1.** to have (an arrested person) set free by giving bail **2.** to help out of financial or other difficulty Often with *out* —**bail'a·ble** *adj.*

bail² (bāl) *n.* [ME. *baille*, bucket] a bucket for dipping up water from a boat —*vi., vt.* to dip out (water) from (a boat) —**bail out** to parachute from an aircraft —**bail'er** *n.*

bail³ (bāl) *n.* [< ON. *beygla*] a hoop-shaped handle for a bucket, etc.

bai·liff (bā'lif) *n.* [< L. *bajulus*, porter] **1.** a deputy sheriff **2.** a court officer who guards the jurors, keeps order in the court, etc. **3.** in England, *a*) a district administrative official *b*) a steward of an estate

bai·li·wick (bā'lə wik) *n.* [ME. < *bailif*, bailiff + *wik* < OE. *wic*, village] **1.** a bailiff's district **2.** one's particular area of activity, authority, etc.

bails·man (bālz'mən) *n., pl.* **-men** a person who gives bail for someone

bairn (bern) *n.* [Scot.] a child

bait (bāt) *vt.* [< ON. *beita*, make bite] **1.** to set dogs on for sport *[to bait bears]* **2.** to torment or harass with unprovoked attacks **3.** to put food, etc. on (a hook or trap) as a lure for animals or fish **4.** to lure; entice —*n.* **1.** food, etc. put on a hook or trap as a lure **2.** any lure; enticement —**bait'er** *n.*

baize (bāz) *n.* [< L. *badius*, brown] a feltlike, thick woolen cloth used to cover billiard tables

Ba·ja Ca·li·for·nia (bä'hä kä'lē fôr'nyä) peninsula in Mexico, between the Pacific & the Gulf of California

bake (bāk) *vt.* **baked, bak'ing** [OE. *bacan*] **1.** to cook (food) by dry heat, esp. in an oven **2.** to dry and harden (pottery) by heat; fire —*vi.* **1.** to bake bread, etc. **2.** to become baked —*n.* **1.** a baking **2.** a social affair at which a baked food is served

Ba·ke·lite (bā'kə līt') [after L. H. *Baekeland* (1863–1944), U.S. chemist] *a trademark for* a synthetic resin and plastic —*n.* [b-] this resin

bak·er (bāk'ər) *n.* **1.** one whose work or business is baking bread, etc. **2.** a small, portable oven

baker's dozen thirteen

bak'er·y *n.* **1.** *pl.* **-ies** a place where bread, pastries, etc. are baked or sold **2.** baked goods

baking powder a leavening agent containing baking soda and an acid substance

baking soda sodium bicarbonate, $NaHCO_3$, used as a leavening agent and as an antacid

bak·sheesh, bak·shish (bak'shēsh) *n.* [< Per. *bakhshidan*, give] in Turkey, India, etc., a tip, gratuity, or alms

Ba·ku (bä kōō') capital of the Azerbaijan S.S.R., on the Caspian Sea: pop. 1,224,000

bal. balance

Ba·laam (bā'ləm) *Bible* a prophet rebuked by his donkey after he had beaten it

bal·a·lai·ka (bal'ə lī'kə) *n.* [Russ.] a Russian stringed instrument somewhat like a guitar

bal·ance (bal'əns) *n.* [< LL. *bilanx*, having two scales] **1.** an instrument for weighing, esp. one with two matched pans hanging from either end of a poised lever **2.** a state of equilibrium in weight, value, etc. **3.** bodily or mental stability **4.** harmonious proportion of elements in a design, etc. **5.** a weight, value, etc. that counteracts another or causes equilibrium **6.** equality of debits and credits, or the difference between them **7.** a remainder **8.** a balancing **9.** *same as* BALANCE WHEEL —*vt.* **-anced, -anc·ing 1.** to weigh in or as in a balance **2.** to compare as to relative value, etc. **3.** to counterpoise or counteract; offset **4.** to put or keep in a state of equilibrium; poise **5.** to make or be equal to in weight, value, etc. **6.** to find any difference between, or to equalize, the debits and credits of (an account) —*vi.* **1.** to be in equilibrium **2.** to be equal in weight, value, etc. **3.** to have the credits and debits equal —**in the balance** not yet settled —**bal'ance·a·ble** *adj.* —**bal'anc·er** *n.*

balance sheet a statement summarizing the financial status of a business

balance wheel a wheel to regulate the movement of a timepiece, etc.

Bal·bo·a (bal bō'ə; *Sp.* bäl bō'ä), **Vas·co Nú·ñez de** (vas'kō nōō'nyeth *the*) 1475?–1517?; Sp. explorer: first European to discover the Pacific Ocean

bal·brig·gan (bal brig'ən) *n.* [after *Balbriggan*, town in Ireland] a knitted cotton material used for hosiery, underwear, etc.

bal·co·ny (bal'kə nē) *n., pl.* **-nies** [< It., akin to OHG. *balcho*, a beam] **1.** a platform projecting from a building

and enclosed by a railing **2.** an upper floor of seats in a theater, etc. often jutting out over the main floor

bald (bôld) *adj.* [ME. *balled* < ?] **1.** having white fur or feathers on the head, as some animals and birds **2.** lacking hair on the head **3.** not covered by natural growth **4.** plain or blunt —**bald'ly** *adv.* —**bald'ness** *n.*

bald eagle a large, strong eagle of N. America, with a white-feathered head and neck

bal·der·dash (bôl'dər dash') *n.* [orig. a senseless mixture of liquids] nonsensical talk or writing

bald·faced (bôld'fāst') *adj.* brazen; shameless

bald'ing *adj.* becoming bald

bal·dric (bôl'drik) *n.* [< OFr., ult. < L. *balteus*, a girdle] a belt worn over one shoulder to support a sword, etc.

bale¹ (bāl) *n.* [< OHG. *balla*, a ball] a large bundle, esp. a standardized quantity of goods, as of cotton, hay, etc., compressed and bound —*vt.* **baled, bal'ing** to make into bales —**bal'er** *n.*

bale² (bāl) *n.* [OE. *bealu*] [Poetic] **1.** evil; harm **2.** sorrow; woe

Bal·e·ar·ic Islands (bal'ē er'ik) group of Sp. islands in the Mediterranean, east of Spain

ba·leen (bə lēn') *n.* [< L. *ballaena*, a whale] *same as* WHALEBONE

bale·ful (bāl'fəl) *adj.* harmful or evil; sinister —**bale'ful·ly** *adv.* —**bale'ful·ness** *n.*

Ba·li (bä'lē) island of Indonesia —**Ba·li·nese** (bä'lə nēz') *adj., n.*

balk (bôk) *n.* [OE. *balca*, a ridge] **1.** a ridge of unplowed land between furrows **2.** a roughly hewn piece of timber **3.** a check, hindrance, etc. **4.** *Baseball* an illegal motion by the pitcher entitling base runners to advance one base —*vt.* to obstruct or foil —*vi.* **1.** to stop and refuse to move or act **2.** to make a balk in baseball —**balk'er** *n.*

Bal·kan (bôl'kən) *adj.* of the Balkans, their people, etc. — **the Balkans** countries of the Balkan Peninsula (Yugoslavia, Bulgaria, Albania, Greece, & the European part of Turkey) & Romania: also **Balkan States**

Balkan Mountains mountain range extending across C Bulgaria, from Yugoslavia to the Black Sea

Balkan Peninsula peninsula in SE Europe, between the Adriatic & Black seas

balk·y (bôk'ē) *adj.* **-i·er, -i·est** stubbornly resisting; balking —**balk'i·ness** *n.*

ball¹ (bôl) *n.* [ME. *bal*] **1.** any round object; sphere; globe **2.** *a*) a round or egg-shaped object used in various games *b*) any of several such games, esp. baseball **3.** a throw or pitch of a ball *[a fast ball]* **4.** a missile for a cannon, rifle, etc. **5.** a rounded part of the body **6.** *Baseball* a pitched ball that is not struck at and is not a strike —*vi., vt.* to form into a ball —**ball up** [Slang] to muddle or confuse — **be on the ball** [Slang] to be alert; be efficient —**play ball 1.** to begin or resume playing a ball game **2.** [Colloq.] to cooperate

ball² (bôl) *n.* [< Fr. < Gr. *ballein*, to throw] **1.** a formal social dance **2.** [Slang] a good time

bal·lad (bal'əd) *n.* [< OFr. *ballade*, dancing song] **1.** a sentimental song with the same melody for each stanza **2.** a narrative song or poem, usually anonymous and handed down orally, having short stanzas, simple words, and a refrain **3.** a slow, sentimental popular song —**bal'·lad·eer'** *n.* —**bal'lad·ry** *n.*

bal·last (bal'əst) *n.* [< ODan. *bar*, bare + *last*, a load] **1.** anything heavy carried in a ship, vehicle, etc. to give stability **2.** anything giving stability, as to character, etc. **3.** crushed rock or gravel, used in railroad beds, etc. —*vt.* to furnish with ballast

ball bearing 1. a bearing in which the moving parts revolve on freely rolling metal balls **2.** any of these balls

bal·le·ri·na (bal'ə rē'nə) *n.* [It. < L.: see BALL²] a woman ballet dancer

bal·let (bal'ā, ba lā') *n.* [< Fr. < It. *ballo*, a dance] **1.** an intricate group dance using pantomime and conventionalized movements to tell a story **2.** ballet dancers

ballistic missile a long-range missile guided automatically in flight, but a free-falling projectile at its target

bal·lis·tics (bə lis'tiks) *n.pl.* [*with sing. v.*] **1.** the science dealing with the motion and impact of projectiles **2.** the study of the effects of firing on a firearm, bullet, etc. — **bal·lis'tic** *adj.*

bal·loon (bə lōōn') *n.* [< Fr. < It. *palla*, a ball] **1.** a large, airtight bag that rises when filled with a gas lighter than air **2.** such a bag with a gondola for passengers or instruments **3.** an inflatable rubber bag, used as a toy —*vt.* to cause to swell like a balloon —*vi.* **1.** to ride in a balloon **2.** to swell; expand —*adj.* like a balloon —**bal·loon′ist** *n.*

bal·lot (bal′ət) *n.* [< It. *palla*, ball] **1.** a ticket, paper, etc. by which a vote is registered **2.** act, method, or right of voting, esp. by secret ballots **3.** the total number of votes cast **4.** a list of candidates for office; ticket —*vi.* to vote

ball·park (bôl′pärk′) *n.* a baseball stadium —*adj.* [Colloq.] designating an estimate, etc. that is thought to be reasonably accurate —**in the ballpark** [Colloq.] **1.** reasonably accurate **2.** fairly close to what is required

ball′play′er *n.* a baseball player

ball point pen a fountain pen with a small ball bearing instead of a point

ball′room′ *n.* a large hall for dancing

bal·lute (ba l<del>oo</del>t′) *n.* [BALL(OON) + (PARACH)UTE] a heat-resistant balloonlike device inflated by stored gas and used to slow down a spacecraft reentering the atmosphere

bal·ly·hoo (bal′ē h<del>oo</del>′) *n.* [< ?] loud talk, sensational advertising, etc. —*vt.*, *vi.* **-hooed′**, **-hoo′ing** [Colloq.] to promote with ballyhoo

balm (bäm) *n.* [< Gr. *balsamon*] **1.** an aromatic resin obtained from certain trees and used in medicine; balsam **2.** a fragrant ointment or oil **3.** anything healing or soothing **4.** any of various aromatic plants similar to mint

balm′y *adj.* **-i·er**, **-i·est 1.** soothing, mild, etc. **2.** [Brit. Slang] crazy or foolish —**balm′i·ly** *adv.* —**balm′i·ness** *n.*

ba·lo·ney (bə lō′nē) *n.* [< ? *bologna*] **1.** *same as* BOLOGNA **2.** [Slang] nonsense

bal·sa (bôl′sə) *n.* [Sp.] **1.** a tropical American tree yielding an extremely light, buoyant wood **2.** the wood

bal·sam (bôl′səm) *n.* [see BALM] **1.** an aromatic resin obtained from certain trees **2.** any of various aromatic, resinous oils or fluids **3.** balm **4.** any of various trees yielding balsam —**bal·sam·ic** (bôl sam′ik) *adj.*

balsam fir an evergreen tree of Canada and the northern U.S., with a soft wood used for pulpwood

Bal·tic (bôl′tik) *adj.* **1.** of the Baltic Sea **2.** of the Baltic States —*n.* the Baltic Sea

Baltic Sea sea in N Europe, west of the U.S.S.R.

Baltic States former independent countries of Latvia, Lithuania, & Estonia

Bal·ti·more (bôl′tə môr′) seaport in N Md.: pop. 906,000 (met. area 2,071,000)

Baltimore oriole a N. American oriole having an orange body with black on the head, wings, and tail

bal·us·ter (bal′əs tər) *n.* [< Fr. < Gr. *balaustion*, flower of the wild pomegranate: from the shape] any of the small posts of a railing, as on a staircase

bal·us·trade (bal′ə strād′) *n.* a railing held up by balusters

Bal·zac (bäl zäk′; *E.* bôl′zak), **Ho·no·ré de** (ô nô rä′ də) 1799–1850; Fr. novelist

bam·bi·no (bam bē′nō) *n., pl.* **-nos**, **-ni** (-nē) [It. dim. of *bambo*, childish] **1.** a child; baby **2.** an image of the infant Jesus

bam·boo (bam b<del>oo</del>′) *n.* [Malay *bambu*] a treelike tropical grass with woody, jointed, often hollow stems, used for furniture, canes, etc.

bam·boo·zle (bam b<del>oo</del>′z'l) *vt.* **-zled**, **-zling** [< ?] **1.** to trick; cheat **2.** to confuse —**bam·boo′zle·ment** *n.*

ban (ban) *vt.* **banned**, **ban′ning** [OE. *bannan*, summon] to prohibit or forbid, esp. officially —*n.* **1.** a condemnation by church authorities **2.** a curse **3.** an official prohibition **4.** strong public disapproval

ba·nal (bā′n'l; bə nal′) *adj.* [Fr.] trite; hackneyed —**ba·nal·i·ty** (bə nal′ə tē) *n., pl.* **-ties** —**ba′nal·ly** *adv.*

ba·nan·a (bə nan′ə) *n.* [Sp. & Port.] **1.** a treelike tropical plant with large clusters of edible fruit **2.** the narrow, somewhat curved fruit, having a creamy flesh and a yellow or red skin

band¹ (band) *n.* [ON.] **1.** something that binds, ties, or encircles, as a strip or ring of wood, rubber, metal, etc. **2.** a stripe **3.** a narrow strip of cloth used to line, decorate, etc. [*hatband*] **4.** a division on a long-playing phonograph record **5.** a range of radiation wavelengths or frequencies —*vt.* to put a band on or around

band² (band) *n.* [< Fr. < Goth. *bandwa*, a sign] **1.** a group of people united for a common purpose **2.** a group of musicians playing together, esp. upon wind and percussion instruments [a dance *band*] —*vi.*, *vt.* to unite for a common purpose

band·age (ban′dij) *n.* [Fr. < *bande*, a strip] a strip of cloth or other dressing used to bind or cover an injury —*vt.* **-aged**, **-ag·ing** to put a bandage on

Band-Aid (ban′dād′) [BAND(AGE) + AID] *a trademark for* a small prepared bandage of gauze and adhesive tape —*n.* [b- a-] a bandage of this type: also **band′aid′**

ban·dan·na, ban·dan·a (ban dan′ə) *n.* [Hindi *bāndhnū*, method of dyeing] a large, colored handkerchief, usually with a printed pattern

band·box (band′bäks′) *n.* a light box, as of pasteboard, to hold hats, small articles, etc.

ban·deau (ban dō′, ban′dō) *n., pl.* **-deaux′** (-dōz′, -dōz) [Fr.] **1.** a narrow ribbon **2.** a narrow brassiere with little support

ban·de·role, ban·de·rol (ban′də rōl′) *n.* [Fr. < It.] a narrow flag or pennant

ban·di·coot (ban′di k<del>oo</del>t′) *n.* [< native name] **1.** a very large rat of India and Ceylon **2.** a ratlike marsupial of Australia

ban·dit (ban′dit) *n., pl.* **-dits**, **ban·dit·ti** (ban dit′ē) [< It. *bandito*] **1.** a robber; highwayman **2.** anyone who cheats, steals, etc. —**ban′dit·ry** *n.*

band′mas′ter *n.* the leader of a musical band

ban·do·leer, ban·do·lier (ban′də lir′) *n.* [< Fr. < Sp. *banda*, scarf] a broad shoulder belt with pockets for carrying ammunition, etc.

band saw a power saw consisting of an endless, toothed steel belt running over pulleys

bands·man (bandz′mən) *n., pl.* **-men** a member of a band of musicians

band′stand′ *n.* a platform for a musical band, esp. one for outdoor concerts

band′wag′on *n.* a wagon for the band to ride in, as in a parade —**on the bandwagon** [Colloq.] on the popular or apparently winning side

ban·dy¹ (ban′dē) *vt.* **-died**, **-dy·ing** [Fr. *bander*, bandy at tennis] **1.** to toss or hit (a ball, etc.) back and forth **2.** to pass (gossip, etc.) about carelessly **3.** to exchange (words), as in arguing

ban·dy² (ban′dē) *adj.* [< Fr. *bander*, to bend] bent or curved outward

ban·dy-leg·ged (-leg′id, -legd′) *adj.* bowlegged

bane (bān) *n.* [OE. *bana*, slayer] **1.** the cause of harm, death, etc. **2.** deadly poison: now obs. except in *ratsbane*, etc. —**bane′ful** *adj.* —**bane′ful·ly** *adv.*

bane·ber·ry (bān′ber′ē) *n., pl.* **-ries 1.** a plant with poisonous berries **2.** the berry

bang¹ (baŋ) *vt.* [ON. *banga*, to pound] to hit, shut, etc. hard and noisily —*vi.* **1.** to make a sharp, loud noise **2.** to strike sharply (*against, into*, etc.) —*n.* **1.** a hard blow or loud knock **2.** a sudden, loud noise **3.** [Colloq.] a burst of vigor **4.** [Slang] a thrill —*adv.* **1.** hard and noisily **2.** suddenly —**bang up** to damage

bang² (baŋ) *vt.* [< ?] to cut (hair) short and straight across —*n.* [*usually pl.*] banged hair worn across the forehead

Bang·kok (baŋ′käk) seaport and capital of Thailand: pop. 1,669,000

Ban·gla·desh (bäŋ′glə desh′) country in S Asia, on the Bay of Bengal: 55,134 sq. mi.; pop. 50,840,000; cap. Dacca

ban·gle (baŋ′g'l) *n.* [Hindi *bangrī*] **1.** a decorative bracelet or anklet **2.** a disk-shaped ornament

bang-up (baŋ′up′) *adj.* [Colloq.] excellent

ban·ish (ban′ish) *vt.* [< OFr. *banir*] **1.** to exile **2.** to drive away; get rid of —**ban′ish·ment** *n.*

ban·is·ter (ban′əs tər) *n.* [< BALUSTER] [*often pl.*] a handrail, specif. one with balusters

ban·jo (ban′jō) *n., pl.* **-jos**, **-joes** [of Afr. origin] a musical instrument with a long neck, circular body, and strings that are plucked —**ban′jo·ist** *n.*

bank¹ (baŋk) *n.* [ult. < OHG. *bank*, a bench] **1.** *a*) an establishment for receiving or lending money *b*) its building **2.** the fund held, as by the dealer, in some gambling games **3.** a reserve supply, as of blood —*vi.* to put money in or do business with a bank —*vt.* to deposit (money) in a bank —**bank on** [Colloq.] to rely on

BANJO

bank² (baŋk) *n.* [< ON. *bakki*] **1.** a long mound or heap **2.** a steep slope **3.** a stretch of rising land at the edge of a stream, etc. **4.** a shallow place, as in a sea **5.** the lateral, slanting turn of an aircraft —*vt.* **1.** to heap dirt around for protection **2.** to cover (a fire) with ashes and fuel so that it will burn longer **3.** to pile up so as to form a bank **4.** to slope (a curve in a road, etc.) **5.** to slope (an aircraft) laterally on a turn **6.** to strike (a billiard ball) so that it recoils from a cushion —*vi.* **1.** to form a bank or banks **2.** to bank an airplane

bank³ (baŋk) *n.* [< OHG. *bank*, bench] **1.** a row of oars **2.** a row or tier of objects **3.** a row of keys in a keyboard — *vt.* to arrange in a bank

bank account money deposited in a bank and credited to the depositor

bank′book′ *n.* a book in which a bank depositor's account is recorded; passbook

bank′er *n.* a person who owns or manages a bank

bank′ing *n.* the business of a bank

bank note a promissory note issued by a bank: it is a form of paper money

bank′roll′ *n.* a supply of money —*vt.* [Colloq.] to finance

bank·rupt (baŋk′rupt′) *n.* [< Fr. < It. *banca*, bench + *rotta*, broken] a person legally declared unable to pay his debts: his property is divided among his creditors —*adj.* **1.** that is bankrupt; insolvent **2.** lacking in some quality [morally *bankrupt*] —*vt.* to make bankrupt —**bank′rupt′cy** *n., pl.* **-cies**

ban·ner (ban′ər) *n.* [< OFr. *baniere*] **1.** a piece of cloth bearing a design, motto, etc. **2.** a flag **3.** a headline extending across a newspaper page —*adj.* foremost; leading

ban·nis·ter (ban′əs tər) *n. same as* BANISTER

banns (banz) *n.pl.* [see BAN] the proclamation, generally made in church on three successive Sundays, of an intended marriage

ban·quet (baŋ′kwit) *n.* [Fr. < It. *banca*, table] **1.** a feast **2.** a formal dinner —*vt.* to honor with a banquet —*vi.* to feast —**ban′quet·er** *n.*

ban·quette (baŋ ket′) *n.* [Fr. < Du. *bank*, bench] **1.** a gunners' platform inside a trench or parapet **2.** an upholstered bench along a wall

ban·shee, ban·shie (ban′shē) *n.* [< Ir. *bean*, woman + *sith*, fairy] *Ir. & Scot. Folklore* a female spirit whose wailing warns of impending death

ban·tam (ban′təm) *n.* [< *Bantam*, former Du. residency in Java] **1.** [*often* B-] any of several breeds of small domestic fowl **2.** a small, aggressive person

ban′tam·weight′ *n.* a boxer or wrestler between a flyweight and lightweight (in boxing, between 113–118 lbs.)

ban·ter (ban′tər) *vt.* [17th-c. slang] to tease playfully —*vi.* to exchange banter (*with* someone) —*n.* genial teasing —**ban′ter·er** *n.* —**ban′ter·ing·ly** *adv.*

Ban·tu (ban′tōō) *n.* [Bantu *ba-ntu*, mankind] **1.** *pl.* **-tus,** **-tu** any member of a large group of Negroid tribes of equatorial and southern Africa **2.** any of the languages of these peoples —*adj.* of the Bantus or their languages

ban·yan (ban′yən) *n.* [from a tree of this kind under which the *banians* (Hindu merchants) had built a pagoda] an East Indian fig tree whose branches take root and become new trunks

ban·zai (bän′zī′) *interj.* a Japanese greeting or cry, meaning "May you live ten thousand years!"

ba·o·bab (bä′ō bab′, bä′-) *n.* [< native name] a tall tree of Africa and India, with edible, gourdlike fruit

bap·tism (bap′tiz′m) *n.* [< Gr. *baptizein*, to immerse] **1.** the rite of admitting a person into a Christian church by dipping him in water or sprinkling water on him **2.** an experience or trial that initiates, tests, etc. —**bap·tis′mal** (-tiz′m′l) *adj.*

Bap′tist (-tist) *n.* **1.** a member of a Protestant denomination practicing baptism by immersion **2.** JOHN THE BAPTIST

bap′tis·ter·y (-tis trē) *n., pl.* **-ies** a place, esp. in a church, for baptizing: also **bap′tis·try,** *pl.* **-tries**

bap·tize (bap′tīz, bap tīz′) *vt.* **-tized, -tiz·ing 1.** to administer baptism to **2.** to initiate **3.** to christen

bar¹ (bär) *n.* [< ML. *barra,* barrier] **1.** any piece of wood, metal, etc. longer than it is wide or thick, often used as a barrier, lever, etc. **2.** an oblong piece [*bar* of soap] **3.** anything that obstructs or hinders **4.** a band, broad line, etc. **5.** a law court, esp. that part enclosed by a railing where the judges or lawyers sit, or where prisoners are brought to trial **6.** lawyers collectively **7.** the legal profession **8.** a counter at which alcoholic drinks are served **9.** a place with such a counter **10.** *Music a)* a vertical line dividing a staff into measures *b)* a measure —*vt.* **barred, bar′ring 1.** to fasten as with a bar **2.** to obstruct; close **3.** to oppose; prevent **4.** to except —*prep.* excluding [the best, *bar* none] —**cross the bar** to die

bar² (bär) *n.* [G. < Gr. *baros,* weight] a metric unit of pressure, equal to one million dynes per sq. cm.

barb (bärb) *n.* [< L. *barba,* beard] **1.** a beardlike growth near the mouth of certain animals **2.** a sharp point projecting away from the main point of a fishhook, arrow, etc. **3.** a cutting remark —*vt.* to provide with a barb — **barbed** *adj.*

Bar·ba·dos (bär bā′dōz, -dōs) country on the easternmost island of the West Indies: a member of the British Commonwealth: 166 sq. mi.; pop. 253,000; cap. Bridgetown

bar·bar·i·an (bär ber′ē ən) *n.* [see BARBAROUS] **1.** a member of a people considered primitive, savage, etc. **2.** a coarse or unmannerly person; boor **3.** a savage, cruel person; brute —*adj.* uncivilized, cruel, etc. —**bar·bar′i·an·ism** *n.*

bar·bar·ic (-ik) *adj.* **1.** uncivilized; primitive **2.** wild, crude, etc. —**bar·bar′i·cal·ly** *adv.*

bar·bar·ism (bär′bər iz′m) *n.* **1.** *a)* the use of words and expressions not standard in a language *b)* a word or expression of this sort (Ex.: "youse" for "you") **2.** the state of being primitive or uncivilized **3.** a barbarous act, custom, etc.

bar·bar·i·ty (bär ber′ə tē) *n., pl.* **-ties 1.** cruel or brutal behavior **2.** a cruel or brutal act **3.** a barbarous act, custom, etc.

bar·ba·rize (bär′bə rīz′) *vt., vi.* **-rized′, -riz′ing** to make or become barbarous —**bar′ba·ri·za′tion** *n.*

bar′ba·rous (-bər əs) *adj.* [< Gr. *barbaros,* foreign] **1.** uncivilized **2.** crude, coarse, etc. **3.** cruel; brutal **4.** characterized by substandard usages of words —**bar′ba·rous·ly** *adv.*

Bar·ba·ry (bär′bər ē) region in N Africa, west of Egypt: its coast (**Barbary Coast**) was once a center of piracy

bar·be·cue (bär′bə kyōō′) *n.* [< Sp. < Haitian Creole *barbacoa,* framework] **1.** *a)* a hog, steer, etc. roasted whole over an open fire *b)* any meat broiled over an open fire **2.** a party or picnic at which such meat is served **3.** a portable outdoor grill —*vt.* **-cued′, -cu′ing** to roast or broil (meat) over an open fire, often with a highly seasoned sauce (**barbecue sauce**)

barbed wire twisted wire with barbs at close intervals, used for barriers: also **barb′wire′** *n.*

bar·bel (bär′b'l) *n.* [see BARB] a threadlike growth from the lips or jaws of certain fishes: it is an organ of touch

bar·bell (bär′bel′) *n.* [BAR¹ + (DUMB)BELL] a metal bar with varying weights attached at each end, used for weight-lifting exercises: also **bar bell**

bar·ber (bär′bər) *n.* [see BARB] a person whose work is cutting hair, shaving and trimming beards, etc. —*vt., vi.* to cut the hair (of), shave, etc.

bar·ber·ry (bär′ber′ē) *n., pl.* **-ries** [< Ar. *barbāris*] **1.** a spiny shrub with sour, red berries **2.** the berry

bar·bi·tal (bär′bi tôl′) *n.* [BARBIT(URIC ACID) + -AL] a drug in the form of a white powder, used to induce sleep

bar·bi·tu·rate (bär bich′ər it, bär′bə tyoor′it) *n.* any salt or ester of barbituric acid, used as a sedative

bar·bi·tu·ric acid (bär′bə tyoor′ik, -toor′-) [< G. *barbitursäure* + -IC] a crystalline acid, $C_4H_4O_3N_2$, derivatives of which are used as sedatives, etc.

bar·ca·role, bar·ca·rolle (bär′kə rōl′) *n.* [Fr. < It. *barca,* a boat] **1.** a song sung by Venetian gondoliers **2.** a piece of music imitating this

Bar·ce·lo·na (bär′sə lō′nə) seaport in NE Spain: pop. 1,697,000

bard (bärd) *n.* [Gael. & Ir.] **1.** an ancient Celtic poet **2.** any poet —**bard′ic** *adj.*

bare (ber) *adj.* [OE. *bær*] **1.** *a)* without the customary covering [*bare* floors] *b)* without clothing; naked **2.** without equipment or furnishings; empty **3.** simple; plain **4.** mere [a *bare* wage] —*vt.* **bared, bar′ing** to make bare; uncover —**lay bare** to uncover; expose —**bare′ness** *n.*

bare′back′ *adv., adj.* on a horse with no saddle

bare′faced′ *adj.* **1.** with the face uncovered **2.** unconcealed; open **3.** shameless; brazen —**bare′fac′ed·ly** (-fās′id lē) *adv.*

bare′foot′ *adj., adv.* without shoes and stockings —**bare′foot′ed** *adj.*

bare′hand′ed *adj., adv.* **1.** with hands uncovered **2.** without weapons or tools

bare′head′ed *adj., adv.* wearing no head covering

bare′leg′ged (-leg′id, -legd′) *adj., adv.* with the legs bare

bare′ly *adv.* **1.** openly; plainly **2.** only just; scarcely **3.** scantily [*barely* furnished]

bar·fly (bär′flī′) *n., pl.* **-flies′** [Slang] one who spends much time drinking in barrooms

bar·gain (bär′g'n) *n.* [< OFr. *bargaignier,* to haggle] **1.** a mutual agreement or contract between parties **2.** such an agreement in terms of its worth to one of the parties [a bad *bargain*] **3.** something sold at a price favorable to the buyer —*vi.* **1.** to haggle **2.** to make a bargain —**bargain**

for (or on) to expect; count on —**into the bargain** in addition; besides —**bar′gain·er** n.

barge (bärj) n. [< ML. *barga*] **1**. a large, flat-bottomed boat for carrying freight on rivers, etc. **2**. a large pleasure boat, used for pageants, etc. —vt. **barged, barg′ing** to carry by barge —vi. **1**. to move slowly and clumsily **2**. to come or go (*in* or *into*) in a rude, abrupt way **3**. to collide (*into*) —**barge′man** n., pl. **-men**

bar graph a graph with parallel bars representing in proportional lengths the figures given in the data

bar·ite (ber′īt) n. [< Gr. *barys*, weighty + -ITE] a white, crystalline mineral, barium sulfate

bar·i·tone (bar′ə tōn′) n. [< Gr. *barys*, deep + *tonos*, tone] **1**. the range of a male voice between bass and tenor **2**. a singer or instrument with such a range **3**. a musical part for a baritone

bar·i·um (ber′ē əm) n. [< Gr. *barys*, heavy] a silvery-white metallic chemical element: symbol, Ba; at. wt., 137.34; at. no., 56

bark[1] (bärk) n. [ON. *borkr*] the outside covering of trees and woody plants —vt. **1**. to take the bark off (a tree) **2**. [Colloq.] to scrape some skin off [to *bark* one's shins]

bark[2] (bärk) vi. [OE. *beorcan*] **1**. to make the sharp, abrupt cry of a dog **2**. to make a sound like this **3**. to speak sharply; snap **4**. [Colloq.] to cough —vt. to say with a bark or shout —n. a sound made in barking —**bark up the wrong tree** to misdirect one's attack, energies, etc.

bark[3] (bärk) n. [< Gr. *baris*, Egyptian barge] **1**. [Poet.] any boat **2**. a sailing vessel with its two forward masts square-rigged and its rear mast rigged fore-and-aft: also sp. **barque**

bar′keep′er n. **1**. a bar owner **2**. a bartender

bark·en·tine (bär′kən tēn′) n. [< BARK[3]] a sailing vessel with its foremast square-rigged and its other two masts rigged fore-and-aft

bark′er n. one that barks; esp., a person who attracts customers to a sideshow, etc. by loud talk

bar·ley (bär′lē) n. [< OE. *bere*] **1**. a cereal grass **2**. its grain, used in making malts, soups, etc.

bar′ley·corn′ n. barley or a grain of barley

barm (bärm) n. [OE. *beorma*] the foamy yeast that appears on the surface of fermenting malt liquors

bar′maid′ n. a woman bartender

bar mitz·vah (bär mits′və) [< Heb., son of the commandment] **1**. a Jewish boy who has arrived at the age of religious responsibility, 13 years **2**. a ceremony celebrating this —**bat** (or **bas**) **mitzvah** (bät, bäs) *fem.*

barm·y (bär′mē) adj. **-i·er, -i·est 1**. full of barm; foamy **2**. [Brit. Slang] silly; idiotic

barn (bärn) n. [< OE. *bere*, barley + *ærn*, a building] a farm building for sheltering harvested crops, livestock, etc.

bar·na·cle (bär′nə k'l) n. [Fr. *bernicle*] a saltwater shellfish that attaches itself to ship bottoms, pilings, etc.

barn owl a brown and gray owl frequenting barns

barn·storm (bärn′stôrm′) vi., vt. to tour small towns and rural areas, giving plays, speeches, etc.

barn swallow a common swallow with a long, deeply forked tail: it usually nests in barns

Bar·num (bär′nəm), P(hineas) T(aylor) 1810–91; U.S. showman & circus operator

barn′yard′ n. the yard near a barn —adj. of, like, or fit for a barnyard

bar·o·graph (bar′ə graf′) n. [< Gr. *baros*, weight + -GRAPH] a barometer that automatically records variations in atmospheric pressure

ba·rom·e·ter (bə räm′ə tər) n. [< Gr. *baros*, weight + -METER] **1**. an instrument for measuring atmospheric pressure, used in forecasting weather **2**. anything that indicates change —**bar·o·met·ric** (bar′ə met′rik), **bar′o·met′ri·cal** adj.

bar·on (bar′ən) n. [OFr., man] **1**. a member of the lowest rank of the British hereditary peerage **2**. a powerful businessman or industrialist; magnate —**ba·ro·ni·al** (bə rō′nē əl) adj.

bar·on·age (bar′ə nij) n. **1**. barons as a class **2**. the peerage **3**. the rank, title, etc. of a baron

bar·on·ess (-nis) n. **1**. a baron's wife or widow **2**. a lady with a barony in her own right

bar·on·et (-nit, -net′) n. a man holding the lowest hereditary British title, below a baron but above a knight — **bar′on·et·cy** (-sē) n., pl. **-cies**

bar·on·y (-nē) n., pl. **-ies 1**. a baron's domain **2**. the rank or title of a baron

ba·roque (bə rōk′) adj. [Fr. < Port. *barroco*, imperfect pearl] **1**. *a*) very ornate and full of curved lines, as much

art and architecture of about 1550–1750 *b*) full of highly embellished melodies, fugues, etc., as much music of that time **2**. overdecorated —n. baroque style, baroque art, etc.

ba·rouche (bə rōōsh′) n. [< G. < LL. *bi-*, two + *rota*, wheel] a four-wheeled carriage with a collapsible hood and two double seats behind the driver

bar·racks (bar′iks) n.pl. [*often with sing.* v.] [< Fr. < Sp. *barro*, clay] **1**. a building or buildings for housing soldiers **2**. any large, plain building

bar·ra·cu·da (bar′ə kōō′də) n., pl. **-da, -das** [Sp.] a fierce pikelike fish of tropical seas

bar·rage (bə räzh′) n. [Fr. < *barrer*, to stop] **1**. a curtain of artillery fire laid down to keep enemy forces from moving, or to cover one's own forces, esp. in attack **2**. a prolonged attack of words —vt., vi. **-raged′, -rag′ing** to lay down a barrage (against)

bar·ra·try (bar′ə trē) n. [< ON. *baratta*, quarrel] negligence or fraud on the part of a ship's officers or crew that results in a loss to the owners

barred (bärd) adj. **1**. having bars or stripes **2**. closed off with bars **3**. forbidden or excluded

bar·rel (bar′əl) n. [< ML. *barillus*] **1**. a large, wooden, cylindrical container with slightly bulging sides and flat ends **2**. the capacity of a standard barrel (in the U.S., usually 31 1/2 gal.) **3**. any somewhat similar cylinder, as the straight tube of a gun —vt. **-reled** or **-relled, -rel·ing** or **-rel·ling** to put in barrels —vi. [Slang] to go at a high speed

barrel organ a mechanical musical instrument played by turning a crank

bar·ren (bar′ən) adj. [< OFr. *baraigne*] **1**. that cannot produce offspring; sterile **2**. without vegetation; unfruitful **3**. unproductive; unprofitable **4**. boring; dull —n. [*usually pl.*] an area of relatively unproductive land, often with shrubs, brush, etc. —**bar′ren·ly** adv. —**bar′ren·ness** n.

bar·rette (bə ret′) n. [Fr.] a bar or clasp for holding a girl's or woman's hair in place

bar·ri·cade (bar′ə kād′; *also, esp. for* v., bar′ə kād′) n. [Fr. < It. *barricare*, to fortify] a barrier, esp. one put up hastily for defense —vt. **-cad′ed, -cad′ing 1**. to shut in or keep out with a barricade **2**. to block or obstruct

Bar·rie (bar′ē), Sir **James** M(atthew) 1860–1937; Scot. novelist & playwright

bar·ri·er (bar′ē ər) n. [< OFr. *barre*, BAR[1]] **1**. an obstruction, as a fence or wall **2**. anything that holds apart or separates [racial *barriers*]

bar·ring (bär′iŋ) prep. excepting

bar·ris·ter (bar′is tər) n. [< BAR[1] (n. 5) + -*ister*, as in MINISTER] in England, a lawyer who pleads cases in court

bar′room′ n. a room with a bar at which alcoholic drinks are sold

bar·row[1] (bar′ō) n. [< OE. *beran*, BEAR[1]] *same as:* **1**. HANDBARROW **2**. WHEELBARROW

bar·row[2] (bar′ō) n. [< OE. *beorg*, hill] a heap of earth or rocks marking an ancient grave

Bart. Baronet

bar·tend·er (bär′ten′dər) n. one who mixes and serves alcoholic drinks at a bar

bar·ter (bär′tər) vi., vt. [< ON. *baratta*, quarrel] to trade by exchanging (goods or services) without using money — n. **1**. a bartering **2**. anything bartered —**bar′ter·er** n.

Bar·ton (bär′t'n), **Clara** 1821–1912; U.S. philanthropist: founder of the American Red Cross

bar·y·on (bar′ē än) n. [< Gr. *barys*, heavy + (ELECTR)ON] any of certain heavy atomic particles, as the proton

ba·ry·tes (bə rīt′ēz) n. *same as* BARITE

bar·y·tone (bar′ə tōn′) n. *same as* BARITONE

bas·al (bā′s'l) adj. **1**. of or at the base **2**. basic; fundamental

basal metabolism the quantity of energy used by any organism at rest

ba·salt (bə sôlt′, bās′ôlt) n. [L. *basaltes*, dark marble] a dark, tough, heavy volcanic rock

bas·cule (bas′kyōōl) n. [Fr., a seesaw] a device so balanced that when one end is lowered, the other is raised

base[1] (bās) n., pl. **bas′es** (-əz) [see BASIS] **1**. the thing or part on which something rests; foundation **2**. the main part, as of a system, on which the rest depends **3**. the principal or essential ingredient **4**. the part of a word to which affixes are attached **5**. a basis **6**. any of the four goals a baseball player must reach to score a run **7**. a headquarters or source of supply **8**. *Chem.* a substance that forms a salt when it reacts with an acid **9**. *Geom.* the line or plane upon which a figure is thought of as resting —adj. forming a base —vt. **based, bas′ing 1**. to make a base for **2**. to establish

base² (bās) *adj.* [< VL. *bassus,* low] **1.** with little or no honor, courage, etc.; contemptible **2.** menial; servile **3.** inferior in quality **4.** not precious *[iron is a base metal]* — **base′ly** *adv.* —**base′ness** *n.*

base′ball′ *n.* **1.** a game played with a ball and bat by two opposing teams on a field with four bases forming a diamond **2.** the ball used in this game

base′board′ *n.* a molding at the base of an interior wall

base hit *Baseball* a hit by which the batter gets safely on base without an error and without forcing a runner

base′less *adj.* having no basis in fact; unfounded —**base′less·ness** *n.*

base line 1. a line serving as a base **2.** *Baseball* the lane between any two consecutive bases **3.** the back line at each end of a tennis court

base·ment (bās′mənt) *n.* the story of a building just below the main floor, usually below the ground

base on balls *Baseball same as* WALK

bash (bash) *vt.* [echoic] [Colloq.] to strike with a violent blow —*n.* **1.** [Colloq.] a blow **2.** [Slang] a party

bash·ful (bash′fəl) *adj.* [(A)BASH + -FUL] timid; shy; easily embarrassed —**bash′ful·ly** *adv.* —**bash′ful·ness** *n.*

bas·ic (bā′sik) *adj.* **1.** of or forming a base; fundamental **2.** *Chem.* of or containing a base; alkaline —*n.* a basic principle, factor, etc.: *usually used in pl.* —**bas′i·cal·ly** *adv.*

Basic English a copyrighted form of English for international communication and for first steps into full English, devised by C. K. Ogden (1889–1957)

bas·il (baz′'l) *n.* [< Gr. *basilikon,* royal] a fragrant herb of the mint family, used for flavoring

ba·sil·i·ca (bə sil′i kə) *n.* [< Gr. *basilikē* (*stoa*), royal (portico)] **1.** a church with a broad nave, side aisles, and an apse **2.** *R.C.Ch.* a church with special ceremonial rights

bas·i·lisk (bas′ə lisk′) *n.* [< Gr. *basileus,* king] a mythical, lizardlike monster whose glance and breath were fatal

ba·sin (bās′'n) *n.* [< VL. *bacca,* water vessel] **1.** a wide, shallow container for liquid **2.** its contents or capacity **3.** a sink **4.** any shallow hollow, esp. water-filled, as a pond **5.** *same as* RIVER BASIN

ba·sis (bā′sis) *n., pl.* **-ses** (-sēz) [Gr., pedestal] **1.** the base or foundation of anything **2.** a principal constituent **3.** a basic principle or theory

bask (bask) *vi.* [ME. *basken,* to wallow] **1.** to warm oneself pleasantly, as in sunlight **2.** to enjoy any pleasant or warm feeling

bas·ket (bas′kit) *n.* [ME.] **1.** a container made of interwoven cane, strips of wood, etc. **2.** its contents **3.** anything like a basket **4.** *Basketball* a) the goal, a round, open net hanging from a ring b) a scoring toss of the ball through this

bas′ket·ball′ *n.* **1.** a game played by two teams of five players each, in a zoned floor area: points are scored by tossing a ball through a basket at the opponent's end of the playing court **2.** a large, round, inflated ball used in this game

basket weave a weave of fabrics that resembles the weave used in basket making

Basque (bask) *n.* **1.** a member of a people living in the W Pyrenees **2.** their unique language —*adj.* of the Basques or their language

bas-re·lief (bä′rə lēf′) *n.* [Fr. < It.: see BASS¹ & RELIEF] sculpture in which figures carved in a flat surface project only a little

bass¹ (bās) *n.* [< VL. *bassus,* low] **1.** the range of the lowest male voice **2.** a singer or instrument with this range; specif., *same as* DOUBLE BASS —*adj.* of, in, for, or having this range

bass² (bas) *n., pl.* **bass, bass′es** [OE. *bærs*] **1.** a North American freshwater food and game fish **2.** any of various saltwater fishes

bass clef (bās) *Music* a sign on a staff, indicating the position of F below middle C on the fourth line

bass drum (bās) the largest and lowest-toned of the double-headed drums

bas·set (bas′it) *n.* [< OFr. *bas,* low] a hunting hound with a long body, short legs, and long ears

bass horn (bās) *same as* TUBA

bas·si·net (bas′ə net′) *n.* [< Fr. *berceau,* a cradle] an infant's basketlike bed, often hooded and on wheels

bas·so (bas′ō, bäs′ō) *n., pl.* **-sos** [It.] a bass voice or singer

bas·soon (bə sōōn′, ba-) *n.* [< Fr.] a double-reed bass woodwind musical instrument —**bas·soon′ist** *n.*

bass viol (bās) *same as* DOUBLE BASS

bass·wood (bas′wood′) *n.* **1.** any of several trees with light, soft wood **2.** the wood

bast (bast) *n.* [OE. *bæst*] plant fiber used in ropes, mats, etc.

bas·tard (bas′tərd) *n.* [< OFr. < ?] **1.** an illegitimate child **2.** anything spurious, inferior, or not standard —*adj.* **1.** of illegitimate birth **2.** inferior, spurious, etc. —**bas′tard·ly** *adv.* —**bas′tard·y** *n.*

BASSOON

bas′tard·ize′ *vt.* **-ized′, -iz′ing 1.** to make, declare, or show to be a bastard **2.** to make corrupt; debase —**bas′tard·i·za′tion** *n.*

baste¹ (bāst) *vt.* **bast′ed, bast′ing** [OHG. *bastjan,* sew with bast] to sew temporarily with long, loose stitches until properly sewed —**bast′er** *n.*

baste² (bāst) *vt.* **bast′ed, bast′ing** [< OFr. *bassiner,* moisten] to moisten (roasting meat) with melted butter, drippings, etc. —**bast′er** *n.*

baste³ (bāst) *vt.* **bast′ed, bast′ing** [ON. *beysta*] **1.** to beat soundly **2.** to attack with words; abuse

bas·tille, bas·tile (bas tēl′) *n.* [Fr.: see BASTION] a prison —**the Bastille** a prison in Paris destroyed (July 14, 1789) in the French Revolution

bas·ti·na·do (bas′tə nä′dō, -nā′-) *n., pl.* **-does** [< Sp. *bastón,* a stick] **1.** a beating with a stick, usually on the soles of the feet **2.** a rod or stick

bast·ing (bās′tiŋ) *n.* **1.** the act of sewing with loose, temporary stitches **2.** such stitches

bas·tion (bas′chən) *n.* [Fr. < Gmc. *bastjan,* make with bast, build] **1.** a projection from a fortification **2.** any strong defense —**bas′tioned** *adj.*

bat¹ (bat) *n.* [OE. *batt*] **1.** a stout club **2.** a club used to strike the ball in baseball and cricket **3.** a turn at batting **4.** [Colloq.] a blow or hit **5.** [Old Slang] a spree —*vt.* **bat′ted, bat′ting 1.** to hit as with a bat **2.** to have a batting average of —*vi.* to take a turn at batting —**bat around** [Slang] to discuss (an idea, plan, etc.) —**go to bat for** [Colloq.] to defend —**(right) off the bat** [Colloq.] immediately

bat² (bat) *n.* [< Scand.] a nocturnal, mouselike, flying mammal with a furry body and membranous wings —**blind as a bat** quite blind

bat³ (bat) *vt.* **bat′ted, bat′ting** [see BATTER¹] [Colloq.] to wink —**not bat an eye (or eyelash)** [Colloq.] not show surprise

Ba·ta·vi·a (bə tā′vē ə) *former name of* JAKARTA

batch (bach) *n.* [OE. *bacan,* bake] **1.** the amount (of bread, etc.) produced at one baking **2.** the quantity of anything needed for or made in one operation or lot **3.** a group of things or persons

BAT
(3 1/2 in. long)

bate (bāt) *vt., vi.* **bat′ed, bat′ing** [< ABATE] to lessen —**with bated breath** with the breath held in because of fear, excitement, etc.

bath (bath) *n., pl.* **baths** (ba*th*z, baths) [OE. *bæth*] **1.** a washing, esp. of the body, in water **2.** water or other liquid for bathing or for dipping or soaking something **3.** a bathtub **4.** a bathroom **5.** a bathhouse (sense 1) **6.** *[often pl.]* a resort where bathing is part of the medical treatment —*vt., vi.* [Brit.] *same as* BATHE —**take a bath** [Slang] to suffer a financial loss

bathe (bā*th*) *vt.* **bathed, bath′ing** [see prec.] **1.** to put into a liquid; immerse **2.** to give a bath to **3.** to moisten **4.** to cover as with a liquid *[bathed in moonlight]* —*vi.* **1.** to take a bath **2.** to swim, cool oneself, etc. in water **3.** to soak oneself in something —*n.* [Brit.] a swim —**bath′er** *n.*

bath′house′ *n.* **1.** a public building for bathing **2.** a building used by bathers for changing clothes

Bath′i·nette′ (-ə net′) [after BASSINET] *a trademark for* a portable folding bathtub for babies

bathing suit a garment worn for swimming

bath′mat′ *n.* a mat used in or next to a bathtub

ba·thos (bā′thäs) *n.* [Gr., depth] **1.** an abrupt change from the lofty to the trivial; anticlimax **2.** false pathos **3.** triteness —**ba·thet·ic** (bə thet′ik) *adj.*
bath′robe′ *n.* a long, loose coat for wear to and from the bath, in lounging, etc.
bath′room′ *n.* a room with a bathtub, toilet, etc.
bath′tub′ *n.* a tub to bathe in, esp. in a bathroom
bath·y·sphere (bath′ə sfir′) *n.* [< Gr. *bathys*, deep + SPHERE] a round, watertight observation chamber lowered by cables into sea depths
ba·tik (bə tēk′) *n.* [Malay] **1.** a method of dyeing designs on cloth by waxing the parts not to be dyed **2.** cloth thus decorated or a design thus made —*adj.* of or like batik
ba·tiste (ba tēst′, bə-) *n.* [Fr.: < supposed original maker, *Baptiste*] a fine, thin cloth of cotton, linen, etc.
ba·ton (bə tän′) *n.* [Fr.] **1.** a staff serving as a symbol of office **2.** a slender stick used in directing music **3.** a metal rod twirled by a drum major
Ba·ton Rouge (bat′'n rōōzh′) capital of La., on the Mississippi: pop. 166,000
bat·tal·ion (bə tal′yən) *n.* [< Fr. < VL. *battalia*, BATTLE] **1.** a large group of soldiers arrayed for battle **2.** any large group joined together in some activity **3.** a tactical military unit forming part of a division
bat·ten[1] (bat′'n) *n.* [var. of BATON] **1.** a sawed strip of wood **2.** a strip of wood put over a seam between boards as a fastening or covering **3.** a strip used to fasten canvas over a ship's hatchways —*vt.* to fasten or supply with battens
bat·ten[2] (bat′'n) *vi.* [ON. *batna*, improve] to grow fat; thrive —*vt.* to fatten up
bat·ter[1] (bat′ər) *vt.* [< L. *battuere*, to beat] **1.** to strike with blow after blow; pound **2.** to injure by hard wear or use —*vi.* to pound noisily
bat·ter[2] (bat′ər) *n.* the baseball or cricket player whose turn it is to bat: also, in cricket, **bats′man** (-mən), *pl.* **-men**
bat·ter[3] (bat′ər) *n.* [see BATTER¹] a flowing mixture of flour, milk, etc. for making cakes, waffles, etc.
bat′ter·ing ram 1. an ancient military machine having a heavy beam for battering down walls, etc. **2.** anything used like this
bat·ter·y (bat′ər ē) *n., pl.* **-ies** [< Fr.: see BATTER¹] **1.** a battering or beating **2.** a set of things used together **3.** *Baseball* the pitcher and the catcher **4.** *Elec.* a cell or group of cells storing an electrical charge and able to furnish a current **5.** *Law* an illegal beating of another person: see ASSAULT AND BATTERY **6.** *Mil.* **a)** a set of heavy guns, rockets, etc. **b)** the men who operate such a set
bat·ting (bat′iŋ, -'n) *n.* [< BAT¹] cotton, wool, etc. fibers wadded into sheets and used in bandages, etc.
bat·tle (bat′'l) *n.* [< L. *battuere*, to beat] **1.** a large-scale fight between armed forces **2.** armed fighting; combat **3.** any fight or conflict —*vt., vi.* **-tled, -tling** to fight —**give** (or **do**) **battle** to engage in battle; fight —**bat′tler** *n.*
bat′tle-ax′, bat′tle-axe′ *n.* **1.** a heavy ax formerly used as a weapon **2.** [Slang] a harsh, domineering woman
battle cry a cry or slogan used to encourage those in a battle, struggle, contest, etc.
bat·tle·dore (bat′'l dôr′) *n.* [< ? Pr. *batedor*, beater] **1.** a paddle or racket used to hit a shuttlecock back and forth in a game (called **battledore and shuttlecock**) like badminton **2.** this game
bat′tle·field′ *n.* **1.** the place where a battle is fought or was fought **2.** any area of conflict Also **bat′tle-ground′**
bat′tle·ment (-mənt) *n.* [< OFr. *batailler*, fortify] a low wall, as on top of a tower, with open spaces for shooting
bat′tle·ship′ *n.* any of a class of large warships with the biggest guns and very heavy armor
bat·ty (bat′ē) *adj.* **-ti·er, -ti·est** [< BAT² + -Y²] [Slang] **1.** insane; crazy **2.** odd; eccentric
bau·ble (bô′b'l) *n.* [< L. *bellus*, pretty] a showy trifle; trinket
baulk (bôk) *n., vt., vi. same as* BALK
baux·ite (bôk′sīt) *n.* [Fr. < (*Les*) *Baux*, town in SE France] the claylike ore from which aluminum is obtained
Ba·var·i·a (bə ver′ē ə) state of S West Germany: cap. Munich —**Ba·var′i·an** *adj., n.*
bawd (bôd) *n.* [< ? Frank. *bald*, bold] [Now Literary] **1.** a woman who keeps a brothel **2.** a prostitute
bawd·y (bô′dē) *adj.* **-i·er, -i·est** indecent, obscene, etc. — **bawd′i·ly** *adv.* —**bawd′i·ness** *n.*
bawl (bôl) *vi., vt.* [< ML. *baulare*, to bark] **1.** to shout or call out noisily; bellow **2.** to weep loudly —*n.* **1.** a bellow **2.** a noisy weeping —**bawl out** [Slang] to scold angrily
bay[1] (bā) *n.* [< ML. *baia*] a wide inlet of a sea or lake, indenting the shoreline

bay[2] (bā) *n.* [< VL. *batare*, gape] **1.** *a)* an alcove marked off by columns, etc. *b)* a recess in a wall, as for a window *c) same as* BAY WINDOW **2.** a compartment for storing or holding something
bay[3] (bā) *vi.* [< VL. *batare*, gape] to bark in long, deep tones —*n.* **1.** the sound of baying **2.** the situation of a hunted animal forced to turn and fight —**at bay 1.** with escape cut off **2.** held off *[a fear kept at bay]* —**bring to bay** to force into a situation that makes escape impossible
bay[4] (bā) *n.* [< L. *baca*, berry] **1.** the laurel tree **2.** *[pl.]* honor; fame
bay[5] (bā) *adj.* [< L. *badius*] reddish-brown: said esp. of horses —*n.* **1.** a horse, etc. of this color **2.** reddish brown
bay·ber·ry (bā′ber′ē) *n., pl.* **-ries 1.** *a)* any of several shrubs, as the wax myrtle, with small, wax-coated berries *b)* any of the berries **2.** a tropical tree yielding an oil used in bay rum
bay leaf the aromatic leaf of the laurel tree, dried and used as a spice in cooking
bay·o·net (bā′ə nit, -net′) *n.* [< Fr. < *Bayonne*, city in France] a detachable blade put on a rifle muzzle, for hand-to-hand fighting —*vt., vi.* **-net′ed** or **-net′ted, -net′-ing** or **-net′ting** to stab or kill with a bayonet
bay·ou (bi′ōō) *n.* [< AmInd.] in the southern U.S., a marshy inlet or outlet of a lake, river, etc.
bay rum an aromatic liquid formerly obtained from leaves of a bayberry tree: it is used in medicines and cosmetics
bay window 1. a window or set of windows jutting out from a wall **2.** [Slang] a large, protruding belly
ba·zaar (bə zär′) *n.* [Per. *bāzār*] **1.** in Oriental countries, a marketplace **2.** a shop for selling various kinds of goods **3.** a benefit sale of various articles, for a club, church, etc.
ba·zoo·ka (bə zōōk′ə) *n.* [< name of a comic musical horn] a portable weapon of metal tubing, for launching armor-piercing rockets
bbl. *pl.* **bbls.** barrel
BB (shot) [designation of size] a size of shot (diameter, .18 in.) for an air rifle (**BB gun**) or shotgun
B.C. 1. before Christ **2.** British Columbia
bd. *pl.* **bds. 1.** board **2.** bond
B.D. Bachelor of Divinity
bdl. *pl.* **bdls.** bundle
be (bē, bi) *vi.* **was** or **were, been, be′ing** [OE. *beon*] **1.** to exist; live *[Ceasar is no more]* **2.** to happen or occur *[the party is tonight]* **3.** to remain or continue *[will he be here long?]* *Note: be* is used to link its subject to a predicate complement *[she is brave, let x be y]* or as an auxiliary: (1) with a past participle: *a)* to form the passive voice *[he will be paid] b)* to form a perfect tense *[Christ is risen]* (2) with a present participle to express continuation *[the motor is running]* (3) with a present participle or infinitive to express futurity, possibility, obligation, intention, etc. *[he is going next week, she is to walk the dog] Be* is conjugated in the present indicative: (I) *am,* (he, she, it) *is,* (we, you, they) *are;* in the past indicative: (I, he, she, it) *was,* (we, you, they) *were*
be- [OE. < *be,* about] *a prefix meaning:* **1.** around *[beset]* **2.** completely *[bedeck]* **3.** away *[betake]* **4.** about *[bemoan]* **5.** make *[besot]* **6.** furnish with, affect by *[becloud]*
Be *Chem.* beryllium
B/E, b.e. bill of exchange
beach (bēch) *n.* [E. dial., pebbles] a sandy shore —*vt., vi.* to ground (a boat) on a beach
beach′comb′er (-kō′mər) *n.* one who loafs on beaches or wharves, living on what he can beg or find
beach′head′ (-hed′) *n.* a position established by invading troops on an enemy shore
bea·con (bēk′'n) *n.* [OE. *beacen*] **1.** a light for warning or guiding: often used figuratively **2.** a lighthouse **3.** a radio transmitter sending signals to guide aircraft —*vi.* to serve as a beacon
bead (bēd) *n.* [< OE. *biddan,* pray] **1.** a small ball of glass, wood, etc., pierced for stringing **2.** *[pl.] a)* a string of beads *b)* a rosary **3.** any small, round object, as the front sight of a rifle **4.** a drop or bubble **5.** foam, as on beer **6.** a narrow, half-round molding —*vt.* to decorate with beads —*vi.* to form a bead or beads —**say** (or **tell** or **count**) **one's beads** to say prayers with a rosary — **bead′ed** *adj.*
bead′ing *n.* **1.** decorative work in beads **2.** a molding resembling a row of beads **3.** a narrow, half-round molding
bea·dle (bē′d'l) *n.* [< Frank. *bidal,* messenger] formerly, a minor parish officer in the Church of England
bead′y *adj.* **-i·er, -i·est 1.** small, round, and glittering like a bead **2.** decorated with beads

bea·gle (bē'g'l) *n.* [< ? Fr. *bégueule*, wide-throat] a small hound with a smooth coat, short legs, and drooping ears

beak (bēk) *n.* [< L. *beccus*] 1. a bird's bill 2. the beaklike mouthpart of various insects, fishes, etc.

beak·er (bē'kər) *n.* [< L. *bacar*, wine glass] 1. a goblet 2. a glass or metal container used by chemists, druggists, etc.

beam (bēm) *n.* [OE.] 1. a long, thick piece of wood, or of metal or stone, used in building 2. the crossbar of a balance 3. a ship's breadth at its widest point 4. a slender shaft of light, etc. 5. a radiant look, smile, etc. 6. a steady radio or radar signal for guiding aircraft or ships —*vt.* 1. to give out (shafts of light) 2. to direct (a radio signal, etc.) —*vi.* 1. to shine brightly 2. to smile warmly —**off the beam** 1. not following a guiding beam, as an airplane 2. [Colloq.] wrong —**on the beam** 1. following a guiding beam 2. [Colloq.] functioning well —**beam'ing** *adj.* —**beam'ing·ly** *adv.*

BEAKER

bean (bēn) *n.* [OE.] 1. a plant of the legume family, with edible, kidney-shaped seeds 2. any such seed 3. a pod with such seeds 4. any beanlike seed 5. [Slang] the head or brain 6. [*pl.*] [Slang] even a small amount [it's not worth *beans*] —*vt.* [Slang] to hit on the head —**spill the beans** [Colloq.] to tell a secret

bear[1] (ber) *vt.* bore, borne or born, bear'ing [OE. *beran*] 1. to carry; transport 2. to have or show [it *bore* his signature] 3. to give birth to 4. to produce or yield 5. to support or sustain 6. to withstand or endure [to *bear* torture] 7. to require [this *bears* watching] 8. to carry or conduct (oneself) 9. to carry over or hold [to *bear* a grudge] 10. to bring and tell (a message, etc.) 11. to give [to *bear* witness] —*vi.* 1. to be productive 2. to lie, point, or move in a given direction 3. to be relevant (with *on*) 4. to put up patiently (with) —**bear down** (on) 1. to exert pressure or effort (on) 2. to approach —**bear out** to confirm —**bear up** to endure —**bear'er** *n.*

bear[2] (ber) *n.* [OE. *bera*] 1. a large, heavy mammal with shaggy fur and a very short tail 2. [B-] either of two N constellations (**Great Bear** and **Little Bear**) 3. one who is clumsy, rude, etc. 4. one who sells stocks, etc., hoping to buy them back later at a lower price —*adj.* falling in price [a *bear* market]

bear'a·ble *adj.* that can be endured —**bear'a·bly** *adv.*

beard (bird) *n.* [OE.] 1. the hair growing on the lower part of a man's face 2. any beardlike part, as the awn of certain grains —*vt.* 1. to oppose courageously 2. to provide with a beard —**beard'ed** *adj.* —**beard'less** *adj.*

bear·ing (ber'iŋ) *n.* 1. way of carrying and conducting oneself; carriage 2. a supporting part 3. a producing or the ability to produce 4. an enduring 5. [*often pl.*] relative position or direction 6. [*pl.*] awareness of one's situation [to lose one's *bearings*] 7. relation; relevance 8. a part of a machine on which another part revolves, slides, etc. 9. *Heraldry* any figure in a coat of arms —*adj.* that bears, or supports, weight

bear'ish *adj.* 1. like a bear; rude, surly, etc. 2. directed toward or causing a lowering of prices in the stock exchange —**bear'ish·ly** *adv.*

bear'skin' *n.* 1. the skin of a bear 2. a rug, coat, etc. made of this

beast (bēst) *n.* [< L. *bestia*] 1. any large, four-footed animal 2. a person who is brutal, gross, etc.

beast'ly *adj.* -li·er, -li·est 1. of or like a beast; bestial, brutal, etc. 2. [Colloq.] disagreeable; unpleasant —**beast'·li·ness** *n.*

beast of burden any animal used for carrying things

beast of prey any animal that hunts and kills other animals for food

beat (bēt) *vt.* beat, beat'en, beat'ing [OE. *beatan*] 1. to strike repeatedly; pound 2. to punish by so striking; flog 3. to dash repeatedly against 4. to form (a path) as by repeated treading 5. to shape by hammering; forge 6. to mix by hard stirring 7. to move (esp. wings) up and down 8. to hunt through; search 9. to outdo or defeat 10. to mark (time) by tapping 11. [Colloq.] to puzzle 12. [Colloq.] to cheat 13. [Slang] to escape the penalties of —*vi.* 1. to strike repeatedly 2. to throb, pulsate, etc. —*n.* 1. a beating, as of the heart 2. any of a series of strokes 3. a throb 4. a habitual route 5. the unit of musical rhythm 6. the accent of the rhythm in verse or music —*adj.* 1. [Slang] tired; exhausted 2. of a group of young persons, esp. of the 1950's, expressing social disillusionment by un-

conventional dress, actions, etc. —**beat down** 1. to shine with intense light and heat 2. to put down; suppress —**beat it!** [Slang] go away! —**beat off** to drive back —**beat up** (on) to give a beating to —**beat'er** *n.*

beat'en (-'n) *adj.* 1. struck with repeated blows 2. shaped by hammering 3. flattened by treading 4. defeated —**off the beaten track** (or **path**) unusual, unfamiliar, etc.

be·a·tif·ic (bē'ə tif'ik) *adj.* 1. making blissful or blessed 2. full of bliss or joy

be·at·i·fy (bē at'ə fī') *vt.* -fied', -fy'ing [< Fr. < L. *beatus*, happy + *facere*, make] 1. to make blissfully happy 2. *R.C.Ch.* to declare one who has died to be among the blessed in heaven —**be·at'i·fi·ca'tion** *n.*

beat'ing *n.* 1. the act of one that beats 2. a whipping 3. a throbbing 4. a defeat

be·at·i·tude (bē at'ə tood') *n.* [< Fr. < L. *beatus*, happy] perfect blessedness or happiness —**the Beatitudes** the pronouncements in the Sermon on the Mount, which begin "Blessed are the poor in spirit"

beat·nik (bēt'nik) *n.* a member of the beat group

beat'-up' *adj.* [Slang] worn-out, shabby, etc.

beau (bō) *n., pl.* **beaus, beaux** (bōz) [Fr. < L. *bellus*, pretty] a woman's sweetheart

Beau·mont (bō'mänt) city in SE Tex.: pop. 116,000

beau·te·ous (byoot'ē əs) *adj. same as* BEAUTIFUL —**beau'te·ous·ly** *adv.*

beau·ti·cian (byoo tish'ən) *n.* a person who does hair styling, manicuring, etc. in a beauty shop

beau·ti·ful (byoot'ə fəl) *adj.* having beauty —**beau'ti·ful·ly** *adv.*

beau'ti·fy' (-fī') *vt., vi.* -fied', -fy'ing to make or become beautiful —**beau'ti·fi·ca'tion** *n.* —**beau'ti·fi'er** *n.*

beau·ty (byoot'ē) *n., pl.* -ties [< L. *bellus*, pretty] 1. the quality of being very pleasing, as in form, color, tone, behavior, etc. 2. a thing having this quality 3. good looks 4. a very good-looking woman

beauty shop (or **salon** or **parlor**) a place where women go for hair styling, manicuring, etc.

bea·ver[1] (bē'vər) *n.* [OE. *beofor*] 1. an amphibious animal with webbed hind feet and a flat, broad tail 2. its soft, brown fur 3. a man's high silk hat 4. [Colloq.] a hard-working, conscientious person

bea·ver[2] (bē'vər) *n.* [< OFr. *bave*, saliva] the visor of a helmet

Bea·ver·board (bē'vər bôrd') *a trademark for* artificial board made of wood fiber, used for walls, etc. —*n.* [b-] fiberboard of this kind

be·calm (bi käm') *vt.* 1. to make calm 2. to make (a ship) motionless from lack of wind

be·came (bi kām') *pt. of* BECOME

be·cause (bi kôz', -kuz') *conj.* [< ME. *bi*, by + *cause*] for the reason that; since —**because of** on account of

beck (bek) *n.* a beckoning gesture of the hand, head, etc. —**at the beck and call of** obedient to the wishes of

beck·on (bek''n) *vt., vi.* [< OE. *beacen*, a beacon] 1. to summon by a gesture 2. to lure; entice

be·cloud (bi kloud') *vt.* to cloud over; obscure

be·come (bi kum') *vi.* -came', -come', -com'ing [OE. *becuman*] to come or grow to be —*vt.* to suit; be right for [that hat *becomes* her] —**become of** to happen to

be·com'ing *adj.* 1. appropriate; seemly 2. suitable to the wearer —**be·com'ing·ly** *adv.*

bed (bed) *n.* [OE.] 1. a piece of furniture for sleeping on 2. a plot of soil where plants are raised 3. the bottom of a river, lake, etc. 4. any flat surface used as a foundation 5. a geological layer —*vt.* bed'ded, bed'ding 1. to provide with a sleeping place 2. to put to bed 3. to embed 4. to plant in a bed of earth 5. to arrange in layers —*vi.* 1. to go to bed; sleep 2. to stratify

be·daub (bi dôb') *vt.* to make daubs on; smear

be·daz·zle (bi daz''l) *vt.* -zled, -zling to bewilder, confuse

bed'bug' *n.* a small, wingless, reddish-brown bloodsucking insect that infests beds, etc.

bed'cham'ber *n. same as* BEDROOM

bed'clothes' (-klōz', -klōthz') *n.pl.* sheets, blankets, etc. used on a bed

bed'ding (-iŋ) *n.* 1. mattresses and bedclothes 2. straw, etc. used to bed animals 3. a bottom layer

be·deck (bi dek') *vt.* to adorn

be·dev·il (bi dev''l) *vt.* -iled or -illed, -il·ing or -il·ling 1. to plague; torment 2. to confuse; bewilder —**be·dev'il·ment** *n.*

be·dew (bi doo') *vt.* to make wet as with dew

bed'fast' (-fast') *adj. same as* BEDRIDDEN

---

bed·fel′low (-fel′ō) *n.* **1.** a person who shares one's bed **2.** any associate

be·dight (bi dīt′) *adj.* [< ME. *bi-*, BE- + *dighten*, set in order < L. *dicere*, speak] [Archaic] bedecked; arrayed

be·dim (bi dim′) *vt.* -dimmed′, -dim′ming to make (the eyes or vision) dim; darken or obscure

be·di·zen (bi di′z'n, -diz′'n) *vt.* [BE- + archaic *dizen* < LG. *diesse*, bunch of flax] [Now Rare] to dress in a cheap, showy way —**be·di′zen·ment** *n.*

bed·lam (bed′ləm) *n.* [< (the old London mental hospital of St. Mary of) *Bethlehem*] any noisy, confused place or condition

bed linen bed sheets, pillowcases, etc.

bed of roses [Colloq.] an easy life or situation

Bed·ou·in (bed′ōō win) *n., pl.* -ins, -in [< Fr. < Ar. *badāwīn*, desert dwellers] **1.** an Arab of the desert tribes of Arabia, Syria, or North Africa **2.** any wanderer

bed′pan′ *n.* a shallow pan used as a toilet by one who is bedridden

be·drag·gle (bi drag′'l) *vt.* -gled, -gling to make wet, limp, and dirty, as by dragging through mire

bed′rid′den (-rid′'n) *adj.* confined to bed, usually for a long time, by illness, infirmity, etc.

bed′rock′ *n.* **1.** solid rock beneath the soil and superficial rock **2.** a secure foundation **3.** the very bottom **4.** basic principles

bed′roll′ *n.* a portable roll of bedding, generally for sleeping outdoors

bed′room′ *n.* a room to sleep in

bed′side′ *n.* the space beside a bed —*adj.* beside a bed

bed′sore′ *n.* a body sore on a bedridden person, caused by chafing or pressure

bed′spread′ *n.* an ornamental cover spread over the blanket on a bed

bed′spring′ *n.* a framework of springs in a bed to support the mattress

bed′stead′ (-sted′) *n.* a framework for supporting the springs and mattress of a bed

bed′time′ *n.* the time when one usually goes to bed

bee¹ (bē) *n.* [OE. *beo*] a four-winged, hairy insect that gathers pollen and nectar —**have a bee in one's bonnet** to be obsessed by an idea

bee² (bē) *n.* [< OE. *ben*, service] a meeting of people to work together or to compete

beech (bēch) *n.* [OE. *boece*] **1.** a tree with smooth, gray bark, hard wood, and edible nuts **2.** its wood —*adj.* of this tree or its wood —**beech′en** *adj.*

beech′nut′ *n.* the small, three-cornered nut of the beech

beef (bēf) *n., pl.* **beeves**; also, and for 5 always, **beefs** [< L. *bos*, ox] **1.** a full-grown ox, cow, bull, or steer, esp. one bred for meat **2.** meat from such an animal **3.** such animals collectively **4.** [Colloq.] human muscle; strength **5.** [Slang] a complaint —*vi.* [Slang] to complain —**beef up** [Colloq.] to strengthen

beef′steak′ (-stāk′) *n.* a thick cut of beef for broiling or frying

beef′y *adj.* -i·er, -i·est fleshy and solid; brawny —**beef′i·ness** *n.*

bee·hive (bē′hīv′) *n.* **1.** a shelter for a colony of bees **2.** a place of great activity

bee′line′ *n.* a straight, direct route —**make a beeline for** [Colloq.] to go straight toward

Be·el·ze·bub (bē el′zə bub′) *Bible* the chief devil; Satan

been (bin, ben; *chiefly Brit.* bēn) *pp. of* BE

beep (bēp) *n.* [echoic] the brief, high-pitched sound of a horn or electronic signal —*vi., vt.* to make or cause to make such a sound

beer (bir) *n.* [OE. *beor*] **1.** an alcoholic, fermented drink made from malt, hops, etc. **2.** a soft drink made from extracts of roots, etc. [ginger *beer*]

Beer·she·ba (bir shē′bə) city in S Israel: pop. 70,000

bees′wax′ *n.* wax secreted and used by bees to build their honeycombs

beet (bēt) *n.* [< L. *beta*] **1.** a plant with a thick, white or red root **2.** this root, used as a vegetable or as a source of sugar

Bee·tho·ven (bā′tō vən), **Lud·wig van** (lōōt′vikh vän) 1770–1827; Ger. composer

bee·tle¹ (bēt′'l) *n.* [< OE. *bitan*, to bite] an insect with hard front wings that cover the membranous hind wings when these are folded

bee·tle² (bēt′'l) *vi.* -tled, -tling [prob. < BEETLE-BROWED] to project or jut; overhang —*adj.* jutting; overhanging: also **bee′tling**

bee·tle-browed (bēt′'l broud′) *adj.* [ME. < ? *bitel*, sharp + *brouwe*, brow] **1.** having bushy or overhanging eyebrows **2.** frowning; scowling

beet sugar sugar extracted from sugar beets

beeves (bēvz) *n. pl. of* BEEF

be·fall (bi fôl′) *vi., vt.* -fell′, -fall′en, -fall′ing [< OE. be- + *feallan*, fall] to happen or occur (to)

be·fit (bi fit′) *vt.* -fit′ted, -fit′ting to be suitable or proper for —**be·fit′ting** *adj.* —**be·fit′ting·ly** *adv.*

be·fog (bi fôg′, -fäg′) *vt.* -fogged′, -fog′ging **1.** to envelop in fog **2.** to obscure; confuse

be·fore (bi fôr′) *adv.* [< OE. *be-*, by + *foran*, before] **1.** ahead; in front **2.** in the past **3.** earlier; sooner —*prep.* **1.** ahead of in time, space, or order **2.** in the sight or presence of [to stand *before* a judge] **3.** being considered by [a bill *before* Congress] **4.** earlier than **5.** in preference to [death *before* dishonor] —*conj.* **1.** earlier than the time that [call *before* you leave] **2.** rather than [I'd starve *before* I ate that]

be·fore′hand′ (-hand′) *adv., adj.* **1.** ahead of time **2.** in anticipation

be·foul (bi foul′) *vt.* to dirty or sully

be·friend (bi frend′) *vt.* to act as a friend to

be·fud·dle (bi fud′'l) *vt.* -dled, -dling to confuse or stupefy, as with alcoholic liquor —**be·fud′dle·ment** *n.*

beg (beg) *vt., vi.* begged, beg′ging [< MDu. *beggaert*, beggar] **1.** to ask for (alms) [he *begged* a dime] **2.** to ask earnestly; entreat —**beg off** to ask to be released from — **go begging** to be unwanted

be·gan (bi gan′) *pt. of* BEGIN

be·get (bi get′) *vt.* -got′ or archaic -gat′ (-gat′), -got′ten or -got′, -get′ting [< OE. *begitan*, acquire] **1.** to be the father of **2.** to cause; produce —**be·get′ter** *n.*

beg·gar (beg′ər) *n.* **1.** a person who begs **2.** a very poor person **3.** a person [a cute little *beggar*] —*vt.* **1.** to make poor; impoverish **2.** to make seem useless [beauty which *beggars* description]

beg′gar·ly *adj.* very poor, inadequate, etc. —**beg′gar·li·ness** *n.*

be·gin (bi gin′) *vi.* -gan′, -gun′, -gin′ning [OE. *beginnan*] **1.** to start doing something **2.** to come into being —*vt.* **1.** to cause to start **2.** to originate

be·gin′ner *n.* one who is just beginning to do or learn something; novice

be·gin′ning *n.* **1.** a starting **2.** the time or place of starting; origin **3.** the first part **4.** [*usually pl.*] an early stage

be·gird (bi gurd′) *vt.* -girt′ (-gurt′) or -gird′ed, -girt′, -gird′ing **1.** to gird **2.** to encircle

be·gone (bi gôn′, -gän′) *interj., vi.* (to) be gone; go away; get out

be·gon·ia (bi gōn′yə) *n.* [< M. *Bégon* (1638–1710), Fr. patron of science] a plant with showy flowers and ornamental leaves

be·got (bi gät′) *pt. & alt. pp. of* BEGET

be·got′ten (-'n) *pp. of* BEGET

be·grime (bi grīm′) *vt.* -grimed′, -grim′ing to cover with grime; soil

be·grudge (bi gruj′) *vt.* -grudged′, -grudg′ing **1.** to resent another's possession of (something) **2.** to give with reluctance [he *begrudges* her every cent] —**be·grudg′ing·ly** *adv.*

be·guile (bi gīl′) *vt.* -guiled′, -guil′ing **1.** to mislead by guile **2.** to deprive (of) by deceit **3.** to pass (time) pleasantly **4.** to charm or delight —**be·guile′ment** *n.* —**be·guil′er** *n.* —**be·guil′ing·ly** *adv.*

be·gun (bi gun′) *pp. of* BEGIN

be·half (bi haf′) *n.* [< OE. *be*, by + *healf*, side] support or interest [speaking in her *behalf*] —**in** (or **on**) **behalf of** in the interest of; for

be·have (bi hāv′) *vt., vi.* -haved′, -hav′ing [see BE- & HAVE] **1.** to conduct (oneself) in a specified way **2.** to conduct (oneself) properly

be·hav·ior (bi hāv′yər) *n.* way of behaving; conduct or action: also, Brit. sp. **behaviour** —**be·hav′ior·al** *adj.*

behavioral science any of the sciences, as sociology or psychology, that study human behavior

be·hav·ior·ism the doctrine that observed behavior provides the only valid data of psychology —**be·hav′ior·ist** *n., adj.* —**be·hav′ior·is′tic** *adj.*

be·head (bi hed′) *vt.* to cut off the head of

be·held (bi held′) *pt. & pp. of* BEHOLD

be·he·moth (bi hē′məth, bē′ə-) *n.* [< Heb. *behēmāh*, beast] **1.** *Bible* a huge animal, assumed to be the hippopotamus **2.** any huge animal or thing

BEEF CUTS

be·hest (bi hest′) *n.* [OE. *behæs*, a vow] an order or earnest request

be·hind (bi hīnd′) *adv.* [OE. *behindan*] 1. in or to the rear 2. in a former time, place, etc. 3. below standard 4. in or into arrears 5. slow; late —*prep.* 1. in back of [sit *behind* me] 2. lower than in rank, achievement, etc. 3. later than [*behind* schedule] 4. beyond [*behind* the next hill] 5. supporting [Congress is *behind* the plan] 6. hidden by [what's *behind* his smile?] —*adj.* that follows [the person *behind*] —*n.* [Colloq.] the buttocks

be·hind'hand' (-hand′) *adv.*, *adj.* late or slow in payment, time, or progress

be·hold (bi hōld′) *vt.* **-held′**, **-held′** or archaic **-hold′en**, **-hold'ing** [OE. *bihealdan*, to hold] to look at; regard —*interj.* look! see! —**be·hold'er** *n.*

be·hold'en (-ən) *adj.* obliged to feel grateful; indebted

be·hoof (bi hōof′) *n.* [OE. *behof*, profit] behalf, benefit, interest, sake, etc.

be·hoove (bi hōōv′) *vt.* **-hooved′**, **-hoov'ing** [OE. *behofian*, to need] to be necessary for or incumbent upon [it *behooves* you to go]

beige (bāzh) *n.* [Fr.] grayish tan —*adj.* grayish-tan

be·ing (bē′iŋ) *n.* [see BE] 1. existence; life 2. essential nature 3. one that lives or exists [a human *being*] —being as (or that) [Dial. or Colloq.] since; because —for the time being for now

Bei·rut (bā rōōt′) capital of Lebanon: pop. 500,000

be·jew·el (bi jōō′əl) *vt.* **-eled** or **-elled**, **-el·ing** or **-el·ling** to decorate with or as with jewels

be·la·bor (bi lā′bər) *vt.* 1. to beat severely 2. to attack verbally 3. popularly, *same as* LABOR, *vt.*

be·lat·ed (bi lāt′id) *adj.* late or too late; tardy —**be·lat'ed·ly** *adv.* —**be·lat'ed·ness** *n.*

be·lay (bi lā′) *vt.*, *vi.* **-layed′**, **-lay'ing** [< OE. *belecgan*, make fast] 1. to make (a rope) secure by winding around a pin (belaying pin), cleat, etc. 2. [Naut. Colloq.] to hold; stop

belch (belch) *vi.*, *vt.* [OE. *bealcian*] 1. to expel (gas) through the mouth from the stomach 2. to throw forth violently [the volcano *belched* flames] —*n.* a belching

bel·dam, bel·dame (bel′dəm) *n.* [see BELLE & DAME] an old woman, esp. a very ugly one

be·lea·guer (bi lē′gər) *vt.* [< Du. *leger*, a camp] 1. to besiege by encircling 2. to beset; harass

Be·lém (be len′) seaport in NE Brazil: pop. 402,000

Bel·fast (bel′fast) seaport & capital of Northern Ireland: pop. 398,000

bel·fry (bel′frē) *n.*, *pl.* **-fries** [ult. < OHG. *bergen*, protect + *frid*, peace] 1. a bell tower 2. the part of a tower that holds the bell(s)

Belg. 1. Belgian 2. Belgium

Bel·gium (bel′jəm) kingdom in W Europe: 11,779 sq. mi.; pop. 9,660,000; cap. Brussels —**Bel'gian** (-jən) *adj.*, *n.*

Bel·grade (bel′grād, -gräd) capital of Yugoslavia: pop. 598,000

be·lie (bi lī′) *vt.* **-lied′**, **-ly'ing** 1. to disguise or misrepresent [his words *belie* his thoughts] 2. to leave unfulfilled 3. to show to be untrue

be·lief (bə lēf′) *n.* [OE. *geleafa*] 1. conviction that certain things are true 2. religious faith 3. trust or confidence 4. a creed, tenet, etc. 5. an opinion; expectation

be·lieve (bə lēv′) *vt.* **-lieved′**, **-liev'ing** [OE. *geliefan*] 1. to take as true, real, etc. 2. to have confidence in a statement or promise of 3. to suppose or think —*vi.* 1. to have confidence (*in*) 2. to have religious faith 3. to suppose or think —**be·liev'a·bil'i·ty** *n.* —**be·liev'a·ble** *adj.* —**be·liev'a·bly** *adv.* —**be·liev'er** *n.*

be·lit·tle (bi lit′'l) *vt.* **-tled**, **-tling** to make seem little, less important, etc. —**be·lit'tle·ment** *n.* —**be·lit'tler** *n.*

bell (bel) *n.* [OE. *belle*] 1. a hollow, cuplike object, as of metal, which rings when struck 2. the sound of a bell 3. anything shaped like a bell 4. *Naut.* a bell rung every half hour to mark the periods of the watch —*vt.* to attach a bell to —*vi.* to flare out like a bell

Bell (bel), **Alexander Gra·ham** (grā′əm) 1847–1922; U.S. inventor of the telephone, born in Scotland

bel·la·don·na (bel′ə dän′ə) *n.* [< It., beautiful lady: from cosmetic use] 1. a poisonous plant of the nightshade family: source of atropine 2. atropine

bell'-bot'tom *adj.* designating trousers flaring at the ankles

bell'boy' *n.* *same as* BELLMAN

bell buoy a buoy with a warning bell rung by the motion of the waves

belle (bel) *n.* [Fr., fem. of BEAU] a pretty woman or girl, esp. the prettiest one [the *belle* of the ball]

belles-let·tres (bel let′rə) *n.pl.* [Fr.] nontechnical or nonscientific literature, as fiction, poetry, drama, etc. —**bel·let·rist** (bel let′rist) *n.* —**bel'le·tris'tic** (-lə tris′tik) *adj.*

bell·hop (bel′häp′) *n.* *same as* BELLMAN

bel·li·cose (bel′ə kōs′) *adj.* [< L. *bellicus*, of war] quarrelsome; warlike —**bel'li·cose'ly** *adv.* —**bel'li·cos'i·ty** (-käs′ə tē) *n.*

bel·lig·er·ent (bə lij′ər ənt) *adj.* [< L. *bellum*, war + *gerere*, carry on] 1. at war 2. of war 3. warlike 4. ready to fight or quarrel —*n.* a belligerent person or nation —**bel·lig'er·ence, bel·lig'er·en·cy** *n.* —**bel·lig'er·ent·ly** *adv.*

bell'man (-mən) *n.*, *pl.* **-men** a man or boy employed by a hotel, etc. to carry luggage and do errands

bel·low (bel′ō) *vi.* [OE. *bylgan*] 1. to roar with a reverberating sound, as a bull 2. to cry out loudly, as in anger —*vt.* to utter loudly or powerfully —*n.* a bellowing sound

bel·lows (bel′ōz) *n. sing. & pl.* [see BELLY] 1. a device that produces a stream of air when its sides are pumped together: used for blowing fires, in pipe organs, etc. 2. anything like a bellows, as the folding part of some cameras

bells (belz) *n.pl.* [Colloq.] bell-bottom trousers

bell·weth·er (bel′weth′ər) *n.* a male sheep that leads the flock: it usually wears a bell

bel·ly (bel′ē) *n.*, *pl.* **-lies** [OE. *belg*, leather bag] 1. the part of the body between the chest and thighs; abdomen 2. the underside of an animal's body 3. the stomach 4. the deep interior [the *belly* of a ship] —*vt.*, *vi.* **-lied**, **-ly·ing** to swell out

bel'ly·ache' (-āk′) *n.* pain in the abdomen —*vi.* **-ached′**, **-ach'ing** [Slang] to complain —**bel'ly·ach'er** *n.*

bel'ly·but'ton (-but′'n) *n.* [Colloq.] the navel: also **belly button**

belly dance a dance characterized by a twisting of the abdomen, sinuous hip movements, etc. —**bel'ly-dance'** *vi.* **-danced′**, **-danc'ing** —**belly dancer**

belly laugh [Colloq.] a hearty laugh

be·long (bi lôŋ′) *vi.* [< ME.] 1. to have a proper place [it *belongs* here] 2. to be related (*to*) 3. to be a member (with *to*) 4. to be owned (with *to*)

be·long'ing *n.* 1. a thing that belongs to one 2. [*pl.*] possessions 3. close relationship

be·lov·ed (bi luv′id, -luvd′) *adj.* dearly loved —*n.* a dearly loved person

be·low (bi lō′) *adv.*, *adj.* [see BE- & LOW¹] 1. in or to a lower place; beneath 2. at a later place (in a book, etc.) 3. in or to hell 4. on earth 5. in or to a lesser rank, function, etc. —*prep.* 1. lower than, as in rank or worth 2. unworthy of

Bel·shaz·zar (bel shaz′ər) *Bible* the last king of Babylon

belt (belt) *n.* [< L. *balteus*, a belt] 1. a band of leather, etc. worn around the waist 2. any encircling thing like this 3. an endless band, as for transferring motion from one wheel to another 4. a distinctive area [the corn *belt*] 5. [Slang] a hard blow; punch 6. [Slang] *a*) a gulp of liquor *b*) a thrill —*vt.* 1. to encircle or fasten as with a belt 2. *a*) to hit with a belt *b*) [Slang] to hit hard 3. [Colloq.] to sing (*out*) lustily —below the belt unfair(ly) —under one's belt as part of one's experience

belt'ing *n.* 1. material for making belts 2. belts regarded collectively 3. [Slang] a beating

be·lu·ga (bə lōō′gə) *n.*, *pl.* **-ga, -gas** [< Russ. *byeli*, white] a large, white dolphin of northern seas

be·mire (bi mīr′) *vt.* **-mired′**, **-mir'ing** 1. to dirty as with mire 2. to cause to bog down in mud

be·moan (bi mōn′) *vt.*, *vi.* to lament

be·muse (bi myōoz′) *vt.* **-mused′**, **-mus'ing** [BE- + MUSE] 1. to confuse 2. to preoccupy —**be·muse'ment** *n.*

bench (bench) *n.* [OE. *benc*] 1. a long, hard seat 2. the place where judges sit in a court 3. [*sometimes* B-] *a*) the status of a judge *b*) judges collectively *c*) a law court 4. *same as* WORKBENCH 5. *Sports a*) a seat where members of a team sit when not in the game *b*) auxiliary players collectively —*vt.* *Sports* to take (a player) out of a game —on the bench 1. presiding in a law court 2. *Sports* not taking part in the game

bench mark 1. a surveyor's mark made on a landmark for use as a reference point 2. a standard in judging quality, value, etc. Also **bench'mark'** *n.*

bench warrant an order issued by a judge or law court for the arrest of a person

bend (bend) *vt.* **bent**, **bend'ing** [OE. *bendan*, to bind] 1.

to make curved or crooked 2. to turn from a straight line 3. to make submit 4. *Naut.* to fasten (sails or ropes) —*vi.* 1. to turn from a straight line 2. to yield by curving, as from pressure 3. to curve the body; stoop (*over* or *down*) 4. to give in; yield *[he bent to her wishes]* —*n.* 1. a bending or being bent 2. a curving part 3. any of various knots —**bend′a·ble** *adj.*

bend′er *n.* 1. one that bends 2. [Slang] a drinking bout

be·neath (bi nēth′) *adv., adj.* [< OE. be- + neothan, down] in a lower place; below; underneath —*prep.* 1. lower than; below 2. underneath 3. unworthy of *[it is beneath* him to cheat*]*

Ben·e·dict (ben′ə dikt′), Saint 480?–543? A.D.; It. monk: founded the Benedictine order

ben·e·dict (ben′ə dikt′) *n.* [< *Benedick,* in Shakespeare's *Much Ado About Nothing*] a newly married man, esp. one who seemed a confirmed bachelor

Ben·e·dic·tine (ben′ə dik′tin; *also, and for n. 2 usually,* -tēn) *adj.* designating or of the monastic order founded by Saint Benedict —*n.* 1. a Benedictine monk or nun 2. [b-] a liqueur, originally made by Benedictine monks

ben·e·dic·tion (ben′ə dik′shən) *n.* [< L. *bene,* well + *dicere,* speak] 1. a blessing 2. an invocation of divine blessing, esp. at the end of a church service —**ben′e·dic′to·ry** *adj.*

ben·e·fac·tion (ben′ə fak′shən, ben′ə fak′-) *n.* [< L. *bene,* well + *facere,* do] 1. the act of helping those in need 2. money or help freely given

ben·e·fac·tor (ben′ə fak′tər) *n.* one who has given financial or other help; patron —**ben′e·fac′tress** (-tris) *n.fem.*

ben·e·fice (ben′ə fis) *n.* [see BENEFACTION] 1. an endowed church office providing a living for a vicar, rector, etc. 2. its income —*vt.* -ficed, -fic·ing to provide with a benefice

be·nef·i·cence (bə nef′ə s'ns) *n.* [see BENEFACTION] 1. a being kind or doing good 2. a charitable act or generous gift

be·nef·i·cent (-s'nt) *adj.* showing beneficence; doing or resulting in good —**be·nef′i·cent·ly** *adv.*

ben·e·fi·cial (ben′ə fish′əl) *adj.* producing benefits; advantageous; favorable —**ben′e·fi′cial·ly** *adv.*

ben·e·fi·ci·ar·y (ben′ə fish′ē er′ē, -fish′ər ē) *n., pl.* -ar′-ies 1. anyone receiving benefit 2. a person named to receive an inheritance, income from insurance, etc.

ben·e·fit (ben′ə fit) *n.* [see BENEFACTION] 1. anything helping to improve conditions; advantage 2. [*often pl.*] payments made by an insurance company, public agency, etc. as during sickness or retirement 3. a public performance, dance, etc. whose proceeds go to help some person or cause —*vt.* -fit·ed, -fit·ing to help; aid —*vi.* to receive advantage; profit

be·nev·o·lence (bə nev′ə ləns) *n.* [< L. *bene,* well + *velle,* to wish] 1. an inclination to do good; kindness 2. a kindly, charitable act —**be·nev′o·lent** *adj.* —**be·nev′o·lent·ly** *adv.*

Ben·gal (ben gôl′), Bay of part of the Indian Ocean, between India and Burma

be·night·ed (bi nīt′id) *adj.* 1. surrounded by darkness 2. unenlightened; ignorant

be·nign (bi nīn′) *adj.* [< *bene,* well + *genus,* birth] 1. good-natured; kindly 2. favorable; beneficial 3. *Med.* not malignant —**be·nign′ly** *adv.*

be·nig·nant (bi nig′nənt) *adj.* [< prec.] 1. kindly or gracious 2. beneficial —**be·nig′nant·ly** *adv.*

be·nig·ni·ty (-nə tē) *n., pl.* -ties 1. kindliness 2. a kind act

Be·nin (be nēn′) country in WC Africa, on the Atlantic: 44,696 sq. mi.; pop. 3,029,000; cap. Porto Novo

ben·i·son (ben′ə z'n, -s'n) *n.* [see BENEDICTION] a blessing

bent¹ (bent) *pt. and pp. of* BEND —*adj.* 1. curved or crooked 2. strongly determined (with *on*) *[bent on going]* —*n.* 1. a tendency 2. a mental leaning; propensity *[a bent for art]* —**to** (or **at**) **the top of one's bent** to (or at) the limit of one's ability

bent² (bent) *n.* [OE. *beonot*] any of various low-growing grasses: also called **bent′grass**

be·numb (bi num′) *vt.* 1. to make numb 2. to deaden the mind or feelings of

Ben·ze·drine (ben′zə drēn′) *a trademark for* AMPHETAMINE —*n.* [b-] this drug

ben·zene (ben′zēn) *n.* [< BENZOIN] a flammable liquid, C_6H_6, obtained from coal tar and used as a solvent for fats and in making varnishes, dyes, etc.

ben·zine (ben′zēn) *n.* [< BENZOIN] a flammable liquid obtained from petroleum and used as a motor fuel, in dry cleaning, etc.

ben·zo·ate (ben′zō āt′) *n.* a salt or ester of benzoic acid

ben·zo·caine (ben′zə kān′) *n.* [BENZO(IN) + (CO)CAINE] a white powder used in ointments as an anesthetic and to protect against sunburn

ben·zo·ic acid (ben zō′ik) [< BENZOIN] a white, crystalline acid, C_6H_5COOH, used as an antiseptic, preservative, etc.

ben·zo·in (ben′zō in, -zoin) *n.* [< Fr. < Ar. *lubān jāwi,* incense of Java] a resin from certain tropical Asiatic trees, used in medicine, perfumes, etc.

ben·zol (ben′zōl, -zôl) *n. same as* BENZENE

Be·o·wulf (bā′ə woolf′) the hero of the Old English folk epic of that name (c.700 A.D.)

be·queath (bi kwēth′, -kwēth′) *vt.* [< OE. be- + cwethan, to say] 1. to leave (property) to another by one's will 2. to hand down; pass on —**be·queath′al** *n.*

be·quest (bi kwest′) *n.* 1. a bequeathing 2. anything bequeathed

be·rate (bi rāt′) *vt.* -rat′ed, -rat′ing [BE- + RATE²] to scold or rebuke severely

Ber·ber (bur′bər) *n.* 1. any of a Muslim people living in N Africa 2. their language

be·reave (bi rēv′) *vt.* -reaved′ or -reft′ (-reft′), -reav′ing [< OE. be- + reafian, rob] 1. to deprive: now usually in the pp. (**bereft**) *[bereft of hope]* 2. to leave in a sad or lonely state, as by death —**be·reave′ment** *n.*

be·ret (bə rā′) *n.* [< Fr. < L. *birrus,* a hood] a flat, round cap of felt, wool, etc.

berg (burg) *n. same as* ICEBERG

ber·ga·mot (bur′gə mät′) *n.* [< Fr. < Turk. *beg-armûdi,* prince's pear] 1. a pear-shaped citrus fruit yielding an oil used in some perfumes 2. this oil 3. an herb of the mint family

BERET

Ber·gen (ber′gən; *E.* bur′-) sea-port in SW Norway: pop. 117,000

ber·i·ber·i (ber′ē ber′ē) *n.* [Singh. *beri,* weakness] a disease caused by lack of thiamine (vitamin B_1) and characterized by nerve disorders, edema, etc.

Ber·ing Sea (ber′iŋ, bir′-) part of the N Pacific, between Siberia & Alaska

Bering Strait strait between Siberia & Alaska

Berke·ley (bur′klē) city in Calif., near San Francisco: pop. 117,000

berke·li·um (bur′klē əm) *n.* [< prec.] a radioactive chemical element: symbol, Bk; at. wt., 248(?); at. no., 97

Ber·lin (bər lin′) city in E Germany: capital of Germany until 1945: now divided into EAST BERLIN and WEST BERLIN

Ber·li·oz (ber′lē ōz′), (**Louis**) **Hector** 1803–69; Fr. composer

berm, berme (burm) *n.* [Fr. < MDu. *baerm*] a ledge or shoulder, as along the edge of a paved road

Ber·mu·da (bər myōō′də) self-governing Brit. colony on a group of islands in the W Atlantic

Bermuda onion a large onion with a mild flavor, grown in Texas, California, etc.

Bermuda shorts knee-length trousers

Bern, Berne (burn; *Fr.* bern) capital of Switzerland: pop. 167,000

ber·ry (ber′ē) *n., pl.* -ries [OE. *berie*] 1. any small, fleshy fruit, as a raspberry 2. the dry seed of various plants, as a coffee bean 3. *Bot.* a fleshy fruit with a soft wall and thin skin, as the tomato or grape —*vi.* -ried, -ry·ing 1. to bear berries 2. to pick berries

ber·serk (bər surk′, -zurk′) *adj., adv.* [ON. *berserkr,* warrior] in or into a violent rage or frenzy

berth (burth) *n.* [< base of BEAR¹] 1. a place where a ship anchors 2. a position, job, etc. 3. a built-in bed on a ship, train, etc. —*vt.* to put into or furnish with a berth —*vi.* to occupy a berth —**give a wide berth to** to keep well clear of

ber·yl (ber′əl) *n.* [< Gr. *bēryllos*] beryllium aluminum silicate, a very hard mineral, of which emerald and aquamarine are two varieties

be·ryl·li·um (bə ril′ē əm) *n.* [< prec.] a hard, rare, metallic chemical element: symbol, Be; at. wt., 9.0122; at. no., 4

be·seech (bi sēch′) *vt.* -sought′ or -seeched′, -seech′ing [< OE. be-, + secan, seek] to ask (for) earnestly; entreat; beg —**be·seech′ing·ly** *adv.*

be·seem (bi sēm′) *vi.* to be suitable or appropriate (to)

be·set (bi set′) *vt.* -set′, -set′ting [< OE. be- + settan, to set] 1. to set thickly with 2. to attack from all sides; harass 3. to surround

be·set·ting *adj.* constantly harassing or attacking

be·side (bi sīd′) *prep.* [OE. *bi sidan*] **1.** at the side of; near **2.** in comparison with *[beside* his, her share seems tiny*]* **3.** in addition to **4.** aside from *[who is going beside us?]* —**beside oneself** wild or upset with fear, rage, etc.

be·sides (bi sīdz′) *adv.* **1.** in addition **2.** except for that mentioned **3.** moreover —*prep.* **1.** in addition to **2.** other than; except

be·siege (bi sēj′) *vt.* -**sieged′**, -**sieg′ing 1.** to hem in with armed forces; lay siege to **2.** to close in on **3.** to overwhelm *[besieged* with requests*]* —**be·sieg′er** *n.*

be·smear (bi smir′) *vt.* to smear over; soil

be·smirch (bi smurch′) *vt.* [BE- + SMIRCH] **1.** to soil **2.** to bring dishonor to; sully

be·som (bē′zəm) *n.* [OE. *besma*] a broom, esp. one made of twigs

be·sot (bi sät′) *vt.* -**sot′ted**, -**sot′ting 1.** to make a sot of; stupefy, as with liquor **2.** to make silly or foolish —**be·sot′ted** *adj.*

be·sought (bi sôt′) *pt. and pp. of* BESEECH

be·span·gle (bi spaŋ′g'l) *vt.* -**gled**, -**gling** to cover with or as with spangles

be·spat·ter (bi spat′ər) *vt.* to spatter, as with mud or slander

be·speak (bi spēk′) *vt.* -**spoke′**, -**spok′en** or -**spoke′**, -**speak′ing 1.** to speak for or engage in advance; reserve **2.** to be indicative of; show

be·spread (bi spred′) *vt.* -**spread′**, -**spread′ing** to spread over or cover

Bes·se·mer process (bes′ə mər) [< H. *Bessemer*, 19th-c. Eng. inventor] a method of making steel by blasting air through molten iron in a large container (**Bessemer converter**) to remove impurities

best (best) *adj. superl. of* GOOD [OE. *betst*] **1.** most excellent **2.** most suitable, desirable, etc. **3.** largest *[the best* part of an hour*]* —*adv. superl. of* WELL² **1.** in the most excellent or most suitable manner **2.** in the highest degree —*n.* **1.** the most excellent person, thing, condition, etc. **2.** the utmost **3.** one's finest clothes —*vt.* to defeat or outdo —**all for the best** ultimately fortunate —**at best** under the most favorable conditions —**get** (or **have**) **the best of 1.** to defeat **2.** to do as well as one can with

bes·tial (bes′chəl, -tyəl) *adj.* [< L. *bestia*, beast] like a beast; savage, brutal, etc. —**bes′ti·al′i·ty** (-chē al′ə tē) *n.*, *pl.* -**ties** —**bes′tial·ly** *adv.*

be·stir (bi stur′) *vt.* -**stirred′**, -**stir′ring** to stir to action; busy (oneself)

best man the principal attendant of the bridegroom at a wedding

be·stow (bi stō′) *vt.* [see BE- & STOW] **1.** to present as a gift (often with *on* or *upon*) **2.** to apply; devote **3.** [Archaic] to put or place —**be·stow′al** *n.*

be·strew (bi strō′) *vt.* -**strewed′**, -**strewed′** or -**strewn′**, -**strew′ing 1.** to strew **2.** to scatter or lie scattered over or about

be·stride (bi strīd′) *vt.* -**strode′** (-strōd′), -**strid′den** (-strid′'n), -**strid′ing 1.** to sit on, mount, or stand astride **2.** [Archaic] to stride over

best seller a book, phonograph record, etc. currently outselling most others

bet (bet) *n.* [prob. < ABET] **1.** an agreement that the person proved wrong about something will do or pay what is stipulated **2.** the thing or sum thus staked **3.** a person or thing likely to bring about a desired result —*vt.*, *vi.* **bet** or **bet′ted**, **bet′ting 1.** to declare as in a bet **2.** to stake (money, etc.) in a bet

be·ta (bāt′ə) *n.* **1.** the second letter of the Greek alphabet (B, β) **2.** the second of a series

be·take (bi tāk′) *vt.* -**took′**, -**tak′en**, -**tak′ing** to go (used reflexively)

beta particle an electron or positron ejected from the nucleus of an atom during radioactive disintegration

beta ray a stream of beta particles

be·ta·tron (bāt′ə trän′) *n.* [BETA (RAY) + (ELEC)TRON] an electron accelerator that uses a rapidly changing magnetic field to accelerate the particles to high velocities

be·tel (bēt′'l) *n.* [Port. < Malay *vettilai*] a tropical Asian climbing plant: its leaf, along with lime and the fruit (**betel nut**) of a palm (**betel palm**), is chewed by some Asians

Be·tel·geuse, Be·tel·geux (bet′'l jōōz′, bēt′-) [< Fr. < Ar. *bayt al jauza*, house of the twins] a very large red star in the constellation Orion

Beth·a·ny (beth′ə nē) ancient town in Palestine, near Jerusalem

beth·el (beth′əl) *n.* [< Heb. *bēth 'ēl*, house of God] a church or other place of worship for seamen

be·think (bi thiŋk′) *vt.* -**thought′**, -**think′ing** to think of, consider, or recollect; remind (oneself)

Beth·le·hem (beth′lə hem′, -lē əm) ancient town in Judea: birthplace of Jesus

be·tide (bi tīd′) *vi.*, *vt.* -**tid′ed**, -**tid′ing** [< BE- + OE. *tid*, time] to happen (to); befall

be·times (bi tīmz′) *adv.* [ME. < *bi-*, by + TIME] **1.** early or early enough **2.** [Archaic] promptly

be·to·ken (bi tō′k'n) *vt.* **1.** to be a token or sign of **2.** to show beforehand

be·tray (bi trā′) *vt.* [ult. < L. *tradere*, hand over] **1.** to help the enemy of (one's country, etc.) **2.** to fail to uphold *[to betray* a trust*]* **3.** to lead astray; specif., to seduce and then desert **4.** to reveal unknowingly **5.** to reveal or disclose —**be·tray′al** *n.* —**be·tray′er** *n.*

be·troth (bi trōth′, -trôth′) *vt.* [< ME. < *be-* + OE. *treowth*, truth] to promise in marriage —**be·troth′al** *n.*

be·trothed′ (-trōthd′, -trôth′) *adj.* engaged to be married —*n.* the person to whom one is betrothed

bet·ter (bet′ər) *adj. compar. of* GOOD [< OE. *betera*] **1.** more excellent **2.** more suitable, desirable, etc. **3.** larger *[the better* part of a day*]* **4.** improved in health —*adv. compar. of* WELL² **1.** in a more excellent or more suitable manner **2.** in a higher degree **3.** more *[it took better* than an hour*]* —*n.* **1.** a person superior in position, etc. **2.** a more excellent thing, condition, etc. —*vt.* **1.** to outdo; surpass **2.** to improve —**better off** in a better condition —**get** (or **have**) **the better of 1.** to outdo **2.** to outwit

better half [Slang] one's wife or husband

bet′ter·ment (-mənt) *n.* a bettering; improvement

bet·tor, bet·ter (bet′ər) *n.* one who bets

be·tween (bi twēn′) *prep.* [< OE. *be*, by + *tweon(um)*, by twos] **1.** in the space, time, etc. separating (two things) **2.** that connects *[a bond between* friends*]* **3.** in the combined possession or action of *[we had ten dollars between us]* **4.** from one or the other of *[choose between* love and duty*]* —*adv.* in an intermediate space, function, etc.

be·twixt (bi twikst′) *prep.*, *adv.* [< OE. *betwix*] between: archaic except in **betwixt and between**, not altogether one nor altogether the other

bev·el (bev′'l) *n.* [< ?] **1.** a tool that is a rule with a movable arm, for measuring or marking angles, etc. **2.** an angle other than a right angle **3.** a sloping edge between parallel surfaces —*adj.* sloped; beveled —*vt.* -**eled** or -**elled**, -**el·ing** or -**el·ling** to cut to an angle other than a right angle —*vi.* to slope at an angle

bevel gear a gearwheel meshed with another so that their shafts are at an angle

bev·er·age (bev′rij, -ər ij) *n.* [< L. *bibere*, imbibe] any liquid for drinking, esp. other than plain water

bev·y (bev′ē) *n.*, *pl.* -**ies** [see BEVERAGE] **1.** a group, esp. of girls or women **2.** a flock; now chiefly of quail

be·wail (bi wāl′) *vt.* to wail over or complain about; lament; mourn —**be·wail′er** *n.*

BEVEL GEAR

be·ware (bi wer′) *vi.*, *vt.* -**wared′**, -**war′ing** [prob. < OE. < *be-* + *warian*, be wary] to be wary or careful (of); be on one's guard (against)

be·wil·der (bi wil′dər) *vt.* [BE- + archaic *wilder*, to lose one's way] to confuse hopelessly; befuddle —**be·wil′dered** *adj.* —**be·wil′der·ing** *adj.* —**be·wil′der·ment** *n.*

be·witch (bi wich′) *vt.* [< OE. *wicce*, witch] **1.** to cast a spell over **2.** to enchant; fascinate —**be·witch′ing** *adj.*

be·witch′ment (-mənt) *n.* **1.** power to bewitch **2.** a spell Also **be·witch′er·y** (-ər ē), *pl.* -**er·ies**

bey (bā) *n.* [Turk.] **1.** formerly, the governor of a Turkish province **2.** a Turkish title of respect and former title of rank

be·yond (bi yänd′) *prep.* [< OE. *be-* + *geond*, yonder] **1.** farther on than **2.** later than **3.** outside the reach of *[beyond* help*]* **4.** more or better than —*adv.* **1.** farther away **2.** in addition —**the (great) beyond** whatever follows death

bez·el (bez′'l) *n.* [< OFr. *biais*, bias] **1.** a sloping cutting edge, as of a chisel **2.** the slanting face of a cut jewel **3.** the groove and flange holding a gem or a watch crystal in place

bf, b.f. boldface

---

fat, āpe, cär; ten, ēven; is, bīte; gō, hôrn, tōōl, look; oil, out; up, fur; thin, *th*en; zh, leisure; ŋ, ring; ə for *a* in *ago*; ' as in *able* (ā′b'l); ë, Fr. coeur; ö, Fr. feu; Fr. mon; ü, Fr. duc; r, Fr. cri; kh, G. doch, ich. ‡ foreign; < derived from

bhang (baŋ) *n.* [Hindi < Sans. *bhangā*] 1. the hemp plant 2. its dried leaves and flowers, which have intoxicating properties

Bhu·tan (bōō tän′) country in the Himalayas: c.18,000 sq. mi.; pop. 750,000 —**Bhu·tan·ese** (bōōt′'n ēz′) *adj., n., pl.* **-ese′**

bi- [L.] *a prefix meaning:* 1. having two 2. doubly 3. happening every two 4. happening twice during every 5. using two or both 6. joining or involving two

Bi *Chem.* bismuth

bi·an·gu·lar (bī aŋ′gyoo lər) *adj.* having two angles

bi·an′nu·al (-an′yoo wəl, -yool) *adj.* coming twice a year; semiannual —**bi·an′nu·al·ly** *adv.*

bi·as (bī′əs) *n., pl.* **bi′as·es** [Fr. *biais*, a slant] 1. a slanting or diagonal line, cut or sewn across the weave of cloth 2. a mental leaning; partiality; prejudice —*adj.* slanting; diagonal —*adv.* diagonally —*vt.* **-ased** or **-assed, -as·ing** or **-as·sing** to cause to have a bias; prejudice —**on the bias** diagonally

bib (bib) *n.* [< L. *bibere*, to drink] 1. an apronlike cloth tied under a child's chin at meals 2. the front upper part of an apron or overalls

Bib. 1. Bible 2. Biblical

Bibl., bibl. 1. Biblical 2. bibliographical

Bi·ble (bī′b'l) *n.* [< Gr. *biblos*, papyrus] 1. the sacred book of Christianity; Old Testament and New Testament 2. the Holy Scriptures of Judaism; Old Testament 3. [b-] any book regarded as authoritative —**Bib·li·cal, bib·li·cal** (bib′li k'l) *adj.*

biblio- [< Gr. *biblion*, book] *a combining form meaning* book, of books

bib·li·og·ra·phy (bib′lē äg′rə fē) *n., pl.* **-phies** 1. the study of the editions, dates, authorship, etc. of books and other writings 2. a list of writings on a given subject, by a given author, etc. —**bib′li·og′ra·pher** *n.* —**bib′li·o·graph′ic** (-ə graf′ik), **bib′li·o·graph′i·cal** *adj.*

bib·li·o·phile′ (-ə fīl′) *n.* one who loves or collects books

bib·u·lous (bib′yoo ləs) *adj.* [< L. *bibere*, to drink] 1. highly absorbent 2. fond of alcoholic liquor

bi·cam·er·al (bī kam′ər əl) *adj.* [< BI- + L. *camera*, chamber] having two legislative chambers

bi·car·bon·ate (bī kär′bə nit, -nāt′) *n.* an acid salt of carbonic acid containing the radical HCO₃

bicarbonate of soda *same as* SODIUM BICARBONATE

bi·cen·te·nar·y (bī′sen ten′ər ē, bī sen′tə ner′ē) *adj., n., pl.* **-nar·ies** *same as* BICENTENNIAL

bi·cen·ten·ni·al (bī′sen ten′ē əl) *adj.* 1. happening once every 200 years 2. lasting for 200 years —*n.* a 200th anniversary or its celebration

bi·ceps (bī′seps) *n., pl.* **-ceps** or **-ceps·es** [L. < *bis*, two + *caput*, head] a muscle with two points of origin; esp., the large muscle in the front of the upper arm

bi·chlo·ride (bī klôr′īd) *n.* 1. a binary compound containing two atoms of chlorine for each atom of another element 2. *same as* MERCURIC CHLORIDE

bichloride of mercury *same as* MERCURIC CHLORIDE

bick·er (bik′ər) *vi., n.* [ME. *bikeren*] squabble; quarrel —**bick′er·er** *n.*

bi·col·or (bī′kul′ər) *adj.* of two colors: also **bi′col′ored**

bi·cus·pid (bī kus′pid) *adj.* [< BI- + L. *cuspis*, pointed end] having two points —*n.* any of eight adult teeth with two-pointed crowns

bi·cy·cle (bī′si k'l) *n.* [Fr.: see BI- & CYCLE] a vehicle consisting of a metal frame on two large wheels, one behind the other, and having handlebars, a saddlelike seat, and, usually, foot pedals —*vi., vt.* **-cled, -cling** to ride on a bicycle —**bi′cy·clist, bi′cy·cler** *n.*

bid (bid) *vt.* **bade** (bad) or **bid, bid′den** or **bid,** ̄**bid′ding** [< OE. *biddan*, to urge & *beodan*, to command] 1. to command, ask, or tell 2. *pt. & pp.* **bid** *a)* to offer (an amount) as the price for *b)* *Card Games* to state (a number of tricks) and declare (trump) 3. to declare openly *[to bid defiance]* 4. to express in greeting or taking leave *[to bid farewell]* —*vi. pt. & pp.* **bid** to make a bid —*n.* 1. a bidding of an amount 2. the amount bid 3. a chance to bid 4. an attempt or try (*for*) 5. [Colloq.] an invitation —**bid fair** to seem likely —**bid′der** *n.*

bid′ding *n.* 1. a command or request 2. an invitation or summons 3. the bids in a card game or auction

bid·dy (bid′ē) *n., pl.* **-dies** 1. a hen 2. [Slang] an elderly, gossipy woman

bide (bīd) *vi.* **bode** (bad) or **bid′ed, bid′ed, bid′ing** [OE. *bidan*] [Archaic or Dial.] 1. to stay; continue 2. to dwell 3. to wait —*vt.* [Archaic or Dial.] to endure —**bide one's time** *pt.* **bid′ed** to wait patiently for an opportunity

bi·det (bi dā′) *n.* [Fr.] a low, bowl-shaped bathroom fixture with running water, used for bathing the crotch

bi·en·ni·al (bī en′ē əl) *adj.* [< L. *bis*, twice + *annus*, year + -AL] 1. happening every two years 2. lasting for two years —*n.* 1. a biennial event 2. *Bot.* a plant that lasts two years, usually producing flowers and seed the second year —**bi·en′ni·al·ly** *adv.*

bier (bir) *n.* [OE. *bær*, a bed] a portable framework on which a coffin or corpse is placed

bi·fo·cal (bī fō′k'l, bī′fō′k'l) *adj.* adjusted to two different focal lengths —*n.* a lens with one part ground to adjust the eyes for close focus, and the rest ground for distant focus

bi′fo′cals *n.pl.* a pair of glasses with bifocal lenses

bi·fur·cate (bī′fər kāt′, bī fur′kāt) *adj.* [< L. *bi-* + *furca*, fork] having two branches; forked —*vt., vi.* **-cat′ed, -cat′ing** to divide into two branches —**bi′fur·ca′tion** *n.*

big (big) *adj.* **big′ger, big′gest** [akin to L. *bucca*, puffed cheek] 1. of great size, capacity, force, etc. 2. *a)* full-grown *b)* elder *[his big* sister*]* 3. loud 4. important or outstanding 5. boastful; extravagant *[big* talk*]* 6. noble *[a big* heart*]* —*adv.* [Colloq.] 1. boastfully *[to* talk *big]* 2. impressively 3. in a broad way; showing imagination *[think big!]* —**big′ness** *n.*

big·a·my (big′ə mē) *n., pl.* **-mies** [< LL. *bis*, twice + Gr. *gamos*, marriage] the crime of marrying a second time while a previous marriage is still legally in effect —**big′a·mist** *n.* —**big′a·mous** *adj.*

Big Dipper a dipper-shaped group of stars in the constellation Ursa Major (Great Bear)

big game 1. large wild animals hunted for sport, as lions, etc. 2. the object of any important or dangerous undertaking

big′heart′ed *adj.* generous or magnanimous

big′horn′ *n.* an animal with large horns, esp. a large wild sheep of the Rocky Mountains

bight (bīt) *n.* [ME. *byht*] 1. a loop or slack part in a rope 2. *a)* a curve in a river, coastline, etc. *b)* a bay formed by such a curve

big mouth [Slang] a person who talks too much

big·ot (big′ət) *n.* [Fr. < OFr., a term of insult used of Normans] a narrow-minded person who is intolerant of other creeds, opinions, etc. —**big′ot·ed** *adj.* —**big′ot·ry** (-ə trē) *n., pl.* **-ries**

big shot [Slang] an important, influential person: also **big noise, big wheel,** etc.

bi·jou (bē′zhōō) *n., pl.* **-joux** (-zhōōz) [Fr. < Bret. *biz*, a finger] 1. a jewel 2. an exquisite trinket

bike (bīk) *n., vt., vi.* **biked, bik′ing** [Colloq.] 1. bicycle 2. motorcycle

bi·ki·ni (bi kē′nē) *n.* [< *Bikini*, atoll in the Marshall Islands] an extremely brief two-piece bathing suit for women

bi·la·bi·al (bī lā′bē əl) *adj. Phonet.* made by stopping or constricting the airstream with the lips, as *p* and *b* —*n.* a bilabial sound

bi·lat·er·al (bī lat′ər əl) *adj.* 1. of, on, or having two sides, factions, etc. 2. affecting both sides equally; reciprocal 3. symmetrical on both sides of an axis —**bi·lat′er·al·ism** *n.*

Bil·ba·o (bil bä′ō) seaport in N Spain: pop. 372,000

bil·ber·ry (bil′ber′ē) *n., pl.* **-ries** [ult. < ON. *bollr*, BALL¹ + *ber*, berry] a N. American blueberry or its fruit

bile (bīl) *n.* [Fr. < L. *bilis*] 1. the bitter, greenish fluid secreted by the liver and found in the gallbladder: it helps in digestion 2. [< ancient belief in bile as the humor causing anger] bitterness of spirit; anger

bilge (bilj) *n.* [var. of BULGE] 1. the rounded, lower part of a ship's hold 2. stagnant water that gathers there: also **bilge water** 3. nonsense

bil·i·ar·y (bil′ē er′ē) *adj.* 1. of the bile 2. bile-carrying 3. bilious

bi·lin·gual (bī liŋ′gwəl) *adj.* [< L. *bis*, two + *lingua*, tongue] of, in, or speaking two languages —**bi·lin′gual·ism** *n.* —**bi·lin′gual·ly** *adv.*

bil·ious (bil′yəs) *adj.* 1. of the bile 2. having or resulting from some ailment of the liver 3. bad-tempered; cross —**bil′ious·ness** *n.*

bilk (bilk) *vt.* [? altered < BALK] to cheat or swindle; defraud —*n.* a bilking or being bilked —**bilk′er** *n.*

bill¹ (bil) *n.* [< ML. *bulla*, sealed document] 1. a statement of charges for goods or services 2. a list, as a menu or theater program 3. a poster or handbill 4. a draft of a proposed law 5. a bill of exchange 6. any promissory note 7. a piece of paper money 8. *Law* a written declaration of charges and complaints filed —*vt.* 1. to make out a bill of (items) 2. to present a statement of charges to 3. *a)* to advertise by bills *b)* to book (a performer) —**fill the bill** [Colloq.] to meet the requirements —**bill′a·ble** *adj.*

bill² (bil) *n.* [OE. *bile*] **1.** a bird's beak **2.** a beaklike mouthpart, as of a turtle —*vi.* **1.** to touch bills together **2.** to caress lovingly: now only in **bill and coo**, to kiss, talk softly, etc. in a loving way

bill'board' *n.* a large signboard, usually outdoors, for advertising posters

bil·let¹ (bil'it) *n.* [see BILL¹] **1.** *a*) a written order to provide lodging for military personnel, as in private buildings *b*) the lodging **2.** a position or job —*vt.* to assign to lodging by billet

bil·let² (bil'it) *n.* [< OFr. *bille*, tree trunk] **1.** a short, thick piece of firewood **2.** a small, unfinished metal bar

bil·let-doux (bil'ē dōō') *n., pl.* **bil·lets-doux** (bil'ē dōōz') [Fr.] a love letter

bill'fold' (bil'fōld') *n. same as* WALLET

bill'head' *n.* a letterhead used for statements of charges

bil·liards (bil'yərdz) *n.* [Fr. *billard*; orig., a cue] a game played with hard balls driven by a cue on an oblong table with raised, cushioned edges

bill·ing (bil'iŋ) *n.* the listing or order of listing of actors' names on a playbill, marquee, etc.

bil·lings·gate (bil'iŋz gāt') *n.* [< a London fish market] foul, vulgar, abusive talk

bil·lion (bil'yən) *n.* [Fr. < *bi-*, BI- + MILLION] **1.** a thousand millions (1,000,000,000) **2.** an indefinite but very large number —**bil'lionth** *adj., n.*

bill of exchange a written order to pay a certain sum of money to the person named

bill of fare a menu

bill of health a certificate stating whether there is infectious disease on a ship or in a port —**clean bill of health 1.** a bill of health certifying the absence of infectious disease **2.** [Colloq.] good record

bill of lading a receipt issued to a shipper by a carrier, listing the goods received for shipment

bill of rights a list of the rights and freedoms of a people **2.** [B- R-] the first ten amendments to the Constitution of the U.S., which guarantee civil liberties

bill of sale a written statement transferring ownership by sale

bil·low (bil'ō) *n.* [ON. *bylgja*] **1.** a large wave **2.** any large, swelling mass or surge, as of smoke —*vi., vt.* to surge, swell, or cause to swell like or in a billow —**bil'low·y** *adj. ·i·er, ·i·est*

bil·ly (bil'ē) *n., pl.* **-lies** [< BILLET²] a club or heavy stick, esp. one carried by a policeman

billy goat a male goat

bi·me·tal·lic (bi'mə tal'ik) *adj.* **1.** containing or using two metals **2.** of or based on bimetallism

bi·met·al·lism (bi met'l iz'm) *n.* the use of two metals, esp. gold and silver, as the monetary standard, with fixed values in relation to each other —**bi·met'al·list** *n.*

bi·month·ly (bi munth'lē) *adj., adv.* **1.** once every two months **2.** loosely, twice a month —*n., pl.* **-lies** a publication appearing once every two months

bin (bin) *n.* [OE., manger] a box, crib, etc. space for storing foods, fuel, etc. —*vt.* binned, bin'ning to store in a bin

bi·na·ry (bi'nər ē) *adj.* [< L. *bis*, double] **1.** made up of two parts or things; twofold **2.** designating or of a number system that has 2 as its base —*n., pl.* **-ries** something made up of two parts or things

bin·au·ral (bi nôr'əl) *adj.* [see BI- & AURAL] **1.** involving the use of both ears **2.** of sound recording that gives a stereophonic effect

bind (bind) *vt.* bound, bind'ing [< OE. *bindan*] **1.** to tie together, as with rope **2.** to hold or restrain **3.** to encircle with a belt, etc. **4.** to bandage (often with *up*) **5.** to make stick together **6.** to constipate **7.** to reinforce with a band, as of tape **8.** to fasten together sheets of (a book) and enclose within a cover **9.** to obligate, as by duty **10.** to compel, as by legal restraint —*vi.* to be obligatory —*n.* [Colloq.] a difficult situation

bind'er *n.* **1.** one who binds **2.** a substance that binds, as tar **3.** a cover for holding sheets of paper together **4.** a device attached to a reaper, for tying grain in bundles

bind·er·y (bin'dər ē, -drē) *n., pl.* **-ies** a place where books are bound

bind'ing *n.* anything that binds, as *a*) the fastenings of a ski for the boot *b*) a band, tape, etc. *c*) the covers and backing of a book —*adj.* that binds; esp., that holds one to an agreement, promise, etc. —**bind'ing·ly** *adv.*

binge (binj) *n.* [? < dial. *binge*, to soak] [Colloq.] a drunken or unrestrained spree

bin·go (biŋ'gō) *n.* [< ?] a gambling game, like lotto

bin·na·cle (bin'ə k'l) *n.* [ult. < L. *habitaculum*, dwelling] the case enclosing a ship's compass

bin·oc·u·lar (bi näk'yə lər, bi-) *adj.* [< L. *bini*, double + *oculus*, an eye] using, or for, both eyes —*n.* [*usually pl.*] a binocular instrument, as field glasses

bi·no·mi·al (bi nō'mē əl) *n.* [< *bi-* + Gr. *nomos*, law] *Math.* an expression consisting of two terms connected by a plus or minus sign —*adj.* of a binomial

bio- [Gr. < *bios*, life] *a combining form meaning* life, of living things, biological *[biography]*

bi·o·chem·is·try (bi'ō kem'is trē) *n.* the branch of chemistry that deals with the life processes of plants and animals —**bi'o·chem'i·cal** *adj.* —**bi'o·chem'i·cal·ly** *adv.* —**bi'o·chem'ist** *n.*

bi'o·feed'back' *n.* a technique of seeking to control one's emotions by using electronic devices to train oneself to modify involuntary body functions, such as heartbeat

biog. 1. biographical **2.** biography

bi·og·ra·phy (bi äg'rə fē, bē-) *n.* [< Gr.: see BIO- & -GRAPHY] **1.** *pl.* **-phies** an account of a person's life written by another **2.** such accounts collectively —**bi·og'ra·pher** *n.* —**bi·o·graph·i·cal** (bi'ə graf'i k'l) *adj.*

biol. 1. biological **2.** biology

bi·o·log·i·cal (bi'ə läj'i k'l) *adj.* **1.** of biology; of plants and animals **2.** used in or produced by practical biology Also **bi'o·log'ic** —*n.* a biological product —**bi'o·log'i·cal·ly** *adv.*

biological warfare the use of disease-spreading microorganisms, etc. in war

bi·ol·o·gy (bi äl'ə jē) *n.* [BIO- + -LOGY] the science that deals with the origin, history, life processes, structure, etc. of plants and animals —**bi·ol'o·gist** *n.*

bi·o·med·i·cine (bi'ō med'ə s'n) *n.* a branch of medicine combined with research in biology —**bi'o·med'i·cal** *adj.*

bi·on·ic (bi än'ik) *adj.* **1.** of bionics **2.** having an artificial bodily part or parts, as in science fiction, so as to enhance strength, abilities, etc. **3.** very strong, skillful, etc.

bi·on·ics (bi än'iks) *n.pl.* [*with sing. v.*] [< Gr. *bion*, living + -ICS] the science of designing instruments or systems modeled closely after living organisms

bi·o·phys·ics (bi'ō fiz'iks) *n.pl.* [*with sing. v.*] the study of biological phenomena in relation to physics —**bi'o·phys'i·cal** *adj.*

bi·op·sy (bi'äp'sē) *n., pl.* **-sies** [< BIO- + Gr. *opsis*, a sight] *Med.* the removal of living body tissue, etc. for diagnosis

bi·o·rhythm (bi'ō rith''m) *n.* any of three hypothetical biological cycles that determine the regular rise and fall of a person's energy levels

bi·o·tin (bi'ə tin) *n.* [< Gr. *bios*, life] a factor of the vitamin B group, found in liver, egg yolk, and yeast

bi·par·ti·san (bi pär'tə z'n) *adj.* of or representing two parties —**bi·par'ti·san·ship'** *n.*

bi·par·tite (bi pär'tit) *adj.* [< L. *bi-*, two + *partire*, to divide] **1.** having two parts **2.** involving two

bi·ped (bi'ped) *n.* [< L. *bi-*, two + *pes*, foot] any two-footed animal —*adj.* two-footed: also **bi·ped'al**

bi·plane (bi'plān') *n.* an airplane with two sets of wings, one above the other

bi·ra·cial (bi rā'shəl) *adj.* consisting of or involving two races, esp. Negroes and whites

birch (burch) *n.* [OE. *beorc*] **1.** a tree having smooth bark in thin layers, and hard, closegrained wood **2.** this wood **3.** a bunch of birch twigs used for whipping —*vt.* to beat with a birch —*adj.* of birch

bird (burd) *n.* [OE. *bridd*, young bird] **1.** any of a group of warmblooded, two-legged, egg-laying vertebrates with feathers and wings **2.** [Slang] a person, esp. an eccentric one —**bird in the hand** something sure because already in one's possession: opposed to **bird in the bush**, something unsure, etc. —**birds of a feather** people with like traits or tastes —**for the birds** [Slang] foolish, worthless, etc.

bird·ie (bur'dē) *n. Golf* a score of one stroke under par for a hole

bird'lime' (-lim') *n.* a sticky substance spread on twigs to catch birds

bird of paradise any of a number of brightly colored birds found in and near New Guinea

bird of passage any migratory bird

bird of prey any bird, as the hawk, owl, etc., that kills and eats mammals and other birds

bird's'-eye' *adj.* **1.** *a*) seen from above *b*) general **2.** having markings like birds' eyes

bi·ret·ta (bə ret′ə) *n.* [< It. < L. *birrus*, a hood] a square cap with three projections on top, worn by Roman Catholic clergy

Bir·ming·ham (bur′miŋ əm) **1.** city in C England: pop. 1,075,000 **2.** (-ham′) city in NC Ala.: pop. 301,000 (met. area 739,000)

birth (burth) *n.* [< OE. *beran*, to bear] **1.** the act of bringing forth offspring **2.** a being born **3.** origin or descent **4.** the beginning of anything **5.** natural inclination or talent [an actor by *birth*] —**give birth to 1.** to bring forth (offspring) **2.** to originate

BIRETTA

birth′day′ *n.* the anniversary of the day of a person's birth or a thing's beginning

birth′mark′ *n.* a skin blemish present at birth

birth′place′ *n.* the place of one's birth or a thing's origin

birth′rate′ *n.* the number of births per year per thousand of population in a given group

birth′right′ *n.* any rights that a person has by birth

birth′stone′ *n.* a gem symbolizing the month of one's birth

Bis·cay, Bay of (bis′kā) part of the Atlantic, north of Spain & west of France

bis·cuit (bis′kit) *n., pl.* -**cuits, -cuit** [< L. *bis*, twice + *co-quere*, to cook] **1.** [Chiefly Brit.] a cracker or cookie **2.** a quick bread baked in small pieces

bi·sect (bī sekt′, bī′sekt) *vt.* [< BI- + L. *secare*, to cut] **1.** to cut in two **2.** *Geom.* to divide into two equal parts —*vi.* to divide; fork —**bi·sec′tion** *n.* —**bi·sec′tion·al** *adj.* —**bi·sec′tor** *n.*

bi·sex·ual (bī sek′shoo wəl) *adj.* of, or sexually attracted by, both sexes —*n.* one that is bisexual

bish·op (bish′əp) *n.* [< Gr. *epi-*, upon + *skopein*, to look] **1.** a high-ranking Christian clergyman, head of a diocese or church district **2.** a chessman that can move only diagonally

bish·op·ric (bish′ə prik) *n.* the district, office, rank, etc. of a bishop

Bis·marck (biz′märk) capital of N.Dak.: pop. 35,000

Bis·marck (biz′märk), Prince **Otto von** 1815–98; Prussian chancellor of Germany (1871–90)

bis·muth (biz′məth) *n.* [< G.] a hard, brittle, metallic chemical element used in low-melting alloys: symbol, Bi; at. wt., 208.980; at. no., 83

bi·son (bis′n) *n., pl.* -**sons** [Fr. < Gmc.] a four-legged bovine mammal with a shaggy mane and a humped back, as the American buffalo

bisque (bisk) *n.* [Fr.] a thick, creamy soup made from shellfish, fowl, vegetables, etc.

bis·tro (bis′trō) *n., pl.* -**tros** [Fr.] a small nightclub or bar

bit[1] (bit) *n.* [< OE. *bite*, a bite] **1.** the metal mouthpiece on a bridle, used for controlling the horse **2.** anything that curbs or controls **3.** a drilling or boring tool for use in a brace, etc. —*vt.* **bit′ted, bit′ting** to put a bit into the mouth of (a horse)

bit[2] (bit) *n.* [< OE. *bita*, a piece] **1.** *a)* a small piece or quantity *b)* a limited degree [a *bit* of a bore] *c)* a short time **2.** [Colloq.] 12 1/2 cents, as in *two bits* —*adj.* very small [a *bit* role] —**bit by bit** gradually —**do one's bit** to do one's share

bitch (bich) *n.* [< OE. *bicce*] **1.** the female of the dog, fox, etc. **2.** a bad-tempered, malicious, etc. woman: a coarse term of contempt —*vi.* [Slang] to complain —**bitch′i·ness** *n.* —**bitch′y** *adj.* -**i·er, -i·est**

bite (bīt) *vt.* **bit** (bit), **bit·ten** (bit′n) or **bit, bit′ing** [< OE. *bitan*] **1.** to seize or cut with or as with the teeth **2.** to cut into, as with a sharp weapon **3.** to sting, as an insect **4.** to hurt in a sharp, stinging way **5.** to eat into; corrode **6.** to seize or possess —*vi.* **1.** to press or snap the teeth (*into, at,* etc.) **2.** to cause a biting sensation **3.** to grip **4.** to seize a bait **5.** to be caught, as by a trick —*n.* **1.** a biting **2.** biting quality; sting **3.** a wound or sting from biting **4.** *a)* a mouthful *b)* a light meal **5.** a tight hold or grip **6.** [Colloq.] an amount removed —**put the bite on** [Slang] to press for a loan, bribe, etc. —**bit′er** *n.*

bit·ing (bīt′iŋ) *adj.* **1.** cutting; sharp **2.** sarcastic —**bit′ing·ly** *adv.*

bitt (bit) *n.* [< ?] *Naut.* any of the deck posts, usually in pairs, to which ropes, etc. are fastened —*vt.* to wind around a bitt

bit·ter (bit′ər) *adj.* [< OE. < base of *bitan*, to bite] **1.** having a sharp, often unpleasant taste; acrid **2.** causing or showing sorrow, pain, etc. **3.** sharp; harsh; piercing **4.** characterized by hatred, etc. —*n.* something bitter —**bit′ter·ly** *adv.* —**bit′ter·ness** *n.*

bit·tern (bit′ərn) *n.* [prob. < L. *butio*] a wading bird of the heron family

bit′ters *n.pl.* a liquor containing bitter herbs, etc., used as a tonic and in some cocktails

bit′ter·sweet′ *n.* **1.** a N. American woody vine with orange fruits and red seeds **2.** an old-world climbing vine with purple flowers and poisonous, red berries —*adj.* **1.** both bitter and sweet **2.** pleasant with sad overtones

bi·tu·men (bi too′mən, -tyoo′-) *n.* [L. < Celt.] any of several substances obtained as residue in the distillation of coal tar, petroleum, etc., or occurring as natural asphalt — **bi·tu′mi·nous** *adj.*

bituminous coal coal that yields pitch or tar when it burns; soft coal

bi·va·lent (bī vā′lənt, biv′ə-) *adj.* **1.** having two valences **2.** having a valence of two

bi·valve (bī′valv′) *n.* any mollusk having a shell of two parts, or valves, hinged together, as a clam —*adj.* having such a shell: also **bi′valved′**

biv·ou·ac (biv′wak, -oo wak′) *n.* [Fr. < OHG. *bi-*, by + *wacht*, a guard] a temporary encampment (esp. of soldiers) in the open —*vi.* -**acked, -ack·ing** to encamp in the open

bi·week·ly (bī wēk′lē) *adj., adv.* **1.** once every two weeks **2.** twice a week; semiweekly —*n., pl.* -**lies** a publication that appears once every two weeks

bi·zarre (bi zär′) *adj.* [Fr. < Basque *bizar*, a beard] odd; grotesque; eccentric —**bi·zarre′ly** *adv.* —**bi·zarre′ness** *n.*

Bi·zet (bē zā′), **Georges** (zhôrzh) 1838–75; Fr. composer

Bk *Chem.* berkelium

bk. *pl.* **bks. 1.** bank **2.** book

bl. 1. bale(s) **2.** barrel(s)

B/L *pl.* **BS/L** bill of lading

B.L. Bachelor of Laws

blab (blab) *vt., vi.* **blabbed, blab′bing** [echoic] **1.** to give away (a secret) in idle chatter **2.** to chatter —*n.* **1.** gossip **2.** one who blabs

black (blak) *adj.* [OE. *blæc*] **1.** opposite to white; of the color of coal: see COLOR **2.** having dark-colored skin and hair; esp., Negro **3.** without light; dark **4.** without cream, milk, etc.: said of coffee **5.** soiled; dirty **6.** wearing black clothing **7.** evil; wicked **8.** sad; dismal **9.** sullen or angry —*n.* **1.** black pigment, color, etc. **2.** black clothes, esp. for mourning **3.** [*also* B-] a Negro: *black* is now the generally preferred term —*vt., vi.* **1.** to blacken **2.** to polish with blacking —**black out 1.** to cause a blackout in **2.** to lose consciousness —**in the black** operating at a profit —**black′-ish** *adj.* —**black′ly** *adv.* —**black′ness** *n.*

black′-and-blue′ *adj.* discolored, as by a bruise

black art *same as* BLACK MAGIC

black′ball′ *n.* a secret vote against —*vt.* **1.** to vote against **2.** to ostracize

black bass a freshwater game fish of N. America

black′ber′ry *n., pl.* -**ries 1.** the dark, edible fruit of various brambles of the rose family **2.** a bush or vine bearing this fruit

black′bird′ *n.* any of various birds the male of which is almost all black

black′board′ *n.* a smooth surface as of slate, on which to write with chalk

Black Death a disease, probably bubonic plague, which devastated Europe and Asia in the 14th cent.

black′en (′n) *vi.* to become black or dark —*vt.* **1.** to make black; darken **2.** to slander; defame —**black′en·er** *n.*

black eye a discoloration of the skin around an eye, caused by a blow

black′-eyed′ Susan a N. American wildflower with yellow rays about a dark center

black flag the flag of piracy, usually black with a white skull and crossbones

black·guard (blag′ərd, -ärd) *n.* a scoundrel; villain —*adj.* vulgar, abusive, etc. —*vt.* to revile —**black′guard·ly** *adj., adv.*

black′head′ *n.* a black-tipped plug of dried fatty matter in a skin pore

black′heart′ed *adj.* wicked; evil

black′ing *n.* a black polish, as for shoes

black′jack′ (-jak′) *n.* **1.** a small, leather-covered bludgeon with a flexible handle **2.** the card game TWENTY-ONE —*vt.* to hit with a blackjack

black′list′ *n.* a list of censured persons being discriminated against —*vt.* to put on a blacklist

black lung (disease) a disease of the lungs caused by the continual inhalation of coal dust

black magic magic with an evil purpose; sorcery

black′mail′ (-māl′) *n.* [lit., black rent < ON. *mal*, discussion] **1.** payment extorted to prevent disclosure of information that could bring disgrace **2**. extortion of such payment —*vt*. **1**. to get or try to get blackmail from **2**. to coerce (*into*) as by threats —**black′mail′er** *n*.

black mark an unfavorable item in one's record

black market a place or system for selling goods illegally, esp. in violation of rationing —**black′-mar′ket** *vt*., *vi*. — **black mar·ket·eer** (mär′kə tir′)

Black Muslim a member of a militant Islamic sect of American blacks

black′out′ *n*. **1**. the extinguishing of all stage lights to end a scene, etc. **2**. a concealing of all lights that might be visible to enemy aircraft at night **3**. temporary unconsciousness

black power political and economic power sought by black Americans in the struggle for civil rights

Black Sea sea surrounded by the European U.S.S.R., Asia Minor, & the Balkan Peninsula

black sheep a person regarded as not so respectable as the rest of his family or group

black′smith′ (-smith′) *n*. one who works in iron, making and fitting horseshoes, etc.

black′snake′ *n*. a slender, harmless, dark-colored snake of the U.S.

black′thorn′ *n*. a thorny shrub with blue-black, plumlike fruit; sloe

black′top′ *n*. a bituminous mixture, usually asphalt, used as a surface for roads, etc. —*vt*. **-topped′**, **-top′ping** to cover with blacktop

black widow an American spider the female of which has a black body with red underneath, and a poisonous bite: the female sometimes eats its mate

blad·der (blad′ər) *n*. [OE. *blæddre*] **1**. a sac in the pelvic cavity, which holds urine flowing from the kidneys **2**. a bag, etc. resembling this

blade (blād) *n*. [OE. *blæd*] **1**. *a*) the leaf of a plant, esp. of grass *b*) the flat part of a leaf **2**. a broad, flat surface, as of an oar **3**. the cutting part of a knife, tool, etc. **4**. the metal runner of an ice skate **5**. a sword or swordsman **6**. a gay, dashing young man —**blad′ed** *adj*.

Blake (blāk), **William** 1757–1827; Eng. poet & artist

blam·a·ble, blame·a·ble (blām′ə b'l) *adj*. that deserves blame —**blam′a·bly** *adv*.

blame (blām) *vt*. **blamed, blam′ing** [see BLASPHEME] **1**. to accuse of being at fault; condemn (*for*) **2**. to put the responsibility of (an error, etc. on) —*n*. **1**. a blaming **2**. responsibility for a fault —**be to blame** to be blamable — **blame′less** *adj*. —**blame′less·ly** *adv*. —**blame′less·ness** *n*.

blame′wor′thy (-wur′thē) *adj*. deserving to be blamed — **blame′wor′thi·ness** *n*.

blanch (blanch) *vt*. [see BLANK] **1**. to make white; bleach **2**. to make pale **3**. to scald (vegetables, etc.) —*vi*. to turn pale

blanc·mange (blə mänzh′) *n*. [Fr.] a sweet, jellylike dessert made with starch or gelatin, milk, etc.

bland (bland) *adj*. [< L. *blandus*, mild] **1**. agreeable; suave **2**. *a*) mild and soothing *b*) tasteless, dull, etc. — **bland′ly** *adv*. —**bland′ness** *n*.

blan·dish (blan′dish) *vt*., *vi*. [see BLAND] to flatter or coax; cajole —**blan′dish·ment** *n*.

blank (blaŋk) *adj*. [< Frank.] **1**. not written on [a *blank* paper] **2**. having an empty or vacant look **3**. empty of thought **4**. utter; complete [a *blank* denial] —*n*. **1**. an empty space, esp. one to be filled out in a printed form **2**. such a printed form **3**. an empty place or time **4**. a piece of metal, etc. to be finished by stamping or marking **5**. a powder-filled cartridge without a bullet —*vt*. to hold (an opponent) scoreless —**draw a blank** [Colloq.] **1**. to be unsuccessful **2**. to be unable to remember something — **blank′ly** *adv*. —**blank′ness** *n*.

blank check a check carrying a signature only and allowing the bearer to fill in any amount

blan·ket (blaŋ′kit) *n*. [< OFr. dim. of *blanc*, white] **1**. a large, soft piece of cloth used for warmth, esp. as a bed cover **2**. anything like this [a *blanket* of snow] —*adj*. including many or all items [a *blanket* insurance policy] — *vt*. **1**. to cover, as with a blanket **2**. to apply uniformly to: said of rates **3**. to suppress; obscure

blank verse unrhymed verse, esp. that with five iambic feet per line

blare (bler) *vt*., *vi*. **blared, blar′ing** [ME. *bleren*, to bellow] to sound or exclaim loudly —*n*. a loud, brassy sound

blar·ney (blär′nē) *n*. [< *Blarney* stone in Ireland, traditionally kissed to gain skill in flattery] smooth talk used in flattery —*vt*., *vi*. **-neyed, -ney·ing** to use blarney (on)

bla·sé (blä zā′) *adj*. [Fr.] satiated and bored

blas·pheme (blas fēm′) *vt*. **-phemed′, -phem′ing** [< Gr. *blasphēmein*, speak evil of] **1**. to speak profanely of or to (God or sacred things) **2**. to curse —*vi*. to utter blasphemy —**blas·phem′er** *n*.

blas′phe·my (-fə mē) *n*., *pl*. **-mies 1**. words or actions showing disrespect for God or sacred things **2**. any irreverent remark or action —**blas′phe·mous** *adj*.

blast (blast) *n*. [< OE. *blæst*] **1**. a strong rush of air **2**. the sound of a sudden rush of air, as through a horn **3**. the current of air forced into a blast furnace **4**. a blight **5**. *a*) an explosion, as of dynamite *b*) a charge of explosive causing this **6**. [Slang] a gay, hilarious time —*vi*. **1**. to make a loud, harsh sound **2**. to set off explosives, etc. — *vt*. **1**. to blight; wither **2**. to blow up; explode **3**. [Colloq.] to criticize sharply —**blast off** to take off: said of a rocket or missile —**(at) full blast** at full speed

blast furnace a smelting furnace in which a blast of air produces the intense heat

blast′off′, blast′-off′ *n*. the launching of a rocket, space vehicle, etc.

bla·tant (blāt′'nt) *adj*. [prob. < L. *blaterare*, to babble] **1**. disagreeably loud; noisy **2**. glaringly conspicuous or obtrusive —**bla′tan·cy** *n*., *pl*. **-cies** —**bla′tant·ly** *adv*.

blath·er (blath′ər) *n*. [ON. *blathr*] foolish talk —*vi*., *vt*. to chatter foolishly —**blath′er·er** *n*.

blaze[1] (blāz) *n*. [< OE. *blæse*] **1**. a brilliant burst of flame; fire **2**. any very bright light **3**. a spectacular outburst [a *blaze* of oratory] **4**. a vivid display —*vi*. **blazed, blaz′ing 1**. to burn rapidly or shine brightly **2**. to be stirred, as with anger —**blaze away** to fire a gun rapidly several times

blaze[2] (blāz) *n*. [< ON. *blesi*] **1**. a white spot on an animal's face **2**. a mark made on a tree by cutting off a piece of bark —*vt*. **blazed, blaz′ing** to mark (a tree or trail) with blazes

blaze[3] (blāz) *vt*. **blazed, blaz′ing** [< OE. or ON.] to make known publicly

blaz·er (blā′zər) *n*. a lightweight sports jacket, often brightly colored

bla·zon (blā′z'n) *n*. [OFr. *blason*, a shield] **1**. a coat of arms **2**. showy display —*vt*. **1**. to make widely known; proclaim **2**. to adorn —**bla′zon·ry** *n*.

bldg. building

bleach (blēch) *vt*., *vi*. [< OE. *blac*, pale] to make or become white or colorless —*n*. a substance for bleaching

bleach′ers *n.pl*. [< *bleach*: in reference to the effects of exposure] seats or benches in tiers without a roof, for spectators at sporting events

bleak (blēk) *adj*. [< ON. *bleikr*, pale] **1**. exposed to wind and cold; bare **2**. cold and cutting; harsh **3**. cheerless; gloomy —**bleak′ly** *adv*. —**bleak′ness** *n*.

blear (blir) *adj*. [< ME. *bleren*, to have watery eyes] **1**. made dim by tears, mucus, etc.: said of eyes **2**. blurred — *vt*. **1**. to dim with tears, etc. **2**. to blur —**blear′y** *adj*.

blear′y-eyed′ (-īd′) *adj*. having bleary eyes

bleat (blēt) *vi*. [< OE. *blætan*] **1**. to make the cry of a sheep, goat, or calf **2**. to make a sound like this cry —*vt*. to say in a bleating voice —*n*. a bleating cry or sound

bleed (blēd) *vi*. **bled** (bled), **bleed′ing** [< OE. *blod*, blood] **1**. to emit or lose blood **2**. to feel pain, grief, or sympathy **3**. to ooze sap, juice, etc. **4**. to run together, as dyes in wet cloth **5**. to come through a covering coat of paint — *vt*. **1**. to draw blood from **2**. to ooze (sap, juice, etc.) **3**. [Colloq.] to extort money from

bleed′er *n*. one who bleeds profusely; hemophiliac

bleeding heart a plant with fernlike leaves and drooping clusters of pink, heart-shaped flowers

bleep (blēp) *n*., *vi*. [echoic] same as BEEP —*vt*. to censor (something said), as in a telecast, by substituting a beep

blem·ish (blem′ish) *vt*. [< OFr. *blesmir*, injure] to mar — *n*. a mark, flaw, defect, etc.

blench[1] (blench) *vt*., *vi*. [var. of BLANCH] to whiten

blench[2] (blench) *vi*. [< OE. *blencan*, deceive] to shrink back, as in fear; flinch

blend (blend) *vt*. **blend′ed** or **blent, blend′ing** [< OE. *blendan*] **1**. to mix or mingle (varieties of tea, tobacco, etc.) **2**. to mix thoroughly —*vi*. **1**. to mix or merge **2**. to shade gradually into each other, as colors **3**. to harmonize —*n*. **1**. a blending **2**. a mixture of varieties [a *blend* of coffee]

blended whiskey whiskey that is blended with other whiskey or with neutral spirits

---

blen·ny (blen′ē) *n., pl.* **-nies, -ny** [< Gr. *blenna,* slime] a small ocean fish covered with a slimy substance

bless (bles) *vt.* **blessed** or **blest, bless′ing** [< OE. *bletsian,* consecrate with blood] **1.** to make holy **2.** to ask divine favor for **3.** to endow (*with*) [*blessed* with health] **4.** to make happy **5.** to praise **6.** to make the sign of the cross over **7.** to protect from evil, harm, etc.

bless·ed (bles′id, blest) *adj.* **1.** holy; sacred **2.** blissful; fortunate **3.** beatified **4.** bringing joy —**bless′ed·ness** *n.*

bless′ing *n.* **1.** an invocation or benediction **2.** a grace said at meals **3.** the gift of divine favor **4.** good wishes or approval **5.** a special benefit

blew (blōō) *pt. of* BLOW¹ & BLOW³

blight (blīt) *n.* [? < ON. *blikja,* turn pale] **1.** any insect, disease, etc. that destroys or stunts plants **2.** anything that destroys, frustrates, etc. —*vt.* **1.** to wither **2.** to destroy **3.** to frustrate

blimp (blimp) *n.* [echoic coinage] [Colloq.] a small, non-rigid or semirigid airship

blind (blīnd) *adj.* [OE.] **1.** without the power of sight **2.** of or for sightless persons **3.** not able or willing to understand **4.** done without directions or knowledge [a *blind* search] **5.** hard to see; hidden **6.** closed at one end **7.** not controlled by reason [*blind* fate] **8.** *Aeron.* by the use of instruments only [*blind* flying] —*vt.* **1.** to make sightless **2.** to dazzle **3.** to deprive of insight **4.** to obscure —*n.* **1.** anything that obscures sight or keeps out light, as a window shade **2.** a place of concealment **3.** a decoy —**blind′ly** *adv.* —**blind′ness** *n.*

blind date [Colloq.] **1.** a date arranged for a man and a woman previously unacquainted **2.** either of these persons

blind′er *n.* either of two flaps on a horse's bridle that shut out the side view

blind′fold′ (-fōld′) *vt.* [< ME. *blindfeld,* struck blind] to cover the eyes of, as with a cloth —*n.* something used to cover the eyes —*adj.* **1.** with the eyes covered **2.** reckless

blind′man's buff (buf′) [*buff,* contr. < BUFFET¹] a game in which a blindfolded player has to catch and identify another: also **blind′man's bluff′** (bluf′)

blind spot 1. the small area, insensitive to light, in the retina where the optic nerve enters **2.** a prejudice or ignorance that one has but is often unaware of

blink (bliŋk) *vi.* [see BLENCH²] **1.** to wink rapidly **2.** to flash on and off; twinkle —*vt.* to cause (eyes, light, etc.) to wink or blink —*n.* **1.** a blinking **2.** a glimmer —**blink at** to ignore —**on the blink** [Slang] out of order

blink′er *n.* **1.** a flashing warning light **2.** *same as* BLINDER

blintz (blints) *n.* [< Yid. < Russ. *blin,* pancake] a thin pancake rolled with a filling of cottage cheese, etc.

bliss (blis) *n.* [OE. *bliths*] **1.** great joy or happiness **2.** spiritual joy —**bliss′ful** *adj.* —**bliss′ful·ly** *adv.* —**bliss′ful-ness** *n.*

blis·ter (blis′tər) *n.* [< ON. *blastr*] **1.** a raised patch of skin filled with watery matter and caused by burning or rubbing **2.** anything like a blister —*vt.* **1.** to raise blisters on **2.** to lash with words —*vi.* to form blisters

blithe (blīth) *adj.* [OE.] gay; carefree —**blithe′ly** *adv.* —**blithe′ness** *n.*

blith·er·ing (blith′ər iŋ) *adj.* [*blither,* var. of BLATHER] jabbering

blithe·some (blīth′səm) *adj.* blithe; gay

blitz (blits) *n.* [< BLITZKRIEG] a sudden, overwhelming attack —*vt.* to subject to a blitz; overwhelm

blitz′krieg (-krēg′) *n.* [G. < *blitz,* lightning + *krieg,* war] sudden, swift, large-scale offensive warfare

bliz·zard (bliz′ərd) *n.* [dial. *bliz,* violent blow + -ARD] a violent snowstorm with very cold winds

bloat (blōt) *vt., vi.* [< ON. *blautr,* soaked] **1.** to swell, as with water or air **2.** to puff up, as with pride

blob (bläb) *n.* [echoic] a small drop or mass

bloc (bläk) *n.* [Fr. < LowG. *block,* log] a bipartisan group of legislators, or a group of nations, acting together in a common cause

block (bläk) *n.* [see BLOC] **1.** a solid piece of wood, stone, or metal **2.** a heavy stand on which chopping, etc. is done **3.** an auctioneer's platform **4.** a mold upon which hats, etc. are shaped **5.** an obstruction or hindrance **6.** a pulley in a frame **7.** *a)* a city square *b)* one side of a city square **8.** a group of buildings **9.** any number of things regarded as a unit **10.** *Printing* a piece of engraved wood, etc. with a design **11.** *Sports* a legal thwarting of an opponent's play —*vt.* **1.** to obstruct; hinder **2.** to shape or mold on a block **3.** to strengthen or support with blocks **4.** to

BLOCKS
(sense 6)

sketch roughly (often with *out*) **5.** *Sports* to hinder (an opponent or a play) —**on the block** up for sale or auction —**block′age** *n.* —**block′er** *n.*

block·ade (blä kād′) *n.* [BLOCK + -ADE] **1.** a shutting off of a place by troops or ships to prevent passage **2.** any strategic barrier —*vt.* **-ad′ed, -ad′ing** to subject to a blockade —**run the blockade** to go through a blockade —**block·ad′er** *n.*

block and tackle pulley blocks and ropes, used for lifting large, heavy objects

block·bust·er (bläk′bus′tər) *n.* [Colloq.] a successful, heavily promoted movie, novel, etc.

block′bust′ing (-bus′tiŋ) *n.* the inducing of owners to sell their homes out of fear that a minority group may move into their neighborhood

block′head′ (-hed′) *n.* a stupid person

block′house′ (-hous′) *n.* **1.** formerly, a wooden fort with openings from which to shoot **2.** a reinforced structure for observers, as of missile launches

bloke (blōk) *n.* [< ?] [Chiefly Brit. Slang] a fellow

blond (bländ) *adj.* [Fr. < ? Gmc.] **1.** having light-colored hair and skin **2.** yellowish: said of hair **3.** light-colored Also sp. **blonde** —*n.* a blond person —**blonde** *n.fem.*

blood (blud) *n.* [< OE. *blod*] **1.** the red fluid circulating in the arteries and veins of vertebrates **2.** bloodshed **3.** the essence of life; life **4.** the sap of a plant **5.** passion, temperament, etc. **6.** parental heritage; lineage **7.** kinship; family relationship **8.** a dandy **9.** people, esp. youthful people —**bad blood** anger; hatred —**in cold blood 1.** with cruelty **2.** deliberately —**make one's blood boil** to make one angry —**make one's blood run cold** to terrify one

blood bank a supply of blood stored for future use in transfusion

blood count the number of red and white corpuscles in a given volume of blood

blood·cur·dling (blud′kurd′liŋ) *adj.* very frightening; causing terror

blood′ed (-id) *adj.* **1.** having (a specified kind of) blood [*hot-blooded*] **2.** of fine breed

blood′hound′ *n.* any of a breed of large, keen-scented dogs used in tracking fugitives, etc.

blood′less *adj.* **1.** without bloodshed **2.** anemic or pale **3.** having little energy —**blood′less·ly** *adv.*

blood′let′ting (-let′iŋ) *n.* the opening of a vein to remove blood; bleeding

blood′mo·bile (-mō bēl′) *n.* a mobile unit for collecting blood from donors for blood banks

blood money 1. money paid to a hired killer **2.** money paid as compensation for a murder

blood poisoning a diseased condition of the blood, due to certain microorganisms or their toxins

blood pressure the pressure of the blood against the inner walls of the blood vessels

blood relation (or **relative**) a person related by birth

blood′root′ *n.* a N. American plant related to the poppy, with a rootstock that yields a red juice

blood′shed′ *n.* killing; slaughter

blood′shot′ *adj.* tinged with red because the small blood vessels are broken: said of an eye

blood′stone′ *n.* a semiprecious, dark-green variety of quartz spotted with red jasper

blood′stream′ *n.* the blood flowing through the circulatory system of the body

blood′suck′er *n.* **1.** an animal that sucks blood, esp. a leech **2.** a person who extorts from others all that he can —**blood′suck′ing** *adj., n.*

blood′thirst′y *adj.* murderous; cruel

blood vessel a tube through which the blood circulates in the body; artery, vein, or capillary

blood′y *adj.* **-i·er, -i·est 1.** of, containing, or covered with blood **2.** involving bloodshed **3.** bloodthirsty **4.** [Brit. Slang] cursed; damned —*adv.* [Brit. Slang] very —*vt.* **-ied, -y·ing** to cover or stain with blood —**blood′i·ly** *adv.* —**blood′i·ness** *n.*

bloom (blōōm) *n.* [< ON. *blomi,* flowers] **1.** a flower; blossom **2.** the state or time of flowering **3.** a period of most health, vigor, etc. **4.** a youthful, healthy glow, as of the cheeks **5.** the powdery coating on some fruits or leaves —*vi.* **1.** to blossom **2.** to be in one's prime **3.** to glow as with health, etc.

bloom·ers (blōō′mərz) *n.pl.* [< Amelia *Bloomer,* U.S. feminist] **1.** baggy trousers gathered at the knee, formerly worn by women for athletics **2.** an undergarment somewhat like this

bloom′ing *adj.* **1.** blossoming **2.** flourishing **3.** [Colloq.] complete

bloop·er (blōōp′ər) *n.* [< imitation of a vulgar noise]

[Slang] **1.** a stupid mistake **2.** *Baseball* a fly that falls just beyond the infield for a hit

blos·som (bläs'əm) *n.* [< OE. *blostma*] **1.** a flower, esp. of a fruit-bearing plant **2.** a state or time of flowering —*vi.* **1.** to have or open into blossoms **2.** to begin to flourish

blot (blät) *n.* [< ?] **1.** a spot or stain, esp. of ink **2.** anything that spoils or mars **3.** a moral stain —*vt.* **blot′ted, blot′ting 1.** to spot; stain **2.** to disgrace **3.** to erase, obscure, or get rid of (with *out*) **4.** to dry, as with blotting paper —*vi.* **1.** to make blots **2.** to become blotted **3.** to be absorbent

blotch (bläch) *n.* [? < prec.] **1.** a discoloration on the skin **2.** any large blot or stain —*vt.* to mark with blotches — **blotch′y** *adj.* **-i·er, -i·est**

blot′ter *n.* **1.** a piece of blotting paper **2.** a book for recording events as they occur [a police *blotter* is a record of arrests, etc.]

blotting paper a soft, absorbent paper used to dry a surface freshly written on in ink

blouse (blous, blouz) *n.* [Fr., workman's smock] **1.** a shirtlike garment worn by women and children **2.** a uniform coat worn by soldiers, etc. —*vt., vi.* **bloused, blous′ing** to gather in and drape, as at the waistline

blow¹ (blō) *vi.* **blew, blown, blow′ing** [< OE. *blawan*] **1.** to move with some force, as the wind **2.** to send forth air, as with the mouth **3.** to pant **4.** to sound by blowing or being blown **5.** to spout water and air, as whales do **6.** to be carried by the wind [my hat *blew* off] **7.** to be stormy **8.** to burst suddenly (often with *out*) **9.** [Colloq.] to brag **10.** [Slang] to go away —*vt.* **1.** to force air from, into, onto, or through **2.** to drive by blowing **3.** to sound by blowing **4.** to shape or form by blown air or gas **5.** to burst by an explosion (often with *up* or *out*) **6.** to melt (a fuse, etc.) **7.** [Colloq.] to spend (money) freely **8.** [Slang] to leave **9.** [Slang] to bungle —*n.* **1.** a blowing **2.** a blast or gale —*n.* [Colloq.] to release emotions, as by shouting —**blow over** to be forgotten —**blow up 1.** to arise and become intense, as a storm **2.** to enlarge (a photograph) **3.** [Colloq.] to lose one's temper —**blow′er** *n.*

blow² (blō) *n.* [ME. *blowe*] **1.** a hard hit, as with the fist **2.** a sudden attack **3.** a sudden calamity; shock —**at a (or one) blow** by one action —**come to blows** to begin fighting

blow³ (blō) *vi.* **blew, blown, blow′ing** [OE. *blowan*] [Poet.] to bloom; blossom —*n.* a mass of blossoms

blow-by-blow (blō′bī′blō′) *adj.* detailed; full

blow′-dry′ *vt.* **-dried′, -dry′ing** to dry (wet hair) with an electric device (**blow′-dry′er**) that sends out a stream of heated air —*n.* the act of blow-drying the hair

blow′fly′ *n., pl.* **-flies′** a fly that lays its eggs on meat, in wounds, etc.

blow′gun′ *n.* a long, tubelike weapon through which darts or pellets are blown

blow′hole′ *n.* **1.** a nostril in the top of the head of whales, etc., used for breathing **2.** a hole through which gas or air can escape

blow′out′ *n.* **1.** the bursting of a tire **2.** [Slang] a party, celebration, etc.

blow′pipe′ *n.* a tube for forcing air into a flame to increase its heat

blow′torch′ *n.* a small gasoline torch that shoots out a hot flame, used to melt metal, etc.

blow′up′ *n.* **1.** an explosion **2.** an enlarged photograph **3.** [Colloq.] a hysterical outburst

blow′y *adj.* **-i·er, -i·est** windy

blowz·y (blou′zē) *adj.* **-i·er, -i·est** [< obs. *blouze*, wench] **1.** fat, ruddy, and coarse-looking **2.** slovenly; sloppy Also **blows′y**

BLOWTORCH

blub·ber (blub′ər) *n.* [ME. *blober*, a bubble] **1.** the fat of the whale and other sea mammals **2.** loud weeping —*vi.* to weep loudly —*vt.* to say while blubbering —**blub′ber·er** *n.*

blub′ber·y *adj.* **1.** of, full, or like blubber **2.** swollen, as by blubbering

blu·cher (bloo′chər, -kər) *n.* [< von *Blücher* (1742–1819), Prussian field marshal] a kind of shoe in which the vamp is of one piece with the tongue

bludg·eon (bluj′n) *n.* [? < MFr. *bouge*, a club] a short club with a thick or heavy end —*vt., vi.* **1.** to strike with a bludgeon **2.** to bully or coerce

blue (bloo) *adj.* [< Frank. *blao*] **1.** of the color of the clear sky **2.** livid: said of the skin **3.** gloomy **4.** puritanical **5.**

[Colloq.] indecent —*n.* **1.** the color of the clear sky **2.** any blue pigment **3.** anything colored blue **4.** [*pl.*] [Colloq.] a depressed feeling (with *the*) **5.** [*pl., also with sing. v.*] Negro folk music having, usually, a slow tempo, melancholy words, etc. (often with *the*) —*vt.* **blued, blu′ing** or **blue′ing 1.** to make blue **2.** to use bluing on or in —**once in a blue moon** very seldom —**out of the blue** unexpectedly —**the blue 1.** the sky **2.** the sea —**blue′ness** *n.*

blue baby a baby born with cyanosis

Blue′beard′ a legendary character who married and murdered one wife after another

blue′bell′ *n.* any of various plants with blue, bell-shaped flowers

blue′ber′ry *n., pl.* **-ries 1.** a small, edible, blue-black berry **2.** the shrub on which it grows

blue′bird′ *n.* a small N. American songbird, the male of which has a bluish back

blue blood 1. descent from nobility **2.** a nobleman; aristocrat: also **blue′blood′** *n.* —**blue′-blood′ed** *adj.*

blue book a book listing socially prominent people

blue′bot′tle *n.* **1.** a plant with blue, bottle-shaped flowers, as the cornflower **2.** a large blowfly with a steel-blue abdomen and a hairy body

blue cheese a cheese similar to Roquefort

blue′-col′lar *adj.* designating or of industrial workers, esp. the semiskilled and unskilled

blue′fish′ *n., pl.*: see FISH a bluish food fish of the Atlantic coast of N. America

blue flu [from the traditional color of police uniforms] a sickout, esp. by police officers

blue′grass′ *n.* **1.** a forage grass, as **Kentucky bluegrass 2.** [*often* B-] Southern folk music played on guitars, fiddles, banjos, etc.

blue′jack′et *n.* an enlisted man in the U.S. or British navy

blue jay a noisy, often crested, American bird with a bluish upper part: also **blue′jay′** *n.*

blue law a puritanical law, esp. one prohibiting certain activities on Sunday

blue′nose′ *n.* [Colloq.] a puritanical person

blue′-pen′cil *vt.* **-ciled** or **-cilled, -cil·ing** or **-cil·ling** to edit, cut, or correct as with a blue pencil

blue′point′ *n.* [< *Blue Point*, Long Island] a small oyster, usually eaten raw

blue′print′ *n.* **1.** a photographic reproduction in white on a blue background, as of architectural plans **2.** any detailed plan or outline —*vt.* to make a blueprint of

blue ribbon first prize in a competition

Blue Ridge Mountains easternmost range of the Appalachians, extending from S Pa. to N Ga.

blue′stock′ing *n.* a learned or pedantic woman

blu·et (bloo′it) *n.* [< Fr. dim. of *bleu*, blue] a small plant having little, pale-blue flowers

bluff¹ (bluf) *vt., vi.* [prob. < Du. *bluffen*, to baffle] to mislead or frighten by a false, bold front —*n.* **1.** a bluffing **2.** one who bluffs: also **bluff′er** *n.*

bluff² (bluf) *adj.* [< Du. *blaf*, flat] **1.** having a flat front that slopes steeply **2.** having a rough, frank manner —*n.* a high, steep bank or cliff —**bluff′ly** *adv.* —**bluff′ness** *n.*

blu·ing (bloo′iŋ) *n.* a blue rinse used on white fabrics to prevent yellowing: also sp. **blue′ing**

blu·ish (-ish) *adj.* somewhat blue: also sp. **blue′ish**

blun·der (blun′dər) *vi.* [< ON. *blunda*, shut the eyes] **1.** to move clumsily **2.** to make a foolish mistake —*vt.* **1.** to say stupidly; blurt (*out*) **2.** to do poorly; bungle —*n.* a foolish mistake —**blun′der·er** *n.*

blun′der·buss′ (-bus′) *n.* [Du. *donderbus*, thunder box] an obsolete short gun with a broad muzzle

blunt (blunt) *adj.* [< ?] **1.** slow to perceive; dull **2.** having a dull edge or point **3.** plain-spoken and abrupt — *vt., vi.* to make or become dull or insensitive —**blunt′ly** *adv.* —**blunt′ness** *n.*

BLUNDERBUSS

blur (blur) *vt., vi.* **blurred, blur′ring** [? akin to BLEAR] **1.** to smear; blot **2.** to make or become indistinct in shape, etc. **3.** to dim —*n.* **1.** a being blurred **2.** an obscuring stain **3.** anything indistinct —**blur′ri·ness** *n.* —**blur′ry** *adj.*

blurb (blurb) *n.* [arbitrary coinage] [Colloq.] an exaggerated statement or advertisement, as on a book jacket

blurt (blurt) *vt.* [prob. echoic] to say suddenly, without stopping to think (with *out*)

blush (blush) *vi.* [< OE. *blyscan*, to shine] **1.** to become red in the face, as from embarrassment **2.** to be ashamed (*at* or *for*) **3.** to become rosy —*n.* **1.** a reddening of the face, as from shame **2.** a rosy color —*adj.* rosy —**at first blush** at first sight —**blush′er** *n.* —**blush′ful** *adj.* —**blush′-ing·ly** *adv.*

blus·ter (blus′tər) *vi.* [< LowG. *blüstern*] **1.** to blow stormily: said of wind **2.** to speak or act in a noisy or swaggering manner —*n.* **1.** noisy commotion **2.** noisy or swaggering talk —**blus′ter·er** *n.* —**blus′ter·ing·ly** *adv.* —**blus′ter·y, blus′ter·ous** *adj.*

blvd. boulevard

BM [Colloq.] bowel movement

BO, B.O. body odor

bo·a (bō′ə) *n.* [L.] **1.** a tropical snake that crushes its prey in its coils, as the python **2.** a woman's long, fluffy scarf, as of feathers

boa constrictor a species of boa which reaches a length of 10 to 15 feet

boar (bôr) *n.* [OE. *bar*] **1.** an uncastrated male hog or pig **2.** a wild hog

board (bôrd) *n.* [< OE. *bord*, plank] **1.** a long, flat piece of sawed wood **2.** a flat piece of wood, etc. for some special use [a bulletin *board*] **3.** pasteboard **4.** *a*) a table for meals *b*) meals, esp. as provided regularly for pay **5.** a group of administrators; council **6.** the side of a ship [overboard] —*vt.* **1.** to cover (*up*) with boards **2.** to provide with meals, or room and meals, regularly for pay **3.** to come onto the deck of (a ship) **4.** to get on (an airplane, bus, etc.) —*vi.* to receive meals, or room and meals, regularly for pay —**across the board** *Horse Racing* to win, place, and show: said of betting —**go by the board** to be got rid of, lost, etc. —**on board** on or in a ship, aircraft, etc. —**the boards** the stage (of a theater)

board·er (bôr′dər) *n.* one who boards at a boardinghouse, etc.

board foot *pl.* **board feet** a unit of measure of lumber equal to a board one foot square and one inch thick

board′ing·house′ *n.* a house where meals, or room and meals, can be had for pay: also **boarding house**

boarding school a school providing lodging and meals for the pupils

board′walk′ *n.* a walk made of thick boards, esp. one elevated and placed along a beach

boast (bōst) *vi.* [< Anglo-Fr.] to talk, esp. about oneself, with too much pride; brag —*vt.* **1.** to brag about **2.** to glory in having or doing (something) —*n.* **1.** a boasting **2.** anything boasted of —**boast′er** *n.* —**boast′ful** *adj.* — **boast′ful·ly** *adv.* —**boast′ful·ness** *n.* —**boast′ing·ly** *adv.*

boat (bōt) *n.* [OE. *bat*] **1.** a small, open watercraft **2.** loosely, a ship **3.** a boat-shaped dish —*vt.* to lay or carry in the boat —**in the same boat** in the same unfavorable situation —**boat′man** (-mən) *n., pl.* -**men**

boat·er (bōt′ər) *n.* a stiff straw hat with a flat crown and brim

boat′house′ *n.* a building for storing boats

boat′ing *n.* rowing, sailing, etc.

boat·swain (bō′s′n) *n.* a ship's petty officer in charge of the deck crew, rigging, etc.

bob¹ (bäb) *n.* [ME. < *bobbe*, hanging cluster; 3 & 4 < the *v.*] **1.** any knoblike hanging weight **2.** a woman's or girl's short haircut **3.** a quick, jerky motion **4.** a float on a fishing line —*vt.* **bobbed, bob′bing** [ME. *bobben*, knock against] **1.** to make move, esp. up and down, with short, jerky motions **2.** to cut (hair, etc.) short —*vi.* to move with short, jerky motions —**bob up** to appear suddenly

bob² (bäb) *n., pl.* **bob** [< ?] [Brit. Slang] a shilling

bob·bin (bäb′in) *n.* [< Fr. *bobiner*, to wind] a spool for thread, etc. used in spinning, machine sewing, etc.

bob·ble (bäb′'l) *n.* [Colloq.] *Sports* an awkward juggling of the ball —*vt.* -**bled, -bling** [Colloq.] to make a bobble with (a ball)

bob·by (bäb′ē) *n., pl.* -**bies** [after Sir Robert (*Bobby*) Peel (1788–1850), who reorganized the London police force] [Brit. Colloq.] a policeman

bobby pin [from use with *bobbed* hair] a small metal hairpin with the sides pressing close together

bobby socks (or **sox**) [< BOB¹ (*vt.* 2)] [Colloq.] girls' socks that reach just above the ankle

bob′cat′ *n.* a wildcat of the E U.S.

bob·o·link (bäb′ə liŋk′) *n.* a migratory songbird of N. America

bob′sled′ *n.* a long racing sled —*vi.* -**sled′ded, -sled′ding** to ride or race on a bobsled

bob′tail′ *n.* **1.** a tail cut short **2.** an animal with a bobtail —*adj.* **1.** having a bobtail **2.** cut short —*vt.* **1.** to dock the tail of **2.** to cut short

bob·white (bäb′hwīt′) *n.* [echoic] a small N. American quail

Boc·cac·cio (bō kä′chē ō′), **Gio·van·ni** (jô vän′nē) 1313–75; It. writer

bock (**beer**) (bäk) [< *Einbeck*, German city where first brewed] a dark beer

bode¹ (bōd) *vt.* **bod′ed, bod′ing** [< OE. *boda*, messenger] to be an omen of; presage —**bode ill** (or **well**) to be a bad (or good) omen

bode² (bōd) *pt.* of BIDE

bod·ice (bäd′is) *n.* [alt. < *bodies*, pl. of *body*] the upper part of a woman's dress

bod·ied (bäd′ēd) *adj.* having a body or substance, esp. of a specified kind [able-*bodied*]

bod′i·less (-ē lis) *adj.* without a body; having no material substance

bod′i·ly (-'l ē) *adj.* **1.** physical **2.** of, in, by, or to the body —*adv.* **1.** in person **2.** as a single body

bod·kin (bäd′k'n) *n.* [ME. *boidekyn* < ?] **1.** a pointed instrument for making holes in cloth **2.** a thick, blunt needle **3.** [Obs.] a dagger

bod·y (bäd′ē) *n., pl.* **bod′ies** [< OE. *bodig*, cask] **1.** the whole physical substance of a person, animal, or plant **2.** the trunk of a man or animal **3.** a corpse **4.** [Colloq.] a person **5.** a group regarded as a unit [an advisory *body*] **6.** the main part of anything **7.** a mass of matter [a *body* of water] **8.** density or consistency, as of a liquid **9.** richness of tone or flavor —*vt.* -**ied, -y·ing** to give a body or substance to —**body forth** to give shape or form to

bod′y·guard′ *n.* a person or persons assigned to guard someone

body politic the people who collectively constitute a political unit under a government

body stocking a tightfitting garment, usually of one piece, that covers the torso and, sometimes, the legs

Boer (bôr, boor, bō′ər) *n.* [Du. *boer*, peasant] a South African whose ancestors were Dutch colonists —*adj.* of the Boers

bog (bäg, bôg) *n.* [< Gael. & Ir. *bog*, soft, moist] wet, spongy ground; a small marsh —*vt., vi.* **bogged, bog′ging** to sink in or as in a bog (often with *down*) —**bog′gy** *adj.* -**gi·er, -gi·est**

bo·gey (bō′gē) *n., pl.* -**geys 1.** *same as* BOGY **2.** [after an imaginary Colonel *Bogey*] *Golf* one stroke more than par on a hole: also sp. **bo′gie**

bog·gle (bäg′'l) *vi.* -**gled, -gling** [< Scot. *bogle*, specter] **1.** to be startled; shy away (*at*) **2.** to hesitate (*at*); have scruples **3.** to equivocate (*at*) —*vt.* to bungle; botch —*n.* a boggling

Bo·go·tá (bō′gə tä′) capital of Colombia: pop. 2,148,000

bo·gus (bō′gəs) *adj.* [< ?] not genuine; spurious; counterfeit

bo·gy (bō′gē, boog′ē) *n., pl.* -**gies** [see BOGGLE] an imaginary evil spirit; goblin: also sp. **bo′gie**

bo·gy·man, bo·gey·man (bō′gē man′, boog′ē-) *n., pl.* -**men′** an imaginary frightful being

Bo·he·mi·a (bō hē′mē ə) region and former province of Czechoslovakia: a former kingdom

Bo·he′mi·an *n.* **1.** a native of Bohemia **2.** *same as* CZECH (*n.* 2) **3.** [*often* b-] an artist, poet, etc. who lives unconventionally —*adj.* **1.** of Bohemia, its people, etc. **2.** [*often* b-] like a Bohemian (*n.* 3) —**Bo·he′mi·an·ism** *n.*

boil¹ (boil) *vi.* [< L. *bulla*, a bubble] **1.** to bubble up and vaporize by being heated **2.** to seethe like boiling liquids **3.** to be agitated, as with rage **4.** to cook in boiling liquid —*vt.* **1.** to heat to the boiling point **2.** to cook in boiling liquid —*n.* the act or state of boiling —**boil down 1.** to lessen in quantity by boiling **2.** to condense; summarize —**boil over 1.** to come to a boil and spill over the rim **2.** to lose one's temper

boil² (boil) *n.* [< OE. *byl*] an inflamed, painful, pus-filled swelling on the skin, caused by infection

boil′er *n.* **1.** a container in which things are boiled or heated **2.** a tank in which water is turned to steam for heat or power **3.** a tank for heating water and storing it

boil′ing point the temperature at which a liquid boils: for water, usually 212°F. or 100°C

Boi·se (boi′sē, -zē) capital of Ida.: pop. 75,000

bois·ter·ous (bois′tər əs) *adj.* [ME. *boistreous*, crude] **1.** rough and stormy; turbulent **2.** *a*) noisy and unruly *b*) loud and exuberant —**bois′ter·ous·ly** *adv.* —**bois′ter·ous·ness** *n.*

bold (bōld) *adj.* [< OE. *beald*] **1.** daring; fearless **2.** taking liberties; impudent **3.** steep or abrupt **4.** prominent and clear —**make bold** to dare (*to*) —**bold′ly** *adv.* —**bold′ness** *n.*

bold′face′ *n. Printing* type with heavy, dark lines

bold′faced′ (-fāst′) *adj.* impudent; forward in manner
bole (bōl) *n.* [ON. *bolr*] a tree trunk
bo·le·ro (bə ler′ō) *n., pl.* **-ros** [Sp.] 1. a Spanish dance in 3/4 time 2. music for this 3. a short, open vest, sometimes with sleeves
Bol·i·var (bō lē′vär), **Si·món** (sē mōn′) 1783–1830; S. American general & revolutionary leader
Bo·liv·i·a (bə liv′ē ə) country in WC S. America: 424,000 sq. mi.; pop. 4,804,000; capitals, La Paz & Sucre —**Bo·liv′i·an** *adj., n.*
boll (bōl) *n.* [< OE. *bolla,* a bowl] the roundish seed pod of a plant, esp. of cotton or flax
boll weevil a small weevil whose larvae destroy the cotton bolls in which they are hatched
bo·lo (bō′lō) *n., pl.* **-los** [Sp.] a large, single-edged knife used in the Philippines
bo·lo·gna (bə lō′nē, -nyə) *n.* [< *Bologna,* It. city] a large, smoked sausage of various meats: also **bologna sausage**
bolo tie a man's string tie held together with a slide device
Bol·she·vik (bōl′shə vik′, bäl′-) *n., pl.* **-viks′, -vi′ki** (-vē′kē) [Russ. < *bolshe,* the majority] [*also* b-] 1. a member of a majority faction that came into power in Russia in 1917 2. a Communist, esp. of the Soviet Union 3. loosely, any radical —*adj.* [*also* b-] of or like the Bolsheviks or Bolshevism —**Bol′she·vism** *n.* —**Bol′she·vist** *n., adj.*
bol·ster (bōl′stər) *n.* [OE.] 1. a long, narrow pillow 2. any bolsterlike object or support —*vt.* to prop up as with a bolster; support (often with *up*)
bolt¹ (bōlt) *n.* [OE.] 1. a short, blunt arrow used with a crossbow 2. a flash of lightning, etc. 3. a sudden dash 4. a sliding bar for locking a door, etc. 5. a similar bar in a lock, moved by a key 6. a metal rod with a head, threaded and used with a nut to hold parts together 7. a roll (*of* cloth, paper, etc.) 8. a withdrawal from one's party or group —*vt.* 1. to say suddenly; blurt (*out*) 2. to swallow (food) hurriedly 3. to fasten as with a bolt 4. to abandon (a party, group, etc.) —*vi.* 1. to spring away suddenly; dart 2. to withdraw support from one's party, etc. —*adv.* erectly [to sit *bolt* upright]
bolt² (bōlt) *vt.* [< OFr. *buleter*] 1. to sift (flour, grain, etc.) 2. to examine closely —**bolt′er** *n.*
bo·lus (bō′ləs) *n., pl.* **bo′lus·es** [< Gr. *bōlos*] 1. a small, round lump 2. a large pill
bomb (bäm) *n.* [< Gr. *bombos,* hollow sound] 1. a container filled with an explosive, incendiary, etc. for dropping or hurling, or for detonation by a timing mechanism 2. a sudden, surprising occurrence 3. an aerosol container 4. [Slang] a complete failure —*vt.* to attack or destroy with bombs —*vi.* [Slang] to have a complete failure
bom·bard (bäm bärd′) *vt.* [< Fr. *bombarde,* mortar] 1. to attack with artillery or bombs 2. to attack with questions, etc. 3. to direct particles against the atomic nuclei of (an element) —**bom·bard′ment** *n.*
bom·bar·dier (bäm′bə dir′) *n.* one who releases the bombs in a bomber
bom·bast (bäm′bast) *n.* [< Per. *pambak,* cotton] pompous, high-sounding talk or writing —**bom·bas′tic** *adj.* —**bom·bas′ti·cal·ly** *adv.*
Bom·bay (bäm′bā′) seaport in W India, on the Arabian Sea: pop. 4,152,000
bomb·er (bäm′ər) *n.* 1. an airplane for dropping bombs 2. a person who uses bombs
bomb′proof′ *adj.* that can withstand the force of ordinary bombs
bomb′shell′ *n. same as* BOMB (*n.* 1, 2)
bomb′sight′ *n.* an instrument for aiming bombs dropped from aircraft
bo·na fi·de (bō′nə fīd′ *or* fī′dē) [L.] in good faith; without fraud
bo·nan·za (bə nan′zə) *n.* [Sp., prosperity] 1. a rich vein of ore 2. any source of wealth
Bo·na·parte (bō′nə pärt′) *see* NAPOLEON I
bon·bon (bän′bän′) *n.* [Fr. *bon,* good] a small piece of candy, esp. one with a creamy filling
bond (bänd) *n.* [ult. < Gothic *bindan,* bind] 1. anything that binds, fastens, or unites 2. [*pl.*] fetters; shackles 3. a binding agreement 4. the status of goods kept in a warehouse until taxes are paid 5. an interest-bearing certificate issued by a government or business, redeemable on a specified date 6. a written obligation to pay specified sums, do or not do specified things, etc. 7. an amount paid as surety or bail —*vt.* 1. to fasten or unite 2. to fur-

nish a bond, or bail, and thus become a surety for (someone) 3. to place (goods) under bond 4. to put under bonded debt —**bottled in bond** bottled and stored in bonded warehouses for the length of time stated on the label
bond·age (bän′dij) *n.* [ult. < ON. *bua,* inhabit] 1. serfdom; slavery 2. subjection to some force
bond′man (-mən) *n., pl.* **-men** 1. a feudal serf 2. a male slave —**bond′wom′an** *n.fem., pl.* **-wom′en**
bonds·man (bändz′mən) *n., pl.* **-men** 1. *same as* BONDMAN 2. one who furnishes bond, or surety
bone (bōn) *n.* [OE. *ban*] 1. any of the pieces of hard tissue forming the skeleton of most vertebrates 2. this hard tissue 3. [*pl.*] the skeleton 4. a bonelike substance or thing 5. [*pl.*] [Colloq.] dice —*vt.* **boned, bon′ing** to remove the bones from —*vi.* [Slang] to study hard (usually with *up*) —**feel in one's bones** to be certain without any real reason —**have a bone to pick** to have cause to quarrel —**make no bones about** [Colloq.] to admit freely —**bone′less** *adj.* —**bone′like′** *adj.*
bone′dry′ *adj.* very dry
bone meal crushed or ground bones, used as feed or fertilizer
bon·er (bōn′ər) *n.* [Slang] a stupid blunder
bon·fire (bän′fīr′) *n.* [ME. *banefyre,* bone fire, pyre] a large, outdoor fire
bong (bôŋ, bäŋ) *n.* [echoic] a deep ringing sound, as of a bell —*vi.* to make this sound
bon·go (bäŋ′gō) *n., pl.* **-gos** [AmSp. < ?] either of a pair of small joined drums, of different pitch, struck with the fingers: in full **bongo drum**
bo·ni·to (bə nēt′ō) *n., pl.* **-tos, -toes, -to** [Sp.] any of several saltwater fishes related to the tuna
‡**bon jour** (bôn zhōōr′) [Fr.] good day; hello

BONGO DRUMS

bon mot (bōn′ mō′) *pl.* **bons mots** (bōn BONGO DRUMS mōz′) [Fr., lit., good word] an apt, clever, or witty remark
Bonn (bän) capital of West Germany, on the Rhine: pop. 138,000
bon·net (bän′it) *n.* [OFr. *bonet*] 1. a flat, brimless cap, worn by men and boys in Scotland 2. a hat with a chin ribbon, worn by children and women 3. *short for* WAR BONNET —*vt.* to put a bonnet on
bon·ny, bon·nie (bän′ē) *adj.* **-ni·er, -ni·est** [< L. *bonus,* good] [Chiefly Scot.] 1. handsome or pretty, with a healthy glow 2. fine; pleasant
bon·sai (bän sī′) *n., pl.* **-sai** [Jpn.] a tree or shrub grown in a pot and dwarfed by pruning, etc.
bo·nus (bō′nəs) *n., pl.* **-nus·es** [L., good] anything given in addition to the usual or required amount
bon voy·age (bän′ voi äzh′) [Fr.] pleasant journey
bon·y (bō′nē) *adj.* **bon′i·er, bon′i·est** 1. of, like, or having bones 2. thin; emaciated —**bon′i·ness** *n.*
boo (bōō) *interj., n., pl.* **boos** a sound made to show disapproval, scorn, etc., or to startle —*vi., vt.* **booed, boo′ing** to make this sound
boob (bōōb) *n.* [Slang] a foolish person
boo-boo, boo·boo (bōō′bōō′) *n., pl.* **-boos′** [Slang] a stupid mistake
boo·by (bōō′bē) *n., pl.* **-bies** [prob. < Sp. *bobo*] 1. a stupid or foolish person 2. a tropical, diving sea bird related to the gannet 3. the one doing worst in a game, contest, etc.
booby prize a prize, usually ridiculous, given to whoever does the worst in a game, race, etc.
booby trap 1. any device for tricking a person unawares 2. a mine set to be exploded by some action of the unsuspecting victim
boo·dle (bōō′d'l) *n.* [< Du. *boedel,* property] [Slang] 1. something given as a bribe; graft 2. loot
boo·gie-woo·gie (boog′ē woog′ē) *n.* [? echoic] a style of jazz piano characterized by repeated bass figures in 8/8 rhythm
book (book) *n.* [OE. *boc*] 1. a printed work on sheets of paper bound together, usually between hard covers 2. a main division of a literary work 3. a record or account 4. a libretto 5. a booklike package, as of matches 6. a record of bets, as on horse races 7. *Bridge,* etc. a specified number of tricks that must be won before scoring can take place —*vt.* 1. to record in a book; list 2. to engage (rooms, etc.) ahead of time 3. to record charges against on a po-

lice record —*adj.* in, from, or according to books or accounts —**bring to book 1.** to force to explain **2.** to reprimand —**by the book** according to the rules —**keep books** to keep a record of business transactions —**the (Good) Book** the Bible —**book′er** *n.*

book′bind′ing *n.* the art or work of binding books — **book′bind′er** *n.* —**book′bind′er·y** *n., pl.* -**ies**

book′case′ *n.* a set of shelves for holding books

book′end′ *n.* a weight or bracket that keeps a row of books upright

book′ie (-ē) *n.* [Slang] *same as* BOOKMAKER (sense 2)

book′ing *n.* an engagement, as for a lecture, performance, etc.

book′ish (-ish) *adj.* **1.** inclined to read and study **2.** having mere book learning; pedantic

book′keep′ing *n.* the work of keeping a systematic record of business transactions —**book′keep′er** *n.*

book′let (-lit) *n.* a small, often paper-covered book

book′mak′er *n.* **1.** a maker of books **2.** a person in the business of taking bets, as on horse races

book′mark′ *n.* anything slipped between the pages of a book to mark a place

book′mo·bile′ (-mō bēl′) *n.* a traveling lending library moved from place to place in a truck

book′plate′ *n.* a label pasted in a book to identify its owner

book′worm′ *n.* **1.** an insect larva that harms books by feeding on the binding, paste, etc. **2.** one who reads or studies much

boom¹ (bōōm) *vi., vt.* [echoic] to make, or say with, a deep hollow sound —*n.* this sound

boom² (bōōm) *n.* [Du., a beam] **1.** a spar extending from a mast to hold the bottom of a sail outstretched **2.** a long beam extending as from an upright to lift and guide something **3.** a barrier, as of logs, to prevent floating logs from dispersing —*vi.* to sail at top speed (usually with *along*)

boom³ (bōōm) *vi.* [< prec. *vi.*] to increase or grow rapidly —*vt.* **1.** to cause to flourish **2.** to promote vigorously —*n.* a period of business prosperity, etc. —*adj.* of or resulting from such a period

boom·er·ang (bōōm′ə raŋ′) *n.* [< Australian native name] **1.** a flat, curved stick that can be thrown so that it will return to the thrower **2.** a scheme, etc. that goes awry, to the disadvantage of the schemer —*vi.* to act as a boomerang

boon¹ (bōōn) *n.* [ON. *bon,* a petition] **1.** a welcome benefit; blessing **2.** [Archaic] a request or favor

boon² (bōōn) *adj.* [< L. *bonus,* good] merry; convivial: now only in **boon companion**

boon·docks (bōōn′däks′) *n.pl.* [< Tag. *bundok,* mountain] [Colloq.] **1.** a wild, heavily wooded area; wilderness **2.** any remote rural region Used with *the*

boon·dog·gle (bōōn′dôg′′l) *vi.* -**gled,** -**gling** [Colloq.] to do trifling, pointless work —*n.* trifling, pointless work — **boon′dog′gler** *n.*

Boone (bōōn), **Daniel** 1734-1820; Am. frontiersman

boor (boor) *n.* [Du. *boer,* peasant] **1.** orig., a peasant **2.** a rude, awkward, or ill-mannered person —**boor′ish** *adj.* — **boor′ish·ly** *adv.* —**boor′ish·ness** *n.*

boost (bōōst) *vt.* [< ?] **1.** to raise as by a push from below **2.** to urge others to support **3.** to increase —*n.* **1.** a push upward or forward **2.** an increase —**boost′er** *n.*

booster shot (or **injection**) a later injection of a vaccine for maintaining immunity

boot¹ (bōōt) *n.* [OFr. *bote*] **1.** a covering of leather, rubber, etc. for the foot and part of the leg **2.** a patch for the inside of an automobile tire **3.** a kick **4.** [Colloq.] a thrill **5.** [Slang] a navy or marine recruit —*vt.* **1.** to put boots on **2.** to kick **3.** [Slang] to dismiss —**the boot** [Slang] dismissal; discharge

boot² (bōōt) *n., vt., vi.* [< OE. *bot,* advantage] [Archaic] profit —**to boot** besides; in addition

boot′black′ *n.* one whose work is shining shoes, etc.

boot·ee, boot·ie (bōōt′ē, bōō tē′) *n.* **1.** a short boot worn by women and children **2.** a baby's soft, knitted or cloth shoe

Bo·ö·tes (bō ō′tēz) a N constellation including the star Arcturus

booth (bōōth) *n., pl.* **booths** (bōōthz) [< ON. *bua,* dwell] **1.** a stall for the sale or display of goods, as at a market **2.** a small enclosure for voting at elections **3.** a small structure for housing a public telephone **4.** a small compartment, as at restaurants

boot′leg′ *vt., vi.* -**legged′,** -**leg′ging** [< hiding objects in a boot] to make or sell (esp. liquor) illegally —*adj.* bootlegged; illegal —*n.* bootlegged liquor —**boot′leg′ger** *n.*

boot′less *adj.* [BOOT² + -LESS] useless —**boot′less·ly** *adv.* —**boot′less·ness** *n.*

boot′lick′ (-lik′) *vt., vi.* [Colloq.] to try to gain favor with (someone) by fawning, servility, etc. —**boot′lick′er** *n.*

boo·ty (bōōt′ē) *n., pl.* -**ties** [< MLowG. *bute*] **1.** spoils of war **2.** any loot **3.** any prize

booze (bōōz) *vi.* boozed, booz′ing [< Du. *buizen*] [Colloq.] to drink too much alcoholic liquor —*n.* [Colloq.] alcoholic liquor —**booz′y** *adj.* -i·er, -i·est

bop (bäp) *n., vt.* bopped, bop′ping [Slang] hit

bo·rac·ic (bə ras′ik) *adj. same as* BORIC

bo·rate (bôr′āt) *n.* a salt or ester of boric acid —*vt.* -rat·ed, -rat·ing to treat with borax or boric acid

bo·rax (bôr′aks) *n.* [< Per. *būrah*] a white, crystalline salt, $Na_2B_4O_7$, used in glass, soaps, etc.

Bor·deaux (bôr dō′) seaport in SW France: pop. 267,000 —*n.* red or white wine from near Bordeaux

bor·der (bôr′dər) *n.* [< OHG. *bord,* margin] **1.** an edge or a part near an edge; margin **2.** a dividing line between countries, etc. **3.** a narrow strip along an edge —*vt.* **1.** to provide with a border **2.** to bound —*adj.* of or near a border —**border on** (or **upon**) **1.** to be next to **2.** to be like — **bor′dered** *adj.*

bor′der·land′ *n.* **1.** land near a border **2.** a vague, uncertain condition

bor′der·line′ *n.* a boundary —*adj.* on the boundary of what is acceptable, normal, etc.

bore¹ (bôr) *vt.* bored, bor′ing [< OE. *bor,* auger] **1.** to make a hole in with a drill, etc. **2.** to make (a hole, tunnel, etc.) as by drilling **3.** to weary by being dull —*vi.* to bore a hole or passage —*n.* **1.** a hole made as by boring **2.** *a)* the hollow part of a tube, gun barrel, etc. *b)* its inside diameter **3.** a tiresome, dull person or thing —**bor′er** *n.*

bore² (bôr) *pt. of* BEAR¹

bo·re·al (bôr′ē əl) *adj.* [< *Boreas*] **1.** northern **2.** of the north wind

Bo·re·as (bôr′ē əs) **1.** *Gr. Myth.* the god of the north wind **2.** the north wind personified

bore·dom (bôr′dəm) *n.* the condition of being bored or uninterested

bo·ric (bôr′ik) *adj.* of or containing boron

boric acid a white, crystalline, weakly acid compound, H_3BO_3, used as a mild antiseptic

born (bôrn) *alt. pp. of* BEAR¹ —*adj.* **1.** brought into life or being **2.** by birth **3.** natural *[a born athlete]*

born-a·gain (bôrn′ə gen′) *adj.* having undergone a spiritual conversion, esp. to evangelical Christianity

borne (bôrn) *pp. of* BEAR¹

Bor·ne·o (bôr′nē ō) large island in the Malay Archipelago: the S part is in Indonesia & the N part has a British-protected sultanate and part of Malaysia

bo·ron (bôr′än) *n.* [< BORAX] a nonmetallic chemical element occurring in borax, etc.: symbol, B; at. wt., 10.811; at. no., 5

bor·ough (bur′ō) *n.* [< OE. *burg,* town] **1.** a self-governing, incorporated town **2.** any of the five administrative units of New York City

bor·row (bär′ō, bôr′ō) *vt., vi.* [< OE. *borgian,* borrow] **1.** to take or receive (something) with the intention of returning it **2.** to adopt (an idea, etc.) as one's own — **bor′row·er** *n.*

borsch (bôrsh) *n.* [Russ. *borshch*] beet soup, served hot or cold, usually with sour cream: also **borsht** (bôrsht)

bor·zoi (bôr′zoi) *n.* [Russ., swift] a large dog with a narrow head, long legs, and silky coat

bosh (bäsh) *n., interj.* [Turk., empty] [Colloq.] nonsense

bosk·y (bäs′kē) *adj.* covered with trees or shrubs

bo's'n (bōs′′n) *n. contracted form of* BOATSWAIN

bos·om (booz′əm, bōō′zəm) *n.* [OE. *bosm*] **1.** the human breast **2.** a thing like this *[the bosom of the sea]* **3.** the breast regarded as the source of feelings **4.** the interior; midst *[in the bosom of one's family]* **5.** the part of a garment that covers the breast —*adj.* close; intimate *[a bosom companion]*

bos′om·y (-ē) *adj.* having large breasts

Bos·po·rus (bäs′pər əs) strait between the Black Sea & Sea of Marmara: also **Bos′pho·rus** (-far əs)

boss¹ (bôs) *n.* [Du. *baas,* a master] **1.** an employer or supervisor **2.** one who controls a political organization —*vt.* **1.** to act as boss of **2.** [Colloq.] to order (a person) about —*adj.* **1.** [Colloq.] chief **2.** [Slang] excellent; fine

boss² (bôs) *n.* [< OFr. *boce,* a swelling] a protruding ornament or decorative knob —*vt.* to decorate with knobs, studs, etc.

boss′ism *n.* control by bosses, esp. of a political party

boss′y *adj.* -i·er, -i·est [Colloq.] domineering —**boss′i·ly** *adv.* —**boss′i·ness** *n.*

Bos·ton (bôs't'n) capital of Mass.: pop. 641,000 (met. area 2,754,000) —**Bos·to'ni·an** (-tō'nē ən) *adj., n.*

Boston terrier a small dog having a smooth, dark coat with white markings

bo·sun (bōs''n) *n. same as* BOATSWAIN

Bos·well (bäz'wel), **James** 1740–95; Scot. writer; biographer of Samuel Johnson

bot·a·ny (bät''n ē) *n.* [< Gr. *botanē*, a plant] the science that deals with plants and plant life —**bo·tan·i·cal** (bə tan'i k'l), **bo·tan'ic** *adj.* —**bot'a·nist** *n.*

botch (bäch) *vt.* [< ? Du. *botsen*, to patch] 1. to patch clumsily 2. to bungle —*n.* a bungled piece of work — **botch'er** *n.* —**botch'y** *adj.*

both (bōth) *adj., pron.* [< OE. *ba tha*, both these] the two [*both* birds sang] —*conj., adv.* together; equally (with *and*) [*both* tired and sick]

both·er (bäth'ər) *vt., vi.* [prob. < *pother*] 1. to worry; harass 2. to concern (oneself) —*n.* 1. worry; trouble 2. one who gives trouble —**both'er·some** (-səm) *adj.*

Bot·swa·na (bät swä'nə) country in S Africa: 222,000 sq. mi.; pop. 629,000

Bot·ti·cel·li (bät'ə chel'ē), **San·dro** (sän'drō) 1445?–1510; It. Renaissance painter

bot·tle (bät''l) *n.* [< LL. *buttis*, a cask] 1. a narrow-necked container, esp. for liquids, usually of glass 2. its contents —*vt.* -**tled, -tling** to put into a bottle —**bottle up** 1. to restrain 2. to suppress (emotions) —**hit the bottle** [Slang] to drink much alcoholic liquor —**bot'tler** *n.*

bot·tle·neck' *n.* 1. a narrow passage or road which retards traffic 2. any hindrance to progress

bot·tom (bät'əm) *n.* [< OE. *botm*, ground] 1. the lowest part or place 2. the part on which something rests 3. the side underneath 4. the seat of a chair 5. the ground beneath a body of water 6. [*often pl.*] *same as* BOTTOM LAND 7. a ship's keel 8. basic meaning or cause; source 9. [Colloq.] the buttocks —*adj.* of, at, or on the bottom; lowest, last, etc. —*vt.* 1. to provide with a bottom 2. to base (*on* or *upon*) —*vi.* 1. to reach the bottom 2. to be based — **at bottom** fundamentally; actually —**bottom out** to level off at a low point —**bot'tom·less** *adj.*

bottom land low land through which a river flows, rich in alluvial deposits

bottom line 1. [Colloq.] profits or losses, as of a business 2. [Slang] *a)* the most important factor, consideration, etc. *b)* the final statement, decision, etc.

bot·u·lism (bäch'ə liz'm) *n.* [< L. *botulus*, sausage] poisoning resulting from the toxin produced by a bacillus sometimes found in improperly preserved foods

bou·clé, bou·cle (bōō klā') *n.* [Fr., curled] 1. a curly yarn that gives the fabric made from it a knotted texture 2. fabric made from this yarn

bou·doir (bōōd'wär) *n.* [Fr., lit., pouting room] a woman's bedroom, dressing room, etc.

bouf·fant (bōō fänt') *adj.* [< Fr. *bouffer*, puff out] puffed out; full, as some skirts

bou·gain·vil·le·a, bou·gain·vil·lae·a (bōō'gən vil'ē ə) *n.* [ModL.] a woody tropical vine having flowers with large, purple or red bracts

bough (bou) *n.* [OE. *bog*, shoulder] a branch of a tree, esp. a main branch

bought (bôt) *pt. & pp. of* BUY

bouil·lon (bōōl'yän, -yən) *n.* [Fr. < *bouillir*, to boil] a clear broth, esp. of beef

boul·der (bōl'dər) *n.* [< ME. *bulderstan* < Scand.] any large rock worn round by weather and water

boul·e·vard (bool'ə värd') *n.* [Fr. < MDu. *bolwerc*, bulwark] a broad street, often lined with trees

bounce (bouns) *vi.* **bounced, bounc'ing** [ME. *bounsen*, to thump] 1. to spring back after impact; rebound 2. to jump; leap 3. [Slang] to be returned: said of a worthless check —*vt.* 1. to cause (a ball, etc.) to bounce 2. [Slang] to put (a person) out by force 3. [Slang] to fire from a job —*n.* 1. a bouncing; rebound 2. a leap or jump 3. capacity for bouncing 4. [Colloq.] energy; zest —**the bounce** [Slang] dismissal —**bounc'y** *adj.*

bounc'er *n.* [Slang] a man hired to remove disorderly people from a nightclub, etc.

bounc'ing *adj.* big, healthy, strong, etc.

bound[1] (bound) *vi.* [Fr. *bondir*, to leap] 1. to move with a leap or leaps 2. to bounce or rebound —*vt.* to cause to bound or bounce —*n.* 1. a jump; leap 2. a bounce; rebound

bound[2] (bound) *pt. & pp. of* BIND —*adj.* 1. tied 2. closely connected 3. certain [*bound* to win] 4. obliged [legally

bound to pay] 5. having a binding, as a book 6. [Colloq.] determined; resolved —**bound up in** (or **with**) 1. devoted to 2. involved in

bound[3] (bound) *adj.* [< ON. *bua*, prepare] going; headed [*bound* for home]

bound[4] (bound) *n.* [< ML. *bodina*, boundary] 1. a boundary 2. [*pl.*] an area near a boundary —*vt.* 1. to limit; confine 2. to be a limit or boundary to 3. to name the boundaries of —*vi.* to have a boundary (*on*) —**out of bounds** 1. beyond the boundaries 2. forbidden —**bound'less** *adj.*

bound·a·ry (boun'drē, -dər ē) *n., pl.* -**ries** anything marking a limit; bound; border

bound'en (-dən) *adj.* [old pp. of BIND] 1. under obligation 2. obligatory [*bounden* duty]

bound'er *n.* [< BOUND[1]] [Chiefly Brit. Colloq.] an ill-mannered fellow; cad

boun·te·ous (boun'tē əs) *adj.* [see BOUNTY] 1. generous 2. abundant Also **boun'ti·ful** (-tə f'l)

boun'ty (-tē) *n., pl.* -**ties** [< L. *bonus*, good] 1. generosity 2. a generous gift 3. a reward or premium

bou·quet (bō kā', bōō-) *n.* [Fr.] 1. a bunch of cut flowers 2. aroma, esp. of wine or brandy

bour·bon (bur'bən, boor'-) *n.* [< *Bourbon* County, Ky.] [*sometimes* B-] a whiskey distilled from corn mash and aged for not less than two years

bour·geois (boor zhwä') *n., pl.* -**geois'** [< LL. *burgus*, castle] a member of the bourgeoisie —*adj.* of the bourgeoisie; conventional, smug, etc.

bour·geoi·sie (boor'zhwä'zē') *n.* [*with sing. or pl. v.*] the social class between the very wealthy and the working class; middle class

bourn[1], **bourne**[1] (bôrn, boorn) *n.* [OE. *burna*, a stream] a brook or stream

bourn[2], **bourne**[2] (bôrn, boorn) *n.* [< ML. *bodina*, boundary] [Archaic] 1. a boundary 2. a goal 3. a domain

bout (bout) *n.* [< OE. *bugan*, to bend] 1. a contest or match 2. a period of activity, illness, etc.

bou·tique (bōō tēk') *n.* [Fr., ult. < Gr. *apo-*, away + *tithenai*, put] a small, elegant shop

bou·ton·niere, bou·ton·nière (bōōt''n ir', -yer') *n.* [Fr., buttonhole] a flower worn in a buttonhole

hou·var·di·a (bōō vär'dē ə) *n.* [< C. *Bouvard*, 17th-c. Fr. physician] a showy flower related to madders

bo·vine (bō'vīn) *adj.* [< L. *bos*, ox] 1. of or like an ox or cow 2. slow, dull, etc. —*n.* an ox or related animal

bow[1] (bou) *vi.* [OE. *bugan*, to bend] 1. to bend the head or body in respect, agreement, etc. 2. to submit; yield — *vt.* 1. to bend (the head), as in respect 2. to weigh (*down*); overwhelm —*n.* a bending of the head or body, as in respect

bow[2] (bō) *n.* [see prec.] 1. anything curved 2. a flexible, curved strip, as of wood, with a taut cord connecting the ends, designed to shoot arrows 3. a slender stick strung with horsehairs, used in playing a violin, cello, etc. 4. *same as* BOWKNOT —*vt., vi.* 1. to curve like a bow (sense 2) 2. to play, as a violin, with a bow

bow[3] (bou) *n.* [< LowG. or Scand.] the front part of a ship or boat —*adj.* of or near the bow

bowd·ler·ize (boud'lə rīz') *vt.* -**ized'**, -**iz'ing** [< Thomas *Bowdler*, who published an expurgated Shakespeare (1818)] to expurgate —**bowd'ler·i·za'tion** *n.*

bow·el (bou'əl) *n.* [< L. *botulus*, sausage] 1. an intestine 2. [*pl.*] the inside [the *bowels* of the earth] —**move one's bowels** to defecate

bowel movement 1. defecation 2. feces

bow·er (bou'ər) *n.* [OE. *bur*, a dwelling] a place enclosed by leafy boughs or by vines; arbor

Bow·er·y (bou'ər ē) a street in New York City, characterized by flophouses, saloons, etc.

bow·ie knife (bōō'ē, bō'ē) [< Col. J. *Bowie*, Am. frontiersman] a long, single-edged knife of steel, orig. carried as a weapon by frontiersmen

bow·knot (bō'nät') *n.* a decorative knot, usually with two loops, untied by pulling the ends

bowl[1] (bōl) *n.* [OE. *bolla*] 1. a deep, rounded dish 2. a large drinking cup 3. a bowllike thing or part, as a stadium or as the bowllike end of a spoon or smoking pipe 4. the contents of a bowl

BOWIE KNIFE

bowl[2] (bōl) *n.* [< L. *bulla*, a bubble] 1. a heavy ball used in the game of bowls 2. a roll of the ball in bowling or bowls —*vt., vi.* 1. to roll (a ball) or participate in bowling or bowls 2. to move swiftly and smoothly **3.** *Cricket* to throw (a ball) to the batter —**bowl over 1.** to knock over **2.** [Colloq.] to astonish —**bowl′er** *n.*

bowl·der (bōl′dər) *n. alt. sp. of* BOULDER

bow·leg (bō′leg′) *n.* a leg that has an outward curvature —**bow′leg′ged** (-leg′id, -legd′) *adj.*

bowl·er (bōl′ər) *n.* [< *Bowler*, a 19th-c. London hat manufacturer] [Brit.] a derby hat

bow·line (bō′lin, -līn′) *n.* [ME. *boueline*] **1.** a rope to keep the sail taut when a ship is sailing into the wind **2.** a knot to fix a loop in place

bowl′ing *n.* **1.** a game in which a heavy ball is bowled along a wooden lane (**bowling alley**) at large, wooden pins **2.** *same as* BOWLS

bowls (bōlz) *n.* **1.** a game played on a smooth lawn (**bowling green**) with wooden balls rolled to stop near a target ball **2.** ninepins or tenpins

bow·man (bō′mən) *n., pl.* **-men** an archer

bow′shot′ *n.* the distance traveled by an arrow

bow·sprit (bou′sprit, bō′-) *n.* [prob. < Du.] a tapered spar extending forward from the bow of a sailing ship

bow tie (bō) a necktie tied in a bowknot

box¹ (bäks) *n.* [< Gr. *pyxos*, boxwood] **1.** a container made of wood, cardboard, or other stiff material, usually rectangular and with a lid **2.** its contents **3.** the driver's seat on a coach **4.** a boxlike thing, as a booth, stall, or compartment; specifically, a small, enclosed section of seats as in a theater **5.** a reserved or special area or space; specifically, *Baseball*, such an area as for the batter —*vt.* to put into a box —*adj.* **1.** boxlike **2.** packaged in a box —**box in** (or **up**) to shut in or confine

box² (bäks) *n.* [< ?] a blow struck with the hand, esp. on the ear —*vt., vi.* **1.** to strike with such a blow **2.** to fight in a boxing match

box³ (bäks) *n.* [< Gr. *pyxos*] an evergreen shrub or small tree with small, leathery leaves

box′car′ *n.* a fully enclosed railroad freight car

box′er *n.* **1.** one that fights in boxing matches; pugilist or prizefighter **2.** a medium-sized, smooth-coated, sturdy dog, brown in color

box′ing *n.* the skill or sport of fighting with the fists, esp. using padded leather mittens (**boxing gloves**)

box office 1. a place selling admission tickets, as in a theater **2.** [Colloq.] drawing power of a show or performer as measured by ticket sales

box score a statistical summary of a baseball game, showing the hits, runs, errors, etc.

box spring a boxlike, cloth-enclosed framework containing rows of springs in coil form: it is put on a bedstead to support the mattress

box·wood (bäks′wood′) *n.* **1.** the wood of the box (the shrub or tree) **2.** the shrub or tree producing this: see BOX³

box′y *adj.* **-i·er, -i·est** like a box (container)

boy (boi) *n.* [ME. *boie*] **1.** a male child from birth to physical maturity **2.** an immature man **3.** any man: familiar term **4.** a male servant, porter, etc.: patronizing term **5.** a bellboy, messenger boy, etc. **6.** [Colloq.] a son —*interj.* [Slang] an exclamation of pleasure, surprise, etc.: often **oh, boy!** —**boy′ish** *adj.* —**boy′ish·ly** *adv.* —**boy′ish·ness** *n.*

boy·cott (boi′kät) *vt.* [< a Captain *Boycott* of Ireland, so treated in 1880] **1.** to join together in refusing to deal with, so as to punish, coerce, etc. **2.** to refuse to buy, sell, or use (something) —*n.* the act of boycotting

boy′friend′ *n.* [Colloq.] **1.** a sweetheart or escort of a girl or woman **2.** a boy who is one's friend

boy′hood′ *n.* **1.** the time or state of being a boy **2.** boys collectively

boy scout a member of the **Boy Scouts**, a worldwide boys' organization that stresses outdoor life and service to others

boy·sen·ber·ry (boi′z'n ber′ē, bois′'n-) *n., pl.* **-ries** [< R. *Boysen*, U.S. horticulturist] a large, purple berry, developed by crossing the raspberry, loganberry, and blackberry

Br *Chem.* bromine

Br. 1. Breton **2.** Britain **3.** British

br. 1. branch **2.** bronze **3.** brother **4.** brown

bra (brä) *n.* an undergarment worn by women to support and shape the breasts; brassiere

brace (brās) *vt.* **braced, brac′ing** [< Gr. *brachiōn*, an arm] **1.** to tie or bind **2.** to tighten **3.** to strengthen or make firm as by supporting or propping up **4.** to equip with braces **5.** to ready as for a shock **6.** to stimulate **7.** to get a firm hold with (the hands or feet) —*n.* **1.** a couple; pair **2.** a device that clasps or connects; fastener **3.** [*pl.*] [Brit.] suspenders **4.** a device to maintain tension **5.** either of

the signs { } , used to connect words, lines, etc. **6.** a device that supports, props up, etc.; specif., [*often pl.*], a device to correct faulty growth of the teeth **7.** a device for holding and rotating a drilling bit —**brace up** [Colloq.] to call forth one's courage, resolution, etc.

brace and bit a tool for boring, consisting of a removable drill (*bit*) in a rotating handle (*brace*)

brace·let (brās′lit) *n.* [see BRACE] **1.** an ornamental, circular strip or series of links for wearing about the wrist or arm **2.** [Colloq.] a handcuff

brac·er (brā′sər) *n.* **1.** one that braces **2.** [Slang] a drink of alcoholic liquor

bra·chi·o·pod (brā′kē ə päd′, brak′ē-) *n.* [< Gr. *brachiōn*, an arm + -POD] a marine animal with hinged upper and lower shells and two armlike parts

bra·chi·um (brā′kē əm, brak′ē-) *n., pl.* **-chi·a** (-ə) [L.] the part of the arm from shoulder to elbow

brac·ing (brās′iŋ) *adj.* invigorating;  BRACE AND BIT stimulating

brack·en (brak′'n) *n.* [< ON.] **1.** any large, coarse fern **2.** a growth of these

brack·et (brak′it) *n.* [< Gaul. *braca*, pants] **1.** an architectural support projecting from a wall **2.** any angle-shaped support **3.** either of the signs [ ], used to enclose words, figures, etc. **4.** the part of a classified grouping that falls within specified limits [a $5 to $10 price *bracket*] —*vt.* **1.** to support with brackets **2.** to enclose in brackets **3.** to classify together

brack·ish (brak′ish) *adj.* [< MDu. *brak*, salty] **1.** rather briny **2.** unpleasant or nauseating in taste

bract (brakt) *n.* [L. *bractea*, thin metal plate] a usually small, scalelike leaf at the base of a flower —**brac·te·al** (brak′tē əl) *adj.*

brad (brad) *n.* [ON. *broddr*, a spike] a thin wire nail —*vt.* **brad′ded, brad′ding** to fasten with such

brae (brā) *n.* [ON. *bra*, eyelid, brow] [Scot.] a sloping bank; hillside

brag (brag) *vt., vi.* **bragged, brag′ging** [prob. < OFr. *braguer*, to boast] to boast —*n.* **1.** boastful talk or manner **2.** [Colloq.] anything boasted of; boast —**brag′ger** *n.*

brag·ga·do·ci·o (brag′ə dō′shē ō, -shō) *n., pl.* **-os** [< BRAG + It. ending] **1.** a braggart **2.** a bragging

brag·gart (brag′ərt) *n.* one that brags offensively

Brah·ma (brä′mə) the chief member of the Hindu trinity (Brahma, Vishnu, and Siva) and creator of the universe — *n.* (brä′-) *same as* BRAHMAN (sense 2)

Brah·man (brä′mən) *n., pl.* **-mans** [< Sans., worship] **1.** a member of the priestly Hindu caste, the highest **2.** (brä′-) a breed of domestic cattle developed from the zebu of India

Brah·min (brä′mən) *n.* **1.** *same as* BRAHMAN (sense 1) **2.** a cultured, upper-class person

Brahms (brämz), **Jo·han·nes** (yō hän′əs) 1833–1897; Ger. composer

braid (brād) *vt.* [OE. *bregdan*, move quickly] **1.** to interweave three or more strands of (hair, straw, etc.) **2.** to make thus **3.** to trim or bind with braid —*n.* **1.** a braided band or strip **2.** a woven band, as of ribbon, for binding or decorating

Braille (brāl) *n.* [< L. *Braille*, its 19th-c. Fr. inventor] [*also* b-] **1.** a system of printing for the blind, using raised dots to be touched **2.** the symbols so made —*vt.* **Brailled, Brail′ling** [*also* b-] to print or write in such symbols

brain (brān) *n.* [OE. *brægen*] **1.** the mass of nerve tissue in the cranium **2.** [*often pl.*] intelligence **3.** [Colloq.] a very intelligent person **4.** [Colloq.] the main planner or organizer —*vt.* to dash out the brains of —**beat** (or **rack, cudgel,** etc.) **one's brains** to try hard to remember, understand, etc.

brain′case′ *n. same as* BRAINPAN

brain′child′ *n.* [Colloq.] an idea one has thought up

brain′less *adj.* foolish or stupid

CEREBRUM
CEREBELLUM
MEDULLA OBLONGATA
SPINAL CORD

BRAIN OF MAN

brain′pan′ *n.* the skull part enclosing the brain

brain′storm′ *n.* [Colloq.] a sudden inspiration

brain′wash′ *vt.* [Colloq.] to indoctrinate so intensively as to make change radically in mind

brain'y *adj.* -i·er, -i·est [Colloq.] highly intellectual; very intelligent —**brain'i·ness** *n.*

braise (brāz) *vt.* **braised, brais'ing** [< Gmc. *brasa,* live coals] to brown (meat) in fat and then simmer in a covered pan with only a little liquid

brake[1] (brāk) *n.* [prob. taken as sing. of BRACKEN] a large, coarse fern; bracken

brake[2] (brāk) *n.* [< MLowG. or ODu.] 1. a device to beat out the fiber from flax or hemp 2. a device used in a vehicle or machine to slow or stop movement —*vt., vi.* **braked, brak'ing** 1. to beat (flax or hemp) 2. to slow or stop as with a brake

brake[3] (brāk) *n.* [MLowG., stumps] a clump of brushwood, briers, etc.

brake'man *n., pl.* -men a brake operator on a train, now chiefly an assistant to the conductor

bram·ble (bram'b'l) *n.* [OE. *brom,* broom] a prickly shrub, specif., one related to the rose

bran (bran) *n.* [OFr. *bren*] the husks separated from grains of wheat, rye, oats, etc.

branch (branch) *n.* [< LL. *branca,* a paw] 1. a woody extension from a tree or shrub, as from the trunk of a tree 2. something branchlike; specif., *a*) a division or tributary of a river *b*) a subsidiary part or extension as of an organization, family, or field of study —*vi.* 1. to put forth branches 2. to emerge as a branch —*vt.* to separate into branches —**branch off** to extend, diverge, or separate as a branch —**branch out** to extend interests, activities, etc.

branch water 1. water from a small stream or brook 2. ordinary water used for mixing as with whiskey

brand (brand) *n.* [OE.] 1. a burning or partially burned stick 2. a mark burned on the skin with a hot iron, as on cattle to show ownership; also, the iron used 3. a mark of disgrace; stigma 4. *a*) an identifying mark or label on a product; trademark *b*) the kind or make of a commodity [*a brand* of cigars] *c*) a special kind or variety [*a brand* of comedy] —*vt.* to mark with a brand

bran·dish (bran'dish) *vt.* [< Gmc. *brand,* sword] to wave, shake, or show in a menacing, challenging, or exultant way; flourish —*n.* a brandishing

brand name the name by which a brand or make of commodity is known —**brand'-name'** *adj.*

brand'-new' *adj.* [orig., fresh from the fire] 1. altogether new 2. recently acquired

bran·dy (bran'dē) *n., pl.* -dies [< Du. *brandewijn,* distilled wine] 1. an alcoholic liquor distilled from wine 2. a similar liquor distilled from fermented fruit juice —*vt.* -died, -dy·ing to flavor, mix, or preserve with brandy

brant (brant) *n.* [< ?] a small wild goose, dark in color, of Europe and N. America

brash (brash) *adj.* [< ?] 1. reckless 2. impudent

Bra·sí·lia (brə zē'lyə) capital of Brazil, in the EC part: pop. 400,000

brass (bras) *n.* [OE. *bræs*] 1. a yellowish metal, an alloy of copper and zinc 2. things made of brass 3. [*often pl.*] brass-wind musical instruments 4. [Colloq.] bold impudence 5. [*often with pl. v.*] [Slang] high-ranking officers or officials —*adj.* of or containing brass

bras·siere, bras·sière (brə zir') *n.* [ult. < Fr. *bras,* an arm] *same as* BRA

brass knuckles linked metal rings or a metal bar with finger holes, worn for rough fighting

brass tacks [Colloq.] basic facts; practical details

brass winds (windz) musical instruments made of coiled metal tubes and having a cup-shaped mouthpiece, as the trumpet and tuba —**brass'-wind'** *adj.*

brass'y *adj.* -i·er, -i·est 1. of, like, or decorated with brass 2. cheap and showy 3. blaring 4. impudent —**brass'i·ly** *adv.* —**brass'i·ness** *n.*

brat (brat) *n.* [< Gael. *bratt,* cloth] a child, esp. when impudent and unruly: scornful or playful term

brat·wurst (brat'wərst; G. brät'voorsht) *n.* [G. < OHG. < *brato,* lean meat + *wurst,* sausage] highly seasoned, fresh sausage of veal and pork

bra·va·do (brə vä'dō) *n.* [< Sp. < *bravo,* BRAVE] pretended courage or feigned confidence

brave (brāv) *adj.* **brav'er, brav'est** [Fr. < It. < L. *barbarus,* barbarous] 1. not afraid; courageous 2. having a fine appearance —*n.* 1. a brave man 2. a N. American Indian warrior —*vt.* **braved, brav'ing** 1. to face with courage 2. to defy; dare —**brave'ly** *adv.* —**brave'ness** *n.*

brav·er·y (brā'vər ē) *n.* braveness; courage

bra·vo (brä'vō) *interj.* [It.] well done! excellent! —*n., pl.* -vos a shout of "bravo!"

bra·vu·ra (brə vyoor'ə) *n.* [It. < *bravo,* brave] 1. a display of daring; dash 2. *Music a*) a passage or piece displaying the performer's skill *b*) brilliant technique

brawl (brôl) *vi.* [< ? Du. *brallen,* to boast] to quarrel or fight noisily —*n.* 1. a noisy quarrel or fight 2. [Slang] a noisy party —**brawl'er** *n.*

brawn (brôn) *n.* [< Frank. *brado,* meat] 1. strong, well-developed muscles 2. muscular strength —**brawn'i·ness** *n.* —**brawn'y** *adj.* -i·er, -i·est

bray (brā) *vi.* [< VL. *bragire,* cry out] to make the loud, harsh cry of a donkey —*vt.* to utter thus —*n.* such a cry

braze[1] (brāz) *vt.* **brazed, braz'ing** [Fr. *braser,* to solder < Gmc. *brasa,* live coals] to solder with a metal having a high melting point

braze[2] (brāz) *vt.* **brazed, braz'ing** [< OE. *bræs,* brass] 1. to cover with brass 2. to make hard like brass

bra·zen (brā'z'n) *adj.* [see prec.] 1. of or like brass 2. shameless 3. harsh and piercing —**brazen it out** to behave as if not ashamed —**bra'zen·ly** *adv.* —**bra'zen·ness** *n.*

bra·zier[1] (brā'zhər) *n.* [see BRAISE] a metal container to hold live coals

bra·zier[2] (brā'zhər) *n.* a person who works in brass

Bra·zil (brə zil') country in C & NE S. America; 3,287,000 sq. mi.; pop. 90,990,000; cap. Brasilia —**Bra·zil'ian** *adj., n.*

Brazil nut 1. a hard-shelled, three-sided, oily, edible seed of a tall S. American tree 2. the tree

breach (brēch) *n.* [< OE. *brecan,* to break] 1. a violation or infraction as of a law, contract, or proper form of behavior 2. an opening broken through a wall, line of defense, etc. 3. a break in friendly relations —*vt.* to make a breach in

breach of promise a breaking of a promise to marry

bread (bred) *n.* [OE., crumb, morsel] 1. a food baked from a leavened, kneaded dough made with flour or meal, water, yeast, etc. 2. one's livelihood: also **bread and butter** 3. [Slang] money —*vt.* to cover with bread crumbs before cooking —**break bread** to eat

bread-and-butter letter a letter of thanks sent to one's host after a visit

bread'bas'ket *n.* [Slang] the stomach

bread'fruit' *n.* a large, round, starchy fruit of the tropics, breadlike when baked

bread line a line of people waiting to be given food as government relief or private charity

bread'stuff' *n.* 1. ground grain or flour for making bread 2. bread

breadth (bredth) *n.* [< OE. *brad,* broad] 1. width 2. lack of narrowness or limitation; broadness

bread'win'ner *n.* one working to support dependents

break (brāk) *vt.* **broke, bro'ken, break'ing** [OE. *brecan*] 1. to split or crack into pieces by force; smash 2. to cut open the surface of (soil, the skin, etc.) 3. to check or end by force [to *break* a strike] 4. to make useless or ruin as by cracking or shattering 5. to tame as with force 6. *a*) to cause to get rid (*of* a habit) *b*) to get rid of (a habit) 7. to demote 8. to make poor or bankrupt 9. to surpass (a record) 10. to violate, as a law 11. to get into or out of by force 12. to disrupt, as the order of ranks 13. to interrupt (a journey, electric circuit, etc.) 14. to lessen the force of, as a fall, by interrupting 15. to end suddenly, as a tie score 16. to penetrate, as darkness 17. to disclose 18. to decipher or solve 19. to exchange (a bill or coin) for smaller units —*vi.* 1. to become split or cracked into pieces 2. to separate or scatter [*break* and run] 3. to force one's way (*through*) 4. to stop associating (*with*) 5. to become useless or ruined 6. to shift or change suddenly [his voice *broke*] 7. to move away or apart suddenly 8. to move suddenly into doing something [*break* into song] 9. to become disclosed 10. to begin to appear [dawn *broke*] 11. to stop activity temporarily 12. to fall apart, disintegrate, or collapse 13. [Colloq.] to happen —*n.* 1. a breaking 2. a broken place 3. a beginning to appear [the *break* of day] 4. an interruption of regularity 5. an interval, gap, or rest 6. a sudden change 7. an escape 8. [Slang] a piece of luck —**break down** 1. to go out of working order 2. to collapse physically or emotionally 3. to analyze —**break in** 1. to enter forcibly 2. to interrupt 3. to train (a beginner) 4. to get the stiffness out of —**break off** 1. to stop abruptly 2. to stop being friendly —**break out** 1. to begin suddenly 2. to escape 3. to get pimples or a rash —**break up** 1. to separate; disperse 2. to stop 3. [Colloq.] to end a relationship 4. [Colloq.] to upset; distress 5. [Colloq.] to laugh or make laugh uncontrollably —**break'a·ble** *adj.*

break'age (-ij) *n.* 1. a breaking 2. things or quantity broken 3. loss or damage due to breaking 4. the sum allowed for this

break'down' *n.* 1. a breaking down 2. an analysis

break'er *n.* 1. one that breaks 2. a wave breaking into foam against a shore or reef

break'-e'ven *adj.* designating that point at which profits and losses are equal

break·fast (brek'fəst) *n.* the first meal of the day —*vi.* to eat this —*vt.* to give breakfast to

break·front (brāk'frunt') *adj.* having a front with a projecting section —*n.* such a cabinet

break'-in' *n.* forcible entry, as into a building, esp. so as to commit burglary —*adj.* of the period of initial use of something new

break'neck' *adj.* dangerously fast

break'through' *n.* 1. the act or place of breaking through against resistance 2. a strikingly important advance or discovery

break'up' *n.* a breaking up; specif., *a)* dispersion *b)* disintegration *c)* collapse *d)* termination

break'wa'ter *n.* a barrier against wave impact

bream (brēm, brim) *n., pl.* **bream, breams** [< Frank. *brahsima*] 1. a European freshwater fish related to minnows 2. any of various saltwater fishes 3. any of various freshwater sunfishes

breast (brest) *n.* [OE. *breost*] 1. either of two milk-secreting glands at the upper, front part of a woman's body 2. a corresponding gland in many animals 3. the upper, front part of the body 4. the part of a shirt, dress, etc. covering the breast 5. the breast regarded as the center of emotion —*vt.* to face firmly —**make a clean breast of** to confess (crimes, faults, etc.) fully

breast'bone' *n. same as* STERNUM

breast'-feed' *vt.* **-fed'**, **-feed'ing** to feed (a baby) milk from the breast; suckle

breast'pin' *n.* an ornamental pin or brooch worn on a dress, near the throat

breast'plate' *n.* a piece of armor for the breast

breast stroke a swimming stroke in which both arms are brought out sideways from the chest

breast'work' *n.* a low wall put up quickly as a defense, esp. to protect gunners

breath (breth) *n.* [OE. *brǣth*, odor] 1. air taken into and let out of the lungs 2. respiration 3. power to breathe easily 4. life; spirit 5. a fragrant odor 6. a slight movement of air 7. a whisper; murmur —**below** (or **under**) **one's breath** in a whisper —**catch one's breath** 1. to gasp 2. to pause so as to breathe normally —**out of breath** gasping, as from running —**take one's breath away** to thrill

breathe (brēth) *vi., vt.* **breathed, breath'ing** [see prec.] 1. to take (air) into the lungs and let out again; inhale and exhale 2. to live 3. to instill 4. to speak or sing softly; whisper 5. to rest

breath·er (brē'thər) *n.* 1. one that breathes 2. [Colloq.] a pause as for rest

breath·less (breth'lis) *adj.* 1. lacking breath 2. dead 3. gasping 4. devoid of the slightest movement of air — **breath'less·ly** *adv.*

breath'tak'ing *adj.* very exciting

breath·y (breth'ē) *adj.* **-i·er, -i·est** of or marked by audible emission of breath —**breath'i·ly** *adv.*

bred (bred) *pt. & pp. of* BREED

breech (brēch) *n.* [OE. *brec*] 1. the buttocks 2. the part of a gun behind the barrel

breech'cloth' *n. same as* LOINCLOTH

breech·es (brich'iz) *n.pl.* 1. trousers reaching to the knees 2. [Colloq.] any trousers

breeches buoy a rescue device consisting of a ring-shaped life preserver that is suspended from a rope run as between two ships and that has a trouserlike canvas piece attached so as to carry a person seated in it

breed (brēd) *vt.* **bred, breed'ing** [< OE. *brod*, fetus] 1. to bring forth (offspring) 2. to originate; produce 3. to raise (animals) 4. to rear; train —*vi.* 1. to be produced 2. to reproduce —*n.* 1. a stock; strain 2. a sort; type —**breed'er** *n.*

BREECHES BUOY

breed'ing *n.* 1. the act of one that breeds 2. good upbringing or training

breeze (brēz) *n.* [< Fr. *brise*] 1. a gentle wind 2. [Colloq.] a thing easy to do —*vi.* **breezed, breez'ing** [Slang] to move or go quickly, jauntily, etc.

breeze'way' *n.* a covered passageway, as between a home and a garage

breez·y (brēz'ē) *adj.* **-i·er, -i·est** 1. with breezes 2. light and gay —**breez'i·ly** *adv.* —**breez'i·ness** *n.*

Bre·men (brem'ən; *G.* brā'mən) seaport in N West Germany: pop. 604,000

Bren·ner Pass (bren'ər) mountain pass across the Alps at the border between Italy & Austria

breth·ren (breth'rən) *n.pl.* brothers: now chiefly in religious use

Bret·on (bret''n) *adj.* of Brittany, its people, or their language —*n.* 1. a native or inhabitant of Brittany 2. the Celtic language of the Bretons

breve (brev, brēv) *n.* [It. < L. *brevis*, brief] 1. a mark (˘) put over a short vowel or short or unstressed syllable 2. *Music* a note equal to two whole notes

bre·vet (brə vet'; *chiefly Brit.* brev'it) *n.* [< OFr., a note < L. *brevis*, brief] *Mil.* a commission giving an officer a higher honorary rank without more pay —*adj.* held by brevet —*vt.* **-vet'ted** or **-vet'ed, -vet'ting** or **-vet'ing** to give a brevet to —**bre·vet'cy** *n., pl.* **-cies**

bre·vi·ar·y (brē'vē er'ē, brev'yər ē) *n., pl.* **-ies** [< L. *brevis*, brief] *R.C.Ch.* a book of prayers, hymns, etc. to be said daily by priests and other clerics

brev·i·ty (brev'ə tē) *n.* [< L. *brevis*, brief] the quality of being brief; conciseness

brew (broo) *vt.* [OE. *breowan*] 1. to make (beer, ale, etc.) from malt and hops by steeping, boiling, and fermenting 2. to make (tea, coffee, etc.) by steeping or boiling 3. to plot; scheme —*vi.* 1. to brew beer, ale, etc. 2. to begin to form: said of a storm, trouble, etc. —*n.* a brewed beverage —**brew'er** *n.*

brew'er·y (-ər ē) *n., pl.* **-er·ies** an establishment where beer, ale, etc. are brewed

Brezh·nev (brezh'nef, -nev), **Le·o·nid I**(lich) (lā'ô nyēt') 1906– ; general secretary of the Communist Party of the U.S.S.R. (1964–)

bri·ar¹ (brī'ər) *n. same as* BRIER¹ —**bri'ar·y** *adj.*

bri·ar² (brī'ər) *n.* 1. *same as* BRIER² (senses 1 & 2) 2. a tobacco pipe made of brierroot

bri'ar·root' *n. same as* BRIERROOT Also **bri'ar·wood'**

bribe (brīb) *n.* [< OFr. *briber*, beg] anything given or promised as an inducement, esp. to do something illegal or wrong —*vt.* **bribed, brib'ing** 1. to offer or give a bribe to 2. to get or influence thus —**brib'a·ble** *adj.* —**brib'er** *n.* —**brib'er·y** *n.*

bric-a-brac (brik'ə brak') *n.* [< Fr. *à bric et à brac*, by hook or crook] small, ornamental objects set about as on shelves, to decorate a room

brick (brik) *n.* [< MDu. *breken*] 1. an oblong block of baked clay, used as in building; also, such blocks collectively, or the material used 2. anything bricklike in shape 3. [Colloq.] a fine fellow —*adj.* of or like brick —*vt.* to build or cover with brick

brick'bat' *n.* 1. a piece of brick, esp. when used as a missile 2. an unfavorable remark

brick'lay'ing *n.* the act or work of building or covering with bricks —**brick'lay'er** *n.*

brid·al (brīd''l) *adj.* [OE. *bryd ealo*, marriage feast] of a bride or wedding

bridal wreath a shrub with many small, white flowers, related to the rose

bride (brīd) *n.* [OE. *bryd*] a woman just married or about to be married

bride'groom' *n.* [< OE. *bryd*, bride + *guma*, man] a man just married or about to be married

brides·maid (brīdz'mād') *n.* a young woman attending the bride at a wedding

bridge¹ (brij) *n.* [OE. *brycge*] 1. a structure built over a river, railroad, etc. to provide a way across 2. a thing providing connection, contact, etc. 3. the bony part of the nose 4. a thin arch over which strings as of a violin are stretched 5. a raised platform on a ship 6. a mounting for artificial teeth —*vt.* **bridged, bridg'ing** to build or provide a bridge over or between

bridge² (brij) *n.* [< ? Russ.] any of various card games developed from whist, as contract bridge

bridge'head' *n.* a fortified position established by an attacking force in enemy territory

Bridge·port (brij'pôrt') seaport in SW Conn., on Long Island Sound: pop. 155,000

bridge'work' *n.* a dental bridge or bridges

bri·dle (brīd''l) *n.* [< OE. *bregdan*, to pull] 1. a head harness for guiding a horse 2. anything that controls or restrains —*vt.* **-dled, -dling 1.** to put a bridle on **2.** to hold in check; restrain —*vi.* to draw one's head back as in anger

bridle path a path for horseback riding

brief (brēf) *adj.* [< L. *brevis*] **1.** short in duration or extent **2.** concise **3.** curt —*n.* **1.** a summary **2.** *Law* a concise statement of the main points of a case **3.** *R.C.Ch.* a papal letter less formal than a bull **4.** [*pl.*] legless underpants —*vt.* **1.** to summarize **2.** to supply with all pertinent information —**hold a brief for** to argue for; support —**in brief** in a few words —**brief'ing** *n.* —**brief'ly** *adv.* — **brief'ness** *n.*

brief'case' *n.* a flat, flexible case for carrying papers, books, etc.

bri·er[1] (brī'ər) *n.* [OE. *brer*] **1.** a thorny bush, as a bramble **2.** a growth of such —**bri'er·y** *adj.*

bri·er[2] (brī'ər) *n.* [Fr. *bruyère*] **1.** a heath of S Europe: its root is used in making tobacco pipes **2.** this root; brierroot **3.** *same as* BRIAR[2] (sense 2)

bri'er·root' *n.* **1.** the root of the brier used in making tobacco pipes **2.** a pipe made from this Also **bri'er·wood'**

brig[1] (brig) *n.* [< It. *brigantino*, pirate ship] a two-masted ship with square sails

brig[2] (brig) *n.* [< ?] **1.** a prison on a U.S. warship **2.** [Mil. Slang] the guardhouse; prison

bri·gade (bri gād') *n.* [Fr. < It. *briga*, strife] **1.** a large unit of soldiers **2.** a military unit composed of two or more battalions **3.** a group of people organized as a unit to do work [a fire *brigade*] —*vt.* **-gad'ed, -gad'ing** to organize into a brigade

brig·a·dier (brig'ə dir') *n.* a brigade commander

brigadier general *pl.* **brigadier generals** *U.S. Mil.* an officer ranking just above a colonel

brig·and (brig'ənd) *n.* [see BRIGADE] a bandit, esp. one of a roving band —**brig'and·age** (-ən dij) *n.*

bright (brīt) *adj.* [OE. *bryht*] **1.** radiating, reflecting, or full of much light **2.** clear or brilliant in color or sound **3.** lively; vivacious **4.** mentally quick; clever **5.** giving, showing, or marked by hope, confidence, joy, etc. **6.** favorable; auspicious **7.** illustrious —*adv.* in a bright way —**bright'ly** *adv.* —**bright'ness** *n.*

bright'en (-'n) *vt., vi.* to make or become bright or brighter

Brigh·ton (brīt''n) resort city in S England, on the English Channel: pop. 165,000

Bright's disease (brīts) [< R. *Bright*, 19th-c. Eng. physician] *see* NEPHRITIS

bril·liance (bril'yəns) *n.* the quality or state of being brilliant: also **bril'lian·cy**

bril·liant (bril'yənt) *adj.* [Fr. < It. *brillare*, to sparkle] **1.** shining brightly **2.** vivid **3.** very splendid or distinguished **4.** keenly intelligent or very talented, skillful, etc. —*n.* a gem, esp. a diamond, cut with many facets to increase its sparkle —**bril'liant·ly** *adv.*

brim (brim) *n.* [OE., sea] **1.** the topmost edge of a cup, bowl, glass, etc. **2.** a projecting rim, as of a hat —*vt., vi.* **brimmed, brim'ming** to fill or be full to the brim

brim'ful' *adj.* full to the brim

brim·stone (brim'stōn') *n.* [< OE. *biernan*, to burn + *stan*, a stone] *same as* SULFUR

brin·dle (brin'd'l) *adj. same as* BRINDLED —*n.* **1.** a brindled color **2.** a brindled animal

brin'dled (-d'ld) *adj.* [prob. < ME. *brennen*, to burn] gray or tawny, along with darker markings

brine (brīn) *n.* [OE.] **1.** water full of salt **2.** sea water **3.** the sea or ocean —*vt.* **brined, brin'ing** to soak in or treat with brine

bring (brin) *vt.* **brought, bring'ing** [OE. *bringan*] **1.** to carry or lead "here" or to where the speaker will be **2.** to make happen, be, appear, etc. **3.** to lead to an action or belief **4.** to sell for [to *bring* a high price] **5.** *Law* to present, as charges, or advance, as evidence —**bring about** to effect —**bring forth** to give birth to or produce —**bring off** to accomplish —**bring out 1.** to make clear; reveal **2.** to present publicly, as a new book or play —**bring to 1.** to revive (one unconscious) **2.** to make (a ship) stop —**bring up 1.** to rear (a child) **2.** to introduce, as into discussion **3.** to cough or vomit up

brink (brink) *n.* [MLowG. or Dan., shore] the edge, esp. at the top of a steep place; verge

brin·y (brīn'ē) *adj.* **-i·er, -i·est** of or like brine; very salty —**brin'i·ness** *n.*

bri·oche (brē ōsh', -ōsh') *n.* [Fr.] a light, rich roll made with flour, butter, eggs, and yeast

bri·quette, bri·quet (bri ket') *n.* [Fr.] a brick as of compressed coal dust, for fuel or kindling

Bris·bane (briz'bān, -bən) seaport on the E coast of Australia: pop. 719,000

brisk (brisk) *adj.* [< ? Fr. *brusque*, brusque] **1.** quick in manner; energetic **2.** cool, dry, and bracing [*brisk* air] **3.** pungent, sharp, etc. [a *brisk* taste] **4.** active; busy [*brisk* trading] —**brisk'ly** *adv.* —**brisk'ness** *n.*

bris·ket (bris'kit) *n.* [ME. *brusket*] **1.** the breast of an animal **2.** meat cut from this part

bris·tle (bris''l) *n.* [OE. *byrst*] a short, stiff, prickly hair; esp., such a hair, as of a hog, or an artificial imitation of such a hair, used in brushes —*vi.* **-tled, -tling 1.** to stand up stiffly, as the bristles do when an animal is frightened or irritated **2.** to have the bristles stand up thus **3.** to stiffen as with fear or anger **4.** to be thickly covered (*with*) [a fort *bristling* with guns] —*vt.* to stiffen like or cover with bristles

bris·tly (bris'lē) *adj.* **-tli·er, -tli·est 1.** having bristles **2.** bristlelike —**bris'tli·ness** *n.*

Bris·tol (bris't'l) seaport in the SW part of England: pop. 428,000

Brit. 1. Britain **2.** Britannia **3.** British

Brit·ain (brit''n) *same as* GREAT BRITAIN

Bri·tan·ni·a (bri tan'yə) **1.** *Roman name for* GREAT BRITAIN **2.** *same as* BRITISH EMPIRE

Bri·tan'nic (-ik) *adj.* of Britain

britch·es (brich'iz) *n.pl.* [Colloq.] *same as* BREECHES (sense 2)

Brit·i·cism (brit'ə siz'm) *n.* a word, phrase, or idiom characteristic of British English

Brit·ish (brit'ish) *adj.* **1.** of Great Britain or its people **2.** of the British Commonwealth —*n.* English as spoken and written in England —**the British** the people of Great Britain

British Columbia province of SW Canada: 366,255 sq. mi.; pop. 1,874,000; cap. Victoria

British Commonwealth (of Nations) confederation of independent nations, including the United Kingdom, united under the British crown

British Empire formerly, the United Kingdom and the British dominions, colonies, etc.: term also still sometimes used for the British Commonwealth of Nations

Brit'ish·er (-ər) *n.* a native of Great Britain, esp. an Englishman

British Honduras Brit. colony in Central America

British Isles group of islands consisting of Great Britain, Ireland, & adjacent islands

British thermal unit the quantity of heat (about 252 calories) required to raise the temperature of one pound of water one degree Fahrenheit

Brit·on (brit''n) *n.* **1.** a member of an early Celtic people of S Britain **2.** a native or inhabitant of Great Britain, esp. an Englishman

Brit·ta·ny (brit''n ē) peninsula & former province of NW France

brit·tle (brit''l) *adj.* [< OE. *breotan*, to break] **1.** easily shattered because hard and inflexible **2.** hard and sharp in quality, as speech **3.** stiff and unbending in manner — *n.* a brittle, crunchy candy with nuts in it —**brit'tle·ness** *n.*

bro. *pl.* **bros.** brother

broach (brōch) *n.* [< ML. *brocca*, a spike] **1.** a tapered bit for enlarging holes **2.** *same as* BROOCH —*vt.* **1.** to make a hole in so as to let out liquid **2.** to start a discussion of

broad (brôd) *adj.* [OE. *brad*] **1.** of large extent from side to side; wide **2.** spacious [*broad* prairies] **3.** clear; open; full [*broad* daylight] **4.** obvious [a *broad* hint] **5.** coarse or ribald [a *broad* joke] **6.** tolerant; liberal **7.** wide in range; not limited **8.** main or general; not detailed —*n.* **1.** the broad part of anything **2.** [Slang] a woman —**broad'ly** *adv.* —**broad'ness** *n.*

broad'ax', broad'axe' *n.* a broad-bladed ax

broad'cast' (-kast') *vt., vi.* **-cast'** or, in radio, occas. **-cast'ed, -cast'ing 1.** to scatter or spread widely **2.** to transmit by radio or television —*adj.* **1.** widely scattered **2.** of, for, or by radio or television broadcasting —*n.* **1.** a broadcasting **2.** a radio or television program —*adv.* far and wide —**broad'cast'er** *n.*

broad'cloth' *n.* a fine, smooth cloth of wool, cotton, or silk

broad'en (-'n) *vt., vi.* to widen; expand

broad jump earlier term for LONG JUMP

broad'loom' *adj.* woven on a broad loom, as rugs

broad'-mind'ed *adj.* tolerant as of unconventional ideas or behavior; liberal —**broad'-mind'ed·ly** *adv.* —**broad'-mind'ed·ness** *n.*

broad'side' *n.* **1.** the side of a ship above the waterline **2.** the firing of all guns at once on one side of a ship **3.** a heavy critical attack **4.** a large printed sheet, as of advertising —*adv.* **1.** with the side facing **2.** indiscriminately

broad'sword' *n.* a broad-bladed sword for slashing

Broad·way (brôd'wā') street in New York City, center of the city's main theater section

bro·cade (brō kād') *n.* [< It. *broccare*, embroider] a rich cloth with a raised design woven into it —*vt.* **-cad'ed**, **-cad'ing** to weave such a design into

broc·co·li (bräk'ə lē) *n.* [< ML. *brocca*, a spike] a kind of cauliflower, with loose heads of tiny buds

bro·chure (brō shoor') *n.* [Fr. < *brocher*, to stitch] a pamphlet

bro·gan (brō'g'n) *n.* [Ir. *brōg*, a shoe] a heavy work shoe, fitting high on the ankle

brogue' (brōg) *n.* [prob. < Ir. *barrōg*, a hold] dialectal pronunciation, esp. that of English by the Irish

brogue² (brōg) *n.* [Ir. *brōg*, a shoe] a man's heavy oxford shoe

broil' (broil) *vt.* [< OFr. *bruillir*] **1.** to cook by exposing to direct heat **2.** to expose directly to intense heat —*vi.* **1.** to become broiled **2.** to get angry —*n.* a broiling

broil² (broil) *n.* [< OFr. *brouillier*, to dirty] a noisy quarrel; brawl —*vi.* to quarrel; brawl

broil·er (broil'ər) *n.* **1.** a pan, stove part, etc. for broiling **2.** a chicken suitable for broiling

broke (brōk) *pt.* of BREAK —*adj.* [Colloq.] **1.** having no money **2.** bankrupt —**go for broke** [Slang] to risk everything in a venture

bro·ken (brō'k'n) *pp.* of BREAK —*adj.* **1.** splintered, fractured, etc. **2.** not in working order **3.** violated, as a promise **4.** disrupted as by divorce [a *broken* home] **5.** weakened or beaten **6.** interrupted; discontinuous **7.** not complete [*broken* sizes] **8.** imperfectly spoken [*broken* English] **9.** tamed —**bro'ken·ly** *adv.* —**bro'ken·ness** *n.*

bro'ken-down' *adj.* **1.** sick or worn out, as by old age or disease **2.** out of order; useless

bro'ken·heart'ed *adj.* crushed by sorrow, grief, etc.

bro·ker (brō'kər) *n.* [< OFr. *brochier*, to broach] **1.** an agent for contracts or sales **2.** a stockbroker

bro'ker·age (-ij) *n.* **1.** a broker's business **2.** a broker's fee

bro·mide (brō'mīd) *n.* **1.** a compound of bromine with another element or a radical **2.** potassium bromide, KBr, used as a sedative **3.** a trite saying

bro·mid'ic (-mid'ik) *adj.* trite; dull; tiresome

bro·mine (brō'mēn) *n.* [< Gr. *brōmos*, stench] a chemical element, usually a reddish-brown, corrosive liquid: symbol, Br; at. wt., 79.909; at. no., 35

bron·chi (brän'kī) *n. pl.* of BRONCHUS

bron'chi·al (-kē əl) *adj.* of or pertaining to the bronchi or bronchioles

bronchial tubes the bronchi and branching tubes

bron'chi·ole (-ōl') *n.* any of the small subdivisions of the bronchi

bron·chi'tis (-kīt'is) *n.* inflammation of the bronchial tubes —**bron·chit'ic** (-kit'ik) *adj.*

bron'cho·scope' (-kə skōp') *n.* an instrument to examine, treat, or clear the bronchi

bron·chus (brän'kəs) *n., pl.* **-chi** (-kī) [< Gr. *bronchos*, windpipe] either of the two main branches of the trachea, or windpipe

bron·co (brän'kō) *n., pl.* **-cos** [< Sp., rough] a wild or partially tamed horse or pony of the western U.S.: also sp. **bron'cho**, *pl.* **-chos**

bron'co·bust'er (-bus'tər) *n.* [Colloq.] a cowboy who tames broncos —**bron'co·bust'ing** *n.*

Bron·të (brän'tē) **1. Charlotte**, 1816–55; Eng. novelist **2. Emily Jane**, 1818–48; Eng. novelist: sister of *prec.*

bron·to·sau·rus (brän'tə sôr'əs) *n., pl.* **-rus·es**, **-ri** (-ī) [< Gr. *brontē*, thunder + *sauros*, lizard] a huge, plant-eating American dinosaur

Bronx (bränks) northernmost borough of New York City: pop. 1,472,000

bronze (bränz) *n.* [< ML. *bronzium*] **1.** an alloy of copper and tin **2.** anything made of bronze **3.** a reddish-brown color —*adj.* of or like bronze —*vt.* **bronzed**, **bronz'ing** to make bronze in color

BRONTOSAURUS
(to 75 ft. long)

brooch (brōch, brooch) *n.* [see BROACH] a large ornamental pin with a clasp

brood (brood) *n.* [OE. *brod*] **1.** a group of birds hatched at one time **2.** the children in a family —*vt.* **1.** to sit on and hatch (eggs) **2.** to hover over or protect (offspring, etc.) as with wings **3.** to ponder in a troubled or morbid way [*brooding* revenge] —*vi.* **1.** to brood eggs or offspring **2.** to keep thinking about something in a troubled way (often with *on*, *over*, or *about*)

brood'er *n.* **1.** one that broods **2.** a heated shelter for raising fowl

brook' (brook) *n.* [OE. *broc*] a small stream

brook² (brook) *vt.* [OE. *brucan*, to use] to put up with; endure [I can't *brook* his insolence]

brook'let *n.* a little brook

Brook·lyn (brook'lən) borough of New York City, on W Long Island: pop. 2,602,000

brook trout a trout native to NE N. America

broom (broom, broom) *n.* [OE. *brom*, brushwood] **1.** a flowering shrub related to peas, beans, etc. **2.** a sweeping device consisting of a bundle of fibers or straws attached to a long handle —*vt.* to sweep with a broom

broom'stick' *n.* the handle of a broom

bros. brothers

broth (brôth) *n.* [OE.] a clear, thin soup made by boiling meat or vegetables or cereals in water

broth·el (brôth'əl, bräth'-) *n.* [< OE. *broethan*, waste away] a house of prostitution

broth·er (bruth'ər) *n., pl.* **broth'ers**; chiefly religious, **breth'ren** [OE. *brothor*] **1.** a male as related to other children of his parents **2.** a brotherlike friend **3.** a male of the same ancestry, ethnic background, profession, etc. as one's own **4.** a lay member of a men's religious order

broth'er·hood' (-hood') *n.* **1.** the state of being a brother or brothers **2.** an association of men united in a common interest, work, creed, etc.

broth'er-in-law' *n., pl.* **broth'ers-in-law'** **1.** the brother of one's husband or wife **2.** the husband of one's sister **3.** the husband of the sister of one's wife or husband

broth'er·ly *adj.* **1.** of or like a brother **2.** friendly, kind, loyal, etc. —**broth'er·li·ness** *n.*

brougham (broom, broo'əm) *n.* [< Lord *Brougham*, 19th-c. Brit. statesman] **1.** a closed, four-wheeled carriage with the driver's seat outside **2.** any of certain early types of automobile

brought (brôt) *pt. & pp.* of BRING

brow (brou) *n.* [OE. *bru*] **1.** the eyebrow **2.** the forehead **3.** the facial expression [an angry *brow*] **4.** a projecting edge, as of a cliff

brow'beat' (-bēt') *vt.* **-beat'**, **-beat'en**, **-beat'ing** to intimidate with harsh, stern looks and talk

brown (broun) *adj.* [OE. *brun*] **1.** having the color of chocolate or coffee, a mixture of red, black, and yellow **2.** tanned or dark-skinned —*n.* brown color —*vt., vi.* to make or become brown, as by exposure to sunlight or heat — **brown'ish** *adj.* —**brown'ness** *n.*

Brown, John 1800–59; U.S. abolitionist: hanged for treason

brown·ie (broun'ē) *n.* **1.** a small helpful elf in folk tales **2.** [B] a Girl Scout of the youngest group, those seven and eight years old **3.** any of the small bars cut from a flat, rich chocolate cake with nuts in it

Brown·ing (broun'iŋ) **1. Elizabeth Bar·rett** (bar'it), 1806–61; Eng. poet **2. Robert**, 1812–89; Eng. poet: husband of *prec.*

brown'out' *n.* a turning off of some lights in a city, as during an electric power shortage

brown'stone' *n.* a reddish-brown sandstone, used for building

brown study deep thought; reverie

brown sugar sugar whose crystals retain a brown coating of syrup

browse (brouz) *n.* [< OS. *brustian*, to sprout] leaves, shoots, etc. which animals feed on —*vt., vi.* **browsed**, **brows'ing** **1.** to nibble at (leaves, shoots, etc.) **2.** to examine (a book, articles for sale, etc.) in a casual way — **brows'er** *n.*

Bruce (broos), **Robert (the)**, 1274–1329; king of Scotland (1306–29)

Bru·in (broo'in) *n.* [Du., brown] [also b-] *a name for* the bear in fable and folklore

bruise (brooz) *vt.* **bruised**, **bruis'ing** [< OE. *brysan*, to crush] **1.** to injure and discolor (body tissue) without breaking the skin **2.** to injure the surface of (fruit, etc.) **3.** to hurt (the feelings, spirit, etc.) —*vi.* to be or become bruised —*n.* a bruised area, as of tissue

bruis'er *n.* [< prec.] a strong, pugnacious man

bruit (broot) *vt.* [< OFr. *bruire,* to rumble] to spread (*about*) a rumor of

brunch (brunch) *n.* [BR(EAKFAST) + (L)UNCH] [Colloq.] a meal combining breakfast and lunch

bru·net (broo net′) *adj.* [Fr. < OHG. *brun,* brown] **1.** having black or dark-brown hair, often with dark eyes and complexion **2.** having a dark color: said of hair, eyes, or skin —*n.* a brunet person

bru·nette′ (-net′) *adj.* [Fr., fem. of prec.] *same as* BRUNET —*n.* a brunette woman or girl

Brünn·hil·de (broon hil′də) in Wagner's *Die Walküre,* a Valkyrie whom Siegfried sets free

brunt (brunt) *n.* [< ? ON. *bruni,* heat] **1.** the shock (of an attack) or the impact (of a blow) **2.** the heaviest or hardest part

brush¹ (brush) *n.* [< OFr. *broce,* bush] **1.** *same as* BRUSHWOOD **2.** sparsely settled, scrubby country **3.** a device for cleaning, painting, etc., having bristles, hairs, or wires fastened into a back **4.** the act of brushing **5.** a light, grazing stroke **6.** a bushy tail, esp. that of a fox **7.** [Slang] *same as* BRUSHOFF **8.** *Elec.* a conductor of carbon, copper, etc. used between an external circuit and a revolving part —*vt.* **1.** to clean, paint, etc. with a brush **2.** to apply, remove, etc. as with a brush **3.** to touch or graze in passing —*vi.* to graze past something —**brush off** [Slang] to dismiss —**brush up** to refresh one's memory —**brush′y** *adj.*

brush² (brush) *vi.* [ME. *bruschen*] to move with a rush; hurry —*n.* a short, quick fight

brush′off′ *n.* [Slang] an abrupt dismissal: esp. in the phrase **give (or get) the brushoff**

brush′wood′ *n.* **1.** chopped-off tree branches **2.** a thick growth of small trees and shrubs

brusque (brusk) *adj.* [< ML. *bruscus,* brushwood] rough or abrupt in manner or speech; curt: also **brusk** — **brusque′ly** *adv.* —**brusque′ness** *n.*

Brus·sels (brus′lz) capital of Belgium, in the C part: pop. 1,079,000

Brussels sprouts 1. a plant with small cabbagelike heads on an erect stem **2.** these edible heads

bru·tal (broot′'l) *adj.* **1.** like a brute; savage, ruthless, etc. **2.** very harsh —**bru′tal·ly** *adv.*

bru·tal·i·ty (broo tal′ə tē) *n.* **1.** the quality of being brutal **2.** *pl.* **-ties** a brutal act

bru·tal·ize (broot′'l īz′) *vt., vi.* **-ized′, -iz′ing** to make or become brutal —**bru′tal·i·za′tion** *n.*

brute (broot) *adj.* [< L. *brutus,* irrational] **1.** lacking the ability to reason *[a brute beast]* **2.** lacking consciousness *[the brute force of nature]* **3.** of or like an animal; brutal, cruel, stupid, etc. —*n.* **1.** an animal **2.** a brutal person

brut·ish (broot′ish) *adj.* of or like a brute; savage, stupid, etc. —**brut′ish·ly** *adv.* —**brut′ish·ness** *n.*

Bru·tus (broot′əs), (Marcus Junius) 85?-42 B.C.; Rom. statesman: one of the assassins of Julius Caesar

Bry·an (brī′ən), **William Jen·nings** (jen′iŋz), 1860–1925; U.S. statesman and orator

Bry·ant (brī′ənt), **William Cul·len** (kul′ən), 1794–1878; U.S. poet & journalist

B.S., B.Sc. Bachelor of Science

b.s. 1. balance sheet **2.** bill of sale

B.t.u. British thermal unit(s): also **B.T.U.,** Btu

bu. 1. bureau **2.** bushel(s)

bub·ble (bub′'l) *n.* [echoic] **1.** a very thin film of liquid forming a ball around air or gas *[soap bubbles]* **2.** a tiny ball of air or gas in a liquid or solid **3.** a plausible scheme that proves worthless —*vi.* **-bled, -bling 1.** to rise in bubbles; boil; foam **2.** to make a gurgling sound —*vt.* to form bubbles in; make bubble —**bubble over 1.** to overflow, as boiling liquid **2.** to be unrestrained in one's enthusiasm, etc. —**bub′bly** *adj.*

bubble gum a kind of chewing gum that can be blown into large bubbles

bu·bo (byoo′bō) *n., pl.* **-boes** [< Gr. *boubōn,* groin] an inflamed swelling of a lymph gland, esp. in the groin

bu·bon·ic plague (-bän′ik) a contagious disease characterized by buboes, fever, and delirium: fleas from infected rats are the carriers

buc·cal (buk′'l) *adj.* [L. *bucca,* cheek + -AL] **1.** of the cheek or cheeks **2.** of the mouth

buc·ca·neer (buk′ə nir′) *n.* [Fr. *boucanier*] a pirate or sea robber

Bu·chan·an (byoo kan′ən), **James** 1791–1868; 15th president of the U.S. (1857–61)

Bu·cha·rest (boo′kə rest′) capital of Romania, in the S part: pop. 1,415,000

buck¹ (buk) *n.* [OE. *bucca,* male goat] **1.** a male deer, goat, etc. **2.** the act of bucking **3.** [Colloq.] a young man: sometimes a patronizing term —*vi.* **1.** to rear upward quickly in an attempt to throw off a rider: said of a horse **2.** [Colloq.] to resist something as if plunging against it — *vt.* **1.** to charge against, as in football **2.** to throw by bucking **3.** [Colloq.] to resist stubbornly —**buck for** [Slang] to work eagerly for (a promotion, etc.) —**buck up** [Colloq.] to cheer up —**buck′er** *n.*

buck² (buk) *n.* [Du. *zaagbok*] **1.** a sawbuck; sawhorse **2.** a gymnastic apparatus somewhat like a sawhorse, with a padded top, for vaulting over

buck³ (buk) *n.* [< ?] [Slang] a dollar —**pass the buck** [Colloq.] to shift the blame or responsibility to another

buck·a·roo (buk′ə roo′, buk′ə roo′) *n., pl.* **-roos′** [< Sp. *vaquero*] a cowboy

buck′board′ *n.* [< ?] an open carriage whose floor boards rest directly on the axles

buck·et (buk′it) *n.* [< OE. *buc,* pitcher] **1.** a round container with a curved handle, for carrying water, coal, etc. **2.** the amount held by a bucket: also **buck′et·ful′,** *pl.* **-fuls′ 3.** a thing shaped like a bucket, as the scoop on a steam shovel — **kick the bucket** [Slang] to die

BUCKBOARD

bucket seat a single contoured seat with a movable back, as in some sports cars

buck·eye (buk′ī′) *n.* [BUCK¹ + EYE: from the appearance of the seed] **1.** a tree with large, spiny capsules enclosing shiny brown seeds **2.** the seed **3.** [B-] [Colloq.] a native or inhabitant of Ohio (the **Buckeye State**)

Buck·ing·ham Palace (buk′iŋ əm) the official residence in London of British sovereigns

buck·le¹ (buk′'l) *n.* [< L. *buccula,* cheek strap of a helmet] **1.** a clasp for fastening a strap, belt, etc. **2.** a clasplike ornament, as for shoes —*vt., vi.* **-led, -ling** to fasten with a buckle —**buckle down** to apply oneself energetically

buck·le² (buk′'l) *vt., vi.* **-led, -ling** [prob. < Du. *bukken,* to bend] to bend, warp, or crumple —*n.* a bend, bulge, etc. —**buckle under** to give in; yield; submit

buck·ler (buk′lər) *n.* [OFr. *bocler*] **1.** a small, round shield worn on the arm **2.** a protection or defense

buck′-pass′er *n.* [Colloq.] one who regularly shifts blame or responsibility to someone else —**buck′-pass′ing** *n.*

buck·ram (buk′rəm) *n.* [prob. < *Bukhara,* city in Uzbek S.S.R.] a coarse, stiffened cloth used in bookbinding, etc.

buck·saw (buk′sô′) *n.* [see BUCK²] a saw set in a frame and held with both hands in cutting wood

buck′shot′ *n.* a large lead shot for shooting deer and other large game

buck′skin′ *n.* **1.** a soft yellowish-gray leather made from the skins of deer or sheep **2.** [*pl.*] clothes made of buckskin —*adj.* made of buckskin

buck′tooth′ *n., pl.* **-teeth′** a projecting front tooth — **buck′toothed′** *adj.*

buck′wheat′ *n.* [< OE. *boc,* beech + WHEAT] **1.** a plant with beechnut-shaped seeds **2.** a dark flour made from the seeds

bu·col·ic (byoo käl′ik) *adj.* [< Gr. *boukolos,* herdsman] **1.** of shepherds; pastoral **2.** of country life; rustic —*n.* a pastoral poem —**bu·col′i·cal·ly** *adv.*

bud¹ (bud) *n.* [ME. *budde*] **1.** a small swelling on a plant, from which a shoot, leaf, or flower develops **2.** an early stage of development —*vi.* **bud′ded, bud′ding 1.** to put forth buds **2.** to begin to develop —*vt.* to cause to bud — **nip in the bud** to check at the earliest stage

bud² (bud) *n.* [Slang] *short for* BUDDY: used in addressing a man or boy

Bu·da·pest (boo′də pest′) capital of Hungary, on the Danube: pop. 1,990,000

Bud·dha (bood′ə, boo′də) a religious leader who lived in India 563?-483? B.C.: founder of Buddhism

Bud·dhism (bood′iz'm, boo′diz'm) *n.* a religion of Asia teaching that by right living and right thinking one achieves Nirvana —**Bud′dhist** *n., adj.*

bud·dy (bud′ē) *n., pl.* **-dies** [< ? Brit. dial.] [Colloq.] a comrade

budge (buj) *vt., vi.* **budged, budg′ing** [Fr. *bouger,* to move] to move even a little

budg·er·i·gar (buj′ə ri gär′) *n.* [native name] a greenish-yellow Australian parakeet: also [Colloq.] **budg′ie**

budg·et (buj′it) *n.* [< L. *bulga*, a bag] **1.** a stock of items **2.** a plan adjusting expenses to income **3.** the estimated cost of living, operating, etc. —*vt.* **1.** to put on a budget **2.** to schedule *[budget* your time*]* —**budg′et·ar′y** *adj.* —**budg′et·er** *n.*

Bue·nos Ai·res (bwā′nəs er′ēz, ī′rēz) capital of Argentina: pop. 2,972,000

buff (buf) *n.* [< It. *bufalo*, BUFFALO] **1.** a heavy, soft, brownish-yellow leather made from the skin of a buffalo, ox, etc. **2.** a military coat made of this **3.** a stick or wheel (**buffing wheel**) covered with leather or cloth, used for cleaning or shining **4.** a dull brownish yellow **5.** [Colloq.] a devotee; fan *[a* jazz *buff]* —*adj.* **1.** made of buff **2.** of the color buff —*vt.* to clean or shine with a buff —**in the buff** naked —**buff′er** *n.*

Buf·fa·lo (buf′ə lō′) city in W N.Y., on Lake Erie: pop. 463,000 (met. area 1,349,000)

buf·fa·lo (buf′ə lō′) *n., pl.* **-loes′, -los′, -lo′** [< It. < Gr. *bous*, ox] **1.** any of various wild oxen sometimes domesticated, as the water buffalo of India **2.** popularly, the American bison — *vt.* **-loed′, -lo′ing** [Slang] to baffle, bluff, etc.

BUFFALO
(55–70 in. high
at shoulder)

buff·er (buf′ər) *n.* [< OFr. *buffe*, a blow] anything that lessens shock, as of collision, antagonism, etc.

buf·fet¹ (buf′it) *n.* [OFr. < *buffe*, a blow] a blow or shock —*vt.* **1.** to punch or slap **2.** to struggle against —*vi.* to struggle

buf·fet² (bə fā′, boo-) *n.* [Fr.] **1.** a piece of furniture with drawers and cupboards for dishes, silver, etc. **2.** a sideboard or table at which guests serve themselves food **3.** a meal served thus

‡buf·fo (boof′fô; *E.* boo͞o′fô) *n., pl.* **-fi** (-fē) [It., comic: see BUFFOON] an opera singer, generally a bass, who plays a comic role

buf·foon (bə foon′) *n.* [< Fr. < It. *buffare*, to jest] a person who is always trying to be funny; clown —**buf·foon′er·y** *n.*

bug (bug) *n.* [prob. < W. *bwg*, hobgoblin] **1.** an insect with sucking mouthparts and forewings thickened toward the base **2.** any insect **3.** [Colloq.] a germ or virus **4.** [Slang] a defect, as in a machine **5.** [Slang] a hidden microphone —*vt.* **bugged, bug′ging** [Slang] **1.** to hide a microphone in (a room, etc.) **2.** to annoy, anger, etc.

bug·a·boo (bug′ə boo͞o′) *n., pl.* **-boos′** a bugbear

bug′bear′ *n.* [BUG + BEAR²] **1.** an imaginary terror **2.** a cause of needless fear

bug′-eyed′ *adj.* [Slang] with bulging eyes

bug·gy¹ (bug′ē) *n., pl.* **-gies** [< ?] **1.** a light, one-horse carriage with one seat **2.** a small carriage for a baby

bug·gy² (bug′ē) *adj.* **-gi·er, -gi·est 1.** infested or swarming with bugs **2.** [Slang] mentally ill

bug′house′ *n.* [Slang] an insane asylum

bu·gle (byoo͞o′g'l) *n.* [< L. *buculus*, young ox] a brass-wind instrument like a small trumpet, usually without valves — *vi., vt.* **-gled, -gling** to signal by blowing a bugle —**bu′gler** *n.*

bugs (bugz) *adj.* [Slang] mentally ill

build (bild) *vt.* **built, build′ing** [< OE. *bold*, a house] **1.** to make by putting together material, parts, etc.; construct **2.** to establish; base *[build* a theory on facts*]* —*vi.* **1.** *a)* to put up buildings *b)* to have a house, etc. built **2.** to grow or intensify —*n.* form or figure *[a* stocky *build]* —**build′er** *n.*

build′ing *n.* **1.** anything that is built; structure **2.** the work or business of making houses, etc.

build′up′, build′-up′ *n.* [Colloq.] **1.** favorable publicity or praise **2.** growth or expansion

built′-in′ *adj.* **1.** made as part of a building **2.** inherent

bulb (bulb) *n.* [< Gr. *bolbos*] **1.** an underground bud with roots and a short, scaly stem, as in a lily or onion **2.** a corm, tuber, or tuberous root resembling a bulb, as in a crocus **3.** a plant that grows from a bulb **4.** anything shaped like a bulb —**bul·bar** (bul′bər) *adj.* —**bul′bous** *adj.*

Bul·gar·i·a (bəl ger′ē ə, bool-) country in S Europe, south of Romania: 42,796 sq. mi.; pop. 7,614,000; cap. Sofia — **Bul·gar′i·an** *adj., n.*

bulge (bulj) *n.* [< L. *bulga*, a bag] **1.** an outward swelling; protuberance **2.** a projecting part —*vi., vt.* **bulged, bulg′-ing** to swell out —**bulg′y** *adj.*

bulk (bulk) *n.* [ON. *bulki*, a heap] **1.** size, mass, or volume, esp. if great **2.** the main mass; largest part —*vi.* to have, or to increase in, size or importance —*vt.* to cause

to bulk —*adj.* **1.** total; aggregate **2.** not packaged —in **bulk 1.** not packaged **2.** in large amounts

bulk·head (bulk′hed′) *n.* [< ON. *balkr*, partition + HEAD] **1.** an upright partition, as in a ship, for protection against fire or leakage **2.** a wall for holding back earth, water, etc.

bulk′y *adj.* **-i·er, -i·est 1.** of great bulk; massive **2.** awkwardly large; big and clumsy —**bulk′i·ly** *adv.* —**bulk′i·ness** *n.*

bull¹ (bool) *n.* [OE. *bula*, a steer] **1.** the adult male of any bovine animal, as the ox, or of certain other large animals, as the elephant, whale, etc. **2.** a person who buys stocks, etc. expecting, or seeking to bring about, a rise in their prices **3.** a large, noisy, or strong person **4.** [Slang] insincere talk; nonsense —[B-] *same as* TAURUS —*vt.* to make (one's way) with force —*adj.* **1.** male **2.** like a bull in size, strength, etc. **3.** rising in price *[a* bull market*]* — **shoot the bull** [Slang] to talk idly —**take the bull by the horns** to deal boldly with danger or difficulty —**bull′ish** *adj.*

bull² (bool) *n.* [< LL. *bulla*, a seal] an official document from the Pope

bull′dog′ *n.* a short-haired, square-jawed, heavily built dog noted for its stubborn grip — *adj.* like a bulldog; stubborn —*vt.* **-dogged′, -dog′ging** to throw (a steer) by seizing its horns and twisting its neck

BULLDOG
(18 in. high
at shoulder)

bull′doze′ (-dōz′) *vt.* **-dozed′, -doz′ing** [< *bull*, a flogging + DOSE] **1.** [Colloq.] to force or frighten by threatening; intimidate **2.** to move, push, etc. with a bulldozer

bull′doz′er *n.* a tractor with a large, shovellike blade in front for pushing earth, debris, etc.

bul·let (bool′it) *n.* [< L. *bulla*, a knob] a small, shaped piece of metal to be shot from a firearm

bul·le·tin (bool′ət 'n) *n.* [Fr. < It. < LL. *bulla*, a seal] **1.** a brief statement of late news **2.** a regular publication, as for members of a society

bulletin board a board or wall area on which notices or displays are put up

bul′let·proof′ *adj.* that bullets cannot pierce —*vt.* to make bulletproof

bull′fight′ (-fīt′) *n.* a public show in which a bull is provoked in various ways and then usually killed with a sword by a matador —**bull′fight′er** *n.*

bull′finch′ (-finch′) *n.* a small European songbird

bull′frog′ *n.* a large N. American frog with a deep, loud croak

bull′head′ *n.* any of various N. American freshwater catfishes

bull′head′ed (-hed′id) *adj.* blindly stubborn —**bull′head′-ed·ness** *n.*

bull′horn′ *n.* a portable electronic voice amplifier

bul·lion (bool′yən) *n.* [< OFr. *billon*, small coin] ingots or bars of gold or silver

bull′ish *adj.* **1.** of or like a bull **2.** rising, or causing a rise, in price on the stock exchange **3.** optimistic

bull·ock (bool′ək) *n.* [< OE. dim. of *bula*, steer] a castrated bull; steer

bull′pen′ *n.* **1.** [Colloq.] a temporary detention room in a jail **2.** *Baseball* a practice area for relief pitchers

Bull Run small stream in NE Va.: site of two Union defeats (1861 & 1862) in the Civil War

bull′s-eye (boolz′ī′) *n.* **1.** the central mark of a target **2.** a direct hit

bull terrier a strong, lean, white dog, developed by crossing the bulldog and the terrier

bull′whip′ *n.* a long, heavy whip, formerly used by cattle drivers, etc.

bul·ly¹ (bool′ē) *n., pl.* **-lies** [< MHG. *buole*, lover; later infl. by BULL¹] one who hurts or browbeats those who are weaker —*vt., vi.* **-lied, -ly·ing** to act the bully (toward) — *adj., interj.* [Colloq.] fine; very good

bul·ly² (bool′ē) *n.* [< Fr. *bouillir*, to boil] canned or corned beef: also **bully beef**

bul·rush (bool′rush′) *n.* [< OE. *bol*, tree trunk + *risc*, a rush] **1.** a marsh plant of the sedge family **2.** *Bible* papyrus

bul·wark (bool′wərk) *n.* [MDu. *bolwerc*] **1.** a defensive wall; rampart **2.** a defense or protection **3.** [*usually pl.*] a ship's side above the deck —*vt.* to provide or be a bulwark for

bum (bum) *n.* [prob. < G. *bummeln,* go slowly] [Colloq.] 1. a vagrant; beggar; loafer 2. a devotee, as of golf or tennis —*vi.* bummed, bum'ming [Colloq.] to live as a bum or by begging —*vt.* [Slang] to get by sponging; cadge —*adj.* bum'mer, bum'mest [Slang] 1. poor in quality 2. false 3. lame —on the bum [Colloq.] 1. living as a vagrant 2. out of repair

bum·ble·bee (bum'b'l bē') *n.* [< ME. *bomblen,* to buzz] a large, hairy, yellow-and-black social bee

bum·bling (bum'bliŋ) *adj.* [< obs. *bumble,* buzz] self-important in a blundering way

bum·mer (bum'ər) *n.* [Slang] an unpleasant experience, esp. with drugs

bump (bump) *vt., vi.* [echoic] 1. to collide (with); hit against 2. [Slang] to displace, as from a job —*n.* 1. a light blow; jolt 2. a swelling, esp. one caused by a blow —**bump into** [Colloq.] to meet unexpectedly —**bump off** [Slang] to murder

bump·er[1] (bump'ər) *n.* a device for absorbing the shock of a collision; esp. a bar at the front or back of an automobile

bump·er[2] (bump'ər) *n.* [prob. < obs. *bombard,* liquor jug] a cup or glass filled to the brim —*adj.* unusually abundant *[a bumper crop]*

bump·kin (bump'kən) *n.* [prob. < MDu. *bommekijn,* small cask] an awkward or simple person from the country

bump'tious (-shəs) *adj.* [prob. < BUMP] disagreeably conceited or forward —**bump'tious·ly** *adv.* —**bump'tious·ness** *n.*

bump·y (bump'pē) *adj.* -i·er, -i·est full of bumps; rough —**bump'i·ly** *adv.* —**bump'i·ness** *n.*

bun (bun) *n.* [prob. < OFr. *buigne,* a swelling] 1. a small roll, often sweetened or spiced 2. hair worn in a roll or knot on a woman's head or neck

bunch (bunch) *n.* [< Fl. *boudje,* little bundle] 1. a cluster of similar things growing or grouped together 2. [Colloq.] a group of people —*vt., vi.* to collect in loose folds, wads, etc. —**bunch'i·ness** *n.* —**bunch'y** *adj.*

bun·co (buŋ'kō) *n., pl.* -cos [< Sp. *banca,* card game] [Colloq.] a swindle; confidence game —*vt.* -coed, -co·ing [Colloq.] to swindle Also **bun'ko**

bun·combe (buŋ'kəm) *n.* [< *Buncombe* county, N.C., loquaciously represented in 16th Congress] [Colloq.] empty, insincere talk: also **bun'kum**

bun·dle (bun'd'l) *n.* [prob. < MDu. *bondel*] 1. a number of things bound together 2. a package 3. a bunch; collection —*vt.* -dled, -dling 1. to make into a bundle 2. to send hastily (*away, off, out,* or *into*) —*vi.* to move or go hastily —**bundle up** to put on plenty of warm clothing

bung (buŋ) *n.* [< MDu. *bonge*] 1. a cork or other stopper for the hole in a barrel, cask, or keg 2. a bunghole —*vt.* 1. to close (a bunghole) with a stopper 2. [Slang] to bruise or damage (with *up*)

bun·ga·low (buŋ'gə lō') *n.* [< Hindi *bāṅglā,* thatched house] a small, one-storied house

bung·hole (buŋ'hōl') *n.* a hole in a barrel or keg through which liquid can be drawn out

bun·gle (buŋ'g'l) *vt., vi.* -gled, -gling [< ?] to spoil by clumsy work; botch —*n.* 1. a bungling 2. a clumsy piece of work —**bun'gler** *n.*

bun·ion (bun'yən) *n.* [prob. < OFr.: see BUN] an inflammation and swelling at the base of the big toe

bunk[1] (buŋk) *n.* [prob. < Scand. cognate of BENCH] 1. a shelflike bed built against a wall, as in a ship 2. [Colloq.] any sleeping place —*vi.* to sleep in a bunk —*vt.* to provide a sleeping place for

bunk[2] (buŋk) *n.* [Slang] *same as* BUNCOMBE

bunk'er *n.* [Scot. < ?] 1. a large bin, as for a ship's fuel 2. an underground fortification 3. a sand trap or mound of earth serving as an obstacle on a golf course —*vt.* Golf to hit (a ball) into a bunker

Bun·ker Hill (buŋ'kər) hill in Boston, Mass., near which a battle of the American Revolution was fought in 1775

bunk'house' *n.* barracks for ranch hands, etc.

bun·ny (bun'ē) *n., pl.* -nies [dim. of dial. *bun*] a rabbit: a child's term

Bun·sen burner (bun's'n) [< R. W. *Bunsen,* 19th-c. G. chemist] a small, tubular gas burner that produces a hot, blue flame

bunt (bunt) *vt., vi.* [< ? Bret. *bounta,* to butt] *Baseball* to bat (a pitched ball) lightly so that it does not go beyond the infield —*n.* 1. the act of bunting 2. a bunted ball

bunt·ing[1] (bun'tiŋ) *n.* [< ? ME. *bonting,* sifting (cloth)] 1. a thin cloth used in making flags, etc. 2. decorative flags 3. a soft, warm, baby's garment in the form of a hooded blanket

bunt·ing[2] (bun'tiŋ) *n.* [< ?] any of various small, brightly colored birds having a stout bill

Bun·yan (bun'yən) 1. John, 1628–88; Eng. writer & preacher 2. *see* PAUL BUNYAN

Buo·na·parte (bwô'nä pär'te) *It. sp. of* BONAPARTE

buoy (boo'ē, boi) *n.* [< L. *boia,* fetter] 1. a floating object anchored in water to warn of rocks, etc. or to mark a channel 2. *short for* LIFE BUOY —*vt.* 1. to mark with a buoy 2. to keep afloat 3. to lift up in spirits; encourage

buoy·an·cy (boi'ən sē, boo'yən-) *n.* [< BUOYANT] 1. the ability to float in liquid or air 2. the power to keep something afloat 3. cheerfulness

buoy·ant (boi'ənt, boo'yənt) *adj.* [< ? Sp. *boyar,* to float] having buoyancy —**buoy'ant·ly** *adv.*

bur (bur) *n.* [< Scand.] 1. a rough, prickly seed capsule of certain plants 2. a plant with burs 3. *same as* BURR[1] & BURR[2] 4. *Dentistry* a cutting or drilling bit

bur·bot (bur'bət) *n., pl.* -bot, -bots [< L. *barba,* a beard] a freshwater fish of the cod family, having chin barbels

bur·den[1] (burd'n) *n.* [< OE. *beran,* to bear] 1. anything that is carried; load 2. a heavy load, as of work, care, etc. 3. the carrying of loads *[a beast of burden]* 4. the carrying capacity of a ship or the weight of its cargo —*vt.* to put a burden on; load; oppress —**bur'den·some** *adj.*

bur·den[2] (burd'n) *n.* [< OFr. *bourdon,* a humming] 1. a chorus or refrain of a song 2. a repeated, central idea; theme

bur·dock (bur'däk) *n.* [BUR + DOCK[3]] a plant with purplish flower heads bearing prickles

bu·reau (byoor'ō) *n., pl.* -reaus, -reaux (-ōz) [Fr., desk] 1. [Brit.] a desk with drawers 2. a chest of drawers for clothing, etc. 3. an agency *[travel bureau]* 4. a government department

bu·reauc·ra·cy (byoo rä'krə sē) *n., pl.* -cies 1. government by departmental officials following an inflexible routine 2. the officials collectively 3. governmental officialism or inflexible routine 4. the concentration of authority in a complex structure of administrative bureaus —**bu·reau·crat** (byoor'ə krat') *n.* —**bu'reau·crat'ic** *adj.*

bu·reauc'ra·tize (-tīz') *vt., vi.* -tized', -tiz'ing to develop into a bureaucracy —**bu·reauc'ra·ti·za'tion** *n.*

bu·rette, bu·ret (byoo ret') *n.* [Fr.] a graduated glass tube with a valve at the bottom, for measuring small amounts of liquid or gas

burg (burg) *n.* [var. of BOROUGH] [Colloq.] a city or town, esp. one regarded as quiet, dull, etc.

bur·geon (bur'jən) *vi.* [< OFr. *burjon,* a bud] 1. to put forth buds, etc. 2. to develop rapidly

-burger [< (HAM)BURGER] *a combining form meaning:* 1. a sandwich of ground meat, etc. *[turkeyburger]* 2. hamburger and *[cheeseburger]*

bur·gess (bur'jis) *n.* [< LL. *burgus,* castle] a member of the lower house of the legislature of colonial Maryland or Virginia

burgh (burg) *n.* [Scot. var. of BOROUGH] 1. [Brit.] a borough 2. in Scotland, a chartered town

burgh'er *n.* a citizen of a town

bur·glar (bur'glər) *n.* [< OFr. *burgeor*] one who commits burglary

bur'glar·ize' *vt.* -ized', -iz'ing [Colloq.] to commit burglary in

bur'gla·ry *n., pl.* -ries the act of breaking into a dwelling at night to commit theft or other felony

bur·gle (bur'g'l) *vt., vi.* -gled, -gling [Colloq.] to commit burglary (in)

bur·go·mas·ter (bur'gə mas'tər) *n.* [< MDu. *burg,* town + *meester,* master] the mayor of a town in the Netherlands, Flanders, Austria, or Germany

Bur·gun·dy (bur'gən dē) *n., pl.* -dies [*occas.* b-] a red or white wine, orig. made in Burgundy, a region in SE France —**Bur·gun·di·an** (bər gun'dē ən) *adj., n.*

bur·i·al (ber'ē əl) *n.* the burying of a dead body; interment —*adj.* of or connected with burial

Burke (burk), Edmund 1729–97; Brit. statesman, orator, & writer, born in Ireland

burl (burl) *n.* [< LL. *burra,* ragged garment] 1. a knot in wool, thread, yarn, etc. that gives a nubby appearance to cloth 2. a kind of knot on some tree trunks —**burled** *adj.*

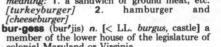

BURETTE

bur·lap (bur'lap) *n.* [< ? ME. *borel*] a coarse cloth made of jute or hemp, used for making bags, etc.

bur·lesque (bər lesk') *n.* [Fr. < It. *burla*, a jest] **1.** any broadly comic or satirical imitation; parody **2.** a sort of vaudeville characterized by low comedy, striptease acts, etc. —*adj.* **1.** parodying **2.** of or connected with burlesque (sense 2) —*vt., vi.* **-lesqued', -lesqu'ing** to imitate comically

bur·ley (bur'lē) *n.* [< ? a proper name] [*also* B-] a thin-leaved tobacco grown esp. in Kentucky

bur·ly (bur'lē) *adj.* **-li·er, -li·est** [ME. *borlich*, excellent] **1.** big and strong **2.** hearty in manner; bluff —**bur'li·ness** *n.*

Bur·ma (bur'mə) country in SE Asia: area 261,789 sq. mi.; pop. 26,980,000; cap. Rangoon —**Bur·mese** (bər mēz') *adj., n., pl.* **-mese'**

burn' (burn) *vt.* **burned** or **burnt, burn'ing** [OE. *biernan*] **1.** to set on fire **2.** to destroy by fire **3.** to injure by fire, friction, or acid **4.** to consume as a fuel **5.** to sunburn **6.** to cause (a hole, etc.) as by fire **7.** to cause a sensation of heat in —*vi.* **1.** to be on fire; blaze **2.** to undergo combustion **3.** to give out light or heat; glow **4.** to be destroyed or injured by fire or heat **5.** to feel hot **6.** to be excited —*n.* **1.** an injury caused by fire, heat, etc. **2.** the process or result of burning —**burn down** to burn to the ground —**burn up** [Slang] to make or become angry —**burn'a·ble** *adj., n.*

burn² (burn) *n.* [OE. *burna*] [Scot.] a brook

burn'er *n.* **1.** the part of a stove, furnace, etc. from which the flame comes **2.** an apparatus for burning fuel or trash

burn'ing *adj.* **1.** that burns **2.** critical

bur·nish (bur'nish) *vt., vi.* [< OFr. *brun*, brown] to make or become shiny by rubbing —*n.* a gloss or polish —**bur'nish·er** *n.*

bur·noose (bər nōōs') *n.* [< Fr. < Ar. *burnus*] a long cloak with a hood, worn by Arabs and Moors

Burns (burnz), **Robert** 1759–96; Scot. poet

burn·sides (burn'sīdz') *n.pl.* [< A. E. *Burnside*, Union general in the Civil War] a style of beard with full side whiskers and mustache

burnt (burnt) *alt. pt. and pp. of* BURN¹

burnt sienna *see* SIENNA

burnt umber *see* UMBER

burp (burp) *n., vi.* [echoic] [Colloq.] belch —*vt.* to cause (a baby) to belch

burr' (bur) *n.* [var. of BUR] **1.** a rough edge left on metal, etc. by drilling or cutting **2.** *same as* BUR (senses 1, 2, 4) —*vt.* **1.** to form a rough edge on **2.** to remove burrs from (metal)

burr² (bur) *n.* [prob. echoic] **1.** the trilling of *r* as in Scottish speech **2.** a whirring sound —*vi.* **1.** to speak with a burr **2.** to make a whir —*vt.* to pronounce with a burr

Burr (bur), **Aaron** 1756–1836; U.S. political leader: killed Alexander Hamilton in a duel

bur·ro (bur'ō) *n., pl.* **-ros** [Sp. < LL. *burricus*, small horse] a donkey

bur·row (bur'ō) *n.* [see BOROUGH] **1.** a hole dug in the ground by an animal **2.** any similar hole —*vi.* **1.** to make a burrow **2.** to live or hide in or as in a burrow **3.** to delve or search, as if by digging —*vt.* **1.** to make burrows in **2.** to make by burrowing

bur·sa (bur'sə) *n., pl.* **-sae** (-sē), **-sas** [< Gr. *byrsa*, a hide] *Anat.* a sac or cavity with a lubricating fluid, as between a tendon and bone

bur·sar (bur'sər) *n.* [< ML. *bursa*, a purse] a college treasurer

bur·si·tis (bər sīt'əs) *n.* [< BURSA + -ITIS] inflammation of a bursa

burst (burst) *vi.* **burst, burst'ing** [OE. *berstan*] **1.** to come apart suddenly and violently; explode **2.** to give sudden expression; break (*into* tears, laughter, etc.) **3.** to appear, start, etc. suddenly **4.** to be as full or crowded as possible —*vt.* to cause to burst —*n.* **1.** a bursting **2.** a break; rupture **3.** a sudden action; spurt **4.** a volley of shots

bur·then (bur'thən) *n., vt.* [Archaic] burden

Bu·run·di (boo roon'dē) country in EC Africa, east of Zaire: 10,745 sq. mi.; pop. 3,475,000

bur·y (ber'ē) *vt.* **-ied, -y·ing** [OE. *byrgan*] **1.** to put (a dead body) into the earth, a tomb, etc. **2.** to hide or cover **3.** to put away **4.** to immerse

bus (bus) *n., pl.* **bus'es, bus'ses** [< (OMNI)BUS] a large motor coach for many passengers, usually along a regular route —*vt.* **bused** or **bussed, bus'ing** or **bus'sing** to transport by bus —*vi.* **1.** to go by bus **2.** to do the work of a busboy

bus. business

bus'boy' *n.* a waiter's assistant who clears tables, brings water, etc.

bush (boosh) *n.* [ME.] **1.** a low woody plant with spreading branches; shrub **2.** anything like a bush **3.** uncleared land —*vi.* to grow thickly —**beat around the bush** to talk around a subject without getting to the point

bushed (boosht) *adj.* [Colloq.] tired; fatigued

bush·el (boosh'l) *n.* [< OFr. *boisse*, grain measure] **1.** a unit of dry measure equal to 4 pecks or 32 quarts **2.** a container with this capacity

bush·ing (boosh'iŋ) *n.* [< ML. *buxis*, a box] a removable metal sleeve for reducing friction on a bearing or for decreasing the diameter of a hole

bush league [Slang] *Baseball* a small or second-rate minor league —**bush'-league'** *adj.* —**bush leaguer**

bush'man *n., pl.* **-men** one who lives in the Australian bush

bush'mas'ter (-mas'tər) *n.* a large poisonous snake of Central and South America

bush'whack' *vi.* [prob. < BUSH + WHACK] **1.** to cut one's way through bushes **2.** to engage in guerrilla fighting —*vt.* to ambush —**bush'whack'er** *n.*

bush'y *adj.* **-i·er, -i·est 1.** covered with bushes **2.** spreading like bushes —**bush'i·ness** *n.*

bus·i·ly (biz'ə lē) *adv.* in a busy manner

busi·ness (biz'nis) *n.* [OE. *bisignes*: see BUSY] **1.** one's work; profession; occupation **2.** rightful concern **3.** a matter or affair **4.** the buying and selling of goods; commerce **5.** a commercial or industrial establishment —*adj.* of or for business —**mean business** [Colloq.] to be in earnest

business college (or **school**) a school offering instruction in secretarial skills, etc.

busi'ness·like' *adj.* efficient, methodical, etc.

busi'ness·man' *n., pl.* **-men'** a man in business, esp. as an owner or executive —**busi'ness·wom'an** *n.fem., pl.* **-wom'en**

bus·ing, bus·sing (bus'iŋ) *n.* the transporting of children by bus to a school outside of their neighborhood, esp. in order to desegregate the schools

bus·kin (bus'kin) *n.* [< ? MDu. *brosekin*, small boot] **1.** a boot reaching to the calf or knee, worn long ago **2.** a high, laced boot worn in ancient tragedy **3.** tragic drama

buss (bus) *n., vt., vi.* [< ?] [Archaic or Dial.] kiss

bust' (bust) *n.* [< Fr. < It. *busto*] **1.** a sculpture of a person's head and shoulders **2.** a woman's bosom

bust² (bust) *vt., vi.* [< BURST] [Slang] **1.** to burst or break **2.** to make or become bankrupt or demoted **3.** to hit **4.** to arrest —*n.* [Slang] **1.** a failure **2.** a financial collapse **3.** a punch **4.** a spree **5.** an arrest —**bust'ed** *adj.*

BUSKINS

bus·tle' (bus'l) *vi., vt.* **-tled, -tling** [< ME. *busken*, prepare] to hurry busily —*n.* busy and noisy activity

bus·tle² (bus'l) *n.* [< ? G. *buschel*, a pad] a framework or padding worn at the back by women to puff out the skirt

bus·y (biz'ē) *adj.* **-i·er, -i·est** [OE. *bisig*] **1.** active; at work **2.** full of activity **3.** in use, as a telephone **4.** meddlesome **5.** too detailed —*vt.* **-ied, -y·ing** to make or keep busy —**bus'y·ness** *n.*

bus'y·bod'y (-bäd'ē) *n., pl.* **-ies** a meddler in the affairs of others

but (but) *prep.* [OE. *butan*, without] except; save [nobody came but me] —*conj.* **1.** yet; still [it's good, but not great] **2.** on the contrary [I am old, but he is young] **3.** unless [it never rains but it pours] **4.** that [I don't doubt but you're right] **5.** that...not [I never gamble but I lose] —*adv.* **1.** only [if I had but known] **2.** merely [he is but a child] **3.** just [I heard it but now] —*pron.* who...not; which...not [not a man but felt it] —**but for** if it were not for

BUSTLE

bu·ta·di·ene (byōōt'ə dī'ēn, -dī ēn') *n.* [< BUTANE] a hydrocarbon, C_4H_6, used to make a synthetic rubber

bu·tane (byōō'tān) *n.* [< L. *butyrum*, butter] either of two hydrocarbons, C_4H_{10}, used as a fuel, etc.

butch·er (booch'ər) *n.* [< Frank. *bukk*, he-goat] **1.** one whose work is killing and dressing animals for meat **2.** one who cuts meat for sale **3.** a brutal killer —*vt.* **1.** to kill or dress (animals) for meat **2.** to kill brutally **3.** to botch —**butch'er·y** *n., pl.* **-ies**

but·ler (but'lər) *n.* [< OFr. *bouteille*, a bottle] a manservant, usually the head servant of a household

But·ler (but'lər) **1. Samuel,** 1612–80; Eng. satirical poet **2. Samuel,** 1835–1902; Eng. novelist
butt¹ (but) *n.* [< ?] **1.** the thick end of anything **2.** a stub or stump, as the unsmoked end of a cigar **3.** a mound of earth behind a target **4.** an object of ridicule or criticism **5.** [Slang] a cigarette —*vt., vi.* to join end to end
butt² (but) *vt., vi.* [< OFr. *buter,* to thrust against] **1.** to ram with the head **2.** to abut on —*n.* a butting —**butt in(to)** [Slang] to mix into (another's business, etc.)
butt³ (but) *n.* [< LL. *bottis,* cask] a large cask, as for wine
butte (byōōt) *n.* [Fr., mound] a steep hill standing alone on a plain
but·ter (but'ər) *n.* [< L. *butyrum* < Gr. *bous,* cow + *tyros,* cheese] **1.** the solid, yellowish, edible fat obtained by churning cream **2.** any substance somewhat like butter —*vt.* **1.** to spread with butter **2.** [Colloq.] to flatter (often with *up*)
butter bean *same as:* **1.** LIMA BEAN **2.** WAX BEAN
but'ter·cup' *n.* a plant with yellow, cup-shaped flowers
but'ter·fat' *n.* the fatty part of milk from which butter is made
but'ter·fin'gers *n.* one who often fumbles and drops things
but'ter·fly' *n., pl.* **-flies'** [OE. *buttorfleoge*] an insect with a slender body and four broad, usually brightly colored wings
but'ter·milk' *n.* the liquid left after churning butter from milk or cream
but'ter·nut' *n.* **1.** a walnut tree of E N. America **2.** its edible, oily nut
but'ter·scotch' (-skäch') *n.* **1.** a hard, sticky candy made with brown sugar, butter, etc. **2.** a syrup flavored with this
but·ter·y¹ (but'ər ē, but'rē) *n., pl.* **-ies** [< LL. *bottis,* cask] **1.** a storeroom for wine, etc. **2.** a pantry
but·ter·y² (but'ər ē) *adj.* **1.** like butter **2.** containing or spread with butter **3.** adulatory
but·tock (but'ək) *n.* [OE. *buttuc,* end] **1.** either of the two fleshy, rounded parts at the back of the hips **2.** [*pl.*] the rump
but·ton (but'n) *n.* [OFr. *boton*] **1.** any small disk or knob used as a fastening, ornament, etc. on a garment **2.** anything small and shaped like a button **3.** a knob for operating a doorbell, electric lamp, etc. —*vt., vi.* to fasten with buttons
but'ton·hole' *n.* a slit or loop through which a button can be fastened —*vt.* **-holed', -hol'ing 1.** to make buttonholes in **2.** to make (a person) listen to one, as if by grasping his coat by a buttonhole
but'ton·wood' *n. same as* PLANE¹
but·tress (but'ris) *n.* [< OFr. *buter:* see BUTT²] **1.** a projecting structure built against a wall to support or reinforce it **2.** a support; prop —*vt.* **1.** to support with a buttress **2.** to bolster
bux·om (buk'səm) *adj.* [ME., humble] healthy, comely, plump, etc.: specif. said of a full-bosomed woman —**bux'om·ness** *n.*
buy (bī) *vt.* **bought, buy'ing** [< OE. *bycgan*] **1.** to get by paying money; purchase **2.** to get by an exchange **3.** to bribe **4.** [Slang] to accept as true [I can't *buy* his excuse] —*vi.* to be a buyer —*n.* **1.** a buying **2.** anything bought **3.** [Colloq.] a bargain —**buy off** to bribe —**buy out** to buy all the stock, rights, etc. —**buy up** to buy all that is available of

buy'er *n.* **1.** one who buys; consumer **2.** one whose work is to buy merchandise for a retail store
buzz (buz) *vi.* [echoic] **1.** to hum like a bee **2.** to gossip **3.** to be filled wih noisy activity or talk —*vt.* to fly an airplane low over —*n.* a sound like a bee's hum —**buzz about** (or **around**) to scurry about
buz·zard (buz'ərd) *n.* [< L. *buteo,* a kind of hawk] **1.** any of various hawks that are slow and heavy in flight **2.** *same as* TURKEY BUZZARD
buzz'er *n.* an electrical device that makes a buzzing sound as a signal
buzz saw a circular saw rotated by machinery
bx. box
by (bī) *prep.* [OE. *be, bi*] **1.** near; at [stand *by* the wall] **2.** *a*) in or during [to travel *by* night] *b*) for a fixed time [to work *by* the hour] *c*) not later than [back *by* noon] **3.** *a*) through; via [to Boston *by* Route 6] *b*) past; beyond [he walked right *by* me] **4.** in behalf of [he did well *by* me] **5.** through the agency of [gained *by* fraud] **6.** *a*) according to [by the book] *b*) in [to grow dark *by* degrees] *c*) following in series [march two *by* two] **7.** *a*) in or to the amount of [apples *by* the peck] *b*) and in another dimension [two *by* four] *c*) using (the given number) as multiplier or divisor —*adv.* **1.** close at hand [stand *by*] **2.** away; aside [put money *by*] **3.** past [he sped *by*] **4.** at someone's place [stop *by*] —**by and by** after a while —**by and large** considering everything —**by the by** incidentally
by- *a prefix meaning:* **1.** close by; near **2.** secondary
by'-and-by' *n.* a future time
bye (bī) *n.* [see BY] the advantage obtained by an unpaired contestant in a tournament, who advances to the next round without playing —*adj.* incidental —**by the bye** incidentally
bye'-bye' *n., interj.* goodbye
by'-e·lec'tion *n.* [Chiefly Brit.] a special election between general elections
Bye·lo·rus·sian Soviet Socialist Republic (bye'lō rush'ən) republic of the U.S.S.R., in the W European part: also **Bye'lo·rus'sia**
by·gone (bī'gôn') *adj.* past; former —*n.* anything gone or past —**let bygones be bygones** to let past offenses be forgotten
by·law (bī'lô') *n.* [< ME. *bī,* town + *laue,* law] any of a set of rules adopted by an organization for governing its meetings or affairs
by'line' *n.* a line above a newspaper article, etc. telling who wrote it
by'pass' *n.* a way, pipe, channel, etc. between two points that avoids or is auxiliary to the main way —*vt.* **1.** to detour **2.** to furnish with a bypass **3.** to ignore
by'path', by'-path' *n.* a side path; byway
by'play' *n.* action, gestures, etc. going on aside from the main action, as in a play
by'prod'uct, by'-prod'uct *n.* anything produced, as from residues, in the course of making another thing
by'road' *n.* a side road
By·ron (bī'rən), **George Gordon** 1788–1824; Eng. poet
by'stand'er *n.* a person who stands near but does not participate
by'way' *n.* a side road or path
by'word' *n.* **1.** a proverb **2.** a person or thing proverbial as being contemptible or ridiculous
By·zan·tine Empire (biz'n tēn') empire (395–1453) in SE Europe & SW Asia

C

C, c (sē) *n., pl.* **C's, c's** the third letter of the English alphabet —*adj.* third in a sequence or group
C (sē) *n.* **1.** a Roman numeral for 100 **2.** a grade indicating average work **3.** *Chem.* carbon **4.** *Music* the first tone in the scale of C major
C, C. 1. Celsius or centigrade **2.** Central
C. 1. Catholic **2.** Congress **3.** Corps
C., c. 1. carat **2.** catcher **3.** cent **4.** center **5.** centimeter

6. century **7.** circa **8.** college **9.** copyright **10.** cycle
Ca *Chem.* calcium
CA California
cab (kab) *n.* [< CABRIOLET] **1.** a carriage for public hire **2.** *short for* TAXICAB **3.** the place in a locomotive, truck, etc. where the operator sits
ca·bal (kə bal') *n.* [Fr., intrigue] **1.** a small group joined in a secret intrigue **2.** such an intrigue

fat, āpe, cär; ten, ēven; is, bīte; gō, hôrn, tōol, look; oil, out; up, fur; thin, *then*; zh, leisure; ŋ, ring; ə for *a* in *ago*; ' as in *able* (ā'b'l); ë, Fr. coeur; ö, Fr. feu; Fr. mon; ü, Fr. duc; r, Fr. cri; kh, G. doch, ich. ‡ foreign; < derived from

cab·a·la (kab′ə lə, kə bäl′ə) *n.* [< Heb. *qabbālāh*, received lore] **1.** an occult rabbinical philosophy based on a mystical interpretation of the Scriptures **2.** any secret doctrine —cab′a·lis′tic *adj.*

ca·bal·le·ro (kab′ə ler′ō, -əl yer′ō) *n., pl.* -ros [Sp. < L. *caballus*, horse] **1.** a Spanish gentleman **2.** [Southwest] *a)* a horseman *b)* a lady's escort

ca·ba·na (kə bän′ə, -ban′ə) *n.* [< Sp. < LL. *capanna*] **1.** a cabin or hut **2.** a small shelter for swimmers at a beach, pool, etc.

cab·a·ret (kab′ə rā′) *n.* [Fr.] a café with dancing, singing, etc. as entertainment

cab·bage (kab′ij) *n.* [? < L. *caput*, head] a vegetable with thick leaves formed into a round, compact head

cab·driv·er (kab′drīv′ər) *n.* one who drives a cab: also [Colloq.] **cab′by, cab′bie** (-ē), *pl.* -bies

cab·in (kab′'n) *n.* [< LL. *capanna*, hut] **1.** a small, crudely or simply built house **2.** a room on a ship or boat **3.** the space for passengers in an aircraft

cabin cruiser a motorboat with a cabin, equipped for living on board

cab·i·net (kab′ə nit) *n.* [Fr. < ?] **1.** a case with drawers or shelves to hold or store things **2.** a boxlike enclosure for the components of a record player, radio, etc. **3.** [often C-] a body of official advisers to a chief executive

cab′i·net·mak′er *n.* a workman who makes fine furniture —cab′i·net·mak′ing *n.*

cab′i·net·work′ *n.* articles made by a cabinetmaker: also **cab′i·net·ry** (-rē)

ca·ble (kā′b'l) *n.* [< L. *capere*, take hold] **1.** a thick, heavy rope, often of wire strands **2.** a bundle of insulated wires to carry an electric current **3.** a cablegram —*vt.* -bled, -bling **1.** to fasten with a cable **2.** to transmit by undersea cable **3.** to send a cablegram to —*vi.* to send a cablegram

cable car a car drawn by a moving cable, as up a steep incline

ca′ble·gram′ (-gram′) *n.* a message sent by undersea cable

cable length a unit of nautical measure equal (in the U.S. Navy) to 720 feet

ca·boo·dle (kə bōō′d'l) *n.* [< BOODLE] [Colloq.] lot; group [the whole *caboodle*]

ca·boose (kə bōōs′) *n.* [MDu. *kabuys*, cabin house] the trainmen's car at the rear of a freight train

Cab·ot (kab′ət), **John** 1450?–98; It. explorer in the service of England: discovered N. America (1497)

cab·ri·o·let (kab′rē ə lā′) *n.* [< Fr. *cabriole*, a leap] a light, two-wheeled carriage drawn by one horse

cab·stand (kab′stand′) *n.* a place where cabs are stationed for hire

ca·ca·o (kə kā′ō, -kä′ō) *n., pl.* -os [Sp. < MexInd. *cacauatl*] **1.** the seed of a tropical American tree, from which cocoa and chocolate are made: also **cacao bean 2.** this tree

cac·cia·to·re (kach′ə tôr′ē) *adj.* [It., lit., a hunter] cooked in a casserole with olive oil and tomatoes, onions, spices, etc.

cache (kash) *n.* [Fr. < L. *coactare*, constrain] **1.** a place in which stores of food, supplies, etc. are hidden **2.** anything so hidden —*vt.* cached, cach′ing to place in a cache

ca·chet (ka shā′) *n.* [Fr. < *cacher*, to hide] **1.** a stamp or seal on an official document **2.** *a)* a mark showing that something is genuine or of superior quality *b)* prestige **3.** a commemorative design, slogan, advertisement, etc. stamped on mail

cack·le (kak′'l) *vi.* -led, -ling [echoic] **1.** to make the shrill, broken sounds of a hen **2.** to laugh or chatter with similar sounds —*vt.* to utter in a cackling manner —*n.* a cackling

ca·coph·o·ny (kə käf′ə nē) *n., pl.* -nies [< Gr. *kakos*, bad + *phōnē*, voice] harsh, jarring sound; dissonance —ca·coph′o·nous *adj.*

cac·tus (kak′təs) *n., pl.* -tus·es, -ti (-tī) [< Gr. *kaktos*, kind of thistle] any of various desert plants with fleshy stems and spinelike leaves

cad (kad) *n.* [< CADET] a man whose behavior is not gentlemanly

ca·dav·er (kə dav′ər) *n.* [L., prob. < *cadere*, to fall] a dead body; corpse, as for dissection

ca·dav′er·ous (-əs) *adj.* of or like a cadaver; pale, gaunt, haggard, etc.

cad·die (kad′ē) *n.* [Scot. form of Fr. *cadet:* see CADET] **1.** one who attends a golfer, carrying his clubs, etc. **2.** a small, wheeled cart —*vi.* -died, -dy·ing to act as a caddie

cad·dish (kad′ish) *adj.* like or characteristic of a cad; ungentlemanly —cad′dish·ly *adv.* —cad′dish·ness *n.*

cad·dy¹ (kad′ē) *n., pl.* -dies [< Malay *kati*, unit of weight] a small container, specif. one used for tea

cad·dy² (kad′ē) *n., vi. same as* CADDIE

-cade [< (CAVAL)CADE] *a suffix meaning* procession, parade *[motorcade]*

ca·dence (kād′'ns) *n.* [< L. *cadere*, to fall] **1.** fall of the voice in speaking **2.** a rhythmic flow of sound **3.** measured movement, as in marching **4.** *Music* the harmonic ending, final trill, etc. of a phrase or movement —ca′denced *adj.*

ca·den·za (kə den′zə) *n.* [It.: see prec.] **1.** an elaborate passage for the solo instrument in a concerto **2.** any brilliant flourish in an aria, etc.

ca·det (kə det′) *n.* [Fr. < L. dim. of *caput*, the head] **1.** a student in training at an armed forces academy **2.** any trainee, as a practice teacher —ca·det′ship *n.*

cadge (kaj) *vt., vi.* cadged, cadg′ing [ME. *caggen*, to tie] to beg or get by begging —cadg′er *n.*

ca·di (kä′dē) *n.* [Ar. *qādī*] a minor Muslim magistrate or judge

Cá·diz (kə diz′) seaport in SW Spain: pop. 133,000

cad·mi·um (kad′mē əm) *n.* [< L. *cadmia*, zinc ore (in which it occurs)] a blue-white, metallic chemical element used in alloys, electroplating, etc.: symbol, Cd; at. wt., 112.40; at. no., 48

ca·dre (kad′rē) *n.* [Fr. < L. *quadrum*, a square] a nucleus around which an expanded organization, as a military unit, can be built

ca·du·ce·us (kə dōō′sē əs) *n., pl.* -ce·i′ (-sē ī′) [L.] the winged staff with two serpents twined about it, carried by Mercury: now a symbol of the medical profession

cae·cum (sē′kəm) *n., pl.* -ca (-kə) *same as* CECUM

Cae·sar (sē′zər) *n.* [< J. CAESAR] **1.** the title of the Roman emperors from Augustus to Hadrian **2.** any emperor or dictator

Cae·sar (sē′zər), **(Gaius) Julius** 100?–44 B.C.; Roman general & statesman

Cae·sar·e·an section (si zer′ē ən) [< J. CAESAR, supposedly born in this way] [*also* c- s-] an operation for delivering a baby by cutting through the mother's abdominal and uterine walls

CADUCEUS

cae·su·ra (si zhoor′ə, -zyoor′ə) *n., pl.* -ras, -rae (-ē) [L. < *caedere*, to cut] a break or pause in a line of verse, usually in the middle

ca·fé, ca·fe (ka fā′) *n.* [Fr. < It. *caffè*, coffee] a small restaurant or a barroom, nightclub, etc.

café curtains short, straight curtains hung from a rod by means of sliding rings

caf·e·te·ri·a (kaf′ə tir′ē ə) *n.* [AmSp., coffee store] a restaurant in which food is displayed on counters and patrons serve themselves

caf·feine, caf·fein (kaf′ēn, ka fēn′) *n.* [< G. < It. *caffè*, coffee + *-in*, -INE³] the alkaloid present in coffee, tea, etc.: it is a stimulant

caf·tan (kaf′tən, käf tän′) *n.* [Turk. *gaftān*] a long-sleeved robe worn in eastern Mediterranean countries

cage (kāj) *n.* [< L. *cavus*, hollow] **1.** a structure of wires, bars, etc. for confining birds or animals **2.** any openwork structure, as some elevator cars —*vt.* caged, cag′ing to put in a cage

ca·gey, ca·gy (kā′jē) *adj.* -gi·er, -gi·est [< ?] [Colloq.] **1.** sly; tricky; cunning **2.** cautious —ca′gi·ly *adv.* —ca′gi·ness *n.*

ca·hoots (kə hōōts′) *n.pl.* [< ?] [Slang] partnership; league: implying scheming in the phrase **in cahoots**

cai·man (kā′mən) *n., pl.* -mans [Sp. < Carib native name] a reptile of tropical America similar to the alligator and crocodile

Cain (kān) *Bible* the oldest son of Adam and Eve: he killed his brother Abel —raise Cain [Slang] to cause a great commotion or much trouble

cairn (kern) *n.* [Scot. < Gael. *carn*, elevation] a conical heap of stones built as a monument or landmark

Cai·ro (kī′rō) capital of Egypt: pop. 3,346,000

cais·son (kā′sän) *n.* [Fr. < It. < L. *capsa*, a box] **1.** a two-wheeled wagon with a chest for ammunition **2.** a watertight box for underwater construction work

cai·tiff (kāt′if) *n.* [< L. *captivus*, CAPTIVE] a mean, evil, or cowardly person —*adj.* mean, evil, or cowardly

ca·jole (kə jōl′) *vt., vi.* -joled′, -jol′ing [< Fr.] to coax with flattery and insincere talk —ca·jol′er *n.* —ca·jol′er·y *n.*

Ca·jun, Ca·jan (kā′jən) *n.* [< Acadian Fr.] **1.** a native of Louisiana descended from Acadian French immigrants:

sometimes used contemptuously 2. the dialect of the Cajuns

cake (kāk) *n.* [< ON.] 1. a small, flat mass of baked or fried dough, batter, or hashed food 2. a baked mixture of flour, eggs, sugar, etc., often covered with icing 3. a shaped solid mass, as of soap 4. a hard crust or deposit — *vt., vi.* **caked, cak′ing** to form into a hard mass or a crust —**take the cake** [Slang] to win the prize: often used ironically

Cal. 1. California 2. large calorie(s)

cal. 1. caliber 2. small calorie(s)

cal·a·bash (kal′ə bash′) *n.* [< Fr. < Sp. *calabaza* < ?] 1. the gourdlike fruit of a tropical American tree 2. the bottle-shaped gourd of a tropical American vine, or a smoking pipe made from it

cal·a·boose (kal′ə bōōs′) *n.* [Sp. *calabozo*] [Slang] a jail

Cal·ais (ka lā′, kal′ā) seaport in N France, on the Strait of Dover: pop. 75,000

cal·a·mine (kal′ə mīn′) *n.* [Fr. < L. *cadmia*, zinc ore] a zinc-oxide powder used in skin lotions and ointments

ca·lam·i·tous (kə lam′ə təs) *adj.* bringing or causing calamity —**ca·lam′i·tous·ly** *adv.* —**ca·lam′i·tous·ness** *n.*

ca·lam′i·ty (-tē) *n., pl.* **-ties** [< Fr. < L. *calamitas*] a great misfortune; disaster

cal·car·e·ous (kal ker′ē əs) *adj.* [< L. *calx*, lime] of or like calcium carbonate, calcium, or lime

cal·cif·er·ous (kal sif′ər əs) *adj.* [< L. *calx*, lime + -FEROUS] producing or containing calcite

cal·ci·fy (kal′sə fī′) *vt., vi.* **-fied′, -fy′ing** [< L. *calx*, lime + -FY] to change into a hard, stony substance by the deposit of lime or calcium salts —**cal·ci·fi·ca′tion** *n.*

cal′ci·mine′ (-mīn′) *n.* [< L. *calx*, lime] a white or colored liquid used as a wash for plastered walls —*vt.* **-mined′, -min′ing** to cover with calcimine

cal·cine (kal′sīn) *vt., vi.* **-cined, -cin·ing** [< ML. *calcinare*] to change into an ashy powder by heat

cal·cite (kal′sīt) *n.* calcium carbonate, CaCO₃, a mineral found as limestone, chalk, and marble

cal·ci·um (kal′sē əm) *n.* [< L. *calx*, lime] a soft, silver-white metallic chemical element found combined in limestone, chalk, etc.: symbol, Ca; at. wt., 40.08; at. no., 20

calcium carbide a dark-gray, crystalline compound, CaC₂, used in making acetylene

calcium carbonate a white powder or crystalline compound, CaCO₃, found in limestone, chalk, and marble, and in bones, shells, etc.: used in making lime

calcium chloride a white, crystalline compound, CaCl₂, used in making ice, for dehydrating, etc.

calcium oxide a white, soft, caustic solid, CaO, prepared by heating calcium carbonate; lime

cal·cu·late (kal′kyə lāt′) *vt.* **-lat′ed, -lat′ing** [< L. *calculare*, reckon] 1. to determine by using mathematics; compute 2. to determine by reasoning; estimate 3. to plan; intend [words *calculated* to mislead us] —*vi.* 1. to make a computation 2. to rely (*on*) —**cal′cu·la·ble** (-lə b'l) *adj.*

cal′cu·lat′ed *adj.* deliberately planned or carefully considered

cal′cu·lat′ing *adj.* shrewd or scheming

cal′cu·la′tion *n.* 1. a calculating 2. something deduced by calculating 3. careful planning or forethought, esp. with selfish motives

cal′cu·la′tor *n.* 1. one who calculates 2. a machine for doing arithmetic rapidly: also **calculating machine**

cal·cu·lus (kal′kyə ləs) *n., pl.* **-li′** (-lī′), **-lus·es** [L., pebble used in counting] 1. an abnormal stony mass in the body 2. a method of calculation or analysis in higher mathematics

Cal·cut·ta (kal kut′ə) seaport in NE India: pop. 2,927,000

cal·dron (kôl′drən) *n.* [< L. *calidus*, warm] a large kettle or boiler

Cal·e·do·ni·a (kal′ə dōn′yə, -dō′nē ə) [L.] *poetic name for* SCOTLAND —**Cal′e·do′ni·an** *adj., n.*

cal·en·dar (kal′ən dər) *n.* [< L. *calendarium*, account book] 1. a system of determining the length and divisions of a year 2. a table that shows the days, weeks, and months of a given year 3. a schedule, as of pending court cases —*vt.* to enter in a calendar; schedule

calendar year the period of time from Jan. 1 through Dec. 31

cal·en·der (kal′ən dər) *n.* [< Fr. < Gr. *kylindein*, to roll] a machine with rollers for giving paper, cloth, etc. a smooth or glossy finish —*vt.* to process (paper, etc.) in a calender

cal·ends (kal′əndz) *n.pl.* [*often with sing. v.*] [< Gr. *kalein*, proclaim] the first day of each month in the ancient Roman calendar

ca·len·du·la (kə len′jə lə) *n.* [< L. *kalendae*, calends: prob. because plant blooms in most months] a plant with yellow or orange, daisylike flowers

calf¹ (kaf) *n., pl.* **calves**; *esp. for 3,* **calfs** [OE. *cealf*] 1. a young cow or bull 2. the young of some other large animals, as the elephant, seal, etc. 3. leather from a calf's hide —**kill the fatted calf** to make a feast of welcome

calf² (kaf) *n., pl.* **calves** [ON. *kalfi*] the fleshy back part of the leg below the knee

calf′skin′ *n.* 1. the skin of a calf 2. leather made from this

Cal·ga·ry (kal′gər ē) city in S Alberta, Canada: pop. 331,000

cal·i·ber, cal·i·bre (kal′ə bər) *n.* [< Fr. & Sp. < Ar. *qālib*, a mold] 1. the diameter of a cylindrical body, esp. of a bullet or shell 2. the diameter of the bore of a gun 3. quality or ability

cal·i·brate (kal′ə brāt′) *vt.* **-brat′ed, -brat′ing** 1. to determine the caliber of 2. to fix or correct the scale of (a measuring instrument) —**cal′i·bra′tion** *n.* —**cal′i·bra′tor** *n.*

cal·i·co (kal′ə kō′) *n., pl.* **-coes′, -cos′** [< *Calicut*, city in India] a kind of coarse, printed cotton cloth —*adj.* 1. of calico 2. spotted like calico

Cal·i·for·ni·a (kal′ə fôr′nyə, -nē ə) 1. State of the SW U.S., on the Pacific coast: 158,693 sq. mi.; pop. 19,953,000; cap. Sacramento: abbrev. **Calif., CA, Cal.** 2. Gulf of, arm of the Pacific, between Baja California and the Mexican mainland —**Cal′i·for′ni·an** *adj., n.*

cal·i·for·ni·um (kal′ə fôr′nē əm) *n.* [< Univ. of *California*] a radioactive chemical element: symbol, Cf; at. wt., 251 (?); at. no., 98

cal·i·per (kal′ə pər) *n.* [var. of CALIBER] [*usually pl.*] instrument consisting of a pair of hinged legs, for measuring thickness or diameter —*vt., vi.* to measure with calipers

ca·liph (kā′lif, kal′if) *n.* [< Ar. *khalīfa*] supreme ruler: the title taken by Mohammed's successors as heads of Islam: also **ca′lif** —**cal·iph·ate** (kal′ə fāt′, -fit) *n.*

cal·is·then·ics (kal′əs then′iks) *n.pl.* [< Gr. *kallos*, beauty + *sthenos*, strength] exercises to develop a strong, trim body —**cal′is·then′ic** *adj.*

calk¹ (kôk) *vt. same as* CAULK —**calk′er** *n.*

calk² (kôk) *n.* [< L. *calx*, a heel] a metal plate put on the bottom of a shoe or horseshoe to prevent slipping —*vt.* to fasten calks on

call (kôl) *vt.* [< ON. *kalla*] 1. to say in a loud tone; shout 2. to summon 3. to convoke [to *call* a meeting] 4. to give or apply a name to 5. to declare to be as specified [I *call* it silly] 6. to awaken 7. to communicate with by telephone 8. to give orders for 9. to stop (a game, etc.) 10. to demand payment of (a loan, etc.) 11. *Poker* to require (a player) to show his hand by equaling his bet —*vi.* 1. to shout 2. to utter its characteristic cry, as a bird 3. to visit for a short while 4. to telephone 5. *Poker* to require a player to show his hand by equaling his bet —*n.* 1. a calling 2. a loud utterance 3. the distinctive cry of an animal or bird 4. a summons to a meeting, etc. 5. an economic demand, as for a product 6. need [no *call* for tears] 7. a demand for payment 8. a brief visit 9. *Sports* an official's decision —**call down** [Colloq.] to scold sharply —**call for** 1. to demand 2. to come and get —**call off** to cancel (a scheduled event) —**call on** 1. to visit briefly 2. to ask (a person) to speak —**call out** to shout —**call up** 1. to make one remember 2. to summon, esp. for military duty 3. to telephone —**on call** available when summoned

cal·la (kal′ə) *n.* [< L., a kind of plant] a plant with a conspicuous spathe surrounding a yellow spadix: also **calla lily**

call′er *n.* 1. a person or thing that calls 2. a person who makes a short visit

call girl a prostitute who is called by telephone to make assignations

cal·lig·ra·phy (kə lig′rə fē) *n.* [< Gr. *kallos*, beauty + *graphein*, to write] 1. beautiful handwriting 2. handwriting —**cal·lig′ra·pher** *n.* —**cal·li·graph·ic** (kal′ə graf′ik) *adj.*

call′ing *n.* 1. the act of one that calls 2. one's occupation, profession, or trade

calling card a small card with one's name and, sometimes, one's address, used in making visits

cal·li·o·pe (kə lī′ə pē′, kal′ē ōp′) *n.* [< Gr. *kallos*, beauty

+ *ops*, voice] a musical instrument with a series of steam whistles, played like an organ

cal·lis·then·ics (kal'əs then'iks) *n.pl. same as* CALISTHENICS

call letters the letters that identify a radio or TV station

cal·los·i·ty (ka läs'ə tē, kə-) *n.* 1. a being callous, hardened, or unfeeling 2. *pl.* **-ties** a hardened, thickened place on skin or bark; callus

cal·lous (kal'əs) *adj.* [< L. *callum*, hard skin] 1. hardened 2. unfeeling; insensitive —*vt., vi.* to make or become callous —**cal'lous·ly** *adv.* —**cal'lous·ness** *n.*

cal·low (kal'ō) *adj.* [OE. *calu*, bald] 1. still lacking the feathers needed for flying 2. young and inexperienced — **cal'low·ness** *n.*

cal·lus (kal'əs) *n., pl.* **-lus·es** [L., var. of *callum*, hard skin] 1. a hardened, thickened place on the skin 2. a mass of cells that develops over a wound on a plant —*vi., vt.* to develop or cause to develop a callus

calm (käm) *n.* [< Gr. *kauma*, heat] 1. stillness 2. lack of excitement; tranquillity —*adj.* 1. still; quiet 2. not excited; tranquil —*vt., vi.* to make or become calm (often with *down*) —**calm'ly** *adv.* —**calm'ness** *n.*

cal·o·mel (kal'ə mel', -məl) *n.* [Fr. < Gr. *kalos*, beautiful + *melas*, black] a white, tasteless powder, HgCl, formerly used as a cathartic, etc.

ca·lor·ic (kə lôr'ik, -lär'-) *adj.* [see CALORIE] 1. of heat 2. of calories —**ca·lor'i·cal·ly** *adv.*

cal·o·rie (kal'ə rē) *n.* [Fr. < L. *calor*, heat] 1. the amount of heat needed to raise the temperature of one gram of water one degree centigrade: also **small calorie** 2. [*occas.* C-] the amount of heat needed to raise the temperature of one kilogram of water one degree centigrade: also **large calorie** 3. a unit equal to the large calorie, used for measuring energy produced by food when oxidized in the body Also sp. **cal'o·ry**, *pl.* **-ries**

cal·o·rif·ic (kal'ə rif'ik) *adj.* [< Fr. < L. *calor*, heat + *facere*, to make] producing heat

cal·o·rim·e·ter (kal'ə rim'ə tər) *n.* [< L. *calor*, heat + -METER] an apparatus for measuring heat

cal·u·met (kal'yə met') *n.* [Fr. < L. *calamus*, a reed] a long-stemmed ceremonial pipe smoked by N. American Indians as a token of peace

ca·lum·ni·ate (kə lum'nē āt') *vt., vi.* **-at'ed, -at'ing** [see CALUMNY] to slander —**ca·lum'ni·a'tion** *n.* —**ca·lum'ni·a'tor** *n.*

cal·um·ny (kal'əm nē) *n., pl.* **-nies** [< Fr. < L. *calumnia*, slander] a false and malicious statement; slander

CALUMET

Cal·va·ry (kal'vər ē) [< L. *calvaria*, skull; transl. of Aram. *gūlgūlthā*, Golgotha, lit., skull] *Bible* the place where Jesus was crucified

calve (kav) *vi., vt.* **calved, calv'ing** to give birth to (a calf)

calves (kavz) *n. pl. of* CALF

Cal·vin (kal'vin), **John** 1509–64; Fr. Protestant reformer

Cal'vin·ism (-iz'm) *n.* the theological system of John Calvin and his followers: it emphasizes predestination and salvation solely by God's grace —**Cal'vin·ist** *n., adj.* — **Cal'vin·is'tic** *adj.*

ca·lyp·so (kə lip'sō) *adj.* [< ?] designating or of highly syncopated, satirical ballads improvised and sung, originally, by natives of Trinidad

ca·lyx (kā'liks, kal'iks) *n., pl.* **-lyx·es, -ly·ces'** (-lə sēz') [L., pod] the outer whorl of protective leaves, or sepals, of a flower

cam (kam) *n.* [Du. *cam*, orig., a comb] a wheel, projection on a wheel, etc. which gives an irregular motion as to a wheel or shaft, or receives such motion from it

ca·ma·ra·de·rie (käm'ə räd'ər ē) *n.* [Fr.] loyalty and friendly feeling among comrades

cam·ber (kam'bər) *n.* [< L. *camur*, arched] 1. a slight convex curve of a surface, as of a road 2. a slight tilt given to each of a pair of automobile wheels so that the bottoms are closer together than the tops —*vt., vi.* to arch slightly

cam·bi·um (kam'bē əm) *n.* [LL., change] a layer of formative cells between the wood and bark in woody plants, from which new wood and bark grow

Cam·bo·di·a (kam bō'dē ə) *former name of* KAMPUCHEA —**Cam·bo'di·an** *adj., n.*

cam·bric (kām'brik) *n.* [< *Cambrai*, Fr. city] a fine linen or cotton cloth

Cam·bridge (kām'brij) 1. city in EC England: pop. 100,000 2. city in E Mass.: pop. 100,000

Cam·den (kam'dən) city in SW N.J.: pop. 103,000

came (kām) *pt. of* COME

cam·el (kam''l) *n.* [< Heb. *gāmāl*] a large, domesticated animal with a humped back and long neck: because it can store water in its body, it is used in Asian and African deserts: see BACTRIAN CAMEL and DROMEDARY

ca·mel·li·a (kə mēl'yə) *n.* [< G. *Kamel* (d. 1706), missionary to the Far East] 1. an Asiatic evergreen tree or shrub with glossy, dark-green leaves and waxy, roselike flowers 2. the flower

ca·mel·o·pard (kə mel'ə pärd') *n.* [< Gr. *kamelos*, camel + *pardalis*, leopard: from its neck and spots] *early name for the* GIRAFFE

Cam·e·lot (kam'ə lät') the legendary English town where King Arthur had his court

camel's hair 1. the hair of the camel 2. cloth made of this hair, sometimes mixed with wool, etc.: it is usually light tan and very soft —**cam'el's-hair', cam'el-hair'** *adj.*

Cam·em·bert (cheese) (kam'əm ber') [< *Camembert*, Fr. village] a soft, creamy, rich cheese

cam·e·o (kam'ē ō') *n., pl.* **-os'** [< It. < ML. *camaeus*] 1. a carving in relief on certain stratified gems or shells 2. a gem, shell, etc. carved with a figure or design raised in relief 3. a choice bit role, esp. when played by a noted actor

cam·er·a (kam'ər ə, kam'rə) *n.* [L., a vault] 1. a device for taking photographs, a closed box containing a sensitized plate or film on which an image is formed when light enters through a lens 2. *TV* that part of the transmitter which receives the image to be televised and transforms it into electrical signals —**in camera** 1. in a judge's private office 2. in privacy or secrecy

Cam·e·roun (kam'ə rōōn') country in WC Africa, on the Atlantic: 183,000 sq. mi.; pop. 5,562,000; cap. Yaoundé: also sp. **Cameroon** —**Cam'e·roun'i·an** *adj., n.*

cam·i·sole (kam'ə sōl') *n.* [Fr. < VL. *camisia*, shirt] 1. a woman's sleeveless underwaist 2. a woman's short negligee

cam·o·mile (kam'ə mīl', -mēl') *n. same as* CHAMOMILE

cam·ou·flage (kam'ə fläzh', -fläj') *n.* [Fr. < *camoufler*, to disguise] 1. the disguising of ships, guns, etc. to conceal them from the enemy, as by the use of paint, nets, etc. 2. a disguise of this kind 3. any device or action used to conceal or mislead; deception —*vt., vi.* **-flaged', -flag'ing** to disguise (a thing or person) in order to conceal

camp (kamp) *n.* [< Fr. < L. *campus*, field] 1. *a)* a place where tents, huts, etc. are put up temporarily, as for soldiers *b)* a group of such tents, etc. 2. the supporters of a particular cause or opinion 3. a recreational place in the country for vacationers, esp. children 4. the people living in a camp 5. [Slang] banality, artifice, etc. so extreme as to amuse or have a perversely sophisticated appeal —*adj.* [Slang] characterized by camp (*n.* 5) —*vi.* 1. to set up a camp 2. to live or stay in a camp (often with *out*) —**break camp** to pack up camping gear and depart

cam·paign (kam pān') *n.* [< Fr. < L. *campus*, field] 1. a series of military operations with a particular objective 2. a series of planned actions, as for electing a candidate — *vi.* to participate in a campaign —**cam·paign'er** *n.*

cam·pa·ni·le (kam'pə nē'lē) *n., pl.* **-les, -li** (-lē) [It. < LL. *campana*, a bell] a bell tower

camp chair a lightweight folding chair

camp'er *n.* 1. one who vacations at a camp 2. a motor vehicle or trailer equipped for camping out

camp'fire' *n.* 1. an outdoor fire at a camp 2. a social gathering around such a fire

campfire girl a member of the Camp Fire Girls, an organization to provide healthful, character-building activities for girls

camp'ground' *n.* 1. a place where a camp is set up 2. a place where a camp meeting is held

cam·phor (kam'fər) *n.* [< Sans. *karpurah*, camphor tree] a crystalline substance, $C_{10}H_{16}O$, with a strong odor, derived chiefly from an Oriental evergreen tree (**camphor tree**): used to repel moths, in medicine as a stimulant, etc. —**cam'phor·ic** (-fôr'ik) *adj.*

cam'phor·ate' (-fə rāt') *vt.* **-at'ed, -at'ing** to put camphor in or on [*camphorated oil*]

camp meeting a religious gathering held outdoors or in a tent, etc.

camp'site' *n.* 1. any site for a temporary camp 2. a camping area in a park, often equipped with water, toilets, etc.

cam·pus (kam'pəs) *n., pl.* **-pus·es** [L., field] the grounds, sometimes including the buildings, of a school or college —*adj.* of a school or college

can¹ (kan, kən) *vi. pt.* **could** [OE. *cunnan*, know] **1.** to know how to **2.** to be able to **3.** to be likely to *[can* it be true?*]* **4.** to have the right to **5.** [Colloq.] to be permitted to; may —**can but** can only

can² (kan) *n.* [OE. *canne*, a cup] **1.** a container, usually metal, with a separate cover *[a garbage can]* **2.** a tinned metal container in which foods, etc. are sealed for preservation **3.** the contents of a can **4.** [Slang] *a)* a prison *b)* a toilet —*vt.* **canned, can'ning 1.** to put up in airtight cans or jars for preservation **2.** [Slang] to dismiss

Can. 1. Canada **2.** Canadian: also **Canad.**

Ca·naan (kā'nən) Promised Land of the Israelites, a region between the Jordan & the Mediterranean —**Ca'naan·ite'** (-īt') *n.*

Can·a·da (kan'ə də) country in N North America: 3,852,000 sq. mi.; pop. 20,015,000; cap. Ottawa —**Ca·na·di·an** (kə nā'dē ən) *adj., n.*

Canada goose a large wild goose of Canada and the northern U.S., gray, with black head and neck

ca·naille (kə nāl') *n.* [Fr. < L. *canis*, a dog] the mob; rabble

ca·nal (kə nal') *n.* [< L. *canalis*, a channel] **1.** an artificial waterway for transportation or irrigation **2.** *Anat.* a tubular passage or duct —*vt.* **-nalled'** or **-naled', -nal'ling** or **-nal'ing** to build a canal through

ca·nal·ize (kə nal'īz, kan'ə līz') *vt.* **-ized, -iz·ing 1.** to make a canal through **2.** to provide an outlet for, esp. by directing into a specific channel

Canal Zone strip of land in Panama under perpetual lease to the U.S.: it extends about 5 miles on either side of the Panama Canal: 362 sq. mi.; pop. 45,000

ca·na·pé (kan'ə pē, -pā') *n.* [Fr.] a cracker, etc. spread with spiced meat, fish, cheese, etc., served as an appetizer

ca·nard (kə närd') *n.* [Fr., a duck, hoax] a false, esp. malicious, report

ca·nar·y (kə ner'ē) *n., pl.* **-ies** [< *Canary* Islands] **1.** a yellow songbird of the finch family **2.** a light yellow: also **canary yellow**

Canary Islands group of Spanish islands in the Atlantic, off NW Africa

ca·nas·ta (kə nas'tə) *n.* [Sp., basket] a double-deck card game for two to six players

Can·ber·ra (kan'bər ə) capital of Australia: pop. 92,000

can·can (kan'kan') *n.* [Fr.] a lively dance with much high kicking, performed by woman entertainers

can·cel (kan's'l) *vt.* **-celed** or **-celled, -cel·ing** or **-cel·ling** [< L. *cancelli*, lattice] **1.** to cross out, as with lines **2.** to make invalid; annul **3.** to do away with; abolish **4.** to neutralize or balance (often with *out*) **5.** *Math.* to remove (a common factor, equivalents, etc.) —*n.* a canceling —**can'cel·la'tion** *n.* —**can'cel·er, can'cel·ler** *n.*

can·cer (kan'sər) [< L., a crab] **1.** [C-] a N constellation **2.** [C-] the fourth sign of the zodiac: see ZODIAC, illus. —*n.* **1.** a malignant tumor: cancers tend to spread **2.** anything evil that spreads and destroys —**can'cer·ous** *adj.*

can·de·la·brum (kan'də lä'brəm, -lab'rəm) *n., pl.* **-bra** (-brə), **-brums** [< L. *candela*, candle] a large branched candlestick: also **can'de·la'bra** (-brə) *pl.* **-bras**

can·did (kan'did) *adj.* [< L. *candidus*, white, sincere] **1.** honest or frank **2.** unposed and informal *[a candid photograph]* —**can'did·ly** *adv.* —**can'did·ness** *n.*

can·di·da·cy (kan'də də sē) *n., pl.* **-cies** the fact or state of being a candidate

can·di·date (kan'də dāt', -dit) *n.* [L. *candidatus*, white-robed: Roman office seekers wore white gowns] one seeking, or proposed for, an office, award, etc.

can·died (kan'dēd) *adj.* **1.** cooked in sugar **2.** crystallized into sugar **3.** sugary

can·dle (kan'd'l) *n.* [< L. *candela*] **1.** a cylinder of tallow or wax with a wick through it, which gives light when burned **2.** a unit of luminous intensity —*vt.* **-dled, -dling** to examine (eggs) for freshness, fertilization, etc. by holding in front of a light —**burn the candle at both ends** to work or play so hard that one's energy is dissipated —**not hold a candle to** to be not nearly so good as —**can'dler** *n.*

can·dle·pow'er *n.* the luminous intensity of a light source expressed in candles

can·dle·stick' *n.* a holder for a candle or candles

can·dor (kan'dər) *n.* [L., whiteness, openness] **1.** open-mindedness **2.** honesty or frankness in expressing oneself Also, Brit. sp., **can'dour**

can·dy (kan'dē) *n., pl.* **-dies** [< Per. *qand*, cane sugar] **1.** a sweet food, usually made of sugar or syrup, in small pieces, with flavoring, nuts, fruits, etc. **2.** a piece of this —

vt. **-died, -dy·ing 1.** to cook in sugar or syrup, esp. to preserve or glaze **2.** to crystallize into sugar **3.** to sweeten; make pleasant

can'dy-striped' *adj.* having diagonal, colored stripes

cane (kān) *n.* [< Gr. *kanna*] **1.** the slender, jointed stem of certain plants, as bamboo **2.** a plant with such a stem, as sugar cane **3.** the woody stem of a fruiting plant **4.** a stick used for flogging **5.** *same as* WALKING STICK **6.** split rattan —*vt.* **caned, can'ing 1.** to flog with a cane **2.** to make or furnish (chairs, etc.) with cane (*n.* 6)

cane·brake (kān'brāk') *n.* [CANE + BRAKE³] a dense growth of cane plants

cane sugar sugar from sugar cane

ca·nine (kā'nīn) *adj.* [< L. *canis*, a dog] **1.** of or like a dog **2.** of the family of animals that includes dogs, wolves, and foxes —*n.* **1.** a dog or other canine animal **2.** any of the four sharp-pointed teeth next to the incisors: in full **canine tooth**

can·is·ter (kan'is tər) *n.* [< Gr. *kanistron*, wicker basket] a small box or can for coffee, tea, etc.

can·ker (kaŋ'kər) *n.* [< L.: see CANCER] **1.** an ulcerlike, spreading sore, esp. in the mouth **2.** anything causing decay or rot —*vt., vi.* to attack or be attacked with canker —**can'ker·ous** *adj.*

can'ker·worm' (-wurm') *n.* a moth larva harmful to trees

can·na·bis (kan'ə bis) *n.* [L., hemp] **1.** hemp **2.** the female flowering tops of the hemp

canned (kand) *adj.* **1.** preserved in cans or jars **2.** [Slang] recorded for reproduction, as on radio

can·nel (coal) (kan''l) [< ? *candle coal*] a variety of bituminous coal that burns with a bright flame

can·ner·y (kan'ər ē) *n., pl.* **-ies** a factory where foods are canned

can·ni·bal (kan'ə b'l) *n.* [Sp. *canibal*] **1.** a person who eats human flesh **2.** an animal that eats its own kind —*adj.* of or like cannibals —**can'ni·bal·ism** *n.* —**can'ni·bal·is'tic** *adj.*

can'ni·bal·ize' (-īz') *vt., vi.* **-ized', -iz'ing** to strip parts from (old equipment) for use in other units —**can'ni·bal·i·za'tion** *n.*

can·ning (kan'iŋ) *n.* the process of preserving foods in cans or jars

can·non (kan'ən) *n., pl.* **-nons, -non** [< L. *canna*, a cane] **1.** a large, mounted piece of artillery **2.** an automatic gun mounted on an aircraft **3.** *same as* CANNON BONE —*vt., vi. same as* CANNONADE

can'non·ade' (-ād') *n.* a continuous firing of artillery —*vt., vi.* **-ad'ed, -ad'ing** to fire artillery (at)

can'non·ball' *n.* a heavy metal ball formerly used as a projectile in cannons: also **cannon ball**

cannon bone the bone between the hock or knee and fetlock in four-legged, hoofed animals

can'non·eer' (-ir') *n.* an artilleryman

can'non·ry (-rē) *n., pl.* **-ries 1.** cannons collectively **2.** cannon fire

can·not (kan'ät, kə nät') can not —**cannot but** have no choice but to; must

can·ny (kan'ē) *adj.* **-ni·er, -ni·est** [< CAN¹] **1.** clever and cautious **2.** wise and well-informed —**can'ni·ly** *adv.* —**can'ni·ness** *n.*

ca·noe (kə nōō') *n.* [< Sp. *canoa* < AmInd.] a narrow, light boat moved by paddles —*vi.* **-noed', -noe'ing** to paddle, or go in, a canoe —*vt.* to transport by canoe —**ca·noe'ist** *n.*

can·on (kan'ən) *n.* [< L., a rule] **1.** a law or body of laws of a church **2.** a basic rule, principle, or criterion **3.** *a)* a list of books of the Bible officially accepted as genuine *b)* a list of the works of an author **4.** a clergyman serving in a cathedral **5.** *Music* a polyphonic composition in which a melody is repeated at intervals

ca·ñon (kan'yən) *n. same as* CANYON

ca·non·i·cal (kə nän'i k'l) *adj.* **1.** of or according to church law **2.** authoritative; accepted **3.** of or belonging to a canon —**ca·non'i·cal·ly** *adv.*

ca·non'i·cals (-k'lz) *n.pl.* the prescribed clothes for a clergyman conducting services

can·on·ic·i·ty (kan'ə nis'ə tē) *n.* the fact or condition of being canonical

can·on·ize (kan'ə nīz') *vt.* **-ized, -iz'ing 1.** to declare (a dead person) to be a saint **2.** to glorify **3.** to give church sanction to —**can'on·i·za'tion** *n.*

canon law the laws governing the ecclesiastical affairs of a Christian church

---

fat, āpe, cär; ten, ēven; is, bīte; gō, hôrn, tōōl, look; oil, out; up, fur; thin, then; zh, leisure; ŋ, ring; ə for *a* in *ago*; ' as in *able* (ā'b'l); ë, Fr. coeur; ö, Fr. feu; Fr. mon; ü, Fr. duc; r, Fr. cri; kh, G. doch, ich. ‡ foreign; < derived from

can·o·py (kan'ə pē) *n., pl.* **-pies** [< Gr. *kōnōpeion*, bed with mosquito nets] **1.** a covering of cloth, etc. fastened above a bed, throne, etc. or held over a person **2.** a rooflike projection —*vt.* **-pied, -py·ing** to place or form a canopy over

canst (kanst, kənst) *archaic 2d pers. sing., pres. indic., of* CAN[1]: *used with* thou

cant[1] (kant) *n.* [< L. *canere*, sing] **1.** the secret slang of beggars, thieves, etc.; argot **2.** the special vocabulary of those in a certain occupation; jargon **3.** insincere talk, esp. when pious or moral —*vi.* to use cant —*adj.* having the nature of cant

cant[2] (kant) *n.* [< L. *cant(h)us*, tire of a wheel] **1.** an outside angle **2.** a beveled edge **3.** a tilt, slant, turn, etc. —*vt., vi.* to tilt; slant —*adj.* slanting

can't (kant) cannot

can·ta·bi·le (kän tä'bi lä') *adj., adv.* [< It. < L. *cantare*, sing] *Music* in an easy, flowing manner; songlike —*n.* music in this style

can·ta·loupe, can·ta·loup (kan'tə lōp') *n.* [< Fr. < It. *Cantalupo*, near Rome, where first grown in Europe] a muskmelon, esp. one with a hard, rough rind and juicy, orange flesh

can·tan·ker·ous (kan taŋ'kər əs) *adj.* [prob. < ME. *contakour*, troublemaker] bad-tempered; quarrelsome —**can·tan'ker·ous·ly** *adv.* —**can·tan'ker·ous·ness** *n.*

can·ta·ta (kən tät'ə) *n.* [It. < *cantare*, sing] a choral composition telling a story that is sung but not acted

can·teen (kan tēn') *n.* [< Fr. < It. *cantina*, wine cellar] **1.** *same as* POST EXCHANGE **2.** *a)* a place where refreshments can be obtained, as by employees *b)* such a place serving as a social center *[a youth canteen]* **3.** a small flask for carrying water

can·ter (kan'tər) *n.* [< *Canterbury gallop*, a riding pace] a moderate gallop —*vi., vt.* to ride at a canter

Can·ter·bur·y (kan'tər ber'ē, -bər ē) city in SE England: site of a famous cathedral: pop. 33,000

cant hook [see CANT[2]] a pole with a movable hook near one end, for catching hold of logs and rolling them

can·ti·cle (kan'ti k'l) *n.* [< L. *canere*, sing] **1.** a song or chant **2.** a liturgical hymn with words from the Bible

Can'ti·cles *same as* SONG OF SOLOMON: also (in the Douay Bible) **Canticle of Canticles**

can·ti·le·ver (kan't'l ē'vər, -ev'ər) *n.* [< ?] **1.** a bracket or block projecting as a support **2.** a projecting structure supported only at one end, which is anchored to a pier or wall —*vt.* to support by means of cantilevers

CANT HOOK

cantilever bridge a bridge with its span formed by two cantilevers projecting toward each other

can·tle (kan't'l) *n.* [< L. *cantus*: see CANT[2]] the upward-curving rear part of a saddle

can·to (kan'tō) *n., pl.* **-tos** [It. < L. *canere*, sing] any of the main divisions of certain long poems

Can·ton (kan tän') **1.** former name of KWANGCHOW **2.** (kan'tən) city in EC Ohio: pop. 110,000

can·ton (kan'tən, kan tän') *n.* [Fr. < LL. *cantus*, corner] any of the political divisions of a country; specif., any of the states in the Swiss Republic —*vt.* to divide into cantons

Can·ton·ese (kan'tə nēz') *adj.* of Canton, China, or its people —*n.* **1.** *pl.* **-ese'** a native or inhabitant of Canton, China **2.** the Chinese dialect spoken there

can·ton·ment (kan tän'mənt, -tōn'-) *n.* [< Fr.: see CANTON] **1.** the assignment of troops to temporary quarters **2.** the quarters assigned

can·tor (kan'tər) *n.* [L., singer] a singer of liturgical solos in a synagogue

can·vas (kan'vəs) *n.* [< L. *cannabis*, hemp] **1.** a coarse cloth of hemp, cotton, etc., used for tents, sails, etc. **2.** a sail, tent, etc. **3.** an oil painting on canvas —**under canvas 1.** in tents **2.** with sails unfurled

can'vas·back' *n.* a N. American wild duck with a grayish back

can·vass (kan'vəs) *vt., vi.* [< *canvas*: ? because used for sifting] to go through (places) or among (people) asking for (votes, opinions, orders, etc.) —*n.* a canvassing, esp. in an effort to estimate the outcome of an election, sales campaign, etc. —**can'vass·er** *n.*

can·yon (kan'yən) *n.* [Sp. *cañón*, tube < L. *canna*, reed] a long, narrow valley between high cliffs

cap (kap) *n.* [< LL. *cappa*, a cloak] **1.** any closefitting head covering, brimless or visored **2.** a caplike thing; cover or top —*vt.* **capped, cap'ping 1.** to put a cap on **2.** to cover the top or end of **3.** to match or surpass —**cap the climax** to be or do more than could be expected

cap. 1. capacity **2.** *pl.* **caps.** capital

ca·pa·ble (kā'pə b'l) *adj.* [Fr. < L. *capere*, take] able; skilled; competent —**capable of 1.** admitting of **2.** having the qualities necessary for **3.** able or ready to —**ca'pa·bil'·i·ty** (-bil'ə tē) *n., pl.* **-ties** —**ca'pa·bly** *adv.*

ca·pa·cious (kə pā'shəs) *adj.* [< L. *capere*, take] roomy; spacious —**ca·pa'cious·ly** *adv.* —**ca·pa'cious·ness** *n.*

ca·pac·i·tance (kə pas'ə təns) *n.* [CAPACIT(Y) + -ANCE] the quantity of electric charge that can be stored in a capacitor

ca·pac'i·tor (-tər) *n.* a device for storing an electric charge; condenser

ca·pac·i·ty (kə pas'ə tē) *n., pl.* **-ties** [< L. *capere*, take] **1.** the ability to contain, absorb, or receive **2.** content or volume **3.** ability **4.** maximum output **5.** position; function *[acting in the capacity of an adviser]*

ca·par·i·son (kə par'ə s'n) *n.* [< Fr. < LL. *cappa*, cloak] an ornamented covering for a horse; trappings —*vt.* to adorn, as with trappings or rich clothing

cape[1] (kāp) *n.* [Fr. < LL. *cappa*, cloak] a sleeveless garment fastened at the neck and hanging over the back and shoulders

cape[2] (kāp) *n.* [< L. *caput*, head] a piece of land projecting into a body of water

ca·per[1] (kā'pər) *vi.* [prob. < Fr. *capriole*, a leap] to skip about in a playful manner —*n.* **1.** a gay, playful leap **2.** a prank **3.** [Slang] a robbery —**cut a caper** (or **capers**) **1.** to caper **2.** to play tricks

ca·per[2] (kā'pər) *n.* [< Gr. *kapparis*] the green flower bud of a Mediterranean bush, pickled and used as a seasoning

Cape Town seat of the legislature of South Africa, a seaport on the SW coast: pop. 807,000

Cape Verde Islands (vurd) island country in the Atlantic, off the NW coast of Africa: 1,557 sq. mi.; pop. 272,000

cap·il·lar·i·ty (kap'ə ler'ə tē) *n.* **1.** the property of exerting or having capillary attraction **2.** *same as* CAPILLARY ATTRACTION

cap·il·lar·y (kap'ə ler'ē) *adj.* [< L. *capillus*, hair] **1.** very slender **2.** having a very small bore **3.** in or of capillaries —*n., pl.* **-ies 1.** a tube with a very small bore: also **capillary tube 2.** any of the tiny blood vessels connecting arteries with veins

capillary attraction a force that is the resultant of adhesion, cohesion, and surface tension in liquids in contact with solids, as in a capillary tube, causing the liquid surface to rise or fall: also **capillary action**

cap·i·tal (kap'ə t'l) *adj.* [< L. *caput*, head] **1.** involving or punishable by death **2.** principal; chief **3.** being the seat of government **4.** of capital, or wealth **5.** excellent —*n.* **1.** *same as* CAPITAL LETTER **2.** a city that is the seat of government of a state, nation, etc. **3.** money or property owned or used in business **4.** an accumulation of such wealth **5.** [*often* C-] capitalists collectively **6.** the top part of a column —**make capital of** to make the most of; exploit

cap'i·tal·ism (-iz'm) *n.* **1.** the economic system in which the means of production and distribution are privately owned and operated for profit **2.** the principles, power, etc. of capitalists

cap'i·tal·ist *n.* **1.** an owner of wealth used in business **2.** an upholder of capitalism **3.** a wealthy person —**cap'i·tal·is'tic** *adj.* —**cap'i·tal·is'ti·cal·ly** *adv.*

cap'i·tal·i·za'tion (-ə zā'shən) *n.* **1.** the act or process of capitalizing **2.** the total capital funds of a corporation, represented by stocks, bonds, etc.

cap'i·tal·ize' (-īz') *vt.* **-ized', -iz'ing 1.** to use as or convert into capital **2.** to establish the capital stock of (a business) at a certain figure **3.** to supply capital to or for **4.** to print or write in capital letters, or begin (a word) with a capital letter —**capitalize on (something)** to use (something) to one's own advantage

capital letter a large letter of a kind used to begin a sentence or proper name, as A, B, C, etc.

cap'i·tal·ly *adv.* in an excellent manner; very well

capital punishment penalty of death for a crime

capital stock the capital of a corporation, divided into shares

Cap·i·tol (kap'ə t'l) [< L. *Capitolium*, temple of Jupiter] **1.** the temple of Jupiter in Rome **2.** the building in which the U.S. Congress meets, at Washington, D.C. —*n.* [*usually* c-] the building in which a State legislature meets

ca·pit·u·late (kə pich'ə lāt') *vi.* -lat'ed, -lat'ing [< LL. *capitulare,* arrange conditions] 1. to give up (*to* an enemy) on prearranged conditions 2. to stop resisting

ca·pit·u·la'tion *n.* 1. a statement of the main parts of a subject 2. a capitulating 3. a document containing terms of surrender, etc.; treaty

ca·pon (kā'pän) *n.* [< L. *capo*] a castrated rooster fattened for eating

Ca·pri (ka prē') island near the entrance to the Bay of Naples: 5 sq. mi.

ca·price (kə prēs') *n.* [Fr. < It.] 1. a sudden, impulsive change in thought or action 2. a capricious quality

ca·pri·cious (kə prish'əs) *adj.* subject to caprices —**ca·pri'cious·ly** *adv.* —**ca·pri'cious·ness** *n.*

Cap·ri·corn (kap'rə kôrn') [< L. *caper,* goat + *cornu,* horn] 1. a S constellation 2. the tenth sign of the zodiac: see ZODIAC, illus.

caps. capitals (capital letters)

cap·si·cum (kap'sə kəm) *n.* [< L. *capsa,* a box] 1. any of various red peppers whose pungent, fleshy pods become commercial peppers 2. these pods used as condiments or as a gastric stimulant

cap·size (kap'sīz) *vt., vi.* -sized, -siz·ing [< ?] to overturn or upset: said esp. of a boat

cap·stan (kap'stən) *n.* [< L. *capere,* take] an upright cylinder, mainly on ships, around which cables are wound, by machinery or by hand, for hoisting anchors, etc.: when operated by hand, a capstan is turned by poles (**capstan bars**) inserted and used as levers

cap·stone (kap'stōn') *n.* the uppermost stone of a structure

CAPSTAN

cap·sule (kap's'l) *n.* [< L. *capsa,* chest] 1. a small, soluble gelatin container for enclosing a dose of medicine 2. a detachable compartment to hold men, instruments, etc. in a rocket 3. *Anat.* a sac or membrane enclosing a part 4. *Bot.* a case, pod, or fruit containing seeds, spores, or carpels —*adj.* in a concise form — **cap'su·lar** *adj.*

cap'sul·ize' (-īz') *vt.* -ized', -iz'ing 1. to enclose in a capsule 2. to condense

cap·tain (kap'tən) *n.* [< L. *caput,* the head] 1. a chief or leader 2. the master of a ship 3. the chief pilot of a commercial airplane 4. the leader of a team, as in sports 5. *U.S. Mil.* an officer ranking just above a first lieutenant 6. *U.S. Navy* an officer ranking just above a commander Abbrev. **Capt.** —*vt.* to be captain of —**cap'tain·cy** (-sē), *pl.* **-cies, cap'tain·ship'** *n.*

cap·tion (kap'shən) *n.* [< L. *capere,* take] 1. a heading, as of a newspaper article, or a legend, as under an illustration 2. *same as* SUBTITLE (*n.* 2) —*vt.* to supply a caption for

cap·tious (kap'shəs) *adj.* [see prec.] 1. made for the sake of argument, as an objection 2. quick to find fault —**cap'tious·ly** *adv.* —**cap'tious·ness** *n.*

cap·ti·vate (kap'tə vāt') *vt.* -vat'ed, -vat'ing to capture the attention or affection of —**cap'ti·vat'ing·ly** *adv.* — **cap'ti·va'tion** *n.* —**cap'ti·va'tor** *n.*

cap·tive (kap'tiv) *n.* [< L. *capere,* take] a prisoner, or one captivated, as by love —*adj.* 1. taken or held prisoner 2. obliged to listen [*a captive* audience] 3. captivated —**cap·tiv'i·ty** *n., pl.* **-ties**

cap·tor (kap'tər) *n.* [L.] one who captures

cap·ture (kap'chər) *vt.* -tured, -tur·ing [< L. *capere,* take] 1. to take or seize by force, surprise, etc. 2. to represent in a more permanent form [a picture *capturing* her charm] —*n.* 1. a capturing or being captured 2. that which is captured

Cap·u·chin (kap'yoo shin, -chin) *n.* [< Fr. *capuce,* cowl] 1. a monk of a strict Franciscan order 2. [c-] a new-world monkey with a hoodlike crown of hair

car (kär) *n.* [< L. *carrus,* chariot] 1. any vehicle on wheels 2. a vehicle that moves on rails 3. an automobile 4. *same as* ELEVATOR (*n.* 2)

ca·ra·bao (kär'ə bou') *n., pl.* **-baos', -bao'** [Sp. < Malay *karbau*] *same as* WATER BUFFALO

car·a·bi·neer, car·a·bi·nier (kar'ə bə nir') *n.* [Fr. *carabinier*] a cavalryman armed with a carbine

Ca·ra·cas (kə räk'əs) capital of Venezuela: pop. 1,000,000

car·a·cul (kar'ə kəl) *n. same as* KARAKUL

ca·rafe (kə raf') *n.* [Fr.] a bottle of glass or metal for water, coffee, etc.

car·a·mel (kar'ə m'l, kär'm'l) *n.* [Fr.] 1. burnt sugar used to color or flavor food 2. a chewy candy made from sugar, milk, etc.

car·a·pace (kar'ə pās') *n.* [Fr. < Sp. *carapacho*] an upper case or shell, as of the turtle

car·at (kar'ət) *n.* [Fr. < Gr. *keration*] 1. a unit of weight for precious stones, equal to 200 milligrams 2. *same as* KARAT

car·a·van (kar'ə van') *n.* [< Per. *kārwān*] 1. a company of people traveling together for safety, as through a desert 2. *same as* VAN²

car·a·van·sa·ry (kar'ə van'sə rē) *n., pl.* **-ries** [< Per. *kārwān,* caravan + *sarāi,* palace] in the Orient, an inn for caravans

car·a·vel (kar'ə vel') *n.* [< Fr. < Gr. *karabos,* kind of light ship] a fast, small sailing ship used in the 16th cent.

car·a·way (kar'ə wā') *n.* [< Ar. *karawiyā'*] the spicy seeds of an herb, used to flavor bread, cheese, etc.

car·bide (kär'bīd) *n.* a compound of an element, usually a metal, with carbon

car·bine (kär'bīn, -bēn) *n.* [< Fr. *scarabée,* beetle] 1. a short-barreled rifle 2. *U.S. Armed Forces* a semiautomatic or automatic .30-caliber rifle

carbo- *a combining form meaning* carbon: also **carb-**

car·bo·hy·drate (kär'bō hī'drāt) *n.* [CARBO- + HYDRATE] an organic compound, as a sugar or starch, composed of carbon, hydrogen, and oxygen

car·bol·ic acid (kär bäl'ik) *same as* PHENOL

car·bon (kär'bən) *n.* [< Fr. < L. *carbo,* coal] 1. a nonmetallic chemical element found esp. in all organic compounds: diamond and graphite are pure carbon: symbol, C; at. wt., 12.01; at. no., 6: a radioactive isotope (**carbon 14**) is used in dating fossils, etc. 2. carbon paper 3. a copy made with carbon paper: in full **carbon copy** —*adj.* of carbon

car·bo·na·ceous (kär'bə nā'shəs) *adj.* of, consisting of, or containing carbon

car·bon·ate (kär'bə nit) *n.* a salt or ester of carbonic acid —*vt.* (-nāt') -at'ed, -at'ing to charge with carbon dioxide —**car'bon·a'tion** *n.*

carbon black finely divided carbon produced by the incomplete burning of oil or gas, used in ink, etc.

car'bon-date' (-dāt') *vt.* -dat'ed, -dat'ing to establish the approximate age of (fossils, etc.) by measuring the carbon 14 content

carbon dioxide a colorless, odorless gas, CO_2: it passes out of the lungs in respiration

car·bon·ic (kär bän'ik) *adj.* of, containing, or obtained from carbon or carbon dioxide

carbonic acid a weak, colorless acid, H_2CO_3, formed by the solution of carbon dioxide in water

car·bon·if·er·ous (kär'bə nif'ər əs) *adj.* [< CARBON + -FEROUS] producing or containing carbon or coal

car'bon·ize' (-nīz') *vt.* -ized', -iz'ing 1. to change into carbon, as by partial burning 2. to treat or combine with carbon —**car'bon·i·za'tion** *n.*

carbon monoxide a colorless, odorless, highly poisonous gas, CO, produced by the incomplete combustion of carbon

carbon paper thin paper coated on one side, as with a carbon preparation, used to make copies of letters, etc.

carbon tet·ra·chlo·ride (tet'rə klôr'īd) a nonflammable, colorless liquid, CCl_4, used in fire extinguishers, cleaning mixtures, etc.

Car·bo·run·dum (kär'bə run'dəm) [CARB(ON) + (C)ORUNDUM] *a trademark for* a hard abrasive, esp. a carbide of silicon, used in grindstones, etc.

car·boy (kär'boi) *n.* [< Per. *qarābah*] a large glass bottle enclosed in basketwork or in a wooden crate, used as a container for corrosive liquids

car·bun·cle (kär'buŋ k'l) *n.* [< L. dim. of *carbo,* coal] 1. a smooth, convex-cut garnet 2. a painful, pus-bearing inflammation of tissue beneath the skin, more severe than a boil —**car·bun'cu·lar** (-kyoo lər) *adj.*

car·bu·ret (kär'bə rāt', -ret'; -byoo-) *vt.* -ret'ed or -ret'ted, -ret'ing or -ret'ting [< obs. *carburet,* carbide] to combine or mix with carbon or volatile carbon compounds — **car'bu·re'tion** (-rā'shən) *n.*

car·bu·ret·or (kär'bə rāt'ər, -byoo-) *n.* a device for mixing air with gasoline spray to make an explosive mixture in an internal-combustion engine: Brit. sp. **car'bu·ret'tor** (-byoo ret'ər)

car·ca·jou (kär'kə joo', -zhoo') *n.* [CanadFr.] *same as* WOLVERINE

car·cass (kär'kəs) *n.* [< Fr. *carcasse*] **1.** the dead body of an animal **2.** the human body: scornful or humorous usage **3.** a framework or shell Also, Brit. var., **car'case**

car·cin·o·gen (kär sin'ə jən) *n.* [CARCINO(MA) + -GEN] any substance that produces cancer —**car'ci·no·gen'ic** *adj.*

car·ci·no·ma (kär'sə nō'mə) *n., pl.* **-mas, -ma·ta** (-mə tə) [L. < Gr. *karkinos,* a crab] a cancerous growth made up of epithelial cells

car coat a short overcoat, mid-thigh in length

card[1] (kärd) *n.* [< Gr. *chartēs,* leaf of paper] **1.** a flat, stiff piece of paper or pasteboard; specif., *a)* one of a pack of playing cards *b)* a card identifying a person, esp. as a member, agent, etc. *c)* a post card *d)* a card bearing a greeting *e)* any of a series of cards on which information is recorded **2.** an attraction *[a drawing card]* **3.** [Colloq.] a comical person —*vt.* **1.** to provide with a card **2.** to put or list on cards —**in** (or **on**) **the cards** likely to happen —**put** (or **lay**) **one's cards on the table** to reveal something frankly

card[2] (kärd) *n.* [< L. *carere,* to card] a metal comb or a machine with wire teeth for combing fibers of wool, cotton, etc. —*vt.* to use a card on (fibers) in preparation for spinning —**card'ing** *n., adj.*

car·da·mom (kär'də məm) *n.* [< Gr. *kardamon,* cress + *amōmon,* spice plant] **1.** an Asiatic plant with aromatic seeds **2.** its seeds, used in medicine and as a spice Also **car'da·mon** (-mən)

card'board' *n.* stiff, thick paper, or pasteboard, used for cards, boxes, etc.

card file cards containing data or records, arranged systematically: also **card catalog**

car·di·ac (kär'dē ak') *adj.* [< Gr. *kardia,* heart] of or near the heart

Car·diff (kär'dif) seaport in SE Wales: pop. 287,000

car·di·gan (kär'də gən) *n.* [< 7th Earl of *Cardigan*] a sweater or jacket, usually knitted, that opens down the front: also **cardigan sweater** (or **jacket**)

car·di·nal (kärd'n əl) *adj.* [< L. *cardo,* hinge] **1.** principal; chief **2.** bright-red —*n.* **1.** an official appointed by the Pope to his council **2.** bright red **3.** a bright-red American songbird: in full **cardinal bird 4.** *same as* CARDINAL NUMBER

cardinal flower a N. American plant that grows in wet ground and has bright-red flowers

cardinal number any number used in counting or showing how many (e.g., two, forty, 627, etc.): distinguished from ORDINAL NUMBER

cardinal points the four principal points of the compass; north, south, east, and west

card index *same as* CARD FILE

cardio- [< Gr. *kardia,* heart] *a combining form meaning* of the heart

car·di·o·gram (kär'dē ə gram') *n. same as* ELECTROCARDIOGRAM —**car'di·o·graph'** (-graf') *n.*

car'di·ol'o·gy (-äl'ə jē) *n.* the branch of medicine dealing with the heart —**car'di·ol'o·gist** *n.*

cards (kärdz) *n.pl.* **1.** any game played with a deck of cards, as poker **2.** card playing

card'sharp' *n.* [Colloq.] a professional cheater at cards: also **card shark**

care (ker) *n.* [< OE. *caru,* sorrow] **1.** *a)* worry or concern *b)* a cause of this **2.** close attention; heed **3.** a liking or regard (*for*) **4.** charge; protection **5.** something to watch over or attend to —*vi.* **cared, car'ing 1.** to feel concern **2.** to feel love or liking (*for*) **3.** to look after; provide (*for*) **4.** to wish (*for*); want —**have a care** to be careful: also **take care —(in) care of** at the address of —**take care of 1.** to be responsible for **2.** to provide for

ca·reen (kə rēn') *vi., vt.* [< L. *carina,* keel] to lean or cause to lean sideways; tip; tilt; lurch —*n.* a careening

ca·reer (kə rir') *n.* [< Fr. < It. *carro,* car] **1.** a swift course **2.** one's progress through life **3.** a profession or occupation —*adj.* pursuing a normally temporary activity as a lifework —*vi.* to rush wildly

ca·reer'ist *n.* a person interested exclusively or selfishly in his own professional ambitions

care·free (ker'frē') *adj.* without care or worry

care'ful *adj.* **1.** cautious; wary **2.** accurately or thoroughly done; painstaking —**care'ful·ly** *adv.* —**care'ful·ness** *n.*

care'less *adj.* **1.** carefree; untroubled **2.** not paying enough attention; inconsiderate **3.** done without enough attention, precision, etc. —**care'less·ly** *adv.* —**care'less·ness** *n.*

ca·ress (kə res') *vt.* [ult. < L. *carus,* dear] to touch lovingly or gently —*n.* an affectionate touch, kiss, etc. —**ca·ress'ing·ly** *adv.*

car·et (kar'it, ker'-) *n.* [L., lit., there is lacking] a mark (∧) used to show where something is to be added in a written or printed line

care'tak'er *n.* a person hired to take care of something, as a house, estate, etc.

care'worn' *adj.* showing the effects of troubles and worry; haggard

car·fare (kär'fer') *n.* the price of a ride on a streetcar, bus, etc.

car·go (kär'gō) *n., pl.* **-goes, -gos** [< Sp. *cargar,* to load] the load carried by a ship, truck, etc.

car'hop' *n.* [CAR + (BELL)HOP] one who serves customers in cars at a drive-in restaurant

Car·ib (kar'ib) *n.* a member of an Indian people of the S West Indies and the N coast of S. America —**Car'ib·an** *adj., n.*

Car·ib·be·an (kar'ə bē'ən, kə rib'ē ən) part of the Atlantic, bounded by the West Indies, Central America, & South America: also **Caribbean Sea**

car·i·bou (kar'ə bōō') *n.* [CanadFr.] a large, northern N. American deer

car·i·ca·ture (kar'ə kə chər) *n.* [Fr. < It. *caricare,* exaggerate] **1.** the exaggerated imitation of a person, literary style, etc. for satirical effect **2.** a picture, etc. in which this is done —*vt.* **-tured, -tur·ing** to depict as in a caricature —**car'i·ca·tur·ist** *n.*

car·ies (ker'ēz) *n.* [L., decay] decay of bones, or, esp., of teeth

car·il·lon (kar'ə län') *n.* [Fr., chime of four bells, ult. < L. *quattuor,* four] a set of bells tuned to the chromatic scale

car·i·ole (kar'ē ōl') *n.* [< It. *carro,* car] **1.** a small one-horse carriage **2.** a light, covered cart

car·i·ous (kar'ē əs) *adj.* having caries; decayed

car'load' *n.* a load that fills a car

Car·lyle (kär līl', kär'līl), **Thomas** 1795–1881; Brit. writer, born in Scotland

car·min·a·tive (kär min'ə tiv) *adj.* [< L. *carminare,* cleanse] causing gas to be expelled from the stomach and intestines —*n.* a carminative medicine

car·nage (kär'nij) *n.* [< Fr. < L. *caro,* flesh] bloody and extensive slaughter; massacre

car'nal (-n'l) *adj.* [< L. *caro,* flesh] **1.** of the flesh; material or worldly **2.** sensual; sexual —**car·nal'i·ty** (-nal'ə tē) *n., pl.* **-ties** —**car'nal·ly** *adv.*

car·na·tion (kär nā'shən) *n.* [< L. *caro,* flesh] a plant related to the pink family, with white, pink, or red flowers that smell like cloves

Car·ne·gie (kär'nə gē', kär nā'gē), **Andrew** 1835–1919; U.S. industrialist & philanthropist

car·nel·ian (kär nēl'yən) *n.* [< L. *carnis,* of flesh (color)] a red variety of chalcedony, used as a gem

car·ni·val (kär'nə vəl) *n.* [< Fr. or It.] **1.** the period of feasting and revelry just before Lent **2.** a reveling; festivity **3.** a traveling entertainment with rides, games, etc.

car·ni·vore (kär'nə vôr') *n.* a carnivorous animal or plant: opposed to HERBIVORE

car·niv·o·rous (kär niv'ə rəs) *adj.* [< L. *caro,* flesh + *vorare,* eat] **1.** flesh-eating: opposed to HERBIVOROUS **2.** insect-eating, as certain plants **3.** of the carnivores —**car·niv'o·rous·ness** *n.*

car·ol (kar'əl) *n.* [< OFr. *carole,* kind of dance] a song of joy or praise; esp., a Christmas song —*vi., vt.* **-oled** or **-olled, -ol·ing** or **-ol·ling** to sing; warble —**car'ol·er, car'ol·ler** *n.*

Car·o·li·na (kar'ə lī'nə) English colony including what is now N. Carolina, S. Carolina, Ga., & N Fla. —**the Carolinas** N. Carolina & S. Carolina

Car·o·line Islands (kar'ə līn', -lən) a group of islands in the W Pacific: a U.S. trust territory

car·om (kar'əm) *n.* [< Sp. *carambola*] **1.** *Billiards* a shot in which the cue ball successively hits the two object balls **2.** a hitting and rebounding —*vi.* **1.** to make a carom **2.** to hit and rebound

ca·rot·id (kə rät'id) *adj.* [Gr. *karōtis*] designating, of, or near either of the two main arteries, one on each side of the neck, which convey the blood to the head —*n.* a carotid artery

ca·rous·al (kə rou'zəl) *n. same as* CAROUSE

ca·rouse (kə rouz') *vi.* **-roused', -rous'ing** [< G. *gar aus(trinken),* (to drink) quite out] to engage in a noisy drinking party —*n.* a noisy drinking party —**ca·rous'er** *n.*

carp[1] (kärp) *n., pl.* **carp, carps** [< Gmc. *carpa*] an edible freshwater fish living in ponds

carp[2] (kärp) *vi.* [< ON. *karpa,* brag] to find fault in a petty or nagging way —**carp'er** *n.*

car·pal (kär'pəl) *adj.* [ModL. *carpalis*] of the carpus —*n.* a bone of the carpus: also **car·pa'le** (-pā'lē), *pl.* **-li·a** (-ə)

Car·pa·thi·an Mountains (kär pā'thē ən) mountain system in C Europe, extending from S Poland into NE Romania: also **Car·pa'thi·ans**

car·pel (kär'pəl) *n.* [< Gr. *karpos,* fruit] a simple pistil, regarded as a modified leaflike structure

CARPEL

car·pen·ter (kär'pən tər) *n.* [< L. *carpentum,* a cart] a workman who builds and repairs wooden articles, buildings, etc. —*vi.* to do a carpenter's work — **car'pen·try** (-trē) *n.*

car·pet (kär'pit) *n.* [< L. *carpere,* to card] 1. a heavy fabric for covering a floor, stairs, etc. 2. anything like a carpet *[a carpet* of snow] —*vt.* to cover as with a carpet —**on the carpet** being reprimanded

car'pet·bag' *n.* an old-fashioned traveling bag, made of carpeting —*vi.* **-bagged'**, **-bag'ging** to act as a carpetbagger

car'pet·bag'ger *n.* a Northerner who went South to take advantage of unsettled conditions after the Civil War: contemptuous term

carpet beetle (or **bug**) a small beetle whose larvae feed on furs and woolens, esp. carpets

car'pet·ing *n.* carpets or carpet fabric

car pool an arrangement by a group to rotate the use of their cars, as for going to work

car·port (kär'pôrt') *n.* a shelter for an automobile, built as a roof at the side of a building

car·pus (kär'pəs) *n., pl.* **-pi** (-pī) [< Gr. *karpos,* wrist] the wrist, or the wrist bones

car·rel, car·rell (kar'əl) *n.* [< ML. *carula*] a small enclosure in a library, for privacy in studying

car·riage (kar'ij) *n.* [ult. < L. *carrus,* wagon] 1. a carrying; transportation 2. manner of carrying the head and body; bearing 3. *a)* a four-wheeled, horse-drawn passenger vehicle *b) same as* BABY CARRIAGE 4. a wheeled support *[a gun carriage]* 5. a moving part (as on a typewriter) that supports and shifts something

car·ri·er (kar'ē ər) *n.* 1. one that carries 2. one in the transportation business 3. something in or on which something else is carried 4. one that transmits disease germs 5. *same as* AIRCRAFT CARRIER 6. *Electronics* the steady, transmitted wave whose amplitude, frequency, or phase is modulated by the signal

carrier pigeon *same as* HOMING PIGEON

car·ri·on (kar'ē ən) *n.* [ult. < L. *caro,* flesh] decaying flesh of a dead body

Car·roll (kar'əl), **Lewis** (pseud. of *Charles Lutwidge Dodgson*) 1832–98; Eng. writer

car·rot (kar'ət) *n.* [< Gr. *karōton*] 1. a plant with an edible, fleshy, orange-red root 2. the root —**car'rot·y** *adj.*

car·rou·sel (kar'ə sel', -zel') *n.* [Fr. < It. dial. *carusiello*] *same as* MERRY-GO-ROUND

car·ry (kar'ē) *vt.* **-ried**, **-ry·ing** [< L. *carrus,* car] 1. to hold or support 2. to take from one place to another 3. to lead or impel 4. to transmit *[air carries* sounds] 5. to transfer or extend *[to carry* a pipe to a sewer] 6. to involve; imply 7. to bear (oneself) in a specified way 8. *a)* to gain support for *b)* to win (an election, debate, etc.) 9. *a)* to keep in stock *b)* to keep on one's account books, etc. —*vi.* 1. to act as a conductor, bearer, etc. 2. to cover a range, as a voice —*n., pl.* **-ries** 1. the distance covered by a gun, ball, etc. 2. a portage —**be** (or **get**) **carried away** to become very emotional or enthusiastic —**carry off** 1. to win (a prize, etc.) 2. to handle (a situation), esp. with success —**carry on** 1. to engage in; conduct 2. to continue 3. [Colloq.] to behave wildly or childishly —**carry out** (or **through**) 1. to put (plans, etc.) into practice 2. to accomplish —**carry over** to postpone; continue

car'ry·all' *n.* [< CARIOLE] a light, covered carriage with seats for several people

car'ry·all'² *n.* a large bag, basket, etc.

carrying charge interest paid on the balance owed in installment buying

car'ry·o'ver *n.* something carried over, as a remainder of crops or goods

car'sick' *adj.* nauseated from riding in an automobile, bus, etc. —**car'sick'ness** *n.*

Car·son City (kär's'n) capital of Nev., in the W part: pop. 15,000

cart (kärt) *n.* [< ON. *kartr*] a small, often two-wheeled, wagon —*vt., vi.* to carry in a cart, truck, etc.; transport — **cart'er** *n.*

cart·age (kär'tij) *n.* 1. the work of carting 2. the charge for this

carte blanche (kärt' blänsh') [Fr., blank card] 1. full authority 2. freedom to do as one thinks best

car·tel (kär tel') *n.* [G. *kartell* < Fr. *cartel:* see CARD¹] an association of business firms establishing a national or international monopoly

Car·ter (kär'tər), **Jimmy** (legal name *James Earl Carter, Jr.*) 1924– ; 39th president of the U.S. (1977–)

Car·thage (kär'thij) ancient city-state in N Africa, destroyed by the Romans, 146 B.C. —**Car'tha·gin'i·an** (-thə jin'ē ən) *adj., n.*

car·ti·lage (kärt'l ij) *n.* [< L. *cartilago*] a tough, elastic tissue forming part of the skeleton; gristle —**car'ti·lag'i·nous** (-aj'ə nəs) *adj.*

car·tog·ra·phy (kär täg'rə fē) *n.* [see CARD¹ & -GRAPHY] the art or work of making maps or charts —**car·tog'ra·pher** *n.* —**car'to·graph'ic** (-tə graf'ik) *adj.*

car·ton (kärt''n) *n.* [Fr. < It. *carta,* card] a cardboard box or container

car·toon (kär tōōn') *n.* [< Fr.: see prec.] 1. a drawing that caricatures some person or event 2. *same as* COMIC STRIP 3. *same as* ANIMATED CARTOON —*vi., vt.* to draw cartoons (of) —**car·toon'ist** *n.*

car·tridge (kär'trij) *n.* [< Fr. < It. *carta,* card] 1. a cylindrical case of cardboard, metal, etc. containing the charge and primer, and usually the projectile, for a firearm 2. a small container, as for camera film, a phonograph needle, etc.

cart·wheel (kärt'hwēl', -wēl') *n.* a kind of handspring performed sideways

carve (kärv) *vt.* **carved, carv'ing** [< OE. *ceorfan*] 1. to make or shape by or as by cutting 2. to decorate the surface of with cut designs 3. to divide by cutting; slice —*vi.* 1. to carve statues or designs 2. to carve meat —**carv'er** *n.* —**carv'ing** *n.*

car·vel (kär'vəl) *n. same as* CARAVEL

carving knife a large knife for carving meat

car·wash (kär'wôsh', -wäsh') *n.* a facility for washing and polishing automobiles

car·y·at·id (kar'ē at'id) *n., pl.* **-ids**, **-i·des'** (-ə dēz') [< Gr. *karyatides,* priestesses of Karyai, in ancient Greece] a supporting column having the form of a draped female figure

ca·sa·ba (kə sä'bə) *n.* [< *Kassaba,* town in Asia Minor] a cultivated melon with a yellow rind

Ca·sa·blan·ca (kas'ə blaŋ'kə, kä'sə blän'-) seaport in NW Morocco: pop. 1,177,000

Ca·sa·no·va (kas'ə nō'və, kaz'-), **Gio·van·ni** (jô vän'nē) 1725–98; It. adventurer and writer

cas·cade (kas kād') *n.* [Fr. < L. *cadere,* to fall] 1. a small, steep waterfall 2. a shower, as of sparks, etc. —*vt., vi.* **-cad'ed, -cad'ing** to fall or drop in a cascade

cas·car·a (kas ker'ə) *n.* [Sp., bark] 1. a small buckthorn of the U.S. Pacific coast 2. a laxative made from its bark

CARYATID

case¹ (kās) *n.* [< L. *casus,* accident, pp. of *cadere,* to fall] 1. an example or instance *[case* of measles] 2. a person being helped by a doctor, social worker, etc. 3. any matter requiring study 4. a statement of the facts, as in a law court 5. convincing arguments *[he has no case]* 6. a lawsuit 7. a form taken by a noun, pronoun, or adjective to show its relation to neighboring words —*vt.* **cased, cas'ing** [Slang] to look over carefully, esp. for intended robbery —**in any case** anyhow —**in case** in the event that; if —**in case of** in the event of —**in no case** by no means; never

case² (kās) *n.* [< L. *capsa,* a box] 1. a container, as a box 2. a protective cover *[a watch case]* 3. a full box or its contents 4. a frame, as for a window —*vt.* **cased, cas'ing** 1. to put in a container 2. to cover or enclose

ca·se·fy (kā'sə fī') *vt., vi.* **-fied', -fy'ing** [< L. *caseus,* cheese + -FY] to make or become cheeselike

case'hard'en *vt.* 1. to form a hard, thin surface on (an iron alloy) 2. to make callous or unfeeling

case history (or **study**) collected information about an individual or group, for use in sociological, medical, or psychiatric studies

ca·se·in (kā'sē in, kā'sēn) *n.* [< L. *caseus,* cheese] a protein that is one of the chief constituents of milk and the basis of cheese

case·load (kās'lōd') *n.* the number of cases being handled by a court, caseworker, etc.

case'mate' (-māt') *n.* [Fr. < Gr. *chasma*, chasm] an armored enclosure with openings for guns, as in a fortress — **case'mat'ed** *adj.*

case'ment (-mənt) *n.* [< OFr. *encassement*, a frame] 1. a hinged window frame that opens outward: a **casement window** has two such frames, opening like French doors 2. a casing; covering

ca·se·ous (kā'sē əs) *adj.* [< L. *caseus*, cheese] of or like cheese

case'work' *n.* social work in which guidance is given in cases of personal and family maladjustment — **case'work'er** *n.*

cash (kash) *n.* [< Fr. *caisse*, money box] 1. money that one actually has; esp., ready money 2. bills and coins 3. money, a check, etc. paid at the time of purchase — *vt.* to give or get cash for — *adj.* of or for cash — **cash in** 1. to turn into cash 2. [Slang] to die — **cash in on** to profit from

cash'-and-car'ry *adj.* with cash payments and no deliveries

cash'book' *n.* a book in which all receipts and payments of money are entered

cash discount a discount allowed a purchaser paying within a specified period

cash·ew (kash'ōō, kə shōō') *n.* [< Fr. < Tupi *acajú*] 1. a tropical tree bearing edible, kidney-shaped nuts 2. the nut: also **cashew nut**

cash·ier' (ka shir') *n.* [Fr. *caissier*] a person in charge of cash transactions for a bank, store, etc.

cash·ier² (ka shir') *vt.* [< LL. *cassare*, destroy] to dismiss in dishonor, from a position of trust

cash·mere (kazh'mir, kash'-) *n.* [< *Kashmir*, region in India] 1. a fine carded wool from goats of N India and Tibet 2. a soft, twilled cloth as of this wool

cash register a device usually with a money drawer, that registers visibly the amount of a sale

cas·ing (kās'iŋ) *n.* 1. a protective covering, as the skin of a sausage or the outer covering of a pneumatic tire 2. a frame, as for a door or window

ca·si·no (kə sē'nō) *n., pl.* **-nos** [It. < L. *casa*, cottage] 1. a room or building for dancing, gambling, etc. 2. *same as* CASSINO

cask (kask) *n.* [< Sp. < L. *quassare*, shatter] 1. a barrel of any size, esp. one for liquids 2. the contents of a full cask

cas·ket (kas'kit) *n.* [prob. < OFr. *casse*, box] 1. a small box or chest, as for valuables 2. a coffin

Cas·pi·an Sea (kas'pē ən) inland sea between Caucasia and Asiatic U.S.S.R. — **Cas'pi·an** *adj.*

Cas·san·dra (kə san'drə) *Gr. Myth.* a Trojan prophetess of doom whose prophecies, Apollo decreed, should never be believed

cas·sa·va (kə sä'və) *n.* [< Fr. < WInd. *casávi*] 1. a tropical American plant with edible, starchy roots 2. a starch taken from the root, used to make bread and tapioca

cas·se·role (kas'ə rōl') *n.* [Fr. < Gr. *kyathos*, a bowl] 1. a covered baking dish in which food can be cooked and served 2. food baked in such a dish

cas·sette (ka set', kə-) *n.* [Fr. < L. *capsa*, a box] 1. a case with roll film in it, for loading a camera quickly 2. a similar case with magnetic tape, for use in a tape recorder

cas·sia (kash'ə) *n.* [ult. < Heb. *qeṣī'āh*] 1. *a*) the bark (**cassia bark**) of a tree of SE Asia: used as a source of cinnamon *b*) this tree 2. any of various tropical plants of the legume family: the pods (**cassia pods**) of some have a laxative pulp (**cassia pulp**); others yield senna

cas·si·mere (kas'ə mir') *n.* [var. of CASHMERE] a woolen cloth, twilled or plain, used for men's suits

cas·si·no (kə sē'nō) *n.* [see CASINO] a simple card game for two to four players

Cas·si·o·pe·ia (kas'ē ə pē'ə) 1. *Gr. Myth.* Andromeda's mother 2. a N constellation near Andromeda

cas·sock (kas'ək) *n.* [< Fr. < Per. *kazh*, raw silk] a long, closefitting vestment, worn by clergymen

cas·so·war·y (kas'ə wer'ē) *n., pl.* **-ies** [Malay *kasuāri*] a large, flightless bird of Australia and New Guinea, somewhat like an ostrich, but smaller

cast (kast) *vt.* **cast, cast'ing** [< ON. *kasta*, to throw] 1. to throw with force; fling; hurl 2. to deposit (a ballot or vote) 3. to direct [to *cast* one's eyes] 4. to project [to *cast* light] 5. to throw out (a fly, etc.) at the end of a fishing line 6. to throw off; shed (a skin, etc.) 7. *a*) to form (molten metal, etc.) by pouring into a mold *b*) to make by such a method 8. to select (an actor) for a role or play — *vi.* 1. to throw dice 2. to throw out a fly, etc. on a fishing line — *n.* 1. a casting; throw; also, a way of casting or the distance thrown 2. a throw of dice; also, the number thrown 3. *a*) something formed in a mold, as a statue *b*) the mold 4. a plaster form for immobilizing a broken limb 5. the set of actors in a play or movie 6. an appearance, as of features 7. kind; quality 8. tinge; shade — **cast about** 1. to search (*for*) 2. to devise — **cast aside** (or **away**) to discard — **cast down** 1. to turn downward 2. to sadden; discourage — **cast off** 1. to discard 2. to free a ship from a dock, etc. — **cast up** 1. to turn upward 2. to add up

cas·ta·nets (kas'tə nets') *n.pl.* [< Sp. < L. *castanea*, chestnut: from the shape] a pair of small, hollow pieces of hard wood, ivory, etc. held in the hand and clicked together in time to music

cast·a·way (kas'tə wā') *n.* 1. a person or thing cast off 2. a shipwrecked person — *adj.* 1. discarded 2. shipwrecked

caste (kast) *n.* [Fr. < L. *castus*, pure] 1. any of the hereditary Hindu social classes of a formerly segregated system of India 2. any exclusive social or occupational group 3. class distinction based on birth, wealth, etc. — **lose caste** to lose social status

CASTANETS

cas·tel·lat·ed (kas'tə lāt'id) *adj.* [see CASTLE] built with turrets and battlements, like a castle — **cas'tel·la'tion** *n.*

cast'er *n.* 1. a person or thing that casts 2. *a*) a small container for serving vinegar, salt, etc. at the table *b*) a stand for holding such containers 3. a wheel, etc. set in a frame and attached to a leg or corner of a piece of furniture for ease in moving

cas·ti·gate (kas'tə gāt') *vt.* **-gat'ed, -gat'ing** [< L. *castigare*] to rebuke severely, esp. by public criticism — **cas'ti·ga'tion** *n.* — **cas'ti·ga'tor** *n.*

Cas·tile (kas tēl') region and former kingdom in N and C Spain

Castile soap [< *Castile*, where first made] [*also* **c- s-**] a fine, mild, hard soap made from olive oil and sodium hydroxide

cast'ing *n.* 1. the action of one that casts 2. anything, esp. of metal, cast in a mold

cast'-i'ron *adj.* 1. made of cast iron 2. very hard, rigid, strong, healthy, etc.

cast iron a hard, unmalleable alloy of iron made by casting: it has a high proportion of carbon

cas·tle (kas''l) *n.* [< L. *castrum*, fort] 1. a large building or group of buildings fortified as a stronghold 2. any massive dwelling like this 3. *Chess same as* ROOK² — *vt.* **-tled, -tling** *Chess* to move (a king) two squares to either side and then set the castle in the square skipped by the king — *vi.* to castle a king

cast'off' *adj.* thrown away; discarded — *n.* a person or thing cast off

Cas·tor (kas'tər) 1. *Gr. & Rom. Myth.* the mortal twin of Pollux 2. one of the two bright stars in the constellation Gemini

cas·tor (kas'tər) *n. same as* CASTER (senses 2 & 3)

cas·tor-oil plant (kas'tər oil') [< Gr. *kastōr*, beaver] a tropical plant with large, beanlike seeds (**castor beans**) from which oil (**castor oil**) is extracted: this oil is used as a cathartic and lubricant

cas·trate (kas'trāt) *vt.* **-trat·ed, -trat·ing** [< L. *castrare*] 1. to remove the testicles of; emasculate 2. to mutilate, expurgate, etc. — **cas·tra'tion** *n.*

cas·u·al (kazh'ōō wəl) *adj.* [< L. *casus*, chance] 1. happening by chance; not planned 2. occasional [a *casual* worker] 3. careless or cursory 4. nonchalant 5. informal, or for informal use — *n.* 1. one who does something only occasionally; esp., a casual worker 2. [*pl.*] shoes, clothes, etc. for informal occasions 3. *Mil.* a person temporarily attached to a unit — **cas'u·al·ly** *adv.* — **cas'u·al·ness** *n.*

cas·u·al·ty (kazh'əl tē, -ōō wəl-) *n., pl.* **-ties** 1. an accident, esp. a fatal one 2. a member of the armed forces killed, wounded, captured, etc. 3. anyone hurt or killed in an accident

cas·u·ist (kazh'ōō wist) *n.* [< Fr. < L. *casus*, CASE¹] an expert in casuistry — **cas'u·is'tic, cas'u·is'ti·cal** *adj.*

cas'u·ist·ry (-wis trē) *n., pl.* **-ries** subtle but false reasoning, esp. about moral issues; sophistry

cat (kat) *n.* [OE.] 1. a small, soft-furred animal, often kept as a pet or for killing mice 2. any flesh-eating mammal related to this, as the lion, tiger, leopard, etc. 3. a spiteful woman 4. *same as* CAT-O'-NINE-TAILS 5. [Slang] a person, esp. a man — *vt.* **cat'ted, cat'ting** to hoist (an anchor) to the cathead — **let the cat out of the bag** to let a secret be found out

ca·tab·o·lism (kə tab'ə liz'm) *n.* [< Gr. *kata*, down + *ballein*, to throw + -ISM] the biological process by which living tissue is changed into waste products —**cat·a·bol·ic** (kat'ə bäl'ik) *adj.*

cat·a·clysm (kat'ə kliz'm) *n.* [< Gr. *kata-*, down + *klyzein*, to wash] **1.** a great flood **2.** any sudden, violent change, as in war —**cat'a·clys'mic** (-kliz'mik), **cat'a·clys'-mal** *adj.*

cat·a·comb (kat'ə kōm') *n.* [< L. *cata*, by + *tumba*, tomb] a gallery in an underground burial place: *usually used in pl.*

cat·a·falque (kat'ə falk', -fôlk') *n.* [Fr. < L. *cata-*, by + *fala*, scaffold] a wooden framework, usually draped, on which the body in a coffin lies in state

cat·a·lep·sy (kat'l ep'sē) *n.* [< Gr. *katalēpsis*, a seizing] a condition of muscle rigidity and sudden, temporary loss of consciousness, as in epilepsy —**cat'a·lep'tic** *adj., n.*

cat·a·log, cat·a·logue (kat'l ôg') *n.* [< Fr. < Gr. *kata-*, down + *legein*, to count] a complete list, as an alphabetical card file of the books in a library, a list of articles for sale, etc. —*vt., vi.* **-loged'** or **-logued'**, **-log'ing** or **-logu'-ing 1.** to enter in a catalog **2.** to make a catalog of —**cat'-a·log'er** or **cat'a·logu'er** *n.*

ca·tal·pa (kə tal'pə) *n.* [< AmInd.] a tree with large, heart-shaped leaves and slender beanlike pods

ca·tal·y·sis (kə tal'ə sis) *n., pl.* **-ses'** (-sēz') [< Gr. *katal-ysis*, dissolution] the speeding up or, sometimes, slowing down of the rate of a chemical reaction by adding a substance which itself is not changed thereby —**cat·a·lyt·ic** (kat'l it'ik) *adj., n.* —**cat'a·lyt'i·cal·ly** *adv.*

cat·a·lyst (kat'l ist) *n.* **1.** any substance serving as the agent in catalysis **2.** a stimulus in producing results

cat·a·lyze (-īz') *vt.* **-lyzed'**, **-lyz'ing** to change or bring about as a catalyst —**cat'a·lyz'er** *n.*

cat·a·ma·ran (kat'ə mə ran') *n.* [< Tamil *kattu*, tie + *maram*, log] **1.** a narrow log raft propelled by sails or paddles **2.** a boat with two parallel hulls

cat·a·mount (kat'ə mount') *n.* [< CAT + obs. *a*, of + MOUNT(AIN)] **1.** the puma; cougar **2.** the lynx

cat·a·pult (kat'ə pult') *n.* [< Gr. *kata-*, down + *pallein*, hurl] **1.** an ancient military device for throwing stones, etc. **2.** a device for launching an airplane, rocket missile, etc. as from a deck or ramp —*vt.* to shoot as from a catapult —*vi.* to leap

cat·a·ract (kat'ə rakt') *n.* [< Gr. *kata-*, down + *rhēg-nynai*, to break] **1.** a large waterfall **2.** a strong flood of water **3.** *a)* an eye disease in which the lens becomes opaque, causing partial or total blindness *b)* the opaque area

ca·tarrh (kə tär') *n.* [< Gr. *kata-*, down + *rhein*, to flow] inflammation of the mucous membrane of the nose or throat: an old-fashioned term —**ca·tarrh'al** *adj.*

ca·tas·tro·phe (kə tas'trə fē) *n.* [< Gr. *kata-*, down + *strephein*, to turn] **1.** the culminating event of a drama, by which the plot is resolved; denouement **2.** any sudden, great disaster —**cat·a·stroph·ic** (kat'ə sträf'ik) *adj.*

cat·a·ton·ic (kat'ə tän'ik) *adj.* [< Gr. *kata-*, down + *tonos*, tension] of or in a state of schizophrenia marked esp. by stupor or catalepsy

Ca·taw·ba (kə tô'bə) *n.* [*often* c-] **1.** a reddish grape of the E U.S. **2.** a wine made from this grape

cat·bird (kat'burd') *n.* a slate-gray N. American songbird that makes a mewing sound like a cat

cat'boat' *n.* a sailboat with a single sail and mast set well forward

cat'call' *n.* a shrill shout or whistle expressing derision, etc. —*vt., vi.* to make catcalls (at)

catch (kach) *vt.* **caught, catch'ing** [< L. *capere*, to take] **1.** to seize and hold; capture **2.** to take by or as by a trap, snare, etc. **3.** to deceive **4.** to surprise **5.** to get to in time *[to catch a bus]* **6.** to lay hold of; grab *[to catch a ball]* **7.** to get *[to catch a glimpse]* **8.** to become infected with *[to catch a cold]* **9.** to understand **10.** to captivate; charm **11.** to get entangled **12.** [Colloq.] to see, hear, etc. —*vi.* **1.** to become held, fastened, etc. **2.** to burn **3.** to keep hold, as a lock **4.** to act as a catcher —*n.* **1.** a catching **2.** a thing that catches **3.** a person, thing, or amount caught **4.** one worth catching as a husband or wife **5.** a snatch or fragment, as of a tune **6.** a break in the voice **7.** [Colloq.] a tricky qualification **8.** *Music* a round for three or more voices —*adj.* **1.** tricky **2.** attracting attention —**catch at** to reach for eagerly —**catch on 1.** to understand **2.** to become popular —**catch up 1.** to snatch **2.** to show to be in error **3.** to come up even; overtake

catch'all' (-ôl') *n.* a place for holding all sorts of things *[one drawer was a catchall]*

catch'er *n.* **1.** one that catches **2.** *Baseball* the player behind home plate, who catches pitched balls

catch'ing *adj.* **1.** contagious **2.** attractive; catchy

catch'pen'ny (-pen'ē) *adj.* cheap and flashy; worthless — *n., pl.* **-nies** a catchpenny commodity

catch·up (kech'əp, kach'-) *n. same as* KETCHUP

catch'word' *n.* **1.** a word so placed as to catch attention, as either of the words at the top of this page **2.** a word or phrase repeated so often that it becomes a slogan

catch'y *adj.* **-i·er, -i·est 1.** easily taken up and remembered *[a catchy tune]* **2.** tricky

cat·e·chism (kat'ə kiz'm) *n.* [< Gr. *kata-*, thoroughly + *ēchein*, to sound] **1.** a handbook of questions and answers for teaching the principles of a religion **2.** a close questioning —**cat'e·chis'tic** (-kis'tik), **cat'e·chis'ti·cal** *adj.*

cat'e·chist (-kist) *n.* a person who catechizes

cat'e·chize' (-kīz') *vt.* **-chized'**, **-chiz'ing** [see CATECHISM] to question searchingly: also **cat'e·chise'** —**cat'e·chi·za'-tion** *n.* —**cat'e·chiz'er** *n.*

cat·e·gor·i·cal (kat'ə gôr'i k'l) *adj.* **1.** unqualified; positive; explicit: said of a statement, etc. **2.** of, as, or in a category Also **cat'e·gor'ic** —**cat'e·gor'i·cal·ly** *adv.*

cat·e·go·rize (kat'ə gə rīz') *vt.* **-rized'**, **-riz'ing** to place in a category; classify

cat'e·go'ry (-gôr'ē) *n., pl.* **-ries** [< Gr. *katēgorein*, assert] a class or division in a scheme of classification

ca·ter (kā'tər) *vi.* [< L. *ad-*, to + *capere*, to take] **1.** to provide food and service, as for parties **2.** to seek to gratify another's desires (with *to*) —**ca'ter·er** *n.*

cat·er·cor·nered (kat'ē kôr'nərd) *adj.* [< Fr. *catre*, four + CORNERED] diagonal —*adv.* diagonally Also **cat'er·cor'-ner**

cat·er·pil·lar (kat'ər pil'ər) *n.* [< L. *catta pilosus*, hairy cat] the wormlike larva of a butterfly, moth, etc. —[C-] *a trademark for* a tractor having an endless roller belt on each side, for moving over rough ground

cat·er·waul (kat'ər wôl') *vi.* [prob. echoic] to make a shrill, howling sound like that of a cat; wail —*n.* such a sound

cat'fish' *n., pl.:* see FISH a scaleless fish with long, whiskerlike barbels around the mouth

cat'gut' *n.* a tough thread made from dried intestines, as of sheep, and used for surgical sutures, etc.

Cath. Catholic

ca·thar·sis (kə thär'sis) *n.* [< Gr. *katharos*, pure] **1.** purgation, esp. of the bowels **2.** a relieving of the emotions, esp. by art or psychotherapy

ca·thar'tic *adj.* purging —*n.* a medicine to stimulate evacuation of the bowels; laxative

Ca·thay (ka thā') *poet. or archaic name of* CHINA

cat'head' *n.* a projecting beam near the bow of a ship, to which the anchor is fastened

ca·the·dra (kə thē'drə) *n.* [< Gr. *kathedra*, a seat] **1.** the bishop's throne in a cathedral **2.** the episcopal see See also EX CATHEDRA

ca·the·dral (kə thē'drəl) *n.* **1.** the main church of a bishop's see **2.** loosely, any large, imposing church —*adj.* **1.** of, like, or containing a cathedra **2.** official **3.** of or like a cathedral

Cath·er·ine II (kath'rin, -ər in) 1729-96; empress of Russia (1762-96): called Catherine the Great

cath·e·ter (kath'ə tər) *n.* [< Gr. *kata-*, down + *hienai*, send] a slender tube inserted into a body passage, etc., as for draining urine from the bladder —**cath'e·ter·ize'** (-īz') *vt.* **-ized', -iz'ing**

cath·ode (kath'ōd) *n.* [< Gr. *kata-*, down + *hodos*, way] **1.** the negative electrode in an electrolytic cell, electron tube, etc. **2.** the positive terminal in a battery

cathode rays streams of electrons projected from a cathode: they produce X-rays on striking solids

cath·o·lic (kath'ə lik, kath'lik) *adj.* [< Gr. *kata-*, completely + *holos*, whole] **1.** all-inclusive; universal **2.** broad in sympathies, tastes, etc.; liberal **3.** [*often* C-] of the universal Christian church **4.** [C-] of the Christian church headed by the Pope; Roman Catholic —*n.* **1.** [*often* C-] a member of the universal Christian church **2.** [C-] *same as* ROMAN CATHOLIC —**ca·thol·i·cal·ly** (kə thäl'i k'l ē, -ik lē) *adv.*

Ca·thol·i·cism (kə thäl'ə siz'm) *n.* the doctrine, faith, practice, and organization of a Catholic church, esp. of the Roman Catholic Church

cath·o·lic·i·ty (kath'ə lis'ə tē) *n.* **1.** broadness of taste, sympathy, etc. **2.** universality **3.** [C-] Catholicism

cat·i·on (kat'ī'ən) *n.* [< Gr. *kata-*, down + *ienai*, to go] a positive ion: in electrolysis, cations move toward the cathode —**cat·i·on·ic** (kat'ī än'ik) *adj.*

cat·kin (kat'kin) *n.* [< Du. dim. of *katte*, cat] a drooping, scaly spike of flowers without petals, as on poplars or walnuts

cat·nap (kat'nap') *n.* a short, light sleep — *vi.* **-napped'**, **-nap'ping** to take a catnap

cat'nip' (-nip') *n.* [CAT + *nip* (dial. for *catnip*) < L. *nepeta*] a plant of the mint family: cats like its odor

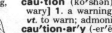

Ca·to (kāt'ō) **1.** 234–149 B.C.; Rom. statesman: called *the Elder* **2.** 95–46 B.C.; Rom. statesman & philosopher: great-grandson of prec.: called *the Younger*

CATKIN

cat-o'-nine-tails (kat'ə nīn'tālz') *n., pl.* **-tails'** a whip made of nine knotted cords attached to a handle

Cats·kill Mountains (kat'skil') mountain range in SE N.Y.: also **Cats'kills'**

cat's-paw (kats'pô') *n.* a person used by another to do distasteful or unlawful work; dupe

cat·sup (kech'əp, kat'səp) *n. same as* KETCHUP

cat·tail (kat'tāl') *n.* a tall marsh plant with long, brown, fuzzy spikes

cat'tish *adj.* **1.** like a cat; feline **2.** *same as* CATTY — **cat'tish·ly** *adv.* —**cat'tish·ness** *n.*

cat·tle (kat''l) *n.* [ult. < L. *caput*, the head] **1.** [Archaic] farm animals **2.** cows, bulls, steers, or oxen **3.** people in the mass: contemptuous term

cat·ty (kat'ē) *adj.* **-ti·er**, **-ti·est 1.** of or like a cat **2.** spiteful, mean, malicious, etc. —**cat'ti·ly** *adv.* —**cat'ti·ness** *n.*

cat'ty-cor'nered *adj., adv. same as* CATER-CORNERED: also **cat'ty-cor'ner**

cat·walk (kat'wôk') *n.* a high, narrow walk, as along a bridge or over an engine room

Cau·ca·sian (kô kā'zhən) *adj.* **1.** of the Caucasus, its people, etc. **2.** *same as* CAUCASOID —*n.* **1.** a native of the Caucasus **2.** *same as* CAUCASOID

Cau·ca·soid (kôk'ə soid') *adj.* designating or of one of the major groups of mankind: loosely called the *white race* —*n.* a member of the Caucasoid group

Cau·ca·sus (kô'kə səs) mountain range in SE Europe, between the Black Sea and the Caspian

cau·cus (kôk'əs) *n.* [< ?] a private meeting of a party to decide on policy, candidates, etc. —*vi.* **-cused** or **-cussed**, **-cus·ing** or **-cus·sing** to hold, or take part in, a caucus

cau·dal (kôd''l) *adj.* [< L. *cauda*, tail] of, like, at, or near the tail

cau·date (kô'dāt) *adj.* [< L. *cauda*, tail] having a tail or taillike part: also **cau'dat·ed**

caught (kôt) *pt. & pp. of* CATCH

caul (kôl) *n.* [OE. *cawl*, net] a membrane sometimes enveloping the head of a child at birth

caul·dron (kôl'drən) *n. same as* CALDRON

cau·li·flow·er (kôl'ə flou'ər, käl'-) *n.* [< It. < L. *caulis*, cabbage] **1.** a variety of cabbage with a compact white head of fleshy flower stalks **2.** the head of this plant, eaten as a vegetable

caulk (kôk) *vt.* [< L. *calx*, a heel] **1.** to make (a boat, etc.) watertight by filling the seams with oakum, tar, etc. **2.** to stop up (cracks) with a filler —**caulk'er** *n.*

caus·al (kôz''l) *adj.* **1.** of, like, being, or expressing a cause **2.** relating to cause and effect —**cau·sal·i·ty** (kô zal'ə tē) *n.* —**caus'al·ly** *adv.*

cau·sa·tion (kô zā'shən) *n.* **1.** the act of causing **2.** anything producing an effect; cause

caus·a·tive (kôz'ə tiv) *adj.* **1.** producing an effect; causing **2.** expressing causation, as the verb *fell* (to cause to fall) —*n.* a causative word or form —**caus'a·tive·ly** *adv.*

cause (kôz) *n.* [< L. *causa*] **1.** anything bringing about an effect or result **2.** a reason or motive for some action, feeling, etc. **3.** any objective or movement that people are interested in and support **4.** an action or question to be resolved by a court of law —*vt.* **caused**, **caus'ing** to be the cause of; bring about; effect —**cause'less** *adj.*

cause·way (kôz'wā') *n.* [ult. < L. *calx*, limestone + WAY] **1.** a raised path or road, as across a marsh **2.** a paved way or road; highway

caus·tic (kôs'tik) *adj.* [< Gr. *kaiein*, to burn] **1.** that can burn or destroy tissue by chemical action; corrosive **2.** cutting or sarcastic —*n.* a caustic substance —**caus'ti·cal·ly** *adv.* —**caus·tic'i·ty** (-tis'ə tē) *n.*

caustic soda *same as* SODIUM HYDROXIDE

cau·ter·ize (kôt'ər īz') *vt.* **-ized'**, **-iz'ing** [< Gr. *kautēr*, branding iron] to burn with a hot iron or needle, or with a caustic, so as to destroy dead tissue, etc. —**cau'ter·i·za'tion** *n.*

cau·ter·y (kôt'ər ē) *n., pl.* **-ies 1.** an instrument or substance for cauterizing **2.** a cauterizing

cau·tion (kô'shən) *n.* [< L., same base as *cavere*, be wary] **1.** a warning; admonition **2.** prudence; wariness — *vt.* to warn; admonish

cau'tion·ar'y (-er'ē) *adj.* urging caution

cau·tious (kô'shəs) *adj.* full of caution; careful to avoid danger; wary —**cau'tious·ly** *adv.* —**cau'tious·ness** *n.*

cav·al·cade (kav''l kād') *n.* [Fr. < L. *caballus*, horse] a procession, as of horsemen or carriages

cav·a·lier (kav'ə lir') *n.* [Fr. < L. *caballus*, horse] **1.** an armed horseman; knight **2.** a gallant gentleman, esp. one serving as a lady's escort **3.** [C-] a partisan of Charles I of England in his struggles with Parliament —*adj.* **1.** [C-] of the Cavaliers **2.** *a)* free and easy; gay *b)* casual toward matters of some importance *c)* haughty; arrogant —**cav'a·lier'ly** *adv., adj.*

cav·al·ry (kav''l rē) *n., pl.* **-ries** [< Fr.: see CAVALIER] combat troops mounted originally on horses but now often on motorized armored vehicles —**cav'al·ry·man** *n., pl.* **-men**

cave (kāv) *n.* [< L. *cavus*, hollow] a hollow place inside the earth; cavern —*vt., vi.* **caved**, **cav'ing** to collapse or make collapse (with *in*)

ca·ve·at emp·tor (kā'vē at' emp'tôr) [L.] let the buyer beware (i.e., one buys at his own risk)

cave'-in' *n.* **1.** a caving in **2.** a place where the ground, a mine, etc. has caved in

cave man 1. a prehistoric human being of the Stone Age who lived in caves: also **cave dweller 2.** a man who is rough and crudely direct

cav·ern (kav'ərn) *n.* [< L. *cavus*, hollow] a cave, esp. a large cave —**cav'ern·ous** *adj.*

cav·i·ar, cav·i·are (kav'ē är') *n.* [Fr. < Per. *khāviyār*] the salted eggs of sturgeon, salmon, etc. eaten as an appetizer

cav·il (kav''l) *vi.* **-iled** or **-illed**, **-il·ing** or **-il·ling** [< L. *cavilla*, a jest] to object unnecessarily; carp (*at* or *about*) —*n.* a trivial objection; quibble —**cav'il·er, cav'il·ler** *n.*

cav·i·ty (kav'ə tē) *n., pl.* **-ties** [< L. *cavus*, hollow] **1.** a hole or hollow place, as in a tooth **2.** a natural hollow place within the body *[the abdominal cavity]*

ca·vort (kə vôrt') *vi.* [< ?] **1.** to leap about; prance **2.** to romp happily; frolic

ca·vy (kā'vē) *n., pl.* **-vies** [< Carib *cabiai*] any of several short-tailed S. American rodents, as the guinea pig

caw (kô) *n.* [echoic] the harsh cry of a crow or raven —*vi.* to make this sound

Cax·ton (kak'stən), **William** 1422?–91; 1st Eng. printer

cay (kā, kē) *n.* [Sp. *cayo:* see KEY²] a low island, coral reef, or sandbank off a mainland

cay·enne (kī en', kā-) *n.* [< Tupi *kynnha*] a very hot red pepper made from the dried fruit of a pepper plant: also **cayenne pepper**

cay·man (kā'mən) *n., pl.* **-mans** *same as* CAIMAN

Ca·yu·ga (kā yōō'gə, kī-) *n., pl.* **-gas, -ga** a member of a tribe of Iroquoian Indians who lived in W N.Y.

cay·use (kī'ōōs, kī ōōs') *n.* [< AmInd.] a small Western horse used by cowboys

CB (sē'bē') *adj.* [*citizens' band*] designating or of short-wave radio frequencies set aside by the FCC for local use by private persons —*n., pl.* **CB's** a shortwave radio using such frequencies

cc, c.c. cubic centimeter(s)

Cd *Chem.* cadmium

Ce *Chem.* cerium

cease (sēs) *vt., vi.* **ceased**, **ceas'ing** [< L. *cedere*, to yield] to end; stop —*n.* a ceasing: chiefly in **without cease**

cease'-fire' *n.* a temporary cessation of warfare; truce

cease'less (-lis) *adj.* unceasing; continual —**cease'less·ly** *adv.*

ce·cro·pi·a moth (si krō'pē ə) the largest moth of the U.S., with wide wings

ce·cum (sē'kəm) *n., pl.* **-ca** (-kə) [< L. *caecus*, blind] the pouch at the beginning of the large intestine

ce·dar (sē'dər) *n.* [< Gr. *kedros*] **1.** a coniferous tree having durable, fragrant wood **2.** any of various trees like this **3.** the wood of any of these

Cedar Rapids city in EC Iowa: pop. 109,000

cedar waxwing a brownish-gray, crested American bird with red, waxlike tips on its secondary wing feathers: also **ce'dar·bird'** *n.*

cede (sēd) *vt.* **ced'ed**, **ced'ing** [< L. *cedere*, to yield] **1.** to give up one's rights in **2.** to transfer the ownership of

ce·dil·la (si dil'ə) *n.* [Fr. < Sp. dim. of *zeda*, the zeta] a mark put under *c* in some French words (Ex.: *façade*) to show that it has an *s* sound

ceil (sēl) *vt.* [< L. *celare*, to hide] **1.** to build a ceiling in or over **2.** to cover (the ceiling or walls of a room) with plaster or boards

ceil'ing (-iŋ) *n.* [< prec.] **1.** the inside top part of a room, opposite the floor **2.** an upper limit *[a wage ceiling]* **3.** *Aeron. a)* a cloud cover limiting vertical visibility, or the height of its lower surface *b)* the highest that an aircraft can normally fly —**hit the ceiling** [Slang] to lose one's temper

cel·an·dine (sel'ən dīn') *n.* [< Gr. *chelidōn*, a swallow] **1.** a weedy plant related to the poppy, with yellow flowers **2.** a plant of the buttercup family, with yellow flowers

Cel·e·bes (sel'ə bēz') island of Indonesia, east of Borneo: 69,277 sq. mi.

cel·e·brant (sel'ə brənt) *n.* **1.** one who performs a religious rite, as the priest officiating at Mass **2.** a celebrator

cel'e·brate' (-brāt') *vt.* **-brat'ed, -brat'ing** [< L. *celebrare*, to honor] **1.** to perform (a ritual, etc.) **2.** to commemorate (an anniversary, etc.) with ceremony or festivity **3.** to honor publicly —*vi.* **1.** to observe a holiday, etc. with festivities **2.** to perform a religious ceremony **3.** [Colloq.] to have a good time

cel'e·brat'ed (-id) *adj.* famous; renowned

cel'e·bra'tion *n.* **1.** a celebrating **2.** that which is done to celebrate

ce·leb·ri·ty (sə leb'rə tē) *n.* **1.** fame **2.** *pl.* **-ties** a celebrated person

ce·ler·i·ty (sə ler'ə tē) *n.* [< L. *celer*, swift] swiftness in acting or moving; speed

cel·e·ry (sel'ər ē) *n.* [< Fr. < Gr. *selinon*, parsley] a plant with long, crisp leafstalks eaten as a vegetable

ce·les·ta (sə les'tə) *n.* [< Fr. < *celeste*, celestial] a small keyboard instrument with hammers that strike metal plates to make bell-like tones

ce·les·tial (sə les'chəl) *adj.* [< L. *caelum*, heaven] **1.** of the heavens, or sky **2.** *a)* of heaven; divine *b)* highest; perfect —**ce·les'tial·ly** *adv.*

celestial equator the great circle of the celestial sphere formed by projecting the plane of the earth's equator on the celestial sphere

celestial sphere an imaginary sphere of infinite diameter containing the whole universe and on which all celestial bodies appear to be projected

cel·i·ba·cy (sel'ə bə sē) *n.* **1.** the state of being unmarried **2.** complete sexual abstinence

cel·i·bate (sel'ə bət) *adj.* [< L. *caelebs*, unmarried] of or in a state of celibacy —*n.* a celibate person

cell (sel) *n.* [< L. *cella*] **1.** a small room, as in a convent or prison **2.** a small hollow, as in a honeycomb **3.** a small unit of an organization **4.** a small unit of protoplasm: all plants and animals are made up of one or more cells **5.** a receptacle for generating electricity by chemical reactions or for decomposing compounds by electrolysis

cel·lar (sel'ər) *n.* [see prec.] a room or rooms below ground level and usually under a building

cel'lar·age (-ij) *n.* **1.** space of or in a cellar **2.** the fee for storage in a cellar

cel·lar·et (sel'ə ret') *n.* [CELLAR + -ET] a cabinet for wine, liquor, glasses, etc.

Cel·li·ni (chə lē'nē), **Ben·ve·nu·to** (ben'və n<del></del>o'tō) 1500–71; It. sculptor & goldsmith

cel·lo (chel'ō) *n., pl.* **-los, -li** (-ē) [< VIOLONCELLO] an instrument of the violin family, between the viola and double bass in size and pitch: also sp. **'cel'lo —cel'list** *n.*

CELLO

cel·lo·phane (sel'ə fān') *n.* [< CELLULOSE + Gr. *phainein*, appear] a thin, transparent material made from cellulose, used as a moistureproof wrapping

cel·lu·lar (sel'yoo lər) *adj.* of, like, or containing a cell or cells

Cel·lu·loid (sel'yoo loid') [CELLUL(OSE) + -OID] *a trademark for* a flammable plastic substance made from pyroxylin and camphor —*n.* [c-] this substance

cel·lu·lose (sel'yoo lōs') *n.* [Fr. < L. *cella*, cell + -OSE[1]] the chief substance in the cell walls or fibers of all plants, used in making paper, textiles, etc.

cellulose acetate a cellulose resin used in making acetate fiber, plastics, lacquers, etc.

Cel·si·us (sel'sē əs) *adj.* [< A. *Celsius* (1701–44), Swed. astronomer] designating or of a thermometer on which 0° is the freezing point and 100° is the boiling point of water; centigrade: abbrev. **C**

Celt (selt, kelt) *n.* [< L.] a person who speaks Celtic: the Bretons, Irish, Welsh, and Highland Scots are Celts

Cel·tic (sel'tik, kel'-) *adj.* of the Celts, their languages, etc. —*n.* an Indo-European group of languages including Gaelic, Manx, Welsh, and Breton

ce·ment (si ment') *n.* [< L. *caementum*, rough stone] **1.** a powdered substance of lime and clay, mixed with water, etc. to make mortar or concrete: it hardens upon drying **2.** any adhesive substance, as glue **3.** anything that joins or unites; bond —*vt.* **1.** to join as with cement **2.** to cover with cement —*vi.* to be cemented —**ce·ment'er** *n.* —**ce·ment'like'** *adj.*

ce·men·tum (si men'təm) *n.* [see prec.] the hard, bony, outer tissue of the root of a tooth

cem·e·ter·y (sem'ə ter'ē) *n., pl.* **-ies** [< Gr. *koiman*, put to sleep] a place for the burial of the dead; graveyard

cen·o·bite (sen'ə bīt') *n.* [< Gr. *koinos*, common + *bios*, life] a member of a religious order in a monastery or convent

cen·o·taph (sen'ə taf') *n.* [< Gr. *kenos*, empty + *taphos*, tomb] a monument honoring a dead person whose body is somewhere else

Ce·no·zo·ic (sē'nə zō'ik, sen'ə-) *adj.* [< Gr. *kainos*, recent + *zō(o)*- + -IC] designating or of the geologic era beginning c.65,000,000 years ago and including the present, during which the various mammals have developed — **the Cenozoic** the Cenozoic Era

cen·ser (sen'sər) *n.* [see INCENSE[1]] a container in which incense is burned

cen·sor (sen'sər) *n.* [L. < *censere*, to value] **1.** one of two Roman magistrates appointed to take the census and, later, to supervise public morals **2.** an official with the power to examine literature, mail, etc. and remove or prohibit anything considered obscene, objectionable, etc. —*vt.* to act as a censor of (a book, writer, etc.) —**cen'sor·ship'** *n.*

cen·so·ri·ous (sen sôr'ē əs) *adj.* inclined to find fault; critical —**cen·so'ri·ous·ly** *adv.*

cen·sure (sen'shər) *n.* [see CENSOR] strong disapproval; condemnation —*vt.* **-sured, -sur·ing** to condemn as wrong —**cen'sur·a·ble** *adj.* —**cen'sur·er** *n.*

cen·sus (sen'səs) *n.* [L.: see CENSOR] **1.** in ancient Rome, a count of the people and evaluation of their property for taxation **2.** an official, usually periodic, count of population and recording of economic status, age, sex, etc.

cent (sent) *n.* [< L. *centum*, a hundred] a 100th part of a dollar, or a coin of this value; penny

cent. 1. centigrade **2.** centimeter **3.** century

cen·taur (sen'tôr) *n.* [< Gr. *Kentauros*] *Gr. Myth.* a monster with a man's head, trunk, and arms, and a horse's body and legs

cen·ta·vo (sen tä'vō) *n., pl.* **-vos** [Sp.: see CENT] a small coin of the Philippines, Mexico, and some S. American countries; one 100th of a peso

cen·te·nar·i·an (sen'tə ner'ē ən) *adj.* of a centenary or a centenarian —*n.* a person at least 100 years old

cen·te·nar·y (sen ten'ər ē, sen'tə ner'ē) *adj.* [< L. *centum*, a hundred] **1.** of a century **2.** of a centennial —*n., pl.* **-ies 1.** a century **2.** *same as* CENTENNIAL

cen·ten·ni·al (sen ten'ē əl) *adj.* [< L. *centum*, a hundred + *annus*, year] **1.** of 100 years **2.** happening once in 100 years **3.** 100 years old **4.** of a 100th anniversary —*n.* a 100th anniversary or its celebration —**cen·ten'ni·al·ly** *adv.*

cen·ter (sen'tər) *n.* [< Gr. *kentron*, a point] **1.** a point equally distant from all points on the circumference of a circle or surface of a sphere **2.** the point around which anything revolves; pivot **3.** a place at which an activity is carried on or to which many people are attracted **4.** the approximate middle point or part of anything **5.** a group of nerve cells regulating a particular function **6.** *Sports* a player at the center of a line, floor, etc. **7.** *Mil.* that part of an army between the flanks **8.** [often C-] *Politics* a position between the left (liberals) and right (conservatives) —*vt.* **1.** to place in or near the center **2.** to gather to one place —*vi.* to be centered

cen'ter·board' *n.* a movable, keellike board lowered through a slot in the floor of a sailboat to prevent drifting

center of gravity that point in a body or system around which its weight is evenly balanced

cen'ter·piece' *n.* an ornament, bowl of flowers, etc. for the center of a table

cen·tes·i·mal (sen tes'ə məl) *adj.* [< L. *centum*, a hundred] **1.** hundredth **2.** of or divided into hundredths

---

centi- [L.] *a combining form meaning:* **1.** hundred **2.** a 100th part of

cen·ti·grade (sen'tə grād') *adj.* [Fr. < L. *centum*, a hundred + *gradus*, a degree] **1.** consisting of or divided into 100 degrees **2.** *same as* CELSIUS

cen'ti·gram' (-gram') *n.* [Fr.: see CENTI- & GRAM] a unit of weight, equal to 1/100 gram: chiefly Brit. sp. **cen'ti·gramme'**

cen'ti·li·ter (-lēt'ər) *n.* [Fr.: see CENTI- & LITER] a unit of capacity, equal to 1/100 liter: chiefly Brit. sp. **cen'ti·li're**

cen·time (sän'tēm) *n.* [Fr.] the 100th part of a franc

cen·ti·me·ter (sen'tə mēt'ər) *n.* [< Fr.: see CENTI- & METER[1]] a unit of measure, equal to 1/100 meter: chiefly Brit. sp. **cen'ti·me'tre**

cen'ti·me'ter-gram'-sec'ond *adj.* designating or of a system of measurement in which the centimeter, gram, and second are used as the units of length, mass, and time, respectively

cen·ti·pede (sen'tə pēd') *n.* [Fr. < L. *centum*, a hundred + *pes*, foot] a many-segmented arthropod with a pair of legs to each segment

cen·tral (sen'trəl) *adj.* **1.** in or near the center **2.** of or forming the center **3.** equally accessible from various points **4.** main; basic **5.** of a single source that controls all activity in an organization **6.** designating that part of a nervous system consisting of the brain and spinal cord — *n.* formerly, a telephone exchange or operator —**cen·tral'·i·ty** (-tral'ə tē) *n.* —**cen'tral·ly** *adv.*

Central African Empire country in C Africa: 238,224 sq. mi.; pop. 2,370,000; cap. Bangui

Central America part of N. America between Mexico and S. America —**Central American**

central city the crowded, industrial central area of a large city

cen'tral·ize' (-trə līz') *vt.* -ized', -iz'ing to organize under one control —*vi.* to become centralized —**cen'tral·i·za'tion** *n.* —**cen'tral·iz'er** *n.*

Central Powers in World War I, Germany, Austria-Hungary, Turkey, and Bulgaria

cen·tre (sen'tər) *n., vt., vi.* -tred, -tring *chiefly Brit. sp.* of CENTER

centri- *same as* CENTRO-

cen·tric (sen'trik) *adj.* **1.** central **2.** of or having a center

cen·trif·u·gal (sen trif'yə gəl) *adj.* [< CENTRI- + L. *fugere*, flee] **1.** moving or tending to move away from a center **2.** using or acted on by centrifugal force —*n.* a centrifuge —**cen·trif'u·gal·ly** *adv.*

centrifugal force the force tending to pull a thing outward when it is rotating rapidly around a center

cen·tri·fuge (sen'trə fyōōj') *n.* a machine using centrifugal force to separate particles of varying density

cen·trip·e·tal (sen trip'ət 'l) *adj.* [< CENTRI- + L. *petere*, seek] **1.** moving or tending to move toward a center **2.** using or acted on by centripetal force —**cen·trip'e·tal·ly** *adv.*

centripetal force the force tending to pull a thing inward when it is rotating rapidly around a center

cen·trist (sen'trist) *n.* a member of a political party of the center

centro- [< L. *centrum*, CENTER] *a combining form meaning* center

cen·tu·ri·on (sen tyoor'ē ən) *n.* [see CENTURY] in ancient Rome, the commanding officer of a military unit, originally of 100 men

cen·tu·ry (sen'chər ē) *n., pl.* -ries [< L. *centum*, a hundred] any period of 100 years, esp. as reckoned from 1 A.D.

century plant a tropical American agave that blooms once in 10 to 30 years

ce·phal·ic (sə fal'ik) *adj.* [< Gr. *kephalē*, the head] **1.** of the head or skull **2.** in, on, or near the head

ceph·a·lo·pod (sef'ə lə päd') *n.* [< Gr. *kephalē*, head + -POD] a mollusk having a distinct head with tentacles about the mouth, as the octopus, squid, etc.

ce·ram·ic (sə ram'ik) *adj.* [< Gr. *keramos*, clay] **1.** of pottery, tile, porcelain, etc. **2.** of ceramics —*n.* **1.** [*pl. with sing. v.*] the art or work of making objects of baked clay **2.** such an object —**ce·ram·ist** (sə ram'ist, ser'ə mist), **ce·ram'i·cist** (-ə sist) *n.*

Cer·ber·us (sur'bər əs) *Gr. & Rom. Myth.* the three-headed dog guarding the gate of Hades

ce·re·al (sir'ē əl) *adj.* [< L. *Cerealis*, of Ceres] of grain — *n.* **1.** any grain used for food, as wheat, oats, etc. **2.** any grass producing such grain **3.** food made from grain, as oatmeal

cer·e·bel·lum (ser'ə bel'əm) *n., pl.* -lums, -la (-ə) [L., dim. of *cerebrum*, the brain] the section of the brain be-

hind and below the cerebrum: it is the coordinating center for muscular movement

cer·e·bral (ser'ə brəl, sə rē'-) *adj.* of the brain or the cerebrum —**cer·e'bral·ly** *adv.*

cerebral palsy any of several disorders of the central nervous system resulting from brain damage and characterized by spastic paralysis

cer·e·brate (ser'ə brāt') *vi.* -brat'ed, -brat'ing [see CEREBELLUM & -ATE[1]] to use one's brain; think —**cer'e·bra'tion** *n.*

cer·e·bro·spi·nal (ser'ə brō spī'n'l) *adj.* of or affecting the brain and the spinal cord

cer·e·brum (ser'ə brəm, sə rē'-) *n., pl.* -brums, -bra (-brə) [L.] the upper, main part of the brain, controlling conscious and voluntary processes in man

cer·e·ment (ser'ə mənt, sir'mənt) *n.* [< Gr. *kēros*, wax] **1.** a shroud **2.** [*usually pl.*] any burial clothes

cer·e·mo·ni·al (ser'ə mō'nē əl) *adj.* of, for, or consisting of ceremony; formal —*n.* **1.** a set system of forms or rites; ritual **2.** a rite —**cer'e·mo'ni·al·ism** *n.* —**cer'e·mo'ni·al·ly** *adv.*

cer·e·mo·ni·ous (-nē əs) *adj.* **1.** full of ceremony **2.** very polite or formal —**cer'e·mo'ni·ous·ly** *adv.*

cer·e·mo·ny (ser'ə mō'nē) *n., pl.* -nies [L. *caerimonia*] **1.** a set of formal acts proper to a special occasion, as a religious rite **2.** behavior that follows rigid etiquette **3.** formality **4.** meaningless formality —**stand on ceremony** to insist on formality

Ce·res (sir'ēz) *Rom. Myth.* the goddess of agriculture: identified with the Greek goddess Demeter

ce·rise (sə rēs', -rēz') *n., adj.* [Fr., a cherry] bright red; cherry red

ce·ri·um (sir'ē əm) *n.* [< the asteroid *Ceres*] a gray, metallic chemical element: symbol, Ce; at. wt., 140.12; at. no., 58

cer·tain (surt''n) *adj.* [< L. *cernere*, decide] **1.** fixed; settled **2.** inevitable **3.** reliable; dependable **4.** sure; positive **5.** not named, though definite [a *certain* person] **6.** some [to a *certain* extent] —**for certain** without doubt

cer'tain·ly (-lē) *adv.* beyond a doubt; surely

cer'tain·ty (-tē) *n.* **1.** the state or fact of being certain **2.** *pl.* -ties anything certain

cer·tif·i·cate (sur tif'ə kit) *n.* [see CERTIFY] a written statement testifying to a fact, qualification, ownership, etc. —*vt.* (-kāt') -cat'ed, -cat'ing to issue a certificate to or for

cer·ti·fied (sur'tə fīd') *adj.* **1.** guaranteed **2.** having, or attested to by, a certificate

certified mail a postal service which provides a receipt to the sender of first-class mail and a record of its delivery; also, mail sent by this

cer·ti·fy (sur'tə fī') *vt.* -fied', -fy'ing [< L. *certus*, certain + *facere*, to make] **1.** to declare (a thing) true, accurate, etc. by formal statement **2.** to guarantee; vouch for **3.** to issue a certificate to —*vi.* to testify (*to*) —**cer'ti·fi·ca'tion** *n.*

cer·ti·tude (sur'tə tōōd', -tyōōd') *n.* **1.** a feeling absolutely sure **2.** inevitability

ce·ru·le·an (sə rōō'lē ən) *adj.* [< L., prob. < *caelum*, heaven] sky-blue; azure

ce·ru·men (sə rōō'mən) *n.* [< L. *cera*, wax] *same as* EARWAX

Cer·van·tes (ther vän'tes; *E.* sər van'tēz), **Mi·guel de** (mē gel' *the*) 1547–1616; Sp. writer

cer·vix (sur'viks) *n., pl.* -vi·ces' (-və sēz'), -vix·es [L., the neck] **1.** the neck **2.** a necklike part, esp. of the uterus — **cer'vi·cal** (-vi kəl) *adj.*

ce·si·um (sē'zē əm) *n.* [< L. *caesius*, bluish-gray] a soft, silver-white metallic chemical element: symbol, Cs; at. wt., 132.905; at. no., 55

ces·sa·tion (se sā'shən) *n.* [< L. *cessare*, to cease] a ceasing, either final or temporary; stop

ces·sion (sesh'ən) *n.* [< L. *cedere*, to yield] a ceding or giving up (of rights, etc.) to another

cess·pool (ses'pōōl') *n.* [< It. < L. *secessus*, place of retirement] a tank or deep hole in the ground to receive drainage or sewage from sinks, toilets, etc.

ce·ta·cean (si tā'shən) *n.* [< Gr. *kētos*, whale] any of a group of fishlike water mammals including whales and dolphins —*adj.* of the cetaceans

Cey·lon (sə län') *former name of* SRI LANKA

Cé·zanne (sā zan'), **Paul** 1839–1906; Fr. painter

Cf *Chem.* californium

cf. [L. *confer*] compare

cg, cg., cgm, cgm. centigram(s)

cgs, c.g.s., C.G.S. centimeter-gram-second

Ch., ch. 1. chapter **2.** church

Chad (chad) **1.** country in NC Africa: 495,000 sq. mi.; pop. 3,361,000; cap. N'Djamena **2. Lake**, lake at the junction of the Chad, Niger, and Nigerian borders

chafe (chāf) *vt.* **chafed, chaf′ing** [< L. *calere*, be warm + *facere*, to make] **1.** to rub so as to make warm **2.** to wear away or make sore by rubbing **3.** to annoy; irritate —*vi.* **1.** to rub (*on* or *against*) **2.** to be irritated or impatient — *n.* an injury caused by rubbing —**chafe at the bit** to be impatient

chaff (chaf) *n.* [OE. *ceaf*]. **1.** threshed or winnowed husks of grain **2.** anything worthless **3.** teasing; banter —*vt., vi.* to tease —**chaff′y** *adj.* **-i·er, -i·est**

chaf·finch (chaf′finch′) *n.* [OE. *ceaffinc*] a small European songbird, often kept in a cage as a pet

chaf·ing dish (chāf′iŋ) [see CHAFE] a pan with a heating apparatus beneath it, to cook food at the table or to keep food hot

cha·grin (shə grin′) *n.* [Fr., grief] a feeling of embarrassment and distress caused by failure or disappointment — *vt.* **-grined′, -grin′ing** to cause to feel chagrin

chain (chān) *n.* [< L. *catena*] **1.** a flexible series of joined links **2.** [*pl.*] *a)* bonds, shackles, etc. *b)* captivity; bondage **3.** a chainlike measuring instrument: a *surveyor's chain* is 66 feet; an *engineer's chain* is 100 feet **4.** a connected series of things or events **5.** *Chem.* a linking of atoms in a molecule —*vt.* **1.** to fasten or shackle with chains **2.** to hold down, restrain, etc.

chain gang a gang of prisoners chained together, as when working

chain mail flexible armor made of metal links

chain′-re·act′ (-rē akt′) *vi.* to be involved in or subjected to a chain reaction

chain reaction 1. a self-sustaining series of chemical or nuclear reactions in which the products of the reaction keep the process going **2.** any sequence of events, each of which results in the following

chain saw a portable power saw with an endless chain carrying cutting teeth

chain′-smoke′ (-smōk′) *vt., vi.* **-smoked′, -smok′ing** to smoke (cigarettes) one right after the other —**chain smoker, chain′-smok′er** *n.*

chain stitch a fancy stitch in which the loops are connected in a chainlike way —**chain′-stitch′** *vt.*

chain store any of a chain of retail stores

chair (cher) *n.* [< L. *cathedra*: see CATHEDRAL] **1.** a piece of furniture with a back, for one person to sit on **2.** an important or official position **3.** a chairman —*vt.* **1.** to seat **2.** to preside over as chairman

chair′lift′ (-lift′) *n.* a line of seats suspended from a power-driven endless cable, used to carry skiers up a slope

chair′man (-mən) *n., pl.* **-men** a person who presides at a meeting or heads a committee, board, etc. —**chair′man·ship′** *n.* —**chair′wom′an** *n.fem., pl.* **-wom′en**

chair′per·son (-pur′s'n) *n.* same as CHAIRMAN: used to avoid the masculine implication of *chairman*

chaise (shāz) *n.* [Fr.] **1.** a lightweight carriage having two or four wheels **2.** same as CHAISE LONGUE

chaise longue (shāz′ lôŋ′, louŋj′) *pl.* **chaise** (or **chaises**) **longues** (shāz′ lôŋz′, louŋ′jəz) [Fr., long chair] a couch-like chair with a long seat to support the outstretched legs: also **chaise lounge**

chal·ced·o·ny (kal sed′'n ē, kal′sə dō′nē) *n., pl.* **-nies** [< Gr. *chalkēdōn*, a precious stone] a kind of colored quartz with the luster of wax

Chal·de·a (kal dē′ə) **1.** ancient province of Babylonia, on the Persian Gulf **2.** Babylonia: so called in the 6th cent. B.C. —**Chal·de′an** *adj., n.*

cha·let (sha lā′, shal′ē) *n.* [Swiss-Fr.] **1.** a Swiss house with overhanging eaves **2.** any building in this style

chal·ice (chal′is) *n.* [< L. *calix*, a cup] **1.** a cup; goblet **2.** the cup for the wine of Holy Communion **3.** a cup-shaped flower

chalk (chôk) *n.* [< L. *calx*, limestone] **1.** a soft, whitish limestone, composed mainly of minute seashells **2.** a piece of chalk or chalklike substance used for writing on a blackboard —*adj.* made with chalk —*vt.* **1.** to smear with chalk **2.** to mark with chalk —**chalk out 1.** to mark out **2.** to plan —**chalk up 1.** to score, get, or achieve **2.** to charge or credit —**chalk′i·ness** *n.* —**chalk′y** *adj.* **-i·er, -i·est**

chalk′board′ same as BLACKBOARD

chal·lenge (chal′ənj) *n.* [< L. *calumnia*, CALUMNY] **1.** a demand for identification [a sentry gave the *challenge*] **2.** a calling into question [a *challenge* to an assertion] **3.** a call to a duel, contest, etc. **4.** anything that calls for special effort **5.** an exception to a vote or to someone's right to vote **6.** *Law* a formal objection —*vt.* **-lenged, -leng·ing 1.** to call to a halt for identification **2.** to make an objection to; question **3.** to call to a duel, contest, etc. **4.** to make demands on [to *challenge* the imagination] **5.** to object to (a vote or voter) as not being valid or qualified — *vi.* to issue a challenge —**chal′lenge·a·ble** *adj.* —**chal′leng·er** *n.*

chal·lis, chal·lie (shal′ē) *n.* [< ?] a lightweight, usually printed fabric of cotton, wool, etc.

cham·ber (chām′bər) *n.* [< L. *camera*, a vault] **1.** a room in a house, esp. a bedroom **2.** [*pl.*] [Brit.] a suite of rooms **3.** [*pl.*] a judge's office near the courtroom **4.** an assembly hall **5.** a legislative or judicial body **6.** a council [a *chamber* of commerce] **7.** an enclosed space in the body **8.** the part of a gun that holds the charge or cartridge —*vt.* to provide a chamber for —**cham′bered** *adj.*

cham′ber·lain (-lin) *n.* [< OHG. *chamarlinc*] **1.** an officer in charge of the household of a ruler or lord **2.** a high official in certain royal courts **3.** [Brit.] a treasurer

cham′ber·maid′ (-mād′) *n.* a woman whose work is taking care of bedrooms, as in hotels

chamber music music for performance by a small group, as a string quartet, orig. in a small hall

chamber of commerce an association established to further the business interests of its community

cham·bray (sham′brā) *n.* [< *Cambrai*, Fr. city] a cotton fabric made by weaving white threads across a colored warp

cha·me·le·on (kə mēl′yən, -mē′lē ən) *n.* [< Gr. *chamai*, on the ground + *leōn*, lion] **1.** any of various lizards that can change the color of their skin **2.** a changeable or fickle person

cham·fer (cham′fər) *n.* [< L.: see CANT² & FRAGILE] a beveled edge or corner

cham·ois (sham′ē) *n., pl.* **-ois** [Fr.] **1.** a small, goatlike antelope of the mountains of Europe and the Caucasus **2.** a soft leather made from the skin of chamois, sheep, etc.: also sp. **cham′my,** *pl.* **-mies** —*adj.* **1.** made of chamois **2.** yellowish-brown

cham·o·mile (kam′ə mīl′, -mēl′) *n.* [< Gr. *chamai*, on the ground + *mēlon*, apple] any of several plants with strong-smelling foliage; esp., a plant whose dried flowers have been used in a medicinal tea

champ¹ (champ) *vt., vi.* [prob. echoic] to chew hard and noisily; munch —*n.* the act of champing —**champ at the bit 1.** to bite upon its bit repeatedly and restlessly: said of a horse **2.** to be restless

CHAMOIS
(30–32 in. high
at shoulder)

champ² (champ) *n.* [Slang] same as CHAMPION

cham·pagne (sham pān′) *n.* **1.** an effervescent white wine, specif. one from Champagne, a region in NE France **2.** pale, tawny yellow

cham·paign (sham pān′) *n.* [< L. *campus*, field] flat, open country

cham·pi·on (cham′pē ən) *n.* [< LL. *campio*, gladiator] **1.** one who fights for another or for a cause; defender **2.** a winner of first place in a competition —*adj.* excelling all others —*vt.* to fight for; defend —**cham′pi·on·ship′** *n.*

Cham·plain (sham plān′), **Lake** lake between N.Y. and Vt.

chance (chans) *n.* [< L. *cadere*, to fall] **1.** the happening of events without apparent cause; luck **2.** an accidental happening **3.** a risk or gamble **4.** a ticket in a lottery or raffle **5.** an opportunity [a *chance* to go] **6.** a possibility or probability —*adj.* accidental —*vi.* **chanced, chanc′ing** to have the fortune (*to*) —*vt.* to risk —**by chance** accidentally —**chance on** (or **upon**) to find by chance —**on the** (**off**) **chance** relying on the (remote) possibility

chan·cel (chan′s'l) *n.* [< L. *cancelli*, lattices] that part of a church around the altar, reserved for clergy and the choir: it is sometimes set off by a railing

chan·cel·ler·y (chan′sə lə rē) *n., pl.* **-ies 1.** the position of a chancellor **2.** a chancellor's office or the building that houses it

chan′cel·lor (-lər) *n.* [< LL. *cancellarius*, secretary] **1.** the title of the president or a high officer in some universities **2.** the prime minister in certain countries **3.** a chief judge of a court of chancery or equity in some States **4.** a high church official —**chan′cel·lor·ship′** *n.*

chan·cer·y (chan′sər ē) *n., pl.* **-ies** [< ML. *cancellaria*] **1.** a court of equity **2.** equity law **3.** a court of record **4.**

same as CHANCELLERY (sense 2) —**in chancery 1.** in litigation in a court of equity **2.** in a helpless situation

chan·cre (shaŋ′kər) *n.* [Fr.: see CANCER] a venereal sore or ulcer; primary lesion of syphilis —**chan′crous** (-krəs) *adj.*

chanc·y (chan′sē) *adj.* **-i·er, -i·est** risky; uncertain

chan·de·lier (shan′də lir′) *n.* [Fr. < L. *candela,* candle] a lighting fixture hanging from a ceiling, with branches for candles, electric bulbs, etc.

chan·dler (chan′dlər) *n.* [< L. *candela,* candle] **1.** a maker of candles **2.** a retailer of supplies, equipment, etc. —**chan′dler·y** *n., pl.* **-ies**

Chang·chun (chäŋ′chōōn′) city in NE China: pop. 1,800,000

change (chānj) *vt.* **changed, chang′ing** [< L. *cambire,* to barter < Celt.] **1.** to put or take (a thing) in place of something else; substitute [to *change* one's clothes] **2.** to exchange [let's *change* seats] **3.** to make different; alter **4.** to give or receive the equivalent of (a coin or bank note) in currency of lower denominations or in foreign money **5.** to put a fresh covering on —*vi.* **1.** to alter; vary [the scene *changes*] **2.** to leave one train, bus, etc. and board another **3.** to put on other clothes **4.** to make an exchange —*n.* **1.** a substitution, alteration, or variation **2.** variety **3.** another set of clothes **4.** *a)* money returned as the difference between the purchase price and the sum given in payment *b)* coins or bills that together equal the larger value of a single coin or bill *c)* small coins **5.** a place where merchants meet to do business; exchange —**ring the changes 1.** to ring a set of bells with all possible variations **2.** to do or say a thing in many ways —**chang′er** *n.*

change′a·ble *adj.* **1.** that can change or be changed; alterable **2.** having a changing appearance or color —**change′a·bil′i·ty, change′a·ble·ness** *n.*

change′less *adj.* unchanging; immutable

change′ling (-liŋ) *n.* a child secretly exchanged for another, esp. in folk tales

change of life *same as* MENOPAUSE

change′o′ver *n.* a complete change, as in goods produced, equipment, etc.

chan·nel (chan′'l) *n.* [see CANAL] **1.** the bed of a river, etc. **2.** the deeper part of a river, harbor, etc. **3.** a body of water joining two larger ones **4.** a tubelike passage for liquids **5.** any means of passage or transmission **6.** [*pl.*] the official course of action [to request through army *channels*] **7.** a long groove **8.** a frequency band within which a radio or television station must keep its signal —*vt.* **-neled** or **-nelled, -nel·ing** or **-nel·ling 1.** to make a channel in **2.** to send through a channel

Channel Islands a group of Brit. islands in the English Channel, off the coast of Normandy

‡**chan·son** (shän sôn′) *n., pl.* **-sons′** (-sôn′) [Fr.] a song

chant (chant) *n.* [Fr. < L. *canere,* sing] **1.** a song, esp. one in which a number of words are sung to each tone **2.** words, as of a psalm, to be sung in this way **3.** a singsong way of speaking —*vi., vt.* to sing or say in a chant

chan·teuse (shan tœz′) *n.* [Fr.] a woman singer

chan·tey (shan′tē, chan′-) *n., pl.* **-teys** a song that sailors sing in rhythm with their motions while working: also **chan′ty,** *pl.* **-ties**

chan·ti·cleer (chan′tə klir′) *n.* [see CHANT & CLEAR] a rooster

cha·os (kā′äs) *n.* [Gr.] **1.** the disorder of formless matter and infinite space, supposed to have existed before the ordered universe **2.** extreme confusion or disorder

cha·ot·ic (-ät′ik) *adj.* in a state of chaos; in a completely confused or disordered condition —**cha·ot′i·cal·ly** *adv.*

chap[1] (chäp, chap) *n.* [prob. < ME. *cheppe* < ?] *same as* CHOP[2]

chap[2] (chap) *n.* [< Brit. *chapman,* peddler] [Colloq.] a man or boy; fellow

chap[3] (chap) *vt., vi.* **chapped** or **chapt, chap′ping** [ME. *chappen,* to cut] to crack open or roughen, as skin —*n.* a chapped place in the skin

chap. 1. chaplain **2.** chapter

chap·ar·ral (chap′ə ral′, shap′-) *n.* [Sp. < *chaparro,* evergreen oak] [Southwest] a thicket of shrubs, bushes, etc.

cha·peau (sha pō′) *n., pl.* **-peaus′, -peaux′** (-pōz′) [Fr. < LL. *cappa,* hood] a hat

chap·el (chap′'l) *n.* [< LL. *cappa,* hood] **1.** a place of Christian worship smaller than a church **2.** a small or private place of worship, as in a school

chap·er·on, chap·er·one (shap′ə rōn′) *n.* [Fr., hood] a person, esp. an older woman, who accompanies young unmarried people for propriety —*vt., vi.* **-oned′, -on′ing** to act as chaperon (to)

chap·lain (chap′lən) *n.* [see CHAPEL] **1.** a clergyman attached to a chapel **2.** a clergyman serving in a religious capacity with the armed forces —**chap′lain·cy,** *pl.* **-cies, chap′lain·ship′** *n.*

chap·let (chap′lit) *n.* [see CHAPEAU] **1.** a garland for the head **2.** a string of beads, esp. prayer beads

chaps (chaps, shaps) *n.pl.* [< MexSp. *chaparejos*] leather trousers without a seat, worn over ordinary trousers by cowboys to protect their legs

chap·ter (chap′tər) *n.* [< L. *caput,* head] **1.** a main division, as of a book **2.** a thing like a chapter; part **3.** a local branch of an organization

char[1] (chär) *vt., vi.* **charred, char′ring** [< CHARCOAL] **1.** to burn to charcoal **2.** to scorch

char[2] (chär) *n.* [< CHARWOMAN] [Brit.] a charwoman —*vi.* **charred, char′ring** [Chiefly Brit.] to work as a charwoman

char[3] (chär) *n.* [< Gael. *ceara,* red] a kind of red-bellied trout

char·ac·ter (kar′ik tər) *n.* [< Gr. *charattein,* engrave] **1.** any figure, letter, or symbol used in writing and printing **2.** a distinctive trait **3.** kind or sort **4.** behavior typical of a person or group **5.** moral strength **6.** reputation **7.** status; position **8.** a personage **9.** a person in a play, novel, etc. **10.** [Colloq.] an eccentric person —**in** (or **out**) **of character** consistent (or inconsistent)

char′ac·ter·is′tic (-tə ris′tik) *adj.* of or constituting the character; typical; distinctive —*n.* a distinguishing trait or quality —**char′ac·ter·is′ti·cal·ly** *adv.*

char′ac·ter·ize′ (-rīz′) *vt.* **-ized′, -iz′ing 1.** to describe the particular traits of **2.** to be the distinctive character of; distinguish —**char′ac·ter·i·za′tion** *n.*

cha·rade (shə rād′) *n.* [Fr. < Pr. *charrar,* to gossip] [*often pl.*] a game in which words to be guessed are acted out in pantomime, often by syllables

char·coal (chär′kōl′) *n.* [prob. < ME. *charren,* to turn + *cole,* coal] **1.** a form of carbon made by partially burning wood or other organic matter in the absence of air **2.** a pencil made of this **3.** a drawing made with such a pencil **4.** a very dark gray or brown

chard (chärd) *n.* [< Fr. < L. *carduus,* thistle] a kind of beet with edible leaves and stalks

chare (cher) *n.* [< OE. *cierran,* to turn] a chore, esp. a household chore —*vi.* **chared, char′ing 1.** to do chores **2.** *same as* CHAR[2]

charge (chärj) *vt.* **charged, charg′ing** [< L. *carrus,* car] **1.** to load or fill (*with* something) **2.** to add an electrical charge to (a battery, etc.) **3.** to give as a duty, command, etc. to; instruct **4.** to accuse; censure [*charged* with negligence] **5.** to make liable for (an error, etc.) **6.** to ask as a price [to *charge* $20 for labor] **7.** to put as a debt [*charge* it to my account] **8.** to attack vigorously —*vi.* **1.** to ask payment (*for*) [to *charge* for a service] **2.** to attack vigorously —*n.* **1.** the amount used to load something **2.** the amount of electrical energy stored in a battery, etc. **3.** responsibility or care (*of*) **4.** a person or thing entrusted to one's care **5.** instruction or command, esp. instructions given by a judge to a jury **6.** accusation; indictment **7.** cost **8.** a debt **9.** *same as* CHARGE ACCOUNT **10.** *a)* an attack, as by troops *b)* the signal for this **11.** *Heraldry* a bearing —**in charge** having the responsibility or control —**charge′a·ble** *adj.*

charge account an arrangement by which a customer may pay for purchases within a specified future period

charg′er *n.* **1.** a person or thing that charges **2.** a horse ridden in battle or on parade

char·i·ot (char′ē ət) *n.* [see CHARGE] a horse-drawn, two-wheeled cart used in ancient times for war, racing, etc.

char′i·ot·eer′ (-ə tir′) *n.* a chariot driver

cha·ris·ma (kə riz′mə) *n., pl.* **-ma·ta** (-mə tə) [Gr.] **1.** a divinely inspired gift **2.** a special, inspiring quality of leadership —**char·is·mat·ic** (kar′iz mat′ik) *adj.*

CHARIOT

char·i·ta·ble (char′i tə b'l) *adj.* **1.** generous to those in need **2.** of or for charity **3.** kind and forgiving in judging others —**char′i·ta·bly** *adv.*

char·i·ty (-ə tē) *n., pl.* **-ties** [< L. *caritas,* affection] **1.** *Christian Theol.* love for one's fellow men **2.** an act of good will **3.** benevolence **4.** kindness in judging others **5.** a giving of money, etc. to those in need **6.** a welfare institution, organization, etc.

cha·ri·va·ri (shə riv′ə rē′, shiv ə rē′) *n.* [Fr. < Gr. *karēbaria,* heavy head] **1.** *same as* SHIVAREE **2.** loud noise din

char·la·tan (shär′lə t′n) *n.* [Fr. < It. < LL. *cerretanus,* seller of papal indulgences] a fake; mountebank —**char′la·tan·ism, char′la·tan·ry** *n.*

Char·le·magne (shär′lə mān′) 742–814 A.D.; king of the Franks (768–814); emperor of the Holy Roman Empire (800–814)

Charles (chärlz) **1. Charles I** 1600–49; king of England, Scotland, & Ireland (1625–49) **2. Charles II** 1630–85; king of England, Scotland, & Ireland (1660–85)

Charles·ton (chärl′stən) capital of W.Va.: pop. 72,000

char·ley horse (chär′lē) [Colloq.] a cramp in the leg or arm muscles, caused by strain

Char·lotte (shär′lət) city in S N.C.: pop. 241,000

Charlotte A·ma·lie (ə mäl′yə, ə mäl′ē) capital of the Virgin Islands of the U.S.: pop. 12,000

charlotte russe (rōōs) [Fr., lit., Russian charlotte] a dessert made of whipped cream, custard, etc. in a mold lined with spongecake

charm (chärm) *n.* [< L. *carmen*] **1.** an object, action, or words assumed to have magic power **2.** a trinket on a bracelet, necklace, etc. **3.** a quality or feature that attracts or delights —*vt., vi.* **1.** to act on as if by magic **2.** to please greatly; fascinate; delight —**charm′er** *n.*

charm′ing *adj.* attractive; fascinating; delightful

char·nel (house) (chär′n′l) *n.* [< LL. *carnale,* graveyard] a building, etc. used for corpses and bones

Cha·ron (ker′ən) *Gr. Myth.* the boatman who ferried the souls of the dead across the river Styx

chart (chärt) *n.* [< Gr. *chartēs,* leaf of paper] **1.** a map, esp. one for use in navigation **2.** an information sheet with tables, graphs, etc. **3.** a table, graph, etc. —*vt.* **1.** to make a chart of **2.** to plan (a course of action) **3.** to show as by a chart

char·ter (chär′tər) *n.* [see prec.] **1.** a franchise or written grant of specified rights given by a government to a person, corporation, etc. **2.** a written statement of basic laws or principles; constitution, as of a city **3.** written permission to form a local chapter of a society **4.** the hire or lease of a ship, bus, etc. —*vt.* **1.** to grant a charter to **2.** to hire (a bus, plane, etc.) for exclusive use

charter member one of the founders or original members of an organization

char·treuse (shar trōōz′) *n.* [Fr.] pale, yellowish green

char′wom′an (chär′-) *n., pl.* -wom′en [see CHORE] a woman who does cleaning or scrubbing

char·y (cher′ē) *adj.* -i·er, -i·est [< OE. *cearu,* care] **1.** not taking chances; cautious **2.** not giving freely; sparing —**char′i·ly** *adv.* —**char′i·ness** *n.*

Cha·ryb·dis (kə rib′dis) whirlpool off the NE coast of Sicily: see SCYLLA

chase¹ (chās) *vt.* chased, chas′ing [ult. < L. *capere,* take] **1.** to follow so as to catch **2.** to run after; follow **3.** to drive away **4.** to hunt **5.** [Slang] to court; woo —*vi.* **1.** to go in pursuit **2.** [Colloq.] to go hurriedly; rush —*n.* **1.** a chasing; pursuit **2.** the hunting of game for sport **3.** anything hunted; quarry —**give chase** to pursue

chase² (chās) *n.* [ult. < L. *capsa,* a box] **1.** a groove; furrow **2.** a rectangular metal frame in which pages or columns of type are locked —*vt.* chased, chas′ing to make a groove or furrow in

chase³ (chās) *vt.* chased, chas′ing [< Fr. *enchâsser,* enshrine] to ornament (metal) by engraving, etc.

chas′er *n.* [Colloq.] a mild drink, as water, taken after or with whiskey, rum, etc.

chasm (kaz′m) *n.* [< Gr. *chasma*] **1.** a deep crack in the earth's surface; abyss **2.** any break or gap **3.** a rift —**chas′mal, chas′mic** *adj.*

chas·sis (chas′ē, shas′ē) *n., pl.* -sis (-ēz) [Fr. < L. *capsa,* a box] **1.** the frame, wheels, etc. of a motor vehicle, but not the body and engine **2.** the frame supporting the body of an airplane **3.** *Radio & TV a*) the framework to which the parts of a receiver, amplifier, etc. are attached *b*) the assembled frame and parts

chaste (chāst) *adj.* [< L. *castus,* pure] **1.** not indulging in unlawful sexual activity **2.** celibate **3.** decent; modest **4.** simple in style —**chaste′ly** *adv.*

chas·ten (chās′'n) *vt.* [< L. *castigare,* punish] **1.** to punish so as to correct; chastise **2.** to restrain from excess; subdue **3.** to refine in style

chas·tise (chas tīz′) *vt.* -tised′, -tis′ing [see prec.] **1.** to punish, esp. by beating **2.** to scold or condemn sharply —**chas·tise′ment** *n.* —**chas·tis′er** *n.*

chas·ti·ty (chas′tə tē) *n.* **1.** virtuousness **2.** sexual abstinence **3.** decency **4.** simplicity of style

chas·u·ble (chaz′yoo b′l, chas′-) *n.* [< ML. *casubla,* hooded garment] a sleeveless outer vestment worn over the alb by priests at Mass

chat (chat) *vi.* chat′ted, chat′ting [< CHATTER] to talk in a light, informal manner —*n.* **1.** a light, informal conversation **2.** any of various birds with a chattering call

châ·teau (sha tō′) *n., pl.* -teaux′ (-tōz′, -tō′), -teaus′ [Fr. < L. *castellum,* castle] **1.** a French feudal castle **2.** a large country house and estate, esp. in France Also **cha·teau′**

chat·e·laine (shat′'l ān′) *n.* [Fr., ult. < L. *castellum,* castle] **1.** the mistress of a castle or of any large household **2.** a woman's ornamental chain or clasp worn at the waist

Chat·ta·noo·ga (chat′ə nōō′gə) city in SE Tenn.: pop. 119,000

chat·tel (chat′'l) *n.* [see CATTLE] **1.** a movable item of personal property, as a piece of furniture **2.** [Archaic] a slave

chattel mortgage a mortgage on personal property

chat·ter (chat′ər) *vi.* [echoic] **1.** to make short, indistinct, rapid sounds, as birds, apes, etc. **2.** to talk much and foolishly **3.** to click together rapidly as teeth do from cold —*n.* **1.** a chattering **2.** rapid, foolish talk —**chat′ter·er** *n.*

chat′ter·box′ (-bäks′) *n.* an incessant talker

chat·ty (chat′ē) *adj.* -ti·er, -ti·est **1.** fond of chatting **2.** light and informal: said of talk —**chat′ti·ly** *adv.*

Chau·cer (chô′sər), **Geoffrey** 1340?–1400; Eng. poet

chauf·feur (shō′fər, shō fur′) *n.* [Fr., lit., stoker] a person hired to drive a private automobile for someone else —*vt.* to act as a chauffeur to

chau·tau·qua (shə tô′kwə) *n.* [< the summer schools inaugurated at Chautauqua, N.Y., in 1874] an educational and recreational assembly

chau·vin·ism (shō′və niz'm) *n.* [< N. *Chauvin,* fanatical Fr. patriot] **1.** militant and fanatical patriotism **2.** unreasoning devotion to one's race, sex, etc. —**chau′vin·ist** *n.,* *adj.* —**chau′vin·is′tic** *adj.*

chaw (chô) *n.* [Now Dial.] *same as* CHEW

cheap (chēp) *adj.* [< OE. *ceap,* a bargain] **1.** low in price **2.** charging low prices **3.** spending little **4.** worth more than the price **5.** easily got **6.** of little value **7.** contemptible **8.** [Colloq.] stingy —*adv.* at a low cost —**cheap′ly** *adv,* —**cheap′ness** *n*

cheap′en *vt., vi.* to make or become cheap or cheaper

cheap′skate′ *n.* [Slang] a stingy person

cheat (chēt) *n.* [< L. *ex-,* out + *cadere,* fall] **1.** a fraud; swindle **2.** a swindler —*vt.* **1.** to defraud; swindle **2.** to foil or elude *[to cheat death]* —*vi.* **1.** to be dishonest or deceitful **2.** [Slang] to be sexually unfaithful (often with *on*) —**cheat′er** *n.*

check (chek) *n.* [< OFr. *eschec,* a check at chess] **1.** a sudden stop **2.** any restraint of action **3.** one that restrains **4.** a supervision or test of accuracy, etc. **5.** a mark (√) to show verification of something **6.** an identification ticket, token, etc. *[a hat check]* **7.** one's bill, as at a restaurant **8.** a written order to a bank to pay a sum of money **9.** a pattern of squares like that of a chessboard, or one of the squares **10.** *Chess* the state of a king that is in danger and must be put into a safe position —*interj.* **1.** [Colloq.] agreed! right! OK! **2.** *Chess* a call meaning the opponent's king is in check —*vt.* **1.** to stop suddenly **2.** to hold back; restrain **3.** to test, verify, etc. by investigation or comparison (often with *out*) **4.** to mark with a check (often with *off*) **5.** to mark with a pattern of squares **6.** to deposit temporarily **7.** to clear (esp. luggage) for shipment **8.** *Chess* to place (an opponent's king) in check —*vi.* **1.** to agree with one another, item for item (often with *out*) **2.** to investigate or verify (often with *on, up on*) —*adj.* **1.** used to check or verify **2.** having a crisscross pattern —**check in 1.** to register at a hotel, etc. **2.** [Colloq.] to present oneself, as at work —**check out 1.** to pay and leave a hotel, etc. **2.** to add up the prices of (items selected) for payment **3.** to prove to be accurate, etc. —**in check** under control —**check′er** *n.*

check′book′ *n.* a book containing forms for writing checks on a bank

check′er *n.* [see CHECK] **1.** a small square, as on a chessboard **2.** a pattern of such squares **3.** *a*) [*pl., with sing. v.*] a game played on a checkerboard by two players, each with 12 flat, round pieces to move *b*) any of these pieces —*vt.* **1.** to mark off in squares **2.** to break the uniformity of, as with varied features, changes in fortune, etc.

check′er·board′ *n.* a board with 64 squares of two alternating colors, used in checkers and chess

check′ered (-ərd) *adj.* **1.** having a pattern of squares **2.** varied

checking account a bank account against which the depositor can draw checks

check′list′ *n.* a list of things, names, etc. to be checked off or referred to: also **check list**

check′mate′ (-māt′) *n.* [ult. < Per. *shāh māt,* the king is dead] **1.** *Chess a)* the winning move that puts the opponent's king in a position where it cannot be saved *b)* this position **2.** total defeat, frustration, etc. —*interj.* *Chess* a call indicating checkmate —*vt.* **-mat′ed, -mat′ing** to subject to checkmate

check′off′ *n.* the withholding of dues for the union by the employer

check′out′ *n.* **1.** the act or place of checking out purchases **2.** the time by which one must check out of a hotel, etc. Also **check′-out′**

check′point′ *n.* a place on a road, etc. where traffic is inspected

check′rein′ *n.* a short rein attached to the bridle to keep a horse's head up

check′room′ *n.* a room in which to check (*vt.* 6) hats, coats, parcels, etc.

check′up′ *n.* a medical examination

Ched·dar (cheese) (ched′ər) [< *Cheddar,* England, where orig. made] [*often* c-] a hard, smooth cheese

cheek (chēk) *n.* [OE. *ceoke,* jaw] **1.** either side of the face, below the eye **2.** either of the buttocks **3.** [Colloq.] sauciness; impudence —(**with**) **tongue in cheek** in a humorously ironic or insincere way

cheek′bone′ *n.* the bone of the upper cheek, just below the eye

cheek′y *adj.* **-i·er, -i·est** [Colloq.] saucy; impudent — **cheek′i·ly** *adv.* —**cheek′i·ness** *n.*

cheep (chēp) *n.* [echoic] the short, shrill sound of a young bird; chirp —*vt., vi.* to chirp

cheer (chir) *n.* [< Gr. *kara,* the head] **1.** a state of mind or feeling; spirit [be of good *cheer*] **2.** gladness; joy **3.** festive food or entertainment **4.** encouragement **5.** *a)* a glad, excited shout to urge on, greet, etc. *b)* a rallying cry —*vt.* **1.** to comfort or gladden (often with *up*) **2.** to urge on, greet, etc. with cheers —*vi.* **1.** to become cheerful (usually with *up*) **2.** to shout cheers

cheer′ful *adj.* **1.** full of cheer; joyful **2.** bright and attractive **3.** willing [a *cheerful* helper] —**cheer′ful·ly** *adv.* —**cheer′ful·ness** *n.*

cheer′i·o (-ē ō′) *interj., n., pl.* **-os′** [Brit. Colloq.] **1.** goodbye **2.** good health: a toast

cheer′lead′er (-lē′dər) *n.* one who leads others in cheering for a football team, etc.

cheer′less *adj.* not cheerful; dismal —**cheer′less·ly** *adv.* —**cheer′less·ness** *n.*

cheer′y *adj.* **-i·er, -i·est** cheerful; lively —**cheer′i·ly** *adv.* —**cheer′i·ness** *n.*

cheese (chēz) *n.* [ult. < L. *caseus*] **1.** a solid food made from milk curds **2.** a shaped mass of this

cheese′burg′er (-bur′gər) *n.* a hamburger topped with melted cheese

cheese′cake′ *n.* **1.** a cake made with cottage cheese or cream cheese **2.** [Slang] photographic display of the figure, esp. the legs, of a pretty girl

cheese′cloth′ *n.* [from its use as cheese wrapping] a thin cotton cloth with a loose weave

chees′y (-ē) *adj.* **-i·er, -i·est** **1.** like cheese **2.** [Slang] inferior; poor —**chees′i·ness** *n.*

chee·tah (chēt′ə) *n.* [< Hindi < Sans. *citra,* spotted] a swift, leopardlike animal of Africa and S Asia

chef (shef) *n.* [Fr. < *chef de cuisine,* head of the kitchen] **1.** a head cook **2.** any cook

‡chef-d'oeu·vre (she dē′vr′) *n., pl.* **chefs-d'oeu′vre** (she dē′vr′) [Fr., principal work] a masterpiece, as in art or literature

Che·khov (chek′ôf), **An·ton (Pavlovich)** (än tôn′) 1860–1904; Russ. writer: also sp. **Chekov**

che·la (kē′lə) *n., pl.* **-lae** (-lē) [< Gr. *chēlē,* claw] a pincerlike claw of a crab, scorpion, etc. —**che′late** (-lāt) *adj.*

chem. **1.** chemical(s) **2.** chemist **3.** chemistry

chem·i·cal (kem′i k'l) *adj.* **1.** of, made by, or used in chemistry **2.** made with or operated by chemicals —*n.* any substance used in or obtained by a chemical process —**chem′i·cal·ly** *adv.*

chemical engineering the science or profession of applying chemistry to industrial uses

chemical warfare warfare using poisonous gases, etc.

che·mise (shə mēz′) *n.* [< VL. *camisia,* shirt] **1.** a woman's undergarment somewhat like a loose, short slip **2.** a straight, loose dress

chem·ist (kem′ist) *n.* [< (AL)CHEMIST] **1.** a specialist in chemistry **2.** [Brit.] a pharmacist, or druggist

chem·is·try (kem′is trē) *n., pl.* **-tries** [< CHEMIST] the science dealing with the composition and properties of substances, and with the reactions by which substances are produced from or converted into other substances

chem·o·ther·a·py (kem′ō ther′ə pē) *n.* the use of chemical drugs in medicine

chem·ur·gy (kem′ər jē) *n.* [< CHEM(ISTRY) + -URGY] the branch of chemistry dealing with the industrial use of organic products, esp. from farms —**chem·ur′gic** (-ur′jik) *adj.*

che·nille (shi nēl′) *n.* [Fr., caterpillar] **1.** a tufted, velvety yarn used for trimming, etc. **2.** a fabric filled or woven with this, as for rugs

cheque (chek) *n. Brit. sp. of* CHECK (*n.* 8)

cheq·uer (chek′ər) *n., vt. Brit. sp. of* CHECKER

Cher·bourg (sher′boorg) seaport in NW France: pop. 37,000

cher·ish (cher′ish) *vt.* [< L. *carus,* dear] **1.** to hold dear; feel or show love for **2.** to protect; foster [to *cherish* one's rights] **3.** to cling to the idea of

Cher·o·kee (cher′ə kē′) *n., pl.* **-kees′, -kee′** a member of a tribe of Iroquoian Indians of the SW U.S.

che·root (shə root′) *n.* [< Tamil *churuṭṭu,* a roll] a cigar with both ends cut square

cher·ry (cher′ē) *n., pl.* **-ries** [< Gr. *kerasion*] **1.** a small, fleshy fruit with a smooth, hard pit **2.** the tree that it grows on **3.** the wood of this tree **4.** a bright red —*adj.* **1.** bright-red **2.** of cherry wood **3.** made with cherries

cher·ub (cher′əb) *n., pl.* **-ubs;** for 1 usually **-u·bim** (-ə bim, -yoo bim) [< Heb. *kerūbh*] **1.** any of an order of angels, often represented as a chubby, rosy-faced child with wings **2.** an innocent or lovely child —**che·ru·bic** (chə rōō′bik) *adj.*

cher·vil (chur′vəl) *n.* [< Gr. *chairein,* to rejoice + *phyllon,* leaf] a plant related to the parsley, with leaves used to flavor soups, etc.

Ches·a·peake Bay (ches′ə pēk′) arm of the Atlantic extending into Va. & Md.

Chesh·ire cat (chesh′ir, -ər) a proverbial grinning cat from Cheshire, England, esp. one described in Lewis Carroll's *Alice's Adventures in Wonderland*

chess (ches) *n.* [< OFr. *eschec,* a check at chess] a game for two, each with 16 pieces (**chessmen**) moved variously on a checkerboard

chest (chest) *n.* [< Gr. *kistē,* a box] **1.** a box with a lid and, often, a lock **2.** a public fund [community *chest*] **3.** a cabinet with drawers; bureau **4.** a cabinet with shelves **5.** the part of the body enclosed by the ribs and breastbone —**get (something) off one's chest** [Colloq.] to unburden oneself of (some trouble, etc.) by talking about it

Ches·ter·field (ches′tər fēld′), **4th Earl of,** (*Philip Dormer Stanhope*) 1694–1773; Eng. statesman & writer

ches·ter·field (ches′tər fēld′) *n.* [< 19th-c. Earl of *Chesterfield*] a single-breasted topcoat, usually with a velvet collar

chest·nut (ches′nut′) *n.* [< Gr. *kastaneia*] **1.** the edible nut of a tree of the beech family **2.** this tree, or its wood **3.** reddish-brown **4.** a reddish-brown horse **5.** [Colloq.] an old, stale joke, story, etc. —*adj.* reddish-brown

chest·y (ches′tē) *adj.* **-i·er, -i·est** [Colloq.] boastful; proud

che·val glass (shə val′) [Fr. *cheval,* horse, support] a full-length mirror on swivels in a frame

chev·a·lier (shev′ə lir′) *n.* [see CAVALIER] a cavalier; gallant

chev·i·ot (shev′ē ət) *n.* [< *Cheviot* Hills, between England and Scotland] a rough, twilled wool fabric

chev·ron (shev′rən) *n.* [< OFr., rafter] a V-shaped bar on the sleeves of a uniform, showing rank

chew (chōō) *vt.* [< OE. *ceowan*] **1.** to bite and crush with the teeth **2.** to think over **3.** [Slang] to rebuke severely (often with *out*) —*vi.* to do chewing —*n.* **1.** a chewing **2.** something chewed or for chewing —**chew′y** *adj.* **-i·er, -i·est**

chewing gum a sweet, flavored substance, as chicle, used for chewing

che·wink (chi wiŋk′) *n.* [echoic] the eastern towhee of N. America, with the iris of the eye bright red

CHEVRON

Chey·enne′ (shī en′, -an′) *n., pl.* **-ennes′, -enne′** a member of a tribe of Algonquian Indians now of Montana and Oklahoma

Chey·enne² (shī an′, -en′) capital of Wyo., in the SE part: pop. 41,000

chg. *pl.* **chgs.** charge

chi (kī) *n.* the 22d letter of the Greek alphabet (X, χ)

Chiang Kai-shek (chan′kī shek′) 1888–1975; Chin. head of government on Taiwan (1950–75)

Chi·an·ti (kē än′tē, -an′-) *n.* [It.] a dry, red wine

chi·a·ro·scu·ro (kē är′ə skyoor′ō) *n., pl.* -ros [It. < L. *clarus*, clear + *obscurus*, dark] 1. treatment of light and shade in a painting, drawing, etc., as to produce an illusion of depth 2. a style or a painting, etc. emphasizing this

chic (shēk) *n.* [Fr. < MLowG. *schick*, skill] smart elegance of style and manner —*adj.* **chic·quer** (shēk′ər), **chic′quest** (-ist) smartly stylish

Chi·ca·go (shə kä′gō, -kô′-) city and port in NE Ill., on Lake Michigan: pop. 3,367,000 (met. area 6,979,000)

chi·can·er·y (shi kān′ər ē) *n., pl.* -ies [< Fr.] 1. the use of clever but tricky talk or action to deceive, evade, etc. 2. an instance of this

Chi·ca·no (chi kä′nō) *n., pl.* -nos [< AmSp.] [*also* c-] [Southwest] a U.S. citizen or inhabitant of Mexican descent

chi·chi, chi-chi (shē′shē, chē′chē) *adj.* [Fr.] extremely chic, esp. in an affected or showy way

chick (chik) *n.* [< CHICKEN] 1. a young chicken 2. any young bird 3. a child 4. [Slang] a young woman

chick·a·dee (chik′ə dē′) *n.* [echoic] a small black, gray, and white bird related to the titmouse

chick·en (chik′ən) *n.* [< OE. *cycen*, lit., little cock] 1. a common farm bird raised for its edible eggs or flesh; hen or rooster, esp. a young one 2. its flesh 3. any young bird —*adj.* 1. made of chicken 2. small and tender [*a chicken lobster*] 3. [Slang] timid or cowardly —*vi.* [Slang] to lose courage and abandon a plan, action, etc. (usually with *out*)

chicken feed [Slang] a petty sum of money

chick′en-heart′ed *adj.* timid; cowardly: also **chick′en-liv′ered**

chicken pox an acute, contagious virus disease, esp. of children, with fever and skin eruptions

chicken wire light, pliable wire fencing

chick′pea′ *n.* [< L. *cicer*, pea] 1. a bushy annual plant with hairy pods 2. the edible seeds

chick′weed′ *n.* a low-growing plant often found as a lawn weed

chic·le (chik′'l) *n* [< MexInd.] a gumlike substance made from the sapodilla, used in chewing gum

chic·o·ry (chik′ə rē) *n., pl.* -ries [< Gr. *kichora*] 1. a weedy plant with blue flowers: the leaves are used for salad 2. its root, ground for mixing with coffee or as a coffee substitute

chide (chīd) *vt., vi.* **chid′ed** or **chid** (chid), **chid′ed** or **chid** or **chid·den** (chid′'n), **chid′ing** [OE. *cidan*] to scold; now, to reprove mildly —**chid′ing·ly** *adv.*

chief (chēf) *n.* [< L. *caput*, the head] the head or leader of a group, organization, etc. —*adj.* 1. highest in rank, office, etc. 2. main; principal —**in chief** in the chief position

chief justice the presiding judge of a court made up of several judges

chief′ly *adv.* 1. most of all 2. mainly —*adj.* of or like a chief

chief′tain (-tən) *n.* [< L. *caput*, the head] a leader, esp. of a clan or tribe —**chief′tain·cy, chief′tain·ship′** *n.*

chif·fon (shi fän′, shif′än) *n.* [Fr. < *chiffe*, a rag] a sheer, lightweight fabric of silk, nylon, etc. —*adj.* 1. made of chiffon 2. made fluffy as with beaten egg whites

chif·fo·nier, chif·fon·nier (shif′ə nir′) *n.* [Fr. < prec.] a narrow, high bureau or chest of drawers, often with a mirror attached

chig·ger (chig′ər) *n.* [of Afr. origin] 1. the tiny, red larva of certain mites, whose bite causes severe itching 2. *same as* CHIGOE

chi·gnon (shēn′yän) *n.* [Fr. < L. *catena*, a chain] a coil of hair sometimes worn at the back of the neck by women

chig·oe (chig′ō) *n., pl.* -oes (-ōz) [< WInd. native name] 1. a flea of tropical S. America and Africa: the female burrows into the skin, causing painful sores 2. *same as* CHIGGER

Chi·hua·hua (chi wä′wä) *n.* [< *Chihuahua*, a Mex. state] a breed of tiny dog with large, pointed ears, orig. from Mexico

chil·blain (chil′blān′) *n.* [CHIL(L) + *blain* < OE. *blegen*, a sore] a painful swelling or sore on the foot or hand, caused by exposure to cold

child (chīld) *n., pl.* **chil′dren** [< OE. *cild*] 1. an infant 2. a boy or girl before puberty 3. a son or daughter 4. a

product [*a child* of the Renaissance] —**with child** pregnant —**child′less** *adj.*

child′bed′ *n.* the condition of a woman giving birth to a child

child′birth′ *n.* the act of giving birth to a child

child′hood′ *n.* the state or time of being a child

child′ish *adj.* 1. of or like a child 2. immature; silly — **child′ish·ly** *adv.* —**child′ish·ness** *n.*

child′like′ *adj.* like a child, esp. in being innocent, trusting, etc. —**child′like′ness** *n.*

chil·dren (chil′drən) *n. pl. of* CHILD

child's play anything simple to do

Chil·e (chil′ē) country on the SW coast of S. America: 286,397 sq. mi.; pop. 9,566,000; cap. Santiago —**Chil′e·an** *adj., n.*

chil·i (chil′ē) *n., pl.* -ies [MexSp.] 1. the very hot dried pod of red pepper, often ground (**chili powder**) 2. a highly seasoned dish of beef, chilies or chili powder, beans, and often tomatoes: in full, **chili con car·ne** (kən kär′nē) Also **chile**

chili sauce a spiced sauce of chopped tomatoes, sweet peppers, onions, etc.

chill (chil) *n.* [OE. *ciele*] 1. a feeling of coldness that makes one shiver 2. a moderate coldness 3. a discouraging influence 4. a sudden fear, etc. 5. unfriendliness —*adj. same as* CHILLY —*vi.* 1. to become cool 2. to shiver from cold, fear, etc. —*vt.* 1. to make cold 2. to cause a chill in 3. to depress; dispirit 4. *Metallurgy* to harden (metal) by rapid cooling —**chill′er** *n.* —**chill′ing·ly** *adv.*

chill factor the combined effect of low temperature and high winds on loss of body heat

chill′y (-ē) *adj.* -i·er, -i·est 1. moderately cold 2. chilling 3. unfriendly 4. depressing —**chill′i·ness** *n.*

chime (chīm) *n.* [< L. *cymbalum*, cymbal] 1. [*usually pl.*] *a*) a set of tuned bells or metal tubes *b*) the musical sounds produced by these 2. a single bell in a clock, etc. 3. harmony —*vi.* **chimed, chim′ing** 1. to sound as a chime 2. to sound in harmony, as bells 3. to harmonize; agree —*vt.* to indicate (time) by chiming —**chime in** 1. to join in 2. to agree —**chim′er** *n.*

Chi·me·ra (ki mir′ə, kī-) [< Gr. *chimaira*, she-goat] *Gr. Myth.* a fire-breathing monster with a lion's head, goat's body, and serpent's tail —*n.* [c-] an impossible or foolish fancy

chi·mer·i·cal (-mir′i k'l, -mer′-) *adj.* 1. imaginary; unreal 2. visionary Also **chi·mer′ic**

chim·ney (chim′nē) *n., pl.* -neys [ult. < Gr. *kaminos*, oven] 1. the passage or structure through which smoke escapes from a fire, often extending above the roof 2. a glass tube around the flame of a lamp 3. a fissure or vent, as in a cliff or volcano

chimney sweep one who cleans soot from chimneys

chimney swift a sooty-brown, swallow-like N. American bird that makes nests in unused chimneys

chim·pan·zee (chim′pan zē′, chim pan′zē) *n.* [< Afr. native name] a medium-sized anthropoid ape of Africa, with black hair and large ears: also [Colloq.] **chimp** (chimp)

chin (chin) *n.* [OE. *cin*] the part of the face below the lower lip; projecting part of the lower jaw —*vt.* **chinned, chin′ning** to pull (oneself) up, while hanging by the hands from a bar, until the chin is just above the bar —*vi.* 1. to chin oneself 2. [Slang] to chat, gossip, etc.

Chin. 1. China 2. Chinese

Chi·na (chī′nə) country in E Asia: 3,691,000 sq. mi.; pop. 732,000,000; cap. Peking

CHIMPANZEE
(35–60 in. high)

chi·na (chī′nə) *n.* 1. *a*) porcelain, orig. from China *b*) vitrified ceramic ware *c*) any earthenware 2. dishes, ornaments, etc. made of this Also **chi′na·ware′**

Chi′na·town′ *n.* the Chinese quarter of a city

chinch (bug) (chinch) [< Sp. < L. *cimex*, bug] a small, white-winged, black bug that damages grain plants

chin·chil·la (chin chil′ə) *n.* [prob. dim. of Sp. *chinche*, chinch] 1. *a*) a small rodent of the Andes *b*) its expensive, soft, pale-gray fur 2. a heavy, nubby wool cloth used for making overcoats

Chi·nese (chī nēz′, -nēs′) *n., pl.* -nese [< China] 1. *pl.* -nese a native of China or one of Chinese descent 2. the language of the Chinese —*adj.* of China, its people, etc.

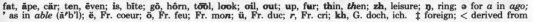

chink¹ (chiŋk) *n.* [OE. *cine*] a crack; fissure —*vt.* to close up the chinks in

chink² (chiŋk) *n.* [echoic] a sharp, clinking sound —*vi., vt.* to make or cause to make this sound

chi·no (chē′nō, shē′-) *n.* [< ?] **1.** a strong, twilled cotton cloth **2.** [*pl.*] men's pants of chino

Chi·nook (chi nŏok′, -nook′) *n.* **1.** *pl.* **-nooks′, -nook′** any of a family of Indian tribes, formerly of the Columbia River valley **2.** their language **3.** [*usually* c-] a warm, moist SW wind blowing onto the coast of the NW U.S. and SW Canada; also, a dry wind of the E Rockies

chin·qua·pin (chiŋ′kə pin′) *n.* [of Algonquian origin] **1.** the dwarf chestnut tree **2.** a related evergreen tree **3.** the edible nut of either of these trees

chintz (chints) *n.* [< Hindi *chhīnt*] a cotton cloth printed in colored designs and usually glazed

chintz′y *adj.* **-i·er, -i·est 1.** like chintz **2.** [Colloq.] cheap, stingy, etc.

chip (chip) *vt.* **chipped, chip′ping** [< OE.] to break or cut off small pieces from —*vi.* to break off in small pieces —*n.* **1.** a small piece of wood, etc. cut or broken off **2.** a place where a small piece has been chipped off **3.** a fragment of dried animal dung used as fuel **4.** a worthless thing **5.** a small, round disk used in poker, etc. as a counter **6.** a thin slice of food [*a potato chip*] **7.** *same as* INTEGRATED CIRCUIT —**chip in** [Colloq.] to contribute (money, etc.) — **chip off the old block** a person much like his father — **chip on one's shoulder** [Colloq.] an inclination to fight — **in the chips** [Slang] wealthy

chip′munk′ (-muŋk′) *n.* [< AmInd.] a small, striped N. American squirrel that lives mainly on the ground

chipped beef shavings of dried or smoked beef

Chip·pen·dale (chip′'n dāl′) *adj.* [< T. *Chippendale* (1718?–79), Eng. cabinetmaker] designating or of an 18th-cent. Eng. style of furniture with graceful lines and, often, rococo ornamentation

chip′per *adj.* [< Brit. dial.] [Colloq.] in good spirits; lively

Chip·pe·wa (chip′ə wô′, -wä′, -wə) *n., pl.* **-was, -wa** *var.* of OJIBWA: also **Chip′pe·way′** (-wā′)

chiro- [< Gr. *cheir*, the hand] *a combining form meaning* hand

chi·rop·o·dy (kə räp′ə dē, kī-) *n.* [CHIRO- + -POD + -Y³] *same as* PODIATRY —**chi·rop′o·dist** *n.*

chi·ro·prac·tic (kī′rə prak′tik) *n.* [< CHIRO- + Gr. *praktikos*, practical] a method of treating disease by manipulation of the body joints, esp. of the spine —**chi′ro·prac′tor** *n.*

chirp (churp) *vi., vt.* [echoic] to make, or utter in, short, shrill tones, as some birds or insects do —*n.* a short, shrill sound —**chirp′er** *n.*

chirr (chur) *n.* [echoic] a shrill, trilled sound, as of some insects or birds —*vi.* to make such a sound

chir·rup (chur′əp, chir′-) *vi.* [var. of CHIRP] to chirp repeatedly —*n.* a chirruping sound

chis·el (chiz′'l) *n.* [< L. *caedere*, to cut] a sharp-edged tool for cutting or shaping wood, stone, etc. —*vi., vt.* **-eled** *or* **-elled, -el·ing** *or* **-el·ling 1.** to cut or shape with a chisel **2.** [Colloq.] to take advantage of (someone) or get (something) by cheating, sponging, etc. —**chis′el·er, chis′el·ler** *n.*

chit¹ (chit) *n.* [ME. *chitte*, kitten] **1.** a child **2.** an immature or childish girl

chit² (chit) *n.* [< Hindi] **1.** [Chiefly Brit.] a memorandum **2.** a voucher of a small sum owed for food, drink, etc.

CHISEL

chit·chat (chit′chat′) *n.* [< CHAT] **1.** light, informal talk **2.** gossip

chi·tin (kīt′'n) *n.* [< Gr. *chitōn*, tunic] a tough, horny substance forming the outer covering of insects, crustaceans, etc. —**chi′tin·ous** *adj.*

chit·ter·lings, chit·lins, chit·lings (chit′lənz) *n.pl.* [< Gmc. base] the small intestines of pigs, used for food

chiv·al·rous (shiv′'l rəs) *adj.* **1.** having the attributes of an ideal knight; gallant, courteous, etc. **2.** of chivalry Also **chiv·al·ric** (shi val′rik, shiv′'l-) —**chiv′al·rous·ly** *adv.*

chiv·al·ry (shiv′'l rē) *n.* [< OFr. *chevaler*, a knight] **1.** medieval knighthood **2.** the qualities of an ideal knight, as courage, honor, courtesy, etc. **3.** the demonstration of any of these qualities

chives (chīvz) *n.pl.* [< L. *cepa*, onion] [*often with sing. v.*] a plant with small, hollow leaves having a mild onion odor, used for flavoring

chlo·ral (klôr′əl) *n.* **1.** a thin, oily, colorless, pungent liquid made from chlorine and alcohol **2.** *same as* CHLORAL HYDRATE

chloral hydrate a colorless, crystalline compound used as a sedative

chlo·rate (klôr′āt) *n.* a salt of chloric acid

chlor·dane (klôr′dān) *n.* a chlorinated, poisonous, volatile oil used as an insecticide: also **chlor′dan** (-dan)

chlo·ric (klôr′ik) *adj.* **1.** of or containing chlorine with a higher valence than in corresponding chlorous compounds **2.** designating or of a colorless acid, $HClO_3$, whose salts are chlorates

chlo·ride (-īd) *n.* a compound in which chlorine is combined with another element or radical

chlo·ri·nate (klôr′ə nāt′) *vt.* **-nat′ed, -nat′ing** to treat (water or sewage) with chlorine for purification —**chlo′ri·na′tion** *n.* —**chlo′ri·na′tor** *n.*

chlo·rine (klôr′ēn, -in) *n.* [CHLOR(O)- + -INE³] a greenish-yellow, poisonous, gaseous chemical element with a disagreeable odor, used in bleaching, water purification, etc.: symbol, Cl; at. wt., 35.453; at. no., 17

chlo·rite (-īt) *n.* a salt of chlorous acid

chloro- [< Gr. *chlōros*, pale green] *a combining form meaning:* **1.** green [*chlorophyll*] **2.** chlorine [*chloroform*]

chlo·ro·form (klôr′ə fôrm′) *n.* [< Fr.: see CHLORO- & FORMIC] a sweetish, colorless, volatile liquid, $CHCl_3$, used as a general anesthetic and as a solvent —*vt.* to anesthetize or kill with chloroform

Chlo·ro·my·ce·tin (klôr′ə mī sēt′'n) [CHLORO- + Gr. *mykēs*, mushroom + -IN¹] *a trademark for* an antibiotic drug used against some viruses, rickets, etc.

chlo·ro·phyll, chlo·ro·phyl (klôr′ə fil′) *n.* [< Gr. *chlōros*, green + *phyllon*, leaf] the green pigment of plants: it is involved in photosynthesis

chlo·rous (klôr′əs) *adj.* **1.** of or containing chlorine with a lower valence than in corresponding chloric compounds **2.** designating or of an acid, $HClO_2$, a strong oxidizing agent

chock (chäk) *n.* [ONormFr. *choque*, a block] **1.** a block or wedge placed under a wheel, etc. to prevent motion **2.** *Naut.* a block with two hornlike projections through which a rope may be run —*vt.* to wedge fast as with chocks —*adv.* as close or tight as can be

chock′-full′ *adj.* as full as possible

choc·o·late (chôk′lət, chäk′-; -ə lət) *n.* [< MexInd. *chocolatl*] **1.** a paste, powder, etc. made from roasted and ground cacao seeds **2.** a drink or candy made with chocolate **3.** reddish brown —*adj.* **1.** made of or flavored with chocolate **2.** reddish-brown

Choc·taw (chäk′tô) *n.* **1.** *pl.* **-taws, -taw** a member of a tribe of N. American Indians originally of the Southeast **2.** the language of this tribe

choice (chois) *n.* [< OFr. < Gothic *kausjan*, to taste] **1.** a choosing; selection **2.** the right or power to choose **3.** a person or thing chosen **4.** the best part **5.** a variety from which to choose **6.** a supply well chosen **7.** an alternative —*adj.* **choic′er, choic′est 1.** of special excellence **2.** carefully chosen —**choice′ly** *adv.* —**choice′ness** *n.*

choir (kwīr) *n.* [< OFr. < L. *chorus*: see CHORUS] **1.** a group of singers trained to sing together, esp. in church **2.** the part of the church they occupy

choke (chōk) *vt.* **choked, chok′ing** [< OE. *aceocian*] **1.** to prevent from breathing by blocking the windpipe; strangle; suffocate **2.** to obstruct by clogging **3.** to hinder the growth or action of **4.** to fill up **5.** to cut off some air from the carburetor of (a gasoline engine) so as to make a richer gasoline mixture —*vi.* **1.** to be suffocated **2.** to be obstructed —*n.* **1.** the act or sound of choking **2.** the valve that chokes a carburetor —**choke back** to hold back (feelings, sobs, etc.) —**choke down** to swallow with difficulty —**choke off** to bring to an end —**choke up** [Colloq.] to be unable to speak, act efficiently, etc., as because of fear, tension, etc.

choke′cher′ry *n., pl.* **-ries 1.** a N. American wild cherry tree **2.** its astringent fruit

choke′damp′ (-damp′) *n.* a suffocating gas, a mixture of carbon monoxide and nitrogen, found in mines

chok′er *n.* a closely fitting necklace

chol·er (käl′ər) *n.* [< Gr. *cholē*, bile] [Now Rare] anger or ill humor

chol·er·a (käl′ər ə) *n.* [see prec.] any of several intestinal diseases; esp., an acute, severe, infectious disease (**Asiatic cholera**) characterized by profuse diarrhea, intestinal pain, and dehydration

chol′er·ic *adj.* [see CHOLER] easily angered

cho·les·ter·ol (kə les′tə rōl′, -rôl′) *n.* [< Gr. *cholē*, bile + *stereos*, solid] a crystalline alcohol found esp. in animal fats, blood, and bile

chomp (chämp) *vt., vi. same as* CHAMP¹

choose (chooz) *vt., vi.* **chose, cho′sen, choos′ing** [OE. *ceosan*] **1.** to take as a choice; select **2.** to decide or prefer [to *choose* to go] —**cannot choose but** cannot do otherwise than —**choos′er** *n.*

choos′y, choos′ey *adj.* **-i·er, -i·est** [Colloq.] fussy in choosing

chop¹ (chäp) *vt.* **chopped, chop′ping** [ME. *choppen*] **1.** to cut by blows with an ax or other sharp tool **2.** to cut into small bits **3.** to say abruptly —*vi.* **1.** to make quick, cutting strokes with a sharp tool **2.** to act with a quick, jerky motion —*n.* **1.** a short, sharp blow or stroke **2.** a slice of lamb, pork, veal, etc. cut from the rib, loin, or shoulder **3.** a short, broken movement of waves

chop² (chäp) *n.* [var. of CHAP¹] **1.** a jaw **2.** a cheek

chop³ (chäp) *vi.* **chopped, chop′ping** [OE. *ceapian*, to bargain] to shift or veer suddenly, as the wind

Cho·pin (shō′pan), **Fré·dé·ric** (frä dā rēk′) 1810–49; Pol. composer & pianist, in France after 1831

chop·per (chäp′ər) *n.* **1.** one that chops **2.** [*pl.*] [Slang] teeth **3.** [Colloq.] *a*) a helicopter *b*) a motorcycle

chop′py (-ē) *adj.* **-pi·er, -pi·est** [< CHOP¹] **1.** rough with short, broken waves, as the sea **2.** making abrupt starts and stops; jerky —**chop′pi·ness** *n.*

chops (chäps) *n.pl.* [see CHAP¹] the mouth and lower cheeks

chop·sticks (chäp′stiks′) *n.pl.* [PidE. for Chin. *k'wai-tsze*, the quick ones] two small sticks held together in one hand and used in some Asian countries to lift food to the mouth

chop su·ey (chäp′ sōō′ē) [< Chin. *tsa-sui*, lit., various pieces] a Chinese-American dish of meat, bean sprouts, celery, mushrooms, etc. cooked together in a sauce and served with rice

cho·ral (kôr′əl) *adj.* [Fr.] of, for, sung by, or recited by a choir or chorus —**cho′ral·ly** *adv.*

cho·rale, cho·ral (kə ral′, kô-) *n.* [< G. *choral* (*gesang*), choral (song)] **1.** a hymn tune **2.** a choir

chord¹ (kôrd) *n.* [alt. (after L. *chorda*) < CORD] **1.** a feeling or emotion thought of as being played on like the string of a harp [to strike a sympathetic *chord*] **2.** *Anat.* same as CORD (sense 5) **3.** *Geom.* a straight line joining any two points on an arc, curve, or circumference

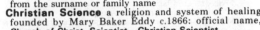

CHORDS (AC, AO)

chord² (kôrd) *n.* [< ACCORD] *Music* a combination of three or more tones sounded together in harmony

chore (chôr) *n.* [< OE. *cierr*, job] **1.** a routine task: *often used in pl.* **2.** a hard or unpleasant task

cho·re·a (kô rē′ə) *n.* [< Gr. *choreia*, choral dance] a nervous disorder characterized by jerking movements caused by involuntary muscular contractions

chor·e·o·graph (kôr′ē ə graf′) *vt., vi.* [see ff.] to design or plan the movements of (a dance) —**chor′e·o·graph′ic** *adj.*

chor·e·og·ra·phy (kôr′ē äg′rə fē) *n.* [< Gr. *choreia*, dance + -GRAPHY] **1.** ballet dancing **2.** the art of devising dances or ballets —**chor′e·og′ra·pher** *n.*

chor·is·ter (kôr′is tər) *n.* [see CHORUS] a member of a choir

chor·tle (chôr′t'l) *vi., vt.* **-tled, -tling** [coined by Lewis Carroll, prob. < CHUCKLE + SNORT] to make, or utter with, a gleeful chuckling or snorting sound —*n.* such a sound —**chor′tler** *n.*

cho·rus (kôr′əs) *n.* [< Gr. *choros*] **1.** in ancient Greek drama, a group whose singing, dancing, and narration supplement the main action **2.** a group of dancers and singers performing together as in an opera **3.** the part of a drama, song, etc. performed by a chorus **4.** a group singing or speaking something together **5.** a simultaneous utterance by many [a *chorus* of protest] **6.** music written for group singing **7.** the refrain of a song, following each verse —*vt., vi.* to sing, speak, or say in unison —**in chorus** in unison

chose (chōz) *pt. of* CHOOSE

Cho·sen (chō′sen′) *Japanese name of* KOREA

cho·sen (chō′z'n) *pp. of* CHOOSE —*adj.* selected; choice

Chou En-lai (jō′ en′lī′) 1898–1976; Chin. Communist leader; prime minister (1949–76)

chow (chou) *n.* [< Chin.] **1.** any of a breed of medium-sized dog, originally from China, with a thick, brown or black coat **2.** [Slang] food

chow·der (chou′dər) *n.* [< Fr. *chaudière*, a pot] a thick soup of onions, potatoes, etc. and, often, clams and milk

chow mein (chou mān′) [Chin. *ch'ao*, to fry + *mien*, flour] a Chinese-American stew of meat, celery, bean sprouts, etc., served with fried noodles

chrism (kriz′m) *n.* [< Gr. *chriein*, anoint] consecrated oil used in baptism and other sacraments

Christ (krīst) [< Gr. *christos*, the anointed] Jesus of Nazareth, regarded by Christians as the Messiah prophesied in the Old Testament

chris·ten (kris′n) *vt.* [OE. *cristnian*] **1.** to take into a Christian church by baptism; baptize **2.** to give a name to, esp. at baptism **3.** [Colloq.] to use for the first time —**chris′ten·ing** *n.*

Chris·ten·dom (kris′n dəm) *n.* **1.** Christians collectively **2.** those parts of the world where most of the inhabitants profess Christianity

Chris·tian (kris′chən) *n.* a believer in Jesus as the Christ, or in the religion based on the teachings of Jesus —*adj.* **1.** of Jesus Christ **2.** of or professing the religion based on his teachings **3.** having the qualities taught by Jesus, as love, kindness, etc. **4.** of Christians or Christianity

Christian Era the era beginning with the year formerly thought to be that of the birth of Jesus Christ (born probably c.8–4 B.C.)

Chris·ti·an·i·ty (kris′chē an′ə tē) *n.* **1.** Christians collectively **2.** the Christian religion **3.** the state of being a Christian

Chris·tian·ize (kris′chə nīz′) *vt.* **-ized′, -iz′ing 1.** to convert to Christianity **2.** to cause to conform with Christian character or precepts

Christian name the baptismal name, as distinguished from the surname or family name

Christian Science a religion and system of healing founded by Mary Baker Eddy c.1866: official name, **Church of Christ, Scientist** —**Christian Scientist**

chris·tie, chris·ty (kris′tē) *n., pl.* **-ties** [< *Christiania*, former name of Oslo] a high-speed turn in skiing with skis kept parallel

Christ′like′ *adj.* like Jesus Christ, esp. in character or spirit

Christ·mas (kris′məs) *n.* [see CHRIST & MASS] a holiday on Dec. 25 celebrating the birth of Jesus Christ: also **Christmas Day**

chro·mate (krō′māt) *n.* a salt of chromic acid

chro·mat·ic (krō mat′ik) *adj.* [< Gr. *chrōma*, color] **1.** of or having color or colors **2.** *Music* using or progressing by semitones —**chro·mat′i·cal·ly** *adv.*

chromatic scale the musical scale made up of thirteen successive semitones to the octave

chro·ma·tin (krō′mə tin) *n.* [< Gr. *chrōma*, color] an easily stained, protoplasmic substance in the nucleus of living cells: it forms the chromosomes

chrome (krōm) *n.* [Fr. < Gr. *chrōma*, color] chromium or chromium alloy —*adj.* designating any of various pigments (**chrome red, chrome yellow**, etc.) made from chromium compounds —*vt.* **chromed, chrom′ing** to plate with chromium

-chrome [< Gr. *chrōma*, color] *a suffix meaning:* **1.** color or coloring agent **2.** chromium

chro·mic (krō′mik) *adj.* designating or of compounds containing trivalent chromium

chromic acid an acid, H_2CrO_4, existing only in solution or known in the form of its salts

chro·mi·um (krō′mē əm) *n.* [see CHROME] a very hard metallic chemical element resistant to corrosion: symbol, Cr; at. wt., 51.996; at. no., 24

chromo- [< Gr. *chrōma*, color] *a combining form meaning* color or pigment [*chromosome*] : also **chrom-**

chro·mo·some (krō′mə sōm′) *n.* [CHROMO- + -SOME²] any of the microscopic rod-shaped bodies into which the chromatin separates during cell division: they carry the genes that convey hereditary characteristics —**chro′mo·so′mal** *adj.*

chro·mous (krō′məs) *adj.* designating or of compounds containing bivalent chromium

chron·ic (krän′ik) *adj.* [< Gr. *chronos*, time] **1.** lasting a long time or recurring often: said of a disease **2.** having had an ailment for a long time **3.** perpetual **4.** habitual —**chron′i·cal·ly** *adv.*

chron·i·cle (krän′i k'l) *n.* [< Gr. *chronika*, annals] **1.** a historical record of events in the order of occurrence **2.** a narrative; history —*vt.* **-cled, -cling** to tell the history of —**chron′i·cler** *n.*

Chron′i·cles either of two books of the Bible, I and II Chronicles: abbrev. **Chron.**

chrono- [Gr. < *chronos*, time] *a combining form meaning* time: also chron-

chron·o·log·i·cal (krän'ə läj'i k'l) *adj.* arranged in the order of occurrence: also **chron'o·log'ic** —**chron'o·log'i·cal·ly** *adv.*

chro·nol·o·gy (krə näl'ə jē) *n., pl.* **-gies** [CHRONO- + -LOGY] **1.** the science of measuring time and of dating events **2.** an arrangement or list of events in the order of occurrence —**chro·nol'o·gist** *n.*

chro·nom·e·ter (krə näm'ə tər) *n.* [CHRONO- + -METER] a highly accurate kind of clock or watch

chrys·a·lis (kris'l əs) *n., pl.* **-lis·es** [< Gr. *chrysallis*] **1.** the pupa of a butterfly, encased in a cocoon **2.** the cocoon Also **chrys'a·lid** (-id)

chrys·an·the·mum (kri san'thə məm) *n.* [< Gr. *chrysos*, gold + *anthemon*, a flower] **1.** a late-blooming plant of the composite family, with showy flowers **2.** the flower

chrys·o·prase (kris'ə prāz') *n.* [< Gr. *chrysos*, gold + *prason*, leek] a light-green chalcedony sometimes used as a semiprecious stone

chub (chub) *n.* [ME. *chubbe*] a small, freshwater fish related to the minnow and carp

chub'by *adj.* **-bi·er, -bi·est** [< prec.] round and plump — **chub'bi·ness** *n.*

chuck[1] (chuk) *vt.* [< ? Fr. *choquer*, strike against] **1.** to tap playfully, esp. under the chin **2.** to toss **3.** [Slang] *a)* to get rid of *b)* to vomit (often with *up*) —*n.* **1.** a light tap under the chin **2.** a toss

chuck[2] (chuk) *vt.* [? var. of CHOCK] **1.** a cut of beef from around the neck and shoulder blade **2.** a clamplike holding device, as on a lathe

chuck'-full' *adj. same as* CHOCK-FULL

chuck'hole' *n.* [see CHOCK & HOLE] a rough hole in a road, made by wear and weathering

chuck·le (chuk'l) *vi.* **-led, -ling** [prob. < *chuck*, to cluck] to laugh softly in a low tone —*n.* a soft, low-toned laugh —**chuck'ler** *n.*

chuck wagon a wagon equipped as a kitchen for feeding cowboys or other outdoor workers

chug (chug) *n.* [echoic] a puffing or explosive sound, as of a steam locomotive —*vi.* **chugged, chug'ging** to make, or move with, such sounds

chuk·ka (boot) (chuk'ə) [< CHUKKER] a man's ankle-length, bootlike shoe, often fleece-lined

chuk·ker, chuk·kar (chuk'ər) *n.* [< Sans. *cakra*, wheel] any of the periods of play, 7 1/2 minutes each, of a polo match

chum (chum) *n.* [prob. < *chamber* (*mate*)] [Colloq.] a close friend —*vi.* **chummed, chum'ming** [Colloq.] to be close friends

chum'my *adj.* **-mi·er, -mi·est** [Colloq.] intimate; friendly —**chum'mi·ly** *adv.* —**chum'mi·ness** *n.*

chump (chump) *n.* [< ?] **1.** a heavy block of wood **2.** a thick, blunt end **3.** [Colloq.] a stupid person

Chung·king (chōōŋ'kiŋ') city in SC China, on the Yangtze: pop. 4,070,000

chunk (chuŋk) *n.* [< ? CHUCK[2]] **1.** a short, thick piece **2.** a fair portion

chunk'y *adj.* **-i·er, -i·est 1.** short and thick **2.** stocky — **chunk'i·ness** *n.*

church (church) *n.* [< Gr. *kyriakē* (*oikia*), Lord's (house)] **1.** a building for public worship, esp. one fŏr Christian worship **2.** religious service **3.** [*usually* C-] *a)* all Christians *b)* a particular Christian denomination **4.** ecclesiastical, as opposed to secular, government **5.** the profession of the clergy —*adj.* of a church or of organized Christian worship

church'go'er *n.* a person who attends church, esp. regularly —**church'go'ing** *n., adj.*

Church·ill (chur'chil), Sir **Winston** (**Leonard Spencer**) 1874–1965; Brit. statesman and writer; prime minister (1940–45; 1951–55)

church'ly *adj.* of or fit for a church —**church'li·ness** *n.*

church'man (-mən) *n., pl.* **-men 1.** a clergyman **2.** a member of a church

Church of England the episcopal church of England; Anglican Church: it is an established church with the sovereign as its head

church'ward'en (-wôr'd'n) *n.* a lay officer who attends to the secular affairs of a church

church'yard' *n.* the yard adjoining a church, often used as a cemetery

churl (churl) *n.* [OE. *ceorl*, freeman] **1.** a peasant **2.** a surly, ill-bred, or miserly person —**churl'ish** *adj.* —**churl'ish·ness** *n.*

churn (churn) *n.* [OE. *cyrne*] a container in which milk or cream is shaken to form butter —*vt., vi.* **1.** to stir and shake (milk or cream) in a churn **2.** to make (butter) thus **3.** to stir up or move vigorously

chute[1] (shōōt) *n.* [Fr., a fall] **1.** a waterfall or rapids **2.** an inclined or vertical trough down which things may slide or drop [a coal *chute*]

chute[2] (shōōt) *n.* [Colloq.] a parachute

chut·ney (chut'nē) *n., pl.* **-neys** [Hindi *chatnī*] a relish of fruits, spices, and herbs: also sp. **chut'nee**

chyle (kīl) *n.* [< Gr. *chylos* < *cheein*, pour] a milky fluid composed of lymph and emulsified fats: it is formed from chyme in the small intestine and is passed into the blood —**chy'lous** *adj.*

chyme (kīm) *n.* [< Gr. *chymos*, juice < *cheein*, pour] the semifluid mass resulting from digestion of food —**chy'mous** *adj.*

CIA, C.I.A. Central Intelligence Agency

ci·ca·da (si kā'də, -kä'-) *n., pl.* **-das, -dae** (-dē) [L.] a large flylike insect with transparent wings: the male makes a loud, shrill sound

cic·a·trix (sik'ə triks) *n., pl.* **ci·cat·ri·ces** (si kat'rə sēz', sik'ə trī'sēz) [L.] **1.** the contracted tissue at the place where a wound heals **2.** the scar on a stem where a branch was once attached Also **cic'a·trice** (-tris)

cic'a·trize' (-trīz') *vt., vi.* **-trized', -triz'ing** to heal with the formation of a scar —**cic'a·tri·za'tion** *n.*

Cic·er·o (sis'ə rō'), (**Marcus Tullius**) 106–43 B.C.: Rom. statesman & orator —**Cic'e·ro'ni·an** *adj.*

-cide [< L. *caedere*, to kill] *a suffix meaning:* **1.** killer **2.** killing

ci·der (sī'dər) *n.* [ult. < Heb. *shēkār*, strong liquor] the juice pressed from apples, used as a beverage or for making vinegar: **sweet cider** is unfermented, **hard cider** is fermented

ci·gar (si gär') *n.* [< Sp. *cigarro*] a compact roll of tobacco leaves for smoking

cig·a·rette, cig·a·ret (sig'ə ret') *n.* [Fr., dim. of *cigare*, cigar] a small roll of finely cut tobacco wrapped in thin paper for smoking

cig'a·ril'lo (-ril'ō) *n., pl.* **-los** [Sp.] a small, thin cigar

cil·i·a (sil'ē ə) *n.pl., sing.* **-i·um** (-əm) [L.] **1.** the eyelashes **2.** *Biol.* small hairlike processes —**cil'i·ate** (-it, -āt')

cil'i·ar'y (-er'ē) *adj.* of, like, or having cilia

cinch (sinch) *n.* [< Sp. < L. *cingulum*, a girdle] **1.** a saddle or pack girth **2.** [Colloq.] a firm grip **3.** [Slang] a sure or easy thing —*vt.* **1.** to tighten a girth on **2.** [Slang] to make sure of

cin·cho·na (sin kō'nə) *n.* [< 17th-c. Peruv. Countess del *Chinchón*] **1.** a tropical tree with a bitter bark **2.** the bark, from which quinine is made

Cin·cin·nat·i (sin'sə nat'ē, -ə) city in SW Ohio, on the Ohio River: pop. 453,000 (met. area 1,385,000)

cinc·ture (siŋk'chər) *n.* [L. *cinctura*] a belt or girdle —*vt.* **-tured, -tur·ing** to encircle with a belt

cin·der (sin'dər) *n.* [OE. *sinder*] **1.** a minute piece of partly burned wood or coal **2.** [*pl.*] ashes from wood or coal —**cin'der·y** *adj.*

Cin·der·el·la (sin'də rel'ə) in a fairy tale, a household drudge who eventually marries a prince

cin·e·ma (sin'ə mə) *n.* [< Gr. *kinēma*, motion] [Chiefly Brit.] **1.** a motion picture **2.** a motion-picture theater — **the cinema** motion pictures collectively —**cin'e·mat'ic** *adj.* —**cin'e·mat'i·cal·ly** *adv.*

cin·e·rar·i·um (sin'ə rer'ē əm) *n., pl.* **-rar'i·a** (-ə) [L. < *cinis*, ashes] a place to keep the ashes of cremated bodies —**cin'e·rar'y** *adj.*

cin·na·bar (sin'ə bär') *n.* [< Gr. *kinnabari*] **1.** mercuric sulfide, HgS, a heavy, bright-red mineral, the principal ore of mercury **2.** artificial mercuric sulfide, used as a red pigment **3.** brilliant red

cin·na·mon (sin'ə mən) *n.* [< Heb. *qinnāmōn*] **1.** the light-brown spice made from the inner bark of a laurel tree of the East Indies **2.** this bark

cinque·foil (siŋk'foil') *n.* [< L. *quinque*, five + *folium*, leaf] **1.** a plant related to the rose, having compound leaves, often with five leaflets **2.** *Archit.* a circular design of five converging arcs

CIO, C.I.O. Congress of Industrial Organizations: see AFL-CIO

ci·pher (sī'fər) *n.* [< Ar. *sifr*, nothing] **1.** the symbol 0; naught; zero **2.** a nonentity **3.** *a)* secret writing based on a key *b)* a message in such writing *c)* the key to such a sys-

CINQUEFOIL

tem **4.** a monogram **5.** an Arabic numeral —*vt.*, *vi.* [Now Rare] to do, or solve by, arithmetic

cir·ca (sur′kə) *prep.* [L.] about: used before an approximate date, figure, etc. *[circa 1650]*

Cir·ce (sur′sē) in Homer's *Odyssey*, an enchantress who turned men into swine

cir·cle (sur′k'l) *n.* [< Gr. *kirkos*] **1.** a plane figure bounded by a single curved line every point of which is equally distant from the center **2.** this curved line **3.** anything like a circle, as a ring **4.** a complete or recurring series; cycle **5.** a group of people with common interests **6.** extent; scope, as of influence —*vt.* **-cled, -cling 1.** to form a circle around **2.** to move around, as in a circle —*vi.* to go around in a circle

cir′clet (-klit) *n.* **1.** a small circle **2.** a circular band for the finger, head, etc.

cir·cuit (sur′kit) *n.* [< L. *circum-*, around + *ire*, to go] **1.** a boundary line or its length **2.** the area bounded **3.** a going around something **4.** *a)* the regular journey of a person through a district in his work *b)* such a district **5.** a chain or association, as of theaters or resorts **6.** a path over which electric current may flow —*vi.* to go in a circuit —*vt.* to make a circuit about

circuit breaker a device that automatically interrupts the flow of an electric current

cir·cu·i·tous (sər kyōō′ə təs) *adj.* roundabout; indirect — **cir·cu′i·tous·ly** *adv.* —**cir·cu′i·ty** *n.*

cir·cuit·ry (sur′kə trē) *n.* the scheme, system, or components of an electric circuit

cir·cu·lar (sur′kyə lər) *adj.* **1.** in the shape of a circle; round **2.** relating to a circle **3.** moving in a circle **4.** roundabout; circuitous **5.** intended for circulation among a number of people —*n.* a circular letter, advertisement, etc. —**cir′cu·lar′i·ty** (-ler′ə tē) *n.* —**cir′cu·lar·ly** *adv.*

cir′cu·lar·ize′ (-lə rīz′) *vt.* **-ized′, -iz′ing 1.** to make circular **2.** to send circulars to **3.** to canvass —**cir′cu·lar·i·za′tion** *n.*

cir·cu·late (sur′kyə lāt′) *vi.* **-lat′ed, -lat′ing** [< L. *circulari*, form a circle] **1.** to move in a circle or circuit and return, as the blood **2.** to go from person to person or from place to place —*vt.* to make circulate —**cir′cu·la′tor** *n.* —**cir′cu·la·to′ry** (-lə tôr′ē) *adj.*

cir·cu·la′tion *n.* **1.** a circulating or moving around, as of the blood through the arteries and veins **2.** the passing of something, as money, news, etc., from person to person **3.** *a)* the distribution of newspapers, magazines, etc. *b)* the average number of newspapers, etc. distributed

circum- [< L. *circum*] a prefix meaning around, about, surrounding

cir·cum·am·bi·ent (sur′kəm am′bē ənt) *adj.* [CIRCUM- + AMBIENT] surrounding

cir·cum·cise (sur′kəm sīz′) *vt.* **-cised′, -cis′ing** [< L. *circum-*, around + *caedere*, to cut] to cut off all or part of the foreskin of —**cir′cum·ci′sion** (-sizh′ən) *n.*

cir·cum·fer·ence (sər kum′fər ens, -frəns) *n.* [< L. *circum-*, around + *ferre*, to carry] **1.** the line bounding a circle or other rounded surface **2.** the distance measured by this line

cir·cum·flex (sur′kəm fleks′) *n.* [< L. *circum-*, around + *flectere*, to bend] a mark (ˆ, ˆ, ˜) used over certain vowels in some languages to indicate a specific sound —*adj.* **1.** of or marked by a circumflex **2.** bending around; curved —*vt.* to bend or twist around

cir′cum·lo·cu′tion (-lō kyōō′shən) *n.* [< L.: see CIRCUM- & LOCUTION] a roundabout or lengthy way of expressing something

cir′cum·nav′i·gate′ (-nav′ə gāt′) *vt.* **-gat′ed, -gat′ing** [< L.: see CIRCUM- & NAVIGATE] to sail or fly around (the earth, an island, etc.) —**cir′cum·nav′i·ga′tion** *n.*

cir′cum·scribe′ (-skrīb′) *vt.* **-scribed′, -scrib′ing** [< L.: see CIRCUM- & SCRIBE] **1.** to trace a line around; encircle **2.** to limit **3.** to restrict **4.** *Geom. a)* to draw a figure around (another figure) so as to touch it at as many points as possible *b)* to be thus drawn around —**cir′cum·scrip′tion** (-skrip′shən) *n.*

cir′cum·spect′ (-spekt′) *adj.* [< L. *circum-*, around + *specere*, to look] cautious; discreet —**cir′cum·spec′tion** *n.* —**cir′cum·spect′ly** *adv.*

cir′cum·stance′ (-stans′) *n.* [< L. *circum-*, around + *stare*, to stand] **1.** a fact or event, esp. one accompanying another, either incidentally or as a determining factor **2.** [*pl.*] conditions affecting a person, esp. financial conditions **3.** ceremony; show *[pomp and circumstance]* —*vt.* **-stanced′, -stanc′ing** to place in certain circumstances —

under no circumstances never —**under the circumstances** conditions being what they are or were

cir′cum·stan′tial (-stan′shəl) *adj.* **1.** having to do with, or depending on, circumstances **2.** incidental **3.** detailed; complete —**cir′cum·stan′tial·ly** *adv.*

circumstantial evidence *Law* evidence offered to prove certain circumstances from which the fact at issue may be inferred

cir′cum·stan′ti·ate′ (-stan′shē āt′) *vt.* **-at′ed, -at′ing** to give detailed proof or support of

cir′cum·vent′ (-vent′) *vt.* [< L. *circum-*, around + *venire*, come] **1.** to go around **2.** to get the better of or prevent by craft or ingenuity —**cir′cum·ven′tion** *n.*

cir·cus (sur′kəs) *n.* [L., a circle] **1.** in ancient Rome, an amphitheater, used for games, races, etc. **2.** a traveling show of acrobats, trained animals, clowns, etc. **3.** [Colloq.] any riotously entertaining person, event, etc.

cir·rho·sis (sə rō′sis) *n.* [< Gr. *kirrhos*, tawny + -OSIS] a degenerative disease, esp. of the liver, marked by excess formation of connective tissue —**cir·rhot′ic** (-rät′ik) *adj.*

cir·ro·cu·mu·lus (sir′ō kyōō′myə ləs) *n.* a high formation of clouds in small, white puffs, flakes, or streaks

cir′ro·stra′tus (-strāt′əs) *n.* a high formation of clouds in a thin, whitish veil

cir·rus (sir′əs) *n., pl.* **-ri** (-ī) ; for 2 **-rus** [L., a curl] **1.** *Biol. a)* a plant tendril *b)* a threadlike appendage, as a feeler.**2.** a formation of clouds in wispy filaments or feathery tufts

Cis·ter·cian (sis tur′shən) *adj.* [< ML. *Cistercium* (now *Cîteaux*, France)] designating or of a monastic order following the Benedictine rule strictly —*n.* a Cistercian monk or nun

cis·tern (sis′tərn) *n.* [< L. *cista*, chest] a large receptacle for storing water, esp. rain water

cit·a·del (sit′ə d'l, -del′) *n.* [< L. *civitas*, city] **1.** a fortress **2.** a stronghold **3.** a refuge

cite (sīt) *vt.* **cit′ed, cit′ing** [< L. *citare*, summon] **1.** to summon to appear before a court of law **2.** to quote (a passage, book, etc.) **3.** to mention by way of example, proof, etc. **4.** to mention in an official report for meritorious service —**ci·ta′tion** *n.*

cit·i·fied (sit′i fīd′) *adj.* having the manners, dress, etc. attributed to city people

cit·i·zen (sit′ə zən) *n.* [< L. *civis*, citizen] **1.** formerly, an inhabitant of a city **2.** a member of a state or nation who owes allegiance to it by birth or naturalization and is entitled to full civil rights **3.** a civilian

cit′i·zen·ry (-rē) *n.* all citizens as a group

cit′i·zen·ship′ *n.* **1.** the status of a citizen **2.** one's conduct as a citizen

cit·rate (si′trāt) *n.* a salt or ester of citric acid

citric acid (si′trik) an acid, $C_6H_8O_7$, obtained from citrus fruits, used in making dyes, citrates, etc.

cit·rine (si′trin) *adj.* lemon-yellow —*n.* lemon yellow

cit′ron (-trən) *n.* [Fr., lemon: see CITRUS] **1.** a yellow, thick-skinned fruit resembling a lemon **2.** its rind candied

cit·ron·el·la (si′trə nel′ə) *n.* [ModL.] a sharp-smelling oil used in perfume, insect repellents, etc.

cit·rus (si′trəs) *n.* [L.] **1.** any of the trees that bear oranges, lemons, limes, etc. **2.** any such fruit —*adj.* of these trees: also **cit′rous** (-trəs)

cit·y (sit′ē) *n., pl.* **-ies** [< L. *civis*, citizen] **1.** a large, important town **2.** in the U.S., an incorporated municipality whose boundaries, powers, etc. are defined by State charter **3.** in Canada, a large urban municipality **4.** all the people of a city —*adj.* of or in a city

city chicken skewered pieces of pork or veal breaded and braised or baked

city hall 1. a building housing a municipal government **2.** the municipal government

cit′y-state′ *n.* a state made up of an independent city and its territories, as in ancient Greece

civ·et (siv′it) *n.* [< Ar. *zabād*] **1.** the musky secretion of a catlike, flesh-eating mammal (**civet cat**) of Africa and S Asia: used in some perfumes **2.** the civet cat or its fur

civ·ic (siv′ik) *adj.* [< L. *civis*, citizen] of a city, citizens, or citizenship —**civ′i·cal·ly** *adv.*

civ′ics (-iks) *n.pl.* [*with sing. v.*] the study of civic affairs and the rights and duties of citizenship

civ·il (siv′'l) *adj.* [see CIVIC] **1.** of a citizen or citizens **2.** of a community of citizens *[civil affairs]* **3.** civilized **4.** polite **5.** not military or religious **6.** *Law* relating to private rights —**civ′il·ly** *adv.*

civil disobedience nonviolent opposition to a law by refusing to comply with it, on the grounds of conscience

---

fat, āpe, cär; ten, ēven; is, bīte; gō, hôrn, tōōl, look; oil, out; up, fur; thin, then; zh, leisure; ŋ, ring; ə for *a* in *ago*; ' as in *able* (ā′b'l); ë, Fr. coeur; ö, Fr. feu; Fr. mon; ü, Fr. duc; r, Fr. cri; kh, G. doch, ich. ‡ foreign; < derived from

civil engineering engineering dealing with the construction of bridges, roads, etc. —**civil engineer**

ci·vil·ian (sə vil′yən) *n.* [see CIVIC] a person not an active member of the armed forces or of an official force having police power —*adj.* of or for civilians

ci·vil·i·ty (sə vil′ə tē) *n., pl.* **-ties 1.** politeness, esp. of a merely formal kind **2.** a civil act or utterance

civ·i·li·za·tion (siv′ə lə zā′shən) *n.* **1.** a civilizing or becoming civilized **2.** the condition of being civilized; social organization of a high order **3.** the total culture of a people, period, etc. **4.** the peoples considered to have reached a high social development

civ·i·lize (siv′ə līz′) *vt.* **-lized′, -liz′ing** [see CIVIC] **1.** to bring out of a primitive or savage condition **2.** to improve in habits or manners; refine —**civ′i·lized′** *adj.*

civil law the body of law concerning private rights

civil liberties liberties guaranteed to the individual by law and custom; rights of thinking, speaking, and acting as one likes without hindrance except in the interests of public welfare

civil marriage a marriage performed by a public official, not by a clergyman

civil rights those rights guaranteed to the individual by the 13th, 14th, 15th, and 19th Amendments to the U.S. Constitution

civil service those employed in government service, esp. through public competitive examination

civil war war between different factions of the same nation —**the Civil War** the war between the North and the South in the U.S. (1861–1865)

civ·vies, civ·ies (siv′ēz) *n.pl.* [Colloq.] civilian clothes

ck. *pl.* **cks. 1.** cask **2.** check

Cl *Chem.* chlorine

cl. 1. centiliter(s) **2.** claim **3.** class **4.** clause

clab·ber (klab′ər) *n.* [Ir. *clabar*] [Dial.] curdled sour milk —*vi., vt.* to curdle

clack (klak) *vi., vt.* [prob. echoic < ON.] **1.** to make or cause to make a sudden, sharp sound **2.** to chatter —*n.* **1.** a clacking sound **2.** chatter —**clack′er** *n.*

clad (klad) *alt. pt. & pp. of* CLOTHE —*adj.* **1.** clothed **2.** having a layer of metal bonded to another metal

claim (klām) *vt.* [< L. *clamare*, cry out] **1.** to demand as rightfully belonging to one; assert one's right to **2.** to require; deserve *[to claim attention]* **3.** to assert; maintain —*n.* **1.** a demand for something rightfully due **2.** a right to something **3.** something claimed, as land **4.** an assertion —**claim′a·ble** *adj.* —**claim′ant, claim′er** *n.*

clair·voy·ance (kler voi′əns) *n.* [Fr. < *clair*, clear + *voir*, see] the supposed ability to perceive things not in sight —**clair·voy′ant** *n., adj.*

clam (klam) *n.* [OE. *clamm*, fetter] a hard-shelled bivalve mollusk —*vi.* **clammed, clam′ming** to dig for clams —**clam up** [Colloq.] to refuse to talk

clam′bake′ *n.* **1.** a picnic at which steamed or baked clams, corn, and other foods are served **2.** [Colloq.] any large, noisy party

clam·ber (klam′bər) *vi., vt.* [ME. *clambren*] to climb clumsily or with effort, using both hands and feet —*n.* a hard or clumsy climb

clam·my (klam′ē) *adj.* **-mi·er, -mi·est** [prob. < OE. *clam*, clay] unpleasantly moist, cold, and sticky —**clam′mi·ness** *n.*

clam·or (klam′ər) *n.* [< L. *clamare*, cry out] **1.** a loud outcry; uproar **2.** a noisy demand or complaint **3.** a loud, sustained noise —*vi.* to make a clamor —*vt.* to express with clamor Also, Brit. sp., **clam′our** —**clam′or·ous** *adj.*

clamp (klamp) *n.* [< MDu. *klampe*] a device for clasping or fastening things together —*vt.* to fasten or brace with a clamp —**clamp down (on)** to become more strict (with)

clan (klan) *n.* [< Gael. < L. *planta*, offshoot] **1.** a group of families descended from a common ancestor **2.** a group of people with interests in common —**clans·man** (klanz′mən) *n., pl.* **-men** —**clans′wom′an** *n.fem., pl.* **-wom′en**

clan·des·tine (klan des′t′n) *adj.* [< L. *clam*, secret] secret or hidden; underhand —**clan·des′tine·ly** *adv.*

clang (klaŋ) *vi., vt.* [echoic] to make or cause to make a loud, sharp, ringing sound, as by striking metal —*n.* this sound

clan·gor (klaŋ′ər) *n.* [L. < *clangere*, to clang] a continuous clanging sound —*vi.* to make a clangor Also, Brit. sp., **clan′gour** —**clan′gor·ous** *adj.* —**clan′gor·ous·ly** *adv.*

clank (klaŋk) *n.* [echoic] a sharp metallic sound —*vi., vt.* to make or cause to make this sound

clan′nish *adj.* **1.** of a clan **2.** tending to associate closely and to avoid others —**clan′nish·ly** *adv.* —**clan′nish·ness** *n.*

clap (klap) *vi.* **clapped, clap′ping** [OE. *clæppan*, to beat] **1.** to make the explosive sound of two flat surfaces struck together **2.** to strike the hands together, as in applause —*vt.* **1.** to strike together briskly and loudly **2.** to strike with an open hand **3.** to put, move, etc. swiftly *[clapped into jail]* **4.** to put together hastily —*n.* **1.** the sound or act of clapping **2.** a sharp slap

clap·board (klab′ərd, klap′bôrd′) *n.* [partial transl. of MDu. *klapholt* < *klappen*, to fit + *holt*, wood] a thin board with one edge thicker than the other, used as siding —*vt.* to cover with clapboards

clap′per *n.* **1.** a person who claps **2.** a thing that makes a clapping sound, as the tongue of a bell

clap′trap′ *n.* [CLAP + TRAP] insincere, empty talk intended to get applause —*adj.* showy and cheap

claque (klak) *n.* [Fr. < *claquer*, to clap] **1.** a group of people paid to applaud at a play, opera, etc. **2.** a group of fawning followers

clar·et (klar′it) *n.* [< L. *clarus*, clear] **1.** a dry red wine **2.** purplish red —*adj.* purplish-red

clar·i·fy (klar′ə fī′) *vt., vi.* **-fied′, -fy′ing** [< L. *clarus*, clear + *facere*, make] **1.** to make or become clear and free from impurities **2.** to make or become easier to understand —**clar′i·fi·ca′tion** *n.*

clar·i·net (klar′ə net′) *n.* [< Fr.; ult. < L. *clarus*, clear] a single-reed woodwind instrument played by means of holes and keys —**clar′i·net′ist, clar′i·net′tist** *n.*

clar·i·on (klar′ē ən) *n.* [< L. *clarus*, clear] a trumpet of the Middle Ages producing clear, sharp, shrill tones —*adj.* clear, sharp, and ringing *[a clarion call]*

CLARINET

clar·i·ty (klar′ə tē) *n.* [< L. *clarus*, clear] clearness

clash (klash) *vi.* [echoic] **1.** to collide wih a loud, harsh, metallic noise **2.** to conflict; disagree —*vt.* to strike with a clashing noise —*n.* **1.** the sound of clashing **2.** conflict

clasp (klasp) *n.* [ME. *claspe*] **1.** a fastening, as a hook, to hold things together **2.** a grasping; embrace **3.** a grip of the hand —*vt.* **1.** to fasten with a clasp **2.** to grasp firmly; embrace **3.** to grip with the hand **4.** to cling to —**clasp′er** *n.*

class (klas) *n.* [< L. *classis*] **1.** a number of people or things grouped together because of likenesses; kind; sort **2.** social or economic status *[the middle class]* **3.** *a)* a group of students taught together *b)* a meeting of such a group *c)* a group of students graduating together **4.** grade or quality *[travel first class]* **5.** [Slang] excellence **6.** *Biol.* a group of animals or plants ranking below a phylum and above an order —*vt.* to classify —*vi.* to be classed —**in a class by itself (or oneself)** unique

class. 1. classic **2.** classification **3.** classified

clas·sic (klas′ik) *adj.* [< L. *classis*, class] **1.** being an excellent model of its kind **2.** of the art, literature, etc. of the ancient Greeks and Romans **3.** balanced, formal, restrained, etc. **4.** famous as traditional or typical —*n.* **1.** a writer, artist, etc. or a literary or artistic work recognized as excellent, authoritative, etc. **2.** a famous traditional event —**the classics** ancient Greek and Roman literature

clas·si·cal (-i k′l) *adj.* **1.** *same as* CLASSIC (senses 1, 2, 3) **2.** versed in Greek and Roman culture, literature, etc. **3.** designating or of music that conforms to certain standards of form, complexity, etc. **4.** standard and traditional *[classical economics]* —**clas·si·cal′i·ty** (-kal′ə tē) *n.* —**clas·si·cal·ly** *adv.*

clas·si·cism (klas′ə siz′m) *n.* **1.** the aesthetic principles or qualities of ancient Greece and Rome **2.** adherence to these principles **3.** knowledge of classical art and literature —**clas′si·cist** *n.*

clas·si·fi·ca·tion (klas′ə fi kā′shən) *n.* a systematic arrangement into classes or groups

classified advertising advertising under such listings as *help wanted, lost and found,* etc. —**classified advertisement**

clas·si·fy (klas′ə fī′) *vt.* **-fied′, -fy′ing 1.** to arrange in classes according to some system or principle **2.** to designate (government documents, etc.) as secret or confidential —**clas′si·fi′a·ble** *adj.* —**clas′si·fi′er** *n.*

class'mate' *n.* a member of the same class at a school or college

class'room' *n.* a room in a school or college in which classes are taught

class'y *adj.* -i·er, -i·est [Slang] first-class, esp. in style; elegant

clat·ter (klat'ər) *vi., vt.* [ME. *clateren*] to make or cause to make a clatter —*n.* **1.** a rapid succession of loud, sharp noises **2.** a tumult; hubbub —**clat'ter·er** *n.*

clause (klôz) *n.* [< L. *claudere*, to close] **1.** a group of words containing a subject and a verb: cf. MAIN CLAUSE, SUBORDINATE CLAUSE **2.** a particular article or provision in a document

claus·tro·pho·bi·a (klôs'trə fō'bē ə) *n.* [< L. *claustrum*, enclosure + -PHOBIA] an abnormal fear of being in an enclosed or confined space

clav·i·chord (klav'ə kôrd') *n.* [< L. *clavis*, key + *chorda*, a string] a stringed musical instrument with a keyboard, predecessor of the piano

clav·i·cle (klav'ə k'l) *n.* [< Fr. < L. *clavis*, key] a bone connecting the sternum with the shoulder blade; collarbone

cla·vi·er (klə vir'; *for 1 also* klav'ē ər) *n.* [Fr. < L. *clavis*, a key] **1.** the keyboard of an organ, piano, etc. **2.** any stringed keyboard instrument

claw (klô) *n.* [OE. *clawu*] **1.** a sharp, hooked nail on the foot of a bird and many reptiles and mammals **2.** a foot with such nails **3.** the pincers of a crab, etc. **4.** the forked end of a claw hammer —*vt., vi.* to scratch, clutch, etc. as with claws

claw hammer a hammer with one end of the head forked for pulling nails

clay (klā) *n.* [OE. *clæg*] **1.** a firm, plastic earth used in making pottery, etc. **2.** *a)* earth *b)* the human body — **clay'ey** *adj.* **clay'i·er, clay'i·est** —**clay'ish** *adj.*

Clay (klā), **Henry** 1777–1852; U.S. statesman

clay·more (klā'môr') *n.* [Gael. *claidheamhmor*, great sword] a large, two-edged broadsword formerly used by Scottish Highlanders

clay pigeon a disk of baked clay thrown from a trap as a target in trapshooting

clean (klēn) *adj.* [OE. *clæne*] **1.** free from dirt or impurities; unsoiled **2.** producing little immediate fallout: said of nuclear weapons **3.** recently laundered **4.** morally pure **5.** sportsmanlike **6.** neat and tidy **7.** trim **8.** skillful **9.** free from flaws; clear **10.** complete; thorough —*adv.* completely —*vt., vi.* to make clean —**clean out** to empty — **clean up 1.** to make clean or neat **2.** [Colloq.] to finish **3.** [Slang] to make much profit —**come clean** [Slang] to confess —**clean'ly** *adv.* —**clean'ness** *n.*

clean'-cut' *adj.* **1.** clearly outlined **2.** well-formed **3.** trim, neat, etc.

clean'er *n.* a person or thing that cleans; esp,. one who dry-cleans

clean·ly (klen'lē) *adj.* -li·er, -li·est **1.** having clean habits **2.** always kept clean —**clean'li·ness** *n.*

cleanse (klenz) *vt.* **cleansed, cleans'ing** [OE. *clænsian*] to make clean, pure, etc. —**cleans'er** *n.*

clean'up' *n.* **1.** a cleaning up **2.** elimination of crime, vice, etc. **3.** [Slang] profit; gain

clear (klir) *adj.* [< L. *clarus*, clear] **1.** free from clouds or mist; bright **2.** transparent; not turbid **3.** easily seen or heard; distinct **4.** keen or logical *[a clear* mind] **5.** not obscure; obvious **6.** certain; positive **7.** free from guilt **8.** free from deductions; net **9.** free from debt **10.** free from obstruction; open —*adv.* in a clear manner —*vt.* **1.** to make clear **2.** to free from impurities, obstructions, etc. **3.** to make lucid **4.** to open *[clear* a path] **5.** to get rid of **6.** to prove the innocence of **7.** to pass or leap over, by, etc. **8.** to make as profit —*vi.* **1.** to become clear **2.** *Banking* to exchange checks, etc. and balance accounts, through a clearinghouse —**clear away** (or off) **1.** to remove so as to leave a cleared space **2.** to go away —**clear out** [Colloq.] to depart —**clear the air** to get rid of emotional tensions, etc. —**clear up** to make or become clear —**in the clear 1.** in the open **2.** [Colloq.] guiltless —**clear'ly** *adv.* —**clear'ness** *n.*

clear'ance (-əns) *n.* **1.** the clear space between an object and that which it is passing **2.** *Banking* the adjustment of accounts in a clearinghouse

clear'-cut' *adj.* **1.** clearly outlined **2.** distinct

clear'head'ed (-hed'id) *adj.* having a clear mind; rational

clear'ing *n.* **1.** an area of land cleared of trees **2.** *Banking* same *as* CLEARANCE

clear'ing·house' *n.* an office maintained by several banks as a center for exchanging checks, etc.

clear'sight'ed *adj.* **1.** seeing clearly **2.** understanding or thinking clearly —**clear'sight'ed·ness** *n.*

cleat (klēt) *n.* [ME.] a piece of wood or metal, often wedge-shaped, fastened to something to strengthen it or give secure footing

cleav·age (klē'vij) *n.* **1.** a cleaving; splitting; dividing **2.** a cleft; fissure

cleave¹ (klēv) *vt.* **cleaved** or **cleft** or **clove, cleaved** or **cleft** or **clo'ven, cleav'ing** [OE. *cleofan*] **1.** to divide by a blow; split **2.** to pierce

cleave² (klēv) *vi.* **cleaved, cleav'ing** [OE. *cleofian*] **1.** to adhere; cling (*to*) **2.** to be faithful (*to*)

cleav'er *n.* a heavy cleaving tool with a broad blade, used by butchers

CLEATS

clef (klef) *n.* [Fr. < L. *clavis*, a key] a symbol used in music to indicate the pitch of the notes on the staff

cleft (kleft) *alt. pt. & pp. of* CLEAVE¹ —*adj.* split; divided — *n.* **1.** an opening made by cleaving; crack; crevice **2.** a hollow between two parts

clem·a·tis (klem'ə tis) *n.* [< Gr. *klēma*, vine] a vine related to the buttercup, with bright-colored flowers

clem·en·cy (klem'ən sē) *n., pl.* -cies [see CLEMENT] **1.** leniency; mercy **2.** mildness, as of weather

Clem·ens (klem'ənz), **Samuel Lang·horne** (laŋ'hôrn) (pseud. *Mark Twain*) 1835–1910; U.S. writer

clem·ent (klem'ənt) *adj.* [L. *clemens*] **1.** lenient; merciful **2.** mild, as weather —**clem'ent·ly** *adv.*

clench (klench) *vt.* [< OE. *(be)clencan*, make cling] **1.** to close (the teeth or fist) firmly **2.** to grip tightly —*n.* a firm grip —**clench'er** *n.*

Cle·o·pa·tra (klē'ə pat'rə, -pā'trə) 69?–30 B.C.; queen of Egypt (51–49; 48–30)

clere·sto·ry (klir'stôr'ē) *n., pl.* -ries [< ME. *cler,* clear + *storie,* STORY²] **1.** the wall of a church rising above the roofs of the flanking aisles and containing windows **2.** any similar windowed wall

cler·gy (klur'jē) *n., pl.* -gies [see CLERK] ministers, priests, etc. collectively

cler'gy·man (-mən) *n., pl.* -men a member of the clergy; minister, priest, rabbi, etc.

cler·ic (kler'ik) *n.* [see CLERK] a clergyman —*adj.* of a clergyman or the clergy

cler'i·cal (-i k'l) *adj.* **1.** of a clergyman or the clergy **2.** of office clerks or their work —**cler'i·cal·ly** *adv.*

cler'i·cal·ism (-iz'm) *n.* political influence or power of the clergy —**cler'i·cal·ist** *n.*

clerk (klurk) *n.* [< Gr. *klērikos,* priest] **1.** a layman with minor duties in a church **2.** an office worker who keeps records, types, files, etc. **3.** a public official who keeps the records of a court, town, etc. **4.** a salesclerk —*vi.* to work as a salesclerk

Cleve·land (klēv'lənd) city in NE Ohio, on Lake Erie: pop. 751,000 (met. area 2,064,000)

Cleve·land (klēv'lənd), **(Stephen) Gro·ver** (grō'vər) 1837–1908; 22d and 24th president of the U.S. (1885–89; 1893–97)

clev·er (klev'ər) *adj.* [? < Norw. *klöver*] **1.** skillful; adroit; dexterous **2.** intelligent, quick-witted, facile, etc. —**clev'-er·ly** *adv.* —**clev'er·ness** *n.*

clev·is (klev'is) *n.* [ult. akin to CLEAVE²] a U-shaped piece of iron with holes in the ends through which a pin is run to attach things

clew (kloo) *n.* [< OE. *cliwen*] **1.** a ball of thread or yarn **2.** something that leads out of a maze or helps to solve a problem: usually sp. **clue 3.** a metal loop in the corner of a sail

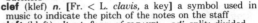

CLEVIS

cli·ché (klē shā') *n.* [Fr. < *clicher,* to stereotype] a trite expression or idea

click (klik) *n.* [echoic] a slight, sharp sound like that of a door latch snapping into place —*vi., vt.* to make or cause to make a click —**click'er** *n.*

cli·ent (klī'ənt) *n.* [< L. *cliens,* follower] **1.** a person or company in whose behalf a lawyer, accountant, etc. works **2.** a customer

cli·en·tele (klī'ən tel') *n.* [Fr. < L. *clientela*] all one's clients or customers, collectively

cliff (klif) *n.* [OE. *clif*] a high, steep face of rock, esp. on a coast; precipice

cliff'hang'er (-haŋ'ər) *n.* a suspenseful movie, story, situation, etc.

cli·mac·ter·ic (klī mak'tər ik, klī'mak ter'ik) *n.* [< Gr. *klimax*, ladder] a crucial period in life, esp. the menopause —*adj.* crucial

cli·mate (klī'mət) *n.* [< Gr. *klima*, region] 1. the prevailing weather conditions of a place 2. a region with reference to its prevailing weather 3. any prevailing conditions affecting life, activity, etc. —**cli·mat'ic** (-mat'ik) *adj.*

cli·ma·tol·o·gy (klī'mə täl'ə jē) *n.* the science dealing with climate and climatic phenomena —**cli'ma·to·log'i·cal** (-tə läj'i k'l) *adj.* —**cli'ma·tol'o·gist** *n.*

cli·max (klī'maks) *n.* [< Gr. *klimax*, ladder] 1. the final, culminating element in a series; highest point of interest, excitement, etc. 2. the turning point of action in a drama, etc. —*vi., vt.* to reach, or bring to, a climax —**cli·mac'tic** (-mak'tik) *adj.*

climb (klīm) *vi., vt.* [OE. *climban*] 1. to go up by using the feet and often the hands 2. to rise gradually; mount 3. to move (*down, over, along*, etc.) using the hands and feet 4. to grow upward on by winding around or clinging —*n.* 1. a climbing 2. a place to be climbed —**climb'er** *n.*

clime (klīm) *n.* [see CLIMATE] [Poet.] a region, esp. with reference to its climate

clinch (klinch) *vt.* [var. of CLENCH] 1. to fasten (a driven nail, etc.) by bending the projecting end 2. to settle (an argument, bargain, etc.) definitely —*vi.* 1. *Boxing* to grip the opponent's body with the arms 2. [Slang] to embrace —*n.* a clinching

clinch'er *n.* 1. one that clinches 2. a decisive point, argument, act, etc.

cling (kliŋ) *vi.* clung, cling'ing [OE. *clingan*] 1. to adhere; hold fast, as by embracing 2. to be or stay near 3. to be emotionally attached —*adj., n.* same as CLINGSTONE

cling'stone' *adj.* having a stone that clings to the fleshy part: said of some peaches —*n.* a peach of this sort

clin·ic (klin'ik) *n.* [< Gr. *klinē*, a bed] 1. the teaching of medicine by treating patients in the presence of students 2. a place where specialist physicians practice as a group 3. an outpatient department, as of a hospital

clin'i·cal (-i k'l) *adj.* 1. of or connected with a clinic 2. having to do with the treatment and observation of patients, as distinguished from experimental study 3. scientifically impersonal —**clin'i·cal·ly** *adv.*

clinical thermometer a thermometer with which the body temperature is measured

cli·ni·cian (kli nish'ən) *n.* an expert in or practitioner of clinical medicine, psychology, etc.

clink (kliŋk) *vi., vt* [echoic] to make or cause to make a slight, sharp sound, as of glasses striking together —*n.* 1. such a sound 2. [Colloq.] a jail

clink'er *n.* 1. a hard mass of fused matter, as from burned coal 2. [Slang] a mistake

cli·nom·e·ter (klī näm'ə tər) *n.* [< Gr. *klinein*, to slope + -METER] an instrument for measuring angles of slope or inclination

Cli·o (klī'ō) *Gr. Myth.* the Muse of history

clip' (klip) *vt.* clipped, clip'ping [ON. *klippa*] 1. to cut as with shears 2. to cut short 3. to cut the hair of 4. [Colloq.] to hit with a quick, sharp blow 5. [Slang] to cheat —*vi.* 1. to clip something 2. to move rapidly —*n.* 1. the act of clipping 2. a thing clipped 3. a rapid pace 4. [Colloq.] a quick, sharp blow 5. same as CLIPPED FORM

clip² (klip) *vi., vt.* clipped, clip'ping [OE. *clyppan*, to embrace] 1. to grip tightly; fasten 2. *Football* to block (an opponent who is not carrying the ball) from behind: an illegal act —*n.* 1. any device that clips or fastens things together 2. a container for cartridges, inserted in certain automatic weapons 3. *Football* a clipping

clip'board' *n.* a writing board with a clip at the top to hold papers

clipped form (or **word**) a shortened form of a word, as *pike* (for *turnpike*)

clip·per (klip'ər) *n.* 1. one who cuts, trims, etc. 2. [*usually pl.*] a tool for cutting or trimming 3. a sailing ship built for great speed

clip'ping *n.* a piece cut out or off, as an item clipped from a newspaper

clique (klēk, klik) *n.* [Fr. < *cliquer*, make a noise] a small, exclusive circle of people; snobbish or narrow coterie — **cliqu'ish** (-ish) *adj.* —**cliqu'ish·ly** *adv.* —**cliqu'ish·ness** *n.*

cli·to·ris (klīt'ər əs, klīt'-) *n.* [< Gr. *kleitys*, hill] a small, erectile organ at the upper end of the vulva

clo·a·ca (klō ā'kə) *n., pl.* **-cae** (-sē, -kē), **-cas** [L. < *cluere*, cleanse] 1. a sewer 2. a cesspool 3. *Zool.* the cavity into which the intestinal and genitourinary tracts empty in reptiles, birds, amphibians, and many fishes —**clo·a·cal** *adj.*

cloak (klōk) *n.* [< ML. *clocca*, a bell: from its shape] 1. a loose, usually sleeveless outer garment 2. something that covers or conceals —*vt.* 1. to cover as with a cloak 2. to hide; conceal

cloak'room' *n.* a room where hats, coats, umbrellas, etc. can be left temporarily

clob·ber (kläb'ər) *vt.* [< ?] [Slang] to beat or hit repeatedly; maul

cloche (klōsh) *n.* [Fr. < ML. *clocca*, bell] a closefitting, bell-shaped hat for women

clock' (kläk) *n.* [ME. *clokke*, orig., clock with bells < ML. *clocca*, bell] a device for measuring and indicating time, usually by means of pointers moving over a dial —*vt.* to record the time of (a race, etc.) with a stopwatch

clock² (kläk) *n.* [< ? prec., because orig. bell-shaped] a woven or embroidered ornament on the side of a stocking, going up from the ankle

clock'wise' (-wīz') *adv., adj.* in the direction in which the hands of a clock rotate

clock'work' (-wurk') *n.* 1. the mechanism of a clock 2. any similar mechanism, with springs and gears —**like clockwork** regularly and precisely

clod (kläd) *n.* [OE.] 1. a lump, esp. of earth or clay 2. a dull, stupid fellow —**clod'dish** *adj.* —**clod'dish·ness** *n.*

clod'hop'per *n.* [CLOD + HOPPER] 1. a plowman 2. a clumsy, stupid fellow 3. a coarse, heavy shoe

clog (kläg) *n.* [ME. *clogge*, lump of wood] 1. anything that hinders or obstructs 2. a shoe with a thick, usually wooden sole —*vt.* clogged, clog'ging 1. to hinder 2. to obstruct (a passage); stop up —*vi.* to become stopped up

clog dance a dance in which clogs are worn to beat out the rhythm —**clog dancing**

cloi·son·né (kloi'zə nā') *adj.* [Fr., lit., partitioned] denoting enamel work in which the surface decoration is set in hollows formed by thin wires

clois·ter (klois'tər) *n.* [< L. *claudere*, to close] 1. a place of religious seclusion; monastery or convent 2. a covered walk along an inside wall with a columned opening along one side —*vt.* to confine as in a cloister —**clois'tered** *adj.* —**clois'tral** *adj.*

close' (klōs) *adj.* clos'er, clos'est [see ff.] 1. confined or confining [*close* quarters] 2. hidden; secluded 3. secretive; reserved 4. miserly; stingy 5. restricted, as in membership 6. oppressively warm and stuffy 7. not readily available [credit is *close*] 8. with little space between; near together 9. compact; dense [a *close* weave] 10. near to the surface [a *close* shave] 11. intimate; familiar [a *close* friend] 12. strict; thorough; careful [*close* attention] 13. nearly alike [*close* in age] 14. nearly even [a *close* contest] —*adv.* in a close manner —**close'ly** *adv.* —**close'ness** *n.*

close² (klōz) *vt.* closed, clos'ing [< L. *claudere*, to close] 1. to shut 2. to block (an opening, passage, etc.) 3. to bring together; unite 4. to finish; conclude —*vi.* 1. to become shut 2. to come to an end 3. to come close or together —*n.* an end; conclusion —**close down** (or **up**) to shut or stop entirely —**close in** to surround, cutting off escape —**close out** to sell out (goods), as in ending a business

close call (klōs) [Colloq.] a narrow escape from danger: also **close shave**

closed circuit a system for telecasting by cable only to receivers connected in the circuit —**closed'-cir'cuit** *adj.*

closed shop a factory, business, etc. operating under a contract with a labor union by which only members of the union may be employed

close'fist·ed (klōs'fis'tid) *adj.* stingy; miserly

close'fit'ting *adj.* fitting tightly to the body

close'hauled' (-hôld') *adj.* with the sails set for heading as nearly as possible into the wind

close'mouthed' (-mouthd', -moutht') *adj.* not talking much; taciturn: also **close'lipped'** (-lipt')

clos·et (kläz'it) *n.* [< L. *claudere*, to close] 1. a small room or cupboard for clothes, supplies, etc. 2. same as WATER CLOSET —*adj.* private or secret —*vt.* to shut up in a private room for confidential discussion

close-up (klōs'up') *n.* a photograph, or a movie or TV shot, made at very close range

clo·sure (klō'zhər) *n.* [< L. *claudere*, to close] 1. a closing or being closed 2. a finish; end 3. anything that closes 4. same as CLOTURE

clot (klät) *n.* [OE. *clott*] a thickened mass or lump [a blood *clot]* —*vt., vi.* **clot'ted, clot'ting** to form into a clot or clots; coagulate

cloth (klôth) *n., pl.* **cloths** (klôthz, klôths) [OE. *clath*] 1. a woven, knitted, or pressed fabric of fibrous material, as cotton, wool, silk, etc. 2. a piece of such fabric for a special use *[washcloth]* —*adj.* made of cloth —**the cloth** 1. professional dress 2. the clergy

clothe (klōth) *vt.* **clothed** or **clad, cloth'ing** [OE. *clathian* < *prec.*] 1. to provide with or dress in clothes 2. to cover *[clothed* in glory*]*

clothes (klōz, klōthz) *n.pl.* [OE. *clathas*] 1. clothing; wearing apparel 2. bedclothes

clothes'horse' *n.* 1. a frame for airing or drying clothes 2. [Slang] a person who pays too much attention to his clothes

clothes'pin' *n.* a small clip, as of plastic or wood, for fastening clothes on a line

clothes'press' *n.* a closet, wardrobe, etc. in which to keep clothes

clothes tree an upright pole with branching hooks or pegs near the top to hold coats and hats

cloth·ier (klōth'yər) *n.* a dealer in clothes or cloth

cloth·ing (klō'thiŋ) *n.* 1. clothes; wearing apparel 2. a covering

clo·ture (klō'chər) *n.* [see CLOSURE] the parliamentary procedure by which debate is closed and the measure put to an immediate vote

cloud (kloud) *n.* [OE. *clud,* mass of rock] 1. a visible mass of vapor in the sky 2. a mass of smoke, dust, steam, etc. 3. a great number of moving things close together *[a cloud* of bees*]* 4. a murkiness or dimness 5. anything that darkens, obscures, etc. —*vt.* 1. to darken or obscure as with clouds 2. to make foggy or gloomy 3. to sully (a reputation, etc.) —*vi.* to become cloudy, gloomy, etc. —**in the clouds** 1. impractical 2. in a daydream —**under a cloud** under suspicion —**cloud'less** *adj.*

cloud'burst' *n.* a sudden heavy rain

cloud'y *adj.* -**i·er, -i·est** 1. covered with clouds; overcast 2. of or like clouds 3. opaque or foggy 4. obscure 5. gloomy; troubled —**cloud'i·ness** *n.*

clout (klout) *n.* [OE. *clut,* a patch] [Colloq.] a blow, as with the hand —*vt.* [Colloq.] to strike, as with the hand; hit

clove' (klōv) *n.* [< L. *clavus,* nail: from its shape] 1. the dried flower bud of a tropical evergreen tree, used as a pungent, fragrant spice 2. the tree

clove² (klōv) *n.* [OE. *clufu]* a segment of a bulb, as of garlic

clove³ (klōv) *alt. pt. of* CLEAVE¹

clo·ven (klō'v'n) *alt. pp. of* CLEAVE¹ —*adj.* split

clo·ver (klō'vər) *n.* [OE. *clafre]* any of various low-growing herbs related to the pea, with leaves of three leaflets (or occasionally four) and with small flowers in dense heads —**in clover** living in ease and luxury

clo'ver·leaf' (-lēf') *n., pl.* -**leafs'** a multiple highway interchange suggestive in form of a four-leaf clover and designed to let traffic flow freely in any of four directions through use of an overpass and curving ramps

clown (kloun) *n.* [ult. < ? L. *colere,* cultivate] 1. orig., a peasant or farmer 2. a clumsy, boorish person 3. a jester or buffoon, as in a medieval court 4. a comedian, typically made up and costumed in a comically grotesque way, who entertains with outlandish antics, absurd remarks, etc., as in a circus 5. a person playing practical jokes, acting silly, etc. —*vi.* to be, act like, or perform as a clown —**clown'ish** *adj.*

CLOVERLEAF

cloy (kloi) *vt., vi.* [< L. *clavus,* a nail] to weary or displease by providing too much, esp. of something sweet, rich, etc. —**cloy'ing·ly** *adv.*

club (klub) *n.* [< ON. *klumba,* mass] 1. a heavy stick used as a weapon 2. any stick used in a game, as golf 3. *a)* a group of people associated for a common purpose *b)* its meeting place 4. *a) [pl.]* a suit of playing cards marked with a black figure like a leaf of clover (♣) *b)* a card of this suit —*vt.* **clubbed, club'bing** to strike as with a club —*vi.* to unite for a common purpose

club'foot' *n., pl.* -**feet'** a congenitally misshapen, often clublike foot —**club'foot'ed** *adj.*

club'house' *n.* 1. a building used by a club 2. a locker room used by an athletic team

club sandwich a sandwich of several layers, often toasted, containing chicken, bacon, lettuce, etc.

club soda *same as* SODA WATER

cluck (kluk) *vi.* [echoic] to make one or more low, sharp sounds, as of a hen calling her chicks —*n.* 1. such a sound 2. [Slang] a dull, stupid person

clue (klōo) *n.* [see CLEW] a fact, object, etc. that helps solve a mystery or problem —*vt.* **clued, clu'ing** 1. to indicate as by a clue 2. [Colloq.] to provide with information needed (often with *in*)

clump (klump) *n.* [< LowG. *klump*] 1. a lump; mass 2. a cluster, as of trees 3. the sound of heavy footsteps —*vi.* 1. to walk heavily 2. to form clumps —*vt.* to group together in a cluster

clum·sy (klum'zē) *adj.* -**si·er, -si·est** [ME. *clumsid,* numb] 1. lacking grace or skill; awkward 2. awkwardly shaped or made —**clum'si·ly** *adv.* —**clum'si·ness** *n.*

clung (kluŋ) *pt. & pp. of* CLING

clunk (kluŋk) *n.* [echoic] 1. a dull, metallic sound 2. [Colloq.] a heavy blow —*vi., vt.* to move or strike with a clunk or clunks

clunk'er (-ər) *n.* [Slang] a battered old machine or automobile

clus·ter (klus'tər) *n.* [OE. *clyster*] 1. a number of things, all of the same sort, gathered or growing together 2. any group of persons, animals, or things close together —*vi., vt.* to form or make into a cluster

clutch' (kluch) *vt.* [OE. *clyccan,* to clench] 1. to grasp or snatch with a hand or claw 2. to grasp or hold eagerly or tightly —*vi.* to snatch or seize (*at*) —*n.* 1. *[usually pl.]* power; control 2. a clutching; grasp; grip 3. a device for engaging or disengaging a motor or engine 4. a device for gripping or holding 5. a woman's small handbag

clutch² (kluch) *n.* [< ON. *klekja,* to hatch] 1. a nest of eggs 2. a brood of chicks 3. a cluster

clut·ter (klut'ər) *n.* [< CLOT] a jumble; confusion —*vt.* to make untidy; litter (often with *up*)

Cly·tem·nes·tra (klīt'əm nes'trə) *Gr. Myth.* the wife of Agamemnon

Cm *Chem.* curium

cm, om. centimeter(s)

co- *a prefix shortened from* COM-, *meaning:* 1. together with *[cooperation]* 2. joint *[coauthor]* 3. equally *[coextensive]*

Co *Chem.* cobalt

CO Colorado

Co., co. *pl.* **Cos., cos.** 1. company 2. county

C/O, c.o. care of

C.O., CO Commanding Officer

coach (kōch) *n.* [< *Kócs,* village in Hungary] 1. a large, covered, four-wheeled carriage with an open, raised seat in front for the driver 2. a railroad passenger car with the lowest-priced seating accommodations 3. the lowest-priced class of airline accommodations 4. a bus 5. a tutor for a student 6. an instructor or trainer as of athletes or actors —*vt., vi.* to tutor, instruct, or train (someone)

coach dog *same as* DALMATIAN

coach'man (-mən) *n., pl.* -**men** the driver of a coach, or carriage

co·ad·ju·tor (kō aj'ə tər, kō'ə jōot'ər) *n.* an assistant, esp. to a bishop

co·ag·u·late (kō ag'yoo lāt') *vt.* -**lat'ed, -lat'ing** [< L. *co-,* together + *agere,* to drive] to cause (a liquid) to become a soft, semisolid mass; clot —*vi.* to become coagulated —**co·ag'u·lant** *n.* —**co·ag'u·la'tion** *n.* —**co·ag'·u·la'tive** *adj.* —**co·ag'u·la'tor** *n.*

coal (kōl) *n.* [OE. *col,* ember] 1. a black, combustible, mineral solid formed from vegetable matter, used as a fuel 2. pieces or a piece of this 3. an ember 4. charcoal —*vt., vi.* to provide with or take in a supply of coal —**haul** (or **rake, drag, call**) **over the coals** to criticize sharply

coal'er *n.* a ship, railroad car (also **coal car**), etc. that transports or supplies coal

co·a·lesce (kō'ə les') *vi.* -**lesced', -lesc'ing** [< L. *co-,* together + *alescere,* grow up] 1. to grow together 2. to unite into a single body or group —**co'a·les'cence** *n.* —**co'a·les'cent** *adj.*

co·a·li·tion (kō'ə lish'ən) *n.* [see *prec.*] a combination or union, esp. a temporary one

coal oil 1. kerosene 2. crude petroleum

coal tar a black, thick liquid obtained by the distillation of coal, used as in dyes and medicines

coam·ing (kō′miŋ) *n.* [< ?] a raised border as around a hatchway, to keep out water

coarse (kôrs) *adj.* **coars′er, coars′est** [< COURSE ("usual way")] **1.** of inferior or poor quality **2.** consisting of rather large particles **3.** not fine or delicate in texture, form, etc. **4.** for rough or crude work or results [a *coarse* file] **5.** not refined; not in good taste; crude [a *coarse* joke] —**coarse′ly** *adv.* —**coarse′ness** *n.*

coars′en *vt., vi.* to make or become coarse

coast (kōst) *n.* [< L. *costa*, rib, side] **1.** land along the sea; seashore **2.** a slide or ride down an incline, as on a sled — *vi.* **1.** to sail near or along a coast **2.** to slide or ride down an incline, as on a sled **3.** to continue moving by momentum alone —*vt.* to sail near or along the coast of —**the coast is clear** there is no apparent danger or hindrance —**coast′al** *adj.*

coast′er *n.* **1.** one that coasts **2.** a small mat, disk, etc. put under a glass or bottle to protect the surface as of a table

coast guard a governmental force employed to defend a nation's coast, aid vessels in distress, etc.; specif., [C- G-] such a branch of the U.S. armed forces —**coast guards′-man** (-mən), **coast guard′man,** *pl.* **-men**

coast′line′ *n.* the outline of a coast

coat (kōt) *n.* [< ML. *cota*, tunic] **1.** a sleeved outer garment opening down the front **2.** the natural covering of an animal or plant **3.** a layer, as of paint, over a surface —*vt.* to cover with a coat

co·a·ti (kō ät′ē) *n., pl.* **-tis** [SAmInd. name] a small, flesh-eating, tree-dwelling mammal of Mexico and Central and South America, having a long, flexible snout

coat·ing (kōt′iŋ) *n.* **1.** *same as* COAT (sense 3) **2.** cloth for making coats

coat of arms [< Fr. *cotte d'armes*, garment worn over armor] a design, as on a shield, used as the individualized symbol of a person, family, etc.

coat of mail *pl.* **coats of mail** a suit of armor made of linked metal rings or overlapping plates

coat′tail′ (-tāl′) *n.* the back part of a coat below the waist; esp., either hanging part formed by division of this back part —**ride (or hang,** etc.) **on (someone's) coattails** to have one's success dependent on that of someone else

co·au·thor (kō ô′thər) *n.* a joint author

coax (kōks) *vt., vi.* [< obs. slang *cokes*, a fool] to urge or get with soft words, flattery, etc.

co·ax·i·al (kō ak′sē əl) *adj.* having a common axis: also **co·ax′al**

cob (käb) *n.* [prob. < LowG.] **1.** a corncob **2.** a male swan **3.** a short, thickset horse

co·balt (kō′bôlt) *n.* [< G. *kobold*, goblin] a hard, steel-gray metallic chemical element: symbol, Co; at. wt., 58.9332; at. no., 27

cobalt blue dark blue

cob·ble′ (käb′'l) *vt.* **-bled, -bling** [ME.] **1.** to mend or patch (shoes, etc.) **2.** to mend or put together clumsily or crudely

cob·ble² (käb′'l) *n.* [< ?] *same as* COBBLESTONE —*vt.* **-bled, -bling** to pave with cobblestones

cob·bler′ (käb′lər) *n.* [< ?] **1.** a sugared iced drink of wine, whiskey, or rum, garnished as with a slice of orange **2.** a deep-dish pie made with fruit

cob·bler² (käb′lər) *n.* [see COBBLE¹] a person whose work is mending shoes

cob·ble·stone (käb′'l stōn′) *n.* [ME. *cobel ston*] a rounded stone formerly much used for paving streets

co·bra (kō′brə) *n.* [Port.] a very poisonous snake of Asia and Africa: when the snake is excited, loose skin about its neck expands into a hood

cob·web (käb′web′) *n.* [ME. *coppe*, spider + WEB] **1.** a web spun by a spider **2.** a thread of this **3.** anything flimsy, ensnaring, etc. like such a web

co·ca (kō′kə) *n.* [< SAmInd. name] **1.** any of certain S. American shrubs, esp. a species whose dried leaves yield cocaine **2.** these dried leaves

co·caine, co·cain (kō kān′) *n.* [< COCA] a crystalline alkaloid, $C_{17}H_{21}NO_4$, obtained from a species of coca: it is a narcotic and local anesthetic

coc·cus (käk′əs) *n., pl.* **coc·ci** (käk′sī) [< Gr. *kokkos*, berry] a spherical bacterium

coc·cyx (käk′siks) *n., pl.* **coc·cy′ges** (-sī′jēz) [< Gr. *kokkyx*, cuckoo: because shaped like its beak] a small, triangular bone at the lower end of the vertebral column — **coc·cyg′e·al** (-sij′ē al) *adj.*

coch·i·neal (käch′ə nēl′) *n.* [< L. *coccum*, a (red) berry] a red dye from certain insects feeding on cactus

coch·le·a (käk′lē ə) *n., pl.* **-le·ae′** (-ē′), **-le·as** [< Gr. *kochlias*, snail] the spiral-shaped part of the internal ear

cock¹ (käk) *n.* [OE. *coc*] **1.** a rooster or other male bird **2.** a weathercock **3.** a leader; chief **4.** a faucet or valve **5.** a firearm hammer or its position for firing **6.** a jaunty tilt, as of a hat —*vt.* **1.** to tilt jauntily **2.** to raise or turn alertly **3.** to set the hammer of (a gun) in firing position —*vi.* to get cocked

cock² (käk) *n.* [ME. *cokke*] a small, cone-shaped pile, as of hay —*vt.* to pile in cocks

cock·ade (kä kād′) *n.* [< Fr. < *coq*, a cock] a rosette or the like worn on the hat as a badge

cock·a·ma·mie (käk′ə mā′mē) *adj.* [< DECALCOMANIA] [Slang] of poor quality; inferior

cock-and-bull story (käk′'n bool′) an absurd tale

cock·a·too (käk′ə tōō′) *n., pl.* **-toos′** [< Du. < Malay *kakatua*] a crested parrot of Australia and the East Indies, usually with white plumage

cock·a·trice (käk′ə tris′) *n.* [< L. *calcare*, to tread] a mythical serpent supposedly killing by a look

cock·boat (käk′bōt′) *n.* [ME. *cokbote*] a small boat

cock·crow (käk′krō′) *n.* the break of day; dawn

cocked hat a three-cornered hat — **knock into a cocked hat** [Slang] to ruin

cock·er·el (käk′ər əl) *n.* a rooster under a year old

cock·er (spaniel) (käk′ər) [because a woodcock hunter] a small spaniel with silky hair and drooping ears

cock·eyed (käk′īd′) *adj.* [< COCK¹ *v.* + EYE] **1.** cross-eyed **2.** [Slang] *a)* silly *b)* drunk *c)* awry

cock·fight (käk′fīt′) *n.* a fight between gamecocks usually fitted with metal spurs —**cock′fight′ing** *n.*

cock·le′ (käk′'l) *n.* [< Gr. *konchē*, mussel] **1.** an edible shellfish with two heart-shaped, radially ridged shells **2.** a cockleshell **3.** a wrinkle; pucker —*vi., vt.* **-led, -ling** to wrinkle; pucker —**cockles of one's heart** one's deepest emotions

cock·le² (käk′'l) *n.* [OE. *coccel*] any of various weeds that grow in grainfields

cock′le·bur′ *n.* a coarse plant related to the daisy, bearing burs and growing commonly as a weed

cock′le·shell′ *n.* **1.** the shell of a cockle **2.** loosely, a scallop shell or the like **3.** a small boat

cock·ney (käk′nē) *n., pl.* **-neys** [ME. *cokenei*, spoiled child] [*often* C-] **1.** a native of the East End, London, speaking a characteristic dialect **2.** this dialect —*adj.* [*often* C-] of cockneys or their dialect

cock·pit (käk′pit′) *n.* **1.** an enclosed space for cockfighting **2.** in small vessels, at the stern, a space as for the steersman **3.** in a small airplane, the space for the pilot and, sometimes, passengers, or, in a large plane, for the pilot and crew

cock·roach (käk′rōch′) *n.* [Sp. *cucaracha*] an insect with long feelers and a flat, soft body: a common household pest

cocks·comb (käks′kōm′) *n.* **1.** the red, fleshy growth on the head of a rooster **2.** *same as* COXCOMB **3.** a plant related to the amaranth

cock·sure (käk′shoor′) *adj.* [< COCK¹ + SURE] absolutely sure or self-confident, esp. in an arrogant way

cock·swain (käk′s'n, -swān′) *n. same as* COXSWAIN

cock·tail (käk′tāl′) *n.* [< ?] **1.** an alcoholic drink made of a distilled liquor mixed with a wine, fruit juice, etc. **2.** an appetizer, as fruit juice, diced fruits, or seafood

cocktail table a low table, typically in a living room, for serving refreshments; coffee table

cock·y (käk′ē) *adj.* **-i·er, -i·est** [< COCK¹ + -Y²] [Colloq.] jauntily conceited or too self-confident —**cock′i·ly** *adv.* — **cock′i·ness** *n.*

co·co (kō′kō) *n., pl.* **-cos** [Sp. < L. < Gr. *kokkos*, berry] **1.** *same as* COCONUT PALM **2.** *same as* COCONUT

co·coa (kō′kō) *n.* [see CACAO] **1.** powder made from roasted, ground cacao seeds **2.** a drink made by adding sugar and hot water or milk to this **3.** a reddish-yellow brown

cocoa butter a yellowish fat prepared from cacao seeds: used in pharmacy and in cosmetics

co·co·nut, co·coa·nut (kō′kə nut′) *n.* the fruit of the coconut palm, a thick, brown, oval husk over edible white meat: the hollow center contains a sweet, milky fluid **(coconut milk)**

coconut palm (or **tree**) a tall tropical palm tree that bears coconuts: also **coco palm**

COCKATOO
(12–20 in. long)

co·coon (kə kōōn′) *n.* [< Fr. < ML. *coco,* shell] the protective silky case that certain insect larvae spin about themselves before the pupa stage

cod (käd) *n., pl.* **cod, cods** any of a family of food fishes of northern seas

C.O.D., c.o.d. cash (or collect) on delivery

Cod (käd), **Cape** peninsula in E Mass.

co·da (kō′də) *n.* [It. < L. *cauda,* a tail] *Music* a passage formally ending a composition or section

cod·dle (käd′'l) *vt.* **-dled, -dling** [< ?] **1.** to cook (esp. eggs) gently in water not quite boiling **2.** to treat tenderly; pamper

code (kōd) *n.* [< L. *codex,* wooden tablet] **1.** a body of laws arranged systematically **2.** any set of principles **3.** a set of signals for sending messages as by telegraph **4.** a system or set of symbols used as in secret writing —*vt.* **cod′ed, cod′ing** to put into a code

co·deine (kō′dēn) *n.* [< Gr. *kōdeia,* poppy head] an alkaloid derived from opium, used for pain relief and in cough medicines: also **co′dein**

co·dex (kō′deks) *n., pl.* **co·di·ces** (kō′də sēz′, käd′ə-) [see CODE] an ancient manuscript

cod′fish′ *n., pl.:* see FISH *same as* COD

codg·er (käj′ər) *n.* [< ?] [Colloq.] an eccentric, esp. elderly, fellow

cod·i·cil (käd′i s′l) *n.* [see CODE] **1.** *Law* an addition to a will to change, explain, revoke, or add provisions **2.** an appendix or supplement

cod·i·fy (käd′ə fī′, kō′də fī′) *vt.* **-fied′, -fy′ing** to put, as a body of laws, into systematic form —**cod′i·fi·ca′tion** *n.* —**cod′i·fi′er** *n.*

cod·ling[1] (käd′liŋ) *n., pl.* **-ling, -lings** a young cod

cod·ling[2] (käd′liŋ) *n.* [< Fr. *coeur de lion,* lion heart] **1.** a variety of elongated apple **2.** a small, unripe apple

codling (or **codlin**) **moth** a small moth whose larva destroys apples, pears, quinces, etc.

cod′-liv′er oil oil, rich in vitamins A and D, from the liver of the cod and related fishes

co·ed, co-ed (kō′ed′) *n.* [Colloq.] a girl attending a coeducational college or university —*adj.* [Colloq.] **1.** coeducational **2.** of a coed

co·ed·u·ca·tion (kō′ej ə kā′shən) *n.* the educational system in which students of both sexes attend classes together —**co′ed·u·ca′tion·al** *adj.*

co·ef·fi·cient (kō′ə fish′ənt) *n.* [co- + EFFICIENT] **1.** a factor that contributes to produce a result **2.** *Math.* a number or symbol used as a multiplier of a variable or unknown quantity **3.** *Physics* a number, constant for a given substance, used as a multiplier in measuring the change in some property of the substance under given conditions

coe·len·ter·ate (si len′tə rāt′, -tər it) *n.* [< Gr. *koilos,* hollow + *enteron,* intestine] any of a large group of marine animals, as a sea anemone, having a large central cavity with a single opening

co·e·qual (kō ē′kwəl) *adj., n.* equal —**co′e·qual′i·ty** (-i kwäl′ə tē) *n.* —**co·e′qual·ly** *adv.*

co·erce (kō urs′) *vt.* **-erced′, -erc′ing** [< L. *co-,* together + *arcere,* to confine] **1.** to restrain or constrain by force; curb **2.** to force; compel **3.** to enforce —**co·er′ci·ble** (-ur′sə b′l) *adj.* —**co·er′cion** (-ur′shən) *n.* —**co·er′cive** (-ur′siv) *adj.*

co·e·val (kō ē′v′l) *adj., n.* [< L. *co-,* together + *aevum,* an age] contemporary —**co·e′val·ly** *adv.*

co·ex·ist (kō′ig zist′) *vi.* **1.** to exist together at the same time or in the same place **2.** to live together without conflict, despite differences —**co′ex·ist′ence** *n.* —**co′ex·ist′ent** *adj.*

co′ex·tend′ (-ik stend′) *vt., vi.* to extend equally in space or time —**co′ex·ten′sion** *n.* —**co′ex·ten′sive** *adj.*

cof·fee (kôf′ē) *n.* [< It. < Ar. *qahwa*] **1.** a dark-brown aromatic drink made by brewing in water the roasted and ground beanlike seeds of a tall tropical shrub related to the madder **2.** these seeds: also **coffee beans 3.** the shrub **4.** the color of coffee with milk or cream in it; brown

coffee break a brief respite from work, when coffee or other refreshment is usually taken

cof′fee·cake′ *n.* a kind of cake or roll baked especially for eating with coffee, as at breakfast

cof′fee·house′ (-hous′) *n.* an establishment featuring coffee and used especially as a gathering place

coffee klatch (or **klatsch**) *same as* KAFFEEKLATSCH

cof′fee·pot′ *n.* a container with a lid and spout, for making and serving coffee

coffee shop an informal restaurant, as in a hotel, where light refreshments or meals are served

coffee table a low table, typically in a living room, for serving refreshments; cocktail table

cof·fer (kôf′ər) *n.* [see COFFIN] **1.** a strongbox for money, jewelry, etc. **2.** [*pl.*] a treasury; funds —*vt.* to enclose in a coffer

cof·fin (kôf′in) *n.* [< Gr. *kophinos,* basket] the case or box in which a corpse is buried

cog (käg) *n.* [< Scand.] **1.** one of the teeth of a cogwheel **2.** a cogwheel

co·gent (kō′jənt) *adj.* [< L. *co-,* together + *agere,* to drive] forceful and to the point, as a reason or argument; compelling —**co′gen·cy** *n.*

cog·i·tate (käj′ə tāt′) *vi., vt.* **-tat′ed, -tat′ing** [< L. *cogitari,* ponder] to think seriously and deeply (about); ponder —**cog′i·ta′tion** *n.* —**cog′i·ta′tive** *adj.* —**cog′i·ta′tor** *n.*

co·gnac (kōn′yak, kän′-, kôn′-) *n.* [Fr.] **1.** a brandy of Cognac, France **2.** loosely, any brandy

cog·nate (käg′nāt) *adj.* [< L. *co-,* together + (*g*)*nasci,* to be born] **1.** related by family **2.** derived from a common original form **3.** having the same nature —*n.* **1.** a person related to another **2.** a cognate word, language, or thing

cog·ni·tion (käg nish′ən) *n.* [< L. *co-,* together + (*g*)*noscere,* know] **1.** the process of knowing **2.** knowledge gained; perception —**cog′ni·tive** *adj.*

cog·ni·za·ble (käg′ni zə b′l, käg ni′-) *adj.* **1.** that can be known or perceived **2.** *Law* within the jurisdiction of a court

cog·ni·zance (käg′nə zəns) *n.* **1.** perception; knowledge **2.** authority over something **3.** *Law* a) a court hearing b) jurisdiction —**take cognizance of** to notice or recognize

cog′ni·zant (-zənt) *adj.* **1.** having authority or jurisdiction **2.** aware or informed (*of* something)

cog·no·men (käg nō′mən) *n.* [L. < *co-,* with + *nomen,* a name] **1.** a surname **2.** any name; esp., a nickname

cog′wheel′ *n.* a wheel rimmed with teeth that mesh with those of another wheel or of a rack to transmit or receive motion

co·hab·it (kō hab′it) *vi.* [< L. *co-,* together + *habitare,* dwell] to live together as husband and wife, esp. when not legally married —**co·hab′·i·ta′tion** *n.*

COGWHEELS

co·heir (kō′er′) *n.* a person who inherits jointly with another or others —**co′heir′ess** *n.fem.*

co·here (kō hir′) *vi.* **-hered′, -her′ing** [< L. *co-,* together + *haerere,* to stick] **1.** to stick together **2.** to be connected logically or naturally

co·her′ence (-əns) *n.* **1.** a cohering; cohesion **2.** logical consistency Also **co·her′en·cy**

co·her′ent (-ənt) *adj.* **1.** sticking together **2.** logically consistent —**co·her′ent·ly** *adv.*

co·he·sion (kō hē′zhən) *n.* **1.** a cohering; tendency to stick together **2.** *Physics* the force by which the molecules of a substance are held together —**co·he′sive** (-hēs′iv) *adj.* —**co·he′sive·ly** *adv.* —**co·he′sive·ness** *n.*

co·ho (kō′hō) *n., pl.* **-ho, -hos** [< ?] a small Pacific salmon, now also in N U.S. fresh waters

co·hort (kō′hôrt) *n.* [< L. *cohors,* enclosure] **1.** an ancient Roman military unit, one tenth of a legion **2.** a band of soldiers **3.** any group or band **4.** an associate, colleague, or supporter

coif (koif) *n.* [< LL. *cofea,* a cap] **1.** a cap that fits the head closely **2.** (*usually* kwäf) [< COIFFURE] a style of arranging the hair —*vt.* **coifed, coif′ing;** also, and for 2 usually, **coiffed, coif′fing 1.** to cover with a coif (sense 1) **2.** (*usually* kwäf) a) to style the hair b) to give a coiffure to

coif·feur (kwä fur′) *n.* [Fr.: see prec.] a male hairdresser —**coif·feuse′** (-fooz′) *n.fem.*

coif·fure (kwä fyoor′) *n.* [Fr. < *coiffe,* COIF] **1.** a headdress **2.** a style of arranging the hair —*vt.* **-fured′, -fur′ing** to coif (sense 2)

coign of vantage (koin) [see COIN] an advantageous position

coil (koil) *vt., vi.* [< L. *com-,* together + *legere,* gather] to wind around and around or gather into a circular or spiral form —*n.* **1.** anything so wound or gathered; also, the series of windings or spirals so formed, or one single turn **2.** a series of connected pipes in rows or coils **3.** *Elec.* a spiral or loop of wire or other conducting element used as an inductor, heating element, etc.

coin (koin) *n.* [< L. *cuneus,* a wedge] **1.** *archaic var. of* QUOIN **2.** *a)* a piece of stamped metal, issued by a government as money *b)* such pieces collectively **3.** [Slang] money —*vt.* **1.** to make (coins) by stamping (metal) **2.** to make up or invent (esp. a new word, phrase, etc.) —*vi.* to make coins —**coin money** [Colloq.] to make money fast — **coin′er** *n.*

coin′age (-ij) *n.* a coining or a thing coined

co·in·cide (kō′in sīd′) *vi.* **-cid′ed, -cid′ing** [< Fr. < L. *co-,* together + *in-,* upon + *cadere,* to fall] **1.** to take up the same place in space **2.** to occur at the same time **3.** to correspond or agree exactly —**co·in′ci·dent** (-sə dənt) *adj.* —**co·in′ci·den′tal·ly** *adv.*

co·in·ci·dence (kō in′sə dəns) *n.* **1.** a coinciding **2.** a striking but merely accidental occurrence of events, ideas, etc. at the same time —**co·in′ci·den′tal** (-den′t′l) *adj.* — **co·in′ci·den′tal·ly** *adv.*

co·i·tus (kō′it əs) *n.* [< L. *co-,* together + *ire,* to go] sexual intercourse: also **co·i·tion** (kō ish′ən) —**co′i·tal** *adj.*

coke (kōk) *n.* [ME. *colke,* a core] coal with most of its gases removed by heating: it burns with intense heat and little smoke —*vt., vi.* **coked, cok′ing** to change into coke

col- *same as* COM-: used before *l*

Col. **1.** Colonel **2.** Colorado **3.** Colossians

col. **1.** colony **2.** color(ed) **3.** column

co·la (kō′lə) *n.* [< WAfr. name] **1.** an African tree bearing nuts that contain caffeine and yield an extract used in soft drinks and medicine **2.** a sweet, carbonated soft drink flavored with this extract

col·an·der (kul′ən dər, käl′-) *n.* [prob. < L. *colum,* strainer] a perforated pan to drain off liquids

cold (kōld) *adj.* [OE. *cald*] **1.** of a temperature much lower than that of the human body **2.** lacking proper heat or warmth **3.** dead **4.** chilled or chilling **5.** not cordial **6.** objective; detached *[cold logic]* **7.** designating or having colors that suggest cold, as tones of blue, green, or gray **8.** faint or stale, as a scent in hunting **9.** [Colloq.] unprepared *[to enter a game cold]* **10.** [Slang] perfectly mastered, as a role **11.** [Slang] unconscious *[knocked cold]* —*adv.* altogether; completely *[cold sober]* —*n.* **1.** absence of heat or warmth, or the sensation produced **2.** a condition characterized by inflamed respiratory passages, a nasal discharge, etc., probably of viral origin —**catch (or take) cold** to get ill with a cold —**have (or get) cold feet** [Colloq.] to be (or become) timid —**in the cold** neglected —**cold′ly** *adv.* —**cold′ness** *n.*

cold′blood′ed *adj.* **1.** having a body temperature that varies with the surrounding air, water, or land, as reptiles or fish **2.** pitiless; cruel

cold cream a creamy preparation for softening and cleansing the skin

cold cuts a variety of sliced cold meats

cold duck [transl. of G. *kalte ente*] a drink made of mixed sparkling Burgundy and champagne

cold front *Meteorol.* the forward edge of a cold air mass advancing into a warmer air mass

cold shoulder [Colloq.] a reaction indicating lack of interest in or rejection of a person, idea, etc.: often with *the* —**cold′-shoul′der** *vt.*

cold sore one or more of the little blisters often appearing about the mouth during a cold or fever

cold turkey [Slang] **1.** abrupt and total withdrawal of drugs from an addict, as in an attempted cure **2.** with blunt directness *[to talk cold turkey]*

cold war sustained hostility without actual warfare

cold wave **1.** an onset of weather colder than normal **2.** a permanent wave in which the hair is set with a liquid preparation instead of with heat

cole (kōl) *n.* [< L. *caulis,* cabbage] any of various plants of the mustard family; esp., rape

co·le·op·ter·ous (kō′lē äp′tər əs) *adj.* [< Gr. *koleos,* sheath + *pteron,* a wing] of an order of insects, including beetles, that have horny front wings covering membranous hind wings

Cole·ridge (kōl′rij, -ər ij), **Samuel Taylor** 1772–1834; Eng. poet and critic

cole·slaw (kōl′slô′) *n.* [< Du. *kool,* cabbage + *sla,* salad] a salad of shredded raw cabbage: also **cole slaw**

cole·wort (kōl′wurt′) *n.* [COLE + WORT²] any cabbage whose leaves do not form a compact head

col·ic (käl′ik) *n.* [< Gr. *kōlon,* colon] acute abdominal pain caused by various abnormal conditions in the bowels —*adj.* **1.** of colic **2.** of the colon —**col′ick·y** (-i kē) *adj.*

co·li·form (kō′lə fôrm′, käl′ə-) *adj.* designating, of, or like bacilli normally in the colon

col·i·se·um (käl′ə sē′əm) *n.* [see COLOSSEUM] [C-] *same as* COLOSSEUM —*n.* a large building or stadium for sports events, shows, etc.

co·li·tis (kō līt′is) *n.* [< Gr. *kolon* + -ITIS] inflammation of the large intestine

coll. **1.** collect **2.** collection **3.** college

col·lab·o·rate (kə lab′ə rāt′) *vi.* **-rat′ed, -rat′ing** [< L. *com-,* with + *laborare,* to work] **1.** to work together, esp. in literary, artistic, or scientific projects **2.** to cooperate with the enemy —**col·lab′o·ra′tion** *n.* —**col·lab′o·ra′tive** *adj.* —**col·lab′o·ra′tor** *n.*

col·lab′o·ra′tion·ist *n.* a person who cooperates with the enemy

col·lage (kə läzh′) *n.* [Fr. < Gr. *kolla,* glue] **1.** an art form in which bits of objects are pasted on a surface **2.** a composition so made

col·la·gen (käl′ə jen′) *n.* [< Gr. *kolla,* glue + -GEN] a fibrous protein in bone, cartilage, etc.

col·lapse (kə laps′) *vi.* **-lapsed′, -laps′ing** [< L. *com-,* together + *labi,* to fall] **1.** to fall down or to pieces **2.** to break down suddenly **3.** to fold together compactly —*vt.* to make collapse —*n.* a collapsing —**col·laps′i·ble** *adj.*

col·lar (käl′ər) *n.* [< L. *collum,* neck] **1.** a garment part encircling the neck **2.** an ornamental band for the neck **3.** a band, as of leather, for the neck of a dog, cat, etc. **4.** a harness part fitting over the neck of a load-pulling animal, as for a horse **5.** a ring or flange, as on a pipe **6.** a band distinctive as in color and encircling the neck of an animal, bird, etc. **7.** foam formed at the top of a glass of beer or ale —*vt.* **1.** to put a collar on **2.** to grab by the collar **3.** [Colloq.] *a)* to seize; capture *b)* to stop and detain by talking to

col′lar·bone′ *n.* the clavicle

col·lard (käl′ərd) *n.* [contr. < COLEWORT] a kind of kale with coarse leaves borne in tufts

col·late (kä lāt′, käl′āt) *vt.* **-lat′ed, -lat′ing** [< L. *com-,* together + *latus,* brought] **1.** to compare (texts, data, etc.) critically **2.** *a)* to bring (book sections) together in proper order for binding *b)* to examine (such sections) to see that all pages, plates, etc. are present and in proper order —**col·la′tor** *n.*

col·lat·er·al (kə lat′ər əl) *adj.* [< L. *com-,* together + *latus,* a side] **1.** side by side; parallel **2.** being in addition to or corroborating the main thing **3.** of the same ancestry but in a different line **4.** *a)* designating or of security given as a pledge for meeting an obligation *b)* secured or guaranteed by property, as stocks, bonds, etc. *[a collateral loan]* —*n.* **1.** a collateral relative **2.** collateral security — **col·lat′er·al·ly** *adv.*

col·la·tion (kä lā′shən) *n.* **1.** the act or result of collating **2.** a light meal

col·league (käl′ēg) *n.* [< Fr. < L. *com-,* together + *legare,* deputize] a fellow worker; associate

col·lect (kə lekt′) *vt.* [< L. *com-,* together + *legere,* gather] **1.** to gather together **2.** to gather (stamps, books, etc.) as a hobby **3.** to call for and receive (money) for (bills, rent, etc.) **4.** to regain control of (oneself or one's wits) —*vi.* **1.** to assemble *[a crowd collected]* **2.** to accumulate *[water collects in the basement]* **3.** to collect payments, etc. —*adj., adv.* with payment to be made by the receiver *[to telephone collect]* —*n.* (käl′ekt) *[also* C-*]* a short prayer in certain church services —**col·lect′a·ble, col·lect′i·ble** *adj.* —**col·lec′tor** *n.*

col·lect′ed *adj.* **1.** gathered **2.** composed; calm —**col·lect′ed·ly** *adv.* —**col·lect′ed·ness** *n.*

col·lec′tion *n.* **1.** a collecting **2.** things collected **3.** an accumulation **4.** a sum collected

col·lec′tive *adj.* **1.** formed by collecting **2.** of or as a group *[collective effort]* **3.** designating or of any enterprise in which people work together as a group *[a collective farm]* **4.** *Gram.* designating a noun, as *crowd,* singular in form but meaning a group —*n.* **1.** a collective enterprise or the people in it **2.** *Gram.* a collective noun —**col·lec′-tive·ly** *adv.*

collective bargaining negotiations between organized workers and their employer or employers concerning wages, hours, and working conditions

col·lec·tiv·ism (kə lek′tə viz′m) *n.* ownership and control, by the people collectively, of the means of production and distribution —**col·lec′tiv·ist** *n., adj.* —**col·lec′tiv·is′tic** *adj.*

col·leen (käl′ēn, kə lēn′) *n.* [< Ir. *caile,* girl] [Irish] a girl

col·lege (käl′ij) *n.* [see COLLEAGUE] **1.** an association of individuals with certain powers, duties, etc. *[the electoral college]* **2.** an institution of higher education granting degrees; specif., *a)* a specialized school of a university *b)* the undergraduate division of a university **3.** a school for a specialized occupation *[a secretarial college]*

col·le·gi·al (kə lē′jē əl) *adj.* **1.** with authority shared equally among colleagues 2. *same as* COLLEGIATE —col·le′gi·al′i·ty (-al′ə tē) *n.*

col·le·gian (kə lē′jən) *n.* a college student

col·le′giate (-jət) *adj.* of or like a college or collegians

col·lide (kə līd′) *vi.* -lid′ed, -lid′ing [< L. *com-*, together + *laedere*, to strike] 1. to strike violently together 2. to clash

col·lie (käl′ē) *n.* [< ?] a large, long-haired Scottish sheep dog with a long, narrow head

col·lier (käl′yər) *n.* [see COAL & -IER] [Chiefly Brit.] 1. a coal miner 2. a ship for carrying coal

col′lier·y *n., pl.* -ies [Chiefly Brit.] a coal mine

col·li·mate (käl′ə māt′) *vt.* -mat′ed, -mat′ing [< L. *com-*, with + *linea*, a line] 1. to make parallel, as light rays 2. to adjust the line of sight of, as a telescope

col·li·sion (kə lizh′ən) *n.* a colliding

col·lo·cate (käl′ə kāt′) *vt.* -cat′ed, -cat′ing [< L. *com-*, together + *locus*, a place] to place together, esp. side by side —col′lo·ca′tion *n.*

col·lo·di·on (kə lō′dē ən) *n.* [< Gr. *kolla*, glue + *eidos*, a form] a quick-drying, highly flammable solution of nitrated cellulose: it forms a tough, elastic film

col·loid (käl′oid) *n.* [< Gr. *kolla*, glue + -OID] a substance made up of tiny, insoluble, nondiffusible particles that remain suspended in a medium of different matter —col·loi′dal *adj.*

colloq. 1. colloquial(ly) 2. colloquialism

col·lo·qui·al (kə lō′kwē əl) *adj.* [see COLLOQUY] 1. of or like conversation 2. designating or of the words, phrases, etc. characteristic of informal speech and writing —col·lo′qui·al·ism *n.* —col·lo′qui·al·ly *adv.*

col·lo·qui·um (-əm) *n., pl.* -qui·a (-ə), -qui·ums [see COLLOQUY] an organized discussion or seminar

col·lo·quy (käl′ə kwē) *n., pl.* -quies [< L. *com-*, together + *loqui*, speak] 1. a talking together; conversation 2. a conference or discussion

col·lu·sion (kə lōō′zhən) *n.* [< L. *com-*, with + *ludere*, to play] a secret agreement to do something illegal or fraudulent —col·lu′sive (-siv) *adj.*

Colo. Colorado

Co·logne (kə lōn′) city in W West Germany, on the Rhine: pop. 854,000

co·logne (kə lōn′) *n. same as* EAU DE COLOGNE

Co·lom·bi·a (kə lum′bē ə) country in NW S. America: 455,335 sq. mi.; pop. 20,463,000; cap. Bogotá —Co·lom′bi·an *adj., n.*

Co·lom·bo (kə lum′bō) capital of Sri Lanka: seaport on the W coast: pop. 512,000

Co·lón (kə lōn′) seaport in Panama, at the Caribbean entrance to the Panama Canal: pop. 64,000

co·lon¹ (kō′lən) *n.* [< Gr. *kôlon*, limb] a mark of punctuation (:) used as before a long quotation or after the salutation of a formal letter

co·lon² (kō′lən) *n., pl.* -lons, -la (-lə) [< Gr. *kolon*] the part of the large intestine from the cecum to the rectum —co·lon·ic (kə län′ik) *adj.*

colo·nel (kur′n'l) *n.* [Fr. < It. < L. *columna*, column] 1. a military officer ranking above a lieutenant colonel 2. an honorary title in some southern or western States —colo′nel·cy (-sē) *n., pl.* -cies

co·lo·ni·al (kə lō′nē əl) *adj.* 1. of or in a colony or colonies 2. [*often* C-] of or in the thirteen British colonies that became the U.S. 3. made up of or having colonies — *n.* an inhabitant of a colony —co·lo′ni·al·ly *adv.*

co·lo′ni·al·ism *n.* a system of having colonies, esp. for exploitation —co·lo′ni·al·ist *n., adj.*

col·o·nist (käl′ə nist) *n.* 1. any of the original settlers of a colony 2. an inhabitant of a colony

col·o·nize (käl′ə nīz′) *vt., vi.* -nized′, -niz′ing 1. to found a colony (in) 2. to settle in a colony —col′o·ni·za′tion *n.* —col′o·niz′er *n.*

col·on·nade (käl′ə nād′) *n.* [Fr. < It. < L. *columna*, column] *Archit.* a series of regularly spaced columns

col·o·ny (käl′ə nē) *n., pl.* -nies [< L. *colere*, cultivate] 1. a group of settlers in a distant land, under the jurisdiction of their native land 2. the region settled 3. any territory ruled by a distant state 4. a community of the same nationality or pursuits, as within a city 5. *Biol.* a group of similar animals or plants living or growing together

col·o·phon (käl′ə fän′) *n.* [< Gr. *kolophōn*, top] a publisher's distinctive emblem, as on a book cover

col·or (kul′ər) *n.* [L.] 1. the property of reflecting light of a particular wavelength: the distinct colors of the spectrum are red, orange, yellow, green, blue, indigo, and vio-

let, its *primary colors* being red, green, and blue 2. any coloring matter; pigment; dye; paint: here the *primary colors* are red, yellow, and blue; these, mixed variously, produce the *secondary colors* (orange, green, etc.); black, white, and gray are *achromatic colors* 3. facial color, esp. a healthy rosiness or a blush 4. the color of the skin of a non-Caucasoid person 5. [*pl.*] an identifying colored badge, costume, etc. 6. [*pl.*] a flag 7. semblance; likeness 8. plausibility or apparent justification 9. vividness 10. *Music* timbre —*vt.* 1. to give color to; paint, dye, etc. 2. to change the color of 3. to alter or influence, as by distorting [*prejudice colored his views*] —*vi.* 1. to become colored 2. to change color 3. to flush or blush —show one's colors to reveal one's true self —under color of under the pretext of

col′or·a·ble *adj.* 1. that can be colored 2. specious; deceptive

Col·o·ra·do (käl′ə rad′ō, -rä′dō) 1. State of the W U.S., one of the Mountain States: 104,247 sq. mi.; pop. 2,207,000; cap. Denver: abbrev. Colo., CO 2. river flowing from N Colo. southwest into the Gulf of California —Col′o·rad′an, Col′o·rad′o·an *adj., n.*

Colorado Springs city in C Colo.: pop. 135,000

col·or·ant (kul′ər ənt) *n.* [Fr.] a coloring agent, as a pigment or dye

col′or·a′tion *n.* 1. a being colored 2. the way a thing is colored 3. the technique of using colors

col·o·ra·tu·ra (kul′ər ə toor′ə, -tyoor′ə) *n.* [It. < L. *colorare*, to color] 1. brilliant runs, trills, etc. displaying a singer's skill 2. music with such ornamentation 3. a soprano who can sing such music: in full coloratura soprano

col′or·blind′ *adj.* 1. unable to perceive colors or to distinguish between certain colors, as red and green 2. not influenced by considerations of race —col′or·blind′ness *n.*

col′or·cast′ *n.* a television broadcast in color —*vt., vi.* -cast′ or -cast′ed, -cast′ing to televise in color

col′ored *adj.* 1. having color 2. non-Caucasoid; specif., Negro 3. altered or influenced

col′or·fast′ (-fast′) *adj.* that will keep its color without fading or running —col′or·fast′ness *n.*

col′or·ful *adj.* 1. full of color 2. varied, vivid, etc. —col′or·ful·ly *adv.* —col′or·ful·ness *n.*

col′or·ing *n.* 1. the applying of colors 2. something that imparts color 3. the way a thing is colored 4. false appearance 5. alteration or influence

col′or·less *adj.* 1. lacking color 2. dull, vapid, etc. —col′or·less·ly *adv.* —col′or·less·ness *n.*

color line a barrier of social, political, or economic restrictions imposed on Negroes or other nonwhites

co·los·sal (kə läs′'l) *adj.* 1. like a colossus in size; huge; gigantic 2. [Colloq.] stupendous; extraordinary —co·los′sal·ly *adv.*

Col·os·se·um (käl′ə sē′əm) [< L. *colosseus*, huge] an amphitheater in Rome, built c.75–80 A.D. —*n.* [c-] *same as* COLISEUM

Co·los·sians (kə läsh′ənz) a book of the New Testament: an epistle of the Apostle Paul

co·los·sus (kə läs′əs) *n., pl.* -los′si (-ī), -los′sus·es [< Gr. *kolossos*] 1. a huge statue; esp., [C-] that of Apollo, set at the harbor of Rhodes c.280 B.C. 2. any huge or important person or thing

col·our (kul′ər) *n., vt., vi.* Brit. sp. of COLOR

colt (kōlt) *n.* [OE.] 1. a young male horse, donkey, etc.; specif., a male racehorse four years of age or under 2. a young, inexperienced person

col·ter (kōl′tər) *n.* [< L. *culter*, plowshare] a blade or disk on a plow, to cut soil vertically

colt′ish *adj.* of or like a colt; esp., frisky

Co·lum·bi·a (kə lum′bē ə) 1. [Poet.] the United States 2. capital of S. Carolina: pop. 114,000 3. river flowing from SE British Columbia, through Washington, into the Pacific —Co·lum′bi·an *adj.*

col·um·bine (käl′əm bīn′) *n.* [< L. *columba*, a dove] a plant related to the buttercup, with spurred flowers of various colors

Co·lum·bus (kə lum′bəs) 1. capital of Ohio, in the C part: pop. 540,000 (met. area 916,000) 2. city in W Georgia: pop. 154,000

Co·lum·bus (kə lum′bəs), Christopher 1451?–1506; It. explorer in the service of Spain; discovered America (1492)

Columbus Day a legal holiday in the U.S. commemorating the discovery of America by Columbus and observed on the second Monday in October

---

fat, āpe, cär; ten, ēven; is, bīte; gō, hôrn, tōōl, look; oil, out; up, fur; thin, *then*; zh, leisure; ŋ, ring; ə for *a* in *ago*; ' as in *able* (ā′b'l); ë, Fr. coeur; ö, Fr. feu; Fr. mon; ü, Fr. duc; r, Fr. cri; kh, G. doch, ich. ‡ foreign; < derived from

col·umn (käl′əm) *n.* [< L. *columna*] **1.** a slender, upright, usually cylindrical structure, typically a supporting or ornamental member in a building; pillar **2.** anything columnlike **3.** a formation in file, as of troops **4.** a relatively narrow, vertical section as of printed material on a page, bounded from a similar section or the rest of the page typically by a ruled line or blank space **5.** a regular feature article, as in a newspaper —**co·lum·nar** (kə lum′nər), **col′umned** (-əmd) *adj.*

col·um·nist (-əm nist, -ə mist) *n.* a person who writes or conducts a column, as in a newspaper

com- [L. < *cum*, with] *a prefix meaning* with, together [*combine*] : also used as an intensive [*command*]

CAPITAL

SHAFT

BASE

COLUMN

Com. 1. Commander **2.** Commission(er) **3.** Committee

com. 1. commerce **2.** common **3.** communication

co·ma¹ (kō′mə) *n.* [< Gr. *kōma*, deep sleep] a state of deep, prolonged unconsciousness, as from injury

co·ma² (kō′mə) *n., pl.* **-mae** (-mē) [< Gr. *komē*, hair] a globular, cloudlike mass around a comet nucleus

co·make (kō′māk′) *vt.* **-made′, -mak′ing** *same as* COSIGN —**co′mak′er** *n.*

Co·man·che (kə man′chē) *n., pl.* **-ches, -che** a member of a tribe of American Indians now of Oklahoma, formerly ranging from the Platte River to the Mexican border

co·ma·tose (kō′mə tōs′, käm′ə-) *adj.* **1.** of, like, or in a coma or stupor **2.** lethargic; torpid

comb (kōm) *n.* [OE. *camb*] **1.** a thin strip of plastic, metal, hard rubber, etc. with teeth, used to arrange or clean the hair or to hold the hair in place **2.** anything used like or suggestive of a comb; specif., *a*) a tool for carding wool, cotton, etc. *b*) a red, fleshy outgrowth as on a rooster's head **3.** a honeycomb —*vt.* **1.** to arrange, straighten, clean, etc. with or as if with a comb **2.** to remove with or as if with a comb (often with *out*) **3.** to search thoroughly —*vi.* to roll over; break: said of waves

com·bat (kəm bat′, käm′bat) *vi., vt.* **-bat′ed** or **-bat′ted, -bat′ing** or **-bat′ting** [< Fr. < L. *com-*, with + *battuere*, to beat, fight] to fight; struggle (against) —*n.* (käm′bat, kum′-) a battle; conflict

com·bat·ant (käm′bə tənt, kəm bat′′nt) *adj.* **1.** fighting **2.** ready or prepared to fight —*n.* one in combat; fighter

combat fatigue a psychoneurotic condition characterized by anxiety, irritability, depression, etc., as after long combat in warfare

com·bat·ive (kəm bat′iv, käm′bə tiv) *adj.* disposed to fight; belligerent; pugnacious

comb·er (kō′mər) *n.* **1.** one that combs **2.** a large wave rolling over and breaking as on a beach

com·bi·na·tion (käm′bə nā′shən) *n.* **1.** a combining or being combined **2.** a thing formed by combining **3.** an association for a common purpose **4.** the series of numbers or letters to which the dial of a special lock (**combination lock**) is turned to open the lock **5.** a one-piece undergarment combining undershirt and drawers

com·bine (kəm bīn′) *vt., vi.* **-bined′, -bin′ing** [< L. *com-*, together + *bini*, two by two] **1.** to bring or come into union; unite; join **2.** to unite to form a chemical compound **3.** (käm′bīn′) to harvest and thresh with a combine —*n.* (käm′bīn′) **1.** a machine for harvesting and threshing grain **2.** an association, as of corporations, for purposes often unethical —**com·bin′er** *n.*

comb·ings (kō′miŋz) *n.pl.* loose hair, wool, etc. removed in combing

combining form a word form occurring only in compounds or derivatives (Ex.: *cardio-* in *cardiograph*)

com·bo (käm′bō) *n., pl.* **-bos** [Colloq.] a combination; specif., a small jazz ensemble

com·bus·ti·ble (kəm bus′tə b′l) *adj.* **1.** easily igniting and burning; flammable **2.** easily aroused or excited —*n.* a flammable substance —**com·bus′ti·bil′i·ty** *n.* —**com·bus′ti·bly** *adv.*

com·bus′tion (-chən) *n.* [< L. *com-*, intens. + *urere*, to burn] **1.** the act or process of burning **2.** agitation; tumult —**com·bus′tive** (-tiv) *adj.*

come (kum) *vi.* **came, come, com′ing** [OE. *cuman*] **1.** to move from "there" to "here" **2.** to arrive or appear **3.** to extend; reach **4.** to happen; occur [*success came* to her] **5.** to take form in the mind [*her name came* to him] **6.** to have a certain place or order [*after* 1 *comes* 2] **7.** to have a certain descent or origin **8.** to result **9.** to be due or owed [*you'll get what's coming* to you] **10.** to move

along; go; pass **11.** to get to be [*it came loose*] **12.** to be available [*it comes* in two sizes] **13.** to amount —*interj.* now, now!: used as from impatience —**come about 1.** to occur **2.** to turn about —**come across 1.** to find by chance **2.** [Colloq.] to be effective, understood, etc. **3.** [Slang] to give or do what is wanted —**come around** (or **round**) **1.** to revive or recover **2.** to turn about **3.** to give in; yield —**come by 1.** to acquire **2.** to drop in for a visit —**come in 1.** to enter **2.** to arrive **3.** to come into fashion —**come into 1.** to enter **2.** to inherit —**come off 1.** to get detached **2.** to occur **3.** to end up a certain way **4.** [Colloq.] to prove effective, successful, etc. —**come off it!** [Slang] stop that! —**come on 1.** to progress **2.** to find or encounter by chance **3.** to enter, appear, begin to function, etc. —**come on!** [Colloq.] **1.** get started! hurry! **2.** stop that! **3.** please be nice, agreeable, etc.! —**come out 1.** to be disclosed **2.** to appear, be published, etc. **3.** to make a debut **4.** to end up —**come out for** to announce one's approval or endorsement of —**come out with 1.** to disclose **2.** to bring out, as a new book, for sale, exhibition, etc. —**come through 1.** to complete or endure something successfully **2.** [Slang] to give or do what is wanted —**come through with** [Slang] to provide (what is wanted) —**come to** to recover consciousness —**come up** to emerge for consideration, voting, on, etc. —**come upon** to find or encounter by chance —**come up to** to meet (expectations, standards, etc.) —**come up with** to suggest, produce, find, etc. —**how come?** [Colloq.] why?

come′back′ *n.* [Colloq.] **1.** a return to a previous position of success, power, etc. **2.** a retort

co·me·di·an (kə mē′dē ən) *n.* **1.** an actor who plays comic parts **2.** an entertainer who tells jokes, sings comic songs, etc. **3.** one who amuses by behaving comically —**co·me′di·enne′** (-en′) *n.fem.*

come′down′ *n.* a loss of status or position

com·e·dy (käm′ə dē) *n., pl.* **-dies** [< Gr. *kōmos*, festival + *aeidein*, sing] **1.** orig., a drama or narrative with a happy ending or nontragic theme **2.** *a*) a humorous play or motion picture with a happy ending *b*) such plays collectively *c*) the writing, acting, or theory of these **3.** a comic novel or other narrative **4.** the comic element in a literary work, or in life **5.** an amusing event or series of events —**cut the comedy** [Slang] to stop joking —**co·me·dic** (kə mē′dik, -med′ik) *adj.*

come·ly (kum′lē) *adj.* **-li·er, -li·est** [OE. *cymlic*] **1.** pleasant to look at; fair **2.** [Archaic] seemly; decorous; proper —**come′li·ness** *n.*

come′-on′ *n.* [Slang] an inducement

com·er (kum′ər) *n.* a person that comes [a contest open to all *comers*]

co·mes·ti·ble (kə mes′tə b′l) *n.* [Fr. < L. *com-*, intens. + *edere*, eat] [*usually pl.*] food

com·et (käm′ət) *n.* [< Gr. *komē*, hair] a heavenly body with a starlike nucleus and usually a long, luminous tail: comets orbit the sun

come·up·pance (kum′up′′ns) *n.* [< COME + UP¹ + -ANCE] [Colloq.] deserved punishment; retribution

com·fit (kum′fit) *n.* [< L. *com-*, with + *facere*, to make] a candy; sweetmeat

com·fort (kum′fərt) *vt.* [< L. *com-*, intens. + *fortis*, strong] to soothe in distress or sorrow; console —*n.* **1.** relief from distress, grief, etc. **2.** one that comforts **3.** a state of ease and quiet enjoyment; also, something contributing to this —**com′fort·ing** *adj.* —**com′fort·less** *adj.*

com·fort·a·ble (kumf′tər b′l, kum′fər tə b′l) *adj.* **1.** providing comfort **2.** having comfort; at ease **3.** [Colloq.] sufficient to satisfy, as a salary —**com′fort·a·bly** *adv.*

com′fort·er *n.* **1.** one that comforts **2.** a quilted blanket

comfort station a public toilet; restroom

com·fy (kum′fē) *adj.* **-fi·er, -fi·est** [Colloq.] comfortable

com·ic (käm′ik) *adj.* **1.** of comedy **2.** amusing; funny —*n.* **1.** a comedian **2.** the humorous part of art or life **3.** *a*) *same as* COMIC STRIP or COMIC BOOK *b*) [*pl.*] a section of comic strips

com′i·cal *adj.* amusing; funny —**com′i·cal′i·ty** (-kal′ə tē) *n.* —**com′i·cal·ly** *adv.*

comic book a booklet of comic strips

comic opera opera with humorous situations, usually some spoken dialogue, and a happy ending

comic strip a series of cartoons, as in a newspaper, telling a humorous or adventurous story

com′ing *adj.* **1.** approaching; next **2.** on the way to becoming successful, popular, important, etc. [it's the *coming* thing] —*n.* arrival; advent

com·i·ty (käm′ə tē) *n., pl.* **-ties** [< L. *comis*, polite] courteous behavior; politeness

comm. 1. commission **2.** committee

com·ma (käm'ə) *n.* [< Gr. *koptein,* cut off] a mark of punctuation (,) used to indicate a slight separation of sentence elements

com·mand (kə mand') *vt.* [< L. *com-,* intens. + *mandare,* commit] 1. to give an order to; direct 2. to have authority over; control 3. to have ready for use *[to command* a huge vocabulary*]* 4. to deserve and get *[to command* respect*]* 5. to control or look out over from a higher position —*vi.* to exercise authority —*n.* 1. an order; direction 2. authority to command 3. power to control by position 4. mastery 5. a military or naval force, or district, under a specified authority

com·man·dant (käm'ən dant', -dänt') *n.* a commanding officer, as of a fort

com·man·deer (käm'ən dir') *vt.* [< Fr. *commander,* to command] 1. to seize (property) for military or governmental use 2. [Colloq.] to take forcibly

com·mand'er *n.* 1. one who commands 2. *U.S. Navy* an officer ranking just above a lieutenant commander

commander in chief *pl.* **commanders in chief** the supreme commander of a nation's armed forces

commanding officer the officer in command of any of certain military units or installations

com·mand'ment *n.* a command or order; specif., any of the Ten Commandments

com·man·do (kə man'dō) *n., pl.* **-dos, -does** [Afrik. < Port.] a member of a small force trained to raid enemy territory

com·mem·o·rate (kə mem'ə rāt') *vt.* **-rat'ed, -rat'ing** [< L. *com-,* intens. + *memorare,* remind] 1. to honor the memory of, as by a ceremony 2. to serve as a memorial to —**com·mem'o·ra'tion** *n.* —**com·mem'o·ra·tive** (-ər ə tiv, -ə rāt'iv) *adj.*

com·mence (kə mens') *vi., vt.* **-menced', -menc'ing** [< L. *com-,* together + *initiare,* begin] to begin; start —**com·menc'er** *n.*

com·mence'ment *n.* 1. a beginning; start 2. the ceremonies at which degrees or diplomas are conferred at a school 3. the day this takes place

com·mend (kə mend') *vt.* [see COMMAND] 1. to put in the care of another; entrust 2. to recommend 3. to praise —**com·mend'a·ble** *adj.* —**com·mend'a·bly** *adv.* —**com·men·da·tion** (käm'ən dā'shən) *n.*

com·mend'a·to'ry (-ə tôr'ē) *adj.* 1. expressing praise or approval 2. recommending

com·men·su·ra·ble (kə men'shər ə b'l, -sər-) *adj.* [see COMMENSURATE] measurable by the same standard or measure

com·men'su·rate (-shər it, -sər-) *adj.* [< L. *com-,* together + *mensura,* measurement] 1. equal in measure or size 2. proportionate 3. *same as* COMMENSURABLE —**com·men'su·rate·ly** *adv.*

com·ment (käm'ent) *n.* [< L. *com-,* intens. + *meminisse,* remember] 1. an explanatory or critical note on something written or said 2. a remark or observation 3. talk; gossip —*vi.* to make a comment or comments (*on* or *upon*)

com·men·tar·y (käm'ən ter'ē) *n., pl.* **-ies** 1. a series of remarks, observations, or explanatory notes 2. something with the force of a comment or remark

com'men·tate' (-tāt') *vi.* **-tat'ed, -tat'ing** to perform as a commentator

com'men·ta'tor (-tāt'ər) *n.* one who reports and analyzes news events, trends, etc., as on radio or TV

com·merce (käm'ərs) *n.* [Fr. < L. *com-,* together + *merx,* merchandise] 1. the buying and selling of goods on a large scale; trade 2. social intercourse

com·mer·cial (kə mur'shəl) *adj.* 1. of or connected with commerce or trade 2. made or done primarily for profit 3. offering training in business skills, etc. —*n. Radio & TV* a paid advertisement —**com·mer'cial·ly** *adv.*

com·mer'cial·ism *n.* the practices and spirit of commerce or business, esp. in seeking profits

com·mer'cial·ize' (-īz') *vt.* **-ized', -iz'ing** 1. to put on a business basis, esp. so as to make profit 2. to imbue with commercialism —**com·mer'cial·i·za'tion** *n.*

com·min·gle (kə miŋ'g'l) *vt., vi.* **-gled, -gling** to mingle together; blend

com·mis·er·ate (kə miz'ə rāt') *vt.* **-at'ed, -at'ing** [< L. *com-,* intens. + *miserari,* to pity] to feel or show pity for —*vi.* to condole (*with*) —**com·mis'er·a'tion** *n.*

com·mis·sar (käm'ə sär') *n.* [< Russ. < L. *committere,* commit] the head of a commissariat (sense 2): now called *minister*

com·mis·sar·i·at (käm'ə ser'ē ət) *n.* [Fr. < L.: see

COMMIT] 1. the branch of an army providing food and supplies for the troops 2. formerly, a government department in the U.S.S.R.: now called *ministry*

com·mis·sar·y (käm'ə ser'ē) *n., pl.* **-ies** [< L. *committere,* commit] 1. formerly, an army officer in charge of food and supplies 2. a store, as in an army camp, where food and supplies are sold

com·mis·sion (kə mish'ən) *n.* [see COMMIT] 1. an authorization to take on certain duties or powers 2. a document granting this 3. the state of being so authorized 4. authority to act for another, or that which one is authorized to do 5. a committing, as of a crime 6. *a)* a group of people chosen to perform specified duties *b)* an administrative agency of the government 7. a percentage of money from sales, allotted to the agent 8. *Mil. a)* an official certificate conferring rank as an officer *b)* the rank conferred —*vt.* 1. to give a commission to 2. to authorize 3. *Naut.* to put (a vessel) into service —**in** (or **out of**) **commission** 1. in (or not in) use 2. in (or not in) working order

com·mis'sion·er *n.* 1. a member of a commission 2. an official in charge of a government bureau, commission, etc. 3. a person selected to regulate and control a professional sport

com·mit (kə mit') *vt.* **-mit'ted, -mit'ting** [< L. *com-,* together + *mittere,* send] 1. to give in charge; consign 2. to put in custody or confinement *[committed to prison]* 3. to do or perpetrate (an offense or crime) 4. to bind as by a promise; pledge —**commit to memory** to memorize

com·mit'ment *n.* 1. a committing or being committed 2. consignment of a person to prison, a mental institution, etc. 3. a pledge or promise Also **com·mit'tal**

com·mit·tee (kə mit'ē) *n.* [see COMMIT] a group of people chosen to report or act upon a certain matter —**in committee** under consideration by a committee, as a bill —**com·mit'tee·man** (-mən) *n., pl.* **-men** —**com·mit'tee·wom'an** *n.fem., pl.* **-wom'en**

com·mode (kə mōd') *n.* [Fr. < L.: see COM- & MODE] 1. a chest of drawers 2. a movable washstand 3. a chair enclosing a chamber pot 4. a toilet

com·mo·di·ous (kə mō'dē əs) *adj.* [see prec.] spacious; roomy —**com·mo'di·ous·ly** *adv.*

com·mod·i·ty (kə mäd'ə tē) *n., pl.* **-ties** [see COMMODE] 1. any useful thing 2. anything bought and sold

com·mo·dore (käm'ə dôr') *n.* [< Fr.: see COMMAND] 1. *U.S. Navy* an officer ranking just above a captain 2. a courtesy title, as of a yacht club president

com·mon (käm'ən) *adj.* [< L. *communis,* shared by all or many] 1. belonging to or shared by each or all 2. belonging to the community; public 3. general; widespread 4. familiar; usual 5. not of the upper classes 6. having no rank *[a common* soldier*]* 7. below ordinary 8. vulgar; coarse 9. designating a noun that refers to any of a group, as *book* 10. *Math.* belonging equally to two or more quantities *[a common* denominator*]* —*n.* [*sometimes pl.*] land owned or used by all the inhabitants of a place —**in common** equally with another or all concerned —**com'mon·ly** *adv.* —**com'mon·ness** *n.*

com'mon·al·ty (-əl tē) *n., pl.* **-ties** the common people; public

common carrier a person or company in the business of transporting people or goods for a fee

com'mon·er *n.* one of the common people

common fraction a fraction with both numerator and denominator whole numbers

common law the law of a country based on custom, usage, and judicial decisions

com'mon-law' marriage a marriage not solemnized by religious or civil ceremony but effected by agreement to live together as husband and wife

common market an association of nations formed to effect a closer economic union; specif., **[C- M-]** *same as* EUROPEAN ECONOMIC COMMUNITY

com'mon·place' *n.* 1. a trite remark; platitude 2. anything common or ordinary —*adj.* obvious or ordinary —**com'mon·place'ness** *n.*

common pleas *Law* in some States, a court having jurisdiction over civil and criminal trials

com·mons (käm'ənz) *n.pl.* 1. the common people 2. [*often with sing. v.*] **[C-]** *same as* HOUSE OF COMMONS 3. [*often with sing. v.*] a dining room, as at a college

common sense ordinary good sense or sound practical judgment —**com'mon-sense'** *adj.*

common stock ordinary capital stock in a company, without the privileges of preferred stock

com'mon·weal' (-wēl') *n.* the public good; the general welfare

com'mon·wealth' (-welth') *n.* 1. the people of a nation or state 2. a democracy or republic 3. a federation of states —**the Commonwealth** *same as* BRITISH COMMONWEALTH (OF NATIONS)

com·mo·tion (kə mō'shən) *n.* [< L. *com-*, together + *movere*, to move] 1. violent motion; turbulence 2. confusion; bustle

com·mu·nal (käm'yoon 'l, kə myoon''l) *adj.* 1. of a commune 2. of the community; public 3. characterized by common ownership of property —**com·mu'nal·ly** *adv.*

com·mune' (kə myoon') *vi.* -muned', -mun'ing [< OFr. *comuner*, to share] 1. to talk together intimately 2. to be in close rapport *[to commune with nature]*

com·mune² (käm'yoon) *n.* [< L. *communis*, common] 1. the smallest administrative district of local government in some European countries, as France 2. a small group of people living communally

com·mu·ni·ca·ble (kə myoo'ni kə b'l) *adj.* that can be communicated, as an idea, or transmitted, as a disease —**com·mu'ni·ca·bil'i·ty** *n.*

com·mu'ni·cant (-kənt) *n.* one who receives Holy Communion

com·mu·ni·cate (kə myoo'nə kāt') *vt.* -cat'ed, -cat'ing [< L. *communicare*] 1. to impart; transmit 2. to give (information, etc.) —*vi.* 1. to give or exchange information, etc. by talk, writing, etc. 2. to be connected, as rooms —**com·mu'ni·ca'tor** *n.*

com·mu·ni·ca·tion *n.* 1. a transmitting 2. a giving or exchanging of information, etc. by talk, writing, etc. 3. a message, letter, etc. 4. *[often pl.]* a means of communicating 5. *[often pl., with sing. v.]* a) the art of expressing ideas b) the science of transmitting information

com·mu·ni·ca·tive (kə myoo'nə kāt'iv, -ni kə tiv) *adj.* 1. giving information readily 2. of communication

com·mun·ion (kə myoon'yən) *n.* [see COMMON] 1. possession in common 2. a communing 3. a Christian denomination 4. [C-] a celebrating of Holy Communion

com·mu·ni·qué (kə myoo'nə kā') *n.* [Fr.] an official communication

com·mu·nism (käm'yə niz'm) *n.* [see COMMON] 1. a theory or system of the ownership of all property by the community 2. *[often C-]* a) socialism as formulated by Marx, Lenin, etc. b) any government or political movement supporting this

com'mu·nist (-nist) *n.* 1. an advocate or supporter of communism 2. [C-] a member of a Communist party —*adj.* 1. of or like communism or communists 2. advocating or supporting communism 3. [C-] designating or of a political party advocating Communism —**com'mu·nis'tic** *adj.* —**com'mu·nis'ti·cal·ly** *adv.*

com·mu·ni·ty (kə myoo'nə tē) *n., pl.* -ties [see COMMON] 1. a) all the people living in the same district, city, etc. b) the district, city, etc. where they live 2. a group of people having interests, work, etc. in common 3. society; the public 4. ownership or participation in common 5. a group of animals and plants living together and having close interactions

community chest a fund collected annually in many cities to support local welfare agencies

community college a junior college serving a certain community and partly supported by it

com·mu·nize (käm'yə nīz') *vt.* -nized', -niz'ing 1. to place under communal ownership 2. to make communistic —**com'mu·ni·za'tion** *n.*

com·mu·tate (käm'yə tāt') *vt.* -tat'ed, -tat'ing [< COMMUTATION] to change the direction of (an electric current) —**com'mu·ta'tor** *n.*

com·mu·ta·tion (käm'yə tā'shən) *n.* [see COMMUTE] 1. an exchange; substitution 2. the act of traveling as a commuter 3. a change of sentence or punishment to a less severe one

com·mute (kə myoot') *vt.* -mut'ed, -mut'ing [< L. *com-*, intens. + *mutare*, to change] 1. to exchange; substitute 2. to change (an obligation, punishment, etc.) to one that is less severe —*vi.* 1. to be a substitute 2. to travel as a commuter

com·mut'er *n.* one who travels regularly, esp. by train, bus, etc., between two points at some distance

Com·o·ros (käm'ə rōs') country on a group of islands off the SE coast of Africa: 700 sq. mi.; pop. 292,000

comp. 1. comparative 2. compound

com·pact (kəm pakt', käm'pakt) *adj.* [< L. *com-*, together + *pangere*, fasten] 1. closely and firmly packed; solid 2. taking little space 3. not wordy; terse 4. designating or of a small, light model of automobile —*vt.* 1. to

pack or join firmly together 2. to make by putting together —*n.* (käm'pakt) 1. a small cosmetic case, usually containing face powder and a mirror 2. a compact automobile 3. an agreement; covenant —**com·pact'ly** *adv.* —**com·pact'ness** *n.*

com·pac'tor (-pak'tər) *n.* a device that compresses trash into small bundles for easy disposal

com·pan·ion (kəm pan'yən) *n.* [< L. *com-*, with + *panis*, bread] 1. an associate; comrade 2. a person paid to live or travel with another 3. one of a pair or set —**com·pan'ion·ship'** *n.*

com·pan'ion·a·ble *adj.* sociable; warm and friendly —**com·pan'ion·a·bly** *adv.*

com·pan'ion·ate (-it) *adj.* of or like companions

com·pan'ion·way' *n.* a stairway from one deck of a ship to another

com·pa·ny (kum'pə nē) *n., pl.* -nies [see COMPANION] 1. companionship; society 2. a group of people gathered or associated for some purpose *[a business company]* 3. a guest or guests 4. companions 5. a military unit, normally composed of two or more platoons 6. a ship's crew —**keep company** 1. to associate (*with*) 2. to go together, as a couple intending to marry —**part company** to stop associating (*with*)

com·pa·ra·ble (käm'pər ə b'l) *adj.* 1. that can be compared 2. worthy of comparison —**com'pa·ra·bil'i·ty** *n.* —**com'pa·ra·bly** *adv.*

com·par·a·tive (kəm par'ə tiv) *adj.* 1. involving comparison as a method *[comparative linguistics]* 2. relative 3. *Gram.* designating the second degree of comparison of adjectives and adverbs —*n. Gram.* the comparative degree *[finer is the comparative of fine]* —**com·par'a·tive·ly** *adv.*

com·pare (kəm per') *vt.* -pared', -par'ing [< L. *com-*, with + *par*, equal] 1. to liken (*to*) 2. to examine for similarities or differences 3. *Gram.* to form the degrees of comparison of —*vi.* 1. to be worth comparing (*with*) 2. to make comparisons —**beyond** (or **past** or **without**) **compare** without equal

com·par·i·son (kəm par'ə s'n) *n.* 1. a comparing or being compared 2. likeness; similarity 3. *Gram.* change in an adjective or adverb to show the positive, comparative, and superlative degrees —**in comparison with** compared with

com·part·ment (kəm pärt'mənt) *n.* [< Fr. < L. *com-*, intens. + *partiri*, divide] 1. any of the divisions into which a space is partitioned off 2. a separate section, part, or category —*vt. same as* COMPARTMENTALIZE —**com·part'men'tal** (-men't'l) *adj.*

com·part·men'tal·ize' (-men'tə līz') *vt.* -ized', -iz'ing to put into separate compartments, divisions, or categories

com·pass (kum'pəs) *vt.* [< L. *com-*, together + *passus*, step] 1. to go around 2. to surround 3. to understand 4. to achieve or contrive —*n.* 1. *[often pl.]* an instrument having two pivoted legs, for drawing circles, taking measurements, etc. 2. a boundary 3. an enclosed area 4. range; scope 5. an instrument for showing direction, esp. one with a swinging magnetic needle that points to the magnetic north —**com'pass·a·ble** *adj.*

DRAWING COMPASS

com·pas·sion (kəm pash'ən) *n.* [< L. *com-*, together + *pati*, suffer] sorrow for the sufferings of another, with the urge to help; deep sympathy

com·pas·sion·ate (-it) *adj.* feeling or showing compassion —**com·pas·sion·ate·ly** *adv.*

com·pat·i·ble (kəm pat'ə b'l) *adj.* [see COMPASSION] getting along or going well together —**com·pat'i·bil'i·ty** *n.* —**com·pat'i·bly** *adv.*

com·pa·tri·ot (kəm pā'trē ət) *n.* [see COM- & PATRIOT] a fellow countryman

com·peer (käm'pir) *n.* [< L. *com-*, with + *par*, an equal] 1. an equal; peer 2. a companion; comrade

com·pel (kəm pel') *vt.* -pelled', -pel'ling [< L. *com-*, together + *pellere*, to drive] to force or get by force —**com·pel'ler** *n.* —**com·pel'ling·ly** *adv.*

com·pen·di·ous (kəm pen'dē əs) *adj.* [see COMPENDIUM] containing all the essentials in brief form; concise but comprehensive —**com·pen'di·ous·ly** *adv.*

com·pen·di·um (kəm pen'dē əm) *n., pl.* -ums, -a (-ə) [< L. *com-*, together + *pendere*, weigh] a concise but comprehensive summary

com·pen·sate (käm'pən sāt') *vt.* -sat'ed, -sat'ing [< L. *com-*, with + *pendere*, to weigh] 1. to make up for; counterbalance 2. to recompense; pay —*vi.* to make amends (for) —com′pen·sa′tor n. —com·pen·sa·to·ry (kəm pen′sə tôr′ē) adj.

com′pen·sa′tion (-sā′shən) n. 1. a compensating or being compensated 2. anything given as an equivalent, or to make amends

com·pete (kəm pēt′) vi. -pet′ed, -pet′ing [< L. com-, together + petere, seek] to be in rivalry; contend; vie (in a contest, etc.)

com·pe·tence (käm′pə təns) n. [see prec.] 1. sufficient means for one's needs 2. ability; fitness; specif., legal capability or jurisdiction Also com′pe·ten·cy

com′pe·tent (-tənt) adj. [see COMPETE] 1. capable; fit 2. sufficient; adequate 3. legally qualified or fit —com′pe·tent·ly adv.

com·pe·ti·tion (käm′pə tish′ən) n. 1. a competing; rivalry, esp. in business 2. a contest or match 3. the person or persons against whom one competes

com·pet·i·tive (kəm pet′ə tiv) adj. of, involving, or based on competition —com·pet′i·tive·ly adv. —com·pet′i·tive·ness n.

com·pet′i·tor (-tər) n. one who competes, as a business rival

com·pile (kəm pīl′) vt. -piled′, -pil′ing [< L. com-, together + pilare, to compress] 1. to gather together (statistics, facts, etc.) in an orderly form 2. to compose (a book, etc.) of materials from various sources —com·pi·la·tion (käm′pə lā′shən) n. —com·pil′er n.

com·pla·cen·cy (kəm plās′'n sē) n. [< L. com-, intens. + placere, please] quiet satisfaction; often, specif., self-satisfaction, or smugness: also com·pla′cence —com·pla′·cent adj.

com·plain (kəm plān′) vi. [< L. com-, intens. + plangere, strike (the breast)] 1. to express pain, displeasure, etc. 2. to find fault 3. to make an accusation or a formal charge —com·plain′er n. com·plain′ing·ly adv.

com·plain′ant (-ənt) n. one who files a charge or makes a complaint in court; plaintiff

com·plaint (kəm plānt′) n. 1. an utterance of pain, displeasure, etc. 2. a cause for complaining 3. an ailment 4. Law a formal charge

com·plai·sant (kəm plā′z'nt, -s'nt) adj. [see COMPLACENCY] willing to please; obliging —com·plai′·sance n. —com·plai′sant·ly adv.

com·plect·ed (kəm plek′tid) adj. [< COMPLEXIONED] [Dial. or Colloq.] same as COMPLEXIONED

com·ple·ment (käm′plə mənt) n. [see COMPLETE] 1. that which completes or perfects 2. the amount needed to fill or complete 3. a complete set 4. either of two parts that complete each other 5. Gram. a word or words completing the meaning of the predicate 6. Math. the number of degrees added to an angle or arc to make it equal 90 degrees —vt. (-ment′) to be a complement to

com′ple·men′ta·ry (-men′tər ē) adj. 1. acting as a complement; completing 2. mutually making up what is lacking —com′ple·men·tar′i·ty (-ter′ə tē) n.

complementary colors any two colors of the spectrum that combine to form white light

com·plete (kəm plēt′) adj. [< L. com-, intens. + plere, to fill] 1. lacking no parts; entire 2. finished 3. thorough; absolute —vt. -plet′ed, -plet′ing 1. to finish 2. to make whole or perfect —com·plete′ly —adv. —com·plete′ness n.

com·ple·tion (kəm plē′shən) n. 1. a completing, or finishing 2. the state of being completed

com·plex (kəm pleks′, käm′pleks) adj. [< L. com-, with + plectere, to weave] 1. consisting of two or more related parts 2. complicated —n. (käm′pleks) 1. a complex whole 2. a unified grouping, as of buildings 3. Psychoanalysis a) a group of mostly unconscious impulses and attitudes toward something, strongly influencing behavior b) loosely, an obsession —com·plex′ly adv. —com·plex′ness n.

complex fraction a fraction with a fraction in its numerator or denominator, or in both

com·plex·ion (kəm plek′shən) n. [see COMPLEX] 1. the color, texture, etc. of the skin, esp. of the face 2. nature; character; aspect

com·plex′ioned adj. having a (specified) complexion [light-complexioned]

com·plex·i·ty (kəm plek′sə tē) n. 1. a complex condition or quality 2. pl. -ties anything complex or intricate; complication

complex sentence a sentence consisting of a main clause and one or more subordinate clauses

com·pli·ance (kəm plī′əns) n. 1. a complying with a request, demand, etc. 2. a tendency to give in to others —in compliance with complying with

com·pli′ant adj. complying; yielding; submissive —com·pli′ant·ly adv.

com·pli·cate (käm′plə kāt′) vt., vi. -cat′ed, -cat′ing [< L. com-, together + plicare, to fold] to make or become intricate, difficult, or involved

com′pli·cat′ed adj. intricately involved; hard to solve, analyze, etc. —com′pli·cat′ed·ly adv.

com′pli·ca′tion n. 1. a complicating 2. a complicated condition 3. a complicating factor 4. Med. a second disease or abnormal condition occurring in the course of a primary disease

com·plic·i·ty (kəm plis′ə tē) n., pl. -ties [see COMPLEX] partnership in wrongdoing

com·pli·ment (käm′plə mənt) n. [Fr. < L.: see COMPLETE] 1. a formal act of courtesy 2. something said in praise 3. [pl.] respects —vt. (-ment′) to pay a compliment to

com′pli·men′ta·ry (-men′tər ē) adj. 1. paying or containing a compliment 2. given free as a courtesy [a complimentary ticket]

com·ply (kəm plī′) vi. -plied′, -ply′ing [see COMPLETE] to act in accordance (with a request, order, etc.) —com·pli′er n.

com·po·nent (kəm pō′nənt) adj. [< L. com-, together + ponere, put] serving as one of the parts of a whole —n. a part, element, or ingredient

com·port (kəm pôrt′) vt. [< L. com-, together + portare, bring] to behave (oneself) in a specified manner —vi. to agree or accord (with) —com·port′ment n.

com·pose (kəm pōz′) vt. -posed′, -pos′ing [< OFr. com-, with + poser, to place] 1. to make up; constitute 2. to put in proper form 3. to create (a musical or literary work) 4. to adjust or settle [to compose differences] 5. to make calm 6. to set (type) —vi. 1. to create musical or literary works 2. to set type

com·posed′ adj. calm; self-possessed —com·pos′ed·ly (-pō′zid lē) adv.

com·pos′er n. a person who composes, esp. one who composes music

com·pos·ite (kəm päz′it) adj. [< L. com-, together + ponere, put] 1. formed of distinct parts 2. designating a family of plants, as the daisy, with flower heads composed of clusters of small flowers —n. a composite thing —com·pos′ite·ly adv.

com·po·si·tion (käm′pə zish′ən) n. 1. a composing; specif., a) the art of writing b) the creation of musical works 2. the makeup of a thing or person 3. something composed, as a piece of writing or a musical work 4. an aesthetically unified arrangement of parts 5. the work of setting type

com·pos·i·tor (kəm päz′ə tər) n. a person who sets type; typesetter

com·post (käm′pōst) n. [see COMPOSITE] a mixture of decomposing vegetation, manure, etc. for fertilizing soil

com·po·sure (kəm pō′zhər) n. [see COMPOSE] calmness; self-possession

com·pote (käm′pōt) n. [Fr.: see COMPOSITE] 1. a dish of stewed fruits 2. a long-stemmed dish for candy, fruit, etc.

com·pound¹ (käm pound′, kəm-) vt. [see COMPOSITE] 1. to mix or combine 2. to make by combining parts 3. to intensify by adding new elements 4. to compute (interest) as compound interest —adj. (käm′pound, käm pound′) made up of two or more parts —n. (käm′pound) 1. a thing formed by combining parts 2. a substance containing two or more elements chemically combined in fixed proportions 3. a word composed of two or more base morphemes —compound a felony (or crime) to agree, for payment, not to prosecute a felony (or crime)

com·pound² (käm′pound) n. [Malay kampong] in the Orient, an enclosed space with one or more buildings in it, esp. if occupied by foreigners

compound fraction same as COMPLEX FRACTION

compound fracture a fracture in which the broken bone pierces the skin

compound interest interest paid on both the principal and the accumulated unpaid interest

compound leaf a leaf divided into two or more leaflets with a common stalk

compound sentence a sentence consisting of two or more independent, coordinate clauses

com·pre·hend (käm′prə hend′) vt. [< L. com-, with +

prehendere, seize] **1.** to grasp mentally; understand **2.** to include; comprise —**com'pre·hen'si·ble** (-hen'sə b'l) *adj.* —**com'pre·hen'si·bly** *adv.*

com'pre·hen'sion (-hen'shən) *n.* **1.** an including or comprising **2.** the act of or capacity for understanding

com'pre·hen'sive *adj.* **1.** including much; inclusive **2.** able to understand fully —**com'pre·hen'sive·ly** *adv.* —**com'pre·hen'sive·ness** *n.*

com·press (kəm pres') *vt.* [< L. *com-*, together + *premere*, to press] **1.** to press together and make more compact **2.** to put (air, gas, etc.) under pressure —*n.* (käm'pres) a pad of folded cloth, often medicated or wet, applied to a part of the body —**com·pressed'** *adj.* —**com·pres'si·bil'i·ty** *n.* —**com·pres'si·ble** *adj.*

com·pres·sion (kəm presh'ən) *n.* **1.** a compressing or being compressed **2.** the compressing of a working fluid in an engine, as of the mixture in an internal-combustion engine just before ignition

com·pres'sor (-pres'ər) *n.* **1.** one that compresses **2.** a muscle that compresses a part **3.** a machine for compressing air, gas, etc.

com·prise (kəm prīz') *vt.* -**prised'**, -**pris'ing** [see COMPREHEND] **1.** to include; contain **2.** to consist of **3.** to make up; form: considered a loose usage by some —**com·pris'al** *n.*

com·pro·mise (käm'prə mīz') *n.* [< L. *com-*, together + *promittere*, to promise] **1.** a settlement in which each side makes concessions **2.** the result of such a settlement **3.** something midway **4.** exposure, as of one's reputation, to criticism or disgrace —*vt.* -**mised'**, -**mis'ing 1.** to settle by compromise **2.** to lay open to criticism or disgrace **3.** to weaken (one's principles, etc.) —*vi.* to make a compromise —**com'pro·mis'er** *n.*

comp·trol·ler (kən trō'lər) *n.* [altered (after Fr. *compte*, an account) < CONTROLLER] *same as* CONTROLLER (sense 1) —**comp·trol'ler·ship'** *n.*

com·pul·sion (kəm pul'shən) *n.* **1.** a compelling or being compelled; coercion **2.** a driving force **3.** *Psychol.* an irresistible, irrational impulse to perform some act —**com·pul'sive** (-siv) *adj.* —**com·pul'sive·ly** *adv.* —**com·pul'sive·ness** *n.*

com·pul·so·ry (-sər ē) *adj.* **1.** obligatory; required **2.** compelling —**com·pul'so·ri·ly** *adv.*

com·punc·tion (kəm puŋk'shən) *n.* [< L. *com-*, intens. + *pungere*, to prick] an uneasy feeling prompted by guilt —**com·punc'tious** *adj.*

com·pu·ta·tion (käm'pyoo tā'shən) *n.* **1.** a computing; calculation **2.** a result obtained in computing —**com'pu·ta'tion·al** *adj.*

com·pute (kəm pyōōt') *vt.*, *vi.* -**put'ed**, -**put'ing** [< L. *com-*, with + *putare*, reckon] to determine (an amount, etc.) by reckoning; calculate —**com·put'a·ble** *adj.*

com·put·er (kəm pyōōt'ər) *n.* a person or thing that computes; specif., an electronic machine that performs rapid, often complex calculations or compiles, correlates, and selects data

com·put·er·ize' (-īz') *vt.* -**ized'**, -**iz'ing** to equip with, or operate, produce, control, etc. by or as by means of, an electronic computer —**com·put'er·i·za'tion** *n.*

com·rade (käm'rad) *n.* [< Sp. *camarada*, chamber mate < L. *camera*, room] **1.** a friend; close companion **2.** an associate —**com'rade·ly** *adv.* —**com'rade·ship'** *n.*

con¹ (kän) *adv.* [< L. *contra*, against /pro and con/ —*n.* a reason, vote, etc. in opposition

con² (kän) *vt.* **conned**, **con'ning** [< OE. *cunnan*, know] to study carefully

con³ (kän) *n.*, *vt.* **conned**, **con'ning** *same as* CONN

con⁴ (kän) *adj.* [Slang] *same as* CONFIDENCE /a con man/ —*vt.* **conned**, **con'ning** [Slang] **1.** to swindle (a victim) by first gaining his confidence **2.** to trick, esp. by glib, persuasive talk

con⁵ (kän) *n.* [Slang] a convict

con- *same as* COM-: used before *c*, *d*, *g*, *j*, *n*, *q*, *s*, *t*, and *v*

con·cat·e·na·tion (kän kat''n ā'shən) *n.* [< L. *com-*, together + *catena*, a chain] a connected series, as of events, regarded as causally connected

con·cave (kän kāv', kän'kāv) *adj.* [< L. *com-*, intens. + *cavus*, hollow] hollow and curved like the inside half of a hollow ball —*n.* (*usually* kän'kāv) a concave surface, line, etc. —**con·cave'ly** *adv.* —**con·cav'i·ty** (-kav'ə tē) *n.*, *pl.* -**ties**

con·ceal (kən sēl') *vt.* [< L. *com-*, together + *celare*, to hide] **1.** to hide **2.** to keep secret —**con·ceal'ment** *n.*

con·cede (kən sēd') *vt.* -**ced'ed**, -**ced'ing** [< L. *com-*, with + *cedere*, cede] **1.** to admit as true or certain **2.** to grant as a right —*vi.* **1.** to make a concession **2.** to acknowledge defeat in an election

con·ceit (kən sēt') *n.* [see CONCEIVE] **1.** an exaggerated opinion of oneself, one's merits, etc.; vanity **2.** a fanciful or witty expression or notion

con·ceit'ed *adj.* having an exaggerated opinion of oneself; vain —**con·ceit'ed·ly** *adv.*

con·ceiv·a·ble (kən sē'və b'l) *adj.* that can be understood, imagined, or believed —**con·ceiv'a·bil'i·ty** *n.* —**con·ceiv'a·bly** *adv.*

con·ceive (kən sēv') *vt.* -**ceived'**, -**ceiv'ing** [< L. *com-*, together + *capere*, take] **1.** to become pregnant with **2.** to form in the mind **3.** to imagine **4.** to understand —*vi.* **1.** to become pregnant **2.** to form an idea (*of*) —**con·ceiv'er** *n.*

con·cen·trate (kän'sən trāt') *vt.* -**trat'ed**, -**trat'ing** [< L. *com-*, together + *centrum*, center + -ATE¹] **1.** to focus (one's thoughts, efforts, etc.) **2.** to increase the strength, density, etc. of —*vi.* to fix one's attention (*on* or *upon*) —*n.* a substance that has been concentrated —*adj.* concentrated —**con'cen·tra'tor** *n.*

con'cen·tra'tion *n.* **1.** a concentrating or being concentrated **2.** close or fixed attention **3.** strength or density, as of a solution

concentration camp a place of confinement for political dissidents, members of minority ethnic groups, etc.

con·cen·tric (kən sen'trik) *adj.* [< L. *com-*, together + *centrum*, center] having a center in common, as circles —**con·cen'tri·cal·ly** *adv.*

con·cept (kän'sept) *n.* [see CONCEIVE] an idea, esp. a generalized idea of a class of objects

con·cep·tion (kən sep'shən) *n.* **1.** a conceiving or being conceived in the womb **2.** the beginning, as of a process **3.** the formulation of ideas **4.** a concept **5.** an original idea or design —**con·cep'tive** *adj.*

con·cep'tu·al (-chōō wəl) *adj.* of conception or concepts —**con·cep'tu·al·ly** *adv.*

con·cep'tu·al·ize' (-īz') *vt.* -**ized'**, -**iz'ing** to form a concept or idea of; conceive —**con·cep'tu·al·i·za'tion** *n.*

con·cern (kən surn') *vt.* [< L. *com-*, with + *cernere*, sift] **1.** to have a relation to **2.** to engage or involve **3.** to make uneasy —*n.* **1.** a matter of importance to one **2.** interest in or regard for a person or thing **3.** relation; reference **4.** worry; anxiety **5.** a business firm —**as concerns** in regard to —**concern oneself 1.** to busy oneself **2.** to be worried

con·cerned' *adj.* **1.** involved or interested (often with *in*) **2.** uneasy or anxious

con·cern'ing *prep.* relating to; about

con·cert (kän'sərt) *n.* [< L. *com-*, with + *certare*, strive] **1.** mutual agreement; concord **2.** a program of vocal or instrumental music —*adj.* of or for concerts —**in concert** in unison

con·cert·ed (kən sur'tid) *adj.* mutually arranged or agreed upon; combined —**con·cert'ed·ly** *adv.*

con·cer·ti·na (kän'sər tē'nə) *n.* [< CONCERT] a small accordion

con·cert·ize (kän'sər tīz') *vi.* -**ized'**, -**iz'ing** to perform as a soloist in concerts, esp. on a tour

con·cer·to (kən cher'tō) *n.*, *pl.* -**tos**, -**ti** (-tē) [It.] a composition, usually in three movements, for one or more solo instruments and an orchestra

con·ces·sion (kən sesh'ən) *n.* **1.** a conceding **2.** a thing conceded; acknowledgment, as of an argument **3.** a privilege granted by a government, company, etc., as the right to sell food at a park —**con·ces'sive** (-ses'iv) *adj.*

con·ces'sion·aire' (-ə ner') *n.* [< Fr.] the holder of a concession (sense 3): also **con·ces'sion·er**

conch (käŋk, känch) *n.*, *pl.* **conchs** (käŋks), **conch'es** (kän'chəz) [< Gr. *konchē*] **1.** the spiral, one-piece shell of various sea mollusks **2.** such a mollusk

con·ci·erge (kän'sē urzh'; *Fr.* kôn syerzh') *n.* [Fr.] a custodian, as of an apartment house

con·cil·i·ar (kən sil'ē ər) *adj.* of, from, or by means of a council

con·cil·i·ate (kən sil'ē āt') *vt.* -**at'ed**, -**at'ing** [see COUNCIL] to win over; make friendly; placate —**con·cil'i·a'tion** *n.* —**con·cil'i·a'tor** *n.*

con·cil'i·a·to'ry (-ə tôr'ē) *adj.* tending to conciliate: also **con·cil'i·a'tive** (-āt'iv)

con·cise (kən sīs') *adj.* [< L. *com-*, intens. + *caedere*, to cut] brief and to the point; short and clear —**con·cise'ly** *adv.* —**con·cise'ness**, **con·ci'sion** (-sizh'ən) *n.*

con·clave (kän'klāv, käŋ'-) *n.* [< L. *com-*, with + *clavis*, a key] a private meeting, specif. one held by the cardinals to elect a pope

CONCH

con·clude (kən klōōd') *vt., vi.* **-clud'ed, -clud'ing** [< L. *com-*, together + *claudere*, to shut] **1.** to bring or come to an end; finish **2.** to infer; deduce **3.** to decide; determine **4.** to arrange (a treaty, etc.)

con·clu·sion (kən klōō'zhən) *n.* **1.** the end or last part **2.** a judgment or opinion formed after thought **3.** an outcome **4.** a concluding (*of* a treaty, etc.) —**in conclusion** lastly; in closing

con·clu'sive (-siv) *adj.* that settles a question; decisive; final —**con·clu'sive·ly** *adv.* —**con·clu'sive·ness** *n.*

con·coct (kən käkt', kän-) *vt.* [< L. *com-*, together + *coquere*, to cook] **1.** to make by combining ingredients **2.** to devise; plan —**con·coc'tion** *n.*

con·com·i·tance (kən käm'ə təns, kän-) *n.* the fact of being concomitant: also **con·com'i·tan·cy**

con·com·i·tant (kən käm'ə tənt, kän-) *adj.* [< L. *com-*, together + *comes*, companion] accompanying; attendant —*n.* a concomitant condition, thing, etc. —**con·com'i·tant·ly** *adv.*

Con·cord (käŋ'kərd) **1.** capital of N.H.: pop. 30,000 **2.** town in E Mass.: site of one of the 1st battles of the Revolutionary War: pop. 16,000 —*n.* a large, dark-blue grape: in full, **Concord grape**

con·cord (kän'kôrd, käŋ'-) *n.* [< L. *com-*, together + *cor*, heart] **1.** agreement; harmony **2.** peaceful relations, as between nations **3.** a treaty establishing this

con·cord·ance (kən kôr'd'ns, kän-) *n.* **1.** agreement; harmony **2.** an alphabetical list of the words in a book, with references to the passages where they occur

con·cord'ant *adj.* agreeing; harmonious

con·cor·dat (kən kôr'dat, kän-) *n.* [see CONCORD] **1.** a compact; formal agreement **2.** an agreement between a pope and a government on church matters

con·course (kän'kôrs, käŋ'-) *n.* [see CONCUR] **1.** a crowd; throng **2.** an open space where crowds gather, as in an airport terminal **3.** a broad boulevard

con·crete (kän krēt', kän'krēt) *adj.* [< L. *com-*, together + *crescere*, to grow] **1.** having a material existence; real; actual **2.** specific, not general or abstract **3.** made of concrete —*n.* (*usually* kän'krēt) **1.** a concrete thing, idea, etc. **2.** a hard building material made of sand and gravel bonded together with cement —*vt.* **-cret'ed, -cret'ing 1.** to solidify **2.** (*usually* kän'krēt) to cover with concrete —*vi.* to solidify —**con·crete'ly** *adv.* —**con·crete'ness** *n.*

con·cre·tion (kän krē'shən, kən-) *n.* **1.** a solidifying or being solidified **2.** a solidified mass

con·cu·bine (käŋ'kyə bīn', kän'-) *n.* [< L. *com-*, with + *cubare*, to lie down] **1.** a woman who cohabits with a man although not legally married to him **2.** in some societies, a secondary wife having inferior status

con·cu·pis·cence (kän kyōōp'ə s'ns) *n.* [< L. *com-*, intens. + *cupere*, to desire] strong desire, esp. sexual desire; lust —**con·cu'pis·cent** *adj.*

con·cur (kən kur') *vi.* **-curred', -cur'ring** [< L. *com-*, together + *currere*, to run] **1.** to occur at the same time; coincide **2.** to act together **3.** to agree

con·cur'rence *n.* **1.** a happening together in time or place **2.** a combining to bring about something **3.** agreement; accord

con·cur'rent *adj.* **1.** occurring at the same time **2.** acting together; cooperating **3.** in agreement **4.** *Law* exercised equally over the same area

con·cus·sion (kən kush'ən) *n.* [< L. *com-*, together + *quatere*, to shake] **1.** a violent shaking; shock, as from impact **2.** impaired functioning, esp. of the brain, caused by a violent blow or impact —**con·cus'sive** (-kus'iv) *adj.*

con·demn (kən dem') *vt.* [< L. *com-*, intens. + *damnare*, to harm] **1.** to disapprove of strongly; censure **2.** to declare guilty; convict **3.** to inflict a penalty upon **4.** to doom **5.** to appropriate (property) for public use **6.** to declare unfit for use —**con·demn'er** *n.*

con·dem·na·tion (kän'dem nā'shən) *n.* **1.** a condemning or being condemned **2.** a cause for condemning

con·dem·na·to·ry (kən dem'nə tôr'ē) *adj.* expressing condemnation

con·den·sa·tion (kän'dən sā'shən) *n.* **1.** a condensing or being condensed **2.** a product of condensing

con·dense (kən dens') *vt.* **-densed', -dens'ing** [< L. *com-*, intens. + *densus*, dense] **1.** to make more dense or compact **2.** to express in fewer words **3.** to change to a denser form, as from a gas to a liquid —*vi.* to become condensed —**con·dens'a·ble, con·dens'i·ble** *adj.*

condensed milk a thick milk made by evaporating part of the water from cow's milk and adding sugar

con·dens'er *n.* one that condenses; specif., *a*) an apparatus for liquefying gases *b*) a lens for concentrating light rays on an area *c*) *Elec. same as* CAPACITOR

con·de·scend (kän'də send') *vi.* [< L. *com-*, together + *descendere*, descend] **1.** to be graciously willing to do something regarded as beneath one's dignity **2.** to deal with others patronizingly —**con'de·scen'sion** *n.*

con·dign (kən dīn') *adj.* [< L. *com-*, intens. + *dignus*, worthy] deserved; suitable: said esp. of punishment

con·di·ment (kän'də mənt) *n.* [< L. *condire*, to pickle] a seasoning or relish for food, as pepper, mustard, etc.

con·di·tion (kən dish'ən) *n.* [< L. *com-*, together + *dicere*, speak] **1.** anything required before the performance, completion, or existence of something else; provision or prerequisite **2.** anything that modifies the nature of something else [good business *conditions*] **3.** state of being **4.** *a*) [Colloq.] an illness [a heart *condition*] *b*) a healthy state [athletes out of *condition*] **5.** social position; rank —*vt.* **1.** to stipulate **2.** to impose a condition on **3.** to be a condition of **4.** to bring into fit condition **5.** to make accustomed (*to*) —**on condition that** provided that —**con·di'tion·er** *n.*

con·di'tion·al *adj.* containing, expressing, or dependent on a condition; qualified —**con·di'tion·al·ly** *adv.*

con·do (kän'dō) *n., pl.* **-dos, -does** *clipped form of* CONDOMINIUM (sense 2)

con·dole (kən dōl') *vi.* **-doled', -dol'ing** [< L. *com-*, with + *dolere*, to grieve] to express sympathy; commiserate —**con·dol'er** *n.*

con·do'lence (-dō'ləns) *n.* expression of sympathy with another in grief: also **con·dole'ment**

con·do·min·i·um (kän'də min'ē əm) *n.* [ModL. < L. *com-*, together + *dominium*, dominion] **1.** joint rule by two or more states **2.** *pl.* **-i·ums, -i·a** (-ə) an apartment building or multiple-dwelling-unit complex in which each tenant owns his own unit

con·done (kən dōn') *vt.* **-doned', -don'ing** [< L. *com-*, intens. + *donare*, give] to forgive, pardon, or overlook (an offense) —**con·don'a·ble** *adj.* —**con·do·na·tion** (kän'dō nā'shən) *n.* —**con·don'er** *n.*

con·dor (kän'dər) *n.* [Sp. < PeruvInd. *cuntur*] **1.** a large vulture of the S. American Andes, with a bare head **2.** a similar vulture of California

con·duce (kən dōōs') *vi.* **-duced', -duc'ing** [< L. *com-*, together + *ducere*, to lead] to tend or lead (*to* an effect); contribute —**con·du'cive** *adj.*

con·duct (kän'dukt'; *for v.* kən dukt') *n.* [see *prec.*] **1.** management; handling **2.** the way one acts; behavior —*vt.* **1.** to lead **2.** to manage or control **3.** to direct (an orchestra, etc.) **4.** to behave (oneself) **5.** to be able to transmit [copper *conducts* electricity] —*vi.* **1.** to lead **2.** to act as a conductor

con·duc·tion (kən duk'shən) *n.* **1.** a conveying **2.** *Physics a*) transmission (*of* electricity, heat, etc.) by the passage of energy from particle to particle *b*) *same as* CONDUCTIVITY

con·duc·tive (-tiv) *adj.* having conductivity

con·duc·tiv·i·ty (kän'duk tiv'ə tē) *n.* the property of conducting heat, electricity, etc.

con·duc·tor (kən duk'tər) *n.* **1.** one who conducts; leader **2.** the director of an orchestra, etc. **3.** one in charge of passengers on a train, etc. **4.** a thing that conducts electricity, heat, etc.

con·duit (kän'dit, -dōō wit) *n.* [see CONDUCE] **1.** a pipe or channel for conveying fluids **2.** a tube for electric wires

cone (kōn) *n.* [< Gr. *kōnos*] **1.** *a*) a solid with a circle for its base and a curved surface tapering evenly to a point *b*) a surface described by a moving straight line passing through a fixed point and tracing a fixed curve, as a circle, at another point **2.** any object shaped like a cone **3.** a reproductive structure of certain lower plants, with a central axis bearing overlapping scales, bracts, etc. which produce pollen or ovules —*vt.* **coned, con'ing** to shape like a cone

CONE (blue spruce)

co·ney (kō'nē) *n., pl.* **-neys, -nies** [< L. *cuniculus*] **1.** a rabbit **2.** rabbit fur

Co·ney Island (kō'nē) beach & amusement park in Brooklyn, N.Y.

con·fab (kän'fab') *n.* [ult. < L. *com-*, together + *fabulari*, to talk] [Colloq.] an informal talk; chat

con·fec·tion (kən fek'shən) *n.* [< L. *com-*, with + *facere*, to make] any candy or other sweet preparation, as ice cream —**con·fec'tion·ar'y** *adj.*

---

fat, āpe, cär; ten, ēven; is, bīte; gō, hôrn, tōol, look; oil, out; up, fur; thin, *th*en; zh, leisure; ŋ, ring; ə for *a* in *ago*; ' as in *able* (ā'b'l); ë, Fr. coeur; ö, Fr. feu; Fr. mo*n*; ü, Fr. duc; *r*, Fr. cri; kh, G. doch, ich. ‡ foreign; < derived from

con·fec'tion·er *n.* one who makes or sells candy and other confections

confectioners' sugar very fine powdered sugar

con·fec'tion·er'y (-er'ē) *n., pl.* **-ies** 1. confections or candy, collectively 2. the business, work, or shop of a confectioner

con·fed·er·a·cy (kən fed'ər ə sē) *n., pl.* **-cies** a league or alliance of people or nations united for a common purpose —**the Confederacy** the league of eleven Southern States that seceded from the U.S. in 1860 & 1861: official name **Confederate States of America**

con·fed·er·ate (kən fed'ər it) *adj.* [< L. *com-*, together + *foedus*, a league] 1. united in an alliance 2. [C-] of the Confederacy —*n.* 1. an ally; associate 2. an accomplice 3. [C-] a Southern supporter of the Confederacy —*vt., vi.* (-ə rāt') -at'ed, -at'ing to unite in a confederacy; ally

con·fed·er·a'tion (-ə rā'shən) *n.* 1. a uniting or being united in a league or alliance 2. nations or states joined in a league —**the Confederation** the United States from 1781 to 1789

con·fer (kən fur') *vt.* -ferred', -fer'ring [< L. *com-*, together + *ferre*, bring] to give; bestow —*vi.* to have a conference —**con·fer'ment, con·fer'ral** *n.*

con·fer·ee (kän'fə rē') *n.* 1. a participant in a conference 2. one on whom an honor is conferred

con·fer·ence (kän'fər əns, -frəns) *n.* 1. a formal meeting for discussion 2. an association, as of colleges or athletic teams

con·fess (kən fes') *vt., vi.* [< L. *com-*, together + *fateri*, acknowledge] 1. to admit or acknowledge (a fault, crime, belief, etc.) 2. *a)* to tell (one's sins) to God *b)* to hear the confession of (a person): said of a priest —**confess to** to acknowledge

con·fes·sion (kən fesh'ən) *n.* 1. a confessing; admission of guilt or sin 2. something confessed 3. a statement of religious beliefs 4. a sect; communion

con·fes'sion·al *n.* an enclosure in a church, where a priest hears confessions —*adj.* of or for confession

con·fes'sor *n.* 1. one who confesses 2. a priest authorized to hear confessions

con·fet·ti (kən fet'ē) *n.pl.* [*with sing. v.*] [It.] bits of colored paper scattered about at celebrations, etc.

con·fi·dant (kän'fə dant') *n.* a close, trusted friend —**con'fi·dante'** *n.fem.*

con·fide (kən fīd') *vi.* -fid'ed, -fid'ing [< L. *com-*, intens. + *fidere*, to trust] to trust (*in* someone), esp. by sharing secrets —*vt.* 1. to tell about as a secret 2. to entrust (*to*) —**con·fid'er** *n.*

con·fi·dence (kän'fə dəns) *n.* 1. firm belief; trust; reliance 2. certainty; assurance 3. belief in one's own abilities; self-confidence 4. the belief that another will keep a secret [told in strict *confidence*] 5. something told as a secret —*adj.* swindling or used to swindle

confidence game a swindle effected by one (**confidence man**) who first gains the confidence of his victim

con·fi·dent (-dənt) *adj.* full of confidence; specif., *a)* certain *b)* sure of oneself —**con'fi·dent·ly** *adv.*

con·fi·den'tial (-den'shəl) *adj.* 1. secret 2. of or showing confidence 3. entrusted with private matters [a *confidential* agent] —**con'fi·den'tial·ly** *adv.*

con·fid·ing (kən fīd'iŋ) *adj.* trustful or inclined to trust —**con·fid'ing·ly** *adv.*

con·fig·u·ra·tion (kən fig'yə rā'shən) *n.* [< L. *com-*, together + *figurare*, to form] 1. arrangement of parts 2. form, contour, or structure; outline

con·fine (kən fīn'; *for n.* kän'fīn) *n.* [< L. *com-*, with + *finis*, an end] [*usually pl.*] a boundary or bounded region; border —*vt.* -fined', -fin'ing 1. to keep within limits; restrict 2. to keep shut up, as in prison, a sickbed, etc. —**con·fine'ment** *n.*

con·firm (kən furm') *vt.* [< L. *com-*, intens. + *firmus*, firm] 1. to make firm; strengthen 2. to make valid by formal approval; ratify 3. to prove to be true; verify 4. to cause to undergo religious confirmation —**con·firm'a·ble** *adj.*

con·fir·ma·tion (kän'fər mā'shən) *n.* 1. a confirming or being confirmed 2. something that confirms 3. a ceremony admitting a person to full church membership

con·firmed' *adj.* 1. firmly established; habitual [a *confirmed* liar] 2. corroborated; proved

con·fis·cate (kän'fə skāt') *vt.* -cat'ed, -cat'ing [< L. *com-*, together + *fiscus*, treasury] 1. to seize (private property) for the public treasury 2. to seize as by authority; appropriate —**con'fis·ca'tion** *n.*

con·fis·ca·to·ry (kən fis'kə tôr'ē) *adj.* 1. of, constituting, or effecting confiscation [a *confiscatory* tax] 2. confiscating

con·fla·gra·tion (kän'flə grā'shən) *n.* [< L. *com-*, intens. + *flagrare*, burn] a big, destructive fire

con·flict (kən flikt'; *for n.* kän'flikt) *vi.* [< L. *com-*, together + *fligere*, to strike] to be antagonistic, incompatible, or contradictory; clash —*n.* 1. a fight or struggle; war 2. sharp disagreement, as of interests or ideas 3. emotional disturbance

con·flu·ence (kän'flōō əns) *n.* [< L. *com-*, together + *fluere*, to flow] 1. a flowing together, esp. of streams 2. the place of this 3. a coming together, as of people; crowd —**con'flu·ent** *adj.*

con·form (kən fôrm') *vt.* [< L. *com-*, together + *formare*, to form] 1. to make similar 2. to bring into agreement; adapt —*vi.* 1. to be or become similar 2. to be in agreement 3. to act in accordance with rules, customs, etc. —**con·form'ist** *n.*

con·form'a·ble *adj.* 1. that conforms; specif., *a)* similar *b)* in agreement *c)* adapted 2. quick to conform; obedient —**con·form'a·bly** *adv.*

con·for·ma·tion (kän'fôr mā'shən) *n.* 1. a symmetrical arrangement of the parts of a thing 2. the structure or form of a thing as determined by the arrangement of its parts; specif., the shape or outline

con·form·i·ty (kən fôr'mə tē) *n., pl.* -ties 1. agreement; correspondence 2. a conforming to rules, customs, etc. Also **con·form'ance**

con·found (kən found', kän-) *vt.* [< L. *com-*, together + *fundere*, pour] 1. to mix up indiscriminately 2. to confuse; bewilder 3. to damn: a mild oath

con·found'ed *adj.* 1. confused; bewildered 2. damned: a mild oath —**con·found'ed·ly** *adv.*

con·fra·ter·ni·ty (kän'frə tur'nə tē) *n., pl.* -ties [see COM- & FRATERNITY] 1. a brotherhood 2. a group of men associated for some purpose, often religious

con·frere (kän'frer, kōn'-) *n.* [OFr.] a colleague; associate

con·front (kən frunt') *vt.* [< L. *com-*, together + *frons*, front] 1. to face, esp. boldly or defiantly 2. to bring face to face (*with*) —**con·fron·ta·tion** (kän'frən tā'shən) *n.*

Con·fu·cian·ism (kən fyōō'shən iz'm) *n.* the ethical teachings of Confucius, emphasizing devotion to parents, ancestor worship, and the maintenance of justice and peace —**Con·fu'cian·ist** *n., adj.*

Con·fu·cius (kən fyōō'shəs) 551?-479? B.C.; Chin. philosopher & teacher —**Con·fu'cian** *adj., n.*

con·fuse (kən fyōōz') *vt.* -fused', -fus'ing [see CONFOUND] 1. to mix up; put into disorder 2. to bewilder; perplex 3. to embarrass; disconcert 4. to mistake the identity of —**con·fus'ed·ly** *adv.*

con·fu·sion (kən fyōō'zhən) *n.* a confusing or being confused; specif., disorder, bewilderment, etc.

con·fute (kən fyōōt') *vt.* -fut'ed, -fut'ing [< L. *confutare*] to prove (a person, statement, etc.) to be in error or false —**con·fu·ta·tion** (kän'fyoo tā'shən) *n.*

Cong. 1. Congress 2. Congressional

con·geal (kən jēl') *vt., vi.* [< L. *com-*, together + *gelare*, freeze] 1. to solidify or thicken by cooling or freezing 2. to thicken; coagulate; jell —**con·geal'a·ble** *adj.* —**congeal'ment** *n.*

con·gen·ial (kən jēn'yəl) *adj.* [see COM- & GENIAL] 1. kindred; compatible 2. of the same temperament; sympathetic 3. suited to one's needs; agreeable —**con·ge'ni·al'·i·ty** (-jēn'ē al'ə tē) *n.* —**con·gen'ial·ly** *adv.*

con·gen·i·tal (kən jen'ə t'l) *adj.* [< L.: see COM- & GENITAL] existing as such at birth [a *congenital* disease] —**con·gen'i·tal·ly** *adv.*

con·ger (**eel**) (käŋ'gər) [< Gr. *gongros*] a large, edible saltwater eel

con·gest (kən jest') *vt.* [< L. *com-*, together + *gerere*, carry] 1. to cause too much blood to accumulate in the vessels of (a part of the body) 2. to fill to excess; overcrowd —*vi.* to become congested —**con·ges'tion** *n.* —**con·ges'tive** *adj.*

con·glom·er·ate (kən gläm'ə rāt'; *for adj. & n.* -ər it) *vt., vi.* -at'ed, -at'ing [< L. *com-*, together + *glomus*, ball] to form into a rounded mass —*adj.* 1. formed into a rounded mass 2. made up of separate substances collected into a single mass 3. *Geol.* made up of rock fragments or pebbles cemented together by clay, silica, etc. —*n.* 1. a conglomerate mass; cluster 2. a large corporation formed by merging many diverse companies 3. *Geol.* a conglomerate rock —**con·glom'er·a'tion** *n.*

Con·go (käŋ'gō) 1. river in C Africa, flowing into the Atlantic: c.2,900 mi. 2. country in WC Africa, west of Zaire: 132,046 sq. mi.; pop. 826,000; cap. Brazzaville 3. *former name of* ZAIRE —**Con'go·lese'** (-gə lēz') *adj., n.*

congo eel (or **snake**) an eellike amphibious animal with two pairs of small, weak legs, of the SE U.S.

con·grat·u·late (kən grach′ə lāt′) *vt.* -lat′ed, -lat′ing [< L. *com-*, together + *gratulari*, wish joy] to express to (a person) one's pleasure at his good fortune, success, etc. — **con·grat′u·la′tor** *n.* —**con·grat′u·la·to′ry** (-lə tôr′ē) *adj.*

con·grat·u·la·tion (kən grach′ə lā′shən) *n.* 1. a congratulating 2. [*pl.*] expressions of pleasure over another's good fortune or success

con·gre·gate (käŋ′grə gāt′) *vt., vi.* -gat′ed, -gat′ing [< L. *com-*, together + *grex*, a flock] to gather into a mass or crowd; assemble —*adj.* (-git) 1. assembled 2. collective —**con′gre·ga′tive** *adj.*

con·gre·ga·tion *n.* 1. a gathering; assemblage 2. an assembly of people for religious worship 3. the members of a particular place of worship

con·gre·ga·tion·al *adj.* 1. of or like a congregation 2. [C-] of Congregationalism or Congregationalists

con·gre·ga·tion·al·ism *n.* 1. a form of church organization in which each congregation governs itself 2. [C-] the faith and organization of a Protestant denomination in which each member church governs itself —**Con′gre·ga′tion·al·ist** *n., adj.*

con·gress (käŋ′grəs) *n.* [< L. *com-*, together + *gradi*, to walk] 1. an association or society 2. an assembly or conference 3. a legislature, esp. of a republic 4. [C-] the legislature of the U.S., consisting of the Senate and the House of Representatives —**con·gres·sion·al** (kən gresh′ən 'l) *adj.*

con′gress·man (-mən) *n., pl.* -men [*often* C-] a member of Congress, esp. of the House of Representatives —**con′gress·wom′an** *n.fem.* (a former usage)

con·gru·ent (käŋ′grσσ wənt) *adj.* [< L. *congruere*, agree] 1. in agreement; harmonious 2. *Geom.* of the same shape and size —**con′gru·ence, con′gru·en·cy** *n.* —**con′gru·ent·ly** *adv.*

con·gru·ous (käŋ′grσσ wəs) *adj.* 1. *same as* CONGRUENT 2. fitting; suitable; appropriate —**con·gru·i·ty** (kən grσσ′ə tē) *n., pl.* -ties —**con′gru·ous·ly** *adv.*

con·i·cal (kän′i k'l) *adj.* of or like a cone: also **con′ic** — **con′i·cal·ly** *adv.*

co·ni·fer (kän′ə fər, kō′nə-) *n.* [< L. *conus*, cone + *ferre*, to bear] any of a group of cone-bearing trees and shrubs, mostly evergreens, as the pine, fir, etc. —**co·nif·er·ous** (kə nif′ər əs) *adj.*

conj. 1. conjugation 2. conjunction

con·jec·tur·al (kən jek′chər əl) *adj.* 1. based on or involving conjecture 2. inclined to make conjectures —**con·jec′tur·al·ly** *adv.*

con·jec·ture (kən jek′chər) *n.* [< L. *com-*, together + *jacere*, to throw] an inferring, theorizing, or predicting from incomplete evidence; guesswork 2. a guess —*vt., vi.* -tured, -tur·ing to guess

con·join (kən join′) *vt., vi.* [< L. *com-*, together + *jungere*, join] to join together; unite

con·joint′ *adj.* 1. joined together; united 2. of or involving two or more together in association; joint —**con·joint′ly** *adv.*

con·ju·gal (kän′jə gəl) *adj.* [< L. *conjunx*, spouse] of marriage or the relation between husband and wife —**con′ju·gal·ly** *adv.*

con·ju·gate (kän′jə gət, -gāt′) *adj.* [< L. *com-*, together + *jugare*, join] 1. joined together, esp. in a pair 2. *Gram.* derived from the same base —*n.* a conjugate word —*vt.* (-gāt′) -gat′ed, -gat′ing 1. [Archaic] to join together; couple 2. *Gram.* to give in order the inflectional forms of (a verb) —*vi.* to conjugate a verb —**con′ju·ga′tive** *adj.*

con′ju·ga′tion *n.* 1. a conjugating or being conjugated 2. *Gram. a)* a methodical arrangement of the inflectional forms of a verb *b)* a class of verbs with similar inflectional forms

con·junc·tion (kən juŋk′shən) *n.* [see CONJOIN] 1. a joining together; union; combination 2. coincidence 3. a word used to connect words, phrases, or clauses (Ex.: *and, but, if,* etc.) 4. *Astron.* the apparent closeness of two or more heavenly bodies

con·junc·ti·va (kän′jəŋk tī′və) *n., pl.* -vas, -vae (-vē) [ModL.] the mucous membrane lining the inner surface of the eyelids and covering the front part of the eyeball

con·junc·tive (kən juŋk′tiv) *adj.* 1. connective 2. united; combined 3. *Gram.* used as a conjunction —*n.* a conjunctive word; esp., a conjunction —**con·junc′tive·ly** *adv.*

con·junc·ti·vi·tis (kən juŋk′tə vīt′is) *n.* [see -ITIS] inflammation of the conjunctiva

con·ju·ra·tion (kän′jə rā′shən) *n.* 1. a conjuring; invocation 2. a magic spell

con·jure (kän′jər, kun′-; *for vt. 1* kən joor′) *vi.* -jured, -jur·ing [< L. *com-*, together + *jurare*, swear] 1. to summon a demon, spirit, etc. by magic 2. to practice magic — *vt.* 1. to entreat solemnly 2. to cause to appear, come (*up*), etc. as by magic

con·jur·er, con·ju·ror (kän′jər ər, kun′-) *n.* a magician; sorcerer

conk (käŋk) *n., vt.* [< CONCH] [Slang] hit on the head — **conk out** [Slang] 1. to fail suddenly in operation 2. to become very tired and, usually, fall asleep

conn (kän) *vt.* conned, con′ning [see CONDUCE] *Naut.* to direct the course of (a vessel) —*n.* a conning

con·nect (kə nekt′) *vt.* [< L. *com-*, together + *nectere*, fasten] 1. to join (two things together, or one thing *with* or *to* another); link; couple 2. to show or think of as related; associate —*vi.* to be joined or related —**con·nec′tor, con·nect′er** *n.*

Con·nect·i·cut (kə net′ə kət) New England State of the U.S.: 5,009 sq. mi.; pop. 3,032,000; cap. Hartford: abbrev. **Conn., CT**

con·nec·tion (kə nek′shən) *n.* 1. a joining or being joined 2. a thing that joins 3. a relation; association 4. *a)* a relative, esp. by marriage *b)* an influential associate, etc.: *usually used in pl.* 5. [*usually pl.*] a transferring from one bus, airplane, etc. to another Brit. sp., **con·nex′ion**

con·nec′tive (-tiv) *adj.* connecting —*n.* that which connects, esp. a connecting word, as a conjunction

conn·ing tower (kän′iŋ) [prp. of CONN] 1. an armored pilothouse of a warship 2. on submarines, a low observation tower

con·nip·tion (fit) (kə nip′shən) [pseudo-Latin] [Colloq.] [*often pl.*] a fit of anger, hysteria, etc.

con·nive (kə nīv′) *vi.* -nived′, -niv′ing [< L. *conivere*, to wink, connive] 1. to pretend not to look (*at* crime, etc.), thus giving tacit consent 2. to cooperate secretly (*with* someone), esp. in wrongdoing —**con·niv′ance** *n.* —**con·niv′er** *n.*

con·nois·seur (kän′ə sur′) *n.* [< Fr. < L. *cognoscere,* know] one who has expert knowledge and keen discrimination in some field, esp. in the fine arts

con·note (kə nōt′) *vt.* -not′ed, -not′ing [< L. *com-,* together + *notare,* to mark] to suggest or convey (associations, overtones, etc.) in addition to the explicit, or denoted, meaning —**con·no·ta·tion** (kän′ə tā′shən) *n.* — **con′no·ta′tive** *adj.*

con·nu·bi·al (kə nōō′bē əl, -nyōō′-) *adj.* [< L. *com-,* together + *nubere,* marry] of marriage; conjugal

con·quer (käŋ′kər) *vt.* [< L. *com-,* intens. + *quaerere,* seek] 1. to get control of as by winning a war 2. to overcome; defeat —*vi.* to win; be victorious —**con′quer·a·ble** *adj.* —**con′quer·or** *n.*

con·quest (kän′kwest, kän′-) *n.* 1. a conquering 2. something conquered 3. *a)* a winning of someone's love *b)* one whose love has been won

con·quis·ta·dor (kän kwis′tə dôr′, -kēs′-) *n., pl.* -dors′, -dores′ [Sp., conqueror] any of the Spanish conquerors of Mexico, Peru, or other parts of America in the 16th century

Con·rad (kän′rad), **Joseph** 1857–1924; Eng. novelist, born in Poland

con·san·guin·e·ous (kän′saŋ gwin′ē əs) *adj.* [see COM- & SANGUINE] having the same ancestor; closely related — **con′san·guin′i·ty** *n.*

con·science (kän′shəns) *n.* [< L. *com-,* with + *scire,* know] an awareness of right and wrong, with a compulsion to do right —**on one's conscience** causing one to feel guilty —**con′science·less** *adj.*

con·sci·en·tious (kän′shē en′shəs) *adj.* 1. governed by one's conscience; scrupulous 2. painstaking —**con′sci·en′tious·ly** *adv.* —**con′sci·en′tious·ness** *n.*

conscientious objector one who for reasons of conscience refuses to take part in warfare

con·scious (kän′shəs) *adj.* [see CONSCIENCE] 1. having an awareness (*of* or *that*) 2. able to feel and think; awake 3. aware of oneself as a thinking being 4. intentional [*conscious* humor] 5. known to or felt by oneself —**con′scious·ly** *adv.*

con′scious·ness *n.* 1. the state of being conscious; awareness 2. the totality of one's thoughts, feelings, and impressions; conscious mind

con·script (kən skript′; *for adj. & n.* kän′skript) *vt.* [< L. *com-,* with + *scribere,* to write] to enroll for compulsory service in the armed forces; draft —*adj.* conscripted —*n.* a conscripted person; draftee —**con·scrip′tion** *n.*

---

fat, āpe, cär; ten, ēven; is, bīte; gō, hôrn, tōōl, lϭϭk; oil, out; up, fur; thin, *th*en; zh, leisure; ŋ, ring; ə for *a* in *ago;* ' as in *able* (ā′b'l); ë, Fr. coeur; ö, Fr. feu; Fr. mon; ü, Fr. duc; r, Fr. cri; kh, G. doch, ich. ‡ foreign; < derived from

con·se·crate (kän'sə krāt') *vt.* -crat'ed, -crat'ing [< L. *com-*, together + *sacer*, sacred] **1.** to set apart as holy; declare sacred for religious use **2.** to devote; dedicate — **con'se·cra'tion** *n.* —**con'se·cra'tor** *n.*

con·sec·u·tive (kən sek'yə tiv) *adj.* [see CONSEQUENCE] **1.** following in order, without interruption; successive **2.** proceeding in logical order —**con·sec'u·tive·ly** *adv.*

con·sen·sus (kən sen'səs) *n.* [see CONSENT] **1.** an opinion held by all or most **2.** general agreement

con·sent (kən sent') *vi.* [< L. *com-*, with + *sentire*, to feel] to agree, permit, or assent —*n.* **1.** permission, approval, or assent **2.** agreement [by common *consent*]

con·se·quence (kän'sə kwens') *n.* [< L. *com-*, with + *sequi*, follow] **1.** a result; effect **2.** a logical result or conclusion **3.** importance —**in consequence (of)** as a result (of) —**take the consequences** to accept the results of one's actions

con'se·quent' (-kwent', -kwənt) *adj.* **1.** following as a result; resulting **2.** proceeding in logical sequence —*n.* anything that follows —**consequent on (or upon) 1.** following as a result of **2.** inferred from

con·se·quen·tial (kän'sə kwen'shəl) *adj.* **1.** following as an effect **2.** important —**con'se·quen'tial·ly** *adv.*

con'se·quent'ly *adv.* as a result; therefore

con·ser·va·tion (kän'sər vā'shən) *n.* **1.** a conserving **2.** the official care and protection of natural resources, as forests —**con'ser·va'tion·ist** *n.*

conservation of energy the principle that energy is never consumed but only changes form, and that the total energy in the universe remains fixed

con·ser·va·tive (kən sur'və tiv) *adj.* **1.** tending to conserve **2.** tending to preserve established institutions, etc.; opposed to change **3.** [C-] designating or of the major right-wing political party of Great Britain or Canada **4.** moderate; cautious —*n.* **1.** a conservative person **2.** [C-] a member of a Conservative party —**con·ser'va·tism** *n.* — **con·ser'va·tive·ly** *adv.*

con·ser·va·tor (kän'sər vāt'ər, kən sur'və tər) *n.* a protector, guardian, or custodian

con·ser·va·to·ry (kən sur'və tôr'ē) *n., pl.* -ries **1.** a greenhouse **2.** a school of music, art, etc.

con·serve (kən surv') *vt.* -served', -serv'ing [< L. *com-*, with + *servare*, to guard] **1.** to keep from being damaged, lost, or wasted **2.** to make (fruit) into preserves —*n.* (*usually* kän'sərv) [*often pl.*] a preserve of two or more fruits —**con·serv'a·ble** *adj.* —**con·serv'er** *n.*

con·sid·er (kən sid'ər) *vt.* [< L. *com-*, with + *sidus*, a star] **1.** to think about in order to understand or decide **2.** to keep in mind **3.** to be thoughtful of (others) **4.** to regard as; think to be —*vi.* to think seriously

con·sid'er·a·ble *adj.* **1.** worth considering; important **2.** much or large —**con·sid'er·a·bly** *adv.*

con·sid·er·ate (-it) *adj.* having or showing regard for others and their feelings; thoughtful

con·sid·er·a'tion (-ə rā'shən) *n.* **1.** the act of considering; deliberation **2.** thoughtful regard for others **3.** something considered in making a decision **4.** an opinion produced by considering **5.** a recompense; fee —**take into consideration** to keep in mind —**under consideration** being thought over

con·sid'ered (-ərd) *adj.* arrived at after careful thought

con·sid'er·ing *prep.* in view of; taking into account — *adv.* [Colloq.] all things considered

con·sign (kən sīn') *vt.* [< L. *consignare*, to seal] **1.** to hand over; deliver **2.** to entrust **3.** to assign; relegate **4.** to send or deliver (goods) —**con·sign'a·ble** *adj.* —**con·sign·ee** (kän'sī nē', kən sī'nē') *n.* —**con·sign'or, con·sign'er** *n.*

con·sign'ment (-mənt) *n.* **1.** a consigning or being consigned **2.** a shipment of goods sent to an agent for sale, etc. —**on consignment** with payment due after sale of the consignment

con·sist (kən sist') *vi.* [< L. *com-*, together + *sistere*, to stand] **1.** to be formed or composed (*of*) **2.** to be contained or inherent (*in*) **3.** to exist in harmony (*with*)

con·sis·ten·cy (-ən sē) *n., pl.* -cies **1.** *a)* firmness or thickness, as of a liquid *b)* degree of this **2.** agreement; harmony **3.** conformity with previous practice Also **con·sis'tence**

con·sis'tent (-ənt) *adj.* **1.** in harmony or agreement; compatible **2.** holding to the same principles or practice — **con·sis'tent·ly** *adv.*

con·sis·to·ry (kən sis'tər ē) *n., pl.* -ries [see CONSIST] **1.** a church council or court, as the papal senate **2.** a session of such a body

con·so·la·tion (kän'sə lā'shən) *n.* **1.** a consoling or being consoled; solace **2.** one that consoles

con·sol·a·to·ry (kən sōl'ə tôr'ē) *adj.* consoling or tending to console; comforting

con·sole' (kən sōl') *vt.* -soled', -sol'ing [< Fr. < L. *com-*, with + *solari*, to solace] to make feel less sad or disappointed; comfort —**con·sol'a·ble** *adj.* —**con·sol'ing·ly** *adv.*

con·sole² (kän'sōl) *n.* [Fr.] **1.** an ornamental bracket for supporting a shelf, bust, cornice, etc. **2.** *same as* CONSOLE TABLE **3.** the desklike frame containing the keys, stops, etc. of an organ **4.** a radio, television, or phonograph cabinet designed to stand on the floor **5.** a control panel for operating aircraft, computers, electronic systems, etc.

console table a small table with legs resembling consoles, placed against a wall

con·sol·i·date (kən säl'ə dāt') *vt.,* vi. -dat'ed, -dat'ing [< L. *com-*, together + *solidus*, solid] **1.** to combine into one; unite **2.** to make or become strong, stable, etc. [the troops *consolidated* their position] —**con·sol'i·da'tion** *n.* —**con·sol'i·da'tor** *n.*

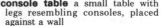

CONSOLE (sense 3)

con·som·mé (kän'sə mā') *n.* [Fr.] a clear, strained meat soup

con·so·nance (kän'sə nəns) *n.* [< L. *com-*, with + *sonus*, sound] harmony, esp. of musical tones

con·so·nant (-nənt) *adj.* **1.** in harmony or agreement **2.** harmonious in tone —*n.* a letter representing a speech sound made by obstructing the breath stream as *p, t, l, f,* etc. —**con'so·nant·ly** *adv.*

con·so·nan·tal (kän'sə nant'l) *adj.* of, being, or having a consonant or consonants

con·sort (kän'sôrt; *for v.* kən sôrt') *n.* [< L. *com-*, with + *sors*, a share] a wife or husband, esp. of a reigning king or queen —*vi.* **1.** to associate **2.** to agree; be in accord —*vt.* to associate; join

con·sor·ti·um (kən sôr'shē əm) *n., pl.* -ti·a (-ə) [see prec.] an international alliance, as of business firms

con·spec·tus (kən spek'təs) *n.* [see CONSPICUOUS] **1.** a general view; survey **2.** a summary; digest

con·spic·u·ous (kən spik'yoo wəs) *adj.* [< L. *com-*, intens. + *specere*, to see] **1.** easy to see; obvious **2.** outstanding; striking —**con·spic'u·ous·ly** *adv.*

con·spir·a·cy (kən spir'ə sē) *n., pl.* -cies **1.** a conspiring, esp. in an unlawful plot **2.** such a plot **3.** the group taking part in such a plot

con·spire (kən spīr') *vi.* -spired', -spir'ing [< L. *com-*, together + *spirare*, to breathe] **1.** to plan and act together secretly, esp. in order to commit a crime **2.** to work together for any purpose or effect —**con·spir'a·tor** (-spir'ə tər) *n.*

con·sta·ble (kän'stə b'l, kun'-) *n.* [< LL. *comes stabuli,* lit., count of the stable] [Chiefly Brit.] a policeman

con·stab·u·lar·y (kən stab'yə ler'ē) *n., pl.* -ies **1.** constables, collectively **2.** a militarized police force

con·stant (kän'stənt) *adj.* [< L. *com-*, together + *stare,* to stand] **1.** not changing; specif., *a)* resolute *b)* faithful *c)* regular; stable **2.** continual; persistent —*n.* anything that does not change or vary —**con'stan·cy** *n.* —**con'stant·ly** *adv.*

Con·stan·tine I (kän'stən tēn', -tīn') 280?-337 A.D.; emperor of Rome (306–337): called *the Great*

Con·stan·ti·no·ple (kän'stan tə nō'p'l) *former name* (330 A.D.–1930) *of* ISTANBUL

con·stel·la·tion (kän'stə lā'shən) *n.* [< L. *com-*, with + *stella,* a star] **1.** a group of fixed stars, usually named after a figure that they supposedly suggest in outline **2.** the part of the heavens occupied by such a group **3.** any brilliant cluster

con·ster·na·tion (kän'stər nā'shən) *n.* [< L. *consternare,* terrify] great fear or shock

con·sti·pate (kän'stə pāt') *vt.* -pat'ed, -pat'ing [< L. *com-*, together + *stipare,* cram] to cause constipation in —**con'sti·pa'tion** *n.* infrequent and difficult movement of the bowels

con·stit·u·en·cy (kən stich'oo wən sē) *n., pl.* -cies **1.** the voters in a district **2.** the district of such voters

con·stit'u·ent (-wənt) *adj.* [see CONSTITUTE] **1.** necessary to the whole; component **2.** that can elect **3.** authorized to make or revise a constitution —*n.* **1.** a voter in a district **2.** a component

con·sti·tute (kän'stə tōōt', -tyōōt') *vt.* -tut'ed, -tut'ing [< L. *com-*, together + *statuere,* etc.] **1.** to establish (a law, government, etc.) **2.** to set up (an assembly, etc.) in a legal form **3.** to appoint **4.** to make up; compose

con·sti·tu·tion (-tōō'shən, -tyōō'-) *n.* **1.** a constituting; establishment **2.** structure; organization **3.** the physical makeup of a person **4.** *a)* the system of basic laws and principles of a government, society, etc. *b)* a document stating these; specif., [C-] the Constitution of the U.S.

con·sti·tu·tion·al *adj.* **1.** of or in one's constitution; basic; essential **2.** for improving one's constitution **3.** of or in accordance with the constitution of a nation, society, etc. —*n.* a walk or other exercise taken for one's health — **con'sti·tu·tion·al'i·ty** (-shə nal'ə tē) *n.* —**con'sti·tu'tion·al·ly** *adv.*

con·strain (kən strān') *vt.* [< L. *com-*, together + *stringere*, draw tight] **1.** to confine **2.** to restrain **3.** to compel *[constrained* to agree] —**con·strained'** *adj.* —**con·strain'ed·ly** (-strā'nid lē) *adv.*

con·straint' *n.* **1.** confinement or restriction **2.** compulsion or coercion **3.** forced, unnatural manner

con·strict (kən strikt') *vt.* [see CONSTRAIN] **1.** to make smaller or narrower by squeezing, etc. **2.** to limit —**con·stric'tion** *n.* —**con·stric'tive** *adj.*

con·stric'tor *n.* **1.** that which constricts **2.** a snake that kills by coiling around its prey and squeezing

con·struct (kən strukt') *vt.* [< L. *com-*, together + *struere*, pile up] to build, form, or devise by fitting parts together systematically —*n.* (kän'strukt) something built or put together systematically —**con·struc'tor, con·struct'er** *n.*

con·struc·tion (kən struk'shən) *n.* **1.** a constructing or manner of being constructed **2.** a structure **3.** an interpretation, as of a statement **4.** the arrangement of words in a sentence —**con·struc'tion·al** *adj.*

con·struc'tive *adj.* **1.** helping to construct; leading to improvements *[constructive* criticism] **2.** of construction **3.** inferred or implied by interpretation —**con·struc'tive·ly** *adv.* —**con·struc'tive·ness** *n.*

con·strue (kən strōō') *vt., vi.* -**strued'**, -**stru'ing** [see CONSTRUCT] **1.** to analyze the grammatical construction of (a sentence, etc.) **2.** to translate **3.** to explain or deduce the meaning (of); interpret *[her* silence was *construed* as agreement] **4.** to combine in syntax —**con·stru'a·ble** *adj.*

con·sul (kän's'l) *n.* [< L. *consulere*, to deliberate] **1.** a chief magistrate of ancient Rome **2.** a government official appointed to live in a foreign city and serve his country's citizens and business interests there —**con'su·lar** *adj.* —**con'sul·ship'** *n.*

con'su·late (-it) *n.* **1.** the position, powers, etc. of a consul **2.** the office or residence of a consul

con·sult (kən sult') *vi.* [< L. *consulere*, to deliberate] to talk things over; confer —*vt.* **1.** to ask advice or information from **2.** to consider *[consult* your own wishes] —**con·sult'er** *n.*

con·sult'ant *n.* **1.** a person who consults another **2.** one who gives professional or technical advice

con·sul·ta·tion (kän's'l tā'shən) *n.* **1.** a consulting **2.** a conference —**con·sul·ta·tive** (kən sul'tə tiv), **con·sul'ta·to'ry** (-tôr'ē) *adj.*

con·sume (kən sōōm') *vt.* -**sumed'**, -**sum'ing** [< L. *com-*, together + *sumere*, to take] **1.** to destroy, as by fire **2.** to use up; waste (time, money, etc.) **3.** to eat or drink up **4.** to engross or obsess *[consumed* with envy] —**con·sum'a·ble** *adj.*

con·sum'er *n.* a person or thing that consumes; specif., a person who buys goods or services for his own needs rather than to produce other goods

con·sum'er·ism (-iz'm) *n.* a movement for protecting the consumer against defective products, misleading business practices, etc.

con·sum·mate (kən sum'it) *adj.* [< L. *com-*, together + *summa*, a sum] **1.** complete or perfect **2.** highly expert — *vt.* (kän'sə māt') -**mat'ed**, -**mat'ing 1.** to complete; finish **2.** to make (a marriage) actual by sexual intercourse — **con·sum'mate·ly** *adv.* —**con'sum·ma'tion** *n.* —**con'sum·ma'tor** *n.*

con·sump·tion (kən sump'shən) *n.* **1.** *a)* a consuming or being consumed; specif., the using up of goods or services *b)* the amount consumed **2.** a wasting disease; esp., tuberculosis of the lungs

con·sump'tive (-tiv) *adj.* **1.** consuming or tending to consume **2.** of or having tuberculosis of the lungs —*n.* one who has tuberculosis of the lungs

cont. 1. containing **2.** continued

con·tact (kän'takt) *n.* [< L. *com-*, together + *tangere*, to touch] **1.** a touching or meeting **2.** the state of being in touch or association (*with*) **3.** an acquaintance; connection **4.** *Elec.* a connection between two conductors in a circuit —*vt.* **1.** to place in contact **2.** to get in touch with —*vi.* to come into contact

contact lens a tiny, thin correctional lens placed in the fluid over the cornea of the eye

con·ta·gion (kən tā'jən) *n.* [see CONTACT] **1.** the spreading of disease by contact **2.** a contagious disease **3.** the spreading of an emotion, idea, etc.

con·ta'gious (-jəs) *adj.* **1.** spread by contact: said of diseases **2.** carrying the causative agent of such a disease **3.** spreading from person to person —**con·ta'gious·ly** *adv.* —**con·ta'gious·ness** *n.*

con·tain (kən tān') *vt.* [< L. *com-*, together + *tenere*, to hold] **1.** to have in it; hold or include **2.** to have the capacity for holding **3.** to hold back or restrain within fixed limits **4.** to be divisible by, esp. without a remainder *[10 contains* 5 and 2] —**con·tain'a·ble** *adj.*

con·tain'er *n.* a thing for containing something; box, can, jar, etc.

con·tain'er·ize' (-īz') *vt.* -**ized'**, -**iz'ing** to pack (cargo) in large, standardized containers for shipment —**con·tain'er·i·za'tion** *n.*

con·tain'ment *n.* the policy of attempting to prevent the influence of an opposing nation or political system from spreading

con·tam·i·nant (kən tam'ə nənt) *n.* a substance that contaminates another substance, the air, etc.

con·tam'i·nate' (-nāt') *vt.* -**nat'ed**, -**nat'ing** [< L. *com-*, together + *tangere*, to touch] to make impure, corrupt, radioactive, etc. by contact; pollute; taint —**con·tam'i·na'tion** *n.* —**con·tam'i·na'tor** *n.*

contd. continued

con·temn (kən tem') *vt.* [< L. *com-*, intens. + *temnere*, to scorn] to treat with contempt; scorn —**con·temn'er**, **con·tem'nor** (-tem'ər, -tem'nər) *n.*

con·tem·plate (kän'təm plāt') *vt.* -**plat'ed**, -**plat'ing** [< L. *contemplari*, observe] **1.** to gaze at intently **2.** to think about intently; study **3.** to expect or intend —*vi.* to meditate or muse —**con'tem·pla'tion** *n.* —**con·tem·pla·tive** (kən tem'plə tiv, kän'təm plāt'iv) *adj., n.*

con·tem·po·ra·ne·ous (kən tem'pə rā'nē əs) *adj.* existing or happening in the same period of time —**con·tem'po·ra'ne·ous·ly** *adv.*

con·tem·po·rar·y (kən tem'pə rer'ē) *adj.* [< L. *com-*, with + *tempus*, time] **1.** living or happening in the same period **2.** of about the same age **3.** modern —*n., pl.* -**ies** one of the same period or about the same age as another or others

con·tempt (kən tempt') *n.* [see CONTEMN] **1.** the feeling of a person toward someone or something he considers low, worthless, etc. **2.** the condition of being despised **3.** *Law* a showing disrespect for the dignity of a court (or legislature): in full **contempt of court** (or **congress**, etc.)

con·tempt'i·ble *adj.* deserving contempt or scorn; despicable —**con·tempt'i·bly** *adv.*

con·temp·tu·ous (kən temp'choo wəs) *adj.* full of contempt; scornful —**con·temp'tu·ous·ly** *adv.*

con·tend (kən tend') *vi.* [< L. *com-*, together + *tendere*, stretch] **1.** to fight **2.** to argue **3.** to compete; vie —*vt.* to assert —**con·tend'er** *n.*

con·tent' (kən tent') *adj.* [see CONTAIN] **1.** satisfied **2.** assenting —*vt.* to satisfy —*n.* contentment

con·tent² (kän'tent) *n.* [see CONTAIN] **1.** *[usually pl.]* *a)* all that is contained in something *b)* all that is dealt with in a writing or speech **2.** meaning or substance **3.** the amount contained

con·tent'ed *adj.* satisfied —**con·tent'ed·ly** *adv.*

con·ten·tion (kən ten'shən) *n.* [see CONTEND] **1.** strife, struggle, dispute, etc. **2.** a point that one argues for as true or valid —**con·ten'tious** *adj.*

con·tent'ment *n.* the state or fact of being contented

con·ter·mi·nous (kən tur'mə nəs) *adj.* [< L. *com-*, together + *terminus*, end] **1.** having a common boundary **2.** contained within the same boundaries or limits

con·test (kən test') *vt.* [< L. *com-*, together + *testis*, witness] **1.** to try to disprove; dispute *[to contest* a will] **2.** to fight for (a position, etc.) —*vi.* to struggle (*with* or *against*) —*n.* (kän'test) **1.** a fight, struggle, or controversy **2.** a competitive race, game, etc. —**con·test'a·ble** *adj.* — **con·test'er** *n.*

con·test'ant *n.* [Fr.] **1.** a competitor in a contest **2.** one who contests a claim, decision, etc.

con·text (kän'tekst) *n.* [< L. *com-*, together + *texere*, to weave] the parts of a sentence, paragraph, etc. just before

---

and after a word or passage, that determine its meaning —**con·tex·tu·al** (kən teks'chōō wəl) *adj.* —**con·tex'tu·al·ly** *adv.*

con·tig·u·ous (kən tig'yōō wəs) *adj.* [see CONTACT] **1.** in contact; touching **2.** near or adjacent —**con·ti·gu·i·ty** (kän'tə gyōō'ə tē) *n., pl.* -**ties** —**con·tig'u·ous·ly** *adv.*

con·ti·nence (känt''n əns) *n.* [see CONTAIN] **1.** self-restraint **2.** self-restraint in sexual activity; esp., total abstinence

con·ti·nent (-ənt) *adj.* **1.** self-restrained **2.** self-restrained, esp. totally abstinent, in sexual activity —*n.* any of the main large land areas of the earth (Africa, Asia, Australia, Europe, N. America, S. America, and, sometimes, Antarctica) —**the Continent** the mainland of Europe — **con'ti·nent·ly** *adv.*

con·ti·nen·tal (-en't'l) *adj.* **1.** of a continent **2.** [*sometimes* C-] European **3.** [C-] of the American colonies at the time of the American Revolution —*n.* **1.** [*usually* C-] a European **2.** [C-] a soldier of the American Revolutionary army

Continental Congress either of the two assemblies of representatives from the American colonies during the Revolutionary period

con·tin·gen·cy (kən tin'jən sē) *n., pl.* -**cies 1.** a being contingent; dependence on chance **2.** a possible or chance event Also **con·tin'gence**

con·tin'gent *adj.* [see CONTACT] **1.** possible **2.** accidental **3.** dependent (*on* or *upon* an uncertainty); conditional — *n.* **1.** a chance happening **2.** a share or quota, as of troops **3.** a part of a large group

con·tin·u·al (kən tin'yōō wəl) *adj.* **1.** repeated often **2.** continuous —**con·tin'u·al·ly** *adv.*

con·tin'u·ance *n.* **1.** a continuing **2.** duration **3.** an unbroken succession **4.** *Law* postponement or adjournment

con·tin'u·a'tion (-wā'shən) *n.* **1.** a continuing or being continued **2.** a beginning again; resumption **3.** a part added; supplement, sequel, etc.

con·tin·ue (kən tin'yōō) *vi.* -**ued**, -**u·ing** [< L. *continuare*, join] **1.** to last; endure **2.** to go on in a specified action or condition; persist **3.** to extend **4.** to stay **5.** to resume after an interruption —*vt.* **1.** to go on with **2.** to extend **3.** to resume **4.** to cause to remain, as in office; retain **5.** *Law* to postpone or adjourn to a later date

con·ti·nu·i·ty (kän'tə nōō'ə tē, -nyōō'-) *n., pl.* -**ties 1.** a continuous state or quality **2.** an unbroken, coherent whole **3.** the script for a motion picture, television program, etc.

con·tin·u·ous (kən tin'yōō wəs) *adj.* going on without interruption; unbroken —**con·tin'u·ous·ly** *adv.*

con·tin'u·um (-yōō wəm) *n., pl.* -**u·a** (-wə), -**u·ums** [L.] a continuous whole, quantity, or series

con·tort (kən tôrt') *vt., vi.* [< L. *com-*, together + *torquere*, to twist] to twist or wrench out of shape; distort — **con·tor'tion** *n.*

con·tor'tion·ist *n.* one who can twist his body into unnatural positions

con·tour (kän'tōōr) *n.* [Fr. < L. *com-*, intens. + *tornare*, to turn] the outline of a figure, land, etc. —*vt.* to shape to the contour of —*adj.* conforming to or following the shape or contour of something

contour map a map with lines (**contour lines**) connecting all points of the same elevation

contr. contraction

contra- [< L. *contra*] *a prefix meaning* against, opposite, opposed to

con·tra·band (kän'trə band') *n.* [< Sp. < It.] **1.** smuggled goods, forbidden by law to be imported and exported **2.** war material which, by international law, may be seized by a belligerent when shipped to the other by a neutral: in full **contraband of war** —*adj.* illegal to import or export

con·tra·bass (kän'trə bās') *adj.* [see CONTRA- & BASS¹] having its pitch an octave lower than the normal bass

con·tra·cep·tion (kän'trə sep'shən) *n.* [CONTRA- + (CON)CEPTION] prevention of the fertilization of the human ovum —**con'tra·cep'tive** *adj., n.*

con·tract (kän'trakt *for n. & usually for vt.* 1. *& vi.* 1; kən trakt' *for v. generally*) *n.* [< L. *com-*, together + *trahere*, draw] **1.** an agreement, esp. a written one enforceable by law **2.** a formal agreement of marriage **3.** a document containing the terms of an agreement **4.** *Bridge a*) the number of tricks bid by the highest bidder *b*) same as CONTRACT BRIDGE —*vt.* **1.** to undertake by contract **2.** to get or incur **3.** to reduce in size; shrink **4.** to shorten (a word or phrase) by the omission of a letter or sound —*vi.* **1.** to make a contract **2.** to become smaller —**contract out** to assign (a job) by contract —**con·tract'i·ble** *adj.*

con·tract bridge (kän'trakt) a form of auction bridge: only the tricks bid may be counted toward a game

con·trac·tile (kən trak't'l) *adj.* having the power of contracting

con·trac'tion (-shən) *n.* **1.** a contracting or being contracted **2.** the drawing up and thickening of a muscle in action **3.** the shortened form of a word or phrase (Ex.: *aren't* for *are not*)

con·trac·tor (kän'trak tər, kən trak'-) *n.* one who contracts to supply certain materials or do certain work for a stipulated sum

con·trac·tu·al (kən trak'chōō wəl) *adj.* of or constituting a contract —**con·trac'tu·al·ly** *adv.*

con·tra·dict (kän'trə dikt') *vt.* [< L. *contra-*, against + *dicere*, speak] **1.** to assert the opposite of (a statement) **2.** to deny the statement of (a person) **3.** to be contrary to —**con'tra·dict'a·ble** *adj.* —**con'tra·dic'tor, con'tra·dict'er** *n.*

con'tra·dic'tion *n.* **1.** a contradicting or being contradicted **2.** a statement in opposition to another; denial **3.** inconsistency; discrepancy

con'tra·dic'to·ry *adj.* **1.** involving a contradiction; inconsistent **2.** inclined to contradict or deny

con'tra·dis·tinc'tion (-dis tiŋk'shən) *n.* distinction by contrast —**con'tra·dis·tinc'tive** *adj.*

con·tral·to (kən tral'tō) *n., pl.* -**tos**, -**ti** (-tē) [It.: < CONTRA- & ALTO] **1.** the range of the lowest female voice **2.** a voice or singer with such a range **3.** a part for this voice —*adj.* of or for a contralto

con·trap·tion (kən trap'shən) *n.* [< ?] [Colloq.] a contrivance or gadget

con·tra·pun·tal (kän'trə pun't'l) *adj.* [< It. *contrapunto*, counterpoint] **1.** of or characterized by counterpoint **2.** according to the principles of counterpoint —**con'tra·pun'tal·ly** *adv.*

con·trar·i·wise (kän'trer ē wīz'; *for 3, often* kən trer'-) *adv.* **1.** on the contrary **2.** in the opposite way, order, direction, etc. **3.** perversely

con·trar·y (kän'trer ē; *for 4, often* kən trer'ē) *adj.* [< L. *contra*, against] **1.** in opposition **2.** opposite in nature, order, etc.; altogether different **3.** unfavorable [*contrary winds*] **4.** always resisting; perverse —*n., pl.* -**ies** the opposite —*adv.* in a contrary way —**on the contrary** as opposed to what has been said —**to the contrary** to the opposite effect —**con'trar·i·ly** *adv.* —**con'trar·i·ness** *n.*

con·trast (kən trast') *vt.* [< L. *contra*, against + *stare*, to stand] to compare so as to point out the differences —*vi.* to show differences when compared —*n.* (kän'trast) **1.** a contrasting or being contrasted **2.** a striking difference between things being compared **3.** a person or thing showing differences when compared with another —**con·trast'·ive** *adj.*

con·tra·vene (kän'trə vēn') *vt.* -**vened'**, -**ven'ing** [< L. *contra*, against + *venire*, come] **1.** to go against; violate **2.** to disagree with; contradict —**con'tra·ven'tion** (-ven'shən) *n.*

con·tre·temps (kōn'trə tän') *n., pl.* -**temps'** (-tän') [Fr.] a confusing or embarrassing occurrence

con·trib·ute (kən trib'yōōt) *vt., vi.* -**ut·ed**, -**ut·ing** [< L.: see COM- & TRIBUTE] **1.** to give jointly with others to a common fund **2.** to write (an article, poem, etc.) for a magazine, newspaper, etc. **3.** to furnish (ideas, etc.) — **contribute to** to have a share in bringing about —**con·trib'u·tor** *n.* —**con·trib'u·to'ry** (-yoo tôr'ē) *adj.*

con·tri·bu·tion (kän'trə byōō'shən) *n.* **1.** a contributing **2.** something contributed, as money to a charity or a poem to a magazine

con·trite (kən trīt') *adj.* [< L. *com-*, together + *terere*, to rub] feeling or showing remorse or guilt —**con·trite'ly** *adv.* —**con·trite'ness, con·tri'tion** (-trish'ən) *n.*

con·triv·ance (kən trī'vəns) *n.* **1.** the act or way of contriving **2.** something contrived; device, etc.

con·trive (kən trīv') *vt.* -**trived'**, -**triv'ing** [ult. < VL. *contropare*, compare] **1.** to devise; plan **2.** to construct skillfully; fabricate **3.** to bring about, as by a scheme —*vi.* to form plans; scheme —**con·triv'er** *n.*

con·trol (kən trōl') *vt.* -**trolled'**, -**trol'ling** [< ML. *contrarotulus*, a register] **1.** to regulate (financial affairs) **2.** to exercise authority over; direct **3.** to restrain —*n.* **1.** power to direct or regulate **2.** a being directed; restraint **3.** a means of controlling; check **4.** [*usually pl.*] an apparatus to regulate a mechanism —**con·trol'la·ble** *adj.*

con·trol'ler *n.* **1.** a person in charge of expenditures, as in business, government (usually sp. **comptroller**), etc. **2.** a person or device that controls —**con·trol'ler·ship'** *n.*

con·tro·ver·sial (kän'trə vur'shəl) *adj.* of, subject to, or stirring up controversy; debatable

con·tro·ver·sy (kän′trə vur′sē) *n., pl.* **-sies** [< L. *contra,* against + *vertere,* to turn] **1.** a discussion in which opinions clash; debate **2.** a quarrel

con′tro·vert′ (-vurt′) *vt.* **1.** to argue against; deny **2.** to argue about; debate —**con′tro·vert′i·ble** *adj.*

con·tu·ma·cy (kän′tōo mə sē) *n., pl.* **-cies** [< L. *contumax,* stubborn] stubborn resistance to authority; disobedience —**con′tu·ma′cious** (-mā′shəs) *adj.*

con·tu·me·ly (kän′tōo mə lē, -tyōo–) *n., pl.* **-lies** [< L. *contumelia,* reproach] humiliating treatment or scornful insult —**con′tu·me′li·ous** (-mē′lē əs) *adj.*

con·tuse (kən tōoz′, -tyōoz′) *vt.* **-tused′, -tus′ing** [< L. *com-,* intens. + *tundere,* to beat] to bruise without breaking the skin

con·tu′sion (-tōo′zhən, -tyōo′-) *n.* a bruise

co·nun·drum (kə nun′drəm) *n.* [pseudo-L.] **1.** a riddle whose answer is a pun **2.** any puzzling problem

con·va·lesce (kän′və les′) *vi.* **-lesced′, -lesc′ing** [< L. *com-,* intens. + *valere,* be strong] to recover gradually from illness; regain strength and health

con′va·les′cence *n.* **1.** a gradual recovery of health after illness **2.** the period of this —**con′va·les′cent** *adj., n.*

con·vec·tion (kən vek′shən) *n.* [< L. *com-,* together + *vehere,* carry] **1.** a transmitting **2.** *a)* movement of parts of a fluid within the fluid because of differences in heat, etc. *b)* heat transference by such movement —**con·vec′-tion·al** *adj.* —**con·vec′tive** *adj.*

con·vene (kən vēn′) *vi., vt.* **-vened′, -ven′ing** [< L. *com-,* together + *venire,* come] to assemble for a meeting

con·ven·ience (kən vēn′yəns) *n.* [see CONVENE] **1.** the quality of being convenient **2.** personal comfort **3.** anything that adds to one's comfort or saves work —**at one's convenience** at a time, place, etc. that suits one

con·ven′ient (-yənt) *adj.* **1.** favorable to one's comfort; easy to do, use, or get to; handy **2.** [Colloq.] easily accessible (*to*); near (*to*) —**con·ven′ient·ly** *adv.*

con·vent (kän′vənt, -vent) *n.* [see CONVENE] **1.** a community of nuns or, sometimes, monks, living under strict religious vows **2.** the place where they live

con·ven·ti·cle (kən ven′ti k'l) *n.* [see CONVENE] **1.** a religious assembly, esp. an illegal or secret one **2.** a place where such an assembly meets

con·ven·tion (kən ven′shən) *n.* **1.** an assembly, often periodical, or the delegates to it **2.** *a)* an agreement between persons, nations, etc. *b)* general agreement on the usages and practices of social life **3.** a customary practice, rule, etc.

con·ven′tion·al (-'l) *adj.* **1.** having to do with a convention **2.** sanctioned by or following custom or usage; customary **3.** *a)* formal; not natural or spontaneous *b)* ordinary —**con·ven′tion·al·ism** *n.* —**con·ven′tion·al·ly** *adv.*

con·ven′tion·al′i·ty (-shə nal′ə tē) *n., pl.* **-ties 1.** a being conventional **2.** conventional behavior or act **3.** a conventional form, usage, or rule

con·ven′tion·al·ize′ (-īz′) *vt.* **-ized′, -iz′ing** to make conventional —**con·ven′tion·al·i·za′tion** *n.*

con·verge (kən vurj′) *vi., vt.* **-verged′, -verg′ing** [< L. *com-,* together + *vergere,* to turn] to come or bring together at a point

con·ver′gence *n.* **1.** the act or fact of converging **2.** the point at which things converge —**con·ver′gent** *adj.*

con·ver·sant (kən vur′s'nt, kän′vər-) *adj.* [see CONVERSE[1]] familiar or acquainted (*with*); versed (*in*)

con·ver·sa·tion (kän′vər sā′shən) *n.* a talking together; specif., informal talk

con′ver·sa′tion·al *adj.* **1.** of or for conversation **2.** given to conversation —**con′ver·sa′tion·al·ist** *n.* —**con′ver·sa′-tion·al·ly** *adv.*

conversation piece an unusual article of furniture, etc. that attracts attention or invites comment

con·verse[1] (kən vurs′) *vi.* **-versed′, -vers′ing** [< L. *conversari,* to live with] to hold a conversation; talk —*n.* (kän′vərs) conversation

con·verse[2] (kän′vərs, kən vurs′) *adj.* [see CONVERT] reversed in position, order, etc.; opposite; contrary —*n.* (kän′vərs) a thing related in a converse way; the opposite —**con·verse′ly** *adv.*

con·ver·sion (kən vur′zhən) *n.* a converting or being converted

con·vert (kən vurt′) *vt.* [< L. *com-,* together + *vertere,* to turn] **1.** to change; transform **2.** to change from one belief, religion, etc. to another **3.** to exchange for something equal in value **4.** *Law* to take and use (another's property) unlawfully —*vi.* **1.** to be converted **2.** *Football* to score the extra point or points after a touchdown —*n.* (kän′vərt) a person converted, as to a religion

con·vert′er *n.* a person or thing that converts; specif., a furnace for converting pig iron into steel: also sp. **con·ver′tor**

con·vert·i·ble (kən vur′tə b'l) *adj.* that can be converted —*n.* an automobile with a folding top —**con·vert′i·bil′i·ty** *n.*

con·vex (kän veks′, kän′veks) *adj.* [< L. *com-,* together + *vehere,* bring] curving outward, like the surface of a sphere —*n.* (*usually* kän′veks) a convex surface, object, etc. —**con·vex′i·ty** *n., pl.* **-ties** —**con·vex′ly** *adv.*

con·vey (kən vā′) *vt.* [< L. *com-,* together + *via,* way] **1.** to take from one place to another; transport; carry **2.** to transmit **3.** to communicate **4.** to transfer, as title to property, to another person —**con·vey′a·ble** *adj.*

CONVEX LENSES
(A, plano-convex;
B, convexo-concave;
C, convexo-convex)

con·vey′ance *n.* **1.** a conveying **2.** a means of conveying, esp. a vehicle **3.** *a)* the transfer of real property from one person to another *b)* a deed

con·vey′or, con·vey′er *n.* one that conveys; esp., a mechanical contrivance, as a continuous chain or belt (**conveyor belt**)

con·vict (kən vikt′) *vt.* [see CONVINCE] to prove or find (a person) guilty —*n.* (kän′vikt) a convicted person serving a prison sentence

con·vic′tion (-vik′shən) *n.* **1.** a convicting or being convicted **2.** a being convinced **3.** a strong belief

con·vince (kən vins′) *vt.* **-vinced′, -vinc′ing** [< L. *com-,* intens. + *vincere,* conquer] to persuade by argument or evidence; make feel sure —**con·vinc′er** *n.* —**con·vinc′-ing·ly** *adv.*

con·viv·i·al (kən viv′ē əl) *adj.* [< L. *com-,* together + *vivere,* to live] **1.** festive **2.** fond of eating, drinking, and good company; sociable —**con·viv′i·al′i·ty** *n.*

con·vo·ca·tion (kän′və kā′shən) *n.* **1.** a convoking **2.** an assembly —**con′vo·ca′tion·al** *adj.*

con·voke (kən vōk′) *vt.* **-voked′, -vok′ing** [< L. *com-,* together + *vocare,* to call] to call together; assemble

con·vo·lut·ed (kän′və lōot′id) *adj.* **1.** coiled **2.** involved; complicated

con·vo·lu′tion (-lōo′shən) *n.* [< L. *com-,* together + *volvere,* to roll] **1.** a twisting, coiling, or winding together **2.** a convoluted condition **3.** any of the irregular folds or ridges on the surface of the brain

con·voy (kän′voi, kən voi′) *vt.* [see CONVEY] to escort in order to protect —*n.* (kän′voi) **1.** the act of convoying **2.** a protecting escort, as for ships or troops **3.** ships, vehicles, etc. traveling together for mutual protection

con·vulse (kən vuls′) *vt.* **-vulsed′, -vuls′ing** [< L. *com-,* together + *vellere,* to pluck] **1.** to shake violently; agitate **2.** to cause to shake with laughter, rage, etc. —**con·vul′-sive** *adj.* —**con·vul′sive·ly** *adv.*

con·vul′sion (-vul′shən) *n.* **1.** a violent, involuntary contraction or spasm of the muscles: *often used in pl.* **2.** a fit of laughter **3.** any violent disturbance

co·ny (kō′nē) *n., pl.* **-nies** *same as* CONEY

coo (kōo) *vi.* [echoic] **1.** to make the soft, murmuring sound of pigeons or doves **2.** to speak gently and lovingly: now only in *bill and coo* —*vt.* to say lovingly, as with a coo —*n.* a cooing sound —**coo′ing·ly** *adv.*

cook (kook) *n.* [< L. *coquere,* to cook] one who prepares food —*vt.* **1.** to prepare (food) by boiling, baking, frying, etc. **2.** [Slang] to spoil —*vi.* **1.** to act as a cook **2.** to undergo cooking —**cook up** [Colloq.] to concoct; devise —**cook′er** *n.*

cook′book′ *n.* a book with recipes and other information about preparing food

cook′er·y (-ər ē) *n.* [Chiefly Brit.] the art or practice of cooking

cook·ie, cook·y (kook′ē) *n., pl.* **-ies** [prob. < Du. *koek,* a cake] a small, sweet cake, usually flat

cook′out′ *n.* a meal cooked and eaten outdoors

cool (kōol) *adj.* [OE. *col*] **1.** moderately cold **2.** tending to reduce the effects of heat [*cool clothes*] **3.** *a)* not excited; composed *b)* restrained [*cool jazz*] **4.** [Slang] dispassionate **5.** showing dislike or indifference **6.** calmly bold **7.** [Colloq.] without exaggeration [*a cool thousand dollars*] **8.** [Slang] pleasing —*n.* **1.** a cool time, place, etc. [*the cool of* the night] 2. [Slang] dispassionate manner —*adv.* in a cool manner —*vt., vi.* to make or become cool —**cool′ly** *adv.* —**cool′ness** *n.*

cool′ant (-ənt) *n.* a fluid or other substance for cooling engines, etc.

cool′er *n.* 1. a place for keeping things cool 2. anything that cools 3. [Slang] a jail

Coo·lidge (kōō′lij), (**John**) **Calvin** 1872–1933; 30th president of the U.S. (1923–29)

coo·lie (kōō′lē) *n.* [Hindi *qūlī,* servant] an unskilled native laborer, esp. formerly, in China, India, etc.

coon (kōōn) *n. clipped form of* RACCOON

coop (kōōp) *n.* [ult. < L. *cupa,* cask] 1. a small cage, pen, or building for poultry, etc. 2. any place of confinement; specif., [Slang] a jail —*vt.* to confine as in a coop —**fly the coop** [Slang] to escape

co-op (kō′äp) *n.* [Colloq.] a cooperative

coop·er (kōōp′ər) *n.* [see COOP] one whose work is making or repairing barrels and casks —*vt., vi.* to make or repair (barrels and casks) —**coop′er·age** (-ij) *n.*

Coop·er (kōōp′ər), **James Fen·i·more** (fen′ə môr′) 1789–1851; U.S. novelist

co·op·er·ate, co-op·er·ate (kō äp′ə rāt′) *vi.* -at′ed, -at′ing [< L. *co-,* with + *opus,* work] to act or work together with another or others for a common purpose: also **co·öp′er·ate** —**co·op·er·a′tion, co-op′er·a′tion** *n.*

co·op·er·a·tive, co-op·er·a·tive (kō äp′ər ə tiv, -ə rāt′iv) *adj.* 1. cooperating or inclined to cooperate 2. designating or of an organization, apartment house, etc. owned collectively by members who share in its benefits —*n.* a cooperative society, store, etc. Also **co·öp′er·a·tive** —**co·op′er·a·tive·ness, co-op′er·a·tive·ness** *n.*

co-opt (kō äpt′) *vt.* [< L. *co-,* with + *optare,* choose] 1. to elect or appoint as an associate 2. to persuade or lure (an opponent) to join one's own system, party, etc.

co·or·di·nate, co-or·di·nate (kō ôr′d'n it, -də nāt′) *adj.* [< L. *co-,* with + *ordo,* order] 1. of equal order, rank, or importance [*coordinate* clauses in a sentence] 2. of coordination or coordinates —*n.* 1. a coordinate person or thing 2. any of a system of numbers used to define the position of a point, line, etc. —*vt.* (-də nāt′) -nat′ed, -nat′ing 1. to make coordinate 2. to bring into proper order or relation; adjust; harmonize —*vi.* to become coordinate Also **co·ör′di·nate** —**co·or′di·na′tor, co-or′di·na′tor** *n.*

coordinating conjunction a conjunction that connects coordinate words, phrases, or clauses (Ex.: *and, but, for*)

co·or′di·na′tion, co-or′di·na′tion *n.* 1. a coordinating or being coordinated 2. harmonious adjustment or action, as of muscles Also **co·ör′di·na′tion**

coot (kōōt) *n.* [< ? MDu. *koet*] 1. a ducklike bird 2. [Colloq.] a foolish or senile person

coot·ie (kōōt′ē) *n.* [< Polynesian *kutu,* parasitic insect] [Slang] a louse

cop (käp) *vt.* **copped, cop′ping** [? ult. < L. *capere,* to take] [Slang] to seize, win, steal, etc. —*n.* [Slang] a policeman —**cop out** [Slang] 1. to confess to the police 2. *a*) to renege *b*) to quit

co·part·ner (kō pärt′nər) *n.* a partner —**co·part′ner·ship′** *n.*

cope¹ (kōp) *vi.* **coped, cop′ing** [< OFr. *coup,* a blow] 1. to fight or contend (*with*) successfully 2. to deal with problems, troubles, etc.

cope² (kōp) *n.* [< ML. *cappa*] 1. a large, capelike vestment worn by priests 2. anything that covers like this, as a canopy —*vt.* **coped, cop′ing** to cover with a cope

Co·pen·ha·gen (kō′pən hā′gən, -hä′-) capital of Denmark: pop. 874,000 (met. area 1,378,000)

Co·per·ni·cus (kō pur′ni kəs), **Nic·o·la·us** (nik′ə lā′əs) 1473–1543; Pol. astronomer —**Co·per′ni·can** *adj., n.*

cop·i·er (käp′ē ər) *n.* 1. one who copies; imitator, transcriber, etc. 2. a duplicating machine

co·pi·lot (kō′pī′lət) *n.* the assistant pilot of an aircraft

cop·ing (kō′piŋ) *n.* [< COPE²] the top layer of a masonry wall

coping saw a saw with a narrow blade in a U-shaped frame, esp. for cutting curved outlines

co·pi·ous (kō′pē əs) *adj.* [< L. *copia,* abundance] plentiful; abundant —**co′pi·ous·ly** *adv.* —**co′pi·ous·ness** *n.*

cop-out (käp′out′) *n.* [Slang] a copping out, as by confessing, backing down, or quitting

cop·per (käp′ər) *n.* [< LL. *cuprum*] 1. a reddish-brown, ductile metallic element: symbol,

COPING SAW

Cu; at. wt., 63.546; at. no., 29 2. [Now chiefly Brit.] a copper coin, as a penny 3. reddish brown —*adj.* 1. of copper 2. reddish-brown —**cop′per·y** *adj.*

cop·per·as (käp′ər əs) *n.* [< ML. *cuprosa*] ferrous sulfate, a green, crystalline compound used in dyeing, the making of ink, etc.

cop′per·head′ *n.* 1. a poisonous N. American snake 2. [**C-**] a Northerner who sympathized with the South during the Civil War

cop′per·plate′ *n.* 1. a sheet of copper etched or engraved for printing 2. a print made from this 3. copperplate printing or engraving

co·pra (kō′prə, käp′rə) *n.* [Port. < Hindi *khoprā*] dried coconut meat, the source of coconut oil

copse (käps) *n.* [< OFr. *couper,* to cut] a thicket of small trees or shrubs: also **cop·pice** (käp′is)

Copt (käpt) *n.* a native of Egypt descended from the ancient inhabitants of that country

Cop·tic (käp′tik) *adj.* of the Copts, their language, etc. — *n.* the Afro-Asiatic language of the Copts

cop·u·la (käp′yə lə) *n., pl.* **-las** [L. < *co-,* together + *apere,* to join] something that connects or links together; specif., *same as* LINKING VERB

cop′u·late′ (-lāt′) *vi.* **-lat′ed, -lat′ing** [see COPULA] to have sexual intercourse —**cop′u·la′tion** *n.*

cop′u·la·tive (-lāt′iv, -lə tiv) *adj.* 1. coupling 2. *Gram. a*) connecting coordinate words, phrases, or clauses *b*) of connected words or clauses *c*) being a copula [*a copulative verb*] 3. of or for copulating —*n.* a copulative word

cop·y (käp′ē) *n., pl.* **-ies** [< L. *copia,* plenty] 1. a thing made just like another 2. any of a number of books, magazines, etc. having the same contents 3. a manuscript to be set in type 4. subject matter for a writer 5. the words of an advertisement —*vt., vi.* **-ied, -y·ing** 1. to make a copy of 2. to imitate

cop′y·ist (-ist) *n.* 1. one who makes written copies; transcriber 2. one who imitates

cop′y·right′ *n.* the exclusive legal right to the publication, sale, etc. of a literary or artistic work —*vt.* to protect (a book, etc.) by copyright —*adj.* protected by copyright

cop′y·writ′er *n.* a writer of copy, esp. for advertisements

co·quet (kō ket′) *vi.* **-quet′ted, -quet′ting** [< Fr. *coq,* rooster] 1. to flirt 2. to trifle (*with*) —**co·quet·ry** (kōk′ə trē, kō ket′rē) *n., pl.* **-ries**

co·quette (kō ket′) *n.* [Fr.: see COQUET] a girl or woman flirt —*vi.* **-quet′ted, -quet′ting** to flirt —**co·quet′tish** *adj.* —**co·quet′tish·ly** *adv.*

Cor. Corinthians

cor- *same as* COM-: used before *r*

cor·al (kôr′əl) *n.* [< Gr. *korallion*] 1. the hard, stony skeleton of some marine polyps, often in masses forming reefs and atolls in tropical seas 2. any of such polyps 3. a piece of coral 4. yellowish red —*adj.* 1. made of coral 2. yellowish-red

cor·bel (kôr′bəl) *n.* [< L. *corvus,* raven] a bracket of stone, wood, etc. projecting from a wall to support a cornice, etc. —*vt.* **-beled** or **-belled, -bel·ing** or **-bel·ling** to provide with corbels

CORBEL

cord (kôrd) *n.* [< Gr. *chordē*] 1. thick string 2. any force acting as a tie or bond 3. a measure of wood cut for fuel (128 cu. ft.) 4. *a*) a rib on the surface of a fabric *b*) corduroy *c*) [*pl.*] corduroy trousers 5. *Anat.* any part like a cord [the spinal *cord*] : also **chord** 6. *Elec.* a slender, insulated cable with a plug —*vt.* 1. to fasten with a cord 2. to stack (wood) in cords

cord′age (-ij) *n.* 1. cords and ropes collectively 2. the amount of wood, in cords, in an area

cor·date (kôr′dāt) *adj.* [< L. *cor,* heart] heart-shaped

cor·dial (kôr′jəl) *adj.* [< L. *cor,* heart] warm and friendly; hearty —*n.* 1. [Rare] a stimulating medicine, food, or drink 2. an aromatic, alcoholic drink —**cor·di·al·i·ty** (kôr′jē al′ə tē, kôr jal′-) *n., pl.* **-ties** —**cor′dial·ly** *adv.*

cor·dil·le·ra (kôr′dil yer′ə, kôr dil′ər ə) *n.* [Sp. < L. *chorda,* a cord] a chain of mountains

cord·ite (kôr′dīt) *n.* [< CORD: it is stringy] a smokeless explosive made of nitroglycerin, guncotton, etc.

cord·less (kôrd′lis) *adj.* operated by batteries rather than by current from an outlet

cor·don (kôr′d'n) *n.* [see CORD] 1. a line or circle of police, ships, etc. guarding an area 2. a cord, ribbon, or braid worn as a decoration

cor·do·van (kôr′də vən) *n.* [< *Córdoba,* Spain] 1. a fine-grained, colored leather, usually of split horsehide 2. [*pl.*] shoes made of this —*adj.* made of cordovan

cor·du·roy (kôr'də roi') *n.* [prob. < CORD + obs. *duroy*, coarse fabric] **1.** a heavy, ribbed cotton fabric **2.** [*pl.*] trousers made of this —*adj.* **1.** made of, or ribbed like, corduroy **2.** made of logs laid crosswise [a corduroy road]

core (kôr) *n.* [prob. < L. *cor*, heart] **1.** the central part of an apple, pear, etc. **2.** the central part of anything **3.** the most important part **4.** *Elec.* a mass of iron inside a wire coil: it increases the magnetic field —*vt.* **cored, cor'ing** to remove the core of —**cor'er** *n.*

co·re·spond·ent (kō'ri spän'dənt) *n.* [CO- + RESPONDENT] *Law* a person charged with having committed adultery with the wife or husband from whom a divorce is being sought

co·ri·an·der (kôr'ē an'dər) *n.* [< Gr. *koriandron*] **1.** a European herb of the parsley family **2.** its strong-smelling, seedlike fruit, used as a flavoring

Cor·inth (kôr'inth) ancient city in S Greece

Co·rin·thi·an (kə rin'thē ən) *adj.* **1.** of Corinth, its people, or culture **2.** dissolute and loving luxury **3.** designating or of an order of Greek architecture, distinguished by a bell-shaped capital with a design of acanthus leaves —*n.* a native or inhabitant of Corinth

Co·rin'thi·ans either of two books of the New Testament, epistles from the Apostle Paul to the Christians of Corinth

cork (kôrk) *n.* [< Sp. < L. *quercus*, oak] **1.** the light, thick, elastic outer bark of an oak tree, the **cork oak 2.** a piece of cork; esp., a stopper for a bottle, etc. **3.** any stopper **4.** the outer bark of woody plants —*vt.* **1.** to stop with a cork **2.** to blacken with burnt cork

cork'er *n.* [Slang] a remarkable person or thing

cork'ing *adj., adv., interj.* [Chiefly Brit. Slang] very good

cork'screw' *n.* a spiral-shaped device for pulling corks out of bottles —*adj.* shaped like a corkscrew —*vi., vt.* to twist

cork'y *adj.* **-i·er, -i·est 1.** of or like cork **2.** tasting of the cork: said of wine

corm (kôrm) *n.* [< Gr. *kormos*, a log] the fleshy, underground stem of certain plants, as the gladiolus

cor·mo·rant (kôr'mə rənt) *n.* [< L. *corvus*, raven + *marinus*, marine] **1.** a large, voracious, diving bird with webbed toes **2.** a greedy person

corn¹ (kôrn) *n.* [OE.] **1.** a small, hard seed, esp. of a cereal grass; kernel **2.** a grain borne on cobs enclosed in husks; maize **3.** [Brit.] grain **4.** the leading cereal crop, as wheat in England or oats in Scotland and Ireland **5.** [Slang] ideas, humor, etc. considered old-fashioned, trite, etc. —*vt.* to pickle (meat, etc.) in brine —**corned** *adj.*

corn² (kôrn) *n.* [< L. *cornu*, a horn] a hard, thick growth of skin, esp. on a toe

corn'cob' (-käb') *n.* **1.** the woody core of an ear of corn **2.** a tobacco pipe (**corncob pipe**) with a bowl made of a hollowed piece of such a core

cor·ne·a (kôr'nē ə) *n.* [< L. *cornu*, a horn] the transparent outer coat of the eyeball —**cor'ne·al** *adj.*

cor·ner (kôr'nər) *n.* [< L. *cornu*, horn] **1.** the point or place where lines or surfaces join and form an angle **2.** the angle so formed **3.** the tip of any angle formed at a street intersection **4.** something used to form, protect, or decorate a corner **5.** a remote or secluded spot **6.** region; quarter [every *corner* of America] **7.** an awkward position from which escape is difficult **8.** a monopoly acquired on a stock or commodity to raise the price —*vt.* **1.** to force into a corner (sense 7) **2.** to get a monopoly on —*vi.* **1.** to be on a corner: said of buildings, etc. **2.** to turn corners: said of a vehicle —*adj.* at, on, or for a corner —**cut corners** to cut down expenses, time, etc. —**cor'nered** *adj.*

cor'ner·stone' (-stōn') *n.* **1.** a stone laid in the corner of a building, esp. at a ceremony for beginning a building **2.** the basic part; foundation

cor·net (kôr net') *n.* [< L. *cornu*, a horn] **1.** a brass-wind musical instrument of the trumpet class **2.** *a)* a cone-shaped paper for candy, etc. *b)* a cone-shaped pastry — **cor·net'ist, cor·net'tist** *n.*

corn·flakes (kôrn'flāks') *n.pl.* a breakfast cereal of crisp flakes made from hulled corn

corn'flow'er *n.* an annual plant of the composite family, with white, pink, or blue flowers

CORNET

cor·nice (kôr'nis) *n.* [Fr. < Gr. *korōnis*, a wreath] **1.** a horizontal molding projecting along the top of a wall, etc. **2.** the top part of an entablature

Cor·nish (kôr'nish) *adj.* of Cornwall, its people, etc. —*n.* the Celtic language formerly spoken in Cornwall

corn'meal' *n.* meal made from maize

corn'starch' (-stärch') *n.* a starch made from maize, used in cooking

cor·nu·co·pi·a (kôr'nə kō'pē ə, -nyōō-) *n.* [L. *cornu copiae*, horn of plenty] **1.** a horn-shaped container overflowing with fruits, flowers, and grain; horn of plenty **2.** an abundance

Corn·wall (kôrn'wôl) county at the SW tip of England

Corn·wal·lis (kôrn wôl'is), **Charles**, 1st Marquis Cornwallis, 1738–1805; a commander of Brit. forces in the Am. Revolution

CORNUCOPIA

corn·y (kôr'nē) *adj.* **-i·er, -i·est 1.** of corn **2.** [Colloq.] unsophisticated, trite, etc. —**corn'i·ness** *n.*

co·rol·la (kə räl'ə, -rōl'-) *n.* [< L. *corona*, crown] the petals of a flower

cor·ol·lar·y (kôr'ə ler'ē) *n., pl.* **-ies** [< L. *corollarium*, a gift] **1.** a proposition following from one already proved **2.** an inference or deduction **3.** a normal result

co·ro·na (kə rō'nə) *n., pl.* **-nas, -nae** (-nē) [L., crown] **1.** a crown **2.** *Anat.* the upper part of a tooth, skull, etc. **3.** *Astron. a)* the outermost part of the sun's atmosphere, seen during a total eclipse *b)* a ring of colored light around the sun or moon **4.** *Bot.* the cuplike part on the inner side of the corolla **5.** *Elec.* a sometimes visible electric discharge around a conductor —**cor·o'nal** *adj.*

Co·ro·na·do (kôr'ə nä'dō; *Sp.* kō'rô nä'thô), **Fran·cis·co Vás·quez de** (frän thes'kô väs'keth *the*) 1510?–54?; Sp. explorer in SW N. America

cor·o·nar·y (kôr'ə ner'ē) *adj.* **1.** of or like a crown **2.** of the arteries supplying blood to the heart muscle —*n., pl.* **-ies** *same as* CORONARY THROMBOSIS

coronary thrombosis the formation of an obstructing clot in a coronary artery

cor·o·na·tion (kôr'ə nā'shən) *n.* the crowning of a sovereign

cor·o·ner (kôr'ə nər) *n.* [ME., officer of the crown] a public officer who must determine by inquest before a jury the causes of any deaths not obviously due to natural causes

cor·o·net (kôr'ə net') *n.* [< OFr. *corone*, crown] **1.** a small crown worn by nobility **2.** a band of jewels, flowers, etc. worn around the head

Co·rot (kə rō'; *Fr.* kô rō'), **Jean** (zhän) 1796–1875; Fr. painter

corp., corpn. corporation

cor·po·ral¹ (kôr'pər əl) *n.* [< Fr. < It. < L. *caput*, the head] the lowest-ranking noncommissioned officer, just below a sergeant: abbrev. **Corp., Cpl**

cor·po·ral² (kôr'pər əl) *adj.* [< L. *corpus*, body] of the body —**cor'po·ral'i·ty** (-pə ral'ə tē) *n.* —**cor'po·ral·ly** *adv.*

corporal punishment punishment inflicted directly on the body, as flogging

cor·po·rate (kôr'pər it) *adj.* [< L. *corpus*, body] **1.** incorporated **2.** of a corporation **3.** shared by all in a group — **cor'po·rate·ly** *adv.*

cor·po·ra·tion (kôr'pə rā'shən) *n.* a group of people organized, as to operate a business, under a charter granting them as a body some of the legal rights and liabilities of an individual

cor·po·re·al (kôr pôr'ē əl) *adj.* [< L. *corpus*, body] **1.** of or for the body **2.** material; physical —**cor·po're·al'i·ty** (-al'ə tē) *n.* —**cor·po're·al·ly** *adv.*

corps (kôr) *n., pl.* **corps** (kôrz) [< L. *corpus*, body] **1.** a body of people associated in some work, organization, etc. **2.** *Mil. a)* a specialized branch of the armed forces [Signal Corps] *b)* a tactical subdivision of an army

corpse (kôrps) *n.* [see CORPS] a dead body, esp. of a person

cor·pu·lence (kôr'pyoo ləns) *n.* [< L. *corpus*, body] fatness; obesity: also **cor'pu·len·cy** —**cor'pu·lent** *adj.*

cor·pus (kôr'pəs) *n., pl.* **-po·ra** (-pər ə) [L.] **1.** a body, esp. a dead one: mainly used facetiously **2.** a complete collection, as of laws or writings of a specified type **3.** the substance of anything

Corpus Christ·i (kris'tē) city in SE Tex.: pop. 205,000

cor·pus·cle (kôr′pəs 'l, -pus″l) *n.* [< L. *corpus,* body] **1.** a very small particle **2.** any of the erythrocytes (**red corpuscles**) or leukocytes (**white corpuscles**) in the blood, lymph, etc. of vertebrates —**cor·pus′cu·lar** (-kyoo lər) *adj.*

corpus de·lic·ti (di lik′tī) [ModL., lit., body of the crime] **1.** the facts constituting or proving a crime **2.** loosely, the body of a murder victim

cor·ral (kə ral′) *n.* [Sp. < L. *currere,* to run] an enclosure for horses, cattle, etc.; pen —*vt.* **-ralled′, -ral′ling 1.** to drive into or confine in a corral **2.** to surround or capture; round up

cor·rect (kə rekt′) *vt.* [< L. *com-,* together + *regere,* lead straight] **1.** to make right **2.** to mark the errors of **3.** to make conform to a standard **4.** to scold or punish **5.** to cure or counteract (a defect) —*adj.* **1.** conforming to an established standard **2.** true; accurate; right —**cor·rec′tive** *adj., n.* —**cor·rect′ly** *adv.* —**cor·rect′ness** *n.* —**cor·rec′tor** *n.*

cor·rec·tion (kə rek′shən) *n.* **1.** a correcting or being corrected **2.** a change that corrects a mistake; rectification **3.** punishment to correct faults —**cor·rec′tion·al** *adj.*

cor·re·late (kôr′ə lāt′) *n.* [see COM- & RELATE] either of two interrelated things —*adj.* closely and naturally related —*vi., vt.* **-lat′ed, -lat′ing** to be in or bring into mutual relation —**cor′re·la′tion** *n.*

cor·rel·a·tive (kə rel′ə tiv) *adj.* **1.** having a mutual relationship **2.** *Gram.* expressing mutual relation and used in pairs, as the conjunctions *neither...nor* —*n.* **1.** a correlate **2.** a correlative word —**cor·rel′a·tive·ly** *adv.*

cor·re·spond (kôr′ə spänd′) *vi.* [< L. *com-,* together + *respondere,* to answer] **1.** to be in agreement (*with* something); match **2.** to be similar or equal (*to*) **3.** to communicate by letters —**cor′re·spond′ing·ly** *adv.*

cor′re·spond′ence *n.* **1.** agreement; conformity **2.** similarity; analogy **3.** *a*) communication by exchange of letters *b*) the letters written or received

correspondence school a school that gives courses of instruction (**correspondence courses**) by mail

cor′re·spond′ent *adj.* corresponding —*n.* **1.** a thing that corresponds **2.** one who exchanges letters with another **3.** one hired by a newspaper to send news regularly from a distant place

cor·ri·dor (kôr′ə dər, -dôr′) *n.* [Fr. < L. *currere,* to run] **1.** a long passageway or hall **2.** a strip of land providing passage through foreign-held land

cor·rob·o·rate (kə räb′ə rāt′) *vt.* **-rat′ed, -rat′ing** [< L. *com-,* intens. + *robur,* strength] to confirm; bolster; support —**cor·rob′o·ra′tion** *n.* —**cor·rob′o·ra′tor** *n.*

cor·rob′o·ra′tive *adj.* corroborating; confirmatory: also **cor·rob′o·ra·to′ry** (-ər ə tôr′ē)

cor·rode (kə rōd′) *vt., vi.* **-rod′ed, -rod′ing** [< L. *com-,* intens. + *rodere,* to gnaw] to eat into or wear away gradually, as by rusting

cor·ro·sion (-rō′zhən) *n.* **1.** a corroding or being corroded **2.** a substance formed by corroding —**cor·ro′sive** (-siv) *adj., n.*

cor·ru·gate (kôr′ə gāt′) *vt., vi.* **-gat′ed, -gat′ing** [< L. *com-,* intens. + *rugare,* to wrinkle] to shape into parallel grooves and ridges; furrow *[corrugated* iron] —**cor′ru·ga′tion** *n.*

cor·rupt (kə rupt′) *adj.* [< L. *com-,* together + *rumpere,* to break] **1.** morally debased; evil; depraved **2.** taking bribes —*vt., vi.* to make or become corrupt —**cor·rupt′er** *n.* —**cor·rupt′i·ble** *adj.* —**cor·rup′tive** *adj.* —**cor·rupt′ness** *n.*

cor·rup′tion *n.* **1.** a making, becoming, or being corrupt **2.** depravity **3.** bribery **4.** decay **5.** something corrupted

cor·sage (kôr säzh′) *n.* [Fr.: see CORPS & -AGE] a small bouquet for a woman to wear, as at the waist or shoulder

cor·sair (kôr′ser) *n.* [< Fr. < L. *cursus,* a COURSE] **1.** a privateer **2.** a pirate **3.** a pirate ship

corse·let (kôrs′lət) *n.* [see CORPS] **1.** a medieval piece of body armor: also sp. **cors′let 2.** (kôr′sə let′) a woman's lightweight corset: also sp. **cor′se·lette′**

cor·set (kôr′sit) *n.* [see CORPS] [*sometimes pl.*] a closefitting undergarment worn, chiefly by women, to give support to or shape the torso —*vt.* to dress in, or fit with, a corset

Cor·si·ca (kôr′si kə) Fr. island in the Mediterranean, west of Italy —**Cor′si·can** *adj., n.*

cor·tege, cor·tège (kôr tezh′, -tāzh′) *n.* [Fr. < L.: see COURT] **1.** a group of attendants; retinue **2.** a ceremonial procession

Cor·tés (kôr tez′), **Her·nan·do** (hər nan′dō) 1485–1547; Sp. explorer: conqueror of Mexico: also sp. **Cortez**

cor·tex (kôr′teks) *n., pl.* **-ti·ces** (-tə sēz′) [L., bark of a tree] **1.** *a*) the outer part of an internal organ, as of the kidney *b*) the layer of gray matter over most of the brain **2.** the bark or rind of a plant —**cor′ti·cal** (-ti k'l) *adj.*

cor·ti·sone (kôrt′ə sōn′, -zōn′) *n.* [< CORTEX (of adrenals)] an adrenal-gland hormone used in treating adrenal insufficiency and various inflammatory and allergic diseases

co·run·dum (kə run′dəm) *n.* [< Sans. *kuruvinda,* ruby] a hard mineral, aluminum oxide, Al_2O_3, used for grinding and polishing

cor·us·cate (kôr′əs kāt′) *vi.* **-cat′ed, -cat′ing** [< L. *coruscus,* vibrating] to glitter; sparkle —**cor′us·ca′tion** *n.*

cor·vette (kôr vet′) *n.* [Fr., prob. ult. < L. *corbis,* basket] **1.** formerly, a warship smaller than a frigate **2.** a small, fast British warship used esp. for convoy duty

cor·ymb (kôr′im, -imb) *n.* [< Gr. *korymbos*] a broad, flat cluster of flowers in which the outer stems are long and those toward the center progressively shorter

co·ry·za (kə rī′zə) *n.* [< Gr. *koryza,* catarrh] a cold in the head; acute nasal congestion

Cos., cos. 1. companies **2.** counties

co·se·cant (kō sē′kənt) *n. Trigonometry* the ratio between the hypotenuse and the side opposite a given acute angle in a right triangle

co·sign (kō′sīn′) *vt., vi.* **1.** to sign (a promissory note) along with the maker, thus becoming responsible if the maker defaults **2.** to sign jointly —**co′sign′er** *n.*

co·sig·na·to·ry (kō sig′nə tôr′ē) *n., pl.* **-ries** one of two or more joint signers

co·sine (kō′sīn) *n. Trigonometry* the ratio between the side adjacent to a given acute angle in a right triangle and the hypotenuse

cos·met·ic (käz met′ik) *adj.* [< Gr. *kosmos,* order] designed to beautify the complexion, hair, etc. —*n.* any cosmetic preparation, as lipstick —**cos·met′i·cal·ly** *adv.*

cos·mic (käz′mik) *adj.* [< Gr. *kosmos,* order] **1.** of the cosmos **2.** vast —**cos′mi·cal·ly** *adv.*

cosmic rays streams of highly penetrating charged particles that bombard the earth from outer space

cos·mog·o·ny (käz mäg′ə nē) *n.* [< Gr. *kosmos,* universe + *gignesthai,* to produce] **1.** the origin of the universe **2.** *pl.* **-nies** a theory of this

cos·mol·o·gy (-mäl′ə jē) *n.* [< Gr. *kosmos,* universe + -LOGY] the study of the physical nature, form, etc. of the universe as a whole

cos·mo·naut (käz′mə nôt′) *n.* [< Russ. < Gr. *kosmos,* universe + *nautēs,* sailor] *same as* ASTRONAUT

cos·mo·pol·i·tan (käz′mə päl′ə t'n) *adj.* [< Gr. *kosmos,* world + *polis,* city] **1.** representative of all or many parts of the world **2.** at home in all countries or places —*n.* a cosmopolitan person

cos·mop·o·lite (käz mäp′ə līt′) *n.* a cosmopolitan person

cos·mos (käz′məs, -mōs) *n.* [Gr. *kosmos,* universe] **1.** the universe considered as an orderly system **2.** any complete and orderly system **3.** (-məs) *pl.* **cos′mos** a tropical American plant with white, pink, or purple flowers

co·spon·sor (kō′spän′sər) *n.* a joint sponsor, as of a proposed piece of legislation —*vt.* to be a cosponsor of —**co′spon′sor·ship′** *n.*

Cos·sack (käs′ak, -ək) *n.* a member of a people of S Russia, famous as horsemen

cost (kôst) *vt.* **cost, cost′ing** [< L. *com-,* together + *stare,* to stand] **1.** to be obtained for (a certain price) **2.** to require the expenditure, loss, etc. of **3.** *Business* to estimate the cost of producing (often with *out*) —*n.* **1.** the amount of money, labor, etc. required to get a thing; price **2.** loss; sacrifice **3.** [*pl.*] *Law* court expenses of a lawsuit —**at all costs** by any means required: also **at any cost**

Cos·ta Ri·ca (käs′tə rē′kə, kôs′-) country in Central America: 19,575 sq. mi.; pop. 1,685,000; cap. San José —**Cos′ta Ri′can**

cost′ly *adj.* **-li·er, -li·est 1.** costing much; dear **2.** magnificent; sumptuous —**cost′li·ness** *n.*

cost of living the average cost of the necessities of life, as food, shelter, and clothes

cos·tume (käs′tōom) *n.* [Fr. < L. *consuetudo,* custom] **1.** *a*) the style of dress typical of a certain period, people, etc. *b*) a set of such clothes **2.** a set of outer clothes —*vt.* **-tumed, -tum·ing** to provide with a costume

co·sy (kō′zē) *adj.* **-si·er, -si·est** & *n., pl.* **-sies** *same as* COZY

cot¹ (kät) *n.* [< Hindi *khāt* < Sans.] a narrow bed, as one made of canvas on a folding frame

cot² (kät) *n.* [OE.] **1.** a small shelter **2.** a sheath, as for a hurt finger

co·tan·gent (kō tan′jənt) *n. Trigonometry* the ratio between the side adjacent to a given acute angle in a right triangle and the side opposite

cote (kōt) *n.* [see COT²] **1.** a small shelter for sheep, doves, etc. **2.** [Dial.] a cottage

co·te·rie (kōt′ər ē) *n.* [Fr. < OE. *cot,* hut] a close circle of friends with common interests

co·til·lion (kō til′yən, kə-) *n.* [< Fr.] **1.** a dance with many intricate figures and the continual changing of partners **2.** a formal ball Also sp. **co·til′lon**

cot·tage (kät′ij) *n.* [< OFr. *cote* or ME. *cot,* hut] a small house, now often a summer home

cottage cheese a soft, white cheese made from the curds of sour milk

cot·ter¹, cot·tar (kät′ər) *n.* [see COT²] [Scot.] a tenant farmer

cot·ter² (kät′ər) *n.* [< ?] **1.** a bolt or wedge put through a slot to hold together parts of machinery **2.** *same as* COTTER PIN

cotter pin a split pin used as a cotter, fastened by spreading apart its ends after insertion

cot·ton (kät′'n) *n.* [< Ar. *quṭun*] **1.** the soft, white, fibrous substance around the seeds of certain mallow plants **2.** such a plant or plants **3.** the crop of such plants **4.** thread or cloth made of cotton —*adj.* of cotton —**cotton to** [Colloq.] **1.** to take a liking to **2.** to become aware of (a situation) —**cot′ton·y** *adj.*

COTTER PIN

cotton gin a machine for separating cotton fibers from the seeds

cot′ton·mouth′ *n.* [from its whitish mouth] *same as* WATER MOCCASIN

cot′ton·seed′ *n.* the seed of the cotton plant, yielding an oil (**cottonseed oil**) used in margarine, cooking oil, etc.

cot′ton·tail′ *n.* a common American rabbit with a short, fluffy tail

cot′ton·wood′ *n.* **1.** a poplar that has seeds covered with cottony hairs **2.** its wood

cot·y·le·don (kät′'l ēd′'n) *n.* [< Gr. *kotylē,* a cavity] the first leaf or a leaf of the first pair produced by the embryo of a flowering plant

couch (kouch) *n.* [< OFr. *couchier,* lie down] **1.** an article of furniture on which one may sit or lie down; sofa **2.** any resting place —*vt.* **1.** to lay as on a couch **2.** to bring down; esp., to lower (a spear, etc.) to an attacking position **3.** to put in words, express —*vi.* **1.** to lie down on a bed; recline **2.** to lie in hiding or ambush

couch′ant (-ənt) *adj.* [see prec.] *Heraldry* lying down

cou·gar (koo′gər) *n.* [< Fr. < SAmInd.] a large, tawny-brown animal of the cat family

cough (kôf) *vi.* [ME. *coughen*] to expel air suddenly and noisily from the lungs —*vt.* to expel by coughing —*n.* **1.** a coughing **2.** a condition, as of the lungs or throat, causing frequent coughing

cough drop a small, flavored, medicated tablet for the relief of coughs, hoarseness, etc.

could (kood) *v.* **1.** *pt.* of CAN¹ **2.** an auxiliary generally equivalent to *can,* expressing esp. a shade of doubt [it *could* be so]

could·n't (kood′'nt) could not

couldst (koodst) *archaic or poetic 2d pers. sing., past indic.,* of CAN¹: *used with* thou

cou·lee (koo′lē) *n.* [Fr. < L. *colum,* a strainer] **1.** a stream of lava **2.** [Northwest] a deep ravine, usually dry in summer

cou·lomb (koo läm′) *n.* [< C. A. de *Coulomb* (1736–1806), Fr. physicist] the charge transported through a conductor by a current of one ampere flowing for one second

coun·cil (koun′s'l) *n.* [< L. *com-,* with + *calere,* to call] **1.** a group of people called together for consultation, advice, etc. **2.** an administrative or legislative body [a city *council*] **3.** a church assembly to discuss points of doctrine, etc.

coun′cil·man (-mən) *n., pl.* **-men** a member of a city council —**coun′cil·man′ic** (-man′ik) *adj.*

coun·ci·lor (-ər) *n.* a member of a council: also [Chiefly Brit.] **coun′cil·lor**

coun·sel (koun′s'l) *n.* [< L. *consilium*] **1.** a mutual exchange of ideas, opinions, etc.; discussion **2.** advice **3.** *a)* a lawyer or group of lawyers *b)* a consultant —*vt.* **-seled** or **-selled, -sel·ing** or **-sel·ling 1.** to give advice to **2.** to recommend (a plan, etc.) —*vi.* to give or take advice — **keep one's own counsel** to be silent —**take counsel** to consult

coun′se·lor, coun′sel·lor (-ər) *n.* **1.** an adviser **2.** a law-

yer, esp. one who conducts cases in court: in full, **counselor-at-law 3.** a group worker in a children's camp

count¹ (kount) *vt.* [< L. *computare,* compute] **1.** to name numbers in regular order to (a certain number) [to *count* five] **2.** to add up, so as to get a total **3.** to check by numbering off; inventory **4.** to take account of; include **5.** to believe to be; consider —*vi.* **1.** to name numbers or items in order **2.** to be taken into account; have importance **3.** to have a specified value (often *with for*) **4.** to rely or depend (*on* or *upon*) —*n.* **1.** a counting, or adding up **2.** the total number **3.** a reckoning **4.** *Law* any of the charges in an indictment —**count off** to separate into equal divisions by counting —**count out** to disregard; omit

count² (kount) *n.* [< L. *comes,* companion] a European nobleman equal in rank to an English earl

count′down′ *n.* the schedule of operations just before the firing of a rocket, etc.; also, the counting off, in reverse order, of units of time in such a schedule

coun·te·nance (koun′tə nəns) *n.* [< L. *continentia,* bearing] **1.** the facial expression **2.** the face; facial features **3.** approval; support **4.** calm control; composure — *vt.* **-nanced, -nanc·ing** to give support to; approve —**in countenance** calm; composed —**put out of countenance** to disconcert

count′er¹ *n.* **1.** a small piece of metal, wood, etc. for keeping score in some games **2.** an imitation coin **3.** a long table, board, etc. as in a store or kitchen, for displaying goods, serving, etc. **4.** one that counts

coun·ter² (koun′tər) *adv.* [< L. *contra,* against] in a contrary direction, manner, etc. —*adj.* opposed; contrary —*n.* **1.** the opposite **2.** an opposing action **3.** a stiff leather piece around the heel of a shoe **4.** the part of a ship's stern between the waterline and the curved part **5.** *Boxing* a blow given while parrying an opponent's blow —*vt., vi.* **1.** to oppose or check (a person or thing) **2.** to say or do (something) in reply **3.** *Boxing* to strike one's opponent while parrying (his blow)

counter- [< L. *contra-,* against] *a combining form meaning:* **1.** contrary to [*counterclockwise*] **2.** in retaliation [*counterplot*] **3.** complementary [*counterpart*]

coun′ter·act′ *vt.* to act against; neutralize the effect of — **coun′ter·ac′tion** *n.*

coun′ter·at·tack′ *n.* an attack made in opposition to another attack —*vt., vi.* to attack in opposition

coun′ter·bal′ance *n.* a weight, force, or influence that balances another —*vt.* **-anced, -anc·ing** to be a counterbalance to; offset

coun′ter·claim′ *n.* an opposing claim to offset another — *vt., vi.* to make a counterclaim (of)

coun′ter·clock′wise′ *adj., adv.* in a direction opposite to that in which the hands of a clock move

coun′ter·es′pi·on·age′ *n.* actions to prevent or thwart enemy espionage

coun·ter·feit (koun′tər fit) *adj.* [< OFr. *contre-,* counter- + *faire,* to make] **1.** made in imitation of something genuine so as to defraud; forged [*counterfeit* money] **2.** pretended; sham —*n.* an imitation made to deceive —*vt., vi.* **1.** to make an imitation of (money, etc.) in order to defraud **2.** to pretend —**coun′ter·feit′er** *n.*

coun·ter·mand (koun′tər mand′) *vt.* [< L. *contra,* against + *mandare,* to command] **1.** to cancel (a command) **2.** to order back by a contrary order

coun′ter·march′ *n.* a march back or in the opposite direction —*vi., vt.* to march back

coun′ter·move′ *n.* a move made in opposition or retaliation —*vi., vt.* **-moved′, -mov′ing** to move in opposition or retaliation

coun′ter·of·fen′sive (-ə fen′siv) *n.* an attack by troops who have been defending a position

coun′ter·pane′ (-pān′) *n.* [ult. < L. *culcita puncta,* embroidered quilt] a bedspread

coun′ter·part′ *n.* **1.** a person or thing that closely resembles another **2.** a copy or duplicate

coun′ter·plot′ *n.* a plot to defeat another plot —*vt., vi.* **-plot′ted, -plot′ting** to plot against (a plot); defeat (a plot) with another

coun′ter·point′ *n.* [< Fr. < It.: see COUNTER- & POINT, *n.*] **1.** a melody accompanying another melody note for note **2.** the art of adding related but independent melodies to a basic melody, according to the rules of harmony

coun′ter·poise′ (-poiz′) *n.* [see COUNTER² & POISE] **1.** *same as* COUNTERBALANCE **2.** a state of balance —*vt.* **-poised′, -pois′ing** *same as* COUNTERBALANCE

coun′ter·rev′o·lu′tion *n.* **1.** a political movement to restore the system overthrown by a revolution **2.** a movement to combat revolutionary tendencies —**coun′ter·rev′o·lu′tion·ar′y** *adj., n.* —**coun′ter·rev′o·lu′tion·ist** *n.*

coun′ter·shaft′ *n.* an intermediate shaft that transmits motion from the main shaft of a machine to a working part

coun′ter·sign′ *n.* **1.** a signature added to a previously signed document for confirmation **2.** *Mil.* a secret signal which must be given to a sentry in order to pass —*vt.* to confirm by signing —**coun′ter·sig′na·ture** *n.*

coun′ter·sink′ *vt.* **-sunk′, -sink′ing 1.** to enlarge the top part of (a hole in metal, wood, etc.) to make the head of a bolt, screw, etc. fit into it **2.** to sink (a bolt, screw, etc.) into such a hole —*n.* a tool for countersinking holes

coun′ter·ten′or *n.* **1.** the range of the highest male voice, above tenor **2.** a singer with this range

coun′ter·weigh′ *vt.* same as COUNTERBALANCE —**coun′ter·weight′** *n.*

count·ess (koun′tis) *n.* **1.** the wife or widow of a count or earl **2.** a noblewoman whose rank is equal to that of a count or earl

count′ing·house′ *n.* [Now Rare] an office where a firm keeps accounts, etc.

count′less (-lis) *adj.* too many to count; innumerable; myriad

coun·tri·fied (kun′tri fīd′) *adj.* **1.** rural; rustic **2.** having the appearance, etc. attributed to country people Also sp. **coun′try·fied′**

coun·try (kun′trē) *n., pl.* **-tries** [< VL. *contrata*, that which is beyond] **1.** an area; region **2.** the whole territory or people of a nation **3.** the land of one's birth or citizenship **4.** land with farms and small towns; rural region — *adj.* rural; rustic

country club a social club in the outskirts of a city, with a clubhouse, golf course, etc.

coun′try-dance′ *n.* an English folk dance, esp. one in which partners form two facing lines

coun′try·man (-mən) *n., pl.* **-men 1.** a man who lives in the country **2.** a man of one's own country; compatriot — **coun′try·wom′an** *n.fem., pl.* **-wom′en**

country music rural folk music, esp. of the Southern U.S.

coun′try·side′ *n.* a rural region or its inhabitants

coun·ty (koun′tē) *n., pl.* **-ties** [< L. *comitatus*, jurisdiction of a count] **1.** a small administrative district; esp., a subdivision of a State **2.** the people in a county

county commissioner a member of an elected governing board in the counties of certain States

county seat a town or city that is the seat of government of a county

coup (ko͞o) *n., pl.* **coups** (ko͞oz; *Fr.* ko͞o) [Fr. < L. *colaphus*, a blow] **1.** literally, a blow **2.** a sudden, successful move or action; brilliant stroke **3.** same as COUP D'ÉTAT

‡coup de grâce (ko͞o də gräs′) [Fr., lit., stroke of mercy] **1.** the blow, shot, etc. that brings death to a sufferer **2.** a finishing stroke

‡coup d'é·tat (dā tä′) [Fr., lit., stroke of state] the sudden overthrow of a government

coupe (ko͞op) *n.* [< Fr. *couper*, to cut] a closed, two-door automobile with a body smaller than that of a sedan: also **cou·pé** (ko͞o pā′)

cou·ple (kup′'l) *n.* [< L. *copula*, a link] **1.** anything joining two things together; link **2.** two things or persons of the same sort who are somehow associated **3.** a man and woman who are engaged, married, etc. **4.** [Colloq.] a few —*vt.* **-pled, -pling** to link; connect —*vi.* **1.** to pair; unite **2.** to copulate

cou·pler (kup′lər) *n.* a person or thing that couples; specif., a pneumatic device for coupling two railroad cars

cou·plet (kup′lit) *n.* two successive, rhyming lines of poetry

cou′pling (-liŋ) *n.* **1.** a joining together **2.** a mechanical device for joining parts or things together

cou·pon (ko͞o′pän, kyo͞o′-) *n.* [Fr. < *couper*, to cut] **1.** a detachable printed statement on a bond, specifying the interest due at a given time **2.** a certificate, ticket, etc. entitling the holder to cash, gifts, a reduced purchase price, etc. or to be used as in ordering goods or samples

COUPLING

cour·age (kur′ij) *n.* [< L. *cor*, heart] the quality of being brave; fearlessness; valor

cou·ra·geous (kə rā′jəs) *adj.* having or showing courage; brave —**cou·ra′geous·ly** *adv.*

cou·ri·er (koor′ē ər, kur′-) *n.* [< L. *currere*, to run] a messenger sent in haste or on a regular schedule with important messages

course (kôrs) *n.* [< L. *currere*, to run] **1.** an onward movement; progress **2.** a way, path, or channel **3.** the direction taken **4.** a regular manner of procedure [the law takes its *course*] **5.** a series of like things in order **6.** a part of a meal served at one time **7.** a horizontal layer, as of bricks, in a building **8.** *Educ. a)* a complete series of studies *b)* any of the studies —*vi.* coursed, cours′ing to run or race —in due course in the usual sequence (of events)·—in the course of during —of course 1. naturally 2. certainly

cours·er (kôr′sər) *n.* [Poet.] a graceful, spirited, or swift horse

court (kôrt) *n.* [< L. *cohors*, enclosure] **1.** an uncovered space surrounded by buildings or walls **2.** a short street **3.** a playing area, as for tennis **4.** the palace, or the family and attendants, of a sovereign **5.** a sovereign and his councilors as a governing body **6.** any formal gathering held by a sovereign **7.** attention paid to someone in order to get something **8.** courtship **9.** *Law a)* a judge or judges *b)* a place where trials are held, investigations made, etc. *c)* a judicial assembly —*vt.* **1.** to pay attention to (a person) in order to get something **2.** to try to get the love of; woo **3.** to seek [to *court* favor] —*vi.* to woo — *adj.* of or fit for a court —pay court to to court, as for favor or love

cour·te·ous (kur′tē əs) *adj.* [see COURT & -EOUS] polite and gracious —**cour′te·ous·ly** *adv.*

cour·te·san (kôr′tə zən, kur′-) *n.* [< Fr.] **1.** a prostitute **2.** formerly, a mistress of a king, nobleman, etc. Also **cour′te·zan**

cour·te·sy (kur′tə sē) *n., pl.* **-sies 1.** courteous behavior **2.** a polite or considerate act or remark **3.** a favor

court·house (kôrt′hous′) *n.* **1.** a building in which law courts are held **2.** a building that houses the offices of a county government

cour·ti·er (kôr′tē ər, -tyər) *n.* an attendant at a royal court

court′ly *adj.* **-li·er, -li·est** suitable for a king's court, as in being dignified and elegant —*adv.* in a courtly manner

court′-mar′tial (-mär′shəl) *n., pl.* **courts′-mar′tials**; for 2, now often **court′-mar′tials 1.** a court of personnel in the armed forces to try offenses against military law **2.** a trial by a court-martial —*vt.* **-tialed** or **-tialled, -tial·ing** or **-tial·ling** to try by a court-martial

court′room′ *n.* a room in which a law court is held

court′ship′ *n.* the act, process, or period of courting, or wooing

court′yard′ *n.* a space enclosed by walls, adjoining or in a large building

cous·in (kuz′'n) *n.* [< L. *com-*, with + *soror*, sister] **1.** the son or daughter of one's uncle or aunt: also called **cous′in-ger′man** (-jur′mən), first (or full) cousin **2.** loosely, any relative by blood or marriage —**cous′in·ly** *adj., adv.*

cou·tu·ri·er (ko͞o toor′ē ā′) *n.* [Fr.] a dress designer

cove (kōv) *n.* [< OE. *cofa*, cave, cell] **1.** a sheltered nook **2.** a small bay or inlet **3.** a concave molding

cov·en (kuv′ən, kō′vən) *n.* [see CONVENE] a gathering or meeting, esp. of witches

cov·e·nant (kuv′ə nənt) *n.* [< L. *convenire*, CONVENE] **1.** a binding agreement made by two or more parties; compact **2.** *Law* a formal, sealed contract **3.** *Theol.* the promises made by God to man, as recorded in the Bible —*vt., vi.* to promise by or in a covenant —**cov′e·nant·er, cov′e·nan·tor** *n.*

Cov·en·try (kuv′ən trē, käv′-) city in C England: pop. 335,000 —*n.* ostracism [to send someone to *Coventry*]

cov·er (kuv′ər) *vt.* [< L. *co-*, intens. + *operire*, to hide] **1.** to place something on or over **2.** to extend over; overlay **3.** to clothe **4.** to conceal; hide **5.** to protect as by shielding **6.** to protect financially [to *cover* a loss, debt, etc.] **7.** to take into account **8.** to travel over **9.** to deal with **10.** to point a firearm at **11.** *Journalism* to get news, pictures, etc. of —*vi.* **1.** to spread over a surface, as a liquid **2.** to provide an alibi or excuse (for) —*n.* **1.** anything that covers, as a lid, top, etc. **2.** a shelter or a hiding place **3.** a tablecloth and a place setting for one person **4.** same as COVER-UP **5.** an envelope or wrapper for mail —cover up 1. to cover entirely 2. to conceal —take cover to seek protective shelter —under cover in secrecy or concealment

cov′er·age (-ij) *n.* the amount, extent, etc. covered by something

cov′er·all′ *n.* [usually pl.] a one-piece garment with sleeves and legs, worn like overalls

cover charge a fixed charge added to the cost of food and drink at a nightclub or restaurant

cover crop a crop, as vetch or clover, grown to protect soil from erosion and to keep it fertile

covered wagon a large wagon with an arched cover of canvas, used by American pioneers

cov·er·ing n. anything that covers

cov·er·let (kuv'ər lit) n. [< OFr. *covrir*, COVER + *lit*, a bed] a bedspread: also **cov'er·lid**

cov·ert (kuv'ərt) adj. [see COVER] concealed, hidden, or disguised —n. 1. a protected place; shelter 2. a hiding place for game —**cov'ert·ly** adv.

cov·er-up' n. something used for hiding one's real activities, etc.

cov·et (kuv'it) vt., vi. [< L.: see CUPIDITY] to desire ardently (something that another has)

cov'et·ous (-əs) adj. greedy; avaricious —**cov'et·ous·ly** adv. —**cov'et·ous·ness** n.

cov·ey (kuv'ē) n., pl. **-eys** [< OFr. *cover*, to hatch] a small flock of birds, esp. partridges or quail

cow[1] (kou) n., pl. **cows**; archaic **kine** (kīn) [OE. *cu*] the mature female of domestic cattle, valued for its milk, or of certain other animals, as the buffalo or elephant: the male of such animals is called a *bull*

cow[2] (kou) vt. [< ON. *kūga*, to subdue] to make timid and submissive; overawe

cow·ard (kou'ərd) n. [ult. < L. *cauda*, tail] one who lacks courage or is shamefully afraid —adj. cowardly

cow'ard·ice (-is) n. a shameful lack of courage

cow'ard·ly adj. of or like a coward; shamefully afraid — adv. in the manner of a coward —**cow'ard·li·ness** n.

cow·bell (kou'bel') n. a bell hung from a cow's neck so she can be found by its clanking

cow'boy' (-boi') n. a ranch worker who rides horseback and herds cattle: also **cow'hand'**

cow'catch'er n. a metal frame on the front of a locomotive or streetcar for clearing the tracks

cow·er (kou'ər) vi. [prob. < ON.] to crouch or huddle up, as from fear or cold; shrink; cringe

cow'herd' n. a person who tends grazing cattle

cow'hide' n. 1. the hide of a cow 2. leather made from it 3. a whip made of this

cowl (koul) n. [< L. *cucullus*, hood] 1. a monk's hood 2. a monk's cloak with a hood 3. a cover for the top of a chimney, to increase the draft 4. the top front part of an automobile body, to which the windshield is attached —vt. to cover as with a cowl

COWL

cow'lick' n. [< its looking as if licked by a cow] a tuft of hair that cannot easily be combed flat

cowl'ing n. [see COWL] a detachable metal covering as for an airplane engine

cow'man n., pl. **-men** 1. the owner or operator of a cattle ranch 2. a cowherd

co-work·er (kō'wur'kər) n. a fellow worker

cow'pea' n. 1. a leguminous forage plant with seeds in slender pods 2. its edible seed

cow·pox (kou'päks') n. a disease of cows: its virus is used in vaccination against smallpox

cow'punch'er n. [from the prodding of animals in herding] [Colloq.] a cowboy

cow·rie, cow·ry (kou'rē) n., pl. **-ries** [< Sans. *kaparda*] the shell of a mollusk of warm seas, formerly used as money in parts of Africa and S Asia

cow'shed' n. a shelter for cows

cow·slip (kou'slip') n. 1. a European primrose with yellow or purple flowers 2. same as MARSH MARIGOLD

cox (käks) n., pl. **cox'es** [Colloq.] a coxswain —vt., vi. to be coxswain for (a boat or crew)

cox·comb (käks'kōm') n. [for *cock's comb*] a silly, vain, foppish fellow; dandy

cox·swain (käk's'n, -swān') n. [< *cock* (a small boat) + SWAIN] one who steers a boat or racing shell

coy (koi) adj. [< L. *quietus*: see QUIET] 1. bashful; shy 2. pretending to be innocent or shy, often coquettishly — **coy'ly** adv. —**coy'ness** n.

coy·o·te (kī ōt'ē, kī'ōt) n. [< MexInd.] a small wolf of western N. American prairies

coy·pu (koi'pōō) n. [< AmSp. < native name] same as NUTRIA

coz·en (kuz''n) vt., vi. [< ME. *cosin*, fraud] to cheat, defraud, or deceive

co·zy (kō'zē) adj. **-zi·er**, **-zi·est** [< Scot., prob. < Scand.] warm and comfortable; snug —n., pl. **-zies** a padded cover to keep a teapot hot —**play it cozy** [Slang] to act cautiously —**co'zi·ly** adv. —**co'zi·ness** n.

CPA, C.P.A. Certified Public Accountant

Cpl, Cpl. Corporal

CPO, C.P.O. Chief Petty Officer

Cr *Chem.* chromium

cr. 1. credit 2. creditor 3. crown

crab[1] (krab) n. [< OE. *crabba*] 1. any of various crustaceans with four pairs of legs and a pair of pincers 2. a machine for hoisting heavy weights —[C-] Cancer, the constellation and zodiac sign —vi. **crabbed**, **crab'bing** to fish for or catch crabs —**catch a crab** Rowing to unbalance the boat by a faulty stroke —**crab'ber** n.

crab[2] (krab) n. [akin ? to Scot. *scrabbe*, wild apple] 1. same as CRAB APPLE 2. a sour-tempered person —adj. of a crab apple —vi. **crabbed**, **crab'bing** [Colloq.] to complain peevishly —**crab one's act (the deal, etc.)** [Colloq.] to spoil one's scheme (the deal, etc.) —**crab'ber** n.

crab apple 1. a small, very sour apple, used as for making jellies 2. a tree bearing crab apples: also **crab tree**

crab·bed (krab'id) adj. [< CRAB[2]] 1. peevish; cross 2. hard to understand 3. hard to read; illegible —**crab'bed·ness** n.

crab'by adj. **-bi·er**, **-bi·est** [< CRAB[2]] peevish; cross — **crab'bi·ly** adv. —**crab'bi·ness** n.

crab grass a coarse, weedy grass that spreads quickly

crack (krak) vi. [< OE. *cracian*, to resound] 1. to make a sudden, sharp breaking noise 2. to break or split, usually without complete separation of parts 3. to rasp, as the voice 4. [Colloq.] to break down /to crack under the strain/ —vt. 1. to cause to make a sharp, sudden noise 2. to cause to break or split 3. to subject (petroleum) to cracking: see CRACKING 4. [Colloq.] to hit with a sudden, sharp blow 5. to manage to solve 6. [Colloq.] to break open or into 7. [Slang] to make (a joke) n. 1. a sudden, sharp noise 2. a break, usually partial 3. a chink; fissure 4. an erratic shift of vocal tone 5. [Colloq.] a sudden, sharp blow 6. [Colloq.] an attempt; try 7. [Slang] a joke —adj. [Colloq.] excelling; first-rate —**crack down (on)** to become strict (with) —**cracked up to be** [Colloq.] alleged or believed to be —**crack up 1.** to crash 2. [Colloq.] a) to break down physically or mentally b) to break into laughter or tears

crack·brained (krak'brānd') adj. crazy

cracked (krakt) adj. 1. broken without complete separation into parts 2. harsh /a *cracked* voice/ 3. [Colloq.] crazy

crack'er n. 1. one that cracks 2. a firecracker 3. a thin, crisp wafer

crack·er·jack (krak'ər jak') adj. [Slang] excellent —n. [Slang] an excellent person or thing

crack'ing n. the process of breaking down heavier hydrocarbons, as of petroleum, by heat and pressure into lighter hydrocarbons, as of gasoline

crack·le (krak''l) vi. **-led**, **-ling** [< CRACK] 1. to make slight, sharp, popping sounds 2. to develop a finely cracked surface —vt. 1. to crush or break with crackling sounds 2. to produce a finely cracked surface on —n. 1. crackling sounds 2. fine, irregular surface cracks, as on old oil paintings

crack·ling (krak'liŋ) n. 1. the making of slight, sharp, popping noises 2. (krak'lin) [pl.] crisp bits left when hot fat is rendered

crack'pot' (-pät') n. [Colloq.] a crazy or eccentric person —adj. [Colloq.] crazy or eccentric

crack'up' n. 1. a crash, esp. of an aircraft 2. [Colloq.] a mental or physical collapse

-cracy [< Gr. *kratos*, rule] a combining form meaning a (specified) type of government; rule by /autocracy/

cra·dle (krā'd'l) n. [OE. *cradol*] 1. a baby's small bed, usually on rockers 2. infancy 3. the place of a thing's beginning 4. a framework for support or protection 5. a frame on a scythe (**cradle scythe**) for laying the grain evenly as it is cut 6. a boxlike device on rockers for washing out gold from gold-bearing sand —vt. **-dled**, **-dling** to place, rock, or hold in or as in a cradle

craft (kraft) n. [OE. *cræft*, power] 1. a special skill or art 2. an occupation requiring this; esp., any manual art 3. the members of a skilled trade 4. guile; slyness 5. pl. **craft** a boat, ship, or aircraft —vt. to make with skill

crafts·man (krafts'mən) n., pl. **-men** a skilled workman; artisan —**crafts'man·ship'** n.

---

fat, āpe, cär; ten, ēven; is, bīte; gō, hôrn, tōol, look; oil, out; up, fur; thin, *th*en; zh, leisure; ŋ, ring; ə for a in ago; ' as in able (ā'b'l); ë, Fr. coeur; ö, Fr. feu; Fr. mo*n*; ü, Fr. duc; r, Fr. cri; kh, G. doch, ich. ‡ foreign; < derived from

craft'y *adj.* **craft'i·er, craft'i·est** sly; cunning —**craft'i·ly** *adv.* —**craft'i·ness** *n.*

crag (krag) *n.* [< Celt.] a steep rock projecting from a rock mass —**crag'gy** -**gi·er, -gi·est, crag'ged** (-id) *adj.* —**crag'gi·ness** *n.*

cram (kram) *vt.* **crammed, cram'ming** [OE. *crammian,* to stuff] **1.** to pack full or too full **2.** to stuff; force **3.** to feed to excess —*vi.* **1.** to eat too much or too quickly **2.** to study a subject in a hurried, intensive way, for an examination —*n.* **1.** a crowded condition **2.** a cramming —**cram'mer** *n.*

cramp¹ (kramp) *n.* [< OFr. *crampe,* bent] **1.** a sudden, painful contraction of muscles, as from chill or strain **2.** [*usually pl.*] abdominal spasms and pain —*vt.* to cause a cramp in

cramp² (kramp) *n.* [MDu. *krampe,* lit., bent in] **1.** a metal bar with both ends bent, for holding together timbers, etc.: also **cramp iron 2.** a clamp **3.** anything that confines or hampers —*vt.* **1.** to fasten as with a cramp **2.** to confine or hamper **3.** to turn (the wheels as of a car) sharply

cramped (krampt) *adj.* **1.** confined; restricted **2.** irregular and crowded, as some handwriting

cram·pon (kram'pän, -pən) *n.* either of a pair of spiked iron plates fastened on shoes to prevent slipping

cran·ber·ry (kran'ber'ē, -bər ē) *n., pl.* **-ries** [< Du. *kranebere*] **1.** a firm, sour, edible, red berry of an evergreen shrub **2.** this shrub

crane (krān) *n.* [OE. *cran*] **1.** a large wading bird with very long legs and neck **2.** any of various herons or storks **3.** a machine for lifting and moving heavy weights, using a movable projecting arm or a horizontal traveling beam **4.** any device with a swinging arm, as to hold a kettle —*vt., vi.* **craned, cran'ing 1.** to raise or move as by a crane **2.** to stretch (the neck)

Crane (krān) **1. Hart,** 1899–1932; U.S. poet **2. Stephen,** 1871–1900; U.S. writer

cra·ni·ol·o·gy (krā'nē äl'ə jē) *n.* the scientific study of skulls

cra·ni·om'e·try (-äm'ə trē) *n.* the science of measuring skulls; cranial measurement

cra·ni·um (krā'nē əm) *n., pl.* **-ni·ums, -ni·a** (-ə) [< Gr. *kranion*] the skull, esp. the part containing the brain —**cra'ni·al** *adj.*

crank (kraŋk) *n.* [< OE. *cranc-,* as in *crancstæf,* yarn comb] **1.** a handle or arm at right angles to the shaft of a machine, to transmit or change motion **2.** [Colloq.] an eccentric or irritable person —*vt.* to start or operate by a crank —*vi.* to turn a crank

crank'case' *n.* the metal casing of the crankshaft of an internal-combustion engine

crank'shaft' *n.* a shaft having one or more cranks for transmitting or changing motion

crank'y *adj.* **crank'i·er, crank'i·est 1.** out of order **2.** irritable; cross **3.** eccentric —**crank'i·ness** *n.*

cran·ny (kran'ē) *n., pl.* **-nies** [< LL. *crena,* a notch] a crevice; crack —**cran'nied** (-ēd) *adj.*

crap¹ (krap) *n.* **1.** *same as* CRAPS **2.** a losing throw at craps

crap² (krap) *n.* [< OFr., ordure] [Vulgar Slang] **1.** nonsense, insincerity, etc. **2.** trash; junk —**crap'py** *adj.* -**pi·er, -pi·est**

crape (krāp) *n.* crepe; esp., black crepe as a sign of mourning

crape'hang'er *n.* [Slang] a pessimist

crap·pie (krap'ē) *n.* [< ?] a small sunfish of eastern and central U.S.

craps (kraps) *n.pl.* [with sing. v.] a gambling game played with two dice: also **crap'shoot'ing**

crash¹ (krash) *vi.* [prob. echoic] **1.** to fall, collide, or break with a loud, smashing noise **2.** to move with such a noise **3.** to fall and be damaged or destroyed: said of an aircraft **4.** to collapse; fail —*vt.* **1.** to smash **2.** to cause to crash **3.** to force or impel with a crashing noise (with *in, out,* etc.) **4.** [Colloq.] to get into (a party, etc.) without an invitation —*n.* **1.** a loud, smashing noise **2.** a crashing **3.** a sudden collapse —*adj.* [Colloq.] using all possible resources and effort

crash² (krash) *n.* [prob. < Russ. *krashenina,* colored linen] a coarse cloth of plain, loose weave

crash'ing (-iŋ) *adj.* [Colloq.] thorough; complete

crass (kras) *adj.* [L. *crassus,* gross] grossly stupid, dull, or obtuse —**crass'ly** *adv.* —**crass'ness, cras'si·tude'** (-ə tōōd') *n.*

-crat [< Gr. *kratos,* rule] *a combining form meaning* member or supporter of (a specified kind of) government or ruling body [*democrat, aristocrat*]

crate (krāt) *n.* [< L. *cratis,* wickerwork] **1.** a packing case made of slats of wood **2.** [Slang] an old, decrepit car or plane —*vt.* **crat'ed, crat'ing** to pack in a crate

cra·ter (krāt'ər) *n.* [< Gr. *kratēr,* bowl] **1.** a bowl-shaped cavity, as at the mouth of a volcano or on the moon **2.** a pit, as one made by an exploding bomb

cra·vat (krə vat') *n.* [< Fr. *Cravate,* Croatian: from scarves worn by Croatian soldiers] **1.** a neckerchief or scarf **2.** a necktie

crave (krāv) *vt.* **craved, crav'ing** [OE. *crafian*] **1.** to ask for earnestly; beg **2.** to long for; desire eagerly **3.** to need greatly —*vi.* to have an eager longing (*for*) —**crav'er** *n.*

cra·ven (krā'vən) *adj.* [< L. *crepare,* to creak] very cowardly —*n.* a thorough coward —**cra'ven·ly** *adv.* —**cra'ven·ness** *n.*

crav·ing (krā'viŋ) *n.* an intense desire or longing, as for affection or a food, drug, etc.

craw (krô) *n.* [ME. *craue*] **1.** the crop of a bird or insect **2.** the stomach of any animal

craw·fish (krô'fish') *n., pl.:* see FISH *same as* CRAYFISH

crawl (krôl) *vi.* [< ON. *krafla*] **1.** to move slowly by drawing the body along the ground, like a worm **2.** to go on hands and knees **3.** to move slowly **4.** to act abjectly servile **5.** to swarm (*with* crawling things) **6.** to feel as if insects were crawling on one —*n.* **1.** the act of crawling **2.** an overarm swimming stroke, face downward

cray·fish (krā'fish') *n., pl.:* see FISH [< OFr. *crevice,* akin to CRAB¹] **1.** a freshwater crustacean somewhat like a little lobster **2.** *same as* SPINY LOBSTER

cray·on (krā'ən, -än') *n.* [Fr. < *craie,* chalk] **1.** a small stick of chalk, colored wax, etc. used for drawing, coloring, or writing **2.** a crayon drawing —*vt.* to draw or color with crayons —**cray'on·ist** *n.*

craze (krāz) *vt.* **crazed, craz'ing** [ME. *crasen,* to crack < Scand.] **1.** to make insane **2.** to produce small cracks in the surface or glaze of (pottery, etc.) —*vi.* to become finely cracked, as pottery glaze —*n.* **1.** a mania **2.** a fad

CRAYFISH
(to 5 in. long)

cra·zy (krā'zē) *adj.* **-zi·er, -zi·est** [< CRAZE] **1.** flawed, cracked, etc. **2.** mentally unbalanced **3.** [Colloq.] *a)* foolish or fantastic *b)* enthusiastic **4.** [Slang] fine —**cra'zi·ly** *adv.* —**cra'zi·ness** *n.*

crazy bone *same as* FUNNY BONE

crazy quilt a patchwork quilt with no regular design

creak (krēk) *vi., vt.* [see CROAK] to make, cause to make, or move with a harsh, grating, or squeaking sound —*n.* such a sound —**creak'i·ly** *adv.* —**creak'i·ness** *n.* —**creak'y** *adj.* **creak'i·er, creak'i·est**

cream (krēm) *n.* [OFr. < LL. *chrisma,* oil] **1.** the oily, yellowish part of milk **2.** any food made of cream or having a creamy consistency **3.** a creamy cosmetic or emulsion **4.** the best part **5.** yellowish white —*adj.* of, with, or like cream; creamy, cream-colored, etc. —*vi.* to form cream or a creamy foam —*vt.* **1.** to take cream from **2.** to add cream to **3.** to cook with cream or a cream sauce **4.** to make creamy as by beating **5.** [Slang] to defeat soundly —**cream of** creamed purée of

cream cheese a soft, white cheese made of cream or of milk enriched with cream

cream'er *n.* a small pitcher for cream

cream'er·y (-ər ē) *n., pl.* **-er·ies** a place where dairy products are processed or sold

cream of tartar a white, acid, crystalline substance, used as in baking powder

cream sauce a sauce made of butter and flour cooked together with milk or cream

cream'y *adj.* **cream'i·er, cream'i·est 1.** full of cream **2.** like cream in consistency or color —**cream'i·ness** *n.*

crease (krēs) *n.* [see CREST] **1.** a line made by folding and pressing **2.** a fold; wrinkle —*vt.* **creased, creas'ing 1.** to make a crease in **2.** to graze with a bullet —*vi.* to become creased

cre·ate (krē āt') *vt.* **-at'ed, -at'ing** [< L. *creare*] **1.** to bring into being; originate, design, invent, etc. **2.** to bring about; cause **3.** to invest with a new rank, function, etc. **4.** *Theater* to be the first to portray (a role)

cre·a'tion (-ā'shən) *n.* **1.** a creating or being created **2.** the universe **3.** anything created, esp. something original —**the Creation** *Theol.* God's creating of the world

cre·a'tive (-āt'iv) *adj.* **1.** creating or able to create **2.** inventive **3.** stimulating inventiveness —**cre·a'tive·ly** *adv.* —**cre·a'tive·ness, cre·a·tiv·i·ty** (krē'ā tiv'ə tē) *n.*

cre·a'tor (-āt'ər) *n.* **1.** one who creates **2.** [C-] God

crea·ture (krē'chər) *n.* [< L. *creatura*] **1.** anything created **2.** a living being, animal or human **3.** one completely dominated by another

crèche (kresh, krāsh) *n.* [Fr.] a display of a stable with figures, representing a scene at the birth of Jesus

cre·dence (krēd'ns) *n.* [< L. *credere*, believe] belief, esp. in the testimony of another

cre·den·tial (kri den'shəl, -chəl) *n.* **1.** that which entitles to credit, confidence, etc. **2.** [*usually pl.*] a letter or certificate showing one's right to a certain position or authority

cre·den·za (kri den'zə) *n.* [It.] a type of buffet, or sideboard

cred·i·ble (kred'ə b'l) *adj.* [< L. *credere*, believe] that can be believed; reliable —**cred'i·bil'i·ty, cred'i·ble·ness** *n.* — **cred'i·bly** *adv.*

cred·it (kred'it) *n.* [< L. *credere*, believe] **1.** belief; confidence **2.** good reputation **3.** praise or approval; commendation **4.** acknowledgment of work done or help given **5.** the amount in a bank account **6.** *a)* the entry in an account of payment on a debt *b)* the right-hand side of an account, where such entries are made *c)* the sum of such entries **7.** *a)* trust in one's ability to meet payments *b)* the time allowed for payment **8.** *Educ. a)* certification of a successfully completed unit or course of study *b)* a unit so certified —*vt.* **1.** to believe; trust **2.** to give credit to or praise for **3.** to give credit as in a bank account —**on credit** with the agreement to pay later

cred'it·a·ble (-ə b'l) *adj.* **1.** praiseworthy **2.** ascribable (*to*) —**cred'it·a·bil'i·ty** *n.* —**cred'it·a·bly** *adv.*

cred'i·tor (-ər) *n.* a person who extends credit or to whom money is owed

cre·do (krē'dō, krā'dō) *n., pl.* **-dos** [L., I believe] **1.** same as CREED **2.** [*usually* C-] the Apostles' Creed or the Nicene Creed

cre·du·li·ty (krə dōō'lə tē, -dyōō'-) *n.* a tendency to believe too readily

cred·u·lous (krej'oo ləs) *adj.* [< L. *credere*, believe] **1.** tending to believe too readily **2.** showing this tendency — **cred'u·lous·ly** *adv.* —**cred'u·lous·ness** *n.*

creed (krēd) *n.* [< L. *credo*, lit., I believe] **1.** a brief statement of religious belief, esp. one accepted by a church **2.** any statement of belief, principles, or the like

creek (krēk, krik) *n.* [< ON. *-kriki*, a winding] a small stream, somewhat larger than a brook

creel (krēl) *n.* [< OFr. *grail:* see GRIDDLE] a wicker basket for fishermen to carry fish caught

creep (krēp) *vi.* **crept, creep'ing** [OE. *creopan*] **1.** to move with the body close to the ground, as on hands and knees **2.** to come on or move slowly, gradually, or stealthily **3.** to grow along the ground or a wall, as some plants —*n.* **1.** a creeping **2.** [Slang] an annoying person —**the creeps** [Colloq.] a feeling of fear, repugnance, etc.

creep'er *n.* **1.** one that creeps **2.** a plant whose stem puts out tendrils for creeping along a surface **3.** [*pl.*] a baby's one-piece garment

creep'y *adj.* **-i·er, -i·est 1.** creeping **2.** having or causing a feeling of fear or repugnance

cre·mate (krē'māt, kri māt') *vt.* **-mat·ed, -mat·ing** [< L. *cremare*, to burn] to burn (a dead body) to ashes —**crema'tion** *n.*

cre·ma·to·ry (krē'mə tôr'ē, krem'ə-) *n., pl.* **-ries 1.** a furnace for cremating **2.** a building with such a furnace in it Also **cre'ma·to'ri·um** (-ē əm), *pl.* **-ri·ums, -ri·a** (-ə) —*adj.* of or for cremation: also **cre'ma·to'ri·al**

crème de ca·ca·o (krem' də kə kä'ō, də kō'kō) [Fr.] a sweet, chocolate-flavored liqueur

crème de menthe (də mänt', menth') [Fr.] a sweet, mint-flavored liqueur, green or colorless

cre·nate (krē'nāt) *adj.* [< VL. *crena*, a notch] having a scalloped edge, as certain leaves

cren·el·ate, cren·el·late (kren'l āt') *vt.* **-el·at'ed** or **-el·lat'ed, -el·at'ing** or **-el·lat'ing** to furnish with squared notches, or battlements —**cren'el·a'tion, cren'el·la'tion** *n.*

Cre·ole, cre·ole (krē'ōl) *n.* [< Fr. < Sp. < L. *creare*, to create] **1.** orig., a person of European parentage born in Latin America or the Gulf States **2.** *a)* a descendant of French settlers in Louisiana or of Spanish settlers in the Gulf States *b)* a person of mixed Creole and Negro descent **3.** French as spoken by Creoles —*adj.* **1.** of Creoles or their languages **2.** [*usually* c-] made with tomatoes, peppers, onions, etc.

cre·o·sote (krē'ə sōt') *n.* [< Gr. *kreas*, flesh + *sōzein*, to save] a transparent, pungent, oily liquid distilled from wood tar or coal tar: used as an antiseptic and a wood preservative —*vt.* **-sot'ed, -sot'ing** to treat with creosote

crepe, crêpe (krāp) *n.* [Fr. < L. *crispus*, curly] **1.** a thin, crinkled cloth, as of silk or wool; crape **2.** same as CRAPE **3.** thin paper crinkled like crepe: also **crepe paper 4.** soft rubber with a wrinkled surface, used for some shoe soles: also **crepe rubber 5.** (*also* krep) a very thin pancake, often with a filling: usually **crêpe**

crêpes su·zette (krāp' soo zet'; *Fr.* krep sü-) [Fr.] crêpes in a hot, orange-flavored sauce, usually served in flaming brandy

crep·i·tate (krep'ə tāt') *vi.* **-tat'ed, -tat'ing** [< L. *crepare*, to creak] to crackle —**crep'i·tant** *adj.* —**crep'i·ta'tion** *n.*

crept (krept) *pt. & pp. of* CREEP

cre·pus·cu·lar (kri pus'kyoo lər) *adj.* [< L. *creper*, dark] of, like, or active at, twilight

cre·scen·do (krə shen'dō) *adj., adv.* [It. < L.: see ff.] *Music* gradually getting louder —*n., pl.* **-dos** a gradual increase in loudness

cres·cent (kres'nt) *n.* [< OFr. < L. *crescere*, to grow] **1.** the shape of the moon in its first or last quarter **2.** anything shaped like this —*adj.* **1.** [Poet.] increasing; growing **2.** shaped like a crescent

cress (kres) *n.* [OE. *cressa*] a plant, as watercress, with pungent leaves used in salads

crest (krest) *n.* [< L. *crista*] **1.** a comb, tuft, etc. on the head of some animals or birds **2.** a plume or emblem on a helmet **3.** a heraldic device as used on a coat of arms, note paper, etc. **4.** top; ridge **5.** the highest point or level —*vt.* **1.** to provide with a crest **2.** to reach the top of —*vi.* to form or reach a crest —**crest'ed** *adj.*

crest·fall·en (krest'fôl'ən) *adj.* **1.** with drooping crest or bowed head **2.** dejected or humbled

cre·ta·ceous (kri tā'shəs) *adj.* [< L. *creta*, chalk] of, like, or containing chalk

Crete (krēt) Greek island in the E Mediterranean —**Cre'tan** *adj., n.*

cre·tin (krēt'n) *n.* [< Fr. *chrétien*, Christian, hence human being] a person suffering from cretinism

cre'tin·ism *n.* a congenital thyroid deficiency with resulting deformity and idiocy

cre·tonne (krē'tän, kri tän') *n.* [< Fr. < *Creton*, village in Normandy] a heavy, printed cotton or linen cloth, used as for curtains

cre·vasse (kri vas') *n.* [Fr. < OFr. *crevace*, CREVICE] **1.** a deep crack or fissure, esp. in a glacier **2.** a break in a river levee —*vt.* **-vassed', -vas'sing** to make crevasses in

crev·ice (krev'is) *n.* [< OFr. < L. *crepare*, to creak] a narrow opening caused by a crack or split; fissure; cleft — **crev'iced** *adj.*

crew[1] (krōō) *n.* [< L. *crescere*, to grow] a group of people working together, as all the seamen on a ship

crew[2] (krōō) *alt. pt. of* CROW[2] (sense 1)

crew·el (krōō'əl) *n.* [LME. *crule*] a fine worsted yarn used in embroidery —**crew'el·work'** *n.*

crib (krib) *n.* [OE.] **1.** a rack, trough, or box for fodder; manger **2.** a small, crude house or room **3.** a small bed with high sides, for a baby **4.** a wooden enclosure as for storing grain **5.** a structure anchored under water, serving as a water intake, pier, etc. **6.** [Colloq.] a translation or other aid used, often dishonestly, in doing schoolwork — *vt.* **cribbed, crib'bing 1.** to confine **2.** to provide with a crib **3.** [Colloq.] to plagiarize —*vi.* [Colloq.] to do schoolwork dishonestly, as by using a crib —**crib'ber** *n.*

crib·bage (krib'ij) *n.* [< CRIB + -AGE] a card game in which the object is to form combinations that count for points recorded by inserting pegs in a board

crick[1] (krik) *n.* [prob. ON.] a painful cramp in the neck or back —*vt.* to cause a crick in

crick[2] (krik) *n.* [Dial.] same as CREEK (sense 1)

crick·et[1] (krik'it) *n.* [< OFr. *criquer*, to creak] a leaping insect related to the grasshoppers: the males produce a chirping noise

crick·et[2] (krik'it) *n.* [prob. MDu. *cricke*, a stick] **1.** an outdoor game played by two teams of eleven players each, in which a ball, bats, and wickets are used **2.** [Colloq.] fair play; sportsmanship —*vi.* to play cricket —**crick'et·er** *n.*

CRICKET
(to 1 inch)

cried (krīd) *pt. & pp. of* CRY

cri·er (krī'ər) *n.* **1.** a person who

cries 2. a person who shouts out news, proclamations, etc.

crime (krīm) *n.* [< L. *crimen*, offense] 1. an act committed or omitted in violation of a law 2. a sin 3. criminal acts, collectively 4. [Colloq.] something regrettable or deplorable; shame

Cri·me·a (krī mē′ə) peninsula in southwestern U.S.S.R., extending into the Black Sea —**Cri·me′an** *adj.*

crim·i·nal (krim′ə n'l) *adj.* 1. having the nature of crime 2. relating to or guilty of crime 3. [Colloq.] deplorable —*n.* a person guilty of a crime —**crim′i·nal′i·ty** *n., pl.* -ties —**crim′i·nal·ly** *adv.*

crim·i·nol·o·gy (krim′ə näl′ə jē) *n.* the scientific study of crime and criminals —**crim′i·no·log′i·cal** *adj.* —**crim′i·nol′o·gist** *n.*

crimp (krimp) *vt.* [< MDu. *crimpen*, to wrinkle] 1. to press into narrow, regular folds; pleat 2. to make (hair) wavy or curly 3. to pinch together 4. [Colloq.] to hamper —*n.* 1. a crimping 2. anything crimped

crimp′y *adj.* -i·er, -i·est curly; wavy; frizzly —**crimp′i·ness** *n.*

crim·son (krim′z'n) *n.* [< Ar. *qirmiz*] deep red —*adj.* 1. deep-red 2. bloody —*vt., vi.* to make or become crimson

cringe (krinj) *vi.* cringed, cring′ing [< OE. *cringan*, to fall (in battle)] 1. to draw back; crouch, as when afraid; cower 2. to act servilely; fawn —*n.* a cringing —**cring′er** *n.*

crin·kle (kriŋ′k'l) *vi., vt.* -kled, -kling [see CRINGE] 1. to wrinkle; ripple 2. to rustle, as paper when crushed —*n.* a wrinkle, ripple, etc. —**crin′kly** *adj.* -kli·er, -kli·est

cri·noid (krī′noid, krin′oid) *adj.* [< Gr. *krinon*, lily] 1. lily-shaped 2. designating or of a small, flower-shaped marine animal, generally anchored by a stalk —*n.* such an animal

crin·o·line (krin′'l in) *n.* [Fr. < L. *crinis*, hair + *linum*, thread] 1. a coarse, stiff cloth used as a lining in garments 2. a hoop skirt

crip·ple (krip′'l) *n.* [< OE. *creopan*, to creep] one who is lame or otherwise disabled —*vt.* -pled, -pling to lame or disable —**crip′pler** *n.*

cri·sis (krī′sis) *n., pl.* -ses (-sēz) [< Gr. *krinein*, to separate] 1. the turning point in a disease, when it becomes clear whether the patient will recover or die 2. any turning point 3. a time of great trouble

crisp (krisp) *adj.* [OE. < L. *crispus*, curly] 1. brittle; easily crumbled 2. fresh and firm, as celery 3. fresh and tidy, as a uniform 4. sharp and clear 5. lively; animated 6. bracing *[crisp* air*]* 7. curly and wiry —*vt., vi.* to make or become crisp —**crisp′ly** *adv.* —**crisp′ness** *n.*

crisp′y *adj.* -i·er, -i·est *same as* CRISP —**crisp′i·ness** *n.*

criss·cross (kris′krôs′) *n.* [ME. *Christcros*, Christ's cross] a mark or pattern made of crossed lines —*adj.* marked by crossings —*vt., vi.* to mark with or move in crossing lines —*adv.* 1. crosswise 2. awry

cri·ter·i·on (krī tir′ē ən) *n., pl.* -i·a (-ə), -i·ons [< Gr. *kritēs*, judge] a standard, rule, or test by which something can be judged

crit·ic (krit′ik) *n.* [< Gr. *krinein*, discern] 1. one who writes judgments of books, plays, music, etc. professionally 2. one who finds fault

crit·i·cal (krit′i k'l) *adj.* 1. tending to find fault 2. characterized by careful analysis 3. of critics or criticism 4. of or forming a crisis; decisive 5. dangerous or risky 6. designating the point at which a nuclear chain reaction becomes self-sustaining —**crit′i·cal′i·ty** (-kal′ə tē), **crit′i·cal·ness** *n.* —**crit′i·cal·ly** *adv.*

crit·i·cism (krit′ə siz′m) *n.* 1. the act, art, or principles of criticizing, esp. literary or artistic work 2. a review, article, etc. expressing this 3. faultfinding; disapproval

crit·i·cize (krit′ə sīz′) *vi., vt.* -cized′, -ciz′ing 1. to analyze and judge as a critic 2. to find fault (with); censure Brit. sp. **criticise** —**crit′i·ciz′er** *n.*

cri·tique (kri tēk′) *n.* [Fr.] a critical analysis or evaluation of a literary or artistic work

crit·ter, crit·tur (krit′ər) *n. dial. var. of* CREATURE

croak (krōk) *vi.* [echoic] 1. to make a deep, hoarse sound *[frogs croak]* 2. [Slang] to die —*vt.* to utter in deep, hoarse tones —*n.* a deep, hoarse sound —**croak′er** *n.* —**croak′y** *adj.*

Cro·at (krō′at, -ət; krōt) *n.* 1. a native or inhabitant of Croatia 2. *same as* CROATIAN (*n.* 2) —*adj. same as* CROATIAN

Cro·a·tia (krō ā′shə) republic of Yugoslavia, in the NW part

Cro·a′tian (-shən) *adj.* of Croatia, the Croats, or their language —*n.* 1. a Croat 2. Serbo-Croatian as spoken and written in Croatia

cro·chet (krō shā′) *n.* [Fr., small hook] needlework in which loops of thread or yarn are interwoven with a

hooked needle (**crochet hook**) —*vi., vt.* -cheted′ (-shād′), -chet′ing to do crochet or make by crochet —**cro·chet′er** *n.*

crock (kräk) *n.* [OE. *crocca*] an earthenware pot or jar

crock·er·y (kräk′ər ē) *n.* earthenware pots, jars, dishes, etc.

Crock·ett (kräk′it), **David** (called *Davy Crockett*) 1786–1836; Am. frontiersman & politician

croc·o·dile (kräk′ə dīl′) *n.* [< Gr. ? *krokē*, pebble + *drilos*, worm] a large, lizardlike reptile of tropical streams, with a thick skin, a long tail, and a long, narrow head with massive jaws

crocodile tears insincere tears

croc·o·dil·i·an (kräk′ə dil′ē ən) *adj.* of a group of reptiles including the crocodile, alligator, cayman, etc. —*n.* any reptile of this group

cro·cus (krō′kəs) *n., pl.* cro′cus·es, cro′ci (-sī) [< Gr. *krokos*, saffron] any of a genus of spring-blooming plants with fleshy corms and a yellow, purple, or white flower

Croe·sus (krē′səs) last king of Lydia (560–546 B.C.), known for his great wealth —*n.* a very rich man

croft (krôft) *n.* [OE.] [Brit.] 1. a small enclosed field 2. a small farm, esp. one worked by a renter

crois·sant (krə sänt′) *n.* [Fr., lit., CRESCENT] a rich, flaky bread roll in the shape of a crescent

‡**croix de guerre** (krwä də ger′) [Fr., cross of war] a French military decoration for bravery

Cro-Ma·gnon (krō mag′nən, -man′yən) *adj.* [< *Cro-Magnon* cave in France, where remains were found] belonging to a prehistoric, Caucasoid type of man, tall and erect, who lived on the European continent —*n.* a member of this group

Crom·well (kräm′wel, -wəl), **Oliver**, 1599–1658; Eng. revolutionary leader & Protector of the Commonwealth (1653–58)

crone (krōn) *n.* [prob. < MDu. *kronje*, old ewe] an ugly, withered old woman; hag

Cro·nus (krō′nəs) *Gr. Myth.* a Titan who overthrew his father, Uranus, and was himself overthrown by his son Zeus: identified with the Roman Saturn

cro·ny (krō′nē) *n., pl.* -nies [< ? Gr. *chronios*, long-continued] a close companion

crook (krook) *n.* [< ON. *krōkr*, hook] 1. a hooked or curved staff, crosier, etc. 2. a bend or curve 3. [Colloq.] a swindler; thief —*vt., vi.* crooked (krookt), crook′ing to bend or curve

crook·ed (krookt; *for* 2 & 3 krook′id) *adj.* 1. having a crook or hook 2. not straight; bent 3. dishonest —**crook′ed·ly** *adv.* —**crook′ed·ness** *n.*

croon (krōōn) *vi., vt.* [< MDu. *cronen*, to growl] 1. to sing or hum in a low, gentle tone 2. to sing (popular songs) in a soft, sentimental manner —*n.* a low, gentle singing or humming —**croon′er** *n.*

crop (kräp) *n.* [OE. *croppa*, a cluster, crop of bird] 1. a saclike part of a bird's gullet, in which food is stored before digestion; craw 2. any agricultural product, growing or harvested, as wheat, fruit, etc. 3. the yield of any product in one season or place 4. a group or collection 5. the handle of a whip 6. a short whip with a looped lash 7. hair cut close to the head —*vt.* cropped, crop′ping 1. to cut or bite off the tops or ends of 2. to grow or harvest as a crop 3. to cut short —*vi.* to bear or grow a crop —**crop out** (or **up**) to appear unexpectedly

crop-dust·ing (kräp′dust′iŋ) *n.* the spraying of growing crops with pesticides from an airplane

crop′per *n.* 1. one that crops 2. a sharecropper —**come a cropper** [Colloq.] 1. to fall heavily 2. to fail

crop rotation a system of growing different crops successively, as to prevent soil depletion

cro·quet (krō kā′) *n.* [Fr.: see CROTCHET] an outdoor game in which the players use mallets to drive a wooden ball through hoops in the ground

cro·quette (krō ket′) *n.* [Fr. < *croquer*, to crunch] a small mass of chopped meat, fish, etc., coated with crumbs and fried in deep fat

cro·sier (krō′zhər) *n.* [< OFr. *croce*] the staff of a bishop or abbot, symbol of his office

cross (krôs) *n.* [< L. *crux*] 1. an upright post with another across it, on which criminals were once executed 2. a representation of a cross as a symbol of the crucifixion of Jesus, and hence of the Christian religion 3. any trouble or affliction 4. a mark made by intersecting lines 5. a crossing of varieties or breeds 6. the result of such mixing; hybrid —*vt.* 1. to make the sign of the cross over or upon 2. to place across or crosswise 3. to intersect 4. to draw a line or lines across 5. to go or extend across 6. to thwart; oppose 7. to interbreed; hybridize —*vi.* 1. to intersect 2. to go or extend from one side to the other 3. to pass each other —*adj.* 1. lying or passing across 2. contrary; opposed 3. cranky; irritable 4. of mixed variety or breed —**cross off** (or **out**) to cancel as by drawing lines across —**cross one's mind** to come suddenly to one's mind —**the Cross** 1. the cross on which Jesus died 2. Christianity —**cross'ly** *adv.* —**cross'ness** *n.*

cross'bar' *n.* a bar, line, or stripe placed crosswise —*vt.* -barred', -bar'ring to furnish or mark with crossbars

cross'beam' *n.* a beam placed across another or from one wall to another

cross'bones' *n.* a picture of two bones placed across each other: see SKULL AND CROSSBONES

cross'bow' (-bō') *n.* a medieval weapon consisting of a bow set transversely on a notched wooden stock

cross'breed' *vt., vi.* -bred', -breed'ing same as HYBRIDIZE —*n.* same as HYBRID —**cross'bred'** *adj.*

CROSSBOW

cross'-coun'try *adj., adv.* 1. across open country or fields, not by roads 2. across a country

cross'cut' *adj.* 1. used for cutting across [a *crosscut* saw] 2. cut across —*n.* a cut across —*vt., vi.* -cut', -cut'ting to cut across

cross'-ex·am'ine *vt., vi.* -ined, -in·ing 1. to question closely 2. *Law* to question (a witness already questioned by the opposing side) to determine the validity of his testimony —**cross'-ex·am'i·na'tion** *n.*

cross'-eye' *n.* an abnormal condition in which the eyes are turned toward each other —**cross'-eyed'** *adj.*

cross'-fer'ti·lize' *vt., vi.* -lized', -liz'ing to fertilize or be fertilized by pollen from another plant or variety —**cross'-fer'ti·li·za'tion** *n.*

cross'-grained' *adj.* 1. having an irregular or transverse grain: said of wood 2. contrary

cross'hatch' *vt., vi* to shade with two sets of crossing parallel lines

cross'ing *n.* 1. the act of passing across, thwarting, interbreeding, etc. 2. an intersection, as of lines, streets, etc. 3. a place where a street, river, etc. may be crossed

cross'patch' *n.* [CROSS + dial. *patch*, fool] [Colloq.] a cross, bad-tempered person

cross'piece' *n.* a piece lying across another

cross'pol'li·nate' *vt., vi.* -nat'ed, -nat'ing to transfer pollen from the anther of (one flower) to the stigma of (another) —**cross'-pol'li·na'tion** *n.*

cross'-pur'pose *n.* a contrary or conflicting purpose —**at cross-purposes** having a misunderstanding as to each other's purposes

cross'-ques'tion *vt.* to cross-examine

cross'-re·fer' *vt., vi.* -ferred', -fer'ring to refer from one part to another

cross-ref·er·ence (-ref'ər əns, -ref'rəns) *n.* a reference from one part of a book, index, etc. to another part

cross'road' *n.* 1. a road that crosses another 2. a road that connects main roads 3. [*usually pl.*] the place where roads intersect

cross section 1. *a)* a cutting through something, esp. at right angles to its axis *b)* a piece so cut off *c)* a drawing of a plane surface as exposed by such a cutting 2. a sample with enough of each kind to show what the whole is like —**cross'-sec'tion** *vt.* —**cross'-sec'tion·al** *adj.*

cross'-stitch' *n.* 1. a stitch made by crossing two stitches in the form of an X 2. needlework made with this stitch —*vt., vi.* to sew or embroider with this stitch

cross'-town' *adj.* going across the main avenues of a city [a *cross-town* bus]

cross'trees' (-trēz') *n.pl.* two short, horizontal bars across a ship's masthead, which spread the rigging that supports the mast

cross'walk' *n.* a lane marked off for pedestrians to use in crossing a street

cross'wise' (-wīz') *adv.* 1. [Archaic] in the form of a cross 2. so as to cross; across Also **cross'ways'** (-wāz')

cross'word' puzzle an arrangement of numbered squares to be filled in with words whose synonyms or definitions are given as clues

crotch (kräch) *n.* [OE. *crycce*, a staff] 1. a pole forked on top 2. a place where two branches fork from a tree 3. *a)* the place where the legs fork from the human body *b)* the part of a garment covering this

crotch·et (kräch'it) *n.* [< OFr. *croc*, a hook] 1. [Archaic] a small hook 2. a peculiar whim; stubborn notion 3. *Music* [Brit.] a quarter note (♩)

crotch'et·y *adj.* full of peculiar whims or stubborn notions —**crotch'et·i·ness** *n.*

crouch (krouch) *vi.* [< OFr. *croc*, a hook] 1. to stoop low, as an animal ready to pounce 2. to cringe in a servile manner —*n.* a crouching posture

croup¹ (krōop) *n.* [< obs. *croup*, speak hoarsely] an inflammation of the respiratory passages, with labored breathing and hoarse coughing —**croup'y** *adj.*

croup² (krōop) *n.* [OFr. *croupe*] the rump of a horse, etc.

crou·pi·er (krōo'pē ā', -ər) *n.* [Fr.] a person in charge of a gambling table, who rakes in and pays out the money

crou·ton (krōo'tän, krōo tän') *n.* [< Fr.: see CRUST] any of the small pieces of toasted bread served in soup, salads, etc.

Crow (krō) *n., pl.* **Crows, Crow** a member of a tribe of Siouan Indians living near the Yellowstone River

crow¹ (krō) *n.* [OE. *crawa*] a large, glossy-black bird with a harsh call —**as the crow flies** in a direct line —**eat crow** [Colloq.] to admit an error, recant, etc.

crow² (krō) *vi.* **crowed** or for 1, chiefly Brit. **crew** (krō), **crowed, crow'ing** [OE. *crawan*] 1. to make the shrill cry of a rooster 2. to boast in triumph 3. to make a sound of pleasure —*n.* a crowing sound

crow·bar (krō'bär') *n.* a long, metal bar used as a lever for prying, etc.

crowd (kroud) *vi.* [OE. *crudan*] 1. to push one's way (*into*) 2. to throng —*vt.* 1. to press or push 2. to fill too full; cram —*n.* 1. a large number of people or things gathered closely together 2. the common people 3. [Colloq.] a set; clique —**crowd'ed** *adj.*

crow'foot' *n., pl.* -**foots'** a plant related to the buttercup, with leaves resembling a crow's foot

crown (kroun) *n.* [< Gr. *korōnē*, wreath] 1. a wreath worn on the head in victory 2. a reward; honor 3. the head covering of a monarch 4. [*often* C-] *a)* the power of a monarch *b)* the monarch 5. the top part, as of the head, a hat, etc. 6. a British coin equal to five shillings 7. the highest quality, point, state, etc. of anything 8. *a)* the part of a tooth projecting beyond the gum line *b)* an artificial substitute for this —*vt.* 1. to put a crown on 2. to make (a person) a monarch 3. to honor or reward 4. to be at the top of 5. to be the highest part of 6. to put the finishing touch on 7. [Slang] to hit on the head 8. *Checkers* to make a king of —**crown'er** *n.*

crown prince the male heir apparent to a throne

crow's-foot (krōz'foot') *n., pl.* -**feet'** any of the wrinkles that often develop at the outer corners of the eyes: *usually used in pl.*

crow's'-nest' (-nest') *n.* 1. a lookout platform high on a ship's mast 2. any platform like this

cro·zier (krō'zhər) *n. same as* CROSIER

cru·cial (krōo'shəl) *adj.* [Fr. < L. *crux*, a cross] 1. decisive; critical 2. extremely trying —**cru'cial·ly** *adv.*

cru·ci·ble (krōo'sə b'l) *n.* [< ML. *crucibulum*, lamp, crucible] 1. a heat-resistant container for melting ores, metals, etc. 2. a severe test or trial

cru·ci·fix (krōo'sə fiks') *n.* [< L. *crux*, a cross + *figere*, fasten] 1. a representation of a cross with the figure of Jesus crucified on it 2. the cross as a Christian symbol

cru·ci·fix'ion (-fik'shən) *n.* 1. a crucifying 2. [C-] the crucifying of Jesus, or a representation of this

CROW'S-NEST

cru'ci·form' (-fôrm') *adj.* cross-shaped

cru·ci·fy (-fī') *vt.* -fied', -fy'ing [see CRUCIFIX] 1. to execute by nailing or binding to a cross and leaving to die of exposure 2. to torment; torture —**cru'ci·fi'er** *n.*

crude (krōod) *adj.* [L. *crudus*, raw] 1. in a raw or natural state 2. lacking grace, taste, etc.; uncultured 3. roughly made —**crude'ly** *adv.* —**cru·di·ty** (krōo'də tē), **crude'ness** *n.*

cru·el (krōo'əl) *adj.* [see prec.] 1. enjoying others' suffering; merciless 2. causing pain, distress, etc. —**cru'el·ly** *adv.* —**cru'el·ty,** *pl.* -**ties, cru'el·ness** *n.*

cru·et (krōo'it) *n.* [< OFr. *crue*, earthen pot] a small glass bottle to hold vinegar, oil, etc. for the table

cruise (krōoz) *vi.* **cruised, cruis'ing** [< Du. *kruisen,* to cross] to sail or drive about from place to place, as for

---

fat, āpe, cär; ten, ēven; is, bīte; gō, hôrn, tōol, look; oil, out; up, fur; thin, *th*en; zh, leisure; ŋ, ring; ə for *a* in *ago*; ' as in *able* (ā'b'l); ë, Fr. coeur; ö, Fr. feu; Fr. mon; ü, Fr. duc; r, Fr. cri; kh, G. doch, ich. ‡ foreign; < derived from pleasure —*vt.* to sail or journey over or about —*n.* a cruising voyage

cruis·er *n.* **1.** one that cruises, as a squad car **2.** a fast warship smaller than a battleship **3.** *same as* CABIN CRUISER

crul·ler (krul′ər) *n.* [Du. < *krullen,* ιο curl] a kind of twisted doughnut made with a rich dough

crumb (krum) *n.* [OE. *cruma*] **1.** a small piece broken off something, as of bread **2.** any bit or scrap *[crumbs* of knowledge*]* **3.** [Slang] a worthless person: also **crum′bum′** —*vt.* **1.** to clear (a table) of crumbs **2.** *Cooking* to cover or thicken with crumbs —**crumb′y** *adj.* -i·er, -i·est

crum·ble (krum′b'l) *vt.* -bled, -bling [< prec.] to break into crumbs or small pieces —*vi.* to fall to pieces; decay —**crum′bly** *adj.* -bli·er, -bli·est

crum·my (krum′ē) *adj.* -mi·er, -mi·est [Slang] cheap, shabby, inferior, etc. —**crum′mi·ness** *n.*

crum·pet (krum′pit) *n.* [prob. < OE. *crompeht,* flat cake] a batter cake baked on a griddle, usually toasted before serving

crum·ple (krum′p'l) *vt., vi.* -pled, -pling [< ME. *crimplen,* to wrinkle] **1.** to crush together into wrinkles **2.** to break down; collapse —**crum′ply** *adj.*

crunch (krunch) *vi., vt.* [echoic] to chew, press, grind, etc. with a noisy, crackling or crushing sound —*n.* **1.** the act or sound of crunching **2.** [Slang] *a)* a showdown *b)* a tight situation —**crunch′y** *adj.* -i·er, -i·est

crup·per (krup′ər, kroop′-) *n.* [< OFr. *crope,* rump] **1.** a leather strap attached to a harness and passed under a horse's tail **2.** a horse's rump

cru·sade (krōō sād′) *n.* [ult. < L. *crux,* a cross] **1.** [often C-] any of the Christian military expeditions (11th–13th cent.) to recover the Holy Land from the Muslims **2.** vigorous, concerted action for some cause or against some abuse —*vi.* -sad′ed, -sad′ing to engage in a crusade —**cru·sad′er** *n.*

cruse (krōōz, krōōs) *n.* [OE. *cruse*] a small container for water, oil, honey, etc.

crush (krush) *vt.* [< OFr. *croisir,* to break] **1.** to press with force so as to break or put out of shape **2.** to grind or pound into small bits **3.** to subdue; overwhelm **4.** to extract by squeezing —*vi.* to become crushed —*n.* **1.** a crushing **2.** a crowded mass of people **3.** [Colloq.] an infatuation —**crush′a·ble** *adj.* —**crush′er** *n.*

crust (krust) *n.* [< L. *crusta*] **1.** the hard, outer part of bread **2.** a piece of this **3.** any dry, hard piece of bread **4.** the pastry shell of a pie **5.** any hard surface layer, as of snow **6.** [Slang] insolence **7.** *Geol.* the solid outer shell of the earth —*vt., vi.* to cover or become covered with a crust

crus·ta·cean (krus tā′shən) *n.* [see prec.] any of a class of arthropods, including shrimps, crabs, lobsters, etc., that have a hard outer shell —*adj.* of crustaceans: also **crus·ta′ceous**

crust′y *adj.* -i·er, -i·est **1.** having or resembling a crust **2.** bad-tempered; surly —**crust′i·ly** *adv.* —**crust′i·ness** *n.*

crutch (kruch) *n.* [OE. *crycce,* staff] **1.** a staff with a top crosspiece that fits under the armpit, used by the lame as an aid in walking **2.** any prop, support, etc. —*vt.* to support as with a crutch; prop up

crux (kruks) *n., pl.* **crux′es, cru·ces** (krōō′sēz) [L., a cross] **1.** a difficult problem **2.** the essential or deciding point

cry (krī) *vi.* **cried, cry′ing** [< L. *quiritare,* to wail] **1.** to make a loud vocal sound or utterance, as for help **2.** to sob and shed tears; weep **3.** to plead *(for),* or show a great need *(for)* **4.** to utter its characteristic call; said of an animal —*vt.* **1.** to beg for *[to cry* quarter*]* **2.** to utter loudly; shout **3.** to call out (wares for sale, etc.) —*n., pl.* **cries 1.** a crying; call; shout **2.** an announcement called out publicly **3.** an urgent appeal; plea **4.** a rallying call **5.** public outcry **6.** a fit of weeping **7.** the characteristic vocal sound of an animal —**a far cry** a great distance or difference —**cry down** to belittle

cry′ba·by *n., pl.* -bies one who complains when he fails to win or get his own way

cry′ing *adj.* **1.** that cries **2.** demanding immediate notice *[a crying* shame*]*

cry·o·gen·ics (krī′ə jen′iks) *n.pl.* [with *sing. v.*] [< Gr. *kryos,* cold + -GEN + -ICS] the science that deals with the effects of very low temperatures on the properties of matter

cry·o·sur·ger·y (krī′ə sur′jə rē) *n.* [< Gr. *kryos,* cold + SURGERY] surgery in which tissues are destroyed by freezing

crypt (kript) *n.* [< Gr. *kryptein*] an underground chamber; esp., a vault under the main floor of a church, used as a burial place

cryp·tic (krip′tik) *adj.* **1.** hidden or mysterious **2.** obscure and curt Also **cryp′ti·cal** —**cryp′ti·cal·ly** *adv.*

cryp·to·gam (krip′tə gam′) *n.* [< Gr. *kryptos,* hidden + *gamos,* marriage] a plant that bears no flowers or seeds but propagates by means of spores, as algae, mosses, etc. —**cryp′to·gam′ic, cryp·tog′a·mous** (-täg′ə məs) *adj.*

cryp·to·gram (krip′tə gram′) *n.* [< Gr. *kryptos,* hidden + -GRAM] something written in code or cipher: also **cryp′to·graph′** (-graf′)

cryp·tog·ra·phy (krip täg′rə fē) *n.* [< Gr. *kryptos,* hidden + -GRAPHY] **1.** the art of writing or deciphering messages in code **2.** a code system —**cryp·tog′ra·pher** *n.* —**cryp′to·graph′ic** (-tə graf′ik) *adj.*

crys·tal (kris′t'l) *n.* [< Gr. *kryos,* frost] **1.** a clear, transparent quartz **2.** a very clear, brilliant glass **3.** articles made of such glass, as goblets, bowls, etc. **4.** the transparent covering over a watch face **5.** anything clear like crystal **6.** a solidified form of a substance having plane faces arranged in a symmetrical, three-dimensional pattern —*adj.* **1.** of crystal **2.** like crystal; clear

crys·tal·line (-tə lin) *adj.* **1.** made of crystal **2.** consisting of crystals **3.** like crystal in clearness, structure, etc.

crys·tal·lize (-līz′) *vi., vt.* -lized′, -liz′ing **1.** to become or cause to become crystalline **2.** to take on or cause to take on a definite form —**crys′tal·liz′a·ble** *adj.* —**crys′tal·li·za′tion** *n.*

crys·tal·log·ra·phy (-läg′rə fē) *n.* [see CRYSTAL & -GRAPHY] the science of the form, structure, and classification of crystals

crys′tal·loid′ (-loid′) *adj.* **1.** like a crystal **2.** having the nature of a crystalloid —*n.* a substance, usually crystallizable, which, when in solution, readily passes through vegetable and animal membranes —**crys′tal·loi′dal** *adj.*

Cs *Chem.* cesium

cs. case; cases

CST, C.S.T. Central Standard Time

CT Connecticut

ct. 1. *pl.* **cts.** cent **2.** court

Cu [L. *cuprum*] *Chem.* copper

cu. cubic

cub (kub) *n.* [< ? OIr. *cuib,* whelp] **1.** a young fox, bear, lion, whale, etc. **2.** an inexperienced youth **3.** a novice or beginner

Cu·ba (kyōō′bə) island country in the West Indies, south of Fla.: 44,218 sq. mi.; pop. 8,074,000; cap. Havana —**Cu′ban** *adj., n.*

cub·by·hole (kub′ē hōl′) *n.* [< Brit. dial. *cub,* little shed + HOLE] a small, enclosed space: also **cub′by**

cube (kyōōb) *n.* [< Gr. *kybos*] **1.** a solid with six equal, square sides **2.** the product obtained by multiplying a given number by its square *[the cube* of 3 is 27*]* —*vt.* **cubed, cub′ing 1.** to obtain the cube of (a number) **2.** to cut or shape into cubes —**cu′bi·form′** *adj.*

cu·beb (kyōō′beb) *n.* [< Fr. < Ar. *kabābah*] the spicy berry of an East Indian vine, formerly used medicinally in cigarettes

cube root the number of which a given number is the cube *[the cube root* of 8 is 2*]*

cu·bic (kyōō′bik) *adj.* **1.** having the shape of a cube: also **cu′bi·cal 2.** having three dimensions: a cubic foot is the volume of a cube one foot in length, width, and breadth **3.** relating to the cubes of numbers —**cu′bi·cal·ly** *adv.*

cu·bi·cle (kyōō′bi k'l) *n.* [< L. *cubare,* lie down] **1.** a small sleeping compartment, as in a dormitory **2.** any small compartment

cubic measure a system of measuring volume in cubic units, esp. that in which 1,728 cubic inches = 1 cubic foot and 1,000 cubic millimeters = 1 cubic centimeter

cub·ism (kyōō′biz'm) *n.* a school of modern art characterized by the use of cubes and other geometric forms —**cu′bist** *n., adj.* —**cu·bis′tic** *adj.*

cu·bit (kyōō′bit) *n.* [< L. *cubitum*] an ancient measure of length, about 18–22 inches

cuck·old (kuk′'ld) *n.* [see CUCKOO] a man whose wife has committed adultery —*vt.* to make a cuckold of —**cuck′old·ry** (-rē) *n.*

cuck·oo (kōō′kōō′, kook′ōō′) *n.* [< OFr. *cucu,* echoic] **1.** a brown bird with a long, slender body: the European species lays its eggs in the nests of other birds **2.** its call —*adj.* [Slang] crazy; silly

cu·cum·ber (kyōō′kum bər) *n.* [< L. *cucumis*] **1.** a long fruit with green rind and firm white flesh, used in salads or preserved as pickles **2.** the vine on which it grows, related to the gourd

cud (kud) *n.* [OE. *cudu*] a mouthful of swallowed food regurgitated from the first stomach of cattle and other ruminants and chewed a second time

cud·dle (kud′'l) *vt.* -dled, -dling [< ?] to embrace and fondle —*vi.* to lie close and snug; nestle —*n.* **1.** a cuddling **2.** an embrace; hug —**cud′dle·some, cud′dly** *adj.* -dli·er, -dli·est

cudg·el (kuj′əl) *n.* [OE. *cycgel*] a short, thick stick or club —*vt.* -eled or -elled, -el·ing or -el·ling to beat with a cudgel —**cudgel one's brains** to think hard —**take up the cudgels (for)** to defend

cue[1] (kyoo) *n.* [< *q, Q* (? for L. *quando*, when) found on 16th-c. plays] **1.** a signal in dialogue, music, etc. for an actor's entrance or speech **2.** any signal to do something **3.** an indirect suggestion; hint —*vt.* cued, cu′ing or cue′ing to give a cue to

cue[2] (kyoo) *n.* [< *queue*] **1.** *same as* QUEUE **2.** a long, tapering rod used in billiards and pool to strike the ball —*vt.* cued, cu′ing or cue′ing to braid (hair, etc.)

cuff (kuf) *n.* [< ME. *cuffe*, glove] **1.** a band at the wrist end of a sleeve **2.** a turned-up fold at the bottom of a trouser leg **3.** a handcuff **4.** a slap —*vt.* **1.** to put a cuff on **2.** to slap —**off the cuff** [Slang] in an offhand manner —**on the cuff** [Slang] on credit

cuff link a pair of linked buttons or any similar device for keeping a shirt cuff closed

cui·rass (kwi ras′) *n.* [ult. < L. *corium*, leather] **1.** a piece of armor for protecting the breast and back **2.** the breastplate of such armor

cui·sine (kwi zēn′) *n.* [Fr. < L. *coquere*, to cook] **1.** a style of cooking or preparing food **2.** the food prepared, as at a restaurant

cul-de-sac (kul′də sak′) *n., pl.* -sacs′ [Fr., lit., bottom of a sack] a passage with only one outlet

-cule [< Fr. or L.] *a suffix meaning* small

cu·lex (kyoo′leks) *n.* [L., gnat] the most common mosquito of N. America and Europe

cu·li·nar·y (kyoo′lə ner′ē, kul′ə-) *adj.* [< L. *culina*, kitchen] of the kitchen or of cooking

cull (kul) *vt.* [< L. *colligere*, collect] to pick out; select and gather —*n.* something picked out; esp., something rejected as not being up to standard

cul·len·der (kul′ən dər) *n. same as* COLANDER

culm[1] (kulm) *n.* [< ME. *colme*] waste material from coal screenings or washings

culm[2] (kulm) *n.* [< L. *culmus*, stem] the jointed stem of various grasses, usually hollow —*vi.* to grow or develop into a culm

cul·mi·nate (kul′mə nāt′) *vi.* -nat′ed, -nat′ing [< L. *culmen*, peak] to reach its highest point or climax —*vt.* to bring to its climax

cul·mi·na′tion *n.* **1.** a culminating **2.** the highest point or climax

cu·lotte (koo lät′, kyoo-) *n.* [Fr.] [*often pl.*] trousers made full in the legs to resemble a skirt, worn by women

cul·pa·ble (kul′pə b'l) *adj.* [< L. *culpa*, fault] deserving blame —**cul′pa·bil′i·ty** *n.* —**cul′pa·bly** *adv.*

cul·prit (kul′prit) *n.* [< early law Fr. *culpable*, guilty + *prit*, ready (to prove)] a person accused, or found guilty, of a crime

cult (kult) *n.* [< L. *cultus*, care] **1.** a system of religious worship **2.** devoted attachment to a person, principle, etc. **3.** a sect —**cult′ist** *n.*

cul·ti·vate (kul′tə vāt′) *vt.* -vat′ed, -vat′ing [see prec.] **1.** to prepare (land) for growing crops; till **2.** to grow (plants) **3.** to loosen the soil and kill weeds around (plants) **4.** to develop or improve [*cultivate* your mind] **5.** to seek to become familiar with —**cul′ti·va·ble** (-və b'l) *adj.* —**cul′ti·vat′ed** *adj.*

cul·ti·va′tion *n.* **1.** the act of cultivating **2.** refinement, or culture

cul′ti·va′tor *n.* **1.** one who cultivates **2.** a tool or machine for loosening the soil around plants

cul·ture (kul′chər) *n.* [see CULT] **1.** cultivation of the soil **2.** development or improvement of some plant or animal **3.** a growth of bacteria, etc. in a specially prepared substance (**culture medium**) **4.** improvement of the mind, manners, etc. **5.** development by special training or care **6.** the skills, arts, etc. of a given people in a given period; civilization —*vt.* -tured, -tur·ing to cultivate —**cul′tur·al** *adj.* —**cul′tur·al·ly** *adv.*

cul′tured *adj.* **1.** produced by cultivation **2.** having culture or refinement

CULTIVATOR

cul·vert (kul′vərt) *n.* [< ?] a drain or conduit under a road or embankment

cum·ber (kum′bər) *vt.* [< OFr. *combre*, obstruction] **1.** to hinder; hamper **2.** to burden; trouble

cum′ber·some (-səm) *adj.* burdensome; unwieldy: also **cum′brous** (-brəs)

cum·in (kum′in) *n.* [< Gr. *kyminon*] **1.** a plant related to the parsley **2.** its aromatic fruits, used for flavoring pickles, soups, etc. Also sp. **cum′min**

‡cum lau·de (koom lou′de, kum lô′dē) [L.] with praise: phrase signifying graduation with honors

cum·mer·bund (kum′ər bund′) *n.* [Hindi & Per. *kamarband*, loin band] a wide sash worn as a waistband, esp. with men's formal dress

cu·mu·la·tive (kyoom′yə lāt′iv, -lə tiv) *adj.* increasing in effect, size, etc. by successive additions —**cu′mu·la′tive·ly** *adv.* —**cu′mu·la′tive·ness** *n.*

cu·mu·lus (kyoom′yə ləs) *n., pl.* -li′ (-lī′) [L., a heap] a thick cloud type with a dark, horizontal base and dome-like upper parts —**cu′mu·lous** *adj.*

cu·ne·i·form (kyoo nē′ə fôrm′) *adj.* [< L. *cuneus*, a wedge + -FORM] wedge-shaped, as the characters used in ancient Assyrian and Babylonian inscriptions —*n.* cuneiform characters

GOD   SUN   MAN

CUNEIFORM

cun·ning (kun′iŋ) *adj.* [< ME. *cunnen*, know] **1.** sly; crafty **2.** made with skill **3.** pretty; cute —*n.* slyness; craftiness —**cun′ning·ly** *adv.*

cup (kup) *n.* [< L. *cupa*, tub] **1.** a small, bowl-shaped container for beverages, often with a handle **2.** the bowl part of a drinking vessel **3.** a cup and its contents **4.** a cupful **5.** anything shaped like a cup **6.** an ornamental cup given as a prize **7.** the wine chalice at Communion; also, the wine **8.** one's portion **9.** something served in a cup **10.** *Golf* the hole in each putting green —*vt.* **cupped, cup′ping 1.** to shape like a cup **2.** to take or put in a cup —**in one's cups** drunk —**cup′like** *adj.*

cup′bear′er (-ber′ər) *n.* a person who fills and serves cups of wine, as in a king's palace

cup·board (kub′ərd) *n.* a closet or cabinet with shelves for holding cups, plates, food, etc.

cup′cake′ *n.* a little cake baked in a cup-shaped mold

cup′ful′ *n., pl.* -fuls′ as much as a cup will hold; specif., eight ounces

Cu·pid (kyoo′pid) the Roman god of love, son of Venus: identified with the Greek god Eros —*n.* [c-] a representation of Cupid as a naked, winged cherub with bow and arrow

cu·pid·i·ty (kyoo pid′ə tē) *n.* [< L. *cupere*, to desire] strong desire for wealth; greed

cu·po·la (kyoo′pə lə) *n.* [It. < L. *cupa*, a tub] **1.** a rounded roof or ceiling **2.** a small dome or similar structure on a roof —**cu′po·laed** (-ləd) *adj.*

cu·pre·ous (kyoo′prē əs) *adj.* [< L. *cuprum*, copper] of, like, or containing copper

cu′pric (-prik) *adj. Chem.* of or containing copper with a valence of two

cu′pro·nick′el (-prō nik′'l) *n.* an alloy of copper and nickel, used in some coins

cu′prous (-prəs) *adj. Chem.* of or containing copper with a valence of one

cur (kur) *n.* [prob. < ON. *kurra*, to growl] **1.** a dog of mixed breed **2.** a contemptible person

cur·a·ble (kyoor′ə b'l) *adj.* that can be cured —**cur′a·bil′i·ty** *n.* —**cur′a·bly** *adv.*

Cu·ra·çao (kyoor′ə sô′, koor′ə sou′) largest island of the Netherlands Antilles —*n.* [c-] a liqueur flavored with orange peel

cu·ra·cy (kyoor′ə sē) *n., pl.* -cies the position, office, or work of a curate

cu·ra·re, cu·ra·ri (kyoo rä′rē, koo-) *n.* [< native (Tupi) name] **1.** a black, resinous substance prepared from certain S. American plants, used by some Indians to poison arrows and in medicine to relax muscles **2.** any of these plants

cu·rate (kyoor′it) *n.* [< L. *cura*, care (of souls)] a clergyman who assists a vicar or rector

cur·a·tive (kyoor′ə tiv) *adj.* curing or having the power to cure —*n.* a remedy

cu·ra·tor (kyoo rāt′ər, kyoor′āt′ər) *n.* [< L. *curare*, take care of] a person in charge of a museum, library, etc. —**cu·ra·to·ri·al** (kyoor′ə tôr′ē əl) *adj.*

curb (kurb) *n.* [< L. *curvus,* bent] **1.** a chain or strap attached to a horse's bit, used to check the horse **2.** anything that checks or restrains **3.** a raised margin along an edge, to strengthen or confine **4.** a stone or concrete edging along a street **5.** a market dealing in stocks and bonds not listed on the exchange —*vt.* **1.** to restrain; control **2.** to lead (a dog) to the curb to pass its waste matter **3.** to provide with a curb

curb'ing *n.* **1.** material for curbstones **2.** a curb (sense 4)

curb service service offered to customers who wish to remain in their cars

curb'stone' *n.* the stone or stones making up a curb

curd (kurd) *n.* [< ME. *crud,* coagulated substance] [*often pl.*] the coagulated part of sour milk, from which cheese is made —*vt., vi.* to curdle —**curd'y** *adj.*

cur·dle (kur'd'l) *vt., vi.* -dled, -dling to form into curd; coagulate —**curdle one's blood** to horrify or terrify one

cure (kyoor) *n.* [< L. *cura,* care] **1.** a healing or being healed **2.** a remedy **3.** a method of medical treatment **4.** *same as* CURACY **5.** a process for curing meat, fish, tobacco, etc. —*vt.* cured, cur'ing **1.** to restore to health **2.** to get rid of (an ailment, evil, etc.) **3.** *a)* to preserve (meat, fish, etc.), as by salting or smoking *b)* to process (tobacco, leather, etc.), as by drying —*vi.* **1.** to bring about a cure **2.** to undergo curing —**cur'er** *n.*

cu·ré (kyoo rā') *n.* [Fr. < L. *cura,* care] in France, a parish priest

cure'-all' *n.* something supposed to cure all ailments or evils

cu·ret·tage (kyoor'ə täzh') *n.* [Fr. < L. *cura,* care] the process of cleaning and scraping the walls of a body cavity with a spoonlike instrument

cur·few (kur'fyoo) *n.* [< OFr. *covrir,* to hide < *feu,* fire] **1.** *a)* in the Middle Ages, a signal every evening for people to cover fires and retire *b)* the bell rung as this signal *c)* the time of this signal **2.** a time in the evening beyond which children, etc. may not appear on the streets

cu·ri·a (kyoor'ē ə) *n., pl.* -ae' (-ē') [L.] **1.** a medieval judicial court held in the king's name **2.** [C-] the administrative body of the Roman Catholic Church, with various courts, officials, etc. under the Pope's authority: in full, **Curia Ro·ma·na** (rō mä'nə, -mä'-) —**cu'ri·al** *adj.*

Cu·rie (kyoo rē', kyoor') **1. Marie,** 1867-1934; Pol. chemist & physicist in France **2. Pierre** (pē er') 1859-1906; Fr. physicist: husband of *prec.*

cu·rie (kyoor'ē, kyoo rē') *n.* [< Marie CURIE] the unit used in measuring radioactivity

cu·ri·o (kyoor'ē ō') *n., pl.* -os' [contr. of CURIOSITY] any unusual or rare article

cu·ri·os·i·ty (kyoor'ē äs'ə tē) *n., pl.* -ties **1.** a desire to learn or know **2.** anything curious or rare

cu·ri·ous (kyoor'ē əs) *adj.* [< L. *curiosus,* careful] **1.** eager to learn or know; prying or inquisitive **2.** unusual; strange —**cu'ri·ous·ly** *adv.* —**cu'ri·ous·ness** *n.*

cu·ri·um (kyoor'ē əm) *n.* [< Marie & Pierre CURIE] a radioactive chemical element of the actinide series: symbol, Cm; at. wt., 247(?); at. no., 96

curl (kurl) *vt.* [< ME. *crul,* curly] **1.** to twist (hair, etc.) into ringlets **2.** to cause to bend around —*vi.* to become curled —*n.* **1.** a ringlet of hair **2.** anything with a curled shape **3.** a curling or being curled —**curl up 1.** to gather into spirals or curls **2.** to sit or lie with the legs drawn up —**curl'er** *n.* —**curl'y** *adj.* -i·er, -i·est

cur·lew (kur'loo) *n.* [echoic] a large, brownish wading bird with long legs

curl·i·cue (kur'li kyoo') *n.* [< CURLY + CUE²] a fancy curve, flourish, etc., as in a design

curl·ing (kur'liŋ) *n.* a game played on ice by sliding a heavy disk (**curling stone**) toward a target circle

cur·mudg·eon (kər muj'ən) *n.* [< ?] a surly, ill-mannered person

cur·rant (kur'ənt) *n.* [ult. < CORINTH] **1.** a small, seedless raisin from the Mediterranean region **2.** *a)* the sour berry of a large group of hardy shrubs, used for jellies and jams *b)* the shrub

cur·ren·cy (kur'ən sē) *n., pl.* -cies [see CURRENT] **1.** circulation **2.** the money in circulation in any country **3.** general use or acceptance

cur·rent (kur'ənt) *adj.* [< L. *currere,* to run] **1.** now going on; of the present time **2.** circulating **3.** commonly accepted; in general use —*n.* **1.** a flow of water or air in a definite direction **2.** a general tendency or drift **3.** the flow or rate of flow of electricity in a conductor —**cur'rent·ly** *adv.*

cur·ric·u·lum (kə rik'yə ləm) *n., pl.* -la (-lə), -lums [L., a course for racing] **1.** a series of required studies **2.** all the courses offered in a school —**cur·ric'u·lar** *adj.*

cur·ry¹ (kur'ē) *vt.* -ried, -ry·ing [< OFr. *correier,* put in order] **1.** to rub down and clean the coat of (a horse, etc.) with a currycomb or brush **2.** to prepare (tanned leather) by soaking, cleaning, beating, etc. —**curry favor** to try to win favor by flattery, fawning, etc. —**cur'ri·er** *n.*

cur·ry² (kur'ē) *n., pl.* -ries [Tamil *kari*] **1.** a powder (**curry powder**) prepared from turmeric and various spices **2.** a sauce made with curry powder **3.** a stew made with curry —*vt.* -ried, -ry·ing to prepare with curry powder

cur'ry·comb' *n.* a comb with teeth or ridges, to curry a horse —*vt.* to curry with this

curse (kurs) *n.* [OE. *curs*] **1.** a calling on God or the gods to bring evil on some person or thing **2.** a profane or obscene oath **3.** a thing cursed **4.** evil that seems to come in answer to a curse **5.** any cause of evil or injury — *vt.* cursed or curst, curs'ing **1.** to call evil down on **2.** to swear at **3.** to bring evil or injury on; afflict —*vi.* to swear; blaspheme —**be cursed with** to suffer from — curs'er *n.*

CURRYCOMB

curs·ed (kur'sid, kurst) *adj.* **1.** under a curse **2.** deserving to be cursed; evil —**curs'ed·ly** *adv.*

cur·sive (kur'siv) *adj.* [ult. < L. *currere,* to run] designating or of writing in which the letters are joined —*n.* **1.** a cursive character **2.** *Printing* a typeface that looks like handwriting

cur·so·ry (kur'sər ē) *adj.* [< L. *cursor,* runner] hastily, often superficially, done —**cur'so·ri·ly** *adv.* —**cur'so·ri·ness** *n.*

curt (kurt) *adj.* [L. *curtus,* short] so brief as to be rude; brusque —**curt'ly** *adv.* —**curt'ness** *n.*

cur·tail (kər tāl') *vt.* [< L. *curtus,* short] to cut short; reduce; abridge —**cur·tail'ment** *n.*

cur·tain (kur't'n) *n.* [< L. *cors,* a court] **1.** a piece of cloth, etc. hung at a window, in front of a stage, etc. to decorate or conceal **2.** anything that conceals or shuts off —*vt.* to provide or shut off as with a curtain

curtain call 1. a call, usually by applause, for performers to return to the stage **2.** such a return

curt·sy (kurt'sē) *n., pl.* -sies [var. of COURTESY] a woman's bow of greeting, respect, etc. made by bending the knees and dipping the body slightly —*vi.* -sied, -sy·ing to make a curtsy Also sp. **curt'sey**

cur·va·ceous (kər vā'shəs) *adj.* [< CURVE] [Colloq.] having a full, shapely figure: said of a woman

cur·va·ture (kur'və chər) *n.* **1.** a curving or being curved **2.** a curve or curved part

curve (kurv) *n.* [L. *curvus,* bent] **1.** a line having no straight part; bend with no angles **2.** something shaped like, or moving in, a curve **3.** a curving **4.** *Baseball* a ball pitched so that it curves before crossing the plate —*vt., vi.* curved, curv'ing **1.** to form a curve by bending **2.** to move in a curve —**curv'y** *adj.* -i·er, -i·est

cur·vet (kur'vit) *n.* [< It. < L. *curvus,* bent] an upward leap by a horse, raising its hind legs just before its forelegs come down —*vi.* (*usually* kər vet') -vet'ted or -vet'ed, -vet'ting or -vet'ing **1.** to make a curvet **2.** to frolic —*vt.* to cause to curvet

cur·vi·lin·e·ar (kur'və lin'ē ər) *adj.* consisting of or enclosed by curved lines: also **cur'vi·lin'e·al**

cush·ion (koosh'ən) *n.* [< ML. *coxinum*] **1.** a pillow or pad **2.** a thing like this in shape or use **3.** something that absorbs shock, as the inner rim of a billiard table —*vt.* **1.** to provide with a cushion **2.** to absorb (shock or noise)

cush·y (koosh'ē) *adj.* -i·er, -i·est [< Hindi *khush,* pleasant] [Slang] easy; comfortable [*a cushy job*]

cusp (kusp) *n.* [L. *cuspis,* a point] **1.** a pointed end **2.** any of the elevations on the chewing surface of a tooth **3.** either horn of a crescent moon

cus·pid (kus'pid) *n.* a canine tooth: see CANINE

cus·pi·date (kus'pə dāt') *adj.* having a cusp or cusps; pointed: also **cus'pi·dat'ed**

cus·pi·dor (kus'pə dôr') *n.* [< Port. *cuspir,* to spit] *same as* SPITTOON

cuss (kus) *n.* [Colloq.] **1.** a curse **2.** a person or animal regarded as queer or annoying —*vt., vi.* [Colloq.] to curse — **cuss'ed** *adj.* —**cuss'ed·ly** *adv.*

cus·tard (kus'tərd) *n.* [< L. *crusta,* crust] **1.** a mixture of eggs, milk, sugar, etc. boiled or baked **2.** *same as* FROZEN CUSTARD

Cus·ter (kus'tər), **George Armstrong** 1839-76; U.S. army officer and Indian fighter

cus·to·di·an (kus tō'dē ən) *n.* **1.** one who has the custody or care of something; keeper **2.** a janitor —**cus·to'di·an·ship'** *n.*

cus·to·dy (kus'tə dē) *n., pl.* **-dies** [< L. *custos*, a guard] a guarding or keeping safe; care **—in custody** under arrest — **take into custody** to arrest **—cus·to'di·al** (-tō'dē əl) *adj.*

cus·tom (kus'təm) *n.* [< L. *com-*, intens. + *suere*, to accustomed] **1.** a usual practice; habit **2.** social conventions carried on by tradition **3.** [*pl.*] *a*) duties or taxes imposed on imported goods *b*) [*with sing. v.*] the agency in charge of collecting these duties **4.** the regular patronage of a business **5.** *Law* such usage as by long-established practice has taken on the force of law **—adj. 1.** made to order **2.** making things to order

cus'tom·ar'y (-tə mer'ē) *adj.* in keeping with custom; usual **—cus'tom·ar'i·ly** *adv.*

cus'tom-built' *adj.* built to order, according to the customer's specifications

cus'tom·er *n.* **1.** a person who buys, esp. one who buys regularly **2.** [Colloq.] a person with whom one has to deal [he's a rough *customer*]

cus'tom·house' *n.* an office where customs or duties are paid: also **cus'toms·house'**

cus'tom·ize' (-īz') *vt., vi.* **-ized', -iz'ing** to make according to individual specifications

cus'tom-made' *adj.* made to order, according to the customer's specifications

cut (kut) *vt., vi.* **cut, cut'ting** [ME. *cutten*] **1.** to make an opening in with a sharp-edged instrument; gash **2.** to pierce sharply so as to hurt **3.** to hurt the feelings of **4.** to have (a new tooth) grow through the gum **5.** to divide into parts with a sharp-edged instrument; sever **6.** to carve (meat) **7.** to hew **8.** to reap **9.** to pass across; intersect **10.** to divide (a pack of cards) at random before dealing **11.** to reduce; curtail *[prices were cut]* **12.** to trim; pare **13.** to dilute (alcohol, etc.) **14.** to dissolve the fat globules of *[lye cuts grease]* **15.** to make or do by or as by cutting; specif., *a*) to make (an opening, clearing, etc.) *b*) to perform *[to cut* a caper*] c*) to hit or throw (a ball) so that it spins *d*) to make a recording of on (a phonograph record) **16.** [Colloq.] to pretend not to recognize (a person) **17.** [Colloq.] to stay away from (a school class, etc.) **18.** [Slang] to stop **—vi. 1.** to pierce, sever, gash, etc. **2.** to take cutting *[pine cuts easily]* **3.** to go (*across* or *through*) **4.** to swing a bat, etc. (at a ball) **5.** to change direction suddenly **—adj. 1.** that has been cut **2.** made or formed by cutting **—n. 1.** a cutting or being cut **2.** a stroke or opening made by a sharp-edged instrument **3.** the omission of a part **4.** a piece cut off, as of meat **5.** a reduction; decrease **6.** a passage or channel cut out **7.** the style in which a thing is cut; fashion **8.** an act, remark, etc. that hurts one's feelings **9.** a block or plate engraved for printing, or the impression from this **10.** [Colloq.] a snub **11.** [Colloq.] an unauthorized absence from school, etc. **12.** [Slang] a share, as of profits **—a cut above** [Colloq.] somewhat better than **—cut and dried 1.** arranged beforehand **2.** lifeless; dull **—cut down (on)** to reduce; lessen **—cut it out** [Colloq.] to stop what one is doing **—cut off 1.** to sever **2.** to stop abruptly; shut off **3.** to interrupt **4.** to intercept **5.** to disinherit **—cut out 1.** to remove or omit **2.** to eliminate and take the place of (a rival) **3.** to make or form as by cutting **4.** [Colloq.] to discontinue; stop **—cut out for** suited for **—cut up 1.** to cut into pieces **2.** [Slang] to clown, joke, etc.

cu·ta·ne·ous (kyōō tā'nē əs) *adj.* [< L. *cutis*, skin] of or on the skin

cut'a·way' *n.* a man's formal coat cut so as to curve back to the tails

cut'back' *n.* a reduction or discontinuance, as of production

cute (kyōōt) *adj.* **cut'er, cut'est** [< ACUTE] [Colloq.] **1.** clever; shrewd **2.** pretty or attractive, esp. in a dainty way **—cute'ly** *adv.* **—cute'ness** *n.*

cut glass glass shaped or ornamented by grinding and polishing **—cut'-glass'** *adj.*

cu·ti·cle (kyōōt'i k'l) *n.* [L. *cuticula*, skin] **1.** the outer layer of the skin; epidermis **2.** hardened skin, as at the base and sides of a fingernail

cut·lass, cut·las (kut'ləs) *n.* [< L. *culter*, CUTAWAY knife] a short, thick, curved sword

cut·ler·y (kut'lər ē) *n.* [see prec.] **1.** cutting implements, as knives **2.** eating implements

cut·let (kut'lit) *n.* [< L. *costa*, a rib] **1.** a small slice of meat from the ribs or leg, for frying or broiling **2.** a small, flat croquette of chopped meat or fish

cut'off' *n.* **1.** the limit set for a process, activity, etc. **2.** a road or passage that is a shortcut **3.** any device for cutting off the flow of a fluid, a connection, etc.

cut'out' *n.* **1.** a device for breaking or closing an electric circuit **2.** a device for letting the exhaust gases of an internal-combustion engine pass directly into the air instead of through a muffler **3.** a design to be cut out

cut'-rate' *adj.* selling or on sale at a lower price

cut·ter (kut'ər) *n.* **1.** a person or thing that cuts **2.** a small, swift vessel; specif., *a*) a boat carried by large ships as a communications tender: also **ship's cutter** *b*) an armed motor ship used by the Coast Guard: also **Coast Guard cutter 3.** a small, light sleigh

cut'throat' *n.* a murderer **—adj. 1.** murderous **2.** merciless; ruthless

cut·ting (kut'iŋ) *n.* **1.** the act of one that cuts **2.** a piece cut off **3.** a shoot cut away from a plant for rooting or grafting **—adj. 1.** that cuts; sharp **2.** chilling or piercing **3.** sarcastic; harsh **—cut'ting·ly** *adv.*

cut·tle·bone (kut''l bōn') *n.* the internal shell of cuttlefish, used as food for caged birds and, when powdered, as a polishing agent

cut'tle·fish' (-fish') *n., pl.:* see FISH [OE. *cudele*] a sea mollusk with ten sucker-bearing arms and a hard internal shell: when in danger, some cuttlefish eject an inky fluid

cut'worm' *n.* any of various caterpillars that feed on young plants of cabbage, corn, etc., cutting them off at ground level

cwt. hundredweight

-cy [< Gr. *-kia*] a suffix meaning: **1.** quality, condition, or fact of being *[hesitancy]* **2.** position, rank, or office of *[captaincy]*

cy·an·ic (sī an'ik) *adj.* **1.** of or containing cyanogen **2.** blue

cyanic acid a colorless, poisonous acid, HOCN

cy·a·nide (sī'ə nīd') *n.* a highly poisonous, white, crystal-line compound containing the cyanogen radical

cy·an·o·gen (sī an'ə jən) *n.* [< Gr. *kyanos*, blue + -GEN] **1.** a colorless, poisonous, flammable gas, C_2N_2 **2.** the univalent radical –CN, in cyanides

cy·a·no·sis (sī'ə nō'sis) *n.* [< Gr. *kyanos*, blue] a bluish skin color caused by lack of oxygen in the blood **—cy'a·not'ic** (-nät'ik) *adj.*

cy·ber·na·tion (sī'bər nā'shən) *n.* [CYBERN(ETICS) + -ATION] the use of computers in connection with automation **—cy'ber·nate'** *vt.* **-nat'ed, -nat'ing**

cy·ber·net·ics (sī'bər net'iks) *n.pl.* [*with sing. v.*] [< Gr. *kybernētēs*, helmsman] the comparative study of complex electronic computers and the human nervous system — **cy'ber·net'ic** *adj.*

cy·cad (sī'kad) *n.* [ult. < Gr. *koix*, palm] a large, tropical plant with a crown of leathery, fernlike leaves

cy·cla·mate (sī'klə māt', sik'lə-) *n.* a complex organic compound with an extremely sweet taste

cy·cla·men (sī'klə mən, sik'lə-) *n., pl.* **-mens** [< Gr. *kyklaminos*] a plant related to the primrose, with heart-shaped leaves

cy·cle (sī'k'l) *n.* [< Gr. *kyklos*, circle] **1.** *a*) a period of time within which a round of regularly recurring events is completed *b*) a complete set of such events **2.** a very long period of time **3.** a series of poems or songs on the same theme **4.** a bicycle, motorcycle, etc. **5.** *Elec.* one complete period of the reversal of an alternating current **—vi.** **-cled, -cling 1.** to occur in cycles **2.** to ride a bicycle, etc.

cy·clic (sī'klik, sik'lik) *adj.* **1.** of or having the nature of a cycle; moving or occurring in cycles **2.** *Chem.* arranged in a ring or closed-chain structure: said of atoms Also **cy'cli·cal**

cy·clist (sī'klist) *n.* a person who rides a cycle

cyclo- [< Gr. *kyklos*, circle] a combining form meaning of a circle or wheel, cyclic: also **cycl-**

cy·clom·e·ter (sī kläm'ə tər) *n.* [CYCLO- + -METER] an instrument that records the revolutions of a wheel, for measuring distance traveled

cy·clone (sī'klōn) *n.* [< Gr. *kyklos*, circle] **1.** loosely, a tornado or hurricane **2.** *Meteorol.* a storm with strong winds rotating about a moving center of low atmospheric pressure **—cy·clon'ic** (-klän'ik) *adj.* **—cy·clon'i·cal·ly** *adv.*

cy·clo·pe·di·a, cy·clo·pae·di·a (sī'klə pē'dē ə) *n.* same as ENCYCLOPEDIA **—cy'clo·pe'dic, cy'clo·pae'dic** *adj.* — **cy'clo·pe'dist, cy'clo·pae'dist** *n.*

Cy·clops (sī'kläps) *n., pl.* **Cy·clo·pes** (sī klō'pēz) [< Gr. *kyklos*, circle + *ōps*, eye] *Gr. Myth.* any of a race of one-eyed giants

cy·clo·ra·ma (sī'klə ram'ə) *n.* [CYCLO- + Gr. *horama*, sight] **1.** a series of large pictures, as of a landscape, put on the wall of a circular room so as to suggest natural perspective to a viewer **2.** a large, curved curtain used as a backdrop for stage sets

cy·clo·tron (sī'klə trän') *n.* [CYCLO- + (ELEC)TRON] an apparatus for giving high energy to particles, as protons and deuterons: used in atomic research

cyg·net (sig'nət) *n.* [< Gr. *kyknos,* swan] a young swan

cyl·in·der (sil'ən dər) *n.* [< Gr. *kylindein,* to roll] **1.** a solid figure described by the edge of a rectangle rotated around the parallel edge as axis **2.** anything with this shape; specif., *a)* the turning part of a revolver, containing chambers for the cartridges *b)* the chamber in which the piston moves in an engine *c)* the barrel of a pump — **cy·lin·dri·cal** (sə lin'dri k'l) *adj.*

cym·bal (sim'b'l) *n.* [< Gr. *kymbē,* hollow of a vessel] *Music* a concave brass plate that makes a sharp, ringing sound when struck with a drumstick, etc., or together in pairs —**cym'bal·ist** *n.*

Cym·ric (kim'rik, sim'-) *adj.* [< W. *Cymru,* Wales] of the Celtic people of Wales or their language

Cym'ry (-rē) *n.pl.* the Cymric Celts; the Welsh

CYMBALS

cyn·ic (sin'ik) *n.* [see CYNICAL] **1.** [C-] a member of a school of ancient Greek philosophers who held virtue to be the only good and stressed independence from worldly needs and pleasures **2.** a cynical person —*adj.* **1.** [C-] of or like the Cynics **2.** *same as* CYNICAL

cyn·i·cal (-i k'l) *adj.* [< Gr. *kyōn,* dog] **1.** denying the sincerity of people or the value of life **2.** sarcastic, sneering, etc. —**cyn'i·cal·ly** *adv.*

cyn·i·cism (-ə siz'm) *n.* **1.** [C-] the philosophy of the Cynics **2.** the attitude or beliefs of a cynic **3.** a cynical remark, idea, or action

cy·no·sure (sī'nə shoor', sin'ə-) *n.* [< Gr. *kynosoura,* dog's tail] a center of attention or interest

Cyn·thi·a (sin'thē ə) **1.** Artemis, goddess of the moon **2.** the moon personified

cy·pher (sī'fər) *n., vt., vi. Brit. var.* of CIPHER

cy·press (sī'prəs) *n.* [< Gr. *kyparissos*] **1.** any of a group of dark-foliaged, cone-bearing evergreens **2.** any of various related trees **3.** their wood

cyp·ri·noid (sip'rə noid') *adj.* [< Gr. *kyprinos,* carp] of or like fishes related to the carp, including the carps, minnows, dace, etc. —*n.* a cyprinoid fish

Cy·prus (sī'prəs) country on an island in the E Mediterranean: 3,572 sq. mi.; pop. 630,000; cap. Nicosia —**Cyp·ri·ot** (sip'rē ət) *adj., n.*

Cy·rus (sī'rəs) ?-529 B.C.; Persian king: founded Persian Empire: called *the Great*

cyst (sist) *n.* [< Gr. *kystis,* sac] any of certain saclike structures in plants or animals, esp. one filled with diseased matter —**cyst'ic** *adj.*

cystic fibrosis a disease of children, characterized by fibrosis and malfunctioning of the pancreas

cy·tol·o·gy (sī täl'ə jē) *n.* [< Gr. *kytos,* a hollow + -LOGY] the branch of biology dealing with cells

cy·to·plasm (sīt'ə plaz'm) *n.* [< Gr. *kytos,* a hollow + -PLASM] the protoplasm of a cell, exclusive of the nucleus: also **cy'to·plast'** —**cy'to·plas'mic** *adj.*

C.Z., CZ Canal Zone

czar (zär) *n.* [< Russ. < L. *Caesar*] **1.** the title of any of the former emperors of Russia **2.** an autocrat; despot — **cza·ri·na** (zä rē'nə) *n.fem.* —**czar'ism** *n.* —**czar'ist** *adj., n.*

Czech (chek) *n.* **1.** a member of a Slavic people of central Europe **2.** the West Slavic language of the Czechs —*adj.* of Czechoslovakia, its people, or their language

Czech·o·slo·vak (chek'ə slō'väk) *adj.* of Czechoslovakia, its people, etc. —*n.* a Czech or Slovak living in Czechoslovakia Also **Czech·o·slo·vak'i·an** (-vä'kē ən)

Czech·o·slo·va·ki·a (chek'ə slō vä'kē ə) country in C Europe: 49,367 sq. mi.; pop. 14,445,000; cap. Prague

D

D, d (dē) *n., pl.* **D's, d's** the fourth letter of the English alphabet

D (dē) *n.* **1.** a Roman numeral for 500 **2.** a grade for below-average work **3.** *Chem.* deuterium **4.** *Music* the second tone in the scale of C major **5.** *Physics the symbol for* density

D. 1. December **2.** Democrat(ic) **3.** Dutch

d. 1. day(s) **2.** degree **3.** diameter **4.** died **5.** [L. *denarius,* pl. *denarii*] penny; pence

'd 1. *contracted auxiliary form of* had *or* would *[I'd, they'd]* **2.** contraction of -ed *[foster'd]*

D.A. District Attorney

dab (dab) *vt., vi.* **dabbed, dab'bing** [ME. *dabben,* to strike] **1.** to touch lightly and quickly; pat **2.** to put on (paint, etc.) with light, quick strokes —*n.* **1.** a tap; pat **2.** a soft or moist bit of something *[a dab of rouge]* —**dab'ber** *n.*

dab·ble (dab''l) *vt.* **-bled, -bling** [< Du. *dabben,* to strike] to spatter or splash —*vi.* **1.** to play in water, as with the hands **2.** to do something superficially (with *in* or *at*) — **dab'bler** *n.*

dace (dās) *n., pl.* **dace, dac'es** [< VL. *darsus*] a small freshwater fish of the carp family

dachs·hund (däks'hoond) *n.* [G. *dachs,* a badger + *hund,* a dog] a small dog of German breed, with a long body and short legs

Da·cron (dā'krän, dak'rän) *a trademark for* a synthetic wrinkle-resistant fabric —*n.* [*also* d-] this fabric

DACHSHUND
(8–10 in. high
at shoulder)

dac·tyl (dak't'l) *n.* [< Gr. *daktylos,* a finger] a metrical foot of three syllables, the first accented and the others unaccented —**dac·tyl'ic** *adj.*

dad (dad) *n.* [< child's cry *dada*] [Colloq.] father: also **dad'dy** (dad'ē), *pl.* **-dies**

dad'dy-long'legs' *n., pl.* **-long'legs'** a spiderlike animal with long legs

da·do (dā'dō) *n., pl.* **-does** [It. < L. *datum,* a die] **1.** the part of a pedestal between the cap and the base **2.** the lower part of a wall if decorated differently from the upper part

Daed·a·lus (ded''l əs, dēd'-) *Gr. Myth.* the builder of the Labyrinth in Crete from which, by means of wings he fabricated, he and Icarus escaped

dae·mon (dē'mən) *n.* [< Gr. *daimōn*] **1.** *Gr. Myth.* a secondary deity **2.** a guardian spirit **3.** *same as* DEMON — **dae·mon·ic** (di män'ik) *adj.*

daf·fo·dil (daf'ə dil') *n.* [< Gr. *asphodelos*] a narcissus with a yellow flower and a large crown

daf·fy (daf'ē) *adj.* **-fi·er, -fi·est** [see DAFT] [Colloq.] crazy; foolish; silly —**daf'fi·ness** *n.*

daft (daft) *adj.* [< OE. *(ge)dæfte,* mild, gentle] **1.** silly; foolish **2.** insane; crazy

da Gam·a (də gam'ə), **Vas·co** (väs'kō) 1469?–1524; Port. navigator

dag·ger (dag'ər) *n.* [< ML. *daggarius*] **1.** a weapon with a short, pointed blade, used for stabbing **2.** *Printing* a reference mark (†)

da·guerre·o·type (də ger'ə tīp') *n.* [< L. J. M. *Daguerre,* 19th-c. Fr. inventor] a photograph made by an early method on a plate of chemically treated metal or glass — *vt.* **-typed', -typ'ing** to photograph by this method

dahl·ia (dal'yə, däl'-) *n.* [< A. *Dahl,* 18th-c. Swed. botanist] **1.** a perennial plant with large, showy flowers **2.** the flower

Da·ho·mey (də hō'mē) *former name of* BENIN

Dail Eir·eann (dôl' er'ən) [Ir. *dáil,* assembly + *Eireann,* gen. of *Eire,* Ireland] the lower house of the legislature of Ireland

dai·ly (dā'lē) *adj.* done, happening, or published every (week)day —*n., pl.* **-lies** a daily newspaper —*adv.* every day; day after day

daily double a bet, the success of which depends on choosing both winners in two specified races on the same program

dain·ty (dān'tē) n., pl. **-ties** [< L. dignitas, worth] a delicacy —adj. **-ti·er, -ti·est 1.** delicious and choice **2.** delicately pretty **3.** a) of refined taste; fastidious b) overly fastidious; squeamish —**dain'ti·ly** adv. —**dain'ti·ness** n.

dai·qui·ri (dak'ər ē) n. [after Daiquiri, village in Cuba] a cocktail made of rum, sugar, and lime or lemon juice

dair·y (der'ē) n., pl. **dair'ies** [< ME. daie, dairymaid] **1.** a place where milk and cream are made into butter, cheese, etc. **2.** a farm that produces, or a store that sells, milk and milk products

dair'y·maid' n. a girl or woman who milks cows or works in a dairy

dair'y·man n., pl. **-men** a man who works in or for a dairy or who owns a dairy

da·is (dā'is, dī'-) n., pl. **da'is·es** [< ML. discus, table] a raised platform at one end of a room, etc.

dai·sy (dā'zē) n., pl. **-sies** [< OE. dæges eage, lit., day's eye] a plant of the composite family, bearing flowers with white rays around a yellow disk

Da·kar (dä kär') capital and seaport of Senegal: pop. 474,000

Da·ko·ta (də kō'tə) n. **1.** pl. **-tas, -ta** a member of a group of Indian tribes (also called Sioux) of the northern plains of the U.S. **2.** their Siouan language —adj. of the Dakota Indians or their language

Da·lai La·ma (dä lī' lä'mə) [Mongol. dalai, ocean + blama, high priest] the traditional high priest of the Lamaist religion: see LAMAISM

dale (dāl) n. [OE. dæl] a valley

Dal·las (dal'əs) city in NE Tex.: pop. 844,000 (met. area 1,556,000)

dal·ly (dal'ē) vi. **-lied, -ly·ing** [< OFr. dalier, to trifle] **1.** to make love in a playful way **2.** to deal lightly or carelessly (with)/3. to waste time; loiter —**dal'li·ance** (-ē əns) n.

Dal·ma·tian (dal mā'shən) n. a large, short-haired dog with dark spots on a white coat

dam[1] (dam) n. [ME.] **1.** a barrier built to hold back flowing water **2.** the water thus kept back —vt. **dammed, dam'ming 1.** to build a dam in **2.** to keep back or confine as by a dam (usually with up)

dam[2] (dam) n. [see DAME] the female parent of any four-legged animal

dam·age (dam'ij) n. [< L. damnum] **1.** injury or harm resulting in a loss **2.** [pl.] Law money compensating for injury, loss, etc. —vt. **-aged, -ag·ing** to do damage to —**dam'age·a·ble** adj.

dam·a·scene (dam'ə sēn', dam'ə sēn') vt. **-scened', -scen'ing** [L. Damascenus, of Damascus] to decorate (steel, etc.) with wavy markings

Da·mas·cus (də mas'kəs) capital of Syria, a very ancient city in the SC part: pop. 530,000

dam·ask (dam'əsk) n. [< It. < prec.] **1.** a reversible fabric in figured weave, used for table linen, etc. **2.** steel decorated with wavy lines **3.** deep pink or rose —adj. **1.** made of or like damask **2.** deep-pink or rose —vt. to damascene

damask rose a very fragrant rose important as a source of attar of roses

dame (dām) n. [< L. domina, lady] **1.** a lady **2.** [D-] in Great Britain, the title of a woman who has received an order of knighthood **3.** [Slang] a woman

damn (dam) vt. **damned, damn'ing** [< L. damnare, condemn] **1.** to condemn to an unhappy fate or, Theol., to hell **2.** to condemn as bad, inferior, etc. **3.** to swear at by saying "damn" —vi. to swear —n. the saying of "damn" as a curse —adj., adv. [Colloq.] clipped form of DAMNED —interj. an expression of anger, etc. —**damn with faint praise** to condemn by praising mildly —**not give (or care) a damn** [Colloq.] not care at all

dam·na·ble (dam'nə b'l) adj. **1.** deserving damnation **2.** deserving to be sworn at; outrageous —**dam'na·bly** adv.

dam·na'tion (-nā'shən) n. a damning or being damned —interj. an expression of anger, etc. —**dam'na·to'ry** adj.

damned (damd) adj. **1.** condemned or deserving condemnation **2.** [Colloq.] deserving cursing; outrageous [a damned shame] —adv. [Colloq.] very —**the damned** Theol. souls doomed to eternal punishment

Dam·o·cles (dam'ə klēz') Gr. Legend a man whose king seated him under a sword hanging by a hair to show him the perils of a ruler's life —**sword of Damocles** any imminent danger

Da·mon and Pyth·i·as (dā'mən ən pith'ē əs) Classical Legend two very devoted friends

damp (damp) n. [MDu., vapor] **1.** a slight wetness; moisture **2.** any harmful gas in a mine —adj. somewhat moist or wet —vt. **1.** to make damp **2.** to reduce or check (energy, action, etc.) —**damp'ish** adj. —**damp'ly** adv. —**damp'ness** n.

damp'-dry' vt. **-dried', -dry'ing** to dry (laundry) so that some moisture is retained —adj. designating or of laundry so treated

damp'en vt. **1.** to make damp; moisten **2.** to deaden, depress, or reduce —vi. to become damp —**damp'en·er** n.

damp'er n. **1.** anything that deadens or depresses **2.** a valve in a flue to control the draft **3.** a device to check vibration in the strings of a piano, etc.

dam·sel (dam'z'l) n. [see DAME] [Archaic] a girl; maiden

dam·son (dam'z'n) n. [< DAMASCUS] a variety of small, purple plum

Dan (dan) Bible a) the fifth son of Jacob b) the tribe of Israel descended from him

Dan. Danish

Da·na·i·des, Da·na·i·des (də nā'ə dēz') n.pl., sing. **Dan·a·id, Dan·a·id** (dan'ē id) Gr. Myth. the fifty daughters of Danaus (dan'ē əs) : forty-nine murdered their husbands at their father's command

dance (dans) vi. **danced, danc'ing** [< OFr. danser] **1.** to move the body and feet in rhythm, ordinarily to music **2.** to move rapidly, lightly, gaily, etc. —vt. **1.** to perform (a dance) **2.** to cause to dance —n. **1.** rhythmic movement, ordinarily to music **2.** a particular kind of dance **3.** the art of dancing **4.** a party for dancing **5.** a piece of music for dancing **6.** rapid, lively movement —**danc'er** n.

dan·de·li·on (dan'də lī'ən) n. [< OFr. dent, tooth + de, of + lion, lion] a common weed with yellow flowers and jagged leaves

dan·der (dan'dər) n. [< ?] [Colloq.] anger or temper —**get one's dander up** [Colloq.] to become or make angry

dan·di·fy (dan'də fī') vt. **-fied', -fy'ing** to dress up like a dandy

dan·dle (dan'd'l) vt. **-dled, -dling** [< ?] to dance (a child) up and down on the knee or in the arms

dan·druff (dan'drəf) n. [< earlier dandro + dial. hurf, scab] little scales of dead skin on the scalp

dan·dy (dan'dē) n., pl. **-dies** [< ?] **1.** a man overly attentive to his clothes and appearance; fop **2.** [Colloq.] something very good —adj. **-di·er, -di·est** [Colloq.] very good —**dan'dy·ish** adj.

Dane (dān) n. a native or inhabitant of Denmark

dan·ger (dān'jər) n. [ult. < L. dominus, a master] **1.** liability to injury, damage, loss, or pain **2.** a thing that may cause injury, pain, etc.

dan'ger·ous adj. full of danger; unsafe —**dan'ger·ous·ly** adv. —**dan'ger·ous·ness** n.

dan·gle (daŋ'g'l) vi. **-gled, -gling** [< Scand.] **1.** to hang swinging loosely **2.** Gram. to lack clear connection as one sentence element modifying another [a dangling participle] —vt. to cause to dangle

Dan·iel (dan'yəl) Bible **1.** a Hebrew prophet whose faith saved him in the lion's den **2.** the book containing his story

Dan·ish (dā'nish) adj. of Denmark, the Danes, or their language —n. **1.** the language of the Danes **2.** [also d-] rich, flaky pastry filled with fruit, cheese, etc.: in full **Danish pastry**

dank (daŋk) adj. [ME.] disagreeably damp —**dank'ly** adv. —**dank'ness** n.

Dan·te (Alighieri) (dän'tā, dan'tē) 1265–1321; It. poet: wrote The Divine Comedy —**Dan'te·an** adj., n.

Dan·ube (dan'yōōb) river flowing from SW Germany eastward into the Black Sea: c.1,770 mi.

Dan·zig (dan'sig) German name of GDAŃSK

Daph·ne (daf'nē) Gr. Myth. a nymph who escaped from Apollo by becoming a laurel tree

dap·per (dap'ər) adj. [< ? MDu.] **1.** small and active **2.** trim, neat, or smart —**dap'per·ly** adv.

dap·ple (dap''l) adj. [< ON. depill, a spot] marked with spots; mottled: also **dap'pled** —n. **1.** a spotted condition **2.** an animal whose skin is spotted —vt., vi. **-pled, -pling** to cover or become covered with spots

DAR, D.A.R. Daughters of the American Revolution

Dar·da·nelles (där'də nelz') strait between the Aegean Sea & the Sea of Marmara: c.40 mi. long; 1–4 mi. wide

fat, āpe, cär; ten, ēven; is, bīte; gō, hôrn, tōol, look; oil, out; up, fur; thin, then; zh, leisure; ŋ, ring; ə for a in ago; ' as in able (ā'b'l); ë, Fr. coeur; ö, Fr. feu; Fr. mon; ü, Fr. duc; r, Fr. cri; kh, G. doch, ich. ‡ foreign; < derived from

dare (der) *vt., vi.* **dared** or archaic **durst** (durst), **dared, dar'ing** [OE. *durran*] **1.** to have enough courage for (some act) **2.** to oppose and defy **3.** to challenge (someone) to do something —*n.* a challenge —**dare say** to think probable —**dar'er** *n.*

dare'dev'il (-dev'l) *adj.* bold and reckless —*n.* a bold, reckless person

Dar es Sa·laam (där' es sə läm') capital of Tanzania, on the Indian Ocean: pop. 373,000

dar·ing (der'iŋ) *adj.* fearless; bold —*n.* bold courage —**dar'ing·ly** *adv.*

Da·ri·us I (də rī'əs) 550?–486? B.C.; king of Persia (521–486?): called *the Great*

dark (därk) *adj.* [< OE. *deorc*] **1.** entirely or partly without light **2.** almost black **3.** not light in color or complexion **4.** hidden; secret **5.** gloomy **6.** sullen **7.** evil; sinister **8.** ignorant; unenlightened —*n.* **1.** the state of being dark **2.** night **3.** a dark color or shade —**in the dark** uninformed —**dark'ish** *adj.* —**dark'ly** *adv.* —**dark'ness** *n.*

Dark Ages the Middle Ages, esp. the earlier part

dark'en *vi., vt.* to make or become dark or darker

dark horse [Colloq.] **1.** an unexpected, almost unknown winner, as in a horse race **2.** *Politics* a person who gets or may get the nomination unexpectedly

dark·ling (därk'liŋ) *adv.* [DARK + -LING] [Poet.] in the dark —*adj.* [Poet.] dark, dim, obscure, etc.

dark'room' *n.* a darkened room for developing photographs

dar·ling (där'liŋ) *n.* [OE. *deorling*] a person much loved by another —*adj.* **1.** very dear; beloved **2.** [Colloq.] cute; attractive [*a darling dress*]

darn¹ (därn) *vt., vi.* [< MFr. dial. *darner*] to mend (cloth, etc.) by sewing a network of stitches across the gap —*n.* a darned place in fabric —**darn'er** *n.*

darn² (därn) *vt., vi., n., adj., adv., interj.* [Colloq.] *a euphemism for* DAMN (the curse) —**darned** *adj., adv.*

dar·nel (där'n'l) *n.* [< Fr. dial. *darnelle*] a weedy rye grass which can become poisonous

darn'ing needle **1.** a large needle for darning **2.** *same as* DRAGONFLY

dart (därt) *n.* [< OFr.] **1.** a small, pointed missile for throwing or shooting **2.** a sudden, quick movement **3.** a short, tapered seam —*vt., vi.* to throw, shoot, send out, move, etc. suddenly and fast

dart'er *n.* **1.** a thing or animal that darts **2.** a tropical diving bird **3.** a small, brightly colored freshwater fish of N. America

Dar·von (där'vän) *a trademark for* a pain-killing drug containing aspirin, etc.

Dar·win (där'win), **Charles Robert** 1809–82; Eng. naturalist —**Dar·win'i·an** (-win'ē ən) *adj., n.*

Darwinian theory Darwin's theory of evolution, which holds that all plants and animals developed from earlier forms, those forms surviving which are best adapted to the environment (*natural selection*): also called **Dar'win·ism** —**Dar'win·ist** *adj., n.*

dash (dash) *vt.* [< Scand.] **1.** to smash; destroy **2.** to strike (something) violently (*against*) **3.** to throw, thrust, etc. (with *away, down,* etc.) **4.** to splash —*vi.* **1.** to strike violently (*against* or *on*) **2.** to rush —*n.* **1.** a smash **2.** a splash **3.** a bit of something added **4.** a sudden rush **5.** a short, fast race **6.** vigor; spirit **7.** the mark of punctuation (—) used to indicate a break, omission, etc. **8.** a long sound or signal, as in Morse code —**dash off** **1.** to do, write, etc. hastily **2.** to rush away —**dash'er** *n.*

dash'board' *n.* a panel with instruments and gauges on it, as in an automobile

dash'ing *adj.* **1.** full of dash or spirit; lively **2.** showy; stylish —**dash'ing·ly** *adv.*

das·tard (das'tərd) *n.* [ME.] a sneaky, cowardly evildoer

das'tard·ly (-lē) *adj.* [see prec.] mean, sneaky, cowardly, etc. —**das'tard·li·ness** *n.*

dat. dative

da·ta (dāt'ə, dat'ə) *n.pl.* [*often with sing. v.*] [see DATUM] things known or assumed; facts or figures from which conclusions can be inferred

data processing the recording and handling of information by mechanical or electronic means

date¹ (dāt) *n.* [< L. *dare*, give] **1.** a statement on a writing, coin, etc. of when it was made **2.** the time at which a thing happens or is done **3.** the day of the month **4.** *a)* an appointment *b)* a social engagement with a person of the opposite sex *c)* this person —*vt.* **dat'ed, dat'ing** **1.** to mark (a letter, etc.) with a date **2.** to find out or give the date of **3.** to make seem old-fashioned **4.** to have a social engagement with —*vi.* **1.** to belong to a definite period in the past (usually with *from*) **2.** to date persons of the op-

posite sex —**out of date** old-fashioned —**up to date** modern —**dat'er** *n.*

date² (dāt) *n.* [< Gr. *daktylos*, lit., a finger] the sweet, fleshy fruit of a palm (**date palm**)

date'less *adj.* **1.** without a date **2.** without end **3.** still good or interesting though old

date'line' *n.* **1.** the date and place of writing, as given in a line in a newspaper, etc. **2.** *same as* DATE LINE —*vt.* **-lined', -lin'ing** to give a dateline to

date line an imaginary line through the Pacific, largely along the 180th meridian: at this line, by international agreement, each calendar day begins at midnight, so that when it is Sunday just west of the line, it is Saturday just east of it

da·tive (dāt'iv) *adj.* [< L. *dare*, give] designating or of that case which expresses the indirect object of a verb —*n.* **1.** the dative case **2.** a word or phrase in this case

da·tum (dāt'əm, dat'-) *n. sing. of* DATA

daub (dôb) *vt., vi.* [< L. *de-*, intens. + *albus*, white] **1.** to cover or smear with sticky, soft matter, as plaster, grease, etc. **2.** to paint badly —*n.* **1.** anything daubed on **2.** a daubing stroke **3.** a poorly painted picture —**daub'er** *n.*

daugh·ter (dôt'ər) *n.* [< OE. *dohtor*] **1.** a girl or woman as she is related to either or both parents **2.** a female descendant **3.** a female thought of as if in relation to a parent [*a daughter* of France]

daugh'ter-in-law' *n., pl.* **daugh'ters-in-law'** the wife of one's son

daunt (dônt, dänt) *vt.* [< L. *domare*, to tame] to frighten or discourage; dishearten

daunt'less *adj.* that cannot be daunted or intimidated; fearless —**daunt'less·ly** *adv.*

dau·phin (dô'fin) *n.* [Fr., dolphin] the eldest son of the king of France: a title used from 1349 to 1830

dav·en·port (dav'ən pôrt') *n.* [< ?] a large sofa, sometimes one convertible into a bed

Da·vid (dā'vid) *Bible* the second king of Israel

da Vin·ci (də vin'chē), **Le·o·nar·do** (lē'ə när'dō) 1452–1519; It. painter, sculptor, & scientist

Da·vis (dā'vis), **Jefferson** 1808–89; U.S. statesman; president of the Confederacy (1861–65)

dav·it (dav'it) *n.* [< OFr. dim. of *David*] either of a pair of uprights projecting over the side of a ship for suspending, lowering, or raising a boat

Da·vy Jones (dā'vē jōnz') the spirit of the sea: humorous name given by sailors

Davy Jones's Locker the bottom of the sea; grave of those drowned or buried at sea

daw (dô) *n.* [ME. *dawe*] *same as* JACKDAW

daw·dle (dôd''l) *vi., vt.* **-dled, -dling** [< ?] to waste (time) in trifling; loiter —**daw'dler** *n.*

DAVITS

dawn (dôn) *vi.* [< OE. *dæg*, day] **1.** to begin to be day; grow light **2.** to begin to appear, develop, etc. **3.** to begin to be understood or felt [the meaning *dawned* on me] —*n.* **1.** daybreak **2.** the beginning (of something)

day (dā) *n.* [< OE. *dæg*] **1.** the period of light between sunrise and sunset **2.** daylight **3.** the time (24 hours) that it takes the earth to revolve once on its axis **4.** [*often* D-] a particular day [Memorial *Day*] **5.** [*also pl.*] a period of time; era **6.** a period of power, glory, etc. [he's had his *day*] **7.** the time one works each day [an eight-hour *day*] **8.** [*pl.*] one's lifetime —**call it a day** [Colloq.] to stop working for the day —**day after day** every day: also **day in, day out**

day'bed' *n.* a couch that can also be used as a bed

day'book' *n.* **1.** a diary or journal **2.** *Bookkeeping* a book used to record daily transactions

day'break' *n.* the time in the morning when light first appears; dawn

day'-care' center *same as* DAY NURSERY

day'dream' *n.* **1.** a pleasant, dreamlike thinking or wishing; reverie **2.** a pleasing but visionary notion —*vi.* to have daydreams —**day'dream'er** *n.*

day laborer an unskilled worker paid by the day

day'light' *n.* **1.** the light of day **2.** dawn **3.** daytime **4.** understanding or knowledge

day'light'-sav'ing time time that is one hour later than standard time, generally used in the summer

day nursery a nursery school for the daytime care of preschool children, as of working mothers

day'time' *n.* the period of daylight

day'-to-day' *adj.* daily; routine

Day·ton (dāt''n) city in SW Ohio: pop. 244,000 (met. area 850,000)

daze (dāz) *vt.* dazed, daz'ing [< ON. *dasi*, tired] **1.** to stun or bewilder **2.** to dazzle —*n.* a dazed condition

daz·zle (daz''l) *vt., vi.* daz'zled, daz'zling [< prec.] **1.** to overpower or be overpowered by the glare of bright light **2.** to surprise or arouse admiration with brilliant qualities, display, etc. —*n.* a dazzling —**daz'zler** *n.* —**daz'zling·ly** *adv.*

DC, D.C., d.c. direct current

D.C., DC District of Columbia

D.D. Doctor of Divinity

D-day (dē'dā') *n.* the day for beginning a military operation

D.D.S. Doctor of Dental Surgery

DDT a powerful insecticide effective upon contact

de- [< Fr. *de-* or L. *de*] *a prefix meaning:* **1.** away from, off [*derail*] **2.** down [*decline*] **3.** entirely [*defunct*] **4.** reverse the action of [*decode*]

dea·con (dēk''n) *n.* [< Gr. *diakonos*, servant] **1.** a cleric ranking just below a priest **2.** a church officer who helps the minister —**dea'con·ess** *n.fem.*

de·ac·ti·vate (dē ak'tə vāt') *vt.* -vat'ed, -vat'ing **1.** to make (an explosive, chemical, etc.) inactive **2.** *Mil.* to place (troops, etc.) on nonactive status —**de·ac'ti·va'tion** *n.*

dead (ded) *adj.* [OE.] **1.** no longer living **2.** without life **3.** deathlike **4.** lacking vitality, interest, warmth, etc. **5.** without feeling, motion, or power **6.** extinguished or extinct **7.** slack, stagnant, etc. **8.** no longer used; obsolete **9.** barren [*dead* soil] **10.** unerring [a *dead* shot] **11.** exact **12.** complete [a *dead* stop] **13.** [Colloq.] very tired —*n.* the time of greatest darkness, most intense cold, etc. [the *dead* of night] —*adv.* **1.** completely **2.** directly —**the dead** those who have died —**dead'ness** *n.*

dead·beat (ded'bēt') *n.* [Slang] **1.** one who evades paying his debts, etc. **2.** a lazy, idle person

dead·en (ded''n) *vt.* **1.** to lessen the vigor or intensity of **2.** to make numb or soundproof —*vi.* to become as if dead

dead end 1. an end of a street, etc. that has no regular exit **2.** an impasse —**dead' end'** *adj.*

dead heat a race in which two or more contestants reach the finish line at exactly the same time; tie

dead letter 1. a rule, law, etc. no longer enforced **2.** an unclaimed letter

dead'line' *n.* the latest time by which something must be done or completed

dead'lock' (-läk') *n.* a standstill resulting from the action of equal and opposed forces —*vt., vi.* to bring or come to a deadlock

dead'ly *adj.* -li·er, -li·est **1.** causing or likely to cause death **2.** to the death [*deadly* combat] **3.** typical of death [*deadly* pallor] **4.** extreme **5.** very boring **6.** very accurate —*adv.* **1.** as if dead **2.** extremely —**dead'li·ness** *n.*

dead'pan' (-pan') *n.* [Slang] an expressionless face —*adj., adv.* [Slang] without expression

dead reckoning the finding of a ship's position by an estimate based on data recorded in the log rather than by taking astronomical observations

Dead Sea inland body of salt water between Israel and Jordan: 1,290 ft. below sea level

dead weight 1. the weight of an inert person or thing **2.** the weight of a vehicle without a load

dead'wood' (-wood') *n.* **1.** dead wood on trees **2.** anything useless or burdensome

deaf (def) *adj.* [OE.] **1.** unable to hear **2.** unwilling to hear or listen, as to a plea —**deaf'ly** *adv.* —**deaf'ness** *n.*

deaf'en (-'n) *vt.* **1.** to make deaf **2.** to overwhelm with noise **3.** to soundproof with insulation —**deaf'en·ing** *adj., n.* —**deaf'en·ing·ly** *adv.*

deaf'-mute' (-myōōt') *n.* a person who is deaf and has not learned to speak

deal¹ (dēl) *vt.* dealt (delt), deal'ing [OE. *dǣlan*] **1.** to portion out or distribute **2.** to give or administer (a blow) —*vi.* **1.** to have to do (*with*) [books *dealing* with fish] **2.** to act or conduct oneself [to *deal* fairly with others] **3.** to consider or attend to [to *deal* with a problem] **4.** to do business; trade (*with* or *in*) **5.** to distribute playing cards to the players —*n.* **1.** *a)* the act of distributing playing cards *b)* a player's turn to deal *c)* the playing of one deal of cards **2.** a business transaction **3.** an agreement, esp. when secret or underhanded **4.** [Colloq.] treatment or conduct toward another [a square *deal*] —**deal'er** *n.*

deal² (dēl) *n.* [OE. *dæl*, a part] an indefinite or considerable amount —**a good** (or **great**) **deal 1.** a large amount **2.** very much

deal³ (dēl) *n.* [MDu. *dele*] a fir or pine board

deal'er·ship' (-ship') *n.* a franchise to market a product in an area, or a distributor holding this

deal'ing *n.* **1.** distribution **2.** behavior **3.** [*usually pl.*] transactions or relations

dean (dēn) *n.* [< LL. *decanus*, head of ten (monks, etc.)] **1.** the presiding official of a cathedral **2.** a college official in charge of the students or faculty **3.** the senior member of a group —**dean'ship'** *n.*

dear (dir) *adj.* [OE. *deore*] **1.** much loved **2.** esteemed: a polite form of address [*Dear* Sir] **3.** high-priced; costly **4.** earnest [our *dearest* wish] —*adv.* **1.** with deep affection **2.** at a high cost —*n.* a loved person; darling —*interj.* an expression of surprise, pity, etc. —**dear'ly** *adv.* —**dear'ness** *n.*

Dear·born (dir'bərn, -bôrn') city in SE Mich.: suburb of Detroit: pop. 104,000

dearth (durth) *n.* [< ME. *dere*, dear] **1.** famine **2.** any scarcity or lack

death (deth) *n.* [OE.] **1.** the act or fact of dying; ending of life **2.** [D-] the personification of death, usually as a skeleton holding a scythe **3.** the state of being dead **4.** any end resembling dying; total destruction **5.** the cause of death **6.** murder or bloodshed —**put to death** to kill —**to death** very much [worried *to death*] —**death'like'** *adj.*

death'bed' *n.* the bed on which a person dies or spends his last hours of life —*adj.* done in one's last hours of life [a *deathbed* will]

death'blow' *n.* **1.** a blow that kills **2.** a thing destructive or fatal (*to* something)

death'less *adj.* that cannot die; immortal —**death'less·ly** *adv.* —**death'less·ness** *n.*

death'ly *adj.* **1.** causing death; deadly **2.** like or characteristic of death —*adv.* **1.** in a deathlike way **2.** extremely [*deathly* ill]

death's'-head' *n.* a human skull symbolizing death

death'trap' *n.* an unsafe building, vehicle, etc.

Death Valley dry, hot desert basin in E Calif. & S. Nev.: 282 ft. below sea level

death warrant 1. an official order to put a person to death **2.** anything that makes inevitable the destruction or end of a person or thing

death'watch' *n.* **1.** a vigil beside a dead or dying person **2.** a guard set over a person to be executed

deb (deb) *n.* [Colloq.] *short for* DEBUTANTE

de·ba·cle (di bäk''l, -bak'-) *n.* [< Fr. *débâcler*, break up] **1.** a breaking up of ice in a river, etc. **2.** a rush of debris-filled waters **3.** an overwhelming defeat **4.** a total, often ludicrous, failure

de·bar (dē bär') *vt.* -barred', -bar'ring [< Anglo-Fr.: see DE- & BAR¹] **1.** to exclude (*from* something); bar **2.** to prevent or prohibit —**de·bar'ment** *n.*

de·bark (di bärk') *vt., vi.* [< Fr.: see DE- & BARK³] to unload from or leave a ship or aircraft —**de·bar·ka·tion** (dē'bär kā'shən) *n.*

de·base (di bās') *vt.* -based', -bas'ing. [DE- + (A)BASE] to make lower in value, quality, dignity, etc. —**de·base'ment** *n.* —**de·bas'er** *n.*

de·bate (di bāt') *vi.* -bat'ed, -bat'ing [< OFr.: see DE- & BATTER¹] **1.** to discuss opposing reasons; argue **2.** to take part in a debate (*n.* 2) —*vt.* **1.** to dispute about, esp. in a meeting or legislature **2.** to argue (a question) or argue with (a person) formally **3.** to consider reasons for and against —*n.* **1.** discussion of opposing reasons; argument **2.** a formal contest of skill in reasoned argument between opposing teams —**de·bat'a·ble** *adj.* —**de·bat'er** *n.*

de·bauch (di bôch') *vt.* [Fr. *débaucher*, seduce] to lead astray morally; corrupt —*vi.* to dissipate —*n.* **1.** debauchery **2.** an orgy —**de·bauch'er** *n.*

deb·au·chee (di bôch'ē'; deb'ô chē', -shē') *n.* a dissipated person

de·bauch·er·y (di bôch'ər ē) *n., pl.* -er·ies **1.** extreme indulgence of one's appetites; dissipation **2.** [*pl.*] orgies **3.** a leading astray morally

de·ben·ture (di ben'chər) *n.* [< L.: see DEBT] **1.** a voucher acknowledging a debt **2.** an interest-bearing bond, often issued without security

de·bil·i·tate (di bil'ə tāt') *vt.* -tat'ed, -tat'ing [< L. *debilis*, weak] to make weak; enervate —**de·bil'i·ta'tion** *n.*

de·bil'i·ty (-tē) *n., pl.* -ties [< L. *debilis*, weak] bodily weakness; feebleness

deb·it (deb'it) *n.* [< L. *debere*, owe] **1.** an entry in an account of money owed **2.** the total of such entries —*vt.* to enter as a debit or debits

deb·o·nair, deb·o·naire (deb'ə ner') *adj.* [< OFr. *de bon aire*, of good breed] **1.** genial; affable **2.** carefree; jaunty —**deb'o·nair'ly** *adv.*

de·bouch (di boosh') *vi.* [< Fr. < *dé-*, DE- + *bouche*, the mouth] **1.** *Mil.* to come forth from a narrow or shut-in place into open country **2.** to emerge

de·bris, dé·bris (də brē') *n.* [Fr. < OFr. *desbrisier*, break apart] **1.** broken pieces of stone, wood, etc.; rubble **2.** bits of rubbish; litter **3.** a heap of rock fragments, as from a glacier

Debs (debz), **Eugene V(ictor)** (1855-1926); U.S. labor leader & Socialist candidate for president

debt (det) *n.* [< L. *debere*, owe] **1.** something owed to another **2.** an obligation to pay or return something **3.** the condition of owing *[to be in debt]* **4.** *Theol.* a sin

debt of honor a gambling or betting debt

debt'or (-ər) *n.* one that owes a debt

de·bug (dē bug') *vt.* **-bugged', -bug'ging** [DE- + BUG] **1.** [Slang] to find and correct defects, etc. in **2.** [Slang] to find and remove hidden listening devices from (a room, etc.)

de·bunk (di buŋk') *vt.* [DE- + BUNK²] [Colloq.] to expose the false or exaggerated claims, etc. of

De·bus·sy (də bü sē'; *E.* deb'yoo sē'), **Claude** 1862-1918; Fr. composer

de·but, dé·but (di byoo', dā'byoo) *n.* [Fr. < *débuter*, lead off] **1.** the first appearance before the public, as of an actor **2.** the formal introduction of a girl into society

deb·u·tante (deb'yoo tänt', deb'yoo tänt') *n.* [< Fr.] a girl making a debut, esp. into society

Dec. December

dec. **1.** deceased **2.** decimeter

deca- [< Gr. *deka*, ten] *a combining form meaning ten:* also **dec-**

dec·ade (dek'ād) *n.* [< Gr. *deka*, ten] **1.** a group of ten **2.** a period of ten years

dec·a·dence (dek'ə dəns, di kā'd'ns) *n.* [Fr. < L. *de-*, from + *cadere*, to fall] a process, condition, or period of decline, as in morals, art, etc.; deterioration —**dec'a·dent** *adj., n.*

dec·a·gon (dek'ə gän') *n.* [see DECA- & -GON] a plane figure with ten sides and ten angles

dec·a·gram' (-gram') *n.* [see DECA- & GRAM] a measure of weight, equal to 10 grams: chiefly Brit. sp. **dec'a·gramme'** (-gram')

dec·a·he·dron (dek'ə hē'drən) *n.,* pl. **-drons, -dra** (-drə) [see DECA- & -HEDRON] a solid figure with ten plane surfaces —**dec'a·he'dral** (-drəl) *adj.*

de·cal (di kal', dē'kal) *n. same as* DECALCOMANIA

de·cal·co·ma·ni·a (di kal'kə mā'nē ə) *n.* [< Fr. < *dé-*, DE- + *calquer*, to copy + *manie*, mania] **1.** the transferring of pictures or designs from prepared paper onto glass, wood, etc. **2.** a picture or design of this kind

dec·a·li·ter (dek'ə lēt'ər) *n.* [see DECA- & LITER] a measure of capacity, equal to 10 liters: chiefly Brit. sp. **dec'a·li'tre** (-lēt'ər)

Dec·a·logue, Dec·a·log (dek'ə lôg') *n.* [< Gr.: see DECA- & -LOGUE] [*sometimes* d-] *same as* TEN COMMANDMENTS

dec·a·me·ter (dek'ə mēt'ər) *n.* [see DECA- & METER¹] a measure of length, equal to 10 meters: chiefly Brit. sp. **dec'a·me'tre** (-mēt'ər)

de·camp (di kamp') *vi.* [< Fr.: see DE- & CAMP] **1.** to break camp **2.** to go away suddenly and secretly

de·cant (di kant') *vt.* [< Fr. < L. *de-*, from + *canthus*, tire of a wheel] to pour off (a liquid) gently without stirring up the sediment

de·cant'er *n.* a decorative glass bottle, used for serving wine, etc.

de·cap·i·tate (di kap'ə tāt') *vi.* **-tat'ed, -tat'ing** [Fr. < L. *de-*, off + *caput*, the head] to cut off the head of; behead —**de·cap'i·ta'tion** *n.*

dec·a·pod (dek'ə päd') *adj.* [see DECA- & -POD] ten-legged —*n.* any crustacean with ten legs

dec·a·syl·la·ble (dek'ə sil'ə b'l) *n.* a line of verse with ten syllables —**dec'a·syl·lab'ic** (-si lab'ik) *adj.*

de·cath·lon (di kath'län) *n.* [DEC(A)- + Gr. DECANTER *athlon*, a contest] an athletic contest in which each contestant takes part in ten track and field events

de·cay (di kā') *vi.* [see DECADENCE] **1.** to lose strength, prosperity, etc. gradually; deteriorate **2.** to rot **3.** to undergo radioactive disintegration —*vt.* to cause to decay —

n. **1.** deterioration **2.** a rotting or rottenness **3.** the spontaneous disintegration of radioactive atoms

de·cease (di sēs') *n.* [< L. *de-*, from + *cedere*, go] death —*vi.* **-ceased', -ceas'ing** to die

de·ceased (di sēst') *adj.* dead —**the deceased** the dead person or persons

de·ce·dent (di sēd''nt) *n. Law* a deceased person

de·ceit (di sēt') *n.* **1.** a deceiving or lying **2.** a dishonest action; lie **3.** a deceitful quality

de·ceit'ful *adj.* **1.** apt to lie or cheat **2.** deceptive; false —**de·ceit'ful·ly** *adv.* —**de·ceit'ful·ness** *n.*

de·ceive (di sēv') *vt.* **-ceived', -ceiv'ing** [< L. *de-*, from + *capere*, to take] to make (a person) believe what is not true; mislead —*vi.* to use deceit —**de·ceiv'er** *n.* —**de·ceiv'ing·ly** *adv.*

de·cel·er·ate (dē sel'ə rāt') *vt., vi.* **-at'ed, -at'ing** [DE- + (AC)CELERATE] to slow down —**de·cel'er·a'tion** *n.*

De·cem·ber (di sem'bər) *n.* [< L. *decem*, ten: tenth month in Rom. calendar] the twelfth and last month of the year, having 31 days

de·cen·cy (dē's'n sē) *n., pl.* **-cies** a being decent; propriety; proper behavior, modesty, etc.

de·cen·ni·al (di sen'ē əl) *adj.* [< L. *decem*, ten + *annus*, year] **1.** of or lasting ten years **2.** occurring every ten years —*n.* a tenth anniversary

de·cent (dē's'nt) *adj.* [< L. *decere*, befit] **1.** proper and fitting **2.** not obscene **3.** conforming to approved social standards; respectable **4.** adequate *[decent wages]* **5.** fair and kind —**de'cent·ly** *adv.*

de·cen·tral·ize (dē sen'trə līz') *vt.* **-ized', -iz'ing** to break up a concentration of (governmental authority, etc.) and distribute more widely —**de·cen'tral·i·za'tion** *n.*

de·cep·tion (di sep'shən) *n.* **1.** a deceiving or being deceived **2.** an illusion or fraud

de·cep'tive *adj.* deceiving or meant to deceive —**de·cep'tive·ly** *adv.* —**de·cep'tive·ness** *n.*

deci- [Fr. < L. *decem*, ten] *a combining form meaning one tenth [decigram]*

dec·i·bel (des'ə bel') *n.* [DECI- + *bel* (after A. G. *Bell*)] a numerical expression of the relative loudness of a sound

de·cide (di sīd') *vt.* **-cid'ed, -cid'ing** [< L. *de-*, off + *caedere*, to cut] **1.** to end (a contest, dispute, etc.) by giving one side the victory **2.** to reach a decision about —*vi.* to arrive at a judgment or decision

de·cid'ed *adj.* **1.** definite; clear-cut **2.** unhesitating; determined —**de·cid'ed·ly** *adv.*

de·cid·u·ous (di sij'oo wəs) *adj.* [< L. *de-*, off + *cadere*, fall] **1.** falling off at a certain season, as some leaves or antlers **2.** shedding leaves annually

dec·i·gram (des'ə gram') *n.* [see DECI- & GRAM] a metric weight, equal to 1/10 gram: chiefly Brit. sp. **dec'i·gramme'**

dec·i·li·ter (des'ə lēt'ər) *n.* [see DECI- & LITER] a metric measure of volume, equal to 1/10 liter: chiefly Brit. sp. **dec'i·li'tre** (-lēt'ər)

dec·i·mal (des'ə m'l) *adj.* [< L. *decem*, ten] of or based on the number 10; progressing by tens —*n.* a fraction with an unwritten denominator of 10 or some power of ten, shown by a point (**decimal point**) before the numerator (Ex.: .5 = 5/10): in full **decimal fraction** —**dec'i·mal·ly** *adv.*

dec·i·mate (des'ə māt') *vt.* **-mat'ed, -mat'ing** [< L. *decem*, ten] to destroy or kill a large part of —**dec'i·ma'tion** *n.* —**dec'i·ma'tor** *n.*

dec·i·me·ter (des'ə mēt'ər) *n.* [see DECI- & METER¹] a metric measure of length, equal to 1/10 meter: chiefly Brit. sp. **dec'i·me'tre** (-mēt'ər)

de·ci·pher (di sī'fər) *vt.* [DE- + CIPHER] **1.** *same as* DECODE **2.** to make out the meaning of (a scrawl, etc.) —**de·ci'pher·a·ble** *adj.*

de·ci·sion (di sizh'ən) *n.* **1.** the act of deciding or settling a dispute or question **2.** the act of making up one's mind **3.** a judgment or conclusion **4.** determination; firmness of mind

de·ci·sive (di sī'siv) *adj.* **1.** that settles a dispute, question, etc. **2.** crucial **3.** showing decision —**de·ci'sive·ly** *adv.* —**de·ci'sive·ness** *n.*

deck¹ (dek) *n.* [prob. < MLowG. *verdeck*] **1.** a floor of a ship **2.** a pack of playing cards —**clear the decks** to get ready for action

deck² (dek) *vt.* [MDu. *decken*, to cover] to array or adorn

deck'hand' *n.* a common sailor

deck·le edge (dek''l) [< G. *deckel*, a cover] a rough, irregular edge sometimes given to a sheet of paper

de·claim (di klām') *vi., vt.* [< L. *de-*, intens. + *clamare*, to shout] to recite or speak in a studied, dramatic, or impassioned way —**de·claim'er** *n.*

dec·la·ma·tion (dek'lə mā'shən) *n.* **1.** a declaiming **2.** a speech, poem, etc. that is or can be declaimed —**de·clam·a·to·ry** (di klam'ə tôr'ē) *adj.*

dec·la·ra·tion (dek'lə rā'shən) *n.* **1.** a declaring; announcement **2.** a formal statement **3.** a statement of taxable goods **4.** *Bridge* the winning bid

Declaration of Independence a formal statement adopted July 4, 1776, by the Second Continental Congress, declaring the thirteen American colonies free and independent of Great Britain

de·clar·a·tive (di klar'ə tiv) *adj.* making a statement or assertion: also **de·clar·a·to·ry** (-ə tôr'ē)

de·clare (di kler') *vt.* **-clared', -clar'ing** [< L. *de-*, intens. + *clarus*, clear] **1.** to announce openly, formally, etc. **2.** to show or reveal **3.** to say emphatically **4.** to make a statement of (taxable goods) **5.** *Card Games* to establish (trump or no-trump) by a successful bid —*vi.* **1.** to make a declaration **2.** to state openly a choice, opinion, etc. —**declare oneself 1.** to state strongly one's opinion **2.** to reveal one's true character, etc. —**de·clar'er** *n.*

de·clas·si·fy (dē klas'ə fī') *vt.* **-fied', -fy'ing** to make (secret documents) available to the public

de·clen·sion (di klen'shən) *n.* [see DECLINE] **1.** a sloping; descent **2.** a declining **3.** *Gram.* the inflection of nouns, pronouns, or adjectives

dec·li·na·tion (dek'lə nā'shən) *n.* **1.** a bending or sloping downward **2.** the angle formed by a magnetic needle with the line pointing to true north **3.** a polite refusal **4.** *Astron.* the angular distance of a heavenly body north or south from the celestial equator

de·cline (di klīn') *vi.* **-clined', -clin'ing** [< L. *de-*, from + *-clinare*, to bend] **1.** to bend or slope downward **2.** to deteriorate **3.** to refuse something —*vt.* **1.** to cause to bend or slope downward **2.** to refuse, esp. politely **3.** *Gram.* to give the inflected forms of (a noun, pronoun, or adjective) —*n.* **1.** a declining; deterioration; decay **2.** a period of decline **3.** a downward slope —**de·clin'a·ble** *adj.*

de·cliv·i·ty (di kliv'ə tē) *n., pl.* **-ties** [< L. *de-*, down + *clivus*, a slope] a downward slope

de·coct (di käkt') *vt.* [< L. *de-*, down + *coquere*, to cook] to extract the essence, flavor, etc. of by boiling —**de·coc'tion** *n.*

de·code (dē kōd') *vt.* **-cod'ed, -cod'ing** to translate (a coded message) into understandable language

dé·col·le·té (dā käl'ə tā') *adj.* [Fr. < L. *de*, from + *collum*, neck] **1.** cut low so as to bare the neck and shoulders **2.** wearing a décolleté dress, etc.

de·col·o·ni·za·tion (dē käl'ə nə zā'shən) *n.* a freeing or being freed from colonialism or colonial status —**de·col'o·nize'** (-nīz') *vt., vi.* **-nized', -niz'ing**

de·com·pose (dē'kəm pōz') *vt., vi.* **-posed', -pos'ing** [< Fr.: see DE- & COMPOSE] **1.** to break up into basic components or parts **2.** to rot —**de'com·po·si'tion** (-käm pə zish'ən) *n.*

de·com·press (dē'kəm pres') *vt.* to free from pressure, esp. from air pressure —**de'com·pres'sion** *n.*

de·con·gest·ant (dē'kən jes'tənt) *n.* a medication that relieves congestion, as in the nasal passages

de·con·tam·i·nate (-tam'ə nāt') *vt.* **-nat'ed, -nat'ing** to rid of a harmful substance, as radioactive products —**de'·con·tam'i·na'tion** *n.*

dé·cor, de·cor (dā kôr') *n.* [Fr. < L. *decere*, to befit] a decorative scheme, as of a room

dec·o·rate (dek'ə rāt') *vt.* **-rat'ed, -rat'ing** [< L. *decus*, an ornament] **1.** to adorn; ornament **2.** to paint or wallpaper **3.** to give a medal or similar honor to —**dec'o·ra·tive** (-ər ə tiv, -ə rāt'iv) *adj.* —**dec'o·ra·tive·ly** *adv.* —**dec'o·ra'tor** *n.*

dec'o·ra'tion *n.* **1.** a decorating **2.** an ornament **3.** a medal or similar honor

Decoration Day *same as* MEMORIAL DAY

dec·o·rous (dek'ər əs, di kôr'əs) *adj.* having or showing decorum, good taste, etc. —**dec'o·rous·ly** *adv.*

de·co·rum (di kôr'əm) *n.* [< L. *decorus*, fit, proper] **1.** whatever is suitable or proper **2.** propriety in behavior, speech, etc.

de·coy (di koi'; *for n. also* dē'koi) *n.* [< Du. *de kooi*, the cage] **1.** an artificial or trained bird or animal used to lure game within gun range **2.** a thing or person used to lure into a trap —*vt., vi.* to lure or be lured into a trap, danger, etc.

de·crease (di krēs'; *esp. for n.* dē'krēs) *vi., vt.* **-creased', -creas'ing** [< L. *de-*, from + *crescere*, to grow] to become or cause to become gradually less, smaller, etc.; diminish —*n.* **1.** a decreasing; lessening **2.** amount of decreasing —**on the decrease** decreasing —**de·creas'ing·ly** *adv.*

de·cree (di krē') *n.* [< L. *de-*, from + *cernere*, see] an official order or decision —*vt.* **-creed', -cree'ing** to order, decide, or appoint by decree

de·crep·it (di krep'it) *adj.* [< L. *de-*, intens. + *crepare*, creak] broken down or worn out by old age or long use —**de·crep'i·tude'** (-ə tōōd') *n.*

de·cre·scen·do (dē'krə shen'dō) *adj., adv.* [It.] *Music* with a gradual decrease in loudness —*n., pl.* **-dos** *Music* a gradual decrease in loudness

de·crim·i·nal·ize (dē krim'ə n'l īz') *vt.* **-ized', -iz'ing** to eliminate or reduce the penalties for (a crime)

de·cry (di krī') *vt.* **-cried', -cry'ing** [< Fr.: see DE- & CRY] to speak out against openly; denounce

de·cum·bent (di kum'bənt) *adj.* [< L. *de-*, down + *-cumbere*, recline] **1.** lying down **2.** *Bot.* trailing on the ground and rising at the tip, as some stems

ded·i·cate (ded'ə kāt') *vt.* **-cat'ed, -cat'ing** [< L. *de-*, intens. + *dicare*, proclaim] **1.** to devote to a sacred purpose **2.** to devote to some work, duty, etc. **3.** to address (a book, etc.) to someone as a sign of honor —**ded'i·ca'tor** *n.*

ded·i·ca·tion (ded'ə kā'shən) *n.* **1.** a dedicating or being dedicated **2.** an inscription in a book, etc. dedicating it to someone —**ded'i·ca·to'ry** *adj.*

de·duce (di dōōs', -dyōōs') *vt.* **-duced', -duc'ing** [< L. *de-*, down + *ducere*, to lead] **1.** to trace the course or derivation of **2.** to infer or conclude by reasoning —**de·duc'i·ble** *adj.*

de·duct (di dukt') *vt.* [see prec.] to take away or subtract (a quantity) —**de·duct'i·ble** *adj.*

de·duc·tion (-duk'shən) *n.* **1.** a deducting or being deducted **2.** the amount deducted **3.** *a)* reasoning from the general to the specific *b)* a conclusion reached by such reasoning —**de·duc'tive** *adj.*

deed (dēd) *n.* [OE. *dæd*] **1.** a thing done; act **2.** a feat of courage, skill, etc. **3.** action; actual performance **4.** a legal document which transfers a property —*vt.* to transfer (property) by such a document —**in deed** in fact; really

deem (dēm) *vt., vi.* [OE. *deman*, to judge] to think, believe, or judge

de·em·pha·size (dē em'fə sīz') *vt.* **-sized', -siz'ing** to lessen the importance of —**de·em'pha·sis** (-sis) *n.*

deep (dēp) *adj.* [OE. *deop*] **1.** extending far downward, inward, or backward **2.** located far down or back **3.** coming from or going far down or back **4.** hard to understand; abstruse **5.** grave or serious **6.** strongly felt **7.** intellectually profound **8.** dark and rich *[a deep red]* **9.** absorbed by *[deep in thought]* **10.** intense **11.** of low pitch —*n.* **1.** a deep place **2.** the part that is darkest, etc. *[the deep of the night]* —*adv.* far down, far back, etc. —**the deep** [Poet.] the ocean —**deep'ly** *adv.* —**deep'ness** *n.*

deep'-dish' pie a pie baked in a deep dish and having only a top crust

deep'en (-'n) *vt., vi.* to make or become deep or deeper

deep'-fry' *vt.* **-fried', -fry'ing** to fry in a deep pan of boiling fat

deep'-root'ed *adj.* **1.** having deep roots **2.** firmly fixed

deep'-seat'ed *adj.* **1.** buried deep **2.** firmly fixed

deep'-set' *adj.* **1.** deeply set **2.** firmly fixed

deer (dir) *n., pl.* **deer**, *occas.* **deers** [OE. *deor*, wild animal] any of a family of hoofed, cud-chewing animals, as the mule deer, moose, reindeer, etc., the males of which usually bear antlers that are shed annually: popularly used only of the smaller species

deer'skin' *n.* **1.** the hide of a deer **2.** leather or a garment made from this

de·es·ca·late (dē es'kə lāt') *vi., vt.* **-lat'ed, -lat'ing** to reduce in scope, magnitude, etc. —**de·es'ca·la'tion** *n.*

def. 1. defendant **2.** deferred **3.** definition

de·face (di fās') *vt.* **-faced', -fac'ing** [see DE- & FACE] to spoil the appearance of; mar —**de·face'ment** *n.* —**de·fac'er** *n.*

de fac·to (di fak'tō, dā) [L.] actually existing though not officially recognized

de·fal·cate (di fal'kāt) *vi.* **-cat·ed, -cat·ing** [< L. *defalcare*, to cut off] to steal or misuse funds entrusted to one; embezzle —**de·fal·ca·tion** (di'fal kā'shən) *n.* —**de·fal'ca·tor** *n.*

de·fame (di fām') *vt.* **-famed', -fam'ing** [< L. *dis-*, from + *fama*, fame] to attack the reputation of; slander or libel —**def·a·ma·tion** (def'ə mā'shən) *n.* —**de·fam·a·to·ry** (di fam'ə tôr'ē) *adj.* —**de·fam'er** *n.*

de·fault (di fôlt') *n.* [< L. *de-*, away + *fallere*, fail] failure to do or appear as required; specif., *a*) failure to pay money due *b*) failure to take part in or finish a contest — *vi.*, *vt.* **1.** to fail to do, pay, etc. (something) when required **2.** to lose (a contest) by default

de·feat (di fēt′) *vt.* [< L. *dis-*, from + *facere*, do] **1.** to win victory over **2.** to bring to nothing; frustrate —*n.* a defeating or being defeated

de·feat′ist *n.* [< Fr.] one who too readily accepts defeat —*adj.* of or like a defeatist —**de·feat′ism** *n.*

def·e·cate (def′ə kāt′) *vi.* -cat′ed, -cat′ing [< L. *de-*, from + *faex*, dregs] to excrete waste matter from the bowels —**def′e·ca′tion** *n.*

de·fect (dē′fekt, di fekt′) *n.* [< L. *de-*, from + *facere*, do] **1.** lack of something necessary for completeness **2.** an imperfection; fault —*vi.* (di fekt′) to forsake a party, cause, etc., esp. so as to join the opposition —**de·fec′tion** *n.* —**de·fec′tor** *n.*

de·fec·tive (di fek′tiv) *adj.* **1.** having defects; imperfect; faulty **2.** subnormal in intelligence —*n.* a person with some mental or physical defect —**de·fec′tive·ly** *adv.* —**de·fec′tive·ness** *n.*

de·fend (di fend′) *vt.* [< L. *de-*, away + *fendere*, to strike] **1.** to guard from attack; protect **2.** to support or justify **3.** *Law a*) to oppose (an action, etc.) *b*) to act as lawyer for (an accused) —*vi.* to make a defense —**de·fend′er** *n.*

de·fend·ant (di fen′dənt) *n. Law* the person sued or accused

de·fense (di fens′, dē′fens) *n.* **1.** a defending against attack **2.** something that defends **3.** justification by speech or writing **4.** self-protection, as by boxing **5.** the side that is defending in any contest **6.** *a*) the arguments of a defendant *b*) the defendant and his counsel Brit. sp. **de·fence** —**de·fense′less** *adj.* —**de·fense′less·ly** *adv.* —**de·fense′less·ness** *n.*

de·fen·si·ble (di fen′sə b'l) *adj.* that can be defended or justified —**de·fen′si·bly** *adv.*

de·fen′sive *adj.* **1.** defending **2.** of or for defense **3.** *Psychol.* feeling under attack and thus quick to justify one's actions —*n.* a position of defense: chiefly in **on the defensive,** in a position that makes defense necessary —**de·fen′sive·ly** *adv.* —**de·fen′sive·ness** *n.*

de·fer¹ (di fur′) *vt.*, *vi.* -ferred′, -fer′ring [see DIFFER] **1.** to postpone; delay **2.** to postpone the induction of (a person) into compulsory military service —**de·fer′ment,** **de·fer′ral** *n.*

de·fer² (di fur′) *vi.* -ferred′, -fer′ring [< L. *de-*, down + *ferre*, to bear] to give in to the wish or judgment of another

def·er·ence (def′ər əns) *n.* [< Fr.] **1.** a yielding in opinion, judgment, etc. **2.** courteous respect

def·er·en·tial (-ə ren′shəl) *adj.* showing deference; very respectful —**def′er·en′tial·ly** *adv.*

de·fi·ance (di fī′əns) *n.* a defying; open, bold resistance to authority —**in defiance of** in spite of —**de·fi′ant** *adj.* —**de·fi′ant·ly** *adv.*

de·fi·cien·cy (di fish′ən sē) *n.* **1.** a being deficient; incompleteness **2.** *pl.* -cies a shortage

de·fi·cient (-ənt) *adj.* [see DEFECT] **1.** lacking in some essential; incomplete **2.** inadequate in amount, quality, etc.

def·i·cit (def′ə sit) *n.* [L. < *deficere,* to lack] the amount by which a sum of money is less than the required amount

de·file¹ (di fīl′) *vt.* -filed′, -fil′ing [< OFr. *defouler,* tread underfoot] **1.** to make filthy **2.** to corrupt **3.** to profane or sully —**de·file′ment** *n.* —**de·fil′er** *n.*

de·file² (di fīl′, dē′fīl) *vi.* -filed′, -fil′ing [< Fr. *dé-,* from + *fil,* a thread] to march in single file —*n.* a narrow passage, valley, etc.

de·fine (di fīn′) *vt.* -fined′, -fin′ing [< L. *de-*, from + *finis,* boundary] **1.** to determine the limits or nature of; describe exactly **2.** to state the meaning of (a word, etc.) —**de·fin′a·ble** *adj.*

def·i·nite (def′ə nit) *adj.* [see prec.] **1.** having exact limits **2.** precise in meaning; explicit **3.** certain; positive **4.** *Gram.* limiting or specifying [''the'' is the *definite* article] —**def′i·nite·ly** *adv.* —**def′i·nite·ness** *n.*

def·i·ni·tion (def′ə nish′ən) *n.* **1.** a defining or being defined **2.** a statement of the meaning of a word, etc. **3.** clarity of outline, sound, etc.

de·fin·i·tive (di fin′ə tiv) *adj.* **1.** decisive; conclusive **2.** most nearly complete and accurate **3.** serving to define —**de·fin′i·tive·ly** *adv.*

de·flate (di flāt′) *vt.*, *vi.* -flat′ed, -flat′ing [DE- + (IN)FLATE] **1.** to collapse by letting out air or gas **2.** to lessen in size or importance **3.** to cause deflation of (currency, prices, etc.)

de·fla′tion *n.* **1.** a deflating or being deflated **2.** a lessening of the amount of money in circulation, making it rise in value —**de·fla′tion·ar′y** *adj.*

de·flect (di flekt′) *vt.*, *vi.* [< L. *de-*, from + *flectere,* to bend] to turn or make go to one side —**de·flec′tion** *n.* —**de·flec′tive** *adj.* —**de·flec′tor** *n.*

de·flow·er (di flou′ər) *vt.* [see DE- & FLOWER] **1.** to make (a woman) no longer a virgin **2.** to ravage or spoil **3.** to remove flowers from (a plant)

De·foe (di fō′), Daniel 1660?–1731; Eng. writer

de·fo·li·ant (dē fō′lē ənt) *n.* [< L. *de-*, from + *folium,* a leaf] a chemical spray that strips growing plants of their leaves —**de·fo′li·ate′** (-āt′) *vt.* -at′ed, -at′ing

de·for·est (dē fôr′ist, -fär′-) *vt.* to clear (land) of forests or trees —**de·for′est·a′tion** *n.*

de·form (di fôrm′) *vt.* [< L. *de-*, from + *forma,* form] **1.** to impair the form of **2.** to make ugly —**de·for·ma·tion** (dē′fôr mā′shən, def′ər-) *n.*

de·formed′ *adj.* misshapen

de·form·i·ty (di fôr′mə tē) *n., pl.* -ties **1.** a deformed part, as of the body **2.** ugliness or depravity

de·fraud (di frôd′) *vt.* to take property, rights, etc. from by fraud; cheat —**de·frau·da·tion** (dē′frô dā′shən) *n.*

de·fray (di frā′) *vt.* [Fr. *défrayer*] to pay (the cost or expenses) —**de·fray′al, de·fray′ment** *n.*

de·frost (di frôst′) *vt.* **1.** to rid of frost or ice by thawing **2.** to cause (frozen foods) to become unfrozen —*vi.* to become defrosted

de·frost′er *n.* a device for melting ice and frost, as on a windshield

deft (deft) *adj.* [see DAFT] skillful in a quick, sure way —**deft′ly** *adv.* —**deft′ness** *n.*

de·funct (di funkt′) *adj.* [< L. *defungi,* to finish] no longer existing; dead or extinct

de·fy (di fī′) *vt.* -fied′, -fy′ing [< L. *dis-*, from + *fidus,* faithful] **1.** to resist boldly or openly **2.** to resist completely in a baffling way **3.** to dare (someone) to do or prove something

De·gas (də gä′), Ed·gar (ed gär′) 1834–1917; Fr. painter

de Gaulle (də gôl′), Charles 1890–1970; Fr. general; president of France (1959–69)

de·gen·er·ate (di jen′ər it) *adj.* [< L. *de-*, from + *genus,* race] having sunk below a former or normal condition, etc.; deteriorated —*n.* a degenerate person, esp. one who is sexually perverted —*vi.* (-āt′) -at′ed, -at′ing to lose former normal or higher qualities —**de·gen′er·a·cy** (-ə sē) *n.* —**de·gen′er·a′tion** *n.* —**de·gen′er·a·tive** *adj.*

de·grade (di grād′) *vt.* -grad′ed, -grad′ing [< L. *de-*, down + *gradus,* a step] **1.** to demote **2.** to lower in quality, moral character, etc. **3.** to dishonor; debase **4.** *Chem.* to convert (an organic compound) into a simpler compound —**deg·ra·da·tion** (deg′rə dā′shən) *n.*

de·gree (di grē′) *n.* [see prec.] **1.** any of the successive steps in a process **2.** a step in the direct line of descent **3.** social or official rank **4.** relative condition; manner or respect **5.** extent, amount, or intensity [sad to a slight *degree*] **6.** rank as determined by the sum of an algebraic term's exponents **7.** a rank given by a college or university to one who has completed a course of study, or to a distinguished person as an honor **8.** a grade of comparison of adjectives and adverbs [the superlative *degree* of ''good'' is ''best''] **9.** *Law* the seriousness of a crime [murder in the first *degree*] **10.** a unit of measure for angles or arcs, 1/360 of the circumference of a circle **11.** a unit of measure for temperature —**by degrees** gradually —**to a degree** somewhat

de·his·cence (di his′'ns) *n.* [< L. *de-*, off + *hiscere,* to gape] a bursting open, as of a seedpod to discharge its contents —**de·his′cent** *adj.*

de·hu·man·ize (dē hyōo′mə nīz′) *vt.* -ized′, -iz′ing to deprive of human qualities; make inhuman or machinelike —**de·hu′man·i·za′tion** *n.*

de·hu·mid·i·fy (dē′hyōo mid′ə fī′) *vt.* -fied′, -fy′ing to remove moisture from (the air, etc.) —**de·hu·mid′i·fi′er** *n.*

de·hy·drate (dē hī′drāt) *vt.* -drat·ed, -drat·ing to remove water from; dry —*vi.* to lose water; become dry —**de·hy·dra′tion** *n.* —**de·hy′dra·tor** *n.*

de·ice (dē īs′) *vt.* -iced′, -ic′ing to melt ice from or keep free of ice —**de·ic′er** *n.*

de·i·fy (dē′ə fī′) *vt.* -fied′, -fy′ing [< L. *deus,* god + *facere,* to make] **1.** to make a god of **2.** to look upon as a god —**de′i·fi·ca′tion** (-fi kā′shən) *n.*

deign (dān) *vi.* [< L. *dignus,* worthy] to condescend (*to do* something)

de·ism (dē′iz'm) *n.* [< Fr. < L. *deus,* god] the belief that God exists and created the world but thereafter assumed no control over it —**de′ist** *n.*

de·i·ty (dē′ə tē) *n., pl.* **-ties** [< L. *deus,* god] **1**. the state of being a god **2**. a god or goddess —**the Deity** God

de·ject (di jekt′) *vt.* [< L. *de-,* down + *jacere,* to throw] to dishearten; depress —**de·jec′tion** *n.*

de·ject′ed *adj.* in low spirits; depressed —**de·ject′ed·ly** *adv.* —**de·ject′ed·ness** *n.*

Del·a·ware (del′ə wer′) **1**. E State of the U.S.: 2,057 sq. mi.; pop. 548,000; cap. Dover: abbrev. **Del., DE 2**. river flowing southward from S N.Y. into the Atlantic —**Del′a·war′e·an** *adj., n.*

de·lay (di lā′) *vt.* [< OFr. *de-,* intens. + *laier,* to leave] **1**. to put off; postpone **2**. to make late; detain —*vi.* to stop for a while; linger —*n.* a delaying or being delayed

de·lec·ta·ble (di lek′tə b'l) *adj.* [see DELIGHT] delightful or delicious —**de·lec′ta·bly** *adv.*

de·lec·ta·tion (dē′lek tā′shən) *n.* [see DELIGHT] delight; enjoyment

del·e·gate (del′ə gāt′; *also, for n.,* -git) *n.* [< L. *de-,* from + *legare,* send] a person authorized to act for others; representative —*vt.* **-gat′ed, -gat′ing 1**. to appoint as a delegate **2**. to entrust (authority, etc.) to another

del·e·ga′tion *n.* **1**. a delegating or being delegated **2**. a group of delegates

de·lete (di lēt′) *vt.* **-let′ed, -let′ing** [< L. *delere,* destroy] to take out (a printed or written letter, word, etc.); cross out —**de·le′tion** *n.*

del·e·te·ri·ous (del′ə tir′ē əs) *adj.* [< Gr. *dēleisthai,* injure] harmful to health, well-being, etc.; injurious

delft·ware (delft′wer′) *n.* [< *Delft,* city in the Netherlands] glazed earthenware, usually blue and white: also **delft, delf**

Del·hi (del′ē) city in N India: pop. 2,062,000: see also NEW DELHI

del·i (del′ē) *n. clipped form of* DELICATESSEN

de·lib·er·ate (di lib′ər it) *adj.* [< L. *de-,* intens. + *librare,* weigh] **1**. carefully thought out, or done on purpose **2**. not rash or hasty **3**. unhurried and methodical —*vi., vt.* (-āt′) **-at′ed, -at′ing** to consider carefully —**de·lib′er·ate·ly** *adv.* —**de·lib′er·ate·ness** *n.* —**de·lib′er·a′tor** *n.*

de·lib·er·a′tion *n.* **1**. a deliberating **2**. [*often pl.*] consideration of alternatives **3**. carefulness; slowness

de·lib′er·a′tive *adj.* **1**. of or for deliberating [a *deliberative* assembly] **2**. marked by deliberation

del·i·ca·cy (del′i kə sē) *n., pl.* **-cies 1**. the quality or state of being delicate; fineness, weakness, sensitivity, tact, etc. **2**. a choice food

del·i·cate (del′i kit) *adj.* [< L. *delicatus,* delightful] **1**. pleasantly mild, light, etc. **2**. beautifully fine in texture, workmanship, etc. **3**. slight and subtle **4**. easily damaged, spoiled, etc. **5**. frail in health **6**. *a)* needing careful handling *b)* showing tact, consideration, etc. **7**. finely sensitive —**del′i·cate·ly** *adv.* —**del′i·cate·ness** *n.*

del·i·ca·tes·sen (del′i kə tes′'n) *n.* [< G. pl. < Fr. *délicatesse,* delicacy] **1**. prepared cooked meats, fish, cheeses, salads, etc., collectively **2**. a shop where such foods are sold

de·li·cious (di lish′əs) *adj.* [see DELIGHT] **1**. very enjoyable **2**. very pleasing to taste or smell —*n.* [D-] a sweet, red winter apple —**de·li′cious·ly** *adv.* —**de·li′cious·ness** *n.*

de·light (di līt′) *vt.* [< L. *de-,* from + *lacere,* entice] to give great pleasure to —*vi.* **1**. to give great pleasure **2**. to be highly pleased —*n.* **1**. great pleasure **2**. something giving great pleasure —**de·light′ed** *adj.* —**de·light′ed·ly** *adv.*

de·light′ful *adj.* giving delight; very pleasing —**de·light′ful·ly** *adv.* —**de·light′ful·ness** *n.*

De·li·lah (di lī′lə) *Bible* the mistress and betrayer of Samson

de·lim·it (di lim′it) *vt.* to set the limits or boundaries of —**de·lim′i·ta′tion** *n.*

de·lin·e·ate (di lin′ē āt′) *vt.* **-at′ed, -at′ing** [< L. *de-,* from + *linea,* a line] **1**. to draw; sketch **2**. to depict in words; describe —**de·lin′e·a′tion** *n.* —**de·lin′e·a′tor** *n.*

de·lin·quent (di liŋ′kwənt) *adj.* [< L. *de-,* from + *linquere,* to leave] **1**. failing to do what duty or law requires **2**. overdue, as taxes —*n.* a delinquent person; esp., *same as* JUVENILE DELINQUENT —**de·lin′quen·cy** *n., pl.* **-cies** —**de·lin′quent·ly** *adv.*

del·i·quesce (del′ə kwes′) *vi.* **-quesced′, -quesc′ing** [< L. *de-,* from + *liquere,* be liquid] **1**. to melt away **2**. to become liquid by absorbing moisture from the air —**del′i·ques′cence** *n.* —**del′i·ques′cent** *adj.*

de·lir·i·ous (di lir′ē əs) *adj.* **1**. in a state of delirium **2**. of or caused by delirium **3**. wildly excited —**de·lir′i·ous·ly** *adv.*

de·lir·i·um (-əm) *n., pl.* **-ums, -a** (-ə) [< L. *de-,* from + *lira,* a line] **1**. a temporary mental disturbance, as during a fever, marked by confused speech and hallucinations **2**. uncontrollably wild excitement

delirium tre·mens (trē′mənz) [ModL., lit., trembling delirium] a violent delirium resulting chiefly from excessive drinking of alcoholic liquor

de·liv·er (di liv′ər) *vt.* [< L. *de-,* from + *liberare,* to free] **1**. to set free or save from evil, danger, etc. **2**. to assist at the birth of **3**. to utter (a speech, etc.) **4**. to hand over; transfer **5**. to distribute (mail, etc.) **6**. to strike (a blow) **7**. to throw [the pitcher *delivered* a curve] —*vi.* to make deliveries, as of merchandise —**be delivered of** to give birth to —**deliver oneself of** to express; utter —**de·liv′er·a·ble** *adj.* —**de·liv′er·er** *n.*

de·liv′er·ance *n.* **1**. a freeing or being freed **2**. an opinion, etc. publicly expressed

de·liv′er·y *n., pl.* **-ies 1**. a handing over; transfer **2**. a distributing, as of mail **3**. a giving birth; childbirth **4**. any giving forth **5**. the act or manner of giving a speech, throwing a ball, etc. **6**. something delivered

dell (del) *n.* [OE. *del*] a small, secluded valley or glen, usually a wooded one

de·louse (dē lous′, -louz′) *vt.* **-loused′, -lous′ing** to rid of lice

Del·phi (del′fī) ancient city in C Greece: site of an oracle of Apollo —**Del′phic** (-fik) *adj.*

del·phin·i·um (del fin′ē əm) *n.* [< Gr. *delphin,* dolphin] a tall plant bearing spikes of irregular flowers, usually blue; larkspur

del·ta (del′tə) *n.* **1**. the fourth letter of the Greek alphabet (Δ, δ) **2**. a deposit of soil, usually triangular, formed at the mouth of some rivers

DELTA

del·toid (del′toid) *adj.* triangular —*n.* a large, triangular muscle of the shoulder

de·lude (di lōōd′) *vt.* **-lud′ed, -lud′ing** [< L. *de-,* from + *ludere,* to play] to mislead; deceive

del·uge (del′yōōj) *n.* [< L. *dis-,* off + *lavere,* to wash] **1**. a great flood **2**. a heavy rainfall **3**. an overwhelming rush of anything —*vt.* **-uged, -ug·ing 1**. to flood **2**. to overwhelm —**the Deluge** *Bible* the great flood in Noah's time

de·lu·sion (di lōō′zhən) *n.* **1**. a deluding or being deluded **2**. a false belief or opinion **3**. *Psychiatry* a false, persistent belief not substantiated by objective evidence —**de·lu′sive** (-lōōs′iv), **de·lu′so·ry** (-lōō′sə rē) *adj.*

de·luxe (di luks′, -looks′) *adj.* [Fr., lit., of luxury] of extra fine quality; elegant —*adv.* in a deluxe manner

delve (delv) *vi.* **delved, delv′ing** [OE. *delfan*] **1**. [Archaic] to dig **2**. to investigate for information; search (*into* books, the past, etc.) —**delv′er** *n.*

Dem. 1. Democrat **2**. Democratic

de·mag·net·ize (dē mag′nə tīz′) *vt.* **-ized′, -iz′ing** to deprive of magnetic properties

dem·a·gogue, dem·a·gog (dem′ə gäg′, -gôg′) *n.* [< Gr. *dēmos,* the people + *agōgos,* leader] one who tries to stir up people's emotions in order to gain power —**dem′a·gog′ic** (-gäj′ik, -gäg′-, -gō′jik), *adj.* —**dem′a·gog′y** (-gō′jē, -gäg′ē), **dem′a·gogu′er·y** (-gäg′ər ē) *n.*

de·mand (di mand′) *vt.* [< L. *de-,* from + *mandare,* entrust] **1**. to ask for boldly or urgently **2**. to ask for as a right or with authority **3**. to require [the work *demands* great care] —*vi.* to make a demand —*n.* **1**. a demanding **2**. a thing demanded **3**. a strong request **4**. an urgent requirement **5**. *Econ.* the desire for a commodity together with ability to pay for it; also, the amount people are ready to buy at a certain price —**in demand** asked for —**on demand** when presented for payment

de·mand′ing *adj.* making difficult demands on one's patience, energy, etc. —**de·mand′ing·ly** *adv.*

de·mar·ca·tion, de·mar·ka·tion (dē′mär kā′shən) *n.* [< Sp. *de-,* from + *marcar,* to mark] **1**. the act of setting and marking boundaries **2**. a limit or boundary

de·mean′ (di mēn′) *vt.* [DE- + MEAN²] to degrade; lower [to *demean* oneself by lying]

de·mean² (di mēn′) *vt.* [see DEMEANOR] to behave or conduct (oneself)

de·mean·or (di mēn′ər) *n.* [< OFr. *demener,* to lead] outward behavior; conduct; deportment: Brit. sp. **de·mean′our**

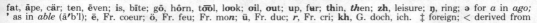

fat, āpe, cär; ten, ēven; is, bīte; gō, hôrn, tool, look; oil, out; up, fur; thin, then; zh, leisure; ŋ, ring; ə for *a* in *ago*; ' as in *able* (ā′b'l); ë, Fr. coeur; ö, Fr. feu; Fr. mon; ü, Fr. duc; r, Fr. cri; kh, G. doch, ich. ‡ foreign; < derived from

de·ment·ed (di ment′id) *adj.* [see DEMENTIA] mentally deranged; insane —**de·ment′ed·ly** *adv.*

de·men·tia (di men′shə) *n.* [< L. *de-*, out from + *mens,* the mind] loss or impairment of mental powers due to organic causes

de·mer·it (di mer′it) *n.* [< L. *de-,* intens. + *merere,* deserve, with *de-* taken as negative] **1.** a fault; defect **2.** a mark recorded against a student, etc. for poor conduct or work

de·mesne (di mān′, -mēn′) *n.* [see DOMAIN] **1.** *Law* possession (of real estate) in one's own right **2.** the land around a mansion **3.** a region or domain

De·me·ter (di mēt′ər) *Gr. Myth.* the goddess of agriculture: identified with the Roman goddess Ceres

demi- [< L. *dimidius,* half] *a prefix meaning:* **1.** half **2.** less than usual in size, power, etc. *[demigod]*

dem·i·god (dem′ē gäd′) *n.* **1.** a minor deity **2.** a godlike person

dem′i·john′ (-jän′) *n.* [Fr. *dame-jeanne*] a large bottle of glass or earthenware in a wicker casing

de·mil·i·ta·rize (dē mil′ə tə rīz′) *vt.* -rized′, -riz′ing to free from military control or from militarism —**de·mil′i·ta·ri·za′tion** *n.*

dem·i·monde (dem′ē mänd′) *n.* [Fr. < *demi-,* DEMI- + *monde,* world] the class of women who have lost social standing because of sexual promiscuity

de·mise (di mīz′) *n.* [< Fr. < L. *de-,* down + *mittere,* send] **1.** *Law* a transfer of an estate by lease **2.** death — *vt.* -mised′, -mis′ing to transfer (an estate) by lease

dem·i·tasse (dem′ē tas′, -täs′) *n.* [Fr. < *demi-,* DEMI- + *tasse,* cup] a small cup of or for after-dinner black coffee

de·mo·bi·lize (dē mō′bə līz′) *vt.* -lized′, -liz′ing **1.** to disband (troops) **2.** to discharge from the armed forces —**de·mo′bi·li·za′tion** *n.*

de·moc·ra·cy (di mäk′rə sē) *n., pl.* -cies [< Fr. < Gr. *dēmos,* the people + *kratein,* to rule] **1.** government by the people, either directly or through representatives **2.** a country, state, etc. with such government **3.** majority rule **4.** equality of rights, opportunity, and treatment

dem·o·crat (dem′ə krat′) *n.* **1.** one who supports or practices democracy **2.** [D-] a member of the Democratic Party

dem′o·crat′ic *adj.* **1.** of or upholding (a) democracy **2.** of or for all or most people **3.** treating people of all classes in the same way **4.** [D-] of or belonging to the Democratic Party —**dem′o·crat′i·cal·ly** *adv.*

Democratic Party one of the two major political parties in the U.S., since about 1830

de·moc·ra·tize (di mäk′rə tīz′) *vt., vi.* -tized′, -tiz′ing to make or become democratic

de·mod·u·la·tion (dē mäj′oo lā′shən) *n. Radio* the recovery, at the receiver, of a signal that has been modulated on a carrier wave

de·mog·ra·phy (di mäg′rə fē) *n.* [< Gr. *dēmos,* the people + -GRAPHY] the statistical study of populations —**de·mog′ra·pher** *n.* —**de·mo·graph·ic** (dē′mə graf′ik, dem′ə-) *adj.*

de·mol·ish (di mäl′ish) *vt.* [< Fr. < L. *de-,* down + *moliri,* to build] to tear down; destroy; ruin —**dem·o·li·tion** (dem′ə lish′ən, dē′mə-), **de·mol′ish·ment** *n.*

de·mon (dē′mən) *n.* [< L. *daemon*] **1.** *same as* DAEMON **2.** a devil; evil spirit **3.** a person or thing regarded as evil, cruel, etc. **4.** a person who has great energy —**de·mon·ic** (di män′ik) *adj.*

de·mon·e·tize (dē män′ə tīz′) *vt.* -tized′, -tiz′ing **1.** to deprive (currency) of its standard value **2.** to stop using as a monetary standard

de·mo·ni·ac (di mō′nē ak′) *adj.* of or like a demon; fiendish: also **de·mo·ni·a·cal** (dē′mə nī′ə k′l)

de·mon·ol·o·gy (dē′mə näl′ə jē) *n.* the study of demons or of beliefs about them

de·mon·stra·ble (di män′strə b′l) *adj.* that can be demonstrated, or proved —**de·mon′stra·bly** *adv.*

dem·on·strate (dem′ən strāt′) *vt.* -strat′ed, -strat′ing [< L. *de-,* from + *monstrare,* to show] **1.** to show by reasoning; prove **2.** to explain by using examples, experiments, etc. **3.** to show the working of **4.** to show (feelings) plainly —*vi.* to show feelings or views publicly by taking part in meetings, parades, etc. —**dem′on·stra′tor** *n.*

dem′on·stra′tion *n.* **1.** a proving **2.** an explanation by example, experiment, etc. **3.** a showing of how something works **4.** a display *[a demonstration of affection]* **5.** a public show of opinion, etc., as by a mass meeting

de·mon·stra·tive (di män′strə tiv) *adj.* **1.** showing clearly **2.** giving proof (*of*) **3.** showing feelings openly **4.** *Gram.* pointing out *["this" is a demonstrative pronoun]* — **de·mon′stra·tive·ly** *adv.* —**de·mon′stra·tive·ness** *n.*

de·mor·al·ize (di môr′ə līz′) *vt.* -ized′, -iz′ing **1.** to lower the morale of **2.** to throw into confusion —**de·mor′al·i·za′tion** *n.*

De·mos·the·nes (di mäs′thə nēz′) 384?-322 B.C.; Athenian orator & statesman

de·mote (di mōt′) *vt.* -mot′ed, -mot′ing [DE- + (PRO)MOTE] to reduce to a lower grade; lower in rank — **de·mo′tion** *n.*

de·mot·ic (di mät′ik) *adj.* [< Gr. *dēmos,* the people] of the people; popular

de·mul·cent (di mul′s′nt) *adj.* [< L. *de-,* down + *mulcere,* to stroke] soothing —*n.* a soothing ointment

de·mur (di mur′) *vi.* -murred′, -mur′ring [< L. *de-,* from + *mora,* a delay] to hesitate, as because of doubts; object —*n.* a demurring: also **de·mur′ral**

de·mure (di myoor′) *adj.* [< *de-* (prob. intens.) + OFr. *mëur,* mature] **1.** modest; reserved **2.** affectedly modest; coy —**de·mure′ly** *adv.* —**de·mure′ness** *n.*

de·mur·rage (di mur′ij) *n.* [see DEMUR] **1.** the delaying of a ship, freight car, etc., as by failure to load, unload, etc. within the time allowed **2.** the compensation paid for this

de·mur·rer (di mur′ər) *n.* [see DEMUR] **1.** a plea for the dismissal of a lawsuit on the grounds that the statements of the opposition, even if true, do not sustain the claim **2.** an objection

den (den) *n.* [OE. *denn*] **1.** the lair of a wild animal **2.** a haunt, as of thieves **3.** a small, cozy room where one can be alone to read, work, etc.

de·nar·i·us (di nar′ē əs) *n., pl.* -nar′i·i′ (-ī′) [< L. < *decem,* ten] an ancient Roman silver coin, the penny of the New Testament

de·na·ture (dē nā′chər) *vt.* -tured, -tur·ing **1.** to change the nature of **2.** to make (alcohol, etc.) unfit for human consumption without spoiling for other uses

den·drite (den′drīt) *n.* [< Gr. *dendron,* a tree] the branched part of a nerve cell that carries impulses toward the cell body

de·ni·al (di nī′əl) *n.* **1.** a denying; saying "no" (to a request, etc.) **2.** a statement in opposition to another **3.** a disowning; repudiation *[the denial of one's family]* **4.** a refusal to believe or accept (a doctrine, etc.) **5.** *same as* SELF-DENIAL

de·nier¹ (den′yər) *n.* [< L. *deni,* by tens] a unit of weight for measuring the fineness of threads of silk, nylon, etc.

de·ni·er² (di nī′ər) *n.* a person who denies

den·i·grate (den′ə grāt′) *vt.* -grat′ed, -grat′ing [< L. *de-,* intens. + *nigrare,* blacken] to disparage the character of; defame —**den′i·gra′tion** *n.* —**den′i·gra′tor** *n.*

den·im (den′əm) *n.* [< Fr. (*serge*) *de Nîmes,* (serge) of Nîmes, Fr. town] a coarse, twilled cotton cloth used for overalls, uniforms, etc.

den·i·zen (den′i zən) *n.* [< L. *de intus,* from within] an inhabitant or frequenter of a particular place

Den·mark (den′märk) country in Europe, on a peninsula & several islands in the North & Baltic seas: 16,615 sq. mi.; pop. 4,870,000; cap. Copenhagen: abbrev. **Den.**

de·nom·i·nate (di näm′ə nāt′) *vt.* -nat′ed, -nat′ing [< L. *de-,* intens. + *nominare,* to name] to name; call

de·nom′i·na′tion (-nā′shən) *n.* **1.** the act of denominating **2.** a name **3.** a class or kind having a specific name or value *[coins of different denominations]* **4.** a religious sect

de·nom′i·na′tion·al *adj.* of, or under the control of, a religious sect

de·nom′i·na′tor (-nāt′ər) *n.* **1.** a shared characteristic **2.** *Math.* the term below the line in a fraction, indicating the number of equal parts into which the whole is divided

de·note (di nōt′) *vt.* -not′ed, -not′ing [< L. *de-,* down + *notare,* to mark] **1.** to be a sign of; indicate **2.** to signify explicitly; mean: cf. CONNOTE —**de·no·ta·tion** (dē′nō tā′shən) *n.* —**de·no·ta·tive** *adj.*

de·noue·ment, dé·noue·ment (dā noo′män) *n.* [Fr.] **1.** the outcome or unraveling of a plot in a drama, story, etc. **2.** any final outcome

de·nounce (di nouns′) *vt.* -nounced′, -nounc′ing [see DENUNCIATION] **1.** to accuse publicly; inform against **2.** to condemn strongly **3.** to give formal notice of the ending of (a treaty, etc.) —**de·nounce′ment** *n.* —**de·nounc′er** *n.*

dense (dens) *adj.* **dens′er, dens′est** [L. *densus,* compact] **1.** packed tightly together **2.** difficult to get through **3.** stupid —**dense′ly** *adv.* —**dense′ness** *n.*

den·si·ty (den′sə tē) *n., pl.* -ties **1.** the condition of being dense **2.** number per unit, as of area **3.** the ratio of the mass of an object to its volume

dent (dent) *n.* [ME., var. of DINT] **1.** a slight hollow made in a surface by a blow **2.** a slight impression —*vt.* to make a dent in —*vi.* to become dented

den·tal (den′t'l) *adj.* [< L. *dens*, tooth] **1.** of or for the teeth or dentistry **2.** *Phonet.* formed by placing the tip of the tongue against or near the upper front teeth —*n. Phonet.* a dental consonant

dental floss thin, strong thread for removing food particles from between the teeth

dental hygienist a dentist's assistant, who cleans teeth, takes dental X-rays, etc.

den·tate (den′tāt) *adj.* [see DENTAL] having teeth or toothlike projections; toothed or notched

den·ti·frice (den′tə fris) *n.* [< L. *dens*, tooth + *fricare*, to rub] any preparation for cleaning teeth

den·tin (den′tin) *n.* [see DENTAL] the hard, calcareous tissue under the enamel of a tooth: also **den′tine** (-tēn, -tin)

den·tist (den′tist) *n.* [< Fr. < L. *dens*, tooth] one whose profession is the care of teeth, the replacement of missing teeth with artificial ones, etc.

den′tist·ry *n.* the profession or work of a dentist

den·ti·tion (den tish′ən) *n.* [see DENTAL] the number, kind, and arrangement of teeth

den·ture (den′chər) *n.* [Fr. < L. *dens*, tooth] a set of artificial teeth

de·nude (di nōōd′, -nyōōd′) *vt.* -nud′ed, -nud′ing [< L. *de-*, off + *nudare*, to strip] to make bare or naked; strip

de·nun·ci·a·tion (di nun′sē ā′shən) *n.* [< L. *de-*, intens. + *nuntiare*, announce] the act of denouncing

Den·ver (den′vər) capital of Colo.: pop. 515,000 (met. area 1,228,000)

de·ny (di nī′) *vt.* -nied′, -ny′ing [< L. *de-*, intens. + *negare*, deny] **1.** to declare (a statement) untrue **2.** to refuse to accept as true or right **3.** to refuse to acknowledge as one's own **4.** to refuse to give **5.** to refuse the request of —**deny oneself** to do without desired things

de·o·dor·ant (dē ō′dər ənt) *adj.* that can counteract undesired odors —*n.* any deodorant preparation, esp. one used on the body

de·o′dor·ize′ (-də rīz′) *vt.* -ized′, -iz′ing to counteract the odor of or in —**de·o′dor·iz′er** *n.*

dep. 1. department **2.** deposit **3.** deputy

de·part (di pärt′) *vi.* [< L. *dis-*, apart + *partire*, divide] **1.** to go away (*from*); leave **2.** to set out; start **3.** to die **4.** to deviate (*from* something)

de·part′ed *adj.* **1.** gone away **2.** dead —**the departed** the dead person or persons

de·part·ment (di pärt′mənt) *n.* **1.** a separate part or division, as of a government or business **2.** a field of knowledge or activity —**de·part′men′tal** (-men′t'l) *adj.* —**de·part′men′tal·ly** *adv.*

de·part′men′tal·ize′ (-men′tə līz′) *vt.* -ized′, -iz′ing to organize into departments —**de·part′men′tal·i·za′tion** *n.*

department store a retail store for the sale of many kinds of goods arranged in departments

de·par·ture (di pär′chər) *n.* **1.** a departing **2.** a starting out, as on a trip **3.** a deviation (*from* something)

de·pend (di pend′) *vi.* [< L. *de-*, down + *pendere*, hang] **1.** to be determined by something else; be contingent (*on*) **2.** to be sure; rely (*on*) **3.** to rely (*on*) for support or aid

de·pend′a·ble *adj.* trustworthy; reliable —**de·pend′a·bil′-i·ty** *n.* —**de·pend′a·bly** *adv.*

de·pend′ence *n.* **1.** a being dependent **2.** reliance (*on* another) for support or aid **3.** reliance; trust

de·pend′en·cy *n., pl.* -cies **1.** *same as* DEPENDENCE **2.** something dependent **3.** a territory geographically distinct from the country governing it

de·pend′ent *adj.* **1.** hanging down **2.** influenced or determined by something else **3.** relying (*on* another) for support or aid **4.** subordinate —*n.* one who depends on another for support, etc. Also sp., esp. for *n.,* **de·pend′ant**

de·per·son·al·ize (dē pur′s'n ə līz′) *vt.* -ized′, -iz′ing **1.** to treat impersonally **2.** to cause to lose one's sense of personal identity —**de·per′son·al·i·za′tion** *n.*

de·pict (di pikt′) *vt.* [< L. *de-*, intens. + *pingere*, to paint] **1.** to represent in a drawing, painting, etc. **2.** to picture in words; describe —**de·pic′tion** *n.* —**de·pic′tor** *n.*

de·pil·a·to·ry (di pil′ə tôr′ē) *adj.* [< L. *de-*, from + *pilus*, hair] serving to remove unwanted hair —*n., pl.* -ries a depilatory substance or device

de·plane (dē plān′) *vi.* -planed′, -plan′ing to get out of an airplane after it lands

de·plete (di plēt′) *vt.* -plet′ed, -plet′ing [< L. *de-*, from + *plere*, fill] **1.** to use up (resources, funds, etc.) **2.** to empty wholly or partly —**de·ple′tion** *n.*

de·plor·a·ble (di plôr′ə b'l) *adj.* to be deplored; regrettable or wretched —**de·plor′a·bly** *adv.*

de·plore (di plôr′) *vt.* -plored′, -plor′ing [< Fr. < L. *de-*, intens. + *plorare*, weep] **1.** to regret deeply; lament **2.** to regard as unfortunate or wretched

de·ploy (dē ploi′) *vt., vi.* [< L. *dis-*, apart + *plicare*, to fold] *Mil.* **1.** to spread out so as to form a wider front **2.** to station or move in accordance with a plan —**de·ploy′-ment** *n.*

de·po·lar·ize (dē pō′lə rīz′) *vt.* -ized′, -iz′ing to destroy or counteract the polarization of

de·pon·ent (di pō′nənt) *n.* [< L. *de-*, down + *ponere*, put] *Law* one who gives written testimony under oath

de·pop·u·late (dē päp′yə lāt′) *vt.* -lat′ed, -lat′ing to reduce the population of, esp. by violence, pestilence, etc. —**de·pop′u·la′tion** *n.*

de·port (di pôrt′) *vt.* [< L. *de-*, from + *portare*, carry] **1.** to behave (oneself) in a specified way **2.** to expel (an alien) from a country

de·por·ta·tion (dē′pôr tā′shən) *n.* expulsion, as of an undesirable alien, from a country

de·port·ment (di pôrt′mənt) *n.* conduct; behavior

de·pose (di pōz′) *vt.* -posed′, -pos′ing [< OFr. *de-*, from + *poser*, cease] **1.** to remove from office or a position of power; oust **2.** *Law* to state under oath but out of court

de·pos·it (di päz′it) *vt.* [< L. *de-*, down + *ponere*, put] **1.** to place (money, etc.) for safekeeping, as in a bank **2.** to give as a pledge or partial payment **3.** to set down **4.** to leave (sediment, etc.) lying —*n.* **1.** something placed for safekeeping, as money in a bank **2.** a pledge or part payment **3.** something left lying

de·pos·i·tar·y (di päz′ə ter′ē) *n., pl.* -ies **1.** a person, firm, etc. entrusted with something for safekeeping; trustee **2.** a storehouse; depository

dep·o·si·tion (dep′ə zish′ən) *n.* **1.** a deposing or being deposed **2.** a testifying **3.** testimony, esp. sworn written testimony **4.** something deposited

de·pos·i·tor (di päz′ə tər) *n.* one who deposits something, esp. money in a bank

de·pos·i·to·ry (di päz′ə tôr′ē) *n., pl.* -ries **1.** a place where things are put for safekeeping; storehouse **2.** a trustee; depositary

de·pot (dē′pō; *military & Brit.* dep′ō) *n.* [< Fr.: see DEPOSIT] **1.** a warehouse **2.** a railroad or bus station **3.** a storage place for military supplies

de·prave (di prāv′) *vt.* -praved′, -prav′ing [< L. *de-*, intens. + *pravus*, crooked] to make morally bad; corrupt —**de·praved′** *adj.*

de·prav·i·ty (di prav′ə tē) *n.* **1.** a depraved condition; wickedness **2.** *pl.* -ties a depraved act

dep·re·cate (dep′rə kāt′) *vt.* -cat′ed, -cat′ing [< L. *de-*, off + *precari*, pray] **1.** to express disapproval of **2.** to belittle —**dep′re·cat′ing·ly** *adv.* —**dep′re·ca′tion** *n.*

dep′re·ca·to·ry (-kə tôr′ē) *adj.* **1.** deprecating **2.** apologetic Also **dep′re·ca′tive**

de·pre·ci·ate (di prē′shē āt′) *vt., vi.* -at′ed, -at′ing [< L. *de-*, from < *pretiare*, to value] **1.** to lessen in value **2.** to belittle

de·pre′ci·a′tion *n.* **1.** a decrease in value of property through wear, etc. **2.** a decrease in the purchasing power of money **3.** a belittling

dep·re·da·tion (dep′rə dā′shən) *n.* [< L. *de-*, intens. + *praedari*, to plunder] a plundering or laying waste

de·press (di pres′) *vt.* [< L. *de-*, down + *premere*, to press] **1.** to press down **2.** to make gloomy; sadden **3.** to make less active **4.** to lower in value, price, etc. —**de·press′ing** *adj.* —**de·press′ing·ly** *adv.* —**de·pres′sor** (-ər) *n.*

de·pres′sant (-ənt) *adj.* lowering the rate of muscular or nervous activity —*n.* a depressant drug, etc.

de·pressed′ *adj.* **1.** pressed down **2.** lowered in intensity, amount, etc. **3.** flattened or hollowed, as if pressed down **4.** gloomy; sad **5.** characterized by widespread unemployment, poverty, etc.

de·pres·sion (di presh′ən) *n.* **1.** a depressing or being depressed **2.** a hollow or low place **3.** low spirits; dejection **4.** a decrease in force, activity, etc. **5.** a period of reduced business activity, much unemployment, etc. —**de·pres′-sive** (-pres′iv) *adj.*

de·prive (di prīv′) *vt.* -prived′, -priv′ing [< L. *de-*, intens. + *privare*, to separate] **1.** to take away from forcibly **2.** to keep from having, using, etc. —**dep·ri·va·tion** (dep′rə vā′shən) *n.*

dept. 1. department **2.** deputy

depth (depth) *n.* [< ME. *dep*, deep + -TH[1]] **1.** the distance from the top downward, or from front to back **2.** deepness **3.** intensity **4.** profundity **5.** lowness of pitch **6.**

[*usually pl.*] the deepest or inmost part —**in depth** comprehensively

depth charge an explosive charge that explodes under water: used esp. against submarines

dep·u·ta·tion (dep'yoo tā'shən) *n.* **1.** a deputing or being deputed **2.** a delegation

de·pute (di pyōōt') *vt.* -put'ed, -put'ing [< L. *de-*, + *putare*, cleanse] **1.** to give (authority, etc.) to a deputy **2.** to appoint as one's substitute

dep·u·tize (dep'yə tīz') *vt.* -tized', -tiz'ing to appoint as deputy —*vi.* to act as deputy

dep·u·ty (dep'yə tē) *n., pl.* -ties [see DEPUTE] **1.** a person appointed to act for another **2.** a member of a legislature called a Chamber of Deputies —*adj.* acting as deputy

de·rail (di rāl') *vi., vt.* to go or cause to go off the rails: said of a train, etc. —**de·rail'ment** *n.*

de·rail·leur (di rā'lər) *n.* [Fr. *dérailleur*, derailer] a gearshifting device on a bicycle: it shifts the sprocket chain from one to another of a set of different-sized sprocket wheels

de·range (di rānj') *vt.* -ranged', -rang'ing [< Fr. < OFr. *des-*, apart + *rengier*, to range] **1.** to upset the order or working of **2.** to make insane —**de·range'ment** *n.*

Der·by (dur'bē; *Brit.* där'-) *n., pl.* -bies **1.** any of certain famous horse races, as the one founded by an Earl of Derby and held annually in Epsom, England, or the one (**Kentucky Derby**) held annually in Louisville, Kentucky **2.** [d-] a stiff felt hat with a round crown

de·reg·u·late (dē reg'yə lāt') *vt.* -lat'ed, -lat'ing to remove regulations governing —**de·reg'u·la'tion** *n.*

der·e·lict (der'ə likt') *adj.* [< L. *de-*, intens. + *relinquere*: see RELINQUISH] **1.** deserted by the owner; abandoned **2.** negligent —*n.* **1.** a ship deserted at sea **2.** a destitute and rejected person

DERBY

der·e·lic'tion (-lik'shən) *n.* **1.** an abandoning or being abandoned **2.** a neglect of, or failure in, duty

de·ride (di rīd') *vt.* -rid'ed, -rid'ing [< L. *de-*, down + *ridere*, to laugh] to laugh at in contempt or scorn; ridicule —**de·ri'sion** (-rizh'ən) *n.*

de·ri·sive (-rī'siv) *adj.* showing derision; ridiculing: also **de·ri'so·ry** (-sə rē) —**de·ri'sive·ly** *adv.*

der·i·va·tion (der'ə vā'shən) *n.* **1.** a deriving or being derived **2.** the source or origin of something **3.** the origin and development of a word

de·riv·a·tive (də riv'ə tiv) *adj.* **1.** derived **2.** not original —*n.* **1.** something derived **2.** a word derived from another **3.** a substance derived from another by chemical change

de·rive (di rīv') *vt.* -rived', -riv'ing [< L. *de-*, from + *rivus*, a stream] **1.** to get or receive (*from* a source) **2.** to deduce or infer **3.** to trace from or to a source **4.** *Chem.* to obtain (a compound) from another compound by replacing one element with another —*vi.* to come (*from* a source)

der·ma (dur'mə) *n.* [< Gr. *derma*, the skin] *same as* DERMIS —**der'mal, der'mic** *adj.*

der·ma·ti·tis (-tīt'is) *n.* [< Gr. *derma*, the skin + -ITIS] inflammation of the skin

der·ma·tol·o·gy (-täl'ə jē) *n.* [< Gr. *derma*, the skin + -LOGY] the branch of medicine dealing with the skin and its diseases —**der'ma·tol'o·gist** *n.*

der·mis (dur'mis) *n.* [< LL. *epidermis*, EPIDERMIS] the layer of skin just below the epidermis

der·o·gate (der'ə gāt') *vi., vt.* -gat'ed, -gat'ing [< L. *de-*, from + *rogare*, ask] to detract or disparage —**der'o·ga'tion** *n.*

de·rog·a·to·ry (di räg'ə tôr'ē) *adj.* [see prec.] **1.** detracting **2.** disparaging; belittling Also **de·rog'a·tive**

der·rick (der'ik) *n.* [orig., a gallows, after T. *Derrick*, 17th-c. London hangman] **1.** a large apparatus for lifting and moving heavy objects **2.** a tall framework, as over an oil well, to support drilling machinery, etc.

der·ri·ère (der'ē er') *n.* [Fr., back part < L. *de-*, from + *retro*, back] the buttocks

der·ring-do (der'iŋ dōō') *n.* [ME. *derrynge do*, daring to do] daring action; reckless courage

der·rin·ger (der'in jər) *n.* [< Henry *Deringer*, 19th-c. U.S. gunsmith] a small, short-barreled pistol of large caliber

DERRICK (sense 2)

der·vish (dur'vish) *n.* [< Per. *darvēsh*, a beggar] a member of any of various Muslim ascetic orders: some whirl, howl, etc. for religious reasons

de·sal·i·na·tion (dē sal'ə nā'shən) *n.* [DE- + SALIN(E) + -ATION] the removal of salt, esp. from sea water to make it drinkable: also **de·sal'i·ni·za'tion** —**de·sal'i·nate'** *vt.* -nat'ed, -nat'ing

des·cant (des'kant) *n.* [< L. *dis-*, apart + *cantus*, song] *Medieval Music* **1.** singing in which there is a fixed melody and a subordinate melody added above **2.** this added melody —*vi.* (*also* des kant') **1.** to discourse (*on* or *upon*) **2.** to sing

Des·cartes (dā kärt'), **Re·né** (rə nā') 1596-1650; Fr. philosopher & mathematician

de·scend (di send') *vi.* [< L. *de-*, down + *scandere*, to climb] **1.** to move down to a lower place **2.** to pass from an earlier to a later time, from greater to less, etc. **3.** to slope downward **4.** to come down (*from* a source) **5.** to pass by inheritance or heredity **6.** to stoop (*to* some act) **7.** to make a sudden visit or attack (*on* or *upon*) —*vt.* to move down, down along, or through

de·scend'ant *adj.* descending: also **de·scend'ent** —*n.* an offspring of a certain ancestor, family, group, etc.

de·scent (di sent') *n.* **1.** a descending, or coming or going down **2.** ancestry **3.** a downward slope **4.** a way down **5.** a sudden attack **6.** a decline

de·scribe (di skrīb') *vt.* -scribed', -scrib'ing [< L. *de-*, from + *scribere*, write] **1.** to tell or write about **2.** to picture in words **3.** to trace the outline of —**de·scrib'er** *n.*

de·scrip·tion (di skrip'shən) *n.* **1.** the act or technique of describing **2.** a statement or passage that describes **3.** sort or variety

de·scrip·tive (-tiv) *adj.* of or characterized by description —**de·scrip'tive·ly** *adv.* —**de·scrip'tive·ness** *n.*

de·scry (di skrī') *vt.* -scried', -scry'ing [< OFr. *descrier*, proclaim] **1.** to catch sight of (distant or obscure objects); discern **2.** to detect

des·e·crate (des'ə krāt') *vt.* -crat'ed, -crat'ing [DE- + (CON)SECRATE] to violate the sacredness of; profane —**des'e·crat'er, des'e·cra'tor** *n.* —**des'e·cra'tion** *n.*

de·seg·re·gate (dē seg'rə gāt') *vt., vi.* -gat'ed, -gat'ing to abolish racial segregation in (public schools, etc.) —**de·seg're·ga'tion** *n.*

de·sen·si·tize (dē sen'sə tīz') *vt.* -tized', -tiz'ing to make insensitive or less sensitive

de·sert' (di zurt') *vt., vi.* [Fr. < L. *de-*, from + *serere*, join] **1.** to forsake (someone or something that one ought not to leave) **2.** to leave (one's military post, etc.) without permission and with no intent to return —**de·sert'er** *n.* —**de·ser'tion** (-zur'shən) *n.*

des·ert² (dez'ərt) *n.* [see prec.] **1.** an uncultivated, uninhabited region; wilderness **2.** a dry, barren, sandy region —*adj.* **1.** of a desert **2.** wild and uninhabited

de·sert³ (di zurt') *n.* [see DESERVE] **1.** the fact of deserving reward or punishment **2.** [*often pl.*] deserved reward or punishment

de·serve (di zurv') *vt., vi.* -served', -serv'ing [< L. *de-*, intens. + *servire*, serve] to be worthy (of); merit (reward, punishment, etc.)

de·serv'ed·ly *adv.* rightfully; justly

de·serv'ing *adj.* worthy (*of* help, reward, etc.) —**de·serv'ing·ly** *adv.*

des·ha·bille (dez'ə bēl', des'-) *n. same as* DISHABILLE

des·ic·cate (des'i kāt') *vt., vi.* -cat'ed, -cat'ing [< L. *de-*, intens. + *siccus*, dry] to dry up completely —**des'ic·ca'tion** *n.*

de·sid·er·a·tum (di sid'ə rāt'əm, -zid'-) *n., pl.* -ta (-ə) [see DESIRE] something needed and wanted

de·sign (di zīn') *vt.* [< L. *de-*, out + *signum*, a mark] **1.** to make preliminary sketches of or a pattern for **2.** to form (plans, etc.) in the mind; contrive **3.** to plan and work out (something) creatively; devise **4.** to have as, or intend for, a specific purpose —*vi.* to make original plans, patterns, etc. —*n.* **1.** a plan; scheme **2.** purpose; intention **3.** [*pl.*] a secret, underhanded scheme (often with *on*) **4.** a plan or sketch to work from; pattern **5.** arrangement of form, parts, color, etc.; artistic invention —**by design** purposely

des·ig·nate (dez'ig nāt') *vt.* -nat'ed, -nat'ing [see prec.] **1.** to point out; specify **2.** to name **3.** to appoint —*adj.* (*also* -nit) appointed but not yet in office

des'ig·na'tion *n.* **1.** a pointing out or marking out **2.** appointment to an office, etc. **3.** a distinguishing name, title, etc.

de·sign·ed·ly (di zī'nid lē) *adv.* purposely

de·sign·er (di zī'nər) *n.* one who designs, or makes original plans, patterns, etc. [a dress *designer*]

de·sign'ing (-niŋ) *adj.* scheming; artful —*n.* the art of creating designs, patterns, etc.

de·sir·a·ble (di zir'ə b'l) *adj.* worth having; pleasing —**de·sir'a·bil'i·ty** *n.* —**de·sir'a·bly** *adv.*

de·sire (di zīr') *vt.* -**sired'**, -**sir'ing** [< L. *desiderare*] 1. to wish or long for; crave 2. to ask for; request 3. to want sexually —*n.* 1. a strong wish or craving 2. sexual appetite 3. a request 4. a thing desired

de·sir'ous (-əs) *adj.* desiring; wanting

de·sist (di zist') *vi.* [< L. *de-*, from + *stare*, to stand] to cease; stop (often with *from*)

desk (desk) *n.* [< ML. *desca*, a table] 1. a kind of table with drawers and a flat top for writing, etc. 2. the place in a hotel where guests register

Des Moines (də moin') capital of Iowa, in the C part: pop. 201,000

des·o·late (des'ə lit) *adj.* [< L. *de-*, intens. + *solus*, alone] 1. lonely; solitary 2. uninhabited; deserted 3. laid waste 4. forlorn; wretched —*vt.* (-lāt') -**lat'ed**, -**lat'ing** 1. to rid of inhabitants 2. to lay waste 3. to forsake 4. to make forlorn

des'o·la'tion (-lā'shən) *n.* 1. a making desolate 2. a desolate condition or place 3. misery 4. loneliness

De So·to (di sōt'ō), **Her·nan·do** (hər nan'dō) 1500?-42; Sp. explorer in America: also **de Soto**

de·spair (di sper') *vi.* [< L. *de-*, without + *sperare*, to hope] to lose or give up hope —*n.* 1. loss of hope 2. a person or thing causing despair —**de·spair'ing** *adj.* —**de·spair'ing·ly** *adv.*

des·patch (di spach') *vt., n. same as* DISPATCH

des·per·a·do (des'pə rä'dō, -rä'-) *n., pl.* -**does**, -**dos** [OSp. < L.: see DESPAIR] a dangerous, reckless criminal; bold outlaw

des·per·ate (des'pər it) *adj.* 1. rash or violent because of despair 2. having a very great need 3. very serious 4. drastic —**des'per·ate·ly** *adv.*

des·per·a·tion (des'pə rā'shən) *n.* 1. a being desperate 2. recklessness resulting from despair

des·pi·ca·ble (des'pik ə b'l, di spik'-) *adj.* deserving to be despised; contemptible —**des'pi·ca·bly** *adv.*

de·spise (di spīz') *vt.* -**spised'**, -**spis'ing** [< L. *de-*, down + *specere*, look at] to regard with scorn or great dislike

de·spite (di spīt') *n.* [see prec.] 1. malice; spite 2. [Ar-chaic] contempt —*prep.* in spite of; notwithstanding —**in despite of** in spite of

de·spoil (di spoil') *vt.* [< L. *de-*, intens. + *spoliare*, to strip] to rob; plunder —**de·spoil'er** *n.* —**de·spoil'ment, de·spo'li·a'tion** (-pō'lē ā'shən) *n.*

de·spond (di spänd') *vi.* [< L. *de-*, from + *spondere*, to promise] to lose courage or hope —*n.* despondency: now chiefly in **slough of despond**

de·spond'en·cy *n.* loss of courage or hope; dejection: also **de·spond'ence** —**de·spond'ent** *adj.*

des·pot (des'pət) *n.* [< Gr. *despotēs*, a master] 1. an absolute ruler 2. anyone in charge who acts like a tyrant —**des'pot·ism** *n.*

des·pot·ic (de spät'ik) *adj.* of or like a despot; autocratic; tyrannical —**des·pot'i·cal·ly** *adv.*

des·sert (di zurt') *n.* [< OFr. *desservir*, to clear the table < L.] a course, as of pudding, pie, cake, or fruit, served at the end of a meal

de·sta·bi·lize (dē stā'bə līz') *vt.* -**lized'**, -**liz'ing** to upset the stability of; unbalance

des·ti·na·tion (des'tə nā'shən) *n.* 1. the end for which something or someone is destined 2. the place to which a person or thing is going

des·tine (des'tin) *vt.* -**tined**, -**tin·ing** [< L. *de-*, intens. + *stare*, to stand] 1. to predetermine, as by fate 2. to set apart for a particular purpose; intend —**destined for** 1. bound for 2. intended for

des·tin·y (des'tə nē) *n., pl.* -**ies** [see prec.] 1. the seemingly inevitable succession of events or the power supposed to determine this 2. (one's) fate

des·ti·tute (des'tə tōōt', -tyōōt') *adj.* [< L. *de-*, down + *statuere*, to set] 1. lacking (with *of*) 2. living in complete poverty —**des'ti·tu'tion** *n.*

de·stroy (di stroi') *vt.* [< L. *de-*, down + *struere*, build] 1. to tear down; demolish 2. to spoil completely; ruin 3. to put an end to 4. to kill

de·stroy'er *n.* 1. one that destroys 2. a small, fast warship

de·struct (di strukt', dē'strukt') *n.* a deliberate destruction, as of a launched, malfunctioning missile —*vt., vi.* to destroy or be destroyed automatically

de·struct·i·ble (di struk'tə b'l) *adj.* that can be destroyed —**de·struct'i·bil'i·ty** *n.*

de·struc·tion (di struk'shən) *n.* 1. a destroying or being destroyed 2. a cause or means of destroying

de·struc'tive *adj.* 1. destroying or tending to destroy 2. not helpful; negative [*destructive* criticism] —**de·struc'-tive·ly** *adv.* —**de·struc'tive·ness** *n.*

destructive distillation decomposition of coal, wood, etc. by heat in the absence of air, and the recovery of the volatile products

des·ue·tude (des'wi tōōd', -tyōōd') *n.* [< L. *de-*, from + *suescere*, to be accustomed] disuse

des·ul·to·ry (des''l tôr'ē) *adj.* [< L. *de-*, from + *salire*, to leap] 1. passing from one thing to another in an aimless way 2. random —**des'ul·to'ri·ly** *adv.* —**des'ul·to'ri·ness** *n.*

de·tach (di tach') *vt.* [< Fr.: see DE- & ATTACH] 1. to unfasten and remove; disconnect; disengage 2. to send (some soldiers, etc.) on a special mission —**de·tach'a·ble** *adj.*

de·tached' *adj.* 1. not connected; separate 2. aloof; disinterested; impartial

de·tach'ment *n.* 1. a detaching; separation 2. a unit of troops, etc. sent on special service 3. the state of being detached or aloof

de·tail (di tāl', dē'tāl) *n.* [< Fr. < *dé-*, from + *tailler*, to cut] 1. a dealing with things item by item 2. a minute account 3. a small part; item or particular 4. *a)* one or more soldiers, etc. on special duty *b)* the duty —*vt.* 1. to tell, item by item 2. to assign to special duty —**de·tailed'** *adj.*

de·tain (di tān') *vt.* [< L. *de-*, off + *tenere*, hold] 1. to keep in custody; confine 2. to keep from going on; hold back —**de·tain'er** *n.* —**de·tain'ment** *n.*

de·tect (di tekt') *vt.* [< L. *de-*, from + *tegere*, to cover] to discover (something hidden or not easily noticed) —**de·tect'a·ble, de·tect'i·ble** *adj.*

de·tec'tion *n.* 1. a finding out or being found out 2. *same as* DEMODULATION —**de·tec'tor** *n.*

de·tec'tive *n.* a person, usually on a police force, whose work is investigating crimes, getting needed evidence, etc. —*adj.* of detectives and their work

dé·tente, de·tente (dā tänt') *n.* [Fr.] a lessening of tension or hostility, esp. between nations

de·ten·tion (di ten'shən) *n.* a detaining or being detained; forced delay or confinement

detention home a place where juvenile offenders are held in custody

de·ter (di tur') *vt.* -**terred'**, -**ter'ring** [< L. *de-*, from + *terrere*, frighten] to keep or discourage (a person) from some action through fear, doubt, etc.

de·ter·gent (di tur'jənt) *adj.* [< L. *de-*, off + *tergere*, wipe] cleansing —*n.* a soaplike cleansing substance not made from fats and lye

de·te·ri·o·rate (di tir'ē ə rāt') *vt., vi.* -**rat'ed**, -**rat'ing** [< L. *deterior*, worse] to make or become worse —**de·te'ri·o·ra'tion** *n.*

de·ter·mi·nant (di tur'mi nənt) *adj.* determining —*n.* a thing or factor that determines Also **de·ter'mi·na'tive** (-mə nā'tiv, -nə tiv)

de·ter·mi·nate (-nit) *adj.* clearly determined; fixed; settled

de·ter·mi·na·tion (di tur'mə nā'shən) *n.* 1. a determining or being determined 2. a firm intention 3. firmness of purpose

de·ter·mine (di tur'mən) *vt.* -**mined**, -**min·ing** [< L. *de-*, from + *terminus*, a limit] 1. to set limits to; define 2. to settle conclusively 3. to decide or decide upon 4. to establish the nature, kind, or quality of [genes *determine* heredity] 5. to find out exactly —*vi.* to decide; resolve —**de·ter'mi·na·ble** *adj.* —**de·ter'min·er** *n.*

de·ter'mined (-mənd) *adj.* 1. having one's mind set; resolved 2. firm and unwavering

de·ter'min·ism (-mə niz'm) *n.* the doctrine that everything, esp. one's choice of action, is determined by a sequence of causes independent of one's will —**de·ter'min·ist** *n., adj.*

de·ter·rent (di tur'ənt) *adj.* deterring —*n.* a thing that deters —**de·ter'rence** *n.*

de·test (di test') *vt.* [< L. *detestari*, to curse by the gods] to dislike intensely; hate —**de·test'a·ble** *adj.* —**de·test'a·bly** *adv.*

de·tes·ta·tion (dē'tes tā'shən) *n.* 1. intense dislike; hatred 2. something detested

de·throne (dē thrōn′) *vt.* -throned′, -thron′ing to remove from a throne; depose

det·o·nate (det′'n āt′) *vi.*, *vt.* -nat′ed, -nat′ing [< L. *de-*, intens. + *tonare*, to thunder] to explode violently —**det′o·na′tion** *n.*

det′o·na′tor (-āt′ər) *n.* a fuse, percussion cap, etc. for setting off explosives

de·tour (dē′toor, di toor′) *n.* [< Fr. < *détourner*, to turn aside: see DE- & TURN] 1. a roundabout way 2. a route used when the regular route is closed to traffic —*vi.*, *vt.* to go or route on a detour

de·tract (di trakt′) *vt.* [< L. *de-*, from + *trahere*, to draw] to take away —*vi.* to take something desirable away (*from*) —**de·trac′tion** *n.* —**de·trac′tor** *n.*

det·ri·ment (det′rə mənt) *n.* [< L. *de-*, off + *terere*, to rub] 1. damage; injury; harm 2. anything that causes this —**det′ri·men′tal** *adj.*

de·tri·tus (di trīt′əs) *n.* [L., a rubbing away: see prec.] rock fragments, etc. produced by disintegration or erosion; debris —**de·tri′tal** (-′l) *adj.*

De·troit (di troit′) city & port in SE Mich.: pop. 1,511,000 (met. area 4,200,000)

deuce (dōōs, dyōōs) *n.* [L. *duo*, two] 1. a playing card or side of a die with two spots 2. *Tennis* a tie score after which one side must score twice in a row to win 3. the devil: used as a mild oath or in exclamations of annoyance, surprise, etc.

deu·ced (dōō′sid, dyōō′-; dōōst) *adj.* devilish; extreme —*adv.* extremely; very: also **deu′ced·ly**

deu·te·ri·um (dōō tir′ē əm, dyōō-) *n.* [< Gr. *deuteros*, second] a heavy isotope of hydrogen, having an atomic weight of 2.0141: symbol, D

Deu·ter·on·o·my (dōōt′ər än′ə mē, dyōōt′-) [< Gr. *deuteros*, second + *nomos*, law] the fifth book of the Pentateuch in the Bible

deut·sche mark (doi′chə märk′) *pl.* mark′, Eng. marks′ the monetary unit of West Germany

de·val·ue (dē val′yōō) *vt.* -ued, -u·ing 1. to lessen the value of 2. to lower the exchange value of (a currency) in relation to other currencies Also **de·val′u·ate′** (-yōō wāt′) -at′ed, -at′ing —**de·val′u·a′tion** *n.*

dev·as·tate (dev′ə stāt′) *vt.* -tat′ed, -tat′ing [< L. *de-*, intens. + *vastare*, to make empty] 1. to lay waste; ravage; destroy 2. to overwhelm —**dev′as·tat′ing·ly** *adv.* —**dev′as·ta′tion** *n.*

de·vel·op (di vel′əp) *vt.* [< Fr. < *dé-*, apart + OFr. *voloper*, to wrap] 1. to make fuller, larger, better, stronger, etc. 2. to bring into being and work out gradually; evolve 3. to come to have 4. to make (housing, highways, etc.) more extensive 5. *Photog.* to put (an exposed film, etc.) in chemical solutions so as to make the picture visible —*vi.* 1. to come into being or activity 2. to become fuller, larger, etc.; grow or evolve 3. to become known — **de·vel′op·a·ble** *adj.*

de·vel·op·er (-ər) *n.* a person or thing that develops; esp., *Photog.* a chemical used to develop film, etc.

de·vel·op·ment (-mənt) *n.* 1. a developing or being developed 2. a stage in growth, advancement, etc. 3. an event or happening 4. a thing that is developed, as a tract of land with newly built homes, etc. —**de·vel′op·men′tal** (-men′t′l) *adj.*

de·vi·ant (dē′vē ənt) *adj.* deviating, esp. from what is considered normal —*n.* a person whose behavior is deviant —**de′vi·ance, de′vi·an·cy** *n.*

de·vi·ate (dē′vē āt′) *vi.*, *vt.* -at′ed, -at′ing [< L. *de-*, from + *via*, road] to turn aside (*from* a course, standard, etc.) —*adj.* (-it) *same as* DEVIANT —*n.* (-it) a deviant; esp., one whose sexual behavior is deviant —**de′vi·a′tor** *n.*

de·vi·a′tion *n.* 1. a deviating or being deviant, as in behavior, political ideology, etc. 2. amount of difference from a specified value

de·vice (di vīs′) *n.* [see DEVISE] 1. a plan, scheme, or trick devised to bring about a specified result 2. a mechanical invention or contrivance 3. something used for artistic effect [a rhetorical *device*] 4. a design or emblem, as on a shield or badge —**leave to one's own devices** to allow to do as one wishes

dev·il (dev′'l) *n.* [ult. < Gr. *diabolos*, slanderer] 1. [often D-] *Theol. a*) the chief evil spirit; Satan (with *the*) *b*) any demon of hell 2. a very wicked person 3. a person who is mischievous, lively, reckless, etc. 4. a wretched person [that poor *devil*] —*vt.* -iled or -illed, -il·ing or -il·ling 1. to prepare (food, often finely chopped) with hot seasoning 2. to annoy, tease, or torment —**a devil of a** (time, etc.) a very bad (time, etc.) —**give the devil his due** to acknowledge the good qualities of a wicked or unpleasant person —**the devil to pay** trouble as a consequence

dev′il·fish′ *n.*, *pl.*: see FISH 1. a large ray whose pectoral fins are hornlike when rolled up 2. an octopus

dev·il·ish (dev′'l ish, dev′lish) *adj.* 1. of or like a devil; diabolic 2. mischievous; reckless 3. [Colloq.] very bad; extreme —*adv.* [Colloq.] extremely; very —**dev′il·ish·ly** *adv.* —**dev′il·ish·ness** *n.*

DEVILFISH
(to 20 ft. across)

dev′il·may·care′ *adj.* reckless or carefree

dev′il·ment *n.* mischief or mischievous action

devil's advocate a person who upholds the wrong side for argument's sake

dev′il's-food′ cake reddish-brown chocolate cake

dev′il·try (-trē) *n.*, *pl.* -tries reckless mischief, fun, etc.: also **dev′il·ry**, *pl.* -ries

de·vi·ous (dē′vē əs) *adj.* [< L. *de-*, off + *via*, road] 1. roundabout; winding 2. straying from what is right or usual 3. not straightforward; deceiving —**de′vi·ous·ly** *adv.* —**de′vi·ous·ness** *n.*

de·vise (di vīz′) *vt.*, *vi.* -vised′, -vis′ing [< L. *dividere*, to divide] 1. to work out (something) by thinking; plan; invent 2. to bequeath (real property) by will —*n.* a bequest of real property —**de·vis′al** (-vī′z′l) *n.* —**de·vis′er**, *Law* **de·vi′sor** *n.*

de·vi·tal·ize (dē vīt′'l īz′) *vt.* -ized′, -iz′ing to lower in vitality —**de·vi′tal·i·za′tion** *n.*

de·void (di void′) *adj.* [see DE- & VOID] completely without; empty (*of*)

de·volve (di välv′) *vt.*, *vi.* -volved′, -volv′ing [< L. *de-*, down + *volvere*, to roll] to pass (*on*) to another: said of duties, responsibilities, etc.

de·vote (di vōt′) *vt.* -vot′ed, -vot′ing [< L. *de-*, from + *vovere*, to vow] to set apart for or give up to some purpose, activity, or person; dedicate [to *devote* one's life to teaching; *devote* time to study]

de·vot·ed *adj.* very loving, loyal, or faithful —**de·vot′ed·ly** *adv.*

dev·o·tee (dev′ə tē′, -tā′) *n.* a person strongly devoted to something or someone

de·vo·tion (di vō′shən) *n.* 1. a devoting or being devoted 2. piety 3. religious worship 4. [*pl.*] prayers 5. loyalty or deep affection —**de·vo′tion·al** *adj.*, *n.*

de·vour (di vour′) *vt.* [< L. *de-*, intens. + *vorare*, swallow whole] 1. to eat up hungrily or greedily 2. to consume, engulf, or destroy 3. to take in greedily, as with the eyes 4. to absorb completely

de·vout (di vout′) *adj.* [see DEVOTE] 1. very religious; pious 2. showing reverence 3. earnest; sincere —**de·vout′ly** *adv.* —**de·vout′ness** *n.*

dew (dōō, dyōō) *n.* [OE. *deaw*] 1. the moisture in the air that condenses in drops on cool surfaces at night 2. anything like dew, as in form, purity, freshness, etc. —**dew′y** *adj.* -i·er, -i·est

dew′ber′ry *n.*, *pl.* -ries 1. any of various trailing blackberry vines 2. their fruit

dew′claw′ (-klô′) *n.* a functionless digit as on the inner side of a dog's leg

dew′drop′ *n.* a drop of dew

Dew·ey (dōō′ē, dyōō′ē) 1. George, 1837–1917; U.S. admiral in the Spanish-American War 2. John, 1859–1952; U.S. philosopher & educator

dew′lap′ *n.* [OE. *deaw*, dew + *laeppa*, a fold] a loose fold of skin hanging from the throat of cattle, etc.

DEW line (dōō, dyōō) [D(*istant*) E(*arly*) W(*arning*)] a line of radar stations near the 70th parallel in N. America

dew point the temperature at which dew starts to form or vapor to condense into liquid

dex·ter·i·ty (dek ster′ə tē) *n.* [see DEXTEROUS] skill in using one's hands, body, or mind

dex·ter·ous (dek′strəs, -stər əs) *adj.* [< L. *dexter*, right] having or showing skill in using the hands, body, or mind: also **dex′trous** —**dex′ter·ous·ly** *adv.*

dex·trin (dek′strin) *n.* [< L. *dexter*, right: it turns the plane of polarized light to the right] a soluble, gummy substance obtained from starch and used as an adhesive, etc.

dex·trose (dek′strōs) *n.* [see prec.] a glucose, $C_6H_{12}O_6$, found in plants and animals

di-¹ [Gr. *di-* < *dis*, twice] *a prefix meaning* twice, double, twofold

di-² *same as* DIS-

di·a·be·tes (dī′ə bēt′is, -ēz) *n.* [< Gr. *dia-*, through + *bainein*, to go] a chronic disease involving an insulin deficiency and marked by excess sugar in the blood and urine, hunger, thirst, etc.: in full **diabetes mel·li·tus** (mə līt′is) —**di′a·bet′ic** (-bet′ik) *adj., n.*

di·a·bol·ic (dī′ə bäl′ik) *adj.* [see DEVIL] very wicked or cruel; fiendish; devilish: also **di′a·bol′i·cal** —**di′a·bol′i·cal·ly** *adv.*

di·ac·o·nate (dī ak′ə nit) *n.* **1.** the rank or office of a deacon **2.** a group of deacons —**di·ac′o·nal** (-n′l)

di·a·crit·ic (dī′ə krit′ik) *adj.* [< Gr. *dia-*, across + *krinein*, to separate] distinguishing: also **di′a·crit′i·cal** — *n.* a mark, as a macron or cedilla, added to a letter or symbol to show its pronunciation, etc.: in full, **diacritical mark**

di·a·dem (dī′ə dem′, -dəm) *n.* [< Gr. *dia-*, through + *dein*, to bind] **1.** a crown **2.** any band worn on the head as an ornament

di·ag·nose (dī′əg nōs′, -nōz′) *vt., vi.* **-nosed′, -nos′ing** to make a diagnosis (of)

di·ag·no·sis (dī′əg nō′sis) *n., pl.* **-ses** (-sēz) [< Gr. *dia-*, through + *gignōskein*, know] **1.** the act or process of deciding the nature of a disease, problem, etc. by examination and analysis **2.** the resulting decision —**di′ag·nos′tic** (-näs′tik) *adj.* —**di′ag·nos·ti′cian** (-näs tish′ən) *n.*

di·ag·o·nal (dī ag′ə n′l) *adj.* [< Gr. *dia-*, through + *gōnia*, an angle] **1.** slanting from one corner to the opposite corner, as of a rectangle **2.** having a slanting direction or slanting markings, lines, etc. —*n.* a diagonal line, plane, course, part, etc. —**di·ag′o·nal·ly** *adv.*

DIAGONAL (AB)

di·a·gram (dī′ə gram′) *n.* [< Gr. *dia-*, through + *graphein*, write] a sketch, plan, graph, etc. that explains a thing, as by outlining its parts and their relationships —*vt.* **-gramed′** or **-grammed′, -gram′ing** or **-gram′ming** to make a diagram of —**di′a·gram·mat′ic** (-grə mat′ik) *adj.*

di·al (dī′əl, dīl) *n.* [< L. *dies*, day] **1.** the face of a watch, clock, or sundial **2.** the face of a meter, gauge, etc., on which a pointer indicates an amount, degree, etc. **3.** a graduated disk or strip on a radio or television set, for tuning in stations **4.** a rotating disk on a telephone, for making connections automatically —*vt., vi.* **-aled** or **-alled, -al·ing** or **-al·ling 1.** to measure, select, tune in, etc. with a dial **2.** to call on a telephone by using a dial or other automatic device

dial. 1. dialect(al) **2.** dialectic(al)

di·a·lect (dī′ə lekt′) *n.* [< Gr. *dia-*, between + *legein*, to talk] **1.** the form of a spoken language peculiar to a region, social group, occupational group, etc. **2.** any language as a member of a related group of languages [English is a West Germanic *dialect*] —**di′a·lec′tal** *adj.*

di·a·lec′tic (-lek′tik) *n.* **1.** [*often pl.*] a logical examination of ideas, often by question and answer, so as to determine their validity **2.** logical argumentation —**di′a·lec′ti·cal** *adj.*

di·a·lec·ti′cian (-lek tish′ən) *n.* **1.** an expert in dialectic **2.** a specialist in dialects

di·a·logue, di·a·log (dī′ə lôg′) *n.* [see DIALECT] **1.** a talking together; conversation **2.** interchange of ideas by open discussion, for mutual understanding **3.** the passages of talk in a play, story, etc.

Dialogue Mass *R.C.Ch.* a Mass at which the congregation makes the responses aloud

dial tone a low buzzing sound heard on a telephone when the line is open for dialing a number

di·al·y·sis (dī al′ə sis) *n., pl.* **-ses′** (-sēz′) [< Gr. *dia-*, apart + *lyein*, to loose] the separation of crystalloids from colloids in solution through a semipermeable membrane, as in an apparatus for removing impurities from the blood during kidney failure —**di·a·lyze** (dī′ə līz′) *vt., vi.* **-lyzed′, -lyz′ing** —**di′a·lyz′er** *n.*

diam. diameter

di·am·e·ter (dī am′ət ər) *n.* [< Gr. *dia-*, through + *metron*, a measure] **1.** a straight line passing through the center of a circle, sphere, etc. from one side to the other **2.** the length of such a line

di·a·met·ri·cal (dī′ə met′ri k′l) *adj.* **1.** of or along a diameter **2.** designating an opposite altogether such; complete Also **di′a·met′ric** —**di′a·met′ri·cal·ly** *adv.*

di·a·mond (dī′mənd, -ə mənd) *n.* [< Gr. *adamas*, adamant] **1.** a nearly pure, brilliant, crystalline carbon, the hardest mineral known: used for gems, phonograph-needle tips, cutting tools, etc. **2.** a gem, etc. cut from this mineral **3.** *a)* the plane figure (♦) *b)* any of a suit of play-

ing cards marked with this figure in red *c)* [*pl.*] this suit **4.** *Baseball* the infield or the whole field

di′a·mond·back′ *n.* a large, poisonous rattlesnake of the S U.S.

Di·an·a (dī an′ə) *Rom. Myth.* the goddess of the moon and of hunting: identified with the Greek goddess Artemis

di·a·pa·son (dī′ə pāz′′n) *n.* [< Gr. *dia-*, through + *pas*, all] **1.** an organ stop covering the instrument's complete range **2.** a swelling burst of harmony

di·a·per (dī′pər, dī′ə pər) *n.* [< ML. *diasprum*, flowered cloth] a soft, absorbent cloth folded around a baby's loins —*vt.* to put a diaper on (a baby)

di·aph·a·nous (dī af′ə nəs) *adj.* [< Gr. *dia-*, through + *phainein*, to show] gauzy or sheer

di·a·phragm (dī′ə fram′) *n.* [< Gr. *dia-*, through + *phragma*, a fence] **1.** the partition of muscles and tendons between the chest cavity and the abdominal cavity **2.** a device to regulate the amount of light entering a camera lens **3.** a vibrating disk that makes or receives sound waves, as in a loudspeaker or microphone **4.** a fitted, vaginal contraceptive device

di·ar·rhe·a, di·ar·rhoe·a (dī′ə rē′ə) *n.* [< Gr. *dia-*, through + *rhein*, to flow] too frequent and loose bowel movements

di·a·ry (dī′ə rē) *n., pl.* **-ries** [< L. *dies*, day] **1.** a daily written record of one's own experiences, thoughts, etc. **2.** a book for this —**di′a·rist** *n.*

di·a·stase (dī′ə stās′) *n.* [< Gr. *dia-*, apart + *histanai*, to stand] an enzyme that changes starches into maltose and later into dextrose

di·as·to·le (dī as′tə lē′) *n.* [< Gr. *dia-*, apart + *stellein*, to put] the rhythmic dilation of the heart following each contraction, or systole —**di·a·stol·ic** (dī′ə stäl′ik) *adj.*

di·a·ther·my (dī′ə thur′mē) *n.* [< Gr. *dia-*, through + *thermē*, heat] medical treatment in which heat is produced in the tissues beneath the skin by a high-frequency electric current —**di′a·ther′mic** *adj.*

di·a·tom (dī′ə täm′, -ət əm) *n.* [< Gr. *diatomos*, cut in two: from shape of cell walls] any of a number of related microscopic algae that are an important source of food for marine life

di·a·ton·ic (dī′ə tän′ik) *adj.* [< Gr. *dia-*, through + *teinein*, to stretch] *Music* designating or of any standard major or minor scale of eight tones

di·a·tribe (dī′ə trīb′) *n.* [< Gr. *dia-*, through + *tribein*, to rub] a bitter, abusive denunciation

di·bas·ic (dī bās′ik) *adj.* denoting or of an acid with two hydrogen atoms which can be replaced by basic radicals or atoms to form a salt

dib·ble (dib′′l) *n.* [ME. *dibbel*, prob. < *dibben*, to dip] a pointed tool used to make holes in the soil for seeds, bulbs, etc.

dice (dīs) *n.pl., sing.* **die** or **dice** [see DIE²] small cubes marked on each side with from one to six dots and used, usually in pairs, in games of chance —*vi.* **diced, dic′ing** to play with dice —*vt.* to cut (vegetables, etc.) into small cubes —**no dice** [Colloq.] **1.** no: used in refusing a request **2.** no success, luck, etc.

DIBBLE

di·chot·o·my (dī kät′ə mē) *n., pl.* **-mies** [< Gr. *dicha*, in two + *temnein*, to cut] division into two usually opposed parts —**di·chot′o·mous** *adj.*

di·chro·mat·ic (dī′krō mat′ik) *adj.* [DI-¹ + CHROMATIC] **1.** having two colors **2.** *Biol.* having two varieties of coloration that are independent of sex or age

dick·ens (dik′′nz) *n., interj.* [Colloq.] the devil: a mild oath

Dick·ens (dik′′nz), **Charles** 1812–70; Eng. novelist

dick·er (dik′ər) *vi.* [< earlier *dicker*, ten hides (as a unit of barter)] to bargain or haggle

dick·ey (dik′ē) *n., pl.* **-eys** [< nickname *Dick*] **1.** a kind of bib or shirt front, often with a collar, worn under a suit or on a dress **2.** a small bird: in full **dickey bird** Also **dick′y,** *pl.* **-ies**

Dick·in·son (dik′in s′n), **Emily** 1830–86; U.S. poet

di·cot·y·le·don (dī′kät ′l ēd′′n) *n.* a flowering plant with two seed leaves (cotyledons) —**di′cot·y·le′don·ous** *adj.*

dict. 1. dictator **2.** dictionary

Dic·ta·phone (dik′tə fōn′) [DIC(TATE) + -PHONE] *a trademark for* a machine that records and plays back speech for typed transcripts, etc. —*n.* this machine

dic·tate (dik′tāt, dik tāt′) *vt., vi.* **-tat·ed, -tat·ing** [< L. *dicere*, speak] **1.** to speak (something) aloud for someone else to write down **2.** to command expressly **3.** to give (orders) with authority or arbitrarily —*n.* (dik′tāt) **1.** an authoritative command **2.** a guiding principle

dic·ta′tion *n.* **1.** the dictating of words to be transcribed **2.** the words dictated **3.** the giving of orders or commands

dic′ta·tor *n.* one who dictates; esp., a ruler or tyrant with absolute power —**dic·ta′tor·ship′** *n.*

dic·ta·to·ri·al (dik′tə tôr′ē əl) *adj.* of or like a dictator; overbearing; tyrannical

dic·tion (dik′shən) *n.* [< L. *dictio*, a speaking] **1.** manner of expression in words; choice of words **2.** enunciation

dic·tion·ar·y (dik′shə ner′ē) *n., pl.* **-ies** [see prec.] **1.** a book of alphabetically listed words in a language, with definitions, pronunciations, etc. **2.** such a book of words in one language with their equivalents in another

dic·tum (dik′təm) *n., pl.* **-tums, -ta** (-tə) [L. < *dicere*, speak] a formal statement of fact, opinion, principle, etc.; pronouncement

did (did) *pt. of* DO¹

di·dac·tic (dī dak′tik) *adj.* [< Gr. *didaskein*, teach] **1.** intended for instruction **2.** morally instructive **3.** boringly pedantic Also **di·dac′ti·cal**

di·dac′tics *n.pl.* [*usually with sing. v.*] the art or science of teaching; pedagogy

did·dle (did′'l) *vi., vt.* **-dled, -dling** [< ?] [Colloq.] **1.** to cheat or swindle **2.** to waste (time) in trifling —**did′dler** *n.*

did·n't (did′'nt) did not

di·do (dī′dō) *n., pl.* **-does, -dos** [< ?] [Colloq.] a mischievous trick; prank

didst (didst) *archaic 2d pers. sing., past indic., of* DO: *used with* thou

di·dym·i·um (dī dim′ē əm) *n.* [< Gr. *didymos*, twin] a mixture of certain rare-earth elements

die¹ (dī) *vi.* **died, dy′ing** [< ON. *deyja*] **1.** to stop living; become dead **2.** to stop functioning; end **3.** to lose force or activity **4.** to fade or wither away **5.** to suffer extreme agony **6.** [Colloq.] to wish very much [I'm *dying* to go] —**die away** (or **down**) to weaken and end gradually —**die off** to die one by one until all are gone —**die out** to stop existing

die² (dī) *n.* [< L. *dare*, give] **1.** *sing. of* DICE **2.** *pl.* **dies** (dīz) any of various tools for stamping, cutting, or shaping metal —*vt.* **died, die′ing** to stamp, cut, or shape with a die —**the die is cast** the irrevocable decision has been made

die casting 1. the process of making a casting by forcing molten metal into a metallic mold **2.** a casting made in this way —**die caster**

die′-hard′, die′hard′ *n.* a person stubbornly resistant to new ideas or reform —*adj.* very stubborn

diel·drin (dēl′drin) *n.* a highly toxic pesticide

di·e·lec·tric (dī′ə lek′trik) *n.* [< Gr. *dia-*, across + ELECTRIC] a substance, as rubber, glass, etc., that does not conduct electricity —*adj.* nonconducting

di·er·e·sis (dī er′ə sis) *n., pl.* **-ses′** (-sēz′) [< Gr. *dia-*, apart + *hairein*, to take] a mark (¨) placed over the second of two consecutive vowels to show that it is pronounced separately: now usually replaced by a hyphen or omitted The mark is also used in pronunciation symbols of vowels, as in (ä)

die·sel (dē′z'l, -s'l) *n.* [< R. *Diesel*, Ger. inventor] [*often* D-] **1.** an internal-combustion engine that burns fuel oil ignited by heat from air compression: also **diesel engine** (or **motor**) **2.** a locomotive, truck, etc. powered by such an engine

die·sink·er (dī′siŋ′kər) *n.* a maker of dies used in stamping or shaping —**die′sink′ing** *n.*

‡Di·es I·rae (dē′ez ir′ā) [L., Day of Wrath] a medieval Latin hymn about Judgment Day, a part of the Requiem Mass

di·et¹ (dī′ət) *n.* [Gr. *diaita*, way of life] **1.** what a person or animal usually eats or drinks **2.** a regimen of special or limited food and drink, as for one's health or for losing weight —*vi.* to eat special or limited food, esp. for losing weight —**di′e·tar′y** (-ə ter′ē) *adj.* —**di′et·er** *n.*

di·et² (dī′ət) *n.* [< ML. *dieta*] a formal assembly

di·e·tet·ic (dī′ə tet′ik) *adj.* of or for a particular diet of food and drink

di·e·tet′ics *n.pl.* [*with sing. v.*] the study of the kinds and quantities of food needed for health

di·e·ti·tian, di·e·ti·cian (dī′ə tish′ən) *n.* a specialist in planning meals or diets

dif·fer (dif′ər) *vi.* [< L. *dis-*, apart + *ferre*, carry] **1.** to be unlike; be different (*from*) **2.** to have opposite or unlike opinions; disagree

dif·fer·ence (dif′ər əns, dif′rəns) *n.* **1.** a being different or not alike **2.** the way in which people or things are different **3.** a differing in opinions; disagreement or quarrel **4.** the amount by which one quantity is greater or less than another

dif′fer·ent *adj.* **1.** not alike; dissimilar (with *from*, or, esp. colloquially, *than*, and, in Brit. usage, *to*) **2.** not the same; distinct **3.** various **4.** unusual —**dif′fer·ent·ly** *adv.*

dif·fer·en·tial (dif′ə ren′shəl) *adj.* of, showing, or constituting a difference —*n.* **1.** a differentiating amount, degree, factor, etc. **2.** a gear arrangement that connects two axles in the same line and lets the outside wheel turn faster around a curve than the inside wheel: in full **differential gear 3.** *Math.* an infinitesimal difference between values of a variable quantity

dif·fer·en·ti·ate (-ren′shē āt′) *vt.* **-at′ed, -at′ing 1.** to constitute a difference in or between **2.** to make unlike **3.** to distinguish the difference between —*vi.* **1.** to become different or differentiated **2.** to note a difference —**dif′fer·en′ti·a′tion** *n.*

dif·fi·cult (dif′i kəlt, -kult′) *adj.* **1.** hard to do, understand, etc. **2.** hard to satisfy, please, etc.

dif·fi·cul′ty *n., pl.* **-ties** [< L. *dis-*, not + *facilis*, easy] **1.** a being difficult **2.** something difficult; problem, obstacle, etc. **3.** trouble **4.** disagreement —**in difficulties** in distress, esp. financially

dif·fi·dent (dif′ə dənt) *adj.* [< L. *dis-*, not + *fidere*, to trust] lacking confidence in oneself; timid; shy —**dif′fi·dence** *n.* —**dif′fi·dent·ly** *adv.*

dif·fract (di frakt′) *vt.* [< L. *dis-*, apart + *frangere*, to break] to break into parts; specif., to cause to undergo diffraction

dif·frac′tion *n.* **1.** the breaking up of a ray of light into dark and light bands or into the colors of the spectrum, as when it is deflected at the edge of an opaque object **2.** a similar breaking up of other waves, as of sound —**dif·frac′tive** *adj.*

dif·fuse (di fyoos′) *adj.* [< L. *dis-*, apart + *fundere*, pour] **1.** spread out; not concentrated **2.** using more words than are needed —*vt., vi.* (-fyooz′) **-fused′, -fus′ing 1.** to pour or spread in every direction **2.** to mix by diffusion, as gases or liquids —**dif·fuse′ly** *adv.* —**dif·fus′i·ble** *adj.* —**dif·fu′sive** *adj.*

dif·fu·sion (di fyoo′zhən) *n.* **1.** a diffusing; spreading, as of knowledge or of light rays by reflection or by dispersion through frosted glass **2.** an intermingling of the molecules of liquids, gases, etc. **3.** wordiness

dig (dig) *vt.* dug or *archaic* digged, dig′ging [< OFr. *digue*, dike < Du. *dijk*] **1.** to turn up or remove (ground, etc.) with a spade, the hands, etc. **2.** to make (a hole, etc.) by doing this **3.** to get from the ground in this way **4.** to find out, as by careful study [to *dig* out the truth] **5.** to jab; prod **6.** [Slang] *a*) to understand *b*) to like —*vi.* **1.** to excavate **2.** [Colloq.] to work or study hard —*n.* **1.** an archaeological excavation **2.** [Colloq.] *a*) a poke, nudge, etc. *b*) a sarcastic remark; gibe

di·gest (dī′jest) *n.* [< L. *di-*, apart + *gerere*, to bear] a summary or synopsis, as of scientific, legal, or literary material —*vt.* (di jest′, dī-) **1.** to summarize **2.** to change (food), esp. in the stomach and intestines, into a form that can be absorbed by the body **3.** to absorb mentally —*vi.* to be digested —**di·gest′i·ble** *adj.*

di·ges·tion (di jes′chən, dī-) *n.* **1.** the act or process of digesting food **2.** the ability to digest **3.** the absorption of ideas —**di·ges′tive** *adj.*

dig·ger (dig′ər) *n.* a person or thing that digs; specif., any tool or machine for digging

dig·gings *n.pl.* **1.** materials dug out **2.** [*often with sing. v.*] a place where digging or mining is carried on **3.** [Slang] one's lodgings

dig·it (dij′it) *n.* [L. *digitus*, a finger, toe] **1.** a finger or toe **2.** any number from 0 to 9

dig′i·tal (-'l) *adj.* **1.** of, like, or having digits **2.** using numbers that are digits to represent all the variables involved in calculation **3.** showing the figure of the moment in a row of digits, as a timepiece or thermometer

digital computer a computer that uses numbers to perform calculations, usually in a binary system

dig·i·tal·is (dij′ə tal′is) *n.* [see DIGIT: from its flowers] **1.** any of a genus of plants with long spikes of thimblelike flowers; foxglove **2.** the dried leaves of the purple foxglove **3.** a medicine made from these leaves, used as a heart stimulant

dig·i·tate (dij′ə tāt′) *adj.* [see DIGIT] **1.** having separate fingers or toes **2.** fingerlike

dig·ni·fied (dig′nə fīd′) *adj.* having or showing dignity or stateliness —**dig′ni·fied′ly** *adv.*

dig·ni·fy (dig′nə fī′) *vt.* **-fied′, -fy′ing** [< L. *dignus,* worthy + *facere,* make] to give dignity to; honor, ennoble, make seem worthy, etc.

dig′ni·tar′y (-ter′ē) *n., pl.* **-ies** a person holding a high, dignified position or office

dig·ni·ty (dig′nə tē) *n., pl.* **-ties** [< L. *dignus,* worthy] **1.** the quality of being worthy of esteem or honor **2.** high repute; honor **3.** the degree of worth or honor **4.** a high position, rank, or title **5.** stately appearance or manner **6.** self-respect

di·graph (dī′graf) *n.* two letters that together represent one sound, as *ea* in *read* or *sh* in *show*

di·gress (dī gres′, di-) *vi.* [< L. *dis-,* apart + *gradi,* to go] to depart temporarily from the main subject in talking or writing —**di·gres′sion** (-gresh′ən) *n.* —**di·gres′sive** *adj.*

di·he·dral (dī hē′drəl) *adj.* [< DI-¹ + Gr. *hedra,* a seat] having or formed by two intersecting plane faces —*n.* a dihedral angle

dike (dīk) *n.* [OE. *dic,* ditch] an embankment or dam to prevent flooding by the sea or by a river —*vt.* **diked, dik′ing** to protect with a dike

di·lap·i·dat·ed (di lap′ə dāt′id) *adj.* [< L. *dis-,* apart + *lapidare,* throw stones at] falling to pieces; broken down; in disrepair —**di·lap′i·da′tion** *n.*

di·late (dī lāt′, dī-) *vt., vi.* **-lat′ed, -lat′ing** [< L. *dis-,* apart + *latus,* wide] to make or become wider or larger; expand —**di·la′tion, dil·a·ta·tion** (dil′ə tā′shən) *n.* —**di·la′tor** *n.*

dil·a·to·ry (dil′ə tôr′ē) *adj.* [< L. *dilator,* one who delays] **1.** causing delay **2.** inclined to delay; slow; tardy —**dil′a·to′ri·ness** *n.*

di·lem·ma (di lem′ə) *n.* [< Gr. *di-,* two + *lēmma,* proposition] any situation in which one must choose between unpleasant alternatives

dil·et·tante (dil′ə tänt′, -tän′tē, -tan′tē) *n., pl.* **-tantes′, -tan′ti** (-tän′tē) [It. < L. *delectare,* to delight] one who dabbles in art, literature, etc. without serious study, interest, etc. —**dil′et·tant′ish** *adj.* —**dil′et·tant′ism** *n.*

dil·i·gent (dil′ə jənt) *adj.* [< L. *di-,* apart + *legere,* choose] **1.** persevering and careful in work; industrious **2.** done with careful, steady effort —**dil′i·gence** *n.* —**dil′i·gent·ly** *adv.*

dill (dil) *n.* [OE. *dile*] a plant with bitter seeds and aromatic leaves, used to flavor pickles, etc.

dil·ly (dil′ē) *n., pl.* **-lies** [? < DEL(IGHTFUL) + -Y¹] [Slang] a remarkable person or thing

dil·ly·dal·ly (dil′ē dal′e) *vi.* **-lied, -ly·ing** [reduplicated form of DALLY] to waste time in hesitation; loiter or dawdle

DILL

di·lute (di lo͞ot′, dī-) *vt.* **-lut′ed, -lut′ing** [< L. dis-, off + *lavere,* to wash]: to thin down or weaken as by mixing with water or adding something —*vi.* to become diluted —*adj.* diluted —**di·lu′tion** *n.*

di·lu·vi·al (di lo͞o′vē əl) *adj.* [< L. *diluvium,* a deluge] of a flood, esp. the Deluge: also **di·lu′vi·an**

dim (dim) *adj.* **dim′mer, dim′mest** [OE. *dimm*] **1.** not bright; darkish or dull **2.** not clearly seen, heard, or understood; vague, faint, indistinct, etc. **3.** not clearly seeing, understanding, etc. **4.** not favorable *[dim prospects]* —*vt., vi.* **dimmed, dim′ming** to make or grow dim —**dim′ly** *adv.* —**dim′ness** *n.*

dim. 1. diminuendo **2.** diminutive

dime (dīm) *n.* [< L. *decem,* ten] a coin of the U.S. and Canada equal to 10 cents

di·men·sion (də men′shən) *n.* [< L. *dis-,* off + *metiri,* to measure] **1.** any measurable extent, as length, width, depth, etc. **2.** *[pl.]* measurements in length, width, and often depth **3.** *[often pl.]* size or scope —**di·men′sion·al** *adj.*

dime store same as FIVE-AND-TEN-CENT STORE

di·min·ish (də min′ish) *vt., vi.* [< L. *de-,* from + *minuere,* lessen] to make or become smaller; lessen in size, degree, importance, etc.; decrease —**dim·i·nu·tion** (dim′ə nyo͞o′shən, -no͞o′-) *n.*

di·min·u·en·do (də min′yoo wen′dō) *adj., adv.* [It.] *Music* with gradually diminishing volume

di·min·u·tive (də min′yoo tiv) *adj.* [see DIMINISH] **1.** very small; little **2.** *Gram.* expressing smallness —*n.* a word having a suffix expressing smallness, endearment, etc., as *booklet* or *Jackie*

dim·i·ty (dim′ə tē) *n., pl.* **-ties** [< Gr. *dis-,* two + *mitos,* a thread] a thin, strong, corded cotton cloth

dim′mer *n.* a device for dimming electric lights

dim·ple (dim′p'l) *n.* [ME. *dimpel*] a small, natural hollow, as on the cheek or chin —*vt., vi.* **-pled, -pling** to form dimples (in) —**dim′ply** (-plē) *adj.*

dim′wit′ *n.* [Slang] a stupid person; simpleton —**dim′wit′ted** *adj.*

din (din) *n.* [OE. *dyne*] a loud, continuous noise; confused clamor —*vt.* **dinned, din′ning 1.** to beset with a din **2.** to repeat insistently or noisily —*vi.* to make a din

dine (dīn) *vi.* **dined, din′ing** [ult. < L. *dis-,* away + *jejunus,* fasting] to eat dinner —*vt.* to provide a dinner for — **dine out** to dine away from home

din·er (dī′nər) *n.* **1.** a person eating dinner **2.** a railroad car equipped to serve meals: also **dining car 3.** a small restaurant built to look like a dining car

din·ette (dī net′) *n.* an alcove or small room used as a dining room

ding (diŋ) *vi.* [ME. *dingen,* to strike < Scand.] to make a sound like that of a bell; ring —*n.* the sound of a bell: also **ding′-dong′** (-dôŋ′)

din·ghy (diŋ′gē) *n., pl.* **-ghies** [< Hindi] any of various small boats, as a ship's tender

din·gle (diŋ′g'l) *n.* [ME. *dingel,* abyss] a small, deep, wooded valley

din·go (diŋ′gō) *n., pl.* **-goes** [native name] the Australian wild dog

ding·us (diŋ′əs) *n.* [Du. *dinges*] [Colloq.] any device; gadget

din·gy (din′jē) *adj.* **-gi·er, -gi·est** [< ? DUNG + -Y²] **1.** having a dull, dirty look; not bright or clean **2.** dismal; shabby —**din′gi·ness** *n.*

din·key (diŋ′kē) *n., pl.* **-keys** [prob. < DINKY] [Colloq.] **1.** a small locomotive used in a railroad yard **2.** a small trolley car

din·ky (diŋ′kē) *adj.* **-ki·er, -ki·est** [< Scot. *dink,* trim] [Colloq.] small and unimportant —*n., pl.* **-kies** *same as* DINKEY

din·ner (din′ər) *n.* [see DINE] **1.** the chief meal of the day, whether eaten in the evening or about noon **2.** a banquet honoring a person or event **3.** a complete meal at a set price, table d'hôte

dinner jacket a tuxedo jacket

din′ner·ware′ (-wer′) *n.* **1.** plates, cups, saucers, etc. collectively **2.** a set of such dishes

di·no·saur (dī′nə sôr′) *n.* [< Gr. *deinos,* terrible + *sauros,* lizard] any of a group of extinct, often huge, four-limbed reptiles of the Mesozoic Era

dint (dint) *n.* [OE. *dynt*] **1.** force; exertion: now chiefly in **by dint of 2.** a dent

di·oc·e·san (dī äs′ə s'n) *adj.* of a diocese —*n.* the bishop of a diocese

di·o·cese (dī′ə sis, -sēs′) *n.* [< Gr. *dioikein,* keep house] the district under a bishop's jurisdiction

di·ode (dī′ōd) *n.* [DI-¹ + -ODE] an electron tube or semiconductor with two terminals, used as a rectifier

di·oe·cious (dī ē′shəs) *adj.* [< DI-¹ + Gr. *oikos,* house] *Biol.* having the male reproductive organs in one individual and the female organs in another

Di·og·e·nes (dī äj′ə nēz′) 412?–323? B.C.: Gr. Cynic philosopher

Di·o·ny·sus, Di·o·ny·sos (dī′ə nī′səs) *n.* the Greek god of wine and revelry; Bacchus —**Di′o·ny′sian** (-nish′ən, -nis′ē ən, -nī′sē ən) *adj.*

di·o·ra·ma (dī′ə ram′ə) *n.* [< Gr. *dia-,* through + *horama,* a view] a scenic display, as of three-dimensional figures against a painted background

di·ox·ide (dī äk′sīd) *n.* an oxide with two atoms of oxygen per molecule

dip (dip) *vt.* **dipped, dip′ping** [OE. *dyppan*] **1.** to put into liquid for a moment **2.** to make (a candle) by putting a wick repeatedly into melted tallow or wax **3.** to take out as by scooping up **4.** to lower (a flag, etc.) and immediately raise again —*vi.* **1.** to go down into a liquid and quickly come out again **2.** to sink or seem to sink suddenly *[the sun dipped into the lake]* **3.** to drop slightly, esp. for a short time *[sales dipped in May]* **4.** to slope down **5.** to go (*into*) so as to dip something out *[to dip into savings]* **6.** to look into or study something superficially (with *into*) —*n.* **1.** a dipping or being dipped **2.** a brief plunge into water, etc. **3.** a liquid, sauce, etc. into which something is dipped **4.** something scooped or dipped out **5.** a downward slope or drop

diph·the·ri·a (dif thir'ē ə, dip-) *n.* [< Gr. *diphthera*, leather] an acute infectious disease marked by high fever and the formation in the air passages of a membranelike obstruction to breathing

diph·thong (dif'thôŋ, dip'-) *n.* [< Gr. *di-*, two + *phthongos*, sound] a sound made by gliding from one vowel to another in one syllable, as (oi) in *boy*, formed by (ô) + (ē)

di·plo·ma (di plō'mə) *n.* [L., state letter of recommendation < Gr. *diplōma*, folded letter] 1. a certificate conferring honors, privileges, etc. 2. a certificate issued by a school, college, etc. indicating graduation or conferring a degree

di·plo·ma·cy (di plō'mə sē) *n., pl.* **-cies** [< Fr.: see ff.] 1. the conducting of relations between nations 2. tact in dealing with people

dip·lo·mat (dip'lə mat') *n.* [< Fr., ult. < L. *diploma*, DIPLOMA] 1. a representative of a government who conducts relations with another government 2. a tactful person

dip'lo·mat'ic *adj.* 1. of diplomacy 2. tactful and adroit in dealing with people —**dip'lo·mat'i·cal·ly** *adv.*

di·pole (antenna) (dī'pōl') a straight antenna separated at its center by a line to a transmitter or receiver

dip·per (dip'ər) *n.* 1. a long-handled cup, etc. for dipping 2. [D-] either of two groups of stars in the shape of a dipper: see BIG DIPPER, LITTLE DIPPER

dip·so·ma·ni·a (dip'sə mā'nē ə) *n.* [< Gr. *dipsa*, thirst + *mania*, madness] an abnormal and insatiable craving for alcoholic drink —**dip'so·ma'ni·ac'** ('-ak'-) *n.*

dip·ter·ous (dip'tər əs) *adj.* [< Gr. *di-*, two + *pteron*, a wing] having two wings, as some insects, or two winglike appendages, as some seeds

dire (dīr) *adj. also* **dir'er**, **dir'est** [L. *dirus*] 1. dreadful; terrible 2. urgent *[dire need]*

di·rect (di rekt', dī-) *adj.* [< L. *dirigere*, put straight] 1. by the shortest way; straight 2. straightforward; frank 3. with nothing or no one between; immediate 4. in unbroken line of descent; lineal 5. exact; complete *[the direct opposite]* 6. in the exact words *[a direct quote]* 7. by popular vote instead of through representatives *[direct primary election]* —*vt.* 1. to manage; guide; conduct 2. to order; command 3. to turn or point; aim 4. to tell (a person) the way to a place 5. to address (words, etc.) to a specific person or group 6. to supervise the action of (a play, etc.) 7. to rehearse and conduct (a choir, orchestra, etc.) —*vi.* 1. to give directions 2. to be a director —*adv.* directly —**di·rect'ness** *n.*

direct current an electric current flowing in one direction

di·rec·tion (də rek'shən, dī-) *n.* 1. a directing; management; supervision 2. [*usually pl.*] instructions for doing, using, etc. 3. an order or command 4. the point toward which one faces or line along which one moves or lies 5. an aspect, trend, etc.

di·rec'tion·al *adj.* 1. of, aimed at, or indicating (a specific) direction 2. designed for radiating or receiving radio signals effectively in one or more particular directions

di·rec'tive (-tiv) *adj.* directing —*n.* a general instruction or order issued authoritatively

di·rect'ly *adv.* 1. in a direct way or line; straight 2. with nothing coming between 3. exactly *[directly opposite]* 4. right away

direct object the word or words denoting the receiver of the action of a verb (Ex.: *me* in *he hit me*)

di·rec'tor *n.* one who directs a school, corporation, etc. or a play, choir, etc. —**di·rec'tor·ship'** *n.*

di·rec'tor·ate (-it) *n.* 1. the position of a director 2. a board of directors

di·rec·to·ry (də rek'tə rē, dī-) *adj.* directing or advising —*n., pl.* **-ries** a book listing the names, addresses, etc. of a specific group of persons

dire·ful (dīr'fəl) *adj.* dreadful; terrible

dirge (durj) *n.* [< L. *dirige* (direct), first word of a funeral hymn] a song, poem, etc. expressing grief or mourning

dir·i·gi·ble (dir'i jə b'l, də rij'ə-) *adj.* [see DIRECT & -IBLE] that can be steered —*n. same as* AIRSHIP

dirk (durk) *n.* [< ?] a short, straight dagger

dirn·dl (durn'd'l) *n.* [< G. *dirne*, girl] 1. a kind of dress with a full skirt, gathered waist, and closefitting bodice 2. such a skirt

dirt (durt) *n.* [< ON. *dritr*, excrement] 1. any unclean matter, as mud, trash, etc.; filth 2. earth or garden soil 3. dirtiness, corruption, etc. 4. obscenity 5. malicious gossip

dirt'y *adj.* **-i·er**, **-i·est** 1. soiled or soiling with dirt; unclean 2. obscene; pornographic 3. mean; nasty 4. unfair; dishonest 5. rough, as weather —*vt., vi.* **-ied**, **-y·ing** to make or become dirty; soil —**dirt'i·ly** *adv.* —**dirt'i·ness** *n.*

Dis (dis) *Rom. Myth.* 1. the god of the lower world: identified with the Greek Pluto 2. Hades

dis- [< L.] *a prefix denoting* separation, negation, or reversal *[dismiss, dishonest, disown]*

dis·a·bil·i·ty (dis'ə bil'ə tē) *n., pl.* **-ties** 1. a disabled condition 2. that which disables, as illness 3. a legal disqualification

dis·a'ble (-ā'b'l) *vt.* **-bled**, **-bling** 1. to make unable or unfit 2. to disqualify legally —**dis·a'ble·ment** *n.*

dis·a·buse (dis'ə byōōz') *vt.* **-bused'**, **-bus'ing** to rid of false ideas; undeceive

dis'ad·van'tage (-əd van'tij) *n.* 1. an unfavorable situation; drawback; handicap 2. detriment —*vt.* **-taged**, **-taging** to act to the disadvantage of —**at a disadvantage** in an unfavorable situation —**dis·ad'van·ta'geous** (-ad'vən tā'jəs) *adj.*

dis'ad·van'taged *adj.* underprivileged

dis·af·fect (dis'ə fekt') *vt.* to make unfriendly, discontented, or disloyal —**dis'af·fec'tion** *n.*

dis·a·gree' (-ə grē') *vi.* **-greed'**, **-gree'ing** 1. to fail to agree; be different 2. to differ in opinion; specif., to quarrel or dispute 3. to give distress *[corn disagrees with me]*

dis·a·gree'a·ble *adj.* 1. unpleasant; offensive 2. quarrelsome —**dis'a·gree'a·ble·ness** *n.* —**dis'a·gree'a·bly** *adv.*

dis·a·gree'ment *n.* 1. refusal to agree 2. difference; discrepancy 3. difference of opinion 4. a quarrel or dispute

dis·al·low' (-ə lou') *vt.* to refuse to allow; reject as invalid or illegal

dis·ap·pear' (-ə pir') *vi.* 1. to cease to be seen; go out of sight 2. to cease being —**dis'ap·pear'ance** *n.*

dis·ap·point' (-ə point') *vt.* 1. to fail to satisfy the hopes or expectations of 2. to frustrate (hopes, etc.)

dis·ap·point'ment (-mənt) *n.* 1. a disappointing or being disappointed 2. a person or thing that disappoints

dis·ap·pro·ba·tion (dis ap'rə bā'shən) *n.* disapproval

dis·ap·prov·al (dis'ə prōōv''l) *n.* 1. failure or refusal to approve 2. unfavorable opinion

dis'ap·prove' (-prōōv') *vt., vi.* **-proved'**, **-prov'ing** 1. to have or express an unfavorable opinion (of) 2. to refuse to approve —**dis'ap·prov'ing·ly** *adv.*

dis·arm (dis ärm') *vt.* 1. to take away weapons from 2. to make harmless 3. to overcome the hostility of —*vi.* to reduce or do away with armed forces and armaments

dis·ar'ma·ment (-är'mə mənt) *n.* 1. a disarming 2. the reduction of armed forces and armaments, as to a limitation set by treaty

dis·arm'ing *adj.* removing fears, hostility, etc.

dis·ar·range (dis'ə rānj') *vt.* **-ranged'**, **-rang'ing** to make less neat; disorder —**dis'ar·range'ment** *n.*

dis·ar·ray' (-ə rā') *vt.* to throw into disorder or confusion; upset —*n.* 1. disorder; confusion 2. a state of disorderly or insufficient dress

dis·as·sem·ble (-ə sem'b'l) *vt.* **-bled**, **-bling** to take apart —**dis'as·sem'bly** *n.*

dis·as·so·ci·ate' (-ə sō'shē āt', -sē-) *vt.* **-at'ed**, **-at'ing** to sever association with; separate

dis·as·ter (di zas'tər) *n.* [< L. *dis-* + *astrum*, a star] any event causing great harm or damage; calamity

dis·as'trous (-trəs) *adj.* being or causing a disaster; calamitous —**dis·as'trous·ly** *adv.*

dis·a·vow (dis'ə vou') *vt.* to deny any knowledge of or responsibility for; disclaim —**dis'a·vow'al** *n.*

dis·band (dis band') *vt., vi.* to break up as an organization —**dis·band'ment** *n.*

dis·bar' (-bär') *vt.* **-barred'**, **-bar'ring** to deprive (a lawyer) of the right to practice law —**dis·bar'ment** *n.*

dis·be·lieve' *vt., vi.* **-lieved'**, **-liev'ing** to refuse to believe (in) —**dis'be·lief'** *n.*

dis·bur'den *vt.* to relieve of a burden or of anything burdensome

dis·burse' (-burs') *vt.* **-bursed'**, **-burs'ing** [< OFr. *desbourser*] to pay out; expend —**dis·burse'ment** *n.* —**dis·burs'er** *n.*

disc (disk) *n.* 1. *same as* DISK 2. a phonograph record 3. *Biol.* any disk-shaped part

dis·card (dis kärd') *vt.* [< OFr.: see DIS- & CARD[1]] 1. *Card Games* to throw away (undesired cards) 2. to get rid of as no longer useful —*vi. Card Games* to make a discard —*n.* (dis'kärd) 1. a discarding or being discarded 2. something discarded 3. *Card Games* the card or cards discarded

dis·cern (di surn', -zurn') *vt., vi.* [< L. *dis-*, apart + *cernere*, to separate] 1. to perceive or recognize clearly 2. to distinguish; differentiate —**dis·cern'i·ble** *adj.* —**dis·cern'i·bly** *adv.*

dis·cern'ing *adj.* having good judgment or understanding —**dis·cern'ing·ly** *adv.*

dis·cern'ment *n.* **1.** a discerning **2.** keen perception or judgment; insight

dis·charge (dis chärj') *vt.* -charged', -charg'ing [< L. *dis-,* from + *carrus,* wagon] **1.** to release or dismiss **2.** to unload (a cargo) **3.** to shoot (a gun or projectile) **4.** to emit *[to discharge* pus] **5.** to pay (a debt) or perform (a duty) **6.** *Elec.* to remove stored energy from (a battery, etc.) —*vi.* **1.** to get rid of a load, etc. **2.** to be released or thrown off **3.** to go off, as a gun **4.** to emit waste matter, as a wound —*n.* (*usually* dis'chärj) **1.** a discharging or being discharged **2.** that which discharges, as an order for release from military service **3.** that which is discharged **4.** a flow of electric current across a gap, as in a spark — **dis·charge'a·ble** *adj.* —**dis·charg'er** *n.*

dis·ci·ple (di sī'p'l) *n.* [< L. *dis-,* apart + *capere,* to hold] **1.** a pupil or follower of any teacher or school **2.** an early follower of Jesus, esp. one of the Apostles —**dis·ci'ple·ship'** *n.*

dis·ci·pli·nar·i·an (dis'ə pli ner'ē ən) *n.* one who believes in or enforces strict discipline

dis·ci·pline (dis'ə plin) *n.* [see DISCIPLE] **1.** training that develops self-control, efficiency, etc. **2.** strict control to enforce obedience **3.** orderly conduct **4.** a system of rules, as for a monastic order **5.** treatment that corrects or punishes —*vt.* -plined, -plin·ing **1.** to train; control **2.** to punish —**dis'ci·pli·nar'y** (-pli ner'ē) *adj.* —**dis'ci·plin·er** *n.*

disc jockey one who conducts a radio program of recorded music

dis·claim (dis klām') *vt.* **1.** to give up any claim to **2.** to repudiate —*vi.* to make a disclaimer

dis·claim'er *n.* **1.** a denial or renunciation, as of a claim or title **2.** a disavowing

dis·close (-klōz') *vt.* -closed', -clos'ing **1.** to bring into view; uncover **2.** to reveal; make known —**dis·clo'sure** (-klō'zhər) *n.*

dis·coid (dis'koid) *adj.* [< Gr. *diskos,* a disk + *eidos,* form] shaped like a disk

dis·col'or *vt., vi.* to change in color by fading, streaking, or staining —**dis·col'or·a'tion** *n.*

dis·com·fit (dis kum'fit) *vt.* [< L. *dis-* + *conficere,* prepare] **1.** orig., to defeat **2.** to frustrate the plans of **3.** to make uneasy; disconcert —**dis·com'fi·ture** (-fi chər) *n*

dis·com'fort *n.* **1.** lack of comfort; uneasiness **2.** anything causing this —*vt.* to cause discomfort to

dis·com·mode (dis'kə mōd') *vt.* -mod'ed, -mod'ing [< DIS- + L. *commodare,* make suitable] to cause bother to; inconvenience

dis·com·pose' (-kəm pōz') *vt.* -posed', -pos'ing **1.** to disturb; fluster; disconcert **2.** [Now Rare] to disarrange — **dis'com·po'sure** (-pō'zhər) *n.*

dis·con·cert' (-kən surt') *vt.* **1.** to upset (plans, etc.) **2.** to upset the composure of —**dis'con·cert'ing** *adj.* —**dis'·con·cert'ing·ly** *adv.*

dis·con·nect' (-kə nekt') *vt.* to break or undo the connection of; detach, unplug, etc. —**dis'con·nec'tion** *n.*

dis·con·nect'ed *adj.* **1.** separated, detached, etc. **2.** incoherent —**dis'con·nect'ed·ly** *adv.*

dis·con·so·late (dis kän'sə lit) *adj.* [see DIS- & CONSOLE¹] **1.** so unhappy that nothing will console **2.** causing dejection; cheerless

dis·con·tent (dis'kən tent') *adj. same as* DISCONTENTED —*n.* dissatisfaction: also **dis'con·tent'ment** —*vt.* to make discontented

dis·con·tent'ed *adj.* not contented; wanting something different —**dis'con·tent'ed·ly** *adv.*

dis·con·tin·ue (dis'kən tin'yōō) *vt., vi.* -ued, -u·ing **1.** to stop; cease; give up **2.** *Law* to stop (a suit) prior to trial —**dis'con·tin'u·ance, dis'con·tin'u·a'tion** *n.*

dis'con·tin'u·ous *adj.* not continuous; broken —**dis·con'·ti·nu'i·ty** (-kän'tə nōō'ə tē) *n.* —**dis'con·tin'u·ous·ly** *adv.*

dis·cord (dis'kôrd) *n.* [< L. *dis-,* apart + *cor,* heart] **1.** disagreement **2.** a harsh or confused noise **3.** *Music* a lack of harmony in tones sounded together —*vi.* (dis kôrd') to disagree; clash

dis·cord'ant *adj.* **1.** disagreeing; conflicting **2.** not in harmony; dissonant —**dis·cord'ance, dis·cord'an·cy** *n.* —**dis·cord'ant·ly** *adv.*

dis·count (dis'kount) *n.* [see DIS- & COMPUTE] **1.** a reduction from the usual or list price **2.** the rate of interest charged on a discounted bill —*vt.* (*also* dis kount') **1.** to pay or receive the value of (a promissory note, etc.) minus a deduction for interest **2.** to deduct an amount from (a bill, price, etc.) **3.** to sell at less than the regular price **4.** *a)* to allow for exaggeration, bias, etc. in (a story, etc.) *b)*

to disregard **5.** to reckon with in advance —**at a discount** below the regular price —**dis'count·a·ble** *adj.*

dis·coun·te·nance (dis koun'tə nəns) *vt.* -nanced, -nanc·ing **1.** to make ashamed or embarrassed **2.** to refuse approval or support to

discount house (or **store**) a retail store that sells goods for less than regular or list prices

dis·cour·age (dis kur'ij) *vt.* -aged, -ag·ing **1.** to deprive of courage; dishearten **2.** to persuade (a person) to refrain **3.** to try to prevent by disapproving —**dis·cour'age·ment** *n.* —**dis·cour'ag·ing** *adj.* —**dis·cour'ag·ing·ly** *adv.*

dis·course (dis'kôrs) *n.* [< L. *dis-,* from + *currere,* to run] **1.** talk; conversation **2.** a formal treatment of a subject, spoken or written —*vi.* (dis kôrs') -coursed', -cours'-ing **1.** to converse; talk **2.** to speak or write (*on* or *upon* a subject) formally

dis·cour·te·ous (dis kur'tē əs) *adj.* impolite; ill-mannered —**dis·cour'te·ous·ly** *adv.*

dis·cour·te·sy (-tə sē) *n.* **1.** impoliteness; rudeness **2.** *pl.* -sies a rude or impolite act or remark

dis·cov·er (dis kuv'ər) *vt.* [see DIS- & COVER] **1.** *a)* to be the first to find, see, or know about *b)* to be the first non-native person to come to, see, etc. **2.** to find out —**dis·cov'er·a·ble** *adj.* —**dis·cov'er·er** *n.*

dis·cov'er·y *n., pl.* -ies **1.** a discovering **2.** anything discovered

dis·cred·it (dis kred'it) *vt.* **1.** to reject as untrue **2.** to cast doubt on **3.** to disgrace —*n.* **1.** loss of belief; doubt **2.** disgrace **3.** something that causes disgrace —**dis·cred'it·a·ble** *adj.* —**dis·cred'it·a·bly** *adv.*

dis·creet (dis krēt') *adj.* [see DISCERN] careful about what one says or does; prudent —**dis·creet'ly** *adv.* —**dis·creet'·ness** *n.*

dis·crep·an·cy (dis krep'ən sē) *n., pl.* -cies [< L. *dis-,* from + *crepare,* to rattle] lack of agreement, or an instance of this; inconsistency —**dis·crep'ant** *adj.* —**dis·crep'ant·ly** *adv.*

dis·crete (dis krēt') *adj.* [see DISCERN] **1.** separate and distinct **2.** made up of distinct parts —**dis·crete'ly** *adv.* —**dis·crete'ness** *n.*

dis·cre·tion (dis kresh'ən) *n.* **1.** the freedom to make decisions **2.** the quality of being discreet; prudence —**at one's discretion** as one wishes —**dis·cre'tion·ar'y** (-er'ē) *adj.*

dis·crim·i·nate (dis krim'ə nāt') *vt.* -nat'ed, -nat'ing [see DISCERN] **1.** to differentiate **2.** to distinguish —*vi.* **1.** to distinguish (*between* things) **2.** to be discerning **3.** to show partiality or prejudice —*adj.* (-nit) distinguishing carefully —**dis·crim'i·nat'ing** *adj.* —**dis·crim'i·na'tive** *adj.*

dis·crim'i·na'tion *n.* **1.** the act of discriminating, or distinguishing differences **2.** the ability to do this **3.** a showing of partiality or prejudice in treatment

dis·crim'i·na·to'ry (-nə tôr'ē) *adj.* showing discrimination or bias

dis·cur·sive (dis kur'siv) *adj.* [see DISCOURSE] wandering from one topic to another; rambling —**dis·cur'sive·ly** *adv.* —**dis·cur'sive·ness** *n.*

dis·cus (dis'kəs) *n., pl.* **dis'cus·es, dis·ci** (dis'ī) [< Gr. *diskos*] a heavy disk, as of metal and wood, thrown in a contest of strength and skill

dis·cuss (dis kus') *vt.* [< L. *dis-,* apart + *quatere,* to shake] to talk or write about; consider the pros and cons of

dis·cus·sion (dis kush'ən) *n.* talk or writing in which the pros and cons of a subject are considered —**under discussion** being discussed

dis·dain (dis dān') *vt.* [< L. *dis-,* not + *dignari,* deign] to regard as beneath one's dignity; scorn —*n.* aloof contempt —**dis·dain'ful** *adj.*

DISCUS THROWER

dis·ease (di zēz') *n.* [see DIS- & EASE] **1.** illness in general **2.** a particular destructive process in an organism; specific illness **3.** a harmful condition —*vt.* -eased', -eas'ing to cause disease in —**dis·eased'** *adj.*

dis·em·bark (dis'im bärk') *vt., vi.* to leave, or unload from, a ship, etc. —**dis'em·bar·ka'tion** *n.*

dis·em·bod'y (-im bäd'ē) *vt.* -ied, -y·ing to free from bodily existence —**dis'em·bod'i·ment** *n.*

dis·em·bow'el (-im bou'əl) *vt.* -eled or -elled, -el·ing or -el·ling to take out the bowels of; eviscerate —**dis'em·bow'el·ment** *n.*

---

dis·en·chant' (-in chant') *vt.* to free from an enchantment or illusion —**dis'en·chant'ment** *n.*

dis·en·cum'ber (-in kum'bər) *vt.* to free from a burden or hindrance

dis·en·gage' (-in gāj') *vt., vi.* -gaged', -gag'ing to release or get loose from something that binds, holds, etc. —**dis'en·gage'ment** *n.*

dis·en·tan'gle (-in taŋ'g'l) *vt.* -gled, -gling to free from something that entangles, confuses, etc.; extricate; untangle —*vi.* to get free from a tangle —**dis'en·tan'gle·ment** *n.*

dis'es·tab'lish (-ə stab'lish) *vt.* **1.** to deprive of the status of being established **2.** to deprive (a state church) of official support by the government —**dis'es·tab'lish·ment** *n.*

dis'es·teem' (-ə stēm') *vt.* to hold in low esteem —*n.* lack of esteem; disfavor

dis·fa'vor (dis fā'vər) *n.* **1.** an unfavorable opinion; dislike; disapproval **2.** the state of being disliked or disapproved of —*vt.* to regard or treat unfavorably

dis·fig'ure (-fig'yər) *vt.* -ured, -ur·ing to hurt the appearance of; deface —**dis·fig'ure·ment, dis·fig'u·ra'tion** *n.*

dis·fran·chise (-fran'chīz) *vt.* -chised, -chis·ing to deprive of a right, privilege, etc., esp. of the right to vote: also **dis'en·fran'chise** —**dis·fran'chise·ment** *n.*

dis·gorge' (-gôrj') *vt., vi.* -gorged', -gorg'ing [< OFr.: see DIS- & GORGE] **1.** to vomit **2.** to pour forth (its contents)

dis·grace' (-grās') *n.* [< It. *dis-*, not + *grazia*, favor] **1.** loss of favor or respect; dishonor; shame **2.** a person or thing bringing shame —*vt.* -graced', -grac'ing to bring shame upon

dis·grace'ful *adj.* causing or characterized by disgrace; shameful —**dis·grace'ful·ly** *adv.*

dis·grun'tle (-grun't'l) *vt.* -tled, -tling [ult. < DIS- & GRUNT] to make peevishly discontented

dis·guise' (-gīz') *vt.* -guised', -guis'ing [< OFr.: see DIS- & GUISE] **1.** to make appear, sound, etc. so different as to be unrecognizable **2.** to hide the real nature of —*n.* **1.** any clothes, manner, etc. used for disguising **2.** the state of being disguised **3.** the act or practice of disguising

dis·gust' (-gust') *n.* [< DIS- + L. *gustus*, taste] a sickening dislike; deep aversion; repugnance —*vt.* to cause to feel disgust —**dis·gust'ed** *adj.* —**dis·gust'ing** *adj.*

dish (dish) *n.* [see DISCUS] **1.** *a)* a shallow, concave container for holding food *b)* [*pl.*] plates, bowls, cups, etc. collectively **2.** a particular kind of food **3.** as much as a dish will hold —*vt.* **1.** to serve in a dish (with *up* or *out*) **2.** to make concave

dis·ha·bille (dis'ə bēl') *n.* [< Fr. < *dés-*, DIS- + *habiller*, to dress] the state of being dressed only partially or in night clothes

dis·har·mo·ny (dis här'mə nē) *n.* lack of harmony; discord

dish'cloth' *n.* a cloth for washing dishes

dis·heart·en (dis härt'n) *vt.* to discourage; depress —**dis·heart'en·ing** *adj.* —**dis·heart'en·ment** *n.*

di·shev·el (di shev'l) *vt.* -eled or -elled, -el·ing or -el·ling [< OFr. *des-*, DIS- + *chevel*, hair] to cause (hair, clothes, etc.) to become disarranged; rumple —**di·shev'el·ment** *n.*

dis·hon'est *adj.* not honest; lying, cheating, etc. —**dis·hon'est·ly** *adv.*

dis·hon'es·ty *n.* **1.** a being dishonest **2.** *pl.* -ties a dishonest act or statement

dis·hon'or *n.* **1.** *a)* loss of honor, respect, etc. *b)* shame; disgrace **2.** a cause of dishonor **3.** a refusal or failure to pay a check, draft, etc. —*vt.* **1.** to treat disrespectfully **2.** to disgrace **3.** to refuse or fail to pay (a check, draft, etc.)

dis·hon'or·a·ble *adj.* causing or deserving dishonor; shameful —**dis·hon'or·a·bly** *adv.*

dish'pan' *n.* a pan in which dishes are washed

dis'il·lu'sion *vt.* **1.** to free from illusion or false ideas **2.** to take away the idealism of and make bitter, etc. —*n.* a disillusioning or being disillusioned: also **dis'il·lu'sion·ment**

dis·in·cline (dis'in klīn') *vt.* -clined', -clin'ing to make unwilling —**dis·in'cli·na'tion** *n.*

dis'in·fect' (-in fekt') *vt.* to destroy the harmful bacteria, viruses, etc. in or on —**dis'in·fec'tion** *n.*

dis'in·fect'ant (-ənt) *adj.* disinfecting —*n.* anything that disinfects

dis·in·gen·u·ous (dis'in jen'yoo wəs) *adj.* not straightforward; insincere

dis'in·her'it (-in her'it) *vt.* to deprive of an inheritance —**dis'in·her'it·ance** *n.*

dis·in·te·grate (dis in'tə grāt') *vt., vi.* -grat'ed, -grat'ing to separate into parts or fragments; break up —**dis·in'te·gra'tion** *n.* —**dis·in'te·gra'tive** *adj.* —**dis·in'te·gra'tor** *n.*

dis·in·ter (dis'in tur') *vt.* -terred', -ter'ring **1.** to dig up from a grave, etc.; exhume **2.** to bring to light —**dis'in·ter'ment** *n.*

dis·in·ter·est·ed (dis in'trist id, -tər ist-) *adj.* **1.** impartial; unbiased **2.** uninterested —**dis·in'ter·est·ed·ly** *adv.*

dis·join' (-join') *vt.* to separate or detach

dis·joint' (-joint') *vt.* **1.** to pull out of joint; dislocate **2.** to dismember **3.** to destroy the unity, connections, etc. of —*vi.* to come apart at the joints —**dis·joint'ed** *adj.* —**dis·joint'ed·ly** *adv.*

dis·junc'tive (-juŋk'tiv) *adj.* **1.** separating or causing to separate **2.** *Gram.* indicating a contrast or an alternative ["or" and "but" are *disjunctive* conjunctions] —**dis·junc'tive·ly** *adv.*

disk (disk) *n.* [see DISCUS] **1.** a thin, flat, circular thing **2.** *same as* DISC; specif., *a)* the disk-shaped center of certain composite flowers *b)* a layer of connective tissue between vertebrae

disk jockey *same as* DISC JOCKEY

dis·like' *vt.* -liked', -lik'ing to have a feeling of not liking —*n.* a feeling of not liking; distaste —**dis·lik'a·ble, dis·like'a·ble** *adj.*

dis·lo·cate (dis'lō kāt', dis lō'kāt) *vt.* -cat'ed, -cat'ing **1.** to displace (a bone) from its proper position at a joint **2.** to disarrange —**dis'lo·ca'tion** *n.*

dis·lodge' *vt., vi.* -lodged', -lodg'ing to force from or leave a place where lodged, hiding, etc. —**dis·lodg'ment** *n.*

dis·loy'al *adj.* not loyal or faithful —**dis·loy'al·ly** *adv.* —**dis·loy'al·ty** *n., pl.* -ties

dis·mal (diz'm'l) *adj.* [< ML. *dies mali*, evil days] **1.** causing gloom or misery **2.** dark and gloomy; dreary —**dis'mal·ly** *adv.*

dis·man·tle (dis man't'l) *vt.* -tled, -tling [see DIS- & MANTLE] **1.** to strip of covering **2.** to strip (a house, etc.) as of furniture **3.** to take apart —**dis·man'tle·ment** *n.*

dis·may' (-mā') *vt.* [< Anglo-Fr.] to make discouraged at the prospect of trouble; daunt —*n.* a loss of courage

dis·mem'ber (-mem'bər) *vt.* [see DIS- & MEMBER] **1.** to cut or tear the limbs from **2.** to cut or pull to pieces —**dis·mem'ber·ment** *n.*

dis·miss' (-mis') *vt.* [< L. *dis-*, from + *mittere*, to send] **1.** to cause or allow to leave **2.** to discharge from an office, employment, etc. **3.** to put out of one's mind **4.** *Law* to reject (a claim or action) —**dis·miss'al** *n.*

dis·mount' *vi.* to get off, as from a horse —*vt.* **1.** to remove (a thing) from its mounting **2.** to cause to get off **3.** to take apart

dis·o·be·di·ence (dis'ə bē'dē əns) *n.* refusal to obey; insubordination —**dis'o·be'di·ent** *adj.* —**dis'o·be'di·ent·ly** *adv.*

dis'o·bey' *vt., vi.* to refuse or fail to obey

dis'o·blige' *vt.* -bliged', -blig'ing **1.** to refuse to oblige **2.** to slight; offend —**dis'o·blig'ing** *adj.*

dis·or'der *n.* **1.** a lack of order; confusion **2.** a breach of public peace; riot **3.** irregularity **4.** an upset of normal function; ailment —*vt.* **1.** to throw into disorder **2.** to upset the normal functions of

dis·or'der·ly *adj.* **1.** not orderly; untidy; unsystematic **2.** unruly; riotous **3.** violating public peace, safety, etc. —**dis·or'der·li·ness** *n.*

dis·or·gan·ize (dis ôr'gə nīz') *vt.* -ized', -iz'ing to break up the order or system of; throw into disorder —**dis·or'gan·i·za'tion** *n.*

dis·o'ri·ent' (-ôr'ē ent') *vt.* **1.** to cause to lose one's bearings **2.** to confuse mentally Also **dis·o'ri·en·tate'** (-ən tāt') -tat'ed, -tat'ing —**dis·o'ri·en·ta'tion** *n.*

dis·own' *vt.* to refuse to acknowledge as one's own; cast off

dis·par'age (-par'ij) *vt.* -aged, -ag·ing [< OFr. *des-* (see DIS-) + *parage*, rank] **1.** to lower in esteem; discredit **2.** to belittle —**dis·par'age·ment** *n.* —**dis·par'ag·ing** *adj.*

dis·pa·rate (dis'pər it) *adj.* [< L. *dis-*, not + *par*, equal] distinct or different in kind; unequal —**dis·par'i·ty** (-par'ə tē) *n., pl.* -ties

dis·pas'sion·ate *adj.* free from passion, emotion, or bias; calm; impartial —**dis·pas'sion** *n.* —**dis·pas'sion·ate·ly** *adv.*

dis·patch (-pach') *vt.* [< L. *dis-*, not + LL. *impedicare*, to entangle] **1.** to send promptly, as on an errand **2.** to kill **3.** to finish quickly —*n.* **1.** a sending off **2.** a killing **3.** speed; promptness **4.** a message, esp. an official message **5.** a news story sent to a newspaper, etc., as by a reporter —**dis·patch'er** *n.*

dis·pel' (-pel') *vt.* -pelled', -pel'ling [< L. *dis-*, away + *pellere*, to drive] to scatter and drive away; disperse

dis·pen'sa·ble (-pen'sə b'l) *adj.* **1.** that can be given out **2.** that can be dispensed with

dis·pen'sa·ry (-sə rē) *n., pl.* **-ries** a room or place where medicines and first aid are available

dis·pen·sa'tion (-pən sā'shən) *n.* 1. a dispensing; distribution 2. anything distributed 3. an administrative system 4. a release from an obligation 5. *R.C.Ch.* an exemption from a specific church law 6. *Theol. a)* the ordering of events under divine authority *b)* any religious system —**dis'pen·sa'tion·al** *adj.*

dis·pen·sa·to·ry (dis pen'sə tôr'ē) *n., pl.* **-ries** a handbook on medicines

dis·pense (-pens') *vt.* **-pensed', -pens'ing** [< L. *dis-*, out + *pendere*, weigh] 1. to give out; distribute 2. to prepare and give out (medicines, etc.) 3. to administer [to *dispense* the law] 4. to exempt; excuse —**dispense with** 1. to get rid of 2. to do without —**dis·pen'ser** *n.*

dis·perse (-pʉrs') *vt.* **-persed', -pers'ing** [< L. *dis-*, out + *spargere*, strew] 1. to break up and scatter 2. to dispel (mist, etc.) 3. to break up (light) into its component colored rays —*vi.* to scatter —**dis·per'sal** *n.* —**dis·pers'er** *n.* —**dis·per'sion** *n.*

dis·pir·it (di spir'it) *vt.* to depress; deject —**dis·pir'it·ed** *adj.* —**dis·pir'it·ed·ly** *adv.*

dis·place *vt.* **-placed', -plac'ing** 1. to move from its usual place 2. to discharge 3. to replace

displaced person one forced from his country, esp. in war, and left homeless elsewhere

dis·place'ment *n.* 1. a displacing or being displaced 2. the weight or volume of air, water, or other fluid displaced by a floating object

dis·play' (-plā') *vt.* [< L. *dis-*, apart + *plicare*, to fold] 1. to unfold; spread out 2. to show off; exhibit 3. to disclose; reveal —*n.* 1. an exhibition 2. anything displayed 3. ostentation; show —**dis·play'er** *n.*

dis·please' *vt., vi.* **-pleased', -pleas'ing** to fail to please; offend

dis·pleas'ure (-plezh'ər) *n.* a being displeased; dissatisfaction, annoyance, etc.

dis·port' (-pôrt') *vi.* [< OFr. *des-* (see DIS-) + *porter*, carry] to play; frolic —*vt.* to amuse (oneself)

dis·pos'al (-pō'z'l) *n.* 1. a disposing; specif., *a)* arrangement *b)* a settling of affairs *c)* a giving away; transfer *d)* a getting rid of 2. the power to dispose 3. *same as* DISPOSER —**at one's disposal** available for use as one wishes

dis·pose (-pōz') *vt.* **-posed', -pos'ing** [see DIS- & POSITION] 1. to place in a certain order; arrange 2. to settle (affairs) 3. to make willing —*vi.* to have the power to settle affairs —**dispose of** 1. to deal with; settle 2. to give away or sell 3. to get rid of —**dis·pos'a·ble** *adj.*

dis·pos'er *n.* a garbage-grinding device installed in a sink drain

dis·po·si·tion (dis'pə zish'ən) *n.* 1. orderly arrangement 2. management of affairs 3. a selling or giving away 4. the power to dispose 5. an inclination or tendency 6. one's temperament

dis'pos·sess' *vt.* to deprive of the possession of land, a house, etc.; oust —**dis'pos·ses'sion** *n.* —**dis'pos·ses'sor** *n.*

dis·praise (dis prāz') *vt.* **-praised', -prais'ing** to disparage; censure —*n.* a dispraising; blame

dis·proof' *n.* 1. a disproving; refutation 2. evidence that disproves

dis'pro·por'tion *n.* lack of proportion —*vt.* to cause to be disproportionate

dis'pro·por'tion·ate (-it) *adj.* not in proportion —**dis'pro·por'tion·ate·ly** *adv.*

dis·prove' *vt.* **-proved', -prov'ing** to prove to be false or in error —**dis·prov'a·ble** *adj.*

dis·pu·ta·tion (dis'pyoo tā'shən) *n.* 1. a disputing; dispute 2. debate

dis'pu·ta'tious (-shəs) *adj.* inclined to dispute; fond of arguing —**dis'pu·ta'tious·ly** *adv.*

dis·pute (dis pyoot') *vi.* **-put'ed, -put'ing** [< L. *dis-*, apart + *putare*, think] 1. to argue; debate 2. to quarrel —*vt.* 1. to argue or debate (a question) 2. to doubt 3. to oppose in any way —*n.* 1. a disputing; argument 2. a quarrel —**in dispute** not settled —**dis·pu'ta·ble** *adj.* —**dis·pu'tant** *adj., n.*

dis·qual'i·fy' *vt.* **-fied', -fy'ing** to make or declare unqualified, unfit, or ineligible —**dis·qual'i·fi·ca'tion** (-fi kā'shən) *n.*

dis·qui'et (-kwī'ət) *vt.* to make anxious or restless; disturb —*n.* restlessness; anxiety: also **dis·qui'e·tude'** (-ə tood', -tyood')

dis·qui·si·tion (dis'kwə zish'ən) *n.* [< L. *dis-*, apart + *quaerere*, seek] a formal discourse; treatise

Dis·rae·li (diz rā'lē), **Benjamin** 1804–81; Eng. prime minister

dis·re·gard' *vt.* 1. to pay little or no attention to 2. to treat without due respect; slight —*n.* 1. lack of attention 2. lack of due regard or respect —**dis·re·gard'ful** *adj.*

dis·re·pair' *n.* the condition of needing repairs; state of neglect

dis·rep'u·ta·ble *adj.* 1. having or causing a bad reputation 2. not fit to be seen —**dis·rep'u·ta·bly** *adv.*

dis·re·pute' *n.* lack or loss of repute; bad reputation; disgrace

dis·re·spect' *n.* lack of respect; discourtesy —*vt.* to have or show a lack of respect for —**dis·re·spect'ful** *adj.* —**dis're·spect'ful·ly** *adv.*

dis·robe (dis rōb') *vt., vi.* **-robed', -rob'ing** to undress —**dis·rob'er** *n.*

dis·rupt' (-rupt') *vt., vi.* [< L. *dis-*, apart + *rumpere*, to break] 1. to break apart 2. to disturb or interrupt —**dis·rup'tion** *n.* —**dis·rup'tive** *adj.*

dis·sat·is·fy' *vt.* **-fied', -fy'ing** to fail to satisfy; discontent —**dis·sat'is·fac'tion** *n.*

dis·sect (di sekt', dī-) *vt.* [< L. *dis-*, apart + *secare*, to cut] 1. to cut apart piece by piece, as a body for purposes of study 2. to analyze closely —**dis·sec'tion** *n.* —**dis·sec'tor** *n.*

dis·sem·ble (di sem'b'l) *vt.* **-bled, -bling** [< OFr. *dessembler*] 1. to conceal (the truth, one's feelings, etc.) under a false appearance 2. to feign —*vi.* to conceal the truth, one's true feelings, etc. by pretense —**dis·sem'·blance** *n.* —**dis·sem'bler** *n.*

dis·sem·i·nate (di sem'ə nāt') *vt.* **-nat'ed, -nat'ing** [< L. *dis-*, apart + *seminare*, to sow] to scatter about; spread widely —**dis·sem'i·na'tion** *n.* —**dis·sem'i·na'tor** *n.*

dis·sen·sion (di sen'shən) *n.* 1. a dissenting; disagreement 2. violent quarreling

dis·sent (di sent') *vi.* [< L. *dis-*, apart + *sentire*, to feel] 1. to disagree 2. to reject the doctrines of an established church —*n.* a dissenting —**dis·sent'er** *n.* —**dis·sent'ing** *adj.*

dis·sen'tient (-sen'shənt) *adj.* dissenting, esp. from the majority opinion —*n.* one who dissents

dis·ser·ta·tion (dis'ər tā'shən) *n.* [< L. *dis-*, apart + *serere*, join] a formal discourse or treatise; thesis

dis·serv·ice (dis sʉr'vis) *n.* harm; injury

dis·sev·er (di sev'ər) *vt.* 1. to sever 2. to divide into parts —*vi.* to separate

dis·si·dence (dis'ə dəns) *n.* [< L. *dis-*, apart + *sidere*, sit] disagreement; dissent —**dis'si·dent** *adj., n.*

dis·sim·i·lar (di sim'ə lər) *adj.* not similar; different —**dis·sim'i·lar'i·ty** (-lar'ə tē) *n., pl.* **-ties** —**dis·sim'i·lar·ly** *adv.*

dis·si·mil·i·tude (dis'si mil'ə tood', -tyood') *n.* dissimilarity; difference

dis·sim·u·late (di sim'yə lāt') *vt., vi.* **-lat'ed, -lat'ing** [see DIS- & SIMULATE] to dissemble —**dis·sim'u·la'tion** *n.* —**dis·sim'u·la'tor** *n.*

dis·si·pate (dis'ə pāt') *vt.* **-pat'ed, -pat'ing** [< L. *dis-*, apart + *supare*, to throw] 1. to scatter 2. to make disappear 3. to waste or squander —*vi.* 1. to vanish 2. to indulge in pleasure to the point of harming oneself —**dis'si·pat'ed** *adj.* —**dis'si·pat'er, dis'si·pa'tor** *n.*

dis'si·pa'tion *n.* a dissipating or being dissipated; dispersion, squandering, dissoluteness, etc.

dis·so·ci·ate (di sō'shē āt', -sē-) *vt., vi.* **-at'ed, -at'ing** [< L. *dis-*, apart + *sociare*, join] 1. to sever association (with); disunite 2. to undergo or cause to undergo dissociation

dis·so'ci·a'tion *n.* 1. a dissociating or being dissociated 2. *Chem.* the breaking up of a compound into simpler components

dis·sol·u·ble (di säl'yoo b'l) *adj.* that can be dissolved —**dis·sol'u·bil'i·ty** *n.*

dis·so·lute (dis'ə loot') *adj.* [see DISSOLVE] dissipated and immoral; debauched —**dis'so·lute'ly** *adv.* —**dis'so·lute'·ness** *n.*

dis·so·lu·tion (dis'ə loo'shən) *n.* a dissolving or being dissolved; specif., *a)* a breaking up or into parts; disintegration *b)* a termination *c)* death

dis·solve (di zälv', -zôlv') *vt., vi.* **-solved', -solv'ing** [< L. *dis-*, apart + *solvere*, loosen] 1. to make or become liquid; melt 2. to pass or make pass into solution 3. to break up; decompose 4. to end as by breaking up; terminate 5. to disappear or make disappear —**dis·solv'a·ble** *adj.* —**dis·solv'er** *n.*

dis·so·nance (dis'ə nəns) *n.* [< L. *dis-*, apart + *sonus*, a sound] 1. an inharmonious combination of sounds 2. any lack of harmony or agreement —**dis'so·nant** *adj.* —**dis'so·nant·ly** *adv.*

dis·suade (di swād') *vt.* **-suad'ed, -suad'ing** [< L. *dis-*, away + *suadere*, persuade] to turn (a person) aside (*from* a course, etc.) by persuasion or advice —**dis·sua'sion** *n.* —**dis·sua'sive** *adj.*

dist. 1. distance 2. district

dis·taff (dis'taf) *n.* [< OE. *dis-*, flax + *stæf*, a staff] 1. a staff on which flax, wool, etc. is wound for use in spinning 2. woman's work or concerns 3. woman, or women in general —*adj.* female

DISTAFF

dis·tance (dis'təns) *n.* [< L. *dis-*, apart + *stare*, to stand] 1. a being separated in space or time; remoteness 2. an interval between two points in space or time 3. a remoteness in relationship or in behavior 4. a remote point in space or time —*vt.* **-tanced, -tanc·ing** to leave behind; outdistance

dis'tant (-tənt) *adj.* 1. far away in space or time 2. away [ten miles *distant*] 3. far apart in relationship [a *distant* cousin] 4. cool in manner; aloof 5. from or at a distance —**dis'tant·ly** *adv.*

dis·taste (dis tāst') *n.* dislike or aversion (*for*)

dis·taste'ful *adj.* unpleasant; disagreeable —**dis·taste'ful·ly** *adv.* —**dis·taste'ful·ness** *n.*

dis·tem·per (dis tem'pər) *vt.* [< L. *dis-*, apart + *temperare*, to mix in proportion] to derange; disorder —*n.* 1. a mental or physical disorder; disease 2. an infectious virus disease of young dogs 3. civil disorder

dis·tend (dis tend') *vt., vi.* [< L. *dis-*, apart + *tendere*, to stretch] 1. to stretch out 2. to make or become swollen —**dis·ten'si·ble** *adj.* —**dis·ten'tion, dis·ten'sion** *n.*

dis·tich (dis'tik) *n.* [< Gr. *di-*, two + *stichos*, a row] two lines of verse regarded as a unit; couplet

dis·till, dis·til (dis til') *vt., vi.* **-tilled', -till'ing** [< L. *de-*, down + *stillare*, to drip] 1. to fall or let fall in drops 2. to undergo, subject to, or produce by distillation —**dis·till'er** *n.*

dis·til·late (dis'tə lāt', -t'l it) *n.* 1. a liquid obtained by distilling 2. the essence of anything

dis·til·la·tion (dis'tə lā'shən) *n.* 1. a distilling 2. the process of heating a mixture and condensing the resulting vapor to produce a more nearly pure substance 3. a distillate

dis·till'er·y *n., pl.* **-ies** a place where distilling is carried on

dis·tinct (dis tiŋkt') *adj.* [see DISTINGUISH] 1. not alike; different 2. separate 3. clearly marked off; plain 4. unmistakable —**dis·tinct'ly** *adv.* —**dis·tinct'ness** *n.*

dis·tinc'tion (-tiŋk'shən) *n.* 1. the act of making or keeping distinct 2. difference 3. a quality or feature that differentiates 4. fame; eminence 5. the quality that makes one seem superior 6. a mark of honor

dis·tinc'tive *adj.* making distinct; characteristic —**dis·tinc'tive·ly** *adv.* —**dis·tinc'tive·ness** *n.*

dis·tin·gué (dis taŋ gā') *adj.* [Fr.] having an air of distinction: also, sometimes, **dis·tin·guée'** *fem.*

dis·tin·guish (dis tiŋ'gwish) *vt.* [< L. *dis-*, apart + *-stinguere*, to prick] 1. to perceive or show the difference in 2. to characterize 3. to perceive clearly 4. to classify 5. to make famous or eminent —*vi.* to make a distinction (*between* or *among*) —**dis·tin'guish·a·ble** *adj.* —**dis·tin'guish·a·bly** *adv.*

dis·tin'guished *adj.* 1. celebrated; famous 2. having an air of distinction

dis·tort (dis tôrt') *vt.* [< L. *dis-*, intens. + *torquere*, to twist] 1. to twist out of shape 2. to misrepresent —**dis·tort'er** *n.* —**dis·tor'tion** *n.*

dis·tract (dis trakt') *vt.* [< L. *dis-*, apart + *trahere*, to draw] 1. to draw (the mind, etc.) away in another direction; divert 2. to create conflict and confusion in —**dis·tract'ed** *adj.* —**dis·tract'ing** *adj.*

dis·trac'tion *n.* 1. a distracting or being distracted; confusion 2. anything that distracts confusingly or amusingly; diversion 3. great mental distress

dis·trait (dis trā') *adj.* [see DISTRACT] absent-minded; inattentive

dis·traught' (-trôt') *adj.* [var. of prec.] 1. very troubled or confused 2. driven mad; crazed

dis·tress (dis tres') *vt.* [< L. *dis-*, apart + *stringere*, to stretch] to cause misery or suffering to —*n.* 1. pain, suffering, etc. 2. an affliction 3. a state of danger or trouble —**dis·tress'ful** *adj.* —**dis·tress'ing** *adj.*

dis·tressed' *adj.* 1. full of distress 2. given an antique appearance, as by having the finish marred 3. designating an area having much poverty

dis·trib·ute (dis trib'yoot) *vt.* **-ut·ed, -ut·ing** [< L. *dis-*, apart + *tribuere*, allot] 1. to give out in shares 2. to spread out 3. to classify 4. to put (things) in various distinct places —**dis·trib'ut·a·ble** *adj.*

dis·tri·bu·tion (dis'trə byoo'shən) *n.* 1. a distributing or being distributed 2. the process by which commodities get to consumers 3. anything distributed

dis·trib·u·tive (dis trib'yoo tiv) *adj.* 1. distributing or tending to distribute 2. *Gram.* referring to each member of a group regarded individually —**dis·trib'u·tive·ly** *adv.*

dis·trib'u·tor *n.* one that distributes; specif., *a*) a dealer that distributes goods to consumers *b*) a device for distributing electric current to spark plugs

dis·trict (dis'trikt) *n.* [Fr. < L. *dis-*, apart + *stringere*, to stretch] 1. a geographic or political division made for a specific purpose 2. any region

district attorney the prosecuting attorney for the State or Federal government in a specified district

District of Columbia Federal district of the U.S., on the Potomac: 69 sq. mi.; pop. 757,000; coextensive with the city of Washington: abbrev. *D.C., DC*

dis·trust (dis trust') *n.* a lack of trust; doubt —*vt.* to have no trust in; doubt —**dis·trust'ful** *adj.*

dis·turb (dis turb') *vt.* [< L. *dis-*, intens. + *turbare*, to disorder] 1. to break up the quiet or settled order of 2. to make uneasy 3. to interrupt

dis·turb'ance *n.* 1. a disturbing or being disturbed 2. anything that disturbs 3. commotion; disorder

dis·un·ion (dis yoon'yən) *n.* 1. the ending of union; separation 2. lack of unity; discord

dis·u·nite (dis'yoo nīt') *vt.* **-nit'ed, -nit'ing** to destroy the unity of; separate —*vi.* to become separated —**dis·u'ni·ty** (-yoo'nə tē) *n.*

dis·use (dis yoos') *n.* lack of use

ditch (dich) *n.* [OE. *dic*] a long, narrow channel dug into the earth, as for drainage —*vt.* 1. to make a ditch in 2. [Slang] to get rid of or away from —*vi.* to dig a ditch

dith·er (dith'ər) *vi.* [prob. akin to ME. *daderen*, dodder] to be nervously excited or confused —*n.* an excited state

dith·y·ramb (dith'ə ram', -ramb') *n.* [< Gr. *dithyrambos*] 1. in ancient Greece, a wild choral hymn in honor of Dionysus 2. any wildly emotional speech or writing —**dith'y·ram'bic** *adj., n.*

dit·to (dit'ō) *n., pl.* **-tos** [It. < L. *dicere*, speak] 1. the same (as above or before) 2. *same as* DITTO MARK —*adv.* as said before —*vt.* **-toed, -to·ing** 1. to duplicate 2. to repeat

ditto mark a mark (") used in lists or tables to show that the item above is to be repeated

dit·ty (dit'ē) *n., pl.* **-ties** [< L. *dicere*, speak] a short, simple song

ditty bag (or **box**) [< ? obs. *dutty*, coarse calico] a small bag (or box) used as by sailors for carrying sewing equipment, toilet articles, etc.

di·u·ret·ic (dī'yoo ret'ik) *adj.* [< Gr. *dia-*, through + *ourein*, urinate] increasing the flow of urine —*n.* a diuretic drug or substance

di·ur·nal (dī ur'n'l) *adj.* [< L. *dies*, day] 1. daily 2. of or in the daytime —**di·ur'nal·ly** *adv.*

div. 1. dividend 2. division 3. divorced

di·va (dē'və) *n., pl.* **-vas** [It. < L., goddess] a prima donna in grand opera

di·va·lent (dī vā'lənt) *adj. Chem. same as* BIVALENT

di·van (dī'van, di van') *n.* [< Per. *dīwān*] a large, low couch or sofa

dive (dīv) *vi.* **dived** or **dove, dived, div'ing** [OE. *dyfan*] 1. to plunge headfirst into water 2. to submerge 3. to plunge suddenly into something 4. to make a steep descent, as an airplane —*n.* 1. a plunge into water 2. any sudden plunge 3. a sharp descent, as of an airplane 4. [Colloq.] a cheap, disreputable bar, etc.

dive bomber an airplane that releases bombs while diving at a target —**dive'bomb'** *vt., vi.*

div'er *n.* one that dives; specif., *a*) one who works or explores under water *b*) a diving bird

di·verge (də vurj', dī-) *vi.* **-verged', -verg'ing** [< L. *dis-*, apart + *vergere*, to turn] 1. to branch off or go in different directions 2. to take on gradually a different form [customs *diverge*] 3. to differ, as in opinion —**di·ver'gence** *n.* —**di·ver'gent** *adj.*

di·vers (dī'vərz) *adj.* [OFr.: see DIVERSE] various

di·verse (dī vurs', də-) *adj.* [< L. *dis-*, apart + *vertere*, to turn] 1. different 2. varied —**di·verse'ly** *adv.* —**di·verse'ness** *n.*

di·ver·si·fy (də vur′sə fī′) *vt.* **-fied′, -fy′ing** to make diverse; vary —**di·ver′si·fi·ca′tion** *n.*

di·ver·sion (də vur′zhən, dī-) *n.* **1.** a diverting, or turning aside **2.** distraction of attention **3.** a pastime

di·ver′sion·ar′y *adj.* serving to divert or distract *[diversionary military tactics]*

di·ver·si·ty (də vur′sə tē, dī-) *n., pl.* **-ties 1.** difference **2.** variety

di·vert′ (-vurt′) *vt.* [see DIVERSE] **1.** to turn aside; deflect **2.** to amuse —**di·vert′ing** *adj.*

‡**di·ver·tisse·ment** (dē ver tês män′) *n.* [Fr.] **1.** a diversion; amusement **2.** a short ballet, etc.

di·vest (də vest′, dī-) *vt.* [< L. *dis-*, from + *vestire*, to dress] **1.** to strip (*of* clothing, etc.) **2.** to deprive (*of* rank, rights, etc.) **3.** to rid (*of* something)

di·vide (də vīd′) *vt.* **-vid′ed, -vid′ing** [< L. *dividere*] **1.** to separate into parts; split up **2.** to classify **3.** to make or keep separate **4.** to apportion **5.** to cause to disagree **6.** *Math.* to separate into equal parts by a divisor **7.** *Mech.* to mark off the divisions of —*vi.* **1.** to be or become separate **2.** to disagree **3.** to share **4.** *Math.* to do division —*n.* a ridge that divides two drainage areas —**di·vid′er** *n.*

di·vid′ed *adj.* **1.** separated into parts **2.** having distinct indentations, as some leaves **3.** disagreeing

div·i·dend (div′ə dend′) *n.* **1.** the number or quantity to be divided **2.** *a*) a sum to be divided among stockholders, etc. *b*) a single share of this **3.** a bonus

div·i·na·tion (div′ə nā′shən) *n.* [see DIVINE] the practice of trying to foretell the future or the unknown

di·vine (də vīn′) *adj.* [< L. *divus*, a god] **1.** of, like, or from God or a god **2.** devoted to God; religious **3.** supremely great, good, etc. —*n.* a clergyman —*vt.* -vined′, -vin′ing **1.** to prophesy **2.** to guess **3.** to find out by intuition —**di·vine′ly** *adv.* —**di·vin′er** *n.*

Divine Comedy a long narrative poem in Italian, written (c.1307–21) by Dante Alighieri

diving bell a large, hollow, air-filled apparatus in which divers can work under water

diving board a board projecting horizontally over a swimming pool, lake, etc., for diving

divining rod a forked stick alleged to dip downward when held over underground water or minerals

di·vin·i·ty (də vin′ə tē) *n., pl.* **-ties 1.** a being divine **2.** a god **3.** theology —**the Divinity** God

di·vis·i·ble (də viz′ə b'l) *adj.* that can be divided, esp. without leaving a remainder —**di·vis′i·bil′i·ty** *n.*

di·vi·sion (də vizh′ən) *n.* **1.** a dividing or being divided **2.** a sharing **3.** a difference of opinion **4.** anything that divides; partition **5.** a segment, section, department, class, etc. **6.** the process of finding out how many times a number (the *divisor*) is contained in another (the *dividend*) **7.** a major military unit **8.** a major taxonomic category in botany —**di·vi′sion·al** *adj.*

division sign (or **mark**) the symbol (÷) indicating that the preceding number is to be divided by the following number (Ex.: 8÷4=2)

di·vi·sor (də vī′zər) *n. Math.* the number or quantity by which the dividend is divided

di·vorce (də vôrs′) *n.* [< L. *dis-*, apart + *vertere*, to turn] **1.** legal dissolution of a marriage **2.** any complete separation —*vt.* -vorced′, -vorc′ing **1.** to dissolve legally a marriage between **2.** to separate from (one's spouse) by divorce **3.** to separate; disunite —*vi.* to get a divorce —**di·vorce′ment** *n.*

di·vor·cée, di·vor·cee (də vôr′sā′, -sē′) *n.* [Fr.] a divorced woman —**di·vor′cé′** *n.masc.*

div·ot (div′ət) *n.* [Scot.] a lump of turf dislodged by a golf club in making a stroke

di·vulge (də vulj′) *vt.* -vulged′, -vulg′ing [< L. *dis-*, apart + *vulgare*, make public] to make known; reveal —**di·vul′-gence** *n.* —**di·vul′ger** *n.*

div·vy (div′ē) *vt., vi.* -vied, -vy·ing [Slang] to share; divide (*up*)

Dix·ie (dik′sē) *n.* the Southern States of the U.S.

Dix·ie·land′ *adj.* in, of, or like the style of jazz associated with New Orleans

diz·zy (diz′ē) *adj.* -zi·er, -zi·est [OE. *dysig*, foolish] **1.** feeling giddy or unsteady **2.** causing dizziness **3.** confused **4.** [Colloq.] silly —*vt.* -zied, -zy·ing to make dizzy —**diz′zi·ly** *adv.* —**diz′zi·ness** *n.*

D.J., DJ disc jockey

Dji·bou·ti (ji bōot′ē) country in E Africa: 8,500 sq. mi.; pop. 180,000

DNA [< *d(eoxyribo)n(ucleic) a(cid)*] an essential compo-

nent of all living matter and the basic chromosomal material transmitting the hereditary pattern

Dne·pr (nē′pər) river in W U.S.S.R., flowing into the Black Sea: 1,420 mi.

Dnes·tr (nēs′tər) river in SW U.S.S.R., flowing into the Black Sea: c.850 mi.

do¹ (dōō) *vt.* **did, done, do′ing** [OE. *don*] **1.** to perform (an action, etc.) **2.** to finish; complete **3.** to cause *[it does no harm]* **4.** to exert *[do* your best*]* **5.** to deal with as required *[do* the ironing*]* **6.** to have as one's occupation; work at **7.** to work out; solve *[do* a problem*]* **8.** to produce (a play, etc.) **9.** to cover (distance) *[to do a* mile in four minutes*]* **10.** to be convenient to; suit *[this will do* me very well*]* **11.** [Colloq.] to cheat **12.** [Colloq.] to serve (a jail term) **13.** [Slang] to take; use *[to do drugs]* —*vi.* **1.** to behave *[he does* well when praised*]* **2.** to be active *[do, don't talk]* **3.** to get along; fare *[the patient is doing* well*]* **4.** to be adequate *[that necktie will do]* **5.** to take place *[anything doing* tonight?*]* Auxiliary uses of *do:* **1.** to give emphasis *[please do* stay*]* **2.** to ask a question *[did* you go?*]* **3.** to serve as a substitute verb *[love me as I do* (love) you*]* —**do in** [Slang] to kill —**do over** [Colloq.] to redecorate —**do up** [Colloq.] to wrap up —**do with** to make use of —**do without** to get along without —**have to do with 1.** to be related to **2.** to deal with —**make do** to get along with what is available

do² (dō) *n.* [It.] *Music* a syllable representing the first or last tone of the diatonic scale

do. ditto

do·a·ble (dōō′ə b'l) *adj.* that can be done

dob·bin (däb′in) *n.* [< *Dobbin*, nickname for Robert] a horse, esp. a plodding, patient one

Do·ber·man pin·scher (dō′bər mən pin′shər) [< G.] a large dog with smooth dark hair and tan markings

doc·ile (däs′'l) *adj.* [Fr. < L. *docere*, teach] easy to discipline; tractable —**do·cil·i·ty** (dä sil′ə tē) *n.*

dock¹ (däk) *n.* [< It. *doccia*, canal] **1.** a large excavated basin for receiving ships between voyages **2.** a landing pier; wharf **3.** the water between two piers **4.** a platform for loading and unloading trucks, etc. —*vt.* to pilot (a ship) to a dock —*vi.* to come into a dock

dock² (däk) *n.* [< Fl. *dok*, cage] the place where the accused stands or sits in court

dock³ (däk) *n.* [OE. *docce*] a coarse weed related to buckwheat, with large leaves

dock⁴ (däk) *n.* [< ON. *dockr*] the solid part of an animal's tail —*vt.* **1.** to cut off the end of (a tail); bob **2.** to deduct from (wages, etc.)

dock·age (-ij) *n.* **1.** docking accommodations **2.** the fee for this **3.** the docking of ships

dock·et (däk′it) *n.* [earlier *doggette*, a register] **1.** a list of cases to be tried by a law court **2.** any list of things to be done —*vt.* to enter in a docket

dock′yard′ *n.* a place with docks, machinery, etc. for repairing or building ships

doc·tor (däk′tər) *n.* [L., teacher] **1.** a person on whom a university has conferred a high degree, as a Ph.D. **2.** a physician or surgeon (M.D.) **3.** a person licensed to practice any of the healing arts —*vt.* [Colloq.] **1.** to try to heal **2.** to mend **3.** to tamper with —**doc′tor·al** *adj.*

doc′tor·ate (-it) *n.* the degree of doctor conferred by a university

doc·tri·naire (däk′trə ner′) *adj.* [Fr.] adhering to a doctrine in an unyielding, dogmatic way

doc·trine (däk′trən) *n.* [see DOCTOR] something taught as the principles of a religion, political party, etc.; tenet or tenets; dogma —**doc′tri·nal** *adj.*

doc·u·ment (däk′yə mənt) *n.* [< L. *documentum*, proof] anything written, printed, etc., relied upon to record or prove something —*vt.* (-ment′) to provide with or support by documents —**doc′u·men·ta′tion** *n.*

doc′u·men′ta·ry (-men′tə rē) *adj.* **1.** of or supported by documents **2.** dramatically showing or analyzing news events, social conditions, etc. in nonfictional form —*n., pl.* **-ries** a documentary film, TV show, etc.

dod·der (däd′ər) *vi.* [ME. *daderen*] **1.** to shake or tremble, as from old age **2.** to totter —**dod′der·ing** *adj.*

Do·dec·a·nese (dō dek′ə nēz′, -nēs′) group of Greek islands in the Aegean

dodge (däj) *vi., vt.* **dodged, dodg′ing** [? akin to Scot. *dod*, to jog] **1.** to move quickly aside, or avoid by so moving **2.** to use tricks or evasions, or evade by so doing —*n.* **1.** a dodging **2.** a trick used in evading or cheating —**dodg′er** *n.*

do·do (dō′dō) *n., pl.* **-dos, -does** [Port. *doudo*, lit., stupid] a large flightless bird, now extinct

doe (dō) *n.* [OE. *da*] the female of the deer, antelope, rabbit, etc.

do·er (dōō′ər) *n.* **1.** one who does something **2.** one who gets things done

does (duz) *3d pers. sing., pres. indic., of* DO¹

doe·skin (dō′skin′) *n.* **1.** leather from the skin of a female deer **2.** a soft wool cloth

does·n't (duz′nt) does not

doff (däf, dôf) *vt.* [see DO¹ & OFF] **1.** to take off (one's clothes); esp., to remove or raise (one's hat) **2.** to discard

DODO
(2 ft. high)

dog (dôg) *n.* [OE. *docga*] **1.** a domesticated animal related to the fox, wolf, and jackal **2.** a mean, contemptible fellow **3.** a mechanical device for holding or grappling **4.** [*pl.*] [Slang] feet **5.** [Slang] an unsatisfactory person or thing —*vt.* **dogged, dog′ging** to follow or hunt like a dog —*adv.* very [*dog*-tired] —**dog eat dog** ruthless competition —**go to the dogs** [Colloq.] to deteriorate —**put on the dog** [Slang] to make a show of being elegant, wealthy, etc.

dog′cart′ *n.* **1.** a small cart drawn by dogs **2.** an open carriage with two seats back to back

dog days hot, humid days in July and August

doge (dōj) *n.* [It. < L. *dux*, leader] the chief magistrate in the former republics of Venice and Genoa

dog′-ear′ *n.* a turned-down corner of the leaf of a book — *vt.* to turn down the corner of (a leaf or leaves in a book) —**dog′-eared′** *adj.*

dog′fight′ *n.* combat as between fighter planes at close quarters

dog′fish′ *n., pl.:* see FISH any of various small sharks

dog·ged (dôg′id) *adj.* persistent; stubborn —**dog′ged·ly** *adv.* —**dog′ged·ness** *n.*

dog·ger·el (dôg′ər əl) *n.* [prob. < It. *doga*, barrel stave] trivial verse, poorly constructed and usually comic

dog′gone′ *interj.* damn! darn! —*vt.* **-goned′, -gon′ing** [Colloq.] to damn —*adj.* [Colloq.] damned

dog·gy, dog·gie (dôg′ē) *n., pl.* **-gies** a little dog: a child's word —*adj.* **-gi·er, -gi·est** of or like a dog

dog′house′ *n.* a dog's shelter —**in the doghouse** [Slang] in disfavor

do·gie, do·gy (dō′gē) *n., pl.* **-gies** [< ?] in the western U.S., a stray or motherless calf

dog·ma (dôg′mə) *n., pl.* **-mas, -ma·ta** (-mə tə) [< Gr. *dokein*, think] **1.** a doctrine; belief; esp., a body of theological doctrines authoritatively affirmed **2.** a positive, arrogant assertion of opinion

dog·mat·ic (-mat′ik) *adj.* **1.** of or like dogma **2.** asserted without proof **3.** stating opinion in a positive or arrogant manner: also **dog·mat′i·cal** —**dog·mat′i·cal·ly** *adv.*

dog·ma·tism (-tiz′m) *n.* dogmatic assertion of opinion, usually without evidence —**dog′ma·tist** *n.*

dog′ma·tize′ (-tīz′) *vt., vi.* **-tized′, -tiz′ing** to speak or write dogmatically

dog sled (or **sledge**) a sled (or sledge) drawn by dogs

Dog Star **1.** a star in the constellation Canis Major, the brightest star in the sky; Sirius **2.** Procyon

dog tag **1.** a license tag for a dog **2.** [Slang] a military identification tag worn about the neck

dog′tooth′ violet a small N. American plant with mottled leaves and white lilylike flowers

dog′trot′ *n.* a slow, easy trot

dog′watch′ *n.* *Naut.* a duty period, either from 4 to 6 P.M. or from 6 to 8 P.M.

dog′wood′ *n.* a small tree of the eastern U.S., with groups of small flowers surrounded by four large white or pink bracts

doi·ly (doi′lē) *n., pl.* **-lies** [after a 17th-c. London draper] a small mat, as of lace or paper, used to protect or decorate a surface

do·ings (dōō′iŋz) *n.pl.* things done; actions

dol·drums (däl′drəmz, dōl′-) *n.pl.* [< ? DULL] **1.** low spirits **2.** sluggishness **3.** equatorial ocean regions noted for dead calms

dole (dōl) *n.* [OE. *dal*] **1.** money or food given in charity **2.** anything given sparingly **3.** money paid by a government to the unemployed —*vt.* **doled, dol′ing** to give sparingly or as a dole —**on the dole** receiving a dole (sense 3)

dole·ful (dōl′fəl) *adj.* [< L. *dolere*, suffer] sad; mournful — **dole′ful·ly** *adv.* —**dole′ful·ness** *n.*

doll (däl) *n.* [< nickname for *Dorothy*] **1.** a child's toy made to resemble a human being **2.** a pretty but silly young woman **3.** [Slang] any attractive or lovable person

—*vt., vi.* [Colloq.] to dress stylishly or showily (with *up*)

dol·lar (däl′ər) *n.* [< G. *thaler*] **1.** the monetary unit of the U.S., equal to 100 cents **2.** the monetary unit of various other countries, as Canada **3.** a coin or paper bill of the value of a dollar

dol·lop (däl′əp) *n.* [< ?] **1.** a soft mass **2.** a quantity, often a small one

dol·ly (däl′ē) *n., pl.* **-lies** **1.** a doll: child's word **2.** a low, flat, wheeled frame for moving heavy objects

dol·men (däl′mən) *n.* [Fr. < Bret. *taol*, a table + *men*, stone] a prehistoric monument formed by a large, flat stone laid across upright stones

do·lo·mite (dō′lə mīt′) *n.* [< *Dolomieu*, 18th-c. Fr. geologist] a common rock-forming mineral

do·lor (dō′lər) *n.* [< L. *dolere*, suffer] [Poetic] sorrow

do·lor·ous (dō′lər əs, däl′ər-) *adj.* **1.** sorrowful; sad **2.** painful —**do′lor·ous·ly** *adv.*

dol·phin (däl′fən) *n.* [< Gr. *delphis*] any of several water-dwelling mammals, often with a beaklike snout

dolt (dōlt) *n.* [< ? DULL] a stupid, slow-witted person — **dolt′ish** *adj.*

-dom [OE. *dom*, state] *a suffix meaning:* **1.** the rank, position, or dominion of [*kingdom*] **2.** fact or state of being [*martyrdom*] **3.** a total of all who are [*officialdom*]

do·main (dō mān′, də-) *n.* [< L. *dominus*, master] **1.** territory under one government or ruler **2.** land belonging to one person; estate **3.** field of activity or influence

dome (dōm) *n.* [< Gr. *dōma*, housetop] **1.** a rounded roof or ceiling **2.** any dome-shaped structure —*vt.* **domed, dom′ing 1.** to cover as with a dome **2.** to form into a dome —*vi.* to swell out like a dome

do·mes·tic (də mes′tik) *adj.* [< L. *domus*, house] **1.** of the home or family **2.** of or made in one's country **3.** tame: said of animals **4.** home-loving —*n.* a servant for the home, as a maid —**do·mes′ti·cal·ly** *adv.*

do·mes′ti·cate′ (-tə kāt′) *vt.* **-cat′ed, -cat′ing 1.** to accustom to home life **2.** to tame for man's use —*vi.* to become domestic —**do·mes′ti·ca′tion** *n.*

do·mes·tic·i·ty (dō′mes tis′ə tē) *n., pl.* **-ties 1.** home life, or devotion to it **2.** [*pl.*] household affairs

dom·i·cile (däm′ə sīl′, -sil; dō′mə-) *n.* [< L. *domus*, house] a home; residence —*vt.* **-ciled′, -cil′ing** to establish (oneself or another) in a domicile

dom·i·nant (däm′ə nənt) *adj.* **1.** dominating; ruling; prevailing **2.** *Genetics* designating or of that one of a pair of alleles that predominates over the other and appears in the organism **3.** *Music* of or based upon the fifth note of a diatonic scale —*n.* *Music* the fifth note of a diatonic scale —**dom′i·nance** *n.* —**dom′i·nant·ly** *adv.*

dom′i·nate′ (-nāt′) *vt., vi.* **-nat′ed, -nat′ing** [< L. *dominus*, master] **1.** to rule or control by superior power **2.** to rise high above (the surroundings, etc.) —**dom′i·na′tion** *n.*

dom·i·neer (däm′ə nir′) *vt., vi.* [< Du. < L.: see prec.] to rule (*over*) in a harsh or arrogant way; tyrannize

dom′i·neer′ing *adj.* overbearing

Dom·i·nic (däm′ə nik), Saint 1170–1221; Sp. priest: founder of the Dominican order

Dom·i·ni·ca (däm′ə nē′kə, də min′i kə) island country in the West Indies: 290 sq. mi.; pop. 80,000

Do·min·i·can (də min′i kən) *adj.* **1.** of Saint Dominic or of a mendicant order founded by him **2.** of the Dominican Republic —*n.* **1.** a friar or nun of one of the Dominican orders **2.** a native or inhabitant of the Dominican Republic

Dominican Republic country occupying the E part of Hispaniola: 18,816 sq. mi.; pop. 4,012,000; cap. Santo Domingo

dom·i·nie (däm′ə nē) *n.* [see DOMINATE] **1.** in Scotland, a schoolmaster **2.** [Colloq.] a clergyman

do·min·ion (də min′yən) *n.* [see DOMAIN] **1.** rule or power to rule **2.** a governed territory **3.** [D-] formerly, any of certain self-governing member nations of the British Commonwealth of Nations

Dominion Day in Canada, July 1, a legal holiday, the anniversary of the proclamation in 1867 of the establishment of the Dominion of Canada

dom·i·no (däm′ə nō′) *n., pl.* **-noes′, -nos′** [Fr. & It.] **1.** a loose cloak with a hood and mask, worn at masquerades **2.** a mask for the eyes **3.** a small oblong tile marked with dots **4.** [*pl., with sing. v.*] a game played with such pieces

Don (dän) river of the C European R.S.F.S.R., flowing south into the Sea of Azov: c.1,200 mi.

don¹ (dän) *n.* [Sp. < L. *dominus*, master] **1.** [D-] Sir; Mr.: a Spanish title of respect **2.** a Spanish gentleman **3.** [Colloq.] a tutor at a British college

don² (dän) *vt.* **donned, don′ning** [contr. of *do on*] to put on (a garment, etc.)

‡**do·ña** (dô'nyä) *n., pl.* **-ñas** (-nyäs) [Sp. < L. *domina,* mistress] a lady: as a title [**D-**], equivalent to *Lady, Madam*

do·nate (dō'nāt) *vt., vi.* **-nat·ed, -nat·ing** [prob. < DONATION] to give or contribute —**do'na·tor** *n.*

do·na'tion *n.* [< L. *donum,* gift] **1.** the act of donating **2.** a gift or contribution

done (dun) *pp.* of DO¹ —*adj.* **1.** completed **2.** sufficiently cooked **3.** socially acceptable —**done** (**for**) [Colloq.] dead, ruined, etc. —**done in** [Colloq.] exhausted

don·jon (dun'jən, dän'-) *n.* [old sp. of DUNGEON] the heavily fortified inner tower of a castle

Don Ju·an (dän' jōo'ən, dän' wän') **1.** *Sp. Legend* a dissolute nobleman and seducer of women **2.** any man who seduces women; libertine

don·key (däŋ'kē, dôŋ'-, duŋ'-) *n., pl.* **-keys** [< ?] **1.** a domesticated ass **2.** a stupid or stubborn person **3.** a small steam engine: in full **donkey engine**

‡**don·na** (dôn'nä) *n., pl.* **-ne** (-ne) [It. < L. *domina,* mistress] a lady: as a title [**D-**], equivalent to *Lady, Madam*

Donne (dun), **John** 1573–1631; Eng. poet

do·nor (dō'nər) *n.* one who donates

Don Qui·xo·te (dän' kē hōt'ē, dän' kwik'sət) **1.** a satirical romance by Cervantes **2.** the chivalrous, unrealistic hero of this romance

don't (dōnt) do not

doo·dad (dōo'dad') *n.* [Colloq.] a trinket or gadget

doo·dle (dōo'd'l) *vi.* **-dled, -dling** [G. *dudeln,* to trifle] to scribble aimlessly —*n.* a mark made in aimless scribbling —**doo'dler** *n.*

doo·dle·bug (-bug') *n.* the larva of the ant lion

doom (dōom) *n.* [OE. *dom*] **1.** a judgment; esp., a sentence of condemnation **2.** fate **3.** ruin or death —*vt.* **1.** to condemn **2.** to destine to a tragic fate

dooms·day (dōomz'dā') *n.* Judgment Day

door (dôr) *n.* [OE. *duru*] **1.** a movable structure for opening or closing an entrance **2.** *same as* DOORWAY —**out of doors** outdoors

door'bell' *n.* a bell rung by someone wishing to enter a building or room

door'man' (-man', -mən) *n., pl.* **-men'** a man whose work is opening the door of a building, hailing taxicabs, etc.

door'mat' *n.* a mat to wipe the shoes on before entering a house, etc.

door'nail' *n.* a large-headed nail used in studding some doors —**dead as a doornail** absolutely dead

door'step' *n.* a step leading from an outer door to a path, lawn, etc.

door'way' *n.* **1.** an opening in a wall that can be closed by a door **2.** any means of access

door'yard' *n.* a yard onto which a door of a house opens

dope (dōp) *n.* [Du. *doop,* sauce] **1.** any thick liquid or paste used as a lubricant, etc. **2.** a varnish or filler, as for protecting the cloth covering of airplane wings **3.** [Slang] any drug or narcotic **4.** [Slang] a stupid person **5.** [Slang] information —*vt.* **doped, dop'ing** to drug —**dope out** [Colloq.] to solve

dop·ey, dop·y (dō'pē) *adj.* **-i·er, -i·est** [Slang] **1.** under the influence of a narcotic **2.** lethargic or stupid —**dop'i·ness** *n.*

Dor·ic (dôr'ik) *adj.* [< Gr. *Dōris,* ancient region of Greece] designating or of a Greek style of architecture marked by fluted columns with simple capitals

dorm (dôrm) *n.* [Colloq.] a dormitory

dor·mant (dôr'mənt) *adj.* [< L. *dormire,* to sleep] **1.** sleeping **2.** inactive **3.** *Biol.* in a resting or torpid state — **dor'man·cy** *n.*

dor·mer (dôr'mər) *n.* [see prec.] **1.** a window set upright in a sloping roof **2.** the roofed projection in which this window is set Also **dormer window**

dor·mi·to·ry (dôr'mə tôr'ē) *n., pl.* **-ries** [see DORMANT] **1.** a room with beds for a number of people **2.** a building, as at a college, with many rooms providing sleeping and living accommodations

dor·mouse (dôr'mous') *n., pl.* **-mice'** (-mīs') [< ? OFr. *dormeuse,* sleepy] a small old-world rodent that resembles a squirrel

DORMER

dor·sal (dôr's'l) *adj.* [< L. *dorsum,* the back] of, on, or near the back —**dor'sal·ly** *adv.*

do·ry (dôr'ē) *n., pl.* **-ries** [AmInd. (Central America) *dori,* a dugout] a small, flat-bottomed fishing boat with high sides

dose (dōs) *n.* [< Gr. *dosis,* a giving] **1.** an amount of medicine to be taken at one time **2.** amount of punishment or other unpleasant experience undergone at one time —*vt.* **dosed, dos'ing** to give doses to —**dos'age** *n.*

dos·si·er (däs'ē ā', dôs'-) *n.* [Fr.] a collection of documents about some person or matter

dost (dust) *archaic 2d pers. sing., pres. indic.,* of DO¹: *used with* thou

Dos·to·ev·ski (dôs'tô yef'skē), **Feo·dor** (Mikhailovich) (fyô'dôr) 1821–81; Russ. novelist

dot (dät) *n.* [OE. *dott,* head of a boil] **1.** a tiny speck or mark **2.** a small, round spot **3.** the short sound in Morse code —*vt.* **dot'ted, dot'ting** to mark as with a dot or dots —**on the dot** [Colloq.] at the exact time

dot·age (dōt'ij) *n.* [ME. < *doten,* to dote] **1.** feeble and childish state due to old age **2.** excessive affection

do·tard (dō'tərd) *n.* [see prec.] a foolish and doddering old person

dote (dōt) *vi.* **dot'ed, dot'ing** [ME. *doten*] **1.** to be weak-minded, esp. because of old age **2.** to be excessively fond (with *on* or *upon*) —**dot'ing** *adj.*

doth (duth) *archaic 3d pers. sing., pres. indic.,* of DO¹: chiefly in auxiliary uses

dot·ty (dät'ē) *adj.* **-ti·er, -ti·est** **1.** covered with dots **2.** [Colloq.] feeble-minded or crazy

Dou·ay Bible (dōo ā') [< *Douai,* in France, where it was published in part (1609–10)] an English translation of the Bible, for Roman Catholics: also **Douay Version**

dou·ble (dub''l) *adj.* [< L. *duplus*] **1.** twofold; duplex **2.** having two layers; folded in two **3.** having two of one kind; repeated **4.** being of two kinds [a *double* standard] **5.** having two meanings; ambiguous **6.** twice as much, as many, etc. **7.** of extra size, value, etc. **8.** made for two [a *double* bed] **9.** two-faced; deceiving **10.** having a tone an octave lower [*double* bass] **11.** *Bot.* having more than one set of petals —*adv.* **1.** twofold **2.** two together; in pairs — *n.* **1.** anything twice as much, as many, etc. as normal **2.** a duplicate; counterpart **3.** a stand-in, as in motion pictures **4.** a fold; second ply **5.** a sharp shift of direction **6.** a trick; shift **7.** [*pl.*] a game of tennis, handball, etc. with two players on each side **8.** *Baseball* a hit on which the batter reaches second base **9.** *Bridge* the doubling of an opponent's bid —*vt.* **-bled, -bling** **1.** to make twice as much or as many **2.** to fold **3.** to repeat or duplicate **4.** to be the double of **5.** *Bridge* to increase the point value or penalty of (an opponent's bid) —*vi.* **1.** to become double **2.** to turn sharply backward [to *double* on one's tracks] **3.** to serve as a double, serve two purposes, etc. **4.** *Baseball* to hit a double —**double up 1.** to clench (one's fist) **2.** to bend over, as in pain **3.** to share a room, etc. with someone

double agent a spy who infiltrates an enemy espionage organization in order to betray it

dou'ble-bar'reled *adj.* **1.** having two barrels, as a kind of shotgun **2.** having a double purpose or meaning

double bass (bās) the largest and deepest-toned instrument of the violin family

double boiler a cooking utensil with an upper pan for food, fitting into a lower pan in which water is boiled

dou'ble-breast'ed *adj.* overlapping across the breast, as a coat

double chin a fold of flesh beneath the chin

dou'ble-cross' *vt.* [Colloq.] to betray —**dou'ble-cross'er** *n.*

double cross [Colloq.] a betrayal; treachery

double dagger a mark (‡) used in printing and writing to indicate a note or cross reference

double date [Colloq.] a social engagement shared by two couples —**dou'ble-date'** *vi., vt.* **-dat'ed, -dat'ing**

dou'ble-deal'ing *n.* duplicity

dou'ble-edged' *adj.* **1.** having two cutting edges **2.** applicable both ways, as an argument

dou·ble-en·ten·dre (dōo'blän tän'drə, dub''l än-) *n.* [Fr. (now obs.), double meaning] a word or phrase with two meanings, esp. when one of them is risqué

double entry a system of bookkeeping in which each transaction is entered as a debit and a credit

double exposure *Photog.* the making of two exposures on the same film or plate

double feature two full-length motion pictures on the same program

---

fat, āpe, cär; ten, ēven; is, bīte; gō, hôrn, tōol, look; oil, out; up, fur; thin, *th*en; zh, leisure; ŋ, ring; ə for *a* in *ago*; ' as in *able* (ā'b'l); ë, Fr. coeur; ö, Fr. feu; Fr. mon; ü, Fr. duc; r, Fr. cri; kh, G. doch, ich. ‡ foreign; < derived from

dou'ble-head'er *n.* a pair of games played in succession on the same day

double indemnity a clause in some insurance policies providing for the payment of twice the face value of the contract for accidental death

dou'ble-joint'ed *adj.* having joints that permit limbs, fingers, etc. to bend at other than the usual angles

dou'ble-park' *vt., vi.* to park (a vehicle) parallel to another parked alongside a curb

double play *Baseball* a play in which two players are put out

dou'ble-quick' *adj.* very quick —*n.* a very quick marching pace; specif., *same as* DOUBLE TIME —*adv.* at this pace

dou'ble-reed' *adj.* designating or of a woodwind instrument, as the oboe, having two reeds separated by a narrow opening —*n.* a double-reed instrument

double standard a system, code, etc. applied unequally; specif., one that is stricter for women than for men, esp. in matters of sex

dou·blet (dub'lit) *n.* [< OFr. *double,* orig., something folded] 1. a man's closefitting jacket of the 14th to 16th cent. 2. either of a pair 3. a pair

double take a delayed, startled reaction to some remark, situation, etc., following initial, unthinking acceptance

double talk 1. ambiguous and deceptive talk 2. deliberately confusing talk made up of a mixture of real words and meaningless syllables

double time a marching cadence of 180 three-foot steps a minute

dou·bloon (du blōōn') *n.* [< Fr. < Sp. < L. *duplus,* double] an obsolete Spanish gold coin

dou·bly (dub'lē) *adv.* 1. twice 2. two at a time

DOUBLET

doubt (dout) *vi.* [< L. *dubitare*] to be uncertain or undecided —*vt.* 1. to be uncertain about 2. to be inclined to disbelieve —*n.* 1. a lack of conviction or trust 2. a condition of uncertainty 3. an unsettled point or matter — **beyond** (or **without**) **doubt** certainly —**no doubt** 1. certainly 2. probably —**doubt'er** *n.* —**doubt'ing·ly** *adv.*

doubt'ful *adj.* 1. uncertain 2. giving rise to doubt 3. feeling doubt; unsettled —**doubt'ful·ly** *adv.* —**doubt'ful·ness** *n.*

doubt'less *adv.* 1. certainly 2. probably —**doubt'less·ly** *adv.*

douche (dōōsh) *n.* [Fr. < It. *doccia*] 1. a jet of liquid applied externally or internally to some part of the body 2. a bath or treatment of this kind 3. a device for douching —*vt., vi.* **douched, douch'ing** to apply a douche (to)

dough (dō) *n.* [OE. *dag*] 1. a mixture of flour, liquid, etc. worked into a soft, thick mass for baking 2. any pasty mass like this 3. [Slang] money

dough·boy (dō'boi') *n.* [Colloq.] a U.S. infantryman, esp. of World War I

dough'nut' *n.* a small, usually ring-shaped cake, fried in deep fat

dough·ty (dout'ē) *adj.* **-ti·er, -ti·est** [< OE. *dugan,* to avail] valiant; brave: now used with a consciously archaic flavor —**dough'ti·ly** *adv.* —**dough'ti·ness** *n.*

dough·y (dō'ē) *adj.* **-i·er, -i·est** of or like dough; soft, pasty, etc. —**dough'i·ness** *n.*

Doug·las (dug'ləs), **Stephen A**(rnold) 1813–61; U.S. politician

Douglas fir (or **spruce, pine, hemlock**) [< David *Douglas,* 19th-c. Scot. botanist] a tall, evergreen, timber tree, found in W N. America

dour (door, dōōr, dour) *adj.* [< L. *durus,* hard] 1. [Scot.] severe; stern 2. sullen; gloomy —**dour'ly** *adv.* —**dour'ness** *n.*

douse¹ (dous) *vt.* **doused, dous'ing** [?] 1. *Naut.* to lower (sails) quickly 2. [Colloq.] to put out (a light or fire) quickly

douse² (dous) *vt.* **doused, dous'ing** [< ? prec.] 1. to thrust suddenly into liquid 2. to drench

dove¹ (duv) *n.* [< ? ON. *dūfa*] 1. a bird of the pigeon family, with a cooing cry: a symbol of peace 2. a person regarded as gentle or innocent 3. an advocate of peaceful international relationships

dove² (dōv) *alt. pt. of* DIVE

dove·cote (duv'kōt') *n.* a small box with compartments for nesting pigeons: also **dove'cot'** (-kät')

Do·ver (dō'vər) 1. seaport in SE England, on the Strait of Dover: pop. 36,000 2. capital of Del.: pop. 17,000 3. **Strait** (or **Straits**) **of,** strait between France and England

dove·tail (duv'tāl') *n.* a projecting part that fits into a corresponding indentation to form a joint —*vt., vi.* to join or fit together closely or by means of dovetails

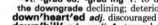

DOVETAIL

dow·a·ger (dou'ə jər) *n.* [ult. < L. *dos,* dowry] 1. a widow with a title or property derived from her dead husband 2. an elderly woman of wealth and dignity

dow·dy (dou'dē) *adj.* **-di·er, -di·est** [< ME. *doude,* plain woman] not neat in dress; shabby —**dow'di·ly** *adv.* —**dow'di·ness** *n.*

dow·el (dou'əl) *n.* [ME. *doule*] a peg of wood, etc., usually fitted into corresponding holes in two pieces to fasten them together —*vt.* **-eled** or **-elled, -el·ing** or **-el·ling** to fasten with dowels

dow·er (dou'ər) *n.* [< L. *dos,* dowry] 1. that part of a man's property which his widow inherits for life 2. a dowry —*vt.* to endow (*with*)

down¹ (doun) *adv.* [OE. *adune,* from the hill] 1. to, in, or on a lower place or level 2. in or to a lower condition, amount, etc. 3. from an earlier to a later period 4. seriously [get *down* to work] 5. out of one's hands [put it *down*] 6. completely [loaded *down*] 7. in cash [$5 *down*] 8. in writing [take *down* his name] —*adj.* 1. descending 2. in a lower place 3. gone, brought, pulled, etc. down 4. dejected; discouraged 5. ill 6. finished [four *down,* six to go] 7. in cash [a *down* payment] —*prep.* down toward, along, through, into, or upon —*vt.* to put or throw down —*n.* 1. a misfortune [ups and *downs*] 2. *Football* one of a series of plays in which a team tries to advance the ball —**down and out** penniless, ill, etc. —**down on** [Colloq.] angry with —**down with!** do away with!

down² (doun) *n.* [< ON. *dūnn*] 1. soft, fine feathers 2. soft, fine hair

down³ (doun) *n.* [OE. *dun,* hill] open, high, grassy land: *usually used in pl.*

down'beat' *n.* *Music* a downward stroke made by a conductor to show the first beat of each measure

down'cast' *adj.* 1. directed downward 2. sad; dejected

Down East New England, esp. Maine: also **down east** — **down'-east'** *adj.*

down'fall' *n.* 1. *a)* a sudden fall, as from power *b)* the cause of this 2. a sudden, heavy fall, as of snow

down'grade' *n.* a downward slope —*adj., adv.* downward —*vt.* **-grad'ed, -grad'ing** 1. to demote 2. to belittle —**on the downgrade** declining; deteriorating

down'heart'ed *adj.* discouraged

down'hill' *adv., adj.* 1. toward the bottom of a hill 2. to a poorer condition, status, etc.

Down·ing Street (doun'iŋ) a street in London containing some of the chief British government offices

down'pour' *n.* a heavy rain

down'range' *adv., adj.* along the course away from the launching site

down'right' *adv.* thoroughly; utterly —*adj.* 1. absolute; utter 2. plain; frank

Down's syndrome (dounz) [< J. *Down* (1828–96), Eng. physician] a congenital disease marked by mental deficiency, a broad face, slanting eyes, etc.

down'stage' *adj., adv.* of or toward the front of the stage

down'stairs' *adv.* 1. down the stairs 2. on or to a lower floor —*adj.* on a lower floor —*n.* a lower floor

down'state' *adj., adv.* in, to, or from the southerly part of a State

down'stream' *adv., adj.* in the direction of the current of a stream

down'swing' *n.* 1. a downward swing, as of a golf club 2. a downward trend

down'-to-earth' *adj.* realistic or practical

down'town' *adj., adv.* in or toward the main business section of a city —*n.* the downtown section

down'trod'den *adj.* oppressed

down'turn' (-turn') *n.* a decline, as in business

down'ward (-wərd) *adv., adj.* toward a lower place, position, etc.: also **down'wards** *adv.*

down·y (doun'ē) *adj.* **-i·er, -i·est** 1. covered with soft, fine feathers or hair 2. soft and fluffy, like down —**down'i·ness** *n.*

dow·ry (dou'rē) *n., pl.* **-ries** [see DOWER] 1. the property that a woman brings to her husband at marriage 2. a natural talent, gift, etc.

dowse (douz) *vi.* **dowsed, dows'ing** [< ?] to search for a source of water or minerals with a divining rod (**dowsing rod**) —**dows'er** *n.*

dox·ol·o·gy (däk säl′ə jē) *n., pl.* **-gies** [< Gr. *doxa,* praise + *legein,* speak] a hymn of praise to God; specif., *a)* the **greater doxology,** which begins "Glory to God in the highest" *b)* the **lesser doxology,** which begins "Glory to the Father" *c)* a hymn beginning "Praise God from whom all blessings flow"

Doyle (doil), Sir **Arthur Co·nan** (kō′nən) 1859–1930; Eng. writer of *Sherlock Holmes* stories

doz. dozen; dozens

doze (dōz) *vi.* **dozed, doz′ing** [prob. < Scand.] to sleep fitfully; nap —*n.* a light sleep; nap

doz·en (duz′'n) *n., pl.* **-ens** or, esp. after a number, **-en** [< L. *duo,* two + *decem,* ten] a set of twelve —**doz′enth** *adj.*

DP, D.P. displaced person

dpt. 1. department 2. deponent

Dr. 1. Doctor 2. Drive

dr. 1. debtor 2. dram; drams

drab[1] (drab) *n.* [< Fr. < VL. *drappus,* cloth] a dull yellowish brown —*adj.* **drab′ber, drab′best** 1. dull yellowishbrown 2. dull; monotonous —**drab′ness** *n.*

drab[2] (drab) *n.* [< Celt.] 1. a slovenly woman 2. a prostitute

drachm (dram) *n. same as:* 1. DRACHMA 2. DRAM

drach·ma (drak′mə) *n., pl.* **-mas, -mae** (-mē), **-mai** (-mī) [< Gr. *drachmē,* a handful] 1. an ancient Greek silver coin 2. the monetary unit of modern Greece

draft (draft) *n.* [< OE. *dragan,* to draw] 1. a drawing, as of a vehicle or load 2. *a)* a drawing in of a fish net *b)* the amount of fish caught in one draw 3. *a)* a drinking or the amount taken at one drink *b)* [Colloq.] a portion of beer, etc. drawn from a cask 4. an inhalation 5. a preliminary or tentative piece of writing 6. a plan or drawing of a work to be done 7. a current of air 8. a device for regulating the current of air in a heating system 9. a written order for payment of money; check 10. *a)* the taking of persons for a special purpose, esp. for compulsory military service *b)* those so taken 11. the depth of water that a ship displaces —*vt.* 1. to take, as for military service, by drawing from a group 2. to make a sketch of or plans for —*adj.* 1. used for pulling loads 2. drawn from a cask [*draft beer*]

draft·ee (draf tē′) *n.* a person drafted, esp. for service in the armed forces

drafts·man (drafts′mən) *n., pl.* **-men** one who draws plans of structures or machinery —**drafts′man·ship′** *n.*

draft′y *adj.* **-i·er, -i·est** letting in, having, or exposed to a draft or drafts of air —**draft′i·ly** *adv.* —**draft′i·ness** *n.*

drag (drag) *vt., vi.* **dragged, drag′ging** [OE. *dragan*] 1. to pull or be pulled with effort, esp. along the ground 2. to pull a grapnel, net, etc. over the bottom of (a river, etc.) in searching for something 3. to draw a harrow over (land) 4. to draw (something) out over a period of time; move or pass too slowly —*n.* 1. something dragged along the ground, as a harrow 2. a grapnel, dragnet, etc. 3. anything that hinders 4. a dragging 5. [Slang] influence 6. [Slang] a puff of a cigarette, etc. 7. [Slang] street [the main *drag*] 8. [Slang] a dull person, situation, etc. —**drag on** (or **out**) to prolong or be prolonged tediously —**drag′gy** *adj.* **-gi·er, -gi·est**

drag·gle (drag′'l) *vt., vi.* **-gled, -gling** [< DRAG] to make or become wet or dirty by dragging in mud or water

drag′net′ *n.* 1. a net dragged along a lake bottom, etc., as for catching fish 2. an organized system or network for catching criminals

drag·o·man (drag′ə mən) *n., pl.* **-mans, -men** [< Ar. *targumān*] in the Near East, an interpreter

drag·on (drag′ən) *n.* [< Gr. *drakōn*] a mythical monster, typically a large, winged reptile breathing out fire and smoke

drag′on·fly′ *n., pl.* **-flies′** a large, long-bodied insect with narrow, transparent wings

dra·goon (drə gōōn′) *n.* [Fr.: see DRAGON] a heavily armed cavalryman —*vt.* to force (into) doing something; coerce

drag race [Slang] a race between hot-rod cars accelerating from a standstill on a short, straight course (**drag strip**) — **drag′-race′** *vi.* **-raced′, -rac′ing**

drain (drān) *vt.* [< OE. *dryge,* dry] 1. to draw off (liquid) gradually 2. to draw liquid from gradually 3. to exhaust (strength, resources, etc.) gradu-

DRAGONFLY
(to 5 in. long)

ally —*vi.* 1. to flow off; trickle 2. to become dry by draining 3. to discharge its waters —*n.* 1. a channel, pipe, etc. for draining 2. a draining —**drain′er** *n.*

drain′age (-ij) *n.* 1. a draining 2. a system of pipes, etc. for carrying off waste matter 3. that which is drained off 4. an area drained, as by a river

drain′pipe′ *n.* a large pipe used to carry off water, sewage, etc.

drake (drāk) *n.* [ME.] a male duck

Drake (drāk), Sir **Francis** 1540?-96; Eng. admiral, navigator, & buccaneer

dram (dram) *n.* [< Gr. *drachma,* a handful] 1. *Apothecaries′ Weight* a unit equal to 1/8 ounce 2. *Avoirdupois Weight* a unit equal to 1/16 ounce 3. *same as* FLUID DRAM 4. a small amount of anything

dra·ma (drä′mə, dram′ə) *n.* [< Gr.] 1. a literary composition to be performed by actors; play 2. the art of writing, acting, or producing plays 3. plays collectively 4. a series of events as interesting, vivid, etc. as a play 5. the quality of being dramatic

Dram·a·mine (dram′ə mēn′) *a trademark for* a drug to relieve motion sickness

dra·mat·ic (drə mat′ik) *adj.* 1. of or connected with drama 2. like a play 3. vivid, exciting, etc. —**dra·mat′i·cal·ly** *adv.*

dra·mat′ics *n.pl.* 1. [*usually with sing. v.*] the art of performing or producing plays 2. plays presented by amateurs 3. dramatic effect

dram·a·tis per·so·nae (dram′ə tis pər sō′nē) [ModL.] the characters in a play

dram·a·tist (dram′ə tist) *n.* a playwright

dram·a·tize′ (-tīz′) *vt.* **-tized′, -tiz′ing** 1. to make into a drama 2. to regard or present in a dramatic manner —**dram·a·ti·za′tion** *n.*

drank (draŋk) *pt. & often colloq. pp. of* DRINK

drape (drāp) *vt.* **draped, drap′ing** [< VL. *drappus,* cloth] 1. to cover or hang as with cloth in loose folds 2. to arrange (a garment, cloth, etc.) in folds or hangings —*n.* cloth hanging in loose folds; esp., a drapery: *usually used in pl.*

drap·er (drā′pər) *n.* [Brit.] a dealer in dry goods

drap′er·y *n., pl.* **-ies** 1. hangings, etc. arranged in loose folds 2. [*pl.*] curtains of heavy material

dras·tic (dras′tik) *adj.* [< Gr. *drastikos,* active] having a violent effect; severe; harsh —**dras′ti·cal·ly** *adv.*

draught (draft) *n., vt., adj. now chiefly Brit. sp. of* DRAFT

draughts (drafts) *n.pl.* [Brit.] the game of checkers

draught·y (draf′tē) *adj.* **-i·er, -i·est** *Brit. sp. of* DRAFTY

Dra·vid·i·an (drə vid′ē ən) *n.* 1. any of a group of intermixed races chiefly in S India and N Sri Lanka 2. the family of non-Indo-European languages spoken by these people, including Tamil —*adj.* of the Dravidians or their languages: also **Dra·vid′ic**

draw (drô) *vt.* **drew, drawn, draw′ing** [OE. *dragan*] 1. to make move toward one; pull; drag 2. to pull up, down, back, in, or out 3. to need (a specified depth of water) to float in: said of a ship 4. to attract; charm 5. to breathe in 6. to elicit (a reply, etc.) 7. to bring on; provoke 8. to receive [to *draw* a salary] 9. to withdraw (money) held in an account 10. to write (a check or draft) 11. to deduce 12. to stretch 13. to make (lines, pictures, etc.) as with a pencil 14. to take out (a liquid, etc.) 15. to disembowel 16. to bring (a game or contest) to a tie —*vi.* 1. to draw something (in various senses of the *vt.*) 2. to be drawn or have a drawing effect 3. to come; move [to *draw* near] 4. to shrink 5. to allow a draft, as of smoke, to move through —*n.* 1. a drawing or being drawn 2. the result of drawing 3. a thing drawn 4. a tie; stalemate 5. a thing that attracts 6. a gully or ravine that water drains into —**draw away** to move away or ahead —**draw on** (or **nigh**) to approach —**draw out** 1. to extend 2. to get (a person) to talk —**draw up** 1. to arrange in order 2. to compose (a document) in proper form 3. to stop

draw′back′ *n.* anything that lessens or prevents full satisfaction; shortcoming

draw′bridge′ *n.* a bridge that can be raised, lowered, or drawn aside

draw′ee′ (-ē′) *n.* the person on whom an order for the payment of money is drawn

draw·er (drô′ər) *n.* 1. a person or thing that draws 2. one who draws an order for the payment of money 3. (drôr) a sliding box in a table, chest, etc.

drawers (drôrz) *n.pl.* an undergarment for the lower part of the body

---

fat, āpe, cär; ten, ēven; is, bīte; gō, hôrn, tōōl, lŏŏk; oil, out; up, fur; thin, *th*en; zh, leisure; ŋ, ring; ə for *a* in *ago;* ′ as in *able* (ā′b'l); ë, Fr. coeur; ö, Fr. feu; Fr. mon; ü, Fr. duc; r, Fr. cri; kh, G. doch, ich. ‡ foreign; < derived from

draw'ing *n.* **1.** the act of one that draws; specif., the art of representing something by lines made on a surface with a pencil, pen, etc. **2.** a picture, design, etc. thus made **3.** a lottery

drawing card an entertainer, show, etc. that draws a large audience

drawing room [< *withdrawing room*: guests withdrew there after dinner] **1.** a room where guests are received or entertained **2.** a private compartment on a railroad car

draw'knife' *n., pl.* **-knives'** a knife with a handle at each end: the user draws it toward him in shaving a surface: also **drawing knife, draw'shave'** (-shāv')

drawl (drôl) *vt., vi.* [prob. < DRAW] to speak slowly, prolonging the vowels —*n.* a manner of speaking thus — **drawl'er** *n.* —**drawl'ing·ly** *adv.*

drawn (drôn) *pp. of* DRAW —*adj.* **1.** disemboweled **2.** tense; haggard

drawn butter melted butter

drawn'work' *n.* ornamental work done on textiles by pulling out threads to produce a lacelike design

draw'string' *n.* a string that tightens or closes an opening, as of a bag, when drawn

dray (drā) *n.* [< OE. *dragan*, to draw] a low, sturdy cart with detachable sides, for carrying heavy loads —*vt.* to carry or haul on a dray —*vi.* to drive a dray

dray'age (-ij) *n.* **1.** the hauling of a load by dray **2.** the charge for this

dray'man *n., pl.* **-men** a man who drives a dray

dread (dred) *vt.* [< OE. *ondrædan*] to anticipate with great fear, misgiving, or distaste —*n.* **1.** intense fear **2.** fear mixed with awe —*adj.* **1.** dreaded or dreadful **2.** inspiring awe

dread'ful *adj.* **1.** inspiring dread; terrible or awesome **2.** [Colloq.] very bad, offensive, etc. —**dread'ful·ly** *adv.* — **dread'ful·ness** *n.*

dread'nought', dread'naught' (-nôt') *n.* a large, heavily armored battleship with big guns

dream (drēm) *n.* [< OE., joy, music] **1.** a sequence of images, thoughts, etc. passing through a sleeping person's mind **2.** a daydream; reverie **3.** a fond hope **4.** anything dreamlike —*vi., vt.* **dreamed** or **dreamt** (dremt), **dream'ing** **1.** to have a dream or dreams (of) **2.** to have a remote idea (of) —**dream up** [Colloq.] to conceive or devise —**dream'er** *n.* —**dream'less** *adj.* —**dream'like'** *adj.*

dream'y *adj.* **-i·er, -i·est** **1.** filled with dreams **2.** visionary; impractical **3.** shadowy; vague **4.** soothing **5.** [Slang] wonderful —**dream'i·ly** *adv.* —**dream'i·ness** *n.*

drear (drir) *adj.* [Poet.] dreary; melancholy

drear'y *adj.* **-i·er, -i·est** [< OE. *dreorig*, sad] gloomy; dismal —**drear'i·ly** *adv.* —**drear'i·ness** *n.*

dredge' (drej) *n.* [prob. < MDu. *dregge*] **1.** a net on a frame, dragged along the bottom of a river, bay, etc. to gather shellfish, etc. **2.** an apparatus for scooping up mud, etc., as in deepening or clearing channels, harbors, etc. — *vt., vi.* **dredged, dredg'ing** **1.** to search (*for*) or gather (*up*) as with a dredge **2.** to enlarge or clean out with a dredge

dredge² (drej) *vt.* **dredged, dredg'ing** [< ME. *dragge, sweetmeat*] to coat (food) with flour or the like

dregs (dregz) *n.pl.* [< ON. *dregg*] **1.** the particles that settle at the bottom of a liquid **2.** the most worthless part [*dregs* of society] —**dreg'gy** *adj.* **-gi·er, -gi·est**

Drei·ser (drī'sər, -zər), **Theodore** 1871–1945; U.S. novelist

drench (drench) *vt.* [< OE. *drincan*, to drink] **1.** to make (a horse, cow, etc.) swallow a medicinal liquid **2.** to make wet all over; soak —*n.* **1.** a large liquid dose, esp. for a sick animal **2.** a drenching; soaking **3.** a solution for soaking

Dres·den (drez'dən) city in SC East Germany, on the Elbe: pop. 500,000 —*n.* a fine porcelain or chinaware made near Dresden

dress (dres) *vt.* **dressed** or **drest, dress'ing** [< L. *dirigere*, lay straight] **1.** to put clothes on; clothe **2.** to trim; adorn **3.** to arrange or do up (the hair) **4.** to arrange (troops, etc.) in straight lines **5.** to apply medicines and bandages to (a wound, etc.) **6.** to prepare for use, esp. for cooking [to *dress* a fowl] **7.** to cultivate (fields or plants) **8.** to smooth or finish (leather, stone, etc.) —*vi.* **1.** to put on or wear clothes **2.** to dress in formal clothes **3.** to get into a straight line —*n.* **1.** clothes **2.** the usual outer garment of women, generally of one piece with a skirt **3.** external covering or appearance —*adj.* **1.** of or for dresses [*dress material*] **2.** worn on formal occasions [a *dress* suit] — **dress down** to scold severely —**dress up** to dress in formal or elegant clothes

dres·sage (drə säzh') *n.* [Fr., training] horsemanship in which slight movements are used to control the horse

dress'er *n.* **1.** one who dresses (in various senses) **2.** a chest of drawers for clothes, with a mirror

dress'ing *n.* **1.** the act of one that dresses **2.** bandages, etc. applied to a wound **3.** a sauce for salads, etc. **4.** a stuffing for roast fowl

dress'ing-down' *n.* a sound scolding

dressing gown a loose robe for wear when one is undressed or lounging

dress'mak'er *n.* one who makes women's dresses, suits, etc. to order —*adj.* not cut on severe, mannish lines — **dress'mak'ing** *n.*

dress parade a military parade in dress uniform

dress rehearsal a final rehearsal, as of a play, performed exactly as it is to take place

dress'y *adj.* **-i·er, -i·est** **1.** showy in dress or appearance **2.** elegant; smart —**dress'i·ness** *n.*

drew (drōō) *pt. of* DRAW

drib·ble (drib''l) *vi., vt.* **-bled, -bling** [< DRIP] **1.** to flow, or let flow, in drops or driblets; trickle **2.** to slaver; drool **3.** in certain games, to move (the ball or puck) along by repeated bouncing, kicking, or tapping —*n.* **1.** dribbling **2.** a very small amount: also **drib'let** (-lit)

dried (drīd) *pt. & pp. of* DRY

dri·er (drī'ər) *n.* **1.** a substance added to paint, etc. to make it dry fast **2.** *same as* DRYER —*adj. compar. of* DRY

dri'est (-ist) *adj. superl. of* DRY

drift (drift) *n.* [< OE. *drifan*, to drive] **1.** a being driven along, as by a current **2.** the course on which something is driven **3.** the deviation of a ship, etc. from its course, caused by side currents or winds **4.** a slow ocean current **5.** a tendency or trend **6.** general meaning; intent **7.** a heap of snow, etc. piled up by the wind **8.** gravel, etc. deposited by a glacier —*vi.* **1.** to be carried, as by a current **2.** to go along aimlessly **3.** to pile up in drifts —*vt.* to cause to drift —**drift'er** *n.*

drift'age *n.* **1.** a drifting **2.** deviation caused by drifting **3.** that which has drifted

drift'wood' *n.* wood drifting in the water, or that has been washed ashore

drill' (dril) *n.* [Du. *drillen*, to bore] **1.** a tool for boring holes in wood, metal, etc. **2.** systematic military or physical training **3.** the method or practice of teaching by repeated exercises —*vt., vi.* **1.** to bore with a drill **2.** to train in, or teach by means of, drill

drill² (dril) *n.* [< ?] a planting machine for making holes or furrows and dropping seeds into them

drill³ (dril) *n.* [< G. < L. *trilix*, three-threaded] a linen or cotton twill, used for work clothes, etc.

drill⁴ (dril) *n.* [< ? Fr. *drill*, a soldier] a bright-cheeked monkey native to W Africa

drill'mas'ter *n.* **1.** an instructor in military drill **2.** one who teaches by drilling

drill press a machine tool for drilling holes

dri·ly (drī'lē) *adv. same as* DRYLY

drink (drink) *vt.* **drank** or archaic **drunk, drunk** or now colloq. **drank** or archaic **drunk'en, drink'ing** [OE. *drincan*] **1.** to swallow (liquid) **2.** to absorb (liquid or moisture) **3.** to swallow the contents of —*vi.* **1.** to swallow liquid **2.** to drink alcoholic liquor, esp. to excess —*n.* **1.** any liquid for drinking **2.** alcoholic liquor —**drink in** to take in eagerly with the senses or mind —**drink to** to drink a toast to — **drink'a·ble** *adj.* —**drink'er** *n.*

drip (drip) *vi., vt.* **dripped** or **dript, drip'ping** [OE. *dryppan*] to fall, or let fall, in drops —*n.* **1.** a falling in drops **2.** [Slang] a person regarded as dull, insipid, etc.

drip'-dry' *adj.* designating or of garments that dry quickly when hung wet and need little or no ironing —*vi.* **-dried', -dry'ing** to launder as a drip-dry garment does

drip'pings *n.* the juices that drip from roasting meat

drive (drīv) *vt.* **drove, driv'en, driv'ing** [OE. *drifan*] **1.** to force to go; push forward **2.** to force into or from a state or act **3.** to force to work, usually to excess **4.** to hit (a ball) hard **5.** to make penetrate **6.** to produce by penetrating **7.** to control the movement of (a vehicle) **8.** to transport in a vehicle **9.** to push (a bargain, etc.) through —*vi.* **1.** to advance violently **2.** to try hard **3.** to drive a blow, ball, etc. **4.** to be driven: said of a motor vehicle **5.** to operate, or go in, a motor vehicle, etc. —*n.* **1.** a driving **2.** a trip in a vehicle **3.** *a)* a road for automobiles, etc. *b)* a driveway **4.** a rounding up of animals **5.** a campaign to achieve some purpose **6.** energy and initiative **7.** a strong impulse or urge **8.** the propelling mechanism of a machine, etc. —**drive at** **1.** to aim at **2.** to mean; intend — **drive in** **1.** to force in, as by a blow **2.** *Baseball* to cause (a runner) to score or (a run) to be scored

drive'-in' *n.* a restaurant, movie theater, bank, etc. designed to serve people seated in their cars

driv·el (driv'l) *vi., vt.* **-eled** or **-elled, -el·ing** or **-el·ling** [< OE. *dreflian*] **1.** to let (saliva) flow from the mouth; slobber **2.** to speak or say in a silly, stupid way —*n.* silly, stupid talk

driv'er *n.* a person or thing that drives, as *a)* one who drives an automobile, etc. *b)* one who herds cattle *c)* a wooden-headed golf club used in hitting the ball from the tee

drive'way' *n.* a path for cars, leading from a street to a garage, house, etc.

driz·zle (driz''l) *vi., vt.* **-zled, -zling** [prob. < ME.] to rain or let fall in fine, misty drops —*n.* a fine, misty rain — **driz'zly** *adj.*

droll (drōl) *adj.* [< Fr. < MDu. *drol*, stout fellow] amusing in an odd or wry way —**droll'ly** *adv.*

droll'er·y (-ər ē) *n., pl.* **-ies 1.** a droll act, remark, story, etc. **2.** the act of joking **3.** wry humor

drom·e·dar·y (dräm'ə der'ē) *n., pl.* **-ies** [< Gr. *dramein*, to run] the one-humped or Arabian camel

drone' (drōn) *n.* [< OE. *dran*] **1.** a male honeybee, which does no work **2.** an idle parasite or loafer

drone² (drōn) *vi.* **droned, dron'ing** [< prec.] **1.** to make a continuous humming sound **2.** to talk in a monotonous way —*vt.* to utter in a monotonous tone —*n.* **1.** a droning sound **2.** a bagpipe

DROMEDARY

drool (drōōl) *vi.* [< DRIVEL] **1.** to let saliva flow from one's mouth **2.** to flow from the mouth, as saliva —*vt.* to let drivel from the mouth —*n.* saliva running from the mouth

droop (drōōp) *vi.* [< ON. *drūpa*] **1.** to sink, hang, or bend down **2.** to lose vitality **3.** to become dejected —*vt.* to let sink or hang down —*n.* a drooping —**droop'y** *adj.* **-i·er, -i·est**

drop (dräp) *n.* [OE. *dropa*] **1.** a small quantity of liquid somewhat roundish, as when falling **2.** [*pl.*] liquid medicine taken in drops **3.** a very small quantity of anything **4.** anything like a drop in shape, size, etc. **5.** a sudden fall, descent, slump, etc. **6.** something that drops, as a curtain, trapdoor, etc. **7.** the distance between a higher and lower level —*vi.* **dropped, drop'ping 1.** to fall in drops **2.** *a)* to fall suddenly down *b)* to fall exhausted, wounded, or dead **3.** to pass into a specified state [to *drop* off to sleep] **4.** to come to an end [let the matter *drop*] **5.** to become lower or less, as prices, etc. —*vt.* **1.** to let or make fall **2.** to utter (a hint, etc.) casually **3.** to send (a letter) **4.** to stop, end, or dismiss **5.** to lower **6.** [Colloq.] to deposit at a specified place —**at the drop of a hat** immediately —**drop back** to be outdistanced: also **drop behind** — **drop in** (or **over, by,** etc.) to pay a casual visit —**drop out** to stop participating

drop'-forge' (-fôrj') *vt.* **-forged', -forg'ing** to pound (heated metal) between dies with a drop hammer or a press —**drop'-forg'er** *n.* —**drop forging**

drop hammer 1. a machine for pounding metal into shape, with a heavy weight that is dropped on the metal **2.** this weight Also **drop press**

drop kick *Football* a kick in which the ball is dropped to the ground and kicked just as it rebounds —**drop'-kick'** *vt., vi.* —**drop'-kick'er** *n.*

drop'let (-lit) *n.* a very small drop

drop'out' (-out') *n.* a person who withdraws from school, esp. high school, before graduating

drop'per *n.* **1.** a person or thing that drops **2.** a small tube with a hollow rubber bulb at one end, used to release a liquid in drops

drop·sy (dräp'sē) *n.* [< Gr. *hydōr*, water] *an earlier term for* EDEMA —**drop'si·cal** (-si k'l) *adj.*

drosh·ky (dräsh'kē) *n., pl.* **-kies** [Russ. *drozhki*] a low, open, four-wheeled Russian carriage: also **dros'ky** (dräs'-, drôs'-) *pl.* **-kies**

dro·soph·i·la (drə säf'ə lə) *n., pl.* **-lae'** (-lē') [< Gr. *drosos*, dew + *philos*, loving] a tiny fly used in laboratory experiments in heredity

dross (drôs) *n.* [OE. *dros*, dregs] **1.** a scum formed on the surface of molten metal **2.** waste matter; rubbish — **dross'y** *adj.* **-i·er, -i·est**

drought (drout, drouth) *n.* [< OE. *drugian*, dry up] prolonged dry weather: also **drouth** (drouth, drout)

drove' (drōv) *n.* [< OE. *drifan*, drive] **1.** a number of cattle, sheep, etc. driven or moving as a group; flock; herd **2.** a moving crowd of people

drove² (drōv) *pt. of* DRIVE

dro·ver (drō'vər) *n.* one who herds animals, esp. to market

drown (droun) *vi.* [< ON. *drukna*] to die by suffocation in water or other liquid —*vt.* **1.** to kill by such suffocation **2.** to flood **3.** to be so loud as to overcome (another sound): usually with *out*

drowse (drouz) *vi.* **drowsed, drows'ing** [< OE. *drusian*, become sluggish] to sleep lightly; doze —*vt.* to spend (time) in drowsing —*n.* a drowsing; doze

drow·sy (drou'zē) *adj.* **-si·er, -si·est 1.** being or making sleepy or half asleep **2.** brought on by sleepiness —**drow'si·ly** *adv.* —**drow'si·ness** *n.*

drub (drub) *vt.* **drubbed, drub'bing** [< Ar. *darb*, a beating] **1.** to beat as with a stick **2.** to defeat soundly in a fight, contest, etc. —**drub'bing** *n.*

drudge (druj) *n.* [prob. < OE. *dreogan*, suffer] a person who does hard, menial, or tedious work —*vi.* **drudged, drudg'ing** to do such work

drudg'er·y *n., pl.* **-ies** work that is hard, menial, or tiresome

drug (drug) *n.* [< OFr. *drogue*] **1.** any substance used as or in a medicine **2.** a narcotic, hallucinogen, etc. —*vt.* **drugged, drug'ging 1.** to put a harmful drug in (a drink, etc.) **2.** to stupefy as with a drug —**drug on the market** a thing in much greater supply than demand

drug'gist (-ist) *n.* **1.** a dealer in drugs, medical equipment, etc. **2.** a pharmacist **3.** a drugstore owner or manager

drug'store' *n.* a store where drugs, medical supplies, and various items are sold and prescriptions are filled

dru·id (drōō'id) *n.* [Fr. < Celt.] [*often* D-] a member of a Celtic religious order in ancient Britain, Ireland, and France —**dru·id'ic, dru·id'i·cal** *adj.*

drum (drum) *n.* [< Du. *trom*] **1.** a percussion instrument consisting of a hollow cylinder or hemisphere with a membrane stretched tightly over the end or ends **2.** the sound produced by beating a drum **3.** any drumlike cylindrical object, as a barrellike metal container for oil, etc. **4.** *same as: a)* MIDDLE EAR *b)* EARDRUM —*vi.* **drummed, drum'ming 1.** to beat a drum **2.** to tap continually, as with the fingers —*vt.* **1.** to play (a rhythm, etc.) as on a drum **2.** to instill (ideas, facts, etc. *into*) by continued repetition —**drum out of** to expel from in disgrace —**drum up to** get (business) by soliciting

drum·lin (drum'lin) *n.* [< Ir. *druim*, a ridge] a long ridge formed by glacial drift

drum major a person who twirls a baton at the head of a marching band —**drum ma'jor·ette'** (-et') *fem.*

drum'mer *n.* **1.** a drum player **2.** [Colloq.] a traveling salesman

drum'stick' *n.* **1.** a stick for beating a drum **2.** the lower half of the leg of a cooked fowl

drunk (druŋk) *pp. of* DRINK —*adj.* **1.** overcome by alcoholic liquor; intoxicated **2.** [Colloq.] *same as* DRUNKEN (sense 2) —*n.* [Slang] **1.** a drunken person **2.** a drinking spree

drunk·ard (druŋ'kərd) *n.* a person who often gets drunk

drunk'en *adj.* [*used before the noun*] **1.** intoxicated **2.** caused by or occurring during intoxication —**drunk'en·ly** *adv.* —**drunk'en·ness** *n.*

drupe (drōōp) *n.* [< Gr. *dryppa*, olive] any fruit with a soft, fleshy part around an inner stone that contains the seed, as an apricot, cherry, etc. —**dru·pa·ceous** (drōō pā'shəs) *adj.*

drupe'let *n.* a small drupe: a single blackberry consists of many drupelets

dry (drī) *adj.* **dri'er, dri'est** [OE. *dryge*] **1.** not under water [*dry* land] **2.** not wet or damp **3.** lacking rain or water; arid **4.** thirsty **5.** not yielding milk **6.** solid; not liquid **7.** not sweet [*dry* wine] **8.** prohibiting or opposed to the sale of alcoholic liquors **9.** funny in a quiet but sharp way [*dry* wit] **10.** dull or boring —*n., pl.* **drys** [Colloq.] a prohibitionist —*vt., vi.* **dried, dry'ing** to make or become dry — **dry up 1.** to make or become thoroughly dry **2.** to make or become unproductive **3.** [Slang] to stop talking —**dry'ly** *adv.* —**dry'ness** *n.*

dry·ad (drī'ad) *n.* [< Gr. *drys*, tree] [*also* D-] *Classical Myth.* a tree nymph

dry battery 1. an electric battery made up of several connected dry cells **2.** a dry cell

dry cell a voltaic cell containing an absorbent so that its contents cannot spill

dry'-clean' *vt.* to clean (garments, etc.) with some solvent other than water, as naphtha or gasoline —**dry cleaner**

Dry·den (drīd''n), **John** 1631–1700; Eng. poet, critic, & playwright

dry dock a dock from which the water can be emptied, used for building and repairing ships

dry'er *n.* **1.** a person or thing that dries **2.** *same as* DRIER

dry'-eyed' (-īd') *adj.* shedding no tears

dry farming farming in an almost rainless region without irrigation: done by conserving the soil moisture and planting drought-resistant crops

dry goods cloth, cloth products, thread, etc.

dry ice carbon dioxide solidified and compressed into snowlike cakes, used as a refrigerant

dry measure a system of measuring the volume of dry things, as grain, etc., in which 2 pints = 1 quart, 8 quarts = 1 peck, and 4 pecks = 1 bushel

dry point **1.** a needle for engraving on copper without using acid **2.** a print from such a plate

dry rot a fungous decay causing seasoned timber to crumble to powder

dry run [Slang] a simulated or practice performance; rehearsal

dry wall a wall made of wallboard, etc. without using wet plaster —**dry'wall'** *adj.*

D.S.C., DSC Distinguished Service Cross

D.S.T., DST Daylight Saving Time

D.T.'s, d.t.'s (dē'tēz') [Slang] *same as* DELIRIUM TREMENS

Du. **1.** Duke **2.** Dutch

du·al (dōō'əl, dyōō'-) *adj.* [< L. *duo,* two] **1.** of two **2.** double; twofold —**du·al'i·ty** (-al'ə tē) *n.* —**du'al·ly** *adv.*

du·al·ism *n.* **1.** the state of being dual **2.** any theory or doctrine based on a twofold distinction, as the theory that the world is composed of mind and matter —**du'al·ist** *n.* —**du'al·is'tic** *adj.*

dub¹ (dub) *vt.* **dubbed, dub'bing** [< OE. *dubbian,* to strike] **1.** to confer a title or name upon **2.** to make smooth, as by hammering, scraping, etc. **3.** [Slang] to bungle (a golf stroke, etc.)

dub² (dub) *vt.* **dubbed, dub'bing** [< DOUBLE] to insert (dialogue, etc.) in the sound track of a film, etc. (often with *in*)

du Bar·ry (dōō bar'ē), **Countess** 1743?–93; mistress of Louis XV of France

du·bi·e·ty (dōō bī'ə tē, dyōō-) *n.* [LL. *dubietas*] **1.** a being dubious **2.** *pl.* **-ties** a doubtful thing

du·bi·ous (dōō'bē əs, dyōō'-) *adj.* [< L. *dubius,* uncertain] **1.** causing doubt **2.** feeling doubt; skeptical **3.** questionable —**du'bi·ous·ly** *adv.*

Dub·lin (dub'lən) capital of Ireland: pop. 569,000

du·cal (dōō'k'l, dyōō'-) *adj.* [< LL. *ducalis,* of a leader] of a duke or dukedom —**du'cal·ly** *adv.*

duc·at (duk'ət) *n.* [see DUCHY] **1.** any of several former European coins **2.** [Slang] a ticket

duch·ess (duch'is) *n.* **1.** the wife or widow of a duke **2.** a woman who, like a duke, rules a duchy

duch'y (-ē) *n., pl.* **-ies** [< L. *dux,* leader] the territory ruled by a duke or duchess

duck¹ (duk) *n.* [< OE. *duce,* lit., diver] **1.** a swimming bird with a flat bill, short neck, and webbed feet **2.** a female duck: opposed to DRAKE **3.** the flesh of a duck as food —**like water off a duck's back** with no effect or reaction

duck² (duk) *vt., vi.* [ME. *douken*] **1.** to plunge or dip under water for a moment **2.** to lower or move (the head, body, etc.) suddenly, as in avoiding a blow **3.** [Colloq.] to avoid (a task, person, etc.) **4.** [Slang] to run (*in* or *out*) — *n.* a ducking

duck³ (duk) *n.* [Du. *doek*] a cotton or linen cloth like canvas but finer and lighter in weight

duck'bill' *n. same as* PLATYPUS

duck'ling *n.* a young duck

duck'pins' *n.pl.* [*with sing. v.*] **1.** a game like bowling, played with smaller pins and balls **2.** these pins

duck'weed' *n.* a minute flowering plant that floats on ponds and sluggish streams

duck'y *adj.* **-i·er, -i·est** [Slang] pleasing, delightful, etc.

duct (dukt) *n.* [< L. *ducere,* to lead] **1.** a tube or channel through which a fluid moves **2.** a tube in the body for the passage of excretions or secretions **3.** a pipe, etc. enclosing wires —**duct'less** *adj.*

duc·tile (duk't'l) *adj.* [see prec.] **1.** that can be drawn and hammered thin without breaking: said of metals **2.** easily molded **3.** easily led; tractable —**duc·til'i·ty** (-til'ə tē) *n.*

ductless gland an endocrine gland

dud (dud) *n.* [prob. < Du. *dood,* dead] [Colloq.] **1.** a bomb or shell that fails to explode **2.** a failure

dude (dōōd) *n.* [< ?] **1.** a dandy; fop **2.** [Western Slang] a city fellow or tourist **3.** [Slang] any man

dude ranch a ranch or farm operated as a vacation resort, with horseback riding, etc.

dudg·eon (duj'ən) *n.* [prob. < Anglo-Fr. *en digeon,* at the dagger hilt] anger or resentment: now chiefly in **in high dudgeon,** very angry or resentful

duds (dudz) *n.pl.* [prob. < ON. *dutha,* wrap up] [Colloq.] **1.** clothes **2.** belongings

due (dōō, dyōō) *adj.* [< L. *debere,* owe] **1.** owed or owing as a debt; payable **2.** suitable; proper **3.** enough *[due care]* **4.** expected or scheduled to arrive —*adv.* exactly; directly *[due west]* —*n.* anything due; specif., *[pl.]* fees or other charges *[membership dues]* —**become** (or **fall**) **due** to become payable as previously arranged —**due to 1.** caused by **2.** [Colloq.] because of

du·el (dōō'əl, dyōō'-) *n.* [< ML. *duellum,* war] **1.** a prearranged fight between two persons armed with deadly weapons **2.** any contest like this —*vi., vt.* **-eled** or **-elled, -el·ing** or **-el·ling** to fight a duel (with) —**du'el·ist** or **du'el·list, du'el·er** or **du'el·ler** *n.*

du·en·na (dōō en'ə, dyōō-) *n.* [< L. *domina,* mistress] **1.** an elderly woman who has charge of the young unmarried women of a Spanish or Portuguese family **2.** a chaperon or governess

due process (of law) the course of legal proceedings established to protect individual rights

du·et (dōō et', dyōō-) *n.* [< L. *duo,* two] *Music* **1.** a composition for two voices or instruments **2.** the two performers of such a composition

duff (duf) *n.* [dial. var. of DOUGH] a thick flour pudding boiled in a cloth bag

duf·fel, duf·fle (duf'l) *n.* [< *Duffel,* town in Belgium] **1.** a coarse woolen cloth **2.** *same as* DUFFEL BAG

duffel (or **duffle**) **bag** a large, cylindrical cloth bag for carrying clothing and personal belongings

duf·fer (duf'ər) *n.* [< thieves' slang *duff,* to fake] [Slang] an awkward or incompetent person

dug¹ (dug) *pt. & pp. of* DIG

dug² (dug) *n.* [< Dan. *dægge,* suckle] a female animal's nipple or teat

du·gong (dōō'gôŋ) *n.* [Malay *dūyung*] a large, whalelike mammal of tropical seas

dug'out' *n.* **1.** a boat hollowed out of a log **2.** a shelter, as in warfare, dug in the ground or hillside **3.** a covered shelter near a baseball diamond for the players to sit in

duke (dōōk, dyōōk) *n.* [< L. *ducere,* to lead] **1.** the ruler of an independent duchy **2.** a nobleman next in rank to a prince —**duke'dom** *n.*

dul·cet (dul'sit) *adj.* [< L. *dulcis,* sweet] soothing or pleasant to hear; melodious

dul·ci·mer (dul'sə mər) *n.* [< L. *dulce,* sweet + *melos,* a song] **1.** a musical instrument with metal strings, which are struck with two small hammers **2.** a violin-shaped stringed instrument of the southern Appalachians, plucked with a plectrum

DULCIMER

dull (dul) *adj.* [< OE. *dol,* stupid] **1.** mentally slow; stupid **2.** lacking sensitivity; unfeeling **3.** physically slow; sluggish **4.** lacking spirit; listless **5.** boring; tedious **6.** not sharp; blunt **7.** not felt keenly **8.** not vivid **9.** not glossy —*vt., vi.* to make or become dull —**dull'ness** *n.* —**dul'ly** *adv.*

dull'ard (-ərd) *n.* a stupid person

dulse (duls) *n.* [Ir. & Gael. *duileasq*] any of several edible marine algae with large, red fronds

Du·luth (də lōōth') city in NE Minn.: pop. 101,000

du·ly (dōō'lē, dyōō'-) *adv.* in due manner; specif., *a)* as due; rightfully *b)* when due *c)* as required

Du·mas (dü mä'), **Alexandre** 1802–70; Fr. writer

dumb (dum) *adj.* [OE.] **1.** lacking the power of speech; mute **2.** silent **3.** [G. *dumm*] [Colloq.] stupid —**dumb'ly** *adv.* —**dumb'ness** *n.*

dumb·bell (dum'bel') *n.* **1.** a device used in pairs for muscular exercise: each one has round weights joined by a short bar **2.** [Slang] a stupid person

dumb·found, dum·found (dum'found') *vt.* [DUMB + (CON)FOUND] to make speechless by shocking; amaze

dumb show 1. formerly, a part of a play done in pantomime **2.** gestures without speech

dumb'wait'er *n.* a small elevator for sending food, trash, etc. from one floor to another

dum·dum (**bullet**) (dum′dum′) [< *Dumdum,* arsenal near Calcutta, India] a soft-nosed bullet that expands when it hits, inflicting a large wound

dum·my (dum′ē) *n., pl.* **-mies 1.** a figure made in human form, as for displaying clothing **2.** an imitation or sham **3.** [Slang] a stupid person **4.** *Bridge,* etc. the declarer's partner, whose hand is exposed on the board and played by the declarer —*adj.* sham

dump (dump) *vt.* [prob. < ON.] **1.** to unload in a heap or mass **2.** to throw away (rubbish, etc.) **3.** to sell (a commodity) in a large quantity at a low price, esp. abroad —*n.* **1.** a rubbish pile or a place for dumping **2.** *Mil.* a temporary storage center **3.** [Slang] a place that is unpleasant, ugly, etc. —(**down**) **in the dumps** in low spirits; depressed

dump′ling (-liŋ) *n.* [< ?] **1.** a small piece of dough, steamed or boiled and served with meat or soup **2.** a crust of baked dough filled with fruit

dump truck a truck that is unloaded by tilting the truck bed backward with the tailgate open

dump·y (dum′pē) *adj.* **-i·er, -i·est 1.** short and thick; squat **2.** [Slang] ugly, run-down, etc. —**dump′i·ly** *adv.* —**dump′i·ness** *n.*

dun[1] (dun) *adj., n.* [OE.] dull grayish brown

dun[2] (dun) *vt., vi.* **dunned, dun′ning** [? dial. var. of DIN] to ask (a debtor) repeatedly for payment —*n.* an insistent demand for payment of a debt

dunce (duns) *n.* [< *Dunsman,* follower of *Duns* Scotus, 13th-c. Scot. scholar] a dull, ignorant person

dunce cap a cone-shaped hat which children slow at learning were formerly forced to wear in school

dun·der·head (dun′dər hed′) *n.* [< Du. *donder,* thunder] a stupid person; dunce

dune (dōōn, dyōōn) *n.* [Fr. < ODu. *duna*] a rounded hill or ridge of sand heaped by the wind

dune buggy [orig. used on sand dunes] a small, light automobile made from a standard, compact chassis and a prefabricated body

dung (duŋ) *n.* [OE.] animal excrement; manure —**dung′y** *adj.* **-i·er, -i·est**

dun·ga·ree (duŋ′gə rē′) *n.* [Hindi *dungrī*] **1.** a coarse cotton cloth; specif., blue denim **2.** [*pl.*] work trousers or overalls of this cloth

dun·geon (dun′jən) *n.* [< OFr. *donjon*] a dark, underground cell or prison

dung′hill′ *n.* **1.** a heap of dung **2.** anything filthy

dunk (duŋk) *vt.* [G. *tunken*] **1.** to dip (bread, cake, etc.) into coffee, etc. before eating it **2.** to immerse briefly

Dun·kirk (dun′kərk) seaport in N France: scene of evacuation of Allied troops under fire (May, 1940)

dun·lin (dun′lin) *n.* [< DUN[1] + -LING] a small sandpiper with a reddish back and a black belly patch

dun·nage (dun′ij) *n.* [< ?] **1.** bulky material put around cargo to protect it **2.** personal belongings

du·o (dōō′ō, dyōō′ō) *n., pl.* **du′os, du′i** (-ē) [It.] **1.** *same as* DUET (esp. sense 2) **2.** a pair; couple

du·o·dec·i·mal (dōō′ə des′ə m'l, dyōō′-) *adj.* [< L. *duo,* two + *decem,* ten] relating to twelve or twelfths —*n.* **1.** one twelfth **2.** [*pl.*] *Math.* a system of numeration with twelve as its base

du′o·dec′i·mo′ (-mō′) *n., pl.* **-mos′** [< L. *in duodecimo,* in twelve] **1.** a page size (about 5 by 7 1/2 in.), 1/12 of a printer's sheet **2.** a book with pages of this size —*adj.* with pages of this size

du·o·de·num (dōō′ə dē′nəm, dyōō′-) *n., pl.* **-de′na** (-nə), **-de′nums** [< L. *duodeni,* twelve each: its length is about twelve fingers' breadth] the first section of the small intestine, below the stomach —**du′o·de′nal** *adj.*

dup. duplicate

dupe (dōōp, dyōōp) *n.* [Fr. < L. *upupa,* stupid bird] a person easily tricked or fooled —*vt.* **duped, dup′ing** to deceive or cheat

du·ple (dōō′p'l, dyōō′-) *adj.* [L. *duplus:* see DOUBLE] **1.** double **2.** *Music* having an even number of beats to the measure

du·plex (dōō′pleks, dyōō′-) *adj.* [< L. *duo,* two + *-lex,* -fold] double —*n. same as* DUPLEX HOUSE or DUPLEX APARTMENT

duplex apartment an apartment with rooms on two floors and a private inner stairway

duplex house a house of two separate family units

du·pli·cate (dōō′plə kit, dyōō′-; *for v.* -kāt′) *adj.* [< L. *duplicare,* to double] **1.** double **2.** corresponding exactly **3.** designating a game of bridge, etc. in which the same

hands are played again by other players —*n.* **1.** an exact copy; facsimile **2.** a duplicate game of bridge, etc. —*vt.* **-cat′ed, -cat′ing 1.** to make an exact copy of **2.** to cause to happen again —**du′pli·ca′tion** *n.*

duplicating machine a machine for making copies of a letter, drawing, etc.: also **du′pli·ca′tor** *n.*

du·plic·i·ty (dōō plis′ə tē, dyōō-) *n., pl.* **-ties** [< LL. *duplicitas*] hypocritical cunning or deception; double-dealing

du·ra·ble (door′ə b'l, dyoor′-) *adj.* [< L. *durare,* to last] **1.** lasting in spite of hard wear or frequent use **2.** stable —**du′ra·bil′i·ty** *n.* —**du′ra·bly** *adv.*

dur·ance (door′əns, dyoor′-) *n.* [see prec.] imprisonment: mainly in phrase **in durance vile**

du·ra·tion (doo rā′shən, dyoo-) *n.* [see DURABLE] the time that a thing continues or lasts

Dü·rer (dü′rər), **Al·brecht** (äl′brekht) 1471–1528; Ger. painter & wood carver

du·ress (doo res′, dyoo-) *n.* [< L. *durus,* hard] **1.** imprisonment **2.** the use of force or threats

dur·ing (door′iŋ, dyoor′-) *prep.* [see DURABLE] **1.** throughout the entire time of **2.** in the course of

durst (dûrst) *archaic pt. of* DARE

du·rum (**wheat**) (door′əm, dyoor′-) [L. < *durus,* hard] a hard wheat that yields flour and semolina used in macaroni, spaghetti, etc.

dusk (dusk) *n.* [< OE. *dox,* dark-colored] **1.** the dim part of twilight **2.** gloom; dusky quality —*vt., vi.* to make or become dusky or shadowy

dusk′y *adj.* **-i·er, -i·est 1.** somewhat dark in color **2.** lacking light; dim **3.** gloomy —**dusk′i·ly** *adv.* —**dusk′i·ness** *n.*

dust (dust) *n.* [OE.] **1.** powdery earth or any finely powdered matter **2.** earth **3.** disintegrated mortal remains **4.** a humble or abject condition **5.** anything worthless —*vt.* **1.** to sprinkle with dust, powder, etc. **2.** to rid of dust, as by wiping —*vi.* to remove dust, as from furniture —**bite the dust** to be killed, esp. in battle —**dust′less** *adj.*

dust bowl a region where eroded topsoil is blown away by winds during droughts

dust′er *n.* **1.** a person or thing that dusts **2.** a short, loose, lightweight housecoat

dust jacket a detachable paper cover for protecting the binding of a book

dust′pan′ *n.* a shovellike receptacle into which dust or debris is swept from a floor

dust storm a windstorm that sweeps up clouds of dust when passing over an arid region

dust′y *adj.* **-i·er, -i·est 1.** covered with or full of dust **2.** like dust; powdery **3.** dust-colored —**dust′i·ly** *adv.* —**dust′i·ness** *n.*

Dutch (duch) *adj.* **1.** of the Netherlands, its people, language, etc. **2.** [Slang] German —*n.* the language of the Netherlands —**go Dutch** [Colloq.] to have each pay his own expenses —**in Dutch** [Colloq.] in trouble or disfavor —**the Dutch** the people of the Netherlands —**Dutch′man** *n., pl.* **-men**

Dutch door a door with upper and lower halves that can be opened separately

Dutch·man's-breech·es (duch′mənz brich′iz) *n., pl.* **-breech′es** a spring wildflower with pinkish, double-spurred flowers, found in E U.S.

Dutch oven a heavy metal pot with an arched lid, for cooking pot roasts, etc.

Dutch treat [Colloq.] any entertainment, etc. at which each participant pays his own expenses

Dutch uncle [Colloq.] a person who bluntly and sternly lectures or scolds someone else

du·te·ous (dōōt′ē əs, dyōōt′-) *adj.* dutiful; obedient —**du′te·ous·ly** *adv.* —**du′te·ous·ness** *n.*

du·ti·a·ble (dōōt′ē ə b'l, dyōōt′-) *adj.* necessitating payment of a duty or tax, as imported goods

du′ti·ful (-ə fəl) *adj.* **1.** showing, or resulting from, a sense of duty **2.** obedient —**du′ti·ful·ly** *adv.*

du·ty (dōōt′ē, dyōōt′ē) *n., pl.* **-ties** [see DUE & -TY] **1.** obedience or respect to parents, elders, etc. **2.** conduct based on moral or legal obligation **3.** any action required by one's position **4.** a sense of obligation **5.** service, esp. military service **6.** a tax imposed on imports, etc. —**on** (or **off**) **duty** at (or having time off from) one's work or duty

du·ve·tyne, du·ve·tyn (dōō′və tēn′) *n.* [< Fr. *duvet,* eiderdown] a soft, velvetlike textile, originally made of cotton and silk

Dvo·řák (dvôr′zhäk), **An·ton** (än′tôn) 1841–1904; Czech composer

dwarf (dwôrf) *n., pl.* **dwarfs, dwarves** (dwôrvz) [OE. *dweorg*] any abnormally small person, animal, or plant — *vt.* **1.** to stunt the growth of **2.** to make seem small by comparison —*vi.* to become stunted or dwarfed —*adj.* undersized; stunted —**dwarf′ish** *adj.*

dwell (dwel) *vi.* dwelt or dwelled, dwell′ing [OE. *dwellan*, lead astray, hinder] to make one's home; reside —**dwell on** (or **upon**) to linger over in thought or speech — **dwell′er** *n.*

dwell′ing (**place**) a residence; abode

DWI, D.W.I. driving while intoxicated

dwin·dle (dwin′d'l) *vi., vt.* -dled, -dling [< OE. *dwinan*, wither] to become or make smaller or less; diminish; shrink

dwt. [*d(enarius) w(eigh)t*] pennyweight(s)

Dy *Chem.* dysprosium

dyb·buk (dib′ək) *n.* [Heb. *dibbūq*] *Jewish Folklore* a spirit of one deceased that enters the body of a person

dye (dī) *n.* [OE. *deag*] a substance or solution for coloring fabric, hair, etc.; also, the color produced —*vt., vi.* dyed, dye′ing to color as with dye —**dye′ing** *n.* —**dy′er** *n.*

dyed′-in-the-wool′ *adj.* **1.** dyed before being woven **2.** thoroughgoing; unchanging

dye′stuff′ *n.* any substance constituting or yielding a dye

dy·ing (dī′iŋ) *prp.* of DIE¹ —*adj.* **1.** about to die or end **2.** at death —*n.* a ceasing to live or exist

dyke (dīk) *n., vt.* same as DIKE

dy·nam·ic (dī nam′ik) *adj.* [< Gr. *dynasthai*, be able] **1.** relating to energy or physical force in motion **2.** relating to dynamics **3.** energetic; vigorous; forceful —**dy·nam′i·cal·ly** *adv.*

dy·nam′ics *n.pl.* [*with sing. v. for* 1] **1.** the branch of mechanics dealing with the motions of material bodies under the action of forces **2.** the various forces operating in any field

dy·na·mism (dī′nə miz′m) *n.* a dynamic quality

dy·na·mite (dī′nə mīt′) *n.* [see DYNAMIC] a powerful explosive made with nitroglycerin —*vt.* -mit′ed, -mit′ing to blow up with dynamite

dy·na·mo (dī′nə mō′) *n., pl.* -mos′ [< *dynamoelectric machine*] **1.** earlier term for GENERATOR **2.** a dynamic person

dynamo- [see DYNAMIC] *a combining form meaning* power [*dynamoelectric*]

dy·na·mo·e·lec·tric (dī′nə mō i lek′trik) *adj.* having to do with the production of electrical energy from mechanical energy, or the reverse process

dy·na·mom·e·ter (dī′nə mäm′ə tər) *n.* an apparatus for measuring force or power

dy·nas·ty (dī′nəs tē) *n., pl.* -ties [< Gr. *dynasthai*, be strong] a succession of rulers, members of the same family —**dy·nas′tic** (-nas′tik) *adj.*

dyne (dīn) *n.* [Fr. < Gr. *dynamis*, power] the amount of force that imparts to a mass of one gram an acceleration of one centimeter per second per second

dys- [Gr.] *a prefix meaning* bad, ill, difficult, etc.

dys·en·ter·y (dis′'n ter′ē) *n.* [< Gr. *dys-*, bad + *entera*, bowels] a painful intestinal inflammation characterized by diarrhea with bloody, mucous feces —**dys′en·ter′ic** *adj.*

dys·pep·si·a (dis pep′shə, -sē ə) *n.* [< Gr. *dys-*, bad + *peptein*, to digest] indigestion —**dys·pep′tic** *adj., n.*

dys·pro·si·um (dis prō′sē əm, -zē-, -shē-) *n.* [< Gr. *dysprositos*, difficult of access] a chemical element of the rare-earth group: symbol, Dy; at. wt., 162.50; at. no., 66: it is one of the most magnetic of all known substances

dz. dozen; dozens

E

E, e (ē) *n., pl.* **E's, e's** the fifth letter of the English alphabet

E (ē) *n.* **1.** *Music* the third tone in the scale of C major **2.** *Physics* the symbol for energy

e- *a prefix meaning* out, from, etc.: see EX-

E, E., e, e. 1. east **2.** eastern

each (ēch) *adj., pron.* [< OE. *ælc*] every one of two or more considered separately —*adv.* apiece [ten cents *each*] Abbrev. **ea.**

ea·ger (ē′gər) *adj.* [< L. *acer*, keen] keenly desiring; impatient or anxious —**ea′ger·ly** *adv.* —**ea′ger·ness** *n.*

ea·gle (ē′g'l) *n.* [< L. *aquila*] **1.** a large, strong bird of prey having sharp vision and powerful wings **2.** a representation of the eagle, esp. as the emblem of the U.S. **3.** a former U.S. $10 gold coin **4.** *Golf* a score of two below par on any hole

ea′gle-eyed′ *adj.* having keen vision

ea·glet (ē′glit) *n.* a young eagle

ear¹ (ir) *n.* [OE. *eare*] **1.** the part of the body that perceives sound; organ of hearing **2.** the external part of the ear **3.** the sense of hearing **4.** the ability to recognize slight differences in sound, esp. in musical tones **5.** anything like an ear —**be all ears** to listen attentively —**give** (or **lend**) **ear** to give attention; heed —**play by ear** to play (music) without using notation —**play it by ear** [Colloq.] to improvise

ear² (ir) *n.* [< OE. *ær*] the grain-bearing spike of a cereal plant [an *ear* of corn] —*vi.* to sprout ears

ear′ache′ *n.* an ache in an ear

ear′drum′ *n.* same as TYMPANIC MEMBRANE

earl (url) *n.* [OE. *eorl*, warrior] a British nobleman ranking just above a viscount —**earl′dom** *n.*

ear·ly (ur′lē) *adv., adj.* -li·er, -li·est [< OE. *ær*, before + *-lice*, -ly] **1.** near the beginning of a given period of time or of a series, as of events **2.** before the expected or usual time **3.** in the distant past **4.** in the near future —**ear′li·ness** *n.*

early bird [Colloq.] a person who arrives early or gets up early in the morning

ear′mark′ *n.* **1.** an identification mark put on the ear of an animal **2.** an identifying mark or feature —*vt.* **1.** to set a distinctive mark upon **2.** to reserve for a special purpose

ear′muffs′ (-mufs′) *n.pl.* cloth or fur coverings for the ears in cold weather

earn (urn) *vt.* [OE. *earnian*] **1.** to receive (wages, etc.) for one's work **2.** to get as a result of something done **3.** to gain (interest, etc.) as profit —**earn′er** *n.*

ear·nest¹ (ur′nist) *adj.* [OE. *eornoste*] **1.** serious and intense; not joking **2.** important —**in earnest 1.** serious **2.** in a determined manner —**ear′nest·ly** *adv.* —**ear′nest·ness** *n.*

ear·nest² (ur′nist) *n.* [ult. < Heb. *'ērābōn*] money, etc. given as a pledge in binding a bargain

earn′ings *n.pl.* **1.** wages or other recompense **2.** profits, interest, dividends, etc.

ear′phone′ *n.* a receiver for radio, etc. held to, or put into, the ear

ear′ring′ *n.* a ring or other small ornament for the lobe of the ear

ear′shot′ (-shät′) *n.* the distance within which a sound can be heard

earth (urth) *n.* [OE. *eorthe*] **1.** [*occas.* E-] the planet we live on, the fifth largest of the solar system: see PLANET **2.** this world, as distinguished from heaven and hell **3.** land, as distinguished from sea or sky **4.** ground; soil **5.** [Poet.] worldly matters **6.** *Chem.* any of the metallic oxides which are reduced with difficulty —**down to earth** practical; realistic —**run to earth** to hunt down

earth′bound′ (-bound′) *adj.* **1.** confined to or by the earth or earthly things **2.** headed for the earth

earth′en *adj.* made of earth or of baked clay

earth′en·ware′ *n.* the coarser sort of containers, tableware, etc. made of baked clay

earth′ly *adj.* **1.** terrestrial **2.** worldly **3.** temporal **4.** conceivable —**earth′li·ness** *n.*

earth′nut′ *n.* the root, tuber, or underground pod of various plants, as the peanut

HUMAN EAR
(A, external ear;
B, middle ear;
C, inner ear)

AUDITORY CANAL
SEMICIRCULAR CANAL
HAMMER ANVIL
VESTIBULE
COCHLEA
STAPES
EUSTACHIAN TUBE
AUDITORY NERVES

earth′quake′ (-kwāk′) *n.* a shaking of the crust of the earth, caused by underground shifting of rock

earth′ward (-wərd) *adv., adj.* toward the earth: also **earth′wards** *adv.*

earth′work′ *n.* **1.** a defensive embankment made by piling up earth **2.** *Engineering* the work of excavating or building embankments

earth′worm′ *n.* a round, segmented worm that burrows in the soil

earth′y (ur′thē) *adj.* **-i·er, -i·est 1.** of or like earth or soil **2.** coarse; unrefined **3.** simple and natural

ear trumpet a trumpet-shaped tube formerly used as a hearing aid by the partially deaf

ear′wax′ *n.* the yellowish, waxlike secretion in the canal of the outer ear; cerumen

ear′wig′ (-wig′) *n.* [< OE. *eare*, ear + *wicga*, beetle] any of a group of insects with short, horny forewings and a pair of forceps at the tail end

ease (ēz) *n.* [< L. *adjacens*, lying nearby] **1.** freedom from pain or trouble; comfort **2.** natural manner; poise **3.** freedom from difficulty; facility **4.** affluence —*vt.* **eased, eas′ing 1.** to free from pain or trouble; comfort **2.** to lessen (pain, anxiety, etc.) **3.** to facilitate **4.** to reduce the strain or pressure of **5.** to move by careful shifting, etc. —*vi.* to lessen in tension, pain, etc.

ea·sel (ē′z'l) *n.* [ult. < L. *asinus*, ass] an upright frame to hold an artist's canvas, etc.

ease·ment (ēz′mənt) *n.* **1.** an easing or being eased **2.** *Law* a right that one may have in another's land

eas·i·ly (ē′z'l ē) *adv.* **1.** in an easy manner **2.** without a doubt; by far **3.** very likely

east (ēst) *n.* [OE. *east*] **1.** the direction in which sunrise occurs (90° on the compass, opposite west) **2.** a region in or toward this direction **3.** [E-] Asia and the nearby islands; the Orient —*adj.* **1.** in, of, or toward the east **2.** from the east —*adv.* in or toward the east —**the East** the eastern part of the U.S.

East Berlin E section of Berlin; capital of East Germany: pop. 1,084,000

East China Sea part of the Pacific Ocean, between China & Japan

East·er (ēs′tər) *n.* [< OE. *Eastre*, dawn goddess] an annual Christian festival in the spring celebrating the resurrection of Jesus, held on the first Sunday after the first full moon on or after March 21

Easter egg a colored egg or an egg-shaped candy, etc., used as an Easter gift or ornament

Easter Island Chilean island in the South Pacific

east′er·ly *adj., adv.* **1.** toward the east **2.** from the east

east′ern *adj.* **1.** in, of, or toward the east **2.** from the east **3.** [E-] of the East —**east′ern·most′** *adj.*

Eastern Church 1. the Christian Church in the Byzantine Empire **2.** the Orthodox Eastern Church

east′ern·er *n.* a native or inhabitant of the east, specif. [E-] of the eastern part of the U.S.

Eastern Hemisphere that half of the earth that includes Europe, Africa, Asia, and Australia

East Germany E section of Germany; a country in NC Europe: 41,800 sq. mi.; pop. 17,084,000; cap. East Berlin

East Indies Malay Archipelago —**East Indian**

east-north·east (ēst′nôrth′ēst′; *nautical* -nôr′-) *n.* the direction halfway between due east and northeast —*adj., adv.* in, toward, or from this direction

east′-south′east′ (-south′ēst′; *nautical* -sou′-) *n.* the direction halfway between due east and southeast —*adj., adv.* in, toward, or from this direction

east′ward (-wərd) *adv., adj.* toward the east: also **east′wards** *adv.* —*n.* an eastward direction, point, or region —**east′ward·ly** *adv., adj.*

eas·y (ē′zē) *adj.* **-i·er, -i·est** [see EASE] **1.** not difficult **2.** free from anxiety, pain, etc. **3.** comfortable; restful **4.** not stiff or awkward **5.** not strict; lenient **6.** compliant **7.** unhurried **8.** gradual —*adv.* [Colloq.] easily —**take it easy** [Colloq.] **1.** to refrain from anger, haste, etc. **2.** to relax; rest —**eas′i·ness** *n.*

easy chair a stuffed or padded armchair

eas′y·go′ing *adj.* dealing with things in a relaxed or lenient way

eat (ēt) *vt.* **ate, eat′en, eat′ing** [OE. *etan*] **1.** to chew and swallow (food) **2.** to consume or ravage (with *away* or *up*) **3.** to destroy, as acid does; corrode **4.** to make by eating [acid *eats* holes in cloth] **5.** [Slang] to worry or bother —*vi.* to eat food; have a meal —**eat one's words** to retract something said earlier —**eat′er** *n.*

eat′a·ble *adj.* fit to be eaten —*n.* a thing fit to be eaten: *usually in pl.*

eat′er·y *n., pl.* **-ies** [Colloq.] a restaurant

eats (ēts) *n.pl.* [Colloq.] food; meals

eau de Co·logne (ō′ də kə lōn′) [Fr., lit., water of Cologne] a perfumed toilet water, with aromatic oils

eaves (ēvz) *n.pl.* [< OE. *efes*] the projecting lower edge or edges of a roof

eaves′drop′ (-dräp′) *vi.* **-dropped′, -drop′ping** [prob. < *eavesdropper*, one standing under eaves to overhear] to listen secretly to a private conversation —**eaves′drop′per** *n.*

ebb (eb) *n.* [OE. *ebba*] **1.** the flow of the tide back toward the sea **2.** a lessening; decline —*vi.* **1.** to recede, as the tide **2.** to lessen; decline

ebb tide the outgoing or falling tide

eb·on·y (eb′ən ē) *n., pl.* **-ies** [< Gr. *ebenos*] the hard, heavy, dark wood of certain tropical trees —*adj.* **1.** of ebony **2.** like ebony; black; dark

e·bul·lient (i bool′yənt, -bul′-) *adj.* [< L. *e-*, out + *bulire*, to boil] **1.** boiling; bubbling **2.** enthusiastic; exuberant —**e·bul′lience, e·bul′lien·cy** *n.*

e·bul·li·tion (eb′ə lish′ən) *n.* **1.** a boiling or bubbling up **2.** a sudden outburst, as of emotion

ec·cen·tric (ik sen′trik) *adj.* [< Gr. *ek-*, out of + *kentron*, center] **1.** not having the same center, as two circles **2.** having its axis off center **3.** not exactly circular **4.** odd, as in conduct; unconventional —*n.* **1.** a disk set off center on a shaft, for converting circular motion into back-and-forth motion **2.** an eccentric person —**ec·cen′tri·cal·ly** *adv.*

ec·cen·tric·i·ty (ek′sen tris′ə tē, -sən-) *n., pl.* **-ties 1.** a being eccentric **2.** deviation from the norm; oddity

Ec·cle·si·as·tes (i klē′zē as′tēz) [< Gr. *ek-*, out + *kalein*, to call] a book of the Bible, written as though by Solomon: abbrev. **Eccles., Eccl.**

ec·cle·si·as·tic (i klē′zē as′tik) *adj.* [see prec.] *same as* ECCLESIASTICAL —*n.* a clergyman

ec·cle·si·as′ti·cal *adj.* of the church or the clergy —**ec·cle′si·as′ti·cal·ly** *adv.*

ECG electrocardiogram

ech·e·lon (esh′ə län′) *n.* [< Fr. < L. *scala*, ladder] **1.** a steplike formation of ships, troops, aircraft, etc. **2.** a subdivision of a military force **3.** any of the levels of responsibility in an organization

e·chid·na (i kid′nə) *n.* [< Gr. *echidna*, adder] a small, egg-laying Australasian mammal with a long snout

e·chi·no·derm (i kī′nə durm′, ek′ə nə-) *n.* [< Gr. *echinos*, sea urchin + *derma*, skin] a sea animal with a hard, spiny skeleton and radial body, as the starfish

ech·o (ek′ō) *n., pl.* **-oes** [< Gr. *ēchō*] **1.** the repetition of a sound by reflection of the sound waves from a surface **2.** a sound so produced **3.** *a)* any repetition or imitation of another's words, style, ideas, etc. *b)* a person who does this —*vi.* **-oed, -o·ing 1.** to reverberate **2.** to make an echo —*vt.* to repeat (another's words, etc.)

e·cho·ic (e kō′ik) *adj.* **1.** like an echo **2.** imitative in sound, as the word *buzz* —**ech′o·ism** *n.*

é·clair (ā kler′, ē-) *n.* [Fr., lit., lightning] an oblong, frosted pastry shell filled with custard, etc.

é·clat (ā klä′) *n.* [Fr. < *éclater*, to burst (out)] **1.** brilliant success **2.** striking effect **3.** acclaim; fame

ec·lec·tic (i klek′tik, e-) *adj.* [< Gr. *ek-*, out + *legein*, to pick] selecting or selected from various sources —*n.* one who uses eclectic methods —**ec·lec′ti·cal·ly** *adv.* —**ec·lec′ti·cism** *n.*

e·clipse (i klips′) *n.* [< Gr. *ek-*, out + *leipein*, to leave] **1.** the obscuring of the sun when the moon comes between it and the earth (**solar eclipse**), or of the moon when the earth's shadow is cast upon it (**lunar eclipse**) **2.** any obscuring of light, or of fame, glory, etc. —*vt.* **e·clipsed′, e·clips′ing 1.** to cause an eclipse of **2.** to overshadow; surpass

e·clip·tic (i klip′tik) *n.* the sun's apparent annual path, or orbit; great circle of the celestial sphere —*adj.* of eclipses or the ecliptic

ec·logue (ek′lôg) *n.* [see ECLECTIC] a short pastoral poem

e·co·cide (ē′kō sīd′, ek′ō-) *n.* [< Gr. *oikos*, house + -CIDE] the destruction of the environment, as by defoliants, pollutants, etc. —**e′co·ci′dal** *adj.*

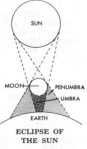

SUN

MOON · PENUMBRA
· UMBRA

EARTH

ECLIPSE OF THE SUN

---

fat, āpe, cär; ten, ēven; is, bīte; gō, hôrn, tōol, look; oil, out; up, fur; thin, *then*; zh, leisure; ŋ, ring; ə for *a* in *ago*; ′ as in *able* (ā′b'l); ë, Fr. coeur; ö, Fr. feu; ü, Fr. mon; ü, Fr. duc; r, Fr. cri; kh, G. doch, ich. ‡ foreign; < derived from

e·col·o·gy (ē käl'ə jē) *n.* [< Gr. *oikos*, house + *-logia*, -LOGY] the interrelationship of organisms and their environment, or the study of this —**ec·o·log·i·cal** (ek'ə läj'i k'l, ē'kə-), **ec'o·log'ic** *adj.* —**ec'o·log'i·cal·ly** *adv.* — **e·col'o·gist** *n.*

econ. 1. economic 2. economics 3. economy

e·co·nom·ic (ē'kə näm'ik, ek'ə-) *adj.* 1. of the management of income, expenditures, etc. of a business, community, etc. 2. of economics 3. of the satisfaction of the material needs of people

e'co·nom'i·cal *adj.* 1. not wasting money, time, etc.; thrifty 2. of economics —**e'co·nom'i·cal·ly** *adv.*

e'co·nom'ics *n.pl.* [*with sing. v.*] 1. the science that deals with the production, distribution, and consumption of wealth 2. economic factors

e·con·o·mist (i kän'ə mist) *n.* a specialist in economics

e·con'o·mize (-mīz') *vi.* -**mized'**, -**miz'ing** to reduce waste or expenses —*vt.* to manage or use with thrift — **e·con'o·miz'er** *n.*

e·con·o·my (-mē) *n., pl.* -**mies** [< Gr. *oikos*, house + *nomos*, managing] 1. the management of the income, expenditures, etc. of a household, government, etc. 2. careful management of wealth, etc.; thrift 3. an instance of thrift 4. an economic system of a specified kind, place, etc.

e·co·sys·tem (ē'kō sis'təm, ek'ō-) *n.* [< Gr. *oikos*, house + SYSTEM] a community of animals and plants and the environment with which it is interrelated

ec·ru (ek'rōō) *adj., n.* [< Fr. < L. *ex-*, intens. + *crudus*, raw] light tan; beige

ec·sta·sy (ek'stə sē) *n., pl.* -**sies** [< Gr. *ek-*, out + *histanai*, to place] a state or feeling of overpowering joy; rapture —**ec·stat·ic** (ik stat'ik) *adj.* —**ec·stat'i·cal·ly** *adv.*

ecto- [< Gr. *ektos*, outside] *a combining form meaning* outside, external: also **ect-**

ec·to·derm (ek'tə durm') *n.* [< ECTO- + Gr. *derma*, skin] the outer layer of cells of an embryo in its early stage

-ectomy [< Gr. *ek-*, out + *temnein*, to cut] *a combining form meaning* a surgical excision of *[appendectomy]*

ec·to·plasm (ek'tə plaz'm) *n.* [ECTO- + -PLASM] 1. the outer layer of the cytoplasm of a cell 2. a luminous substance believed by spiritualists to emanate from the medium in a trance

Ec·ua·dor (ek'wə dôr') country on the NW coast of S. America: 104,506 sq. mi.; pop. 5,840,000; cap. Quito

ec·u·men·i·cal (ek'yoo men'i k'l) *adj.* [< Gr. *oikoumenē* (*gē*), the inhabited (world)] 1. general or universal; esp., of the Christian church as a whole 2. furthering religious unity, esp. among Christian churches Also **ec'u·men'ic** — **ec'u·men·i·cal·ism** *n.* —**ec'u·men'i·cal·ly** *adv.*

ec'u·men·ism (-mə niz'm, e kyōo'-) *n.* the ecumenical movement, esp. among Christian churches

ec·ze·ma (ek'sə mə, eg'zə-; ig zē'mə) *n.* [< Gr. *ek-*, out + *zein*, to boil] a skin disease characterized by inflammation, itching, and scaliness

-ed [OE.] a suffix used: 1. to form the past tense and past participle of many verbs 2. to form adjectives from nouns or verbs *[cultured]*

ed. 1. edited 2. *pl.* **eds.** *a)* edition *b)* editor

E·dam (cheese) (ē'dəm) [< *Edam*, Netherlands] a round, mild, yellow cheese

ed·dy (ed'ē) *n., pl.* -**dies** [prob. < ON. *itha*] a little whirlpool or whirlwind —*vi.* -**died**, -**dy·ing** to move as in an eddy; whirl

Ed·dy (ed'ē), **Mary Baker** 1821–1910; U.S. founder of Christian Science

e·del·weiss (ā'd'l vīs') *n.* [G. < *edel*, noble + *weiss*, white] a small, flowering plant, esp. of the Alps, with white, woolly leaves

e·de·ma (i dē'mə) *n.* [< Gr. *oidēma*, swelling] an abnormal accumulation of fluid in body tissues

E·den (ē'd'n) *Bible* the garden where Adam and Eve first lived; Paradise —*n.* any delightful place

e·den·tate (ē den'tāt) *adj.* [< L. *e-*, out + *dens*, tooth] 1. without teeth 2. of the edentates —*n.* any of a group of mammals with molars only or no teeth at all, as sloths and anteaters

edge (ej) *n.* [OE. *ecg*] 1. the sharp, cutting part of a blade 2. sharpness; keenness 3. the brink or verge, as of a cliff 4. a border; margin 5. [Colloq.] advantage *[you have the edge on me]* —*vt., vi.* **edged**, **edg'ing** 1. to form an edge (on) 2. to make (one's way) sideways 3. to move gradually —**on edge** irritable or impatient —**take the edge off** to dull the force or pleasure of —**edg'er** *n.*

edge'ways' (-wāz') *adv.* with the edge foremost: also **edge'wise'** (-wīz')

edg'ing *n.* trimming along an edge

edg·y (ej'ē) *adj.* -**i·er**, -**i·est** 1. having an edge; sharp 2. on edge; irritable —**edg'i·ly** *adv.* —**edg'i·ness** *n.*

ed·i·ble (ed'ə b'l) *adj.* [< L. *edere*, eat] fit to be eaten —*n.* [*usually pl.*] food —**ed'i·bil'i·ty** *n.*

e·dict (ē'dikt) *n.* [< L. *e-*, out + *dicere*, speak] a public order issued by authority; decree

ed·i·fice (ed'ə fis) *n.* [see EDIFY] a building, esp. a large, imposing one

ed·i·fy (ed'ə fī') *vt.* -**fied'**, -**fy'ing** [< L. *aedificare*, build] to instruct; esp., to instruct or improve morally —**ed'i·fi·ca'tion** *n.* —**ed'i·fi'er** *n.*

Ed·in·burgh (ed''n bur'ə, -ō) capital of Scotland: pop. 468,000

Ed·i·son (ed'ə s'n), **Thomas A.** 1847–1931; U.S. inventor

ed·it (ed'it) *vt.* [< EDITOR] 1. to prepare (a manuscript, etc.) for publication by arranging, revising, etc. 2. to control the policy and contents of (a newspaper, etc.) 3. to prepare (a film, tape, etc.) for presentation by cutting, dubbing, etc.

edit. 1. edited 2. edition 3. editor

e·di·tion (i dish'ən) *n.* [see EDITOR] 1. the size or form in which a book is published 2. the total number of copies of a book, etc. published at one time 3. one of these copies

ed·i·tor (ed'i tər) *n.* [L. < *e-*, out + *dare*, give] 1. one who edits 2. the head of a department of a newspaper, etc. —**ed'i·tor·ship'** *n.*

ed·i·to·ri·al (ed'ə tôr'ē əl) *adj.* of or by an editor —*n.* a statement of opinion in a newspaper, etc. or on radio or TV by an editor or publisher —**ed'i·to'ri·al·ly** *adv.*

ed'i·to'ri·al·ize' (-īz') *vt., vi.* -**ized'**, -**iz'ing** to express editorial opinions about (something) or in (an article, etc.)

editor in chief *pl.* **editors in chief** the editor who heads the editorial staff of a publication

Ed·mon·ton (ed'mən tən) capital of Alberta, Canada: pop. 377,000

educ. 1. education 2. educational

ed·u·ca·ble (ej'ə kə b'l) *adj.* that can be educated or trained —**ed'u·ca·bil'i·ty** *n.*

ed·u·cate (ej'ə kāt') *vt.* -**cat'ed**, -**cat'ing** [< L. *e-*, out + *ducere*, to lead] 1. to train, teach, instruct, or develop, esp. by formal schooling 2. to pay for the schooling of — **ed'u·ca'tor** *n.*

ed·u·ca'tion *n.* 1. the process of educating; teaching 2. knowledge, etc. thus developed 3. formal schooling —**ed'u·ca'tion·al**, **ed'u·ca'tive** *adj.* —**ed'u·ca'tion·al·ly** *adv.*

e·duce (i dōos', ē-) *vt.* **e·duced'**, **e·duc'ing** [see EDUCATE] 1. to draw out; elicit 2. to deduce

-ee [< Anglo-Fr. pp. ending] *a suffix designating:* 1. the recipient of an action *[appointee]* 2. one in a specified condition *[absentee]*

EEG electroencephalogram

eel (ēl) *n.* [OE. *æl*] a long, slippery, snakelike fish, without pelvic fins —**eel'like'**, **eel'y** *adj.*

eel'grass' *n.* an underwater flowering plant with long, grasslike leaves

e'en (ēn) *adv.* [Poet.] even —*n.* [Poet.] even(ing)

e'er (er, ar) *adv.* [Poet.] ever

-eer [< L. *-arius*] *a suffix denoting* a person involved with or an action involving *[auctioneer, electioneer]*

ee·rie, ee·ry (ir'ē) *adj.* -**ri·er**, -**ri·est** [< OE. *earg*, timid] mysterious, uncanny, or weird —**ee'ri·ness** *n.*

ef- *same as* EX-: used before *f* *[efferent]*

ef·face (i fās', e-) *vt.* -**faced'**, -**fac'ing** [< L. *ex*, out + *facies*, face] 1. to blot out; erase *[time effaced the memory]* 2. to make (oneself) inconspicuous —**ef·face'a·ble** *adj.* — **ef·face'ment** *n.*

ef·fect (i fekt', i-) *n.* [< L. *ex-*, out + *facere*, do] 1. anything brought about by a cause; result 2. the power to cause results 3. influence or action *[the drug's effect]* 4. meaning; purport *[he spoke to this effect]* 5. the impression made on the mind, as by artistic design 6. the condition or fact of being operative or in force 7. [*pl.*] belongings; property —*vt.* to bring about; accomplish —**in effect** 1. actually 2. virtually 3. in operation —**take effect** to become operative

ef·fec'tive *adj.* 1. producing a desired effect; efficient 2. in effect; operative 3. striking; impressive —*n.* a soldier, unit, etc. equipped and ready for combat: *usually used in pl.* —**ef·fec'tive·ly** *adv.* —**ef·fec'tive·ness** *n.*

ef·fec·tu·al (ə fek'choo wəl, i-) *adj.* 1. producing, or able to produce, the desired effect 2. having legal force; valid —**ef·fec'tu·al'i·ty** (-wal'ə tē) *n.* —**ef·fec'tu·al·ly** *adv.*

ef·fec'tu·ate' (-wāt') *vt.* -**at'ed**, -**at'ing** to bring about; make happen; effect —**ef·fec'tu·a'tion** *n.*

ef·fem·i·nate (i fem'ə nit) *adj.* [< L. *ex-*, out + *femina*, woman] showing qualities attributed to women, as weakness, delicacy, etc.; unmanly —**ef·fem'i·na·cy** (-nə sē) *n.* —**ef·fem'i·nate·ly** *adv.*

ef·fer·ent (ef'ər ənt) *adj.* [< L. *ex-*, out + *ferre*, to bear] *Physiol.* carrying away; specif., designating nerves carrying impulses away from a nerve center: opposed to AFFERENT

ef·fer·vesce (ef'ər ves') *vi.* -vesced', -vesc'ing [< L. *ex-*, out + *fervere*, to boil] **1.** to give off gas bubbles, as soda water; bubble **2.** to be lively and high-spirited —**ef'fer·ves'cence** *n.* —**ef'fer·ves'cent** *adj.*

ef·fete (e fēt', i-) *adj.* [< L. *ex-*, out + *fetus*, productive] **1.** no longer able to produce; sterile **2.** decadent; overrefined —**ef·fete'ly** *adv.* —**ef·fete'ness** *n.*

ef·fi·ca·cious (ef'ə kā'shəs) *adj.* [see EFFECT & -OUS] that produces the desired effect —**ef'fi·ca'cious·ly** *adv.* —**ef'fi·ca·cy** (-kə sē), *pl.* —**ef'fi·ca'cious·ness** *n.*

ef·fi·cient (ə fish'ənt, i-) *adj.* [see EFFECT] producing the desired result with a minimum of effort, expense, or waste —**ef·fi'cien·cy** *n.*, *pl.* -cies —**ef·fi'cient·ly** *adv.*

ef·fi·gy (ef'ə jē) *n.*, *pl.* -gies [< L. *ex-*, out + *fingere*, to form] a statue or other image; esp., a crude representation (for hanging or burning) of one who is hated

ef·flo·resce (ef'lô res') *vi.* -resced', -resc'ing [< L. *ex-*, out + *florescere*, to blossom] **1.** to blossom; flower **2.** *Chem. a)* to change from crystals to a powder through loss of the water of crystallization *b)* to develop a powdery crust by evaporation or chemical change —**ef'flo·res'cence** *n.* —**ef'flo·res'cent** *adj.*

ef·flu·ence (ef'loo wəns) *n.* [< L. *ex-*, out + *fluere*, to flow] **1.** a flowing out **2.** a thing that flows out —**ef'flu·ent** *adj.*, *n.*

ef·flu·vi·um (e floo'vē əm, i-) *n.*, *pl.* -vi·a (-ə), -vi·ums [see prec.] **1.** an aura **2.** a disagreeable or noxious vapor or odor —**ef·flu'vi·al** *adj.*

ef·fort (ef'ərt) *n.* [< L. *ex-*, intens. + *fortis*, strong] **1.** the use of energy to do something **2.** a try; attempt **3.** a result of working or trying —**ef'fort·less** *adj.* —**ef'fort·less·ly** *adv.*

ef·fron·ter·y (e frun'tər ē, i-) *n.*, *pl.* -ies [< L. *ex-*, from + *frons*, forehead] unashamed boldness; impudence; audacity

ef·ful·gence (e ful'jəns, i-) *n.* [< L. *ex-*, forth + *fulgere*, to shine] great brightness; radiance —**ef·ful'gent** *adj.*

ef·fuse (e fyooz', i-) *vt.*, *vi.* -fused', -fus'ing [< L. *ex-*, out + *fundere*, to pour] **1.** to pour out or forth **2.** to spread; diffuse

ef·fu·sion (-fyoo'zhən) *n.* **1.** a pouring forth **2.** unrestrained expression in speaking or writing

ef·fu·sive (-siv) *adj.* overly demonstrative; gushy —**ef·fu'sive·ly** *adv.* —**ef·fu'sive·ness** *n.*

eft (eft) *n.* [OE. *efeta*] same as NEWT

e.g. [L. *exempli gratia*] for example

e·gad (i gad', ē-) *interj.* [prob. < *oh God*] a softened oath

e·gal·i·tar·i·an (i gal'ə ter'ē ən) *adj.* [< Fr. *égalité*, equality] advocating full political and social equality for all people —*n.* one advocating this

egg¹ (eg) *n.* [ON.] **1.** the oval body laid by a female bird, fish, etc., containing the germ of a new individual **2.** a female reproductive cell; ovum **3.** a hen's egg, raw or cooked **4.** something like an egg **5.** [Slang] a person [she's a good *egg*]

egg² (eg) *vt.* [< ON. *eggja*, to give edge to] to urge or incite (with *on*)

egg'beat'er *n.* a kitchen utensil for beating eggs, cream, etc.

egg foo yong (or **young**) (eg' foo yuŋ') a Chinese-American dish of eggs beaten and cooked with bean sprouts, onions, minced pork, etc.

egg'head' *n.* [Slang] an intellectual: usually a term of derision as used by anti-intellectuals

egg'nog' (-näg') *n.* [EGG¹ + *nog*, strong ale] a drink made of eggs, milk, sugar, and, often, whiskey

egg'plant' *n.* **1.** a plant with a large, purple-skinned fruit, eaten as a vegetable **2.** the fruit

egg roll a fried roll of thin egg dough enclosing minced vegetables, meat, etc.: a Chinese-American dish

e·gis (ē'jis) *n. same as* AEGIS

eg·lan·tine (eg'lən tīn', -tēn') *n.* [< L. *aculeus*, a sting] a pink, European rose with sweet-scented leaves

e·go (ē'gō) *n.*, *pl.* -gos [L., I] **1.** the individual as aware of himself; the self **2.** egotism; conceit **3.** *Psychoanalysis* the part of the psyche which governs action rationally

e'go·cen'tric (-sen'trik) *adj.* viewing everything in relation to oneself —*n.* an egocentric person

e'go·ism *n.* **1.** selfishness; self-interest **2.** conceit —**e'go·ist** *n.* —**e'go·is'tic, e'go·is'ti·cal** *adj.*

e·go·tism (ē'gə tiz'm) *n.* **1.** excessive reference to oneself in speaking or writing **2.** conceit —**e'go·tist** *n.* —**e'go·tis'tic, e'go·tis'ti·cal** *adj.*

ego trip an experience, activity, etc. that is self-fulfilling or increases one's vanity

e·gre·gious (i grē'jəs) *adj.* [< L. *e-*, out + *grex*, a herd] remarkably bad; flagrant —**e·gre'gious·ly** *adv.*

e·gress (ē'gres) *n.* [< L. *e-*, out + *gradi*, go] **1.** a going out **2.** the right to go out **3.** a way out; exit

e·gret (ē'grit, eg'rit) *n.* [OFr. *aigrette*] **1.** a heronlike bird with long, white plumes **2.** an aigrette (sense 1)

E·gypt (ē'jipt) country in NE Africa, on the Mediterranean: 386,000 sq. mi.; pop. 35,619,000; cap. Cairo

E·gyp·tian (i jip'shən, ē-) *adj.* of Egypt, its people, etc. —*n.* **1.** a native or inhabitant of Egypt **2.** the language of the ancient Egyptians

eh (ā, e) *interj.* a sound expressing: **1.** surprise **2.** doubt or inquiry

EHF extremely high frequency

ei·der (ī'dər) *n.* [ult. < ON. *æthr*] **1.** a large duck of northern regions: often **eider duck 2.** *same as* EIDERDOWN

ei'der·down' *n.* the soft, fine down of the eider duck, used as a stuffing for quilts, pillows, etc.

Eif·fel Tower (ī'f'l) [< A. *Eiffel* (1832–1923), Fr. designer] tower of iron framework in Paris, built for the Exposition of 1889: 984 ft. high

eight (āt) *adj.*, *n.* [OE. *eahta*] one more than seven; 8; VIII

eight ball a black ball with the number eight on it, used in playing pool —**behind the eight ball** [Slang] in a very unfavorable position

eight·een (ā'tēn') *adj.*, *n.* eight more than ten; 18; XVIII —**eight'eenth'** (-tēnth') *adj.*, *n.*

eighth (ātth, āth) *adj.* **1.** preceded by seven others in a series; 8th **2.** designating any of eight equal parts —*n.* **1.** the one following the seventh **2.** any of the eight equal parts of something; 1/8

eighth note *Music* a note (♪) having one eighth the duration of a whole note

eight·y (āt'ē) *adj.*, *n.*, *pl.* -ies eight times ten; 80; LXXX —**the eighties** the numbers or years, as of a century, from 80 through 89 —**eight'i·eth** (-ith) *adj.*, *n.*

Ein·stein (īn'stīn), **Albert** 1879–1955; U.S. physicist, born in Germany: formulated theory of relativity

ein·stein·i·um (īn stī'nē əm) *n.* [< prec.] a radioactive chemical element: symbol, Es; at. wt., 252(?); at. no., 99

Eir·e (er'ə) *Gaelic name of* IRELAND (sense 2)

Ei·sen·how·er (ī'z'n hou'ər), **Dwight David** 1890–1969; U.S. general & 34th president of the U.S. (1953–1961)

ei·ther (ē'thər, ī'-) *adj.* [OE. *æghwæther*] **1.** one or the other (of two) **2.** each (of two) —*pron.* one or the other —*conj.* a correlative used with *or* to denote a choice of alternatives [*either* go *or* stay] —*adv.* any more than the other; also [if you don't go, he won't *either*]

e·jac·u·late (i jak'yə lāt') *vt.*, *vi.* -lat'ed, -lat'ing [see EJECT] **1.** to eject (esp. semen) **2.** to utter suddenly; exclaim —**e·jac'u·la'tion** *n.* —**e·jac'u·la·to'ry** (-lə tôr'ē) *adj.*

e·ject (e jekt') *vt.* [< L. *e-*, out + *jacere*, to throw] to throw or drive out; expel; discharge —**e·ject'a·ble** *adj.* —**e·jec'tion** *n.* —**e·jec'tor** *n.*

eke (ēk) *vt.* eked, ek'ing [OE. *eacan*, to increase] **1.** to supplement (with *out*) **2.** to make (a living) with difficulty (with *out*)

EKG electrocardiogram

e·kis·tics (i kis'tiks) *n.pl.* [with sing. v.] [< Gr. *oikos*, house + -ICS] the science of city and area planning to meet both individual and community needs

e·lab·o·rate (i lab'ər it) *adj.* [< L. *e-*, out + *labor*, work] developed in great detail; complicated —*vt.* (-ə rāt') -rat'ed, -rat'ing to work out in detail —*vi.* to add more details (usually with *on* or *upon*) —**e·lab'o·rate·ly** *adv.* —**e·lab'o·rate·ness** *n.* —**e·lab'o·ra'tion** *n.*

é·lan (ā län') *n.* [Fr. < *élancer*, to dart] spirited self-assurance; dash

e·lapse (i laps') *vi.* e·lapsed', e·laps'ing [< L. *e-*, out + *labi*, to glide] to slip by; pass: said of time

e·las·mo·branch (i laz'mə braŋk', -las'-) *adj.* [< Gr. *elasmos*, beaten metal + L. *branchia*, gills] of a group of fishes with cartilaginous skeletons, horny scales, and no air bladders —*n.* any fish of this group, as the shark

e·las·tic (i las'tik) *adj.* [< Gr. *elaunein*, set in motion] **1.** able to return immediately to its original size, shape, etc.

after being stretched, squeezed, etc.; flexible **2.** able to recover easily, as from dejection; buoyant **3.** adaptable — *n.* an elastic band or fabric —**e·las'ti·cal·ly** *adv.* —**e·las'tic'i·ty** (-tis'ə tē) *n.*

e·las'ti·cize' (-tə sīz') *vt.* -cized', -ciz'ing to make (fabric) elastic

e·late (i lāt', ē-) *vt.* -lat'ed, -lat'ing [< L. *ex-*, out + *ferre*, to bear] to raise the spirits of; make very proud, happy, etc. —**e·la'tion** *n.*

El·ba (el'bə) It. island between Corsica & Italy: site of Napoleon's first exile (1814–15)

El·be (el'bə, elb) river flowing from NW Czechoslovakia through Germany into the North Sea

el·bow (el'bō) *n.* [see ELL² & BOW²] **1.** the joint between the upper and lower arm; esp., the outer angle made by a bent arm **2.** anything bent like an elbow —*vt., vi.* to shove as with the elbows —**out at (the) elbows** shabby; poor —**rub elbows with** to associate or mingle with

elbow grease [Colloq.] hard work

el'bow·room' *n.* sufficient space or room

eld·er¹ (el'dər) *adj.* [< OE. *ald*, old] **1.** older **2.** of superior rank, position, etc. **3.** earlier; former —*n.* **1.** an older person, esp. one with authority in a tribe or community **2.** an ancestor **3.** any of certain church officers, esp. in some Protestant churches

el·der² (el'dər) *n.* [OE. *ellern*] a shrub or tree with clusters of white flowers and red or purple berries

el'der·ber'ry *n., pl.* -ries **1.** *same as* ELDER² **2.** its berry, used for making wines, jellies, etc.

eld'er·ly *adj.* somewhat old; approaching old age

eld·est (el'dist) *adj.* oldest

El Do·ra·do, El·do·ra·do (el'də rä'dō) *pl.* -dos [Sp., the gilded] any place supposed to be rich in gold, opportunity, etc.

elec., elect. **1.** electric(al) **2.** electricity

e·lect (i lekt') *adj.* [< L. *e-*, out + *legere*, choose] **1.** chosen **2.** elected but not yet installed in office *[mayor-elect]* **3.** *Theol.* chosen by God for salvation and eternal life —*vt., vi.* **1.** to select for an office by voting **2.** to choose

e·lec·tion (i lek'shən) *n.* **1.** a choosing or choice **2.** a choosing or being chosen for office by vote

e·lec'tion·eer' (-shə nir') *vi.* to canvass votes for a candidate, party, etc. in an election

e·lec'tive *adj.* **1.** filled by election *[an elective office]* **2.** chosen by election **3.** having the power to choose **4.** optional —*n.* an optional course or subject in a school curriculum

e·lec'tor (-tər) *n.* **1.** one who elects; specif., a qualified voter **2.** a member of the electoral college **3.** *[usually E-]* any of the German princes of the Holy Roman Empire who elected the emperor —**e·lec'tor·al** *adj.*

electoral college an assembly elected by the voters to perform the formal duty of electing the president and vice president of the U.S.

e·lec'tor·ate (-it) *n.* all those qualified to vote in an election

E·lec·tra (i lek'trə) *Gr. Myth.* a daughter of Agamemnon: she incited her brother to kill their mother

e·lec·tric (i lek'trik) *adj.* [< Gr. *ēlektron*, amber: from the effect of friction on amber] **1.** of or charged with electricity **2.** producing, or produced by, electricity **3.** operated by electricity **4.** electrifying; exciting —*n.* a train, car, etc. run by electricity

e·lec'tri·cal *adj.* **1.** *same as* ELECTRIC **2.** connected with the science of electricity *[an electrical engineer]* —**e·lec'tri·cal·ly** *adv.*

electric chair a chair used in electrocuting those sentenced to death

electric eel a large, eel-shaped fish of S. America, with special organs that can give electric shocks

electric eye *same as* PHOTOELECTRIC CELL

e·lec·tri·cian (i lek'trish'ən) *n.* a person whose work is the installation or repair of electric apparatus

e·lec'tric'i·ty (-tris'ə tē) *n.* **1.** a property of certain fundamental particles of all matter, as electrons (negative charges) and protons or positrons (positive charges): electric charge is generated by friction, induction, or chemical change **2.** an electric current **3.** the branch of physics dealing with electricity **4.** electric current as a public utility for lighting, heating, etc.

e·lec·tri·fy (i lek'trə fī') *vt.* -fied', -fy'ing **1.** to charge with electricity **2.** to excite; thrill **3.** to equip for the use of electricity —**e·lec'tri·fi·ca'tion** *n.* —**e·lec'tri·fi'er** *n.*

electro- *a combining form meaning* electric, electricity

e·lec·tro·car·di·o·gram (i lek'trō kär'dē ə gram') *n.* [ELECTRO- + CARDIO- + -GRAM] a tracing showing the

changes in electric potential produced by the contractions of the heart

e·lec'tro·car'di·o·graph' (-graf') *n.* an instrument for making electrocardiograms

e·lec'tro·chem'is·try *n.* the science dealing with chemical changes produced by electrical energy or with electrical energy produced by chemical changes

e·lec·tro·cute (i lek'trə kyōōt') *vt.* -cut'ed, -cut'ing [ELECTRO- + (EXE)CUTE] to kill or execute with electricity —**e·lec'tro·cu'tion** *n.*

e·lec·trode (i lek'trōd) *n.* [ELECTR(O)- + -ODE] any terminal that conducts electricity into or away from a battery, etc. or that controls the flow of electrons in an electron tube

e·lec·tro·dy·nam·ics (i lek'trō dī nam'iks) *n.pl.* [*with sing. v.*] the branch of physics dealing with the phenomena of electric currents and associated magnetic forces —**e·lec'tro·dy·nam'ic** *adj.*

e·lec'tro·en·ceph'a·lo·gram' (-en sef'ə lə gram') *n.* [< ELECTRO- + Gr. *enkephalos,* brain + -GRAM] a tracing showing the changes in electric potential produced by the brain

e·lec'tro·en·ceph'a·lo·graph' (-graf') *n.* an instrument for making electroencephalograms

e·lec·trol·o·gist (i lek'träl'ə jist) *n.* a practitioner of electrolysis (sense 2)

e·lec·trol'y·sis (-ə sis) *n.* [ELECTRO- + -LYSIS] **1.** the decomposition of an electrolyte by the action of an electric current passing through it **2.** the eradication of unwanted hair with an electrified needle

e·lec·tro·lyte (i lek'trə līt') *n.* [ELECTRO- + -LYTE] any substance which in solution can conduct an electric current by the movement of its dissociated ions to electrodes, where they are deposited as a coating, liberated as a gas, etc. —**e·lec'tro·lyt'ic** (-lit'ik) *adj.*

e·lec'tro·lyze' (-līz') *vt.* -lyzed', -lyz'ing to subject to electrolysis

e·lec'tro·mag'net *n.* a soft iron core that becomes a magnet when an electric current flows through a coil surrounding it

electromagnetic wave a wave propagated through space or matter by the oscillating electric and magnetic field generated by an oscillating electric charge

e·lec'tro·mag'net·ism (-nə tiz'm) *n.* **1.** magnetism produced by an electric current **2.** the branch of physics dealing with the relations between electricity and magnetism —**e·lec'tro·mag·net'ic** *adj.*

e·lec·trom·e·ter (i lek'träm'ə tər) *n.* a device for detecting or measuring differences of potential by means of electrostatic or mechanical forces

e·lec·tro·mo·tive (i lek'trə mōt'iv) *adj.* producing an electric current through differences in potential

electromotive force the force that causes a current to flow in a circuit, equivalent to the potential difference between the terminals

e·lec·tron (i lek'trän) *n.* [see ELECTRIC] any of the negatively charged particles that form a part of all atoms

e·lec·tro·neg·a·tive (i lek'trō neg'ə tiv) *adj.* **1.** having a negative electric charge **2.** able to attract electrons, as the atoms of nonmetallic elements

e·lec·tron·ic (i lek'trän'ik) *adj.* **1.** of electrons **2.** operating, produced, or done by the action of electrons —**e·lec'tron'i·cal·ly** *adv.*

electronic music music in which the sounds are originated by electronic devices and recorded on tape

e·lec·tron'ics *n.pl.* [*with sing. v.*] the science that deals with the behavior of electrons and with the use of electron tubes, transistors, etc.

electron microscope a device that focuses a beam of electrons to form a greatly enlarged image of an object, as on a fluorescent screen

electron tube a sealed glass or metal tube with two or more electrodes and a gas or vacuum inside, through which electrons can flow

e·lec·tro·plate (i lek'trə plāt') *vt.* -plat'ed, -plat'ing to deposit a coating of metal on by electrolysis —*n.* anything so plated

e·lec'tro·pos'i·tive *adj.* **1.** having a positive electrical charge **2.** able to give up electrons, as the atoms of certain metallic elements

e·lec'tro·scope' (-skōp') *n.* an instrument for detecting very small charges of electricity, and indicating whether they are positive or negative

e·lec'tro·shock' therapy shock therapy using electricity

e·lec'tro·stat'ics (-stat'iks) *n.pl.* [*with sing. v.*] the branch of physics dealing with the phenomena connected with static electricity

e·lec′tro·ther′a·py (-ther′ə pē) *n.* the treatment of disease by means of electricity, as by diathermy

e·lec′tro·type′ (-tīp′) *n. Printing* a facsimile plate made by electroplating a wax or plastic impression of the surface to be reproduced —**e·lec′tro·typ′er** *n.*

el·ee·mos·y·nar·y (el i mäs′ə ner′ē, el′ē ə-) *adj.* [< Gr. *eleēmosynē* pity] of, for, or supported by charity

el·e·gant (el′ə gənt) *adj.* [< Fr. < L. *e-*, out + *legere*, choose] 1. having dignified richness and grace, as of manner, design, dress, etc.; tastefully luxurious 2. fastidious in manners and taste 3. [Colloq.] excellent —**el′e·gance** *n.* — **el′e·gant·ly** *adv.*

el·e·gi·ac (el′ə jī′ək, i lē′jē ak′) *adj.* 1. of, like, or fit for an elegy 2. sad; mournful

el·e·gy (el′ə jē) *n., pl.* **-gies** [< Gr. *elegos,* a lament] a mournful poem, esp. of lament and praise for the dead

el·e·ment (el′ə mənt) *n.* [< L. *elementum*] 1. any of the four substances—earth, air, fire, water—formerly believed to constitute all physical matter 2. the natural or suitable environment for a person or thing 3. a component part or quality, often one that is basic or essential 4. the wire coil, etc. that becomes glowing hot in an electric oven, appliance, etc. 5. *Chem.* any substance that cannot be separated into different substances except by radioactive decay or by nuclear reactions: all matter is composed of such substances 6. [*pl.*] *Eccles.* the bread and wine of Communion —**the elements** 1. the first principles; rudiments 2. wind, rain, etc.; the forces of the atmosphere

el·e·men·tal (el′ə men′t′l) *adj.* 1. of or like basic, natural forces; primal 2. *same as* ELEMENTARY (sense 2) 3. being an essential part or parts

el′e·men′ta·ry (-tər ē, -trē) *adj.* 1. *same as* ELEMENTAL 2. of first principles or fundamentals; basic; simple

elementary particle a subatomic particle, as a neutron, proton, electron, etc.

elementary school a school of the first six (or eight) grades, where basic subjects are taught

el·e·phant (el′ə fənt) *n.* [< Gr. *elephas*] a huge, thick-skinned mammal with a long, flexible snout, or trunk, and, usually, two ivory tusks

el·e·phan·ti·a·sis (el′ə fən tī′ə sis) *n.* a chronic disease of the skin causing enlargement of certain bodily parts

el·e·phan·tine (el′ə fan′tēn, -tīn) *adj.* like an elephant; huge, slow, clumsy, etc.

el·e·vate (el′ə vāt′) *vt.* **-vat′ed, -vat′ing** [< L. *e-*, out + *levare,* to lift] 1. to lift up; raise 2. to raise in rank or position 3. to raise to a higher moral or intellectual level 4. to elate; exhilarate

ELEPHANTS
(shoulder height:
African, 10–13 ft.;
Indian, 8 1/2–10 ft.)

el·e·va′tion *n.* 1. an elevating or being elevated 2. a high place or position 3. height above the surface of the earth or above sea level 4. a scale drawing of the front, rear, or side of a structure

el′e·va′tor *n.* 1. one that elevates, or lifts up 2. a suspended cage or enclosed boxlike structure for hoisting or lowering people or things 3. a warehouse for storing and discharging grain 4. a device like a horizontal rudder, for making an aircraft go up or down

e·lev·en (i lev′ən) *adj., n.* [OE. *endleofan*] one more than ten; 11; XI —**e·lev′enth** (-ənth) *adj., n.*

elf (elf) *n., pl.* **elves** (elvz) [OE. *ælf*] 1. *Folklore* a tiny, often mischievous fairy 2. a small, often mischievous child —**elf′in, elf′ish** *adj.*

El Grec·o (el grek′ō) 1541?–1614?; painter in Italy & Spain, born in Crete

e·lic·it (i lis′it) *vt.* [< L. *e-*, out + *lacere,* entice] to draw forth; evoke (a response, etc.) —**e·lic′i·ta′tion** *n.*

e·lide (i līd′) *vt.* **e·lid′ed, e·lid′ing** [< L. *e-*, out + *laedere,* to strike] to leave out; esp., to slur over (a letter, etc.) in pronunciation —**e·li·sion** (i lizh′ən) *n.*

el·i·gi·ble (el′i jə b′l) *adj.* [see ELECT] 1. fit to be chosen; qualified 2. desirable, esp. for marriage —*n.* an eligible person —**el′i·gi·bil′i·ty** *n.*

E·li·jah (i lī′jə) *Bible* a prophet of Israel in the 9th cent. B.C.

e·lim·i·nate (i lim′ə nāt′) *vt.* **-nat′ed, -nat′ing** [< L. *e-*, out + *limen,* threshold] 1. to get rid of; remove 2. to leave out of consideration; omit 3. to excrete 4. *Algebra*

to get rid of (an unknown quantity) by combining equations —**e·lim′i·na′tion** *n.* —**e·lim′i·na′tor** *n.*

El·i·ot (el′ē ət) 1. **George,** (pseud. of *Mary Ann Evans*) 1819–80; Eng. novelist 2. **T(homas) S(tearns),** 1888–1965; Brit. poet & critic, born in the U.S.

E·li·sha (i lī′shə) *Bible* a prophet of Israel, who succeeded Elijah

e·lite, é·lite (i lēt′, ā-) *n.* [Fr. < L.: see ELECT] [*also used with pl. v.*] the group or part of a group regarded as the best, most powerful, etc.

e·lit′ism *n.* government or control by an elite —**e·lit′ist** *adj., n.*

e·lix·ir (i lik′sər) *n.* [Ar. *al-iksīr*] 1. a hypothetical substance sought for by medieval alchemists to prolong life indefinitely: in full, **elixir of life** 2. a panacea 3. a medicine made of drugs in alcoholic solution

E·liz·a·beth¹ (i liz′ə bəth) 1. **Elizabeth I** 1533–1603; queen of England (1558–1603) 2. **Elizabeth II** 1926– ; queen of Great Britain and Northern Ireland (1952–)

E·liz·a·beth² (i liz′ə bəth) city in NE N.J.: pop. 113,000

E·liz′a·be′than (-bē′thən, -beth′ən) *adj.* of or characteristic of the time of Elizabeth I —*n.* an English person, esp. a writer, of that time

elk (elk) *n., pl.* **elk, elks** [OE. *eolh*] 1. a large, mooselike deer of N Europe and Asia 2. *same as* WAPITI

ell¹ (el) *n.* something L-shaped; specif., an extension or wing at right angles to the main structure

ell² (el) *n.* [OE. *eln,* a forearm] a former English measure of length, mainly for cloth, equal to 45 in.

el·lipse (i lips′) *n., pl.* **-lip′ses** (-lip′siz) [< Gr. *elleipein,* to fall short] *Geom.* the path of a point that moves so that the sum of its distances from two fixed points is constant

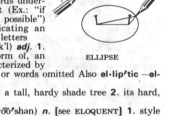

FOCUS   FOCUS
PENCIL   STRING

ELLIPSE

el·lip·sis (i lip′sis) *n., pl.* **-ses** (-sēz) [see prec.] 1. the omission of a word or words understood in the context (Ex.: "if possible" for "if it is possible") 2. a mark (...) indicating an omission of words or letters

el·lip·ti·cal (i lip′ti k′l) *adj.* 1. of, or having the form of, an ellipse 2. of or characterized by ellipsis; with a word or words omitted Also **el·lip′tic** —**el·lip′ti·cal·ly** *adv.*

elm (elm) *n.* [OE.] 1. a tall, hardy shade tree 2. its hard, heavy wood

el·o·cu·tion (el′ə kyōo′shən) *n.* [see ELOQUENT] 1. style or manner of speaking or reading in public 2. the art of public speaking —**el′o·cu′tion·ist** *n.*

e·lon·gate (i lôn′gāt) *vt., vi.* **-gat·ed, -gat·ing** [< L. *e-*, out + *longus,* long] to make or become longer; lengthen —*adj.* lengthened; stretched —**e·lon′ga′tion** *n.*

e·lope (i lōp′) *vi.* **e·loped′, e·lop′ing** [prob. < OE. *a-*, away + *hleapan,* to run] to run away secretly, esp. in order to get married —**e·lope′ment** *n.*

el·o·quent (el′ə kwənt) *adj.* [< L. *e-*, out + *loqui,* speak] 1. vivid, forceful, fluent, etc. in speech or writing 2. vividly expressive —**el′o·quence** *n.* —**el′o·quent·ly** *adv.*

El Pas·o (el pas′ō) city in westernmost Tex.: pop. 322,000

El Sal·va·dor (el sal′və dôr′) country in Central America, on the Pacific: 8,260 sq. mi.; pop. 3,390,000; cap. San Salvador

else (els) *adj.* [OE. *elles*] 1. different; other [*somebody else*] 2. in addition [*is there anything else?*] —*adv.* 1. differently; otherwise [*where else* can I go?] 2. if not [*study,* (or) *else* you will fail]

else′where′ (-hwer′, -wer′) *adv.* in or to some other place; somewhere else

e·lu·ci·date (i lōo′sə dāt′) *vt., vi.* **-dat′ed, -dat′ing** [< L. *e-*, out + *lucidus,* clear] to make (something) clear; explain —**e·lu′ci·da′tion** *n.*

e·lude (i lōod′) *vt.* **e·lud′ed, e·lud′ing** [< L. *e-*, out + *ludere,* to play] 1. to avoid or escape from by quickness, cunning, etc.; evade 2. to escape notice or understanding by —**e·lud′er** *n.* —**e·lu·sion** (i lōo′zhən) *n.*

e·lu·sive (i lōo′siv) *adj.* 1. tending to elude 2. hard to grasp or retain mentally; baffling —**e·lu′sive·ly** *adv.* — **e·lu′sive·ness** *n.*

el·ver (el′vər) *n.* [for *eelfare,* upstream passage of eels] a young eel

elves (elvz) *n. pl. of* ELF

elv·ish (el′vish) *adj.* of or like an elf

E·ly·si·um (i lizh′ē əm, -liz′-) *Gr. Myth.* the place where virtuous people dwell after death —*n.* any state of ideal bliss; paradise —**E·ly·sian** (i lizh′ən, -ē ən) *adj.*

em (em) *n.* 1. the letter M, m 2. *Printing* a square of any type body, used as a unit of measure, as of column width

'em (əm, ′m) *pron.* [Colloq.] them

em- *same as* EN-: used before *p, b,* or *m*

e·ma·ci·ate (i mā′shē āt′, -sē-) *vt.* -at′ed, -at′ing [< L. *e-*, out + *macies*, leanness] to cause to become abnormally lean; make lose much weight —**e·ma′ci·a′tion** *n.*

em·a·nate (em′ə nāt′) *vi.* -nat′ed, -nat′ing [< L. *e-*, out + *manare*, to flow] to come forth; issue, as from a source —em′a·na′tion *n.*

e·man·ci·pate (i man′sə pāt′) *vt.* -pat′ed, -pat′ing [< L. *e-*, out + *manus*, the hand + *capere*, to take] 1. to set free (a slave, etc.) 2. to free from restraint —**e·man′ci·pa′tion** *n.* —**e·man′ci·pa′tor** *n.*

e·mas·cu·late (i mas′kyə lāt′) *vt.* -lat′ed, -lat′ing [< L. *e-*, out + *masculus*, male] 1. to castrate 2. to destroy the strength or vigor of; weaken —**e·mas′cu·la′tion** *n.* —**e·mas′cu·la′tor** *n.*

em·balm (im bäm′) *vt.* [see EN- & BALM] 1. to preserve (a dead body) with various chemicals 2. to preserve in memory —**em·balm′er** *n.*

em·bank (im baŋk′) *vt.* to protect, support, or enclose with a bank of earth, rubble, etc.

em·bank′ment *n.* 1. an embanking 2. a bank (of earth, rubble, etc.) used to keep back water, hold up a roadway, etc.

em·bar·go (im bär′gō) *n., pl.* -**goes** [Sp. < L. *in-*, in + ML. *barra*, a bar] 1. a government order prohibiting the entry or departure of commercial ships at its ports 2. any legal restriction of commerce 3. any restriction or restraint —*vt.* -**goed**, -**go·ing** to put an embargo on

em·bark (im bärk′) *vt.* [Fr. < Sp. < L. *in-*, in + *barca*, small boat] to put or take aboard a ship, airplane, etc. —*vi.* 1. to go aboard a ship, airplane, etc. 2. to begin a journey 3. to get started in an enterprise —**em·bar·ka·tion** (em′bär kā′shən) *n.*

em·bar·rass (im ber′əs) *vt.* [Fr. < Sp. < It. *in-*, in + *barra*, a bar] 1. to cause to feel self-conscious 2. to hinder 3. to cause to be in debt 4. to complicate —**em·bar′rass·ing** *adj.* —**em·bar′rass·ing·ly** *adv.* —**em·bar′rass·ment** *n.*

em·bas·sy (em′bə sē) *n., pl.* -**sies** [see AMBASSADOR] 1. the official residence or offices of an ambassador 2. an ambassador and his staff 3. a person or group sent on an official mission

em·bat·tle[1] (im bat′'l) *vt.* -**tled**, -**tling** to provide with battlements; build battlements on

em·bat·tle[2] (im bat′'l) *vt.* -**tled**, -**tling** [< OFr.] [Rare, except in pp.] to prepare for battle

em·bed (im bed′) *vt.* -**bed′ded**, -**bed′ding** to set or fix firmly in a surrounding mass

em·bel·lish (im bel′ish) *vt.* [< OFr. *em-*, in + *bel*, beautiful] 1. to decorate; adorn 2. to improve (a story, etc.) by adding details, often fictitious —**em·bel′lish·er** *n.* —**em·bel′lish·ment** *n.*

em·ber[1] (em′bər) *n.* [OE. *æmerge*] 1. a glowing piece of coal, wood, etc. 2. [*pl.*] the smoldering remains of a fire

em·ber[2] (em′bər) *adj.* [< OE. *ymbryne*, circuit] [*often* E-] designating or of three days set aside in each season of the year for prayer and fasting: observed in the Roman Catholic and other churches

em·bez·zle (im bez′'l) *vt.* -**zled**, -**zling** [< OFr. *en-*, in + *besillier*, destroy] to steal (money, etc. entrusted to one) —**em·bez′zle·ment** *n.* —**em·bez′zler** *n.*

em·bit·ter (im bit′ər) *vt.* to make bitter or resentful —**em·bit′ter·ment** *n.*

em·bla·zon (im blā′z'n) *vt.* [see BLAZON] 1. to decorate (*with* coats of arms, etc.) 2. to display brilliantly 3. to extol —**em·bla′zon·ment** *n.*

em·blem (em′bləm) *n.* [< Gr. *en-*, in + *ballein*, to throw] a visible symbol of a thing, idea, etc.; sign; badge —**em′blem·at′ic** (-blə mat′ik) *adj.*

em·bod·y (im bäd′ē) *vt.* -**ied**, -**y·ing** 1. to give bodily form to 2. to give definite form to 3. to form into, or make part of, an organized whole; incorporate —**em·bod′i·ment** *n.*

em·bold·en (im bōl′d'n) *vt.* to give courage to; cause to be bold or bolder

em·bo·lism (em′bə liz'm) *n.* the obstruction of a blood vessel by an embolus

em·bo·lus (em′bə ləs) *n., pl.* -**li′** (-lī′) [< Gr. *en-*, in + *ballein*, to throw] any foreign matter, as a blood clot or air bubble, in the bloodstream

em·bos·om (im booz′əm, -bōō′zəm) *vt.* 1. to embrace; cherish 2. to enclose; surround; shelter

em·boss (im bôs′, -bäs′) *vt.* [see EN- & BOSS[2]] 1. to decorate with raised designs, etc. 2. to raise (a design, etc.) in relief —**em·boss′ment** *n.*

em·bou·chure (äm′boo shoor′) *n.* [Fr. < L. *in*, in + *bucca*, the cheek] 1. the mouthpiece of a wind instrument 2. the way of applying the lips to a mouthpiece

em·bow·er (im bou′ər) *vt.* to enclose or shelter in or as in a bower

em·brace (im brās′) *vt.* -**braced′**, -**brac′ing** [< L. *im-*, in + *brachium*, an arm] 1. to clasp in the arms lovingly; hug 2. to accept readily 3. to take up (a profession, etc.) 4. to encircle 5. to include —*vi.* to clasp each other in the arms —*n.* an embracing; hug —**em·brace′a·ble** *adj.*

em·bra·sure (im brā′zhər) *n.* [Fr. < obs. *embraser*, widen an opening] 1. an opening (for a door or window) wider on the inside than on the outside 2. an opening in a wall for a gun, with the sides slanting outward

em·bro·cate (em′brō kāt′) *vt.* -**cat′ed**, -**cat′ing** [< Gr. *en-*, in + *brechein*, to wet] to moisten and rub (a part of the body) with an oil, liniment, etc. —**em′bro·ca′tion** *n.*

em·broi·der (im broi′dər) *vt., vi.* [< OFr. *en-*, in + *brosder*, embroider] 1. to make (a design, etc.) on (fabric) with needlework 2. to embellish (a story, etc.); exaggerate —**em·broi′der·er** *n.*

em·broi·der·y *n., pl.* -**ies** 1. the art of embroidering 2. embroidered work or fabric 3. embellishment, as of a story

em·broil (im broil′) *vt.* [see EN- & BROIL[2]] 1. to confuse (affairs, etc.); muddle 2. to draw into a conflict or fight; involve in trouble —**em·broil′ment** *n.*

em·bry·o (em′brē ō′) *n., pl.* -**os**′ [< Gr. *en-*, in + *bryein*, to swell] 1. an animal in the earliest stages of its development in the uterus 2. the rudimentary plant contained in a seed 3. *a*) an early stage of something *b*) anything in such a stage —*adj. same as* EMBRYONIC

em′bry·ol′o·gy (-äl′ə jē) *n.* [< EMBRYO + -LOGY] the branch of biology dealing with the formation and development of embryos —**em′bry·o·log′ic** (-ə läj′ik), **em′bry·o·log′i·cal** *adj.* —**em′bry·ol′o·gist** *n.*

em′bry·on′ic (-än′ik) *adj.* 1. of or like an embryo 2. in an early stage; rudimentary

em·cee (em′sē′) *vt., vi.* -**ceed′**, -**cee′ing** [< M.C., sense 1] [Colloq.] to act as master of ceremonies (for) —*n.* [Colloq.] a master of ceremonies

e·mend (i mend′) *vt.* [< L. *e-*, out + *mendum*, a fault] to make scholarly corrections or improvements in (a text) —**e·men·da·tion** (ē′mən dā′shən, em′ən-) *n.*

em·er·ald (em′ər əld) *n.* [< Gr. *smaragdos*] 1. a bright-green, transparent precious stone; green beryl 2. bright green —*adj.* bright-green

Emerald Isle Ireland

e·merge (i murj′) *vi.* **e·merged′**, **e·merg′ing** [< L. *e-*, out + *mergere*, to dip] 1. to rise as from a fluid 2. to become visible or apparent 3. to evolve —**e·mer′gence** *n.* —**e·mer′gent** *adj.*

e·mer·gen·cy (i mur′jən sē) *n., pl.* -**cies** [orig. sense, an emerging] a sudden, generally unexpected occurrence demanding immediate action —*adj.* for use in an emergency

e·mer·i·tus (i mer′ə təs) *adj.* [L. < *e-*, out + *mereri*, to serve] retired from active service, usually for age, but retaining one's rank or title [professor *emeritus*]

Em·er·son (em′ər sən), **Ralph Waldo** 1803–82; U.S. essayist, philosopher, and poet

em·er·y (em′ər ē) *n.* [< Gr. *smyris*] a dark, impure variety of corundum used for grinding, etc.

e·met·ic (i met′ik) *adj.* [< Gr. *emein*, to vomit] causing vomiting —*n.* an emetic substance

E.M.F., e.m.f., EMF, emf electromotive force

-emia [< Gr. *haima*, blood] *a suffix meaning* a (specified) condition of the blood [*leukemia*]

em·i·grate (em′ə grāt′) *vi.* -**grat′ed**, -**grat′ing** [< L. *e-*, out + *migrare*, to move] to leave one country or region to settle in another —**em′i·grant** (-grənt) *adj., n.* —**em′i·gra′tion** *n.*

é·mi·gré, e·mi·gré (em′ə grā′, ā′mə grā′) *n.* [Fr.] 1. an emigrant 2. a person forced to flee his country for political reasons

em·i·nence (em′ə nəns) *n.* [< L. *eminere*, stand out] 1. high place, thing, etc. 2. superiority in rank, position, etc.; greatness 3. [E-] a title of honor of a cardinal: preceded by *His* or *Your*

em′i·nent *adj.* [see prec.] 1. high; lofty 2. projecting; prominent 3. exalted; distinguished 4. outstanding —**em·i·nent·ly** *adv.*

eminent domain the right of a government to take private property for public use, just compensation usually being given to the owner

e·mir (i mir′) *n.* [< Ar. *amara*, to command] in certain Muslim countries, a ruler

em·is·sar·y (em′ə ser′ē) *n., pl.* **-ies** [see EMIT] a person, esp. a secret agent, sent on a specific mission —*adj.* of or serving as an emissary

e·mis·sion (i mish′ən) *n.* **1.** an emitting; issuance **2.** something emitted; discharge —**e·mis′sive** *adj.*

e·mit (i mit′) *vt.* **e·mit′ted**, **e·mit′ting** [< L. *e-*, out + *mittere*, send] **1.** to send out; give forth **2.** to utter (sounds, etc.) **3.** to transmit (a signal) as by radio waves **4.** to give off (electrons)

e·mol·lient (i mäl′yənt) *adj.* [< L. *e-*, out + *mollire*, soften] softening; soothing —*n.* an emollient preparation, esp. for the surface tissues of the body

e·mol·u·ment (i mäl′yoo mənt) *n.* [< L. *e-*, out + *molere*, to grind] gain from employment; salary, fees, etc.

e·mote (i mōt′) *vi.* **e·mot′ed**, **e·mot′ing** [Colloq.] to display one's emotions dramatically

e·mo·tion (i mō′shən) *n.* [Fr. < L. *e-*, out + *movere*, to move] **1.** strong feeling; excitement **2.** any specific feeling, as love, hate, fear, anger, etc.

e·mo·tion·al *adj.* **1.** of or showing emotion **2.** easily aroused to emotion **3.** appealing to the emotions —**e·mo′-tion·al·ly** *adv.*

e·mo·tion·al·ism *n.* **1.** the tendency to be emotional. display of emotion **3.** an appeal to emotion

Emp. **1.** Emperor **2.** Empire **3.** Empress

em·pan·el (im pan′'l) *vt.* **-eled** or **-elled**, **-el·ing** or **-el·ling** *same as* IMPANEL

em·pa·thy (em′pə thē) *n.* [< Gr. *en-*, in + *pathos*, feeling] intellectual or emotional identification with another —**em·path·ic** (im path′ik), **em·pa·thet·ic** (em′pə thet′ik) *adj.*

em·per·or (em′pər ər) *n.* [< L. *imperare*, to command] the supreme ruler of an empire

em·pha·sis (em′fə sis) *n., pl.* **-ses′** (-sēz′) [< Gr. *en-*, in + *phainein*, to show] **1.** force of expression, action, etc. **2.** special stress given to a syllable, word, etc. in speaking **3.** importance; stress

em′pha·size′ (-sīz′) *vt.* **-sized′**, **-siz′ing** to give emphasis or special force to; stress

em·phat·ic (im fat′ik) *adj.* **1.** felt or done with emphasis **2.** using emphasis in speaking, etc. **3.** forcible; striking —**em·phat′i·cal·ly** *adv.*

em·phy·se·ma (em′fə sē′mə) *n.* [< Gr. *en-*, in + *physaein*, to blow] a disease of the lungs in which the air sacs become distended and lose elasticity

em·pire (em′pīr; *for adj., usually* äm pir′) *n.* [see EMPEROR] **1.** supreme rule; absolute authority **2.** government by an emperor or empress **3.** a group of states or territories under one sovereign power —*adj.* [E-] of or characteristic of the first French Empire (1804–15)

em·pir·i·cal (em pir′i k'l) *adj.* [< Gr. *en-*, in + *peira*, a trial] **1.** relying or based on experiment and observation **2.** relying on practical experience

em·pir′i·cism (-ə siz′m) *n.* **1.** the act or method of seeking knowledge by observation and experiment **2.** *Philos.* the theory that experience is the only source of knowledge —**em·pir′i·cist** *n.*

em·place·ment (im plās′mənt) *n.* **1.** a placing in position **2.** the prepared position from which a heavy gun or guns are fired

em·ploy (im ploi′) *vt.* [< L. *in-*, in + *plicare*, to fold] **1.** to use **2.** to keep busy or occupied **3.** to engage the services of; hire —*n.* employment

em·ploy′a·ble *adj.* physically and mentally fit to be hired for work

em·ploy·ee, em·ploy·e (im ploi′ē, em′ploi ē′) *n.* a person employed by another for wages or salary

em·ploy′er *n.* one who employs others for wages or salary

em·ploy′ment *n.* **1.** an employing or being employed **2.** work; occupation; job **3.** the number or percentage of persons gainfully employed

em·po·ri·um (em pôr′ē əm) *n., pl.* **-ri·ums, -ri·a** (-ə) [< Gr. *en-*, in + *poros*, way] a large store with a wide variety of things for sale

em·pow·er (im pou′ər) *vt.* **1.** to give power to; authorize **2.** to enable; permit —**em·pow′er·ment** *n.*

em·press (em′pris) *n.* **1.** the wife of an emperor **2.** a woman ruler of an empire

emp·ty (emp′tē) *adj.* **-ti·er, -ti·est** [< OE. *æmettig*, unoccupied] **1.** having nothing or no one in it; unoccupied **2.** worthless [*empty* pleasures] **3.** insincere [*empty* promises] **4.** [Colloq.] hungry —*vt.* **-tied, -ty·ing** **1.** to make empty **2.** to remove (the contents) of something —*vi.* **1.** to become empty **2.** to pour out; discharge —*n., pl.* **-ties** an empty truck, bottle, etc. —**empty of** lacking; devoid of —**emp′ti·ness** *n.*

emp′ty-hand′ed *adj.* bringing or carrying away nothing

emp′ty-head′ed *adj.* silly and ignorant

em·pur·ple (im pur′p'l) *vt., vi.* **-pled, -pling** to make or become purple

em·pyr·e·al (em pir′ē əl, em′pī rē′əl) *adj.* [< Gr. *en-*, in + *pyr*, a fire] of the empyrean; heavenly

em·py·re·an (em′pī rē′ən, em pir′ē ən) *n.* [see prec.] **1.** the highest heaven **2.** the sky —*adj. same as* EMPYREAL

e·mu (ē′myōō) *n.* [prob. < Port. *ema*, a crane] a large, nonflying Australian bird, similar to the ostrich but somewhat smaller

em·u·late (em′yə lāt′) *vt.* **-lat′ed, -lat′ing** [< L. *aemulus*, trying to equal] **1.** to try to equal or surpass **2.** to rival successfully —**em′u·la′tion** *n.* —**em′u·la′tive** *adj.* —**em′-u·la′tor** *n.*

em′u·lous (-ləs) *adj.* desirous of equaling or surpassing —**em′u·lous·ly** *adv* —**em′u·lous·ness** *n.*

e·mul·si·fy (i mul′sə fī′) *vt., vi.* **-fied′, -fy′ing** to form into an emulsion —**e·mul′-si·fi·ca′tion** *n.*

EMU
(5 ft. high)

e·mul·sion (i mul′shən) *n.* [< L. *e-*, out + *mulgere*, to milk] a fluid, as milk, formed by the suspension of one liquid in another; specif., *a*) *Pharmacy* a preparation of an oily substance held in suspension in a watery liquid *b*) *Photog.* a suspension of a salt of silver in gelatin or collodion, used to coat plates and film —**e·mul′-sive** *adj.*

en (en) *n.* **1.** the letter N, n **2.** *Printing* a space half the width of an em

en- [< L. *in-*, in] *a prefix meaning:* **1.** to put or get into or on [*entrain*] **2.** to make, cause to be [*endanger, enfeeble*] **3.** in or into [*enclose*]

-en [< OE.] *a suffix:* **1.** *meaning: a*) to become or cause to be [*weaken*] *b*) to cause to have [*strengthen*] **2.** used to form [*woolen*] **2.** *used to form plurals* [*children*] **3.** *used to form diminutives* [*chicken*]

en·a·ble (in ā′b'l) *vt.* **-bled, -bling** to make able; provide with means, opportunity, power, etc. (*to do something*)

en·act (in akt′) *vt.* **1.** to make (a bill, etc.) into a law; pass (a law); decree **2.** to represent as in a play

en·act′ment *n.* **1.** an enacting or being enacted **2.** something enacted, as a law

en·am·el (i nam′'l) *n.* [< OFr. *esmail*] **1.** a glassy, opaque substance fused to metal or the like as a protective coating **2.** any hard, glossy coating like enamel **3.** the hard, white, glossy coating of teeth **4.** anything enameled **5.** paint or varnish producing a hard, glossy surface —*vt.* **-eled** or **-elled**, **-el·ing** or **-el·ling** to coat with enamel —**en·am′el·er, en·am′el·ler, en·am′el·ist, en·am′el·list** *n.*

en·am′el·ware′ (-wer′) *n.* kitchen utensils, etc. made of enameled metal

en·am·or (in am′ər) *vt.* [ult. < L. *in-*, in + *amor*, love] to fill with love and desire; charm: mainly in the passive voice, with *of* [*enamored* of her]

en bloc (en bläk′) [Fr., lit., in a block] in one lump; as a whole; all together

enc., encl. enclosure

en·camp (in kamp′) *vt., vi.* to set up, or put in, a camp —**en·camp′ment** *n.*

en·cap·su·late (in kap′sə lāt′, -syoo-) *vt.* **-lat′ed, -lat′ing** **1.** to enclose in a capsule **2.** to condense; abridge Also **en·cap′sule -suled, -sul·ing** —**en·cap′su·la′tion** *n.*

en·case (in kās′) *vt.* **-cased′, -cas′ing** **1.** to cover completely; enclose **2.** to put into a case

en·caus·tic (en kôs′tik) *n.* [< Gr. *en-*, in + *kaiein*, to burn] a method of painting in which colors in wax are fused to a surface with hot irons

-ence [< L.] *a suffix meaning* act, fact, quality, state, result, or degree [*conference, excellence*]

en·ceph·a·li·tis (en sef′ə līt′is, en′sef-) *n.* [< Gr. *enkephalos*, brain + -ITIS] inflammation of the brain

en·ceph·a·lon (en sef′ə län′) *n., pl.* **-la** (-lə) [< Gr. *en-*, in + *kephalē*, the head] *Anat.* the brain

en·chain (in chān′) *vt.* **1.** to bind with chains **2.** to captivate —**en·chain′ment** *n.*

en·chant (in chant′) *vt.* [< L. *in-*, in + *cantare*, sing] **1.** to cast a spell over, as by magic **2.** to charm greatly; delight —en·chant'er *n.* —en·chant'ing *adj.* —en·chant'ing·ly *adv.* —en·chant'ment *n.* —en·chant'ress *n.fem.*

en·chi·la·da (en'chə lä'də) *n.* [AmSp.] a tortilla usually rolled with meat inside and served with a chili-flavored sauce

en·cir·cle (in sur'k'l) *vt.* -cled, -cling 1. to make a circle around 2. to move in a circle around —en·cir'cle·ment *n.*

en·clave (en'klāv) *n.* [Fr. < L. *in,* in + *clavis,* a key] territory surrounded by another country's territory

en·close (in klōz') *vt.* -closed', -clos'ing 1. to shut in all around; fence in; surround 2. to insert in an envelope, wrapper, etc., often along with something else 3. to contain

en·clo'sure (-klō'zhər) *n.* 1. an enclosing or being enclosed 2. something that encloses 3. something enclosed, as in an envelope or by a wall

en·code (in kōd') *vt.* -cod'ed, -cod'ing to put (information, etc.) into code —en·cod'er *n.*

en·co·mi·ast (en kō'mē ast') *n.* one who speaks or writes encomiums; eulogist

en·co'mi·um (-əm) *n., pl.* -mi·ums, -mi·a (-ə) [< Gr. *en-,* in + *kōmos,* a revel] high praise; eulogy

en·com·pass (in kum'pəs) *vt.* 1. to enclose; surround 2. to contain; include —en·com'pass·ment *n.*

en·core (äŋ'kôr) *interj.* [Fr.] again; once more —*n.* 1. a demand by an audience, shown by applause, for further performance 2. such further performance

en·coun·ter (in koun'tər) *vt.* [< L. *in,* in + *contra,* against] 1. to meet unexpectedly 2. to meet in conflict —*n.* 1. a direct meeting, as in conflict or battle 2. an unexpected meeting —*adj.* designating or of a small group meeting to explore personal relationships through an open exchange of intimate feelings, release of inhibitions, etc.

en·cour·age (in kur'ij) *vt.* -aged, -ag·ing 1. to give courage, hope, or confidence to 2. to give support to; help —en·cour'ag·ing *adj.*

en·cour'age·ment *n.* 1. an encouraging or being encouraged 2. something that encourages

en·croach (in krōch') *vi.* [< OFr. *en-,* in + *croc,* a hook] to trespass or intrude (*on* or *upon*) —en·croach'ment *n.*

en·crust (in krust') *vt., vi. same as* INCRUST —en'crus·ta'tion *n.*

en·cum·ber (in kum'bər) *vt.* [see EN- & CUMBER] 1. to hold back the motion or action of; hinder 2. to load down; burden

en·cum'brance (-brəns) *n.* 1. a hindrance; burden 2. *Law same as* INCUMBRANCE

-ency [L. *-entia*] *a suffix meaning* act, fact, quality, state, result, or degree [*dependency, efficiency*]

ency., encyc., encycl. encyclopedia

en·cyc·li·cal (in sik'li k'l, -sī'kli-) *n.* [< Gr. *en-,* in + *kyklos,* a circle] a letter from the Pope to the bishops, usually dealing with doctrine

en·cy·clo·pe·di·a, en·cy·clo·pae·di·a (in sī'klə pē'dē ə) *n.* [< Gr. *enkyklios,* general + *paideia,* education] a book or set of books with alphabetically arranged articles on all branches, or on one field, of knowledge —en·cy'clo·pe'dic, en·cy'clo·pae'dic *adj.*

en·cyst (en sist') *vt., vi.* to enclose or become enclosed in a cyst, capsule, or sac —en·cyst'ment *n.*

end (end) *n.* [OE. *ende*] 1. a boundary; limit 2. the last part of anything; finish; conclusion 3. a ceasing to exist; death or destruction 4. the part at or near an extremity; tip 5. a purpose; intention 6. an outcome; result 7. a remnant 8. *Football* a player at either end of the line —*vt., vi.* to bring or come to an end; finish; stop —*adj.* at the end; final —make (both) ends meet to keep one's expenses within one's income —no end [Colloq.] extremely —put an end to 1. to stop 2. to do away with

en·dan·ger (in dān'jər) *vt.* to expose to danger, harm, or loss; imperil —en·dan'ger·ment *n.*

en·dear (in dir') *vt.* to make dear or beloved —en·dear'ing *adj.*

en·dear'ment *n.* 1. affection 2. an expression of affection

en·deav·or (in dev'ər) *vt.* [< EN- + OFr. *deveir,* duty] to try (*to* do something) —*n.* an earnest attempt or effort Brit. sp. **en·deav'our**

en·dem·ic (en dem'ik) *adj.* [< Fr. < Gr. *en-,* in + *dēmos,* people] 1. native to a particular country, etc. 2. restricted to and present in a particular country, etc.: said of a disease

end·ing (en'diŋ) *n.* 1. *a)* the last part; finish *b)* death 2. *Gram.* the final letter or letters added to a word base to make a derivative or inflectional form [*-ed* is the *ending* in *wanted*]

en·dive (en'dīv, än'dēv) *n.* [< Gr. *entybon*] a plant with curled, narrow leaves used in salads

end·less (end'lis) *adj.* 1. having no end; eternal; infinite 2. lasting too long [*an endless speech*] 3. with the ends joined to form a closed unit [*an endless belt*] —end'less·ly *adv.* —end'less·ness *n.*

end'most' *adj.* at the end; farthest; last

endo- [< Gr. *endon,* within] *a combining form meaning* within, inner: also **end-**

en·do·carp (en'də kärp') *n.* [< ENDO- + Gr. *karpos,* fruit] the inner layer of the wall of a ripened ovary or fruit, as the pit of a plum

en·do·crine (en'də krin, -krīn') *adj.* [ENDO- + Gr. *krinein,* to separate] designating or of any gland producing an internal secretion carried by the blood to some body part whose functions it regulates —*n.* any such gland or its secretion, as the thyroid, adrenal, and pituitary glands

en·do·derm (en'də durm') *n.* [< ENDO- + Gr. *derma,* skin] the inner layer of cells of the embryo in its early stage

en·dog·e·nous (en däj'ə nəs) *adj.* [ENDO- + -GENOUS] developing from within

en·do·plasm (en'də plaz'm) *n.* [ENDO- + -PLASM] the inner part of the cytoplasm of a cell —en'do·plas'mic *adj.*

end organ any structure at the end of nerve fibers having either sensory or motor functions

en·dorse (in dôrs') *vt.* -dorsed', -dors'ing [< L. *in,* on + *dorsum,* the back] 1. to write on the back of (a document); specif., to sign (one's name) as payee on the back of (a check, etc.) 2. to sanction —en·dorse'ment *n.* —en·dors'er *n.*

en·do·sperm (en'də spurm') *n.* [ENDO- + SPERM] a tissue which surrounds the developing embryo of a seed and provides food for its growth

en·dow (in dou') *vt.* [ult. < L. *in,* in + *dotare,* endow] 1. to provide with some talent, quality, etc. [*endowed* with courage] 2. to give money or property to (a college, etc.)

en·dow'ment *n.* 1. an endowing 2. that with which something is endowed 3. talent, ability, etc.

end product the final result of any series of changes, processes, or chemical reactions

end table a small table placed beside a chair, etc.

en·due (in d$\overline{oo}$', -dy$\overline{oo}$') *vt.* -dued', -du'ing [< L. *in-,* in + *ducere,* to lead] to provide (*with* qualities)

en·dur·ance (in door'əns, -dyoor'-) *n.* 1. an enduring 2. ability to last, continue, or remain 3. ability to stand pain, fatigue, etc. 4. duration

en·dure (in door', -dyoor') *vt.* -dured', -dur'ing [< L. *in-,* in + *durus,* hard] 1. to stand (pain, fatigue, etc.) 2. to tolerate —*vi.* 1. to last; continue 2. to bear pain, etc. without flinching —en·dur'a·ble *adj.* —en·dur'a·bly *adv.*

en·dur'ing *adj.* lasting; permanent

end'ways' (-wāz') *adv.* 1. on end; upright 2. with the end foremost 3. lengthwise 4. end to end Also **end'wise'** (-wīz')

-ene [after Gr. *-enos,* adj. suffix] a suffix used to form names for some hydrocarbons [*benzene*]

ENE, E.N.E., e.n.e. east-northeast

en·e·ma (en'ə mə) *n.* [< Gr. *en-,* in + *hienai,* send] the injection of a liquid, as a purgative, medicine, etc., into the colon through the anus

en·e·my (en'ə mē) *n., pl.* -mies [< L. *in-,* not + *amicus,* friend] 1. a person who hates another and wishes to injure him 2. *a)* a nation hostile to another *b)* a soldier, citizen, etc. of a hostile nation 3. one hostile to an idea, cause, etc. 4. anything injurious —*adj.* of an enemy

en·er·get·ic (en'ər jet'ik) *adj.* of, having, or showing energy; vigorous —en'er·get'i·cal·ly *adv.*

en·er·gize (en'ər jīz') *vt.* -gized', -giz'ing to give energy to; activate —en'er·giz'er *n.*

en·er·gy (en'ər jē) *n., pl.* -gies [< Gr. *en-,* in + *ergon,* work] 1. force of expression 2. *a)* inherent power; capacity for action *b)* [*often pl.*] such power, esp. in action 3. effective power 4. *Physics* the capacity for doing work and overcoming resistance

en·er·vate (en'ər vāt') *vt.* -vat'ed, -vat'ing [< L. *e-,* out + *nervus,* a nerve] to deprive of strength, force, etc.; debilitate —en'er·va'tion *n.*

‡en·fant ter·ri·ble (än fän te rē'bl') [Fr.] 1. an unmanageable, mischievous child 2. a person who causes trouble or embarrassment by his imprudent remarks or actions

en·fee·ble (in fē'b'l) *vt.* -bled, -bling to make feeble

en·fi·lade (en'fə läd', en'fə läd') *n.* [Fr. < *enfiler,* to thread] gunfire directed from either flank along the length of a line of troops —*vt.* -lad'ed, -lad'ing to direct such gunfire at (a column, etc.)

en·fold (in fōld') *vt.* 1. to wrap in folds; envelop 2. to embrace —en·fold'er *n.*

en·force (in fôrs′) *vt.* **-forced′, -forc′ing 1.** to give force to **2.** to impose by force *[to enforce* one's will*]* **3.** to compel observance of (a law, etc.) **—en·force′a·ble** *adj.* **—en·force′ment** *n.* **—en·forc′er** *n.*

en·fran·chise (in fran′chīz) *vt.* **-chised, -chis·ing 1.** to free from slavery **2.** to admit to citizenship, esp. to the right to vote **—en·fran′chise·ment** (-chiz mənt, -chīz-) *n.* **—en·fran′chis·er** *n.*

Eng. 1. England **2.** English

eng. 1. engineer(ing) **2.** engraved **3.** engraving

en·gage (in gāj′) *vt.* **-gaged′, -gag′ing** [see EN- & GAGE¹] **1.** to pledge (oneself); specif. (now only in the passive), to bind by a promise of marriage **2.** to hire **3.** to arrange for the use of *[to engage* a hotel room*]* **4.** to involve, as in conversation **5.** to attract and hold (the attention, etc.) **6.** to enter into conflict with (the enemy) **7.** to mesh (gears, etc.) together **—vi. 1.** to pledge oneself **2.** to involve oneself **3.** to enter into conflict **4.** to mesh

en·gaged′ *adj.* **1.** pledged; esp., betrothed **2.** occupied; employed **3.** involved in combat, as troops **4.** meshed

en·gage′ment *n.* an engaging or being engaged; specif., *a)* a betrothal *b)* an appointment or commitment *c)* employment *d)* a conflict; battle *e)* state of being in gear

en·gag′ing *adj.* attractive; charming **—en·gag′ing·ly** *adv.*

‡en garde (än gärd′) [Fr.] *Fencing* on guard

En·gels (en′əls), **Frie·drich** (frē′drikh) 1820–95; Ger. socialist theoretician (with Karl Marx)

en·gen·der (in jen′dər) *vt.* [< L. *in-,* in + *generare,* beget] to bring into being; cause; produce

en·gine (en′jən) *n.* [< L. *in-,* in + base of *gignere,* to produce] **1.** any machine that uses energy to develop mechanical power; esp., a machine for starting motion in some other machine **2.** a railroad locomotive **3.** any instrument or machine

en·gi·neer (en′jə nir′) *n.* **1.** one skilled in some branch of engineering **2.** one who operates or supervises the operation of engines or technical equipment *[a locomotive engineer]* **—vt. 1.** to plan, construct, etc. as an engineer **2.** to manage skillfully

en′gi·neer′ing *n.* **1.** the putting of scientific knowledge in various branches to practical uses **2.** the planning, designing, construction, etc. of machinery, roads, etc.

Eng·land (iŋ′glənd) division of the United Kingdom, in S Great Britain: 50,331 sq. mi.; pop. 47,023,000; cap. London

Eng·lish (iŋ′glish) *adj.* **1.** of England, its people, etc. **2.** of their language **—n. 1.** the language of the people of England, the official language of the British Commonwealth, the U.S., etc. **2.** the English language of a specific period: see OLD ENGLISH, MIDDLE ENGLISH, MODERN ENGLISH **3.** [*sometimes* e-] a spinning motion given to a ball **—the English** the people of England

English Channel arm of the Atlantic, between England & France: 21–150 mi. wide

English horn a double-reed instrument of the woodwind family

Eng′lish·man (-mən) *n., pl.* **-men** a native or inhabitant of England; a man **— Eng′lish·wom′an** *n.fem., pl.* **-wom′en**

ENGLISH HORN

English sparrow the common sparrow, a small, brownish-gray, finchlike bird of European origin

English walnut 1. an Asiatic walnut tree now grown in Europe and North America **2.** its nut

en·gorge (in gôrj′) *vt., vi.* **-gorged′, -gorg′ing 1.** to eat gluttonously; gorge **2.** *Med.* to congest with blood or other fluid **—en·gorge′ment** *n.*

engr. 1. engineer **2.** engraved **3.** engraver

en·graft (in graft′) *vt.* **1.** to graft (a shoot, etc.) from one plant onto another **2.** to implant

en·grave (in grāv′) *vt.* **-graved′, -grav′ing** [< Fr. *en-,* in + *graver,* to incise] **1.** to cut or etch (letters, designs, etc.) in or on (a metal plate, wooden block, etc.) **2.** to print from such a plate, etc. **3.** to impress deeply **—en·grav′er** *n.*

en·grav′ing *n.* **1.** the act or art of one who engraves **2.** an engraved plate, design, etc. **3.** a print made from an engraved surface

en·gross (in grōs′) *vt.* [< OFr. *engrossier,* become thick] to take the entire attention of; occupy wholly **—en·gross′ing** *adj.* **—en·gross′ment** *n.*

en·gulf (in gulf′) *vt.* [EN- + GULF] to swallow up; overwhelm

en·hance (in hans′) *vt.* **-hanced′, -hanc′ing** [ult. < L. *in,* in + *altus,* high] to make greater; heighten **—en·hance′ment** *n.* **—en·hanc′er** *n.*

e·nig·ma (ə nig′mə) *n., pl.* **-mas** [< Gr. *ainigma*] **1.** a riddle **2.** a perplexing or baffling matter, person, etc. **—e·nig·mat·ic** (en′ig mat′ik, ē′nig-), **e′nig·mat′i·cal** *adj.* **—e′nig·mat′i·cal·ly** *adv.*

en·join (in join′) *vt.* [< L. *in-,* in + *jungere,* to join] **1.** to order; enforce **2.** to prohibit, esp. by legal injunction

en·joy (in joi′) *vt.* [< OFr. *en-,* in + *joir,* rejoice] **1.** to get joy or pleasure from; relish **2.** to have the use or benefit of **—enjoy oneself** to have a good time **—en·joy′a·ble** *adj.* **—en·joy′a·bly** *adv.*

en·joy′ment *n.* **1.** an enjoying **2.** something enjoyed **3.** pleasure; gratification; joy

en·kin·dle (en kin′d'l) *vt.* **-dled, -dling 1.** to set on fire; make blaze up **2.** to stir up; arouse

en·lace (in lās′) *vt.* **-laced′, -lac′ing 1.** to wind about as with a lace **2.** to entangle **—en·lace′ment** *n.*

en·large (in lärj′) *vt.* **-larged′, -larg′ing 1.** to make larger; expand **2.** *Photog.* to reproduce on a larger scale **— vi. 1.** to become larger; increase **2.** to discuss at greater length (with *on* or *upon*) **—en·large′ment** *n.* **—en·larg′er** *n.*

en·light·en (in līt′'n) *vt.* **1.** to free from ignorance, prejudice, etc. **2.** to inform; instruct **—en·light′en·er** *n.* **—en·light′en·ment** *n.*

en·list (in list′) *vt., vi.* **1.** to enroll in some branch of the armed forces **2.** to engage in a cause or movement **—en·list′ee′** *n.* **—en·list′ment** *n.*

enlisted man any man in the armed forces who is not a commissioned officer or warrant officer

en·liv·en (in lī′v'n) *vt.* to make active, vivacious, interesting, or cheerful **—en·liv′en·ment** *n.*

en masse (en mas′) [Fr., lit., in mass] in a group; as a whole; all together

en·mesh (en mesh′) *vt.* to catch in or as in the meshes of a net; entangle

en·mi·ty (en′mə tē) *n., pl.* **-ties** [see ENEMY] the attitude or feelings of an enemy or enemies; hostility

en·no·ble (i nō′b'l) *vt.* **-bled, -bling** to give a noble quality to; dignify **—en·no′ble·ment** *n.* **—en·no′bler** *n.*

en·nui (än′wē) *n.* [Fr.: see ANNOY] weariness and dissatisfaction resulting from inactivity or lack of interest; boredom

e·nor·mi·ty (i nôr′mə tē) *n., pl.* **-ties** [< Fr. < L. *e-,* out + *norma,* rule] **1.** great wickedness **2.** an outrageous act **3.** loosely, enormous size or extent

e·nor·mous (i nôr′məs) *adj.* [see prec.] of great size, number, etc.; huge; vast **—e·nor′mous·ly** *adv.* **—e·nor′mous·ness** *n.*

e·nough (i nuf′) *adj.* [OE. *genoh*] as much or as many as necessary; sufficient **—n.** the amount needed **—adv. 1.** sufficiently **2.** fully; quite *[oddly enough]* **3.** just adequately; tolerably

e·now (i nou′) *adj., n., adv.* [Archaic] enough

en·plane (en plān′) *vi.* **-planed′, -plan′ing** to board an airplane

en·quire (in kwīr′) *vt., vi.* **-quired′, -quir′ing** same as INQUIRE **—en·quir′y** *n., pl.* **-ies**

en·rage (in rāj′) *vt.* **-raged′, -rag′ing** to put into a rage; infuriate **—en·rage′ment** *n.*

en·rap·ture (in rap′chər) *vt.* **-tured, -tur·ing** to fill with great pleasure or delight

en·rich (in rich′) *vt.* to make rich or richer; specif., *a)* to give more wealth to *b)* to give greater value or effectiveness to *[to enrich* a curriculum*]* *c)* to decorate; adorn *d)* to fertilize (soil) *e)* to add vitamins, minerals, etc. to (bread, etc.) for more food value **—en·rich′ment** *n.*

en·roll, en·rol (in rōl′) *vt., vi.* **-rolled′, -roll′ing 1.** to record or be recorded in a roll or list **2.** to enlist **3.** to make or become a member **—en·roll′ment, en·rol′ment** *n.*

en route (än rōōt′, en) [Fr.] on or along the way

Ens. Ensign

en·sconce (in skäns′) *vt.* **-sconced′, -sconc′ing** [EN- + SCONCE²] to place or settle snugly or securely

en·sem·ble (än säm′b'l) *n.* [Fr. < L. *in-,* in + *simul,* at the same time] **1.** all the parts considered as a whole; total effect **2.** a whole costume of matching parts **3.** *Music a)* a small group of musicians playing or singing together *b)* the performance of such a group, or of an orchestra, chorus, etc.

en·shrine (in shrīn′) *vt.* -shrined′, -shrin′ing 1. to enclose in or as in a shrine 2. to hold as sacred; cherish —en·shrine′ment *n.*

en·shroud′ (-shroud′) *vt.* to cover as if with a shroud; hide; obscure

en·sign (en′sīn; *also, and for 3 always,* -s′n) *n.* [see INSIGNIA] 1. a badge, symbol, or token of office or authority 2. a flag or banner 3. *U.S. Navy* a commissioned officer of the lowest rank —en′sign·ship′, en′sign·cy *n.*

en·si·lage (en′s'l ij) *n.* [Fr.] 1. the preserving of green fodder by storage in a silo 2. green fodder so preserved

en·slave (in slāv′) *vt.* -slaved′, -slav′ing 1. to make a slave of 2. to subjugate —en·slave′ment *n.* —en·slav′er *n.*

en·snare′ (-sner′) *vt.* -snared′, -snar′ing to catch in or as in a snare; trap —en·snare′ment *n.*

en·sue (in sōō′, -syōō′) *vi.* -sued′, -su′ing [< L. *in-*, in + *sequi,* follow] 1. to follow immediately 2. to happen as a consequence; result

en·sure (in shoor′) *vt.* -sured′, -sur′ing 1. to make sure 2. to protect

-ent [< L. *-ens,* prp. ending] *a suffix meaning:* 1. that has, shows, or does *[insistent]* 2. a person or thing that *[superintendent, solvent]*

en·tab·la·ture (en tab′lə chər) *n.* [< It. *in-*, in + *tavola,* table] *Archit.* a horizontal superstructure supported by columns and composed of architrave, frieze, and cornice

en·tail (in tāl′) *vt.* [< OFr. *taillier,* to cut] 1. *Law* to limit the inheritance of (property) to a specific line of heirs 2. to cause or require as a necessary consequence; necessitate —*n.* 1. an entailing or being entailed 2. an entailed inheritance 3. the order of descent for an entailed inheritance —en·tail′ment *n.*

en·tan·gle (in taŋ′g'l) *vt.* -gled, -gling 1. to involve in a tangle 2. to involve in difficulty 3. to confuse 4. to complicate —en·tan′gle·ment *n.*

en·tente (än tänt′) *n.* [Fr. < OFr. *entendre,* understand] 1. an understanding or agreement, as between nations 2. the parties to this

en·ter (en′tər) *vt.* [< L. *intra,* within] 1. to come or go in or into 2. to force a way into 3. to insert 4. to write down in a list, etc. 5. to become a member of or participant in 6. to get (someone) admitted 7. to start upon; begin 8. *Law* to place on record formally or before a law court —*vi.* 1. to come or go into some place 2. to pierce; penetrate —enter into 1. to take part in 2. to form a part of —enter on (or upon) to begin; start

en·ter·ic (en ter′ik) *adj.* [< Gr. *enteron,* intestine] intestinal: also **en·ter·al** (en′tər əl)

en·ter·prise (en′tər prīz′) *n.* [ult. < L. *inter,* in + *prehendere,* to take] 1. an undertaking, esp. a bold, hard, or important one 2. energy and initiative

en′ter·pris′ing *adj.* showing enterprise; full of energy and initiative; venturesome

en·ter·tain (en′tər tān′) *vt.* [ult. < L. *inter,* between + *tenere,* to hold] 1. to amuse; divert 2. to have as a guest 3. to have in mind; consider —*vi.* to have guests

en′ter·tain′er *n.* one who entertains; esp., a popular singer, dancer, comedian, etc.

en′ter·tain′ing *adj.* interesting and pleasurable; amusing —en′ter·tain′ing·ly *adv.*

en′ter·tain′ment *n.* 1. an entertaining or being entertained 2. something that entertains; esp., a show or performance

en·thrall, en·thral (in thrôl′) *vt.* -thralled′, -thrall′ing [see EN- & THRALL] to fascinate; captivate; enchant —en·thrall′ment, en·thral′ment *n.*

en·throne (-thrōn′) *vt.* -throned′, -thron′ing 1. to place on a throne 2. to revere; exalt —en·throne′ment *n.*

en·thuse (-thōōz′, -thyōōz′) *vi.* -thused′, -thus′ing [Colloq.] to express enthusiasm —*vt.* [Colloq.] to make enthusiastic

en·thu·si·asm (in thōō′zē az′m, -thyōō′-) *n.* [< Gr. *enthous,* inspired] intense or eager interest; zeal

en·thu·si·ast′ (-ast′) *n.* one full of enthusiasm; an ardent supporter, a devotee, etc.

en·thu·si·as′tic *adj.* of, having, or showing enthusiasm; ardent —en·thu′si·as′ti·cal·ly *adv.*

en·tice (in tīs′) *vt.* -ticed′, -tic′ing [< L. *in,* in + *titio,* a firebrand] to attract by offering hope of reward or pleasure —en·tice′ment *n.* —en·tic′er *n.* —en·tic′ing·ly *adv.*

en·tire (in tīr′) *adj.* [< L. *integer,* whole] 1. *a)* not lacking any of the parts; whole *b)* complete 2. unbroken; intact 3. being wholly of one piece 4. not castrated 5. *Bot.* having an unbroken margin, as some leaves —en·tire′ly *adv.*

en·tire′ty (-tē) *n., pl.* -ties 1. the state or fact of being entire; wholeness 2. an entire thing; whole —in its entirety as a whole

en·ti·tle (in tīt′'l) *vt.* -tled, -tling 1. to give a title or name to 2. to give a right or legal title to

en·ti·ty (en′tə tē) *n., pl.* -ties [ult. < L. *esse,* to be] 1. being; existence 2. a thing that has definite, individual existence in reality or in the mind

en·tomb (in tōōm′) *vt.* to place in a tomb or grave; bury —en·tomb′ment *n.*

en·to·mol·o·gy (en′tə mäl′ə jē) *n.* [< Gr. *entomon,* insect + -LOGY] the branch of zoology that deals with insects — en′to·mo·log′i·cal (-mə läj′i k'l) *adj.* —en′to·mol′o·gist *n.*

en·tou·rage (än′tōō räzh′) *n.* [Fr. < *entourer,* to surround] a group of associates or attendants; retinue

en·tr'acte (än trakt′, än′trakt) *n.* [Fr. < *entre-,* between + *acte,* an act] 1. the interval between two acts of a play, opera, etc.; intermission 2. music, a dance, etc. performed during this interval

en·trails (en′trālz, -trəlz) *n.pl.* [< L. *interaneus,* internal] the inner organs of men or animals; specif., the intestines; viscera; guts

en·train (in trān′) *vt.* to put aboard a train —*vi.* to go aboard a train —en·train′ment *n.*

en·trance[1] (en′trəns) *n.* 1. the act of entering 2. a place for entering; door, gate, etc. 3. permission or right to enter; admission

en·trance[2] (in trans′) *vt.* -tranced′, -tranc′ing 1. to put into a trance 2. to enchant; charm —en·trance′ment *n.* —en·tranc′ing·ly *adv.*

en·trant (en′trənt) *n.* a person who enters

en·trap (in trap′) *vt.* -trapped′, -trap′ping 1. to catch as in a trap 2. to trick into difficulty —en·trap′ment *n.*

en·treat (in trēt′) *vt., vi.* [< OFr. *en-,* in + *traiter:* see TREAT] to ask earnestly; beseech; implore —en·treat′ing·ly *adv.*

en·treat′y *n., pl.* -ies an earnest request; plea

en·tree, en·trée (än′trā) *n.* [< Fr. < OFr. *entrer,* ENTER] 1. the right to enter 2. the main course of a meal 3. formerly, and still in some countries, a dish served between the main courses

en·trench (in trench′) *vt.* 1. to surround or fortify with a trench or trenches 2. to establish securely —*vi.* to encroach or infringe (*on* or *upon*) —en·trench′ment *n.*

en·tre·pre·neur (än′trə prə nur′) *n.* [Fr.: see ENTERPRISE] one who organizes a business undertaking, assuming the risk for the sake of profit

en·tro·py (en′trə pē) *n.* [< G. < Gr. *entropē,* a turning toward] 1. a measure of the energy unavailable for useful work in a system 2. the tendency of an energy system to run down

en·trust (in trust′) *vt.* 1. to charge with a trust or duty 2. to assign the care of; turn over for safekeeping —en·trust′ment *n.*

en·try (en′trē) *n., pl.* -tries [< OFr.: see ENTER] 1. an entering; entrance 2. a way by which to enter 3. an item or a note recorded in a list, journal, etc. 4. one entered in a race, competition, etc. 5. a term defined, or a person, place, etc. identified, in a dictionary 6. *Law* the taking possession of buildings, land, etc. by entering them

en·twine (in twīn′) *vt., vi.* -twined′, -twin′ing to twine or twist together or around

e·nu·mer·ate (i nōō′mə rāt′, -nyōō′-) *vt.* -at′ed, -at′ing [< L. *e-,* out + *numerare,* to count] 1. to count 2. to name one by one; specify, as in a list —e·nu′mer·a′tion *n.* —e·nu′mer·a′tor *n.*

e·nun·ci·ate (i nun′sē āt′, -shē-) *vt., vi.* -at′ed, -at′ing [< L. *e-,* out + *nuntiare,* announce] 1. to state definitely 2. to announce 3. to pronounce (words) —e·nun′ci·a′tion *n.* —e·nun′ci·a′tor *n.*

e·nu·re·sis (en′yoo rē′sis) *n.* [< Gr. *enourein,* to urinate in] inability to control urination, esp. during sleep —en′u·ret′ic (-ret′ik) *adj.*

en·vel·op (in vel′əp) *vt.* [< OFr.: see EN- & DEVELOP] 1. to wrap up; cover completely 2. to surround 3. to conceal; hide —en·vel′op·ment *n.*

en·ve·lope (en′və lōp′, än′-) *n.* 1. a thing that envelops; covering 2. a folded paper container for letters, etc., usually with a gummed flap

en·ven·om (in ven′əm) *vt.* 1. to put venom or poison on or into 2. to fill with hate; embitter

en·vi·a·ble (en′vē ə b'l) *adj.* worthy to be envied or desired —en′vi·a·bly *adv.*

en·vi·ous (en′vē əs) *adj.* feeling or showing envy —en′vi·ous·ly *adv.*

en·vi·ron (in vī′rən) *vt.* [see ENVIRONS] to surround; encircle

en·vi·ron·ment (in vī′rən mənt, -ərn mənt) *n.* [see ENVIRONS] 1. surroundings 2. all the conditions, circumstances, etc. surrounding, and affecting the development of, an organism —**en·vi·ron·men'tal** (-men't'l) *adj.* —**en·vi'ron·men'tal·ly** *adv.*

en·vi'ron·men·tal·ist *n.* a person working to solve environmental problems, as air and water pollution

en·vi·rons (in vī'rənz) *n.pl.* [< OFr. *en-*, in + *viron*, a circuit] 1. the districts surrounding a city; suburbs 2. surrounding area; vicinity

en·vis·age (en viz'ij) *vt.* **-aged, -ag·ing** [< Fr.: see EN- & VISAGE] to form an image of in the mind; visualize

en·voy (en'voi, än'-) *n.* [< Fr. < L. *in*, in + *via*, way] 1. a messenger; agent 2. a diplomatic agent ranking just below an ambassador

en·vy (en'vē) *n., pl.* **-vies** [< L. *invidia*] 1. discontent and ill will over another's advantages, possessions, etc. 2. desire for something that another has 3. an object of such feeling —*vt.* **-vied, -vy·ing** to feel envy toward or because of —**en'vi·er** *n.*

en·wrap (en rap') *vt.* **-wrapped', -wrap'ping** to wrap; envelop

en·zyme (en'zīm) *n.* [< G. < Gr. *en-*, in + *zymē*, leaven] a proteinlike substance, formed in plant and animal cells, that acts as an organic catalyst in chemical reactions —**en'zy·mat'ic** (-zī mat'ik) *adj.*

e·o·lith·ic (ē'ə lith'ik) *adj.* [< Gr. *ēōs*, dawn + *lithos*, a stone] designating or of the early part of the Stone Age, during which crude stone tools were first used

e·on (ē'ən, ē'än) *n.* [< Gr. *aiōn*, an age] an extremely long, indefinite period of time

E·os (ē'äs) *Gr. Myth.* the goddess of dawn: identified with the Roman Aurora

e·o·sin (ē'ə sin) *n.* [< Gr. *ēōs*, dawn + -IN¹] a rose-colored dye used as an industrial pigment and as a stain for microscopic study

-eous [< L. *-eus*] *a suffix meaning* having the nature of, like [*beauteous*]

EPA Environmental Protection Agency

ep·au·let, ep·au·lette (ep'ə let') *n.* [< Fr.: see SPATULA] a shoulder ornament, as on military uniforms

e·pee, é·pée (e pā', ā-) *n.* [Fr. < Gr. *spathē*, blade] a sword, esp. a thin, pointed sword without a cutting edge, used in fencing

Eph. Ephesians: also **Ephes.**

e·phed·rine (i fed'rin) *n.* [< Gr. *ephedra*, the plant horsetail] an alkaloid used to relieve nasal congestion and asthma

EPAULETS

e·phem·er·al (i fem'ər əl) *adj.* [< Gr. *epi-*, upon + *hēmera*, a day] 1. lasting only one day 2. short-lived; transitory —**e·phem'er·al·ly** *adv.*

e·phem'er·id (-id) *n.* [see prec.] *same as* MAYFLY

E·phe·sians (i fē'zhənz) a book of the New Testament: an epistle of the Apostle Paul

E·phra·im (ē'frē əm) *Bible* 1. the younger son of Joseph 2. the tribe of Israel descended from this son 3. the kingdom of Israel

epi- [< Gr. *epi*, at, on] *a prefix meaning* on, upon, over, beside [*epiglottis, epidemic, epidermis*]

ep·ic (ep'ik) *n.* [< Gr. *epos*, a word, song] 1. a long narrative poem in a dignified style about the deeds of a hero or heroes, as the *Iliad* 2. a story, play, etc. with epic qualities —*adj.* of or like an epic; heroic; grand: also **ep'i·cal**

ep·i·can·thus (ep'ə kan'thəs) *n.* [< EPI- + Gr. *kanthos*, corner of the eye] a small fold of skin sometimes covering the inner corner of the eye

ep·i·carp (ep'ə kärp') *n.* [< EPI- + Gr. *karpos*, fruit] *same as* EXOCARP

ep·i·cen·ter (ep'ə sen'tər) *n.* 1. the area of the earth's surface directly above the place of origin of an earthquake 2. a focal or central point

ep·i·cure (ep'i kyoor') *n.* [< *Epicurus*, ancient Gr. philosopher] one who enjoys and has a discriminating taste for fine foods and drinks

Ep·i·cu·re·an (ep'i kyoo rē'ən) *adj.* 1. of the philosophy of Ep'i·cu'rus, an ancient Greek philosopher who held that the goal of man should be a life of calm pleasure regulated by morality, temperance, serenity, etc. 2. [e-] fond of sensuous pleasure *b*) having to do with an epicure —*n.* 1. a follower of the philosophy of Epicurus 2. [e-] an epicure —Ep'i·cu·re'an·ism, ep'i·cu·re'an·ism *n.*

ep·i·dem·ic (ep'ə dem'ik) *adj.* [< Fr. < Gr. *epi-*, among + *dēmos*, people] prevalent and spreading rapidly among many individuals in a community, as a contagious disease —*n.* 1. an epidemic disease 2. the spreading of such a disease —**ep'i·dem'i·cal·ly** *adv.*

ep·i·der·mis (ep'ə dur'mis) *n.* [< Gr. *epi-*, upon + *derma*, the skin] 1. the outermost layer of the skin 2. the outermost layer of cells covering seed plants and ferns —**ep'i·der'mal** *adj.*

ep·i·glot·tis (ep'ə glät'is) *n.* [see EPI- & GLOTTIS] the thin lid of cartilage that folds back over the opening of the windpipe during swallowing

ep·i·gram (ep'ə gram') *n.* [< Gr. *epi-*, upon + *graphein*, write] 1. a short poem with a witty or satirical point 2. any terse, witty, pointed statement —**ep·i·gram·mat·ic** (ep'i grə mat'ik) *adj.*

ep·i·lep·sy (ep'ə lep'sē) *n.* [< Gr. *epi-*, upon + *lambanein*, seize] a chronic nervous disease, characterized by convulsions and unconsciousness

ep'i·lep'tic (-tik) *adj.* of or having epilepsy —*n.* a person who has epilepsy

ep·i·logue (ep'ə lôg') *n.* [< Gr. *epi-*, upon + *legein*, speak] 1. a closing section of a novel, play, etc., providing further comment; specif., a speech to the audience by an actor 2. the actor who speaks this

ep·i·neph·rine (ep'ə nef'rin) *n.* [< EPI- + Gr. *nephros*, kidney + -INE³] a hormone secreted by the adrenal gland, that stimulates the heart, etc.: it is produced from animal adrenals or synthetically

E·piph·a·ny (i pif'ə nē) *n., pl.* **-nies** [< Gr. *epi-*, upon + *phainein*, to show] a Christian festival (Jan. 6) commemorating the revealing of Jesus as the Christ to the Gentiles

e·pis·co·pa·cy (i pis'kə pə sē) *n., pl.* **-cies** [< Gr. *epi-*, upon + *skopein*, to look] 1. church government by bishops 2. *same as* EPISCOPATE

e·pis·co·pal (-p'l) *adj.* 1. of or governed by bishops 2. [E-] designating or of any of various churches so governed, as the Protestant Episcopal Church

E·pis·co·pa'li·an (-pāl'yən, -pā'lē ən) *adj. same as* EPISCOPAL —*n.* a member of the Protestant Episcopal Church

e·pis'co·pate (-pit, -pāt') *n.* 1. the position, rank, or term of office of a bishop 2. a bishop's see 3. bishops collectively

ep·i·sode (ep'ə sōd') *n.* [< Gr. *epi-*, upon + *eisodos*, entrance] 1. any part of a novel, poem, etc. that is complete in itself; incident 2. any event or series of events complete in itself —**ep'i·sod'ic** (-säd'ik), **ep'i·sod'i·cal** *adj.* —**ep'i·sod'i·cal·ly** *adv.*

e·pis·tle (i pis''l) *n.* [< Gr. *epi-*, to + *stellein*, send] 1. a letter, esp. a formal, instructive one 2. [E-] any of the letters of the Apostles in the New Testament

e·pis'to·lar'y (-tə ler'ē) *adj.* 1. of or suitable to letters 2. contained in or conducted by letters

ep·i·taph (ep'ə taf') *n.* [< Gr. *epi-*, upon + *taphos*, tomb] an inscription, as on a tomb, in memory of the person buried there

ep·i·the·li·um (ep'ə thē'lē əm) *n., pl.* **-li·ums, -li·a** (-ə) [< Gr. *epi-*, upon + *thēlē*, nipple] cellular tissue covering surfaces, forming glands, and lining most cavities of the body —**ep'i·the'li·al** *adj.*

ep·i·thet (ep'ə thet') *n.* [< Gr. *epi-*, on + *tithenai*, put] a word or phrase characterizing some person or thing (Ex.: Philip the Fair)

e·pit·o·me (i pit'ə mē) *n., pl.* **-mes** [< Gr. *epi-*, upon + *temnein*, to cut] 1. an abstract; summary 2. a person or thing that typifies a whole class

e·pit'o·mize' (-mīz') *vt.* **-mized', -miz'ing** to make or be an epitome of —**e·pit'o·miz'er** *n.*

ep·i·zo·ot·ic (ep'ə zō ät'ik) *adj.* [< Gr. *epi-*, upon + *zōion*, animal] epidemic among animals —*n.* an epizootic disease

‡e plu·ri·bus u·num (ē' ploor'ə bəs yōō'nəm) [L.] out of many, one: a motto of the U.S.

ep·och (ep'ək) *n.* [< Gr. *epi-*, upon + *echein*, to hold] 1. the start of a new period of something [radio marked an *epoch* in communication] 2. a period of time in terms of noteworthy events, persons, etc. 3. a subdivision of a geologic period —**ep'och·al** *adj.*

ep·ox·y (e päk'sē) *adj.* [EP(I)- + OXYGEN] designating a compound, specif. a resin used in glues, etc., in which an oxygen atom is joined to each of two connected carbon atoms —*n., pl.* **-ies** an epoxy resin

ep·si·lon (ep'sə län') *n.* the fifth letter of the Greek alphabet (E, ε)

Ep·som salts (or **salt**) (ep'səm) [< *Epsom,* town in England] a white, crystalline salt, magnesium sulfate, used as a cathartic

eq·ua·ble (ek'wə b'l) *adj.* [see EQUAL] 1. steady; uniform 2. even; serene —**eq'ua·bil'i·ty** *n.* —**eq'ua·bly** *adv.*

e·qual (ē'kwəl) *adj.* [< L. *aequus,* even] 1. of the same quantity, size, value, etc. 2. having the same rights, ability, rank, etc. 3. evenly proportioned 4. having the necessary ability, strength, etc. (with *to*) —*n.* any person or thing that is equal —*vt.* e'qualed or e'qualled, e'qual·ing or e'qual·ling 1. to be equal to 2. to do or make something equal to —**e'qual·ly** *adv.*

e·qual·i·ty (i kwäl'ə tē, -kwôl'-) *n., pl.* **-ties** state or instance of being equal

e·qual·ize (ē'kwə līz') *vt.* **-ized'**, **-iz'ing** to make equal or uniform —**e'qual·i·za'tion** *n.* —**e'qual·iz'er** *n.*

equal sign (or **mark**) the arithmetical sign (=), indicating equality (Ex.: 2 + 2 = 4)

e·qua·nim·i·ty (ek'wə nim'ə tē, ē'kwə-) *n.* [< L. *aequus,* even + *animus,* the mind] calmness of mind; composure

e·quate (i kwāt') *vt.* **e·quat'ed, e·quat'ing** 1. to make equal 2. to treat, regard, or express as equal

e·qua·tion (i kwā'zhən) *n.* 1. an equating or being equated 2. a statement of equality between two quantities, as shown by the equal sign (=) 3. an expression in which symbols and formulas are used to represent a chemical reaction (Ex.: $SO_3 + H_2O = H_2SO_4$)

e·qua·tor (i kwāt'ər) *n.* 1. an imaginary circle around the earth, equally distant from the North Pole and the South Pole 2. *same as* CELESTIAL EQUATOR

e·qua·to·ri·al (ē'kwə tôr'ē əl, ek'wə-) *adj.* 1. of or near the earth's equator 2. like conditions near the earth's equator *[equatorial heat]*

Equatorial Guinea country in C Africa, including a mainland section & two islands in the Atlantic: 10,832 sq. mi.; pop. 286,000; cap. Santa Isabel

eq·uer·ry (ek'wər ē) *n., pl.* **-ries** [< OFr. *escuerie,* status of a squire] 1. formerly, an officer in charge of the horses of a noble household 2. a personal attendant on some member of a royal family

e·ques·tri·an (i kwes'trē ən) *adj.* [< L. *equus,* horse] 1. of horses or horsemanship 2. on horseback —*n.* a rider on horseback, as in a circus —**e·ques'tri·enne'** (-en') *n.fem.*

equi- *a combining form meaning* equal, equally *[equidistant]*

e·qui·an·gu·lar (ē'kwə aŋ'gyə lər) *adj.* having all angles equal

e'qui·dis'tant *adj.* equally distant —**e'qui·dis'tance** *n.* — **e'qui·dis'tant·ly** *adv.*

e'qui·lat'er·al (-lat'ər əl) *adj.* [< L. *aequus,* equal + *latus,* side] having all sides equal —*n.* a figure having equal sides

e·quil·i·brate (i kwil'ə brāt', ē'kwə lī'brāt) *vt., vi.* **-brat'ed, -brat'ing** to bring into or be in equilibrium — **e·quil'i·bra'tion** *n.*

e·qui·lib·ri·um (ē'kwə lib'rē əm) *n., pl.* **-ri·ums, -ri·a** (-ə) [< L. *aequus,* equal + *libra,* a balance] a state of balance between opposing forces

e·quine (ē'kwīn, ek'wīn) *adj.* [< L. *equus,* horse] of or like a horse —*n.* a horse

e·qui·noc·tial (ē'kwə näk'shəl) *adj.* 1. relating to either of the equinoxes 2. occurring at about the time of an equinox *[an equinoctial storm]* —*n.* 1. *same as* CELESTIAL EQUATOR 2. an equinoctial storm

e·qui·nox (ē'kwə näks') *n.* [< L. *aequus,* equal + *nox,* night] the time when the sun crosses the equator, making night and day of equal length in all parts of the earth: the **vernal equinox** occurs about March 21, the **autumnal equinox** about September 22

e·quip (i kwip') *vt.* **e·quipped', e·quip'ping** [< OFr. *es-quiper,* embark] to provide with what is needed

eq·ui·page (ek'wə pij) *n.* 1. the equipment of a ship, army, etc. 2. a carriage with horses and liveried servants

e·quip·ment (i kwip'mənt) *n.* 1. an equipping or being equipped 2. whatever one is equipped with; supplies, resources, etc.

eq·ui·poise (ek'wə poiz', ē'kwə-) *n.* [EQUI- + POISE] 1. equal distribution of weight 2. counterbalance

eq·ui·ta·ble (ek'wit ə b'l) *adj.* fair; just —**eq'ui·ta·bly** *adv.*

eq·ui·ty (ek'wət ē) *n., pl.* **-ties** [< L. *aequus,* equal] 1. fairness; impartiality; justice 2. anything that is fair or equitable 3. the value of property beyond the amount owed on it 4. *Law* a system of doctrines supplementing common and statute law

e·quiv·a·lent (i kwiv'ə lənt) *adj.* [< L. *aequus,* equal + *valere,* be strong] 1. equal in quantity, value, force, mean-ing, etc. 2. *Chem.* having the same valence 3. *Geom.* equal in area or volume but not of the same shape —*n.* an equivalent thing —**e·quiv'a·lence, e·quiv'a·len·cy** *n.* — **e·quiv'a·lent·ly** *adv.*

e·quiv·o·cal (i kwiv'ə k'l) *adj.* [see EQUIVOCATE] 1. having two or more meanings; purposely ambiguous 2. uncertain; doubtful 3. suspicious; questionable —**e·quiv'o·cal·ly** *adv.*

e·quiv'o·cate' (-kāt') *vi.* **-cat'ed, -cat'ing** [< L. *aequus,* equal + *vox,* voice] to use equivocal terms in order to deceive, hedge, etc. —**e·quiv'o·ca'tion** *n.* —**e·quiv'o·ca'tor** *n.*

-er [< OE.] 1. *a suffix meaning:* a) a person or thing having to do with *[hatter]* b) a person living in *[New Yorker]* c) a person or thing that *[sprayer]* d) repeatedly *[flicker]* 2. *a suffix forming the comparative degree [greater]*

Er *Chem.* erbium

e·ra (ir'ə, er'-) *n.* [LL. *aera*] 1. a period of time measured from some occurrence or date 2. a period of time in terms of noteworthy events, persons, etc. 3. any of the five main divisions of geologic time

e·rad·i·cate (i rad'ə kāt') *vt.* **-cat'ed, -cat'ing** [< L. *e-,* out + *radix,* root] to uproot; wipe out; destroy —**e·rad'i·ca·ble** (-kə b'l) *adj.* —**e·rad'i·ca'tion** *n.* —**e·rad'i·ca'tor** *n.*

e·rase (i rās') *vt.* **e·rased', e·ras'ing** [< L. *e-,* out + *radere,* to scrape] 1. to rub, scrape, or wipe out (writing, etc.) 2. to remove (something recorded) from (magnetic tape) 3. to obliterate, as from the mind —**e·ras'a·ble** *adj.*

e·ras'er *n.* a thing that erases; specif., a rubber device for erasing ink or pencil marks, or a pad for removing chalk marks from a blackboard

E·ras·mus (i raz'məs), **Des·i·der·i·us** (des'ə dir'ē əs) 1466?–1536; Du. humanist & scholar

e·ra·sure (i rā'shər) *n.* 1. an erasing 2. the place where a word, mark, etc. has been erased

er·bi·um (ur'bē əm) *n.* [< (*Ytt*)*erby,* Sweden] a metallic chemical element of the rare-earth group: symbol, Er; at. wt., 167.28; at. no., 68

ere (er) *prep.* [< OE. *ær*] [Archaic or Poet.] before (in time) —*conj.* [Archaic or Poet.] 1. before 2. rather than

Er·e·bus (er'ə bəs) *Gr. Myth.* the dark place that the dead went through to reach Hades

e·rect (i rekt') *adj.* [< L. *e-,* up + *regere,* make straight] 1. upright; vertical 2. bristling; stiff —*vt.* 1. to construct (a building, etc.) 2. to set in an upright position 3. to put together 4. *Geom.* to draw (a perpendicular, figure, etc.) upon a base line —**e·rec'tion** *n.* —**e·rect'ly** *adv.* —**e·rect'ness** *n.* —**e·rec'tor** *n.*

ere·long (er'lôŋ') *adv.* [Archaic] before long

er·e·mite (er'ə mīt') *n.* [see HERMIT] a religious recluse; hermit

erg (urg) *n.* [< Gr. *ergon,* work] *Physics* a unit of work or energy, being the work done by one dyne acting through a distance of one centimeter

‡er·go (ur'gō) *conj., adv.* [L.] therefore

er·got (ur'gət) *n.* [Fr. < OFr. *argot,* rooster's spur] 1. a disease of rye and other cereal plants caused by a fungus growing on the grains 2. this fungus dried and used as a drug, as to stop bleeding

ERMINE
(to 16 in. long)

Er·ics·son (er'ik sən), **Leif** (lāf) fl. 1000; Norw. explorer: discovered what is now believed to be part of N. America: also sp. **Ericson**

E·rie (ir'ē) 1. port on Lake Erie, in NW Pa.: pop. 129,000 2. **Lake,** one of the Great Lakes, between Lake Huron and Lake Ontario

E·rin (er'in) [Poet.] Ireland

E·rin·y·es (i rin'ē ēz') *n.pl., sing.* **E·rin·ys** (i rin'is) *Gr. Myth. same as* FURIES

E·ris (ir'is, er'-) *Gr. Myth.* the goddess of strife

Er·i·tre·a (er'ə trē'ə) province of Ethiopia, on the Red Sea: 45,000 sq. mi. —**Er'i·tre'an** *adj., n.*

er·mine (ur'mən) *n.* [OFr.; prob. < OHG. *harmo,* weasel] 1. a weasel whose fur is white in winter 2. its white fur

erne, ern (urn) *n.* [OE. *earn*] the European white-tailed eagle, which lives near the sea

e·rode (i rōd') *vt.* **e·rod'ed, e·rod'ing** [< L. *e-,* out + *rodere,* to gnaw] 1. to wear away 2. to form by wearing away gradually *[the stream eroded a gully]* —*vi.* to become eroded

E·ros (er'äs, ir'-) *Gr. Myth.* the god of love, son of Aphrodite: identified with the Roman Cupid

e·ro·sion (i rō'zhən) *n.* an eroding or being eroded — **e·ro'sive** *adj.*

e·rot·ic (i rät'ik) *adj.* [< Gr. *erōs,* love] of or arousing sexual feelings or desires; amatory —**e·rot'i·cal·ly** *adv.*

e·rot'i·cism (-ə siz'm) *n.* **1.** erotic quality **2.** sexual excitement or behavior **3.** preoccupation with sex Also, and for 2 usually, **er·o·tism** (er'ə tiz'm)

err (ur, er) *vi.* [< L. *errare,* wander] **1.** to be wrong or mistaken **2.** to deviate from the established moral code

er·rand (er'ənd) *n.* [OE. *ærende*] **1.** a short trip to do a thing, as for another **2.** the thing to be done

er·rant (er'ənt) *adj.* **1.** [< L. *iter,* a journey] roving or wandering in search of adventure **2.** [see ERR] erring; wrong —**er'rant·ly** *adv.* —**er'rant·ry** *n.*

er·rat·ic (i rat'ik) *adj.* [< L. *errare,* wander] **1.** having no fixed course; irregular **2.** eccentric; queer —*n.* an erratic person —**er·rat'i·cal·ly** *adv.*

er·ra·tum (e rät'əm, -rāt'-) *n., pl.* **-ta** (-tə) [L. < *errare,* wander] an error in printing or writing

er·ro·ne·ous (ə rō'nē əs) *adj.* containing or based on error; wrong —**er·ro'ne·ous·ly** *adv.*

er·ror (er'ər) *n.* [< L. *errare,* wander] **1.** the state of believing what is untrue **2.** a wrong belief **3.** something incorrect or wrong; mistake **4.** a transgression **5.** *Baseball* any misplay in fielding

er·satz (ur'zäts, er'-) *n., adj.* [G.] substitute: the word usually suggests inferior quality

Erse (urs) *adj., n.* [ME. *Erish,* var. of *Irisc,* Irish] *same as* GAELIC

erst (urst) *adv.* [< OE. *ær,* ere] [Archaic] formerly —*adj.* [Obs.] first

erst'while' (-hwil') *adv.* [Archaic] formerly; some time ago —*adj.* former

e·ruct (i rukt') *vt., vi.* [< L. *e-,* out + *ructare,* to belch] to belch: also **e·ruc'tate** (-tāt), **-tat·ed, -tat·ing** —**e·ruc'ta'tion** *n.*

er·u·dite (er'yoo dīt', -oo-) *adj.* [< L. *e-,* out + *rudis,* rude] learned; scholarly —**er'u·dite'ly** *adv.*

er'u·di'tion (-dish'ən) *n.* learning acquired by reading and study; scholarship

e·rupt (i rupt') *vi.* [< L. *e-,* out + *rumpere,* to break] **1.** to burst forth or out [the lava *erupted*] **2.** to throw forth lava, water, etc. **3.** to break out in a rash —*vt.* to cause to burst forth

e·rup·tion (i rup'shən) *n.* **1.** a bursting forth or out **2.** a throwing forth of lava, water, etc. **3.** *a)* a breaking out in a rash *b)* a rash —**e·rup'tive** *adj.*

-ery [< LL. *-aria*] a suffix meaning: **1.** a place to [*tannery*] **2.** a place for [*nunnery*] **3.** the practice or act of [*surgery*] **4.** the product of [*pottery*] **5.** a collection of [*crockery*] **6.** the condition of [*drudgery*] **7.** the qualities of [*tomfoolery*]

er·y·sip·e·las (er'ə sip''l əs, ir'-) *n.* [< Gr. *erythros,* red + *-pelas,* skin] an acute, infectious skin disease with local inflammation and fever

e·ryth·ro·cyte (i rith'rə sīt') *n.* [< Gr. *erythros,* red + *kytos,* a hollow] a cell of human blood whose red pigment, hemoglobin, carries oxygen to the body tissues

-es [< OE.] a suffix used: **1.** to form certain plurals [*fishes*] **2.** to form the third person singular, present indicative, of verbs [(he) *kisses*]

E·sau (ē'sô) *Bible* Isaac's son, who sold his birthright to his brother, Jacob

es·ca·drille (es'kə dril') *n.* [Fr. < Sp. < *escuadra,* squad] a squadron of airplanes

es·ca·lade (es'kə lād') *n.* [< L. *scala,* ladder] the act of climbing the walls of a fortified place by ladders —*vt.* **-lad'ed, -lad'ing** to climb (a wall, etc.) or enter (a fortified place) by ladders

es·ca·late (es'kə lāt') *vi.* **-lat'ed, -lat'ing** **1.** to rise as on an escalator **2.** to expand, as from a limited conflict into a general war **3.** to increase rapidly, as prices

es'ca·la'tor (-ər) *n.* [< L. *scala,* ladder] a moving stairway on an endless belt

es·cal·lop, es·cal·op (e skäl'əp, -skal'-) *n., vt. same as* SCALLOP

es·ca·pade (es'kə pād') *n.* [Fr.] a reckless adventure or prank

es·cape (ə skāp', e-) *vi.* **-caped', -cap'ing** [< L. *ex-,* out of + *cappa,* cloak] **1.** to get free; get away **2.** to avoid harm, injury, etc. **3.** to leak away [gas is *escaping*] —*vt.* **1.** to get away from; flee **2.** to avoid [to *escape* death] **3.** to come from involuntarily [a scream *escaped* his lips] **4.** to slip away from [his name *escapes* me] —*n.* **1.** an escaping or state of having escaped **2.** a means of escape **3.** a leakage **4.** a temporary mental release from reality —*adj.* providing an escape —**es·cap'er** *n.*

es·cap·ee (ə skā'pē', e-) *n.* a person who has escaped, esp. from confinement

es·cape'ment *n.* **1.** a notched wheel with a detaining catch to control the speed and regularity of the balance wheel or pendulum of a clock or watch **2.** the mechanism in typewriters that regulates the horizontal movement of the carriage

es·cap'ism (-iz'm) *n.* a tendency to escape from reality, responsibilities, etc., esp. through the imagination —**es·cap'ist** *adj., n.*

es·ca·role (es'kə rōl') *n.* [Fr. < L. *esca,* food] a kind of endive with wide leaves

es·carp·ment (e skärp'mənt) *n.* [< Fr.] **1.** a steep slope or cliff **2.** a steep slope of ground on the exterior of a fortification

-escence *a noun suffix corresponding to the adjective suffix* -ESCENT [*obsolescence*]

-escent [< L. *-escens*] *an adjective suffix meaning:* **1.** starting to be, being, or becoming [*convalescent*] **2.** giving off light or color [*phosphorescent*]

es·cheat (es chēt') *n.* [< L. *ex-,* out + *cadere,* to fall] **1.** the reverting of property to the lord of the manor or to the government when there are no legal heirs **2.** property so reverting —*vt., vi.* to confiscate or revert by escheat

es·chew (es chōō') *vt.* [< OHG. *sciuhan,* to fear] to keep away from; shun

es·cort (es'kôrt) *n.* [< L. *ex-,* out + *corrigere,* set right] **1.** one or more persons (or cars, ships, etc.) accompanying another to protect it or show honor **2.** a man accompanying a woman —*vt.* (i skôrt') to go with as an escort

es·cri·toire (es'krə twär') *n.* [< L. *scribere,* write] a writing desk or table

es·crow (es'krō) *n.* [OFr. *escroue,* scroll] *Law* the state of a bond, deed, etc. put in the care of a third party until certain conditions are fulfilled

es·cu·do (es kōō'dō) *n., pl.* **-dos** [Sp., a shield < L. *scutum*] **1.** any of several obsolete coins of Spain and Portugal **2.** the monetary unit of Chile and Portugal

es·cu·lent (es'kyoo lənt) *adj.* [< L. *esca,* food] edible —*n.* something fit for food, esp. a vegetable

es·cutch·eon (i skuch'ən) *n.* [< L. *scutum,* shield] a shield on which a coat of arms is displayed

Es·dras (ez'drəs) *Douay Bible name for* EZRA

-ese [< L. *-ensis*] *a suffix meaning:* **1.** (a native or inhabitant) of [*Portuguese*] **2.** (in) the language of [*Chinese*]

ESE, E.S.E., e.s.e. east-southeast

Es·ki·mo (es'kə mō') *n.* [< Fr. < Algonquian] **1.** *pl.* **-mos', -mo'** a member of a native N. American people living in Greenland, N Canada, Alaska, etc. **2.** either of the two languages of the Eskimos —*adj.* of the Eskimos, their language, etc. —**Es'ki·mo'an** *adj.*

Eskimo dog a strong breed of dog used by the Eskimos to pull sleds

e·soph·a·gus (i säf'ə gəs) *n., pl.* **-gi'** (-jī') [< Gr. *oisein,* to be going to carry + *phagein,* eat] the passage for food from the pharynx to the stomach

es·o·ter·ic (es'ə ter'ik) *adj.* [< Gr. *esōteros,* inner] **1.** *a)* understood by only a chosen few *b)* beyond the understanding of most people; abstruse **2.** confidential; private

ESP extrasensory perception

esp., espec. especially

es·pa·drille (es'pə dril') *n.* [Fr. < Sp. *esparto,* coarse grass] a casual shoe with a canvas upper and a rope or rubber sole

es·pal·ier (es pal'yər) *n.* [Fr. < L. *spatula,* spatula] **1.** a lattice or trellis on which trees and shrubs are trained to grow flat **2.** a plant, tree, etc. so trained —*vt.* to train on an espalier

es·pe·cial (ə spesh'əl) *adj.* special; particular; exceptional —**es·pe'cial·ly** *adv.*

Es·pe·ran·to (es'pə rän'tō, -ran'-) *n.* [after pseudonym of its inventor] an artificial language for international use

es·pi·o·nage (es'pē ə näzh', -nij') *n.* [< Fr. < It. *spia,* a spy] **1.** the act of spying **2.** the use of spies, esp. for military purposes

es·pla·nade (es'plə nād', -näd') *n.* [Fr. < It. < L. *explanare,* to level] a level, open space of ground; esp., a public walk or roadway; promenade

es·pous·al (i spou'z'l) *n.* **1.** [*often pl.*] a wedding **2.** an espousing (of some cause, idea, etc.)

ESPALIER

---

fat, āpe, cär; ten, ēven; is, bīte; gō, hôrn, tōōl, look; oil, out; up, fur; thin, *th*en; zh, leisure; ŋ, ring; ə for a in *ago;* ' as in able (ā'b'l); ë, Fr. coeur; ö, Fr. feu; Fr. mon; ü, Fr. duc; r, Fr. cri; kh, G. doch, ich. ‡ foreign; < derived from

es·pouse (i spouz′) *vt.* -poused′, -pous′ing [see SPOUSE] 1. to marry 2. to support or advocate (some cause, idea, etc.) —**es·pous′er** *n.*

es·pres·so (es pres′ō) *n., pl.* -sos [It.] coffee made by forcing steam through finely ground coffee beans

es·prit (es prē′) *n.* [Fr.] 1. spirit 2. lively wit

esprit de corps (də kôr′) [Fr.] group spirit; sense of pride, honor, etc. in shared activities

es·py (ə spī′, es pī′) *vt.* -pied′, -py′ing [see SPY] to catch sight of; spy

-esque [Fr. < It. -*esco*] a suffix meaning: 1. in the manner or style of 2. like [*picturesque*]

es·quire (es′kwīr, ə skwīr′) *n.* [< LL. *scutarius*, shield-bearer] 1. formerly, an attendant for a knight 2. in England, a member of the gentry ranking just below a knight 3. [E-] a title of courtesy, usually abbrev. **Esq., Esqr.,** placed after a man's surname

-ess [< Gr.] a suffix meaning female [*lioness*]

es·say (e sā′) *vt.* [< L. *exagium*, a weighing] to try —*n.* 1. (es′ā, e sā′) an attempt; trial 2. (es′ā) a short, personal literary composition of an analytical or interpretive kind —**es′say·ist** *n.*

Es·sen (es′'n) city in W West Germany: pop. 705,000

es·sence (es′'ns) *n.* [< L. *esse*, to be] 1. the basic nature (of something) 2. *a*) a concentrated substance that keeps the flavor, fragrance, etc. of the plant, drug, etc. from which it is extracted *b*) a solution of such a substance in alcohol *c*) a perfume

es·sen·tial (ə sen′shəl) *adj.* 1. of or constituting the essence of something; basic 2. absolutely necessary; indispensable —*n.* something necessary or fundamental —**es·sen′tial·ly** *adv.*

essential oil any volatile oil that gives distinctive odor, flavor, etc. to a plant, flower, or fruit

-est [< OE.] a suffix forming the superlative degree [*greatest*]

EST, E.S.T. Eastern Standard Time

est. 1. established 2. estimate 3. estimated

es·tab·lish (ə stab′lish) *vt.* [< L. *stabilis*, stable] 1. to order, ordain, or enact (a law, statute, etc.) permanently 2. to found (a nation, business, etc.) 3. to bring about 4. to set up in business or a profession 5. to make a state institution of (a church) 6. to cause (a theory, precedent, etc.) to be accepted 7. to prove; demonstrate

es·tab′lish·ment *n.* 1. an establishing or being established 2. a thing established, as a business

es·tate (ə stāt′) *n.* [< OFr. *estat*, state] 1. a condition or stage of life 2. property; possessions 3. an individually owned piece of land containing a residence 4. *Law a*) the degree, nature, and extent of ownership that one has in land, etc. *b*) all the property, real or personal, owned by one

es·teem (ə stēm′) *vt.* [< L. *aestimare*, to value] 1. to value highly; respect 2. to hold to be; consider —*n.* favorable opinion; high regard

es·ter (es′tər) *n.* [G. < *essig*, vinegar + *äther*, ether] an organic compound, comparable to an inorganic salt, formed by the reaction of an acid and an alcohol, or a phenol

Es·ther (es′tər) *Bible* 1. the Jewish wife of a Persian king: she saved her people from slaughter 2. the book telling her story: abbrev. **Esth.**

es·thete (es′thēt′) *n. same as* AESTHETE —**es·thet′ic** (-thet′ik) *adj.*

es·thet·ics (-thet′iks) *n.pl. same as* AESTHETICS

es·ti·ma·ble (es′tə mə b'l) *adj.* worthy of esteem —**es′ti·ma·bly** *adv.*

es·ti·mate (es′tə māt′) *vt.* -mat′ed, -mat′ing [see ESTEEM] 1. to form an opinion about 2. to determine generally (size, cost, etc.) —*vi.* to make an estimate —*n.* (-mit) 1. a general calculation; esp., an approximate computation of probable cost 2. an opinion or judgment —**es′ti·ma′tor** *n.*

es′ti·ma′tion *n.* 1. an estimating 2. an opinion or judgment 3. esteem; regard

Es·to·ni·a (es tō′nē ə) republic of the U.S.S.R., in NE Europe: in full **Estonian Soviet Socialist Republic** —**Es·to′ni·an** *adj., n.*

es·trange (ə strānj′) *vt.* -tranged′, -trang′ing [< L. *ex-traneus*, strange] 1. to keep apart or away 2. to turn (a person) from an affectionate or friendly attitude to an indifferent or hostile one; alienate —**es·trange′ment** *n.*

es·tro·gen (es′trə jən) *n.* [< Gr. *oistros*, frenzy] any of several female sex hormones

es·trus (es′trəs, ēs′-) *n.* [< Gr. *oistrus*, frenzy] the sexual excitement, or heat, of most female placental mammals, or the period of this —**es′trous** *adj.*

es·tu·ar·y (es′choo wer′ē) *n., pl.* -ies [< L. *aestus*, the tide] an arm of the sea; esp., the mouth of a river, where the tide meets the current

-et [< OFr.] a suffix meaning little [*islet*]

e·ta (āt′ə, ēt′ə) *n.* the seventh letter of the Greek alphabet (H, η)

et al. [L. *et alii*] and others

et cet·er·a (et set′ər ə, set′rə) [L.] and others; and so forth: abbrev. etc.

etch (ech) *vt.* [< MHG. *etzen*, to eat] 1. to make (a drawing, design, etc.) on metal, glass, etc. by the action of an acid 2. to engrave (a metal plate, glass, etc.) in this way for use in printing such drawings, etc. 3. to impress sharply —**etch′er** *n.*

etch′ing *n.* 1. an etched plate, drawing, etc. 2. a print made from an etched plate 3. the art of making such drawings, etc.

e·ter·nal (i tur′n'l) *adj.* [< L. *aevum*, an age] 1. without beginning or end; everlasting 2. forever the same; unchanging 3. seeming never to stop —**the Eternal God** —**e·ter′nal·ly** *adv.* —**e·ter′nal·ness** *n.*

e·ter·ni·ty (i tur′nə tē) *n., pl.* -ties 1. the state or fact of being eternal 2. infinite time 3. a long period of time that seems endless 4. the endless time after death

eth·ane (eth′ān) *n.* [< ETHYL] an odorless, colorless, gaseous hydrocarbon, C_2H_6: it is found in natural gas and is used as a fuel, etc.

e·ther (ē′thər) *n.* [< Gr. *aithein*, to burn] 1. the upper regions of space 2. a volatile, colorless, highly flammable liquid, $(C_2H_5)_2O$: it is used as an anesthetic and a solvent 3. an invisible substance once thought to pervade space

e·the·re·al (i thir′ē əl) *adj.* 1. of or like the ether, or upper regions of space 2. very light; airy; delicate 3. heavenly —**e·the′re·al·ly** *adv.*

e·the′re·al·ize (-ə līz′) *vt.* -ized′, -iz′ing to make, or treat as being, ethereal

e·ther·ize (ē′thə rīz′) *vt.* -ized′, -iz′ing to anesthetize as by causing to inhale ether fumes

eth·i·cal (eth′i k'l) *adj.* [< Gr. *ēthos*, character] 1. having to do with ethics or morality; of or conforming to moral standards 2. conforming to professional standards of conduct —**eth′i·cal′i·ty** (-kal′ə tē) *n.* —**eth′i·cal·ly** *adv.*

eth·ics (eth′iks) *n.pl.* [see prec.] 1. [*with sing. v.*] the study of standards of conduct and moral judgment 2. the system of morals of a particular person, religion, group, etc.

E·thi·o·pi·a (ē′thē ō′pē ə) country in E Africa: 457,000 sq. mi.; pop. 24,769,000; cap. Addis Ababa —**E′thi·o′pi·an** *adj., n.*

eth·nic (eth′nik) *adj.* [< Gr. *ethnos*, nation] of any of the basic divisions of mankind or of a heterogeneous population, as distinguished by customs, language, etc.: also **eth′ni·cal** —*n.* a member of a minority or nationality group that is part of a larger community —**eth′ni·cal·ly** *adv.*

eth·nol·o·gy (eth näl′ə jē) *n.* [< Gr. *ethnos*, nation + -LOGY] the branch of anthropology that deals with the distribution, characteristics, culture, etc. of various peoples —**eth′no·log′i·cal** (-nə läj′i k'l) *adj.* —**eth′no·log′i·cal·ly** *adv.* —**eth·nol′o·gist** *n.*

eth·yl (eth′'l) *n.* [< ETHER] the hydrocarbon radical, C_2H_5, which forms the base of common alcohol, ether, etc.

ethyl alcohol *same as* ALCOHOL (sense l)

eth·yl·ene (eth′ə lēn′) *n.* [< ETHYL] a colorless, flammable, gaseous hydrocarbon with a disagreeable odor

e·ti·ol·o·gy (ēt′ē äl′ə jē) *n., pl.* -gies [< Gr. *aitia*, cause + -LOGY] 1. the science of causes or origins 2. *Med.* the causes of a disease —**e′ti·o·log′ic** (-ə läj′ik), **e′ti·o·log′i·cal** *adj.*

et·i·quette (et′i kət, -ket′) *n.* [Fr. *étiquette*, a ticket] the forms, manners, etc. conventionally acceptable or required in social relations

Et·na (et′nə) volcanic mountain in E Sicily

E·ton (ēt′'n) a private preparatory school for boys near London, England: in full **Eton College** —**E·to·ni·an** (ē tō′nē ən) *adj., n.*

E·trus·can (i trus′kən) *adj.* of an ancient country (Etruria) in what is now WC Italy

et seq. [L. *et sequens*] and the following

-ette [Fr.] a suffix meaning: 1. little [*dinette*] 2. female [*majorette*]

é·tude (ā′tood, -tyood) *n.* [Fr., STUDY] a musical composition for a solo instrument, designed to give practice in some special point of technique

ETV educational television

et·y·mol·o·gy (et′ə mäl′ə jē) *n., pl.* -gies [< Gr. *etymos*, true + -LOGY] 1. the origin and development of a word,

phrase, etc. **2.** the branch of linguistics dealing with this
Abbrev. etym. —et′y·mo·log′i·cal (-mə läj′ə k'l) *adj.* —
et′y·mo·log′i·cal·ly *adv.* —et′y·mol′o·gist *n.*

eu- [Fr. < Gr.] *a prefix meaning* good, well [*eugenic*]

Eu *Chem.* europium

eu·ca·lyp·tus (yōō′kə lip′təs) *n., pl.* -tus·es, -ti (-tī) [<
EU- + Gr. *kalyptos*, covered] a tall, chiefly Australian
evergreen related to the myrtle, valued for its timber,
gum, and oil (**eucalyptus oil**) which is used as an antiseptic and expectorant

Eu·cha·rist (yōō′rist) *n.* [< Gr. *eucharistia*, gratitude]
1. *same as* HOLY COMMUNION **2.** the consecrated bread
and wine used in Holy Communion —**Eu′cha·ris′tic** *adj.*

eu·chre (yōō′kər) *n.* [< ?] a card game played with
thirty-two cards —*vt.* -chred, -chring [Colloq.] to outwit

Eu·clid (yōō′klid) fl. 300 B.C.; Gr. mathematician: author
of a basic work in geometry —**Eu·clid′e·an, Eu·clid′i·an**
(-ē ən) *adj.*

eu·gen·ic (yoo jen′ik) *adj.* [see EU- & GENESIS] **1.** relating
to the bearing of sound offspring **2.** of or relating to eu-
genics Also **eu·gen′i·cal** —**eu·gen′i·cal·ly** *adv.*

eu·gen′i·cist (-ə sist) *n.* a specialist in or advocate of eu-
genics

eu·gen·ics (yoo jen′iks) *n.pl.* [*with sing. v.*] the movement devoted to improving the human species by control
of hereditary factors in mating

eu·lo·gize (yōō′lə jīz′) *vt.* -gized′, -giz′ing to praise as in
a eulogy —**eu′lo·gist** *n.*

eu′lo·gy (-jē) *n., pl.* -gies [< Gr. *eulegein*, speak well of]
1. speech or writing in praise of a person or thing; esp., a
funeral oration **2.** high praise —**eu′lo·gis′tic** (-jis′tik) *adj.*
—**eu′lo·gis′ti·cal·ly** *adv.*

Eu·men·i·des (yoo men′ə dēz′) *n.pl.* [< Gr. *Eumenides*,
lit., the gracious ones: a propitiatory euphemism] *same as*
FURIES

eu·nuch (yōō′nək) *n.* [< Gr. *eunē*, a bed + *echein*, keep]
a castrated man, esp. one in charge of a harem

eu·pep·si·a (yoo pep′shə, -sē ə) *n.* [< Gr. *eupepsia*,
digestibility] good digestion —**eu·pep′tic** *adj.*

eu·phe·mism (yōō′fə miz′m) *n.* [< Gr. *eu-*, good +
phanai, speak] **1.** the use of a less direct word or phrase
for one considered offensive **2.** a word or phrase so substituted (Ex.: *remains* for *corpse*) —**eu′phe·mis′tic** *adj.* —
eu′phe·mis′ti·cal·ly *adv.*

eu·pho·ni·ous (yoo fō′nē əs) *adj.* having a pleasant
sound; harmonious —**eu·pho′ni·ous·ly** *adv.*

eu·pho′ni·um (-əm) *n.* a brass-wind instrument having a
mellow tone

eu·pho·ny (yōō′fə nē) *n., pl.* -nies [< Gr. *eu-*, well +
phōnē, voice] a pleasant combination of agreeable sounds,
as in speech

eu·pho·ri·a (yoo fôr′ē ə) *n.* [< Gr. *eu-*, well + *pherein*, to
bear] a feeling of well-being or high spirits —**eu·phor′ic**
adj.

Eu·phra·tes (yoo frät′ēz) river flowing from EC Turkey
through Syria & Iraq: c.1,700 mi.

eu·phu·ism (yōō′fyoo wiz′m) *n.* [< *Euphues*, character in
works by J. Lyly, 16th-c. Eng. author] **1.** an artificial,
high-flown style of speaking or writing **2.** an instance of
this

Eur. **1.** Europe **2.** European

Eur·a·sia (yoo rā′zhə) land mass made up of the continents of Europe & Asia

Eur·a′sian *adj.* **1.** of Eurasia **2.** of mixed European and
Asian descent —*n.* a person of Eurasian descent

eu·re·ka (yoo rē′kə) *interj.* [< Gr.] I have found (it): an
exclamation of triumphant achievement

Eu·rip·i·des (yoo rip′ə dēz′) 479?-406? B.C.; Gr. writer of
tragedies

Eu·rope (yoor′əp) continent between Asia & the Atlantic
Ocean: c.3,750,000 sq. mi.; pop. c.637,366,000 —**Eu′ro-
pe′an** (-ə pē′ən) *adj., n.*

European Economic Community the European common market formed in 1958 by Belgium, France, West
Germany, Italy, Luxembourg, and the Netherlands

European plan a system of hotel operation in which the
charge to guests covers rooms and service but not meals

eu·ro·pi·um (yoo rō′pē əm) *n.* [ModL. < EUROPE] a
chemical element of the rare-earth group: symbol, Eu; at.
wt., 151.96; at. no., 63

Eu·ryd·i·ce (yoo rid′ə sē′) see ORPHEUS

eu·ryth·mics (yoo rith′miks) *n.pl.* [*with sing. v.*] [< Gr.
eu-, well + *rhythmos*, rhythm] the art of performing
bodily movements in rhythm

Eu·sta·chi·an tube (yoo stā′shən, -kē ən) [after B. *Eus-
tachio*, 16th-c. It. anatomist] a slender tube between the
middle ear and the pharynx

Eu·ter·pe (yoo tur′pē) *Gr. Myth.* the Muse of music and
lyric poetry

eu·tha·na·sia (yōō′thə nā′zhə) *n.* [< Gr. *eu-*, well +
thanatos, death] **1.** a painless death **2.** act of causing
death painlessly to end suffering: advocated by some in
cases of incurable, painful diseases

Eux·ine Sea (yōōk′sən, -sīn) *ancient name of the* BLACK
SEA

e·vac·u·ate (i vak′yoo wāt′) *vt.* -at′ed, -at′ing [< L. *e-*,
out + *vacuus*, empty] **1.** to make empty **2.** to discharge
(bodily waste) **3.** to withdraw from; remove —*vi.* **1.** to
withdraw, as from a danger area **2.** to discharge bodily
waste —**e·vac′u·a′tion** *n.* —**e·vac′u·ee′** (-wē′) *n.*

e·vade (i vād′) *vt.* -vad′ed, -vad′ing [< L. *e-*, out
+ *vadere*, to go] **1.** to avoid or escape (from) by deceit or
cleverness **2.** to avoid doing or answering directly —
e·vad′er *n.*

e·val·u·ate (i val′yoo wāt′) *vt.* -at′ed, -at′ing [ult. < L.
ex-, out + *valere*, be worth] **1.** to find the value or
amount of **2.** to appraise —**e·val′u·a′tion** *n.*

ev·a·nesce (ev′ə nes′) *vi.* -nesced′, -nesc′ing [< L. *e-*,
out + *vanescere*, vanish] to fade from sight; vanish

ev′a·nes′cent (-nes′'nt) *adj.* tending to fade away; vanishing; fleeting —**ev′a·nes′cence** *n.*

e·van·gel (i van′jəl) *n.* **2.** [< Gr. *eu-*, well + *angelos*,
messenger] **1.** the gospel **2.** [E-] any of the four Gospels
3. an evangelist

e·van·gel·i·cal (ē′van jel′i k'l, ev′ən-) *adj.* **1.** of or ac-
cording to the Gospels or the New Testament **2.** of those
Protestant churches that emphasize salvation by faith
Also **e′van·gel′ic** —**e′van·gel′i·cal·ly** *adv.*

e·van·gel·ism (i van′jə liz′m) *n.* a preaching or spreading
of the gospel, as in revival meetings —**e·van′gel·is′tic** *adj.*

e·van′gel·ist *n.* **1.** [E-] any of the four writers of the
Gospels **2.** anyone who evangelizes; esp., a traveling
preacher; revivalist

e·van′gel·ize *vt.* -ized′, -iz′ing **1.** to preach the gospel
to **2.** to convert to Christianity —*vi.* to preach the gospel

Ev·ans·ville (ev′ənz vil′) city in SW Ind.: pop. 139,000

e·vap·o·rate (i vap′ə rāt′) *vt.* -rat′ed, -rat′ing [< L. *e-*,
out + *vapor*, vapor] **1.** to change (a liquid or solid) into
vapor **2.** to remove moisture from (milk, etc.), as by heating, so as to get a concentrated product —*vi.* **1.** to become
vapor **2.** to give off vapor **3.** to vanish —**e·vap′o·ra′tion**
n. —**e·vap′o·ra′tor** *n.*

evaporated milk canned, unsweetened milk thickened by
evaporation

e·va·sion (i vā′zhən) *n.* **1.** an evading; specif., an avoiding of a duty, question, etc. by deceit or cleverness **2.** a
way of doing this; subterfuge

e·va′sive (-siv) *adj.* **1.** tending or seeking to evade; not
straightforward; tricky **2.** elusive —**e·va′sive·ly** *adv.* —
e·va′sive·ness *n.*

Eve (ēv) *Bible* Adam's wife, the first woman

eve (ēv) *n.* [< OE. *æfen*, evening] **1.** [Poet.] evening **2.**
[*often* E-] the evening or day before a holiday **3.** the
period immediately before some event

e·ven¹ (ē′vən, -v'n) *adj.* [OE. *efne, efen*] **1.** flat; level;
smooth **2.** not varying; constant [an *even* tempo] **3.** calm;
tranquil [an *even* temper] **4.** in the same plane or line
[*even* with the rim] **5.** equally balanced **6.** owing and
being owed nothing **7.** revenged **8.** just; fair [an *even*
trade] **9.** equal in number, quantity, etc. **10.** exactly divisible by two **11.** exact [an *even* mile] —*adv.* **1.** however
improbable; indeed **2.** exactly; just [it happened *even* as I
expected] **3.** still; yet [*even* worse] —*vt., vi.* to make,
become, or be even —**break even** [Colloq.] to finish as neither a winner nor a loser —**even if** though —**e′ven·ly** *adv.*
—**e′ven·ness** *n.*

e·ven² (ē′vən) *n.* [see EVE] [Poet.] evening

e′ven·hand′ed (-han′did) *adj.* impartial; fair

eve·ning (ēv′niŋ) *n.* [< OE. *æfen*] **1.** the last part of day
and early part of night **2.** [Dial.] the period from noon
through sunset **3.** the last period, as of life —*adj.* in, for,
or of the evening

evening primrose a plant having yellow flowers that
open in the evening

evening star a bright planet, esp. Venus, seen in the
western sky soon after sunset

e′ven·song′ (-sôŋ′) *n.* **1.** *R.C.Ch.* vespers (see VESPER,
sense 2) **2.** *Anglican Ch.* the evening worship service

---

fat, āpe, cär; ten, ēven; is, bīte; gō, hôrn, tōōl, look; oil, out; up, fur; thin, *then*; zh, leisure; ŋ, ring; ə for *a* in *ago*;
′ as in *able* (ā′b'l); ë, Fr. coeur; ö, Fr. feu; Fr. mo*n*; ü, Fr. duc; *r*, Fr. cri; kh, G. doch, ich. ‡ foreign; < derived from

e·vent (i vent′) *n.* [< L. *e*-, out + *venire*, come] **1.** an occurrence, esp. when important **2.** a result **3.** a particular contest in a program of sports —**in any event** in any case —**in the event of** in case of

e·vent′ful *adj.* **1.** full of outstanding events **2.** having an important outcome —**e·vent′ful·ly** *adv.* —**e·vent′ful·ness** *n.*

e·ven·tide (ē′vən tīd′) *n.* [Archaic] evening

e·ven·tu·al (i ven′chŏo wəl) *adj.* happening in the end; ultimate —**e·ven′tu·al·ly** *adv.*

e·ven′tu·al′i·ty (-wal′ə tē) *n., pl.* **-ties** a possible event, outcome, or condition

e·ven′tu·ate′ (-wāt′) *vi.* **-at′ed, -at′ing** to happen in the end; result

ev·er (ev′ər) *adv.* [< OE. *æfre*] **1.** always [*ever* the same] **2.** at any time [do you *ever* see her?] **3.** at all; by any chance [how can I *ever* repay you?] **4.** [Colloq.] truly [was she *ever* tired!] —**ever so** [Colloq.] very

Ev·er·est (ev′ər ist, ev′rist), **Mount** peak of the Himalayas between Nepal & Tibet: highest known mountain in the world: 29,028 ft.

ev′er·glade′ (-glād′) *n.* swampland —**the Everglades** large tract of swampland in S Florida

ev′er·green′ (-grēn′) *adj.* having green leaves throughout the year —*n.* an evergreen plant or tree

ev′er·last′ing *adj.* **1.** lasting forever; eternal **2.** going on for a long time **3.** going on too long —*n.* **1.** eternity **2.** any of various plants whose blossoms keep their color and shape when dried —**the Everlasting** God —**ev′er·last′ing·ly** *adv.*

ev′er·more′ *adv.* forever; constantly

e·vert (ē vurt′) *vt.* [< L. *e*-, out + *vertere*, to turn] to turn outward or inside out —**e·ver′sion** *n.*

ev·er·y (ev′rē, -ər ē) *adj.* [< OE. *æfre ælc*] **1.** each, individually and separately **2.** all possible [he was given *every* chance] **3.** each interval of [a pill *every* three hours] —**every now and then** from time to time: also [Colloq.] **every so often** —**every other** each alternate, as the first, third, fifth, etc. —**every which way** [Colloq.] in complete disorder

ev′er·y·bod′y (-bäd′ē, -bud′ē) *pron.* every person; everyone

ev′er·y·day′ (-dā′) *adj.* **1.** daily **2.** suitable for ordinary days [*everyday* shoes] **3.** usual; common

ev′er·y·one (-wən, -wun′) *pron.* everybody

every one every person or thing of those named

ev′er·y·thing *pron.* every thing; all

ev′er·y·where *adv.* in or to every place

e·vict (i vikt′) *vt.* [see EVINCE] to remove (a tenant) from leased premises by legal procedure —**e·vic′tion** *n.*

ev·i·dence (ev′ə dəns) *n.* **1.** the state of being evident **2.** something that makes another thing evident; sign **3.** something that tends to prove **4.** *Law* a statement by a witness, an object, etc. bearing on or establishing the point in question in a court —*vt.* **-denced, -denc·ing** to make evident —**in evidence** plainly visible

ev′i·dent (-dənt, -dent′) *adj.* [< L. *e*-, from + *videre*, see] easy to see or perceive; clear —**ev′i·dent·ly** *adv.*

ev′i·den′tial (-den′shəl) *adj.* of, serving as, or providing evidence

e·vil (ē′v′l) *adj.* [OE. *yfel*] **1.** morally bad or wrong; wicked **2.** harmful; injurious **3.** unlucky; disastrous —*n.* **1.** wickedness; sin **2.** anything causing harm, pain, etc. —**e′vil·ly** *adv.*

e′vil·do′er (-dŏo′ər) *n.* one who does evil, esp. habitually —**e′vil·do′ing** *n.*

evil eye a look which, in superstitious belief, is able to harm the one stared at

e′vil-mind′ed *adj.* having an evil mind; specif., *a)* malicious *b)* lewd —**e′vil-mind′ed·ness** *n.*

e·vince (i vins′) *vt.* **e·vinced′, e·vinc′ing** [< L. *e*-, intens. + *vincere*, conquer] to show plainly (a quality, feeling, etc.) —**e·vin′ci·ble** *adj.*

e·vis·cer·ate (i vis′ə rāt′) *vt.* **-at′ed, -at′ing** [< L. *e*-, out + *viscera*, VISCERA] **1.** to remove the entrails from **2.** to deprive of an essential part —**e·vis′cer·a′tion** *n.*

e·voke (i vōk′) *vt.* **e·voked′, e·vok′ing** [< L. *e*-, out + *vox*, the voice] to call forth; elicit (a response, etc.) —**ev·o·ca·tion** (ev′ə kā′shən) *n.* —**e·voc·a·tive** (i väk′ə tiv) *adj.*

ev·o·lu·tion (ev′ə lōō′shən) *n.* [see EVOLVE] **1.** an unfolding; process of development **2.** a thing evolved **3.** a movement that is part of a series **4.** *Biol. a)* the development of a species, organism, etc. from its original to its present state *b)* a theory that all species of plants and animals developed from earlier forms: see DARWINIAN THEORY **5.** *Mil.* any maneuver by which troops, ships, etc. change formation —**ev′o·lu′tion·ar′y** *adj.*

ev′o·lu′tion·ist *n.* one who accepts the theory of evolution —*adj.* of this theory

e·volve (i välv′) *vt., vi.* **e·volved′, e·volv′ing** [< L. *e*-, out + *volvere*, to roll] **1.** to unfold; develop gradually **2.** to develop by evolution

ewe (yōō) *n.* [OE. *eowu*] a female sheep

ew·er (yōō′ər) *n.* [< L. *aqua*, water] a large, wide-mouthed water pitcher

ex (eks) *prep.* [L.] without [*ex* interest] —*n., pl.* **ex′es** [Colloq.] one's divorced husband or wife

ex- [< OFr. or L.] *a prefix meaning:* **1.** from, out [*expel*] **2.** beyond [*excess*] **3.** thoroughly [*exterminate*] **4.** upward [*exalt*] **5.** former [*ex-president*]

Ex. Exodus

EWER

ex. **1.** example **2.** except(ed)

ex·ac·er·bate (ig zas′ər bāt′) *vt.* **-bat′ed, -bat′ing** [< L. *ex*-, intens. + *acerbus*, harsh] **1.** to aggravate (disease, pain, etc.) **2.** to irritate —**ex·ac′er·ba′tion** *n.*

ex·act (ig zakt′) *adj.* [< L. *ex*-, out + *agere*, to do] **1.** characterized by or requiring accuracy; methodical; correct **2.** without variation; precise —*vt.* **1.** to extort **2.** to demand and get by authority or force **3.** to require —**ex·act′ness** *n.*

ex·act′ing *adj.* **1.** making severe demands; strict **2.** demanding great care, effort, etc.; arduous —**ex·act′ing·ly** *adv.*

ex·ac′tion (-zak′shən) *n.* **1.** an exacting **2.** an extortion **3.** an exacted tax, fee, etc.

ex·ac′ti·tude′ (-tə tōōd′, -tyōōd′) *n.* the quality of being exact; accuracy

ex·act′ly *adv.* in an exact manner; accurately: also used as a reply to mean "I agree," "quite true"

ex·ag·ger·ate (ig zaj′ə rāt′) *vt., vi.* **-at′ed, -at′ing** [< L. *ex*-, out + *agger*, a heap] **1.** to think or tell of (something) as greater than it is; overstate **2.** to enlarge abnormally —**ex·ag′ger·a′tion** *n.* —**ex·ag′ger·a′tor** *n.*

ex·alt (ig zôlt′) *vt.* [< L. *ex*-, out + *altus*, high] **1.** to raise in status, dignity, etc. **2.** to praise; glorify **3.** to fill with joy, pride, etc.; elate —**ex·al·ta·tion** (eg′zôl tā′shən) *n.* —**ex·alt′ed·ly** *adv.*

ex·am (ig zam′) *n.* [Colloq.] examination

ex·am·i·na·tion (ig zam′ə nā′shən) *n.* **1.** an examining or being examined **2.** a set of questions asked in testing; test

ex·am·ine (ig zam′ən) *vt.* **-ined, -in·ing** [< L. *examinare*, weigh] **1.** to look at critically or methodically; investigate; inspect **2.** to test by questioning to find out the knowledge, etc. of —**ex·am′i·nee′** *n.* —**ex·am′in·er** *n.*

ex·am·ple (ig zam′p'l) *n.* [< L. *eximere*, take out] **1.** something selected to show the character of the rest; sample **2.** a case that serves as a warning **3.** a model; pattern **4.** an instance that illustrates a principle —**set an example** to behave so as to be a model for others —**without example** having no precedent

ex·as·per·ate (ig zas′pə rāt′) *vt.* **-at′ed, -at′ing** [< L. *ex*-, out + *asper*, rough] to irritate or annoy very much; vex —**ex·as′per·a′tion** *n.*

ex ca·the·dra (eks′ kə thē′drə, kath′i-) [ModL., lit., from the chair] with the authority of one's rank or office: often used of certain papal pronouncements on faith or morals

ex·ca·vate (eks′kə vāt′) *vt.* **-vat′ed, -vat′ing** [< L. *ex*-, out + *cavus*, hollow] **1.** to make a hole or cavity in **2.** to form (a tunnel, etc.) by hollowing out **3.** to unearth **4.** to dig out (earth, etc.) —**ex′ca·va′tion** *n.* —**ex′ca·va′tor** *n.*

ex·ceed (ik sēd′) *vt.* [< L. *ex*-, out + *cedere*, go] **1.** to go or be beyond (a limit, etc.) **2.** to be more or greater than; surpass

ex·ceed′ing *adj.* surpassing; extraordinary; extreme —**ex·ceed′ing·ly** *adv.*

ex·cel (ik sel′) *vi., vt.* **-celled′, -cel′ling** [< L. *ex*-, out of + *-cellere*, to rise] to be better or greater than (another or others)

ex·cel·lence (ek′s'l əns) *n.* **1.** the fact or state of excelling; superiority **2.** something in which a person or thing excels **3.** [E-] *same as* EXCELLENCY

ex′cel·len·cy (-ən sē) *n., pl.* **-cies** **1.** [E-] a title of honor for certain dignitaries, as an ambassador, bishop, etc. **2.** *same as* EXCELLENCE

ex′cel·lent *adj.* [see EXCEL] outstandingly good of its kind; of exceptional merit —**ex′cel·lent·ly** *adv.*

ex·cel·si·or (ek sel′sē ôr′) *interj.* [see EXCEL] onward and upward! —*n.* (ik sel′sē ər) long, thin wood shavings used for packing

ex·cept (ik sept′) *vt.* [< L. *ex*-, out + *capere*, take] to leave out or take out; exclude —*prep.* other than; but —

conj. [Colloq.] were it not that; only —**except for** if it were not for

ex·cept'ing *prep., conj. same as* EXCEPT

ex·cep'tion *n.* **1.** an excepting **2.** a person or thing different from others of the same class; case to which a rule does not apply **3.** an objection —**take exception** to object

ex·cep'tion·a·ble *adj.* liable to exception; open to objection —**ex·cep'tion·a·bly** *adv.*

ex·cep'tion·al *adj.* **1.** unusual; esp., unusually good **2.** requiring special education, as because mentally handicapped —**ex·cep'tion·al·ly** *adv.*

ex·cerpt (ik surpt', ek'surpt') *vt.* [< L. *ex-*, out + *carpere*, to pick] to select or quote (passages from a book, etc.); extract —*n.* (ek'surpt') a passage selected or quoted; extract

ex·cess (ik ses', ek'ses') *n.* [see EXCEED] **1.** action that goes beyond a reasonable limit **2.** intemperance **3.** an amount greater than is necessary **4.** the amount by which one thing exceeds another; surplus —*adj.* (*usually* ek'ses') extra or surplus —**in excess of** more than —**to excess** too much

ex·ces'sive *adj.* being too much; immoderate —**ex·ces'sive·ly** *adv.* —**ex·ces'sive·ness** *n.*

ex·change (iks chānj') *vt., vi.* -**changed'**, -**chang'ing** [see EX- & CHANGE] **1.** to give or receive (something) *for* another thing; trade; barter **2.** to interchange (similar things) —*n.* **1.** an exchanging; interchange, trade, etc. **2.** a thing exchanged **3.** a place for exchanging [a stock *exchange*] **4.** a central office providing telephone service **5.** the value of one currency in terms of another —**exchange'a·ble** *adj.*

ex·cheq·uer (iks chek'ər, eks'chek-) *n.* [< ML. *scaccarium*, chessboard; accounts of revenue were kept on a squared board] **1.** [*often* E-] the British state department in charge of the national revenue **2.** a treasury **3.** money in one's possession; funds

ex·cise' (ek'sīz) *n.* [ult. < L. *assidere*, assist (in office)] a tax on various commodities, as tobacco, within a country: also **excise tax** —*vt.* (ik sīz') -**cised'**, -**cis'ing** to put an excise on

ex·cise² (ik sīz') *vt.* -**cised'**, -**cis'ing** [< L. *ex-*, out + *caedere*, to cut] to remove (a tumor, etc.) by cutting away —**ex·ci'sion** (-sizh'ən) *n.*

ex·cit·a·ble (ik sīt'ə b'l) *adj.* easily excited —**ex·cit'a·bil'i·ty** *n.* —**ex·cit'a·bly** *adv.*

ex·ci·ta·tion (ek'sī tā'shən) *n.* an exciting or being excited

ex·cite (ik sīt') *vt.* -**cit'ed**, -**cit'ing** [< L. *ex-*, out + *ciere*, to call] **1.** to make active; stimulate **2.** to arouse; provoke **3.** to arouse the feelings of

ex·cit'ed *adj.* emotionally aroused; agitated —**ex·cit'ed·ly** *adv.*

ex·cite'ment *n.* **1.** an exciting or being excited **2.** something that excites

ex·cit'ing *adj.* causing excitement; stirring, thrilling, etc. —**ex·cit'ing·ly** *adv.*

ex·claim (iks klām') *vi., vt.* [< Fr. < L. *ex-*, out + *clamare*, to shout] to cry out; speak or say suddenly and excitedly, as in surprise

ex·cla·ma·tion (eks'klə mā'shən) *n.* **1.** an exclaiming **2.** something exclaimed; interjection —**ex·clam·a·to·ry** (iks klam'ə tôr'ē) *adj.*

exclamation mark (or **point**) a mark (!) used in punctuating to show surprise, strong feeling, etc.

ex·clude (iks klōōd') *vt.* -**clud'ed**, -**clud'ing** [< L. *ex-*, out + *claudere*, to close] **1.** to refuse to admit, consider, etc.; reject **2.** to put out; force out; expel

ex·clu'sion (-klōō'zhən) *n.* **1.** an excluding or being excluded **2.** a thing excluded —**to the exclusion of** so as to keep out, bar, etc.

ex·clu'sive (-siv) *adj.* **1.** excluding all others **2.** not shared or divided; sole [an *exclusive* right] **3.** excluding certain people, as for social reasons —**exclusive of** not including —**ex·clu'sive·ly** *adv.* —**ex·clu'sive·ness**, **ex·clu·siv·i·ty** (eks'klōō siv'ə tē) *n.*

ex·com·mu·ni·cate (eks'kə myōō'nə kāt'; *for adj. and n., usually* -kit) *vt.* -**cat'ed**, -**cat'ing** to exclude from communion with a church —*adj.* excommunicated —*n.* an excommunicated person —**ex'com·mu'ni·ca'tion** *n.*

ex·co·ri·ate (ik skôr'ē āt') *vt.* -**at'ed**, -**at'ing** [< L. *ex-*, off + *corium*, the skin] to denounce harshly —**ex·co'ri·a'tion** *n.*

ex·cre·ment (eks'krə mənt) *n.* waste matter excreted from the bowels —**ex'cre·men'tal** (-men't'l) *adj.*

ex·cres·cence (iks kres''ns) *n.* [< L. *ex-*, out + *crescere*, grow] an abnormal outgrowth, as a bunion —**ex·cres'cent** *adj.*

ex·cres'cen·cy (-'n sē) *n.* **1.** a being excrescent **2.** *pl.* -**cies** *same as* EXCRESCENCE

ex·cre·ta (eks krēt'ə) *n.pl.* waste matter excreted from the body, esp. sweat or urine

ex·crete (iks krēt') *vt., vi.* -**cret'ed**, -**cret'ing** [< L. *ex-*, out of + *cernere*, sift] to eliminate (waste matter) from the body —**ex·cre'tion** *n.* —**ex·cre·to·ry** (eks'krə tôr'ē) *adj.*

ex·cru·ci·at·ing (iks krōō'shē āt'iŋ) *adj.* [< L. *ex-*, intens. + *cruciare*, crucify] **1.** intensely painful; agonizing **2.** intense or extreme [*excruciating* care] —**ex·cru'ci·at'ing·ly** *adv.*

ex·cul·pate (eks'kəl pāt') *vt.* -**pat'ed**, -**pat'ing** [< L. *ex-*, out + *culpa*, fault] to free from blame; prove guiltless —**ex'cul·pa'tion** *n.*

ex·cur·sion (ik skur'zhən) *n.* [< L. *ex-*, out + *currere*, to run] **1.** a short trip, as for pleasure **2.** a round trip at reduced rates **3.** a group taking such a trip **4.** a digression —*adj.* for an excursion —**ex·cur'sion·ist** *n.*

ex·cur'sive (-siv) *adj.* rambling; digressive —**ex·cur'sive·ly** *adv.* —**ex·cur'sive·ness** *n.*

ex·cuse (ik skyōōz') *vt.* -**cused'**, -**cus'ing** [< L. *ex-*, from + *causa*, a charge] **1.** to try to free (a person) of blame **2.** to apologize or give reasons for **3.** to overlook (an offense or fault) **4.** to release from an obligation, etc. **5.** to permit to leave **6.** to justify —*n.* (-skyōōs') **1.** a defense of some action; apology **2.** a release from obligation, etc. **3.** something that excuses **4.** a pretext —**excuse oneself 1.** to apologize **2.** to ask for permission to leave —**ex·cus'a·ble** *adj.* —**ex·cus'a·bly** *adv.*

exec. 1. executive **2.** executor

ex·e·cra·ble (ek'si krə b'l) *adj.* [see EXECRATE] abominable; detestable —**ex'e·cra·bly** *adv.*

ex·e·crate (ek'si krāt') *vt.* -**crat'ed**, -**crat'ing** [< L. *ex-*, out + *sacrare*, consecrate] **1.** to denounce scathingly **2.** to loathe; abhor —**ex'e·cra'tion** *n.*

ex·e·cute (ek'sə kyōōt') *vt.* -**cut'ed**, -**cut'ing** [< L. *ex-*, intens. + *sequi*, follow] **1.** to carry out; do **2.** to administer (laws, etc.) **3.** to put to death in accordance with a legal sentence **4.** to create in accordance with a plan, etc. **5.** to make valid (a deed, will, etc.)

ex'e·cu'tion *n.* **1.** an executing; specif., *a)* a carrying out, doing, etc. *b)* a putting to death in accordance with a legal sentence **2.** the manner of doing or performing something

ex'e·cu'tion·er *n.* one who carries out a court-imposed death penalty

ex·ec·u·tive (ig zek'yə tiv) *adj.* **1.** of or capable of carrying out duties, functions, etc. **2.** empowered to administer (laws, government affairs, etc.) **3.** of managerial personnel or functions —*n.* **1.** the branch of government administering the laws and affairs of a nation **2.** one who administers or manages affairs

Executive Mansion 1. the White House (in Washington, D.C.), official home of the President of the U.S. **2.** the official home of the governor of a State

ex·ec·u·tor (ig zek'yə tər) *n.* a person appointed to carry out the provisions of another's will

ex·e·ge·sis (ek'sə jē'sis) *n., pl.* -**ses** (-sēz) [< Gr. *ex-*, out + *hēgeisthai*, to guide] analysis or interpretation of a word, passage, etc., as in the Bible

ex·em·plar (ig zem'plär, -plər) *n.* [< L. *exemplum*, EXAMPLE] **1.** a model; pattern **2.** a typical specimen

ex·em·pla·ry (-plə rē) *adj.* **1.** serving as a model or example [an *exemplary* life] **2.** serving as a warning [*exemplary* punishment] **3.** serving as a sample

ex·em·pli·fy (ig zem'plə fī') *vt.* -**fied'**, -**fy'ing** [< L. *exemplum*, example + *facere*, to make] to show by example —**ex·em'pli·fi·ca'tion** *n.*

ex·empt (ig zempt') *vt.* [< L. *ex-*, out + *emere*, take] to free from a rule or obligation which applies to others —*adj.* freed from a usual rule, duty, etc. —**ex·emp'tion** *n.*

ex·er·cise (ek'sər sīz') *n.* [< L. *exercere*, to put to work] **1.** active use or operation **2.** performance (of duties, etc.) **3.** activity for developing the body or mind **4.** a series of movements to strengthen some part of the body **5.** a task to be worked out for developing some skill **6.** [*pl.*] a program of speeches, etc. —*vt.* -**cised'**, -**cis'ing 1.** to use; employ **2.** to put into use so as to develop or train **3.** to worry or perplex **4.** to exert (influence, etc.) —*vi.* to do exercises —**ex'er·cis'er** *n.*

ex·ert (ig zurt′) *vt.* [< L. *exserere*, stretch out] **1.** to put into action **2.** to apply (oneself) with great effort
ex·er′tion *n.* **1.** the act or fact of exerting **2.** effort
ex·hale (eks hāl′) *vt., vi.* -haled′, -hal′ing [< Fr. < L. *ex-*, out + *halare*, breathe] **1.** to breathe forth (air) **2.** to give off (vapor, etc.) —**ex·ha·la·tion** (eks′hə lā′shən) *n.*
ex·haust (ig zôst′) *vt.* [< L. *ex-*, out + *haurire*, to draw] **1.** to draw off or let out (air, gas, etc.), as from a container **2.** to use up **3.** to empty completely; drain **4.** to tire out **5.** to deal with thoroughly —*n.* **1.** the discharge of used steam, gas, etc. from an engine **2.** the pipe through which such steam, etc. is released **3.** fumes, etc. given off —**ex·haust′i·ble** *adj.*
ex·haus·tion (ig zôs′chən) *n.* **1.** an exhausting **2.** the state of being exhausted; esp., great fatigue
ex·haus′tive *adj.* leaving nothing out [*exhaustive research*] —**ex·haus′tive·ly** *adv.* —**ex·haus′tive·ness** *n.*
ex·hib·it (ig zib′it) *vt.* [< L. *ex-*, out + *habere*, to hold] **1.** to show; display **2.** to present to public view —*vi.* to put art objects, etc. on public display —*n.* **1.** a display **2.** a thing exhibited **3.** *Law* an object produced as evidence in court —**ex·hib′i·tor, ex·hib′it·er** *n.*
ex·hi·bi·tion (ek′sə bish′ən) *n.* **1.** an exhibiting **2.** that which is exhibited **3.** a public showing
ex′hi·bi′tion·ism *n.* **1.** a tendency to call attention to oneself or to show off **2.** *Psychol.* a tendency to expose parts of the body that are conventionally concealed —**ex′hi·bi′tion·ist** *n.*
ex·hil·a·rate (ig zil′ə rāt′) *vt.* -rat′ed, -rat′ing [< L. *ex-*, intens. + *hilaris*, glad] **1.** to make merry or lively **2.** to stimulate —**ex·hil′a·ra′tion** *n.*
ex·hort (ig zôrt′) *vt., vi.* [< L. *ex-*, out + *hortari*, to urge] to urge earnestly; entreat —**ex·hor·ta·tion** (eg′zôr tā′shən, ek′sər-) *n.*
ex·hume (ig zyōōm′) *vt.* -humed′, -hum′ing [< L. *ex-*, out + *humus*, the ground] to dig out of the earth; disinter —**ex·hu·ma·tion** (eks′hyoo mā′shən) *n.*
ex·i·gen·cy (ek′sə jən sē) *n., pl.* -cies [< L. *ex-*, out + *agere*, to do] **1.** urgency **2.** a situation calling for immediate attention **3.** [*pl.*] pressing needs —**ex′i·gent** *adj.*
ex·ig·u·ous (eg zig′yoo wəs) *adj.* [L. *exiguus*, small] scanty; meager
ex·ile (eg′zīl, ek′sīl) *n.* [< L. *exul*, an exile] **1.** a prolonged living away from one's country, usually enforced **2.** a person in exile —*vt.* -iled, -il·ing to force into exile
ex·ist (ig zist′) *vi.* [< Fr. < L. *ex-*, forth + *sistere*, to set, place] **1.** to have reality or being; be **2.** to occur or be present (*in*) **3.** to continue being; live —**ex·ist′ent** *adj.*
ex·ist′ence *n.* **1.** the state or fact of being **2.** life; living **3.** occurrence **4.** a manner of existing **5.** a thing that exists; being
ex·is·ten·tial (eg′zis ten′shəl) *adj.* **1.** of or based on existence **2.** of or relating to existentialism
ex′is·ten′tial·ism *n.* a philosophical movement stressing individual existence and holding that man is totally free and responsible for his acts —**ex′is·ten′tial·ist** *adj., n.*
ex·it (eg′zit, ek′sit) *n.* [< L. *ex-*, out + *ire*, go] **1.** an actor's departure from the stage **2.** a going out; departure **3.** a way out —*vi.* to leave a place; depart
exo- [< Gr. *exō*] *a prefix meaning* outside, outer, outer part
ex·o·carp (ek′sō kärp′) *n.* [< EXO- & Gr. *karpos*, fruit] the outer layer of a ripened fruit; peel
ex·o·dus (ek′sə dəs) *n.* [< Gr. *ex-*, out + *hodos*, way] a going out or forth —[E-] **1.** the departure of the Israelites from Egypt (with *the*) **2.** the second book of the Pentateuch, which describes this: abbrev. Ex., Exod.
ex of·fi·ci·o (eks′ ə fish′ē ō′) [L., lit., from office] by virtue of one's office, or position
ex·og·e·nous (ek säj′ə nəs) *adj.* [EXO- + -GENOUS] **1.** originating externally **2.** *Biol.* of or relating to external factors that affect an organism
ex·on·er·ate (ig zän′ə rāt′) *vt.* -at′ed, -at′ing [< L. *ex-*, out + *onerare*, to load] to declare or prove blameless —**ex·on′er·a′tion** *n.*
ex·or·bi·tant (ig zôr′bə tənt) *adj.* [< L. *ex-*, out + *orbita*, a track] going beyond what is reasonable, just, etc.; excessive —**ex·or′bi·tance** *n.* —**ex·or′bi·tant·ly** *adv.*
ex·or·cise, ex·or·cize (ek′sôr sīz′) *vt.* -cised′ or -cized′, -cis′ing or -ciz′ing [< Gr. *ex-*, out + *horkos*, oath] **1.** to expel (an evil spirit) by ritual, incantation, etc. **2.** to free from such a spirit
ex′or·cism (-siz′m) *n.* **1.** an exorcising **2.** a formula or ritual used in exorcising —**ex′or·cist** *n.*
ex·or·di·um (ig zôr′dē əm) *n., pl.* -ums, -a (-ə) [< L. *ex-*, from + *ordiri*, begin] **1.** a beginning **2.** the opening part of a speech, treatise, etc.

ex·ot·ic (ig zät′ik) *adj.* [< Gr. *exō*, outside] **1.** foreign **2.** strangely beautiful, enticing, etc. —**ex·ot′i·cal·ly** *adv.* —**ex·ot′i·cism** (-ə siz′m) *n.*
exp. 1. expenses **2.** export **3.** express
ex·pand (ik spand′) *vt., vi.* [< L. *ex-*, out + *pandere*, to spread] **1.** to spread out; unfold **2.** to increase in size; enlarge **3.** to develop (a topic, etc.) in detail
ex·panse (ik spans′) *n.* a large, open area or unbroken surface; wide extent
ex·pan′si·ble *adj.* that can be expanded: also **ex·pand′a·ble**
ex·pan′sion *n.* **1.** an expanding or being expanded; enlargement **2.** an expanded thing or part **3.** the extent or degree of expansion **4.** a development, as of a topic
expansion bolt a bolt with an attachment that expands in use to act as a wedge
ex·pan′sive *adj.* **1.** that can expand **2.** broad; extensive **3.** demonstrative; open and friendly —**ex·pan′sive·ly** *adv.* —**ex·pan′sive·ness** *n.*
ex·pa·ti·ate (ik spā′shē āt′) *vi.* -at′ed, -at′ing [< L. *ex(s)patiari*, wander] to speak or write at length (*on* or *upon*) —**ex·pa′ti·a′tion** *n.*
ex·pa·tri·ate (eks pā′trē āt′; *for adj. & n., usually* -it) *vt.* -at′ed, -at′ing [< L. *ex*, out of + *patria*, fatherland] **1.** to exile **2.** to withdraw (oneself) from one's native land —*adj.* expatriated —*n.* an expatriated person —**ex·pa′tri·a′tion** *n.*
ex·pect (ik spekt′) *vt.* [< L. *ex-*, out + *spectare*, to look] **1.** to look for as likely to occur or appear **2.** to look for as proper or necessary **3.** [Colloq.] to suppose; guess —**be expecting** [Colloq.] to be pregnant
ex·pect′an·cy *n., pl.* -cies **1.** *same as* EXPECTATION **2.** that which is expected, esp. on a statistical basis
ex·pect′ant *adj.* expecting; specif., *a*) having or showing expectation *b*) waiting, as for the birth of a child —**ex·pect′ant·ly** *adv.*
ex·pec·ta·tion (ek′spek tā′shən) *n.* **1.** an expecting **2.** a thing looked forward to **3.** [*also pl.*] a reason for expecting something —**in expectation** in the state of being looked for
ex·pec·to·rant (ik spek′tər ənt) *adj.* stimulating expectoration —*n.* an expectorant medicine
ex·pec·to·rate (ik spek′tə rāt′) *vt., vi.* -rat′ed, -rat′ing [< L. *ex-*, out + *pectus*, breast] **1.** to cough up and spit out (phlegm, mucus, etc.) **2.** to spit —**ex·pec′to·ra′tion** *n.*
ex·pe·di·en·cy (ik spē′dē ən sē) *n., pl.* -cies **1.** a being expedient; suitability for a given purpose **2.** the doing of what is of selfish advantage rather than what is just or right; self-interest **3.** an expedient Also **ex·pe′di·ence**
ex·pe′di·ent (-ənt) *adj.* [see EXPEDITE] **1.** useful for effecting a desired result; convenient **2.** based on or guided by self-interest —*n.* an expedient thing; means to an end —**ex·pe′di·ent·ly** *adv.*
ex·pe·dite (ek′spə dīt′) *vt.* -dit′ed, -dit′ing [< L. *expedire*, lit., to free the feet] **1.** to speed up the progress of; facilitate **2.** to do quickly
ex′pe·dit′er *n.* one employed to expedite urgent or involved projects
ex·pe·di·tion (ek′spə dish′ən) *n.* [see EXPEDITE] **1.** a journey, voyage, etc., as for exploration or battle **2.** those on such a journey **3.** efficient speed —**ex′pe·di′tion·ar′y** *adj.*
ex′pe·di′tious (-dish′əs) *adj.* efficient and speedy; prompt —**ex′pe·di′tious·ly** *adv.*
ex·pel (ik spel′) *vt.* -pelled′, -pel′ling [< L. *ex-*, out + *pellere*, to thrust] **1.** to drive out by force **2.** to dismiss by authority [*expelled* from college] —**ex·pel′la·ble** *adj.* —**ex·pel′ler** *n.*
ex·pend (ik spend′) *vt.* [< L. *ex-*, out + *pendere*, weigh] **1.** to spend **2.** to use up
ex·pend′a·ble *adj.* **1.** that can be expended **2.** *Mil.* designating equipment (or men) expected to be used up (or sacrificed) in service —**ex·pend·a·bil′i·ty** *n.*
ex·pend·i·ture (ik spen′də chər) *n.* **1.** an expending of money, time, etc. **2.** the amount expended
ex·pense (ik spens′) *n.* [see EXPEND] **1.** financial cost; fee **2.** any cost or sacrifice **3.** [*pl.*] charges met with in one's work **4.** a cause of spending
ex·pen′sive *adj.* costly; high-priced —**ex·pen′sive·ly** *adv.* —**ex·pen′sive·ness** *n.*
ex·pe·ri·ence (ik spir′ē əns) *n.* [< L. *experiri*, to try] **1.** the act of living through an event **2.** anything or everything observed or lived through **3.** *a*) training and personal participation *b*) knowledge, skill, etc. resulting from this —*vt.* -enced, -enc·ing to have experience of; undergo
ex·pe′ri·enced *adj.* **1.** having had much experience **2.** having learned from experience

ex·pe′ri·en′tial (-en′shəl) *adj.* of or based on experience —**ex·pe′ri·en′tial·ly** *adv.*

ex·per·i·ment (ik sper′ə mənt) *n.* [see EXPERIENCE] a test or trial undertaken to discover or demonstrate something —*vi.* (*also* -ment′) to make an experiment —**ex·per′·i·men·ta′tion** (-mən tā′shən) *n.* —**ex·per′i·ment′er** *n.*

ex·per′i·men′tal *adj.* 1. based on, tested by, or having the nature of, experiment 2. used for experiments —**ex·per′i·men′tal·ly** *adv.*

ex·pert (ek′spərt, ik spurt′) *adj.* [see EXPERIENCE] 1. very skillful 2. of or from an expert —*n.* (ek′spərt) one who is very skillful or well-informed in some special field —**ex′·pert·ly** *adv.* —**ex′pert·ness** *n.*

ex·pert·ise (ek′spər tēz′) *n.* [Fr.] the skill, knowledge, judgment, etc. of an expert

ex·pi·ate (ek′spē āt′) *vt.* -at′ed, -at′ing [< L. *ex*-, out + *piare*, appease] to make amends for (wrongdoing or guilt); atone for —**ex′pi·a′tion** *n.* —**ex′pi·a′tor** *n.*

ex′pi·a·to′ry (-ə tôr′ē) *adj.* that expiates or is meant to expiate

ex·pire (ik spīr′) *vt.* -pired′, -pir′ing [< L. *ex*-, out + *spirare*, breathe] to breathe out (air from the lungs) —*vi.* 1. to breathe out; exhale 2. to die 3. to come to an end —**ex·pi·ra·tion** (ek′spə rā′shən) *n.*

ex·plain (ik splān′) *vt.* [< L. *ex*-, out + *planus*, level] 1. to make plain or understandable 2. to give the meaning of; expound 3. to account for —*vi.* to give an explanation —**ex·plain′a·ble** *adj.*

ex·pla·na·tion (eks′plə nā′shən) *n.* 1. an explaining 2. something that explains 3. the interpretation, meaning, etc. given in explaining

ex·plan·a·to·ry (ik splan′ə tôr′ē) *adj.* explaining or intended to explain

ex·ple·tive (eks′plə tiv) *n.* [< L. *ex*-, out + *plere*, to fill] 1. an oath or exclamation 2. a word, phrase, etc. used merely to fill out a sentence or metrical line

ex·pli·ca·ble (eks′pli kə b′l, iks plik′ə-) *adj.* [see EXPLICATE] that can be explained

ex·pli·cate (eks′pli kāt′) *vt.* -cat′ed, -cat′ing [< L. *ex*-, out + *plicare*, to fold] to make clear or explicit (something obscure or implied); explain fully —**ex′pli·ca′·tion** *n.* —**ex′pli·ca′tor** *n.*

ex·plic·it (ik splis′it) *adj.* [see prec.] 1. clearly stated; definite 2. outspoken 3. plain to see —**ex·plic′it·ly** *adv.* —**ex·plic′it·ness** *n.*

ex·plode (ik splōd′) *vt.* -plod′ed, -plod′ing [orig., to drive off the stage < L. *ex*-, off + *plaudere*, applaud] 1. to expose as false 2. to make burst with a loud noise 3. to cause a rapid, violent change in, as by chemical reaction —*vi.* 1. to burst noisily 2. to break forth noisily [to *explode* with anger] 3. to increase very rapidly

ex·ploit (eks′ploit) *n.* [see EXPLICATE] a daring act; bold deed —*vt.* (*usually* ik sploit′) 1. to make use of; utilize 2. to make unethical use of for one's own profit —**ex′ploi·ta′tion** *n.* —**ex·ploit′a·tive** *adj.* —**ex·ploit′er** *n.*

ex·plore (ik splôr′) *vt., vi.* -plored′, -plor′ing [< L. *ex*-, out + *plorare*, to cry out] 1. to examine (something) carefully; investigate 2. to travel in (a little-known region) for discovery —**ex·plo·ra·tion** (eks′plə rā′shən) *n.* —**ex·plor′a·to′ry** (-ə tôr′ē) *adj.* —**ex·plor′er** *n.*

ex·plo·sion (ik splō′zhən) *n.* 1. an exploding; esp., a blowing up 2. the noise made by exploding 3. a noisy outburst 4. a sudden, widespread increase

ex·plo′sive (-siv) *adj.* 1. of, causing, or like an explosion 2. tending to explode —*n.* a substance that can explode, as gunpowder —**ex·plo′sive·ly** *adv.* —**ex·plo′sive·ness** *n.*

ex·po·nent (ik spō′nənt) *n.* [see EXPOUND] 1. one who expounds or promotes (principles, etc.) 2. a person or thing that is an example or symbol (*of* something) 3. (*usually* ek′spō′nənt) *Algebra* a symbol placed at the upper right of another symbol to show how many times the latter is to be used as a factor (Ex.: b² = b x b) —**ex·po·nen·tial** (eks′pō nen′shəl) *adj.*

ex·port (ik spôrt′, eks′pôrt) *vt.* [< L. *ex*-, out + *portare*, carry] to send (goods, etc.) to another country, esp. for sale —*n.* (eks′pôrt) 1. something exported 2. an exporting Also **ex′por·ta′tion** —*adj.* (eks′pôrt) of or for exporting or exports —**ex·port′a·ble** *adj.* —**ex·port′er** *n.*

ex·pose (ik spōz′) *vt.* -posed′, -pos′ing [see EXPOUND] 1. to lay open (*to* danger, attack, etc.) 2. to reveal; exhibit; make known 3. *Photog.* to subject (a sensitized film or plate) to actinic rays

ex·po·sé (eks′pō zā′) *n.* [Fr.] a public disclosure of a scandal, crime, etc.

ex·po·si·tion (eks′pə zish′ən) *n.* [see EXPOUND] 1. a detailed explanation 2. writing or speaking that explains 3. a large public exhibition

ex·pos′i·tor (ik späz′ə tər) *n.* one who expounds or explains

ex·pos′i·to′ry (-tôr′ē) *adj.* of or containing exposition; explanatory

ex post fac·to (eks pōst fak′tō) [L., from (the thing) done afterward] done or made afterward, esp. when having retroactive effect

ex·pos·tu·late (ik späs′chə lāt′) *vi.* -lat′ed, -lat′ing [< L. *ex*-, intens. + *postulare*, to demand] to reason with a person earnestly, objecting to his actions or intentions —**ex·pos′tu·la′tion** *n.* —**ex·pos′tu·la′tor** *n.*

ex·po·sure (ik spō′zhər) *n.* 1. an exposing or being exposed 2. facing position of a house, etc. /an eastern *exposure*/ 3. frequent appearance before the public 4. the time during which photographic film is exposed 5. a section of film for one picture

ex·pound (ik spound′) *vt.* [< L. *ex*-, out + *ponere*, put] 1. to set forth; state in detail 2. to explain

ex·press (ik spres′) *vt.* [< L. *ex*-, out + *premere*, to press] 1. to squeeze out (juice, etc.) 2. to put into words; state 3. to reveal; show 4. to signify or symbolize 5. to send by express —*adj.* 1. expressed; stated; explicit 2. specific 3. exact 4. fast and direct [an *express* bus, highway, etc.] 5. related to express (*n.* 2) —*adv.* by express —*n.* 1. an express train, bus, etc. 2. a service for transporting goods rapidly 3. the things sent by express —**express oneself** 1. to state one's thoughts 2. to give expression to one's feelings, talents, etc. —**ex·press′er** *n.* —**ex·press′i·ble** *adj.*

ex·pres·sion (-spresh′ən) *n.* 1. a putting into words; stating 2. a manner of expressing, esp. with eloquence 3. a particular word or phrase 4. a showing of feeling, character, etc. 5. a look, intonation, etc. that conveys meaning 6. a mathematical symbol or set of symbols —**ex·pres′sion·less** *adj.*

ex·pres′sion·ism *n.* an early 20th-cent. movement in art, drama, etc., using symbols, stylization, etc. to express inner experience —**ex·pres′sion·ist** *adj., n.* —**ex·pres′sion·is′tic** *adj.*

ex·pres′sive *adj.* 1. that expresses; indicative (*of*) 2. full of meaning or feeling —**ex·pres′sive·ly** *adv.* —**ex·pres′sive·ness** *n.*

ex·press′ly *adv.* 1. plainly; definitely 2. especially; particularly

ex·press′way *n.* a divided highway for high-speed, through traffic, generally with overpasses or underpasses at intersections

ex·pro·pri·ate (eks prō′prē āt′) *vt.* -at′ed, -at′ing [< L. *ex*-, out + *proprius*, one's own] to take (land, property, etc.) from its owner, esp. for public use —**ex·pro′pri·a′tion** *n.* —**ex·pro′pri·a′tor** *n.*

ex·pul·sion (ik spul′shən) *n.* an expelling or being expelled —**ex·pul′sive** (-siv) *adj.*

ex·punge (ik spunj′) *vt.* -punged′, -pung′ing [< L. *ex*-, out + *pungere*, to prick] to erase or remove completely; delete

ex·pur·gate (eks′pər gāt′) *vt.* -gat′ed, -gat′ing [< L. *ex*-, out + *purgare*, cleanse] to remove passages considered obscene, etc. from (a book, etc.) —**ex′pur·ga′tion** *n.*

ex·qui·site (eks′kwi zit, ik skwiz′it) *adj.* [< L. *ex*-, out + *quaerere*, ask] 1. carefully or elaborately done 2. very beautiful, esp. in a delicate way 3. of highest quality 4. very intense; keen [exquisite pain] —**ex′qui·site·ly** *adv.* —**ex′qui·site·ness** *n.*

ext. 1. extension 2. external 3. extract

ex·tant (ek′stənt, ik stant′) *adj.* [< L. *ex*-, out + *stare*, to stand] still existing

ex·tem·po·ra·ne·ous (ik stem′pə rā′nē əs) *adj.* [see EXTEMPORE] 1. done or spoken with little preparation; offhand 2. speaking without preparation 3. makeshift —**ex·tem′po·ra′ne·ous·ly** *adv.*

ex·tem·po·re (ik stem′pə rē) *adv., adj.* [L. < *ex*, out of + *tempus*, time] with little preparation; offhand

ex·tem′po·rize′ (-rīz′) *vi., vt.* -rized′, -riz′ing to speak, perform, etc. extempore; improvise —**ex·tem′po·ri·za′tion** *n.* —**ex·tem′po·riz′er** *n.*

ex·tend (ik stend′) *vt.* [< L. *ex*-, out + *tendere*, to stretch] 1. to make longer; stretch out; prolong 2. to enlarge in area, scope, etc.; expand 3. to stretch forth 4. to offer; grant 5. to make (oneself) work or try hard —*vi.* 1. to be extended 2. to reach or stretch —**ex·tend′ed** *adj.* —**ex·tend′er** *n.*

---

fat, āpe, cär; ten, ēven; is, bīte; gō, hôrn, tōol, look; oil, out; up, fur; thin, *th*en; zh, leisure; ŋ, ring; ə for *a* in *ago*; ′ as in *able* (ā′b'l); ë, Fr. coeur; ö, Fr. feu; Fr. mo*n*; ü, Fr. duc; r, Fr. cri; kh, G. doch, ich. ‡ foreign; < derived from

ex·ten'si·ble (-sten'sə b'l) *adj.* that can be extended: also **ex·tend'i·ble**

ex·ten'sion (-sten'shən) *n.* **1.** an extending or being extended **2.** range; extent **3.** a part forming a continuation or addition **4.** a branch of a university away from the university proper **5.** an extra telephone on the same line as the main telephone **6.** *Physics* that property of a body by which it occupies space —**ex·ten'sion·al** *adj.*

ex·ten'sive (-siv) *adj.* having great extent; vast; comprehensive; far-reaching —**ex·ten'sive·ly** *adv.* —**ex·ten'sive·ness** *n.*

ex·ten'sor (-sər) *n.* a muscle that extends or straightens a limb or some other part of the body

ex·tent (ik stent') *n.* **1.** the space, amount, or degree to which a thing extends; size **2.** scope; limits **3.** an extended space; vast area

ex·ten·u·ate (ik sten'yoo wāt') *vt.* -at'ed, -at'ing [< L. *ex-*, out + *tenuis*, thin] to make (an offense, guilt, etc.) seem less serious by giving excuses or serving as an excuse —**ex·ten'u·a'tion** *n.*

ex·te·ri·or (ik stir'ē ər) *adj.* [see EXTERNAL] **1.** on the outside; outer **2.** for use on the outside **3.** coming from without *[exterior* forces] —*n.* **1.** an outside or outside surface **2.** an outward appearance

exterior angle any of the four angles formed on the outside of two straight lines by a straight line cutting across them

ex·ter·mi·nate (ik stur'mə nāt') *vt.* -nat'ed, -nat'ing [< L. *ex-*, out + *terminus*, boundary] to destroy entirely, as by killing; wipe out — **ex·ter'mi·na'tion** *n.*

ex·ter'mi·na'tor *n.* one that exterminates; esp., a person whose work is exterminating rats, insects, etc.

ex·ter·nal (ik stur'n'l) *adj.* [< L. *externus*] **1.** on the outside; outer **2.** on, or for use on, the outside of the body **3.** existing apart from the mind; material **4.** coming from without **5.** superficial **6.** foreign —*n.* an outside surface or part —**ex·ter'nal·ly** *adv.*

EXTERIOR ANGLES (CEL, LER, ADT, TDF)

ex·tinct (ik stiŋkt') *adj.* [see EXTINGUISH] **1.** having died down or burned out **2.** no longer active **3.** no longer in existence

ex·tinc'tion *n.* **1.** an extinguishing **2.** a destroying or being destroyed **3.** a dying out, as of a species of animal

ex·tin·guish (ik stiŋ'gwish) *vt.* [< L. *ex-*, out + *stinguere*, to extinguish] **1.** to put out (a fire, etc.) **2.** to destroy —**ex·tin'guish·er** *n.* —**ex·tin'guish·ment** *n.*

ex·tir·pate (ek'stər pāt') *vt.* -pat'ed, -pat'ing [< L. *ex-*, out + *stirps*, root] **1.** to pull up by the roots **2.** to destroy completely —**ex'tir·pa'tion** *n.*

ex·tol, ex·toll (ik stōl') *vt.* -tolled', -tol'ling [< L. *ex-*, up + *tollere*, raise] to praise highly; laud

ex·tort (ik stôrt') *vt.* [< L. *ex-*, out + *torquere*, to twist] to get (money, etc.) *from* someone by force or threats — **ex·tort'er** *n.*

ex·tor'tion (-stôr'shən) *n.* **1.** an extorting **2.** something extorted —**ex·tor'tion·ate** *adj.* —**ex·tor'tion·er, ex·tor'tion·ist** *n.*

ex·tra (eks'trə) *adj.* [< L. *extra*, more than] more or better than normal, expected, necessary, etc.; additional —*n.* an extra person or thing; specif., *a)* formerly, a special newspaper edition for important news *b)* an extra benefit *c)* an actor hired by the day for a minor part —*adv.* more than usually *[extra* hot]

extra- [see EXTERNAL] *a prefix meaning* outside, beyond, besides

ex·tract (ik strakt') *vt.* [< L. *ex-*, out + *trahere*, draw] **1.** to draw out by effort *[to extract* teeth, to *extract* a promise] **2.** to obtain by pressing, distilling, etc. **3.** to deduce; derive **4.** to copy out or quote (a passage from a book, etc.) —*n.* (eks'trakt) something extracted; specif., *a)* a concentrate *[vanilla extract] b)* an excerpt; quotation — **ex·trac'tor** *n.*

ex·trac'tion *n.* **1.** an extracting; specif., the extracting of a tooth **2.** origin; descent

ex·tra·cur·ric·u·lar (eks'trə kə rik'yə lər) *adj.* not part of the required curriculum

ex·tra·dite (eks'trə dīt') *vt.* -dit'ed, -dit'ing [< L. *ex*, out + *traditio*, a surrender] to turn over (an alleged criminal, a fugitive, etc.) to the jurisdiction of another country, State, etc. —**ex'tra·di'tion** (-dish'ən) *n.*

ex·tra·ne·ous (ik strā'nē əs) *adj.* [< L. *extraneus*, foreign] **1.** coming from outside; foreign **2.** not essential **3.** not pertinent; irrelevant —**ex·tra'ne·ous·ly** *adv.* —**ex·tra'ne·ous·ness** *n.*

ex·traor·di·nar·y (ik strôr'd'n er'ē) *adj.* [< L. *extra ordinem*, out of the usual order] **1.** not usual or ordinary **2.** very unusual; exceptional; remarkable —**ex·traor'di·nar'·i·ly** *adv.*

ex·trap·o·late (ik strap'ə lāt') *vt., vi.* -lat'ed, -lat'ing [see EXTRA- & INTERPOLATE] to estimate (something unknown) on the basis of known facts —**ex·trap'o·la'tion** *n.*

ex·tra·sen·so·ry (eks'trə sen'sər ē) *adj.* apart from, or in addition to, normal sense perception

ex'tra·ter'ri·to'ri·al *adj.* outside the territorial limits or jurisdiction of the country, State, etc. —**ex'tra·ter'ri·to'ri·al'i·ty** (-al'ə tē) *n.*

ex·trav·a·gance (ik strav'ə gəns) *n.* **1.** a going beyond reasonable or proper limits; excess **2.** unnecessary spending; wastefulness **3.** an instance of excess in spending, behavior, or speech

ex·trav·a·gant (ik strav'ə gənt) *adj.* [< L. *extra*, beyond + *vagari*, wander] **1.** going beyond reasonable limits; excessive **2.** costing or spending too much; wasteful —**ex·trav'a·gant·ly** *adv.*

ex·trav·a·gan·za (ik strav'ə gan'zə) *n.* [< It. *estravaganza*, extravagance] a spectacular, elaborate theatrical production

ex·treme (ik strēm') *adj.* [< L. *exterus*, outer] **1.** farthest away; utmost **2.** very great; excessive **3.** unconventional or radical, as in politics **4.** very severe; drastic —*n.* **1.** either of two things that are as different or as far as possible from each other **2.** an extreme act, degree, state, etc. —**go to extremes** to be immoderate in speech or action —**in the extreme** to the utmost degree —**ex·treme'ly** *adv.* —**ex·treme'ness** *n.*

extreme unction *same as* ANOINTING OF THE SICK

ex·trem'ism (-iz'm) *n.* a being extreme, esp. in politics —**ex·trem'ist** *n.*

ex·trem·i·ty (ik strem'ə tē) *n., pl.* -ties **1.** the outermost part; end **2.** the greatest degree **3.** a state of extreme need, danger, etc. **4.** an extreme measure **5.** [*pl.*] the hands and feet

ex·tri·cate (eks'trə kāt') *vt.* -cat'ed, -cat'ing [< L. *ex-*, out + *tricae*, vexations] to set free; disentangle (*from* a net, difficulty, etc.) —**ex'tri·ca·ble** *adj.* —**ex'tri·ca'tion** *n.*

ex·trin·sic (ek strin'sik) *adj.* [< L. *exter*, without + *secus*, following] **1.** not essential; not inherent **2.** extraneous; external —**ex·trin'si·cal·ly** *adv.*

ex·tro·vert (eks'trə vurt') *n.* [< L. *extra-*, outside + *vertere*, to turn] one who directs his interest to things outside himself rather than to his own feelings; an active, expressive person —**ex'tro·ver'sion** (-vur'zhən) *n.* —**ex'tro·vert'ed** *adj.*

ex·trude (ik strood') *vt.* -trud'ed, -trud'ing [< L. *ex-*, out + *trudere*, to thrust] to push or force out, as through a small opening —*vi.* to be extruded; esp., to protrude —**ex·tru'sion** (-stroo'zhən) *n.*

ex·u·ber·ance (ig zoo'bər əns, -zyoo'-) *n.* [< Fr. < L. *ex-*, intens. + *uberare*, bear abundantly] **1.** the state or quality of being exuberant **2.** an instance of this; esp., action or speech showing high spirits Also **ex·u'ber·an·cy,** *pl.* -cies

ex·u'ber·ant *adj.* **1.** growing profusely; luxuriant **2.** full of life, vitality, or high spirits —**ex·u'ber·ant·ly** *adv.*

ex·ude (ig zood', -zyood') *vt., vi.* -ud'ed, -ud'ing [< L. *ex-*, out + *sudare*, to sweat] **1.** to pass out in drops, as through pores; ooze **2.** to seem to radiate *[to exude* joy] —**ex·u·da·tion** (eks'yə dā'shən) *n.*

ex·ult (ig zult') *vi.* [< Fr. < L. *ex-*, intens. + *saltare*, to leap] to rejoice greatly; be jubilant; glory —**ex·ul·ta·tion** (eg'zəl tā'shən, ek'səl-) *n.*

ex·ult'ant *adj.* exulting; triumphant; jubilant —**ex·ult'ant·ly** *adv.*

ex·ur·bi·a (eks ur'bē ə) *n.* [EX- + (SUB)URBIA] the semirural communities beyond the suburbs, lived in by upper-income families —**ex·ur'ban** *adj.* —**ex·ur'ban·ite'** *n., adj.*

eye (ī) *n.* [OE. *eage*] **1.** the organ of sight in man and animals **2.** *a)* the eyeball *b)* the iris *[blue eyes]* **3.** the area around the eye *[a black eye]* **4.** [*often pl.*] sight; vision **5.** a look; glance **6.** attention; observation **7.** the power of judging, etc. by eyesight *[an eye* for distances] **8.** [*often pl.*] judgment; opinion *[in the eyes* of the law] **9.** a thing like an eye in shape or function **10.** [Slang] a detective: esp. in **private eye 11.** *Meteorol.* the calm center (of a hurricane) —*vt.* **eyed, eye'ing** or **ey'ing** to look at; observe —**catch one's eye** to attract one's attention —**feast one's eyes on** to look at with pleasure —**have an eye for** to have a keen appreciation of —**keep an eye on** to look after —**keep an eye out for** to be watchful for —**lay (or set**

or clap) **eyes on** to see; look at —**make eyes at** to look at flirtatiously —**see eye to eye** to agree completely —**with an eye to** paying attention to; considering

eye′ball′ *n.* the ball-shaped part of the eye, enclosed by the socket and eyelids

eye′brow′ *n.* the bony arch over each eye, or the hair growing on this

eye′-catch′er *n.* something that especially attracts one's attention —**eye′-catch′ing** *adj.*

eye′ful′ (-fool′) *n.* **1.** a full look at something **2.** [Slang] a person or thing that looks striking

eye′glass′ *n.* **1.** a lens to help faulty vision **2.** [*pl.*] a pair of such lenses in a frame; glasses

eye′lash′ *n.* any of the hairs on the edge of the eyelid

eye′less (-lis) *adj.* without eyes; blind

eye′let (-lit) *n.* **1.** a small hole for receiving a cord, hook, etc. **2.** a metal ring, etc. for lining such a hole **3.** a small hole edged by stitching in embroidered work

eye′lid′ *n.* either of the two folds of flesh that cover and uncover the eyeball

eye liner a cosmetic applied in a thin line to the eyelid at the base of the eyelashes

eye′-o′pen·er (-ō′p'n ər) *n.* a surprising piece of news, sudden realization, etc.

eye′piece′ *n.* in a telescope, microscope, etc., the lens or lenses nearest the viewer's eye

eye shadow a cosmetic, usually green or blue, applied to the upper eyelids

eye′sight′ *n.* **1.** the power of seeing; sight **2.** the range of vision

eye′sore′ *n.* a thing that is unpleasant to look at

eye′strain′ *n.* a tired or strained condition of the eye muscles, caused by too much use or an incorrect use of the eyes

eye′tooth′ *n., pl.* **-teeth′** a canine tooth of the upper jaw

eye′wit′ness *n.* one who has himself seen a specific thing happen

ey·rie, ey·ry (er′ē, ir′ē) *n., pl.* **-ries** *same as* AERIE

E·zek·i·el (i zē′kē əl) *Bible* **1.** a Hebrew prophet of the 6th cent. B.C. **2.** the book containing his writings: abbrev. **Ezek.**

Ez·ra (ez′rə) *Bible* **1.** a prophet and religious reformer of the 5th cent. B.C. **2.** the book telling of his life and teachings: abbrev. **Ez.**

F

F, f (ef) *n., pl.* **F's, f's** the sixth letter of the English alphabet

F (ef) *n.* **1.** a grade indicating failing work or, sometimes, fair or average work **2.** *Chem.* fluorine **3.** *Music* the fourth tone in the scale of C major

F, F. 1. Fahrenheit **2.** Friday

F., f. 1. feminine **2.** folio(s) **3.** following **4.** *Music* forte **5.** franc(s)

fa (fä) *n.* [< ML.] *Music* a syllable representing the fourth tone of the diatonic scale

fa·ble (fā′b'l) *n.* [< L. *fabula*, a story] **1.** a fictitious story, usually about animals, meant to teach a moral lesson **2.** a myth or legend **3.** a falsehood

fa′bled *adj.* **1.** told of in fables; legendary **2.** unreal

fab·ric (fab′rik) *n.* [< L. *fabrica*, workshop] **1.** a framework or structure **2.** a material made from fibers or threads by weaving, felting, etc.

fab·ri·cate (fab′rə kāt′) *vt.* **-cat′ed, -cat′ing** [see prec.] **1.** to make, construct, etc.; manufacture **2.** to make up (a story, reason, etc.); invent —**fab′ri·ca′tion** *n.* —**fab′ri·ca′tor** *n.*

fab·u·lous (fab′yoo ləs) *adj.* [see FABLE] **1.** of or like a fable; imaginary, fictitious, etc. **2.** incredible **3.** [Colloq.] wonderful —**fab′u·lous·ly** *adv.*

fa·çade, fa·cade (fə säd′) *n.* [Fr. < It.: see FACE] **1.** the front of a building **2.** an imposing appearance concealing something inferior

face (fās) *n.* [< L. *facies*] **1.** the front of the head **2.** the expression of the countenance **3.** the main or front surface **4.** any of the surfaces of a crystal **5.** the surface that is marked, as of a clock or playing card **6.** appearance; outward aspect **7.** dignity; self-respect: usually in **lose** (or **save**) **face 8.** the functional or striking surface (of a tool, etc.) —*vt.* **faced, fac′ing 1.** to turn, or have the face turned, toward **2.** to confront with courage, etc. **3.** to cover with a new surface —*vi.* to turn, or have the face turned, in a specified direction —**face to face 1.** confronting each other **2.** in the presence (with *with*) —**face up to** to confront with courage —**in the face of 1.** in the presence of **2.** in spite of —**make a face** to grimace —**on the face of it** apparently

face card any king, queen, or jack in a deck of cards

face′less (-lis) *adj.* **1.** lacking a face **2.** lacking a distinct character; anonymous

face lifting 1. plastic surgery for removing wrinkles, etc. from the face **2.** an altering, repairing, etc., as of a building's exterior Also **face lift**

face′-off′ *n. Hockey* the start or resumption of play when the referee drops the puck between two opposing players

face powder a cosmetic applied to the face

face′-sav′ing *adj.* preserving or meant to preserve one's dignity or self-respect

fac·et (fas′it) *n.* [see FACE] **1.** any of the polished plane surfaces of a cut gem **2.** any of the sides or aspects, as of a personality —*vt.* **-et·ed** or **-et·ted, -et·ing** or **-et·ting** to cut or make facets on

fa·ce·tious (fə sē′shəs) *adj.* [< Fr. < L. *facetus*, witty] straining to be funny, esp. at the wrong time —**fa·ce′tious·ly** *adv.* —**fa·ce′tious·ness** *n.*

face value 1. the value shown as on a bill or bond **2.** the seeming value [took his words at *face value*]

fa·cial (fā′shəl) *adj.* of or for the face —*n.* a cosmetic treatment for the skin of the face

facial tissue a soft paper tissue designed esp. for wiping the face, blowing the nose, etc.

fac·ile (fas′'l) *adj.* [Fr. < L. *facere*, do] **1.** easily done, achieved, etc. **2.** effortless; quick [a *facile* wit] **3.** glib **4.** too superficial

fa·cil·i·tate (fə sil′ə tāt′) *vt.* **-tat′ed, -tat′ing** [see prec.] to make easy or easier

fa·cil′i·ty *n., pl.* **-ties 1.** absence of difficulty **2.** ready ability; skill **3.** [*usually pl.*] the means to do something **4.** a room, etc. for an activity

fac·ing (fās′iŋ) *n.* **1.** a lining along a garment edge **2.** exterior covering as on a wall surface

fac·sim·i·le (fak sim′ə lē) *n.* [< L. *facere*, make + *simile*, like] (an) exact reproduction or copy

fact (fakt) *n.* [< L. *facere*, do] **1.** a deed; act **2.** an actual or true thing **3.** reality; truth **4.** something taken to be true, real, etc. —**as a matter of fact** really: also **in fact**

fac·tion (fak′shən) *n.* [< L. *facere*, do] **1.** a group that is part of a larger group but that opposes the views of it or of other member groups **2.** the resultant dissension —**fac′tion·al** *adj.* —**fac′tion·al·ism** *n.* —**fac′tion·al·ist** *n., adj.*

fac′tious (-shəs) *adj.* of, characterized by, or producing faction —**fac′tious·ly** *adv.*

fac·ti·tious (fak tish′əs) *adj.* [< L. *facere*, do] forced or artificial —**fac·ti′tious·ly** *adv.*

fac·tor (fak′tər) *n.* [< L. *facere*, do] **1.** one transacting business for another **2.** anything contributing to a result **3.** *Math.* any of the quantities forming a product when multiplied together —*vt. Math.* to resolve into factors

fac·to·ry (fak′tə rē) *n., pl.* **-ries** [< Fr.: see prec.] one or more buildings where manufacturing is done

fac·to·tum (fak tōt′əm) *n.* [< L. *facere*, do + *totum*, all] one hired to do all sorts of work

fac·tu·al (fak′choo wəl) *adj.* of fact or facts; real, actual, true, etc. —**fac′tu·al·ly** *adv.*

fac·ul·ty (fak′'l tē) *n., pl.* **-ties** [< L. *facere*, do] **1.** any natural or specialized power of a living organism **2.** a special aptitude 3. the teaching staff of a school 4. an authorization

fad (fad) *n.* [< Brit. dial.] an activity, fashion, etc. of widespread but brief popularity —**fad'dish** *adj.*

fade (fād) *vi.* **fad'ed, fad'ing** [< OFr. *fade,* pale] 1. to lose color, intensity, power, etc. 2. to wane, wither away, or die out —*vt.* to make fade —**fade in** (or **out**) *Motion Pictures, Radio & TV* to grow or make grow more (or less) distinct, as a scene

fade'-in' *n. Motion Pictures,* etc. a fading in

fade'-out' *n. Motion Pictures,* etc. a fading out

faer·ie, faer·y (fer'ē) *n.* [Archaic] 1. fairyland 2. *pl.* -**ies** a fairy

fag (fag) *vt., vi.* **fagged, fag'ging** [< ?] to make or become very tired by hard work —*n.* [Slang] a male homosexual: also **fag'got**

fag end [< ME. *fagge,* broken thread] 1. the frayed end of a cloth or rope 2. any last, worst part

fag·ot, fag·got (fag'ət) *n.* [ult. < Gr. *phakelos,* a bundle] a bundle of twigs, esp. for a fire

fag·ot·ing, fag·got·ing (fag'ət iŋ) *n.* a decorative pattern of stitches, as across a seam

FAGOTING
(A, bar; B, crisscross)

Fahr·en·heit (fer'ən hīt', fär'-) *adj.* [< G. D. *Fahrenheit,* 18th-c. G. physicist] designating or of a thermometer on which 32° is the freezing point and 212° is the boiling point of water: abbrev. F, Fah., Fahr.

fail (fāl) *vi.* [< L. *fallere,* deceive] 1. to be or become insufficient or lacking 2. to weaken; die away 3. to stop functioning 4. to be deficient in meeting an obligation, expectation, etc.; default 5. to be unsuccessful in gaining or achieving something 6. to become bankrupt 7. *Educ.* to get a less than passing grade —*vt.* 1. to be useless to or less than adequate for 2. to give no support or less than adequate support to 3. to be wholly or partly deficient in (an expected or desired action, function, etc.) *[the motor failed to start]* 4. *Educ. a)* to give a less than passing grade to *b)* to get a less than passing grade in —**without fail** without any possibility of the contrary; for sure; for certain

fail'ing *n.* 1. a failure 2. a weakness, defect, or fault —*prep.* without; lacking

faille (fīl, fāl) *n.* [Fr.] a ribbed, soft fabric of silk or rayon, for dresses, coats, etc.

fail'-safe' *adj.* so designed as to exclude unintended or faulty operation, as a nuclear device

fail·ure (fāl'yər) *n.* 1. the act, state, or fact of failing 2. a person or thing that fails 3. *Educ.* a failing to pass, or a grade showing this

fain (fān) *adj.* [OE. *fægen,* glad] [Archaic] 1. glad; ready 2. reluctantly willing —*adv.* [Archaic] gladly or willingly

faint (fānt) *adj.* [see FEIGN] 1. weak; feeble 2. timid 3. halfhearted 4. undergoing a sensation of weakness and dizziness 5. dim; indistinct —*n.* a condition of brief unconsciousness resulting from inadequate flow of blood to the brain —*vi.* to fall into a faint —**faint'ly** *adv.* —**faint'ness** *n.*

faint'heart'ed *adj.* cowardly; timid

fair[1] (fer) *adj.* [OE. *fæger*] 1. attractive or beautiful 2. unblemished *[a fair name]* 3. light in color; blond 4. clear and sunny 5. clear and easy to read *[write a fair hand]* 6. just and honest; impartial 7. not violating the rules as of a game 8. likely *[in a fair way to succeed]* 9. pleasant, as in manner 10. favorable *[a fair wind]* 11. sizable *[a fair number]* 12. average in quality *[a fair movie]* —*adv.* 1. in a fair way *[play fair]* 2. squarely *[struck fair in the face]* —**fair and square** [Colloq.] with justice and honesty —**fair'ness** *n.*

fair[2] (fer) *n.* [< L. *feriae,* festivals] 1. orig., a regular gathering of people for the barter and sale of goods 2. a festival featuring entertainment and things for sale 3. an exhibition, as of farm products, manufactured goods, or international displays, usually also with various amusements

fair'ground' *n.* [often *pl.*] an area for a fair

fair'-haired' *adj.* 1. having blond hair 2. [Colloq.] favorite *[the fair-haired boy of the family]*

fair'ly *adv.* 1. justly 2. moderately 3. distinctly 4. completely or really *[fairly filled the room]*

fair'-mind'ed *adj.* just; impartial

fair play observance of the rules, as in sports, or of justice, honesty, etc., as in business

fair sex women collectively: used with *the*

fair shake [Colloq.] fair, just, or equitable treatment

fair'-spo'ken *adj.* speaking or spoken politely

fair'-trade' *adj.* designating or of an agreement whereby the seller of a product charges no less than the minimum price set by the producer

fair'way' (-wā') *n.* on a golf course, the mowed part between a tee and a green

fair'-weath'er *adj.* 1. suitable for fair weather 2. existent, available, dependable, etc. only when things are going well *[fair-weather friends]*

fair·y (fer'ē) *n., pl.* -**ies** [< OFr. *feie*] 1. *Folklore* a tiny, graceful being in human form, with magic powers 2. [Slang] a male homosexual

fair'y·land' *n.* 1. the imaginary land where fairies live 2. a lovely, enchanting place

fairy tale 1. a story about fairies, giants, etc. 2. an unbelievable or untrue story

‡fait ac·com·pli (fe tä kôn plē') [Fr.] a thing undeniably already done

faith (fāth) *n.* [< L. *fidere,* to trust] 1. unquestioning belief, esp. in God, religion, etc. 2. a particular religion 3. complete trust or reliance 4. loyalty —**good** (or **bad**) **faith** (in)sincerity or (dis)honesty —**in faith** indeed; truly

faith'ful (-fəl) *adj.* 1. loyal 2. conscientious 3. accurate; exact —**the faithful** the true believers or loyal followers —**faith'ful·ly** *adv.* —**faith'ful·ness** *n.*

faith'less (-lis) *adj.* 1. disloyal 2. unreliable —**faith'less·ly** *adv.* —**faith'less·ness** *n.*

fake (fāk) *vt., vi.* **faked, fak'ing** [< ? G. *fegen,* to clean] to practice deception by giving a false indication or appearance of (something); feign —*n.* a person or thing that is not genuine; fraud; sham; counterfeit —*adj.* not genuine; false; counterfeit —**fak'er** *n.*

fa·kir (fə kir') *n.* [Ar. *faqīr,* lit., poor] 1. one of a Muslim holy sect of beggars 2. a Hindu ascetic 3. a Muslim or Hindu itinerant beggar, often one claiming to perform miracles

Fa·lange (fā'lanj) *n.* [Sp., lit., phalanx] the fascist political party in Spain since 1934

fal·cate (fal'kāt) *adj.* [< L. *falx,* sickle] shaped like a sickle; curved; hooked

fal·chion (fôl'chən, -shən) *n.* [see prec.] a medieval sword with a short, broad, slightly curved blade

fal·con (fal'kən, fôl'-, fô'-) *n.* [prob. < L. *falx,* sickle] 1. a hawk trained to hunt small game 2. any of several hawklike birds

fal'con·er (-ər) *n.* a person who hunts with falcons —**fal'con·ry** (-rē) *n.*

fal·de·ral (fôl'də rôl', fal'də ral') *n.* nonsense

Falk·land Islands (fôk'lənd) group of Brit. islands, east of the S tip of S. America

fall (fôl) *vi.* **fell, fall'en, fall'ing** [OE. *feallan*] 1. to come down by gravity, as when dropped 2. to come down suddenly from an upright position; tumble or collapse 3. to be wounded or killed in battle 4. to take a downward direction 5. to become lower, less, weaker, etc. 6. to lose power, status, etc. 7. to do wrong; sin 8. to be captured or conquered 9. to take on a sad look *[his face fell]* 10. to take place; occur 11. to come by inheritance, lot, etc. 12. to pass into a specified condition *[to fall ill]* 13. to be directed, esp. by chance 14. to hit; strike *[to fall wide of the mark]* 15. to hang down —*n.* 1. a dropping; descending 2. a coming down suddenly from an upright position 3. a downward direction or slope 4. a becoming lower or less 5. a capturing, overthrow, etc. 6. a loss of power, status, virtue, etc. 7. something fallen, as snow, or the amount of this 8. autumn 9. the distance something falls 10. [*usually pl., often with sing. v.*] water falling as over a cliff 11. a long tress of hair, added to a woman's hairdo —*adj.* of autumn —**fall back** to withdraw; retreat —**fall back on** (or **upon**) to turn, or return, to for help —**fall flat** to fail to have the desired effect —**fall for** [Colloq.] 1. to fall in love with 2. to be tricked by —**fall in** 1. to agree 2. to line up in formation —**fall off** to become smaller, worse, etc. —**fall on** (or **upon**) 1. to attack 2. to be the duty of —**fall out** 1. to quarrel 2. to happen 3. to leave one's place in line —**fall through** to come to nothing; fail —**fall to** to begin; esp., to begin eating

fal·la·cious (fə lā'shəs) *adj.* [see FALLACY] 1. containing a fallacy 2. misleading or deceptive —**fal·la'cious·ly** *adv.*

fal·la·cy (fal'ə sē) *n., pl.* -**cies** [< L. *fallere,* deceive] 1. aptness to mislead 2. a mistaken idea; error 3. an error in reasoning

fall·en (fôl'ən) *adj.* that fell; dropped, prostrate, overthrown, ruined, etc.

fall guy [Slang] a person left to face the consequences as of a scheme that has miscarried

fal·li·ble (fal'ə b'l) *adj.* [see FALLACY] capable of making mistakes or of being wholly or partly in error —**fal'li·bil'·i·ty** *n.* —**fal'li·bly** *adv.*

fall'ing-out' *n.* a quarrel

falling star *same as* METEOR (sense 1)

fall'off' *n.* a becoming less or worse; decline

Fal·lo·pi·an tube (fə lō'pē ən) [< G. *Fallopius*, 16th-c. It. anatomist] either of two slender tubes that carry ova from the ovaries to the uterus

fall'out' *n.* 1. the descent to earth of radioactive particles, as after a nuclear explosion 2. these particles

fal·low' (fal'ō) *adj.* [OE. *fealh*] 1. plowed but unplanted 2. untrained or inactive, as the mind

fal·low² (fal'ō) *adj.* [OE. *fealo*] pale-yellow

fallow deer a small European deer with a yellowish coat spotted with white in summer

false (fôls) *adj.* **fals'er, fals'est** [< L. *fallere*, deceive] 1. not true or correct; wrong 2. untruthful; lying 3. disloyal; unfaithful 4. misleading 5. not real; artificial 6. not properly so named 7. based on mistaken ideas 8. *Mech.* temporary, not essential, or added on as for disguise [a *false* drawer] 9. *Music* pitched inaccurately —*adv.* in a false way —**false'ly** *adv.* —**false'ness** *n.*

false'face' *n.* a facelike mask, typically with comical or grotesque features

false'heart'ed *adj.* disloyal or deceitful

false'hood' *n.* 1. falsity 2. a lie or the telling of lies 3. a false belief, idea, etc.

false ribs the five lower ribs on each side of the body, not directly attached to the breastbone

fal·set·to (fôl set'ō) *n., pl.* **-tos** [It.: see FALSE] an artificially high vocal register —*adj., adv.* in this register

fal·si·fy (fôl'sə fī') *vt.* **-fied', -fy'ing** 1. to make false, as by lying or altering 2. to show to be untrue or wrong —*vi.* to tell a lie or lies —**fal'si·fi·ca'tion** *n.* —**fal'si·fi'er** *n.*

fal·si·ty (fôl'sə tē) *n., pl.* **-ties** 1. the condition or quality of being false 2. a lie

Fal·staff (fôl'staf), Sir **John** a character in some Shakespearean plays: he is a fat, jovial knight

fal·ter (fôl'tər) *vi.* [ME. *faltren*] 1. to move uncertainly or unsteadily 2. to stumble or hesitate in speech 3. to show uncertainty; waver —*vt.* to say in a stumbling or hesitant way *n.* 1. a faltering 2. a faltering sound

fame (fām) *n.* [< L. *fama*] 1. reputation, esp. for good 2. widespread public recognition, usually highly favorable; renown; glory

famed (fāmd) *adj.* famous

fa·mil·ial (fə mil'yəl) *adj.* of a family

fa·mil·iar (fə mil'yər) *adj.* [see FAMILY] 1. friendly; close; intimate [a *familiar* companion] 2. too friendly; unduly intimate 3. closely acquainted (*with*) 4. common; ordinary —*n.* a close friend —**fa·mil'iar·ly** *adv.*

fa·mil·i·ar·i·ty (fə mil'yar'ə tē, -mil'ē ar'-) *n., pl.* **-ties** 1. informality or intimacy, either acceptable or excessive, or an instance of such 2. close acquaintance (*with*)

fa·mil·iar·ize (fə mil'yə rīz') *vt.* **-ized', -iz'ing** 1. to make commonly known 2. to make fully acquainted —**fa·mil'iar·i·za'tion** *n.*

fam·i·ly (fam'ə lē) *n., pl.* **-lies** [< L. *famulus*, servant] 1. orig., all the people living in the same house 2. *a*) a social unit consisting of parents and their children *b*) the children of the same parents 3. a group of people related by ancestry or marriage 4. a group of related or similar things; specif., *Biol.* a taxonomic category ranking above a genus and below an order

family name a surname

family room a room in a home, set apart for relaxation and recreation

fam·ine (fam'ən) *n.* [< L. *fames*, hunger] an acute and general shortage or lack, specif. of food

fam·ish (fam'ish) *vt., vi.* [see prec.] to make or be very hungry

fa·mous (fā'məs) *adj.* 1. having fame, or widespread recognition; renowned 2. [Colloq.] very good or excellent —**fa'mous·ly** *adv.*

fan¹ (fan) *n.* [< L. *vannus*, basket to winnow grain] 1. a device producing a current of air for ventilating or cooling; specif., *a*) a flat hand-moved surface *b*) a folding device, as of paper, that opens as a sector of a circle *c*) a motor-driven device with revolving blades 2. anything shaped like a fan (sense 1 *b*) —*vt., vi.* **fanned, fan'ning** 1. to move (air) as with a fan 2. to direct air toward as with a fan 3. to stir up; excite 4. *Baseball* to strike out — **fan out** to spread out like a fan (*n.* 1 *b*) —**fan'like'** *adj.*

fan² (fan) *n.* [< FANATIC] [Colloq.] a person enthusiastic about a sport, performer, etc.

fa·nat·ic (fə nat'ik) *adj.* [< L. *fanum*, temple] unreasonably enthusiastic; overly zealous: also **fa·nat'i·cal** —*n.* a fanatic person —**fa·nat'i·cal·ly** *adv.* —**fa·nat'i·cism** *n.*

fan·cied (fan'sēd) *adj.* imaginary; imagined

fan·ci·er (fan'sē ər) *n.* one especially interested in and knowledgeable about something [a dog *fancier*]

fan·ci·ful (fan'si fəl) *adj.* 1. full of fancy; imaginative 2. not real; imaginary —**fan'ci·ful·ly** *adv.* —**fan'ci·ful·ness** *n.*

fan·cy (fan'sē) *n., pl.* **-cies** [< FANTASY] 1. imagination, now esp. when light, playful, etc. 2. a mental image 3. a whim; caprice; notion 4. an inclination or fondness —*adj.* **-ci·er, -ci·est** 1. whimsical; capricious 2. extravagant [a *fancy* price] 3. far from plain; highly decorated, elaborate, etc. 4. not at all simple; intricate 5. superior in quality and high-priced —*vt.* **-cied, -cy·ing** 1. to imagine 2. to like 3. to suppose —**fan'ci·ly** *adv.* —**fan'ci·ness** *n.*

fan'cy-free' *adj.* 1. free to fall in love; unattached; uncommitted 2. carefree

fan'cy·work' *n.* ornamental needlework

fan·dan·go (fan daŋ'gō) *n., pl.* **-gos** [Sp.] 1. a lively Spanish dance in rhythm varying from slow to quick 3/4 time 2. music for this

fan·dom (fan'dəm) *n.* fans, collectively, as of a sport or entertainer

fane (fān) *n.* [L. *fanum*] [Archaic or Poet.] a temple or church

fan·fare (fan'fer) *n.* [Fr.] 1. a loud blast of trumpets 2. noisy or showy display

fang (faŋ) *n.* [OE. < *fon*, seize] 1. one of the long, pointed teeth of meat-eating animals 2. one of the long, venom-injecting teeth of some snakes

fan'jet' *n.* a jet aircraft with a turbofan engine

fan'light' *n.* a semicircular window, fanlike in shape, as over a door

fan'tail' *n.* 1. a part or tail spread out like a fan 2. *Naut.* the part of the main deck at the stern 3. *Zool.* a pigeon or goldfish with a fantail

fan-tan (fan'tan') *n.* [< Chin.] 1. a Chinese gambling game 2. a card game in which the aim is to discard all cards in sequence Also **fan tan**

fan·ta·si·a (fan tā'zhə, -zē ə; fan'tə zē'ə) *n.* [see FANTASY] 1. a musical composition of no fixed form 2. a medley of familiar tunes

fan·ta·size (fan'tə sīz') *vt., vi.* **-sized', -siz'ing** to evoke (mental images, illusions, etc.) in fantasy or in a daydreaming way

fan·tas·tic (fan tas'tik) *adj.* 1. existing in fantasy; imaginary; unreal 2. grotesque; odd 3. capricious; eccentric 4. beyond or almost beyond belief; incredible Also **fan·tas'ti·cal** —**fan·tas'ti·cal·ly** *adv.*

fan·ta·sy (fan'tə sē, -zē) *n., pl.* **-sies** [< Gr. *phainein*, to show] 1. imagination or fancy, esp. when unrestrained 2. an odd or illusory mental image 3. a whim; caprice 4. a highly imaginative poem, play, etc. —*vt., vi.* **-sied, -sy·ing** to form a fantasy or fantasies (about something)

FAO Food and Agriculture Organization (of the UN)

far (fär) *adj.* **far'ther, far'thest** [OE. *feorr*] 1. distant in space or time 2. extending a long way [a *far* journey] 3. more distant [the *far* side of the room] —*adv.* 1. at or to a point distant in space or time 2. very much [*far* better] —**as far as** 1. to the distance, extent, or degree that 2. [Colloq.] in regard to —**by far** very much: also **far and away** —(in) so far as to the extent that —**so far** up to this point

far·ad (far'ad, -əd) *n.* [< M. FARADAY] a unit of capacitance, equal to the amount that permits the storing of one coulomb of charge for each volt of applied potential

Far·a·day (far'ə dā'), **Michael** 1791–1867; Eng. scientist: noted esp. for his work in electricity

far'a·way' *adj.* 1. distant in space or time 2. mentally withdrawn or preoccupied; abstracted

farce (färs) *n.* [Fr., stuffing < L. *farcire*, to stuff] 1. (an) exaggerated comedy based on highly unlikely situations 2. (a) ridiculous display, pretense, etc. —**far'ci·cal** *adj.*

fare (fer) *vi.* **fared, far'ing** [OE. *faran*, go] 1. [Poet.] to travel; go 2. to happen or result 3. to get along or progress in a certain way [to *fare* worse] 4. to eat —*n.* 1. the charge for passenger conveyance as in a taxi, bus, or plane; also, a passenger so conveyed 2. food offered, esp.

regularly, as in restaurants **3**. material offered as for entertainment, esp. regularly, as in theaters

Far East E Asia, including China, Japan, etc.

fare·well (fer'wel'; *for adj.* -wel') *interj.* goodbye —*n.* **1**. the expression of good wishes at parting **2**. a departure — *adj.* accompanying a departure; parting *[a farewell gesture]*

far-fetched (fär'fecht') *adj.* strained, as a comparison; forced; artificial

far'-flung' *adj.* extending over a wide area

fa·ri·na (fə rē'nə) *n.* [< L., meal] flour or meal made as from whole wheat or nuts and cooked to make a cereal or cereallike food

far·i·na·ceous (far'ə nā'shəs) *adj.* [see prec.] **1**. of or made from flour or meal **2**. mealy **3**. starchy

farm (färm) *n.* [< ML. *firma*, fixed payment] **1**. a piece of land (with houses, barns, etc.) on which crops or animals are raised **2**. any area of land or water where certain things are raised *[a fish farm]* **3**. a minor-league team owned by or associated with a major-league team —*vt.* **1**. to cultivate (land) **2**. to turn over to another for a fee — *vi.* to work on or operate a farm —**farm out 1**. to let out (work or workers) on contract to outsiders **2**. to assign to a farm (*n.* 3)

farm'er *n.* one who operates or works on a farm

farm'hand' *n.* a hired farm worker

farm'house' *n.* a house on a farm

farm'ing *n.* the business of operating a farm

farm'stead' (-sted') *n.* **1**. a farm **2**. the main building or cluster of buildings on a farm

farm'yard' *n.* the yard surrounding or enclosed by the buildings on a farm

far·o (fer'ō) *n.* [Fr. *pharaon*] a gambling game played with cards

far-off (fär'ôf') *adj.* distant; remote

far·ra·go (fə rä'gō, -rä'-) *n., pl.* **-goes** [L., mixed fodder] a confused mixture; jumble

far'-reach'ing *adj.* reaching widely, as an effect

far·ri·er (far'ē ər) *n.* [< L. *ferrum*, iron] [Brit.] a shoer of horses —**far'ri·er·y** *n., pl.* **-ies**

far·row (far'ō) *n.* [OE. *fearh*, young pig] a litter of pigs — *vt., vi.* to give birth to (a litter of pigs)

far'see'ing *adj.* farsighted (senses 1 & 2)

far'sight'ed *adj.* **1**. capable of seeing far **2**. prudent and provident **3**. seeing distant objects better than near ones —**far'sight'ed·ness** *n.*

far·ther (fär'thər) *compar. of* FAR —*adj.* **1**. more distant **2**. additional; more —*adv.* **1**. at or to a greater distance **2**. to a greater degree **3**. in addition Cf. FURTHER

far'ther·most' *adj.* most distant; farthest

far'thest (fär'thist) *superl. of* FAR —*adj.* most distant — *adv.* **1**. at or to the greatest distance **2**. to the greatest degree

far·thing (fär'thiŋ) *n.* [OE. *feorthing*, fourth part] a former British coin worth 1/4 penny

far·thin·gale (fär'thiŋ gāl') *n.* [< Sp. < *verdugo*, hoop] a skirt spread out and down over a hoop or other support extending horizontally from the waist, worn by women in the 16th and 17th centuries

fas·ces (fas'ēz) *n.pl.* [L., pl. of *fascis*, a bundle] a bundle of rods bound about an ax, a symbol of authority of ancient Roman magistrates

fas·ci·cle (fas'i k'l) *n.* [< L. dim. of *fascis*, a bundle] one part of a book published in parts

fas·ci·nate (fas'ə nāt') *vt.* **-nat'ed, -nat'ing** [< L. *fascinum*, an enchanting] to hold spellbound; esp., to grip as by irresistible charm or interest — **fas'ci·nat'ing·ly** *adv.* —**fas'ci·na'tion** *n.*

fas·cism (fash'iz'm) *n.* [< It. < L.: see FASCES] *[occas.* F-] a system of government characterized by dictatorship, belligerent nationalism, militarism, etc.: first instituted in Italy (1922–43) —**fas'cist** *n., adj.*

FASCES

fash·ion (fash'ən) *n.* [ult. < L. *facere*, make] **1**. form or shape **2**. way or manner **3**. current style, as of dress —*vt.* **1**. to make; form **2**. to adapt (*to*) —**after** (or **in**) **a fashion** to some extent

fash'ion·a·ble *adj.* **1**. in fashion; stylish **2**. of stylish people —**fash'ion·a·bly** *adv.*

fast¹ (fast) *adj.* [OE. *fæst*] **1**. firm, fixed, or stuck **2**. tightly fastened or shut **3**. loyal; devoted **4**. unfading *[fast colors]* **5**. speedy **6**. ahead of time **7**. wild, dissolute, etc. **8**. sexually promiscuous **9**. [Colloq.] glib —*adv.* **1**. firmly; fixedly **2**. sound *[fast asleep]* **3**. speedily **4**. ahead of time **5**. wildly, dissolutely, etc.

fast² (fast) *vi.* [OE. *fæstan*] to abstain from or do without food, food and drink, or one or more kinds of food or

drink, wholly or partly —*n.* **1**. a fasting **2**. a time of fasting

fas·ten (fas''n) *vt.* [see FAST¹] **1**. to attach; connect **2**. to make secure, as by locking or buttoning **3**. to fix (the attention, gaze, etc.) *on* a person or thing —*vi.* to become fastened —**fas'ten·er** *n.*

fas'ten·ing *n.* anything, as a clasp, used to fasten

fast'-food' *adj.* designating a business, as a hamburger stand, offering food prepared and served quickly

fas·tid·i·ous (fas tid'ē əs) *adj.* [< L. *fastus*, disdain + *taedium:* see TEDIUM] **1**. not easy to please **2**. overly refined and easily disgusted —**fas·tid'i·ous·ly** *adv.* —**fas·tid'i·ous·ness** *n.*

fast·ness (fast'nis) *n.* **1**. the quality or condition of being fast **2**. a secure place; stronghold

fast'-talk' *vt.* [Colloq.] to persuade with fast, smooth, often deceitful talk

fast time *same as* DAYLIGHT-SAVING TIME

fat (fat) *adj.* **fat'ter, fat'test** [OE. *fætt*] **1**. containing fat; oily; greasy **2**. *a)* fleshy; plump *b)* obese **3**. thick; broad **4**. fertile *[fat* land] **5**. profitable *[a fat* job] **6**. plentiful — *n.* **1**. an oily material in animal tissue or plant seeds **2**. fleshiness **3**. the richest part of anything —*vt., vi.* **fat'ted, fat'ting** *same as* FATTEN —**a fat chance** [Slang] very little chance —**chew the fat** [Slang] to chat —**fat'ness** *n.*

fa·tal (fāt''l) *adj.* **1**. fateful; decisive **2**. bringing death **3**. disastrous; ruinous —**fa'tal·ly** *adv.*

fa'tal·ism *n.* the belief that all events are determined by fate and hence inevitable —**fa'tal·ist** *n.* —**fa'tal·is'tic** *adj.*

fa·tal·i·ty (fə tal'ə tē, fā-) *n., pl.* **-ties 1**. subjection to fate **2**. inevitable liability to disaster **3**. deadliness **4**. a death caused as by an accident, fire, etc.

fat'back' *n.* fat from a hog's back, usually dried and salted in strips

fat cat [Slang] a wealthy person

fate (fāt) *n.* [< L. *fatum*, oracle] **1**. a supposed inexorable power making everything happen in a predetermined, inevitable way; destiny **2**. anything so predetermined **3**. the lot or destiny of anyone or anything **4**. final outcome or disposition **5**. adverse destiny, esp. the final one, as ruin, destruction, or death —*vt.* **fat'ed, fat'ing** to destine: now usually in passive —**the Fates** *Gr. & Rom. Myth.* three goddesses controlling human destiny

fat·ed (fāt'id) *adj.* **1**. destined **2**. doomed

fate'ful (-fəl) *adj.* **1**. prophetic **2**. full of consequences; crucial **3**. controlled as if by fate **4**. bringing death or destruction —**fate'ful·ly** *adv.* —**fate'ful·ness** *n.*

fat·head (fat'hed') *n.* [Slang] a stupid person; blockhead —**fat'head'ed** *adj.*

fa·ther (fä'thər) *n.* [OE. *fæder*] **1**. a male parent **2**. a male guardian or protector **3**. [F-] God **4**. a male ancestor **5**. a male originator, founder, or inventor **6**. a male leader, as of a city **7**. *[often* F-] *a)* any of certain important early Christian religious writers *b)* a Christian priest —*vt.* **1**. to be the father of **2**. to act as a father toward — **fa'ther·hood'** *n.* —**fa'ther·less** *adj.*

fa'ther-in-law' *n., pl.* **fa'thers-in-law'** the father of one's wife or husband

fa'ther·land' *n.* a person's native land or, sometimes, that of his ancestors

fa'ther·ly *adj.* of or like a father; kindly, protective, etc. —**fa'ther·li·ness** *n.*

fath·om (fath'əm) *n.* [OE. *fæthm*, the two arms outstretched] a nautical unit of depth or length, equal to 6 feet —*vt.* **1**. to measure the depth of **2**. to understand thoroughly —**fath'om·a·ble** *adj.* —**fath'om·less** *adj.*

fa·tigue (fə tēg') *n.* [Fr. < L. *fatigare*, to weary] **1**. exhaustion; weariness **2**. *a)* labor, other than drill or instruction, assigned to soldiers: also **fatigue duty** *b)* *[pl.]* special clothes worn for this **3**. the tendency of a material, as metal, to break or weaken under stress —*vt., vi.* **-tigued', -tigu'ing** to weary; tire

Fat·i·ma (fat'i mə, fät'-; fə tē'mə) 606?–632 A.D.; daughter of Mohammed

fat·ling (fat'liŋ) *n.* a calf, lamb, kid, or young pig fattened before being slaughtered

fat·ten (fat''n) *vt., vi.* to make or become fat

fat'ty *adj.* **-ti·er, -ti·est** of, like, or full of fat —*n.* [Colloq.] a fleshy person —**fat'ti·ness** *n.*

fatty acid any of a series of organic acids having the general formula $C_nH_{2n+1}COOH$

fa·tu·i·ty (fə tōō'ə tē, -tyōō'-; fa-) *n., pl.* **-ties 1**. smug stupidity; asininity **2**. something fatuous

fat·u·ous (fach'oo wəs) *adj.* [L. *fatuus*] smugly stupid; asinine —**fat'u·ous·ly** *adv.*

fau·ces (fô'sēz) *n.pl.* [L., throat] the passage from the back of the mouth to the pharynx

fau·cet (fô′sit) *n.* [prob. < OFr. *faulser,* to breach] a device with a valve for regulating the flow of liquid as from a pipe; tap

Faulk·ner (fôk′nər), **William** 1897–1962; U.S. novelist

fault (fôlt) *n.* [< L. *fallere,* deceive] **1.** something that mars; flaw; defect **2.** a misdeed or mistake **3.** responsibility for something wrong; blame **4.** *Geol.* a fracture and displacement in rock strata —*vt.* **1.** to blame **2.** *Geol.* to cause a fault in —*vi. Geol.* to develop a fault —**at fault** in the wrong —**find fault (with)** to criticize — **to a fault** excessively

FAULT (sense 4)

fault′find′ing *n., adj.* criticizing — **fault′find′er** *n.*

fault′less *adj.* perfect —**fault′less·ly** *adv.*

fault′y *adj.* **-i·er, -i·est** having a fault or faults; imperfect —**fault′i·ly** *adv.* —**fault′i·ness** *n.*

faun (fôn) *n.* [< L. *faunus*] any of a class of minor Roman deities, half man and half goat

fau·na (fô′nə) *n., pl.* **-nas, -nae** (-nē) [< LL. *Fauna,* Roman goddess] the animals of a specified region or time

Faust (foust) in legend and literature, a man who sold his soul to the devil for knowledge and power

FAUN

faux pas (fō′ pä′) *pl.* **faux pas** (fō′ päz′) [Fr., lit., false step] a social blunder

fa·vor (fā′vər) *n.* [< L. *favere,* to favor] **1.** friendly regard; approval **2.** partiality **3.** a kind act **4.** a small gift or token —*vt.* **1.** to approve or like **2.** to be partial to **3.** to support; advocate **4.** to make easier; help **5.** to do a kindness for **6.** to resemble *[he favors his father]* Brit. sp. **favour** —**in favor of 1.** approving **2.** to the advantage of

fa·vor·a·ble *adj.* **1.** approving **2.** helpful **3.** pleasing —**fa′vor·a·bly** *adv.*

fa′vored *adj.* **1.** treated with favor **2.** having (specified) features *[ill-favored]*

fa·vor·ite (fā′vər it) *n.* **1.** a person or thing especially liked **2.** a contestant viewed as most likely to win —*adj.* highly regarded; preferred

fa′vor·it·ism *n.* partiality; bias

fawn[1] (fôn) *vi.* [< OE. *fægen,* glad] **1.** to show affection as by licking the hand: said of a dog **2.** to cringe and flatter —**fawn′ing·ly** *adv.*

fawn[2] (fôn) *n.* [< L. *fetus,* FETUS] **1.** a deer less than a year old **2.** a pale, yellowish brown —*adj.* of this color

fay (fā) *n.* [see FATE] a fairy

faze (fāz) *vt.* **fazed, faz′ing** [< OE. *fesan,* to drive] [Colloq.] to disturb; disconcert

FBI, F.B.I. Federal Bureau of Investigation

FCC, F.C.C. Federal Communications Commission

FDA, F.D.A. Food and Drug Administration

FDIC, F.D.I.C. Federal Deposit Insurance Corporation

Fe [L. *ferrum*] *Chem.* iron

fe·al·ty (fē′əl tē) *n., pl.* **-ties** [< L. *fidelitas,* fidelity] loyalty, esp. as owed to a feudal lord

fear (fir) *n.* [OE. *fær,* danger] **1.** anxiety over real or possible danger, pain, etc.; fright **2.** awe; reverence **3.** apprehension; concern **4.** a cause for fear —*vt., vi.* **1.** to have fear (of) **2.** to be in awe (of) **3.** to expect with misgiving —**fear′less** *adj.* —**fear′less·ness** *n.*

fear′ful *adj.* **1.** causing, feeling, or showing fear **2.** [Colloq.] very bad, great, etc. —**fear′ful·ly** *adv.* —**fear′ful·ness** *n.*

fear′some *adj.* **1.** causing fear **2.** frightened

fea·si·ble (fē′zə b'l) *adj.* [< L. *facere,* do] **1.** possible **2.** likely; probable **3.** suitable —**fea′si·bil′i·ty** *n.* —**fea′si·bly** *adv.*

feast (fēst) *n.* [< L. *festus,* festal] **1.** a festival **2.** a rich, elaborate meal —*vi.* to dine richly —*vt.* **1.** to give a feast to **2.** to delight *[to feast one's eyes on a sight]*

feat (fēt) *n.* [< L. *factum,* a deed] a deed of unusual daring or skill

feath·er (feth′ər) *n.* [OE. *fether*] **1.** any of the soft, light outgrowths covering the body of a bird **2.** *[pl.] a)* plumage *b)* attire **3.** class; kind *[birds of a feather]* —*vt.* **1.** to provide or adorn as with feathers **2.** to turn (an oar or propeller blade) so that the edge is foremost —**feather in one's cap** a distinctive achievement —**in fine** (or **high** or **good**) **feather** in very good humor, health, or form — **feath′er·y** *adj.*

feath′er·bed′ding (-bed′iŋ) *n.* the limitation of work output or the requiring of extra workers so as to provide more jobs and prevent unemployment

feath′er·brain′ *n.* a brainless person

feath′er·weight′ *n.* **1.** a boxer weighing over 118 but not over 126 pounds **2.** a wrestler weighing over 123 but not over 134 pounds

fea·ture (fē′chər) *n.* [< L. *facere,* to make] **1.** *a)* [*pl.*] facial form or appearance *b)* any facial part **2.** a distinct or outstanding part or quality of something **3.** something given special emphasis as in an entertainment, at a sale, etc. **4.** a special story, article, etc., as in a newspaper **5.** a full-length motion picture —*vt.* **-tured, -tur·ing 1.** to emphasize or have as a special part of something **2.** to be a feature of **3.** [Slang] to imagine —*vi.* to be featured

feb·ri·fuge (feb′rə fyōōj′) *n.* [< L. *febris,* fever + *fugere,* flee] something for reducing fever

fe·brile (fē′brəl, -brīl) *adj.* [< L. *febris,* fever] of or characterized by fever; feverish

Feb·ru·ar·y (feb′rə wer′ē, feb′yoo wer′ē) *n.* [< L. *Februarius* (*mensis*), orig. month of expiation] the second month of the year, having 28 days (or 29 days in leap years): abbrev. **Feb., F.**

fe·ces (fē′sēz) *n.pl.* [< L. *faeces,* dregs] excrement —**fe′cal** (-kəl) *adj.*

feck·less (fek′lis) *adj.* [Scot. < *feck,* effect + -LESS] **1.** weak; ineffective **2.** careless

fe·cund (fē′kənd, fek′ənd) *adj.* [< L. *fecundus*] fertile; prolific —**fe·cun·di·ty** (fi kun′də tē) *n.*

fe·cun·date (fē′kən dāt′, fek′ən-) *vt.* **-dat′ed, -dat′ing 1.** to make fecund **2.** to fertilize; impregnate; pollinate —**fe′-cun·da′tion** *n.*

fed (fed) *pt. & pp. of* FEED —**fed up** [Colloq.] having had enough to become disgusted, bored, etc.

Fed. 1. Federal **2.** Federated **3.** Federation

fed·a·yeen (fed′ä yēn′) *n.pl.* [Ar., lit., self-sacrificers] Arab guerrillas in the Middle East

fed·er·al (fed′ər əl) *adj.* [< L. *foedus,* a league] **1.** designating or of a union of states, groups, etc. in which each member subordinates its power to a central authority **2.** designating or of such a central authority, specif. [*usually* F-] that of the U.S. government **3.** [F-] of or for the Federalist Party **4.** [F-] of or for the U.S. government in the Civil War —*n.* **1.** [F-] a Federalist **2.** [F-] a supporter of the U.S. government in the Civil War **3.** [F-] a Federal agent or officer

fed·er·al·ism *n.* **1.** the federal principle, or support of this **2.** Federalist Party principles

fed·er·al·ist *n.* **1.** one supporting federalism **2.** [F-] a member or supporter of the Federalist Party —*adj.* **1.** of federalism **2.** [F-] of the Federalist Party

Federalist (or **Federal**) **Party** a U.S. political party (1789–1816) advocating the Constitution and a strong, centralized government

fed′er·al·ize′ *vt.* **-ized′, -iz′ing 1.** to unite in a federal union **2.** to put under the authority of a federal government —**fed′er·al·i·za′tion** *n.*

fed·er·ate (fed′ə rāt′) *vt., vi.* **-at′ed, -at′ing** to unite in a federal union —**fed′er·a′tion** *n.*

fe·do·ra (fə dôr′ə) *n.* [Fr.] a soft felt hat with the crown creased lengthwise and a curved brim

fee (fē) *n.* [< OFr. *feu,* fief & OE. *feoh,* cattle] **1.** a charge for professional services, licenses, tuition, etc. **2.** *Law* an inheritance in land

fee·ble (fē′b'l) *adj.* **-bler, -blest** [< L. *flere,* weep] lacking strength, force, vitality, effectiveness, etc.; weak —**fee′ble·ness** *n.* —**fee′bly** *adv.*

fee′ble·mind′ed *adj.* mentally subnormal

feed (fēd) *vt.* **fed, feed′ing** [OE. *fedan*] **1.** to give food to or provide food for **2.** to provide as food *[to feed oats to horses]* **3.** to supply with what maintains or furthers growth, development, operation, etc. —*vi.* **1.** to eat: said chiefly of animals **2.** to flow steadily, as fuel into a machine —*n.* **1.** fodder, or the amount of this **2.** material supplied to a machine, or a machine part supplying it **3.** [Colloq.] a meal —**feed on** (or **upon**) **1.** to take or use as food; eat: said chiefly of animals **2.** to get satisfaction, support, etc. from —**feed′er** *n.*

feed′back′ *n.* **1.** transfer of some output back to the input, as in radio **2.** modification of the causative factors by the result produced

feel (fēl) *vt.* **felt, feel′ing** [OE. *felan*] **1.** to touch or handle and so examine **2.** to sense physically, mentally, or emotionally **3.** to experience or react strongly to (an emotion or condition) **4.** to think or believe, often for unanalyzed reasons —*vi.* **1.** to have physical sensation **2.** to make a specified sensory impression *[the rug feels soft]* **3.** to elicit a specified emotional response *[it feels good to be home]* **4.** to grope **5.** to be aware of being in a certain condition *[to feel happy]* **6.** to be moved to sympathy, pity, etc. —*n.* **1.** the act of feeling **2.** the sense of touch **3.** the sensory impression made or emotional response elicited by something **4.** instinctive ability, insight, etc. *[a feel for design]* —**feel like** [Colloq.] to have an inclination or desire for —**feel out** to try cautiously to find out the opinions of —**feel strongly about** to have decided opinions about —**feel up to** [Colloq.] to feel capable of

feel'er *n.* **1.** a specialized organ of touch, as the antenna of an insect **2.** a remark, offer, etc. made to find out another's attitude

feel'ing *n.* **1.** the sense of touch **2.** ability to experience physical sensation **3.** awareness **4.** emotion **5.** *[pl.]* sensibilities **6.** sympathy or pity **7.** an opinion or sentiment **8.** general impression given; spirit; air *[the lonely feeling of a deserted house]* **9.** sensitivity

feet (fēt) *n. pl. of* FOOT

feign (fān) *vt., vi.* [< L. *fingere*, to shape] **1.** to make up (a story, excuse, etc.) **2.** to pretend

feint (fānt) *n.* [see prec.] **1.** pretense **2.** a misleading movement designed to confuse one's opponent —*vt., vi.* to make (a feint)

feist·y (fīst'ē) *adj.* **-i·er, -i·est** [ME. *fīst*, a breaking of wind] [Colloq.] **1.** lively; energetic **2.** hot-tempered and full of fight; pugnacious

feld·spar (feld'spär') *n.* [< G. *feld*, field + *spath*, spar] any of several crystalline and usually glassy minerals made up of aluminum silicates with sodium, potassium, or calcium

fe·lic·i·tate (fə lis'ə tāt') *vt.* **-tat'ed, -tat'ing** [< L. *felix*, happy] to congratulate —**fe·lic'i·ta'tion** *n.*

fe·lic'i·tous (-təs) *adj.* [< FELICITY] **1.** smoothly appropriate; apt **2.** speaking or writing smoothly and aptly —**fe·lic'i·tous·ly** *adv.* —**fe·lic'i·tous·ness** *n.*

fe·lic'i·ty *n., pl.* **-ties** [< L. *felix*, happy] **1.** happiness, or a cause of it **2.** felicitousness

fe·line (fē'līn) *adj.* [< L. *felis*, cat] **1.** of a cat or the cat family **2.** catlike —*n.* any animal of the cat family

fell[1] (fel) *pt. of* FALL

fell[2] (fel) *vt.* [OE. *fellan*] **1.** to knock down **2.** to cut down (a tree)

fell[3] (fel) *adj.* [< ML. *fello*] **1.** fierce; savage; cruel **2.** vile; base; wicked; criminal

fell[4] (fel) *n.* [OE. *fel*] an animal's hide or skin

fel·low (fel'ō, -ə) *n.* [OE. *feolaga*, partner] **1.** a companion; associate **2.** one of the same class or rank; equal **3.** either of a pair; mate **4.** a graduate student holding a fellowship in a university or college **5.** a member of a learned society **6.** [Colloq.] a man or boy —*adj.* having the same position, work, etc. *[fellow workers]*

fel'low·ship' *n.* **1.** companionship **2.** mutual sharing **3.** a group of people with the same interests **4.** an endowment to support a person doing advanced study; also, the rank or position of such a person

fellow traveler a nonmember supporting a party

fel·on (fel'ən) *n.* [< ML. *felo*] one guilty of felony

fel'o·ny (-ə nē) *n., pl.* **-nies** [< ML. *felonia*, treason] some major crime, as murder, arson, or rape —**fe·lo·ni·ous** (fə lō'nē əs) *adj.*

felt[1] (felt) *n.* [OE.] a fabric of wool, often mixed as with fur or cotton, the fibers being worked together as by pressure and heat —*adj.* of felt —*vt.* **1.** to make into or cover with felt **2.** to mat (fibers) together —*vi.* to become so matted

felt[2] (felt) *pt. and pp. of* FEEL

fem. feminine

fe·male (fē'māl) *adj.* [< L. *femina*, woman] **1.** designating or of the sex bearing offspring **2.** of or suitable to this sex **3.** having a hollow part for receiving an inserted part, as an electric socket **4.** *Bot.* having a pistil and no stamens —*n.* a female person, animal, or plant

fem·i·nine (fem'ə nin) *adj.* [see prec.] **1.** of women or girls **2.** having qualities viewed as typical of or suitable to women and girls **3.** *Gram.* designating or of the gender of words referring to females or things orig. regarded as female —*n. Gram.* **1.** the feminine gender **2.** a word or form in this gender —**fem'i·nin'i·ty** *n.*

fem'i·nism *n.* the movement to win political, economic, and social equality for women —**fem'i·nist** *n., adj.*

fe·mur (fē'mər) *n., pl.* **fe'murs, fem·o·ra** (fem'ər ə) [L., thigh] *same as* THIGHBONE —**fem'o·ral** *adj.*

fen (fen) *n.* [OE.] an area of low, flat, marshy land; swamp; bog

fence (fens) *n.* [< ME. *defens*, defense] **1.** a protective or confining barrier as of posts, wire, etc. **2.** one who deals in stolen goods —*vt.* **fenced, fenc'ing** **1.** to enclose as with a fence (often with *in, off*, etc.) **2.** to keep (*out*) as by a fence **3.** to sell (stolen goods) —*vi.* **1.** to practice the art of fencing **2.** to be evasive **3.** to deal in stolen goods — **on the fence** neutral; uncommitted —**fenc'er** *n.*

fenc'ing *n.* **1.** the art of fighting with a foil or other sword **2.** material for making fences **3.** a system of fences

fend (fend) *vi.* [< ME. *defenden*, defend] to resist; parry —**fend for oneself** to get along without help from others —**fend off** to ward off; turn aside

fend'er *n.* anything that fends off or protects something else, as any of the metal frames over the wheels of an automobile or other vehicle

fen·nel (fen'l) *n.* [< L. *fenum*, hay] an herb with aromatic seeds used in cooking, related to parsley

fe·ral (fir'əl) *adj.* [< L. *ferus*, fierce] **1.** untamed; wild **2.** savage; brutal

fer-de-lance (fer'də läns') *n.* [Fr., iron tip of a lance] a large, poisonous snake of tropical America, related to the rattlesnake

fer·ment (fur'ment) *n.* [< L. *fervere*, to boil] **1.** something causing fermentation, as yeast or bacteria **2.** excitement; agitation —*vt.* (fər ment') **1.** to cause fermentation in **2.** to excite; agitate —*vi.* **1.** to undergo fermentation **2.** to be excited or agitated

fer·men·ta·tion (fur'mən tā'shən, -men-) *n.* **1.** the breakdown of complex molecules in organic compounds, caused by a ferment, as in the curdling of milk **2.** excitement; agitation

fer·mi·um (fer'mē əm) *n.* [< E. *Fermi* (1901–54), It. physicist] a radioactive chemical element: symbol, Fm; at. wt., 257(?); at. no., 100

fern (furn) *n.* [OE. *fearn*] any of a widespread class of nonflowering plants that have roots, stems, and fronds and that reproduce by spores

fe·ro·cious (fə rō'shəs) *adj.* [< L. *ferus*, wild] **1.** violently cruel; fierce; savage **2.** [Colloq.] very great *[a ferocious appetite]* —**fe·ro'cious·ly** *adv.* —**fe·roc'i·ty** (-räs'ə tē), **fe·ro'cious·ness** *n.*

-ferous [< L. *ferre*, to bear] a suffix meaning bearing, yielding *[coniferous]*

fer·ret (fer'it) *n.* [< L. *fur*, thief] a weasellike animal, tamed for hunting rabbits, rats, etc. —*vt.* **1.** to force out of hiding with a ferret **2.** to search (*out*) — *vi.* **1.** to hunt with ferrets **2.** to search around —**fer'ret·er** *n.*

Fer·ris wheel (fer'is) [< G. *Fer-ris* (1859–1896), U.S. engineer] a large, upright wheel revolving on a fixed axle and having suspended seats: used as an amusement ride

FERRET (19 1/2–21 in. long, including tail)

ferro- [< L. *ferrum*, iron] a combining form meaning: **1.** iron **2.** iron and

fer·rous (fer'əs) *adj.* [< L. *ferrum*, iron] of, containing, or derived from iron: also **fer'ric** (-ik)

fer·rule (fer'əl, -ool) *n.* [< L. *viriae*, bracelets] a metal ring or cap put around the end of a cane, tool handle, etc. to give added strength

fer·ry (fer'ē) *vt., vi.* **-ried, -ry·ing** [OE. *ferian*, carry] **1.** to take across or cross (a river, etc.) in a boat **2.** to deliver (airplanes) by flying them **3.** to transport by airplane — *n., pl.* **-ries** **1.** a system for carrying people, goods, etc. across a river, etc. by boat **2.** a boat (**ferryboat**) used for this, or the place where the boat docks on either shore — **fer'ry·man** (-mən) *n., pl.* **-men**

fer·tile (fur't'l) *adj.* [< L. *ferre*, to bear] **1.** producing abundantly; fruitful **2.** able to produce young, seeds, fruit, pollen, spores, etc. **3.** fertilized; impregnated —**fer·til·i·ty** (fər til'ə tē) *n.*

fer'til·ize' (-īz') *vt.* **-ized', -iz'ing** **1.** to make fertile **2.** to spread fertilizer on **3.** to make (the female cell or female) fruitful by introducing the male germ cell; impregnate — **fer'til·i·za'tion** *n.*

fer'til·iz'er *n.* manure, chemicals, etc. used to enrich the soil

fer·ule (fer'əl, -ool) *n.* [< L. *ferula*, a whip, rod] a flat stick or ruler used for punishing children

fer·vent (fur'vənt) *adj.* [< L. *fervere*, to glow] **1.** hot; burning **2.** showing great warmth of feeling; intensely earnest —**fer'ven·cy** *n.* —**fer'vent·ly** *adv.*

fer·vid (fur'vəd) *adj.* [see prec.] **1.** hot; burning **2.** impassioned; fervent —**fer'vid·ly** *adv.*

fer·vor (fur'vər) *n.* [see FERVENT] **1.** intense heat **2.** great warmth of emotion; ardor; zeal

fes·cue (fes'kyōō) *n.* [< L. *festuca*, straw] a tough grass used for pasture or lawns

-fest [< G. *fest*, a feast] *a combining form meaning* an occasion of much [*gabfest*]

fes·tal (fes't'l) *adj.* [< L. *festum*, feast] of or like a joyous celebration; festive —**fes'tal·ly** *adv.*

fes·ter (fes'tər) *n.* [< L. *fistula*, ulcer] a small sore filled with pus —*vi.* **1.** to form pus **2.** to rankle

fes·ti·val (fes'tə v'l) *n.* [see FESTIVE] **1.** a time or day of feasting or celebration **2.** a celebration or series of performances **3.** merrymaking —*adj.* of or for a festival

fes·tive (fes'tiv) *adj.* [< L. *festum*, feast] of or for a feast or festival; merry; joyous —**fes'tive·ly** *adv.* —**fes'tive·ness** *n.*

fes·tiv·i·ty (fes tiv'ə tē) *n., pl.* **-ties 1.** merrymaking; gaiety **2.** a festival **3.** [*pl.*] things done in celebration

fes·toon (fes tōōn') *n.* [< It. *festa*, feast] a garland of flowers, etc. hanging in a curve —*vt.* to adorn with festoons —**fes·toon'er·y** *n.*

fet·a (cheese) (fet'ə) *n.* [< ModGr. < It. *fetta*, a slice] a white, soft cheese made in Greece

fe·tal (fēt''l) *adj.* of or like a fetus

fetch (fech) *vt.* [OE. *feccan*] **1.** to go after and bring back; get **2.** to cause to come **3.** to sell for **4.** [Colloq.] to deliver (a blow, etc.) —*vi.* to go after things and bring them back

fetch'ing *adj.* attractive; charming

fete, fête (fāt) *n.* [Fr. *fête:* see FEAST] a festival; entertainment, esp. outdoors —*vt.* **fet'ed** or **fêt'ed, fet'ing** or **fêt'ing** to honor with a fete

fet·id (fet'id, fēt'-) *adj.* [< L. *f(o)etere*, to stink] having a bad smell; stinking —**fet'id·ness** *n.*

fet·ish (fet'ish, fēt'-) *n.* [< Port. *feitiço*] **1.** any object believed to have magic power **2.** anything to which one is irrationally devoted **3.** any nonsexual object that abnormally excites erotic feelings Also **fet'ich** —**fet'ish·ism** *n.* — **fet'ish·ist** *n.* —**fet'ish·is'tic** *adj.*

fet·lock (fet'läk') *n.* [< ME. *fet*, feet + *lok*, LOCK²] **1.** a tuft of hair on the back of a horse's leg above the hoof **2.** the joint bearing this tuft

fet·ter (fet'ər) *n.* [< OE. *fot*, foot] **1.** a shackle or chain for the feet **2.** any check or restraint —*vt.* **1.** to bind with fetters **2.** to restrain

fet·tle (fet''l) *n.* [ME. *fetlen*, make ready] condition; state [he is in fine *fettle*]

fe·tus (fēt'əs) *n., pl.* **-tus·es** [L., a bringing forth] **1.** the unborn young of an animal while still in the uterus or egg, esp. in its later stages **2.** in man, the offspring in the womb from the fourth month until birth

feud (fyōōd) *n.* [< OFr.] a long-continued, deadly quarrel, esp. between clans or families —*vi.* to carry on a feud

feu·dal (fyōōd''l) *adj.* [< OHG. *feho*, property] of or like feudalism —**feu'dal·ly** *adv.*

feu·dal·ism *n.* the economic and social system in medieval Europe, in which land, worked by serfs, was held by vassals in exchange for military and other services to overlords: also **feudal system** —**feu'dal·is'tic** *adj.*

fe·ver (fē'vər) *n.* [< L. *febris*] **1.** an abnormally increased body temperature, often along with a quickened pulse, delirium, etc. **2.** any disease marked by a high fever **3.** a restless excitement —*vt.* to cause fever in —**fe'vered** *adj.*

fever blister (or **sore**) *same as* COLD SORE

fe'ver·ish *adj.* **1.** having fever, esp. slight fever **2.** of, like, or caused by fever **3.** causing fever **4.** greatly excited — **fe'ver·ish·ly** *adv.*

few (fyōō) *adj.* [OE. *feawe*, pl.] not many —*pron., n.* a small number —**quite a few** [Colloq.] a rather large number —**the few** the minority

fey (fā) *adj.* [OE. *fæge*] **1.** [Archaic] fated **2.** strange or unusual

fez (fez) *n., pl.* **fez'zes** [< *Fez*, city in Morocco] a tapering felt hat, usually red with a black tassel: worn, esp. formerly, by Turkish men

ff. 1. folios **2.** following (pages, lines, etc.)

FHA Federal Housing Administration

fi·an·cé (fē'än sā') *n.* [Fr. < OFr. *fiance*, a promise] the man to whom a woman is engaged to be married

fi·an·cée (fē'än sā') *n.* [Fr.: see prec.] the woman to whom a man is engaged to be married

fi·as·co (fē as'kō) *n., pl.* **-coes, -cos** [Fr. < It. (*far*) *fiasco*, to fail] a complete, ridiculous failure

FEZ

fi·at (fī'at, -ət) *n.* [L., let it be done] **1.** an order issued by legal authority; decree **2.** a sanction

fiat money paper currency made legal tender by fiat, although not necessarily redeemable in coin

fib (fib) *n.* [? < *fable*] a lie about something unimportant —*vi.* **fibbed, fib'bing** to tell a fib —**fib'ber** *n.*

fi·ber, fi·bre (fī'bər) *n.* [< L. *fibra*] **1.** a threadlike structure combining with others to form animal or vegetable tissue **2.** any substance that can be separated into threadlike parts for weaving, etc. **3.** a threadlike root **4.** texture **5.** character; nature —**fi'brous** (-brəs) *adj.*

fi'ber·board' *n.* a boardlike material made from pressed fibers of wood, etc., used in building

fi'ber·fill' *n.* a lightweight, fluffy filling for quilts, etc., made of synthetic fibers

Fi'ber·glas' (-glas') *a trademark for* finespun filaments of glass made into textiles or insulating material —*n.* [f-] this substance: usually **fiberglass, fiber glass**

fi·bril (fī'brəl) *n.* a small fiber

fi·bril·la·tion (fib'rə lā'shən) *n.* [< FIBRIL + -ATION] a rapid series of contractions of the heart, causing weak, irregular heartbeats

fi·brin (fī'brən) *n.* an elastic, threadlike, insoluble protein formed in the clotting of blood

fi·brin·o·gen (fī brin'ə jən) *n.* [< prec. + -GEN] a protein in the blood from which fibrin is formed

fi·broid (fī'broid) *adj.* like or composed of fibrous tissue, as a tumor

fi·bro·sis (fī brō'sis) *n.* an abnormal increase in the amount of fibrous connective tissue in an organ or tissue —**fi·brot'ic** (-brät'ik) *adj.*

fib·u·la (fib'yoo lə) *n., pl.* **-lae** (-lē'), **-las** [L., a clasp] the long, thin outer bone of the lower leg

-fic [< L. *facere*, make] *a suffix meaning* making, creating [*terrific*]

FICA Federal Insurance Contributions Act

-fication [see -FIC] *a suffix meaning* a making, creating [*glorification*]

fich·u (fish'ōō) *n.* [Fr.] a three-cornered lace or muslin cape worn over the shoulders by women

fick·le (fik'l) *adj.* [OE. *ficol*] changeable or unstable in affection, interest, etc —**fick'le·ness** *n.*

fic·tion (fik'shən) *n.* [< L. *fingere*, to form] **1.** an imaginary statement, story, etc. **2.** any literary work with imaginary characters and events, as a novel, play, etc. **3.** such works collectively —**fic'tion·al, fic'tive** *adj.* —**fic'tion·al·ly** *adv.*

fic'tion·al·ize' (-'l īz') *vt.* **-ized', -iz'ing** to deal with (historical events) as fiction

fic·ti·tious (fik tish'əs) *adj.* **1.** of or like fiction; imaginary **2.** pretended; false **3.** assumed for disguise [a *fictitious* name] —**fic·ti'tious·ly** *adv.*

fid·dle (fid''l) *n.* [OE. *fithele*] any stringed instrument played with a bow, esp. the violin —*vt.* **-dled, -dling** [Colloq.] to play (a tune) on a fiddle —*vi.* **1.** [Colloq.] to play on a fiddle **2.** to tinker (*with*) nervously —**fiddle away** to waste (time) —**fid'dler** *n.*

fiddler crab a small, burrowing crab

fid'dle·sticks' *interj.* nonsense!

fi·del·i·ty (fə del'ə tē, fī-) *n., pl.* **-ties** [< L. *fides*, faith] **1.** faithful devotion to duty; loyalty **2.** accuracy of description, sound reproduction, etc.

fidg·et (fij'it) *n.* [< ME. *fichen*] a restless or nervous state, esp. in the phrase **the fidgets** —*vi.* to make restless or nervous movements —**fidg'et·y** *adj.*

fi·du·ci·ar·y (fi dōō'shē er'ē) *adj.* [< L. *fiducia*, trust] holding or held in trust —*n., pl.* **-ies** a trustee

fie (fī) *interj.* for shame!

fief (fēf) *n.* [Fr.: see FEE] in feudalism, heritable land held by a vassal

FIDDLER CRAB (width to 1 2/3 in.; length to 1 in.)

field (fēld) *n.* [OE. *feld*] **1.** a wide stretch of open land **2.** a piece of cleared land for crops or pasture **3.** a piece of land used for a particular purpose [a landing *field*] **4.** any wide, unbroken expanse [a *field* of ice] **5.** *a*) a battlefield *b*) a battle **6.** a realm of knowledge or work **7.** the background, as on a flag **8.** an area where athletic events are held, or a part of it used for contests in jumping, the shot put, etc. **9.** all the entrants in a contest **10.** *Physics* a space within which magnetic or electrical lines of force are active —*adj.* of, in, on, or growing in a field —*vt.* 1. to stop or catch and return (a baseball, etc.) 2. to put (a player) into active play —*vi.* to play a defensive position in baseball, etc. —**play the field** to expand one's activities to a broad area —**field'er** *n.*

field day 1. a day of military exercises, or of athletic events 2. a day of enjoyably exciting events or highly successful activity

field glass a small, portable, binocular telescope: *usually used in pl.* (**field glasses**)

field goal 1. *Basketball* a basket toss made from play, scoring two points 2. *Football* a goal kicked from the field, scoring three points

field hand a hired farm laborer

field hockey *same as* HOCKEY (sense 2)

Field·ing (fēl'diŋ), **Henry** 1707–54; Eng. novelist

field marshal in some armies, an officer of the highest rank

field'-test' *vt.* to test (a device, method, etc.) under operating conditions

field'work' *n.* 1. any temporary fortification made by troops in the field 2. the work of collecting scientific data in the field —**field'work'er** *n.*

fiend (fēnd) *n.* [OE. *feond*] 1. an evil spirit; devil 2. an inhumanly wicked person 3. [Colloq.] an addict *[a dope fiend, fresh-air fiend]*

fiend'ish *adj.* inhumanly wicked or cruel; devilish —**fiend'ish·ly** *adv.* —**fiend'ish·ness** *n.*

fierce (firs) *adj.* **fierc'er, fierc'est** [< L. *ferus*, wild] 1. violently cruel; savage 2. violent; uncontrolled 3. intensely eager 4. [Colloq.] very disagreeable —**fierce'ly** *adv.* —**fierce'ness** *n.*

fi·er·y (fī'ər ē) *adj.* **-i·er, -i·est** 1. containing or consisting of fire 2. like fire; glaring, hot, etc. 3. ardent 4. excitable —**fi'er·i·ness** *n.*

fi·es·ta (fi es'tə) *n.* [Sp. < L. *festus*, festal] 1. a religious festival 2. any gala celebration; holiday

fife (fīf) *n.* [G. *pfeife*] a small, shrill musical instrument like a flute —*vt., vi.* **fifed, fif'ing** to play on a fife —**fif'er** *n.*

fif·teen (fif'tēn') *adj., n.* [OE. *fiftene*] five more than ten; 15; XV —**fif'teenth'** (-tēnth') *adj., n.*

fifth (fifth) *adj.* [< OE. *fif*, five] 1. preceded by four others in a series; 5th 2. designating any of five equal parts —*n.* 1. the one following the fourth 2. any of the five equal parts of something; 1/5 3. a fifth of a gallon

Fifth Amendment the fifth amendment to the U.S. Constitution; specif., the clause protecting a person from being compelled to be a witness against himself

fifth column [orig. (1936) applied to those inside Madrid sympathetic to four columns of Franco's troops besieging it] a group of people within a country who secretly aid the enemy —**fifth columnist**

fifth wheel any superfluous person or thing

fif·ty (fif'tē) *adj., n., pl.* **-ties** [OE. *fiftig*] five times ten; 50; L —**the fifties** the numbers or years, as of a century, from 50 through 59 —**fif'ti·eth** (-ith) *adj., n.*

fif'ty-fif'ty *adj.* [Colloq.] even; equal —*adv.* [Colloq.] equally

fig (fig) *n.* [< L. *ficus*] 1. a small, sweet, pear-shaped fruit 2. the tree it grows on 3. a trifle *[not worth a fig]*

fig. 1. figurative(ly) 2. figure(s)

fight (fīt) *vi.* **fought, fight'ing** [OE. *feohtan*] to take part in a struggle, contest, etc., esp. against a foe or for a cause —*vt.* 1. to oppose physically or in battle 2. to struggle against 3. to engage in (a war, etc.) 4. to gain (one's way) by struggle —*n.* 1. any struggle, contest, or quarrel 2. power or readiness to fight —**fight it out** to fight until one side is defeated

fight'er *n.* 1. one that fights; esp., a prizefighter 2. a fast, highly maneuverable combat airplane

fig·ment (fig'mənt) *n.* [< L. *fingere*, make] something merely imagined or made up in the mind

fig·u·ra·tion (fig'yə rā'shən) *n.* 1. a forming; shaping 2. form; appearance 3. an ornamenting with figures or symbols —**fig'u·ra'tion·al** *adj.*

fig·u·ra·tive (fig'yər ə tiv) *adj.* 1. representing by means of a figure or symbol 2. not in its usual or exact sense; metaphorical 3. using figures of speech —**fig'u·ra·tive·ly** *adv.*

fig·ure (fig'yər) *n.* [< L. *fingere*, to form] 1. an outline or shape; form 2. the human form 3. a person thought of in a specified way *[a historical figure]* 4. a likeness of a person or thing 5. an illustration; diagram 6. a design; pattern 7. a pattern of musical notes 8. the symbol for a number *[the figure 5]* 9. [*pl.*] arithmetic 10. a sum of money 11. a figure of speech 12. *Geom.* a surface or

space bounded by lines or planes —*vt.* **-ured, -ur·ing** 1. to represent in definite form 2. to imagine 3. to ornament with a design 4. to compute with figures 5. [Colloq.] to believe; consider —*vi.* 1. to be conspicuous 2. to do arithmetic —**figure in** to include —**figure on** 1. to rely on 2. to plan on —**figure out** 1. to solve 2. to understand —**figure up** to add; total

fig'ured *adj.* 1. shaped; formed 2. having a design

fig'ure-head' *n.* 1. a carved figure on the bow of a ship 2. one put in a position of leadership, but having no real power or authority

figure of speech an expression, as a metaphor or simile, using words in an unusual or nonliteral sense to give beauty or vividness of style

figure skating ice skating in which the performer traces various elaborate figures on the ice

fig·u·rine (fig'yə rēn') *n.* [Fr.] a small sculptured or molded figure; statuette

Fi·ji (fē'jē) country on a group of islands (**Fiji Islands**) in the SW Pacific, north of New Zealand: c.7,000 sq. mi.; pop. 535,000; cap. Suva

fil·a·ment (fil'ə mənt) *n.* [< L. *filum*, thread] a very slender thread or threadlike part; specif., the fine wire in a light bulb or electron tube

fil·bert (fil'bərt) *n.* [ME. *filberde*] the cultivated hazelnut or the tree it grows on

filch (filch) *vt.* [ME. *filchen*] to steal (usually something small or petty); pilfer —**filch'er** *n.*

file¹ (fīl) *vt.* **filed, fil'ing** [< L. *filum*, thread] 1. to put (papers, etc.) in order for future reference 2. to dispatch (a news story) 3. to register (an application, etc.) 4. to put on public record 5. to initiate (a legal action) —*vi.* 1. to move in a line 2. to register or apply (*for*) —*n.* 1. a folder, cabinet, etc. for keeping papers in order 2. an orderly arrangement of papers, etc. 3. a line of persons or things, one behind another —**on file** kept as in a file for reference —**fil'er** *n.*

file² (fīl) *n.* [OE. *feol*] a steel tool with a ridged surface for smoothing or grinding —*vt.* **filed, fil'ing** to smooth or grind, as with a file —**fil'er** *n.*

fi·let (fi lā', fil'ā) *n.* [see FILLET] 1. a net or lace with a simple pattern on a square mesh background 2. *same as* FILLET (*n.* 2) —*vt.* **-leted'** (-lād'), **-let'ing** (-lā'iŋ) *same as* FILLET

fi·let mi·gnon (fi lā' min yōn') [Fr., lit., tiny fillet] a thick, round cut of lean beef tenderloin broiled

fil·i·al (fil'ē əl, fil'yəl) *adj.* [< L. *filius*, son] of, suitable to, or due from a son or daughter

fil·i·bus·ter (fil'ə bus'tər) *n.* [< Sp. < MDu. *vrijbuiter*, freebooter] 1. a member of a legislature who obstructs a bill by making long speeches 2. such obstruction of a bill —*vt., vi.* to obstruct (a bill) by such methods

fil·i·gree (fil'ə grē') *n.* [< Fr. < It. < L. *filum*, thread + *granum*, grain] 1. lacelike ornamental work of intertwined wire of gold, silver, etc. 2. any delicate work like this —*adj.* like or made of filigree —*vt.* **-greed', -gree'ing** to ornament with filigree

fil·ing (fīl'iŋ) *n.* a small piece scraped off with a file: *usually used in pl.*

Fil·i·pi·no (fil'ə pē'nō) *n., pl.* **-nos** [Sp.] a native of the Philippines —*adj.* Philippine

fill (fil) *vt.* [OE. *fyllan*] 1. to put as much as possible into 2. to occupy wholly *[the crowd filled the room]* 3. to occupy (a position, etc.) 4. to put a person into (a position, etc.) 5. to supply the things called for in (an order, etc.) 6. to close or plug (holes, cracks, etc.) 7. to satisfy the hunger of —*vi.* to become full —*n.* 1. enough to make full or to satisfy 2. anything that fills —**fill in** 1. to fill with some substance 2. to complete by supplying something 3. to be a substitute —**fill out** 1. to make or become larger, etc. 2. to make (a document, etc.) complete by inserting data —**fill up** to make or become completely full —**fill'er** *n.*

fil·let (fil'it; *for n. 2 & v. usually* fil'ā, fi lā') *n.* [< L. *filum*, thread] 1. a thin strip or band, as a headband for the hair 2. a boneless, lean piece of meat or fish —*vt.* to bone and slice (meat or fish)

fill'-in' *n.* 1. one that fills a vacancy or gap 2. [Colloq.] a brief summary of the pertinent facts

fill'ing *n.* a substance used to fill something, as gold put into a prepared cavity in a tooth

filling station *same as* SERVICE STATION

fil·lip (fil'əp) *n.* [< FLIP¹] 1. a snap made by a finger held down by the thumb and then suddenly released 2. something stimulating —*vt.* to strike or snap with a fillip

Fill·more (fil'môr), **Mill·ard** (mil'ərd) 1800–74; 13th president of the U.S. (1850–53)

fil·ly (fil'ē) *n., pl.* **-lies** [< ON. *fylja*] **1.** a young female horse **2.** [Colloq.] a vivacious girl

film (film) *n.* [OE. *filmen*] **1.** a fine, thin skin, coating, etc. **2.** a flexible cellulose material covered with a substance sensitive to light and used in photography **3.** a haze or blur **4.** a motion picture —*vt., vi.* **1.** to cover or be covered as with a film **2.** to make a motion picture (of) —**film'er** *n.*

film·ic (fil'mik) *adj.* of or concerning motion pictures

film'strip' *n.* a strip of film with stills of pictures, charts, etc. arranged in a sequence for projection separately and used in teaching, etc.

film'y *adj.* **-i·er, -i·est 1.** hazy, gauzy, etc. **2.** covered as with a film —**film'i·ness** *n.*

fil·ter (fil'tər) *n.* [< ML. *filtrum,* FELT¹] **1.** a device or substance for straining out solid particles, impurities, etc. from a liquid or gas passed through it **2.** a device for absorbing certain light rays [a color *filter* for a camera lens] —*vt., vi.* **1.** to pass through or as through a filter **2.** to remove with a filter

fil'ter·a·ble *adj.* that can be filtered: also **fil'tra·ble** (-trə b'l) —**fil'ter·a·bil'i·ty** *n.*

filter tip 1. a cigarette with a tip of cellulose, cotton, etc. for filtering the smoke **2.** such a tip

filth (filth) *n.* [OE. *fylthe*] **1.** foul dirt **2.** obscenity —**filth'i·ness** *n.* —**filth'y** *adj.* **-i·er, -i·est**

fil·trate (fil'trāt) *vt.* **-trat·ed, -trat·ing** to filter —*n.* a filtered liquid —**fil·tra'tion** *n.*

fin (fin) *n.* [OE. *finn*] **1.** any of several winglike, membranous organs on the body of a fish, dolphin, etc., used in swimming **2.** anything like this

fi·na·gle (fə nā'g'l) *vi., vt.* **-gled, -gling** [< ?] [Colloq.] to use, or get by, craftiness or trickery —**fi·na'gler** *n.*

fi·nal (fī'n'l) *adj.* [< L. *finis,* end] **1.** of or coming at the end; last **2.** deciding; conclusive —*n.* **1.** anything final **2.** [*pl.*] the last of a series of contests **3.** a final examination —**fi·nal'i·ty** (-nal'ə tē) *n., pl.* **-ties** —**fi'nal·ly** *adv.*

fi·na·le (fə nä'lē) *n.* [It.] the concluding part of a musical work, etc.

fi'nal·ist *n.* a contestant who competes in the finals

fi'nal·ize' *vt.* **-ized', -iz'ing** to make final; complete —**fi'nal·i·za'tion** *n.*

fi·nance (fə nans', fī'nans) *n.* [< L. *finis,* end] **1.** [*pl.*] money resources, income, etc. **2.** the science of managing money matters —*vt.* **-nanced', -nanc'ing** to supply or get money for —**fi·nan'cial** (-nan'shəl) *adj.* —**fi·nan'cial·ly** *adv.*

fin·an·cier (fin'ən sir', fī'nan-) *n.* [Fr.] one skilled in finance

finch (finch) *n.* [OE. *finc*] any of a group of small songbirds, including the canary, sparrow, etc.

find (fīnd) *vt.* **found, find'ing** [OE. *findan*] **1.** to discover by chance; come upon **2.** to get by searching **3.** to perceive; learn **4.** to recover (something lost) **5.** to consider; think **6.** to reach; attain **7.** to decide and declare to be [to *find* him guilty] —*vi.* to announce a decision [the jury *found* for the accused] —*n.* **1.** a finding **2.** something found —**find out** to discover; learn

find'er *n.* **1.** one that finds **2.** a camera device that shows what will appear in the photograph

find'ing *n.* **1.** discovery **2.** something found **3.** [*often pl.*] the verdict of a judge, scholar, etc.

fine (fīn) *adj.* **fin'er, fin'est** [< L. *finis,* end] **1.** very good; excellent **2.** with no impurities; refined **3.** containing a specified proportion of pure metal: said of gold or silver **4.** clear and bright [*fine* weather] **5.** not heavy or coarse [*fine* sand] **6.** very thin or small [*fine* print] **7.** sharp [a *fine* edge] **8.** subtle; delicate [a *fine* distinction] **9.** too elegant —*adv.* **1.** in a fine manner **2.** [Colloq.] very well —*n.* a sum of money paid as a penalty —*vt.* **fined, fin'ing** to order to pay a fine —**fine'ly** *adv.* —**fine'ness** *n.*

fine art any of the art forms that include drawing, painting, sculpture, and ceramics, or, occasionally, architecture, literature, music, etc.: *usually used in pl.*

fin·er·y (fīn'ər ē) *n., pl.* **-ies** showy, elaborate decoration, esp. clothes, jewelry, etc.

fi·nesse (fi nes') *n.* [Fr.: see FINE] **1.** adroitness or skill **2.** the ability to handle delicate situations diplomatically **3.** cunning; craft **4.** *Bridge* an attempt to take a trick with a lower card while holding a higher card not in sequence with it —*vt., vi.* **-nessed', -ness'ing 1.** to manage by or use finesse **2.** *Bridge* to make a finesse with (a card)

fin·ger (fiŋ'gər) *n.* [OE.] **1.** any of the five jointed parts extending from the palm of the hand, esp. one other than

the thumb **2.** anything like a finger in shape or use —*vt.* **1.** to touch with the fingers; handle **2.** to play (an instrument) by using the fingers on strings, keys, etc. —**have (or keep) one's fingers crossed** to hope for something —**put one's finger on** to ascertain exactly

fin'ger·board' *n.* the part of a stringed instrument against which the strings are pressed to produce the tones

fin'gered *adj.* having fingers (of a specified kind or number) [thick-*fingered*]

fin'ger·ling (-liŋ) *n.* **1.** any small object **2.** a small fish about the length of a finger

fin'ger·nail' *n.* the horny substance on the upper part of the end joint of a finger

finger painting a painting done by using the fingers, hand, or arm to spread paints made of starch, glycerin, and pigments (**finger paints**) on wet paper —**fin'ger·paint'** *vi., vt.*

fin'ger·print' *n.* an impression of the lines and whorls on a finger tip, used to identify a person —*vt.* to take the fingerprints of

finger tip the tip of a finger —**have at one's finger tips** to have available for instant use

fin·i·al (fin'ē əl) *n.* [ult. < L. *finis,* end] a decorative part at the tip of a spire, lamp-shade support, etc.

fin·ick·y (fin'i kē) *adj.* [< FINE] too particular; fussy: also **fin'i·cal** (-k'l), **fin'icking**

fi·nis (fin'is, fī'nis) *n., pl.* **-nis·es** [L.] the end; finish

fin·ish (fin'ish) *vt.* [< L. *finis,* end] **1.** to bring to an end **2.** to come to the end of **3.** to use up; consume **4.** to give final touches to; perfect **5.** to give a desired surface effect to —*vi.* to come to an end — FINIAL
n. **1.** the last part; end **2.** *a)* anything used to finish a surface, etc. *b)* the finished effect **3.** means or manner of completing or perfecting **4.** polish in manners, speech, etc. —**finish off 1.** to end **2.** to kill or ruin —**finish with** to bring to an end —**fin'ished** *adj.* —**fin'ish·er** *n.*

fi·nite (fī'nīt) *adj.* [< L. *finis,* end] **1.** having definable limits; not infinite **2.** *Gram.* having limits of person, number, and tense: said of a verb that can be used in a predicate —**fi'nite·ly** *adv.*

fink (fiŋk) *n.* [< ?] [Slang] an informer or strikebreaker

Fin·land (fin'lənd) country in N Europe: 130,119 sq. mi.; pop. 4,696,000; cap. Helsinki

Finn (fin) *n.* a native or inhabitant of Finland

Finn. Finnish

fin·nan had·die (fin'ən had'ē) [prob. < *Findhorn* (Scotland) *haddock*] smoked haddock: also **finnan haddock**

Finn·ish (fin'ish) *adj.* of Finland, its people, their language, etc. —*n.* the language of the Finns

fiord (fyôrd) *n.* [Norw. < ON. *fjörthr*] a narrow inlet of the sea bordered by steep cliffs

fir (fur) *n.* [OE. *fyrh*] **1.** a cone-bearing evergreen tree related to the pine **2.** its wood

fire (fīr) *n.* [OE. *fyr*] **1.** the flame, heat, and light of combustion **2.** something burning, as fuel in a furnace **3.** a destructive burning [a forest *fire*] **4.** strong feeling; ardor **5.** a discharge of firearms —*vt., vi.* **fired, fir'ing 1.** to start burning **2.** to supply with fuel **3.** to bake (bricks, etc.) in a kiln **4.** to excite or become excited **5.** to shoot (a gun, bullet, etc.) **6.** to hurl or direct with force [to *fire* questions] **7.** to dismiss from a job; discharge —**catch (on) fire** to ignite —**on fire 1.** burning **2.** greatly excited —**under fire** under attack —**fir'er** *n.*

fire'arm' *n.* any hand weapon from which a shot is fired by explosive force, as a rifle or pistol

fire'base' *n.* a military base in a combat zone, from which artillery, rockets, etc. are fired

fire'bomb' *n.* an incendiary bomb —*vt.* to attack or damage with a firebomb

fire'brand' *n.* **1.** a piece of burning wood **2.** one who stirs up others to revolt or strife

fire'break' *n.* a strip of land cleared to stop the spread of fire, as in a forest

fire'brick' *n.* a brick made of clay (**fire clay**) that can withstand great heat, used to line furnaces, etc.

fire'bug' *n.* [Colloq.] one who deliberately sets fire to buildings, etc.; pyromaniac

fire'crack'er *n.* a roll of paper containing an explosive, set off as a noisemaker at celebrations, etc.

fire'damp' *n.* a gas, largely methane, formed in coal mines, explosive when mixed with air

fire'dog' *n. same as* ANDIRON

fire engine a motor truck with equipment for fighting fires

fire escape a ladder, outside stairway, etc. for escape from a burning building

fire extinguisher a portable device containing chemicals for spraying on a fire to put it out

fire'fight'er *n.* a person who helps fight fires —**fire'fight'-ing** *n.*

fire'fly' *n., pl.* -**flies'** a winged beetle whose abdomen glows with a luminescent light

fire'man (-mən) *n., pl.* -**men** 1. a man whose work is fighting fires 2. a man who tends a fire in a furnace, etc.

fire'place' *n.* a place for a fire, esp. an open place built in a wall

fire'plug' *n.* a street hydrant to which a hose can be attached for fighting fires

fire'proof' *adj.* not easily destroyed by fire —*vt.* to make fireproof

fire sale a sale of goods damaged in a fire

fire'side' *n.* 1. the space around a fireplace 2. home or home life

fire'storm' *n.* an intense fire over a wide area, as one caused by an atomic explosion

fire tower a tower used as a lookout for forest fires

fire'trap' *n.* a building easily set afire or hard to escape from in case of fire

fire'wa'ter *n.* [Colloq.] alcoholic liquor

fire'wood' *n.* wood used as fuel

fire'works' *n.pl.* 1. firecrackers, rockets, etc., used for noisy or brilliant displays, as in celebrations: *sometimes used in sing.* 2. a display of or as of fireworks

firing line 1. the line from which gunfire is directed at the enemy 2. any vulnerable front position

firm[1] (furm) *adj.* [< L. *firmus*] 1. solid; hard 2. not moved easily; fixed 3. not fluctuating; steady 4. resolute; constant *[a firm faith]* 5. showing determination; strong 6. definite; final *[a firm contract]* *vt., vi.* to make or become firm —**firm'ly** *adv.* —**firm'ness** *n.*

firm[2] (furm) *n.* [< It. < L. *firmus*, firm] a business company

fir·ma·ment (fur'mə mənt) *n.* [< L. *firmus*, firm] the sky, viewed poetically as a solid arch or vault

first (furst) *adj.* [OE. *fyrst*] 1. before any others; 1st 2. earliest 3. foremost in rank, importance, etc. —*adv.* 1. before any other person or thing 2. for the first time 3. sooner; preferably —*n.* 1. any person or thing that is first 2. the beginning 3. the winning place, as in a race 4. low gear

first aid emergency treatment for injury, etc. before regular medical aid is available —**first'-aid'** *adj.*

first'born' *adj.* born first in a family; oldest —*n.* the first-born child

first'-class' *adj.* 1. of the highest class, quality, etc. 2. designating or of the most expensive accommodations 3. designating or of the most expensive regular class of sealed mail —*adv.* 1. with first-class accommodations 2. by first-class mail

first finger the finger next to the thumb

first'hand' *adj., adv.* from the original producer or source; direct

first lady [*often* F- L-] the wife of the U.S. president

first lieutenant *U.S. Mil.* an officer ranking above a second lieutenant

first'ly *adv.* in the first place; first

first mate a merchant ship's officer next in rank below the captain: also **first officer**

first person that form of a pronoun (as *I* or *we*) or verb (as *do*) that refers to the speaker

first'-rate' *adj.* of the highest quality, class, etc.; excellent —*adv.* [Colloq.] very well

first'-string' *adj.* [Colloq.] *Sports* that is the first choice for regular play at the specified position

firth (furth) *n.* [< ON. *fjörthr*] a narrow inlet or arm of the sea

fis·cal (fis'kəl) *adj.* [< L. *fiscus*, public chest] 1. relating to the public treasury or revenues 2. financial —**fis'cal·ly** *adv.*

fish (fish) *n., pl.* **fish**: in referring to different species, **fish'es** [OE. *fisc*] 1. any of a large group of coldblooded animals living in water and having backbones, gills for breathing, and fins 2. the flesh of a fish used as food —*vi.* 1. to catch or try to catch fish 2. to try to get something indirectly (often with *for*) —*vt.* to grope for, find, and bring to view (often with *out*)

fish'er *n.* 1. a fisherman 2. a flesh-eating animal related to the marten, larger than a weasel

fish'er·man (-mən) *n., pl.* -**men** 1. a person who fishes for sport or for a living 2. a ship used in fishing

fish'er·y *n., pl.* -**ies** 1. the business of catching fish 2. a place where fish are caught or bred

fish'eye' lens a camera lens designed for a full 180° field of vision

fish'hook' *n.* a hook, usually barbed, for catching fish

fish'ing *n.* the catching of fish for sport or for a living

fishing rod a slender pole with an attached line, hook, and usually a reel, used in fishing

fish'mon'ger (-muŋ'gər) *n.* a dealer in fish

fish'wife' *n., pl.* -**wives'** a coarse, scolding woman

fish'y *adj.* -**i·er**, -**i·est** 1. like a fish in odor, taste, etc. 2. dull; without expression *[a fishy stare]* 3. [Colloq.] questionable; odd —**fish'i·ness** *n.*

fis·sion (fish'ən) *n.* [< L. *findere*, to split] 1. a splitting apart; cleavage 2. *same as* NUCLEAR FISSION 3. *Biol.* a form of asexual reproduction in which the parent organism divides into two or more parts, each becoming an independent individual —**fis'sion·a·ble** *adj.*

fis·sure (fish'ər) *n.* [see prec.] 1. a cleft or crack 2. a dividing or breaking into parts —*vt., vi.* -**sured**, -**sur·ing** to crack or split apart

fist (fist) *n.* [OE. *fyst*] a hand with the fingers closed tightly into the palm

fist·ic (fis'tik) *adj.* [Colloq.] having to do with boxing; pugilistic

fis·ti·cuffs (fis'ti kufs') *n.pl.* a fight, or the art of fighting, with the fists

fis·tu·la (fis'choo lə) *n., pl.* -**las**, -**lae'** (-lē') [L.] an abnormal hollow passage, as from an abscess, cavity, etc. to the skin —**fis'tu·lous** *adj.*

fit[1] (fit) *vt.* **fit'ted** or **fit**, **fit'ted**, **fit'ting** [ME. *fitten*] 1. to be suitable to 2. to be the proper size, shape, etc. for 3. to make or adjust so as to fit 4. to make suitable or qualified 5. to equip; outfit —*vi.* 1. to be suitable or proper 2. to have the proper size or shape —*adj.* **fit'ter**, **fit'test** 1. suited to some purpose, function, etc. 2. proper; right 3. healthy —*n.* the manner of fitting *[a tight fit]* —**fit'ly** *adv.* —**fit'ness** *n.* —**fit'ter** *n.*

fit[2] (fit) *n.* [OE. *fitt*, conflict] 1. any sudden, uncontrollable attack *[a fit of coughing]* 2. a temporary outburst, as of feeling, activity, etc. 3. a seizure involving convulsions or loss of consciousness —**by fits (and starts)** in an irregular way —**have** (or **throw**) **a fit** [Colloq.] to become very angry or upset

fit'ful (-fəl) *adj.* characterized by intermittent activity; spasmodic —**fit'ful·ly** *adv.*

fit'ting *adj.* suitable; proper —*n.* 1. an adjustment or trying on of clothes, etc. for fit 2. a part used to join or adapt other parts 3. *[pl.]* fixtures

five (fiv) *adj., n.* [OE. *fif*] one more than four; 5; V

five'-and-ten'-cent' store a store that sells a wide variety of inexpensive merchandise: also **five'-and-ten'** *n.*

fix (fiks) *vt.* [< L. *figere*, fasten] 1. to fasten firmly 2. to set firmly in the mind 3. to direct (one's eyes) steadily at something 4. to make rigid 5. to make permanent 6. to establish (a date, etc.) definitely 7. to set in order; adjust 8. to repair; mend 9. to prepare (food or meals) 10. [Colloq.] to influence the result or action of (a race, jury, etc.) as by bribery 11. [Colloq.] to punish —*vi.* 1. to become fixed 2. [Dial.] to prepare or intend —*n.* 1. the position of a ship, etc. determined from the bearings of two known positions 2. [Colloq.] a predicament 3. [Slang] a situation that has been fixed (sense 10) 4. [Slang] an injection of a narcotic by an addict —**fix on** (or **upon**) to choose —**fix up** [Colloq.] 1. to repair 2. to set in order; arrange —**fix'a·ble** *adj.* —**fix'er** *n.*

fix·a·tion (fik sā'shən) *n.* 1. a fixing or being fixed 2. an exaggerated preoccupation 3. a remaining at an early stage of libidinal development

fix·a·tive (fik'sə tiv) *adj.* that is able to or tends to make permanent, prevent fading, etc. —*n.* a fixative substance

fixed (fikst) *adj.* 1. firmly in place 2. clearly established 3. steady; resolute 4. obsessive *[a fixed idea]* —**fix·ed·ly** (fik'sid lē) *adv.*

fix·ings (fik'siŋz) *n.pl.* [Colloq.] accessories or trimmings

fix·i·ty (fik'sə tē) *n.* 1. a being fixed; steadiness; permanence 2. *pl.* -**ties** anything fixed

fix·ture (fiks'chər) *n.* [see FIX] 1. anything firmly in place 2. any attached piece of equipment in a house, etc. 3. a person long-established in a place or job

fizz (fiz) *n.* [echoic] 1. a hissing, bubbling sound 2. an effervescent drink —*vi.* **fizzed**, **fizz'ing** 1. to make a bubbling sound 2. to effervesce

fiz·zle (fiz'l) *vi.* **-zled, -zling** [< ME.] **1.** to make a hissing or sputtering sound **2.** [Colloq.] to fail, esp. after a good start —*n.* **1.** a hissing or sputtering sound **2.** [Colloq.] a failure

fjord (fyôrd) *n. same as* FIORD

fl. 1. [L. *floruit*] (he or she) flourished **2.** fluid

Fla., FL Florida

flab (flab) *n.* [< FLABBY] [Colloq.] sagging flesh

flab·ber·gast (flab'ər gast') *vt.* [< ? FLABBY + AGHAST] [Colloq.] to amaze; dumbfound

flab·by (flab'ē) *adj.* **-bi·er, -bi·est** [< FLAP] **1.** lacking firmness; limp and soft **2.** lacking force; weak —**flab'bi·ly** *adv.* —**flab'bi·ness** *n.*

flac·cid (flak'sid, flas'id) *adj.* [< L. *flaccus*] **1.** limp and soft; flabby **2.** weak; feeble —**flac·cid'i·ty** *n.* —**flac'cid·ly** *adv.*

‡**fla·con** (flä kôn') *n.* [Fr.] a small flask with a stopper, for perfume, etc.

flag¹ (flag) *n.* [< ? FLAG⁴, to flutter] a cloth with colors, patterns, etc. used as a symbol of a nation, state, organization, etc., or as a signal —*vt.* **flagged, flag'ging** to signal as with a flag; esp., to signal to stop (often with *down*) —**flag'ger** *n.*

flag² (flag) *n.* [< ON. *flaga*, slab of stone] *same as* FLAGSTONE —*vt.* **flagged, flag'ging** to pave with flagstones

flag³ (flag) *n.* [ME. *flagge*] any of various irises with white, blue, or yellow flowers

flag⁴ (flag) *vi.* **flagged, flag'ging** [< ? ON. *flakka*, to flutter] **1.** to become limp **2.** to grow weak or tired

flag·el·lant (flaj'ə lənt) *n.* [see FLAGELLATE] one who whips himself or has himself whipped as for religious discipline —*adj.* engaging in flagellation

flag·el·late (flaj'ə lāt') *vt.* **-lat'ed, -lat'ing** [< L. *flagellum*, a whip] to whip; flog —*adj.* having flagella or shaped like a flagellum —**flag'el·la'tion** *n.*

fla·gel·lum (flə jel'əm) *n., pl.* **-la** (-ə), **-lums** [L.: see prec.] **1.** *Biol.* a whiplike part serving as an organ of locomotion in certain cells, bacteria, etc. **2.** *Bot.* a threadlike shoot or runner

flag·ging¹ (flag'iŋ) *adj.* weakening or drooping

flag·ging² (flag'iŋ) *n.* flagstones or a pavement made of flagstones

fla·gi·tious (flə jish'əs) *adj.* [< L. < *flagitare*, to demand] shamefully wicked; vile and scandalous —**fla·gi'tious·ly** *adv.* —**fla·gi'tious·ness** *n.*

flag·on (flag'ən) *n.* [< LL. *flasca*] a container for liquids, with a handle, a spout, and, often, a lid

flag'pole' *n.* a pole on which a flag is raised and flown: also **flag'staff'**

fla·grant (flā'grənt) *adj.* [< L. *flagrare*, to blaze] glaringly bad; notorious; outrageous —**fla'gran·cy** (-grən sē) **fla'grance** *n.* —**fla'grant·ly** *adv.*

flag'ship' *n.* the ship that carries the commander of a fleet or squadron and displays his flag

flag'stone' *n.* a flat piece of hard stone used in paving

flail (flāl) *n.* [< L. *flagellum*, a whip] a farm tool for threshing grain by hand —*vt., vi.* **1.** to thresh with a flail **2.** to beat **3.** to move (one's arms) like flails

flair (fler) *n.* [< L. *fragrare*, to smell] **1.** keen, natural discernment **2.** an aptitude; knack **3.** [Colloq.] smartness in style; dash

flak (flak) *n.* [G. acronym] **1.** the fire of antiaircraft guns **2.** strong criticism: also **flack**

flake (flāk) *n.* [< Scand.] **1.** a small, thin mass [a *flake* of snow] **2.** a thin piece split off; chip —*vt., vi.* **flaked, flak'ing 1.** to form into flakes **2.** to chip off in flakes —**flak'er** *n.*

flak'y *adj.* **-i·er, -i·est 1.** containing or made up of flakes **2.** breaking easily into flakes **3.** [Slang] very eccentric —**flak'i·ness** *n.*

FLAIL

‡**flam·bé** (flän bā') *adj.* [Fr.] served with a brandy or rum sauce set afire to flame —*n.* a dessert so served

flam·beau (flam'bō) *n., pl.* **-beaux** (-bōz), **-beaus** [Fr. < L. *flamma*, a flame] a lighted torch

flam·boy·ant (flam boi'ənt) *adj.* [Fr.: see prec.] **1.** flame-like or brilliant **2.** too showy; ornate **3.** *Archit.* characterized by flamelike tracery and florid decoration —**flam·boy'ance** *n.* —**flam·boy'ant·ly** *adv.*

flame (flām) *n.* [< L. *flamma*] **1.** the burning gas of a fire, appearing as a tongue of light **2.** the state of burning with a blaze **3.** a thing like a flame **4.** an intense emotion **5.** a sweetheart: now humorous —*vi.* **flamed, flam'ing 1.** to burst into flame **2.** to grow red or hot **3.** to become excited —**flame up** (or **out**) to burst out as in flames —**flam'ing** *adj.*

fla·men·co (flə meŋ'kō) *n.* [Sp.] **1.** Spanish gypsy style of music or dancing **2.** *pl.* **-cos** a song or dance in this style

flame'out' *n.* a failure of combustion in a jet engine during flight

flame thrower a military weapon for shooting a stream of flaming gasoline, oil, etc.

fla·min·go (flə miŋ'gō) *n., pl.* **-gos, -goes** [Port. < Sp. *flama*, flame] a tropical wading bird with long legs, a long neck, and bright pink or red feathers

flam·ma·ble (flam'ə b'l) *adj.* easily set on fire: term now preferred to INFLAMMABLE —**flam'ma·bil'i·ty** *n.*

Flan·ders (flan'dərz) region in NW Europe, in France, Belgium, & the Netherlands

flange (flanj) *n.* [< ? ME.] a projecting rim on a wheel, rail, etc., to hold it in place, give strength, etc. —*vt.* **flanged, flang'ing** to put a flange on

FLANGE

flank (flaŋk) *n.* [< OFr. *flanc*] **1.** the fleshy side of an animal between the ribs and the hip **2.** a cut of beef from this part **3.** the side of anything **4.** the right or left side of a military force —*vt.* **1.** to be at the side of **2.** to attack, or pass around, the side of (enemy troops) —*vi.* to be located at the side (with *on* or *upon*) —**flank'er** *n.*

flan·nel (flan''l) *n.* [prob. < W. *gwlan*, wool] **1.** a soft, loosely woven cloth of wool or cotton **2.** [*pl.*] trousers, etc. made of flannel

flan·nel·ette, flan·nel·et (flan'ə let') *n.* a soft, fleecy, cotton cloth

flap (flap) *n.* [ME. *flappe*] **1.** anything flat and broad hanging loose from one end [the *flap* of a pocket] **2.** the motion or sound of a swinging flap [the *flap* of an awning] **3.** a slap **4.** [Slang] a commotion; stir **5.** *Aeron.* a movable airfoil —*vt.* **flapped, flap'ping 1.** to slap **2.** to move back and forth or up and down, as wings

flap'jack' *n.* a pancake

flap·per (flap'ər) *n.* **1.** one that flaps **2.** [Colloq.] in the 1920's, a bold, unconventional young woman

flare (fler) *vi.* **flared, flar'ing** [ME. *fleare*] **1.** *a)* to blaze brightly *b)* to burn unsteadily **2.** to burst out suddenly, as in anger (often with *up* or *out*) **3.** to curve outward, as the lip of a bell —*vt.* to make flare —*n.* **1.** a bright, unsteady blaze **2.** a brightly flaming light for signaling, etc. **3.** an outburst, as of emotion **4.** a curving outward

flare'-up' *n.* a sudden outburst of flame or of anger, trouble, etc.

flash (flash) *vi.* [ME. *flashen*, to splash] **1.** to send out a sudden, brief light **2.** to sparkle **3.** to come or pass suddenly —*vt.* **1.** to cause to flash **2.** to send (news, etc.) swiftly —*n.* **1.** a sudden, brief light **2.** a brief moment **3.** a sudden, brief display [a *flash* of wit] **4.** a brief news item sent by radio, etc. **5.** a gaudy display —*adj.* happening swiftly or suddenly —**flash'er** *n.*

flash'back' *n.* an interruption in the continuity of a story, etc by telling or showing an earlier episode

flash'bulb' *n.* an electric light bulb giving a brief, dazzling light, for taking photographs

flash'cube' *n.* a rotating cube containing a flashbulb in each of four sides

flash flood a sudden flood

flash'-for'ward *n.* an interruption in the continuity of a story, etc. by telling or showing a future episode

flash'ing *n.* sheets of metal used to weatherproof joints, edges, etc., esp. of a roof

flash'light' *n.* **1.** a portable electric light, usually operated by batteries **2.** a brief, dazzling light for taking photographs at night or indoors

flash'y *adj.* **-i·er, -i·est 1.** dazzling for a little while **2.** gaudy; showy —**flash'i·ly** *adv.* —**flash'i·ness** *n.*

flask (flask) *n.* [< LL. *flasca*, bottle] **1.** any of various bottles used in laboratories, etc. **2.** a small, flat pocket container for liquor, etc.

flat¹ (flat) *adj.* **flat'ter, flat'test** [< ON. *flatr*] **1.** having a smooth, level surface **2.** lying spread out **3.** broad, even, and thin **4.** absolute [a *flat* denial] **5.** not fluctuating [a *flat* rate] **6.** tasteless; insipid [a *flat* drink] **7.** not interesting; dull **8.** emptied of air *[a flat tire]* **9.** without gloss *[flat paint]* **10.** *Art a)* lacking relief or perspective *b)* uniform in tint **11.** *Music* below the true pitch —*adv.* **1.** in a flat manner or position **2.** exactly *[ten seconds flat]* **3.** *Music* below the true pitch —*n.* **1.** a flat surface or part **2.** an expanse of level land **3.** a deflated tire **4.** *Music a)* a note one half step below another *b)* the symbol (♭) for such a note —*vt., vi.* **flat′ted, flat′ting** to make or become flat —**fall flat** to arouse no response —**flat′ly** *adv.* —**flat′ness** *n.*

flat² (flat) *n.* [< Scot. dial. *flet,* a floor] an apartment or suite of rooms

flat′boat′ *n.* a flat-bottomed boat, for carrying freight in shallow waters or on rivers

flat′car′ *n.* a railroad car without sides or roof, for carrying certain freight

flat′fish′ *n., pl.:* see FISH a flat-bodied fish with both eyes on the uppermost side, as the flounder

flat′foot′ *n.* **1.** a condition in which the instep arch of the foot has been flattened **2.** *pl.* **-foots′** [Slang] a policeman —**flat′-foot′ed** *adj.*

flat′i·ron *n. same as* IRON (sense 2)

flat′ten (-′n) *vt., vi.* to make or become flat or flatter

flat·ter (flat′ər) *vt.* [< Frank. *flat,* to smooth] **1.** to praise insincerely **2.** to try to please, as by praise **3.** to make seem more attractive than is so *[his portrait flatters him]* **4.** to gratify the vanity of —*vi.* to use flattery —**flatter** oneself to be smug or deluded in thinking *(that)* —**flat′-ter·er** *n.* —**flat′ter·ing·ly** *adv.*

flat′ter·y *n., pl.* **-ies 1.** a flattering **2.** insincere praise

flat′top′ *n.* [Slang] an aircraft carrier

flat·u·lent (flach′ə lənt, -yoo-) *adj.* [ult. < L. *flare,* to blow] **1.** of, having, or producing gas in the stomach or intestines **2.** windy in speech; pompous —**flat′u·lence,** **flat′u·len·cy** *n.* —**flat′u·lent·ly** *adv.*

flat′ware′ *n.* flat tableware

flat′worm′ *n.* any of a group of flattened worms with a soft, unsegmented body, as the tapeworm

Flau·bert (flō ber′), **Gus·tave** (güs täv′) 1821–80; Fr. novelist

flaunt (flônt) *vi., vt.* [< ? dial. *flant,* to strut] to show off proudly or defiantly —**flaunt′ing·ly** *adv.*

flau·tist (flôt′ist) *n.* [It. *flautista*] *same as* FLUTIST

fla·vor (flā′vər) *n.* [ult. < L. *flare,* to blow] **1.** *a)* the combined taste and smell of something *b)* taste in general **2.** *same as* FLAVORING **3.** characteristic quality —*vt.* to give flavor to Brit. sp. **fla′vour** —**fla′vor·ful** *adj.* —**fla′vor·less** *adj.*

fla′vor·ing *n.* an essence, extract, etc. that adds flavor to food or drink

flaw (flô) *n.* [prob. < Scand.] **1.** a break, scratch, crack, etc. that spoils something; blemish **2.** a defect; fault —*vt., vi.* to make or become faulty —**flaw′less** *adj.* —**flaw′-less·ly** *adv.* —**flaw′less·ness** *n.*

flax (flaks) *n.* [OE. *fleax*] **1.** a slender, erect plant with delicate, blue flowers: the seed (**flax′seed′**) yields linseed oil, and the fibers of the stem are spun into linen thread **2.** these fibers

flax′en (-′n) *adj.* **1.** of or made of flax **2.** pale-yellow

flay (flā) *vt.* [OE. *flean*] **1.** to strip off the skin of **2.** to criticize harshly —**flay′er** *n.*

flea (flē) *n.* [OE. *fleah*] a small, wingless, jumping insect that is a bloodsucking parasite as an adult

flea′bag′ *n.* [Slang] a very cheap hotel

flea′-bit′ten *adj.* **1.** bitten by or infested with fleas **2.** wretched; shabby

flea market an outdoor bazaar dealing mainly in cheap, secondhand goods

fleck (flek) *n.* [ON. *flekkr*] a spot, speck, or flake —*vt.* to spot; speckle

FLEA
(to 1/8 in. long)

fled (fled) *pt. & pp. of* FLEE

fledge (flej) *vi.* **fledged, fledg′ing** [< OE. *(un)flycge,* (un)fledged] to grow the feathers needed for flying —*vt.* **1.** to rear (a young bird) until it is able to fly **2.** to supply with feathers

fledg·ling (flej′lin) *n.* **1.** a young bird just fledged **2.** a young, inexperienced person Chiefly Brit. **fledge′ling**

flee (flē) *vi., vt.* **fled, flee′ing** [OE. *fleon*] **1.** to go swiftly or escape, as from danger, etc. **2.** to vanish

fleece (flēs) *n.* [OE. *fleos*] **1.** the wool covering a sheep or similar animal **2.** the amount of wool cut from a sheep at one shearing **3.** a soft, warm, napped fabric —*vt.* **fleeced, fleec′ing 1.** to shear fleece from **2.** to swindle —**fleec′er** *n.*

fleec′y *adj.* **-i·er, -i·est** made of, covered with, or like fleece —**fleec′i·ly** *adv.* —**fleec′i·ness** *n.*

fleet¹ (flēt) *n.* [OE. *fleot*] **1.** a number of warships under one command **2.** any group of ships, trucks, airplanes, etc. under one control

fleet² (flēt) *adj.* [< OE. *fleotan,* to float] swift; rapid — **fleet′ly** *adv.* —**fleet′ness** *n.*

fleet′ing *adj.* passing swiftly —**fleet′ing·ly** *adv.*

Flem·ing (flem′in) *n.* **1.** a native of Flanders **2.** a Flemish-speaking Belgian

Flem·ish (flem′ish) *adj.* of Flanders, the Flemings, or their language —*n.* the Low German language of Flanders

flesh (flesh) *n.* [OE. *flæsc*] **1.** the soft substance of the body; esp., the muscular tissue **2.** the pulpy part of fruits and vegetables **3.** meat **4.** the human body, as distinguished from the soul **5.** all mankind **6.** yellowish pink — **in the flesh 1.** alive **2.** in person —**one′s (own) flesh and blood** one's close relatives

flesh′ly *adj.* **1.** of the body **2.** sensual

flesh′pot′ *n.* **1.** orig., a pot for cooking meat **2.** *[pl.]* a place where luxuries and sensual pleasures are provided

flesh′y *adj.* **-i·er, -i·est 1.** plump; fat **2.** of or like flesh **3.** pulpy, as some fruits —**flesh′i·ness** *n.*

fleur-de-lis (flur′də lē′) *n., pl.* **fleurs-de-lis** (flur′də lēz′) [< OFr., flower of the lily] **1.** *same as* IRIS (sense 2) **2.** a lilylike emblem, the coat of arms of the kings of France

flew (floo) *pt. of* FLY¹

flex (fleks) *vt., vi.* [< L. *flectere,* to bend] **1.** to bend, as an arm **2.** to contract, as a muscle

flex·i·ble (flek′sə b′l) *adj.* **1.** able to bend without breaking **2.** easily influenced **3.** adjustable to change — **flex′i·bil′i·ty** *n.* —**flex′i·bly** *adv.*

flib·ber·ti·gib·bet (flib′ər tē jib′it) *n.* [< ?] an irresponsible, flighty person

FLEUR-DE-LIS

flick¹ (flik) *n.* [echoic] a light, quick stroke —*vt.* to strike, remove, etc. with a light, quick stroke

flick² (flik) *n.* [< FLICKER¹] [Slang] a movie —**the flicks** *n.* showing of a movie

flick·er¹ (flik′ər) *vi.* [OE. *flicorian*] **1.** to move with a quick, light, wavering motion **2.** to burn or shine unsteadily —*vt.* to make flicker —*n.* **1.** a flickering **2.** a flame or light that flickers **3.** a quick, passing look or feeling

flick·er² (flik′ər) *n.* [echoic of its cry] a woodpecker with wings colored golden on the underside

fli·er (flī′ər) *n.* **1.** a thing that flies **2.** an aviator **3.** a bus, train, etc. on a fast schedule **4.** a widely distributed handbill **5.** [Colloq.] a reckless gamble

flight¹ (flīt) *n.* [OE. *flyht*] **1.** the act, manner, or power of flying **2.** the distance flown **3.** a group of things flying together **4.** an airplane scheduled to fly a certain trip **5.** a trip by airplane **6.** a soaring above the ordinary *[a flight of fancy]* **7.** a set of stairs, as between landings

flight² (flīt) *n.* [< OE. *fleon,* to flee] a fleeing, as from danger —**put to flight** to force to flee

flight′less *adj.* not able to fly

flight′y *adj.* **-i·er, -i·est 1.** given to sudden whims; frivolous **2.** foolish; silly —**flight′i·ness** *n.*

flim·sy (flim′zē) *adj.* **-si·er, -si·est** [< ?] **1.** easily broken or damaged; fragile **2.** weak or inadequate *[a flimsy excuse]* —*n.* a sheet of thin paper —**flim′si·ly** *adv.* —**flim′-si·ness** *n.*

flinch (flinch) *vi.* [< OFr. *flenchir*] **1.** to draw back, as from a blow, difficulty, etc. **2.** to wince, as because of pain —*n.* a flinching

flin·ders (flin′dərz) *n.pl.* [< Scand.] splinters or fragments: chiefly in **break** (or **fly**) **into flinders**

fling (flin) *vt.* **flung, fling′ing** [< ON. *flengja,* to whip] **1.** to throw, esp. with force; hurl **2.** to put abruptly or violently **3.** to move (one's limbs, head, etc.) suddenly —*n.* **1.** a flinging **2.** a brief time of self-indulgence **3.** a spirited dance *[the Highland fling]* **4.** [Colloq.] a try

Flint (flint) city in SE Mich.: pop. 193,000

flint (flint) *n.* [OE.] **1.** a fine-grained, very hard, siliceous rock that makes sparks when struck with steel **2.** a piece of this, used to start a fire, etc. **3.** anything very hard

flint′lock′ *n.* **1.** a gunlock in which the powder is exploded by a spark produced by the striking of a flint against a metal plate **2.** an old-fashioned gun with such a lock

flint′y *adj.* **-i·er, -i·est 1.** of or containing flint **2.** like flint; very hard —**flint′i·ness** *n.*

flip¹ (flip) *vt.* **flipped, flip'ping** [echoic] **1.** to move with a quick jerk **2.** to snap (a coin) into the air with the thumb **3.** to turn or turn over —*vi.* **1.** to move jerkily **2.** [Slang] to lose self-control: also **flip one's lid** —*n.* a flipping

flip² (flip) *n.* [prob. < prec.] a sweetened drink of wine or liquor with egg, spices, etc.

flip³ (flip) *adj.* **flip'per, flip'pest** [contr. < FLIPPANT] [Colloq.] flippant; saucy; impertinent

flip'-flop' (-fläp') **1.** an acrobatic spring backward from feet to hands to feet **2.** an abrupt change, as to the opposite opinion —*vi.* **-flopped', -flop'ping** to do a flip-flop

flip'pant (-ənt) *adj.* [prob. < FLIP¹] frivolous and disrespectful; saucy —**flip'pan·cy** *n., pl.* **-cies**

flip·per (flip'ər) *n.* [< FLIP¹] **1.** a broad, flat limb, as of a seal, adapted for swimming **2.** a paddlelike rubber piece worn on each foot as a help in swimming

flip side [Colloq.] the reverse side (of a phonograph recording), esp. the less important side

flirt (flurt) *vt.* [< ?] to move jerkily *[the bird flirted its tail]* —*vi.* **1.** to make love without serious intentions **2.** to toy, as with an idea —*n.* **1.** a quick, jerky movement **2.** one who plays at love

flir·ta·tion (flər tā'shən) *n.* a flirting, or playing at love — **flir·ta·tious** *adj.* —**flir·ta'tious·ly** *adv.*

flit (flit) *vi.* **flit'ted, flit'ting** [< ON. *flytja*] to pass or fly lightly and rapidly; dart

flitch (flich) *n.* [OE. *flicce*] the cured and salted side of a hog; side of bacon —*vt.* to cut into flitches

fliv·ver (fliv'ər) *n.* [< ?] [Old Slang] a small, cheap automobile, esp. an old one

float (flōt) *n.* [< OE. *fleotan*, to float] **1.** anything that stays on the surface of a liquid, as a raft, a fishing-line cork, etc. **2.** a platform on wheels that carries a display or exhibit in a parade —*vi.* **1.** to stay on the surface of a liquid **2.** to drift gently on water, in air, etc. **3.** to move about aimlessly —*vt.* **1.** to cause to float **2.** to put into circulation *[float a bond issue]* **3.** to arrange for (a loan)

float'er *n.* **1.** one that floats **2.** one who illegally votes at several polling places **3.** one who changes his place of residence or work often

float'ing *adj.* **1.** that floats **2.** not fixed; moving about **3.** designating an unfunded, short-term debt **4.** *Med.* displaced and more movable *[a floating kidney]*

floating ribs the eleventh and twelfth pairs of ribs, not attached to the breastbone or other ribs

flock¹ (fläk) *n.* [OE. *flocc*, a troop] **1.** a group of certain animals, as sheep, birds, etc., living, eating, etc. together **2.** any group, as of church members —*vi.* to assemble or travel in a flock

flock² (fläk) *n.* [< L. *floccus*] **1.** a tuft of wool, cotton, etc. **2.** wool or cotton waste used as stuffing **3.** tiny fibers put on wallpaper, etc., to form a velvety surface or design

flock'ing (-iŋ) *n.* **1.** *same as* FLOCK² (sense 3) **2.** a material or surface with flock on it

floe (flō) *n.* [prob. < Norw. *flo*, layer] *same as* ICE FLOE

flog (fläg, flôg) *vt.* **flogged, flog'ging** [< ? L. *flagellare*] to beat with a stick, whip, etc. —**flog'ger** *n.*

flood (flud) *n.* [OE. *flod*] **1.** an overflowing of water on an area normally dry; deluge **2.** the rising of the tide **3.** a great outpouring, as of words —*vt.* **1.** to cover or fill, as with a flood **2.** to put too much water, fuel, etc. on or in —*vi.* **1.** to gush out in a flood **2.** to become flooded —**the Flood** *Bible* the great flood in Noah's time

flood'gate' *n.* **1.** a gate in a stream or canal, to control the flow of water **2.** anything like this in controlling an outburst

flood'light' *n.* **1.** a lamp that casts a broad beam of bright light **2.** such a light —*vt.* **-light'ed** or **-lit', -light'-ing** to illuminate by a floodlight

flood tide the rising tide

floor (flôr) *n.* [OE. *flor*] **1.** the inside bottom surface of a room **2.** any bottom surface *[the ocean floor]* **3.** a story in a building **4.** the part of a legislative chamber, stock exchange, etc. occupied by members **5.** the right to speak in an assembly **6.** a lower limit set on anything —*vt.* **1.** to furnish with a floor **2.** to knock down **3.** [Colloq.] *a)* to defeat *b)* to shock, confuse, etc. **4.** [Colloq.] to press (a car accelerator) to the floor

floor'board' *n.* **1.** a board in a floor **2.** the floor of an automobile, etc.

floor'ing *n.* **1.** a floor or floors **2.** material for making a floor

floor leader a member of a legislature chosen by his political party to direct its actions on the floor

floor plan a scale drawing of the layout of rooms, halls, etc. on one floor of a building

floor show a show presenting singers, dancers, etc. in a restaurant, nightclub, etc.

floor'walk'er *n.* formerly, a department store employee supervising sales, etc.: now often **floor manager**

floo·zy, floo·zie (flōō'zē) *n., pl.* **-zies** [Slang] a loose, disreputable woman

flop (fläp) *vt.* **flopped, flop'ping** [var. of FLAP] to flap or throw noisily and clumsily —*vi.* **1.** to move, drop, or flap around loosely or clumsily **2.** [Colloq.] to be a failure —*n.* **1.** the act or sound of flopping **2.** [Colloq.] a failure — **flop'py** *adj.* **-pi·er, -pi·est**

flop'house' *n.* [Colloq.] a cheap hotel

flo·ra (flôr'ə) *n.* [< L. *flos*, a flower] the plants of a specified region or time

flo'ral (-əl) *adj.* of, made of, or like flowers

Flor·ence (flôr'əns) city in C Italy: pop. 455,000 —**Flor'en·tine'** (-ən tēn') *adj., n.*

flo·res·cence (flô res''ns) *n.* [< L. *florere*, to bloom] a blooming or flowering —**flo·res'cent** *adj.*

flo·ret (flôr'it) *n.* [< L. *flos*, a flower] **1.** a small flower **2.** any of the small flowers making up the head of a composite plant

flo·ri·cul·ture (flôr'ə kul'chər) *n.* the cultivation of flowers —**flo'ri·cul'tur·al** *adj.*

flor·id (flôr'id) *adj.* [< L. *flos*, a flower] **1.** ruddy: said of the complexion **2.** showy; ornate —**flo·rid·i·ty** (flô rid'ə tē) *n.* —**flor'id·ly** *adv.*

Flor·i·da (flôr'ə də) SE State of the U.S.: 58,560 sq. mi.; pop. 6,789,000; cap. Tallahassee: abbrev. **Fla., FL** —**Flo·rid·i·an** (flô rid'ē ən) *adj., n.*

flor·in (flôr'in) *n.* [< L. *flos*, a flower] any of various European or S. African silver or gold coins

flo·rist (flôr'ist) *n.* [< L. *flos*, a flower] one who cultivates or sells flowers

floss (flôs, fläs) *n.* [prob. < L. *floccus*, tuft of wool] **1.** the soft, downy waste fibers of silk **2.** a soft thread or yarn, as of silk, used in embroidery **3.** a substance like this **4.** *same as* DENTAL FLOSS —*vt., vi.* to clean (the teeth) with dental floss —**floss'y** *adj.* **-i·er, -i·est**

flo·ta·tion (flō tā'shən) *n.* a floating; specif., the financing of a business, etc., as by selling an entire issue of bonds

flo·til·la (flō til'ə) *n.* [Sp., dim. of *flota*, a fleet] **1.** a small fleet **2.** a fleet of boats or small ships

flot·sam (flät'səm) *n.* [< MDu. *vloten*, to float] the wreckage of a ship or its cargo floating at sea: chiefly in **flotsam and jetsam**

flounce¹ (flouns) *vi.* **flounced, flounc'ing** [prob. < Scand.] to move with quick, flinging motions of the body, as in anger —*n.* the act of flouncing

flounce² (flouns) *n.* [< OFr. *froncir*, to wrinkle] a wide, ornamental ruffle, as on a skirt —*vt.* **flounced, flounc'ing** to trim with a flounce

floun·der¹ (floun'dər) *vi.* [? var. of FOUNDER] **1.** to struggle awkwardly, as in deep mud **2.** to speak or act in an awkward, confused way

floun·der² (floun'dər) *n.* [< Scand.] any of various fishes caught for food, as the halibut

flour (flour) *n.* [orig. flower (i.e., best) of meal] **1.** a fine, powdery substance produced by grinding and sifting grain, esp. wheat **2.** any finely powdered substance —*vt.* to put flour on or in —**flour'y** *adj.*

flour·ish (flur'ish) *vi.* [ult. < L. *flos*, a flower] **1.** to grow vigorously; thrive; prosper **2.** to be at the peak of development, etc. **3.** to make showy, wavy motions —*vt.* to brandish (a sword, etc.) —*n.* **1.** anything done in a showy way **2.** a brandishing **3.** decorative lines in writing **4.** a musical fanfare —**flour'ish·ing** *adj.*

flout (flout) *vt., vi.* [prob. < ME. *flouten*, play the flute] to show scorn or contempt (for) —*n.* a flouting

flow (flō) *vi.* [OE. *flowan*] **1.** to move as a liquid does **2.** to move gently and smoothly **3.** to pour out **4.** to be derived; proceed **5.** to hang loose *[flowing hair]* **6.** to rise, as the tide **7.** to be plentiful —*n.* **1.** a flowing, or the manner or rate of this **2.** anything that flows **3.** a continuous production

flow·er (flou'ər, flour) *n.* [< L. *flos*] **1.** the seed-producing structure of a flowering plant; blossom **2.** a plant cultivated for its blossoms **3.** the best or finest part —*vi.* **1.** to produce blossoms **2.** to reach the best period —**in flower** flowering

flow'er·et (-it) *n. same as* FLORET

flow'er·pot' *n.* a container in which to grow plants

flow'er·y *adj.* **-i·er, -i·est** 1. covered or decorated with flowers 2. full of ornate expressions and fine words — **flow'er·i·ness** *n.*

flown (flōn) *pp. of* FLY¹

flu (flōō) *n.* 1. *short for* INFLUENZA 2. popularly, a respiratory or intestinal infection caused by a virus

flub (flub) *vt., vi.* **flubbed, flub'bing** [< ? FL(OP) + (D)UB¹] [Colloq.] to botch (a job, chance, etc.) —*n.* [Colloq.] a blunder

fluc·tu·ate (fluk'chōō wāt') *vi.* **-at'ed, -at'ing** [< L. *fluctus,* a wave] to be continually varying in an irregular way —**fluc'tu·a'tion** *n.*

flue (flōō) *n.* [< ? OFr. *fluie,* a flowing] a shaft for the passage of smoke, hot air, etc., as in a chimney

flu·ent (flōō'ənt) *adj.* [< L. *fluere,* to flow] 1. flowing smoothly 2. able to write or speak easily, expressively, etc.

fluff (fluf) *n.* [? blend of *flue,* soft mass + PUFF] 1. soft, light down 2. a loose, soft mass, as of dust —*vt.* 1. to shake or pat until loose and fluffy 2. to bungle (one's lines), as in acting

fluff'y (-ē) *adj.* **-i·er, -i·est** like, or covered with, fluff; soft and feathery —**fluff'i·ness** *n.*

flu·id (flōō'id) *adj.* [< L. *fluere,* to flow] 1. that can flow; not solid 2. not settled or fixed [*fluid* plans] 3. moving gracefully 4. available for investment or as cash —*n.* a liquid or gas —**flu·id'i·ty, flu'id·ness** *n.* —**flu'id·ly** *adv.*

fluid dram a liquid measure equal to 1/8 fluid ounce

fluid ounce a liquid measure equal to 1/16 pint

fluke¹ (flōōk) *n.* [OE. *floc*] 1. a flatfish; esp., a flounder 2. a flatworm parasitic in internal organs of vertebrates

fluke² (flōōk) *n.* [prob. < prec.] 1. either of the pointed blades on an anchor, which catch in the ground 2. a barb or barbed head of an arrow, harpoon, etc. 3. either of the lobes of a whale's tail

fluke³ (flōōk) *n.* [< ?] [Colloq.] a lucky or unlucky outcome

fluk'y, fluk'ey *adj.* **-i·er, -i·est** [Colloq.] resulting from chance

flume (flōōm) *n.* [< L. *flumen,* river] 1. an inclined chute for carrying water to transport logs, etc. 2. a narrow gorge with a stream running through it

flung (fluŋ) *pt. & pp. of* FLING

flunk (fluŋk) *vt., vi.* [< ?] [Colloq.] to fail, as in schoolwork —**flunk out** [Colloq.] to send or be sent away from school because of failure

flun·ky (fluŋ'kē) *n., pl.* **-kies** [orig. Scot.] 1. one who obeys superiors in a servile way 2. one having minor or menial tasks Also **flun'key**

flu·o·resce (flōō'ə res', floo res') *vi.* **-resced', -resc'ing** to show or undergo fluorescence

flu·o·res·cence (-'ns) *n.* [ult. < L. *fluor,* flux] 1. the property of a substance, as fluorite, of producing light when acted upon by radiant energy 2. light so produced —**flu'o·res'cent** *adj.*

fluorescent lamp (or **tube**) a glass tube coated on the inside with a fluorescent substance that gives off light (**fluorescent light**) when mercury vapor in the tube is acted upon by a stream of electrons

fluor·i·date (flôr'ə dāt', floor'-) *vt.* **-dat'ed, -dat'ing** to add fluorides to (a water supply) in order to reduce tooth decay —**fluor'i·da'tion** *n.*

flu·o·ride (floor'īd, flōō'ə rīd') *n.* a compound of fluorine with another element or radical

flu·o·rine (floor'ēn; flōō'ə rēn', -rin) *n.* [< L. *fluor,* flux] a corrosive, greenish-yellow, gaseous chemical element: symbol, F; at. wt., 18.9984; at. no., 9

flu·o·rite (floor'īt, flōō'ə rīt') *n.* [see prec.] calcium fluoride, CaF_2, a transparent, crystalline mineral of various colors: also **flu·or** (flōō'ər), **fluor spar**

fluor·o·scope (floor'ə skōp') *n.* a machine for examining internal structures by viewing the shadows cast on a fluorescent screen by objects through which X-rays are directed —*vt.* **-scoped', -scop'ing** to examine with a fluoroscope —**fluor'o·scop'ic** (-skäp'ik) *adj.*

flur·ry (flur'ē) *n., pl.* **-ries** [< ?] 1. a sudden, brief rush of wind or fall of snow 2. a sudden commotion —*vt.* **-ried, -ry·ing** to confuse; agitate

flush¹ (flush) *vi.* [blend of FLASH & ME. *flusshen,* fly up suddenly] 1. to flow rapidly 2. to blush or glow 3. to be washed out with a sudden flow of water 4. to start up from cover: said of birds —*vt.* 1. to make flow 2. to clean or empty with a sudden flow of water, etc. 3. to make blush or glow 4. to excite 5. to drive (birds) from cover — *n.* 1. a rapid flow, as of water 2. a sudden, vigorous growth [the first *flush* of youth] 3. sudden excitement 4.

a blush; glow 5. a sudden feeling of heat, as in a fever — *adj.* 1. well supplied, esp. with money 2. abundant 3. ruddy 4. level or even (*with*) 5. direct; full [a blow *flush* in the face] —*adv.* 1. so as to be level 2. directly

flush² (flush) *n.* [< L. *fluere,* to flow] a hand of cards all in the same suit

flus·ter (flus'tər) *vt., vi.* [prob. < Scand.] to get confused or nervous —*n.* a flustered state

flute (flōōt) *n.* [< Pr. *flaüt*] 1. a high-pitched wind instrument consisting of a long, slender tube with finger holes and keys 2. an ornamental groove —*vi., vt.* **flut'ed, flut'ing** 1. to sing, speak, etc. in a flutelike tone 2. to play on a flute 3. to make ornamental grooves (in)

flut'ing *n.* 1. a series of ornamental grooves, as in a column 2. the act of one that flutes

flut'ist *n.* a flute player; flautist

FLUTE

flut·ter (flut'ər) *vi.* [< OE. *fleotan,* to float] 1. to flap the wings rapidly 2. to wave, move, or vibrate rapidly and irregularly —*vt.* to cause to flutter —*n.* 1. a fluttering movement 2. a state of excitement or confusion —**flut'ter·y** *adj.*

flu·vi·al (flōō'vē əl) *adj.* [< L. *fluere,* to flow] of, found in, or produced by a river

flux (fluks) *n.* [< L. *fluere,* to flow] 1. a flowing 2. a coming in of the tide 3. continual change 4. any abnormal discharge from the body 5. a substance used to help fuse metals together, as in soldering 6. *Physics* the rate of flow of energy, etc. over a surface —*vt.* to fuse (metals)

fly¹ (flī) *vi.* **flew, flown, fly'ing** [OE. *fleogan*] 1. to move through the air by using wings, as a bird, or in an aircraft 2. to be propelled through the air or through space, as a missile 3. to operate an aircraft 4. to wave or float in the air 5. to move or go swiftly 6. to flee 7. **flied, fly'ing** *Baseball* to hit a fly —*vt.* 1. to cause to float in air 2. to operate (an aircraft) 3. to travel over in an aircraft 4. to carry in an aircraft 5. to flee from —*n., pl.* **flies** 1. a flap that conceals a zipper, buttons, etc. in a garment 2. a flap serving as a tent door 3. *Baseball* a ball batted high 4. [*pl.*] *Theater* the space above a stage —**fly at** to attack by or as by springing forward —**fly out** *Baseball* to be put out by hitting a fly that is caught —**let fly (at)** 1. to shoot or throw (at) 2. to unleash a verbal attack (at) —**on the fly** [Colloq.] while in a hurry

fly² (flī) *n., pl.* **flies** [OE. *fleoge*] 1. any of a large group of insects with two transparent wings; esp., the housefly 2. a hooked lure for fishing, made to resemble an insect

fly'a·ble *adj.* suitable for flying

fly'-by-night' *adj.* not trustworthy, esp. financially —*n.* a fly-by-night person

fly'-cast' *vi.* **-cast', -cast'ing** to fish by casting artificial flies

fly'catch'er *n.* any of various small birds, as the pewee, that catch insects in flight

fly'er *n. same as* FLIER

fly'ing *adj.* 1. that flies or can fly 2. moving swiftly 3. hasty and brief 4. of or for aircraft or aviators —*n.* the action of one that flies

flying boat an airplane with a hull that permits it to land on and take off from water

flying buttress a buttress connected with a wall by an arch, serving to resist outward pressure

flying colors notable success

flying fish a fish with winglike pectoral fins that enable it to glide through the air

flying saucer *same as* UFO

fly'leaf' *n., pl.* **-leaves'** a blank leaf at the beginning or end of a book

fly'pa'per *n.* a sticky or poisonous paper set out to catch flies

fly'speck' *n.* 1. a speck of fly excrement 2. any tiny spot or petty flaw

fly'trap' *n.* a plant that catches insects

fly'weight' *n.* a boxer who weighs 112 pounds or less —*adj.* of flyweights

fly'wheel' *n.* a heavy wheel attached to a machine so as to regulate its speed and motion

FLYING BUTTRESS

Fm *Chem.* fermium

FM frequency modulation

foal (fōl) *n.* [OE. *fola*] a young horse, mule, etc.; colt or filly —*vt., vi.* to give birth to (a foal)

foam (fōm) *n.* [OE. *fam*] 1. the whitish mass of bubbles formed on or in liquids by agitation, fermentation, etc. 2.

something like foam, as frothy saliva **3.** a rigid or spongy cellular mass, made from liquid rubber, plastic, etc. *—vi.* to produce foam; froth *—vt.* to cause to foam **—foam at the mouth** to rage **—foam′y** *adj.* **-i·er, -i·est**

foam rubber rubber treated to form a firm, spongy foam, used as in upholstered seats or in mattresses

fob (fäb) *n.* [prob. < dial. G. *fuppe*, a pocket] **1.** a short ribbon or chain attached to a pocket watch **2.** any ornament worn on such a chain, etc.

F.O.B., f.o.b. free on board

fo·cal (fō′k'l) *adj.* of or at a focus **—fo′cal·ly** *adv.*

focal length the distance from the optical center of a lens to the point where the light rays converge

fo′c's'le (fōk′s'l) *n. phonetic spelling of* FORECASTLE

fo·cus (fō′kəs) *n., pl.* **-cus·es, -ci** (-sī) [L., hearth] **1.** the point where rays of light, heat, etc. come together; specif., the point where rays of reflected or refracted light meet **2.** *same as* FOCAL LENGTH **3.** an adjustment of this length to make a clear image **4.** any center of activity, attention, etc. *—vt.* **-cused** *or* **-cussed, -cus·ing** *or* **-cus·sing 1.** to bring into focus **2.** to adjust the focal length of (the eye, a lens, etc.) so as to make a clear image **3.** to concentrate *[focus* one's attention] *—vi.* **1.** to come to a focus **—in focus** clear; distinct **—out of focus** blurred

fod·der (fäd′ər) *n.* [< OE. *foda*, food] coarse food for cattle, horses, etc., as hay and straw

foe (fō) *n.* [OE. *fah*, hostile] an enemy; opponent

foe·tus (fēt′əs) *n. same as* FETUS

fog (fôg, fäg) *n.* [prob. < Scand.] **1.** a large mass of water vapor condensed to fine particles, just above the earth's surface **2.** a state of mental confusion **3.** a blur on a photograph or film *—vt., vi.* **fogged, fog′ging** to make or become foggy, blurred, etc.

fog bank a dense mass of fog

fog′gy (-ē) *adj.* **-gi·er, -gi·est 1.** full of fog **2.** dim; blurred **3.** confused **—fog′gi·ness** *n.*

fog′horn′ *n.* a horn blown to give warning to ships in a fog

fo·gy (fō′gē) *n., pl.* **-gies** [< ?] one who is old-fashioned or highly conservative: also **fo′gey,** *pl.* **-geys**

foi·ble (foi′b'l) *n.* [< Fr. *faible*, feeble] a small weakness in character; frailty

foil¹ (foil) *vt.* [< OFr. *fuler*, trample] to thwart

foil² (foil) *n.* [< L. *folium*, a leaf] **1.** a very thin sheet of metal *[gold foil]* **2.** one that sets off or enhances another by contrast **3.** [etym. unc.] a long, thin, blunted fencing sword

foist (foist) *vt.* [prob. < dial. Du. *vuisten*, to hide in the hand] to put in slyly; palm off (*on* or *upon*)

fold¹ (fōld) *vt.* [OE. *faldan*] **1.** to bend or press (something) so that one part is over another **2.** to draw together and intertwine *[to fold* the arms] **3.** to embrace **4.** to wrap up; envelop *—vi.* **1.** to be or become folded **2.** [Colloq.] *a)* to fail, as a play, business, etc. *b)* to collapse, as from exhaustion *—n.* **1.** a folded part **2.** a hollow or crease made by folding

fold² (fōld) *n.* [OE. *fald*] **1.** a pen for sheep **2.** a flock of sheep **3.** a group of people, esp. in a church

-fold [OE. *-feald*] *a suffix meaning:* **1.** having (a specified number of) parts *[tenfold]* **2.** (a specified number of) times as many or as much

fold′er *n.* **1.** a person or thing that folds **2.** a sheet of heavy paper folded as a holder for papers **3.** an unstitched, folded booklet

fo·li·a·ceous (fō′lē ā′shəs) *adj.* [< L. *folium,* a leaf] **1.** of or like the leaf of a plant **2.** having leaflike layers

fo·li·age (fō′lē ij) *n.* [< L. *folium,* a leaf] leaves, as of a plant or tree

fo·li·a·tion (fō′lē ā′shən) *n.* [see prec.] **1.** a growing or developing into a leaf or leaves **2.** the state of being in leaf **3.** a leaflike decoration

fo·li·o (fō′lē ō′) *n., pl.* **-os′** [< L. *folium,* a leaf] **1.** a large sheet of paper folded once **2.** a book (the largest regular size) made of sheets so folded **3.** a leaf of a book, etc. numbered on only one side **4.** the number of a page in a book *—adj.* of folio size

folk (fōk) *n., pl.* **folk, folks** [OE. *folc*] **1.** *a)* a people; nation *b)* the common people of a nation **2.** [*pl.*] people; persons *—adj.* of the common people **—(one's) folks** [Colloq.] (one's) family

folk dance 1. a traditional dance of the common people of a country **2.** music for this

folk′lore′ *n.* the traditional beliefs, legends, etc. of a people

folk′-rock′ *n.* music with a rock-and-roll beat combined with words in a folk-song style

folk song a song made and handed down among the common people, or one like it if known authorship

folk′sy (-sē) *adj.* **-si·er, -si·est** [Colloq.] friendly or sociable in a simple and direct or overly familiar manner

folk tale (or **story**) a story, often legendary, made and handed down orally among the common people

folk′way′ *n.* any way of thinking, behaving, etc. characteristic of a certain social group

fol·li·cle (fäl′i k'l) *n.* [ult. < L. *follis*, bellows] any small sac, cavity, or gland [a hair *follicle*]

fol·low (fäl′ō) *vt.* [< OE. *folgian*] **1.** to come or go after **2.** to chase; pursue **3.** to go along *[follow* the road] **4.** to take up; engage in (a trade, etc.) **5.** to result from **6.** to take as a model; imitate **7.** to obey **8.** to watch or listen to closely **9.** to understand the continuity or logic of *—vi.* **1.** to come or go after something else in place, time, etc. **2.** to result **—follow out** (or **up**) to carry out fully **—follow through** to continue and complete a stroke or action

fol′low·er *n.* one that follows; specif., *a)* one that follows another's teachings; disciple *b)* an attendant

fol′low·ing *adj.* that follows; next after *—n.* a group of followers *—prep.* after *[following* dinner he left]

fol′low-up′ *n.* a letter, visit, etc. that follows as a review or addition

fol·ly (fäl′ē) *n., pl.* **-lies** [see FOOL] **1.** a lack of sense; foolishness **2.** a foolish action or belief

fo·ment (fō ment′) *vt.* [< L. *fovere*, keep warm] to stir up; incite **—fo′men·ta′tion** *n.*

fond (fänd) *adj.* [< ME. *fonnen*, be foolish] **1.** tender and affectionate; loving or doting **2.** greatly cherished **—fond of** having a liking for **—fond′ly** *adv.* **—fond′ness** *n.*

fon·dant (fän′dənt) *n.* [< Fr. *fondre*, to melt] a soft, creamy candy made of sugar, used esp. as a filling for other candies

fon·dle (fän′d'l) *vt.* **-dled, -dling** [< obs. *fond, v.*] to stroke lovingly; caress

fon·due, fon·du (fän dōō′) *n.* [Fr. < *fondre,* to melt] melted cheese, etc., used for dipping cubes of bread

font¹ (fänt) *n.* [< L. *fons,* fountain] **1.** a bowl to hold the water used in baptism **2.** a basin for holy water **3.** a source; origin

font² (fänt) *n.* [see FOUND³] *Printing* a complete assortment of type in one size and style

food (fōōd) *n.* [OE. *foda*] **1.** any substance taken in and assimilated by a plant or animal to enable it to live and grow **2.** solid substances of this sort: distinguished from *drink* **3.** anything that nourishes or stimulates

food poisoning sickness resulting from eating food contaminated by bacteria, chemicals, etc.

food stamp any of the Federal stamps allotted to unemployed or low-income persons for use in buying food

food′stuff′ *n.* any material made into or used as food

fool (fōōl) *n.* [< L. *follis*, windbag] **1.** a silly person; simpleton **2.** a jester **3.** a dupe *—vi.* **1.** to act like a fool; be silly **2.** to joke **3.** [Colloq.] to meddle (*with*) *—vt.* to trick; deceive **—fool around** [Colloq.] to trifle **—fool away** [Colloq.] to squander

fool′er·y *n., pl.* **-ies** foolish activity

fool′har′dy *adj.* **-di·er, -di·est** foolishly daring; rash **— fool′har′di·ly** *adv.* **—fool′har′di·ness** *n.*

fool′ish *adj.* **1.** silly; unwise **2.** absurd **—fool′ish·ly** *adv.* **— fool′ish·ness** *n.*

fool′proof′ *adj.* so harmless, simple, etc. as not to be mishandled, injured, etc. even by a fool

fools·cap (fōōlz′kap′) *n.* [< former watermark] a size of writing paper: in the U.S., 13 by 16 in.

fool's gold iron pyrites or copper pyrites

foot (foot) *n., pl.* **feet** [OE. *fot*] **1.** the end part of the leg, on which one stands **2.** the base or bottom *[the foot* of a page] **3.** the last of a series **4.** the end, as of a bed, toward which the feet are directed **5.** the part of a stocking, etc. covering the foot **6.** a measure of length, equal to 12 inches: symbol ′ **7.** [Brit.] infantry **8.** a group of syllables serving as a unit of meter in verse *—vi.* **1.** to dance **2.** to walk *—vt.* **1.** to add (a column of figures) **2.** [Colloq.] to pay (costs, etc.) **—foot it** [Colloq.] to dance, walk, or run **—on foot** walking **—put one's foot down** [Colloq.] to be firm **—under foot** in the way

foot·age (foot′ij) *n.* a length expressed in feet

foot′-and-mouth′ disease a contagious disease of cattle, deer, etc. characterized by fever and blisters in the mouth and around the hoofs

foot'ball' *n.* **1.** a field game played with an inflated leather ball by two teams **2.** the ball used

foot'board' *n.* **1.** a board or small platform for supporting the feet **2.** a vertical piece across the foot of a bed

foot'bridge' *n.* a narrow bridge for use by pedestrians

foot'-can'dle *n.* a unit of illumination, equal to the amount of direct light thrown by one candle (*n.* 2) on a square foot of surface one foot away

foot'ed (-id) *adj.* having a foot or feet, esp. of a specified number or kind [four-*footed*]

foot'fall' *n.* the sound of a footstep

foot'hill' *n.* a low hill at or near the foot of a mountain or mountain range

foot'hold' *n.* **1.** a place to put a foot down securely, as in climbing **2.** a secure position

foot'ing *n.* **1.** a secure placing of the feet **2.** *a*) the condition of a surface for walking, running, etc. *b*) same as FOOTHOLD **3.** a basis for relationship

foot'lights' *n.pl.* a row of lights along the front of a stage floor —**the footlights** the theater, or acting as a profession

foot'loose' *adj.* free to go where or do as one likes

foot'man (-mən) *n.*, *pl.* -**men** a male servant who assists the butler in a large household

foot'note' *n.* a note of comment or reference at the bottom of a page —*vt.* -**not'ed**, -**not'ing** to add such a note or notes to

foot'path' *n.* a narrow path for pedestrians

foot'-pound' *n.* a unit of energy, equal to the amount of energy needed to raise a one-pound weight a distance of one foot

foot'print' *n.* a mark left by a foot

foot'sie, foot'sy (-sē) *n.*, *pl.* -**sies** the foot: a child's term —**play footsie** (**with**) [Colloq.] to flirt (with) or have surreptitious dealings (with)

foot soldier an infantryman

foot'sore' *adj.* having sore or tender feet, as from much walking

foot'step' *n.* **1.** the distance covered in a step **2.** the sound of a step **3.** a footprint —**follow in** (**someone's**) **footsteps** to follow (someone's) example, vocation, etc.

foot'stool' *n.* a low stool for supporting the feet of a seated person

foot'wear' *n.* foot coverings, as shoes, boots, etc.

foot'work' *n.* the act or manner of using the feet, as in walking, boxing, dancing, etc.

fop (fäp) *n.* [ME. *foppe*, a fool] *same as* DANDY (*n.* 1) — **fop'per·y** *n.*, *pl.* -**ies** —**fop'pish** *adj.*

for (fôr, fər) *prep.* [OE.] **1.** in place of [use a rope *for* a belt] **2.** in the interest of [acting *for* another] **3.** in favor of [vote *for* the levy] **4.** in honor of [a party *for* him] **5.** in order to have, get, keep, find, reach, etc. [walk *for* exercise, start *for* home] **6.** meant to be received by a specified person or used in a specified way [flowers *for* a girl, money *for* expenses] **7.** suitable to [a room *for* sleeping] **8.** with regard to [an ear *for* music] **9.** as being [know *for* a fact] **10.** considering the nature of [cool *for* July] **11.** because of [to cry *for* pain] **12.** in spite of [stupid *for* all her learning] **13.** to the length, amount, or duration of **14.** at the price of [two *for* a dollar] —*conj.* because —O! **for** I wish that I had

for- [OE.] *a prefix meaning* away, apart, off, etc. [*forbid, forgo*]

for·age (fôr'ij, fär'-) *n.* [< Frank. *fodr*, food] **1.** food for domestic animals; fodder **2.** a search for food or provisions —*vi.* -**aged**, -**ag·ing** to search for food, provisions, etc. —*vt.* to get or take food, provisions, etc. from; raid — **for'ag·er** *n.*

fo·ra·men (fō rā'mən) *n.*, *pl.* -**ram'i·na** (-ram'ə nə), -**ra'mens** [L., a hole] a small opening, as in a bone

for·as·much (fôr'əz much') *conj.* inasmuch (as)

for·ay (fôr'ā) *vt.*, *vi.* [< OFr. *forrer*, to forage] to plunder —*n.* a sudden raid, as for spoils

for·bear' (fôr ber') *vt.* -**bore'**, -**borne'**, -**bear'ing** [see FOR- & BEAR¹] to refrain from (doing, saying, etc.) —*vi.* **1.** to refrain or abstain **2.** to control oneself

for·bear² (fôr'ber') *n. same as* FOREBEAR

for·bear'ance (-əns) *n.* **1.** the act of forbearing **2.** self-control; patient restraint

for·bid (fər bid', fôr-) *vt.* -**bade'** (-bad') or -**bad'**, -**bid'-den**, -**bid'ding** [see FOR- & BID] **1.** to order (a person) not to do (something); prohibit **2.** to prevent

for·bid'ding *adj.* looking dangerous, threatening, or disagreeable; repellent —**for·bid'ding·ly** *adv.*

force (fôrs) *n.* [< L. *fortis*, strong] **1.** strength; power **2.** physical coercion against a person or thing **3.** the power to control, persuade, etc.; effectiveness **4.** military power **5.** any group of people organized for some activity [a

sales *force*] **6.** *Law* binding power **7.** *Physics* the cause that starts or stops motion in bodies or alters their motion —*vt.* **forced**, **forc'ing** **1.** to make do something by force; compel **2.** to break open, into, or through by force **3.** to take by force; extort **4.** to drive as by force; impel **5.** to impose as by force (with *on* or *upon*) **6.** to produce as by force [to *force* a smile] **7.** to cause (plants, etc.) to develop faster by artificial means —**in force 1.** in full strength **2.** in effect; valid

forced (fôrst) *adj.* **1.** compulsory [*forced* labor] **2.** produced by unusual effort; strained [a *forced* smile] **3.** due to an emergency [a *forced* landing]

force'-feed' *vt.* -**fed'**, -**feed'ing** to feed as by a tube through the throat to the stomach

force'ful (-fəl) *adj.* full of force; powerful; vigorous; effective —**force'ful·ly** *adv.* —**force'ful·ness** *n.*

force'meat' *n.* [< *farce* (obs.), to stuff] meat chopped up and seasoned, usually for stuffing

for·ceps (fôr'səps) *n.*, *pl.* **for'ceps** [L. < *formus*, warm + *capere*, to take] tongs or pincers for grasping, pulling, etc., used esp. by surgeons and dentists

for·ci·ble (fôr'sə b'l) *adj.* **1.** done by force **2.** having force —**for'ci·bly** *adv.*

FORCEPS

ford (fôrd) *n.* [OE.] a shallow place in a stream, etc. that can be crossed by wading —*vt.* to cross (a stream) in this way —**ford'a·ble** *adj.*

Ford (fôrd) **1.** **Gerald R(udolph), Jr.**, 1913– ; 38th president of the U.S. (1974–77) **2.** **Henry**, 1863–1947; U.S. automobile manufacturer

fore (fôr) *adv.*, *adj.* [OE.] at, in, or toward the front part, as of a ship —*n.* the front —*interj.* *Golf* a shout of warning that one is about to hit the ball

'fore (fôr) *prep.* [Poet.] before

fore- [OE.] *a prefix meaning:* **1.** before in time, place, etc. [*forenoon*] **2.** the front part of [*forearm*]

fore'-and-aft' *adj.* *Naut.* from the bow to the stern; set lengthwise, as a rig

fore·arm¹ (fôr'ärm') *n.* the part of the arm between the elbow and the wrist

fore·arm² (fôr ärm') *vt.* to arm in advance

fore'bear' (-ber') *n.* [< FORE + BE + -ER] an ancestor

fore·bode (-bōd') *vt.*, *vi.* -**bod'ed**, -**bod'ing** [see FORE- & BODE¹] **1.** to foretell; predict (esp. something bad or harmful) **2.** to have a presentiment of (something bad or harmful) —**fore·bod'ing** *n.*

fore'cast' *vt.* -**cast'** or -**cast'ed**, -**cast'ing** **1.** to predict (weather, etc.) **2.** to serve as a prediction of —*n.* a prediction —**fore'cast'er** *n.*

fore·cas·tle (fōk's'l; fôr'kas·'l *is a sp. pronun.*) *n.* [FORE- + CASTLE] **1.** the upper deck of a ship in front of the foremast **2.** the front part of a merchant ship, where the sailors' quarters are located

fore·close (fôr klōz') *vt.* -**closed'**, -**clos'ing** [< OFr. *fors*, outside + *clore*, CLOSE²] to take away the right to redeem (a mortgage, etc.) —**fore·clo'sure** (-klō'zhər) *n.*

fore·doom' *vt.* to doom in advance

fore·fa'ther *n.* an ancestor

fore'fin'ger *n.* the finger nearest the thumb; index

fore'foot' *n.*, *pl.* -**feet'** either of the front feet of an animal with four or more feet

fore'front' *n.* **1.** the extreme front **2.** the position of most activity, importance, etc.

fore·go¹ (fôr gō') *vt.*, *vi.* -**went'**, -**gone'**, -**go'ing** to precede

fore·go² (fôr gō') *vt. same as* FORGO

fore'go'ing *adj.* previously said, written, etc.; preceding

fore·gone' *adj.* **1.** previous **2.** *a*) previously determined *b*) inevitable: said of a conclusion

fore'ground' *n.* the part of a scene, etc. nearest the viewer

fore'hand' *n.* a kind of stroke, as in tennis, made with the palm of the hand turned forward —*adj.* done as with a forehand

fore·hand'ed *adj.* **1.** making provision for the future; thrifty; prudent **2.** prosperous; well-off

fore·head (fôr'id, fär'-; fôr'hed', fär'-) *n.* the part of the face between the eyebrows and the hairline

for·eign (fôr'in, fär'-) *adj.* [< L. *foras*, out-of-doors] **1.** situated outside one's own country, locality, etc. **2.** of, from, or characteristic of another country **3.** concerning the relations of one country to another [*foreign* affairs] **4.** not characteristic of or belonging —**for'eign·ness** *n.*

for'eign-born' *adj.* born in some other country

for'eign·er *n.* a person born in another country; alien

foreign office in some countries, the office of government in charge of foreign affairs

fore·know *vt.* -knew′, -known′, -know′ing to know beforehand —fore′knowl′edge (-näl′ij) *n.*

fore′leg′ *n.* either of the front legs of an animal with four or more legs

fore′lock′ *n.* a lock of hair growing just above the forehead

fore′man (-mən) *n., pl.* -men 1. the chairman of a jury 2. a man in charge of a group of workers, as in a factory

fore′mast′ *n.* the mast nearest the bow of a ship

fore′most′ *adj.* first in place, time, rank, etc. —*adv.* first

fore′named′ *adj.* named or mentioned before

fore′noon′ *n.* the time from sunrise to noon

fo·ren·sic (fə ren′sik) *adj.* [< L. *forum,* marketplace] of or suitable for a law court or public debate —**fo·ren′si·cal·ly** *adv.*

fore′or·dain′ *vt.* to ordain beforehand; predestine —**fore′or·di·na′tion** *n.*

fore′paw′ *n.* a front paw

fore′quar′ter *n.* the front half of a side of beef, pork, etc.

fore′run′ner *n.* 1. a messenger sent or going before; herald 2. a sign that tells or warns of something to follow 3. *a)* a predecessor *b)* an ancestor

fore′sail′ (-sāl′, -s′l) *n.* the main sail on the foremast

fore·see *vt.* -saw′, -seen′, -see′ing to see or know beforehand —**fore·see′a·ble** *adj.*

fore·shad′ow *vt.* to indicate or suggest beforehand; presage —**fore·shad′ow·er** *n.*

fore·short′en *vt. Drawing, Painting,* etc. to shorten some lines of (an object) to give the illusion of proper relative size

fore·show′ *vt.* ·showed′, -shown′ or -showed′, -show′-ing to indicate beforehand; foretell

fore′sight′ *n.* 1. *a)* a foreseeing *b)* the power to foresee 2. prudent regard or provision for the future —**fore′sight′ed** *adj.* —**fore′sight′ed·ness** *n.*

fore′skin′ *n.* the fold of skin that covers the end of the penis; prepuce

for·est (fôr′ist, fär′-) *n.* [< L. *foris,* out-of-doors] a thick growth of trees and underbrush covering a large tract of land —*adj.* of or in a forest —*vt.* to plant with trees

fore·stall (fôr stôl′) *vt.* [< OE. *foresteall,* ambush] 1. to prevent by doing something beforehand 2. to act in advance of; anticipate

for·est·a·tion (fôr′is tā′shən, fär′-) *n.* the planting or care of forests

for·est·er *n.* one trained in forestry or charged with the care of a forest

for′est·ry *n.* the science of planting and taking care of forests

fore′taste′ *n.* a preliminary taste; anticipation

fore·tell′ *vt.* -told′, -tell′ing to tell or indicate beforehand; prophesy; predict

fore′thought′ *n.* 1. a thinking or planning beforehand 2. foresight; prudence

fore·to·ken (fôr′tō′kən) *n.* a prophetic sign; omen —*vt.* (fôr tō′kən) to be an omen of; foreshadow

fore′top (fôr′täp′, -təp) *n.* the platform at the top of a ship's foremast

for·ev·er (fər ev′ər, fôr-) *adv.* 1. for always; endlessly 2. always; at all times Also **for·ev′er·more′**

fore·warn′ *vt.* to warn beforehand

fore′word′ *n.* an introductory remark or preface

for·feit (fôr′fit) *n.* [< ML. *forisfacere,* to do wrong] 1. a fine or penalty for some crime, fault, or neglect 2. the act of paying a forfeit —*adj.* lost or taken away as a forfeit —*vt.* to lose or be deprived of as a forfeit

for′fei·ture (-fə chər) *n.* 1. a forfeiting 2. anything forfeited; penalty or fine

for·gath·er (fôr gath′ər) *vi.* to come together; assemble; also **fore·gath′er**

for·gave (fər gāv′, fôr-) *pt.* of FORGIVE

forge[1] (fôrj) *n.* [< L. *faber,* workman] 1. a furnace for heating metal to be wrought 2. a place where metal is heated and wrought; smithy —*vt., vi.* forged, forg′ing 1. to shape (metal) by heating and hammering 2. to form; shape 3. to imitate (a signature, etc.) fraudulently; counterfeit (a check, etc.) —**forg′er** *n.*

forge[2] (fôrj) *vt., vi.* forged, forg′ing [prob. altered < FORCE] 1. to move forward steadily, as if against difficulties 2. to move in a sudden spurt

for·ger·y *n., pl.* -ies 1. the act or legal offense of forging documents, signatures, etc. to deceive 2. anything forged

for·get (fər get′, fôr-) *vt., vi.* -got′, -got′ten or -got′, -get′ting [OE. *forgitan*] 1. to be unable to remember 2. to overlook or neglect —**for·get′ter** *n.*

for·get′ful *adj.* 1. apt to forget; having a poor memory 2. negligent —**for·get′ful·ly** *adv.* —**for·get′ful·ness** *n.*

for·get′-me-not′ *n.* a plant with clusters of tiny blue, white, or pink flowers

for·give (fər giv′, fôr-) *vt., vi.* -gave′, -giv′en, -giv′ing [OE. *forgiefan*] 1. to give up resentment against or the desire to punish; pardon (an offense or offender) 2. to cancel (a debt) —**for·giv′a·ble** *adj.* —**for·giv′er** *n.*

for·give′ness *n.* 1. a forgiving; pardon 2. inclination to forgive

for·giv′ing *adj.* inclined to forgive

for·go (fôr gō′) *vt.* -went′, -gone′, -go′ing [OE. *forgan*] to do without; abstain from; give up

for·got (fər gät′, fôr-) *pt. & alt. pp.* of FORGET

for·got′ten (-′n) *pp.* of FORGET

fork (fôrk) *n.* [< L. *furca*] 1. an instrument with prongs at one end, for picking up or spearing 2. something like a fork in shape 3. the place where a road, etc. divides into branches 4. any of these branches —*vi.* to divide into branches —*vt.* to use a fork on —**fork over** (or out, up) [Colloq.] to pay out; hand over —**forked** *adj.*

fork·lift (fôrk′lift′) *n.* a device with projecting prongs, usually on a truck, for lifting heavy objects

for·lorn (fər lôrn′, fôr-) *adj.* [< OE. *forleosan,* to lose utterly] 1. abandoned or deserted 2. wretched; miserable 3. without hope —**for·lorn′ly** *adv.*

form (fôrm) *n.* [< L. *forma*] 1. shape; general structure 2. the figure of a person or animal 3. a mold 4. the combination of qualities making something what it is 5. arrangement; style 6. a way of doing something 7. a customary way of behaving; ceremony 8. a fixed order of words 9. a printed document with blanks to be filled in 10. a particular kind or type 11. condition of mind or body 12. a grade or class in school 13. *Gram.* any of the changes in a word to show inflection, etc. 14. *Printing* type, etc. locked in a frame for printing —*vt.* 1. to shape; fashion 2. to train; instruct 3. to develop (habits) 4. to think of; conceive 5. to organize into 6. to make up; create —*vi.* 1. to be formed 2. to take form

-form [< L. *-formis*] a suffix meaning having the form of [cuneiform]

for·mal (fôr′məl) *adj.* [< L. *formalis*] 1. according to fixed customs, rules, etc. 2. stiff in manner; not relaxed 3. designed for wear at ceremonies, balls, etc. 4. done or made in explicit, definite form [a *formal* contract] 5. of or belonging to that level of language usage characterized by expanded vocabulary, close adherence to grammatical rules, complex sentences, etc. —*n.* 1. a dance requiring formal clothes 2. a woman's evening dress —**for′mal·ly** *adv.*

form·al·de·hyde (fôr mal′də hīd′, fər-) *n.* [FORM(IC) + ALDEHYDE] a colorless, pungent gas, HCHO, used in solution as a disinfectant and preservative

for′mal·ism *n.* strict attention to outward forms and customs —**for′mal·is′tic** *adj.*

for·mal·i·ty (fôr mal′ə tē) *n., pl.* -ties 1. *a)* an observing of customs, rules, etc.; propriety *b)* too careful attention to regularity, convention, etc.; stiffness 2. a formal act; ceremony

for·mal·ize (fôr′mə līz′) *vt.* -ized′, -iz′ing 1. to shape 2. to make formal or official —*vi.* to be formal —**for′mal·i·za′tion** *n.*

for·mat (fôr′mat) *n.* [< L. *formatus,* formed] 1. the size, shape, and arrangement of a book, magazine, etc. 2. general plan, as of a television program

for·ma·tion (fôr mā′shən) *n.* 1. a forming or being formed 2. a thing formed 3. the way in which something is formed or arranged; structure 4. an arrangement as of troops, ships, a football team, etc. 5. *Geol.* a rock unit distinguished by composition, origin, etc.

form·a·tive (fôr′mə tiv) *adj.* helping or involving formation or development [*formative* years]

for·mer (fôr′mər) *adj.* [< OE. *formest,* foremost] 1. previous; earlier; past 2. first mentioned of two: used as a noun with *the*

for′mer·ly *adv.* at or in a former time; in the past

for·mic (fôr′mik) *adj.* [< L. *formica,* an ant] designating a colorless acid, HCOOH, found in ants, etc.

for·mi·da·ble (fôr′mə də b′l) *adj.* [< L. *formidare,* to dread] 1. causing fear, dread, or awe 2. hard to handle or overcome —**for′mi·da·bly** *adv.*

form′less adj. shapeless; amorphous —**form′less·ly** adv. — **form′less·ness** n.

form letter one of a number of duplicated letters, with the date, address, etc. filled in separately

For·mo·sa (fôr mō′sə, -zə) former (Portuguese) name of TAIWAN —**For·mo′san** adj., n.

for·mu·la (fôr′myə lə) n., pl. **-las, -lae′** (-lē′) [L. < forma, form] **1.** a fixed form of words, esp. a conventional expression **2.** any conventional rule for doing something **3.** a prescription for a baby's food, a medicine, etc. **4.** a set of symbols expressing a mathematical rule **5.** Chem. an expression of the composition, as of a compound, using symbols and figures

for·mu·lar·y (-ler′ē) n., pl. **-ies 1.** a collection of prescribed forms, as of prayers **2.** a formula

for·mu·late (-lāt′) vt. **-lat′ed, -lat′ing 1.** to express in a formula **2.** to express in a definite way —**for′mu·la′tion** n. —**for′mu·la′tor** n.

for·ni·cate (fôr′nə kāt′) vi. **-cat′ed, -cat′ing** [< L. fornix, brothel] to commit fornication —**for′ni·ca′tor** n.

for·ni·ca·tion n. voluntary sexual intercourse between unmarried persons

for·sake (fər sāk′, fôr-) vt. **-sook′** (-sook′), **-sak′en, -sak′-ing** [< OE. forsacan] **1.** to give up (a habit, etc.) **2.** to abandon; desert —**for·sak′en** adj.

for·sooth (fər sooth′, fôr-) adv. [< OE. for + soth, truth] [Archaic] no doubt; indeed

for·swear (fôr swer′) vt. **-swore′, -sworn′, -swear′ing 1.** to swear or promise earnestly to give up **2.** to deny earnestly or on oath —**forswear oneself** to perjure oneself

for·syth·i·a (fər sith′ē ə, fôr-) n. [< W. Forsyth, 18th-c. Eng. botanist] a shrub with yellow, bell-shaped flowers in early spring

fort (fôrt) n. [< L. fortis, strong] a fortified place for military defense

forte¹ (fôrt) n. [< Fr.: see FORT] that which one does particularly well

for·te² (fôr′tā, -tē) adj., adv. [It. < L. fortis, strong] Music loud —n. a forte note or passage

forth (fôrth) adv. [OE.] **1.** forward; onward **2.** out; into view —**and so forth** et cetera

Forth (fôrth), **Firth of** the estuary of the Forth River, in SE Scotland

forth′com′ing adj. **1.** about to appear; approaching **2.** ready when needed —n. an appearance or approach

forth′right′ adj. straightforward; direct; frank —adv. straight forward; directly onward —**forth′right′ly** adv. — **forth′right′ness** n.

forth′with′ adv. without delay

for·ti·fi·ca·tion (fôr′tə fi kā′shən) n. **1.** the act or science of fortifying **2.** a fort, defensive earthwork, etc. **3.** a fortified place

for·ti·fy (fôr′tə fī′) vt. **-fied′, -fy′ing** [< L. fortis, strong + facere, make] **1.** to strengthen physically, emotionally, etc. **2.** to strengthen against attack, as with forts **3.** to support; corroborate **4.** to strengthen (wine, etc.) by adding alcohol **5.** to add vitamins, minerals, etc. to (milk, etc.) —vi. to build military defenses

for·tis·si·mo (fôr tis′ə mō′) adj., adv. [It. superl. of FORTE²] Music very loud

for·ti·tude (fôr′tə tood′, -tyood′) n. [< L. fortis, strong] firm courage; patient endurance of trouble, pain, etc.

Fort Lau·der·dale (lô′dər dāl′) city on the SE coast of Fla.: pop. 140,000 (met. area 620,000)

fort·night (fôrt′nīt′) n. [lit., fourteen nights] [Chiefly Brit.] two weeks

fort′night′ly adv., adj. [Chiefly Brit.] (happening or appearing) once in every fortnight

for·tress (fôr′trəs) n. [< L. fortis, strong] a fortified place; fort

for·tu·i·tous (fôr too′ə təs, -tyoo′-) adj. [< L. fors, luck] **1.** happening by chance; accidental **2.** bringing, or happening by, good luck; fortunate —**for·tu′i·tous·ly** adv.

for·tu·i·ty n., pl. **-ties** chance; accident

for·tu·nate (fôr′chə nit) adj. **1.** having good luck **2.** coming by good luck —**for′tu·nate·ly** adv.

for·tune (fôr′chən) n. [< L. fors, luck] **1.** luck; chance; fate **2.** one's future lot, good or bad **3.** good luck; success **4.** wealth; riches

for′tune-tell′er n. one who professes to foretell events in other people's lives —**for′tune-tell′ing** n., adj.

Fort Wayne (wān) city in NE Ind.: pop. 178,000

Fort Worth (wurth) city in N Tex.: pop. 393,000 (met. area 762,000)

for·ty (fôr′tē) adj., n., pl. **-ties** [OE. feowertig] four times ten; 40; XL —**the forties** the numbers or years, as of a century, from 40 through 49 —**for′ti·eth** (-ith) adj., n.

for′ty-nin′er, For′ty-Nin′er (-nīn′ər) n. [Colloq.] a participant in the California gold rush of 1849

forty winks [Colloq.] a short sleep; nap

fo·rum (fôr′əm) n., pl. **-rums, -ra** (-ə) [L.] **1.** the public square or marketplace of an ancient Roman city **2.** a law court; tribunal **3.** an assembly for the discussion of public matters

for·ward (fôr′wərd) adj. [OE. foreweard] **1.** at, toward, or of the front **2.** advanced **3.** onward **4.** prompt; ready **5.** bold; presumptuous **6.** of or for the future —adv. **1.** toward the front; ahead **2.** toward the future —n. Basketball, Hockey, etc. a player in a front position —vt. **1.** to promote **2.** to send on; transmit [to forward mail] —**for′-ward·er** n. —**for′ward·ness** n.

for′wards adv. same as FORWARD

fos·sil (fäs′'l, fôs′-) n. [< L. fossilis, dug up] **1.** any hardened remains or traces of a plant or animal of a previous geological period, preserved in the earth's crust **2.** a person who has outmoded, fixed ideas —adj. **1.** of or like a fossil **2.** obtained from the earth [coal is a fossil fuel] **3.** antiquated

fos′sil·if′er·ous adj. containing fossils

fos′sil·ize′ (-īz′) vt. **-ized′, -iz′ing 1.** to change into a fossil; petrify **2.** to make out of date, rigid, etc. —vi. to become fossilized —**fos′sil·i·za′tion** n.

fos·ter (fôs′tər, fäs′-) vt. [OE. fostrian, nourish] **1.** to bring up; rear **2.** to help to develop; promote **3.** to cherish —adj. having a specified status in a family but not by birth [a foster brother]

Fos·ter (fôs′tər, fäs′-), **Stephen Collins** 1826–64; U.S. composer of songs

fought (fôt) pt. & pp. of FIGHT

foul (foul) adj. [OE. ful] **1.** stinking; loathsome **2.** extremely dirty **3.** clogged with dirt, etc. **4.** indecent; profane **5.** wicked; abominable **6.** stormy [foul weather] **7.** tangled [a foul rope] **8.** not within the limits or rules set **9.** designating lines setting limits on the playing field **10.** dishonest **11.** [Colloq.] unpleasant, disagreeable, etc. — adv. in a foul way —n. Sports a hit, blow, move, etc. that is foul (adj. 8) —vt. **1.** to make filthy **2.** to dishonor; disgrace **3.** to obstruct [grease fouls sink drains] **4.** to entangle, as a rope **5.** to make a foul against in a contest or game **6.** Baseball to bat (the ball) foul —vi. **1.** to be or become fouled **2.** to break the rules of a game **3.** Baseball to bat a foul ball —**foul up** [Colloq.] to bungle —**foul′ly** adv. —**foul′ness** n.

fou·lard (foo lärd′) n. [Fr.] **1.** a lightweight fabric of silk, rayon, etc., usually printed with small figures **2.** a necktie, scarf, etc. of this fabric

foul play 1. unfair play **2.** treacherous action or violence

found¹ (found) pt. & pp. of FIND

found² (found) vt. [< L. fundus, bottom] **1.** to base [founded on fact] **2.** to begin to build or organize; establish —**found′er** n.

found³ (found) vt. [< L. fundere, pour] **1.** to melt and pour (metal) into a mold **2.** to make by pouring molten metal into a mold; cast

foun·da·tion (foun dā′shən) n. **1.** a founding or being founded; establishment **2.** an endowment to maintain an institution **3.** an institution so endowed **4.** basis **5.** the base of a wall, house, etc.

foun·der (foun′dər) vi. [< L. fundus, bottom] **1.** to stumble, fall, or go lame **2.** to fill with water and sink: said of a ship **3.** to break down

found·ling (found′liŋ) n. an infant of unknown parents, found abandoned

found·ry (foun′drē) n., pl. **-ries 1.** the work of founding metals; casting **2.** metal castings **3.** a place where metal is cast

fount (fount) n. [< L. fons] **1.** [Poet.] a fountain or spring **2.** a source

foun·tain (foun′t'n) n. [< L. fons] **1.** a natural spring of water **2.** a source **3.** an artificial jet of water, or the device, basin, etc. where this flows **4.** a reservoir, as for ink

foun′tain·head′ n. the source, as of a stream

fountain pen a pen in which a nib at the end is fed ink from its own reservoir or cartridge

four (fôr) adj., n. [OE. feower] one more than three; 4; IV —**on all fours 1.** on all four feet **2.** on hands and knees

four′flush′er (-flush′ər) n. [< FLUSH²] [Colloq.] one who bluffs or attempts to deceive

four′-foot′ed adj. having four feet; quadruped

four′-in-hand′ n. a necktie tied in a slipknot with the ends left hanging

four-leaf clover a clover leaf of four leaflets, popularly supposed to bring good luck

four-post·er (fôr'pōs'tər) *n.* a large bed with tall corner posts that sometimes support a canopy

four'score' *adj., n.* four times twenty; eighty

four'some (-səm) *n.* a group of four persons

four'square' *adj.* **1.** square **2.** unyielding; firm **3.** frank; forthright —*adv.* in a square form or manner

four'teen' (-tēn') *adj., n.* [OE. *feowertyne*] four more than ten; 14; XIV —*four'teenth' adj., n.*

fourth (fôrth) *adj.* [OE. *feortha*] **1.** preceded by three others in a series; 4th **2.** designating any of four equal parts —*n.* **1.** the one following the third **2.** any of the four equal parts of something; 1/4

fourth'-class' *adj.* designating a class of mail consisting of merchandise or printed matter; parcel post

fourth dimension a dimension in addition to those of length, width, and depth: in the theory of relativity, time is regarded as this dimension

Fourth of July Independence Day

fowl (foul) *n.* [OE. *fugol*] **1.** orig., any bird [fish or *fowl*] **2.** any of the domestic birds used as food, as the chicken, duck, etc. **3.** the flesh of these birds used for food —*vi.* to hunt wild birds for food or sport —*fowl'er n.* —*fowl'ing adj., n.*

fox (fäks) *n.* [OE.] **1.** a small, wild mammal of the dog family, considered sly and crafty **2.** its fur **3.** a sly, crafty person —*vt.* to trick by craftiness

fox'glove' *n.* common name for DIGITALIS (sense 1)

fox'hole' *n.* a hole dug in the ground as protection for one or two soldiers against enemy gunfire or tanks

FOX (average length 42 in., including tail)

fox'hound' *n.* a strong, swift hound with a keen scent, bred to hunt foxes

fox terrier a small, active terrier, sometimes wire-haired, formerly trained to drive foxes out of hiding

fox trot a ballroom dance in 4/4 time, or music for it —*fox'-trot' vi. -trot'ted, -trot'ting*

fox'y *adj.* -i·er, -i·est foxlike; crafty; sly —*fox'i·ly adv.* —*fox'i·ness n.*

foy·er (foi'ər, foi yā') *n.* [Fr. < L. *focus*, hearth] an entrance hall or lobby, as in a theater or hotel

f.p., fp 1. foot-pound(s) **2.** freezing point

FPO *U.S. Navy* Fleet Post Office

Fr *Chem.* francium

Fr. 1. Father **2.** France **3.** French **4.** Friday

Fra (frä) *n.* [It. < L. *frater*] brother: title given to an Italian friar or monk

fra·cas (frā'kəs) *n.* [Fr. < It. < *fracassare*, smash] a noisy dispute; brawl

frac·tion (frak'shən) *n.* [< L. *frangere*, to break] **1.** a small part, amount, etc.; fragment **2.** *Math. a)* a quantity less than a whole, expressed as a decimal or with a numerator and denominator *b)* any quantity expressed by a numerator and denominator, as 13/4 —*frac'tion·al adj.*

frac·tious (frak'shəs) *adj.* [< ?] **1.** unruly; rebellious **2.** irritable —*frac'tious·ly adv.*

frac·ture (frak'chər) *n.* [< L. *frangere*, to break] a breaking or break, esp. of a bone —*vt., vi.* -tured, -tur·ing to break, crack, or split

frag·ile (fraj'l) *adj.* [< L. *frangere*, to break] easily broken or damaged; frail; delicate —*fra·gil·i·ty* (frə jil'ə tē) *n.*

frag·ment (frag'mənt) *n.* [< L. *frangere*, to break] **1.** a part broken away **2.** an incomplete part, as of a novel —*frag'men·ta'tion n.*

frag'men·tar'y (-mən ter'ē) *adj.* made up of fragments; not complete

fra·grance (frā'grəns) *n.* a fragrant smell; pleasant odor: also [Now Rare] *fra'gran·cy, pl.* -cies

fra·grant (frā'grənt) *adj.* [< L. *fragrare*, emit a smell] having a pleasant odor —*fra'grant·ly adv.*

frail (frāl) *adj.* [see FRAGILE] **1.** easily broken; fragile **2.** slender and delicate **3.** easily tempted; morally weak —*frail'ly adv.* —*frail'ness n.*

frail'ty (-tē) *n.* **1.** a being frail; esp., moral weakness **2.** *pl.* -ties a fault arising from such weakness

frame (frām) *vt.* framed, fram'ing [< OE. *framian*, be helpful] **1.** to form according to a pattern [to *frame* laws] **2.** to construct **3.** to compose; put into words **4.** to adjust; fit **5.** to enclose in a border, as a picture, etc. **6.** [Colloq.] to make appear guilty, as by falsifying evidence —*n.* **1.** a basic structure around which a thing is built;

framework, as of a house **2.** body structure; build **3.** *a)* the structural case into which a window, door, etc. is set *b)* the framework supporting an automobile chassis **4.** a border, as of a picture **5.** the way that anything is constructed; form **6.** mood; temper [a good *frame* of mind] **7.** an established order or system **8.** one exposure in a filmstrip or motion picture film **9.** *Bowling,* etc. any of the divisions of a game —*adj.* having a wooden framework [a *frame* house] —*fram'er n.*

frame'-up' *n.* [Colloq.] **1.** a falsifying of evidence to make a person seem guilty **2.** a secret, deceitful scheme

frame'work' *n.* **1.** a structure to hold together or to support something **2.** a basic structure or system

franc (fraŋk) *n.* [Fr. < L. *Francorum rex,* king of the French, formerly on the coin] the monetary unit of France, Belgium, Switzerland, Luxembourg, etc.

France (frans, fräns) country in W Europe: 212,821 sq. mi.; pop. 50,620,000; cap. Paris

France (frans, fräns), **A·na·tole** (an'ə tōl') 1844–1924; Fr. writer & literary critic

fran·chise (fran'chīz) *n.* [< OFr. *franc,* free] **1.** any special right or privilege granted by a government **2.** the right to vote; suffrage **3.** the right to sell a product or service in an area

Fran·cis·can (fran sis'kən) *adj.* of Saint Francis of Assisi or the religious order founded by him in 1209 —*n.* any member of this order

Fran·cis of As·si·si (fran'sis əv ə sēs'ē), Saint 1181?–1226; It. founder of the Franciscan Order

fran·ci·um (fran'sē əm) *n.* [< FRANCE] a radioactive metallic chemical element of the alkali group: symbol, Fr; at. wt., 223(?); at. no., 87

Franck (fränk), **Cé·sar** (**Auguste**) (sä zär') 1822–90; Fr. composer, born in Belgium

Fran·co (fraŋ'kō), **Fran·cis·co** (fran sis'kō) 1892–1975; dictator of Spain (1939–75)

Franco- *a combining form meaning:* **1.** of France or the French **2.** France and; the French and

fran·gi·ble (fran'jə b'l) *adj.* [< L. *frangere,* to break] breakable —*fran'gi·bil'i·ty n.*

Frank (fraŋk) *n.* a member of the Germanic tribes whose 9th-cent. empire extended over what is now Franoo, Ger many, and Italy

frank (fraŋk) *adj.* [< OFr. *franc,* free] free in expressing oneself; candid —*vt.* **1.** to send (mail) free of postage **2.** to mark (mail) so that it can be sent free —*n.* **1.** the privilege of sending mail free **2.** a mark indicating this right —*frank'ly adv.* —*frank'ness n.*

Frank·en·stein (fraŋ'kən stīn') the title character in a novel (1818), creator of a monster that destroys him —*n.* popularly, the monster

Frank·fort (fraŋk'fərt) capital of Ky., in the NC part: pop. 21,000

Frank·furt (fraŋk'fərt) city in C West Germany, on the Main River: pop. 662,000

frank·furt·er, frank·fort·er (fraŋk'fər tər) *n.* [G. < FRANKFURT] a smoked sausage of beef or beef and pork, etc.; wiener: also **frank'furt, frank'fort,** [Colloq.] frank

frank·in·cense (fraŋ'kən sens') *n.* [see FRANK & INCENSE[1]] a gum resin burned as incense

Frank·ish (fraŋ'kish) *n.* the West Germanic language of the Franks

frank·lin (fraŋk'lin) *n.* [see FRANK] in England in the 14th & 15th cent., a landowner of free but not noble birth

Frank·lin (fraŋk'lin), **Benjamin** 1706–90; Am. statesman, scientist, inventor, & writer

fran·tic (fran'tik) *adj.* [< Gr. *phrenitis,* madness] wild with anger, worry, etc. —*fran'ti·cal·ly adv.*

frap·pé (fra pā') *n.* [Fr. < *frapper,* to strike] **1.** a dessert made of partly frozen fruit juices, etc. **2.** a beverage poured over shaved ice **3.** [Eastern] a milkshake Also, esp. for 3, **frappe** (frap)

frat (frat) *n.* [Colloq.] a fraternity, as at a college

fra·ter·nal (frə tur'n'l) *adj.* [< L. *frater,* brother] **1.** of brothers; brotherly **2.** of or like a fraternal order or a fraternity **3.** designating either of a pair of twins (**fraternal twins**) developed from separately fertilized ova

fraternal order (or **society, association**) a society, often secret, organized for fellowship or for work toward a common goal

fra·ter·ni·ty (frə tur'nə tē) *n., pl.* -ties **1.** brotherliness **2.** a group of men joined together by common interests, for fellowship, etc., as in some colleges **3.** a group of people with the same beliefs, work, etc.

frat·er·nize (frat'ər nīz') *vi.* -nized', -niz'ing to associate in a brotherly manner —**frat'er·ni·za'tion** *n.*

frat·ri·cide (frat'rə sīd') *n.* [< L. *frater*, brother + *caedere*, to kill] the act of killing one's own brother or sister —**frat'ri·ci'dal** *adj.*

‡**Frau** (frou) *n., pl.* **Frau'en** (-ən) [G.] a married woman; lady: as a title, equivalent to *Mrs.* or *Madam*

fraud (frôd) *n.* [< L. *fraus*] 1. deceit; trickery 2. *Law* intentional deception 3. a trick 4. a person who is not what he pretends to be

fraud·u·lent (frô'jə lənt) *adj.* 1. based on or using fraud 2. done or obtained by fraud —**fraud'u·lence** *n.* —**fraud'u·lent·ly** *adv.*

fraught (frôt) *adj.* [< MDu. *vracht*, a load] filled (*with*) [a situation *fraught* with danger]

‡**Fräu·lein** (froi'līn) *n., pl.* -lein [G.] an unmarried woman or girl; young lady: as a title, equivalent to *Miss*

fray[1] (frā) *n.* [< AFFRAY] a noisy quarrel or fight

fray[2] (frā) *vt., vi.* [< L. *fricare*, to rub] 1. to make or become worn or ragged 2. to make or become weak

fraz·zle (fraz''l) *vt., vi.* -zled, -zling [< dial. *fazle*] [Colloq.] 1. to wear to tatters 2. to tire out —*n.* [Colloq.] a being frazzled

freak (frēk) *n.* [< ?] 1. an odd notion; whim 2. an unusual happening 3. any abnormal animal, person, or plant 4. [Slang] *a*) a user of a specified narcotic, etc. *b*) a devotee [a rock *freak*] —*adj.* queer; abnormal —**freak out** [Slang] 1. to experience extreme reactions as from a psychedelic drug 2. to become a hippie —**freak'ish**, **freak'y** *adj.*

freak'out' *n.* [Slang] an instance of freaking out

freck·le (frek''l) *n.* [< Scand.] a small, brownish spot on the skin, esp. as a result of exposure to the sun —*vt., vi.* -led, -ling to make or become spotted with freckles —**freck'led**, **freck'ly** *adj.*

Fred·er·ick the Great (fred'ər ik) 1712–86; king of Prussia (1740–86)

free (frē) *adj.* **fre'er**, **fre'est** [OE. *freo*] 1. not under the control or power of another; having liberty; independent 2. having civil liberties 3. able to move in any direction; loose 4. not burdened by obligations, discomforts, constraints, etc. 5. not confined to the usual rules [*free* verse] 6. not exact [a *free* translation] 7. generous; profuse [*free* spending] 8. with no charge or cost 9. exempt from taxes, duties, etc. 10. clear of obstructions [a *free* road] 11. frank; straightforward 12. open to all [a *free* port] 13. not fastened —*adv.* 1. without cost 2. in a free manner —*vt.* **freed**, **free'ing** to make free; specif., *a*) to release from bondage, arbitrary power, obligation, etc. *b*) to clear of obstruction, etc. —**free and easy** informal —**free from** (or **of**) without —**make free with** to use freely —**set free** to release; liberate —**free'ly** *adv.*

free·bie, **free·by** (frē'bē) *n., pl.* -**bies** [Slang] something given or gotten free of charge

free'board' *n.* the height of a ship's side from the main deck or gunwale to the waterline

free'boot'er (-bōōt'ər) *n.* [< Du. *vrij*, free + *buit*, plunder] a pirate; buccaneer

free'born' *adj.* 1. born free, not in slavery 2. of or fit for a free person

free city a city that is an autonomous state

freed·man (frēd'mən) *n., pl.* -**men** a man legally freed from slavery or bondage

free·dom (frē'dəm) *n.* 1. a being free 2. a civil or political liberty [*freedom* of speech] 3. exemption from a specified obligation, discomfort, etc. 4. a being able to act, use, move, etc. without hindrance 5. ease of movement; facility 6. a being free from the usual rules, patterns, etc. 7. frankness

free enterprise the economic doctrine of permitting private industry to operate with a minimum of control by the government

free'-for-all' *n.* a disorganized, general fight; brawl —*adj.* open to anyone

free'hand' *adj.* drawn by hand without the use of instruments, measurements, etc.

free'hand'ed *adj.* generous; liberal

free'hold' *n.* 1. an estate in land held for life or with the right to pass it on through inheritance 2. the holding of land in this way —**free'hold'er** *n.*

free lance a writer, artist, etc. who sells his services to individual buyers —**free'-lance'** *adj., vi.* -lanced', -lanc'ing

free'man (-mən) *n., pl.* -**men** 1. a person not in slavery or bondage 2. a citizen

Free·ma·son (frē'mās''n) *n.* a member of a secret society based on brotherliness, charity, and mutual aid; Mason —**Free'ma'son·ry** *n.*

free on board delivered aboard the train, ship, etc. at the point of shipment, without extra charge

free silver the free coinage of silver, esp. at a fixed ratio to the gold coined in the same period

Free'-Soil' *adj.* [also f- s-] opposed to the extension of slavery into U.S. Territories before the Civil War

free'-spo'ken *adj.* frank; outspoken

free'stone' *n.* a peach, etc. in which the pit does not cling to the pulp —*adj.* having such a pit

free'think'er *n.* one who forms his opinions about religion independently —**free'think'ing** *n., adj.*

free trade trade conducted without quotas on imports or exports, protective tariffs, etc.

free verse poetry not adhering to regular metrical, rhyming, or stanzaic forms

free'way' *n.* an expressway with interchanges for fully controlled access

free'will' *adj.* voluntary; spontaneous

free will one's freedom of decision or choice

freeze (frēz) *vi.* **froze**, **fro'zen**, **freez'ing** [OE. *freosan*] 1. to be formed into, or become covered or clogged with, ice 2. to become very cold 3. to be damaged or killed by cold 4. to become motionless 5. to be made speechless from strong emotion 6. to become formal or unfriendly —*vt.* 1. to change into or cover or clog with ice 2. to make very cold 3. to preserve (food) by bringing it rapidly below the freezing point 4. to kill or damage by cold 5. to make motionless 6. to make formal or unfriendly 7. to fix (prices, etc.) at a given level by authority —*n.* 1. a freezing or being frozen 2. a period of freezing weather —**freeze out** [Colloq.] to force out by a cold manner, competition, etc.

freeze'-dry' *vt.* -**dried'**, -**dry'ing** to quick-freeze (food, vaccines, etc.) and then dry under high vacuum at low temperature

freez'er *n.* 1. an electric or hand-cranked device for making ice cream 2. a refrigerator, compartment, etc. for freezing and storing frozen foods

freezing point the temperature at which a liquid freezes: for water, it is 32°F or 0°C

freight (frāt) *n.* [< MDu. *vracht*, a load] 1. the transportation of goods by water, land, or air 2. the cost for such transportation 3. the goods transported 4. a railroad train for transporting goods: in full **freight train** 5. any load or burden —*vt.* 1. to load with freight 2. to load; burden 3. to transport by freight

freight'age (-ij) *n.* 1. the charge for transporting goods 2. freight; cargo 3. transportation of goods

freight car a railroad car for transporting freight

freight'er *n.* a ship or aircraft for carrying freight

Fre·mont (frē'mänt) city in W Calif.: pop. 101,000

French (french) *adj.* of France, its people, language, etc. —*n.* the language of France —**the French** the people of France —**French'man** *n., pl.* -**men** —**French'wom'an** *n.fem.*, *pl.* -**wom'en**

French Canadian a Canadian of French ancestry

French cuff a double cuff turned back on itself and fastened with a link

French doors two adjoining doors with glass panes from top to bottom, hinged at opposite sides of a doorway and opening in the middle

French dressing a salad dressing made of vinegar, oil, and various seasonings

French fry [*often* **f- f-**] to fry in very hot, deep fat until crisp: **French fried potatoes** (colloquially, **French fries**) are first cut into strips

French Guiana French possession in NE S. America

French horn a brass-wind instrument with a long, coiled tube ending in a wide, flaring bell

French leave an unauthorized departure; act of leaving secretly or in haste

French Revolution the revolution (1789–99) of the people of France against the monarchy

French toast sliced bread dipped in a batter of egg and milk and fried

fre·net·ic (frə net'ik) *adj.* [< Gr. *phrenētikos*, mad] frantic; frenzied: also **fre·net'i·cal** —**fre·net'i·cal·ly** *adv.*

fren·zy (fren'zē) *n., pl.* -**zies** [< Gr. *phrenitis*, madness] wild excitement; brief delirium —*vt.* -**zied**, -**zy·ing** to make frantic; drive mad —**fren'zied** —**fren'zied·ly** *adv.*

fre·quen·cy (frē'kwən sē) *n., pl.* -**cies** 1. frequent occurrence 2. the number of times an event, value, etc. occurs in a given period or group 3. *Physics* the number of vibrations, waves, etc. in a unit of time

frequency modulation the changing of the frequency of the transmitting radio wave in accordance with the sound being broadcast

fre·quent (frē′kwənt) *adj.* [< L. *frequens,* crowded] **1.** occurring often **2.** constant; habitual —*vt.* (frē kwent′) to go to or be in habitually —**fre·quent′er** *n.* —**fre′quent·ly** *adv.*

fres·co (fres′kō) *n., pl.* **-coes, -cos** [It., fresh] **1.** the art of painting with watercolors on wet plaster **2.** a painting or design so made —*vt.* to paint in fresco

fresh[1] (fresh) *adj.* [OE. *fersc*] **1.** recently made, grown, etc. *[fresh* coffee*]* **2.** not spoiled **3.** not tired; lively **4.** not worn, soiled, etc. **5.** new; recent **6.** additional *[a fresh* start*]* **7.** inexperienced **8.** cool and refreshing *[a fresh* day*]* **9.** brisk: said of wind **10.** not salt: said of water —**fresh′ly** *adv.* —**fresh′ness** *n.*

fresh[2] (fresh) *adj.* [< G. *frech,* bold] [Slang] saucy; impudent —**fresh′ly** *adv.* —**fresh′ness** *n.*

fresh′en (-ən) *vt., vi.* to make or become fresh

fresh′et (-it) *n.* **1.** a rush of fresh water flowing into the sea **2.** a flooding of a stream because of melting snow or heavy rain

fresh′man (-mən) *n., pl.* **-men 1.** a beginner **2.** a first-year student in a high school or college —*adj.* of or for first-year students

fresh′wa′ter *adj.* **1.** of or living in water that is not salty **2.** sailing only on inland waters **3.** unskilled

Fres·no (frez′nō) city in C Calif.; pop. 166,000

fret[1] (fret) *vt., vi.* **fret′ted, fret′ting** [OE. *fretan,* eat up] **1.** to gnaw, chafe, wear away, etc. **2.** to make or become rough **3.** to irritate or be irritated; worry —*n.* irritation; worry

fret[2] (fret) *n.* [< OFr. *frete* & OE. *frætwa*] an ornamental pattern of straight bars joining one another at right angles to form a design —*vt.* **fret′ted, fret′ting** to furnish with frets

fret[3] (fret) *n.* [OFr. *frette,* a band] any of the ridges across the fingerboard of a banjo, guitar, etc. to regulate the fingering

FRETS

fret′ful *adj.* tending to fret; peevish —**fret′ful·ly** *adv.* —**fret′ful·ness** *n.*

fret′work′ *n.* decorative open-work or carving

Freud (froid), **Sigmund** 1856–1939; Austrian physician & neurologist: founder of psychoanalysis

Freud·i·an (froi′dē ən) *adj.* of or according to Freud or his theories —*n.* a follower of Freud or his theories —**Freud′i·an·ism** *n.*

Fri. Friday

fri·a·ble (frī′ə b'l) *adj.* [< L. *friare,* to rub] easily crumbled into powder —**fri′a·bil′i·ty** *n.*

fri·ar (frī′ər) *n.* [< L. *frater,* brother] *R.C.Ch.* a member of any of several mendicant orders

fri′ar·y *n., pl.* **-ies 1.** a monastery where friars live **2.** a brotherhood of friars

fric·as·see (frik′ə sē′) *n.* [< Fr. *fricasser,* to cut up and fry] meat cut into pieces, stewed or fried, and served in its own gravy —*vt.* **-seed′, -see′ing** to prepare as a fricassee

fric·tion (frik′shən) *n.* [< L. *fricare,* to rub] **1.** a rubbing of one object against another **2.** conflict, as because of differing opinions **3.** the resistance to motion of surfaces that touch —**fric′tion·al** *adj.*

Fri·day (frī′dē, -dā) *n.* [< *Frig,* Norse goddess] **1.** the sixth day of the week **2.** [< the devoted servant of ROBINSON CRUSOE] a faithful helper: usually **man** (or **girl**) **Friday**

fried (frīd) *pt. & pp. of* FRY[1]

fried·cake (frīd′kāk′) *n.* a small cake fried in deep fat; doughnut or cruller

friend (frend) *n.* [OE. *freond*] **1.** a person whom one knows well and is fond of **2.** an ally, supporter, or sympathizer **3.** [F-] a member of a Christian sect, the Society of Friends; Quaker —**be** (or **make**) **friends with** to be (or become) a friend of —**friend′less** *adj.*

friend′ly *adj.* **-li·er, -li·est 1.** of or like a friend; kindly **2.** not hostile; amicable **3.** supporting —*adv.* in a friendly way —**friend′li·ness** *n.*

friend′ship′ *n.* **1.** the state of being friends **2.** friendly feeling or attitude

fri·er (frī′ər) *n. same as* FRYER

frieze (frēz) *n.* [< ML. *frisium*] **1.** an ornamental band around a room, building, etc. **2.** a horizontal band, usually decorated with sculpture, between the architrave and cornice of a building

frig·ate (frig′it) *n.* [< It. *fregata*] a fast, medium-sized sailing warship of the 18th & 19th cent.

fright (frīt) *n.* [OE. *fyrhto*] **1.** sudden fear; alarm **2.** an ugly or startling person or thing

fright′en *vt.* **1.** to make suddenly afraid; scare **2.** to drive (*away, off,* etc.) by frightening —**fright′ened** *adj.* —**fright′en·ing·ly** *adv.*

fright′ful *adj.* **1.** causing fright; alarming **2.** shocking **3.** [Colloq.] *a*) unpleasant; annoying *b*) great *[a frightful* bore*]* —**fright′ful·ly** *adv.* —**fright′ful·ness** *n.*

frig·id (frij′id) *adj.* [< L. *frigus,* coldness] **1.** extremely cold **2.** without warmth of feeling or manner **3.** sexually unresponsive: said of a woman —**fri·gid′i·ty, frig′id·ness** *n.* —**frig′id·ly** *adv.*

Frigid Zone either of two zones (**North** or **South Frigid Zone**) between the polar circles and the poles

fri·jol (frē′hōl) *n., pl.* **fri·jo·les** (frī′hōlz, frē hō′lēz) [Sp. *frijol*] a bean, esp. the kidney bean, used for food in Mexico and the SW U.S.: also **fri·jo·le** (frē hō′lē)

frill (fril) *n.* [< ?] **1.** an unnecessary ornament **2.** a ruffle —**frill′y** *adj.* **-i·er, -i·est**

fringe (frinj) *n.* [< L. *fimbria*] **1.** a border of cords or threads, hanging loose or tied in bunches **2.** an outer edge; border **3.** a minor part —*vt.* **fringed, fring′ing** to be or make a fringe for —*adj.* **1.** at the outer edge **2.** additional **3.** minor

frip·per·y (frip′ər ē) *n., pl.* **-ies** [< OFr. *frepe,* rag] **1.** cheap, gaudy clothes **2.** showy display in dress, manners, speech, etc.

Fris·bee (friz′bē) *a trademark for* a plastic disk tossed back and forth in a game —*n.* [f-] such a disk

fri·sé (fri zā′) *n.* [Fr. < *friser,* to curl] a type of upholstery fabric with a thick pile of loops

Fri·sian (frizh′ən) *n.* the West Germanic language spoken on islands (**Frisian Islands**) off the coast of N Netherlands, West Germany, & Denmark

frisk (frisk) *vi.* [< OHG. *frisc,* lively] to frolic —*vt.* [Slang] to search (a person) for weapons, etc. by passing the hands quickly over his clothing

frisk′y *adj.* **-i·er, -i·est** lively; frolicsome —**frisk′i·ly** *adv.* —**frisk′i·ness** *n.*

frit·ter[1] (frit′ər) *vt.* [< L. *frangere,* to break] to waste (money, time, etc.) bit by bit on petty things

frit·ter[2] (frit′ər) *n.* [< VL. *frigere,* to fry] a small cake of fried batter, usually containing corn, fruit, etc.

fri·vol·i·ty (fri väl′ə tē) *n.* **1.** a frivolous quality **2.** *pl.* **-ties** a frivolous act or thing

friv·o·lous (friv′ə ləs) *adj.* [L. *frivolus*] **1.** trifling; trivial **2.** silly and light-minded; giddy —**friv′o·lous·ly** *adv.*

frizz, friz (friz) *vt., vi.* **frizzed, friz′zing** [Fr. *friser*] to form into small, tight curls —*n.* something frizzed, as hair

friz·zle[1] (friz′'l) *vt., vi.* **-zled, -zling** [< FRY[1]] to make or cause to make a sputtering, hissing noise, as in frying

friz·zle[2] (friz′'l) *n., vt., vi.* **-zled, -zling** *same as* FRIZZ

friz′zly *adj.* **-zli·er, -zli·est** full of or covered with small, tight curls: also **friz′zy, -zi·er, -zi·est**

fro (frō) *adv.* [< ON. *frā*] backward: now only in *to and fro,* back and forth

frock (fräk) *n.* [OFr. *froc*] **1.** a robe worn by friars, monks, etc. **2.** a dress; gown —*vt.* to clothe in a frock

frock coat a man's double-breasted dress coat reaching to the knees, common in the 19th cent.

frog (frôg, fräg) *n.* [OE. *frogga*] **1.** a tailless, leaping, four-legged amphibian with webbed feet **2.** a horny pad on the sole of a horse's foot **3.** a braided loop used as a fastener on clothing **4.** a device for keeping railroad cars on the proper rails at switches or intersections —**frog in the throat** hoarseness

frog′man′ *n., pl.* **-men** a person trained and equipped, as with scuba gear, for underwater work

frol·ic (fräl′ik) *n.* [< Du. < MDu. *vrō,* merry] **1.** a prank or trick **2.** a lively party or game **3.** merriment —*vi.* **-icked, -ick·ing 1.** to make merry; have fun **2.** to romp **frol′ic·some** (-səm) *adj.* full of gaiety; playful; merry: also **frol′ick·y**

from (frum, främ) *prep.* [OE.] **1.** beginning at; starting with *[he walked from* the door*]* **2.** out of *[from* a closet*]* **3.** originating with *[a letter from* me*]* **4.** out of the possibility or use of *[kept from* going*]* **5.** at a place not near to *[far from* home*]* **6.** out of the whole of *[take two from* four*]* **7.** as not being like *[to know good from* evil*]* **8.** because of *[to shake from* fear*]*

frond (fränd) *n.* [L. *frons,* leafy branch] the leaf of a fern or palm

---

front (frunt) *n.* [< L. *frons,* forehead] **1.** *a)* outward behavior *[a bold front]* *b)* [Colloq.] an appearance of social standing, wealth, etc. **2.** the part facing forward **3.** the first part; beginning **4.** a forward or leading position **5.** the land bordering a lake, street, etc. **6.** the advanced battle area in warfare **7.** a broad coalition of parties, groups, etc. as for political purposes **8.** a person or group used to hide another's activity **9.** *Meteorol.* the boundary between two differing masses of air *[a cold front]* —*adj.* at, to, in, on, or of the front —*vt., vi.* **1.** to face **2.** to serve as a front *(for)* —**in front of** before

front'age (-ij) *n.* **1.** the front part of a building **2.** the front boundary line of a lot or the length of this line **3.** land bordering a street, river, etc.

fron'tal (-'l) *adj.* **1.** of, in, on, or at the front **2.** of or for the forehead —**fron'tal·ly** *adv.*

fron·tier (frun tir') *n.* [see FRONT] **1.** the border between two countries **2.** the part of a country which borders an unexplored region **3.** any new field or area of learning, etc. *[the frontiers of medicine]* —*adj.* of or on the frontier

fron·tiers'man (-tirz'mən) *n., pl.* **-men** a man who lives on the frontier

fron·tis·piece (frun'tis pēs') *n.* [< L. *frons,* front + *specere,* to look] an illustration facing the first page or title page of a book

front·let (frunt'lit) *n.* [ult. < L. *frons,* front] a phylactery worn on the forehead

front office the management or administration, as of a company

frost (frôst, fräst) *n.* [OE. < *freosan,* freeze] **1.** a freezing or being frozen **2.** a temperature low enough to cause freezing **3.** frozen dew or vapor —*vt.* **1.** to cover with frost **2.** to damage or kill by freezing **3.** to cover with frosting **4.** to give a frostlike surface to (glass)

Frost (frôst, fräst), **Robert** (**Lee**) 1874–1963; U.S. poet

frost'bite' *vt.* **-bit'**, **-bit'ten**, **-bit'ing** to injure the tissues of (a body part) by exposure to intense cold —*n.* injury caused by such exposure

frost'ing *n.* **1.** a mixture of sugar, butter, eggs, etc. for covering a cake; icing **2.** a dull, frostlike finish on glass, metal, etc.

frost'y *adj.* **-i·er, -i·est 1.** cold enough to produce frost; freezing **2.** covered as with frost **3.** unfriendly —**frost'i·ly** *adv.* —**frost'i·ness** *n.*

froth (frôth, fräth) *n.* [ON. *frotha*] **1.** foam **2.** foaming saliva **3.** light, trifling talk, ideas, etc. —*vi., vt.* to foam or cause to foam —**froth'y** *adj.*

frou-frou (frōō'frōō') *n.* [Fr.] **1.** a rustling, as of a skirt **2.** [Colloq.] excessive ornateness

fro·ward (frō'ərd, -wərd) *adj.* [see FRO & -WARD] not easily controlled; willful —**fro'ward·ness** *n.*

frown (froun) *vi.* [< OFr. *froigne,* sullen face] **1.** to contract the brows, as in displeasure or concentration **2.** to show disapproval (with *on* or *upon*) —*n.* a frowning

frow·zy (frou'zē) *adj.* **-zi·er, -zi·est** [< ?] dirty and untidy; slovenly: also sp. **frow'sy** —**frow'zi·ly** *adv.* —**frow'zi·ness** *n.*

froze (frōz) *pt.* of FREEZE

fro'zen (-'n) *pp.* of FREEZE —*adj.* **1.** turned into or covered with ice **2.** damaged or killed by freezing **3.** preserved by freezing, as food **4.** as if turned into ice *[frozen with terror]* **5.** without warmth or affection **6.** kept at a fixed level **7.** not readily converted into cash *[frozen assets]*

frozen custard a food like ice cream, but with less butterfat content and a looser consistency

fruc·ti·fy (fruk'tə fī') *vi., vt.* **-fied'**, **-fy'ing** [< L. *fructificare*] to bear or cause to bear fruit

fruc·tose (fruk'tōs, frook'-) *n.* [< L. *fructus,* fruit + (GLUC)OSE] a crystalline sugar found in sweet fruits and in honey

fru·gal (frōō'g'l) *adj.* [< L. *frugi,* fit for food] **1.** not wasteful; thrifty **2.** inexpensive or meager —**fru·gal'i·ty** (-gal'ə tē) *n., pl.* **-ties** —**fru'gal·ly** *adv.*

fruit (frōōt) *n.* [< L. *fructus*] **1.** any plant product, as grain, vegetables, etc.: *usually used in pl.* **2.** a sweet and edible plant structure, consisting of a fruit (sense 4), usually eaten raw or as a dessert **3.** the result or product of any action *[the fruit of labor]* **4.** *Bot.* the mature ovary of a flowering plant, along with its contents, as the whole peach —*vi., vt.* to bear or cause to bear fruit

fruit'cake' *n.* a rich cake containing nuts, preserved fruit, citron, spices, etc.

fruit fly 1. a small fly whose larvae feed on fruits and vegetables **2.** *same as* DROSOPHILA

fruit'ful *adj.* **1.** bearing much fruit **2.** productive; prolific **3.** producing results; profitable —**fruit'ful·ly** *adv.* —**fruit'-ful·ness** *n.*

fru·i·tion (frōō ish'ən) *n.* **1.** the bearing of fruit **2.** a coming to fulfillment; realization

fruit'less *adj.* **1.** without results; unsuccessful **2.** bearing no fruit; sterile —**fruit'less·ly** *adv.*

fruit'y *adj.* **-i·er, -i·est 1.** like fruit in taste or smell **2.** rich or mellow in tone, as a voice

frump (frump) *n.* [< Du. *rompelen,* rumple] a dowdy, unattractive woman —**frump'ish, frump'y** *adj.*

frus·trate (frus'trāt) *vt.* **-trat·ed, -trat·ing** [< L. *frustra,* in vain] **1.** to cause to have no effect; nullify **2.** to keep from an objective or from gratifying certain desires —**frus·tra'tion** *n.*

frus·tum (frus'təm) *n., pl.* **-tums, -ta** (-tə) [L., a piece] the solid figure formed when the top of a cone or pyramid is cut off by a plane parallel to the base

fry¹ (frī) *vt., vi.* **fried, fry'ing** [< L. *frigere*] to cook or be cooked, usually in hot fat or oil, over direct heat —*n., pl.* **fries 1.** a fried food; esp., *[pl.]* fried potatoes **2.** a social gathering where food is fried and eaten

fry² (frī) *n., pl.* **fry** [< OFr. *freier,* to spawn] **1.** young fish **2.** offspring —**small fry 1.** children **2.** trivial people or things

fry'er *n.* **1.** a utensil for deep-frying foods **2.** a chicken young and tender enough to fry

ft. foot; feet

fuch·sia (fyōō'shə) *n.* [< L. *Fuchs,* 16th-c. G. botanist] **1.** a shrubby plant with drooping pink, red, or purple flowers **2.** purplish red

fud·dle (fud'l) *vt.* **-dled, -dling** [< ?] to confuse or stupefy as with alcoholic liquor —*n.* a fuddled condition

fud·dy-dud·dy (fud'ē dud'ē) *n., pl.* **-dies** [Slang] a fussy, critical, or old-fashioned person

fudge (fuj) *n.* [? echoic] **1.** nonsense **2.** [< ?] a soft candy made of butter, milk, sugar, flavoring, etc. —*vt.* **fudged, fudg'ing** to make dishonestly or carelessly —*vi.* **1.** to refuse to commit oneself **2.** to cheat

fu·el (fyōō'əl, fyōōl) *n.* [ult. < L. *focus,* fireplace] **1.** coal, oil, gas, wood, etc. burned to supply heat or power **2.** material from which atomic energy can be obtained **3.** anything that intensifies strong feeling —*vt., vi.* **-eled or -elled, -el·ing** or **-el·ling** to supply with or get fuel

fuel cell any of various devices that convert chemical energy directly into electrical energy

fu·gi·tive (fyōō'jə tiv) *adj.* [< L. *fugere,* flee] **1.** fleeing or having fled, as from danger, justice, etc. **2.** passing quickly; fleeting **3.** roaming; shifting —*n.* one who flees or has fled from danger, justice, etc.

fugue (fyōōg) *n.* [Fr. < L. *fugere,* flee] a musical composition in which a subject is announced by one voice and then developed contrapuntally by each of usually two or three other voices —**fu'gal** *adj.*

‡Füh·rer, Fueh·rer (fü'rər; E. fyōōr'ər) *n.* [G. < *führen,* to lead] leader: title used by A. Hitler

Fu·ji (fōō'jē) extinct volcano near Tokyo, Japan: also **Fu'-ji·ya'ma** (-yä'mə)

-ful [< FULL¹] *a suffix meaning:* **1.** full of, having *[joyful]* **2.** having the qualities of or tendency to *[helpful]* **3.** pl. **-fuls** the quantity that fills *[handful]*

ful·crum (fool'krəm, ful'-) *n., pl.* **-crums, -cra** (-krə) [L., a support] the support on which a lever turns in raising something

ful·fill, ful·fil (fool fil') *vt.* **-filled', -fill'ing** [OE. *fullfyllan*] **1.** to carry out (something promised, etc.) **2.** to do (something required) **3.** to satisfy (a condition) **4.** to complete —**fulfill oneself** to realize completely one's ambitions, potentialities, etc. —**ful·fill'ment, ful·fil'ment** *n.*

FULCRUM

ful·gent (ful'jənt, fool'-) *adj.* [< L. *fulgere,* to flash] [Now Rare] very bright; radiant

full¹ (fool) *adj.* [OE.] **1.** having in it all there is space for; filled **2.** having eaten all that one wants **3.** occupying all of a given space *[a full load]* **4.** having a great deal or number *(of)* **5.** complete *[a full dozen]* **6.** having reached the greatest size, extent, etc. **7.** having clearness, volume, and depth *[a full tone]* **8.** plump; round **9.** with loose, wide folds; flowing *[a full skirt]* —*n.* the greatest amount, extent, etc. —*adv.* **1.** completely **2.** directly **3.** very *[full well]* —**in full 1.** to or for the full amount, etc. **2.** not abbreviated —**full'ness, ful'ness** *n.*

full² (fool) *vt., vi.* [< L. *fullo,* cloth fuller] to shrink and thicken (wool cloth) —**full'er** *n.*

full'back' *n.* *Football* a member of the offensive backfield, the back farthest behind the line

full'-blood'ed *adj.* **1.** of unmixed breed or race; purebred: also **full'-blood' 2.** vigorous **3.** rich and full

full′-blown′ adj. 1. in full bloom; open 2. fully developed; mature

full dress formal clothes; esp., formal evening clothes — **full′-dress′** adj.

full·er's earth (fool′ərz) a highly absorbent clay used to remove grease from cloth in fulling, etc.

full′-fledged′ adj. completely developed or trained; of full rank or status

full house a poker hand containing three of a kind and a pair, as three jacks and two fives

full moon the phase of the moon when its entire illuminated hemisphere is seen as a full disk

full′-scale′ adj. 1. according to the original or standard scale 2. to the utmost limit, degree, etc.

full′y adv. 1. completely; entirely 2. abundantly; amply 3. at least

ful·mi·nate (ful′mə nāt′) vi., vt. -nat′ed, -nat′ing [< L. fulmen, lightning] 1. to explode with violence; detonate 2. to shout forth (denunciations, etc.) —n. any highly explosive compound —ful′mi·na′tion n. —ful′mi·na′tor n.

ful·some (fool′səm, ful′-) adj. [see FULL¹ & -SOME¹, but infl. by ME. ful, foul] disgusting, esp. because excessive or insincere —ful′some·ly adv.

Ful·ton (fool′t'n), **Robert** 1765-1815; U.S. inventor: designer of the 1st successful U.S. steamboat

fum·ble (fum′b'l) vi., vt. -bled, -bling [prob. < ON. famla, grope] 1. to grope (for) or handle (a thing) clumsily 2. to lose one's grasp on (a football, etc.) —n. a fumbling — **fum′bler** n.

fume (fyoōm) n. [< L. fumus] [often pl.] a gas, smoke, or vapor, esp. if offensive or suffocating —vi. fumed, fum′ing 1. to give off fumes 2. to show anger

fu·mi·gate (fyoo′mə gāt′) vt. -gat′ed, -gat′ing [< L. fumus, smoke + agere, make] to expose to fumes, esp. in order to disinfect or kill the vermin in —fu′mi·ga′tion n. —fu′mi·ga′tor n.

fum·y (fyoo′mē) adj. -i·er, -i·est full of or producing fumes; vaporous

fun (fun) n. [< ME. fonne, a fool] 1. a) lively, gay play or playfulness b) pleasure 2. a source of amusement —vi. funned, fun′ning [Colloq.] to play or joke —for (or in) fun playfully —like fun [Slang] not at all —make fun of to ridicule

func·tion (fuŋk′shən) n. [< L. fungi, perform] 1. the normal or characteristic action of anything 2. a special duty required in work 3. a formal ceremony or social occasion 4. a thing that depends on and varies with something else 5. Math. a quantity whose value depends on that of another quantity or quantities —vi. 1. to act in a required manner; work 2. to be used (as)

func′tion·al adj. 1. of a function 2. performing a function 3. Med. affecting a function of some organ without apparent organic changes [a functional disease] —func′tion·al·ly adv.

func′tion·ar′y (-er′ē) n., pl. -ies an official performing some function

fund (fund) n. [L. fundus, bottom] 1. a supply that can be drawn on; store [a fund of good humor] 2. a) a sum of money set aside for a purpose b) [pl.] ready money —vt. 1. to put or convert into a long-term debt that bears interest 2. to provide for with a fund

fun·da·men·tal (fun′də men′t'l) adj. [see FUND] of or forming a foundation or basis; basic —n. a principle, law, etc. serving as a basis —fun′da·men′tal·ly adv.

fun′da·men′tal·ism n. [sometimes F-] religious beliefs based on a literal interpretation of the Bible —fun′da·men′tal·ist n., adj.

undamental particle same as ELEMENTARY PARTICLE

un·dy (fun′dē), **Bay of** arm of the Atlantic, between New Brunswick & Nova Scotia, Canada

u·ner·al (fyoo′nər əl) n. [< L. funus] the ceremonies connected with burial or cremation of the dead —adj. of or for a funeral

uneral director the manager of an establishment (**funeral home** or **parlor**) where funeral services can be held

u·ne·re·al (fyoo nir′ē əl) adj. suitable for a funeral; sad and solemn; gloomy —fu·ne′re·al·ly adv.

un·gi·cide (fun′jə sīd′) n. [< FUNGUS & -CIDE] any substance that kills fungi —fun′gi·ci′dal adj.

un·gous (fuŋ′gəs) adj. of, like, or caused by a fungus or fungi

un·gus (fuŋ′gəs) n., pl. fun·gi (fun′jī, fuŋ′gī), fun′gus·es [L.] any of various plants, as molds, mildews, mushrooms,

etc., that lack chlorophyll and leaves and reproduce by spores —adj. of, like, or caused by a fungus

fu·nic·u·lar (fyoo nik′yoo lər) n. [< L. funis, a rope] a mountain railway on which cars are moved by cables: also **funicular railway**

funk (fuŋk) n. [< ? Fl. fonck, dismay] [Colloq.] 1. a cowering through fear; panic 2. a depressed mood —vi. [Colloq.] to be in a funk —vt. [Colloq.] 1. to be afraid of 2. to shrink from in fear

fun·ky (fuŋ′kē) adj. -ki·er, -ki·est [orig., earthy] Jazz having an earthy style derived from early blues —fun′ki·ness n.

fun·nel (fun′'l) n. [ult. < L. fundere, to pour] 1. a slender tube with a cone-shaped mouth, for pouring things into containers with small openings 2. a cylindrical smokestack of a steamship —vi., vt. -neled or -nelled, -nel·ing or -nel·ling to move or pour as through a funnel

fun·ny (fun′ē) adj. -ni·er, -ni·est 1. causing laughter; humorous 2. [Colloq.] a) strange; queer b) tricky —n., pl. -nies [Colloq.] same as COMIC STRIP: usually in pl. —fun′ni·ly adv. —fun′ni·ness n.

funny bone a place on the elbow where a sharp impact on a nerve causes a tingling sensation

fur (fur) n. [< OFr. fuerre, sheath] 1. the soft, thick hair covering certain animals 2. a processed skin bearing such hair 3. any garment made of such skins 4. any fuzzy coating, as on the tongue —adj. of fur —vt. furred, fur′ring to line, cover, or trim with fur

fur·be·low (fur′bə lō′) n. [var. of Fr. falbala] 1. a flounce or ruffle 2. [usually pl.] showy trimming —vt. to decorate with furbelows

fur·bish (fur′bish) vt. [< OFr. forbir] 1. to polish; burnish 2. to renovate —fur′bish·er n.

Fu·ries (fyoor′ēz) Gr. & Rom. Myth. three female spirits who punished doers of unavenged crimes

fu·ri·ous (fyoor′ē əs) adj. [< L. furiosus] 1. full of fury; violently angry 2. violently overpowering 3. very great; intense —fu′ri·ous·ly adv.

furl (furl) vt. [< L. firmus, FIRM¹ + ligare, to tie up] to roll up tightly and securely, as a flag —n. 1. a roll of something furled 2. a furling

fur·long (fur′lôŋ) n. [< OE. furh, a furrow + lang, LONG¹] a measure of distance equal to 1/8 of a mile, or 220 yards

fur·lough (fur′lō) n. [< Du. verlof] a leave of absence; esp., a leave granted to military enlisted personnel —vt. to grant a furlough to

fur·nace (fur′nəs) n. [< L. fornus, oven] 1. an enclosed structure in which heat is produced for heating a building, reducing ores and metals, etc. 2. any extremely hot place

fur·nish (fur′nish) vt. [< OFr. furnir] 1. to supply with furniture, etc. 2. to supply; provide

fur′nish·ings n.pl. 1. the furniture, carpets, etc. as for a house 2. things to wear [men's furnishings]

fur·ni·ture (fur′ni chər) n. [Fr. fourniture] 1. the movable things in a room, etc. which equip it for living, as chairs, beds, etc. 2. the necessary equipment of a ship, trade, etc.

fu·ror (fyoor′ôr) n. [< L. furor] 1. fury; rage 2. a) a widespread enthusiasm; craze b) a commotion or uproar

furred (furd) adj. 1. made, trimmed, or lined with fur 2. having fur 3. wearing fur

fur·ri·er (fur′ē ər) n. 1. a dealer in furs 2. one who processes furs

fur·ring (fur′iŋ) n. 1. thin strips of wood fixed on a wall, floor, etc. before adding boards or plaster 2. the act of trimming, lining, etc. with fur

fur·row (fur′ō) n. [OE. furh] 1. a narrow groove made in the ground by a plow 2. anything like this, as a wrinkle —vt. to make furrows in —vi. to become wrinkled

fur·ry (fur′ē) adj. -ri·er, -ri·est 1. of or like fur 2. covered with fur —fur′ri·ness n.

fur·ther (fur′thər) adj. [OE. furthra] 1. additional; more 2. more distant; farther —adv. 1. to a greater degree or extent 2. in addition 3. at or to a greater distance in space or time In sense 2 of the adj. and sense 3 of the adv., FARTHER is more commonly used —vt. to give aid to; promote —fur′ther·ance n. —fur′ther·er n.

fur′ther·more′ adv. besides; moreover; in addition

fur·thest (fur′thist) adj. most distant; farthest: also **fur′ther·most′** —adv. at or to the greatest distance or degree

fur·tive (fur′tiv) adj. [< Fr. < L. fur, thief] done or acting in a stealthy manner; sneaky —fur′tive·ly adv. —fur′tive·ness n.

fu·ry (fyoor′ē) n., pl. -ries [< L. furere, to rage] 1. violent anger; wild rage **2.** violence; vehemence **3.** a violent, vengeful person —**like fury** [Colloq.] violently, swiftly, etc.

furze (furz) *n.* [OE. *fyrs*] a prickly evergreen shrub with yellow flowers, native to Europe

fuse[1] (fyōoz) *vt., vi.* **fused, fus′ing** [< L. *fundere*, to shed] **1.** to melt or to join by melting, as metals **2.** to unite or blend together

fuse[2] (fyōoz) *n.* [< It. < L. *fusus*, hollow spindle] **1.** a tube or wick filled with combustible material for setting off an explosive charge **2.** *Elec.* a strip of easily melted metal placed in a circuit: it melts and breaks the circuit if the current becomes too strong

fu·see (fyōo zē′) *n.* [Fr. *fusee*, a rocket: see prec.] **1.** formerly, a friction match with a large head **2.** a colored flare used as a signal by railroaders, etc.

fu·se·lage (fyōo′sə läzh′) *n.* [Fr. < *fuselé*, tapering] the body of an airplane, exclusive of the wings, tail, and engines

fu·sel oil (fyōo′z′l, -s′l) [G. *fusel*, inferior liquor] an oily, acrid, poisonous liquid occurring in insufficiently distilled alcoholic products

fu·si·ble (fyōo′zə b′l) *adj.* that can be fused or easily melted —**fu′si·bil′i·ty** *n.*

fu·sil·ier, fu·sil·eer (fyōo′zə lir′) *n.* formerly, a soldier armed with a light flintlock musket: certain British regiments are still called *Fusiliers*

fu·sil·lade (fyōo′sə lād′) *n.* [Fr. < *fusiller*, to shoot] **1.** a simultaneous discharge of many firearms **2.** a thing like this *[a fusillade of questions]* —*vt.* **-lad′ed, -lad′ing** to shoot down with a fusillade

fu·sion (fyōo′zhən) *n.* **1.** a fusing or melting together **2.** a blending; coalition *[a fusion of political parties]* **3.** anything made by fusing **4.** *same as* NUCLEAR FUSION

fuss (fus) *n.* [prob. echoic] **1.** nervous, excited activity **2.** a nervous state **3.** [Colloq.] a quarrel **4.** [Colloq.] a showy display of approval, etc. —*vi.* **1.** to bustle about or worry over trifles **2.** to whine, as a baby —*vt.* [Colloq.] to bother unnecessarily

fuss′budg′et (-buj′it) *n.* [FUSS + BUDGET] [Colloq.] a fussy person: also **fuss′pot′** (-pät′)

fuss′y *adj.* **-i·er, -i·est 1.** bustling about or worrying over trifles **2.** hard to please **3.** whining, as a baby **4.** showing or needing careful attention **5.** full of unnecessary details —**fuss′i·ness** *n.*

fus·tian (fus′chən) *n.* [< L. *fustis*, wooden stick] **1.** orig., a coarse cloth of cotton and linen **2.** pompous, pretentious talk or writing; bombast —*adj.* pompous; pretentious

fus·ty (fus′tē) *adj.* **-ti·er, -ti·est** [< OFr. *fust*, cask] **1.** musty; moldy **2.** old-fashioned —**fus′ti·ness** *n.*

fut. future

fu·tile (fyōot′′l) *adj.* [Fr. < L. *futilis*, that easily pours out] **1.** useless; vain **2.** trifling; unimportant —**fu′tile·ly** *adv.* —**fu·til·i·ty** (fyōo til′ə tē), *pl.* **-ties, fu′tile·ness** *n.*

fu·ture (fyōo′chər) *adj.* [< L. *futurus*, about to be] **1.** that is to be or come **2.** indicating time to come *[future* tense*]* —*n.* **1.** the time that is to come **2.** what is going to be **3.** prospective condition **4.** [*usually pl.*] a contract for a commodity bought or sold for delivery at a later date **5.** *Gram.* the future tense —**fu′tur·is′tic** *adj.*

future perfect 1. a tense indicating an action or state as completed in relation to a specific time in the future **2.** a verb form in this tense (Ex.: will have gone)

fu·tu·ri·ty (fyōo toor′ə tē, -tyoor′-) *n., pl.* **-ties 1.** the future **2.** a future condition or event **3.** the quality of being future

fu·tur·ol·o·gy (fyōo′chər äl′ə jē) *n.* [< FUTUR(E) + -LOGY] a system of stating the probable form of future conditions by making assumptions based on known facts and observations —**fu′tur·ol′o·gist** *n.*

fuze[1] (fyōoz) *vt., vi.* **fuzed, fuz′ing** *same as* FUSE[1]

fuze[2] (fyōoz) *n. same as* FUSE[2]

fu·zee (fyōo zē′) *n. same as* FUSEE

fuzz (fuz) *n.* [< ?] loose, light particles of down, wool, etc.; fine hairs or fibers —**the fuzz** [Slang] a policeman or the police

fuzz′y *adj.* **-i·er, -i·est 1.** of, like, or covered with fuzz **2.** not clear, distinct, or precise[:] —**fuzz′i·ly** *adv.* —**fuzz′i·ness** *n.*

-fy [< L. *facere*, do] a suffix meaning: **1.** to make *[liquefy]* **2.** to cause to have *[glorify]* **3.** to become *[putrefy]*

G

G, g (jē) *n., pl.* **G's, g's 1.** the seventh letter of the English alphabet **2.** *Physics* gravity

G (jē) *n.* *Music* the fifth tone in the scale of C major

G general audience: a motion-picture rating meaning that the film is considered suitable for persons of all ages

G. German

G., g. 1. gauge **2.** gram(s) **3.** gulf

Ga *Chem.* gallium

Ga., GA Georgia

gab (gab) *vi.* **gabbed, gab′bing** [< ON. *gabba*, to mock] [Colloq.] to talk much or idly; chatter —*n.* [Colloq.] idle talk; chatter —**gab′ber** *n.*

gab·ar·dine (gab′ər dēn′) *n.* [< OFr. *gaverdine*, kind of cloak] a twilled cloth of wool, cotton, etc., with a fine, diagonal weave: also [Brit.] **gab′er·dine**

gab·ble (gab′′l) *vi., vt.* **-bled, -bling** [< GAB] to talk or utter rapidly and incoherently —*n.* rapid, incoherent talk —**gab′bler** *n.*

gab′by *adj.* **-bi·er, -bi·est** [Colloq.] talkative

gab′fest′ (-fest′) *n.* [Colloq.] an informal gathering of people to talk with one another

ga·ble (gā′b′l) *n.* [< Gmc.] the triangular wall enclosed by the sloping ends of a ridged roof —*vt.* **-bled, -bling** to put a gable or gables on

Ga·bon (gä bōn′) country on the W coast of Africa: 103,089 sq. mi.; pop. 480,000

Ga·bri·el (gā′brē əl) *Bible* an archangel, the herald of good news

Gad (gad) *interj.* [euphemism for GOD] [*also* g-] a mild oath or expression of surprise

gad[1] (gad) *vi.* **gad′ded, gad′ding** [? < OE. *gædeling*, companion] to wander about restlessly or idly

gad[2] (gad) *n.* [ON. *gaddr*] *same as* GOAD

gad′a·bout′ *n.* [Colloq.] one who gads about, looking for fun, excitement, etc. —*adj.* fond of gadding

gad′fly′ *n., pl.* **-flies′** [GAD[2] + FLY[2]] **1.** a large fly that bites livestock **2.** one who annoys others

gadg·et (gaj′it) *n.* [< ?] any small mechanical device — **gadg′e·teer′** *n.* —**gadg′et·ry** *n.*

gad·o·lin·i·um (gad′′l in′ē əm) *n.* [< J. *Gadolin* (1760–1852), Finn. chemist] a metallic chemical element of the rare-earth group: symbol, Gd; at. wt., 157.25; at. no., 64

Gae·a (jē′ə) *Gr. Myth.* the earth personified as a goddess

Gael (gāl) *n.* a Celt of Scotland, Ireland, or the Isle of Man; esp., a Celt of the Scottish Highlands

Gael′ic (-ik) *adj.* of the Gaels or any of their Celtic languages —*n.* any Celtic language spoken by the Gaels: Abbrev. **Gael.**

gaff (gaf) *n.* [< Pr. *gaf* or Sp. *gafa*] **1.** a large hook on a pole for landing large fish **2.** a spar supporting a fore-and-aft sail —*vt.* to strike or land (a fish) with a gaff —**stand the gaff** [Slang] to bear up well under difficulties, punishment, etc.

gaffe (gaf) *n.* [Fr.] a blunder

gaf·fer (gaf′ər) *n.* [altered < GODFATHER] an old man: now usually humorous

gag (gag) *vt.* **gagged, gag′ging** [echoic] **1.** to cause to retch **2.** to keep from speaking, as by stopping the mouth of —*vi.* to retch —*n.* **1.** something put into the mouth to prevent talking, etc. **2.** any restraint of free speech **3.** a joke

gage[1] (gāj) *n.* [< OFr., a pledge] **1.** something given as a pledge; security **2.** a glove, etc. thrown down as a challenge to fight **3.** a challenge

gage[2] (gāj) *n., vt.* **gaged, gag′ing** *same as* GAUGE

gag·gle (gag′′l) *n.* [< ME. *gagelen*, to cackle] **1.** a flock of geese **2.** any group or cluster

gai·e·ty (gā′ə tē) *n., pl.* **-ties 1.** the quality of being gay; cheerfulness **2.** merrymaking **3.** showy brightness

gai·ly (gā′lē) *adv.* in a gay manner; specif., *a*) happily; merrily *b*) brightly

gain (gān) *n.* [< OFr. *gaaignier*, earn] **1.** an increase; specif., *a*) [*often pl.*] profit *b*) an increase in advantage **2.** acquisition —*vt.* **1.** to earn **2.** to win **3.** to get as an addition, profit, or advantage **4.** to make an increase in **5.** to get to; reach —*vi.* **1.** to make progress; improve, as in health **2.** to become heavier —**gain on** to draw nearer to (an opponent in a race, etc.) —**gain over** to win over to one's side —**gain'er** *n.*

gain'ful *adj.* producing gain; profitable —**gain'ful·ly** *adv.*

gain·say (gān′sā′) *vt.* **-said'** (-sed′, -sād′), **-say'ing** [< OE. *gegn*, against + *secgan*, to say] **1.** to deny **2.** to contradict **3.** to oppose —**gain'say'er** *n.*

Gains·bor·ough (gānz′bur′ō, -bər ə), **Thomas** 1727–88; Eng. painter

'gainst, gainst (genst, gānst) *prep. poet. clipped form of* AGAINST

gait (gāt) *n.* [< ON. *gata*, path] **1.** manner of walking or running **2.** any of various foot movements of a horse, as a trot, canter, etc. —**gait'ed** *adj.*

gai·ter (gāt′ər) *n.* [< Fr. *guêtre*] a cloth or leather covering for the instep, ankle, and lower leg

gal (gal) *n.* [Colloq.] a girl

Gal. Galatians

gal. gallon; gallons

ga·la (gā′lə, gal′ə) *n.* [It. < OFr. *gale*, enjoyment] a festive occasion; festival —*adj.* festive

ga·lac·tic (gə lak′tik) *adj.* [< Gr. *gala*, milk] of the Milky Way or some other galaxy

Gal·a·had (gal′ə had′) in Arthurian legend, a knight who was successful in the quest for the Holy Grail because of his purity and noble spirit

Ga·lá·pa·gos Islands (gə lä′pə gōs′) group of islands in the Pacific, on the equator, belonging to Ecuador

Gal·a·te·a (gal′ə tē′ə) *see* PYGMALION

Ga·la·tians (gə lā′shənz) a book of the New Testament, an epistle of the Apostle Paul

gal·ax·y (gal′ək sē) [< Gr. *gala*, milk] [*often* G-] *same as* MILKY WAY —*n., pl.* **-ies** **1.** any similar group of stars **2.** a group of illustrious people

gale (gāl) *n.* [< ?] **1.** a strong wind; specif., *Meteorol.* one ranging in speed from 32 to 63 miles an hour **2.** an outburst [*a gale* of laughter]

Ga·len (gā′lən) 130?–200? A.D.; Gr. physician & writer on philosophy

ga·le·na (gə lē′nə) *n.* [L., lead ore] native lead sulfide, PbS, a lustrous, lead-gray mineral: it is the principal ore of lead: also **ga·le′nite** (-nīt)

Gal·i·le·an (gal′ə lē′ən) *adj.* of Galilee or its people —*n.* a native or inhabitant of Galilee —**the Galilean** Jesus

Gal·i·lee (gal′ə lē′) **1.** region of N Israel **2. Sea of,** lake of NE Israel, on the Syria border

Gal·i·le·o (gal′ə lē′ō, -lā′-) 1564–1642; It. astronomer & physicist —**Gal′i·le'an** *adj.*

gall[1] (gôl) *n.* [OE. *galla*] **1.** bile, the bitter, greenish fluid secreted by the liver **2.** something distasteful **3.** bitter feeling **4.** [Colloq.] impudence

gall[2] (gôl) *n.* [see GALL[3]] **1.** a sore on the skin caused by chafing **2.** annoyance, or a cause of this —*vt.* **1.** to make sore by rubbing; chafe **2.** to annoy

gall[3] (gôl) *n.* [< L. *galla*, gallnut] a tumor on plant tissue caused by stimulation by fungi, insects, or bacteria

gal·lant (gal′ənt; *for adj. 3 & n., usually* gə lant′ *or* -länt′) *adj.* [< OFr. *gale*, enjoyment] **1.** stately; imposing **2.** brave and noble **3.** polite and attentive to women —*n.* [Now Rare] **1.** a high-spirited, stylish man **2.** a man attentive and polite to women

gal'lant·ry *n., pl.* **-ries** **1.** heroic courage **2.** the courtly manner of a gallant **3.** an act or speech characteristic of a gallant

gall·blad·der (gôl′blad′ər) *n.* a membranous sac attached to the liver, in which excess gall, or bile, is stored

gal·le·on (gal′ē ən) *n.* [see GALLEY] a large Spanish ship of the 15th and 16th cent., with three or four decks at the stern

gal·ler·y (gal′ə rē) *n., pl.* **-ies** [< ML. *galeria*] **1.** a covered walk or porch open at one side **2.** a long, narrow balcony on the outside of a building **3.** a platform at the stern of an early sailing ship **4.** *a*) a balcony in a theater, etc.; esp., the highest balcony with the cheapest seats *b*) the people in these seats **5.** a group of spectators, as at a sporting event **6.** a long, narrow corridor or room **7.** an establishment for the exhibition of art works

gal·ley (gal′ē) *n., pl.* **-leys** [< MGr. *galaia*, a kind of ship] **1.** a long, low ship of ancient times, propelled by oars and sails **2.** a ship's kitchen **3.** *Printing a*) a shallow tray for holding composed type *b*) proof printed from such type: in full **galley proof**

GALLEY

galley slave 1. a slave or convict sentenced or compelled to pull an oar on a galley **2.** a drudge

Gal·lic (gal′ik) *adj.* **1.** of ancient Gaul or its people **2.** French

gal·lic acid (gal′ik) [< Fr.: see GALL[3]] an acid prepared from gallnuts, tannin, etc. and used in photography and in making inks, dyes, etc.

Gal·li·cism (gal′ə siz′m) *n.* [*also* g-] a French idiom, expression, custom, trait, etc.

Gal'li·cize' (-sīz′) *vt., vi.* **-cized'**, **-ciz'ing** [*also* g-] to make or become French or like the French in thought, language, etc.

gal·li·na·ceous (gal′ə nā′shəs) *adj.* [< L. *gallus*, a cock] of or belonging to a group of birds that nest on the ground, including poultry, grouse, etc.

gall'ing (gôl′iŋ) *adj.* that galls; very annoying

gal·li·um (gal′ē əm) *n.* [< L. *Gallia*, Gaul] a soft, bluish-white metallic chemical element with a low melting point: symbol, Ga; at. wt., 69.72; at. no., 31

gal·li·vant (gal′ə vant′) *vi.* [arbitrary elaboration of GALLANT] to go about in search of amusement

gall·nut (gôl′nut′) *n.* a nutlike gall, esp. on oaks

gal·lon (gal′ən) *n.* [< ML. *galo*, jug] a liquid measure, equal to 4 quarts

gal·lop (gal′əp) *vi., vt.* [< OFr. *galoper*] to go, or cause to go, at a gallop —*n.* the fastest gait of a horse, etc., consisting of a succession of leaping strides

gal·lows (gal′ōz) *n., pl.* **-lows·es, -lows** [OE. *galga*] an upright frame with a crossbeam and a rope, for hanging condemned persons

gall·stone (gôl′stōn′) *n.* a small, solid mass sometimes formed in the gallbladder or bile duct

gal·op (gal′əp) *n.* [Fr.: see GALLOP] a lively round dance in 2/4 time —*vi.* to dance a galop

ga·lore (gə lôr′) *adv.* [Ir. *go leór*, enough] in abundance; plentifully

ga·losh, ga·loshe (gə läsh′) *n.* [< OFr. *galoche*] an overshoe, esp. a high overshoe of rubber and fabric

Gals·wor·thy (gôlz′wur′thē, galz′-), **John** 1867–1933; Eng. novelist & playwright

gal·van·ic (gal van′ik) *adj.* **1.** of or producing an electric current, esp. from a battery **2.** startling

gal·va·nism (gal′və niz′m) *n.* [< Fr. < L. *Galvani*, 18th-c. It. physicist] electricity produced by chemical action

gal'va·nize' (-nīz′) *vt.* **-nized'**, **-niz'ing 1.** to apply an electric current to **2.** to startle; excite **3.** to plate (metal) with zinc —**gal'va·ni·za'tion** *n.*

gal'va·nom'e·ter (-näm′ə tər) *n.* an instrument for detecting and measuring a small electric current

gam (gam) *n.* [< dial. Fr. *gambe* < Gr. *kampē*, a joint] [Slang] a leg; esp., a woman's shapely leg

Gama, Vasco da *see* DA GAMA

Gam·bi·a (gam′bē ə) country on the W coast of Africa: c.4,000 sq. mi.; pop. 357,000

gam·bit (gam′bit) *n.* [Fr. < Sp. *gambito*, a tripping] **1.** *Chess* an opening in which a pawn or other piece is sacrificed to get an advantage in position **2.** a maneuver or action intended to gain an advantage

gam·ble (gam′b'l) *vi.* **-bled, -bling** [OE. *gamenian*, to play] **1.** to play games of chance for money, etc. **2.** to take a risk in order to gain some advantage —*vt.* to bet; wager —*n.* an undertaking involving risk —**gam′bler** *n.*

gam·bol (gam′b'l) *n.* [< Fr. < It. *gamba*, leg] a gamboling; frolic —*vi.* **-boled** or **-bolled, -bol·ing** or **-bol·ling** to jump and skip about in play; frolic

gam·brel (gam′brəl) *n.* [< OFr. *gambe*: see GAM] **1.** the hock of a horse, etc. **2.** *same as* GAMBREL ROOF

gambrel roof a roof with two slopes on each side, the lower steeper than the upper

game[1] (gām) *n.* [OE. *gamen*] **1.** any form of play; amusement **2.** *a*) an amusement or sport involving competition under specific rules *b*) a single contest in such a competition **3.** the number of points required for winning **4.** a set of equipment for a com-

GAMBREL ROOF

petitive amusement **5.** a project; scheme **6.** wild birds or animals hunted for sport or food **7.** [Colloq.] any object of pursuit: usually in **fair game 8.** [Colloq.] a business or vocation, esp. a risky one —*vi.* **gamed, gam'ing** to play cards, etc. for stakes; gamble —*adj.* **1.** designating or of wild birds or animals hunted for sport or food **2.** *a)* plucky; courageous *b)* enthusiastic; ready (*for*) —**make game of** to make fun of —**the game is up** failure is certain —**game'ly** *adv.* —**game'ness** *n.*

game² (gām) *adj.* [< ?] [Colloq.] lame or injured: said esp. of a leg

game'cock' *n.* a specially bred rooster trained for cockfighting

game'keep'er *n.* a person who takes care of game birds and animals, as on an estate

game plan a long-range strategy to reach a goal

games·man·ship (gāmz'mən ship') *n.* skill in using ploys to gain a victory or advantage over another

game·ster (gām'stər) *n.* a gambler

gam·ete (gam'ēt, gə mēt') *n.* [< Gr. *gamos,* marriage] a reproductive cell that unites with another to form the cell that develops into a new individual

gam·in (gam'ən) *n.* [Fr.] **1.** a neglected child left to roam the streets **2.** a girl with a roguish, saucy charm: also **ga·mine** (ga mēn')

gam·ing (gā'miŋ) *n.* the practice of gambling

gam·ma (gam'ə) *n.* the third letter of the Greek alphabet (Γ, γ)

gamma glob·u·lin (gläb'yə lin) that fraction of blood serum which contains most antibodies

gamma ray an electromagnetic radiation emitted by the nucleus of a radioactive substance: similar to an X-ray, but shorter in wavelength

gam·mon (gam'ən) *n.* [see GAM] a smoked or cured ham

gam·ut (gam'ət) *n.* [< Gr. letter *gamma,* for the lowest note of the medieval scale] **1.** *a)* the entire series of recognized notes of modern music *b)* any complete musical scale, esp. the major scale **2.** the entire range or extent, as of emotions

gam·y (gā'mē) *adj.* **-i·er, -i·est 1.** having the strong flavor of cooked game **2.** slightly tainted **3.** plucky **4.** risqué —**gam'i·ness** *n.*

gan·der (gan'dər) *n.* [OE. *gan(d)ra*] **1.** a male goose **2.** [Slang] a look

Gan·dhi (gän'dē, gan'-), **Mo·han·das K.** (mō hän'dəs) 1869–1948; Hindu nationalist leader: called *Mahatma Gandhi* —**Gan'dhi·an** *adj.*

gang (gaŋ) *n.* [< OE. *gang,* a going] a group of people working or acting together [a *gang* of criminals, a neighborhood *gang*] —*vi.* to form a gang (with *up*) —*vt.* [Colloq.] to attack as a gang —**gang up on** [Colloq.] to attack as a group

Gan·ges (gan'jēz) river in N India & Bangladesh, flowing into the Bay of Bengal: c.1,560 mi.

gan·gling (gaŋ'gliŋ) *adj.* [< ?] tall, thin, and awkward; lanky: also **gang'gly**

gan·gli·on (gaŋ'glē ən) *n., pl.* **-gli·a** (-ə), **-gli·ons** [ult. < Gr., tumor] a mass of nerve cells from which impulses are transmitted —**gan'gli·on'ic** (-än'ik) *adj.*

gang'plank' *n.* a narrow, movable platform by which to board or leave a ship

gan·grene (gaŋ'grēn, gaŋ grēn') *n.* [< Fr. < Gr. *gran,* gnaw] decay of body tissue when the blood supply is obstructed as by injury —**gan'gre·nous** (-grə nəs) *adj.*

gang·ster (gaŋ'stər) *n.* a member of a gang of criminals —**gang'ster·ism** *n.*

gang'way' *n.* [OE. *gangweg*] a passageway; specif., *a)* an opening in a ship's side for freight or passengers *b)* a gangplank —*interj.* make room!

gan·net (gan'it) *n., pl.* **-nets, -net** [OE. *ganot*] a large, web-footed sea bird

gan·oid (gan'oid) *n.* [< Fr. < Gr. *ganos,* brightness] any of a group of fishes covered by rows of hard, glossy scales or plates, as the sturgeons and gars

gant·let (gônt'lit, gant'-) *n.* [< Sw. *gata,* lane + *lopp,* a run] **1.** a former punishment in which the offender ran between two rows of men who struck him **2.** a series of troubles or difficulties Now sp. equally **gaunt'let** —**run the gantlet** to proceed while under attack from both sides

gan·try (gan'trē) *n., pl.* **-tries** [< L. *canterius,* beast of burden] **1.** a framework that spans a distance, as one on wheels that carries a traveling crane **2.** a wheeled framework with a crane, platforms, etc. for readying a rocket to be launched

Gan·y·mede (gan'ə mēd) *Gr. Myth.* a beautiful youth who was cupbearer to the gods

gaol (jāl) *n. Brit. sp. of* JAIL —**gaol'er** *n.*

gap (gap) *n.* [< ON. *gapa,* to gape] **1.** a hole or opening made by breaking or parting **2.** a mountain pass or ravine **3.** a blank space **4.** a disparity; lag

gape (gāp) *vi.* **gaped, gap'ing** [< ON. *gapa*] **1.** to open the mouth wide, as in yawning **2.** to stare with the mouth open, as in wonder **3.** to open wide, as a chasm — *n.* **1.** a gaping **2.** a wide opening

gar (gär) *n., pl.* **gar, gars** [< OE. *gar,* a spear] a long fish with a beaklike snout: also **gar'fish'**

G.A.R. Grand Army of the Republic

ga·rage (gə räzh', -räj') *n.* [Fr. < *garer,* protect] **1.** a shelter for automobiles **2.** a business place where automobiles are repaired, stored, etc. —*vt.* **-raged', -rag'ing** to put or keep in a garage

Gar·and rifle (gar'ənd, gə rand') [< J. *Garand,* U.S. inventor of it, c.1930] a semiautomatic, rapid-firing, .30-caliber rifle

garb (gärb) *n.* [< It. *garbo,* elegance] **1.** clothing; style of dress **2.** external appearance —*vt.* to clothe

gar·bage (gär'bij) *n.* [ME., entrails of fowls] spoiled or waste food that is thrown away

gar·ban·zo (gär ban'zō) *n., pl.* **-zos** [Sp.] *same as* CHICK-PEA

gar·ble (gär'b'l) *vt.* **-bled, -bling** [< It. < Ar. *ghirbāl,* a sieve] to distort or confuse (a story, etc.) so as to mislead or misrepresent

‡**gar·çon** (gär sōn') *n., pl.* **-çons'** (-sōn') [Fr.] **1.** a boy or young man **2.** a waiter or servant

gar·den (gär'd'n) *n.* [< Frank.] **1.** a piece of ground for growing flowers, vegetables, etc. **2.** an area of fertile land **3.** [*often pl.*] a public parklike place, sometimes having displays of animals or plants —*vi.* to make, or work in, a garden —*adj.* of, for, or grown in a garden —**gar'den·er** *n.*

gar·de·nia (gär dēn'yə) *n.* [< A. *Garden,* 18th-c. Am. botanist] any of a group of plants with glossy leaves and fragrant, white or yellow, waxy flowers

Gar·field (gär'fēld), **James A(bram)** 1831–81; 20th president of the U.S. (1881): assassinated

Gar·gan·tu·a (gär gan'choo wə) a giant king in a satire by Rabelais —**Gar·gan'tu·an, gar·gan'tu·an** *adj.*

gar·gle (gär'g'l) *vt., vi.* **-gled, -gling** [< Fr. < *gargouille,* throat] to rinse (the throat) with a liquid kept in motion by the slow expulsion of air from the lungs —*n.* a liquid for gargling

gar·goyle (gär'goil) *n.* [see prec.] a waterspout formed like a fantastic creature, projecting from the gutter of a building

Gar·i·bal·di (gar'ə bôl'dē), **Giu·sep·pe** (jōō zep'pe) 1807–82; It. patriot & general

gar·ish (ger'ish) *adj.* [prob. < ME. *gauren,* to stare] too bright or gaudy; showy —**gar'ish·ly** *adv.* —**gar'ish·ness** *n.*

GARGOYLE

gar·land (gär'lənd) *n.* [< OFr. *garlande*] a wreath of flowers, leaves, etc. —*vt.* to decorate with garlands

gar·lic (gär'lik) *n.* [< OE. *gar,* a spear + *leac,* a leek] **1.** a plant of the lily family **2.** its strong-smelling bulb, used as seasoning —**gar'lick·y** *adj.*

gar·ment (gär'mənt) *n.* [see GARNISH] any article of clothing —*vt.* to clothe

gar·ner (gär'nər) *n.* [< L. *granum,* grain] a granary —*vt.* to gather up and store

gar·net (gär'nit) *n.* [< ML. *granatum*] **1.** any of a group of hard silicate minerals, chiefly crystalline: red varieties are used as gems **2.** a deep red

gar·nish (gär'nish) *vt.* [< OFr. *garnir,* furnish] **1.** to decorate; trim **2.** to decorate (food) with something that adds color or flavor **3.** to garnishee —*n.* **1.** a decoration **2.** something used to garnish food, as parsley

gar·nish·ee (gär'nə shē') *n. Law* a person served with a garnishment —*vt.* **-eed', -ee'ing** *Law* to attach (a debtor's property, wages, etc.) so that it can be used to pay the debt

gar'nish·ment *n.* **1.** a decoration; embellishment **2.** *Law* a notice ordering a person not to dispose of a defendant's property or money in his possession pending settlement of the lawsuit

gar·ni·ture (gär'ni chər) *n.* garnish; decoration

gar·ret (gar'it) *n.* [< OFr. *garite,* watchtower] an attic

gar·ri·son (gar'ə s'n) *n.* [< OFr. *garir,* to watch] **1.** troops stationed in a fort **2.** a military post or station —*vt.* to station (troops) in (a fortified place) for its defense

gar·rote (gə rät', -rōt') *n.* [Sp.] **1.** a method of execution, as formerly in Spain, by strangling with an iron collar **2.** a cord, thong, etc. used in strangling a person **3.** strangulation with a cord, thong, etc. —*vt.* **-rot'ed** or **-rot'ted,**

-rot'ing or -rot'ting to execute or attack by such strangling Also sp. **ga·rotte'**, **gar·rotte'** —**gar·rot'er** n.

gar·ru·lous (gar'ə ləs, gar'yoo-) adj. [< L. garrire, to chatter] talking much, esp. about unimportant things — **gar·ru·li·ty** (gə rōō'lə tē), **gar'ru·lous·ness** n. —**gar'ru·lous·ly** adv.

gar·ter (gär'tər) n. [< OFr. garet, the back of the knee] an elastic band or strap for holding a stocking in place — vt. to fasten with a garter

garter belt a wide belt, usually of elastic fabric, with garters suspended from it, worn by women

garter snake any of various small, harmless, striped snakes common in N. America

Gar·y (ger'ē) city in NW Ind.: pop. 175,000

gas (gas) n. [coined < Gr. chaos, chaos] 1. the fluid form of a substance in which it can expand indefinitely; vapor 2. any mixture of flammable gases used for heating or lighting 3. any gas used as an anesthetic 4. any poisonous substance dispersed in the air, as in war 5. [Colloq.] a) gasoline b) the accelerator in an automobile, etc. —vt. **gassed**, **gas'sing** to attack or kill by gas —vi. [Slang] to talk idly or boastfully —adj. of or using gas

gas·e·ous (gas'ē əs) adj. of, like, or in the form of gas

gash (gash) vt. [< OFr. garser] to make a long, deep cut in; slash —n. a long, deep cut

gas·i·fy (gas'ə fī') vt., vi. -**fied**, -**fy'ing** to change into gas —**gas'i·fi·ca'tion** n.

gas·ket (gas'kit) n. [prob. < OFr. garcette, small cord] a piece or ring of rubber, metal, etc. placed around a piston or joint to make it leakproof

gas mask a filtering mask to protect against breathing in poisonous gases

gas·o·line, gas·o·lene (gas'ə lēn', gas'ə lēn') n. [< GAS + L. oleum, oil] a volatile, flammable liquid distilled from petroleum and used chiefly as a fuel in internal-combustion engines

gas·om·e·ter (gas äm'ə tər) n. a container for holding and measuring gas

gasp (gasp) vi. [< ON. geispa, to yawn] to inhale suddenly, as in surprise, or breathe with effort, as in choking —vt. to say with gasps —n. a gasping

gas station same as SERVICE STATION

gas'sy adj. -**si·er**, -**si·est** 1. full of, containing, or producing gas 2. like gas 3. [Colloq.] full of talk

gas·tric (gas'trik) adj. [GASTR(O)- + -IC] of, in, or near the stomach

gastric juice the acid digestive fluid produced by glands in the stomach lining

gas·tri·tis (gas trīt'is) n. [GASTR(O)- + -ITIS] inflammation of the stomach, esp. of the stomach lining

gastro- [< Gr. gastēr] a combining form meaning the stomach (and)

gas'tro·in·tes'ti·nal (-in tes'tə n'l) adj. of the stomach and the intestines

gas·tron·o·my (gas trän'ə mē) n. [< Gr. gastēr, the stomach + nomos, a rule] the art of good eating —**gas'tro·nom'ic** (-trə näm'ik), **gas'tro·nom'i·cal** adj.

gas·tro·pod (gas'trə päd') n. [GASTRO- + -POD] any of a large group of mollusks having a single, straight or spiral shell, as snails, limpets, etc., or no shell, as certain slugs: most gastropods move by means of a broad, muscular, ventral foot

gate (gāt) n. [< OE. geat] 1. a movable structure controlling passage through an opening in a fence or wall 2. a gateway 3. a movable barrier 4. a structure controlling the flow of water, as in a canal 5. the total amount or number of paid admissions to a performance or exhibition —**to give (someone) the gate** [Slang] to get rid of

gate'way' n. 1. an entrance in a wall, etc. fitted with a gate 2. a means of access

gath·er (gath'ər) vt. [< OE. gad(e)rian] 1. to bring together in one place or group 2. to get gradually; accumulate 3. to collect by picking; harvest 4. to infer; conclude 5. to draw into folds or pleats —vi. 1. to assemble 2. to increase 3. to form pus, as a boil —n. a pleat — **gath'er·er** n.

gath·er·ing n. 1. the act of one that gathers 2. what is gathered; specif., a meeting; crowd

gauche (gōsh) adj. [Fr. < MFr. gauchir, become warped] awkward; tactless —**gauche'ness** n.

gau·che·rie (gō'shə rē') n. gauche behavior or a gauche act

gau·cho (gou'chō) n., pl. -**chos** [AmSp.] a cowboy living on the S. American pampas

gaud (gôd) n. [ME. gaude, a trinket] a cheap, showy ornament

gaud'y adj. -**i·er**, -**i·est** bright and showy, but in bad taste —**gaud'i·ly** adv. —**gaud'i·ness** n.

gauge (gāj) n. [< ONormFr. gaugier, to gauge] 1. a standard measure or criterion 2. any device for measuring something, as the thickness of wire, steam pressure, etc. 3. the distance between the rails of a railway 4. the size of the bore of a shotgun 5. the thickness of sheet metal, wire, etc. —vt. **gauged**, **gaug'ing** 1. to measure the size, amount, etc. of 2. to estimate; judge —**gaug'er** n.

WIRE GAUGE

Gau·guin (gō gan'), **Paul** 1848-1903; Fr. painter, in Tahiti after 1891

Gaul (gôl) ancient division of the Roman Empire in W Europe —n. any of the people of Gaul

Gaul'ish n. the Celtic language spoken in ancient Gaul

gaunt (gônt) adj. [ME. gawnte, gant] 1. thin and bony; haggard, as from great hunger or age 2. looking grim or forbidding —**gaunt'ly** adv. —**gaunt'ness** n.

gaunt·let[1] (gônt'lit, gänt'-) n. [< OFr. gant, a glove] 1. a medieval armored glove 2. a long glove with a flaring cuff —**take up the gauntlet** to accept a challenge —**throw down the gauntlet** to challenge, as to combat

gaunt·let[2] (gônt'lit, gänt'-) n. same as GANTLET

gauze (gôz) n. [Fr. gaze] any very thin, transparent, loosely woven material, as of cotton or silk

gauz'y adj. -**i·er**, -**i·est** thin, light, and transparent, like gauze —**gauz'i·ness** n.

gave (gāv) pt. of GIVE

gav·el (gav'l) n. [< OE. gafol, a tool] a small mallet rapped on the table by a chairman, judge, etc. to call for attention or silence

ga·votte (gə vät') n. [Fr.] 1. a 17th-c. dance like the minuet, but livelier 2. the music for this, in 4/4 time

Ga·wain (gä'win, -wān) Arthurian Legend a knight of the Round Table, nephew of King Arthur

gawk (gôk) n. [prob. < gowk, a simpleton] a clumsy, stupid fellow vi. to stare stupidly

gawk·y (gô'kē) adj. -**i·er**, -**i·est** clumsy; ungainly —**gawk'i·ly** adv. —**gawk'i·ness** n.

gay (gā) adj. [OFr. gai] 1. joyous and lively; merry 2. bright; brilliant [gay colors] 3. homosexual —n. a homosexual —**gay'ness** n.

gay·e·ty (gā'ə tē) n., pl. -**ties** same as GAIETY

gay·ly (gā'lē) adv. same as GAILY

gaze (gāz) vi. **gazed**, **gaz'ing** [< Scand.] to look steadily; stare —n. a steady look —**gaz'er** n.

ga·ze·bo (gə zē'bō, -zā'-) n., pl. -**bos**, -**boes** [< ?] a balcony, summerhouse, etc. with a commanding or extensive view

ga·zelle (gə zel') n. [Fr. < Ar. ghazāl] a small, swift antelope of Africa and Asia, with spirally twisted horns and large, lustrous eyes

ga·zette (gə zet') n. [Fr. < It. dial. gazeta, a small coin, price of a newspaper] 1. a newspaper 2. in England, an official publication —vt. -**zet'ted**, -**zet'ting** [Chiefly Brit.] to announce or list in a gazette

gaz·et·teer (gaz'ə tir') n. a dictionary or index of geographical names

G.B. Great Britain

Gd Chem. gadolinium

Gdańsk (g'dänsk') seaport in N Poland, on the Baltic Sea: pop. 330,000

Ge Chem. germanium

gear (gir) n. [prob. < ON. gervi, preparation] 1. clothing 2. equipment for some task, as a workman's tools, a harness, etc. 3. a) [often pl.] a system of toothed wheels, disks, etc. meshed together so that the motion of one is passed on to the others b) a gearwheel c) a specific adjustment of gears: in motor-vehicle transmissions, high gear provides greatest speed and low gear greatest power d) a part of a mechanism performing a specific function [the steering gear] —vt. 1. to connect by or furnish with gears 2. to adapt (one thing) to conform with another [to gear supply to demand] —**in (or out of) gear** 1. (not) connected to the motor 2. (not) in proper working order

GEARS

gear'ing n. a system of gears or other parts for transmitting motion

gear'shift' *n.* a device for connecting or disconnecting any of a number of sets of transmission gears to a motor, etc.

gear'wheel' *n.* a toothed wheel in a system of gears

geck·o (gek'ō) *n., pl.* **-os, -oes** [Malay *gekok,* echoic of its cry] a soft-skinned, tropical lizard

gee' (jē) *interj., n.* a word of command to a horse, etc. meaning "turn right!" —*vt., vi.* **geed, gee'ing** to turn to the right

gee² (jē) *interj.* [euphemistic contr. < JE(SUS)] [Slang] an exclamation of surprise, wonder, etc.

geese (gēs) *n. pl.* of GOOSE

gee·zer (gē'zər) *n.* [< GUISE] [Slang] an eccentric old man

Ge·hen·na (gi hen'ə) *Bible* a valley where refuse was burned: translated in the New Testament as "hell" —*n.* any place of torment

Gei·ger counter (gī'gər) [< H. *Geiger,* Ger. physicist] an instrument for detecting and counting ionizing particles, as from radioactive ores

gei·sha (gā'shə) *n., pl.* **-sha, -shas** [Jpn.] a Japanese girl trained as an entertainer to serve as a hired companion to men

gel (jel) *n.* [< GELATIN] a jellylike substance formed by a colloidal solution in its solid phase —*vi.* **gelled, gel'ling** to form a gel

gel·a·tin, gel·a·tine (jel'ət 'n) *n.* [< L. *gelare,* to freeze] **1.** a tasteless, odorless substance extracted by boiling bones, hoofs, etc., or a similar vegetable substance: dissolved and cooled, it forms a jellylike substance used in food, photographic film, etc. **2.** a jelly made with gelatin

ge·lat·i·nous (jə lat'n əs) *adj.* **1.** of or containing gelatin **2.** like gelatin or jelly

geld (geld) *vt.* **geld'ed** or **gelt, geld'ing** [< ON. *geldr,* barren] to castrate (esp. a horse)

geld'ing *n.* a gelded animal, esp. a horse

gel·id (jel'id) *adj.* [< L. *gelu,* frost] extremely cold; icy

gem (jem) *n.* [< L. *gemma*] **1.** a precious stone, cut for use as a jewel **2.** a highly valued person or thing —*vt.* **gemmed, gem'ming** to adorn with gems

gem·i·nate (jem'ə nāt') *adj.* [< L. *geminare,* to double] growing or combined in pairs —*vt., vi.* **-nat'ed, -nat'ing** to double; arrange or be arranged in pairs —**gem'i·na'tion** *n.*

Gem·i·ni (jem'ə nī', -nē') [L., twins] **1.** a N constellation containing the stars Castor and Pollux **2.** the third sign of the zodiac: see ZODIAC, illus.

gems·bok (gemz'bäk') *n., pl.* **-bok', -boks'** [Afrik. < G. *gemse,* chamois + *bock,* a buck] a large antelope of S Africa, with long, straight horns

-gen [< Gr. *gignesthai,* be born] *a suffix meaning:* **1.** something that produces [oxygen] **2.** something produced (in a specified way)

Gen. 1. General **2.** Genesis

gen·darme (zhän'därm) *n.* [Fr., ult. < L. *gens,* a people + *de,* of + *arma,* arms] an armed policeman in France, Belgium, etc.

gen·der (jen'dər) *n.* [< L. *genus,* origin] **1.** *Gram.* the classification by which words are grouped as masculine, feminine, or neuter **2.** [Colloq.] sex

gene (jēn) *n.* [see -GEN] any of the units occurring at specific points on the chromosomes, by which hereditary characters are transmitted and determined

ge·ne·al·o·gy (jē'nē äl'ə jē, -al'-) *n., pl.* **-gies** [< Gr. *genea,* race + *-logia,* -LOGY] **1.** a recorded history of the ancestry of a person **2.** the study of family descent **3.** descent from an ancestor; lineage —**ge'ne·a·log'i·cal** (-ə läj'i k'l) *adj.* —**ge'ne·al'o·gist** *n.*

gen·er·a (jen'ər ə) *n. pl.* of GENUS

gen·er·al (jen'ər əl, jen'rəl) *adj.* [< L. *genus,* class] **1.** of, for, or from all; not particular or specialized **2.** of or for a whole genus, kind, etc. **3.** widespread [general unrest] **4.** most common; usual **5.** not precise; vague [in general terms] **6.** highest in rank [an attorney general] —*n.* **1.** the head of a religious order **2.** any of various military officers ranking above a colonel —**in general 1.** usually **2.** without specific details

general assembly 1. in some States of the U.S., the legislative assembly **2.** [G- A-] the legislative assembly of the United Nations

general election 1. an election to choose from among candidates previously nominated **2.** a nationwide or Statewide election

gen·er·al·is·si·mo (jen'ər ə lis'ə mō') *n., pl.* **-mos'** [It.] in some countries, the commander in chief of all the armed forces

gen·er·al·i·ty (jen'ə ral'ə tē) *n., pl.* **-ties 1.** the quality of being general **2.** a nonspecific statement, idea, etc. **3.** the bulk; main body

gen·er·al·i·za·tion (jen'ər ə li zā'shən) *n.* **1.** a generalizing **2.** an idea, statement, etc. resulting from this

gen'er·al·ize' (-ə līz') *vt.* **-ized', -iz'ing 1.** to state in terms of a general law **2.** to infer from (particular instances) **3.** to emphasize the general character of —*vi.* **1.** to formulate general principles **2.** to talk in generalities

gen'er·al·ly *adv.* **1.** widely; popularly **2.** usually **3.** not specifically

general practitioner a practicing physician who does not specialize in a particular field of medicine

gen'er·al·ship' *n.* **1.** *a)* the rank, tenure, or authority of a general *b)* the military skill of a general **2.** leadership

general staff *Mil.* a group of high-ranking army officers who plan military operations

gen·er·ate (jen'ə rāt') *vt.* **-at'ed, -at'ing** [< L. *genus,* race] **1.** to produce (offspring); beget **2.** to bring into being; produce —**gen'er·a·tive** (-ər ə tiv) *adj.*

gen·er·a'tion *n.* **1.** the producing of offspring **2.** production **3.** a single stage in the succession of descent **4.** the average time (c. 30 years) between human generations **5.** all the people born and living at about the same time

gen'er·a'tor *n.* **1.** a machine for producing gas or steam **2.** a machine for changing mechanical energy into electrical energy; dynamo

ge·ner·ic (jə ner'ik) *adj.* [see GENUS & -IC] **1.** inclusive or general **2.** that is not a trademark **3.** of or characteristic of a genus —**ge·ner'i·cal·ly** *adv.*

gen·er·os·i·ty (jen'ə räs'ə tē) *n.* **1.** the quality of being generous **2.** *pl.* **-ties** a generous act

gen·er·ous (jen'ər əs) *adj.* [< L. *generosus,* noble] **1.** noble-minded; magnanimous **2.** willing to give or share; unselfish **3.** large; ample **4.** full-flavored: said of wine —**gen'er·ous·ly** *adv.*

gen·e·sis (jen'ə sis) *n., pl.* **-ses'** (-sēz') [< Gr. *gignesthai,* be born] a beginning; origin —[G-] the first book of the Bible, telling of the creation of the universe

genetic code the order in which four chemical constituents are arranged in DNA molecules for transmitting genetic information to the cells

ge·net·ics (jə net'iks) *n.pl.* [with sing. v.] [< GENESIS] the branch of biology that deals with heredity and variation in animal and plant species —**ge·net'ic** *adj.* —**ge·net'i·cal·ly** *adv.* —**ge·net'i·cist** (-ə sist) *n.*

Ge·ne·va (jə nē'və) **1.** city in Switzerland, on Lake Geneva: pop. 171,000 **2.** **Lake** (of), lake in SW Switzerland, on the border of France: 224 sq. mi.

Gen·ghis Khan (geŋ'gis kän', jeŋ'-) 1162?–1227; Mongol conqueror of C Asia

ge·nial (jēn'yəl, jē'nē əl) *adj.* [see GENIUS] **1.** promoting life and growth [a genial climate] **2.** cheerful, friendly, and sympathetic; amiable —**ge·ni·al·i·ty** (jē'nē al'ə tē) *n.* —**ge'nial·ly** *adv.*

ge·nie (jē'nē) *n.* [Fr. *génie*] same as JINNI

gen·i·tal (jen'ə t'l) *adj.* [< L. *genere,* to beget] of reproduction or the sexual organs

gen'i·tals *n.pl.* the reproductive organs; esp., the external sex organs: also **gen'i·ta'li·a** (-tāl'yə)

gen·i·tive (jen'ə tiv) *adj.* [< Gr. *genos,* genus] designating or in a grammatical case expressing possession, source, etc. —*n.* the genitive case

ge·nius (jēn'yəs) *n.* [L., guardian spirit] **1.** *a)* [often G-] the guardian spirit of a person, place, etc. *b)* either of two spirits, one good and one evil, supposed to influence one's destiny *c)* a person considered as having strong influence over another **2.** particular spirit of a nation, place, age, etc. **3.** a great natural ability or strong inclination (for) **4.** *a)* great mental and inventive ability *b)* a person having such ability

Gen·o·a (jen'ə wə) seaport in NW Italy: pop. 844,000 — **Gen'o·ese'** (-wēz') *adj., n.* —**Gen'o·ese'**, **-ese'**

gen·o·cide (jen'ə sīd') *n.* [< Gr. *genos,* race + -CIDE] the systematic killing of a whole national or ethnic group — **gen'o·ci'dal** *adj.*

-genous [-GEN + -OUS] *a suffix meaning* producing, produced by, generated in [exogenous]

gen·re (zhän'rə) *n.* [Fr. < L. *genus,* kind] **1.** a kind, or type, as of literature **2.** painting in which subjects from everyday life are treated realistically

gent (jent) *n.* [Colloq.] a gentleman

gen·teel (jen tēl') *adj.* [< Fr. *gentil*] **1.** formerly, elegant or fashionable **2.** affectedly refined, polite, etc. —**gen·teel'ly** *adv.* —**gen·teel'ness** *n.*

gen·tian (jen'shən) *n.* [< L. *gentiana*] a plant with blue, white, red, or yellow flowers

gen·tile (jen'tīl) *n.* [< L. *gentilis,* of the same clan] [also G-] **1.** any person not a Jew **2.** formerly, among Christians, a heathen or pagan **3.** among Mormons, any person not a Mormon —*adj.* [*also* G-] **1.** not Jewish **2.** heathen; pagan **3.** not Mormon

gen·til·i·ty (jen til′ə tē) *n., pl.* **-ties** [see GENTLE] **1.** the condition of belonging by birth to the upper classes **2.** the quality of being genteel

gen·tle (jent′'l) *adj.* **-tler, -tlest** [< L. *gentilis,* of the same clan] **1.** of the upper classes **2.** refined; polite **3.** generous; kind **4.** tame [*a gentle dog*] **5.** kindly; patient **6.** not violent or harsh [*a gentle tap*] **7.** gradual [*a gentle slope*] **8.** [Archaic] chivalrous [*a gentle knight*] —*vt.* **-tled, -tling** to tame or calm —**gen′tle·ness** *n.* —**gen′tly** *adv.*

gen′tle·folk′ *n.pl.* people of high social standing: also **gen′tle·folks′**

gen′tle·man (-mən) *n., pl.* **-men 1.** orig., a man born into a family of high social standing **2.** a courteous, gracious, and honorable man **3.** any man: polite term, as (chiefly in pl.) of address —**gen′tle·man·ly** *adj.* —**gen′tle·wom′an** *n.fem., pl.* **-wom′en**

gentlemen's (or **gentleman's**) **agreement** an unwritten agreement secured only by the parties' pledge of honor

gen·try (jen′trē) *n.* [see GENTLE] **1.** people of high social standing **2.** people of a particular class or group

gen·u·flect (jen′yə flekt′) *vi.* [< L. *genu,* the knee + *flectere,* to bend] to bend the knee, as in worship —**gen′u·flec′tion, gen′u·flex′ion** *n.*

gen·u·ine (jen′yoo wən) *adj.* [< L. *genuinus,* inborn] **1.** really being what it is said to be; true **2.** sincere —**gen′u·ine·ly** *adv.* —**gen′u·ine·ness** *n.*

ge·nus (jē′nəs) *n., pl.* **gen·er·a** (jen′ər ə), sometimes **ge′nus·es** [L., race, kind] **1.** a class; kind; sort **2.** *Biol.* a classification of related plants or animals: a genus is the main subdivision of a family and includes one or more species

geo- [< Gr. *gē*] *a combining form meaning* earth, of the earth [*geology*]

ge·o·cen·tric (jē′ō sen′trik) *adj.* [GEO- + CENTRIC] **1.** viewed as from the center of the earth **2.** having the earth as a center Also **ge′o·cen′tri·cal**

ge·o·des·ic (jē′ə des′ik, -dē′sik) *adj.* **1.** *same as* GEODETIC (sense 1) **2.** designating the shortest line between two points on a curved surface —*n.* a geodesic line

ge·od·e·sy (jē äd′ə sē) *n* [< Gr. *gē,* the earth ǀ *daiein,* to divide] the branch of mathematics concerned with measuring the earth and its surface

ge·o·det·ic (jē′ə det′ik) *adj.* **1.** of or determined by geodesy **2.** *same as* GEODESIC (sense 2)

ge·og·ra·phy (jē äg′rə fē) *n., pl.* **-phies** [< Gr. *gē,* earth + *graphein,* to write] **1.** the science dealing with the earth's surface, continents, climates, plants, animals, resources, etc. **2.** the physical features of a region —**ge·og′-ra·pher** *n.* —**ge′o·graph′i·cal** (-ə graf′i k'l), **ge′o·graph′ic** *adj.* —**ge′o·graph′i·cal·ly** *adv.*

ge·ol·o·gy (jē äl′ə jē) *n., pl.* **-gies** [see GEO- & -LOGY] **1.** the science dealing with the development of the earth's crust, its rocks and fossils, etc. **2.** the structure of the earth's crust in a given place —**ge′o·log′ic** (-ə läj′ik), **ge′-o·log′i·cal** *adj.* —**ge′o·log′i·cal·ly** *adv.* —**ge·ol′o·gist** *n.*

ge·om·e·trid (jē äm′ə trid) *n.* [see GEOMETRY] any of a group of moths whose larvae move by looping the body

ge·om·e·try (jē äm′ə trē) *n., pl.* **-tries** [< Gr. *gē,* earth + *metrein,* to measure] the branch of mathematics dealing with the properties, measurement, and relationships of points, lines, planes, and solids —**ge′o·met′ric** (-ə met′-rik), **ge′o·met′ri·cal** *adj.* —**ge′o·met′ri·cal·ly** *adv.*

ge·o·phys·ics (jē′ō fiz′iks) *n.pl.* [*with sing. v.*] the science dealing with the effects of weather, winds, tides, etc. on the earth —**ge′o·phys′i·cal** *adj.* —**ge′o·phys′i·cist** *n.*

ge·o·pol·i·tics (jē′ō päl′ə tiks) *n.pl.* [*with sing. v.*] [< G. *geopolitik*] the interrelationship of politics and geography, or the study of this

George (jôrj) **1. George III** 1738–1820; king of Great Britain and Ireland (1760–1820) **2. George VI** 1895–1952; king of Great Britain and Northern Ireland (1936–52) **3.** Saint, d. 303?A.D.; patron saint of England

geor·gette (jôr jet′) *n.* [< *Georgette* de la Plante, Fr. modiste] a kind of thin crepe fabric, used for dresses, etc.: also **georgette crepe**

Geor·gia (jôr′jə) **1.** Southern State of the SE U.S.: 58,876 sq. mi.; pop. 4,590,000; cap. Atlanta: abbrev **Ga., GA 2.** republic of the U.S.S.R., on the Black Sea: in full, **Georgian Soviet Socialist Republic**

Ger. 1. German **2.** Germany

ge·ra·ni·um (jə rā′nē əm) *n.* [< Gr. *geranion,* crane's-bill: its seed capsule is beaked] **1.** a plant with showy red, pink, or white flowers and many-lobed leaves **2.** a related wildflower

ger·bil (jur′b'l) *n.* [Fr. *gerbille,* ult. < Ar.] a small rodent with long hind legs

ger·i·at·rics (jer′ē at′riks) *n.pl.* [*with sing. v.*] [< Gr. *gēras,* old age + -IATRICS] the branch of medicine dealing with the diseases and hygiene of old age —**ger′i·at′ric** *adj.*

germ (jurm) *n.* [< L. *germen,* sprout] **1.** the rudimentary form from which a new organism is developed; seed, bud, etc. **2.** any microscopic, disease-causing organism, esp. one of the bacteria **3.** an origin

Ger·man (jur′mən) *adj.* of Germany, its people, language, etc. —*n.* **1.** a native or inhabitant of Germany **2.** the language of the Germans

ger·man (jur′mən) *adj.* [< L. *germanus*] **1.** having the same parents [a brother-*german*] **2.** being a first cousin [a cousin-*german*]

ger·mane (jər mān′) *adj.* [var. of GERMAN] truly relevant; pertinent

Ger·man·ic (jər man′ik) *adj.* **1.** German **2.** designating or of the original language of the German peoples or the languages descended from it —*n.* **1.** the original language of the Germanic peoples **2.** a branch of languages descended from this, including Swedish, Dutch, English, etc.

ger·ma·ni·um (jər mā′nē əm) *n.* [< L. *Germania,* Germany] a rare, grayish-white, metallic chemical element: symbol, Ge; at. wt., 72.59; at. no., 32

German measles *same as* RUBELLA

German shepherd dog a dog of wolflike form and size, used in police work, as a guide for the blind, etc.: also **(German) police dog**

German silver *same as* NICKEL SILVER

Ger·ma·ny (jur′mə nē) former country in NC Europe: divided (1945) into EAST GERMANY and WEST GERMANY

germ cell a cell from which a new organism can develop; egg or sperm cell

ger·mi·cide (jur′mə sīd′) *n.* [< GERM + -CIDE] anything used to destroy germs —**ger′mi·ci′dal** *adj.*

ger·mi·nal (jur′mə n'l) *adj.* **1.** of or like germs or germ cells **2.** in the first stage, as of growth

ger·mi·nate (-nat′) *vi., vt.* **-nat′ed, -nat′ing** [< L. *germen,* a sprout] to start developing; sprout, as from a seed —**ger′mi·na′tion** *n.*

ger·on·tol·o·gy (jer′ən täl′ə jē) *n.* [< Gr. *gerōn,* old man + -LOGY] the scientific study of aging and the problems of aged people

ger·ry·man·der (jer′i man′dər, ger′-) *vt., vi.* [< E. *Gerry,* governor of Mass. (1812) + SALAMANDER (the shape of the redistricted county)] to divide (a voting area) so as to give unfair advantage to one political party —*n.* redistricting of this kind

ger·und (jer′ənd) *n.* [< L. *gerere,* to do or carry out] *Gram.* a verbal noun ending in *-ing*

Ge·sta·po (gə stä′pō) *n.* [< G. *Ge*(*heime*) *Sta*(*ats*)*po*(*lizei*), secret state police] the secret police force of the German Nazi state

ges·tate (jes′tāt) *vt.* **-tat·ed, -tat·ing** [< L. *gerere,* to bear] to carry in the uterus during pregnancy —**ges·ta′-tion** *n.*

ges·tic·u·late (jes tik′yə lāt′) *vi.* **-lat′ed, -lat′ing** [see GESTURE] to make or use gestures, as in adding force to one's speech —*vt.* to express by gesticulating —**ges·tic′u·la′tive** *adj.* —**ges·tic′u·la′tor** *n.*

ges·tic′u·la′tion *n.* **1.** a gesticulating **2.** a gesture

ges·ture (jes′chər) *n.* [< L. *gerere,* to bear] **1.** a movement of part of the body, to express or emphasize ideas, emotions, etc. **2.** any act or remark conveying a state of mind, intention, etc., often made merely for effect —*vi.* **-tured, -tur·ing** to make or use gestures —**ges′tur·er** *n.*

get (get) *vt.* **got, got** or **got′ten, get′ting** [< ON. *geta*] **1.** to come into the state of having; receive, obtain, etc. **2.** to arrive at [to *get* home early] **3.** to go and bring [*get* your books] **4.** to catch; capture **5.** to learn **6.** to persuade [*get* him to go] **7.** to cause to be [he *got* his hands dirty] **8.** to prepare [to *get* lunch] **9.** [Colloq.] to be obliged to (with *have* or *has*) [he's *got* to pass] **10.** [Colloq.] to possess (with *have* or *has*) [he's *got* red hair] **11.** [Colloq.] *a*) to baffle or defeat *b*) to wound or kill *c*) to strike; hit **12.** [Colloq.] to understand **13.** [Slang] to cause an emotional response in [her singing *gets* me] **14.** [Slang] to notice —*vi.* **1.** to come or arrive [to *get* to work on time] **2.** to come to be [I *got* into trouble] **3.** to contrive [to *get* to do something/ *Get* is used as an auxiliary for emphasis in passive constructions [we *got* beaten/ —*n.* the young of an animal —**get across** [Colloq.] to succeed, as in making oneself understood —**get after** [Colloq.] to pursue or goad —**get around 1.** to move from place to place; circulate: also **get about 2.** to circumvent **3.** to influence as by flattery —**get away 1.** to go away **2.** to escape —**get away with** [Slang] to succeed in doing or taking without being discovered or punished —**get back 1.** to return **2.** to recover **3.** [Slang] to get revenge (with *at*) —**get by** [Colloq.] to survive; manage —**get down to** to begin to consider or act on —**get in 1.** to enter **2.** to arrive **3.** to put in —**get off 1.** to come off, down, or out of **2.** to leave **3.** to take off **4.** to escape or help to escape **5.** to have time off —**get on 1.** to go on or into **2.** to put on **3.** to proceed **4.** to grow older **5.** to succeed **6.** to agree —**get out 1.** to go out or away **2.** to take out **3.** to become no longer a secret **4.** to publish —**get over 1.** to recover from **2.** to forget —**get through 1.** to finish **2.** to manage to survive —**get together 1.** to assemble **2.** [Colloq.] to reach an agreement —**get up 1.** to rise (from a chair, from sleep, etc.) **2.** to contrive; organize —**get'ter** *n.*

get'a·way' *n.* **1.** the act of starting, as in a race **2.** the act of escaping

Geth·sem·a·ne (geth sem'ə nē) *Bible* a garden outside Jerusalem, scene of the agony, betrayal, and arrest of Jesus

get'-to·geth'er *n.* an informal social gathering

Get·tys·burg (get'iz burg') town in S Pa.: site of a crucial battle (July, 1863) of the Civil War

get'-up' *n.* [Colloq.] **1.** general arrangement or composition **2.** costume; dress

gew·gaw (gyōō'gô, gōō'-) *n.* [< ME.] something showy but useless; trinket

gey·ser (gī'zər, -sər) *n.* [< ON. *gjosa*, to gush] a spring from which columns of boiling water and steam gush into the air at intervals

Gha·na (gä'nə) country in W Africa: a member of the Commonwealth: 91,843 sq. mi.; pop. 8,600,000; cap. Accra

ghast·ly (gast'lē) *adj.* **-li·er, -li·est** [< OE. *gast*, ghost] **1.** horrible; frightful **2.** ghostlike; pale; haggard **3.** [Colloq.] very bad or unpleasant —*adv.* in a ghastly manner —**ghast'li·ness** *n.*

ghat, ghaut (gôt, gät) *n.* [Hindi *ghāt*] in India, **1.** a mountain pass **2.** a flight of steps leading down to a river landing for ritual bathers

Ghent (gent) city in NW Belgium: pop. 156,000

gher·kin (gur'kin) *n.* [< Du. *gurken*, ult. < Per. *angārah*] a small pickled cucumber

ghet·to (get'ō) *n., pl.* **-tos, -toes** [It.] **1.** a section of some European cities to which Jews were formerly restricted **2.** any section of a city in which many members of some minority group live, or to which they are restricted by discrimination

ghost (gōst) *n.* [OE. *gast*] **1.** the supposed disembodied spirit of a dead person, appearing as a pale, shadowy apparition **2.** a faint semblance [not a *ghost* of a chance/ **3.** *Optics & TV* an unwanted secondary image —**give up the ghost** to die —**ghost'like'** *adj.* —**ghost'li·ness** *n.* —**ghost'ly** *adj.* **-li·er, -li·est**

ghost'writ'er (-rīt'ər) *n.* one who writes speeches, articles, etc. for another who professes to be the author —**ghost'write'** *vt., vi.* **-wrote', -writ'ten, -writ'ing**

ghoul (gōōl) *n.* [< Ar. *ghâla*, to seize] **1.** *Oriental Folklore* an evil spirit that robs graves and feeds on the dead **2.** a robber of graves **3.** one who does or enjoys horrible things —**ghoul'ish** *adj.* —**ghoul'ish·ly** *adv.* —**ghoul'ish·ness** *n.*

GHQ, G.H.Q. General Headquarters

GI (jē'ī') *adj.* **1.** government issue: designating clothing, etc. issued to military personnel **2.** [Colloq.] of or characteristic of the U.S. armed forces —*n., pl.* **GI's, GIs** [Colloq.] a U.S. enlisted soldier

gi·ant (jī'ənt) *n.* [< Gr. *gigas*] **1.** an imaginary being of human form but of superhuman size **2.** a person or thing of great size, intellect, etc. —*adj.* of great size, strength, etc. —**gi'ant·ess** *n.fem.*

gib·ber (jib'ər, gib'-) *vi., vt.* [echoic] to speak or utter rapidly and incoherently; chatter —*n.* gibberish

gib'ber·ish *n.* unintelligible chatter

gib·bet (jib'it) *n.* [< Frank. *gibb*, forked stick] **1.** a gallows **2.** a structure from which bodies of executed criminals were hung and exposed to public scorn —*vt.* **1.** to hang on a gibbet **2.** to expose to public scorn

gib·bon (gib'ən) *n.* [Fr.] a small, slender, long-armed ape of India, S China, and the East Indies: see illustration at top of next column

Gib·bon (gib'ən), **Edward** 1737–94; Eng. historian

gib·bous (gib'əs) *adj.* [< L. *gibba*, a hump] **1.** rounded and bulging **2.** designating the moon or a planet when more than half, but not all, of the disk is illuminated **3.** humpbacked

gibe (jīb) *vi., vt.* **gibed, gib'ing** [< ? OFr. *giber*, handle roughly] to jeer; taunt —*n.* a jeer; taunt —**gib'er** *n.*

gib·let (jib'lit) *n.* [< OFr. *gibelet*, stew made of game] any of the edible internal parts of a fowl, as the heart, gizzard, etc.

Gi·bral·tar (ji brôl'tər) **1.** Brit. territory occupying a peninsula consisting mostly of a rocky hill (**Rock of Gibraltar**) at the S tip of Spain **2. Strait of,** strait between Spain & Morocco, joining the Atlantic & the Mediterranean

GIBBON (18 1/2–25 in. long, head & body)

gid·dy (gid'ē) *adj.* **-di·er, -di·est** [OE. *gydig*, insane] **1.** having or causing a whirling, dazed sensation; dizzy **2.** frivolous; flighty —*vt., vi.* **-died, -dy·ing** to make or become giddy —**gid'di·ness** *n.*

Gid·e·on (gid'ē ən) *Bible* a judge of Israel and victorious leader in battle

gie (gē) *vt., vi.* **gied, gi·en** (gē'ən), **gie'ing** [Scot. & Brit. Dial.] to give

gift (gift) *n.* [< OE. *giefan*, to give] **1.** something given; present **2.** the act, power, or right of giving **3.** a natural ability; talent —*vt.* to present with or as a gift

gift'ed *adj.* **1.** talented **2.** having superior intelligence

gig¹ (gig) *n.* [prob. < Scand.] **1.** a light, two-wheeled, open carriage drawn by one horse **2.** a long, light ship's boat

gig² (gig) *n.* [< ?] [Slang] a job to play or sing jazz, rock, etc.

gi·gan·tic (jī gan'tik) *adj.* [see GIANT] **1.** of, like, or fit for a giant **2.** huge; enormous; immense

gig·gle (gig''l) *vi.* **-gled, -gling** [prob. < Du. *giggelen*] to laugh with rapid, high-pitched sounds, suggestive of foolishness, etc. —*n.* such a laugh —**gig'gly** *adj.*

gig·o·lo (jig'ə lō) *n., pl.* **-los** [Fr.] a man paid by a woman to be her escort

Gi·la monster (hē'lə) [< the *Gila* River, Ariz.] a stout, poisonous, black-and-orange lizard found in deserts of the SW U.S.

Gil·bert (gil'bərt), **Sir William** 1836–1911; Eng. librettist of comic operas: collaborated with A. SULLIVAN

gild (gild) *vt.* **gild'ed** or **gilt, gild'ing** [OE. *gyldan*] **1.** *a)* to overlay with a thin layer of gold *b)* to coat with a gold color **2.** to make (something) seem more attractive or valuable than it is —**gild'er** *n.* —**gild'ing** *n.*

gill¹ (gil) *n.* [prob. < Anglo-N.] the organ for breathing of most animals that live in water, as fish

gill² (jil) *n.* [< LL. *gillo*, cooling vessel] a liquid measure, equal to 1/4 pint

gilt (gilt) *alt. pt. & pp.* of GILD —*adj.* overlaid with gilding —*n.* gold leaf or a substance like gold

gilt'-edged' *adj.* **1.** having gilded edges **2.** of the highest quality or value [gilt-edged securities] Also **gilt'-edge'**

gim·bals (gim'b'lz, jim'-) *n.pl.* [with sing. v.] [< L. *geminus*, twin] a pair of rings pivoted so that one is free to swing within the other: a ship's compass suspended in gimbals will stay horizontal

gim·crack (jim'krak') *adj.* [< ME. *gibbecrak*, an ornament] showy but cheap and useless —*n.* a showy, useless thing; knickknack

gim·let (gim'lit) *n.* [< MDu. *wimmel*, wimble] a small boring tool with a spiral, pointed cutting edge

gim·mick (gim'ik) *n.* [< ? GIMCRACK] [Slang] **1.** an attention-getting feature for promoting a product, etc. **2.** any clever little gadget or ruse

gimp (gimp) *n.* [< ?] [Colloq.] **1.** a lame person **2.** a limp —**gimp'y** *adj.*

gin¹ (jin) *n.* [< L. *juniperus*, juniper] a strong alcoholic liquor distilled from grain and usually flavored with juniper berries

gin² (jin) *n.* [< OFr. *engin*, engine] **1.** a snare or trap, as for game **2.** short for COTTON GIN —*vt.* ginned, gin'ning **1.** to catch in a trap **2.** to remove seeds from (cotton) with a gin

GIMLET

gin³ (jin) *n. same as* GIN RUMMY —*vi.* ginned, gin'ning to win in gin rummy with no unmatched cards left in one's hand

gin·ger (jin′jər) *n.* [< L. *zingiber*] 1. an Asiatic plant with rhizomes that are used as a spice and in medicine 2. the spice made from the rhizome 3. [Colloq.] vigor; spirit —**gin′ger·y** *adj.*

ginger ale a carbonated, sweet soft drink flavored with ginger

ginger beer a drink like ginger ale but with a stronger flavor

gin′ger·bread′ *n.* 1. a cake flavored with ginger and molasses 2. showy ornamentation

gin′ger·ly *adv.* very carefully or cautiously —*adj.* very careful; cautious —**gin′ger·li·ness** *n.*

gin′ger·snap′ *n.* a crisp, spicy cookie flavored with ginger and molasses

ging·ham (giŋ′əm) *n.* [< Malay *ginggang*, striped] a cotton cloth, usually in stripes, checks, or plaids

gin·gi·vi·tis (jin′jə vīt′əs) *n.* [< L. *gingiva*, the gum + -ITIS] inflammation of the gums

gink (giŋk) *n.* [? < dial. *gink*, a trick] [Slang] a man or boy, esp. one regarded as odd

gink·go (giŋ′kō) *n., pl.* -**goes** [Jpn. *ginkyo* < Chin.] an Asiatic tree with fan-shaped leaves and yellow seeds: also **ging′ko**, *pl.* -**koes**

gin rummy a variety of the card game rummy

gin·seng (jin′seŋ) *n.* [Chin. *jen shen*] a perennial plant with a thick, aromatic root, used medicinally: some species are found in China and N. America

Giot·to (jôt′tō; *E.* jät′ō) 1266?-1337; Florentine painter & architect

gip (jip) *n., vt., vi.* same as GYP

Gip·sy (jip′sē) *n.* same as Gypsy

gi·raffe (jə raf′) *n.* [Fr. < Ar. *zarāfa*] a large, cud-chewing animal of Africa, with a very long neck and legs: the tallest of existing animals

gird (gurd) *vt.* **gird′ed** or **girt, gird′ing** [OE. *gyrdan*] 1. to encircle or fasten with a belt 2. to encircle 3. to prepare (oneself) for action

gird′er *n.* a large beam of timber or steel, for supporting the joists of a floor, a framework, etc.

gir·dle (gur′d′l) *n.* [OE. *gyrdel*] 1. a belt for the waist 2. anything that surrounds 3. an elasticized undergarment for supporting the waist and hips —*vt.* -**dled, -dling** 1. to bind, as with a girdle 2. to encircle —**gir′dler** *n.*

girl (gurl) *n.* [ME. *girle*, youngster] 1. a female child 2. a young, unmarried woman 3. a female servant 4. [Colloq.] a woman of any age 5. [Colloq.] a sweetheart —**girl′ish** *adj.* —**girl′ish·ly** *adv.* —**girl′ish·ness** *n.*

girl′hood′ (-hood′) *n.* 1. the state or time of being a girl 2. girls collectively

girl scout a member of the **Girl Scouts**, a U.S. organization to provide character-building activities for girls

girt¹ (gurt) *alt. pt. & pp. of* GIRD

girt² (gurt) *vt.* [var. of GIRD] 1. to gird 2. to fasten with a girth

girth (gurth) *n.* [< ON. *gjörth*] 1. a band put around the belly of a horse, etc. to hold a saddle or pack 2. the circumference, as of a tree trunk or person's waist —*vt.* 1. to encircle 2. to bind with a girth

gist (jist) *n.* [< OFr. *giste*, point at issue] the essence or main point, as of an article or argument

give (giv) *vt.* **gave, giv′en, giv′ing** [OE. *giefan*] 1. to make a gift of 2. to hand or pass over [he *gave* the porter his bag] 3. to sell (goods, etc.) or pay (a price) for goods, etc. 4. to relay [*give* my regards] 5. to cause to have 6. to confer 7. to act as host of (a party, etc.) 8. to produce; supply [cows *give* milk] 9. to sacrifice 10. to concede; yield 11. to offer 12. to perform [to *give* a concert] 13. to inflict (punishment, etc.) —*vi.* to bend, move, etc. from force or pressure —*n.* 1. a bending, moving, etc. under pressure 2. resiliency —**give away** 1. to make a gift of 2. to present (the bride) ritually to the bridegroom 3. [Colloq.] to reveal —**give back** to return —**give forth** (or **off**) to emit —**give in** to yield —**give it to** [Colloq.] to beat or scold —**give out** 1. to emit 2. to make public 3. to distribute 4. to become worn out, etc. —**give up** 1. to relinquish 2. to stop 3. to stop trying 4. to lose hope for 5. to devote wholly —**giv′er** *n.*

give′-and-take′ *n.* 1. a mutual yielding and conceding 2. an exchange of remarks or retorts

give′a·way′ *n.* [Colloq.] 1. an unintentional revelation 2. something given free or sold cheap 3. a radio or television program giving prizes

giv·en (giv′n) *pp. of* GIVE —*adj.* 1. bestowed 2. accustomed [*given* to lying] 3. stated 4. assumed; granted

given name the first name of a person, as distinguished from the surname

giz·mo, gis·mo (giz′mō) *n., pl.* -**mos** [< ?] [Slang] 1. any gadget 2. a gimmick

giz·zard (giz′ərd) *n.* [< L. *gigeria*, cooked entrails of poultry] the second stomach of a bird

Gk. Greek

gla·brous (glā′brəs) *adj.* [< L. *glaber*, bald] without hair, down, or fuzz; bald

gla·cé (gla sā′) *adj.* [Fr.] 1. having a smooth, glossy surface 2. candied or glazed, as fruits —*vt.* -**céed′, -cé′ing** to glaze (fruits)

gla·cial (glā′shəl) *adj.* 1. of ice or glaciers 2. of or produced by a glacial epoch 3. freezing; frigid 4. cold and unfriendly 5. having an icelike appearance —**gla′cial·ly** *adv.*

glacial epoch any extent of geologic time when large parts of the earth were covered with glaciers

gla·ci·ate (glā′shē āt′) *vt.* -**at′ed, -at′ing** 1. to cover over with ice or a glacier 2. to expose to or change by glacial action —**gla′ci·a′tion** *n.*

gla·cier (glā′shər) *n.* [Fr. < L. *glacies*, ice] a large mass of ice and snow moving slowly down a mountain or valley

glad¹ (glad) *adj.* **glad′der, glad′dest** [OE. *glæd*] 1. happy; pleased 2. causing joy; making happy 3. very willing [I'm *glad* to help] 4. bright or beautiful —**glad′ly** *adv.* —**glad′ness** *n.*

glad² (glad) *n.* [Colloq.] same as GLADIOLUS

glad′den (-'n) *vt., vi.* to make or become glad

glade (glād) *n.* [ME., prob. < *glad*, GLAD¹] 1. an open space in a forest 2. an everglade

glad hand [Slang] a cordial, effusive, or demonstrative welcome —**glad′-hand′** *vt., vi.*

glad·i·a·tor (glad′ē āt′ər) *n.* [L. < *gladius*, sword] in ancient Rome, a slave or paid performer who fought other men or animals in an arena as a public show —**glad′i·a·to′ri·al** (-ə tôr′ē əl) *adj.*

glad·i·o·lus (glad′ē ō′ləs) *n., pl.* -**lus·es, -li** (-lī) [< L. *gladius*, sword] a plant with swordlike leaves and tall spikes of funnel-shaped flowers in various colors: also **glad′i·o′la** (-lə)

glad′some (-səm) *adj.* joyful or cheerful —**glad′some·ly** *adv.*

Glad·stone (glad′stōn), **William** 1809-98; English prime minister

Gladstone (bag) [after prec.] a traveling bag hinged to open flat

glair (gler) *n.* [< L. *clarus*, clear] 1. raw white of egg, used in sizing 2. a size or glaze made from this —**glair′y** *adj.*

glam·or·ize (glam′ə rīz′) *vt.* -**ized′, -iz′ing** to make glamorous —**glam′or·i·za′tion** *n.*

glam·our, glam·or (glam′ər) *n.* [Scot. var. of *grammar*, magic] seemingly mysterious allure; bewitching charm —**glam′or·ous, glam′our·ous** *adj.*

glance (glans) *vi.* **glanced, glanc′ing** [ME. *glansen*] 1. to strike obliquely and go off at an angle 2. to flash or gleam 3. to take a quick look —*n.* 1. a glancing off 2. a flash or gleam 3. a quick look

gland (gland) *n.* [< L. *glans*, acorn] any organ that separates certain elements from the blood and secretes them for the body to use or throw off —**glan·du·lar** (glan′jə lər) *adj.*

glan·ders (glan′dərz) *n.pl.* [with sing. v.] [OFr. *glandres*, glands] a contagious disease of horses, mules, etc. characterized by fever, swelling of glands beneath the jaw, etc.

glans (glanz) *n., pl.* **glan·des** (glan′dēz) [L., lit., acorn] 1. the head of the penis: in full **glans penis** 2. the tip of the clitoris

glare¹ (gler) *vi.* **glared, glar′ing** [ME. *glaren*] 1. to shine with a steady, dazzling light 2. to be too bright or showy 3. to stare fiercely —*vt.* to express with a glare —*n.* 1. a steady, dazzling light 2. a too showy display 3. a fierce or angry stare

glare² (gler) *n.* [prob. < prec.] a smooth, bright, glassy surface, as of ice —*adj.* smooth, bright, and glassy

glar′ing *adj.* 1. dazzlingly bright 2. too showy 3. staring fiercely 4. flagrant [a *glaring* mistake]

Glas·gow (glas′kō, glaz′gō) seaport in SC Scotland: pop. 961,000

glass (glas) *n.* [OE. *glæs*] 1. a hard, brittle substance, usually transparent, made by fusing silicates with soda, lime, etc. 2. same as GLASSWARE 3. *a)* an article made of glass, as a drinking container, mirror, etc. *b)* [*pl.*] eyeglasses or binoculars 4. the quantity contained in a drinking glass —

vt. to equip with glass —*adj.* of or made of glass —**glass'ful'** *n., pl.* **glass'fuls'**

glass blowing the art or process of shaping molten glass by blowing air into a mass of it at the end of a tube — **glass blower**

glass'ware' *n.* articles made of glass

glass'y *adj.* **-i·er, -i·est** 1. like glass, as in smoothness or transparency 2. expressionless or lifeless *[a glassy stare]* — **glass'i·ly** *adv.* —**glass'i·ness** *n.*

glau·co·ma (glô kō′mə, glou-) *n.* [see GLAUCOUS] a disease of the eye marked by increased pressure in the eyeball: it leads to a gradual loss of sight

glau·cous (glô′kəs) *adj.* [< Gr. *glaukos*, gleaming] 1. bluish-green or yellowish-green 2. *Bot.* covered with a whitish bloom that can be rubbed off, as grapes

glaze (glāz) *vt.* **glazed, glaz'ing** [< ME. *glas*, glass] 1. to fit (windows, etc.) with glass 2. to give a hard, glossy finish to (pottery, etc.) 3. to cover (foods) with a coating of sugar syrup, etc. —*vi.* to become glassy or glossy —*n.* a glassy finish or coating —**glaz'ing** *n.*

gleam (glēm) *n.* [OE. *glæm*] 1. a flash or beam of light 2. a faint light 3. a faint manifestation, as of hope, etc. —*vi.* 1. to shine with a gleam 2. to appear suddenly

glean (glēn) *vt., vi.* [< Celt.] 1. to collect (grain left by reapers) 2. to collect (facts, etc.) gradually —**glean'er** *n.*

glean'ings *n.pl.* that which is gleaned

glee (glē) *n.* [OE. *gleo*] 1. lively joy; merriment 2. a part song for three or more voices —**glee'ful** *adj.* —**glee'ful·ly** *adv.* —**glee'ful·ness** *n.*

glee club a group singing part songs

glen (glen) *n.* [< ScotGael.] a narrow, secluded valley

Glen·dale (glen′dāl) city in SW Calif.: suburb of Los Angeles: pop. 133,000

Glen·gar·ry (glen gar′ē) *n., pl.* **-ries** [< *Glengarry*, in Scotland [*sometimes* g-] a Scottish cap for men, creased lengthwise across the top: also **Glengarry bonnet** (or **cap**)

glib (glib) *adj.* **glib'ber, glib'best** [< or akin to Du. *glibberig*, slippery] speaking or spoken in a smooth, fluent manner, often in a way too smooth to be convincing — **glib'ly** *adv.* —**glib'ness** *n.*

glide (glīd) *vi.* **glid'ed, glid'ing** [OE. *glidan*] 1. to move smoothly and easily 2. *Aeron. a)* to fly in a glider *b)* to descend at a normal angle with little or no engine power 3. *Music* to make a glide —*vt.* to cause to glide —*n.* 1. the act of gliding 2. a small disk or ball attached under furniture, etc. to allow easy sliding 3. *Music* loosely, a slur

glid'er *n.* 1. one that glides 2. an engineless aircraft that is carried along by air currents 3. a porch swing suspended in a frame

glim·mer (glim′ər) *vi.* [< OE. *glæm*, gleam] 1. to give a faint, flickering light 2. to appear faintly —*n.* 1. a faint, flickering light 2. a faint manifestation —**glim′mer·ing** *n.*

glimpse (glimps) *vt.* **glimpsed, glimps'ing** [see GLIMMER] to catch a quick view of —*vi.* to look quickly —*n.* 1. a faint, fleeting appearance 2. a quick view

glint (glint) *vi.* [prob. < Scand.] to gleam; flash —*n.* a gleam, flash, or glitter

glis·sade (gli säd′, -säd′) *n.* [Fr. < *glisser*, to slide] 1. an intentional slide by a mountain climber down a steep, snow-covered slope 2. *Ballet* a gliding step

glis·san·do (gli sän′dō) *n., pl.* **-di** (-dē), **-dos** [as if It. < Fr. *glisser*, to slide] *Music* a sliding effect, with tones sounded in rapid succession —*adj., adv.* (performed) with such an effect

glis·ten (glis′'n) *vi.* [OE. *glisnian*] to shine or sparkle with reflected light —*n.* a glistening

glit·ter (glit′ər) *vi.* [prob. < ON. *glitra*] 1. to shine brightly; sparkle 2. to be showy and bright —*n.* 1. bright, sparkling light 2. showiness; brightness 3. bits of glittering material —**glit′ter·y** *adj.*

gloam·ing (glō′miŋ) *n.* [< OE. *glom*] evening dusk; twilight

gloat (glōt) *vi.* [prob. < ON. *glotta*, grin scornfully] to gaze or think with malicious pleasure

glob (gläb) *n.* [prob. < GLOBULE] a rounded mass or lump, as of mud

glob·al (glō′b'l) *adj.* worldwide —**glob′al·ly** *adv.*

glob′al·ism *n.* a policy, outlook, etc. that is worldwide in scope —**glob′al·ist** *n., adj.*

globe (glōb) *n.* [< L. *globus*] 1. any ball-shaped thing; sphere 2. the earth 3. a spherical model of the earth 4. anything shaped like a globe —*vt., vi.* **globed, glob'ing** to form or gather into a globe

globe′fish′ *n., pl.:* see FISH a tropical fish that can puff itself into a globular form

globe′-trot′ter *n.* one who travels widely about the world, esp. for pleasure or sightseeing

glob·u·lar (gläb′yə lər) *adj.* 1. shaped like a globe or ball; spherical 2. made up of globules

glob′ule (-yōōl) *n.* [< L. *globus*, ball] a tiny ball; very small drop

glock·en·spiel (gläk′ən spēl′) *n.* [G. < *glocke*, bell + *spiel*, play] a musical instrument with tuned metal bars in a frame, played with hammers

glom·er·ate (gläm′ər it) *adj.* [< L. *glomus*, a ball] formed into a rounded mass —**glom′er·a′tion** *n.*

gloom (glōōm) *n.* [prob. < Scand.] 1. darkness; dimness 2. sadness; dejection —*vi., vt.* to make or become gloomy, dark, sad, etc.

gloom′y *adj.* **-i·er, -i·est** 1. enveloped in darkness or dimness 2. sad; dejected 3. causing gloom; dismal —**gloom′i·ly** *adv.* —**gloom′i·ness** *n.*

GLOCKENSPIEL

glop (gläp) *n.* [< ? GL(UE) + (SL)OP] [Slang] any soft, gluey substance

Glo·ri·a (glôr′ē ə) *n.* [L., glory] any of several Latin hymns beginning with this word

glo·ri·fy (glôr′ə fī′) *vt.* **-fied′, -fy′ing** [< L. *gloria*, glory + *facere*, make] 1. to give glory to 2. to exalt as in worship 3. to honor; extol 4. to make seem better, greater, etc. than is so —**glo′ri·fi·ca′tion** *n.* —**glo′ri·fi′er** *n.*

glo·ri·ous (-ē əs) *adj.* 1. full of glory 2. receiving or deserving glory 3. splendid; magnificent 4. [Colloq.] very delightful —**glo′ri·ous·ly** *adv.*

glo·ry (glôr′ē) *n., pl.* **-ries** [< L. *gloria*] 1. great honor or fame 2. anything bringing this 3. worship; adoration 4. great splendor, prosperity, success, etc. 5. heaven or heavenly bliss 6. *same as* HALO (n. 1 & 2) —*vi.* **-ried, -ry·ing** to exult (*in*) —**in one's glory** at one's best, happiest, etc.

gloss¹ (glôs) *n.* [< ? Scand.] 1. the luster of a polished surface 2. a deceptive outward appearance —*vt.* 1. to give a shiny surface to 2. to hide (an error, etc.) or make seem right or trivial —**gloss′i·ness** *n.* —**gloss′y** *adj.* **-i·er, -i·est**

gloss² (glôs) *n.* [< Gr. *glōssa*, tongue] a note of comment or explanation, as in a footnote —*vt.* to furnish (a text) with glosses

glos·sa·ry (gläs′ə rē, glôs′-) *n., pl.* **-ries** [see prec.] a list of difficult terms with explanations, as for a book, author, etc.

glos·so·la·li·a (gläs′ə lā′lē ə, glôs′-) *n.* [< Gr. *glōssa*, tongue + *lalein*, to speak] an uttering of unintelligible sounds, as in a religious ecstasy

glot·tal (glät′'l) *adj.* of or produced in or at the glottis

glot·tis (glät′is) *n.* [< Gr. *glōssa*, tongue] the opening between the vocal cords in the larynx

glove (gluv) *n.* [OE. *glof*] 1. a covering for the hand, with separate sheaths for the fingers and thumb 2. a baseball player's mitt 3. a boxing glove —*vt.* **gloved, glov'ing** to cover as with a glove

glov'er *n.* a maker or seller of gloves

glow (glō) *vi.* [OE. *glowan*] 1. to give off a bright light due to great heat 2. to give out a steady light 3. to be or feel hot 4. to be enlivened by emotion 5. to be bright with color —*n.* 1. light given off, due to great heat 2. steady, even light 3. brightness of color 4. a sensation of warmth and well-being 5. warmth of emotion —**glow'ing** *adj.* —**glow'ing·ly** *adv.*

glow·er (glou′ər) *vi.* [prob. < ON.] to stare with sullen anger —*n.* a sullen, angry stare; scowl

glow'worm' *n.* a wingless insect or insect larva that gives off a luminescent light; esp., the wingless female or the larva of the firefly

glox·in·i·a (gläk sin′ē ə) *n.* [< B. P. *Gloxin*, 18th-c. Ger. botanist] a cultivated tropical plant with bell-shaped flowers of various colors

gloze (glōz) *vt.* **glozed, gloz'ing** [see GLOSS²] to explain away

glu·cose (glōō′kōs) *n.* [Fr. < Gr. *gleúkos*, sweetness] a crystalline sugar, $C_6H_{12}O_6$, occurring naturally in fruits, honey, etc.: prepared commercially as a sweet syrup by the hydrolysis of starch

glu'co·side' (-kə sīd′) *n.* [GLUCOS(E) + -IDE] a compound that yields glucose on hydrolysis

glue (glōō) *n.* [< LL. *glus*] 1. a sticky, viscous liquid made from animal gelatin, used as an adhesive 2. any similar substance —*vt.* **glued, glu'ing** to make stick as with glue

glu'y *adj.* **glu'i·er, glu'i·est** 1. like glue; sticky 2. covered with or full of glue

glum (glum) *adj.* **glum'mer, glum'mest** [prob. < ME. *glomen*, look morose] gloomy; sullen —**glum'ly** *adv.* —**glum'-ness** *n.*

glut (glut) *vi.* **glut′ted, glut′ting** [< L. *gluttire,* to swallow] to eat to excess —*vt.* **1.** to feed, fill, etc. to excess **2.** to supply (the market) beyond demand —*n.* **1.** a glutting or being glutted **2.** a supply that is greater than the demand

glu·ten (gloōt′'n) *n.* [L., glue] a gray, sticky, nutritious protein substance found in wheat, etc. —**glu′ten·ous** *adj.*

glu·te·us (glōō tē′əs) *n., pl.* **-te′i** (-ī) [Gr. *gloutos,* rump] any of the three muscles that form each of the buttocks —**glu·te′al** *adj.*

glu·ti·nous (glōōt′'n əs) *adj.* [< L. *gluten,* glue] gluey; sticky —**glu′ti·nous·ly** *adv.*

glut·ton (glut′'n) *n.* [see GLUT] **1.** one who eats too much **2.** one who has a great capacity for something —**glut′ton·ous** *adj.* —**glut′ton·ous·ly** *adv.*

glut′ton·y *n., pl.* **-ies** the habit or act of eating too much

glyc·er·in, glyc·er·ine (glis′ər in) *n.* [< Fr. < Gr. *glykeros,* sweet] *popular and commercial name for* GLYCEROL

glyc·er·ol (glis′ər ōl′, -ôl′) *n.* [< prec.] a colorless, syrupy liquid made from fats and oils: used in skin lotions, in making explosives, etc.

gly·co·gen (glī′kə jən) *n.* [see GLYCERIN] a starchlike substance produced in animal tissues, that is changed into a simple sugar as needed by the body

gm. gram; grams

Gmc. Germanic

gnarl (närl) *n.* [< ME. *knorre*] a knot on a tree trunk or branch —*vt.* to make knotted; twist —**gnarled, gnarl′y** *adj.*

gnash (nash) *vi., vt.* [prob. < ON.] to grind (the teeth) together, as in anger —*n.* a gnashing

gnat (nat) *n.* [OE. *gnæt*] any of various small, two-winged insects that bite or sting

gnaw (nô) *vt., vi.* [< OE. *gnagen*] **1.** to bite and wear away bit by bit; consume **2.** to torment, as by constant pain —**gnaw′ing** *n., adj.*

gneiss (nīs) *n.* [< OHG. *gneisto,* a spark] a granitelike rock formed of layers of feldspar, quartz, mica, etc.

gnome (nōm) *n.* [Fr. < Gr. *gnōmē,* thought] *Folklore* a dwarf who dwells in the earth and guards its treasures — **gnom′ish** *adj.*

gno·mon (nō′män) *n.* [< Gr. *gignōskein,* know] a column, pin on a sundial, etc., that casts a shadow indicating the time of day

GNP gross national product

gnu (nōō) *n.* [< the native name] a large African antelope with an oxlike head and horns and a horselike mane

go (gō) *vi.* **went, gone, go′ing** [OE. *gan*] **1.** to move along; travel; proceed **2.** to work properly; operate [the clock won't *go*] **3.** to act, sound, etc. as specified [the balloon went "pop"] **4.** to turn out; result [the game went badly] **5.** to pass: said of time **6.** to be in a certain state [he *goes* in rags] **7.** to become [to go mad] **8.** to be expressed, sung, etc. [as the saying *goes*] **9.** to harmonize; agree [blue goes with gold] **10.** to be accepted, valid, etc. **11.** to leave; depart **12.** to fail [his hearing went] **13.** to be allotted or sold **14.** to reach, extend, etc. [this road goes to the lake] **15.** to attend [he goes to college] **16.** to be able to pass (through), fit (into), etc. **17.** to be a divisor (into) [5 goes into 10 twice] **18.** to belong [socks go in this drawer] —*vt.* **1.** to travel or proceed along [to go the wrong way] **2.** [Colloq.] *a)* to put up with *b)* to furnish (bail) for an arrested person —*n., pl.* **goes 1.** a success [make a go of marriage] **2.** [Colloq.] energy; animation **3.** [Colloq.] a try; attempt —**go along 1.** to continue **2.** to agree **3.** to accompany —**go around 1.** to surround **2.** to be enough for each **3.** to circulate —**go back on** [Colloq.] **1.** to betray **2.** to break (a promise, etc.) —**go beyond** to exceed —**go by 1.** to pass **2.** to be guided by **3.** to be known by (the name of) —**go for 1.** to try to get **2.** [Colloq.] to be attracted by —**go hard with** to cause trouble to —**go in for** [Colloq.] to engage or indulge in —**go in with** to share expenses, etc. with; join —**go off 1.** to depart **2.** to explode —**go out 1.** to be extinguished, become outdated, etc. **2.** to attend social affairs, etc. —**go over 1.** to examine thoroughly **2.** to do again **3.** [Colloq.] to be successful —**go through 1.** to endure; experience **2.** to search —**go through with** to complete —**go together 1.** to harmonize **2.** [Colloq.] to be sweethearts —**go under** to fail, as in business —**let go 1.** to let escape **2.** to release one's hold —**let oneself go** to be unrestrained —**on the go** [Colloq.] in constant motion or action —**to go** [Colloq.] **1.** to be taken out: said of food in a restaurant **2.** still to be done, etc.

goad (gōd) *n.* [OE. *gad*] **1.** a sharp-pointed stick used in driving oxen **2.** any driving impulse; spur —*vt.* to drive as with a goad; spur on

go′-a·head′ *n.* permission or a signal to proceed: usually with *the*

goal (gōl) *n.* [ME. *gol,* boundary] **1.** the place at which a race, trip, etc. is ended **2.** an end that one strives to attain **3.** in some games, *a)* the line, net, etc. over or into which the ball or puck must go to score *b)* a scoring in this way *c)* the score made

goal′keep′er *n.* in some games, a player stationed at a goal to prevent the ball or puck from crossing or entering it: also **goal′ie** (-ē), **goal′tend′er**

goat (gōt) *n.* [OE. *gat*] **1.** a cud-chewing mammal with hollow horns, related to the sheep **2.** a lecherous man **3.** [Colloq.] a scapegoat —[G-] the constellation Capricorn — **get one's goat** [Colloq.] to irritate one

goat·ee (gō tē′) *n.* a pointed beard on a man's chin

goat′herd′ *n.* one who herds goats

goat′skin′ *n.* the hide of a goat, or leather made from this

goat′suck′er *n.* a large-mouthed, nocturnal bird that feeds on insects, as the whippoorwill

gob[1] (gäb) *n.* [< OFr. *gobe,* mouthful] **1.** a soft lump or mass **2.** [pl.] [Colloq.] a large quantity

gob[2] (gäb) *n.* [< ?] [Slang] a sailor in the U.S. Navy

gob·ble[1] (gäb′'l) *n.* [echoic] the throaty sound made by a male turkey —*vi.* **-bled, -bling** to make this sound

gob·ble[2] (gäb′'l) *vt., vi.* **-bled, -bling** [prob. < OFr. *gobe,* mouthful] **1.** to eat quickly and greedily **2.** to snatch (*up*)

gob′ble·dy·gook′ (-dē gook′) *n.* [? echoic] [Slang] pompous and wordy talk or writing

gob·bler (gäb′lər) *n.* a male turkey

go-be·tween (gō′bi twēn′) *n.* one who makes arrangements between each of two sides; intermediary

Go·bi (gō′bē) large desert plateau in E Asia, chiefly in Mongolia

gob·let (gäb′lit) *n.* [< OFr. *gobel*] a drinking glass with a base and stem

gob·lin (gäb′lin) *n.* [< ML. *gobelinus*] *Folklore* an evil or mischievous sprite

go-by (gō′bī′) *n.* [Colloq.] an intentional disregard or slight: chiefly in *give* (or *get*) *the go-by* to slight (or be slighted)

go′-cart′ *n.* **1.** a small, low baby carriage **2.** *same as* KART

god (gäd) *n.* [OE.] **1.** any of various beings conceived of as supernatural, immortal, and having power over people or nature; deity, esp. a male one **2.** an idol **3.** a person or thing deified or excessively honored —[G-] in monotheistic religions, the creator and ruler of the universe; Supreme Being —**god′like′** *adj.*

god′child′ *n., pl.* **-chil′dren** the person for whom a godparent is sponsor

god′daugh′ter *n.* a female godchild

god′dess *n.* **1.** a female god **2.** a woman greatly admired, as for her beauty

god′fa′ther *n.* a male godparent

god′head′ (-hed′) *n.* **1.** *same as* GODHOOD **2.** [G-] God (usually with *the*)

god′hood′ (-hood′) *n.* the state of being a god

Go·di·va (gə dī′və) *Eng. Legend* an 11th-cent. noblewoman who rode naked through the streets on condition that her husband would abolish a heavy tax

god′less *adj.* **1.** denying the existence of God; irreligious **2.** wicked —**god′less·ly** *adv.* —**god′less·ness** *n.*

god′ly *adj.* **-li·er, -li·est** devoted to God; devout —**god′li·ness** *n.*

god′moth′er *n.* a female godparent

god′par′ent *n.* a person who sponsors a newborn child and assumes responsibility for its faith

god′send′ *n.* anything that comes unexpectedly and when needed or desired, as if sent by God

god′son′ *n.* a male godchild

God′speed′ *n.* [contr. of *God speed you*] success; good luck: a wish made for travelers

God·win Austen (gäd′win) mountain in N Jammu & Kashmir: second highest in the world: 28,250 ft.

Goe·the (gö′tə; *E.* gur′tə), **Jo·hann Wolf·gang von** (yō′hän vôlf′gäŋ fôn) 1749–1832; Ger. poet

go-get·ter (gō′get′ər) *n.* [Colloq.] an enterprising and aggressive person

gog·gle (gäg′'l) *vi.* **-gled, -gling** [ME. *gogelen*] **1.** to stare with bulging eyes **2.** to bulge or roll: said of the eyes —*n.* **1.** a staring with bulging eyes **2.** [pl.] large spectacles to protect the eyes against dust, wind, etc. —*adj.* bulging: said of the eyes —**gog'gle-eyed'** (-īd') *adj.*

go-go (gō'gō') *adj.* [< Fr. *à gogo*, in plenty] of rock-and-roll dancing performed in cafés, often in topless costumes

go-ing (gō'iŋ) *n.* **1.** a departure **2.** the condition of the ground or land as it affects traveling, walking, etc. —*adj.* **1.** moving; working **2.** commonly accepted —**be going to** will or shall

go'ing-o'ver *n.* [Colloq.] **1.** a thorough inspection **2.** a severe scolding or beating

go'ings-on' *n.pl.* [Colloq.] actions or events, esp. when regarded with disapproval

goi-ter, goi-tre (goit'ər) *n.* [< L. *guttur*, throat] an enlargement of the thyroid gland, often seen as a swelling in the front of the neck

gold (gōld) *n.* [OE.] **1.** a heavy, yellow metallic chemical element: it is a precious metal and is used in coins, jewelry, etc.: symbol, Au; at. wt., 196.967; at. no., 79 **2.** money; wealth **3.** bright yellow —*adj.* **1.** made of or like gold **2.** bright-yellow

gold'brick' *n.* **1.** [Colloq.] anything worthless passed off as valuable **2.** [Mil. Slang] one who tries to avoid work; shirker: also **gold'brick'er** —*vi.* [Mil. Slang] to avoid work; shirk

gold'en *adj.* **1.** made of or containing gold **2.** bright-yellow **3.** very valuable; excellent **4.** flourishing

golden ag·er (āj'ər) [Colloq.] [*also* G- A-] an elderly person, esp. one 65 or older and retired

Golden Fleece *Gr. Myth.* the fleece of gold captured by Jason

Golden Gate strait between San Francisco Bay and the Pacific

golden mean the safe, prudent way between extremes; moderation

gold'en·rod' *n.* a N. American plant with long, branching stalks bearing clusters of small, yellow flowers

golden rule the precept that one should act toward others as he would want them to act toward him

golden wedding a 50th wedding anniversary

gold'-filled' *adj.* made of a base metal overlaid with gold

gold'finch' *n.* [OE. *goldfinc*] **1.** a small American finch, the male of which has a yellow body **2.** a European songbird with yellow-streaked wings

gold'fish' *n., pl.:* see FISH a small, golden-yellow or orange fish, often kept in aquariums

gold leaf gold beaten into very thin sheets, used for gilding —**gold'-leaf'** *adj.*

gold'smith' *n.* a skilled worker who makes articles of gold

Gold·smith (gōld'smith'), **Oliver** 1728–74; Brit. poet, playwright, and novelist, born in Ireland

gold standard a monetary standard whose basic currency unit equals a specified quantity of gold

golf (gôlf, gälf) *n.* [< ? Scot. *gowf*, to strike] an outdoor game played on a tract of land (**golf course** or **golf links**) with a small, hard ball and a set of long-handled clubs, the object being to hit the ball into each of 9 or 18 holes in turn, with the fewest possible strokes —*vi.* to play golf —**golf'er** *n.*

Gol·go·tha (gäl'gə thə) [see CALVARY] the place where Jesus was crucified; Calvary

Go·li·ath (gə lī'əth) *Bible* the Philistine giant killed by David with a stone from a sling

gol·ly (gäl'ē) *interj.* an exclamation of surprise, etc.

Go·mor·rah, Go·mor·rha (gə môr'ə) *see* SODOM

-gon [< Gr. *gōnia*, an angle] *a combining form meaning* a figure having a (specified number of) angles

go·nad (gō'nad) *n.* [< Gr. *gonē*, seed] an animal organ that produces reproductive cells; ovary or testicle —**go·nad'al** *adj.*

gon·do·la (gän'də lə) *n.* [It.] **1.** a long, narrow boat used on the canals of Venice **2.** a railroad freight car with low sides and no top: also **gondola car 3.** a cabin suspended under a dirigible or balloon

gon'do·lier' (-lir') *n.* a man who rows or poles a gondola

gone (gôn, gän) *pp. of* GO —*adj.* **1.** departed **2.** ruined **3.** lost **4.** dead **5.** faint; weak **6.** consumed **7.** ago; past —**far gone** deeply involved

GONDOLA

gon'er *n.* [Colloq.] a person or thing certain to die, be ruined, etc.

gong (gôŋ, gäŋ) *n.* [< Malay; echoic] a slightly convex metallic disk that gives a loud, resonant tone when struck

gon·or·rhe·a, gon·or·rhoe·a (gän'ə rē'ə) *n.* [< Gr. *gonos*, semen + *rheein*, to flow] a venereal disease with inflammation of the genital organs

goo (gōō) *n.* [Slang] **1.** anything sticky, or sticky and sweet **2.** sentimentality —**goo'ey** *adj.* **-i·er, -i·est**

goo·ber (gōō'bər) *n.* [< Afr. *nguba*] [Chiefly South] a peanut

good (good) *adj.* **bet'ter, best** [OE. *god*] **1.** suitable to a purpose [a *good* lamp] **2.** beneficial [*good* exercise] **3.** valid; real [*good* money] **4.** healthy or sound [*good* eyesight] **5.** honorable [one's *good* name] **6.** enjoyable, pleasant, etc. **7.** dependable [*good* advice] **8.** thorough [did a *good* job] **9.** virtuous, devout, kind, dutiful, etc. **10.** skilled [a *good* cook] **11.** considerable [a *good* many] —*n.* something good; specif., *a*) worth; virtue [the *good* in a person] *b*) benefit [for the *good* of all] *c*) something desirable See also GOODS —*interj.* an exclamation of satisfaction, pleasure, etc. —*adv.* [Dial. or Colloq.] well; fully —**as good as** virtually; nearly —**for good (and all)** permanently —**good and** [Colloq.] very or altogether —**good for 1.** able to endure or be used for (a period of time) **2.** worth **3.** able to pay or give —**make good 1.** to repay or replace **2.** to fulfill **3.** to succeed —**no good** useless; worthless —**to the good** as a profit or advantage

good'bye', good'-bye' (-bī') *interj., n., pl.* **-byes'** [contr. of *God be with ye*] farewell: term used at parting: also **good'by', good'-by'**

Good Friday the Friday before Easter Sunday, commemorating the crucifixion of Jesus

good'-heart'ed *adj.* kind; generous —**good'-heart'ed·ly** *adv.* —**good'-heart'ed·ness** *n.*

Good Hope, Cape of cape at the SW tip of Africa

good humor a cheerful, agreeable mood —**good'-hu'mored** *adj.* —**good'-hu'mored·ly** *adv.*

good'ish *adj.* **1.** fairly good **2.** fairly large

good'-look'ing *adj.* beautiful or handsome

good looks attractive personal appearance

good'ly *adj.* **-li·er, -li·est 1.** of good appearance or quality **2.** rather large; ample —**good'li·ness** *n.*

good nature a pleasant, agreeable, or kindly disposition —**good'-na'tured** *adj.* —**good'-na'tured·ly** *adv.*

good'ness *n.* the state or quality of being good; virtue, kindness, etc. —*interj.* an exclamation of surprise

goods (goodz) *n.pl.* **1.** movable personal property **2.** merchandise; wares **3.** fabric; cloth —**get (or have) the goods on** [Slang] to discover (or know) something incriminating about

good Sa·mar·i·tan (sə mer'ə t'n) anyone who pities and helps others unselfishly: Luke 10:30–37

good'-sized' *adj.* fairly big; ample

good'-tem'pered *adj.* not easily angered or annoyed; amiable —**good'-tem'pered·ly** *adv.*

good turn a friendly, helpful act

good will 1. benevolence **2.** willingness **3.** the value of a business in patronage, reputation, etc. beyond its tangible assets Also **good'will'** *n.*

good'y *n., pl.* **-ies** [Colloq.] something good to eat, as a candy —*interj.* a child's exclamation of delight

good'y-good'y *adj.* [Colloq.] affectedly moral or pious —*n.* [Colloq.] a goody-goody person

goof (gōōf) *n.* [Slang] **1.** a stupid person **2.** a mistake; blunder —*vi.* [Slang] **1.** to err or blunder **2.** to waste time, shirk duties, etc. (with *off* or *around*) —**goof'y** *adj.* —**goof'i·ness** *n.*

gook (gook, gōōk) *n.* [GOO + (GUN)K] [Slang] any sticky or slimy substance

goon (gōōn) *n.* [Slang] **1.** a ruffian or thug, esp. one hired as a strikebreaker **2.** a stupid person

goop (gōōp) *n.* [GOO + (SOU)P] [Slang] any sticky, semiliquid substance —**goop'y** *adj.*

goose (gōōs) *n., pl.* **geese** [OE. *gos*] **1.** a long-necked, web-footed bird like a duck but larger, esp. the female **2.** its flesh, used for food **3.** a silly person **4.** *pl.* **goos'es** [Slang] a sudden, playful prod in the backside —*vt.* **goosed, goos'ing** [Slang] **1.** to prod in the backside so as to startle **2.** to feed gasoline to (an engine) in irregular spurts —**cook one's goose** [Colloq.] to spoil one's chances

goose'ber'ry *n., pl.* **-ries 1.** a small, round, sour berry used in preserves, pies, etc. **2.** the shrub it grows on

goose flesh (or **bumps** or **pimples**) a roughened condition of the skin, caused by cold, fear, etc.

goose'neck' *n.* any of various mechanical devices shaped like a goose's neck, as a flexible support for a desk lamp

goose step a marching step in which the legs are raised high and kept unbent —**goose'-step'** *vi.* **-stepped', -step'-ping**

GOP, G.O.P. Grand Old Party (Republican Party)

go·pher (gō′fər) *n.* [< ? Fr. *gaufre*, honeycomb: from its burrowing] **1.** a burrowing rodent, about the size of a large rat, with wide cheek pouches **2.** a striped ground squirrel of the prairies

gore¹ (gôr) *n.* [OE. *gor*, filth] blood from a wound; esp., clotted blood

gore² (gôr) *vt.* **gored, gor′ing** [OE. *gar*, a spear] **1.** to pierce as with a horn or tusk **2.** to insert a gore or gores in —*n.* a tapering piece of cloth inserted in a skirt, sail, etc. to give it fullness

gorge (gôrj) *n.* [< L. *gurges*, whirlpool] **1.** the gullet **2.** what has been swallowed **3.** a deep, narrow pass between steep heights —*vi., vt.* **gorged, gorg′ing** to stuff (oneself) with food; glut —**make one's gorge rise** to make one disgusted, angry, etc.

gor·geous (gôr′jəs) *adj.* [< OFr. *gorgias*] **1.** brilliantly colored; magnificent **2.** [Slang] beautiful, delightful, etc. —**gor′geous·ly** *adv.*

Gor·gon (gôr′gən) *Gr. Myth.* any of three sisters with snakes for hair, so horrible that the beholder was turned to stone

Gor·gon·zo·la (gôr′gən zō′lə) *n.* [< *Gorgonzola*, Italy] a white Italian cheese similar to Roquefort

go·ril·la (gə ril′ə) *n.* [< WAfr.] **1.** the largest and most powerful of the manlike apes, native to Africa **2.** [Slang] a person regarded as like a gorilla

Gor·ki, Gor·kiy, Gor·ky (gôr′kē) city in E European R.S.F.S.R., on the Volga: pop. 1,139,000

Gor·ki (gôr′kē), **Max·im** (mak′sim) 1868–1936; Russian novelist & playwright: also sp. **Gor′ky**

gor·mand·ize (gôr′mən dīz′) *vi., vt.* **-ized′, -iz′ing** [< Fr. *gourmandise*, gluttony] to eat like a glutton —**gor′-mand·iz′er** *n.*

GORILLA
(50–70 in. high)

gorse (gôrs) *n.* [OE. *gorst*] *same as* FURZE —**gors′y** *adj.*

gor·y (gôr′ē) *adj.* **-i·er, -i·est 1.** covered with gore; bloody **2.** with much bloodshed —**gor′i·ness** *n.*

gosh (gäsh) *interj.* an exclamation of surprise, wonder, etc.: a euphemism for God

gos·hawk (gäs′hôk′) *n.* [< OE.: see GOOSE & HAWK¹] a large, swift hawk with short wings

Go·shen (gō′shən) *Bible* the fertile land assigned to the Israelites in Egypt —*n.* a land of plenty

gos·ling (gäz′liŋ) *n.* a young goose

gos·pel (gäs′p'l) *n.* [OE. *gōdspel*, good news] **1.** [*often* G-] the teachings of Jesus and the Apostles **2.** [G-] any of the first four books of the New Testament **3.** anything proclaimed or accepted as the absolute truth: also **gospel truth 4.** any doctrine widely maintained

gos·sa·mer (gäs′ə mər) *n.* [ME. *gossomer*, lit., goose summer] **1.** a filmy cobweb **2.** a very thin, filmy cloth —*adj.* light, thin, and filmy

gos·sip (gäs′əp) *n.* [< OE. *godsibbe*, godparent] **1.** one who chatters idly about others, esp. about their private affairs **2.** such talk —*vi.* to indulge in gossip —**gos′sip·y** *adj.*

got (gät) *pt.* & *alt. pp. of* GET

Goth (gäth) *n.* any member of a Germanic people that conquered most of the Roman Empire in the 3d, 4th, and 5th centuries A.D.

Goth′ic *adj.* **1.** of the Goths or their language **2.** designating or of a style of architecture developed in W Europe between the 12th and 16th cent., with pointed arches, flying buttresses, etc. **3.** [*sometimes* g-] uncivilized —*n.* **1.** the East Germanic language of the Goths **2.** Gothic architecture **3.** [*often* g-] a printing type having straight lines of even width and lacking serifs Abbrev. **Goth.**

got·ten (gät′'n) *alt. pp. of* GET

gouache (gwäsh) *n.* [Fr. < It. < L. *aqua*, water] **1.** a way of painting with opaque watercolors mixed with gum **2.** such a pigment or a picture so painted

Gou·da (cheese) (gou′də, gōō′-) [< *Gouda*, Netherlands] a mild cheese made from curds, usually coated with red wax

gouge (gouj) *n.* [< LL. *gulbia*] **1.** a chisel for cutting grooves or holes in wood **2.** such a groove or hole —*vt.* **gouged, goug′ing 1.** to scoop out as with a gouge **2.** [Colloq.] to defraud or overcharge —**goug′er** *n.*

gou·lash (gōō′läsh, -lash) *n.* [< Hung. *gulyás*] a beef or veal stew seasoned with paprika

Gou·nod (gōō′nō), **Charles** (shärl) 1818–93; Fr. composer

gourd (gôrd, goord) *n.* [< L. *cucurbita*] **1.** any trailing or climbing plant of a family that includes the squash, melon, etc. **2.** the fruit of one species or its dried, hollowed-out shell, used as a cup, dipper, etc.

gour·mand (goor′mənd, goor mänd′) *n.* [OFr.] one who likes good food and drink, often to excess

gour·met (goor′mā) *n.* [Fr. < OFr., wine taster] one who likes and is an excellent judge of fine foods and drinks

gout (gout) *n.* [< L. *gutta*, a drop] a disease characterized by painful swelling of the joints, esp. in the big toe —**gout′y** *adj.* **-i·er, -i·est**

gov., Gov. 1. government **2.** governor

gov·ern (guv′ərn) *vt., vi.* [< Gr. *kybernan*, to steer] **1.** to exercise authority over; rule, control, etc. **2.** to influence the action or conduct of; guide **3.** to restrain **4.** to be a rule or law for; determine **5.** *Gram.* to require (a word) to be in a certain case or mood —**gov′ern·a·ble** *adj.*

gov′ern·ance (-ər nəns) *n.* the action, function, or power of government

gov′ern·ess (-ər nəs) *n.* a woman employed in a private home to train and teach the children

gov·ern·ment (guv′ər mənt, -ərn mənt) *n.* **1.** the exercise of authority over a state, organization, etc.; control; rule **2.** a system of ruling, political administration, etc. **3.** those who direct the affairs of a state, etc.; administration —**gov′ern·men′tal** *adj.* —**gov′ern·men′tal·ly** *adv.*

gov·er·nor (guv′ə nər, -ər nər) *n.* **1.** one who governs; esp., *a*) one appointed to govern a province, etc. *b*) the elected head of any State of the U.S. **2.** a mechanical device for automatically controlling the speed of an engine, as by regulating fuel intake —**gov′er·nor·ship′** *n.*

governor general *pl.* **governors general, governor generals** a governor with deputy governors under him: also, Brit., **gov′er·nor-gen′er·al** *n.*

govt., Govt. government

gown (goun) *n.* [< LL. *gunna*] **1.** a woman's long, usually formal dress **2.** a dressing gown **3.** a nightgown **4.** a long, flowing robe worn by judges, clergymen, scholars, etc.

Go·ya (gô′yä), **Fran·cis·co** (frän thēs′kô) 1746–1828; Sp. painter

Gr. Greek

gr. 1. grain(s) **2.** gram(s) **3.** gross

grab (grab) *vt.* **grabbed, grab′bing** [prob. < MDu. *grabben*] **1.** to snatch suddenly **2.** to get by unscrupulous methods **3.** [Slang] to affect; impress —*vi.* to try to grab something (with *at, for,* etc.) —*n.* a grabbing —**grab′ber** *n.*

grab bag a container holding wrapped or bagged articles sold unseen at a fixed price

grab·by (grab′ē) *adj.* **-bi·er, -bi·est** grasping; avaricious

grace (grās) *n.* [< L. *gratus*, pleasing] **1.** beauty or charm of form, movement, or expression **2.** an attractive quality, manner, etc. **3.** decency **4.** good will; favor **5.** a delay granted for payment of an obligation **6.** a short prayer of thanks for a meal **7.** [G-] a title of an archbishop, duke, or duchess **8.** the love and favor of God toward man —*vt.* **graced, grac′ing 1.** to decorate **2.** to dignify —**in the good** (or **bad**) **graces** of in favor (or disfavor) with

grace′ful *adj.* having beauty of form, movement, or expression —**grace′ful·ly** *adv.* —**grace′ful·ness** *n.*

grace′less *adj.* **1.** lacking any sense of what is proper **2.** clumsy —**grace′less·ly** *adv.* —**grace′less·ness** *n.*

grace note a musical note not necessary to the melody, added only for ornamentation

gra·cious (grā′shəs) *adj.* **1.** having or showing kindness, charm, courtesy, etc. **2.** compassionate **3.** polite to those held to be inferiors **4.** marked by luxury, ease, etc. [*gracious living*] —*interj.* an expression of surprise —**gra′cious·ly** *adv.* —**gra′cious·ness** *n.*

grack·le (grak′'l) *n.* [< L. *graculus*, jackdaw] any of various blackbirds somewhat smaller than a crow

grad (grad) *n.* [Colloq.] a graduate

gra·da·tion (grā dā′shən) *n.* **1.** an arranging in grades, or stages **2.** a gradual change by stages **3.** a step or degree in a graded series

grade (grād) *n.* [Fr. < L. *gradus*] **1.** a stage or step in a progression **2.** *a*) a degree in a scale of quality, rank, etc. *b*) a group of people of the same rank, merit, etc. **3.** the degree of slope, as of a highway **4.** a sloping part **5.** any of the divisions in a school curriculum, by years **6.** a mark or rating in an examination, etc. —*vt.* **grad′ed, grad′ing 1.** to classify by grades of quality, etc.; sort **2.** to give a grade (sense 6) to **3.** to make (ground) level or evenly sloped, as for a road —*vi.* to change gradually —**make the grade** to succeed

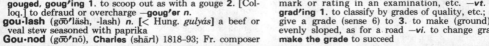

fat, āpe, cär; ten, ēven; is, bīte; gō, hôrn, tōōl, look; oil, out; up, fur; thin, *then*; zh, leisure; ŋ, ring; ə for *a* in *ago*; ′ as in *able* (ā′b'l); ë, Fr. coeur; ö, Fr. feu; ô, Fr. mon; ü, Fr. duc; r, Fr. cri; kh, G. doch, ich. ‡ foreign; < derived from

grade crossing a place where a railroad intersects another railroad or a roadway on the same level

grad'er *n.* **1.** one that grades **2.** a pupil in a specified grade at school

grade school *same as* ELEMENTARY SCHOOL

gra·di·ent (grā'dē ənt) *adj.* [< L. *gradi,* to step] ascending or°descending with a uniform slope —*n.* **1.** a slope, as of a road **2.** the degree of slope

grad·u·al (graj'ōō wəl) *adj.* [< L. *gradus,* a step] taking place by degrees; developing little by little —*n.* a set of verses, esp. from the Psalms, following the Epistle at Mass —**grad'u·al·ly** *adv.* —**grad'u·al·ness** *n.*

grad'u·al·ism *n.* the principle of promoting gradual rather than rapid change

grad·u·ate (graj'ōō wit; *for v.,* -wāt') *n.* [< L. *gradus,* a step] **1.** one who has completed a course of study at a school or college and received a degree or diploma **2.** a container marked off for measuring the contents —*vt.* -at'ed, -at'ing **1.** to give a degree or diploma to upon completion of a course of study **2.** to mark with degrees for measuring **3.** to grade or sort by size, quality, etc. —*vi.* **1.** to become a graduate of a school, etc. **2.** to change by degrees —*adj.* **1.** graduated from a school, etc. **2.** of or for graduates

grad'u·a'tion *n.* **1.** a graduating from a school or college **2.** the ceremony connected with this

graf·fi·to (grə fēt'ō) *n., pl.* -ti (-ē) [It. < L. *graphium,* stylus] a crude inscription or drawing on a wall or other public surface

graft (graft) *n.* [< Gr. *grapheion,* stylus] **1.** a shoot or bud of one plant or tree inserted into another, where it grows permanently **2.** the inserting of such a shoot **3.** the transplanting of skin, bone, etc. by surgery **4.** *a)* the dishonest use of one's position to gain money, etc., as in politics *b)* anything so gained —*vt., vi.* **1.** to insert (a graft) **2.** to obtain (money, etc.) by graft —**graft'er** *n.*

gra·ham (grā'əm) *adj.* [< S. *Graham,* 19th-c. U.S. dietary reformer] designating or made of finely ground, whole-wheat flour *[graham crackers]*

Grail (grāl) [< ML. *gradalis,* cup] *Medieval Legend* the cup used by Jesus at the Last Supper

grain (grān) *n.* [< L. *granum*] **1.** the small, hard seed of any cereal plant, as wheat, corn, etc. **2.** cereal plants **3.** a tiny, solid particle, as of salt or sand **4.** a tiny bit **5.** the smallest unit in the system of weights of the U.S. and Great Britain, equal to 0.0648 gram **6.** *a)* the arrangement of fibers, particles, etc. of wood, leather, etc. *b)* the markings or texture due to this **7.** disposition; nature — *vt.* **1.** to form into grains **2.** to paint or finish in imitation of the grain of wood, marble, etc. —**against the** (or **one's**) **grain** contrary to one's feelings, nature, etc.

grain alcohol ethyl alcohol, esp. if from grain

grain'y *adj.* -i·er, -i·est **1.** having a clearly defined grain, as wood **2.** coarsely textured; granular —**grain'i·ness** *n.*

gram (gram) *n.* [< Fr. < Gr. *gramma,* small weight] the basic unit of weight in the metric system, equal to about 1/28 of an ounce: chiefly Brit. sp. **gramme**

-gram [< Gr. *gramma,* writing] *a combining form meaning* something written *[telegram]*

gram. **1.** grammar **2.** grammatical

gram·mar (gram'ər) *n.* [< Gr. *gramma,* writing] **1.** language study dealing with the forms of words and with their arrangement in sentences **2.** a system of rules for speaking or writing a given language **3.** a book of such rules **4.** one's manner of speaking or writing as judged by such rules

gram·mar·i·an (grə mer'ē ən) *n.* a specialist or expert in grammar

grammar school **1.** *earlier name for* ELEMENTARY SCHOOL **2.** in England, a secondary school

gram·mat·i·cal (grə mat'i k'l) *adj.* **1.** of grammar **2.** conforming to the rules of grammar

gram molecule *same as* MOLE⁴

gram·o·phone (gram'ə fōn') *n.* [inversion of *phonogram,* a shorthand symbol] *chiefly Brit. var. of* PHONOGRAPH

gram·pus (gram'pəs) *n., pl.* -pus·es [< L. *crassus,* fat + *piscis,* fish] a small, black, fierce whale, related to the dolphins

Gra·na·da (grə nä'də) a city in S Spain: pop. 162,000

gran·a·ry (gran'ər ē, grā'nər ē) *n., pl.* -ries [< L. *granum,* grain] a building for storing grain

grand (grand) *adj.* [< L. *grandis,* large] **1.** higher in rank than others *[a grand duke]* **2.** most important; main *[the grand ballroom]* **3.** imposing in size, beauty, extent, etc. **4.** distinguished; illustrious **5.** overall; comprehensive *[the grand total]* **6.** [Colloq.] very good; delightful —*n.* [Slang] a thousand dollars —**grand'ly** *adv.*

grand- *a combining form meaning* of the generation older (or younger) than *[grandfather, grandson]*

gran·dam (gran'dam, -dəm) *n.* [see prec. & DAME] [Archaic] a grandmother or old woman

grand'aunt' *n. same as* GREAT-AUNT

Grand Banks (or **Bank**) large shoal southeast of Newfoundland: noted fishing grounds

Grand Canyon deep gorge of the Colorado River, in NW Ariz.: over 200 mi. long; 1 mi. deep

grand'child' *n., pl.* -chil'dren a child of one's son or daughter

grand'daugh'ter *n.* a daughter of one's son or daughter

grand duke **1.** a nobleman ranking just below a king and ruling a certain territory (**grand duchy**) **2.** in czarist Russia, a prince of the royal family —**grand duchess**

gran·dee (gran dē') *n.* [< Sp. & Port.: see GRAND] **1.** a Spanish or Portuguese nobleman of the highest rank **2.** a man of high rank

gran·deur (gran'jər, -joor) *n.* [see GRAND] **1.** splendor; magnificence **2.** nobility; dignity

grand'fa'ther *n.* **1.** the father of one's father or mother **2.** a forefather

gran·dil·o·quent (gran dil'ə kwənt) *adj.* [< L. *grandis,* grand + *loqui,* speak] using pompous, bombastic words — **gran·dil'o·quence** *n.*

gran·di·ose (gran'dē ōs') *adj.* [Fr. < L. *grandis,* great] **1.** having grandeur; imposing **2.** pompous and showy — **gran'di·os'i·ty** (-äs'ə tē) *n.*

grand jury a jury that investigates accusations against persons charged with crime and indicts them for trial if there is sufficient evidence

grand·ma (gran'mä) *n.* [Colloq.] grandmother

grand'moth'er *n.* **1.** the mother of one's father or mother **2.** a female ancestor

grand'neph'ew *n. same as* GREAT-NEPHEW

grand'niece' *n. same as* GREAT-NIECE

grand opera opera, generally on a serious theme, in which the whole text is set to music

grand·pa (gran'pä) *n.* [Colloq.] grandfather

grand'par'ent *n.* a grandfather or grandmother

grand piano a large piano with strings set horizontally in a harp-shaped case

Grand Rapids city in SW Mich.: pop. 198,000

grand·sire (gran'sīr') *n.* [Archaic] **1.** a grandfather **2.** a male ancestor **3.** an old man

grand slam **1.** *Baseball* a home run hit when there is a runner on each base **2.** *Bridge* the winning of all the tricks in a deal

grand'son' *n.* a son of one's son or daughter

grand'stand' *n.* the main seating structure for spectators at a sporting event, etc.

grand'un'cle *n. same as* GREAT-UNCLE

grange (grānj) *n.* [< L. *granum,* grain] **1.** a farm **2.** [G-] an association of farmers or a local lodge of this

gran·ite (gran'it) *n.* [< It. < L. *granum,* grain] a hard, crystalline rock consisting chiefly of feldspar and quartz — **gra·nit·ic** (grə nit'ik) *adj.*

gran·ny, gran·nie (gran'ē) *n., pl.* -nies [Colloq.] **1.** a grandmother **2.** an old woman **3.** any fussy person **4.** *same as* GRANNY KNOT

granny knot a knot like a square knot but with the ends crossed the wrong way, forming an awkward, insecure knot: also **granny's knot**

gran·o·la (grə nō'lə) *n.* [? < L. *granum,* grain] a breakfast cereal of rolled oats, wheat germ, sesame seeds, brown sugar or honey, nuts or dried fruit, etc.

grant (grant) *vt.* [< L. *credere,* believe] **1.** to give (what is requested, as permission, etc.) **2.** to give or transfer by legal procedure **3.** to admit as true; concede —*n.* **1.** a granting **2.** something granted, as property, etc. —**take for granted** to accept as a matter of course —**grant·ee'** *n.* — **grant'er,** *Law* **grant'or** *n.*

Grant (grant), **Ulysses S.** 1822–85; 18th president of the U.S. (1869–77); commander of Union forces in the Civil War

gran·u·lar (gran'yə lər) *adj.* **1.** containing or consisting of grains **2.** like grains or granules

gran'u·late' (-lāt') *vt., vi.* -lat'ed, -lat'ing to form into grains or granules —**gran'u·la'tion** *n.*

gran·ule (gran'yool) *n.* [< L. *granum,* grain] a small grain or particle

grape (grāp) *n.* [< OFr. *graper,* gather with a hook] **1.** a small, round, juicy berry, growing in clusters on a woody vine **2.** a grapevine **3.** a dark purplish red

grape'fruit' *n.* a large, round citrus fruit with a yellow rind and a somewhat sour pulp

grape sugar *same as* DEXTROSE

grape'vine' *n.* **1.** a woody vine bearing grapes **2.** a secret means of spreading information **3.** a rumor

graph (graf) *n.* [short for *graphic formula*] a diagram representing the successive changes in the value of a variable quantity or quantities —*vt.* to represent by a graph

-graph [< Gr. *graphein*, write] *a combining form meaning:* **1.** something that writes or records [*telegraph*] **2.** something written [*autograph*]

graph·ic (graf'ik) *adj.* [< Gr. *graphein*, write] **1.** describing or described in realistic detail **2.** of those arts (**graphic arts**) that include any form of visual artistic representation, esp. painting, drawing, etching, etc. Also **graph'i·cal** —**graph'i·cal·ly** *adv.*

graph·ite (graf'īt) *n.* [< G. < Gr. *graphein*, write] a soft, black form of carbon used in pencils, lubricants, etc.

graph·ol·o·gy (gra fäl'ə jē) *n.* [< Fr.: see GRAPHIC & -LOGY] the study of handwriting, esp. as a clue to character, attitudes, etc. —**graph·ol'o·gist** *n.*

-graphy [< Gr. *graphein*, write] *a combining form meaning:* **1.** a process or method of writing, or graphically representing [*lithography*] **2.** a descriptive science [*geography*]

grap·nel (grap'n'l) *n.* [< Pr. *grapa*, a hook] **1.** a small anchor with several flukes **2.** an iron bar with claws at one end for grasping things

grap·ple (grap''l) *n.* [OFr. *grapil*] **1.** *same as* GRAPNEL (sense 2) **2.** a hand-to-hand fight —*vt.* **-pled, -pling** to grip and hold — *vi.* **1.** to use a grapnel (sense 2) **2.** to wrestle **3.** to try to cope (*with*)

grappling iron (or **hook**) *same as* GRAPNEL (sense 2)

GRAPNEL

grasp (grasp) *vt.* [ME. *graspen*] **1.** to grip, as with the hand **2.** to take hold of eagerly; seize **3.** to comprehend —*vi.* **1.** to try to seize (with *at*) **2.** to accept eagerly (with *at*) —*n.* **1.** a grasping; grip **2.** control; possession **3.** the power to hold or seize **4.** comprehension

grasp'ing *adj.* greedy; avaricious

grass (gras) *n.* [OE. *græs*] **1.** any of a family of plants with long, narrow leaves, jointed stems, and seedlike fruit, as wheat, rye, sugar cane, etc. **2.** any of various green plants with narrow leaves, growing densely in meadows, lawns, etc. **3.** pasture or lawn **4.** [Slang] marijuana **grass'y** *adj.*

grass'hop'per *n.* any of a group of insects with two pairs of wings and powerful hind legs for jumping

grass'land' *n.* **1.** land with grass growing on it, used for grazing **2.** prairie

grass roots [Colloq.] **1.** the common people **2.** a basic source or support, as of a political movement

grass widow a woman divorced or separated from her husband —**grass widower**

grate[1] (grāt) *vt.* **grat'ed, grat'ing** [< OFr. *grater*] **1.** to grind into particles by scraping **2.** to rub against (an object) or grind (the teeth) together, with a harsh sound **3.** to irritate; annoy —*vi.* **1.** to rub with or make a rasping sound **2.** to be irritating —**grat'er** *n.*

grate[2] (grāt) *n.* [< L. *cratis*, a hurdle] **1.** *same as* GRATING[1] **2.** a frame of metal bars for holding fuel in a fireplace **3.** a fireplace —*vt.* **grat'ed, grat'ing** to provide with a grate

grate·ful (grāt'fəl) *adj.* [obs. *grate* (< L. *gratus*), pleasing] **1.** feeling or showing gratitude; thankful **2.** causing gratitude; welcome —**grate'ful·ly** *adv.*

grat·i·fy (grat'ə fī') *vt.* **-fied', -fy'ing** [< Fr. < L. *gratus*, pleasing + *facere*, make] **1.** to please or satisfy **2.** to indulge; humor —**grat'i·fi·ca'tion** *n.*

grat·ing[1] (grāt'iŋ) *n.* a framework of bars set in a window, door, or other opening

grat·ing[2] (grāt'iŋ) *adj.* **1.** harsh and rasping **2.** irritating; annoying —**grat'ing·ly** *adv.*

gra·tis (grat'is, grāt'-) *adv., adj.* [L. < *gratia*, a favor] free of charge

grat·i·tude (grat'ə tood', -tyood') *n.* [< Fr. < L. *gratus*, thankful] a feeling of thankful appreciation for favors received

gra·tu·i·tous (grə too'ə təs, -tyoo'-) *adj.* [< L. *gratus*, pleasing] **1.** given free of charge **2.** uncalled-for —**gra·tu'i·tous·ly** *adv.*

gra·tu·i·ty (-tē) *n., pl.* **-ties** a gift of money, etc., esp. for a service rendered; tip

grave[1] (grāv) *adj.* **grav'er, grav'est** [Fr. < L. *gravis*, heavy] **1.** important **2.** serious [a *grave* illness] **3.** solemn **4.** somber; dull —**grave'ly** *adv.* —**grave'ness** *n.*

grave[2] (grāv) *n.* [< OE. *grafan*, to dig] **1.** *a)* a place in the ground where a dead body is buried *b)* any burial place; tomb **2.** death —*vt.* **graved, grav'en** or **graved, grav'ing 1.** to carve or engrave **2.** to impress sharply —**grav'er** *n.*

grave accent a mark (`) showing the quality of a vowel or stress, a full pronunciation of a syllable (as in *lovèd*), etc.

grav·el (grav''l) *n.* [< OFr. *grave*, coarse sand] a loose mixture of pebbles and rock fragments coarser than sand —*vt.* **-eled** or **-elled, -el·ing** or **-el·ling** to cover with gravel

grav·el·ly (-ē) *adj.* **1.** full of or like gravel **2.** harsh or rasping [a *gravelly* voice]

grav·en (grāv''n) *alt. pp. of* GRAVE[2]

grave'stone' *n.* a tombstone

grave'yard' *n.* a cemetery

grav·i·tate (grav'ə tāt') *vi.* **-tat'ed, -tat'ing 1.** to move or tend to move in accordance with the force of gravity **2.** to be attracted or tend to move (*toward*)

grav'i·ta'tion *n.* **1.** a gravitating **2.** *Physics* the force by which every mass or particle of matter attracts and is attracted by every other mass or particle —**grav'i·ta'tion·al** *adj.*

grav·i·ty (grav'ə tē) *n., pl.* **-ties** [< L. *gravis*, heavy] **1.** the condition of being grave, or serious **2.** weight [specific *gravity*] **3.** gravitation; esp., the force that tends to draw all bodies in the earth's sphere toward the center of the earth

gra·vy (grā'vē) *n., pl.* **-vies** [< ?] **1.** the juice given off by meat in cooking **2.** a sauce made with this juice combined with flour, seasoning, etc. **3.** [Slang] *a)* money easily obtained *b)* any extra benefit

gravy boat a boat-shaped dish for serving gravy

gray (grā) *n.* [< OE. *græg*] **1.** a color made by mixing black and white **2.** an animal or thing having this color —*adj.* **1.** of the color gray **2.** *a)* darkish *b)* dreary; dismal **3.** having hair that is gray **4.** being of a vague, intermediate nature —*vt., vi.* to make or become gray —**gray'ness** *n.*

Gray (grā), **Thomas** 1716–71; Eng. poet

gray'beard' *n.* an old man

gray'ish *adj.* somewhat gray

gray'ling (-liŋ) *n., pl.* **-ling, -lings** a freshwater game fish related to the salmon

gray matter 1. grayish nerve tissue of the brain and spinal cord **2.** [Colloq.] intelligence

graze[1] (grāz) *vt.* **grazed, graz'ing** [< OE. *græs*, grass] **1.** to feed on (growing grass, pasture, etc.) **2.** to put (livestock) into pasture to graze —*vi.* to feed on growing grass, etc.

graze[2] (grāz) *vt., vi.* **grazed, graz'ing** [prob. < prec.] to scrape or rub lightly in passing —*n.* a grazing, or a scratch, etc. caused by it

graz'ing *n.* land to graze on; pasture

Gr. Brit., Gr. Br. Great Britain

grease (grēs) *n.* [< OFr. < L. *crassus*, fat] **1.** melted animal fat **2.** any thick, oily substance or lubricant —*vt.* (*also* grēz) **greased, greas'ing** to smear or lubricate with grease

grease'paint' *n.* greasy coloring matter used by performers in making up

greas·y (grē'sē, -zē) *adj.* **-i·er, -i·est 1.** smeared with grease **2.** containing or like grease; oily —**greas'i·ness** *n.*

great (grāt) *adj.* [OE. *great*] **1.** of much more than ordinary size, extent, etc. **2.** much above the average; esp., *a)* intense [a *great* pain] *b)* very much of a [a *great* reader] *c)* eminent [a *great* writer] *d)* very impressive [*great* ceremony] *e)* noble or grand **3.** most important; main [the *great* seal] **4.** designating a relationship one generation removed [*great*-grandmother] **5.** [Colloq.] skillful [*great* at tennis] **6.** [Colloq.] excellent; fine —**great'ly** *adv.* —**great'ness** *n.*

great'-aunt' *n.* an aunt of one's father or mother

Great Bear the constellation Ursa Major

Great Britain 1. island including England, Scotland, and Wales **2.** popularly, the United Kingdom

great circle any circle described on the surface of a sphere by a plane which passes through the sphere's center: the shortest course between any two points on the earth's surface is one plotted along a great circle of the earth

Great Dane a large, powerful dog with short, smooth hair

great'-grand'child' *n.* a child of any of one's grandchildren —**great'-grand'daugh'ter** *n.* —**great'-grand'son** *n.*

great'-grand'par'ent *n.* a parent of any of one's grandparents —**great'-grand'fa'ther** *n.* —**great'-grand'moth'er** *n.*

great'heart'ed *adj.* **1.** brave; fearless **2.** generous; unselfish

Great Lakes chain of freshwater lakes in EC N. America: Lakes Superior, Michigan, Huron, Erie, & Ontario

great'-neph'ew *n.* a son of one's nephew or niece

great'-niece' *n.* a daughter of one's nephew or niece

Great Plains sloping region of valleys & plains in WC N. America, east of the base of the Rockies

Great Salt Lake a saltwater lake in NW Utah

great seal the chief seal of a nation, state, etc., with which official papers are stamped

Great Smoky Mountains mountain range of the Appalachians, along the Tenn.-N.C. border

great'-un'cle *n.* an uncle of one's father or mother

grebe (grēb) *n.* [Fr. *grèbe*] a diving and swimming bird related to the loons

Gre·cian (grē'shən) *adj., n.* Greek

Greco- *a combining form meaning:* **1.** Greek or Greeks **2.** Greek and or Greece and

Greece (grēs) country in the S Balkan Peninsula, including many nearby islands: 50,534 sq. mi.; pop. 8,835,000; cap. Athens

greed (grēd) *n.* [< *greedy*] excessive desire, esp. for wealth; avarice

greed'y *adj.* **-i·er, -i·est** [OE. *grædig*] **1.** wanting or taking more than one needs or deserves; avaricious **2.** gluttonous; voracious **3.** intensely eager —**greed'i·ly** *adv.* —**greed'i·ness** *n.*

Greek (grēk) *n.* **1.** a native or inhabitant of ancient or modern Greece **2.** the language, ancient or modern, of Greece —*adj.* of ancient or modern Greece, its people, language, or culture

Greek (Orthodox) Church 1. the established church of Greece, an autonomous part of the Orthodox Eastern Church **2.** *popular name for* ORTHODOX EASTERN CHURCH

Gree·ley (grē'lē), **Horace** 1811–72; U.S. journalist & political leader

green (grēn) *adj.* [OE. *grene*] **1.** of the color of growing grass **2.** covered with green plants or foliage **3.** sickly or bilious **4.** not ripe or mature **5.** not trained; inexperienced **6.** naive **7.** not dried, seasoned, or cured **8.** fresh; new **9.** flourishing; vigorous **10.** [Colloq.] jealous —*n.* **1.** the color of growing grass **2.** any green pigment **3.** anything colored green **4.** [*pl.*] green leafy vegetables **5.** an area of smooth turf [village *green*, putting *green*] —*vt., vi.* to make or become green —**green'ish** *adj.* —**green'ness** *n.*

green'back' *n.* any piece of U.S. paper money printed in green on the back

green bean the edible, immature green pod of the kidney bean

green'er·y *n., pl.* **-ies** green leaves, plants, branches, etc.

green'-eyed' *adj.* very jealous

green'gro'cer *n.* [Brit.] a retail dealer in fresh vegetables and fruit —**green'gro'cer·y** *n.*

green'horn' *n.* a beginner, novice, or newcomer

green'house' *n.* a heated building, mainly of glass, for growing plants

Green·land (grēn'lənd) island of Denmark, northeast of N. America: the world's largest island

green light 1. the green phase of a traffic light, a direction to go ahead **2.** permission to proceed with some undertaking: usually in **give** (or **get**) **the green light**

green onion an immature onion with green leaves, eaten raw; scallion

green pepper the green, immature fruit of the sweet red pepper, eaten as a vegetable

green power money, as the source of power

Greens·bo·ro (grēnz'bur'ō) city in north central N.C.: pop. 144,000

greens fee a fee paid to play golf

greens'keep'er *n.* the person in charge of maintaining a golf course

green'sward' (-swôrd') *n.* green turf

green thumb a knack for growing plants

Green·wich (mean) time (gren'ich, grin'ij) mean solar time of the prime meridian, which passes through Greenwich, a borough of London: used as the basis for standard time

Green·wich Village (gren'ich) section of New York City, a center for artists, writers, etc.

green'wood' *n.* a forest in leaf

greet (grēt) *vt.* [OE. *gretan*] **1.** to address with expressions of friendliness, respect, etc. **2.** to meet or receive (a person, event, etc.) in a specified way **3.** to present itself to [music *greeted* his ears] —**greet'er** *n.*

greet'ing *n.* **1.** the act or words of one who greets **2.** [*often pl.*] a message of regards

greeting card a decorated card bearing a greeting for some occasion, as a birthday

gre·gar·i·ous (grə ger'ē əs) *adj.* [< L. *grex*, herd] **1.** living in herds or flocks **2.** fond of the company of others; sociable —**gre·gar'i·ous·ness** *n.*

Gre·go·ri·an calendar (grə gôr'ē ən) the calendar now widely used, introduced by Pope Gregory XIII in 1582

grem·lin (grem'lən) *n.* [prob. < Dan. hyp. *græmling*, an imp < obs. *gram*, a devil] an imaginary small creature humorously blamed when things fail to work

Gre·na·da (grə nä'də) country on a group of islands in the Windward group of the West Indies: 133 sq. mi.; pop. 95,000

gre·nade (grə nād') *n.* [Fr. < L. *granatus*, seedy] a small bomb detonated by a fuse and usually thrown by hand

gren·a·dier (gren'ə dir') *n.* [Fr. < *grenade*] **1.** orig., a soldier who threw grenades **2.** a member of a special regiment

gren·a·dine (gren'ə dēn') *n.* [Fr.] a syrup made from pomegranate juice

grew (grōō) *pt. of* GROW

grey (grā) *n., adj., vt., vi. Brit. sp. of* GRAY

grey'hound' *n.* a tall, slender, swift hound

grid (grid) *n.* [< GRIDIRON] **1.** a gridiron or grating **2.** a network of crossing parallel lines, as on graph paper **3.** a metallic plate in a storage battery **4.** an electrode, as of wire mesh, for controlling the flow of electrons in an electron tube

grid·dle (grid'l) *n.* [< L. *craticula*, gridiron] a heavy, flat metal pan for cooking pancakes, etc.

grid'dle·cake' *n.* a pancake

grid·i·ron (grid'ī'ərn) *n.* [see GRIDDLE] **1.** a framework of metal bars or wires for use in broiling **2.** anything resembling this, as a football field

grief (grēf) *n.* [see GRIEVE] **1.** intense emotional suffering caused by loss, disaster, etc.; deep sorrow **2.** a cause of such suffering —**come to grief** to fail or be ruined

Grieg (grēg), **Ed·vard** (ed'värt) 1843–1907; Norw. composer

griev·ance (grē'vəns) *n.* **1.** a circumstance thought to be unjust and ground for complaint **2.** complaint against a real or imagined wrong

grieve (grēv) *vi., vt.* **grieved, griev'ing** [< L. *gravis*, heavy] to feel or cause to feel grief

griev·ous (grē'vəs) *adj.* **1.** causing grief **2.** showing or full of grief **3.** severe **4.** deplorable; atrocious —**griev'ous·ly** *adv.* —**griev'ous·ness** *n.*

grif·fin (grif'ən) *n.* [< Gr.] a mythical animal, part eagle and part lion: also sp. **grif'fon** (-ən)

grift·er (grif'tər) *n.* [prob. < *grafter*] [Slang] a petty swindler, as an operator of a dishonest gambling device

grill' (gril) *n.* [see GRIDDLE] **1.** a gridiron (sense 1) **2.** a large griddle **3.** grilled food **4.** a restaurant or dining room that specializes in grilled foods: also **grill'room'** —*vt.* **1.** to broil **2.** to question relentlessly

grill² (gril) *n. same as* GRILLE

GRIFFIN

grille (gril) *n.* [see GRIDDLE] an open grating forming a screen to a door, window, etc.

grilse (grils) *n., pl.* **grilse, grils'es** [< ? OFr.] a salmon on its first return from sea to river

grim (grim) *adj.* **grim'mer, grim'mest** [OE. *grimm*] **1.** fierce; cruel **2.** hard and unyielding; stern **3.** appearing forbidding, harsh, etc. **4.** repellent; frightful; ghastly —**grim'ly** *adv.* —**grim'ness** *n.*

gri·mace (gri mās', grim'əs) *n.* [Fr.] a distortion of the face, as in expressing pain, disgust, etc.; wry look —*vi.* **-maced', -mac'ing** to make grimaces

grime (grīm) *n.* [prob. < Fl. *grijm*] dirt or soot rubbed into or covering a surface, as of the skin —*vt.* **grimed, grim'ing** to soil with grime —**grim'y** *adj.* **-i·er, -i·est**

Grimm (grim), **Ja·kob** (yä'kōp) 1785–1863 & **Wil·helm** (vil'helm) 1786–1859; Ger. brother philologists & collectors of folk tales

grin (grin) *vi.* **grinned, grin'ning** [< OE. *grennian*] to draw back the lips and show the teeth, as in a big or foolish smile —*n.* such a smile

grind (grīnd) *vt.* **ground, grind'ing** [OE. *grindan*] **1.** to crush into fine particles; pulverize **2.** to oppress **3.** to sharpen or smooth by friction **4.** to press down or rub together harshly or gratingly [to *grind* one's teeth] **5.** to operate by turning the crank of (—). **1.** a grinding **2.** the fineness of the particles ground **3.** long, difficult work or study **4.** [Colloq.] a student who studies very hard —**grind out** to produce by steady, often uninspired effort

grind'er *n.* **1.** a person or thing that grinds, or sharpens, crushes, etc. **2.** any of the molar teeth **3.** *same as* HERO SANDWICH

grind'stone' *n.* a revolving stone disk for sharpening tools or shaping and polishing things —**keep one's nose to the grindstone** to work steadily

grip (grip) *n.* [OE. *gripe,* a grasp, *gripa,* handful] **1.** a secure grasp; firm hold **2.** a special or secret handshake **3.** the way one holds a bat, golf club, etc. **4.** the power of grasping firmly **5.** mental grasp **6.** firm control; mastery **7.** a handle **8.** a small traveling bag —*vt.* **gripped** or **gript, grip'ping 1.** to take firmly and hold fast **2.** *a)* to get and hold the attention of *b)* to have a strong emotional impact on —**come to grips** to struggle (*with*) —**grip'per** *n.*

gripe (grīp) *vt.* **griped, grip'ing** [OE. *gripan,* seize] **1.** formerly, to oppress or afflict **2.** to cause sudden, sharp pain in the bowels of **3.** [Slang] to annoy; irritate —*vi.* [Slang] to complain —*n.* **1.** a sharp pain in the bowels: *usually used in pl.* **2.** [Slang] a complaint —**grip'er** *n.*

grippe (grip) *n.* [Fr., lit., a seizure] *earlier term for* INFLUENZA: also sp. **grip**

gris-gris (grē'grē) *n., pl.* **gris'-gris** [of Afr. origin] a voodoo amulet, charm, or spell

gris·ly (griz'lē) *adj.* **-li·er, -li·est** [OE. *grislic*] terrifying; ghastly

grist (grist) *n.* [OE.] grain that is to be or has been ground

gris·tle (gris'l) *n.* [OE.] cartilage, now esp. as found in meat —**gris'tly** *adj.*

grist'mill' *n.* a mill for grinding grain

grit (grit) *n.* [OE. *greot*] **1.** rough, hard particles of sand, etc. **2.** a coarse sandstone **3.** stubborn courage; pluck —*vt.* **grit'ted, grit'ting** to clench or grind (the teeth) in anger or determination —**grit'ty** *adj.* **-ti·er, -ti·est**

grits (grits) *n.pl.* [OE. *grytte*] coarsely ground grain, esp. corn

griz·zled (griz'ld) *adj.* [< OFr. *gris,* gray] **1.** gray or streaked with gray **2.** having gray hair

griz·zly (griz'lē) *adj.* **-zli·er, -zli·est** grayish; grizzled —*n., pl.* **-zlies** *same as* GRIZZLY BEAR

grizzly bear a large, ferocious bear of W N. America, with brownish, grayish, or yellowish fur

groan (grōn) *vi.* [OE. *granian*] **1.** to utter a deep sound expressing pain, distress, etc. **2.** to make a creaking sound, as from strain **3.** to be loaded down to the point of strain —*n.* a groaning sound

gro·cer (grō'sər) *n.* [< OFr. *grossier*] a storekeeper who sells food and various household supplies

gro'cer·y *n., pl.* **-ies 1.** a grocer's store **2.** [*pl.*] the food and supplies sold by a grocer

grog (gräg) *n.* [< Old *Grog,* nickname of an 18th-c. Brit. admiral] **1.** rum mixed with water **2.** any alcoholic liquor

grog'gy *adj.* **-gi·er, -gi·est** [< prec.] **1.** orig., intoxicated **2.** shaky or dizzy —**grog'gi·ly** *adv.*

groin (groin) *n.* [< ? OE. *grynde,* abyss] **1.** the hollow or fold where the abdomen joins either thigh **2.** the sharp, curved edge where two ceiling vaults meet

grom·met (gräm'it, grum'-) *n.* [< obs. Fr. *gromette,* a curb] **1.** a ring of rope or metal used to fasten a sail to its stay **2.** an eyelet of metal or plastic

GROIN

groom (grōōm) *n.* [ME. *grom,* boy] **1.** one whose work is tending horses **2.** a bridegroom —*vt.* **1.** to clean and curry (a horse, dog, etc.) **2.** to make neat and trim **3.** to train (a person) for a particular purpose

groove (grōōv) *n.* [< ON. *grof,* a pit] **1.** a long, narrow furrow or hollow formed on or cut or worn into a surface **2.** a habitual way of doing things; settled routine —*vt.* **grooved, groov'ing** to make a groove in —*vi.* [Slang] to enjoy, appreciate, etc. in a relaxed, unthinking way (usually with *on*)

groov'y *adj.* **-i·er, -i·est** [Slang] very pleasing

grope (grōp) *vi.* **groped, grop'ing** [< OE. *grapian,* to touch] to feel or search about blindly or uncertainly —*vt.* to seek or find (one's way) by groping —**grop'er** *n.*

gros·beak (grōs'bēk') *n.* [< Fr.: see GROSS & BEAK] a finchlike bird with a thick, conical bill

gros·grain (grō'grān') *n.* [Fr., lit., coarse grain] a ribbed silk or rayon fabric for ribbons, etc.

gross (grōs) *adj.* [< LL. *grossus,* thick] **1.** fat and coarse-looking **2.** flagrant; very bad **3.** dense; thick **4.** lacking fineness, fine distinctions, etc. **5.** coarse, vulgar, unrefined, etc. **6.** total; with no deductions [*gross* income] —*n.* **1.** *pl.* **gross'es** overall total **2.** *pl.* **gross** twelve dozen —*vt., vi.* [Colloq.] to earn (a specified total amount) before expenses are deducted —**in the gross** in bulk; as a whole —**gross'ly** *adv.* —**gross'ness** *n.*

gross national product the total value of a nation's annual output of goods and services

gross weight the total weight of a commodity, including the weight of the wrapper or container

gro·tesque (grō tesk') *adj.* [< It. *grotta,* grotto: from designs in Roman caves] **1.** distorted or fantastic in appearance, shape, etc. **2.** ridiculous; absurd —*n.* a grotesque design, thing, etc. —**gro·tesque'ly** *adv.* —**gro·tesque'ness** *n.*

grot·to (grät'ō) *n., pl.* **-toes, -tos** [< It. < L. *crypta,* crypt] **1.** a cave **2.** a cavelike shrine, summerhouse, etc.

grouch (grouch) *vi.* [< ME. *grucchen:* see GRUDGE] to grumble or complain sulkily —*n.* **1.** a person who grouches continually **2.** a grumbling or sulky mood **3.** a complaint —**grouch'y** *adj.* **-i·er, -i·est**

ground[1] (ground) *n.* [OE. *grund,* bottom] **1.** the solid surface of the earth **2.** soil; earth **3.** [*often pl.*] a tract of land [the *grounds* of an estate] **4.** area, as of discussion **5.** [*often pl.*] *a)* basis; foundation *b)* valid reason or motive **6.** the basic surface or background in a painting, design, etc. **7.** [*pl.*] dregs; sediment [coffee *grounds*] **8.** the connection of an electrical conductor with the ground —*adj.* **1.** of, on, or near the ground **2.** growing or living on or in the ground —*vt.* **1.** to set on the ground **2.** to cause to run aground **3.** to base; found; establish **4.** to instruct in the basic principles of a subject **5.** to keep (an aircraft or pilot) from flying **6.** *Elec.* to connect (a conductor) with the ground —*vi.* **1.** to run ashore **2.** *Baseball a)* to hit a grounder *b)* to be put out on a grounder (with *out*) —**break ground 1.** to dig or plow **2.** to start building —**from the ground up** thoroughly —**gain** (or **lose**) **ground** to gain (or lose) in achievement, strength, etc. —**give ground** to retreat; yield —**hold** (or **stand**) **one's ground** to keep one's position against opposition —**run into the ground** [Colloq.] to overdo

ground[2] (ground) *pt. & pp. of* GRIND

ground control personnel, electronic equipment, etc. on the ground for guiding aircraft or spacecraft in takeoff, flight, and landing operations

ground cover ivy, myrtle, etc. used instead of grass for covering ground

ground crew a group of workers who repair and maintain aircraft

ground'er *n. Baseball* a batted ball that travels along the ground: also **ground ball**

ground floor that floor of a building more or less level with the ground; first floor —**in on the ground floor** in at the start of an enterprise

ground'hog' *n. same as* WOODCHUCK

Groundhog Day February 2, when, according to folklore, if the groundhog sees his shadow, he returns to his hole for six more weeks of winter

ground'less *adj.* without reason or cause

ground rule 1. *Baseball* any of a set of rules adapted to a specific ballpark **2.** any basic rule

ground squirrel any of various small, burrowing animals related to the tree squirrels and chipmunks

ground'swell' *n.* a rapidly growing wave of public opinion or feeling: also **ground swell**

ground'work' *n.* foundation; basis

group (grōōp) *n.* [< It. *gruppo*] **1.** a number of persons or things appearing or classified together **2.** *Chem. same as* RADICAL —*vt., vi.* to form into a group or groups

group'er (grōōp'ər) *n.* [Port. *garoupa*] any of several large fishes found in warm seas

group'ie (-ē) *n.* [Colloq.] a girl fan of rock groups or other popular personalities, who follows them about

group therapy a form of psychotherapy for a group of patients with similar emotional problems, as by mutual criticism under a therapist's direction

grouse[1] (grous) *n., pl.* **grouse** [< ?] a game bird with a round, plump body and mottled feathers

grouse[2] (grous) *vi.* **groused, grous'ing** [< ?] [Colloq.] to complain —**grous'er** *n.*

grove (grōv) *n.* [OE. *graf*] **1.** a small wood or group of trees **2.** an orchard of fruit or nut trees

grov·el (gruv'l, gräv'l) *vi.* **-eled** or **-elled, -el·ing** or **-el·ling** [ME. *grufelinge,* down on one's face] **1.** to lie or crawl in a prostrate position, esp. abjectly **2.** to behave in a very humble or cringing manner

grow (grō) *vi.* **grew, grown, grow'ing** [OE. *growan*] **1.** to come into being; spring up **2.** to exist, develop, or thrive, as a living thing **3.** to increase in size, quantity, degree, etc. **4.** to come to be; become *[to grow weary]* —*vt.* to cause to or let grow; raise; cultivate —**grow on** to become gradually more acceptable, likable, etc. —**grow up** to mature —**grow'er** *n.*

growl (groul) *vi.* [< ? OFr. *grouler*] to make a rumbling, menacing sound such as a dog makes —*vt.* to utter in an angry or surly way —*n.* the act or sound of growling — **growl'er** *n.*

grown (grōn) *pp.* of GROW —*adj.* fully mature

grown-up (grōn'up'; *for n.* -up') *adj.* **1.** adult **2.** of or for adults —*n.* an adult: also **grown'up'**

growth (grōth) *n.* **1.** a growing or developing **2.** degree or extent of increase in size, etc. **3.** something that grows or has grown **4.** an abnormal mass of tissue, as a tumor

grub (grub) *vi.* **grubbed, grub'bing** [ME. *grubben*] **1.** to dig in the ground **2.** to work hard, esp. at menial or tedious jobs —*vt.* **1.** to clear (ground) of roots and stumps **2.** to uproot —*n.* **1.** a short, fat, wormlike larva, esp. of a beetle **2.** [Slang] food —**grub'ber** *n.*

grub'by *adj.* **-bi·er, -bi·est** dirty; messy —**grub'bi·ness** *n.*

grub'stake' (-stāk') *n.* [GRUB, *n.* 2 + STAKE] [Colloq.] money or supplies advanced as to a prospector

grudge (gruj) *vt.* **grudged, grudg'ing** [< OFr. *grouchier* *same as* BEGRUDGE —*n.* resentment or ill will against someone over a grievance —**grudg'ing·ly** *adv.*

gru·el (grōō'əl) *n.* [OFr., coarse meal] a thin broth of meal cooked in water or milk

gru'el·ing, gru'el·ling *adj.* [prp. of obs. v. *gruel*, punish] very trying; exhausting

grue·some (grōō'səm) *adj.* [< dial. *grue*, to shudder + -SOME[1]] causing horror or loathing; grisly

gruff (gruf) *adj.* [Du. *grof*] **1.** rough or surly; brusque **2.** harsh and throaty; hoarse —**gruff'ly** *adv.* —**gruff'ness** *n.*

grum·ble (grum'b'l) *vi.* **-bled, -bling** [prob. < Du. *grommelen*] **1.** to growl or rumble **2.** to mutter or complain in a surly way —*vt.* to express by grumbling —*n.* a grumbling —**grum'bler** *n.*

grump·y (grum'pē) *adj.* **-i·er, -i·est** [prob. echoic] grouchy; peevish —**grump'i·ness** *n.*

grun·gy (grun'jē) *adj.* **-gi·er, -gi·est** [Slang] dirty, messy, slovenly, etc.

grun·ion (grun'yən) *n., pl.* **-ions, -ion** [prob. < Sp.] a sardine-shaped fish that spawns on sandy beaches of California during certain spring tides

grunt (grunt) *vi.* [OE. *grunnettan*] to make the short, deep, hoarse sound of a hog or a sound like this —*vt.* to express by grunting —*n.* **1.** a grunting sound **2.** a saltwater fish that makes this sound

Gru·yère (cheese) (grōō yer', grē-) [< *Gruyère*, Switzerland] a light-yellow Swiss cheese, rich in butterfat

gr. wt. gross weight

G-string (jē'strin') *n.* [< ?] **1.** a narrow loincloth **2.** a similar band worn by striptease dancers

G-suit (jē'sōōt') *n.* [G for *gravity*] an astronaut's or pilot's garment, pressurized to counteract the effects as of rapid acceleration or deceleration

Gt. Brit., Gt. Br. Great Britain

Gua·da·la·ja·ra (gwä'd'l ə här'ə) city in W Mexico: pop. 1,352,000

Guam (gwäm) island in the W Pacific: a possession of the U.S.

gua·na·co (gwə nä'kō) *n., pl.* **-cos** [Sp. < SAmInd.] a woolly, reddish-brown, wild animal of the Andes, related to the camel and llama

gua·no (gwä'nō) *n., pl.* **-nos** [Sp. < SAmInd.] manure of sea birds, used as fertilizer

guar·an·tee (gar'ən tē', gär'-) *n.* **1.** *same as* GUARANTY (sense 1) **2.** *a)* a pledge that something will be replaced if it is not as represented *b)* assurance that something will be done as specified **3.** a guarantor —*vt.* **-teed', -tee'ing** **1.** to give a guarantee for **2.** to state confidently; promise

guar·an·tor (gar'ən tôr', -tər; gär'-) one who makes or gives a guaranty or guarantee

guar'an·ty (-tē) *n., pl.* **-ties** [< OFr. *garant*, a warrant] **1.** a pledge or security for another's debt or obligation **2.** an agreement that secures the existence or maintenance of something

guard (gärd) *vt.* [< OFr. *garder*] **1.** to watch over and protect; defend **2.** *a)* to keep from escape or trouble *b)* to hold in check; control **3.** *Sports* to cover (a goal or area) in defensive play —*vi.* **1.** to keep watch (*against*) **2.** to act as a guard —*n.* **1.** defense; protection **2.** a posture of defense, as in boxing, fencing, etc. **3.** any device that protects against injury or loss **4.** a person or group that

guards, as a sentinel or sentry, a special unit of troops, etc. **5.** either of two of the five players making up a basketball team **6.** an offensive football lineman —**on (one's) guard** vigilant —**stand guard** to do sentry duty

guard'ed *adj.* **1.** watched over **2.** cautious; noncommittal —**guard'ed·ly** *adv.*

guard'house' *n. Mil.* **1.** a building used by the members of a guard when not walking a post **2.** a jail for temporary confinement

guard'i·an (-ē ən) *n.* **1.** one who guards or takes care of another person, property, etc. **2.** a person legally placed in charge of a minor or of someone incapable of managing his own affairs —*adj.* protecting —**guard'i·an·ship'** *n.*

guards·man (gärdz'mən) *n., pl.* **-men** a member of a National Guard or of any military guard

Gua·te·ma·la (gwä'tə mä'lə) **1.** country in Central America: 42,042 sq. mi.; pop. 5,014,000 **2.** its capital: pop. 577,000: also **Guatemala City** —**Gua'te·ma'lan** *adj., n.*

gua·va (gwä'və) *n.* [< SAmInd.] a yellow, pear-shaped tropical fruit, used for jelly, preserves, etc.

gu·ber·na·to·ri·al (gōō'bər nə tôr'ē əl) *adj.* [L. *gubernator*, governor] of a governor or his office

guck (guk) *n.* [< ? G(OO) + (M)UCK] [Slang] any thick sticky or slimy substance

Guern·sey (gurn'zē) *n., pl.* **-seys** [< *Guernsey*, one of the Channel Islands] any of a breed of dairy cattle, usually fawn-colored with white markings

guer·ril·la, gue·ril·la (gə ril'ə) *n.* [Sp., dim. of *guerra*, war] a member of a small group of fighters not part of the regular army, who make surprise raids behind an invading enemy's lines

guess (ges) *vt., vi.* [prob. < MDu. *gessen*] **1.** to form a judgment or estimate of (something) without actual knowledge; surmise **2.** to judge correctly by doing this **3.** to think or suppose *[I guess you're bored]* —*n.* **1.** a guessing **2.** something guessed; conjecture

guess'work' *n.* **1.** a guessing **2.** a judgment, result, etc. arrived at by guessing

guest (gest) *n.* [< ON. *gestr*] **1.** a person entertained at the home of another or at a restaurant, theater, etc. by another acting as host **2.** any paying customer of a hotel, restaurant, etc. **3.** a person who appears on a program by special invitation —*adj.* **1.** for guests **2.** performing by special invitation *[a guest artist]*

guff (guf) *n.* [echoic] [Slang] nonsensical, brash, or insolent talk

guf·faw (gə fô') *n.* [echoic] a loud and rough laugh —*vi.* to laugh in this way

Gui·a·na (gē an'ə, -ä'nə) region in N S. America, including Guyana, Surinam, & French Guiana

guid·ance (gīd''ns) *n.* **1.** a guiding; direction; leadership **2.** advice or assistance, as that given by counselors **3.** the process of directing the course of a spacecraft, missile, etc.

guide (gīd) *vt.* **guid'ed, guid'ing** [< OFr. *guier*] **1.** to point out the way for; lead **2.** to direct the course or motion of **3.** to direct (the policies, actions, etc.) of; manage; regulate —*n.* **1.** one whose work is conducting tours, etc. **2.** a person or thing that controls, directs, or instructs; specif., a controlling device, handbook, guidebook, etc. — **guid'a·ble** *adj.*

guide'book' *n.* a book containing directions and information for tourists

guided missile a military missile whose course is controlled by radio signals, radar, etc.

guide dog a dog trained to lead a blind person

guide'line' *n.* a principle by which to determine a course of action

guide'post' *n.* **1.** a post at a roadside, with a sign giving directions to places **2.** anything serving as a guide, standard, etc.

guild (gild) *n.* [< ON. *gildi* and OE. *gyld*] **1.** in medieval times, an association of men in the same craft or trade **2.** any association of people with common aims and interests

guil·der (gil'dər) *n.* [< MDu. *gulden*, golden] the monetary unit and a coin of the Netherlands

guile (gīl) *n.* [OFr.] slyness and cunning in dealing with others —**guile'ful** *adj.* —**guile'less** *adj.*

guil·le·mot (gil'ə mät') *n.* [Fr., dim. of *Guillaume*, William] any of various narrow-billed, northern diving birds

guil·lo·tine (gil'ə tēn') *n.* [Fr. < J. *Guillotin*, who advocated its use in the 18th c.] an instrument for beheading, having a heavy blade dropped between two grooved uprights —*vt.* (gil'ə tēn') **-tined', -tin'ing** to behead with a guillotine

guilt (gilt) *n.* [OE. *gylt*, a sin] **1.** the fact or state of having done a wrong or committed an offense **2.** a feeling of

self-reproach from believing that one has done a wrong —
guilt'less *adj.*

guilt'y *adj.* **-i·er, -i·est** 1. having guilt 2. legally judged an offender 3. of, involving, or showing guilt *[a guilty look]* —**guilt'i·ly** *adv.* —**guilt'i·ness** *n.*

Guin·ea (gin'ē) country on the W coast of Africa: 94,925 sq. mi.; pop. 3,702,000; cap. Conakry

guin·ea (gin'ē) *n.* [< former Eng. gold coin, orig. made of gold from *Guinea*] the sum of 21 English shillings

Guin·ea-Bis·sau (-bi sou') country just north of Guinea, on the W coast of Africa: formerly a Port. territory: 15,050 sq. mi.; pop. 487,000

guinea fowl [orig. from region of *Guinea*] a domestic fowl with a rounded body and speckled feathers

guinea hen a guinea fowl, esp. a female

guinea pig [prob. orig. brought to England by ships plying between England, *Guinea* coast, and S. America] 1. a small, fat rodent used in biological experiments 2. any person or thing used in an experiment

Guin·e·vere (gwin'ə vir') *Arthurian Legend* the wife of King Arthur and mistress of Lancelot

guise (gīz) *n.* [OFr. < OHG. *wisa*, manner] 1. manner of dress; garb 2. semblance 3. a false appearance; pretense

gui·tar (gi tär') *n.* [< Sp. < Gr. *kithara*, lyre] a musical instrument with strings, usually six, that are plucked or strummed with the fingers or a plectrum —**gui·tar'ist** *n.*

gulch (gulch) *n.* [prob. < dial. *gulch*, swallow greedily] a deep, narrow ravine

gulf (gulf) *n.* [ult. < Gr. *kolpos*, bosom] 1. an area of ocean larger than a bay, indenting a coastline 2. a wide, deep chasm 3. a vast separation

Gulf States States on the Gulf of Mexico; Fla., Ala., Miss., La., & Tex.

Gulf Stream warm ocean current flowing from the Gulf of Mexico northeastward to Europe

gull' (gul) *n.* [< Celt.] a water bird with large wings, webbed feet, and white and gray feathers

gull² (gul) *n.* [< ?] a person easily tricked; dupe —*vt.* to cheat; trick

Gul·lah (gul'ə) *n.* [< ? *Gola* or < ? *Ngola*, tribal groups in W Africa] 1. any of a group of Negroes living in coastal S. Carolina and Georgia and esp. on nearby islands 2. their English dialect

gul·let (gul'ət) *n.* [< L. *gula*, throat] 1. the esophagus 2. the throat

gul·li·ble (gul'ə b'l) *adj.* easily gulled or tricked; credulous —**gul'li·bil'i·ty** *n.* —**gul'li·bly** *adv.*

gul·ly (gul'ē) *n., pl.* **-lies** [see GULLET] a channel worn by running water; small, narrow ravine

gulp (gulp) *vt.* [prob. < Du. *gulpen*] 1. to swallow hastily or greedily 2. to choke back as if swallowing —*vi.* to gasp *(for* air) —*n.* 1. a gulping or swallowing 2. the amount swallowed at one time

gum' (gum) *n.* [< L. *gumma*] 1. a sticky substance found in certain trees and plants and used in adhesives, emollients, foodstuffs, etc. 2. any similar plant secretion, as resin 3. any of various sticky substances or deposits 4. *same as:* a) GUM TREE b) GUMWOOD 5. *same as* CHEWING GUM —*vt.* **gummed, gum'ming** to coat or unite with gum —*vi.* to become sticky or clogged —**gum up** [Slang] to cause to go awry; spoil; ruin —**gum'my** *adj.*

gum² (gum) *n.* [OE. *goma*] [often *pl.*] the firm flesh surrounding the base of the teeth —*vt.* **gummed, gum'ming** to chew with toothless gums

gum arabic a gum from certain acacia trees, used in medicine, candy, etc.

gum·bo (gum'bō) *n.* [< Bantu name for okra] 1. a soup made thick with unripe okra pods 2. a fine, silty soil of the Western prairies, which becomes sticky when wet: also **gumbo soil**

gum'drop' *n.* a small, firm candy made of sweetened gum arabic or gelatin

gump·tion (gump'shən) *n.* [< Scot. dial.] [Colloq.] courage and initiative; enterprise and boldness

gum resin a mixture of gum and resin, given off by certain trees and plants

gum tree any of various trees that yield gum, as the sour gum, eucalyptus, etc.

gum'wood' *n.* the wood of a gum tree

gun (gun) *n.* [< ME. *gonnilde*, cannon < ON.] 1. any of various weapons, as a cannon, rifle, pistol, etc., having a metal tube from which a projectile is discharged by the force of an explosive 2. anything like this that shoots or squirts something *[air gun, spray gun]* 3. a discharge of a

gun in signaling or saluting —*vi.* **gunned, gun'ning** to shoot or hunt with a gun —*vt.* 1. [Colloq.] to shoot (a person) 2. [Slang] to advance the throttle of (an engine) so as to increase the speed —**gun for** to seek in order to shoot, harm, etc. —**jump the gun** [Slang] to begin before the proper time —**stick to one's guns** to be firm under attack

gun'boat' *n.* a small armed ship used to patrol rivers, harbors, etc.

gun'cot'ton *n.* nitrocellulose in a highly nitrated form, used as an explosive

gun'fight' *n.* a fight between persons using pistols or revolvers

gun'fire' *n.* the firing, or shooting, of guns

gung-ho (guŋ'hō') *adj.* [< Chin.] overly enthusiastic, enterprising, etc.

gunk (guŋk) *n.* [< ? G(OO) + (J)UNK¹] [Slang] thick, messy matter

gun'lock' *n.* in some guns, the mechanism by which the charge is set off

gun'man (-mən) *n., pl.* **-men** an armed gangster or hired killer

gun'met'al *n.* 1. bronze with a dark tarnish 2. its dark-gray color

gun'ner *n.* 1. a soldier, etc. who helps fire artillery 2. a naval warrant officer in charge of a ship's guns

gun'ner·y *n.* the science of making or firing heavy guns

gun·ny (gun'ē) *n.* [< Sans. *gōnī*, a sack] a coarse, heavy fabric of jute or hemp

gun'ny·sack' *n.* a sack made of gunny

gun'play' *n.* an exchange of gunshots, as between gunmen and police

gun'point' *n.* the muzzle of a gun —**at gunpoint** under threat of being shot with a gun

gun'pow'der *n.* an explosive powder used in guns, for blasting, etc.

gun'run'ning *n.* the smuggling of guns and ammunition into a country —**gun'run'ner** *n.*

gun'ship' *n.* a heavily armed helicopter used to assault enemy ground forces

gun'shot' *n.* 1. shot fired from a gun 2. the range of fire

gun'smith' *n.* one who makes or repairs small guns

gun·wale (gun''l) *n.* [first applied to bulwarks supporting a ship's guns] the upper edge of the side of a ship or boat

gup·py (gup'ē) *n., pl.* **-pies** [< R. *Guppy*, of Trinidad] a tiny, brightly colored tropical fish

gur·gle (gɜr'g'l) *vi.* **-gled, -gling** [prob. echoic] 1. to flow with a bubbling sound 2. to make such a sound in the throat —*n.* a gurgling sound

gu·ru (goor'ōō, goo rōō') *n.* [< Sans. *guru-ḥ*, venerable] in Hinduism, one's spiritual adviser or teacher

gush (gush) *vi.* [akin to ON. *gjosa*] 1. to flow out suddenly and plentifully 2. to have a sudden flow 3. to talk or write with exaggerated enthusiasm or feeling —*vt.* to emit in a sudden flow —*n.* 1. a sudden, heavy flow 2. gushing talk or writing

gush'er *n.* 1. one who gushes 2. an oil well from which oil spouts without being pumped

gush'y *adj.* **-i·er, -i·est** given to or full of exaggerated feeling; effusive —**gush'i·ness** *n.*

gus·set (gus'it) *n.* [< OFr. *gousset*] a triangular or diamond-shaped piece inserted to make a garment stronger or roomier

gus·sie, gus·sy (gus'ē) *vt., vi.* **-sied, -sy·ing** [< *Gussie*, girl's name] [Slang] to dress *(up)* in a fine or showy way

gust (gust) *n.* [< ON. *gustr*] 1. a sudden, strong rush of wind, or of smoke, rain, etc. 2. a sudden outburst of laughter, rage, etc. —**gust'y** *adj.* **-i·er, -i·est**

gus·ta·to·ry (gus'tə tôr'ē) *adj.* [< L. *gustus*, taste] of or having to do with the sense of taste

GUSSET

gus·to (gus'tō) *n.* [see prec.] 1. taste; liking 2. zest; relish 3. great vigor

gut (gut) *n.* [OE. *guttas*, pl.] 1. [*pl.*] the bowels or entrails 2. the stomach or belly 3. the intestine 4. tough cord made of animal intestines 5. [*pl.*] [Colloq.] the basic or inner parts 6. [*pl.*] [Slang] daring, courage, etc. or bold impudence, effrontery, etc. —*vt.* **gut'ted, gut'ting** 1. to remove the entrails from 2. to destroy the interior of, as by fire —*adj.* [Slang] basic or immediate

Gu·ten·berg (goot''n burg'), **Jo·hann** (yō'hän) 1400?-68; Ger. printer, innovator in movable type

gut·ta·per·cha (gut'ə pur'chə) *n.* [< Malay] a rubberlike gum produced from the latex of certain Asian trees, used in insulation, dentistry, etc.

gut·ter (gut'ər) *n.* [< L. *gutta*, a drop] a trough or channel to carry off water, as along the eaves of a roof or the side of a street —*vi.* to melt fast, with the wax running down in channels: said of a candle

gut·tur·al (gut'ər əl) *adj.* [< L. *guttur*, throat] 1. of the throat 2. produced in the throat; rasping

guy¹ (gī) *n.* [< OFr. *guier*, to guide] a wire, rope, etc. attached to something to steady or guide it

guy² (gī) *n.* [< *Guy* Fawkes, Eng. conspirator] [Slang] 1. a man or boy 2. any person —*vt.* to make fun of; tease

Guy·a·na (gī an'ə, -ä'nə) country in NE S. America, on the Atlantic: 83,000 sq. mi.; pop. 763,000 —**Guy'a·nese'** (-ə nēz') *adj., n., pl.* **-nese'**

guz·zle (guz''l) *vi., vt.* **-zled, -zling** [< ? OFr. *gosier*, throat] to drink greedily or immoderately —**guz'zler** *n.*

gym (jim) *n.* [Colloq.] *same as:* 1. GYMNASIUM 2. PHYSICAL EDUCATION

gym·na·si·um (jim nā'zē əm) *n., pl.* **-si·ums, -si·a** (-ə) [< Gr. *gymnos*, naked] a room or building equipped for physical training and sports

gym·nast (jim'nast) *n.* an expert in gymnastics

gym·nas·tics (-nas'tiks) *n.pl.* exercises that develop and train the body and the muscles —**gym·nas'tic** *adj.*

gym·no·sperm (jim'nə spurm') *n.* [< Gr. *gymnos*, naked + *sperma*, seed] a plant having the ovules borne on open scales, usually in cones, as on pines and cedars

gyn·e·col·o·gy (gī'nə käl'ə jē, jin'ə-, jī'nə-) *n.* [< Gr. *gynē*, woman + -LOGY] the branch of medicine dealing with the specific functions, diseases, etc. of women —**gyn'e·col'o·gist** *n.*

gyp (jip) *n.* [prob. < GYPSY] [Colloq.] 1. a swindle 2. a swindler: also **gyp'per** —*vt., vi.* **gypped, gyp'ping** [Colloq.] to swindle; cheat

gyp·sum (jip'səm) *n.* [< Gr. *gypsos*] a sulfate of calcium used to make plaster of Paris, to treat soil, etc.

Gyp·sy (jip'sē) *n., pl.* **-sies** [< earlier *Egipcien*, Egyptian: orig. thought to be from Egypt] 1. [*also* g-] a member of a wandering Caucasoid people, prob. orig. from India, with dark skin and black hair 2. their language 3. [g-] one who looks or lives like a Gypsy —*adj.* of or like a Gypsy or Gypsies

gypsy moth a European moth, common in the E U.S.: its larvae feed on leaves of trees and plants

gy·rate (jī'rāt) *vi.* **-rat·ed, -rat·ing** [< Gr. *gyros*, a circle] to move in a circular or spiral path; whirl —**gy·ra'tion** *n.* —**gy'ra'tor** *n.*

gyro- [< Gr. *gyros*, a circle] *a combining form meaning:* 1. gyrating [*gyroscope*] 2. gyroscope

gy·ro·com·pass (jī'rō kum'pəs) *n.* a compass consisting of a motor-operated gyroscope whose rotating axis points to the geographic north pole

gy·ro·scope (jī'rə skōp') *n.* [GYRO- + -SCOPE] a wheel mounted in a ring so that its axis is free to turn in any direction: when the wheel is spun rapidly, it will keep its original plane of rotation —**gy'ro·scop'ic** (-skäp'ik) *adj.*

gy·ro·sta·bi·liz·er (jī'rō stā'bə lī'zər) *n.* a device consisting of a gyroscope spinning in a vertical plane, used to stabilize the side-to-side rolling of a ship

gyve (jīv) *n., vt.* **gyved, gyv'ing** [< Anglo-Fr. *gyves*, pl.] [Archaic or Poet.] fetter; shackle

GYROSCOPE

H

H, h (āch) *n., pl.* **H's, h's** the eighth letter of the English alphabet

H 1. *Chem.* hydrogen 2. *Physics* henry

H., h. 1. height 2. high 3. *Baseball* hits 4. hour(s)

ha (hä) *interj.* an exclamation of wonder, surprise, anger, triumph, etc.

Ha·bak·kuk (hab'ə kuk, hə bak'ək) *Bible* 1. a Hebrew prophet 2. the book containing his prophecies: abbrev. **Hab.**

‡**ha·be·as cor·pus** (hā'bē əs kôr'pəs) [L., (that) you have the body] *Law* a writ requiring that a detained person be brought before a court to decide the legality of his detention or imprisonment

hab·er·dash·er (hab'ər dash'ər) *n.* [< ME.] a dealer in men's hats, shirts, gloves, etc.

hab·er·dash·er·y *n., pl.* **-ies** 1. things sold by a haberdasher 2. a haberdasher's shop

ha·bil·i·ment (hə bil'ə mənt) *n.* [< MFr. *habiller*, clothe] 1. [*usually pl.*] clothing; dress 2. [*pl.*] furnishings or equipment; trappings

hab·it (hab'it) *n.* [< L. *habere*, have] 1. a distinctive costume, as for a religious order 2. character, disposition, etc. 3. a thing done often and, hence, easily; custom 4. a usual way of doing 5. an addiction, esp. to narcotics

hab'it·a·ble *adj.* fit to be lived in

hab'it·ant *n.* an inhabitant; resident

hab·i·tat (hab'ə tat') *n.* [L., it inhabits] 1. native environment 2. the place where a person or thing is ordinarily found

hab·i·ta·tion (-tā'shən) *n.* 1. an inhabiting 2. a dwelling; home

hab'it-form'ing *adj.* resulting in the formation of a habit or addiction

ha·bit·u·al (hə bich'oo wəl) *adj.* 1. done or acquired by habit 2. steady; inveterate [a *habitual* smoker] 3. much seen, done, or used; usual —**ha·bit'u·al·ly** *adv.*

ha·bit'u·ate' (-wāt') *vt.* **-at·ed, -at·ing** to accustom (to) —**ha·bit'u·a'tion** *n.*

hab·i·tude (hab'ə tōōd') *n.* 1. habitual condition of mind or body; disposition 2. custom

ha·bit·u·é (hə bich'oo wā') *n.* [Fr.] a person who frequents a certain place

ha·ci·en·da (hä'sē en'də) *n.* [Sp. < L. *facere*, do] in Spanish America, 1. a large estate, ranch, etc. 2. the main dwelling on any of these

hack¹ (hak) *vt.* [OE. *haccian*] 1. to chop or cut roughly 2. to break up (land) with a hoe, etc. —*vi.* 1. to make rough cuts 2. to give harsh, dry coughs —*n.* 1. a tool for hacking 2. a gash or notch 3. a harsh, dry cough —**hack'er** *n.*

hack² (hak) *n.* [< HACKNEY] 1. a horse for hire 2. an old, worn-out horse 3. a literary drudge 4. a coach for hire 5. [Colloq.] a taxicab —*vi.* [Colloq.] to drive a taxicab —*adj.* 1. employed as, or done by, a hack 2. stale; trite

hack·le (hak''l) *n.* [ME. *hechele*] 1. all or any of the neck feathers of a rooster, pigeon, etc. 2. *Fishing* an artificial fly made with hackles 3. [*pl.*] the bristling hairs on a dog's neck and back

hack·ney (hak'nē) *n., pl.* **-neys** [< *Hackney*, England] 1. a horse for ordinary driving or riding 2. a carriage for hire

hack'neyed (-nēd') *adj.* made trite by overuse

hack·saw (hak'sô') *n.* a fine-toothed saw for cutting metal: also **hack saw**

had (had) *pt. & pp. of* HAVE

had·dock (had'ək) *n., pl.* **-dock, -docks** [ME. *hadok*] an Atlantic food fish, related to the cod

HACKSAW

Ha·des (hā'dēz) *Gr. Myth.* the home of the dead —*n.* [*often* h-] [Colloq.] hell: a euphemism

had·n't (had''nt) had not

Ha·dri·an (hā'drē ən) 76–138 A.D.; Roman emperor (117–138)

hadst (hadst) *archaic 2d pers. sing., past indic., of* HAVE: *used with* thou

haf·ni·um (haf'nē əm) *n.* [< L. *Hafnia*, Roman name of Copenhagen] a metallic chemical element resembling zirconium: symbol, Hf; at. wt., 178.49; at. no., 72

haft (haft) *n.* [OE. *hæft*] a handle or hilt of a knife, ax etc. —*vt.* to fit with a haft

hag (hag) *n.* [< OE. *haga*, a hedge] 1. a witch 2. an ugly often vicious old woman —**hag'gish** *adj.*

Ha·gar (hā'gär) *Bible* a concubine of Abraham and slave of his wife Sarah

Hag·ga·da, Hag·ga·dah (hə gä′də) *n., pl.* **-dot′** (-dōt′) [Heb. < *higgid,* to tell] **1.** [*often* **h-**] in the *Talmud,* a story explaining some point of law **2.** the part of the Talmud devoted to such narratives

Hag·ga·i (hag′ē ī′, hag′ī) *Bible* **1.** a Hebrew prophet **2.** the book attributed to him: abbrev. **Hag.**

hag·gard (hag′ərd) *adj.* [MFr. *hagard,* untamed] having a wild, wasted, worn look; gaunt

hag·gis (hag′is) *n.* [ME. *hagas,* kind of pudding] a Scottish dish made of the lungs, heart, etc. of a sheep or calf, mixed with suet, seasoning, and oatmeal and boiled in the animal's stomach

hag·gle (hag′'l) *vi.* **-gled, -gling** [< Scot. *hag,* to cut] to argue about terms, price, etc. —*n.* a haggling —**hag′gler** *n.*

Hague (hāg), **The** political capital of the Netherlands: pop. 576,000

hah (hä) *interj. same as* HA

Hai·fa (hī′fə) seaport in NW Israel: pop. 210,000

hail¹ (hāl) *vt.* [< ON. *heill,* whole, sound] **1.** to greet with cheers; acclaim **2.** to salute as **3.** to call out to, as in summoning —*n.* a greeting —*interj.* an exclamation of tribute, greeting, etc. —**hail** from to be from —**hail′er** *n.*

hail² (hāl) *n.* [OE. *hægel*] **1.** frozen raindrops falling during thunderstorms **2.** a shower of or like hail —*vt., vi.* to pour down like hail

hail′stone′ *n.* a pellet of hail

hail′storm′ *n.* a storm with hail

hair (her) *n.* [OE. *hær*] **1.** any of the threadlike outgrowths from the skin **2.** a growth of these, as on the human head **3.** an extremely small space, degree, etc. **4.** a threadlike growth on a plant —*adj.* of or for hair —**get in one's hair** [Slang] to annoy one —**split hairs** to quibble —**hair′less** *adj.*

hair′breadth′ (-bredth′) *n.* a very small space or amount —*adj.* very narrow; close Also **hairs′breadth′**

hair′cloth′ *n.* cloth woven from horsehair, camel's hair, etc.: used esp. for upholstery

hair′cut′ *n.* the act of, or a style of, cutting the hair

hair′do′ *n., pl.* **-dos′** the style in which (a woman's) hair is arranged; coiffure

hair′dress′er *n.* a person whose work is dressing (women's) hair —**hair′dress′ing** *n., adj.*

hair′line′ *n.* **1.** a very thin line **2.** the outline of the hair on the head, esp. above the forehead

hair′piece′ *n.* a toupee or wig

hair′pin′ *n.* a small, usually U-shaped, piece of wire, etc. for keeping the hair in place —*adj.* U-shaped [a hairpin turn]

hair′-rais′ing *adj.* [Colloq.] terrifying or shocking

hair′split′ting *adj., n.* making petty distinctions; quibbling —**hair′split′ter** *n.*

hair′spring′ *n.* a slender, hairlike coil that controls the balance wheel in a watch or clock

hair trigger a trigger so delicately adjusted that slight pressure on it discharges the firearm

hair′y *adj.* **-i·er, -i·est** **1.** of, like, or covered with hair **2.** [Slang] difficult —**hair′i·ness** *n.*

Hai·ti (hāt′ē) country in the W portion of Hispaniola: 10,714 sq. mi.; pop. 4,768,000; cap. Port-au-Prince —**Haitian** (hā′shən, hāt′ē ən) *adj., n.*

hake (hāk) *n., pl.* **hake, hakes** [prob. < ON.] a marine food fish related to the cod

hal·berd (hal′bərd) *n.* [< MHG. *helmbarte*] a combination spear and battle-ax used in the 15th and 16th cent.: also **hal′bert** (-bərt) —**hal′berd·ier′** (-bər dir′) *n.*

hal·cy·on (hal′sē ən) *n.* [< Gr. *alkyōn,* kingfisher (fabled calmer of the sea)] tranquil, happy, idyllic, etc.: esp. in phrase **halcyon days**

hale¹ (hāl) *adj.* **hal′er, hal′est** [OE. *hal*] sound in body; vigorous and healthy —**hale′ness** *n.*

hale² (hāl) *vt.* **haled, hal′ing** [< OFr. *haler*] to force (one) to go [*haled* him into court]

Hale (hāl), **Nathan** 1755–76; Am. soldier in the Revolutionary War: hanged by the British as a spy

half (haf) *n., pl.* **halves** [OE. *healf*] **1.** either of the two equal parts of something **2.** either of the two equal periods of some games —*adj.* **1.** being a half **2.** incomplete; partial —*adv.* **1.** to the extent of a half **2.** [Colloq.] partly [*half* convinced] **3.** [Colloq.] at all: used with *not* [not *half* bad] —**by half** very much

half′-and-half′ *n.* something half one thing and half another, as a mixture of equal parts of milk and cream — *adj.* combining two things equally —*adv.* in two equal parts

half′back′ *n. Football* either of two backs, in addition to the fullback and the quarterback

half′-baked′ *adj.* **1.** only partly baked **2.** not completely thought out **3.** not very intelligent

half′-blood′ *n.* **1.** a person related to another through one parent only **2.** *same as* HALF-BREED —**half′-blood′ed** *adj.*

half′-breed′ *n.* one whose parents are of different races: also **half′-caste′**

half brother a brother through one parent only

half′-cocked′ *adj.* thoughtless or too hasty —**go off half-cocked** to speak or act thoughtlessly

half dollar a coin of the U.S. and Canada, worth 50 cents

half′heart′ed *adj.* with little enthusiasm, determination, interest, etc. —**half′heart′ed·ly** *adv.*

half hitch a knot made by passing the end of the rope around the rope and through the loop thus made

half′-life′ *n.* the period required for the disintegration of half of the atoms in a sample of some radioactive substance: also **half life**

half′-mast′ *n.* the position of a flag lowered about halfway down its staff, as in public mourning —*vt.* to hang (a flag) at half-mast

half′-moon′ *n.* **1.** the moon when only half its disk is clearly seen **2.** anything shaped like this

half note *Music* a note (♩) having one half the duration of a whole note

half·pen·ny (hāp′pə nē, hāp′nē) *n., pl.* **-pence** (-pens), **-pen·nies** a former British coin equal to half a penny — *adj.* worth a halfpenny, or very little

half sister a sister through one parent only

half sole a sole (of a shoe or boot) from the arch to the toe

half step **1.** a short marching step **2.** *Music same as* SEMITONE

half′tone′ *n.* **1.** *Art* a shading between light and dark **2.** *Music same as* SEMITONE **3.** *Photoengraving a)* a technique of shading by the use of dots *b)* a photoengraving so made

half′track′ *n.* an army truck, armored vehicle, etc. with a continuous tread instead of rear wheels

half′way′ *adj.* **1.** midway between two points, etc. **2.** partial [*halfway* measures] —*adv.* **1.** to the midway point **2.** partially —**meet halfway** to be willing to compromise with

half′-wit′ *n.* a stupid, silly, or imbecilic person; fool — **half′-wit′ted** *adj.*

hal·i·but (hal′ə bət) *n., pl.* **-but, -buts** [ME. *hali,* holy + *butt,* a flounder: eaten on holidays] a large, edible flatfish found in northern seas

Hal·i·fax (hal′ə faks′) capital of Nova Scotia: pop. 87,000

hal·ite (hal′īt, hā′līt) *n.* [< Gr. *hals,* salt + -ITE] native sodium chloride; rock salt

hal·i·to·sis (hal′ə tō′sis) *n.* [< L. *halitus,* breath] bad-smelling breath

hall (hôl) *n.* [OE. *heall*] **1.** the dwelling of a baron, squire, etc. **2.** a public building with offices, etc. **3.** a large room for gatherings, exhibits, etc. **4.** a college or university building **5.** a vestibule at the entrance of a building **6.** a passageway

hal·le·lu·jah, hal·le·lu·iah (hal′ə lōō′yə) *interj.* [< Heb. *hallelū,* praise + *yāh,* Jehovah] praise (ye) the Lord! —*n.* a hymn of praise to God

Hal·ley's comet (hal′ēz) a comet, last seen in 1910, whose periodic reappearance (c.75 years) was predicted by E. Halley (1656–1742), Eng. astronomer

hall·mark (hôl′märk′) *n.* **1.** an official mark stamped on gold and silver articles orig. at Goldsmiths' Hall in London **2.** a mark or symbol of genuineness or high quality

hal·loo (hə lōō′) *vi., vt.* **-looed′, -loo′ing** **1.** to call out in order to attract attention **2.** to shout —*interj., n.* a shout

hal·low (hal′ō) *vt.* [OE. *halgian*] to make or regard as holy

hal·lowed (hal′ōd; *in liturgy, often* hal′ə wid) *adj.* **1.** made holy or sacred **2.** honored as sacred

Hal·low·een, Hal·low·e'en (hal′ə wen′, häl′-) *n.* [contr. < *all hallow even*] the evening of October 31, which is followed by All Saints' Day

hal·lu·ci·nate (hə lōō′sə nāt′) *vi., vt.* **-nat′ed, -nat′ing** [< L. *hallucinari,* wander mentally] to have or cause to have hallucinations

hal·lu·ci·na·tion (hə lōō′sə nā′shən) *n.* **1.** the apparent perception of sights, sounds, etc. that are not actually present **2.** the imaginary thing apparently seen, heard, etc. —**hal·lu′ci·na·to′ry** (-nə tôr′ē) *adj.*

hal·lu·ci·no·gen (-nə jen, hal'yōō sin'ə jen) *n.* a drug or other substance that produces hallucinations —**hal·lu·ci·no·gen'ic** *adj.*

hall·way (hôl'wā') *n.* a passageway; corridor

ha·lo (hā'lō) *n., pl.* **-los, -loes** [< Gr. *halōs,* circular threshing floor] 1. a ring of light, as around the sun 2. a symbolic ring of light around the head of a saint in pictures 3. the glory attributed to a person or thing idealized —*vt.* **-loed, -lo·ing** to encircle with a halo

hal·o·gen (hal'ə jən) *n.* [< Gr. *hals,* salt] any of the very active chemical elements, fluorine, chlorine, bromine, astatine, and iodine

Hals (häls), **Frans** (fräns) 1580?–1666; Du. painter

halt[1] (hôlt) *n., vi., vt.* [< Fr. *faire halte* and G. *halt machen*] stop —**call a halt** to order a stop

halt[2] (hôlt) *vi.* [< OE. *healt*] 1. [Archaic] to limp 2. to hesitate —*adj.* limping; lame —**the halt** those who are lame —**halt'ing·ly** *adv.*

hal·ter (hôl'tər) *n.* [OE. *hælftre*] 1. *a)* a rope, strap, etc. for tying or leading an animal *b)* a bitless bridle, with or without a lead rope 2. a hangman's noose 3. a woman's upper garment, held up by a loop around the neck —*vt.* to put a halter on (an animal)

halve (hav) *vt.* **halved, halv'ing** 1. to divide into two equal parts 2. to reduce to half

halves (havz) *n. pl. of* HALF —**by halves** 1. halfway; imperfectly 2. halfheartedly —**go halves** to share expenses, etc. equally

HALTER
(sense 1*b*)

hal·yard (hal'yərd) *n.* [< ME. *halier* (see HALE[2])] a rope or tackle for raising or lowering a flag, sail, etc.: also sp. **halliard**

Ham (ham) *Bible* Noah's second son

ham (ham) *n.* [OE. *hamm*] 1. the part of the leg behind the knee 2. the back of the thigh 3. the upper part of a hog's hind leg, salted, smoked, etc. 4. [Colloq.] an amateur radio operator 5. [Slang] an actor who overacts —**ham'my** *adj.* **-mi·er, -mi·est**

Ham·burg (ham'bərg) seaport in N West Germany: pop. 1,833,000

ham·burg·er (ham'bʉr'gər) *n.* [< prec.] 1. ground beef 2. a cooked patty of such meat, often eaten as a sandwich Also **ham'burg**

Ham·il·ton (ham'əl t'n) city & port in SE Ontario: pop. 298,000

Ham·il·ton (ham'əl t'n), **Alexander** 1757–1804; Am. statesman; 1st secretary of the U.S. treasury (1789–95)

Ham·it·ic (ha mit'ik) *adj.* designating or of a group of African languages, including ancient Egyptian

Ham·let (ham'lit) the title hero of a tragedy by Shakespeare

ham·let (ham'lit) *n.* [< LowG. *hamm,* enclosed area] a very small village

ham·mer (ham'ər) *n.* [OE. *hamor*] 1. a tool for pounding, having a metal head and a handle 2. a thing like this in shape or use, as the part of a gun that strikes the firing pin 3. a bone of the middle ear —*vt., vi.* 1. to strike repeatedly as with a hammer 2. to drive, force, or shape as with hammer blows —**hammer (away) at** to keep emphasizing

ham'mer·head' *n.* 1. the head of a hammer 2. a shark with a mallet-shaped head

ham'mer·toe' *n.* a toe that is deformed, with its first joint bent downward

ham·mock (ham'ək) *n.* [Sp. *hamaca* < WInd.] a bed of canvas, etc. swung from ropes at both ends

Ham·mond (ham'ənd) city in NW Ind., near Chicago: pop. 108,000

ham·per[1] (ham'pər) *vt.* [ME. *hampren*] to hinder; impede; encumber

ham·per[2] (ham'pər) *n.* [< OFr. *hanap,* a cup] a large basket, usually with a cover

Hamp·ton (hamp'tən) seaport in SE Va.: pop. 121,000

ham·ster (ham'stər) *n.* [G.] a ratlike animal, often used in scientific research

ham·string (ham'striŋ') *n.* 1. a tendon at the back of the knee 2. the great tendon at the back of the hock in a four-legged animal —*vt.* **-strung', -string'ing** to disable, as by cutting a hamstring

Han·cock (han'käk), **John** 1737–93; Am. statesman; 1st signer of the Declaration of Independence

hand (hand) *n.* [OE.] 1. the part of the arm below the wrist, used for grasping 2. a side or direction [at my right *hand*] 3. possession or care [the land is in my *hands*] 4.

control [to strengthen one's *hand*] 5. an active part [take a *hand* in the work] 6. a promise to marry 7. skill 8. one having a special skill 9. handwriting 10. applause 11. help [to lend a *hand*] 12. one whose chief work is with his hands, as a farm laborer 13. a source [to get news at first *hand*] 14. anything like a hand, as a pointer on a clock 15. the breadth of a hand, about four inches 16. *Card Games a)* the cards held by a player at one time *b)* a round of play —*adj.* of, for, or controlled by the hand —*vt.* 1. to give as with the hand 2. to help or conduct with the hand —**at hand** near —**by hand** not by machines but with the hands —**change hands** to pass to another's ownership —**from hand to mouth** with just enough for immediate needs —**hand down** 1. to bequeath 2. to announce (a verdict, etc.) —**hand in** to give; submit —**hand in hand** together —**hand it to** [Slang] to give deserved credit to —**hand out** to distribute —**hand over** to give up; deliver —**hand over fist** [Colloq.] easily and in large amounts —**hands down** easily —**hands off!** don't touch! —**on hand** 1. near 2. available 3. present —**on one's hands** in one's care —**on the one** (or **other**) **hand** from one (or the opposed) point of view

hand'bag' *n.* 1. a woman's purse 2. a small suitcase

hand'ball' *n.* 1. a game in which players bat a small ball against a wall or walls with the hand 2. this ball

hand'bar'row *n.* a frame carried by two people, each holding a pair of handles at either end

hand'bill' *n.* a small printed notice, advertisement, etc. to be passed out by hand

hand'book' *n.* 1. a compact reference book on some subject; manual 2. a guidebook

hand'breadth' *n.* the breadth of the human palm, about four inches

hand'cart' *n.* a small cart, often with only two wheels, pulled or pushed by hand

hand'clasp' *n.* a clasping of each other's hand in greeting, farewell, etc.

hand'cuff' *n.* either of a pair of connected rings that can be locked about the wrists, as in shackling a prisoner: *usually used in pl.* —*vt.* to put handcuffs on; manacle

hand'ed *adj.* having or involving (a specified kind or number of) hands [right-*handed,* two-*handed*]

Han·del (han'd'l), **George Frederick** 1685–1759; Eng. composer, born in Germany

hand'ful' *n., pl.* **-fuls'** 1. as much or as many as the hand will hold 2. a small number or amount 3. [Colloq.] someone or something hard to manage

hand'gun' *n.* any firearm that is held and fired with one hand, as a pistol

hand·i·cap (han'dē kap') *n.* [< *hand in cap,* former kind of lottery] 1. a competition in which difficulties are imposed on, or advantages given to, the various contestants to equalize their chances 2. such a difficulty or advantage 3. any hindrance —*vt.* **-capped', -cap'ping** 1. to give a handicap to 2. to hinder —**the handicapped** those who are physically disabled or mentally retarded —**hand'i·cap'per** *n.*

hand·i·craft (han'dē kraft') *n.* 1. skill with the hands 2. work calling for this, as weaving

hand'i·work' *n.* 1. *same as* HANDWORK 2. anything made or done by a particular person

hand·ker·chief (haŋ'kər chif) *n.* 1. a small, square piece of cloth for wiping the nose, face, etc. 2. a kerchief

han·dle (han'd'l) *n.* [OE. < *hand*] 1. that part of a tool, etc. by which it is held, turned, etc. 2. a thing like a handle —*vt.* **-dled, -dling** 1. to touch, lift, operate, etc. with the hand 2. to manage, control, etc. 3. to deal with or treat 4. to sell or deal in 5. to behave toward; treat —*vi.* to respond to control [the car *handles* well] —**fly off the handle** [Colloq.] to become violently angry

han'dle·bar' *n.* [*often pl.*] a curved metal bar with handles on the ends, for steering a bicycle, etc.

han·dler (han'dlər) *n.* a person or thing that handles; specif., a boxer's trainer and second

hand'made' *adj.* made by hand, not by machine

hand'maid'en *n.* [Archaic] a woman or girl servant: also **hand'maid'**

hand'-me-down' *n.* [Colloq.] a used article of clothing etc. which is passed along to someone else

hand organ *same as* BARREL ORGAN

hand'out' *n.* 1. a gift of food, clothing, etc., as to a beggar 2. a leaflet handed out 3. an official news release

hand'pick' *vt.* 1. to pick (fruit or vegetables) by hand 2. to choose with care —**hand'picked'** *adj.*

hand'rail' *n.* a rail serving as a guard or hand support, as along a stairway

hand'saw' *n.* a saw used with one hand

hand'set' *n.* a telephone mouthpiece and receiver in a single unit, held in one hand

hand'shake' *n.* a gripping of each other's hand in greeting, agreement, etc.

hand·some (han'səm) *adj.* [orig., easily handled] **1.** large; considerable **2.** generous; gracious **3.** good-looking, esp. in a manly or dignified way —**hand'some·ly** *adv.*

hand'spring' *n.* a spring in which one turns over in mid-air with one or both hands touching the ground

hand'-to-hand' *adj.* in close contact: said of fighting

hand'-to-mouth' *adj.* barely subsisting

hand'work' *n.* work done or made by hand

hand'writ'ing *n.* **1.** writing done by hand, with pen, pencil, etc. **2.** a style of such writing —**hand'writ'ten** *adj.*

hand'y *adj.* -i·er, -i·est **1.** close at hand; easily reached **2.** easily used; convenient **3.** clever with the hands —**hand'i·ly** *adv.* —**hand'i·ness** *n.*

han·dy·man *n., pl.* -men' a man who does odd jobs

hang (haŋ) *vt.* hung, hang'ing; for vt. 3 & vi. 5 hanged is preferred pt. & pp. [OE. *hangian*] **1.** to attach from above with no support from below; suspend **2.** to attach (a door, etc.) so as to move freely **3.** to kill by suspending from a rope about the neck **4.** to paste (wallpaper) to walls **5.** to ornament [to *hang* a room with pictures] **6.** to let (one's head) droop downward **7.** to deadlock (a jury) —*vi.* **1.** to be suspended **2.** to hover in the air **3.** to swing, as on a hinge **4.** to drape, as cloth **5.** to die by hanging **6.** to droop; bend **7.** to hesitate —*n.* the way a thing hangs —**get (or have) the hang of 1.** to learn (or have) the knack of **2.** to understand the meaning or idea of —**hang around (or about)** [Colloq.] to loiter around —**hang back (or off)** to be reluctant, as from shyness —**hang on 1.** to persevere **2.** to depend on **3.** to listen attentively to —**hang out** [Slang] to frequent —**hang up 1.** to put on a hanger, hook, etc. **2.** to end a telephone call by replacing the receiver **3.** to delay

hang·ar (haŋ'ər) *n.* [Fr., a shed] a repair shed or shelter for aircraft

Hang·chow (haŋ'chou') river & canal port in E China: pop. 784,000

hang'dog' *adj.* **1.** sneaking or abject **2.** ashamed

hang'er *n.* **1.** one who hangs things **2.** a thing on which objects, as garments, are hung

hang'er-on' *n., pl.* hang'ers-on' a follower, esp. one who attaches himself to others although not wanted

hang gliding the sport of gliding through the air while hanging by a harness from a large type of kite (**hang glider**)

hang'ing *adj.* that hangs —*n.* **1.** a putting to death by hanging **2.** something hung, as a drapery

hang'man (-mən) *n., pl.* -men an executioner who hangs convicted criminals

hang'nail' *n.* [< OE. *angnægl*, a corn] a bit of torn skin hanging next to a fingernail

hang'out' *n.* [Slang] a place frequented by some person or group

hang'o'ver *n.* **1.** a survival **2.** nausea, headache, etc. from drinking much alcoholic liquor

hang'-up' *n.* [Slang] an emotional problem that cannot easily be resolved

hank (haŋk) *n.* [prob. < Scand.] **1.** a loop of something flexible **2.** a length of coiled thread or yarn

hank·er (haŋ'kər) *vi.* [prob. < Du. or LowG.] to crave or long (for) —**hank'er·ing** *n.*

han·ky-pan·ky (haŋ'kē paŋ'kē) *n.* [altered < HOCUS-POCUS] [Colloq.] trickery or deception

Han·ni·bal (han'ə b'l) 247?–183? B.C.; Carthaginian general: crossed the Alps to invade Italy

Ha·noi (hä noi') the capital of Vietnam in the N part: pop. 644,000

Han·o·ver (han'ō vər) ruling family of England (1714–1901)

han·som (cab) (han'səm) [< J. A. *Hansom*, Eng. inventor] a two-wheeled covered carriage pulled by one horse, with the driver's seat behind

Ha·nu·ka (khä'noō kä', -kə; hä'-) *n.* [< Heb., dedication] a Jewish festival in early winter commemorating the rededication of the Temple by the Maccabees in 165 B.C.: also **Ha'nuk·kah', Ha'nuk·ka'**

HANSOM

hap (hap) *n.* [< ON. *happ*] chance; luck —*vi.* happed, hap'ping to occur by chance; happen

hap·haz·ard (hap'haz'ərd) *adj.* [prec. + HAZARD] not planned; casual —*adv.* by chance; casually —**hap'haz'-ard·ly** *adv.*

hap·less (hap'lis) *adj.* unfortunate; unlucky

hap'ly *adv.* [Archaic] by chance

hap·pen (hap''n) *vi.* [ME. *happenen*] **1.** to take place; occur **2.** to be or occur by chance **3.** to have the luck or occasion; chance [I *happened* to see it] —**happen on (or upon)** to meet or find by chance

hap'pen·ing *n.* something that happens; occurrence

hap·py (hap'ē) *adj.* -pi·er, -pi·est [< HAP] **1.** lucky; fortunate **2.** having, showing, or causing a feeling of pleasure, joy, etc. **3.** suitable and clever [a *happy* suggestion] —**hap'pi·ly** *adv.* —**hap'pi·ness** *n.*

hap'py-go-luck'y *adj.* easygoing; trusting to luck —*adv.* haphazardly; by chance

Haps·burg (haps'burg') former ruling family of Austria-Hungary, Spain, & the Holy Roman Empire

ha·ra·ki·ri (hä'rə kir'ē) [Jpn. *hara*, belly + *kiri*, a cutting] ritual suicide by disembowelment, done by high-ranking Japanese to avoid facing disgrace

ha·rangue (hə raŋ') *n.* [< OIt. *aringo*, site for public assemblies] a long, blustering speech; tirade —*vt., vi.* -rangued', -rangu'ing to speak or address in a harangue

har·ass (hə ras', har'əs) *vt.* [< Fr. < OFr. *harer*, set a dog on] **1.** to worry or torment, as with cares, debts, etc. **2.** to trouble by repeated raids or attacks —**har·ass'ment** *n.*

Har·bin (här'bin) city in NE China: pop. 1,552,000

har·bin·ger (här'bin jər) *n.* [< OFr. *herberge*, a shelter] a forerunner; herald —*vt.* to be a harbinger of

har·bor (här'bər) *n.* [< OE. *here*, army + *beorg*, a shelter] **1.** a shelter **2.** a protected inlet of a sea, lake, etc., for anchoring ships; port —*vt.* **1.** to shelter or house **2.** to hold in the mind [to *harbor* a grudge] —*vi.* to take shelter Brit. sp. **har'bour**

hard (härd) *adj.* [OE. *heard*] **1.** firm and unyielding to the touch; solid and compact **2.** powerful [a *hard* blow] **3.** difficult to do, understand, or deal with **4.** *a)* unfeeling [a *hard* heart] *b)* unfriendly [*hard* feelings] **5.** practical and shrewd **6.** *a)* aggressively firm *b)* actual [*hard* facts] **7.** harsh; severe **8.** having mineral salts that interfere with lathering: said of water **9.** energetic [a *hard* worker] **10.** strongly alcoholic [*hard* liquor] **11.** [Colloq.] designating any drug, as heroin, that is addictive and harmful **12.** popularly, designating *c* and *g* as sounded in *can* and *gun* —*adv.* **1.** energetically [work *hard*] **2.** with strength [hit *hard*] **3.** with difficulty [*hard*-earned] **4.** firmly **5.** close; near [we live *hard* by] **6.** so as to be solid [frozen *hard*] **7.** sharply [turn *hard* right] —**hard and fast** invariable; strict —**hard of hearing** partially deaf —**hard put** to it having considerable difficulty —**hard up** [Colloq.] in great need of something, esp. money —**hard'ness** *n.*

hard'-bit'ten *adj.* tough; dogged

hard'-boiled' *adj.* **1.** boiled until solid: said of an egg **2.** [Colloq.] unfeeling; callous; tough

hard coal same as ANTHRACITE

hard'-core' *adj.* absolute; unqualified

hard'-cov'er *adj.* designating any book bound in a relatively stiff cover: also **hard'-bound'**

hard·en (här'd'n) *vt., vi.* to make or become hard —**hard'-en·er** *n.*

hard'fist'ed *adj.* stingy; miserly

hard hat 1. a protective helmet worn by construction workers, miners, etc. **2.** [Slang] such a worker

hard'head'ed *adj.* **1.** shrewd and unsentimental; practical **2.** stubborn —**hard'head'ed·ness** *n.*

hard'heart'ed *adj.* unfeeling; pitiless —**hard'heart'ed·ly** *adv.* —**hard'heart'ed·ness** *n.*

har·di·hood (här'dē hood') *n.* **1.** boldness, daring, fortitude, etc. **2.** impudence; insolence

Har·ding (här'diŋ), **Warren G.** 1865–1923; 29th president of the U.S. (1921–23)

hard'ly (härd'lē) *adv.* **1.** with difficulty **2.** severely; harshly **3.** only just; scarcely: often ironic for "not at all" **4.** probably not; not likely

hard'-nosed' *adj.* [Slang] **1.** tough; stubborn **2.** shrewd and practical —**hard'nose'** *n.*

hard palate the bony part of the roof of the mouth

hard'pan' *n.* a layer of hard, clayey soil

hard sauce a creamy mixture of butter, sugar, and flavoring, served with plum pudding, etc.

hard sell high-pressure salesmanship

fat, āpe, cär; ten, ēven; is, bīte; gō, hôrn, tōōl, look; oil, out; up, fur; thin, *th*en; zh, leisure; ŋ, ring; ə for *a* in *ago*; ' as in *able* (ā'b'l); ë, Fr. coeur; ö, Fr. feu; Fr. mon; ü, Fr. duc; r, Fr. cri; kh, G. doch, ich. ‡ foreign; < derived from

hard'-shell' *adj.* **1.** having a hard shell, as a crab: also **hard'-shelled'** **2.** [Colloq.] strict; uncompromising

hard'ship' *n.* **1.** hard circumstances of life **2.** a thing hard to bear, as poverty, pain, etc.

hard'tack' (-tak') *n.* unleavened bread made in very hard, large wafers: traditionally a part of army and navy rations

hard'top' *n.* an automobile like a convertible but having a fixed metal top

hard'ware' (-wer') *n.* **1.** articles made of metal, as tools, nails, fittings, etc. **2.** the mechanical, magnetic, and electronic devices of a computer

hard'wood' *n.* any tough, heavy timber with a compact texture

har·dy (här'dē) *adj.* -di·er, -di·est [< OFr. *hardir,* make bold] **1.** bold and resolute **2.** too bold; rash **3.** robust; vigorous —**har'di·ly** *adv.* —**har'di·ness** *n.*

hare (her) *n.* [OE. *hara*] a swift mammal related to the rabbit, with long ears, soft fur, etc.

hare'brained' *adj.* reckless, giddy, rash, etc.

hare'lip' *n.* a congenital deformity consisting of a cleft of the upper lip

ha·rem (her'əm) *n.* [Ar. *harīm,* prohibited (place)] **1.** that part of a Muslim's household in which the women live **2.** the women in a harem Also **ha·reem** (hä rēm')

ha·ri·ka·ri (her'ē ker'ē) *n. same as* HARA-KIRI

hark (härk) *vi.* [< ? OE. *heorcnian,* hearken] to listen carefully: usually in the imperative —**hark back** to go back; revert

hark·en (här'k'n) *vi. same as* HEARKEN

Har·lem (här'ləm) section of New York City

Har·le·quin (här'lə kwin, -kin) a traditional comic character in pantomime, who wears a mask and gay, spangled tights —*n.* [h-] a clown; buffoon —*adj.* [h-] **1.** comic; ludicrous **2.** of many colors; colorful

har·lot (här'lət) *n.* [OFr., rogue] a prostitute

har'lot·ry (-rē) *n.* **1.** prostitution **2.** prostitutes, collectively

harm (härm) *n.* [OE. *hearm*] **1.** hurt; injury; damage **2.** moral wrong; evil —*vt.* to do harm to; hurt, damage, etc. —**harm'er** *n.*

harm'ful *adj.* causing or able to cause harm; hurtful —**harm'ful·ly** *adv.* —**harm'ful·ness** *n.*

harm'less *adj.* causing no harm; inoffensive —**harm'less·ly** *adv.* —**harm'less·ness** *n.*

har·mon·ic (här män'ik) *adj. Music* **1.** of or in harmony **2.** pertaining to an overtone —*n. same as* OVERTONE (sense 1)

har·mon'i·ca (-i kə) *n.* a small wind instrument with a series of metal reeds that produce tones when air is blown or sucked across them

har·mon'ics *n.pl.* [*with sing. v.*] the physical science dealing with musical sounds

har·mo·ni·ous (här mō'nē əs) *adj.* **1.** having parts combined in an orderly or pleasing arrangement **2.** having similar feelings, ideas, interests, etc. **3.** having musical tones combined to give a pleasing effect —**har·mo'ni·ous·ly** *adv.*

har·mo'ni·um (-əm) *n.* a small kind of reed organ

har·mo·nize (här'mə nīz') *vi.* -nized', -niz'ing to be or sing in harmony —*vt.* **1.** to make harmonious **2.** to add chords to (a melody) so as to form a harmony —**har'mo·niz'er** *n.*

har·mo·ny (här'mə nē) *n., pl.* -nies [< Gr. *harmos,* a fitting] **1.** pleasing agreement of parts in color, size, shape, etc. **2.** agreement in feeling, action, ideas, etc.; peaceable or friendly relations **3.** agreeable sounds; music **4.** *Music a)* the pleasing combination of tones in a chord *b)* structure in the arrangement of chords

har·ness (här'nis) *n.* [< OFr. *harneis,* armor] the leather straps and metal pieces by which a horse, mule, etc. is fastened to a vehicle, plow, etc. —*vt.* **1.** to put harness on **2.** to control so as to use the power of —**in harness** at one's routine work

harp (härp) *n.* [OE. *hearpe*] a musical instrument with strings stretched across a triangular frame, played by plucking with the fingers —*vi.* **1.** to play a harp **2.** to persist in talking or writing tediously (*on* or *upon* something) —**harp'er** *n.*

harp·ist (här'pist) *n.* a harp player

har·poon (här pōōn') *n.* [< ON. *harpa,* to squeeze] a barbed spear with an attached line, used for spearing whales, etc. —*vt.* to strike or kill with a harpoon —**harpoon'er** *n.*

harp·si·chord (härp'si kôrd') *n.* [< obs. Fr. or < It.: see HARP & CHORD] a stringed musical instrument with a keyboard, predecessor of the piano

Har·py (här'pē) *n., pl.* -pies [< Gr. *harpazein,* seize] **1.** *Gr. Myth.* any of several hideous, winged monsters with the head and trunk of a woman and the tail and legs of a bird **2.** [h-] a greedy person

har·ri·dan (har'i d'n) *n.* [prob. < Fr. *haridelle,* worn-out horse] a disreputable, shrewish old woman

har·ri·er (har'ē ər) *n.* [< HARE + -IER] **1.** a small dog used for hunting hares **2.** a cross-country runner

har·ri·er² (har'ē ər) *n.* **1.** one who harries **2.** a hawk that preys on small mammals, reptiles, etc.

Har·ris (har'is), **Joel Chan·dler** (chan'dlər) 1848–1908; U.S. writer

Har·ris·burg (har'is burg') capital of Pa., on the Susquehanna: pop. 68,000

Har·ri·son (har'ə s'n) **1. Benjamin,** 1833–1901; 23d president of the U.S. (1889–93) **2. William Henry,** 1773–1841; 9th president of the U.S. (1841): grandfather of *prec.*

har·row (har'ō) *n.* [prob. < ON. *harfr*] a heavy frame with spikes or disks, used for leveling and breaking up plowed ground, etc. —*vt.* **1.** to draw a harrow over (land) **2.** to cause mental distress to; vex —**har'row·ing** *adj.*

har·ry (har'ē) *vt.* -ried, -ry·ing [< OE. *here,* army] **1.** to raid and ravage or rob **2.** to torment; harass

harsh (härsh) *adj.* [ME. *harsk*] **1.** unpleasantly rough to the ear, eye, taste, or touch **2.** unpleasantly crude or abrupt **3.** excessively severe; cruel —**harsh'ly** *adv.* —**harsh'ness** *n.*

hart (härt) *n.* [OE. *heorot*] a male of the European red deer, esp. after its fifth year; stag

Harte (härt), **Bret** (bret) 1836–1902; U.S. writer

har·te·beest (här'tə bēst', härt'bēst') *n.* [obs. Afrik. < *harte,* hart + *beest,* beast] a large, swift South African antelope

Hart·ford (härt'fərd) capital of Conn., in the C part: pop. 158,000 (met. area 644,000)

harts·horn (härts'hôrn') *n.* [Now Rare] ammonium carbonate, used in smelling salts: orig. obtained from deer's antlers

har·um-scar·um (her'əm sker'əm) *adj.* [< ? HARE + SCARE + 'EM] acting or done in a reckless or rash way —*adv.* in a reckless or rash manner

har·vest (här'vist) *n.* [OE. *hærfest*] **1.** the time of the year when grain, fruit, etc. are gathered in **2.** a season's crop **3.** the gathering in of a crop **4.** the outcome of any effort —*vt., vi.* **1.** to gather in (a crop, etc.) **2.** to gather the crop from (a field) —**har'vest·a·ble** *adj.* —**har'vest·er** *n.*

har'vest·man (-mən) *n., pl.* -men **1.** a man who harvests **2.** a spiderlike animal with long legs

harvest moon the full moon at or about the time of the autumnal equinox, September 22 or 23

Har·vey (här'vē), **William** 1578–1657; Eng. physician: discovered the circulation of the blood

has (haz) *3d pers. sing., pres. indic., of* HAVE

has'-been' *n.* [Colloq.] a person or thing whose popularity or effectiveness is past

ha·sen·pfef·fer (has''n fef'ər) *n.* [G. < *hase,* rabbit + *pfeffer,* pepper] a German dish of rabbit meat marinated in vinegar and stewed in the marinade

hash (hash) *vt.* [Fr. *hacher,* to chop] **1.** to chop (meat or vegetables) into small pieces for cooking **2.** [Colloq.] to bungle —*n.* **1.** a chopped mixture of cooked meat and vegetables, usually baked **2.** a mixture **3.** a muddle; mess —**hash out** [Colloq.] to settle by long discussion —**hash over** [Colloq.] to discuss at length —**settle someone's hash** [Colloq.] to overcome or subdue someone

hash house [Slang] a cheap restaurant

hash·ish (hash'ēsh, -ish) *n.* [Ar. *hashīsh,* dried hemp] a drug obtained from the resin in the flowering tops of Indian hemp, chewed or smoked for its intoxicating or euphoric effects: also **hash'eesh** (-ēsh)

has·n't (haz''nt) has not

hasp (hasp) *n.* [OE. *hæpse*] a hinged metal fastening for a door, window, etc.; esp., a metal piece fitted over a staple and fastened by a bolt or padlock

has·sle (has''l) *n.* [< ?] [Colloq.] **1.** a heated argument **2.** a troublesome situation —*vi.* -sled, -sling [Colloq.] to have a heated argument —*vt.* [Slang] to annoy, harass, etc.

has·sock (has'ək) *n.* [OE. *hassuc*] **1.** [Now Rare] a thick clump of grass **2.** a firmly stuffed cushion used as a footstool or seat

HASP

hast (hast) *archaic 2d pers. sing., pres. indic., of* HAVE: *used with* thou

haste (hāst) *n.* [OFr.] quickness of motion; hurrying —*vt., vi.* **hast′ed, hast′ing** [Rare] *same as* HASTEN —**in haste 1.** in a hurry **2.** in too great a hurry —**make haste** to hasten

has·ten (hās′n) *vt.* to cause to be or come faster; speed up —*vi.* to move swiftly; hurry

hast·y (hās′tē) *adj.* **-i·er, -i·est 1.** done with haste; hurried **2.** done or made too quickly or rashly **3.** impetuous or impatient —**hast′i·ly** *adv.* —**hast′i·ness** *n.*

hasty pudding 1. mush made of cornmeal **2.** [Brit.] mush made of flour or oatmeal

hat (hat) *n.* [OE. *hætt*] a head covering, usually with a brim and a crown —*vt.* **hat′ted, hat′ting** to cover or provide with a hat —**pass the hat** to take up a collection — **talk through one's hat** [Colloq.] to talk nonsense —**under one's hat** [Colloq.] secret

hatch¹ (hach) *vt.* [ME. *hacchen*] **1.** to bring forth (young) from (an egg or eggs) **2.** to contrive (a plan, plot, etc.) — *vi.* **1.** to bring forth young: said of eggs **2.** to emerge from the egg —*n.* the process of hatching

hatch² (hach) *n.* [OE. *hæcc*, grating] **1.** *same as* HATCH-WAY **2.** a lid for a hatchway

hatch³ (hach) *vt.* [< OFr. *hache*, an ax] to mark or engrave with fine, crossed or parallel lines so as to indicate shading —**hatch′ing** *n.*

hatch′er·y *n., pl.* **-ies** a place for hatching eggs, esp. those of fish or poultry

hatch·et (hach′it) *n.* [< OFr. *hache*, an ax] a small, short-handled ax —**bury the hatchet** to make peace

hatchet job [Colloq.] a biased, malicious attack on another's character

hatch′way′ *n.* a covered opening in a ship's deck, or in a floor or roof

hate (hāt) *vt.* **hat′ed, hat′ing** [OE. *hatian*] **1.** to have strong dislike or ill will for **2.** to wish to avoid *[to hate arguments]* —*vi.* to feel hatred —*n.* **1.** a strong feeling of dislike or ill will **2.** a person or thing hated —**hat′er** *n.*

hate′ful *adj.* **1.** [Now Rare] feeling or showing hate **2.** causing or deserving hate —**hate′ful·ly** *adv.* —**hate′ful·ness** *n.*

hath (hath) *archaic 3d pers. sing., pres. indic., of* HAVE

hat′rack′ *n.* a rack to hold hats

ha·tred (hā′trid) *n.* strong dislike or ill will; hate

hat·ter (hat′ər) *n.* one who makes or sells hats

hau·berk (hô′bərk) *n.* [< Frank. *hals*, neck + *borgan*, protect] a medieval coat of armor, usually of chain mail

haugh·ty (hôt′ē) *adj.* **-ti·er, -ti·est** [< OFr. *haut*, high] having or showing great pride in oneself and contempt for others; arrogant —**haugh′ti·ly** *adv.* —**haugh′ti·ness** *n.*

haul (hôl) *vt., vi.* [< ODu. *halen*, fetch] **1.** to move by pulling; drag **2.** to transport by wagon, truck, etc. **3.** *Naut.* to change the course of (a ship) by setting the sails —*n.* **1.** the act of hauling **2.** the amount gained, caught, etc. at one time **3.** the distance or route covered in transporting or traveling **4.** a load transported —**haul off** [Colloq.] to draw the arm back before hitting —**haul up 1.** to sail nearer the direction of the wind **2.** to stop —**in (or over) the long haul** over a long period of time —**haul′er** *n.*

haunch (hônch, hänch) *n.* [< OFr. *hanche* < Gmc.] **1.** the hip, buttock, and upper thigh together **2.** an animal's loin and leg together

haunt (hônt, hänt) *vt.* [< OFr. *hanter*, to frequent] **1.** to visit (a place) often or continually **2.** to recur repeatedly to *[memories haunted her]* —*n.* a place often visited

haunt′ed *adj.* supposedly frequented by ghosts

haunt′ing *adj.* recurring often to the mind *[a haunting melody]* —**haunt′ing·ly** *adv.*

haut·boy (hō′boi′, ō′-) *n.* [< Fr. *haut*, high + *bois*, wood] *earlier name for* OBOE

hau·teur (hō tur′) *n.* [Fr. < *haut*, high, proud] disdainful pride; haughtiness; snobbery

Ha·va·na (hə van′ə) capital of Cuba; pop. 788,000 —*n.* a cigar made of Cuban tobacco

have (hav) *vt.* **had, hav′ing** [OE. *habban*] **1.** to hold; own; possess *[to have wealth]* **2.** to possess as a part, characteristic, etc. **3.** to experience *[have a visit]* **4.** to hold in mind *[to have an idea]* **5.** to state *[so gossip has it]* **6.** to get, take, or obtain *[have some tea]* **7.** to beget (offspring) **8.** to engage in *[to have an argument]* **9.** to cause to; cause to be *[have her leave]* **10.** to be in a certain relation to *[to have a wife]* **11.** to permit; tolerate *[I won't have this noise]* **12.** [Colloq.] *a)* to take at a disadvantage *b)* to deceive; cheat **Have** is used as an auxiliary to express completed action, as in the perfect tenses

(Ex.: I *had* left) and with infinitives to express obligation or necessity (Ex.: we *have* to go) **Have got** often replaces *have:* see GET **Have** is conjugated in the present indicative: (I) *have,* (he, she, it) *has,* (we, you, they) *have* —*n.* a wealthy person or nation —**have at** to attack; strike — **have it out** to settle a disagreement by fighting or discussion —**have on** to be wearing

ha·ven (hā′vən) *n.* [OE. *hæfen*] **1.** a port; harbor **2.** any sheltered place; refuge

have-not (hav′nät′) *n.* a person or nation with little wealth or resources

have·n't (hav′nt) have not

hav·er·sack (hav′ər sak′) *n.* [< Fr. < G. *habersack,* lit., sack of oats] a canvas bag for rations, worn over the shoulder, as by soldiers and hikers

hav·oc (hav′ək) *n.* [< OFr. *havot,* plunder] great destruction and devastation —**play havoc with** to devastate; ruin

haw¹ (hô) *n.* [OE. *haga*] **1.** the berry of the hawthorn **2.** *same as* HAWTHORN

haw² (hô) *interj., n.* a command to a horse, ox, etc., meaning "turn left!" —*vt., vi.* to turn to the left

haw³ (hô) *vi.* [echoic] to hesitate in speaking; falter: usually in HEM AND HAW (see HEM²) —*n.* a conventionalized expression of the sound often made by a speaker when hesitating briefly

Ha·wai·i (hə wä′ē, -yē, -yə) **1.** State of the U.S., consisting of a group of islands (**Hawaiian Islands**) in the N Pacific: 6,424 sq. mi.; pop. 769,000; cap. Honolulu: abbrev. **HI 2.** the largest of these islands —**Ha·wai′ian** (-yən) *adj., n.*

hawk¹ (hôk) *n.* [< OE. *hafoc*] **1.** a bird of prey with short, rounded wings, a long tail, and a hooked beak and claws **2.** an advocate of war —*vi.* to hunt birds with the help of hawks

hawk² (hôk) *vt., vi.* [< HAWKER] to advertise or peddle (goods) in the street by shouting

hawk³ (hôk) *vi.* [echoic] to clear the throat audibly —*vt.* to bring up (phlegm) by coughing —*n.* an audible clearing of the throat

hawk′er *n.* [ult. < MLowG. *hoken,* peddle] one who hawks goods

hawk′-eyed′ *adj.* keen-sighted like a hawk

hawk′moth′ (-môth′) *n.* a moth with a thick body and a long feeding tube for sucking the nectar of flowers

hawks·bill (turtle) (hôks′bil′) a medium-sized turtle of warm seas, from which tortoise shell is obtained

haw·ser (hô′zər) *n.* [< L. *altus,* high] a rope or cable by which a ship is anchored, towed, etc.

haw·thorn (hô′thôrn′) *n.* [< OE. *haga,* hedge + *thorn*] a thorny shrub or small tree related to the rose, with white or pinkish flowers and red fruits (*haws*)

Haw·thorne (hô′thôrn′), **Nathaniel** 1804–64; U.S. novelist & short-story writer

hay (hā) *n.* [OE. *hieg*] grass, clover, etc. cut and dried for fodder —*vi.* to mow and dry grass, etc. for hay —**hit the hay** [Slang] to go to bed

hay′cock′ (-käk′) *n.* a small, conical heap of hay drying in a field

Hay·dn (hīd′n), **Franz Jo·seph** (fränts yō′zef) 1732–1809; Austrian composer

Hayes (hāz), **Ruth·er·ford B(irchard)** (ruth′ər fərd) 1822–93; 19th president of the U.S. (1877–81)

hay fever an acute inflammation of the eyes and upper respiratory tract: an allergic reaction to some pollens

hay′field′ *n.* a field of grass, alfalfa, etc. to be made into hay

hay′loft′ *n.* a loft, or upper story, in a barn or stable, for storing hay

hay′mak′er *n.* **1.** a person who cuts hay and spreads it out to dry **2.** [Slang] a powerful blow with the fist

hay′mow′ (-mou′) *n.* **1.** hay stored in a barn **2.** *same as* HAYLOFT

hay′ride′ *n.* a pleasure ride taken by a group in a wagon partly filled with hay

hay′seed′ *n.* **1.** grass seed shaken from mown hay **2.** [Old Slang] a rustic; yokel

hay′stack′ *n.* a large heap of hay piled up outdoors: also **hay′rick′** (-rik′)

hay′wire′ *n.* wire for tying up bales of hay, etc. —*adj.* [Slang] **1.** out of order; confused **2.** crazy: usually in **go haywire,** to become crazy

haz·ard (haz′ərd) *n.* [OFr. *hasard,* game of dice] **1.** an early game of chance played with dice **2.** chance **3.** risk; danger **4.** an obstacle on a golf course —*vt.* to risk

---

haz'ard·ous *adj.* risky; dangerous —**haz'ard·ous·ly** *adv.*

haze[1] (hāz) *n.* [prob. < HAZY] 1. a thin vapor of fog, smoke, dust, etc. in the air 2. slight vagueness of mind — *vi., vt.* **hazed, haz'ing** to make or become hazy (often with *over*)

haze[2] (hāz) *vt.* **hazed, haz'ing** [< ? OFr. *haser*, to irritate] to initiate or discipline (fellow students) by forcing to do humiliating or painful things

ha·zel (hā'z'l) *n.* [OE. *hæsel*] 1. a tree or shrub related to the birch, bearing edible nuts 2. a light brown —*adj.* light-brown

ha'zel·nut' *n.* the small, edible, roundish nut of the hazel; filbert

ha·zy (hā'zē) *adj.* **-zi·er, -zi·est** [prob. < OE. *hasu,* dusky] 1. somewhat foggy or smoky 2. vague, obscure, or indefinite —**ha'zi·ly** *adv.* —**ha'zi·ness** *n.*

H-bomb (āch'bäm') *n. same as* HYDROGEN BOMB

hdqrs. headquarters

he (hē) *pron. for pl. see* THEY [OE.] 1. the man, boy, or male animal previously mentioned 2. anyone *[he* who laughs last laughs best*]* —*n., pl.* **hes** a man, boy, or male animal

He *Chem.* helium

head (hed) *n.* [OE. *heafod*] 1. the part of the body containing the brain, and the jaws, eyes, ears, nose, and mouth 2. the mind; intelligence 3. a person *[dinner at five dollars a head]* 4. *pl.* **head** a unit of counting *[ten head* of cattle*]* 5. *[often pl.]* the main side of a coin 6. the uppermost part or thing; top 7. the topic or title of a section, chapter, etc. 8. a headline 9. froth, as on newly poured beer 10. the foremost or projecting part; front 11. the part designed for holding, striking, etc. *[the head* of a nail*]* 12. a projecting place, as in a boil, where pus is about to break through 13. the part of a tape recorder that records or plays back the magnetic signals on a tape 14. the membrane stretched across the end of a drum 15. the source of a river, etc. 16. the pressure in an enclosed fluid, as steam 17. a position of leadership or honor 18. a leader, ruler, etc. 19. a large compact bud *[a head* of cabbage*]* 20. [Slang] a habitual user of marijuana, LSD, etc. —*adj.* 1. most important; principal 2. at the top or front 3. striking against the front *[head* winds] —*vt.* 1. to be chief of or in charge of 2. to lead; precede 3. to cause to go in a specified direction —*vi.* to set out; travel *[to head* eastward*]* —**come to a head** 1. to be about to suppurate, as a boil 2. to culminate —**give one his head** to let one do as he likes —**go to one's head** 1. to confuse or intoxicate one 2. to make one vain —**head off** to get ahead of and intercept —**head over heels** deeply; completely —**heads up!** [Colloq.] look out! be careful! —**keep (or lose) one's head** to keep (or lose) one's poise, self-control, etc. —**make head or tail of** to understand —**on (or upon) one's head** as one's responsibility or misfortune —**over one's head** 1. too difficult to understand 2. to a higher authority —**turn one's head** to make one vain

head'ache' (-āk') *n.* 1. a continuous pain in the head 2. [Colloq.] a cause of worry, trouble, etc.

head'board' *n.* a board that forms the head of a bed

head'cheese' *n.* a loaf of jellied, seasoned meat made from the head and feet of hogs

head'dress' *n.* 1. a covering or decoration for the head 2. a style of arranging the hair

-headed *a combining form meaning* having a head or heads *[clearheaded, two-headed]*

head'er *n.* 1. a person or device that puts heads on nails, pins, etc. 2. [Colloq.] a headlong fall or dive

head'first' *adv.* 1. with the head in front; headlong 2. recklessly Also **head'fore'most'** (-mōst')

head'gear' *n.* a hat, cap, bonnet, etc.

head'hunt'er *n.* a member of any of certain primitive tribes who remove and preserve the heads of slain enemies —**head'hunt'ing** *n.*

head'ing *n.* 1. something forming the head, top, front, etc. 2. the title, topic, etc., as of a chapter 3. the direction in which a ship, plane, etc. is moving: expressed as a compass reading

head'land' *n.* a point of land reaching out into the water; promontory

head'light' *n.* a light with a reflector and lens, at the front of a vehicle: also **head'lamp'**

head'line' *n.* printed lines at the top of a newspaper article, giving the topic —*vt.* **-lined', -lin'ing** 1. to provide with a headline 2. to give featured billing to

head'long' (-lôn') *adv., adj.* 1. with the head first 2. with uncontrolled speed and force 3. reckless(ly); impetuous(ly)

head'man (-mən) *n., pl.* **-men** a leader; chief

head'mas'ter *n.* the principal of a private school, esp. a private school for boys —**head'mis'tress** *n.fem.*

head'-on' *adj., adv.* with the head or front foremost

head'phone' *n.* a telephone or radio receiver held to the ear by a band over the head

head'piece' *n.* a protective covering for the head

head'pin' *n.* the front pin of a triangle of bowling pins

head'quar'ters (-kwôr'tərz) *n.pl.* [often with sing. v.] 1. the main office, or center of operations, of one in command, as in an army 2. the main office in any organization

head'rest' *n.* a support for the head

head'room' *n.* space overhead, as in a doorway

head'set' *n.* an earphone or earphones

heads·man (hedz'mən) *n., pl.* **-men** an executioner who beheads those condemned to die

head start an early start or other competitive advantage

head'stock' *n.* the part of a lathe supporting the spindle

head'stone' *n.* a stone marker placed at the head of a grave

head'strong' *adj.* determined to do as one pleases

head'wa'ters *n.pl.* the small streams that are the sources of a river

head'way' *n.* 1. forward motion 2. progress in work, etc.

head wind a wind blowing in a direction directly opposite the course of a ship or aircraft

head'work' *n.* mental effort; thought

head·y (hed'ē) *adj.* **-i·er, -i·est** 1. impetuous; rash 2. intoxicating —**head'i·ness** *n.*

heal (hēl) *vt., vi.* [OE. *hælan*] 1. to make or become well or healthy again 2. to cure (a disease) or mend, as a wound —**heal'er** *n.*

health (helth) *n.* [OE. *hælth*] 1. physical and mental well-being; freedom from disease, etc. 2. condition of body or mind *[good health]* 3. a wish for a person's health and happiness, as in a toast 4. soundness, as of a society

health food food considered especially healthful; often, specif., such food when organically grown and free of chemical additives

health'ful *adj.* helping to produce or maintain health —**health'ful·ly** *adv.* —**health'ful·ness** *n.*

health·y (hel'thē) *adj.* **-i·er, -i·est** 1. having good health 2. showing or resulting from good health *[a healthy* appetite*]* 3. *same as* HEALTHFUL —**health'i·ness** *n.*

heap (hēp) *n.* [OE. *heap,* a troop] 1. a pile or mass of things jumbled together 2. [Colloq.] a large amount —*vt.* 1. to make a heap of 2. to give in large amounts 3. to fill (a plate, etc.) full or to overflowing —*vi.* to rise in a heap

hear (hir) *vt.* **heard** (hurd), **hear'ing** [OE. *hieran*] 1. to perceive or sense (sounds) by the ear 2. to listen to 3. to conduct a hearing of (a law case, etc.) 4. to be informed of; learn —*vi.* 1. to be able to hear sounds 2. to be told *(of or about)* —**hear from** to get a letter, telegram, etc. from —**not hear of** to refuse to consider —**hear'er** *n.*

hear'ing *n.* 1. the act or process of perceiving sounds 2. the ability to hear 3. opportunity to speak, sing, etc. 4. an appearance before a judge, investigative body, etc. 5. the distance a sound will carry *[within hearing]*

heark·en (här'k'n) *vi.* [OE. *heorcnian*] to pay careful attention; listen carefully

hear·say (hir'sā') *n.* rumor; gossip —*adj.* based on hearsay

hearse (hurs) *n.* [< L. *hirpex,* a harrow] a vehicle used in a funeral for carrying the corpse

heart (härt) *n.* [OE. *heorte*] 1. the hollow, muscular organ that circulates the blood by alternate dilation and contraction 2. any place or part centrally located like the heart *[the heart* of the city*]* 3. the central, vital, or main part; core 4. the human heart considered as the center of emotions, personality attributes, etc.; specif., *a)* inmost thought and feeling *b)* love, sympathy, etc. *c)* mood; feeling *d)* spirit or courage 5. a conventionalized design of a heart (♥) 6. *a)* any of a suit of playing cards marked with such symbols in red *b)* *[pl.]* this suit of cards —**after one's own heart** that pleases one perfectly —**at heart** in one's innermost nature —**break one's heart** to overwhelm one with grief and disappointment —**by heart** by or from memorization —**change of heart** a change of mind, affections, etc. —**set one's heart on** to have a fixed desire for —**take heart** to cheer up —**take to heart** 1. to consider seriously 2. to be troubled by

heart'ache' *n.* sorrow or grief

heart attack any sudden instance of heart failure; esp., as CORONARY THROMBOSIS

heart'beat' *n.* one full contraction and dilation of the heart

heart block defective transmission of impulses regulating the heartbeat

heart′break′ *n.* overwhelming sorrow, grief, or disappointment —**heart′break′ing** *adj.* —**heart′bro′ken** *adj.*

heart′burn′ *n.* a burning, acid sensation beneath the breastbone, in the esophagus

heart′en (-'n) *vt.* to cheer up; encourage

heart failure the inability of the heart to pump enough blood through the body tissues

heart′felt′ *adj.* sincere; genuine

hearth (härth) *n.* [OE. *heorth*] **1.** the stone or brick floor of a fireplace **2.** *a)* the fireside *b)* the home

hearth′stone′ *n.* **1.** the stone forming the hearth **2.** the home, or home life

heart′less *adj.* unkind; unfeeling —**heart′less·ly** *adv.* —**heart′less·ness** *n.*

heart′-rend′ing *adj.* causing much grief or mental anguish —**heart′-rend′ing·ly** *adv.*

heart′sick′ *adj.* sick at heart; extremely unhappy or despondent: also **heart′sore′**

heart′-strick′en *adj.* deeply grieved or greatly dismayed: also **heart′-struck′**

heart′strings′ *n.pl.* deepest feelings or affections

heart′-to-heart′ *adj.* intimate and candid

heart′warm′ing *adj.* such as to cause genial feelings

heart′wood′ *n.* the hard wood at the core of a tree trunk

heart′y (-ē) *adj.* **-i·er, -i·est** **1.** warm and friendly; cordial **2.** strongly felt or expressed *[a hearty dislike]* **3.** strong and healthy **4.** *a)* nourishing and plentiful *[a hearty meal] b)* liking plenty of food *[a hearty eater]* —*n., pl.* **-ies** [Archaic] a friend; esp., a fellow sailor —**heart′i·ly** *adv.* —**heart′i·ness** *n.*

heat (hēt) *n.* [OE. *hætu*] **1.** the quality of being hot; hotness, or the perception of this **2.** much hotness **3.** degree of hotness or warmth **4.** hot weather or climate **5.** the warming of a house, etc. **6.** *a)* strong feeling; ardor, anger, etc. *b)* the period of this **7.** a single effort, bout, or trial **8.** the period of sexual excitement in animals, esp. females **9.** [Slang] coercion or pressure —*vt., vi.* **1.** to make or become warm or hot **2.** to make or become excited

heat′ed *adj.* **1.** hot **2.** vehement or angry —**heat′ed·ly** *adv.*

heat′er *n.* a stove, furnace, radiator, etc. for heating a room, a car, water, etc.

heat exhaustion a mild form of heatstroke

heath (hēth) *n.* [OE. *hæth*] **1.** a tract of open wasteland, esp. in the British Isles, covered with heather, low shrubs, etc. **2.** any of various shrubs growing on heaths, as heather

hea·then (hē′thən) *n., pl.* **-thens, -then** [OE. *hæthen*] **1.** anyone not a Jew, Christian, or Muslim **2.** a person regarded as uncivilized, irreligious, etc. —*adj.* **1.** of heathens; pagan **2.** irreligious —**hea′then·ish** *adj.* —**hea′then·ism** *n.*

heath·er (heth′ər) *n.* [ME. *haddyr*] a low-growing shrub common in the British Isles, with small, purplish flowers

heat lightning lightning without thunder, seen near the horizon, esp. on summer evenings

heat′stroke′ *n.* a condition resulting from exposure to intense heat, characterized by high fever and collapse

heat wave **1.** unusually hot weather **2.** a period of such weather

heave (hēv) *vt.* **heaved** or (esp. *Naut.*) **hove, heav′ing** [< OE. *hebban*] **1.** to lift, esp. with effort **2.** to lift in this way and throw **3.** to utter (a sigh, etc.) with great effort **4.** *Naut.* to raise, haul, etc. by pulling with a rope or cable —*vi.* **1.** to swell up **2.** to rise and fall rhythmically **3.** *a)* to vomit *b)* to pant; gasp **4.** *Naut.* to tug or haul (on or at a cable, rope, etc.) —*n.* the act or effort of heaving —**heave ho!** pull hard! —**heave to** *Naut.* to stop

heav·en (hev′'n) *n.* [OE. *heofon*] **1.** [*usually pl.*] the space surrounding the earth; firmament **2.** *Theol.* [H-] *a)* the dwelling place of God and his angels, where the blessed go after death *b)* God **3.** any place or state of great happiness

heav′en·ly *adj.* **1.** of or in the heavens *[the sun is a heavenly body]* **2.** causing or marked by great happiness, beauty, etc. **3.** [Colloq.] very pleasing, attractive, etc. **4.** *Theol.* of or in heaven; divine

heav′en·ward *adv., adj.* toward heaven: also **heav′en·wards** *adv.*

heav·y (hev′ē) *adj.* **-i·er, -i·est** [OE. *hefig*] **1.** hard to lift because of its weight **2.** of concentrated weight for the

size **3.** above the usual or defined weight **4.** larger, greater, or more intense than usual *[a heavy blow, a heavy vote, heavy applause]* **5.** to an unusual extent *[a heavy drinker]* **6.** serious; grave *[a heavy responsibility]* **7.** hard to endure *[heavy demands]* **8.** hard to do *[heavy work]* **9.** sorrowful *[a heavy heart]* **10.** burdened with sleep, etc. *[heavy eyelids]* **11.** hard to digest *[a heavy meal]* **12.** clinging; penetrating *[a heavy odor]* **13.** cloudy; gloomy *[a heavy sky]* **14.** doughy *[a heavy cake]* **15.** using massive machinery to produce basic materials, as steel —*adv.* heavily —*n., pl.* **-ies** *Theater* a villain —**hang heavy** to pass tediously —**heav′i·ly** *adv.* —**heav′i·ness** *n.*

heav′y-du′ty *adj.* made to withstand great strain, bad weather, etc.

heav′y-hand′ed *adj.* **1.** clumsy; tactless **2.** oppressive; tyrannical —**heav′y-hand′ed·ness** *n.*

heav′y-heart′ed *adj.* sad; depressed

heavy hydrogen *same as* DEUTERIUM

heav′y-set′ *adj.* stout or stocky in build

heav′y·weight′ *n.* **1.** a person or animal weighing much more than average **2.** a boxer or wrestler who weighs over 175 pounds

Heb. 1. Hebrew **2.** Hebrews

He·bra·ic (hi brā′ik) *adj.* of or characteristic of the Hebrews, their language, culture, etc.; Hebrew

He·bra·ism (hē′bri iz'm) *n.* **1.** a Hebrew idiom **2.** Hebrew character, thought, etc.

He·brew (hē′brōō) *n.* **1.** *a)* a member of an ancient Semitic people; Israelite *b)* a Jew **2.** *a)* the ancient Semitic language of the Israelites *b)* its modern form, the language of Israel —*adj.* of Hebrew or the Hebrews

He′brews (-brōōz) *Bible* the Epistle to the Hebrews, a book of the New Testament

Heb·ri·des (heb′rə dēz′) Scottish island group off W Scotland

Hec·a·te (hek′ə tē) *Gr. Myth.* a goddess of the moon, earth, and underworld, later regarded as the goddess of sorcery

heck (hek) *interj., n.* [Colloq.] *a euphemism for* HELL

heck·le (hek′'l) *vt.* **-led, -ling** [< ME. *hechele*] to annoy or harass (a speaker, etc.) by interrupting with questions or taunts —**heck′ler** *n.*

hec·tare (hek′ter) *n.* [Fr.] a metric measure of area, equal to 10,000 square meters or 2.471 acres

hec·tic (hek′tik) *adj.* [< Gr. *hektikos*, habitual] **1.** feverish; flushed **2.** confused, rushed, excited, etc. —**hec′ti·cal·ly** *adv.*

hec·to·graph (hek′tə graf′) *n.* [< Gr. *hekaton*, hundred + -GRAPH] a duplicating device by which copies are taken from a sheet of gelatin —*vt.* to duplicate by means of a hectograph

Hec·tor (hek′tər) *Gr. Myth.* a Trojan hero killed by Achilles: he was Priam's son

hec·tor (hek′tər) *vt., vi.* [< prec.] to bully

he'd (hēd) **1.** he had **2.** he would

hedge (hej) *n.* [OE. *hecg*] **1.** a dense row of bushes, shrubs, etc. forming a boundary **2.** any fence or barrier **3.** a hedging —*vt.* **hedged, hedg′ing 1.** to put a hedge around **2.** to hinder or guard as with a barrier **3.** to try to avoid loss in (a bet, risk, etc.) as by making counterbalancing bets, etc. —*vi.* to refuse to commit oneself; avoid direct answers

hedge′hog′ *n.* **1.** a small insect-eating mammal of the Old World, with sharp spines on the back **2.** the American porcupine

hedge′hop′ *vi.* **-hopped′, -hop′ping** [Colloq.] to fly an airplane very close to the ground

hedge′row′ *n.* a row of shrubs, etc. forming a hedge

he·do·nism (hēd′'n iz'm) *n.* [< Gr. *hēdonē*, pleasure] the doctrine that pleasure is the principal good —**he′do·nist** *n.* —**he′do·nis′tic** *adj.*

-hedron [Gr.] *a combining form meaning* a figure or crystal with (a specified number of) surfaces

heed (hēd) *vt., vi.* [OE. *hedan*] to pay close attention (to) —*n.* close attention; careful notice —**heed′ful** *adj.* —**heed′less** *adj.* —**heed′less·ly** *adv.* —**heed′less·ness** *n.*

hee·haw (hē′hô′) *n., vi.* [echoic] *same as* BRAY

heel′ (hēl) *n.* [OE. *hela*] **1.** the back part of the foot, under the ankle **2.** that part of a stocking, etc. that covers the heel **3.** anything like a heel in location, shape, or

HEDGEHOG
(5–10 in. long)

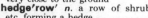

function 4. [Colloq.] a despicable person —*vt.* 1. to furnish with a heel 2. to follow closely 3. [Colloq.] to provide (a person) with money —*vi.* to follow along at the heels of someone —**down at the heel(s)** shabby; seedy — **kick up one's heels** to have fun —**on** (or **upon**) **the heels** of close behind —**take to one's heels** to run away

heel² (hēl) *vi.* [OE. *hieldan*] to lean to one side; list: said esp. of a ship —*vt.* to make (a ship) list

heft (heft) *n.* [< base of HEAVE] [Colloq.] 1. weight; heaviness 2. importance; influence —*vt.* [Colloq.] 1. to lift or heave 2. to estimate the weight of by lifting —*vi.* [Colloq.] to weigh

heft·y (hef'tē) *adj.* **-i·er, -i·est** [Colloq.] 1. heavy 2. large and powerful —**heft'i·ness** *n.*

He·gel (hā'gəl), **Ge·org** (gā ôrkh') 1770–1831; German philosopher

he·gem·o·ny (hi jem'ə nē) *n., pl.* **-nies** [< Gr. *hēgemōn*, leader] leadership or dominance, esp. that of one nation over others

he·gi·ra (hi jī'rə) *n.* [< Ar. *hijrah*, flight] 1. [often H-] the flight of Mohammed from Mecca in 622 A.D. 2. any journey for safety or escape

Hei·del·berg (hīd'l burg') city in SW West Germany: pop. 122,000: site of a university

heif·er (hef'ər) *n.* [OE. *heahfore*] a young cow that has not borne a calf

height (hīt) *n.* [< OE. *heah*, high] 1. the topmost point 2. the highest limit; extreme 3. the distance from bottom to top 4. elevation above a given level; altitude 5. a relatively great distance above a given level 6. [often *pl.*] an eminence; hill

height'en (-'n) *vt., vi.* 1. to bring or come to a higher position 2. to make or become larger, greater, etc.

Hei·ne (hī'nə), **Hein·rich** (hīn'rikh) 1797–1856; German poet & essayist

hei·nous (hā'nəs) *adj.* [< OFr. *haine*, hatred] outrageously evil; vile —**hei'nous·ly** *adv.*

heir (er) *n.* [< L. *heres*] one who inherits or is entitled to inherit another's property, title, etc.

heir apparent the heir whose right to inherit cannot be denied if he outlives the ancestor

heir'ess (-is) *n.* a woman or girl who is an heir, esp. to great wealth

heir'loom' (-lōōm') *n.* [HEIR + LOOM¹] any possession handed down from generation to generation

heir presumptive an heir whose right to inherit will be lost if someone more closely related is born before the ancestor dies

heist (hīst) *n.* [< HOIST] [Slang] a robbery —*vt.* [Slang] to rob or steal

held (held) *pt. & pp.* of HOLD¹

Hel·e·na (hel'i nə) capital of Mont.: pop. 23,000

Helen of Troy *Gr. Legend* the beautiful wife of the king of Sparta: the Trojan War was started because Paris abducted her and took her to Troy

hel·i·cal (hel'i kəl) *adj.* of, or having the form of, a helix; spiral —**hel'i·cal·ly** *adv.*

Hel·i·con (hel'ə kän', -kən) mountain group in SC Greece: in Greek mythology, the home of the Muses

hel·i·cop·ter (hel'ə käp'tər, hē'lə-) *n.* [< Gr. *helix*, a spiral + *pteron*, wing] a kind of aircraft lifted, moved, or kept hovering by revolving blades mounted horizontally

he·li·o·cen·tric (hē'lē ō sen'trik) *adj.* [< Gr. *hēlios*, the sun] having or regarding the sun as the center

He·li·os (hē'lē äs') *Gr. Myth.* the sun god

he·li·o·trope (hē'lē ə trōp') *n.* [< Gr. *hēlios*, the sun + *trepein*, to turn] 1. a plant with fragrant clusters of small, white or reddish-purple flowers 2. reddish purple —*adj.* reddish-purple

hel·i·port (hel'ə pôrt') *n.* [HELI(COPTER) + (AIR)PORT] a flat place where helicopters land and take off

he·li·um (hē'lē əm) *n.* [< Gr. *hēlios*, the sun] a chemical element, a very light, inert gas: it is used for inflating balloons, etc.: symbol, He; at. wt., 4.0026; at. no., 2

he·lix (hē'liks) *n., pl.* **-lix·es, -li·ces'** (hel'ə sēz') [Gr., a spiral] 1. any spiral, as the thread of a screw, bolt, etc. 2. the folded rim of cartilage around the outer ear

hell (hel) *n.* [< OE. *helan*, to hide] 1. [often H-] *Christianity* the place to which sinners and unbelievers go after death for punishment 2. any place or state of pain, cruelty, etc. —**catch** (or **get**) **hell** [Slang] to receive a severe scolding, punishment, etc.

he'll (hēl) 1. he will 2. he shall

hell'bend'er *n.* a large, edible salamander

hell'bent' *adj.* [Slang] 1. recklessly determined 2. moving fast

hell'cat' *n.* an evil, spiteful woman

hel·le·bore (hel'ə bôr') *n.* [< Gr. *helleboros*] any of various plants related to the lily, whose dried rhizomes and roots were formerly used in medicine

Hel·lene (hel'ēn) *n.* [< Gr.] a Greek

Hel·len·ic (hə len'ik) *adj.* 1. Greek 2. of the language, culture, etc. of the ancient Greeks

Hel·len·ism (hel'ən iz'm) *n.* 1. a Greek phrase, custom, etc. 2. the culture and ethics of ancient Greece 3. the adoption of the Greek language, customs, etc. —**Hel'len·ist** *n.*

Hel'len·is'tic *adj.* 1. of or characteristic of Hellenism 2. of Greek history, culture, etc. after the death of Alexander the Great (323 B.C.)

Hel·les·pont (hel'əs pänt') *ancient name of the* DARDANELLES

hel·lion (hel'yən) *n.* [Colloq.] a person fond of deviltry; troublemaker

hell·ish (hel'ish) *adj.* 1. devilish; fiendish 2. [Colloq.] very unpleasant; detestable —**hell'ish·ly** *adv.*

hel·lo (he lō', hel'ō) *interj.* 1. an exclamation of greeting 2. an exclamation to attract attention —*n., pl.* **-los'** a saying of "hello" —*vt., vi.* **-loed', -lo'ing** to say "hello" (to)

helm (helm) *n.* [OE. *helma*] 1. the wheel or tiller by which a ship is steered 2. the complete steering gear 3. control or leadership, as of an organization —*vt.* to guide

hel·met (hel'mət) *n.* [< OFr. *helme*] a protective, rigid head covering, variously designed for use in combat, certain sports, etc.

helms·man (helmz'mən) *n., pl.* **-men** one who steers a ship

hel·ot (hel'ət) *n.* [< Gr. *Heilōtes*, serfs] a serf or slave

help (help) *vt.* [OE. *helpan*] 1. to make things easier or better for (a person); aid; assist 2. to make it easier for something to exist, happen, etc. 3. to remedy [this will *help* your cough] 4. *a)* to keep from; avoid [she can't *help* crying] *b)* to stop; prevent [faults that can't be *helped*] 5. to serve or wait on (a customer, client, etc.) —*vi.* to give assistance; be useful —*n.* 1. a helping; aid; assistance 2. remedy 3. *a)* a hired helper, as a servant, farmhand, etc. *b)* hired helpers —**help oneself to** 1. to serve oneself with (food, etc.) 2. to steal —**help out** to help in getting or doing something —**help'er** *n.*

help'ful (-fəl) *adj.* giving help; useful —**help'ful·ly** *adv.* —**help'ful·ness** *n.*

help'ing (-iŋ) *n.* 1. a giving of aid 2. a portion of food served to one person

help'less *adj.* 1. not able to help oneself; weak 2. lacking help or protection 3. incompetent —**help'less·ly** *adv.* —**help'less·ness** *n.*

help'mate' *n.* [< HELPMEET] a helpful companion; specif., a wife or husband

help'meet' *n.* [misreading of "an *help meet* (suitable) for him" (Gen. 2:18)] same as HELPMATE

Hel·sin·ki (hel'siŋ kē) capital of Finland: pop. 527,000

hel·ter-skel·ter (hel'tər skel'tər) *adv.* [arbitrary formation] in haste and confusion —*adj.* confused and disorderly

helve (helv) *n.* [OE. *helfe*] the handle of a tool, esp. of an ax or hatchet —*vt.* **helved, helv'ing** to put a helve on

Hel·ve·tian (hel vē'shən) *adj., n.* Swiss

hem¹ (hem) *n.* [OE.] the border on a garment or piece of cloth, made by folding and sewing down the edge —*vt.* **hemmed, hem'ming** to fold back the edge of and sew down —**hem in** (or **around** or **about**) 1. to surround 2. to confine —**hem'mer** *n.*

hem² (hem) *interj., n.* the sound made in clearing the throat —*vi.* **hemmed, hem'ming** 1. to make this sound, as to get attention 2. to grope about in speech for the right words: usually in **hem and haw**

he-man (hē'man') *n.* [Colloq.] a strong, virile man

hem·a·tite (hem'ə tīt', hē'mə-) *n.* [< Gr. *haima*, blood] a brownish-red to black mineral, Fe₂O₃, an important iron ore

he·ma·tol·o·gy (hē'mə täl'ə jē) *n.* [< Gr. *haima*, blood + -LOGY] the study of the blood and its diseases —**he'ma·tol'o·gist** *n.*

hemi- [Gr. *hēmi-*] *a prefix meaning* half [hemisphere]

Hem·ing·way (hem'iŋ wā'), **Ernest** 1899–1961; U.S. novelist & short-story writer

he·mip·ter·an (hi mip'tər ən) *n.* [< HEMI- + Gr. *pteron*, wing] any of a group of insects, including bedbugs, lice, etc., with piercing and sucking mouthparts —**he·mip'ter·ous** *adj.*

hem·i·sphere (hem'ə sfir') *n.* 1. half of a sphere or globe 2. any of the halves (northern, southern, eastern, or western) of the earth —**hem'i·spher'i·cal** (-sfer'i kəl), **hem'i·spher'ic** *adj.*

hem·line (hem'līn') *n.* the bottom edge of a dress, coat, skirt, etc.

hem·lock (hem'läk) *n.* [OE. *hemlic*] **1.** a poisonous European plant, with small, white flowers: also **poison hemlock 2.** a poison made from this plant **3.** an evergreen tree related to the pine **4.** the wood of this tree

hemo- [< Gr. *haima*] *a combining form meaning* blood

he·mo·glo·bin (hē'mə glō'bin) *n.* [< prec. + GLOBULE] the red coloring matter of the red blood corpuscles: it carries oxygen from lungs to tissues

he·mo·phil·i·a (hē'mə fil'ē ə) *n.* [see HEMO- & -PHILE] a hereditary condition in which the blood fails to clot normally, causing prolonged bleeding from even minor injuries —**he'mo·phil'i·ac** (-ak) *n.*

hem·or·rhage (hem'ər ij, hem'rij) *n.* [< Gr. *haima*, blood + *rhēgnynai*, to break] the escape of blood from a blood vessel; heavy bleeding —*vi.* **-rhaged, -rhag·ing** to have a hemorrhage —**hem'or·rhag'ic** (-ə raj'ik) *adj.*

hem·or·rhoid (hem'ə roid') *n.* [< Gr. *haima*, blood + *rhein*, to flow] a painful swelling of a vein in the region of the anus, often with bleeding: *usually used in pl.* —**hem'or·rhoid'al** *adj.*

he·mo·stat (hē'mə stat', hem'ə-) *n.* [HEMO- + -STAT] anything used to stop bleeding; specif., a clamplike instrument used in surgery

hemp (hemp) *n.* [OE. *hænep*] **1.** a tall Asiatic plant having tough fiber in its stem **2.** this fiber, used to make rope, sailcloth, etc. **3.** a substance, as marijuana, hashish, etc., made from the leaves and flowers of this plant — **hemp'en** *adj.*

hem·stitch (hem'stich') *n.* **1.** an ornamental stitch, used esp. at a hem, made by pulling out several parallel threads and tying the cross threads into small bunches **2.** needlework done with this stitch —*vt.* to put hemstitches on —**hem'stitch'er** *n.* —**hem'stitch'ing** *n.*

hen (hen) *n.* [OE. *henn*] **1.** the female of the chicken (the domestic fowl) **2.** the female of various other birds

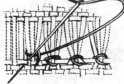

HEMSTITCH

hen·bane (hen'bān') *n.* a coarse, hairy, foul-smelling, poisonous plant, related to nightshade and formerly used in medicine

hence (hens) *adv.* [< OE. *heonan*, from here] **1.** from this place; away *[go hence]* **2.** from this time *[a year hence]* **3.** as a result; therefore **4.** [Archaic] from this origin or source —*interj.* [Archaic] go away!

hence'forth' *adv.* from this time on: also **hence'for'ward**

hench·man (hench'mən) *n., pl.* **-men** [OE. *hengest*, stallion + *-man*] a trusted helper or follower

hen·e·quen (hen'ə kin) *n.* [< Sp. < native name] **1.** a tropical American agave, cultivated for its fiber **2.** this fiber, used for rope, twine, etc.

hen'house' *n.* a shelter for poultry

hen·na (hen'ə) *n.* [Ar. *hinnā'*] **1.** an old-world plant with white or red flowers **2.** a dye extracted from its leaves, used to tint the hair auburn **3.** reddish brown —*adj.* reddish-brown —*vt.* **-naed, -na·ing** to tint with henna

hen·peck (hen'pek') *vt.* to nag and domineer over (one's husband) —**hen'pecked'** *adj.*

Hen·ry (hen'rē) **1.** Henry VIII 1491–1547; king of England (1509–1547) **2.** O., (pseud. of *William Sydney Porter*) 1862–1910; U.S. short-story writer **3.** Patrick, 1786–99; Am. patriot & orator

hen·ry (hen'rē) *n., pl.* **-rys, -ries** [< J. *Henry* (1797–1878), U.S. physicist] the unit of inductance in which variation of the current at the rate of one ampere per second induces an electromotive force of one volt

he·pat·ic (hi pat'ik) *adj.* [< Gr. *hēpar*, liver] **1.** of or affecting the liver **2.** like the liver in color or shape

he·pat·i·ca (-i kə) *n.* [see prec.: its leaves are liver-shaped] a small plant with white, pink, blue, or purple flowers

hep·a·ti·tis (hep'ə tīt'is) *n.* [< Gr. *hēpar*, liver + -ITIS] inflammation of the liver

He·phaes·tus (hi fes'təs) *Gr. Myth.* the god of fire and forge: identified with the Roman Vulcan

Hep·ple·white (hep''l hwīt') *adj.* [after G. *Hepplewhite* (?–1786), Eng. cabinetmaker] designating or of a style of furniture with graceful curves

hepta- [< Gr. *hepta*, seven] *a combining form meaning* seven: also **hept-**

hep·ta·gon (hep'tə gän') *n.* [< Gr.: see HEPTA- & -GON] a plane figure with seven angles and seven sides —**hep·tag'o·nal** (-tag'ə n'l) *adj.*

her (hur) *pron.* [OE. *hire*] *objective case of* SHE —*poss. pronominal adj.* of, belonging to, or done by her

He·ra (hir'ə) *Gr. Myth.* the wife of Zeus and queen of the gods: identified with the Roman Juno

Her·a·kles, Her·a·cles (her'ə klēz') *same as* HERCULES

her·ald (her'əld) *n.* [< OFr. *herault*] **1.** formerly, an official who made proclamations, carried state messages, etc. **2.** in England, an official in charge of genealogies, heraldic arms, etc. **3.** a person who announces significant news **4.** a forerunner; harbinger —*vt.* to announce, foretell, etc.

he·ral·dic (hə ral'dik) *adj.* of heraldry or heralds

her'ald·ry *n., pl.* **-ries 1.** the science dealing with coats of arms, genealogies, etc. **2.** heraldic devices **3.** ceremony or pomp

herb (urb, hurb) *n.* [< L. *herba*] **1.** any seed plant whose stem withers away annually **2.** any plant used as a medicine, seasoning, etc., as mint or sage —**her·ba·ceous** (hər bā'shəs, ər-) *adj.*

herb·age (ur'bij, hur'-) *n.* **1.** herbs collectively, esp. those used as pasturage; grass **2.** the green foliage and juicy stems of herbs

herb'al (hur'b'l, ur'-) *adj.* of herbs

herb'al·ist *n.* one who collects or deals in herbs

her·bar·i·um (hər ber'ē əm, ər-) *n., pl.* **-i·ums, -i·a** (-ə) [< L. *herba*, herb] **1.** a collection of dried plants used for botanical study **2.** a place for keeping such a collection

Her·bert (hur'bərt), Victor 1859–1924; U.S. composer & conductor, born in Ireland

her·bi·cide (hur'bə sīd', ur'-) *n.* any chemical substance used to destroy plants, esp. weeds —**her'bi·ci'dal** *adj.*

her'bi·vore' (-vôr') *n.* [Fr.] a herbivorous animal: opposed to CARNIVORE

her·biv·o·rous (hər biv'ər əs) *adj.* [< L. *herba*, herb + *vorare*, devour] feeding chiefly on plants: opposed to CARNIVOROUS

her·cu·le·an (hur'kyə lē'ən, hər kyōō'lē ən) *adj.* [*sometimes* H-] **1.** having the great size and strength of Hercules **2.** calling for great strength, size, or courage

Her·cu·les (hur'kyə lēz') *Gr. & Rom. Myth.* a hero famous for feats of strength —*n.* [h-] any very strong man

herd' (hurd) *n.* [OE. *heord*] **1.** a number of cattle or other large animals feeding or living together **2.** a crowd **3.** the common people; masses: contemptuous term —*vt., vi.* to form into or move as a herd

herd² (hurd) *n.* [OE. *hierde*] a herdsman: now chiefly in combination *[cowherd]* —*vt.* to tend or drive as a herdsman —**herd'er** *n.*

herds·man (hurdz'mən) *n., pl.* **-men** one who keeps or tends a herd

here (hir) *adv.* [OE. *her*] **1.** at or in this place: often used as an intensive *[John here is a good player]* **2.** to or into this place *[come here]* **3.** at this point; now **4.** in earthly life —*n.* this place —**neither here nor there** irrelevant

here'a·bout' *adv.* in this general vicinity: also **here'a·bouts'**

here·af'ter *adv.* **1.** from now on; in the future **2.** following this —*n.* **1.** the future **2.** the state after death

here'by' *adv.* by this means

he·red·i·ta·ble (hə red'i tə b'l) *adj. same as* HERITABLE

he·red·i·tar·y (hə red'ə ter'ē) *adj.* **1.** *a)* of, or passed down by, inheritance from an ancestor *b)* having title, etc. by inheritance **2.** of or passed down by heredity

he·red·i·ty (hə red'ə tē) *n., pl.* **-ties** [< L. *heres*, heir] **1.** the transmission of characteristics from parents to offspring by means of genes **2.** the characteristics transmitted in this way

Her·e·ford (hur'fərd, her'ə-) *n.* any of a breed of beef cattle having a white face and a red body with white markings

here·in (hir in') *adv.* **1.** in here **2.** in this writing **3.** in this matter, detail, etc.

here'in·af'ter *adv.* in the following part (of this document, speech, etc.)

here·of' *adv.* of or concerning this

here's to! here's a toast to! I wish joy, etc. to!

her·e·sy (her'ə sē) *n., pl.* **-sies** [< Gr. *hairesis*, selection, sect] **1.** a religious belief opposed to the orthodox doctrines of a church **2.** any opinion opposed to established views

her·e·tic (her′ə tik) *n.* one who professes a heresy; esp., a church member who holds beliefs opposed to church dogma —**he·ret·i·cal** (hə ret′i k′l) *adj.* —**he·ret′i·cal·ly** *adv.*

here·to′ *adv.* to this (document, etc.)

here′to·fore′ *adv.* up to now; before this

here′up·on′ *adv.* **1.** immediately following this **2.** concerning this

here·with′ *adv.* **1.** along with this **2.** by this method or means

her·it·a·ble (her′it ə b′l) *adj.* **1.** that can be inherited **2.** that can inherit —**her′it·a·bil′i·ty** *n.*

her·it·age (her′ət ij) *n.* **1.** property that is or can be inherited **2.** a tradition, etc. handed down from one's ancestors or the past

her·maph·ro·dite (hər maf′rə dīt′) *n.* [< *Hermaphroditos,* son of Hermes and Aphrodite, united in a single body with a nymph] a person, animal, or plant with the sexual organs of both the male and the female —**her·maph′ro·dit′ic** (-dit′ik) *adj.*

Her·mes (hur′mēz) *Gr. Myth.* a god who served as messenger of the other gods: identified with the Roman Mercury

her·met·ic (hər met′ik) *adj.* [< prec. (reputed founder of alchemy)] airtight: also **her·met′i·cal** —**her·met′i·cal·ly** *adv.*

her·mit (hur′mit) *n.* [< Gr. *erēmos,* solitary] one who lives by himself in a secluded spot; recluse

her′mit·age (-ij) *n.* a secluded retreat, as the place where a hermit lives

hermit crab a soft-bellied crab that lives in the empty shells of certain mollusks, as snails

her·ni·a (hur′nē ə) *n., pl.* **-as, -ae′** (-ē′) [L.] the protrusion of an organ, esp. a part of the intestine, through a tear in the wall of the surrounding structure; rupture —**her′ni·al** *adj.*

her′ni·ate′ (-āt′) *vi.* **-at′ed, -at′ing** to protrude so as to form a hernia —**her′ni·a′tion** *n.*

he·ro (hir′ō, hē′rō) *n., pl.* **-roes** [< Gr. *hērōs*] **1.** a man of great courage, nobility, etc., or one admired for his exploits **2.** the central male character in a novel, play, etc.

Her·od An·ti·pas (her′əd an′ti pas′) ?-40? A.D.; ruler of Galilee (4? B.C.–39 A.D.)

He·rod·o·tus (hə räd′ə təs) 485?-425? B.C.; Gr. historian: called the *Father of History*

he·ro·ic (hi rō′ik) *adj.* **1.** of or like a hero **2.** of or about heroes and their deeds **3.** exalted; eloquent **4.** daring and risky **5.** *Art* larger than life-size Also **he·ro′i·cal** —*n.* [*pl.*] extravagant talk or action —**he·ro′i·cal·ly** *adv.*

heroic couplet a pair of rhymed lines in iambic pentameter

her·o·in (her′ə win) *n.* [G., orig. a trademark] a habit-forming narcotic derived from morphine

her·o·ine (her′ə win) *n.* a girl or woman hero in life or literature

her′o·ism (-wiz′m) *n.* the qualities and actions of a hero or heroine; great bravery, nobility, etc.

her·on (her′ən) *n.* [< OFr. *hairon*] a wading bird with a long neck, long legs, and a long bill

hero sandwich a large roll sliced lengthwise and filled with cold meats, cheeses, etc.

her·pes (hur′pēz) *n.* [< Gr. *herpein,* to creep] a virus disease causing small blisters on the skin

her·pe·tol·o·gy (hur′pə täl′ə jē) *n.* [< Gr. *herpeton,* reptile + -LOGY] the branch of zoology dealing with reptiles and amphibians —**her′pe·tol′o·gist** *n.*

‡Herr (her) *n., pl.* **Her′ren** (-ən) [G.] a man; gentleman: a title, equivalent to *Mr.* or *Sir*

her·ring (her′iŋ) *n.* [OE. *hæring*] a small food fish of the N Atlantic

her′ring·bone′ *n.* **1.** the spine of a herring with ribs extending in rows of parallel, slanting lines **2.** anything having such a pattern

hers (hurz) *pron.* that or those belonging to her [*hers* are better]

her·self (hər self′) *pron.* **1.** *the intensive form of* SHE [she went *herself*] **2.** *the reflexive form of* SHE [she hurt *herself*] **3.** her true self [she's not *herself* today]

hertz (hurts) *n., pl.* **hertz** [< H. R. *Hertz* (1857-94), G. physicist] the international unit of frequency, equal to one cycle per second

he's (hēz) **1.** he is **2.** he has

hes·i·tant (hez′ə tənt) *adj.* hesitating or undecided; doubtful —**hes′i·tan·cy,** *pl.* **-cies, hes′i·tance** *n.* —**hes′i·tant·ly** *adv.*

hes·i·tate (hez′ə tāt′) *vi.* **-tat′ed, -tat′ing** [< L. *haerere,* to stick] **1.** to stop in indecision; waver **2.** to pause **3.** to

be reluctant [I *hesitate* to ask] **4.** to pause continually in speaking —**hes′i·ta′tion** *n.*

Hes·per·i·des (hes per′ə dēz′) *n.pl. Gr. Myth.* **1.** the nymphs who guarded the golden apples of Hera **2.** the garden in which the apples grew

Hesse (hes, hes′i) former region in WC Germany, now a state of West Germany

Hes·sian (hesh′ən) *adj.* of Hesse —*n.* **1.** a native of Hesse **2.** any of the Hessian mercenaries who fought for the British in the Revolutionary War

Hessian fly a small, two-winged fly whose larvae destroy wheat crops

hetero- [Gr. < *heteros,* the other] *a combining form meaning* other, another, different

het·er·o·dox (het′ar ə däks′) *adj.* [< Gr. *hetero-,* other + *doxa,* opinion] opposed to the usual beliefs, esp. in religion; unorthodox

het′er·o·dox′y (-däk′sē) *n., pl.* **-ies 1.** the quality of being heterodox **2.** a heterodox belief

het·er·o·ge·ne·ous (het′ar ə jē′nē əs) *adj.* [< Gr. *hetero-,* other + *genos,* a kind] **1.** differing in structure, quality, etc.; dissimilar **2.** composed of unlike parts —**het′er·o·ge·ne′i·ty** (-jə nē′ə tē) *n.*

het·er·o·sex·u·al (het′ar ə sek′shoo wəl) *adj.* **1.** of or having sexual desire for those of the opposite sex **2.** *Biol.* of different sexes —*n.* a heterosexual individual

het up (het) [*het,* dial. *pt. & pp. of heat*] [Slang] excited or angry

heu·ris·tic (hyoo ris′tik) *adj.* [< Gr. *heuriskein,* invent] helping to learn, as by a method of self-teaching

hew (hyoo) *vt.* **hewed, hewed** or **hewn, hew′ing** [OE. *heawan*] **1.** to chop or cut with an ax, knife, etc. **2.** to make or shape thus —*vi.* to conform (*to* a line, rule, etc.) —**hew′er** *n.*

HEW (Department of) Health, Education, and Welfare

hex (heks) *n.* [< G. *hexe,* witch] something supposed to bring bad luck —*vt.* to cause to have bad luck

hexa- [< Gr. *hex,* six] *a combining form meaning* six

hex·a·gon (hek′sə gän′) *n.* [< Gr. *hex,* six + *gōnia,* an angle] a plane figure with six angles and six sides —**hex·ag′o·nal** (-sag′ə n′l) *adj.*

hex·am·e·ter (hek sam′ə tər) *n.* [see HEXA- & -METER¹] **1.** a line of verse containing six metrical feet **2.** verse consisting of hexameters

hex·a·pod (hek′sə päd′) *n.* [see HEXA- & -POD] *same as* INSECT (sense 1) —*adj.* having six legs

hey (hā) *interj.* an exclamation used to attract attention, express surprise, etc.

hey·day (hā′dā′) *n.* [prob. < ME. *hey,* high + *dei,* day] the time of greatest vigor, success, etc.; prime

Hez·e·ki·ah (hez′ə kī′ə) *Bible* a king of Judah: II Kings 18–20

Hf *Chem.* hafnium

HF, hf high frequency

hf. half

Hg [L. *hydrargyrum*] *Chem.* mercury

hi (hī) *interj.* an exclamation of greeting

HI Hawaii

hi·a·tus (hī āt′əs) *n., pl.* **-tus·es, -tus** [L. < *hiare,* to gape] a break or gap, as where a part is missing; lacuna

hi·ba·chi (hi bä′chē) *n., pl.* **-chis** [Jpn. < *hi,* fire + *bachi,* bowl] a charcoal-burning brazier and grill

hi·ber·nate (hī′bər nāt′) *vi.* **-nat′ed, -nat′ing** [< L. *hibernus,* wintry] to spend the winter in a dormant state —**hi′ber·na′tion** *n.*

Hi·ber·ni·a (hī bur′nē ə) [L.] *poetic name for* IRELAND —**Hi·ber′ni·an** *adj., n.*

hi·bis·cus (hī bis′kəs, hi-) *n.* [< L.] a plant or shrub related to the mallow, with large, colorful flowers

hic·cup (hik′əp) *n.* [echoic] an involuntary contraction of the diaphragm that closes the glottis at the moment of breathing in so that a sharp sound is produced —*vi.* **-cuped** or **-cupped, -cup·ing** or **-cup·ping** to make a hiccup Also **hic·cough** (hik′əp)

hick (hik) *n.* [< *Richard*] [Colloq.] an awkward, unsophisticated person regarded as typical of rural areas: somewhat contemptuous term —*adj.* [Colloq.] of or like a hick

hick·o·ry (hik′ər ē) *n., pl.* **-ries** [< AmInd. *pawcohiccora*] **1.** a N. American tree related to the walnut: its nut (**hickory nut**) is smooth-shelled and edible **2.** its hard, tough wood

hi·dal·go (hi dal′gō) *n., pl.* **-gos** [Sp.] a Spanish nobleman of secondary rank

hide¹ (hīd) *vt.* **hid** (hid), **hid·den** (hid′'n) or **hid, hid′ing** [OE. *hydan*] **1.** to put or keep out of sight; conceal **2.** to keep secret **3.** to keep from sight by covering, obscuring, etc. —*vi.* **1.** to be concealed **2.** to conceal oneself

hide² (hīd) *n.* [OE. *hid*] an animal skin or pelt, either raw or tanned

hide′a·way′ (-ə wā′) *n.* [Colloq.] a place where one can hide, be secluded, etc.

hide′bound′ *adj.* obstinately conservative and narrow-minded

hid·e·ous (hid′ē əs) *adj.* [< OFr. *hide*, fright] horrible; very ugly or revolting —**hid′e·ous·ly** *adv.* —**hid′e·ous·ness** *n.*

hide′-out′ *n.* [Colloq.] a hiding place, as for gangsters

hie (hī) *vi., vt.* **hied, hie′ing** or **hy′ing** [OE. *higian*] to hurry or hasten

hi·er·ar·chy (hī′ə rär′kē) *n., pl.* **-chies** [< Gr. *hieros*, sacred + *archos*, ruler] **1.** church government by clergy in graded ranks **2.** the highest officials in such a system **3.** a group of persons or things arranged in order of rank, grade, etc. —**hi′er·ar′chi·cal, hi′er·ar′chic** *adj.*

hi·er·at·ic (hī′ə rat′ik) *adj.* [< Gr. *hieros*, sacred] of or used by priests; priestly

hi·er·o·glyph·ic (hī′ər ə glif′ik, hī′rə-) *n.* [< Gr. *hieros*, sacred + *glyphein*, carve] **1.** a picture or symbol representing a word, sound, etc., in a system used by the ancient Egyptians and others **2.** [*usually pl.*] writing using hieroglyphics **3.** a sign, symbol, etc. hard to understand —*adj.* of or like hieroglyphics

hi-fi (hī′fī′) *n.* **1.** *same as* HIGH FIDELITY **2.** a radio, phonograph, etc. having high fidelity —*adj.* of or having high fidelity of sound reproduction

hig·gle·dy-pig·gle·dy (hig′'l dē pig′'l dē) *adv.* [prob. < PIG] in disorder —*adj.* jumbled

high (hī) *adj.* [OE. *heah*] **1.** lofty; tall **2.** extending upward a (specified) distance **3.** reaching to, situated at, or done from a height **4.** above others in rank, position, etc.; superior **5.** grave; very serious [*high* treason] **6.** greater in size, amount, cost, etc. than usual [*high* prices] **7.** luxurious [*high* living] **8.** raised or acute in pitch; shrill **9.** slightly tainted, as meat **10.** elated [*high* spirits] **11.** [Slang] *a)* drunk *b)* under the influence of a drug —*adv.* in or to a high level, degree, rank, etc. —*n.* **1.** a high level, place, etc. **2.** an area of high barometric pressure **3.** that gear of a motor vehicle, etc. producing the greatest speed **4.** [Slang] a euphoric state induced as by drugs —**high and dry** stranded —**high and low** everywhere —**high on** [Colloq.] enthusiastic about —**on high 1.** high above **2.** in heaven

high′ball′ *n.* whiskey or brandy mixed with water, soda water, etc. and served with ice in a glass

high′born′ *adj.* of noble birth

high′boy′ *n.* a high chest of drawers mounted on legs

high′brow′ *n.* [Colloq.] one having or affecting highly cultivated, intellectual tastes; intellectual —*adj.* [Colloq.] of or for highbrows

high′chair′ *n.* a baby's chair with an attached tray, mounted on long legs

High Church that party of the Anglican Church which emphasizes the importance of the priesthood and of traditional rituals and doctrines

high′er-up′ *n.* [Colloq.] a person of higher rank or position

high·fa·lu·tin(g) (hī′fə lōōt′'n) *adj.* [Colloq.] pretentious or pompous

HIGHBOY

high fidelity in radio, sound recording, etc., nearly exact reproduction of a wide range of sound waves

high′-flown′ (-flōn′) *adj.* **1.** extravagantly ambitious **2.** bombastic

high frequency any radio frequency between 3 and 30 megahertz

High German the West Germanic dialects spoken in C and S Germany

high′-grade′ *adj.* of superior quality

high′hand′ed *adj.* overbearing and arbitrary —**high′-hand′ed·ly** *adv.* —**high′hand′ed·ness** *n.*

high′-hat′ *vt.* **-hat′ted, -hat′ting** [Slang] to snub

high′land (-lənd) *n.* a region higher than adjacent land and containing many hills or mountains —**the Highlands** mountainous region occupying most of N Scotland —**High′land·er** *n.*

highland fling a lively dance of the Highlands

high life the way of life of fashionable society

high′light′ *n.* **1.** a part on which light is or is represented as brightest **2.** the most important or interesting part,

scene, etc. —*vt.* **1.** to give highlights to **2.** to give prominence to

high′ly *adv.* **1.** in a high office or rank **2.** very much **3.** favorably **4.** at a high wage, salary, etc.

High Mass *R.C.Ch.* a sung Mass, usually celebrated with the complete ritual, at which the celebrant is assisted by a deacon and subdeacon

high′-mind′ed *adj.* having high ideals, principles, etc. —**high′-mind′ed·ness** *n.*

high′ness *n.* **1.** height **2.** [H-] a title used in speaking to or of royalty

high′-pres′sure *adj.* **1.** having or withstanding high pressure **2.** using forcefully persuasive or insistent methods —*vt.* **-sured, -sur·ing** [Colloq.] to urge with such methods

high′-rise′ *n.* a tall apartment house, office building, etc. of many stories

high′road′ *n.* **1.** [Chiefly Brit.] a main road; highway **2.** an easy or direct way

high school a secondary school that includes grades 10, 11, and 12, and sometimes grade 9

high seas open ocean waters outside the territorial limits of any nation

high′-sound′ing *adj.* sounding pretentious or impressive

high′-spir′it·ed *adj.* **1.** courageous or noble **2.** lively; spirited —**high′-spir′it·ed·ly** *adv.*

high′-strung′ *adj.* nervous and tense; excitable

high′-ten′sion *adj.* having or carrying a high voltage

high′-test′ *adj.* vaporizing at a low temperature: said of gasoline

high tide 1. the highest level to which the tide rises **2.** the time when the tide is at this level **3.** any culminating point or time

high time 1. none too soon **2.** [Slang] an exciting time

high′-toned′ (-tōnd′) *adj.* **1.** dignified; lofty **2.** [Colloq.] of or imitating upper-class manners, etc.

high′way′ *n.* **1.** a public road **2.** a main road

high′way·man (-mən) *n., pl.* **-men** one who robs travelers on a highway

hi·jack (hī′jak′) *vt.* [Colloq.] **1.** to steal (goods in transit, a truck and its contents, etc.) by force **2.** to force the pilot of (an aircraft) to fly to a nonscheduled landing point —**hi′jack′er** *n.*

hike (hīk) *vi.* **hiked, hik′ing** [< dial. *heik*] to take a long, vigorous walk; tramp —*vt.* [Colloq.] **1.** to pull up; hoist **2.** to raise (prices, etc.) —*n.* **1.** a long, vigorous walk **2.** [Colloq.] a moving upward; rise —**hik′er** *n.*

hi·lar·i·ous (hi ler′ē əs, hī-) *adj.* [< Gr. *hilaros*, cheerful] **1.** noisily merry **2.** very funny —**hi·lar′i·ous·ly** *adv.* —**hi·lar′i·ty** (-ə tē) *n.*

hill (hil) *n.* [OE. *hyll*] **1.** a natural raised part of the earth's surface, smaller than a mountain **2.** a small heap or mound [an *anthill*] **3.** a mound of soil heaped around plant roots [a *hill* of beans]

hill′bil′ly *n., pl.* **-lies** [< nickname *Billy*] [Colloq.] one who lives in or comes from the mountains or backwoods, esp. of the South: somewhat contemptuous term —*adj.* [Colloq.] of hillbillies

hill′ock (-ək) *n.* a small hill; mound

hill′side′ *n.* the side of a hill

hill′top′ *n.* the top of a hill

hill′y *adj.* **-i·er, -i·est 1.** full of hills **2.** like a hill; steep —**hill′i·ness** *n.*

hilt (hilt) *n.* [OE.] the handle of a sword, dagger, tool, etc. —**(up) to the hilt** thoroughly; entirely

hi·lum (hī′ləm) *n., pl.* **-la** (-lə) [< L., little thing] *Bot.* a scar on a seed, marking the place where it was attached to the seed stalk

him (him) *pron.* [OE.] *objective case of* HE

Hi·ma·la·yas (him′ə lā′əz, hi mäl′yəz) mountain system in SC Asia, along the India-Tibet border —**Hi′ma·la′yan** *adj.*

him·self′ *pron.* **1.** *the intensive form of* HE [he went *himself*] **2.** *the reflexive form of* HE [he hurt *himself*] **3.** his true self [he is not *himself* today]

hind¹ (hīnd) *adj.* **hind′er, hind′most′** or **hind′er·most′** [prob. < HINDER²] back; rear; posterior

hind² (hīnd) *n.* [OE.] the female of the red deer

hind′brain′ *n.* the hindmost part of the brain

hin·der¹ (hin′dər) *vt.* [OE. *hindrian*] **1.** to keep back; restrain; stop **2.** to thwart

hind′er² (hīn′dər) *adj.* [OE., behind] rear; posterior

Hin·di (hin′dē) *n.* the main (and official) language of India

hind′most′ *adj.* farthest back; last

hind′quar′ter *n.* the hind half of a side of veal, beef, lamb, etc.

hin·drance (hin′drəns) *n.* **1.** the act of hindering **2.** a person or thing that hinders; obstacle

hind′sight′ *n.* ability to see, after the event, what should have been done

Hin·du (hin′dōō) *n.* **1.** any of the peoples of India that speak an Indic language **2.** a follower of Hinduism —*adj.* **1.** of the Hindus, their language, etc. **2.** of Hinduism

Hin′du·ism *n.* the religion and social system of the Hindus

Hin·du·stan (hin′dōō stan′) **1.** region in N India **2.** the Indian peninsula **3.** the republic of India

Hin·du·sta·ni (hin′dōō stan′ē, -stä′nē) *n.* a dialect of Western Hindi, used as a trade language in N India

hinge (hinj) *n.* [< ME. *hengen*, hang] **1.** a joint on which a door, lid, etc. swings **2.** a natural joint, as of the shell of a clam —*vt.* **hinged, hing′ing** to attach by a hinge —*vi.* to depend (*on*)

hint (hint) *n.* [< OE. *hentan*, seize] a slight indication; indirect allusion —*vt.*, *vi.* to give a hint (of) —**hint at** to suggest indirectly —**take a hint** to perceive and act on a hint

hin·ter·land (hin′tər land′) *n.* [G. < *hinter*, back + *land*, land] **1.** the land behind that bordering a coast or river **2.** a remote area

hip[1] (hip) *n.* [OE. *hype*] **1.** the part of the body around the joint formed by each thighbone and the pelvis **2.** the angle formed by the meeting of two sloping sides of a roof

hip[2] (hip) *n.* [OE. *heope*] the fleshy fruit of the rose

hip[3] (hip) *adj.* **hip′per, hip′pest** [< ?] [Slang] **1.** sophisticated; knowing **2.** fashionable **3.** of hippies —**get** (or **be**) **hip to** [Slang] to become (or be) informed about

hip·pie (hip′ē) *n.* [< HIP[3] + -IE] [Slang] a young person who, in his alienation from conventional society, has turned to mysticism, psychedelic drugs, communal living, etc.: also **hip′py**, *pl.* **-pies**

hip·po (hip′ō) *n.*, *pl.* **-pos** [Colloq.] *same as* HIPPOPOTAMUS

Hip·poc·ra·tes (hi päk′rə tēz′) 460?–370? B.C.; Gr. physician: called the *Father of Medicine*

Hip·po·crat·ic oath (hip′ə krat′ik) the oath, attributed to Hippocrates, generally taken by medical graduates: it sets forth their ethical code

hip·po·drome (hip′ə drōm′) *n.* [< Fr. < Gr. *hippos*, horse + *dromos*, a course] an arena for a circus, games, etc.

hip·po·pot·a·mus (hip′ə pät′ə məs) *n.*, *pl.* **-mus·es, -mi′** (-mī′) [< Gr. *hippos*, horse + *potamos*, river] a large, plant-eating mammal with a heavy, thick-skinned body: it lives in or near rivers in Africa

hip roof a roof with sloping ends and sides

hire (hīr) *n.* [OE. *hyr*] **1.** the amount paid for the services of a person or the use of a thing **2.** a hiring —*vt.* **hired, hir′ing 1.** to pay for the services of (a person) or the use of (a thing) **2.** to give the use of for payment (often with *out*) —**hire out** to work for payment

HIP ROOF

hire′ling *n.* one who will follow anyone's orders for pay; mercenary

Hi·ro·shi·ma (hir′ə shē′mə) seaport in SW Honshu, Japan: largely destroyed (Aug. 6, 1945) by a U.S. atomic bomb, the first used in warfare: pop. 504,000

hir·sute (hur′sōōt, hir′-) *adj.* [L. *hirsutus*] hairy; shaggy

his (hiz) *pron.* [OE.] that or those belonging to him [*his* are better] —*poss. pronominal adj.* of, belonging to, or done by him

His·pan·io·la (his′pən yō′lə) island in the West Indies, divided between Haiti & the Dominican Republic

hiss (his) *vi.* [echoic] **1.** to make a sound like that of a prolonged *s* **2.** to show disapproval by hissing —*vt.* to say or indicate by hissing —*n.* the act or sound of hissing

hist (st, hist) *interj.* be quiet!

his·ta·mine (his′tə mēn′, -mən) *n.* [< Gr. *histos*, tissue + AMINE] an amine, $C_5H_9N_3$, released by the tissues in allergic reactions

his·tol·o·gy (his täl′ə jē) *n.* [< Gr. *histos*, tissue + -LOGY] the branch of biology concerned with the microscopic study of the structure of tissues

his·to·ri·an (his tôr′ē ən) *n.* a writer of, or authority on, history

his·tor·ic (his tôr′ik) *adj.* **1.** *same as* HISTORICAL **2.** famous in history

his·tor′i·cal (-i k′l) *adj.* **1.** of or concerned with history **2.** based on people or events of the past **3.** established by history; factual —**his·tor′i·cal·ly** *adv.*

historical present the present tense used in telling about past events: also **historic present**

his·to·ric·i·ty (his′tə ris′ə tē) *n.* the condition of having actually occurred in history

his·to·ri·og·ra·phy (his tôr′ē äg′rə fē) *n.* the study of the techniques of historical research

his·to·ry (his′tə rē, his′trē) *n.*, *pl.* **-ries** [< Gr. *histōr*, learned] **1.** an account of what has happened, esp. in the life of a people, country, etc. **2.** all recorded past events **3.** the branch of knowledge that deals with the recording, analysis, etc. of past events **4.** a known past [this coat has a *history*] —**make history** to do something important enough to be recorded

his·tri·on·ic (his′trē än′ik) *adj.* [< L. *histrio*, actor] **1.** of acting or actors **2.** overacted or overacting

his′tri·on′ics *n.pl.* [*sometimes with sing. v.*] **1.** dramatics **2.** an artificial or affected manner or outburst

hit (hit) *vt.*, *vi.* **hit, hit′ting** [< ON. *hitta*, meet with] **1.** to come against (something) with force; bump; knock **2.** to give a blow (to); strike **3.** to strike (something) with a missile **4.** to affect (a person or thing) strongly [a town hard *hit* by floods] **5.** to come (*on* or *upon*) by accident or after a search **6.** to arrive at [stocks *hit* a new high] **7.** [Slang] to apply oneself to diligently [to *hit* the books] **8.** [Slang] to demand of [he *hit* me for a loan] **9.** *Baseball* to get (a base hit) —*n.* **1.** a blow that strikes its mark **2.** a collision **3.** a successful and popular song, play, etc. **4.** *Baseball same as* BASE HIT —**hit it off** to get along well together —**hit or miss** in a haphazard way —**hit the road** [Slang] to leave; go away —**hit′ter** *n.*

hit′-and-run′ *adj.* hitting with a vehicle, usually an automobile, and then fleeing: also **hit′-skip′**

hitch (hich) *vi.* [ME. *hicchen*] **1.** to move jerkily **2.** to become fastened or caught **3.** [Slang] to hitchhike —*vt.* **1.** to move, pull, etc. with jerks **2.** to fasten with a hook, knot, etc. **3.** [Slang] to hitchhike —*n.* **1.** a tug; jerk **2.** a limp **3.** a hindrance; obstacle **4.** a catching or fastening **5.** [Slang] a period of time served, as of military service **6.** *Naut.* a kind of knot that can be easily undone —**without a hitch** smoothly and successfully

hitch′hike′ (-hīk′) *vi.* **-hiked′, -hik′ing** to travel by asking for rides from motorists along the way —*vt.* to get (a ride) or make (one's way) by hitchhiking —**hitch′hik′er** *n.*

hith·er (hith′ər) *adv.* [OE. *hider*] to this place; here —*adj.* nearer

hith′er·to′ *adv.* until this time

Hit·ler (hit′lər), **Adolf** 1889–1945; Nazi dictator of Germany (1933–45)

hit man [< underworld slang *hit*, murder] [Slang] a hired murderer

Hit·tite (hit′īt) *n.* any of an ancient people of Asia Minor and Syria (fl. 1700–700 B.C.) —*adj.* of the Hittites, their language, or culture

hive (hīv) *n.* [OE. *hyf*] **1.** a shelter for a colony of domestic bees; beehive **2.** the bees of a hive **3.** a crowd of busy people **4.** a place of great activity —*vt.* **hived, hiv′ing** to gather (bees) into a hive —*vi.* to enter a hive

hives (hīvz) *n.* [orig. Scot. dial.] an allergic skin condition characterized by itching and smooth, raised patches

H.M.S. 1. His (or Her) Majesty's Service **2.** His (or Her) Majesty's Ship

ho (hō) *interj.* an exclamation of surprise, derision, etc.: also used to attract attention

Ho *Chem.* holmium

hoa·gy, hoa·gie (hō′gē) *n.*, *pl.* **-gies** [< ?] *same as* HERO SANDWICH

hoard (hôrd) *n.* [OE. *hord*] a supply stored up and hidden or kept in reserve —*vt.*, *vi.* to accumulate and store away (money, goods, etc.) —**hoard′er** *n.*

hoar·frost (hôr′frôst′) *n.* white, frozen dew on the ground, leaves, etc.; rime

hoarse (hôrs) *adj.* **hoars′er, hoars′est** [OE. *has*] **1.** harsh and grating in sound **2.** having a rough, husky voice —**hoarse′ly** *adv.* —**hoarse′ness** *n.*

hoar·y (hôr′ē) *adj.* **-i·er, -i·est 1.** white or gray **2.** having white or gray hair from old age **3.** very old; ancient Also **hoar** —**hoar′i·ness** *n.*

hoax (hōks) *n.* [< ? HOCUS-POCUS] a trick or fraud; esp., a practical joke —*vt.* to deceive with a hoax

hob[1] (häb) *n.* [< ?] a ledge at the back or side of a fireplace, for keeping a kettle, pan, etc. warm

hob[2] (häb) *n.* [< *Robin* or *Robert*] [Eng. Dial.] an elf or goblin —**play** (or **raise**) **hob** with to make trouble for

Hobbes (häbz), **Thomas** 1588–1679; English philosopher

hob·ble (häb′l) *vi.* **-bled, -bling** [ME. *hobelen*] to go haltingly; limp —*vt.* **1.** to cause to limp **2.** to hamper the movement of (a horse, etc.) by tying two legs together to hinder —*n.* **1.** a limp **2.** a rope, strap, etc. used to hobble a horse

hob·by (häb'ē) *n., pl.* **-bies** [ME. *hoby*] **1.** *same as* HOBBYHORSE **2.** something that a person likes to do in his spare time —**hob'by·ist** *n.*

hob'by·horse' *n.* **1.** a child's toy consisting of a stick with a horse's head **2.** *same as* ROCKING HORSE

hob·gob·lin (häb'gäb'lin) *n.* [HOB² + GOBLIN] **1.** an elf or goblin **2.** a bugbear

hob'nail' *n.* [*hob*, a peg + NAIL] a broad-headed nail put on the soles of heavy shoes to prevent wear or slipping —*vt.* to put hobnails on —**hob'nailed'** *adj.*

hob'nob' (-näb') *vi.* **-nobbed', -nob'bing** [< ME. *habben*, have + *nabben*, not have] to be on close terms (*with*)

ho·bo (hō'bō) *n., pl.* **-bos, -boes 1.** a migratory worker **2.** a vagrant; tramp

hock¹ (häk) *n.* [OE. *hoh*, the heel] the joint bending backward in the hind leg of a horse, ox, etc.

hock² (häk) *vt., n.* [< Du. *hok*, prison, debt] [Slang] *same as* PAWN¹

HOBNAILS

hock·ey (häk'ē) *n.* [prob. < OFr. *hoquet*, bent stick] **1.** a team game played on ice skates, in which the players, using curved sticks (**hockey sticks**), try to drive a rubber disk (*puck*) into their opponents' goal **2.** a similar game played on foot on a field with a small ball

hock'shop' *n.* [Slang] a pawnshop

ho·cus-po·cus (hō'kəs pō'kəs) *n.* [imitation L.] **1.** meaningless words used as a formula by conjurers **2.** *same as* SLEIGHT OF HAND **3.** trickery

hod (häd) *n.* [prob. < MDu. *hodde*] **1.** a long-handled wooden trough used for carrying bricks, mortar, etc. on the shoulder **2.** a coal scuttle

hodge·podge (häj'päj') *n.* [< OFr. *hochepot*, a stew] a jumbled mixture; mess

Hodg·kin's disease (häj'kinz) [< Dr. T. *Hodgkin* (1798–1866)] a disease characterized by progressive enlargement of the lymph nodes

hoe (hō) *n.* [< OHG. *houwan*, hew] a tool with a thin blade set across the end of a long handle, for weeding, loosening soil, etc. —*vt., vi.* **hoed, hoe'ing** to dig, cultivate, weed, etc. with a hoe

hoe'cake' (-kāk') *n.* a thin bread made of cornmeal

hoe'down' (-doun') *n.* [prob. of U.S. Negro origin] **1.** a lively dance, often a square dance **2.** music for this **3.** a party at which hoedowns are danced

hog (hôg, häg) *n.* [OE. *hogg*] **1.** a pig, esp. a full-grown pig raised for its meat **2.** [Colloq.] a selfish, greedy, or filthy person —*vt.* **hogged, hog'ging** [Slang] to take all or an unfair share of —**go (the) whole hog** [Slang] to go all the way —**high on (or off) the hog** [Colloq.] in a luxurious or costly way —**hog'gish** *adj.* —**hog'gish·ly** *adv.*

ho·gan (hō'gôn, -gän) *n.* [< AmInd.] a Navaho Indian dwelling built of earth walls supported by timbers

Ho·garth (hō'gärth), **William** 1697–1764; Eng. painter & engraver

hogs·head (hôgz'hed', hägz'-) *n.* **1.** a large barrel or cask holding from 63 to 140 gallons **2.** a liquid measure, esp. one equal to 63 gallons

hog'tie' *vt.* **-tied', -ty'ing or -tie'ing 1.** to tie the four feet or the hands and feet of **2.** [Colloq.] to make incapable of effective action

hog'wash' (-wôsh', -wäsh') *n.* **1.** refuse fed to hogs; swill **2.** insincere talk, writing, etc.

hoi pol·loi (hoi' pə loi') [Gr., the many] the common people; the masses: usually patronizing

hoist (hoist) *vt.* [< Du. *hijschen*] to raise aloft; lift, esp. with a pulley, crane, etc. —*n.* **1.** a hoisting **2.** an apparatus for lifting; elevator or tackle

hoke (hōk) *vt.* **hoked, hok'ing** [< HOKUM] [Slang] to treat in a too sentimental or crudely comic way: usually with *up* —*n.* *same as* HOKUM —**hok'ey** *adj.*

Hok·kai·do (hō kī'dō) one of the four main islands of Japan

ho·kum (hō'kəm) *n.* [< HOCUS-POCUS] [Slang] **1.** crudely comic or mawkishly sentimental elements in a story, play, etc. **2.** nonsense; humbug

Hol·bein (hōl'bīn), **Hans** (häns) **1.** 1460?–1524; Ger. painter **2.** 1497?–1543; Ger. painter: son of *prec.*

hold¹ (hōld) *vt.* **held, hold'ing** [OE. *haldan*] **1.** to keep in the hands, arms, etc.; grasp **2.** to keep in a certain position or condition **3.** to restrain or control; keep back **4.** to

possess; occupy [*to hold* an office] **5.** to guard; defend [to *hold* the fort] **6.** to carry on (a meeting, etc.) **7.** to contain [the jar *holds* a pint] **8.** to regard; consider [I *hold* the story to be true] **9.** *Law* to decide; decree —*vi.* **1.** to go on being firm, loyal, etc. **2.** to remain unbroken or unyielding [the rope *held*] **3.** to be true or valid [a rule which still *holds*] **4.** to continue [the wind *held* steady] — *n.* **1.** a grasping or seizing; grip **2.** a thing to hold on by **3.** a controlling force [to have a *hold* over someone] **4.** an order reserving something —**get (catch, lay, or take) hold of** to take, seize, acquire, etc. —**hold forth 1.** to preach; lecture **2.** to offer —**hold off 1.** to keep at a distance **2.** to keep from doing something —**hold one's own** to persist in spite of obstacles —**hold out 1.** to last; endure **2.** to stand firm **3.** to offer **4.** [Colloq.] to refuse to give (what is to be given) —**hold over 1.** to postpone **2.** to keep or stay for an additional period —**hold up 1.** to prop up **2.** to show **3.** to last; endure **4.** to stop; delay **5.** to stop forcibly and rob —**hold with** to agree with —**hold'er** *n.*

hold² (hōld) *n.* [< HOLE or MDu. *hol*] **1.** the interior of a ship below decks, in which cargo is carried **2.** the compartment for cargo in an aircraft

hold'ing *n.* **1.** land, esp. a farm, rented from another **2.** [*usually pl.*] property owned, esp. stocks and bonds

holding company a corporation organized to own bonds or stocks of other corporations, which it usually controls

hold'out' *n.* a player in a professional sport who delays signing his contract because he wants better terms

hold'o'ver *n.* [Colloq.] one staying on from a previous period

hold'up' *n.* **1.** a delay **2.** the act of stopping forcibly and robbing

hole (hōl) *n.* [OE. *hol*] **1.** a hollow place; cavity **2.** an animal's burrow **3.** a small, dingy, squalid place **4.** an opening in anything; gap; tear; rent **5.** a flaw [*holes* in an argument] **6.** [Colloq.] an embarrassing situation **7.** *Golf a*) a small cup sunk into a green, into which the ball is to be hit *b*) the tee, fairway, etc. leading to this —*vt.* **holed, hol'ing** to put or drive into a hole —**hole in one** *Golf* the act of getting the ball into the hole on the shot from the tee —**hole up** [Colloq.] **1.** to hibernate, as in a hole **2.** to shut oneself in —**in the hole** [Colloq.] financially embarrassed or behind —**hole'y** *adj.*

hol·i·day (häl'ə dā') *n.* **1.** a religious festival; holy day **2.** a day of freedom from labor, often one set aside by law to celebrate some event **3.** [*often pl.*] [Chiefly Brit.] a vacation —*adj.* of or suited to a holiday; joyous; gay

ho·li·er-than-thou (hō'lē ər *than* thou') *adj.* annoyingly self-righteous

ho·li·ness (hō'lē nis) *n.* **1.** a being holy **2.** [H-] a title of the Pope (with *His* or *Your*)

Hol·land (häl'ənd) *same as the* NETHERLANDS —**Hol'land·er** *n.*

hol·lan·daise sauce (häl'ən dāz') [Fr., of Holland] a creamy sauce, as for vegetables, made of butter, egg yolks, lemon juice, etc.

hol·ler (häl'ər) *vi., vt., n.* [Colloq.] shout; yell

hol·low (häl'ō) *adj.* [OE. *holh*] **1.** having a cavity inside; not solid **2.** shaped like a bowl; concave **3.** sunken [*hollow* cheeks] **4.** empty or worthless [*hollow* praise] **5.** hungry **6.** deep-toned and muffled —*adv.* in a hollow manner —*n.* **1.** a hollow place; cavity **2.** a valley —*vt., vi.* to make or become hollow —**hol'low·ness** *n.*

hol·ly (häl'ē) *n., pl.* **-lies** [OE. *holegn*] **1.** an evergreen shrub with glossy leaves and red berries **2.** the leaves and berries, used as decorations

hol·ly·hock (häl'ē häk') *n.* [< OE. *halig*, holy + *hoc*, mallow] a tall plant related to the mallow, with large, showy flowers

Hol·ly·wood (häl'ē wood') **1.** section of Los Angeles: once the site of many U.S. motion-picture studios; hence, the U.S. motion-picture industry **2.** city on the SE coast of Fla.: pop. 107,000

Holmes (hōmz, hōlmz), **Oliver Wendell** 1841–1935; associate justice, U.S. Supreme Court (1902–32)

hol·mi·um (hōl'mē əm) *n.* [< ModL. *Holmia*, Stockholm] a metallic chemical element of the rare-earth group: symbol, Ho; at. wt., 164.930; at. no., 67

holm oak (hōm) [< OE. *holegn*, holly] an evergreen oak of S Europe, with hollylike leaves

HOLLYHOCK

hol·o·caust (häl′ə kôst′, hō′lə-) *n.* [< Gr. *holos,* whole + *kaustos,* burnt] great destruction of life, esp. by fire —**the Holocaust** [also h-] the systematic destruction of over six million Jewish Jews by the Nazis

hol·o·graph (häl′ə graf′) *adj.* [< Fr. < Gr. *holos,* whole + *graphein,* write] written in the handwriting of the person under whose name it appears —*n.* a holograph document, letter, etc. —**hol′o·graph′ic** *adj.*

Hol·stein (hōl′stēn, -stīn) *n.* [< Schleswig-*Holstein,* Germany] any of a breed of black-and-white dairy cattle

hol·ster (hōl′stər) *n.* [Du.] a pistol case, usually of leather and attached to a belt

ho·ly (hō′lē) *adj.* **-li·er, -li·est** [< OE. *hal,* sound, whole] **1.** dedicated to religious use; sacred **2.** spiritually pure; sinless **3.** deserving deep respect or reverence —*n., pl.* **-lies** a holy thing or place

Holy Communion a Christian rite in which bread and wine are consecrated and received as (symbols of) the body and blood of Jesus

Holy Ghost the third person of the Trinity

Holy Land *same as* PALESTINE (sense 1)

holy of holies 1. the innermost part of the Jewish tabernacle and Temple, where the ark of the covenant was kept **2.** any most sacred place

holy orders 1. the sacrament or rite of ordination **2.** the position of being an ordained minister or priest **3.** ranks of the Christian ministry

Holy Roman Empire empire of WC Europe, from the 8th or 9th century A.D. until 1806

Holy See the office, power, or court of the Pope

Holy Spirit the spirit of God; specif., the third person of the Trinity

Holy Week the week before Easter

hom·age (häm′ij, äm′-) *n.* [< L. *homo,* a man] anything given or done to show reverence, honor, etc. [to do *homage* to a hero]

hom·bre (äm′brā, -brē) *n.* [Sp. < L. *homo,* a man] [Slang] a man; fellow

hom·burg (häm′bərg) *n.* [< *Homburg,* Prussia] a man's felt hat with the crown dented front to back and a stiff, upturned brim

home (hōm) *n.* [OE. *ham*] **1.** the place where one lives **2.** the city, state, etc. where one was born or reared **3.** a place where one likes to be **4.** a household and its affairs **5.** an institution for orphans, the aged, etc. **6.** the natural environment of an animal, plant, etc. **7.** the place of origin **8.** in many games, the goal; esp., the home plate in baseball —*adj.* **1.** of one's home or country; domestic **2.** central [the *home* office] —*adv.* **1.** at, to, or in the direction of home **2.** to the point aimed at [to drive a nail *home*] **3.** to the heart of the matter —**at home 1.** in one's home **2.** at ease —**bring (something) home to** to impress upon —**home (in) on** to be directed as by radar to (a destination) —**home′less** *adj.* —**home′like** *adj.*

home′com′ing (-kum′iŋ) *n.* in many colleges, an annual celebration attended by alumni

home economics the science and art of homemaking, including nutrition, budgeting, etc.

home′land′ *n.* the country in which one was born or makes one's home

home′ly *adj.* **-li·er, -li·est 1.** suitable for home life; simple or plain **2.** crude **3.** not good-looking —**home′li·ness** *n.*

home′made′ *adj.* made, or as if made, at home

home′mak′er (-māk′ər) *n.* a person who manages a home; esp., a housewife —**home′mak′ing** *n.*

ho·me·op·a·thy (hō′mē äp′ə thē) *n.* [< Gr. *homos,* same + *pathos,* feeling] a system of medical treatment of certain diseases with small doses of drugs which in a healthy person and in large doses would produce symptoms like those of the disease: opposed to ALLOPATHY —**ho′me·o·path′ic** (-ə path′ik) *adj.*

home plate *Baseball* the slab that the batter stands beside: it is the last base touched in scoring a run

Ho·mer (hō′mər) semilegendary Gr. epic poet of c. 8th cent. B.C.: reputed author of the *Iliad* and the *Odyssey*

ho·mer (hō′mər) *n.* [Colloq.] *same as* HOME RUN

Ho·mer·ic (hō mer′ik) *adj.* of or characteristic of Homer, his poems, or the world they describe

home rule local self-government

home run *Baseball* a safe hit that allows the batter to touch all the bases and score a run

home′sick′ *adj.* longing for home —**home′sick′ness** *n.*

home′spun′ *n.* **1.** cloth made of yarn spun at home **2.** coarse cloth like this —*adj.* **1.** spun at home **2.** made of homespun **3.** plain; homely

home′stead′ (-sted′) *n.* **1.** a place where a family makes its home, including the land and buildings **2.** a 160-acre

tract of U.S. public land granted to a settler to develop as a farm —*vi., vt.* to settle on (as) a homestead —**home′stead′er** *n.*

home′stretch′ (-strech′) *n.* **1.** the part of a race track between the last turn and the finish line **2.** the final part of any undertaking

home′ward (-wərd) *adv., adj.* toward home: also **home′wards** *adv.*

home′work′ *n.* **1.** work done at home **2.** schoolwork to be done outside the classroom **3.** study or research in preparation for some project, activity, etc.: usually in **do one's homework**

home′y (-ē) *adj.* **hom′i·er, hom′i·est** comfortable, familiar, cozy, etc. —**home′y·ness** *n.*

hom·i·cide (häm′ə sīd′, hō′mə-) *n.* [< L. *homo,* man + *caedere,* to kill] **1.** the killing of one person by another **2.** a person who kills another —**hom′i·ci′dal** *adj.*

hom·i·let·ics (häm′ə let′iks) *n.pl.* [with sing. v.] [see HOMILY] the art of writing and preaching sermons —**hom′i·let′ic** *adj.*

hom·i·ly (häm′ə lē) *n., pl.* **-lies** [< Gr. *homilos,* assembly] **1.** a sermon **2.** a solemn, moralizing talk or writing

homing pigeon a pigeon trained to find its way home from distant places

hom·i·ny (häm′ə nē) *n.* [< AmInd.] dry corn hulled and coarsely ground: it is boiled for food

homo- [< Gr. *homos*] *a combining form meaning* same, equal, like

ho·mo·ge·ne·ous (hō′mə jē′nē əs, häm′ə-; -jēn′yəs) *adj.* [< Gr. *homos,* same + *genos,* kind] **1.** similar or identical in structure, quality, etc. **2.** composed of similar or identical parts —**ho′mo·ge·ne′i·ty** (-jə nē′ə tē) *n.*

ho·mog·e·nize (hə mäj′ə nīz′) *vt.* **-nized′, -niz′ing 1.** to make homogeneous **2.** to make more uniform throughout; specif., to process (milk) so that fat particles are so well emulsified that the cream does not separate

hom·o·graph (häm′ə graf′, hō′mə-) *n.* [HOMO- + -GRAPH] a word with the same spelling as another but with a different meaning and origin

ho·mol·o·gous (hō mäl′ə gəs) *adj.* [< Gr. *homos,* same + *legein,* to say] matching in structure, position, origin, etc.

ho·mol·o·gy (hō mäl′ə jē) *n., pl.* **-gies 1.** the quality or state of being homologous **2.** a homologous correspondence or relationship

hom·o·nym (häm′ə nim) *n.* [< Fr. < Gr. *homos,* same + *onyma,* a name] a word with the same pronunciation as another but with a different meaning, origin, and, usually, spelling (Ex.: *bore* and *boar*)

hom·o·phone (häm′ə fōn′) *n.* [< Gr. *homos,* same + *phōnē,* a sound] *same as* HOMONYM

ho·mop·ter·ous (hō mäp′tər əs) *adj.* [< Gr. *homos,* same + *pteron,* wing] belonging to an order of insects with two pairs of wings of uniform thickness throughout, as aphids

Ho·mo sa·pi·ens (hō′mō sā′pē enz′) [ModL. *homo,* man + *sapiens,* prp. of *sapere,* know] man; human being

ho·mo·sex·u·al (hō′mə sek′shoo wəl) *adj.* of or having sexual desire for those of one's own sex —*n.* a homosexual person —**ho′mo·sex′u·al′i·ty** *n.*

Hon., hon. 1. honorable **2.** honorary

Hon·du·ras (hän door′əs, -dyoor′-) country in Central America: 43,227 sq. mi.; pop. 2,495,000; cap. Tegucigalpa —**Hon·du′ran** *adj., n.*

hone (hōn) *n.* [< OE. *han,* a stone] a hard stone used to sharpen cutting tools —*vt.* **honed, hon′ing** to sharpen as with a hone

hon·est (än′əst) *adj.* [< L. *honor,* honor] **1.** trustworthy; truthful **2.** *a)* showing fairness and sincerity [an *honest* effort] *b)* gained by fair methods [an *honest* living] **3.** being what it seems; genuine **4.** frank and open [an *honest* face] —*adv.* [Colloq.] honestly; truly: an intensive

hon′est·ly *adv.* **1.** in an honest manner **2.** truly; really: an intensive [*honestly,* it is so]

hon·es·ty (än′əs tē) *n.* truthfulness, sincerity, etc.

hon·ey (hun′ē) *n., pl.* **-eys** [OE. *hunig*] **1.** a sweet, syrupy substance that bees make as food from the nectar of flowers **2.** sweetness **3.** darling **4.** [Colloq.] something excellent of its kind —*adj.* of or like honey

hon′ey·bee′ (-bē′) *n.* a bee that makes honey

hon′ey·comb′ (-kōm′) *n.* **1.** the structure of six-sided wax cells made by bees to hold their honey, eggs, etc. **2.** anything like this —*vt.* **1.** to fill with holes like a honeycomb **2.** to permeate or undermine —*adj.* of or like a honeycomb

hon′ey·dew′ melon (-dōō′) a variety of melon with a smooth, whitish rind and sweet, green flesh

hon·eyed (hun′ēd) *adj.* **1.** sweetened with honey **2.** sweet as honey; flattering [*honeyed* words]

honey locust a N. American tree with thorny branches, featherlike foliage, and large, twisted pods

hon'ey·moon' *n.* **1.** the vacation spent together by a newly married couple **2.** a brief period of apparent agreement —*vi.* to have or spend a honeymoon —**hon'ey·moon'er** *n.*

hon'ey·suck'le (-suk''l) *n.* any of a group of plants with small, fragrant flowers of red, yellow, or white

Hong Kong (häŋ' käŋ', hôŋ' kôŋ') Brit. colony in SE China: also **Hong'kong'**

honk (hôŋk, häŋk) *n.* [echoic] **1.** the call of a wild goose **2.** a similar sound, as of an automobile horn —*vi.*, *vt.* to make or cause to make such a sound

hon·ky-tonk (hôŋ'kē tôŋk', häŋ'kē täŋk') *n.* [< ?] [Slang] a cheap, noisy nightclub

Hon·o·lu·lu (hän'ə lo͞o'lo͞o) capital of Hawaii, on Oahu: pop. 325,000 (met. area 631,000)

hon·or (än'ər) *n.* [L.] **1.** high regard or respect; esp., *a)* glory; fame *b)* good reputation **2.** adherence to principles considered right; integrity **3.** chastity **4.** high rank; distinction **5.** [H-] a title of certain officials, as judges (with *His, Her,* or *Your*) **6.** something done or given as a token of respect **7.** a source of respect and fame —*vt.* **1.** to respect greatly **2.** to show high regard for **3.** to do something in honor of **4.** to accept as good for payment, credit, etc. *[to honor all major credit cards]* —*adj.* of or showing honor *[honor roll]* —**do honor to 1.** to show great respect for **2.** to bring honor to —**do the honors** to act as host or hostess

hon'or·a·ble *adj.* **1.** worthy of being honored; specif., having a position of high rank: used as a title of courtesy **2.** honest; upright **3.** bringing honor *[honorable mention]* —**hon'or·a·bly** *adv.*

hon·o·ra·ri·um (än'ə rer'ē əm) *n.*, *pl.* **-ri·ums, -ri·a** (-ə) [L.] a payment as to a professional person for services on which no fee is set

hon·or·ar·y (än'ə rer'ē) *adj.* **1.** given as an honor only *[an honorary degree]* **2.** designating or in an office held as an honor only, without service or pay

hon·our (än'ər) *n.*, *vt.*, *adj.* Brit. var. of HONOR

Hon·shu (hän'sho͞o') largest of the islands forming Japan

hooch (ho͞och) *n.* [< Alaskan Ind. *hoochinoo,* crude alcoholic liquor] [Slang] alcoholic liquor

hood (ho͝od) *n.* [OE. *hod]* **1.** a covering for the head and neck, often part of a cloak **2.** anything like a hood, as the metal cover over an automobile engine —*vt.* to cover as with a hood —**hood'ed** *adj.*

-hood [< OE. *had,* order, rank] a suffix meaning: **1.** state or quality *[childhood]* **2.** the whole group of *[priesthood]*

hood·lum (ho͞od'ləm) *n.* [prob. < G. dial. *hudilump,* wretch] a wild, lawless person, often a member of a gang of criminals

hoo·doo (ho͞o'do͞o) *n.*, *pl.* **-doos** [var. of VOODOO] **1.** same as VOODOO **2.** [Colloq.] bad luck or a person or thing that causes it —*vt.* [Colloq.] to bring bad luck to

hood·wink (ho͝od'wiŋk') *vt.* [HOOD + WINK] **1.** orig., to blindfold **2.** to deceive; trick

hoo·ey (ho͞o'ē) *interj.*, *n.* [echoic] [Slang] nonsense

hoof (ho͝of, ho͞of) *n.*, *pl.* **hoofs, hooves** [OE. *hof]* the horny covering on the feet of cattle, horses, etc., or the entire foot —*vt.*, *vi.* [Colloq.] to walk —**hoofed** *adj.*

hoof'beat' (-bēt') *n.* the sound made by the hoof of an animal when it runs, walks, etc.

hoof'er *n.* [Slang] a professional dancer

hook (ho͝ok) *n.* [OE. *hoc]* **1.** a bent piece as of metal, used to catch, hold, or pull something **2.** something hooklike in shape **3.** *a)* the path of a hit ball that curves away to the left from a right-handed player or to the right from a left-handed player *b)* a ball that follows such a path **4.** *Boxing* a short blow delivered with the arm bent —*vt.* **1.** to catch, fasten, etc. with a hook **2.** to hit (a ball) in a hook —*vi.* **1.** to curve as a hook does **2.** to be fastened or caught by a hook —**by hook or by crook** by any means, honest or dishonest —**hook up** to connect, as a radio —**off the hook** [Colloq.] out of trouble —**on one's own hook** [Colloq.] by oneself; without help

hook·ah, hook·a (ho͝ok'ə) *n.* [Ar. *ḥuqqah]* an Oriental tobacco pipe with a long tube by means of which the smoke is drawn through water so as to be cooled

hooked *adj.* **1.** like, having, or made by a hook **2.** [Slang] *a)* addicted (often with *on) b)* married

hook'er *n.* [Slang] a prostitute

hook'up' *n.* **1.** the arrangement and connection of parts, circuits, etc., as in (a) radio **2.** [Colloq.] an alliance

hook'worm' *n.* a small, parasitic roundworm with hooks around the mouth, infesting the small intestine

hook'y (-ē) *n. see* PLAY HOOKY

hoo·li·gan (ho͞o'li gən) *n.* [< ? *Hooligan,* family name] [Slang] a hoodlum —**hoo'li·gan·ism** *n.*

hoop (ho͞op) *n.* [OE. *hop]* **1.** a circular band to hold barrel staves together **2.** anything similarly shaped, as a ring in a hoop skirt

hoop·la (ho͞op'lä) *n.* [< ?] [Colloq.] **1.** great excitement **2.** showy publicity; ballyhoo

hoop skirt a skirt worn over a framework of hoops, or rings, to make it spread out

hoo·ray (ho͝o rā', ho͞o-) *interj.*, *n.*, *vi.*, *vt.* hurrah

hoose·gow, hoos·gow (ho͞os'gou) *n.* [< Sp. *juzgado,* a court] [Slang] a jail

Hoo·sier (ho͞o'zhər) *n.* [Colloq.] a native or inhabitant of Indiana

hoot (ho͞ot) *vi.* [echoic] **1.** to utter its characteristic hollow sound: said of an owl **2.** to make any such sound **3.** to cry out, as in scorn —*vt.* **1.** to express, as scorn, by hooting **2.** to express scorn, disapproval, etc. of by hooting **3.** to drive or chase away by hooting —*n.* **1.** the cry of an owl **2.** any similar sound **3.** a crying out, as in scorn

Hoo·ver (ho͞o'vər), **Herbert Clark,** 1874–1964; 31st president of the U.S. (1929–33)

hooves (ho͝ovz, ho͞ovz) *n. alt. pl. of* HOOF

hop¹ (häp) *vi.* **hopped, hop'ping** [OE. *hoppian]* **1.** to make a short leap or leaps on one foot **2.** to leap on both or all feet, as a bird or frog does **3.** [Colloq.] to move quickly or in bounces —*vt.* **1.** to jump over **2.** to jump onto —*n.* **1.** a hopping **2.** [Colloq.] *a)* a dance *b)* a short flight in an airplane —**hop on** (or **all over**) [Slang] to rebuke

hop² (häp) *n.* [< MDu. *hoppe]* **1.** a twining vine with cone-shaped flowers **2.** [*pl.*] the dried cones, used as for flavoring beer —**hop up** [Slang] **1.** to stimulate as with drugs **2.** to supercharge (an engine)

hope (hōp) *n.* [OE. *hopa]* **1.** a feeling that what is wanted will happen **2.** the object of this **3.** a reason for hope **4.** one on which hope may be based —*vt.* **hoped, hop'ing 1.** to want and expect **2.** to want very much —*vi.* to have hope (*for*) —**hope against hope** to continue hoping though it seems baseless

hope chest a chest in which a young woman hoping to get married collects linen, clothing, etc.

hope'ful *adj.* hoping or giving hope —*n.* one hoping or likely to succeed —**hope'ful·ness** *n.*

hope'ful·ly *adv.* **1.** in a hopeful way **2.** it is to be hoped (that): regarded by some as a loose usage

hope'less *adj.* **1.** devoid of hope **2.** impossible to solve, deal with, etc. —**hope'less·ness** *n.*

Ho·pi (hō'pē) *n.*, *pl.* **-pis, -pi** a member of a Pueblo tribe of Indians in NE Arizona

hop·per (häp'ər) *n.* **1.** one that hops **2.** a box, tank, etc. allowing slow, even emptying

hop·sack·ing (häp'sak'iŋ) *n.* [lit., sacking for hops] **1.** a coarse material for bags **2.** a fabric somewhat like this, used as for suits Also **hop'sack'**

hop·scotch (häp'skäch') *n.* [HOP¹ + *scotch,* line] a children's game, each player hopping to successive sections of a figure traced on the ground

Hor·ace (hôr'is) 65–8 B.C.; Roman poet

horde (hôrd) *n.* [Fr., ult. < Tatar *urdu,* a camp] a large, swarming crowd; throng; multitude

hore·hound (hôr'hound') *n.* [< OE. *har,* white + *hune,* horehound] **1.** a white-leaved, bitter plant related to the mint **2.** cough medicine or candy made from the juice of the leaves

ho·ri·zon (hə rī'z'n) *n.* [< Gr. *horos,* boundary] **1.** the line where the sky seems to meet the earth **2.** [usually *pl.*] one's limit as of experience

hor·i·zon·tal (hôr'ə zän't'l) *adj.* **1.** parallel to the plane of the horizon; not vertical **2.** flat and even; level —*n.* a horizontal line, plane, etc. —**hor'i·zon'tal·ly** *adv.*

hor·mone (hôr'mōn) *n.* [< Gr. *hormē,* impulse] a substance formed in a bodily organ, as in the pituitary gland, and having a specific effect on some other organ or tissue to which it is carried —**hor·mo'nal** *adj.*

horn (hôrn) *n.* [OE.] **1.** a hard, bony or keratinous projection growing on the head of certain hoofed animals **2.** anything suggestive of this **3.** the substance horns are made of **4.** an instrument made of horn and sounded by blowing; also, a brass-wind instrument or, *Jazz,* any wind instrument **5.** a signaling device producing a sound like that of a horn (sense 4), used esp. to give a warning —*adj.* made of horn —**horn in (on)** [Colloq.] to intrude or meddle (in) —**horned** *adj.* —**horn′less** *adj.*

Horn, Cape southernmost point of S. America

horn·blende (hôrn′blend′) *n.* [G.] a black, rock-forming mineral common in some granites

horn′book′ *n.* **1.** an early rudimentary learning device for children: it consisted of a small board and handle, a sheet of parchment or paper (with the alphabet, numbers, etc. shown on it) being mounted on the board and overlaid with clear horn **2.** an elementary treatise

hor·net (hôr′nit) *n.* [OE. *hyrnet*] any of several large, yellow-and-black social wasps

horn of plenty same as CORNUCOPIA

horn′pipe′ *n.* **1.** a lively dance formerly popular with sailors **2.** music for this

horn′y *adj.* -i·er, -i·est **1.** of or like horn **2.** having horns **3.** toughened and calloused **4.** [Slang] sexually keyed up; lustful; lascivious

ho·rol·o·gy (hō räl′ə jē) *n.* [< Gr. *hōra*, hour + -LOGY] the science or art of measuring time or making timepieces —**hor·o·log·ic** (hôr′ə läj′ik), **hor′o·log′i·cal** *adj.* —**ho·rol′·o·gist** *n.*

hor·o·scope (hôr′ə skōp′, här′-) *n.* [Fr. < Gr. *hōra*, hour + *skopein*, to view] a zodiacal chart by which astrologers profess to tell a person's future

hor·ren·dous (hô ren′dəs, hə-) *adj.* [see HORROR] horrible; frightful —**hor·ren′dous·ly** *adv.*

hor·ri·ble (hôr′ə b'l, här′-) *adj.* [see HORROR] **1.** causing horror; terrible; dreadful **2.** [Colloq.] very bad, ugly, unpleasant, etc. —**hor′ri·bly** *adv.*

hor·rid (hôr′id, här′-) *adj.* **1.** causing horror; terrible; revolting **2.** very bad, ugly, unpleasant, etc. —**hor′rid·ly** *adv.* —**hor′rid·ness** *n.*

hor·ri·fy (hôr′ə fī′, här′-) *vt.* -fied′, -fy′ing **1.** to cause to feel horror **2.** [Colloq.] to shock greatly

hor·ror (hôr′ər, här′-) *n.* [< L. *horrere*, to bristle] **1.** the strong feeling caused by something frightful or shocking; terror and repugnance **2.** strong dislike **3.** something causing horror

hors d'oeu·vre (ôr′ durv′, duv′), *pl.* **hors′ d'oeuvres′** (durvz′, duvz′) [Fr., lit., outside of work] an appetizer, as a canapé, served before a meal

horse (hôrs) *n.* [OE. *hors*] **1.** a large, four-legged, solid-hoofed animal with flowing mane and tail, domesticated for drawing loads, carrying riders, etc. **2.** a supporting frame with legs **3.** *Gym.* a padded block used as for vaulting **4.** *Mil.* [*with pl. v.*] cavalry — *vt.* **horsed, hors′ing** to supply with a horse or horses; put on horseback —*adj.* of or on horses —**horse around** [Slang] to engage in horseplay —**on one's high horse** [Colloq.] arrogant

HORSE (sense 3)

horse′back′ *n.* a horse's back —*adv.* on horseback

horse chestnut 1. a flowering tree with large leaves and glossy brown seeds **2.** one of the seeds

horse′fly′ *n., pl.* -flies′ a large fly, the female of which sucks the blood of horses, cattle, etc.

horse′hair′ *n.* **1.** hair, or a hair, from the mane or tail of a horse **2.** a stiff fabric of such hair

horse′hide′ *n.* **1.** the hide of a horse **2.** leather made from this

horse′laugh′ *n.* a loud, coarse laugh; guffaw

horse′man (-mən) *n., pl.* -men **1.** a man who rides horseback **2.** a man skilled in the riding or care of horses — **horse′man·ship′** *n.* —**horse′wom′an** *n.fem.*

horse′play′ *n.* rough, boisterous fun

horse′pow′er *n.* a unit for measuring the power of motors or engines, equal to 746 watts or to a rate of 33,000 foot-pounds per minute

horse′rad′ish *n.* **1.** a plant of the mustard family, with a pungent, white root **2.** a relish made by grating this root

horse sense [Colloq.] ordinary common sense

horse′shoe′ *n.* **1.** a flat, U-shaped, protective metal plate nailed to a horse's hoof **2.** anything so shaped **3.** [*pl.*] a game in which horseshoes are tossed at a stake

horse′tail′ *n.* **1.** a horse's tail **2.** a rushlike plant with hollow, jointed stems

horse′whip′ *n.* a whip for driving horses —*vt.* -whipped′, -whip′ping to lash with this

hors·y (hôr′sē) *adj.* -i·er, -i·est **1.** of or like a horse **2.** of or like people fond of horses, horse racing, etc. Also **hors′ey**

hor·ta·to·ry (hôr′tə tôr′ē) *adj.* [< L. *hortari*, incite] exhorting; advising: also **hor′ta·tive**

hor·ti·cul·ture (hôr′tə kul′chər) *n.* [< L. *hortus*, a garden + *cultura*, culture] the art or science of growing flowers, fruits, etc. —**hor′ti·cul′tur·al** *adj.* —**hor′ti·cul′tur·ist** *n.*

ho·san·na (hō zan′ə) *n., interj.* [< Heb. *hōshī′āh nnā*, save, we pray] an exclamation of praise to God

hose (hōz) *n., pl.* **hose;** for 3, usually **hos′es** [OE. *hosa*] **1.** orig., a man's tightfitting outer garment covering the hips, legs, and feet **2.** [*pl.*] stockings or socks **3.** a flexible tube to convey fluid, esp. water from a hydrant —*vt.* **hosed, hos′ing** to water or drench with a hose

Ho·se·a (hō zā′ə, -zē′ə) *Bible* **1.** a Hebrew prophet, 8th cent. B.C. **2.** the book of his writings

ho·sier (hō′zhər) *n.* [Chiefly Brit.] a person who makes or sells hosiery

ho′sier·y (-ē) *n.* **1.** hose; stockings and socks **2.** [Chiefly Brit.] similar knitted or woven goods

hos·pice (häs′pis) *n.* [Fr. < L. *hospes*, host, guest] a place of shelter for travelers

hos·pi·ta·ble (häs′pi tə b'l, häs pit′ə-) *adj.* [see prec.] **1.** friendly and solicitous toward guests **2.** favoring health, comfort, etc., as a climate **3.** receptive or open, as to ideas —**hos′pi·ta·bly** *adv.*

hos·pi·tal (häs′pi t'l) *n.* [see HOSPICE] an institution for the treatment and care of the ill or injured

hos·pi·tal·i·ty (häs′pə tal′ə tē) *n., pl.* -ties the act, practice, or quality of being hospitable

hos·pi·tal·ize (häs′pi t'l īz′) *vt.* -ized′, -iz′ing to put in a hospital —**hos′pi·tal·i·za′tion** *n.*

host¹ (hōst) *n.* [< L. *hostia*, sacrifice] a wafer of the Eucharist; esp., [H-] a consecrated wafer

host² (hōst) *n.* [see HOSPICE] **1.** *a*) a man entertaining guests in his own home or at his own expense *b*) *Radio & TV* the key personality conducting a show that typically features informal talk, conversations with guests, etc. **2.** a man who keeps an inn or hotel **3.** any organism on or in which another (called a *parasite*) lives —*vi., vt.* to act as host (to)

host³ (hōst) *n.* [< L. *hostis*, army] **1.** an army **2.** a multitude; great number

hos·tage (häs′tij) *n.* [< OFr.] a person kept or given as a pledge for the fulfillment of certain terms

hos·tel (häs′t'l) *n.* [see HOSPICE] a lodging place; inn: also **hos′tel·ry** (-rē), *pl.* -ries

host·ess (hōs′tis) *n.* **1.** a woman entertaining guests in her own home or at her own expense; often, a host's wife **2.** a woman innkeeper **3.** *a*) a stewardess, as on an airplane *b*) a woman employed in a restaurant to supervise waitresses, seating, etc. *c*) a paid woman partner at a public dance hall

hos·tile (häs′t'l; chiefly Brit. -tīl) *adj.* [< L. *hostis*, enemy] **1.** of or characteristic of an enemy **2.** unfriendly; antagonistic **3.** not hospitable, as a climate; adverse —**hos′tile·ly** *adv.*

hos·til·i·ty (häs til′ə tē) *n., pl.* -ties **1.** a feeling of enmity, ill will, etc. **2.** *a*) a hostile act *b*) [*pl.*] acts of war

hos·tler (häs′lər, äs′-) *n.* [contr. of *hosteler*, innkeeper] one who takes care of horses as at an inn

hot (hät) *adj.* **hot′ter, hot′test** [OE. *hat*] **1.** of a temperature much higher than that of the human body **2.** having a relatively high temperature **3.** producing a burning sensation [*hot* pepper] **4.** full of intense feeling or activity, as *a*) excitable [a *hot* temper] *b*) violent or angry [a *hot* battle, *hot* words] *c*) lustful *d*) controversial **5.** following closely [*hot* pursuit] **6.** *a*) electrically charged [a *hot* wire] *b*) highly radioactive **7.** designating or having colors that suggest heat, as intense red or orange **8.** [Colloq.] *a*) recent; fresh [*hot* news] *b*) very popular [a *hot* recording] **9.** [Slang] *a*) recently stolen or smuggled *b*) sought by the police *c*) risky for use as a hiding place **10.** [Slang] excellent, good, funny, etc. **11.** *Jazz* exciting, as in rhythm or tonal effects —*adv.* in a hot manner —**make it hot for** [Colloq.] to make things uncomfortable for —**hot′ly** *adv.* —**hot′ness** *n.*

hot air [Slang] empty or pretentious talk

hot′bed′ *n.* **1.** a bed of earth covered with glass and kept warm to make plants grow faster **2.** any place that fosters rapid growth or much activity

hot′-blood′ed *adj.* excitable, fiery, reckless, etc.

hot cake a pancake —**sell like hot cakes** [Colloq.] to be sold rapidly in large quantities

hot dog [Colloq.] a frankfurter or wiener, esp. one served in a soft roll

ho·tel (hō tel′) *n.* [< Fr.: see HOSPICE] an establishment providing lodging and often meals, as for travelers

hot′foot′ *adv.* [Colloq.] in great haste —*vi.* [Colloq.] to hasten: with *it*

hot′head′ *n.* a hotheaded person

hot′head′ed *adj.* 1. easily angered 2. impetuous; rash
hot′house′ *n. same as* GREENHOUSE
hot line a telephone or telegraph line for immediate communication in a crisis
hot pepper any of various pungent peppers
hot plate a small gas or electric stove for cooking
hot rod [Slang] 1. an old automobile with a supercharged engine 2. its driver: also **hot rod′der**
hot′-tem′pered *adj.* easily angered
Hot·ten·tot (hät′'n tät′) *n.* 1. a member of a nomadic people of SW Africa 2. their language
hound (hound) *n.* [OE. *hund*] a dog; specif., any of several breeds of hunting dog —*vt.* 1. to hunt or chase as with hounds 2. to urge on
hour (our) *n.* [< Gr. *hōra*] 1. a division (sixty minutes) of time, one of the twenty-four parts of a day 2. the time, or one of the periods of time, during which something is done *[the dinner hour]* 3. the time of day *[the hour* is 2:30*]* 4. *Educ.* a class session of about one hour: each hour of a course per week is a unit of academic credit
hour′glass′ *n.* an invertible device measuring time by the flow of sand from an upper glass bulb to a lower bulb through a narrow interconnecting neck
hou·ri (hoor′ē, hou′rē) *n., pl.* -**ris** [< Ar.] a beautiful nymphlike maiden of the Muslim paradise
hour·ly (our′lē) *adj., adv.* of, at, for, or throughout each hour or any hour

HOUR-
GLASS

house (hous) *n., pl.* **hous·es** (hou′ziz) [OE. *hus*] 1. a building or other shelter to live or stay in 2. a section of this so used as by one or more occupants or groups of occupants 3. the occupants of a house 4. a family, including kin, ancestors, and descendants 5. a building or other shelter for storing things 6. *a)* a theater *b)* the audience in it 7. a business firm 8. *[often* H-] a legislative assembly —*vt.* (houz) **housed, hous′ing** 1. to provide a house, or lodging, for 2. to store, shelter, etc. —**keep house** to take care of the affairs of a home; run a house —**on the house** given free, at the expense of the establishment
house′boat′ *n.* a large, flat-bottomed boat with a houselike superstructure, used as a residence
house′break′ *vt.* -**broke′**, -**bro′ken**, -**break′ing** to train (a dog, cat, etc.) to void in the proper place —**house′bro′ken** *adj.*
house′break′ing *n.* a breaking into another's house to commit theft or some other felony
house′coat′ *n.* a woman's long, loose garment for casual wear at home
house′dress′ *n.* a cheap dress worn for housework
house′fly′ *n., pl.* -**flies′** a two-winged fly found in and about houses: it feeds esp. on garbage
house′ful′ *n.* all that a house can hold
house′hold′ *n.* 1. all those living in one house 2. the home and its affairs
house′hold′er *n.* 1. one who owns or maintains a house 2. the head of a household
household word a very familiar word or saying
house′keep′er *n.* one who manages a home, esp. a woman hired to do so —**house′keep′ing** *n.*
house′maid′ *n.* a maid to do housework
house′moth′er *n.* a woman in charge of a sorority house, dormitory, etc., often as housekeeper
House of Commons the lower branch of the legislature of Great Britain or Canada
House of Delegates the lower branch of the legislature of Maryland, Virginia, or West Virginia
House of Lords the upper branch of the legislature of Great Britain
House of Representatives the lower branch of the U.S. legislature or of most States of the U.S.
house′top′ *n.* the top of a house; roof
house′wares′ *n.pl.* articles for household use, esp. in the kitchen, as dishes or pots and pans
house′warm′ing *n.* a party given for or by someone moving into a new home
house′wife′ *n., pl.* -**wives′** a married woman whose principal occupation is her household
house′work′ *n.* the work involved in housekeeping, as cleaning or cooking
hous·ing (hou′zin) *n.* 1. provision of or accommodation in houses, apartments, etc. 2. houses collectively 3. a shelter 4. a covering 5. an enclosing recess, frame, box, etc.

Hous·ton (hyōōs′tən) city in SE Tex.: pop. 1,233,000 (met. area 1,985,000)
Hous·ton (hyōōs′tən), **Samuel** 1793–1863; U.S. general & statesman
hove (hōv) *alt. pt. & pp. of* HEAVE
hov·el (huv′'l, häv′-) *n.* [ME.] a small, miserable dwelling; hut
hov·er (huv′ər, häv′-) *vi.* [ME. *hoveren*] 1. to stay suspended or flutter in the air near one place 2. to linger close by 3. to waver —*n.* a hovering
how (hou) *adv.* [OE. *hu*] 1. in what manner or way 2. in what state or condition 3. for what reason 4. to what effect 5. to what extent, degree, etc. 6. at what price 7. [Colloq.] what? Also used as an intensive —*n.* the way of doing —**how about** what is your thought or feeling concerning?
how·be·it (hou bē′it) *adv.* [Archaic] however it may be; nevertheless
how·dah (hou′də) *n.* [< Ar. *haudaj*] a canopied seat for riding on the back of an elephant or camel
Howe (hou), **E·li·as** (i lī′əs) 1819–67; U.S. inventor of a sewing machine
how·ev·er (hou ev′ər) *adv.* 1. in whatever way 2. to whatever degree or extent 3. nevertheless
how·itz·er (hou′it sər) *n.* [< Czech *haufnice*, a sling] a short cannon with a high trajectory
howl (houl) *vi.* [ME. *houlen*] 1. to utter the long, wailing cry of wolves, dogs, etc. 2. to make a similar cry or sound, as in pain; shriek or yell, as with mirth or rage —*vt.* 1. to utter with a howl 2. to drive or effect by howling —*n.* 1. a howling 2. [Colloq.] something hilarious
howl′er *n.* 1. one that howls 2. [Colloq.] a ludicrous blunder
howl′ing *adj.* 1. that howls 2. [Slang] great *[a howling success]*
how·so·ev·er (hou′sō ev′ər) *adv.* 1. to whatever degree or extent 2. in whatever way
hoy·den (hoid′'n) *n.* [< ?] a bold, boisterous girl
Hoyle (hoil) *n.* a book of rules for card games, orig. compiled by E. Hoyle (1672–1769) —**according to Hoyle** according to the rules and regulations
HP, H.P., hp, h.p. horsepower
HQ, H.Q., hq, h.q. headquarters
hr. *pl.* **hrs.** hour(s)
H.R. House of Representatives
h.r., hr, HR home run
H.R.H. His (or Her) Royal Highness
H.S., h.s. high school
ht. 1. heat 2. *pl.* **hts.** height
hua·ra·ches (ha rä′chēz, wə rä′ches) *n.pl.* [MexSp.] flat sandals with straps or woven strips for uppers
hub (hub) *n.* [< ?] 1. the wheel part attached to or turning on an axle 2. a center, as of activity
hub·bub (hub′ub′) *n.* [< ?] an uproar; tumult
hu·bris (hyōō′bris) *n.* [Gr. *hybris*] arrogance
huck·le·ber·ry (huk′'l ber′ē) *n., pl.* -**ries** [< ?] 1. a shrub of the heath family, with dark-blue berries 2. one of these berries
huck·ster (huk′stər) *n.* [< MDu.] 1. a peddler 2. an aggressive merchant —*vt.* to peddle or sell
HUD (Department of) Housing and Urban Development
hud·dle (hud′'l) *vi.* -**dled, -dling** [< ?] 1. to crowd close together 2. to draw oneself together, as from cold 3. [Colloq.] to confer privately 4. *Football* to gather in a huddle —*vt.* 1. to crowd close together 2. to draw (oneself) together 3. to do, put, etc. with careless haste —*n.* 1. a confused crowd or heap 2. [Colloq.] a private, informal conference 3. *Football* a grouping to get signals before a play
Hud·son (hud′s'n) river in E N.Y., flowing southward into the Atlantic at New York City: c. 315 mi.
Hud·son (hud′s'n), **Henry** ?–1611; Eng. explorer, esp. of the waters about NE N. America
Hudson Bay inland sea in NE Canada
Hudson seal muskrat fur treated to resemble seal
hue[1] (hyōō) *n.* [OE. *heow*] 1. color 2. a certain shade or tint of color —**hued** *adj.*
hue[2] (hyōō) *n.* [< OFr.] a shouting: now only in **hue and cry**, a loud outcry; clamor
huff (huf) *vt.* [prob. echoic] to offend or anger —*vi.* to blow; puff —*n.* a condition of smoldering anger or resentment
huff′y *adj.* -**i·er, -i·est** 1. easily offended; touchy 2. piqued; ruffled —**huff′i·ly** *adv.*

---

fat, āpe, cär; ten, ēven; is, bīte; gō, hôrn, tōōl, look; oil, out; up, fur; thin, *then*; zh, leisure; ŋ, ring; ə for *a* in *ago*; ′ as in *able* (ā′b'l); ë, Fr. coeur; ö, Fr. feu; ö, Fr. mo*n*; ü, Fr. duc; r, Fr. cri; kh, G. doch, ich. ‡ foreign; < derived from

hug (hug) *vt.* **hugged, hug'ging** [prob. < ON. *hugga,* to comfort] **1.** to put the arms around and hold closely, esp. affectionately **2.** to cling to (a belief, opinion, etc.) **3.** to keep close to [the bus *hugged* the curb] —*vi.* to embrace —*n.* an embrace

huge (hyōōj, yōōj) *adj.* [OFr. *ahuge*] very large; gigantic; immense —**huge'ly** *adv.* —**huge'ness** *n.*

Hu·go (hyōō'gō), **Victor Marie** 1802–85; Fr. poet, novelist, & playwright

Hu·gue·not (hyōō'gə nät') *n.* a French Protestant of the 16th or 17th century

huh (hu, huN) *interj.* an exclamation used to express contempt, surprise, etc. or to ask a question

hu·la (hōō'lə) *n.* [Haw.] a native Hawaiian dance using flowing gestures: also **hu'la-hu'la**

hulk (hulk) *n.* [OE. *hulc*] **1.** the body of a ship, esp. if old and dismantled **2.** a deserted wreck **3.** a big, clumsy person or thing

hulk'ing *adj.* bulky: also **hulk'y**

hull (hul) *n.* [OE. *hulu*] **1.** *a)* an outer covering, specif. that of a seed or fruit, as a husk, pod, or nutshell *b)* the calyx as of a strawberry **2.** the frame or main body as of a ship —*vt.* to remove the hull or hulls from (a seed or seeds, etc.)

hul·la·ba·loo (hul'ə bə lōō') *n.* [echoic] hubbub

hum (hum) *vi.* **hummed, hum'ming** [echoic] **1.** to make a low, murmuring, continuous sound **2.** to produce a musical note or notes vocally, not using words and letting the breath pass only through the nose **3.** [Colloq.] to be full of activity —*vt.* to sound, as a note, by humming —*n.* a humming

hu·man (hyōō'mən, yōō'-) *adj.* [< L. *humanus*] of, characteristic of, or produced by people or mankind —*n.* a person: also **human being** —**hu'man·ly** *adv.*

hu·mane (hyōō mān', yōō-) *adj.* [see prec.] **1.** kind, sympathetic, merciful, etc. **2.** civilizing; refining —**hu·mane'ly** *adv.* —**hu·mane'ness** *n.*

hu·man·ism (hyōō'mə niz'm, yōō'-) *n.* **1.** any system seeking to advance mankind, esp. without recourse to the supernatural **2.** study of the humanities —**hu'man·ist** *n., adj.* —**hu'man·is'tic** *adj.*

hu·man·i·tar·i·an (hyōō man'ə ter'ē ən, yōō-) *n.* one devoted to promoting human welfare; philanthropist —*adj.* philanthropic —**hu·man'i·tar'i·an·ism** *n.*

hu·man·i·ty (hyōō man'ə tē, yōō-) *n., pl.* **-ties 1.** the fact or quality of being human or humane **2.** the human race —**the humanities** branches of learning other than the sciences, as literature, art, etc.

hu·man·ize (hyōō'mə niz', yōō'-) *vt., vi.* **-ized', -iz'ing** to make or become human or humane

hu'man·kind' *n.* the human race

hu'man·oid' (-oid') *adj.* nearly human —*n.* a nearly human creature

hum·ble (hum'b'l, um'-) *adj.* **-bler, -blest** [< L. *humilis,* low] **1.** having or showing awareness of one's defects; not proud; not self-assertive **2.** low in condition or rank; lowly —*vt.* **-bled, -bling 1.** to lower in condition or rank **2.** to lessen or obliterate the pride of; make humble —**hum'bly** *adv.*

humble pie [< L. *lumbus,* loin] formerly, a pie made of the inner parts of a deer —**eat humble pie** to undergo humiliation, esp. of admitting one's error

hum·bug (hum'bug') *n.* [< ?] **1.** *a)* fraud; sham *b)* misleading or empty talk **2.** an impostor **3.** a spirit of trickery —*vt.* **-bugged', -bug'ging** to dupe; deceive —*interj.* nonsense!

hum·ding·er (hum'diŋ'ər) *n.* [Slang] a person or thing considered excellent of its kind

hum·drum (hum'drum') *adj.* [echoic] monotonous; boring; dull

hu·mec·tant (hyōō mek'tənt) *n.* [< L. *umere,* be moist] a moisture-retaining substance, as glycerol

hu·mer·us (hyōō'mər əs) *n., pl.* **-mer·i'** (-ī') [L.] the bone of the upper arm or forelimb, extending from the shoulder to the elbow —**hu'mer·al** *adj.*

hu·mid (hyōō'mid, yōō'-) *adj.* [< Fr. < L. *umere,* be moist] full of water vapor; damp; moist

hu·mid·i·fy' (-ə fī') *vt.* **-fied', -fy'ing** to make humid —**hu·mid'i·fi'er** *n.*

hu·mid·i·ty (-tē) *n., pl.* **-ties** humid condition; specif., the amount of water vapor in the air

hu·mi·dor (hyōō'mə dôr') *n.* a jar, case, etc., as for tobacco, designed to keep the contents moist

hu·mil·i·ate (hyōō mil'ē āt') *vt.* **-at'ed, -at'ing** [< L. *humilis,* low] to hurt the pride or dignity of by making seem foolish or contemptible; mortify —**hu·mil'i·a'tion** *n.*

hu·mil'i·ty (-ə tē) *n.* the state or quality of being humble

hum·ming·bird (hum'iŋ burd') *n.* any of a large family of very small, brightly colored new-world birds feeding on nectar and having narrow wings that vibrate rapidly, often with a humming sound

hum·mock (hum'ək) *n.* [< ?] **1.** a low, rounded hill; knoll **2.** a ridge or rise in an ice field

hu·mor (hyōō'mər, yōō'-) *n.* [< L. *umor,* fluid, from former belief that four body fluids controlled one's disposition] **1.** mood; state of mind **2.** whim; caprice **3.** the quality of being funny **4.** *a)* ability to appreciate or express what is funny *b)* expression in speech or action of what is funny **5.** a bodily fluid, as lymph —*vt.* to comply with the mood or whim of Brit. sp. **humour** —**out of humor** not in a good mood

HUMMINGBIRD (4 1/4–4 3/4 in. long)

hu·mor·esque (hyōō'mə resk') *n.* a light, fanciful or playful musical composition

hu'mor·ist *n.* a person quick to appreciate or skilled in expressing what is funny

hu'mor·ous *adj.* funny —**hu'mor·ous·ly** *adv.*

hump (hump) *n.* [prob. < LowG. *humpe,* thick piece] **1.** a rounded, protruding lump, as on a camel's back **2.** a hummock —*vt.* to hunch; arch

hump'back' *n.* **1.** a humped, deformed back **2.** a person having a humped back —**hump'backed'** *adj.*

humph (humf: *conventionalized pronun.*) *interj., n.* a snort or grunt expressing disdain, disgust, etc.

hu·mus (hyōō'məs) *n.* [L., earth] the brown or black organic part of the soil, resulting from the partial decay of plant and animal matter

Hun (hun) *n.* **1.** a member of an Asiatic people invading Europe in the 4th and 5th centuries A.D. **2.** [*often* **h-**] a vandal or savage

hunch (hunch) *vt.* [< ?] to arch into a hump —*vi.* **1.** to move along jerkily **2.** to sit or stand with the back arched —*n.* **1.** a hump **2.** a chunk **3.** [Colloq.] a more or less vague but compelling feeling that something is so or is going to happen

hunch'back' *n.* a humpback —**hunch'backed'** *adj.*

hun·dred (hun'drid, -dərd) *adj., n.* [OE.] ten times ten; 100; C —**hun'dredth** (-dridth) *adj., n.*

hun'dred·fold' *adj., adv., n.* a hundred times as much or as many

hun'dred·weight' *n.* a unit of weight equal to 100 pounds in the U.S. and to 112 pounds in England

hung (huŋ) *pt. & pp.* of HANG —**hung over** [Slang] having an alcoholic hangover —**hung up (on)** [Slang] emotionally disturbed, frustrated, or obsessed (by)

Hun·gar·i·an (huŋ ger'ē ən) *adj.* of Hungary, its people, etc. —*n.* **1.** a native or inhabitant of Hungary **2.** the language of the Hungarians

Hun·ga·ry (huŋ'gər ē) country in SC Europe: 35,919 sq. mi.; pop. 10,331,000; cap. Budapest

hun·ger (huŋ'gər) *n.* [OE. *hungor*] **1.** *a)* discomfort caused by a need for food *b)* famine; starvation **2.** a need or appetite for food **3.** any strong desire —*vi.* **1.** to have hunger **2.** to crave

hunger strike a refusal, as of a protester, to eat, designed to force the granting of demands

hun·gry (huŋ'grē) *adj.* **-gri·er, -gri·est** having or showing hunger —**hun'gri·ly** *adv.*

hunk (huŋk) *n.* [Fl. *hunke*] [Colloq.] a chunk

hun·ker (huŋ'kər) *vi.* [prob. < ON. *hokra,* to creep] to settle down on one's haunches; squat

hun·ky-do·ry (huŋ'kē dôr'ē) *adj.* [< Du. *honk,* goal + *-dory* < ?] [Slang] all right; fine; OK

hunt (hunt) *vt., vi.* [OE. *huntian*] **1.** to chase (game) for food or sport **2.** to search for; seek **3.** to pursue —*n.* **1.** a hunting **2.** a group of people hunting together **3.** a search —**hunt'er** *n.* —**hunt'ress** *n.fem.* —**hunts'man** *n., pl.* **-men**

Hun·ting·ton Beach (hun'tiŋ tən) city in SW Calif.: suburb of Los Angeles: pop. 116,000

Hunts·ville (hunts'vil') city in N Ala.: pop. 138,000

hur·dle (hur'd'l) *n.* [OE. *hyrdel*] **1.** a framelike barrier to be leaped in a race **2.** an obstacle —*vt.* **-dled, -dling** to leap over (a barrier or obstacle) —**hur'dler** *n.*

hur·dy-gur·dy (hur'dē gur'dē) *n., pl.* **-gur'dies** [prob. echoic] *same as* BARREL ORGAN

hurl (hurl) *vt.* [prob. < ON.] **1.** to throw hard **2.** to drive or thrust with great force **3.** to utter vehemently **4.** [Colloq.] *Baseball* to pitch —*vi.* **1.** to move with great force; hurtle **2.** [Colloq.] *Baseball* to pitch —**hurl'er** *n.*

hurl·y-burl·y (hur'lē bur'lē) *n., pl.* **-burl'ies** [prob. < archaic *hurly*] uproar; turmoil

Hu·ron (hyōōr'ən, -än) *n.* **1.** *pl.* **-rons, -ron** a member of a confederation of Indian tribes that lived east of Lake Huron and now live in Oklahoma and Quebec **2.** their Iroquoian language

Huron, Lake second largest of the Great Lakes, between Mich. & Ontario, Canada: 24,328 sq. mi.; 247 mi. long

hur·rah (hə rô', -rä') *interj., n.* [echoic] a shout of joy, approval, etc. —*vi.* to shout "hurrah" Also **hur·ray'** (-rā')

hur·ri·cane (hur'ə kān', -kən) *n.* [< WInd. *huracan*] a tropical cyclone with winds of 73 or more miles per hour, usually of West Indian origin

hur·ry (hur'ē) *vt.* **-ried, -ry·ing** [prob. akin to HURL] **1.** to move or send with haste **2.** to make occur or be done with haste **3.** to make act with haste —*vi.* to move or act with haste —*n.* haste —**hur'ried** *adj.* —**hur'ried·ly** *adv.*

hur·ry-scur·ry, hur·ry-skur·ry (-skur'ē) *n.* [< prec.] disorderly confusion —*adj., adv.* with disorderly confusion

hurt (hurt) *vt.* **hurt, hurt'ing** [< OFr. *hurter,* to hit] **1.** to cause pain or injury to **2.** to harm or damage **3.** to offend or distress —*vi.* **1.** to cause pain, injury, etc. **2.** to have pain; be sore —*n.* **1.** a pain or injury **2.** harm or damage **3.** something that wounds the feelings

hurt'ful *adj.* causing hurt; harmful —**hurt'ful·ly** *adv.*

hur·tle (hurt''l) *vi., vt.* **-tled, -tling** [ME. *hurtlen*] to move or throw with great speed or force

hus·band (huz'bənd) *n.* [< ON. *hūs,* house + *bondi,* freeholder] a married man —*vt.* to manage thriftily

hus'band·man (-mən) *n., pl.* **-men** [Archaic] a farmer

hus'band·ry *n.* **1.** thrifty care **2.** farming

hush (hush) *vt., vi.* [ME. *huscht,* quiet] **1.** to make or become quiet **2.** to calm —*n.* quiet; silence —*interj.* silence! —**hush up 1.** to keep quiet **2.** to keep from being told; suppress

hush'-hush' *adj.* [Colloq.] very secret

hush money money paid to keep something secret

hush puppy [South] a cornmeal fritter

husk (husk) *n.* [prob. < MDu. *huus,* a house] **1.** the dry outer covering of various fruits or seeds, as of an ear of corn **2.** any dry, rough, or useless covering —*vt.* to remove the husk from

hus·ky[1] (hus'kē) *n., pl.* **-kies** [< ? ESKIMO] [*sometimes* H-] a hardy dog used for pulling sleds in the Arctic

husk·y[2] (hus'kē) *adj.* **-i·er, -i·est 1.** of, like, or full of husks **2.** not loud, lacking resonance, and somewhat breathy or rough in tone; hoarse **3.** big and strong; robust —**husk'i·ly** *adv.* —**husk'i·ness** *n.*

hus·sar (hoo zär', hə-) *n.* [< Serb. *husar*] a European light-armed cavalryman, brilliantly uniformed

hus·sy (huz'ē, hus'-) *n., pl.* **-sies** [ME. *huswife,* housewife] **1.** a woman of low morals **2.** an impudent girl

hus·tings (hus'tiŋz) *n.pl.* [*usually with sing. v.*] [< ON. *hūs,* a house + *thing,* assembly] the process of, or a place for, political campaigning

hus·tle (hus''l) *vt.* **-tled, -tling** [< MDu. *hutsen,* to shake] **1.** to jostle **2.** to force hurriedly **3.** [Colloq.] to get done, sent, made, etc. hurriedly **4.** [Slang] to get, sell, obtain, etc. by aggressive effort or questionable tactics —*vi.* **1.** to move hurriedly **2.** [Colloq.] to work or act rapidly or energetically **3.** [Slang] *a)* to seek or get money, customers, etc. aggressively or by questionable tactics *b)* to work as a prostitute —*n.* **1.** a hustling **2.** [Colloq.] energetic action or effort; drive —**hus'tler** *n.*

hut (hut) *n.* [< OHG. *hutta*] a crude little house

hutch (huch) *n.* [< ML. *hutica,* chest] **1.** a storage chest or bin **2.** a china cabinet with open shelves on top **3.** a coop for small animals **4.** a hut

Hux·ley (huks'lē), **Thomas Henry,** 1825-95; Eng. biologist and writer

Hwang Ho (hwäŋ' hō') river in N China, flowing from Tibet into the Yellow Sea: c.2,900 mi.

hwy. highway

hy·a·cinth (hī'ə sinth') *n.* [< Gr. *hyakinthos*] **1.** *a)* anciently, a certain blue gem, probably the sapphire *b)* a reddish-orange or brownish variety as of zircon, used as a semiprecious stone **2.** a plant related to the lily, with spikes of fragrant, bell-shaped flowers **3.** a bluish purple

hy·brid (hī'brid) *n.* [L. *hybrida*] **1.** the offspring of two animals or plants of different species, varieties, etc. **2.** anything of mixed origin —*adj.* of or being a hybrid

hy'brid·ize (-brə dīz') *vi., vt.* **-ized, -iz'ing** to produce or cause to produce hybrids

Hyde Park (hīd) **1.** public park in London **2.** village in SE N.Y.: site of the estate & burial place of F. D. Roosevelt

Hy·der·a·bad (hī'dər ə bad') city in SC India: pop. 1,119,000

hydr- *same as* HYDRO-: used before vowels

Hy·dra (hī'drə) [< Gr. *hydra,* water serpent] *Gr. Myth.* a nine-headed serpent slain by Hercules: each head grew back double when cut off —*n., pl.* **-dras, -drae** (-drē) [h-] **1.** any persistent or growing evil **2.** a small freshwater polyp with a soft, tubelike body and a mouth surrounded by tentacles

HYDRA
(1/4-1/2
inch in
length)

hy·dran·ge·a (hī drān'jə, -dran'-; -jē ə) *n.* [< HYDR- + Gr. *angeion,* vessel] any of certain shrubby plants with large, showy clusters of white, blue, or pink flowers

hy·drant (hī'drənt) *n.* [< Gr. *hydōr,* water] a large discharge pipe with a valve for drawing water from a water main; fireplug

hy·drate (hī'drāt) *n.* [HYDR- + -ATE[1]] a chemical compound of water and another substance —*vt., vi.* **-drat·ed, -drat·ing 1.** to become or cause to become a hydrate **2.** to combine with water —**hy·dra'tion** *n.*

hy·drau·lic (hī drô'lik) *adj.* [< Gr. *hydōr,* water + *aulos,* tube] **1.** of hydraulics **2.** operated by the movement and pressure of liquid [*hydraulic* brakes] —**hy·drau'li·cal·ly** *adv.*

hy·drau'lics *n.pl.* [*with sing. v.*] the science dealing with the mechanical properties of liquids, as water, and their application in engineering

hy·dride (hī'drīd) *n.* [HYDR- + -IDE] a compound of hydrogen with another element or radical

hydro- [< Gr. *hydōr,* water] *a combining form meaning:* **1.** water [*hydrofoil*] **2.** hydrogen [*hydride*]

hy·dro·car·bon (hī'drə kär'bən) *n.* any compound containing only hydrogen and carbon

hy'dro·chlo'ric acid (-klôr'ik) a strong, highly corrosive acid, HCl, a solution of hydrogen chloride in water

hy'dro·cy·an'ic acid (-sī an'ik) a weak, highly poisonous acid, HCN, a colorless liquid with an almond odor

hy'dro·e·lec'tric *adj.* producing, or relating to the production of, electricity by water power

hy·dro·fluor·ic acid (hī'drə flôr'ik, -floor'-) [HYDRO- + FLUOR(INE) + -IC] an acid, HF, existing as a colorless, fuming, corrosive liquid

hy·dro·foil (hī'drə foil') *n.* [HYDRO- + (AIR)FOIL] **1.** a winglike structure on the hull of some watercraft: at high speeds the craft skims along on the hydrofoils **2.** a craft with hydrofoils

hy·dro·gen (hī'drə jən) *n.* [< Fr.: see HYDRO- & -GEN] a flammable, colorless, odorless gaseous chemical element, the lightest known substance: symbol, H; at. wt., 1.00797; at. no., 1 —**hy·drog·e·nous** (hī dräj'ə nəs) *adj.*

hy·dro·gen·ate (hī'drə jə nāt', hī dräj'ə-) *vt.* **-at'ed, -at'ing** to combine or treat with hydrogen, as in producing a solid fat —**hy'dro·gen·a'tion** *n.*

hydrogen bomb an extremely destructive bomb operating by fusion of the atoms of heavy isotopes of hydrogen through explosion of a nuclear-fission unit

hydrogen peroxide an unstable, colorless, syrupy liquid, H_2O_2, often used diluted as for bleaching

hy·drol·y·sis (hī dräl'ə sis) *n., pl.* **-ses'** (-sēz') [HYDRO- + -LYSIS] the breaking up of a substance into other substances by reaction with water

hy·drom·e·ter (hī dräm'ə tər) *n.* [HYDRO- + -METER] an instrument, typically a graduated, weighted tube, used for measuring the specific gravity of liquids

hy·dro·pho·bi·a (hī'drə fō'bē ə) *n.* [see HYDRO- & -PHOBIA] **1.** abnormal fear of water **2.** rabies

hy·dro·plane (hī'drə plān') *n.* [HYDRO- + PLANE[4]] a small, high-speed motorboat with hydrofoils or with a flat bottom rising in steps to the stern

hy·dro·pon·ics (hī'drə pän'iks) *n.pl.* [*with sing. v.*] [< HYDRO- + Gr. *ponos,* labor + -ICS] the science of growing plants by keeping the roots in nutrient solutions rather than in soil

hy·dro·sphere (hī'drə sfir') *n.* [HYDRO- + SPHERE] **1.** all the water on the surface of the earth **2.** the moisture in the atmosphere of the earth

hy·dro·stat·ics (hī'drə stat'iks) *n.pl.* [*with sing. v.*] [< Fr.: see HYDRO- & STATICS] the science dealing with the pressure and equilibrium of liquids, as water —**hy'dro·stat'ic** *adj.* —**hy'dro·stat'i·cal·ly** *adv.*

hy'dro·ther'a·py (-ther'ə pē) *n.* [HYDRO- + THERAPY] use of baths, compresses, etc. in physical therapy

hy·drous (hī′drəs) *adj.* [HYDR- + -OUS] containing water, as certain chemical compounds

hy·drox·ide (hī dräk′sīd) *n.* [HYDR- + OXIDE] a compound consisting of an element or radical combined with the hydroxyl radical (OH)

hy·drox·yl (-sil) *n.* [HYDR- + OX(YGEN) + -YL] the univalent radical OH, present in all hydroxides

hy·dro·zo·an (hī′drə zō′ən) *adj.* [< HYDRA + ZO(O)- + -AN] of a class of coelenterate animals with a saclike body and with a mouth that opens directly into the body cavity —*n.* an animal of this class

hy·e·na (hī ē′nə) *n.* [< Gr. *hys,* a hog] a carrion-eating mammal of Africa and Asia, having a bristly mane and short hind legs

hy·giene (hī′jēn) *n.* [< Fr. < Gr. *hygiēs,* healthy] 1. a system of principles and practices to preserve health 2. application of such principles and practices —**hy·gi·en·ic** (hī′jē en′ik, -jē′nik, -jen′-) *adj.* —**hy′gi·en′i·cal·ly** *adv.*

hy·gi·en·ist (hī′jē ə nist, -jē nist; hī jē′nist) *n.* a specialist in hygiene

hy·grom·e·ter (hī gräm′ə tər) *n.* [< Fr. < Gr. *hygros,* wet + -METER] an instrument for measuring humidity

hy·gro·scope (hī′grə skōp′) *n.* [< Gr. *hygros,* wet + -SCOPE] an instrument that indicates, without actually measuring, changes in atmospheric humidity

hy·gro·scop·ic (hī′grə skäp′ik) *adj.* 1. of a hygroscope 2. *a)* absorbing moisture from the air *b)* changed by the absorption of moisture

hy·ing (hī′iŋ) *alt. prp. of* HIE

Hy·men (hī′mən) *Gr. Myth.* the god of marriage

hy·men (hī′mən) *n.* [Gr. *hymen,* membrane] a thin mucous membrane closing the vaginal opening partially —**hy′men·al** *adj.*

hy·me·ne·al (hī′mə nē′əl) *adj.* [see HYMEN] of marriage

hy·me·nop·ter·an (hī′mə näp′tər ən) *n.* [< Gr. *hymēn,* membrane + *pteron,* a wing + -AN] any of a large order of highly specialized insects, as wasps, bees, or ants: when winged, they have four membranous wings

hymn (him) *n.* [< Gr. *hymnos*] a song of praise, esp. in honor of God —*vt.* to express or praise in a hymn

hym′nal (-nəl) *n.* a collection of religious hymns: also **hymn′book′** —*adj.* of hymns

hym′nist (-nist) *n.* a composer of hymns

hym′no·dy (-nə dē) *n.* [see HYMN & ODE] 1. the singing of hymns 2. hymns collectively 3. *same as* HYMNOLOGY —**hym′no·dist** *n.*

hym·nol′o·gy (-näl′ə jē) *n.* [see HYMN & -LOGY] 1. the study of hymns, their history, etc. 2. the composition of hymns —**hym·nol′o·gist** *n.*

hype (hīp) *n.* [Slang] 1. *same as* HYPODERMIC 2. a drug addict 3. deception; esp., exaggerated promotion —*vt.* **hyped, hyp′ing** [Slang] 1. to stimulate, enliven, etc. artificially, by or as by drug injection: usually with *up* 2. to promote in a sensational way

hyper- [Gr. *hyper,* over] *a prefix meaning* over, above, excessive [*hypercritical*]

hy·per·a·cid·i·ty (hī′pər ə sid′ə tē) *n.* excessive acidity, as of the gastric juice

hy′per·ac′tive (-ak′tiv) *adj.* excessively active

hy·per·bo·la (hī pur′bə la) *n., pl.* **-las, -lae′** (-lē′) [< Gr. *hyper-,* over + *ballein,* to throw] a curve formed by the section of a cone cut by a plane more steeply inclined to the base than to the side of the cone

hy·per′bo·le (-bə lē) *n.* [L. < Gr.: see prec.] exaggeration for effect, not to be taken literally —**hy·per·bol·ic** (hī′pər bäl′ik) *adj.*

hy·per·bo·re·an (hī′pər bôr′ē ən) *adj.* [< Gr. *hyperboreos,* beyond the north wind] 1. of the far north 2. very cold —*n.* [H-] *Gr. Myth.* an inhabitant of a region of sunshine and eternal spring, beyond the north wind

hy·per·crit·i·cal (hī′pər krit′i k'l) *adj.* too critical

hy·per·me·tro·pi·a (hī′pər mi trō′pē ə) *n.* [< Gr. *hypermetros,* excessive + *ōps,* eye] farsightedness

hy·per·sen·si·tive (hī′pər sen′sə tiv) *adj.* excessively sensitive —**hy′per·sen′si·tiv′i·ty** *n.*

hy·per·son·ic (hī′pər sän′ik) *adj.* designating, of, or moving at a speed equal to about five times the speed of sound or greater: see SONIC

hy·per·ten·sion (hī′pər ten′shən) *n.* abnormally high blood pressure

hy·per·thy·roid·ism (hī′pər thī′roid iz'm) *n.* excessive activity of the thyroid gland, causing nervousness, rapid pulse, etc. —**hy′per·thy′roid** *adj., n.*

hy·per·tro·phy (hī pur′trə fē) *n.* [< HYPER- + Gr. *trophein,* nourish] an abnormal increase in the size of an organ or tissue —*vi., vt.* **-phied, -phy·ing** to undergo or cause to undergo hypertrophy

hy·phen (hī′f'n) *n.* [< Gr. *hypo-,* under + *hen,* one] a mark (-) used between the parts of a compound word or the syllables of a divided word, as at the end of a line —*vt. same as* HYPHENATE

hy′phen·ate′ (-āt′) *vt.* **-at′ed, -at′ing** 1. to connect by a hyphen 2. to write with a hyphen —*adj.* hyphenated —**hy′phen·a′tion** *n.*

hyp·no·sis (hip nō′sis) *n., pl.* **-ses** (-sēz) [< Gr. *hypnos,* sleep + -OSIS] a sleeplike condition artificially induced, in which the subject is in a state of altered consciousness and responds to the suggestions of the hypnotist

hyp·not·ic (hip nät′ik) *adj.* 1. causing sleep; soporific 2. of, like, or inducing hypnosis 3. easily hypnotized —*n.* 1. any agent causing sleep 2. a hypnotized person or one easily hypnotized —**hyp·not′i·cal·ly** *adv.*

hyp·no·tism (hip′nə tiz'm) *n.* the act or practice of inducing hypnosis —**hyp′no·tist** *n.*

hyp′no·tize′ (-tīz′) *vt.* **-tized′, -tiz′ing** 1. to induce hypnosis in 2. to spellbind as by hypnotism

hy·po¹ (hī′pō) *n., pl.* **-pos** (-pōz) *short for* HYPODERMIC

hy·po² (hī′pō) *n. a popular name for* a white, crystalline sodium salt used as a fixing agent in photography, etc.

hypo- [Gr. *hypo,* under] *a prefix meaning:* 1. under, beneath [*hypodermic*] 2. less than, deficient in [*hypothyroid*]

hy·po·chlo·rous acid (hī′pə klôr′əs) [HYPO- + CHLOROUS] an unstable acid, HClO, known only in solution and used as a bleach and oxidizer

hy·po·chon·dri·a (hī′pə kän′drē ə) *n.* [LL., pl., abdomen (supposed seat of this condition)] abnormal anxiety over one's health, often with imaginary illnesses

hy′po·chon′dri·ac′ (-ak′) *adj.* of or having hypochondria: also **hy′po·chon·dri′a·cal** (-kən drī′ə k'l) —*n.* a person who has hypochondria

hy·poc·ri·sy (hi päk′rə sē) *n., pl.* **-sies** [< Gr. *hypokrisis,* acting a part] a pretending to be what one is not, or to feel what one does not feel; esp., a pretense of virtue, piety, etc.

hyp·o·crite (hip′ə krit) *n.* [see prec.] one who pretends to be better than he really is, or to be pious, virtuous, etc. without really being so —**hyp′o·crit′i·cal** *adj.* —**hyp′o·crit′i·cal·ly** *adv.*

hy·po·der·mic (hī′pə dur′mik) *adj.* [< HYPO- + Gr. *derma,* skin] 1. injected under the skin 2. of the parts under the skin —*n. same as:* 1. HYPODERMIC INJECTION 2. HYPODERMIC SYRINGE —**hy′po·der′mi·cal·ly** *adv.*

hypodermic injection the injection of a medicine or drug under the skin

hypodermic syringe a syringe as of glass, attached to a hollow metal needle (**hypodermic needle**), used for giving hypodermic injections

hy·pot·e·nuse (hī pät′'n ōōs′, -yōōs′) *n.* [< Gr. *hypo-,* under + *teinein,* to stretch] the side of a right-angled triangle opposite the right angle: also **hy·poth′e·nuse′** (hī päth′-)

hy·poth·e·sis (hī päth′ə sis, hi-) *n., pl.* **-ses′** (-sēz′) [Gr. < *hypo-,* under + *tithenai,* to place] an unproved theory, etc. tentatively accepted to explain certain facts

HYPOTENUSE / SIDE / BASE

hy·poth′e·size′ (-sīz′) *vi.* **-sized′, -siz′ing** to make a hypothesis —*vt.* to assume; suppose

hy·po·thet·i·cal (hī′pə thet′i k'l) *adj.* 1. based on a hypothesis; assumed; supposed 2. given to the use of hypotheses 3. *Logic* conditional Also **hy′po·thet′ic** —**hy′po·thet′i·cal·ly** *adv.*

hy·po·thy·roid·ism (hī′pō thī′roid iz'm) *n.* deficient activity of the thyroid gland, causing sluggishness, puffiness, etc. —**hy′po·thy′roid** *adj., n.*

hys·sop (his′əp) *n.* [< Heb. *ēzōbh*] a fragrant, blueflowered plant related to the mint

hys·ter·ec·to·my (his′tə rek′tə mē) *n., pl.* **-mies** [< Gr. *hystera,* uterus + -ECTOMY] surgical removal of all or part of the uterus

hys·te·ri·a (his tir′ē ə, -ter′-) *n.* [< Gr. *hystera,* uterus: orig. attributed to disturbances of the uterus] 1. a psychiatric condition characterized by excitability, sensory and motor disturbances, or the unconscious simulation of organic disorders 2. any outbreak of wild, uncontrolled behavior

hys·ter·ic (his ter′ik) *adj. same as* HYSTERICAL —*n.* 1. [*usually pl., occas. with sing. v.*] a hysterical fit 2. a person subject to hysteria

hys·ter′i·cal *adj.* 1. of or like hysteria 2. having or subject to hysteria

Hz, hz hertz

I

I, i (ī) *n., pl.* **I's, i's** the ninth letter of the English alphabet
I¹ (ī) *n.* **1.** a Roman numeral for 1 **2.** *Chem.* iodine
I² (ī) *pron. for pl. see* WE [OE. *ic*] the person speaking or writing —*n., pl.* **I's** the ego; the self
I., i. 1. island(s) **2.** isle(s)
Ia., IA Iowa
I·a·go (ē ä′gō) the villain in Shakespeare's *Othello*
-ial [L. *-ialis, -iale*] *same as* -AL (senses 1, 2)
i·amb (ī′amb, -am) *n.* [< Fr. < Gr. *iambos*] a metrical foot of two syllables, the first unaccented and the other accented: also **i·am′bus** (-bəs), *pl.* **-bus·es, -bi** (-bī)
i·am·bic (ī am′bik) *adj.* of or made up of iambs —*n.* **1.** an iamb **2.** an iambic verse
-ian [< L. *-ianus*] *same as* -AN [*reptilian, Grecian*]
-iatrics [< Gr. *iatros,* physician] *a combining form meaning* treatment of disease [*pediatrics*]
-iatry [< Gr. *iatreia,* healing] *a combining form meaning* medical treatment [*psychiatry*]
I·be·ri·a (ī bir′ē ə) peninsula in SW Europe, comprising Spain & Portugal· also **Iberian Peninsula I·be′ri·an** *adj., n.*
i·bex (ī′beks) *n., pl.* **i′bex·es, i·bi·ces** (ib′ə sēz′, ī′bə-) [L.] a wild goat of Europe, Asia, or Africa: the male has large, backward-curved horns
ibid. [L. *ibidem*] in the same place: used in citing again the book, page, etc. cited ·just before
-ibility *pl.* **-ties** [< L. *-ibilitas*] *a suffix used to form nouns from adjectives ending in* -IBLE [*sensibility*]
i·bis (ī′bis) *n.* [< Egypt.· *hīb*] a large wading bird related to the heron
-ible [L. *-ibilis*] *same as* -ABLE [*legible*]
Ib·sen (ib′s'n), **Hen·rik** (hen′rik) 1828–1906; Norw. playwright & poet
-ic [< Gr. *-ikos*] *a suffix meaning:* **1.** *a)* of, having to do with [*volcanic*] *b)* like [*angelic*] *c)* produced by [*photographic*] *d)* consisting of, containing [*alcoholic*] *e) Chem.* of a higher valence than the compound ending in *-ous* [*nitric*] **2.** a person or thing *a)* having [*paraplegic*] *b)* supporting [*Socratic*] *c)* producing [*hypnotic*] Also **-ical**
Ic·a·rus (ik′ə rəs) *Gr. Myth.* the son of Daedalus: he fell to his death in the sea when he flew too high and the sun melted the wax in the wings his father made for him
ICBM intercontinental ballistic missile
ICC, I.C.C. Interstate Commerce Commission
ice (īs) *n.* [OE. *is*] **1.** water frozen solid by cold **2.** anything like frozen water in appearance, etc. **3.** a frozen dessert, usually of water, fruit juice, and sugar **4.** [Slang] diamonds —*vt.* **iced, ic′ing 1.** to change into ice; freeze **2.** to cool with ice **3.** to cover with ice or icing —*vi.* to freeze (often with *up* or *over*) —**break the ice** to make a start, as in getting acquainted —**cut no ice** [Colloq.] to have no effect —**on thin ice** [Colloq.] in a risky situation
Ice. 1. Iceland **2.** Icelandic
ice age *same as* GLACIAL EPOCH
ice bag a bag, as of rubber, for holding ice, applied to the body, as to reduce a swelling
ice′berg′ (-burg′) *n.* [prob. < Du. *ijsberg,* lit., ice mountain] a great mass of ice broken off from a glacier and floating in the sea
ice′boat′ *n.* a light, boatlike frame equipped with runners and driven over ice by a sail, propeller, etc.
ice′bound′ *adj.* **1.** held fast by ice, as a boat **2.** made inaccessible by ice, as a port
ice′box′ *n.* a cabinet with ice in it for keeping foods, etc. cold; also, any refrigerator
ice′break′er *n.* a sturdy boat for breaking a channel through ice
ice′cap′ *n.* a mass of glacial ice that spreads slowly out from a center
ice cream a sweet, frozen food made from flavored cream or milk —**ice′-cream′** *adj.*

ice floe an extensive area of floating sea ice
ice hockey *same as* HOCKEY (sense 1)
Ice·land (īs′lənd) island country in the N. Atlantic, southeast of Greenland: 39,768 sq. mi.; pop. 204,000; cap. Reykjavik —**Ice′land·er** *n.*
Ice·lan·dic (īs lan′dik) *adj.* of Iceland, its people, etc. —*n.* the Germanic language of the Icelanders
ice·man (īs′man′, -mən) *n., pl.* **-men′** a person who sells or delivers ice
ice pack 1. a large, floating expanse of ice masses frozen together **2.** a bag, etc. filled with crushed ice and applied to the body, as to reduce swelling
ice skate a skate for skating on ice: see SKATE¹ (sense 1) —**ice′skate′** *vi.* **-skat′ed, -skat′ing**
ich·neu·mon fly (ik nyōō′mən, -nōō′-) [< Gr. *ichneumōn,* lit., tracker] a hymenopteran insect whose larvae live as parasites in or on other insect larvae
ich·thy·ol·o·gy (ik′thē äl′ə jē) *n.* [< Gr. *ichthys,* a fish + -LOGY] the branch of zoology dealing with fishes —**ich′-thy·ol′o·gist** *n.*
i·ci·cle (ī′si k'l) *n.* [< OE. *is,* ice + *gicel,* piece of ice] a hanging piece of ice, formed by the freezing of dripping water —**i′ci·cled** *adj.*
ic·ing (ī′siŋ) *n.* a mixture, as of sugar, butter, flavoring, etc., as for covering a cake; frosting
ick·y (ik′ē) *adj.* **-i·er, -i·est** [< STICKY] [Slang] **1.** unpleasantly sticky or sweet **2.** very distasteful
i·con (ī′kän) *n.* [< Gr. *eikōn,* image] **1.** an image; figure **2.** *Orthodox Eastern Ch.* an image or picture of Jesus, Mary, a saint, etc., venerated as sacred
i·con·o·clast (ī kän′ə klast′) *n.* [< LGr. *eikōn,* image + *klaein,* to break] one who attacks or ridicules traditional or venerated institutions or ideas —**i·con′o·clasm** *n.* —**i·con′o·clas′tic** *adj.*
-ics [see -IC] *a suffix meaning* art, science, study [*physics, economics*]
i·cy (ī′sē) *adj.* **i′ci·er, i′ci·est 1.** full of or covered with ice **2.** of ice **3.** like ice; slippery or very cold **4.** cold in manner; unfriendly —**i′ci·ly** *adv.* —**i′ci·ness** *n.*
id (id) *n.* [L., it] *Psychoanalysis* that part of the psyche which is the source of the instinctual drives
ID, I.D. identification
id. [L. *idem*] the same
I'd (īd) **1.** I had **2.** I would **3.** I should
I·da·ho (ī′də hō′) State of the NW U.S., one of the Mountain States: 83,557 sq. mi.; pop. 713,000; cap. Boise: abbrev. **Ida., ID** —**I′da·ho′an** *adj., n.*
-ide [< (OX)IDE] *a suffix added to part of the name of* the nonmetallic or electronegative element or radical in a binary compound [*sodium chloride*] *or used in forming the name of* a class of related compounds [*glucoside*]
i·de·a (ī dē′ə) *n.* [< Gr. *idea,* appearance of a thing] **1.** a thought; mental conception or image **2.** an opinion or belief **3.** a plan or scheme **4.** a vague impression **5.** meaning or significance
i·de·al (ī dē′əl, ī dēl′) *adj.* [see prec.] **1.** existing as an idea, model, etc. **2.** thought of as perfect **3.** existing only in the mind; imaginary **4.** *Philos.* of idealism —*n.* **1.** a conception of something in its most excellent form **2.** a perfect model **3.** a goal or principle
i·de′al·ism *n.* **1.** behavior or thought based on a conception of things as one thinks they should be **2.** a striving to achieve one's ideals **3.** *Philos.* any theory which holds that things exist only as ideas in the mind or·that things are really imperfect imitations of unchanging forms existing independently of the material world —**i·de′al·ist** *n.* —**i′de·al·is′tic** *adj.* —**i′de·al·is′ti·cal·ly** *adv.*
i·de·al·ize (ī dē′ə līz′) *vt.* **-ized′, -iz′ing** to regard or show as perfect or more nearly perfect than is true —**i·de′al·i·za′tion** *n.*
i·de′al·ly *adv.* **1.** in an ideal manner; perfectly **2.** in theory

‡**i·dée fixe** (ē dā fēks′) [Fr.] a fixed idea; obsession

i·den·ti·cal (ī den′ti k′l) *adj.* [< L. *idem*, the same] **1.** the very same **2.** exactly alike —**i·den′ti·cal·ly** *adv.*

i·den·ti·fi·ca·tion (ī den′tə fi kā′shən) *n.* **1.** an identifying or being identified **2.** anything by which a person or thing can be identified

i·den·ti·fy (ī den′tə fī′) *vt.* -**fied′**, -**fy′ing 1.** to make identical; treat as the same **2.** to fix the identity of **3.** to connect or associate closely —*vi.* to understand and share another's feelings; sympathize (*with*) —**i·den′ti·fi′a·ble** *adj.*

i·den·ti·ty (-tē) *n., pl.* -**ties 1.** the state or fact of being the same **2.** *a*) the state or fact of being a specific person or thing; individuality *b*) the state of being as described

id·e·ol·o·gy (ī′dē äl′ə jē, id′ē-) *n., pl.* -**gies** [< Gr. *idea*, idea + *logos*, word] the doctrines, opinions, or way of thinking of an individual, class, etc. —**i′de·o·log′i·cal** (-ə läj′i k′l) *adj.*

ides (īdz) *n.pl.* [*often with sing. v.*] [Fr. < L. *idus*] in the ancient Roman calendar, the 15th day of March, May, July, or October, or the 13th of the other months

id·i·o·cy (id′ē ə sē) *n.* **1.** the state of being an idiot **2.** great foolishness or stupidity **3.** *pl.* -**cies** an idiotic act or remark

id·i·om (id′ē əm) *n.* [< Fr. < Gr. *idios*, one's own] **1.** the dialect of a people, region, etc. **2.** the usual way in which words of a language are joined together to express thought **3.** an accepted phrase or expression having a meaning different from the literal **4.** a characteristic style, as in art or music

id·i·o·mat·ic (id′ē ə mat′ik) *adj.* **1.** characteristic of a particular language **2.** of, like, or using idioms —**id′i·o·mat′i·cal·ly** *adv.*

id·i·o·syn·cra·sy (id′ē ə siŋ′krə sē) *n., pl.* -**sies** [< Gr. *idio-*, one's own + *synkrasis*, a mixture] any personal peculiarity, mannerism, etc. —**id′i·o·syn·crat′ic** (-sin krat′ik) *adj.*

id·i·ot (id′ē ət) *n.* [< Gr. *idiōtēs*, ignorant person] **1.** a person having severe mental retardation: an obsolescent term **2.** a very foolish or stupid person

id·i·ot·ic (id′ē ät′ik) *adj.* very foolish or stupid —**id′i·ot′i·cal·ly** *adv.*

i·dle (ī′d'l) *adj.* **i′dler, i′dlest** [OE. *idel*, empty] **1.** worthless; futile **2.** unfounded [*idle* rumors] **3.** *a*) unemployed *b*) not in use **4.** lazy —*vi.* **i′dled, i′dling 1.** to move slowly or aimlessly **2.** to be unemployed or inactive **3.** to operate without transmitting any power, esp. with disengaged gears —*vt.* **1.** to waste; squander **2.** to cause (a motor, etc.) to idle **3.** to make inactive or unemployed —**i′dle·ness** *n.* —**i′dler** *n.* —**i′dly** *adv.*

i·dol (ī′d'l) *n.* [< Gr. *eidōlon*, an image] **1.** an image of a god, used as an object of worship **2.** an object of excessive devotion or admiration

i·dol·a·ter (ī däl′ə tər) *n.* **1.** a worshiper of idols **2.** a devoted admirer; adorer —**i·dol′a·tress** (-tris) *n.fem.*

i·dol·a·try (-trē) *n., pl.* -**tries 1.** worship of idols **2.** excessive devotion or reverence —**i·dol′a·trous** *adj.*

i·dol·ize (ī′d'l īz′) *vt.* -**ized′**, -**iz′ing 1.** to make an idol of **2.** to love or admire excessively —**i′dol·i·za′tion** *n.*

i·dyll, i·dyl (ī′d'l) *n.* [< Gr. *eidos*, a form] **1.** a short poem or prose work describing a simple, pleasant scene of rural or pastoral life **2.** a scene or incident suitable for such a work —**i·dyl·lic** (ī dil′ik) *adj.*

-ie [earlier form of -Y¹] *a suffix meaning:* **1.** small, little [*lassie*] **2.** one that is as specified [*softie*]

i.e. [L. *id est*] that is (to say)

-ier [< L. *-arius*] *a suffix meaning* a person concerned with (a specified action or thing) [*bombardier*]

if (if) *conj.* [OE. *gif*] **1.** on condition that; in case that [*if* I come, I'll see him] **2.** granting that [*if* he was there, I didn't see him] **3.** whether [ask him *if* he knows her] —*n.* **1.** a supposition **2.** a condition —**as if** as the situation would be if

if·fy (if′ē) *adj.* [Colloq.] full of uncertainty

ig·loo (ig′lōō) *n., pl.* -**loos** [Esk. *igdlu*, snow house] an Eskimo house or hut, usually dome-shaped and built of blocks of packed snow

Ig·na·tius (of) Loy·o·la (ig nā′shəs loi ō′lə), Saint 1491–1556; Sp. founder of the Jesuit order

ig·ne·ous (ig′nē əs) *adj.* [< L. *ignis*, a fire] **1.** of, like, or containing fire **2.** produced by volcanic action or intense heat [*igneous* rock]

IGLOO

ig·nis fat·u·us (ig′nis fach′oo wəs) *pl.* **ig·nes fat·u·i** (ig′nēz fach′oo wī′) [< L. *ignis*, a fire + *fatuus*, foolish] a light seen at night moving over swamps, etc.: popularly called *will-o′-the-wisp*

ig·nite (ig nīt′) *vt., vi.* -**nit′ed**, -**nit′ing** [< L. *ignis*, a fire] **1.** to start burning **2.** to get excited —**ig·nit′a·ble, ig·nit′i·ble** *adj.* —**ig·nit′er, ig·ni′tor** *n.*

ig·ni·tion (ig nish′ən) *n.* **1.** an igniting or means of igniting **2.** the system for igniting the explosive mixture in the cylinder of an internal-combustion engine

ig·no·ble (ig nō′b'l) *adj.* [< L. *in-*, not + (*g*)*nobilis*, known] not noble; base; mean —**ig·no′bly** *adv.*

ig·no·min·i·ous (ig′nə min′ē əs) *adj.* **1.** shameful; disgraceful **2.** despicable **3.** degrading —**ig′no·min′i·ous·ly** *adv.*

ig·no·min·y (ig′nə min′ē) *n., pl.* -**ies** [< Fr. < L. *in-*, without + *nomen*, name] **1.** loss of reputation; shame; disgrace **2.** shameful quality or action

ig·no·ra·mus (ig′nə rā′məs, -ram′əs) *n., pl.* -**mus·es** an ignorant person

ig·no·rance (ig′nər əns) *n.* the condition or quality of being ignorant; lack of knowledge

ig′no·rant *adj.* [see IGNORE] **1.** lacking knowledge or experience **2.** caused by or showing lack of these **3.** unaware (*of*) —**ig′no·rant·ly** *adv.*

ig·nore (ig nôr′) *vt.* -**nored′**, -**nor′ing** [< Fr. < L. *in-*, not + *gnarus*, knowing] to disregard deliberately; pay no attention to —**ig·nor′er** *n.*

I·go·rot (ig′ə rōt′, ē′gə-) *n.* **1.** *pl.* -**rots′**, -**rot′** a member of a Malayan people of Luzon, in the Philippines **2.** their Indonesian language

i·gua·na (i gwä′nə) *n.* [Sp. < SAmInd. *iuana*] a large, harmless, tropical American lizard

IHS a contraction misread from the Greek word for Jesus, used as a symbol or monogram

i·kon (ī′kän) *n. var. of* ICON

il- *same as:* **1.** IN-¹ **2.** IN-² Used before *l*

il·e·um (il′ē əm) *n., pl.* **il′e·a** (-ə) [< L., flank, groin (var. of *ilium*)] the lowest part of the small intestine

i·lex (ī′leks) *n.* [L.] *same as:* **1.** HOLLY **2.** HOLM OAK

Il·i·ad (il′ē əd) [< Gr. *Ilios*, Troy] a long Greek epic poem, ascribed to Homer, about the final part of the Trojan War

LAND IGUANA
(to 5 ft. long)

-ility *pl.* -**ties** *a suffix used in nouns formed from adjectives ending in* -ile, -il

il·i·um (il′ē əm) *n., pl.* **il′i·a** (-ə) [see ILEUM] the flat, uppermost section of the innominate bone

ilk (ilk) *n.* [< OE. *ilca*, same] kind; sort; class: only in **of that** (or **his, her,** etc.) **ilk**

ill (il) *adj.* **worse, worst** [< ON. *illr*] **1.** bad [*ill* repute, *ill* will, an *ill* omen, etc.] **2.** not healthy; sick **3.** improper [*ill* breeding] —*n.* anything causing harm, pain, etc.; evil —*adv.* **worse, worst 1.** badly **2.** scarcely —**ill at ease** uneasy; uncomfortable

I'll (īl) **1.** I shall **2.** I will

Ill. Illinois

ill. 1. illustrated **2.** illustration

ill′-ad·vised′ *adj.* resulting from a lack of sound advice or proper consideration; unwise

ill′-bred′ *adj.* badly brought up; rude

ill′-con·sid′ered *adj.* not properly considered; not suitable or wise

il·le·gal (i lē′gəl) *adj.* not lawful; against the law —**il·le·gal·i·ty** (il′ē gal′ə tē) *n., pl.* -**ties** —**il·le′gal·ly** *adv.*

il·leg·i·ble (i lej′ə b'l) *adj.* difficult or impossible to read because badly written or printed —**il·leg′i·bil′i·ty** *n.* —**il·leg′i·bly** *adv.*

il·le·git·i·mate (il′ə jit′ə mit) *adj.* **1.** born of parents not married to each other **2.** not lawful **3.** unsanctioned —**il′le·git′i·ma·cy** (-mə sē) *n., pl.* -**cies** —**il′le·git′i·mate·ly** *adv.*

ill′-fat′ed *adj.* **1.** having or sure to have an evil fate or unlucky end **2.** unlucky

ill′-fa′vored *adj.* ugly or unpleasant

ill′-found′ed *adj.* not supported by facts or sound reasons

ill′-got′ten *adj.* obtained by evil, unlawful, or dishonest means [*ill-gotten* gains]

ill humor a disagreeable, cross, or sullen mood —**ill′-hu′mored** *adj.* —**ill′-hu′mored·ly** *adv.*

il·lib·er·al (i lib′ər əl) *adj.* **1.** narrow-minded **2.** miserly

il·lic·it (i lis′it) *adj.* not allowed by law, custom, etc.; unlawful —**il·lic′it·ly** *adv.*

il·lim·it·a·ble (i lim′it ə b′l) *adj.* without limit or bounds —**il·lim′it·a·bly** *adv.*

Il·li·nois (il′ə noi′; *occas.* -noiz′) Middle Western State of the U.S.: 56,400 sq. mi.; pop. 11,114,000; cap. Springfield: abbrev. Ill., IL —Il′li·nois′an *adj., n.*

il·lit·er·ate (i lit′ər it) *adj.* uneducated; esp., not knowing how to read or write —*n.* an illiterate person —**il·lit′er·a·cy** (-ə sē) *n.* —**il·lit′er·ate·ly** *adv.*

ill′-man′nered *adj.* rude; impolite

ill nature an unpleasant, disagreeable, or mean disposition —**ill′-na′tured** *adj.*

ill′ness *n.* the condition of being ill; sickness

il·log·i·cal (i läj′i k′l) *adj.* not logical; using or based on faulty reasoning —**il·log′i·cal·ly** *adv.*

ill′-starred′ *adj.* unlucky; doomed

ill′-tem′pered *adj.* bad-tempered

ill′-timed′ *adj.* inopportune

ill′-treat′ *vt.* to treat unkindly, cruelly, or unfairly; abuse —**ill′-treat′ment** *n.*

il·lu·mi·nant (i lōō′mə nənt) *adj.* giving light; illuminating —*n.* something that gives light

il·lu′mi·nate′ (-nāt′) *vt.* **-nat′ed, -nat′ing** [< L. *in-*, in + *luminare*, to light] **1.** to give light to; light up **2.** *a*) to make clear; explain *b*) to inform **3.** to decorate with lights **4.** to decorate (an initial letter, etc.) with designs of gold, bright colors, etc. —**il·lu′mi·na′tive** *adj.*

il·lu′mi·na′tion *n.* **1.** an illuminating or being illuminated **2.** the intensity of light per unit of area **3.** the designs used in illuminating manuscripts

il·lu′mine (-min) *vt.* **-mined, -min·ing** *same as* ILLUMINATE —**il·lu′mi·na·ble** *adj.*

illus., illust. illustration

ill-us·age (il′yōō′sij, -zij) *n.* unfair, unkind, or cruel treatment; abuse: also **ill usage**

ill′-use′ (-yōōz′) *vt.* **-used′, -us′ing** to subject to ill-usage —*n.* (-yōōs′) *same as* ILL-USAGE

il·lu·sion (i lōō′zhən) *n.* [< L. *illudere*, to mock] **1.** a false idea or conception **2.** an unreal or misleading appearance or image **3.** a false perception of what one sees —**il·lu′so·ry** (-sər ē), **il·lu′sive** (-siv) *adj.*

il·lu′sion·ist *n.* an entertainer who performs sleight-of-hand tricks

il·lus·trate (il′ə strāt′, i lus′trāt) *vt.* **-trat′ed, -trat′ing** [< L. *in-*, in + *lustrare*, illuminate] **1.** to make clear or explain, as by examples or comparisons **2.** to furnish (books, etc.) with explanatory or decorative drawings, pictures, etc. —**il′lus·tra′tor** *n.*

il′lus·tra′tion *n.* **1.** an illustrating or being illustrated **2.** an explanatory example, story, etc. **3.** an explanatory or decorative picture, diagram, etc.

il·lus·tra·tive (i lus′trə tiv) *adj.* serving to illustrate —**il·lus′tra·tive·ly** *adv.*

il·lus·tri·ous (i lus′trē əs) *adj.* [< L. *illustris*, bright] very distinguished; famous; eminent —**il·lus′tri·ous·ly** *adv.* —**il·lus′tri·ous·ness** *n.*

ill will hostility; hate; dislike

I'm (īm) I am

im- *same as:* **1.** IN-1 **2.** IN-2 Used before *b, m,* and *p*

im·age (im′ij) *n.* [< L. *imago*] **1.** a representation of a person or thing; esp., a statue **2.** the visual impression of something in a lens, mirror, etc. **3.** a copy; likeness **4.** a mental picture; idea **5.** a type; embodiment *[the image of laziness]* **6.** a figure of speech —*vt.* **-aged, -ag·ing 1.** to portray; delineate **2.** to reflect **3.** to imagine

im·age·ry (im′ij rē) *n., pl.* **-ries 1.** mental images **2.** descriptions and figures of speech

i·mag·i·na·ble (i maj′ə nə b′l) *adj.* that can be imagined —**i·mag′i·na·bly** *adv.*

i·mag′i·nar′y (-ner′ē) *adj.* existing only in the imagination; unreal

i·mag·i·na′tion (-nā′shən) *n.* **1.** *a*) the act or power of forming mental images of what is not actually present *b*) the act or power of creating new ideas by combining previous experiences **2.** responsiveness to the imaginative creations of others **3.** resourcefulness in dealing with new experiences

i·mag′i·na·tive (-nə tiv) *adj.* **1.** having, using, or showing imagination **2.** of or resulting from imagination —**i·mag′i·na·tive·ly** *adv.*

i·mag·ine (i maj′in) *vt., vi.* **-ined, -in·ing** [< L. *imago*, image] **1.** to make a mental image (of); conceive in the mind **2.** to suppose; think

im·be·cile (im′bə s′l) *n.* [< Fr. < L. *imbecilis*, feeble] **1.** an adult mentally equal to a child between three and

eight: an obsolescent term **2.** a foolish or stupid person —*adj.* foolish or stupid: also **im′be·cil′ic** (-sil′ik) —**im′be·cil′i·ty** *n.*

im·bed (im bed′) *vt. same as* EMBED

im·bibe (im bīb′) *vt.* **-bibed′, -bib′ing** [< L. *in-*, in + *bibere*, drink] **1.** *a*) to drink (esp. alcoholic liquor) *b*) to drink in **2.** to absorb (moisture) —*vi.* to drink, esp. alcoholic liquor —**im·bib′er** *n.*

im·bro·glio (im brōl′yō) *n., pl.* **-glios** [It. < *imbrogliare*, embroil] **1.** an involved and confusing situation **2.** a confused misunderstanding or disagreement

im·brue (im brōō′) *vt.* **-brued′, -bru′ing** [< L. *imbibere*: see IMBIBE] to wet or stain, esp. with blood

im·bue (im byōō′) *vt.* **-bued′, -bu′ing** [< L. *imbuere*, to wet] **1.** to fill with color; dye **2.** to permeate or inspire *(with* principles, ideas, etc.)

im·i·tate (im′ə tāt′) *vt.* **-tat′ed, -tat′ing** [< L. *imitari*, imitate] **1.** to follow the example of **2.** to act the same as; mimic **3.** to copy the form, color, etc. of **4.** to resemble —**im′i·ta·tor** *n.*

im′i·ta′tion *n.* **1.** an imitating **2.** the result of imitating; copy —*adj.* made to resemble something usually superior or genuine *[imitation* leather*]*

im′i·ta′tive *adj.* **1.** formed from a model **2.** given to imitating

im·mac·u·late (i mak′yə lit) *adj.* [< L. *in-*, not + *macula*, a spot] **1.** perfectly clean **2.** without flaw **3.** pure; innocent; sinless —**im·mac′u·late·ly** *adv.* —**im·mac′u·late·ness** *n.*

Immaculate Conception *R.C.Ch.* the doctrine that the Virgin Mary was from the moment of conception free from original sin

im·ma·nent (im′ə nənt) *adj.* [< L. *in-*, in + *manere*, remain] **1.** remaining or operating within; inherent **2.** present throughout the universe: said of God —**im′ma·nence** *n.* —**im′ma·nent·ly** *adv.*

Im·man·u·el (i man′yoo wəl) a name given to the Messiah (Isa. 7:14), often applied to Jesus (Matt. 1:23)

im·ma·te·ri·al (im′ə tir′ē əl) *adj.* **1.** spiritual **2.** unimportant

im·ma·ture (im′ə toor′, -choor′, -tyoor′) *adj.* **1.** not mature or ripe; not completely developed **2.** not finished or perfected —**im′ma·tu′ri·ty** *n.*

im·meas·ur·a·ble (i mezh′ər ə b′l) *adj.* not measurable; boundless; vast —**im·meas′ur·a·bly** *adv.*

im·me·di·a·cy (i mē′dē ə sē) *n.* a being immediate; esp., direct relevance to the present time, etc.

im·me′di·ate (-it) *adj.* [see IN-2 & MEDIATE] **1.** not separated in space or time; closest **2.** without delay; instant **3.** next in order **4.** directly or closely related **5.** directly affecting; direct —**im·me′di·ate·ly** *adv.*

im·me·mo·ri·al (im′ə môr′ē əl) *adj.* back beyond memory or record —**im′me·mo′ri·al·ly** *adv.*

im·mense (i mens′) *adj.* [Fr. < L. *in-*, not + *metiri*, to measure] very large; vast; huge —**im·mense′ly** *adv.* —**im·mense′ness** *n.*

im·men′si·ty *n., pl.* **-ties 1.** great size or extent **2.** infinite space or being

im·merse (i murs′) *vt.* **-mersed′, -mers′ing** [< L. *immergere*] **1.** to plunge into or as if into a liquid **2.** to baptize by dipping under water **3.** to absorb deeply; engross *[immersed* in study*]* —**im·mer′sion** *n.*

im·mi·grant (im′ə grənt) *n.* one that immigrates —*adj.* immigrating

im′mi·grate′ (-grāt′) *vi.* **-grat′ed, -grat′ing** [see IN-1 & MIGRATE] to come into a new country, etc. in order to settle there —**im′mi·gra′tion** *n.*

im·mi·nent (im′ə nənt) *adj.* [< L. *in-*, on + *minere*, to project] likely to happen soon: said of danger, evil, etc. —**im′mi·nence** *n.* —**im′mi·nent·ly** *adv.*

im·mis·ci·ble (i mis′ə b′l) *adj.* [< IN-2 + MISCIBLE] that cannot be mixed, as oil and water —**im·mis′ci·bil′i·ty** *n.*

im·mo·bile (i mō′b′l) *adj.* **1.** firmly placed; stable **2.** motionless —**im′mo·bil′i·ty** *n.*

im·mo′bi·lize′ (-bə līz′) *vt.* **-lized′, -liz′ing 1.** to make immobile **2.** to prevent the movement of (a limb or joint) with splints or a cast —**im·mo′bi·li·za′tion** *n.*

im·mod·er·ate (i mäd′ər it) *adj.* without restraint; excessive —**im·mod′er·ate·ly** *adv.*

im·mod·est (i mäd′ist) *adj.* **1.** indecent; improper **2.** bold; forward —**im·mod′est·ly** *adv.* —**im·mod′es·ty** *n.*

im·mo·late (im′ə lāt′) *vt.* **-lat′ed, -lat′ing** [< L. *immolare*, sprinkle with sacrificial meal] to kill as a sacrifice —**im′mo·la′tion** *n.*

im·mor·al (i môr′əl) *adj.* not moral; specif., unchaste; lewd —**im·mor′al·ly** *adv.*

im·mo·ral·i·ty (im′ə ral′ə tē) *n.* **1.** a being immoral **2.** immoral behavior **3.** *pl.* **-ties** an immoral act or practice

im·mor·tal (i môr′t'l) *adj.* **1.** not mortal; living or lasting forever **2.** enduring **3.** having lasting fame —*n.* an immortal being —**im′mor·tal′i·ty** (-tal′ə tē) *n.* —**im·mor′tal·ly** *adv.*

im·mor′tal·ize (i môr′tə līz′) *vt.* **-ized′, -iz′ing** to make immortal; esp., to give lasting fame to

im·mov·a·ble (i mōōv′ə b'l) *adj.* **1.** firmly fixed **2.** motionless **3.** unyielding; steadfast **4.** unemotional; impassive —*n.* [*pl.*] *Law* immovable objects or property, as land, buildings, etc. —**im·mov′a·bly** *adv.*

im·mune (i myōōn′) *adj.* [< L. *in-*, without + *munia*, duties] **1.** exempt from or protected against something disagreeable or harmful **2.** not susceptible to a specified disease

immune body *same as* ANTIBODY

im·mu·ni·ty (i myōōn′ə tē) *n., pl.* **-ties 1.** exemption from something burdensome, as a legal obligation **2.** resistance to a specified disease

im·mu·nize (im′yə nīz′) *vt.* **-nized′, -niz′ing** to give immunity to —**im′mu·ni·za′tion** *n.*

im·mu·nol·o·gy (im′yoo näl′ə jē) *n.* the branch of medicine dealing with immunity to disease or with allergic reactions —**im′mu·nol′o·gist** *n.*

im·mure (i myoor′) *vt.* **-mured′, -mur′ing** [< L. *im-*, in + *murus*, a wall] to shut up as within walls; confine

im·mu·ta·ble (i myōōt′ə b'l) *adj.* unchangeable —**im·mu′ta·bil′i·ty** *n.* —**im·mu′ta·bly** *adv.*

imp (imp) *n.* [< Gr. *em-*, in + *phyton*, a plant] **1.** a young demon **2.** a mischievous child

imp. 1. imperative **2.** imperfect **3.** import **4.** imprimatur

im·pact (im pakt′) *vt.* [< L. *impingere*, press firmly together] to force tightly together —*n.* (im′pakt) **1.** a striking together **2.** the force of a collision; shock **3.** a shocking effect —**im·pac′tion** *n.*

im·pact′ed (-pak′tid) *adj.* abnormally lodged in the jaw: said of a tooth unable to erupt

im·pair (im per′) *vt.* [< L. *in-*, in-tens. + *pejor*, worse] to make worse, less, etc.; damage —**im·pair′ment** *n.*

im·pa·la (im pä′lə) *n., pl.* **-la, -las** a medium-sized, reddish antelope of C and S Africa

im·pale (im pāl′) *vt.* **-paled′, -pal′ing** [< Fr. < L. *in-*, on + *palus*, a pole] **1.** to pierce through with, or fix on, something pointed **2.** to torture by fixing on a stake **3.** to make helpless, as if fixed on a stake [*impaled* by her glance*]* —**im·pale′ment** *n.*

IMPACTED TOOTH

im·pal·pa·ble (im pal′pə b'l) *adj.* **1.** not perceptible to the touch **2.** too subtle to be easily understood

im·pan·el (im pan′'l) *vt.* **-eled** or **-elled, -el·ing** or **-el·ling 1.** to enter the name or names of on a jury list **2.** to choose (a jury) from such a list

im·part (im pärt′) *vt.* [see IN-¹ & PART] **1.** to give a share of; give **2.** to tell; reveal

im·par·tial (im pär′shəl) *adj.* without bias; fair —**im·par′ti·al′i·ty** (-shē al′ə tē) *n.* —**im·par′tial·ly** *adv.*

im·pass·a·ble (im pas′ə b'l) *adj.* that cannot be passed, crossed, or traveled over

im·passe (im′pas, im pas′) *n.* [Fr.] a situation offering no escape; deadlock

im·pas·si·ble (im pas′ə b'l) *adj.* [< L. *im-*, not + *pati*, suffer] **1.** that cannot feel pain or be injured **2.** that cannot be moved emotionally

im·pas·sioned (im pash′ənd) *adj.* passionate; fiery; ardent —**im·pas′sioned·ly** *adv.*

im·pas·sive (im pas′iv) *adj.* **1.** not feeling pain **2.** not feeling or showing emotion; calm —**im·pas′sive·ly** *adv.* —**im·pas·siv·i·ty** (im′pə siv′ə tē) *n.*

im·pa·tience (im pā′shəns) *n.* **1.** annoyance because of delay, opposition, etc. **2.** restless eagerness to do something

im·pa′tient (-shənt) *adj.* feeling or showing impatience —**im·pa′tient·ly** *adv.*

im·peach (im pēch′) *vt.* [< L. *in-*, in + *pedica*, a fetter] **1.** to discredit (a person's honor, etc.) **2.** to bring (a public official) before the proper tribunal on a charge of wrongdoing —**im·peach′a·ble** *adj.* —**im·peach′ment** *n.*

im·pec·ca·ble (im pek′ə b'l) *adj.* [< L. *in-*, not + *peccare*, to sin] without defect or error; flawless —**im·pec′ca·bil′i·ty** *n.* —**im·pec′ca·bly** *adv.*

im·pe·cu·ni·ous (im′pi kyōō′nē əs) *adj.* [< L. *in-*, not + *pecunia*, money] having no money; poor

im·ped·ance (im pēd′'ns) *n.* [IMPED(E) + -ANCE] the total opposition in an electric circuit to the flow of an alternating current of a single frequency

im·pede (im pēd′) *vt.* **-ped′ed, -ped′ing** [< L. *in-*, in + *pes*, foot] to hinder the progress of; obstruct

im·ped·i·ment (im ped′ə mənt) *n.* anything that impedes; specif., a speech defect

im·ped·i·men·ta (im ped′ə men′tə) *n.pl.* [L.] things hindering progress, as on a trip; esp., baggage, supplies, etc.

im·pel (im pel′) *vt.* **-pelled′, -pel′ling** [< L. *in-*, on + *pellere*, to drive] **1.** to push, drive, or move forward; propel **2.** to force, compel, or urge

im·pend (im pend′) *vi.* [< L. *in-*, in + *pendere*, hang] to be about to happen; threaten [*impending* disaster*]*

im·pen·e·tra·ble (im pen′i trə b'l) *adj.* **1.** that cannot be penetrated **2.** that cannot be solved or understood **3.** unreceptive to ideas, influences, etc. —**im·pen′e·tra·bil′i·ty** *n.* —**im·pen′e·tra·bly** *adv.*

im·pen·i·tent (im pen′ə tənt) *adj.* without regret, shame, or remorse —**im·pen′i·tence** *n.* —**im·pen′i·tent·ly** *adv.*

im·per·a·tive (im per′ə tiv) *adj.* [< L. *imperare*, to order] **1.** of or indicating power or authority; commanding **2.** absolutely necessary; urgent **3.** *Gram.* designating or of a verb mood expressing a command, etc. —*n.* **1.** a command **2.** *Gram. a)* the imperative mood *b)* a verb in this mood —**im·per′a·tive·ly** *adv.*

im·pe·ra·tor (im′pə rāt′ər) *n.* [L. < *imperare*, to command] in ancient Rome, a title of honor for generals and, later, emperors

im·per·cep·ti·ble (im′pər sep′tə b'l) *adj.* not easily perceived by the senses or mind; very slight, subtle, etc. —**im′per·cep′ti·bly** *adv.*

im·per·fect (im pur′fikt) *adj.* **1.** not complete **2.** not perfect **3.** *Gram.* designating or of a verb tense indicating an incomplete or continuous past action: "was writing" is a form in the imperfect tense —*n. Gram.* **1.** the imperfect tense **2.** a verb in this tense —**im·per′fect·ly** *adv.* —**im·per′fect·ness** *n.*

im·per·fec·tion (im′pər fek′shən) *n.* **1.** a being imperfect **2.** a shortcoming; defect

im·per·fo·rate (im pur′fər it, -fə rāt′) *adj.* **1.** having no holes or openings **2.** having a straight edge without perforations: said of a postage stamp —**im·per′fo·ra′tion** *n.*

im·pe·ri·al (im pir′ē əl) *adj.* [< L. *imperium*, empire] **1.** of an empire, emperor, or empress **2.** having supreme authority **3.** majestic; august **4.** of great size or superior quality **5.** of a British system of weights and measures —*n.* a pointed tuft of beard on the lower lip and chin —**im·pe′ri·al·ly** *adv.*

im·pe′ri·al·ism *n.* **1.** imperial state, authority, or government **2.** the policy of forming and maintaining an empire by conquest, colonization, economic domination, etc. —**im·pe′ri·al·ist** *n., adj.* —**im·pe′ri·al·is′tic** *adj.*

im·per·il (im per′əl) *vt.* **-iled** or **-illed, -il·ing** or **-il·ling** to put in peril —**im·per′il·ment** *n.*

im·pe·ri·ous (im pir′ē əs) *adj.* [< L. *imperium*, empire] **1.** arrogant; domineering **2.** urgent —**im·pe′ri·ous·ly** *adv.*

im·per·ish·a·ble (im per′ish ə b'l) *adj.* that will not die or decay; indestructible; immortal —**im·per′ish·a·bly** *adv.*

im·per·ma·nent (im pur′mə nənt) *adj.* not permanent; not lasting; temporary —**im·per′ma·nence** *n.*

im·per·me·a·ble (im pur′mē ə b'l) *adj.* not permeable; not permitting passage, esp. of fluids —**im·per′me·a·bil′i·ty** *n.* —**im·per′me·a·bly** *adv.*

im·per·son·al (im pur′s'n əl) *adj.* **1.** without reference to any particular person [an *impersonal* comment*]* **2.** not existing as a person **3.** *Gram.* designating or of a verb occurring only in the third person singular (Ex.: "it is snowing") —**im·per·son·al·i·ty** (-al′ə tē) *n.* —**im·per′son·al·ly** *adv.*

im·per·son·ate (im pur′sə nāt′) *vt.* **-at′ed, -at′ing** to assume the role of, theatrically or fraudulently; mimic —**im·per′son·a′tion** *n.* —**im·per′son·a′tor** *n.*

im·per·ti·nence (im pur′t'n əns) *n.* **1.** a being impertinent; specif., *a)* irrelevance *b)* insolence **2.** an impertinent act, remark, etc. Also **im·per′ti·nen·cy,** *pl.* **-cies**

im·per′ti·nent (-ənt) *adj.* **1.** not pertinent; irrelevant **2.** insolent —**im·per′ti·nent·ly** *adv.*

im·per·turb·a·ble (im′pər tur′bə b'l) *adj.* that cannot be perturbed or excited —**im·per·turb′a·bly** *adv.*

im·per·vi·ous (im pur′vē əs) *adj.* **1.** not pervious; impermeable **2.** not affected by (with *to*) —**im·per′vi·ous·ly** *adv.* —**im·per′vi·ous·ness** *n.*

im·pe·ti·go (im′pə tī′gō) *n.* [L.: see IMPETUS] a contagious skin disease with eruption of pustules

im·pet·u·os·i·ty (im pech′ōō wäs′ə tē) *n.* **1.** the quality of being impetuous **2.** *pl.* **-ties** an impetuous action or feeling

im·pet·u·ous (im pech′ōō wəs) *adj.* [see IMPETUS] **1.** rushing **2.** acting or done suddenly with little thought; impulsive —**im·pet′u·ous·ly** *adv.*

im·pe·tus (im′pə təs) *n., pl.* **-tus·es** [< L. *in-*, in + *petere*, rush at] **1.** the force with which a body moves against resistance **2.** a stimulus to action; incentive

im·pi·e·ty (im pī′ə tē) *n.* **1.** lack of piety, esp. toward God **2.** *pl.* **-ties** an impious act or remark

im·pinge (im pinj′) *vi.* **-pinged′, -ping′ing** [< L. *in-*, in + *pangere*, to strike] **1.** to strike or hit (*on, upon,* etc.) **2.** to encroach (*on* or *upon*)

im·pi·ous (im′pē əs) *adj.* not pious; lacking reverence for God —**im·pi·ous·ly** *adv.*

imp·ish (im′pish) *adj.* of or like an imp; mischievous — **imp′ish·ly** *adv.* —**imp′ish·ness** *n.*

im·plac·a·ble (im plak′ə b'l, -plā′kə-) *adj.* that cannot be appeased or pacified —**im·plac′a·bil′i·ty** *n.* —**im·plac′a·bly** *adv.*

im·plant (im plant′) *vt.* **1.** to plant firmly; embed **2.** to fix firmly in the mind; instill

im·plau·si·ble (im plô′zə b'l) *adj.* not plausible —**im·plau′si·bly** *adv.*

im·ple·ment (im′plə mənt) *n.* [< L. *in-*, in + *plere*, fill] any tool, instrument, etc. used or needed in a given activity —*vt.* (-ment′) **1.** to fulfill; accomplish **2.** to provide with implements —**im′ple·men·ta′tion** *n.*

im·pli·cate (im′plə kāt′) *vt.* **-cat′ed, -cat′ing** [see IMPLY] **1.** to cause to be involved in or associated with a crime, etc. **2.** to imply

im′pli·ca′tion *n.* **1.** an implicating or being implicated **2.** an implying or being implied **3.** something implied

im·plic·it (im plis′it) *adj.* [see IMPLY] **1.** suggested though not plainly expressed; implied **2.** necessarily involved though not apparent; inherent **3.** without reservation; absolute —**im·plic′it·ly** *adv.*

im·plied (im plīd′) *adj.* involved, suggested, or understood without being directly expressed

im·plode (im plōd′) *vt., vi.* **-plod′ed, -plod′ing** [< IN-¹ + (EX)PLODE] to burst inward —**im·plo′sion** (-plō′zhən) *n.*

im·plore (im plôr′) *vt.* **-plored′, -plor′ing** [< L. *in-*, intens. + *plorare*, cry out] **1.** to ask earnestly for **2.** to beg (a person) to do something —**im·plor′ing·ly** *adv.*

im·ply (im plī′) *vt.* **-plied′, -ply′ing** [< L. *in-*, in + *plicare*, to fold] **1.** to have as a necessary part, condition, or effect [war *implies* killing] **2.** to indicate indirectly; hint; suggest

im·po·lite (im′pə līt′) *adj.* not polite; discourteous; rude —**im′po·lite′ly** *adv.* —**im′po·lite′ness** *n.*

im·pol·i·tic (im päl′ə tik) *adj.* not politic; unwise; injudicious —**im·pol′i·tic·ly** *adv.*

im·pon·der·a·ble (im pän′dər ə b'l) *adj.* **1.** that cannot be weighed or measured **2.** that cannot be explained conclusively —*n.* anything imponderable

im·port (im pôrt′; *also, and for n. always,* im′pôrt) *vt.* [< L. *in-*, in + *portare*, carry] **1.** to bring (goods) from another country, esp. for selling **2.** to mean; signify —*vi.* to be of importance; matter —*n.* **1.** the importing of goods **2.** something imported **3.** meaning **4.** importance —**im·port′er** *n.*

im·por·tance (im pôr′t'ns) *n.* a being important; significance; consequence

im·por′tant (-t'nt) *adj.* [see IMPORT] **1.** meaning a great deal; having much significance or consequence **2.** having, or acting as if having, power, authority, etc. —**im·por′tant·ly** *adv.*

im·por·ta·tion (im′pôr tā′shən) *n.* **1.** an importing, as of goods **2.** something imported

im·por·tu·nate (im pôr′chə nit) *adj.* persistent in asking or demanding —**im·por′tu·nate·ly** *adv.*

im·por·tune (im′pôr tōōn′, -tyōōn′) *vt., vi.* **-tuned′, -tun′ing** [< Fr. < L. *importunus*, troublesome] to urge or entreat persistently and repeatedly —**im′por·tune′ly** *adv.*

im′por·tu′ni·ty *n., pl.* **-ties** an importuning; persistence in requesting or demanding

im·pose (im pōz′) *vt.* **-posed′, -pos′ing** [< Fr. < L. *in-*, on + *ponere*, to place] **1.** to place (a burden, tax, etc. *on* or *upon*) **2.** to force (oneself) on another **3.** to pass off by deception —**impose** on (or upon) **1.** to put to trouble or use unfairly for one's own benefit **2.** to cheat; defraud

im·pos·ing *adj.* impressive because of great size, strength, dignity, etc. —**im·pos′ing·ly** *adv.*

im·po·si·tion (-pə zish′ən) *n.* **1.** an imposing or imposing on; specif., a taking advantage of friendship **2.** something imposed, as a tax, burden, etc.

im·pos·si·bil·i·ty (im päs′ə bil′ə tē) *n.* **1.** a being impossible **2.** *pl.* **-ties** something that is impossible

im·pos·si·ble (im päs′ə b'l) *adj.* **1.** not capable of being, being done, or happening **2.** not capable of being endured, used, etc. because disagreeable or unsuitable —**im·pos′si·bly** *adv.*

im·post¹ (im′pōst) *n.* [< L. *in-*, on + *ponere*, to place] **1.** a tax; esp., a duty on imported goods **2.** the weight assigned to a horse in a handicap race —*vt.* to classify (imported goods) for taxing

im·post² (im′pōst) *n.* [< L.: see prec.] the top part of a pillar, pier, etc. supporting an arch

im·pos·tor (im päs′tər) *n.* [see IMPOSE] one who deceives by pretending to be what he is not; cheat

im·pos′ture (-chər) *n.* the act or practice of an impostor; fraud

im·po·tent (im′pə tənt) *adj.* **1.** lacking physical strength **2.** ineffective; powerless **3.** unable to engage in sexual intercourse: said of males —**im′po·tence, im′po·ten·cy** *n.* —**im′po·tent·ly** *adv.*

im·pound (im pound′) *vt.* **1.** to shut up (an animal) in a pound **2.** to take into legal custody

im·pov·er·ish (im päv′ər ish) *vt.* [< L. *in-*, in + *pauper*, poor] **1.** to make poor **2.** to deprive of strength, resources, etc. —**im·pov′er·ish·ment** *n.*

im·prac·ti·ca·ble (im prak′ti kə b'l) *adj.* **1.** not capable of being carried out in practice **2.** not capable of being used —**im·prac′ti·ca·bly** *adv.*

im·prac·ti·cal (im prak′ti k'l) *adj.* not practical —**im·prac′ti·cal′i·ty** *n.*

im·pre·cate (im′prə kāt′) *vt.* **-cat′ed, -cat′ing** [< L. *in-*, on + *precari*, to PRAY] to invoke (evil, a curse, etc.) —**im′pre·ca′tion** *n.*

im·preg·na·ble (im preg′nə b'l) *adj.* **1.** that cannot be captured or entered by force **2.** unyielding —**im·preg′na·bil′i·ty** *n.* —**im·preg′na·bly** *adv.*

im·preg·nate (im preg′nāt) *vt.* **-nat·ed, -nat·ing** **1.** to make pregnant; fertilize **2.** to saturate **3.** to imbue (*with* ideas, etc.) —**im·preg′na·ble** *adj* —**im′preg·na′tion** *n.*

im·pre·sa·ri·o (im′prə sär′ē ō) *n., pl.* **-os** [It.] the manager of an opera, concert series, etc.

im·pre·scrip·ti·ble (im′pri skrip′tə b'l) *adj.* that cannot rightfully be taken away or revoked; inviolable —**im′pre·scrip′ti·bly** *adv.*

im·press¹ (im pres′) *vt.* [< IN-¹ + PRESS²] **1.** to force (a person) into military service **2.** to seize (property, etc.) for public use —**im·press′ment** *n.*

im·press² (im pres′) *vt.* [see IN-¹ & PRESS¹] **1.** to stamp; imprint **2.** to affect strongly the mind or emotions of **3.** to win the approval of **4.** to fix in the memory, etc. —*n.* (im′pres) **1.** an impressing **2.** any mark, imprint, etc. **3.** an effect produced by a strong influence —**im·press′i·ble** *adj.*

im·pres·sion (im presh′ən) *n.* **1.** an impressing **2.** *a)* a mark, imprint, etc. *b)* an effect produced on the mind **3.** a vague notion **4.** an amusing impersonation **5.** *Printing a)* a printed copy *b)* all the copies printed at one time

im·pres·sion·a·ble *adj.* easily impressed or influenced; sensitive

im·pres·sion·ism *n.* a theory of art, music, etc. whose aim is to reproduce the immediate impression or mood — **im·pres·sion·ist** *n., adj.* —**im·pres′sion·is′tic** *adj.* —**im·pres′sion·is′ti·cal·ly** *adv.*

im·pres·sive (im pres′iv) *adj.* tending to affect strongly the mind or emotions —**im·pres′sive·ly** *adv.*

im·pri·ma·tur (im′pri mät′ər, -mät′-) *n.* [ModL., let it be printed] license to publish or print a book, article, etc.; specif., *R.C.Ch.* permission granted by an ecclesiastical censor

im·print (im print′) *vt.* [< L. *in-*, on + *premere*, to PRESS¹] **1.** to mark or fix as by pressing or stamping; impress **2.** to fix in the memory —*n.* (im′print) **1.** a mark made by imprinting **2.** a characteristic effect **3.** a note in a book giving facts of its publication

im·pris·on (im priz′'n) *vt.* to put in or as in prison —**im·pris′on·ment** *n.*

im·prob·a·ble (im präb′ə b'l) *adj.* not probable; unlikely to happen or be true —**im′prob·a·bil′i·ty** *n., pl.* **-ties** —**im·prob′a·bly** *adv.*

im·promp·tu (im prämp′tōō) *adj., adv.* [Fr. < L. *in promptu*, in readiness] without preparation; offhand —*n.* an impromptu speech, etc.

im·prop·er (im präp′ər) *adj.* **1.** not suitable; unfit **2.** incorrect **3.** not in good taste; indecent —im·prop′er·ly *adv.*
improper fraction a fraction in which the denominator is less than the numerator (Ex.: 5/3)
im·pro·pri·e·ty (im′prə prī′ə tē) *n., pl.* **-ties 1.** a being improper **2.** an improper action, usage, etc.
im·prove (im prōōv′) *vt.* **-proved′, -prov′ing** [< L. *in-*, in + *prodesse*, to profit] **1.** to use (time, etc.) profitably **2.** to make better **3.** to add value to, as by cultivation —*vi.* to become better —**improve on** (or **upon**) to do or make better than —im·prov′a·ble *adj.*
im·prove′ment *n.* **1.** an improving or being improved **2.** a change that improves or adds value to something
im·prov·i·dent (im präv′ə dənt) *adj.* failing to provide for the future; lacking foresight or thrift —im·prov′i·dence *n.* —im·prov′i·dent·ly *adv.*
im·pro·vise (im′prə vīz′) *vt., vi.* **-vised′, -vis′ing** [< Fr. < L. *in-*, not + *providere*, foresee] **1.** to compose and perform without preparation **2.** to make or do with whatever is at hand —im·prov·i·sa·tion (im präv′ə zā′shən) *n.* —im′pro·vis′er, im′pro·vi′sor *n.*
im·pru·dent (im prōōd′′nt) *adj.* not prudent; rash —im·pru′dence *n.* —im·pru′dent·ly *adv.*
im·pu·dent (im′pyoo dənt) *adj.* [< L. *in-*, not + *pudere*, feel shame] shamelessly bold; insolent —im′pu·dence *n.* —im′pu·dent·ly *adv.*
im·pugn (im pyōōn′) *vt.* [< L. *in-*, against + *pugnare*, to fight] to oppose or challenge as false —im·pug·na·tion (im′pəg nā′shən) *n.*
im·pulse (im′puls) *n.* [see IMPEL] **1.** *a)* a driving forward *b)* an impelling force; impetus *c)* the motion or effect caused by such a force **2.** *a)* incitement to action arising from a state of mind or an external stimulus *b)* a sudden inclination to act, without conscious thought **3.** *Physiol.* a stimulus transmitted in a muscle or nerve
im·pul·sion (im pul′shən) *n.* **1.** an impelling or being impelled **2.** an impelling force; impetus
im·pul·sive (-siv) *adj.* **1.** driving forward **2.** likely to act on impulse **3.** resulting from impulse [an *impulsive* remark] —im·pul′sive·ly *adv.* —im·pul′sive·ness *n.*
im·pu·ni·ty (im pyōō′nə tē) *n.* [< Fr. < L. *in-*, without + *poena*, punishment] exemption from punishment, penalty, or harm
im·pure (im pyoor′) *adj.* **1.** unclean; dirty **2.** immoral; obscene **3.** mixed with foreign matter; adulterated —im·pure′ly *adv.*
im·pu′ri·ty *n.* **1.** a being impure **2.** *pl.* **-ties** an impure thing or part
im·pute (im pyōōt′) *vt.* **-put′ed, -put′ing** [< L. *in-*, to + *putare*, to estimate] to attribute (esp. a fault or misconduct) to another; charge with —im′pu·ta′tion *n.*
in (in) *prep.* [OE.] **1.** contained by [in the room] **2.** wearing [in formal dress] **3.** during [done in a day] **4.** at the end of [due in an hour] **5.** perceptible to [in sight] **6.** amidst [in a storm] **7.** affected by [in trouble] **8.** employed at [in business] **9.** with regard to [in my opinion] **10.** using [paint in oil, speak in French] **11.** because of; for [to cry in pain] **12.** by way of [in recompense] **13.** belonging to [not in his nature] **14.** into [come in the house] —*adv.* **1.** to the inside **2.** so as to be contained by a certain space, condition, etc. **3.** so as to be agreeing or involved [he fell in with our plans] **4.** so as to form a part —*adj.* **1.** that is in power [the in group] **2.** inner; inside **3.** ingoing [the in door] **4.** [Colloq.] currently smart [an in joke] —*n.* **1.** a person or group in power: *usually used in pl.* **2.** [Colloq.] special influence, power, etc. —**have it in for** [Colloq.] to hold a grudge against —**in for** certain to have [he's in for a shock] —**ins and outs** all the parts, details, and intricacies —**in that** because; since —**in with** associated with
in-[1] [< the prep. IN or L. *in*, in] *a prefix meaning* in, into, within, on, toward [infer, induct] : also used as an intensive [instigate, inflame]
in-[2] [< L. *in-*] *a prefix meaning* no, not, without, non-. The following list includes some common compounds formed with *in-* that do not have special meanings; they will be understood if *not* or *lack of* is used with the meaning of the base word:

inability	inapplicable	incivility
inaccuracy	inappropriate	incombustible
inaccurate	inaptitude	incommensurable
inaction	inartistic	incommensurate
inactive	inaudible	incommunicable
inadequacy	inauspicious	incomprehensible
inadmissible	incapable	inconceivable
inadvisable	incautious	inconclusive
inanimate	incertitude	inconsonant

incontrovertible	ineffectual	inhospitable
incorporeal	inefficacious	inhumane
incorrect	inefficacy	injudicious
incurable	inelastic	inoperable
incurious	inelegant	inopportune
indecipherable	ineligible	insanitary
indecorous	inequality	insensitive
indefinable	inequitable	insentient
indehiscent	inequity	inseparable
indiscernible	ineradicable	insoluble
indisputable	inessential	insolvable
indistinct	inexact	insufficiency
indistinguishable	inexcusable	insufficient
indivisible	inexpedient	insurmountable
inedible	inexpressive	insusceptible
ineffective	infertile	invariable

-in[1] [see -INE[3]] a suffix used in forming the names of various compounds [albumin, Chloromycetin]
-in[2] a combining form used in terms formed by analogy with SIT-IN [teach-in]
In *Chem.* indium
IN Indiana
in. inch; inches
in ab·sen·ti·a (in əb sen′shə, ab sen′shē ə) [L., lit., in absence] although not present
in·ac·ces·si·ble (in′ək ses′ə b'l) *adj.* **1.** impossible to reach or enter **2.** that cannot be seen, talked to, etc. **3.** not obtainable —in′ac·ces·si·bil′i·ty *n.* —in′ac·ces·si·bly *adv.*
in·ac·ti·vate (in ak′tə vāt′) *vt.* **-vat′ed, -vat′ing 1.** to make inactive **2.** *Chem.* to destroy the activity of (a substance), as by heat —in·ac′ti·va′tion *n.*
in·ad·vert·ent (in′əd vur′tənt) *adj.* **1.** not attentive; negligent **2.** due to oversight —in′ad·vert′ence *n.* —in′ad·vert′ent·ly *adv.*
in·al·ien·a·ble (in āl′yən ə b'l) *adj.* [see ALIEN] that may not be taken away or transferred —in·al′ien·a·bil′i·ty *n.* —in·al′ien·a·bly *adv.*
in·am·o·ra·ta (in am′ə rät′ə, in′am-) *n.* [It.] one's sweetheart or mistress
in·ane (in ān′) *adj.* [L. *inanis*] **1.** empty **2.** lacking sense; silly —in·ane′ly *adv.*
in·an·i·ty (in an′ə tē) *n.* **1.** emptiness or silliness **2.** *pl.* **-ties** a silly act, remark, etc.
in·ar·tic·u·late (in′är tik′yə lit) *adj.* **1.** without the articulation of normal speech [an *inarticulate* cry] **2.** unable to speak; mute **3.** unable to speak clearly or expressively —in′ar·tic′u·late·ly *adv.* —in′ar·tic′u·late·ness *n.*
in·as·much as (in′əz much′ əz) **1.** seeing that; since; because **2.** to the extent that
in·at·ten·tion (in′ə ten′shən) *n.* failure to pay attention; heedlessness; negligence —in′at·ten′tive *adj.* —in′at·ten′tive·ly *adv.* —in′at·ten′tive·ness *n.*
in·au·gu·ral (in ô′gyə rəl) *adj.* [Fr.] of an inauguration —*n.* an inaugural ceremony or address
in·au·gu·rate′ (-rāt′) *vt.* **-rat′ed, -rat′ing** [< L. *inaugurare*, to practice augury] **1.** to induct into office with a formal ceremony **2.** to make a formal beginning of **3.** to celebrate formally the first public use of —in·au′gu·ra′tion *n.* —in·au′gu·ra′tor *n.*
in·board (in′bôrd′) *adv., adj.* **1.** inside the hull of a ship or boat **2.** close to the fuselage of an aircraft —*n.* a marine motor mounted inboard
in·born (in′bôrn′) *adj.* present in the organism at birth; innate; natural
in′bound′ *adj.* traveling or going inward
in·bred (in′bred′) *adj.* **1.** innate or deeply instilled **2.** resulting from inbreeding
in·breed (in′brēd′) *vt.* **-bred′, -breed′ing** to breed by continual mating of individuals of the same or closely related stocks —*vi.* to engage in such breeding
inc. 1. including **2.** inclusive **3.** incorporated **4.** increase
In·ca (iŋ′kə) *n.* any member of the highly civilized Indian people that dominated Peru until the Spanish conquest —In′can *adj.*
in·cal·cu·la·ble (in kal′kyə lə b'l) *adj.* **1.** that cannot be calculated; too great or too many to be counted **2.** unpredictable —in·cal′cu·la·bly *adv.*
in·can·des·cent (in′kən des′'nt) *adj.* [< L. *in-*, in + *candere*, to shine] **1.** glowing with intense heat; red-hot or, esp., white-hot **2.** very bright —in′can·des′cence *n.*
incandescent lamp a lamp having a filament contained in a vacuum and heated to incandescence by an electric current
in·can·ta·tion (in′kan tā′shən) *n.* [< L. *in-*, to + *cantare*, to chant] **1.** words chanted in magic spells or rites **2.** the chanting of these words

in·ca·pac·i·tate (in'kə pas'ə tāt') *vt.* **-tat'ed, -tat'ing 1.** to make unable or unfit; disable **2.** *Law* to disqualify — **in'ca·pac'i·ta'tion** *n.*

in'ca·pac'i·ty (-tē) *n., pl.* **-ties 1.** lack of capacity, power, or fitness; disability **2.** legal ineligibility

in·car·cer·ate (in kär'sə rāt') *vt.* **-at'ed, -at'ing** [< L. *in-*, in + *carcer*, prison] **1.** to imprison **2.** to confine —**in·car'cer·a'tion** *n.*

in·car·na·dine (in kär'nə din', -dēn') *adj., n.* [see INCARNATE] (of) the color of flesh or blood —*vt.* **-dined', -din'ing** to make incarnadine

in·car·nate (in kär'nit) *adj.* [< L. *in-*, in + *caro*, flesh] endowed with a human body; personified —*vt.* **(-nāt) -nat·ed, -nat·ing 1.** to give bodily form to; embody **2.** to give actual form to; make real **3.** to be the type or embodiment of

in·car·na·tion (in'kär nā'shən) *n.* **1.** endowment with a human body **2.** [I-] the taking on of human form and nature by Jesus as the Son of God **3.** any person or thing serving as the embodiment of a quality, spirit, etc.

in·case (in kās') *vt.* **-cased', -cas'ing** *same as* ENCASE

in·cen·di·ar·y (in sen'dē er'ē) *adj.* [< L. *incendium*, a fire] **1.** having to do with willful destruction of property by fire **2.** designed to cause fires, as certain bombs **3.** willfully stirring up strife, riot, etc. —*n., pl.* **-ies 1.** one who willfully destroys property by fire **2.** one who willfully stirs up strife, riot, etc. **3.** an incendiary bomb, substance, etc. —**in·cen'di·a·rism** (-ə riz'm) *n.*

in·cense[1] (in'sens) *n.* [see INCENSE[2]] **1.** any substance burned for its pleasant odor **2.** the fragrance from this **3.** any pleasant odor —*vt.* **-censed, -cens·ing** to burn or offer incense to

in·cense[2] (in sens') *vt.* **-censed', -cens'ing** [< L. *in-*, in + *candere*, to burn] to make very angry; enrage

in·cen·tive (in sen'tiv) *adj.* [< L. *in-*, on + *canere*, to sing] stimulating to action —*n.* a stimulus; motive

in·cep·tion (in sep'shən) *n.* [see INCIPIENT] a beginning; start; commencement

in·ces·sant (in ses''nt) *adj.* [< L. *in-*, not + *cessare*, cease] never ceasing; continuing or repeated endlessly; constant —**in·ces'sant·ly** *adv.*

in·cest (in'sest) *n.* [< L. *in-*, not + *castus*, chaste] sexual intercourse between persons too closely related to marry legally —**in·ces·tu·ous** (in ses'choo wəs) *adj.* —**in·ces'tu·ous·ly** *adv.*

inch (inch) *n.* [< L. *uncia*, a twelfth] a measure of length equal to 1/12 foot: symbol, " —*vt., vi.* to move by degrees or very slowly —**every inch** in all respects —**within an inch of** very close to

inch'meal' *adv.* [cf. PIECEMEAL] gradually; inch by inch: also **by inchmeal**

in·cho·ate (in kō'it) *adj.* [< L. *inchoare*, to begin] **1.** just begun **2.** not yet clearly formed —**in·cho'ate·ly** *adv.*

inch'worm' *n. same as* MEASURING WORM

in·ci·dence (in'si dəns) *n.* **1.** the act, fact, or manner of falling upon or influencing **2.** the degree or range of occurrence or effect; extent of influence

in'ci·dent (-dənt) *adj.* [< L. *in-*, on + *cadere*, to fall] **1.** likely to happen in connection with **2.** falling upon or affecting —*n.* **1.** something that happens; event **2.** a minor episode, as in a play **3.** an apparently minor conflict, etc. that may have serious results

in'ci·den'tal (-den't'l) *adj.* **1.** happening in connection with something more important; casual **2.** secondary or minor —*n.* **1.** something incidental **2.** [pl.] miscellaneous items

in'ci·den'tal·ly (-dent'lē, -den't'l ē) *adv.* **1.** in an incidental manner **2.** as a new but related point; by the way

in·cin·er·ate (in sin'ə rāt') *vt., vi.* **-at'ed, -at'ing** [< L. *in*, to + *cinis*, ashes] to burn to ashes; burn up —**in·cin'er·a'tion** *n.*

in·cin'er·a'tor (-rāt'ər) *n.* a furnace for burning trash

in·cip·i·ent (in sip'ē ənt) *adj.* [< L. *in-*, on + *capere*, to take] just beginning to exist or appear —**in·cip'i·ence** *n.* —**in·cip'i·ent·ly** *adv.*

in·cise (in siz') *vt.* **-cised', -cis'ing** [< L. *in-*, into + *caedere*, to cut] to cut into with a sharp tool; specif., to engrave or carve —**in·cised'** *adj.*

in·ci·sion (in sizh'ən) *n.* **1.** the act or result of incising; cut **2.** incisive quality **3.** *Surgery* a cut made into a tissue or organ

in·ci·sive (in si'siv) *adj.* **1.** cutting into **2.** sharp; keen; acute —**in·ci'sive·ly** *adv.*

in·ci·sor (in si'zər) *n.* any of the front cutting teeth between the canines in either jaw

in·cite (in sit') *vt.* **-cit'ed, -cit'ing** [< L. *in-*, on + *citare*, to urge] to urge to action; rouse —**in·cite'ment** *n.* —**in·cit'er** *n.*

incl. 1. inclosure **2.** including **3.** inclusive

in·clem·ent (in klem'ənt) *adj.* [< L. *in-*, not + *clemens*, lenient] **1.** rough; stormy **2.** lacking mercy; harsh —**in·clem'en·cy** *n., pl.* **-cies** —**in·clem'ent·ly** *adv.*

in·cli·na·tion (in'klə nā'shən) *n.* **1.** an inclining, leaning, bowing, etc. **2.** a slope; slant **3.** the degree of incline from the horizontal or vertical **4.** the angle made by two lines or planes **5.** *a)* a bias; tendency *b)* a preference; liking

in·cline (in klin') *vi.* **-clined', -clin'ing** [< L. *in-*, on + *clinare*, to lean] **1.** to lean; slope **2.** to bow the body or head **3.** to have a tendency **4.** to have a preference or liking —*vt.* **1.** to cause to lean, slope, etc. **2.** to make willing; influence —*n.* (in'klin, in klin') a slope; grade —**incline one's ear** to listen willingly —**in·clined'** *adj.*

inclined plane any plane surface set at an angle against a horizontal surface

in·cli·nom·e·ter (in'klə näm'ə tər) *n.* [< INCLINE + -METER] an instrument for indicating the inclination of an aircraft or ship from the horizontal

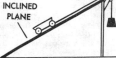

INCLINED PLANE

in·close (in klōz') *vt.* **-closed', -clos'ing** *same as* ENCLOSE —**in·clo'sure** (-klō'zhər) *n.*

in·clude (in klood') *vt.* **-clud'ed, -clud'ing** [< L. *in-*, in + *claudere*, to close] **1.** to enclose **2.** to have as part of a whole; contain; comprise **3.** to put in a total, category, etc.

in·clu·sion (in kloo'zhən) *n.* **1.** an including or being included **2.** something included

in·clu·sive (-kloo'siv) *adj.* **1.** taking everything into account **2.** including the terms or limits mentioned [the first to the tenth *inclusive*] —**in·clu'sive·ly** *adv.* —**in·clu'sive·ness** *n.*

in·cog·ni·to (in'käg nēt'ō, in käg'ni tō') *adv., adj.* [It. < L. *in-*, not + *cognitus*, known] disguised under an assumed name, rank, etc. —*n., pl.* **-tos 1.** a person who is incognito **2.** *a)* the state of being incognito *b)* the disguise assumed

in·co·her·ent (in'kō hir'ənt) *adj.* **1.** not logically connected; disjointed **2.** characterized by incoherent speech, thought, etc. —**in'co·her'ence** *n.* —**in'co·her'ent·ly** *adv.*

in·come (in'kum') *n.* the money or other gain received for labor or services, or from property, investments, etc.

income tax a tax on net income or on that part of income which exceeds a certain amount

in'com'ing *adj.* coming in or about to come in

in·com·mode (in'kə mōd') *vt.* **-mod'ed, -mod'ing** [< Fr. < L. *in-*, not + *commodus*, convenient] to inconvenience; put to some trouble; bother

in·com·mu·ni·ca·do (in'kə myoo'nə kä'dō) *adj.* [Sp.] unable or not allowed to communicate with others

in·com·pa·ra·ble (in käm'pər ə b'l) *adj.* **1.** having no basis of comparison **2.** beyond comparison; matchless — **in·com'pa·ra·bly** *adv.*

in·com·pat·i·ble (in'kəm pat'ə b'l) *adj.* **1.** unable to live together harmoniously **2.** not suitable for being used together —*n.* an incompatible person or thing —**in'com·pat'i·bil'i·ty** *n., pl.* **-ties** —**in'com·pat'i·bly** *adv.*

in·com·pe·tent (in käm'pə tənt) *adj.* **1.** without adequate ability, knowledge, fitness, etc. **2.** not legally qualified —*n.* an incompetent person —**in·com'pe·tence** *n.* — **in·com'pe·tent·ly** *adv.*

in·com·plete (in'kəm plēt') *adj.* **1.** lacking a part or parts **2.** unfinished; not concluded **3.** not perfect —**in'com·plete'ly** *adv.* —**in'com·plete'ness** *n.*

in·con·gru·ous (in käŋ'groo wəs) *adj.* **1.** lacking harmony or agreement of parts, etc. **2.** unsuitable; inappropriate —**in·con·gru·i·ty** (in'kän groo'ə tē) *n.*

in·con·se·quen·tial (in kän'sə kwen'shəl) *adj.* of no consequence; unimportant —*n.* something inconsequential — **in·con'se·quen'tial·ly** *adv.*

in·con·sid·er·a·ble (in'kən sid'ər ə b'l) *adj.* trivial; small —**in'con·sid'er·a·bly** *adv.*

in·con·sid·er·ate (in'kən sid'ər it) *adj.* without thought or consideration for others; thoughtless —**in'con·sid'er·ate·ly** *adv.* —**in·con·sid'er·ate·ness, in'con·sid'er·a'tion** *n.*

in·con·sis·tent (in'kən sis'tənt) *adj.* **1.** not in harmony or accord **2.** self-contradictory *[inconsistent* testimony] **3.** changeable *[inconsistent* behavior] —in'con·sis'ten·cy *n., pl.* -cies —in'con·sis'tent·ly *adv.*

in·con·sol·a·ble (in'kən sōl'ə b'l) *adj.* that cannot be consoled —in'con·sol'a·bly *adv.*

in·con·spic·u·ous (in'kən spik'yoo wəs) *adj.* attracting little attention —in'con·spic'u·ous·ly *adv.* —in'con·spic'·u·ous·ness *n.*

in·con·stant (in kän'stənt) *adj.* not constant; changeable, fickle, irregular, etc. —in·con'stan·cy *n.*

in·con·test·a·ble (in'kən tes'tə b'l) *adj.* unquestionable; indisputable

in·con·ti·nent (in känt''n ənt) *adj.* **1.** without self-restraint, esp. in regard to sexual activity **2.** unable to restrain a natural discharge, as of urine —in·con'ti·nence *n.*

in·con·ven·ience (in'kən vēn'yəns) *n.* **1.** lack of comfort, ease, etc. **2.** anything inconvenient —*vt.* -ienced, -ienc·ing to trouble; bother

in'con·ven'ient (-yənt) *adj.* not favorable to one's comfort; causing bother, etc. —in'con·ven'ient·ly *adv.*

in·cor·po·rate (in kôr'pə rāt') *vt.* -rat'ed, -rat'ing [see IN-¹ & CORPORATE] **1.** to combine; embody **2.** to bring together into a single whole; merge **3.** to form into a corporation **4.** to give material form to —*vi.* **1.** to unite into a single whole **2.** to form a corporation —in·cor'po·ra'tion *n.*

in·cor·ri·gi·ble (in kôr'i jə b'l) *adj.* [see IN-² & CORRECT] that cannot be corrected or reformed, esp. because set in bad habits —*n.* an incorrigible person —in·cor'ri·gi·bil'i·ty *n.* —in·cor'ri·gi·bly *adv.*

in·cor·rupt·i·ble (in'kə rup'tə b'l) *adj.* that cannot be corrupted, esp. morally —in'cor·rupt'i·bil'i·ty *n.* —in'cor·rupt'i·bly *adv.*

in·crease (in krēs') *vi., vt.* -creased', -creas'ing [< L. *in-,* in + *crescere,* grow] to become or cause to become greater in size, amount, etc. —*n.* (in'krēs) **1.** an increasing or becoming increased **2.** the result or amount of an increasing —on the increase increasing

in·creas'ing·ly *adv.* more and more

in·cred·i·ble (in kred'ə b'l) *adj.* not credible; seeming too unusual to be possible —in·cred'i·bil'i·ty *n.* —in·cred'i·bly *adv.*

in·cred·u·lous (in krej'oo ləs) *adj.* **1.** unwilling to believe; doubting **2.** showing doubt or disbelief —in·cre·du·li·ty (in'krə dōō'lə tē) *n.* —in·cred'u·lous·ly *adv.*

in·cre·ment (in'krə mənt, iŋ'-) *n.* **1.** a becoming greater or larger; increase **2.** amount of increase —in'cre·men'tal (-men't'l) *adj.*

in·crim·i·nate (in krim'ə nāt') *vt.* -nat'ed, -nat'ing [< L. *in-,* in + *crimen,* offense] **1.** to accuse of a crime **2.** to involve in, or make appear guilty of, a crime or fault —in·crim'i·na'tion *n.* —in·crim'i·na·to'ry *adj.*

in·crust (in krust') *vt.* **1.** to cover as with a crust **2.** to decorate, as with gems —*vi.* to form a crust —in'crus·ta'tion *n.*

in·cu·bate (iŋ'kyə bāt') *vt.* -bat'ed, -bat'ing [< L. *in-,* on + *cubare,* to lie] **1.** to sit on and hatch (eggs) **2.** to keep (eggs, embryos, etc.) in a favorable environment for hatching or developing —*vi.* to undergo incubation —in'cu·ba'tion *n.*

in'cu·ba'tor *n.* **1.** a heated container for hatching eggs **2.** a similar apparatus in which premature babies are kept for a period

in·cu·bus (iŋ'kyə bəs) *n., pl.* -bus·es, -bi' (-bī') [LL.] **1.** a spirit or demon thought in medieval times to lie on sleeping women **2.** a nightmare **3.** an oppressive burden

in·cul·cate (in kul'kāt, in'kul kāt') *vt.* -cat·ed, -cat·ing [< L. *in-,* in + *calcare,* trample underfoot] to impress upon the mind by repetition or persistent urging —in'cul·ca'tion *n.*

in·cul·pate (in kul'pāt, in'kul pāt') *vt.* -pat·ed, -pat·ing [< L. *in-,* on + *culpa,* blame] *same as* INCRIMINATE —in'·cul·pa'tion *n.* —in·cul'pa·to'ry *adj.*

in·cum·ben·cy (in kum'bən sē) *n., pl.* -cies **1.** a duty or obligation **2.** *a)* the holding and administering of a position *b)* a term of office

in·cum'bent (-bənt) *adj.* [< L. *in-,* on + *cubare,* lie down] **1.** resting (*on* or *upon* one) as a duty or obligation **2.** currently in office —*n.* one who is currently in office

in·cum·ber (in kum'bər) *vt. same as* ENCUMBER

in·cum'brance (-brəns) *n.* **1.** *Law* a lien, mortgage, etc. on property **2.** *same as* ENCUMBRANCE

in·cu·nab·u·la (in'kyoo nab'yə lə) *n.pl., sing.* -u·lum (-ləm) [< L. *in-,* in + *cunabula,* neut. pl., a cradle] **1.** beginnings **2.** early printed books; esp., books printed before 1500

in·cur (in kur') *vt.* -curred', -cur'ring [< L. *in-,* in + *currere,* to run] to acquire or bring upon oneself (something undesirable)

in·cur·sion (in kur'zhən) *n.* [see INCUR] an invasion or raid; inroad

Ind. 1. India **2.** Indian **3.** Indiana **4.** Indies

ind. 1. independent **2.** index **3.** industrial

in·debt·ed (in det'id) *adj.* **1.** in debt **2.** obliged; owing gratitude

in·debt'ed·ness *n.* **1.** a being indebted **2.** the amount owed; all one's debts

in·de·cen·cy (in dē's'n sē) *n.* **1.** a being indecent **2.** *pl.* -cies an indecent act or remark

in·de·cent (-s'nt) *adj.* not decent; specif., *a)* improper *b)* morally offensive —in·de'cent·ly *adv.*

in·de·ci·sion (in'di sizh'ən) *n.* inability to decide or a tendency to change the mind frequently

in'de·ci'sive (-sī'siv) *adj.* **1.** not decisive **2.** showing indecision; hesitating or vacillating —in'de·ci'sive·ly *adv.* —in'de·ci'sive·ness *n.*

in·deed (in dēd') *adv.* certainly; truly —*interj.* an exclamation of surprise, doubt, sarcasm, etc.

in·de·fat·i·ga·ble (in'di fat'i gə b'l) *adj.* [< L. *in-,* not + *defatigare,* tire out] not tiring; tireless

in·de·fen·si·ble (in'di fen'sə b'l) *adj.* **1.** that cannot be defended **2.** that cannot be justified

in·def·i·nite (in def'ə nit) *adj.* **1.** having no exact limits **2.** not precise in meaning; vague **3.** not sure; uncertain **4.** *Gram.* not limiting or specifying [*a* and *an* are *indefinite* articles] —in·def'i·nite·ly *adv.*

in·del·i·ble (in del'ə b'l) *adj.* [< L. *in-,* not + *delere,* destroy] **1.** that cannot be erased, washed out, etc.; permanent **2.** leaving an indelible mark [*indelible* ink]

in·del·i·cate (in del'i kit) *adj.* lacking propriety or modesty; coarse —in·del'i·ca·cy *n., pl.* -cies —in·del'i·cate·ly *adv.*

in·dem·ni·fy (in dem'nə fī') *vt.* -fied', -fy'ing [< L. *in·demnis,* unhurt + -FY] **1.** to insure against loss, damage, etc. **2.** to repay for (loss or damage) —in·dem'ni·fi·ca'tion *n.*

in·dem'ni·ty (-tē) *n., pl.* -ties **1.** insurance against loss, damage, etc. **2.** repayment for loss, damage, etc. **3.** legal exemption from penalties incurred by one's actions

in·dent (in dent') *vt., vi.* [< L. *in,* in + *dens,* tooth] **1.** to notch **2.** to make jagged in outline **3.** to space (the beginning of a paragraph, etc.) in from the regular margin —in'den·ta'tion *n.*

in·den·ture (in den'chər) *n.* **1.** a written contract **2.** [*often pl.*] a contract binding one person to work for another —*vt.* -tured, -tur·ing to bind by indenture

In·de·pend·ence (in'di pen'dəns) city in W Mo.: suburb of Kansas City: pop. 112,000

in·de·pend·ence (in'di pen'dəns) *n.* a being independent; freedom from the control of another

Independence Day the Fourth of July, the anniversary of the American colonies' adoption of the Declaration of Independence on July 4, 1776

in'de·pend'ent (-dənt) *adj.* **1.** free from the influence or control of others; specif., *a)* self-governing *b)* self-confident; self-reliant *c)* not adhering to any political party *d)* not connected with others [an *independent* grocer] **2.** *a)* not depending upon another for financial support *b)* of or having an income large enough to enable one to live without working —*n.* one who is independent in thinking, action, etc.; specif., [*often* I-] a voter not an adherent of any political party —independent of apart from; regardless of —in'de·pend'ent·ly *adv.*

in·de·scrib·a·ble (in'di skrī'bə b'l) *adj.* beyond the power of description —in'de·scrib'a·bly *adv.*

in·de·struct·i·ble (in'di struk'tə b'l) *adj.* that cannot be destroyed —in'de·struct'i·bil'i·ty *n.*

in·de·ter·mi·na·ble (in'di tur'mi nə b'l) *adj.* that cannot be decided or ascertained

in'de·ter'mi·nate (-nit) *adj.* **1.** indefinite; vague **2.** unsettled; inconclusive —in'de·ter'mi·na'tion *n.*

in·dex (in'deks) *n., pl.* -dex·es, -di·ces' (-də sēz') [L.: see INDICATE] **1.** the forefinger: also **index finger 2.** a pointer, as the needle on a dial **3.** an indication [an *index* of ability] **4.** *a)* an alphabetical list of names, subjects, etc. indicating pages where found, as in a book *b)* a catalog [a library *index*] **5.** a figure showing ratio or relative change **6.** [I-] *R.C.Ch.* formerly, a list of books forbidden to be read —*vt.* **1.** to make an index of or for **2.** to include in an index

In·di·a (in'dē ə) **1.** a large peninsula of S Asia **2.** republic in C & S India: 1,177,000 sq. mi.; pop. 536,984,000; cap. New Delhi

India ink a black ink made of lampblack mixed with a gelatinous substance

In·di·an (in′dē ən) *n.* **1.** a native of India or the East Indies **2.** a member of any of the aboriginal peoples of N. America, S. America, or the West Indies: also **American Indian 3.** any of the languages spoken by American Indians —*adj.* **1.** of India or the East Indies, their people, etc. **2.** of the American Indians or their culture

In·di·an·a (in′dē an′ə) Middle Western State of the U.S.: 36,291 sq. mi.; pop. 5,194,000; cap. Indianapolis; abbrev. Ind., IN —In′di·an′i·an *adj., n.*

In·di·an·ap·o·lis (in′dē ə nap′ə lis) capital of Indiana: pop. 745,000 (met. area 1,110,000)

Indian club a club of wood, metal, etc. shaped like a tenpin and swung in the hand for exercise

Indian corn *same as* CORN¹ (sense 2)

Indian file *same as* SINGLE FILE

Indian giver [Colloq.] a person who gives something and then asks for it back

Indian Ocean ocean south of Asia, between Africa & Australia

Indian pipe a leafless, fleshy plant, bearing a single, nodding, white flower

Indian summer mild, warm, hazy weather following the first frosts of late autumn

India paper a thin, strong, opaque printing paper, used for some Bibles, dictionaries, etc.

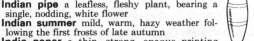
INDIAN CLUB

In·dic (in′dik) *adj.* **1.** of India **2.** of a branch of the Indo-European languages, including many languages of India

indic. indicative

in·di·cate (in′də kāt′) *vt.* -cat′ed, -cat′ing [< L. *in-*, in + *dicare*, declare] **1.** to direct attention to; point out **2.** to be a sign of; signify **3.** to show the need for **4.** to state briefly

in′di·ca′tion *n.* **1.** an indicating **2.** something that indicates **3.** the amount registered by an indicator

in·dic·a·tive (in dik′ə tiv) *adj.* **1.** giving an indication or intimation; signifying **2.** designating that mood of a verb used to express an act, state, etc. as actual, or to ask a question —*n.* **1.** the indicative mood **2.** a verb in this mood

in·di·ca·tor (in′də kāt′ər) *n.* **1.** a person or thing that indicates; specif., a gauge, dial, etc. that measures something **2.** any substance used to indicate acidity or alkalinity, a chemical reaction, etc. by change in color

in·di·ces (in′də sēz′) *n. alt. pl. of* INDEX

in·dict (in dīt′) *vt.* [ult. < L. *in*, against + *dicere*, speak] to charge with a crime; esp., to make formal accusation against on the basis of positive legal evidence —in·dict′er, in·dict′or *n.*

in·dict′ment *n.* **1.** an indicting or being indicted **2.** a charge; specif., a formal accusation charging someone with a crime, presented by a grand jury to the court

In·dies (in′dēz) *same as:* **1.** EAST INDIES **2.** WEST INDIES

in·dif·fer·ence (in dif′ər əns, -dif′rəns) *n.* **1.** lack of concern or interest **2.** lack of importance or meaning

in·dif′fer·ent *adj.* **1.** having or showing no bias; neutral **2.** unconcerned; apathetic **3.** of no importance **4.** fair; average **5.** not particularly good —in·dif′fer·ent·ly *adv.*

in·dig·e·nous (in dij′ə nəs) *adj.* [< OL. *indu*, in + *gignere*, be born] born or growing naturally in a region or country; native

in·di·gent (in′di jənt) *adj.* [< OL. *indu*, in + *egere*, to need] poor; needy —in′di·gence *n.* —in′di·gent·ly *adv.*

in·di·gest·i·ble (in′di jes′tə b′l, -dī-) *adj.* not easily digested —in′di·gest′i·bil′i·ty *n.*

in·di·ges·tion (in′di jes′chən) *n.* difficulty in digesting food, or the discomfort caused by this

in·dig·nant (in dig′nənt) *adj.* [< L. *in-*, not + *dignus*, worthy] feeling or expressing indignation —in·dig′nant·ly *adv.*

in·dig·na·tion (in′dig nā′shən) *n.* anger or scorn that is a reaction to injustice or meanness

in·dig·ni·ty (in dig′nə tē) *n., pl.* -ties an insult or affront to one's dignity or self-respect

in·di·go (in′di gō′) *n., pl.* -gos′, -goes′ [Sp. < Gr. *Indikos*, Indian] **1.** a blue dye obtained from certain plants or made synthetically **2.** a deep violet-blue: also **indigo blue** —*adj.* deep violet-blue: also **in′di·go′-blue′**

indigo bunting (or **bird**) a small finch of the eastern U.S.: the male is indigo, the female brown

in·di·rect (in′di rekt′, -dī-) *adj.* **1.** not straight **2.** not straight to the point **3.** dishonest *[indirect* dealing*]* **4.** not immediate; secondary *[an indirect* result*]* —in′di·rect′ly *adv.* —in′di·rect′ness *n.*

in′di·rec′tion *n.* **1.** roundabout act, procedure, or means **2.** deceit; dishonesty

indirect lighting lighting reflected, as from a ceiling, or diffused so as to avoid glare

indirect object *Gram.* the person or thing indirectly affected by the action of the verb (Ex.: *us* in *give us time*)

in·dis·creet (in′dis krēt′) *adj.* not discreet; lacking prudence; unwise —in′dis·creet′ly *adv.*

in·dis·cre·tion (in′dis kresh′ən) *n.* **1.** lack of discretion **2.** an indiscreet act or remark

in·dis·crim·i·nate (in′dis krim′ə nit) *adj.* **1.** random or promiscuous **2.** not making careful choices or distinctions —in′dis·crim′i·nate·ly *adv.* —in′dis·crim′i·nate·ness *n.*

in·dis·pen·sa·ble (in′dis pen′sə b′l) *adj.* absolutely necessary —in′dis·pen′sa·bly *adv.*

in′dis·posed′ *adj.* **1.** slightly ill **2.** unwilling; disinclined —in′dis·po·si′tion *n.*

in·dis·sol·u·ble (in′di säl′yoo b′l) *adj.* that cannot be dissolved or destroyed; lasting

in·dite (in dīt′) *vt.* -dit′ed, -dit′ing [ME. *enditen*, to write down] to compose and write —in·dite′ment *n.*

in·di·um (in′dē əm) *n.* [< L. *indicum*, indigo: from its spectrum] a silver-white, metallic chemical element: symbol, In; at. wt., 114.82; at. no., 49

in·di·vid·u·al (in′di vij′oo wəl) *adj.* [< L. *individuus*, not divisible] **1.** existing as a separate thing or being; single **2.** of, for, by, or characteristic of a single person or thing **3.** unique or striking —*n.* **1.** a single thing or being **2.** a person

in′di·vid′u·al·ism *n.* **1.** the leading of one's life in one's own way **2.** individuality **3.** the doctrine that the state exists for the individual —in′di·vid′u·al·ist *n., adj.* —in′di·vid′u·al·is′tic *adj.*

in′di·vid′u·al′i·ty (-wal′ə tē) *n., pl.* -ties **1.** the sum of the characteristics that set one person or thing apart **2.** separate existence

in′di·vid′u·al·ize′ (-vij′oo wə līz′) *vt.* -ized′, -iz′ing **1.** to mark as different from others **2.** to make suitable for a certain individual **3.** to consider individually

in′di·vid′u·al·ly *adv.* **1.** one at a time; separately **2.** personally **3.** distinctively

In·do·chi·na (in′dō chī′nə) **1.** peninsula in SE Asia, including Burma, Thailand, Indochina (sense 2), & Malaya **2.** E part of this peninsula, consisting of Laos, Cambodia, & Vietnam Also written **Indo-China** —In′do·chi·nese′, In′do-Chi·nese′ *adj., n., pl.* -nese′

in·doc·tri·nate (in däk′trə nāt′) *vt.* -nat′ed, -nat′ing **1.** to instruct in doctrines, theories, or beliefs **2.** to teach —in·doc′tri·na′tion *n.*

In·do-Eu·ro·pe·an (in′dō yoor′ə pē′ən) *adj.* designating a family of languages without most of those of Europe and some of those of Asia —*n.* this family of languages

in·do·lent (in′də lənt) *adj.* [< L. *in-*, not + *dolere*, to feel pain] avoiding work; idle; lazy —in′do·lence *n.* —in′do·lent·ly *adv.*

in·dom·i·ta·ble (in däm′it ə b′l) *adj.* [< L. *in-*, not + *domare*, to tame] not easily discouraged or defeated

In·do·ne·sia (in′də nē′zhə, -shə) republic in the Malay Archipelago, consisting of Java, Sumatra, most of Borneo, Celebes, West Irian, & smaller islands: 736,510 sq. mi.; pop. 113,721,000; cap. Jakarta —In′do·ne′sian *adj., n.*

in·door (in′dôr′) *adj.* living, belonging, or carried on within a house or building

in·doors (in′dôrz′) *adv.* in or into a building

in·dorse (in dôrs′) *vt.* -dorsed′, -dors′ing *same as* ENDORSE

in·du·bi·ta·ble (in doo′bi tə b′l, -dyoo′-) *adj.* that cannot be doubted; unquestionable —in·du′bi·ta·bly *adv.*

in·duce (in doos′, -dyoos′) *vt.* -duced′, -duc′ing [< L. *in-*, in + *ducere*, to lead] **1.** to persuade **2.** to bring on *[to induce* vomiting with an emetic*]* **3.** to draw (a conclusion) from particular facts **4.** to bring about (an electric or magnetic effect) in a body by placing it within a field of force

in·duce′ment *n.* **1.** an inducing or being induced **2.** a motive; incentive

in·duct (in dukt′) *vt.* [see INDUCE] **1.** to place formally in an office, society, etc. **2.** to enroll (esp. a draftee) in the armed forces

in·duct′ance (-duk′təns) *n.* the property of an electric circuit by which a varying current in it induces voltages in that circuit or in one nearby

---

fat, āpe, cär; ten, ēven; is, bīte; gō, hôrn, ttool, look; oil, out; up, fur; thin, *then*; zh, leisure; ŋ, ring; ə for *a* in *ago*; ′ as in *able* (ā′b′l); ë, Fr. coeur; ö, Fr. feu; Fr. mon; ü, Fr. duc; r, Fr. cri; kh, G. doch, ich.　‡ foreign; < derived from

in·duct·ee (in duk′tē′) *n.* a person being inducted
in·duc·tion (in duk′shən) *n.* **1.** an inducting or being inducted **2.** reasoning from particular facts to a general conclusion **3.** the inducing of an electric or magnetic effect by the influence of a field of force —**in·duc′tive** *adj.*
induction coil an apparatus made up of a primary and a secondary coil: interruptions of the direct current in the primary induce a high-voltage alternating current in the secondary
in·duc′tor (-tər) *n.* a device designed to introduce inductance into an electric circuit
in·due (in dōō′, -dyōō′) *vt.* -**dued′**, -**du′ing** *same as* ENDUE
in·dulge (in dulj′) *vt.* -**dulged′**, -**dulg′ing** [L. *indulgere*, be kind to] **1.** to satisfy (a desire) **2.** to gratify the wishes of; humor —*vi.* to give way to one's desires —**in·dulg′er** *n.*
in·dul′gence (-dul′jəns) *n.* **1.** an indulging or being indulgent **2.** a thing indulged in **3.** a favor or privilege **4.** *R.C.Ch.* a remission of punishment still due for a sin after the guilt has been forgiven
in·dul′gent *adj.* indulging or inclined to indulge; kind or lenient, often to excess —**in·dul′gent·ly** *adv.*
in·du·rate (in′dōō rāt′, -dyōō-) *vt.*, *vi.* -**rat′ed**, -**rat′ing** [< L. *in-*, in + *durare*, harden] **1.** to harden **2.** to make or become callous or unfeeling —*adj.* **1.** hardened **2.** unfeeling —**in′du·ra′tion** *n.*
In·dus (in′dəs) river in S Asia, flowing from SW Tibet into the Arabian Sea: c.1,900 mi.
in·dus·tri·al (in dus′trē əl) *adj.* **1.** of, connected with, or resulting from industries **2.** of or concerned with people working in industries **3.** working in industries **4.** for use by industries: said of products —**in·dus′tri·al·ly** *adv.*
industrial arts the mechanical and technical skills used in industry, esp. as taught in schools
in·dus′tri·al·ism *n.* economic and social organization characterized by large industries, etc.
in·dus′tri·al·ist *n.* one who owns or manages an industrial enterprise
in·dus′tri·al·ize′ *vt.* -**ized′**, -**iz′ing** **1.** to develop industrialism in **2.** to organize as an industry —**in·dus′tri·al·i·za′tion** *n.*
industrial relations relations between industrial employers and their employees
in·dus·tri·ous (in dus′trē əs) *adj.* characterized by earnest, steady effort; hard-working —**in·dus′tri·ous·ly** *adv.* —**in·dus′tri·ous·ness** *n.*
in·dus·try (in′dəs trē) *n.*, *pl.* -**tries** [< L. *industrius*, active] **1.** earnest, steady effort **2.** systematic work **3.** any branch of production, esp. manufacturing, or all of these collectively **4.** the owners and managers of industry
-ine′ [< L. -*inus*] *a suffix meaning* of, having the nature of, like [*divine, crystalline*]
-ine² [< L. -*ina*] *a suffix used to form certain abstract nouns* [*medicine, doctrine*]
-ine³ [< L. -*inus*] *a suffix used to form the chemical names of: a)* halogens [*iodine*] *b)* alkaloids or nitrogen bases [*morphine*] Often used to form commercial names [*Vaseline*]
in·e·bri·ate (in ē′brē āt′) *vt.* -**at′ed**, -**at′ing** [ult. < L. *in-*, intens. + *ebrius*, drunk] **1.** to make drunk; intoxicate **2.** to excite; exhilarate —*n.* (-it) a drunkard —**in·e′bri·at′ed** *adj.* —**in·e′bri·a′tion**, **in·e·bri·e·ty** (in′ē brī′ə tē) *n.*
in·ef·fa·ble (in ef′ə b'l) *adj.* [< L. *in-*, not + *effabilis*, utterable] **1.** too overwhelming to be expressed in words **2.** too sacred to be spoken —**in·ef′fa·bly** *adv.*
in·ef·fi·cient (in′ə fish′ənt) *adj.* not producing the desired effect with a minimum of energy, time, etc. **2.** incapable —**in′ef·fi′cien·cy** *n.*
in·ept (in ept′) *adj.* [< L. *in-*, not + *aptus*, fit] **1.** unsuitable; unfit **2.** absurd; foolish **3.** clumsy; inefficient —**in·ept′ly** *adv.* —**in·ept′ness** *n.*
in·ept·i·tude (in ep′tə tōōd′, -tyōōd′) *n.* **1.** a being inept **2.** an inept act, remark, etc.
in·ert (in urt′) *adj.* [< L. *in-*, not + *ars*, skill] **1.** without power to move or act **2.** inactive; dull; slow **3.** with few or no active properties —**in·ert′ly** *adv.* —**in·ert′ness** *n.*
in·er·tia (in ur′shə) *n.* [see INERT] **1.** *Physics* the tendency of matter to remain at rest (or continue in a fixed direction) unless affected by an outside force **2.** disinclination to move or act
in·es·cap·a·ble (in′ə skāp′ə b'l) *adj.* that cannot be escaped or avoided —**in′es·cap′a·bly** *adv.*
in·es·ti·ma·ble (in es′tə mə b'l) *adj.* too great to be properly estimated —**in·es′ti·ma·bly** *adv.*
in·ev·i·ta·ble (in ev′ə tə b'l) *adj.* [< L. *in-*, not + *evitabilis*, avoidable] that cannot be avoided; certain to happen —**in·ev′i·ta·bil′i·ty** *n.* —**in·ev′i·ta·bly** *adv.*

in·ex·haust·i·ble (in′ig zôs′tə b'l) *adj.* **1.** that cannot be exhausted or used up **2.** tireless
in·ex·o·ra·ble (in ek′sər ə b'l) *adj.* [< L. *in-*, not + *exorare*, move by entreaty] **1.** that cannot be influenced by persuasion or entreaty; unrelenting **2.** that cannot be altered, checked, etc. —**in·ex′o·ra·bil′i·ty** *n.* —**in·ex′o·ra·bly** *adv.*
in·ex·pen·sive (in′ik spen′siv) *adj.* not expensive; low-priced; cheap —**in′ex·pen′sive·ly** *adv.*
in·ex·pe·ri·ence (in′ik spir′ē əns) *n.* lack of experience or of the knowledge or skill resulting from experience —**in′ex·pe′ri·enced** *adj.*
in·ex·pert (in ek′spərt, in′ik spurt′) *adj.* not expert; unskillful —**in·ex′pert·ly** *adv.*
in·ex·pi·a·ble (in ek′spē ə b'l) *adj.* that cannot be expiated or atoned for [*an inexpiable sin*]
in·ex·pli·ca·ble (in eks′pli kə b'l) *adj.* that cannot be explained —**in·ex′pli·ca·bly** *adv.*
in·ex·press·i·ble (in′ik spres′ə b'l) *adj.* that cannot be expressed —**in′ex·press′i·bly** *adv.*
in·ex·tin·guish·a·ble (in′ik stiŋ′gwish ə b'l) *adj.* that cannot be put out or stopped
‡in ex·tre·mis (in′ ik strē′mis) [L., in extremity] at the point of death
in·ex·tri·ca·ble (in eks′tri kə b'l) *adj.* **1.** that one cannot extricate himself from **2.** that cannot be disentangled or untied **3.** insolvable —**in·ex′tri·ca·bly** *adv.*
inf. 1. infantry: also **Inf. 2.** infinitive
in·fal·li·ble (in fal′ə b'l) *adj.* [see IN-² & FALLIBLE] **1.** incapable of error **2.** not liable to fail, go wrong, etc.; reliable; sure **3.** *R.C.Ch.* incapable of error in setting forth doctrine on faith and morals —**in·fal′li·bil′i·ty** *n.* —**in·fal′li·bly** *adv.*
in·fa·mous (in′fə məs) *adj.* **1.** having a bad reputation; notorious **2.** causing a bad reputation; scandalous —**in′fa·mous·ly** *adv.*
in·fa·my (in′fə mē) *n.*, *pl.* -**mies** **1.** very bad reputation; disgrace **2.** great wickedness **3.** an infamous act
in·fan·cy (in′fən sē) *n.*, *pl.* -**cies** **1.** the state or period of being an infant **2.** the earliest stage of anything **3.** *Law* the state of being a minor
in·fant (in′fənt) *n.* [< L. *in-*, not + *fari*, speak] **1.** a very young child; baby **2.** *Law* a minor —*adj.* **1.** of or for infants **2.** in a very early stage
in·fan·ta (in fan′tə) *n.* [Sp. & Port., fem. of *infante*: see INFANTE] **1.** any daughter of a king of Spain or Portugal **2.** the wife of an infante
in·fan·te (in fan′tā) *n.* [Sp. & Port.: see INFANT] any son of a king of Spain or Portugal, except the heir to the throne
in·fan·ti·cide (in fan′tə sīd′) *n.* [< L. *infans*, child + *caedere*, to kill] the murder of a baby
in·fan·tile (in′fən tīl′, -til) *adj.* **1.** of infants **2.** like an infant; babyish
infantile paralysis *same as* POLIOMYELITIS
in·fan·try (in′fən trē) *n.*, *pl.* -**tries** [< It. *infante*, a youth] that branch of an army consisting of soldiers trained to fight on foot —**in′fan·try·man** (-mən) *n.*, *pl.* -**men**
in·farct (in färkt′) *n.* [< L. *in-*, in + *farcire*, to stuff] an area of dying or dead tissue caused by obstruction of blood vessels: also **in·farc′tion** (-färk′shən)
in·fat·u·ate (in fach′ōō wāt′) *vt.* -**at′ed**, -**at′ing** [< L. *in-*, intens. + *fatuus*, foolish] to inspire with foolish love or affection —**in·fat′u·a′tion** *n.*
in·fat′u·at′ed *adj.* completely carried away by foolish love or affection
in·fect (in fekt′) *vt.* [< L. *inficere*, to stain] **1.** to contaminate, or cause to become diseased, with a germ or virus **2.** to imbue with one's feelings or beliefs, esp. so as to harm
in·fec·tion (in fek′shən) *n.* **1.** an infecting or being infected **2.** an infectious disease **3.** anything that infects
in·fec′tious (-shəs) *adj.* **1.** likely to cause infection **2.** designating a disease caused by the presence in the body of certain microorganisms **3.** tending to spread to others —**in·fec′tious·ly** *adv.*
in·fer (in fur′) *vt.* -**ferred′**, -**fer′ring** [< L. *in-*, in + *ferre*, bring] **1.** to conclude by reasoning from something known or assumed **2.** to imply: still sometimes regarded as a loose usage
in·fer·ence (in′fər əns) *n.* **1.** an inferring **2.** something inferred; logical conclusion
in·fer·en·tial (in′fə ren′shəl) *adj.* of or based on inference —**in′fer·en′tial·ly** *adv.*
in·fe·ri·or (in fir′ē ər) *adj.* [< L. *inferus*, low] **1.** lower in space **2.** lower in order, status, quality, etc. (with *to*) **3.** poor in quality; below average —*n.* an inferior person or thing —**in·fe′ri·or′i·ty** (-ôr′ə tē) *n.*

inferiority complex *Psychol.* a neurotic condition resulting from various feelings of inferiority

in·fer·nal (in fur'n'l) *adj.* [< L. *inferus*, below] **1.** of hell or Hades **2.** hellish; fiendish **3.** [Colloq.] hateful; outrageous —**in·fer'nal·ly** *adv.*

in·fer·no (in fur'nō) *n., pl.* -nos [It. < L.: see prec.] hell or any place suggesting hell

in·fest (in fest') *vt.* [< Fr. < L. *infestus*, hostile] **1.** to overrun in large numbers, usually so as to be harmful **2.** to be parasitic in or on —**in'fes·ta'tion** *n.*

in·fi·del (in'fə d'l) *n.* [< L. *in-*, not + *fidelis*, faithful] **1.** one who does not believe in a particular, esp. the prevailing, religion **2.** one who has no religion —*adj.* **1.** that is an infidel **2.** of infidels

in·fi·del·i·ty (in'fə del'ə tē) *n., pl.* -ties **1.** unfaithfulness, esp. in marriage **2.** an unfaithful or disloyal act

in·field (in'fēld') *n.* **1.** the area enclosed by the four base lines on a baseball field **2.** the infielders collectively

in'field'er *n. Baseball* a player whose position is in the infield; shortstop, first baseman, second baseman, or third baseman

in'fight'ing *n.* **1.** fighting, esp. boxing, at close range **2.** intense personal conflict within a group

in·fil·trate (in fil'trāt, in'fil trāt') *vi., vt.* -trat·ed, -trat·ing **1.** to filter or pass gradually through or into **2.** to penetrate (enemy lines, a region, etc.) gradually or stealthily, so as to attack or seize control from within — **in'fil·tra'tion** *n.*

in·fi·nite (in'fə nit) *adj.* [see IN-² & FINITE] **1.** lacking limits; endless **2.** very great; vast —*n.* something infinite —**the Infinite (Being)** God —**in'fi·nite·ly** *adv.*

in·fin·i·tes·i·mal (in'fin ə tes'ə məl) *adj.* [< L. *infinitus*, infinite] too small to be measured; very minute —*n.* an infinitesimal quantity —**in'fin·i·tes'i·mal·ly** *adv.*

in·fin·i·tive (in fin'ə tiv) *n.* [see INFINITE] the form of a verb without reference to person, number, or tense: usually following *to* (*to go*) or another verb form (*can he go*) —**in·fin'i·ti'val** (-tī'vəl) *adj.*

in·fin'i·tude' (-tood', -tyood') *n.* **1.** a being infinite **2.** an infinite quantity or extent

in·fin'i·ty (-tē) *n., pl.* -ties [< L. *infinitas*] **1.** the quality of being infinite **2.** unlimited space, time, etc. **3.** an indefinitely large quantity

in·firm (in furm') *adj.* **1.** weak; feeble **2.** not firm; unstable —**in·firm'ly** *adv.* —**in·firm'ness** *n.*

in·fir·ma·ry (in fur'mə rē) *n., pl.* -ries a place for the care of the sick, injured, or infirm; hospital

in·fir'mi·ty (-mə tē) *n., pl.* -ties **1.** physical weakness or defect **2.** moral weakness

in·fix (in fiks') *vt.* **1.** to fix firmly in **2.** to instill; teach — *n.* (in'fiks') one or more syllables placed within the body of a word to modify its meaning

in·flame (in flām') *vt., vi.* -flamed', -flam'ing [see IN-¹ & FLAME] **1.** to arouse, excite, etc. or become aroused, excited, etc. **2.** to undergo or cause to undergo inflammation

in·flam·ma·ble (in flam'ə b'l) *adj.* **1.** *same as* FLAMMABLE **2.** easily excited —*n.* anything flammable —**in·flam'ma·bil'i·ty** *n.* —**in·flam'ma·bly** *adv.*

in·flam·ma·tion (in'flə mā'shən) *n.* **1.** an inflaming or being inflamed **2.** redness, pain, heat, and swelling in some part of the body, caused by injury or disease

in·flam·ma·to·ry (in flam'ə tôr'ē) *adj.* **1.** rousing or likely to rouse excitement, anger, etc. **2.** of or caused by inflammation

in·flate (in flāt') *vt.* -flat'ed, -flat'ing [< L. *in-*, in + *flare*, to blow] **1.** to blow full with air or gas **2.** to puff up with pride **3.** to increase beyond what is normal; specif., to cause inflation of (money, credit, etc.) —*vi.* to become inflated —**in·flat'a·ble** *adj.* —**in·flat'er, in·fla'tor** *n.*

in·fla'tion *n.* **1.** an inflating or being inflated **2.** an increase in the currency in circulation or a marked expansion of credit, resulting in a fall in currency value and a sharp rise in prices —**in·fla'tion·ar'y** *adj.*

in·flect (in flekt') *vt.* [< L. *in-*, in + *flectere*, to bend] **1.** to bend **2.** to vary the tone of (the voice) **3.** to change the form of (a word) by inflection, as in conjugating or declining

in·flec·tion (in flek'shən) *n.* **1.** a bend **2.** a change in the tone of the voice **3.** the change in form of a word to indicate number, case, gender, tense, etc. Brit. sp. **in·flex'ion** —**in·flec'tion·al** *adj.*

in·flex·i·ble (in flek'sə b'l) *adj.* not flexible; specif., *a)* rigid *b)* firm in mind; stubborn *c)* unalterable —**in·flex'i·bil'i·ty** *n.* —**in·flex'i·bly** *adv.*

in·flict (in flikt') *vt.* [< L. *in-*, on + *fligere*, to strike] **1.** to cause (wounds, pain, etc.) as by striking **2.** to impose (a punishment, etc. *on* or *upon*) —**in·flict'er, in·flic'tor** *n.* —**in·flic'tion** *n.*

in·flight (in'flīt') *adj.* done, shown, etc. while an aircraft is in flight

in·flo·res·cence (in'flô res''ns) *n.* [see IN-¹ & FLORESCENCE] *Bot.* **1.** a flowering **2.** the arrangement of flowers on a stem **3.** a single flower cluster **4.** flowers collectively

in·flu·ence (in'floo wəns) *n.* [< L. *in-*, in + *fluere*, to flow] **1.** *a)* the power to affect others *b)* the effect of such power **2.** the ability to produce effects because of wealth, high position, etc. **3.** one that has influence —*vt.* -enced, -encing to have influence or an effect on

INFLORESCENCES (left, raceme; right, spadix)

in'flu·en'tial (-wen'shəl) *adj.* exerting influence, esp. great influence —**in'flu·en'tial·ly** *adv.*

in·flu·en·za (in'floo wen'zə) *n.* [It., an influence] an acute, contagious virus infection, characterized by inflammation of the respiratory tract, fever, muscular pain, etc.

in·flux (in'fluks') *n.* [Fr.: see INFLUENCE] **1.** a flowing in or streaming in **2.** the point where a river joins another body of water

in·fold (in fōld') *vt. same as* ENFOLD

in·form (in fôrm') *vt.* [see IN-¹ & FORM] to give knowledge of something to —*vi.* to give information, esp. in accusing another —**in·form'er** *n.*

in·for·mal (in fôr'məl) *adj.* not formal; specif., *a)* not according to fixed customs, rules, etc. *b)* casual, relaxed, etc. *c)* not requiring formal dress *d)* colloquial —**in'for·mal'i·ty** (-mal'ə tē) *n., pl.* -ties —**in·for'mal·ly** *adv.*

in·form·ant (in fôr'mənt) *n.* a person who gives information

in·for·ma·tion (in'fər mā'shən) *n.* **1.** an informing or being informed **2.** something told or facts learned; news or knowledge **3.** a person or agency answering questions as a service to others **4.** data stored in or retrieved from a computer —**in'for·ma'tion·al** *adj.*

in·form·a·tive (in fôr'mə tiv) *adj.* giving information; instructive

infra- [< L.] *a prefix meaning* below

in·frac·tion (in frak'shən) *n.* [see INFRINGE] a violation of a law, pact, etc.

in·fran·gi·ble (in fran'jə b'l) *adj.* [see IN-² & FRANGIBLE] unbreakable or inviolable

in·fra·red (in'frə red') *adj.* designating or of those invisible rays just beyond the red of the visible spectrum: they have a penetrating heating effect

in'fra·struc'ture *n.* the basic facilities on which a city, state, etc. depends, as roads or schools

in·fre·quent (in frē'kwənt) *adj.* not frequent; happening seldom; rare —**in·fre'quen·cy, in·fre'quence** *n.* —**in·fre'quent·ly** *adv.*

in·fringe (in frinj') *vt.* -fringed', -fring'ing [< L. *in-*, in + *frangere*, to break] to break or violate (a law or pact) — **infringe on** (or **upon**) to encroach on (the rights, etc. of others) —**in·fringe'ment** *n.* —**in·fring'er** *n.*

in·fu·ri·ate (in fyoor'ē āt') *vt.* -at'ed, -at'ing [< L. *in-*, in + *furia*, rage] to make very angry; enrage —**in·fu'ri·a'tion** *n.*

in·fuse (in fyooz') *vt.* -fused', -fus'ing [< L. *in-*, in + *fundere*, pour] **1.** to instill or impart (qualities, etc.) **2.** to fill; inspire **3.** to steep (tea leaves, etc.) to extract the essence —in·fu'sion (-fyoo'zhən) *n.*

in·fu'si·ble *adj.* that cannot be fused or melted

in·fu·so·ri·an (in'fyoo sôr'ē ən) *n.* [from their occurrence in infusions] any of certain protozoans having cilia that permit free movement —*adj.* of these protozoans: also **in'·fu·so'ri·al**

-ing [< OE.] *a suffix used to form the present participle or verbal nouns* [*talking, painting*]

in·gen·ious (in jēn'yəs) *adj.* [< L. *in-*, in + *gignere*, to produce] **1.** clever, resourceful, etc. **2.** made or done in a clever or original way —**in·gen'ious·ly** *adv.* —**in·gen'ious·ness** *n.*

in·gé·nue (an'zhə noo', -jə-) *n.* [Fr., ingenuous] *Theater* **1.** the role of an innocent, inexperienced young woman **2.** an actress playing such a role

in·ge·nu·i·ty (in'jə noo'ə tē) *n.* ingenious quality; cleverness

in·gen·u·ous (in jen'yoo wəs) *adj.* [< L. *in-*, in + *gignere*, to produce] **1.** frank; open **2.** simple; naive —**in·gen'u·ous·ly** *adv.* —**in·gen'u·ous·ness** *n.*

in·gest (in jest') *vt.* [< L. *in-*, into + *gerere*, carry] to take (food, etc.) into the body, as by swallowing —**in·ges'tion** *n.* —**in·ges'tive** *adj.*

in·glo·ri·ous (in glôr'ē əs) *adj.* shameful; disgraceful —**in·glo'ri·ous·ly** *adv.*

in·got (iŋ'gət) *n.* [prob. < OPr. *lingo*, tongue] a mass of metal cast into a bar or other convenient shape

in·grained (in grānd') *adj.* **1.** firmly established, as habits **2.** inveterate *[an ingrained* liar]

in·grate (in'grāt) *n.* [< L. *in-*, not + *gratus*, grateful] an ungrateful person

in·gra·ti·ate (in grā'shē āt') *vt.* -at'ed, -at'ing [< L. *in-*, in + *gratia*, favor] to bring (oneself) into another's favor —**in·gra'ti·at'ing·ly** *adv.* —**in·gra'ti·a'tion** *n.*

in·grat·i·tude (in grat'ə tōōd', -tyōōd') *n.* lack of gratitude; ungratefulness

in·gre·di·ent (in grē'dē ənt) *n.* [see INGRESS] any of the things that make up a mixture; component

in·gress (in'gres) *n.* [< L. *in-*, into + *gradi*, go] **1.** the act of entering **2.** the right to enter **3.** an entrance

in·grown (in'grōn') *adj.* grown inward, esp. into the flesh, as a toenail

in·gui·nal (iŋ'gwə n'l) *adj.* [< L. *inguen*, groin] of or near the groin

in·gulf (in gulf') *vt.* *same as* ENGULF

in·hab·it (in hab'it) *vt.* [< L. *in-*, in + *habitare*, dwell] to live in —**in·hab'it·a·ble** *adj.*

in·hab·it·ant (-i tənt) *n.* a person or animal that inhabits a specified place

in·hal·ant (in hāl'ənt) *adj.* used in inhalation —*n.* a medicine to be inhaled as a vapor

in·ha·la·tor (in'hə lāt'ər) *n.* **1.** an apparatus used in inhaling medicinal vapors **2.** *same as* RESPIRATOR (sense 2)

in·hale (in hāl') *vt., vi.* -haled', -hal'ing [< L. *in-*, in + *halare*, breathe] to breathe in (air or smoke) —**in·ha·la·tion** (in'hə lā'shən) *n.*

in·hal'er *n.* **1.** one who inhales **2.** *same as: a)* RESPIRATOR (sense 1) *b)* INHALATOR (sense 1)

in·here (in hir') *vi.* -hered', -her'ing [< L. *in-*, in + *haerere*, to stick] to be inherent

in·her·ent (in hir'ənt, -her'-) *adj.* [see prec.] existing in someone or something as a natural and inseparable quality, right, etc. —**in·her'ence** *n.* —**in·her'ent·ly** *adv.*

in·her·it (in her'it) *vt., vi.* [< L. *in*, in + *heres*, heir] **1.** to receive (property, etc.) as an heir **2.** to have (certain characteristics) by heredity —**in·her'i·tor** *n.*

in·her·it·a·ble *adj.* **1.** capable of inheriting **2.** that can be inherited

in·her·it·ance *n.* **1.** the action of inheriting **2.** something inherited or to be inherited; legacy **3.** right to inherit

in·hib·it (in hib'it) *vt.* [< L. *in-*, in + *habere*, to hold] to hold back; check or repress —**in·hib'i·tive, in·hib'i·to'ry** (-i tôr'ē) *adj.* —**in·hib'it·or, in·hib'it·er** *n.*

in·hi·bi·tion (in'hi bish'ən, in'ə-) *n.* **1.** an inhibiting or being inhibited **2.** a mental process that restrains an action, emotion, or thought

in·hu·man (in hyōō'mən) *adj.* not having worthy human characteristics; heartless, cruel, brutal, etc.

in·hu·man·i·ty (in'hyōō man'ə tē) *n.* **1.** a being inhuman **2.** *pl.* -ties an inhuman act or remark

in·im·i·cal (in im'i k'l) *adj.* [< L. *in-*, not + *amicus*, friend] **1.** hostile; unfriendly **2.** in opposition; adverse —**in·im'i·cal·ly** *adv.*

in·im·i·ta·ble (in im'ə tə b'l) *adj.* that cannot be imitated; matchless —**in·im'i·ta·bly** *adv.*

in·iq·ui·ty (in ik'wə tē) *n.* [< L. *in-*, not + *aequus*, equal] **1.** wickedness; sin **2.** *pl.* -ties a wicked or unjust act —**in·iq'ui·tous** *adj.* —**in·iq'ui·tous·ly** *adv.*

in·i·tial (i nish'əl) *adj.* [< L. *in-*, in + *ire*, go] of or at the beginning; first —*n.* the first letter of a name —*vt.* -tialed or -tialled, -tial·ing or -tial·ling to mark with initials —**in·i'tial·ly** *adv.*

in·i·ti·ate (i nish'ē āt') *vt.* -at'ed, -at'ing [see INITIAL] **1.** to bring into practice or use **2.** to teach the fundamentals of a subject to **3.** to admit as a member into a fraternity, club, etc., esp. with a special or secret ceremony —*n.* (*usually* -it) one who has recently been, or is about to be, initiated —**in·i'ti·a'tion** *n.* —**in·i'ti·a·tor** *n.*

in·i·ti·a·tive (i nish'ē ə tiv, -nish'ə-) *n.* **1.** the action of taking the first step or move **2.** ability in originating new ideas or methods **3.** the introduction of proposed legislation, as to popular vote, by voters' petitions

in·i'ti·a·to'ry (-tôr'ē) *adj.* **1.** beginning; introductory **2.** of or used in an initiation

in·ject (in jekt') *vt.* [< L. *in-*, in + *jacere*, to throw] **1.** to force (a fluid) into a vein, tissue, etc by means of a syringe, etc. **2.** to introduce (a remark, quality, etc.) —**in·jec'tion** *n.* —**in·jec'tor** *n.*

in·junc·tion (in juŋk'shən) *n.* [< L. *in-*, in + *jungere*, join] **1.** a command; order **2.** a court order prohibiting a person or group from carrying out a given action, or ordering a given action to be done —**in·junc'tive** *adj.*

in·jure (in'jər) *vt.* -jured, -jur·ing [see INJURY] **1.** to do physical harm to; hurt **2.** to wrong or offend **3.** to weaken (a reputation, etc.)

in·ju·ri·ous (in joor'ē əs) *adj.* **1.** injuring or likely to injure; harmful **2.** offensive; abusive —**in·ju'ri·ous·ly** *adv.* —**in·ju'ri·ous·ness** *n.*

in·ju·ry (in'jər ē) *n., pl.* -ries [< L. *in-*, not + *jus*, right] **1.** physical harm to a person, etc. **2.** an injurious act

in·jus·tice (in jus'tis) *n.* **1.** a being unjust **2.** an unjust act; wrong

ink (iŋk) *n.* [< Gr. *en-*, in + *kaiein*, to burn] a colored liquid used for writing, printing, etc. —*vt.* to cover, mark, or color with ink

ink'blot' *n.* any of the patterns made by blots of ink that are used in the RORSCHACH TEST

ink·ling (iŋk'liŋ) *n.* [ME. *ingkiling*] **1.** a hint; suggestion **2.** a vague notion

ink'stand' *n.* **1.** a small stand holding an inkwell, pens, etc. **2.** *same as* INKWELL

ink'well' *n.* a container for ink

ink'y *adj.* -i·er, -i·est **1.** like very dark ink in color; black **2.** covered with ink —**ink'i·ness** *n.*

in·laid (in'lād', in lād') *adj.* set into a surface or formed, decorated, etc. by inlaying

in·land (in'lənd; *for n. & adv. usually* -land') *adj.* of or in the interior of a country —*n.* inland areas —*adv.* into or toward the interior

in·law (in'lô') *n.* [< (MOTHER)-IN-LAW, etc.] [Colloq.] a relative by marriage

in·lay (in'lā'; *for v., also in* lā') *vt.* -laid', -lay'ing **1.** *a)* to set (pieces of wood, metal, etc.) into, and level with, a surface to make a design *b)* to decorate thus **2.** to add extra silverplating to —*n., pl.* -lays' **1.** inlaid decoration or material **2.** a filling for a tooth made from a mold and cemented in —**in'lay'er** *n.*

in·let (in'let) *n.* **1.** a narrow strip of water extending into a body of land, or between islands **2.** an entrance, as to a culvert

in·mate (in'māt') *n.* a person living with others in the same building, now esp. one confined with others in a prison, etc.

in me·mo·ri·am (in mə môr'ē əm) [L.] in memory (of)

in·most (in'mōst') *adj.* **1.** located farthest within **2.** most intimate or secret *[inmost* thoughts*]*

inn (in) *n.* [OE.] **1.** a small hotel **2.** a restaurant or tavern

in·nards (in'ərdz) *n.pl.* [< INWARDS] [Colloq.] inner organs or parts

in·nate (i nāt', in'āt) *adj.* [< L. *in-*, in + *nasci*, be born] inborn; natural —**in·nate'ly** *adv.*

in·ner (in'ər) *adj.* **1.** located farther within; interior **2.** of the mind or spirit **3.** more intimate or secret *[the inner* emotions*]*

inner circle the small, exclusive, most influential part of a group

inner city the central sections of a large city, esp. when crowded or blighted

in'ner·most' *adj.* *same as* INMOST

in'ner·spring' mattress a mattress with built-in coil springs

in·ning (in'iŋ) *n.* [< OE. *innung*, getting in] **1.** *Baseball* & (*pl.*) *Cricket a)* a team's turn at bat *b)* a numbered round of play in which both teams have a turn at bat **2.** [*often pl.*] the period of action, exercise of authority, etc.

inn'keep'er *n.* the owner of an inn

in·no·cence (in'ə səns) *n.* a being innocent; specif., *a)* freedom from sin or guilt *b)* guilelessness; simplicity *c)* naiveté *d)* harmlessness

in·no·cent (in'ə sənt) *adj.* [< L. *in-*, not + *nocere*, to harm] **1.** free from sin, evil, etc.; specif., not guilty of a specific crime **2.** harmless **3.** knowing no evil **4.** without guile; artless **5.** naive —*n.* an innocent person, as a child —**in'no·cent·ly** *adv.*

in·noc·u·ous (i näk'yoo wəs) *adj.* [see prec.] harmless —**in·noc'u·ous·ly** *adv.*

in·nom·i·nate bone (i näm'ə nit) [< LL. *innominatus*, unnamed + BONE] either of two large, irregular bones of the pelvis; hipbone

in·no·vate (in'ə vāt') *vi.* -vat'ed, -vat'ing [< L. *in-*, in + *novus*, new] to introduce new methods, devices, etc. —*vt.*

to bring in as an innovation —**in′no·va′tive** *adj.* —**in′no·va′tor** *n.*

in·no·va·tion (-vā′shən) *n.* **1.** an innovating **2.** a new method, practice, device, etc.

in·nu·en·do (in′yoo wen′dō) *n., pl.* **-does, -dos** [L. < *in-,* in + *-nuere,* to nod] a hint or sly remark, usually derogatory; insinuation

in·nu·mer·a·ble (i noo′mər ə b′l) *adj.* too numerous to be counted —**in·nu′mer·a·bly** *adv.*

in·oc·u·late (i näk′yoo lāt′) *vt.* **-lat′ed, -lat′ing** [< L. *in-,* in + *oculus,* eye] to inject a serum or vaccine into, esp. in order to create immunity —**in·oc′u·la′tion** *n.* —**in·oc′u·la′tor** *n.*

in·of·fen·sive (in′ə fen′siv) *adj.* causing no harm or annoyance; unobjectionable —**in′of·fen′sive·ly** *adv.* —**in′of·fen′sive·ness** *n.*

in·op·er·a·tive (in äp′ər ə tiv, -ə rāt′iv) *adj.* not working or functioning

in·or·di·nate (in ôr′d′n it) *adj.* [< L. *in-,* not + *ordo,* an order] **1.** too great or too many; immoderate **2.** disordered —**in·or′di·nate·ly** *adv.*

in·or·gan·ic (in′ôr gan′ik) *adj.* not organic; specif., *a)* designating or of matter not animal or vegetable; not living *b)* designating a chemical compound not organic —**in′·or·gan′i·cal·ly** *adv.*

in·put (in′poot′) *n.* what is put in, as power into a machine, information into a computer, etc.

in·quest (in′kwest) *n.* [see INQUIRE] a judicial inquiry, esp. when held before a jury, as a coroner's investigation of a death

in·qui·e·tude (in kwī′ə tood′, -tyood′) *n.* restlessness; uneasiness

in·quire (in kwīr′) *vi.* **-quired′, -quir′ing** [< L. *in-,* into + *quaerere,* seek] **1.** to ask a question or questions **2.** to investigate (usually with *into*) —*vt.* to seek information about —**inquire after** to pay respects by asking about the health of —**in·quir′er** *n.* —**in·quir′ing·ly** *adv.*

in·quir·y (in′kwə rē, in kwīr′ē) *n., pl.* **-ies 1.** an inquiring; investigation **2.** a question

in·qui·si·tion (in′kwə zish′ən) *n.* **1.** an inquiry or investigation **2.** [I-] *R.C.Ch.* formerly, the tribunal for suppressing heresy and heretics **3.** any harsh suppression of nonconformity **4.** any relentless questioning —**in′qui·si′tion·al** *adj.*

in·quis·i·tive (in kwiz′ə tiv) *adj.* **1.** inclined to ask many questions **2.** unnecessarily curious; prying —**in·quis′i·tive·ly** *adv.* —**in·quis′i·tive·ness** *n.*

in·quis·i·tor (in kwiz′ə tər) *n.* **1.** an investigator **2.** [I-] an official of the Inquisition —**in·quis′i·to′ri·al** (-tôr′ē əl) *adj.* —**in·quis′i·to′ri·al·ly** *adv.*

in re (in rē, rā) [L.] in the matter (of); concerning

in·res′i·dence *adj.* having specific duties, often as a teacher, but given time to work at one's profession

I.N.R.I. [L. *Iesus Nazarenus, Rex Iudaeorum*] Jesus of Nazareth, King of the Jews

in·road (in′rōd′) *n.* **1.** a sudden invasion or raid **2.** [*usually pl.*] any injurious encroachment

in′rush′ *n.* a rushing in

ins. 1. inches **2.** insurance

in·sane (in sān′) *adj.* **1.** mentally ill or deranged; mad **2.** of or for insane people **3.** very foolish; senseless —**insane′ly** *adv.*

in·san·i·ty (in san′ə tē) *n., pl.* **-ties 1.** mental illness: a term used formally in law **2.** great folly

in·sa·ti·a·ble (in sā′shə b′l, -shē ə-) *adj.* [see IN-[2] & SATIATE] that cannot be satisfied —**in·sa′ti·a·bly** *adv.*

in·scribe (in skrīb′) *vt.* **-scribed′, -scrib′ing** [< L. *in-,* in + *scribere,* write] **1.** to mark or engrave (words, symbols, etc.) on (a surface) **2.** to add (a person's name) to a list **3.** *a)* to dedicate (a book, etc.) informally *b)* to autograph **4.** to fix in the mind **5.** *Geom.* to draw (a figure) inside another figure so that their boundaries touch at as many points as possible —**in·scrib′er** *n.*

in·scrip·tion (in skrip′shən) *n.* **1.** an inscribing **2.** something inscribed **3.** an informal dedication in a book, etc. —**in·scrip′tive** *adj.*

in·scru·ta·ble (in skroot′ə b′l) *adj.* [< L. *in-,* not + *scrutari,* examine] not easily understood; enigmatic —**in·scru′ta·bil′i·ty** *n.* —**in·scru′ta·bly** *adv.*

in·seam (in′sēm′) *n.* the inner seam from the crotch to the bottom of a trouser leg

in·sect (in′sekt) *n.* [< L. *insectum,* lit., notched] **1.** any of a large group of small arthropod animals, as beetles, flies, wasps, etc., having three pairs of legs and, usually, wings

2. popularly, any of a group of small animals, usually wingless, including spiders, centipedes, ticks, mites, etc.

in·sec·ti·cide (in sek′tə sīd′) *n.* any substance used to kill insects —**in·sec′ti·ci′dal** *adj.*

in·sec′ti·vore′ (-vôr′) *n.* [Fr.] any animal or plant that feeds on insects

in′sec·tiv′o·rous (-tiv′ər əs) *adj.* [< INSECT + L. *vorare,* devour] feeding chiefly on insects

in·se·cure (in′si kyoor′) *adj.* **1.** not safe from danger **2.** feeling anxiety **3.** not firm or dependable —**in′se·cure′ly** *adv.* —**in′se·cu′ri·ty** *n., pl.* **-ties**

in·sem·i·nate (in sem′ə nāt′) *vt.* **-nat′ed, -nat′ing** [< L. *in-,* in + *semen,* seed] **1.** to impregnate with semen **2.** to imbue (with ideas, etc.) —**in·sem′i·na′tion** *n.*

in·sen·sate (in sen′sāt, -sit) *adj.* **1.** not feeling sensation **2.** foolish; stupid **3.** without feeling for others; cold

in·sen·si·ble (in sen′sə b′l) *adj.* **1.** unable to perceive with the senses **2.** unconscious **3.** unaware; indifferent **4.** so slight as to be virtually imperceptible —**in·sen′si·bil′i·ty** *n.* —**in·sen′si·bly** *adv.*

in·sert (in surt′) *vt.* [< L. *in-,* in + *serere,* join] to put or fit (something) into something else —*n.* (in′sərt) anything inserted or to be inserted —**in·ser′tion** *n.*

in·set (in set′) *vt.* **-set′, -set′ting** to set in; insert —*n.* (in′set) something inserted

in·shore (in′shôr′, in shôr′) *adv., adj.* **1.** in toward the shore **2.** near the shore

in·side (in′sīd′, -sīd′; *for prep. & adv., usually* in′sīd′) *n.* **1.** the inner side, surface, or part **2.** [*pl.*] [Colloq.] the viscera —*adj.* **1.** of or on the inside; internal **2.** known only to insiders; secret —*adv.* **1.** on or in the inside; within **2.** indoors —*prep.* in or within —**inside of** within the space or time of —**inside out 1.** with the inside where the outside should be **2.** [Colloq.] thoroughly

in′sid′er *n.* **1.** a person inside a given place or group **2.** one having secret or confidential information

in·sid·i·ous (in sid′ē əs) *adj.* [< L. *insidiae,* an ambush] **1.** characterized by treachery or slyness **2.** more dangerous than seems evident —**in·sid′i·ous·ly** *adv.*

in·sight (in′sīt′) *n.* **1.** the ability to see and understand clearly the inner nature of things, esp. by intuition **2.** an instance of such understanding

in·sig·ni·a (in sig′nē ə) *n.pl., sing.* **-sig′ni·a, -sig′ne** (-nē) [ult. < L. *in-,* in + *signum,* mark] distinguishing marks, as emblems of rank, membership, etc.

in·sig·nif·i·cant (in′sig nif′ə kənt) *adj.* **1.** meaningless **2.** unimportant; trivial **3.** small; unimposing —**in′sig·nif′i·cance** *n.* —**in′sig·nif′i·cant·ly** *adv.*

in·sin·cere (in′sin sir′) *adj.* not sincere; deceptive or hypocritical —**in′sin·cere′ly** *adv.* —**in′sin·cer′i·ty** (-ser′ə tē) *n.*

in·sin·u·ate (in sin′yoo wāt′) *vt.* **-at′ed, -at′ing** [< L. *in-,* in + *sinus,* a curve] **1.** to introduce or work into gradually, indirectly, etc. **2.** to hint or suggest indirectly; imply —**in·sin′u·a′tor** *n.*

in·sin·u·a·tion (-wā′shən) *n.* **1.** an insinuating **2.** something insinuated; specif., *a)* a sly hint *b)* an act or remark intended to win favor

in·sip·id (in sip′id) *adj.* [< Fr. < L. *in-,* not + *sapidus,* savory] **1.** without flavor; tasteless **2.** not exciting; dull —**in′si·pid′i·ty** *n.* —**in·sip′id·ly** *adv.*

in·sist (in sist′) *vi.* [< L. *in-,* on + *sistere,* to stand] to take and maintain a stand (often with *on* or *upon*) —*vt.* **1.** to demand strongly **2.** to declare firmly

in·sist′ent *adj.* **1.** insisting or demanding **2.** demanding attention [*an insistent rhythm]* —**in·sist′ence** *n.* —**in·sist′ent·ly** *adv.*

in·snare (in sner′) *vt.* **-snared′, -snar′ing** *same as* ENSNARE

in·so·far (in′sə fär′) *adv.* to such a degree or extent (usually with *as*)

in·sole (in′sōl′) *n.* **1.** the inside sole of a shoe **2.** a removable sole put inside a shoe for comfort

in·so·lent (in′sə lənt) *adj.* [< L. *in-,* not + *solere,* be accustomed] boldly disrespectful; impudent —**in′so·lence** *n.* —**in′so·lent·ly** *adv.*

INSOLE

in·sol·vent (in säl′vənt) *adj.* not solvent; unable to pay debts; bankrupt —**in·sol′ven·cy** *n.*

in·som·ni·a (in säm′nē ə) *n.* [< L. *in-,* without + *somnus,* sleep] abnormal inability to sleep —**in·som′ni·ac′** (-ak′) *n.*

in·so·much (in'sō much') *adv.* **1.** to such a degree or extent; so (with *that*) **2.** inasmuch (*as*)

in·sou·ci·ant (in sōō'sē ənt) *adj.* [Fr. < *in-*, not + *soucier*, to care] calm and unbothered; carefree —**in·sou'ci·ance** *n.* —**in·sou'ci·ant·ly** *adv.*

in·spect (in spekt') *vt.* [< L. *in-*, at + *specere*, look at] **1.** to look at carefully **2.** to examine or review officially —**in·spec'tion** *n.*

in·spec'tor *n.* **1.** one who inspects; official examiner **2.** an officer on a police force, ranking next below a superintendent

in·spi·ra·tion (in'spə rā'shən) *n.* **1.** an inhaling **2.** an inspiring or being inspired mentally or emotionally **3.** *a)* any stimulus to creative thought or action *b)* an inspired idea, action, etc. —**in'spi·ra'tion·al** *adj.*

in·spire (in spīr') *vt.* -spired', -spir'ing [< L. *in-*, in + *spirare*, breathe] **1.** to inhale **2.** to stimulate or impel, as to some creative effort **3.** to motivate by divine influence **4.** to arouse (a thought or feeling) in (someone) **5.** to cause to be written or said —*vi.* **1.** to inhale **2.** to give inspiration —**in·spir'er** *n.* —**in·spir'ing·ly** *adv.*

in·spir·it (in spir'it) *vt.* to put spirit or life into

Inst. 1. Institute **2.** Institution

in·sta·bil·i·ty (in'stə bil'ə tē) *n.* lack of firmness, steadiness, determination, etc.

in·stall, in·stal (in stôl') *vt.* -stalled', -stall'ing [< ML. *in-*, in + *stallum*, a place] **1.** to place in an office, rank, etc. with formality **2.** to establish in a place **3.** to fix in position for use [to *install* new fixtures] —**in·stal·la·tion** (in'stə lā'shən) *n.* —**in·stall'er** *n.*

in·stall'ment, in·stal'ment *n.* **1.** an installing or being installed **2.** any of the parts of a sum of money to be paid at regular specified times **3.** any of several parts, as of a magazine serial

installment plan a system by which debts, as for purchased articles, are paid in installments

in·stance (in'stəns) *n.* [see INSTANT] **1.** an example; case **2.** a step in proceeding; occasion [in the first *instance*] —*vt.* -stanced, -stanc·ing to give as an example; cite —**at the instance of** at the suggestion of —**for instance** as an example

in·stant (in'stənt) *adj.* [< L. *in-*, upon + *stare*, to stand] **1.** urgent; pressing **2.** of the current month: an old usage [your letter of the 8th *instant*] **3.** imminent **4.** immediate **5.** concentrated or precooked for quick preparation, as a food or beverage —*n.* **1.** a moment **2.** a particular moment —*adv.* [Poet.] at once —**the instant** as soon as

in·stan·ta·ne·ous (in'stən tā'nē əs) *adj.* done or happening in an instant; immediate —**in'stan·ta'ne·ous·ly** *adv.*

in'stant·ly *adv.* immediately —*conj.* as soon as

in·state (in stāt') *vt.* -stat'ed, -stat'ing to put in a particular position or rank —**in·state'ment** *n.*

in·stead (in sted') *adv.* [IN + STEAD] in place of the one mentioned —**instead of** in place of

in·step (in'step') *n.* **1.** the upper surface of the arch of the foot, between the ankle and the toes **2.** that part of a shoe or stocking covering this

in·sti·gate (in'stə gāt') *vt.* -gat'ed, -gat'ing [< L. *in-*, on + *stigare*, to prick] **1.** to urge on to some action **2.** to foment (rebellion, etc.) —**in'sti·ga'tion** *n.* —**in'sti·ga'tor** *n.*

in·still, in·stil (in stil') *vt.* -stilled', -still'ing [< L. *in-*, in + *stilla*, a drop] **1.** to put in drop by drop **2.** to put (an idea, feeling, etc.) in or into gradually —**in'stil·la'tion** *n.* —**in·still'ment, in·stil'ment** *n.*

in·stinct (in'stiŋkt) *n.* [< L. *instinguere*, impel] **1.** (an) inborn tendency to behave in a way characteristic of a species **2.** a natural or acquired tendency; knack —*adj.* (in stiŋkt') filled or charged (*with*) —**in·stinc·tu·al** (in stiŋk'chōō wəl) *adj.*

in·stinc·tive (in stiŋk'tiv) *adj.* **1.** of, or having the nature of, instinct **2.** prompted or done by instinct —**in·stinc'tive·ly** *adv.*

in·sti·tute (in'stə tōōt', -tyōōt') *vt.* -tut'ed, -tut'ing [< L. *in-*, in + *statuere*, set up] **1.** to set up; establish **2.** to start; initiate —*n.* something instituted; specif., *a)* an established principle or law *b)* an organization for the promotion of art, science, etc. *c)* a school or college specializing in some field

in·sti·tu·tion (-tōō'shən, -tyōō'-) *n.* **1.** an instituting or being instituted **2.** an established law, custom, etc. **3.** *a)* an organization having a social, educational, or religious purpose, as a school, church, etc. *b)* the building housing it **4.** [Colloq.] a well-established person or thing —**in'sti·tu'tion·al** *adj.*

in'sti·tu'tion·al·ize' *vt.* -ized', -iz'ing **1.** to make into an institution **2.** to make institutional **3.** to place in an institution, as for treatment —**in'sti·tu'tion·al·i·za'tion** *n.*

in·struct (in strukt') *vt.* [< L. *in-*, in + *struere*, pile up] **1.** to teach; educate **2.** to inform **3.** to order or direct

in·struc'tion (-struk'shən) *n.* **1.** an instructing; education **2.** something taught **3.** [*pl.*] orders or directions —**in·struc'tion·al** *adj.*

in·struc'tive *adj.* instructing; giving knowledge

in·struc'tor *n.* **1.** a teacher **2.** a college teacher ranking below an assistant professor —**in·struc'tor·ship'** *n.*

in·stru·ment (in'strə mənt) *n.* [see INSTRUCT] **1.** a thing by means of which something is done; means **2.** a tool or implement **3.** any of various devices for indicating, measuring, controlling, etc. **4.** any of various devices producing musical sound **5.** *Law* a formal document

in'stru·men'tal (-men't'l) *adj.* **1.** serving as a means; helpful **2.** of, performed on, or written for a musical instrument or instruments **3.** of or performed with an instrument or tool —**in'stru·men'tal·ly** *adv.*

in'stru·men'tal·ist *n.* one who performs on a musical instrument

in'stru·men·tal'i·ty (-tal'ə tē) *n., pl.* -ties a means; agency

in'stru·men·ta'tion (-tā'shən) *n.* **1.** the writing or scoring of music for instruments **2.** use of, or equipment with, instruments

instrument panel (or **board**) a panel or board with instruments, gauges, etc. mounted on it, as in an automobile or airplane

in·sub·or·di·nate (in'sə bôr'd'n it) *adj.* not submitting to authority; disobedient —**in'sub·or'di·nate·ly** *adv.* —**in'·sub·or'di·na'tion** *n.*

in·sub·stan·tial (in'səb stan'shəl) *adj.* not substantial; specif., *a)* unreal; imaginary *b)* flimsy

in·suf·fer·a·ble (in suf'ər ə b'l) *adj.* not sufferable; intolerable; unbearable —**in·suf'fer·a·bly** *adv.*

in·su·lar (in'sə lər) *adj.* [< L. *insula*, island] **1.** of or like an island or islanders **2.** narrow-minded; illiberal —**in'su·lar'i·ty** (-lar'ə tē), **in'su·lar·ism** *n.* —**in'su·lar·ly** *adv.*

in'su·late' (-lāt') *vt.* -lat'ed, -lat'ing [< L. *insula*, island] **1.** to set apart; isolate **2.** to separate or cover with a nonconducting material in order to prevent the escape of electricity, heat, sound, etc. —**in'su·la'tor** *n.*

in'su·la'tion *n.* **1.** an insulating or being insulated **2.** any material used to insulate

in·su·lin (in'sə lin) *n.* [< L. *insula*, island: referring to islands of tissue in the pancreas] **1.** a hormone secreted by the pancreas, which helps the body use carbohydrates **2.** an extract from the pancreas of sheep, oxen, etc., used in the treatment of diabetes

in·sult (in sult') *vt.* [< L. *in-*, on + *salire*, to leap] to treat or speak to with scorn, insolence, or disrespect —*n.* (in'sult) an insulting act, remark, etc. —**in·sult'ing** *adj.* —**in·sult'ing·ly** *adv.*

in·su·per·a·ble (in sōō'pər ə b'l) *adj.* [< L. *in-*, not + *superare*, overcome] that cannot be overcome —**in·su'per·a·bil'i·ty** *n.*

in·sup·port·a·ble (in'sə pôrt'ə b'l) *adj.* not supportable; incapable of being borne, upheld, proved, etc.

in·sur·ance (in shoor'əns) *n.* **1.** an insuring or being insured **2.** a contract (**insurance policy**) whereby compensation is guaranteed to the insured for a specified loss by fire, death, etc. **3.** the amount for which something is insured **4.** the premium paid for an insurance policy **5.** the business of insuring against loss

in·sure (in shoor') *vt.* -sured', -sur'ing [see IN-1 & SURE] **1.** to take out or issue insurance on (something or someone) **2.** *same as* ENSURE —*vi.* to give or take out insurance —**in·sur'a·ble** *adj.*

in·sured' *n.* one whose life, property, etc. is insured against loss

in·sur'er *n.* a person or company that insures others against loss or damage

in·sur·gent (in sur'jənt) *adj.* [< L. *in-*, upon + *surgere*, to rise] rising up against established authority —*n.* an insurgent person —**in·sur'gence** *n.* —**in·sur'gent·ly** *adv.*

in·sur·rec·tion (in'sə rek'shən) *n.* [see prec.] a rising up against established authority; rebellion; revolt —**in'sur·rec'tion·ar'y** *adj., n., pl.* -ies —**in'sur·rec'tion·ist** *n.*

int. 1. interest **2.** interior **3.** international

in·tact (in takt') *adj.* [< L. *in-*, not + *tactus*, touched] unimpaired or uninjured; kept or left whole

in·tagl·io (in tal'yō) *n., pl.* -ios [It. < *in-*, in + *tagliare*, to cut] **1.** a design carved or engraved below the surface **2.** a gem ornamented in this way

in·take (in'tāk') *n.* **1.** a taking in **2.** amount taken in **3.** a place in a pipe, etc. where a fluid enters

in·tan·gi·ble (in tan'jə b'l) *adj.* **1.** that cannot be touched; incorporeal **2.** representing value, but either without material being or without intrinsic value, as good will or stocks **3.** that cannot be easily defined; vague —*n.* something intangible —in·tan'gi·bil'i·ty *n.* —in·tan'gi·bly *adv.*

in·te·ger (in'tə jər) *n.* [L., whole] **1.** anything complete in itself; whole **2.** any whole number (as 5 or 10, or –5 or –10) or zero

in'te·gral (-grəl) *adj.* [see prec.] **1.** necessary for completeness; essential **2.** whole or complete **3.** made up of parts forming a whole **4.** *Math.* of or having to do with integers —*n.* a whole —in'te·gral·ly *adv.*

in'te·grate' (-grāt') *vt., vi.* -grat'ed, -grat'ing [< L. *integer*, whole] **1.** to make or become whole or complete **2.** to bring (parts) together into a whole **3.** *a)* to remove barriers imposing segregation upon (racial groups) *b)* to abolish segregation in —in'te·gra'tion *n.* —in'te·gra'tion·ist *n., adj.*

integrated circuit an electronic circuit with many interconnected circuit elements formed on a single body of semiconductor material

in·teg·ri·ty (in teg'rə tē) *n.* [see INTEGER] **1.** completeness; wholeness **2.** unimpaired condition; soundness **3.** honesty, sincerity, etc.

in·teg·u·ment (in teg'yoo mənt) *n.* [< L. *in-*, upon + *tegere*, to cover] an outer covering; skin, shell, etc.

in·tel·lect (in't'l ekt') *n.* [< L. *inter-*, between + *legere*, choose] **1.** the ability to reason or understand **2.** high intelligence **3.** a very intelligent person

in·tel·lec·tu·al (in't'l ek'choo wəl) *adj.* **1.** of, involving, or appealing to the intellect **2.** requiring intelligence **3.** showing high intelligence —*n.* one who has intellectual interests or does intellectual work —in'tel·lec'tu·al'i·ty *n.* — in'tel·lec'tu·al·ly *adv.*

in'tel·lec'tu·al·ism *n.* devotion to intellectual matters

in'tel·lec'tu·al·ize' (-īz') *vt.* -ized', -iz'ing to examine rationally, often without regard for emotional considerations

in·tel·li·gence (in tel'ə jəns) *n.* [see INTELLECT] **1.** *a)* the ability to learn or understand *b)* the ability to cope with a new situation **2.** news or information **3.** *a)* the gathering of secret, esp. military, information *b)* those engaged in this

intelligence quotient a number indicating a person's level of intelligence: mental age (as shown by intelligence tests) times 100 divided by chronological age

intelligence test a series of problems intended to test the intelligence of an individual

in·tel·li·gent (-jənt) *adj.* having or showing intelligence; bright; clever —in·tel'li·gent·ly *adv.*

in·tel'li·gent'si·a (-jent'sē ə) *n.* [< Russ.] intellectuals collectively

in·tel·li·gi·ble (in tel'i jə b'l) *adj.* [see INTELLECT] that can be understood; clear; comprehensible —in·tel'li·gi·bil'i·ty *n.* —in·tel'li·gi·bly *adv.*

in·tem·per·ate (in tem'pər it) *adj.* **1.** not temperate or moderate; excessive **2.** drinking too much alcoholic liquor —in·tem'per·ance *n.* —in·tem'per·ate·ly *adv.*

in·tend (in tend') *vt.* [< L. *in-*, at + *tendere*, to stretch] **1.** to plan; purpose **2.** to mean (something) to be or be used (*for*) **3.** to mean; signify —*vi.* to have a purpose

in·tend·ant (in ten'dənt) *n.* [Fr.: see INTEND] a director, manager, or superintendent

in·tend'ed *n.* [Colloq.] one's prospective wife or husband

in·tense (in tens') *adj.* [see INTEND] **1.** very strong [*an intense* light] **2.** strained to the utmost; strenuous [*intense* thought] **3.** characterized by much action, emotion, etc. — in·tense'ly *adv.*

in·ten·si·fy (in ten'sə fī') *vt., vi.* -fied', -fy'ing to make or become more intense —in·ten'si·fi·ca'tion *n.* —in·ten'si·fi·er *n.*

in·ten'si·ty *n., pl.* -ties **1.** a being intense **2.** great energy or vehemence, as of emotion **3.** the amount of force or energy of heat, light, sound, etc.

in·ten'sive *adj.* **1.** of or characterized by intensity; thorough **2.** designating very attentive hospital care given to patients, as after surgery **3.** *Gram.* giving force or emphasis (Ex.: "very" in "the very same man") —*n.* **1.** anything that intensifies **2.** an intensive word, prefix, etc. — in·ten'sive·ly *adv.*

in·tent (in tent') *adj.* [see INTEND] **1.** firmly directed; earnest **2.** having one's attention or purpose firmly fixed [*intent* on going] —*n.* **1.** an intending **2.** something intended; purpose or meaning —**to all intents and purposes** in almost every respect —in·tent'ly *adv.* —in·tent'ness *n.*

in·ten·tion (in ten'shən) *n.* **1.** a determination to act in a specified way **2.** *a)* anything intended; purpose *b)* [*pl.*] purpose in regard to marriage

in·ten'tion·al *adj.* done purposely; intended —in·ten'tion·al·ly *adv.*

in·ter (in tur') *vt.* -terred', -ter'ring [< L. *in*, in + *terra*, earth] to put (a dead body) into a grave or tomb; bury

inter- [L.] *a combining form meaning:* **1.** between or among [*interstate*] **2.** with or on each other (or one another), mutual [*interact*]

in·ter·act (in'tər akt') *vi.* to act on one another —in'ter·ac'tion *n.* —in'ter·ac'tive *adj.*

in'ter·breed' *vt., vi.* -bred', -breed'ing *same as* HYBRIDIZE

in·ter·cede (-sēd') *vi.* -ced'ed, -ced'ing [< L. *inter-*, between + *cedere*, go] **1.** to plead in behalf of another **2.** to intervene for the purpose of producing agreement; mediate

in'ter·cel'lu·lar (-sel'yoo lər) *adj.* located between or among cells

in·ter·cept (in'tər sept') *vt.* [< L. *inter-*, between + *capere*, take] **1.** to seize, stop, or interrupt on the way [*to intercept* a message] **2.** *Math.* to mark off between two points, lines, or planes —in'ter·cep'tion *n.* —in'ter·cep'tor, in'ter·cept'er *n.*

in'ter·ces·sion (-sesh'ən) *n.* an interceding; mediation or prayer in behalf of another —in'ter·ces'sor (-ses'ər) *n.* — in'ter·ces'so·ry *adj.*

in'ter·change' *vt.* -changed', -chang'ing **1.** to give and take mutually; exchange **2.** to put (each of two things) in the other's place **3.** to alternate —*vi.* to change places with each other —*n.* (in'tər chānj') **1.** an interchanging **2.** a place on a freeway where traffic can enter or depart — in'ter·change'a·ble *adj.* —in'ter·change'a·bly *adv.*

in'ter·col·le'gi·ate *adj.* between or among colleges and universities

in·ter·com (in'tər käm') *n.* a radio or telephone intercommunication system, as between rooms

in'ter·com·mu'ni·cate' *vt., vi.* -cat'ed, -cat'ing to communicate with or to each other or one another —in'ter·com·mu'ni·ca'tion *n.*

in'ter·con·nect' *vt., vi.* to connect with one another — in'ter·con·nec'tion *n.*

in·ter·course (in'tər kôrs') *n.* [see INTER- & COURSE] **1.** communication or dealings between people, countries, etc. **2.** the sexual joining of two individuals; copulation: in full **sexual intercourse**

in'ter·de·nom'i·na'tion·al *adj.* between or involving different religious denominations

in'ter·de·pend'ence *n.* mutual dependence —in'ter·de·pend'ent *adj.* —in'ter·de·pend'ent·ly *adv.*

in·ter·dict (in'tər dikt') *vt.* [< L. *inter-*, between + *dicere*, speak] **1.** to prohibit (an action) **2.** to restrain from doing or using something **3.** *R.C.Ch.* to exclude (a person, parish, etc.) from certain acts or privileges —*n.* (in'tər dikt') an official prohibition or restraint; specif., *R.C.Ch.* an interdicting of a person, parish, etc. —in'ter·dic'tion *n.* —in'ter·dic'to·ry *adj.*

in·ter·est (in'trist, in'tər ist) *n.* [< L. *inter-*, between + *esse*, to be] **1.** a right to, or share in, something **2.** anything in which one has a share **3.** [*often pl.*] welfare; benefit **4.** [*usually pl.*] those having a common concern in some industry, cause, etc. [the steel *interests*] **5.** *a)* a feeling of concern, curiosity, etc. about something *b)* the power of causing this feeling *c)* something causing this feeling **6.** importance [a matter of little *interest*] **7.** *a)* money paid for the use of money *b)* the rate of such payment —*vt.* **1.** to involve or excite the interest or attention of **2.** to cause to have an interest, or share, in —**in the interest (or interests) of** for the sake of

in'ter·est·ed *adj.* **1.** having an interest or share **2.** influenced by personal interest; biased **3.** feeling or showing interest —in'ter·est·ed·ly *adv.*

in'ter·est·ing *adj.* exciting interest, curiosity, or attention —in'ter·est·ing·ly *adv.*

in·ter·fere (in'tər fir') *vi.* -fered', -fer'ing [< L. *inter-*, between + *ferire*, to strike] **1.** to clash; collide **2.** *a)* to come between; intervene *b)* to meddle **3.** *Sports* to be guilty of interference —**interfere with** to hinder

in'ter·fer'ence *n.* **1.** an interfering **2.** something that interferes **3.** *Sports* the illegal hindering of an opposing player in any of various ways **4.** *Physics* the mutual action of two waves of vibration, as of sound, light, etc., in reinforcing or neutralizing each other **5.** *Radio & TV* static, unwanted signals, etc. producing a distortion of sounds or images

in'ter·fold' *vt., vi.* to fold together or inside one another

in'ter·fuse' *vt.* **-fused', -fus'ing 1.** to combine by fusing together **2.** to spread itself through —*vi.* to fuse; blend —**in'ter·fu'sion** *n.*

in·ter·im (in'tər im) *n.* [L. < *inter*, between] the period of time between; meantime —*adj.* temporary

in·te·ri·or (in tir'ē ər) *adj.* [< L. *inter*, between] **1.** situated within; inner **2.** inland **3.** private —*n.* **1.** the interior part, as of a room, country, etc. **2.** the domestic affairs of a country

interior decoration the decorating and furnishing of the interior of a room, house, etc.

in·te·ri·or·ize' (-īz') *vt.* **-ized', -iz'ing** to make (a concept, value, etc.) part of one's inner nature

interj. interjection

in·ter·ject (in'tər jekt') *vt.* [< L. *inter-*, between + *jacere*, to throw] to throw in between; insert

in'ter·jec'tion (-jek'shən) *n.* **1.** an interjecting **2.** something interjected **3.** *Gram.* an exclamatory word or phrase (Ex.: ah! well!) —**in'ter·jec'tion·al** *adj.*

in'ter·lace' *vt., vi.* **-laced', -lac'ing 1.** to weave together **2.** to connect intricately

in'ter·lard' *vt.* [see INTER- & LARD] **1.** to intersperse; diversify [to *interlard* a lecture with quotations] **2.** to be intermixed in

in'ter·lay' *vt.* **-laid', -lay'ing** to lay or put between or among

in·ter·leaf (in'tər lēf') *n., pl.* **-leaves'** a leaf, usually blank, bound between the other leaves of a book, for notes, etc. —**in'ter·leave'** *vt.* **-leaved', -leav'ing**

in'ter·line'¹ *vt.* **-lined', -lin'ing** to write or print (something) between the lines of (a text, etc.)

in'ter·line'² *vt.* **-lined', -lin'ing** to put an inner lining under the ordinary lining of (a garment)

in'ter·lin'e·ar (-lin'ē ər) *adj.* **1.** written or printed between the lines **2.** having the same text in different languages printed in alternate lines

in'ter·link' *vt.* to link together

in'ter·lock' *vt., vi.* to lock together; join with one another

in·ter·loc·u·tor (in'tər läk'yə tər) *n.* [< L. *inter*, between + *loqui*, to talk] **1.** a person taking part in a conversation **2.** the master of ceremonies in a minstrel show

in'ter·loc'u·to'ry (-tôr'ē) *adj.* **1.** conversational **2.** *Law* not final, as a decree

in·ter·lop·er (in'tər lō'pər) *n.* [prob. < INTER- + LOPE] one who meddles in others' affairs

in·ter·lude (in'tər lōōd') *n.* [< L. *inter*, between + *ludus*, play] anything that fills time between two events, as music between acts of a play

in'ter·mar'ry *vi.* **-ried', -ry'ing** to become connected by marriage: said of persons of different races, religions, etc. —**in'ter·mar'riage** *n.*

in'ter·me'di·ar'y (-mē'dē er'ē) *adj.* **1.** acting as a mediator **2.** intermediate —*n., pl.* **-ies** a go-between; mediator

in'ter·me'di·ate (-mē'dē it) *adj.* [< L. *inter-*, between + *medius*, middle] being or happening between; in the middle —*n.* **1.** anything intermediate **2.** *same as* INTERMEDIARY

in·ter·ment (in tur'mənt) *n.* burial

in·ter·mez·zo (in'tər met'sō) *n., pl.* **-zos, -zi** (-sē, -zē) [It.] **1.** a short, light musical entertainment between the acts of a play or opera **2.** *Music* a short work, esp. one connecting the main parts of a composition

in·ter·mi·na·ble (in tur'mi nə b'l) *adj.* lasting, or seeming to last, forever; endless —**in·ter'mi·na·bly** *adv.*

in·ter·min·gle (in'tər miŋ'g'l) *vt., vi.* **-gled, -gling** to mix together; mingle

in'ter·mis'sion (-mish'ən) *n.* [< L. *inter*, between + *mittere*, to send] an interval between periods of activity, as between acts of a play

in'ter·mit'tent (-mit''nt) *adj.* [see INTERMISSION] stopping and starting again at intervals; periodic —**in'ter·mit'tent·ly** *adv.*

in'ter·mix' *vt., vi.* to mix together; blend

in·tern (in'tərn) *n.* [< L. *internus*, inward] **1.** a doctor serving as an assistant resident in a hospital, generally just after graduation from medical school **2.** an apprentice teacher, journalist, etc. —*vi.* to serve as an intern —*vt.* (in tʉrn') to detain and confine within an area [to *intern* aliens in time of war] —**in·tern'ment** *n.* —**in'tern·ship'** *n.*

in·ter·nal (in tur'n'l) *adj.* [< L. *internus*] **1.** of or on the inside; inner **2.** to be taken inside the body [*internal* remedies] **3.** intrinsic [*internal* evidence] **4.** domestic [*internal* revenue] —**in·ter'nal·ly** *adv.*

in·ter'nal-com·bus'tion engine an engine, as in an automobile, powered by the explosion of a fuel-and-air mixture within the cylinders

internal ear that part of the ear consisting of the labyrinth and semicircular canals

in·ter'nal·ize' (-īz') *vt.* **-ized', -iz'ing** to make (others' ideas, etc.) a part of one's own way of thinking —**in·ter'nal·i·za'tion** *n.*

internal medicine the branch of medicine dealing with the diagnosis and nonsurgical treatment of diseases

internal revenue governmental income from taxes on income, profits, luxuries, etc.

in·ter·na·tion·al (in'tər nash'ən 'l) *adj.* **1.** between or among nations **2.** concerned with the relations between nations **3.** for the use of all nations **4.** of or for people in various nations —*n.* [I-] any of several international socialist organizations —**in'ter·na'tion·al·ly** *adv.*

international date line *same as* DATE LINE

in'ter·na'tion·al·ism *n.* the principle of international cooperation for the common good

in'ter·na'tion·al·ize' (-īz') *vt.* **-ized', -iz'ing** to make international; bring under international control —**in'ter·na'tion·al·i·za'tion** *n.*

in·terne (in'tərn) *n. same as* INTERN

in·ter·ne·cine (in'tər nē'sin, -sīn) *adj.* [< L. *inter-*, between + *necare*, to kill] mutually destructive

in·ter·nist (in'tər nist, in tur'nist) *n.* a doctor who specializes in internal medicine

in·ter·of·fice (in'tər ôf'is) *adj.* between the offices of an organization

in'ter·pen'e·trate' *vt.* **-trat'ed, -trat'ing** to penetrate thoroughly —*vi.* to penetrate mutually —**in'ter·pen'e·tra'tion** *n.*

in'ter·per'son·al *adj.* between persons

in'ter·plan'e·tar'y (-plan'ə ter'ē) *adj.* **1.** between planets **2.** within the solar system but outside the atmosphere of any planet or the sun

in'ter·play' *n.* action or effect on each other

in·ter·po·late (in tur'pə lāt') *vt.* **-lat'ed, -lat'ing** [< L. *inter-*, between + *polire*, to polish] **1.** to change (a text, etc.) by inserting new material **2.** to insert between or among others **3.** *Math.* to estimate a missing value by taking an average of known values at neighboring points —*vi.* to make interpolations —**in·ter'po·la'tion** *n.*

in·ter·pose (in'tər pōz') *vt., vi.* **-posed', -pos'ing 1.** to place or come between **2.** to intervene (with) **3.** to interrupt (with) —**in'ter·po·si'tion** (-pə zish'ən) *n.*

in·ter·pret (in tur'prit) *vt.* [< L. *interpres*, negotiator] **1.** to explain or translate **2.** to construe **3.** to give one's own conception of, as a role in a play —*vi.* to translate —**in·ter'pret·a·ble** *adj.* —**in·ter'pret·er** *n.* —**in·ter'pre·tive, in·ter'pre·ta'tive** *adj.*

in·ter'pre·ta'tion (-prə tā'shən) *n.* **1.** an interpreting; explanation, translation, etc. **2.** the expression of a person's conception of a work of art, etc. through acting, writing, etc.

in·ter·ra·cial (in'tər rā'shəl) *adj.* between, among, or for persons of different races

in'ter·reg'num (-reg'nəm) *n., pl.* **-nums, -na** (-nə) [L. < *inter-*, between + *regnum*, a reign] **1.** an interval between two successive reigns, when the country has no sovereign **2.** any period without the usual ruler, etc. **3.** any break in a series

in'ter·re·late' *vt., vi.* **-lat'ed, -lat'ing** to make, be, or become mutually related —**in'ter·re·la'tion** *n.*

in·ter·ro·gate (in ter'ə gāt') *vt., vi.* **-gat'ed, -gat'ing** [< L. *inter-*, between + *rogare*, ask] to question formally —**in·ter'ro·ga'tion** *n.* —**in·ter'ro·ga'tor** *n.*

interrogation mark (or **point**) *same as* QUESTION MARK

in·ter·rog·a·tive (in'tə räg'ə tiv) *adj.* asking a question —*n.* an interrogative word, element, etc.

in·ter·rupt (in'tə rupt') *vt.* [< L. *inter-*, between + *rumpere*, to break] **1.** to break into (a discussion, etc.) or break in upon (a speaker, worker, etc.) **2.** to make a break in the continuity of —*vi.* to make an interruption —**in'ter·rup'tive** *adj.*

in'ter·rup'tion (-rup'shən) *n.* **1.** an interrupting **2.** anything that interrupts **3.** an intermission

in'ter·scho·las'tic *adj.* between or among schools

in·ter·sect (in'tər sekt') *vt.* [< L. *inter-*, between + *secare*, to cut] to divide into two parts by passing through or across —*vi.* to cross each other

in'ter·sec'tion *n.* **1.** an intersecting **2.** the point or line where two lines, surfaces, roads, etc. meet or cross

in·ter·sperse (in'tər spurs') *vt.* **-spersed', -spers'ing** [< L. *inter-*, among + *spargere*, scatter] **1.** to scatter among other things; put here and there **2.** to decorate or diversify with things scattered here and there —**in'ter-sper'sion** (-spur'zhən, -shən) *n.*

in'ter·state' *adj.* between states of a federal government

in'ter·stel'lar *adj.* between or among the stars

in·ter·stice (in tur'stis) *n., pl.* **-stic·es** (-stis iz) [Fr. < L. *inter-*, between + *sistere*, to set] a crevice; crack —**in·ter·sti·tial** (in'tər stish'əl) *adj.*

in'ter·twine' *vt., vi.* **-twined'**, **-twin'ing** to twine together

in'ter·twist' *vt., vi.* to twist together

in'ter·ur'ban (-ur'bən) *adj.* between cities or towns —*n.* an interurban railway

in·ter·val (in'tər v'l) *n.* [< L. *inter-*, between + *vallum*, a wall] **1.** a space between things **2.** the time between events **3.** the difference in pitch between two tones —**at intervals 1.** now and then **2.** here and there

in·ter·vene (in'tər vēn') *vi.* **-vened'**, **-ven'ing** [< L. *inter-*, between + *venire*, come] **1.** to come or be between **2.** to occur between two events, etc. **3.** to come in to modify, settle, or hinder some action, etc.

in'ter·ven'tion (-ven'shən) *n.* **1.** an intervening **2.** interference, esp. of one state in the affairs of another —**in'ter·ven'tion·ist** *n., adj.*

in'ter·view' (-vyoo') *n.* [see INTER- & VIEW] **1.** a meeting of people face to face, as for evaluating a job applicant **2.** *a)* a meeting in which a person is asked about his views, etc., as by a reporter *b)* a published account of this —*vt.* to have an interview with —**in'ter·view'er** *n.*

in'ter·weave' *vt., vi.* **-wove'**, **-wo'ven**, **-weav'ing 1.** to weave together **2.** to connect closely

in·tes·tate (in tes'tāt, -tit) *adj.* [< L. *in-*, not + *testari*, make a will] **1.** having made no will **2.** not disposed of by a will —*n.* one who has died intestate

in·tes·tine (in tes'tin) *n.* [< L. *intus*, within] [*usually pl.*] the lower part of the alimentary canal, extending from the stomach to the anus and consisting of a convoluted upper part (**small intestine**) and a lower part of greater diameter (**large intestine**); bowel(s) —**in·tes'tin·al** *adj.*

in·thrall, in·thral (in thrôl') *vt.* **-thralled'**, **-thrall'ing** *same as* EN-THRALL

in·ti·ma·cy (in'tə mə sē) *n., pl.* **-cies 1.** a being intimate **2.** an intimate act; esp., [*usually pl.*] illicit sexual intercourse

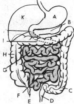

INTESTINE
(A, stomach; B, pancreas; C, descending colon; D, rectum; E, appendix; F, ileum; G, jejunum; H, ascending colon; I, transverse colon; J, duodenum; K, liver)

in·ti·mate (in'tə mit) *adj.* [< L. *intus*, within] **1.** most private or personal **2.** closely associated; very familiar **3.** fundamental **4.** having illicit sexual relations —*n.* an intimate friend —*vt.* (-māt') **-mat'ed**, **-mat'ing** to hint or imply —**in'ti·mate·ly** *adv.* —**in'ti·ma'tion** *n.*

in·tim·i·date (in tim'ə dāt') *vt.* **-dat'ed**, **-dat'ing** [< L. *in-*, in + *timidus*, afraid] to make afraid, as with threats —**in·tim'i·da'tion** *n.*

in·ti·tle (in tīt''l) *vt.* **-tled**, **-tling** *same as* ENTITLE

in·to (in'too, -too, -tə) *prep.* [OE.] **1.** toward and within [*into* a room] **2.** advancing to the midst of [to talk *into* the night] **3.** to the form, substance, or condition of [divided *into* parts] **4.** so as to strike [to run *into* a wall] **5.** [Colloq.] involved in [she's *into* jazz now]

in·tol·er·a·ble (in täl'ər ə b'l) *adj.* unbearable; too severe, painful, etc. to be endured —**in·tol'er·a·bly** *adv.*

in·tol'er·ant (-ənt) *adj.* unwilling to tolerate others' beliefs, etc. or persons of other races, etc.; bigoted —**intolerant of** not able or willing to tolerate —**in·tol'er·ance** *n.* —**in·tol'er·ant·ly** *adv.*

in·to·na·tion (in'tə nā'shən) *n.* **1.** an intoning **2.** the manner of producing tones with regard to accurate pitch **3.** variations in pitch within an utterance

in·tone (in tōn') *vt., vi.* **-toned'**, **-ton'ing** to speak or recite in a singing tone; chant

in to·to (in tō'tō) [L.] as a whole

in·tox·i·cant (in täk'sə kənt) *n.* something that intoxicates; esp., alcoholic liquor —*adj.* intoxicating

in·tox'i·cate' (-kāt') *vt.* **-cat'ed**, **-cat'ing** [< L. *in-*, in + *toxicum*, a poison] **1.** to make drunk **2.** to excite greatly —**in·tox'i·ca'tion** *n.* **1.** a making or becoming drunk **2.** a feeling of wild excitement **3.** *Med.* a poisoning or being poisoned

intra- [L., within] *a combining form meaning* within, inside of

in·trac·ta·ble (in trak'tə b'l) *adj.* **1.** hard to manage; unruly or stubborn **2.** hard to work, cure, etc. —**in·trac'ta·bly** *adv.*

in·tra·dos (in'trə däs', in trā'dōs) *n.* [Fr. < L. *intra*, within + Fr. *dos*, the back] the inside curve of an arch

in·tra·mu·ral (in'trə myoor'əl) *adj.* within the walls or limits of a city, college, etc. [*intramural* sports]

in·tran·si·gent (in tran'sə jənt) *adj.* [ult. < L. *in-*, not + *transigere*, settle] refusing to compromise —*n.* one who is intransigent, esp. in politics —**in·tran'si·gence** *n.* —**in·tran'si·gent·ly** *adv.*

in·tran·si·tive (in tran'sə tiv) *adj.* not transitive; designating a verb that does not require a direct object to complete its meaning —*n.* an intransitive verb —**in·tran'si·tive·ly** *adv.*

in·tra·state (in'trə stāt') *adj.* within a state; esp., within a State of the U.S.

in·tra·u·ter·ine (contraceptive) device (in'trə yoot'ər in) a device, as a coil or loop of plastic, inserted in the uterus as a contraceptive

in'tra·ve'nous (-vē'nəs) *adj.* [INTRA- + VENOUS] in, or directly into, a vein [an *intravenous* injection] —**in'tra·ve'nous·ly** *adv.*

in·trench (in trench') *vt., vi. same as* ENTRENCH

in·trep·id (in trep'id) *adj.* [< L. *in-*, not + *trepidus*, alarmed] bold; fearless; very brave —**in'tre·pid'i·ty** (-trə pid'ə tē) *n.* —**in·trep'id·ly** *adv.*

in·tri·ca·cy (in'tri kə sē) *n.* **1.** an intricate quality or state **2.** *pl.* **-cies** something intricate

in·tri·cate (in'tri kit) *adj.* [< L. *in-*, in + *tricae*, perplexities] **1.** hard to follow or understand because full of puzzling parts, details, etc. **2.** full of elaborate detail —**in'tri·cate·ly** *adv.*

in·trigue (in trēg') *vi.* **-trigued'**, **-trigu'ing** [see INTRICATE] to plot secretly or underhandedly —*vt.* **1.** to get by secret plotting **2.** to excite the interest or curiosity of —*n.* **1.** secret or underhanded plotting **2.** a secret or underhanded plot or scheme **3.** a secret love affair —**in·trigu'er** *n.*

in·trin·sic (in trin'sik) *adj.* [< L. *intra-*, within + *secus*, close] belonging to the real nature of a thing; inherent —**in·trin'si·cal·ly** *adv.*

intro. 1. introduction **2.** introductory

in·tro·duce (in'trə dōōs', -dyōōs') *vt.* **-duced'**, **-duc'ing** [< L. *intro-*, within + *ducere*, to lead] **1.** to put in; insert **2.** to add as a new feature **3.** to bring into use or fashion **4.** *a)* to make acquainted; present (*to*) [*introduce* me to her] *b)* to give experience of [they *introduced* him to music] **5.** to bring forward [*introduce* a bill in Congress] **6.** to begin [to *introduce* a talk with a joke]

in'tro·duc'tion (-duk'shən) *n.* **1.** an introducing or being introduced **2.** anything that introduces, as the preliminary section of a book or speech

in'tro·duc'to·ry (-tər ē) *adj.* used as an introduction; preliminary: also **in'tro·duc'tive**

in·tro·spec·tion (in'trə spek'shən) *n.* [< L. *intro-*, within + *specere*, to look] a looking into one's own mind, feelings, etc. —**in'tro·spec'tive** *adj.*

in·tro·vert (in'trə vurt') *vt.* [< L. *intro*, within + *vertere*, to turn] to direct (one's interest, etc.) upon oneself —*n.* one who is more interested in his own experiences and feelings than in external objects or other persons —**in'tro·ver'sion** (-vur'zhən) *n.*

in·trude (in trōōd') *vt., vi.* **-trud'ed**, **-trud'ing** [< L. *in-*, in + *trudere*, to thrust] to force (oneself) upon others without being asked or welcomed —**in·trud'er** *n.*

in·tru·sion (in trōō'zhən) *n.* an intruding —**in·tru'sive** (-siv) *adj.*

in·trust (in trust') *vt. same as* ENTRUST

in·tu·i·tion (in'tōō wish'ən, -tyoo-) *n.* [< L. *in-*, in + *tueri*, look at] the direct knowing or learning of something without conscious reasoning

in·tu·i·tive (in tōō'i tiv, -tyoo'-) *adj.* **1.** having to do with, having, or perceiving by intuition **2.** perceived by intuition —**in·tu'i·tive·ly** *adv.*

in·un·date (in'ən dāt') *vt.* **-dat'ed**, **-dat'ing** [< L. *in-*, in + *undare*, to flood] to cover as with a flood; deluge —**in'un·da'tion** *n.*

in·ure (in yoor') *vt.* **-ured'**, **-ur'ing** [< ME. *in*, in + *ure*, work] to accustom to difficulty, pain, etc. —*vi.* to take effect —**in·ure'ment** *n.*

in·vade (in vād') *vt.* **-vad'ed**, **-vad'ing** [< L. *in-*, in + *vadere*, go] **1.** to enter forcibly, as to conquer **2.** to crowd

fat, āpe, cär; ten, ēven; is, bīte; gō, hôrn, tōōl, look; oil, out; up, fur; thin, then; zh, leisure; ŋ, ring; ə for *a* in *ago*; ' as in *able* (ā'b'l); ë, Fr. coeur; ö, Fr. feu; ō, Fr. mon; ü, Fr. duc; r, Fr. cri; kh, G. doch, ich. ‡ foreign; < derived from into; throng **3**. to intrude upon; violate —*vi*. to make an invasion —**in·vad′er** *n*.

in·va·lid[1] (in′və lid) *adj*. [< L. *in*-, not + *valere*, be strong] **1**. weak and sickly **2**. of or for invalids —*n*. one who is ill or disabled —*vt*. to disable or weaken —**in′va·lid·ism** *n*.

in·val·id[2] (in val′id) *adj*. not valid; having no force; null or void —**in·va·lid·i·ty** (in′və lid′ə tē) *n*.

in·val′i·date′ (-ə dāt′) *vt*. **-dat′ed**, **-dat′ing** to make invalid; deprive of legal force

in·val·u·a·ble (in val′yoo wə b′l) *adj*. too valuable to be measured; priceless —**in·val′u·a·bly** *adv*.

in·va·sion (in vā′zhən) *n*. **1**. an invading or being invaded, as by an army **2**. an intrusion

in·vec·tive (in vek′tiv) *n*. [see INVEIGH] a violent verbal attack; insults, curses, etc.

in·veigh (in vā′) *vi*. [< L. *in*-, in + *vehere*, carry] to make a violent verbal attack; rail (*against*) —**in·veigh′er** *n*.

in·vei·gle (in vē′g'l, -vā′-) *vt*. **-gled**, **-gling** [< L. *ab*, from + *oculus*, an eye] to entice or trick into doing something —**in·vei′gle·ment** *n*.

in·vent (in vent′) *vt*. [< L. *in*-, on + *venire*, come] **1**. to think up [to *invent* excuses] **2**. to think out or produce (a new device, etc.); originate —**in·ven′tor** *n*.

in·ven′tion (-ven′shən) *n*. **1**. an inventing **2**. the power of inventing; ingenuity **3**. something invented; specif., *a*) a falsehood *b*) a new device

in·ven′tive (-tiv) *adj*. **1**. of or characterized by invention **2**. skilled in inventing —**in·ven′tive·ly** *adv*. —**in·ven′tive·ness** *n*.

in·ven·to·ry (in′vən tôr′ē) *n*., *pl*. **-ries** [see INVENT] **1**. an itemized list of goods, property, etc., as of a business **2**. the store of goods, etc. for such listing; stock **3**. the act of making such a list —*vt*. **-ried**, **-ry·ing** to make an inventory of —**take inventory 1**. to make an inventory of stock on hand **2**. to make an appraisal

in·verse (in vurs′, in′vurs′) *adj*. inverted; directly opposite —*n*. any inverse thing; direct opposite —**in·verse′ly** *adv*.

in·ver·sion (in vur′zhən) *n*. **1**. an inverting or being inverted **2**. something inverted; reversal **3**. a reversal of the normal order of words in a sentence **4**. *Music* the reversal of the tones in an interval or chord, as by raising the lower tone by an octave

in·vert (in vurt′) *vt*. [< L. *in*-, to + *vertere*, to turn] **1**. to turn upside down **2**. to reverse the order, position, direction, etc. of —*n*. (in′vurt′) anything inverted —**in·vert′i·ble** *adj*.

in·ver·te·brate (in vur′tə brit, -brāt′) *adj*. not vertebrate; having no backbone, or spinal column —*n*. any animal without a backbone

in·vest (in vest′) *vt*. [< L. *in*-, in + *vestis*, clothing] **1**. to clothe **2**. *a*) to cover or surround *b*) to endow with attributes, etc. **3**. to install in office with ceremony **4**. to furnish with power, authority, etc. **5**. to put (money) into business, bonds, etc. in order to get a profit —*vi*. to invest money —**in·ves′tor** *n*.

in·ves·ti·gate (in ves′tə gāt′) *vt*., *vi*. **-gat′ed**, **-gat′ing** [< L. *in*-, in + *vestigare*, to track] to search (into); inquire —**in·ves′ti·ga′tive**, **in·ves′ti·ga·to′ry** (-gə tôr′ē) *adj*. —**in·ves′ti·ga′tor** *n*.

in·ves′ti·ga′tion *n*. **1**. an investigating **2**. a careful inquiry

in·ves·ti·ture (in ves′tə chər) *n*. a formal investing with an office, power, authority, etc.

in·vest·ment (in vest′mənt) *n*. **1**. an investing or being invested **2**. *a*) money invested *b*) anything in which money is or may be invested

in·vet·er·ate (in vet′ər it) *adj*. [< L. *in*-, in + *vetus*, old] firmly established; habitual —**in·vet′er·a·cy** *n*. —**in·vet′er·ate·ly** *adv*.

in·vid·i·ous (in vid′ē əs) *adj*. [< L. *invidia*, envy] such as to excite ill will; giving offense, as by discriminating unfairly —**in·vid′i·ous·ly** *adv*. —**in·vid′i·ous·ness** *n*.

in·vig·or·ate (in vig′ə rāt′) *vt*. **-at′ed**, **-at′ing** to give vigor to; fill with energy; enliven —**in·vig′or·a′tion** *n*.

in·vin·ci·ble (in vin′sə b′l) *adj*. [< L. *in*-, not + *vincere*, overcome] that cannot be overcome; unconquerable —**in·vin′ci·bil′i·ty** (-bil′ə tē) *n*. —**in·vin′ci·bly** *adv*.

in·vi·o·la·ble (in vī′ə lə b′l) *adj*. **1**. not to be violated; not to be profaned or injured; sacred **2**. indestructible —**in·vi′o·la·bil′i·ty** (-bil′ə tē) *n*. —**in·vi′o·la·bly** *adv*.

in·vi′o·late (-lit, -lāt′) *adj*. not violated; kept sacred or unbroken

in·vis·i·ble (in viz′ə b′l) *adj*. **1**. not visible; that cannot be seen **2**. out of sight **3**. imperceptible **4**. kept hidden —

n. an invisible thing or being —**the Invisible 1**. God **2**. the unseen world —**in·vis′i·bil′i·ty** *n*. —**in·vis′i·bly** *adv*.

in·vi·ta·tion (in′və tā′shən) *n*. **1**. an inviting **2**. the message or note used in inviting

in′vi·ta′tion·al *adj*. participated in only by those invited, as an art show

in·vite (in vīt′) *vt*. **-vit′ed**, **-vit′ing** [< L. *invitare*] **1**. to ask courteously to come somewhere or do something **2**. to make a request for **3**. to give occasion for [action that *invites* scandal] **4**. to tempt; entice —*n*. (in′vīt) [Colloq.] an invitation

in·vit′ing *adj*. tempting; enticing

in·vo·ca·tion (in′və kā′shən) *n*. **1**. an invoking of God, the Muses, etc. **2**. a formal prayer used in invoking **3**. an incantation

in·voice (in′vois) *n*. [prob. < ME. *envoie*, message] an itemized list of goods shipped to a buyer, stating prices, etc. —*vt*. **-voiced**, **-voic·ing** to present an invoice for or to

in·voke (in vōk′) *vt*. **-voked′**, **-vok′ing** [< L. *in*-, on + *vocare*, to call] **1**. to call on (God, the Muses, etc.) for blessing, help, etc. **2**. to resort to (a law, penalty, etc.) as pertinent **3**. to call forth **4**. to conjure **5**. to ask solemnly for; implore

in·vol·un·tar·y (in väl′ən ter′ē) *adj*. **1**. not done of one's own free will **2**. unintentional **3**. not consciously controlled [sneezing is *involuntary*] —**in·vol′un·tar′i·ly** *adv*.

in·vo·lute (in′və lōōt′) *adj*. [see INVOLVE] **1**. intricate; involved **2**. rolled up or curled in a spiral —**in′vo·lu′tion** *n*.

in·volve (in välv′) *vt*. **-volved′**, **-volv′ing** [< L. *in*-, in + *volvere*, to roll] **1**. to make intricate or complicated **2**. to entangle in difficulty, danger, etc.; implicate **3**. to affect or include [a riot *involving* thousands] **4**. to require [saving *involves* thrift] **5**. to make busy; occupy [involved in research] —**in·volve′ment** *n*.

in·vul·ner·a·ble (in vul′nər ə b′l) *adj*. **1**. that cannot be wounded or injured **2**. proof against attack —**in·vul′ner·a·bil′i·ty** *n*. —**in·vul′ner·a·bly** *adv*.

in·ward (in′wərd) *adj*. **1**. situated within; internal **2**. mental or spiritual **3**. directed toward the inside —*n*. **1**. the inside **2**. [*pl*.] the entrails —*adv*. **1**. toward the inside or center **2**. into the mind or spirit Also **in′wards** *adv*.

in′ward·ly *adv*. **1**. in or on the inside **2**. in the mind or spirit **3**. toward the inside

in′ward·ness *n*. **1**. the inner nature or meaning **2**. spirituality **3**. introspection

in·wrap (in rap′) *vt*. **-wrapped′**, **-wrap′ping** *same as* ENWRAP

in·wrought (in rôt′) *adj*. **1**. worked or woven into a fabric: said of a pattern, etc. **2**. closely blended with other things

i·o·dide (ī′ə dīd′) *n*. a compound of iodine with another element or with a radical

i·o·dine (ī′ə dīn′, -din; *Brit. & Chem.* -dēn′) *n*. [< Gr. *iōdēs*, violetlike] **1**. a nonmetallic chemical element consisting of grayish-black crystals that volatilize into a violet vapor: used in medicine, photography, etc.: symbol, I; at. wt., 126.9044; at. no., 53 **2**. tincture of iodine, used as an antiseptic

i·o·dize (ī′ə dīz′) *vt*. **-dized′**, **-diz′ing** to treat with iodine or an iodide

i·o·do·form (ī ō′də fôrm′) *n*. a yellowish, crystalline compound of iodine, CHI₃, used as an antiseptic

i·on (ī′ən, -än) *n*. [< Gr. *ienai*, go] an electrically charged atom or group of atoms, the electrical charge of which results when a neutral atom or group of atoms loses or gains one or more electrons —**i·on·ic** (ī än′ik) *adj*.

-ion [< L. *-io*] a suffix meaning the act, condition, or result of [translation, correction]

I·o·ni·a (ī ō′nē ə) ancient region along the W coast of Asia Minor, colonized by the Greeks in the 11th cent. B.C. —**I·o′ni·an** *adj*., *n*.

Ionian Sea section of the Mediterranean, between Greece, Sicily, & S Italy

I·on·ic (ī än′ik) *adj*. **1**. Ionian **2**. designating or of an order of Greek architecture distinguished by ornamental scrolls on the capitals

i·on·ize (ī′ə nīz′) *vt*., *vi*. **-ized′**, **-iz′ing** to dissociate into ions, as a salt dissolved in water, or become electrically charged, as a gas under radiation —**i′on·i·za′tion** *n*.

i·on·o·sphere (ī än′ə sfir′) *n*. the outer layers of the earth's atmosphere, with appreciable electron and ion content

IONIC CAPITAL

i·o·ta (ī ōt′ə) *n*. **1**. the ninth letter of the Greek alphabet (I, ι) **2**. a very small quantity; jot

IOU, I.O.U. (ī'ō'yōō') **1.** I owe you **2.** a signed note bearing these letters, acknowledging a debt

-ious [see -OUS] *a suffix used to form adjectives meaning* having, characterized by *[furious]*

I·o·wa (ī'ə wə) Middle Western State of the U.S.: 56,290 sq. mi.; pop. 2,825,000; cap. Des Moines: abbrev. **Ia., IA** — **I'o·wan** *adj., n.*

ip·e·cac (ip'ə kak') *n.* [< SAmInd. name] a preparation made from the dried roots of a S. American plant, used to induce vomiting

‡ip·se dix·it (ip'sē dik'sit) [L., he himself has said (it)] a dogmatic statement

ip·so fac·to (ip'sō fak'tō) [L.] by that very fact

IQ, I.Q. intelligence quotient

ir- *same as:* **1.** IN-[1] **2.** IN-[2] Used before *r*

Ir *Chem.* iridium

Ir. 1. Ireland **2.** Irish

I·ran (i ran', ī-; ē rän') country in SW Asia: formerly called *Persia:* 636,000 sq. mi.; pop. 28,237,000; cap. Tehrán —**I·ra·ni·an** (i rã'nē ən) *adj., n.*

I·raq (i räk', -rak'; ē-) country in SW Asia, at the head of the Persian Gulf: 171,599 sq. mi.; pop. 9,431,000; cap. Baghdad: also sp. **Irak** —**I·ra·qi** (i rã'kē, -rak'ē) *adj., n., pl.* **-qis**

i·ras·ci·ble (i ras'ə b'l) *adj.* [see IRATE] easily angered; quick-tempered —**i·ras'ci·bly** *adv.*

i·rate (ī rãt', ī'rãt) *adj.* [< L. *ira,* ire] angry; wrathful; incensed —**i·rate'ly** *adv.* —**i·rate'ness** *n.*

ire (īr) *n.* [< L. *ira*] anger; wrath —**ire'ful** *adj.*

Ire. Ireland

Ire·land (īr'lənd) **1.** island of the British Isles **2.** republic comprising most of this island: 27,136 sq. mi.; pop. 2,921,000; cap. Dublin

ir·i·des·cent (ir'ə des''nt) *adj.* [< Gr. *iris,* rainbow] having or showing an interplay of rainbowlike colors —**ir'i·des'cence** *n.*

i·rid·i·um (i rid'ē əm, ī-) *n.* [< Gr. *iris,* rainbow] a white, heavy, brittle, metallic chemical element found in platinum ores: symbol, Ir; at. wt., 192.2; at. no., 77

i·ris (ī'ris) *n., pl.* **i'ris·es, ir·i·des** (ir'ə dēz', ī'rə-) [< Gr. *iris,* rainbow] **1.** the round, pigmented membrane surrounding the pupil of the eye **2.** a plant with sword-shaped leaves and showy flowers

I·rish (ī'rish) *adj.* of Ireland, its people, language, etc. —*n.* **1.** *same as* IRISH GAELIC **2.** the English dialect of Ireland —**the Irish** the people of Ireland —**I'rish·man** (-mən) *n., pl.* **-men** — **I'rish·wom'an** *n.fem., pl.* **-wom'en**

Irish Gaelic the Celtic language of Ireland

Irish potato the common white potato

Irish Sea arm of the Atlantic between Ireland & Great Britain

Irish setter any of a breed of setter with long, silky, reddish-brown hair

irk (urk) *vt.* [ME. *irken,* be weary of] to annoy, disgust, tire out, etc.

irk'some (-səm) *adj.* tiresome or annoying

Ir·kutsk (ir kōōtsk') city in S Asiatic R.S.F.S.R.: pop. 428,000

i·ron (ī'ərn) *n.* [OE. *iren*] **1.** a white, malleable, ductile, metallic chemical element, the most common of all the metals: symbol, Fe; at. wt., 55.847; at. no., 26 **2.** any tool, etc. made of iron, as a device with a handle and flat undersurface, used, when heated, for pressing cloth **3.** *[pl.]* iron shackles **4.** firm strength; power **5.** a golf club with a metal head —*adj.* **1.** of iron **2.** like iron; strong **3.** cruel — *vt., vi.* to press (clothes, etc.) with a hot iron —**iron out** to smooth out; eliminate —**strike while the iron is hot** to act at the opportune time

i'ron·clad' (-klad') *adj.* **1.** covered with iron **2.** difficult to change or break *[an ironclad lease]* —*n.* formerly, a warship armored with iron plates

iron curtain secrecy and censorship regarded as forming a barrier, esp. around the Soviet Union

i·ron·i·cal (ī rän'i k'l) *adj.* **1.** meaning the contrary of what is expressed **2.** using irony **3.** opposite to what might be expected Also **i·ron'ic** —**i·ron'i·cal·ly** *adv.*

iron lung a large metal respirator enclosing all of the body but the head

iron pyrites *same as* PYRITE

I'ron·sides' (-sīdz') *nickname of* Oliver CROMWELL —*n.pl.* [i-] *[with sing. v.] same as* IRONCLAD

i'ron·ware (-wer') *n.* things made of iron

i'ron·wood' (-wood') *n.* **1.** any of various trees with extremely hard wood **2.** the wood

i'ron·work' (-wurk') *n.* articles or parts made of iron — **i'ron·work'er** *n.*

i'ron·works' *n.pl.* [*often with sing. v.*] a place where iron is smelted or heavy iron goods are made

i·ro·ny (ī'rən ē, ī'ər nē) *n., pl.* **-nies** [< Gr. *eirōn,* dissembler in speech] **1.** expression in which the intended meaning of the words is the opposite of their usual sense **2.** an event or result that is the opposite of what is expected

Ir·o·quoi·an (ir'ə kwoi'ən) *adj.* of an important linguistic family of N. American Indians, including speakers of Huron, Cherokee, etc. —*n.* a member of an Iroquoian tribe

Ir·o·quois (ir'ə kwoi') *n.* **1.** *pl.* **-quois'** (-kwoi', -kwoiz') a member of a confederation of Iroquoian Indian tribes that lived in New York and Canada **2.** the Iroquoian language family —*adj.* of the Iroquois

ir·ra·di·ate (i rã'dē ãt') *vt.* **-at'ed, -at'ing 1.** to shine upon; light up **2.** to enlighten **3.** to radiate **4.** to expose to X-rays, ultraviolet rays, etc. —*vi.* to emit rays; shine — **ir·ra'di·a'tion** *n.*

ir·ra·tion·al (i rash'ən 'l) *adj.* **1.** lacking the power to reason **2.** senseless; unreasonable; absurd —**ir·ra'tion·al'i·ty** (-ə nal'ə tē) *n., pl.* **-ties** —**ir·ra'tion·al·ly** *adv.*

Ir·ra·wad·dy (ir'ə wä'dē) river flowing from N Burma into the Indian Ocean: c.1,000 mi.

ir·re·claim·a·ble (ir'i klã'mə b'l) *adj.* that cannot be reclaimed —**ir're·claim'a·bly** *adv.*

ir·rec·on·cil·a·ble (i rek'ən sīl'ə b'l, i rek'ən sīl'-) *adj.* that cannot be brought into agreement; incompatible —**ir·rec'on·cil'a·bly** *adv.*

ir·re·cov·er·a·ble (ir'i kuv'ər ə b'l) *adj.* that cannot be recovered, rectified, or remedied —**ir're·cov'er·a·bly** *adv.*

ir·re·deem·a·ble (ir'i dēm'ə b'l) *adj.* **1.** that cannot be bought back **2.** that cannot be converted into coin, as certain paper money **3.** that cannot be changed or reformed —**ir're·deem'a·bly** *adv.*

ir·re·duc·i·ble (ir'i dōōs'ə b'l, -dyōōs'-) *adj.* that cannot be reduced

ir·ref·ra·ga·ble (i ref'rə gə b'l) *adj.* [< L. *in-,* IN-[2] + *refragari,* oppose] that cannot be refuted

ir·re·fu·ta·ble (i ref'yoo tə b'l, ir'i fyōōt'ə b'l) *adj.* indisputable —**ir·ref'u·ta·bly** *adv.*

irreg. 1. irregular **2.** irregularly

ir·re·gard·less (ir'i gärd'lis) *adj., adv.* a substandard or *humorous redundancy for* REGARDLESS

ir·reg·u·lar (i reg'yə lər) *adj.* **1.** not conforming to established rule, standard, etc. **2.** not straight or even; not uniform in shape, design, etc. **3.** uneven in occurrence **4.** having minor flaws: said of merchandise **5.** *Gram.* not inflected in the usual way *[go* is an *irregular* verb] **6.** *Mil.* not belonging to the regularly established army —*n.* a person or thing that is irregular —**ir·reg'u·lar'i·ty** *n., pl.* **-ties** —**ir·reg'u·lar·ly** *adv.*

ir·rel·e·vant (i rel'ə vənt) *adj.* not pertinent; not to the point —**ir·rel'e·vance, ir·rel'e·van·cy** *n., pl.* **-cies** —**ir·rel'e·vant·ly** *adv.*

ir·re·li·gious (ir'i lij'əs) *adj.* **1.** not religious **2.** indifferent or hostile to religion **3.** profane; impious

ir·re·me·di·a·ble (ir'i mē'dē ə b'l) *adj.* that cannot be remedied; incurable —**ir're·me'di·a·bly** *adv.*

ir·re·mis'si·ble (-mis'ə b'l) *adj.* that cannot be excused, pardoned, or shirked

ir·re·mov'a·ble (-mōō'və b'l) *adj.* not removable —**ir're·mov'a·bly** *adv.*

ir·re·par·a·ble (i rep'ər ə b'l) *adj.* that cannot be repaired, mended, remedied, etc.

ir·re·place·a·ble (ir'i plãs'ə b'l) *adj.* not replaceable

ir're·press'i·ble (-pres'ə b'l) *adj.* that cannot be repressed or restrained —**ir're·press'i·bly** *adv.*

ir're·proach'a·ble (-prō'chə b'l) *adj.* blameless; faultless —**ir're·proach'a·bly** *adv.*

ir're·sist'i·ble (-zis'tə b'l) *adj.* that cannot be resisted; too strong, fascinating, etc. to be withstood —**ir're·sist'i·bly** *adv.*

ir·res·o·lute (i rez'ə lōōt') *adj.* not resolute; wavering; indecisive —**ir·res'o·lute'ly** *adv.* —**ir·res·o·lu'tion** *n.*

ir·re·spec·tive (ir'i spek'tiv) *adj.* regardless (*of*)

ir·re·spon·si·ble (ir'i spän'sə b'l) *adj.* **1.** not accountable for actions **2.** lacking a sense of responsibility —**ir're·spon'si·bil'i·ty** *n.* —**ir're·spon'si·bly** *adv.*

ir're·triev'a·ble (-trēv'ə b'l) *adj.* that cannot be retrieved, recovered, restored, etc. —**ir're·triev'a·bly** *adv.*

IRIS

---

at, āpe, cär; ten, ēven; is, bīte; gō, hôrn, tōōl, look; oil, out; up, fur; thin, *then;* zh, leisure; ŋ, ring; ə for *a* in *ago;* as in *able* (ā'b'l); ë, Fr. coeur; ö, Fr. feu; Fr. mon; ü, Fr. duc; r, Fr. cri; kh, G. doch, ich. ‡ foreign; < derived from

ir·rev·er·ence (i rev′ər əns) *n.* **1.** lack of reverence **2.** an act or statement showing this —**ir·rev′er·ent** *adj.* —**ir·rev′er·ent·ly** *adv.*

ir·re·vers·i·ble (ir′i vur′sə b'l) *adj.* not reversible; specif., that cannot be repealed or annulled —**ir′re·vers′i·bly** *adv.*

ir·rev·o·ca·ble (i rev′ə kə b'l) *adj.* that cannot be revoked or undone —**ir·rev′o·ca·bly** *adv.*

ir·ri·ga·ble (ir′i gə b'l) *adj.* that can be irrigated

ir·ri·gate (ir′ə gāt′) *vt.* **-gat′ed, -gat′ing** [< L. *in-*, in + *rigare*, to water] **1.** to supply (land) with water as by means of artificial ditches **2.** *Med.* to wash out (a cavity, wound, etc.) —**ir′ri·ga′tion** *n.*

ir·ri·ta·ble (ir′i tə b'l) *adj.* **1.** easily irritated or provoked **2.** *Med.* excessively sensitive to a stimulus **3.** *Physiol.* able to respond to a stimulus —**ir′ri·ta·bil′i·ty** *n.* —**ir′ri·ta·bly** *adv.*

ir′ri·tant (-tənt) *adj.* causing irritation —*n.* something causing irritation

ir′ri·tate′ (-tāt′) *vt.* **-tat′ed, -tat′ing** [< L. *irritare*, excite] **1.** to provoke to impatience or anger; annoy **2.** to make (a part of the body) inflamed or sore **3.** *Physiol.* to excite (an organ, muscle, etc.) to a characteristic action by a stimulus —**ir′ri·ta′tion** *n.*

ir·rupt (i rupt′) *vi.* [< L. *in-*, in + *rumpere*, to break] **1.** to burst violently (*into*) **2.** *Ecol.* to increase abruptly in size of population —**ir·rup′tion** *n.* —**ir·rup′tive** *adj.*

Ir·ving (ur′viŋ), **Washington** 1783–1859; U.S. writer

is (iz) [OE.] *3d pers. sing., pres. indic.,* of BE

is. 1. island(s) **2.** isle(s)

I·saac (ī′zək) *Bible* one of the patriarchs, son of Abraham and Sarah, and father of Jacob and Esau

Is·a·bel·la I (iz′ə bel′ə) 1451–1504; queen of Castile (1474–1504); gave help to Columbus

I·sa·iah (ī zā′ə) *Bible* **1.** a Hebrew prophet of the 8th cent. B.C. **2.** the book containing his teachings: abbrev. **Isa., Is.**

-ise *chiefly Brit. var. of* -IZE

-ish [OE. *-isc*] *a suffix meaning:* a) of (a specified people) [*Spanish*] b) like [*devilish*] c) tending to [*bookish*] d) somewhat [*tallish*] e) [Colloq.] approximately [*thirtyish*]

Ish·ma·el (ish′mē əl, -mā-) *Bible* the son of Abraham and Hagar: he and his mother were made outcasts —*n.* an outcast

Ish′ma·el·ite′ (-ə līt′) *n.* **1.** a descendant of Ishmael, the traditional progenitor of Arab peoples **2.** an outcast

Ish·tar (ish′tär) the Babylonian and Assyrian goddess of love and fertility

i·sin·glass (ī′z'n glas′, -ziŋ-) *n.* [prob. < MDu. *huizen*, sturgeon + *blas*, bladder] **1.** a gelatin prepared from fish bladders **2.** mica, esp. in thin sheets

I·sis (ī′sis) the Egyptian goddess of fertility

isl. *pl.* **isls. 1.** island **2.** isle

Is·lam (is′läm, iz′-; is läm′) *n.* [Ar. *islām*, lit., submission (to God's will)] **1.** the Muslim religion, a monotheistic religion founded by Mohammed **2.** Muslims collectively or the lands in which they predominate —**Is·lam′ic** (-läm′-, -läm′-) *adj.*

is·land (ī′lənd) *n.* [< OE. *igland*, lit., island land: sp. after *isle*] **1.** a land mass not so large as a continent, surrounded by water **2.** anything like an island in position or isolation **3.** *Anat.* a cluster of cells differing from surrounding tissue in formation, etc.

is′land·er *n.* a native or inhabitant of an island

isle (īl) *n.* [< L. *insula*] an island, esp. a small one

is·let (ī′lit) *n.* a very small island

ism (iz′m) *n.* a doctrine, theory, system, etc., esp. one whose name ends in *-ism*

-ism [< Gr. *-ismos*] *a suffix meaning:* **1.** the act or result of [*terrorism*] **2.** the condition, conduct, or qualities of [*patriotism*] **3.** the theory of [*socialism*] **4.** devotion to [*nationalism*] **5.** an instance of [*witticism*] **6.** an abnormal condition caused by [*alcoholism*]

is·n't (iz′'nt) is not

iso- [< Gr. *isos*, equal] *a combining form meaning* equal, similar, alike: also **is-**

i·so·bar (ī′sə bär′) *n.* [< prec. + Gr. *baros*, weight] **1.** a line on a map connecting points of equal barometric pressure **2.** any of two or more forms of an atom having the same atomic weight but different atomic numbers —**i′so·bar′ic** (-bär′ik) *adj.*

i·so·late (ī′sə lāt′) *vt.* **-lat′ed, -lat′ing** [< It. *isola* (< L. *insula*), island] **1.** to set apart from others; place alone **2.** *Chem.* to separate (an element or compound) in pure form from another compound or mixture **3.** *Med.* to place (a patient with a contagious disease) apart from others —*n.* a person or thing that is isolated —**i′so·la′tion** *n.*

i′so·la′tion·ist *n.* one who believes his country should not take part in international alliances, etc. —*adj.* of isolationists —**i′so·la′tion·ism** *n.*

I·sol·de (i sōl′də, i sōld′) *see* TRISTRAM

i·so·mer (ī′sə mər) *n.* [< Gr. *isos*, equal + *meros*, a part] any of two or more chemical compounds whose molecules contain the same atoms but in different arrangements —**i′so·mer′ic** (-mer′ik) *adj.*

i·so·met·ric (ī′sə met′rik) *adj.* [< Gr. *isos*, equal + *metron*, a measure] **1.** of or having equality of measure: also **i′so·met′ri·cal 2.** of isometrics —*n.* [*pl.*] exercise in which one set of muscles is briefly tensed in opposition to another set of muscles or to an immovable object

i·sos·ce·les (ī säs′ə lēz′) *adj.* [< Gr. *isos*, equal + *skelos*, a leg] designating a triangle with two equal sides

i·so·therm (ī′sə thurm′) *n.* [< Fr. < *iso-*, ISO- + Gr. *thermē*, heat] a line on a map connecting points on the earth's surface having the same mean temperature or the same temperature at a given time —**i′so·ther′mal** *adj.*

ISOSCELES TRIANGLES

i·so·tope (ī′sə tōp′) *n.* [< ISO- + Gr. *topos*, place] any of two or more forms of an element having the same atomic number but different atomic weights —**i′so·top′ic** (-täp′ik, -tō′pik) *adj.*

i·so·trop·ic (ī′sə träp′ik, -trō′pik) *adj.* [ISO- + -TROPIC] having physical properties, as conductivity, elasticity, etc., that are the same regardless of the direction of measurement

Is·ra·el (iz′rē əl) **1.** *Bible* Jacob **2.** the Jewish people **3.** ancient land of the Hebrews at the SE end of the Mediterranean **4.** kingdom in the N part of this region **5.** country between the Mediterranean & the country of Jordan: a Jewish state: 7,992 sq. mi.; pop. 2,889,000; cap. Jerusalem

Is·rae·li (iz rā′lē) *adj.* of modern Israel or its people —*n., pl.* **-lis, -li** a native or inhabitant of modern Israel

Is·ra·el·ite (iz′rē ə līt′) *n.* any of the people of ancient Israel or their descendants; Jew —*adj.* of ancient Israel or the Israelites; Jewish

is·su·ance (ish′oo wəns) *n.* an issuing; issue

is·sue (ish′oo) *n.* [< L. *ex-*, out + *ire*, go] **1.** an outgoing; outflow **2.** an exit; outlet **3.** a result; consequence **4.** offspring **5.** a point under dispute **6.** a sending or giving out **7.** all that is put forth at one time [an *issue* of bonds, a periodical, etc.] **8.** *Med.* a discharge of blood, etc. —*vi.* **-sued, -su·ing 1.** to go or flow out; emerge **2.** to result (*from*) or end (*in*) **3.** to be published —*vt.* **1.** to let out; discharge **2.** to give or deal out (supplies, etc.) **3.** to publish —**at issue** in dispute —**join issue** to meet in conflict, argument, etc. —**take issue** to disagree —**is′su·er** *n.*

-ist [< Gr. *-istēs*] *a suffix meaning:* **1.** one who does, makes, or practices [*satirist*] **2.** one skilled in or occupied with [*druggist, violinist*] **3.** an adherent of [*anarchist*]

Is·tan·bul (is′tan bool′, -tän-) seaport in NW Turkey: pop. 1,751,000

isth·mus (is′məs) *n., pl.* **-mus·es, -mi** (-mī) [< Gr. *isthmos*, a neck] a narrow strip of land having water at each side and connecting two larger bodies of land —**isth′mi·an** *adj.*

-istic [< -IST + -IC] *a suffix used to form adjectives from nouns ending in -ISM and -IST*

is·tle (ist′lē) *n.* [< AmSp.] a fiber of certain tropical American plants, used for baskets, etc.

it (it) *pron. for pl. see* THEY [OE. *hit*] the animal or thing under discussion *It* is used as: a) the subject of an impersonal verb [*it* is snowing] b) a subject or object of indefinite sense in various idiomatic constructions [*it's* all right, he lords *it* over us] c) the grammatical subject of a clause of which the actual subject follows [*it* is well that he can go] d) [Colloq.] an emphatic predicate pronoun referring to something ultimate or final [zero hour is here; this is *it*] —*n.* the player, as in the game of tag, who must do some specific thing —**with it** [Slang] alert, informed, or hip

It., Ital. 1. Italian **2.** Italy

ital. italic (type)

I·tal·ian (i tal′yən) *adj.* of Italy, its people, their language, etc. —*n.* **1.** a native or inhabitant of Italy **2.** the Romance language of the Italians

i·tal·ic (i tal′ik) *adj.* [< its early use in *Italy*] designating a type in which the letters slant upward to the right [*this is italic type*] —*n.* [*usually pl., sometimes with sing. v.*] italic type or print

i·tal·i·cize (i tal′ə sīz′) *vt.* **-cized′, -ciz′ing 1.** to print in italics **2.** to underscore (copy) to indicate that it is to be printed in italics

It·a·ly (it′′l ē) country in S Europe: 116,304 sq. mi.; pop. 54,388,000; cap. Rome

itch (ich) *vi.* [OE. *giccan*] **1.** to feel a tingling of the skin, with the desire to scratch **2.** to have a restless desire —*n.* **1.** an itching on the skin **2.** a restless desire —**the itch** any of various skin disorders with severe irritation of the skin —**itch′i·ness** *n.* —**itch′y** *adj.* **-i·er, -i·est**

-ite [< Gr. *-ītēs*] *a suffix meaning:* **1.** an inhabitant of [*Akronite*] **2.** an adherent of [*laborite*] **3.** a manufactured product [*dynamite*] **4.** a salt or ester of an acid whose name ends in *-ous* [*nitrite*] **5.** a (specified) mineral or rock [*anthracite*]

i·tem (īt′əm) *adv.* [< L. *ita*, so, thus] also: used before each article in a series being enumerated —*n.* **1.** an article; unit; separate thing **2.** a bit of news or information

i′tem·ize′ (-īz′) *vt.* **-ized′, -iz′ing** to specify the items of; set down by items —**i′tem·i·za′tion** *n.*

it·er·ate (it′ə rāt′) *vt.* **-at′ed, -at′ing** [< L. *iterum*, again] to utter or do again or repeatedly —**it′er·a′tion** *n.* —**it′er·a′tive** *adj.*

i·tin·er·ant (ī tin′ər ənt) *adj.* [< L. *iter*, a walk] traveling from place to place —*n.* a traveler

i·tin·er·ar·y (ī tin′ə rer′ē) *n., pl.* **-ies 1.** a route **2.** a record of a journey **3.** a detailed plan for a journey

-ition [< L. *-itionis*] *var. of* -ATION [*nutrition*]

-itious [L. *-itius*] *a suffix that is used to form adjectives from nouns ending in* -ITION *and that means* of, characterized by [*nutritious*]

-itis [< Gr. *-itis*] *a suffix meaning* inflammation of (a specified part or organ) [*sinusitis*]

it′ll (it′′l) **1.** it will **2.** it shall

its (its) *pron.* that or those belonging to it —*possessive pronominal adj.* of, belonging to, or done by it

it′s (its) **1.** it is **2.** it has

it·self (it self′) *pron.* **1.** *the intensive form of* IT [*the work itself* is easy] **2.** *the reflexive form of* IT [*the dog bit itself*] **3.** its true self [*the cat is not itself* today]

it·ty-bit·ty (it′ē bit′ē) *adj.* [alteration < *little bit*] [Colloq.] very small; tiny: also **it·sy-bit·sy** (it′sē bit′sē)

-ity [< L. *-itas*] *a suffix meaning* state, condition [*chastity, possibility*]

IUD intrauterine (contraceptive) device: also **IUCD**

I·van IV (ī′vən; *Russ.* i vän′) 1530–84; 1st czar of Russia (1547–84): called *the Terrible*

I′ve (īv) I have

-ive [< Fr. *-if* < L. *-ivus*] *a suffix meaning:* **1.** of, related to, having the nature of [*substantive*] **2.** tending to [*creative*]

i·vied (ī′vēd) *adj.* covered or overgrown with ivy

i·vo·ry (ī′vər ē, īv′rē) *n., pl.* **-ries** [ult. < Egypt. *āb, ābu*, elephant] **1.** the hard, white substance forming the tusks of elephants, walruses, etc. **2.** a substance like ivory **3.** the color of ivory; creamy white **4.** [*pl.*] [Slang] *a)* piano keys *b)* teeth *c)* dice —*adj.* **1.** of or like ivory **2.** creamy-white

Ivory Coast country on WC coast of Africa: 124,500 sq. mi.; pop. 3,750,000; cap. Abidjan

ivory tower figuratively, a place of mental withdrawal from reality and action

i·vy (ī′vē) *n., pl.* **i′vies** [OE. *ifig*] **1.** a climbing vine with a woody stem and evergreen leaves: also **English ivy 2.** any of various similar plants, as poison ivy

-ization *a suffix used to form nouns from verbs ending in* -IZE [*realization*]

-ize [< Gr. *-izein*] *a suffix meaning:* **1.** to cause to be, make [*sterilize*] **2.** to become (like), change into [*crystallize*] **3.** to subject to, combine with [*oxidize*] **4.** to engage in [*theorize*]

J

J, j (jā) *n., pl.* **J′s, j′s** the tenth letter of the English alphabet

J *Physics symbol for* joule

Ja. January

jab (jab) *vt., vi.* **jabbed, jab′bing** [< ME. *jobben*, to peck] **1.** to poke or thrust, as with a sharp instrument **2.** to punch with short, straight blows —*n.* a quick thrust, blow, or punch

jab·ber (jab′ər) *vi., vt.* [prob. echoic] to talk quickly, incoherently, or nonsensically —*n.* fast, incoherent, nonsensical talk —**jab′ber·er** *n.*

ja·bot (zha bō′, ja-) *n.* [Fr., bird's crop] a trimming or frill, as of lace, attached to the front of a blouse or shirt

ja·cinth (jā′sinth, jas′inth) *n.* [see HYACINTH] *same as* HYACINTH (sense 1 *b*)

jack (jak) *n.* [< the name *Jack*] **1.** [*often* J-] a man or boy **2.** any of various devices used to lift something heavy a short distance [an automobile *jack*] **3.** *Elec.* a plug-in receptacle used to make electric contact **4.** *Games a)* a playing card with a page boy's picture on it *b)* a small pebble or six-pronged metal piece used in playing jacks: see JACKS **5.** *Naut.* a small flag flown on the ship's bow as a signal or to show nationality **6.** [Old Slang] money —*vt.* to raise by means of a jack —**jack up** [Colloq.] to raise (prices, wages, etc.)

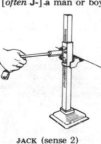

JACK (sense 2)

jack- [see prec.] *a combining form meaning:* **1.** male [*jackass*] **2.** large or strong [*jackboot*] **3.** boy, fellow [*jack-in-the-box*]

jack·al (jak′əl, -ôl) *n.* [< Sans.] **1.** a yellowish-gray wild dog of Asia and N Africa **2.** one who does dishonest or humiliating tasks for another

jack·a·napes (jak′ə nāps′) *n.* [< nickname of a Duke of Suffolk] a conceited, insolent fellow

jack·ass (jak′as′) *n.* [JACK- + ASS] **1.** a male donkey **2.** a stupid or foolish person

jack′boot′ *n.* [JACK- + BOOT¹] a heavy, sturdy military boot that reaches above the knee

jack·daw (jak′dô′) *n.* [JACK- + DAW] a European black bird related to the crow, but smaller

jack·et (jak′it) *n.* [< Ar. *shakk*] **1.** a short coat **2.** an outer covering, as the removable paper cover on a book, the skin of a potato, the cardboard holder of a phonograph record, etc. —*vt.* to put a jacket on

Jack Frost frost or cold weather personified

jack′-in-the-box′ *n., pl.* **-box′es** a toy consisting of a box from which a figure on a spring jumps up when the lid is lifted: also **jack′-in-a-box′**

jack′-in-the-pul′pit (-pool′pit) *n., pl.* **-pits** a plant with a flower spike partly arched over by a hoodlike covering

jack′knife′ *n., pl.* **-knives′** (-nīvz′) **1.** a large pocketknife **2.** a dive in which one keeps the knees unbent, touches the feet with the hands, and then straightens out —*vi.* **-knifed′, -knif′ing** to bend at the middle as in a jackknife dive

jack′-of-all′-trades′ *n., pl.* **jacks′-** [see JACK-] [*often* J-] one who can do many kinds of work acceptably

jack-o′-lan·tern (jak′ə lan′tərn) *n., pl.* **-terns** a hollow pumpkin cut to look like a face and used as a lantern

jack′pot′ *n.* [JACK, *n.* 4 *a* + POT] cumulative stakes, as in a poker game, slot machine, etc. —**hit the jackpot** [Slang] **1.** to win the jackpot **2.** to attain the highest success

jack rabbit a large hare of W N. America, with long ears and strong hind legs

jacks (jaks) *n.pl.* [< JACKSTONE] [*with sing. v.*] a children's game in which pebbles or small, six-pronged metal pieces are tossed and picked up in various ways, esp. while bouncing a small ball

Jack·son (jak′s′n) capital of Miss., in the SW part: pop. 154,200

Jack·son (jak's'n) **1.** Andrew, 1767–1845; 7th president of the U.S. (1829–37) **2. Thomas J.**, (nickname *Stonewall Jackson*) 1824–63; Confederate general in the Civil War
Jack·son·ville (jak's'n vil') port in NE Fla.: pop. 529,000
jack·stone (jak'stōn') *n.* [for dial. *checkstone*, pebble] **1.** same as JACK (*n.* 4 *b*) **2.** [*pl.*, with *sing. v.*] same as JACKS
jack'straw' *n.* [JACK- + STRAW] a narrow strip of wood, plastic, etc. used in a game (**jackstraws**) in which one tries to pick one strip at a time from a jumbled heap of such strips without moving any of the others
Ja·cob (jā'kəb) *Bible* a son of Isaac and father of the founders of the twelve tribes of Israel
Jac·o·be·an (jak'ə bē'ən) *adj.* [< *Jacobus*, Latin for James] of the period (1603–25) when James I was king of England —*n.* a person of this period
Jac·o·bin (jak'ə bin) *n.* [< the Church of St. *Jacques* in Paris] **1.** a member of a group of radical democrats in France during the Revolution of 1789 **2.** a political radical —Jac'o·bin·ism *n.*
Jac·o·bite (jak'ə bīt') *n.* [see JACOBEAN] a supporter of James II of England and his descendants in their claim to the throne, after 1688
Jacob's ladder 1. *Bible* the ladder to heaven that Jacob saw in a dream **2.** a ship's ladder of rope, wire, etc.
jade¹ (jād) *n.* [Fr. < Sp. *piedra de ijada*, stone of the side: from the notion that it cured pains in the side] **1.** a hard, ornamental stone, usually green **2.** a green color of medium hue —*adj.* **1.** made of jade **2.** green like jade
jade² (jād) *n.* [< ON. *jalda*, a mare < Finn.] **1.** a horse, esp. a worn-out, worthless one **2.** a disreputable woman —*vt., vi.* jad'ed, jad'ing to make or become tired, weary, or worn-out
jad·ed (jā'did) *adj.* **1.** tired; worn-out **2.** satiated —jad'·ed·ly *adv.* —jad'ed·ness *n.*
jae·ger (yā'gər) *n.* [< G. *jäger*, huntsman] a sea bird which forces other, weaker birds to give up their prey
Jaf·fa (yä'fə, jaf'ə) *see* TEL AVIV-JAFFA
jag¹ (jag) *n.* [ME. *jagge*] a sharp, toothlike projection —*vt.* jagged, jag'ging to notch or nick (cloth, etc.)
jag² (jag) *n.* [< ?] [Slang] a drunken spree
jag·ged (jag'id) *adj.* having sharp projecting points or notches —jag'ged·ly *adv.* —jag'ged·ness *n.*
jag·uar (jag'wär) *n.* [Port. < SAmInd.] a large, leopardlike cat, yellowish with black spots, found from SW U.S. to Argentina
Jah·veh, Jah·ve, Jah·weh, Jah·we (yä've) *same as* JEHOVAH
jai a·lai (hī'lī', hī'ə lī') [Sp. < Basque *jai*, celebration + *alai*, merry] a Latin-American game like handball, played with a curved basket fastened to the arm, for catching and hurling the ball
jail (jāl) *n.* [ult. < L. *cavea*, a cage] a prison for those awaiting trial or convicted of minor offenses —*vt.* to put or keep in jail
jail'bird' *n.* [Colloq.] **1.** a prisoner in jail **2.** a person often put in jail
jail'break' *n.* a breaking out of jail
jail'er, jail'or *n.* a person in charge of a jail or of prisoners
Ja·kar·ta (jə kär'tə) capital of Indonesia, on the NW coast of Java: pop. c. 4,500,000
ja·lop·y (jə läp'ē) *n., pl.* -ies [< ?] [Slang] an old, ramshackle automobile
jal·ou·sie (jal'ə sē') *n.* [Fr.: see JEALOUS] a window, shade, or door formed of adjustable, horizontal slats of wood, metal, or glass
jam¹ (jam) *vt.* jammed, jam'ming [< ?] **1.** to squeeze into a confined space **2.** to crush **3.** to crowd **4.** to crowd into or block (a passageway, etc.) **5.** to wedge so that it cannot move **6.** to make (radio or radar signals) unintelligible, as by sending out others on the same wavelength —*vi.* **1.** to become wedged or stuck fast, esp. so as to become unworkable **2.** to push against one another in a confined space **3.** [Slang] *Jazz* to improvise —*n.* **1.** a jamming or being jammed **2.** a group of persons or things blocking a passageway, etc. [a traffic *jam*] **3.** [Colloq.] a difficult situation

JALOUSIES

jam² (jam) *n.* [< ? prec.] a food made by boiling fruit with sugar to a thick mixture
Ja·mai·ca (jə mā'kə) country on an island of the West Indies: 4,411 sq. mi.; pop. 1,972,000; cap. Kingston —Ja·mai'can *adj., n.*

jamb (jam) *n.* [< LL. *gamba*, leg] a side post of an opening for a door, window, etc.
jam·bo·ree (jam'bə rē') *n.* [< ?] **1.** [Colloq.] a boisterous party or revel **2.** a large assembly of boy scouts
James (jāmz) **1.** *Bible a)* either of two Christian apostles *b)* a book of the New Testament **2. James I** 1566–1625; king of England (1603–25) **3. James II** 1633–1701; king of England (1685–88): deposed **4. Henry**, 1843–1916; U.S. novelist **5. William**, 1842–1910; U.S. psychologist & philosopher: brother of *Henry*
James·town (jāmz'toun') colonial settlement (1607) in Virginia
Jam·mu and Kashmir (jum'ōō) state of N India, control of which is disputed by Pakistan
jam-packed (jam'pakt') *adj.* tightly packed
jam session an informal gathering of jazz musicians, etc. to play improvisations
jan·gle (jaŋ'g'l) *vi.* -gled, -gling [< OFr. *jangler*] **1.** to make a harsh, inharmonious sound **2.** to quarrel noisily —*vt.* **1.** to cause to jangle **2.** to irritate [to *jangle* one's nerves] —*n.* **1.** noisy talk or arguing **2.** a harsh sound —jan'gler *n.*
jan·i·tor (jan'i tər) *n.* [L., doorkeeper] the custodian of a building, who does routine maintenance —jan'i·to'ri·al (-ə tôr'ē əl) *adj.*
Jan·u·ar·y (jan'yoo wer'ē) *n., pl.* -ies [< L. *Januarius* (*mensis*), (the month) of Janus] the first month of the year, having 31 days: abbrev. Jan., Ja.
Ja·nus (jā'nəs) *Rom. Myth.* the god who was guardian of portals and patron of beginnings and endings: his head is shown with two faces
Jap. 1. Japan **2.** Japanese
Ja·pan (jə pan') island country off the E coast of Asia: 142,726 sq. mi.; pop. 102,833,000; cap. Tokyo
ja·pan (jə pan') *n.* [orig. from Japan] **1.** a varnish giving a hard, glossy finish **2.** objects varnished in the Japanese style —*vt.* -panned', -pan'ning to varnish with japan
Jap·a·nese (jap'ə nēz') *adj.* of Japan, its people, language, culture, etc. —*n.* **1.** *pl.* -nese' a native of Japan **2.** the language of Japan
Japanese beetle a shiny, green-and-brown beetle, orig. from Japan, which eats leaves, fruits, and grasses, and is damaging to crops
jape (jāp) *vi.* japed, jap'ing [ME. *japen*] **1.** to joke **2.** to play tricks —*n.* **1.** a joke **2.** a trick
Ja·pheth (jā'fith) *Bible* the youngest of Noah's three sons
ja·pon·i·ca (jə pän'i kə) *n.* [< Fr. *Japon*, Japan] a popular name for CAMELLIA, etc.
jar¹ (jär) *vi.* jarred, jar'ring [ult. echoic] **1.** to make a harsh sound; grate **2.** to have an irritating effect (*on* one) **3.** to vibrate from an impact **4.** to clash or quarrel sharply —*vt.* **1.** to jolt or shock —*n.* **1.** a harsh, grating sound **2.** a vibration due to sudden impact **3.** a jolt or shock **4.** a sharp clash or quarrel
jar² (jär) *n.* [< Fr. < Ar. *jarrah*, earthen container] **1.** a container made of glass, earthenware, etc., with a large opening and no spout **2.** as much as a jar will hold: also **jar'ful'**
jar·di·niere (jär'd'n ir') *n.* [Fr. < *jardin*, a garden] an ornamental pot or stand for flowers or plants
jar·gon (jär'gən) *n.* [MFr., a chattering] **1.** unintelligible talk **2.** the specialized vocabulary and idioms of those in the same work, profession, etc.
Jas. James
jas·mine, jas·min (jaz'min; *chiefly Brit.* jas'-) *n.* [< Fr. < Per. *yāsamīn*] any of certain plants of warm regions, with fragrant flowers of yellow, red, or white
Ja·son (jās'n) *Gr. Myth.* a prince who led the Argonauts and got the Golden Fleece
jas·per (jas'pər) *n.* [< Gr. *iaspis*] an opaque variety of quartz, usually reddish, yellow, or brown
jaun·dice (jôn'dis) *n.* [ult. < L. *galbus*, yellow] **1.** a diseased condition in which the eyeballs, skin, and urine become abnormally yellow as a result of bile in the blood **2.** bitterness or prejudice caused by jealousy, envy, etc. —*vt.* -diced, -dic·ing **1.** to cause to have jaundice **2.** to make bitter or prejudiced through jealousy, envy, etc.
jaunt (jônt) *vi.* [< ?] to take a short trip for pleasure —*n.* such a trip; excursion
jaun·ty (jônt'ē) *adj.* -ti·er, -ti·est [< Fr. *gentil*, genteel] **1.** in fashion; chic **2.** gay and carefree; sprightly —jaun'ti·ly *adv.* —jaun'ti·ness *n.*
Ja·va (jä'və, jav'ə) large island of Indonesia —*n.* **1.** coffee grown there **2.** [*often* j-] [Slang] any coffee —Jav·a·nese (jav'ə nēz') *adj., n., pl.* -nese'
Java man a type of primitive man (*Homo erectus erectus*) known from fossil remains found in Java

jav·e·lin (jav′lin, jav′ə lin) *n.* [< MFr. *javelot,* a spear] a light spear, esp. one thrown for distance in a contest

jaw (jô) *n.* [< ? OFr. *joue,* cheek] **1.** either of the two bony parts that hold the teeth and frame the mouth **2.** either of two movable parts that grasp or crush something, as in a vise **3.** [*pl.*] the entrance of a canyon, valley, etc. —*vi.* [Slang] to talk —*vt.* [Slang] to scold

jaw′bone′ *n.* a bone of a jaw, esp. of the lower jaw —*vt., vi.* -**boned′, -bon′ing** to try to persuade by using the influence of one's high office

jaw′break′er *n.* **1.** a machine for crushing rocks, ore, etc. **2.** a hard, usually round candy **3.** [Slang] a word that is hard to pronounce

jay (jā) *n.* [< LL. *gaius,* a jay] **1.** any of several birds of the crow family **2.** *same as* BLUE JAY **3.** [Colloq.] a stupid or foolish person

Jay (jā), **John** 1745–1829; Am. statesman & jurist; 1st chief justice of the U.S. (1789–95)

jay·walk (jā′wôk′) *vi.* [JAY, 3 + WALK] to cross a street carelessly without obeying traffic regulations and signals —**jay′walk′er** *n.* —**jay′walk′ing** *n.*

jazz (jaz) *n.* [< ? Creole patois *jass,* sexual term] **1.** a kind of music characterized by syncopation, melodic variations, and unusual tonal effects **2.** [Slang] remarks, acts, etc. regarded as hypocritical, tiresome, etc. —*adj.* of, in, or like jazz —*vt.* **1.** to play as jazz **2.** [Slang] to enliven or embellish (usually with *up*)

jazz′y *adj.* -**i·er, -i·est 1.** of or like jazz **2.** [Slang] lively, flashy, etc. —**jazz′i·ly** *adv.*

jct. junction

Je. June

jeal·ous (jel′əs) *adj.* [see ZEAL] **1.** watchful in guarding [*jealous* of one's rights] **2.** *a)* resentfully suspicious of rivalry [a *jealous* lover] *b)* resentfully envious *c)* resulting from such feelings [a *jealous* rage] **3.** [Now Rare] requiring exclusive loyalty [a *jealous* God] —**jeal′ous·ly** *adv.* —**jeal′ous·ness** *n.*

jeal′ous·y *n., pl.* -**ies** the quality, condition, or feeling of being jealous

jean (jēn) *n.* [< L. *Genua,* Genoa] **1.** a durable, twilled cotton cloth **2.** [*pl.*] trousers of this material or of denim

Jeans (jēnz), **Sir James (Hopwood)** 1877–1946; Eng. physicist, astronomer, & writer

jee (jē) *interj., n., vt., vi. same as* GEE¹

jeep (jēp) *n.* [< a creature in a comic strip by E. C. Segar] a small, rugged military automotive vehicle of World War II

jeer (jir) *vt., vi.* [< ? CHEER] to make fun of in a rude, sarcastic manner; scoff (at) —*n.* a jeering remark —**jeer′ing·ly** *adv.*

Jef·fer·son (jef′ər s'n), **Thomas** 1743–1826; 3d president of the U.S. (1801–09) —**Jef′fer·so′ni·an** (-sō′nē ən) *adj., n.*

Jefferson City capital of Mo.: pop. 32,000

Je·ho·vah (ji hō′və) [< Heb. sacred name for God] God; (the) Lord

Jehovah's Witnesses a proselytizing Christian sect founded by Charles T. Russell (1852–1916)

je·hu (jē′hōō) [< *Jehu* in the Bible: II Kings 9] [Colloq.] a fast, reckless driver

je·june (ji jōōn′) *adj.* [L. *jejunus,* empty] **1.** not interesting or satisfying **2.** not mature; childish

je·ju·num (ji jōō′nəm) *n., pl.* -**na** (-nə) [see prec.] the middle part of the small intestine

jell (jel) *vi., vt.* [< JELLY] **1.** to become or make into jelly **2.** [Colloq.] to take or give definite form; crystallize [the plans didn't *jell*] —*n.* [Dial.] *same as* JELLY

jel·ly (jel′ē) *n., pl.* -**lies** [< L. *gelare,* freeze] **1.** a soft, gelatinous food made from cooked fruit syrup or meat juice **2.** any substance like this —*vi., vt.* -**lied, -ly·ing** to jell (sense 1)

jel′ly·fish′ *n., pl.:* see FISH **1.** an invertebrate sea animal with an umbrella-shaped body of jellylike substance and long tentacles with stinging cells on them **2.** [Colloq.] a weak-willed person

jel′ly·roll′ *n.* a thin sheet of spongecake spread with jelly and rolled to form layers

jen·net (jen′it) *n.* [< Sp. *jinete,* horseman] any of a breed of small Spanish horses

jen·ny (jen′ē) *n., pl.* -**nies** [< *Jenny,* fem. name] **1.** *same as* SPINNING JENNY **2.** *a)* the female of some birds [*jenny* wren] *b)* a female donkey

jeop·ard·ize (jep′ər dīz′) *vt.* -**ized′, -iz′ing** to put in jeopardy; endanger

jeop·ard·y (jep′ər dē) *n., pl.* -**ies** [< OFr. *jeu parti,* lit., a game with even chances] **1.** great danger; peril **2.** *Law* the situation of an accused person on trial for a crime

jer·bo·a (jər bō′ə) *n.* [< Ar. *yarbū*] any of various small, nocturnal, leaping rodents of N Africa and Asia, with very long hind legs

jer·e·mi·ad (jer′ə mī′əd) *n.* a lamentation or tale of woe

Jer·e·mi·ah (jer′ə mī′ə) *Bible* **1.** a Hebrew prophet of the 7th and 6th cent. B.C. **2.** the book containing his prophecies: abbrev. **Jer.**

Jer·i·cho (jer′ə kō′) city in Jordan: site of an ancient city in Canaan: Josh. 6

jerk¹ (jurk) *n.* [< ?] **1.** a sharp, abrupt pull, twist, etc. **2.** a sudden muscular contraction caused by a reflex action **3.** [Slang] a person regarded as stupid, foolish, etc. —*vt., vi.* **1.** to move with a jerk; pull sharply **2.** to twitch

jerk² (jurk) *vt.* [< JERKY²] to preserve (meat) by slicing into strips and drying in the sun

jer·kin (jur′kin) *n.* [< ?] a closefitting, sleeveless jacket of a kind worn in the 16th and 17th cent.

jerk′wa′ter *adj.* [Colloq.] small, unimportant, etc. [a *jerkwater* town]

jerk·y¹ (jurk′ē) *adj.* -**i·er, -i·est 1.** moving by jerks; spasmodic **2.** [Slang] stupid, foolish, etc. —**jerk′i·ly** *adv.*

jer·ky² (jur′kē) *n.* [< Sp. *charqui*] meat, esp. beef, preserved by being sliced into strips and dried, as in the sun

Jerome, Saint 340?–420 A.D.; monk & church scholar: author of the Vulgate

jer·ry-built (jer′ē bilt′) *adj.* [prob. < name *Jerry,* infl. by JURY²] built poorly, of cheap materials

Jer·sey (jur′zē) largest of the Channel Islands —*n., pl.* -**seys 1.** any of a breed of reddish-brown dairy cattle, originally from Jersey **2.** [**j-**] *a)* a soft, elastic, knitted cloth *b)* any closefitting, knitted upper garment

Jersey City city in NE N.J., across the Hudson from New York City: pop. 261,000 (met. area 609,000)

Je·ru·sa·lem (jə rōō′sə ləm) capital of Israel (sense 5), in the C part: pop. 266,000

Jerusalem artichoke [altered (after prec.) < Fr. < It. *girasole,* sunflower] **1.** a tall N. American sunflower with edible potatolike tubers **2.** such a tuber

jest (jest) *n.* [< L. *gerere,* perform] **1.** a mocking remark; taunt **2.** a joke **3.** fun; joking **4.** a thing to be laughed at —*vi.* **1.** to jeer; mock **2.** to joke

jest′er *n.* one who jests; esp., a professional fool employed by a medieval ruler to amuse him

Jes·u·it (jezh′ōō wit, jez′-) *n.* a member of the Society of Jesus, a Roman Catholic religious order for men founded in 1534 —**Jes′u·it′ic** *adj.*

Je·sus (jē′zəs) c.8–4 B.C.–29? A.D.: founder of the Christian religion: also called **Jesus Christ, Jesus of Nazareth**

jet¹ (jet) *vt., vi.* **jet′ted, jet′ting** [< L. *jacere,* to throw] **1.** to gush out in a stream **2.** to travel or convey by a jet airplane —*n.* **1.** a stream of liquid or gas emitted, as from a spout **2.** a spout for emitting a jet **3.** a jet-propelled airplane: in full **jet (air)plane** —*adj.* **1.** jet-propelled **2.** of jet propulsion or jet-propelled aircraft

jet² (jet) *n.* [< Gr. *Gagas,* town in Asia Minor] **1.** a hard, black variety of lignite, used in jewelry **2.** a lustrous black —*adj.* **1.** made of jet **2.** black

jet′lin′er *n.* a commercial jet aircraft for carrying passengers

jet′port′ *n.* an airport with long runways, for use by jet airplanes

jet propulsion a method of propelling airplanes, boats, etc. by the discharge of gases under pressure from a rear vent —**jet′-pro·pelled′** (-prə peld′) *adj.*

jet·sam (jet′səm) *n.* [var. of JETTISON] **1.** cargo thrown overboard to lighten a ship in danger **2.** such cargo washed ashore **3.** discarded things

jet set rich, fashionable people who travel widely for pleasure, esp. in jets

jet·ti·son (jet′ə s'n) *n.* [< L. *jactare,* to throw] **1.** a throwing overboard of goods to lighten a ship, airplane, etc. in an emergency **2.** *same as* JETSAM —*vt.* **1.** to throw (goods) overboard **2.** to discard

jet·ty (jet′ē) *n., pl.* -**ties** [see JET¹] **1.** a wall built out into the water to restrain currents, protect a harbor, etc. **2.** a landing pier

Jew (jōō) *n.* [< Heb. *yehūdī,* member of the tribe of Judah] **1.** a person descended, or regarded as descended, from the ancient Hebrews **2.** a person whose religion is Judaism

jew·el (jōō'əl) *n.* [ult. < L. *jocus,* a joke] **1.** a valuable ring, necklace, etc., esp. one set with gems **2.** a precious stone; gem **3.** any person or thing that is very precious **4.** a small gem used as a bearing in a watch —*vt.* **-eled** or **-elled, -el·ing** or **-el·ling** to decorate or set with jewels

jew·el·er, jew·el·ler (-ər) *n.* one who makes or deals in jewelry, watches, etc.

jew·el·ry *n.* jewels collectively

jew'fish' *n., pl.:* see FISH any of several large fish found in warm seas

Jew·ish (jōō'ish) *adj.* of or having to do with Jews or Judaism —*n.* [Colloq.] *same as* YIDDISH —**Jew'ish·ness** *n.*

Jew'ry (-rē) *n.* Jewish people collectively

jew's-harp, jews'-harp (jōōz'härp') *n.* [< Du. *jeugdtromp,* child's trumpet] a small, metal musical instrument, held between the teeth and played by plucking a projecting piece with the finger

Jez·e·bel (jez'ə bel') *Bible* the wicked woman who married Ahab, king of Israel —*n.* [*also* j-] any shameless, wicked woman

jg, j.g. junior grade

jib¹ (jib) *n.* [< Dan. *gibbe,* to jibe] a triangular sail projecting ahead of the foremast

jib² (jib) *vi.* **jibbed, jib'bing** [prob. < prec.] **1.** to refuse to go forward; balk **2.** to start or shy (*at* something)

jib boom a spar fixed to and extending beyond the bowsprit of a ship: the jib is attached to it

jibe¹ (jīb) *vi.* **jibed, jib'ing** [< Du. *gÿpen*] **1.** to shift from one side of a ship to the other, as a fore-and-aft sail **2.** to change the course of a ship so that the sails jibe **3.** [Colloq.] to be in agreement or accord

jibe² (jīb) *vi., vt. same as* GIBE

jif·fy (jif'ē) *n., pl.* **-fies** [< ?] [Colloq.] a very short time; instant: also **jiff**

jig (jig) *n.* [prob. < MFr. *gigue,* a fiddle] **1.** *a*) a fast, springy dance in triple time *b*) music for such a dance **2.** a fishing lure that is jiggled up and down in the water **3.** a device used as a guide for a tool —*vi., vt.* **jigged, jig'-ging 1.** to dance (a jig) **2.** to move jerkily up and down or to and fro —**in jig time** [Colloq.] very quickly —**the jig is up** [Slang] all chances for success are gone

jig·ger¹ (jig'ər) *n.* [? < Afr.] *same as* CHIGGER

jig·ger² (jig'ər) *n.* **1.** a small glass, usually of 1 1/2 ounces, used to measure liquor **2.** the contents of a jigger

jig·gle (jig''l) *vt., vi.* **-gled, -gling** [< JIG] to move in quick, slight jerks —*n.* a jiggling

jig'saw' *n.* a saw with a narrow blade set in a frame, that moves with an up-and-down motion for cutting along curved or irregular lines: also **jig saw**

jigsaw puzzle a puzzle made by cutting up a picture into pieces of irregular shape, which must be put together again to re-form the picture

JIGSAW

jilt (jilt) *vt.* [< *Jill,* sweetheart] to reject or cast off (a previously accepted lover or sweetheart)

Jim Crow [name of an early Negro minstrel song] [*also* j- c-] [Colloq.] discrimination against or segregation of Negroes —**Jim'-Crow'** *vt., adj.*

jim·my (jim'ē) *n., pl.* **-mies** [< JAMES] a short crowbar, used by burglars to pry open windows, etc. —*vt.* **-mied, -my·ing** to pry open with a jimmy, etc.

jim·son weed (jim's'n) [< JAMESTOWN, Va.] a poisonous weed with foul-smelling leaves and trumpet-shaped flowers

jin·gle (jiŋ'g'l) *vi.* **-gled, -gling** [echoic] **1.** to make light, ringing sounds, as small bells **2.** to have obvious, easy rhythm, simple rhymes, etc., as some poetry and music — *vt.* to cause to jingle —*n.* a jingling sound, verse, etc. — **jin'gly** *adj.*

jin·go·ism (jiŋ'gō iz'm) *n.* [< phr. *by jingo* in a patriotic Brit. song] chauvinistic advocacy of an aggressive, warlike foreign policy —**jin'go·ist** *n.*

jinn (jin) *n. pl. of* JINNI: popularly regarded as a singular with the pl. **jinns**

jin·ni (ji nē', jin'ē) *n., pl.* **jinn** [< Ar.] *Muslim Legend* a supernatural being that can take human or animal form and influence human affairs

jin·rik·i·sha (jin rik'shô, -shä) *n.* [< Jpn. *jin,* a man + *riki,* power + *sha,* carriage] a small, two-wheeled carriage with a hood, pulled by one or two men, esp. formerly in the Orient: also sp. **jin·rick'sha, jin·rik'sha**

jinx (jinks) *n.* [< Gr. *iynx,* the wryneck (bird used in black magic)] [Colloq.] a person or thing supposed to bring bad luck —*vt.* [Colloq.] to bring bad luck to

jit·ney (jit'nē) *n., pl.* **-neys** [c.1903 < ? Fr. *jeton,* a token] a small bus or car that carries passengers for a low fare, originally five cents

jit·ter (jit'ər) *vi.* [? echoic] [Colloq.] to be nervous —**the jitters** [Colloq.] a very uneasy, nervous feeling —**jit'ter·y** *adj.*

jit'ter·bug' *n.* [prec. + BUG] a fast, acrobatic dance for couples, esp. in the 1940's —*vi.* **-bugged', -bug'ging** to dance the jitterbug

jiu·jit·su, jiu·jut·su (jōō jit'sōō) *n. var. of* JUJITSU

jive (jīv) *vt.* **jived, jiv'ing** [altered < JIBE²] [Slang] to speak to in a way that is exaggerated, insincere, etc., esp. in an effort to mislead —*n.* **1.** [Slang] talk used or like that used in jiving someone **2.** *former term* (c.1930–45) *for* JAZZ *or* SWING

Joan of Arc (ärk), Saint 1412–31; Fr. military heroine: burned at the stake

Job (jōb) *Bible* **1.** a man who endured much suffering but did not lose his faith in God **2.** the book telling of him

job (jäb) *n.* [< ?] **1.** a piece of work done for pay **2.** a task; duty **3.** the thing or material being worked on **4.** employment; work **5.** [Colloq.] any happening, affair, etc. —*adj.* hired or done by the job —*vt., vi.* **jobbed, job'bing 1.** to deal in (goods) as a jobber **2.** to sublet (work, etc.) —**odd jobs** miscellaneous pieces of work —**job'less** *adj.*

job·ber (jäb'ər) *n.* **1.** a wholesaler; middleman **2.** a person who does piecework

job'hold'er *n.* a person who has a steady job; specif., a government employee

job lot an assortment of goods for sale as one quantity

jock (jäk) *n. clip for:* **1.** JOCKEY **2.** JOCKSTRAP (sense 2)

jock·ey (jäk'ē) *n., pl.* **-eys** [< Scot. dim. of JACK] one whose job is riding horses in races —*vt., vi.* **-eyed, -ey·ing 1.** to cheat; swindle **2.** to maneuver for position or advantage

jock·strap (jäk'strap') *n.* [*jock,* penis + STRAP] **1.** an elastic belt with a pouch to support the genitals, worn by men **2.** [Slang] an athlete

jo·cose (jō kōs') *adj.* [< L. *jocus,* a joke] joking or playful —**jo·cos'i·ty** (-käs'ə tē) *pl.* **-ties, jo·cose'ness** *n.*

joc·u·lar (jäk'yə lər) *adj.* [< L. *jocus,* a joke] joking; full of fun —**joc'u·lar'i·ty** (-lar'ə tē) *n., pl.* **-ties** —**joc'u·lar·ly** *adv.*

joc·und (jäk'ənd, jō'kənd) *adj.* [< L. *jucundus,* pleasant] cheerful; genial; gay —**jo·cun·di·ty** (jō kun'də tē) *n., pl.* **-ties** —**joc'und·ly** *adv.*

jodh·purs (jäd'pərz) *n.pl.* [after *Jodhpur,* former state in India] riding breeches made loose and full above the knees and closefitting below

Jo·el (jō'əl) *Bible* **1.** a Hebrew prophet, probably of the 5th cent. B.C. **2.** the book of his preachings

joe-pye weed (jō'pī') [< ? Indian name] a tall plant with clusters of pinkish or purple flower heads

jog¹ (jäg) *vt.* **jogged, jog'ging** [ME. *joggen,* to spur] **1.** to give a little shake to **2.** to nudge **3.** to shake up or revive (a person's memory) —*vi.* to move along at a slow, steady, jolting pace —*n.* **1.** a little shake or nudge **2.** a slow, steady, jolting motion —**jog'ger** *n.*

jog² (jäg) *n.* [var. of JAG¹] **1.** a projecting or notched part in a surface or line **2.** a sharp, brief change of direction, as in a road

jog·gle¹ (jäg''l) *vt., vi.* **-gled, -gling** [< JOG¹] to shake or jolt slightly —*n.* a slight jolt

jog·gle² (jäg''l) *n.* [< JOG²] **1.** a joint made with a notch in one surface that fits a projection in the other **2.** the notch or projection —*vt.* **-gled, -gling** to join by joggles

Jo·han·nes·burg (jō han'is burg', yō hän'-) city in South Africa: pop. 1,295,000

John (jän) **1.** 1167?–1216; king of England (1199–1216): forced to sign the Magna Charta **2.** *Bible a*) a Christian apostle, credited with having written the fourth Gospel, the three Epistles of John, and Revelation *b*) the fourth book of the New Testament *c*) *same as* JOHN THE BAPTIST **3.** John XXIII 1881–1963; Pope (1958–63)

john (jän) *n.* [Slang] a toilet

John Bull England, or an Englishman, personified

John Doe (dō) a fictitious name used in legal papers for an unknown person

john·ny·cake (jän'ē kāk') *n.* [< Eng. dial. *jannock,* bread of oatmeal] corn bread baked on a griddle

John'ny-jump'-up' *n.* any of various American violets

John·son (jän's'n) **1. Andrew,** 1808–75; 17th president of the U.S. (1865–69) **2. Lyn·don Baines** (lin'dən bānz), 1908–73; 36th president of the U.S. (1963–69) **3. Samuel,** 1709–84; Eng. lexicographer & writer

John the Baptist *Bible* the forerunner and baptizer of Jesus

join (join) *vt., vi.* [< L. *jungere*] **1.** to bring or come together (with); connect; combine; unite **2.** to become a part or member of (a club, etc.) **3.** to participate (*in* a conversation, etc.) **4.** [Colloq.] to adjoin —*n.* a place of joining, as a seam

join'er *n.* **1.** a carpenter who finishes interior woodwork **2.** [Colloq.] one who joins many organizations

joint (joint) *n.* [< L. *jungere*, join] **1.** a place where, or way in which, two things are joined **2.** one of the parts of a jointed whole **3.** a large cut of meat with the bones still in it **4.** [Slang] *a*) a cheap bar, restaurant, etc. *b*) any building, etc. **5.** [Slang] a marijuana cigarette **6.** *Anat.* a place where two bones, etc. are joined, usually so that they can move **7.** *Bot.* a point where a branch or leaf grows out of the stem —*adj.* **1.** common to two or more [*joint* property] **2.** sharing with another [a *joint* owner] — *vt.* **1.** to fasten together by a joint or joints **2.** to cut (meat) into joints —**out of joint 1.** dislocated **2.** disordered

joint'ly *adv.* in common

joint return a single income tax return filed by a married couple, combining their incomes

joint'-stock' company a business firm owned by the stockholders in shares which each may sell or transfer independently

join-ture (join'chər) *n.* [< L. *jungere*, join] **1.** settlement of property on a wife for use after her husband's death **2.** the property thus settled

joist (joist) *n.* [< OFr. *giste*, a bed] any of the parallel beams that hold up the planks of a floor or the laths of a ceiling

joke (jōk) *n.* [L. *jocus*] **1.** anything said or done to arouse laughter; a funny anecdote **2.** something done or said merely in fun **3.** a person or thing to be laughed at —*vi.* joked, jok'ing to make jokes —jok'ing·ly *adv.*

jok'er *n.* **1.** one who jokes **2.** a hidden provision, as in a legal document, etc. to make it different from what it seems to be **3.** an extra playing card used in some games

JOISTS

jol·li·ty (jäl'ə tē) *n.* a being jolly; gaiety

jol·ly (jäl'ē) *adj.* -li·er, -li·est [OFr. *joli*] **1.** full of high spirits and good humor **2.** [Colloq.] enjoyable; pleasant — *adv.* [Brit. Colloq.] very; altogether —*vt., vi.* -lied, -ly·ing [Colloq.] **1.** to try to make (a person) feel good, as by coaxing (often with *along*) **2.** to make fun of (someone) — jol'li·ly *adv.* —jol'li·ness *n.*

jolly (boat) [< MDu. *jolle*, yawl] a ship's small boat

Jolly Roger a black flag of pirates, with white skull and crossbones

jolt (jōlt) *vt.* [< earlier *jot*] **1.** to shake up or jar, as with a bumpy ride **2.** to shock or surprise —*vi.* to move along in a bumpy manner —*n.* **1.** a sudden jerk, bump, etc. **2.** a shock or surprise

Jo·nah (jō'nə) *Bible* **1.** a Hebrew prophet: thrown overboard in a storm, he was swallowed by a big fish, but later cast up unharmed **2.** the book telling Jonah's story —*n.* any person said to bring bad luck by his presence

Jon·a·than (jän'ə thən) *Bible* Saul's oldest son, a close friend of David —*n.* a late fall variety of apple

Jones (jōnz), **John Paul** 1747–92; Am. naval officer in the Revolutionary War, born in Scotland

jon·gleur (jäŋ'glər) *n.* [Fr.: see JUGGLE] a wandering minstrel in medieval France and England

jon·quil (jäŋ'kwəl, jän'-) *n.* [< Fr. < L. *juncus*, a rush] a variety of narcissus having relatively small yellow flowers and long, slender leaves

Jon·son (jän's'n), **Ben** 1572?–1637; Eng. dramatist & poet

Jor·dan (jôr'd'n) **1.** river in the Near East, flowing into the Dead Sea **2.** country east of Israel: 37,300 sq. mi.; pop. 2,133,000; cap. Amman —**Jor·da'ni·an** (-dā'nē ən) *adj., n.*

Jo·seph (jō'zəf) *Bible* **1.** Jacob's eleventh son, who became a high official in Egypt **2.** the husband of Mary, mother of Jesus

josh (jäsh) *vt., vi.* [< ?] [Colloq.] to ridicule in a good-humored way; banter —josh'er *n.*

Josh·u·a (jäsh'oo wə) *Bible* **1.** Moses' successor, and leader of the Israelites into the Promised Land **2.** the book telling about him

joss (jäs) *n.* [PidE. < Port. *deos* < L. *deus*, a god] a figure of a Chinese god

joss house a Chinese temple

jos·tle (jäs''l) *vt., vi.* -tled, -tling [see JOUST] **1.** to bump or push, as in a crowd **2.** to contend (*with* someone *for* something) —*n.* a jostling

jot (jät) *n.* [< Gr. *iōta*, the smallest letter] a very small amount —*vt.* jot'ted, jot'ting to make a brief note of (usually with *down*) —jot'ter *n.*

jot'ting *n.* a short note jotted down

joule (jōol, joul) *n.* [< J. P. Joule, 19th-c. Eng. physicist] *Physics* a unit of work or energy equal to 10,000,000 ergs

jounce (jouns) *n., vt., vi.* jounced, jounc'ing [< ?] jolt or bounce —jounc'y *adj.*

jour·nal (jur'n'l) *n.* [< L. *diurnalis*, daily] **1.** a daily record of happenings, as a diary **2.** a record of the transactions of a club, etc. **3.** a ship's logbook **4.** a newspaper, magazine, etc. **5.** *Bookkeeping* a book of original entry for recording transactions **6.** *Mech.* the part of a rotatory axle or shaft that turns in a bearing

journal box *Mech.* a housing for a journal

jour·nal·ese (jur'n'l ēz') *n.* a facile style of newspaper writing with many clichés

jour'nal·ism (-iz'm) *n.* the work of gathering, writing, and publishing or disseminating news, as through newspapers, etc. or by radio and TV —jour'nal·ist *n.* —jour'nal·is'tic *adj.*

jour·ney (jur'nē) *n., pl.* -neys [< OFr. *journee*, ult. < L. *dies*, day] a traveling from one place to another; trip —*vi.* -neyed, -ney·ing to travel

jour'ney·man (-mən) *n., pl.* -men [ME. < *journee*, day's work + *man*] **1.** a worker who has learned his trade **2.** an experienced craftsman of only average ability

joust (joust, just) *n.* [< L. *juxta*, beside] a combat with lances between two knights on horseback —*vi.* to engage in a joust —joust'er *n.*

Jove (jōv) *same as* JUPITER —**by Jove!** an exclamation of astonishment, emphasis, etc.

jo·vi·al (jō'vē əl) *adj.* [Fr. < LL. *Jovialis*, of Jupiter: from astrological notion of planet's influence] full of hearty, playful good humor; gay —jo'vi·al'i·ty (-al'ə tē) *n.* —jo'vi·al·ly *adv.*

jowl[1] (joul) *n.* [OE. *ceafl*, jaw] **1.** the lower jaw **2.** the cheek, esp. of a hog

jowl[2] (joul) *n.* [OE. *ceole*, throat] [often *pl.*] the fleshy, hanging part under the jaw —jowl'y *adj.*

joy (joi) *n.* [< L. *gaudium*, joy] **1.** a very glad feeling; happiness; delight **2.** anything causing this

Joyce (jois), **James** 1882–1941; Ir. novelist & poet

joy'ful *adj.* feeling, expressing, or causing joy; glad —joy'ful·ly *adv.* —joy'ful·ness *n.*

joy'less *adj.* without joy; unhappy; sad

joy'ous (-əs) *adj.* joyful; happy; gay —joy'ous·ly *adv.* — joy'ous·ness *n.*

joy ride [Colloq.] an automobile ride merely for pleasure, often at reckless speeds

J.P. justice of the peace

Jpn. Japanese

Jr., jr. junior

ju·bi·lant (jōō'b'l ənt) *adj.* [< L. *jubilum*, wild shout] joyful and triumphant; rejoicing; elated —ju'bi·lance *n.* — ju'bi·lant·ly *adv.*

ju·bi·la·tion (jōō'bə lā'shən) *n.* **1.** a rejoicing, as in triumph **2.** a happy celebration

ju·bi·lee (jōō'bə lē') *n.* [< Heb. *yōbēl*, a ram's horn (trumpet)] **1.** a 50th or 25th anniversary **2.** a time or occasion of rejoicing **3.** jubilation

Ju·dah (jōō'də) **1.** *Bible a*) one of Jacob's sons *b*) the tribe descended from him **2.** kingdom in the S part of ancient Palestine

Ju·da·ic (jōō dā'ik) *adj.* of the Jews or Judaism; Jewish

Ju·da·ism (jōō'də iz'm) *n.* the Jewish religion, a monotheistic religion based on teachings in Scripture and the Talmud

Ju·das (jōō'dəs) *Bible* the disciple who betrayed Jesus: in full **Judas Is·car·i·ot** (is ker'ē ət) —*n.* a traitor or betrayer

Jude (jōōd) *Bible* **1.** a Christian apostle **2.** a book of the New Testament

Ju·de·a (jōō dē'ə) ancient region of S Palestine: also sp. **Ju·dae'a** —**Ju·de'an** *adj., n.*

judge (juj) *n.* [< L. *jus*, law + *dicere*, say] **1.** a public official with authority to hear and decide cases in a court of law **2.** a person designated to determine the winner, settle a controversy, etc. **3.** a person qualified to decide on the relative worth of anything [a good *judge* of music] —*vt., vi.* judged, judg'ing **1.** to hear and pass judgment (on) in a court of law **2.** to determine the winner of (a contest) or settle (a controversy) **3.** to form an opinion about (a matter) **4.** to criticize or censure **5.** to think; suppose — **judge'ship'** *n.*

Judg·es (juj'iz) a book of the Bible telling the history of the Jews from Joshua to Samuel

judg·ment (juj'mənt) *n.* **1.** a judging; deciding **2.** a legal decision; order given by a judge, etc. **3.** a debt resulting from a court order **4.** an opinion or estimate **5.** criticism or censure **6.** the ability to come to opinions about things; understanding **7.** [J-] *short for* LAST JUDGMENT Also sp. **judge'ment** —**judg·men'tal** (-men't'l) *adj.*

Judgment Day *Theol.* the time of God's final judgment of all people

ju·di·ca·to·ry (jōō'di kə tôr'ē) *adj.* [see JUDGE] having to do with administering justice —*n., pl.* **-ries** a law court, or law courts collectively

ju'di·ca·ture (-chər) *n.* **1.** the administering of justice **2.** jurisdiction of a judge or court **3.** judges or courts collectively

ju·di·cial (jōō dish'əl) *adj.* **1.** of judges, courts, or their functions **2.** allowed, enforced, etc. by a court **3.** befitting a judge **4.** fair; unbiased —**ju·di'cial·ly** *adv.*

ju·di·ci·ar·y (jōō dish'ē er'ē, -dish'ər ē) *adj.* of judges or courts —*n., pl.* **-ies 1.** the part of government that administers justice **2.** judges collectively

ju·di·cious (jōō dish'əs) *adj.* [see JUDGE] having or showing sound judgment; wise and careful —**ju·di'cious·ly** *adv.* —**ju·di'cious·ness** *n.*

ju·do (jōō'dō) *n.* [Jpn. < *jū*, soft + *dō*, art] a form of jujitsu, esp. as a means of self-defense

jug (jug) *n.* [a pet form of *Judith* or *Joan*] **1.** a container for liquids, with a small opening and a handle **2.** [Slang] a jail —*vt.* **jugged, jug'ging** to put into a jug

jug·ger·naut (jug'ər nôt') *n.* [< Sans. *Jagannātha*, lord of the world] any terrible, irresistible force

jug·gle (jug''l) *vt.* **-gled, -gling** [< L. *jocus*, a joke] **1.** to perform skillful tricks of sleight of hand with (balls, etc.) **2.** to make awkward attempts to catch or hold (a ball, etc.) **3.** to manipulate so as to cheat or deceive [to *juggle* figures to show a profit] —*vi.* to toss up a number of balls, etc. and keep them in the air —**jug'gler** *n.* —**jug'gler·y** *n.*

jug·u·lar (jug'yoo lər) *adj.* [< L. *jugum*, a yoke] of the neck or throat —*n.* either of two large veins in the neck carrying blood from the head to the heart: in full **jugular vein**

juice (jōōs) *n.* [< L. *jus*, broth] **1.** the liquid part of a plant, fruit, etc. **2.** a liquid in or from animal tissue [gastric *juice*] **3.** [Colloq.] energy; vitality **4.** [Slang] electricity —*vt.* **juiced, juic'ing** to extract juice from —**juice up** to add power, vigor, interest, etc. to

juic·er (jōō'sər) *n.* a device for extracting juice from fruit

juic·y (jōō'sē) *adj.* **-i·er, -i·est 1.** full of juice **2.** [Colloq.] *a)* full of interest; piquant *b)* highly profitable —**juic'i·ly** *adj.* —**juic'i·ness** *n.*

ju·jit·su (jōō jit'sōō) *n.* [< Jpn. < *jū*, soft + *jutsu*, art] a Japanese system of wrestling in which the strength and weight of an opponent are used against him: also sp. **ju·jut'su**

juke·box (jōōk'bäks') *n.* [< Am. Negro *juke*, wicked] a coin-operated electric phonograph: also **juke box**

ju·lep (jōō'ləp) *n.* [< Per. *gul*, rose + *āb*, water] same as MINT JULEP

Jul·ian calendar (jōōl'yən) the calendar introduced by Julius Caesar in 46 B.C.: replaced by the Gregorian calendar

ju·li·enne (jōō'lē en') *adj.* [Fr.] *Cooking* cut into strips: said of vegetables

Ju·li·et (jōōl'yət, jōō'lē et') the heroine of Shakespeare's tragedy *Romeo and Juliet*

Ju·ly (joo lī', jōō-) *n., pl.* **-lies'** [< L. < *Julius* Caesar] the seventh month of the year, having 31 days: abbrev. **Jul.**

jum·ble (jum'b'l) *vt., vi.* **-bled, -bling** [? blend of JUMP + TUMBLE] to mix or be mixed in a confused heap —*n.* a confused mixture or heap

jum·bo (jum'bō) *n., pl.* **-bos** [< Am. Negro *jamba*, elephant] a very large person, animal, or thing —*adj.* very large

jump (jump) *vi.* [< ?] **1.** to spring or leap from the ground, a height, etc. **2.** to jerk; bob **3.** to move or act eagerly (often with *at*) **4.** to start in surprise **5.** to pass suddenly, as to a new topic **6.** to rise suddenly, as prices **7.** *Checkers* to move a piece over an opponent's piece, thus capturing it —*vt.* **1.** *a)* to leap over *b)* to pass over; skip **2.** to cause to leap **3.** to leap upon **4.** to cause (prices, etc.) to rise **5.** [Colloq.] to attack suddenly **6.** to react to prematurely, in anticipation **7.** [Slang] to leave suddenly [to *jump* town] **8.** *Checkers* to capture (an opponent's

piece) —*n.* **1.** a jumping **2.** a distance jumped **3.** a thing to be jumped over **4.** a sudden transition **5.** a sudden rise, as in prices **6.** a sudden, nervous start or jerk —**get (or have) the jump on** [Slang] to get (or have) an advantage over —**jump bail** to forfeit one's bail by running away —**jump on (or all over)** [Slang] to scold; censure

jump·er¹ (jum'pər) *n.* **1.** one that jumps **2.** a short wire used to make a temporary electrical connection

jump·er² (jum'pər) *n.* [< dial. *jump*, short coat] **1.** a loose jacket **2.** a sleeveless dress for wearing over a blouse or sweater

jump suit 1. a coverall worn by paratroops, etc. **2.** any one-piece garment like this

jump'y *adj.* **-i·er, -i·est 1.** moving in jumps, jerks, etc. **2.** easily startled; apprehensive —**jump'i·ness** *n.*

Jun., jun. junior

jun·co (juŋ'kō) *n., pl.* **-cos** [Sp. < L. *juncus*, a rush] a sparrowlike American bird with a gray or black head

junc·tion (juŋk'shən) *n.* [< L. *jungere*, join] **1.** a joining or being joined **2.** a place of joining or crossing, as of highways

junc·ture (juŋk'chər) *n.* **1.** a joining or being joined **2.** a point of joining or connection **3.** a point of time **4.** a crisis **5.** a state of affairs

June (jōōn) *n.* [< L. *Junius*, of Juno] the sixth month of the year, having 30 days: abbrev. **Je.**

Ju·neau (jōō'nō) capital of Alaska, on the SE coast: pop. 6,000

June bug a large beetle found in the N U.S.: also **June beetle**

Jung (yoong), **Carl** 1875–1961; Swiss psychologist & psychiatrist

jun·gle (juŋ'g'l) *n.* [< Hindi *jangal*, desert < Sans.] **1.** land densely covered with trees, vines, etc., as in the tropics: typically inhabited by predatory animals **2.** [Slang] a situation in which people compete ruthlessly

jun·ior (jōōn'yər) *adj.* [L. < *juvenis*, young] **1.** the younger: written *Jr.* after a son's name if it is the same as his father's **2.** of more recent position or lower rank [a *junior* partner] **3.** of juniors —*n.* **1.** one who is younger, of lower rank, etc. **2.** a student in the next-to-last year of a high school or college

junior college a school offering courses two years beyond the high school level

junior high school a school intermediate between elementary school and senior high school: it usually includes the 7th, 8th, and 9th grades

ju·ni·per (jōō'nə pər) *n.* [L. *juniperus*] a small evergreen shrub or tree with berrylike cones

junk¹ (juŋk) *n.* [< ?] **1.** old metal, paper, rags, etc. **2.** [Colloq.] useless stuff; trash **3.** [Slang] a narcotic drug; esp., heroin —*vt.* [Colloq.] to throw away or sell as junk; scrap —**junk'y** *adj.* **-i·er, -i·est**

junk² (juŋk) *n.* [< Javanese *jon*] a Chinese flat-bottomed ship

Junk·er (yoong'kər) *n.* [G.] a Prussian of the militaristic landowning class

junk·er (juŋ'kər) *n.* [Slang] an old, dilapidated car or truck

junk·et (juŋ'kit) *n.* [ME. *joncate*, cream cheese] **1.** milk sweetened, flavored, and thickened into a curd **2.** a picnic **3.** an excursion, esp. one by an official at public expense —*vi.* to go on a junket

junk food any of various snack foods processed as with chemical additives and of low nutritional value

JUNK

junk·ie, junk·y (juŋ'kē) *n., pl.* **-ies** [Slang] a narcotics addict, esp. one addicted to heroin

junk mail advertisements, requests for aid, etc. mailed impersonally to a large number of people

junk'man' *n., pl.* **-men'** a dealer in old metal, paper, etc.

Ju·no (jōō'nō) *Rom. Myth.* wife of Jupiter and queen of the gods: identified with the Greek goddess Hera

jun·ta (hoon'tə, jun'-) *n.* [Sp. < L. *jungere*, join] **1.** a Spanish or Latin-American legislative or administrative body **2.** a group of political intriguers, esp. military men in power after a coup d'état: also **jun·to** (jun'tō), *pl.* **-tos**

Ju·pi·ter (jōō'pə tər) *n.* **1.** the chief Roman god: identified with the Greek god Zeus **2.** the largest planet of the solar system: see PLANET

ju·rid·i·cal (joo rid'i k'l) *adj.* [< L. *jus*, law + *dicere*, declare] of judicial proceedings or of law

ju·ris·dic·tion (joor'is dik'shən) *n.* [see prec.] **1.** the administering of justice; authority to hear and decide cases **2.** authority or its range —**ju'ris·dic'tion·al** *adj.*

ju·ris·pru·dence (joor'is prōō'd'ns) *n.* [< L. *jus*, law + *prudentia*, a foreseeing] **1.** the science or philosophy of law **2.** a division of law [medical *jurisprudence*]
ju·rist (joor'ist) *n.* [< L. *jus*, law] **1.** an expert in law or writer on law **2.** a judge
ju·ris·tic (joo ris'tik) *adj.* of jurists or jurisprudence; relating to law
ju·ror (joor'ər) *n.* a member of a jury; juryman
ju·ry[1] (joor'ē) *n., pl.* **-ries** [< L. *jurare*, swear] **1.** a group of people sworn to hear evidence in a law case and to give a decision **2.** a committee that decides winners in a contest
ju·ry[2] (joor'ē) *adj.* [< ?] *Naut.* for temporary or emergency use [a *jury* mast]
ju·ry·man (-mən) *n., pl.* **-men** same as JUROR
just (just) *adj.* [< L. *jus*, law] **1.** right or fair [a *just* decision] **2.** righteous [a *just* man] **3.** deserved [*just* praise] **4.** lawful **5.** proper, fitting, etc. **6.** correct or true **7.** accurate; exact —*adv.* **1.** exactly [*just* one o'clock] **2.** almost at the point of [*just* leaving] **3.** only [*just* a taste] **4.** barely [*just* missed him] **5.** a very short time ago [she *just* left] **6.** immediately [*just* to my right] **7.** [Colloq.] quite; really [feeling *just* fine] —**just now** a moment ago —**just the same** [Colloq.] nevertheless —**just'ly** *adv.* —**just'ness** *n.*
jus·tice (jus'tis) *n.* **1.** a being righteous **2.** fairness **3.** rightfulness **4.** reward or penalty as deserved **5.** the use of authority to uphold what is just **6.** the administration of law **7.** *same as: a)* JUDGE (sense 1) *b)* JUSTICE OF THE PEACE —**bring to justice** to cause a (wrongdoer) to be tried in court and duly punished —**do justice to** to treat fairly or with due appreciation

justice of the peace a local magistrate who decides minor cases, performs marriages, etc.
jus·ti·fi·a·ble (jus'tə fī'ə b'l) *adj.* that can be justified or defended as correct —**jus'ti·fi'a·bly** *adv.*
jus·ti·fy (jus'tə fī') *vt.* **-fied'**, **-fy'ing** [< L. *justus*, just + *facere*, make] **1.** to show to be just, right, etc. **2.** *Theol.* to free from blame **3.** to supply good grounds for —**jus'ti·fi·ca'tion** (-fi kā'shən) *n.*
Jus·tin·i·an I (jəs tin'ē ən) 483–565 A.D.; Byzantine emperor (527–565): codified Roman law (**Justinian code**)
jus·tle (jus''l) *n., vt., vi.* **-tled**, **-tling** same as JOSTLE
jut (jut) *vi., vt.* **jut'ted**, **jut'ting** [prob. var. of JET[1]] to stick out; project —*n.* a part that juts
Jute (jōot) *n.* a member of any of several early Germanic tribes in Jutland: Jutes settled in England in the 5th cent. A.D.
jute (jōot) *n.* [< Hindi < Sans. *jūta*, matted hair] **1.** a strong fiber used for making burlap, rope, etc. **2.** an East Indian plant yielding this fiber
Jut·land (jut'lənd) peninsula forming the mainland of Denmark
Ju·ve·nal (jōō'və n'l) 60?–140? A.D.; Rom. satirical poet
ju·ven·ile (jōō'və n'l, -nīl') *adj.* [< L. *juvenis*, young] **1.** *a)* young *b)* immature; childish **2.** of, characteristic of, or suitable for young persons —*n.* **1.** a young person; child or youth **2.** an actor who plays youthful roles **3.** a book for children
juvenile delinquency antisocial or illegal behavior by minors, usually 18 or younger —**juvenile delinquent**
jux·ta·pose (juk'stə pōz') *vt.* **-posed'**, **-pos'ing** [< Fr. < L. *juxta*, near + POSE] to put side by side or close together —**jux'ta·po·si'tion** *n.*

K

K, k (kā) *n., pl.* **K's, k's** the eleventh letter of the English alphabet
K 1. *Chess* king **2.** [ModL. *kalium*] *Chem.* potassium
K., k. 1. karat (carat) **2.** kilo **3.** king
Ka·bu·ki (kä bōō'kē) *n.* [Jpn. < *kabu*, music and dancing + *ki*, spirit] [also k-] a form of Japanese drama with formalized pantomime, dance, and song
Ka·bul (kä'bool) capital of Afghanistan: pop. 456,000
kad·dish (käd'ish) *n.* [Aram. *qaddish*, holy] *Judaism* a hymn in praise of God, recited at the daily service or as a mourner's prayer
kaf·fee·klatsch (kä'fā kläch', kô'fē klach') *n.* [G. < *kaffee*, coffee + *klatsch*, gossip] [also K-] an informal gathering to drink coffee and chat
Kaf·fir (kaf'ər) *n.* [Ar. *kāfir*, infidel] a member of a Bantu-speaking tribe in South Africa: also sp. **Kaf'ir**
kaf·ir (kaf'ər) *n.* [see prec.] a grain sorghum grown in dry regions for grain and fodder: also sp. **kaf'fir**
Kaf·ka (käf'kə), **Franz** (fränts) 1883–1924; Austrian writer
kai·ser (kī'zər) *n.* [< L. *Caesar*] emperor: the title [K-] of the former rulers of Austria and of Germany
kale (kāl) *n.* [Scot. var. of COLE] a hardy cabbage with loose, spreading, curled leaves
ka·lei·do·scope (kə lī'də skōp') *n.* [< Gr. *kalos*, beautiful + *eidos*, form + -SCOPE] **1.** a small tube containing bits of colored glass reflected by mirrors to form symmetrical patterns as the tube is rotated **2.** anything that changes constantly —**ka·lei'do·scop'ic** (-skäp'ik) *adj.*
Kam·chat·ka (käm chät'kä) peninsula in NE Siberia
kam·pong (käm'pôn') *n.* [Malay] a small Malay village or cluster of native huts
Kam·pu·che·a (kam'poo chē'ə) country in the S Indochinese peninsula: 69,884 sq. mi.; pop. 6,701,000; cap. Phnom Penh: formerly called *Cambodia* —**Kam'pu·che'an** *adj., n.*
Kan·a·ka (kə nak'ə, kan'ə kə) *n.* [Haw., man] **1.** a Hawaiian **2.** a native of the South Sea Islands
kan·ga·roo (kan'gə rōō') *n.* [< ?] a leaping, plant-eating mammal of Australia and nearby islands, with short forelegs and large, strong hind legs: the female has a pouch in which she carries her young

kangaroo court [Colloq.] an irregular court illegally passing and executing judgment, as among frontiersmen
kangaroo rat a small, jumping, mouselike rodent of desert regions in the SW U.S. and Mexico
Kan·sas (kan'zəs) Middle Western State of the U.S.: 82,264 sq. mi.; pop. 2,249,000; cap. Topeka: abbrev. **Kans., KS** —**Kan'san** *adj., n.*
Kansas City 1. city in W Mo., on the Missouri River: pop. 507,000 **2.** city opposite this, in NE Kans.: pop. 168,000 (Both are in a single met. area, pop. 1,257,000)
Kant (kant; *G.* känt), **Immanuel** 1724–1804; Ger. philosopher
ka·o·lin (kā'ə lin) *n.* [Fr. < Chin. name of hill where found] a white clay used in making porcelain
ka·pok (kā'päk) *n.* [Malay *kapoq*] the silky fibers around the seeds of certain tropical trees: used for stuffing mattresses, sleeping bags, etc.
kap·pa (kap'ə) *n.* the tenth letter of the Greek alphabet (K, κ)
ka·put (kə pōōt') *adj.* [G. *kaputt*] [Slang] ruined, destroyed, etc.
Ka·ra·chi (kə rä'chē) seaport in SW Pakistan: pop. 3,060,000
kar·a·kul (kar'ə kəl) *n.* [< *Kara Kul*, lake in the U.S.S.R.] **1.** a sheep of C Asia **2.** the curly, black fur from the fleece of its newborn lambs
kar·at (kar'ət) *n.* [var. of CARAT] one 24th part (of pure gold)
ka·ra·te (kə rät'ē) *n.* [Jpn. < *kara*, empty + *te*, hand] a Japanese system of self-defense chiefly using sharp, quick blows with the hands and feet
kar·ma (kär'mə) *n.* [Sans., a deed] *Buddhism & Hinduism* a person's actions in one reincarnation thought of as determining his fate in the next
kart (kärt) *n.* [< CART] **1.** any of various small vehicles **2.** a small, 4-wheeled, motorized vehicle: used in racing
Kash·mir (kash'mir) region in SE Asia, between Afghanistan & Tibet: see also JAMMU and KASHMIR
ka·ty·did (kāt'ē did') *n.* [echoic of its shrill sound] a large, green tree insect resembling the grasshopper

kay·ak (kī′ak) *n.* [Esk.] an Eskimo canoe made of skins covering a wooden frame

kay·o (kā′ō′) *vt.* **-oed′, -o′ing** [< KO] [Slang] *Boxing* to knock out —*n.* [Slang] *Boxing* a knockout

Ka·zakh Soviet Socialist Republic (kä zäk′) republic of the U.S.S.R., in W Asia: also **Ka′zakh·stan′** (-stän′)

ka·zoo (kə zōō′) *n.* [echoic] a toy musical instrument consisting of a small tube into which one hums, causing a piece of paper set into it to vibrate and buzz

KAYAK

kc, kc. kilocycle; kilocycles

Keats (kēts), **John** 1795–1821; Eng. poet

ke·bab (kə bäb′) *n.* [Ar. *kabāb*] [*often pl.*] a dish consisting of small pieces of marinated meat broiled on a skewer, often with alternating pieces of onion, tomato, etc.

kedge (kej) *vt., vi.* **kedged, kedg′ing** [ME. *caggen*, to fasten] to move (a ship) by hauling on a rope fastened to an anchor —*n.* a light anchor, esp. for such use: also **kedge anchor**

keel (kēl) *n.* [< ON. *kjǫlr*] **1.** the chief timber or steel piece extending along the length of the bottom of a ship or boat **2.** anything like this in position, appearance, etc. —**keel over** [Colloq.] **1.** to turn over; capsize **2.** to fall over suddenly, as in a faint —**on an even keel** upright and level, steady, stable, etc.

keel′haul′ *vt.* [< Du. < *kiel*, boat + *halen*, haul] to haul (a person) under the keel of a ship as a punishment

keel·son (kel′s'n, kēl′-) *n.* [prob. via Du. < Dan. *kjøl*, keel + *sville*, sill] a beam, set of metal plates, etc. fastened inside a ship's hull along the keel for added strength

keen[1] (kēn) *adj.* [OE. *cene*, wise] **1.** having a sharp edge or point **2.** cutting; piercing [a *keen* wind] **3.** sharp and quick in seeing, hearing, etc.; acute **4.** sharp-witted; shrewd **5.** eager **6.** strong or intense [*keen* enjoyment] **7.** [Slang] good, excellent, etc. —**keen′ly** *adv.* —**keen′ness** *n.*

keen[2] (kēn) *n.* [< Ir. *caoinim*, I wail] [Irish] a wailing for the dead —*vt., vi.* [Irish] to lament or wail for (the dead)

keep (kēp) *vt.* **kept, keep′ing** [OE. *cepan*, behold] **1.** to celebrate; observe [*keep* the Sabbath] **2.** to fulfill (a promise, etc.) **3.** to go on maintaining [*keep* pace] **4.** to protect; guard; take care of; tend **5.** to preserve **6.** to provide for; support **7.** to make regular entries in [to *keep* a diary] **8.** to maintain in a specified state, position, etc. [*keep* prices down] **9.** to hold for future use or for a long time **10.** to have or hold and not let go; detain, withhold, restrain, etc. **11.** to conceal (a secret) **12.** to stay in or at (a course, place, etc.) —*vi.* **1.** to stay in a specified state, position, etc. **2.** to continue; go on (often with *on*) **3.** to refrain [to *keep* from laughing] **4.** to stay fresh; not spoil **5.** to require no immediate attention —*n.* **1.** orig., care or custody **2.** the inner stronghold of a castle **3.** food and shelter; support —**for keeps** [Colloq.] **1.** with the winner keeping what he wins **2.** forever —**keep to 1.** to persevere in **2.** to adhere to **3.** to remain in —**keep to oneself 1.** to avoid others **2.** to refrain from telling —**keep up 1.** to maintain in good condition **2.** to continue **3.** to maintain the pace **4.** to remain informed about (with *on* or *with*)

keep′er *n.* one that keeps; specif., *a*) a guard, as of prisoners *b*) a guardian *c*) a caretaker

keep′ing *n.* **1.** observance (of a rule, holiday, etc.) **2.** care; charge —**in keeping with** in conformity or accord with

keep′sake′ *n.* something kept, or to be kept, in memory of the giver; memento

keg (keg) *n.* [< ON. *kaggi*] **1.** a small barrel **2.** a unit of weight for nails, equal to 100 lbs.

keg·ler (keg′lər) *n.* [G. < *kegel*, (nine)pin] [Colloq.] a person who bowls; bowler

Kel·ly (green) (kel′ē) [*also* k-] a bright, yellowish green

kelp (kelp) *n.* [ME. *culp*] large, coarse, brown seaweed, rich in iodine

Kelt (kelt) *n. same as* CELT —**Kelt′ic** *adj., n.*

ken (ken) *vt., vi.* **kenned, ken′ning** [OE. *cennan*, cause to know] [Scot.] to know (*of* or *about*) —*n.* range of knowledge

Ken·ne·dy (ken′ə dē), **John F.** 1917–63; 35th president of the U.S. (1961–63)

ken·nel (ken′'l) *n.* [< L. *canis*, a dog] **1.** a doghouse **2.** [*often pl.*] a place where dogs are bred or kept —*vt.* **-neled** or **-nelled, -nel·ing** or **-nel·ling** to keep in a kennel

Ken·tuck·y (kən tuk′ē) EC State of the U.S.: 40,395 sq. mi.; pop. 3,219,000; cap. Frankfort: abbrev. **Ky., KY** — **Ken·tuck′i·an** *adj., n.*

Ken·ya (ken′yə, kēn′-) country in EC Africa, on the Indian Ocean: 224,960 sq. mi.; pop. 10,890,000; cap. Nairobi

kep·i (kep′ē) *n., pl.* **-is** [Fr. *képi*] a cap with a flat, round top and a visor, worn by French soldiers

Kep·ler (kep′lər), **Jo·hann** (yō′hän) 1571–1630; Ger. astronomer & mathematician

kept (kept) *pt. & pp. of* KEEP —*adj.* maintained as a mistress [a *kept* woman]

ker·a·tin (ker′ət 'n) *n.* [< Gr. *keras*, horn + -IN[1]] a tough, fibrous protein, the basic substance of hair, nails, horn, etc. —**ke·rat·i·nous** (kə rat′'n əs) *adj.*

kerb (kurb) *n. Brit. sp. of* CURB (*n.* 4)

ker·chief (kur′chif) *n.* [< OFr. *covrir*, to cover + *chef*, the head] **1.** a piece of cloth worn over the head or around the neck **2.** a handkerchief

kerf (kurf) *n.* [< OE. *ceorfan*, carve] the cut made by a saw —*vt.* to make a kerf in

ker·nel (kur′n'l) *n.* [OE. *cyrnel*] **1.** a grain or seed, as of corn **2.** the inner, softer part of a nut, etc. **3.** the central, most important part; essence

ker·o·sene (ker′ə sēn′) *n.* [< Gr. *kēros*, wax] a thin oil distilled from petroleum, used as a fuel, solvent, etc.: also, esp. in science and industry, sp. **ker′o·sine′**

kes·trel (kes′trəl) *n.* [echoic] a small European falcon that can hover in the air against the wind

ketch (kech) *n.* [ME. *cache*] a fore-and-aft-rigged sailing vessel with a mainmast forward and a mizzenmast toward the stern

ketch·up (kech′əp) *n.* [Malay *kēchap*, a fish sauce < Chin.] a sauce for meat, fish, etc.; esp., a thick sauce (**tomato ketchup**) of tomatoes, onions, spices, etc.

ke·tone (kē′tōn) *n.* [< G. *keton*] an organic chemical compound containing the bivalent CO group combined with two hydrocarbon radicals

ket·tle (ket′'l) *n.* [< L. *catinus*, a bowl] **1.** a metal container for boiling or cooking things **2.** a teakettle

ket′tle·drum′ *n.* a percussion instrument consisting of a hollow metal hemisphere and a parchment top that can be tightened or loosened to change pitch

key[1] (kē) *n., pl.* **keys** [OE. *cæge*] **1.** a device for moving the bolt of a lock and thus locking or unlocking something **2.** any somewhat similar device, as a lever pressed down to operate a typewriter, piano, etc. or a device for opening or closing an electric circuit **3.** a thing that explains or solves, as the legend of a map **4.** a controlling person or thing **5.** style or mood of expression **6.** *Music* a system of related tones based on a keynote and forming a given scale —*adj.* controlling; important —*vt.* **keyed, key′ing 1.** to furnish with a key **2.** to regulate the tone or pitch of **3.** to bring into harmony —**key up** to make tense or excited

key[2] (kē) *n., pl.* **keys** [Sp. *cayo*] a reef or low island

Key (kē), **Francis Scott** 1779–1843; U.S. lawyer: wrote "The Star-Spangled Banner"

key′board′ *n.* the row or rows of keys of a piano, typewriter, etc.

key′hole′ *n.* an opening (in a lock) into which a key is inserted

key′note′ *n.* **1.** the lowest, basic note or tone of a musical scale **2.** the basic idea or ruling principle, as of a speech, policy, etc. —*vt.* **-not′ed, -not′ing 1.** to give the keynote of **2.** to give the keynote speech at —**key′not′er** *n.*

keynote speech (or **address**) a speech, as at a convention, setting forth the main line of policy

key punch a machine with a keyboard for recording data by punching holes in cards for use in data processing

key′stone′ *n.* **1.** the central, topmost stone of an arch **2.** the main part or principle

Key West westernmost island of a chain of small islands (**Florida Keys**) off the S tip of Florida

KEYSTONE

kg, kg. kilogram(s)

kha·ki (kak′ē, kä′kē) *adj.* [Hindi *khākī*, dust-colored] **1.** dull yellowish-brown **2.** made of khaki (cloth) —*n., pl.* **-kis 1.** a dull yellowish brown **2.** strong twilled cloth of this color, used esp. for uniforms **3.** [*often pl.*] a khaki uniform or trousers

khan (kän, kan) *n.* [< Turkic *khān*, lord] **1.** a title of Tatar or Mongol rulers in the Middle Ages **2.** a title of various dignitaries in Iran, Afghanistan, etc.

Khar·kov (kär′kôf) city in NE Ukrainian S.S.R.: pop. 1,148,000

Khar·toum (kär tōōm′) capital of Sudan: pop. 185,000 (met. area 490,000)

khe·dive (kə dēv′) *n.* [< Fr. < Per. *khidīw*, prince] the title of the Turkish viceroys of Egypt, from 1867 to 1914

Khy·ber Pass (kī′bər) mountain pass between Afghanistan & Pakistan

kHz kilohertz

Ki. Kings

kib·butz (ki bŏŏts′, -boots′) *n., pl.* **kib·but·zim** (kē′bŏŏ tsēm′) [ModHeb.] an Israeli collective settlement, esp. a collective farm

kib·itz·er (kib′its ər) *n.* [Yid. < G. *kiebitz*] [Colloq.] an onlooker at a card game, etc., esp. one who volunteers advice —**kib′itz** *vi.*

ki·bosh (kī′bäsh) *n.* [< ?] [Slang] orig., nonsense: now usually in **put the kibosh on,** to squelch; veto

kick (kik) *vi.* [ME. *kiken*] **1.** to strike out with the foot or feet **2.** to recoil, as a gun **3.** [Colloq.] to complain **4.** *Football* to kick the ball —*vt.* **1.** to strike with the foot or feet **2.** to drive, force, etc. as by kicking **3.** to score (a goal, etc.) by kicking **4.** [Slang] to get rid of (a habit) —*n.* **1.** a blow with the foot **2.** a method of kicking **3.** a sudden recoil **4.** [Colloq.] a complaint **5.** [Colloq.] a stimulating effect **6.** [Colloq.] [*often pl.*] pleasure; thrill **7.** *Football a*) a kicking of the ball *b*) the kicked ball —**kick around** [Colloq.] **1.** to treat roughly **2.** to move from place to place **3.** to consider or discuss —**kick in** [Slang] to pay (one's share) —**kick off 1.** to put a football into play with a place kick **2.** to start (a campaign, etc.) —**kick out** [Colloq.] to get rid of; expel —**kick over** to start working, as an internal-combustion engine —**kick up** [Colloq.] to cause (trouble, etc.)

kick′back′ *n.* **1.** [Colloq.] a sharp reaction **2.** [Slang] *a*) a giving back of part of money received as payment *b*) the money so returned

kick′er *n.* **1.** one that kicks **2.** [Slang] *a*) a surprise ending *b*) a hidden difficulty

kick′off′ *n.* **1.** *Football* a place kick that puts the ball into play **2.** the start of a campaign, etc.

kick′stand′ *n.* a pivoted metal bar that can be kicked down to support a bicycle, motorcycle, etc. in an upright position

kick·y (kik′ē) *adj.* **-i·er, -i·est** [Slang] **1.** stylish **2.** stimulating; exciting

kid (kid) *n.* [ME. *kide*] **1.** a young goat **2.** leather from the skin of young goats: also **kid′skin′ 3.** [Colloq.] a child or young person —*adj.* **1.** made of kidskin [*kid* gloves] **2.** [Colloq.] younger [*my kid* sister] —*vt., vi.* **kid′ded, kid′ding** [Colloq.] to tease or fool playfully —**kid′der** *n.*

Kidd (kid), Captain (**William**) 1645?–1701; Brit. privateer & pirate: hanged

kid·dy, kid·die (kid′ē) *n., pl.* **-dies** [dim. of KID, *n.* 3] [Colloq.] a child

kid′nap′ (-nap′) *vt.* **-napped′** or **-naped′, -nap′ping** or **-nap′ing** [KID, *n.* 3 + dial. *nap,* to snatch] **1.** to steal (a child) **2.** to seize and hold (a person) by force or fraud, often for ransom —**kid′nap′per, kid′nap′er** *n.*

kid·ney (kid′nē) *n., pl.* **-neys** [ME. *kidenei*] **1.** either of a pair of glandular organs which separate waste products from the blood and excrete them as urine **2.** an animal's kidney used as food **3.** *a*) disposition *b*) kind; sort

kidney bean the kidney-shaped seed of the common garden bean

kidney stone a hard mineral deposit sometimes formed in the kidney

Kiel (kēl) seaport in N West Germany, on a canal (**Kiel Canal**) connecting the North Sea & the Baltic Sea: pop. 270,000

kiel·ba·sa (kēl bä′sə) *n., pl.* **-si** (-sē), **-sas** [Pol.] a smoked Polish sausage flavored with garlic

Ki·ev (kē′ef) capital of the Ukrainian S.S.R., on the Dnepr: pop. 1,476,000

Kil·i·man·ja·ro (kil′ə män jä′rō) mountain in NE Tanzania, the highest in Africa: 19,340 ft.

kill (kil) *vt.* [ME. *killen*] **1.** to cause the death of; slay **2.** to destroy; put an end to **3.** to defeat or veto (legislation) **4.** to spend (time) on trivial matters **5.** to turn off (an engine, light, etc.) **6.** to prevent publication of **7.** [Colloq.] to overcome with laughter, chagrin, etc. —*vi.* to destroy life —*n.* **1.** an act of killing **2.** an animal or animals killed —**kill′er** *n.*

kill·deer (kil′dir′) *n.* [echoic of its cry] a small N. American bird related to the plover

killer whale a small whale that hunts in packs and preys on large fish, seals, and other whales

kill′ing *adj.* **1.** causing death; deadly **2.** exhausting; fatiguing —*n.* **1.** slaughter; murder **2.** [Colloq.] a sudden, great profit

kill′-joy′ *n.* one who destroys or lessens other people's enjoyment: also **kill′joy′**

kiln (kil, kiln) *n.* [< L. *culina,* cooking stove] a furnace or oven for drying, burning, or baking bricks, pottery, grain, etc. —*vt.* to dry, burn, or bake in a kiln

ki·lo (kē′lō, kil′ō) *n., pl.* **-los** [Fr.] *short for:* **1.** KILOGRAM **2.** KILOMETER

kilo- [Fr. < Gr. *chilioi,* thousand] *a combining form meaning* a thousand

kil·o·cy·cle (kil′ə sī′k'l) *n. former name for* KILOHERTZ

kil′o·gram′ (-gram′) *n.* a unit of weight and mass, equal to 1,000 grams (2.2046 lb.): chiefly Brit. sp. **kil′o·gramme′**

kil′o·hertz′ (-hurts′) *n., pl.* **-hertz** one thousand hertz

kil′o·li·ter (-lēt′ər) *n.* a unit of capacity, equal to 1,000 liters, or one cubic meter (264.18 gal.): chiefly Brit. sp. **kil′o·li′tre**

kil·o·me·ter (ki läm′ə tər, kil′ə mēt′ər) *n.* a unit of length or distance, equal to 1,000 meters (3,280.8 ft.): chiefly Brit. sp. **ki·lo′me·tre** —**kil·o·met·ric** (kil′ə met′rik) *adj.*

kil·o·watt (kil′ə wät′) *n.* a unit of electrical power, equal to 1,000 watts

kil′o·watt′-hour′ *n.* a unit of electrical energy or work, equal to that expended or done by one kilowatt acting for one hour

kilt (kilt) *n.* [prob. < Scand.] a knee-length, pleated tartan skirt worn sometimes by men of the Scottish Highlands

kil·ter (kil′tər) *n.* [< ?] [Colloq.] good condition; proper order: now chiefly in **out of kilter**

ki·mo·no (kə mō′nə) *n., pl.* **-nos** [Jpn.] **1.** a loose outer garment with a sash, part of the traditional costume of Japanese men and women **2.** a woman's dressing gown like this

kin (kin) *n.* [OE. *cynn*] relatives; family —*adj.* related, as by blood —**(near) of kin** (closely) related

-kin [< MDu. *-ken*] *a suffix meaning* little [*lambkin*]

KILT

kind (kīnd) *n.* [OE. *cynd*] **1.** a natural group or division **2.** essential character **3.** sort; class —*adj.* **1.** sympathetic, gentle, generous, etc. **2.** cordial [*kind* regards] —**in kind** in the same way —**kind of** [Colloq.] somewhat; rather —**of a kind** alike

kin·der·gar·ten (kin′dər gär′t'n) *n.* [G. < *kinder,* children + *garten,* garden] a school or class for children, usually four to six years old, that develops basic skills and social behavior by means of games, handicraft, etc. —**kin′der·gart′ner, kin′der·gar′ten·er** *n.*

kind′heart′ed *adj.* sympathetic; kindly —**kind′heart′ed·ly** *adv.* —**kind′heart′ed·ness** *n.*

kin′dle (kin′d'l) *vt.* **-dled, -dling** [< ON. *kynda*] **1.** to set on fire; ignite **2.** to excite (interest, feelings, etc.) —*vi.* **1.** to catch fire **2.** to become aroused or excited

kin·dling (kin′dlin) *n.* material, as bits of dry wood, for starting a fire

kind′ly *adj.* **-li·er, -li·est 1.** kind; gracious **2.** agreeable; pleasant —*adv.* **1.** in a kind, gracious manner **2.** agreeably; favorably **3.** please [*kindly* reply] —**take kindly to 1.** to be naturally attracted to **2.** to accept willingly —**kind′li·ness** *n.*

kind′ness *n.* **1.** the state, quality, or habit of being kind **2.** a kind act

kin·dred (kin′drid) *n.* [< OE. *cynn,* kin + *ræden,* condition] **1.** formerly, family relationship **2.** relatives or family; kin —*adj.* of like nature; similar [*kindred* spirits]

kine (kīn) *n.pl.* [< OE. *cy,* cows] [Archaic] cows; cattle

kin·e·scope (kin′ə skōp′) *n.* [< Gr. *kinein,* to move + -SCOPE] a cathode-ray tube used in television receivers, etc. for picture display

ki·net·ic (ki net′ik) *adj.* [< Gr. *kinein,* to move] of or resulting from motion

kin·folk (kin′fōk′) *n.pl.* relatives; kin: also **kin′folks′**

king (kin) *n.* [OE. *cyning*] **1.** the male ruler of a state usually called a kingdom **2.** a man who is supreme in some field **3.** something supreme in its class **4.** a playing card with a picture of a king on it **5.** *Checkers* a piece that has moved the length of the board **6.** *Chess* the chief piece —*adj.* chief (in size, importance, etc.): used often in combination —**king′ly** *adv.* —**king′ship′** *n.*

King (kin), **Martin Luther, Jr.** 1929-68; U.S. clergyman & civil-rights leader

king′bird′ *n.* any of several American flycatchers

king′bolt′ *n.* a vertical bolt connecting the front axle of a wagon, etc., or the truck of a railroad car, with the body

king′dom (-dəm) *n.* 1. a country headed by a king or queen; monarchy 2. a realm; sphere *[the kingdom of poetry]* 3. any of the three divisions into which all natural objects have been classified (the animal, vegetable, and mineral kingdoms)

king′fish′ *n.* 1. *pl.:* see FISH a large food fish of the Atlantic or Pacific coast 2. [Colloq.] a person holding absolute power in some group or place

king′fish′er *n.* a bright-colored bird with a large, crested head and a short tail

King James Version *same as* AUTHORIZED VERSION

King Lear (lir) the title character of a tragedy by Shakespeare

king′mak′er (-mā′kər) *n.* a politically powerful person who is instrumental in getting candidates into office

king′pin′ *n.* 1. *same as* KINGBOLT 2. the headpin or center pin in bowling, etc. 3. [Colloq.] the main or essential person or thing

Kings (kiŋz) either of two books, or, in the Douay Bible, any of four books, in the Old Testament

king′-size′ *adj.* [Colloq.] larger than the usual size: also **king′-sized′**

king snake a large, harmless snake of C and S N. America: it eats rats, lizards, etc.

Kings·ton (kiŋz′tən) seaport & capital of Jamaica: pop. 123,000 (met. area 422,000)

kink (kiŋk) *n.* [< Scand.] 1. a short twist or curl in a rope, hair, etc. 2. a painful cramp, as in the neck 3. a queer notion; eccentricity 4. a defect, as in a plan —*vi., vt.* to form or cause to form a kink or kinks

kin·ka·jou (kiŋ′kə jōō′) *n.* [< Fr. < AmInd. name] a tree-dwelling, raccoonlike mammal of Central and South America, with a long, prehensile tail

kink′y *adj.* **-i·er, -i·est** 1. full of kinks; tightly curled 2. [Slang] weird, bizarre, etc.; specif., sexually abnormal

kins·folk (kinz′fōk′) *n.pl. var. of* KINFOLK

kin·ship (kin′ship′) *n.* 1. family relationship 2. close connection

kins·man (kinz′mən) *n., pl.* **-men** a relative, esp. a male relative —**kins′wom′an** *n.fem., pl.* **-wom′en**

ki·osk (kē′äsk) *n.* [< Fr. < Per. *kūshk,* palace] a small, open structure used as a newsstand, etc.

Kip·ling (kip′liŋ), **Rud·yard** (rud′yərd) 1865–1936; Eng. writer

kip·per (kip′ər) *vt.* [< ?] to cure (herring, salmon, etc.) by salting and drying or smoking —*n.* a kippered herring, salmon, etc.

Kir·ghiz Soviet Socialist Republic (kir gēz′) republic of the U.S.S.R., in SC Asia

kirk (kurk; *Scot.* kirk) *n.* [Scot. & North Eng.] a church

kis·met (kiz′met) *n.* [< Turk. < Ar. *qasama,* to divide] fate; destiny

kiss (kis) *vt., vi.* [OE. *cyssan*] 1. to touch or caress with the lips as an act of affection, greeting, etc. 2. to touch lightly —*n.* 1. an act of kissing 2. a light, gentle touch 3. any of various candies —**kiss′a·ble** *adj.*

kiss′er *n.* 1. a person who kisses 2. [Slang] *a)* the mouth or lips *b)* the face

kit (kit) *n.* [ME. *kyt,* tub] 1. personal equipment, esp. as packed for travel 2. a set of tools, articles for special use, parts to be assembled, etc. 3. a container for such equipment, tools, etc. —**the whole kit and caboodle** [Colloq.] everybody or everything

kitch·en (kich′ən) *n.* [< L. *coquere,* to cook] a room or place for the preparation and cooking of food

kitch′en·ette′ kitch′en·et′ (-et′) *n.* a small, compact kitchen

kitch′en·ware′ (-wer′) *n.* kitchen utensils

kite (kīt) *n.* [OE. *cyta*] 1. a bird related to the hawk, with long, pointed wings 2. a light, wooden frame covered with paper or cloth, to be flown in the wind at the end of a string —*vi.* **kit′ed, kit′ing** [Colloq.] to move lightly and rapidly

kith (kith) *n.* [OE. *cyth*] friends, acquaintances, etc.: now only in **kith and kin,** friends, acquaintances, and relatives; also, often, relatives

kitsch (kich) *n.* [G., gaudy trash] pretentious but shallow art, writing, etc., designed for popular appeal —**kitsch′y** *adj.*

kit·ten (kit′'n) *n.* [< OFr. dim. of *chat,* cat] a young cat

kit′ten·ish (-ish) *adj.* like a kitten; playful; often, playfully coy —**kit′ten·ish·ness** *n.*

kit·ty¹ (kit′ē) *n., pl.* **-ties** 1. a kitten 2. *a pet name for a* cat of any age

kit·ty² (kit′ē) *n., pl.* **-ties** [prob. < KIT] 1. in poker, etc., the stakes 2. money pooled by card players, etc. for some special use

kit·ty-cor·nered (kit′ē kôr′nərd) *adj., adv. same as* CATER-CORNERED: also **kit′ty-cor′ner**

ki·wi (kē′wē) *n., pl.* **-wis** [Maori: echoic of its cry] a tailless New Zealand bird with undeveloped wings and hairlike feathers

K.K.K., KKK Ku Klux Klan

Klan (klan) *n. short for* KU KLUX KLAN —**Klans′man** *n., pl.* **-men**

klatch, klatsch (kläch, klach) *n.* [G. *klatsch,* gossip] [Colloq.] an informal gathering, as to chat

klep·to·ma·ni·a (klep′tə mā′nē ə) *n.* [< Gr. *kleptēs,* thief + -MANIA] an abnormal, persistent impulse to steal —**klep′to·ma′ni·ac′** (-ak′) *n.*

klieg light (klēg) [after A. & J. *Kliegl,* its inventors] a very bright arc light used to light motion-picture sets

Klon·dike (klän′dīk) gold-mining region in W Yukon Territory, Canada

km, km. kilometer(s)

knack (nak) *n.* [ME. *knak,* sharp blow] 1. a clever expedient 2. ability to do something easily

knack·wurst (näk′wurst′) *n.* [G.] a thick, highly seasoned sausage

knap·sack (nap′sak′) *n.* [< Du. *knappen,* eat + *zak,* sack] a leather or canvas bag for carrying equipment or supplies on the back

knave (nāv) *n.* [OE. *cnafa,* boy] 1. a tricky rascal; rogue 2. a jack (the playing card) —**knav′ish** *adj.*

knav·er·y (nāv′ər ē) *n., pl.* **-ies** behavior or an act characteristic of a knave

knead (nēd) *vt.* [OE. *cnedan*] 1. to work (dough, clay, etc.) into a pliable mass by pressing and squeezing 2. to massage

knee (nē) *n.* [OE. *cneow*] 1. the joint between the thigh and the lower leg 2. anything shaped like a knee, esp. like a bent knee 3. the part of a stocking, trouser leg, etc. covering the knee —*vt.* **kneed, knee′ing** to hit or touch with the knee

knee′cap′ (-kap′) *n.* a movable bone at the front of the human knee

knee′hole′ (-hōl′) *n.* a space for the knees, as under a desk top

kneel (nēl) *vi.* **knelt** or **kneeled, kneel′ing** [< OE. *cneow*] to bend or rest on a knee or the knees —**kneel′er** *n.*

knee·pad (nē′pad′) *n.* a pad worn to protect the knee, as by a basketball player

knell (nel) *vi.* [OE. *cnyllan*] 1. to ring slowly; toll 2. to sound ominously —*vt.* to call or announce as by a knell —*n.* 1. the sound of a tolling bell 2. an omen of death, failure, etc.

knelt (nelt) *alt. pt. and pp. of* KNEEL

knew (nōō, nyōō) *pt. of* KNOW

Knick·er·bock·er (nik′ər bäk′ər) *n.* [< Diedrich *Knickerbocker,* fictitious Du. author of Washington Irving's *History of New York*] 1. a New Yorker, esp. one descended from the early Dutch settlers 2. [k-] *[pl.]* short, loose trousers gathered just below the knees

knick·ers (nik′ərz) *n.pl.* [contr. < prec.] *same as* KNICKERBOCKERS

knick·knack (nik′nak′) *n.* [< KNACK] a small ornamental article or contrivance

knife (nif) *n., pl.* **knives** (nīvz) [OE. *cnif*] 1. a cutting instrument with a sharp-edged blade set in a handle 2. a cutting blade, as in a machine —*vt.* **knifed, knif′ing** 1. to cut or stab with a knife 2. [Colloq.] to hurt, defeat, etc. by treachery

knight (nīt) *n.* [OE. *cniht,* boy] 1. in the Middle Ages, a man formally raised to honorable military rank and pledged to chivalrous conduct 2. in Britain, a man who for some achievement is given honorary nonhereditary rank entitling him to use *Sir* before his given name 3. a chessman shaped like a horse's head —*vt.* to make (a man) a knight

knight′-er′rant (-er′ənt) *n., pl.* **knights′-er′rant** 1. a medieval knight wandering in search of adventure 2. a chivalrous or quixotic person

knight′hood′ (-hood′) *n.* 1. the rank or vocation of a knight 2. knightly conduct 3. knights collectively

knight′ly *adj.* 1. of or like a knight; chivalrous, brave, etc. 2. consisting of knights

knit (nit) *vt., vi.* **knit′ted** or **knit, knit′ting** [< OE. *cnotta,* a knot] 1. to make (a fabric) by looping yarn or thread together with special needles 2. to join closely and firmly 3. to draw (the brows) together —**knit′ter** *n.*

knit′ting *n.* knitted work

knitting needle an eyeless, long needle used in pairs, etc. in knitting by hand

knives (nīvz) *n. pl. of* KNIFE

knob (näb) *n.* [< or akin to MLowG. *knobbe,* a knot] **1.** a rounded lump or protuberance **2.** a handle, usually round, of a door, drawer, etc. **3.** a rounded hill or mountain — **knobbed** *adj.*

knob'by *adj.* **-bi·er, -bi·est 1.** covered with knobs **2.** like a knob

knock (näk) *vi.* [OE. *cnocian*] **1.** to strike a blow, as with the fist; esp., to rap on a door **2.** to bump; collide **3.** to make a thumping noise, as an engine **4.** [Colloq.] to find fault —*vt.* **1.** to hit; strike **2.** to make by hitting *[to knock* a hole in the wall] **3.** [Colloq.] to find fault with — *n.* **1.** a knocking **2.** a hit; rap **3.** a thumping noise, as in an engine **4.** [Colloq.] an adverse criticism —**knock about (or around)** [Colloq.] to wander about —**knock down 1.** to strike down **2.** to take apart **3.** to indicate the sale of at an auction —**knock off 1.** [Colloq.] to stop working **2.** [Colloq.] to deduct **3.** [Colloq.] to do **4.** [Slang] to kill, overcome, etc. —**knock out** to make unconscious or exhausted —**knock together** to make or compose hastily or crudely

knock'a·bout' (-ə bout′) *n.* **1.** a small, one-masted yacht with a mainsail, jib, and centerboard **2.** something for knockabout use —*adj.* **1.** rough; boisterous **2.** made for rough use

knock'down' *adj.* **1.** overwhelming **2.** made so as to be easily taken apart *[a knockdown* table] —*n.* **1.** a knocking down **2.** a blow that knocks down

knock'er *n.* one that knocks; specif., a small ring, knob, etc. on a door, for knocking

knock'-kneed' (-nēd′) *adj.* having legs which bend inward at the knee

knock'out' *adj.* that knocks out, as a blow —*n.* **1.** a knocking out or being knocked out **2.** [Slang] a very attractive or striking person or thing **3.** *Boxing* a victory won when the opponent is knocked down and cannot rise before an official count of ten

knock·wurst (näk′wurst′) *n. alt. sp. of* KNACKWURST

knoll (nōl) *n.* [OE. *cnoll*] a hillock; mound

knot (nät) *n.* [OE. *cnotta*] **1.** a lump in a thread, etc. as formed by a tangle **2.** a fastening made by tying together pieces of string, rope, etc. **3.** an ornamental bow of ribbon, etc. **4.** a small group or cluster **5.** something that ties closely; esp., the bond of marriage **6.** a problem; difficulty **7.** a hard lump on a tree where a branch grows out, or a cross section of such a lump in a board **8.** *Naut.* a speed of one nautical mile an hour —*vt., vi.* **knot'ted, knot'ting 1.** to make or form a knot (in) **2.** to entangle or become entangled

knot'hole' *n.* a hole in a board, etc. where a knot has fallen out

knot'ty *adj.* **-ti·er, -ti·est 1.** full of knots *[a knotty* board] **2.** hard to solve; puzzling *[a knotty* problem] —**knot'ti·ness** *n.*

know (nō) *vt.* **knew, known, know'ing** [OE. *cnawan*] **1.** to be well informed about **2.** to be aware of *[to know* that one is loved] **3.** to have securely in the memory *[the actor knows* his lines] **4.** to be acquainted with **5.** to have understanding of or skill in **6.** to distinguish *[to know* right from wrong] —*vi.* **1.** to have knowledge **2.** to be sure or aware —**in the know** [Colloq.] having confidential information —**know'a·ble** *adj.*

know'-how' (-hou′) *n.* [Colloq.] knowledge of how to do something well; technical skill

know'ing *adj.* **1.** having knowledge **2.** shrewd; clever **3.** implying shrewd or secret understanding *[a knowing* look] —**know'ing·ly** *adv.*

knowl·edge (näl′ij) *n.* **1.** the fact or state of knowing **2.** range of information or understanding **3.** what is known; learning **4.** the body of facts, principles, etc. accumulated by mankind —**to (the best of) one's knowledge** as far as one knows

knowl'edge·a·ble (-ə b'l) *adj.* having or showing knowledge or intelligence

known (nōn) *pp. of* KNOW

know'-noth'ing *n.* **1.** an ignoramus **2.** [K- N-] a member of a U.S. secret political party in the 1850's, with a program of excluding all but native-born Americans from public office

Knox (näks), **John** 1505?-72; Scot. Protestant clergyman & religious reformer

Knox·ville (näks′vil) city in E Tenn.: pop. 175,000

knuck·le (nuk′'l) *n.* [< ? MDu. or MLowG. *knokel,* little bone] **1.** a joint of the finger; esp., the joint connecting a finger to the rest of the hand **2.** the knee or hock joint of an animal, used as food **3.** [*pl.*] *same as* BRASS KNUCKLES —*vt.* **-led, -ling** to strike or touch with the knuckles — **knuckle down** to work hard —**knuckle under** to yield; give in

knuck'le·head' (-hed′) *n.* [Colloq.] a stupid person

knurl (nurl) *n.* [prob. < ME. *knur,* a knot + GNARL] **1.** a knot, knob, etc. **2.** any of a series of small beads or ridges, as along the edge of a coin —*vt.* to make knurls on —**knurled** *adj.*

knurl'y *adj.* **-i·er, -i·est** full of knurls, as wood

KO (kā′ō′) *vt.* **KO'd, KO'ing** [Slang] *Boxing* to knock out —*n., pl.* **KO's** [Slang] *Boxing* a knockout Also **K.O., k.o.**

ko·a·la (kō ä′lə) *n.* [< the native name] an Australian tree-dwelling marsupial with thick, gray fur

Ko·be (kō′bē) seaport on the S coast of Honshu, Japan: pop. 1,217,000

ko·di·ak bear (kō′dē ak′) a large brown bear found on an island (**Kodiak Island**) off the SW coast of Alaska

Koh·i·noor, Koh-i-noor (kō′ə noor′) [< Per.] a famous large Indian diamond, now one of the British crown jewels

kohl·ra·bi (kōl′rä′bē, kōl′rä′bē) *n., pl.* **-bies** [G. < It. *cavolo rapa*] a vegetable related to the cabbage, with an edible bulbous stem

ko·la (kō′lə) *n. same as* COLA

KOALA
(27–35 in. long)

ko·lin·sky (kə lin′skē, kō-) *n., pl.* **-skies** **1.** any of several weasels of Asia **2.** its golden-brown fur

kook (kōōk) *n.* [< ? *cuckoo*] [Slang] a person regarded as silly, eccentric, crazy, etc. —**kook'y, kook'ie** *adj.*

ko·peck, ko·pek (kō′pek) *n.* [< Russ.] a monetary unit, and a coin, equal to 1/100 of a ruble

Ko·ran (kō ran′, kō-) *n.* [Ar. *qur'ān,* lit., book] the sacred book of the Muslims: its contents are reported revelations made to Mohammed by Allah

Ko·re·a (kô rē′ə, kō-) peninsula in E Asia: divided (1948) into two countries: *a)* **North Korea,** 47,255 sq. mi.; pop. 11,568,000; cap. Pyongyang, and *b)* **South Korea,** 38,030 sq. mi.; pop. 31,738,000; cap. Seoul —**Ko·re'an** *adj., n.*

ko·ru·na (kô rōō′nä) *n.* [Czech < L. *corona,* a crown] the monetary unit of Czechoslovakia

Kos·ci·us·ko (käs′ē us′kō), **Thad·de·us** (thad′ē əs) 1746–1817; Pol. general: served in the American Revolutionary army

ko·sher (kō′shər) *adj.* [Heb. *kāshēr,* proper] **1.** *Judaism a)* clean or fit to eat according to the dietary laws *b)* dealing in such food **2.** [Slang] all right, proper, etc. —*n.* kosher food

Kos·suth (käs′ōōth), **Louis** 1802–94; Hung. patriot & statesman

kow·tow (kou′tou′, kō′-) *n.* [Chin. *k'o-t'ou,* lit., knock head] the act of kneeling and touching the ground with the forehead to show great deference, etc. —*vi.* **1.** to make a kowtow **2.** to show submissive respect (*to*)

KP, K.P. kitchen police, a detail to assist the cooks in an army kitchen

Kr *Chem.* krypton

kraal (kräl) *n.* [Afrik. < Port. *curral,* pen for cattle] **1.** a village of South African natives, usually surrounded by a stockade **2.** an enclosure for cattle or sheep in South Africa

krait (krīt) *n.* [Hindi *karait*] a very poisonous snake of SC and SE Asia

Kra·ków (krä′kou′) city in S Poland: pop. 535,000

Krem·lin (krem′lin) *n.* [Fr. < Russ. *kreml'*] **1.** the citadel of Moscow, formerly housing Soviet government offices **2.** the government of the Soviet Union

krim·mer (krim′ər) *n.* [G. < *Krim,* Crimea] the grayish, tightly curled fur of Crimean lambs

Krish·na (krish′nə) a Hindu god, an incarnation of Vishnu

Kriss Krin·gle (kris′ krin′g'l) [< G. < *Christ,* Christ + *kind,* child] *same as* SANTA CLAUS

kro·na (krō′nə) *n., pl.* **-nor** (-nôr) [Sw. < L. *corona,* crown] the monetary unit and a coin of Sweden

kro·ne (krō′nə) *n., pl.* **-ner** [Dan. < L. *corona,* crown] the monetary unit and a coin of Denmark or Norway

---

at, āpe, cär; ten, ēven; is, bīte; gō, hôrn, tōōl, look; oil, out; up, fur; thin, *th*en; zh, leisure; ŋ, ring; ə for *a* in *ago;* as in *able* (ā′b'l); ë, Fr. coeur; ö, Fr. feu; Fr. mon; ü, Fr. duc; r, Fr. cri; kh, G. doch, ich. ‡ foreign; < derived from

kryp·ton (krip′tän) *n.* [< Gr. *kryptein,* to hide] a rare, inert gaseous chemical element: symbol, Kr; at. wt., 83.80; at. no., 36
KS Kansas
Kt *Chess* knight
Ku·blai Khan (kōō′blī kän′, -blə) 1216?-94; Mongol emperor of China (1260?-94)
ku·chen (kōō′kən, -khən) *n.* [G., cake] a coffeecake made of yeast dough, often frosted or filled with raisins, nuts, etc.
ku·dos (kōō′däs, -dōs; kyōō′-) *n.* [Gr. *kydos,* glory] [Colloq.] praise for an achievement; glory; fame
ku·du (kōō′dōō) *n.* [Hottentot] a large, grayish-brown African antelope
Ku Klux Klan (kōō′ kluks′ klan′) [< Gr. *kyklos,* a circle] a U.S. secret, terrorist society that is anti-Negro, anti-Semitic, anti-Catholic, etc.
ku·lak (kōō läk′) *n.* [Russ., lit., fist] a well-to-do farmer in Russia who opposed the Soviet collectivization of the land
ku·miss (kōō′mis) *n.* [G. ult. < Tatar *kumiz*] fermented mare's or camel's milk, used as a drink by Tatar nomads
küm·mel (kim′′l) *n.* [G., caraway] a colorless liqueur flavored with caraway seeds, anise, etc.

kum·quat (kum′kwät) *n.* [< Chin. *chin-chü,* golden orange] 1. a small, orange-colored, oval fruit with a sour pulp and a sweet rind 2. a tree that bears this fruit
kung fu (koonʹ fōōʹ, goonʹ) [< Chin.] a Chinese system of self-defense, like karate but emphasizing circular movements
Kuo·min·tang (kwōʹmin taŋʹ) [Chin.] nationalist party of China, organized in 1911
Kurd (kurd) *n.* [Turk. & Ar.] any of a nomadic Muslim people living chiefly in Kurdistan
Kur·dis·tan (kur′di stan′, -stän′) region occupying SE Turkey, N Iraq, & NW Iran
Ku·ril (or **Ku·rile**) **Islands** (kōō′ril, koo rēl′) chain of islands of the U.S.S.R., between Japan and Kamchatka peninsula
Ku·wait (kōō wāt′, -wīt′) independent Arab state in E Arabia, on the Persian Gulf: 6,000 sq. mi.; pop. 555,000
kw. kilowatt(s)
Kwang·chow (kwän′chō′) port in SE China: pop. 2,200,000: also sp. **Kwangchou**
kwh, K.W.H., kw.-hr., kw-hr kilowatt-hour
Ky., KY Kentucky
Kyo·to (kē ōt′ō) city in Japan: pop. 1,365,000
Kyu·shu (kyōō′shōō′) one of the islands forming Japan

L

L, l (el) *n., pl.* **L's, l's** the twelfth letter of the English alphabet
L (el) *n., pl.* **L's** 1. an object shaped like L; esp., an extension of a building that gives the whole a shape resembling L 2. a Roman numeral for 50
L. Latin
L., l. 1. lake 2. latitude 3. left 4. length 5. *pl.* **LL., ll.** line 6. liter 7. [L. *libra(e)*] pound(s)
la (lä) *n.* [< L.] *Music* a syllable representing the sixth tone of the diatonic scale
La *Chem.* lanthanum
La., LA Louisiana
L.A. [Colloq.] Los Angeles
lab (lab) *n.* [Colloq.] a laboratory
la·bel (lā′b′l) *n.* [OFr., a rag] 1. a card, paper, etc. marked and attached to an object to indicate its contents, destination, ownership, etc. 2. a term of generalized classification for a person, group, etc. 3. an identifying brand of a company —*vt.* **-beled** or **-belled, -bel·ing** or **-bel·ling** 1. to attach a label to 2. to classify as; call
la·bi·al (lā′bē əl) *adj.* [see LABIUM] 1. of the lips 2. *Phonet.* formed mainly with the lips, as *b, m,* and *p* —*n.* a labial sound —**la′bi·al·ly** *adv.*
la′bi·ate′ (-āt′, -it) *adj.* [see LABIUM] having, or formed like, a lip or lips
la·bi·um (lā′bē əm) *n., pl.* **-bi·a** (-ə) [L., a lip] *Anat., Bot.,* etc. a lip or liplike organ
la·bor (lā′bər) *n.* [L.] 1. physical or mental exertion; work 2. a specific task 3. all wage-earning, esp. manual, workers 4. labor unions collectively 5. the process of childbirth —*vi.* 1. to work 2. to work hard 3. to move slowly and with difficulty 4. to suffer (*under* a false idea, etc.) 5. to be in childbirth —*vt.* to develop in too great detail
lab·o·ra·to·ry (lab′rə tôr′ē, -ər ə tôr′ē) *n., pl.* **-ries** [see LABOR] 1. a room, building, etc. for scientific work or research 2. a place for preparing chemicals, drugs, etc.
Labor Day the first Monday in September, a legal holiday honoring labor
la·bored (lā′bərd) *adj.* made or done with great effort
la·bor·er (lā′bər ər) *n.* one who labors; esp., a wage-earning worker whose work involves physical exertion
la·bo·ri·ous (lə bôr′ē əs) *adj.* 1. involving much hard work; difficult 2. hard-working —**la·bo′ri·ous·ly** *adv.*
la·bor·ite (lā′bə rīt′) *n.* a member or supporter of a labor party, esp. [L-] of the British Labor Party: Brit. sp. **La′bour·ite′**
labor party 1. a political party organized to protect and further the rights of workers 2. [L- P-] such a party in Great Britain: Brit. sp. **Labour Party**
labor union an association of workers to promote and protect the welfare, interests, and rights of its members, mainly by collective bargaining

la·bour (lā′bər) *n., vi., vt. Brit. sp.* of LABOR
Lab·ra·dor (lab′rə dôr′) 1. region along the E coast of Canada, constituting the mainland part of Newfoundland 2. large peninsula occupied by this region & most of Quebec
Labrador retriever any of a breed of medium-sized hunting dog with a coat of short, thick hair
la·bur·num (lə bur′nəm) *n.* [L.] a small, poisonous tree or shrub of the legume family, with drooping yellow flowers
lab·y·rinth (lab′ə rinth′) *n.* [< Gr. *labyrinthos*] 1. a structure containing winding passages hard to follow without losing one's way; maze 2. [L-] *Gr. Myth.* such a structure built to house the Minotaur 3. a complicated, perplexing arrangement, condition, etc. 4. *Anat.* the inner ear —**lab′y·rin′thine** (-rin′thin) *adj.*
lac (lak) *n.* [< Hindi < Sans. *lākṣā*] 1. a resinous substance secreted on various trees in S Asia by a scale insect: the source of shellac 2. *same as* LAKH
lace (lās) *n.* [< L. *laqueus,* noose] 1. a string, etc. used to draw together and fasten the parts of a shoe, corset, etc. 2. an openwork fabric of linen, silk, etc., woven in ornamental designs —*vt.* **laced, lac′ing** 1. to fasten with a lace 2. to weave together; intertwine 3. to thrash; beat 4. to add a dash of alcoholic liquor to (a beverage) —*vi.* [Colloq.] to attack physically or verbally (with *into*)
lac·er·ate (las′ə rāt′) *vt.* **-at′ed, -at′ing** [< L. *lacer,* mangled] 1. to tear jaggedly; mangle 2. to hurt (someone's feelings, etc.) —*adj.* (*also* -ər it) 1. torn; mangled 2. *Bot.* having jagged edges —**lac′er·a′tion** *n.*
lace′work′ *n.* lace, or any openwork decoration like lace
lach·ry·mal (lak′rə məl) *adj.* [< L. *lacrima,* tear] 1. of or producing tears 2. *same as* LACRIMAL (sense 1)
lach′ry·mose′ (-mōs′) *adj.* 1. inclined to shed tears; tearful 2. causing tears; sad
lac·ing (lās′iŋ) *n.* 1. the act of one who laces 2. a thrashing; beating 3. a cord or lace 4. gold or silver braid used to trim a uniform, etc.
lack (lak) *n.* [< or akin to MLowG. *lak*] 1. the fact or state of not having enough or of not having any 2. the thing that is needed —*vi., vt.* to be deficient in or entirely without
lack·a·dai·si·cal (lak′ə dā′zi k'l) *adj.* [ult. < *alack the day*] showing lack of interest or spirit; listless —**lack′a·dai′si·cal·ly** *adv.*
lack·ey (lak′ē) *n., pl.* **-eys** [< Sp. *lacayo*] 1. a male servant of low rank 2. a servile follower; toady
lack·lus·ter (lak′lus′tər) *adj.* lacking brightness; dull [*lackluster* eyes] : chiefly Brit. sp. **lack′lus′tre**
la·con·ic (lə kän′ik) *adj.* [< Gr. *Lakōn,* a Spartan] terse in expression; using few words —**la·con′i·cal·ly** *adv.*
lac·quer (lak′ər) *n.* [< Fr. < Port. *laca,* gum lac] 1. coating substance made of shellac, gum resins, etc. dis

solved in ethyl alcohol or other solvent that evaporates quickly 2. a resinous varnish obtained from certain Oriental trees 3. a wooden article coated with this —*vt.* to coat with lacquer

lac·ri·mal (lak′rə məl) *adj.* 1. of or near the glands that secrete tears 2. *same as* LACHRYMAL (sense 1)

la·crosse (lə krôs′) *n.* [CanadFr. < Fr. *la*, the + *crosse*, a crutch] a ball game played by two ten-member teams using long-handled, pouched rackets

LACROSSE

lac·tate (lak′tāt) *vi.* -tat·ed, -tat·ing [< L. *lac*, milk] to secrete milk —*n.* any salt or ester of lactic acid

lac·ta′tion *n.* 1. the secretion of milk by a mammary gland 2. the period of such secretion

lac·te·al (lak′tē əl) *adj.* [< L. *lac*, milk] 1. of or like milk; milky 2. containing or carrying chyle —*n.* any of the lymphatic vessels that carry chyle from the small intestine to the blood

lac·tic (lak′tik) *adj.* [< L. *lac*, milk] of or obtained from milk

lactic acid a clear, syrupy acid formed when milk sours

lac·tose (lak′tōs) *n.* [< L. *lac*, milk] a white, crystalline sugar, $C_{12}H_{22}O_{11}$, found in milk

la·cu·na (lə kyōō′nə) *n., pl.* -nas, -nae (-nē) [L., a ditch] a blank space; gap; hiatus

lac·y (lā′sē) *adj.* -i·er, -i·est of or like lace —**lac′i·ness** *n.*

lad (lad) *n.* [ME. *ladde*] a boy or youth

lad·der (lad′ər) *n.* [OE. *hlæder*] 1. a framework of two parallel sidepieces connected by rungs, for use in climbing up or down 2. any means of climbing /the *ladder* of success/ 3. [Chiefly Brit.] a run as in a stocking

lad·die (lad′ē) *n.* [Chiefly Scot.] a young lad

lade (lād) *vt., vi.* lad′ed, lad′ed or lad′en, lad′ing [OE. *hladan*] 1. to load 2. to bail; ladle

lad·en (lād′'n) *alt. pp. of* LADE —*adj.* 1. loaded 2. burdened; afflicted

la-di-da, la-de-da (lä′dē dä′) *adj.* [Colloq.] affectedly refined in speech, manners, etc.

lad·ing (lā′diŋ) *n.* a load, cargo, freight

la·dle (lā′d'l) *n.* [OE. *hlædel*] a long-handled, cuplike spoon for dipping out liquids —*vt.* -dled, -dling to dip out with, or carry in, a ladle —**la′dle·ful′** *n., pl.* -fuls′ —**la′dler** *n.*

la·dy (lā′dē) *n., pl.* -dies [< OE. *hlaf*, loaf + base of *dæge*, kneader] 1. *a*) a woman of high social position *b*) a woman who is polite, refined, etc. 2. any woman 3. [L-] the Virgin Mary (usually with *Our*) 4. [L-] a British title given to women of certain ranks —*adj.* female /a *lady* barber/

la′dy·bug′ *n.* a small, roundish beetle with a spotted back: also **la′dy·bird′ (beetle), lady beetle**

la′dy·fin′ger *n.* a small spongecake shaped somewhat like a finger

la′dy-in-wait′ing *n., pl.* **la′dies-in-wait′ing** a woman attending, or waiting upon, a queen or princess

la′dy·like′ *adj.* like or suitable for a lady; refined; well-bred

la′dy·love′ *n.* a sweetheart

la′dy·ship′ (-ship′) *n.* the rank or position of a lady: used in speaking to or of a titled Lady, preceded by *your* or *her*

la′dy-slip′per *n.* a wild orchid whose flowers somewhat resemble a slipper: also **la′dy's-slip′per**

La·fa·yette (lä′fi yet′), marquis de 1757–1834; Fr. general & statesman: served in the American Revolutionary army

La Fon·taine (lä fōn ten′), **Jean de** (zhän də) 1621–95; Fr. poet & writer of fables

lag (lag) *vi.* lagged, lag′ging [? akin to MDan. *lakke*, go slowly] 1. to fall, move, or stay behind 2. to wane —*n.* 1. a falling behind or being retarded 2. the amount of this

la·ger (beer) (lä′gər) [G. *lagerbier*, lit., storehouse beer] a beer that is aged for several months after it has been brewed

lag·gard (lag′ərd) *n.* [< LAG + -ARD] a slow person, esp. one who is always falling behind —*adj.* slow or late in doing things —**lag′gard·ly** *adv., adj.*

la-gniappe, la-gnappe (lan yap′, lan′yap) *n.* [Creole < Fr. *la*, the + Sp. *ñapa*, lagniappe] 1. [Chiefly South] a small gift given with a purchase 2. a gratuity

la-goon (lə gōōn′) *n.* [< Fr. & It. < L. *lacuna*, lake] 1. a shallow lake or pond, esp. one connected with a larger body of water 2. the water enclosed by a circular coral reef 3. shallow salt water separated from the sea by dunes

lag screw a wood screw with a boltlike head

La·hore (lə hôr′, lä-) city in NE Pakistan: pop. 1,296,000

la·ic (lā′ik) *adj.* [< Gr. *laos*, the people] secular; lay: also **la′i·cal** —*n.* a layman

laid (lād) *pt. & pp. of* LAY[1]

lain (lān) *pp. of* LIE[1]

lair (ler) *n.* [OE. *leger*] the resting place of a wild animal; den

laird (lerd) *n.* [Scot. form of LORD] in Scotland, a landowner, esp. a wealthy one

lais·sez faire (les′ā fer′, lez′-) [Fr., let do] noninterference; specif., absence of governmental control over industry and business

la·i·ty (lā′ət ē) *n., pl.* -ties [< LAY[3]] laymen collectively

lake[1] (lāk) *n.* [< L. *lacus*] 1. a large, inland body of water 2. a pool of oil or other liquid

lake[2] (lāk) *n.* [< Fr.: see LAC] 1. *a*) a dark-red pigment prepared from cochineal *b*) its color 2. an insoluble coloring compound precipitated from a solution of dye by adding a metallic salt

lake trout a large, gray game fish of lakes of the N U.S. and Canada

lakh (lak) *n.* [< Hindi] in India and Pakistan, 1. the sum of 100,000 (rupees) 2. any indefinitely large number

lam[1] (lam) *vt., vi.* lammed, lam′ming [< Scand.] [Slang] to beat; thrash

lam[2] (lam) *n.* [< ? prec.] [Slang] headlong flight —*vi.* lammed, lam′ming [Slang] to flee; escape —**on the lam** [Slang] in flight, as from the police

la·ma (lä′mə) *n.* [Tibetan *blama*] a priest or monk in Lamaism

La·ma·ism (lä′mə iz'm) *n.* a form of Buddhism practiced in Tibet and Mongolia —**La′ma·ist** *adj., n.*

la·ma·ser·y (lä′mə ser′ē) *n., pl.* -ies [< Fr.] a monastery of lamas

lamb (lam) *n.* [OE.] 1. a young sheep 2. its flesh used as food 3. lambskin 4. a gentle, innocent, or gullible person —*vi.* to give birth: said of a ewe —**the Lamb** Jesus

Lamb (lam), **Charles** 1775–1834; Eng. essayist & critic

lam·baste (lam bāst′, -bast′) *vt.* -bast′ed, -bast′ing [LAM[1] + BASTE[3]] [Colloq.] 1. to beat soundly 2. to scold severely

lamb·da (lam′də) *n.* the eleventh letter of the Greek alphabet (Λ, λ)

lam·bent (lam′bənt) *adj.* [< L. *lambere*, to lick] 1. playing lightly over a surface; flickering 2. softly glowing 3. light and graceful /lambent wit/ —**lam′ben·cy** *n.* —**lam′bent·ly** *adv.*

lamb·kin *n.* a little lamb

lamb′skin′ *n.* 1. the skin of a lamb, esp. with the fleece left on it 2. leather made from this skin

lame (lām) *adj.* [OE. *lama*] 1. crippled; esp., having an injured leg or foot that makes one limp 2. stiff and painful 3. poor, ineffectual, etc. /a lame excuse/ —*vt.* lamed, lam′ing to make lame —**lame′ly** *adv.* —**lame′ness** *n.*

la·mé (la mā′) *n.* [< Fr. *lame*, metal plate] a cloth interwoven with metallic threads

lame duck an elected official whose term extends beyond the time of his defeat for reelection

la·mel·la (lə mel′ə) *n., pl.* -lae (-ē), -las [L.] *Biol.* a thin, platelike part, layer, organ, or structure

la·ment (lə ment′) *vi., vt.* [< L. *lamentum*, a wailing] to feel or express deep sorrow (for); mourn —*n.* 1. a lamenting; wail 2. an elegy, dirge, etc. mourning a loss, death, etc.

lam·en·ta·ble (lam′ən tə b'l, lə men′-) *adj.* to be lamented; regrettable; distressing —**lam′en·ta·bly** *adv.*

lam·en·ta·tion (lam′ən tā′shən) *n.* a lamenting

Lam·en·ta′tions a book of the Bible attributed to Jeremiah

lam·i·na (lam′ə nə) *n., pl.* -nae (-nē′), -nas [L.] a thin flake, scale, or layer

lam·i·nate (lam′ə nāt′) *vt.* -nat′ed, -nat′ing 1. to separate into or cover with thin layers 2. to make by building up in thin layers —*vi.* to split into thin layers —*adj.* (-nit) *same as* LAMINATED —**lam′i·na′tion** *n.*

lam′i·nat′ed *adj.* composed of or built in thin sheets or layers, as of fabric, wood, etc., that have been bonded together

lamp (lamp) *n.* [< Gr. *lampein*, to shine] 1. a container with a wick for burning oil, etc. to produce light or heat

2. any device for producing light or therapeutic rays **3.** a holder or base for such a device

lamp'black' *n.* fine soot used as a black pigment

lam·poon (lam pōōn′) *n.* [< Fr. *lampons*, let us drink (used as a refrain)] strongly satirical writing, usually attacking or ridiculing someone —*vt.* to attack in a lampoon —**lam·poon'er, lam·poon'ist** *n.*

lamp'post' *n.* a post supporting a street lamp

lam·prey (lam'prē) *n., pl.* **-preys** [< ML. *lampreda*] an eellike parasitic fish with a funnel-shaped, jawless, sucking mouth

la·nai (lä nī′, la-) *n.* [Haw.] a veranda or open-sided living room of a kind found in Hawaii

Lan·cas·ter (laŋ′kəs tər) ruling family of England (1399-1461) —**Lan·cas'tri·an** (-kas′trē ən) *adj., n.*

lance (lans) *n.* [< L. *lancea*] **1.** a thrusting weapon consisting of a long wooden shaft with a sharp metal head **2.** *same as: a)* LANCER *b)* LANCET **3.** any instrument like a lance —*vt.* **lanced, lanc'ing 1.** to pierce with a lance **2.** to cut open with a lancet

Lan·ce·lot (lan′sə lät′) *Arthurian Legend* the most celebrated of the Knights of the Round Table: he was Guinevere's lover

lan·ce·o·late (lan′sē ə lāt′, -lit) *adj.* [< LL. *lanceola*, little lance] narrow and tapering like the head of a lance, as certain leaves

lanc·er (lan′sər) *n.* a cavalry soldier armed with a lance

lan·cet (lan′sit) *n.* [< OFr. dim. of *lance*, LANCE] a small, pointed surgical knife, usually two-edged

lance'wood' *n.* **1.** a tough, elastic wood **2.** a tropical tree yielding such wood

land (land) *n.* [OE.] **1.** the solid part of the earth's surface **2.** a country or nation **3.** ground or soil **4.** real estate **5.** rural regions —*vt.* **1.** to put on shore from a ship **2.** to bring to a particular place *[it landed* him in jail*]* **3.** to set (an aircraft) down on land or water **4.** to catch **5.** [Colloq.] to get or win **6.** [Colloq.] to deliver (a blow) —*vi.* **1.** to leave a ship and go on shore **2.** to come to a port, etc.: said of a ship **3.** to arrive at a specified place **4.** to alight or come to rest, as after a flight, jump, or fall

lan·dau (lan′dou, -dô) *n.* [< *Landau*, Germany] a four-wheeled carriage with the top in two sections, either of which can be lowered independently

land·ed (lan′did) *adj.* **1.** owning land **2.** consisting of land or real estate *[a landed* estate*]*

land'fall' *n.* **1.** a sighting of land from a ship at sea **2.** the land sighted

land'fill' *n.* the disposal of garbage or rubbish by burying it in the ground

land grant a grant of public land by the government for a railroad, State college, etc.

land'hold'er *n.* an owner or occupant of land —**land'-hold'ing** *adj., n.*

land'ing *n.* **1.** the act of coming to shore **2.** the place where a ship is loaded or unloaded **3.** a platform at the end of a flight of stairs **4.** the act of alighting, as after a flight or jump

landing field a field with a smooth surface to enable airplanes to land and take off easily

landing gear the undercarriage of an aircraft, including wheels, etc.

land'la'dy *n., pl.* **-dies** a woman landlord

land'less *adj.* not owning land

land'locked' *adj.* **1.** surrounded by land, as a bay or a country **2.** cut off from the sea and confined to fresh water *[landlocked* salmon*]*

land'lord' *n.* **1.** a person, esp. a man, who rents or leases land, houses, etc. to others **2.** a man who keeps a rooming house, inn, etc.

land'lub'ber (-lub′ər) *n.* one who has had little experience at sea, and is awkward aboard ship

land'mark' *n.* **1.** an object that marks the boundary of a piece of land **2.** any prominent feature of the landscape, marking a locality **3.** an important event in the development of something

land office a government office that handles the sales of public lands —**land'-of'fice business** [Colloq.] a booming business

Land of Promise *same as* PROMISED LAND

land'own'er *n.* one who owns land

land'scape' (-skāp′) *n.* [< Du. *land*, land + -*schap*, -SHIP] **1.** a picture representing natural, inland scenery **2.** an expanse of natural scenery seen in one view —*vt.* -**scaped', -scap'ing** to make (a plot of ground) more attractive, as by adding lawns, bushes, etc. —**land'scap'er** *n.*

landscape gardening the art or work of arranging

lawns, trees, etc. on a plot of ground to make it more attractive —**landscape gardener**

land'scap'ist *n.* a painter of landscapes

land'slide' *n.* **1.** the sliding of a mass of rocks or earth down a slope **2.** the mass sliding down **3.** an overwhelming victory in an election

lands·man (landz′mən) *n., pl.* **-men 1.** a person who lives on land: distinguished from SEAMAN **2.** a fellow countryman

land'ward (-wərd) *adv., adj.* toward the land: also **land'-wards** *adv.*

lane (lān) *n.* [OE. *lanu*] **1.** a narrow country road or city street **2.** any narrow way, as an opening in a crowd **3.** a path or strip designated, for reasons of safety, for ships, aircraft, automobiles, etc. **4.** any of the parallel courses marked off for contestants in a race

lang. language

lan·guage (laŋ′gwij) *n.* [< L. *lingua*, tongue] **1.** human speech or the written symbols for speech **2.** *a)* any means of communicating *b)* a special set of symbols used in a computer **3.** the speech of a particular nation, etc. *[the French language]* **4.** the verbal expression characteristic of a particular group, writer, etc. **5.** linguistics

lan·guid (laŋ′gwid) *adj.* [< Fr. < L. *languere*, be faint] **1.** without vigor or vitality; weak **2.** listless; indifferent **3.** sluggish; slow —**lan'guid·ly** *adv.*

lan'guish (-gwish) *vi.* [see LANGUID] **1.** to become weak; droop **2.** to become slack or dull **3.** to long; pine **4.** to put on a wistful air —**lan'guish·ing** *adj.* —**lan'guish·ing·ly** *adv.*

lan·guor (laŋ′gər) *n.* [see LANGUID] **1.** a lack of vigor or vitality; weakness **2.** listlessness; sluggishness **3.** tenderness of mood or feeling —**lan'guor·ous** *adj.* —**lan'guor·ous·ly** *adv.*

lank (laŋk) *adj.* [OE. *hlanc*] **1.** long and slender; lean **2.** straight and limp: said of hair —**lank'ness** *n.*

lank'y *adj.* **-i·er, -i·est** awkwardly tall and lean or long and slender —**lank'i·ness** *n.*

lan·o·lin (lan′'l in) *n.* [< L. *lana*, wool + *oleum*, oil] a fatty substance obtained from sheep wool and used in ointments, cosmetics, etc.

Lan·sing (lan′siŋ) capital of Mich.: pop. 132,000

lan·tern (lan′tərn) *n.* [< Gr. *lampein*, to shine] **1.** a transparent case for holding and shielding a light **2.** the room containing the lamp at the top of a lighthouse

lan'tern-jawed' *adj.* having long, thin jaws and sunken cheeks

lan·tha·nide series (lan′thə nīd′) [< LANTHANUM] the rare-earth group of chemical elements from element 58 (cerium) through element 71 (lutetium)

lan'tha·num (-nəm) *n.* [< Gr. *lanthanein*, be concealed] a chemical element of the rare-earth group; symbol, La; at. wt., 138.91; at. no., 57

lan·yard (lan′yərd) *n.* [< OFr. *lasne*, noose] **1.** a short rope used on board ship for holding or fastening something **2.** a cord for firing certain types of cannon

La·os (lä′ōs, lous) country in the NW part of the Indochina peninsula: 91,429 sq. mi.; pop. 2,893,000; cap. Vientiane

Lao-tse (lou′dzu′) 604? B.C.-?; Chin. philosopher: reputed founder of Taoism: also sp. **Lao-tzu, Lao-tsze**

lap¹ (lap) *n.* [OE. *læppa*] **1.** *a)* the front part from the waist to the knees of a sitting person *b)* the part of the clothing covering this **2.** that in which one is cared for, sheltered, etc. **3.** *a)* an overlapping *b)* amount or place of this **4.** one complete circuit around a race track **5.** a lapping —*vt.* **lapped, lap'ping 1.** to fold (*over* or *on*) **2.** to wrap; enfold **3.** to overlap **4.** to get a lap ahead of (an opponent) in a race —*vi.* **1.** to overlap **2.** to extend beyond something in space or time (with *over*)

lap² (lap) *vi., vt.* **lapped, lap'ping** [OE. *lapian*] **1.** to drink (a liquid) by dipping it up with the tongue as a dog does **2.** to strike gently with a light splash, as waves —*n.* **1.** a lapping **2.** the sound of lapping —**lap up** [Colloq.] to take in eagerly

La Paz (lä päs′) city & seat of government of Bolivia: pop. 482,000

lap dog a pet dog small enough to hold in the lap

la·pel (lə pel′) *n.* [dim. of LAP¹] either of the front parts of a coat folded back and forming a continuation of the collar

lap·ful (lap′fool′) *n., pl.* **-fuls'** as much as a lap can hold

lap·i·dar·y (lap′ə der′ē) *n., pl.* **-ies** [< L. *lapis*, a stone] a workman who cuts and polishes precious stones

lap·is laz·u·li (lap′is laz′yoo lī′) [< L. *lapis*, a stone + ML. *lazulus*, azure] an azure-blue, opaque, semiprecious stone

lap joint a joint made by overlapping parts: also **lapped joint** —**lap′-joint′** vt.

Lap·land (lap′land′) region in N Scandinavia, Finland, & the U.S.S.R., inhabited by the Lapps

La Pla·ta (lä plä′tä) seaport in E Argentina: pop. 337,000

Lapp (lap) n. **1.** a member of a Mongoloid people living in Lapland: also **Lapp′land′er 2.** their language

LAP JOINT

lap·pet (lap′it) n. [dim. of LAP¹] a small fold or flap, as of a garment or as of flesh

lapse (laps) n. [< L. *labi*, to slip] **1.** a small error **2.** *a)* a moral slip *b)* a falling into lower condition **3.** a passing, as of time **4.** the termination as of a privilege through failure to meet requirements —vi. **lapsed, laps′ing 1.** to slip into a specified state [to *lapse* into a coma/ **2.** to backslide **3.** to pass away: said of time **4.** to become void because of failure to meet requirements —**laps′a·ble** adj.

lap·wing (lap′wiŋ) n. [< OE. *hleapan*, to leap + *wincian*, wink] an old-world crested plover noted for its irregular, wavering flight

lar·board (lär′bərd) n., adj. [< OE. *hladan*, to lade + *bord*, side] port; left

lar·ce·ny (lär′sə nē) n., pl. **-nies** [< L. *latro*, robber] the unlawful taking of another's property; theft: sometimes differentiated as **grand larceny** (more than a stated amount) and **petit**, or **petty, larceny** (less than this amount) —**lar′ce·nous** adj.

larch (lärch) n. [< L. *larix*] **1.** a tree of the pine family, that sheds its needles annually **2.** its tough wood

lard (lärd) n. [< L. *lardum*] the fat of hogs, melted down and clarified —vt. **1.** to smear with lard, etc.; grease **2.** to put strips of fat pork, bacon, etc. on or in slits in (meat, etc.) **3.** to embellish [a talk *larded* with jokes/

lard′er n. **1.** a place where food supplies are kept; pantry **2.** a supply of food

lar·es and pe·na·tes (ler′ēz ənd pi nāt′ēz) [< L.] the household gods of the ancient Romans

large (lärj) adj. **larg′er, larg′est** [< L. *largus*] **1.** big; great; bulky, spacious, of great extent or amount, etc. **2.** bigger than others of its kind **3.** operating on a big scale [a *large* producer/ —adv. in a large way [write *large*] —**at large 1.** free; not confined **2.** fully; in detail **3.** in general **4.** representing an entire State or area rather than only a subdivision [a congressman *at large*] —**large′ness** n. — **larg′ish** adj.

large′ly adv. **1.** much; in great amounts **2.** for the most part; mainly

large′-scale′ adj. **1.** drawn to a large scale **2.** of wide scope; extensive

lar·gess, lar·gesse (lär jes′, lär′jis) n. [see LARGE] **1.** generous giving **2.** a gift generously given

lar·go (lär′gō) adj., adv. [It., slow] *Music* slow and stately —n., pl. **-gos** a largo movement

lar·i·at (lar′ē it) n. [Sp. *la reata*, the rope] **1.** a rope for tethering grazing horses, etc. **2.** a lasso

lark¹ (lärk) n. [OE. *læwerce*] any of a large family of chiefly old-world songbirds; esp., the skylark

lark² (lärk) vi. [< ? ON. *leika*] to play or frolic —n. a frolic

lark·spur (lärk′spur′) n. a common name for DELPHINIUM

lar·rup (lar′əp) vt. [prob. < Du. *larpen*] [Colloq.] to whip; flog; beat

lar·va (lär′və) n., pl. **-vae** (-vē), **-vas** [L., ghost] the early, free-living, immature form of any animal that changes structurally when it becomes an adult [the caterpillar is the *larva* of the butterfly/ —**lar′val** adj.

la·ryn·ge·al (lə rin′jē əl) adj. **1.** of, in, or near the larynx **2.** used for treating the larynx

lar·yn·gi·tis (lar′ən jīt′əs) n. inflammation of the larynx, often with a temporary loss of voice

lar·ynx (lar′iŋks) n., pl. **lar′ynx·es, la·ryn·ges** (lə rin′jēz) [< Gr.] the structure at the upper end of the trachea, containing the vocal cords

la·sa·gna (lə zän′yə) n. [It., the noodle] a dish of wide noodles baked in layers with cheese, tomato sauce, and ground meat

La Salle (lä säl′; E. lä sal′), **Ro·bert Cave·lier de** (rô ber′ käv lyā′ də) Fr. explorer in N. America

las·civ·i·ous (lə siv′ē əs) adj. [< L. *lascivus*, wanton] **1.** characterized by or expressing lust **2.** tending to excite lust —**las·civ′i·ous·ly** adv.

la·ser (lā′zər) n. [l(ight) a(mplification by) s(timulated) e(mission of) r(adiation)] a device that amplifies focused light waves and concentrates them in a narrow, very intense beam

lash¹ (lash) n. [< ?] **1.** the flexible striking part of a whip **2.** a stroke as with a whip **3.** a sharp rebuke **4.** an eyelash —vt. **1.** to strike or drive as with a whip **2.** to switch energetically [the cat *lashed* its tail/ **3.** to censure or rebuke —vi. to make strokes as with a whip —**lash out 1.** to strike out violently **2.** to speak angrily

lash² (lash) vt. [see LACE] to fasten or tie with a rope, etc.

lash′ing¹ n. **1.** a whipping **2.** a strong rebuke

lash′ing² n. **1.** the act of fastening with a rope, etc. **2.** a rope, etc. so used

lass (las) n. [prob. < ON. *løskr*, weak] a young woman

Las·sa fever (läs′ə) [< *Lassa*, Nigerian village] an acute virus disease endemic to western Africa, causing high fever and inflammation

las·sie (las′ē) n. [Scot.] a young girl

las·si·tude (las′ə tōōd′, -tyōōd′) n. [< L. *lassus*, faint] a state or feeling of being tired or weak

las·so (las′ō, -ōō) n., pl. **-sos, -soes** [< Sp. < L. *laqueus*, noose] a long rope with a sliding noose at one end, used in catching cattle, etc. —vt. **-soed, -so·ing** to catch with a lasso —**las′so·er** n.

last¹ (last) alt. superl. of LATE —adj. **1.** being or coming after all others in place or time; final **2.** only remaining **3.** most recent [last month/ **4.** least likely [the *last* person to suspect/ **5.** conclusive [the *last* word] —adv. **1.** after all others **2.** most recently **3.** finally —n. **1.** the one coming last **2.** end [friends to the *last*/ —**at (long) last** finally — **see the last of** to see for the last time

last² (last) vi. [OE. *læstan*] **1.** to remain in existence or operation; continue; endure **2.** to remain in good condition —vt. **1.** to continue during **2.** to be enough for

last³ (last) n. [< OE. *last*, footstep] a form shaped like a foot, used in making or repairing shoes

last hurrah a final attempt or appearance, as in politics

last′ing adj. that lasts a long time; durable

Last Judgment *Theol.* the final judgment of mankind at the end of the world

last′ly adv. in conclusion; finally

last straw [< the last straw that broke the camel's back in the fable] a final annoyance or trouble that results in a defeat, loss of patience, etc.

Last Supper the last supper eaten by Jesus with his disciples before the Crucifixion

last word 1. *a)* the final word or speech, regarded as settling the argument *b)* final authority **2.** something regarded as perfect **3.** [Colloq.] the very latest style

Las Ve·gas (läs vā′gəs) city in SE Nev.: pop. 126,000

lat. latitude

latch (lach) n. [< OE. *læccan*] a fastening for a door, gate, or window; esp., a bar, etc. that fits into a notch —vt., vi. to fasten with a latch —**latch onto** [Colloq.] to get or obtain

latch′key′ n. a key for drawing back or unfastening the latch of a door

latch′string′ n. a cord fastened to a latch so that it can be raised from the outside

late (lāt) adj. **lat′er** or **lat′ter, lat′est** or **last** [OE. *læt*] **1.** happening, coming, etc. after the usual or expected time, or at a time far advanced in a period [a *late* party, the *late* Middle Ages/ **2.** *a)* recent *b)* having recently died — adv. **lat′er, lat′est** or **last 1.** after the expected time **2.** at or until an advanced time of the day, year, etc. **3.** toward the end of a period **4.** recently —**of late** recently —**late′- ness** n.

la·teen (la tēn′) adj. [< Fr. (*voile*) *latine*, Latin (sail)] **1.** designating or of a triangular sail attached to a long yard suspended from a short mast **2.** having such a sail

late′ly adv. not long ago; recently

la·tent (lā′t'nt) adj. [< L. *latere*, lurk] lying hidden and undeveloped in a person or thing —**la′ten·cy** n. —**la′- tent·ly** adv.

lat·er·al (lat′ər əl) adj. [< L. *latus*, a side] of, at, from, or toward the side; sideways —n. *Football* a short pass more or

LATEEN SAIL

less parallel to the goal line: in full **lateral pass** —**lat′er·al·ly** *adv.*

la·tex (lā′teks) *n.* [L., a fluid] a milky liquid in certain plants and trees: latex is the basis of rubber

lath (lath) *n., pl.* **laths** (la*th*z, laths) [< OE. *lætt*] **1.** any of the thin, narrow strips of wood used as a groundwork for plastering, etc. **2.** any framework for plaster, as wire screening **3.** laths collectively —*vt.* to cover with lath

lathe (lā*th*) *n.* [prob. < MDu. *lade*] a machine for shaping wood, metal, etc. by holding and turning it rapidly against a cutting tool —*vt.* **lathed, lath′ing** to shape on a lathe

lath·er (lath′ər) *n.* [OE. *leathor*, soap] **1.** the foam formed by soap and water **2.** foamy sweat **3.** [Slang] an excited state —*vt., vi.* to cover with or form lather —**lath′er·y** *adj.*

Lat·in (lat′′n) *adj.* [< *Latium*, ancient country in C Italy] **1.** of ancient Rome, its people, their language, etc. **2.** designating or of the languages derived from Latin, the peoples who speak them, their countries, etc. —*n.* **1.** a native or inhabitant of ancient Rome **2.** the language of ancient Rome **3.** a person, as a Spaniard or Italian, whose language is derived from Latin

Latin America that part of the Western Hemisphere south of the U.S. where Spanish, Portuguese, and French are the official languages —**Latin American**

lat·ish (lāt′ish) *adj., adv.* somewhat late

lat·i·tude (lat′ə tōōd′, -tyōōd′) *n.* [< L. *latus*, wide] **1.** extent; scope; range **2.** freedom from narrow restrictions **3.** *a)* distance north or south from the equator, measured in degrees *b)* a region with reference to this distance —**lat′i·tu′di·nal** *adj.*

la·trine (lə trēn′) *n.* [< L. *lavare*, to wash] a toilet for the use of many people, as in an army camp

lat·ter (lat′ər) *adj. alt. compar.* of LATE **1.** *a)* later; more recent *b)* nearer the end or close **2.** being the last mentioned of two: used as a noun with *the*

lat′ter·ly *adv.* lately; recently

lat·tice (lat′is) *n.* [< MHG. *latte*, lath] **1.** an openwork structure of crossed strips of wood, metal, etc. used as a screen, support, etc. **2.** a door, shutter, etc. formed of such a structure —*vt.* **-ticed, -tic·ing 1.** to arrange like a lattice **2.** to furnish with a lattice

lat′tice·work′ *n.* **1.** a lattice **2.** lattices collectively Also **lat′tic·ing**

Lat·vi·a (lat′vē ə) republic of the U.S.S.R., in NE Europe: in full **Latvian Soviet Socialist Republic** —**Lat′vi·an** *adj., n.*

laud (lôd) *n.* [< L. *laus*] praise —*vt.* to praise

laud′a·ble *adj.* praiseworthy —**laud′a·bly** *adv.*

laud·a·num (lôd′′n əm) *n.* [< L. *ladanum*, a dark resin] **1.** formerly, any of various opium preparations **2.** a solution of opium in alcohol

lau·da·tion (lô dā′shən) *n.* praise

laud·a·to·ry (lôd′ə tôr′ē) *adj.* expressing praise; commendatory

laugh (laf) *vi.* [< OE. *hleahhan*] to make the sounds and facial movements that express mirth, ridicule, etc. —*vt.* to cause to be by means of laughter [to *laugh* oneself hoarse] —*n.* **1.** the act or sound of laughing **2.** a cause of laughter —**have the last laugh** to win after apparent defeat —**laugh at 1.** to be amused by **2.** to make fun of —**laugh off** to scorn or reject by laughter or ridicule —**laugh′er** *n.*

laugh′a·ble *adj.* amusing or ridiculous —**laugh′a·bly** *adv.*

laughing gas nitrous oxide used as an anesthetic: inhaling it may cause a reaction of laughter

laugh′ing·stock′ (-stäk′) *n.* an object of ridicule

laugh′ter (-tər) *n.* the action or sound of laughing

launch¹ (lônch) *vt.* [< L. *lancea*, lance] **1.** to hurl or send forth with some force [to *launch* a rocket] **2.** to slide (a vessel) into the water **3.** to set in operation; start [to *launch* an attack] **4.** to start (a person) on some course —*vi.* **1.** *a)* to put to sea *b)* to begin something new With *out* or *forth* **2.** to plunge (*into*) —*n.* a launching of a ship, spacecraft, etc. —*adj.* designating or of facilities, sites, etc. used in launching spacecraft or missiles —**launch′er** *n.*

launch² (lônch) *n.* [Sp. or Port. *lancha*] **1.** formerly, the largest boat carried by a warship **2.** an open, or partly enclosed, motorboat

launch pad the platform from which a rocket, guided missile, etc. is launched: also **launching pad**

launch window a time period during which conditions are favorable for launching a spacecraft

laun·der (lôn′dər) *vt.* [< L. *lavare*, to wash] to wash, or wash and iron, (clothes, etc.) —*vi.* **1.** to withstand washing [this fabric *launders* well] **2.** to do laundry —**laun′der·er** *n.* —**laun′dress** (-dris) *n.fem.*

Laun·dro·mat (lôn′drə mat′) *a service mark for* a self-service laundry —*n.* [l-] such a laundry

laun·dry (lôn′drē) *n., pl.* **-dries 1.** a place for laundering **2.** clothes, etc. laundered or to be laundered

laun′dry·man (-mən) *n., pl.* **-men** a man who works for a laundry, esp. one who collects and delivers laundry

lau·re·ate (lôr′ē it) *adj.* [< L. *laurus*, laurel] honored, as with a crown of laurel —*n. same as* POET LAUREATE —**lau′re·ate·ship′** *n.*

lau·rel (lôr′əl) *n.* [< L. *laurus*] **1.** an evergreen tree or shrub of S Europe, with large, glossy leaves **2.** its foliage, esp. as woven into crowns for victors in contests in ancient Greece **3.** [*pl.*] *a)* fame; honor *b)* victory **4.** a tree or shrub resembling the true laurel, as the mountain laurel —**rest on one's laurels** to be satisfied with what one has already achieved

Lau·ren·tian Mountains (lô ren′shən) mountain range in S Quebec, Canada, extending along the St. Lawrence River valley

la·va (lä′və, lav′ə) *n.* [It. < L. *labi*, to slide] **1.** melted rock issuing from a volcano **2.** such rock when solidified by cooling

lav·a·liere, lav·a·lier (lav′ə lir′, lä′və-) *n.* [< Fr.] an ornament hanging from a chain, worn around the neck

lav·a·to·ry (lav′ə tôr′ē) *n., pl.* **-ries** [< L. *lavare*, to wash] **1.** a washbowl with faucets and drain **2.** a room with a washbowl and a toilet

lave (lāv) *vt., vi.* **laved, lav′ing** [< L. *lavare*] [Poet.] to wash; bathe

lav·en·der (lav′ən dər) *n.* [< ML. *lavandria*] **1.** a fragrant European mint with spikes of pale-purplish flowers that yield an aromatic oil (**oil of lavender**) **2.** its dried flowers and leaves, used to perfume clothes, etc. **3.** a pale purple —*adj.* pale-purple

lav·ish (lav′ish) *adj.* [< OFr. *lavasse*, downpour] **1.** very generous; prodigal **2.** very abundant —*vt.* to give or spend liberally —**lav′ish·ly** *adv.*

law (lô) *n.* [OE. *lagu*] **1.** *a)* all the rules of conduct established by the authority or custom of a nation, etc. *b)* any one of such rules **2.** obedience to such rules **3.** the study of such rules; jurisprudence **4.** the seeking of justice in courts under such rules **5.** the profession of lawyers, judges, etc. **6.** *a)* a sequence of natural events occurring with unvarying uniformity under the same conditions *b)* the stating of such a sequence **7.** any rule expected to be observed [the *laws* of health] **8.** *Eccles.* a divine commandment **9.** *Math.* a general principle [the *laws* of exponents] —**lay down the law 1.** to give orders authoritatively **2.** to give a scolding (*to*) —**the Law 1.** the Mosaic code, or the part of the Bible containing it **2.** [l-] [Colloq.] a policeman or the police

law′-a·bid′ing *adj.* obeying the law

law′break′er *n.* one who violates the law —**law′break′ing** *adj., n.*

law′ful *adj.* **1.** in conformity with the law **2.** recognized by law [lawful debts] —**law′ful·ly** *adv.* —**law′ful·ness** *n.*

law′giv′er *n.* one who draws up a code of laws for a nation or people; lawmaker

law′less *adj.* **1.** not regulated by the authority of law **2.** not in conformity with law; illegal **3.** not obeying the law; unruly —**law′less·ness** *n.*

law′mak′er *n.* one who makes or helps to make laws; esp., a legislator —**law′mak′ing** *adj., n.*

lawn¹ (lôn) *n.* [< OFr. *launde*, heath] land covered with grass kept closely mowed, esp. around a house

lawn² (lôn) *n.* [< *Laon*, city in France] a fine, sheer cloth of linen or cotton

lawn mower a hand-propelled or power-driven machine for cutting the grass of a lawn

lawn tennis *see* TENNIS

law·ren·ci·um (lô ren′sē əm) *n.* [< E. O. *Lawrence* (1901-58), U.S. physicist] a radioactive chemical element produced by nuclear bombardment of californium: symbol, Lr; at. wt., 256(?); at. no., 103

law′suit′ (-sōōt′) *n.* a suit between private parties in a law court

law·yer (lô′yər) *n.* one whose profession is advising others in matters of law or representing them in lawsuits

lax (laks) *adj.* [< L. *laxus*] **1.** loose; slack; not tight **2.** not strict or exact —**lax′ly** *adv.* —**lax′ness** *n.*

lax·a·tive (lak′sə tiv) *adj.* [see LAX] making the bowels loose and relieving constipation —*n.* any laxative medicine

lax′i·ty *n.* lax quality or condition

lay¹ (lā) *vt.* **laid, lay′ing** [< OE. *lecgan*] **1.** to cause to fall with force; knock down **2.** to place or put in a resting position (with *on* or *in*) [lay the pen on the desk] **3.** to put down (bricks, carpeting, etc.) in the correct position or way **4.** to situate; set [the scene is *laid* in France] **5.** to place; put; set [to *lay* emphasis on accuracy] **6.** to produce (an egg) **7.** to allay, overcome, etc. **8.** to bet (a specified sum, etc.) **9.** to devise [to *lay* plans] **10.** to present or assert [to *lay* claim to property] —*n.* the way or position in which something is situated [the *lay* of the land] —**lay aside** to set aside for future use; save: also **lay away, lay by** —**lay for** [Colloq.] to be waiting to attack —**lay in** to get and store away —**lay it on (thick)** [Colloq.] **1.** to exaggerate **2.** to flatter effusively —**lay off 1.** to discharge (an employee), esp. temporarily **2.** [Slang] to cease —**lay open 1.** to cut open **2.** to expose —**lay out 1.** to spend **2.** to arrange according to a plan **3.** to spread out (clothes, etc.) ready for wear —**lay over** to stop a while in a place before going on —**lay up 1.** to store for future use **2.** to confine to a sickbed

lay² (lā) *pt. of* LIE¹

lay³ (lā) *adj.* [< Gr. *laos,* the people] **1.** of a layman **2.** not belonging to a given profession

lay⁴ (lā) *n.* [ME. *lai*] **1.** a short poem, esp. a narrative poem, for singing **2.** [Archaic] a song

lay analyst a psychoanalyst who is not a medical doctor

lay·a·way' plan a method of buying by making a deposit on something which is delivered only after it is paid for in full

lay'er *n.* **1.** a person or thing that lays **2.** a single thickness, coat, fold, etc.

lay·ette (lā et') *n.* [< MDu. *lade,* chest] a complete outfit of clothes, bedding, etc. for a newborn baby

lay·man (lā'mən) *n., pl.* **-men** a person not belonging to the clergy or to a given profession

lay·off (lā'ôf') *n.* a laying off; esp., temporary unemployment, or the period of this

lay'out' *n.* **1.** the manner in which anything is laid out; specif., the makeup of a newspaper, advertisement, etc. **2.** the thing laid out

lay'o'ver *n.* a stop during a journey

Laz·a·rus (laz'ə rəs) *Bible* **a)** a man raised from the dead by Jesus **b)** the diseased beggar in Jesus' parable about the rich man and the beggar

laze (lāz) *vi., vt.* **lazed, laz'ing** to idle; loaf

la·zy (lā'zē) *adj.* **-zi·er, -zi·est** [prob. < MLowG. or MDu.] **1.** not eager or willing to work or exert oneself **2.** slow and heavy; sluggish —**la'zi·ly** *adv.* —**la'zi·ness** *n.*

la'zy·bones' *n.* [Colloq.] a lazy person

Lazy Su·san (soo'z'n) a revolving tray for food

lb. [L. *libra,* pl. *librae*] pound; pounds

lbs. pounds

l.c. 1. [L. *loco citato*] in the place cited **2.** *Printing* lower case

lea (lē) *n.* [OE. *leah*] [Chiefly Poet.] a meadow or grassy field

leach (lēch) *vt.* [prob. < OE. *leccan,* to water] **1.** to wash (wood ashes, etc.) with a filtering liquid **2.** to extract (a soluble substance) from some material —*vi.* **1.** to lose soluble matter through a filtering liquid **2.** to dissolve and be washed away

lead¹ (lēd) *vt.* **led, lead'ing** [OE. *lædan*] **1.** to direct, as by going before or along with, by physical contact, pulling a rope, etc.; guide **2.** to direct by influence to some action or thought **3.** to be the head of (an expedition, orchestra, etc.) **4.** to be at the head of [to *lead* one's class] **5.** to be ahead of in a contest **6.** to guide the course of (water, steam, etc.) **7.** to live; spend [to *lead* a full life] **8.** *Card Games* to begin the play with (a card or suit) —*vi.* **1.** to show the way, as by going before **2.** to tend in a certain direction (with *to, from,* etc.) **3.** to bring as a result (with *to*) [hate *led* to war] **4.** to be or go first **5.** *Card Games* to play the first card —*n.* **1.** the role or example of a leader **2.** first or front place **3.** the amount or distance ahead [to hold a safe *lead*] **4.** anything that leads, as a clue **5.** a principal role in a play, etc. **6.** the opening paragraph of a news story **7.** the right of playing first in cards, or the card played **8.** *Elec.* a wire carrying current in a circuit —*adj.* acting as leader [the *lead* horse] —**lead off** to begin —**lead on** to lure —**lead up to** to prepare the way for

lead² (led) *n.* [OE.] **1.** a heavy, soft, bluish-gray metallic chemical element used for piping, etc.: symbol, Pb; at. wt., 207.19; at. no., 82 **2.** a weight for sounding depths at sea, etc. **3.** bullets **4.** a thin stick of graphite, used in pencils —*adj.* made of or containing lead —*vt.* to cover, line, or weight with lead

lead·en (led''n) *adj.* **1.** made of lead **2.** heavy **3.** sluggish **4.** gloomy **5.** of a dull gray

lead·er (lē'dər) *n.* **1.** a person or thing that leads; guiding head **2.** a pipe for carrying fluid **3.** a featured, low-priced article of trade **4.** a short piece of catgut, etc. attaching the hook, lure, etc. to a fish line —**lead'er·ship'** *n.*

lead-in (lēd'in') *n.* **1.** the wire leading from an aerial or antenna to a receiver or transmitter **2.** an introduction —*adj.* that is a lead-in

lead·ing (lē'diŋ) *n.* direction; guidance —*adj.* **1.** that leads; guiding **2.** principal; chief

lead time (lēd) the period of time needed from the decision to make a product to the start of production

leaf (lēf) *n., pl.* **leaves** (lēvz) [OE.] **1.** any of the flat, thin parts, usually green, growing from the stem of a plant **2.** a petal **3.** leaves collectively [choice tobacco *leaf*] **4.** a sheet of paper **5.** a thin sheet of metal **6.** a hinged or removable section of a table top —*vi.* **1.** to bear leaves **2.** to turn the pages of a book, etc. (with *through*) —**in leaf** with foliage —**turn over a new leaf** to make a new start —**leaf'less** *adj.* —**leaf'like'** *adj.*

leaf'age (-ij) *n.* leaves collectively; foliage

leaf'let (-lit) *n.* **1.** a small or young leaf **2.** a separate sheet of printed matter, often folded

leaf'stalk' (-stôk') *n.* the part of a leaf that supports the blade and is attached to the stem

leaf'y *adj.* **-i·er, -i·est 1.** of or like a leaf **2.** having many leaves **3.** having broad leaves, as spinach —**leaf'i·ness** *n.*

league¹ (lēg) *n.* [< L. *ligare,* bind] **1.** an association of nations, groups, etc. for promoting common interests **2.** *Sports* a group of teams formed to play one another —*vt., vi.* **leagued, leagu'ing** to form into a league —**in league** allied —**leagu'er** *n.*

league² (lēg) *n.* [ult. < Celt.] a measure of distance, about 3 miles

League of Nations an association of nations (1920–46) to promote international cooperation

Le·ah (lē'ə) *Bible* the elder of the sisters who were wives of Jacob

leak (lēk) *vi.* [< ON. *leka,* to drip] **1.** to let a fluid out or in accidentally **2.** to enter or escape in this way, as a fluid **3.** to become known gradually, accidentally, etc. [the truth *leaked* out] —*vt.* **1.** to allow to leak —*n.* **1.** an accidental hole or crack that lets something out or in **2.** any accidental means of escape **3.** leakage **4.** *a)* a loss of electrical charge through faulty insulation *b)* the point where this occurs —**leak'y** *adj.*

leak'age (-ij) *n.* **1.** a leaking; leak **2.** something that leaks in or out **3.** the amount that leaks

lean¹ (lēn) *vi.* **leaned** or **leant** (lent), **lean'ing** [OE. *hlinian*] **1.** to bend or slant from an upright position **2.** to bend the body and rest part of one's weight on something **3.** to rely (*on* or *upon*) **4.** to tend (*toward* or *to*) —*vt.* to cause to lean

lean² (lēn) *adj.* [OE. *hlæne*] **1.** with little flesh or fat; thin; spare **2.** containing little or no fat: said of meat **3.** meager —*n.* meat containing little or no fat —**lean'ness** *n.*

lean'ing *n.* tendency; inclination

lean'-to' *n., pl.* **-tos'** a structure whose sloping roof abuts a wall or building

leap (lēp) *vi.* **leaped** or **leapt** (lept, lēpt), **leap'ing** [OE. *hleapan*] **1.** to jump; spring; bound **2.** to accept eagerly something offered (with *at*) —*vt.* **1.** to pass over by a jump **2.** to cause to leap —*n.* **1.** a jump; spring **2.** the distance covered in a jump **3.** a place that is, or is to be, leaped over or from **4.** a sudden transition —**leap'er** *n.*

leap'frog' *n.* a game in which each player in turn leaps over the bent backs of the others —*vt., vi.* **-frogged', -frog'ging** to leap or jump in or as in this way; skip (*over*)

leap year a year of 366 days, occurring every fourth year: the additional day is February 29

learn (lurn) *vt., vi.* **learned** (lurnd) or **learnt** (lurnt), **learn'ing** [OE. *leornian*] **1.** to get knowledge of or skill in (an art, trade, etc.) by study, experience, etc. **2.** to come to know; hear (*of* or *about*) **3.** to memorize —**learn'er** *n.*

learn·ed (lur'nid) *adj.* **1.** having or showing much learning **2.** of or characterized by study or learning **3.** (lurnd) acquired by study, experience, etc. [a *learned* response] —**learn'ed·ly** *adv.*

learn'ing *n.* **1.** the acquiring of knowledge or skill **2.** acquired knowledge or skill

lease (lēs) *n.* [< L. *laxus,* loose] a contract by which a landlord rents lands, buildings, etc. to a tenant for a specified time —*vt.* **leased, leas'ing** to give or get by a lease

at, āpe, cär; ten, ēven; is, bīte; gō, hôrn, tōōl, look; oil, out; up, fur; thin, *th*en; zh, leisure; ŋ, ring; ə for *a* in *ago*; as in *able* (ā'b'l); ë, Fr. coeur; ö, Fr. feu; ô, Fr. mon; ü, Fr. duc; r, Fr. cri; kh, G. doch, ich. ‡ foreign; < derived from

leash (lēsh) *n.* [< L. *laxus*, loose] a cord, strap, etc. by which a dog or other animal is held in check —*vt.* to check or control as by a leash —**hold in leash** to control

least (lēst) *alt. superl. of* LITTLE —*adj.* [OE. *læst*] smallest in size, degree, etc. —*adv.* in the smallest degree —*n.* the smallest in amount, importance, etc. —**at (the) least 1.** with no less **2.** at any rate —**not in the least** not at all

least'wise' (-wīz') *adv.* [Colloq.] at least; anyway: also **least'ways'**

leath·er (leth'ər) *n.* [< OE. *lether-*] animal skin prepared for use by removing the hair and tanning —*adj.* of or made of leather

leath'ern (-ərn) *adj.* **1.** made of leather **2.** like leather

leath'er·neck' *n.* [< former leather-lined collar] [Slang] a U.S. marine

leath'er·y *adj.* like leather; tough and flexible

leave (lēv) *vt.* **left, leav'ing** [OE. *læfan*, let remain] **1.** to allow to remain [*leave* a sip for me, *leave* it open] **2.** to have remaining behind or after one [he *leaves* a widow] **3.** to bequeath **4.** to go away from **5.** to abandon **6.** to stop working for, belonging to, etc. **7.** [Dial. or Slang] to let or allow [*leave* us go] —*vi.* to go away or set out —**leave off 1.** to stop **2.** to stop doing or using —**leave (one) alone** to refrain from bothering (one) —**leave out** to omit

leave² (lēv) *n.* [OE. *leaf*] **1.** permission **2.** *a)* permission to be absent from duty *b)* the period for which this is granted —**on leave** absent from duty with permission —**take leave of** to say goodbye to —**take one's leave** to depart

leave³ (lēv) *vi.* **leaved, leav'ing** to put forth, or bear, leaves; leaf

leav·en (lev''n) *n.* [< L. *levare*, raise] **1.** a small piece of fermenting dough used to produce fermentation in a fresh batch of dough **2.** *same as* LEAVENING —*vt.* **1.** to make (batter or dough) rise **2.** to spread through, causing a gradual change

leav'en·ing *n.* **1.** a substance, such as yeast, used to make batter or dough rise by forming gas: also **leavening agent 2.** any influence working to cause gradual change

leave of absence a leave from work or duty, esp. for a long time; also, the period of time

leaves (lēvz) *n. pl. of* LEAF

leave'-tak'ing *n.* the act of taking leave, or saying goodbye

leav·ings (lēv'iŋz) *n.pl.* things left over; leftovers, remnants, refuse, etc.

Leb·a·non (leb'ə nən) country in SW Asia, on the Mediterranean: c.4,000 sq. mi.; pop. 2,367,000; cap. Beirut —**Leb'a·nese'** (-nēz') *adj., n., pl.* **-nese'**

lech·er (lech'ər) *n.* [OFr. *lechier*, live debauchedly] a lustful, grossly sensual man —**lech'er·ous** *adj.* —**lech'er·ous·ly** *adv.* —**lech'er·y** *n.*

lec·i·thin (les'ə thin) *n.* [< Gr. *lekithos*, egg yolk] a fatty compound found in nerve tissue, blood, egg yolk, etc. and plant cells: used in medicines, foods, etc.

lec·tern (lek'tərn) *n.* [< L. *legere*, read] **1.** a reading desk in a church **2.** a stand for holding the notes, speech, etc. of a lecturer

lec·ture (lek'chər) *n.* [< L. *legere*, read] **1.** an informative talk given before an audience, class, etc. **2.** a lengthy scolding —*vt., vi.* **-tured, -tur·ing 1.** to give a lecture (to) **2.** to scold —**lec'tur·er** *n.*

led (led) *pt. & pp. of* LEAD¹

ledge (lej) *n.* [ME. *legge*] **1.** a shelf or shelflike projection **2.** a projecting ridge of rocks

ledg·er (lej'ər) *n.* [ME. *legger*] *Bookkeeping* a book of final entry, in which a record of debits, credits, and all money transactions is kept

lee (lē) *n.* [OE. *hleo*, shelter] **1.** shelter **2.** *Naut.* the side or part away from the wind —*adj.* of or on the side away from the wind

Lee (lē), **Robert E.** 1807-70; commander of the Confederate Army

leech (lēch) *n.* [OE. *læce*] **1.** a bloodsucking worm living in water and used, esp. formerly, to bleed patients **2.** a person who is a parasite —*vt.* to bleed with leeches —*vi.* to act as a parasite

leek (lēk) *n.* [OE. *leac*] a vegetable that resembles a thick green onion

leer (lir) *n.* [OE. *hleor*] a sly, sidelong look showing lust, malicious triumph, etc. —*vi.* to look with a leer —**leer'ing·ly** *adv.*

LEECH
(3 in. long)

leer·y (lir'ē) *adj.* **-i·er, -i·est** wary; suspicious

lees (lēz) *n.pl.* [< ML. *lia*] dregs or sediment, as of wine

lee·ward (lē'wərd; *naut.* lōo'ərd) *adj.* in the direction toward which the wind blows —*n.* the lee part or side —*adv.* toward the lee Opposed to WINDWARD

Lee·ward Islands (lē'wərd) N group of islands in the Lesser Antilles of the West Indies

lee·way (lē'wā') *n.* **1.** leeward drift of a ship or aircraft from its course **2.** [Colloq.] *a)* margin of time, money, etc. *b)* room for freedom of action

left¹ (left) *adj.* [< OE. *lyft*, weak] **1.** designating or of that side toward the west when one faces north **2.** closer to the left side of one facing the thing mentioned —*n.* **1.** the left side **2.** *Boxing* a blow with the left hand **3.** [*often* L-] *Politics* a radical or liberal position, party, etc. (often with *the*) —*adv.* on or toward the left hand or side

left² (left) *pt. & pp. of* LEAVE¹

left'-hand' *adj.* **1.** on or directed toward the left **2.** of, for, or with the left hand

left'-hand'ed *adj.* **1.** using the left hand more skillfully than the right **2.** done with or made for use with the left hand **3.** clumsy; awkward **4.** insincere or ambiguous [a *left-handed* compliment] —*adv.* with the left hand [to write *left-handed*] —**left'-hand'ed·ly** *adv.* —**left'-hand'ed·ness** *n.*

left'ist *n., adj.* radical or liberal

left'o·ver *n.* something left over, as from a meal —*adj.* remaining unused, uneaten, etc.

left wing the more radical or liberal section of a political party, group, etc. —**left'-wing'** *adj.* —**left'-wing'er** *n.*

left'y *n., pl.* **-ies** [Slang] a left-handed person: often used as a nickname

leg (leg) *n.* [ON. *leggr*] **1.** one of the parts of the body by means of which men and animals stand and walk **2.** the part of a garment covering the leg **3.** anything like a leg in shape or use, as one of the supports of a piece of furniture **4.** any of the stages of a journey **5.** either of the sides of a triangle other than its base or other than its hypotenuse —*vi.* **legged, leg'ging** [Colloq.] to walk or run: chiefly in the phrase **leg it** —**pull someone's leg** [Colloq.] to make fun of or fool one —**shake a leg** [Slang] to hurry —**stretch one's legs** to walk, esp. after sitting a long time —**leg'less** *adj.*

leg. 1. legal **2.** legislative **3.** legislature

leg·a·cy (leg'ə sē) *n., pl.* **-cies** [ult. < L. *lex*, law] **1.** money or property left to someone by a will **2.** anything handed down as from an ancestor

le·gal (lē'g'l) *adj.* [< L. *lex*, law] **1.** of, based on, or authorized by law **2.** permitted by law **3.** of or for lawyers —**le'gal·ly** *adv.*

le·gal·ese (lē'gə lēz') *n.* the special vocabulary and formulations of legal forms, documents, etc.

legal holiday a holiday set by law

le'gal·ism *n.* strict or too strict adherence to the law —**le'gal·ist** *n.* —**le'gal·is'tic** *adj.*

le·gal·i·ty (li gal'ə tē) *n., pl.* **-ties** quality, condition, or instance of being legal or lawful

le·gal·ize (lē'gə līz') *vt.* **-ized', -iz'ing** to make legal or lawful —**le'gal·i·za'tion** *n.*

legal tender money that may be legally offered and must be accepted in payment of an obligation

leg·ate (leg'it) *n.* [< L. *lex*, law] an envoy, esp. one officially representing the Pope

leg·a·tee (leg'ə tē') *n.* one to whom a legacy is bequeathed

le·ga·tion (li gā'shən) *n.* **1.** a diplomatic minister and his staff, ranking just below an embassy **2.** their headquarters

le·ga·to (li gät'ō) *adj., adv.* [< It. *legare*, to tie] *Music* in a smooth, even style, with no breaks between notes

leg·end (lej'ənd) *n.* [< L. *legere*, read] **1.** a story or body of stories handed down for generations and popularly believed to have a historical basis **2.** a notable person or the stories of his exploits **3.** an inscription on a coin, etc. **4.** a title, key, etc. accompanying an illustration or map

leg·end·ar·y (lej'ən der'ē) *adj.* of, based on, or presented in a legend or legends; traditional

leg'end·ry (-drē) *n.* legends collectively

leg·er·de·main (lej'ər di mān') *n.* [< MFr. *leger de main*, light of hand] **1.** sleight of hand; tricks of a stage magician **2.** trickery

leg·er line (lej'ər) [< *ledger line*] *Music* a short line written above or below the staff, for notes beyond the range of the staff

leg·ged (leg'id, legd) *adj.* having (a specified number of a kind of) legs [long-*legged*]

leg·ging (leg'iŋ) *n.* a covering of canvas, leather, etc. for protecting the leg below the knee

leg·horn (leg′hôrn, -ərn) *n.* [< *Leghorn*, It. seaport] [*often* L-] any of a breed of small chicken

leg·i·ble (lej′ə b'l) *adj.* [< L. *legere*, read] that can be read, esp. easily —**leg′i·bil′i·ty** *n.* —**leg′i·bly** *adv.*

le·gion (lē′jən) *n.* [< L. *legere*, to select] 1. *Rom. History* a military division of from 3,000 to 6,000 foot soldiers, with additional cavalrymen 2. a large group of soldiers; army 3. a large number; multitude —**le′gion·ar′y** *adj., n.*

le′gion·naire′ (-jə ner′) *n.* [< Fr.] a member of a legion

leg·is·late (lej′is lāt′) *vi.* -lat′ed, -lat′ing [see ff.] to make or pass a law or laws —*vt.* to cause to be, go, etc. by making laws —**leg′is·la′tor** *n.*

leg′is·la′tion *n.* [< L. *lex*, law + *latio*, a bringing] 1. the making of laws 2. the law or laws made

leg′is·la′tive *adj.* 1. of legislation or a legislature 2. having the power to make laws —**leg′is·la′tive·ly** *adv.*

leg′is·la′ture (-chər) *n.* a body of persons given the power to make laws for a country, State, etc.

le·git·i·mate (lə jit′ə mit) *adj.* [< L. *lex*, law] 1. born of parents married to each other 2. lawful 3. ruling by the rights of heredity 4. *a*) logically correct; reasonable *b*) justifiable 5. conforming to accepted rules, standards, etc. 6. of stage plays, as distinguished from motion pictures, etc. —*vt.* (-māt′) -mat′ed, -mat′ing *same as* LEGITIMIZE —**le·git′i·ma·cy** (-mə sē) *n.* —**le·git′i·mate·ly** *adv.*

le·git′i·ma·tize (-mə tīz′) *vt.* -tized, -tiz′ing *same as* LEGITIMIZE

le·git′i·mize (-mīz′) *vt.* -mized′, -miz′ing 1. to make or declare legitimate 2. to legalize, authorize, justify, etc.

leg·man (leg′man′) *n., pl.* -men′ a reporter who turns in news from on the scene

leg′room′ *n.* adequate space for the legs while seated, as in a car

leg·ume (leg′yoom, li gyoom′) *n.* [< L. *legere*, gather] 1. any of a large family of plants having seeds growing in pods, including peas, beans, etc. 2. the pod or seed of such a plant —**le·gu·mi·nous** (li gyoo′min əs) *adj.*

leg′work′ *n.* [Colloq.] necessary routine travel as part of a job

Le Ha·vre (lə häv′rə) seaport in NW France, on the English Channel: pop. 200,000

lei (lā, lā′ē) *n., pl.* **leis** [Haw.] in Hawaii, a wreath of flowers and leaves

Leib·niz (līp′nits), Baron Gott·fried Wil·helm von (gôt′frēt vil′helm fôn) 1646-1716; Ger. philosopher: also sp. **Leib′nitz**

Leip·zig (līp′sig) city in SC East Germany: pop. 592,000

lei·sure (lē′zhər, lezh′ər) *n.* [< L. *licere*, be permitted] free time during which one may indulge in rest, recreation, etc. —*adj.* 1. free and unoccupied [*leisure* time] 2. having much leisure [the *leisure* class] —**at leisure** 1. having free time 2. with no hurry 3. not occupied or engaged

lei′sure·ly *adj.* without haste; slow —*adv.* in an unhurried manner —**lei′sure·li·ness** *n.*

leit·mo·tif, leit·mo·tiv (līt′mō tēf′) *n.* [< G. *leiten*, to LEAD[1] + *motiv*, motif] 1. a short musical phrase representing and recurring with a given character, situation, etc. in an opera 2. a dominant theme

lem·ming (lem′iŋ) *n.* [Dan. < ON. *læmingi*] a small arctic rodent with a short tail

lem·on (lem′ən) *n.* [< Per. *līmūn*] 1. a small, sour, pale-yellow citrus fruit 2. the spiny, semitropical tree that it grows on 3. [Slang] something that is defective —*adj.* 1. pale-yellow 2. made with or flavored like lemon —**lem′on·y** *adj.*

lem′on·ade′ (-ə nād′) *n.* a drink made of lemon juice, sugar, and water

le·mur (lē′mər) *n.* [< L. *lemures*, ghosts] a small primate related to the monkeys, with large eyes and soft fur

lend (lend) *vt.* lent, lend′ing [< OE. *læn*, a loan] 1. to let another use or have (a thing) temporarily 2. to let out (money) at interest 3. to give; impart [to *lend* an air of mystery] —*vi.* to make a loan or loans —**lend itself** (or **oneself**) to be useful for or open to —**lend′er** *n.*

lend′-lease′ *n.* in World War II, material aid granted countries whose defense the U.S. deemed vital

length (leŋkth) *n.* [< OE. *lang*, long] 1. the distance from end to end of a thing 2. extent in space or time 3. a long stretch or extent 4. the state or fact of being long 5. a piece of a certain length —**at length** 1. finally 2. in full

length′en *vt., vi.* to make or become longer

length′wise′ (-wīz′) *adv., adj.* in the direction of the length: also **length′ways′** (-wāz′)

length′y *adj.* -i·er, -i·est long; esp., too long —**length′i·ly** *adv.* —**length′i·ness** *n.*

le·ni·ent (lē′ni ənt, lēn′yənt) *adj.* [< L. *lenis*, soft] not harsh or severe; merciful —**le′ni·en·cy, le′ni·ence** *n.* —**le′ni·ent·ly** *adv.*

Len·in (len′in), **V. I.** (also called *Nikolai Lenin*) 1870-1924; Russ. leader of the Communist revolution of 1917; premier of the U.S.S.R. (1917-24)

Len·in·grad (len′in grad′) seaport in NW R.S.F.S.R.: pop. 3,752,000

len·i·tive (len′ə tiv) *adj.* [< L. *lenire*, soften] lessening pain or distress; soothing

lens (lenz) *n.* [L., lentil: < its shape] 1. a curved piece of glass, plastic, etc. for bringing together or spreading rays of light passing through it: used in optical instruments to form an image 2. any device used to focus microwaves, sound waves, etc. 3. a transparent body of the eye: it focuses upon the retina light rays entering the pupil

Lent (lent) *n.* [OE. *lengten*, the spring] *Christianity* the forty weekdays of fasting and penitence, from Ash Wednesday to Easter —**Lent′en, lent′en** *adj.*

lent (lent) *pt. & pp. of* LEND

len·til (lent′'l) *n.* [< L. *lens*] 1. a leguminous plant, with small, edible seeds 2. this seed

len·to (len′tō) *adv., adj.* [It. < L. *lentus*, slow] *Music* slow

Le·o (lē′ō) [L., lion] 1. a N constellation 2. the fifth sign of the zodiac: see ZODIAC, illus.

le·o·nine (lē′ə nīn′) *adj.* [< L. *leo*, lion] of or like a lion

leop·ard (lep′ərd) *n.* [< Gr. *leōn*, lion + *pardos*, panther] 1. a large, wild animal of the cat family, with a black-spotted tawny coat, found in Africa and Asia 2. *same as* JAGUAR

le·o·tard (lē′ə tärd′) *n.* [< J. *Léotard*, 19th-c. Fr. aerial performer] a tightfitting garment for the torso, worn by acrobats, dancers, etc.

lep·er (lep′ər) *n.* [< Gr. *lepros*, scaly] a person having leprosy

lep·i·dop·ter·an (lep′ə däp′tər ən) *n.* [< Gr. *lepis*, a scale + *pteron*, a wing] any of a large group of insects, including the butterflies and moths, having two pairs of broad, membranous wings covered with very fine scales —**lep′i·dop′ter·ous** *adj.*

lep·re·chaun (lep′rə kôn′) *n.* [< OIr. *lu*, little + *corp*, body] *Ir. Folklore* a fairy who can reveal a buried crock of gold to anyone who catches him

lep·ro·sy (lep′rə sē) *n.* [see LEPER] a chronic infectious disease of the skin, flesh, nerves, etc., characterized by ulcers, white scaly scabs, deformities, etc. —**lep′rous** *adj.*

les·bi·an (lez′bē ən) *n.* [< *Lesbos*, Gr. island home of Sappho] a homosexual woman —**les′bi·an·ism** *n.*

lese maj·es·ty (lēz′ maj′is tē) [< Fr.] 1. a crime against the sovereign; treason 2. any lack of proper respect, as toward one in authority

le·sion (lē′zhən) *n.* [< L. *laedere*, to harm] an injury of an organ or tissue resulting in impairment of function

Le·so·tho (le sut′hō, -sō′thō) country in SE Africa: 11,716 sq. mi.; pop. 997,000

less (les) *adj. alt. compar. of* LITTLE [OE. *læs(sa)*] not so much, so great, etc.; smaller; fewer —*adv. compar. of* LITTLE to a smaller extent —*n.* a smaller amount —*prep.* minus —**less and less** decreasingly

-less [OE. *leas*, free] a suffix meaning: 1. without, lacking [*valueless*] 2. that does not [*tireless*] 3. that cannot be [*dauntless*]

les·see (les ē′) *n.* [see LEASE] one to whom a lease is given; tenant

less·en (les′'n) *vt., vi.* to make or become less; decrease, diminish, etc.

less·er (les′ər) *adj. alt. compar. of* LITTLE smaller, less, or less important —*adv.* less

les·son (les′'n) *n.* [< L. *legere*, to read] 1. an exercise for a student to learn 2. something learned for one's safety, etc. 3. [*pl.*] course of instruction 4. a selection read from the Bible 5. a rebuke; reproof

les·sor (les′ôr) *n.* [see LEASE] one who gives a lease; landlord

lest (lest) *conj.* [< OE. *thy læs the*, by the less that] 1. for fear that [speak low *lest* you be overheard] 2. that: used after expressions denoting fear

let[1] (let) *vt.* let, let′ting [OE. *lætan*, leave behind] 1. to leave: now only in **let alone** (or **let be**), to refrain from bothering, etc. 2. *a*) to rent *b*) to assign (a contract) 3. to cause to escape [to *let* blood] 4. to allow; permit Also used as an auxiliary in commands or suggestions [*let* us go] —*vi.* to be rented —**let down 1.** to lower **2.** to slow up **3.** to disappoint —**let off 1.** to give forth **2.** to deal leniently with —**let on** [Colloq.] **1.** to pretend **2.** to indicate one's awareness —**let out 1.** to release **2.** to rent out **3.** to make a garment larger —**let up 1.** to relax **2.** to cease

let² (let) *n.* [< OE. *lettan*, make late] **1.** an obstacle or impediment: used in **without let or hindrance 2.** in tennis, etc., an interference with the ball, making it necessary to play the point over again

-let [< MFr. *-el* + *-et*, dim. suffixes] *a suffix meaning:* **1.** small [*ringlet*] **2.** a small object worn as a band on [*armlet*]

let'down' *n.* **1.** a slowing up **2.** the descent of an airplane about to land **3.** a disappointment

le·thal (lē'thəl) *adj.* [< L. *letum*, death] **1.** causing death; fatal **2.** of or suggestive of death

le·thar·gic (li thär'jik) *adj.* **1.** of or producing lethargy **2.** abnormally drowsy or dull, sluggish, etc. —**le·thar'gi·cal·ly** *adv.*

leth·ar·gy (leth'ər jē) *n., pl.* **-gies** [< Gr. *lēthē*, oblivion + *argos*, idle] **1.** an abnormal drowsiness **2.** sluggishness; apathy

Le·the (lē'thē) [< Gr. *lēthē*, oblivion] *Gr. & Rom. Myth.* the river in Hades whose water produced loss of memory in those who drank it —*n.* oblivion; forgetfulness —**Le·the·an** (lē thē'ən) *adj.*

let's (lets) let us

Lett (let) *n.* a member of a people living in Latvia and adjacent Baltic regions —**Let'tish** *adj., n.*

let·ter (let'ər) *n.* [< L. *littera*] **1.** any character of the alphabet **2.** a written or printed message, usually sent by mail **3.** [*pl.*] *a)* literature *b)* learning; knowledge **4.** literal meaning **5.** the first letter of the name of a school, awarded and worn for superiority in sports, etc. —*vt.* to mark with letters —**to the letter** exactly

letter box *same as* MAILBOX

letter carrier *same as* MAIL CARRIER

let'tered *adj.* **1.** literate **2.** well-educated **3.** marked with letters

let'ter·head' *n.* **1.** the name, address, etc. of a person or firm as a heading on stationery **2.** a sheet of such stationery

let'ter·ing *n.* **1.** the act of making letters or inscribing in or with letters **2.** such letters

letter of credit a letter from a bank asking that the holder of the letter be allowed to draw specified sums of money from other banks or agencies

let'ter-per'fect *adj.* correct in every respect

let'ter·press' *n.* **1.** printing done from raised surfaces, as from set type **2.** matter so printed

letters patent a document granting a patent

let·tuce (let'is) *n.* [< L. *lac*, milk] **1.** a plant with crisp, green leaves **2.** the leaves, much used for salads **3.** [Slang] paper money

let'up' *n.* [Colloq.] **1.** a slackening **2.** a stop; pause

leu·ke·mi·a (lōō kē'mē ə) *n.* [see LEUKOCYTE & -EMIA] a disease of the blood-forming organs, resulting in an abnormal increase in the production of leukocytes: also sp. **leu·kae'mi·a**

leu·ko·cyte (lōō'kə sīt') *n.* [< Gr. *leukos*, white + *kytos*, hollow] a white corpuscle in the blood: it destroys disease-causing organisms

Lev. Leviticus

Le·vant (lə vant') [Fr. *levant*, rising (of the sun) < It. < L. *levare*, to raise] coastal region on the E Mediterranean, between Greece & Egypt

lev·ee¹ (lev'ē) *n.* [< Fr. < L. *levare*, to raise] an embankment to prevent a river from flooding bordering land

lev·ee² (lev'ē, lə vē') *n.* [< Fr. *se lever*, to rise] formerly, a morning reception held by a sovereign

lev·el (lev''l) *n.* [< L. *libra*, a balance] **1.** an instrument for determining the horizontal **2.** a horizontal plane or line [*sea level*] **3.** a horizontal area **4.** normal position with reference to height [*water seeks its level*] **5.** position, rank, etc. in a scale of values [*income level*] —*adj.* **1.** perfectly flat and even **2.** not sloping **3.** even in height (*with*) **4.** not heaping [*a level teaspoonful*] **5.** equal in importance, advancement, quality, etc. **6.** *a)* well-balanced; equable *b)* calm or steady —*vt., vi.* **-eled** or **-elled, -el·ing** or **-el·ling 1.** to make or become level, flat, equal, etc. **2.** to demolish **3.** to raise and aim (a gun, etc.) —**level off 1.** to give a flat surface to **2.** *Aeron.* to come or bring to a horizontal line of flight: also **level out 3.** to become stable or constant —**level with** [Slang] to be honest —**one's level best** [Colloq.] the best one can do —**on the level** [Slang] honest(ly) and fair(ly) —**lev'el·er, lev'el·ler** *n.* — **lev'el·ness** *n.*

lev·el·head·ed *adj.* having an even temper and sound judgment —**lev'el·head'ed·ness** *n.*

lev·er (lev'ər, lē'vər) *n.* [< L. *levare*, raise] **1.** a bar used as a pry **2.** a means to an end **3.** *Mech.* a device consisting of a bar turning about a fixed point, using force at a second point to lift a weight at a third —*vt.* to lift with a lever —*vi.* to use a lever

lev·er·age (-ij) *n.* **1.** the action or mechanical power of a lever **2.** increased means of effecting an aim

Le·vi (lē'vī) *Bible* Jacob's third son: see also LEVITE

le·vi·a·than (lə vī'ə thən) *n.* [< Heb. *liwyāthān*] **1.** *Bible* a sea monster **2.** any huge thing

LEVERS

Le·vi's (lē'vīz) [< *Levi* Strauss, the U.S. maker] *a trademark for* closefitting trousers of heavy denim, reinforced at the seams, etc. with small copper rivets —*n.pl.* such trousers: usually **le'vis**

lev·i·ta·tion (lev'ə tā'shən) *n.* [< L. *levis*, LIGHT²] the illusion of raising a body in the air with no support

Le·vite (lē'vīt) *n. Bible* any member of the tribe of Levi, chosen to assist the priests in the Temple

Le·vit·i·cus (lə vit'i kəs) the third book of the Bible, containing the laws relating to priests and Levites

lev·i·ty (lev'ə tē) *n., pl.* **-ties** [< L. *levis*, LIGHT²] **1.** improper gaiety; frivolity **2.** fickleness

lev·u·lose (lev'yoo lōs') *n. same as* FRUCTOSE

lev·y (lev'ē) *n., pl.* **-ies** [see LEVER] **1.** an imposing and collecting of a tax, fine, etc. **2.** the amount levied **3.** *a)* compulsory enlistment for military service *b)* a group so enlisted —*vt.* **-ied, -y·ing 1.** to impose (a tax, fine, etc.) **2.** to enlist (troops) **3.** to wage (war)

lewd (lōōd) *adj.* [OE. *lǣwede*, unlearned] showing, or intended to excite, lust or sexual desire, esp. offensively — **lewd'ly** *adv.* —**lewd'ness** *n.*

Lew·is (lōō'is) **1.** Mer·i·weth·er (mer'ē weth'ər), 1774–1809; Am. explorer, with William Clark (1770–1838), of the Northwest **2.** Sinclair, 1885–1951; U.S. novelist

lew·is·ite (lōō'ə sīt') *n.* [< W. L. *Lewis* (1878–1943), U.S. chemist] an arsenical compound, used as a blistering poison gas

lex·i·cog·ra·phy (lek'sə käg'rə fē) *n.* [< Gr. *lexikon*, LEXICON + *graphein*, to write] the act, art, or work of writing or compiling a dictionary —**lex'i·cog'ra·pher** *n.* —**lex'-i·co·graph'ic** (-si kə graf'ik), **lex'i·co·graph'i·cal** *adj.*

lex·i·con (lek'si kən, -kän') *n.* [< Gr. *lexis*, a word] **1.** a dictionary, esp. of an ancient language **2.** a special vocabulary

Lex·ing·ton (lek'siŋ tən) **1.** city in NC Ky.: pop. 108,000 **2.** suburb of Boston, in E Mass.: site of one of the 1st battles of the Revolutionary War

Ley·den jar (or **vial**) (līd''n) [< *Leiden*, Netherlands] a condenser for static electricity, consisting of a glass jar with a coat of tinfoil outside and inside and a metallic rod connecting with the inner lining and passing through the lid

LF, lf low frequency

LG., L.G. Low German

LGr., L.Gr. Late Greek

Lha·sa (lä'sə) capital of Tibet: pop. 70,000

Li *Chem.* lithium

L.I. Long Island

li·a·bil·i·ty (lī'ə bil'ə tē) *n., pl.* **-ties 1.** the state of being liable **2.** anything for which a person is liable **3.** [*pl.*] *Accounting* the debts of a person or business **4.** something that works to one's disadvantage

li·a·ble (lī'ə b'l; also, esp. for 3, lī'b'l) *adj.* [< L. *ligare*, to bind] **1.** legally bound; responsible **2.** subject to [*liable* to heart attacks] **3.** likely (*to*) [*liable* to cause hard feelings]

li·ai·son (lē'ə zän', -zōn'; lē ā'zän) *n.* [Fr. < L. *ligare*, bind] **1.** intercommunication, as between units of a military force, to bring about proper coordination of activities **2.** an illicit love affair

li·ar (lī'ər) *n.* a person who tells lies

lib (lib) *n. clipped form of* LIBERATION

lib. 1. [L. *liber*] book **2.** librarian **3.** library

li·ba·tion (lī bā'shən) *n.* [< L. *libare*, pour out] **1.** the ritual of pouring out wine or oil in honor of a god **2.** the liquid poured out **3.** an alcoholic drink: used humorously

li·bel (lī'b'l) *n.* [< L. *liber*, book] **1.** any written or printed matter tending to injure a person's reputation unjustly **2.** the act of publishing such a thing **3.** anything that gives a damaging picture of the subject —*vt.* **-beled** or **-belled, -bel·ing** or **-bel·ling** to make a libel against —**li'bel·er, li'-bel·ler** *n.* —**li'bel·ous, li'bel·lous** *adj.*

lib·er·al (lib′ər əl) *adj.* [< L. *liber*, free] **1.** generous **2.** ample; abundant **3.** not literal or strict **4.** tolerant; broad-minded **5.** favoring reform or progress; specif., favoring political reforms —*n.* **1.** one who favors reform or progress **2.** [L-] a member of a liberal political party —**lib′er·al·ism** *n.* —**lib′er·al·ly** *adv.* —**lib′er·al·ness** *n.*

liberal arts literature, philosophy, languages, history, etc. as courses of study, as distinguished from professional or technical subjects

lib·er·al·i·ty (-ə ral′ə tē) *n., pl.* **-ties 1.** generosity **2.** tolerance; broad-mindedness

lib·er·al·ize (-ər ə līz′) *vt., vi.* **-ized′, -iz′ing** to make or become liberal —**lib′er·al·i·za′tion** *n.*

lib·er·ate (lib′ə rāt′) *vt.* **-at′ed, -at′ing** [< L. *liber*, free] **1.** to release from slavery, enemy occupation, etc. **2.** [Slang] to loot **3.** *Chem.* to free from combination in a compound —**lib′er·a′tor** *n.*

lib·er·a·tion (lib′ə rā′shən) *n.* **1.** a liberating or being liberated **2.** the securing of equal social and economic rights —**lib′er·a′tion·ist** *n.*

Li·ber·i·a (lī bir′ē ə) country on the W coast of Africa: founded by freed slaves from the U.S.: 43,000 sq. mi.; pop. 1,200,000; cap. Monrovia —**Li·ber′i·an** *adj., n.*

lib·er·tar·i·an (lib′ər ter′ē ən) *n.* **1.** a believer in free will **2.** an advocate of full civil liberties

lib·er·tine (lib′ər tēn′) *n.* [< L. *liber*, free] a man who is sexually promiscuous —*adj.* licentious —**lib′er·tin·ism** *n.*

lib·er·ty (lib′ər tē) *n., pl.* **-ties** [< L. *liber*, free] **1.** freedom from slavery, captivity, etc. **2.** a particular right, freedom, etc. **3.** an impertinent attitude **4.** *U.S. Navy* permission for an enlisted person to be absent from duty for 72 hours or less —**at liberty 1.** not confined **2.** allowed (*to*) **3.** not busy or in use —**take liberties 1.** to be too familiar or impertinent in action or speech **2.** to deal (*with* facts, etc.) in a distorting way

Liberty Bell the bell of Independence Hall in Philadelphia, rung July 4, 1776, to proclaim U.S. independence

li·bid·i·nous (li bid′'n əs) *adj.* [see LIBIDO] lustful; lewd; lascivious —**li·bid′i·nous·ly** *adv.*

li·bi·do (li bē′dō, -bi′-) *n.* [L., desire] **1.** the sexual urge **2.** *Psychoanalysis* psychic energy generally; specif., that comprising the positive, loving instincts —**li·bid′i·nal** (-bid′'n əl) *adj.*

Li·bra (lī′brə, lē′-) [L., a balance] **1.** a S constellation between Virgo and Scorpio **2.** the seventh sign of the zodiac: see ZODIAC, illus.

li·brar·i·an (lī brer′ē ən) *n.* a person in charge of a library or trained to work in a library

li·brar·y (lī′brer′ē) *n., pl.* **-ies** [< L. *liber*, book] **1.** a room or building where a collection of books, periodicals, etc. is kept **2.** an institution in charge of the care and circulation of such a collection **3.** a collection of books, periodicals, etc.

li·bret·to (li bret′ō) *n., pl.* **-tos, -ti** (-ē) [It. < L. *liber*, book] **1.** the words, or text, of an opera, oratorio, etc. **2.** a book containing these words —**li·bret′tist** *n.*

Lib·y·a (lib′ē ə) country in N Africa, on the Mediterranean: 679,359 sq. mi.; pop. 1,869,000; caps. Benghazi & Tripoli —**Lib′y·an** *adj., n.*

lice (līs) *n. pl. of* LOUSE

li·cense (līs′'ns) *n.* [< L. *licere*, be permitted] **1.** formal or legal permission to do something specified **2.** a document indicating such permission **3.** freedom to deviate from rule, practice, etc. [poetic *license*] **4.** excessive freedom, constituting an abuse of liberty   Brit. sp. **licence** —*vt.* **-censed, -cens·ing** to permit formally

li′cen·see′ (-'n sē′) *n.* a person to whom a license is granted

li·cen·ti·ate (lī sen′shē it, -āt′) *n.* a person licensed to practice a specified profession

li·cen·tious (lī sen′shəs) *adj.* [see LICENSE] morally unrestrained, esp. in sexual activity; lascivious —**li·cen′tious·ly** *adv.* —**li·cen′tious·ness** *n.*

li·chee (lē′chē′) *n. same as* LITCHI

li·chen (lī′kən) *n.* [< Gr. *leichein*, to lick] a mosslike plant growing in patches on rock, wood, soil, etc.

lic·it (lis′it) *adj.* [< L. *licere*, be permitted] permitted; lawful —**lic′it·ly** *adv.*

lick (lik) *vt.* [OE. *liccian*] **1.** to pass the tongue over **2.** to bring into a certain condition by passing the tongue over [to *lick* one's fingers clean] **3.** to pass lightly over like a tongue **4.** [Colloq.] *a)* to whip *b)* to vanquish —*n.* **1.** a licking with the tongue **2.** a small quantity **3.** *short for* SALT LICK **4.** [Colloq.] *a)* a sharp blow *b)* a short, rapid

burst of activity: also **lick and a promise 5.** [*often pl.*] [Slang] chance; turn [to get one's *licks* in] —**lick up** to consume as by licking

lick·e·ty-split (lik′ə tē split′) *adv.* [Colloq.] at great speed

lick·spit·tle (lik′spit′'l) *n.* a servile flatterer

lic·o·rice (lik′ər ish, lik′rish) *n.* [< Gr. *glykys*, sweet + *rhiza*, root] **1.** the dried root or black flavoring extract of a European plant **2.** candy flavored with this extract

lid (lid) *n.* [OE. *hlid*] **1.** a movable cover, as for a box, etc. **2.** *short for* EYELID **3.** [Colloq.] a restraint **4.** [Slang] a hat —**lid′ded** *adj.*

lie¹ (lī) *vi.* **lay, lain, ly′ing** [OE. *licgan*] **1.** to be or put oneself in a horizontal or reclining position **2.** to rest on a support in a horizontal position **3.** to be in a specified condition **4.** to be situated [Canada *lies* to the north] **5.** to extend [the road *lies* before us] **6.** to exist [love *lies* in her eyes] **7.** to be buried —*n.* the way in which something is situated; lay —**lie down on the job** [Colloq.] to put forth less than one's best efforts

lie² (lī) *vi.* **lied, ly′ing** [OE. *leogan*] to make a statement that one knows to be false —*vt.* to bring, put, accomplish, etc. by lying —*n.* a false statement made with intent to deceive —**give the lie to 1.** to charge with lying **2.** to prove to be false

Liech·ten·stein (lēkh′tən shtīn′) country in WC Europe, on the Rhine: 61 sq. mi.; pop. 21,000

Lie·der·kranz (lē′dər krants′) [G.] *a trademark for* a soft cheese having a strong odor

lief (lēf) *adv.* [OE. *leof*] willingly; gladly: only in **would** (or **had**) **as lief**, etc.

liege (lēj) *adj.* [< OFr.] loyal; faithful —*n. Feudal Law* **1.** a lord or sovereign **2.** a subject or vassal

li·en (lēn, lē′ən) *n.* [Fr. < L. *ligare*, to bind] a legal claim on another's property as security for the payment of a debt

lieu (lōō) *n.* [< L. *locus*, place] place: now chiefly in **in lieu of**, in place of; instead of

lieu·ten·ant (lōō ten′ənt) *n.* [< MFr. *lieu*, place + *tenant*, holding] **1.** one who acts for a superior **2.** *U.S. Mil.* an officer ranking below a captain: see FIRST LIEUTENANT, SECOND LIEUTENANT **3.** *U.S. Navy* an officer ranking just above a lieutenant junior grade Abbrev. **Lieut., Lt.** —**lieu·ten′an·cy** (-ən sē) *n., pl.* **-cies**

lieutenant colonel *U.S. Mil.* an officer ranking above a major

lieutenant commander *U.S. Navy* an officer ranking above a lieutenant

lieutenant general *U.S. Mil.* an officer ranking above a major general

lieutenant governor an elected official of a State who ranks below and substitutes for the governor

lieutenant junior grade *U.S. Navy* an officer ranking above an ensign

life (līf) *n., pl.* **lives** [OE. *lif*] **1.** that property of plants and animals (ending at death) which makes it possible for them to take in food, get energy from it, grow, etc. **2.** the state of having this property **3.** a human being [100 *lives* were lost] **4.** living things collectively [plant *life*] **5.** the time a person or thing is alive or flourishing **6.** one's manner of living [a *life* of ease] **7.** the people and activities of a given time, place, etc. [military *life*] **8.** human existence [to learn from *life*] **9.** *a)* one's lifetime experiences *b)* biography **10.** something essential to the continued existence of something else [freedom of speech is the *life* of democracy] **11.** the source of liveliness [the *life* of the party] **12.** vigor; liveliness —**as large** (or **big**) **as life** life-size —**for dear life** with desperate intensity —**for life** for the duration of one's life —**true to life** true to reality

life belt a life preserver in the form of a belt

life′blood′ *n.* **1.** the blood necessary to life **2.** a vital element or animating influence

life′boat′ *n.* any of the small rescue boats carried by a ship

life buoy *same as* LIFE PRESERVER

life expectancy the average number of years that an individual of a given age may expect to live

life′-giv′ing *adj.* **1.** that gives or can give life **2.** refreshing —**life′-giv′er** *n.*

life′guard′ *n.* an expert swimmer employed at a beach, pool, etc. to prevent drownings

life insurance insurance in which a stipulated sum is paid to the beneficiary at the death of the insured, or to the insured when he reaches a specified age

life jacket (or **vest**) a life preserver in the form of a sleeveless jacket or vest

life′less *adj.* **1.** without life; specif., *a)* inanimate *b)* dead **2.** dull —**life′less·ly** *adv.* —**life′less·ness** *n.*

life′like′ *adj.* resembling real life or a real person or thing

life′line′ *n.* **1.** a rope for saving life **2.** the rope used to raise or lower a diver **3.** a commercial route of vital importance

life′long′ *adj.* lasting or not changing during one's whole life

life net a strong net used by firemen, etc. as to catch people jumping from a burning building

life preserver a buoyant device for saving a person from drowning by keeping his body afloat

lif′er *n.* [Slang] a person sentenced to prison for the remainder of his life

life raft a small, inflatable raft or boat

life′sav′er *n.* **1.** a lifeguard **2.** [Colloq.] a help in time of need —**life′sav′ing** *adj., n.*

life′-size′ *adj.* as big as the person or thing represented, as a statue, etc.: also **life′-sized′**

life style an individual's whole way of living

life′time′ *n.* the length of time that one lives, or that a thing lasts —*adj.* lasting for such a period

life′work′ *n.* the work or task to which a person devotes his life

lift (lift) *vt.* [< ON. *lopt,* air] **1.** to bring up to a higher position; raise **2.** to raise in rank, condition, etc.; exalt **3.** to pay off (a mortgage, debt, etc.) **4.** to end (a blockade, etc.) **5.** to subject to FACE LIFTING (sense 1) **6.** [Colloq.] to plagiarize **7.** [Slang] to steal —*vi.* **1.** to exert strength in raising something **2.** to rise; go up —*n.* **1.** a lifting or rising **2.** the amount lifted **3.** the distance something is lifted **4.** lifting force, influence, etc. **5.** elevation of mood, etc. **6.** elevated position or carriage **7.** a ride in the direction one is going **8.** help of any kind **9.** any layer of leather in the heel of a shoe **10.** [Brit.] an elevator —**lift′er** *n.*

lift′off′ *n.* **1.** the vertical thrust of a spacecraft, missile, etc. at launching **2.** the time of this

lig·a·ment (lig′ə mənt) *n.* [< L. *ligare,* to bind] **1.** a bond or tie **2.** *Anat.* a band of tissue connecting bones or holding organs in place

lig·a·ture (lig′ə chər) *n.* [< L. *ligare,* bind] **1.** a tying or binding together **2.** a tie, bond, etc. **3.** two or more letters united, as *æ, th* **4.** *Music* a slur **5.** *Surgery* a thread used to tie up an artery, etc.

light¹ (līt) *n.* [OE. *leoht*] **1.** *a)* the form of electromagnetic radiation acting on the retina of the eye to make sight possible *b)* ultraviolet or infrared radiation **2.** brightness; illumination **3.** a source of light, as the sun, a lamp, etc. **4.** *same as* TRAFFIC LIGHT **5.** daylight **6.** a thing used to ignite something **7.** a means by which light is let in; window **8.** knowledge; enlightenment **9.** spiritual inspiration **10.** public view **11.** aspect [presented in a favorable *light*] **12.** an outstanding person —*adj.* **1.** having light; bright **2.** pale in color; fair —*adv.* palely [a *light* blue color] —*vt.* **light′ed** or **lit, light′ing 1.** to ignite [to *light* a bonfire] **2.** to cause to give off light **3.** to furnish with light **4.** to brighten; animate —*vi.* **1.** to catch fire **2.** to be lighted (usually with *up*) —**in the light of** considering —**see the light (of day) 1.** to come into existence **2.** to come into public view **3.** to understand

light² (līt) *adj.* [OE. *leoht*] **1.** having little weight; not heavy, esp. for its size **2.** less than the usual in weight, amount, force, etc. [a *light* blow] **3.** of little importance **4.** easy to bear [a *light* tax] **5.** easy to do [*light* work] **6.** gay; happy **7.** dizzy; giddy **8.** not serious [*light* reading] **9.** moderate [a *light* meal] **10.** containing little alcohol [a *light* wine] **11.** soft and spongy [a *light* cake] **12.** moving with ease [*light* on one's feet] **13.** producing small products [*light* industry] **14.** equipped with light weapons, armor, etc. —*adv.* lightly —*vi.* **light′ed** or **lit, light′ing 1.** to come to rest after traveling through the air **2.** to come or happen (*on* or *upon*) **3.** to strike suddenly, as a blow **4.** [Now Dial.] to dismount —**light out** [Colloq.] to depart suddenly —**make light of** to treat as trivial

light air a wind speed of 1 to 3 miles per hour

light breeze a wind speed of 4 to 7 miles per hour

light′en¹ *vt., vi.* **1.** to make or become light or brighter **2.** to shine; flash —**light′en·er** *n.*

light′en² *vt., vi.* **1.** to make or become lighter in weight **2.** to make or become more cheerful

light′er¹ *n.* a person or thing that lights something or starts it burning

light′er² *n.* [< MDu. *licht,* LIGHT²] a large barge used in loading or unloading ships lying offshore

light′face′ *n. Printing* type with thin, light lines

light′-fin′gered *adj.* skillful at stealing, esp. by picking pockets

light′-foot′ed *adj.* stepping lightly and gracefully: also [Poet.] **light′-foot′** —**light′-foot′ed·ly** *adv.*

light′head′ed *adj.* **1.** giddy; dizzy **2.** flighty; frivolous — **light′head′ed·ness** *n.*

light′heart′ed *adj.* free from care; gay —**light′heart′ed·ly** *adv.* —**light′heart′ed·ness** *n.*

light heavyweight a boxer or wrestler between a middleweight and heavyweight (in boxing, 161–175 lbs.)

light′house′ *n.* a tower with a bright light to guide ships at night

light′ing *n.* the act, manner, or art of giving light, or illuminating

light′ly *adv.* **1.** with little weight or pressure; gently **2.** to a small degree or amount **3.** nimbly; deftly **4.** cheerfully **5.** with indifference or neglect

light′-mind′ed *adj.* not serious; frivolous —**light′-mind′ed·ly** *adv.* —**light′-mind′ed·ness** *n.*

light′ness¹ *n.* **1.** the quality or intensity of lighting; brightness **2.** paleness

light′ness² *n.* **1.** the state of being light, not heavy **2.** mildness, nimbleness, delicacy, cheerfulness, etc.

light′ning (-niŋ) *n.* a flash of light in the sky caused by the discharge of atmospheric electricity from one cloud to another or between a cloud and the earth

lightning bug (or **beetle**) *same as* FIREFLY

lightning rod a metal rod placed high on a building and grounded to divert lightning from the structure

light opera a short, amusing musical play

lights (līts) *n.pl.* [from their light weight] [Dial.] the lungs of animals, used as food

light′ship′ *n.* a ship with a bright light, etc., moored in a dangerous place to warn other ships

light′some *adj.* **1.** nimble, graceful, or lively **2.** lighthearted; gay **3.** frivolous

light′weight′ *n.* **1.** one below normal weight **2.** a boxer or wrestler between a featherweight and a welterweight (in boxing, 127–135 lbs.) **3.** [Colloq.] a person of limited influence, intelligence, etc. —*adj.* **1.** light in weight **2.** not serious

light′-year′ *n.* the distance that light travels in a vacuum in one year, c.6 trillion miles

lig·ne·ous (lig′nē əs) *adj.* [< L. *lignum,* wood] of, or having the nature of, wood; woody

lig·nite (lig′nīt) *n.* [Fr. < L. *lignum,* wood] a soft, brownish-black coal with the texture of the original wood

lig·num vi·tae (lig′nəm vīt′ē) [L., wood of life] **1.** a tropical American tree with hard, dense wood **2.** *a commercial name for* the hard wood of this tree

lik·a·ble (līk′ə b'l) *adj.* attractive, pleasant, genial, etc.: also **likeable** —**lik′a·ble·ness, lik′a·bil′i·ty** *n.*

like¹ (līk) *adj.* [OE. *gelic*] having the same characteristics; similar; equal —*adv.* [Colloq.] likely [*like* as not, he'll go] —*prep.* **1.** similar to **2.** similarly to [to sing *like* a bird] **3.** characteristic of [not *like* her to cry] **4.** in the mood for [to feel *like* sleeping] **5.** indicative of [it looks *like* rain] **6.** as for example [fruit, *like* pears and plums] —*conj.* [Colloq.] **1.** as [it's just *like* he said] **2.** as if [it looks *like* he's late] —*n.* an equal or counterpart [the *like* of it] — **and the like** and others of the same kind —**like anything** [Colloq.] very much —**like blazes** (or **crazy, the devil, mad,** etc.) [Colloq.] with furious energy, speed, etc. — **nothing like** not at all like —**something like** almost like; about —**the like** (or **likes**) **of** [Colloq.] any person or thing like

like² (līk) *vi.* **liked, lik′ing** [OE. *lician*] to be so inclined [do as you *like*] —*vt.* **1.** to be pleased with; enjoy **2.** to wish [I'd *like* to go] —*n.* [pl.] preferences or tastes —**lik′er** *n.*

-like *a suffix meaning* like, characteristic of [*doglike, homelike*]

like·li·hood (līk′lē hood′) *n.* (a) probability

like·ly (līk′lē) *adj.* **-li·er, -li·est** [OE. *geliclic*] **1.** credible [a *likely* cause] **2.** reasonably to be expected [*likely* to rain] **3.** suitable [a *likely* man] **4.** promising [a *likely* lad] —*adv.* probably [he will very *likely* go]

like′-mind′ed *adj.* having the same ideas, tastes, etc. — **like′-mind′ed·ness** *n.*

lik·en (līk′n) *vt.* to compare

like′ness *n.* **1.** a being like; similarity **2.** (the same) form or shape **3.** a copy, portrait, etc.

like′wise′ *adv.* [< *in like wise*] **1.** in the same manner **2.** also; too; moreover

lik′ing *n.* **1.** fondness; affection **2.** preference; taste; pleasure

li·lac (lī′lək, -läk) *n.* [Fr. < Per. *nīlak,* bluish] **1.** a shrub with large clusters of tiny, fragrant flowers ranging from white to lavender **2.** a pale-purple color —*adj.* pale-purple

Lil·li·pu·tian (lil′ə pyōo̅′shən) *adj.* [< *Lilliput,* place inhabited by tiny people in J. Swift's *Gulliver's Travels*] **1.** tiny **2.** petty

lilt (lilt) *vt., vi.* [ME. *lilten*] to sing, speak, or play with a light, graceful rhythm —*n.* a light, swingy rhythm or tune

lil·y (lil′ē) *n., pl.* **-ies** [< L. *lilium*] **1.** a plant grown from a bulb and having typically trumpet-shaped flowers, white or colored **2.** its flower **3.** any similar plant, as the waterlily —*adj.* like a lily, as in whiteness, purity, etc.

lil′y-liv′ered (-liv′ərd) *adj.* cowardly; timid

lily of the valley *pl.* **lilies of the valley** a low plant with a spike of fragrant, small, white, bell-shaped flowers

Li·ma (lē′mə) capital of Peru: pop. 1,716,000

li·ma bean (lī′mə) [< LIMA, Peru] [*also* L-b-] **1.** a bean plant with broad pods **2.** its broad, flat, nutritious seed

limb (lim) *n.* [OE. *lim*] **1.** an arm, leg, or wing **2.** a large branch of a tree —**out on a limb** [Colloq.] in a precarious position — **limb′less** *adj.*

limbed (limd) *adj.* having (a specified number or kind of) limbs [four-*limbed*]

LILY OF THE VALLEY

lim·ber[1] (lim′bər) *adj.* [< ? LIMB] **1.** easily bent; flexible **2.** able to bend the body easily —*vt., vi.* to make or become limber

lim·ber[2] (lim′bər) *n.* [< ?] the two-wheeled, detachable front of a gun carriage —*vt., vi.* to attach the limber to (a gun carriage)

lim·bo (lim′bō) *n., pl.* **-bos** [< L. (*in*) *limbo,* (on) the border] **1.** [*often* L-] in some Christian theologies, a region bordering on hell, the abode after death of unbaptized children and righteous people who lived before Jesus **2.** a place or condition of oblivion or neglect **3.** an indeterminate state

Lim·bur·ger (cheese) (lim′bər gər) [< *Limburg,* Belgian province] a semisoft cheese with a strong odor: also **Lim′-burg (cheese)**

lime[1] (līm) *n.* [OE. *lim*] a white substance, calcium oxide, CaO, obtained by the action of heat on limestone and used in mortar and cement and to neutralize acid soil — *vt.* **limed, lim′ing 1.** to smear or catch with birdlime **2.** to treat with lime

lime[2] (līm) *n.* [Fr. < Ar. *līma*] **1.** a small, lemon-shaped, greenish-yellow citrus fruit with a juicy, sour pulp **2.** the semitropical tree it grows on

lime[3] (līm) *n.* [< ME. *lind*] *same as* LINDEN

lime′ade (-ād′) *n.* a drink of lime juice and water, usually sweetened

lime′light′ *n.* **1.** a brilliant light created by the incandescence of lime, formerly used in theaters **2.** a prominent position before the public

lim·er·ick (lim′ər ik) *n.* [prob. < *Limerick,* Ir. county] a rhymed, nonsense poem of five lines

lime′stone′ *n.* rock consisting mainly of calcium carbonate

lime′wa′ter *n.* a solution of calcium hydroxide in water, used to neutralize acids

lim·ey (lī′mē) *n.* [< the LIME[2] juice formerly served to British sailors to prevent scurvy] [Slang] **1.** an English sailor or soldier **2.** any Englishman

lim·it (lim′it) *n.* [< L. *limes*] **1.** the point, line, etc. where something ends or must end; boundary **2.** [*pl.*] bounds **3.** the greatest amount allowed —*vt.* to set a limit to; restrict —**lim′it·er** *n.*

lim·i·ta′tion *n.* **1.** a limiting or being limited **2.** restriction **3.** a period of time, fixed by statute, during which legal action can be brought

lim′it·ed *adj.* **1.** confined within bounds; restricted **2.** making a restricted number of stops: said of a train, bus, etc. —*n.* a limited train, bus, etc.

lim′it·less *adj.* without limits; unbounded; vast

limn (lim) *vt.* [< L. *illuminare,* make light] **1.** to paint or draw **2.** to describe

Li·moges (lē mōzh′) city in WC France —*n.* fine porcelain made there: also **Limoges ware**

lim·ou·sine (lim′ə zēn′) *n.* [Fr., lit., a hood] a large, luxury automobile, esp. one driven by a chauffeur

limp (limp) *vi.* [< OE. *limpan,* befall] **1.** to walk with or as with a lame leg **2.** to move jerkily, laboriously, etc. —*n.*

a halt or lameness in walking —*adj.* lacking firmness; wilted, flexible, etc. —**limp′ly** *adv.* —**limp′ness** *n.*

limp·et (lim′pit) *n.* [< ML. *lempreda*] a mollusk which clings to rocks, timbers, etc.

lim·pid (lim′pid) *adj.* [< Fr. < L. *limpidus*] perfectly clear; transparent —**lim·pid′i·ty** *n.* —**lim′pid·ly** *adv.*

lim·y (lī′mē) *adj.* **-i·er, -i·est 1.** covered with, of, or like birdlime **2.** of, like, or containing lime —**lim′i·ness** *n.*

lin·age (lī′nij) *n.* the number of written or printed lines on a page

linch·pin (linch′pin′) *n.* [< OE. *lynis,* linchpin] a pin that goes through the end of an axle outside the wheel to keep the wheel from coming off

Lin·coln (liŋ′kən) capital of Nebr.: pop. 150,000

Lin·coln (liŋ′kən), **Abraham** 1809–65; 16th president of the U.S. (1861–65): assassinated

Lind·bergh (lind′bərg), **Charles A.** 1902–74; U.S. aviator

lin·den (lin′dən) *n.* [OE.] a tree with dense, heart-shaped leaves

line[1] (līn) *n.* [< L. *linea,* lit., linen thread] **1.** a cord, rope, wire, etc. **2.** any wire, pipe, etc., or system of these, conducting fluid, electricity, etc. **3.** a thin, threadlike mark, as one made by a pencil, etc., or a thin crease on the face **4.** a border or boundary **5.** a limit **6.** outline; contour **7.** [*pl.*] a plan **8.** a row of persons or things, as of printed characters across a page **9.** *same as* LINEAGE[1] **10.** a succession of persons or things **11.** *a*) a transportation system of buses, ships, etc. *b*) a company operating such a system **12.** the course a moving thing takes **13.** a course of conduct, action, explanation, etc. **14.** a person's trade or occupation **15.** a stock of goods **16.** the field of one's special knowledge **17.** a short letter, note, etc. **18.** a verse of poetry **19.** [*pl.*] all the speeches of one character in a play **20.** the forward combat position in warfare **21.** *Football* the players in the forward row **22.** *Math.* the path of a moving point **23.** *Music* any of the long parallel marks forming the staff —*vt.* **lined, lin′ing 1.** to mark with lines **2.** to bring into alignment (often with *up*) **3.** to form a line along —*vi.* to form a line (usually with *up*) — **bring (or come, get) into line** to bring (or come) into alignment —**down the line** completely; entirely —**draw the** (or *a*) **line** to set a limit —**hold the line** to stand firm — **line up** to form, or bring into, a line

line[2] (līn) *vt.* **lined, lin′ing** [< L. *linum,* flax] to put, or be used as, a lining in

lin·e·age[1] (lin′ē ij) *n.* [see LINE[1]] **1.** direct descent from an ancestor **2.** ancestry; family

line·age[2] (lī′nij) *n.* *same as* LINAGE

lin·e·al (lin′ē əl) *adj.* **1.** in the direct line of descent from an ancestor **2.** hereditary **3.** linear —**lin′e·al·ly** *adv.*

lin·e·a·ment (lin′ē ə mənt) *n.* [< L. *linea,* LINE[1]] a distinctive feature, esp. of the face: *usually used in pl.*

lin·e·ar (lin′ē ər) *adj.* **1.** of, made of, or using a line or lines **2.** in a line **3.** *Bot.* narrow

linear measure a system of measuring length in which 12 in. = 1 ft. or in which 100 cm. = 1 m.

line·back·er (līn′bak′ər) *n.* *Football* any player on defense stationed directly behind the line

line drive a baseball hit in a straight line parallel to the ground

line′man (-mən) *n., pl.* **-men 1.** a person who sets up and repairs telephone or electric wires, etc. **2.** *Football* one of the players in the line

lin·en (lin′ən) *n.* [< OE. *lin,* flax: see LINE[2]] **1.** thread or cloth made of flax **2.** [*often pl.*] sheets, tablecloths, etc. of linen, or of cotton, etc.

lin·er[1] (lī′nər) *n.* **1.** a steamship, airplane, etc. in regular service for a specific line **2.** *same as* LINE DRIVE **3.** a cosmetic applied in a fine line, as along the eyelid

lin·er[2] (lī′nər) *n.* **1.** one who makes or attaches linings **2.** a lining **3.** the jacket of a long-playing record

lines·man (līnz′mən) *n., pl.* **-men 1.** *same as* LINEMAN **2.** *Football* a football official who measures and marks the gains or losses in ground

line′up′ *n.* an arrangement of persons or things in or as in a line; specif., the list of a team's players, arranged in a certain order

-ling [OE.] *a suffix meaning:* **1.** small [*duckling*] **2.** contemptible or unimportant [*hireling*]

lin·ger (liŋ′gər) *vi.* [< OE. *lengan,* to delay] **1.** to continue to stay, esp. through reluctance to leave **2.** to loiter —**lin′-ger·er** *n.* —**lin′ger·ing** *adj.*

lin·ge·rie (län′zhə rā′, -rē′; -jə-) *n.* [Fr.] women's underwear of silk, nylon, lace, etc.

lin·go (liŋ′gō) *n., pl.* **-goes** [< L. *lingua*, tongue] language; esp., a dialect, jargon, etc. one is not familiar with: a humorous or disparaging term

lin·gua fran·ca (liŋ′gwə fraŋ′kə) *pl.* **lin′gua fran′cas, lin·guae fran·cae** (liŋ′gwē fran′sē) [It., lit., Frankish language] any hybrid language used for communication between different peoples, as pidgin English

lin·gual (liŋ′gwəl) *adj.* [< L. *lingua*, the tongue] of, or pronounced with, the tongue —*n.* a lingual sound, as *l* or *t* —**lin′gual·ly** *adv.*

lin·guist (liŋ′gwist) *n.* [< L. *lingua*, the tongue] 1. a specialist in linguistics 2. *same as* POLYGLOT

lin·guis′tic (-gwis′tik) *adj.* 1. of language 2. of linguistics —**lin·guis′ti·cal·ly** *adv.*

lin·guis′tics *n.pl.* [*with sing. v.*] 1. the science of language, including morphology, syntax, etc. 2. the study of a particular language

lin·i·ment (lin′ə mənt) *n.* [< L. *linere*, to smear] a medicated liquid to be rubbed on the skin for soothing sore, sprained, or inflamed areas

lin·ing (lī′niŋ) *n.* [see LINE²] the material covering an inner surface

link¹ (liŋk) *n.* [< Scand.] 1. any of the series of loops forming a chain 2. *a*) a section of something resembling a chain [a *link* of sausage] *b*) an element in a series [a weak *link* in the evidence] 3. anything that connects [a *link* with the past] 4. one division (1/100) of a surveyor's chain, equal to 7.92 in. —*vt., vi.* to join; connect

link² (liŋk) *n.* [prob. < L. *lychnus*, a light] a torch made of tow and pitch

link′age *n.* 1. a linking or being linked 2. a series or system of links

linking verb a verb that functions chiefly as a connection between a subject and a predicate complement (Ex.: *be, seem, become,* etc.)

links (liŋks) *n.pl.* [OE. *hlinc*, a slope] a golf course

link′up′ *n.* a linking together

Lin·nae·us (li nē′əs), **Car·o·lus** (kar′ə ləs) 1707–78; Swed. botanist

lin·net (lin′it) *n.* [< L. *linum*, flax: it feeds on flaxseed] a small finch of Europe, Asia, and Africa

li·no·le·um (li nō′lē əm) *n.* [< L. *linum*, flax + *oleum*, oil] a hard, washable floor covering made of a mixture of ground cork and linseed oil on a backing, as of canvas

Lin·o·type (līn′ə tīp′) [< *line of type*] a trademark for a typesetting machine that casts a line of type in one bar —*n.* [*often* l-] a machine of this kind

lin·seed (lin′sēd′) *n.* [OE. *linsæd*] the seed of flax

linseed oil a yellowish oil extracted from flaxseed, used in oil paints, etc.

lin·sey-wool·sey (lin′zē wool′zē) *n., pl.* **-wool′seys** [ME. < *lin,* flax + *wolle,* wool] a coarse cloth made of linen (or cotton) and wool: also **lin′sey**

lint (lint) *n.* [prob. < *lin,* linen] 1. scraped and softened linen formerly used as a dressing for wounds 2. bits of thread, fluff, etc. from cloth or yarn —**lint′y** *adj.*

lin·tel (lin′t'l) *n.* [ult. < L. *limen,* threshold] the horizontal crosspiece over a door, window, etc.

lin·ters (lin′tərz) *n.pl.* the short fibers clinging to cotton seeds after ginning, used in making batting

lin·y (lī′nē) *adj.* **-i·er, -i·est** 1. linelike 2. marked with lines

li·on (lī′ən) *n.* [< Gr. *leōn*] 1. a large, powerful mammal of the cat family, found in Africa and SW Asia 2. a person of great courage or strength 3. a celebrity —**li′on·ess** *n.fem.*

li′on·heart′ed (-här′tid) *adj.* very brave

li·on·ize (lī′ə nīz′) *vt.* **-ized′, -iz′ing** to treat as a celebrity —**li′on·i·za′tion** *n.*

lion's share the biggest and best portion

lip (lip) *n.* [OE. *lippa*] 1. either of the two fleshy folds forming the edges of the mouth 2. anything like a lip, as the rim of a pitcher 3. [Slang] insolent talk —*vt.* **lipped, lip′ping** to touch with the lips —*adj.* spoken, but insincere [*lip* service] —**keep a stiff upper lip** [Colloq.] to avoid showing fright or discouragement —**lip′less** *adj.*

lipped (lipt) *adj.* having a lip or lips: often in compounds [*tight-lipped*]

lip′py *adj.* **-pi·er, -pi·est** [Slang] impudent or insolent —**lip′pi·ness** *n.*

lip reading recognition of a speaker's words, as by the deaf, by watching the movement of his lips —**lip′-read′** *vt., vi.* —**lip reader**

lip′stick′ *n.* a small stick of cosmetic paste, set in a case, for coloring the lips

liq·ue·fy (lik′wə fī′) *vt., vi.* **-fied′, -fy′ing** [< Fr. < L. *liquere,* be liquid + *facere,* make] to change to a liquid —**liq′ue·fac′tion** (-fak′shən) *n.*

li·queur (li kur′) *n.* [Fr.] any of certain sweet, syrupy alcoholic liquors, variously flavored

liq·uid (lik′wid) *adj.* [< L. *liquidus*] 1. readily flowing; fluid 2. clear; limpid 3. flowing smoothly and gracefully, as verse 4. readily convertible into cash —*n.* a substance that, unlike a solid, flows readily but, unlike a gas, does not expand indefinitely —**liq·uid′i·ty, liq′uid·ness** *n.*

liquid air air brought to a liquid state by being subjected to great pressure and then cooled by its own expansion

liq·ui·date (lik′wə dāt′) *vt.* **-dat′ed, -dat′ing** [see LIQUID] 1. to settle the accounts of (a business) by apportioning assets and debts 2. to pay (a debt) 3. to convert into cash 4. to get rid of, as by killing —*vi.* to liquidate debts, accounts, etc. —**liq′ui·da′tion** *n.* —**liq′ui·da′tor** *n.*

liq′uid·ize′ (-dīz′) *vt.* **-ized′, -iz′ing** to cause to have a liquid quality

liquid measure a system of measuring liquids, esp. that in which 2 pt. = 1 qt., 4 qt. = 1 gal., etc.

liq·uor (lik′ər) *n.* [L.] 1. any liquid 2. an alcoholic drink, esp. a distilled drink, as whiskey or rum —*vt., vi.* [Colloq.] to drink or cause to drink alcoholic liquor

li·ra (lir′ə) *n., pl.* **-re** (-ā), *for* 1 **-ras** [It. < L. *libra,* a balance] the monetary unit of 1. Italy 2. Turkey

Lis·bon (liz′bən) capital of Portugal: pop. 826,000 (met. area 1,450,000)

lisle (līl) *n.* [< *Lisle* (now *Lille*), France] 1. a fine, hard, extra-strong cotton thread: in full **lisle thread** 2. a fabric, stockings, etc. woven of this —*adj.* made of lisle

lisp (lisp) *vi.* [< OE. *wlisp*, a lisping] 1. to substitute the sounds (th) and (*th*) for the sounds of *s* and *z* 2. to speak imperfectly —*vt.* to utter with a lisp —*n.* the act, speech defect, or sound of lisping —**lisp′er** *n.* —**lisp′ing·ly** *adv.*

lis·some, lis·som (lis′əm) *adj.* [< *lithesome*] lithe, limber, agile, etc. —**lis′some·ness, lis′som·ness** *n.*

list¹ (list) *n.* [< OE. *liste*, border] a series of names, words, etc. set forth in order —*vt.* to set forth or enter in a list, directory, etc. —*vi.* to be listed for sale (at the price specified)

list² (list) *vt.* [< OE. *lust*, desire] [Archaic] to be pleasing to; suit —*vi.* [Archaic] to wish; like

list³ (list) *vt., vi.* [< prec.] to tilt to one side, as a ship —*n.* a tilting or inclining to one side

list⁴ (list) *vt., vi.* [OE. *hlyst*, hearing] [Archaic] to listen (to)

lis·ten (lis′'n) *vi.* [OE. *hlysnan*] 1. to make a conscious effort to hear 2. to give heed; take advice —*n.* a listening —**lis′ten·er** *n.*

Lis·ter (lis′tər), **Joseph** 1827–1912; Eng. surgeon: introduced antiseptic surgery

list·less (list′lis) *adj.* [LIST² + -LESS] indifferent because of illness, dejection, etc.; languid —**list′less·ly** *adv.* —**list′less·ness** *n.*

list price retail price as given in a list or catalog, discounted in sales to dealers, etc.

lists (lists) *n.pl.* [< ME. *liste*, border] 1. a fenced area where knights jousted 2. any place of struggle

Liszt (list), **Franz** (fränts) 1811–86; Hung. composer & pianist

lit (lit) *alt. pt. & pp. of* LIGHT

lit·a·ny (lit′'n ē) *n., pl.* **-nies** [< Gr. *litaneia*] prayer in which the congregation recites responses

li·tchi (lē′chē′) *n.* [Chin. *li-chih*] 1. a Chinese evergreen tree 2. the dried fruit of this tree (**litchi nut**), with a single seed, a sweet pulp, and a papery shell

li·ter (lēt′ər) *n.* [Fr. *litre* < Gr. *litra*, a pound] the basic unit of capacity in the metric system, equal to 1.0567 liquid quarts or .908 dry quart

lit·er·a·cy (lit′ər ə sē) *n.* the ability to read and write

lit·er·al (lit′ər əl) *adj.* [< L. *littera*, a letter] 1. following the exact words of the original [a *literal* translation] 2. in a .basic or strict sense [the *literal* meaning] 3. prosaic; matter-of-fact 4. restricted to fact; real [the *literal* truth] —**lit′er·al·ly** *adv.* —**lit′er·al·ness** *n.*

lit′er·al·ism *n.* the tendency to take words, statements, etc. in their literal sense

lit·er·ar·y (lit′ə rer′ē) *adj.* 1. of or dealing with literature 2. expressed in the relatively formal language of literature 3. versed in literature 4. making literature a profession

lit·er·ate (lit′ər it) *adj.* [< L. *littera*, a letter] 1. able to read and write 2. well-educated —*n.* a literate person

lit·e·ra·ti (lit′ə rät′ē, -rä′tī) *n.pl.* [It. < L.] men of letters; scholarly or learned people

lit·er·a·ture (lit′ər ə chər) *n.* [< L. *littera*, a letter] 1. the profession of an author 2. *a*) all the writings of a particular time, country, etc., esp. those valued for excellence of form and expression *b*) all the writings on a particular subject 3. [Colloq.] any printed matter

lithe (līth) *adj.* lith′er, lith′est [OE., soft] bending easily; supple; limber: also **lithe′some** (-səm) —**lithe′ly** *adv.* — **lithe′ness** *n.*

lith·i·um (lith′ē əm) *n.* [< Gr. *lithos*, stone] a soft, silver-white metallic chemical element, the lightest known metal: symbol, Li; at. wt., 6.939; at. no., 3

lith·o·graph (lith′ə graf′) *n.* a print made by lithography —*vt., vi.* to make (prints or copies) by lithography —**li·thog·ra·pher** (li thäg′rə fər) *n.*

li·thog·ra·phy (li thäg′rə fē) *n.* [< Gr. *lithos*, stone + -GRAPHY] printing from a flat stone or metal plate, parts of which have been treated to repel ink —**lith·o·graph·ic** (lith′ə graf′ik) *adj.*

lith·o·sphere (lith′ə sfir′) *n.* [< Gr. *lithos*, stone + SPHERE] the solid part of the earth; earth's crust

Lith·u·a·ni·a (lith′oo wā′nē ə) republic of the U.S.S.R., in NE Europe: in full **Lithuanian Soviet Socialist Republic** —**Lith′u·a′ni·an** *adj., n.*

lit·i·gant (lit′ə gənt) *n.* a party to a lawsuit

lit′i·gate′ (-gāt′) *vt., vi.* -gat′ed, -gat′ing [< L. *lis*, dispute + *agere*, do] to contest in a lawsuit —**lit′i·ga·ble** (-i gə b'l) *adj.* —**lit′i·ga′tor** *n.*

lit′i·ga′tion *n.* 1. the carrying on of a lawsuit 2. a lawsuit

lit·mus (lit′məs) *n.* [< ON. *litr*, color + *mosi*, moss] a purple coloring matter obtained from lichens: paper treated with it (**litmus paper**) turns blue in bases and red in acids

li·tre (lē′tər) *n. chiefly Brit. sp. of* LITER

Litt.D. Doctor of Letters; Doctor of Literature

lit·ter (lit′ər) *n.* [< L. *lectus*, a couch] 1. a framework enclosing a couch on which a person can be carried 2. a stretcher for carrying the sick or wounded 3. straw, hay, etc. used as bedding for animals 4. the young borne at one time by a dog, cat, etc. 5. things lying about in disorder, esp. bits of rubbish —*vt.* 1. to bring forth (a number of young animals) at one time 2. to make untidy 3. to scatter about carelessly

lit′ter·bug′ *n.* a person who litters a public place with trash, garbage, etc.

lit·tle (lit′'l) *adj.* lit′tler or less or less′er, lit′tlest or least [OE. *lytel*] 1. small in size, amount, degree, etc. 2. short in duration; brief 3. small in importance or power *[the little man]* 4. narrow-minded *[a little mind]* 5. young: said of children or animals *Little* is sometimes used to express endearment *[bless your little heart]* —*adv.* **less, least** 1. slightly; not much 2. not in the least —*n.* 1. a small amount, degree, etc. 2. a short time or distance — **little by little** gradually —**make** (or **think**) **little of** to treat as unimportant —**not a little** very much; very —**lit′tle·ness** *n.*

Little Bear the constellation URSA MINOR

Little Dipper a dipper-shaped group of stars in the constellation Ursa Minor

Little Rock capital of Ark.: pop. 132,000

little slam *Bridge* the winning of all but one trick

little theater 1. a small theater, as of a college, usually noncommercial and amateur 2. drama produced by such theaters

lit·to·ral (lit′ər əl) *adj.* [< L. *litus*, seashore] of, on, or along the shore —*n.* the region along the shore

lit·ur·gy (lit′ər jē) *n., pl.* -gies [< Fr. < Gr. *leos*, people + *ergon*, work] prescribed ritual for public worship —**li·tur·gi·cal** (li tur′jə k'l) *adj.*

liv·a·ble (liv′ə b'l) *adj.* 1. fit or pleasant to live in, as a house 2. endurable 3. agreeable to live with Also sp. **liveable** —**liv′a·bil′i·ty** *n.*

live (liv) *vi.* **lived, liv′ing** [OE. *libban*] 1. to have life 2. *a*) to remain alive *b*) to endure 3. to pass life in a specified manner 4. to enjoy a full life 5. to maintain life *[to live on a pension]* 6. to feed *[to live on fruits and nuts]* 7. to reside —*vt.* 1. to carry out in one's life *[to live one's faith]* 2. to spend; pass *[to live a useful life]* —**live down** to live so as to wipe out the shame of (a fault, etc.) —**live high** (or **well**) to live in luxury —**live up to** to act in accordance with (ideals, promises, etc.) —**live with** to endure

live² (līv) *adj.* [< ALIVE] 1. having life 2. of the living state or living things 3. warm, vigorous, bright, brilliant, etc. *[a live organization, color, etc.]* 4. of present interest *[a live issue]* 5. still burning *[a live spark]* 6. unexploded *[a live shell]* 7. carrying electrical current *[a live wire]* 8.

a) transmitted during the actual performance *b*) recorded at a public performance *c*) in person 9. *Sports* in play *[a live ball]*

-lived (līvd; *occas.* livd) *a combining form meaning* having (a specified kind of) life *[short-lived]*

live·li·hood (līv′lē hood′) *n.* [< OE. *lif*, life + *-lad*, course] means of supporting life; subsistence

live·long (liv′lôn′) *adj.* [ME. *lefe longe*, lit., lief long: *lief* is merely intens.] long in passing; whole; entire *[the livelong day]*

live·ly (līv′lē) *adj.* -li·er, -li·est [OE. *liflic*] 1. full of life; vigorous 2. full of spirit; exciting 3. gay; cheerful 4. vivid; keen 5. bounding back with great resilience *[a lively ball]* —*adv.* in a lively manner —**live′li·ness** *n.*

liv·en (līv′ən) *vt., vi.* to make or become lively or gay; cheer (*up*) —**liv′en·er** *n.*

liv·er¹ (liv′ər) *n.* [OE. *lifer*] 1. the largest glandular organ in vertebrate animals: it secretes bile and is important in metabolism 2. the liver of cattle, fowl, etc. used as food 3. the reddish-brown color of liver

liv·er² (liv′ər) *n.* a person who lives (in a specified way or place) *[a clean liver]*

liv·er·ied (liv′ər ēd) *adj.* wearing a livery

Liv·er·pool (liv′ər pool′) seaport in NW England: pop. 688,000 —**Liv′er·pud′li·an** (-pud′lē ən) *adj., n.*

liv·er·wort (liv′ər wurt′) *n.* any of a class of plants, often forming dense, green, mosslike mats on rocks, soil, etc. in moist places

liv·er·wurst (liv′ər wurst′) *n.* [< G. *leber*, LIVER¹ + *wurst*, sausage] a sausage containing ground liver

liv·er·y (liv′ər ē, liv′rē) *n., pl.* -ies [< OFr. *livree*, gift of clothes to a servant] 1. an identifying uniform, as of a servant 2. *a*) the care and feeding of horses for a fee *b*) the keeping of horses or vehicles for hire *c*) a stable providing these services: also **livery stable**

liv′er·y·man (-mən) *n., pl.* -men a person who owns or works in a livery stable

lives (līvz) *n. pl. of* LIFE

live·stock (līv′stäk′) *n.* domestic animals kept for use on a farm or raised for sale and profit

live wire 1. a wire carrying an electric current 2. [Colloq.] an energetic and enterprising person

liv·id (liv′id) *adj.* [L. *lividus*] 1. discolored by a bruise, black-and-blue 2. grayish-blue or pale *[livid with rage]*

liv·ing (liv′in) *adj.* 1. alive; having life 2. in active operation or use *[a living language]* 3. of persons alive *[within living memory]* 4. true; lifelike 5. of life *[living conditions]* —*n.* 1. a being alive 2. livelihood 3. manner of existence 4. in England, a church benefice —**the living** those that are still alive

living death a life of unrelieved misery

living room a room in a home with sofas, chairs, etc., used for socializing, entertaining, etc.

living wage a wage sufficient to maintain a person and his family in reasonable comfort

Liv·y (liv′ē) 59 B.C.-17 A.D.; Roman historian

liz·ard (liz′ərd) *n.* [< L. *lacerta*] 1. any of a group of reptiles with a long, slender body and tail, a scaly skin, and four legs, as the chameleon, iguana, and gecko 2. loosely, any similar animal, as the salamander

'll *contraction of* will or shall *[I'll go]*

LL., L.L. Late Latin

ll., ll lines

lla·ma (lä′mə) *n.* [Sp. < Peruv. native name] a S. American beast of burden related to the camel but smaller and without humps

lla·no (lä′nō) *n., pl.* -nos (-nōz) [Sp. < L. *planus*, plain] a grassy plain in the Southwest and in Spanish America

LL.B. Bachelor of Laws

LL.D. Doctor of Laws

lo (lō) *interj.* [OE. *la*] look! see!

load (lōd) *n.* [< OE. *lad*, a course] 1. an amount carried at one time; burden 2. a varying measure of weight or quantity *[a load of wood]* 3. something borne with difficulty 4. the weight borne up by a structure 5. [*often pl.*] [Colloq.] a great amount or number *[loads of friends]* 6. *Elec.* the amount of current supplied by a generator, motor, etc. —*vt.* 1. to put (something to be carried) into or upon (a carrier) 2. to burden; oppress 3. to supply in abundance *[loaded with honors]* 4. to put ammunition into (a firearm), film in (a camera), etc. 5. to weight (dice) unevenly 6. *Baseball* to cause to have runners on (all bases) —*vi.* to put on or take on a load —**get a load of** [Slang] to listen to or look at —**load′ed** *adj.* —**load′er** *n.*

load·stone (lōd′stōn′) *n. var. sp. of* LODESTONE

loaf[1] (lōf) *n., pl.* **loaves** [OE. *hlaf*] **1.** a portion of bread baked in one piece, commonly oblong **2.** any mass of food shaped like a loaf and baked

loaf[2] (lōf) *vi.* [prob. < LOAFER] to loiter or lounge about; idle, dawdle, etc. —*vt.* to spend (time) idly

loaf′er *n.* [prob. < G. *landläufer*, a vagabond] one who loafs; idler —[L-] *a trademark for* a moccasinlike sport shoe; also, [l-] a shoe like this

loam (lōm) *n.* [OE. *lam*] a rich soil of clay, sand, and organic matter —**loam′y** *adj.*

loan (lōn) *n.* [< ON. *lān*] **1.** the act of lending **2.** something lent; esp., a sum of money lent, often at interest —*vt., vi.* to lend —**loan′er** *n.*

loan shark [Colloq.] a person who lends money at exorbitant or illegal rates of interest

loath (lōth) *adj.* [OE. *lath*, hostile] unwilling; reluctant [to be *loath* to depart] —**nothing loath** willing(ly)

loathe (lōth) *vt.* **loathed**, **loath′ing** [< OE. *lathian*, be hateful] to feel intense dislike or disgust for; abhor —**loath′er** *n.*

loath·ing (lōth′iŋ) *n.* intense dislike, disgust, or hatred; abhorrence

loath·some (lōth′səm) *adj.* causing loathing; disgusting —**loath′some·ness** *n.*

loaves (lōvz) *n. pl. of* LOAF[1]

lob (läb) *n.* [ME. *lobbe-*, lit., "heavy, thick"] *Tennis* a stroke in which the ball is sent high into the air —*vt.* **lobbed**, **lob′bing** to send (a ball) into a lob —*vi.* **1.** to move clumsily **2.** to lob a ball —**lob′ber** *n.*

lo·bar (lō′bər, -bär) *adj.* of a lobe or lobes

lo·bate (lō′bāt) *adj.* having or formed into a lobe or lobes —**lo′bate·ly** *adv.*

lob·by (läb′ē) *n., pl.* **-bies** [LL. *lobia*: see LODGE] **1.** an entrance hall, as of a hotel, theater, etc. **2.** a group of lobbyists —*vi.* **-bied**, **-by·ing** to act as a lobbyist

lob′by·ist (-ist) *n.* one who tries to get legislators to support measures to benefit a special-interest group

lobe (lōb) *n.* [Gr. *lobos*] a rounded projection, as the lower end of the ear or any of the divisions of the brain, lung, or liver —**lobed** *adj.*

lob·lol·ly (läb′läl′ē) *n., pl.* **-lies** [prob. < dial. *lob*, to boil + dial. *lolly*, broth] **1.** a common pine of the southeastern U.S., having long needles **2.** its wood Also **loblolly pine**

lob·ster (läb′stər) *n.* [< OE. *lopustre* < *loppe*, spider] an edible sea crustacean with long antennae and five pairs of legs, the first pair being modified into large pincers

lo·cal (lō′k'l) *adj.* [< L. *locus*, a place] **1.** relating to place **2.** of, characteristic of, or confined to a particular place **3.** of or for a particular part of the body **4.** making all stops along its run [a *local* train] —*n.* **1.** a local train, bus, etc. **2.** a branch, as of a labor union —**lo′cal·ly** *adv.*

LOBSTER
(to 24 in. long)

local color behavior, speech, etc. characteristic of a certain region or time, introduced into a novel, play, etc. to supply realism

lo·cale (lō kal′) *n.* [Fr. *local*] a locality, esp. with reference to events, etc. connected with it

lo′cal·ism *n.* **1.** a local custom **2.** an expression, pronunciation, etc. peculiar to one locality

lo·cal·i·ty (lō kal′ə tē) *n., pl.* **-ties** **1.** position with regard to surrounding objects, etc. **2.** a place

lo·cal·ize (lō′kə līz′) *vt.* **-ized′**, **-iz′ing** to limit, confine, or trace to a particular place or locality —**lo′cal·iz′a·ble** *adj.* —**lo′cal·i·za′tion** *n.*

lo·cate (lō′kāt, lō kāt′) *vt.* **-cat·ed**, **-cat·ing** [< L. *locus*, a place] **1.** to establish in a certain place [offices *located* downtown] **2.** to discover the position of **3.** to show the position of [to *locate* Guam on a map] —*vi.* [Colloq.] to settle

lo·ca·tion (lō kā′shən) *n.* **1.** a locating or being located **2.** position; place **3.** an area marked off for a specific purpose **4.** a motion picture set, away from the studio: chiefly in **on location**

loc·a·tive (läk′ə tiv) *adj.* [see LOCATE] *Linguis.* expressing place at which or in which —*n.* the locative case (in Latin, Greek, etc.)

loc. cit. [L. *loco citato*] in the place cited

loch (läk, läkh) *n.* [Gael. & OIr.] [Scot.] **1.** a lake **2.** an inlet of the sea

lock[1] (läk) *n.* [OE. *loc*, a bolt, enclosure] **1.** a mechanical device for fastening a door, strongbox, etc. as with a key or combination **2.** an enclosed part of a canal, etc.

equipped with gates so that the level of the water can be raised or lowered **3.** the mechanism of a firearm that explodes the charge **4.** *Wrestling* a hold in which a part of the opponent's body is firmly gripped —*vt.* **1.** to fasten with a lock **2.** to shut (*up, in,* or *out*); confine **3.** to fit; link [*lock* arms] **4.** to jam together so as to make immovable —*vi.* **1.** to become locked **2.** to interlock —**lock, stock, and barrel** [Colloq.] completely

lock[2] (läk) *n.* [OE. *loc*] **1.** a curl of hair **2.** [*pl.*] [Poet.] the hair of the head **3.** a tuft of wool, etc.

Locke (läk), **John** 1632–1704; Eng. philosopher

lock′er *n.* **1.** a chest, closet, etc. that can be locked, esp. one for individual use **2.** a large compartment for freezing and storing foods

locker room a room equipped with lockers

lock·et (läk′it) *n.* [< OFr. *loc*, a lock] a small, hinged case of gold, silver, etc., for holding a picture, lock of hair, etc.: it is usually worn on a necklace

lock′jaw′ *n. same as* TETANUS

lock′out′ *n.* the refusal by an employer to let his employees come in to work unless they accept his terms

lock′smith′ *n.* a person whose work is making or repairing locks and keys

lock·up (läk′up′) *n.* a jail

lo·co (lō′kō) *n.* [Sp., insane] [Western] *same as:* **1.** LOCOWEED **2.** LOCO DISEASE —*adj.* [Slang] crazy; demented

loco disease a nervous disease of horses, sheep, and cattle, caused by locoweed poisoning

lo·co·mo·tion (lō′kə mō′shən) *n.* [< L. *locus*, a place + MOTION] motion, or the power of moving, from one place to another

lo′co·mo′tive (-mōt′iv) *adj.* of locomotion —*n.* an electric, steam, or diesel engine on wheels, designed to push or pull a railroad train

lo·co·weed (lō′kō wēd′) *n.* a plant of the legume family, of the western U.S.: it causes loco disease in cattle, etc.

lo·cus (lō′kəs) *n., pl.* **-ci** (-sī) [L.] **1.** a place **2.** *Math.* a line, plane, etc. every point of which satisfies a given condition

lo·cust (lō′kəst) *n.* [< L. *locusta*] **1.** a large grasshopper often traveling in swarms and destroying crops **2.** *same as* SEVENTEEN-YEAR LOCUST **3.** a spiny tree of the E and C U.S., having clusters of fragrant white flowers **4.** *same as* HONEY LOCUST

lo·cu·tion (lō kyoo′shən) *n.* [< L. *loqui*, speak] **1.** a word, phrase, or expression **2.** a particular style of speech

LOCUST
(to 2 in. long)

lode (lōd) *n.* [< OE. *lad*, a course] a vein, stratum, deposit, etc. of metallic ore

lode′star′ *n.* a star by which one directs his course; esp., the North Star

lode′stone′ *n.* **1.** a strongly magnetic variety of the mineral magnetite **2.** something that attracts

lodge (läj) *n.* [< OFr. *loge*, arbor < LL. *lobia*] **1.** a small house for special or seasonal use [a hunting *lodge*] **2.** a resort hotel or motel **3.** the local chapter or hall of a fraternal organization **4.** the den of certain animals, as the beaver **5.** the hut or tent of an American Indian —*vt.* **lodged**, **lodg′ing** **1.** to house, esp. temporarily **2.** to rent rooms to **3.** to deposit; place **4.** to bring (a complaint) before legal authorities **5.** to confer (powers) upon (with *in*) —*vi.* **1.** to live in a place for a time **2.** to live (*with* or *in*) as a paying guest **3.** to come to rest (*in*) [a bone *lodged* in her throat]

lodg′er *n.* one who rents a room in another's home

lodg′ing *n.* **1.** a place to live in, esp. temporarily **2.** [*pl.*] a room or rooms rented in a private home

lodging house *same as* ROOMING HOUSE

lodg·ment (läj′mənt) *n.* **1.** a lodging or being lodged **2.** a lodging place **3.** an accumulation of deposited material Also sp. **lodge′ment**

Łódź (looj) city in C Poland: pop. 749,000

lo·ess (les, lō′es) *n.* [< G. *lösch*, loose] a fine-grained, yellowish, very fertile loam deposited by the wind

loft (lôft, läft) *n.* [< ON. *lopt*, upper room, air] **1.** the space just below the roof of a house, barn, etc. **2.** an upper story of a warehouse or factory **3.** a gallery [a choir *loft*] **4.** *Golf a*) the slope of the face of a club *b*) the height of a ball hit in a high curve —*vt., vi.* to give (a ball) loft

loft′y *adj.* **-i·er**, **-i·est** **1.** very high **2.** elevated; noble **3.** haughty; arrogant —**loft′i·ly** *adv.* —**loft′i·ness** *n.*

log¹ (lôg, läg) *n.* [ME. *logge*] **1.** a section of the trunk of a felled tree **2.** a device for measuring the speed of a ship **3.** a daily record of a ship's speed, progress, etc. **4.** a record of an aircraft's flight, a pilot's flying time, etc. **5.** any similar record —*adj.* made of logs —*vt.* **logged, log′ging 1.** to saw (trees) into logs **2.** to enter in a ship's or aircraft's log —*vi.* to cut down trees and remove the logs

log² (lôg, läg) *n. clipped form of* LOGARITHM

lo·gan·ber·ry (lō′gən ber′ē) *n., pl.* **-ries** [< J. H. *Logan* (1841-1928), U.S. horticulturist] **1.** a hybrid bramble developed from the blackberry and the red raspberry **2.** its purplish-red fruit

log·a·rithm (lôg′ə rith′m, läg′-) *n.* [< Gr. *logos*, ratio + *arithmos*, number] the exponent indicating the power to which a fixed number must be raised to produce a given number —**log′a·rith′mic** *adj.*

log′book′ *n. same as* LOG¹ (senses 3, 4, & 5)

loge (lōzh) *n.* [Fr.: see LODGE] **1.** a box in a theater **2.** the forward section of a balcony in a theater

log′ger *n.* a person whose work is logging

log·ger·head (lôg′ər hed′, läg′-) *n.* [< LOG¹ + HEAD] **1.** a tropical sea turtle with a large head: also **loggerhead turtle 2.** [Dial.] a stupid fellow —**at loggerheads** in disagreement

log·gia (lä′jē ə, lä′jə; lô′-) *n., pl.* **-gi·as** [It.: see LODGE] a roofed gallery projecting from the side of a building, often one overlooking an open court

log′ging *n.* the work of felling trees, cutting them into logs, and transporting them to the sawmill

log·ic (läj′ik) *n.* [ult. < Gr. *logos*, word] **1.** the science of correct reasoning **2.** correct reasoning **3.** way of reasoning [poor *logic*] **4.** necessary connection or outcome, as of events **5.** the interconnections in an electronic digital computer

log·i·cal (-i k'l) *adj.* **1.** of or used in the science of logic **2.** according to the principles of logic, or correct reasoning **3.** expected because of what has gone before **4.** using correct reasoning —**log′i·cal′i·ty** (-kal′ə tē) *n.* —**log′i·cal·ly** *adv.*

lo·gi·cian (lō jish′ən) *n.* an expert in logic

lo·gis·tics (lō jis′tiks) *n.pl.* [*with sing. v.*] [< Fr. *loger*, to quarter] the branch of military science having to do with moving, supplying, and quartering troops —**lo·gis′tic, lo·gis′ti·cal** *adj.*

log′jam′ *n.* a piling up of too many items to deal with

log′roll′ *vi.* to take part in logrolling —*vt.* to get passage of (a bill) by logrolling —**log′roll′er** *n.*

log′roll′ing *n.* **1.** mutual aid, esp. among politicians, as by voting for each other's bills **2.** the sport of balancing oneself while revolving a floating log with one's feet

-logue [see LOGIC] *a combining form meaning* a (specified kind of) speaking or writing [*monologue*]: also **-log**

lo·gy (lō′gē) *adj.* **-gi·er, -gi·est** [< ? Du. *log*, dull] [Colloq.] dull or sluggish —**lo′gi·ness** *n.*

-logy [see LOGIC] *a combining form meaning:* **1.** a (specified kind of) speaking [*eulogy*] **2.** science, doctrine, or theory of [*biology, geology*]

loin (loin) *n.* [< L. *lumbus*] **1.** [*usually pl.*] the lower part of the back between the hipbones and the ribs **2.** the front part of the hindquarters of beef, lamb, etc. **3.** [*pl.*] the hips and the lower abdomen regarded as the region of strength and procreative power, etc. —**gird (up) one's loins** to get ready to do something difficult

loin′cloth′ *n.* a cloth worn about the loins, as by some tribes in warm climates

loi·ter (loit′ər) *vi.* [< MDu. *loteren*] **1.** to spend time idly; linger **2.** to move slowly and indolently —*vt.* to spend (time) idly —**loi′ter·er** *n.*

loll (läl) *vi.* [< MDu. *lollen*] **1.** to lean or lounge about in a lazy manner **2.** to droop —*vt.* to let droop —**loll′er** *n.*

lol·li·pop, lol·ly·pop (läl′ē päp′) *n.* [prob. < dial. *lolly*, the tongue + POP¹] a piece of hard candy on the end of a stick; sucker

lol·ly·gag (läl′ē gag′) *vi.* **-gagged′, -gag′ging** [< ?] [Colloq.] to waste time in trifling activity

Lom·bar·dy (läm′bər dē, lum′-) region of N Italy

Lo·mond (lō′mənd), **Loch** lake in WC Scotland

Lon·don (lun′dən) capital of England, the United Kingdom, & the Commonwealth, in SE England: pop. (of Greater London) 11,025,000 —**Lon′don·er** *n.*

Lon·don (lun′dən), **Jack** 1876-1916; U.S. writer

lone (lōn) *adj.* [< ALONE] **1.** by oneself; solitary **2.** lonesome **3.** isolated

lone′ly *adj.* **-li·er, -li·est 1.** alone **2.** *a)* isolated *b)* unfrequented **3.** unhappy at being alone —**lone′li·ness** *n.*

lon·er (lō′nər) *n.* [Colloq.] one who avoids the company of others

lone′some *adj.* **1.** having or causing a lonely feeling **2.** unfrequented —*n.* [Colloq.] self [all by my *lonesome*] —**lone′some·ly** *adv.* —**lone′some·ness** *n.*

long¹ (lôŋ) *adj.* [OE.] **1.** measuring much from end to end in space or time **2.** in length [six feet *long*] **3.** of greater than usual length, quantity, etc. [a *long* list] **4.** tedious; slow **5.** far-reaching [a *long* view of the matter] **6.** well supplied [*long* on excuses] **7.** requiring a relatively long time to pronounce —*adv.* **1.** for a long time **2.** for the duration of [all day *long*] **3.** at a remote time [*long* ago] —*n.* a long time [it won't take *long*] —**as (or so) long as 1.** during the time that **2.** since **3.** provided that —**before long** soon —**long′ish** *adj.*

long² (lôŋ) *vi.* [OE. *langian*] to feel a strong yearning; wish earnestly [to *long* to go home]

long. longitude

Long Beach seaport in SW Calif.: pop. 359,000

long′boat′ *n.* the largest boat on a sailing ship

long′bow′ *n.* a large bow drawn by hand to shoot a long, feathered arrow

long distance a telephone service or system for calls to distant places —**long′-dis′tance** *adj., adv.*

long′-drawn′ *adj.* prolonged: also **long′-drawn′-out′**

lon·gev·i·ty (län jev′ə tē, lôn-) *n.* [< L. *longus*, long + *aevum*, age] **1.** long life **2.** length of service

long′-faced′ *adj.* glum; disconsolate

Long·fel·low (lôŋ′fel′ō), **Henry Wads·worth** (wädz′wurth′) 1807-82; U.S. poet

long′hair′ *adj.* [Colloq.] of intellectuals or intellectual tastes; specif., preferring classical music to jazz, etc. —*n.* [Colloq.] an intellectual

long′hand′ *n.* ordinary handwriting

long′horn′ *n.* any of a breed of long-horned cattle formerly raised in great numbers in the Southwest

long′ing *n.* strong desire; yearning —*adj.* feeling or showing a yearning —**long′ing·ly** *adv.*

Long Island island in SE N.Y., between Long Island Sound & the Atlantic

Long Island Sound arm of the Atlantic, between N Long Island & S Conn.: c.100 mi. long

lon·gi·tude (län′jə tood′, -tyood′) *n.* [< L. *longus*, long] angular distance, measured in degrees, east or west on the earth's surface from the prime meridian, which runs north and south through Greenwich, England

lon·gi·tu·di·nal *adj.* **1.** of or in length **2.** running or placed lengthwise **3.** of longitude

long jump an event in track and field that is a jump for distance rather than height

long-lived (lôŋ′līvd′, -livd′) *adj.* having or tending to have a long life span

long′-play′ing *adj.* designating a phonograph record that plays at 33 1/3 revolutions per minute

long′-range′ *adj.* taking the future into consideration

long′shore′man (-shôr′mən) *n., pl.* **-men** [< (a)*longshore* + MAN] a person whose work is loading and unloading ships

long shot [Colloq.] a betting choice that has little chance of winning and, hence, carries great odds

long′stand′ing *adj.* having continued for a long time

long′-suf′fer·ing *adj.* bearing trouble, etc. patiently for a long time —*n.* long and patient endurance

long′-term′ *adj.* for or extending over a long time

long ton the British ton, equal to 2,240 pounds

long′-wind′ed *adj.* **1.** speaking or writing at great length **2.** tiresomely long —**long′-wind′ed·ness** *n.*

look (look) *vi.* [OE. *lōcian*] **1.** to direct one's eyes in order to see **2.** to search **3.** to appear; seem **4.** to be facing in a specified direction **5.** to direct one's attention —*vt.* **1.** to direct one's eyes on **2.** to express by one's looks [he *looked* his disgust] **3.** to appear to be (some age) —*n.* **1.** the act of looking **2.** outward aspect **3.** [Colloq.] *a)* [*usually pl.*] appearance *b)* [*pl.*] personal appearance —*interj.* **1.** see! **2.** pay attention! —**look after** to take care of —**look alive** [Colloq.] to be alert —**look down on** (or upon) to regard with contempt —**look for** to expect —**look forward to** to anticipate —**look in** (on) to pay a brief visit (to) —**look on 1.** to be an observer **2.** to consider —**look (like) oneself** to seem in normal health, spirits, etc. —**look out** to be careful —**look over** to examine —**look to 1.** to take care of **2.** to rely upon **3.** to expect —**look up 1.** to search for in a reference book **2.** [Colloq.] to visit **3.** [Colloq.] to improve —**look up to** to admire —**look′er** *n.*

look'er-on' *n., pl.* **look'ers-on'** an observer or spectator; onlooker

looking glass a (glass) mirror

look'out' *n.* 1. a careful watching 2. a place for keeping watch 3. a person detailed to watch 4. [Colloq.] concern; worry

loom¹ (lōōm) *n.* [< OE. (ge)*loma*, tool] a machine for weaving thread or yarn into cloth

loom² (lōōm) *vi.* [< ?] to come into sight indistinctly, esp. in a large or threatening form

loon¹ (lōōn) *n.* [< ON. *lomr*] a fish-eating diving bird, noted for its weird cry

loon² (lōōn) *n.* [Scot. *loun*] a stupid or crazy person

loon-y (lōō'nē) *adj.* -i-er, -i-est [< LUNATIC] [Slang] crazy; demented —*n., pl.* -ies [Slang] a loony person Also **loon'ey**

loop (lōōp) *n.* [ME. *loup*] 1. the figure of a line, thread, etc. that curves back to cross itself 2. anything forming this figure 3. a plastic contraceptive device inserted into the uterus (usually with *the*) —*vt.* 1. to make a loop in or of 2. to fasten with a loop —*vi.* to form or move in a loop or loops

LOON
(to 34 in. long, including bill)

loop-hole (lōōp'hōl') *n.* [prob. < MDu. *lupen*, to peer + HOLE] 1. a hole or narrow slit in a wall, for looking or shooting through 2. a means of evading an obligation, a law, etc.

loose (lōōs) *adj.* [< ON.] 1. not confined or restrained; free 2. not put up in a package 3. not firmly fastened 4. not tight or compact 5. not precise; inexact 6. sexually immoral 7. moving freely, as the bowels —*adv.* loosely — *vt.* **loosed, loos'ing** 1. to set free; unbind 2. to make less tight, compact, etc. 3. to relax 4. to release [he loosed the arrow] —*vi.* to become loose —**set** (or **turn**) **loose** to release —**loose'ly** *adv.*

loose'-joint'ed *adj.* 1. having loose joints 2. moving freely; limber —**loose'-joint'ed-ly** *adv.*

loose'-leaf' *adj.* having leaves or sheets that can easily be removed or inserted

loos-en (lōōs''n) *vt., vi.* to make or become loose or looser —**loos'en-er** *n.*

loot (lōōt) *n.* [Hindi *lūt*] goods stolen or taken by force; plunder —*vt., vi.* to plunder —**loot'er** *n.*

lop¹ (läp) *vt.* **lopped, lop'ping** [OE. *loppian*] 1. to trim (a tree, etc.) by cutting off branches or twigs 2. to remove as by cutting off

lop² (läp) *vi.* **lopped, lop'ping** [prob. akin to LOB] 1. to hang down loosely 2. to move in a halting way

lope (lōp) *vi.* **loped, lop'ing** [< ON. *hlaupa*, to leap] to move with a long, swinging stride or in an easy canter — *vt.* to cause to lope —*n.* a loping stride

lop-eared (läp'ird') *adj.* having drooping ears

lop'sid'ed *adj.* (-sīd'id) noticeably heavier, bigger, or lower on one side —**lop'sid'ed-ly** *adv.* —**lop'sid'ed-ness** *n.*

lo-qua-cious (lō kwā'shəs) *adj.* [< L. *loqui*, to speak] very talkative; fond of talking —**lo-qua'cious-ly** *adv.* —**lo-quac'i-ty** (-kwas'ə tē) *n.*

Lor-an (lôr'an) *n.* [*Lo(ng) Ra(nge) N(avigation)*] [*also* l-] a system by which a ship or aircraft can determine its position by radio signals sent from two or more known stations

lord (lôrd) *n.* [< OE. *hlaf*, loaf + *weard*, keeper] 1. a ruler; master 2. the head of a feudal estate 3. [L-] *a)* God *b)* Jesus Christ 4. in Great Britain, a titled nobleman — **lord it (over)** to domineer (over)

lord'ly *adj.* -li-er, -li-est 1. noble; grand 2. haughty —*adv.* in the manner of a lord —**lord'li-ness** *n.*

lord'ship' *n.* 1. the rank or authority of a lord 2. rule; dominion 3. [*also* L-] a title used in speaking of or to a lord: with *his* or *your*

Lord's Prayer the prayer beginning *Our Father*: Matt. 6:9–13

Lord's Supper 1. *same as* LAST SUPPER 2. Holy Communion; Eucharist

lore (lôr) *n.* [OE. *lar*] knowledge or learning; specif., all the knowledge concerning a particular subject, esp. that of a traditional nature

Lor-e-lei (lôr'ə lī') [G.] *German Legend* a siren whose singing on a rock in the Rhine lured sailors to shipwreck on the reefs

lor-gnette (lôr nyet') *n.* [Fr. < OFr. *lorgne*, squinting] a pair of eyeglasses, or an opera glass, attached to a handle

lorn (lôrn) *adj.* [ME. < *losen*, lose] [Archaic] forsaken, forlorn, bereft, or desolate

lor-ry (lôr'ē, lär'-) *n., pl.* **-ries** 1. a low, flat wagon without sides 2. [Brit.] a motor truck

Los An-gel-es (lôs an'jə ləs, läs; an'gə ləs; -lēz') city on the SW coast of Calif.: pop. 2,816,000

lose (lōōz) *vt.* **lost, los'ing** [OE. *leosan*] 1. to become unable to find [I lost my key] 2. to have taken from one by accident, death, removal, etc. 3. to get rid of [to lose weight] 4. to fail to keep [to lose one's temper] 5. *a)* to fail to see, hear, or understand *b)* to fail to keep in sight, mind, etc. 6. to fail to win 7. to fail to have, get, take, etc.; miss 8. to cause the loss of [it lost him his job] 9. to wander from (one's way, etc.) 10. to waste; squander 11. to engross or preoccupy [lost in reverie] —*vi.* 1. to suffer (a) loss 2. to be slow: said of a timepiece —**lose oneself** 1. to go astray 2. to become engrossed

los-er (lōō'zər) *n.* 1. one who reacts to loss as specified [a poor *loser*] 2. [Colloq.] one who seems doomed to lose

los'ing *n.* [*pl.*] losses by gambling —*adj.* 1. that loses 2. resulting in loss

loss (lôs, läs) *n.* [< ? OE. *los*, ruin] 1. a losing or being lost 2. the damage, trouble, etc. caused by losing 3. the person, thing, or amount lost —**at a loss (to)** uncertain (how to)

loss leader any article that a store sells cheaply or below cost to attract customers

lost (lôst, läst) *pt. & pp.* of LOSE —*adj.* 1. ruined; destroyed 2. not to be found; missing 3. no longer held, seen, heard, etc. 4. not gained or won 5. having wandered from the way 6. bewildered 7. wasted —**lost in** engrossed in —**lost on** without effect on

lot (lät) *n.* [OE. *hlot*] 1. the deciding of a matter by chance, as by drawing counters 2. any of the counters so used, or the decision thus arrived at 3. one's share by lot 4. fortune [his unhappy *lot*] 5. a plot of ground 6. a group of persons or things 7. a motion-picture studio 8. [*often pl.*] [Colloq.] a great amount 9. [Colloq.] sort [he's a bad *lot*] —*adv.* very much: also **lots** —**draw** (or **cast**) **lots** to decide by lot

Lot (lät) *Bible* Abraham's nephew who fled from Sodom: his wife was turned into a pillar of salt when she glanced back at its destruction

Lo-thar-i-o (lō ther'ē ō') *n., pl.* -i-os' [< the rake in a play by N. Rowe (1674–1718)] [*often* l-] a lighthearted seducer of women

lo-tion (lō'shən) *n.* [< L. *lavare*, to wash] a liquid preparation used, as on the skin, for washing, soothing, healing, etc.

lot-ter-y (lät'ər ē) *n., pl.* -ies [see LOTTO] a game of chance in which people buy numbered chances on prizes, winners being chosen by lot

lot-to (lät'ō) *n.* [It. < Fr. < MDu. *lot*, lot] a game of chance played on cards with numbered squares: counters are placed on numbers chosen by lot

lo-tus, lo-tos (lōt'əs) *n.* [< Gr. *lōtos*] 1. *Gr. Legend* a plant whose fruit induced forgetfulness 2. any of several tropical waterlilies 3. a plant of the legume family, with yellow, purple, or white flowers

LOTUS (sense 2)

loud (loud) *adj.* [OE. *hlud*] 1. strongly audible: said of sound 2. sounding with great intensity 3. noisy 4. emphatic [loud denials] 5. [Colloq.] *a)* flashy *b)* vulgar —*adv.* in a loud manner —**loud'ly** *adv.* —**loud'ness** *n.*

loud'speak'er *n.* a device for converting electrical energy to sound and amplifying it

Lou-is (lōō'ē) 1. **Louis XIV** 1638–1715; king of France (1643–1715) 2. **Louis XV** 1710–74; king of France (1715–74) 3. **Louis XVI** 1754–93; king of France (1774–92); guillotined

Lou-ise (lōō wēz'), **Lake** small lake in Alberta, Canada

Lou-i-si-an-a (lōō wē'zē an'ə, lōō'ə zē-) Southern State of the U.S.: 48,523 sq. mi.; pop. 3,643,000; cap. Baton Rouge: abbrev. **La., LA** —**Lou-i'si-an'i-an, Lou-i'si-an'an** *adj., n.*

Lou-is-ville (lōō'ē vil) city in N Ky., on the Ohio River: pop. 361,000 (met. area 827,000)

lounge (lounj) *vi.* **lounged, loung'ing** [Scot. dial. < ? *lungis*, laggard] 1. to stand, move, sit, etc. in a relaxed or lazy way 2. to spend time in idleness —*n.* 1. a room with comfortable furniture 2. a couch or sofa —**loung'er** *n.*

lour (lour) *vi., n. same as* LOWER²

Lourdes (loord, loordz) town in SW France: site of a famous Catholic shrine

louse (lous) *n., pl.* **lice** [OE. *lus*] 1. a small, wingless insect parasitic on man and other animals 2. any similar insect parasitic on plants **3.** *pl.* **lous′es** [Slang] a mean, contemptible person —**louse up** [Slang] to botch; spoil; ruin

lous·y (lou′zē) *adj.* **-i·er, -i·est 1.** infested with lice **2.** [Slang] *a)* disgusting *b)* poor; inferior *c)* oversupplied (*with*) —**lous′i·ly** *adv.* —**lous′i·ness** *n.*

lout (lout) *n.* [prob. < ME. *lutien*, to lurk] a clumsy, stupid fellow; boor —**lout′ish** *adj.* —**lout′ish·ness** *n.*

lou·ver (lōō′vər) *n.* [< MDu. *love*, theater gallery] **1.** an opening fitted with sloping slats (**louver boards**) so as to admit light and air but shed rain **2.** any of these slats **3.** any ventilating slit Also **lou′vre** —**lou′vered** *adj.*

Lou·vre (lōō′vrə, lōōv) ancient royal palace in Paris, now an art museum

love (luv) *n.* [OE. *lufu*] **1.** a deep affection or liking for someone or something **2.** a passionate affection of one person for another **3.** the object of this; sweetheart **4.** sexual passion or intercourse **5.** *Tennis* a score of zero — *vt., vi.* **loved, lov′ing** to feel love (for) —**fall in love (with)** to begin to feel love (for) —**for the love of** for the sake of —**in love** feeling love —**make love 1.** to woo, embrace, etc. **2.** to have sexual intercourse —**lov′a·ble, love′a·ble** *adj.* —**love′less** *adj.*

love′bird′ *n.* any of various small parrots, often kept as cage birds: the mates appear to be greatly attached to each other

love′-lies′-bleed′ing *n.* a cultivated amaranth with spikes of small, red flowers

love′lorn′ *adj.* pining from love

love′ly *adj.* **-li·er, -li·est 1.** very pleasing in looks or character; beautiful **2.** [Colloq.] highly enjoyable —**love′li·ness** *n.*

lov·er (luv′ər) *n.* **1.** a sweetheart **2.** [*pl.*] a couple in love with each other **3.** one who greatly enjoys some (specified) thing —**lov′er·ly** *adj., adv.*

love seat a small sofa for two

love′sick′ *adj.* **1.** so much in love as to be unable to act normally **2.** expressive of such a condition —**love′sick′-ness** *n.*

lov′ing *adj.* feeling or expressing love —**lov′ing·ly** *adv.*

loving cup a large drinking cup with two handles, often given as a trophy in sports

lov′ing-kind′ness *n.* kindness expressing love

low¹ (lō) *adj.* [< ON. *lagr*] **1.** not high or tall **2.** below the normal or usual surface or level [*low* ground] **3.** shallow **4.** less in amount, degree, cost, power, etc. than usual [*low* speed] **5.** deep in pitch **6.** depressed; melancholy **7.** not of high rank; humble **8.** vulgar; coarse **9.** poor; unfavorable **10.** not loud **11.** not advanced in evolution **12.** not well supplied with —*adv.* in or to a low level, degree, position, etc. [pitch the ball *low*, speak *low*] —*n.* **1.** a low level, degree, etc. **2.** an arrangement of gears giving the lowest speed and greatest power **3.** *Meteorol.* an area of low pressure —**lay low** to overcome or kill —**lie low** to keep oneself hidden —**low′ness** *n.*

low² (lō) *vi.* [OE. *hlowan*] to make the characteristic sound of a cow; moo —*n.* this sound

low′born′ *adj.* of humble birth

low′boy′ *n.* a chest of drawers mounted on short legs

low′bred′ *adj.* ill-mannered; vulgar

low′brow′ *n.* one considered to lack intellectual tastes —*adj.* [Colloq.] of or for lowbrows

Low Church that party of the Anglican Church which attaches little importance to the priesthood or to traditional rituals, doctrines, etc. —**Low′-Church′** *adj.*

Low Countries, the the Netherlands, Belgium, & Luxembourg

low′down′ *n.* [Slang] the pertinent facts (with *the*) —*adj.* (lō′doun′) [Colloq.] mean; contemptible

Low·ell (lō′əl), **James Russell** 1819–91; U.S. poet, essayist, & editor

low·er¹ (lō′ər) *adj. compar. of* LOW¹ below or farther down in place, rank, etc. —*vt.* **1.** to let or put down [to *lower* a window] **2.** to reduce in height, amount, etc. [to *lower* prices] **3.** to weaken or lessen **4.** to demean **5.** to reduce (a sound) in volume or in pitch —*vi.* **1.** to become lower; sink, fall, etc.

low·er² (lou′ər) *vi.* [ME. *louren*] **1.** to scowl or frown **2.** to appear dark and threatening —*n.* a frowning or threatening look

Lower California *same as* BAJA CALIFORNIA

lower case small-letter type used in printing, as distinguished from capital letters (*upper case*) —**low′er-case′** *adj.* —**low′er-case′** *vt.* **-cased′, -cas′ing**

lower class the working class; proletariat

low′er·class′man *n., pl.* **-men** a student who is a freshman or sophomore

Lower House [*often* l- h-] the larger and more representative branch of a legislature having two branches, as the U.S. House of Representatives

low·er·ing (lou′ər iŋ) *adj.* **1.** scowling; frowning darkly **2.** dark, as if about to rain or snow —**low′er·ing·ly** *adv.*

low′er·most′ *adj.* lowest

lower world 1. *same as* NETHER WORLD **2.** the earth

low frequency any radio frequency between 30 and 300 kilohertz

Low German 1. the Germanic dialects of N Germany **2.** the branch of Germanic languages including English, Dutch, Flemish, etc.

low′-grade′ *adj.* **1.** of inferior quality **2.** of low degree [a *low-grade* infection]

low′-key′ *adj.* of low intensity, tone, etc.; subdued

low·land (lō′lənd, -land′) *n.* land below the level of the surrounding land —**the Lowlands** lowlands of SC Scotland —**low′land·er, Low′land·er** *n.*

Low Latin nonclassical, esp. medieval, Latin

low′ly *adj.* **-li·er, -li·est 1.** of low position or rank **2.** humble; meek —*adv.* **1.** humbly **2.** in a low manner, position, etc. **3.** softly; gently —**low′li·ness** *n.*

Low Mass a Mass said, not sung, less ceremonial than High Mass, and offered by one priest

low′-mind′ed *adj.* having or showing a coarse, vulgar mind —**low′-mind′ed·ness** *n.*

low′-spir′it·ed *adj.* sad; melancholy

low tide 1. the lowest level reached by the ebbing tide **2.** the time when this point is reached

lox (läks) *n.* [< Yid. < G. *lachs*, salmon] a variety of salty smoked salmon

loy·al (loi′əl) *adj.* [Fr.: see LEGAL] **1.** faithful to one's country, friends, ideals, etc. **2.** of or indicating loyalty — **loy′al·ly** *adv.*

loy·al·ist *n.* **1.** one who supports the established government of his country during a revolt **2.** [*often* L-] in the American Revolution, a colonist loyal to England **3.** [L-] in the Spanish Civil War (1936–39), one who remained loyal to the Republic —**loy′al·ism** *n.*

loy·al·ty *n., pl.* **-ties** quality, state, or instance of being loyal; faithful adherence, etc.

loz·enge (läz′′nj) *n.* [OFr. *losenge*] **1.** a diamond-shaped figure **2.** a cough drop, candy, etc., orig. in this shape

LP [*L(ong) P(laying)*] *a trademark for* a long playing record —*n.* a long-playing record

LPN, L.P.N. Licensed Practical Nurse

LSD [*l(y)s(ergic acid) d(iethylamide)*] a psychedelic drug that produces behavior and symptoms, as hallucinations, etc., like those of certain psychoses

Lt. Lieutenant

Ltd., ltd. limited

Lu *Chem.* lutetium

lu·au (lōō ou′, lōō′ou′) *n.* [Haw.] a Hawaiian feast, usually with entertainment

lub·ber (lub′ər) *n.* [< ME. *lobbe-*, heavy] **1.** a big, slow, clumsy person **2.** a landlubber —**lub′ber·li·ness** *n.* —**lub′-ber·ly** *adj., adv.*

Lub·bock (lub′ək) city in NW Tex.: pop. 149,000

lube (lōōb) *n.* **1.** a lubricating oil: also **lube oil 2.** [Colloq.] a lubrication

lu·bri·cant (lōō′brə kənt) *adj.* reducing friction by providing a smooth surface film over parts that move against each other —*n.* a lubricant oil, grease, etc.

lu·bri·cate (-kāt′) *vt.* **-cat·ed, -cat′ing** [< L. *lubricus*, smooth] **1.** to make slippery or smooth **2.** to apply a lubricant to —**lu′bri·ca′tion** *n.* —**lu′bri·ca′tor** *n.*

lu·bric·i·ty (lōō bris′ə tē) *n., pl.* **-ties 1.** slipperiness; smoothness **2.** trickiness **3.** lewdness

lu·cent (lōō′s′nt) *adj.* [< L. *lucere*, to shine] **1.** giving off light; shining **2.** translucent

lu·cid (lōō′sid) *adj.* [< L. *lucere*, to shine] **1.** shining **2.** transparent **3.** sane **4.** readily understood **5.** rational —**lu·cid′i·ty, lu′cid·ness** *n.* —**lu′cid·ly** *adv.*

Lu·ci·fer (lōō′sə fər) [< L. *lux*, LIGHT¹ + *ferre*, to BEAR¹] **1.** [Poet.] the planet Venus when it is the morning star **2.** *Theol.* Satan, esp. as leader of the revolt of the angels before his fall

Lu·cite (lōō′sīt) [< L. *lux*, light + -ITE] *a trademark for* a transparent or translucent acrylic resin or plastic

luck (luk) *n.* [prob. < MDu. *luk* < *gelucke*] **1.** the seemingly chance happening of events which affect one; fortune **2.** good fortune —**down on one's luck** unlucky —**in**

luck lucky —**luck out** [Colloq.] to have things turn out favorably for one —**out of luck** unlucky —**luck′less** adj.

luck′y adj. **-i·er, -i·est 1.** having good luck **2.** resulting fortunately **3.** believed to bring good luck —**luck′i·ly** adv. —**luck′i·ness** n.

lu·cra·tive (lōō′krə tiv) adj. [< L. lucrum, riches] producing wealth or profit; profitable —**lu′cra·tive·ly** adv. —**lu′cra·tive·ness** n.

lu·cre (lōō′kər) n. [< L. lucrum, riches] riches; money: chiefly derogatory, as in **filthy lucre**

Lu·cre·tius (lōō krē′shəs) 96?–55? B.C.; Rom. poet & philosopher

lu·cu·brate (lōō′kyŏŏ brāt′) vi. **-brat′ed, -brat′ing** [< L. lucubrare, to work by candlelight] **1.** to work or study laboriously, esp. late at night **2.** to write in a scholarly manner —**lu′cu·bra′tion** n.

lu·di·crous (lōō′di krəs) adj. [< L. ludus, a game] causing laughter because absurd or ridiculous —**lu′di·crous·ly** adv. —**lu′di·crous·ness** n.

luff (luf) n. [< ODu.] **1.** a sailing close to the wind **2.** the forward edge of a fore-and-aft sail —vi. to turn the bow of a ship toward the wind

lug (lug) vt. **lugged, lug′ging** [prob. < Scand.] to carry or drag with effort —n. **1.** an earlike projection by which a thing is held or supported **2.** a heavy nut used with a bolt to secure a wheel to an axle **3.** a shallow box in which fruit is shipped **4.** [Slang] a lout

luge (lōōzh) n. [Fr.] a racing sled for one or two persons

lug·gage (lug′ij) n. [< LUG + -AGE] suitcases, valises, trunks, etc.; baggage

lug·ger (lug′ər) n. a small vessel equipped with a lugsail or lugsails

lug·sail (lug′s'l, -sāl′) n. [prob. < LUG, v.] a four-sided sail attached to an upper yard that hangs obliquely on the mast

lu·gu·bri·ous (lŏŏ gōō′brē əs, -gyōō′-) adj. [< L. lugere, mourn] mournful, esp. in a way that seems exaggerated or ridiculous —**lu·gu′bri·ous·ly** adv.

Luke (lōōk) Bible **1.** a Christian apostle, the reputed author of the third Gospel **2.** this book

luke·warm (lōōk′wôrm′) adj. [ME. luke, tepid + warm, WARM] **1.** barely or moderately warm **2.** lacking enthusiasm —**luke′warm′ly** adv. —**luke′warm′ness** n.

lull (lul) vt. [ME. lullen] **1.** to calm by gentle sound or motion **2.** to bring into a specified condition by soothing and reassuring **3.** to allay —vi. to become calm —n. a short period of calm

lull·a·by (lul′ə bī′) n., pl. **-bies′** a song for lulling a baby to sleep

lum·ba·go (lum bā′gō) n. [< L. lumbus, loin] pain in the lower back

lum·bar (lum′bər, -bär) adj. [< L. lumbus, loin] of or near the loins; specif., designating the vertebrae, nerves, etc. just below the thoracic part of the body

lum·ber¹ (lum′bər) n. [< ? pawnshop of Lombardy, in Italy] **1.** discarded household articles, furniture, etc. stored or taking up room **2.** timber sawed into beams, boards, etc. —vi. to cut down timber and saw it into lumber —**lum′ber·er** n. —**lum′ber·ing** n.

lum·ber² (lum′bər) vi. [< ? Scand.] to move heavily and noisily —**lum′ber·ing** adj. —**lum′ber·ing·ly** adv.

lum·ber·jack (lum′bər jak′) n. a person whose work is cutting down timber and preparing it for the sawmill; logger

lum′ber·man (-mən) n., pl. **-men 1.** a logger; lumberjack **2.** one who deals in lumber

lum′ber·yard′ n. a place where lumber is kept for sale

lu·men (lōō′mən) n., pl. **-mi·na** (-mi nə), **-mens** [< L., light] a unit of measure for the flow of light equal to the amount of flow from a uniform point source of one candle

lu·mi·nar·y (lōō′mə ner′ē) n., pl. **-ies** [< L. lumen, light] **1.** a body that gives off light, such as the sun **2.** a famous person

lu·mi·nes·cence (lōō′mə nes′'ns) n. [< L. lumen, a light + -ESCENCE] any giving off of light caused by the absorption of radiant energy, etc. and not by incandescence; any cold light —**lu′mi·nes′cent** adj.

lu·mi·nous (lōō′mə nəs) adj. [< L. lumen, a light] **1.** giving off light; bright **2.** glowing in the dark **3.** enlightening; clear —**lu′mi·nos′i·ty** (-näs′ə tē), pl. **-ties, lu′mi·nous·ness** n. —**lu′mi·nous·ly** adv.

lum·mox (lum′əks) n. [< ?] [Colloq.] a clumsy, stupid person

lump¹ (lump) n. [ME. lumpe] **1.** an indefinitely shaped mass of something **2.** a small cube, or oblong piece, as of sugar **3.** a swelling **4.** a large amount; mass **5.** [pl.] [Colloq.] hard blows, criticism, etc.: in **get** (or **take**) one's

lumps —adj. in lumps [lump sugar] —vt. **1.** to put together in a lump or lumps **2.** to treat or deal with in a mass, or collectively —vi. to become lumpy —**lump in one's throat** a tight feeling in the throat, as from restrained emotion

lump² (lump) vt. [Early ModE., to look sour] [Colloq.] to put up with (something disagreeable)

lump′ish adj. **1.** like a lump **2.** clumsy, dull, etc. —**lump′ish·ly** adv. —**lump′ish·ness** n.

lump′y adj. **-i·er, -i·est 1.** full of lumps **2.** covered with lumps **3.** like a lump; heavy; clumsy —**lump′i·ness** n.

lu·na·cy (lōō′nə sē) n., pl. **-cies** [< LUNATIC] **1.** [Now Rare] insanity **2.** utter foolishness

luna moth a large moth of N. America with green wings, the hind pair of which end in long tails

lu·nar (lōō′nər) adj. [see LUNATE] of, on, or like the moon

lunar month the interval from one new moon to the next, equal to about 29 1/2 days

lu·nate (lōō′nāt) adj. [< L. luna, the moon] crescent-shaped: also **lu′nat·ed** —**lu′nate·ly** adv.

lu·na·tic (lōō′nə tik) adj. [< L. luna, the moon] **1.** [Now Rare] a) insane b) of or for insane persons **2.** utterly foolish —n. an insane person

lunatic fringe the minority considered fanatical in any political, social, or other movement

lunch (lunch) n. [? < Sp. lonja, slice of ham] any light meal; esp., the midday meal between breakfast and dinner —vi. to eat lunch —**lunch′er** n.

lunch·eon (lun′chən) n. a lunch; esp., a formal lunch

lunch′eon·ette′ (-chə net′) n. a small restaurant where light lunches can be had

luncheon meat meat processed in loaves, sausages, etc. and ready to eat

lunch′room′ n. a restaurant where light, quick meals are served

lung (lung) n. [OE. lungen] either of the two spongelike breathing organs in the thorax of vertebrates —**at the top of one's lungs** in one's loudest voice

lunge (lunj) n. [< Fr. allonger, lengthen] **1.** a sudden thrust, as with a sword **2.** a sudden plunge forward —vi., vt. **lunged, lung′ing** to move, or cause to move, with a lunge —**lung′er** n.

lung′fish′ n., pl.: see FISH any of various fishes having lungs as well as gills

lu·pine (lōō′pīn) adj. [< L. lupus, wolf] of or like a wolf —n. (-pin) a plant related to the pea, with long spikes of white, rose, or blue flowers

lurch¹ (lurch) vi. [< ?] **1.** to pitch or sway suddenly to one side **2.** to stagger —n. a lurching movement

lurch² (lurch) n. [prob. < OFr. lourche, duped] a difficult situation: only in **leave in the lurch**

lure (loor) n. [< OFr. loirre] **1.** a feathered device on the end of a long cord, used in falconry to recall the hawk **2.** a) the power of attracting or enticing b) anything having this power **3.** a bait used in fishing —vt. **lured, lur′ing** to attract; tempt; entice —**lur′er** n.

lu·rid (loor′id) adj. [L. luridus, ghastly] **1.** glowing through a haze, as flames enveloped by smoke **2.** shocking; sensational; startling **3.** [Rare] deathly pale —**lu′rid·ly** adv. —**lu′rid·ness** n.

lurk (lurk) vi. [ME. lurken] **1.** to stay hidden, ready to attack, etc. **2.** to be present as a latent threat **3.** to move furtively —**lurk′er** n.

lus·cious (lush′əs) adj. [ME. lucius] **1.** highly gratifying to taste or smell; delicious **2.** delighting any of the senses —**lus′cious·ly** adv. —**lus′cious·ness** n.

lush¹ (lush) adj. [< ? OFr. lasche, lax] **1.** tender and full of juice **2.** of or characterized by rich growth [lush vegetation] **3.** rich, abundant, extravagant, etc. —**lush′ly** adv. —**lush′ness** n.

lush² (lush) n. [Slang] an alcoholic

lust (lust) n. [OE., pleasure] **1.** bodily appetite; esp., strong sexual desire **2.** an intense desire [a lust for power] —vi. to feel an intense desire, esp. sexual desire —**lust′ful** adj. —**lust′ful·ly** adv. —**lust′ful·ness** n.

lus·ter (lus′tər) n. [< L. lustrare, illumine] **1.** gloss; sheen **2.** brightness; radiance **3.** brilliant beauty or fame; glory Chiefly Brit. sp. **lustre**

lus′trous (-trəs) adj. having luster; shining —**lus′trous·ly** adv. —**lus′trous·ness** n.

lust·y (lus′tē) adj. **-i·er, -i·est** full of vigor; strong; robust —**lust′i·ly** adv. —**lust′i·ness** n.

lute (lōōt) n. [ult. < Ar. al′ūd, the wood] an early stringed instrument with a rounded back and a long, fretted neck

lu·te·ti·um (lōō tē′shē əm) n. [< L. Lutetia, ancient Rom. name for Paris] a metallic chemical element of the rare-earth group: symbol, Lu; at. wt., 174.97; at. no., 71

Lu·ther (lōō'thər), **Martin** 1483–1546; leader of the Protestant Reformation in Germany
Lu'ther·an *adj.* of the Protestant denomination founded by Martin Luther —*n.* a member of the Lutheran Church —**Lu'ther·an·ism** *n.*
lut·ist (lōōt'ist) *n.* a lute player: also **lu·ta·nist** (lōōt'ʼn ist)
Lux·em·bourg (luk'səm burg') **1.** grand duchy in W Europe, north of France: 998 sq. mi.; pop. 337,000 **2.** its capital: pop. 79,000 Also sp. **Luxemburg**
lux·u·ri·ant (lug zhoor'ē ənt) *adj.* [see LUXURY] **1.** growing with vigor and in abundance; lush; teeming **2.** richly varied, elaborate, etc. —**lux·u'ri·ance** *n.* —**lux·u'ri·ant·ly** *adv.*
lux·u'ri·ate (-āt') *vi.* -at'ed, -at'ing **1.** to live in great luxury **2.** to take great pleasure; revel (*in*)
lux·u'ri·ous *adj.* **1.** fond of or indulging in luxury **2.** full of luxury; rich, comfortable, etc. —**lux·u'ri·ous·ly** *adv.* —**lux·u'ri·ous·ness** *n.*
lux·u·ry (luk'shə rē, lug'zhə-) *n., pl.* -ries [< L. *luxus*] **1.** the enjoyment of the best and most costly things **2.** anything giving such enjoyment, usually something not a necessity
Lu·zon (lōō zän') main island of the Philippines
-ly [< OE. *-lic*] *a suffix meaning:* **1.** like or characteristic of *[manly]* **2.** in a (specified) manner, to a (specified) extent or direction, in or at a (specified) time or place *[harshly, outwardly, hourly]* **3.** in sequence *[thirdly]* **4.** happening (once) every (specified period) *[monthly]*
‡ly·cée (lē sā') *n.* [Fr.] in France, a public, college-preparatory secondary school
ly·ce·um (lī sē'əm, lī'sē-) *n.* [< Gr. *Lykeion,* grove at Athens where Aristotle taught] **1.** a lecture hall **2.** an organization providing public lectures, etc.
Lyd·i·a (lid'ē ə) ancient kingdom in W Asia Minor —**Lyd'i·an** *adj., n.*
lye (lī) *n.* [OE. *leag*] any strongly alkaline substance, used in cleaning and in making soap
ly·ing[1] (lī'iŋ) *prp. of* LIE[1]
ly·ing[2] (lī'iŋ) *prp. of* LIE[2] —*adj.* false; not truthful —*n.* the telling of a lie or lies
ly'ing-in' *n.* confinement in childbirth —*adj.* of or for childbirth *[a lying-in hospital]*

lymph (limf) *n.* [L. *lympha,* spring water] a clear, yellowish fluid resembling blood plasma, found in the lymphatic vessels of vertebrates
lym·phat·ic (lim fat'ik) *adj.* **1.** of, containing, or conveying lymph **2.** sluggish —*n.* a lymphatic vessel
lymph node any of the compact structures lying in groups along the course of the lymphatic vessels
lymph·oid (lim'foid) *adj.* of or like lymph or the tissue of the lymph nodes
lynch (linch) *vt.* [< W. *Lynch,* vigilante in Va. in 1780] to murder (an accused person) by mob action, without lawful trial, as by hanging —**lynch'er** *n.* —**lynch'ing** *n.*
lynx (liŋks) *n.* [< Gr. *lynx*] a wildcat found throughout the N Hemisphere, having a short tail and tufted ears
lynx'-eyed' (-īd') *adj.* having very keen sight
Lyon (lyōn) city in EC France: pop. 528,000
ly·on·naise (lī'ə nāz') *adj.* [Fr., of *Lyon*] prepared with sliced, fried onions *[lyonnaise potatoes]*
lyre (līr) *n.* [< Gr. *lyra*] a small stringed instrument resembling the harp, used by the ancient Greeks
lyr·ic (lir'ik) *adj.* [< Gr. *lyrikos*] **1.** suitable for singing; specif., designating or of poetry expressing the poet's personal emotion **2.** of or having a high voice with a light, flexible quality *[a lyric tenor]* —*n.* **1.** a lyric poem **2.** *[usually pl.]* the words of a song

LYRE

lyr'i·cal (-i k'l) *adj.* **1.** *same as* LYRIC **2.** expressing rapture or great enthusiasm —**lyr'i·cal·ly** *adv.*
lyr·i·cism (lir'ə siz'm) *n.* lyric quality, style, expression, etc.
lyr'i·cist (-sist) *n.* a writer of lyrics, esp. for popular songs
-lysis [< Gr. *lysis,* a loosening] *a combining form meaning* a loosing, dissolution, dissolving, destruction *[electrolysis, paralysis]*
-lyte [see -LYSIS] *a combining form meaning* a substance undergoing decomposition *[electrolyte]*
-lytic *a combining form used to form adjectives corresponding to nouns ending in* -LYSIS *[paralytic]*
-lyze *a combining form used to form verbs corresponding to nouns ending in* -LYSIS *[electrolyze]*

M

M, m (em) *n., pl.* **M's, m's** the thirteenth letter of the English alphabet
M (em) *n.* a Roman numeral for 1,000
M. 1. Monday **2.** *pl.* **MM.** Monsieur
M., m. 1. male **2.** married **3.** masculine **4.** *Physics* mass **5.** mile(s) **6.** minute(s) **7.** month **8.** [L. *meridies*] noon
m., m meter(s)
ma (mä) *n.* [Colloq.] mother
MA Massachusetts
M.A. Master of Arts
ma'am (mam, mäm, məm) *n.* [Colloq.] madam: used in direct address
ma·ca·bre (mə käb'rə, mə käb') *adj.* [Fr. < OFr. (*danse*) *Macabré,* (dance) of death] gruesome; grim and horrible: also **ma·ca'ber** (-kä'bər)
mac·ad·am (mə kad'əm) *n.* [< J. L. *McAdam* (1756–1836), Scot. engineer] **1.** small broken stones used in making roads, usually combined with tar or asphalt **2.** a macadamized road
mac·ad'am·ize' (-ə mīz') *vt.* -ized', -iz'ing to make, repair, or cover (a road) by rolling successive layers of macadam on it
Ma·cao (mə kou') Port. territory in SE China, near Hong Kong
ma·caque (mə käk') *n.* [Fr. < Port. *macaco*] any of a group of monkeys of Asia, Africa, and the East Indies, with a tail that is not prehensile
mac·a·ro·ni (mak'ə rō'nē) *n.* [It. *maccaroni,* ult. < Gr. *makar,* blessed] **1.** pasta in the form of tubes, etc., often

baked with cheese, ground meat, etc. **2.** *pl.* -nies an 18th-cent. English dandy
mac·a·roon (mak'ə rōōn') *n.* [see prec.] a small cookie made of crushed almonds or coconut, and sugar
Ma·cau·lay (mə kô'lē), **Thomas Bab·ing·ton** (bab'iŋ tən) 1800–59; Eng. historian & essayist
ma·caw (mə kô') *n.* [prob. < Braz. native name] a large, bright-colored parrot of Central and South America
Mac·beth (mək beth') the title hero of a tragedy by Shakespeare
Mac·ca·bees (mak'ə bēz') **1.** a family of Jewish patriots who headed a successful revolt against Syria (175–164 B.C.) **2.** two books of the Old Testament Apocrypha that tell of this revolt
Mace (mās) [< MACE[1]] *a trademark for* a chemical compound used as a tear gas and a nerve gas
mace[1] (mās) *n.* [OFr. *masse*] **1.** a heavy, spiked war club, used in the Middle Ages **2.** a staff used as a symbol of authority by certain officials
mace[2] (mās) *n.* [< ML. *macis*] a spice, usually ground, made from the dried husk of the nutmeg
Mac·e·do·ni·a (mas'ə dō'nē ə) ancient kingdom in SE Europe —**Mac'e·do'ni·an** *adj., n.*
mac·er·ate (mas'ə rāt') *vt.* -at'ed, -at'ing [< L. *macerare,* soften] **1.** to soften or separate the parts of by soaking in liquid **2.** loosely, to tear, chop, etc. into bits **3.** to cause to waste away —*vi.* to waste away; grow thin —**mac'er·a'tion** *n.*
mach. 1. machine **2.** machinery

ma·che·te (mə shet′ē, -chet′ē) *n.* [Sp. < L. *marcus*, hammer] a large, heavy-bladed knife used for cutting sugar cane, etc., esp. in Central and South America

Mach·i·a·vel·li (mak′ē ə vel′ē), **Nic·co·lò** (nē′kô lô′) 1469–1527; Florentine statesman & writer

Mach′i·a·vel′li·an *adj.* of or like Machiavelli or the political principles of craftiness and duplicity he advocated —*n.* a follower of such principles

MACHETE

mach·i·na·tion (mak′ə nā′shən) *n.* [< L. *machinari*, to plot] an artful or secret plot or scheme, esp. an evil one: *usually used in pl.*

ma·chine (mə shēn′) *n.* [Fr. < Gr. *mēchos*, contrivance] 1. a vehicle, as an automobile: an old-fashioned term 2. a structure consisting of a framework with various moving parts, for doing some kind of work 3. a person or organization functioning like a machine 4. the controlling group in a political party 5. a device, as the lever or screw, that transmits, or changes the application of, energy —*adj.* 1. of machines 2. done by machinery —*vt.* -chined′, -chin′ing to make, shape, etc. by machinery

machine gun an automatic gun, firing a rapid stream of bullets —**ma·chine′-gun′** *vt.* -gunned′, -gun′ning

machine language the system of signs, symbols, etc. used by a computer

ma·chin·er·y (mə shēn′ər ē, -shēn′rē) *n., pl.* -ies 1. machines collectively 2. the working parts of a machine 3. any means by which something is kept in action [the *machinery* of government]

machine shop a factory for making or repairing machines or machine parts

machine tool a power-driven tool, as an electric lathe or drill —**ma·chine′-tool′** *adj., vt.*

ma·chin′ist *n.* one who makes, repairs, or operates machinery

‡**ma·chis·mo** (mä chēz′mô) *n.* [Sp. < *macho*, masculine] assertive masculinity; virility

Mach (number) (mäk) [< E. *Mach* (1838–1916), Austrian physicist] [*also* m-] a number representing the ratio of the speed of an object to the speed of sound through the same medium, as air

‡**ma·cho** (mä′chō) *adj.* [Sp. < Port., ult. < L. *masculus*, MASCULINE] masculine, virile, courageous, etc.

Mac·ken·zie (mə ken′zē) river in NW Canada: 2,635 mi.

mack·er·el (mak′ər əl) *n., pl.* -el, -els [< OFr. *makerel*] an edible fish of the North Atlantic, with a greenish, blue-striped back and a silvery belly

Mack·i·nac (mak′ə nô′), **Straits of** strait connecting Lake Huron & Lake Michigan

Mack·i·naw coat (mak′ə nô′) [< *Mackinac* Is. in N Lake Huron] a short, heavy, double-breasted coat of wool, usually plaid: also **mackinaw** *n.*

mack·in·tosh (mak′in täsh′) *n.* [< C. *Macintosh* (1766–1843), the Scot. inventor] a waterproof raincoat, or the fabric for it

Ma·con (mā′kən) city in C Ga.: pop. 122,000

mac·ra·mé (mak′rə mā′) *n.* [Fr., ult. < Ar. *miqramah*, a veil] a coarse fringe or lace knotted in designs

macro- [< Gr. *makros*, long] *a combining form meaning* long, large, enlarged or elongated

mac·ro·bi·ot·ics (mak′rō bī ät′iks) *n.pl.* [*with sing. v.*] [< prec. & Gr. *bios*, life] the art of prolonging life, as by a special diet —**mac′ro·bi·ot′ic** *adj.*

mac·ro·cosm (mak′rə käz′m) *n.* [see MACRO- & COSMOS] 1. the universe 2. any large, complex entity

mac·ron (mā′krən, -krän) *n.* [< Gr. *makros*, long] a mark (ˉ) placed over a vowel to indicate its pronunciation

mad (mad) *adj.* **mad′der, mad′dest** [< OE. (ge)*mædan*, make mad] 1. mentally ill; insane 2. frantic [mad with fear] 3. foolish and rash 4. infatuated [she's *mad* about him] 5. wildly amusing 6. having rabies [a *mad* dog] 7. angry —*n.* an angry mood —**mad as a hatter** completely crazy

Mad·a·gas·car (mad′ə gas′kər) country that is an island off the SE coast of Africa: 229,940 sq. mi.; pop. 6,750,000

mad·am (mad′əm) *n., pl.* -ams; for 1, usually **mes·dames** (mā däm′) [< Fr., orig. *ma dame*, my lady] 1. a woman; lady: a polite term of address 2. a woman in charge of a brothel

mad·ame (mad′əm; Fr. mä däm′) *n., pl.* **mes·dames** (mā däm′) [Fr.] a married woman: French title [**M-**] equivalent to *Mrs.*: abbrev. **Mme., Mdme.**

mad′cap′ *n.* [MAD + CAP, fig. for head] a reckless, impulsive person —*adj.* reckless and impulsive

mad·den (mad′'n) *vt., vi.* to make or become mad; make

or become insane, angry, or wildly excited —**mad′den·ing** *adj.* —**mad′den·ing·ly** *adv.*

mad·der (mad′ər) *n.* [OE. *mædere*] 1. any of various plants; esp., a vine with yellow flowers and a red root 2. a red dye made from the root

mad·ding (mad′iŋ) *adj.* [Rare] 1. raving; frenzied ["the *madding* crowd"] 2. making mad

made (mād) *pt. & pp. of* MAKE —*adj.* 1. constructed 2. produced artificially 3. sure of success

Ma·deir·a (mə dir′ə) 1. group of Port. islands in the Atlantic, off the W coast of Morocco 2. largest island of this group —*n.* [*also* m-] a strong white wine made on this island

ma·de·moi·selle (mad′ə mə zel′; Fr. mäd mwä zel′) *n.,* Fr. *pl.* **mesde·moi·selles** (mäd mwä zel′) [Fr. < *ma*, my + *demoiselle*, young lady] an unmarried woman or girl: French title [**M-**] equivalent to *Miss:* abbrev. **Mlle.**

made′-to-or′der *adj.* made to conform to the customer's specifications; custom-made

made′-up′ *adj.* 1. put together 2. invented; false [a *made-up* story] 3. with cosmetics applied

mad′house′ *n.* 1. [Archaic] a place of confinement for the mentally ill 2. any place of turmoil, noise, etc.

Mad·i·son (mad′i s'n) capital of Wis.: pop. 173,000

Mad·i·son (mad′i s'n), **James** 1751–1836; 4th president of the U.S. (1809–17)

mad′ly *adv.* 1. insanely 2. wildly 3. foolishly 4. extremely

mad′man′ *n., pl.* -men′ an insane person; lunatic —**mad′wom′an** *n.fem., pl.* -wom′en

mad′ness *n.* 1. insanity 2. great anger 3. great folly 4. wild excitement 5. rabies

Ma·don·na (mə dän′ə) [It. < *ma*, my + *donna*, lady] Mary, mother of Jesus —*n.* a picture or statue of Mary

Ma·dras (mə dras′, -dräs′) seaport on the SE coast of India: pop. 1,729,000

ma·dras (mad′rəs, mə dras′) *n.* [< prec.] a fine, firm cotton cloth, usually striped or plaid

mad·re·pore (mad′rə pôr′) *n.* [< Fr. < It. *madre*, mother + *poro*, a pore] any of various branching corals that form coral reefs

Ma·drid (mə drid′) capital of Spain, in the C part: pop. 2,867,000

mad·ri·gal (mad′ri gəl) *n.* [< It.] 1. a short poem, usually of love, that can be set to music 2. a part song, without accompaniment, popular in the 15th to 17th cent.

mael·strom (māl′strəm) *n.* [< Du. *malen*, grind + *stroom*, a stream] 1. a large or violent whirlpool 2. a violently agitated state of mind, affairs, etc.

ma·es·to·so (mīs tō′sō; It. mä′e stô′sô) *adj., adv.* [It.] *Music* with majesty or dignity

ma·es·tro (mīs′trō, mä es′-) *n., pl.* -tros, -tri (-trē) [It. < L. *magister*, master] a master in any art; esp., a great composer, conductor, or teacher of music

Ma·fi·a, Maf·fi·a (mä′fē ə) *n.* [It. *maffia*, hostility to law] an alleged secret society of criminals in the U.S. and other countries

mag. 1. magazine 2. magnetism 3. magnitude

mag·a·zine (mag′ə zēn′) *n.* [< Fr. < Ar. *makhzan*, granary] 1. a warehouse or military supply depot 2. a space in which explosives are stored, as in a fort 3. a supply chamber, as in a rifle, camera, etc. 4. a periodical publication containing stories, articles, etc.

Ma·gel·lan (mə jel′ən), **Ferdinand** 1480?–1521; Port. navigator in the service of Spain

Magellan, Strait of channel between the S. American mainland and Tierra del Fuego

ma·gen·ta (mə jen′tə) *n.* [< *Magenta*, town in Italy] 1. a purplish-red dye 2. purplish red —*adj.* purplish-red

mag·got (mag′ət) *n.* [ME. *magotte*] a wormlike larva, as of the housefly —**mag′got·y** *adj.*

Ma·gi (mā′jī) *n.pl., sing.* -gus (-gəs) [< OPer. *magus*, magician] *Douay Bible* the wise men who came bearing gifts to the infant Jesus

mag·ic (maj′ik) *n.* [< Gr. *magikos*, of the Magi] 1. the use of charms, spells, etc. in seeking or pretending to control events or forces; sorcery 2. any mysterious power [the *magic* of love] 3. the art of producing illusions by sleight of hand, etc. —*adj.* 1. of, produced by, or using magic 2. producing extraordinary results, as by magic —**mag′i·cal** *adj.* —**mag′i·cal·ly** *adv.*

ma·gi·cian (mə jish′ən) *n.* [< OFr. *magicien*] an expert in magic; specif., a) a sorcerer; wizard b) a performer skilled in magic (sense 3)

mag·is·te·ri·al (maj′is tir′ē əl) *adj.* 1. of or suitable for a magistrate 2. authoritative 3. domineering

mag·is·trate (maj′is trāt′) *n.* [< L. *magister*, master] 1. a civil officer empowered to administer the law 2. a mino official, as a justice of the peace —**mag′is·tra·cy** (-trə sē) *n.*

mag·ma (mag′mə) *n.* [L.] moıten rock deep in the earth, from which igneous rock is formed

Mag·na Char·ta (or **Car·ta**) (mag′nə kär′tə) [ML., great charter] **1.** the charter, granted in 1215, that guaranteed certain civil and political liberties to the English people **2.** any constitution guaranteeing certain liberties

‡**mag·na cum lau·de** (mäg′nä koom lou′de, mag′nə kum lô′dē) [L.] with great praise: phrase used to signify graduation with high honors

mag·na·nim·i·ty (mag′nə nim′ə tē) *n.* **1.** a magnanimous quality or state **2.** *pl.* **-ties** a magnanimous act

mag·nan·i·mous (mag nan′ə məs) *adj.* [< L. *magnus*, great + *animus*, soul] generous in overlooking injury or insult; rising above pettiness —**mag·nan′i·mous·ly** *adv.*

mag·nate (mag′nāt) *n.* [< L. *magnus*, great] a very influential person, esp. in business

mag·ne·sia (mag nē′zhə, -shə) *n.* [< Gr. *Magnēsia*, district in ancient Greece] a white powder, magnesium oxide, used as a laxative and antacid

mag·ne′si·um (-zē əm, -zhē-) *n.* [< prec.] a light, silverwhite metallic chemical element: symbol, Mg; at. wt., 24.312; at. no., 12

mag·net (mag′nit) *n.* [< Gr. *Magnētis* (*lithos*), (stone) of *Magnēsia*, district in ancient Greece] **1.** any piece of iron, steel, or lodestone that has the property of attracting iron or steel **2.** anything that attracts

mag·net·ic (mag net′ik) *adj.* **1.** having the properties of a magnet **2.** of, producing, or caused by magnetism **3.** of the earth's magnetism **4.** that can be magnetized **5.** powerfully attractive —**mag·net′i·cal·ly** *adv.*

magnetic field a region of space in which there is an appreciable magnetic force

magnetic needle a slender bar of magnetized steel which, when swinging freely on a pivot, points toward the magnetic poles

magnetic north the direction toward which a magnetic needle points, usually not true north

magnetic pole 1. either pole of a magnet **2.** either point on the earth's surface toward which a magnetic needle points: the north and south magnetic poles do not precisely coincide with the geographical poles

magnetic recording the recording of electrical signals by means of changes in areas of magnetization on a tape (*magnetic tape*) or disc

magnetic tape a thin plastic ribbon with a magnetized coating for recording sound, digital computer data, etc.

mag·net·ism (mag′nə tiz′m) *n.* **1.** the property or quality of being magnetic **2.** the force to which this is due **3.** the branch of physics dealing with magnetic phenomena **4.** personal charm

mag′net·ite′ (-tīt′) *n.* a black iron oxide, Fe₃O₄, an important iron ore: called *lodestone* when magnetic

mag′net·ize′ (-tīz′) *vt.* **-ized′, -iz′ing 1.** to give magnetic properties to (steel, iron, etc.) **2.** to charm (a person) —**mag′net·i·za′tion** *n.*

mag·ne·to (mag nēt′ō) *n., pl.* **-tos** a small generator in which one or more permanent magnets produce the magnetic field

mag·ne′to·e·lec′tric (-i lek′trik) *adj.* of or relating to electricity produced by changing magnetic fields in the vicinity of electrical conductors

mag·ne·tom·e·ter (mag′nə täm′ə tər) *n.* an instrument for measuring magnetic forces: one form is used to check airline passengers for concealed metal weapons

mag·ni·fi·ca·tion (mag′nə fi kā′shən) *n.* **1.** a magnifying or being magnified **2.** the power of magnifying **3.** a magnified image or model

mag·nif·i·cent (mag nif′ə s′nt) *adj.* [< L. *magnus*, great + *facere*, do] **1.** beautiful and grand or stately; splendid, as in construction **2.** exalted: said of ideas, etc. **3.** [Colloq.] excellent —**mag·nif′i·cence** *n.* —**mag·nif′i·cent·ly** *adv.*

mag·ni·fy (mag′nə fī′) *vt., vi.* **-fied′, -fy′ing** [see MAGNIFICENT] **1.** to exaggerate **2.** to increase the apparent size of (an object), as (with) a lens —**mag′ni·fi′er** *n.*

mag·nil·o·quent (mag nil′ə kwənt) *adj.* [< L. *magnus*, great + *loqui*, to speak] **1.** pompous or grandiose in talking or writing **2.** boastful —**mag·nil′o·quence** *n.*

mag·ni·tude (mag′nə tood′, -tyood′) *n.* [< L. *magnus*, great] **1.** greatness of size, extent, or influence **2.** *a)* size *b)* importance **3.** the degree of brightness of a fixed star —**of the first magnitude** of the greatest importance

mag·no·li·a (mag nō′lē ə, -nōl′yə) *n.* [< P. *Magnol* (1638–1715), Fr. botanist] **1.** a tree with large, fragrant flowers of white, pink, or purple **2.** the flower

mag·num (mag′nəm) *n.* [< L. *magnus*, great] a wine bottle holding about 2/5 of a gallon

‡**mag·num o·pus** (mag′nəm ō′pəs) [L.] **1.** a great work; masterpiece **2.** a person's greatest work

mag·pie (mag′pī′) *n.* [< *Mag*, dim. of *Margaret* + *pie*, magpie] **1.** a noisy, black-and-white bird related to the crow **2.** one who chatters

mag·uey (mag′wā) *n.* [Sp.] a fleshy-leaved, fiber-yielding agave of the SW U.S., Mexico, and Central America; esp., the century plant

Mag·yar (mag′yär; *Hung.* môd′yär) *n.* **1.** a member of the main ethnic group in Hungary **2.** the Hungarian language —*adj.* of the Magyars, their language, etc.

ma·ha·ra·jah, ma·ha·ra·ja (mä′hə rä′jə) *n.* [< Sans. *mahā*, great + *rājā*, king] formerly in India, a prince, specif. one who ruled any of the chief native states —**ma′ha·ra′ni, ma′ha·ra′nee** (-nē) *n.fem.*

ma·ha·ri·shi (mä′hä rish′ē) *n.* [< Hindi < *mahā*, great + *ṛshi*, sage] a Hindu teacher of mysticism and meditation

ma·hat·ma (mə hat′mə, -hät′-) *n.* [< Sans. *mahā*, great + *ātman*, soul] *Buddhism* any of a class of wise and holy persons held in special regard

Ma·hi·can (mə hē′kən) *n.* **1.** a confederacy of Algonquian Indians of the upper Hudson Valley **2.** an Indian of this confederacy —*adj.* of this confederacy

mah-jongg, mah-jong (mä′jôŋ′) *n.* [< Chin. *ma-ch′iao*, sparrow (a figure on one of the tiles)] a game of Chinese origin, played with small tiles

ma·hog·a·ny (mə häg′ə nē, -hôg′-) *n., pl.* **-nies** [< ?] **1.** any of various tropical trees, esp. one of tropical America, with hard, reddish-brown wood **2.** the wood **3.** reddish brown —*adj.* **1.** made of mahogany **2.** reddish-brown

Ma·hom·et (mə häm′it) *same as* MOHAMMED

ma·hout (mə hout′) *n.* [< Hindi < Sans. *mahāmātra*, lit., great in measure] in India and the East Indies, an elephant driver or elephant keeper

maid (mād) *n.* **1.** *same as* MAIDEN **2.** a girl or woman servant

maid′en (-′n) *n.* [OE. *mægden*] **1.** a girl or young unmarried woman **2.** a virgin —*adj.* **1.** of or suitable for a maiden **2.** unmarried or virgin **3.** untried; new **4.** first or earliest [a *maiden* voyage] —**maid′en·hood′** *n.* —**maid′en·ly** *adj.*

maid′en·hair′ *n.* a fern with delicate fronds and slender stalks: also **maidenhair fern**

maid′en·head′ (-hed′) *n.* **1.** [Archaic] virginity **2.** the hymen

maiden name the surname that a woman had when not yet married

maid of honor an unmarried woman acting as chief attendant to the bride at a wedding

maid′ser′vant *n.* a girl or woman servant

mail¹ (māl) *n.* [< OHG. *malaha*, wallet] **1.** letters, packages, etc. transported and delivered by the post office **2.** [*also pl.*] the postal system —*adj.* of mail —*vt.* to send by mail, as by putting into a mailbox —**mail′a·ble** *adj.* —**mail′er** *n.*

mail² (māl) *n.* [< L. *macula*, mesh of a net] a flexible body armor made of small metal rings, scales, etc. —*vt.* to cover as with mail —**mailed** *adj.*

mail′bag′ *n.* a bag in which a mail carrier carries the mail

mail′box′ *n.* **1.** a box in which mail is put when delivered **2.** a box, as on a street, into which mail is put for collection Also **mail box**

mail carrier one whose work is carrying and delivering mail; mailman; postman

mail′man′ *n., pl.* **-men′** *same as* MAIL CARRIER

mail order an order for goods to be sent through the mail —**mail′-or′der** *adj.*

mail-order house a business establishment that takes mail orders and sends goods by mail

maim (mām) *vt.* [OFr. *mahaigner*] to cripple; mutilate; disable

main (mān) *n.* [OE. *mægen*, strength] **1.** a principal pipe in a distributing system for water, gas, etc. **2.** [Poet.] the ocean **3.** [Archaic] the mainland —*adj.* chief in size, importance, etc.; principal —**by main force** (or **strength**) by

MAIL

sheer force (or strength) —**in the main** mostly; chiefly —**with might and main** with all one's strength

main clause a clause that can function as a complete sentence by itself

main drag [Slang] the principal street of a city or town

Maine (mān) New England State of the U.S.: 33,215 sq. mi.; pop. 994,000; cap. Augusta: abbrev. **Me.**, **ME**

main·land (mān'land', -land) n. the principal land mass of a continent, as distinguished from nearby islands

main'line' n. the principal road, course, etc. —vt. **-lined'**, **-lin'ing** [Slang] to inject (a narcotic drug) directly into a large vein

main'ly adv. chiefly; principally

main'mast (-məst, -mast') n. the principal mast of a vessel

main'sail (-s'l, -sāl') n. the principal sail of a vessel, set from the mainmast

main'spring' n. 1. the principal spring in a clock, watch, etc. 2. the chief motive, incentive, etc.

main'stay' (-stā') n. 1. the supporting line run forward from the mainmast 2. a chief support

main'stream' n. a major trend or line of thought, action, etc.

main·tain (mān tān') vt. [< L. manu tenere, to hold in the hand] 1. to keep or keep up; carry on 2. to keep in continuance or in a certain state, as of repair 3. to defend 4. to affirm or assert 5. to support by aid or influence 6. to provide the means of existence for [to maintain a family] —**main·tain'a·ble** adj. —**main·tain'er** n.

main·te·nance (mān't'n əns) n. 1. a maintaining or being maintained 2. means of support

main'top' n. a platform at the head of the lower section of the mainmast

main'top'mast (-məst) n. the section of the mainmast above the maintop

‡**maî·tre d'hô·tel** (me'tr' dô tel') [Fr., master of the house] 1. a butler or steward 2. a chief waiter

maize (māz) n. [< Sp. < WInd. mahiz] 1. same as CORN¹ (sense 2) 2. the color of ripe corn; yellow

Maj. Major

ma·jes·tic (mə jes'tik) adj. grand; stately; dignified: also **ma·jes'ti·cal** —**ma·jes'ti·cal·ly** adv.

maj·es·ty (maj'is tē) n., pl. **-ties** [< L. magnus, great] 1. [M-] a title used in speaking to or of a sovereign, preceded by His, Her, or Your 2. grandeur or stateliness

ma·jol·i·ca (mə jäl'i kə, -yäl'-) n. [< It. Maiolica, MAJORCA] a variety of Italian pottery, enameled, glazed, and richly decorated

ma·jor (mā'jər) adj. [L., compar. of magnus, great] 1. greater in size, amount, importance, rank, etc. 2. of full legal age 3. Educ. designating a field of study in which a student specializes 4. Music a) designating an interval greater than the corresponding minor interval by a semitone b) characterized by major intervals, scales, etc. [a major key] c) based on the major scale: see MAJOR SCALE —vi. Educ. to specialize (in a field of study) —n. 1. U.S. Mil. an officer ranking just above a captain 2. Educ. a major field of study 3. Music a major interval, key, etc.

Ma·jor·ca (mə jôr'kə) largest of the Balearic Islands

ma'jor-do'mo (-dō'mō) n., pl. **-mos** [< Sp. or It. < L. major, greater + domus, house] a man in charge of a great household; chief steward

major general pl. **major generals** U.S. Mil. an officer ranking just above a brigadier general

ma·jor·i·ty (mə jôr'ə tē, -jär'-) n., pl. **-ties** [< Fr. < L.: see MAJOR] 1. the greater number; more than half of a total 2. the excess of the larger number of votes cast for one candidate, bill, etc. over all the rest of the votes 3. the group or party with the majority of votes 4. full legal age 5. the military rank of a major

major league a principal league in a professional sport —**ma'jor-league'** adj.

major scale one of the two standard diatonic musical scales, with half steps instead of whole steps after the third and seventh tones

make (māk) vt. made, mak'ing [OE. macian] 1. to bring into being; build, create, produce, etc. 2. to cause to be or become [the news made her sad] 3. to prepare for use [make the beds] 4. to amount to [two pints make a quart] 5. to have the qualities of [he made a good doctor] 6. to establish [to make rules] 7. to acquire; earn 8. to cause the success of [that venture made him] 9. to understand [what do you make of that?] 10. to execute, do, etc. [to make a speech] 11. to arrive at; reach [the ship made port] 12. to arrive at; reach [the ship made port] 13. to go; travel [to make 300 miles a day] 14. [Colloq.] to get on or in [he made the team] —vi. 1. to start (to do something)

[she made to go] 2. to behave as specified [to make merry] 3. to cause something to be as specified [make ready] —n. 1. the way in which something is made; style 2. type; sort; brand —**make away with** 1. to steal 2. to kill —**make believe** to pretend —**make for** 1. to go toward 2. to attack 3. to help effect —**make it** [Colloq.] to achieve a certain thing —**make off with** to steal —**make out** 1. to see with difficulty 2. to understand 3. to fill out (a blank form, etc.) 4. to (try to) show or prove to be 5. to succeed; get along —**make over** 1. to change; renovate 2. to transfer the ownership of —**make up** 1. to put together 2. to form; constitute 3. to invent 4. to provide (what is lacking) 5. to compensate (for) 6. to become friends again after a quarrel 7. to put on cosmetics, etc. 8. to decide (one's mind) —**make up to** to try to ingratiate oneself with

make'-be·lieve' n. 1. pretense; feigning 2. a pretender —adj. pretended; feigned

mak·er (māk'ər) n. 1. a person or thing that makes 2. [M-] God

make'shift' (-shift') n. a temporary substitute or expedient —adj. that will do as a makeshift

make'up', make'-up' n. 1. the way something is put together; composition 2. nature; disposition 3. the cosmetics, etc. used by an actor 4. cosmetics generally

make'-work' adj. that serves no useful purpose other than to give an idle or unemployed person something to do

mak·ing (māk'iŋ) n. 1. the act of one that makes or the process of being made 2. the cause of success 3. [often pl.] the material or qualities needed [she has the makings of a good lawyer]

mal- [< L. malus, bad] a prefix meaning bad or badly, wrong, ill

Ma·lac·ca (mə lak'ə) state of Malaya

Mal·a·chi (mal'ə kī') Bible 1. a Hebrew prophet of the 5th cent. B.C. 2. the book containing prophecies attributed to him: abbrev. **Mal.**

mal·a·chite (mal'ə kīt') n. [< Gr. malachē, mallow: from its color] a green mineral, copper carbonate, used for table tops, vases, etc.

mal·ad·just·ed (mal'ə jus'tid) adj. poorly adjusted, esp. to the environment —**mal'ad·just'ment** n.

mal·a·droit (mal'ə droit') adj. [Fr.: see MAL- & ADROIT] awkward; clumsy; bungling —**mal'a·droit'ly** adv. —**mal'a·droit'ness** n.

mal·a·dy (mal'ə dē) n., pl. **-dies** [< VL. male habitus, badly kept] a disease; illness; sickness

Mal·a·gas·y (mal'ə gas'ē) n. 1. pl. **-gas'y, -gas'ies** a native of Madagascar 2. the Indonesian language of the Malagasy

Malagasy Republic former name of MADAGASCAR

ma·laise (ma lāz') n. [Fr. < mal, bad + aise, ease] a vague feeling of physical discomfort or uneasiness

mal·a·mute (mal'ə myōōt') n. [< Malemute, an Eskimo tribe] a strong dog with a thick coat, developed as a sled dog by Eskimos: also sp. **malemute**

mal·a·prop·ism (mal'ə präp iz'm) n. [< Mrs. Malaprop in Sheridan's The Rivals (1775)] a ludicrous misuse of words that sound alike

ma·lar·i·a (mə ler'ē ə) n. [It. < mala aria, bad air] an infectious disease transmitted by the anopheles mosquito, characterized by intermittent chills and fever —**ma·lar'i·al, ma·lar'i·an, ma·lar'i·ous** adj.

ma·lar·key, ma·lar·ky (mə lär'kē) n. [< ? Ir. surname] [Slang] insincere talk; nonsense

mal·a·thi·on (mal'ə thī'än) n. [< chem. names] an organic phosphate used as an insecticide

Ma·la·wi (mä'lä wē) country in SE Africa: 46,066 sq. mi.; pop. 4,530,000; cap. Zomba

Ma·lay (mā'lā, mə lā') n. 1. a member of a large group of brown-skinned peoples living chiefly in the Malay Peninsula and the Malay Archipelago 2. their language —adj. of the Malays, their language, etc. Also **Ma·lay'an**

Ma·lay·a (mə lā'ə) 1. same as MALAY PENINSULA 2. group of states at the S end of the Malay Peninsula constituting a part of Malaysia

Malay Archipelago large group of islands between the mainland of SE Asia & Australia

Malay Peninsula peninsula in SE Asia, including the S part of Thailand and the states of Malaya

Ma·lay·sia (mə lā'zhə, -shə) country in SE Asia, consisting of the states of Malaya and two states on N Borneo: 128,654 sq. mi.; pop. 10,319,000; cap. Kuala Lumpur —**Ma·lay'sian** adj., n.

mal·con·tent (mal'kən tent') adj. [see MAL- & CONTENT¹] dissatisfied or rebellious —n. a malcontent person

Mal·dive Islands (mal'dīv) country on a group of islands in the Indian Ocean, southwest of Sri Lanka: 115 sq. mi.; pop. 104,000; cap. Malé

male (māl) *adj.* [< L. *mas*, a male] **1.** designating or of the sex that fertilizes the ovum of the female **2.** of, like, or suitable for men or boys; masculine **3.** having a part shaped to fit into a corresponding hollow part **4.** *Bot.* designating or of fertilizing bodies, organs, etc. —*n.* a male person, animal, or plant

mal·e·dic·tion (mal'ə dik'shən) *n.* [see MAL- & DICTION] a calling down of evil on someone; curse

mal·e·fac·tor (mal'ə fak'tər) *n.* [< L. *male*, evil + *facere*, do] an evildoer; criminal —**mal'e·fac'tion** *n.*

ma·lef·i·cent (mə lef'ə s'nt) *adj.* [see prec.] harmful; hurtful; evil —**ma·lef'i·cence** *n.*

ma·lev·o·lent (mə lev'ə lənt) *adj.* [< L. *male*, evil + *velle*, to wish] wishing evil or harm to others; malicious —**ma·lev'o·lence** *n.*

mal·fea·sance (mal fē'z'ns) *n.* [< Fr. *mal*, evil + *faire*, do] wrongdoing, esp. by a public official —**mal·fea'sant** *adj.*

mal·for·ma·tion (mal'fôr mā'shən) *n.* faulty or abnormal formation of a body or part —**mal·formed'** *adj.*

mal·func·tion (mal funk'shən) *vi.* to fail to function as it should —*n.* an instance of malfunctioning

Ma·li (mä'lē) country in W Africa: 464,873 sq. mi.; pop. 4,929,000; cap. Bamako

mal·ice (mal'is) *n.* [< L. *malus*, bad] **1.** active ill will; desire to harm another **2.** *Law* evil intent —**malice aforethought** a deliberate intention to do something unlawful

ma·li·cious (mə lish'əs) *adj.* having, showing, or caused by malice; spiteful —**ma·li'cious·ly** *adv.*

ma·lign (mə līn') *vt.* [< L. *male*, ill + *genus*, born] to speak evil of; slander —*adj.* **1.** showing ill will; malicious **2.** evil; sinister **3.** very harmful —**ma·lign'er** *n.*

ma·lig·nan·cy (mə lig'nən sē) *n.* **1.** a being malignant: also **ma·lig'nance 2.** *pl.* **-cies** a malignant tumor

ma·lig'nant (-nənt) *adj.* [see MALIGN] **1.** having an evil influence **2.** wishing evil; malevolent **3.** very harmful **4.** causing or likely to cause death [a *malignant* growth] —**ma·lig'nant·ly** *adv.*

ma·lig·ni·ty (mə lig'nə tē) *n.* **1.** great malice **2.** the quality of being very harmful **3.** *pl.* **-ties** a malignant act, event, or feeling

ma·lin·ger (mə lin'gər) *vi.* [< Fr. *malingre*, sickly] to pretend to be ill in order to escape duty or work; shirk —**ma·lin'ger·er** *n.*

mall (môl, mal) *n.* [< *maul*, mallet: from use in a game on outdoor lanes] **1.** a shaded walk or public promenade **2.** *a)* a shop-lined street for pedestrians only *b)* an enclosed shopping center

mal·lard (mal'ərd) *n.* [< OFr. *malart*] the common wild duck: the male has a green head

mal·le·a·ble (mal'ē ə b'l) *adj.* [< L. *malleus*, a hammer] **1.** that can be hammered, pounded, or pressed into various shapes without breaking **2.** adaptable —**mal'le·a·bil'i·ty** *n.*

mal·let (mal'it) *n.* [see prec.] **1.** a short-handled hammer with a wooden head, for driving a chisel, etc. **2.** *a)* a long-handled hammer used in playing croquet *b)* a longer-handled hammer used in playing polo **3.** a small hammer for playing a xylophone, etc.

mal·low (mal'ō) *n.* [< L. *malva*] any of a family of plants, including the hollyhock, cotton, and okra, having large, showy flowers

malm·sey (mäm'zē) *n.* [< Gr. *Monembasia*, Gr. town] a strong, sweet white wine

MALLET

mal·nour·ished (mal nur'isht) *adj.* improperly nourished

mal·nu·tri·tion (mal'nōō trish'ən) *n.* faulty or inadequate nutrition; poor nourishment

mal·oc·clu·sion (mal'ə klōō'zhən) *n.* a faulty position of the teeth so that they do not meet properly

mal·o·dor·ous (mal ō'dər əs) *adj.* having a bad odor; stinking —**mal·o'dor·ous·ly** *adv.*

mal·prac·tice (mal prak'tis) *n.* professional misconduct or improper practice, esp. by a physician

malt (môlt) *n.* [OE. *mealt*] **1.** barley or other grain softened by soaking and then kiln-dried: used in brewing and distilling certain alcoholic liquors **2.** such liquor, esp. beer, ale, etc. —*adj.* made with malt —*vt.* **1.** to change

(barley, etc.) into malt **2.** to prepare with malt or a sweet extract of malt —**malt'ed** *adj.* —**malt'y** *adj.* **-i·er, -i·est**

Mal·ta (môl'tə) country on a group of islands in the Mediterranean, south of Sicily: 122 sq. mi.; pop. 328,000; cap. Valletta —**Mal·tese'** (-tēz') *adj., n.*

malted milk a drink made by mixing milk and, usually, ice cream with a powder of dried milk and malted cereals

Maltese cat a variety of domestic cat with bluish-gray fur

Maltese cross a cross whose arms look like arrowheads pointing inward

Mal·thus (mal'thəs), **Thomas Robert** 1766–1834; Eng. political economist

malt liquor beer, ale, etc. fermented from malt

malt·ose (môl'tōs) *n.* a white, crystalline sugar, $C_{12}H_{22}O_{11} \cdot H_2O$, obtained by the action of diastase on starch: also called **malt sugar**

mal·treat (mal trēt') *vt.* [< Fr.: see MAL- & TREAT] to treat roughly or brutally —**mal·treat'ment** *n.*

mam·ma¹ (mä'mə; *occas.* mə mä') *n.* mother: a child's word: also **ma'ma**

mam·ma² (mam'ə) *n., pl.* **-mae** (-ē) [L., breast] a gland for secreting milk, present in all female mammals

mam·mal (mam'əl) *n.* [< L. *mamma*, breast] any of a group of vertebrates the females of which have milk-secreting glands for feeding their offspring —**mam·ma·li·an** (mə mā'lē ən) *adj., n.*

mam·ma·ry (mam'ər ē) *adj.* designating or of the milk-secreting glands; of the mammae

mam·mon (mam'ən) *n.* [< Aram. *māmōnā*, riches] [*often* M-] riches regarded as an object of worship and greedy pursuit —**mam'mon·ism** *n.*

mam·moth (mam'əth) *n.* [Russ. *mamont*] an extinct elephant with a hairy skin and long tusks curving upward —*adj.* very big; huge; enormous

man (man) *n., pl.* **men** (men) [OE. *mann*] **1.** a human being; person **2.** the human race; mankind **3.** an adult male human being **4.** an adult male servant, employee, etc. **5.** a husband or lover **6.** a manly person **7.** any of the pieces used in chess, checkers, etc. —*vt.* **manned, man'ning 1.** to furnish with men for work, defense, etc. [to *man* a ship] **2.** to take assigned places in, on, or at [*man* the guns!] **3.** to strengthen; brace —*interj.* [Slang] an exclamation of emphasis —**as a** (or **one**) **man** in unison; unanimously —**to a man** with no one as an exception

-man a combining form meaning man or person of a specified kind, in a specified activity, etc. [*Frenchman, sportsman*]

Man. Manitoba

Man (man), **Isle of** one of the Brit. Isles, between Northern Ireland & England

man·a·cle (man'ə k'l) *n.* [< L. *manus*, hand] **1.** a handcuff **2.** any restraint *Usually used in pl.* —*vt.* **-cled, -cling 1.** to put handcuffs on **2.** to restrain; hamper

man·age (man'ij) *vt.* **-aged, -ag·ing** [It. *maneggiare* < L. *manus*, hand] **1.** to control the movement or behavior of **2.** to have charge of; direct [to *manage* a household] **3.** to get (a person) to do what one wishes **4.** to succeed in accomplishing —*vi.* **1.** to carry on business **2.** to contrive to get along —**man'age·a·ble** *adj.*

man'age·ment *n.* **1.** the act, art, or manner of managing, controlling, etc. **2.** skillful managing **3.** the persons managing a business, institution, etc.

man'ag·er *n.* a person who manages the affairs of a business, institution, team, etc.

man·a·ge·ri·al (man'ə jir'ē əl) *adj.* of a manager or management

‡ma·ña·na (mä nyä'nä) *n.* [Sp.] tomorrow —*adv.* **1.** tomorrow **2.** at some indefinite future time

man-at-arms (man'ət ärmz') *n., pl.* **men'-at-arms'** formerly, a soldier; esp., a heavily armed medieval soldier on horseback

man·a·tee (man'ə tē') *n.* [< Sp. < native (Carib) name] a large, plant-eating aquatic mammal of tropical waters

Man·ches·ter (man'ches'tər) city & port in NW England: pop. 603,000

Man·chu (man chōō') *n.* **1.** *pl.* **-chus', -chu'** a member of a Mongolian people of Manchuria who ruled China from 1644 to 1912 **2.** their language —*adj.* of Manchuria, the Manchus, their language, etc.

Man·chu·ri·a (man choor'ē ə) region of NE China, north of Korea —**Man·chu'ri·an** *adj., n.*

Man·da·lay (man'də lā', man'də lā') city in C Burma: pop. 322,000

man·da·mus (man dā'məs) *n.* [L., we command] *Law* a writ commanding that a specified thing be done, issued by a higher court to a lower one, or to a corporation, agency, official, etc.

man·da·rin (man'də rin) *n.* [< Port. < Sans. *mantra,* counsel] **1.** a high official of the former Chinese Empire **2.** a member of any elite group **3.** [M-] the official or main dialect of Chinese **4.** a small, sweet orange with a loose rind

man·date (man'dāt) *n.* [< L. *mandare,* to command] **1.** an order or command **2.** *a)* formerly, a commission from the League of Nations to a country to administer some region, colony, etc. *b)* the area so administered **3.** the wishes of constituents expressed to a representative, etc. —*vt.* **-dat·ed, -dat·ing** to assign (a region, etc.) as a mandate —**man·da'tor** *n.*

man·da·to·ry (man'də tôr'ē) *adj.* **1.** of, like, or containing a mandate **2.** authoritatively commanded or required; obligatory

man·di·ble (man'də b'l) *n.* [< L. *mandere,* chew] the jaw; specif., *a)* the lower jaw of a vertebrate *b)* either jaw of a beaked animal *c)* either of the biting jaws of an insect

man·do·lin (man'd'l in', man'də lin') *n.* [< Fr. < LGr. *pandoura,* kind of lute] a musical instrument with four or five pairs of strings and a deep, rounded sound box

man·drake (man'drāk) *n.* [< Gr. *mandragoras*] **1.** a poisonous plant of the nightshade family **2.** its thick root, formerly used in medicine as a narcotic Also **man·drag·o·ra** (man drag'ər ə)

man·drel, man·dril (man'drəl) *n.* [prob. < Fr. *mandrin*] a spindle or bar inserted into something to hold it while it is being machined

man·drill (man'dril) *n.* [MAN + DRILL⁴] a large, fierce, strong baboon of W Africa

mane (mān) *n.* [OE. *manu*] the long hair growing from the top or sides of the neck of certain animals, as the horse, lion, etc. —**maned** *adj.*

man'-eat'er *n.* an animal that eats human flesh

ma·nège, ma·nege (ma nezh', -nāzh') *n.* [Fr.: see MANAGE] **1.** the art of riding and training horses **2.** a riding school **3.** the paces of a trained horse

ma·nes (mā'nēz) *n.pl.* [L.] [*often* M-] *Ancient Rom. Religion* the deified souls of the dead, esp. of dead ancestors

ma·neu·ver (mə nōō'vər, -nyōō'-) *n.* [< Fr. < L. *manu operare,* to work by hand] **1.** a planned and controlled movement of troops, warships, etc. **2.** [*pl.*] large-scale practice movements of troops, etc. **3.** a stratagem; scheme —*vi., vt.* **1.** to perform or cause to perform maneuvers **2.** to manage or plan skillfully **3.** to move, get, make, etc. by some stratagem —**ma·neu'ver·a·bil'i·ty** *n.* —**ma·neu'ver·a·ble** *adj.*

man·ful (man'fəl) *adj.* manly; brave, resolute, etc. —**man'ful·ly** *adv.* —**man'ful·ness** *n.*

man·ga·nese (maŋ'gə nēs', -nēz') *n.* [< Fr. < It. < ML. *magnesia*] a grayish-white, metallic chemical element, usually hard and brittle: used in various alloys: symbol, Mn; at. wt., 54.938; at. no., 25

mange (mānj) *n.* [< OFr. *mangeue,* an itch] a skin disease of mammals, causing itching, hair loss, etc.

man·gel-wur·zel (maŋ'g'l wur'z'l) *n.* [G. < *mangold,* beet + *wurzel,* a root] a variety of large beet, used as food for cattle, esp. in Europe: also **mangel**

man·ger (mān'jər) *n.* [< L. *mandere,* to chew] a box or trough to hold hay, etc. for horses or cattle to eat

man·gle¹ (maŋ'g'l) *vt.* **-gled, -gling** [< OFr. *mehaigner,* maim] **1.** to mutilate by roughly cutting, hacking, etc. **2.** to spoil; botch; mar

man·gle² (maŋ'g'l) *n.* [Du. *mangel* < Gr. *manganon,* war machine] a machine for pressing cloth, esp. sheets and other flat pieces, between rollers —*vt.* **-gled, -gling** to press in a mangle —**man'gler** *n.*

man·go (maŋ'gō) *n., pl.* **-goes, -gos** [< Port. < Tamil *mān-kāy*] **1.** a yellow-red, somewhat acid tropical fruit **2.** the tree on which it grows

man·grove (maŋ'grōv) *n.* [< Port. < WInd. name] a tropical tree with branches that spread and send down roots, thus forming more trunks

man·gy (mān'jē) *adj.* **-gi·er, -gi·est 1.** having or caused by the mange **2.** shabby and filthy **3.** mean and low; despicable —**man'gi·ness** *n.*

man'han'dle *vt.* **-dled, -dling** to handle roughly

Man·hat·tan (man hat''n) **1.** island in SE N.Y.: also **Manhattan Island 2.** borough of New York City of which this island forms a major part: pop. 1,525,000 —*n.* [*often* m-] a cocktail made of whiskey and vermouth

man'hole' *n.* a hole through which a man can enter a sewer, conduit, etc., as for repair work

man'hood' *n.* **1.** the state or time of being a man **2.** virility, courage, etc. **3.** men collectively

man'-hour' *n.* a time unit equal to one hour of work done by one person

man'hunt' *n.* a hunt for a man, esp. for a fugitive

ma·ni·a (mā'nē ə) *n.* [Gr.] **1.** wild or violent mental disorder **2.** an excessive enthusiasm; obsession

-mania [see prec.] *a combining form meaning* a (specified) type of mental disorder [*kleptomania*]

ma·ni·ac (mā'nē ak') *adj.* wildly insane; raving —*n.* a violently insane person; lunatic —**ma·ni·a·cal** (mə nī'ə k'l) *adj.*

man·ic (man'ik) *adj.* having, characterized by, or like mania

man'ic-de·pres'sive *adj.* designating, of, or having a psychosis characterized by alternating periods of mania and mental depression —*n.* a person who has this psychosis

man·i·cure (man'ə kyoor') *n.* [Fr. < L. *manus,* a hand + *cura,* care] a trimming, polishing, etc. of the fingernails — *vt.* **-cured', -cur'ing** to trim, polish, etc. (the fingernails) —**man'i·cur'ist** *n.*

man·i·fest (man'ə fest') *adj.* [< L. *manifestus,* lit., struck by the hand] apparent to the senses or the mind; obvious —*vt.* **1.** to show plainly; reveal **2.** to prove; be evidence of —*n.* an itemized list of a craft's cargo or passengers — **man'i·fest'ly** *adv.*

man·i·fes·ta·tion (man'ə fes tā'shən) *n.* **1.** a manifesting or being manifested **2.** something that manifests

man·i·fes·to (man'ə fes'tō) *n., pl.* **-toes** [It. < L.: see MANIFEST] a public declaration of motives and intentions by a government or by an important person or group

man·i·fold (man'ə fōld') *adj.* [see MANY & -FOLD] **1.** having many forms, parts, etc. **2.** of many sorts [*manifold* duties] **3.** being such in many ways [a *manifold* villain] **4.** operating several parts of one kind —*n.* a pipe with several outlets for connecting with other pipes, as the cylinder exhaust system in an automobile —*vt.* to make a number of copies of, as with carbon paper

MANIFOLD
(A, manifold;
B, cylinders)

man·i·kin (man'ə k'n) *n.* [< Du. *manneken*] **1.** a little man; dwarf **2.** *same as* MANNEQUIN

Ma·nil·a (mə nil'ə) capital & seaport of the Philippines, on Luzon: pop. 1,499,000 (met. area 3,100,000)

Manila hemp [*often* m-] a strong fiber from the leafstalk of a Philippine plant, used for rope, etc.

Manila paper [*often* m-] strong, buff-colored paper, orig. made of Manila hemp

man in the street the average person

ma·nip·u·late (mə nip'yə lāt') *vt.* **-lat'ed, -lat'ing** [ult. < Fr. < L. *manus,* a hand + *plere,* to fill] **1.** to work or handle skillfully **2.** to manage artfully or shrewdly, esp. in an unfair way **3.** to alter (figures, accounts, etc.) for one's own purposes —**ma·nip'u·la'tion** *n.* —**ma·nip'u·la'tive** *adj.* —**ma·nip'u·la'tor** *n.*

Man·i·to·ba (man'ə tō'bə) province of SC Canada: 251,000 sq. mi.; pop. 963,000; cap. Winnipeg —**Man'i·to'ban** *adj., n.*

man·kind *n.* **1.** (man'kīnd') the human race **2.** (-kīnd') all human males

man'like' *adj.* **1.** like or characteristic of a man or men **2.** fit for a man; masculine

man'ly *adj.* **-li·er, -li·est 1.** having qualities regarded as befitting a man; strong, brave, etc. **2.** fit for a man [*manly* sports] —*adv.* in a manly way —**man'li·ness** *n.*

man'-made' *adj.* artificial; synthetic

Mann (man; *for 2* män) **1. Horace,** 1796–1859; U.S. educator **2. Thom·as** (G. tō'mäs), 1875–1955; Ger. novelist in the U.S. & Switzerland

man·na (man'ə) *n.* [< Heb. *mān*] **1.** *Bible* food miraculously provided for the Israelites in the wilderness **2.** any help that comes unexpectedly

man·ne·quin (man'ə kin) *n.* [Fr. < Du.: see MANIKIN] **1.** a model of the human body, used by tailors, etc. **2.** a woman who models clothes in stores, etc.

man·ner (man'ər) *n.* [< L. *manus,* a hand] **1.** a way of doing something; mode of procedure **2.** a way, esp. a usual way, of acting; habit **3.** [*pl.*] *a)* ways of social behavior [good *manners*] *b)* polite ways of social behavior [the child lacks *manners*] **4.** characteristic style in art, etc. **5.** kind; sort —**by no manner** definitely not —**in a manner of speaking** in a certain sense or way

man'nered *adj.* **1.** having manners of a specified sort [*ill-mannered*] **2.** artificial or affected

man·ner·ism *n.* **1.** excessive use of some distinctive manner in art, literature, etc. **2.** a habitual peculiarity of manner in behavior, speech, etc.

man'ner·ly *adj.* polite —*adv.* politely

man·ni·kin (man'ə kin) *n. alt. sp. of* MANIKIN

man·nish (man'ish) *adj.* of, like, or fit for a man [she walks with a *mannish* stride] —**man'nish·ness** *n.*

ma·noeu·vre (mə nōō'vər, -nyōō'-) *n., vi., vt.* -vred, -vring *chiefly Brit. sp. of* MANEUVER

man of letters a writer, scholar, etc., esp. in the field of literature

man of the world a man familiar with and tolerant of various sorts of people and their ways

man'-of-war' *n., pl.* **men'-of-war'** an armed naval vessel; warship

ma·nom·e·ter (mə näm'ə tər) *n.* [< Fr. < Gr. *manos*, rare + Fr. -*mètre*, -METER] an instrument for measuring the pressure of gases or liquids

man·or (man'ər) *n.* [< L. *manere*, dwell] **1.** in England, a landed estate **2.** a mansion, as on an estate —**ma·no·ri·al** (mə nôr'ē əl) *adj.*

man'pow'er *n.* **1.** power furnished by human physical strength **2.** the collective strength or availability for work of the people in a given area, nation, etc. Also **man power**

man·sard (roof) (man'särd) [< F. *Mansard*, 17th-c. Fr. architect] a roof with two slopes on each of the four sides, the lower steeper than the upper

manse (mans) *n.* [< L. *manere*, dwell] a parsonage

man'ser'vant *n., pl.* **men'ser'vants** a male servant: also **man servant**

man·sion (man'shən) *n.* [< L. *manere*, dwell] a large, imposing house

man'-sized' *adj.* [Colloq.] of a size fit for a man; big: also **man'-size'**

man'slaugh'ter (-slôt'ər) *n.* the killing of a human being by another, esp. unlawful but without malice

man·tel (man't'l) *n.* [see MANTLE] **1.** the facing about a fireplace, including a shelf or slab above it **2.** the shelf or slab: also **man'tel·piece'**

man·til·la (man til'ə) *n.* [Sp. < L. *mantellum*, a mantle] a woman's scarf worn over the hair and shoulders, as in Spain, Mexico, etc.

man·tis (man'tis) *n., pl.* -tis·es, -tes (-tēz) [< Gr. *mantis*, prophet] an insect with forelegs held as if praying

man·tle (man't'l) *n.* [< L. *mantellum*] **1.** a loose, sleeveless cloak **2.** anything that envelops or conceals **3.** a small, mesh hood which becomes white-hot over a flame and gives off light —*vt.* -tled, -tling to cover as with a mantle —*vi.* **1.** to be or become covered **2.** to blush

man·tra (mun'trə, man'-) *n.* [Sans.] a chant of a Vedic hymn, text, etc.

man·u·al (man'yoo wəl) *adj.* [< L. *manus*, a hand] **1.** of the hands **2.** made, done, or worked by the hands **3.** involving hard work with the hands —*n.* **1.** a handy book of instructions, etc. for use as a guide **2.** a keyboard of an organ console or harpsichord **3.** prescribed drill in the handling of a rifle —**man'u·al·ly** *adv.*

manual training training in practical arts and crafts, as metalworking, etc.

man·u·fac·ture (man'yə fak'chər) *n.* [Fr. < L. *manus*, a hand + *facere*, make] **1.** the making of goods, esp. by machinery and on a large scale **2.** anything so made **3.** the making of something in a mechanical way —*vt.* -tured, -tur·ing **1.** to make, esp. by machinery **2.** to work (wool, steel, etc.) into usable form **3.** to make up (excuses, etc.)

man·u·fac'tur·er *n.* a person or company in the business of manufacturing; esp., a factory owner

man·u·mit (man'yə mit') *vt.* -mit'ted, -mit'ting [< L. *manus*, a hand + *mittere*, send] to free from slavery — **man'u·mis'sion** (-mish'ən) *n.*

ma·nure (mə noor', -nyoor') *vt.* -nured', -nur'ing [< OFr. *manouvrer*, to work with the hands] to put manure on or into (soil) —*n.* animal excrement, etc. used to fertilize soil

man·u·script (man'yə skript') *adj.* [< L. *manus*, hand + *scriptus*, written] **1.** written by hand or typewritten **2.** written with printlike letters —*n.* **1.** a written or typewritten document, book, etc., as submitted to a publisher **2.** writing as distinguished from print

Manx (maŋks) *adj.* of the Isle of Man, its people, etc. —*n.* their language, now nearly extinct —**the Manx** the people of the Isle of Man

Manx cat [*also* m-] any of a breed of domestic cat that has no tail

Manx'man *n., pl.* -men a native or inhabitant of the Isle of Man

man·y (men'ē) *adj.* **more, most** [OE. *manig*] **1.** numerous **2.** relatively numerous (preceded by *as, too,* etc.) —*n.* a large number (of persons or things) —*pron.* many persons or things —**a good many** [*with pl. v.*] quite a large number

man'y-sid'ed *adj.* **1.** having many sides or aspects **2.** having many possibilities, qualities, etc.

Ma·o·ri (mou'rē, mä'ô rē) *n.* **1.** *pl.* -ris, -ri any of a brown-skinned people native to New Zealand, of Polynesian origin **2.** their Polynesian language

Mao Tse-tung (mou' dzu'dōōŋ') 1893–1976; chairman of the Chin. Communist Party (1949–76) —**Mao'ism** *n.* — **Mao'ist** *n.*

map (map) *n.* [< L. *mappa*, napkin] **1.** a representation, usually flat, of all or part of the earth's surface, showing countries, bodies of water, cities, etc. **2.** a representation of the sky, showing stars, etc. —*vt.* mapped, map'ping **1.** to make a map of **2.** to plan [to *map* out a project]

ma·ple (mā'p'l) *n.* [OE. *mapel*(*treo*)] **1.** any of a large group of trees grown for wood, sap, or shade **2.** its hard, light-colored wood **3.** the flavor of the syrup (**maple syrup**) or the sugar (**maple sugar**) made from its sap

mar (mär) *vt.* marred, mar'ring [OE. *mierran*, hinder] to hurt or spoil the looks, perfection, etc. of; impair; damage

Mar. March

mar·a·bou (mar'ə bōō') *n.* [Fr. < Ar. *murābit*, hermit] **1.** a large stork of Africa or India **2.** its plumes, used in millinery

ma·ra·ca (mə rä'kə) *n.* [< Port. < the Braz. native name] a percussion instrument made of a dried gourd or gourd-shaped rattle with loose pebbles in it

mar·a·schi·no (mar'ə skē'nō, -shē'-) *n.* [It. < *marasca*, kind of cherry] a liqueur or cordial made from a kind of black wild cherry

maraschino cherries cherries in a syrup flavored with maraschino

mar·a·thon (mar'ə thän') *n.* [< *Marathon*, in ancient Greece] **1.** a foot race of 26 miles, 385 yards: so called in allusion to the Greek runner who carried word of the victory at Marathon to Athens **2.** any endurance contest

ma·raud (mə rôd') *vi., vt.* [< Fr. *maraud*, vagabond] to raid and plunder —**ma·raud'er** *n.*

mar·ble (mär'b'l) *n.* [< Gr. *marmaros*, white stone] **1.** a hard limestone, white or colored, which takes a high polish **2.** a piece of this stone, used in sculpture, etc. **3.** anything like marble in hardness, coldness, etc. **4.** *a)* a little ball of stone, glass, etc. *b)* [*pl., with sing. v.*] a children's game played with such balls **5.** [*pl.*] [Slang] brains —*adj.* of or like marble —*vt.* -bled, -bling **1.** to make (book edges) look mottled like marble **2.** to cause (meat) to be streaked with fat

mar'ble·ize' *vt.* -ized', -iz'ing to make look like marble

mar·ca·site (mär'kə sīt') *n.* [< Fr. < Ar. *marqashīṭā*] a pale, distinctively crystallized pyrite

mar·cel (mär sel') *n.* [< *Marcel* Grateau, early 20th-c. Fr. hairdresser] a series of even waves put in the hair with a curling iron: also **marcel wave** —*vt.* -celled', -cel'ling to put such waves in (hair)

March (märch) *n.* [< L. *Mars*, Mars] the third month of the year, having 31 days: abbrev. **Mar.**

march[1] (märch) *vi.* [Fr. *marcher*] **1.** to walk with regular steps, as in military formation **2.** to advance or progress steadily —*vt.* to make march or go —*n.* **1.** a marching **2.** a steady advance; progress **3.** a regular, steady step **4.** the distance covered in marching **5.** a piece of music for marching —**on the march** marching —**steal a march on** to get an advantage over secretly —**march'er** *n.*

march[2] (märch) *n.* [< OFr.] a boundary or frontier

March hare a hare in breeding time, proverbially an example of madness

marching orders orders to march, go, or leave

mar·chion·ess (mär'shə nis) *n.* **1.** the wife or widow of a marquess **2.** a lady of the rank of a marquess

march·pane (märch'pān') *n. same as* MARZIPAN

Mar·co·ni (mär kō'nē), **Gu·gliel·mo** (gōō lyel'mô) 1874–1937; It. physicist: developed wireless telegraphy

Marco Polo *see* POLO

Mar·cus Aurelius (mär'kəs) *see* AURELIUS

Mar·di gras (mär'di grä') [Fr., fat Tuesday] Shrove Tuesday, the last day before Lent: a day of carnival, as in New Orleans

---

fat, āpe, cär; ten, ēven; is, bīte; gō, hôrn, tōol, look; oil, out; up, fur; thin, then; zh, leisure; ŋ, ring; ə for *a* in *ago*; ' as in *able* (ā'b'l); ë, Fr. coeur; ö, Fr. feu; Fr. moŋ; ü, Fr. duc; r, Fr. cri; kh, G. doch, ich. ‡ foreign; < derived from

mare¹ (mer) *n.* [OE. *mere*] a fully mature female horse, mule, donkey, etc.

ma·re² (mer′ē, mär′ē) *n., pl.* **-ri·a** (-ē ə) [L., sea] a large, dark area on the moon or Mars

mare's-nest (merz′nest′) *n.* **1.** a hoax **2.** a mess

mar·ga·rine (mär′jə rin) *n.* [Fr.] a spread or cooking fat made of refined vegetable oils processed to the consistency of butter, often churned with pasteurized skim milk: also **mar′ga·rin**

mar·gin (mär′jən) *n.* [L. *margo*] **1.** a border or edge **2.** the blank border of a printed or written page **3.** a limit **4.** *a)* an amount beyond what is needed *b)* provision for increase, advance, etc. **5.** *a)* the difference between the cost and selling price of goods *b)* money deposited with a broker to insure him against loss on contracts which he undertakes for a buyer or seller of stocks, etc. —**mar′gin·al** *adj.*

mar·gue·rite (mär′gə rēt′) *n.* [Fr., a pearl] **1.** *same as* DAISY **2.** a chrysanthemum with a single flower

ma·ri·a·chi (mär′ē ä′chē) *n., pl.* **-chis** [MexSp. < ?] **1** one of a strolling band of musicians in Mexico **2.** such a band **3.** its music

Mar·i·an (mer′ē ən) *adj.* of the Virgin Mary

Ma·ri·an·a Islands (mer′ē an′ə) group of islands in the W Pacific: a U.S. trust territory

Marie An·toi·nette (an′twə net′) 1755-93; wife of Louis XVI: guillotined

mar·i·gold (mar′ə gōld′) *n.* [< Virgin *Mary* + *gold*] **1.** a plant of the composite family, with red, yellow, or orange flowers **2.** its flower

ma·ri·jua·na, ma·ri·hua·na (mar′ə wä′nə) *n.* [AmSp.] **1.** *same as* HEMP (sense 1) **2.** its dried leaves and flowers, smoked for the psychological effects

ma·rim·ba (mə rim′bə) *n.* [< native Afr. name] a kind of xylophone with resonators under the wooden bars

ma·ri·na (mə rē′nə) *n.* [It. & Sp., seacoast < L. *mare*, sea] a small arbor with docks, services, etc. for pleasure craft

mar·i·nade (mar′ə nād′) *n.* [Fr. < Sp. *marinar*, to pickle] **1.** a spiced pickling solution for steeping meat, fish, etc., often before cooking **2.** meat, etc. so steeped —*vt.* **-nad′ed, -nad′ing** *same as* MARINATE

mar·i·nate (mar′ə nāt′) *vt.* **-nat′ed, -nat′ing** [< It. *marinare*, to pickle] to steep (meat, etc.) in a marinade

ma·rine (mə rēn′) *adj.* [< L. *mare*, sea] **1.** of or found in the sea **2.** *a)* maritime; nautical *b)* naval —*n.* **1.** a member of a military force trained for service at sea **2.** [*often* M-] a member of the MARINE CORPS **3.** naval or merchant ships collectively

Marine Corps a branch of the U.S. armed forces trained for land, sea, and aerial combat

mar·i·ner (mar′ə nər) *n.* a sailor

mar·i·o·nette (mar′ē ə net′) *n.* [Fr. < *Marie*, Mary] a little jointed doll moved by strings or wires

mar·i·tal (mar′ə t'l) *adj.* [< L. *maritus*, a husband] of marriage —**mar′i·tal·ly** *adv.*

mar·i·time (mar′ə tīm′) *adj.* [< L. *mare*, sea] **1.** on, near, or living near the sea **2.** of navigation, shipping, etc. [*maritime* law]

Maritime Provinces Canad. provinces of Nova Scotia, New Brunswick, & Prince Edward Island

mar·jo·ram (mär′jər əm) *n.* [? ult. < Gr. *amarakos*] any of various plants of the mint family; esp., **sweet marjoram**, having aromatic leaves used in cooking

Mark (märk) *Bible* **1.** a Christian apostle, the reputed author of the second Gospel **2.** this book

mark¹ (märk) *n.* [OE. *mearc*, boundary] **1.** a spot, scratch, etc. on a surface **2.** a printed or written symbol [*punctuation marks*] **3.** a brand, label, etc. put on an article to show the maker, etc. **4.** an indication of some quality, character, etc. **5.** a grade [*a mark* of B in Latin] **6.** a standard of quality, etc. **7.** impression; influence **8.** an object of known position, serving as a guide **9.** a line, dot, etc. indicating position, as on a graduated scale **10.** a cross, etc. made by a person unable to write his signature **11.** a target or goal **12.** *Sports* the starting line of a race —*vt.* **1.** to put or make a mark or marks on **2.** to identify as by a mark **3.** to indicate by a mark **4.** to show plainly [*a smile marking* heed *[mark* my words] **5.** to distinguish; characterize **6.** to take notice of; heed *[mark* my words] **7.** to grade; rate **8.** to put price tags on **9.** to keep (score, etc.); record —*vi.* to observe; take note —**hit the mark 1.** to achieve one's aim **2.** to be right —**make one's mark** to achieve fame —**mark down (or up)** to mark for sale at a reduced (or an increased) price —**mark time 1.** to keep time while at a halt by lifting the feet as if marching **2.** to suspend progress for a time —**miss the mark 1.** to fail in achieving one's aim **2.** to be inaccurate —**mark′er** *n.*

mark² (märk) *n.* [< ON. *mork*, a half pound of silver] **1.** the monetary unit of East Germany **2.** *same as* DEUTSCHE MARK

mark′down′ *n.* **1.** a marking for sale at a reduced price **2.** the amount of reduction

marked (märkt) *adj.* **1.** having a mark or marks **2.** singled out as an object of hostility, etc. [a *marked* man] **3.** noticeable; distinct [a *marked* change] —**mark·ed·ly** (mär′kid lē) *adv.*

mar·ket (mär′kit) *n.* [ult. < L. *merx*, merchandise] **1.** a gathering of people for buying and selling things **2.** an open space or building with goods for sale from stalls, etc.: also **mar′ket·place′ 3.** a store selling provisions [a meat *market*] **4.** a region where goods can be bought and sold [the European *market*] **5.** buying and selling; trade **6.** demand (for goods, etc.) [a good *market* for tea] —*vt.* **1.** to offer for sale **2.** to sell —*vi.* to buy provisions —**be in the market for** to be seeking to buy —**be (or put) on the market** to be offered (or offer) for sale —**mar′ket·a·bil′i·ty** *n.* —**mar′ket·a·ble** *adj.*

mark′ing *n.* **1.** a mark or marks **2.** the characteristic arrangement of marks, as on fur or feathers

mark·ka (märk′kä) *n., pl.* **-kaa** (-kä) [Finn.] the monetary unit of Finland

marks·man (märks′mən) *n., pl.* **-men** a person who shoots, esp. with skill —**marks′man·ship′** *n.*

mark′up′ *n.* **1.** a marking for sale at an increased price **2.** the amount of increase

marl (märl) *n.* [< L. *marga*] a crumbly mixture of clay, sand, and limestone, usually with shell fragments —*vt.* to fertilize with marl —**marl′y** *adj.*

mar·lin (mär′lin) *n., pl.* **-lin, -lins** [< MARLINESPIKE] a large, slender deep-sea fish related to the sailfish

mar·line·spike, mar·lin·spike (mär′lin spīk′) *n.* [< Du. *marlijn*, small cord + SPIKE¹] a pointed iron instrument used in splicing rope

Mar·lowe (mär′lō), **Christopher** 1564-93; Eng. dramatist & poet

mar·ma·lade (mär′mə lād′) *n.* [ult. < Gr. *meli*, honey + *mēlon*, apple] a jamlike preserve of oranges or some other fruits and sugar

Mar·ma·ra (mär′mə rə), **Sea of** sea between European & Asiatic Turkey: also sp. **Marmora**

mar·mo·set (mär′mə zet′, -set′) *n.* [< OFr. *marmouset*, grotesque figure] a very small monkey of S. and C. America, with thick, soft fur

mar·mot (mär′mət) *n.* [< Fr., prob. < L. *mus montanus*, mountain mouse] any of a group of thick-bodied rodents, as the woodchuck

Marne (märn) river in NE France, flowing into the Seine

ma·roon¹ (mə rōōn′) *n., adj.* [Fr. *marron*, chestnut] dark brownish red

ma·roon² (mə rōōn′) *vt.* [< Fr. < AmSp. *cimarrón*, wild] **1.** to put (a person) ashore in a desolate place and abandon him there **2.** to leave abandoned, helpless, etc.

marque (märk) *n.* [Fr., a sign] an identifying emblem on an automobile

mar·quee (mär kē′) *n.* [< Fr. *marquise*, orig. a canopy over an officer's tent] a rooflike projection or awning over an entrance, as to a theater

mar·quess (mär′kwis) *n.* [see MARQUIS] **1.** a British nobleman ranking above an earl **2.** *same as* MARQUIS

mar·que·try (mär′kə trē) *n.* [< Fr. *marque*, a mark] decorative inlaid work, as in furniture

mar·quis (mär′kwis; *Fr.* mär kē′) *n., pl.* **-quis·es;** Fr. **-quis′** (-kē′) [< ML. *marchisus*, a prefect] in some European countries, a nobleman ranking above an earl or count

mar·quise (mär kēz′) *n.* **1.** the wife or widow of a marquis **2.** a lady of the rank of a marquis

mar·qui·sette (mär′ki zet′, -kwi-) *n.* [see MARQUEE] a thin, meshlike fabric used for curtains

Mar·ra·kech, Mar·ra·kesh (mə rä′kesh, mar′ə kesh′) traditional S capital in C Morocco: pop. 295,000

mar·riage (mar′ij) *n.* **1.** the state of being married; wedlock **2.** a wedding **3.** any close union —**mar′riage·a·ble** *adj.*

mar·ried *adj.* **1.** being husband and wife **2.** having a husband or wife **3.** of marriage —*n.* a married person: chiefly in **young marrieds**

mar·row (mar′ō) *n.* [OE. *mearg*] **1.** the soft, fatty tissue that fills the cavities of most bones **2.** the innermost or essential part —**mar′row·y** *adj.*

mar·ry (mar′ē) *vt.* **-ried, -ry·ing** [< L. *maritus*, a husband] **1.** to join as husband and wife **2.** to take as husband or wife **3.** to unite —*vi.* to get married —**marry off** to give in marriage

Mars (märz) **1.** *Rom. Myth.* the god of war: identified with the Greek god Ares **2.** a planet of the solar system: see PLANET

Mar·seil·laise (mär′sə lāz′; *Fr.* mär se yez′) [Fr., lit., of Marseille] the French national anthem, composed in 1792

Mar·seille (mär se′y′; *E.* mär sā′) seaport in SE France: pop. 889,000

marsh (märsh) *n.* [OE. *merisc*] a tract of low, wet, soft land; swamp —**marsh′y** *adj.* -i·er, -i·est

mar·shal (mär′shəl) *n.* [< OHG. *marah*, horse + *scalh*, servant] **1.** in various foreign armies, a general officer of the highest rank **2.** an official in charge of ceremonies, processions, etc. **3.** in the U.S., *a)* a Federal officer appointed to a judicial district with duties like those of a sheriff *b)* the head of some police or fire departments — *vt.* -shaled or -shalled, -shal·ing or -shal·ling **1.** to arrange (troops, ideas, etc.) in order **2.** *a)* to direct as a marshal *b)* to guide ceremoniously

Mar·shall (mär′shəl) **1.** George C(atlett), 1880–1959; U.S. general & statesman **2.** John, 1755–1835; chief justice of the U.S. (1801–35)

Marshall Islands group of islands in the W Pacific: a U.S. trust territory

marsh·mal·low (märsh′mel′ō, -mal′ō) *n.* [orig. made of the root of the marsh mallow] a soft, spongy confection of sugar, starch, gelatin, etc.

marsh mallow a pink-flowered European plant with a root sometimes used in medicine

marsh marigold a marsh plant with bright-yellow flowers

mar·su·pi·al (mär sōō′pē əl) *adj.* **1.** of or like a marsupium **2.** of a group of mammals whose young are carried by the female for several months after birth in an external pouch of the abdomen —*n.* an animal of this kind, as a kangaroo, opossum, etc.

mar·su′pi·um (-əm) *n.*, *pl.* -pi·a (-ə) [< Gr. *marsypos*, a pouch] the pouch on the abdomen of a female marsupial

mart (märt) *n.* [MDu.] a market

mar·ten (mär′t'n) *n.* [< OFr. *martre*] **1.** a small mammal like a weasel but larger, with soft, thick fur **2.** the fur

Mar·tha (mär′thə) *Bible* a woman rebuked by Jesus for fussing over chores while he talked with her sister Mary

mar·tial (mär′shəl) *adj.* [< L. *martialis*, of Mars] **1.** of or connected with war **2.** warlike; militaristic —**mar′tial·ly** *adv.*

martial law temporary rule by military authorities over civilians, as in time of war

Mar·tian (mär′shən) *adj.* of Mars (god or planet) —*n.* an imagined inhabitant of the planet Mars

MARTEN
(to 3 ft. long, including tail)

mar·tin (mär′t'n) *n.* [Fr.] **1.** a bird of the swallow family **2.** any of various swallowlike birds

mar·ti·net (mär′t'n et′) *n.* [< *Martinet*, 17th-c. Fr. general] a very strict disciplinarian

mar·tin·gale (mär′t'n gāl′) *n.* [Fr.] **1.** the harness strap from head to girth, that keeps the horse from rearing or throwing back its head **2.** a lower stay for the jib boom of a sailing vessel

mar·ti·ni (mär tē′nē) *n.*, *pl.* -nis [< ?] [*also* M-] a cocktail of gin (or vodka) and dry vermouth

Mar·ti·nique (mär′tə nēk′) French island possession in the Windward group of the West Indies

mar·tyr (mär′tər) *n.* [< Gr. *martyr*, a witness] **1.** one tortured or killed because of his faith or beliefs **2.** one suffering great misery a long time —*vt.* to make a martyr of —**mar′tyr·dom** *n.*

mar·vel (mär′v'l) *n.* [< L. *mirari*, admire] a wonderful or astonishing thing —*vi.* -veled or -velled, -vel·ing or -vel·ling to be amazed; wonder —*vt.* to wonder at or about (followed by a clause)

mar·vel·ous (mär′v'l əs) *adj.* **1.** causing wonder; extraordinary, etc. **2.** [Colloq.] fine; splendid Also, chiefly Brit. sp., **mar′vel·lous** —**mar′vel·ous·ly** *adv.*

Marx (märks), Karl 1818–83; Ger. social philosopher & political economist whose doctrines are the basis of modern socialism

Marx·ism (märk′siz'm) *n.* the system of thought developed by Karl Marx, Friedrich Engels, and their followers —**Marx′ist**, **Marx′i·an** *adj.*, *n.*

Mar·y (mer′ē) *Bible* **1.** mother of Jesus **2.** sister of Martha **3.** *same as* MARY MAGDALENE

Mar·y·land (mer′ə lənd) E State of the U.S.: 10,577 sq. mi.; pop. 3,922,000; cap. Annapolis: abbrev. **Md.**, **MD**

Mary Mag·da·lene (mag′də lēn) *Bible* a woman out of whom Jesus cast devils

Mary, Queen of Scots (*Mary Stuart*) 1542–87; queen of Scotland (1542–67): beheaded

mar·zi·pan (mär′zi pan′) *n.* [G. < It. *marzapane*] a confection of various shapes and colors made of a paste of ground almonds, sugar, and egg white

masc., **mas.** masculine

mas·ca·ra (mas kar′ə) *n.* [< Sp. < It. *maschera*] a cosmetic for coloring the eyelashes

mas·cot (mas′kät) *n.* [< Fr. < Pr. *masco*, sorcerer] any person, animal, or thing supposed to bring good luck by being present

mas·cu·line (mas′kyə lin) *adj.* [< L. *mas*, male] **1.** male; of men or boys **2.** suitable for or characteristic of men and boys; strong, vigorous, etc. **3.** mannish: said of women **4.** *Gram.* designating or of the gender of words referring to males or things orig. regarded as male —*n.* **1.** the masculine gender **2.** a word in this gender —**mas′cu·lin′i·ty** *n.*

Mase·field (mās′fēld, māz′-), John 1878–1967; Eng. writer, esp. of poetry

ma·ser (mā′zər) *n.* [m(icrowave) a(mplification by) s(timulated) e(mission of) r(adiation)] a device in which atoms, as in a gas, are raised to a higher energy level and emitted in a very narrow beam

mash (mash) *n.* [< OE. *mascwyrt*] **1.** crushed malt or meal soaked in hot water for making wort **2.** a mixture of bran, meal, etc. in warm water for feeding horses, etc. **3.** any soft mixture or mass —*vt.* **1.** to mix (crushed malt, etc.) in hot water for making wort **2.** to change into a soft mass by beating, crushing, etc. —**mash′er** *n.*

mask (mask) *n.* [< Fr. < It. *maschera*] **1.** a covering to conceal or protect the face **2.** anything that conceals or disguises **3.** a masque or masquerade **4.** *a)* a molded likeness of the face *b)* a grotesque representation of a face, worn to amuse or frighten —*vt.* to conceal, cover, disguise, etc. as with a mask —**masked** *adj.* —**mask′er** *n.*

mask′ing tape an adhesive tape for covering borders, etc., as during painting

mas·och·ism (mas′ə kiz'm, maz′-) *n.* [< L. von Sacher-Masoch, 19th-c. Austrian writer] the getting of pleasure, specif. sexual pleasure, from being dominated or hurt physically or psychologically —**mas′och·ist** *n.* —**mas′och·is′tic** *adj.*

ma·son (mā′s'n) *n.* [< ML. *matio*] **1.** one whose work is building with stone, brick, etc. **2.** [M-] *same as* FREEMASON

Ma·son-Dix·on line (mā′s'n dik′s'n) [< C. *Mason* & J. *Dixon*, who surveyed it, 1763–67] boundary line between Pa. & Md., regarded as separating the North from the South: also **Mason and Dixon's line**

Ma·son·ic (mə sän′ik) *adj.* [*also* m-] of Freemasons or Freemasonry

Ma·son·ite (mā′s'n īt′) [< W. H. *Mason* (1877–1947?), U.S. engineer] *a trademark for* a kind of wood fiberboard, used as building material, etc. —*n.* such fiberboard

ma·son·ry (mā′s'n rē) *n.*, *pl.* -ries **1.** the trade of a mason **2.** something built by a mason; brickwork or stonework **3.** [*usually* M-] *same as* FREEMASONRY

masque (mask) *n.* [see MASK] **1.** *same as* MASQUERADE (sense 1) **2.** a former kind of dramatic entertainment with a mythical or allegorical theme

mas·quer·ade (mas′kə rād′) *n.* [see MASK] **1.** a ball or party at which masks and fancy costumes are worn **2.** a costume for such a ball, etc. **3.** *a)* a disguise *b)* an acting under false pretenses —*vi.* -ad′ed, -ad′ing **1.** to take part in a masquerade **2.** to act under false pretenses —**mas′quer·ad′er** *n.*

Mass (mas) *n.* [< L. *missa* in *ite, missa est* (*contio*), go, (the meeting) is dismissed] [*also* m-] **1.** the service of the Eucharist in the Roman Catholic Church and some other churches **2.** a musical setting for certain parts of this service

mass (mas) *n.* [< Gr. *maza*, barley cake] **1.** a quantity of matter of indefinite shape and size; lump **2.** a large quantity or number [a *mass* of bruises] **3.** bulk; size **4.** the main part **5.** *Physics* the quantity of matter in a body as measured in its relation to inertia —*adj.* **1.** of a large number [*mass* production] **2.** of or for the masses [*mass* education] —*vt., vi.* to gather or form into a mass —**in the mass** collectively —**the masses** the great mass of common people; specif., the working people

Mas·sa·chu·setts (mas′ə chōō′sits) New England State of the U.S.: 8,257 sq. mi.; pop. 5,689,000; cap. Boston: abbrev. **Mass., MA**

mas·sa·cre (mas′ə kər) *n.* [Fr. < OFr. *maçacre,* shambles] the indiscriminate, merciless killing of human beings or animals —*vt.* **-cred, -cr·ing** to kill in large numbers

mas·sage (mə säzh′) *n.* [Fr. < Ar. *massa,* to touch] a rubbing, kneading, etc. of part of the body, as to stimulate circulation —*vt.* **-saged′, -sag′ing** to give a massage to — **mas·sag′er** *n.*

mas·seur (ma sur′) *n.* [Fr.] a man whose work is giving massages —**mas·seuse′** (-sōoz′, -sooz′) *n.fem.*

mas·sive (mas′iv) *adj.* [< Fr.] **1.** forming or consisting of a large mass; big and solid **2.** large and imposing **3.** extensive —**mas′sive·ly** *adv.* —**mas′sive·ness** *n.*

mass media those means of communication that reach and influence large numbers of people, esp. newspapers, magazines, radio, and television

mass meeting a large public meeting to discuss public affairs, demonstrate public approval or disapproval, etc.

mass number the number of neutrons and protons in the nucleus of an atom

mass production quantity production of goods, esp. by machinery and division of labor

mast¹ (mast) *n.* [OE. *mæst*] **1.** a tall vertical spar used to support the sails, yards, etc. on a ship **2.** any vertical pole, as in a crane —*vt.* to put masts on

mast² (mast) *n.* [OE. *mæst*] beechnuts, acorns, chestnuts, etc., esp. as food for hogs

mas·ter (mas′tər) *n.* [< L. *magister*] **1.** a man who rules others or has control over something; specif., *a)* a man who is head of a household *b)* an employer *c)* an owner of an animal or slave *d)* the captain of a merchant ship *e)* [Chiefly Brit.] a male teacher *f)* a victor *g)* a person whose teachings one follows *h)* [M-] Jesus Christ (with *our, the,* etc.) **2.** an expert; specif., *a)* a workman skilled in his trade *b)* an artist regarded as great **3.** [M-] a title applied to: *a)* a boy regarded as too young to be addressed as *Mr. b)* one who is a MASTER OF ARTS (or SCIENCE, etc.) —*adj.* **1.** being a master **2.** of a master **3.** chief; main; controlling —*vt.* **1.** to become master of; control, conquer, etc. **2.** to become an expert in (an art, science, etc.)

mas′ter·ful *adj.* **1.** acting the part of a master; imperious **2.** expert; skillful —**mas′ter·ful·ly** *adv.*

master key a key for opening a set of locks

mas′ter·ly *adj.* expert; skillful —*adv.* in a masterly manner —**mas′ter·li·ness** *n.*

mas′ter·mind′ *n.* a very intelligent person, esp. one with the ability to plan or direct a group project —*vt.* to be the mastermind of (a project)

Master of Arts (or **Science,** etc.) **1.** a degree given by a college or university to one who has completed a prescribed course of graduate study in the humanities (or in science, etc.) **2.** one who has this degree

master of ceremonies a person who presides over an entertainment, introducing the participants, telling jokes, etc.

mas′ter·piece′ *n.* **1.** a thing made or done with masterly skill **2.** the greatest work of a person or group Also **mas′ter·work′**

master sergeant *U.S. Mil.* a noncommissioned officer of high rank

mas′ter·stroke′ *n.* a masterly action, move, or achievement

mas′ter·y *n., pl.* **-ies 1.** control as by a master **2.** ascendancy or victory **3.** expert skill or knowledge

mast′head′ *n.* **1.** the top part of a ship's mast **2.** that part of a newspaper or magazine stating its address, publishers, etc.

mas·tic (mas′tik) *n.* [< Gr. *mastichē*] **1.** a yellowish resin obtained from a Mediterranean evergreen tree, used in making varnish, adhesives, etc. **2.** the tree

mas·ti·cate (mas′tə kāt′) *vt.* **-cat′ed, -cat′ing** [ult. < Gr. *mastax,* mouth] to chew up (food, etc.) —**mas′ti·ca′tion** *n.*

mas·tiff (mas′tif) *n.* [ult. < L. *mansuetus,* tame] a large, powerful, smooth-coated dog with hanging lips and drooping ears

mas·to·don (mas′tə dän′) *n.* [< Fr. < Gr. *mastos,* breast + *odous,* tooth: from the nipplelike processes on its molars] a large, extinct animal resembling the elephant but larger

mas·toid (mas′toid) *adj.* [< Gr. *mastos,* breast + *eidos,* form] designating, of, or near a projection of the temporal bone behind the ear —*n.* **1.** the mastoid projection **2.** [Colloq.] *same as* MASTOIDITIS

mas·toid·i·tis (-toi dīt′is) *n.* inflammation of the mastoid

mas·tur·bate (mas′tər bāt′) *vi.* **-bat′ed, -bat′ing** [< L. *masturbari*] to manipulate the genitals for sexual gratification —**mas′tur·ba′tion** *n.* —**mas′tur·ba′tor** *n.*

mat¹ (mat) *n.* [< LL. *matta*] **1.** a flat piece of cloth, woven straw, rubber, etc., variously used for protection, as under a vase, etc. or on the floor **2.** a thickly padded floor covering, as for wrestling, etc. **3.** anything growing or interwoven in a thick tangle —*vt., vi.* **mat′ted, mat′ting** to interweave or tangle

mat² (mat) *adj.* [Fr. < OFr.] *same as* MATTE —*n.* **1.** *same as* MATTE **2.** a border, as of cardboard or cloth, put around a picture —*vt.* **mat′ted, mat′ting 1.** to produce a dull finish on **2.** to frame (a picture) with a mat

mat·a·dor (mat′ə dôr′) *n.* [Sp. < *matar,* to kill] the bullfighter who kills the bull

match¹ (mach) *n.* [prob. < Gr. *myxa,* lamp wick] a slender piece of wood, cardboard, etc. tipped with a composition that catches fire by friction, sometimes only on a specially prepared surface

match² (mach) *n.* [OE. *(ge)mæcca,* a mate] **1.** *a)* one that is equal or similar *b)* a counterpart or facsimile **2.** two that go well together **3.** a contest or game **4.** a marriage or mating **5.** a suitable mate —*vt.* **1.** to join in marriage; mate **2.** to put in opposition **3.** to be equal or similar to **4.** to make or get the competitor, counterpart, or equivalent of **5.** to suit (one thing) to another **6.** to fit (things) together —*vi.* to be equal, similar, etc.

match′book′ *n.* a folder of paper matches

match′box′ *n.* a small box for holding matches

match′less *adj.* having no equal; peerless

match′lock′ *n.* **1.** an old type of gunlock in which the powder was ignited by a slow-burning wick **2.** a musket with such a gunlock

match′mak′ing *n.* **1.** the arranging of marriages for others **2.** the arranging of wrestling or boxing matches, etc. —**match′mak′er** *n.*

match play *Golf* play in which the score is calculated by holes won rather than by strokes taken

mate¹ (māt) *n.* [MDu.] **1.** a companion or fellow worker **2.** one of a matched pair **3.** *a)* a husband or wife *b)* the male or female of paired animals **4.** *Naut. a)* an officer of a merchant ship, ranking below the captain *b)* an assistant **5.** *U.S. Navy* any of various petty officers —*vt., vi.* **mat′ed, mat′ing 1.** to pair **2.** to couple in marriage or sexually

mate² (māt) *n., interj., vt.* **mat′ed, mat′ing** *same as* CHECKMATE

ma·té, ma·te (mä′tā, mat′ā) *n.* [AmSp. *mate* < Incan *mati,* calabash] **1.** a beverage made from dried leaves of a S. American tree **2.** the tree or leaves

ma·ter (māt′ər) *n.* [L.] [Chiefly Brit. Colloq.] mother

ma·te·ri·al (mə tir′ē əl) *adj.* [< L. *materia,* matter] **1.** of matter; physical **2.** bodily; not spiritual **3.** important, essential, etc. —*n.* **1.** what a thing is made of; elements or parts; constituent substance **2.** data; ideas, notes, etc. **3.** fabric, as cloth **4.** [*pl.*] things used, as tools

ma·te·ri·al·ism (-iz′m) *n.* **1.** the doctrine that everything is explainable in terms of matter **2.** concern with material things rather than with spiritual values —**ma·te′ri·al·ist** *n., adj.* —**ma·te′ri·al·is′tic** *adj.* —**ma·te′ri·al·is′ti·cal·ly** *adv.*

ma·te′ri·al·ize′ (-ə līz′) *vt.* **-ized′, -iz′ing** to give material form to —*vi.* **1.** to become fact **2.** to take on bodily form —**ma·te′ri·al·i·za′tion** *n.*

ma·te′ri·al·ly *adv.* **1.** physically **2.** considerably

ma·te·ri·el, ma·té·ri·el (mə tir′ē el′) *n.* [Fr.: see MATERIAL] necessary materials and tools; specif., military weapons, equipment, supplies, etc.

ma·ter·nal (mə tur′n'l) *adj.* [< L. *mater,* mother] **1.** motherly **2.** of or from a mother **3.** on the mother's side of the family —**ma·ter′nal·ly** *adv.*

ma·ter′ni·ty (-nə tē) *n.* the state of being a mother; motherhood —*adj.* for pregnant women

math (math) *n. clipped form of* MATHEMATICS

math·e·mat·i·cal (math′ə mat′i k'l) *adj.* **1.** of or like mathematics **2.** rigorously exact; absolutely accurate — **math′e·mat′i·cal·ly** *adv.*

math′e·mat′ics (-iks) *n.pl.* [*with sing. v.*] [< Gr. *manthanein,* learn] sciences (arithmetic, geometry, etc.) dealing with quantities, forms, etc. by numbers and symbols —**math′e·ma·ti′cian** (-mə tish′ən) *n.*

mat·in (mat′'n) *n.* [< L. *matutinus,* of the morning] **1.** [*pl.*] [*often* M-] a service of morning prayer **2.** [Poet.] a morning song

mat·i·nee, mat·i·née (mat''n ā') *n.* [see prec.] an afternoon presentation or performance, as of a play

Ma·tisse (mä tēs'), **Hen·ri** (än rē') 1869–1954; Fr. painter

ma·tri·arch (mā'trē ärk') *n.* [< L. *mater,* a mother + -ARCH] a mother ruling her family or tribe; specif., one heading a matriarchy —**ma'tri·ar'chal** *adj.*

ma'tri·ar'chy *n., pl.* -**chies** 1. a form of social organization in which the mother is the head of the family or tribe, descent being traced through the female line 2. rule or domination by women

mat·ri·cide (mat'rə sīd', mā'trə-) *n.* [< L. *mater,* a mother + *caedere,* to kill] 1. the murder of a mother by her son or daughter 2. one committing such a murder — **mat'ri·ci'dal** *adj.*

ma·tric·u·late (mə trik'yoo lāt') *vt., vi.* -**lat'ed,** -**lat'ing** [see MATRIX] to enroll, esp. as a student in a college —**ma·tric'u·la'tion** *n.*

mat·ri·mo·ny (mat'rə mō'nē) *n., pl.* -**nies** [< L. *mater,* a mother] 1. the ceremony or sacrament of marriage 2. married state; wedlock —**mat'ri·mo'ni·al** *adj.*

ma·trix (mā'triks) *n., pl.* -**tri·ces** (mā'trə sēz', mat'rə-), -**trix·es** [ult. < L. *mater,* a mother] that within which something originates or takes form; specif., a die or mold for casting or shaping

ma·tron (mā'trən) *n.* [< L. *mater,* a mother] 1. a wife or widow 2. a woman superintendent of domestic arrangements in an institution 3. a woman attendant or guard, as in a jail —**ma'tron·ly** *adj.*

matron of honor a married woman acting as principal attendant to the bride at a wedding

Matt. Matthew

matte (mat) *n.* [var. of MAT²] a dull surface or finish —*adj.* not shiny; dull Also sp. **matt**

mat·ted (mat'id) *adj.* closely tangled, as hair

mat·ter (mat'ər) *n.* [< L. *materia*] 1. what a thing is made of; constituent material 2. whatever occupies space and is perceptible to the senses 3. a specified substance [coloring *matter*] 4. what is expressed or thought, apart from its style or form; content 5. an amount or quantity [a *matter* of a few days] 6. *a)* a thing or affair [business *matters*] *b)* a cause or occasion [no laughing *matter*] 7. importance [it's of no *matter*] 8. trouble [what's the *matter?*] 9. pus —*vi.* to have importance —**as a matter of fact** in fact; really —**for that matter** as far as that is concerned —**no matter** 1. it is not important 2. regardless of [*no matter* what you say]

Mat·ter·horn (mat'ər hôrn') mountain of the Alps, on the Swiss-Italian border: c.14,700 ft.

mat'ter-of-fact' *adj.* sticking to facts; literal, practical, etc. —**mat'ter-of-fact'ness** *n.*

Mat·thew (math'yoo) *Bible* 1. a Christian apostle, reputed author of the first Gospel 2. this book

mat·ting (mat'iŋ) *n.* 1. a fabric, as of straw, for floor mats, padding, etc. 2. mats collectively

mat·tock (mat'ək) *n.* [OE. *mattuc*] a tool like a pickax but with at least one flat blade, used in loosening the soil, digging up roots, etc.

mat·tress (mat'ris) *n.* [< Ar. *maṭraḥ,* cushion] a casing made of strong fabric, filled with cotton or other soft material, usually containing coiled springs, and used as or on a bed

mat·u·rate (mach'ə rāt') *vi.* -**rat'ed,** -**rat'-ing** [see MATURE] to ripen; mature —**mat'-u·ra'tion** *n.*

ma·ture (mə toor', -tyoor') *adj.* [< L. *maturus,* ripe] 1. fully grown, developed, ripened, etc. 2. due, as a note or bond —*vt., vi.* -**tured', -tur'ing** to make or become mature —**ma·tu'ri·ty** *n.*

mat·zo (mät'sə, -sô) *n., pl.* -**zot,** -**zoth** (-sōt), -**zos** [Heb. *matstsāh,* unleavened] 1. flat, thin, unleavened bread eaten by Jews during Passover 2. a piece of this

maud·lin (môd'lin) *adj.* [< OFr. *Madeleine,* (Mary) Magdalene (often represented as weeping)] foolishly, often tearfully, sentimental

Maugham (môm), **(William) Som·er·set** (sum'ər set') 1874–1965; Eng. novelist and playwright

maul (môl) *n.* [< L. *malleus,* a hammer] a heavy hammer or mallet as for driving stakes —*vt.* 1. to bruise or lacerate 2. to handle roughly

maun·der (môn'dər) *vi.* [Early ModE. *mander,* to growl] to move, act, or talk in a vague, dreamy way

Mau·pas·sant (mō'pə sänt'), **Guy de** (gē də) 1850–93; Fr. writer of novels & short stories

Mau·ri·ta·ni·a (môr'ə tā'nē ə) country in W Africa: 419,230 sq. mi.; pop. 1,120,000

Mau·ri·ti·us (mô rish'ē əs) island country in the Indian Ocean, east of Madagascar: 809 sq. mi.; pop. 810,000

mau·so·le·um (mô'sə lē'əm, -zə-) *n., pl.* -**le'ums, -le'a** (-lē'ə) [< the tomb of King *Mausolus,* in ancient Asia Minor] a large, imposing tomb

mauve (mōv, môv) *n.* [Fr., mallow < L. *malvea,* mallow] a delicate purple —*adj.* of such a color

ma·ven (mā'vən) *n.* [Yid. < LHeb. *mēvin*] an expert or connoisseur, often, specif., a self-proclaimed one

mav·er·ick (mav'ər ik) *n.* [< S. *Maverick,* 19th-c. Texan whose cattle had no brand] 1. an unbranded animal 2. [Colloq.] an independent, as in politics

maw (mô) *n.* [OE. *maga*] 1. orig., the stomach 2. the oral cavity, jaws, or gullet, as of a beast

mawk·ish (mô'kish) *adj.* [< ON. *mathkr,* maggot] sickeningly sentimental —**mawk'ish·ly** *adv.*

max. maximum

maxi- [< MAXIMUM] *a combining form meaning* maximum, very long, very large [*maxicoat*]

max·il·la (mak sil'ə) *n., pl.* -**lae** (-ē) [L.] a jaw; specif., in vertebrates, the upper jaw

max·im (mak'sim) *n.* [< LL. *maxima (propositio),* the greatest (premise)] a concise rule of conduct; precept

max·i·mal (mak'sə m'l) *adj.* greatest possible, permissible, etc.; of or being the maximum —**max'i·mal·ly** *adv.*

max'i·mize (-mīz') *vt.* -**mized', -miz'ing** to increase to the maximum

max'i·mum (-məm) *n., pl.* -**mums, -ma** (-mə) [L., superl. of *magnus,* great] 1. the greatest quantity, number, etc. possible or permissible 2. the highest degree or point reached —*adj.* 1. greatest possible, permissible, or reached 2. of, marking, or setting a maximum

May (mā) *n.* [< L. *Maia,* goddess of increase] the fifth month of the year, having 31 days

may (mā) *v.aux. pt.* **might** [OE. *mæg*] an auxiliary verb expressing: 1. possibility [it *may* rain] 2. permission [you *may* go] 3. purpose, result, etc. [be quiet so that we *may* hear] 4. wish or hope [*may* he win!]

Ma·ya (mä'yə) *n.* 1. *pl.* -**yas, -ya** a member of a tribe of Indians of SE Mexico and Central America who had a highly developed civilization 2. their language —*adj.* of the Mayas —**Ma'yan** *adj., n.*

may·be (mā'bē) *adv.* [ME. *it may be*] perhaps

May Day May 1: a traditional spring festival and, in many countries, a labor holiday

may·flow·er (mā'flou'ər) *n.* any of various plants flowering in May or early spring —[M-] the ship on which the Pilgrims came to America (1620)

may'fly' *n., pl.* -**flies'** [see MAY & FLY²] a slender, short-lived insect with gauzy wings

may·hap (mā'hap', mā'hap') *adv.* [< *it may hap(pen)*] [Archaic] perhaps

may·hem (mā'hem, mā'əm) *n.* [see MAIM] 1. *Law* the offense of maiming a person 2. any violent destruction

may·n't (mā'nt, mānt) may not

may·o (mā'ō) *n.* [Colloq.] clipped form of MAYONNAISE

may·on·naise (mā'ə nāz') *n.* [Fr., prob. < *Mahón,* port on a Sp. island] a creamy salad dressing made with egg yolks, oil, etc.

may·or (mā'ər, mer) *n.* [< L. *major,* greater] the chief administrative official of a municipality —**may'or·al** *adj.*

may'or·al·ty (-əl tē) *n., pl.* -**ties** the office or term of office of a mayor

May'pole' *n.* a high pole with streamers, etc., around which merrymakers dance on May Day

mayst (māst) *archaic 2d pers. sing., pres. indic.,* of MAY: used with thou

maze (māz) *n.* [OE. *amasian,* amaze] 1. a confusing, intricate network of pathways 2. a confused state

‡**maz·el tov** (mä'z'l tōv', tôf') [Heb.] good luck: an expression of congratulation

ma·zur·ka (mə zur'kə) *n.* [Pol.] 1. a lively Polish dance 2. music for it, usually in 3/4 or 3/8 time

M.C. 1. Master of Ceremonies 2. Member of Congress

Mc·Coy (mə koi'), **the (real)** [< *Mackay,* Scottish clan name] [Slang] the real person or thing, not a substitute

Mc·In·tosh (mak'in täsh') *n.* [< J. *McIntosh* of Ontario, its first cultivator] a late-maturing variety of red apple

MATTOCK

MAYFLY
(body to 1 inch)

Mc·Kin·ley (mə kin'lē), **Mount** mountain in SC Alas.: highest peak in N. America: 20,320 ft.

Mc·Kin·ley (mə kin'lē), **William** 1843–1901; 25th president of the U.S. (1897–1901): assassinated

Md *Chem.* mendelevium

Md., MD Maryland

M.D. [L. *Medicinae Doctor*] Doctor of Medicine

Mdlle. *pl.* **Mdlles.** Mademoiselle

Mdme. *pl.* **Mdmes.** Madame

mdse. merchandise

me (mē) *pron.* [OE.] *objective case of* I

ME. Middle English

Me., ME Maine

mead' (mēd) *n.* [OE. *meodu*] an alcoholic drink made of fermented honey and water, often spiced

mead² (mēd) *n.* [OE. *mæd*] [Poet.] a meadow

mead·ow (med'ō) *n.* [OE. *mæd*] a fairly extensive piece of open, grassy land, as a tract of pasture land, typically level and well watered

mead'ow·lark' *n.* either of two N. American songbirds with brown-and-black upper parts and a bright-yellow breast

mea·ger (mē'gər) *adj.* [< L. *macer*, lean] **1.** very thin; emaciated **2.** notably deficient in quantity or extent; inadequate; scanty **3.** notably deficient in richness, productivity, usefulness, etc.   Brit. sp. **mea'gre** —**mea'ger·ly** *adv.* —**mea'ger·ness** *n.*

meal' (mēl) *n.* [OE. *mæl*] **1.** a time of eating; lunch, dinner, etc. **2.** the food then served

meal² (mēl) *n.* [OE. *melu*] **1.** any edible grain, coarsely ground **2.** anything ground or powdered

meal'time' *n.* the usual time for eating a meal

meal·y (mēl'ē) *adj.* **-i·er, -i·est 1.** granular or crumbly, like meal **2.** of, containing, or sprinkled with meal **3.** flecked **4.** pale **5.** mealy-mouthed —**meal'i·ness** *n.*

meal'y-mouthed' (-mouthd', -moutht') *adj.* not simple or direct in speech; evasive and insincere

mean' (mēn) *vt.* **meant** (ment), **mean'ing** [OE. *mænan*] **1.** to have in mind; intend **2.** to intend to express **3.** to denote; signify —*vi.* **1.** to have a purpose in mind: chiefly in **mean well,** to have good intentions **2.** to have a (specified) degree of importance, effect, etc.

mean² (mēn) *adj.* [OE. (ge)*mæne*] **1.** low, as in quality; paltry; poor **2.** shabby in appearance **3.** ignoble; petty **4.** stingy **5.** bad-tempered, nasty, disagreeable, etc. **6.** [Slang] *a*) difficult *b*) expert —**mean'ly** *adv.* —**mean'ness** *n.*

mean³ (mēn) *adj.* [< L. *medius*, middle] **1.** halfway between extremes **2.** average —*n.* **1.** what is between extremes **2.** *Math.* an average or other intermediate quantity

me·an·der (mē an'dər) *vi.* [< Gr. *Maiandros*, a winding river of Asia Minor] to wander; ramble

mean·ie, mean·y (mē'nē) *n., pl.* **-ies** [MEAN² + -IE] [Colloq.] one who is bad-tempered, nasty, etc.

mean'ing *n.* what is meant; significance; import —**mean'ing·ful** *adj.* —**mean'ing·less** *adj.*

means (mēnz) *n.pl.* [< MEAN³, *n.*] **1.** [*with sing. or pl. v.*] that by which something is done or obtained **2.** resources or wealth —**by all means 1.** without fail **2.** certainly —**by means of** by using —**by no means** certainly not

mean (solar) time time having exactly equal divisions

meant (ment) *pt. & pp. of* MEAN¹

mean'time' *adv.* **1.** in or during the intervening time **2.** at the same time —*n.* the intervening time   Also, and for adv. usually, **mean'while'**

mea·sles (mē'z'lz) *n.pl.* [*with sing. v.*] [ME. *maseles*] **1.** an acute, infectious, communicable virus disease, usually of children, characterized by small red spots on the skin, high fever, etc. **2.** any of various similar but milder diseases; esp., rubella

mea·sly (mēz'lē) *adj.* **-sli·er, -sli·est 1.** infected with measles **2.** [Colloq.] contemptibly small, meager, or inferior; wretched

meas·ur·a·ble (mezh'ər ə b'l) *adj.* that can be measured —**meas'ur·a·bil'i·ty** *n.* —**meas'ur·a·bly** *adv.*

meas·ure (mezh'ər) *n.* [< L. *metiri*, to measure] **1.** the extent, dimensions, capacity, etc. of anything **2.** the determining of any of these; measurement **3.** *a*) a unit of measurement *b*) any standard of valuation **4.** a system of measurement **5.** an instrument used for measuring **6.** a definite quantity measured **7.** proportion, quantity, or degree [in large *measure*] **8.** a course of action **9.** a statute; law **10.** a rhythmical pattern or unit; specif., the notes and rests be-

MEASURES

tween two bars on a staff of music —*vt.* **-ured, -ur·ing 1.** to determine the extent, dimensions, etc. of **2.** to get, take, set apart, etc. in units thus determined **3.** to estimate by comparison **4.** to be a measure of **5.** to adjust by a standard —*vi.* **1.** to determine extent, dimensions, etc. **2.** to be of specified extent, dimensions, etc. —**beyond** (or **above**) **measure** exceedingly —**for good measure** as a bonus or something extra —**in a measure** to some extent —**measure up** to prove to be qualified —**measure up to** to meet (qualifications)

meas'ured *adj.* **1.** determined as in extent **2.** regular or uniform **3.** *a*) rhythmical *b*) metrical **4.** calculated, deliberate, etc., as speech

meas'ure·less *adj.* beyond being measured; immense

meas'ure·ment *n.* **1.** a measuring or being measured **2.** extent, dimension, etc. as determined by measuring **3.** a system of measuring

measuring worm the larva of a geometrid

meat (mēt) *n.* [OE. *mete*] **1.** food: archaic except in **meat and drink 2.** animal, esp. mammal, flesh used as food **3.** the edible part, as of a nut **4.** gist

meat'ball' *n.* a small ball of ground meat

meat'pack'ing *n.* the slaughtering of animals and the preparation of the meat for market

meat'y *adj.* **-i·er, -i·est 1.** of, like, or full of meat **2.** containing much to think about; not shallow or trivial

Mec·ca (mek'ə) the religious capital of Saudi Arabia, near the Red Sea: birthplace of Mohammed and a pilgrimage center: pop. c.250,000 —*n.* [*often* m-] a place one yearns to go to —**Mec'can** *adj., n.*

me·chan·ic (mə kan'ik) *n.* [< Gr. *mēchanē*, a machine] a worker skilled in using tools or in making, operating, and repairing machines

me·chan'i·cal *adj.* **1.** involving, or skilled in the use of, machinery or tools **2.** produced or operated by machinery **3.** of the science of mechanics **4.** lacking spirit or expression; machinelike —**me·chan'i·cal·ly** *adv.*

mechanical drawing drawing done, as by a draftsman, with T squares, scales, compasses, etc.

me·chan'ics *n.pl.* [*with sing. v.*] **1.** the science of motion and the action of forces on bodies **2.** knowledge of machinery **3.** the technical aspect

mech·a·nism (mek'ə niz'm) *n.* [see MECHANIC] **1.** the working parts of a machine **2.** any system or process of interrelated parts **3.** any physical or mental process by which a result is produced **4.** the theory that all phenomena can be explained in terms of physics and chemistry —**mech'a·nis'tic** *adj.* —**mech'a·nis'ti·cal·ly** *adv.*

mech'a·nize' (-nīz') *vt.* **-nized', -niz'ing 1.** to make mechanical **2.** to equip with machinery **3.** to equip (a military force) with tanks, self-propelled guns, etc. —**mech'a·ni·za'tion** *n.*

med. 1. medical **2.** medicine **3.** medium

med·al (med''l) *n.* [< LL. *medialis*, medial] a small, flat piece of metal with a design or inscription on it, made in commemoration, given as an award, or used as a religious token

med'al·ist (-ist) *n.* **1.** one who makes medals **2.** one awarded a medal **3.** *Golf* the winner at medal play   Brit. sp. **med'al·list**

me·dal·lion (mə dal'yən) *n.* [< Fr.: see MEDAL] **1.** a large medal **2.** a decorative panel or the like, as in architecture, suggestive of a large medal

medal play *Golf* play in which the score is calculated by totaling the strokes taken

med·dle (med''l) *vi.* **-dled, -dling** [< L. *miscere*, to mix] **1.** to concern oneself with other people's affairs without being asked or needed **2.** to tamper (*with*) —**med'dler** *n.* —**med'dle·some** (-səm) *adj.*

Mede (mēd) *n.* a native or inhabitant of Media

Me·de·a (mi dē'ə) *Gr. Myth.* a sorceress who helped Jason get the Golden Fleece

Me·di·a (mē'dē ə) ancient kingdom in the part of SW Asia that is now NW Iran —**Me'di·an** *adj., n.*

me·di·a (mē'dē ə) *n. alt. pl. of* MEDIUM: see MEDIUM (*n.* 3)

me·di·ae·val (mē'dē ē'v'l, med'ē-, mid'ē-) *adj. alt. sp. of* MEDIEVAL

me·di·al (mē'dē əl) *adj.* [< L. *medius*, middle] **1.** intermediate; middle **2.** average

me·di·an (mē'dē ən) *adj.* [see prec.] **1.** intermediate; middle **2.** designating the middle number in a series —*n.* **1.** a median number, point, etc. **2.** a strip of land between the opposing lanes of a divided highway: in full **median strip**

me·di·ate (mē'dē āt') *vi.* **-at·ed, -at·ing** [see MEDIAL] **1.** to be in an intermediate position **2.** to be an intermediary or conciliator —*vt.* **1.** to settle (a dispute, etc.) through efforts as intermediary or conciliator **2.** to be the medium, or means, for bringing about, carrying, etc. —*adj.* (-it) not direct; mediated —**me'di·a'tion** *n.* —**me'di·a'tor** *n.*

med·ic (med'ik) *n.* [L. *medicus*] [Colloq.] **1.** a physician or surgeon **2.** a medical student or intern **3.** a member of a military medical corps

Med·i·caid (med'i kād') *n.* [*also* m-] a State and Federal public health plan paying certain medical and hospital expenses of persons having a low income or no income

med·i·cal (med'i k'l) *adj.* [< Fr. < L. *medicus*, physician] of or involving medicine or the practice or study of medicine —**med'i·cal·ly** *adv.*

med·i·ca·ment (med'i kə mənt, mə dik'ə-) *n.* [< L. *medicamentum*] a medicine

Med·i·care (med'i ker') *n.* [*also* m-] a Federal health program paying certain medical and hospital expenses esp. of the aged

med·i·cate (med'ə kāt') *vt.* -cat'ed, -cat'ing [< L. *medicari*, heal] to treat with medicine

med·i·ca·tion (med'ə kā'shən) *n.* [L. *medicatio*] **1.** a medicating or being medicated **2.** a medicine

Med·i·ci (med'ə chē') family of rich, powerful bankers, merchants, & rulers of Florence & Tuscany in the 14th, 15th, & 16th cent.

me·dic·i·nal (mə dis''n 'l) *adj.* of, or having the properties of, medicine —**me·dic'i·nal·ly** *adv.*

med·i·cine (med'ə s'n) *n.* [< L. *medicus*, physician] **1.** the science and art of treating and preventing disease **2.** any substance, as a drug, used in treating disease, relieving pain, etc.

medicine ball a large, heavy, leather-covered ball tossed from one person to another for exercise

medicine man among N. American Indians, etc., a man supposed to have supernatural powers to cure disease and control spirits

me·di·e·val (mē'dē ē'v'l, med'ē-, mid'ē-) *adj.* [< L. *medius*, middle + *aevum*, age] of, like, or typical of the Middle Ages —**me'di·e'val·ly** *adv.*

me'di·e'val·ism *n.* **1.** medieval spirit, customs, etc. **2.** devotion to these **3.** a medieval belief, custom, etc.

me'di·e'val·ist *n.* a specialist in, or devotee of, medieval history, literature, customs, etc.

Me·di·na (mə dē'nə) city in NW Saudi Arabia: site of Mohammed's tomb: pop. c.60,000

me·di·o·cre (mē'dē ō'kər) *adj.* [< Fr. < L. *medius*, middle + *ocris*, a peak] **1.** of middle quality; ordinary **2.** not good enough; inferior

me·di·oc·ri·ty (mē'dē äk'rə tē) *n., pl.* -ties **1.** mediocre state, quality, ability, etc. **2.** a mediocre person or thing

med·i·tate (med'ə tāt') *vt.* -tat'ed, -tat'ing [< L. *meditari*] to plan or intend —*vi.* to think deeply —**med'i·ta'tion** *n.* —**med'i·ta'tive** *adj.*

Med·i·ter·ra·ne·an (med'i tə rā'nē ən) *adj.* [< L. *medius*, middle + *terra*, land] of the Mediterranean Sea or nearby regions

Mediterranean (Sea) large sea surrounded by Europe, Africa, & Asia: c.2,300 mi. long

me·di·um (mē'dē əm) *n., pl.* -di·ums: also (except sense 5), and for sense 3 usually, -di·a (-ə) [L. < *medius*, middle] **1.** *a)* something intermediate *b)* a middle state or degree; mean **2.** an intervening thing through which a force acts **3.** any means, agency, etc.; specif., a means of communication, with advertising, directed toward the public: in this sense a singular form **media** (*pl.* **medias**) is sometimes used **4.** a surrounding substance or environment **5.** a person through whom communications are supposedly sent from the dead **6.** any material or technique used in art **7.** a liquid mixed with pigments —*adj.* **1.** intermediate in quality, degree, amount, etc. **2.** neither rare nor well-done: said of meat

medium frequency any radio frequency between 300 kilohertz and 3 megahertz

med·ley (med'lē) *n., pl.* -leys [see MEDDLE] **1.** a mixture of dissimilar things **2.** a musical piece made up of tunes or passages from various works

me·dul·la (mi dul'ə) *n., pl.* -las, -lae (-ē) [L., marrow] **1.** the medulla oblongata **2.** the inner substance of an organ, as of the kidney **3.** bone marrow

medulla ob·lon·ga·ta (äb'lôŋ gät'ə, -gät'-) [ModL., oblong medulla] the lowest part of the brain

Me·du·sa (mə doo'sə, -zə) *Gr. Myth.* a Gorgon slain by Perseus —*n.* [m-] *pl.* -sas, -sae (-sē, -zē) *Zool.* same as JELLYFISH

meed (mēd) *n.* [OE. *med*] [Archaic] a reward

meek (mēk) *adj.* [< ON. *miukr*, gentle] **1.** patient and mild **2.** too submissive —**meek'ly** *adv.*

meer·schaum (mir'shəm, -shôm) *n.* [G. < *meer*, sea + *schaum*, foam] **1.** a white, claylike mineral used for tobacco pipes **2.** a pipe made of this

meet¹ (mēt) *vt.* **met, meet'ing** [OE. *metan*] **1.** to come upon; esp., to come face to face with **2.** to be present at the arrival of [to *meet* a bus] **3.** to come into contact with **4.** to be introduced to **5.** to contend with **6.** to be perceived by (the eye, ear, etc.) **7.** *a)* to satisfy (a demand, etc.) *b)* to pay (a bill, etc.) —*vi.* **1.** to come together, into contact, etc. **2.** to be introduced —*n.* a coming together as for a sports event —*meet* (up) **with** to encounter

meet² (mēt) *adj.* [OE. (ge)*mǽte*] [Now Rare] suitable; proper; fit

meet'ing *n.* **1.** a coming together **2.** a gathering; assembly **3.** a series of horse or dog races held during a period of days at a certain track **4.** a point of contact; junction

meet'ing·house' *n.* a building for public meetings, esp. for public worship, as by Friends, or Quakers

mega- [Gr. < *megas*, great] a combining form meaning: **1.** large, powerful **2.** a million (of)

meg·a·hertz (meg'ə hurts') *n., pl.* -hertz' [MEGA- + HERTZ] one million hertz: formerly **meg'a·cy'cle** (-sī'k'l)

meg·a·lo·ma·ni·a (meg'ə lō mā'nē ə) *n.* [< Gr. *megas*, large + -MANIA] a mental disorder characterized by delusions of grandeur, power, etc. —**meg'a·lo·ma'ni·ac'** (-ak') *adj., n.*

meg·a·lop·o·lis (meg'ə läp'ə ləs) *n.* [Gr., great city] a vast, populous, continuously urban area

meg·a·phone (meg'ə fōn') *n.* [MEGA- + -PHONE] a funnel-shaped device to amplify and direct the voice

meg·a·ton' (-tun') *n.* [MEGA- + TON] the explosive force of a million tons of TNT

mel·a·mine (mel'ə mēn') *n.* [G. *melamin*] a white crystalline compound used to make synthetic resins

mel·an·cho·li·a (mel'ən kō'lē ə) *n.* [see MELANCHOLY] a mental disorder characterized by extreme depression, brooding, and anxiety

mel·an·chol·y (mel'ən käl'ē) *n.* [< Gr. *melas*, black + *cholē*, bile] **1.** sadness and depression of spirits **2.** pensiveness —*adj.* **1.** sad and depressed **2.** causing sadness **3.** pensive

Mel·a·ne·sia (mel'ə nē'zhə) a major division of the Pacific islands, south of the equator & west of the international date line —**Mel'a·ne'sian** *adj., n.*

mé·lange (mā länzh', -länj') *n.* [Fr. < *mêler*, to mix] a mixture or medley; jumble

mel·a·nin (mel'ə nin) *n.* [< Gr. *melas*, black] a brownish-black pigment found in skin, hair, etc.

Mel·ba toast (mel'bə) [< N. *Melba* (1861-1931), Australian soprano] [*also* m-] thin, dry toast

Mel·bourne (mel'bərn) seaport in SE Australia: pop. 2,110,000

meld (meld) *vt., vi.* [G. *melden*, announce] *Card Games* to declare (a card combination), esp. by putting the cards face up on the table —*n.* **1.** a melding **2.** a card combination melded

me·lee, mê·lée (mā'lā, mā lā') *n.* [Fr.] a confused hand-to-hand fight among a number of people

mel·io·rate (mēl'yə rāt') *vt., vi.* -rat'ed, -rat'ing [< L. *melior*, better] to make or become better —**mel'io·ra'tion** *n.* —**mel'io·ra'tive** *adj.*

mel·lif·lu·ous (mə lif'loo wəs) *adj.* [< L. *mel*, honey + *fluere*, to flow] sounding sweet and smooth: also **mel·lif'-lu·ent** (-wənt)

mel·low (mel'ō) *adj.* [prob. < OE. *melu*, MEAL²] **1.** soft, sweet, etc. because ripe: said of fruit **2.** full-flavored: said as of wine **3.** rich, pure, etc.: said as of sound or light **4.** grown gentle and understanding —*vt., vi.* to make or become mellow

me·lod·ic (mə läd'ik) *adj.* **1.** of or like melody **2.** same as MELODIOUS —**me·lod'i·cal·ly** *adv.*

me·lo'di·ous (-lō'dē əs) *adj.* **1.** containing or producing melody **2.** tuneful —**me·lo'di·ous·ly** *adv.*

mel·o·dra·ma (mel'ə drä'mə, -dram'ə) *n.* [< Fr. < Gr. *melos*, song + *drama*, drama] **1.** a shallow drama with stereotyped characters, exaggerated emotions, unconvincing plot twists meant to startle, thrill, or horrify, etc. **2.** anything suggestive of this —**mel'o·dra·mat'ic** (-drə mat'ik) *adj.* —**mel'o·dra·mat'i·cal·ly** *adv.*

mel·o·dy (mel'ə dē) *n., pl.* -dies [< Gr. *melos*, song + *aeidein*, sing] **1.** a sequence of pleasing sounds **2.** *a)* a

at, āpe, cär; ten, ēven; is, bīte; gō, hôrn, tōōl, look; oil, out; up, fur; thin, then; zh, leisure; ŋ, ring; ə for a in ago; as in able (ā'b'l); ë, Fr. coeur; ö, Fr. feu; Fr. mon; ü, Fr. duc; r, Fr. cri; kh, G. doch, ich. ‡ foreign; < derived from tune, song, etc. *b*) the leading part in a harmonic composition

mel·on (mel'ən) *n.* [< Gr. *mēlon*, apple] the large, juicy, many-seeded fruit of certain trailing plants of the gourd family, as the cantaloupe

melt (melt) *vt., vi.* [OE. *m(i)eltan*] **1.** to change from a solid to a liquid state, generally by heat **2.** to dissolve **3.** to disappear or make disappear gradually **4.** to merge; blend **5.** to soften —*n.* a melting

melting point the temperature at which a specified solid becomes liquid

melting pot a place where immigrants of different nationalities and races are assimilated

Mel·ville (mel'vil), **Herman** 1819–91; U.S. novelist

mem·ber (mem'bər) *n.* [< L. *membrum*] **1.** a limb or other part of a person, animal, or plant **2.** a distinct part of a whole **3.** one of the individuals belonging to a group

mem'ber·ship' *n.* **1.** the state of being a member **2.** the members of a group **3.** the total of these

mem·brane (mem'brān) *n.* [< L. *membrum*, member] a thin, soft layer, esp. of animal or plant tissue, covering or lining something such as an organ or other part —**mem'·bra·nous** (-brə nəs) *adj.*

me·men·to (mə men'tō) *n., pl.* -**tos**, -**toes** [< L. *meminisse*, remember] a souvenir or other reminder

mem·o (mem'ō) *n., pl.* -**os** *clipped form of* MEMORANDUM

mem·oir (mem'wär) *n.* [< Fr. < L. *memoria*, memory] **1.** a biography **2.** [*pl.*] an autobiography **3.** [*pl.*] a record of events that is based on the writer's personal knowledge **4.** a scholarly report

mem·o·ra·bil·i·a (mem'ər ə bil'ē ə) *n.pl.* [L.] noteworthy things remembered or collected

mem·o·ra·ble (mem'ər ə b'l) *adj.* of such a kind as to remain clearly in the memory; so remarkable as not to be easily forgotten —**mem'o·ra·bly** *adv.*

mem·o·ran·dum (mem'ə ran'dəm) *n., pl.* -**dums**, -**da** (-də) [L.] **1.** a note written as a reminder **2.** a piece of writing, usually brief and often informal, designed to summarize, review, or announce certain points, seek out information, etc., as within a business office

me·mo·ri·al (mə môr'ē əl) *adj.* [see MEMORY] serving to help people remember some person or event; commemorative —*n.* anything meant to help people remember a person, event, etc., as a monument

Memorial Day a legal holiday in the U.S. (the last Monday in May in most States) in memory of the dead servicemen of all wars

me·mo·ri·al·ize (mə môr'ē ə līz') *vt.* -**ized'**, -**iz'ing** to commemorate

mem·o·rize (mem'ə rīz') *vt.* -**rized'**, -**riz'ing** to commit to memory —**mem'o·ri·za'tion** *n.*

mem·o·ry (mem'ər ē) *n., pl.* -**ries** [< L. *memor*, mindful] **1.** the power or act of remembering **2.** all that one remembers **3.** something remembered **4.** the period over which remembering extends **5.** commemoration **6.** reputation after death

Mem·phis (mem'fis) city in SW Tenn., on the Mississippi: pop. 624,000 (met. area 770,000)

men (men) *n. pl. of* MAN

men·ace (men'is) *n.* [< L. *minari*, threaten] a threat or danger —*vt., vi.* -**aced**, -**ac·ing** to threaten —**men'ac·ing·ly** *adv.*

mé·nage, me·nage (mā nàzh', mə-) *n.* [Fr. < L. *mansio*, a dwelling] a household

me·nag·er·ie (mə naj'ər ē) *n.* [< Fr.: see prec.] **1.** a collection of wild animals kept as in cages for exhibition **2.** a place where such animals are kept

mend (mend) *vt.* [see AMEND] **1.** to repair; fix **2.** to improve; reform —*vi.* **1.** to improve, esp. in health **2.** to heal, as a fracture —*n.* **1.** a mending **2.** a mended place — **on the mend** improving

men·da·cious (men dā'shəs) *adj.* [< L. *mendax*] untruthful —**men·dac'i·ty** (-das'ə tē) *n., pl.* -**ties**

Men·del (men'd'l), **Gre·gor** (grā'gôr) 1822–84; Austrian monk & botanist —**Men·de'li·an** (-dē'lē ən) *adj.*

men·de·le·vi·um (men'də lē'vē əm) *n.* [< D. I. *Mendeleev* (1834–1907), Russ. chemist] a radioactive chemical element: symbol, Md; at. wt., 258(?); at. no., 101

Mendel's laws the basic genetic principles discovered and formulated by Mendel

Men·dels·sohn (men'd'l sən), **Fe·lix** (fā'liks) 1809–47; Ger. composer

men·di·cant (men'di kənt) *adj.* [< L. *mendicare*, beg] begging alms —*n.* **1.** a beggar **2.** a friar living mostly on alms —**men'di·can·cy** *n.*

Men·e·la·us (men'ə lā'əs) *Gr. Myth.* a king of Sparta and husband of Helen of Troy

men'folk', men'folks' *n.pl.* [Dial. or Colloq.] men

men·ha·den (men hād'n) *n., pl.* -**den**, -**dens** [< AmInd.] a sea fish related to the herring, common along the Atlantic coast of the U.S.: it is used for bait or for making oil and fertilizer

me·ni·al (mē'nē əl) *adj.* [< L. *mansio*, a dwelling] **1.** of or fit for servants **2.** servile; low —*n.* **1.** a domestic servant **2.** a servile person

me·nin·ges (mə nin'jēz) *n.pl.* [< Gr. *mēninx*, membrane] the three membranes enveloping the brain and the spinal cord —**me·nin'ge·al** (-jē əl) *adj.*

men·in·gi·tis (men'in jīt'is) *n.* inflammation of the meninges, esp. as the result of infection

Men·non·ite (men'ə nīt') *n.* [< *Menno* Simons (1496?–1561?), a leader] a member of an evangelical Christian sect living and dressing plainly and rejecting military service, oath-taking, etc.

men·o·pause (men'ə pôz') *n.* [< Gr. *mēn*, month + *pauein*, to end] the permanent cessation of menstruation; change of life —**men'o·paus'al** *adj.*

men·o·rah (mə nô'rə, -nôr'ə) *n.* [Heb., lamp stand] *Judaism* a candelabrum with seven (or nine) branches

men·ses (men'sēz) *n.pl.* [L., months] the periodic flow, usually monthly, of blood from the uterus

men·stru·ate (men'stroo wāt', -strāt) *vi.* -**at'ed**, -**at'ing** [< L. *mensis*, month] to have a discharge of the menses — **men'stru·al** (-stroo wəl, -strəl) *adj.* —**men'stru·a'tion** *n.*

men·sur·a·ble (men'shər ə b'l, -sər-) *adj.* [< L. *mensura*, a measure] that can be measured

men·su·ra·tion (men'shə rā'shən, -sə-) *n.* [see prec.] **1.** a measuring **2.** mathematics dealing with the determination of length, area, or volume

-ment [< L. -*mentum*] *a suffix meaning:* **1.** result [*improvement*] **2.** means [*adornment*] **3.** act [*movement*] **4.** state of being [*disappointment*]

men·tal (men't'l) *adj.* [< L. *mens*, the mind] **1.** of, for, by, or in the mind **2.** *a*) ill in mind *b*) for the ill in mind —**men'tal·ly** *adv.*

men'tal·ist *n. same as* MIND READER

men·tal·i·ty (men tal'ə tē) *n., pl.* -**ties** mental capacity, power, or activity

mental retardation congenitally low intelligence

men·ta·tion (men tā'shən) *n.* use of the mind

men·thol (men'thōl, -thôl) *n.* [G. < L. *mentha*, MINT²] a white, waxy, pungent, crystalline alcohol from oil of peppermint, used as in medicine and cosmetics —**men'tho·lat'ed** (-thə lāt'id) *adj.*

men·tion (men'shən) *n.* [< L. *mens*, the mind] **1.** a brief reference **2.** a citing for honor —*vt.* to refer to briefly — **men'tion·a·ble** *adj.*

men·tor (men'tər, -tôr) *n.* [< *Mentor*, friend of Odysseus] **1.** a wise, loyal adviser **2.** a teacher

men·u (men'yōō) *n., pl.* -**us** [Fr. < L. *minutus*, small] **1.** a detailed list of the foods served at a meal, as in a restaurant **2.** the foods served

me·ow, me·ou (mē ou') *n.* [echoic] the characteristic vocal sound of a cat —*vi.* to make this sound

Meph·i·stoph·e·les (mef'ə stäf'ə lēz') in medieval legend, a devil to whom Faust sells his soul for knowledge and power

me·phit·ic (mə fit'ik) *adj.* [< L. *mephitis*, stench] **1.** bad-smelling **2.** poisonous; noxious

mer·can·tile (mur'kən til, -tīl') *adj.* [< Fr. < It. < L. *merx*, wares] of merchants or trade; commercial

Mer·ca·tor projection (mər kāt'ər) [< G. *Mercator*, 16th-c. Flemish cartographer] map-making using equally spaced parallel straight lines for the meridians and, for the parallels of latitude, parallel straight lines increasingly far apart according to distance from the equator

mer·ce·nar·y (mur'sə ner'ē) *adj.* [< L. *merces*, wages] working or done only for payment —*n., pl.* -**ies** a soldier serving for pay in a foreign army

mer·cer (mur'sər) *n.* [< L. *merx*, wares] [Brit.] a dealer in textiles

mer·cer·ize (mur'sə rīz') *vt.* -**ized'**, -**iz'ing** [< J. *Mercer*, 19th-c. Eng. calico dealer] to treat (cotton thread or fabric) with a solution of caustic soda to strengthen it, give it a silky luster, etc.

mer·chan·dise (mur'chən dīz', -dīs') *n.* [see MERCHANT] things bought and sold; goods; wares —*vt., vi.* (-dīz') -**dised'**, -**dis'ing 1.** to buy and sell **2.** to promote the sale of (a product)

mer·chant (mur'chənt) *n.* [< L. *merx*, wares] **1.** one whose business is the buying and selling of goods **2.** a dealer at retail; storekeeper —*adj.* **1.** mercantile **2.** of the merchant marine

mer'chant·man (-mən) *n., pl.* -**men** a merchant ship

merchant marine 1. all the ships of a nation that are used in commerce 2. the personnel of these

‡**mer·ci** (mer sē′) *interj.* [Fr.] thank you

mer·ci·ful (mur′si fəl) *adj.* having or showing mercy — **mer′ci·ful·ly** *adv.* —**mer′ci·ful·ness** *n.*

mer·ci·less *adj.* without mercy; pitiless

mer·cu·ri·al (mər kyoor′ē əl) *adj.* 1. of mercury 2. quick, changeable, fickle, etc.

mer·cu′ric (-ik) *adj.* of mercury, esp. with a valence of two

mercuric chloride a very poisonous, white, crystalline compound, HgCl₂, used in photography and as an insecticide, antiseptic, etc.

Mer·cu·ro·chrome (mər kyoor′ə krōm′) [see MERCURY & -CHROME] *a trademark for* a red solution of a compound of mercury, used as an antiseptic

mer·cu·rous (mər kyoor′əs, mur′kyoo rəs) *adj.* of mercury, esp. with a valence of one

Mer·cu·ry (mur′kyoo rē) *n.* 1. *Rom. Myth.* a god, the messenger of the other gods 2. the smallest planet in the solar system: see PLANET —*n.* [< L. *Mercurius*, Mercury] [m-] a heavy, silver-white metallic chemical element, liquid at ordinary temperatures, used as in thermometers and in dentistry, pharmacy, etc.: symbol, Hg; at. wt., 200.59; at. no., 80

mer·cy (mur′sē) *n., pl.* -cies [< L. *merces*, payment] 1. forbearance, compassion, or restraint with regard to the treatment or punishment of offenders, enemies, etc. 2. a disposition to be kind or to forgive 3. kind or compassionate treatment 4. an event, outcome, etc. to be grateful for —*interj.* a mild exclamation of surprise, annoyance, etc. — **at the mercy of** in the power of

mercy killing *same as* EUTHANASIA

mere (mir) *adj. superl.* **mer′est** [< L. *merus*, pure] being only or simply (what is specified)

mere·ly *adv.* only; simply; just

mer·e·tri·cious (mer′ə trish′əs) *adj.* [< L. *meretrix*, a prostitute] 1. alluring but tawdry 2. specious

mer·gan·ser (mər gan′sər) *n.* [< L. *mergus*, diver + *anser*, goose] a large, fish-eating, diving duck

merge (murj) *vi., vt.* **merged, merg′ing** [< L. *mergere*, to dip] 1. to lose or make lose identity as by absorption 2. to unite; combine

merg′er *n.* a merging; specif., a combining of two or more companies, corporations, etc. into one

me·rid·i·an (mə rid′ē ən) *adj.* [< L. *meridies*, noon] 1. of or at a zenith 2. of or along a meridian —*n.* 1. a zenith 2. *a)* a great circle of the earth passing through the geographical poles and any given point on the earth's surface *b)* any of the lines of longitude

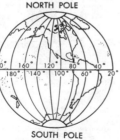

NORTH POLE

SOUTH POLE

MERIDIANS

me·ringue (mə raŋ′) *n.* [Fr.] egg whites mixed with sugar and beaten stiff, spread over a pie, etc.

me·ri·no (mə rē′nō) *n., pl.* -nos [Sp.] 1. one of a breed of sheep with long, fine wool 2. the wool 3. a soft yarn or cloth of such wool

mer·it (mer′it) *n.* [< L. *mereri*, deserve] 1. worth; value; excellence 2. something deserving reward, praise, etc. 3. an award to acknowledge something praiseworthy 4. [pl.] intrinsic rightness or wrongness —*vt.* to deserve

mer·i·toc·ra·cy (mer′ə täk′rə sē) *n., pl.* -cies 1. an intellectual elite, based on academic merit 2. leadership, domination, etc. by such 3. such a system

mer·i·to·ri·ous (-tôr′ē əs) *adj.* meriting reward, praise, etc. —**mer′i·to′ri·ous·ly** *adv.*

Mer·lin (mur′lin) *Arthurian Legend* a magician and seer, helper of King Arthur

mer·maid (mur′mād′) *n.* [OE. *mere*, sea + MAID] an imaginary sea creature, half woman and half fish

mer·ry (mer′ē) *adj.* -ri·er, -ri·est [OE. *myrge*] bubbling over with lighthearted gaiety; cheery —**make merry** to enjoy oneself with carefree abandon; romp; frolic —**mer′ri·ly** *adv.* —**mer′ri·ment** *n.*

mer′ry-go-round′ *n.* 1. an amusement ride consisting of a revolving circular platform with artificial animals, usually moving up and down 2. a round of constant activity

mer′ry·mak′ing *n.* a making merry; joyous festivity — **mer′ry·mak′er** *n.*

me·sa (mā′sə) *n.* [Sp. < L. *mensa*, a table] a small, high plateau with steep sides

mes·cal (mes kal′) *n.* [Sp. *mezcal* < MexInd. *mexcalli*] 1. a colorless alcoholic liquor made from the juice of various agaves 2. an agave yielding juice so used 3. a small cactus with buttonlike tops (**mescal buttons**) causing hallucinations when chewed

mes·ca·line (mes′kə lēn′, -lin) *n.* [< prec.] a psychedelic drug obtained from mescal buttons

mes·dames (mā däm′) *n. pl. of* MADAME, MADAM (sense 1), *or* MRS.

mesde·moi·selles (mād mwä zel′) *n. Fr. pl. of* MADEMOISELLE

mesh (mesh) *n.* [prob. < MDu. *maesche*] 1. any of the open spaces of a net, screen, etc. 2. [pl.] the threads, cords, etc. forming these openings 3. a net or network 4. a netlike material, as for stockings 5. a structure of interlocking metal links 6. anything that entangles or snares —*vt., vi.* 1. to catch or be caught in or as in a net 2. to fit together, as gears; interlock —**in mesh** with the gear teeth engaged

mes·mer·ize (mez′mər īz′, mes′-) *vt.* -ized′, -iz′ing [< Fr. < F. A. *Mesmer*, 18th-c. G. physician] to hypnotize or spellbind —**mes′mer·ism** *n.* —**mes′mer·ist** *n.*

meso- [< Gr. *mesos*, middle] *a combining form meaning* in the middle, intermediate: also **mes-**

mes·o·carp (mes′ə kärp′, mez′-) *n.* [< MESO- + Gr. *karpos*, fruit] the middle layer of the wall of a ripened ovary or fruit, as the flesh of a plum

mes′o·derm′ (-durm′) *n.* [< MESO- + Gr. *derma*, skin] the middle layer of cells of an embryo: also **mes′o·blast′**

mes·on (mes′än, mez′-; mē′sän, -zän) *n.* [MES(O)- + (ELECTR)ON] an unstable particle, between the electron and proton in mass

Mes·o·po·ta·mi·a (mes′ə pə tā′mē ə) ancient country in SW Asia, between the Tigris & Euphrates rivers

Mes·o·zo·ic (mes′ə zō′ik, mez′-) *adj.* [MESO- + ZO(O)- + -IC] designating or of the geologic era (c.230-65 million years ago) characterized by dinosaurs —**the Mesozoic** the Mesozoic Era

mes·quite, mes·quit (mes kēt′) *n.* [< MexInd. *mizquitl*] a thorny tree or shrub of the SW U.S. and Mexico

mess (mes) *n.* [< L. *missus*, course (at a meal)] 1. a serving of soft food, as porridge 2. *a)* a group of people who regularly eat together, as in the army *b)* a meal eaten by such a group, or the place where they eat 3. a jumble; hodgepodge 4. *a)* a state of trouble, confusion, untidiness, etc. *b)* [Colloq.] a person in such a state —*vt.* to make dirty or untidy; also, to bungle; botch: often with *up* —*vi.* 1. to eat as one of a mess 2. to make a mess 3. to putter or meddle (*in, with, around,* etc.)

mes·sage (mes′ij) *n.* [< L. *mittere*, send] 1. a report, request, etc. sent between persons 2. the chief idea that an artist, writer, etc. seeks to communicate in a work —**get the message** [Colloq.] to understand a hint

mes·sen·ger (mes′'n jər) *n.* a person who carries messages or goes on errands

mess hall a room or building where soldiers, etc. regularly have meals

Mes·si·ah (mə sī′ə) [< Heb. *māshīah*, anointed] 1. *Judaism* the expected deliverer of the Jews 2. *Christianity* Jesus —*n.* [m-] any expected savior —**Mes·si·an·ic** (mes′ē an′ik) *adj.*

mes·sieurs (mes′ərz; Fr. mā syö′) *n. pl. of* MONSIEUR

mess kit a compact set of plates, a fork, spoon, etc. carried by a soldier or camper: also **mess gear**

mess′y *adj.* -i·er, -i·est in or like a mess; untidy, dirty, etc. —**mess′i·ly** *adv.* —**mess′i·ness** *n.*

mes·ti·zo (mes tē′zō) *n., pl.* -zos, -zoes [Sp. < L. *miscere*, to mix] a person of mixed parentage, esp. Spanish and American Indian

met (met) *pt. & pp. of* MEET[1]

met. metropolitan

meta- [< Gr. *meta*, after] *a prefix meaning:* 1. changed [*metamorphosis*] 2. after, beyond, higher [*metaphysics*] Also **met-**

me·tab·o·lism (mə tab′ə liz′m) *n.* [< Gr. *meta*, beyond + *ballein*, to throw] the processes in organisms by which food is built up into protoplasm, which is used and broken down into simpler substances or waste matter, with the release of energy for vital processes —**met·a·bol·ic** (met′ə bäl′ik) *adj.*

me·tab'o·lize' (-līz') *vt.*, *vi.* **-lized'**, **-liz'ing** to change by or subject to metabolism

met·a·car·pus (met'ə kär'pəs) *n.*, *pl.* **-pi** (-pī) [< Gr. *meta*, beyond + *karpos*, wrist] the five bones of the hand between the wrist and the fingers —**met'a·car'pal** *adj.*, *n.*

met·al (met''l) *n.* [< L. < Gr. *metallon*, metal, mine] **1.** *a)* any of a class of chemical elements, as iron, gold, copper, etc., that have luster, are malleable, can conduct heat and electricity, etc. *b)* an alloy of such elements, as brass, bronze, etc. **2.** anything consisting of metal **3.** material; stuff —*adj.* made of metal —**me·tal·lic** (mə tal'ik) *adj.*

metal., **metall.** **1.** metallurgical **2.** metallurgy

met·al·lur·gy (met''l ʉr'jē) *n.* [< Gr. *metallon*, metal, mine + *ergon*, work] the science of separating metals from their ores and preparing them for use by smelting, refining, etc. —**met'al·lur'gi·cal**, **met'al·lur'gic** *adj.* —**met'al·lur'gist** *n.*

met·al·work' *n.* **1.** things made of metal **2.** the making of such things: also **met'al·work'ing** —**met'al·work'er** *n.*

met·a·mor·phism (met'ə môr'fiz'm) *n.* **1.** *same as* METAMORPHOSIS **2.** change in the structure of rocks under pressure, heat, etc. —**met'a·mor'phic** *adj.*

met·a·mor·phose (met'ə môr'fōz, -fōs) *vt.*, *vi.* **-phosed**, **-phos·ing** to change in form or nature

met·a·mor·pho·sis (met'ə môr'fə sis, -môr fō'-) *n.*, *pl.* **-ses'** (-sēz') [< Gr. *meta*, over + *morphē*, form] **1.** a change of form as, in myths, by magic **2.** the physical change undergone by some animals, as of tadpole to frog **3.** any marked change, as in character, appearance, or condition

met·a·phor (met'ə fôr', -fər) *n.* [< Fr. < Gr. *meta*, over + *pherein*, to bear] a figure of speech in which one thing is spoken of as if it were another (Ex.: the curtain of night) —**mix metaphors** to use inconsistent metaphors together (Ex.: the storm of protest was nipped in the bud) —**met'a·phor'i·cal**, **met'a·phor'ic** *adj.* —**met'a·phor'i·cal·ly** *adv.*

met·a·phys·i·cal (met'ə fiz'i k'l) *adj.* **1.** of, or having the nature of, metaphysics **2.** very abstract, abstruse, or subtle **3.** supernatural

met·a·phys'ics (-iks) *n.pl.* [*with sing. v.*] [< Gr. *meta* (ta) *physika*, after (the) *Physics* (in Aristotle's work)] **1.** the branch of philosophy that seeks to explain the nature of being and reality **2.** speculative philosophy in general

me·tas·ta·sis (mə tas'tə sis) *n.*, *pl.* **-ses** (-sēz') [< Gr. *meta*, after + *histanai*, to place] the transfer, as of malignant cells, from one part of the body to another, as through the bloodstream —**me·tas'ta·size'** (-sīz') *vi.* **-sized'**, **-siz'ing**

met·a·tar·sus (met'ə tär'səs) *n.*, *pl.* **-si** (-sī) [< Gr. *meta*, over + *tarsos*, flat of the foot] the five bones of the foot between the ankle and the toes —**met'a·tar'sal** *adj.*, *n.*

me·tath·e·sis (mə tath'ə sis) *n.*, *pl.* **-ses'** (-sēz') [< Gr. *meta*, over + *tithenai*, to place] transposition, specif. of letters or sounds in a word

met·a·zo·an (met'ə zō'ən) *n.* [< Gr. *meta*, after + *zōion*, animal] any of the very large division of animals whose bodies are made up of many differentiated cells, arranged into definite organs

mete (mēt) *vt.* **met'ed**, **met'ing** [OE. *metan*] to allot; portion (*out*)

me·tem·psy·cho·sis (mi temp'si kō'sis, met'əm sī-) *n.*, *pl.* **-ses** (-sēz) [< Gr. *meta*, over + *en*, in + *psychē*, soul] transmigration of souls

me·te·or (mēt'ē ər) *n.* [< Gr. *meta*, beyond + *eōra*, a hovering] **1.** the streak of light, the ionized trail, etc. occurring when a meteoroid enters the earth's atmosphere **2.** loosely, a meteoroid or meteorite

me·te·or·ic (mēt'ē ôr'ik, -är'-) *adj.* **1.** of a meteor **2.** like a meteor in brilliance and swiftness

me·te·or·ite (mēt'ē ə rīt') *n.* a stone or metal mass remaining from a meteoroid fallen to earth

me'te·or·oid' (-roid') *n.* a small, solid body traveling through space, seen as a meteor when it enters the earth's atmosphere

me·te·or·ol·o·gy (mēt'ē ə räl'ə jē) *n.* [see METEOR & -LOGY] the science of the atmosphere and atmospheric phenomena; study of weather and climate —**me'te·or·o·log'i·cal** (-ər ə läj'i k'l) *adj.* —**me'te·or·ol'o·gist** *n.*

me·ter' (mēt'ər) *n.* [< Gr. *metron*, measure] **1.** rhythmic pattern in verse; measured arrangement of syllables according to stress **2.** rhythm in music, esp. the division into measures having a uniform number of beats **3.** [Fr.] the basic unit of length in the metric system, equal to 39.37 in.

me·ter² (mēt'ər) *n.* [< words ending in -METER] **1.** an apparatus for measuring and recording the quantity or rate

of flow of gas, water, etc. passing through it **2.** *same as* PARKING METER —*vt.* to measure or record with a meter

-meter [< Fr. < Gr. *metron*, measure] *a suffix meaning*: **1.** a device for measuring (a specified thing) [*barometer*] **2.** having (a specified number of) metrical feet [*pentameter*]

me'ter·kil'o·gram-sec'ond *adj.* designating or of a system of measurement in which the meter, kilogram, and second are used as the units of length, mass, and time, respectively

meth·a·done (meth'ə dōn') *n.* [< its chemical name] a synthetic narcotic drug, less habit-forming than morphine, used in treating morphine addicts

meth·ane (meth'ān) *n.* [< METHYL] a colorless, odorless, flammable gas, CH_4, present in marsh gas, firedamp, and natural gas

meth·a·nol (meth'ə nôl') *n.* [< METHAN(E) + (ALCOH)OL] a poisonous liquid, CH_3OH, used as a fuel, solvent, antifreeze, etc.: also called methyl alcohol

me·thinks (mi thiŋks') *v.impersonal pt.* **me·thought'** [< OE. *me*, to me + *thyncth*, it seems] [Archaic] it seems to me

meth·od (meth'əd) *n.* [< Fr. < Gr. *meta*, after + *hodos*, a way] **1.** a way of doing anything, esp. an orderly way; process **2.** system in doing things or handling ideas

me·thod·i·cal (mə thäd'i k'l) *adj.* characterized by method; orderly; systematic: also **me·thod'ic** —**me·thod'i·cal·ly** *adv.*

Meth·od·ist (meth'ə dist) *n.* a member of a Protestant denomination developed from John Wesley's teachings —**Meth'od·ism** *n.*

meth'od·ize' (-dīz') *vt.* **-ized'**, **-iz'ing** to make methodical; systematize —**meth'od·iz'er** *n.*

meth·od·ol·o·gy (meth'ə däl'ə jē) *n.*, *pl.* **-gies** **1.** the science of method, or orderly arrangement **2.** a system of methods, as in any particular science

Me·thu·se·lah (mə thōō'zə lə, -thyōō'-) *Bible* a patriarch who lived 969 years

meth·yl (meth'əl) *n.* [< Fr. < Gr. *methy*, wine + *hylē*, wood] the hydrocarbon radical CH_3, found in methanol, etc.

me·tic·u·lous (mə tik'yoo ləs) *adj.* [< L. *metus*, fear] very careful or too careful about details; scrupulous or finicky —**me·tic'u·lous·ly** *adv.*

mé·tier (mā tyā') *n.* [Fr.] a trade or occupation; esp., the work that one is particularly suited for

me·ton·y·my (mə tän'ə mē) *n.* [< Gr. *meta*, other + *onyma*, name] use of the name of one thing for that of another associated with it (Ex.: "the press" for "journalists") —**met·o·nym·ic** (met'ə nim'ik) *adj.*

me·tre (mē'tər) *n. chiefly Brit. sp. of* METER¹

met·ric (met'rik) *adj.* **1.** *same as* METRICAL **2.** of or in the metric system: see METRIC SYSTEM

met'ri·cal *adj.* **1.** of or composed in meter or verse **2.** of or used in measurement; metric —**met'ri·cal·ly** *adv.*

met·ri·ca·tion (met'rə kā'shən) *n.* [METRIC + -ATION] a changing over to the metric system of weights and measures —**met'ri·cate'** *vt.* **-cat'ed**, **-cat'ing**

metric system a decimal system of weights and measures in which the basic units are the gram, the meter, and the liter: see TABLES OF WEIGHTS AND MEASURES in Supplements

metric ton a measure of weight equal to 1,000 kilograms or 2,204.62 pounds

met·ro·nome (met'rə nōm') *n.* [< Gr. *metron*, measure + *nomos*, law] a clockwork device that can be set to beat time at different rates of speed, as for piano practice

METRONOME

me·trop·o·lis (mə träp''l is) *n.*, *pl.* **-lis·es** [< Gr. *mētēr*, mother + *polis*, city] **1.** the main city, often the capital, of a country, state, etc. **2.** any large city or center of population, culture, etc.

met·ro·pol·i·tan (met'rə päl'ə t'n) *adj.* **1.** of or constituting a metropolis **2.** of a population area consisting of a central city, or adjacent cities, and smaller surrounding communities —*n.* **1.** a person who lives in and is wise in the ways of a metropolis **2.** *a)* an archbishop of a church province *b)* *Orthodox Eastern Ch.* a bishop ranking just below a Patriarch

-metry [< Gr. *metron*, measure] *a combining form meaning* the process or science of measuring [*anthropometry*]

Met·ter·nich (met'ər nik), Prince **von** 1773–1859; Austrian statesman & diplomat

met·tle (met''l) *n.* [var. of METAL] spirit or courage —**on one's mettle** prepared to do one's best

met'tle·some (-səm) *adj.* full of mettle; spirited, brave, etc.

Meuse (myo͞oz) river in NE France, Belgium, & the Netherlands, flowing into the North Sea: 575 mi.

mew[1] (myo͞o) *n.* [< L. *mutare,* to change] a cage, as for hawks while molting —*vt.* to confine in or as in a cage

mew[2] (myo͞o) *n.* [echoic] the characteristic vocal sound made by a cat —*vi.* to make this sound

mew[3] (myo͞o) *n.* [OE. *mæw*] a sea gull

mewl (myo͞ol) *vi.* [< MEW[2]] to cry weakly, like a baby; whimper —**mewl'er** *n.*

Mex. 1. Mexican **2.** Mexico

Mexican War a war between the U.S. and Mexico (1846–1848)

Mex·i·co (mek'si kō') **1.** country in N. America, south of the U.S.: 760,373 sq. mi.; pop. 48,313,000; cap. Mexico City **2. Gulf of,** arm of the Atlantic, east of Mexico & south of the U.S. —**Mex'i·can** (-kən) *adj., n.*

Mexico City capital of Mexico, in the SC part: pop. 3,484,000

mez·za·nine (mez'ə nēn') *n.* [Fr. < It. *mezzano,* middle] **1.** a low-ceilinged story between two main stories, often a balcony jutting out over the main floor **2.** the lowest balcony section of a theater

mez·zo (met'sō, mez'ō) *adj., adv.* [It. < L. *medius,* middle] *Music* moderate(ly); half

mez'zo-so·pra'no *n., pl.* **-nos, -ni** (-nē) [It.] a voice or singer between soprano and contralto

MF, mf medium frequency

mf *Music* mezzo forte

mfd. manufactured

mfg. manufacturing

mfr. *pl.* **mfrs.** manufacturer

Mg *Chem.* magnesium

mg, mg. milligram; milligrams

Mgr. Manager

MHz, Mhz megahertz

Mi Michigan

mi (mē) *n.* [< ML.] *Music* a syllable representing the third tone of the diatonic scale

mi. 1. mile(s) **2.** mill(s)

Mi·am·i (mī am'ē, -ə) city on the SE coast of Fla.: pop. 335,000 (met. area 1,268,000)

mi·as·ma (mī az'mə, mē-) *n., pl.* **-mas, -ma·ta** (-mə tə) [Gr., pollution] **1.** a vapor as from marshes, formerly supposed to poison the air **2.** any unwholesome or befogging influence —**mi·as'mal, mi·as'mic** *adj.*

mi·ca (mī'kə) *n.* [L., a crumb] a mineral that crystallizes in thin, flexible, easily separated layers resistant to heat and electricity

Mi·cah (mī'kə) *Bible* **1.** a Hebrew prophet of the 8th cent. B.C. **2.** the book containing his prophecies: abbrev. **Mic.**

mice (mīs) *n. pl. of* MOUSE

Mi·chael (mī'k'l) *Bible* one of the archangels

Mi·chel·an·ge·lo (mī'k'l an'jə lō') 1475–1564; It. sculptor and painter

Mich·i·gan (mish'ə gən) **1.** Middle Western State of the U.S.: 58,216 sq. mi.; pop. 8,875,000; cap. Lansing: abbrev. **Mich., MI 2. Lake,** one of the Great Lakes, between Mich. & Wis.

micro- [< Gr. *mikros,* small] *a combining form meaning:* **1.** very small [*microfilm*] **2.** enlarging [*microscope*] **3.** microscopic [*microchemistry*] **4.** one millionth [*microgram*]

mi·crobe (mī'krōb) *n.* [Fr. < Gr. *mikros,* small + *bios,* life] a microorganism, esp. one causing disease —**mi·cro'bic, mi·cro'bi·al** *adj.*

mi·cro·bi·ol·o·gy (mī'krō bī äl'ə jē) *n.* the branch of biology that deals with microorganisms

mi'cro·chem'is·try *n.* the chemistry of microscopic or submicroscopic quantities or objects

mi·cro·cop·y (mī'krə käp'ē) *n., pl.* **-ies** a copy produced in greatly reduced size, on microfilm

mi'cro·cosm (-käz'm) *n.* [see MICRO- & COSMOS] an organism or organization regarded as a world in miniature —**mi'cro·cos'mic** *adj.*

mi'cro·fiche' (-fēsh') *n.* [Fr. < *micro-,* MICRO- + *fiche,* small card] a film card containing many pages of greatly reduced microfilm copy

mi'cro·film' *n.* film on which documents, etc. are photographed in a reduced size for convenience —*vt., vi.* to photograph on microfilm

mi'cro·groove' *n.* a very narrow needle groove, as for a long-playing phonograph record

mi·crom·e·ter (mī kräm'ə tər) *n.* [< Fr.: see MICRO- & -METER] an instrument for measuring very small distances, angles, etc., as in a caliper (**micrometer caliper**) using a finely threaded screw (**micrometer screw**) with a head graduated to show measurements

MICROMETER

mi·cron (mī'krän) *n., pl.* **-crons, -cra** (-krə) [< Gr. *mikros,* small] one millionth of a meter

Mi·cro·ne·sia (mī'krə nē'zhə) a major division of the Pacific islands, north of the equator & west of the international date line —**Mi'cro·ne'sian** *adj., n.*

mi·cro·or·gan·ism (mī'krō ôr'gə niz'm) *n.* any microscopic or ultramicroscopic animal or vegetable organism; esp., any of the bacteria, viruses, etc.

mi·cro·phone (mī'krə fōn') *n.* [MICRO- + -PHONE] an instrument that converts the mechanical energy of sound waves into an electric signal, as for radio

mi'cro·scope' (-skōp') *n.* [see MICRO- & -SCOPE] an instrument using a combination of lenses to make very small objects, as microorganisms, look larger

mi'cro·scop'ic (-skäp'ik) *adj.* **1.** so small as to be invisible or obscure except through a microscope; minute **2.** of, with, or like a microscope —**mi'cro·scop'i·cal·ly** *adv.*

mi·cros·co·py (mī kräs'kə pē) *n.* the use of the microscope to study objects

mi'cro·wave' *n.* an electromagnetic wave between 300,000 megahertz and 300 megahertz in frequency

mic·tu·rate (mik'cho͞o rāt') *vi.* **-rat'ed, -rat'ing** [< L. *mingere*] to urinate —**mic'tu·ri'tion** (-rish'ən) *n.*

mid[1] (mid) *adj.* [OE. *midd-*] middle

mid[2] (mid) *prep.* [Poet.] amid: also **'mid**

mid- *a combining form meaning* middle or middle part of [*midweek*]

mid·air (mid er') *n.* any point in the air not in contact with the ground or other surface

Mi·das (mī'dəs) *Gr. Myth.* a king granted the power to turn everything that he touched into gold

mid'brain' *n.* the middle part of the brain

mid'day' *n., adj.* noon

mid·dle (mid''l) *adj.* [OE. *middel*] **1.** halfway between two given points, times, limits, etc. **2.** in between; intermediate **3.** [M-] in a stage of language development intermediate between *Old* and *Modern [Middle* English] —*n.* **1.** a point or part halfway between the ends; middle point, time, etc. **2.** the middle part of the body; waist

middle age the time of life when a person is neither young nor old —**mid'dle-aged'** *adj.*

Middle Ages the period of European history between ancient and modern times, 476 A.D.–c.1450 A.D.

Middle America the conventional or conservative American middle class, esp. of the Middle West

mid'dle-brow' (-brou') *n.* [Colloq.] one regarded as having conventional, middle-class tastes or opinions

middle C the musical note on the first leger line below the treble staff and the first above the bass staff

middle class the social class between the aristocracy and very wealthy and the lower working class —**mid'dle-class'** *adj.*

middle ear the part of the ear including the eardrum and a cavity containing three small bones; tympanum

Middle East area at the eastern end of the Mediterranean, including the Arabian Peninsula

Middle English the English language as written and spoken between c.1100 and c.1500

mid'dle·man' *n., pl.* **-men'** **1.** a merchant who buys from a producer and sells at wholesale or retail **2.** a go-between

mid'dle·most' *adj. same as* MIDMOST

mid'dle-of-the-road' *adj.* avoiding extremes, esp. of the political left or right

middle school in some school systems, a school with grades variously between 5 and 9

mid'dle·weight' *n.* a boxer or wrestler between a welterweight and a light heavyweight (in boxing, 148–160 lbs.)

Middle West region of the NC U.S. between the Rocky Mountains and the E border of Ohio —**Middle Western**

mid·dling (mid'liŋ) *adj.* of middle size, quality, state, etc.; medium —*adv.* [Colloq.] somewhat —*n.* **1.** [*pl.*] products of medium quality, size, etc. **2.** [*pl.*] coarsely ground grain, often mixed with bran —**fair to middling** [Colloq.] moderately good or well

mid·dy (mid'ē) *n., pl.* **-dies 1.** [Colloq.] a midshipman **2.** a girl's loose blouse with a sailor collar: in full, **middy blouse**

midge (mij) *n.* [OE. *mycg*] a small, two-winged, gnatlike insect

midg·et (mij'it) *n.* [dim. of prec.] **1.** a very small person **2.** anything very small of its kind

mid·land (mid'lənd) *n.* the middle region of a country; interior *—adj.* in or of the midland; inland *—***the Midlands** the middle counties of England

mid'most' *adj.* exactly in the middle, or nearest the middle

mid'night' *n.* twelve o'clock at night *—adj.* of or at midnight *—***burn the midnight oil** to study or work very late at night

midnight sun the sun visible at midnight in the arctic or antarctic regions during the summer

mid'point' *n.* a point at or close to the middle or center

mid'rib' (-rib') *n.* the central vein of a leaf

mid'riff (-rif) *n.* [< OE. *midd*, mid + *hrif*, belly] **1.** *same as* DIAPHRAGM (sense 1) **2.** the middle part of the torso, between the abdomen and the chest

mid'ship' *n.* the middle part of a ship

mid'ship'man (-mən) *n., pl.* **-men** a student at the U.S. Naval Academy at Annapolis

mid'ships' *adv., adj. same as* AMIDSHIPS

midst[1] (midst) *n.* the middle; central part *—***in our** (or **your, their**) **midst** among us (or you, them) *—***in the midst of 1.** in the middle of **2.** during

midst[2] (midst) *prep.* [Poet.] in the middle of; amid

mid'stream' *n.* the middle of a stream

mid'sum'mer *n.* **1.** the middle of the summer **2.** the time of the summer solstice, about June 21 *—adj.* of, in, or like midsummer

mid'term' *adj.* in the middle of the term *—n.* [Colloq.] a midterm examination, as in a college course

mid'-Vic·to'ri·an (-vik tôr'ē ən) *adj.* **1.** of or in the middle of Queen Victoria's reign **2.** old-fashioned, prudish, etc. *—n.* a mid-Victorian person

mid'way' (-wā') *n.* that part of a fair where sideshows and other amusements are located *—adj., adv.* (*also* -wā') in the middle

Midway Islands U.S. territory northwest of Hawaii, consisting of an atoll and two islets

mid'week' *n., adj.* (in) the middle of the week *—***mid'week'ly** *adj., adv.*

Mid'west' *n. same as* MIDDLE WEST *—***Mid'west'ern** *adj.* *—***Mid'west'ern·er** *n.*

mid·wife (mid'wīf') *n., pl.* **-wives'** [OE. *mid*, with + *wif*, wife] a woman who helps women in childbirth *—***mid'wife'ry** (-wī'fə rē, -wīf'rē) *n.*

mid'win'ter *n.* **1.** the middle of the winter **2.** the time of the winter solstice, about Dec. 22 *—adj.* of, in, or like midwinter

mid'year' *adj.* in the middle of the year *—n.* [Colloq.] a midyear examination, as in a college course

mien (mēn) *n.* [< DEMEAN[2]] one's appearance, bearing, or manner

miff (mif) *vt.* [prob. echoic of cry of disgust] [Colloq.] to offend; displease; anger

might[1] (mīt) *v.* [OE. *mihte*] **1.** *pt. of* MAY **2.** *an auxiliary generally equivalent to* MAY *[it might* rain*]*

might[2] (mīt) *n.* [OE. *miht*] great strength, force, or power

might'y *adj.* **-i·er, -i·est 1.** powerful; strong **2.** remarkably large, etc.; great *—adv.* [Colloq.] very *—***might'i·ly** *adv.* *—***might'i·ness** *n.*

mi·gnon·ette (min'yə net') *n.* [< Fr. *mignon*, small] a plant with spikes of small, fragrant flowers

mi·graine (mī'grān) *n.* [Fr. < Gr. *hēmi-*, half + *kranion*, skull] an intense, periodic headache, usually limited to one side of the head

mi·grant (mī'grənt) *adj.* migrating *—n.* a person, bird, or animal that migrates

mi·grate (mī'grāt) *vi.* **-grat·ed, -grat·ing** [< L. *migrare*] **1.** to move from one place to another, esp. to another country **2.** to move from one region to another with the change in seasons, as many birds **3.** to move from place to place to harvest seasonal crops *—***mi'gra·tor** *n.*

mi·gra·tion (mī grā'shən) *n.* **1.** a migrating **2.** a group of people, birds, etc. migrating together

mi·gra·to·ry (mī'grə tôr'ē) *adj.* **1.** migrating *[migratory* birds, *migratory* workers*]* **2.** of migration **3.** roving; wandering

mi·ka·do (mi kä'dō) *n., pl.* **-dos** [Jpn. < *mi*, exalted + *kado*, gate] [*often* M-] the emperor of Japan: title no longer used

mike (mīk) *n.* [Colloq.] a microphone

mil (mil) *n.* [< L. *mille*, thousand] a unit of length, .001 inch, used in measuring the diameter of wire

mil. 1. military **2.** militia

mi·la·dy, mi·la·di (mi lā'dē) *n.* [Fr. < Eng. *my lady*] **1.** an English noblewoman, or gentlewoman **2.** a woman of fashion: advertiser's term

Mi·lan (mi lan') city in NW Italy: pop. 1,684,000

milch (milch) *adj.* [ME. *milche*] kept for milking *[milch* cows*]*

mild (mīld) *adj.* [OE. *milde*] **1.** gentle or moderate in nature, action, or effect; not severe, harsh, extreme, etc. *[a mild* winter, *mild* punishment*]* **2.** having a pleasant flavor that is not strong or sharp: said of tobacco, cheese, etc. *—***mild'ly** *adv.* *—***mild'ness** *n.*

mil·dew (mil'dōō', -dyōō') *n.* [OE. *meledeaw*, lit., honeydew] a fungus that appears as a whitish, furry coating on plants or on damp cloth, paper, etc. *—vt., vi.* to affect or be affected with mildew

mile (mīl) *n.* [< L. *milia* (*passuum*), thousand (paces)] a unit of linear measure, equal to 5,280 ft.

mile·age (mīl'ij) *n.* **1.** an allowance per mile for traveling expenses **2.** total number of miles traveled **3.** rate per mile **4.** the amount of use one can get from something Also sp. **milage**

mile'post' *n.* a signpost showing the distance in miles to or from a specified place

mil'er *n.* one who competes in mile races

mile'stone' 1. a stone set up as a milepost **2.** a significant event in history, in one's life, etc.

mi·lieu (mēl yoo') *n.* [Fr. < L. *medius*, middle + *locus*, a place] environment; esp., social setting

mil·i·tant (mil'i tənt) *adj.* [< L. *miles*, soldier] **1.** fighting **2.** ready to fight; aggressive in support of a cause *—n.* a militant person *—***mil'i·tan·cy** *n.*

mil'i·ta·rism (-tər iz'm) *n.* **1.** military spirit **2.** a policy of maintaining a strong military organization in aggressive preparedness for war *—***mil'i·ta·rist** *n.* *—***mil'i·ta·ris'tic** *adj.*

mil'i·ta·rize (-tə rīz') *vt.* **-rized', -riz'ing** to fill with militarism; equip and prepare for war

mil'i·tar'y (-ter'ē) *adj.* [< Fr. < L. *miles*, soldier] **1.** of, for, or by soldiers or the armed forces **2.** of, for, or fit for war **3.** of the army as apart from the navy *—***the military** the army or the armed forces *—***mil'i·tar'i·ly** *adv.*

military attaché an army officer attached to his nation's embassy or legation in a foreign country

military police soldiers assigned to carry on police duties for the army

mil·i·tate (mil'ə tāt') *vi.* **-tat'ed, -tat'ing** [< L. *militare*, be a soldier] to operate or work (*against*): said of facts, evidence, actions, etc.

mi·li·tia (mə lish'ə) *n.* [< L. *miles*, soldier] an army composed of citizens called out in time of emergency *—***mi·li'tia·man** (-mən) *n., pl.* **-men**

milk (milk) *n.* [OE. *meolc*] **1.** a white liquid secreted by the mammary glands of female mammals for suckling their young **2.** cow's milk, drunk by humans as a food or used to make butter, cheese, etc. **3.** any liquid like this *[coconut milk]* *—vt.* **1.** to squeeze milk from (a cow, goat, etc.) **2.** to extract (something), or extract something from, as if by milking *[to milk* a rich uncle for his money*]* *—***milk'er** *n.*

milk glass a nearly opaque whitish glass

milk'maid' *n.* a girl or woman who milks cows or works in a dairy

milk'man' *n., pl.* **-men'** a man who sells or delivers milk for a dairy

milk of magnesia a milky-white suspension of magnesium hydroxide in water, used as a laxative and antacid

milk'shake' *n.* a drink of milk, flavoring, and ice cream, mixed until frothy

milk snake a harmless snake, gray or reddish with black-rimmed markings: it feeds on mice, etc.

milk'sop' (-säp') *n.* a sissy

milk sugar *same as* LACTOSE

milk tooth any of the temporary, first set of teeth in a child or the young of other mammals

milk'weed' *n.* a plant with a milky juice and pods which when ripe burst to release plumed seeds

milk'y *adj.* **-i·er, -i·est 1.** like milk; esp., white as milk **2.** of or containing milk *—***milk'i·ness** *n.*

Milky Way a broad, faint band of light arching across the night sky, formed by billions of stars in the galaxy containing our solar system

mill[1] (mil) *n.* [< L. *mola*, millstone] **1.** a building with machinery for grinding grain into flour or meal **2.** any of various machines for grinding, crushing, etc. or for cutting, stamping, shaping, etc. **3.** a factory [a steel *mill*] **4.** [Colloq.] a place where something is done in a rapid, mechanical way [a diploma *mill*] —*vt.* **1.** to grind, work, form, etc. by or in a mill **2.** to raise and ridge the edge of (a coin) —*vi.* to move (*around* or *about*) confusedly, as a crowd —**in the mill** in preparation —**through the mill** [Colloq.] through a hard, painful, instructive experience — **milled** *adj.*

mill² (mil) *n.* [< L. *millesimus*, thousandth] 1/10 of a cent: a money of account, used as in taxation in mills (**millage**) per dollar of valuation

Mill (mil), **John Stuart** 1806–73; Eng. philosopher & political economist

Mil·lay (mi lā′), **Edna St. Vincent** 1892–1950; U.S. poet

mil·len·ni·um (mi len′ē əm) *n., pl.* **-ni·ums, -ni·a** (-ə) [< L. *mille*, thousand + *annus*, year] **1.** a period of 1,000 years **2.** *Theol.* the period of 1,000 years during which some believe Christ will reign on earth (with *the*): Rev. 20:1–5 **3.** a period of peace and happiness for everyone — **mil·len′ni·al** *adj.*

mil·ler (mil′ər) *n.* **1.** one who owns or operates a mill, esp. a flour mill **2.** a moth with wings that look dusty like millers' clothes

mil·let (mil′it) *n.* [< L. *milium*] **1.** *a*) a cereal grass whose small grain is used for food in Europe and Asia *b*) the grain **2.** any of several similar grasses used for forage

Mil·let (mi lā′), **Jean** (zhän) 1814–75; Fr. painter

milli- [< L. *mille*, thousand] *a combining form meaning* one thousandth of (a specified unit)

mil·li·gram (mil′ə gram′) *n.* [< Fr.] one thousandth of a gram: chiefly Brit. sp. **milligramme**

mil′li·me′ter (-mēt′ər) *n.* [< Fr.] one thousandth of a meter: chiefly Brit. sp. **millimetre**

mil·li·ner (mil′ə nər) *n.* [< *Milaner*, importer of dress wares from Milan] one who makes or sells women's hats

mil·li·ner·y (mil′ə ner′ē) *n.* **1.** women's hats, headdresses, etc. **2.** the work or business of a milliner

milling machine a machine on which material rests as it is fed against a rotating cutter (**milling cutter**) for cutting, grinding, or shaping

mil·lion (mil′yən) *n., adj.* [< L. *mille*, thousand] **1.** a thousand thousands; 1,000,000 **2.** very many —**mil′lionth** *adj., n.*

mil′lion·aire′ (-yə ner′) *n.* [< Fr.] a person worth at least a million dollars, pounds, etc.

mil·li·pede (mil′ə pēd′) *n.* [< L. *mille*, thousand + *pes*, a foot] a many-legged arthropod with two pairs of legs on each apparent segment

mill′pond′ *n.* a pond from which water flows for driving a mill wheel

mill′race′ *n.* **1.** the current of water that drives a mill wheel **2.** the channel in which it runs

mill′stone′ *n.* **1.** either of a pair of flat, round stones between which grain or the like is ground **2.** a heavy burden

mill′stream′ *n.* a stream used as a millrace

mill wheel the wheel, usually a water wheel, that drives the machinery in a mill

mill′work′ *n.* **1.** doors, windows, etc. made in a planing mill **2.** work done in a mill —**mill′work′er** *n.*

mill′wright′ (-rīt′) *n.* a worker who installs, maintains, or repairs the machinery in a mill

milque·toast (milk′tōst′) *n.* [< a comic-strip character] a timid, apologetic person

milt (milt) *n.* [prob. < Scand.] the sex glands or sperm of male fishes

Mil·ton (mil′t'n), **John** 1608–74; Eng. poet

Mil·wau·kee (mil wô′kē) city in SE Wis., on Lake Michigan: pop. 717,000 (met. area 1,404,000)

mime (mīm) *n.* [< Gr. *mimos*] **1.** the representation of an action, character, mood, etc. by gestures, not words **2.** a mimic or pantomimist —*vt.* **mimed, mim′ing** to mimic or pantomime

mim·e·o·graph (mim′ē ə graf′) *n.* [< Gr. *mimeomai*, I imitate] a machine for making copies of written or typewritten matter by means of a stencil —*vt.* to make (such copies) of (specified matter)

mi·met·ic (mi met′ik, mī-) *adj.* [< Gr. *mimeisthai*, imitate] **1.** imitative **2.** characterized by mimicry

mim·ic (mim′ik) *adj.* [< Gr. *mimos*, a mime] **1.** imitative **2.** make-believe; mock —*n.* an imitator; esp., an actor skilled in mimicry —*vt.* **-icked, -ick·ing** **1.** to imitate in speech or action, often so as to ridicule **2.** to copy or resemble closely

mim′ic·ry *n., pl.* **-ries** **1.** the practice, art, or way of mimicking **2.** close resemblance of one organism to another or to some natural object

mi·mo·sa (mi mō′sə) *n.* [see MIME] a tree, shrub, or herb of warm regions, with heads or spikes of small white, yellow, or pink flowers

min. **1.** minimum **2.** minute(s)

min·a·ret (min′ə ret′) *n.* [Fr. < Ar. *manārah*, lighthouse] a high tower on a mosque, with a balcony from which a crier calls the people to prayer

min·a·to·ry (min′ə tôr′ē) *adj.* [< L. *minari*, threaten] menacing; threatening

mince (mins) *vt.* **minced, minc′ing** [< L. *minutus*, small] **1.** to cut up into small bits; hash **2.** to express or do with affected daintiness **3.** to lessen the force of [to *mince* no words] —*vi.* to speak, act, or walk with affected daintiness —**minc′er** *n.*

mince′meat′ *n.* a mixture of chopped apples, raisins, suet, spices, etc., and sometimes meat, used as a filling for pie (**mince pie**)

mind (mīnd) *n.* [OE. (*ge*)*mynd*] **1.** memory [to bring to *mind*] **2.** what one thinks or intends; opinion, desire, purpose, etc. [to change one's *mind*, have a *mind* to go] **3.** the seat of consciousness, where thinking, perceiving, feeling, etc. take place **4.** intellect **5.** attention [pay him no *mind*] **6.** *same as* PSYCHE (*n.* 2) **7.** sanity [to lose one's *mind*] **8.** an intelligent person [the great minds of today] **9.** way of thinking [the reactionary *mind*] —*vt.* **1.** to pay attention to; heed **2.** to obey **3.** to take care of [*mind* the baby] **4.** to be careful about [*mind* the stairs] **5.** to care about; object to [don't *mind* the noise] —*vi.* **1.** to pay attention **2.** to be obedient **3.** to be careful **4.** to care; object —**bear** (or **keep**) **in mind** to remember —**give** (**someone**) **a piece of one's mind** to criticize or rebuke (someone) sharply —**make up one's mind** to reach a decision —**never mind** don't be concerned —**on one's mind** **1.** occupying one's thoughts **2.** worrying one —**out of one's mind** **1.** insane **2.** frantic (*with* worry, grief, etc.) — **put in mind** to remind

Min·da·na·o (min′də nou′, -nä′ō) 2d largest island of the Philippines, at the S end of the group

mind′ed *adj.* **1.** having a (specified kind of) mind [highminded] **2.** inclined [minded to go]

mind′ful *adj.* having in mind; aware or careful (*of*) — **mind′ful·ly** *adv.* —**mind′ful·ness** *n.*

mind′less *adj.* **1.** without intelligence **2.** heedless (*of*) — **mind′less·ly** *adv.* —**mind′less·ness** *n.*

mind reader one who professes to be able to perceive another's thoughts —**mind reading**

mind's eye the imagination

mine¹ (mīn) *pron.* [OE. *min*] that or those belonging to me [mine are better] —*poss. pronominal adj.* my: mainly archaic [mine eyes] or in direct address after the noun [mother *mine*]

mine² (mīn) *n.* [< MFr. < ? Celt.] **1.** a large excavation made in the earth, from which to extract ores, coal, etc. **2.** a deposit of ore, coal, etc. **3.** any great source of supply **4.** *Mil.* *a*) a tunnel dug under an enemy's fort, etc., in which an explosive is placed *b*) an explosive hidden underground or in the sea, for destroying enemy troops, ships, etc. —*vt., vi.* **mined, min′ing** **1.** to dig (ores, etc.) from (the earth) **2.** to dig or lay military mines in or under (a place) **3.** to undermine

mine detector an electromagnetic device for locating the position of hidden explosive mines

mine field an area where explosive mines have been set

mine′lay′er *n.* a ship that lays explosive mines in the water

min′er *n.* one whose work is digging coal, ore, etc. in a mine

min·er·al (min′ər əl, min′rəl) *n.* [< ML. *minera*, a mine] **1.** an inorganic substance occurring naturally in the earth, as ore, rock, etc.: sometimes applied to organic substances in the earth, such as coal **2.** any substance neither vegetable nor animal —*adj.* of or containing minerals

min·er·al·o·gy (min′ə räl′ə jē, -ral′-) *n.* the scientific study of minerals —**min′er·al′o·gist** *n.*

mineral oil a colorless, tasteless oil derived from petroleum and used as a laxative

mineral water water containing mineral salts or gases

Mi·ner·va (mi nur′və) the Roman goddess of wisdom, etc.: identified with the Greek Athena

mi·ne·stro·ne (min′ə strō′nē) *n.* [It.] a thick vegetable soup in a meat broth

mine sweeper a ship for destroying enemy mines

Ming (miŋ) Chin. dynasty (1368–1644): period noted for scholarly achievements & artistic works

min·gle (miŋ′g'l) vt. **-gled, -gling** [< OE. *mengan*, to mix] to mix together; blend —vi. **1.** to become mixed or blended **2.** to join or unite with others

mini- [< MINI(ATURE)] *a combining form meaning* miniature, very small, very short [*miniskirt*]

min·i·a·ture (min′ē ə chər, min′i chər) n. [It. < L. *miniare*, paint red] **1.** a very small painting, esp. a portrait **2.** a copy or model on a very small scale —adj. that is a miniature; very small —**in miniature** on a very small scale —**min′i·a·tur·ist** n.

min′i·a·tur·ize′ (-īz′) vt. **-ized′, -iz′ing** to make in a small and compact form —**min′i·a·tur′i·za′tion** n.

min·i·bus (min′ē bus′) n. a very small bus

min·im (min′im) n. [< L. *minimus*, least] **1.** the smallest liquid measure, 1/60 fluid dram, or about a drop **2.** [Brit.] *Music* a half note

min·i·mal (min′ə m'l) adj. smallest or least possible; of or being the minimum —**min′i·mal·ly** adv.

min′i·mize′ (-mīz′) vt. **-mized′, -miz′ing** to reduce to or estimate at the minimum; make or make seem as small as possible

min·i·mum (-məm) n., pl. **-mums, -ma** (-mə) [L., least] **1.** the smallest quantity, number, etc. possible or permissible **2.** the lowest degree or point reached or recorded —adj. **1.** smallest possible, permissible, or reached **2.** of, marking, or setting a minimum

minimum wage a wage established by contract or by law as the lowest that may be paid, as for work of a specified kind

min·ing (mī′niŋ) n. the process or work of removing ores, coal, etc. from a mine

min·ion (min′yən) n. [Fr. *mignon*, darling] **1.** a favorite, esp. one who is a servile follower: term of contempt **2.** a subordinate official

minion of the law a policeman

min·i·skirt (min′ē skurt′) n. a very short skirt ending well above the knee

min·is·ter (min′is tər) n. [L., a servant] **1.** a person appointed to head a department of government **2.** a diplomat representing his government in a foreign nation **3.** a person authorized to conduct religious services in a church, esp. a Protestant church; pastor —vi. **1.** to serve as a minister in a church **2.** to give help or service (*to*) —**min′is·trant** (-trənt) adj., n.

min·is·te′ri·al (-tir′ē əl) adj. [< Fr.] **1.** of a minister or (the) ministry **2.** subordinate or instrumental **3.** administrative; executive

min′is·tra′tion (-trā′shən) n. **1.** the giving of help or care **2.** a ministering in religious matters

min·is·try (-trē) n., pl. **-tries 1.** the act of ministering, or serving **2.** a) the office or function of a clergyman b) the clergy **3.** a) the department under a minister of government b) his term of office c) the ministers of a particular government as a group

mink (miŋk) n. [< Scand.] **1.** a kind of weasel that lives in water part of the time **2.** its valuable fur, soft, thick, and white to brown in color

Min·ne·ap·o·lis (min′ē ap′'l is) city in E Minn.: pop. 434,000 (met. area, with adjacent St. Paul, 1,814,000)

min·ne·sing·er (min′i siŋ′ər) n. [G. < MHG. *minne*, love + *senger*, singer] any of a number of German lyric poets and singers of the 12th to 14th cent.

MINK
(17–28 in. long, including tail)

Min·ne·so·ta (min′ə sōt′ə) Middle Western State of the U.S.: 84,068 sq. mi.; pop. 3,805,000; cap. St. Paul: abbrev. Minn., MN —**Min′ne·so′tan** adj., n.

min·now (min′ō) n. [< OE. *myne*] any of a large number of usually small freshwater fishes, commonly used as bait: also [Colloq.] **min′ny** (-ē), pl. **-nies**

Mi·no·an (mi nō′ən) adj. [< *Minos*, mythical king of Crete] of an advanced prehistoric culture in Crete (c.2800–c.1100 B.C.)

mi·nor (mī′nər) adj. [L.] **1.** lesser in size, amount, importance, rank, etc. **2.** under full legal age **3.** *Educ.* designating a field of study in which a student specializes, but to a lesser degree than in his major **4.** *Music* a) designating an interval smaller than the corresponding major interval by a semitone b) characterized by minor intervals, scales, etc.: music in a minor key is often associated with sadness, melancholy, etc. c) based on the minor scale: see MINOR SCALE —vi. *Educ.* to have a secondary field of study (*in*) —n. **1.** a person under full legal age, not yet having all civil rights **2.** *Educ.* a minor field of study **3.** *Music* a minor interval, key, etc.

Mi·nor·ca (mi nôr′kə) 2d largest of the Balearic Islands

mi·nor·i·ty (mə nôr′ə tē, mī-; -när′-) n., pl. **-ties 1.** the smaller number; less than half **2.** a racial, religious, ethnic, or political group that differs from the larger, controlling group **3.** the period or state of being under full legal age

minor league any league in a professional sport other than the major leagues —**mi′nor-league′** adj.

minor scale one of the two standard diatonic musical scales, with half steps instead of whole steps, in ascending, after the second and seventh tones (**melodic minor scale**) or after the second, fifth, and seventh tones (**harmonic minor scale**)

Min·o·taur (min′ə tôr′) *Gr. Myth.* a monster, part man and part bull, kept in a labyrinth in Crete

Minsk (minsk) capital of the Byelorussian S.S.R.: pop. 818,000

min·strel (min′strəl) n. [see MINISTER] **1.** a traveling singer of the Middle Ages **2.** a member of a comic variety show (**minstrel show**) in which the performers blacken their faces

min′strel·sy (-sē) n., pl. **-sies 1.** the art or occupation of a minstrel **2.** a group of minstrels **3.** a collection of their ballads or songs

mint¹ (mint) n. [< L. < Juno *Moneta*, whose temple was the mint] **1.** a place where money is coined by the government **2.** a large amount —adj. new, as if freshly minted [*in mint* condition] —vt. **1.** to coin (money) **2.** to invent or create —**mint′age** n.

mint² (mint) n. [< Gr. *mintha*] **1.** an aromatic plant whose leaves are used for flavoring **2.** a candy flavored with mint

mint julep an iced drink of whiskey or brandy, sugar, and mint leaves

min·u·end (min′yoo wend′) n. [< L. *minuere*, lessen] the number from which another is to be subtracted

min·u·et (min′yoo wet′) n. [< Fr. < *menu*, small: from the small steps taken] **1.** a slow, stately dance for groups of couples **2.** the music for this

mi·nus (mī′nəs) prep. [L. < *minor*, less] **1.** less [four *minus* two] **2.** [Colloq.] without [a cup *minus* a handle] —adj. **1.** involving subtraction [a *minus* sign] **2.** negative [a *minus* quantity] **3.** a little less than [a grade of A *minus*] —n. a sign (–), indicating subtraction or negative quantity: in full **minus sign**

mi·nus·cule (mi nus′kyool, min′ə skyool′) adj. [Fr. < L. *minusculus*] very small

min·ute¹ (min′it) n. [< L. (*pars*) *minuta* (*prima*), (first) small (part)] **1.** the sixtieth part of an hour or of a degree of an arc **2.** a moment **3.** a specific point [time **4.** a measure of distance covered in a minute [ten *minutes* away by car] **5.** [pl.] an official record of a meeting

mi·nute² (mī noot′) adj. [< L. *minutus*, small] **1.** very small **2.** of little importance **3.** of or attentive to tiny details; precise —**mi·nute′ly** adv.

min′ute·man′ n., pl. **-men′** a member of the American citizen army at the time of the Revolution who volunteered to be ready for military service at a minute's notice

minute steak (min′it) a small, thin steak that can be cooked quickly

mi·nu·ti·ae (mi nōō′shi ē′, -nyōō′-) n.pl., sing. **-ti·a** (-shē ə, -shə) [see MINUTE²] small or unimportant details

minx (miŋks) n. [< ?] a pert, saucy young woman

mir·a·cle (mir′ə k'l) n. [< L. *mirus*, wonderful] **1.** an event or action that apparently contradicts known scientific laws **2.** a remarkable thing **3.** a wonderful example [a *miracle* of tact]

miracle play a medieval religious drama dealing with events in the lives of the saints

mi·rac·u·lous (mi rak′yoo ləs) adj. **1.** having the nature of a miracle; supernatural **2.** like a miracle; marvelous **3.** able to work miracles —**mi·rac′u·lous·ly** adv.

mi·rage (mi räzh′) n. [Fr. < VL. *mirare*, look at] **1.** an optical illusion, caused by the refraction of light, in which a distant object appears to be nearby **2.** something that falsely appears to be real

mire (mīr) n. [< ON. *myrr*] **1.** an area of wet, soggy ground **2.** deep mud or slush —vt. **mired, mir′ing 1.** to cause to get stuck as in mire **2.** to soil with mud, etc. —vi. to sink in mud

mir·ror (mir'ər) *n.* [< VL. *mirare*, look at] **1.** a smooth surface that reflects images; esp., a piece of glass coated on one side as with silver **2.** anything that truly pictures or describes —*vt.* to reflect, as in a mirror

mirth (murth) *n.* [< OE. *myrig*, pleasant] joyfulness or gaiety, esp. when marked by laughter —**mirth'ful** *adj.* —**mirth'less** *adj.*

MIRV (murv) *n., pl.* **MIRV's** [*m(ultiple) i(ndependently targeted) r(eentry) v(ehicle)*] an intercontinental ballistic missile whose several warheads can be scattered

mis- [< OE. *mis-* or OFr. *mes-*] *a prefix meaning:* **1.** wrong(ly), bad(ly) [*misrule*] **2.** no, not [*misfire*]

mis·ad·ven·ture (mis'əd ven'chər) *n.* a mishap; bad luck

mis'al·li'ance *n.* an improper alliance; esp., an unsuitable marriage

mis·an·thrope (mis'ən thrōp') *n.* [< Gr. *misein*, to hate + *anthrōpos*, a man] one who hates or mistrusts all people: also **mis·an'thro·pist** (-an'thrə pist) —**mis'an·throp'ic** (-thräp'ik) *adj.*

mis·an·thro·py (mis an'thrə pē) *n.* hatred or mistrust of all people

mis·ap·ply' *vt.* **-plied'**, **-ply'ing** to apply or use badly or improperly —**mis'ap·pli·ca'tion** *n.*

mis·ap·pre·hend (mis'ap rə hend') *vt.* to misunderstand —**mis'ap·pre·hen'sion** (-hen'shən) *n.*

mis'ap·pro'pri·ate' *vt.* **-at'ed**, **-at'ing** to appropriate to a wrong or dishonest use —**mis'ap·pro'pri·a'tion** *n.*

mis'be·got'ten *adj.* wrongly or unlawfully begotten; illegitimate

mis'be·have' *vt., vi.* **-haved'**, **-hav'ing** to behave (oneself) wrongly —**mis'be·hav'ior** (-yər) *n.*

misc. miscellaneous

mis·cal'cu·late' *vt., vi.* **-lat'ed**, **-lat'ing** to calculate incorrectly; miscount or misjudge —**mis'cal·cu·la'tion** *n.*

mis·call' *vt.* to call by a wrong name

mis·car·riage (mis kar'ij) *n.* **1.** failure to carry out what was intended **2.** failure of mail, etc. to reach its destination **3.** the expulsion of a fetus from the womb before it is developed enough to live

mis·car·ry (mis kar'ē) *vi.* **-ried**, **-ry·ing 1.** to go wrong; fail [the plan *miscarried*] **2.** to fail to arrive: said of mail, etc. **3.** to suffer a miscarriage of a fetus

mis·cast' *vt.* **-cast'**, **-cast'ing** to cast (an actor or a play) unsuitably

mis·ce·ge·na·tion (mis'i jə nā'shən, mi sej'ə-) *n.* [coined (c.1863) < L. *miscere*, to mix + *genus*, race] marriage or sexual relations between a man and woman of different races, esp. between a white and a black

mis·cel·la·ne·ous (mis'ə lā'nē əs) *adj.* [< L. *miscere*, to mix] **1.** consisting of various kinds; varied **2.** having various qualities; many-sided —**mis'cel·la'ne·ous·ly** *adv.*

mis·cel·la·ny (mis'ə lā'nē) *n., pl.* **-nies** a miscellaneous collection, esp. of literary works

mis·chance' *n.* bad luck

mis·chief (mis'chif) *n.* [< OFr. *mes-*, mis- + *chief*, end] **1.** harm or damage, esp. that done by a person **2.** a cause of harm or annoyance **3.** *a)* a prank *b)* playful teasing

mis'chief-mak'er *n.* one who causes mischief, esp. by gossiping

mis·chie·vous (mis'chi vəs) *adj.* **1.** causing mischief; harmful **2.** prankish; teasing **3.** inclined to annoy with playful tricks —**mis'chie·vous·ly** *adv.*

mis·ci·ble (mis'ə b'l) *adj.* [< L. *miscere*, to mix] that can be mixed —**mis'ci·bil'i·ty** *n.*

mis·con·ceive (mis'kən sēv') *vt., vi.* **-ceived'**, **-ceiv'ing** to misunderstand —**mis'con·cep'tion** (-sep'shən) *n.*

mis·con·duct (mis kän'dukt) *n.* **1.** bad or dishonest management **2.** improper behavior

mis·con·strue (mis'kən strōō') *vt.* **-strued'**, **-stru'ing** to misinterpret —**mis'con·struc'tion** *n.*

mis·count' *vt.* to count incorrectly —*n.* (*usually* mis'-kount) an incorrect count

mis·cre·ant (mis'krē ənt) *adj.* [< OFr. *mes-*, mis- + *croire*, to believe] villainous; evil —*n.* a criminal; villain

mis·cue' *n.* **1.** *Billiards* a shot spoiled by the cue's slipping off the ball **2.** [Colloq.] a mistake; error —*vi.* **-cued'**, **-cu'ing 1.** to make a miscue **2.** *Theater* to miss one's cue

mis·deal' *vt., vi.* **-dealt'**, **-deal'ing** to deal (playing cards) wrongly —*n.* (mis'dēl') a wrong deal

mis·deed (mis dēd') *n.* a wrong or wicked act; crime, sin, etc.

mis·de·mean·or (mis'di mēn'ər) *n.* [MIS- + DEMEANOR] *Law* any minor offense bringing a lesser punishment than a felony

mis·di·rect' *vt.* to direct wrongly or badly —**mis'di·rec'-tion** *n.*

mis·do' *vt.* **-did'**, **-done'**, **-do'ing** to do wrongly

mis·em·ploy' *vt.* to employ wrongly or badly; misuse

mi·ser (mī'zər) *n.* [L., wretched] a greedy, stingy person who hoards money, even at the expense of his own comfort —**mi'ser·li·ness** *n.* —**mi'ser·ly** *adv.*

mis·er·a·ble (miz'ər ə b'l) *adj.* **1.** in misery; wretched **2.** causing misery, discomfort, etc. **3.** bad; inadequate **4.** pitiable —**mis'er·a·bly** *adv.*

mis·er·y (miz'ər ē) *n., pl.* **-ies** [see MISER] **1.** a condition of great suffering; distress **2.** a cause of such suffering; pain, sorrow, poverty, etc.

mis·fea·sance (mis fē'z'ns) *n.* [< OFr. *mes-*, mis- + *faire*, do] *Law* wrongdoing; specif., the doing of a lawful act in an unlawful manner

mis·file' *vt.* **-filed'**, **-fil'ing** to file (papers, etc.) in the wrong place

mis·fire' (mis fīr') *vi.* **-fired'**, **-fir'ing 1.** to fail to have the fuel ignite properly: said of an internal-combustion engine **2.** to fail to be discharged, as a firearm **3.** to fail to have the desired effect —*n.* a misfiring

mis·fit' *n.* **1.** an improper fit **2.** a person not adjusted to his job, associates, etc.

mis·for·tune *n.* **1.** ill fortune; trouble **2.** an unlucky accident; mishap

mis·give (mis giv') *vt.* **-gave'**, **-giv'en**, **-giv'ing** to cause fear, doubt, etc. in [his heart *misgave* him]

mis·giv·ing (mis giv'iŋ) *n.* [*often pl.*] a disturbed feeling of fear, doubt, etc.

mis·gov'ern *vt.* to govern badly —**mis·gov'ern·ment** *n.*

mis·guide (mis gīd') *vt.* **-guid'ed**, **-guid'ing** to lead into error or misconduct; mislead —**mis·guid'ance** *n.* —**mis·guid'ed·ly** *adv.*

mis·han·dle *vt.* **-dled**, **-dling** to handle badly or roughly; abuse

mis·hap (mis'hap) *n.* an unlucky or unfortunate accident

mish·mash (mish'mash') *n.* a hodgepodge

mis·in·form' *vt.* to give false or misleading information to —**mis'in·for·ma'tion** *n.*

mis·in·ter·pret *vt.* to interpret wrongly; understand or explain incorrectly —**mis'in·ter·pre·ta'tion** *n.*

mis·judge' *vt., vi.* **-judged'**, **-judg'ing** to judge wrongly or unfairly —**mis·judg'ment** *n.*

mis·la'bel *vt.* **-beled** or **-belled**, **-bel·ing** or **-bel·ling** to label incorrectly

mis·lay (mis lā') *vt.* **-laid'**, **-lay'ing 1.** to put in a place afterward forgotten **2.** to put down or install improperly [to *mislay* floor tiles]

mis·lead' *vt.* **-led'**, **-lead'ing 1.** to lead in a wrong direction **2.** to deceive or delude **3.** to lead into wrongdoing —**mis·lead'ing** *adj.* —**mis·lead'ing·ly** *adv.*

mis·man·age *vt., vi.* **-aged**, **-ag·ing** to manage or administer badly —**mis·man'age·ment** *n.*

mis·match' *vt.* to match badly or unsuitably —*n.* a bad or unsuitable match

mis·mate' *vt., vi.* **-mat'ed**, **-mat'ing** to mate badly or unsuitably

mis·name' *vt.* **-named'**, **-nam'ing** to give a wrong or inappropriate name to

mis·no·mer (mis nō'mər) *n.* [< OFr. *mes-*, mis- + *nommer*, to name] a name wrongly applied

mi·sog·a·my (mi säg'ə mē) *n.* [< Gr. *misein*, to hate + *gamos*, marriage] hatred of marriage —**mi·sog'a·mist** *n.*

mi·sog·y·ny (mi säj'ə nē) *n.* [< Gr. *misein*, to hate + *gynē*, woman] hatred of women —**mi·sog'y·nist** *n.* —**mi·sog'y·nous** *adj.*

mis·place' *vt.* **-placed'**, **-plac'ing 1.** to put in a wrong place **2.** to bestow (one's trust, etc.) unwisely **3.** *same as* MISLAY (sense 1) —**mis·place'ment** *n.*

mis·play' *vt., vi.* to play wrongly or badly, as in games or sports —*n.* a wrong or bad play

mis·print' *vt.* to print incorrectly —*n.* (*usually* mis'print') an error in printing

mis·pri·sion (mis prizh'ən) *n.* [< OFr. *mesprendre*, take wrongly] *Law* misconduct or neglect of duty, esp. by a public official

mis'pro·nounce' *vt., vi.* **-nounced'**, **-nounc'ing** to pronounce differently from the accepted pronunciations —**mis'pro·nun'ci·a'tion** *n.*

mis'quote' *vt., vi.* **-quot'ed**, **-quot'ing** to quote incorrectly —**mis'quo·ta'tion** *n.*

mis·read' (-rēd') *vt., vi.* **-read'** (-red'), **-read'ing** to read wrongly, esp. so as to misinterpret or misunderstand

mis·rep·re·sent' *vt.* to represent falsely; give an untrue idea of —**mis'rep·re·sen·ta'tion** *n.*

mis·rule' *vt.* -ruled', -rul'ing to rule badly or unjustly; misgovern —*n.* 1. misgovernment 2. disorder or riot

miss¹ (mis) *vt.* [OE. *missan*] 1. to fail to hit, meet, catch, attend, do, see, hear, etc. 2. to let (a chance, etc.) go by 3. to avoid *[he missed being hit]* 4. to notice, feel, or regret the absence or loss of —*vi.* 1. to fail to hit 2. to fail to be successful 3. to misfire, as an engine —*n.* a failure to hit, obtain, etc.

miss² (mis) *n., pl.* **miss'es** [< MISTRESS] 1. [M-] a title used before the name of an unmarried woman or girl 2. a young, unmarried woman or girl 3. [*pl.*] a series of sizes in clothing for women and girls of average proportions

mis·sal (mis'l) *n.* [< LL. *missa,* Mass] *R.C.Ch.* the official, liturgical book containing the prayers used in celebrating Mass throughout the year

mis·shape' *vt.* -shaped', -shap'ing to shape badly; deform —**mis·shap'en** *adj.*

mis·sile (mis'l) *n.* [< L. *mittere,* send] an object, as a spear, bullet, rocket, etc., designed to be thrown or launched toward a target; often, specif., *same as* GUIDED MISSILE

mis·sile·ry, mis·sil·ry (-rē) *n.* 1. the science of building and launching guided missiles 2. such missiles

miss·ing (mis'iŋ) *adj.* absent; lost; specif., absent after combat, but not definitely known to be dead or taken prisoner

mis·sion (mish'ən) *n.* [< L. *mittere,* send] 1. a sending out or being sent out to perform a special duty 2. *a)* a group of missionaries *b)* its headquarters 3. a diplomatic delegation 4. a group of technicians, specialists, etc. sent to a foreign country 5. the special duty for which someone is sent 6. the special task for which a person is apparently destined in life; calling 7. any charitable or religious organization for aiding the needy 8. *Mil.* an assigned combat operation; esp., a single combat flight by aircraft

mis·sion·ar'y (-er'ē) *adj.* of religious missions or missionaries —*n., pl.* -ies a person sent out by his church to preach and make converts in a foreign country

Mis·sis·sip·pi (mis'ə sip'ē) 1. river in C U.S., flowing from N Minn. to the Gulf of Mexico: 2,348 mi. 2. Southern State of the U.S.: 47,716 sq. mi.; pop. 2,217,000; cap. Jackson: abbrev. **Miss., MS** —**Mis'sis·sip'pi·an** *adj., n.*

mis·sive (mis'iv) *n.* [Fr. < L. *mittere,* send] a letter or written message

Mis·sour·i (mi zoor'ē) 1. river in WC U.S., flowing from NW Mont. to the Mississippi: 2,466 mi. 2. Middle Western State of the C U.S.: 69,686 sq. mi.; pop. 4,677,000; cap. Jefferson City: abbrev. **Mo., MO** —from **Missouri** [Colloq.] not easily convinced —**Mis·sour'i·an** *adj., n.*

mis·spell' *vt., vi.* -spelled' or -spelt', -spell'ing to spell incorrectly

mis·spend' *vt.* -spent', -spend'ing to spend improperly or wastefully

mis·state' *vt.* -stat'ed, -stat'ing to state incorrectly or falsely —**mis·state'ment** *n.*

mis·step' *n.* 1. a wrong or awkward step 2. a mistake in conduct

mist (mist) *n.* [OE.] 1. a large mass of water vapor like a light fog 2. a cloud of dust, gas, etc. 3. a fine spray, as of perfume 4. anything that dims or obscures —*vt., vi.* to make or become misty

mis·take (mi stāk') *vt.* -took', -tak'en, -tak'ing [< ON. *mistaka,* take wrongly] 1. to understand or perceive wrongly 2. to take to be another —*vi.* to make a mistake —*n.* an idea, answer, act, etc. that is wrong; blunder; error —**mis·tak'a·ble** *adj.*

mis·tak'en *adj.* 1. wrong; having an incorrect understanding 2. incorrect: said of ideas, etc. —**mis·tak'en·ly** *adv.*

mis·ter (mis'tər) *n.* [< MASTER] 1. [M-] a title used before the name of a man or his office and usually written *Mr.* 2. [Colloq.] sir 3. [Colloq. or Dial.] one's husband

mis·time' *vt.* -timed', -tim'ing to do or say at an inappropriate time

mis·tle·toe (mis'l tō') *n.* [< OE. *mistel,* mistletoe + *tan,* a twig] 1. a parasitic evergreen plant with yellowish flowers and white, poisonous berries 2. a sprig of this, hung as a Christmas decoration

mis·took (mi stook') *pt. of* MISTAKE

mis·tral (mis'trəl, mi strāl') *n.* [Fr. < Pr., master-wind] a cold, dry north wind that blows over the Mediterranean coast of France and nearby regions

mis·treat' *vt.* to treat wrongly or badly —**mis·treat'ment** *n.*

mis·tress (mis'tris) *n.* [< OFr. fem. of *maistre,* master] 1. a woman who is head of a household or institution 2. a woman, nation, etc. that has control or power 3. a woman with whom a man is having a prolonged affair 4. [M-] formerly, a title used before the name of a woman: now replaced by *Mrs.* or *Miss*

mis·tri·al (mis trī'əl) *n. Law* a trial made void as because of an error in the proceedings or because the jury cannot reach a verdict

mis·trust' *n.* lack of trust or confidence —*vt., vi.* to have no trust in (someone or something); doubt —**mis·trust'ful** *adj.* —**mis·trust'ful·ly** *adv.* —**mis·trust'ful·ness** *n.*

mist·y (mis'tē) *adj.* -i·er, -i·est 1. of, like, or covered with mist 2. blurred, as by mist 3. vague or obscure —**mist'i·ly** *adv.* —**mist'i·ness** *n.*

mis·un·der·stand' *vt.* -stood', -stand'ing to fail to understand or interpret correctly

mis·un·der·stand'ing *n.* 1. a failure to understand; mistake of meaning or intention 2. a quarrel; disagreement

mis·un·der·stood' *adj.* 1. not properly understood 2. not properly appreciated

mis·us·age *n.* 1. incorrect usage, as of words 2. bad or harsh treatment

mis·use (mis yōoz'; *for n.* -yōos') *vt.* -used', -us'ing 1. to use improperly 2. to treat badly or harshly; abuse —*n.* incorrect or improper use

mite (mīt) *n.* [OE.] 1. a tiny arachnid, often parasitic upon animals or plants 2. a very small sum of money 3. a bit; a little 4. a very small creature or object

mi·ter (mīt'ər) *n.* [< Gr. *mitra,* headband] 1. a tall, ornamented cap worn by bishops and abbots 2. *Carpentry* a joint formed by fitting together two pieces beveled so that they form a corner: also **miter joint** —*vt.* 1. to invest with the office of bishop 2. to fit together in a miter

MITER

mit·i·gate (mit'ə gāt') *vt., vi.* -gat'ed, -gat'ing [< L. *mitis,* mild + *agere,* to drive] to make or become less severe, less painful, etc. —**mit'i·ga'tion** *n.*

mi·to·sis (mī tō'sis) *n.* [< Gr. *mitos,* thread] the process by which a cell divides into two so that the nucleus of each new cell has the full number of chromosomes —**mi·tot'ic** (-tät'ik) *adj.*

mitt (mit) *n.* [< MITTEN] 1. a woman's glove covering part of the arm, the hand, and sometimes part of the fingers 2. [Slang] a hand 3. *a) Baseball* a padded glove, usually without separate and distinct sections for the four fingers *b)* a boxing glove

mit·ten (mit''n) *n.* [< OFr. *mitaine*] a glove with a single section for all four fingers

mix (miks) *vt.* mixed or mixt, mix'ing [prob. < Fr. < L. *miscere*] 1. to blend together in a single mass 2. to make by blending ingredients *[to mix a cake]* 3. to combine *[to mix work and play]* —*vi.* 1. to be mixed or blended 2. to get along together —*n.* 1. a mixture, as of ingredients for making something 2. a beverage for mixing with alcoholic liquor —**mix up** 1. to mix thoroughly 2. to confuse 3. to involve (*in* some matter)

mixed (mikst) *adj.* 1. blended 2. made up of different parts, races, sexes, etc. 3. confused

mixed number a number consisting of a whole number and a fraction, as 3 2/3

mix·er (mik'sər) *n.* 1. a person with reference to his sociability 2. a machine or an electric appliance for mixing 3. [Slang] a social gathering for getting people acquainted

mix·ture (miks'chər) *n.* 1. a mixing or being mixed 2. something mixed 3. *Chem.* a substance containing two or more ingredients not chemically united

mix'-up *n.* a confused condition; tangle

miz·zen (miz'n) *adj.* [< L. *medius,* middle] of the mizzenmast —*n.* a fore-and-aft sail set on the mizzenmast

miz'zen·mast (-məst, -mast') *n.* the mast nearest the stern in a ship with two or three masts

mks, m.k.s. meter-kilogram-second

ML. Medieval (or Middle) Latin

Mlle. *pl.* **Mlles.** Mademoiselle

MLowG. Middle Low German

mm, mm. millimeter(s)

MM. Messieurs

Mme. Madame

Mmes. Mesdames

MN Minnesota

Mn *Chem.* manganese

mne·mon·ic (nē män′ik) *adj.* [< Gr. *mnēmōn,* mindful] of or helping the memory

mne·mon′ics *n.pl.* [*with sing. v.*] a technique for improving memory

Mo *Chem.* molybdenum

Mo., MO Missouri

mo. *pl.* **mos.** month

M.O., MO 1. [L. *modus operandi*] mode of operation 2. money order: also **m.o.**

Mo·ab (mō′ab) ancient kingdom east & south of the Dead Sea —**Mo′ab·ite′** (-ə bīt′) *adj., n.*

moan (mōn) *n.* [prob. < OE. *mænan,* complain] 1. a low, mournful sound of sorrow or pain 2. any similar sound, as of the wind —*vt., vi.* 1. to say with or utter a moan 2. to complain or lament (about)

moat (mōt) *n.* [< OFr. *mote*] a deep, broad ditch, often filled with water, dug around a fortress or castle for protection

mob (mäb) *n.* [< L. *mobile* (*vulgus*), movable (crowd)] 1. a disorderly, lawless crowd 2. any crowd 3. the masses: contemptuous term 4. [Slang] a gang of criminals —*vt.* **mobbed, mob′bing** 1. to crowd around and attack, annoy, etc. 2. to throng

Mo·bile (mō bēl′, mō′bēl) seaport in SW Alabama: pop. 190,000

mo·bile (mō′b′l, -bīl, -bēl) *adj.* [< L. *movere,* to move] 1. moving, or able to move, from place to place 2. movable by means of a motor vehicle [a *mobile* X-ray unit] 3. that can change rapidly or easily, as to suit moods or needs — *n.* (*usually* -bēl) an abstract sculpture with parts that can move, as an arrangement of thin forms, rings, etc. suspended in midair —**mo·bil′i·ty** (-bil′ə tē) *n.*

mobile home a large trailer outfitted as a home, to be parked somewhere more or less permanently

mo′bi·lize′ (-bə līz′) *vt., vi.* **-lized′, -liz′ing** to make or become organized and ready, as for war —**mo′bi·li·za′tion** *n.*

mob·ster (mäb′stər) *n.* [Slang] a gangster

moc·ca·sin (mäk′ə s′n) *n.* [< AmInd.] 1. a heelless slipper of soft, flexible leather 2. a similar slipper, but with a hard sole and heel 3. *same as* WATER MOCCASIN

mo·cha (mō′kə) *n.* [< *Mocha,* seaport in Yemen] a choice grade of coffee grown orig. in Arabia —*adj.* flavored with coffee and, often, chocolate

mock (mäk) *vt.* [< OFr. *mocquer*] 1. to ridicule 2. to mimic, as in fun or derision 3. to lead on and disappoint; deceive 4. to defy and make futile —*vi.* to express scorn, ridicule, etc. —*adj.* sham; imitation

mock′er·y *n., pl.* **-ies** 1. a mocking 2. one receiving or deserving ridicule 3. a false or derisive imitation 4. vain effort; futility

mock′ing·bird′ *n.* an American bird that imitates the calls of other birds

mock orange a shrub with fragrant, white flowers like those of the orange

mock-up (mäk′up′) *n.* a scale model, usually a full-sized replica, used for teaching, testing, etc.

mod. 1. moderate 2. modern

mod·al (mōd′′l) *adj.* of or indicating a mode or mood; specif., *Grammar* of or expressing mood —**mo·dal·i·ty** (mō dal′ə tē) *n., pl.* **-ties**

mode (mōd) *n.* [< L. *modus*] 1. a manner or way of acting, doing, or being 2. customary usage or current fashion 3. *Grammar same as* MOOD² 4. *Music* any of various forms of scale arrangement

mod·el (mäd′′l) *n.* [< Fr. < L. *modus,* a measure] 1. *a*) a small representation of a planned or existing object *b*) a hypothetical representation or description 2. a person or thing regarded as a standard of excellence to be imitated 3. a style or design 4. *a*) one who poses for an artist or photographer *b*) one employed to display clothes by wearing them —*adj.* 1. serving as a model 2. representative of others of the same kind [a *model* home] —*vt.* **-eled** or **-elled, -el·ing** or **-el·ling** 1. *a*) to make a model of *b*) to plan or form after a model 2. to display (clothes) by wearing —*vi.* to serve as a model (sense 4)

mod·er·ate (mäd′ər it) *adj.* [< L. *moderare,* restrain] 1. within reasonable limits; avoiding extremes 2. mild; calm 3. of average or medium quality, range, etc. —*n.* one holding moderate opinions, as in politics —*vt., vi.* (-ə rāt′) **-at′ed, -at′ing** 1. to make or become moderate 2. to preside over (a meeting, etc.) —**mod′er·ate·ly** *adv.*

mod′er·a′tion *n.* 1 a moderating 2. avoidance of extremes 3. calmness —**in moderation** to a moderate degree

mod·e·ra·to (mäd′ə rät′ō) *adj., adv.* [It.] *Music* with moderation in tempo

mod·er·a·tor (mäd′ə rāt′ər) *n.* one who presides at a meeting, debate, etc.

mod·ern (mäd′ərn) *adj.* [< Fr. < L. *modo,* just now] 1. of the present or recent times; specif., up-to-date 2. of the period of history from c.1450 A.D. to now 3. [*often* **M-**] designating the most recent form of a language —*n.* a person living in modern times, having modern ideas, etc.

Modern English the English language since about the middle of the 15th century

mod′ern·ism *n.* modern ideas, practices, trends, etc., or sympathy with these —**mod′ern·ist** *n., adj.* —**mod′ern·is′-tic** *adj.* —**mod′ern·is′ti·cal·ly** *adv.*

mo·der·ni·ty (mä dur′nə tē, mə-) *n.* a being modern

mod′ern·ize′ *vt., vi.* **-ized′, -iz′ing** to make or become modern —**mod′ern·i·za′tion** *n.*

mod·est (mäd′ist) *adj.* [< Fr. < L. *modus,* a measure] 1. not vain or boastful; unassuming 2. shy or reserved 3. decorous or decent in dress, behavior, etc. 4. reasonable; not extreme [a *modest* request] 5. unpretentious [a *modest* home] —**mod′est·ly** *adv.* —**mod′es·ty** *n.*

mod·i·cum (mäd′i kəm) *n.* [L., moderate] a small amount; bit

mod·i·fi·ca·tion (mäd′ə fi kā′shən) *n.* a modifying or being modified; specif., *a*) a partial or slight change in form *b*) a product of such a change *c*) a slight reduction *d*) a qualification or limitation of meaning

mod·i·fi·er (mäd′ə fī′ər) *n.* one that modifies; esp., a word, phrase, or clause that limits the meaning of another word or phrase

mod·i·fy (mäd′ə fī′) *vt.* **-fied′, -fy′ing** [< L. *modificare,* to limit] 1. to change slightly or partially in character, form, etc. 2. to limit or lessen slightly 3. *Gram.* to limit in meaning; qualify [“old” *modifies* “man” in “old man”] — *vi.* to be modified

mod·ish (mōd′ish) *adj.* stylish; fashionable —**mod′ish·ly** *adv.* —**mod′ish·ness** *n.*

mo·diste (mō dēst′) *n.* [Fr.: see MODE] a woman who makes or sells fashionable clothing for women

ModL. Modern Latin

mod·u·lar (mäj′ə lər) *adj.* of modules

mod·u·late (mäj′ə lāt′) *vt.* **-lat′ed, -lat′ing** [< L. *modus,* a measure] 1. to regulate or adjust 2. to vary the pitch, intensity, etc. of (the voice) 3. to vary the amplitude, frequency, etc. of (a radio wave, etc.) in accordance with some signal —*vi.* to shift from one key to another within a musical composition —**mod′u·la′tion** *n.* —**mod′u·la′tor** *n.*

mod·ule (mäj′ool) *n.* [Fr. < L. *modus,* a measure] 1. a standard or unit of measurement, as of building materials 2. *a*) any of a set of units designed to be arranged in various ways *b*) a detachable section, unit, etc. with a specific function, as in a spacecraft *c*) *Electronics* a compact assembly functioning as a component of a larger unit

mo·gul (mō′gul, -g′l) *n.* [Per. *Mughul,* Mongol] a powerful or important person

mo·hair (mō′her) *n.* [< Ar. *mukhayyar*] 1. the hair of the Angora goat 2. yarn or a fabric made from this

Mo·ham′med (mō ham′id) 570?-632 A.D.; Arabian prophet: founder of the Muslim religion

Mo·ham′med·an *adj.* of Mohammed or the Muslim religion —*n. same as* MUSLIM

Mo·ham′med·an·ism *n. same as* ISLAM

Mo·hawk (mō′hôk) *n., pl.* **-hawks, -hawk** a member of an Iroquoian Indian tribe of New York & Canada

Mo·he·gan (mō hē′gən) *n.* 1. *pl.* **-gans, -gan** a member of a Mahican tribe of Algonquian Indians who lived in Connecticut 2. *same as* MAHICAN

Mo·hi·can (mō hē′kən) *n., adj. same as* MAHICAN

moi·e·ty (moi′ə tē) *n., pl.* **-ties** [< L. *medius,* middle] 1. a half 2. an indefinite part

moil (moil) *vi.* [< L. *mollis,* soft] to toil —*n.* 1. toil 2. confusion; turmoil

moire (mwär, môr) *n.* [Fr.] a fabric, as silk, having a watered, or wavy, pattern

moi·ré (mwä rā′, mô-) *adj.* [Fr.] having a watered, or wavy, pattern —*n.* 1. a wavy pattern pressed into cloth, etc. 2. *same as* MOIRE

moist (moist) *adj.* [< L. *mucus,* mucus] slightly wet; damp —**moist′ly** *adv.* —**moist′ness** *n.*

mois·ten (mois′′n) *vt., vi.* to make or become moist

mois′ture (-chər) *n.* water or other liquid causing a slight wetness

mois'tur·ize' (-īz') *vt., vi.* -ized', -iz'ing to add or restore moisture (to the skin, air, etc.) —**mois'tur·iz'er** *n.*

Mo·ja·ve Desert (mō hä'vē) desert in SE Calif.: also sp. **Mohave Desert**

mo·lar (mō'lər) *adj.* [< L. *mola*, millstone] designating a tooth or teeth adapted for grinding —*n.* a molar tooth: in man there are twelve molars

mo·las·ses (mə las'iz) *n.* [< L. *mel*, honey] a thick, dark syrup produced during the refining of sugar, or from sorghum, etc.

mold' (mōld) *n.* [< L. *modus*, a measure] 1. a hollow form for shaping something plastic or molten 2. a frame on which something is modeled 3. a pattern; model 4. something formed in or on a mold 5. distinctive character —*vt.* 1. to make or shape in or on, or as if in or on, a mold 2. to influence (opinion, etc.) strongly —**mold'er** *n.*

mold² (mōld) *n.* [ME. *moul*] 1. a fungus producing a furry growth on the surface of organic matter 2. this growth —*vi.* to become moldy

mold³ (mōld) *n.* [OE. *molde*, earth] loose, soft soil, esp. when rich with decayed organic matter

Mol·da·vi·an Soviet Socialist Republic (mäl dā'vē ən) republic of the U.S.S.R., in the W European part: also **Mol·da·vi·a**

mold·board (mōld'bôrd') *n.* a curved iron plate on a plowshare, for turning over the soil

mold·er (mōl'dər) *vi.* [< OE. *molde*, dust] to crumble into dust; decay

mold·ing (mōl'diŋ) *n.* 1. the act of one that molds 2. something molded 3. a shaped strip of wood, etc., as around the upper walls of a room

mold·y (mōl'dē) *adj.* -i·er, -i·est 1. covered with a growth of mold 2. musty or stale, as from age or decay — **mold'i·ness** *n.*

mole' (mōl) *n.* [OE. *mal*] a small, congenital spot on the human skin, usually dark-colored and raised

mole² (mōl) *n.* [ME. *molle*] a small, burrowing mammal with soft fur

mole³ (mōl) *n.* [< Fr. < L. *moles*, a dam] a breakwater

mole⁴ (mōl) *n.* [G. *mol*, short for *mol(ekulargewicht)*, molecular weight] *Chem.* the quantity of a substance having a weight in grams equal to its molecular weight

MOLDINGS

mo·lec·u·lar (mə lek'yə lər) *adj.* of, produced by, or existing between molecules

molecular biology the branch of biology dealing with the chemical and physical structure and activities of the molecules in living matter

molecular weight the sum of the atomic weights of all atoms in a given molecule

mol·e·cule (mäl'ə kyōōl') *n.* [< Fr. < L. *moles*, a mass] 1. the smallest particle of an element or compound that can exist in the free state and still retain the characteristics of the element or compound 2. a small particle

mole'hill' *n.* a small ridge of earth formed by a burrowing mole

mole'skin' *n.* 1. the fur of the mole 2. a strong cotton fabric with a soft nap

mo·lest (mə lest', mō-) *vt.* [< L. *moles*, a burden] 1. to annoy or to meddle with so as to trouble or harm 2. to make improper sexual advances to —**mo·les·ta·tion** (mō'les tā'shən) *n.* —**mo·lest'er** *n.*

Mo·lière (mōl yer') 1622–73; Fr. dramatist

moll (mäl) *n.* [< the name *Molly*] [Slang] a gangster's mistress

mol·li·fy (mäl'ə fī') *vt.* -fied', -fy'ing [< L. *mollis*, soft + *facere*, make] 1. to soothe or appease 2. to make less severe or violent —**mol'li·fi·ca'tion** *n.*

mol·lusk, mol·lusc (mäl'əsk) *n.* [< Fr. < L. *mollis*, soft] any of a group of invertebrates, as oysters, snails, squids, etc., having a soft body often enclosed in a hard shell

mol·ly·cod·dle (mäl'ē käd'l) *n.* [< the name *Molly* + CODDLE] a man or boy used to being coddled —*vt.* -dled, -dling to pamper; coddle

Mo·lo·tov cocktail (mô'lə täf) [< V. *Molotov* (1890–), Russ. statesman) [Slang] a bottle of gasoline, etc., plugged with a rag, ignited, and hurled as a grenade

molt (mōlt) *vi.* [< L. *mutare*, to change] to shed skin, feathers, horns, etc. prior to replacement by a new growth, as reptiles, birds, etc. —*vt.* to shed thus —*n.* 1. a molting 2. the parts shed

mol·ten (mōl't'n) *adj.* [archaic pp. of MELT] 1. melted by heat 2. made by being melted and cast in a mold

mol·to (mōl'tō) *adv.* [It.] *Music* very; much

Mo·luc·cas (mō luk'əz) group of islands in Indonesia: also **Molucca Islands**

mo·lyb·de·num (mə lib'də nəm) *n.* [< Gr. *molybdos*, lead] a soft, silver-white metallic chemical element, used in alloys: symbol, Mo; at. wt., 95.94; at. no., 42

mom (mäm) *n. colloq. var. of* MOTHER¹

mo·ment (mō'mənt) *n.* [< L. *momentum*, movement] 1. an indefinitely brief period of time; instant 2. a definite point in time 3. a brief time of being important 4. importance —**the moment** the present time

mo·men·tar·i·ly (mō'mən ter'ə lē) *adv.* 1. for a short time 2. in an instant 3. at any moment

mo·men·tar·y (mō'mən ter'ē) *adj.* 1. lasting for only a moment; passing 2. likely to occur at any moment

mo·men·tous (mō men'təs) *adj.* of great moment; very important —**mo·men'tous·ly** *adv.* —**mo·men'tous·ness** *n.*

mo·men·tum (mō men'təm) *n., pl.* -tums, -ta (-tə) [L.: see MOMENT] 1. the impetus of or as of a moving object 2. *Physics & Mech.* the quantity of motion of a moving body, equal to the product of its mass and its velocity

mom·my (mäm'ē) *n., pl.* -mies *child's term for* MOTHER¹

Mon. 1. Monday 2. Monsignor

Mon·a·co (män'ə kō, mə nä'kō) principality on the Mediterranean; enclave in SE France: 1/2 sq. mi.; pop. 23,000

mo·nad (mō'nad) *n.* [< Gr. *monos*, alone] 1. something simple and indivisible 2. *Chem.* an atom, element, or radical with a valence of one

mon·arch (män'ərk, -ärk) *n.* [< Gr. *monos*, alone + *archein*, to rule] 1. a hereditary ruler; king, queen, etc. 2. a large, migrating butterfly of N. America

mo·nar·chi·cal (mə när'ki k'l) *adj.* 1. of or like a monarch or monarchy 2. favoring a monarchy

mon·ar·chism (män'ər kiz'm) *n.* monarchical principles, or the advocacy of such principles —**mon'ar·chist** *n., adj.*

mon·ar·chy (män'ər kē) *n., pl.* -chies a government or state headed by a monarch

mon·as·ter·y (män'ə ster'ē) *n., pl.* -ies [< Gr. *monos*, alone] the residence of a group of monks or nuns, esp. monks

mo·nas·tic (mə nas'tik) *adj.* 1. of or characteristic of monasteries 2. of or characteristic of monks or nuns; ascetic Also **mo·nas'ti·cal** —*n.* a monk

mo·nas'ti·cism (-tə siz'm) *n.* the monastic system, state, or way of life

mon·au·ral (män ôr'l) *adj.* [MON(O)- + AURAL] designating or of sound reproduction using a single channel to carry and reproduce sound

Mon·day (mun'dē, -dā) *n.* [OE. *monandæg*, moon's day] the second day of the week

Mo·net (mō nā'), **Claude** 1840–1926; Fr. painter

mon·e·tar·y (män'ə ter'ē, mun'-) *adj.* [< L. *moneta*, a MINT¹] 1. of the coinage or currency of a country 2. of money; pecuniary —**mon'e·tar'i·ly** *adv.*

mon·e·tize (män'ə tiz', mun'-) *vt.* -tized', -tiz'ing [< L. *moneta*, a MINT¹ + -IZE] 1. to coin into money 2. to legalize as money —**mon·e·ti·za'tion** *n.*

mon·ey (mun'ē) *n., pl.* -eys, -ies [< L. *moneta*, a MINT¹] 1. stamped pieces of metal, or any paper note, authorized by a government as a medium of exchange 2. anything used as a medium of exchange 3. property; wealth —**in the money** [Slang] 1. among the winners in a race, contest, etc. 2. wealthy —**make money** to gain profits; become wealthy —**place (or put) money on** to bet on —**put money into** to invest money in

mon'ey·bag' *n.* 1. a bag for money 2. [*pl., with sing. v.*] [Colloq.] a rich person

money belt a belt with a compartment to hold money

mon'ey·chang'er *n.* 1. one whose business is exchanging the currency of different countries 2. a device holding stacked coins for making change

mon·eyed (mun'ēd) *adj.* wealthy; rich

mon'ey·mak'er *n.* 1. one successful at acquiring money 2. something financially profitable —**mon'ey·mak'ing** *adj., n.*

money of account a monetary denomination used in keeping accounts, etc., esp. one not issued as a coin or piece of paper money (e.g., the U.S. mill)

money order an order for the payment of a specified sum of money, as one issued at one post office or bank and payable at another

mon·ger (muŋ'gər, män'-) *n.* [< L. *mango*] [Chiefly Brit.] a dealer or trader: usually in compounds [*fishmonger*]

Mon·gol (män'gəl, -gōl) *adj., n. same as* MONGOLIAN

Mon·go·li·a (män gō'lē ə) *n.* region in EC Asia, consisting of a country (**Mongolian People's Republic**: 592,60[...]

sq. mi.; pop. 1,174,000; cap. Ulan Bator) and a contiguous region in China (**Inner Mongolia**)

Mon·go'li·an *adj.* **1.** of Mongolia, its people, or their culture **2.** *same as:* a) MONGOLOID b) MONGOLIC —*n.* **1.** a native of Mongolia **2.** *same as* MONGOLOID **3.** any Mongolic language

Mon·gol·ic (mäŋ gäl'ik) *adj.* designating or of a subfamily of languages spoken in Mongolia —*n.* any Mongolic language

Mon·gol·ism (mäŋ'gə liz'm) *n.* [*often* m-] *earlier term for* DOWN'S SYNDROME

Mon·gol·oid (mäŋ'gə loid') *adj.* **1.** of or characteristic of the natives of Mongolia **2.** designating or of one of the major groups of mankind, including most of the peoples of Asia **3.** [*often* m-] of or having Down's syndrome —*n.* **1.** a member of the Mongoloid group **2.** a person having Down's syndrome

mon·goose (mäŋ'gōōs) *n.,* pl. **-goos·es** [< native Indian name] a ferretlike, flesh-eating old-world mammal that kills snakes, etc.

mon·grel (muŋ'grəl, mäŋ'-) *n.* [< OE. *mengan,* to mix] an animal or plant, esp. a dog, of mixed breed —*adj.* of mixed breed, race, character, etc.

mon·ied (mun'ēd) *adj. same as* MONEYED

mon·i·ker, mon·ick·er (män'i kər) *n.* [< ?] [Slang] a person's name or nickname

mo·nism (mō'niz'm, män'iz'm) *n.* [< Gr. *monos,* single] *Philos.* the doctrine that there is only one ultimate substance or principle —**mo'nist** *n.*

mo·ni·tion (mō nish'ən) *n.* [< L. *monere,* warn] **1.** admonition; warning **2.** an official notice

mon·i·tor (män'ə tər) *n.* [< L. *monere,* warn] **1.** in some schools, a student chosen to help keep order, record attendance, etc. **2.** a device or instrument used for monitoring **3.** *Radio & TV* a receiver for checking the quality of transmission —*vt., vi.* **1.** to watch or check on (a person or thing) **2.** to regulate the performance of (a machine, aircraft, etc.) **3.** to listen in on (a broadcast, telephone conversation, etc.) **4.** *Radio & TV* to check with a monitor

mon·i·to·ry (män'ə tôr'ē) *adj.* giving monition

monk (muŋk) *n.* [< Gr. *monos,* alone] a man who joins a religious order living in retirement generally under vows of poverty, obedience, and chastity

mon·key (muŋ'kē) *n., pl.* **-keys** [prob. < Fr. or Sp. *mona,* ape + LowG. *-ke, -KIN*] any of the primates except man and the lemurs; specif., any of the smaller, long-tailed primates —*vi.* [Colloq.] to play, trifle, or meddle

monkey business [Colloq.] foolish, mischievous, or deceitful tricks or behavior

mon'key·shine' (-shīn') *n.* [Colloq.] a mischievous trick or prank: *usually used in pl.*

monkey wrench a wrench with an adjustable jaw — **throw a monkey wrench into** [Colloq.] to disrupt the orderly functioning of

monk's cloth a heavy cloth with a basket weave, used for drapes, etc.

monks·hood (muŋks'hood') *n. same as* ACONITE (sense 1)

mon·o (män'ō) *adj. clipped form of* MONOPHONIC —*n. clipped form of* MONONUCLEOSIS

mono- [< Gr. *monos,* single] *a prefix meaning* one, alone, single

mon·o·bas·ic (män'ə bā'sik) *adj.* designating an acid the molecule of which contains one hydrogen atom replaceable by a metal or positive radical

mon·o·cle (män'ə k'l) *n.* [Fr. < Gr. *monos,* single + L. *oculus,* eye] an eyeglass for one eye only

mon·o·cot·y·le·don (män'ə kät''l ē'd'n) *n.* a flowering plant with only one cotyledon —**mon'o·cot'y·le'don·ous** *adj.*

mon·o·dy (män'ə dē) *n., pl.* **-dies** [< Gr. *monos,* alone + *aeidein,* sing] a musical composition in which the melody is carried by one part, or voice

mo·noe·cious (mə nē'shəs, mō-) *adj.* [< MON(O)- + Gr. *oikos,* a house] *Bot.* having separate male flowers and female flowers on the same plant

mo·nog·a·my (mə näg'ə mē) *n.* [< Fr. < Gr. *monos,* single + *gamos,* marriage] the practice or state of being married to only one person at a time —**mo·nog'a·mist** *n.* —**mo·nog'a·mous** *adj.*

mon·o·gram (män'ə gram') *n.* [< Gr. *monos,* single + *gramma,* letter] the initials of a name combined in a single design —*vt.* **-grammed', -gram'ming** to put a monogram on

mon·o·graph (män'ə graf') *n.* [MONO- + -GRAPH] a book, article, etc., esp. a scholarly one, on a single subject

mon·o·lin·gual (män'ə liŋ'gwəl) *adj.* [MONO- + LINGUAL] using or knowing only one language

mon·o·lith (män'ə lith') *n.* [< Fr. < Gr. *monos,* single + *lithos,* stone] **1.** a single large block of stone, as one made into an obelisk, etc. **2.** something like a monolith in being massive, unified, unyielding, etc. —**mon'o·lith'ic** *adj.*

mon·o·logue, mon·o·log (män'ə lôg') *n.* [Fr. < Gr. *monos,* alone + *legein,* speak] **1.** a long speech, esp. one monopolizing a conversation **2.** a soliloquy **3.** a play, skit, etc. for one actor only —**mon'o·logu'ist, mo·nol·o·gist** (mə näl'ə jist) *n.*

mon·o·ma·ni·a (män'ə mā'nē ə) *n.* an excessive interest in or enthusiasm for some one thing; craze —**mon'o·ma'·ni·ac'** (-mā'nē ak') *n.*

mon·o·met·al·ism (män'ə met''l iz'm) *n.* the use of one metal, usually gold or silver, as the monetary standard

Mo·non·ga·he·la (mə nän'gə hē'lə) river in N W.Va. & SW Pa.: 128 mi.: see ALLEGHENY

mon·o·nu·cle·o·sis (män'ə nōō'klē ō'sis) *n.* [MONO- + NUCLE(US) + -OSIS] an acute disease, esp. of young people, characterized by fever, swollen lymph nodes, sore throat, etc.

mon·o·phon·ic (män'ə fän'ik) *adj.* [< MONO- + Gr. *phōnē,* a sound] of sound reproduction using a single channel to carry and reproduce sounds

mo·nop·o·list (mə näp'ə list) *n.* one who has a monopoly or favors monopoly —**mo·nop'o·lis'tic** *adj.*

mo·nop'o·lize (-līz') *vt.* **-lized', -liz'ing 1.** to get, have, or exploit a monopoly of **2.** to get full control of —**mo·nop'o·li·za'tion** *n.*

mo·nop'o·ly (-lē) *n., pl.* **-lies** [< Gr. *monos,* single + *pō·lein,* sell] **1.** exclusive control of a commodity or service in a given market, or control that makes possible the fixing of prices **2.** such control granted by a government **3.** something held as a monopoly **4.** a company that has a monopoly

mon·o·rail (män'ə rāl') *n.* a railway with a single rail serving as a track for cars suspended from it or balanced on it

mon·o·syl·la·ble (män'ə sil'ə b'l) *n.* a word of one syllable —**mon'o·syl·lab'ic** (-si lab'ik) *adj.*

mon·o·the·ism (män'ə thē iz'm) *n.* [MONO- + THEISM] the doctrine or belief that there is only one God —**mon'o·the·ist** *n.* —**mon'o·the·is'tic** *adj.*

mon·o·tone (män'ə tōn') *n.* [see MONO- & TONE] **1.** utterance of successive words without change of pitch or key **2.** tiresome sameness of style, color, etc. **3.** a single, unchanging musical tone **4.** recitation, singing, etc. in such a tone

mo·not·o·nous (mə nät'n əs) *adj.* **1.** going on in the same tone without variation **2.** having little or no variety **3.** tiresome because unvarying —**mo·not'o·nous·ly** *adv.*

mo·not'o·ny (-ē) *n.* **1.** sameness of tone or pitch **2.** lack of variety **3.** tiresome sameness

mon·o·treme (män'ə trēm') *n.* [< Gr. *monos,* single + *trēma,* hole] an egg-laying mammal (either the platypus or echidna) that has a single opening for the excretory and genital organs

mon·o·type (män'ə tīp') *n.* [MONO- + -TYPE] *Printing* type produced by Monotype —[M-] *a trademark for* either of a pair of machines for casting and setting up type in separate characters

mon·o·va·lent (män'ə vā'lənt) *adj. Chem. same as* UNIVALENT

mon·ox·ide (mə näk'sīd) *n.* an oxide with one atom of oxygen in each molecule

Mon·roe (mən rō'), **James** 1758–1831; 5th president of the U.S. (1817–25)

Monroe Doctrine the doctrine, stated by President Monroe, that the U.S. would regard as an unfriendly act any attempt by a European nation to interfere in the affairs of the Americas

Mon·sei·gneur (män'sen yur') *n., pl.* **Mes·sei·gneurs** (mes'en yurz') [Fr., lit., my lord] a French title of honor for persons of high rank, as princes or bishops

mon·sieur (mə syur'; *Fr.* mə syö') *n., pl.* **mes·sieurs** (mes'ərz; *Fr.* mā syö') [Fr., lit., my lord] a man; gentleman: as a title [M-], equivalent to *Mr.* or *Sir*

Mon·si·gnor (män sēn'yər) *n.* [It., lit., my lord] a title for certain Roman Catholic prelates

mon·soon (män sōōn') *n.* [< Ar. *mausim,* a season] **1.** a seasonal wind of the Indian Ocean and S Asia, blowing

fat, āpe, cär; ten, ēven; is, bīte; gō, hôrn, tōōl, look; oil, out; up, fur; thin, *then*; zh, leisure; ŋ, ring; ə for *a* in *ago*; ' as in able (ā'b'l); ë, Fr. coeur; ö, Fr. feu; ô, Fr. mon; ü, Fr. duc; r̄, Fr. cri; kh, G. doch, ich. ‡ foreign; < derived from

from the southwest from April to October and from the northeast the rest of the year **2.** the rainy season, when this wind blows from the southwest

mon·ster (män′stər) *n.* [< L. *monere,* warn] **1.** any greatly malformed plant or animal **2.** any grotesque imaginary creature **3.** any very cruel or wicked person **4.** any huge animal or thing —*adj.* huge; enormous

mon·strance (män′strəns) *n.* [< L. *monstrare,* to show] *R.C.Ch.* a receptacle in which the consecrated Host is exposed for adoration

mon·stros·i·ty (män sträs′ə tē) *n.* **1.** the state of being monstrous **2.** *pl.* **-ties** a monstrous thing

mon·strous (män′strəs) *adj.* **1.** abnormally large; enormous **2.** very unnatural, as in shape **3.** like a monster **4.** horrible; hideous **5.** hideously evil —**mon′strous·ly** *adv.* —**mon′strous·ness** *n.*

mon·tage (män täzh′) *n.* [Fr. < *monter,* MOUNT²] **1.** *a)* the art or process of making a composite picture from a number of different pictures *b)* a picture so made **2.** *Motion Pictures* a rapid sequence of photographic images, often superimposed

Mon·taigne (män tān′), **Mi·chel** (mē shel′) 1533–92; Fr. essayist

Mon·tan·a (män tan′ə) State of the NW U.S., one of the Mountain States: 147,138 sq. mi.; pop. 694,000; cap. Helena: abbrev. **Mont., MT** —**Mon·tan′an** *adj., n.*

Mon·te Car·lo (män′ti kär′lō) town in Monaco: gambling resort: pop. 9,500

Mon·ter·rey (män′tə rā′) city in NE Mexico: pop. 1,012,000

Mon·tes·so·ri method (or **system**) (män′tə sôr′ē) [< Maria *Montessori* (1870–1952), It. educator] a method of teaching young children, emphasizing training of the senses

Mon·te·vid·e·o (män′tə vi dā′ō) capital of Uruguay: pop. 1,204,000

Mon·te·zu·ma II (män′tə zōō′mə) 1479?–1520; Aztec emperor of Mexico (1502–20)

Mont·gom·er·y (mənt gum′ər ē, mänt-) capital of Ala.: pop. 133,000

month (munth) *n.* [OE. *monath*] **1.** any of the twelve divisions of the calendar year **2.** a period of four weeks or 30 days **3.** one twelfth of the solar year

month′ly *adj.* **1.** continuing for a month **2.** done, happening, payable, etc. every month *n., pl.* **-lies** a periodical published once a month —*adv.* once a month; every month

Mon·ti·cel·lo (män′tə sel′ō, -chel′ō) home of Thomas Jefferson, in C Va.

Mont·mar·tre (môn mär′tr′) district in Paris, in N part, famous as an artists' quarter

Mont·pel·ier (mänt pēl′yər) capital of Vt.: pop. 9,000

Mont·re·al (män′trē ôl′) seaport in SW Quebec, on an island in the St. Lawrence River: pop. 1,222,000 (met. area 2,437,000)

mon·u·ment (män′yə mənt) *n.* [< L. *monere,* remind] **1.** something set up to keep alive the memory of a person or event, as a tablet, statue, etc. **2.** a work of enduring significance

mon′u·men′tal (-men′t′l) *adj.* **1.** of or serving as a monument **2.** like a monument; massive, enduring, etc. **3.** of lasting importance **4.** great; colossal *[monumental pride]*

moo (mōō) *n., pl.* **moos** [echoic] the vocal sound made by a cow —*vi.* **mooed, moo′ing** to make this sound; low

mooch (mōōch) *vi., vt.* [ult. < OFr. *muchier,* to hide] [Slang] to get (food, money, etc.) by begging or sponging —**mooch′er** *n.*

mood¹ (mōōd) *n.* [OE. *mod,* mind] **1.** a particular state of mind or feeling **2.** a prevailing feeling or tone **3.** *[pl.]* fits of sullen or uncertain temper

mood² (mōōd) *n.* [< MODE] *Gram.* that aspect of verbs which indicates whether the action or state expressed is a fact (*indicative mood*), supposition (*subjunctive mood*), or command (*imperative mood*)

mood′y *adj.* **-i·er, -i·est** subject to or characterized by gloomy or changing moods —**mood′i·ly** *adv.* —**mood′i·ness** *n.*

moon (mōōn) *n.* [OE. *mona*] **1.** the satellite of the earth, that revolves around it once in 29 1/2 days and shines by reflected sunlight **2.** anything shaped like the moon (i.e., an orb or crescent) **3.** any satellite of a planet —*vi.* to behave in an idle or abstracted way —*vt.* to pass (time) in mooning

moon′beam′ *n.* a ray of moonlight

moon′calf′ *n.* an idiot or fool

moon′light′ *n.* the light of the moon —*adj.* **1.** of moon-

light **2.** lighted by the moon **3.** done or occurring by moonlight, or at night

moon′light′ing *n.* the practice of holding a second regular job, as at night, in addition to one's main job

moon′lit′ *adj.* lighted by the moon

moon′quake′ *n.* a trembling of the moon's surface, as because of internal rock shifting or meteorite impact

moon′shine′ *n.* **1.** the light of the moon **2.** foolish talk, notions, etc. **3.** [Colloq.] whiskey unlawfully made or smuggled

moon′shin′er *n.* [Colloq.] a person who makes and sells alcoholic liquor unlawfully

moon′shot′ *n.* the launching of a rocket to the moon

moon′stone′ *n.* a translucent feldspar with a pearly luster, used as a gem

moon′struck′ *adj.* **1.** crazed; lunatic **2.** romantically dreamy **3.** dazed

moon′y *adj.* **-i·er, -i·est** listless; dreamy

Moor (mōōr) *n.* a member of a Muslim people living in NW Africa: they invaded Spain in the 8th cent. A.D. —**Moor′ish** *adj.*

moor¹ (mōōr) *n.* [OE. *mor*] [Brit.] a tract of open, rolling wasteland, usually covered with heather and often marshy

moor² (mōōr) *vt.* [< ? MDu. *maren,* to tie] **1.** to hold (a ship, etc.) in place by cables or chains as to a pier or buoy **2.** to secure —*vi.* **1.** to moor a ship, etc. **2.** to be secured

moor′ing *n.* **1.** *[often pl.]* the lines, cables, etc. by which a ship is moored **2.** *[pl.]* a place where a ship is moored

moose (mōōs) *n., pl.* **moose** [< AmInd.] the largest animal of the deer family, native to the N U.S. and Canada: the male has huge antlers

moot (mōōt) *adj.* [OE. (*ge*)*mot,* a meeting] **1.** debatable **2.** hypothetical —*vt.* to debate or discuss

moot court a mock court in which hypothetical cases are tried as an exercise for law students

mop (mäp) *n.* [< ? L. *mappa,* napkin] **1.** a bundle of rags, a sponge, etc. at the end of a stick, as for washing floors **2.** anything suggesting this, as a thick head of hair —*vt.* **mopped, mop′ping** to wash, wipe, or remove as with a mop —**mop up** [Colloq.] to finish

MOOSE
(4 1/2–6 ft. high
at shoulder)

mope (mōp) *vi.* **moped, mop′ing** [akin to MDu. *mopen*] to be gloomy and apathetic —*n.* one who mopes **2.** *[pl.]* low spirits —**mop′ey, mop′y, mop′ish** *adj.*

mop·pet (mäp′it) *n.* [< ?] [Colloq.] a little child: a term of affection

mo·raine (mə rān′) *n.* [Fr. < *morre,* a muzzle] a mass of rocks, sand, etc. deposited by a glacier

mor·al (môr′əl, mär′-) *adj.* [< L. *mos,* pl. *mores,* morals] **1.** dealing with, or able to distinguish between, right and wrong conduct **2.** of, teaching, or in accordance with, the principles of right and wrong **3.** good in conduct or character; specif., sexually virtuous **4.** involving sympathy without action *[moral* support] **5.** virtually such because of its effects *[a moral* victory] **6.** based on strong probability *[a moral* certainty] —*n.* **1.** a moral lesson taught by a fable, event, etc. **2.** *[pl.]* principles or standards with respect to right and wrong in conduct; ethics —**mor′al·ly** *adv.*

mo·rale (mə ral′, mô-) *n.* [Fr.] moral or mental condition with respect to courage, discipline, confidence, etc.

mor·al·ist *n.* **1.** one who moralizes **2.** one who adheres to a system of moral teaching —**mor′al·is′tic** *adj.*

mo·ral·i·ty (mə ral′ə tē, mô-) *n., pl.* **-ties 1.** rightness or wrongness, as of an action **2.** a being in accord with moral principles; virtue **3.** principles of right and wrong in conduct; ethics **4.** moral instruction

morality play a kind of allegorical drama of the 15th and 16th cent., with Everyman, Vice, etc. as characters

mor·al·ize (môr′ə līz′, mär′-) *vi.* **-ized′, -iz′ing** [< Fr.] to consider or discuss moral matters, often in a self-righteous way —*vt.* **1.** to draw a moral from **2.** to improve the morals of —**mor′al·i·za′tion** *n.* —**mor′al·iz′er** *n.*

mo·rass (mə ras′, mô-) *n.* [< Du. < Frank. *marisk*] a bog; swamp

mor·a·to·ri·um (môr′ə tôr′ē əm) *n., pl.* **-ri·ums, -ri·a** (-ə) [< L. *mora,* a delay] **1.** a legal authorization to delay payment of money due **2.** the effective period of such an authorization **3.** any authorized delay or stopping of a specified activity

Mo·ra·vi·a (mô rā′vē ə) region in C Czechoslovakia —**Mo·ra′vi·an** *adj., n.*

mo·ray (môr′ā) *n.* [< Port. < Gr. *myraina*] a voracious, brilliantly colored eel: in full, **moray eel**

mor·bid (môr′bid) *adj.* [< L. *morbus*, disease] **1.** of or caused by disease; diseased **2.** having or showing an interest in gruesome matters **3.** gruesome; horrible —**morbid′i·ty**, **mor′bid·ness** *n.* —**mor′bid·ly** *adv.*

mor·dant (môr′d'nt) *adj.* [< L. *mordere*, to bite] **1.** caustic or sarcastic **2.** acting as a mordant —*n.* **1.** a substance used in dyeing to fix the colors **2.** an acid used in etching lines in a surface —**mor′dan·cy** *n.*

more (môr) *adj. superl.* MOST [OE. *mara*] **1.** greater in amount or degree: compar. of MUCH **2.** greater in number: compar. of MANY **3.** additional *[take more tea]* —*n.* **1.** a greater amount or degree **2.** [*with pl. v.*] a greater number (*of*) **3.** something additional [*more* can be said] —*adv. superl.* MOST **1.** in or to a greater degree or extent **2.** in addition —**more or less 1.** somewhat **2.** approximately

more·o·ver (-ō′vər) *adv.* in addition to what has been said; besides

mo·res (môr′ēz, -āz) *n.pl.* [L., customs] folkways that, through general observance, develop the force of law

mor·ga·nat·ic (môr′gə nat′ik) *adj.* [< OHG. *morgengeba*, morning gift (to one's bride, in lieu of a dower)] designating or of a marriage in which a man of royalty or nobility marries a woman of lower social status without giving her or their offspring any claim to his rank or property

morgue (môrg) *n.* [Fr.] **1.** a place where the bodies of unknown dead or those dead of unknown causes are temporarily kept **2.** a newspaper office's reference file of back numbers, pictures, etc.

mor·i·bund (môr′ə bund′) *adj.* [< L. *mori*, die] **1.** dying **2.** coming to an end

Mor·mon (môr′mən) *n.* a member of the Church of Jesus Christ of Latter-day Saints, founded in the U.S. in 1830 by Joseph Smith —*adj.* of the Mormons or their religion —**Mor′mon·ism** *n.*

morn (môrn) *n.* [OE. *morne*] [Poet.] morning

morn·ing (môr′niŋ) *n.* [OE. *morgen*] **1.** the first or early part of the day, from midnight, or esp. dawn, to noon **2.** dawn —*adj.* in, of, or for morning

morning glory a twining annual vine with trumpet-shaped flowers

morning star a planet, esp. Venus, visible in the eastern sky before sunrise

Mo·ro (môr′ō) *n., pl.* **-ros, -ro** [Sp., Moor] a member of a group of Muslim Malay tribes living in the S Philippines

Mo·roc·co (mə räk′ō) kingdom in NW Africa: c.171,300 sq. mi.; pop. 15,102,000; cap. Rabat —*n.* [m-] a fine, soft leather made from goatskins —**Mo·roc′can** *adj., n.*

mo·ron (môr′än) *n.* [coined (1910) < Gr. *mōros*, foolish] **1.** a person who is mentally retarded to a mild degree: an obsolescent term **2.** a very stupid person —**mo·ron′ic** *adj.*

mo·rose (mə rōs′) *adj.* [< L. *mos*, manner] gloomy, sullen, etc. —**mo·rose′ly** *adv.* —**mo·rose′ness** *n.*

mor·pheme (môr′fēm) *n.* [< Fr. < Gr. *morphē*, form] the smallest meaningful language unit, as a base, affix, or inflectional ending

Mor·pheus (môr′fē əs) *Gr. Myth.* the god of dreams

mor·phine (môr′fēn) *n.* [< G. or Fr. < MORPHEUS] a bitter, white or colorless alkaloid derived from opium and used in medicine to relieve pain

mor·phol·o·gy (môr fäl′ə jē) *n.* [< G. < Gr. *morphē*, form + -LOGY] **1.** the branch of biology dealing with the form and structure of animals and plants **2.** the branch of linguistics dealing with the internal structure and forms of words —**mor′pho·log′i·cal** (-fə läj′i k'l) *adj.*

mor·row (mär′ō, môr′ō) *n.* [< OE. *morgen*, morning] [Poet.] **1.** morning **2.** the next day

Morse (môrs), **Samuel F. B.** 1791–1872; U.S. inventor of the telegraph

Morse (code) (môrs) [after S. MORSE] [*often* m-] a code, or alphabet, consisting of a system of dots and dashes, used in telegraphy, etc.

mor·sel (môr′s'l) *n.* [< L. *morsum*, a bite] **1.** a small bite or portion of food **2.** a small amount

mor·tal (môr′t'l) *adj.* [< L. *mors*, death] **1.** that must eventually die **2.** of man as a being who must die **3.** of this world **4.** of death **5.** causing death; fatal **6.** to the death *[mortal combat]* **7.** very intense *[mortal terror]* **8.** *R.C.Ch.* so serious as to cause death of the soul *[a mortal sin]* —*n.* a human being —**mor′tal·ly** *adv.*

mor·tal·i·ty (môr tal′ə tē) *n.* **1.** the mortal nature of man **2.** death on a large scale, as from war **3.** the proportion of deaths to population; death rate

mor·tar (môr′tər) *n.* [< L. *mortarium*] **1.** a bowl in which substances are pulverized with a pestle **2.** [< Fr.] a short-barreled cannon which hurls shells in a high trajectory **3.** a mixture of cement or lime with sand and water, used between bricks or stones, or as plaster

mor′tar·board′ *n.* **1.** a square board with a handle beneath, for carrying mortar **2.** an academic cap with a square, flat top, worn as at commencements

mort·gage (môr′gij) *n.* [< OFr. *mort*, dead + *gage*, pledge] **1.** the pledging of property to a creditor as security for the payment of a debt **2.** the deed by which this is done —*vt.* **-gaged, -gag·ing 1.** to pledge (property) by a mortgage **2.** to put an advance claim on *[he mortgaged his future]* —**mort′ga·gor, mort′-gag·er** *n.*

mort·ga·gee (môr′gə jē′) *n.* a person to whom property is mortgaged

mor·ti·cian (môr tish′ən) *n.* [< L. *mors*, death] *same as* FUNERAL DIRECTOR

mor·ti·fi·ca·tion (môr′tə fi kā′shən) *n.* **1.** a mortifying or being mortified; specif., *a*) the control of physical desires by self-denial, fasting, etc. *b*) shame, humiliation, etc. **2.** something causing shame, humiliation, etc. **3.** [Now Rare] gangrene

mor·ti·fy (môr′tə fī′) *vt.* **-fied′, -fy′ing** [< L. *mors*, death + *facere*, to make] **1.** to control (physical desires) by self-denial, fasting, etc. **2.** to shame, humiliate, etc. —*vi.* [Now Rare] to become gangrenous

mor·tise (môr′tis) *n.* [< Ar. *murtazza*, joined] a notch or hole cut, as in a piece of wood, to receive a projecting part (*tenon*) shaped to fit —*vt.* **-tised, -tis·ing** to join securely, esp. with a mortise and tenon

mor·tu·ar·y (môr′choo wer′ē) *n., pl.* **-ies** [< L. *mortuus*, dead] a place where dead bodies are kept before burial or cremation, as a funeral home —*adj.* **1.** of the burial of the dead **2.** of death

mos. months

Mo·sa·ic (mō zā′ik) *adj.* of Moses or the writings, principles, etc. attributed to him

mo·sa·ic (mō zā′ik) *n.* [< L. *musivus*, artistic < *musa*, MUSE] **1.** the making of pictures or designs by inlaying small bits of colored stone, glass, etc. in mortar **2.** a picture or design so made **3.** anything resembling this —*adj.* of or resembling a mosaic

Mosaic law the ancient Hebrew law, ascribed to Moses and contained mainly in the Pentateuch

Mos·cow (mäs′kou, -kō) capital of the U.S.S.R. & the R.S.F.S.R., in W R.S.F.S.R.: pop. 6,942,000

Mo·ses (mō′ziz) *Bible* the leader who brought the Israelites out of slavery in Egypt and who received the Ten Commandments from God

mo·sey (mō′zē) *vi.* [< var. of VAMOOSE] [Slang] **1.** to amble along **2.** to go away

Mos·lem (mäz′ləm, muz′-, mäs′-) *n., adj. var. of* MUSLIM

mosque (mäsk) *n.* [ult. < Ar. *sajada*, pray] a Muslim place of worship

mos·qui·to (mə skēt′ō) *n., pl.* **-toes, -tos** [Sp. & Port. < L. *musca*, a fly] a two-winged insect, the female of which bites animals and sucks their blood: some varieties transmit malaria and yellow fever

moss (môs, mäs) *n.* [OE. *mos*, a swamp] a very small, green plant growing in velvety clusters on rocks, moist ground, etc. —**moss′y** *adj.*

most (mōst) *adj. compar.* MORE [OE. *mast*] **1.** greatest in amount or degree: superl. of MUCH **2.** greatest in number: superl. of MANY **3.** in the greatest number of instances —*n.* **1.** the greatest amount or degree **2.** [*with pl. v.*] the greatest number (*of*) —*adv. compar.* MORE in or to the greatest degree or extent —**at (the) most** not more than —**make the most of** to take the fullest advantage of

-most [OE. *-mest*] *a suffix used in forming superlatives [foremost, hindmost]*

most′ly *adv.* **1.** for the most part; mainly **2.** chiefly; principally **3.** usually; generally

mot (mō) *n.* [Fr., a word] a witty remark

mote (mōt) *n.* [OE. *mot*] a speck, as of dust

mo·tel (mō tel′) *n.* [MO(TORIST) + (HO)TEL] a hotel for those traveling by car, with an accessible parking area

moth (môth) *n., pl.* **moths** (môthz, môths) [OE. *moththe*] a four-winged, chiefly night-flying insect related to the butterfly but usually smaller and less brightly colored; specif., a moth (**clothes moth**) whose larvae eat holes in woolens, furs, etc.

moth'ball' (-bôl') *n.* a small ball of naphthalene, the fumes of which repel moths, as from woolens, furs, etc. —**in mothballs** put into storage or reserve

moth'-eat'en *adj.* **1.** gnawed away in patches by moths, as cloth **2.** worn-out **3.** outdated

moth·er¹ (mu*th*'ər) *n.* [OE. *modor*] **1.** a female parent **2.** that which is the origin, source, or nurturer of something **3.** *a)* a woman having the responsibility and authority of a mother *b)* a woman who is the head (**mother superior**) of a religious establishment —*adj.* **1.** of or like a mother **2.** native [*mother tongue*] —*vt.* **1.** to be the mother of **2.** to care for as a mother does —**moth'er·hood'** *n.* —**moth'er·less** *adj.*

moth·er² (mu*th*'ər) *n.* [< MDu. *moeder*] same as MOTHER OF VINEGAR

Mother Car·ey's chicken (ker'ēz) [< ?] any of various oceanic petrels; esp., same as STORMY PETREL (sense 1)

Mother Goose the imaginary creator of a collection of English nursery rhymes

moth'er-in-law' (-ən lô') *n., pl.* **moth'ers-in-law'** the mother of one's husband or wife

moth'er·land' *n.* one's native land

mother lode the main vein of ore in a region

moth'er·ly *adj.* of, like, or befitting a mother; maternal —**moth'er·li·ness** *n.*

moth'er-of-pearl' *n.* the hard, pearly internal layer of the shell of the pearl oyster, etc., used to make buttons, etc.; nacre —*adj.* of mother-of-pearl

mother of vinegar [see MOTHER²] a stringy, gummy, slimy substance formed by bacteria in vinegar or on the surface of fermenting liquids

Mother's Day the second Sunday in May, a day set aside (in the U.S.) in honor of mothers

mother tongue 1. one's native language **2.** a language from which another derives

mo·tif (mō tēf') *n.* [Fr.: see MOTIVE] **1.** a theme or subject that is repeated with various changes, as in a piece of music, a book, etc. **2.** a repeated figure in a design

mo·tile (mōt'l) *adj.* [< L. *movere*, to move] *Biol.* capable of or exhibiting spontaneous motion

mo·tion (mō'shən) *n.* [< L. *movere*, to move] **1.** a moving from one place to another **2.** a moving of a part of the body; specif., a gesture **3.** a proposal formally made in an assembly —*vi.* to make a meaningful movement of the hand, etc. —*vt.* to direct by a meaningful gesture —**go through the motions** to do something in a mechanical way —**in motion** moving —**mo'tion·less** *adj.*

motion picture 1. a sequence of photographs or drawings projected on a screen in such rapid succession as to create the illusion of moving persons and objects **2.** a play, etc. in this form

mo·ti·vate (mōt'ə vāt') *vt.* **-vat'ed, -vat'ing** to provide with, or affect as, a motive; incite —**mo'ti·va'tion** *n.*

mo·tive (mōt'iv) *n.* [< L. *movere*, to move] **1.** an inner drive, impulse, etc. that causes one to act; incentive **2.** same as MOTIF —*adj.* of or causing motion

-motive a suffix meaning moving, of motion [*locomotive*]

mot·ley (mät'lē) *adj.* [< ?] **1.** of many colors **2.** of many different elements [*a motley group*]

mo·tor (mōt'ər) *n.* [L. < *movere*, to move] **1.** anything that produces motion **2.** an engine; esp., an internal-combustion engine **3.** a machine for converting electrical energy into mechanical energy —*adj.* **1.** producing motion **2.** of or powered by a motor **3.** of, by, or for motor vehicles **4.** for motorists [*a motor inn*] **5.** designating or of a nerve carrying impulses from the central nervous system to a muscle producing motion **6.** of or involving muscular movements —*vi.* to travel by automobile

mo'tor·boat' *n.* a boat propelled by a motor

mo'tor·cade' (-kād') *n.* [MOTOR + (CAVAL)CADE] a procession of automobiles

mo'tor·car' *n.* same as AUTOMOBILE

mo'tor·cy'cle (-sī'k'l) *n.* a two-wheeled vehicle propelled by an internal-combustion engine —*vi.* **-cled, -cling** to ride a motorcycle —**mo'tor·cy'clist** *n.*

motor hotel same as MOTEL: also **motor court, motor inn, motor lodge**

mo'tor·ist *n.* one who drives an automobile or travels by automobile

mo·tor·ize (mōt'ə rīz') *vt.* **-ized', -iz'ing 1.** to equip with motor-driven vehicles **2.** to equip (a vehicle, etc.) with a motor —**mo'tor·i·za'tion** *n.*

mo'tor·man (-mən) *n., pl.* **-men** one who drives an electric railway car or electric locomotive

motor vehicle a vehicle on wheels having its own motor, as an automobile or bus

mot·tle (mät''l) *vt.* **-tled, -tling** [< MOTLEY] to mark with blotches or streaks of different colors —*n.* a mottled pattern, as of marble —**mot'tled** *adj.*

mot·to (mät'ō) *n., pl.* **-toes, -tos** [It., a word] a word or saying that expresses one's aims, ideals, or guiding rule

mould (mōld) *n., vt., vi. chiefly Brit. sp.* of MOLD (all terms and senses) —**mould'y** *adj.* **-i·er, -i·est**

mould'er *vi. chiefly Brit. sp.* of MOLDER

moult (mōlt) *n., vt., vi. chiefly Brit. sp.* of MOLT

mound (mound) *n.* [< ? MDu. *mond*, protection] a heap or bank of earth, sand, etc., whether built or natural; small hill —*vt.* to heap up in a mound

Mound Builders the early Indian peoples who built burial mounds and earthworks found in the Middle West and the Southeast

mount¹ (mount) *n.* [< L. *mons*] a mountain or hill: now poetic or [M-] before a proper name [*Mount McKinley*]

mount² (mount) *vi.* [< L. *mons*, mountain] **1.** to climb; ascend **2.** to climb up on something, as a horse **3.** to increase in amount —*vt.* **1.** to go up; ascend [*to mount stairs*] **2.** to get up on (a horse, platform, etc.) **3.** to set on or provide with a horse **4.** to fix (a jewel, picture, etc.) on or in the proper support, backing, setting, etc. **5.** to arrange (a dead animal, etc.) for exhibition **6.** *a)* to place (a gun) into position for use *b)* to be armed with [*this ship mounts six cannon*] **7.** to post (a guard) or go on (guard) as a sentry —*n.* **1.** the act of mounting **2.** a horse, bicycle, etc. for riding **3.** the support, setting, etc. on or in which a thing is mounted —**mount'a·ble** *adj.*

moun·tain (moun't'n) *n.* [< L. *mons*] **1.** a natural raised part of the earth, larger than a hill **2.** [*pl.*] a chain or group of such elevations: also **mountain chain, mountain range 3.** a large pile, heap, amount, etc. —*adj.* **1.** of or in mountains **2.** like a mountain

mountain ash a small tree with clusters of white flowers and, later, orange berries

moun'tain·eer' (-ir') *n.* **1.** one who lives in a mountainous region **2.** a mountain climber —*vi.* to climb mountains, as for sport

mountain goat same as ROCKY MOUNTAIN GOAT

mountain laurel an evergreen shrub of E N. America, with pink and white flowers

mountain lion same as COUGAR

moun'tain·ous (-əs) *adj.* **1.** full of mountains **2.** like a mountain; esp., very large

mountain sheep any of various wild sheep found in mountain regions; esp., same as BIGHORN

Mountain State any of the eight States of the W U.S. through which the Rocky Mountains pass

moun·te·bank (moun'tə baŋk') *n.* [< It. *montare*, to mount + *in*, on + *banco*, a bench] **1.** orig., one who sold quack medicines in a public place **2.** any charlatan, or quack —*vi.* to act as a mountebank

mount'ed *adj.* provided with a horse, vehicle, support, etc. [*mounted police*]

Mount·ie, Mount·y (moun'tē) *n., pl.* **-ies** [Colloq.] a member of the Royal Canadian Mounted Police

mount'ing *n.* something serving as a backing, support, setting, etc.

Mount Ver·non (vur'nən) home of George Washington, in N Va., on the Potomac

mourn (môrn) *vi., vt.* [OE. *murnan*] **1.** to feel or express sorrow for (something regrettable) **2.** to grieve for (someone dead) —**mourn'er** *n.*

mourn'ful *adj.* **1.** feeling or expressing grief or sorrow **2.** causing sorrow; melancholy —**mourn'ful·ly** *adv.* —**mourn'ful·ness** *n.*

mourn'ing *n.* **1.** a sorrowing; specif., the expression of grief at someone's death, or the period of this **2.** black clothes, etc., worn as a sign of grief —*adj.* of or expressing mourning

mourning dove a gray, wild dove of the U.S.: so called because of its cooing, regarded as mournful

mouse (mous) *n., pl.* **mice** [OE. *mus*] **1.** any of numerous small rodents, esp. the **house mouse** which infests human dwellings **2.** a timid person **3.** [Slang] a dark, swollen bruise under the eye —*vi.* (mouz) **moused, mous'ing 1.** to hunt for mice **2.** to search for something busily and stealthily

mous·er (mou'zər, -sər) *n.* a cat, dog, etc. with reference to its ability to catch mice

mousse (mōōs) *n.* [Fr., foam] a light chilled or frozen food made with egg white, whipped cream, etc., often combined with fruit or flavoring for dessert

mous·tache (mə stash', mus'tash) *n. var. of* MUSTACHE

mous·y, mous·ey (mou′sē, -zē) *adj.* **-i·er, -i·est 1.** quiet, timid, etc. **2.** infested with mice

mouth (mouth) *n., pl.* **mouths** (mou*th*z) [OE. *muth*] **1.** the opening through which an animal takes in food and through which sounds are uttered **2.** any opening regarded as like the mouth *[the mouth of a river]* —*vt.* (mou*th*) **1.** to say, esp. in an insincere manner **2.** to form (a word) with the mouth soundlessly **3.** to rub with the mouth or lips —**down in** (or **at**) **the mouth** [Colloq.] depressed; unhappy

-mouthed *a combining form meaning* having a (specified kind of) mouth, voice, etc. *[loudmouthed]*

mouth′ful′ *n., pl.* **-fuls′ 1.** as much as the mouth can hold **2.** the usual amount taken into the mouth **3.** a small amount **4.** [Slang] a pertinent remark: chiefly in **say a mouthful**

mouth organ *same as* HARMONICA

mouth′part′ *n.* any of various structures or organs around the mouth in arthropods, used for biting, grasping, etc.: *usually used in pl.*

mouth′piece′ *n.* **1.** a part placed at, or forming, a mouth **2.** the part of a musical instrument held in or to the mouth **3.** a person, periodical, etc. used by others to express their views **4.** [Slang] a criminal's lawyer

mouth′wash′ *n.* a flavored liquid used for rinsing the mouth or gargling

mouth·y (mou′*th*ē, -*th*ē) *adj.* **-i·er, -i·est** overly talkative, esp. in a bombastic or rude way

mou·ton (mōō′tän) *n.* [Fr., sheep] lambskin, processed to resemble beaver, seal, etc.

mov·a·ble (mōō′və b'l) *adj.* **1.** that can be moved from one place to another **2.** changing in date from one year to the next *[movable holidays]* —*n.* **1.** something movable **2.** *[usually pl.] Law* personal property, as furniture Also **move′a·ble** —**mov′a·bil′i·ty** *n.* —**mov′a·bly** *adv.*

move (mōōv) *vt.* **moved, mov′ing** [< L. *movere*] **1.** to change the place or position of **2.** to set or keep in motion **3.** to cause (*to act, do, say,* etc.) **4.** to arouse the emotions, etc. of **5.** to propose formally, as in a meeting —*vi.* **1.** to change place or position **2.** to change one's residence **3.** to be active **4.** to make progress **5.** to take action **6.** to be, or be set, in motion **7.** to make a formal application (*for*) **8.** to evacuate: said of the bowels **9.** [Colloq.] to depart *[let's move on]* **10.** *Commerce* to be sold: said of goods —*n.* **1.** the act of moving **2.** an action toward some goal **3.** a change of residence **4.** *Chess, Checkers,* etc. the act of moving or one's turn to move —**on the move** [Colloq.] moving from place to place

move′ment (-mənt) *n.* **1.** a moving or manner of moving **2.** an evacuation (of the bowels) **3.** a change in the location of troops, ships, etc. **4.** organized action by people working toward some goal **5.** a tendency **6.** the progress of events in a literary work **7.** the effect of motion in painting, sculpture, etc. **8.** the moving parts of a mechanism, as of a clock **9.** *Music a)* any of the principal divisions of an extended composition *b) same as* RHYTHM

mov′er *n.* one that moves; specif., one whose work is moving furniture, etc. for those changing residence

mov·ie (mōō′vē) *n.* [< MOVING PICTURE] **1.** a motion picture **2.** a motion-picture theater —**the movies 1.** the motion-picture industry **2.** a showing of a motion picture

mov′ing *adj.* **1.** changing, or causing to change, place or position **2.** causing motion or action **3.** stirring the emotions **4.** involving a moving motor vehicle *[a moving violation (of a traffic law)]*

moving picture *same as* MOTION PICTURE

mow[1] (mō) *vt., vi.* **mowed, mowed** or **mown, mow′ing** [OE. *mawan*] to cut down (grass, etc.) from (a lawn, etc.) as with a sickle or lawn mower —**mow down 1.** to cause to fall like cut grass **2.** to kill or destroy —**mow′er** *n.*

mow[2] (mou) *n.* [OE. *muga*] **1.** a heap of hay, grain, etc., esp. in a barn **2.** the part of a barn where hay or grain is stored

Mo·zam·bique (mō′zəm bēk′) country on the SE coast of Africa: 302,300 sq. mi.; pop. 7,274,000

Mo·zart (mō′tsärt), **Wolf·gang A·ma·de·us** (vôlf′gäŋk′ ä′mä dā′ōos) 1756–91; Austrian composer

moz·za·rel·la (mät′sə rel′ə) *n.* [It.] a soft, white, mild-flavored Italian cheese

MP, M.P. Military Police

M.P. 1. Member of Parliament **2.** Mounted Police

M.P., m.p. melting point

mpg, m.p.g. miles per gallon

mph, m.p.h. miles per hour

Mr. (mis′tər) *pl.* **Messrs.** (mes′ərz) mister: used before the name or title of a man

Mrs. (mis′iz) *pl.* **Mmes.** (mā däm′) mistress: used as a title before the name of a married woman

MS 1. Mississippi **2.** multiple sclerosis

MS., ms., ms *pl.* **MSS., mss., mss** manuscript

Ms. (miz, em′es′) a title, free of reference to marital status, used before the name of a woman in place of either *Miss* or *Mrs.*

M.S., M.Sc. Master of Science

Msgr. Monsignor

MSgt, M/Sgt. Master Sergeant

MST, M.S.T. Mountain Standard Time

MT Montana

Mt., mt. *pl.* **mts. 1.** mount **2.** mountain

M.T. metric ton

mu (myōō, mōō) *n.* the twelfth letter of the Greek alphabet (M, μ)

much (much) *adj.* **more, most** [OE. *mycel*] great in quantity, degree, etc. —*adv.* **more, most 1.** to a great degree or extent *[much* happier] **2.** nearly *[much* the same] —*n.* **1.** a great amount *[much* of it] **2.** something great, outstanding, etc. *[not much* to look at] —**make much of** to treat or consider as of great importance —**much′ness** *n.*

mu·ci·lage (myōō′s'l ij) *n.* [< L. *mucere,* be moldy] **1.** a thick, sticky substance produced in certain plants **2.** any watery solution of gum, glue, etc. used as an adhesive

mu·ci·lag·i·nous (myōō′sə laj′ə nəs) *adj.* **1.** of or like mucilage; sticky **2.** producing mucilage

muck (muk) *n.* [< ? ON. *myki,* dung] **1.** moist manure **2.** black earth containing decaying matter, used as fertilizer **3.** dirt; filth —*vt.* **1.** to fertilize with muck **2.** [Colloq.] to dirty as with muck —**muck′y** *adj.* **-i·er, -i·est**

muck′rake′ (-rāk′) *vi.* **-raked′, -rak′ing** [see MUCK & RAKE[1]] to search for and expose corruption in politics, business, etc. —**muck′rak′er** *n.*

mu·cous (myōō′kəs) *adj.* **1.** of, containing, or secreting mucus **2.** slimy

mucous membrane a mucus-secreting membrane lining body cavities and canals, as the mouth, etc., connecting with the external air

mu·cus (myōō′kəs) *n.* [L.] the slimy secretion that moistens and protects the mucous membranes

mud (mud) *n.* [prob. < a LowG. source] wet, soft, sticky earth

mud·dle (mud′'l) *vt.* **-dled, -dling** [< MUD] **1.** to mix up; bungle **2.** to confuse, as with liquor —*vi.* to act or think in a confused way —*n.* mess, confusion, etc.

mud′dler (-lər) *n.* a stick to stir mixed drinks

mud′dy (-ē) *adj.* **-di·er, -di·est 1.** full of or spattered with mud **2.** cloudy *[muddy* coffee] **3.** confused, obscure, etc. —*vt., vi.* **-died, -dy·ing** to make or become muddy —**mud′di·ness** *n.*

mud hen any of various birds that live in marshes, as the coot

mud′sling′ing *n.* unscrupulous attacks against an opponent, as in politics —**mud′sling′er** *n.*

Muen·ster (mun′stər, mōōn′-) *n.* [< *Munster,* France] a semisoft, mild cheese

mu·ez·zin (myōō ez′in) *n.* [< Ar. *adhana,* proclaim] a Muslim crier who calls the people to prayer at the proper hours

muff (muf) *n.* [Du. *mof* < Fr. *moufle,* mitten] **1.** a cylindrical covering of fur, etc. for keeping the hands warm **2.** *a) Baseball,* etc. a failure to hold the ball when catching it *b)* any bungling action —*vt., vi.* to do (something) badly or awkwardly

muf·fin (muf′in) *n.* [< ?] a quick bread baked in a small, cup-shaped mold and usually eaten hot

muf·fle (muf′'l) *vt.* **-fled, -fling** [prob. < OFr. *moufle,* mitten] **1.** to wrap so as to hide, keep warm, etc. **2.** to cover so as to deaden sound **3.** to deaden (a sound)

muf′fler (-lər) *n.* **1.** a scarf worn around the throat, as for warmth **2.** a device for silencing noises, as a section in the exhaust pipe of an internal-combustion engine

MUFFLER

muf·ti (muf′tē) *n., pl.* **-tis** [Ar. < *āftā,* to judge] **1.** in Muslim countries, an interpreter of religious law **2.** ordinary clothes, not a uniform

mug (mug) *n.* [prob. < Scand.] **1.** a cup of earthenware or metal, with a handle **2.** as much as a mug will hold **3.** [Slang] *a)* the face *b)* the mouth —*vt.* **mugged, mug′ging 1.** to assault, esp. from behind and usually with intent to rob **2**. [Slang] to photograph, as for police records —**vi**. [Slang] to grimace, esp. in overacting —**mug′ger** n.

mug·gy (mug′ē) adj. **-gi·er, -gi·est** [< ? ON. *mugga*, a drizzle] hot, damp, and close [*muggy* weather] —**mug′gi·ness** n.

mug·wump (mug′wump′) n. [< Algonquian *mugquomp*, chief] an independent, esp. in politics

Muk·den (mook′dən, mook den′) *former name of* SHENYANG

mu·lat·to (mə lat′ō, myoo-) n., pl. **-toes** [Sp. & Port. *mulato*, of mixed breed] **1**. a person who has one black parent and one white parent **2**. popularly, any person with mixed Negro and Caucasoid ancestry

mul·ber·ry (mul′ber′ē, -bər ē) n., pl. **-ries** [OE. *morberie*] **1**. any of several trees with edible fruits resembling the raspberry **2**. this fruit **3**. purplish red

mulch (mulch) n. [ME. *molsh*, soft] leaves, peat, etc., spread on the ground around plants to prevent freezing of roots, etc. —**vt**. to apply mulch to

mulct (mulkt) vt. [< L. *multa*, a fine] **1**. to fine **2**. to extract (money) from (someone), as by fraud —n. a fine

mule¹ (myool) n. [< L. *mulus*] **1**. the (usually sterile) offspring of a male donkey and a female horse **2**. a machine that spins cotton fibers into yarn **3**. [Colloq.] a stubborn person

mule² (myool) n. [Fr. < L. *mulleus*, red shoe] a lounging slipper that does not cover the heel

mule deer a long-eared deer of the western U.S.

mule skinner [Colloq.] a driver of mules

mu·le·teer (myoo′lə tir′) n. [< OFr.] a driver of mules

mul′ish adj. like a mule; stubborn

mull¹ (mul) vt., vi. [ME. *mullen*, to grind] [Colloq.] to ponder (*over*)

mull² (mul) vt. [< ?] to heat, sweeten, and flavor with spices (ale, cider, wine, etc.)

mul·lein (mul′in) n. [< L. *mollis*, soft] a tall plant with spikes of yellow, lavender, or white flowers

mul·let (mul′it) n. [< L. *mullus*] any of a group of edible, spiny-rayed fishes found in fresh and salt waters; specif., the striped (or gray) **mullet**

mul·li·gan (stew) (mul′i g'n) [< ?] [Slang] a stew made of odd bits of meat and vegetables

mul·li·ga·taw·ny (mul′i gə tô′nē) n. [Tamil *milagutannir*, pepper water] an East Indian soup of meat, etc., flavored with curry

mul·lion (mul′yən) n. [prob. < L. *medianus*, middle] a slender, vertical dividing bar between the lights of windows, panels, etc.

multi- [L. < *multus*, much, many] *a combining form meaning:* **1**. having many **2**. more than two **3**. many times more than Also **mult-**

mul·ti·far·i·ous (mul′tə far′ē əs, -fer′-) adj. [< L.] having many kinds of parts or elements

mul·ti·form (mul′tə fôrm′) adj. having many forms, shapes, etc.

mul·ti·lat·er·al (mul′ti lat′ər əl) adj. **1**. many-sided **2**. involving more than two nations, etc. [a *multilateral* treaty] — **mul′ti·lat′er·al·ly** adv.

MULLIONS

mul′ti·mil′lion·aire′ n. a person whose wealth amounts to many millions of dollars, francs, etc.

mul·ti·par·tite (-pär′tīt) adj. **1**. divided into many parts **2**. same as MULTILATERAL (sense 2)

mul·ti·ple (mul′tə p'l) adj. [Fr. < L. *multus*, many + -*plex*, -fold] **1**. having many parts, elements, etc. **2**. *Elec*. designating a circuit with two or more conductors in parallel —n. a number that is a product of some specified number and another number

multiple sclerosis a disease in which there is damage to the central nervous system: it is marked by speech defects, lack of coordination, etc.

mul′ti·plex′ (-pleks′) adj. [L.] **1**. multiple **2**. designating or of a system for transmitting or receiving simultaneously two or more messages or signals over a common circuit, carrier wave, etc.

mul·ti·pli·cand (mul′tə pli kand′) n. a number that is to be multiplied by another

mul′ti·pli·ca′tion (-pli kā′shən) n. a multiplying or being multiplied; specif., the process of finding the quantity obtained by repeating a specified quantity a specified number of times

mul′ti·plic′i·ty (-plis′ə tē) n. **1**. a being manifold or various **2**. a great number

mul′ti·pli′er (-plī′ər) n. **1**. one that multiplies **2**. the number by which another is to be multiplied

mul·ti·ply (mul′tə plī′) vt., vi. **-plied′, -ply′ing** [see MULTIPLE] **1**. to increase in number, degree, etc. **2**. to find the product (of) by multiplication

mul·ti·stage (mul′ti stāj′) adj. having several propulsion systems, used and discarded in sequence: said of a rocket or missile

mul·ti·tude (mul′tə tood′, -tyood′) n. [< L. *multus*, many] **1**. a large number; host, myriad, etc. **2**. the masses (preceded by *the*)

mul′ti·tu′di·nous (-tood′'n əs, -tyood′-) adj. very numerous; many

mul·ti·va·lent (mul′ti vā′lənt) adj. *Chem*. same as POLYVALENT

mum¹ (mum) n. [Colloq.] a chrysanthemum

mum² (mum) adj. [< L. *momme*] silent; not speaking — **mum's the word** say nothing

mum·ble (mum′b'l) vt., vi. **-bled, -bling** [ME. *momelen*] to speak or say indistinctly —n. a mumbled utterance — **mum′bler** n.

mum·ble·ty·peg (mum′b'l tē peg′) n. a game in which a jackknife is tossed in various ways to make it land with the blade in the ground

mum·bo jum·bo (mum′bō jum′bō) [of Afr. orig.] **1**. an idol or fetish **2**. meaningless ritual, etc.

mum·mer (mum′ər) n. [< OFr. *momo*, echoic for grimace] **1**. one who wears a mask or disguise, as for acting out pantomimes **2**. any actor

mum′mer·y n., pl. **-ies 1**. performance by mummers **2**. a hypocritical show or ceremony

mum·mi·fy (mum′ə fī′) vt., vi. **-fied′, -fy′ing** to make or become a mummy

mum·my (mum′ē) n., pl. **-mies** [ult. < Per. *mum*, wax] a well-preserved dead body, esp. one preserved by embalming, as by the ancient Egyptians

mumps (mumps) n.pl. [*with sing*. v.] [pl. of obs. *mump*, a grimace] an acute communicable disease, caused by a virus and characterized by swelling of the salivary glands

mun. municipal

munch (munch) vt., vi. [echoic] to chew steadily, often with a crunching sound

mun·dane (mun dān′, mun′dān) adj. [< L. *mundus*, world] **1**. of the world; worldly **2**. commonplace; everyday

Mu·nich (myoo′nik) city in West Germany; capital of Bavaria: pop. 1,244,000

mu·nic·i·pal (myoo nis′ə p'l) adj. [< L. *munia*, official duties + *capere*, to take] of or having to do with a city, town, etc. or its local government —**mu·nic′i·pal·ly** adv.

mu·nic′i·pal′i·ty (-pal′ə tē) n., pl. **-ties** a city, town, etc. having its own incorporated government

mu·nif·i·cent (myoo nif′ə s'nt) adj. [< L. *munus*, a gift + *facere*, to make] very generous in giving; lavish —**mu·nif′i·cence** n. —**mu·nif′i·cent·ly** adv.

mu·ni·tions (myoo nish′ənz) n.pl. [< L. *munire*, fortify] war supplies; esp., weapons and ammunition

mu·ral (myoor′əl) adj. [Fr. < L. *murus*, a wall] **1**. of, on, or for a wall **2**. like a wall —n. a picture or photograph, esp. a large one, painted or applied directly on a wall — **mu′ral·ist** n.

mur·der (mur′dər) n. [OE. *morthor*] the unlawful and malicious or premeditated killing of a person —**vt**. **1**. to kill unlawfully and with malice **2**. to botch, as in performance [she *murdered* that song] —**vi**. to commit murder —**mur′der·er** n. —**mur′der·ess** n.fem.

mur′der·ous (-əs) adj. **1**. of or characteristic of murder; brutal **2**. capable or guilty of, or intending, murder — **mur′der·ous·ly** adv.

mu·ri·at·ic acid (myoor′ē at′ik) [< L. *muria*, brine] hydrochloric acid: a commercial term

Mu·ril·lo (moo rē′lyō; E. myoo ril′ō), **Bar·to·lo·mé** (bär′tô lô me′) 1617–82; Sp. painter

murk (murk) n. [< ON. *myrkr*, dark] darkness; gloom

murk′y adj. **-i·er, -i·est 1**. dark or gloomy **2**. heavy and obscure with smoke, mist, etc. —**murk′i·ness** n.

mur·mur (mur′mər) n. [< L.: echoic word] **1**. a low, indistinct, continuous sound, as of a stream, far-off voices, etc. **2**. a mumbled complaint **3**. *Med*. an abnormal sound in the body, esp. in the region of the heart —**vi**. to make a murmur —**vt**. to say in a murmur —**mur′mur·ing** adj.

Mur·phy bed (mur′fē) [after W. L. *Murphy*, its U.S. inventor (c.1900)] a bed that swings up or folds into a closet when not in use

mur·rain (mur′in) n. [< L. *mori*, to die] **1**. any of various infectious diseases of cattle **2**. [Archaic] a pestilence; plague

mus. 1. museum **2**. music **3**. musical

mus·cat (mus′kət, -kat) n. [Fr. < LL. *muscus*, musk] a sweet European grape

mus·ca·tel (mus'kə tel') *n.* **1.** a rich, sweet wine made from the muscat **2.** *same as* MUSCAT

mus·cle (mus''l) *n.* [Fr. < L. *mus,* mouse] **1.** any body organ consisting of fibrous tissue that can be contracted and expanded to produce bodily movements **2.** this tissue **3.** muscular strength; brawn —*vi.* **-cled, -cling** [Colloq.] to force one's way (*in*)

mus'cle-bound' *adj.* having some of the muscles enlarged and less elastic, as from too much exercise

Mus·co·vy (mus'kə vē) *former name of* RUSSIA —**Mus'co·vite'** ('-vīt') *n., adj.*

mus·cu·lar (mus'kyə lər) *adj.* **1.** of or done by muscles **2.** having well-developed muscles; strong —**mus'cu·lar'i·ty** (-lar'ə tē) *n.* —**mus'cu·lar·ly** *adv.*

muscular dys·tro·phy (dis'trə fē) [< DYS- + Gr. *trephein,* nourish] a chronic disease characterized by a progressive wasting of the muscles

mus·cu·la·ture (mus'kyə lə chər) *n.* [Fr.] the arrangement of the muscles of a body or of some part of the body; muscular system

Muse (myōoz) *n.* [< Gr. *mousa*] **1.** *Gr. Myth.* any of the nine goddesses who presided over literature and the arts and sciences **2.** [m-] the spirit regarded as inspiring a poet or artist

muse (myōoz) *vi.* mused, mus'ing [< OFr. *muser,* to loiter] to think deeply; meditate —*vt.* to think or say meditatively

mu·se·um (myōo zē'əm) *n.* [ult. < Gr. *mousa,* Muse] a building, room, etc. for preserving and exhibiting artistic, historical, or scientific objects

mush¹ (mush) *n.* [prob. var. of MASH] **1.** a thick porridge of boiled cornmeal **2.** any thick, soft mass **3.** [Colloq.] maudlin sentimentality —**mush'y** *adj.* **-i·er, -i·est**

mush² (mush) *interj.* [? < Fr. *marchons,* let's go] a shout to urge on sled dogs —*vi.* to travel on foot over snow, usually with a dog sled

mush·room (mush'rōom') *n.* [< LL. *mussirio*] any of various fleshy fungi, typically with a stalk capped by an umbrellalike top; esp., any edible variety —*adj.* of or like a mushroom —*vi.* **1.** to grow or spread rapidly **2.** to flatten out at the end so as to resemble a mushroom

mu·sic (myōo'zik) *n.* [< Gr. *mousikē* (*technē*), (art) of the Muses] **1.** the art of combining tones in varying melody, harmony, etc. to form expressive compositions **2.** such compositions **3.** any rhythmic sequence of pleasing sounds, as of birds —**face the music** [Colloq.] to accept the consequences —**set to music** to compose music for (a poem, etc.)

mu·si·cal *adj.* **1.** of or for music **2.** melodious or harmonious **3.** fond of or skilled in music **4.** set to music —*n.* a light play or movie with dialogue, songs, and dances: often **musical comedy** —**mu'si·cal·ly** *adv.*

mu·si·cale (myōo'zə kal') *n.* [Fr.] a party or social affair featuring a musical program

music box a mechanical musical instrument containing a bar with tuned steel teeth that are struck by pins on a revolving cylinder so as to produce a tune

music hall **1.** an auditorium for musical productions **2.** [Brit.] a vaudeville theater

mu·si·cian (myōo zish'ən) *n.* one skilled in music; esp., a professional performer —**mu·si'cian·ship'** *n.*

mu·si·col·o·gy (myōo'zi käl'ə jē) *n.* the study of the science, history, and methods of music —**mu'si·col'o·gist** *n.*

mus·ing (myōo'ziŋ) *adj.* that muses; meditative —*n.* meditation; reflection

musk (musk) *n.* [< Sans. *mus,* mouse] **1.** a substance having a strong odor, obtained from the musk deer: used in making perfumes **2.** the odor of this substance —**musk'i·ness** *n.* —**musk'y** *adj.* **-i·er, -i·est**

musk deer a small, hornless deer of central Asia

mus·kel·lunge (mus'kə lunj') *n., pl.* **-lunge'** [< Ojibwa] a large pike of the cooler fresh waters of N. America: also called **mus'kie** (-kē)

mus·ket (mus'kit) *n.* [< L. *musca,* a fly] a former shoulder firearm, with a smooth bore

mus·ket·eer (mus'kə tir') *n.* a soldier armed with a musket

mus'ket·ry *n.* **1.** the skill of firing muskets and other small arms **2.** muskets or musketeers, collectively

musk'mel'on *n.* any of various sweet, juicy melons, as the cantaloupe

musk ox a hardy ox of arctic America and Greenland with a shaggy coat and long horns

musk·rat (musk'rat') *n.* **1.** a N. American water rodent with brown fur and a musky odor **2.** its fur

Mus·lim (muz'ləm, mōoz'-, mōos'-) *n.* [< Ar. < *aslama,* resign oneself (to God)] an adherent of Islam —*adj.* of Islam or the Muslims

mus·lin (muz'lin) *n.* [< Fr. < *Mosul,* city in Iraq] a strong cotton cloth; esp., a heavy kind used for sheets, etc.

muss (mus) *vt.* [prob. var. of MESS] to make messy or disordered; disarrange —**muss'y** *adj.* **-i·er, -i·est**

MUSKRAT
(16–24 in. long, including tail)

mus·sel (mus''l) *n.* [ult. < L. *musculus*] any of various saltwater or freshwater bivalve mollusks

Mus·so·li·ni (mōos'ə lē'nē), **Be·ni·to** (bə nē'tō) 1883–1945; Fascist dictator of Italy (1922–43): executed

must¹ (must) *v.aux. pt.* must [< OE. *moste*] an auxiliary expressing: **1.** necessity [I *must* go] **2.** probability [it *must* be Joe] **3.** certainty [all *must* die] —*n.* [Colloq.] something that must be done, had, etc. [this book is a *must*]

must² (must) *n.* [< L. *mustum,* new wine] the juice pressed from grapes, etc. before it has fermented

mus·tache (mə stash', mus'tash) *n.* [< Fr. < Gr. *mastax,* mouth] the hair on the upper lip of men

mus·ta·chio (məs tä'shō) *n., pl.* **-chios** [< Sp. or It.] a mustache

mus·tang (mus'taŋ) *n.* [< Sp. *mesteño,* strayed] a small wild horse of the SW plains

mus·tard (mus'tərd) *n.* [< OFr.] **1.** any of several plants with yellow flowers and slender pods **2.** the yellow powder made from its ground seeds, often used in paste form as a condiment **3.** a dark yellow

mustard gas [< its mustardlike odor] a volatile liquid used as a poison gas in war

mustard plaster a plaster made with powdered mustard, applied to the skin as a poultice

mus·ter (mus'tər) *vt.* [< L. *monere,* to warn] **1.** to assemble (troops, etc.) **2.** to collect; summon [to *muster* up strength] —*vi.* to assemble, as troops —*n.* **1.** an assembling, as of troops for inspection **2.** the persons or things assembled —**muster in** (or **out**) to enlist in (or discharge from) military service —**pass muster** to measure up to the required standards

must·n't (mus''nt) must not

mus·ty (mus'tē) *adj.* **-ti·er, -ti·est** [< ? MOIST] **1.** having a stale, moldy smell or taste **2.** stale or trite; antiquated —**mus'ti·ness** *n.*

mu·ta·ble (myōot'ə b'l) *adj.* [< L. *mutare,* to change] **1.** that can be changed **2.** inconstant; fickle —**mu'ta·bil'i·ty** *n.* —**mu'ta·bly** *adv.*

mu·tant (myōot''nt) *adj.* [see prec.] of mutation —*n.* an animal or plant with inheritable characteristics that differ from those of the parents

mu·tate (myōo'tāt) *vi., vt.* **-tat·ed, -tat·ing** [see MUTABLE] to change; specif., to undergo or cause to undergo mutation

mu·ta·tion (myōo tā'shən) *n.* **1.** a change, as in form, nature, etc. **2.** *a*) a sudden variation in some inheritable characteristic of an animal or plant *b*) a mutant

mute (myōot) *adj.* [< L. *mutus*] **1.** not speaking; silent **2.** unable to speak **3.** not pronounced; silent, as the *e* in *mouse* **4.** *Law* refusing to plead when arraigned —*n.* **1.** a deaf-mute **2.** a silent letter **3.** *Music* a device that softens the tone of an instrument —*vt.* **mut'ed, mut'ing** to soften the sound of —**mute'ly** *adv.* —**mute'ness** *n.*

mu·ti·late (myōot''l āt') *vt.* **-lat·ed, -lat·ing** [< L. *mutilus,* maimed] to cut off, damage, or spoil an important part of —**mu'ti·la'tion** *n.*

mu·ti·neer (myōot''n ir') *n.* one guilty of mutiny

mu·ti·ny (myōot''n ē) *n., pl.* **-nies** [ult. < L. *movere,* to move] revolt against constituted authority; esp., rebellion of soldiers or sailors against their officers —*vi.* **-nied, -ny·ing** to revolt —**mu'ti·nous** *adj.*

mutt (mut) *n.* [Slang] a mongrel dog

mut·ter (mut'ər) *vi., vt.* [ME. *moteren*] **1.** to speak or say in low, indistinct tones **2.** to grumble —*n.* **1.** a muttering **2.** something muttered

mut·ton (mut''n) *n.* [< ML. *multo,* sheep] the flesh of sheep, esp. a grown sheep, used as food

mutton chop 1. a piece cut from the rib of a sheep for broiling or frying **2.** [*pl.*] side whiskers shaped like mutton chops

mu·tu·al (myōō'choo wəl) *adj.* [< L. *mutare*, to change] **1.** *a*) done, felt, etc. by each of two or more for or toward the other or others [*mutual* admiration] *b*) of each other [*mutual* enemies] **2.** shared in common [our *mutual* friend] —**mu'tu·al·ly** *adv.*

mutual fund a corporation that invests its shareholders' funds in diversified securities

muu-muu (mōō'mōō) *n.* [Haw.] a long, loose dress of Hawaiian style

muz·zle (muz''l) *n.* [< ML. *musum*] **1.** the mouth, nose, and jaws of a dog, horse, etc. **2.** a device put over the mouth of an animal to prevent its biting or eating **3.** the front end of the barrel of a firearm —*vt.* **-zled, -zling 1.** to put a muzzle on (an animal) **2.** to prevent from talking

muz'zle·load'er *n.* any firearm loaded through the muzzle —**muz'zle·load'ing** *adj.*

my (mī) *possessive pronominal adj.* [OE. *min*] of, belonging to, or done by me —*interj.* an exclamation of surprise, dismay, etc.

my·ce·li·um (mī sē'lē əm) *n., pl.* **-li·a** (-ə) [< Gr. *mykēs*, a mushroom] the vegetative part of a fungus, made of a mass of threadlike tubes

my·col·o·gy (mī käl'ə jē) *n.* [see prec. & -LOGY] the branch of botany dealing with fungi

my·e·li·tis (mī'ə līt'is) *n.* [< Gr. *myelos*, marrow + -ITIS] inflammation of the spinal cord or the bone marrow

My·lar (mī'lär) *a trademark for* a polyester used for recording tapes, fabrics, etc. —*n.* [m-] this substance

my·na, my·nah (mī'nə) *n.* [Hindi *mainā*] any of a group of tropical birds of SE Asia related to the starling: some can mimic human speech

my·o·pi·a (mī ō'pē ə) *n.* [< Gr. *myein*, to close + *ōps*, eye] nearsightedness —**my·op'ic** (-äp'ik) *adj.*

myr·i·ad (mir'ē əd) *n.* [< Gr. *myrias*, ten thousand] a large number of persons or things —*adj.* very many

myr·i·a·pod (mir'ē ə päd') *n.* [see prec. & -POD] an arthropod with many legs, as the centipede

myr·mi·don (mur'mə dän', -dən) *n.* [< name of a Greek tribe led by Achilles] an unquestioning follower

myrrh (mur) *n.* [ult. < Ar. *murr*] a fragrant gum resin from Arabia and E Africa, used in incense, perfume, etc.

myr·tle (mur't'l) *n.* [< Gr. *myrtos*] **1.** an evergreen shrub with white or pink flowers and dark berries **2.** any of various other plants, as the periwinkle

my·self (mī self') *pron.* **1.** *the intensive form of* I [I myself went] **2.** *the reflexive form of* I [I hurt *myself*] **3.** my true self [I am not *myself* today]

mys·te·ri·ous (mis tir'ē əs) *adj.* of, containing, or characterized by mystery —**mys·te'ri·ous·ly** *adv.*

mys·ter·y (mis'tə rē, -trē) *n., pl.* **-ies** [< Gr. *mystērion*, secret rite] **1.** something unexplained, unknown, or kept secret **2.** a novel or play about a secret crime, etc. [a murder *mystery*] **3.** obscurity or secrecy **4.** [*pl.*] secret rites or doctrines known only to the initiated

mystery play any of a class of medieval dramatic representations of Biblical events

mys·tic (mis'tik) *adj.* [< Gr. *mystēs*, one initiated] **1.** *same as* MYSTICAL **2.** mysterious, secret, occult, awe-inspiring, etc. [*mystic* rites, *mystic* powers] —*n.* one professing to undergo profound spiritual experiences

mys'ti·cal *adj.* **1.** of mystics or mysticism **2.** spiritually significant or symbolic **3.** *same as* MYSTIC (sense 2) —**mys'ti·cal·ly** *adv.*

mys·ti·cism (mis'tə siz'm) *n.* **1.** the beliefs or practices of mystics **2.** the doctrine that knowledge of spiritual truths can be acquired by intuition and meditation **3.** obscure thinking or belief

mys'ti·fy' (-fī') *vt.* **-fied', -fy'ing 1.** *a*) to puzzle or perplex *b*) to bewilder deliberately **2.** to involve in mystery —**mys'ti·fi·ca'tion** *n.*

mys·tique (mis tēk') *n.* [Fr., mystic] the quasi-mystical attitudes and feelings surrounding some person, institution, activity, etc.

myth (mith) *n.* [< Gr. *mythos*] **1.** a traditional story serving to explain some phenomenon, custom, etc. **2.** mythology **3.** any fictitious story **4.** any imaginary person or thing —**myth'i·cal** *adj.*

my·thol·o·gy (mi thäl'ə jē) *n., pl.* **-gies 1.** the study of myths **2.** myths collectively; esp., the myths of a specific people —**myth·o·log·i·cal** (mith'ə läj'i k'l) *adj.* —**my·thol'·o·gist** *n.*

N

N, n (en) *n., pl.* **N's, n's** the fourteenth letter of the English alphabet

n (en) *n.* **1.** *Math.* the symbol for an indefinite number **2.** *Physics* the symbol for neutron

N *Chem.* nitrogen

N, N., n, n. 1. north **2.** northern

n. 1. net **2.** neuter **3.** noon **4.** noun **5.** number

Na [L. *natrium*] *Chem.* sodium

N.A. North America

NAACP, N.A.A.C.P. National Association for the Advancement of Colored People

nab (nab) *vt.* **nabbed, nab'bing** [prob. < dial. *nap*, to snatch] [Colloq.] **1.** to seize suddenly; snatch **2.** to arrest or catch (a felon or wrongdoer)

na·bob (nā'bäb) *n.* [< Ar. *nā'ib*, deputy] a very rich man

na·cre (nā'kər) *n.* [Fr. < Ar.] *same as* MOTHER-OF-PEARL

na·dir (nā'dər, -dir) *n.* [< Ar. *nazīr*, opposite] **1.** the point opposite the zenith and directly below the observer **2.** the lowest point

nae (nā) *adv.* [Scot.] no; not —*adj.* no

nag¹ (nag) *vt., vi.* **nagged, nag'ging** [< Scand.] **1.** to annoy by continual scolding, faultfinding, etc. **2.** to keep troubling [*nagged* by doubts] —*n.* one who nags: also **nag'ger**

nag² (nag) *n.* [ME. *nagge*] an inferior horse, esp. an old one

Na·ga·sa·ki (nä'gə sä'kē) seaport in SW Japan: partly destroyed (1945) by a U.S. atomic bomb: pop. 405,000

Na·go·ya (nä'gô yä') seaport in S Honshu, Japan: pop. 1,935,000

Na·hum (nā'əm, -həm) *Bible* **1.** a Hebrew prophet of the 7th cent. B.C. **2.** the book containing his prophecies: abbrev. **Nah.**

nai·ad (nā'ad, nī'-) *n.* [< Gr. *naein*, to flow] [*also* N-] *Gr. & Rom. Myth.* any nymph living in springs, rivers, etc.

na·if, na·ïf (nä ēf') *adj.* [Fr.] *same as* NAIVE

nail (nāl) *n.* [OE. *nægl*] **1.** *a*) the thin, horny substance growing out at the ends of fingers and toes *b*) a claw **2.** a slender, pointed piece of metal driven with a hammer to hold pieces of wood together —*vt.* **1.** to attach, fasten, etc. with nails **2.** to discover or expose (a lie, etc.) **3.** [Colloq.] to catch, capture, etc. **4.** [Colloq.] to hit squarely —**hit the nail on the head** to do or say whatever is exactly right

nail file a small file for shaping the fingernails

nain·sook (nān'sook) *n.* [< Hindi *nain*, the eye + *sukh*, pleasure] a thin, lightweight cotton fabric

Nai·ro·bi (nī rō'bē) capital of Kenya: pop. 479,000

na·ive, na·ïve (nä ēv') *adj.* [Fr. < L. *nativus*, natural] unaffectedly simple; artless; unsophisticated —**na·ive'ly, na·ïve'ly** *adv.* —**na·ive·té', na·ïve·té'** (-tā') *n.*

na·ked (nā'kid) *adj.* [OE. *nacod*] **1.** completely unclothed; nude **2.** without covering [a *naked* sword] **3.** without additions, disguises, etc.; plain [the *naked* truth] **4.** unaided by any optical device [the *naked* eye] —**na'ked·ly** *adv.* —**na'ked·ness** *n.*

nam·by-pam·by (nam'bē pam'bē) *adj.* [< nickname of *Ambrose Philips*, 18th-c. Eng. poet] weakly sentimental; insipid —*n., pl.* **-bies** a namby-pamby person

name (nām) *n.* [OE. *nama*] **1.** a word or phrase by which a person, thing, or class of things is known; title **2.** a word or phrase considered descriptive; epithet **3.** *a*) reputation *b*) good reputation **4.** appearance only, not reality [chief in *name* only] **5.** a famous person —*adj.* well-known —*vt.* **named, nam'ing 1.** to give a name to **2.** to designate by name **3.** to identify by the right name [*name* the oceans] **4.** to appoint to an office, etc. **5.** to specify (a day, price, etc.) —**call names** to swear at —**in the name of 1.** in appeal to **2.** by authority of —**to one's name** belonging to one —**nam′a·ble, name′a·ble** *adj.*

name′less *adj.* **1.** not having a name **2.** left unnamed **3.** not well known **4.** illegitimate **5.** indescribable **6.** too horrible to specify

name′ly *adv.* that is to say; to wit

name′sake′ *n.* a person with the same name as another, esp. if named after another

nan·keen, nan·kin (nan kēn′) *n.* [< ff.] a buff-colored, durable cotton cloth

Nan·king (nan′kiŋ′) city in E China, on the Yangtze River: pop. 2,700,000

nan·ny (nan′ē) *n., pl.* **-nies** [< *Nan,* dim. of *Ann(a)*] [Brit.] a child's nurse

nanny goat [see prec.] [Colloq.] a female goat

nano- [< Gr. *nanos,* dwarf] *a combining form meaning* one billionth part of [*nanosecond*]

Na·o·mi (nā ō′mē) *Bible* the mother-in-law of Ruth

nap[1] (nap) *vi.* **napped, nap′ping** [OE. *hnappian*] **1.** to sleep lightly for a short time **2.** to be careless or unprepared —*n.* a brief, light sleep

nap[2] (nap) *n.* [< or akin to MDu. & MLowG. *noppe*] the downy or hairy surface of cloth formed by short hairs or fibers

na·palm (nā′päm) *n.* [containing *na(phthene)* & *palm(itate)*] a jellylike substance with gasoline in it, used in flame throwers and fire bombs

nape (nāp) *n.* [ME.] the back of the neck

naph·tha (naf′thə, nap′-) *n.* [< Per. *neft,* pitch] a flammable liquid distilled from petroleum, coal tar, etc. and used as a fuel, solvent, etc.

naph′tha·lene′ (-lēn′) *n.* [< prec.] a white, crystalline hydrocarbon obtained from coal tar and used in moth repellents, certain dyes, etc.

nap·kin (nap′kin) *n.* [< L. *mappa,* cloth] **1.** a small cloth or piece of paper used while eating to protect the clothes or wipe the lips and fingers **2.** any small cloth, towel, etc.

Na·ples (nā′p′lz) seaport in SW Italy: pop. 1,236,000

na·po·le·on (nə pō′lē ən) *n.* [after ff.] **1.** a former gold coin of France **2.** a card game **3.** a layered pastry with a custardlike filling

Na·po·le·on I (nə pō′lē ən, -pōl′yən) (full Fr. name *Napoléon Bonaparte*) 1769–1821; Fr. military leader & emperor (1804–15) —**Na·po·le·on′ic** (-än′ik) *adj.*

narc, nark (närk) *n.* [Slang] a police agent who enforces laws dealing with narcotics

nar·cis·sism (när′sə siz′m) *n.* [< ff.] self-love —**nar′cis·sist** *n., adj.*

Nar·cis·sus (när sis′əs) *Gr. Myth.* a youth who fell in love with his own reflection in a pool and was changed into the narcissus —*n.* [n-] *pl.* **-cis′sus, -cis′sus·es, -cis′si** (-ī) a bulbous plant with white, yellow, or orange flowers

nar·co·sis (när kō′sis) *n.* unconsciousness caused by a narcotic

nar·co·syn·the·sis (när′kō sin′thə sis) *n.* a method of treating a neurosis by working with a patient while he is under the influence of a hypnotic drug

nar·cot·ic (när kät′ik) *n.* [< Gr. *narkē,* numbness] **1.** a drug, as opium, used to relieve pain and induce sleep **2.** anything with a soothing, lulling, or dulling effect —*adj.* **1.** of, like, or producing narcosis **2.** of, by, or for narcotic addicts

nar·co·tism (när′kə tiz′m) *n.* **1.** *same as* NARCOSIS **2.** addiction to narcotics

nar′co·tize′ (-tīz′) *vt.* **-tized′, -tiz′ing** to subject to a narcotic —**nar′co·ti·za′tion** *n.*

nar·es (ner′ēz) *n.pl. sing.* **nar′is** (-is) [L.] the nasal passages; esp., the nostrils

nar·ghi·le (när′gə lē′, -lā′) *n.* [< Per.] *same as* HOOKAH: also sp. **nar′gi·le′, nar′gi·leh′**

nar·rate (nar′āt, na rāt′) *vt., vi.* **-rat·ed, -rat·ing** [< L. *narrare,* relate] **1.** to tell (a story) **2.** to give an account of (events) —**nar′ra·tor** *n.*

nar·ra·tion (na rā′shən) *n.* **1.** a narrating **2.** *same as* NARRATIVE **3.** writing or speaking that narrates

nar·ra·tive (nar′ə tiv) *adj.* in story form —*n.* **1.** a story; account **2.** the art or practice of narrating

nar·row (nar′ō, ner′ō) *adj.* [OE. *nearu*] **1.** small in width; not wide **2.** limited in meaning, size, amount, etc. [a *narrow* majority] **3.** limited in outlook; not liberal **4.** close; careful [a *narrow* inspection] **5.** with barely enough space, time, etc. [a *narrow* escape] **6.** limited in means [*narrow* circumstances] —*vi., vt.* to decrease or limit in width, ex-

tent, or scope —*n.* [*usually pl.*] a narrow passage; strait —**nar′row·ly** *adv.* —**nar′row·ness** *n.*

nar′row-mind′ed *adj.* limited in outlook; bigoted; prejudiced —**nar′row-mind′ed·ness** *n.*

nar·whal (när′wəl) *n.* [ON. *nahvalr,* lit., corpse whale: from its white color] a small arctic whale valued for its oil and ivory: the male has a long spiral tusk: also **nar′wal** (-wəl), **nar′whale′** (-hwāl′)

nar·y (ner′ē) *adj.* [< *ne′er a,* never a] [Dial.] not any; no (with *a* or *an*) [*nary* a doubt]

NASA (nas′ə) National Aeronautics and Space Administration

na·sal (nā′z′l) *adj.* [< L. *nasus,* nose] **1.** of the nose **2.** produced by making breath go through the nose —*n.* a nasal sound —**na′sal·ly** *adv.*

NARWHAL
(body 11–16 ft. long; tusk to 9 ft. long)

na′sal·ize′ *vt., vi.* **-ized′, -iz′ing** to pronounce or speak with a nasal sound —**na′sal·i·za′tion** *n.*

nas·cent (nas′′nt, nā′s′nt) *adj.* [< L. *nasci,* be born] **1.** coming into being **2.** beginning to form or develop —**nas′cence, nas′cen·cy** *n.*

Nash·ville (nash′vil) capital of Tenn.: pop. 448,000

Nas·sau (nas′ô) capital of the Bahamas: pop. 81,000

na·stur·tium (nə stur′shəm) *n.* [< L. *nasus,* nose + *torquere,* to twist] **1.** a plant with red, yellow, or orange flowers and a pungent odor **2.** the flower

nas·ty (nas′tē) *adj.* **-ti·er, -ti·est** [< ?] **1.** very dirty; filthy **2.** nauseating **3.** morally offensive; obscene **4.** very unpleasant, mean, or harmful —**nas′ti·ly** *adv.* —**nas′ti·ness** *n.*

nat. 1. national **2.** native **3.** natural

na·tal (nāt′′l) *adj.* [< L. *nasci,* be born] of or connected with one's birth

na·ta·to·ri·um (nāt′ə tôr′ē əm) *n., pl.* **-ri·ums, -ri·a** (-ə) [LL.] a swimming pool

na·tes (nā′tēz) *n.pl.* [L.] the buttocks

na·tion (nā′shən) *n.* [< L. *nasci,* be born] **1.** a community of people with a territory, history, economic life, culture, and language in common **2.** the people of a territory united under a single government; country **3.** a people or tribe

na·tion·al (nash′ə n′l) *adj.* of or affecting a nation as a whole —*n.* a citizen of a nation —**na′tion·al·ly** *adv.*

national bank 1. a bank or system of banks owned and operated by a government **2.** in the U.S., a bank chartered by the Federal government and a member of a centralized banking system

National Guard in the U.S., the organized militia of individual States, part of the U.S. Army when called into active Federal service

na′tion·al·ism *n.* **1.** *a)* patriotism *b)* narrow, jingoist patriotism **2.** the putting of national interests above international considerations **3.** the advocacy of national independence —**na′tion·al·ist** *adj., n.* —**na′tion·al·is′tic** *adj.*

na·tion·al·i·ty (nash′ə nal′ə tē) *n., pl.* **-ties 1.** national character **2.** the status of belonging to a particular nation by birth or naturalization **3.** a national group, esp. of immigrants from some other country

na·tion·al·ize (nash′ə nə līz′) *vt.* **-ized′, -iz′ing 1.** to make national **2.** to transfer ownership or control of (land, industries, etc.) to the nation —**na′tion·al·i·za′tion** *n.*

National Weather Service the division of the Department of Commerce that gathers data on weather conditions, on which weather forecasts are based

na′tion·wide′ *adj.* by or through the whole nation

na·tive (nāt′iv) *adj.* [< L. *nasci,* be born] **1.** inborn; innate **2.** belonging to a locality or country by birth, production, or growth **3.** being, or associated with, the place of one's birth [one's *native* land or language] **4.** found in nature; natural **5.** of or characteristic of the people born in a certain place —*n.* **1.** a person born in the region indicated **2.** an original inhabitant **3.** an indigenous plant or animal **4.** a permanent resident, not a mere visitor —**go native** to adopt a simple way of life —**na′tive·ly** *adv.*

na′tive-born′ *adj.* born in a specified place or country

na·tiv·i·ty (nə tiv′ə tē) *n., pl.* -**ties** [see NATIVE] birth — **the Nativity** 1. the birth of Jesus 2. Christmas Day

natl. national

NATO (nā′tō) North Atlantic Treaty Organization

nat·ty (nat′ē) *adj.* -**ti·er**, -**ti·est** [< ? NEAT] trim and smart in appearance or dress *[a natty suit]* —**nat′ti·ly** *adv.* —**nat′ti·ness** *n.*

nat·u·ral (nach′ər əl, nach′rəl) *adj.* [< L. *naturalis*, by birth] 1. of or arising from nature 2. produced or existing in nature; not artificial 3. innate; not acquired 4. based on instinctive moral feeling *[natural rights]* 5. true to nature; lifelike 6. normal *[a natural result]* 7. customarily expected *[a natural courtesy]* 8. free from affectation 9. illegitimate *[a natural child]* 10. *Music* neither sharped nor flatted —*n.* 1. [Colloq.] a sure success 2. *Music a)* the sign (♮) canceling a preceding sharp or flat *b)* the note affected —**nat′u·ral·ness** *n.*

natural gas a mixture of gaseous hydrocarbons, chiefly methane, occurring naturally in the earth and conveyed through pipes to be used as fuel

natural history the study of the animal, vegetable, and mineral world, esp. in a popular way

nat′u·ral·ism *n.* 1. action or thought based on natural desires or instincts 2. *Literature, Art,* etc. faithful adherence to nature; realism

nat′u·ral·ist *n.* 1. one who studies animals and plants 2. one who believes in or practices naturalism —**nat′u·ral·is′tic** *adj.*

nat′u·ral·ize′ (-ə līz′) *vt.* -**ized′**, -**iz′ing** 1. to confer citizenship upon (an alien) 2. to adopt and make common (a custom, word, etc.) from another locality 3. to adapt (a plant or animal) to a new environment —**nat′u·ral·i·za′tion** *n.*

nat′u·ral·ly *adv.* 1. in a natural manner 2. by nature; innately 3. as one might expect; of course

natural resources the forms of wealth supplied by nature, as coal, oil, water power, etc.

natural science the systematized knowledge of nature, including biology, chemistry, physics, etc.

natural selection see DARWINIAN THEORY

na·ture (nā′chər) *n.* [< L. *nasci*, be born] 1. the quality or qualities that make something what it is; essence 2. inborn character, disposition, or tendencies 3. kind; sort 4. *a)* the entire physical universe *b) [sometimes* N-] the power, force, etc. that seems to regulate this 5. the primitive state of man 6. natural scenery —**by nature** inherently

-natured *a combining form meaning* having or showing a (specified kind of) nature, disposition, or temperament *[good-natured]*

Naug·a·hyde (nôg′ə hīd′) [arbitrary coinage] *a trademark for* a kind of imitation leather, used for upholstery —*n.* [n-] this material

naught (nôt) *n.* [< OE. *na wiht*, no person] 1. nothing 2. *Arith.* the figure zero (0)

naugh·ty (nôt′ē) *adj.* -**ti·er**, -**ti·est** [< obs. *naught*, wicked] 1. not behaving properly; disobedient 2. indelicate —**naugh′ti·ly** *adv.* —**naugh′ti·ness** *n.*

Na·u·ru (nä ōō′rōō) country on an island in the W Pacific: 8 sq. mi.; pop. 7,000

nau·se·a (nô′shə, -sē ə) *n.* [< Gr. *nausia*, seasickness] 1. a feeling of sickness at the stomach, with an urge to vomit 2. disgust

nau·se·ate (nô′shē āt′, -sē-, -zē-) *vt., vi.* -**at′ed**, -**at′ing** to feel or cause to feel nausea

nau·seous (nô′shəs, -zē əs) *adj.* 1. causing nausea; sickening 2. [Colloq.] feeling nausea

naut. nautical

nau·ti·cal (nôt′i k′l) *adj.* [< Fr. < Gr. *naus*, a ship] of sailors, ships, or navigation —**nau′ti·cal·ly** *adv.*

nautical mile an international unit of distance for sea and air navigation, equal to c.6,076 ft.

nau·ti·lus (nôt′′l əs) *n., pl.* -**lus·es**, -**li′** (-ī′) [< Gr. *naus*, a ship] a tropical mollusk with a many-chambered, spiral shell having a pearly interior

Nav·a·ho, Nav·a·jo (nav′ə hō′) *n., pl.* -**hos′**, -**ho′**, -**hoes′** a member of a tribe of Indians now living in Arizona, New Mexico, and Utah

na·val (nā′v′l) *adj.* [< L. *navis*, a ship] of, having, characteristic of, or for a navy, its ships, etc.

Na·varre (nə vär′) region in NE Spain & SW France: formerly a kingdom

NAUTILUS
(shell to 10 in. in diameter)

nave (nāv) *n.* [< L. *navis*, a ship] the main part of a church, from the chancel to the main entrance

na·vel (nā′v′l) *n.* [OE. *nafela*] the small depression in the middle of the abdomen, where the umbilical cord was attached to the fetus

navel orange a seedless orange having a navellike depression containing a small, secondary fruit

nav·i·ga·ble (nav′i gə b′l) *adj.* 1. wide or deep enough to be traveled on by ships 2. that can be steered —**nav′i·ga·bil′i·ty** *n.*

nav·i·gate (nav′ə gāt′) *vt., vi.* -**gat′ed**, -**gat′ing** [< L. *navis*, a ship + *agere*, to lead] 1. to steer or direct (a ship or aircraft) 2. to travel through or over (water, air, etc.) in a ship or aircraft

nav′i·ga′tion (-gā′shən) *n.* a navigating; esp., the science of locating the position and plotting the course of ships and aircraft —**nav′i·ga′tion·al** *adj.*

nav′i·ga′tor *n.* one skilled in the navigation of a ship or aircraft

na·vy (nā′vē) *n., pl.* -**vies** [< L. *navis*, a ship] 1. all the warships of a nation 2. [often N-] the entire sea force of a nation, including its vessels, personnel, etc. 3. very dark blue: also **navy blue**

navy bean [from use in U.S. *Navy*] a small, white variety of kidney bean

nay (nā) *adv.* [< ON. *ne*, not + *ei*, ever] not only that, but beyond that *[he is well-off, nay rich]* —*n.* 1. a refusal or denial 2. a negative vote or voter

Naz·a·rene (naz′ə rēn′, naz′ə rēn′) *adj.* of Nazareth or the Nazarenes —*n.* a native or inhabitant of Nazareth — **the Nazarene** Jesus

Naz·a·reth (naz′ər əth) town in N Israel

Na·zi (nät′sē) *adj.* [G., contr. of the party name] designating or of the German fascist political party that ruled Germany under Hitler (1933–45) —*n.* 1. a member of this party 2. [often n-] a supporter of this party or its ideology; fascist —**Na′zism** (-siz′m), **Na′zi·ism** (-sē iz′m) *n.*

Nb *Chem.* niobium

N.B. New Brunswick

N.B., n.b. [L. *nota bene*] note well

N.C., NC North Carolina

NCO, N.C.O. noncommissioned officer

Nd *Chem.* neodymium

N.D., n.d. no date

N.Dak., ND North Dakota

Ne *Chem.* neon

NE Nebraska

NE, N.E., n.e. 1. northeast 2. northeastern

N.E. New England

Ne·an·der·thal (nē an′dər thôl′, -täl′) *adj.* [< a G. valley where remains were found] designating or of a form of primitive man of the paleolithic period

neap (nēp) *adj.* [OE. *nep-* in *nepflod*, neap tide] designating either of the two lowest monthly tides

Ne·a·pol·i·tan (nē′ə päl′ə t′n) *adj.* of Naples —*n.* a native or inhabitant of Naples

near (nir) *adv.* [OE. *near*, nearer, compar. of *neah*, nigh] 1. at a short distance in space or time 2. almost; nearly *[near* right] 3. closely; intimately —*adj.* 1. close in distance or time 2. close in relationship; akin 3. close in friendship; intimate 4. close in degree *[a near* escape] 5. short or direct *[the near* way] 6. approximating *[near* beer] —*prep.* close to in space, time, degree, etc. —*vt., vi.* to draw near (to); approach —**near at hand** very close in time or space —**near′ness** *n.*

near′by′ *adj., adv.* near; close at hand

Near East 1. countries near the E end of the Mediterranean, including those of SW Asia, NE Africa, &, sometimes, the Balkans 2. [Brit.] the Balkans

near′ly *adv.* almost; not quite

near′sight′ed *adj.* seeing only near objects distinctly; myopic —**near′sight′ed·ly** *adv.* —**near′sight′ed·ness** *n.*

neat (nēt) *adj.* [< L. *nitere*, to shine] 1. trim; tidy; clean and orderly 2. skillful and precise 3. unmixed; straight 4. well-proportioned; shapely 5. cleverly phrased or done; adroit 6. [Slang] nice, pleasing, etc. —**neat′ly** *adv.* —**neat′ness** *n.*

'neath, neath (nēth) *prep.* [Poet.] beneath

neat's-foot oil (nēts′foot′) a light-yellow oil obtained from the shinbones and feet of cattle, used as a dressing for leather

Ne·bras·ka (nə bras′kə) Middle Western State of the U.S.: 77,227 sq. mi.; pop. 1,484,000; cap. Lincoln: abbrev. **Nebr., NE** —**Ne·bras′kan** *adj., n.*

Neb·u·chad·nez·zar (neb′yə kəd nez′ər, neb′ə-) ?-562 B.C.; king of Babylonia (605?–562) who conquered Jerusalem: also **Neb′u·chad·rez′zar** (-rez′ər)

neb·u·la (neb′yə lə) *n., pl.* **-lae′** (-lē′), **-las** [< L., fog] any of the cloudlike patches in the sky consisting of gaseous matter, far distant stars, or external galaxies —**neb′u·lar** *adj.*

neb′u·lous (-ləs) *adj.* **1.** of or like a nebula **2.** unclear; vague; indefinite —**neb′u·lous·ly** *adv.*

nec·es·sar·i·ly (nes′ə ser′ə lē, nes′ə ser′-) *adv.* **1.** because of necessity **2.** as a necessary result

nec′es·sar′y (-ser′ē) *adj.* [< L. *ne-,* not + *cedere,* give way] **1.** essential; indispensable **2.** inevitable **3.** required **4.** that follows logically; undeniable —*n., pl.* **-ies** a thing necessary to life, some purpose, etc.

ne·ces·si·tate (nə ses′ə tāt′) *vt.* **-tat′ed, -tat′ing 1.** to make (something) necessary **2.** to compel

ne·ces·si·tous (nə ses′ə təs) *adj.* needy; destitute

ne·ces′si·ty (-tē) *n., pl.* **-ties** [see NECESSARY] **1.** natural causation; fate **2.** what is required by custom, law, etc. **3.** great need **4.** something that cannot be done without **5.** poverty —**of necessity** necessarily

neck (nek) *n.* [OE. *hnecca*] **1.** that part of a man or animal joining the head to the body **2.** that part of a garment nearest the neck **3.** a necklike part; specif., *a)* a narrow strip of land *b)* the narrowest part of a bottle, vase, etc. *c)* a strait —*vt., vi.* [Slang] to kiss and caress in making love —**neck and neck** very close, as in a contest —**risk one's neck** to put one's life, career, etc. in danger

neck′band′ *n.* **1.** a band worn around the neck **2.** the part of a garment that encircles the neck

neck·er·chief (nek′ər chif, -chēf′) *n.* a kerchief worn around the neck

neck′lace (-lis) *n.* [NECK + LACE, *n.* 1] an ornamental chain of gold, beads, etc. worn around the neck

neck′tie′ *n.* a decorative band for the neck, tied in front in a slipknot or bow

neck′wear′ *n.* articles worn about the neck, as neckties, scarfs, etc.

necro- [< Gr. *nekros,* dead body] *a combining form meaning* death, corpse

ne·crol·o·gy (ne kräl′ə jē) *n., pl.* **-gies** [see prec. & -LOGY] a list of people who have died

nec·ro·man·cy (nek′rə man′sē) *n.* [< Gr. *nekros,* corpse + *manteia,* divination] **1.** divination by alleged communication with the dead **2.** sorcery —**nec′ro·man′cer** *n.*

ne·cro·sis (ne krō′sis) *n., pl.* **-ses** (-sēz) [< Gr. *nekros,* dead body] the death or decay of tissue in a part of a living body or plant —**ne·crot′ic** (-krät′ik) *adj.*

nec·tar (nek′tər) *n.* [< Gr. *nektar,* lit., that overcomes death] **1.** *Gr. Myth.* the drink of the gods **2.** any very delicious beverage **3.** the sweetish liquid in many flowers, made into honey by bees

nec·tar·ine (nek′tə rēn′, nek′tə rēn′) *n.* [< prec.] a smooth-skinned variety of peach

nee, née (nā; *now often* nē) *adj.* [Fr.] born: used to introduce the maiden name of a married woman *[*Mrs. Helen Jones, *nee* Smith*]*

need (nēd) *n.* [OE. *nied*] **1.** necessity **2.** lack of something desired or required *[the need of a rest]* **3.** something required or desired *[one's daily needs]* **4.** *a)* a time or condition when help is required *[a friend in need] b)* poverty; want —*vt.* to have need of; require *Need* is often used as an auxiliary followed by an infinitive with or without *to,* meaning "to be obliged, must" *[he need not come, he needs to be careful]* —*vi.* to be in need —**have need to** to be compelled to —**if need be** if it is required

need′ful *adj.* necessary; required

nee·dle (nēd′'l) *n.* [OE. *nædl*] **1.** a slender, sharp-pointed piece of steel with a hole for thread, used for sewing **2.** *a)* a slender, hooked rod of steel, bone, etc. for crocheting *b)* a similar but hookless rod for knitting **3.** a short, pointed piece of metal, etc. that moves in phonograph-record grooves to transmit vibrations **4.** the pointer of a compass, gauge, etc. **5.** the thin, short leaf of the pine, spruce, etc. **6.** the sharp, slender metal tube at the end of a hypodermic syringe **7.** a needlelike structure or part —*vt.* **-dled, -dling** [Colloq.] **1.** to goad; provoke **2.** to tease or heckle

nee′dle·point′ *n.* **1.** lace made on a paper pattern with a needle **2.** an embroidery of woolen threads on canvas, as in tapestry

need′less *adj.* not needed; unnecessary —**need′less·ly** *adv.* —**need′less·ness** *n.*

nee′dle·work′ *n.* work done with a needle; sewing or fancywork

need′n't (-'nt) need not

needs (nēdz) *adv.* [OE. *nedes*] of necessity; necessarily (with *must*) *[he must needs obey]*

need·y (nēd′ē) *adj.* **-i·er, -i·est** in need; very poor; destitute —**need′i·ness** *n.*

ne′er (ner) *adv.* [Poet.] never

ne′er′-do-well′ *n.* a shiftless, irresponsible person —*adj.* lazy, worthless, etc.

ne·far·i·ous (ni fer′ē əs) *adj.* [< L. *ne-,* not + *fas,* lawful] very wicked —**ne·far′i·ous·ly** *adv.*

neg. **1.** negative **2.** negatively

ne·gate (ni gāt′) *vt.* **-gat′ed, -gat′ing** [< L. *negare,* deny] **1.** to deny the existence or truth of **2.** to make ineffective

ne·ga·tion (ni gā′shən) *n.* **1.** a denying; denial **2.** the lack or opposite of something positive

neg·a·tive (neg′ə tiv) *adj.* [see NEGATE] **1.** expressing denial or refusal; saying "no" **2.** opposite to or lacking what is positive *[a negative personality]* **3.** *Elec. a)* of electricity predominating in a body of resin that has been rubbed with wool *b)* charged with negative electricity *c)* having an excess of electrons **4.** *Math.* designating a quantity less than zero, or one to be subtracted **5.** *Med.* not indicating the presence of symptoms, bacteria, etc. **6.** *Photog.* reversing the relation of light and shade of the original subject —*n.* **1.** a word, phrase, etc. expressing denial, rejection, etc. **2.** the point of view opposing the affirmative **3.** the plate in a voltaic battery where the lower potential is **4.** *Math.* a negative quantity **5.** *Photog.* an exposed and developed negative film from which positive prints are made —*vt.* **-tived, -tiv·ing 1.** *a)* to refuse *b)* to veto **2.** to deny —**in the negative** in refusal or denial of a plan, etc. —**neg′a·tive·ly** *adv.* —**neg′a·tive·ness, neg′a·tiv′i·ty** *n.*

neg′a·tiv·ism (-iz'm) *n. Psychol.* an attitude characterized by ignoring or opposing suggestions or orders from others —**neg′a·tiv·ist** *n., adj.* —**neg′a·tiv·is′tic** *adj.*

neg·lect (ni glekt′) *vt.* [< L. *neg-,* not + *legere,* to gather] **1.** to ignore or disregard **2.** to fail to attend to properly **3.** to leave undone —*n.* **1.** a neglecting or being neglected **2.** lack of proper care

neg·lect′ful *adj.* negligent (often with *of*) —**neg·lect′ful·ly** *adv.* —**neg·lect′ful·ness** *n.*

neg·li·gee (neg′lə zhā′) *n.* [< Fr. *négliger,* to neglect] **1.** a woman's loosely fitting dressing gown **2.** any informal attire

neg·li·gent (neg′li jənt) *adj.* **1.** habitually failing to do the required thing **2.** careless, inattentive, etc. —**neg′li·gence** *n.* —**neg′li·gent·ly** *adv.*

neg′li·gi·ble (-jə b'l) *adj.* that can be neglected or disregarded; trifling —**neg′li·gi·bly** *adv.*

ne·go·ti·a·ble (ni gō′shē ə b'l) *adj.* **1.** legally transferable, as a promissory note **2.** that can be passed, crossed, etc. —**ne·go′ti·a·bil′i·ty** *n.*

ne·go′ti·ate′ (-āt′) *vi.* **-at′ed, -at′ing** [< L. *negotium,* business] to confer or discuss with a view to reaching agreement —*vt.* **1.** to settle (a transaction, treaty, etc.) **2.** to transfer or sell (negotiable paper) **3.** to succeed in crossing, moving through, etc. —**ne·go′ti·a′tor** *n.*

ne·go′ti·a′tion *n.* a negotiating; specif., *[often pl.]* a conferring or bargaining to reach agreement

Ne·gri·to (ni grēt′ō) *n., pl.* **-tos, -toes** [Sp. < *negro,* black] a member of any of various dwarfish Negroid peoples of the East Indies, the Philippines, and Africa

ne·gri·tude (neg′rə tōōd′, nē′grə-) *n.* [Fr. *négritude*] an awareness and affirmation by blacks of their distinctive cultural heritage

Ne·gro (nē′grō) *n., pl.* **-groes** [< Sp. & Port. *negro,* black] **1.** a member of the dominant group of mankind in Africa, characterized generally by a dark skin **2.** a member of the Negroid group **3.** any person with some Negro ancestors See BLACK (*n.* 3) —*adj.* of or for Negroes

Ne′groid (-groid) *adj.* designating or of one of the major groups of mankind, including most of the peoples of Africa south of the Sahara

Ne·he·mi·ah (nē′ə mī′ə) *Bible* **1.** a Hebrew leader of about the 5th cent. B.C. **2.** the book that tells about his work: abbrev. **Neh.**

Neh·ru (nā′rōō), **Ja·wa·har·lal** (jə wä′hər läl′) 1889–1964; prime minister of India (1947–1964)

neigh (nā) *vi.* [OE. *hnægan*] to utter the characteristic cry of a horse —*n.* this cry

neigh·bor (nā′bər) *n.* [OE. *neah,* nigh + *gebur,* farmer] **1.** one that lives or is situated near another **2.** a fellow man —*adj.* nearby —*vt., vi.* to live or be situated near or nearby Brit. sp. **neigh′bour**

neigh'bor·hood' *n.* **1.** a particular community, district, or area **2.** the people living near one another —**in the neighborhood of** [Colloq.] **1.** near (a place) **2.** about; approximately

neigh'bor·ly *adj.* like or appropriate to neighbors; friendly —**neigh'bor·li·ness** *n.*

nei·ther (nē'*th*ər, nī'-) *adj., pron.* [OE. *na-hwæther,* lit., not whether] not either [*neither* boy went, *neither* of them sings] —*conj.* not either [she could *neither* laugh nor cry]

Nel·son (nel's'n), **Horatio** 1758–1805; Eng. admiral

nem·a·tode (nem'ə tōd') *n.* [< Gr. *nēma,* thread + -ODE] any of a group of long, cylindrical worms, as the hookworm

Nem·e·sis (nem'ə sis) [< Gr. *nemein,* deal out] *Gr. Myth.* the goddess of retribution or vengeance —*n.* [*usually* n-] *pl.* **-ses'** (-sēz') **1.** *a)* just punishment *b)* one who imposes it **2.** anyone or anything that seems inevitably to defeat or frustrate one

neo- [< Gr. *neos*] [*often* N-] *a combining form meaning:* **1.** new, recent **2.** in a new or different way

ne·o·clas·sic (nē'ō klas'ik) *adj.* designating or of a revival of classic style in art, literature, etc.: also **ne'o·clas'si·cal**

ne·o·dym·i·um (nē'ə dim'ē əm) *n.* a metallic chemical element of the rare-earth group: symbol Nd; at. wt., 144.24; at. no., 60

ne·o·lith·ic (nē'ə lith'ik) *adj.* [< NEO- + Gr. *lithos,* stone + -IC] designating or of the later part of the Stone Age, when man used polished stone tools

ne·ol·o·gism (nē äl'ə jiz'm) *n.* [< Fr.: see NEO-, -LOGY, & -ISM] **1.** a new word or a new meaning for an established word **2.** the use of these

ne·o·my·cin (nē'ə mī'sin) *n.* [< NEO- + Gr. *mykēs,* fungus + -IN¹] an antibiotic used esp. in treating infections of the skin and eye

ne·on (nē'än) *n.* [< Gr. *neos,* new] a rare, inert gaseous chemical element: symbol, Ne; at. wt., 20.183; at. no., 10

neon lamp a tube containing neon, which glows red when an electric current is sent through it

ne·o·phyte (nē'ə fīt') *n.* [< Gr. *neos,* new + *phyein,* to produce] **1.** a new convert **2.** a beginner; novice

ne'o·plasm (-plaz'm) *n.* [NEO- + -PLASM] an abnormal growth of tissue, as a tumor —**ne'o·plas'tic** *adj.*

ne'o·prene' (-prēn') *n.* a synthetic rubber, highly resistant to oil, heat, light, and oxidation

Ne·pal (ni pôl') country in the Himalayas: 54,362 sq. mi.; pop. 10,845,000; cap. Katmandu —**Nep·a·lese** (nep'ə lēz') *adj., n., pl.* **-lese'**

ne·pen·the (ni pen'thē) *n.* [< Gr. *ne-,* not + *penthos,* sorrow] anything that causes forgetfulness of sorrow

neph·ew (nef'yōō) *n.* [< L. *nepos*] **1.** the son of one's brother or sister **2.** the son of one's brother-in-law or sister-in-law

ne·phri·tis (ne frīt'əs) *n.* [< Gr. *nephros,* kidney + -ITIS] disease of the kidneys, characterized by inflammation, etc.: certain types were formerly called *Bright's disease*

nep·o·tism (nep'ə tiz'm) *n.* [< Fr. < L. *nepos,* nephew] favoritism shown to relatives, esp. in appointment to desirable positions

Nep·tune (nep'tōōn) **1.** *Rom. Myth.* the god of the sea: identified with the Greek god Poseidon **2.** the planet eighth in distance from the sun: see PLANET

nep·tu·ni·um (nep tōō'nē əm) *n.* a radioactive chemical element produced by irradiating uranium atoms: symbol, Np; at. wt., 237; at. no., 93

Ne·re·id (nir'ē id) *n. Gr. Myth.* a sea nymph

Ne·ro (nir'ō) 37–68 A.D.; emperor of Rome (54–68)

nerve (nurv) *n.* [< L. *nervus*] **1.** any of the cordlike fibers carrying impulses between body organs and the central nervous system **2.** courage **3.** strength; vigor **4.** [*pl.*] nervousness **5.** [Colloq.] impudent boldness **6.** *Biol.* a vein in a leaf or insect's wing —*vt.* **nerved, nerv'ing** to give strength or courage to —**get on one's nerves** [Colloq.] to make one irritable

nerve cell *same as* NEURON

nerve gas a poisonous gas causing paralysis of the respiratory and central nervous systems

nerve'less *adj.* **1.** without strength, courage, etc.; weak **2.** not nervous; controlled **3.** *Biol.* without nerves —**nerve'less·ly** *adv.* —**nerve'less·ness** *n.*

nerve'-rack'ing, nerve'-wrack'ing (-rak'iŋ) *adj.* very trying to one's patience or equanimity

nerv·ous (nur'vəs) *adj.* **1.** vigorous in expression **2.** of or made up of nerves **3.** characterized by or having a disordered state of the nerves **4.** emotionally tense, restless, etc. **5.** fearful —**nerv'ous·ly** *adv.* —**nerv'ous·ness** *n.*

nervous system all the nerve cells and nervous tissues in an organism, including, in the vertebrates, the brain, spinal cord, nerves, etc.

nerv'y *adj.* **-i·er, -i·est** **1.** [Brit.] nervous; excitable **2.** full of courage; bold **3.** [Colloq.] brazen; impudent

-ness [OE. *-nes(s)*] *a suffix meaning* state, quality, or instance of being [*sadness*]

nest (nest) *n.* [OE.] **1.** the structure or place where a bird lays its eggs and shelters its young **2.** the place used by hornets, fish, etc. for spawning or breeding **3.** a cozy place; retreat **4.** a resort, haunt, etc. or its frequenters [a *nest* of thieves] **5.** a swarm or colony of birds, insects, etc. **6.** a set of similar things, each fitting within the one next larger —*vi., vt.* **1.** to build or settle in (a nest) **2.** to fit (an object) closely within another

nest egg money, etc. put aside as a reserve or to set up a fund

nes·tle (nes''l) *vi.* **-tled, -tling** [OE. *nestlian*] **1.** to settle down comfortably and snugly **2.** to press close for comfort or in affection **3.** to lie sheltered, as a house among trees —*vt.* **1.** to rest or press snugly **2.** to house as in a nest

nest·ling (nest'liŋ, nes'-) *n.* **1.** a young bird not yet ready to leave the nest **2.** a young child

net¹ (net) *n.* [OE. *nett*] **1.** an openwork fabric, as of string, used to snare birds, fish, etc. **2.** a trap; snare **3.** a meshed fabric used to hold, protect, or mark off something [a *hairnet,* tennis *net*] **4.** a fine, meshed, lacelike cloth —*vt.* **net'ted, net'ting** **1.** to make into a net **2.** to snare as with a net **3.** to shelter or enclose as with a net

net² (net) *adj.* [Fr., clear] remaining after certain deductions or allowances have been made, as for expenses, weight of containers, etc. —*n.* a net amount, profit, weight, etc. —*vt.* **net'ted, net'ting** to gain as profit, etc.

neth·er (neth'ər) *adj.* [OE. *neothera*] lower or under [the *nether* world, *nether* garments]

Neth·er·lands (neth'ər landz) **1.** country in W Europe: 12,978 sq. mi.; pop. 13,033,000; cap. Amsterdam; seat of govt. The Hague **2.** kingdom consisting of the independent states of the Netherlands & Netherlands Antilles Often with *the*

Netherlands Antilles group of islands in the West Indies, together constituting a state of the Netherlands

neth·er·most (neth'ər mōst') *adj.* lowest

nether world *Theol. & Myth.* the world of the dead or of punishment after death; hell

net'ting *n.* netted material

net·tle (net''l) *n.* [OE. *netele*] a weed with stinging hairs —*vt.* **-tled, -tling** **1.** to sting with or as with nettles **2.** to irritate; annoy; vex

net'work' *n.* **1.** an arrangement of parallel wires, threads, etc. crossed at regular intervals by others so as to leave open spaces **2.** anything like this, as a system of interconnected roads, individuals, etc. **3.** *Radio & TV* a chain of transmitting stations operated as a unit

neu·ral (noor'əl, nyoor'-) *adj.* [NEUR(O)- + -AL] of a nerve, nerves, or the nervous system

neu·ral·gia (noo ral'jə, nyoo-) *n.* [see NEURO- & -ALGIA] severe pain along the course of a nerve —**neu·ral'gic** (-jik) *adj.*

neu·ras·the·ni·a (noor'əs thē'nē ə, nyoor'-) *n.* [< NEUR(O)- + Gr. *astheneia,* weakness] a type of neurosis characterized by irritability, fatigue, anxiety, etc. —**neu·ras·then'ic** (-then'ik) *adj., n.*

neu·ri·tis (noo rīt'əs, nyoo-) *n.* [NEUR(O)- + -ITIS] inflammation of a nerve or nerves, accompanied by pain —**neu·rit'ic** (-rit'ik) *adj.*

neuro- [< Gr. *neuron,* nerve] *a combining form meaning* of a nerve or the nervous system: also **neur-**

neu·rol·o·gy (noo räl'ə jē, nyoo-) *n.* [prec. + -LOGY] the branch of medicine dealing with the nervous system and its diseases —**neu·ro·log·i·cal** (noor'ə läj'i k'l, nyoor'-) *adj.* —**neu·rol'o·gist** *n.*

neu·ron (noor'än, nyoor'-) *n.* [< Gr. *neuron,* nerve] the nerve cell body and all its processes

neu'ro·psy·chi'a·try (-ō sə kī'ə trē) *n.* a branch of medicine combining neurology and psychiatry

neu·rop·ter·an (noo räp'tər ən, nyoo-) *n.* [< Gr. *pteron,* wing + -AN] any of a group of insects with four membranous wings and biting mouthparts

neu·ro·sis (noo rō'sis, nyoo-) *n., pl.* **-ses** (-sēz) [see NEURO- & -OSIS] a mental disorde

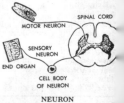

SPINAL CORD
MOTOR NEURON
SENSORY NEURON
END ORGAN
CELL BODY OF NEURON

NEURON

characterized by anxiety, compulsions, obsessions, phobias, depression, etc.

neu·rot·ic (noo rät'ik, nyoo-) *adj.* of or having a neurosis —*n.* a neurotic person —**neu·rot'i·cal·ly** *adv.*

neut. neuter

neu·ter (noot'ər, nyoot'-) *adj.* [< L. *ne-*, not + *uter*, either] **1.** *Biol. a)* having no sexual organs *b)* having undeveloped sexual organs in the adult **2.** *Gram.* designating or of the gender that refers to things regarded as neither male nor female —*n.* **1.** a castrated or spayed animal **2.** *Biol.* a neuter plant or animal **3.** *Gram. a)* the neuter gender *b)* a neuter word —*vt.* to castrate or spay

neu·tral (noo'trəl, nyoo'-) *adj.* [see prec.] **1.** supporting neither side in a quarrel or war **2.** of neither extreme in type, kind, etc.; indifferent **3.** having little or no decided color **4.** *Biol. same as* NEUTER **5.** *Chem.* neither acid nor alkaline **6.** *Elec.* neither negative nor positive **7.** *Phonet.* pronounced as the vowel is in most unstressed syllables, which tends to become (ə) —*n.* **1.** a neutral person or nation **2.** a neutral color **3.** *Mech.* a disengaged position of gears, when they do not transmit power from the engine —**neu'tral·ly** *adv.*

neu'tral·ism *n.* a policy, or the advocacy of a policy, of remaining neutral, esp. in international power conflicts —**neu'tral·ist** *adj., n.*

neu·tral'i·ty (-tral'ə tē) *n.* **1.** a being neutral **2.** the status or policy of a neutral nation

neu'tral·ize (-trə līz') *vt.* **-ized', -iz'ing 1.** to declare (a nation, etc.) neutral in war **2.** to destroy or counteract the effectiveness, force, etc. of **3.** *Chem.* to destroy the active properties of **4.** *Elec.* to make electrically neutral —**neu'tral·i·za'tion** *n.*

neu·tri·no (noo trē'nō, nyoo-) *n., pl.* **-nos** [It., little neutron] *Physics* an uncharged particle with almost no mass

neu·tron (noo'trän, nyoo'-) *n.* [NEUTR(AL) + (ELECTR)ON] an elementary, uncharged particle in the nucleus of an atom

Ne·vad·a (nə vad'ə, -vä'də) State of the W U.S., one of the Mountain States: 110,540 sq. mi.; pop. 489,000; cap. Carson City: abbrev. **Nev., NV** —**Ne·vad'an** *adj., n.*

nev·er (nev'ər) *adv.* [< OE. *ne,* not + *æfre,* ever] **1.** not ever; at no time **2.** not at all; in no case

nev·er·more (nev'ər môr') *adv.* never again

never-never land an unreal or imaginary place or situation

nev·er·the·less (nev'ər *thə* les') *adv.* in spite of that; however

ne·vus (nē'vəs) *n., pl.* **-vi** (-vī) [< L. *naevus*] a colored spot on the skin; birthmark or mole

new (noo) *adj.* [OE. *niwe*] **1.** appearing, thought of, discovered, made, etc. for the first time **2.** *a)* different *[a new* hairdo*] b)* strange; unfamiliar **3.** more or most recent of two or more things of the same class *[the new* library*]* **4.** recently grown; fresh *[new* potatoes*]* **5.** not previously used or worn **6.** modern; recent **7.** more; additional **8.** starting as a repetition of a cycle, series, etc. *[the new* year*]* **9.** having just reached a position, rank, place, etc. *[a new* arrival*]* —*adv.* **1.** again **2.** newly; recently —*n.* something new (with *the*) —**new'ish** *adj.* —**new'ness** *n.*

New·ark (noo'ərk) city in NE N.J.: pop. 382,000 (met. area 1,857,000)

New Bed·ford (bed'fərd) seaport in SE Mass.: pop. 102,000

new blood new people as a potential source of fresh ideas, renewed vigor, etc.

new'born' *adj.* **1.** recently born **2.** reborn

New Bruns·wick (brunz'wik) province of SE Canada: 28,354 sq. mi.; pop. 617,000; cap. Fredericton: abbrev. **N.B.**

New·cas·tle (noo'kas'l, -käs'-) seaport in N England: pop. 254,000; in full **New·cas'tle-up·on-Tyne'** (-tīn') — **carry coals to Newcastle** to do what is superfluous or unneeded

new'com'er *n.* a recent arrival

New Deal the principles and policies adopted by President F. D. Roosevelt in the 1930's to advance economic recovery and social welfare

New Delhi capital of India, adjacent to Delhi: pop. 261,000

new·el (noo'əl) *n.* [ult. < L. *nux,* nut] **1.** the upright pillar around which the steps of a winding staircase turn **2.** the post at the top or bottom of a flight of stairs, supporting the handrail: also **newel post**

New England the six NE States of the U.S.: Me., Vt., N.H., Mass., R.I., and Conn. —**New Englander**

new'fan'gled (-fan'g'ld) *adj.* [< ME. *newe,* new + *-fangel* < OE. *fon,* to take] new; novel: a humorously derogatory term

New·found·land (noo'fənd land', -lənd) **1.** an island off the E coast of Canada **2.** province of E Canada, including this island & Labrador: 156,185 sq. mi.; pop. 493,000; cap. St. John's: abbrev. **Nfld.** —**New'found·land'er** *n.*

Newfoundland dog any of a North American breed of large, powerful, shaggy-haired dogs

New Guinea large island in the East Indies, north of Australia: divided between Indonesia & the country of Papua New Guinea

New Hamp·shire (hamp'shir) New England State of the U.S.: 9,304 sq. mi.; pop. 738,000; cap. Concord: abbrev. **N.H., NH**

New Ha·ven (hā'vən) city in S Conn.: pop. 138,000

New Jersey Eastern State of the U.S.: 7,836 sq. mi.; pop. 7,168,000; cap. Trenton: abbrev. **N.J., NJ**

new·ly *adv.* **1.** recently; lately **2.** anew; afresh

new'ly-wed' *n.* a recently married person

New·man (noo'mən), **John Henry,** Cardinal Newman, 1801–90; Eng. theologian & writer

New Mexico State of the SW U.S., one of the Mountain States: 121,666 sq. mi.; pop. 1,016,000; cap. Santa Fe: abbrev. **N.Mex., NM**

new moon the moon when it is between the earth and the sun, with its dark side toward the earth: it emerges as a crescent curving to the right

New Or·le·ans (ôr'lē ənz, ôr lēnz') city in SE La.: pop. 593,000 (met. area 1,046,000)

New·port News (noo'pôrt) seaport in SE Va.: pop. 138,000

news (nooz) *n.pl.* [with sing. v.] **1.** new information; information previously unknown **2.** reports of recent happenings

news'boy' *n.* a boy who sells or delivers newspapers

news'cast' *n.* a program of news broadcast over radio or TV —**news'cast'er** *n.*

news'deal'er *n.* a retailer of newspapers, magazines, etc.

news'let'ter *n.* a news bulletin issued regularly to a special group

news'man' (-man', -mən) *n., pl.* **-men'** (-men', -mən) **1.** *same as* NEWSDEALER **2.** one who gathers and reports news for a newspaper, TV station, etc.

news'pa'per (-pā'pər) *n.* a regular publication, usually daily or weekly, containing news, opinions, advertisements, etc. —**news'pa'per·man'** *n., pl.* **-men'** —**news'pa'-per·wom'an** *n.fem., pl.* **-wom'en**

news'print' *n.* a cheap paper used for newspapers, etc.

news'reel' *n.* a short motion picture of news events

news'stand' *n.* a stand at which newspapers, magazines, etc. are sold

news'wor'thy (-wur'*thē*) *adj.* timely and important or interesting

news'y *adj.* **-i·er, -i·est** [Colloq.] containing much news

newt (noot) *n.* [by merging of ME. *an eute* < OE. *efeta,* eft] any of various small amphibious salamanders

New Testament the part of the Bible containing the life and teachings of Jesus and his followers

New·ton (noot''n), **Sir Isaac** 1642–1727; Eng. mathematician

New World the Western Hemisphere —**new'-world'** *adj.*

New Year's (Day) January 1

New Year's Eve the evening before New Year's Day

New York 1. State of the NE U.S.: 49,576 sq. mi.; pop. 18,191,000; cap. Albany: abbrev. **N.Y., NY 2.** city in SE N.Y.: often called **New York City:** pop. 7,868,000 (met. area 11,529,000) — **New York'er**

NEWT
(3–4 in. long)

New Zea·land (zē'lənd) country including two large islands in the S Pacific: 103,736 sq. mi.; pop. 2,809,000; cap. Wellington —**New Zea'land·er**

next (nekst) *adj.* [OE. *neahst,* superl. of *neah,* nigh] nearest; immediately preceding or following —*adv.* **1.** in the nearest time, place, rank, etc. **2.** on the first subsequent occasion —*prep.* beside; nearest to *[sit next* the tree*]* —**get next to** [Slang] to become friendly or close to —**next door (to)** in or at the house adjacent (to)

next-door (neks'dôr') *adj.* in or at the next house, building, etc.

next of kin one's nearest relative(s)

nex·us (nek'səs) *n., pl.* **-us·es, nex'us** [L.] **1.** a connection or link **2.** a connected group or series

Nfld., Nfd. Newfoundland

N.G., n.g. [Slang] no good

N.H., NH New Hampshire

Ni *Chem.* nickel

ni·a·cin (nī'ə sin) *n.* [NI(COTINIC) AC(ID) + -IN¹] a white, odorless substance found in protein foods: it is a member of the vitamin B complex, used in treating pellagra

Ni·ag·a·ra (nī ag'rə, -ər ə) river flowing from Lake Erie into Lake Ontario: c.36 mi.

Niagara Falls 1. waterfall on the Niagara River: divided into two falls, Horseshoe, or Canadian, Falls (c.160 ft. high) & American Falls (c.167 ft. high) **2.** city in W N.Y.: pop. 86,000

nib (nib) *n.* [< ME. *nebb*] **1.** a bird's bill or beak **2.** the point of a pen **3.** a point; sharp prong

nib·ble (nib''l) *vt., vi.* **-bled, -bling** [LME. *nebyllen*] **1.** to eat (food) with quick, small bites **2.** to bite at with small, gentle bites —*n.* **1.** a small bite or morsel **2.** a nibbling — **nib'bler** *n.*

Ni·be·lung·en·lied (nē'bə looŋ'ən lēt') a German epic poem by an unknown author of the 13th cent.: see SIEGFRIED

nibs (nibz) *n.* [< ?] [Colloq.] an important, or esp. self-important, person (with *his*)

Nic·a·ra·gua (nik'ə rä'gwə) country in Central America: 54,342 sq. mi.; pop. 1,984,000; cap. Managua —**Nic'a·ra'guan** *adj., n.*

Nice (nēs) seaport in SE France: pop. 322,000

nice (nīs) *adj.* **nic'er, nic'est** [< L. *nescius*, ignorant] **1.** difficult to please; fastidious **2.** delicate; precise; subtle *[a nice distinction]* **3.** calling for care, tact, etc. *[a nice problem]* **4.** *a)* finely discriminating *b)* minutely accurate **5.** *a)* pleasant *b)* attractive *c)* kind *d)* good —**nice'ly** *adv.* —**nice'ness** *n.*

Ni·cene Creed (nī'sēn) [< *Nicaea*, ancient city in Asia Minor] a confession of faith for Christians adopted in 325 A.D.

ni·ce·ty (nī'sə tē) *n., pl.* **-ties 1.** precision; accuracy **2.** fastidiousness; refinement **3.** a subtle or minute detail, distinction, etc. **4.** something choice or dainty —**to a nicety** exactly

niche (nich) *n.* [Fr., ult. < L. *nidus*, a nest] **1.** a recess in a wall for a statue, vase, etc. **2.** an especially suitable place or position

Nich·o·las (nik''l əs) **1. Nicholas II** 1868–1918; last czar of Russia (1894–1917): executed **2.** Saint, 4th cent. A.D.: patron saint of Russia, of Greece, & of young people, sailors, etc.: cf. SANTA CLAUS

nick (nik) *n.* [prob. akin to *nocke*, notch] a small cut, chip, etc. made on a surface —*vt.* **1.** to make a nick or nicks in **2.** *a)* to wound slightly *b)* to strike glancingly **3.** [Slang] to cheat —**in the nick of time** just before it is too late

nick·el (nik''l) *n.* [Sw. < G. *kupfernickel*, copper demon: the copperlike ore contains no copper] **1.** a hard, silver-white, metallic chemical element, used in alloys: symbol, Ni; at. wt., 58.71; at. no., 28 **2.** a U.S. or Canadian coin of nickel and copper, equal to five cents —*vt.* **-eled** or **-elled, -el·ing** or **-el·ling** to plate with nickel

nick·el·o·de·on (nik'ə lō'dē ən) *n.* [< NICKEL + Fr. *odéon*, concert hall] **1.** formerly, a motion-picture theater, etc. where admission was five cents **2.** a coin-operated player piano or early jukebox

nickel plate a thin layer of nickel deposited by electrolysis on metallic objects to prevent rust —**nick'el·plate'** *vt.* **-plat'ed, -plat'ing**

nickel silver a hard, tough alloy of nickel, copper, and zinc

nick·er (nik'ər) *vi., n.* neigh; whinny

nick·nack (nik'nak') *n. same as* KNICKKNACK

nick·name (nik'nām') *n.* [by merging of ME. *an eke-name*, a surname] **1.** a substitute, often descriptive name given in fun, affection, etc., as "Shorty" **2.** a familiar form of a name, as "Dick" for "Richard" —*vt.* **-named', -nam'ing** to give a nickname to

nic·o·tine (nik'ə tēn', -tin) *n.* [Fr. < J. *Nicot*, 16th-c. Fr. diplomat who introduced tobacco into France] a poisonous alkaloid found in tobacco leaves

nic·o·tin·ic acid (-tin'ik, -tē'nik) *same as* NIACIN

nic·ti·tate (nik'tə tāt') *vi.* **-tat'ed, -tat'ing** [< L. *nictare*, to wink] to wink or blink rapidly, as birds and animals with a nictitating membrane

nictitating membrane a transparent third eyelid hinged at the lower lid of the eye of some animals

niece (nēs) *n.* [< L. *neptis*] **1.** the daughter of one's brother or sister **2.** the daughter of one's brother-in-law or sister-in-law

Nie·tzsche (nē'chə), **Frie·drich W.** (frē'drikh) 1844–1900; Ger. philosopher

nif·ty (nif'tē) *adj.* **-ti·er, -ti·est** [prob. < MAGNIFICENT] [Slang] attractive, smart, stylish, etc.

Ni·ger (nī'jər) **1.** river in W Africa, flowing from Guinea into the Atlantic: c.2,600 mi. **2.** country in WC Africa, north of Nigeria: c.458,500 sq. mi.; pop. 4,016,000; cap. Niamey

Ni·ger·i·a (nī jir'ē ə) country in WC Africa, on the Atlantic: 327,186 sq. mi.; pop. 61,450,000; cap. Lagos —**Ni·ger'i·an** *adj., n.*

nig·gard (nig'ərd) *n.* [prob. < Scand.] a stingy person; miser —*adj.* stingy; miserly

nig'gard·ly *adj.* **1.** stingy; miserly **2.** small, few, or scanty *[a niggardly sum]* —*adv.* stingily —**nig'gard·li·ness** *n.*

nig·gle (nig''l) *vi.* **-gled, -gling** [prob. akin to Norw. dial. *nigla*] to work fussily; be finicky —**nig'gler** *n.* —**nig'gling** *adj., n.*

nigh (nī) *adj., adv., prep.* [OE. *neah*] [Chiefly Archaic or Dial.] near

night (nīt) *n.* [OE. *niht*] **1.** the period of darkness between sunset and sunrise **2.** any period or condition of darkness or gloom —**make a night of it** to celebrate all night

night blindness imperfect vision in the dark or in dim light: a symptom of vitamin A deficiency

night'cap' *n.* **1.** a cap worn in bed **2.** [Colloq.] an alcoholic drink taken at bedtime

night clothes clothes to be worn in bed, as pajamas

night'club' *n.* a place of entertainment open at night for eating, drinking, dancing, etc.

night crawler any large earthworm that comes to the surface at night, commonly used as fish bait

night'fall' *n.* the close of day; dusk

night'gown' *n.* a loose gown worn in bed by women or girls

night'hawk' *n.* **1.** any of a group of night birds related to the whippoorwill **2.** *same as* NIGHT OWL

night'ie *n.* [Colloq.] a nightgown

night·in·gale (nīt''n gāl') *n.* [< OE. *niht*, night + *galan*, to sing] a small European thrush known for the melodious singing of the male, esp. at night

Night·in·gale (nīt''n gāl'), **Florence** 1820–1910; Eng. nurse; pioneer in modern nursing

night letter a long telegram sent at night at a cheaper rate

night'ly *adj.* **1.** of or like the night **2.** done or occurring every night —*adv.* **1.** at night **2.** every night

night'mare' (-mer') *n.* [< ME. *niht*, night + *mare*, demon] **1.** a frightening dream **2.** any frightening experience —**night'mar'ish** *adj.*

night owl a person who works at night or otherwise stays up late

nights (nīts) *adv.* on every night or most nights

night school a school held in the evening, as for adults unable to attend by day

night'shade' (-shād') *n.* any of various flowering plants related to the potato and tomato; esp., a poisonous variety, as the belladonna

night'shirt' *n.* a long, loose, shirtlike garment, worn in bed, esp. formerly, by men or boys

night'spot' *n. colloq. var. of* NIGHTCLUB

night stick a heavy club carried by a policeman

night'time' *n.* the period of darkness from sunset to sunrise

night'wear' *n. same as* NIGHT CLOTHES

ni·hil·ism (nī'ə liz'm, nē'-, ni'hi-) *n.* [< L. *nihil*, nothing + -ISM] **1.** *Philos. a)* the denial of the existence of any basis for knowledge *b)* the general rejection of customary beliefs in morality, religion, etc. **2.** *Politics a)* the doctrine that all social, political, and economic institutions must be destroyed *b)* loosely, any revolutionary movement involving the use of terrorism —**ni'hil·ist** *n.* —**ni'hil·is'tic** *adj.*

nil (nil) *n.* [L., contr. of *nihil*] nothing

Nile (nīl) river in NE Africa, flowing through Egypt into the Mediterranean: over 4,000 mi.

nil·gai (nil'gī) *n.* [Per. *nīlgāw*, blue cow] a large, gray Indian antelope: also **nil'gau** (-gô)

nim·ble (nim'b'l) *adj.* **-bler, -blest** [< OE. *niman*, take] **1.** quick-witted; alert **2.** moving quickly and lightly —**nim'ble·ness** *n.* —**nim'bly** *adv.*

nim·bus (nim′bəs) *n., pl.* **-bi** (-bī), **-bus·es** [L.] **1**. orig., any rain-producing cloud **2**. a halo surrounding the head of a saint, etc., as in a picture

Nim·rod (nim′räd) *Bible* a mighty hunter: Gen. 10:8–9

nin·com·poop (nin′kəm pōōp′, niŋ′-) *n.* [< ?] a stupid, silly person; fool

nine (nīn) *adj., n.* [OE. *nigon*] one more than eight; 9; IX

nine′pins′ *n.pl.* [*with sing. v.*] a British version of ten-pins, in which nine pins are used

nine′teen′ (-tēn′) *adj., n.* [OE. *nigontyne*] nine more than ten; 19; XIX —**nine′teenth′** (-tēnth′) *adj., n.*

nine′ty (-tē) *adj., n., pl.* **-ties** nine times ten; 90; XC (or LXXXX) —**the nineties** the numbers or years, as of a century, from 90 through 99 —**nine′ti·eth** (-ith) *adj., n.*

Nin·e·veh (nin′ə və) capital of ancient Assyria

nin·ny (nin′ē) *n., pl.* **-nies** [prob. by merging and contr. of *an innocent*] a fool; dolt

ninth (nīnth) *adj.* **1**. preceded by eight others in a series; 9th **2**. designating any of the nine equal parts —*n.* **1**. the one following the eighth **2**. any of the nine equal parts of something; 1/9

ni·o·bi·um (nī ō′bē əm) *n.* [< *Niobe*, mythical Grecian queen] a gray or white metallic chemical element: symbol, Nb; at. wt., 92.906; at. no., 41

nip¹ (nip) *vt.* **nipped, nip′ping** [prob. < MLowG. *nippen*] **1**. to pinch or bite **2**. to sever (shoots, etc.) as by clipping **3**. to check the growth of **4**. to have a painful or injurious effect on because of cold —*vi.* to give a nip or nips —*n.* **1**. a nipping; pinch; bite **2**. a stinging quality, as in cold air **3**. stinging cold; frost —**nip and tuck** so close as to leave the outcome in doubt

nip² (nip) *n.* [prob. < Du. *nippen*, to sip] a small drink of liquor; sip —*vt., vi.* **nipped, nip′ping** to drink in nips

nip·per (nip′ər) *n.* **1**. anything that nips **2**. [*pl.*] pliers, pincers, etc. **3**. the claw of a crab or lobster

nip·ple (nip′'l) *n.* [prob. < *neb* < OE. *nebb*, bird's beak] **1**. the small protuberance on a breast or udder, through which the milk passes; teat **2**. a teatlike part, as of rubber, for a baby's bottle **3**. any projection or thing resembling a nipple in shape or function

Nip·pon (nip′än, ni pän′) *a Japanese name for* JAPAN **Nip′pon·ese′** (-ə nēz′) *adj., n., pl.* **-ese′**

nip·py (nip′ē) *adj.* **-pi·er, -pi·est** **1**. tending to nip **2**. cold in a stinging way

nir·va·na (nir vä′nə, nər-; -van′ə) *n.* [< Sans.] [*also* N-] **1**. *Buddhism* the state of perfect blessedness achieved by the absorption of the soul into the supreme spirit **2**. great peace or bliss

nit (nit) *n.* [OE. *hnitu*] **1**. the egg of a louse or similar insect **2**. a young louse, etc.

ni·ter (nīt′ər) *n.* [< Gr. *nitron*] *same as:* **1**. POTASSIUM NITRATE **2**. SODIUM NITRATE Also, chiefly Brit., **ni′tre**

nit-pick·ing (nit′pik′iŋ) *adj., n.* paying too much attention to petty details —**nit′-pick′er n.**

ni·trate (nī′trāt) *n.* **1**. a salt or ester of nitric acid **2**. potassium nitrate or sodium nitrate, used as a fertilizer —*vt.* **-trat·ed, -trat·ing** to treat or combine with nitric acid or a nitrate —**ni·tra′tion** *n.*

ni·tric (nī′trik) *adj.* of or containing nitrogen, esp. of a higher valence than in nitrous compounds

nitric acid a colorless, corrosive acid, HNO_3

ni·tri·fy (nī′trə fī′) *vt.* **-fied′, -fy′ing** **1**. to impregnate (soil, etc.) with nitrates **2**. to oxidize (ammonium salts, etc.) to nitrates, as by the action of soil bacteria —**ni′tri·fi·ca′tion** *n.*

ni·tro·cel·lu·lose (nī′trō sel′yōō lōs′) *n.* a substance produced by treating wood, etc. with nitric acid: used for explosives, plastics, etc.

ni·tro·gen (nī′trə jən) *n.* [< Fr.: see NITER & -GEN] a colorless, tasteless, odorless gaseous chemical element forming nearly four fifths of the atmosphere: symbol, N; at. wt., 14.0067; at. no., 7 —**ni·trog·e·nous** (nī träj′ə nəs) *adj.*

ni·tro·glyc·er·in, ni·tro·glyc·er·ine (nī′trə glis′ər in) *n.* a thick, explosive oil, $C_3H_5(ONO_2)_3$, prepared by treating glycerin with nitric and sulfuric acids: used in dynamite, medicine, etc.

ni·trous (nī′trəs) *adj.* **1**. of or containing niter **2**. designating or of compounds in which nitrogen has a lower valence than in nitric compounds

nitrous oxide a colorless, nonflammable gas, N_2O, used as an anesthetic and in aerosols

nit·ty (nit′ē) *adj.* **-ti·er, -ti·est** full of nits

nit′ty-grit′ty (-grit′ē) *n.* [Slang] the actual, basic facts, elements, issues, etc.

nit′wit′ *n.* [? NIT + WIT¹] a stupid or silly person

nix¹ (niks) *n., pl.* **nix′es**, G. **nix′e** (nik′sə) [G.] *Germanic Myth.* a water sprite

nix² (niks) *adv.* [G. *nichts*] [Slang] **1**. no **2**. not at all — *interj.* [Slang] **1**. stop! **2**. I forbid, disagree, etc. —*vt.* [Slang] to disapprove of or stop

Nix·on (nik′s'n), **Richard M.** 1913– ; 37th president of the U.S. (1969–74)

N.J., NJ New Jersey

NLRB, N.L.R.B. National Labor Relations Board

N.Mex., NM New Mexico

NNE, N.N.E., n.n.e. north-northeast

NNW, N.N.W., n.n.w. north-northwest

no (nō) *adv.* [< OE. *ne a*, not ever] **1**. not at all *[no worse]* **2**. nay; not so: the opposite of YES, used to deny, refuse, or disagree —*adj.* not any; not a *[no errors]* —*n., pl.* **noes, nos** **1**. a refusal or denial **2**. a negative vote or voter

No *Chem.* nobelium

No. 1. north **2**. northern **3**. number: also **no.**

no-ac·count (nō′ə kount′) *adj.* [Colloq.] worthless

No·ah (nō′ə) *Bible* the patriarch commanded by God to build the ark: see ARK (sense 1)

no·bel·i·um (nō bel′ē əm) *n.* [< *Nobel* Institute in Stockholm, where discovered] a radioactive chemical element produced by the nuclear bombardment of curium: symbol, No; at. wt., 255(?); at. no., 102

No·bel prizes (nō bel′) [< A. B. *Nobel*, 19th-c. Sw. inventor who established them] annual prizes given for distinction in physics, chemistry, medicine, and literature, and for the promotion of peace

no·bil·i·ty (nō bil′ə tē) *n., pl.* **-ties** **1**. a being noble **2**. high rank in society **3**. the class of people of noble rank

no·ble (nō′b'l) *adj.* **-bler, -blest** [< L. *nobilis*, well-known] **1**. famous or renowned **2**. having high moral qualities **3**. excellent **4**. grand; stately *[a noble view]* **5**. of high rank or title —*n.* one having hereditary rank or title —**no′ble·ness** *n.* —**no′bly** *adv.*

no·ble·man (-mən) *n., pl.* **-men** a member of the nobility; peer —**no′ble·wom′an** *n.fem., pl.* **-wom′en**

no·blesse o·blige (nō bles′ ō blēzh′) [Fr., lit., nobility obliges] the obligation of people of high rank or social position to be kind and generous

no·bod·y (nō′bud′ē, -bäd′ē, -bəd ē) *pron.* not anybody; no one —*n., pl.* **-ies** a person of no importance

noc·tu·id (näk′chōō wid) *n.* [< L. *noctua*, night owl] any of a large group of moths which fly at night

noc·tur·nal (näk tur′n'l) *adj.* [< L. *nox*, night] **1**. of, done, or happening in the night **2**. active during the night —**noc·tur′nal·ly** *adv.*

noc·turne (näk′tərn) *n.* [Fr.] a romantic, dreamy musical composition, appropriate to night

nod (näd) *vi.* **nod′ded, nod′ding** [ME. *nodden*] **1**. to bend the head forward quickly, as in agreement, greeting, etc. **2**. to let the head fall forward because of drowsiness **3**. to be careless; make a slip **4**. to sway back and forth, etc., as plumes —*vt.* **1**. to bend (the head) forward quickly **2**. to signify (assent, etc.) by doing this —*n.* **1**. a nodding **2**. [N-] the imaginary realm of sleep and dreams: usually **land of Nod** —**nod′der** *n.*

nodding acquaintance a slight, not intimate, acquaintance with a person or thing

node (nōd) *n.* [L. *nodus*, knot] **1**. a knot; knob; swelling **2**. that part of a stem from which a leaf starts to grow **3**. *Physics* the point, line, or surface of a vibrating object where there is comparatively no vibration —**nod′al** *adj.*

nod·ule (näj′ōōl) *n.* [L. *nodulus*] **1**. a small knot or rounded lump **2**. a small knot or joint on a stem or root —**nod′u·lar, nod′u·lose′, nod′u·lous** *adj.*

no·el, no·ël (nō el′) *n.* [Fr. < L. *natalis*, natal] **1**. a Christmas carol **2**. [N-] *same as* CHRISTMAS

no-fault (nō′fôlt′) *adj.* **1**. of insurance in which the victim of an accident collects damages although blame for the accident is not established **2**. of a divorce granted without blame being indicated

nog·gin (näg′in) *n.* [prob. < *nog*, strong ale] **1**. a small cup or mug **2**. one fourth of a pint: a measure for ale or liquor **3**. [Colloq.] the head

no′-good′ *adj.* [Slang] contemptible

no′how′ *adv.* [Dial.] in no manner

noise (noiz) *n.* [OFr.] **1**. *a)* loud shouting; clamor *b)* any loud, disagreeable sound **2**. sound —*vt.* **noised, nois′ing** to spread (a report, rumor, etc.)

noise′less *adj.* with little or no noise; silent —**noise′-less·ly** *adv.* —**noise′less·ness** *n.*

noi·some (noi′səm) *adj.* [see ANNOY & -SOME¹] **1.** injurious to health **2.** foul-smelling; offensive —**noi′some·ly** *adv.* —**noi′some·ness** *n.*

nois′y *adj.* **-i·er, -i·est** **1.** making noise **2.** full of noise —**nois′i·ly** *adv.* —**nois′i·ness** *n.*

nom. nominative

no·mad (nō′mad) *n.* [< Gr. *nemein,* to pasture] **1.** any of a people having no permanent home, but moving about constantly in search of food, pasture, etc. **2.** a wanderer —*adj.* wandering: also **no·mad′ic**

no man's land the area on a battlefield separating the combatants

nom de plume (näm′də ploom′) *pl.* **noms′ de plume′** [Fr.] a pen name; pseudonym

Nome (nōm) city in W Alas.: pop. 2,500

no·men·cla·ture (nō′mən klā′chər) *n.* [< L. *nomen,* name + *calare,* to call] the system of names used in a branch of learning, or for the parts of a device

nom·i·nal (näm′i n'l) *adj.* [< L. *nomen,* a name] **1.** of or like a name **2.** in name only, not in fact [the *nominal* leader] **3.** relatively very small [a *nominal* fee] —**nom′i·nal·ly** *adv.*

nom·i·nate (näm′ə nāt′) *vt.* **-nat′ed, -nat′ing** **1.** to appoint to an office or position **2.** to name as a candidate for election, an award, etc. —**nom′i·na′tion** *n.* —**nom′i·na′tor** *n.*

nom·i·na·tive (näm′ə nə tiv) *adj. Gram.* designating or of the case of the subject of a verb and the words that agree with it —*n.* **1.** this case **2.** a word in this case

nom·i·nee (näm′ə nē′) *n.* a person who is nominated

non- [< L. *non*] *a prefix meaning* not: less emphatic than *in-* and *un-,* which often give a word an opposite meaning The following list includes the more common compounds formed with *non-* that do not have special meanings; they will be understood if *not* is used before the meaning of the base word

nonabrasive	nonconstructive	nongaseous
nonabsorbent	noncontagious	nongranular
nonacceptance	noncontiguous	nonhabitable
nonacid	noncontinuous	nonhazardous
nonactive	noncontributory	nonhereditary
nonaddictive	noncontroversial	nonhuman
nonadjacent	nonconvertible	nonhumorous
nonaggressive	noncorroding	nonidentical
nonalcoholic	noncorrosive	noninclusive
nonallergenic	noncritical	nonindependent
non-American	noncrystalline	nonindustrial
non-Anglican	noncumulative	noninfected
nonappearance	nondelivery	noninfectious
nonaquatic	nondemocratic	noninflammable
nonassignable	nondepreciating	noninflationary
nonathletic	nonderivative	noninformative
nonattendance	nondestructive	noninjurious
nonattributive	nondetachable	noninstrumental
nonbasic	nondisciplinary	nonintellectual
nonbeliever	nondivisible	noninterference
nonbelligerent	nondramatic	noninternational
nonblooming	nondrinker	nonintersecting
nonbreakable	nondrying	nonintoxicating
nonburnable	nonedible	nonirritant
noncanonical	noneducational	nonirritating
non-Catholic	noneffective	non-Jewish
noncellular	nonelastic	nonjudicial
nonchargeable	nonelective	nonlegal
nonchemical	nonemotional	nonliterary
non-Christian	nonenforceable	nonmagnetic
noncivilized	non-English	nonmalignant
nonclassifiable	nonexclusive	nonmarrying
nonclerical	nonexempt	nonmartial
nonclinical	nonexistence	nonmechanical
noncollapsible	nonexistent	nonmember
noncollectable	nonexplosive	nonmigratory
noncombining	nonexportable	nonmilitant
noncombustible	nonfactual	nonmilitary
noncommercial	nonfading	nonmortal
non-Communist	nonfat	nonnarcotic
noncompeting	nonfatal	nonnative
noncompetitive	nonfederated	nonnegotiable
noncompliance	nonfiction	nonneutral
noncomplying	nonfictional	nonnutritious
nonconcurrence	nonflammable	nonobligatory
noncondensing	nonflowering	nonobservance
nonconducting	nonfluctuating	nonobservant
nonconflicting	nonflying	nonoccurrence
nonconforming	nonformal	nonodorous
noncongenital	nonfulfillment	nonofficial
nonconsecutive	nonfunctional	nonoperational

nonoperative	nonresidential	nonstructural
nonoxidizing	nonresidual	nonsubscriber
nonpaying	nonrestricted	nonsuccessive
nonpayment	nonreturnable	nonsupporting
nonperformance	nonreversible	nonsustaining
nonperishable	nonrhyming	nonsymbolic
nonpermissible	nonrhythmic	nonsympathizer
nonphysical	nonrigid	nontarnishable
nonpoetic	nonrural	nontaxable
nonpoisonous	nonsalaried	nontechnical
nonpolitical	nonscientific	nonterritorial
nonporous	nonscoring	nonthinking
nonpredictable	nonseasonal	nontoxic
nonpreferential	nonsecular	nontransferable
nonprejudicial	nonsensitive	nontransparent
nonproducer	nonshattering	nontropical
nonprofessional	nonshrinkable	nontypical
nonprofitable	nonsmoker	nonuser
non-Protestant	nonsolid	nonvenomous
nonpunishable	nonsolvent	nonverbal
nonracial	nonspecializing	nonviolation
nonreciprocal	nonspiritual	nonvirulent
nonrecognition	nonstaining	nonvocal
nonrecoverable	nonstandard	nonvocational
nonrecurring	nonstarting	nonvolatile
nonredeemable	nonstatic	nonvoluntary
nonrefillable	nonstrategic	nonvoter
nonreigning	nonstretchable	nonvoting
nonreligious	nonstriking	nonwhite
nonrenewable	nonyielding	

non·age (nän′ij, nō′nij) *n.* [see NON- & AGE] **1.** the state of being under full legal age, usually twenty-one **2.** the period of immaturity

non·a·ge·nar·i·an (nän′ə ji ner′ē ən, nō′nə-) *adj.* [< L. *nonaginta,* ninety] ninety years old, or between the ages of ninety and one hundred —*n.* a person of this age

non·ag·gres·sion pact (nän′ə gresh′ən) an agreement between two nations not to attack each other

non·a·ligned (nän′ə līnd′) *adj.* not aligned with either side in a conflict —**non′a·lign′ment** *n.*

nonce (näns) *n.* [by merging of ME. (*for then*) *ones,* lit., (for the) once] the present use, occasion, or time: chiefly in **for the nonce**

non·cha·lant (nän′shə länt′, nän′shə lənt) *adj.* [Fr., ult. < L. *non,* not + *calere,* be warm] **1.** without warmth or enthusiasm **2.** casually indifferent —**non′cha·lance′** *n.* —**non′cha·lant′ly** *adv.*

non·com (nän′käm′) *n. colloq. clipped form of* NONCOM-MISSIONED OFFICER

non·com·bat·ant (nän käm′bə tənt, nän′kəm bat′ənt) *n.* **1.** a member of the armed forces not engaged in actual combat **2.** any civilian in wartime —*adj.* of noncombatants

non·com·mis·sioned officer (nän′kə mish′ənd) an enlisted person of any of various grades in the armed forces: in the U.S. Army, from corporal to sergeant major inclusive

non·com·mit·tal (nän′kə mit′'l) *adj.* not committing one to any point of view or course of action

non com·pos men·tis (nän′ käm′pəs men′tis) [L.] *Law* not of sound mind; mentally incapable of handling one's own affairs: often **non compos**

non·con·duc′tor *n.* a substance that does not readily transmit electricity, sound, heat, etc.

non·con·form′ist *n.* one who does not conform to prevailing attitudes, behavior, etc.; esp., [N-] in England, a Protestant who is not an Anglican —**non′con·form′ism,** **non′con·form′i·ty** *n.*

non′co·op′er·a′tion *n.* **1.** failure to work together or act jointly **2.** refusal to cooperate with a government, as by nonpayment of taxes: used as a form of protest

non·de·script (nän′di skript′) *adj.* [< L. *non,* not + *describere,* describe] belonging to no definite class or type; hard to classify or describe

none (nun) *pron.* [< OE. *ne,* not + *an,* one] **1.** no one; not anyone **2.** [*usually with pl. v.*] not any [*none* are his] —*n.* no part; nothing [I want *none* of it] —*adv.* not at all [*none* too soon]

non·en·ti·ty (nän en′tə tē) *n., pl.* **-ties** **1.** the state of not existing **2.** something that exists only in the mind **3.** a person of no importance

non·es·sen′tial *adj.* not essential; unnecessary —*n.* a nonessential person or thing

none·such (nun′such′) *n.* a person or thing unrivaled or unequaled; nonpareil

none·the·less (nun′thə les′) *adv.* nevertheless: also **none the less**

non·fer·rous (nän fer'əs) *adj.* **1.** not made of or containing iron **2.** of metals other than iron

non·in·ter·ven'tion *n.* the state or fact of not intervening; esp., a refraining by one nation from interference in the affairs of another

non·met'al *n.* an element lacking the characteristics of a metal, as oxygen, carbon, nitrogen, fluorine, sulfur, etc. — **non'me·tal'lic** *adj.*

non·mor'al *adj.* not connected in any way with morality; not moral and not immoral

non·ob·jec'tive *adj. same as* NONREPRESENTATIONAL

non·pa·reil (nän'pə rel') *adj.* [Fr. < *non,* not + *pareil,* equal] unequaled; peerless —*n.* someone or something unequaled or unrivaled

non·par'ti·san *adj.* not partisan; esp., not connected with any single political party: also **non·par'ti·zan** —**non·par'ti·san·ship'** *n.*

non·plus (nän plus', nän'plus') *vt.* **-plused'** or **-plussed', -plus'ing** or **-plus'sing** [L. *non,* not + *plus,* more] to cause to be so perplexed that one cannot go, speak, or act further

non·pro·duc'tive *adj.* **1.** not productive **2.** not directly related to the production of goods, as salesmen —**non'pro·duc'tive·ness** *n.*

non·prof'it *adj.* not intending or intended to earn a profit

non·rep·re·sen·ta'tion·al *adj.* designating or of art that does not attempt to represent in recognizable form any object in nature; abstract

non·res'i·dent *adj.* not residing in the locality where one works, attends school, etc. —*n.* a nonresident person — **non·res'i·dence** *n.*

non·re·sist'ant *adj.* not resistant; submitting to force or arbitrary authority —*n.* one who believes that force should not be used to oppose arbitrary authority, however unjust —**non're·sist'ance** *n.*

non·re·stric'tive (-ri strik'tiv) *adj. Gram.* designating a clause, phrase, or word felt as not essential to the sense, usually set off by commas (Ex.: John, *who is six feet tall,* is younger than Bill)

non·sched'uled *adj.* licensed for commercial air flights as demand warrants rather than on a schedule

non'sec·tar'i·an (-sek ter'ē ən) *adj.* not sectarian; not confined to any specific religion

non·sense (nän'sens, -səns) *n.* **1.** words, actions, etc. that are absurd or meaningless **2.** things of relatively no importance or value —*interj.* how foolish! how absurd! — **non·sen'si·cal** *adj.*

non se·qui·tur (nän' sek'wi tər) [L., it does not follow] **1.** a conclusion that does not follow from the premises **2.** a remark having no bearing on what has just been said

non'skid' *adj.* so constructed as to reduce skidding: said of a tire tread, etc.

non'stop' *adj., adv.* without a stop

non'sup·port' *n.* failure to provide for a legal dependent

non·un'ion *adj.* **1.** not belonging to a labor union **2.** not made or serviced under labor-union conditions **3.** refusing to recognize a labor union —**non·un'ion·ism** *n.* —**non·un'ion·ist** *n.*

non·vi'o·lence *n.* an abstaining from violence, as in opposing government policy —**non·vi'o·lent** *adj.*

noo·dle[1] (noo'd'l) *n.* [prob. < earlier *noddle,* the head] [Slang] the head

noo·dle[2] (noo'd'l) *n.* [G. *nudel*] a flat, narrow strip of dry dough, usually made with egg and served in soups, etc.

nook (nook) *n.* [ME. *nok*] **1.** a corner, esp. of a room **2.** a small recess or secluded spot

noon (noon) *n.* [< L. *nona (hora),* ninth (hour) (orig. 3:00 P.M.)] **1.** twelve o'clock in the daytime; midday **2.** the highest point or culmination —*adj.* of or at noon Also **noon'day', noon'time'**

no one not anybody; nobody

noose (noos) *n.* [< L. *nodus,* a knot] **1.** a loop formed in a rope, etc. by means of a slipknot so that the loop tightens as the rope is pulled **2.** anything that restricts one's freedom

nor (nôr) *conj.* [ME., contr. of *nother,* neither] and not; and not either *[she neither hears nor sees]*

Nor. 1. North **2.** Norway **3.** Norwegian

Nor·dic (nôr'dik) *adj.* [OE. *north,* north] of a Caucasoid physical type exemplified by the long-headed, tall, blond Scandinavians

Nor·folk (nôr'fək) seaport in SE Va.: pop. 308,000

norm (nôrm) *n.* [< L. *norma,* rule] a standard or model; esp., the standard of achievement of a large group

nor·mal (nôr'm'l) *adj.* **1.** conforming with an acceptable standard or norm; natural; usual; regular **2.** free from disease, disorder, etc.; sound in body or mind —*n.* **1.** anything normal **2.** the usual state, amount, etc. —**nor'mal·cy, nor·mal'i·ty** (-mal'ə tē) *n.*

nor·mal·ize (-mə līz') *vt., vi.* **-ized', -iz'ing** to make or become normal; bring or come into conformity with a standard —**nor'mal·i·za'tion** *n.*

nor·mal·ly *adv.* **1.** in a normal manner **2.** under normal circumstances; ordinarily

Nor·man (nôr'mən) *n.* [< OFr.] **1.** any of the Scandinavians who occupied Normandy in the 10th cent. A.D. **2.** a descendant of the Normans and French who conquered England in 1066 **3.** *same as* NORMAN FRENCH **4.** a native of Normandy —*adj.* of Normandy, the Normans, their language, etc.

Norman Conquest the conquest of England by the Normans under William the Conqueror in 1066

Nor·man·dy (nôr'mən dē) region in NW France, on the English Channel

Norman French the French spoken in England by the Norman conquerors

norm·a·tive (nôr'mə tiv) *adj.* of or establishing a norm, or standard

Norse (nôrs) *adj., n.* [prob. < Du. *noord,* north] Scandinavian, esp. (of) the Norwegian and Icelandic languages —**the Norse** the Scandinavians

Norse'man (-mən) *n., pl.* **-men** a member of the ancient Scandinavian people

north (nôrth) *n.* [OE.] **1.** the direction to the right of one facing the sunset (0° or 360° on the compass, opposite south) **2.** a region in or toward this direction **3.** *[often* N-*]* the northern part of the earth —*adj.* **1.** in, of, or toward the north **2.** from the north —*adv.* in or toward the north —**the North** that part of the U.S. bounded on the south by Maryland, the Ohio River, and S Missouri

North America N continent in the Western Hemisphere: c.9,330,000 sq. mi.; pop. 314,000,000 —**North American**

North Carolina Southern State of the U.S.: 52,712 sq. mi.; pop. 5,082,000; cap. Raleigh: abbrev. **N.C., NC** — **North Car·o·lin·i·an** (kar'ə lin'ē ən)

North Dakota Middle Western State of the U.S.: 70,665 sq. mi.; pop. 618,000; cap. Bismarck: abbrev. **N.Dak., ND** —**North Da·ko'tan**

north·east (nôrth'ēst'; *nautical* nôr-) *n.* **1.** the direction halfway between north and east **2.** a region in or toward this direction —*adj.* **1.** in, of, or toward the northeast **2.** from the northeast —*adv.* in, toward, or from the northeast —**the Northeast** the northeastern part of the U.S., esp. New England —**north'east'er·ly** *adj., adv.* — **north'east'ern** *adj.* —**north'east'ward** (-wərd) *adv., adj.* — **north'east'wards** *adv.*

north·east·er (nôrth'ēs'tər; *nautical* nôr-) *n.* a storm or strong wind from the northeast

north·er (nôr'thər) *n.* a storm or strong wind from the north

north·er·ly (nôr'thər lē) *adj., adv.* **1.** toward the north **2.** from the north

north·ern (nôr'thərn) *adj.* **1.** in, of, or toward the north **2.** from the north **3.** [N-] of the North —**north'ern·most'** *adj.*

north'ern·er *n.* a native or inhabitant of the north, specif. [N-] of the northern part of the U.S.

Northern Hemisphere that half of the earth north of the equator

Northern Ireland division of the United Kingdom, in NE Ireland: 5,462 sq. mi.; pop. 1,512,000; cap. Belfast

northern lights *same as* AURORA BOREALIS

north-north·east (nôrth'nôrth'ēst'; *nautical* nôr'nôr-) *n.* the direction halfway between due north and northeast — *adj., adv.* in, toward, or from this direction

north'-north'west' (-west') *n.* the direction halfway between due north and northwest —*adj., adv.* in, toward, or from this direction

North Pole the northern end of the earth's axis

North Sea arm of the Atlantic, between Great Britain & the European mainland

North Star Polaris, the bright star almost directly above the North Pole

north'ward (-wərd) *adv., adj.* toward the north: also **north'wards** *adv.* —*n.* a northward direction, point, or region —**north'ward·ly** *adv., adj.*

north·west (nôrth'west'; *nautical* nôr-) *n.* **1.** the direction halfway between north and west **2.** a region in or toward this direction —*adj.* **1.** in, of, or toward the northwest **2.** from the northwest —*adv.* in, toward, or from the northwest —**the Northwest** the northwestern part of the U.S., esp. Wash., Oreg., and Ida. —**north′west′er·ly** *adj.*, *adv.* —**north′west′ern** *adj.* —**north′west′ward** (-wərd) *adv.*, *adj.* —**north′west′wards** *adv.*

north·west·er (nôrth′wes′tər; *nautical* nôr-) *n.* a storm or strong wind from the northwest

Northwest Territories division of N Canada: 1,304,903 sq. mi.; pop. 29,000; cap. Yellowknife: abbrev. **N.W.T.**

Norw. 1. Norway **2.** Norwegian

Nor·way (nôr′wā′) country in N Europe: 125,064 sq. mi.; pop. 3,851,000; cap. Oslo

Nor·we·gian (nôr wē′jən) *adj.* of Norway, its people, language, etc. —*n.* **1.** a native or inhabitant of Norway **2.** the language of Norway

Nos., nos. numbers

nose (nōz) *n.* [OE. *nosu*] **1.** the part of the face between the mouth and the eyes, having two openings for breathing and smelling: in animals, the snout, muzzle, etc. **2.** the sense of smell **3.** power to perceive as by scent [a *nose* for news] **4.** anything noselike in shape or position, as a prow, front of an airplane, etc. —*vt.* **nosed, nos′ing 1.** to discover as by smell **2.** to rub with the nose **3.** to push (a way, etc.) with the front forward —*vi.* **1.** to pry inquisitively **2.** to move forward —**nose out** to defeat by a very small margin —**on the nose** [Slang] precisely; exactly —**turn up one's nose at** to sneer at; scorn —**under one's (very) nose** in plain view

nose′bleed′ *n.* a bleeding from the nose

nose cone the cone-shaped foremost part of a rocket or missile, resistant to intense heat

nose dive 1. a swift, downward plunge of an airplane, nose first **2.** any sudden, sharp drop, as in profits or prices —**nose′-dive′** *vi.* **-dived′, -div′ing**

nose drops medication administered through the nose with a dropper

nose′gay′ *n.* [NOSE + GAY (in obs. sense of "gay object")] a small bunch of flowers

nose′piece′ *n.* **1.** that part of a helmet which protects the nose **2.** anything noselike in form or position **3.** the bridge of a pair of eyeglasses

nos·tal·gia (näs tal′jə) *n.* [< Gr. *nostos*, a return + -ALGIA] **1.** homesickness **2.** a longing for something far away or long ago —**nos·tal′gic** (-jik) *adj.* —**nos·tal′gi·cal·ly** *adv.*

nos·tril (näs′trəl) *n.* [< OE. *nosu*, the nose + *thyrel*, hole] either of the openings into the nose

nos·trum (näs′trəm) *n.* [L., ours] **1.** a quack medicine **2.** a patent medicine **3.** a pet scheme for solving some problem

nos·y, nos·ey (nōz′ē) *adj.* **-i·er, -i·est** [Colloq.] prying; inquisitive —**nos′i·ly** *adv.* —**nos′i·ness** *n.*

not (nät) *adv.* [< ME. *nought*] in no manner, degree, etc.: a word expressing negation or the idea of *no*

no·ta·ble (nōt′ə b'l) *adj.* [< L. *notare*, to note] worthy of notice; remarkable —*n.* a famous or well-known person —**no′ta·bly** *adv.*

no·ta·rize (nōt′ə rīz′) *vt.* **-rized′, -riz′ing** to certify or attest (a document) as a notary public —**no′ta·ri·za′tion** *n.*

no·ta·ry (nōt′ər ē) *n., pl.* **-ries** [< L. *notare*, to note] *clipped form of* NOTARY PUBLIC

notary public *pl.* **notaries public, notary publics** an official authorized to certify or attest documents, take affidavits, etc.

no·ta·tion (nō tā′shən) *n.* [< L. *notare*, to note] **1.** the use of a system of signs or symbols for words, quantities, etc. **2.** any such system used in algebra, music, etc. **3.** a brief note **4.** a noting in writing —**no·ta′tion·al** *adj.*

notch (näch) *n.* [by merging of ME. *an oche*, a notch] **1.** a V-shaped cut in an edge or surface **2.** a narrow, deep pass **3.** [Colloq.] a step; degree [a *notch* better] —*vt.* **1.** to cut a notch or notches in **2.** to record, as by means of notches —**notched** *adj.*

note (nōt) *n.* [< L. *nota*, a mark] **1.** a distinguishing feature [a *note* of joy] **2.** importance or distinction [a person of *note*] **3.** a brief writing to aid the memory; memorandum **4.** a comment or explanation; annotation **5.** notice; heed [worthy of *note*] **6.** *a*) a short letter *b*) a formal diplomatic communication **7.** any of certain commercial papers relating to

A   B   C   D   E   F   G

NOTES

(A, whole; B, half; C, quarter; D, eighth; E, sixteenth; F, thirty-second; G, sixty-fourth)

debts or payment of money [a promissory *note*] **8.** a cry or call, as of a bird **9.** a signal or intimation [a *note* of warning] **10.** *Music a*) a tone of definite pitch *b*) a symbol for a tone, indicating pitch and duration *c*) a key of a piano, etc. —*vt.* **not′ed, not′ing 1.** to heed; observe **2.** to set down in writing **3.** to mention specially —**compare notes** to exchange views —**take notes** to write down notes, as during a lecture

note′book′ *n.* a book in which notes, or memorandums, are kept

not·ed (nōt′id) *adj.* distinguished; renowned; eminent

note′wor′thy *adj.* worthy of note; outstanding; remarkable —**note′wor′thi·ness** *n.*

noth·ing (nuth′iŋ) *n.* [OE. *na thing*] **1.** no thing; not anything **2.** nothingness **3.** a thing that does not exist **4.** a person or thing considered of little or no importance **5.** a nought; zero —*adv.* not at all; in no way —**for nothing 1.** free; at no cost **2.** in vain **3.** without reason

noth′ing·ness *n.* **1.** nonexistence **2.** insignificance **3.** unconsciousness

no·tice (nōt′is) *n.* [see NOTE] **1.** an announcement or warning **2.** a short article about a book, play, etc. **3.** a written or printed sign giving some public information, warning, etc. **4.** attention; heed **5.** a formal warning of intention to end an agreement or contract at a certain time —*vt.* **-ticed, -tic·ing 1.** to refer to; mention **2.** to pay attention to; observe —**serve notice** to announce; warn —**take notice** to observe

no′tice·a·ble *adj.* **1.** readily noticed; conspicuous **2.** significant —**no′tice·a·bly** *adv.*

no·ti·fi·ca·tion (nōt′ə fi kā′shən) *n.* **1.** a notifying or being notified **2.** the notice given or received **3.** the letter, form, etc. notifying

no·ti·fy (nōt′ə fī′) *vt.* **-fied′, -fy′ing** [< L. *notus*, known + *facere*, to make] to give notice to; inform —**no′ti·fi′er** *n.*

no·tion (nō′shən) *n.* [see NOTE] **1.** *a*) a mental image *b*) a vague thought **2.** a belief; opinion **3.** an inclination; whim **4.** an intention **5.** [*pl.*] small, useful articles, as needles, thread, etc., sold in a store

no′tion·al *adj.* **1.** of or expressing notions, or concepts **2.** imaginary **3.** visionary; fanciful

no·to·ri·e·ty (nōt′ə rī′ə tē) *n.* the quality or state of being notorious

no·to·ri·ous (nō tôr′ē əs) *adj.* [see NOTE] widely known, esp. unfavorably —**no·to′ri·ous·ly** *adv.*

no′-trump′ *adj. Bridge* with no suit being trumps —*n. Bridge* a no-trump bid or hand

Not·ting·ham (nät′iŋ əm) city in C England: pop. 305,000

not·with·stand·ing (nät′with stan′diŋ, -with-) *prep.* in spite of —*adv.* nevertheless —*conj.* although

nou·gat (nōō′gət) *n.* [Fr. < Pr. < L. *nux*, nut] a confection of sugar paste with nuts

nought (nôt) *n.* [< OE. *ne*, not + *awiht*, aught] **1.** nothing **2.** *Arith.* the figure zero (0)

noun (noun) *n.* [< L. *nomen*, a name] *Gram.* **1.** any of a class of words naming or denoting a person, thing, action, quality, etc. **2.** any word, phrase, or clause so used —**noun′al** *adj.*

nour·ish (nur′ish) *vt.* [< L. *nutrire*] **1.** to feed or sustain with substances necessary to life and growth **2.** to foster; promote —**nour′ish·ing** *adj.*

nour′ish·ment (-mənt) *n.* **1.** a nourishing or being nourished **2.** something that nourishes; food

nou·veau riche (nōō′vō rēsh′) *pl.* **nou·veaux riches** (nōō′vō rēsh′) [Fr., newly rich] a newly rich person: often connoting lack of culture

Nov. November

no·va (nō′və) *n., pl.* **-vae** (-vē), **-vas** [< L. *nova* (*stella*), new (star)] *Astron.* a star that suddenly becomes vastly brighter and then gradually dims

No·va Sco·tia (nō′və skō′shə) province of SE Canada: 21,425 sq. mi.; pop. 756,000; cap. Halifax: abbrev. **N.S.** —**No′va Sco′tian**

nov·el (näv′'l) *adj.* [< L. dim. of *novus*, new] new and unusual —*n.* a relatively long fictional prose narrative with a more or less complex plot

nov·el·ette (näv′ə let′) *n.* a short novel

nov′el·ist *n.* one who writes novels

no·vel·la (nō vel′ə) *n., pl.* **-las, -le** (-ē) [It.] **1.** a short prose narrative **2.** a short novel

nov′el·ty *n., pl.* **-ties 1.** the quality of being novel **2.** something new, fresh, or unusual **3.** a small, often cheap, cleverly made article: *usually used in pl.*

No·vem·ber (nō vem′bər) *n.* [< L. *novem*, nine: 9th month in Roman year] eleventh month of the year, having 30 days: abbrev. **Nov.**

no·ve·na (nō vē'nə) *n.* [< L. *novem,* nine] *R.C.Ch.* a nine-day period of devotions

nov·ice (näv'is) *n.* [< L. *novus,* new] **1.** a person on probation in a religious order before taking vows **2.** a person new to a particular activity, etc.; beginner

no·vi·ti·ate (nō vish'ē it) *n.* **1.** the period or state of being a novice **2.** the quarters of religious novices

No·vo·cain (nō'və kān') [L. *nov(us),* new + (c)OCAIN(E)] *a trademark for* PROCAINE: also sp. **Novocaine**

now (nou) *adv.* [OE. *nu*] **1.** *a)* at the present time *b)* at once **2.** at the time referred to; then; next **3.** very recently [he left just *now*] **4.** with things as they are [now I'll never know] *—conj.* since; seeing that *—n.* the present time [that's all for *now*] *—adj.* of the present time *—interj.* an exclamation of warning, reproach, etc. **—now and then** (or **again**) occasionally

now'a·days' (-ə dāz') *adv.* in these days; at the present time *—n.* the present time

no·way (nō'wā') *adv.* by no means; not at all: now often **no' way'**, used as an interjection: also **no'ways'** (-wāz')

no·where (nō'hwer', -wer') *adv.* not in, at, or to any place **—nowhere near** not nearly

no·wise (nō'wīz') *adv.* in no manner; noway

nox·ious (näk'shəs) *adj.* [< L. *nocere,* to hurt] harmful to health or morals; injurious; unwholesome **—nox'ious·ly** *adv.* **—nox'ious·ness** *n.*

noz·zle (näz'l) *n.* [dim. of NOSE] **1.** the spout at the end of a hose, pipe, etc. **2.** [Slang] the nose

Np *Chem.* neptunium

N.S. Nova Scotia

-n't *a contracted form of* not [aren't]

NT., NT, N.T. New Testament

nth (enth) *adj.* of the indefinitely large or small number represented by *n* **—to the nth degree** (or **power**) **1.** to an indefinite degree or power **2.** to an extreme

nt. wt. net weight

nu (nōō, nyōō) *n.* the thirteenth letter of the Greek alphabet (N, *ν*)

nu·ance (nōō'äns, nyōō'-; nōō äns') *n.* [Fr. < *nuer,* to shade] a slight variation in tone, color, meaning, etc. **— nu'anced** *adj.*

nub (nub) *n.* [var. of *knub,* knob] **1.** a lump or small piece **2.** [Colloq.] the main point; gist

nub·bin (nub'in) *n.* [dim. of NUB] **1.** a small or imperfect ear of Indian corn **2.** a small piece

nub·by (nub'ē) *adj.* **-bi·er, -bi·est** having a rough, knotted surface [a *nubby* fabric]

nu·bile (nōō'b'l, nyōō'-; -bīl) *adj.* [Fr. < L. *nubere,* to marry] marriageable: said of a young woman who seems fully developed sexually

nu·cle·ar (nōō'klē ər, nyōō'-) *adj.* **1.** of, like, or forming a nucleus **2.** of, involving, or using atomic nuclei or atomic energy, bombs, power, etc.

nuclear family a family unit consisting of parents and their children living in one household

nuclear fission the splitting of the nuclei of atoms, with conversion of part of the mass into energy: the principle of the atomic bomb

nuclear fusion the fusion of atomic nuclei into a nucleus of heavier mass, with a resultant loss in the combined mass, which is converted into energy, as in a hydrogen bomb

nuclear physics the branch of physics dealing with the structure of atomic nuclei, nuclear forces, etc.

nuclear reactor a device for creating a controlled nuclear chain reaction in a fissionable fuel, as for the production of energy

nu·cle·ate (nōō'klē it, nyōō'-; *also,* & *for v. always,* -āt') *adj.* having a nucleus *—vt., vi.* **-at'ed, -at'ing** to form into a nucleus **—nu'cle·a'tion** *n.*

nu·cle·ic acid (nōō klē'ik, nyōō-) any of a group of complex organic acids found esp. in the nucleus of all living cells and essential to life

nu·cle·us (nōō'klē əs, nyōō'-) *n., pl.* **-cle·i'** (-ī'), **-cle·us·es** [L., a kernel] **1.** a central thing or part around which others are grouped **2.** any center of growth or development **3.** the central part of an atom, the fundamental particles of which are the proton and neutron **4.** the central mass of protoplasm in most plant and animal cells **5.** a stable arrangement of atoms that may occur in many organic compounds **6.** the bright central part of the head of a comet

nude (nōōd, nyōōd) *adj.* [L. *nudus*] naked; bare *—n.* **1.** a nude human figure, esp. as in painting, sculpture, etc. **2.**

the condition of being nude [in the *nude*] **—nude'ly** *adv.* **—nude'ness, nu'di·ty** *n.*

nudge (nuj) *vt.* **nudged, nudg'ing** [< ?] to push gently, esp. with the elbow, in order to get attention, etc. *—n.* a gentle push with the elbow, etc.

nud'ism *n.* the practice or cult of going nude for hygienic reasons **—nud'ist** *n., adj.*

nu·ga·to·ry (nōō'gə tôr'ē, nyōō'-) *adj.* [< L. *nugari,* to trifle] **1.** trifling; worthless **2.** not operative; invalid

nug·get (nug'it) *n.* [prob. < dial. *nug,* lump] a lump, esp. of native gold

nui·sance (nōō's'ns, nyōō'-) *n.* [< L. *nocere,* annoy] an act, thing, person, etc. causing trouble, annoyance, or inconvenience

null (nul) *adj.* [< L. *nullus,* none] **1.** without legal force; invalid: usually in the phrase **null and void 2.** amounting to nought **3.** of no value, effect, etc.

nul·li·fy (nul'ə fī') *vt.* **-fied', -fy'ing** [< L. *nullus,* none + *facere,* make] **1.** to make legally null **2.** to make valueless **3.** to cancel out **—nul'li·fi·ca'tion** *n.* **—nul'li·fi'er** *n.*

nul·li·ty (nul'ə tē) *n.* **1.** a being null **2.** *pl.* **-ties** anything that is null

numb (num) *adj.* [< ME. *nimen,* take] deadened; insensible [numb with grief] *—vt.* to make numb **—numb'ly** *adv.* **—numb'ness** *n.*

num·ber (num'bər) *n.* [< L. *numerus*] **1.** a symbol or word showing how many or which one in a series (Ex.: 2, 27, four, sixth) **2.** [*pl.*] arithmetic **3.** the sum or total of persons or units **4.** *a)* [often *pl.*] many *b)* [*pl.*] numerical superiority **5.** quantity **6.** *a)* a single issue of a periodical *b)* a single song, dance, etc. in a program of entertainment **7.** [Colloq.] a person or thing singled out [a smart *number*] **8.** *Gram.* the form of a word as indicating either singular or plural **9.** [*pl.*] metrical form or lines *—vt.* **1.** to count; enumerate **2.** to give a number to **3.** to include as one of a group **4.** to limit the number of **5.** to comprise; total *—vi.* to be numbered **—a number of** several or many **—beyond** (or **without**) **number** too numerous to be counted **—the numbers** an illegal lottery based on certain numbers published in newspapers: also **numbers pool** (or **racket**)

num'ber·less *adj.* **1.** too many to be counted; countless **2.** without a number or numbers

Num·bers (num'bərz) the 4th book of the Pentateuch in the Bible: abbrev. **Num.**

nu·mer·a·ble (nōō'mər ə b'l, nyōō'-) *adj.* that can be numbered or counted

nu'mer·al (-mər əl) *adj.* [< L. *numerus,* number] of or denoting a number or numbers *—n.* a figure, letter, or word expressing a number: see ARABIC NUMERALS, ROMAN NUMERALS

nu'mer·ate' (-mə rāt') *vt.* **-at'ed, -at'ing** to count one by one; enumerate

nu'mer·a'tion *n.* **1.** a numbering or counting **2.** a system of numbering

nu·mer·a·tor (nōō'mə rāt'ər, nyōō'-) *n. Math.* the term above the line in a fraction, indicating how many of the specified parts of a unit are taken

nu·mer·i·cal (nōō mer'i k'l, nyōō-) *adj.* **1.** of, or having the nature of, number **2.** in or by numbers **3.** expressed by numbers, not letters **—nu·mer'i·cal·ly** *adv.*

nu·mer·ol·o·gy (nōō'mə räl'ə jē, nyōō'-) *n.* the attributing of occult meanings to numbers, as in birth dates

nu·mer·ous (nōō'mər əs, nyōō'-) *adj.* **1.** consisting of a great number **2.** very many **—nu'mer·ous·ly** *adv.*

Nu·mid·i·a (nōō mid'ē ə, nyōō-) ancient country in N Africa **—Nu·mid'i·an** *adj., n.*

nu·mis·mat·ic (nōō'miz mat'ik, nyōō'-; -mis-) *adj.* [< L. *numisma,* a coin] **1.** of coins or medals **2.** of currency **3.** of numismatics

nu'mis·mat'ics (-iks) *n.pl.* [with *sing. v.*] the study or collection of coins, medals, paper money, etc. **—nu·mis'ma·tist** (-mə tist) *n.*

num·skull, numb·skull (num'skul') *n.* [NUM(B) + SKULL] a stupid person; dunce

nun (nun) *n.* [< LL. *nonna*] a woman devoted to a religious life, esp. one living in a convent under vows

nun·ci·o (nun'shē ō', -sē-) *n., pl.* **-os'** [< It. < L. *nuntius,* messenger] an ambassador of the Pope to a foreign government

nun·ner·y (nun'ər ē) *n., pl.* **-ies** *a former name for* CONVENT

nup·tial (nup'shəl, -chəl) *adj.* [< L. *nubere,* to marry] **1.** of marriage **2.** of mating *—n.* [*pl.*] a wedding

Nu·rem·berg (noor'əm burg', nyoor'-) city in NC Bavaria, West Germany: pop. 472,000

nurse (nurs) *n.* [< L. *nutrire*, nourish] **1.** a woman hired to take care of another's children **2.** a person trained to take care of the sick, assist surgeons, etc. —*vt.* **nursed, nurs'ing 1.** to suckle (an infant) **2.** to take care of (a child, invalid, etc.) **3.** to nourish, foster, etc. **4.** to try to cure [to *nurse* a cold] **5.** to use or handle so as to protect or conserve **6.** to clasp; fondle —*vi.* **1.** to feed at the breast; suckle **2.** to serve as a nurse —**nurs'er** *n.*

nurse'maid' *n.* a woman hired to take care of a child or children: also **nurs'er·y·maid'**

nurs·er·y (nur'sə rē) *n., pl.* **-ies 1.** a room in a home, set aside for the children **2.** *same as:* a) NURSERY SCHOOL b) DAY NURSERY **3.** a place where young trees or plants are raised for sale, etc.

nurs'er·y·man (-mən) *n., pl.* **-men** one who owns, operates, or works for a nursery (sense 3)

nursery rhyme a poem for children

nursery school a prekindergarten school for young children aged usually 3 to 5

nursing home a residence providing care for the infirm, chronically ill, disabled, etc.

nur·ture (nur'chər) *n.* [< L. *nutrire*, nourish] **1.** food **2.** training; rearing —*vt.* **-tured, -tur·ing 1.** to feed or nourish **2.** to train, rear, foster, etc.

nut (nut) *n.* [OE. *hnutu*] **1.** a dry, one-seeded fruit, consisting of a kernel, often edible, in a woody shell, as the walnut **2.** the kernel itself **3.** loosely, any hardshelled, relatively nonperishable fruit, as the peanut **4.** a small, usually metal block with a threaded hole, for screwing onto a bolt, etc. **5.** [Colloq.] the cost that must be recovered before a profit can be made **6.** [Slang] a) a crazy or eccentric person b) a devotee; fan —*vi.* **nut'ted, nut'ting** to hunt for or gather nuts

NUTMEG

nut'crack'er *n.* **1.** a device, usually hinged, for cracking nutshells **2.** a bird related to the crow, that feeds on nuts

nut'hatch' (-hach') *n.* a small, nut-eating bird with a sharp beak and short tail

nut'meat' *n.* the kernel of a nut

nut'meg' (-meg') *n.* [< L. *nux*, nut + LL. *muscus*, musk]

1. the hard, aromatic seed of an East Indian tree: it is grated and used as a spice **2.** the tree

nut'pick' *n.* a small, sharp instrument for digging out the kernels of cracked nuts

nu·tri·a (noo'trē ə, nyoo'-) *n.* [Sp. < L. *lutra*, otter] **1.** a S. American water rodent with webbed feet **2.** its soft, brown fur

nu·tri·ent (noo'trē ənt, nyoo'-) *adj.* [< L. *nutrire*, nourish] nourishing —*n.* anything nutritious

nu'tri·ment (-trə mənt) *n.* anything that nourishes; food

nu·tri·tion (noo trish'ən, nyoo-) *n.* [see NUTRIENT] **1.** a nourishing or being nourished; esp., the process by which an organism takes in and assimilates food **2.** nourishment **3.** the science or study of proper diet —**nu·tri'tion·al** *adj.* —**nu·tri'tion·al·ly** *adv.* —**nu·tri'tion·ist** *n.*

nu·tri'tious (-əs) *adj.* nourishing; of value as food —**nu·tri'tious·ly** *adv.*

nu·tri·tive (noo'trə tiv, nyoo'-) *adj.* **1.** having to do with nutrition **2.** *same as* NUTRITIOUS

nuts (nuts) *adj.* [Slang] crazy; foolish —*interj.* [Slang] an exclamation of disgust, scorn, etc.: often in the phrase **nuts to** (someone or something) —**be nuts about** [Slang] to be very enthusiastic about

nut'shell' *n.* the shell enclosing the kernel of a nut —**in a nutshell** in concise form; in a few words

nut'ty *adj.* **-ti·er, -ti·est 1.** containing or producing nuts **2.** having a nutlike flavor **3.** [Slang] a) very enthusiastic b) queer, crazy, etc. —**nut'ti·ness** *n.*

nuz·zle (nuz'l) *vt., vi.* **-zled, -zling** [< NOSE] **1.** to push (against) or rub with the nose or snout **2.** to nestle; snuggle —**nuz'zler** *n.*

NV Nevada

NW, N.W., n.w. 1. northwest **2.** northwestern

N.W.T. Northwest Territories

N.Y., NY New York

N.Y.C. New York City

ny·lon (nī'län) *n.* [arbitrary coinage] **1.** an elastic, very strong synthetic material made into fiber, bristles, etc. **2.** [pl.] stockings made of this

nymph (nimf) *n.* [< Gr. *nymphē*] **1.** *Gr. & Rom. Myth.* any of a group of minor nature goddesses, represented as beautiful maidens living in rivers, trees, etc. **2.** a lovely young woman **3.** the young of an insect with incomplete metamorphosis

nym·pho·ma·ni·a (nim'fə mā'nē ə) *n.* uncontrollable desire by a woman for sexual intercourse —**nym'pho·ma'·ni·ac'** (-ak') *n., adj.*

N.Z., N.Zeal. New Zealand

O

O, o (ō) *n., pl.* **O's, o's 1.** the fifteenth letter of the English alphabet **2.** the numeral zero **3.** *Physics* the symbol for ohm

O (ō) *interj.* an exclamation used: **1.** in direct address [O Lord!] **2.** to express surprise, fear, etc.: now usually *oh* —*n., pl.* **O's** a use of this exclamation

o' (ə, ō) *prep. an abbreviated form of* of

O 1. *Linguis.* Old [OFr.] **2.** *Chem.* oxygen

O. 1. Ocean **2.** October **3.** Ohio **4.** Ontario

oaf (ōf) *n.* [< ON. *alfr*, elf] a stupid, clumsy fellow; lout —**oaf'ish** *adj.*

O·a·hu (ō ä'hoo) chief island of Hawaii

oak (ōk) *n.* [OE. *ac*] **1.** a large hardwood tree or bush bearing nuts called *acorns* **2.** its wood —*adj.* of oak —**oak'en** *adj.*

Oak·land (ōk'lənd) seaport in W Calif., on San Francisco Bay: pop. 362,000

Oak Ridge city in E Tenn.: center for atomic research: pop. 28,000

oa·kum (ō'kəm) *n.* [< OE. *a-*, out + *camb*, a comb] stringy, hemp fiber got by taking apart old ropes: used in caulking

oar (ôr) *n.* [OE. *ar*] a long pole with a broad blade at one end, used in rowing —*vt., vi.* to row —**rest on one's oars** to stop to rest or relax

oar'lock' *n.* a device, often U-shaped, for holding an oar in place in rowing

oars·man (ôrz'mən) *n., pl.* **-men** a man who rows; esp., an expert at rowing —**oars'man·ship'** *n.*

OAS, O.A.S. Organization of American States

o·a·sis (ō ā'sis) *n., pl.* **-ses** (-sēz) [< Gr. *oasis*] a fertile place in a desert, due to the presence of water

oat (ōt) *n.* [OE. *ate*] [usually pl.] **1.** a hardy cereal grass **2.** its edible grain —**feel one's oats** [Slang] **1.** to be frisky **2.** to feel and act important —**oat'en** *adj.*

oat'cake' *n.* a thin, flat cake made of oatmeal

oath (ōth) *n., pl.* **oaths** (ōthz, ōths) [OE. *ath*] **1.** a) a declaration, as by appeal to God, that one will speak the truth, keep a promise, etc. b) the thing declared **2.** the profane use of God's name, as in anger **3.** a swearword; curse —**take oath** to promise or declare with an oath

oat'meal' *n.* **1.** oats crushed into meal or flakes **2.** a porridge made from this

Ob (ōb; *Russ.* ôb'y') river in W Siberia, flowing into the Arctic Ocean: 2,495 mi.

ob- [< L. *ob*] *a prefix meaning:* **1.** to, toward, before [object] **2.** against [obnoxious] **3.** upon, over [obfuscate] **4.** completely [obsolete] In words of Latin origin, *ob-* assimilates to *o-* before *m*, *oc-* before *c*, *of-* before *f*, and *op-* before *p*

OB, O.B. 1. obstetrician **2.** obstetrics

ob. [L. *obiit*] he (or she) died

O·ba·di·ah (ō'bə dī'ə) *Bible* **1.** a minor Hebrew prophet **2.** the book containing his prophecies: abbrev. **Ob., Obad.**

ob·bli·ga·to (äb′lə gät′ō) *adj*. [It., lit., obliged < L.] *Music* indispensable: said earlier of a required accompaniment but now usually of an optional one —*n., pl.* **-tos, -ti** (-ē) such an accompaniment

ob·du·rate (äb′door ət, -dyoor-) *adj*. [< L. *ob-*, intens. + *durus*, hard] 1. hardhearted 2. hardened and unrepenting 3. stubborn; obstinate —**ob′du·ra·cy** (-ə sē) *n*. —**ob′du·rate·ly** *adv*.

o·be·di·ent (ō bē′dē ənt) *adj*. obeying or willing to obey —**o·be′di·ence** *n*. —**o·be′di·ent·ly** *adv*.

o·bei·sance (ō bā′s′ns, -bē′-) *n*. [< OFr. *obeir*, obey] 1. a gesture of respect, as a bow 2. homage; deference —**o·bei′sant** *adj*.

ob·e·lisk (äb′ə lisk, ō′bə-) *n*. [< Gr. *obelos*, needle] a tall, four-sided stone pillar tapering to its pyramidal top

O·ber·on (ō′bə rän′, -bər ən) in early folklore, the king of fairyland

o·bese (ō bēs′) *adj*. [< L. *ob-* (see OB-) + *edere*, eat] very fat; stout —**o·be′si·ty** (-ə tē) *n*.

o·bey (ō bā′) *vt*. [< L. *ob-* (see OB-) + *audire*, hear] 1. to carry out the orders of 2. to carry out (an order) 3. to be guided by [to *obey* one's conscience] —*vi*. to be obedient

ob·fus·cate (äb′fəs kāt′, äb fus′kāt) *vt*. **-cat′ed, -cat′ing** [< L. *ob-* (see OB-) + *fuscus*, dark] to obscure; confuse; bewilder —**ob′fus·ca′tion** *n*.

o·bi (ō′bē) *n*. [Jpn.] a broad sash with a bow in back, worn with a Japanese kimono

o·bit (ō′bit, äb′it) *n. same as* OBITUARY

o·bit·u·ar·y (ō bich′oo wer′ē) *n., pl.* **-ies** [< L. *obire*, die] a notice of someone's death, usually with a brief biography —*adj*. of or recording a death

obj. 1. object 2. objective

ob·ject (äb′jikt) *n*. [< ML. *objectum*, thing thrown in the way < L. *ob-* (see OB-) + *jacere*, to throw] 1. a thing that can be seen or touched 2. a person or thing to which action, feeling, etc. is directed 3. purpose; goal 4. *Gram*. a noun or substantive that receives the action of a verb, or is governed by a preposition —*vt*. (əb jekt′, äb-) to state in opposition or disapproval —*vi*. to feel or express opposition or disapproval —**ob′ject·less** *adj*. —**ob·jec′tor** *n*.

ob·jec·tion (əb jek′shən, äb-) *n*. 1. a feeling or expression of opposition or disapproval 2. a reason for objecting

ob·jec′tion·a·ble *adj*. 1. open to objection 2. disagreeable; offensive —**ob·jec′tion·a·bly** *adv*.

ob·jec′tive *adj*. 1. existing as an object or fact, independent of the mind; real 2. concerned with the realities of the thing dealt with rather than the thoughts of the artist, writer, speaker, etc. 3. without bias or prejudice 4. *Gram*. designating or of the case of an object of a preposition or verb —*n*. 1. something aimed at 2. the lens in a microscope, telescope, etc. nearest to the object observed: also called **object glass** 3. *Gram*. a) the objective case b) a word in this case —**ob·jec′tive·ly** *adv*. —**ob·jec·tiv·i·ty** (äb′jek tiv′ə tē) *n*.

object lesson an actual or practical demonstration or exemplification of some principle

ob·jet d'art (äb′zhā där′, ub′-) *pl.* **ob·jets d'art** (äb′zhā-, ub′-) [Fr.] a relatively small object of artistic value, as a figurine, vase, etc.

ob·jur·gate (äb′jər gāt′) *vt*. **-gat′ed, -gat′ing** [< L. *ob-* (see OB-) + *jurgare*, chide] to upbraid sharply; rebuke —**ob′jur·ga′tion** *n*.

ob·late (äb′lāt) *adj*. [< ModL. *oblatus*, thrust forward] flattened at the poles [an *oblate* spheroid]

ob·la·tion (ä blā′shən) *n*. [< L. *oblatus*, offered] an offering made to God or a god

ob·li·ga·to (äb′lə gāt′) *vt*. **-gat′ed, -gat′ing** [see OBLIGE] to bind by a contract, promise, sense of duty, etc.

ob′li·ga′tion *n*. 1. an obligating or being obligated 2. a) a legal or moral responsibility b) the thing that such a responsibility binds one to do 3. binding power of a contract, promise, etc. 4. a) indebtedness for a favor, service, etc. b) a favor or service

ob·li·ga·to (äb′lə gät′ō) *adj., n., pl.* **-tos, -ti** (-ē) *same as* OBBLIGATO

ob·lig·a·to·ry (ə blig′ə tôr′ē, äb′lig ə-) *adj*. legally or morally binding; required

o·blige (ə blīj′, ō-) *vt*. **o·bliged′, o·blig′ing** [< L. *ob-* (see OB-) + *ligare*, bind] 1. to compel by moral, legal, or physical force 2. to make indebted for a favor; do a favor for —*vi*. to do a favor

o·blig′ing *adj*. ready to do favors; helpful —**o·blig′ing·ly** *adv*.

ob·lique (ə blēk′, ō-; *also, esp. in mil. use,* -blīk′) *adj*. [< L. *ob-* (see OB-) + *liquis*, awry] 1. neither perpendicular nor horizontal; slanting 2. indirect or evasive —*vi*. **-liqued′, -liqu′ing** to slant —**ob·lique′ly** *adv*. —**ob·liq·ui·ty** (ə blik′wə tē), **ob·lique′ness** *n*.

oblique angle any angle other than a right angle; acute or obtuse angle

ob·lit·er·ate (ə blit′ə rāt′) *vt*. **-at′ed, -at′ing** [< L. *ob-* (see OB-) + *litera*, a letter] 1. to blot out; efface 2. to destroy —**ob·lit′er·a′tion** *n*.

ob·liv·i·on (ə bliv′ē ən) *n*. [< L. *oblivisci*, forget] 1. forgetfulness 2. the state of being forgotten

ob·liv′i·ous *adj*. forgetful or unmindful (usually with *of* or *to*) —**ob·liv′i·ous·ly** *adv*. —**ob·liv′i·ous·ness** *n*.

ob·long (äb′lôn) *adj*. [< L. *ob-* (see OB-) + *longus*, long] longer than broad; specif., rectangular and longer in one direction —*n*. an oblong figure

ob·lo·quy (äb′lə kwē) *n., pl.* **-quies** [< L. *ob-* (see OB-) + *loqui*, speak] 1. verbal abuse; esp., widespread censure 2. disgrace or infamy resulting from this

ob·nox·ious (əb näk′shəs, äb-) *adj*. [< L. *ob-* (see OB-) + *noxa*, harm] very unpleasant; offensive —**ob·nox′ious·ly** *adv*. —**ob·nox′ious·ness** *n*.

o·boe (ō′bō) *n*. [It. < Fr. *haut*, high (pitch) + *bois*, wood] a double-reed woodwind instrument having a high, penetrating tone —**o′bo·ist** *n*.

Obs., obs. obsolete

ob·scene (äb sēn′, əb-) *adj*. [< Fr. < L. *obscenus*, filthy] 1. offensive to modesty or decency; lewd 2. disgusting; repulsive —**ob·scene′ly** *adv*. —**ob·scen′i·ty** (-sen′ə tē) *n., pl.* **-ties**

ob·scu·rant·ism (äb skyoor′ənt iz′m, əb-) *n*. [< L. *obscurans*, obscuring] 1. opposition to human progress or enlightenment 2. a being deliberately obscure or vague —**ob·scu′rant·ist** *n., adj*.

ob·scure (əb skyoor′, äb-) *adj*. [< L. *obscurus*, covered over] 1. dim; dark; murky 2. not easily seen; indistinct 3. vague; ambiguous [an *obscure* answer] 4. inconspicuous; hidden 5. not well-known [an *obscure* actor] —*vt*. **-scured′, -scur′ing** to make obscure; dim, hide, confuse, etc. —**ob·scure′ly** *adv*. —**ob·scu′ri·ty** *n*.

ob·se·quies (äb′sə kwēz) *n.pl.* [< L. *obsequium*, compliance, substituted for L. *exsequiae*, funeral] funeral rites

ob·se·qui·ous (əb sē′kwē əs, äb-) *adj*. [< L. *obsequi*, comply with] showing too great a willingness to serve or obey; fawning —**ob·se′qui·ous·ly** *adv*. —**ob·se′qui·ous·ness** *n*.

ob·serv·a·ble (əb zur′və b′l, äb-) *adj*. 1. that can be observed; visible; noticeable 2. that can or must be kept or celebrated [an *observable* holiday] —**ob·serv′a·bly** *adv*.

ob·serv′ance (-vəns) *n*. 1. the observing of a law, duty, custom, etc. 2. a customary act, rite, etc.

ob·serv′ant *adj*. 1. strict in observing a rule, custom, etc. 2. paying careful attention 3. perceptive or alert —**ob·serv′ant·ly** *adv*.

ob·ser·va·tion (äb′zər vā′shən) *n*. 1. a) the act or power of observing b) something noticed 2. a being seen or noticed 3. a) a noting and recording of facts, as for research b) a fact so noted 4. a comment; remark —**ob′ser·va′tion·al** *adj*.

ob·serv·a·to·ry (əb zur′və tôr′ē, äb-) *n., pl.* **-ries** 1. a building equipped for scientific observation, esp. one with a large telescope for astronomical research 2. any building or place providing an extensive view of the surrounding land

ob·serve (əb zurv′, äb-) *vt*. **-served′, -serv′ing** [< L. *ob-* (see OB-) + *servare*, keep] 1. to adhere to (a law, custom, etc.) 2. to celebrate (a holiday, etc.) 3. a) to notice (something) b) to pay special attention to 4. to arrive at as a conclusion 5. to say casually; remark 6. to examine scientifically —*vi*. 1. to take notice 2. to comment (on or upon) —**ob·serv′er** *n*.

ob·sess (əb ses′, äb-) *vt*. [< L. *ob-* (see OB-) + *sedere*, sit] to haunt or trouble in mind; preoccupy —**ob·ses′sive** *adj*. —**ob·ses′sive·ly** *adv*.

ob·ses′sion (-sesh′ən) *n*. 1. a being obsessed 2. an idea, desire, etc. that obsesses one

ob·sid·i·an (əb sid′ē ən, äb-) *n*. [< one *Obsius*, its alleged discoverer] a hard, dark, volcanic glass

OBELISK

OBOE

ob·so·lesce (äb'sə les') *vi.* -lesced', -lesc'ing to be obsolescent

ob'so·les'cent (-les''nt) *adj.* in the process of becoming obsolete —**ob'so·les'cence** *n.*

ob·so·lete (äb'sə lēt') *adj.* [< L. *ob-* (see OB-) + *solere,* become accustomed] **1.** no longer in use; discarded **2.** out-of-date —**ob'so·lete'ness** *n.*

ob·sta·cle (äb'sti k'l) *n.* [< L. *ob-* (see OB-) + *stare,* to stand] anything that stands in the way; obstruction

ob·ste·tri·cian (äb'stə trish'ən) *n.* a medical doctor who specializes in obstetrics

ob·stet·rics (əb stet'riks, äb-) *n.pl.* [*with sing. v.*] [< L. *obstetrix,* midwife] the branch of medicine concerned with the care and treatment of women during pregnancy and childbirth —**ob·stet'ric, ob·stet'ri·cal** *adj.* —**ob·stet'ri·cal·ly** *adv.*

ob·sti·nate (äb'stə nit) *adj.* [< L. *obstinare,* resolve on] **1.** determined to have one's own way; stubborn **2.** resisting treatment [an *obstinate* fever] —**ob'sti·na·cy** (-nə sē) *n.* —**ob'sti·nate·ly** *adv.*

ob·strep·er·ous (əb strep'ər əs, äb-) *adj.* [< L. *ob-* (see OB-) + *strepere,* to roar] noisy or unruly, esp. in resisting —**ob·strep'er·ous·ly** *adv.* —**ob·strep'er·ous·ness** *n.*

ob·struct (əb strukt', äb-) *vt.* [< L. *ob-* (see OB-) + *struere,* pile up] **1.** to block (a passage); clog **2.** to hinder (progress, etc.); impede **3.** to block (the view) —**ob·struct'er, ob·struc'tor** *n.* —**ob·struc'tive** *adj.*

ob·struc'tion (-struk'shən) *n.* **1.** an obstructing **2.** anything that obstructs; hindrance

ob·struc'tion·ist (-ist) *n.* one who obstructs progress; esp., a member of a legislature who hinders legislation by technical maneuvers —*adj.* of obstructionists: also **obstruc'tion·is'tic** —**ob·struc'tion·ism** *n.*

ob·tain (əb tān', äb-) *vt.* [< L. *ob-* (see OB-) + *tenere,* to hold] to get possession of by effort; procure —*vi.* to prevail [peace will *obtain*] —**ob·tain'a·ble** *adj.* —**ob·tain'ment** *n.*

ob·trude (əb trōōd', äb-) *vt.* -trud'ed, -trud'ing [< L. *ob-* (see OB-) + *trudere,* to thrust] **1.** to push out; eject **2.** to force (oneself, one's opinions, etc.) upon others unasked or unwanted —*vi.* to obtrude oneself (*on* or *upon*) —**ob·tru'sion** (-trōō'zhən) *n.*

ob·tru'sive (-trōō'siv) *adj.* **1.** inclined to obtrude **2.** obtruding itself —**ob·tru'sive·ly** *adv.* —**ob·tru'sive·ness** *n.*

ob·tuse (äb tōōs', əb-; -tyōōs') *adj.* [< L. *ob-* (see OB-) + *tundere,* to strike] **1.** not sharp; blunt **2.** greater than 90 degrees and less than 180 degrees [an *obtuse* angle] **3.** slow to understand or perceive **4.** not acute [an *obtuse* pain] —**ob·tuse'ly** *adv.* —**ob·tuse'ness** *n.*

ob·verse (äb vurs', əb-; äb'vərs) *adj.* [< L. *ob-* (see OB-) + *vertere,* to turn] **1.** turned toward the observer **2.** forming a counterpart —*n.* (äb'vərs) **1.** the side, as of a coin or medal, bearing the main design **2.** the front or main surface of anything **3.** a counterpart —**ob·verse'ly** *adv.*

ob·vi·ate (äb'vē āt') *vt.* -at'ed, -at'ing [see OBVIOUS] to do away with or prevent by effective measures; make unnecessary —**ob'vi·a'tion** *n.*

ob·vi·ous (äb'vē əs) *adj.* [L. *obvius,* in the way: see OB- & VIA] easy to see or understand; evident —**ob'vi·ous·ly** *adv.* —**ob'vi·ous·ness** *n.*

oc- see OB-

oc·a·ri·na (äk'ə rē'nə) *n.* [It. < L. *auca,* a goose] a small, simple wind instrument with finger holes and a mouthpiece: it produces soft, hollow tones

O'Ca·sey (ō kā'sē), Sean (shôn) 1880–1964; Ir. playwright

occas. occasional(ly)

oc·ca·sion (ə kā'zhən) *n.* [< L. *ob-* (see OB-) + *cadere,* to fall] **1.** a favorable time; opportunity **2.** a fact or event that makes something else possible **3.** *a)* a happening *b)* a particular time **4.** a special time or event **5.** need arising from circumstances —*vt.* to cause —**on occasion** sometimes —**rise to the occasion** to meet an emergency

oc·ca'sion·al *adj.* **1.** of or for special occasions **2.** happening now and then; infrequent —**oc·ca'sion·al·ly** *adv.*

oc·ci·dent (äk'sə dənt) *n.* [< L. *occidere,* to fall: with reference to the setting sun] the west: now rare, except [O-] the part of the world west of Asia, esp. Europe and the Americas —**oc'ci·den'tal, Oc'ci·den'tal** *adj., n.*

oc·ci·put (äk'si put') *n., pl.* **oc·cip·i·ta** (-sip'ə tə), **-puts'** [< L. *ob-* (see OB-) + *caput,* head] the back part of the skull or head —**oc·cip·i·tal** (äk sip'ə t'l) *adj.*

oc·clude (ə klōōd') *vt.* -clud'ed, -clud'ing [< L. *ob-* (see OB-) + *claudere,* shut] **1.** to close or block (a passage) **2.** to shut in or out **3.** *Chem.* to retain or absorb (a gas, liquid, or solid) —*vi. Dentistry* to meet with the cusps fitting closely —**oc·clu'sion** (-klōō'zhən) *n.* —**oc·clu'sive** *adj.*

oc·cult (ə kult', ä'kult) *adj.* [< L. *ob-* (see OB-) + *celare,* hide] **1.** hidden **2.** secret **3.** beyond human understanding **4.** of such alleged mystic arts as alchemy, astrology, etc. —**the occult** the occult arts —**oc·cult'ism** *n.*

oc·cu·pan·cy (äk'yə pən sē) *n., pl.* -cies **1.** an occupying; a taking or keeping in possession **2.** *Law* the taking possession of a previously unowned object

oc'cu·pant *n.* **1.** one who occupies a house, post, etc. **2.** one who acquires possession by occupancy

oc·cu·pa·tion (äk'yə pā'shən) *n.* **1.** an occupying or being occupied; specif., the seizure and control of a country or area by military forces **2.** (one's) trade, profession, or business —**oc'cu·pa'tion·al** *adj.*

occupational disease a disease commonly acquired by people in a particular occupation [silicosis is an *occupational disease* of miners]

occupational therapy therapy by work designed to divert the mind or to correct a physical defect

oc·cu·py (äk'yə pi') *vt.* -pied', -py'ing [< L. *ob-* (see OB-) + *capere,* seize] **1.** to take possession of by settlement or seizure **2.** to hold possession of; specif., *a)* to dwell in *b)* to hold (a position or office) **3.** to take up (space, time, etc.) **4.** to busy (oneself, one's mind, etc.) —**oc'cu·pi'er** *n.*

oc·cur (ə kur') *vi.* -curred', -cur'ring [< L. *ob-* (see OB-) + *currere,* to run] **1.** to be found; exist **2.** to present itself; come to mind **3.** to happen

oc·cur'rence *n.* **1.** the act or fact of occurring **2.** an event; incident

o·cean (ō'shən) *n.* [< Gr. *Ōkeanos*] **1.** the great body of salt water that covers about 71% of the earth's surface **2.** any of its five principal divisions: the Atlantic, Pacific, Indian, Arctic, or Antarctic Ocean **3.** a great quantity —**o·ce·an·ic** (ō'shē an'ik) *adj.*

o'cean·aut' (-ôt') *n.* [< OCEAN + Gr. *nautēs,* sailor] same as AQUANAUT

o'cean·go'ing *adj.* of, having to do with, or made for travel on, the ocean

O·ce·an·i·a (ō'shē an'ē ə) islands in the Pacific, including Melanesia, Micronesia, & Polynesia &, sometimes, Australia, New Zealand, & the Malay Archipelago

o'cean·og·ra·phy (ō'shə näg'rə fē, ō'shē ə-) *n.* the study of the environment in the oceans —**o'cean·og'ra·pher** *n.* —**o'cean·o·graph'ic** (-nə graf'ik), **o'cean·o·graph'i·cal** *adj.*

o'cean·ol'o·gy (-näl'ə jē) *n.* **1.** the study of the sea in all its aspects, including oceanography **2.** *same as* OCEANOGRAPHY —**o'cean·ol'o·gist** *n.*

o·cel·lus (ō sel'əs) *n., pl.* -li (-ī) [L. < *oculus,* an eye] the simple eye of certain invertebrates

o·ce·lot (äs'ə lät', ō'sə-) *n.* [Fr. < Mex. *ocelotl,* jaguar] a large, spotted cat of N. and S. America

o·cher (ō'kər) *n.* [< Gr. *ōchros,* pale-yellow] **1.** a yellow or reddish-brown clay colored by iron oxide, used as a pigment **2.** the color of ocher; esp., dark yellow Also sp. **ochre**

-ock [OE. *-oc, -uc,* dim.] *a suffix used orig. to form the diminutive* [hillock]

o'clock (ə kläk', ō-) *adv.* **1.** of or according to the clock **2.** as if on a clock dial

Oct. October

octa- [< Gr. *oktō,* eight] *a combining form meaning eight:* also **oct-**

oc·ta·gon (äk'tə gän') *n.* [< Gr.: see OCTA- & -GON] a plane figure with eight angles and eight sides —**oc·tag'o·nal** (-tag'ə n'l) *adj.*

oc·ta·he·dron (äk'tə hē'drən) *n., pl.* -drons, -dra (-drə) [< Gr.: see OCTA- & -HEDRON] a solid figure with eight plane surfaces —**oc'ta·he'dral** *adj.*

oc·tane (äk'tān) *n.* [< OCT(O)- + -ane, a suffix denoting a hydrocarbon of the paraffin series] an oily paraffin hydrocarbon found in petroleum

octane number (or **rating**) a number representing the antiknock quality of a gasoline, etc.: the higher the number, the greater this quality

oc·tave (äk'tiv, -tāv) *n.* [< L. *octavus,* eighth] *Music* **1.** the eighth full tone above or below a given tone **2.** the interval of eight degrees between a tone and either of its octaves **3.** the series of tones (a full scale) within this interval, or the keys of an instrument producing such a series **4.** a tone and either of its octaves sounded together

oc·ta·vo (äk tā'vō, -tä'-) *n., pl.* -vos [< L. (*in*) *octavo,* (in) eight] **1.** the page size (about 6 by 9 inches) of a book made up of printer's sheets folded into eight leaves **2.** a book of such pages Also written **8vo** or **8°**

oc·tet, oc·tette (äk tet') *n.* [< OCT(O)- + (DU)ET] *Music* **1.** a composition for eight voices or eight instruments **2.** the eight performers of this

octo- [< Gr. *oktō*, eight] *a combining form meaning* eight: also **oct-**

Oc·to·ber (äk tō′bər) *n.* [< L. *octo*, eight: eighth month of the Roman year] the tenth month of the year, having 31 days: abbrev. **Oct., O.**

oc·to·ge·nar·i·an (äk′tə ji ner′ē ən) *adj.* [< L. *octoginta*, eighty] eighty years old, or between the ages of eighty and ninety —*n.* a person of this age

oc·to·pus (äk′tə pəs) *n., pl.* **-pus·es, -pi′** (-pī′) [< Gr. *oktō*, eight + *pous*, a foot] 1. a mollusk with a soft body and eight arms covered with suckers 2. anything suggesting an octopus; esp., a powerful organization with many branches

oc·to·roon (äk′tə rōōn′) *n.* [OCTO- + (QUAD)ROON] the offspring of a white and a quadroon

oc·u·lar (äk′yə lər) *adj.* [< L. *oculus*, the eye] 1. of, for, or like the eye 2. by eyesight —*n.* the eyepiece of an optical instrument

OCTOPUS (diameter from 1 in. to 25 ft.)

oc′u·list (-list) *n.* [< L. *oculus*, the eye] *earlier term for* OPHTHALMOLOGIST

OD, O.D. 1. Officer of the Day 2. overdose

o·da·lisque, o·da·lisk (ōd′l isk) *n.* [Fr. < Turk. *ōdalik*, chambermaid] a female slave or concubine in an Oriental harem

odd (äd) *adj.* [< ON. *oddi*] 1. *a*) remaining from a pair, set, etc. [an odd glove] *b*) remaining after the others are paired, taken, etc. 2. having a remainder of one when divided by two 3. numbered with an odd number [the odd months] 4. left over after taking a round number 5. with a few more [thirty odd years ago] 6. occasional; incidental [odd jobs] 7. *a*) peculiar *b*) queer; eccentric 8. out-of-the-way [in odd corners] —**odd′ly** *adv.* —**odd′ness** *n.*

odd′ball *n.* [Slang] an eccentric or nonconforming person —*adj.* [Slang] strange or unconventional

odd·i·ty (äd′ə tē) *n.* 1. peculiarity 2. *pl.* **-ties** an odd person or thing

odd′ment (-mənt) *n.* a miscellaneous item

odds (ädz) *n.pl.* 1. difference in favor of one side over the other; advantage 2. an equalizing advantage given by a bettor or competitor in proportion to the assumed chances in his favor —**at odds** quarreling —**by (all) odds** by far —**the odds are** the likelihood is

odds and ends scraps; remnants

odds′-on′ *adj.* having better than an even chance of winning [an odds-on favorite]

ode (ōd) *n.* [Fr. < Gr. *ōidē*, song] a lyric poem typically addressed to some person or thing and characterized by lofty feeling and dignified style

-ode [< Gr. *hodos*] *a suffix meaning* way, path

O·der (ō′dər) river in C Europe, flowing through Czechoslovakia & Poland into the Baltic: c.560 mi.

O·des·sa (ō des′ə) seaport in Ukrainian S.S.R., on the Black Sea: pop. 797,000

O·din (ō′din) *Norse Myth.* the chief god

o·di·ous (ō′dē əs) *adj.* [< L. *odium*, hatred] arousing or deserving hatred or loathing; disgusting —**o′di·ous·ly** *adv.*

o′di·um (-əm) *n.* [L. < *odi*, I hate] 1. hatred 2. the disgrace brought on by hateful action

o·dom·e·ter (ō däm′ə tər) *n.* [< Fr. < Gr. *hodos*, way + *metron*, a measure] an instrument for measuring the distance traveled by a vehicle

o·dor (ō′dər) *n.* [L.] a smell, whether pleasant or unpleasant; fragrance, stench, etc.: Brit. sp. **odour** —**be in bad (or ill) odor** to be in ill repute —**o′dor·less** *adj.* —**o′dor·ous** *adj.*

o·dor·if·er·ous (ō′də rif′ər əs) *adj.* giving off an odor, specif., a fragrant one

O·dys·se·us (ō dis′yōōs, -dis′ē əs) the hero of the *Odyssey*, one of the Greek leaders in the Trojan War

Od·ys·sey (äd′ə sē) an ancient Greek epic poem, ascribed to Homer, about the wanderings of Odysseus during the ten years after the fall of Troy —*n.* [*sometimes* o-] *pl.* **-seys** any extended wandering

OE., OE, O.E. Old English

Oed·i·pus (ed′ə pəs, ē′də-) *Gr. Myth.* a king who unwittingly killed his father and married his mother

Oedipus complex *Psychoanalysis* the unconscious tendency of a child, sometimes unresolved in adulthood, to be attached to the parent of the opposite sex and hostile toward the other parent

o′er (ôr) *prep., adv. chiefly poet. contr. of* OVER

of (uv, äv) *prep.* [OE.] 1. from; specif., *a*) coming from [men of Ohio] *b*) as relates to [how wise of her] *c*) resulting from [to die of fever] *d*) at a distance from [east of the city] *e*) by [the poems of Poe] *f*) separated from [robbed of his money] *g*) from the whole constituting [part of the time] *h*) made from [a sheet of paper] 2. belonging to 3. *a*) possessing [a man of wealth] *b*) containing [a bag of nuts] 4. specified as [a height of six feet] 5. characterized by [a man of honor] 6. concerning; about 7. set aside for [a day of rest] 8. during [of late years] 9. before: in telling time [ten of nine] 10. with (something specified) as object, goal, etc. [a reader of books]

of- *see* OB-

off (ôf) *adv.* [LME. variant of *of*, OF] 1. so as to be away or at a distance [to move off] 2. so as to be measured, divided, etc. [to mark off] 3. so as to be no longer on, attached, etc. [take off your hat] 4. (a specified distance) away in space or time· [20 yards off] 5. so as to be no longer in operation, etc. [turn the motor off] 6. so as to be less, etc. [5% off for cash] 7. away from one's work [take a day off] —*prep.* 1. no longer (or not) on, attached, etc. [the car is off the road] 2. away from [to live off the campus] 3. *a*) from the substance of [to live off the land] *b*) at the expense of 4. branching out from [an alley off Main Street] 5. relieved from [off duty] 6. not up to the usual standard, etc. of [off one's game] 7. [Colloq.] no longer using, supporting, etc. [he's off liquor] 8. [Colloq.] from [to buy it off him] —*adj.* 1. not on, attached, in operation, etc. 2. on the way [be off to bed] 3. away from work, etc. [we are off today] 4. not up to the usual standard, etc. [an off day] 5. more remote [on the off chance] 6. in (specified) circumstances [to be well off] 7. not correct [his figures are off] —*interj.* go away! —**off and on** now and then

off. 1. office 2. officer 3. official

of·fal (ôf′l, äf′-) *n.* [ME. *ofall*, lit., off-fall] 1. [*with sing. or pl. v.*] the entrails, etc. of a butchered animal 2. refuse; garbage

off′beat′ *adj.* [< a rhythm in jazz music] [Colloq.] not conforming to the usual pattern or trend; unconventional, unusual, etc.

off′-col′or *adj.* 1. varying from the standard color 2. not quite proper; risqué

of·fend (ə fend′) *vi.* [< L. *ob-* (see OB-) + *fendere*, to hit] 1. to commit a sin or crime 2. to create resentment, anger, etc. —*vt.* 1. to hurt the feelings of; make angry, etc. 2. to be displeasing to (the taste, sense, etc.) —**of·fend′er** *n.*

of·fense (ə fens′, ô′fens) *n.* 1. a sin or crime 2. a creating of resentment, anger, etc. 3. a feeling hurt, angry, etc. 4. something that causes anger, etc. 5. the act of attacking 6. the person, side, army, etc. that is attacking· Brit. sp. **offence** —**give offense** to anger, insult, etc. —**take offense** to become offended; feel hurt, angry, etc.

of·fen′sive *adj.* 1. attacking or for attack 2. unpleasant; disgusting 3. causing resentment, anger, etc. —*n.* 1. attitude or position of attack 2. an attack or hostile action —**of·fen′sive·ly** *adv.* —**of·fen′sive·ness** *n.*

of·fer (ôf′ər, äf′-) *vt.* [< L. *ob-* (see OB-) + *ferre*, bring] 1. to present in an act of worship [to offer prayers] 2. to present for acceptance [to offer help] 3. to express willingness or intention [to offer to go] 4. to show or give signs of [to offer resistance] 5. *a*) to present for sale *b*) to bid (a price, etc.) —*vi.* to occur; present itself —*n.* the act of offering or thing offered

of′fer·ing *n.* 1. the act of making an offer 2. something offered; specif., *a*) a contribution *b*) a presentation made in worship *c*) a theatrical presentation

of′fer·to′ry (-tôr′ē) *n., pl.* **-ries** [*often* O-] 1. that part of Holy Communion during which the Eucharistic bread and wine are offered to God 2. money collected at a church service, or a hymn sung during the collection

off′hand′ *adv.* without prior preparation —*adj.* 1. said or done offhand 2. casual, curt, etc. Also **off′hand′ed**

of·fice (ôf′is, äf′-) *n.* [< L. *opus*, a work + *facere*, to do] 1. a service done for another [he got the job through his uncle's good *offices*] 2. a duty, esp. a part of one's work 3. a position of authority or trust, as in government 4. a main branch of a U.S. government department [the Printing *Office*] 5. a place where work or business that is administrative, professional, etc. is carried on 6. a religious ceremony or rite

office boy a boy doing odd jobs in an office

of′fice·hold′er *n.* a government official

of·fi·cer (ôf′ə sər, äf′-) *n.* **1.** anyone holding an office or position of authority in a government, business, club, etc. **2.** a policeman **3.** one holding a position of authority, esp. by commission, in the armed forces **4.** the captain or any of the mates of a nonnaval ship —*vt.* **1.** to provide with officers **2.** to command; direct

officer of the day the military officer in charge of the interior guard and security of his garrison for any given day

of·fi·cial (ə fish′əl) *adj.* **1.** of or holding an office, or position of authority **2.** authorized or authoritative *[an official request]* **3.** formal —*n.* **1.** a person holding office **2.** *Sports* one who supervises an athletic contest —**of·fi′cial·dom** (-dəm) *n.* —**of·fi′cial·ism** *n.* —**of·fi′cial·ly** *adv.*

of·fi·ci·ate (ə fish′ē āt′) *vi.* **-at′ed, -at′ing 1.** to perform the duties of an office **2.** to perform the functions of a priest, minister, etc. **3.** *Sports* to act as referee, umpire, etc. —**of·fi′ci·a′tion** *n.* —**of·fi′ci·a′tor** *n.*

of·fi·cious (ə fish′əs) *adj.* [see OFFICE] offering unwanted advice or services; meddlesome —**of·fi′cious·ly** *adv.* —**of·fi′cious·ness** *n.*

off·ing (ôf′iŋ) *n.* [< OFF] the distant part of the sea visible from the shore —**in the offing 1.** far but in sight **2.** at some indefinite future time

off′-key′ *adj.* **1.** flat or sharp **2.** not quite in accord with what is fitting, etc.

off′-lim′its *adj.* ruled · a place not to be gone to by a specified group

off·set (ôf′set′) *n.* **1.** anything that balances or compensates for something else **2.** *a)* same as OFFSET PRINTING *b)* an impression made by this process —*vt.* (ôf set′) **-set′, -set′ting** to balance, compensate for, etc.

offset printing a printing process in which the inked impression is first made on a rubber-covered roller, then transferred to paper

off′shoot′ *n.* **1.** a shoot growing from the main stem of a plant **2.** anything that branches off, or derives from, a main source

off′shore′ *adj.* **1.** moving away from the shore **2.** at some distance from shore —*adv.* away from the shore

off′side′ *adj. Sports* not in the proper position for play, as, in football, ahead of the ball before the play has begun —*n.* an offside play

off′spring′ *n., pl.* **-spring′, -springs′ 1.** a child or animal as related to its parent **2.** progeny

off′stage′ *n.* that part of a stage not seen by the audience —*adj.* in or from the offstage —*adv.* **1.** to the offstage **2.** when not appearing before the public

off′-white′ *adj.* grayish-white or yellowish-white

off year 1. a year in which a major election does not take place **2.** a year of little production —**off′-year′** *adj.*

OFr. Old French

oft (ôft) *adv.* [OE.] *chiefly poet. var. of* OFTEN

of·ten (ôf′n, ôf′t′n) *adv.* [ME. var. of prec.] many times; frequently: also **of′ten·times′**

o·gee (ō′jē, ō jē′) *n.* [< OFr. *ogive*] **1.** an S-shaped curve, line, molding, etc. **2.** a pointed arch formed with the curve of an ogee on each side: also **ogee arch**

o·gle (ō′g'l, ä′-) *vi., vt.* **o′gled, o′gling** [prob. < LowG. *oog*, the eye] to keep looking (at) boldly and with desire —*n.* an ogling look —**o′gler** *n.*

o·gre (ō′gər) *n.* [Fr.] **1.** in fairy tales and folklore, a man-eating giant **2.** a hideous or cruel man —**o′gre·ish, o′grish** *adj.* —**o′gress** *n.fem.*

OGEE ARCH

oh (ō) *interj., n., pl.* **oh's, ohs** an exclamation of surprise, fear, wonder, pain, etc.

O. Henry *see* HENRY

OHG, OHG., O.H.G. Old High German

O·hi·o (ō hī′ō) **1.** Middle Western State of the U.S.: 41,222 sq. mi.; pop. 10,652,000; cap. Columbus: abbrev. **O., OH 2.** river flowing from SW Pa. into the Mississippi: 981 mi. —**O·hi′o·an** *adj., n.*

ohm (ōm) *n.* [< G. S. *Ohm* (1789-1854), G. physicist] the unit of electrical resistance, equal to the resistance of a circuit in which one volt maintains a current of one ampere —**ohm′ic** *adj.*

-oid [< Gr. *eidos*, a form] *a suffix meaning* like, resembling *[crystalloid]*

oil (oil) *n.* [< Gr. *elaion*, (olive) oil] **1.** any of various greasy, combustible, normally liquid substances obtained from animal, vegetable, and mineral sources: oils are insoluble in water **2.** *same as* PETROLEUM **3.** *same as: a)* OIL COLOR *b)* OIL PAINTING —*vt.* to lubricate or supply with oil —*adj.* of, from, or like oil —**oiled** *adj.* —**oil′er** *n.*

oil′cloth′ *n.* cloth made waterproof with oil or with heavy coats of paint

oil color paint made by grinding a pigment in oil

oil painting 1. a picture painted in oil colors **2.** the art of painting in oil colors

oil′skin′ *n.* **1.** cloth made waterproof by treatment with oil **2.** *[often pl.]* a garment made of this

oil slick a film of oil on water

oil well a well bored through layers of rock, etc. to a supply of petroleum

oil′y *adj.* **-i·er, -i·est 1.** of, like, or containing oil **2.** greasy **3.** too smooth; unctuous —**oil′i·ly** *adv.* —**oil′i·ness** *n.*

oink (oiŋk) *n.* the grunt of a pig —*vi.* to make this sound

oint·ment (oint′mənt) *n.* [< L. *unguentum*: see UNGUENT] a fatty substance applied to the skin as a salve or cosmetic

O·jib·wa (ō jib′wä) *n., pl.* **-was, -wa** a member of a group of N. American tribes living from Michigan to North Dakota —*adj.* of these tribes Also **O·jib′way** (-wā)

OK, O.K. (ō′kā′) *adj., adv., interj.* [abbrev. for "oll korrect," jocular misspelling of *all correct*] all right; correct —*n.* (ō′kā′) *pl.* **OK's, O.K.'s** approval —*vt.* (ō′kā′) **OK'd** or **O.K.'d, OK'ing** or **O.K.'ing** to put an OK on; approve

OK Oklahoma

o·ka·pi (ō kä′pē) *n.* [native name] an African animal related to the giraffe, but having a much shorter neck

O·khotsk (ō kätsk′), **Sea of** arm of the Pacific, off the E coast of Siberia

O·ki·na·wa (ō′kə nä′wə) largest island of the Ryukyus, northeast of Taiwan

O·kla·ho·ma (ō′klə hō′mə) State of the SC U.S.: 69,919 sq. mi.; pop. 2,559,000; cap. Oklahoma City: abbrev. **Okla., OK** —**O′kla·ho′man** *adj., n.*

Oklahoma City capital of Okla.: pop. 366,000 (met. area 641,000)

o·kra (ō′krə) *n.* [< WAfr. name] **1.** a tall plant with ribbed, sticky green pods **2.** the pods, used as a vegetable

-ol [< (ALCOH)OL] *a suffix meaning* an alcohol or phenol *[menthol]*

old (ōld) *adj.* **old′er** or **eld′er, old′est** or **eld′est** [OE. *ald*] **1.** having lived or existed for a long time; aged **2.** of aged people **3.** of a certain age *[ten years old]* **4.** not new **5.** worn out by age or use **6.** former **7.** experienced *[an old hand]* **8.** ancient **9.** of long standing **10.** designating the earlier or earliest of two or more *[the Old World]* **11.** [Colloq.] dear: a term of affection *[old boy]* Also used as a colloquial intensive *[a fine old time]* —*n.* **1.** time long past *[days of old]* **2.** something old (with *the*) —**old′ish** *adj.* —**old′ness** *n.*

OKRA

old country the country from which an immigrant came, esp. a country in Europe

old·en (ōl′d'n) *adj.* [Poet.] (of) old; ancient

Old English the Germanic language of the Anglo-Saxons, spoken in England from c.400 to c.1100 A.D.

old′-fash′ioned *adj.* suited to or favoring the styles, ideas, etc. of past times —*n.* *[also* O- F-*]* a cocktail made with whiskey, soda water, bitters, sugar, and fruit

Old French the French language as spoken from the 9th to the 16th century

Old Glory the flag of the U.S.

Old Guard [after Napoleon's imperial guard (1804)] **1.** any group that has long defended a cause **2.** the conservative element of a group, party, etc.

old hat [Slang] **1.** old-fashioned **2.** trite

Old High German the High German language from the 8th to the 12th century

old′ie, old′y *n., pl.* **old′ies** [Colloq.] an old joke, song, movie, etc.

old lady [Slang] **1.** one's mother **2.** one's wife

old′-line′ *adj.* **1.** old and well-established **2.** following tradition; conservative

Old Low German the Low German language from its earliest period to the 12th century A.D.

old maid 1. a woman, esp. an older woman, who has never married; spinster **2.** a prim, prudish, fussy person —**old′-maid′ish** *adj.*

old man [Slang] **1.** one's father **2.** one's husband **3.** *[usually* O- M-*]* a man in authority

old master 1. any great European painter before the 18th cent. **2.** a painting by any of these

old moon the moon in its last quarter, when it appears as a crescent curving to the left

Old Nick the Devil; Satan: also **Old Harry**

Old Norse the Germanic language of the Scandinavian peoples before the 14th century

Old Saxon the Low German dialect of the Saxons before the 10th century

old school a group of people who cling to traditional or conservative ideas, methods, etc.

old'ster (-stər) *n.* [Colloq.] an old or elderly person

old style an old style of type with narrow letters

Old Testament *Christian designation for* the Holy Scriptures of Judaism, the first of the two general divisions of the Christian Bible

old'-time' *adj.* 1. of or like past times 2. of long standing or experience

old'-tim'er *n.* [Colloq.] a longtime resident, employee, etc.

old wives' tale a silly story or superstition such as gossipy old women might pass around

Old World the Eastern Hemisphere, often esp. Europe — **old'-world'** *adj.*

o·le·ag·i·nous (ō'lē aj'i nəs) *adj.* [< Fr. < L. *olea*, olive tree] oily; unctuous

o·le·an·der (ō'lē an'dər, ō'lē an'dər) *n.* [ML.] a poisonous evergreen shrub with fragrant white, pink, or red flowers

o·le·o·mar·ga·rine, o·le·o·mar·ga·rin (ō'lē ō mär'jə rin) *n.* [< Fr. < L. *oleum*, an oil + MARGARINE] *full name of* MARGARINE: also **o'le·o'**

o·le·o·res·in (ō'lē ō rez''n) *n.* a mixture of a resin and an essential oil, as turpentine

ol·fac·to·ry (äl fäk'tər ē, -trē) *adj.* [< L. *olere*, have a smell + *facere*, make] of the sense of smell —*n., pl.* -ries [*usually pl.*] an organ of smell

ol·i·garch (äl'ə gärk') *n.* any of the rulers of an oligarchy

ol'i·gar·chy (-gär'kē) *n., pl.* -chies [< Gr. *oligos*, few + -ARCHY] 1. (a) government with the ruling power belonging to a few 2. those ruling —**ol'i·gar'chic** *adj.*

ol·ive (äl'iv) *n.* [< Gr. *elaia*] 1. *a*) an evergreen tree of S Europe and the Near East *b*) its small, oval fruit, eaten green or ripe, or pressed to extract its oil 2. the yellowish-green color of the unripe fruit —*adj.* 1. of the olive 2. olive-colored

olive branch 1. the branch of the olive tree, a symbol of peace 2. any peace offering

olive drab 1. a shade of greenish brown 2. woolen cloth dyed this color and used for U.S. Army uniforms 3. [*pl.*] a uniform of this cloth —**ol'ive-drab'** *adj.*

olive oil a light-yellow oil pressed from ripe olives, used in cooking, soap, etc.

ol·i·vine (äl'ə vēn') *n.* [OLIV(E) + -INE³] a green silicate of magnesium and iron

O·lym·pi·a (ō lim'pē ə) 1. plain in Greece: site of the ancient Olympic games 2. capital of Wash.: pop. 23,000

O·lym'pi·ad' (-ad') *n.* [*often* o-] 1. a four-year period between the ancient Olympic games 2. a celebration of the modern Olympic games

O·lym'pi·an (-ən) *n.* 1. *Gr. Myth.* any of the gods on Mount Olympus 2. a participant in the Olympic games — *adj.* 1. of Olympia or Mount Olympus 2. exalted; majestic

O·lym'pic (-pik) *adj. same as* OLYMPIAN —*n.* [*pl.*] the Olympic games (preceded by *the*)

Olympic games 1. an ancient Greek festival with contests in athletics, music, etc., held every four years at Olympia in honor of Zeus 2. a modern international athletic competition generally held every four years

O·lym'pus (-pəs), **Mount** mountain in N Greece: in Greek mythology, the home of the gods

O·ma·ha (ō'mə hô, -hä) city in E Nebr.: pop. 347,000 (met. area 541,000)

O·mar Khay·yám (ō'mär kī yäm', -yam') ?–1123?; Persian poet

om·buds·man (äm'bədz mən) *n., pl.* -men [Sw.] an appointed public official who investigates citizens' complaints against government agencies that may be infringing on the rights of individuals

o·me·ga (ō mä'gə, -meg'ə, -mē'gə) *n.* the twenty-fourth and final letter of the Greek alphabet (Ω, ω)

om·e·let, om·e·lette (äm'lit, äm'ə let) *n.* [< Fr. < L. *lamella*, small plate] eggs beaten up, often with milk or water, and cooked as a pancake in a pan

o·men (ō'mən) *n.* [L.] a thing or happening supposed to foretell a future event; augury

om·i·cron, om·i·kron (äm'ə krän', ō'mə-) *n.* the fifteenth letter of the Greek alphabet (O, o)

om·i·nous (äm'ə nəs) *adj.* of or serving as an evil omen; threatening —**om'i·nous·ly** *adv.*

o·mis·sion (ō mish'ən) *n.* 1. an omitting or being omitted 2. anything omitted

o·mit (ō mit') *vt.* **o·mit'ted, o·mit'ting** [< L. *ob-* (see OB-) + *mittere*, send] 1. to fail to include; leave out 2. to fail to do; neglect

omni- [L. < *omnis*, all] *a combining form meaning* all, everywhere

om·ni·bus (äm'nə bəs, -ni bus') *n., pl.* -bus'es [Fr. < L., lit., for all] *same as* BUS —*adj.* providing for many things at once

om·nip·o·tent (äm nip'ə tənt) *adj.* [< L. *omnis*, all + *potens*, able] having unlimited power or authority; all-powerful —**the Omnipotent** God —**om·nip'o·tence** *n.*

om·ni·pres·ent (äm'ni prez'*'*nt) *adj.* present in all places at the same time —**om'ni·pres'ence** *n.*

om·nis·cient (äm nish'ənt) *adj.* [< L. *omnis*, all + *scire*, know] knowing all things —**om·nis'cience** *n.*

om·niv·o·rous (äm niv'ər əs) *adj.* [< L.: see OMNI- & -VOROUS] 1. eating any sort of food 2. taking in everything indiscriminately [an *omnivorous* reader]

on (än, ôn) *prep.* [OE.] 1. in contact with, supported by, or covering 2. in the surface of [scars *on* it] 3. near to [*on* my left] 4. at the time of [*on* Monday] 5. connected with [*on* the team] 6. engaged in [*on* a trip] 7. in a state of [*on* parole] 8. as a result of [a profit *on* the sale] 9. in the direction of [light shone *on* us] 10. through the use of [to live *on* bread] 11. concerning [an essay *on* war] 12. coming after [insult *on* insult] 13. [Colloq.] chargeable to [a drink *on* the house] 14. [Slang] using; addicted to [*on* drugs] —*adv.* 1. in a situation of contacting, being supported by, or covering 2. in a direction toward [looked *on*] 3. forward [move *on*] 4. continuously [she sang *on*] 5. into operation or action [turn the light *on*] —*adj.* in action or operation [the TV is *on*] —**and so on** and more like the preceding —**on and off** intermittently —**on and on** continuously —**on to** [Slang] aware of

ON., ON, O.N. Old Norse

o·nan·ism (ō'nə niz'm) *n.* [< *Onan* (Gen. 38:9)] withdrawal in coition before ejaculation

once (wuns) *adv.* [< OE. *an*, one] 1. one time only 2. at any time; ever 3. formerly 4. by one degree [a cousin *once* removed] —*conj.* as soon as; if ever —*n.* one time [go this *once*] —**all at once** all at the same time; suddenly — **at once** 1. immediately 2. at the same time —**once (and) for all** finally —**once in a while** occasionally —**once upon a time** long ago

once'-o'ver *n.* [Colloq.] 1. a swiftly appraising glance 2. a quick going-over

on·com·ing (än'kum'iŋ) *adj.* approaching [*oncoming* traffic] —*n.* approach

one (wun) *adj.* [OE. *an*] 1. being a single thing 2. united 3. designating a particular person or thing [from *one* day to another] 4. being uniquely such [the *one* solution] 5. the same 6. a certain but unnamed [*one* day last week] : also used as an intensive [she's *one* beautiful girl] —*n.* 1. the first and lowest cardinal number; 1; I 2. a single person or thing —*pron.* 1. some or a certain person or thing 2. any person or thing 3. the person or thing previously mentioned —**all one** making no difference —**at one** in accord —**one and all** everybody —**one another** each one the other —**one of those things** something inevitable

one'-horse' *adj.* 1. drawn by or using one horse 2. [Colloq.] small, unimportant, etc.

O·nei·da (ō nī'də) *n., pl.* -das, -da a member of a tribe of Indians orig. of New York State but now also of Wisconsin and Ontario

O'Neill (ō nēl'), **Eugene** 1888–1953; U.S. playwright

one'ness (-nis) *n.* 1. singleness; unity 2. unity of mind, feeling, etc. 3. sameness; identity

one'-night' stand a single appearance in a town by a traveling show, lecturer, etc.

on·er·ous (än'ər əs, ō'nər-) *adj.* [< L. *onus*, a load] burdensome; oppressive —**on'er·ous·ly** *adv.*

one·self (wun'self', wunz'-) *pron.* a person's own self: also **one's self** —**be oneself** 1. to function normally 2. to be natural —**by oneself** alone; unaccompanied —**come to oneself** to recover one's senses

one'-sid'ed (-sīd'id) *adj.* 1. on, having, or involving only one side 2. larger, heavier, etc. on one side 3. unfair; favoring one side 4. unequal [a *one-sided* race] —**one'-sid'ed·ness** *n.*

one'-time' *adj.* at a past time; former

one'-track' adj. 1. having a single track 2. [Colloq.] limited in scope [a one-track mind]

one'-up' adj. [Colloq.] having an advantage (over another): often in **be one-up on**

one'-way' adj. moving, or allowing movement, in one direction only

on·go·ing (än'gō'iŋ) adj. going on; in process

on·ion (un'yən) n. [< L. unio, a kind of single onion] 1. a plant of the lily family, with an edible bulb having a sharp smell and taste 2. the bulb

on'ion·skin' n. a tough, thin, translucent paper

on'look'er n. a spectator —**on'look'ing** adj., n.

on·ly (ōn'lē) adj. [< OE. an, one + -lic, -LY] 1. alone of its or their kind; sole 2. alone in superiority; best —adv. 1. and no other; solely 2. (but) in the end 3. as recently as —conj. [Colloq.] except that; but —if . . . only I wish that —only too very

on·o·mat·o·poe·ia (än'ə mat'ə pē'ə) n. [< Gr. onoma, a name + poiein, make] 1. formation of words by imitating sounds (Ex.: buzz) 2. the use of such words —**on'o·mat·o·poe'ic**, **on'o·mat·o·po·et'ic** (-pō et'ik) adj.

On·on·da·ga (än'ən dô'gə) n., pl. -gas, -ga a member of a tribe of Indians orig. of New York State but now also of Ontario

on'rush' n. a headlong dash forward —**on'rush'ing** adj.

on'set' n. 1. an attack 2. a beginning

on'shore' adj. 1. moving onto or toward the shore 2. on land —adv. landward

on'slaught' (-slôt') n. [< Du. slagen, to strike] a violent, intense attack

On·tar·i·o (än ter'ē ō) 1. province of SC Canada: 412,582 sq. mi.; pop. 6,961,000; cap. Toronto: abbrev. **Ont.** 2. Lake, smallest & easternmost of the Great Lakes, between N.Y. & Ontario, Canada: 7,313 sq. mi.

on·to (än'tōō) prep. 1. to a position on 2. [Slang] aware of [he's onto our schemes] Also **on to**

on·tog·e·ny (än täj'ə nē) n. [< Gr. einai, to be + -geneia, origin] the development of a single organism

o·nus (ō'nəs) n. [L.] 1. a burden, unpleasant duty, etc. 2. blame

on·ward (än'wərd) adv. toward or at a position ahead; forward: also **on'wards** —adj. advancing

on·yx (än'iks) n. [< Gr. onyx, fingernail] a variety of agate with alternate colored layers

oo·dles (ōō'd'lz) n.pl. [< ?] [Colloq.] a great amount

oo·long (ōō'lôŋ) n. [< Chin. wulung, lit., black dragon] a dark Chinese tea

ooze' (ōōz) n. [OE. wos, sap] something that oozes —vi. oozed, ooz'ing to flow or leak out slowly —vt. to exude

ooze² (ōōz) n. [OE. wase] soft mud or slime, as at the bottom of a lake —**oo·zy** (ōō'zē) adj. -zi·er, -zi·est

op- see OB-

o·pac·i·ty (ō pas'ə tē) n. [< Fr.] 1. an opaque state, quality, or degree 2. pl. -ties an opaque thing

o·pal (ō'p'l) n. [< Sans. upala, gem] a silica of various colors, typically iridescent: some varieties are semiprecious

o·pal·es·cent (ō'pə les'nt) adj. iridescent like opal —**o'pal·esce'** vi. -esced', -esc'ing —**o'pal·es·cence** n.

o·paque (ō pāk') adj. [L. opacus, shady] 1. not letting light through 2. not reflecting light or not shining 3. hard to understand; obscure 4. slow in understanding; obtuse —**o·paque'ly** adv. —**o·paque'ness** n.

op. cit. [L. opere citato] in the work cited

OPEC (ō'pek) Organization of Petroleum Exporting Countries

Op'-Ed' adj. [Op(posite) Ed(itorial page)] designating or on a newspaper page featuring a wide variety of articles, letters, etc.

o·pen (ō'p'n) adj. [OE.] 1. not closed, covered, clogged, or shut 2. unenclosed 3. spread out; unfolded 4. having spaces, gaps, etc. [open ranks] 5. a) not excluding anyone b) ready to admit customers, clients, etc. 6. free to be argued [an open question] 7. not prejudiced or narrow-minded 8. generous 9. a) free from legal or discriminatory restrictions [open season, open housing] b) not regulated or organized along traditional lines [open marriage, open education] 10. not already taken [the job is open] 11. not secret; public 12. frank; candid —vt., vi. 1. to cause to be, or to become, open 2. to spread out; expand; unfold 3. to make or become available for use, etc. without restriction 4. to begin; start 5. to start operating —n. [usually O-] any of various golf tournaments for both professionals and amateurs —**open to** 1. willing to receive, discuss, etc. 2. liable to 3. available to —**open up** 1. to make or become open 2. to unfold 3. to begin 4. [Colloq.] to speak freely 5. [Colloq.] to go or make go faster —**the open** 1. any open, clear area 2. the outdoors 3. public

knowledge —**o'pened** adj. —**o'pen·er** n. —**o'pen·ly** adv. —**o'pen·ness** n.

open air the outdoors —**o'pen-air'** adj.

o'pen-and-shut' adj. easily decided; obvious

open city a city left open to enemy occupation to gain immunity from attack

open door 1. unrestricted admission 2. equal, unrestricted opportunity for all nations to trade with a given nation —**o'pen-door'** adj.

o'pen-end'ed adj. 1. unrestricted 2. open to change 3. allowing for a freely formulated answer: said of a question

o'pen-eyed' adj. with the eyes open or wide open, as in awareness or amazement

o'pen-faced' adj. 1. having a frank, honest face 2. designating a sandwich without a top slice of bread: also **o'pen-face'**

o'pen-hand'ed adj. generous —**o'pen-hand'ed·ly** adv. —**o'pen-hand'ed·ness** n.

o'pen-heart'ed adj. 1. not reserved; frank 2. kindly; generous —**o'pen-heart'ed·ly** adv.

o'pen-hearth' adj. designating or using a furnace with a wide hearth and low roof, for making steel

open house informal reception of visitors freely coming and going, at one's home, a school, etc.

o'pen·ing n. 1. a becoming or making open 2. an open place; hole; gap 3. a clearing 4. a) a beginning b) a first performance 5. an opportunity 6. a job available

open letter a letter written to a specific person but published in a newspaper, etc. for all to read

o'pen-mind'ed adj. open to new ideas; not biased —**o'pen-mind'ed·ness** n.

o'pen-mouthed' adj. 1. having the mouth open 2. gaping, as in astonishment

open secret something supposed to be secret but known to almost everyone

open shop a factory, business, etc. employing workers regardless of union membership

open stock merchandise, as dishes, available in sets, with individual pieces kept in stock

o'pen-work' n. ornamental work, as in cloth, with openings in the material

op·er·a¹ (äp'ər ə, äp'rə) n. [It. < L., a work] 1. a play with most or all the text sung to orchestral accompaniment 2. the art of such plays 3. the score, libretto, or performance of an opera 4. a theater for operas

o·pe·ra² (ō'pə rə, äp'ər ə) n. pl. of OPUS

op·er·a·ble (äp'ər ə b'l) adj. [see OPERATE] 1. practicable 2. treatable surgically

opera glasses a small binocular telescope used at the opera, in theaters, etc.

opera hat a man's tall, collapsible silk hat

opera house a theater chiefly for operas

op·er·ate (äp'ə rāt') vi. -at'ed, -at'ing [< L. operari, to work] 1. to be in action; work 2. to produce a certain effect 3. to perform a surgical operation —vt. 1. to put or keep in action 2. to manage

op·er·at·ic (äp'ə rat'ik) adj. of or like the opera —**op'er·at'i·cal·ly** adv.

op·er·a·tion (äp'ə rā'shən) n. 1. the act or method of operating 2. a being in action or at work 3. any of a series of procedures in some work 4. any strategic military movement 5. any specific plan, project, etc. [Operation Cleanup] 6. any surgical procedure to remedy a physical ailment or defect 7. Math. any process involving a change in quantity —**op'er·a'tion·al** adj.

op·er·a·tive (äp'ə rā'tiv, äp'ər ə-) adj. 1. capable of or in operation 2. effective 3. connected with physical work or mechanical action 4. of or resulting from a surgical operation —n. 1. a worker, esp. a skilled industrial worker 2. a detective or spy

op'er·a'tor (-tər) n. one who operates; specif., a) a person who works a machine b) a person engaged in commercial or industrial operations or enterprises

o·per·cu·lum (ō pur'kyoo ləm) n., pl. -la (-lə), -lums [< L. operire, to close] a covering flap or lidlike structure in plants and animals

op·er·et·ta (äp'ə ret'ə) n. [It. < OPERA¹] a light, amusing opera with spoken dialogue

oph·thal·mi·a (äf thal'mē ə) n. [< Gr. ophthalmos, the eye] inflammation of the eyeball or conjunctiva

oph·thal'mic (-mik) adj. of the eye; ocular

oph·thal·mol·o·gy (äf'thal mäl'ə jē; äp'-; -thə-) n. the branch of medicine dealing with the structure, functions, and diseases of the eye —**oph'thal·mol'o·gist** n.

o·pi·ate (ō'pē it, -āt') n. 1. any medicine containing opium or any of its derivatives, and acting as a sedative and narcotic 2. anything quieting

o·pine (ō pīn′) *vt., vi.* **o·pined′**, **o·pin′ing** [< L. *opinari*, think] to hold or express (some opinion): now usually humorous

o·pin·ion (ə pin′yən) *n.* [< L. *opinari*, think] **1.** a belief not based on certainty but on what seems true or probable **2.** an evaluation, estimation, etc. **3.** an expert's formal judgment **4.** a judge's formal statement of the law bearing on a case

o·pin′ion·at′ed (-āt′id) *adj.* holding obstinately to one's opinions —**o·pin′ion·at′ed·ly** *adv.* —**o·pin′ion·at′ed·ness** *n.*

o·pin′ion·a′tive (-āt′iv) *adj.* **1.** of, or of the nature of, opinion **2.** opinionated

o·pi·um (ō′pē əm) *n.* [L. < Gr. *opos*, vegetable juice] a narcotic drug made from the seed of a certain poppy, used as an intoxicant and medicinally to relieve pain and produce sleep

o·pos·sum (ə päs′əm) *n.* [< AmInd.] a small, tree-dwelling American marsupial: it is active at night and pretends to be dead when trapped

opp. 1. opposed **2.** opposite

op·po·nent (ə pō′nənt) *n.* [< L. *ob-* (see OB-) + *ponere*, to set] one who opposes, as in a fight, game, etc.; adversary —*adj.* opposing

OPOSSUM
(body 12–20 in. long; tail 10–21 in. long)

op·por·tune (äp′ər tōōn′, -tyōōn′) *adj.* [< L. *ob-* (see OB-) + *portus*, a port] **1.** right for the purpose: said of time **2.** timely —**op′por·tune′ly** *adv.* —**op′por·tune′ness** *n.*

op′por·tun′ism *n.* the adapting of one's actions, judgments, etc. to circumstances, as in politics, without regard for principles —**op′por·tun′ist** *n.* —**op′por·tun·is′tic** *adj.*

op·por·tu·ni·ty (äp′ər tōō′nə tē, -tyōō′-) *n., pl.* **-ties 1.** a combination of circumstances favorable for the purpose **2.** a good chance

op·pos·a·ble (ə pō′zə b′l) *adj.* **1.** that can be resisted **2.** that can be placed opposite something else

op·pose (ə pōz′) *vt.* **-posed′**, **-pos′ing** [see OB- & POSITION] **1.** to place opposite, in balance or contrast **2.** to contend with; resist

op·po·site (äp′ə zit) *adj.* [see OB- & POSITION] **1.** set against, facing, or back to back **2.** hostile; resistant **3.** entirely different; exactly contrary **4.** *Bot.* growing in pairs, but separated by a stem —*n.* anything opposed or opposite —*prep.* across from —**op′po·site·ly** *adv.*

op′po·si′tion (-zish′ən) *n.* **1.** an opposing **2.** resistance, contrast, etc. **3.** anything that opposes **4.** [often O-] a political party opposing the party in power

op·press (ə pres′) *vt.* [< L. *ob-* (see OB-) + *premere*, to press] **1.** to weigh heavily on the mind, spirits, or senses of **2.** to keep down by the cruel or unjust use of authority —**op·pres′sor** *n.*

op·pres·sion (ə presh′ən) *n.* **1.** an oppressing or being oppressed **2.** a thing that oppresses **3.** physical or mental distress

op·pres·sive (ə pres′iv) *adj.* **1.** hard to put up with **2.** tyrannical **3.** weighing heavily on the mind, etc. —**op·pres′sive·ly** *adv.* —**op·pres′sive·ness** *n.*

op·pro·bri·ous (ə prō′brē əs) *adj.* expressing opprobrium; abusive —**op·pro′bri·ous·ly** *adv.*

op·pro′bri·um (-əm) *n.* [< L. *opprobare*, to reproach] **1.** the disgrace attached to shameful conduct; scorn **2.** anything bringing shame

opt (äpt) *vi.* [< Fr. < L. *optare*] to make a choice

opt. 1. optician **2.** optics

op·ta·tive (äp′tə tiv) *adj.* [< Fr. < L. *optare*, to desire] expressing wish or desire, as a mood in Greek grammar —*n.* the optative mood, or a verb in this mood

op·tic (äp′tik) *adj.* [< Fr. < Gr. *optikos*] of the eye or sense of sight

op′ti·cal (-'l) *adj.* **1.** of the sense of sight; visual **2.** of optics **3.** made to give help in seeing —**op′ti·cal·ly** *adv.*

op·ti·cian (äp tish′ən) *n.* one who makes or sells eyeglasses and other optical instruments

op·tics (äp′tiks) *n.pl.* [with *sing. v.*] the branch of physics dealing with light and vision

op·ti·mism (äp′tə miz′m) *n.* [< Fr. < L. *optimus*, best] **1.** the belief that good ultimately prevails over evil **2.** the tendency to take the most hopeful or cheerful view of matters —**op′ti·mist** *n.* —**op′ti·mis′tic** *adj.* —**op′ti·mis′ti·cal·ly** *adv.*

op′ti·mum (-məm) *n., pl.* **-mums, -ma** (-mə) [< L. *optimus*, best] the best or most favorable degree, condition, amount, etc. —*adj.* best; most favorable: also **op′ti·mal**

op·tion (äp′shən) *n.* [Fr. < L. *optare*, to wish] **1.** a choosing **2.** the right of choosing **3.** something that is or can be chosen **4.** the right to buy or sell something at a set price within a set time

op′tion·al *adj.* left to one's option, or choice; elective —**op′tion·al·ly** *adv.*

op·tom·e·try (äp täm′ə trē) *n.* [< Gr. *optikos*, optic + *metron*, measure] the science or profession of testing the vision and fitting glasses to correct eye defects —**op·tom′·e·trist** *n.*

op·u·lent (äp′yə lənt) *adj.* [< L. *ops*, wealth] **1.** wealthy; rich **2.** abundant —**op′u·lence**, **op′u·len·cy** *n.* —**op′u·lent·ly** *adv.*

o·pus (ō′pəs) *n., pl.* **o·pe·ra** (ō′pə rə, äp′ər ə), **o′pus·es** [L., a work] a work; composition; esp., any of the musical works of a composer numbered in order of composition or publication

or (ôr, ər) *conj.* [< OE. *oththe*] a coordinating conjunction introducing: *a)* an alternative *[red or blue] b)* a synonymous term *[ill, or sick]*

-or [< L. *-or*] a suffix meaning: **1.** a person or thing that *[inventor]* **2.** quality or condition *[error]* : in Brit. usage, often **-our**

OR Oregon

or·a·cle (ôr′ə k'l, är′-) *n.* [< L. *orare*, to pray] **1.** in ancient Greece and Rome, the place where, or medium by which, deities were consulted **2.** the revelation of a medium or priest **3.** *a)* any person of great wisdom *b)* statements of such a person

o·rac·u·lar (ô rak′yoo lər) *adj.* of or like an oracle; wise, mysterious, etc. —**o·rac′u·lar·ly** *adv.*

o·ral (ôr′əl) *adj.* [< L. *os*, mouth] **1.** uttered; spoken **2.** of or using speech **3.** of or near the mouth —*n.* a spoken examination, as in a college —**o′ral·ly** *adv.*

or·ange (ôr′inj, är′-) *n.* [ult. < Ar. < Per. < Sans. *naranga*] **1.** a reddish-yellow, round citrus fruit with a sweet, juicy pulp **2.** the evergreen tree it grows on **3.** reddish yellow —*adj.* **1.** reddish-yellow **2.** of oranges

or′ange·ade′ (-ād′) *n.* a drink made of orange juice and water, usually sweetened

orange pekoe a black tea of Sri Lanka or India

o·rang·u·tan (ô raŋ′oo tan′, ə-; -tan′) *n.* [< Malay *oran*, man + *utan*, forest] a large ape of Borneo and Sumatra, with shaggy, reddish-brown hair, very long arms, and a hairless face: also sp. **o·rang′ou·tang′** (-taŋ′)

o·rate (ô rāt′, ôr′āt) *vi.* **o·rat′ed**, **o·rat′ing** to make an oration; speak pompously: a humorously derogatory term

o·ra·tion (ô rā′shən) *n.* [< L. *orare*, speak] a formal speech, as at a ceremony

or·a·tor (ôr′ət ər, är′-) *n.* **1.** one who delivers an oration **2.** an eloquent public speaker

or·a·to·ri·o (ôr′ə tôr′ē ō′, är′-) *n., pl.* **-os′** [It., small chapel: from performances at a chapel in Rome] a long, dramatic musical work, usually on a religious theme, presented without stage action

or·a·to·ry (ôr′ə tôr′ē, är′-) *n., pl.* **-ries 1.** skill in public speaking **2.** [< L. *orare*, pray] a small chapel, esp. for private prayer —**or′a·tor′i·cal** *adj.* —**or′a·tor′i·cal·ly** *adv.*

orb (ôrb) *n.* [L. *orbis*, a circle] **1.** a globe; sphere **2.** any heavenly sphere, as the sun or moon **3.** [Poet.] the eye

or·bic·u·lar (ôr bik′yoo lər) *adj.* [< L. *orbis*, a circle] **1.** in the form of an orb **2.** *Bot.* round and flat, as some leaves Also **or·bic′u·late** (-lit, -lāt′)

or·bit (ôr′bit) *n.* [< L. *orbis*, a circle] **1.** the eye socket **2.** the path of a heavenly body, artificial satellite, or spacecraft in its revolution around another body **3.** the range of one's activity —*vi., vt.* to go or put into an orbit in space —**or′bit·al** *adj.*

or·chard (ôr′chərd) *n.* [< L. *hortus*, a garden + OE. *geard*, enclosure] **1.** an area of land where fruit trees or nut trees are grown **2.** such trees

or·ches·tra (ôr′kis trə, -kes′-) *n.* [< Gr. *orchēstra*, space for the chorus] **1.** the space in front of the stage, where the musicians sit: in full **orchestra pit 2.** the main floor of a theater **3.** *a)* a group of musicians playing together *b)* their instruments —**or·ches′tral** (-kes′trəl) *adj.* —**or·ches′tral·ly** *adv.*

or′ches·trate′ (-trāt′) *vt., vi.* **-trat′ed**, **-trat′ing 1.** to compose or arrange (music) for an orchestra **2.** to furnish (a ballet, etc.) with an orchestral score —**or′ches·tra′tion** *n.*

or·chid (ôr′kid) *n.* [< Gr. *orchis*, testicle: from the shape of its roots] **1.** a plant having flowers with three petals, one lip-shaped **2.** the flower **3.** a light bluish red —*adj.* of this color

ord. 1. order **2.** ordinal **3.** ordinance

or·dain (ôr dān′) *vt.* [< L. *ordo*, an order] **1.** to decree; establish; enact **2.** to invest with the functions or office of a minister, priest, or rabbi

or·deal (ôr dēl′, -dē′əl) *n.* [OE. *ordal*] **1.** an old method of trial exposing the accused to physical dangers from which he was supposedly protected if innocent **2.** a painful or severe experience

or·der (ôr′dər) *n.* [< L. *ordo*, straight row] **1.** social position **2.** a state of peace; orderly conduct **3.** arrangement of things or events; series **4.** a definite plan; system **5.** a group set off from others by some quality **6.** a military, monastic, or fraternal brotherhood **7.** a condition in which everything is in its place and functioning properly **8.** condition in general [in working *order*] **9.** an authoritative command, instruction, etc. **10.** a class; kind **11.** an established method, as of conduct in meetings, etc. **12.** *a)* a request to supply something *b)* the thing supplied **13.** written instructions to pay money or surrender property **14.** [*pl.*] the position of ordained minister **15.** *Archit.* any of several classical styles of structure, determined chiefly by the type of column **16.** *Biol.* a classification of plants or animals ranking above a family and below a class —*vt., vi.* **1.** to put or keep (things) in order; arrange **2.** to command **3.** to request (something to be supplied) —**call to order** to ask to be quiet —**in** (or **out of**) **order 1.** in (or out of) proper position **2.** in (or not in) working condition —**in order that** so that —**in order to** as a means to —**in short order** without delay —**on order** ordered but not yet supplied —**on the order of** similar to —**to order** as specified by the buyer

or′der·ly *adj.* **1.** neat **2.** systematic **3.** well-behaved; law-abiding —*adv.* in proper order —*n., pl.* **-lies 1.** *Mil.* an enlisted man assigned as a personal attendant or given a specific task **2.** a male hospital attendant —**or′der·li·ness** *n.*

or·di·nal (ôr′d'n əl) *adj.* [< L. *ordo*, an order] **1.** expressing order in a series **2.** of an order of animals or plants — *n.* **1.** *same as* ORDINAL NUMBER **2.** [*often* O-] a book of religious rituals

ordinal number a number used to indicate order (e.g., ninth, 25th, etc.) in a series: distinguished from CARDINAL NUMBER

or·di·nance (ôr′d'n əns) *n.* [< L. *ordo*, an order] a statute, esp. one enacted by a city government

or·di·nar·i·ly (ôr′d'n er′ə lē) *adv.* **1.** usually; as a rule **2.** in an ordinary way

or·di·nar·y (ôr′d'n er′ē) *n., pl.* **-ies** [< L. *ordo*, an order] **1.** an official of church or court with independent powers **2.** [*often* O-] the unvarying part of the Mass —*adj.* **1.** customary; usual **2.** *a)* unexceptional; common *b)* relatively inferior —**out of the ordinary** unusual

or·di·nate (ôr′d'n it, -āt′) *n.* [< L. *ordo*, an order] in a coordinate system, the distance of a point from the horizontal axis as measured along a line parallel to the vertical axis: cf. ABSCISSA

or·di·na·tion (ôr′d'n ā′shən) *n.* an ordaining or being ordained

ord·nance (ôrd′nəns) *n.* [< ORDINANCE] **1.** artillery **2.** all weapons and ammunition used in warfare

or·dure (ôr′jər, -dyoor) *n.* [< OFr. *ord*, filthy] dung; excrement

ore (ôr) *n.* [OE. *ar*, brass, copper] **1.** any natural combination of minerals, esp. one from which a metal or metals can be profitably extracted **2.** a natural substance from which a nonmetallic material, as sulfur, can be extracted

o·reg·a·no (ô reg′ə nō, ə-) *n.* [< Sp., ult. < Gr. *origanon*] a plant with fragrant leaves used for seasoning

Or·e·gon (ôr′i gən, är′-; -gän′) NW State of the U.S.: 96,981 sq. mi.; pop. 2,091,000; cap. Salem: abbrev. **Oreg.**, **OR** —**Or′e·go′ni·an** (-gō′nē ən) *adj., n.*

or·gan (ôr′gən) *n.* [< Gr. *organon*, an instrument] **1.** a keyboard musical instrument with sets of graduated pipes through which compressed air is passed, causing sound by vibration **2.** in animals and plants, a part adapted to perform a specific function **3.** a means for performing some action **4.** a means of communicating ideas, as a periodical

or·gan·dy, or·gan·die (ôr′gən dē) *n., pl.* **-dies** [Fr. *organdi*] a very sheer, crisp cotton fabric

or·gan·ic (ôr gan′ik) *adj.* **1.** of or having to do with an organ **2.** inherent; constitutional **3.** systematically arranged **4.** designating or of any chemical compound containing carbon **5.** of, like, or derived from living organisms **6.** grown with only animal or vegetable fertilizers **7.** *Med.* producing or involving alteration in the structure of an organ [*organic* disease] : cf. FUNCTIONAL —**or·gan′i·cal·ly** *adv.*

or·gan·ism (ôr′gə niz′m) *n.* **1.** any animal or plant with organs and parts that function together **2.** anything with a complex structure —**or′gan·is′mic** *adj.*

or′gan·ist *n.* one who plays the organ

or·gan·i·za·tion (ôr′gə ni zā′shən, -nī-) *n.* **1.** an organizing or being organized **2.** manner of being organized **3.** an organized group, as a club, union, etc. **4.** the administrative or executive structure of a business, party, etc. — **or′gan·i·za′tion·al** *adj.*

or·gan·ize (ôr′gə nīz′) *vt.* **-ized′, -iz′ing 1.** to provide with an organic structure; systematize **2.** to arrange **3.** to establish **4.** [Colloq.] to set (oneself) into an orderly state —*vi.* **1.** to become organized **2.** to form a labor union — **or′gan·iz′er** *n.*

or·gan·za (ôr gan′zə) *n.* [< ?] a stiff, sheer fabric

or·gasm (ôr′gaz'm) *n.* [< Fr. < Gr. *organ*, to swell] the climax of a sexual act —**or·gas′mic** *adj.*

or·gy (ôr′jē) *n., pl.* **-gies** [< Fr. < Gr. *orgia*, secret rites] **1.** [*usually pl.*] in ancient Greece and Rome, wild celebration in worship of certain gods **2.** any wild merrymaking **3.** overindulgence in any activity —**or′gi·as′tic** (-as′tik) *adj.*

o·ri·el (ôr′ē əl) *n.* [< ? ML. *oriolum*, porch] a large window built out from a wall

o·ri·ent (ôr′ē ənt; *also, and for v. usually,* -ent′) *n.* [< L. *oriri*, arise: with reference to the rising sun] the east: now rare, except [O-] the East, or Asia; esp., the Far East —*vt.* **1.** to set (a map or chart) in agreement with the points of the compass **2.** to adjust (oneself) to a particular situation

ORIEL

o·ri·en·tal (ôr′ē en′t'l) *adj.* **1.** [Poet.] eastern **2.** [O-] of the Orient, its people, or their culture —*n.* [*usually* O-] a member of a people native to the Orient

o·ri·en·tate (ôr′ē ən tāt′, -en-) *vt.* **-tat′ed, -tat′ing** *same as* ORIENT —*vi.* **1.** to face east, or in any specified direction **2.** to adjust to a situation —**o′ri·en·ta′tion** *n.*

or·i·fice (ôr′ə fis, är′-) *n.* [Fr. < L. *os*, mouth + *facere*, make] an opening; mouth or outlet

orig. 1. origin **2.** original **3.** originally

o·ri·ga·mi (ôr′ə gä′mē) *n.* [Jpn.] **1.** a traditional Japanese art of folding paper to form figures, flowers, etc. **2.** an object so made

or·i·gin (ôr′ə jin, är′-) *n.* [< L. *oriri*, to rise] **1.** a coming into existence or use; beginning **2.** parentage; birth **3.** source; root

o·rig·i·nal (ə rij′ə n'l) *adj.* **1.** first; earliest **2.** never having been before; new; novel **3.** capable of creating something new; inventive **4.** being that from which copies are made —*n.* **1.** a primary type that has given rise to varieties **2.** an original work, as of art or literature **3.** the person or thing depicted in a painting, etc. —**o·rig′i·nal′i·ty** (-nal′ə tē) *n.* —**o·rig′i·nal·ly** *adv.*

original sin *Christian Theology* sinfulness and depravity regarded as innate in man as a direct result of Adam's sin

o·rig·i·nate (ə rij′ə nāt′) *vt.* **-nat′ed, -nat′ing** to bring into being; esp., to create; invent —*vi.* to come into being; begin; start —**o·rig′i·na′tion** *n.* —**o·rig′i·na′tor** *n.*

O·ri·no·co (ôr′ə nō′kō) river in Venezuela, flowing into the Atlantic: c.1,700 mi.

o·ri·ole (ôr′ē ōl′) *n.* [ult. < L. *aurum*, gold] **1.** any of a group of yellow and black birds found from Europe to Australia **2.** any of a group of American birds, with orange and black plumage, that build hanging nests

O·ri·on (ō rī′ən, ô-) an equatorial constellation, containing the bright star Betelgeuse

or·i·son (ôr′i z'n, är′-) *n.* [< LL.] a prayer

Ork·ney Islands (ôrk′nē) group of islands north of Scotland, constituting a region of Scotland

Or·lon (ôr′län) *a trademark for* a synthetic fiber somewhat similar to nylon, or a fabric made from this fiber

or·mo·lu (ôr′mə lōō′) *n.* [< Fr. *or moulu*, ground gold] imitation gold: an alloy of copper and tin

or·na·ment (ôr′nə mənt) *n.* [< L. *ornare*, adorn] **1.** anything that adorns; decoration **2.** one whose character or talent adds luster to his society, etc. —*vt.* (-ment′) to decorate —**or′na·men′tal** *adj.* —**or′na·men·ta′tion** *n.*

or·nate (ôr nāt′) *adj.* [< L. *ornare*, adorn] **1.** heavily ornamented; overadorned **2.** flowery: said of literary style — **or·nate′ly** *adv.* —**or·nate′ness** *n.*

or·ner·y (ôr′nər ē) *adj.* [< ORDINARY] [Chiefly Dial.] **1.**

having an ugly disposition **2.** obstinate **3.** base; low —**or′·ner·i·ness** *n.*

or·ni·thol·o·gy (ôr′nə thäl′ə jē) *n.* [< Gr. *ornis,* bird + -LOGY] the branch of zoology dealing with birds —**or′ni·tho·log′i·cal** (-thə läj′i k'l) *adj.* —**or′ni·thol′o·gist** *n.*

o·ro·tund (ôr′ə tund′) *adj.* [< L. *os,* mouth + *rotundo,* round] **1.** clear, strong, and deep: said of the voice **2.** bombastic; pompous, as speech

or·phan (ôr′fən) *n.* [< Gr. *orphanos*] a child whose parents are dead —*adj.* **1.** being an orphan **2.** of or for orphans —*vt.* to cause to become an orphan

or′phan·age (-ij) *n.* an institution for orphans

Or·phe·us (ôr′fē əs, -fyōōs) *Gr. Myth.* a musician with magical ability on the lyre: he lost his chance to lead his wife, Eurydice, out from the world of the dead when he looked back at her

Or′phic (-fik) *adj.* **1.** of or characteristic of Orpheus **2.** [*also* o-] mystic; occult

or·ris (ôr′is, är′-) *n.* [prob. < L. *iris,* iris] a European plant of the iris family, having a fragrant rootstock (**or′ris·root′**), ground and used in perfumery, etc.

ortho- [< Gr. *orthos,* straight] *a combining form meaning:* **1.** straight [*orthodontics*] **2.** correct [*orthography*] **3.** *Med.* correction of deformities [*orthopedics*] Also **orth-**

or·tho·don·tics (ôr′thə dän′tiks) *n.pl.* [*with sing. v.*] [< ORTH(O)- + Gr. *odōn,* tooth + -ICS] the branch of dentistry concerned with correcting irregularities of the teeth and poor occlusion: also **or′tho·don′ti·a** —**or′tho·don′tic** *adj.* —**or′tho·don′tist** *n.*

or·tho·dox (ôr′thə däks′) *adj.* [< Fr. < Gr. *orthos,* correct + *doxa,* opinion] **1.** conforming to the usual beliefs or established doctrines, esp. in religion; conventional **2.** conforming to the Christian faith as formulated in the early creeds **3.** [O-] strictly observing the rites and traditions of Judaism **4.** [O-] designating or of any church in the Orthodox Eastern Church —**or′tho·dox′y** *n., pl.* -ies

Orthodox Eastern Church the Christian church dominant in E Europe, W Asia, and N Africa

or·thog·ra·phy (ôr thäg′rə fē) *n., pl.* -phies [see ORTHO- & -GRAPHY] **1.** spelling in accord with accepted usage **2.** any method of spelling **3.** spelling as a subject of study —**or·thog·ra·pher** *n.* —**or·tho·graph·ic** (ôr′thə graf′ik) *adj.*

or·tho·pe·dics, or·tho·pae·dics (ôr′thə pē′diks) *n.pl.* [*with sing. v.*] [< Fr. < ORTHO- + Gr. *pais,* child] the branch of surgery concerned with deformities, diseases, and injuries of the bones, joints, etc. —**or′tho·pe′dic** *adj.* —**or′tho·pe′dist** *n.*

or·thop·ter·an (ôr thäp′tər ən) *n.* [< ORTHO- + *pteron,* wing] any of an order of insects, including crickets, grasshoppers, etc., having biting mouthparts and hard forewings covering membranous hind wings

-ory [< L. *-orius*] *a suffix meaning:* **1.** of, having the nature of [*contradictory*] **2.** a place or thing for [*directory*]

o·ryx (ôr′iks, är′-) *n.* any of a group of large African and Asian antelopes, including the gemsbok, with long horns

Os *Chem.* osmium

OS., OS, O.S. Old Saxon

O·sage orange (ō sāj′) [< *Osage,* AmInd. tribe] **1.** a thorny tree with hard, yellow wood, used for hedges, etc. **2.** its orangelike, inedible fruit

O·sa·ka (ō sä′kə) seaport in S Honshu, Japan: pop. 3,156,000

os·cil·late (äs′ə lāt′) *vi.* -lat′ed, -lat′ing [< L. *oscillare,* to swing] **1.** to swing to and fro **2.** to vacillate **3.** *Physics* to vary between maximum and minimum values, as electric current —**os′cil·la′tion** *n.* —**os′cil·la′tor** *n.*

os·cil·lo·scope (ä sil′ə skōp′, ə-) *n.* [< L. *oscillare,* to swing + -SCOPE] an instrument that visually records an electrical wave on a fluorescent screen, as of a cathode-ray tube

os·cu·late (äs′kyə lāt′) *vt., vi.* -lat′ed, -lat′ing [< L. *osculum,* a kiss] to kiss —**os′cu·la′tion** *n.*

-ose¹ [Fr. < (*gluc*)*ose*] *a suffix designating:* **1.** a carbohydrate [*cellulose*] **2.** the product of a protein hydrolysis

-ose² [L. *-osus*] *a suffix meaning* full of, having the qualities of [*bellicose, morose*]

o·sier (ō′zhər) *n.* [< ML. *ausaria,* bed of willows] **1.** a willow whose wood is used for baskets and furniture **2.** a willow branch used for wickerwork

O·si·ris (ō sī′ris) the ancient Egyptian god of the lower world, brother and husband of Isis

-osis [< Gr. *-ōsis*] *a suffix meaning:* **1.** state, condition, action [*osmosis*] **2.** an abnormal or diseased condition [*neurosis*]

-osity [< L. *-ositas*] *a suffix used to form nouns from adjectives ending in* -OSE² *or* -OUS

Os·lo (äs′lō, äz′-) capital of Norway; seaport in the SE part: pop. 487,000

os·mi·um (äz′mē əm) *n.* [< Gr. *osmē,* odor] a bluish metallic chemical element, occurring as an alloy with platinum and iridium: symbol, Os; at. wt., 190.2; at. no., 76

os·mo·sis (äs mō′sis, äz-) *n.* [< Gr. *ōsmos,* impulse] **1.** the tendency of fluids to pass through a somewhat porous membrane so as to equalize concentrations on both sides **2.** the diffusion of fluids through a porous partition —**os·mot′ic** (-mät′ik) *adj.* —**os·mot′i·cal·ly** *adv.*

os·prey (äs′prē) *n., pl.* -preys [< L. *os,* a bone + *frangere,* to break] a large hawk with a blackish back and white breast, that feeds solely on fish

Os·sa (äs′ə) mountain in Thessaly, NE Greece: see PELION

os·si·fy (äs′ə fī′) *vt., vi.* -fied′, -fy′ing [< L. *os,* a bone + -FY] **1.** to change or develop into bone **2.** to settle or fix rigidly in a practice, custom, etc. —**os′si·fi·ca′tion** *n.*

os·ten·si·ble (äs ten′sə b'l, əs-) *adj.* [Fr. < L. *ostendere,* to show] apparent; seeming —**os·ten′si·bly** *adv.*

os·ten·ta·tion (äs′tən tā′shən) *n.* [see OSTENSIBLE] showy display, as of wealth, knowledge, etc. —**os′ten·ta′tious** *adj.* —**os′ten·ta′tious·ly** *adv.*

osteo- [< Gr. *osteon*] *a combining form meaning* a bone or bones [*osteopath*] : also **oste-**

os·te·o·my·e·li·tis (äs′tē ō mī′ə līt′is) *n.* [see OSTEO- & MYELITIS] infection of bone marrow or structures

os·te·op·a·thy (äs′tē äp′ə thē) *n.* [see OSTEO- & -PATHY] a school of medicine and surgery that emphasizes the relationship of the muscles and bones to all other body systems —**os′te·o·path′** (-path′) *n.* —**os′te·o·path′ic** *adj.*

ost·ler (äs′lər) *n.* same as HOSTLER

os·tra·cize (äs′trə sīz′) *vt.* -cized′, -ciz′ing [< Gr. *ostrakon,* a shell (cast as a ballot)] to banish from society, etc. —**os′tra·cism** *n.*

os·trich (ôs′trich, äs′-) *n.* [< L. *avis,* bird + *struthio,* ostrich] **1.** a swift-running, nonflying bird of Africa and the Near East, the largest living bird **2.** *same as* RHEA (*see* RHEA *n.*)

OT., OT, O.T. Old Testament

O·thel·lo (ə thel′ō, ō-) a tragedy by Shakespeare in which the title character kills his wife because he wrongly believes her unfaithful

oth·er (uth′ər) *adj.* [OE.] **1.** being the remaining one or ones [Bill and the *other* boy(s)] **2.** different or distinct from that or those implied [some *other* girl] **3.** additional [he has no *other* coat] **4.** former [in *other* times] —*pron.* **1.** the other one **2.** some other person or thing [do as *others* do] —*adv.* otherwise [I can't do *other* than go] —**the other day** (or **night,** etc.) not long ago —**oth′er·ness** *n.*

OSTRICH
(to 8 ft. high)

oth·er·wise′ *adv.* **1.** in another manner; differently [to believe *otherwise*] **2.** in all other respects [an *otherwise* intelligent man] **3.** in other circumstances —*adj.* different [his answer could not be *otherwise*]

oth·er·world·ly (-wurld′lē) *adj.* being apart from earthly interests —**oth′er·world′li·ness** *n.*

o·ti·ose (ō′shē ōs′) *adj.* [< L. *otium,* leisure] **1.** idle; indolent **2.** futile **3.** useless

o·ti·tis (ō tīt′əs) *n.* [< Gr. *ous, ōtos,* the ear + -ITIS] inflammation of the ear

Ot·ta·wa¹ (ät′ə wə, -wä′) *n., pl.* -was, -wa a member of a tribe of Indians who lived in SE Canada and in Michigan

Ot·ta·wa² (ät′ə wə, -wä′) capital of Canada, in SE Ontario: pop. 291,000

ot·ter (ät′ər) *n.* [OE. oter] **1.** a furry, swimming mammal related to the weasel and mink **2.** its fur

Ot·to·man (ät′ə mən) *n., pl.* -mans **1.** a Turk **2.** [o-] a low, cushioned seat or footstool *adj.* Turkish

Ottoman Empire empire (c.1300–1918) of the Turks in SE Europe, SW Asia, & NE Africa

ouch (ouch) *interj.* an exclamation of pain

ought¹ (ôt) *v.aux.* [< OE. *agan,* owe] an auxiliary used to express obligation or duty [he *ought* to pay rent] or desirability [you *ought* to rest] or probability [he *ought* to be here soon]

ought² (ôt) *n.* anything whatever; aught —*adv.* [Archaic] to any degree; aught

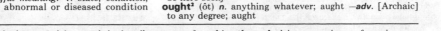

ought³ (ôt) *n.* a nought; the figure zero (0)
ought·n't (ôt′nt) ought not
‡**oui** (wē) *adv.* [Fr.] yes
Oui·ja (wē′jə, -jē) [Fr. *oui*, yes + G. *ja*, yes] *a trademark for* a device consisting of a planchette and a board bearing the alphabet and other symbols, used in fortunetelling, séances, etc.
ounce¹ (ouns) *n.* [< L. *uncia*, a twelfth] **1.** a unit of weight equal to 1/16 pound avoirdupois, or 1/12 pound troy **2.** a fluid ounce, 1/16 pint **3.** any small amount Abbrev. **oz.**
ounce² (ouns) *n.* [< OFr. *l'once* < L. *lynx*, lynx] *same as* SNOW LEOPARD
our (our, är) *possessive pronominal adj.* [OE. *ure*] of, belonging to, made, or done by us
ours (ourz, ärz) *pron.* that or those belonging to us [*ours are better, a friend of ours*]
our·self' (-self′) *pron.* myself: used by a king, queen, etc., as in a formal speech
our·selves' (-selvz′) *pron.* **1.** *the intensive form of* WE [*we went ourselves*] **2.** *the reflexive form of* WE [*we hurt ourselves*] **3.** our true selves [*we are not ourselves today*]
-ous [< L. *-osus*] *a suffix meaning:* **1.** having, full of, characterized by [*outrageous*] **2.** *Chem.* having a lower valence than is indicated by the suffix *-ic* [*nitrous*]
oust (oust) *vt.* [< OFr. *ouster*] to force out; expel, dispossess, etc.
oust·er (ou′stər) *n.* **1.** one that ousts **2.** an ousting or being ousted, esp. from real property
out (out) *adv.* [OE. *ut*] **1.** away or forth from a place, position, etc. **2.** into the open air **3.** into existence or activity [*disease broke out*] **4.** *a)* to a conclusion [*argue it out*] *b)* completely [*tired out*] **5.** into sight or notice [*the moon came out*] **6.** into or in circulation or society **7.** from existence or activity [*fade out*] **8.** aloud [*sing out*] **9.** beyond a regular surface, condition, etc. [*stand out*] **10.** away from the interior or midst **11.** into disuse [*long skirts went out*] **12.** from a number or stock [*pick out*] **13.** [Slang] into unconsciousness **14.** *Baseball*, etc. in a manner producing an out [*to fly out*] —*adj.* **1.** external: usually in combination [*outpost*] **2.** beyond regular limits **3.** away from work, etc. **4.** in error **5.** not in operation, use, etc. **6.** [Colloq.] having suffered a loss [*out five dollars*] **7.** *Baseball* having failed to get on base —*prep.* out of; through to the outside —*n.* **1.** something that is out **2.** a person, group, etc. that is not in power: *usually used in pl.* **3.** [Slang] a way out; means of avoiding **4.** *Baseball* the failure of a batter or runner to reach base safely —*vi.* to come out —*interj.* get out! —**on the outs** [Colloq.] on unfriendly terms —**out and away** by far; without comparison —**out and out** completely; thoroughly —**out for** trying to get or do —**out of 1.** from inside of **2.** from the number of **3.** beyond **4.** from (material, etc.) **5.** because of [*out of spite*] **6.** having no [*out of gas*] **7.** so as to deprive [*cheat out of money*] —**out to** trying to
out- *a combining form meaning:* **1.** at or from a point away, outside [*outbuilding*] **2.** going away or forth, outward [*outbound*] **3.** better or more than [*outdo, outproduce, outscore, outspend*]
out·age (out′ij) *n.* an accidental suspension of operation, as of electric power
out'-and-out' *adj.* complete; thorough
out'back' *n.* [*also* O-] the sparsely settled, flat, arid inland region of Australia
out·bid' *vt.* -bid', -bid'ding to bid or offer more than (another)
out'board' (-bôrd′) *adj., adv.* **1.** outside the hull of a watercraft **2.** away from the fuselage of an aircraft **3.** outside the main body of a spacecraft
outboard motor a portable gasoline engine mounted outboard on a boat to propel it
out'bound' *adj.* outward bound
out'break' *n.* a breaking out; sudden occurrence, as of disease, war, rioting, etc.
out'build'ing *n.* a structure, as a garage, separate from the main building
out'burst' *n.* a sudden release, as of emotion or energy
out'cast' *adj.* driven out; rejected —*n.* a person or thing cast out or rejected
out·class' *vt.* to surpass; excel
out'come' *n.* result; consequence
out'crop' *n.* the emergence of a mineral so as to be exposed on the surface of the earth —*vi.* -cropped', -crop'ping **1.** to emerge in this way **2.** to break forth
out'cry' *n., pl.* -cries' **1.** a crying out **2.** a strong protest or objection

out'dat'ed *adj.* no longer popular; behind the times
out·dis'tance *vt.* -tanced, -tanc·ing to leave behind, as in a race
out·do' *vt.* -did', -done', -do'ing to exceed; surpass — **outdo oneself** to do better than expected
out'door' (-dôr′) *adj.* **1.** being or taking place outdoors **2.** of, or fond of, the outdoors
out'doors' (-dôrz′) *adv.* in or into the open; outside —*n.* the outdoor world
out'er *adj.* farther out; exterior
Outer Mongolia former name of MONGOLIAN PEOPLE'S REPUBLIC: see MONGOLIA
outer space space beyond the earth's atmosphere or beyond the solar system
out'field' (-fēld′) *n. Baseball* **1.** the playing area beyond the infield **2.** the outfielders
out'field'er *n. Baseball* a player whose position is in the outfield
out'fit' *n.* **1.** the equipment used in any craft or activity **2.** clothing worn together **3.** a group of people associated in some activity —*vt.* -fit'ted, -fit'ting to equip —**out'fit'ter** *n.*
out'flank' *vt.* **1.** to go around and beyond the flank of (enemy troops) **2.** to thwart; outwit
out'flow' *n.* **1.** the act of flowing out **2.** *a)* that which flows out *b)* amount flowing out
out'fox' (-fäks′) *vt.* to outwit; outsmart
out·go' (out′gō′) *vt.* -went', -gone', -go'ing to surpass; go beyond —*n.* (out′gō′) *pl.* -goes' that which is paid out; expenditure
out'go'ing *adj.* **1.** going out; leaving **2.** sociable, friendly, etc. —*n.* the act of going out
out'grow' *vt.* -grew', -grown', -grow'ing **1.** to grow faster or larger than **2.** to lose or get rid of by becoming mature **3.** to grow too large for
out'growth' *n.* **1.** a growing out **2.** a result; consequence **3.** an offshoot
out'guess' (-ges′) *vt.* to outwit; anticipate
out'house' *n.* an outbuilding; specif., a small outbuilding with a toilet over a pit; privy
out'ing *n.* **1.** a pleasure trip or holiday away from home **2.** an outdoor walk, ride, etc.
out'land'er (-lan′dər) *n.* a foreigner; stranger
out·land·ish (out lan′dish) *adj.* **1.** very odd; fantastic **2.** remote; secluded
out·last' *vt.* to endure longer than
out·law (out′lô′) *n.* **1.** orig., a person deprived of legal rights and protection **2.** a notorious criminal who is a fugitive from the law —*vt.* **1.** orig., to declare to be an outlaw **2.** to remove the legal force of (contracts, etc.) **3.** to declare illegal **4.** to bar, or ban —**out'law'ry** *n., pl.* -ries
out'lay' (-lā′) *n.* **1.** a spending (of money, energy, etc.) **2.** money, etc. spent —*vt.* (out′lā′) -laid', -lay'ing to spend (money, etc.)
out'let' *n.* **1.** a passage for letting something out **2.** a means of expression [*an outlet for rage*] **3.** a stream, river, etc. that flows out from a lake **4.** *a)* a market for goods *b)* a store, etc. that sells the goods of a specific manufacturer, etc. **5.** a point in a wiring system where electrical current may be taken by inserting a plug
out'line' *n.* **1.** a line bounding the limits of an object **2.** a sketch showing the contours of an object **3.** [*also pl.*] an undetailed general plan **4.** a systematic listing of the important points of a subject —*vt.* -lined', -lin'ing **1.** to draw in outline **2.** to list the main points of
out·live' *vt.* -lived', -liv'ing **1.** to live longer than; survive **2.** to outlast; live through
out'look' *n.* **1.** the view from a place **2.** viewpoint **3.** prospect; probable result
out'ly'ing (-lī′iŋ) *adj.* relatively far out from a certain point; remote
out'ma·neu'ver, out'ma·noeu'vre *vt.* -vered or -vred -ver·ing or -vring to maneuver with better effect than; outwit
out·match' (-mach′) *vt.* to surpass; outdo
out'mod'ed (-mōd′id) *adj.* no longer in fashion or accepted; obsolete
out'num'ber *vt.* to exceed in number
out'-of-date' *adj.* no longer in style or use; outmoded; old-fashioned
out'-of-doors' *adv., n. same as* OUTDOORS
out'-of-the-way' *adj.* **1.** secluded **2.** unusual **3.** not conventional
out'pa'tient *n.* a patient, not an inmate, receiving treatment at a hospital
out'play' *vt.* to play better than
out'point' *vt.* to score more points than

out'post' *n.* **1.** *Mil. a)* a small group stationed at a distance beyond the main force *b)* the station so occupied **2.** a frontier settlement

out'put' *n.* **1.** the work done or amount produced, esp. over a given period **2.** in computers, *a)* information transferred or delivered *b)* the process of transferring or delivering this information **3.** *Elec.* the useful current delivered by amplifiers, generators, etc.

out·rage (out'rāj') *n.* [ult. < L. *ultra*, beyond] **1.** an extremely vicious or violent act **2.** a deep insult or offense **3.** great anger or indignation aroused by such an act or offense —*vt.* **-raged'**, **-rag'ing 1.** to commit an outrage upon **2.** to rape

out·ra'geous (-rā'jəs) *adj.* **1.** involving or doing great injury or wrong **2.** very offensive or shocking **3.** violent in action or disposition —**out·ra'geous·ly** *adv.* —**out·ra'geous·ness** *n.*

out'rank' *vt.* to exceed in rank

‡**ou·tré** (ōō trā') *adj.* [Fr.] **1.** exaggerated **2.** eccentric; bizarre

out·reach (out'rēch') *vt., vi.* **1.** to surpass **2.** to reach out —*n.* (out'rēch') **1.** a reaching out **2.** the extent of reach

out'rid'er *n.* **1.** an attendant on horseback who rides ahead of or beside a carriage **2.** a cowboy who rides over a range to prevent cattle from straying

out'rig'ger *n.* **1.** a timber rigged out from the side of a canoe to prevent tipping **2.** a canoe of this type

out·right (out'rīt') *adj.* **1.** without reservation; downright **2.** straightforward **3.** complete; whole —*adv.* (out'rīt') **1.** entirely **2.** openly **3.** at once —*out'-right'ness n.*

OUTRIGGER

out'run' *vt.* **-ran'**, **-run'**, **-run'ning 1.** to run faster or farther than **2.** to exceed

out'sell' *vt.* **-sold'**, **-sell'ing 1.** to sell in greater amounts than **2.** to excel in salesmanship

out'set' *n.* a setting out; beginning

out'shine' *vt.* **-shone'** or **-shined'**, **-shin'ing 1.** to shine brighter or longer than (another) **2.** to surpass; excel —*vi.* to shine forth

out'side' *n.* **1.** the outer side; exterior **2.** *a)* outward aspect *b)* that which is obvious or superficial **3.** any place or area not inside —*adj.* **1.** outer **2.** coming from or situated beyond given limits [*outside* help] **3.** extreme **4.** slight [*an outside* chance] —*adv.* **1.** on or to the outside **2.** beyond certain limits **3.** outdoors —*prep.* **1.** on or to the outer side of **2.** beyond the limits of —**outside of 1.** outside **2.** [Colloq.] other than

out'sid'er *n.* one not a member of a given group

out'size' *n.* an odd or very large size

out'skirts' (-skurts') *n.pl.* the outer areas, as of a city

out'smart' *vt.* [Colloq.] to overcome by cunning or cleverness; outwit

out'spo'ken *adj.* **1.** unrestrained in speech; frank **2.** spoken boldly or candidly —**out'spo'ken·ness n.**

out'spread' (for *n. & adj.* out'spred') *vt., vi.* **-spread'**, **-spread'ing** to spread out; extend; expand —*n.* a spreading out —*adj.* extended; expanded

out'stand'ing *adj.* **1.** projecting **2.** distinguished **3.** unsettled **4.** unpaid **5.** that have been issued and sold, as stocks, etc. —**out'stand'ing·ly** *adv.*

out'stretch' *vt.* **1.** to extend **2.** to stretch beyond

out'strip' (-strip') *vt.* **-stripped'**, **-strip'ping 1.** to go at a faster pace than **2.** to surpass; excel

out'talk' *vt.* to talk more skillfully, loudly, or forcefully than

out'vote' *vt.* **-vot'ed**, **-vot'ing** to defeat or surpass in voting

out'ward (out'wərd) *adj.* **1.** having to do with the outside; outer **2.** visible **3.** to or toward the outside **4.** superficial —*adv.* **1.** toward the outside; away **2.** visibly Also **out'wards** *adv.* —**out'ward·ly** *adv.* —**out'ward·ness n.**

out'wear' *vt.* **-wore'**, **-worn'**, **-wear'ing 1.** to wear out **2.** to be more lasting than

out'weigh' *vt.* **1.** to weigh more than **2.** to be more important than

out'wit' *vt.* **-wit'ted**, **-wit'ting** to get the better of by cunning or cleverness

ou·zel (ōō'z'l) *n.* [OE. *osle*] any of several brownish or grayish water birds; esp., the WATER OUZEL

o·va (ō'və) *n. pl. of* OVUM

o·val (ō'v'l) *adj.* [< Fr. < L. *ovum*, an egg] **1.** elliptical **2.** having the form of an egg —*n.* anything oval

o·va·ry (ō'vər ē) *n., pl.* **-ries** [< L. *ovum*, an egg] **1.** either of the pair of female reproductive glands producing eggs **2.** *Bot.* the enlarged hollow part of the pistil, containing ovules —**o·var·i·an** (ō ver'ē ən) *adj.*

o·vate (ō'vāt) *adj.* egg-shaped, esp. with the broader end at the base, as some leaves —**o'vate·ly** *adv.*

o·va·tion (ō vā'shən) *n.* [< L. *ovare*, celebrate a triumph] an enthusiastic public welcome, burst of applause, etc.

ov·en (uv'ən) *n.* [OE. *ofen*] a compartment or receptacle for baking, drying, etc. by means of heat

ov'en·bird' *n.* a N. American warbler that builds a dome-like nest on the ground

o·ver (ō'vər) *prep.* [OE. *ofer*] **1.** in, at, or to a position above **2.** across and down from **3.** while engaged in **4.** upon the surface of **5.** so 'as to cover **6.** upon, as an effect or influence **7.** with care, concern, etc. for **8.** above in authority, power, etc. **9.** along or across, or above and to the other side of **10.** through all or many parts of **11.** during [*over* the year] **12.** more than **13.** up to and including [stay *over* Easter] **14.** through the medium of [*over* the radio] —*adv.* **1.** *a)* above, across, or to the other side *b)* across the brim **2.** more; beyond **3.** covering the entire area **4.** from start to finish [read it *over*] **5.** *a)* from an upright position *b)* upside down [turn the cup *over*] **6.** again **7.** at or on the other side **8.** from one side, etc. to another [win him *over*] —*adj.* **1.** upper, outer, superior, excessive, or extra **2.** finished; past **3.** having reached the other side **4.** [Colloq.] as a surplus —*n.* something in addition; surplus —**over again** another time —**over all** from end to end —**over and over (again)** repeatedly

over- *a combining form meaning:* **1.** above in position, outer, upper, superior [*overhead*, *overlord*] **2.** passing across or beyond [*overrun*] **3.** involving a movement downward from above [*overflow*] **4.** excessive(ly), too much [*overload*, *oversell*] : the following list includes some common compounds formed with *over-* that can be understood if *too* or *too much* is added to the meaning of the base word

overabundance	overemotional	overprecise
overactive	overemphasize	overproduce
overambitious	overexercise	overproduction
overanxious	overexert	overrefined
overattentive	overexpansion	overripe
overburden	overexpose	oversell
overcareful	overexposure	oversensitive
overcautious	overfed	oversolicitous
overcompensate	overhasty	overspecialize
overconfident	overheat	overstimulate
overcook	overindulgence	overstock
overcritical	overinflate	overstrict
overcrowd	overload	overtire
overdevelop	overpay	overuse
overeager	overpayment	overwind
overeat	overpopulate	overzealous

o'ver·act' *vt., vi.* to act with exaggeration

o·ver·age' (ō'vər āj') *adj.* **1.** over the age fixed as a standard **2.** too old to be of use

o·ver·age² (ō'vər ij) *n.* a surplus, as of goods

o'ver·all' *adj.* **1.** from end to end **2.** total —*adv.* (ō'vər ôl') **1.** from end to end **2.** in general

o'ver·alls' *n.pl.* loose trousers, often with an attached bib, worn over other clothing as a protection

o'ver·awe' *vt.* **-awed'**, **-aw'ing** to overcome or subdue by inspiring awe

o'ver·bal'ance *vt.* **-anced**, **-anc·ing 1.** to weigh more than; outweigh **2.** to throw off balance —*n.* (ō'vər bal'əns) something that overbalances

o'ver·bear' (-ber') *vt.* **-bore'**, **-borne'**, **-bear'ing 1.** to press down, as by weight **2.** to dominate

o'ver·bear'ing *adj.* **1.** arrogant or domineering **2.** dominant or overriding

o'ver·bid' *vt., vi.* **-bid'**, **-bid'ding 1.** to outbid (another person) **2.** to bid more than the worth of (a thing) —*n.* (ō'vər bid') a higher bid

o·ver·blown' (ō'vər blōn') *adj.* past full bloom

o·ver·blown² (ō'vər blōn') *adj.* **1.** overdone; excessive **2.** pompous; bombastic

o'ver·board' *adv.* **1.** over a ship's side **2.** from a ship into the water —**go overboard** [Colloq.] to go to extremes

o'ver·cast' (-kast') *n.* a covering, esp. of clouds —*adj.* **1.** cloudy: said of the sky or weather **2.** *Sewing* sewn over an edge to prevent raveling

o'ver·charge' vt., vi. -charged', -charg'ing 1. to charge too high a price 2. to overload —n. (ō'vər chärj') 1. an excessive charge 2. too full a load

o'ver·cloud' vt., vi. to make or become cloudy, gloomy, etc.

o'ver·coat' n. a coat, esp. a heavy coat, worn over the usual clothing for warmth

o'ver·come' vt. -came', -come', -com'ing 1. to get the better of in competition, etc. 2. to suppress, prevail over, overwhelm, etc. —vi. to win

o'ver·do' vt. -did', -done', -do'ing 1. to do too much 2. to spoil by exaggerating 3. to cook too long —vi. to do too much

o'ver·dose' n. too large a dose

o'ver·draft' (-draft') n. 1. an overdrawing of money from a bank 2. the amount overdrawn

o'ver·draw' vt. -drew', -drawn', -draw'ing 1. to spoil the effect of by exaggeration 2. to draw on in excess of the amount credited to the drawer

o'ver·dress' vt., vi. to dress too warmly, too showily, or too formally for the occasion

o'ver·drive' (-drīv') n. a gear that automatically reduces an engine's power output without reducing its driving speed

o'ver·due' adj. past or delayed beyond the time set for payment, arrival, etc.

o'ver·es'ti·mate' (-es'tə māt') vt. -mat'ed, -mat'ing to set too high an estimate on or for —n. an estimate that is too high —o'ver·es'ti·ma'tion n.

o'ver·flow' vt. 1. to flow across; flood 2. to flow over the brim of 3. to fill beyond capacity —vi. 1. to run over 2. to be superabundant —n. (ō'vər flō') 1. an overflowing 2. the amount that overflows 3. a vent for overflowing liquids

o'ver·grow' vt. -grew', -grown', -grow'ing to overspread so as to cover, as with foliage —vi. to grow too fast or beyond normal —o'ver·grown' adj. —o'ver·growth' n.

o'ver·hand' adj. 1. done with the hand raised above the shoulder 2. Sewing designating stitches passed over two edges to sew them together —adv. in an overhand manner —n. Sports an overhand stroke

o'ver·hang' vt. -hung', -hang'ing 1. to hang or project over or beyond 2. to impend; threaten —vi. to project out over something —n. (ō'vər haŋ') the projection of one thing over another

o'ver·haul' (-hôl') vt. 1. a) to check thoroughly for needed repairs, adjustments, etc. b) to make such repairs, etc., as on a motor 2. to catch up with —n. (ō'vər hôl') an overhauling

o'ver·head' adj. 1. above the level of the head 2. in the sky 3. on a higher level, with reference to related objects —n. the general, continuing costs of a business, as of rent, maintenance, etc. —adv. (ō'vər hed') above the head; aloft

o'ver·hear' vt. -heard', -hear'ing to hear (something spoken or a speaker) without the speaker's knowledge or intention

o'ver·joy' vt. to give great joy to; delight

o'ver·kill' n. the capacity of a nation's nuclear weapon stockpile to kill many times the total population of any given nation

o'ver·land' adv., adj. by, on, or across land

o'ver·lap' vt., vi. -lapped', -lap'ping to lap over; to extend over (something or each other) so as to coincide in part —n. (ō'vər lap') 1. an overlapping 2. a part that overlaps

o'ver·lay' vt. -laid', -lay'ing 1. to lay or spread over 2. to cover, as with a decorative layer —n. (ō'vər lā') 1. a covering 2. a decorative layer

o'ver·look' vt. 1. to look at from above 2. to give a view of from above 3. to rise above 4. a) to look beyond and not see b) to ignore; neglect 5. to excuse in an indulgent way 6. to supervise —n. (ō'vər look') a height or the view from it

o'ver·lord' n. a lord ranking above other lords

o·ver·ly (ō'vər lē) adv. too much; excessively

o'ver·much' adj., adv., n. too much

o'ver·night' adv. 1. during the night 2. very suddenly —adj. 1. done or going on during the night 2. for one night [an overnight guest] 3. of or for a brief trip [an overnight bag]

o·ver·pass (ō'vər pas') n. a bridge or other passageway over a road, railway, etc.

o'ver·play' vt. 1. to overact or overdo 2. Card Games to overestimate the strength of (one's hand)

o'ver·pow'er vt. 1. to subdue; overwhelm 2. to supply with more power than is needed —o'ver·pow'er·ing adj.

o'ver·pro·tec'tive adj. tending to protect more than is necessary; specif., shielding (one's child, etc.) from normal hurts or conflicts

o'ver·rate' vt. -rat'ed, -rat'ing to rate or estimate too highly

o'ver·reach' vt. 1. to reach beyond or above 2. to reach too far for and miss 3. to cheat —vi. to reach too far — overreach oneself to fail because of trying more than one can do, or because of being too crafty

o'ver·re·act' vi. to react in an extreme, highly emotional way, as by undue use of force

o'ver·ride' vt. -rode', -rid'den, -rid'ing 1. to ride over 2. to trample down 3. to suppress or prevail over 4. to disregard or nullify 5. to fatigue (a horse, etc.) by riding too long

o'ver·rule' vt. -ruled', -rul'ing 1. to rule out or set aside, as by higher authority 2. to prevail over —o'ver·rul'ing adj.

o'ver·run' vt. -ran', -run', -run'ning 1. to spread out over so as to cover 2. to swarm over, as vermin 3. to invade or spread swiftly throughout 4. to run beyond (certain limits) —vi. to overflow —n. (ō'vər run') 1. an overrunning 2. the amount that overruns 3. [usually pl.] the amount by which the cost of something exceeds an estimated cost

o'ver·seas' adv. over or beyond the sea —adj. 1. foreign 2. over or across the sea Chiefly Brit., o'ver·sea'

o'ver·see' vt. -saw', -seen', -see'ing 1. to supervise; superintend 2. to catch sight of accidentally 3. to survey; watch —o'ver·se'er n.

o'ver·shad'ow vt. 1. to cast a shadow over 2. to darken 3. to be more important than

o'ver·shoe' n. a boot of rubber or fabric worn over the regular shoe to protect from cold or dampness

o'ver·shoot' vt. -shot', -shoot'ing 1. to shoot or pass over or beyond 2. to go farther than (an intended limit) —vi. to shoot or go too far

o'ver·shot' adj. with the upper part extending past the lower [an overshot jaw]

o'ver·sight' (-sīt') n. a careless mistake or omission

o'ver·sim'pli·fy' vt., vi. -fied', -fy'ing to simplify so much as to distort, as by ignoring essential details — o'ver·sim'pli·fi·ca'tion n.

o'ver·size' adj. 1. too large 2. larger than the normal or usual —n. a size larger than regular sizes

o'ver·skirt' n. an outer skirt

o'ver·sleep' vi. -slept', -sleep'ing to sleep past the intended time for getting up

o'ver·spread' vt., vi. -spread', -spread'ing to spread or cover over

o'ver·state' (-stāt') vt. -stat'ed, -stat'ing to exaggerate — o'ver·state'ment n.

o'ver·stay' vt. to stay beyond the time or limits of

o'ver·step' (-step') vt. -stepped', -step'ping to go beyond the limits of; exceed

o'ver·strung' adj. too highly strung; tense

o'ver·stuff' vt. 1. to stuff with too much of something 2. to upholster (furniture) with deep stuffing

o'ver·sup·ply' vt. -plied', -ply'ing to supply in excess — n., pl. -plies' too great a supply

o·vert (ō vurt', ō'vurt) adj. [< L. aperire, to open] 1. not hidden; open 2. Law done publicly, without attempt at concealment —o·vert'ly adv.

o·ver·take (ō'vər tāk') vt. -took', -tak'en, -tak'ing 1. to catch up with and, often, go beyond 2. to come upon suddenly

o'ver·tax' vt. 1. to tax too heavily 2. to make excessive demands on

o'ver·the-count'er adj. 1. sold directly rather than through an exchange, as stocks and bonds 2. sold legally without prescription, as some drugs

o'ver·throw' vt. -threw', -thrown', -throw'ing 1. to throw or turn over 2. to conquer; bring to an end —n. (ō'vər thrō') 1. an overthrowing or being overthrown 2. destruction; end

o'ver·time' n. 1. time beyond the established limit, as of working hours 2. pay for work done in such time 3. Sports an extra period added to the game to decide a tie —adj., adv. of, for, or during (an) overtime

o'ver·tone' n. 1. any of the attendant higher tones heard with a fundamental musical tone 2. an implication; nuance: usually used in pl.

o'ver·top' (-täp') vt. -topped', -top'ping 1. to rise above 2. to excel; surpass

o·ver·ture (ō'vər chər, ō'və-) n. [< L. apertura, APERTURE] 1. an introductory offer or proposal 2. a musical introduction to an opera, etc.

o'ver·turn' *vt.* **1.** to turn over **2.** to conquer —*vi.* to tip over; capsize —*n.* (ō'vər turn') an overturning or being overturned

o'ver·view' (-vyōō') *n.* a general survey

o·ver·ween·ing (ō'vər wē'niŋ) *adj.* [< OE. *oferwenan:* see OVER- & WEEN] **1.** arrogant; conceited **2.** excessive

o'ver·weigh' *vt.* **1.** to outweigh **2.** to oppress

o'ver·weight' *n.* extra or surplus weight —*adj.* (ō'vər wāt') above the normal or allowed weight

o·ver·whelm (ō'vər hwelm', -welm') *vt.* [see OVER- & WHELM] **1.** to pour down on and bury beneath **2.** to crush; overpower —**o'ver·whelm'ing** *adj.*

o'ver·work' *vt.* to work or use to excess —*vi.* to work too hard or too long —*n.* work that is severe or burdensome

o'ver·wrought' (-rôt') *adj.* **1.** very nervous or excited **2.** too elaborate; ornate

ovi- [< L. *ovum*, an egg] *a combining form meaning* egg or ovum

Ov·id (äv'id) 43 B.C.–17? A.D.; Roman poet

o·vi·duct (ō'vi dukt') *n.* [see OVI- & DUCT] a duct or tube through which the ovum passes from an ovary to the uterus or to the outside

o·vip·a·rous (ō vip'ər əs) *adj.* [< L. *ovum*, egg + *parere*, produce] producing eggs which hatch after leaving the body —**o·vip'a·rous·ly** *adv.*

o·vi·pos·i·tor (ō'vi päz'i tər) *n.* [< OVI- + L. *positor*, one who places] an organ of many female insects, usually at the end of the abdomen, for depositing eggs

o·void (ō'void) *adj.* [OV(I)- + -OID] egg-shaped: also **o·void'al** —*n.* anything of ovoid form

o·vu·late (ō'vyə lāt', äv'yə-) *vi.* -lat'ed, -lat'ing [ult. < L. *ovum*, egg] to produce and discharge ova from the ovary —**o'vu·la'tion** *n.*

o·vule (ō'vyōōl, äv'yōōl) *n.* [Fr. < L. *ovum*, egg] **1.** *Bot.* the part of a plant which develops into a seed **2.** *Zool.* the immature ovum —**o'vu·lar** *adj.*

o·vum (ō'vəm) *n., pl.* **o·va** (ō'və) [L., an egg] *Biol.* a mature female germ cell

owe (ō) *vt.* **owed, ow'ing** [< OE. *agan*, to own] **1.** to be indebted to (someone) for (a specified amount or thing) **2.** to feel the need to do, give, etc. —*vi.* to be in debt

ow·ing (ō'iŋ) *adj.* **1.** that owes **2.** due; unpaid —**owing to** because of; as a result of

owl (oul) *n.* [OE. *ule*] **1.** a night bird of prey, having a large head, large eyes, and a short, hooked beak **2.** a person of nocturnal habits, solemn appearance, etc. —**owl'ish** *adj.* —**owl'ish·ly** *adv.*

own (ōn) *adj.* [< OE. *agan*, to possess] belonging or relating to oneself or others /his *own* fault/, that which belongs to oneself /the car is her *own*/ —*vt.* **1.** to possess; have **2.** to admit; acknowledge —*vi.* to confess (*to*) —**come into one's own** to receive what properly belongs to one, esp. recognition —**on one's own** [Colloq.] by one's own efforts —**own up (to)** to confess (to) —**own'er** *n.* —**own'er·less** *adj.* —**own'er·ship'** *n.*

ox (äks) *n., pl.* **ox'en** [OE. *oxa*] **1.** any of several bovine mammals, as the buffalo, bison, yak, etc. **2.** a castrated bull, used as a draft animal —**ox'like'** *adj.*

ox·al·ic acid (äk sal'ik) [< Gr. *oxys*, acid] a colorless, poisonous, crystalline acid, found in many plants and used in dyeing, bleaching, etc.

ox·blood (äks'blud') *n.* a deep-red color

ox'bow' (-bō') *n.* **1.** the U-shaped part of an ox yoke which passes under and around the animal's neck **2.** a crescent-shaped bend in a river

ox·eye daisy (äks'ī') *same as* DAISY

Ox·ford (äks'fərd) city in SC England: site of Oxford University: pop. 110,000

ox·ford (äks'fərd) *n.* [< OXFORD] [*sometimes* O-] **1.** a low shoe laced over the instep: also **oxford shoe 2.** a cotton or rayon fabric with a basketlike weave, used for shirts, etc.: also **oxford cloth**

OXBOWS

Oxford gray a very dark gray, nearly black

ox·i·da·tion (äk'sə dā'shən) *n.* an oxidizing or being oxidized —**ox'i·dant** (-dənt) *n.*

ox·ide (äk'sīd) *n.* [< Gr. *oxys*, sour + Fr. *acide*, acid] a binary compound of oxygen with another element or a radical

ox·i·dize (äk'sə dīz') *vt.* -dized', -diz'ing **1.** to unite with oxygen, as in burning or rusting **2.** to increase the positive valence or decrease the negative valence of (an element or ion) —*vi.* to become oxidized —**ox'i·diz'er** *n.*

Ox·o·ni·an (äk sō'nē ən) *adj.* of Oxford (England) or Oxford University —*n.* a student or alumnus of Oxford University

ox·tail (äks'tāl') *n.* the tail of an ox or steer, esp. when skinned and used in soup

oxy- [< Gr. *oxys*, sharp] *a combining form meaning:* **1.** sharp, acid **2.** oxygen

ox·y·a·cet·y·lene (äk'sē ə set''l ēn') *adj.* of or using a mixture of oxygen and acetylene, as for producing a hot flame used in welding

ox·y·gen (äk'si jən) *n.* [< Fr.: see OXY- & -GEN] a colorless, odorless, gaseous chemical element, the most abundant of all elements: it is essential to life processes and to combustion: symbol, O; at. wt., 15.9994; at. no., 8

ox·y·gen·ate (äk'si jə nāt') *vt.* -at'ed, -at'ing to mix or combine with oxygen: also **ox'y·gen·ize' -ized', -iz'ing** —**ox'y·gen·a'tion** *n.* —**ox'y·gen·a'tor** *n.*

oxygen tent a transparent enclosure supplied with oxygen, fitted around a bed patient to help him breathe

ox·y·mo·ron (äk'si môr'än) *n., pl.* -mo'ra (-ə) [< Gr. *oxys*, sharp + *moros*, dull] a figure of speech in which contradictory terms are combined (Ex.: sweet sorrow)

o·yez, o·yes (ō'yez', -yes', -yā') *interj.* [< L. *audire*, hear] hear ye! attention!: used to command silence before a proclamation is made

oys·ter (oi'stər) *n.* [< Gr. *ostreon*] **1.** an edible marine mollusk with an irregular, bivalve shell **2.** any of several similar bivalve mollusks

oyster cracker a small, round, salted soda cracker

oz. *pl.* **oz., ozs.** ounce

O·zark Mountains (ō'zärk) highland region in NW Ark., SW Mo., & NE Okla.: also **Ozarks**

o·zone (ō'zōn) *n.* [Fr. < Gr. *ozein*, to smell] **1.** a pale-blue gas with a strong odor: it is an allotropic form of oxygen, formed by an electrical discharge in air and used as a bleaching agent, water purifier, etc. **2.** [Slang] pure, fresh air —**o·zon'ic** (-zän'ik) *adj.*

P

P, p (pē) *n., pl.* **P's, p's** the sixteenth letter of the English alphabet —**mind one's p's and q's** to be careful what one does

P 1. *Chess* pawn **2.** *Chem.* phosphorus **3.** police

p [Brit.] penny; pennies

p. 1. *pl.* **pp.** page **2.** participle **3.** past **4.** per **5.** pint

pa (pä; *dial. often* pô) *n.* [Colloq.] father; papa

Pa *Chem.* protactinium

Pa., PA Pennsylvania

P.A. public address (system)

Pab·lum (pab'ləm) [< PABULUM] *a trademark for* a soft, bland cereal food for infants —*n.* [p-] any oversimplified or tasteless writing, etc.

pab·u·lum (pab'yōō ləm) *n.* [L.] **1.** food **2.** nourishment for the mind **3.** *same as* PABLUM

pac (pak) *n.* [< AmInd. *pacu*, moccasin] a high, insulated, waterproof, laced boot

pace (pās) *n.* [< L. *passus*, a step] **1.** a step in walking, running, etc. **2.** the length of a step or stride **3.** the rate of speed in walking, etc. **4.** rate of progress, development,

fat, āpe, cär; ten, ēven; is, bīte; gō, hôrn, tōōl, look; oil, out; up, fur; thin, *then*; zh, leisure; ŋ, ring; ə for *a* in *ago*; ' as in able (ā'b'l); ë, Fr. coeur; ö, Fr. feu; Fr. mon; ü, Fr. duc; ȓ, Fr. cri; kh, G. doch, ich. ‡ foreign; < derived from etc. **5.** a gait **6.** the gait of a horse in which both legs on the same side are raised together —*vt.* **paced, pac′ing 1.** to walk back and forth across **2.** to measure by paces **3.** to set the pace for (a runner, etc.) **4.** to go before and lead —*vi.* **1.** to walk with regular steps **2.** to move at a pace: said of a horse —**change of pace** variation in tempo or in speed of delivery —**put through one's paces** to test one's abilities, etc. —**pac′er** *n.*

pace·mak·er (pās′māˊkər) *n.* **1.** a runner, horse, etc. that sets the pace, as in a race: also **pace′setˊter 2.** *Med.* an electronic device implanted in the body to regulate the heartbeat —**pace′makˊing** *n.*

pach·y·derm (pak′ə dʉrm′) *n.* [< Gr. *pachys,* thick + *derma,* skin] a large, thick-skinned, hoofed animal, as the elephant, rhinoceros, etc.

Pa·cif·ic (pə sif′ik) largest of the earth's oceans, between Asia and the American continents —*adj.* of, in, on, or near this ocean

pa·cif·ic (pə sif′ik) *adj.* [see PACIFY] **1.** making or tending to make peace **2.** peaceful; calm; tranquil —**pa·cif′i·cal·ly** *adv.*

pa·cif′i·cate′ (-ə kāt′) *vt.* **-cat′ed, -cat′ing** *same as* PACIFY —**pac·i·fi·ca·tion** (pas′ə fi kā′shən) *n.*

pac·i·fi·er (pas′ə fī′ər) *n.* **1.** a person or thing that pacifies **2.** a nipple or teething ring for babies

pac′i·fism (-fiz′m) *n.* opposition to the use of force under any circumstances; specif., refusal to participate in war —**pac′i·fist** *n., adj.* —**pac′i·fis′tic** *adj.*

pac·i·fy (pas′ə fī′) *vt.* **-fied′, -fy′ing** [< Fr. < L. *pax,* peace + *facere,* make] **1.** to make peaceful or calm; appease **2.** to secure peace in (a nation, etc.) **3.** to seek to win over (people in an occupied area)

pack[1] (pak) *n.* [ult. < MFl. *pac*] **1.** a bundle of things tied up for carrying **2.** a package of a standard number, as cigarettes, playing cards, etc. **3.** a group of wild animals living together **4.** *same as* ICE PACK **5.** *a)* treatment by wrapping a patient in wet or dry, hot or cold sheets *b)* the sheets so used **6.** a cosmetic paste applied to the skin and left to dry **7.** a method of packing or canning —*vt.* **1.** to make a pack of **2.** *a)* to put together in a box, trunk, etc. *b)* to fill (a box, etc.) **3.** to put (food) in (cans, etc.) for preservation **4.** to crowd; cram [to pack the hall] **5.** to fill in tightly, as for prevention of leaks **6.** to carry in a pack **7.** to send (*off*) **8.** [Slang] *a)* to carry (a gun, etc.) *b)* to deliver (a blow) with force —*vi.* **1.** to make up packs **2.** to put one's clothes, etc. into luggage for a trip **3.** to crowd together **4.** to admit of being folded compactly **5.** to settle into a compact mass —*adj.* **1.** used in packing **2.** formed into packs **3.** used for carrying packs, etc. [a pack animal] —**send packing** to dismiss (a person) abruptly

pack[2] (pak) *vt.* to choose (a jury, court, etc.) dishonestly so as to get desired results

pack·age (pak′ij) *n.* **1.** a wrapped or boxed thing; parcel **2.** a box, etc. in which things are packed **3.** a number of items, plans, etc. offered as a unit —*vt.* **-aged, -ag·ing** to put into a package

package store a store where alcoholic liquor is sold by the bottle to be drunk elsewhere

pack′er *n.* one who packs, as in a packing house

pack·et (pak′it) *n.* **1.** a small package **2.** a boat that travels a regular route carrying passengers, freight, and mail: in full **packet boat**

pack′ing *n.* **1.** the act or process of a person or thing that packs **2.** any material used to pack

packing house a plant where meats, fruits, etc. are processed and packed for future sale

pack′sad′dle *n.* a saddle with fastenings to secure the load carried by a pack animal

pack train a procession of pack animals

pact (pakt) *n.* [< L. *pax,* peace] an agreement

pad′[1] (pad) *n.* [echoic, but infl. by Du. *pad,* path] the dull thud of a footstep —*vi.* **pad′ded, pad′ding** to walk, esp. with a soft step

pad[2] (pad) *n.* [prob. var. of POD] **1.** anything soft used to protect from friction, blows, etc.; cushion **2.** folded gauze, etc. used as for dressing on a wound **3.** the cushionlike sole of an animal's paw **4.** the floating leaf of a waterlily **5.** a tablet of paper for writing on **6.** a cushion soaked with ink for inking a rubber stamp **7.** *same as* LAUNCH PAD **8.** [Slang] a bed, or the room or apartment where one lives —*vt.* **pad′ded, pad′ding 1.** to stuff or cover with soft material **2.** to lengthen (a speech, etc.) with unnecessary material **3.** to fill (an expense account, etc.) with fraudulent entries

pad′ding *n.* any material used to pad

pad·dle[1] (pad′'l) *n.* [< ?] **1.** a short oar with a wide blade, used without an oarlock **2.** any similar implement used in flogging, etc. **3.** any of the boards on a paddle wheel —*vt., vi.* **-dled, -dling 1.** to propel (a canoe, etc.) with a paddle **2.** to beat with a paddle; spank —**pad′dler** *n.*

pad·dle[2] (pad′'l) *vi.* **-dled, -dling** [prob. < PAD[1]] to move hands or feet in shallow water; dabble

pad′dle·fish′ *n., pl.:* see FISH a large fish of the Mississippi and Yangtze, with a paddle-shaped snout

paddle wheel a wheel with paddles around it for propelling a steamboat

pad·dock (pad′ək) *n.* [< OE. *pearruc,* enclosure] **1.** a small enclosure near a stable, where horses are exercised **2.** an enclosure near a race track, where horses are assembled before a race

pad·dy (pad′ē) *n., pl.* **-dies** [Malay *padi*] **1.** rice in the husk **2.** rice **3.** a rice field: often **rice paddy**

pad·lock (pad′läk′) *n.* [< ME.] a removable lock with a hinged link to be passed through a staple, chain, or eye —*vt.* to fasten as with a padlock

pa·dre (pä′drā, -drē) *n.* [Sp., It., Port. < L. *pater,* father] **1.** father: the title of a priest in Italy, Spain, Portugal, etc. **2.** [Slang] a chaplain

pae·an (pē′ən) *n.* [< Gr. *Paian,* epithet of Apollo] a song of joy, triumph, praise, etc.

pa·gan (pā′gən) *n.* [< L. *paganus,* a peasant] **1.** anyone not a Christian, Muslim, or Jew; heathen **2.** one who has no religion —*adj.* **1.** of pagans **2.** not religious —**pa′gan·ism** *n.*

page[1] (pāj) *n.* [Fr. < L. *pangere,* to fasten] **1.** *a)* one side of a leaf of a book, newspaper, etc. *b)* the entire leaf **2.** [often *pl.*] a record of events —*vt.* **paged, pag′ing** to number the pages of —*vi.* to turn pages in scanning (*through* a book, etc.)

page[2] (pāj) *n.* [< It. *paggio*] **1.** formerly, a boy training for knighthood **2.** a boy or girl who runs errands, carries messages, etc., as in a hotel, legislature, etc. —*vt.* **paged, pag′ing** to try to find (a person) by calling his name, as a hotel page does

pag·eant (paj′ənt) *n.* [< Anglo-L. *pagina,* stage < L., PAGE[1]] **1.** a spectacular exhibition, parade, etc., as a procession with floats **2.** an outdoor drama celebrating historical events

pag′eant·ry *n., pl.* **-ries 1.** grand spectacle; gorgeous display **2.** empty show or display

pag·i·na·tion (paj′ə nā′shən) *n.* **1.** the numbering of pages **2.** the figures used for numbering pages in sequence

pa·go·da (pə gō′də) *n.* [< Port., prob. < Per. *but,* idol + *kadah,* house] in the Orient, a several-storied temple: a tapering tower with rooflike projections

Pa·go Pa·go (päŋ′ō päŋ′ō, pä′gō pä′gō) main seaport of American Samoa: pop. 2,500

PAGODA

paid (pād) *pt. & pp. of* PAY

pail (pāl) *n.* [ult. < VL. *pagella,* a measure of volume] **1.** a cylindrical container, usually with a handle, for holding liquids, etc.; bucket **2.** the amount held by a pail: also **pail′ful′** *pl.* **-fuls′**

pain (pān) *n.* [< Gr. *poinē,* penalty] **1.** physical or mental suffering caused by injury, disease, tribulation, etc. **2.** [*pl.*] great care [take *pains* with the work] **3.** [Slang] an annoyance —*vt.* to cause pain to —*vi.* to have pain —**on** (or **upon** or **under**) **pain of** with the threat of (penalty) —**pain′less** *adj.* —**pain′less·ly** *adv.*

Paine (pān), **Thomas** 1737–1809; Am. Revolutionary patriot & writer, born in England

pained *adj.* **1.** hurt or distressed **2.** showing hurt feelings or resentment

pain′ful *adj.* **1.** causing or having pain; hurting **2.** irksome —**pain′ful·ly** *adv.* —**pain′ful·ness** *n.*

pains·tak·ing (pānz′tāk′iŋ) *adj.* requiring or showing great care or diligence —**pains′tak′ing·ly** *adv.*

paint (pānt) *vt.* [< L. *pingere*] **1.** *a)* to make (a picture) in colors applied to a surface *b)* to depict with paints **2.** to describe vividly **3.** to cover or decorate with paint **4.** to apply like paint —*vi.* to paint pictures —*n.* **1.** a mixture of pigment with oil, water, etc. used as a covering or coloring **2.** coloring matter used as a cosmetic **3.** [Dial.] a piebald horse —**paint out** to cover up as with a coat of paint

paint′brush′ *n.* a brush used for applying paint

paint′er[1] *n.* **1.** an artist who paints pictures **2.** one whose work is covering surfaces, as walls, with paint

paint′er[2] *n.* [< OFr., ult. < L. *pendere,* to hang] a rope attached to the bow of a boat

paint′ing *n.* **1.** the work or art of one who paints **2.** a picture made with paints

pair (per) *n., pl.* **pairs;** sometimes, after a number, **pair** [< L. *par*, equal] **1.** two corresponding things associated or used together [a *pair* of shoes] **2.** a single thing with two joined corresponding parts [a *pair* of pants] **3.** any two persons or animals regarded as a unit —*vt., vi.* **1.** to form a pair or pairs (of); match **2.** to mate

pais·ley (pāz'lē) *adj.* [< *Paisley*, Scotland, where orig. made] [*also* P-] designating an elaborate, colorful pattern of intricate, curved figures, or cloth made with such a pattern —*n.* [*also* P-] a paisley cloth, shawl, necktie, etc.

pa·ja·mas (pə jam'əz, -jä'məz) *n.pl.* [< Per. *pāi*, leg + *jāma*, garment] a loosely fitting sleeping or lounging suit consisting of jacket and trousers —**pa·ja'ma** *adj.*

Pa·ki·stan (pä'ki stän', pak'i stan') country in S Asia, on the Arabian Sea: 310,403 sq. mi.; pop. 42,900,000; cap. Islamabad —**Pa'ki·stan'i** (-stä'nē) *adj., n.*

pal (pal) *n.* [Eng. Romany < Sans. *bhrātr*, brother] [Colloq.] a close friend; comrade —*vi.* **palled, pal'ling** [Colloq.] to associate as pals

pal·ace (pal'is) *n.* [< L. *Palatium*, the hill in Rome where Augustus lived] **1.** the official residence of a king, etc. **2.** any large, magnificent building

pal·an·quin, pal·an·keen (pal'ən kēn') *n.* [< Port. < Sans.] formerly in eastern Asia, a covered litter for one person, carried by poles on men's shoulders

pal·at·a·ble (pal'it ə b'l) *adj.* **1.** pleasant to the taste; savory **2.** acceptable to the mind —**pal'at·a·bil'i·ty** *n.*

pal·a·tal (pal'it 'l) *adj.* **1.** of the palate **2.** pronounced with the tongue raised against or near the hard palate, as *y* in *yes* —*n.* a palatal sound

pal·ate (pal'it) *n.* [L. *palatum*] **1.** the roof of the mouth, consisting of a bony front part (*hard palate*) and a fleshy back part (*soft palate*) **2.** taste

pa·la·tial (pə lā'shəl) *adj.* [see PALACE] **1.** of, suitable for, or like a palace **2.** large and ornate; magnificent —**pa·la'tial·ly** *adv.*

pa·lat·i·nate (pə lat''n āt', -it) *n.* the territory ruled by a palatine

pal·a·tine (pal'ə tīn', -tin) *adj.* [see PALACE] having royal privileges —*n.* a medieval vassal lord having royal privileges in his own territory

pa·lav·er (pə lav'ər) *n.* [Port. *palavra*, a speech] **1.** talk; esp., idle talk **2.** flattery —*vi.* to talk glibly

pale¹ (pāl) *adj.* [< L. *pallere*, to be pale] **1.** of a whitish or colorless complexion **2.** lacking intensity, as color, light, etc. **3.** feeble —*vi., vt.* **paled, pal'ing** to become or make pale —**pale'ly** *adv.* —**pale'ness** *n.* —**pal'ish** *adj.*

pale² (pāl) *n.* [< L. *palus*, a stake] **1.** a pointed stake used in fences; picket **2.** a boundary; enclosure: now chiefly figurative

pale'face' *n.* a white person: a term allegedly first used by N. American Indians

pa·le·og·ra·phy (pā'lē äg'rə fē) *n.* **1.** ancient forms of writing **2.** the study of ancient writings

pa·le·o·lith·ic (pā'lē ə lith'ik, pal'ē-) *adj.* [< Gr. *palaios*, ancient + *lithos*, stone + -IC] designating or of the middle part of the Stone Age, when man used stone tools

pa'le·on·tol'o·gy (-än täl'ə jē) *n.* [< Gr. *palaios*, ancient + *on*, a being + -LOGY] the branch of geology that deals with prehistoric life through the study of fossils —**pa'le·on·tol'o·gist** *n.*

Pa'le·o·zo'ic (-ə zō'ik) *adj.* [< Gr. *palaios*, ancient + ZO(O)- + -IC] designating or of the geologic era (c.600–230 million years ago) when fish, amphibians, reptiles and land plants appeared —**the Paleozoic** the Paleozoic Era

Pa·ler·mo (pə lur'mō) seaport on the N coast of Sicily: pop. 659,000

Pal·es·tine (pal'əs tīn') **1.** ancient land of the Hebrews on the E coast of the Mediterranean **2.** part of this region now divided into Arab and Jewish states: see ISRAEL —**Pal'es·tin'i·an** (-tin'ē ən) *adj., n.*

pal·ette (pal'it) *n.* [Fr. < L. *pala*, a shovel] **1.** a thin board with a hole for the thumb at one end, on which an artist mixes his paints **2.** the colors used, as by a particular artist

pal·frey (pôl'frē) *n., pl.* **-freys** [ult. < Gr. *para*, beside + L. *veredus*, horse for hire] [Archaic] a saddle horse, esp. one for a woman

pal·ing (pāl'iŋ) *n.* **1.** a fence made of pales **2.** a pale, or pales collectively

pal·i·sade (pal'ə sād') *n.* [< Fr. < L. *palus*, a stake] **1.** any of a row of large pointed stakes set in the ground to form a fence as for fortification **2.** such a fence **3.** [*pl.*] a line of steep cliffs

---

pall¹ (pôl) *vi.* **palled, pall'ing** [ME. *pallen*] **1.** to become cloying, insipid, etc. **2.** to become satiated or bored

pall² (pôl) *n.* [< L. *pallium*, a cover] **1.** a piece of velvet, etc. used to cover a coffin, hearse, or tomb **2.** a dark or gloomy covering

pal·la·di·um (pə lā'dē əm) *n.* [ult. < Gr. *Pallas*, the goddess Athena] a rare, silvery-white, metallic chemical element: it is used as a catalyst or in jewelry: symbol, Pd; at. wt., 106.4; at. no., 46

Pal·las (pal'əs) *Gr. Myth.* Athena, goddess of wisdom: also **Pallas Athena**

pall·bear·er (pôl'ber'ər) *n.* [PALL² + BEARER] one of the persons who bear the coffin at a funeral

pal·let¹ (pal'it) *n.* [see PALETTE] **1.** a wooden tool with a flat blade and a handle, used for smoothing pottery **2.** *same as* PALETTE **3.** a low, portable platform for storing goods in warehouses, etc. **4.** any pawl in a clock which engages the ratchet wheel to regulate the speed

pal·let² (pal'it) *n.* [< L. *palea*, chaff] a small, inferior bed or a mattress filled as with straw and used on the floor

pal·li·ate (pal'ē āt') *vt.* **-at'ed, -at'ing** [< L. *pallium*, a cloak] **1.** to lessen the severity of without curing; alleviate **2.** to make appear less serious or offensive; excuse —**pal'li·a'tive** *adj., n.*

pal·lid (pal'id) *adj.* [< L. *pallidus*, PALE¹] faint in color; pale —**pal'lid·ly** *adv.* —**pal'lid·ness** *n.*

Pall Mall (pel' mel', pal' mal', pôl' môl') a London street, noted for its clubs

pal·lor (pal'ər) *n.* [L. < *pallere*, be pale] unnatural paleness, as of the face

palm¹ (päm; *occas.* pälm) *n.* [< L. *palma*: from its handlike fronds] **1.** any of several tropical or subtropical trees with a tall, branchless trunk and a bunch of large leaves at the top **2.** a leaf of this tree carried as a symbol of victory **3.** victory —**palm'y** *adj.*

palm² (päm; *occas.* pälm) *n.* [< L. *palma*] **1.** the inner surface of the hand between the fingers and wrist **2.** a unit of measure equal to either the width of the hand (3–4 inches) or its length (7–9 inches) **3.** a broad, flat part at the end of an armlike part —*vt.* to hide (something) in the palm, as in a sleight-of-hand trick —**palm off** to pass off by fraud or deceit —**pal·mar** (pal'mər, pä'-) *adj.*

pal·mate (päl'māt, pä'-) *adj.* [see PALM²] shaped like a hand with the fingers spread

pal·met·to (pal met'ō) *n., pl.* **-tos, -toes** a small palm tree with fan-shaped leaves

palm·is·try (päm'is trē, päl'mis-) *n.* [< ME., prob. < *paume*, PALM² + *maistrie*, mastery] the pretended art of telling a person's fortune by the lines, etc. on the palm of the hand —**palm'ist** *n.*

Palm Sunday the Sunday before Easter, commemorating Jesus' triumphal entry into Jerusalem

pal·my·ra (pal mī'rə) *n.* [< Port. < L. *palma*, PALM¹] a palm tree of India, Sri Lanka, and Africa, with leaves used for thatching and durable wood

pal·o·mi·no (pal'ə mē'nō) *n., pl.* **-nos** [AmSp. < Sp., dove-colored, ult. < L. *palumbes*, pigeon] a cream, golden, or light-chestnut horse with white mane and tail

pal·pa·ble (pal'pə b'l) *adj.* [< L. *palpare*, to touch] **1.** that can be touched, felt, etc. **2.** easily perceived by the senses; perceptible **3.** obvious; plain —**pal'pa·bil'i·ty** *n.* —**pal'pa·bly** *adv.*

pal·pi·tate (pal'pə tāt') *vi.* **-tat'ed, -tat'ing** [< L. *palpare*, to feel] **1.** to beat rapidly or flutter, as the heart **2.** to throb; quiver —**pal'pi·ta'tion** *n.*

pal·sy (pôl'zē) *n., pl.* **-sies** [see PARALYSIS] paralysis of any voluntary muscle, sometimes accompanied by uncontrollable tremors —*vt.* **-sied, -sy·ing** to afflict with or as with palsy

pal·ter (pôl'tər) *vi.* [< dial. *palt*, rag] **1.** to talk or act insincerely **2.** to trifle **3.** to quibble

pal·try (pôl'trē) *adj.* **-tri·er, -tri·est** [prob. < LowG. *palte*, rag] trifling; petty —**pal'tri·ness** *n.*

pam·pas (pam'pəz) *n.pl.* [AmSp. < SAmInd. *pampa*, plain] the extensive treeless plains of Argentina —*adj.* (-pəs) of the pampas —**pam·pe·an** (pam'pē ən, pam pē'-) *adj., n.*

pam·per (pam'pər) *vt.* [< LowG.] to be overindulgent with; coddle —**pam'per·er** *n.*

pam·phlet (pam'flit) *n.* [< OFr. *Pamphilet*, popular name of a ML. poem] a small, unbound booklet, often on some topic of current interest

pam'phlet·eer' (-flə tir') *n.* a writer of pamphlets, esp. those dealing with political or social issues

---

Pan (pan) *Gr. Myth.* a god of fields, forests, flocks, and shepherds, represented with the legs of a goat

pan¹ (pan) *n.* [OE. *panne*] **1.** any broad, shallow container used in cooking, etc. **2.** a pan-shaped part or object **3.** *same as* HARDPAN **4.** the part holding the powder in a flintlock **5.** [Slang] a face —*vt., vi.* **panned, pan′ning 1.** [Colloq.] to criticize unfavorably **2.** *Mining* to wash (gravel) in a pan in order to separate (gold, etc.) — **pan out** [Colloq.] to turn out; esp., to turn out well

pan² (pan) *vt., vi.* **panned, pan′ning** [< PAN(ORAMA)] to move (a motion-picture or television camera) so as to get a panoramic effect or follow a moving object —*n.* the act of panning

pan- [< Gr. *pan,* all] *a combining form meaning:* **1.** all [*pantheism*] **2.** [P-] of, comprising, or uniting every [*Pan-American*]

pan·a·ce·a (pan′ə sē′ə) *n.* [< Gr. *pan,* all + *akeisthai,* to cure] a supposed remedy or cure for all ills; cure-all —**pan′a·ce′an** *adj.*

pa·nache (pə nash′) *n.* [Fr., ult. < LL. *pinnaculum,* plume] carefree self-confidence or style

Pan·a·ma (pan′ə mä′, -mô′) **1.** a Central American country: 29,201 sq. mi.; pop. 1,425,000 **2.** its capital: pop. 412,000: also **Panama City 3. Isthmus of,** strip of land connecting South America & Central America —**Pan′a·ma′ni·an** (-mä′nē ən) *adj., n.*

Panama Canal ship canal across Panama, connecting the Caribbean Sea & the Pacific Ocean: 50.7 mi.

Panama (hat) a fine, hand-plaited hat made from leaves of a Central and South American plant

Pan′-A·mer′i·can *adj.* of North, Central, and South America, collectively

pan·a·tel·a, pan·a·tel·la (pan′ə tel′ə) *n.* [AmSp.] a long, slender cigar

Pa·nay (pə nī′) island of the C Philippines

pan·cake (pan′kāk′) *n.* a thin, flat cake of batter fried on a griddle or in a pan

pan·chro·mat·ic (pan′krō mat′ik) *adj.* sensitive to light of all colors [*panchromatic* film]

pan·cre·as (pan′krē əs, paŋ′-) *n.* [< Gr. *pan,* all + *kreas,* flesh] a large gland that secretes a digestive juice into the small intestine: the pancreas of animals, used as food, is called *sweetbread* —**pan′cre·at′ic** (-at′ik) *adj.*

pan·da (pan′də) *n.* [Fr. < native name] **1.** a reddish, raccoonlike mammal of the Himalayas **2.** a black-and-white, bearlike mammal of China and Tibet: also **giant panda**

pan·dem·ic (pan dem′ik) *adj.* [< Gr. *pan,* all + *dēmos,* people] epidemic over a large region

Pan·de·mo·ni·um (pan′də mō′nē əm) [< Gr. *pan-* + *daimōn,* demon] the capital of Hell in Milton's *Paradise Lost* —*n.* [p-] wild disorder or noise, or a place where this exists

pan·der (pan′dər) *n.* [< L. *Pandarus,* lovers' go-between in a medieval story] **1.** a procurer; pimp **2.** one who helps others to satisfy their vices, etc. Also **pan′der·er** —*vi.* to act as pander (*to*)

Pan·do·ra (pan dôr′ə) [< Gr. *pan,* all + *dōron,* a gift] *Gr. Myth.* the first mortal woman: she opened a box letting all human ills into the world

pan·dow·dy (pan dou′dē) *n., pl.* **-dies** [prob. < obs. E. dial. *pandoulde,* custard] deep-dish apple pie, having a top crust only

pane (pān) *n.* [< L. *pannus,* piece of cloth] **1.** a sheet of glass in a window, door, frame, etc. **2.** any of the single divisions of a window, etc.

pan·e·gyr·ic (pan′ə jir′ik) *n.* [< Gr. *panēgyris,* public meeting] **1.** a formal speech or writing praising a person or event **2.** high praise —**pan′e·gyr′i·cal** *adj.*

pan·el (pan′'l) *n.* [see PANE] **1.** *a)* a section or division, usually rectangular, set off on a wall, door, etc. *b)* a board for instruments or controls **2.** a strip inserted in a skirt, etc. **3.** a list of persons summoned for jury duty **4.** a group of persons selected for judging, discussing, etc. —*vt.* **-eled** or **-elled, -el·ing** or **-el·ling** to provide with panels

panel discussion a discussion carried on by a selected group of speakers before an audience

pan′el·ing, pan′el·ling *n.* panels collectively

pan′el·ist *n.* a member of a panel (*n.* 4)

pan′-fry′ *vt.* **-fried′, -fry′ing** to fry in a shallow skillet or frying pan

pang (paŋ) *n.* [< ?] a sudden, sharp, brief pain, physical or emotional

pan·go·lin (paŋ gō′lin) *n.* [Malay *pengulin,* roller] a scaly mammal of Asia and Africa, able to roll into a ball when attacked

pan′han′dle¹ *n.* [*often* P-] a strip of land like the handle of a pan, as the northern extension of Texas

pan′han′dle² *vt., vi.* **-dled, -dling** [Colloq.] to beg (from), esp. on the streets —**pan′han′dler** *n.*

pan·ic (pan′ik) *n.* [< Fr. < Gr. *panikos,* of Pan, as inspirer of sudden fear] **1.** a sudden, unreasoning fear, often spreading quickly **2.** a widespread fear of financial collapse —*adj.* like, showing, or resulting from panic —*vt.* **-icked, -ick·ing 1.** to affect with panic **2.** [Slang] to delight as with comedy —*vi.* to give way to panic —**pan′ick·y** *adj.*

pan·i·cle (pan′i k'l) *n.* [< L. *panus,* a swelling] a loose, irregularly branched flower cluster

pan′ic-strick′en *adj.* stricken with panic; badly frightened: also **panic-struck**

pan·nier, pan·ier (pan′yər, -ē ər) *n.* [< L. *panis,* bread] a large basket for carrying loads on the back, or one of a pair of baskets hung across the back of a horse, mule, etc.

pa·no·cha (pə nō′chə) *n.* [AmSp., ult. < L. *panis,* bread] **1.** a coarse Mexican sugar **2.** *var. of* PENUCHE

pan·o·ply (pan′ə plē) *n., pl.* **-plies** [< Gr. *pan,* all + *hopla,* arms] **1.** a complete suit of armor **2.** any magnificent array —**pan′o·plied** *adj.*

pan·o·ra·ma (pan′ə ram′ə) *n.* [< PAN- + Gr. *horama,* a view] **1.** a picture unrolled in such a way as to give an impression of a continuous view **2.** an open view in all directions **3.** a constantly changing scene —**pan′o·ram′ic** *adj.*

pan·pipe (pan′pīp′) *n.* [*also* P-] a primitive musical instrument made of a row of tubes of graduated lengths, played by blowing across the open ends: also **panpipes, Pan's pipes**

pan·sy (pan′zē) *n., pl.* **-sies** [Fr. *pensée,* a thought] a small, flowering plant with flat, broad, velvety petals in many colors

pant (pant) *vi.* [ult. < L. *phantasia,* nightmare] **1.** to breathe rapidly and heavily, as from running fast **2.** to throb, as the heart **3.** to yearn eagerly (with *for* or *after*) —*vt.* to gasp out —*n.* any of a series of rapid, heavy breaths; gasp

PANPIPE

pan·ta·lets, pan·ta·lettes (pan′t'l ets′) *n.pl.* [dim. of *pantaloon*] long drawers showing below the skirt, worn by women in the 19th cent.

pan·ta·loons (pan′t'l ōōnz′) *n.pl.* [It., ult. after St. *Pantalone*] trousers

pant·dress (pant′dres′) *n.* a woman's garment with the lower part like pants instead of a skirt

pan·the·ism (pan′thē iz′m) *n.* **1.** the belief that God is not a personality but the sum of all beings, things, forces, etc. in the universe **2.** the worship of all gods —**pan′the·ist** *n.* —**pan′the·is′tic** *adj.*

pan·the·on (pan′thē än′) *n.* [< Gr. *pan,* all + *theos,* a god] **1.** a temple for all the gods; esp., [P-] a temple built in Rome in 27 B.C. **2.** [*often* P-] a building in which the famous dead of a nation are entombed

pan·ther (pan′thər) *n.* [< Gr. *panthēr*] **1.** a leopard; esp., a black leopard **2.** a cougar **3.** a jaguar

pant·ies (pan′tēz) *n.pl.* women's or children's short underpants: also **pan′tie** (-tē)

pan·to·graph (pan′tə graf′) *n.* [Fr. < Gr. *pan,* all + -GRAPH] a mechanical device for reproducing a drawing on the same or a different scale

pan·to·mime (pan′tə mīm′) *n.* [< Gr.: see PAN- & MIME] **1.** a drama without words, using actions and gestures only **2.** actions and gestures without words —*vt., vi.* **-mimed′, -mim′ing** to express or act in pantomime —**pan′to·mim′ic** (-mim′ik) *adj.* —**pan′to·mim′ist** (-mī′mist, -mim′ist) *n.*

pan·try (pan′trē) *n., pl.* **-tries** [< L. *panis,* bread] a small room off the kitchen where cooking ingredients and utensils, china, etc. are kept

pants (pants) *n.pl.* [< PANTALOONS] **1.** trousers **2.** drawers or panties As an adjective or in compounds, usually **pant** [*pant* legs, *pantdress*]

pant·suit (pant′sōōt′) *n.* a woman's outfit of a matched jacket and pants: also **pants suit**

pan·ty (pan′tē) *n., pl.* **-ties** *same as* PANTIES

panty hose a woman's undergarment combining panties with hose: also **pan′ty·hose′** (-hōz′) *n.*

pan′ty·waist′ (-wāst′) *n.* [Slang] a sissy

pan·zer (pan′zər; *G.* pän′tsər) *adj.* [G., armor] armored [a *panzer* division]

pap (pap) *n.* [orig. < baby talk] **1.** any soft food for babies or invalids **2.** any oversimplified writing, etc.

pa·pa (pä′pə; *now less freq.* pə pä′) *n.* father: a child's word

pa·pa·cy (pä′pə sē) *n., pl.* **-cies** [< ML. *papa*, pope] **1.** the position or authority of the Pope **2.** the period during which a pope rules **3.** the succession of popes **4.** [P-] the government of the Roman Catholic Church, headed by the Pope

pa·pal (pä′pəl) *adj.* **1.** of the Pope or the papacy **2.** of the Roman Catholic Church

pa·paw (pô′pô, pə pô′) *n.* [prob. < PAPAYA] **1.** a tree of central and southern U.S. bearing a yellowish, edible fruit with many seeds **2.** its fruit

pa·pa·ya (pə pä′yə) *n.* [Sp. < Carib name] **1.** a tropical American tree bearing a large, yellowish-orange fruit like a melon **2.** its fruit

pa·per (pä′pər) *n.* [see PAPYRUS] **1.** a thin, flexible material in sheets, made from rags, wood pulp, etc. and used to write or print on, wrap, etc. **2.** a single sheet of this **3.** an official document **4.** an essay, dissertation, etc. **5.** a written examination, report, etc. **6.** checks, promissory notes, paper money, etc. **7.** a newspaper **8.** wallpaper **9.** [*pl.*] credentials —*adj.* **1.** of, or made of, paper **2.** like paper; thin **3.** existing only in written form; theoretical [*paper* profits] —*vt.* to cover with paper, esp. wallpaper —**on paper 1.** in written or printed form **2.** in theory —**pa′per·like′, pa′per·y** *adj.*

pa′per·back′ *n.* a book bound in paper —**pa′per·backed′, pa′per·bound′** *adj.*

pa′per·boy′ *n.* a boy who sells or delivers newspapers

pa′per·hang′er *n.* a person whose work is covering walls with wallpaper —**pa′per·hang′ing** *n.*

paper money noninterest-bearing notes issued by a government or its banks, circulated as legal tender

pa′per·weight′ *n.* any small, heavy object set on papers to keep them from being scattered

paper work the keeping of records, filing of reports, etc. incidental to some work or task

pa·pier-mâ·ché (pä′pər mə shā′) *n.* [Fr. < *papier*, paper + *mâcher*, to chew] a material made of paper pulp mixed with size, glue, etc. and molded into various objects when moist

pa·pil·la (pə pil′ə) *n., pl.* **-lae** (-ē) [L. < *papula*, pimple] a small bulge of flesh, as at the root of a hair, a developing tooth, etc., or on the surface of the tongue —**pap·il·lar·y** (pap′ə ler′ē) *adj.*

pa·poose (pa pōōs′) *n.* [< AmInd.] a North American Indian baby

pap·py (pap′ē) *n., pl.* **-pies** [Dial. or Colloq.] father

pa·pri·ka (pa prē′kə, pap′ri-) *n.* [Hung. < Gr. *peperi*, pepper] a mild red condiment ground from the fruit of certain peppers

Pap test (pap) [< G. *Papanicolaou*, 20th-c. U.S. anatomist] the examination of a smear (**Pap smear**) taken from a woman's cervix: a test for uterine cancer

Pap·u·a (pap′yoo wə, pä′poo wə) *same as* NEW GUINEA —**Pap′u·an** (-wən) *adj., n.*

Papua New Guinea country occupying the E half of the island of New Guinea & nearby islands: c.180,000 sq. mi.; pop. 2,563,000; cap. Port Moresby

pap·ule (pap′yōōl) *n.* [L. *papula*] a pimple —**pap′u·lar** (-yoo lər) *adj.* —**pap′u·lose′** (-yoo lōs′) *adj.*

pa·py·rus (pə pī′rəs) *n., pl.* **-ri** (-rī), **-rus·es** [< Gr. *papyros*] **1.** a tall water plant of Egypt **2.** a writing material made from the pith of this plant by the ancients

par (pär) *n.* [L., an equal] **1.** the established value of a currency in foreign-exchange rates **2.** an equal status, footing, level, etc.: usually in **on a par** (**with**) **3.** the average state, condition, etc. [work that is above *par*] **4.** the face value of stocks, bonds, etc. **5.** *Golf* the number of strokes established as a skillful score for a hole or course —*adj.* **1.** of or at par **2.** average; normal

par. 1. paragraph **2.** parallel **3.** parenthesis

para- [< Gr. *para*, at the side of] *a prefix meaning:* **1.** beside, beyond [*parapsychology*] **2.** helping in a secondary way, accessory [*paramedical*]

par·a·ble (par′ə b'l) *n.* [< Gr. *para-*, beside + *ballein*, to throw] a short, simple story teaching a moral lesson

pa·rab·o·la (pə rab′ə lə) *n.* [see prec.] *Math.* a plane curve formed by the intersection of a cone with a plane parallel to its side

par·a·bol·ic (par′ə bäl′ik) *adj.* **1.** of, like, or expressed by a parable **2.** of or like a parabola

Par·a·cel·sus (par′ə sel′səs) 1493–1541; Swiss physician & alchemist

par·a·chute (par′ə shōōt′) *n.* [Fr. < *para-*, protecting + *chute*, a fall] a large cloth contrivance, umbrella-shaped when unfolded, used to retard the speed of one dropping from an airplane, etc. —*vt., vi.* **-chut′ed, -chut′ing** to drop by parachute —**par′a·chut′ist** *n.*

pa·rade (pə rād′) *n.* [Fr. < Sp. < L. *parare*, to prepare] **1.** ostentatious display **2.** *a*) a review of troops *b*) a place where troops assemble for review **3.** any organized procession or march, as for display **4.** a public walk or promenade —*vt.* **-rad′ed, -rad′ing 1.** to march or walk through (the streets, etc.), as for display **2.** to show off [he *parades* his knowledge] —*vi.* **1.** to march in a parade **2.** to walk about ostentatiously **3.** to assemble in military formation for review —**pa·rad′er** *n.*

par·a·digm (par′ə dim, -dīm′) *n.* [< Fr. < Gr. *para*, beside + *deigma*, example] **1.** a pattern, example, or model **2.** *Gram.* an example of a declension or conjugation, giving all the inflectional forms of a word

par·a·dise (par′ə dīs′) *n.* [< Gr. *paradeisos*, a garden] **1.** [P-] the garden of Eden **2.** *same as* HEAVEN (sense 2 *a*) **3.** any place or state of perfection, happiness, etc.

par·a·dox (par′ə däks′) *n.* [< Gr. *para-*, beyond + *doxa*, opinion] **1.** a statement that seems contradictory, absurd, etc. but may be true in fact **2.** a statement that contradicts itself and is false —**par′a·dox′i·cal** *adj.* —**par′a·dox′i·cal·ly** *adv.*

par·af·fin (par′ə fin) *n.* [G. < L. *parum*, too little + *affinis*, akin: from its inertness] **1.** a white, waxy substance distilled from petroleum and used for making candles, sealing jars, etc. **2.** *Chem.* any hydrocarbon of the methane series —*vt.* to coat or impregnate with paraffin

par·a·gon (par′ə gän′, -gən) *n.* [< It. *paragone*, touchstone] a model of perfection or excellence

par·a·graph (par′ə graf′) *n.* [< Gr. *para-*, beside + *graphein*, write] **1.** a distinct section of a writing, begun on a new line and often indented **2.** a mark (¶) used to indicate a new paragraph **3.** a brief item in a newspaper or magazine —*vt.* to arrange in paragraphs

Par·a·guay (par′ə gwā′, -gwī′) inland country in SC S. America: 157,042 sq. mi.; pop. 2,303,000; cap. Asunción —**Par′a·guay′an** *adj., n.*

par·a·keet (par′ə kēt′) *n.* [see PARROT] a small, slender parrot with a long, tapering tail

par·al·lax (par′ə laks′) *n.* [< Fr. < Gr. *para-*, beyond + *allassein*, to change] the apparent change in the position of an object, as a heavenly body, resulting from a change in the viewer's position

par·al·lel (par′ə lel′) *adj.* [< Fr. < Gr. *para-*, side by side + *allēlos*, one another] **1.** extending in the same direction and at a constant distance apart, so as never to meet **2.** similar or corresponding, as in purpose, time, etc. —*adv.* in a parallel manner —*n.* **1.** a parallel line, surface, etc. **2.** any person or thing similar to another; counterpart **3.** a being parallel **4.** any comparison showing likeness **5.** *a*) any of the imaginary lines parallel to the equator and representing degrees of latitude *b*) such a line drawn on a map or globe: in full **parallel of latitude** —*vt.* **-leled′** or **-lelled′, -lel′ing** or **-lel′ling 1.** to make parallel **2.** to be parallel with [the road *parallels* the river] **3.** to compare **4.** to match; equal

parallel bars two parallel, horizontal bars set on adjustable upright posts: used in gymnastics

par′al·lel′ism (-iz'm) *n.* **1.** the state of being parallel **2.** close resemblance; similarity

par′al·lel′o·gram (-ə gram′) *n.* a four-sided plane figure having the opposite sides parallel and equal

pa·ral·y·sis (pə ral′ə sis) *n., pl.* **-ses′** (-sēz′) [< Gr. *para-*, beside + *lyein*, to loose] **1.** partial or complete loss of the power of motion or sensation, esp. voluntary motion, in some or all of the body **2.** a condition of helpless inactivity —**par·a·lyt·ic** (par′ə lit′ik) *adj., n.*

PARALLELOGRAM

par·a·lyze (par′ə līz′) *vt.* **-lyzed′, -lyz′ing 1.** to cause paralysis in **2.** to make ineffective or powerless

par·a·me·ci·um (par′ə mē′shē əm, -sē əm) *n., pl.* **-ci·a** (-ə) [< Gr. *paramēkēs*, oval] a one-celled, elongated protozoan that moves by means of cilia

par·a·med·i·cal (par′ə med′i k'l) *adj.* [< Gr. *para-*, beside + MEDICAL] of auxiliary medical personnel, as midwives, aidmen, nurses' aides, etc.

---

fat, āpe, cär; ten, ēven; is, bīte; gō, hôrn, tōol, look; oil, out; up, fur; thin, *th*en; zh, leisure; ŋ, ring; ə for *a* in *ago*; ′ as in *able* (ā′b'l); ë, Fr. coeur; ö, Fr. feu; Fr. mo*n*; ü, Fr. duc; *r*, Fr. cri; kh, G. doch, ich. ‡ foreign; < derived from.

pa·ram·e·ter (pə ram′ə tər) *n.* [< Gr. *para-*, beside + *metron*, a measure] a constant with variable values

par·a·mil·i·tar·y (par′ə mil′ə ter′ē) *adj.* [PARA- + MILITARY] of forces working along with, or in place of, a regular military organization, often as a semiofficial or secret auxiliary

par·a·mount (par′ə mount′) *adj.* [< OFr. *par*, by + *amont*, uphill] ranking higher than any other; chief

par·a·mour (par′ə moor′) *n.* [< OFr. *par amour*, with love] **1.** a lover; esp., the illicit sexual partner of a married person **2.** [Archaic] a sweetheart

Pa·ra·ná (pä′rä nä′) river flowing from S Brazil through NE Argentina: c.2,000 mi.

par·a·noi·a (par′ə noi′ə) *n.* [< Gr. *para-*, beside + *nous*, the mind] a mental disorder characterized by delusions, as of grandeur or, esp., persecution —**par′a·noid′**, **par′a·noi′ac** (-ak) *adj., n.*

par·a·pet (par′ə pit, -pet′) *n.* [Fr. < It. *parare*, to guard + *petto*, breast] **1.** a wall or bank for screening troops from enemy fire **2.** a low wall or railing, as on a balcony or bridge

par·a·pher·na·li·a (par′ə fər nāl′yə, -fə nā′lē ə) *n.pl.* [often with sing. v.] [< Gr. *para-*, beyond + *phernē*, a dowry] **1.** personal belongings **2.** equipment

par·a·phrase (par′ə frāz′) *n.* [Fr. < Gr. *para-*, beyond + *phrazein*, tell] a rewording of the meaning of something spoken or written —*vt., vi.* **-phrased′, -phras′ing** to express in a paraphrase —**par′a·phras′tic** (-fras′tik) *adj.*

par·a·ple·gi·a (par′ə plē′jē ə, -jə) *n.* [< Gr. *para-*, beside + *plēgē*, a stroke] paralysis of the entire lower half of the body —**par′a·ple′gic** (-plē′jik, -plej′ik) *adj., n.*

par′a·psy·chol′o·gy (-sī käl′ə jē) *n.* [PARA- + PSYCHOLOGY] the study of such psychic phenomena as telepathy, ESP, etc.

Pa·rá rubber (pä rä′) [< river in Brazil] crude rubber obtained from several S. American trees

par·a·site (par′ə sīt′) *n.* [< Gr. *para-*, beside + *sitos*, food] **1.** one who lives at others' expense without making any useful return **2.** a plant or animal that lives on or within another from which it derives sustenance —**par′a·sit′ic** (-sit′ik), **par′a·sit′i·cal** *adj.* —**par′a·sit′i·cal·ly** *adv.* —**par′a·sit′ism** (-sīt′iz′m) *n.*

par·a·sol (par′ə sôl′) *n.* [Fr. < It. *parare*, ward off + *sole*, the sun] a light umbrella used as a sunshade

par·a·sym·pa·thet·ic (par′ə sim′pə thet′ik) *adj.* [PARA- + SYMPATHETIC] designating or of that part of the autonomic nervous system whose functions include the slowing of the heartbeat and stimulation of certain digestive glands

par·a·thi·on (par′ə thī′än) *n.* [< Gr. *para-*, alongside + *theion*, sulfur] a poisonous insecticide

par·a·thy·roid (par′ə thī′roid) *adj.* [PARA- + THYROID] designating or of any of four small glands on the thyroid gland whose hormonal secretions help control the body's calcium-phosphorus balance —*n.* a parathyroid gland

par·a·troops (par′ə troops′) *n.pl.* [< PARA(CHUTE) + TROOP] troops trained and equipped to parachute into a combat area —**par′a·troop′er** *n.*

‡par a·vion (pär ä vyôn′) [Fr.] by air mail

par·boil (pär′boil′) *vt.* [< L. *per*, through + *bullire*, to boil: infl. by *part*] to boil until partly cooked, as before roasting

par·cel (pär′s′l) *n.* [see PARTICLE] **1.** a small, wrapped bundle; package **2.** a quantity of items put up for sale **3.** a group; pack [a *parcel* of fools] **4.** a piece, as of land —*vt.* **-celed** or **-celled, -cel·ing** or **-cel·ling** to separate into parts and distribute (with *out*)

parcel post a postal service for carrying and delivering parcels (fourth-class mail)

parch (pärch) *vt.* [< ?] **1.** to expose (corn, etc.) to great heat, so as to dry or roast **2.** to make hot and dry **3.** to make very thirsty —*vi.* to become very hot, dry, thirsty, etc.

Par·chee·si (pär chē′zē) *a trademark for* a game in which moves of pieces around a board are determined by throwing dice —*n.* [p-] this game: also sp. **par·che′si, par·chi′si**

parch·ment (pärch′mənt) *n.* [ult. < L. (*charta*) *Pergamena*, (paper) of *Pergamum*, city in Asia Minor] **1.** the skin of a sheep, goat, etc. prepared as a surface for writing or painting **2.** paper treated to resemble this **3.** a manuscript, etc. on parchment

pard·ner (pärd′nər) *n.* [altered < PARTNER] [Chiefly Dial.] a partner: often clipped to **pard**

par·don (pär′d′n) *vt.* [< L. *per-*, through + *donare*, give] **1.** to release (a person) from punishment **2.** to cancel penalty for (an offense); forgive **3.** to excuse (a person) for (a minor fault, discourtesy, etc.) —*n.* **1.** forgiveness **2.**

an official document granting a pardon —**par′don·a·ble** *adj.* —**par′don·a·bly** *adv.* —**par′don·er** *n.*

pare (per) *vt.* **pared, par′ing** [< L. *parare*, prepare] **1.** to cut or trim away (the rind, skin, etc.) of; peel **2.** to reduce gradually —**par′er** *n.*

par·e·gor·ic (par′ə gôr′ik) *n.* [< Gr. *parēgoros*, consoling] a camphorated tincture of opium, used to relieve diarrhea

pa·ren·chy·ma (pə ren′ki mə) *n.* [< Gr. *para-*, beside + *en-*, in + *cheein*, pour] **1.** *Anat.* the functional tissue of an organ, as distinguished from its connective tissue, etc. **2.** *Bot.* a soft tissue of cells in plant leaves and stems, fruit pulp, etc.

par·ent (per′ənt) *n.* [< L. *parere*, beget] **1.** a father or mother **2.** any organism in relation to its offspring **3.** a source; origin —**pa·ren·tal** (pə ren′t′l) *adj.* —**pa·ren′tal·ly** *adv.* —**par′ent·hood′** *n.*

par′ent·age (-ij) *n.* **1.** descent from parents or ancestors; lineage **2.** the state of being a parent

pa·ren·the·sis (pə ren′thə sis) *n., pl.* **-ses′** (-sēz′) [< Gr. *para-*, beside + *entithenai*, insert] **1.** a word, clause, etc. added as an explanation or comment within a complete sentence, usually set off by curved lines, commas, etc. **2.** either or both of the curved lines ( ) so used —**par·en·thet·i·cal** (par′ən thet′i k′l), **par′en·thet′ic** *adj.*

pa·ren′the·size (-sīz′) *vt.* **-sized′, -siz′ing** to insert in parentheses or as a parenthesis

par·ent·ing (per′ənt in) *n.* the work or skill of a parent in raising a child or children

pa·re·sis (pə rē′sis) *n., pl.* **-ses** (-sēz) [Gr. < *parienai*, relax] **1.** partial paralysis **2.** a syphilitic brain disease marked by paralytic attacks, etc.: in full **general paresis**

par ex·cel·lence (pär ek′sə läns′) [Fr.] in the greatest degree of excellence; beyond comparison

par·fait (pär fä′) *n.* [Fr., perfect] a frozen dessert of cream, eggs, syrup, etc. or ice cream, crushed fruit, etc. in a tall, slender glass

par·he·li·on (pär hē′lē ən, -hēl′yən) *n., pl.* **-li·a** (-ə, -yə) [< Gr. *para-*, beside + *hēlios*, the sun] a bright, colored spot of light on a solar halo

pa·ri·ah (pə rī′ə) *n.* [< Tamil *paraiyan*] **1.** a member of one of the lowest social castes in India **2.** any outcast

pa·ri·e·tal (pə rī′ə t′l) *adj.* [< Fr. < L. *paries*, a wall] *Anat.* of the walls of a cavity; esp., designating either of two bones forming part of the top and sides of the skull

par·i·mu·tu·el (par′ə myōō′choo wəl) *n.* [Fr., lit., a mutual bet] a system of betting on races in which the winning bettors share the net of each pool in proportion to their wagers

par·ing (per′in) *n.* a thin piece or strip pared off

Par·is¹ (par′is) *Gr. Legend* a son of Priam: he kidnapped Helen, thus causing the Trojan War

Par·is² (par′is; *Fr.* pá·rē′) capital of France: pop. 2,591,000 (urbanized area, 8,197,000) —**Pa·ri·sian** (pə rizh′ən, -rē′zhən) *adj., n.*

Paris green a poisonous, bright-green chemical powder used chiefly as an insecticide

par·ish (par′ish) *n.* [< LGr. *paroikia*, diocese] **1.** a part of a diocese under the charge of a priest or minister **2.** the congregation of a church **3.** a civil division in Louisiana, like a county

pa·rish·ion·er (pə rish′ə nər) *n.* a member of a parish

par·i·ty (par′ə tē) *n., pl.* **-ties** [< Fr. < L. *par*, equal] **1.** equality in power, value, etc. **2.** resemblance; similarity **3.** equivalence in value of a currency in terms of another country's currency **4.** equality of value at a given ratio between different kinds of money, etc.

park (pärk) *n.* [< ML. *parricus*] **1.** wooded land held as part of a private estate or as a hunting preserve **2.** an area of public land, with playgrounds, etc., for recreation **3.** *same as* PARKING LOT **4.** *Mil.* an area for storing and servicing vehicles, supplies, etc. —*vt., vi.* **1.** to leave (a vehicle) in a certain place temporarily **2.** to maneuver (a vehicle) into a space for parking **3.** [Colloq.] to put or settle in a certain place

par·ka (pär′kə) *n.* [Aleutian < Russ., fur coat] a hip-length hooded jacket

parking lot an area for parking motor vehicles

parking meter a coin-operated timing device at a parking space to show the length of time that a parked vehicle may occupy that space

Par·kin·son's disease (pär′kin sənz) [< J. *Parkinson* (1755–1824), Eng. physician] a degenerative disease of later life, characterized by a rhythmic tremor and muscular rigidity

park′way′ *n.* a broad roadway edged or divided with plantings of trees, bushes, etc.

Parl. 1. Parliament **2.** Parliamentary

parl·ance (pär′ləns) *n.* [< OFr. *parler*, speak] a style of speaking or writing; idiom [military *parlance*]

par·lay (pär′lā, -lē; *for v., also* pär lā′) *vt., vi.* [< Fr. < It. *paro*, a pair] **1.** to bet (an original wager plus its winnings) on another race, etc. **2.** to exploit (an asset) successfully —*n.* a parlayed bet

par·ley (pär′lē) *vi.* [< Fr. *parler*, speak] to confer, esp. with an enemy —*n., pl.* **-leys** a conference, as to settle a dispute or discuss terms

par·lia·ment (pär′lə mənt) *n.* [< OFr. *parler*, speak] **1.** an official government council **2.** [P-] the national legislative body of certain countries, esp. Great Britain

par′lia·men·tar′i·an (-men ter′ē ən) *n.* a person skilled in parliamentary rules or debate

par′lia·men′ta·ry (-men′tər ē) *adj.* **1.** of or by a parliament **2.** conforming to the rules of a parliament or other public assembly **3.** governed by a parliament

par·lor (pär′lər) *n.* [< OFr. *parler*, speak] **1.** a living room **2.** a small, semiprivate room in a hotel, etc., used as for conferences **3.** a business establishment, esp. one with specialized services [a beauty *parlor*] *Brit.* sp. **parlour**

Par·ma (pär′mə) city in NE Ohio: suburb of Cleveland: pop. 100,000

Par·me·san (cheese) (pär′mə zän′) [Fr. < It. < *Parma*, city in Italy] a hard, dry Italian cheese, usually grated for sprinkling on spaghetti, etc.

Par·nas·sus (pär nas′əs) mountain in C Greece: 8,061 ft.: sacred to Apollo and the Muses in ancient times

Par·nell (pär′n'l, pär nel′), **Charles Stewart** 1846–91; Ir. nationalist leader

pa·ro·chi·al (pə rō′kē əl) *adj.* [see PARISH] **1.** of or in a parish **2.** narrow; provincial —**pa·ro′chi·al·ism** *n.*

parochial school a school supported and controlled by a church

par·o·dy (par′ə dē) *n., pl.* **-dies** [< Fr. < Gr. *para-*, beside + *ōidē*, song] **1.** a nonsensical imitation of a literary or musical work or style **2.** a weak imitation —*vt.* **-died, -dy·ing** to make a parody of —**par′o·dist** *n.*

pa·role (pə rōl′) *n.* [Fr. < LL. *parabola*, speech] **1.** the release of a prisoner before his sentence has expired, on condition of future good behavior **2.** the freedom thus granted, or its duration —*vt.* **-roled′, -rol′ing** to release on parole —**on parole** at liberty under conditions of parole

pa·rol·ee (pə rō′lē′) *n.* a person on parole from prison

pa·rot·id (pə rät′id) *adj.* [< Gr. *para-*, beside + *ous*, ear] designating or of either of the salivary glands below and in front of each ear —*n.* a parotid gland

-parous [< L. *parere*, to bear] *a combining form meaning* producing, bearing [*viviparous*]

par·ox·ysm (par′ək siz′m) *n.* [< Fr. < Gr. *para-*, beyond + *oxynein*, sharpen] **1.** a sudden attack of a disease **2.** a sudden outburst, as of laughter —**par′ox·ys′mal** (-siz′m'l) *adj.*

par·quet (pär kā′) *n.* [Fr. < MFr. *parc*, a park] **1.** the main floor of a theater: usually called *orchestra* **2.** a flooring of parquetry —*vt.* **-queted′** (-kād′), **-quet′ing** (-kā′iŋ) to make (a floor) of parquetry

parquet circle the part of a theater beneath the balcony and behind the parquet

par·quet·ry (pär′kə trē) *n.* [< Fr.] inlaid woodwork in geometric forms: used esp. in flooring

par·ra·keet (par′ə kēt′) *n. alt. sp. of* PARAKEET

par·ri·cide (par′ə sīd′) *n.* [Fr. < L. *paricida*, kin + *caedere*, kill] **1.** one who murders his parent or another near relative **2.** the act of a parricide —**par′ri·ci′dal** *adj.*

par·rot (par′ət) *n.* [Fr. dial. *perrot*] **1.** a bird with a hooked bill and brightly colored feathers: some parrots can learn to imitate human speech **2.** a person who mechanically repeats the words of others —*vt.* to repeat or imitate without understanding

parrot fever *same as* PSITTACOSIS

parrot fish any of various related, brightly colored, tropical ocean fishes with parrotlike jaws

par·ry (par′ē) *vt.* **-ried, -ry·ing** [< L. *parare*, prepare] **1.** to ward off (a blow, etc.) **2.** to evade (a question, etc.) —*vi.* to make a parry —*n., pl.* **-ries** **1.** a warding off **2.** an evasive reply

parse (pärs) *vt., vi.* **parsed, pars′ing** [< L. *pars* (*orationis*), part (of speech)] [Now Rare] to separate (a sentence) into its parts, explaining the grammatical form, function, etc. of each part

Par·see, Par·si (pär′sē, pär sē′) *n.* [Per., a Persian] a member of a Zoroastrian religious sect in India descended from Persian refugees

par·si·mo·ny (pär′sə mō′nē) *n.* [< L. *parcere*, to spare] a tendency to be very careful in spending; stinginess —**par′si·mo′ni·ous** *adj.*

pars·ley (pärs′lē) *n.* [< Gr. *petros*, a rock + *selinon*, celery] a plant with aromatic, often curled leaves used to flavor or garnish some foods

pars·nip (pär′snip) *n.* [< L. *pastinare*, dig up] **1.** a plant with a long, thick, sweet, white root used as a vegetable **2.** its root

par·son (pär′s'n) *n.* [see PERSON] **1.** a clergyman in charge of a parish **2.** any clergyman

par′son·age (-ij) *n.* the dwelling provided by a church for the use of its parson

part (pärt) *n.* [< L. *pars*] **1.** a portion, segment, etc. of a whole [*part* of a book] **2.** an essential, separable element [an automobile *part*] **3.** a share assigned or given; specif., *a*) duty [to do one's *part*] *b*) [*usually pl.*] talent; ability [a man of *parts*] *c*) a role in a play *d*) any voice or instrument in a musical ensemble, or the score for it **4.** a region; esp., [*usually pl.*] a district **5.** one of the sides in a conflict, etc. **6.** the dividing line formed in combing the hair —*vt.* **1.** to break or divide into parts **2.** to comb (the hair) so as to leave a part **3.** to break or hold apart —*vi.* **1.** to break or divide into parts **2.** to separate and go different ways **3.** to cease associating **4.** to go away (*from*) —*adj.* partial —*adv.* partly —**for one's part** as far as one is concerned —**for the most part** mostly —**in part** partly —**part with** to give up; relinquish —**take part** to participate —**take someone's part** to side with someone

part. **1.** participial **2.** participle

par·take (pär tāk′) *vi.* **-took′, -tak′en, -tak′ing** [< *part taker*] **1.** to participate (*in* an activity) **2.** to eat or drink, esp. with others (usually with *of*) **3.** to have some of the qualities (*of*) —**par·tak′er** *n.*

part·ed (pär′tid) *adj.* separated; divided

par·terre (pär ter′) *n.* [Fr. < *par*, on + *terre*, earth] **1.** an ornamental garden area **2.** *same as* PARQUET CIRCLE

par·the·no·gen·e·sis (pär′thə nō jen′ə sis) *n.* [< Gr. *parthenos*, virgin + *genesis*, origin] reproduction by the development of an unfertilized ovum, seed, or spore, as in certain insects, algae, etc.

Par·the·non (pär′thə nän′) [< Gr. *parthenos*, a virgin (i.e., Athena)] the Doric temple of Athena on the Acropolis in Athens

par·tial (pär′shəl) *adj.* [< L. *pars*, a part] **1.** favoring one person, faction, etc. more than another; biased **2.** not complete —**partial to** fond of —**par′ti·al′i·ty** (-shē al′ə tē) *n.* —**par′tial·ly** *adv.*

par·tic·i·pant (pär tis′ə pənt) *adj.* participating —*n.* a person who participates

par·tic′i·pate′ (-pāt′) *vi.* **-pat′ed, -pat′ing** [< L. *pars*, a part + *capere*, to take] to have or take a share with others (*in* an activity, etc.) —**par·tic′i·pa′tion** *n.* —**par·tic′i·pa′tor** *n.* —**par·tic′i·pa·to′ry** (-pə tôr′ē) *adj.*

par·ti·ci·ple (pär′tə sip′'l) *n.* [see prec.] a verbal form having the qualities of both verb and adjective —**par′ti·cip′i·al** (-sip′ē əl) *adj.*

par·ti·cle (pär′ti k'l) *n.* [< L. *pars*, part] **1.** a tiny fragment or trace **2.** a short, uninflected part of speech, as an article, preposition, etc. **3.** *Physics* a piece of matter so small as to be considered without magnitude

par·ti·col·ored (pär′tē kul′ərd) *adj.* [< Fr. *parti*, divided + COLORED] **1.** having different colors in different parts **2.** diversified

par·tic·u·lar (pər tik′yə lər) *adj.* [see PARTICLE] **1.** of or belonging to a single group, person, or thing **2.** regarded separately; specific **3.** unusual **4.** hard to please; exacting —*n.* a distinct fact, item, detail, etc. —**in particular** especially —**par·tic′u·lar′i·ty** (-lar′ə tē) *n., pl.* **-ties**

par·tic′u·lar·ize′ (-lə rīz′) *vt., vi.* **-ized′, -iz′ing** to give particulars or details (of); specify

par·tic′u·lar·ly *adv.* **1.** in detail **2.** especially **3.** specifically

par·tic·u·late (-lit, -lāt′) *adj.* of or formed of small, separate particles

part′ing *adj.* **1.** dividing; separating **2.** departing **3.** given, spoken, etc. at parting —*n.* **1.** a breaking or separating **2.** a leave-taking or departure

par·ti·san (pärt′ə z'n) *n.* [< L. *pars*, part] **1.** a strong supporter of a side, party, etc. **2.** a guerrilla fighter —*adj.* of or like a partisan Also sp. **par′ti·zan** —**par′ti·san·ship′** *n.*

par·tite (pär′tīt) *adj.* [< L. *partire*, to part] in parts: often in compounds [*tripartite*]

par·ti·tion (pär tish'ən) *n.* [< L. *partitio*] **1**. division into parts **2**. something that divides, as a wall separating rooms **3**. a part or section —*vt.* **1**. to divide into parts **2**. to divide by a partition

part'ly *adv.* in part; not fully

part·ner (pärt'nər) *n.* [< ME.] one who takes part in an activity with another or others; specif., *a*) one of two or more persons heading the same business *b*) a spouse *c*) either of two persons dancing together *d*) a player on the same side or team

part'ner·ship' *n.* **1**. the state of being a partner **2**. the relationship of partners; joint interest **3**. *a*) an association of partners in a business *b*) the contract for this

part of speech any of the traditional classes to which the words of a language are assigned according to form, function, meaning, etc.: in English, noun, verb, adjective, adverb, pronoun, preposition, conjunction, and interjection

par·took (pär took') *pt. of* PARTAKE

par·tridge (pär'trij) *n.* [< Gr. *perdix*] any of several game birds, as the grouse, pheasant, etc.

part song a song for several voices singing in harmony, usually without accompaniment: also **part'-song'** *n.*

PARTRIDGE

part'·time' *adj.* of or engaged in work, study, etc. for periods of less time than in a full schedule

part time as a part-time employee, student, etc.

par·tu·ri·ent (pär tyoor'ē ənt, -toor'-) *adj.* [< L. *parturire*, to be in labor] **1**. giving birth or about to give birth to young **2**. of childbirth

par·tu·ri·tion (pär'choo rish'ən) *n.* [see prec.] a giving birth; childbirth

part'way' *adv.* to a degree but not fully

par·ty (pär'tē) *n., pl.* **-ties** [< L. *pars*, part] **1**. a group working to promote a political platform or slate, a cause, etc. **2**. a group acting together to accomplish something *[a surveying party]* **3**. a gathering for social entertainment, or the entertainment itself **4**. one concerned in an action, plan, lawsuit, etc. *[a party to the action]* **5**. [Colloq.] a person —*vi.* **-tied, -ty·ing** to attend social parties —*vt.* to give a party for

party line 1. a single circuit connecting two or more telephone users with the exchange **2**. the policies of a political party —**par'ty·lin'er** *n.*

par·ve·nu (pär'və noo', -nyoo') *n.* [Fr. < L. *parvenire*, arrive] a newly rich person who is considered an upstart

pas (pä) *n., pl.* **pas** (päz; *Fr.* pä) [Fr. < L. *passus*, a step] a step or series of steps in dancing

Pas·a·de·na (pas'ə dē'nə) city in SW Calif.: pop. 113,000

pas·chal (pas'k'l) *adj.* [< Heb. *pesah*, Passover] **1**. of Passover **2**. of Easter

pa·sha (pə shä', pä'shə, pash'ə) *n.* [Turk. *pasha*] formerly, in Turkey, **1**. a title of honor placed after the name **2**. a high official

pass (pas) *vi.* [< L. *passus*, a step] **1**. to go or move forward, through, etc. **2**. to extend; lead **3**. to go or be conveyed from one place, condition, possession, etc. to another **4**. *a*) to cease *b*) to depart **5**. to die (usually with *away, on,* or *out*) **6**. to go by **7**. to elapse *[an hour passed]* **8**. to make a way (*through* or *by*) **9**. to be accepted without question **10**. to be approved, as by a legislative body **11**. to go through a test, course, etc. successfully **12**. to give a sentence, judgment, etc. **13**. to take place; happen **14**. *Card Games* to decline a chance to bid, play, etc. —*vt.* **1**. to go by, beyond, over, or through; specif., *a*) to leave behind *b*) to go through (a test, course, etc.) successfully **2**. to cause or allow to go, move, proceed, etc.; specif., *a*) to ratify; enact *b*) to spend (time) *c*) to excrete *d*) *Baseball* to walk (a batter) **3**. to make move from place to place or person to person; specif., *a*) to hand to another *b*) to put into circulation *c*) to throw or hit (a ball, etc.) from one player to another **4**. to give (an opinion or judgment) —*n.* **1**. an act of passing; passage **2**. a condition or situation *[a strange pass]* **3**. *a*) a ticket, etc. giving one free entry or exit *b*) *Mil.* a brief leave of absence **4**. a motion of the hands **5**. a tentative attempt **6**. a narrow passage, etc., esp. between mountains **7**. [Slang] an overfamiliar attempt to embrace or kiss **8**. *Sports a*) a transfer of a ball, etc. to another player during play *b*) a walk in baseball —**come** (or **bring**) **to pass** to (cause to) happen —**pass for** to be accepted as —**pass off** to be or cause to be accepted as genuine, real, etc. through deceit —**pass out 1**. to distribute **2**. to faint —**pass over** to disregard; ignore —**pass up** [Colloq.] to refuse or let go by —**pass'er** *n.*

pass'a·ble *adj.* **1**. that can be passed, traveled over, etc. **2**. adequate; fair —**pass'a·bly** *adv.*

pas·sage (pas'ij) *n.* **1**. a passing; specif., *a*) migration *b*) transition *c*) the enactment of a law **2**. permission or right to pass **3**. a voyage **4**. passenger accommodations on a ship **5**. a way or means of passing; road, passageway, etc. **6**. an interchange, as of blows **7**. a portion of a book, composition, etc.

pas'sage·way' *n.* a narrow way for passage, as a hall, corridor, or alley

pass'book' *n. same as* BANKBOOK

pas·sé (pa sä') *adj.* [Fr., past] **1**. out-of-date; old-fashioned **2**. rather old

passed ball *Baseball* a pitch that gets by the catcher and allows a base runner to advance

pas·sel (pas''l) *n.* [< PARCEL] [Colloq. or Dial.] a group, esp. a fairly large one

pas·sen·ger (pas'n jər) *n.* [< OFr. *passage*, passage] a person traveling in a vehicle

pass'er-by' *n., pl.* **pass'ers-by'** one who passes by

pass'ing *adj.* **1**. going by, beyond, etc. **2**. fleeting **3**. casual *[a passing remark]* **4**. satisfying requirements *[a passing grade]* —*n.* the act of one that passes; specif., death —**in passing** incidentally

pas·sion (pash'ən) *n.* [< L. *pati*, suffer] **1**. [P-] the suffering of Jesus during the Crucifixion or after the Last Supper **2**. any emotion, as hate, love, etc. **3**. extreme emotion, as rage, enthusiasm, lust, etc. **4**. the object of strong desire or fondness —**pas'sion·less** *adj.*

pas'sion·ate (-it) *adj.* **1**. having or showing strong emotions **2**. hot-tempered **3**. intense; ardent **4**. readily aroused sexually —**pas'sion·ate·ly** *adv.*

pas'sion·flow'er *n.* a plant with variously colored flowers and yellow, egglike fruit

pas·sive (pas'iv) *adj.* [see PASSION] **1**. not active, but acted upon **2**. not resisting; submissive **3**. inactive **4**. *Gram.* denoting the voice of a verb whose subject receives the action —*n.* the passive voice —**pas'sive·ly** *adv.* —**pas'sive·ness, pas·siv'i·ty** *n.*

passive resistance opposition to a government, by refusal to comply or by nonviolent acts, as fasting

pass'key' *n.* **1**. *same as:* **a**) MASTER KEY **b**) SKELETON KEY **2**. any private key

Pass·o·ver (pas'ō'vər) *n.* a Jewish holiday commemorating the ancient Hebrews' deliverance from slavery in Egypt: Ex. 12

pass'port' *n.* a government document issued to a citizen traveling abroad, certifying identity and citizenship

pass'word' *n.* **1**. a secret term used for identification, as in passing a guard **2**. any means of admission

past (past) *rare pp. of* PASS —*adj.* **1**. gone by; ended **2**. of a former time **3**. just gone by *[the past week]* **4**. having served formerly *[a past chairman]* **5**. *Gram.* indicating a time gone by *[the past tense]* —*n.* **1**. time gone by **2**. the history of a person, group, etc.: often used to indicate a hidden or questionable background **3**. *Gram.* the past tense —*prep.* **1**. beyond in time, space, amount, etc. **2**. beyond the extent, power, etc. of *[past belief]* —*adv.* to and beyond

pas·ta (päs'tə) *n.* [It.] **1**. dough made as of semolina and dried in the form of spaghetti, macaroni, etc. **2**. spaghetti, macaroni, etc. cooked in some way

paste (pāst) *n.* [< Gr. *pastē*, barley porridge] **1**. dough for making rich pastry **2**. any soft, moist, smooth preparation *[toothpaste, almond paste]* **3**. a mixture of flour or starch, water, etc. used as an adhesive **4**. a hard, brilliant glass used for artificial gems —*vt.* **past'ed, past'ing 1**. to make adhere, as with paste **2**. [Slang] to hit

paste'board' *n.* a stiff material made of layers of paper pasted together or of pressed paper pulp

pas·tel (pas tel') *n.* [Fr. < LL. *pasta*, paste] **1**. a crayon of ground coloring matter **2**. a picture drawn with such crayons **3**. a soft, pale shade of color —*adj.* soft and pale: said of colors

pas·tern (pas'tərn) *n.* [< OFr. < *pasture*, a tether] the part of a horse's foot between the fetlock and the hoof

Pas·teur (pas tur'), **Louis** 1822–95; Fr. chemist & bacteriologist

pas·teur·ize (pas'chə rīz', -tə-) *vt.* **-ized', -iz'ing** [< prec.] to destroy bacteria in (milk, etc.) by heating to a prescribed temperature for a specified time —**pas'teur·i·za'tion** *n.*

pas·tiche (pas tēsh') *n.* [Fr.] **1**. an artistic composition drawn from various sources **2**. a hodgepodge

pas·tille (pas tēl') *n.* [Fr. < L. *pastillus*,

PASTERN

lozenge] **1.** a small lozenge containing medicine, flavoring, etc. **2.** an aromatic pellet burned for fumigating

pas·time (pas'tīm') *n.* a way of spending spare time pleasantly

past master 1. a former master, as in a lodge **2.** an expert —**past mistress** *fem.*

pas·tor (pas'tər) *n.* [L., a shepherd] a clergyman in charge of a congregation

pas'to·ral *adj.* **1.** of shepherds or their work, etc. **2.** of rural life idealized as peaceful, simple, etc. **3.** of a pastor or his duties —*n.* **1.** a poem, play, etc. having a pastoral setting **2.** a pastoral picture or scene

pas'tor·ate (-it) *n.* **1.** the position, rank, or term of office of a pastor **2.** a group of pastors

past participle a participle used: *a)* to indicate a past time or state (as *gone* in "he has gone") *b)* as an adjective (as *grown* in "a grown man")

past perfect 1. a tense indicating an action as completed before a specified time in the past **2.** a verb form in this tense (Ex.: had gone)

pas·tra·mi (pə strä'mē) *n.* [Yid. < Romanian] highly spiced, smoked beef

pas·try (pās'trē) *n., pl.* **-tries** [see PASTE] **1.** pies, tarts, etc. with crusts baked from flour dough made with shortening **2.** all fancy baked goods

pas·tur·age (pas'chər ij) *n. same as* PASTURE

pas·ture (pas'chər) *n.* [< L. *pascere*, to feed] **1.** grass or growing plants used as food by grazing animals **2.** ground suitable, or a field set aside, for grazing —*vt.* **-tured, -tur·ing** to put (cattle, etc.) out to graze in a pasture —*vi.* to graze

past·y (pās'tē) *adj.* **-i·er, -i·est** of or like paste in color or texture —**past'i·ness** *n.*

pat (pat) *n.* [prob. echoic] **1.** a gentle tap or stroke with a flat surface **2.** the sound made by this **3.** a small lump, as of butter —*vt.* **pat'ted, pat'ting 1.** to tap or stroke gently with the hand or a flat surface **2.** to shape, apply, etc. by patting —*adj.* **1.** apt; timely **2.** exactly suitable *[a pat* hand in poker*]* **3.** so glib as to seem contrived —**have** (**down**) **pat** [Colloq.] to know or have memorized thoroughly —**stand pat** to stick to an opinion, etc.

pat. 1. patent **2.** patented

Pat·a·go·ni·a (pat'ə gō'nē ə) dry region in S Argentina & Chile —**Pat'a·go'ni·an** *adj., n.*

patch (pach) *n.* [ME. *pacche*] **1.** a piece of material to cover or mend a hole or tear or to strengthen a weak spot **2.** a dressing for a wound **3.** a shield worn over an injured eye **4.** a differing part of an area; spot *[patches* of blue sky*]* **5.** a small plot of ground **6.** a scrap; bit —*vt.* **1.** to put a patch on **2.** to produce crudely or hurriedly (often with *up* or *together*) **3.** to make (a quilt, etc.) out of patches —**patch up** to settle (a quarrel, etc.) —**patch'y** *adj.* **-i·er, -i·est**

patch'work' *n.* **1.** anything made of odd, miscellaneous parts **2.** needlework, as a quilt, made of odd patches of cloth

pate (pāt) *n.* [< ?] the top of the head: a humorous term

pâ·té (pä tā') *n.* [Fr.] **1.** a pie **2.** a meat paste

pâ·té de foie gras (pä tā' də fwä' grä') [Fr.] a paste made of the livers of fattened geese

pa·tel·la (pə tel'ə) *n., pl.* **-las, -lae** (-ē) [L., a pan] *same as* KNEECAP —**pa·tel'lar** *adj.*

pat·en (pat''n) *n.* [see prec.] a metal plate, esp. for the Eucharistic bread

pat·ent (pat'nt; *also, for adj. 1 & 2,* pāt'-) *adj.* [< L. *patere,* be open] **1.** open, accessible, unobstructed, etc. **2.** obvious; plain **3.** protected by a patent —*n.* **1.** a document granting the exclusive right to produce or sell an invention, etc. for a certain time **2.** *a)* the right so granted *b)* the thing so protected —*vt.* to get a patent for —**pat·ent·ee** (pat'''n tē') *n.*

patent leather leather with a hard, glossy, usually black finish: formerly patented

patent medicine a trademarked medical preparation obtainable without a prescription

pa·ter (pāt'ər) *n.* [L.] [Chiefly Brit. Colloq.] father

pa·ter·nal (pə tur'n'l) *adj.* [< L. *pater,* father] **1.** fatherly **2.** inherited from a father **3.** on the father's side of the family —**pa·ter'nal·ly** *adv.*

pa·ter'nal·ism *n.* the system of controlling a country, employees, etc. as a father might his children —**pa·ter'nal·is'tic** *adj.*

pa·ter'ni·ty (-nə tē) *n.* **1.** the state of being a father **2.** male parentage **3.** origin in general

pa·ter·nos·ter (pät'ər nôs'tər, pāt'-) *n.* [L., our father] the Lord's Prayer, esp. in Latin: often **Pater Noster**

Pat·er·son (pat'ər s'n) city in NE N.J.: pop. 145,000

path (path) *n.* [OE. *pæth*] **1.** a way worn by footsteps **2.** a walk for use by people on foot **3.** a line of movement **4.** a course of conduct

pa·thet·ic (pə thet'ik) *adj.* [< Gr. *pathos,* suffering] **1.** arousing pity, sympathy, etc.; pitiful **2.** pitifully unsuccessful, etc. —**pa·thet'i·cal·ly** *adv.*

-pathic *a combining form used to form adjectives from nouns ending in* -PATHY

path·o·gen·ic (path'ə jen'ik) *adj.* causing disease

pa·thol·o·gy (pə thäl'ə jē) *n., pl.* **-gies** [< Fr. < Gr. *pathos,* suffering + -LOGY] **1.** the branch of medicine that deals with the nature of disease, esp. with structural and functional effects **2.** any abnormal variation from a sound condition —**path·o·log·i·cal** (path'ə läj'i k'l) *adj.* —**path'o·log'i·cal·ly** *adv.* —**pa·thol'o·gist** *n.*

pa·thos (pā'thäs, -thôs) *n.* [Gr., suffering] the quality in something which arouses pity, sorrow, sympathy, etc.

path'way' *n. same as* PATH

-pathy [< Gr. *pathos,* suffering] *a combining form meaning:* **1.** feeling *[antipathy]* **2.** disease *[osteopathy]*

pa·tience (pā'shəns) *n.* **1.** the state, quality, or fact of being patient **2.** [Chiefly Brit.] any game of solitaire

pa'tient (-shənt) *adj.* [< L. *pati,* suffer] **1.** enduring pain, trouble, etc. without complaint **2.** calmly tolerating insult, delay, confusion, etc. **3.** showing calm endurance *[a patient* face*]* **4.** diligent; persevering —*n.* one receiving medical care —**pa'tient·ly** *adv.*

pat·i·na (pat''n ə, pə tē'nə) *n.* [Fr. < It.] **1.** a fine greenish crust formed by oxidation on bronze or copper **2.** any surface change due to age, as on old wood

pa·ti·o (pat'ē ō') *n., pl.* **-os'** [Sp.] **1.** a courtyard open to the sky **2.** a paved area, as one next to a house, for outdoor lounging, dining, etc.

pat·ois (pat'wä) *n., pl.* **-ois** (-wäz) [Fr.] a nonstandard form of a language, as a provincial dialect

pat. pend. patent pending

pa·tri·arch (pā'trē ärk') *n.* [< Gr. *patēr,* father + *archein,* to rule] **1.** the father and ruler of a family or tribe: in the Bible, Abraham, Isaac, Jacob, and Jacob's sons were patriarchs **2.** one regarded as a founder, as of a religion **3.** a man of great age and dignity **4.** [*often* P-] *a)* R.C.Ch. the Pope or any of certain Eastern bishops *b)* Orthodox Eastern Ch. the highest-ranking bishop at Constantinople, Jerusalem, Moscow, etc. —**pa·tri·ar'chal** *adj.*

pa'tri·arch'ate (-är'kit) *n.* the position, rank, jurisdiction, etc. of a patriarch

pa'tri·ar'chy (-kē) *n., pl.* **-chies 1.** a social organization in which the father is head of the family, descent being traced through the male line **2.** rule or domination by men

pa·tri·cian (pə trish'ən) *n.* [< L. *pater,* father] **1.** in ancient Rome, a member of the nobility **2.** an aristocrat —*adj.* **1.** of or like patricians **2.** noble; aristocratic

pat·ri·cide (pat'rə sīd') *n.* [< L. < Gr. *patēr,* father + -CIDE] **1.** the murder of a father by his son or daughter **2.** one committing such a murder —**pat'ri·ci'dal** *adj.*

Pat·rick (pat'rik), Saint 385?-461? A.D.; Brit. missionary in, and patron saint of, Ireland

pat·ri·mo·ny (pat'rə mō'nē) *n., pl.* **-nies** [< L. *pater,* father] **1.** property inherited from one's father or ancestors **2.** an endowment or inheritance —**pat'ri·mo'ni·al** *adj.*

pa·tri·ot (pā'trē ət) *n.* [< Fr. < Gr. *patris,* fatherland] one who loves and zealously supports his country —**pa'tri·ot'ic** (-ät'ik) *adj.* —**pa'tri·ot'i·cal·ly** *adv.* —**pa'tri·ot·ism** *n.*

pa·tris·tic (pə tris'tik) *adj.* [< G. < L. *pater,* father] of the early leaders, or fathers, of the Christian Church or their writings: also **pa·tris'ti·cal**

pa·trol (pə trōl') *vt., vi.* **-trolled', -trol'ling** [< Fr. < OFr. *patouiller,* to paddle] to make a regular, repeated circuit of in guarding —*n.* **1.** a patrolling **2.** a person or group patrolling **3.** a group of ships, airplanes, etc. used in patrolling **4.** a subdivision of a troop in Boy Scouts or Girl Scouts

pa·trol'man (-mən) *n., pl.* **-men** a policeman assigned to patrol a specific area

pa·tron (pā'trən) *n.* [< L. *pater,* father] **1.** a protector; benefactor **2.** one who sponsors and supports some person, activity, etc. **3.** a regular customer —**pa'tron·ess** *n.fem.*

pa·tron·age (pā'trən ij, pat'rən-) *n.* **1.** support, encouragement, etc. given by a patron **2.** condescension **3.** *a)* customers *b)* business; trade **4.** *a)* the power to grant political favors *b)* such favors

pa·tron·ize (pā'trə nīz', pat'rə-) *vt.* **-ized', -iz'ing 1.** to sponsor; support **2.** to treat kindly but as an inferior **3.** to be a regular customer of (a store, etc.)

patron saint a saint looked upon as the special guardian of a person, place, institution, etc.

pat·ro·nym·ic (pat'rə nim'ik) *n.* [< Gr. *patēr*, father + *onyma*, a name] a name showing descent from a given person (e.g., *Stevenson*, son of Steven)

pat·sy (pat'sē) *n., pl.* **-sies** [< ?] [Slang] a person easily imposed upon or victimized

pat·ter[1] (pat'ər) *vi.* [< PAT] to make, or move so as to make, a patter —*n.* a series of quick, light taps

pat·ter[2] (pat'ər) *vt., vi.* [< PATERNOSTER] to speak rapidly or glibly —*n.* glib, rapid speech, as of salesmen

pat·tern (pat'ərn) *n.* [< OFr. *patron*] **1.** a person or thing worthy of imitation **2.** a model, plan, etc. used in making things **3.** a design **4.** a regular way of acting or doing **5.** a predictable route, movement, etc. —*vt.* to make, do, or plan in imitation of a model or pattern (with *on, upon,* or *after*)

pat·ty (pat'ē) *n., pl.* **-ties** [Fr. *pâté*, a pie] **1.** a small pie **2.** a small, flat cake of ground meat, fish, etc., usually fried **3.** a small disk, as of candy

pau·ci·ty (pô'sə tē) *n.* [< L. *paucus*, few] **1.** fewness; small number **2.** scarcity

Paul (pôl) *n. Bible* the apostle of Christianity to the Gentiles, author of many Epistles; lived ?-67? A.D.: also *Saint Paul* **2. Paul VI** 1897-1978; Pope (1963-78)

Paul Bun·yan (bun'yən) *American Folklore* a giant lumberjack who performed superhuman feats

paunch (pônch) *n.* [< L. *pantex*, belly] the abdomen, or belly; esp., a potbelly —**paunch'y** *adj.*

pau·per (pô'pər) *n.* [L.] an extremely poor person, esp. one who lives on charity —**pau'per·ism** *n.*

pause (pôz) *n.* [< Gr. *pauein*, to stop] **1.** a temporary stop or rest **2.** hesitation; delay —*vi.* paused, paus'ing to make a pause; stop; hesitate —**give one pause** to make one hesitant or uncertain

pave (pāv) *vt.* paved, pav'ing [< L. *pavire*, beat] to cover the surface of (a road, etc.), as with concrete, asphalt, etc. —**pave the way (for)** to prepare the way (for) —**pav'er** *n.*

pave'ment *n.* **1.** a paved surface, as of concrete; specif., a paved street or road **2.** the material used in paving

pa·vil·ion (pə vil'yən) *n.* [< L. *papilio*, tent] **1.** a large tent **2.** a building, often partly open, for exhibits, etc., as at a fair or park **3.** any of a group of related buildings

pav·ing (pā'viŋ) *n.* **1.** a pavement **2.** material for a pavement

paw (pô) *n.* [< OFr. *poue*] **1.** the foot of a four-footed animal having claws **2.** [Colloq.] a hand —*vt., vi.* **1.** to touch, dig, strike, etc. with the paws or feet **2.** to handle clumsily, roughly, or overintimately

pawl (pôl) *n.* [akin ? to Du. *pal*, pole] a device, as a hinged tongue which engages cogs in a wheel, allowing motion in only one direction

pawn[1] (pôn) *n.* [< MFr. *pan*] **1.** anything given as security, as for a debt; pledge **2.** the state of being pledged —*vt.* to give as security —**pawn'er, pawn'nor** *n.*

pawn[2] (pôn) *n.* [< ML. *pedo*, foot soldier] **1.** a chessman of the lowest value **2.** a person used to advance another's purposes

pawn'bro'ker *n.* a person licensed to lend money at interest on personal belongings left with him as security — **pawn'bro'king** *n.*

Paw·nee (pô nē') *n.* **1.** *pl.* **-nees', -nee'** a member of an Indian tribe now living in N Oklahoma **2.** their language

pawn'shop' *n.* a pawnbroker's shop

pawn ticket a receipt for goods in pawn

paw·paw (pô'pô') *n. same as* PAPAW

pay (pā) *vt.* paid, pay'ing [< L. *pacare*, pacify] **1.** to give (a person) what is due, as for goods or services; remunerate **2.** to give (what is due) in return, as for goods or services **3.** to settle (a debt, etc.) **4.** *a)* to give (a compliment, respects, etc.) *b)* to make (a visit, etc.) **5.** to yield [this job *pays* $90] **6.** to be profitable to [it will *pay* him to listen] —*vi.* **1.** to give due compensation **2.** to be profitable —*n.* **1.** a paying or being paid **2.** money paid; esp., wages or salary —*adj.* **1.** operated by depositing a coin [a pay telephone] **2.** designating a service, etc. paid for by fees [pay TV] —**in the pay of** employed and paid by —**pay back 1.** to repay **2.** to retaliate upon —**pay for** to suffer or atone for (a wrong) —**pay off** to pay all that is owed —**pay out** (*pt.* payed out) to let out (a rope, cable, etc.) —**pay up** to pay in full or on time —**pay'er** *n.*

pay'a·ble *adj.* **1.** that can be paid **2.** that is to be paid (on a specified date); due

pay'check' *n.* a check in payment of wages, etc.

pay'day' *n.* the day on which wages, etc. are paid

pay dirt soil, ore, etc. rich enough in minerals to make mining profitable

pay·ee (pā ē') *n.* one to whom a check, note, money, etc. is payable

pay'load' *n.* **1.** the part of a cargo producing income **2.** *a)* the warhead of a ballistic missile, the spacecraft launched by a rocket, etc. *b)* the weight of this

pay'mas'ter *n.* the official in charge of paying employees

pay'ment *n.* **1.** a paying or being paid **2.** something paid **3.** penalty or reward

pay'off' *n.* **1.** settlement, reckoning, or payment **2.** [Colloq.] a bribe **3.** [Colloq.] an unexpected climax

pay·o·la (pā ō'lə) *n.* [Slang] **1.** the paying of bribes for commercial advantage, as to a disc jockey for promoting a song unfairly **2.** such a bribe

pay phone (or **station**) a public telephone, usually coin-operated

pay'roll' *n.* **1.** a list of employees to be paid, with the amount due each **2.** the total amount needed for this

payt., pay't payment

Pb [L. *plumbum*] *Chem.* lead

PBS Public Broadcasting Service

PBX, P.B.X. [< *p(rivate) b(ranch) ex(change)*] a telephone system within an organization, having outside lines

pc. 1. piece **2.** price(s)

p.c. 1. percent: also **pct. 2.** postal card **3.** post card

Pd *Chem.* palladium

pd. paid

P.D. 1. per diem **2.** Police Department

pea (pē) *n., pl.* **peas**, archaic **pease** [< ME. *pese*, a pea, mistaken as *pl.*; ult. < Gr. *pison*] **1.** a climbing plant with green seed pods **2.** its small, round seed, eaten as a vegetable **3.** any similar plant

peace (pēs) *n.* [< L. *pax*] **1.** freedom from war **2.** a treaty or agreement to end war **3.** freedom from public disturbance; law and order **4.** harmony; concord **5.** serenity, calm, or quiet —**at peace** free from war, conflict, etc. — **hold** (or **keep**) **one's peace** to be silent

peace'a·ble *adj.* fond of or promoting peace

peace'ful *adj.* **1.** not quarrelsome **2.** free from disturbance; calm **3.** of or characteristic of a time of peace — **peace'ful·ly** *adv.* —**peace'ful·ness** *n.*

peace'mak'er *n.* one who makes peace, as by settling the quarrels of others

peace officer an officer entrusted with maintaining law and order

peace pipe *same as* CALUMET

peace'time' *n.* a time of peace —*adj.* of or characteristic of such a time

peach[1] (pēch) *n.* [< L. *Persicum (malum)*, Persian (apple)] **1.** a tree with round, juicy, orange-yellow fruit having a fuzzy skin and a rough pit **2.** its fruit **3.** the color of this fruit **4.** [Slang] any person or thing well liked

peach[2] (pēch) *vi.* [see IMPEACH] [Old Slang] to inform against another

peach'y *adj.* **-i·er, -i·est 1.** like a peach, as in color or texture **2.** [Old Slang] fine; excellent

pea·cock (pē'käk') *n.* [< L. *pavo*, peacock] the male of a pheasantlike bird (**pea'fowl'**), with a long, showy tail which can be spread out like a fan —**pea'hen'** *n.fem.*

pea green a light yellowish green

pea jacket [< Du. *pijjekker*] a hip-length, heavy woolen coat, worn by seamen: also **pea'coat'** *n.*

peak (pēk) *n.* [var. of *pike* (summit)] **1.** a pointed end or top, as of a cap, roof, etc. **2.** *a)* the summit of a mountain ending in a point *b)* a mountain with such a summit **3.** the highest or utmost point of anything; maximum —*vt., vi.* to come or bring to a peak

peaked[1] (pēkt) *adj.* having a peak; pointed

peak·ed[2] (pē'kid) *adj.* [< ?] thin and drawn, as from illness

peal (pēl) *n.* [< ME. *apele*, appeal] **1.** the loud ringing of a bell or bells **2.** a set of bells **3.** a loud, prolonged sound as of gunfire, laughter, etc. —*vt., vi.* to ring or resound

pea'nut' *n.* **1.** a vine of the legume family, with underground pods containing edible seeds **2.** the pod or its seed **3.** [*pl.*] [Slang] a trifling sum

peanut butter a paste or spread made by grinding roasted peanuts

pear (per) *n.* [< L. *pirum*] **1.** a tree with soft, juicy fruit, round at the base and narrowing toward the stem **2.** this fruit

pearl (purl) *n.* [ult. < L. *perna*, a sea mussel] **1.** a smooth, hard, usually white or bluish-gray, roundish growth formed within the shell of some oysters and other mollusks: it is used as a gem **2.** *same as* MOTHER-OF-PEARL **3.** anything pearllike in shape, beauty, value, etc. **4.** bluish gray —*adj.* **1.** of or having pearls **2.** like a pearl in shape or color —**pearl'i·ness** *n.* —**pearl'y** *adj.* **-i·er, -i·est**

pearl gray a pale bluish gray

Pearl Harbor inlet on the S coast of Oahu, Hawaii: site of the U.S. naval base bombed by Japan, Dec. 7, 1941

Pear·y (pir'ē), **Robert Edwin** 1856–1920; U.S. arctic explorer: discovered the North Pole

peas·ant (pez'nt) *n.* [< LL. *pagus*, district] **1.** a small farmer or farm laborer, as in Europe or Asia **2.** a person regarded as coarse, boorish, ignorant, etc. —**peas'ant·ry** *n.*

peat (pēt) *n.* [< ML. *peta*, piece of turf] partly decayed plant matter found in ancient swamps, dried and used as for fuel —**peat'y** *adj.* **-i·er, -i·est**

peat moss 1. *same as* SPHAGNUM **2.** peat composed of residues of mosses, used as a mulch

pea·vey (pē'vē) *n., pl.* **-veys** [< J. *Peavey*, said to be its inventor] a wooden lever with a pointed tip and hinged hook near the end: used by lumbermen in handling logs

peb·ble (peb''l) *n.* [< OE. *papol(stan)*, pebble (stone)] a small stone worn smooth and round, as by the action of water —*vt.* **-bled, -bling** to stamp (leather) so as to give it an irregular surface —**peb'bly** *adj.* **-bli·er, -bli·est**

pe·can (pi kan', -kän') *n.* [< AmInd.] **1.** an olive-shaped, edible nut with a thin shell **2.** the N. American tree on which it grows

pec·ca·dil·lo (pek'ə dil'ō) *n., pl.* **-loes, -los** [Sp. < L. *peccare*, to sin] a small fault or offense

pec·ca·ry (pek'ər ē) *n., pl.* **-ries** [< SAmInd. name] a piglike animal of N. and S. America, with sharp tusks

peck¹ (pek) *vt.* [< ME. *picken*, to pick] **1.** to strike, as with a beak **2.** to make by doing this *[to peck a hole]* **3.** to pick up or get by pecking —*vi.* **1.** to make strokes as with a beak —*n.* **1.** a stroke made as with a beak **2.** [Colloq.] a quick, casual kiss —**peck at** to eat very little of

peck² (pek) *n.* [< OFr. *pek*] **1.** a unit of dry measure equal to 1/4 bushel, or 8 quarts **2.** a container holding this amount **3.** [Colloq.] a large amount, as of trouble

pec·tin (pek'tin) *n.* [< Gr. *pēktos*, congealed] a carbohydrate obtained from certain fruits, which yields a gel that is the basis of jellies and jams

pec·to·ral (pek'tər əl) *adj.* [< L. *pectus*, breast] of or located in or on the chest or breast

pec·u·late (pek'yə lāt') *vt., vi.* **-lat·ed, -lat·ing** [< L. *peculari*] to embezzle —**pec'u·la'tion** *n.* —**pec'u·la'tor** *n.*

pe·cul·iar (pi kyōōl'yər) *adj.* [< L. *peculium*, private property] **1.** of only one person, thing, group, etc.; exclusive **2.** particular; special **3.** odd; strange —**pe·cul'·iar·ly** *adv.*

pe·cu·li·ar·i·ty (pi kyōō'lē ar'ə tē) *n.* **1.** a being peculiar **2.** *pl.* **-ties** something that is peculiar, as a trait

pe·cu·ni·ar·y (pi kyōō'nē er'ē) *adj.* [< L. *pecunia*, money] of or involving money

ped·a·gogue, ped·a·gog (ped'ə gäg', -gôg') *n.* [< Gr. *pais*, child + *agein*, to lead] a teacher; often specif., a pedantic teacher

ped'a·go'gy (-gō'jē, -gäj'ē) *n.* the art or science of teaching —**ped'a·gog'ic** (-gäj'ik), **ped'a·gog'i·cal** *adj.* —**ped'a·gog'i·cal·ly** *adv.*

ped·al (ped''l) *adj.* [< L. *pes*, foot] **1.** of the foot or feet **2.** of or operated by a pedal —*n.* a lever operated by the foot, as on a bicycle, organ, etc. —*vt., vi.* **-aled** or **-alled, -al·ing** or **-al·ling** to operate by a pedal or pedals

pedal pushers calf-length pants for women or girls, used originally for bicycle riding

ped·ant (ped''nt) *n.* [< Fr. < It., ult. < Gr. *paidagōgos*, teacher] **1.** one who emphasizes trivial points of learning **2.** a narrow-minded teacher who insists on exact adherence to rules —**pe·dan·tic** (pi dan'tik) *adj.* —**pe·dan'ti·cal·ly** *adv.*

ped·ant·ry (ped''n trē) *n., pl.* **-ries 1.** the qualities, practices, etc. of a pedant **2.** arbitrary adherence to rules

ped·dle (ped''l) *vi., vt.* **-dled, -dling** [< ? ME. *ped*, basket] to go from place to place selling (small articles) —**ped'dler** *n.*

-pede [< L. *pes*, foot] *a combining form meaning* foot or feet *[centipede]* : also **-ped**

ped·er·as·ty (ped'ə ras'tē, pē'də-) *n.* [< Gr. *pais*, boy + *eran*, to love] sodomy between males, esp. by a man with a boy —**ped'er·ast'** *n.*

ped·es·tal (ped'is t'l) *n.* [< Fr. < It. *piè*, foot + *di*, of + *stal*, a rest] the bottom support of a column, statue, etc. —**to put** (or **set**) **on a pedestal** to idolize

pe·des·tri·an (pə des'trē ən) *adj.* [< L. *pes*, foot] **1.** going or done on foot **2.** of or for pedestrians **3.** ordinary and dull; prosaic —*n.* a walker —**pe·des'tri·an·ism** *n.*

pedi- [< L. *pes*, foot] *a combining form meaning* foot or feet *[pedicure]*

ped·i·a·tri·cian (pē'dē ə trish'ən) *n.* a specialist in pediatrics: also **pe'di·at'rist** (-at'rist)

pe·di·at·rics (pē'dē at'riks) *n.pl.* [with sing. v.] [< PED(O)- + -IATRICS] the branch of medicine dealing with the care of infants and children and the treatment of their diseases —**pe'di·at'ric** *adj.*

ped·i·cab (ped'i kab') *n.* [PEDI- + CAB] a 3-wheeled carriage, esp. in SE Asia, pedaled by the driver

pe·dic·u·lo·sis (pi dik'yə lō'sis) *n.* [< L. *pedis*, louse] infestation with lice —**pe·dic'u·lous** *adj.*

ped·i·cure (ped'i kyoor') *n.* [< Fr. < L. *pes*, foot + *cura*, care] a trimming, cleaning, etc. of the toenails

ped·i·gree (ped'ə grē') *n.* [< MFr. *pie de grue*, lit., crane's foot: from the lines in the genealogical tree] **1.** a list of ancestors **2.** descent; lineage **3.** a recorded line of descent, esp. of a purebred animal —**ped'i·greed'** *adj.*

ped·i·ment (ped'ə mənt) *n.* [< earlier *periment*, prob. < PYRAMID] an ornamental gable or triangular piece on the front of a building, over a doorway, etc.

pedo- [< Gr. *pais*, child] *a combining form meaning* child, children: also **ped-**

PEDIMENT

pe·dom·e·ter (pi däm'ə tər) *n.* [< L. *pes*, foot + Gr. *metron*, a measure] an instrument carried to measure the distance walked

pe·dun·cle (pi dun'k'l, pē'dun-) *n.* [< L. *pes*, foot] a stalklike organ or process in some plants, animals, etc.

peek (pēk) *vi.* [< ?] to glance or look quickly and furtively, as through an opening —*n.* such a glance

peek·a·boo (pēk'ə bōō') *n.* a child's game in which one hides one's face, as behind one's hands, and then suddenly reveals it, calling "peekaboo!"

peel (pēl) *vt.* [< L. *pilare*, make bald] to cut away (the skin, rind, etc.) —*vi.* **1.** to shed skin, bark, etc. **2.** to come off in layers or flakes, as old paint —*n.* the rind or skin of fruit —**peel off** Aeron. to veer away from a flight formation abruptly —**peel'er** *n.*

peel'ing *n.* a peeled-off strip, as of apple skin

peen (pēn) *n.* [prob. < Scand.] the part of certain hammerheads opposite to the flat, striking surface: often ball-shaped (**ball peen**) or wedge-shaped —*vt.* to hammer with a peen

peep¹ (pēp) *vi.* [echoic] to make the short, high-pitched cry of a young bird —*n.* a peeping sound

peep² (pēp) *vi.* [ME. *pepen*] **1.** to look through a small opening or from a place of hiding **2.** to appear gradually or partially —*n.* **1.** a brief look; furtive glimpse **2.** the first appearance, as of dawn

peep'hole' *n.* a hole to peep through

peeping Tom [< the legendary English tailor who peeped at Lady Godiva] one who gets sexual pleasure from furtively watching others

peer¹ (pir) *n.* [< L. *par*, an equal] **1.** one that has the same rank, value, etc.; specif., an equal before the law **2.** a noble; esp., a British duke, earl, etc. —**peer'ess** *n.fem.*

peer² (pir) *vi.* [< ? APPEAR] **1.** to look closely, as in trying to see more clearly **2.** to show slightly

peer'age (-ij) *n.* **1.** all the peers of a country **2.** the rank of a peer

peer'less *adj.* without equal

peeve (pēv) *vt.* **peeved, peev'ing** [< ff.] [Colloq.] to make peevish —*n.* [Colloq.] an annoyance

pee'vish *adj.* [< ?] irritable; fretful —**pee'vish·ly** *adv.* —**pee'vish·ness** *n.*

pee·wee (pē'wē') *n.* [prob. < WEE] [Colloq.] an unusually small person or thing

peg (peg) *n.* [ME. *pegge*] **1.** a short pin or bolt used to hold parts together, hang things on, mark the score of a game, etc. **2.** a step or degree **3.** [Colloq.] a throw —*vt.* **pegged, peg'ging 1.** to put a peg or pegs into so as to fasten, mark, etc. **2.** to maintain (prices, etc.) at a fixed level **3.** [Colloq.] to throw (a ball) —**peg away (at)** to work steadily (at) —**take down a peg** to lower the pride of

Peg·a·sus (peg′ə səs) **1.** *Gr. Myth.* a winged horse **2.** a northern constellation

peign·oir (pān wär′, pān′wär; pen-) *n.* [Fr. < L. *pecten*, a comb] a short negligee

pe·jo·ra·tion (pē′jə rā′shən, pej′ə-) *n.* [< L. *pejor*, worse] **1.** a worsening **2.** a change for the worse in the meaning of a word —**pe·jo·ra·tive** (pi jôr′ə tiv) *adj., n.*

Pe·king (pē′kiŋ′; *Chin.* bā′jiŋ′) capital of China in the NE part: pop. c.7,000,000

Pe·king·ese (pē′kə nēz′) *n., pl.* **-ese′** a small dog with long, silky hair, short legs, and a pug nose: also **Pe′kin·ese′**

Peking man a type of early man of c.450,000 B.C., known from fossil remains found near Peking

pe·koe (pē′kō) *n.* [< Chin. *pek-ho*, white down (on the young leaves used)] a black, small-leaved tea of Sri Lanka and India

pe·lag·ic (pi laj′ik) *adj.* [< Gr. *pelagos*, sea] of the open sea or ocean

pelf (pelf) *n.* [akin to MFr. *pelfre*, booty] **1.** orig., booty **2.** wealth regarded with contempt

pel·i·can (pel′i kən) *n.* [< Gr. *pelekan*] a large water bird with webbed feet and an expandable pouch in the lower bill for scooping up fish

Pe·li·on (pē′lē ən) mountain in NE Greece: in Greek mythology, the Titans piled Pelion on Ossa and both on Olympus in an attempt to attack the gods

pel·la·gra (pə lag′rə, -lā′grə) *n.* [It. < *pelle*, skin + *-agra* < Gr. *agra*, seizure] a chronic disease caused by a deficiency of niacin in the diet and characterized by skin eruptions and mental disorders

pel·let (pel′ət) *n.* [< L. *pila*, a ball] **1.** a little ball, as of clay or medicine **2.** a bullet, small lead shot, etc. —*vt.* to shoot or hit with pellets

pell-mell, pell·mell (pel′mel′) *adv., adj.* [< Fr. < OFr. *mesler*, to mix] **1.** in a jumbled, confused mass or manner **2.** in reckless haste —*n.* confusion; disorder

pel·lu·cid (pə lōō′sid) *adj.* [< L. *per*, through + *lucere*, to shine] **1.** transparent; clear **2.** clear and simple in style — **pel·lu′cid·ly** *adv.*

Pel·o·pon·ne·sus, Pel·o·pon·ne·sos (pel′ə pə nē′səs) peninsula forming the S part of the mainland of Greece — **Pel′o·pon·ne′sian** (-shən, -zhən) *adj., n.*

pelt[1] (pelt) *vt.* [? ult. < L. *pillare*, to drive] **1.** to throw things at **2.** to beat repeatedly **3.** to throw (missiles) —*vi.* to strike heavily or steadily, as hard rain —*n.* a blow

pelt[2] (pelt) *n.* [prob. < OFr. *pel*, a skin] the skin of a fur-bearing animal, esp. when stripped from the carcass

pel·vis (pel′vis) *n., pl.* **-vis·es, -ves** (-vēz) [L., a basin] **1.** the basinlike cavity in the posterior part of the trunk in man and many other vertebrates **2.** the bones forming this cavity —**pel′vic** *adj.*

pem·mi·can (pem′i kən) *n.* [< AmInd.] a concentrated food of dried beef, suet, raisins, etc.

pen[1] (pen) *n.* [OE. *penn*] **1.** a small enclosure for domestic animals **2.** any small enclosure —*vt.* **penned** or **pent, pen′ning** to enclose as in a pen

pen[2] (pen) *n.* [< L. *penna*, a feather] **1.** a device used in writing or drawing with ink, often with a metal point split into two nibs **2.** the metal point **3.** writing as a profession —*vt.* **penned, pen′ning** to write as with a pen

pen[3] (pen) *n.* [Slang] a penitentiary

Pen., pen. peninsula

pe·nal (pē′n'l) *adj.* [< L. *poena*, punishment] of, for, constituting, or deserving punishment

penal code a body of law dealing with various crimes and offenses and their legal penalties

pe·nal·ize (pē′n'l īz′, pen′'l-) *vt.* **-ized′, -iz′ing** to impose a penalty on; punish —**pe′nal·i·za′tion** *n.*

pen·al·ty (pen′'l tē) *n., pl.* **-ties 1.** punishment fixed by law, as for a crime **2.** the handicap, fine, etc. imposed on an offender **3.** any unfortunate consequence **4.** *Sports* a loss of yardage, etc. imposed for breaking a rule

pen·ance (pen′əns) *n.* [see PENITENT] **1.** *R.C.Ch.* a sacrament involving confession of sin, repentance, and submission to penalties imposed, followed by absolution **2.** any voluntary suffering to show repentance for wrongdoing

pe·na·tes (pi nāt′ēz) *n.pl.* [L.] the household gods of the ancient Romans: see LARES AND PENATES

pence (pens) *n.* [Brit.] *pl.* of PENNY

pen·chant (pen′chənt) *n.* [Fr. < L. *pendere*, hang] a strong liking; inclination

pen·cil (pen′s'l) *n.* [< L. *penis*, tail] **1.** a pointed, rod-shaped instrument with a core of graphite or crayon, used

for writing, drawing, etc. **2.** something shaped or used like a pencil [a styptic *pencil*] **3.** a series of lines coming to or spreading out from a point —*vt.* **-ciled** or **-cilled, -cil·ing** or **-cil·ling 1.** to write, draw, etc. as with a pencil **2.** to use a pencil on

pend (pend) *vi.* [< L. *pendere*, hang] to await judgment or decision

pend·ant (pen′dənt) *n.* [see prec.] **1.** an ornamental hanging object, as an earring **2.** a decorative piece suspended from a ceiling or a roof —*adj. same as* PENDENT

pend′ent (-dənt) *adj.* [see PEND] **1.** suspended **2.** overhanging **3.** undecided; pending —*n. same as* PENDANT

pend′ing *adj.* **1.** not decided **2.** impending —*prep.* **1.** during **2.** while awaiting; until

pen·drag·on (pen drag′ən) *n.* [W. *pen*, head + *dragon*, leader] supreme chief or leader: a title used in ancient Britain

pen·du·lous (pen′jōō ləs) *adj.* [see PEND] **1.** hanging freely **2.** drooping —**pen′du·lous·ly** *adv.*

pen′du·lum (-ləm) *n.* [see PEND] a body hung from a fixed point so that it can swing freely to and fro: often used to regulate clock movements

Pe·nel·o·pe (pə nel′ə pē) Odysseus' wife, who waited faithfully for his return

pen·e·trate (pen′ə trāt′) *vt., vi.* **-trat′ed, -trat′ing** [< L. *penitus*, inward] **1.** to enter by piercing **2.** to have an effect throughout **3.** to affect deeply **4.** to understand — **pen′e·tra·ble** *adj.*

pen′e·trat′ing *adj.* **1.** that penetrates **2.** sharp; piercing **3.** that has entered deeply **4.** discerning Also **pen′e·tra′·tive** —**pen′e·trat′ing·ly** *adv.*

pen′e·tra′tion *n.* **1.** a penetrating **2.** the depth to which something penetrates **3.** sharp discernment

pen·guin (peŋ′gwin, pen′-) *n.* [prob. < W. *pen gwyn*, lit., white head] a flightless bird of the S Hemisphere with webbed feet and paddlelike flippers for swimming

pen·i·cil·lin (pen′ə sil′in) *n.* [< L. *penicillus*, brush] an antibiotic obtained from certain molds or produced synthetically

pen·in·su·la (pə nin′sə lə, -syoo-) *n.* [< L. *paene*, almost + *insula*, isle] **1.** a land area almost surrounded by water **2.** any land area projecting into the water —**pen·in′su·lar** *adj.*

PENGUIN
(to 4 ft. high)

pe·nis (pē′nis) *n., pl.* **-nis·es, -nes** (-nēz) [L., a tail] the male organ of sexual intercourse: in mammals it is also the organ through which urine is ejected —**pe′nile** (-nīl) *adj.*

pen·i·tent (pen′ə tənt) *adj.* [< L. *paenitere*, repent] sorry for having done wrong and willing to atone —*n.* a penitent person —**pen′i·tence** *n.* —**pen′i·ten′tial** (-ten′shəl) *adj.* —**pen′i·tent·ly** *adv.*

pen·i·ten·tia·ry (pen′ə ten′shə rē) *adj.* making one liable to imprisonment in a penitentiary —*n., pl.* **-ries** a State or Federal prison for persons convicted of serious crimes

pen′knife′ (-nīf′) *n., pl.* **-knives′** (-nīvz′) a small pocket-knife: orig. used in making quill pens

pen′light′, pen′lite′ *n.* a flashlight about the size of a fountain pen

pen′man (-mən) *n., pl.* **-men 1.** one skilled in penmanship **2.** an author

pen′man·ship′ (-ship′) *n.* handwriting as an art or skill

Penn (pen), **William** 1644–1718; Eng. Quaker leader; founder of Pennsylvania

Penn., Penna. Pennsylvania

pen name a pseudonym

pen·nant (pen′ənt) *n.* [< PENNON] **1.** any long, narrow flag **2.** such a flag symbolizing a championship, as in baseball

pen·ni·less (pen′i lis) *adj.* without even a penny; extremely poor

pen·non (pen′ən) *n.* [< L. *penna*, a feather] a flag or pennant; esp., one carried by a knight or lancer

Penn·syl·va·ni·a (pen′s'l vān′yə, -vā′nē ə) State of the NE U.S.: 45,333 sq. mi.; pop. 11,794,000; cap. Harrisburg: abbrev. **Pa., PA** —**Penn′syl·va′ni·an** *adj., n.*

Pennsylvania Dutch 1. the descendants of early German immigrants to Pennsylvania **2.** their High German dialect **3.** their folk art

pen·ny (pen′ē) *n., pl.* **-nies**; for 1 (esp. collectively) **pence** [< OE. *pening*] **1.** in the United Kingdom and certain Commonwealth countries, *a)* formerly, a unit of currency equal to one twelfth shilling *b)* a unit of currency equal to one 100th part of a pound: in full **new penny 2.** a U.S. or Canadian cent **3.** a sum of money —**a pretty penny** [Colloq.] a large sum of money

penny arcade a public amusement hall with coin-operated game and vending machines

penny pincher an extremely frugal or stingy person — **pen′ny-pinch′ing** *n., adj.*

pen′ny·weight′ *n.* a unit of weight equal to 1/20 ounce troy weight

pen′ny-wise′ *adj.* careful or thrifty in small matters — **penny-wise and pound-foolish** thrifty in small matters but wasteful in major ones

pe·nol·o·gy (pē näl′ə jē) *n.* [< Gr. *poinē*, penalty + -LOGY] the study of the rehabilitation of criminals and of prison management —**pe·nol′o·gist** *n.*

pen pal a person, esp. one abroad, with whom one exchanges letters

pen·sion (pen′shən) *n.* [< L. *pensio*, a paying] **1.** a regular payment, not wages, to one who is retired or disabled **2.** (pän′sē än′, *Fr.* pän syön′) in France, etc., *a*) a boardinghouse *b*) room and board —*vt.* to grant a pension to — **pen′sion·er** *n.*

pen·sive (pen′siv) *adj.* [< L. *pensare*, consider] thinking deeply, often of sad or melancholy things —**pen′sive·ly** *adv.* —**pen′sive·ness** *n.*

pent (pent) *alt. pt. & pp.* of PEN[1] —*adj.* held or kept in; penned (often with *up*)

penta- [< Gr. *pente*, five] *a combining form meaning* five: also **pent-**

pen·ta·cle (pen′tə k′l) *n.* [< ML. *pentaculum*] a symbol, usually a five-pointed star, formerly used in magic: also **pen′ta·gram′** (-gram′)

pen·ta·gon (pen′tə gän′) *n.* [< Gr.: see PENTA- & -GON] a plane figure with five angles and five sides —**the Pentagon** the pentagonal office building of the Defense Department, near Washington, D.C. —**pen·tag′o·nal** (-tag′ə n′l) *adj.*

pen·tam·e·ter (pen tam′ə tər) *n.* [see PENTA- & -METER] **1.** a line of verse containing five metrical feet **2.** verse consisting of pentameters

Pen·ta·teuch (pen′tə tŏŏk′) *n.* [< Gr. *pente*, five + *teuchos*, book] the first five books of the Bible

pen·tath·lon (pen tath′län) *n.* [< Gr. *penta-*, five + *athlon*, contest] an athletic contest in which each contestant takes part in five different events

Pen·te·cost (pen′tə kôst′, -käst′) [< Gr. *pentēkostē* (*hēmera*), the fiftieth day after Passover] a Christian festival on the seventh Sunday after Easter, celebrating the descent of the Holy Spirit upon the Apostles; Whitsunday —**Pen′te·cos′tal** *adj.*

pent·house (pent′hous′) *n.* [< L. *appendere*, append] a house or apartment on the roof of a building

Pen·to·thal Sodium (pen′tə thal′) *a trademark for* THIOPENTAL SODIUM

pent′-up′ *adj.* held in check; curbed

pe·nu·che, pe·nu·chi (pə nŏŏ′chē) *n.* [var. of PANOCHA] a fudgelike candy made of brown sugar, etc.

pe·nult (pē′nult) *n.* [< L. *paene*, almost + *ultimus*, last] the one next to the last; specif., the second last syllable in a word —**pe·nul·ti·mate** (pi nul′tə mit) *adj., n.*

pe·num·bra (pi num′brə) *n., pl.* **-brae** (-brē), **-bras** the partly lighted area surrounding the complete shadow of a body, as the moon, in full eclipse

pe·nu·ri·ous (pə nyoor′ē əs, -noor′-) *adj.* miserly; stingy —**pe·nu′ri·ous·ly** *adv.* —**pe·nu′ri·ous·ness** *n.*

pen·u·ry (pen′yə rē) *n.* [< L. *penuria*, want] lack of money, necessities, etc.; destitution

pe·on (pē′än, -ən) *n.* [< Sp. < ML. *pedo*, foot soldier] **1.** in Latin America, a person of the laboring class **2.** an exploited laborer —**pe′on·age** (-ə nij) *n.*

pe·o·ny (pē′ə nē) *n., pl.* **-nies** [< Gr. *Paiōn*, Apollo as god of medicine: from its former medicinal use] **1.** a plant with large pink, white, red, or yellow, showy flowers **2.** the flower

peo·ple (pē′p′l) *n., pl.* **-ple;** for 1 **-ples** [< L. *populus*, nation] **1.** all the persons of a racial, national, religious, linguistic, or cultural group; nation, race, ethnic group, etc. **2.** the persons of a certain place, community, or class **3.** the persons under the leadership or control of a particular person or body **4.** one's relatives; family **5.** the populace **6.** the electorate of a state **7.** persons considered indefinitely [what will *people* say?] **8.** human beings —*vt.* -pled, -pling to populate

Pe·or·i·a (pē ôr′ē ə) city in C Ill.: pop. 127,000

pep (pep) *n.* [< PEPPER] [Colloq.] energy; vigor —*vt.* **pepped, pep′ping** [Colloq.] to fill with pep; invigorate (with *up*) —**pep′py** *adj.* -**pi·er,** -**pi·est**

pep·per (pep′ər) *n.* [< Gr. *peperi*] **1.** *a*) a pungent condiment ground from the dried fruits of an East Indian plant *b*) this plant **2.** the fruit of the red pepper plant, red, yellow, or green, sweet or hot —*vt.* **1.** to season with ground pepper **2.** to pelt with small objects

PEPPER

pep′per·corn′ *n.* the dried berry of the pepper, ground as a condiment

pepper mill a hand mill used to grind peppercorns

pep′per·mint′ *n.* **1.** a plant related to the mint that yields a pungent oil used in flavoring **2.** the oil **3.** a candy flavored with this oil

pep·per·o·ni (pep′ə rō′nē) *n., pl.* **-nis, -ni** [< It. *peperoni*] a highly spiced Italian sausage

pepper pot any of various stews or soups of vegetables, meat, etc. flavored with hot spices

pepper shaker a container for ground pepper, with a perforated top

pep′per·y *adj.* -**i·er,** -**i·est** **1.** of, like, or highly seasoned with pepper **2.** sharp or fiery, as words **3.** hot-tempered — **pep′per·i·ness** *n.*

pep·sin (pep′s'n) *n.* [G. < Gr. *peptein*, to digest] a stomach enzyme, aiding in the digestion of proteins

pep talk a talk, as to an athletic team by its coach, to instill enthusiasm and determination

pep′tic (-tik) *adj.* **1.** of or aiding digestion **2.** caused by digestive secretions [a *peptic* ulcer]

pep·tone (pep′tōn) *n.* [< Gr. *peptos*, digested] any of a group of soluble and diffusible derived proteins formed by the action of enzymes on proteins, as in digestion

Pepys (pēps), **Samuel** 1633–1703; Eng. government official, known for his diary

per (pur, pər) *prep.* [L.] **1.** through; by; by means of **2.** for each [fifty cents *per* yard] **3.** [Colloq.] according to [*per* his instructions]

per- [< L. *per*, through] *a prefix meaning:* **1.** through; throughout **2.** thoroughly

Per. **1.** Persia **2.** Persian

per. **1.** period **2.** person

per·ad·ven·ture (pur′əd ven′chər) *adv.* [< OFr. *par*, by + *aventure*, chance] [Archaic] **1.** possibly **2.** by chance

per·am·bu·late (pər am′byoo lāt′) *vt.* **-lat′ed, -lat′-ing** [< L. *per*, through + *ambulare*, to walk] to walk (through, over, etc.) —**per·am′bu·la′tion** *n.*

per·am′bu·la′tor (-lāt′ər) *n.* [Chiefly Brit.] a baby carriage

per an·num (pər an′əm) [L.] by the year; yearly

per·cale (pər kāl′, -kal′) *n.* [Fr. < Per. *pargāla*] closely woven cotton cloth, used for sheets, etc.

per cap·i·ta (pər kap′ə tə) [ML., lit., by heads] for each person

per·ceive (pər sēv′) *vt., vi.* **-ceived′, -ceiv′ing** [< L. *per*, through + *capere*, take] **1.** to grasp mentally **2.** to become aware (of) through the senses —**per·ceiv′a·ble** *adj.* —**per·ceiv′a·bly** *adv.*

per·cent (pər sent′) *adv., adj.* [< It. < L. *per centum*] in, to, or for every hundred [a twenty *percent* rate means 20 in every hundred] : symbol, %: also **per cent** —*n.* [Colloq.] percentage

per·cent′age (-ij) *n.* **1.** a given part in every hundred **2.** part; portion [a *percentage* of the audience] **3.** [Colloq.] advantage; profit

per·cen·tile (pər sen′til, -sent′'l) *n. Statistics* any of 100 divisions of a series, each of equal frequency

per·cep·ti·ble (pər sep′tə b'l) *adj.* that can be perceived —**per·cep′ti·bil′i·ty** *n.* —**per·cep′ti·bly** *adv.*

per·cep·tion (-shən) *n.* [< L. *percipere*, perceive] **1.** the mental grasp of objects, etc. through the senses **2.** insight or intuition **3.** knowledge, etc. gained by perceiving

per·cep·tive *adj.* **1.** of or capable of perception **2.** able to perceive quickly —**per·cep′tive·ness** *n.*

perch[1] (purch) *n., pl.* **perch, perch′es** [< Gr. *perkē*] **1.** a small, spiny-finned, freshwater food fish **2.** a similar bony, usually saltwater, fish

perch[2] (purch) *n.* [< L. *pertica*, a pole] **1.** a horizontal pole, branch, etc. serving as a roost for birds **2.** any high resting place **3.** *a*) a measure of length, equal to 5 1/2 yards *b*) a measure of area, equal to 30 1/4 square yards —*vt., vi.* to rest or place on or as on a perch

per·chance (pər chans′) *adv.* [< OFr. *par*, by + *chance*, chance] [Archaic] **1.** by chance **2.** perhaps

Per·che·ron (pur'chə rän', -shə-) *n.* [Fr. < *Perche,* region in France] a breed of large draft horses

Per·ci·vale, Per·ci·val (pur'sə v'l) a knight in Arthurian legend, who saw the Holy Grail

per·co·late (pur'kə lāt') *vt.* **-lat'ed, -lat'ing** [< L. *per,* through + *colare,* to strain] **1.** to pass (a liquid) through a porous substance; filter **2.** to brew (coffee) in a percolator —*vi.* to ooze through a porous substance —**per'co·la'tion** *n.*

per'co·la'tor *n.* a coffeepot in which boiling water bubbles up through a tube and filters back down through the ground coffee

per·cus·sion (pər kush'ən) *n.* [< L. *percutere,* to strike] **1.** the hitting of one body against another, as the hammer of a firearm against a powder cap (**percussion cap**) **2.** *Med.* the tapping of the chest, back, etc. with the fingers to determine from the sound produced the condition of internal organs

percussion instrument a musical instrument producing a tone when struck, as a drum, cymbal, etc.

per·cus'sion·ist *n.* a musician who plays percussion instruments

per di·em (pər dē'əm, dī'-) [L.] daily; by the day

per·di·tion (pər dish'ən) *n.* [< L. *perdere,* lose] *Theol.* **1.** the loss of the soul **2.** *same as* HELL

per·e·gri·nate (per'ə gri nāt') *vt., vi.* **-nat'ed, -nat'ing** [see PILGRIM] to travel, esp. walk (along or through) — **per'e·gri·na'tion** *n.*

per·e·grine (falcon) (per'ə grin, -grēn') [see prec.] a very swift European falcon: used in falconry

per·emp·to·ry (pə remp'tər ē) *adj.* [< L. *perimere,* destroy] **1.** *Law* barring further action; final **2.** that cannot be denied, delayed, etc., as a command **3.** intolerantly positive; dogmatic —**per·emp'to·ri·ly** *adv.* —**per·emp'to·ri·ness** *n.*

per·en·ni·al (pə ren'ē əl) *adj.* [< L. *per,* through + *annus,* year] **1.** lasting throughout the whole year **2.** continuing for a long time **3.** living more than two years: said of plants —*n.* a perennial plant —**per·en'ni·al·ly** *adv.*

perf. 1. perfect **2.** perforated

per·fect (pur'fikt; *for v. usually* pər fekt') *adj.* [< L. *per,* through + *facere,* to do] **1.** complete in all respects; flawless **2.** excellent, as in skill or quality **3.** completely accurate; exact **4.** utter; absolute *[a perfect fool]* **5.** *Gram.* expressing a state or action completed at the time of speaking or the time indicated —*vt.* **1.** to complete **2.** to make perfect or more nearly perfect —*n.* **1.** the perfect tense **2.** a verb form in this tense —**per·fect'er** *n.* —**per'fect·ly** *adv.* —**per'fect·ness** *n.*

per·fect·i·ble (pər fek'tə b'l) *adj.* that can become, or be made, perfect or more nearly perfect

per·fec·tion (pər fek'shən) *n.* **1.** the act of perfecting **2.** a being perfect **3.** a person or thing that is the perfect embodiment of some quality —**to perfection** completely; perfectly

per·fec'tion·ist *n.* one who strives for perfection

per·fec·to (pər fek'tō) *n., pl.* **-tos** [Sp., perfect] a cigar of standard shape, thick in the center and tapering to a point at each end

per·fi·dy (pur'fə dē) *n., pl.* **-dies** [< Fr. < L. *per fidem* (*decipi*), (deceive) through faith] betrayal of trust; treachery —**per·fid·i·ous** (pər fid'ē əs) *adj.*

per·fo·rate (pur'fə rāt') *vt., vi.* **-rat'ed, -rat'ing** [< L. *per,* through + *forare,* to bore] **1.** to make a hole or holes through, as by boring **2.** to pierce with holes in a row, as a pattern, computer tape, etc. —*adj.* (-rit, -rāt') pierced with holes: also **per'fo·rat'ed** —**per'fo·ra'tor** *n.*

per'fo·ra'tion *n.* **1.** a perforating or being perforated **2.** any of a series of punched holes, as those between postage stamps on a sheet

per·force (pər fôrs') *adv.* [< OFr.: see PER & FORCE] of necessity; necessarily

per·form (pər fôrm') *vt.* [< OFr. *parfournir*] **1.** to do (a task, process, etc.) **2.** to fulfill (a promise, etc.) **3.** to render or enact (a piece of music, dramatic role, etc.) —*vi.* to execute an action or process; esp., to act in a play, dance, etc. —**per·form'er** *n.*

per·form'ance *n.* **1.** the act of performing **2.** functional effectiveness **3.** a deed or feat **4.** *a)* a formal exhibition or presentation, as a play *b)* one's part in this

performing arts arts, such as drama, dance, and music, for performance before an audience

per·fume (pər fyoom') *vt.* **-fumed', -fum'ing** [< L. *per-,* intens. + *fumare,* to smoke] **1.** to fill with a pleasing odor **2.** to put perfume on —*n.* (*usually* pur'fyoom) **1.** a sweet scent; fragrance **2.** a substance producing a pleasing odor; esp., a volatile oil extracted from flowers

per·fum'er *n.* **1.** one who makes or sells perfumes **2.** one who or that which perfumes

per·fum'er·y (-ər ē) *n., pl.* **-ies 1.** the trade or art of a perfumer **2.** perfumes collectively **3.** a place where perfume is made or sold

per·func·to·ry (pər funk'tər ē) *adj.* [< L. *per-,* intens. + *fungi,* to perform] **1.** done merely as a routine; superficial **2.** without concern; indifferent —**per·func'to·ri·ly** *adv.* — **per·func'to·ri·ness** *n.*

per·go·la (pur'gə lə) *n.* [It. < L. *pergula*] an arbor with a latticework roof

per·haps (pər haps') *adv.* [PER- + pl. of *hap,* chance] possibly; maybe

pe·ri (pir'ē) *n.* [Per. *parī*] Persian Myth. a fairy or elf

peri- [< Gr. *peri*] *a prefix meaning:* **1.** around; about *[periscope]* **2.** near *[perigee]*

per·i·anth (per'ē anth') *n.* [< Gr. *peri-,* around + *anthos,* a flower] the outer envelope of a flower, including the calyx and corolla

per·i·car·di·tis (per'ə kär dīt'is) *n.* inflammation of the pericardium

per·i·car·di·um (-kär'dē əm) *n., pl.* **-di·a** (-ə) [< Gr. *peri-,* around + *kardia,* heart] the thin, membranous sac around the heart

per·i·carp (per'ə kärp') *n.* [< Gr. *peri-,* around + *karpos,* a fruit] *Bot.* the wall of a ripened ovary

Per·i·cles (per'ə klēz') 495?-429 B.C.; Athenian statesman & general —**Per'i·cle'an** (-klē'ən) *adj.*

per·i·gee (per'ə jē') *n.* [< Fr. < Gr. *peri-,* near + *gē,* earth] the point nearest the moon, the earth, or another planet, in the orbit of a satellite or spacecraft around it

per·i·he·li·on (per'ə hē'lē ən) *n., pl.* **-li·ons, -li·a** (-ə) [< Gr. *peri-,* around + *hēlios,* the sun] the point nearest the sun in the orbit around it of a planet, comet, or manmade satellite: cf. APHELION

per·il (per'əl) *n.* [< L. *periculum,* danger] **1.** exposure to harm or injury; danger **2.** something that may cause harm —*vt.* **-iled** or **-illed, -il·ing** or **-il·ling** to expose to danger

per'il·ous *adj.* involving peril or risk; dangerous —**per'il·ous·ly** *adv.* —**per'il·ous·ness** *n.*

pe·rim·e·ter (pə rim'ə tər) *n.* [< Gr. *peri-,* around + *metron,* a measure] **1.** the outer boundary of a figure or area **2.** the total length of this

pe·ri·od (pir'ē əd) *n.* [< Gr. *periodos,* a cycle] **1.** the interval between successive occurrences of an event **2.** a portion of time characterized by certain processes, etc. *[a period of change]* **3.** any of the portions of time into which a game, school day, etc. is divided **4.** the menses **5.** an end or conclusion **6.** *a)* a complete sentence *b)* the pause in speaking or a mark of punctuation (.) used at the end of a sentence *c)* the dot (.) following many abbreviations **7.** a subdivision of a geologic era **8.** *Physics* the interval of time necessary for a complete cycle of a regularly recurring motion

pe·ri·od·ic (pir'ē äd'ik) *adj.* **1.** appearing or recurring at regular intervals **2.** intermittent **3.** of a sentence (**periodic sentence**) in which the essential elements are withheld until the end

pe'ri·od'i·cal *adj.* **1.** *same as* PERIODIC **2.** published at regular intervals, as weekly, monthly, etc. **3.** of a periodical —*n.* a periodical publication —**pe'ri·od'i·cal·ly** *adv.*

pe·ri·o·dic·i·ty (pir'ē ō dis'ə tē) *n., pl.* **-ties** the tendency or fact of recurring at regular intervals

periodic law the law that properties of chemical elements recur periodically when the elements are arranged in order of their atomic numbers

periodic table an arrangement of the chemical elements according to their atomic numbers, to exhibit the periodic law

per·i·o·don·tal (per'ē ə dän't'l) *adj.* [< PERI- + Gr. *odōn,* tooth] occurring around a tooth or affecting the gums

per·i·pa·tet·ic (per'i pə tet'ik) *adj.* [< Fr. < Gr. *peri-,* around + *patein,* to walk] **1.** [P-] of the philosophy or followers of Aristotle **2.** walking or moving about; itinerant

pe·riph·er·y (pə rif'ər ē) *n., pl.* **-ies** [< Gr. *peri-,* around + *pherein,* to bear] **1.** an outer boundary, esp. of a rounded figure **2.** surrounding space or area —**pe·riph'er·al** *adj.*

pe·riph·ra·sis (pə rif'rə sis) *n., pl.* **-ses'** (-sēz') [< Gr. *peri-,* around + *phrazein,* speak] the use of many words where a few would do

per·i·phras·tic (per'ə fras'tik) *adj.* **1.** of or using periphrasis **2.** *Gram.* formed with a particle or auxiliary verb instead of by inflection, as the phrase *did sing* for *sang*

per·i·scope (per′ə skōp′) *n.* [PERI- + -SCOPE] an optical instrument equipped with reflecting elements that allows one to see around or over an obstacle: used on submarines, etc.

per·ish (per′ish) *vi.* [< L. *per-*, intens. + *ire*, go] **1.** to be destroyed or ruined **2.** to die, esp. violently

per′ish·a·ble *adj.* that may perish; esp., liable to spoil, as some foods —*n.* something, esp. a food, liable to spoil or deteriorate —**per′ish·a·bil′i·ty** *n.*

per·i·stal·sis (per′ə stôl′sis, -stal′-) *n.,* PERISCOPE *pl.* **-ses** (-sēz) [< Gr. *peri-*, around + *stellein*, to place] the wavelike contractions and dilations of the walls of the alimentary canal and certain other hollow organs that move the contents onward —**per′i·stal′tic** *adj.*

per·i·to·ne·um (per′it ′n ē′əm) *n., pl.* **-ne′a** (-ə), **-ne′ums** [< Gr. *peri-*, around + *teinein*, to stretch] the serous membrane lining the abdominal cavity and covering the visceral organs

per·i·to·ni·tis (per′it ′n īt′əs) *n.* inflammation of the peritoneum

per·i·wig (per′ə wig′) *n.* [< Fr. *perruque*] a wig worn by men in the 17th and 18th cent.

per·i·win·kle¹ (per′ə wiŋ′k′l) *n.* [< L. *pervinca*] a European creeper with blue, white, or pink flowers

per·i·win·kle² (per′ə wiŋ′k′l) *n.* [OE. *pinewincle*] a small saltwater snail with a thick, cone-shaped shell

per·jure (pur′jər) *vt.* **-jured, -jur·ing** [< L. *per*, through + *jurare*, swear] to make (oneself) guilty of perjury —**per′jur·er** *n.*

per′ju·ry (-jər ē) *n., pl.* **-ries** [< L. *perjurus*, false] the willful telling of a lie while under oath

perk¹ (purk) *vt.* [ME. *perken*] **1.** to raise (the head, ears, etc.) briskly **2.** to make smart in appearance (often with *up*) —*vi.* to become lively (with *up*)

perk² (purk) *vt., vi. colloq.* clip of PERCOLATE

perk·y (pur′kē) *adj.* **-i·er, -i·est 1.** aggressive; self-confident **2.** gay or lively; sprightly —**perk′i·ly** *adv.* —**perk′i·ness** *n.*

per·ma·frost (pur′mə frôst′, -fräst′) *n.* [PERMA(NENT) + FROST] permanently frozen subsoil

per·ma·nent (pur′mə nənt) *adj.* [< L. *per*, through + *manere*, remain] lasting or intended to last indefinitely or for a long time —*n. colloq.* clip of PERMANENT WAVE — **per′ma·nence** *n.* —**per′ma·nent·ly** *adv.*

permanent wave a hair wave produced by use of chemicals or heat and lasting through many washings

per·me·a·ble (pur′mē ə b′l) *adj.* that can be permeated, as by fluids —**per′me·a·bil′i·ty** *n.*

per·me·ate (pur′mē āt′) *vt.* **-at′ed, -at′ing** [< L. *per*, through + *meare*, to glide] to pass into and affect every part of; spread through —*vi.* to spread (*through* or *among*) —**per′me·a′tion** *n.*

per·mis·si·ble (pər mis′ə b′l) *adj.* that can be permitted; allowable —**per·mis′si·bly** *adv.*

per·mis·sion (pər mish′ən) *n.* the act of permitting; esp., formal consent

per·mis·sive (pər mis′iv) *adj.* **1.** that permits **2.** allowing freedom; lenient —**per·mis′sive·ly** *adv.* —**per·mis′sive·ness** *n.*

per·mit (pər mit′) *vt.* **-mit′ted, -mit′ting** [< L. *per*, through + *mittere*, send] **1.** to allow to be done; consent to [smoking is not *permitted*] **2.** to authorize [permit me to go] **3.** to give opportunity for [to *permit* light to enter] —*vi.* to give opportunity [if time *permits*] —*n.* (usually pur′mit) a document granting permission; license

per·mu·ta·tion (pur′myoo tā′shən) *n.* **1.** any radical alteration **2.** *Math.* any of the total number of groupings into which a group of elements can be arranged

per·ni·cious (pər nish′əs) *adj.* [< Fr. L. *per*, thoroughly + *necare*, kill] causing great injury, destruction, etc.; deadly —**per·ni′cious·ly** *adv.* —**per·ni′cious·ness** *n.*

pernicious anemia a form of anemia characterized by a reduction of the red blood cells, nervous disturbances, etc.

per·o·ra·tion (per′ə rā′shən) *n.* [< L. *per*, through + *orare*, speak] the concluding part of a speech, including a summing up

per·ox·ide (pə räk′sīd) *n.* [< L. *per*, through + OXIDE] any oxide containing the oxygen (O_2) group linked by a single bond; specif., hydrogen peroxide —*vt.* **-id·ed, -id·ing** to bleach with hydrogen peroxide

per·pen·dic·u·lar (pur′pən dik′yə lər) *adj.* [< L. *perpendiculum*, plumb line] **1.** at right angles to a given line or plane **2.** exactly upright; vertical —*n.* **1.** a line at right angles to another line or plane **2.** a perpendicular position —**per′pen·dic′u·lar·ly** *adv.*

per·pe·trate (pur′pə trāt′) *vt.* **-trat′ed, -trat′ing** [< L. *per*, thoroughly + *patrare*, to effect] **1.** to do (something evil, criminal, etc.) **2.** to commit (a blunder), impose (a hoax), etc. —**per′pe·tra′tion** *n.* —**per′pe·tra′tor** *n.*

per·pet·u·al (pər pech′oo wəl) *adj.* [< L. *perpetuus*, constant] **1.** lasting forever or for a very long time **2.** continuing without interruption; constant —**per·pet′u·al·ly** *adv.*

perpetual motion the motion of a hypothetical device which, once set in motion, would operate indefinitely by creating its own energy

per·pet′u·ate′ (-wāt′) *vt.* **-at′ed, -at′ing** to make perpetual; cause to continue or be remembered —**per·pet′u·a′tion** *n.*

per·pe·tu·i·ty (pur′pə tōō′ə tē, -tyōō′-) *n.* unlimited time; eternity —**in perpetuity** forever

per·plex (pər pleks′) *vt.* [< L. *per*, through + *plectere*, to twist] to make (a person) uncertain, hesitant, etc.; confuse —**per·plexed′** *adj.* —**per·plex′ing** *adj.* —**per·plex′ing·ly** *adv.*

per·plex′i·ty *n.* **1.** the state of being perplexed **2.** *pl.* **-ties** something that perplexes

per·qui·site (pur′kwə zit) *n.* [< L. *per-*, intens. + *quaerere*, seek] **1.** something in addition to one's regular pay for one's work, as a tip **2.** a privilege or benefit to which a person, institution, etc. is entitled because of status, position, etc.

pers. **1.** person **2.** personal

per se (pur′ sē′, sā′) [L.] by (or in) itself; intrinsically

per·se·cute (pur′sə kyōot′) *vt.* **-cut′ed, -cut′ing** [< L. *per*, through + *sequi*, follow) to afflict constantly so as to injure or distress, esp. for reasons of religion, race, etc. — **per′se·cu′tion** *n.* —**per′se·cu′tor** *n.*

Per·seph·o·ne (pər sef′ə nē) *Gr. Myth.* the daughter of Demeter, abducted by Pluto to be his wife

Per·seus (pur′syoos, -sē əs) *Gr. Myth.* a son of Zeus and the slayer of Medusa

per·se·ver·ance (pur′sə vir′əns) *n.* **1.** the act of persevering **2.** persistence; steadfastness

per·se·vere (pur′sə vir′) *vi.* **-vered′, -ver′ing** [< L. *per-*, intens. + *severus*, severe] to continue in some effort, course of action, etc. in spite of difficulty, opposition, etc.; persist

Per·sia (pur′zhə) *former official name of* IRAN —**Per′sian** *adj., n.*

Persian Gulf arm of the Arabian Sea, between Iran and Arabia

Persian lamb the pelt of karakul lambs

per·si·flage (pur′sə fläzh′) *n.* [Fr. < L. *per*, through + *sifilare*, to whistle] light, frivolous talk or writing

per·sim·mon (pər sim′ən) *n.* [< AmInd.] **1.** a hardwood tree with plumlike fruit **2.** the fruit, sour when green, but sweet and edible when ripe

per·sist (pər sist′, -zist′) *vi.* [< L. *per*, through + *sistere*, cause to stand] **1.** to refuse to give up, esp. when faced with opposition **2.** to continue insistently **3.** to endure; remain; last

per·sist′ent *adj.* **1.** continuing, esp. in the face of opposition, etc. **2.** continuing to exist or endure **3.** constantly repeated —**per·sist′ence, per·sist′en·cy** *n.* —**per·sist′ent·ly** *adv.*

per·snick·e·ty (pər snik′ə tē) *adj.* [< Scot. dial.] [Colloq.] too particular or precise; fussy

per·son (pur′s′n) *n.* [< L. *persona*] **1.** a human being **2.** the human body **3.** personality; self **4.** *Gram.* division into three sets of pronouns, and, usually, corresponding verb forms, to identify the subject: see FIRST PERSON, SECOND PERSON, THIRD PERSON —**in person** actually present

-person *a combining form meaning* person in a specified activity: used to avoid the masculine implications of *-man* [chairperson]

per′son·a·ble (-ə b′l) *adj.* having a pleasing appearance and personality

per′son·age (-ij) *n.* **1.** an important person; notable **2.** any person

per′son·al (-əl) *adj.* **1.** private; individual **2.** done in person **3.** involving human beings **4.** of the body or physical appearance **5.** *a)* having to do with the character, con-

duct, etc. of a certain person [a *personal* remark] b) tending to make personal, esp. derogatory, remarks **6.** of or like a person or rational being **7.** *Gram.* indicating person (sense 4) **8.** *Law* of property (**personal property**) that is movable —*n.* **1.** a local news item about a person or persons **2.** a classified advertisement about a personal matter
personal effects personal belongings, esp. those worn or carried
per·son·al·i·ty (pur'sə nal'ə tē) *n., pl.* -ties **1.** the quality or fact of being a person or a particular person **2.** distinctive individual qualities of a person, considered collectively **3.** *a)* the sum of such qualities as impressing others *b)* personal attractiveness **4.** a notable person **5.** [*pl.*] offensive remarks aimed at a person
per·son·al·ize (pur's'n ə līz') *vt.* -ized', -iz'ing **1.** to apply to a particular person, esp. to oneself **2.** *same as* PERSONIFY **3.** to have marked with one's name or initials
per·son·al·ly *adv.* **1.** in person **2.** as a person [I dislike him *personally*] **3.** in one's own opinion **4.** as though directed at oneself [to take a remark *personally*]
‡**per·so·na non gra·ta** (pər sō'nə nän grät'ə) [L.] a person who is not acceptable
per·son·i·fy (pər sän'ə fī') *vt.* -fied', -fy'ing [< Fr.] **1.** to think of or represent (a thing) as a person **2.** to symbolize (an abstract idea) by a human figure, as in art **3.** to be a perfect example of; typify —**per·son'i·fi·ca'tion** *n.*
per·son·nel (pur'sə nel') *n.* [Fr.] **1.** persons employed in any work, enterprise, service, etc. **2.** a department or office for hiring employees, etc. —*adj.* of or in charge of personnel
per·spec·tive (pər spek'tiv) *n.* [< L. *per*, through + *specere*, to look] **1.** the art of picturing objects so as to show relative distance or depth **2.** the appearance of objects as determined by their relative distance and positions **3.** a specific point of view in judging things or events **4.** the ability to see things in a true relationship
per·spi·ca·cious (pur'spə kā'shəs) *adj.* [see PERSPECTIVE] having keen judgment; discerning —**per'spi·cac'i·ty** (-kas'ə tē) *n.*
per·spic·u·ous (pər spik'yoo wəs) *adj.* [see PERSPECTIVE] easily understood; lucid —**per·spi·cu·i·ty** (pur'spə kyōo'ə tē) *n.*
per·spi·ra·tion (pur'spə rā'shən) *n.* **1.** the act of perspiring **2.** sweat
per·spire (pər spīr') *vt., vi.* -spired', -spir'ing [< Fr. < L. *per*, through + *spirare*, breathe] to sweat
per·suade (pər swād') *vt.* -suad'ed, -suad'ing [< L. *per-*, intens. + *suadere*, to urge] to cause to do or believe something, esp. by reasoning, urging, etc.; convince —**per·suad'er** *n.*
per·sua·sion (pər swā'zhən) *n.* **1.** a persuading or being persuaded **2.** power of persuading **3.** a strong belief **4.** a particular religious belief
per·sua·sive *adj.* having the power, or tending, to persuade —**per·sua'sive·ly** *adv.* —**per·sua'sive·ness** *n.*
pert (purt) *adj.* [< L. *apertus*, open] bold; impudent; saucy —**pert'ly** *adv.* —**pert'ness** *n.*
per·tain (pər tān') *vi.* [< L. *per-*, intens. + *tenere*, to hold] **1.** to belong; be connected or associated **2.** to have reference [laws *pertaining* to the case]
Perth (purth) seaport in W Australia: pop. 626,000
per·ti·na·cious (pur'tə nā'shəs) *adj.* [< L. *per-*, intens. + *tenax*, holding fast] **1.** holding firmly to some purpose, belief, etc. **2.** hard to get rid of —**per'ti·nac'i·ty** (-nas'ə tē) *n.*
per·ti·nent (pur't'n ənt) *adj.* [see PERTAIN] of or connected with the matter at hand; relevant —**per'ti·nence** *n.* —**per'ti·nent·ly** *adv.*
per·turb (pər turb') *vt.* [< L. *per-*, intens. + *turbare*, disturb] to cause to be alarmed, agitated, or upset —**per·tur·ba·tion** (pur'tər bā'shən) *n.*
per·tus·sis (pər tus'is) *n.* [< L. *per-*, intens. + *tussis*, a cough] *same as* WHOOPING COUGH
Pe·ru (pə rōo') country in W S. America: 496,222 sq. mi.; pop. 13,586,000; cap. Lima —**Pe·ru'vi·an** (-vē ən) *adj., n.*
pe·ruke (pə rōok') *n.* [< Fr. *perruque*] *same as* PERIWIG
pe·rus·al (pə rōo'z'l) *n.* a perusing
pe·ruse (pə rōoz') *vt.* -rused', -rus'ing [prob. < L. *per-*, intens. + ME. *usen*, to use] **1.** to read carefully; study **2.** to read
per·vade (pər vād') *vt.* -vad'ed, -vad'ing [< L. *per*, through + *vadere*, go] to spread or be prevalent throughout
per·va·sive (-vā'siv) *adj.* tending to spread throughout —**per·va'sive·ly** *adv.* —**per·va'sive·ness** *n.*
per·verse (pər vurs') *adj.* [see PERVERT] **1.** deviating from what is considered right or good **2.** stubbornly contrary **3.**

obstinately disobedient —**per·verse'ly** *adv.* —**per·verse'·ness**, per·ver'si·ty *n., pl.* -ties
per·ver·sion (-vur'zhən) *n.* **1.** a perverting or being perverted **2.** something perverted **3.** any sexual act or practice considered abnormal
per·vert (pər vurt') *vt.* [< L. *per-*, intens. + *vertere*, to turn] **1.** to lead astray; corrupt **2.** to misuse **3.** to change the meaning of; distort **4.** to debase —*n.* (pur'vərt) a perverted person; esp., one who practices sexual perversion —**per·vert'ed** *adj.*
per·vi·ous (pur'vē əs) *adj.* [< L. *per*, through + *via*, way] allowing passage through; permeable
pe·se·ta (pə sät'ə) *n.* [Sp., dim. of *peso*, PESO] the monetary unit and a coin of Spain
pes·ky (pes'kē) *adj.* -ki·er, -ki·est [prob. < PEST + -Y²] [Colloq.] annoying; troublesome —**pes'ki·ness** *n.*
pe·so (pā'sō) *n., pl.* -sos [Sp. < L. *pendere*, weigh] the monetary unit and a coin of various Spanish-speaking countries
pes·si·mism (pes'ə miz'm) *n.* [< Fr. < L. *pejor*, worse] **1.** the belief that the evil in life outweighs the good **2.** the tendency to expect the worst outcome in any circumstances —**pes'si·mist** *n.* —**pes'si·mis'tic** *adj.* —**pes'si·mis'ti·cal·ly** *adv.*
pest (pest) *n.* [< Fr. < L. *pestis*, a plague] a person or thing that causes trouble, annoyance, etc.; specif., any destructive insect, small animal, weed, etc.
pes·ter (pes'tər) *vt.* [< OFr. *empestrer*, entangle] to annoy repeatedly with petty irritations; vex
pest'hole' *n.* a place infested or likely to be infested with an epidemic disease
pes·ti·cide (pes'tə sīd') *n.* any chemical used for killing insects, weeds, etc.
pes·tif·er·ous (pes tif'ər əs) *adj.* [< L. *pestis*, a plague + *ferre*, to bear] **1.** orig., diseased or carrying disease **2.** dangerous to society **3.** [Colloq.] annoying; bothersome
pes·ti·lence (pes't'l əns) *n.* [< L. *pestis*, a plague] **1.** any virulent, contagious or infectious disease, esp. one of epidemic proportions **2.** anything regarded as harmful —**pes'ti·len'tial** (-tə len'shəl) *adj.*
pes'ti·lent *adj.* [see prec.] **1.** likely to cause death **2.** dangerous to society **3.** annoying
pes·tle (pes''l) *n.* [< L. *pinsere*, to pound] **1.** a tool used to pound or grind substances, esp. in a mortar **2.** a heavy bar for pounding or stamping —*vt., vi.* -tled, -tling to pound, grind, etc. with a pestle
pet¹ (pet) *n.* [orig. Scot. dial.] **1.** an animal that is domesticated and kept as a companion or treated with fondness **2.** a person treated with particular indulgence —*adj.* **1.** kept or treated as a pet **2.** especially liked; favorite **3.** particular [a *pet* peeve] —*vt.* pet'ted, pet'ting **1.** to stroke or pat gently; caress **2.** to pamper —*vi.* [Colloq.] to kiss, embrace, etc. amorously
pet² (pet) *n.* [< ?] a sulky mood
pet·al (pet''l) *n.* [< Gr. *petalos*, outspread] any of the leaflike parts of a blossom —**pet'aled, pet'alled** *adj.*
pe·tard (pi tärd') *n.* [Fr. < L. *pedere*, break wind] an explosive device formerly used to break down gates, walls, etc. —**hoist with** (or **by**) **one's own petard** destroyed by the very thing with which one meant to destroy others
pet·cock (pet'käk') *n.* [< L. *pedere*, break wind + COCK¹] a small valve for draining unwanted water or air from pipes, boilers, etc.
Pe·ter (pēt'ər) **1.** *Bible* one of the twelve Apostles; reputed author of two Epistles; lived ?-64? A.D.: also **Saint Peter 2. Peter I** 1672-1725; czar of Russia (1682-1725): called *Peter the Great*
pe·ter (pēt'ər) *vi.* [< ?] [Colloq.] to become gradually smaller, weaker, etc. and then cease (with *out*)
pet·i·ole (pet'ē ōl') *n.* [< L. *pes*, a foot] *Bot. same as* LEAFSTALK —**pet'i·o·late'** (-ə lāt') *adj.*
pet·it (pet'ē) *adj.* [OFr.] small; petty: now used chiefly in law
pe·tite (pə tēt') *adj.* [Fr.] small and trim in figure: said of a woman
pe·tit four (pet'ē fôr') *pl.* pe·tits fours (pet'ē fôrz'), pe'tit fours' [Fr., lit., small oven] a small cake cut from spongecake, etc. and decorated with icing
pe·ti·tion (pə tish'ən) *n.* [< L. *petere*, ask] **1.** a solemn, earnest request; entreaty **2.** a formal document embodying such a request, often signed by a number of persons **3.** something that is entreated —*vt.* **1.** to address a petition to **2.** to ask for —*vi.* to make a petition —**pe·ti'tion·er** *n.*
petit jury a group of twelve citizens picked to weigh the evidence in and decide the issues of a trial in court
Pe·trarch (pē'trärk) 1304-74; It. poet

pet·rel (pet'rəl) *n.* [< ? St. *Peter:* cf. Matt. 14:29] a small, dark sea bird with long wings

pet·ri·fy (pet'rə fī') *vt.* **-fied'**, **-fy'ing** [< Fr. < L. *petra*, a rock + *facere*, make] **1.** to replace the normal cells of (organic matter) with silica, etc.; re-form as a stony substance **2.** to harden or deaden **3.** to paralyze, as with fear —*vi.* to become petrified —**pet'ri·fac'tion** (-fak'shən), **pet'·ri·fi·ca'tion** (-fi kā'shən) *n.*

pet·ro·chem·i·cal (pet'rō kem'i k'l) *n.* a chemical derived ultimately from petroleum

pet·rol (pet'rəl) *n.* [< Fr.: see PETROLEUM] *Brit. term for* GASOLINE

pet·ro·la·tum (pet'rə lāt'əm) *n.* [< PETROLEUM] a greasy, jellylike substance derived from petroleum and used for ointments, etc.

pe·tro·le·um (pə trō'lē əm) *n.* [< L. *petra*, a rock + *oleum*, oil] an oily, liquid solution of hydrocarbons occurring naturally in certain rock strata: it yields kerosene, gasoline, etc.

petroleum jelly *same as* PETROLATUM

pe·trol·o·gy (pi träl'ə jē) *n.* [< Gr. *petra*, a rock + -LOGY] the study of the composition, structure, and origin of rocks —**pe·trol'o·gist** *n.*

pet·ti·coat (pet'i kōt') *n.* [< PETTY + COAT] a woman's underskirt —*adj.* of or by women

pet·ti·fog·ger (pet'ē fäg'ər, -fôg'-) *n.* [PETTY + obs. *fogger* < ?] **1.** a lawyer who handles petty cases, esp. in an unethical manner **2.** a cheater —**pet'ti·fog'** *vi.* **-fogged'**, **-fog'ging**

pet·tish (pet'ish) *adj.* [< PET²] peevish; petulant —**pet'·tish·ly** *adv.* —**pet'tish·ness** *n.*

pet·ty (pet'ē) *adj.* **-ti·er**, **-ti·est** [OFr. *petit*] **1.** relatively unimportant **2.** narrow-minded, mean, etc. **3.** relatively low in rank —**pet'ti·ness** *n.*

petty cash a cash fund for incidental expenses

petty jury *same as* PETIT JURY

petty officer a naval enlisted man whose grade corresponds to that of a noncommissioned army officer

pet·u·lant (pech'ōō lənt) *adj.* [< L. *petere*, to attack] impatient or irritable, esp. over a petty annoyance —**pet'u·lance** *n.* —**pet'u·lant·ly** *adv.*

pe·tu·ni·a (pə tōōn'yə, -ē ə) *n.* [< Tupi *petun*, tobacco] a plant with variously colored, funnel-shaped flowers

pew (pyōō) *n.* [< Gr. *pous*, foot] any of the benches with a back fixed in rows in a church

pe·wee (pē'wē) *n.* [echoic of its call] any of several small flycatchers

pe·wit (pē'wit, pyōō'it) *n.* [echoic of its call] *same as:* **1.** LAPWING **2.** PEEWEE

pew·ter (pyōō'tər) *n.* [OFr. *peautre*] **1.** a dull, silvery-gray alloy of tin with brass, copper, or, esp., lead **2.** articles made of pewter —*adj.* made of pewter

pe·yo·te (pā ōt'ē) *n.* [AmSp. < AmInd. *peyotl*, caterpillar] *same as* MESCAL (sense 3)

pf., pfd. preferred

Pfc, Pfc., PFC Private First Class

pfen·nig (fen'ig; G. pfen'ikh) *n., pl.* **-nigs,** G. **-ni·ge** (-i gə) [G.] a German unit of currency equal to 1/100 deutsche mark or 1/100 mark

PG parental guidance suggested: a motion-picture rating cautioning parents that they may find the film unsuitable for children

pg. page

pH (pē'āch') [< Fr. *p*(*ouvoir*) *h*(*ydrogène*), hydrogen power] *a symbol for* the degree of acidity or alkalinity of a solution

pha·e·ton, pha·ë·ton (fā'ət 'n) *n.* [< Fr. < Gr. *Phaethōn*, son of Helios, sun god] **1.** a light, four-wheeled carriage **2.** an early type of open automobile

pha·lan·ger (fə lan'jər) *n.* [< Gr. *phalanx*, bone between two joints: from the structure of its hind feet] a small Australian marsupial with a long tail

pha·lanx (fā'laŋks) *n., pl.* **-lanx·es**, **pha·lan·ges** (fə lan'jēz) [Gr., line of battle] **1.** an ancient military formation of infantry in close ranks with shields together **2.** a massed group of individuals **3.** a group of individuals united for a common purpose **4.** *pl.* **-lan'ges** any of the bones of the fingers or toes

phal·lus (fal'əs) *n., pl.* **-li** (-ī), **-lus·es** [< Gr. *phallos*] an image of the penis as the reproductive organ —**phal'lic** *adj.*

phan·tasm (fan'taz'm) *n.* [< Gr. *phantazein*, to show] **1.** a figment of the mind; esp., a specter, or ghost **2.** a deceptive likeness

phan·tas·ma·go·ri·a (fan taz'mə gôr'ē ə) *n.* [< Fr. < Gr. *phantasma*, phantasm + *ageirein*, assemble] a rapidly changing series of things seen or imagined, as in a dream —**phan·tas'ma·go'ri·al, phan·tas'ma·go'ric** *adj.*

phan·ta·sy (fan'tə sē) *n., pl.* **-sies** *same as* FANTASY

phan·tom (fan'təm) *n.* [see FANTASY] **1.** an apparition; specter **2.** an illusion **3.** any mental image —*adj.* of or like a phantom; illusory

Phar·aoh (fer'ō) *n.* the title of the rulers of ancient Egypt

Phar·i·sa·ic (far'ə sā'ik) *adj.* **1.** of the Pharisees **2.** [p-] self-righteous or hypocritical: also **phar'i·sa'i·cal**

Phar·i·see (far'ə sē') *n.* **1.** a member of an ancient Jewish sect that rigidly observed both the written and the oral law **2.** [p-] a pharisaic person —**Phar'i·see'ism** *n.*

phar·ma·ceu·ti·cal (fär'mə sōōt'i k'l, -syōōt'-) *adj.* [< Gr. *pharmakon*, a medicine] **1.** of pharmacy or pharmacists **2.** of or by drugs Also **phar'ma·ceu'tic** —*n.* a drug or medicine

phar'ma·ceu'tics (-iks) *n.pl.* [*with sing. v.*] *same as* PHARMACY (sense 1)

phar·ma·cist (fär'mə sist) *n.* one licensed to practice pharmacy

phar·ma·col·o·gy (-käl'ə jē) *n.* [< Gr. *pharmakon*, a drug] the science dealing with the effect of drugs on living organisms —**phar'ma·co·log'i·cal** (-kə läj'i k'l) *adj.* —**phar'ma·col'o·gist** *n.*

phar·ma·co·pe·ia, phar'ma·co·poe'ia (-kə pē'ə) *n.* [< Gr. *pharmakon*, a drug + *poiein*, to make] an official book listing drugs and medicines, together with the legal standards for their production, etc.

phar·ma·cy (fär'mə sē) *n., pl.* **-cies** [< Gr. *pharmakon*, a drug] **1.** the art or profession of preparing and dispensing drugs and medicines **2.** a drugstore

phar·yn·gi·tis (far'in jīt'əs) *n.* inflammation of the pharynx; sore throat

phar·ynx (far'iŋks) *n., pl.* **phar'ynx·es**, **pha·ryn·ges** (fə rin'jēz) [Gr.] the cavity leading from the mouth and nasal passages to the larynx and esophagus —**pha·ryn·ge·al** (fə rin'jē əl) *adj.*

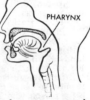

PHARYNX

phase (fāz) *n.* [< Gr. *phasis*] **1.** any stage in the illumination or appearance of the moon or a planet **2.** any stage in a series of changes, as in development **3.** an aspect or side, as of a problem **4.** a solid, liquid, or gaseous homogeneous form [ice is a *phase* of H₂O] **5.** the part of a cycle through which a periodic wave, as of light or sound, has advanced, with reference to a standard position —*vt.* **phased**, **phas'ing** to introduce, carry out, etc. in stages (often with *in, into,* etc.) —**in** (or **out of**) **phase** in (or not in) synchronization —**phase out** to bring to an end, or withdraw from use, by stages

phase'-out' *n.* a phasing out; gradual termination, withdrawal, etc.

Ph.D. Doctor of Philosophy

pheas·ant (fez''nt) *n.* [< Gr. *phasianos*, (bird) of *Phasis*, river in Asia] a chickenlike game bird with a long tail and brightly colored feathers

phen- [< Fr. < Gr. *phainein*, to show] *a combining form meaning* of or derived from benzene: also **pheno-**

phe·no·bar·bi·tal (fē'nə bär'bə tôl') *n.* a white crystalline powder used as a sedative

phe·nol (fē'nōl, -nôl) *n.* a white crystalline compound, corrosive and poisonous, used to make explosives, synthetic resins, etc. and, in dilute solution (*carbolic acid*), as an antiseptic

phe·nol·phthal·ein (fē'nōl thal'ēn, -nôl-) *n.* a white to pale-yellow powder used as a laxative and as an acid-base indicator in chemical analysis

phe·nom·e·nal (fi näm'ə n'l) *adj.* **1.** of or constituting a phenomenon or phenomena **2.** very unusual; extraordinary —**phe·nom'e·nal·ly** *adv.*

phe·nom·e·non (fi näm'ə nän', -nən) *n., pl.* **-na** (-nə); also, esp. for 3 & usually for 4, **-nons'** [< Gr. *phainesthai*, appear] **1.** any observable fact or event that can be scientifically described **2.** the appearance of something as distinguished from the thing in itself **3.** anything extremely unusual **4.** [Colloq.] an extraordinary person; prodigy

phen·yl (fen'il, fē'nil) *n.* [PHEN- + -YL] the monovalent radical C₆H₅, forming the basis of phenol, benzene, aniline, etc.

fat, āpe, cär; ten, ēven; is, bīte; gō, hôrn, tōōl, look; oil, out; up, fur; thin, *th*en; zh, leisure; ŋ, ring; ə for *a* in *ago*; ' as in *able* (ā'b'l); ë, Fr. coeur; ö, Fr. feu; Fr. mon; ü, Fr. duc; r, Fr. cri; kh, G. doch, ich. ‡ foreign; < derived from

phew (fyōō) *interj.* a breathy sound expressing disgust, surprise, etc.

phi (fī, fē) *n.* the 21st letter of the Greek alphabet (Φ, φ)

phi·al (fī'əl) *n.* [< Gr. *phialē*, shallow bowl] a small glass bottle; vial

Phi Be·ta Kap·pa (fī' bāt'ə kap'ə) **1.** an honorary society of U.S. college students of high scholastic rank **2.** a member of this society

Phid·i·as (fid'ē əs) 5th cent. B.C.; Gr. sculptor

Phil·a·del·phi·a (fil'ə del'fē ə) city & port in SE Pa.: pop. 1,949,000 (met. area 4,818,000)

Philadelphia lawyer [Colloq.] a shrewd or tricky lawyer

phi·lan·der (fi lan'dər) *vi.* [< Gr. *philos*, loving + *anēr*, a man] to engage lightly in love affairs: said of a man — **phi·lan'der·er** *n.*

phi·lan·thro·py (fi lan'thrə pē) *n.* [< Gr. *philein*, to love + *anthrōpos*, man] **1.** a desire to help mankind, esp. as shown by gifts to charitable or humanitarian institutions **2.** *pl.* **-pies** a philanthropic act, gift, etc. —**phil·an·throp·ic** (fil'ən thräp'ik) *adj.* —**phi·lan'thro·pist** *n.*

phi·lat·e·ly (fi lat'ʼl ē) *n.* [< Fr. < Gr. *philos*, loving + *ateleia*, exemption from (further) tax (i.e., postage prepaid)] the collection and study of postage stamps, postmarks, etc. —**phil·a·tel·ic** (fil'ə tel'ik) *adj.* —**phi·lat'e·list** *n.*

-phile [< Gr. *philos*, loving] *a combining form meaning* loving, liking

Phi·le·mon (fi lē'mən, fī-) a book of the New Testament: an epistle from the Apostle Paul to his friend Philemon

phil·har·mon·ic (fil'här män'ik) *adj.* [< Fr. < It. < Gr. *philos*, loving + *harmonia*, harmony] loving or devoted to music: used in the title of some symphony orchestras —*n.* **1.** a society sponsoring a symphony orchestra **2.** [Colloq.] such an orchestra

Phil·ip (fil'əp) **1.** *Bible* one of the twelve Apostles **2.** Philip II 382–336 B.C.; king of Macedonia (359–336): father of ALEXANDER THE GREAT

Phi·lip·pi·ans (fi lip'ē ənz) a book of the New Testament, an epistle of the Apostle Paul: abbrev. **Phil.**

Phi·lip·pic (fi lip'ik) *n.* **1.** any of the orations of Demosthenes against Philip, king of Macedonia **2.** [p-] any bitter verbal attack

Phil·ip·pine (fil'ə pēn') *adj.* of the Philippine Islands or their people

Phil·ip·pines (fil'ə pēnz') country consisting of c.7,100 islands (**Philippine Islands**) off the SE coast of Asia: 114,830 sq. mi.; pop. 43,751,000; cap. Manila

Phil·is·tine (fil'is tēn', fi lis'tin) *n.* **1.** any of a non-Semitic people of SW Palestine in Biblical times **2.** [often p-] a person who is smugly conventional, lacking in culture, etc. —*adj.* **1.** of the ancient Philistines **2.** [often p-] smugly conventional, lacking in culture, etc.

phil·o·den·dron (fil'ə den'drən) *n.* [< Gr. *philos*, loving + *dendron*, tree] a tropical American vine, often with heart-shaped leaves

phi·lol·o·gy (fi läl'ə jē) *n.* [< Fr. < Gr. *philein*, to love + *logos*, a word] **1.** the study of literary texts, etc. **2.** *earlier term for* LINGUISTICS —**phil·o·log·i·cal** (fil'ə läj'i k'l) *adj.* —**phi·lol'o·gist** *n.*

philos. philosophy

phi·los·o·pher (fi läs'ə fər) *n.* [< Gr. *philos*, loving + *sophos*, wise] **1.** one who is learned in philosophy **2.** one who lives by or expounds a system of philosophy **3.** one who meets difficulties with calm composure **4.** one given to philosophizing

phil·o·soph·ic (fil'ə säf'ik) *adj.* **1.** of a philosophy or a philosopher **2.** devoted to or learned in philosophy **3.** calm, as in a difficult situation; rational Also **phil'o·soph'i·cal** —**phil'o·soph'i·cal·ly** *adv.*

phi·los·o·phize (fi läs'ə fīz') *vi.* -phized', -phiz'ing **1.** to think or reason like a philosopher **2.** to moralize, express truisms, etc. —**phi·los'o·phiz'er** *n.*

phi·los·o·phy (-fē) *n., pl.* **-phies** [see PHILOSOPHER] **1.** theory or analysis of the principles underlying conduct, thought, knowledge, and the nature of the universe **2.** the general principles of a field of knowledge **3.** a particular system of ethics

phil·ter (fil'tər) *n.* [< Gr. *philein*, to love] a potion or charm thought to arouse sexual love

phle·bi·tis (fli bīt'is) *n.* [< Gr. *phleps*, vein + -ITIS] inflammation of a vein

phle·bot·o·my (fli bät'ə mē) *n.* [< Gr. *phleps*, vein + *temnein*, to cut] the act of bloodletting as a therapeutic measure

phlegm (flem) *n.* [< Gr. *phlegma*, inflammation] **1.** thick mucus discharged from the throat, as during a cold **2.** sluggishness; apathy

phleg·mat·ic (fleg mat'ik) *adj.* [see prec.] sluggish or unexcited —**phleg·mat'i·cal·ly** *adv.*

phlo·em (flō'em) *n.* [G. < Gr. *phloos*, bark] the cell tissue through which food is distributed in a plant

phlox (fläks) *n.* [Gr., a flame] a N. American plant with clusters of white, red, or bluish flowers

Phnom Penh (p'nôm' pen') capital of Kampuchea: pop. c.600,000

-phobe [Fr. < Gr. *phobos*, a fear] *a suffix meaning* one who fears or hates

pho·bi·a (fō'bē ə) *n.* [< Gr. *phobos*, a fear] an irrational, excessive, and persistent fear of some thing or situation —**pho'bic** *adj.*

-phobia [see prec.] *a combining form meaning* fear, dread, hatred [claustrophobia]

Phoe·be (fē'bē) Gr. *Myth.* same as ARTEMIS

phoe·be (fē'bē) *n.* [echoic, with sp. after prec.] a small, crested American bird that catches insects in flight

PHLOX

Phoe·ni·cia (fə nish'ə, -nē'shə) ancient region at the E end of the Mediterranean —**Phoe·ni'cian** *adj., n.*

Phoe·nix (fē'niks) capital of Ariz.: pop. 582,000 (met. area 968,000)

phoe·nix (fē'niks) *n.* [< Gr. *phoinix*] Egyptian *Myth.* a bird which lived for 500 years and then consumed itself in fire, rising renewed from the ashes

phone (fōn) *n., vt., vi.* phoned, phon'ing *colloq. shortened form of* TELEPHONE

-phone [< Gr. *phōnē*, a sound] *a combining form meaning:* **1.** a device producing or transmitting sound **2.** a telephone

pho·neme (fō'nēm) *n.* [< Fr. < Gr. *phōnē*, a voice] a set of similar sounds in a language that are heard as the same sound by native speakers and represented by the same symbol —**pho·ne·mic** (fə nē'mik) *adj.*

pho·ne·mics (fə nē'miks) *n.pl.* [with sing. v.] the study of the phonemes of a language or of phonemic systems

pho·net·ic (fə net'ik) *adj.* [< Gr. *phōnē*, a sound] **1.** of speech sounds **2.** of phonetics **3.** conforming to pronunciation [phonetic spelling] —**pho·net'i·cal·ly** *adv.*

pho·net'ics *n.pl.* [with sing. v.] the study of the production and written representation of speech sounds —**pho·ne·ti·cian** (fō'nə tish'ən) *n.*

phon·ic (fän'ik) *adj.* [< Gr. *phōnē*, a sound] **1.** of sounds; esp., of speech sounds **2.** of phonics

phon'ics *n.pl.* [with sing. v.] a phonetic method of teaching beginners to read

pho·no·graph (fō'nə graf') *n.* [< Gr. *phōnē*, a sound + -GRAPH] an instrument for reproducing sound recorded in a spiral groove on a disk —**pho'no·graph'ic** *adj.*

pho·nol·o·gy (fō näl'ə jē) *n.* [< Gr. *phōnē*, a sound + -LOGY] **1.** the speech sounds of a language **2.** the study of changes in these —**pho·no·log·i·cal** (fō'nə läj'i k'l) *adj.* —**pho·nol'o·gist** *n.*

pho·ny (fō'nē) *adj.* -ni·er, -ni·est [< Brit. thieves' argot *fawney*, gilt ring] [Colloq.] not genuine; false —*n., pl.* **-nies** **1.** something not genuine; fake **2.** one who dissembles, is insincere, etc.; fraud Also sp. **phoney** —**pho'ni·ness** *n.*

phoo·ey (fōō'ē) *interj.* [echoic] an exclamation of scorn, disgust, etc.

phos·phate (fäs'fāt) *n.* [Fr.] **1.** a salt or ester of phosphoric acid **2.** a fertilizer containing phosphates **3.** a flavored carbonated beverage

phos·pho·res·cence (fäs'fə res''ns) *n.* **1.** the property of giving off light without noticeable heat, as phosphorus does **2.** such light —**phos'pho·res'cent** *adj.*

phos·phor·ic (fäs fôr'ik) *adj.* of, like, or containing phosphorus, esp. with a valence of five

phosphoric acid any of several oxygen acids of phosphorus

phos·pho·rous (fäs'fər əs, fäs fôr'-) *adj.* of, like, or containing phosphorus, esp. with a valence of three

phos·pho·rus (fäs'fər əs) *n.* [< Gr. *phōs*, a light + *pherein*, to bear] a nonmetallic chemical element, a phosphorescent, waxy solid that ignites spontaneously at room temperature: symbol, P; at. wt., 30.9738; at. no., 15

pho·to (fōt'ō) *n., pl.* **-tos** clipped form of PHOTOGRAPH

photo- *a combining form meaning:* **1.** [< Gr. *phōs*, a light] of or produced by light **2.** [< PHOTOGRAPH] of photography

pho·to·cop·y (fōt'ə käp'ē) *n., pl.* **-ies** a photographic reproduction, as of a book page, made by a special device (**pho'to·cop'i·er**)

pho·to·e·lec·tric (fōt′ō i lek′trik) *adj.* of or involving the electric effects produced by light or other radiation

photoelectric cell any device in which light controls an electric circuit which operates a mechanical device, as for opening doors

pho·to·en·grav·ing (fōt′ō in grā′viŋ) *n.* **1.** a process by which photographs are reproduced in relief on printing plates **2.** such a plate **3.** a print made from such a plate —**pho′to·en·grave′** *vt.* **-graved′**, **-grav′ing** —**pho′to·en·grav′er** *n.*

photo finish 1. a race finish so close that the winner can be determined only from a photograph of the finish **2.** any close finish of a contest

pho·to·fin·ish·ing (fōt′ō fin′ish iŋ) *n.* the developing and printing of photographs —**pho′to·fin′ish·er** *n.*

pho·to·flash (fōt′ə flash′) *adj.* designating a flashbulb, etc. electrically synchronized with the camera shutter

pho·to·gen·ic (fōt′ə jen′ik) *adj.* [PHOTO- + -GEN + -IC] that looks or is likely to look attractive in photographs

pho·to·graph (fōt′ə graf′) *n.* a picture made by photography —*vt.* to take a photograph of —*vi.* to appear (as specified) in photographs —**pho·tog·ra·pher** (fə täg′rə fər) *n.*

pho·tog·ra·phy (fə täg′rə fē) *n.* [PHOTO- + -GRAPHY] the art or process of producing images of objects upon a surface (as film in a camera) sensitive to the chemical action of light or other radiant energy —**pho·to·graph·ic** (fōt′ə graf′ik) *adj.* —**pho′to·graph′i·cal·ly** *adv.*

pho·to·gra·vure (fōt′ə grə vyoor′) *n.* [Fr.] **1.** a process by which photographs are reproduced on intaglio printing plates **2.** a print made from such a plate

pho·to·li·thog·ra·phy (fōt′ə li thäg′rə fē) *n.* a printing process combining photography and lithography

pho·tom·e·ter (fō täm′ə tər) *n.* [PHOTO- + -METER] a device used to measure the intensity of light

pho·tom′e·try (-trē) *n.* the measurement of the intensity of light —**pho·to·met·ric** (fōt′ə met′rik) *adj.*

pho·to·mon·tage (fōt′ə män täzh′, -mōn-) *n.* montage done in or with photographs

pho·ton (fō′tän) *n.* [PHOT(O)- + (ELECTR)ON] a quantum of electromagnetic energy

pho·to·off·set (fōt′ō ôf′set′) *n.* a method of offset printing in which the text or pictures are photographically transferred to a metal plate from which inked impressions are made on the roller

pho·to·sen·si·tive (fōt′ō sen′sə tiv) *adj.* sensitive to radiant energy, esp. to light —**pho′to·sen′si·tiv′i·ty** *n.* —**pho′to·sen′si·tize′** (-tīz′) *vt.* **-tized′**, **-tiz′ing**

Pho·to·stat (fōt′ə stat′) [PHOTO- + -STAT] *a trademark for* a device for making copies of printed matter, drawings, etc. directly as positives on special paper —*n.* [p-] a copy so made —*vt.* [p-]-**stat′ed** or **-stat′ted**, **-stat′ing** or **-stat′ting** to make a photostat of —**pho′to·stat′ic** *adj.*

pho·to·syn·the·sis (fōt′ə sin′thə sis) *n.* the formation in green plants of organic substances, chiefly sugars, from carbon dioxide and water by the action of light on the chlorophyll

pho′to·syn′the·size′ (-sīz′) *vt., vi.* **-sized′**, **-siz′ing** to carry on, or produce by, photosynthesis

phrase (frāz) *n.* [< Gr. *phrazein*, speak] **1.** a short, colorful expression **2.** a group of words, not a full sentence or clause, conveying a single thought **3.** a short, distinct musical passage —*vt.* **phrased**, **phras′ing** to express in words or in a phrase —**phras·al** (frā′z′l) *adj.*

phra·se·ol·o·gy (frā′zē äl′ə jē) *n., pl.* **-gies** choice and pattern of words

phre·nol·o·gy (fri näl′ə jē) *n.* [< Gr. *phrēn*, mind + -LOGY] a system, now rejected, of analyzing character and mental faculties by studying the shape of the head —**phre·nol′o·gist** *n.*

Phryg·i·a (frij′ē ə) ancient country in WC Asia Minor

Phyfe (fīf), **Duncan** 1768-1854; U.S. cabinetmaker & furniture designer, born in Scotland

phy·lac·ter·y (fi lak′tər ē) *n., pl.* **-ies** [< Gr. *phylassein*, to guard] either of two small, leather cases holding Scripture texts, worn during morning prayer on the forehead and arm by Orthodox Jewish men

phy·log·e·ny (fī läj′ə nē) *n., pl.* **-nies** [< Gr. *phylon*, tribe + *-geneia*, origin] the origin and evolution of a group or race of animals or plants

phy·lum (fī′ləm) *n., pl.* **-la** (-lə) [< Gr. *phylon*, tribe] **1.** a main division of the animal kingdom **2.** sometimes, a main subdivision of the plant kingdom

phys. **1.** physical **2.** physician **3.** physics

phys·ic (fiz′ik) *n.* [< Gr. *physis*, nature] a medicine, esp. a cathartic —*vt.* **-icked**, **-ick·ing** to dose with medicine, esp. with a cathartic

phys·i·cal (fiz′i k′l) *adj.* [see prec.] **1.** of nature and all matter; material **2.** of or according to the laws of nature **3.** of, or produced by the forces of, physics **4.** of the body —*n.* a general medical examination: in full **physical examination** —**phys′i·cal·ly** *adv.*

physical chemistry chemistry dealing with physical properties in relation to chemical properties

physical education instruction in the exercise and care of the body; esp., a course in gymnastics, etc.

physical geography the study of the features and nature of the earth's surface and oceans, climate, etc.

physical science any science dealing with inanimate matter or energy, as physics, chemistry, or astronomy

physical therapy the treatment of disease, injury, etc. by physical means, as exercise, massage, heat, etc., rather than with drugs

phy·si·cian (fə zish′ən) *n.* [see PHYSIC] **1.** a doctor of medicine **2.** a medical doctor other than a surgeon

phys·ics (fiz′iks) *n.pl.* [see PHYSIC] **1.** [*with sing. v.*] the science dealing with the properties, changes, interactions, etc. of matter and energy **2.** physical properties or processes [the *physics* of flight] —**phys′i·cist** (-ə sist) *n.*

phys·i·og·no·my (fiz′ē äg′nə mē) *n., pl.* **-mies** [< Gr. *physis*, nature + *gnōmōn*, one who knows] facial features, esp. as supposedly indicative of character

phys·i·og·ra·phy (fiz′ē äg′rə fē) *n.* [< Gr. *physis*, nature + -GRAPHY] **1.** a description of the features and phenomena of nature **2.** *same as* PHYSICAL GEOGRAPHY —**phys′i·og′ra·pher** *n.*

physiol. **1.** physiological **2.** physiology

phys·i·ol·o·gy (fiz′ē äl′ə jē) *n.* [< Fr. < Gr. *physis*, nature + -LOGY] the science dealing with the functions and vital processes of living organisms or their parts and organs —**phys′i·o·log′i·cal** (-ə läj′i k′l) *adj.* —**phys′i·ol′o·gist** *n.*

phys·i·o·ther·a·py (fiz′ē ō ther′ə pē) *n. same as* PHYSICAL THERAPY —**phys′i·o·ther′a·pist** *n.*

phy·sique (fi zēk′) *n.* [Fr.] the structure, strength, or appearance of the body

pi¹ (pī) *n., pl.* **pies** [see PIE²] **1.** a disordered collection of printing type **2.** any jumble —*vt.* **pied**, **pie′ing** or **pi′ing** to make jumbled

pi² (pī) *n.* **1.** the sixteenth letter of the Greek alphabet (Π, π) **2.** the symbol (π) designating the ratio of the circumference of a circle to its diameter, about 3.1416

pi·a·nis·si·mo (pē′ə nis′ə mō′) *adj., adv.* [It.] *Music* very soft

pi·an·ist (pē an′ist, pyan′-, pē′ən-) *n.* [< Fr.] one who plays the piano

pi·an·o¹ (pē an′ō, pyan′ō) *n., pl.* **-os** [It. < PIANOFORTE] a large, stringed keyboard instrument: each key operates a felt-covered hammer that strikes a corresponding steel wire or set of wires

pi·an·o² (pē ä′nō, pyä′-) *adj., adv.* [It.] *Music* soft

pi·an·o·for·te (pē an′ə fôrt′, pē an′ə fôr′tē) *n.* [It. < *piano*, soft + *forte*, loud] *same as* PIANO¹

pi·as·ter (pē as′tər) *n.* [< Fr. < It., ult. < L. *emplastrum*, plaster] a unit of currency in Egypt, Lebanon, Syria, etc.

pi·az·za (pē az′ə, pyät′-) *n.* [It.] **1.** in Italy, a public square **2.** (pē az′ə) a large, covered porch

pi·broch (pē′bräk) *n.* [< Gael. < *piob*, bagpipe] a piece of music for the bagpipe, usually martial but sometimes dirgelike

pi·ca (pī′kə) *n.* [< ? ML., directory] **1.** a size of type, 12 point **2.** the height of this type, about 1/6 inch

pic·a·dor (pik′ə dôr′) *n.* [Sp. < *picar*, to prick] in bullfighting, a horseman who pricks the bull's neck with a lance to weaken him

pic·a·resque (pik′ə resk′) *adj.* [< Sp. *picaro*, rascal] of or dealing with sharp-witted vagabonds and their adventures [a *picaresque* novel]

Pi·cas·so (pi kä′sō), **Pab·lo** (pä′blō) 1881-1973; Sp. artist in France

pic·a·yune (pik′ē ōōn′) *adj.* [< Fr. *picaillon*, small coin] trivial; petty: also **pic′a·yun′ish**

Pic·ca·dil·ly (pik′ə dil′ē) street in London, a traditional center of fashionable shops, clubs, etc.

pic·ca·lil·li (pik′ə lil′ē) *n.* [prob. < PICKLE] a relish of chopped vegetables, mustard, and spices

pic·co·lo (pik′ə lō′) *n., pl.* **-los** [It., small] a small flute, pitched an octave above the ordinary flute

---

at, āpe, cär; ten, ēven; is, bīte; gō, hôrn, tool, look; oil, out; up, fur; thin, *th*en; zh, leisure; ŋ, ring; ə for *a* in *ago*; as in *able* (ā′b′l); ë, Fr. coeur; ö, Fr. feu; Fr. mo*n*; ü, Fr. duc; r, Fr. cri; kh, G. doch, ich. ‡ foreign; < derived from

pick¹ (pik) *n.* [OE. *pic*, PIKE²] **1.** a heavy tool with a long, pointed metal head set at a right angle to the handle, used in breaking up soil, rock, etc. **2.** any of several pointed tools for picking **3.** *same as* PLECTRUM

pick² (pik) *vt.* [ME. *picken*] **1.** to pierce, dig up, etc. with something pointed **2.** to probe, scratch at, etc. in trying to remove, or to clear something from **3.** to gather (flowers, berries, etc.) **4.** to prepare (a fowl) by removing the feathers **5.** to pull (fibers, rags, etc.) apart **6.** to choose; select **7.** to provoke *[to pick a fight]* **8.** to pluck (the strings) of (a guitar, etc.) **9.** to open (a lock) with a wire, etc. instead of a key **10.** to steal from (another's pocket, etc.) —*vi.* **1.** to use a pick **2.** to select, esp. in a fussy way —*n.* **1.** the act of choosing or the choice made **2.** the best —**pick at 1.** to eat small portions of, esp. in a fussy way **2.** [Colloq.] to find fault with **3.** to toy with; finger —**pick off 1.** to remove by picking **2.** to hit with a carefully aimed shot —**pick on** [Colloq.] **1.** to single out for criticism, abuse, etc. —**pick out 1.** to choose **2.** to single out from a group —**pick over** to examine item by item —**pick up 1.** to grasp and lift **2.** to get or learn, esp. by chance **3.** to stop for and take along **4.** to arrest **5.** to gain (speed) **6.** to improve **7.** to resume (an activity, etc.) after a pause **8.** to bring into range of sight, hearing, etc. **9.** to make (a room, etc.) tidy **10.** [Colloq.] to become acquainted with casually, esp. for lovemaking —**pick'er** *n.*

pick·a·back (pik'ə bak') *adv., adj.* [ult. < PACK¹] *same as* PIGGYBACK

pick·ax, pick·axe (pik'aks') *n.* [< OFr. *picquois*] a pick with a point at one end of the head and a chisellike edge at the other

picked (pikt) *adj.* [< PICK²] carefully selected

pick·er·el (pik'ər əl) *n., pl.* -el, -els [ME. *pik*, PIKE³ + dim. -*rel*] any of various small N. American freshwater fishes related to the pike

pick·et (pik'it) *n.* [Fr. *piquet*] **1.** a pointed stake used as in a fence **2.** a soldier or soldiers stationed to guard against a surprise attack **3.** a person, as a member of a striking labor union, stationed

PICKAX

outside a factory, store, etc. to demonstrate, keep strikebreakers out, etc. —*vt.* **1.** to enclose with a fence of stakes driven into the ground **2.** to hitch (an animal) to an upright stake **3.** to station as, or guard with, a military picket **4.** to station a picket, or serve as a picket, at (a factory, store, etc.) —*vi.* to serve as a picket (sense 3)

pick'ings *n.pl.* **1.** something picked **2.** leftovers; scraps **3.** profit; returns **4.** plunder; spoils

pick·le (pik'l) *n.* [< MDu. *pekel*] **1.** a brine, vinegar, etc. used to preserve or marinate food **2.** a vegetable, specif. a cucumber, so preserved **3.** a chemical bath to clear metal of scale, preserve wood, etc. **4.** [Colloq.] an awkward or difficult situation —*vt.* -led, -ling to preserve in or treat with a pickle solution

pick'pock'et *n.* one who steals from pockets

pick'up' *n.* **1.** a picking up **2.** the process or power of increasing in speed; acceleration **3.** a small delivery truck **4.** [Colloq.] a casual acquaintance, esp. for sexual purposes **5.** [Colloq.] improvement **6.** [Colloq.] *a)* a stimulant *b)* stimulation **7.** a record-player part converting the stylus vibrations into audio-frequency currents; also, the tone arm **8.** *Radio & TV a)* reception of sound or light for conversion into electrical energy in the transmitter *b)* the apparatus used

pick'y *adj.* -i·er, -i·est [Colloq.] fussy

pic·nic (pik'nik) *n.* [Fr. *pique-nique*] **1.** a pleasure outing, with an outdoor meal **2.** [Slang] any pleasant experience —*vi.* -nicked, -nick·ing to hold or attend a picnic —**pic'nick·er** *n.*

pi·cot (pē'kō) *n., pl.* -cots (-kōz) [Fr. < *pic*, a point] any of the small loops forming an ornamental edging on lace, ribbon, etc.

pic·ric acid (pik'rik) [< Fr. < Gr. *pikros*, bitter] a poisonous, yellow, crystalline, bitter acid used in making dyes and explosives

Pict (pikt) *n.* any of an ancient people of Great Britain, driven into Scotland by the Britons and Romans —**Pict'ish** *adj., n.*

pic·to·graph (pik'tə graf') *n.* [< L. *pictus*, painted + -GRAPH] **1.** a picture or picturelike symbol used in a writing system **2.** a diagram or graph using pictures —**pic'to·graph'ic** *adj.*

pic·to·ri·al (pik tôr'ē əl) *adj.* of, in, with, or like a picture or pictures —*n.* a periodical with many pictures —**pic·to'ri·al·ly** *adv.*

pic·ture (pik'chər) *n.* [< L. *pictus*, painted] **1.** a likeness made on a flat surface, as by drawing or photographing **2.** anything closely resembling or perfectly exemplifying something else **3.** anything suggestive of a beautiful painting, drawing, etc. **4.** a mental image; idea **5.** a vivid or detailed description **6.** the whole group of facts or details relating to something **7.** *same as* MOTION PICTURE **8.** the image on a television screen —*vt.* -tured, -tur·ing **1.** to make a picture of **2.** to show visibly or clearly **3.** to describe or explain **4.** to imagine —**in** (or **out of**) **the picture** considered as involved (or as not involved) in a situation

pic'tur·esque' (-chə resk') *adj.* like a picture; scenic, quaint, vivid, etc.

picture window a large window, esp. in a living room, that seems to frame the outside view

pid·dle (pid'l) *vi., vt.* -dled, -dling [< ?] to dawdle or trifle —**pid'dler** *n.* —**pid'dling** *adj.*

pidg·in (pij'in) *n.* [supposed Chin. pronun. of BUSINESS] a jargon for trade purposes, using words and grammar from different languages: **pidgin English** uses English words and Chinese or Melanesian syntax

pie¹ (pī) *n.* [ME.] **1.** a baked dish, as of fruit, with an under or upper crust or both **2.** a layer cake with a filling as of custard **3.** [Slang] something very good or easy —(**as**) **easy as pie** [Colloq.] very easy —**pie in the sky** [Slang] a Utopian plan or project

pie² (pī) *n., vt.* pied, pie'ing [< ? prec.] *chiefly Brit. sp.* of PI¹

pie·bald (pī'bôld') *adj.* [*pie*, magpie + BALD] covered with patches of two colors, esp. white and black —*n.* a piebald horse or other animal

piece (pēs) *n.* [OFr. *pece*] **1.** a part broken or separated from the whole **2.** a part of a whole, regarded as complete in itself **3.** a single thing, as an artistic work, an action, a firearm, a coin, one of a set, etc. **4.** [Archaic or Dial.] an amount of time or space —*vt.* pieced, piec'ing **1.** to add pieces to, as in repairing **2.** to join the pieces of, as in mending —**go to pieces 1.** to fall apart **2.** to lose self-control —**of a** (or **one**) **piece** of the same sort; alike

‡pièce de ré·sis·tance (pyes' də rā zē stäns') [Fr., piece of resistance] **1.** the principal dish of a meal **2.** the main item or event in a series

piece goods *same as* YARD GOODS

piece'meal' (-mēl') *adv.* [< ME. *pece*, a piece + -*mele*, a measure] piece by piece; in small amounts or degrees —*adj.* made or done piecemeal

piece of eight the obsolete Spanish dollar

piece'work' *n.* work paid for at a fixed rate (**piece rate**) per piece of work done

pied (pīd) *adj.* [< *pie*, magpie] covered with patches of two or more colors

Pied·mont (pēd'mänt') hilly region of the E U.S., between the Atlantic coast and the Appalachians

pier (pir) *n.* [< ML. *pera*] **1.** a structure supporting the spans of a bridge **2.** a structure built out over water, supported by pillars, and used as a landing place, pavilion, etc. **3.** *Archit. a)* a heavy supporting column *b)* the wall section between windows or other openings *c)* a buttress

pierce (pirs) *vt.* pierced, pierc'ing [< L. *per*, through + *tundere*, to strike] **1.** to pass into or through as a pointed instrument does; stab **2.** to make a hole in or through; bore **3.** to break into or through **4.** to penetrate with the sight or mind —*vi.* to penetrate —**pierc'ing·ly** *adv.*

Pierce (pirs), **Franklin** 1804–69; 14th president of the U.S. (1853–57)

Pierre (pir) capital of S.Dak.: pop. 10,000

pi·e·tism (pī'ə tiz'm) *n.* religious piety, esp. if exaggerated —**pi'e·tis'tic, pi'e·tis'ti·cal** *adj.*

pi·e·ty (pī'ə tē) *n., pl.* -ties [< L. *pius*, pious] **1.** devotion to religious duties and practices **2.** devotion to parents, family, etc. **3.** a pious act

pi·e·zo·e·lec·tric (pē ā'zō i lek'trik) *adj.* of or pertaining to piezoelectricity

piezoelectric effect the property some crystals have of generating voltage when subjected to pressure and of expanding and contracting when subjected to an electrically charged field

pi·e'zo·e·lec'tric'i·ty (-i lek'tris'ə tē) *n.* [< Gr. *piezein*, to press + ELECTRICITY] electricity resulting from the piezoelectric effect

pif·fle (pif'l) *n.* [< Brit. dial.] [Colloq.] talk, action, etc regarded as insignificant or nonsensical —*interj.* nonsense!

pig (pig) *n.* [ME. *pigge*] **1.** a domesticated animal with a broad snout and a fat body covered with bristles; swine, hog **2.** a young hog of less than c.100 lbs. **3.** pork **4.** a gluttonous or filthy person **5.** an oblong casting of meta poured from the smelting furnace

pi·geon (pij′ən) *n.* [< L. *pipire*, to peep] any of various related birds with a small head, plump body, long, pointed wings, and short legs, typically larger than doves

pi′geon·hole′ *n.* a small, open compartment, as in a desk, for filing papers —*vt.* -holed′, -hol′ing 1. to put in a pigeonhole 2. to put aside indefinitely 3. to classify

pi′geon-toed′ (-tōd′) *adj.* having the toes or feet turned in

pig·gish (pig′ish) *adj.* like a pig; gluttonous or filthy — pig′gish·ly *adv.* —pig′gish·ness *n.*

pig′gy, pig′gie (-ē) *n., pl.* -gies a little pig —*adj.* -gi·er, -gi·est *same as* PIGGISH

pig′gy·back′ (-bak′) *adv., adj.* [alt. of PICKABACK] 1. (carried or carrying) on the shoulders or back 2. of or by the carrying of truck trailers on flatcars —*vt.* to carry piggyback

piggy bank a small savings bank, often shaped like a pig, with a slot for receiving coins

pig′head′ed *adj.* stubborn; obstinate

pig iron [see PIG, sense 5] crude iron, smelted for casting in molds

pig′let (-lit) *n.* a little pig

pig·ment (pig′mənt) *n.* [L. *pigmentum*] 1. coloring matter used to make paints 2. coloring matter in the cells and tissues of animals or plants

pig·men·ta′tion (-mən tā′shən) *n.* coloration in animals or plants through their natural pigment

Pig·my (pig′mē) *adj., n., pl.* -mies *alt. sp. of* PYGMY

pig′pen′ *n.* a pen where pigs are confined

pig′skin′ *n.* 1. leather made from the skin of a pig 2. [Colloq.] a football

pig′sty′ (-stī′) *n., pl.* -sties′ *same as* PIGPEN

pig′tail′ (-tāl′) *n.* a long braid of hair hanging at the back of the head

pike[1] (pīk) *n. clipped form of* TURNPIKE

pike[2] (pīk) *n.* [Fr. *pique*] a former weapon consisting of a metal spearhead on a long wooden shaft

pike[3] (pīk) *n., pl.* **pike, pikes** [ME. *pik*] 1. a voracious freshwater game fish found throughout northern waters: it has a narrow, pointed head and a slender body 2. any of several related fishes, as the muskellunge

pik·er (pī′kər) *n.* [< ? *Pike* County, Mo.] [Slang] a person who is petty, stingy, or too cautious

Pikes Peak (pīks) mountain in C Colo.: 14,110 ft.

pi·laf, pi·laff (pi läf′, pē′läf) *n.* [Per. & Turk. *pilāw*] rice boiled in a seasoned liquid and usually containing meat or fish: also **pi·lau′** (-lô′)

pi·las·ter (pi las′tər) *n.* [< Fr. < It. < L. *pila*, a pile] a columnlike rectangular support projecting partially from a wall

Pi·late (pī′lət), **Pon·tius** (pän′shəs, -chəs) Rom. governor of Judea who condemned Jesus to death

pil·chard (pil′chərd) *n.* [< ?] 1. a small saltwater fish of the herring family, the commercial sardine of W Europe 2. any of several related fishes; esp., the **Pacific sardine**, found off the W U.S. coast

pile[1] (pīl) *n.* [< L. *pila*, pillar] 1. a mass of things heaped together 2. a heap, as of wood, on which a corpse or sacrifice is burned 3. a large building 4. [Colloq.] a large amount 5. *earlier name for* NUCLEAR REACTOR —*vt.* piled, pil′ing 1. to heap up 2. to load —*vi.* 1. to form a pile 2. to move confusedly in a mass (with *in, out, etc.*)

pile[2] (pīl) *n.* [< L. *pilus*, a hair] 1. a soft, velvety, raised surface of yarn loops, as on a rug 2. soft, fine hair, fur, etc. —**piled** *adj.*

pile[3] (pīl) *n.* [OE. *pil*] 1. a long, heavy beam driven into the earth to support a structure 2. any similar supporting member, as of concrete

pile driver (or **engine**) a machine for driving piles by raising and dropping a heavy weight on them

piles (pīlz) *n.pl.* [< L. *pila*, ball] hemorrhoids

pile′up′ *n.* 1. a piling up 2. [Colloq.] a collision involving several vehicles

pil·fer (pil′fər) *vt., vi.* [< MFr. *pelfre*, booty] to steal (esp. small sums or petty objects) —**pil′fer·age** *n.* —**pil′fer·er** *n.*

pil·grim (pil′grəm) *n.* [< L. *peregrinus*, foreigner] 1. a wanderer 2. a traveler to a holy place 3. [P-] one of the English Puritan founders of Plymouth

pil′grim·age (-ij) *n.* 1. a pilgrim's journey, esp. to a holy place 2. any similar long journey

pil·ing (pī′liŋ) *n.* 1. piles (beams) collectively 2. a structure of piles

pill (pil) *n.* [< L. *pila*, ball] 1. a small ball, tablet, etc. of medicine to be swallowed whole 2. [Slang] a baseball, golf ball, etc. 3. [Slang] an unpleasant person —*vi.* to form small balls of fuzz —**the pill** (or **Pill**) [Colloq.] a contraceptive drug taken as a pill by women

pil·lage (pil′ij) *n.* [< MFr. *piller*, rob] 1. a plundering 2. plunder; loot —*vt., vi.* to plunder

pil·lar (pil′ər) *n.* [< L. *pila*, column] 1. a slender, vertical structure used as a support; column 2. a person who is a main support as of an institution

pill′box′ *n.* 1. a small box for pills 2. a low, enclosed gun emplacement of concrete and steel

pil·lion (pil′yən) *n.* [< L. *pellis*, a skin] an extra seat behind the saddle on a horse or motorcycle

pil·lo·ry (pil′ər ē) *n., pl.* -ries [< OFr. *pilori*] a wooden board with holes for the head and hands, in which petty offenders were formerly locked and exposed to public scorn —*vt.* -ried, -ry·ing 1. to put in a pillory 2. to expose to public scorn

pil·low (pil′ō) *n.* [OE. *pyle*] a cloth case filled as with feathers and used as a support, esp. for the head during sleep —*vt.* 1. to rest as on a pillow 2. to be a pillow for — **pil′low·y** *adj.*

pil′low·case′ *n.* a removable cloth case to cover a pillow: also **pil′low·slip′**

pi·lot (pī′lət) *n.* [< Gr. *pēdon*, oar blade] 1. a steersman; specif., one licensed to steer ships as into or out of a harbor 2. an aircraft operator 3. a guide; leader —*vt.* 1. to act as a pilot of 2. to guide —*adj.* serving as a test unit

pilot film (or **tape**) a film (or videotape) of a single segment of a projected television series

pi′lot·house′ *n.* an enclosed place on the upper deck of a ship, for the helmsman

pilot light a small gas burner kept lighted to rekindle a principal burner when needed

pi·men·to (pi men′tō) *n., pl.* -tos [< Sp. < L. *pigmentum*, pigment] 1. a variety of sweet red pepper used as a relish, olive stuffing, etc. 2. *same as* ALLSPICE Also **pi·mien′to** (-myen′-, -men′-)

pimp (pimp) *n.* [< ?] a prostitute's agent —*vi.* to act as a pimp

pim·per·nel (pim′pər nel′, -nəl) *n.* [< L. *piper*, pepper] any of certain related plants with clustered flowers and leafless stems

pim·ple (pim′p'l) *n.* [ME. *pinplis* (pl.)] a small, rounded, usually inflamed elevation of the skin —**pim′ply** *adj.*

pin (pin) *n.* [OE. *pinn*] 1. a peg, as of metal or wood, used as a fastening, support, etc. 2. a little piece of stiff wire with a pointed end and a head, used as a fastening 3. anything pinlike 4. an ornament, badge, or emblem with a pin or clasp for fastening to clothes 5. [Colloq.] one's leg: *usually used in pl.* 6. *Bowling* any of the wooden, bottle-shaped clubs at which the ball is rolled 7. *Golf* a pole with a flag attached, at the hole of a green —*vt.* pinned, pin′ning 1. to fasten as with a pin 2. to hold firmly in one position —**pin down** 1. to get (someone) to be definitive or specific 2. to establish definitely (a fact, details, etc.) —**pin someone's ears back** [Colloq.] to beat, defeat, or scold someone soundly —**pin (something) on someone** [Colloq.] to lay the blame for (something) on someone

pin·a·fore (pin′ə fôr′) *n.* [PIN + AFORE] a sleeveless garment worn over a dress

pin′ball′ machine a game machine with an inclined board having pins, holes, etc. marked with scores that are recorded as a spring-driven ball makes contacts

pince-nez (pans′nā′, pins′-) *n., pl.* **pince′-nez′** (-nāz′) [Fr., nose-pincher] eyeglasses without sidepieces, kept in place by a spring gripping the nose bridge

pin·cers (pin′sərz) *n.pl.* [*occas. with sing. v.*] [< OFr. *pincier*, to pinch] 1. a tool with two pivoted parts used for gripping 2. a grasping claw as of a lobster —**pin′cer·like′** *adj.*

pinch (pinch) *vt.* [see prec.] 1. to squeeze as between finger and thumb 2. to nip off the end of (a plant shoot) 3. to press painfully upon (a bodily part) 4. to cause distress or discomfort to 5. to make thin, cramped, etc., as by hunger or cold 6. to restrict closely; straiten 7. [Slang] *a*) to steal *b*) to arrest —*vi.* 1. to squeeze painfully 2. to be stingy or frugal —*n.* 1. a pinching or being pinched 2. the small amount that can be grasped between finger and thumb 3. an emergency

PINCERS

pinch′ers *n.pl. same as* PINCERS

pinch'-hit' *vi.* -hit', -hit'ting 1. *Baseball* to bat in place of the batter whose turn it is 2. to substitute in an emergency —**pinch hitter**

pin'cush'ion *n.* a small cushion in which pins and needles are stuck to keep them handy

Pin·dar (pin'dər) 522?–438? B.C.; Gr. lyric poet

pine¹ (pīn) *n.* [< L. *pinus*] 1. any of various related evergreen trees with needlelike leaves and woody cones: many pines are valuable for their wood and their resin, from which turpentine, tar, etc. are obtained 2. the wood

pine² (pīn) *vi.* pined, pin'ing [< L. *poena*, a pain] 1. to waste (*away*) from grief, longing, etc. 2. to have intense longing or desire; yearn

pin·e·al body (pin'ē əl) [< Fr. < L. *pinea*, pine cone] a small, cone-shaped body in the brain of vertebrates: its function is obscure

pine·ap·ple (pīn'ap''l) *n.* [ME. *pinappel*, pine cone] 1. a juicy, edible tropical fruit shaped somewhat like a pine cone 2. the plant it grows on

pin'feath'er *n.* a young, emerging feather

ping (piŋ) *n.* [echoic] a sharp sound as of a bullet striking, an engine knocking, etc. —*vi., vt.* to make or cause to make this sound

Ping-Pong (piŋ'pôŋ', -päŋ') [echoic] *a trademark for* table-tennis equipment —*n.* [p- p-] table tennis

pin'head' *n.* 1. the head of a pin 2. a stupid or silly person —**pin'head'ed** *adj.*

pin'hole' *n.* 1. a tiny hole made as by a pin 2. a hole into which a pin or peg goes

pin·ion (pin'yən) *n.* [< Fr. < L. *pinna*, a feather] 1. a cogwheel engaging with a larger one or with a rack 2. the end joint of a bird's wing 3. a wing 4. a wing feather —*vt.* to bind the wings or arms of

pink¹ (piŋk) *n.* [< ?] 1. any of a genus of plants with pink, red, or white flowers 2. such a flower 3. pale red 4. the finest example, degree, etc. 5. [Colloq.] a person of somewhat radical political or economic views —*adj.* 1. pale-red 2. [Colloq.] somewhat radical —**in the pink** [Colloq.] in good physical condition; healthy

pink² (piŋk) *vt.* [ME. *pynken*] 1. to make patterned perforations in or cut a saw-toothed edge on (cloth, paper, etc.) 2. to prick or stab 3. to adorn

pink'eye' *n.* an acute, contagious conjunctivitis, with inflammation also of the eyeball

pink·ie, pink·y (piŋ'kē) *n., pl.* -ies [prob. < Du. *pinkje*] the fifth, or smallest, finger

pink'ing shears shears with notched blades, for pinking the edges of cloth, paper, etc.

pin money money for miscellaneous small expenses

pin·na (pin'ə) *n., pl.* -nae (-ē), -nas [L., a feather] 1. *Anat.* the external ear 2. *Bot.* a leaflet as of a fern 3. *Zool.* a feather, wing, fin, etc.

pin·nace (pin'is) *n.* [< Fr. < Sp. < L. *pinus*, a pine] 1. a small sailing ship 2. a ship's boat

pin·na·cle (pin'ə k'l) *n.* [< L. *pinna*, a wing] 1. a small turret or spire 2. a slender, pointed formation, as a mountain peak 3. the highest point

pin·nate (pin'āt, -it) *adj.* [< L. *pinna*, a feather] 1. resembling a feather 2. *Bot.* with leaflets on each side of a common stem

pi·noch·le, pi·noc·le (pē'nuk''l, -näk''l) *n.* [< G. < Fr. *binocle*, pince-nez] a card game using a double deck of all cards above the eight

pin'point' *vt.* to locate or determine precisely

pin'prick' *n.* 1. a tiny puncture as from a pin 2. a minor irritation or annoyance

pins and needles a prickling feeling as in a numb limb —**on pins and needles** in anxious suspense

pin'set'ter *n.* a person or automatic device that sets up bowling pins on the alley: also **pin'spot'ter**

pin stripe 1. a very narrow stripe, as in some suits 2. a pattern of such stripes in parallel

pint (pīnt) *n.* [ME. *pynte*] a measure of capacity (liquid or dry) equal to 1/2 quart

pin·tle (pin't'l) *n.* [OE. *pintel*, penis] a pin or bolt upon which some other part pivots or turns

pin·to (pin'tō) *n., pl.* -tos [AmSp., spotted] a horse with patches of white and another color

pinto (bean) a mottled kidney bean of the SW U.S.

pint'-size', pint'-sized' *adj.* very small

pin'up' *adj.* 1. designed or suitable for pinning up on a wall 2. [Colloq.] designating an attractive girl whose picture is often pinned up on walls —*n.* [Colloq.] a pinup girl, picture, etc.

PINTLE

pin'wheel' *n.* 1. a toy consisting of an arrangement of little vanes with a pin stuck through their center to a stick so that they whirl in the wind 2. a whirling firework

pin'worm' *n.* a small, unsegmented worm sometimes parasitic in the human large intestine

pi·o·neer (pī'ə nir') *n.* [Fr. *pionnier,* ult. < L. *pes,* foot] one who goes before, preparing the way for others, as an early settler —*vi.* to be a pioneer —*vt.* 1. to prepare or open (a way, area, etc.) 2. to be a pioneer in or of

pi·ous (pī'əs) *adj.* [L. *pius*] 1. of, showing, or prompted by real or feigned religious devotion 2. not secular or profane; sacred —**pi'ous·ly** *adv.*

pip¹ (pip) *n.* [< PIPPIN] a small seed as of an apple

pip² (pip) *n.* [< ?] one of the conventionalized marks or dots used as on playing cards or dominoes

pip³ (pip) *n.* [< L. *pituita,* phlegm] a contagious disease of fowl

pipe (pīp) *n.* [< L. *pipare,* to chirp] 1. a tube into which air is blown to make musical sounds; specif., [*pl.*] *same as: a)* PANPIPE *b)* BAGPIPE 2. a shrill sound, as of a child's voice 3. a tube, as of concrete, for conveying water, oil, etc. 4. a tubular part, organ, etc. 5. a tube with a small bowl at one end, used as for smoking tobacco —*vi.* piped, pip'ing 1. to play a pipe or pipes 2. to make shrill sounds —*vt.* 1. to play (a tune) on a pipe or pipes 2. to utter shrilly 3. to bring, call, etc. as by playing pipes 4. to convey (water, oil, etc.) by pipes 5. to trim (a dress, coat, etc.) with piping —**pipe down** [Slang] to become quiet; stop shouting, talking, etc. —**pip'er** *n.*

pipe dream [Colloq.] a wild idea, vain hope, etc.

pipe fitter a mechanic who installs and maintains pipes used as for plumbing —**pipe fitting**

pipe'line' *n.* 1. a line of pipes as for conveying water 2. any channel of conveyance

pipe organ *same as* ORGAN (sense 1)

pi·pette, pi·pet (pī pet', pi-) *n.* [Fr., dim. of *pipe,* tube] a slender tube for taking up a little liquid by suction, as in transferring the liquid

pip·ing (pīp'iŋ) *n.* 1. music made by pipes 2. a shrill sound 3. a system of pipes 4. a narrow, rounded trimming on seams or edges —*adj.* shrill —**piping hot** so hot as to sizzle, steam, etc.

pip·pin (pip'in) *n.* [< OFr. *pepin,* a seed] any of a number of varieties of apple

pip·squeak (pip'skwēk') *n.* [< *pip,* to chirp + SQUEAK] [Colloq.] one contemptibly insignificant

pi·quant (pē'kənt) *adj.* [Fr. < *piquer,* to prick] 1. agreeably pungent to the taste 2. exciting interest; stimulating —**pi'quan·cy** *n.*

pique (pēk) *n.* [see prec.] resentment; ruffled pride —*vt.* piqued, piqu'ing 1. to make resentful 2. to arouse (one's curiosity, etc.)

pi·qué (pē kā') *n.* [see PIQUANT] a firmly woven cotton fabric with wales: also pi·que'

pi·ra·cy (pī'rə sē) *n., pl.* -cies [see PIRATE] 1. robbery of ships on the high seas 2. unauthorized use of copyrighted or patented work

Pi·ran·del·lo (pir'ən del'ō), **Lu·i·gi** (lōō ē'jē) 1867–1936; It. playwright & novelist

pi·ra·nha (pi rän'yə, -ran'-) *n.* [Braz. Port. < SAmInd. *piro,* a fish + *sainha,* tooth] a small, fierce, voracious freshwater fish of S. America

pi·rate (pī'rət) *n.* [< Gr. *peirān,* to attack] one that practices piracy —*vt., vi.* -rat·ed, -rat·ing 1. to practice piracy (upon) 2. to take (something) by piracy 3. to publish or reproduce (a book, recording, etc.) without authorization, esp. in violation of a copyright

pi·ro·gi (pi rō'gē) *n.pl.* [Russ., pies] small pastry turnovers filled with meat, cheese, etc.: also **pi·rosh'ki** (-räsh'kē), **pi·ro'gen** (-rō'gən)

pi·rogue (pi rōg') *n.* [Fr. < Sp. < WInd. (Carib) name] a canoe made by hollowing out a log

pir·ou·ette (pir'oo wet') *n.* [Fr., spinning top] a whirling on one foot or on the point of the toe —*vi.* -et'ted, -et'ting to do a pirouette

Pi·sa (pē'zə) city in W Italy: pop. 100,000

pis·ca·to·ri·al (pis'kə tôr'ē əl) *adj.* [< L. *piscis,* a fish] of fishermen or fishing: also **pis'ca·to'ry**

Pis·ces (pī'sēz, pis'ēz) [L., pl. of *piscis,* a fish] 1. a N constellation 2. the twelfth sign of the zodiac: see ZODIAC, illus.

pis·mire (pis'mīr', piz'-) *n.* [ME. *pisse,* urine + *mire,* ant] an ant

pis·ta·chi·o (pi stä'shē ō', -stash'ē-, -stash'ō) *n., pl.* -os' [< It. < OPer. *pistah*] 1. a small tree related to the cashew 2. its edible greenish seed (**pistachio nut**) 3. a light yellow-green color

pis·til (pis't'l) *n.* [Fr. < L. *pistillum*, pestle] the seed-bearing organ of a flowering plant

pis·tol (pis't'l) *n.* [< Fr. < G. < Czech *pišt'al*] a small firearm held and fired with one hand

pis'tol-whip' *vt.* -whipped', -whip'-ping to beat with a pistol, esp. about the head

pis·ton (pis't'n) *n.* [Fr. < It. < L. *pin-sere*, to beat] a disk or short cylinder fitted into a hollow cylinder and moved back and forth by the pressure of a fluid to transmit motion to a rod (**piston rod**) or moved by the rod to exert pressure on the fluid

PISTIL

piston ring a split ring placed around a piston to make it fit the cylinder closely

pit[1] (pit) *n.* [Du. < MDu. *pitte*] the hard stone, as of a peach, containing the seed —*vt.* **pit'ted, pit'ting** to remove the pit from

pit[2] (pit) *n.* [< L. *puteus*, a well] **1.** a hole in the ground **2.** an abyss **3.** hell: with *the* **4.** a pitfall **5.** an enclosed area in which animals are kept or made to fight **6.** a small hollow in a surface **7.** the section for the orchestra, in front of the stage **8.** any of various enclosed, often sunken, areas —*vt.* **pit'ted, pit'ting 1.** to put in a pit **2.** to make pits in **3.** to set in competition (*against*) —*vi.* to become marked with pits

pit·a·pat (pit'ə pat') *adv.* [echoic] with rapid beating —*n.* a rapid succession of beats —*vi.* **-pat'ted, -pat'ting** to go pitapat; palpitate

pitch[1] (pich) *n.* [< L. *pix*] **1.** a black, sticky substance formed from coal tar, petroleum, etc. and used as for waterproofing or pavements **2.** any of certain bitumens, as asphalt **3.** a resin from certain evergreen trees

pitch[2] (pich) *vt.* [ME. *picchen*] **1.** to set up [*to pitch* a tent*]* **2.** to throw; toss **3.** to fix at a certain point, level, degree, etc. **4.** *Baseball a)* to throw (the ball) to the batter *b)* to assign (a player) to pitch *c)* to serve as pitcher for (a game) **5.** *Music* to set the key of —*vi.* **1.** to pitch something, as a ball **2.** to plunge forward or dip downward **3.** to rise and fall, as a ship in rough water —*n.* **1.** act or manner of pitching **2.** a throw; toss **3.** anything pitched **4.** a point or degree *[*feelings were at a high *pitch]* **5.** the degree of slope **6.** [Slang] a line of talk for persuading **7.** *Machinery* the distance between corresponding points as on two adjacent screw threads **8.** *Music, Acoustics a)* the highness or lowness of sound determined by frequency vibrations *b)* a standard of pitch for tuning instruments —**make a pitch for** [Slang] to speak in favor of —**pitch in** [Colloq.] to begin working hard —**pitch into** [Colloq.] to attack

pitch'-black' *adj.* very black

pitch'blende' (-blend') *n.* [< G. *pech*, PITCH[1] + *blenden*, deceive] a lustrous mineral, the chief ore of uranium, ranging in color from brown to black

pitch'-dark' *adj.* very dark

pitched battle (picht) **1.** a battle in which positions are previously fixed **2.** a fierce combat

pitch·er[1] (pich'ər) *n.* [< L. *bacar*, wineglass] a container, usually with handle and lip, for holding and pouring liquids —**pitch'er·ful'** *n., pl.* **-fuls'**

pitch·er[2] (pich'ər) *n.* one that pitches; esp., *Baseball* the player pitching to opposing players

pitcher plant a plant with pitcherlike leaves that attract, trap, and digest insects

pitch'fork' *n.* a large, long-handled fork for lifting and tossing hay, straw, etc.

pitch'man (-mən) *n., pl.* **-men 1.** a hawker of goods **2.** [Slang] a high-pressure salesman or advertiser

pitch pipe a small pipe producing a fixed tone used as a guide in determining pitch, esp. for singers

pit·e·ous (pit'ē əs) *adj.* arousing or deserving pity —**pit'e·ous·ly** *adv.* —**pit'e·ous·ness** *n.*

pit'fall' *n.* [ME. *pit*, PIT[2] + *falle*, a trap] **1.** a covered pit to trap animals **2.** a hidden danger

pith (pith) *n.* [OE. *pitha*] **1.** the soft, spongy tissue in the center of certain plant stems **2.** the spongy fibrous tissue under the rind and about the sections of an orange, grapefruit, etc. **3.** gist

pith'y (-ē) *adj.* **-i·er, -i·est 1.** of, like, or full of pith **2.** terse and full of substance or meaning —**pith'i·ly** *adv.*

pit·i·a·ble (pit'ē ə b'l) *adj.* arousing pity sometimes mixed with scorn —**pit'i·a·bly** *adv.*

pit·i·ful (pit'i fəl) *adj.* **1.** arousing or deserving pity **2.** deserving scorn —**pit'i·ful·ly** *adv.*

pit'i·less (-lis) *adj.* without pity; merciless

pi·ton (pē'tän; *Fr.* pē tôn') *n., pl.* **-tons** (-tänz; *Fr.* -tôn') [Fr. < MFr., a spike] a spike that has an eye to which a rope can be secured and that is driven into rock or ice to support a mountain climber

Pitt (pit), **William 1.** 1708–78; Eng. statesman; prime minister (1766–68) **2.** 1759–1806; Eng. statesman; prime minister (1783–1801; 1804–06): son of *prec.*

pit·tance (pit'ns) *n.* [ult. < L. *pius*, pious] a small amount, share, or allotment

pit·ter-pat·ter (pit'ər pat'ər) *n.* [echoic] a rapid succession of light tapping sounds

Pitts·burgh (pits'bərg) city in SW Pa.: pop. 520,000 (met. area 2,401,000)

pi·tu·i·tar·y (pi tōō'ə ter'ē, -tyōō'-) *adj.* [< L. *pituita*, phlegm] of the pituitary gland —*n., pl.* **-ies** *same as* PITUITARY GLAND

pituitary gland (or **body**) a small, oval endocrine gland at the base of the brain: it secretes hormones affecting body growth, metabolism, etc.

pit·y (pit'ē) *n., pl.* **-ies** [ult. < L. *pius*, pious] **1.** sorrow for another's suffering or misfortune **2.** a cause for sorrow or regret —*vt., vi.* **-ied, -y·ing** to feel pity (for) —**pit'y·ing·ly** *adv.*

piv·ot (piv'ət) *n.* [Fr.] **1.** a point, shaft, etc. on which something turns **2.** a person or thing on which something depends **3.** a pivoting movement —*vt.* to provide with a pivot —*vi.* to turn as on a pivot —**piv'ot·al** *adj.*

pix (piks) *n.pl.* [< PIC(TURE)S] [Slang] **1.** motion pictures **2.** photographs

pix·ie, pix·y (pik'sē) *n., pl.* **-ies** [< Brit. dial.] a fairy or sprite —**pix'ie·ish, pix'y·ish** *adj.*

pix·i·lat·ed (pik'sə lāt'id) *adj.* [< prec.] eccentric, slightly demented, puckish, etc.

pi·zazz, piz·zazz (pə zaz') *n.* [< ?] [Slang] **1.** vigor, vitality, etc. **2.** flair, dash, style, etc.

piz·za (pēt'sə) *n.* [It.] an Italian dish made of a thin layer of dough covered with a spiced preparation of tomatoes, cheese, etc. and baked

piz·ze·ri·a (pēt'sə rē'ə) *n.* [It.] a place where pizzas are made and sold

piz·zi·ca·to (pit'sə kät'ō) *adj.* [It.] *Music* plucked: a direction to pluck the strings as of a violin —*adv.* in a pizzicato manner

pk. *pl.* **pks. 1.** pack **2.** park **3.** peak **4.** peck

pkg. package; packages

pkwy. parkway

pl. 1. place **2.** plural

plac·a·ble (plak'ə b'l, plā'kə-) *adj.* that can be placated —**plac'a·bil'i·ty** *n.* —**plac'a·bly** *adv.*

plac·ard (plak'ärd, -ərd) *n.* [< MDu. *placke*, a piece] **1.** a notice for display; poster **2.** a small card or plaque —*vt.* **1.** to put placards on or in **2.** to advertise with placards

pla·cate (plā'kāt, plak'āt) *vt.* **-cat·ed, -cat·ing** [< L. *placare*] to appease; pacify —**pla·ca'tion** *n.*

place (plās) *n.* [< Gr. *plateia*, street] **1.** a city square or court **2.** a short street **3.** space; room **4.** region; locality **5.** *a)* an occupied part of space *b)* situation or state *[*if I were in his *place]* **6.** a city, town, or village **7.** a residence **8.** a building or space devoted to a special purpose **9.** a particular spot, part, position, etc. **10.** a particular passage or page as in a book **11.** a step or point in a sequence **12.** the customary or proper position, time, etc. **13.** a seat, location, etc. reserved for, customarily occupied by, or being used by someone **14.** a job; office; employment **15.** official position **16.** the duties of any position **17.** one's duty or business **18.** *Racing* the first, second, or third position at the finish, specif. the second —*vt.* **placed, plac'ing 1.** *a)* to put or set in a particular place, condition, relation, category, etc. *b)* to put in an assigned or proper place, as in a series *c)* to identify by associating with the correct place or circumstances **2.** to find a place, as a job or residence, for **3.** to appoint to a position **4.** to present or arrange for handling, treatment, consideration, etc. **5.** *a)* to rank *b)* to estimate —*vi.* **1.** to finish in a certain position in a contest; come in *[to place* last*]* **2.** to finish among the first three in a contest; specif., to finish second in a horse or dog race —**in place of** instead of —**take place** to occur —**take the place of** to substitute for

pla·ce·bo (plə sē'bō) *n., pl.* **-bos, -boes** [L., I shall please] *Med.* a neutral preparation given as to humor a patient

place kick *Football* a kick made while the ball is held in place on the ground, as in attempting a field goal — **place'-kick'** *vi.*

place mat a small mat serving as an individual table cover for a person at a meal

place'ment *n.* **1.** a placing or being placed **2.** location or arrangement

pla·cen·ta (plə sen'tə) *n., pl.* **-tas, -tae** (-tē) [< Gr. *plax,* flat object] an organ developed within the uterus and nourishing a fetus through the umbilical cord —**pla·cen'-tal** *adj.*

plac·er (plas'ər) *n.* [AmSp., ult. < Gr. *plateia,* street] a deposit of gravel or sand with particles of gold, platinum, etc. in it that can be washed out

placer mining extraction, as of gold, from placers as by washing or dredging

place setting the china, silverware, etc. for setting one place at a table for a meal

plac·id (plas'id) *adj.* [L. *placidus*] tranquil; calm —**pla·cid·i·ty** (plə sid'ə tē) *n.* —**plac'id·ly** *adv.*

plack·et (plak'it) *n.* [< ?] a slit at the waist as of a skirt to make a garment easy to put on and take off

pla·gia·rize (plā'jə rīz', -jē ə rīz') *vt., vi.* **-rized', -riz'ing** [< L. *plagiarius,* kidnapper] to take (ideas, writings, etc.) from (another) and pass them off as one's own —**pla'gia·rism, pla'gia·ry** *n., pl.* **-ries** —**pla'gia·rist, pla'gia·riz'er** *n.*

plague (plāg) *n.* [< Gr. *plēgē,* misfortune] **1.** any affliction or calamity **2.** any deadly epidemic disease **3.** [Colloq.] a nuisance —*vt.* **plagued, plagu'ing** to afflict, vex, etc.

plaice (plās) *n., pl.* **plaice, plaic'es** [< Gr. *platys,* broad] a kind of American or European flatfish

plaid (plad) *n.* [Gael. *plaide,* a blanket] **1.** cloth with a crossbarred pattern **2.** such a pattern

plain (plān) *adj.* [< L. *planus,* flat] **1.** open; clear *[in plain view]* **2.** evident **3.** direct; frank **4.** not fancy; simple **5.** not good-looking; homely **6.** common; ordinary —*n.* an extent of level country —*adv.* in a plain way —**plain'ly** *adv.* —**plain'ness** *n.*

plain'clothes' man a detective or policeman who wears civilian clothes while on duty: also **plain'clothes'man** (-mən) *n., pl.* **-men**

plains·man (plānz'mən) *n., pl.* **-men** an inhabitant of the plains; esp., an American frontiersman of the western plains

plain'song' *n.* early Christian church music in free rhythm, sung in unison: also **plain'chant'**

plain'-spo'ken *adj.* speaking or spoken in a straightforward way —**plain'-spo'ken·ness** *n.*

plaint (plānt) *n.* [< L. *plangere,* to lament] **1.** [Poet.] lamentation **2.** a complaint

plain·tiff (plān'tif) *n.* [see prec.] one who brings a suit into a court of law; complainant

plain·tive (plān'tiv) *adj.* [see PLAINT] mournful; sad — **plain'tive·ly** *adv.* —**plain'tive·ness** *n.*

plait (plāt; *chiefly Brit.* plat) *n.* [< L. *plicare,* to fold] **1.** *same as* PLEAT **2.** a braid of hair, ribbon, etc. —*vt.* **1.** *same as* PLEAT **2.** to braid

plan (plan) *n.* [Fr.] **1.** a diagram showing the arrangement as of a structure **2.** a scheme for making, doing, or arranging something **3.** any outline or sketch —*vt., vi.* **planned, plan'ning** to make or have in mind a plan of or for (something) —**plan'ner** *n.*

plan·chette (plan chet', -shet') *n.* [Fr.] a small, three-cornered device used on a Ouija board

plane¹ (plān) *n.* [< Gr. *platys,* broad] any of a genus of trees with broad leaves, spherical dry fruits, and bark that sheds in large patches

plane² (plān) *adj.* [L. *planus,* flat] **1.** flat; level **2.** *Math a)* on a surface that is a plane *b)* of such surfaces —*n.* **1.** a surface wholly containing every straight line joining any two points in it **2.** a flat or level surface **3.** a level of existence, development, etc. **4.** an airplane **5.** an airfoil

plane³ (plān) *n.* [< L. *planus,* level] a carpenter's tool for smoothing or leveling wood —*vt.* **planed, plan'ing 1.** to smooth or level as with a plane **2.** to remove as with a plane —*vi.* **1.** to work with a plane **2.** to do the work of a plane —**plan'er** *n.*

plane⁴ (plān) *vi.* **planed, plan'ing** [Fr. *planer*] **1.** to soar or glide **2.** to rise partly out of the water, as a hydroplane (sense 1) does **3.** to travel by airplane

plane geometry the geometry of plane figures

PLANE

plan·et (plan'it) *n.* [< Gr. *planan,* wander] any heavenly body revolving about a star as the earth does about the sun, and shining by light reflected from the star: the major planets, in their order from the sun, are Mercury, Venus, Earth, Mars, Jupiter, Saturn, Uranus, Neptune, and Pluto —**plan'e·tar'y** (-ə ter'ē) *adj.*

plan·e·tar·i·um (plan'ə ter'ē əm) *n., pl.* **-i·ums, -i·a** (-ə) [< LL. *planeta,* planet + L. *(sol)arium,* solarium] a room or building with a large dome on the inner side of which the images of the sun, moon, planets, and stars are optically projected by an instrument that revolves to show celestial motions

plan'et·oid' (-ə toid') *n.* an asteroid (sense 1)

plank (plaŋk) *n.* [< LL. *planca*] **1.** a long, broad, thick board **2.** any of the principles in a platform as of a political party —*vt.* **1.** to cover, lay, etc. with planks **2.** to broil and serve (steak, fish, etc.) on a board or wooden platter **3.** [Colloq.] *a)* to set (*down*) with force *b)* to pay

plank'ing *n.* **1.** the act of laying planks **2.** planks collectively

plank·ton (plaŋk'tən) *n.* [G. < Gr. *planktos,* wandering] floating microscopic animal and plant life used as food by fish —**plank·ton'ic** (-tän'ik) *adj.*

plant (plant) *n.* [< L. *planta,* a sprout] **1.** a living organism that has no sense organs, lacks the power of voluntary movement, and synthesizes food from carbon dioxide; often, specif., a soft-stemmed organism of this kind, as distinguished from a tree or shrub **2.** a young tree, shrub, or herb ready to put into other soil to mature **3.** the machinery, buildings, etc. of a factory or business **4.** the equipment, buildings, etc. of an institution **5.** the apparatus for certain mechanical operations *[a ship's power plant]* **6.** [Slang] a person or thing put somewhere to trick or trap —*vt.* **1.** *a)* to put into the ground to grow *b)* to set plants in (a piece of ground) **2.** to set firmly in position **3.** to fix in the mind **4.** to settle; establish **5.** [Slang] to put (a person or thing) somewhere so as to trick or trap

plan·tain¹ (plan'tin) *n.* [< L. *plantago*] any of various related plants with leaves at the base of the stem and with spikes of tiny, greenish flowers

plan·tain² (plan'tin) *n.* [< Sp. < L. *platanus,* PLANE¹] **1.** a tropical banana plant with a coarse fruit cooked as a vegetable **2.** the fruit

plan·ta·tion (plan tā'shən) *n.* [< L. *plantare,* to plant] **1.** formerly, a colony **2.** an area growing cultivated crops **3.** an estate in a warm climate, cultivated by workers living on it **4.** a large, cultivated planting of trees

plant'er *n.* **1.** a plantation owner **2.** a person or machine that plants **3.** a container for house plants

plant louse *same as* APHID

plaque (plak) *n.* [Fr. < MDu. *placke,* disk] **1.** a thin, flat, decorated or lettered piece as of metal, placed as on a wall **2.** a bacterial film on teeth

plash (plash) *vt., vi., n.* [echoic] *same as* SPLASH

plasm (plaz''m) *n. same as* PLASMA (senses 1 & 2)

-plasm [see PLASMA] *a combining form meaning:* **1.** fluid substance as of an animal cell **2.** protoplasm

plas·ma (plaz'mə) *n.* [G. < Gr. *plassein,* to form] **1.** the fluid part of blood, lymph, etc., as distinguished from suspended elements **2.** protoplasm **3.** a high-temperature, ionized, electrically neutral gas

plas·ter (plas'tər) *n.* [< Gr. *emplassein,* to daub] **1.** a pasty mixture of lime, sand, and water, hard when dry, for coating walls, ceilings, etc. **2.** *same as* PLASTER OF PARIS **3.** a medicinal preparation spread as on cloth for application —*vt.* **1.** to cover as with plaster **2.** to apply like a plaster **3.** to make lie smooth and flat

plas'ter·board' *n.* a thin board formed of layers of plaster of Paris and paper

plaster of Paris calcined gypsum which, combined with water, forms a thick, pasty, quick-setting mixture used as in making casts and statuary

plas·tic (plas'tik) *adj.* [< Gr. *plassein,* to form] **1.** that molds or shapes matter; formative **2.** *a)* that can be molded or shaped *b)* impressionable **3.** dealing with molding or modeling **4.** made of a plastic —*n.* any of various nonmetallic, synthetic compounds that can be molded and hardened —**plas·tic·i·ty** (-tis'ə tē) *n.*

plastic surgery surgery to repair deformed bodily parts as by skin transfer —**plastic surgeon**

plat (plat) *n.* [var. of PLOT] **1.** a small piece of ground **2.** a map or plan as of subdivided land —*vt.* **plat'ted, plat'ting** to make a map or plan of

plate (plāt) *n.* [< Gr. *platys,* flat] **1.** a smooth, flat, thin piece as of metal **2.** *same as* SHEET METAL **3.** an impression taken from engraved metal **4.** a print of a woodcut, lithograph, etc. **5.** dishes, utensils, etc. of, or plated with, gold or silver **6.** a shallow dish **7.** a plateful **8.** the food in a dish; course **9.** food and service for an individual at a meal 10. a receptacle to receive donations, passed as in churches 11. *Anat., Zool.* a thin layer or scale as of bone 12. *Baseball* *short* for HOME PLATE 13. *Dentistry* a denture, specif. the part fitted to the gums 14. *Photog.* a sheet as of glass, with a light-sensitive coating 15. *Printing* a cast made as from a mold of set type —*vt.* plat′ed, plat′ing 1. to coat with metal 2. to cover with protective plates as of metal

pla·teau (pla tō′) *n., pl.* **-teaus′**, **-teaux′** (-tōz′) [Fr. < Gr. *platys*, flat] 1. an elevated tract of level land 2. a period of stability or little progress, as represented by a flat extent on a graph, etc.

plat′ed *adj.* 1. protected with plates, as of armor 2. coated with a metal *[silver-plated]*

plate′ful′ *n., pl.* **-fuls′** as much as a plate will hold

plate glass polished, clear glass in thick sheets, for shop windows, mirrors, etc.

plat·en (plat′'n) *n.* [see PLATE] 1. in a printing press, a flat metal plate which presses the paper against the inked type 2. in a typewriter, the roller against which the keys strike

plat·form (plat′fôrm′) *n.* [Fr. *plate-forme*, lit., flat form] 1. a raised horizontal surface; specif., *a)* a raised flooring beside railroad tracks, etc. *b)* a raised stage for performers, speakers, etc. 2. a statement of principles, as of a political party

plat·ing (plāt′iŋ) *n.* 1. the act or process of one that plates 2. an external layer of metal plates 3. a thin coating of gold, silver, etc.

plat·i·num (plat′'n əm) *n.* [< Sp. *plata*, silver] a steel-gray, metallic chemical element, resistant to corrosion: used as a chemical catalyst, for jewelry, etc.: symbol, Pt; at. wt., 195.09; at. no., 78

plat·i·tude (plat′ə tōōd′, -tyōōd′) *n.* [Fr. < *plat*, flat, after *latitude*, etc.] a trite remark, esp. one uttered as though it were fresh —**plat′i·tu′di·nous** *adj.*

Pla·to (plā′tō) 427?-347? B.C.; Gr. philosopher

Pla·ton·ic (plə tän′ik) *adj.* 1. of Plato or his philosophy 2. [*usually* p-] not sexual, but purely spiritual or intellectual *[platonic love]*

Pla·to·nism (plāt′'n iz'm) *n.* the philosophy of Plato or his school; Platonic idealism —**Pla′to·nist** *n.* —**Pla′to·nis′tic** *adj.*

pla·toon (plə tōōn′) *n.* [Fr. *peloton*, a ball, group] 1. a military unit composed of two or more squads 2. a group like this

Platte (plat) river formed in C Nebr. & flowing east into the Missouri: 310 mi.

plat·ter (plat′ər) *n.* [< OFr. *plat*: see PLATE] a large, shallow dish, usually oval, for serving food

plat·y·pus (plat′ə pəs) *n., pl.* **-pus·es**, **-pi′** (-pī′) [< Gr. *platys*, flat + *pous*, a foot] a small, aquatic, egg-laying mammal of Australia, with webbed feet, a tail like a beaver's, and a bill like a duck's: in full duckbill platypus

PLATYPUS
(16–24 in. long)

plau·dit (plô′dit) *n.* [< L. *plaudere*, applaud] [*usually pl.*] 1. applause 2. any expression of approval

plau·si·ble (plô′zə b'l) *adj.* [< L. *plaudere*, applaud] seemingly true, trustworthy, etc. —**plau′si·bil′i·ty**, **plau′si·ble·ness** *n.* —**plau′si·bly** *adv.*

play (plā) *vi.* [OE. *plegan*] 1. to move lightly, rapidly, etc. *[sunlight playing on the water]* 2. to have fun 3. to take part in a game or sport 4. to gamble 5. to trifle (*with*) 6. to perform on a musical instrument 7. to give out sounds: said of an instrument, phonograph record, etc. 8. to act in a specified way *[to play fair]* 9. to perform on the stage, etc. 10. to impose (*on* another's feelings, etc.) —*vt.* 1. to take part in (a game or sport) 2. to oppose (a person, etc.) in a game 3. to use (a player, etc.) in a game 4. to do, as in fun *[to play tricks]* 5. to bet (on) 6. to cause to move, etc.; wield 7. to cause *[to play havoc]* 8. to perform (music, a drama, etc.) 9. to perform on (an instrument) 10. to act the part of *[to play Iago]* 11. to imitate for amusement *[to play teacher]* 12. to direct repeatedly or continuously, as a light, etc. (with *on*, *over*, or *along*) —*n.* 1. motion or activity, esp. when free and rapid 2. freedom for motion or action 3. sport, games, etc. 4. fun; joking 5. the playing of a game 6. a move or act in a game 7. gambling 8. a dramatic composition or performance; drama —**play at** to work at halfheartedly —**play down** to make seem not too important —**played out 1.** finished 2. exhausted —**play out 1.** to play to the finish 2. to pay out (a rope, etc.) —**play up** to give prominence to —**play up to** [Colloq.] to try to please by flattery

play′back′ *n.* the playing of a phonograph record or tape

play′bill′ *n.* a program of a play

play′boy′ *n.* a man of means who is given to pleasure-seeking, sexual promiscuity, etc.

play′er *n.* 1. one who plays a game, musical instrument, etc. 2. an actor 3. a gambler 4. a thing that plays; specif., a record player

player piano a piano played mechanically

play′ful *adj.* 1. fond of play or fun; frisky 2. said or done in fun —**play′ful·ly** *adv.* —**play′ful·ness** *n.*

play′go′er *n.* one who goes to the theater frequently

play′ground′ *n.* a place, often part of a schoolyard, for outdoor games and play

play hook·y (hook′ē) [prob. < *hook it*, run away] to stay away from school without permission

play′house′ *n.* 1. a theater 2. a small house for children to play in 3. a doll house

playing cards cards used in playing various games, arranged in decks of four suits

play′mate′ *n.* a companion in games and recreation: also **play′fel′low**

play′-off′ *n.* a contest to break a tie or decide a championship

play on words a pun or punning

play′thing′ *n.* a toy

play′time′ *n.* time for play or recreation

play′wright′ (-rīt′) *n.* a writer of plays; dramatist

pla·za (plä′zə, plaz′ə) *n.* [Sp. < L.: see PLACE] 1. a public square in a city or town 2. *same as* SHOPPING CENTER 3. a service area along a superhighway

plea (plē) *n.* [< L. *placere*, please] 1. a statement in defense; excuse 2. an appeal; entreaty 3. *Law* a defendant's statement, answering the charges against him or showing why he should not answer

plea bargaining negotiations before a trial, in which a defendant agrees to plead guilty to a lesser charge in exchange for having more serious charges dropped

plead (plēd) *vi.* **plead′ed** or **pled** or **plead** (pled), **plead′ing** 1. to present a plea in a law court 2. to make an appeal; beg —*vt.* 1. to argue (a law case) 2. to answer (guilty or not guilty) to a charge 3. to offer as an excuse —**plead′a·ble** *adj.* —**plead′er** *n.*

plead′ings *n.pl.* the statements setting forth to the court the claims of the plaintiff and the answer of the defendant

pleas·ance (plez′'ns) *n.* a pleasant area or garden, as on an estate

pleas·ant (-'nt) *adj.* [< MFr. *plaisir*, please] 1. agreeable to the mind or senses; pleasing 2. having an agreeable manner, appearance, etc. —**pleas′ant·ly** *adv.* —**pleas′ant·ness** *n.*

pleas·ant·ry (-'n trē) *n., pl.* **-ries** 1. a humorous remark 2. a polite social remark

please (plēz) *vt.* **pleased**, **pleas′ing** [< L. *placere*] 1. to be agreeable to; satisfy 2. to be the wish of *[it pleased* him to go] —*vi.* 1. to be agreeable; satisfy 2. to have the wish; like *[to do as one pleases] Please* is also used in polite requests *[please* sit down] —**if you please** if you wish or like

pleas′ing *adj.* giving pleasure; agreeable —**pleas′ing·ly** *adv.*

pleas·ur·a·ble (plezh′ər ə b'l) *adj.* pleasant; enjoyable

pleas·ure (plezh′ər) *n.* 1. a pleased feeling; delight 2. one's wish, will, or choice 3. a thing that gives delight or satisfaction 4. sensual satisfaction

pleat (plēt) *n.* [see PLAIT] a flat double fold in cloth, etc., pressed or stitched in place —*vt.* to lay and press (cloth, etc.) in a pleat or pleats

plebe (plēb) *n.* [short for PLEBIAN] a member of the freshman class at the U.S. Military Academy or Naval Academy

ple·be·ian (pli bē′ən) *n.* [< L. *plebs*, common people] 1. a member of the ancient Roman lower class 2. one of the common people 3. a vulgar, coarse person —*adj.* vulgar, coarse, or common

pleb·i·scite (pleb′ə sīt′) *n.* [< Fr. < L. *plebs*, common people + *scitum*, decree] a direct vote of the people on a political issue

plec·trum (plek′trəm) *n., pl.* **-trums**, **-tra** (-tra) [< Gr. *plēssein*, to strike] a thin piece of metal, bone, etc. for plucking the strings of a guitar, mandolin, etc.

pled (pled) *alt. pt. & pp.* of PLEAD

---

fat, āpe, cär; ten, ēven; is, bīte; gō, hôrn, tōol, look; oil, out; up, fur; thin, *then*; zh, leisure; ŋ, ring; ə for *a* in *ago*; ' as in *able* (ā′b'l); ë, Fr. coeur; ö, Fr. feu; Fr. mon; ü, Fr. duc; r, Fr. cri; kh, G. doch, ich.   ‡ foreign; < derived from

pledge (plej) *n.* [prob. < OS. *plegan*, to guarantee] **1.** the condition of being given or held as security for a contract, payment, etc. **2.** a person or thing given or held as such security **3.** a token **4.** the drinking of a toast **5.** a promise or agreement **6.** something promised, esp. money **7.** one undergoing a trial period before initiation into a fraternity —*vt.* **pledged, pledg'ing 1.** to give as security **2.** to drink a toast to **3.** to bind by a promise **4.** to promise to give **5.** to accept tentative membership in (a fraternity) — **take the pledge** to vow not to drink alcoholic liquor — **pledg'er** *n.*

Ple·ia·des (plē′ə dēz′, plī′-) *n.pl., sing.* **Ple′iad** (-ad) **1.** *Gr. Myth.* the seven daughters of Atlas who were placed among the stars **2.** a cluster of stars in the constellation Taurus

ple·na·ry (plē′nə rē, plen′ə-) *adj.* [< L. *plenus*, full] **1.** full; complete **2.** for attendance by all members —**ple′na·ri·ly** (-rə lē) *adv.*

plen·i·po·ten·ti·ar·y (plen′i pə ten′shē er′ē, -shə rē) *adj.* [< L. *plenus*, full + *potens*, powerful] having or giving full authority —*n., pl.* **-ies** a diplomat given full authority

plen·i·tude (plen′ə tōod′, -tyōod′) *n.* [< L. *plenus*, full] **1.** fullness; completeness **2.** abundance; plenty

plen·te·ous (plen′tē əs) *adj.* plentiful; abundant —**plen′te·ous·ly** *adv.* —**plen′te·ous·ness** *n.*

plen·ti·ful (plen′ti fəl) *adj.* **1.** having or yielding plenty **2.** abundant —**plen′ti·ful·ly** *adv.*

plen·ty (plen′tē) *n., pl.* **-ties** [< L. *plenus*, full] **1.** prosperity; opulence **2.** an ample supply **3.** a large number —*adj.* [Colloq.] ample; enough —*adv.* [Colloq.] quite

ple·o·nasm (plē′ə naz′m) *n.* [< Gr. *pleonazein*, be in excess] **1.** the use of more words than are necessary for the meaning **2.** a redundant word or expression

pleth·o·ra (pleth′ə rə) *n.* [< Gr. *plēthos*, fullness] the state of being too full; overabundance

pleu·ra (ploor′ə) *n., pl.* **-rae** (-ē) [< Gr. *pleura*, a rib] the thin serous membrane lining each half of the chest cavity and covering a lung —**pleu′ral** *adj.*

pleu·ri·sy (ploor′ə sē) *n.* inflammation of the pleura, characterized by painful breathing —**pleu·rit·ic** (ploo rit′ik) *adj.*

Plex·i·glas (plek′sə glas′) [< L. *plexus*, a twining + GLASS] *a trademark for* a lightweight, transparent thermoplastic substance —*n.* this material: also **plex′i·glass**

plex·us (plek′səs) *n., pl.* **-us·es, -us** [< L. *plectere*, to twine] a network, as of blood vessels or nerves

pli·a·ble (plī′ə b'l) *adj.* [< L. *plicare*, to fold] **1.** easily bent; flexible **2.** easily influenced or persuaded **3.** adaptable —**pli′a·bil′i·ty, pli′a·ble·ness** *n.*

pli·ant (plī′ənt) *adj.* **1.** easily bent; pliable **2.** compliant —**pli′an·cy** *n.* —**pli′ant·ly** *adv.*

pli·ers (plī′ərz) *n.pl.* [< PLY¹] small pincers for gripping small objects, bending wire, etc.

plight¹ (plīt) *n.* [< OFr. *pleit*, a fold] a condition or state of affairs; esp., an awkward, sad, or dangerous situation

plight² (plīt) *vt.* [< OE. *pliht*, danger] to pledge, or bind by a pledge —**plight one's troth** to promise to marry

plinth (plinth) *n.* [< Gr. *plinthos*, a brick] the square block at the base of a column, pedestal, etc.

PLO, P.L.O. Palestine Liberation Organization

plod (pläd) *vi.* **plod′ded, plod′ding** [prob. echoic] **1.** to move heavily and laboriously; trudge **2.** to work steadily; drudge —**plod′der** *n.*

plop (pläp) *vt., vi.* **plopped, plop′ping** [echoic] **1.** to drop with a sound like that of something flat falling into water **2.** to drop heavily —*n.* the sound of plopping —*adv.* with a plop

plo·sive (plō′siv) *adj.* [< (EX)PLOSIVE] produced by the sudden release of the breath, as the sounds of *k, p,* and *t* used initially —*n.* a plosive sound

plot (plät) *n.* [OE., piece of land] **1.** a small area of ground **2.** a chart or diagram **3.** a secret, usually evil, scheme **4.** the plan of action of a play, novel, etc. —*vt.* **plot′ted, plot′ting 1.** to draw a map, plan, etc. of **2.** to make secret plans for **3.** to plan the action of (a story, etc.) **4.** to form (a curve) on a graph —*vi.* to scheme —**plot′ter** *n.*

plough (plou) *n., vt., vi.* chiefly Brit. sp. of PLOW

plov·er (pluv′ər, plō′vər) *n.* [< L. *pluvia*, rain] a shore bird with a short tail and long, pointed wings

plow (plou) *n.* [OE. *ploh*] **1.** a farm implement used to cut and turn up the soil **2.** anything like this; specif., a

SNOWPLOW —*vt.* **1.** to cut and turn up (soil) with a plow **2.** to make as if by plowing [he *plowed* his way in] —*vi.* **1.** to use a plow **2.** to cut a way (*through* water, etc.) **3.** to plod **4.** to begin work vigorously (with *into*) **5.** to collide forcefully (with *into*)

plow′man (-mən) *n., pl.* **-men 1.** one who guides a plow **2.** a farm worker

plow′share′ (-sher′) *n.* the cutting blade of a plow

ploy (ploi) *n.* [? < (EM)PLOY] an action or maneuver intended to outwit or disconcert another person

pluck (pluk) *vt.* [OE. *pluccian*] **1.** to pull off or out; pick **2.** to pull feathers or hair from [to *pluck* a chicken, *pluck* eyebrows] **3.** to pull at (the strings of a musical instrument) and release quickly —*vi.* to pull (*at*) —*n.* **1.** a pulling **2.** courage —**pluck up** to take heart —**pluck′er** *n.*

pluck′y *adj.* **-i·er, -i·est** brave; spirited; resolute —**pluck′i·ly** *adv.* —**pluck′i·ness** *n.*

plug (plug) *n.* [MDu. *plugge*] **1.** an object used to stop up a hole, drain, etc. **2.** a cake of tobacco **3.** an electrical device, as with prongs, for making contact or closing a circuit **4.** *same as: a)* SPARK PLUG *b)* FIREPLUG **5.** a defective or shopworn article **6.** [Colloq.] a free boost, advertisement, etc. —*vt.* **plugged, plug′ging 1.** to stop up (a hole, etc.) with a plug **2.** to insert a plug of **3.** [Colloq.] to advertise with a plug **4.** [Slang] to shoot a bullet into —*vi.* [Colloq.] to work doggedly —**plug in** to connect electrically by inserting a plug in a socket or jack

plum (plum) *n.* [OE. *plume*] **1.** *a)* a tree bearing a smooth-skinned, edible fruit with a flattened stone *b)* the fruit **2.** a raisin, when used in pudding or cake **3.** the dark bluish-red color of some plums **4.** something choice or desirable

plum·age (plōo′mij) *n.* [< L. *plumbe*, a feather] a bird's feathers

plumb (plum) *n.* [< L. *plumbum*, LEAD²] a lead weight (**plumb bob**) hung at the end of a line (**plumb line**), used to determine how deep water is or whether a wall, etc. is vertical —*adj.* perfectly vertical —*adv.* **1.** straight down **2.** [Colloq.] entirely [*plumb* crazy] —*vt.* **1.** to test or sound with a plumb **2.** to discover the facts of —**out of** (or **off**) **plumb** not vertical

plumb·er (plum′ər) *n.* [< L. *plumbum*, LEAD²] a worker who installs and repairs pipes, fixtures, etc., as of water or gas systems

plumb·ing (plum′iŋ) *n.* **1.** the work of a plumber **2.** the pipes and fixtures with which a plumber works

plume (plōom) *n.* [< L. *pluma*] **1.** *a)* a feather, esp. a large, showy one *b)* a cluster of these **2.** an ornament made of feathers **3.** a prize **4.** something like a plume in shape or lightness —*vt.* **plumed, plum′ing 1.** to adorn with plumes **2.** to preen (its feathers): said of a bird **3.** to pride (oneself)

plum·met (plum′it) *n.* [see PLUMB] **1.** a plumb **2.** a thing that weighs heavily —*vi.* to fall or drop straight downward

plump¹ (plump) *adj.* [< MDu. *plomp*, bulky] full and rounded in form; chubby —*vt., vi.* to fill out (sometimes with *up* or *out*) —**plump′ness** *n.*

plump² (plump) *vi.* [echoic] **1.** to fall or bump (*against*) **2.** to offer strong support (*for*) —*vt.* to drop or put down heavily or suddenly —*n.* a fall or the sound of this —*adv.* **1.** suddenly or heavily **2.** straight down —*adj.* blunt; direct

plum pudding [orig., made with plums] a rich pudding made of raisins, currants, suet, etc., boiled or steamed, as in a linen bag

plum·y (plōo′mē) *adj.* **-i·er, -i·est 1.** covered or adorned with plumes **2.** like a plume; feathery

plun·der (plun′dər) *vt., vi.* [< G. *plunder*, baggage] **1.** to rob by force, esp. in warfare **2.** to take (property) by force or fraud —*n.* **1.** the act of plundering **2.** goods taken by force or fraud —**plun′der·er** *n.*

plunge (plunj) *vt.* **plunged, plung′ing** [< L. *plumbum*, LEAD²] to thrust or throw suddenly (*into*) —*vi.* **1.** to dive or rush **2.** to move violently and rapidly downward or forward **3.** [Colloq.] to gamble heavily —*n.* **1.** *a)* a dive or downward leap *b)* a swim **2.** any plunging motion —**take the plunge** to start on some new and uncertain enterprise

plung′er *n.* **1.** one who plunges **2.** a large, rubber suction cup with a long handle, used to free clogged drains **3.** any cylindrical device that operates with a plunging motion, as a piston

plunk (pluŋk) *vt.* [echoic] **1.** to strum (a banjo, guitar, etc.) **2.** to throw or put down heavily; plump —*vi.* **1.** to give out a twanging sound **2.** to fall heavily —*n.* the act or sound of plunking —*adv.* with a twang or thud —**plunk down** [Colloq.] to pay

PLIERS
(A, slip joint;
B, needle nose)

plu·per·fect (ploo̅ pur'fikt) *adj.* [abbrev. of L. *plus quam perfectum*, more than perfect] designating a tense in certain languages corresponding to the past perfect in English —*n.* a pluperfect tense or form

plu·ral (ploor'əl) *adj.* [< L. *plus*, more] 1. of or including more than one 2. of or involving a plurality of persons or things 3. *Gram.* designating or of more than one (of what is referred to) —*n. Gram.* 1. the plural number 2. the form of a word designating more than one (Ex.: *hands, men*) 3. a word in plural form

plu·ral·i·ty (ploo ral'ə tē) *n., pl.* -ties 1. a being plural or numerous 2. a multitude 3. the excess of votes in an election that the leading candidate has over his nearest rival 4. *same as* MAJORITY

plu·ral·ize (ploor'ə līz') *vt., vi.* -ized', -iz'ing to make or become plural

plus (plus) *prep.* [L., more] 1. added to [2 *plus* 2] 2. in addition to —*adj.* 1. designating a sign (**plus sign**, +) indicating addition 2. positive [a *plus* quantity] 3. higher than [a grade of B *plus*] 4. [Colloq.] and more [personality *plus*] 5. *Elec. same as* POSITIVE [the *plus* terminal] —*n., pl.* **plus'es, plus'ses** 1. a plus sign 2. something added or favorable

plush (plush) *n.* [< L. *pilus*, hair] a fabric with a soft, thick pile —*adj.* [Slang] luxurious —**plush'i·ness** *n.* — **plush'y** *adj.* -i·er, -i·est

Plu·tarch (ploo̅'tärk) 46?-120? A.D.; Gr. biographer & historian

Plu·to (ploot'ō) 1. *Gr. & Rom. Myth.* the god ruling the lower world 2. the outermost planet of the solar system: see PLANET

plu·toc·ra·cy (ploo täk'rə sē) *n., pl.* -cies [< Gr. *ploutos*, wealth + *kratein*, to rule] 1. government by the wealthy 2. a group of wealthy people who control a government

plu·to·crat (ploot'ə krat') *n.* 1. a member of a wealthy ruling class 2. one whose wealth gives him control or influence —**plu'to·crat'ic** *adj.*

plu·to·ni·um (ploo tō'nē əm) *n.* [< *Pluto* (planet)] a radioactive, metallic chemical element: symbol, Pu; at. wt., 239.05; at. no., 94

plu·vi·al (ploo̅'vē əl) *adj.* [< L. *pluvia*, rain] 1. *a)* of or having to do with rain *b)* having much rain 2. *Geol.* formed by the action of rain

ply¹ (plī) *vt.* plied, ply'ing [< L. *plicare*, to fold] [Now Rare] to bend, twist, etc. —*n., pl.* plies 1. a thickness or layer, as of plywood, cloth, etc. 2. a twisted strand in rope, etc. —*adj.* having (a specified number of) layers, strands, etc. [three-*ply*]

ply² (plī) *vt.* plied, ply'ing [contr. < APPLY] 1. to work with (a tool, faculty, etc.) 2. to work at (a trade) 3. to address (someone) urgently (*with* questions, etc.) 4. to keep supplying (*with* gifts, food, etc.) 5. to sail back and forth across —*vi.* 1. to keep busy or work 2. to travel regularly (*between* places): said of ships, buses, etc.

Ply·mouth (plim'əth) village on the coast of Mass.: settled by the Pilgrims (1620) as **Plymouth Colony**

Plymouth Rock 1. boulder at Plymouth, Mass., where the Pilgrims are said to have landed 2. a breed of American chickens

ply'wood' *n.* [PLY¹ + WOOD] a material made of thin layers of wood glued and pressed together

Pm *Chem.* promethium

P.M. 1. Paymaster 2. Postmaster 3. Prime Minister

P.M., p.m., PM [L. *post meridiem*] after noon: used to designate time from noon to midnight

pneu·mat·ic (noo mat'ik, nyoo-) *adj.* [< Gr. *pneuma*, breath] 1. of or containing wind, air, or gases 2. worked by or filled with compressed air —**pneu·mat'i·cal·ly** *adv.*

pneu·mat'ics (-iks) *n.pl.* [*with sing. v.*] the branch of physics dealing with such properties of air and other gases as pressure, density, etc.

pneu·mo·nia (noo mōn'yə, nyoo-) *n.* [< Gr. *pnein*, to breathe] inflammation or infection of the lungs, caused by bacteria, viruses, etc.

Po (pō) river in N Italy: 405 mi.

Po *Chem.* polonium

P.O., p.o. 1. petty officer: also **PO** 2. post office 3. post office box

poach¹ (pōch) *vt.* [< MFr. *poche*, a pocket: the yolk is "pocketed" in the white] to cook (fish, an egg without its shell, etc.) in or over water or other liquid near the boiling point

poach² (pōch) *vt., vi.* [< Fr. < MHG. *puchen*, to plunder] 1. *a)* to trespass on (private property), esp. for hunting or

fishing *b)* to hunt or catch (game or fish) illegally 2. to steal —**poach'er** *n.*

Po·ca·hon·tas (pō'kə hän'təs) 1595?-1617; Am. Indian princess: reputed to have saved Captain John Smith from execution

pock (päk) *n.* [OE. *pocc*] 1. a pustule caused by smallpox, etc. 2. *same as* POCKMARK —**pocked** *adj.*

pock·et (päk'it) *n.* [< OFr. *poque*, a bag] 1. a little bag or pouch, esp. when sewn into or on clothing, for carrying small articles 2. a pouchlike cavity or hollow 3. a small area or group [a *pocket* of poverty] 4. funds [a drain on one's *pocket*] 5. *same as* AIR POCKET 6. *Geol.* a cavity filled with ore, oil, etc. —*adj.* 1. that can be carried in a pocket 2. small —*vt.* 1. to put into a pocket 2. to envelop; enclose 3. to take dishonestly, as money 4. to suppress [*pocket* one's pride] —**out of pocket** from money at hand —**pock'et·ful'** *n., pl.* -fuls'

pock'et·book' *n.* 1. a case for carrying money and papers in one's pocket 2. a woman's purse 3. monetary resources

pock'et·knife' *n., pl.* -knives' a knife with blades that fold into the handle

pocket money cash for small expenses

pocket veto the indirect veto by the President of the U.S. of a bill presented to him by Congress within ten days of its adjournment, by his failing to sign the bill

pock·mark (päk'märk') *n.* a scar or pit left by a pustule, as of smallpox —**pock'marked'** *adj.*

po·co (pō'kō) *adv.* [It.] *Music* somewhat

pod (päd) *n.* [< ?] a dry fruit or seed vessel enclosing one or more seeds, as a legume —**pod'like'** *adj.*

-pod [< Gr. *pous*, a foot] *a combining form meaning:* 1. foot 2. (one) having (a specified number or kind of) feet Also **-pode**

po·di·a·try (pō dī'ə trē, pə-) *n.* [< Gr. *pous*, foot + -IATRY] the profession dealing with the treatment of foot disorders —**po·di'a·trist** *n.*

po·di·um (pō'dē əm) *n., pl.* -di·ums, -di·a (-ə) [< Gr. *pous*, foot] a low platform, esp. for the conductor of an orchestra

Po·dunk (pō'duŋk') [Colloq.] any typically dull small town in the U.S.

Poe (pō), **Edgar Allan** 1809-49; U.S. poet, short-story writer, & critic

po·em (pō'əm) *n.* [< Gr. *poiein*, to make] 1. an arrangement of words written or spoken, traditionally a rhythmical or metrical composition, sometimes rhymed 2. anything suggesting a poem in its effect

po·e·sy (pō'ə sē', -zē') *n. old-fashioned var. of* POETRY

po·et (pō'ət) *n.* 1. one who writes poems 2. one who expresses himself with beauty of thought and language — **po'et·ess** [Now Rare] *n.fem.*

poet. 1. poetic 2. poetry

po·et·as·ter (pō'ə tas'tər) *n.* [< POET + L. *-aster*, dim. suffix] a writer of mediocre verse

po·et·ic (pō et'ik) *adj.* 1. of, like, or for poets or poetry 2. written in verse 3. having the beauty, imagination, etc. of poetry Also **po·et'i·cal** —**po·et'i·cal·ly** *adv.*

poetic justice justice, as in some plays, etc., in which good is rewarded and evil punished

poetic license 1. disregard of strict fact or of rigid form, as by a poet, for artistic effect 2. freedom to do this

po·et·ics (pō et'iks) *n.pl.* [*with sing. v.*] 1. the theory or structure of poetry 2. a treatise on this

poet laureate *pl.* **poets laureate, poet laureates** the official poet of a nation, appointed to write poems celebrating national events, etc.

po·et·ry (pō'ə trē) *n.* 1. the art, theory, or structure of poems 2. poems 3. poetic qualities

po·go stick (pō'gō) [arbitrary coinage] a stilt with pedals and a spring at one end, on which one can move along in a series of bounds

po·grom (pō gräm') *n.* [Russ., devastation] an organized persecution and massacre of a minority group, esp. of Jews (as in Czarist Russia)

poi (poi, pō'ē) *n.* [Haw.] a Hawaiian food made of mashed, fermented taro root

poign·ant (poin'yənt) *adj.* [< L. *pungere*, to prick] 1. *a)* sharp to the smell *b)* keenly affecting the other senses 2. sharply painful to the feelings 3. biting [*poignant* wit] — **poign'an·cy** *n.* —**poign'ant·ly** *adv.*

poin·ci·a·na (poin'sē an'ə, -ā'nə) *n.* [< M. de *Poinci*, a governor of the Fr. West Indies] a small tropical tree with showy red, orange, or yellow flowers

fat, āpe, cär; ten, ēven; is, bīte; gō, hôrn, too̅l, look; oil, out; up, fur; thin, *then*; zh, leisure; ŋ, ring; ə for *a* in *ago*; ' as in *able* (ā'b'l); ë, Fr. coeur; ö, Fr. feu; Fr. mon; ü, Fr. duc; r, Fr. cri; kh, G. doch, ich. ‡ foreign; < derived from

poin·set·ti·a (poin set′ē ə, -set′ə) *n.* [< J. R. *Poinsett,* 19th-c. U.S. ambassador to Mexico] a tropical plant with yellow flowers and petallike red leaves

point (point) *n.* [< L. *pungere,* to prick] **1.** a dot in writing, etc., as a decimal point **2.** position, location, etc. [*all points south*] **3.** the exact moment **4.** a condition, degree, etc. reached [*a boiling point*] **5.** an item [*explain it point by point*] **6.** a distinguishing characteristic **7.** a unit, as of value, game scores, etc. **8.** a sharp end **9.** a projecting piece of land; cape **10.** a branch of a deer's antler **11.** the essential fact or idea **12.** aim; purpose **13.** an impressive argument or fact **14.** a helpful hint **15.** *Ballet* the position of being on the tips of the toes **16.** *Elec.* either of the contacts that make or break the circuit in a distributor **17.** a mark showing direction on a compass **18.** a measuring unit for printing type, about 1/72 of an inch — *vt.* **1.** to sharpen to a point **2.** to give (a story, etc.) emphasis (usually with *up*) **3.** to show (usually with *out*) [*point the way*] **4.** to aim —*vi.* **1.** to direct one's finger or the like (*at* or *to*) **2.** to call attention (*to*) **3.** to be directed (*to* or *toward*) —**at the point of** very close to —**beside the point** irrelevant —**make a point of 1.** to insist on **2.** to call special attention to —**on** (or **upon**) **the point of** on the verge of —**to the point** pertinent; apt: also **in point**

point′-blank′ *adj., adv.* [POINT + *blank,* white center of a target] **1.** (aimed) straight at a mark **2.** direct(ly); blunt(ly)

point′ed *adj.* **1.** having a sharp end **2.** sharp; incisive **3.** aimed at someone, as a remark **4.** very evident —**point′-ed·ly** *adv.* —**point′ed·ness** *n.*

point′er *n.* **1.** a person or thing that points **2.** a long, tapered rod for pointing to things, as on a map **3.** an indicator on a clock, meter, etc. **4.** a large, lean hunting dog with a smooth coat **5.** [Colloq.] a helpful hint

point′less *adj.* **1.** without a point **2.** without meaning or force; senseless —**point′less·ly** *adv.* —**point′less·ness** *n.*

point of order a question as to whether parliamentary procedure is being observed

point of view 1. the way in which something is viewed **2.** a mental attitude

point′y *adj.* **-i·er, -i·est 1.** that comes to a sharp point **2.** having many points

poise (poiz) *n.* [< L. *pendere,* weigh] **1.** balance; stability **2.** ease and dignity of manner **3.** carriage, as of the body —*vt., vi.* **poised, pois′ing 1.** to balance or be balanced **2.** to suspend or be suspended

poi·son (poi′z'n) *n.* [< L. *potio,* potion] a substance which in small quantities can cause illness or death —*vt.* **1.** to harm or destroy with poison **2.** to put poison on or into **3.** to influence wrongfully —*adj.* poisonous or poisoned —**poi′son·er** *n.*

poison ivy 1. a plant with leaves of three leaflets and ivory-colored berries: it can cause a severe rash on contact **2.** such a rash

poison oak *name variously used for:* **1.** POISON IVY **2.** POISON SUMAC

poi′son·ous *adj.* that can injure or kill by or as by poison —**poi′son·ous·ly** *adv.*

poison sumac a swamp plant with leaves made up of 7 to 13 leaflets: it can cause a severe rash on contact

POISON IVY

poke¹ (pōk) *vt.* **poked, pok′ing** [MDu. or LowG. *poken*] **1.** *a)* to jab with a stick, finger, etc. *b)* [Slang] to hit **2.** to make (a hole, etc.) by poking **3.** to thrust forward [*to poke one's head out a window*] —*vi.* **1.** to jab (*at*) **2.** to search (*about* or *around*) **3.** to stick out **4.** to move slowly (*along*) —*n.* **1.** *a)* a jab; thrust *b)* [Slang] a blow with the fist **2.** a poke bonnet —**poke fun (at)** to ridicule

poke² (pōk) *n.* [< Frank.] [Dial.] a sack or bag

poke³ (pōk) *n.* [< AmInd. *puccoon*] *same as* POKEWEED: also **poke′ber′ry** (-ber′ē), *pl.* **-ries**

poke bonnet a bonnet with a wide front brim

pok·er¹ (pō′kər) *n.* [< ?] a card game in which the players bet on the value of their hands, forming a pool to be taken by the winner

pok·er² (pō′kər) *n.* **1.** a person or thing that pokes **2.** a bar, as of iron, for stirring a fire

poker face [Colloq.] an expressionless face, as of a poker player hiding the nature of his hand

poke·weed (pōk′wēd′) *n.* [see POKE³] a N. American plant with reddish-purple berries and poisonous roots

pok·ey (pō′kē) *n., pl.* **-eys, -ies** [< ?] [Slang] a jail: also **pok′y**

pok·y (pō′kē) *adj.* **-i·er, -i·est** [see POKE¹] **1.** slow; dull **2.** small and uncomfortable [*a poky room*] **3.** shabbily dressed Also **pok′ey**

pol (päl) *n.* [Slang] an experienced politician

Pol. 1. Poland **2.** Polish

Po·land (pō′lənd) country in C Europe: 120,625 sq. mi.; pop. 32,807,000; cap. Warsaw

po·lar (pō′lər) *adj.* **1.** of or near the North or South Pole **2.** of a pole or poles **3.** having polarity **4.** opposite in character, direction, etc.

polar bear a large, white bear of the arctic regions

Po·lar·is (pō lar′is) *same as* NORTH STAR

po·lar·i·ty (pō lar′ə tē) *n., pl.* **-ties 1.** the property of having opposite magnetic poles **2.** any tendency to turn, feel, etc. in a certain way, as if magnetized **3.** the having of two contrary qualities, powers, etc. **4.** the condition of being positive or negative with respect to a reference point or object

po·lar·i·za·tion (pō′lər i zā′shən) *n.* **1.** the producing or acquiring of polarity **2.** the accumulation of gases around the electrodes of an electric cell during electrolysis, reducing the current flow **3.** *Optics* a condition, or the production of a condition, of light in which the vibrations of the waves are confined to one plane or one direction

po·lar·ize (pō′lə rīz′) *vt.* **-ized′, -iz′ing** to give polarity to —*vi.* to acquire polarity; specif., to separate into opposed groups, viewpoints, etc.

Po·lar·oid (pō′lə roid′) *a trademark for:* **1.** a transparent material that can polarize light **2.** a camera that develops and prints snapshots: in full **Polaroid (Land) camera**

Pole (pōl) *n.* a native or inhabitant of Poland

pole¹ (pōl) *n.* [< L. *palus,* a stake] **1.** a long, slender piece of wood, metal, etc. **2.** a unit of measure, equal to one rod or one square rod —*vt., vi.* **poled, pol′ing** to propel (a boat or raft) with a pole

pole² (pōl) *n.* [< Gr. *polos*] **1.** either end of any axis, as of the earth **2.** the region around the North Pole or South Pole **3.** either of two opposed forces, parts, etc., as the ends of a magnet, terminals of a battery, etc. —**poles apart** widely separated

pole·cat (pōl′kat′) *n.* [prob. < OFr.: see PULLET & CAT] **1.** a small, weasellike carnivore of Europe **2.** *same as* SKUNK

po·lem·ic (pə lem′ik, pō-) *adj.* [< Fr. < Gr. *polemos,* a war] of or involving dispute: also **po·lem′i·cal** —*n.* an argument or controversial discussion

po·lem′ics *n.pl.* [*with sing. v.*] the art or practice of disputation —**po·lem′i·cist** (-ə sist) *n.*

pole′star′ *n.* **1.** the North Star **2.** a guiding principle

pole vault a leap for height by vaulting over a bar with the aid of a long pole —**pole′-vault′** *vi.*

po·lice (pə lēs′) *n.* [Fr. < Gr. *polis,* city] **1.** the governmental department (of a city, state, etc.) for keeping order, enforcing the law, and investigating crime **2.** [*with pl. v.*] the members of such a department, or of a private organization like this [*security police*] —*vt.* **-liced′, -lic′ing 1.** to control, protect, etc. with police or the like **2.** to keep (a military camp, etc.) clean and orderly

police dog a German shepherd dog

po·lice′man (-mən) *n., pl.* **-men** a member of a police force —**po·lice′wom′an** *n.fem., pl.* **-wom′en**

police state a government that uses a secret police force to suppress political opposition

pol·i·cy¹ (päl′ə sē) *n., pl.* **-cies** [see POLICE] **1.** wise management **2.** any governing principle, plan, etc.

pol·i·cy² (päl′ə sē) *n., pl.* **-cies** [< Gr. *apodeixis,* proof] a written insurance contract

po·li·o (pō′lē ō′) *n. clipped form of* POLIOMYELITIS

po·li·o·my·e·li·tis (pō′lē ō mī′ə līt′əs) *n.* [< Gr. *polios,* gray + *myelos,* marrow] an acute infectious disease, esp. of children, caused by a virus inflammation of the gray matter of the spinal cord, often resulting in muscular paralysis

Po·lish (pō′lish) *adj.* of Poland, its people, their language, etc. —*n.* the Slavic language of the Poles

pol·ish (päl′ish) *vt.* [< L. *polire*] **1.** *a)* to smooth and brighten, as by rubbing *b)* to coat with wax, etc. and make glossy **2.** to refine (manners, etc.) **3.** to complete or embellish —*vi.* to take a polish —*n.* **1.** a surface gloss **2.** elegance; refinement **3.** a substance used for polishing —**polish off** [Colloq.] to finish or get rid of —**pol′ished** *adj.*

po·lite (pə līt′) *adj.* [< L. *polire,* to polish] **1.** cultured; refined **2.** having good manners; courteous —**po·lite′ly** *adv.* —**po·lite′ness** *n.*

pol·i·tic (päl′ə tik) *adj.* [see POLICE] **1.** having practical wisdom; prudent **2.** crafty; unscrupulous **3.** expedient [*a politic plan*] **4.** [Rare] political: see BODY POLITIC —*vi.* **-ticked, -tick·ing** to campaign in politics —**pol′i·tic·ly** *adv.*

po·lit·i·cal (pə lit′i k'l) *adj.* **1.** of, concerned with, or engaged in government, politics, etc. **2.** of or characteristic of political parties or politicians —**po·lit′i·cal·ly** *adv.*

political science the science of the principles, organization, and methods of government

pol·i·ti·cian (päl′ə tish′ən) *n.* one actively engaged in politics, often one holding or seeking political office: often used with implications of seeking personal or partisan gain, scheming, etc.

po·lit·i·co (pə lit′i kō′) *n., pl.* -**cos′** [Sp. or It.] *same as* POLITICIAN

pol·i·tics (päl′ə tiks) *n.pl.* [*with sing. or pl. v.*] **1.** the science of government **2.** political affairs **3.** participation in political affairs **4.** political methods, tactics, etc. **5.** political opinions, principles, etc. **6.** factional scheming for power

pol′i·ty *n., pl.* -**ties** [see POLICE] **1.** the governmental organization of a state, church, etc. **2.** a society or institution with a government; state

Polk (pōk), **James K.** 1795-1849; 11th president of the U.S. (1845-49)

pol·ka (pōl′kə) *n.* [Czech < Pol. *Polak*, a Pole] **1.** a fast dance for couples **2.** music for this dance —*vi.* to dance the polka

pol·ka dot (pō′kə) any of a pattern of small round dots on cloth

poll (pōl) *n.* [ME. *pol*] **1.** the head **2.** a counting, listing, etc. of persons, esp. of voters **3.** the number of votes recorded **4.** [*pl.*] a place where votes are cast **5.** a canvassing of people's opinions on some question —*vt.* **1.** to cut off or cut short **2.** to trim the wool, branches, etc. of **3.** *a*) to register the votes of *b*) to require each member of (a jury, etc.) to declare his vote individually **4.** to receive (a certain number of votes) **5.** to cast (a vote) **6.** to canvass in a poll (sense 5) —*vi.* to vote in an election

pol·len (päl′ən) *n.* [L., dust] the yellow, powderlike male sex cells on the stamens of a flower

pollen count the number of grains of pollen, esp. of ragweed, in a given volume of air at a specified time and place

pol·li·nate (päl′ə nāt′) *vt.* -**nat′ed**, -**nat′ing** to transfer pollen from a stamen to a pistil of (a flower) —**pol′li·na′tion** *n.*

pol·li·wog (päl′ē wäg′, -wôg′) *n.* [< ME.: see POLL & WIGGLE] *same as* TADPOLE: also sp. **pol′ly·wog′**

poll·ster (pōl′stər) *n.* a person whose work is taking public opinion polls

poll tax a tax per head: in some States payment of a poll tax is a prerequisite for voting

pol·lu·tant (pə lōōt′'nt) *n.* something that pollutes, as a harmful chemical discharged into the air

pol·lute (pə lōōt′) *vt.* -**lut′ed**, -**lut′ing** [< L. *polluere*] to make unclean, impure, or corrupt; defile —**pol·lut′er** *n.* —**pol·lu′tion** *n.*

Pol·lux (päl′əks) **1.** *Gr. & Rom. Myth.* the immortal twin of Castor **2.** the brightest star in the constellation Gemini

Pol·ly·an·na (päl′ē an′ə) *n.* [title heroine of a novel (1913)] a persistently optimistic person

po·lo (pō′lō) *n.* [prob. < Tibet. *pulu*, the ball] a game played on horseback by two teams using a wooden ball and long-handled mallets

Po·lo (pō′lō), **Mar·co** (mär′kō) 1254?-1324?; Venetian traveler in E Asia

po·lo·naise (päl′ə nāz′, pō′lə-) *n.* [Fr. < fem. of *polonais*, Polish] **1.** a stately Polish dance in triple time **2.** music for this dance

po·lo·ni·um (pə lō′nē əm) *n.* [< ML. *Polonia*, Poland: coinage of Marie Curie] a radioactive chemical element formed by the disintegration of radium: symbol, Po; at. wt., 210.05; at. no., 84

pol·troon (päl trōōn′) *n.* [< Fr. < It. *poltrone*] a thorough coward

poly- [< Gr. *polys*] *a combining form meaning* much, many

pol·y·an·dry (päl′ē an′drē) *n.* [< Gr. *poly-*, many + *aner*, a man] the practice of having two or more husbands at the same time —**pol′y·an′drous** *adj.*

pol·y·clin·ic (päl′ē klin′ik) *n.* [POLY- + CLINIC] a clinic or hospital treating various kinds of disease

pol·y·es·ter (päl′ē es′tər) *n.* [POLY(MER) + ESTER] any of several polymeric synthetic resins used in making plastics, fibers, etc.

pol·y·eth·yl·ene (päl′ē eth′ə lēn′) *n.* [POLY(MER) + ETHYLENE] a thermoplastic resin used in making plastics, films, etc.

po·lyg·a·my (pə lig′ə mē) *n.* [< Fr. < Gr. *poly-*, many + *gamos*, marriage] the practice of having two or more

wives or husbands at the same time —**po·lyg′a·mist** *n.* —**po·lyg′a·mous** *adj.*

pol·y·glot (päl′i glät′) *adj.* [< Gr. *poly-*, many + *glotta*, tongue] **1.** speaking or writing several languages **2.** written in several languages —*n.* a polyglot person

pol·y·gon (päl′i gän′) *n.* [< Gr.: see POLY- & -GON] a closed plane figure with several angles and sides, usually more than four —**po·lyg·o·nal** (pə lig′ə n'l) *adj.*

pol′y·graph′ (-graf′) *n.* an instrument for recording changes in blood pressure, pulse rate, etc., used on persons suspected of lying

po·lyg·y·ny (pə lij′ə nē) *n.* [< POLY- + Gr. *gynē*, woman] the practice of having two or more wives or concubines at the same time —**po·lyg′y·nous** *adj.*

pol·y·he·dron (päl′i hē′drən) *n., pl.* -**drons**, -**dra** (-drə) [< Gr.: see POLY- & -HEDRON] a solid figure with several plane surfaces, usually more than six —**pol′y·he′dral** *adj.*

pol·y·mer (päl′i mər) *n.* [G. < Gr. *poly-*, many + *meros*, a part] a substance made up of giant molecules formed by polymerization

pol·y·mer·ic (päl′i mer′ik) *adj.* composed of the same chemical elements in the same proportions by weight, but differing in molecular weight

po·lym·er·i·za·tion (pə lim′ər i zā′shən, päl′i mər-) *n.* the process of joining two or more like molecules to form a more complex molecule whose molecular weight is a multiple of the original and whose physical properties are different —**po·lym′er·ize′** (-īz′) *vt., vi.* -**ized′**, -**iz′ing**

pol·y·mor·phous (päl′i môr′fəs) *adj.* [< Gr. *poly-*, many + *morphē*, form] having, occurring in, or passing through several or various forms: also **pol′y·mor′phic**

Pol·y·ne·sia (päl′ə nē′zhə) a major division of the Pacific islands, east of the international date line —**Pol′y·ne′sian** *adj., n.*

pol·y·no·mi·al (päl′i nō′mē əl) *n.* [POLY- + (BI)NOMIAL] *Algebra* an expression consisting of two or more terms (Ex.: $x^3 + 3x + 2$)

pol·yp (päl′ip) *n.* [< Fr. < Gr. *poly-*, many + *pous*, a foot] **1.** any of various coelenterates with a fringe of tentacles at the top of a tubelike body, as the sea anemone, hydra, etc. **2.** a projecting growth of mucous membrane inside the nose, bladder, etc.

POLYP (sense 1)

pol·y·phon·ic (päl′i fän′ik) *adj.* [< Gr. *poly-*, many + *phōnē*, a sound] **1.** having or making many sounds **2.** *Music* of or characterized by polyphony

po·lyph·o·ny (pə lif′ə nē) *n.* **1.** multiplicity of sounds **2.** *Music* a combining of a number of harmonious melodies; counterpoint

pol·y·syl·lab·ic (päl′i si lab′ik) *adj.* **1.** having several, esp. four or more, syllables **2.** characterized by polysyllabic words —**pol′y·syl′la·ble** (-sil′ə b'l) *n.*

pol·y·tech·nic (päl′i tek′nik) *adj.* [< Fr. < Gr. *poly-*, many + *technē*, an art] of or providing instruction in many scientific and technical subjects

pol·y·the·ism (päl′i thē iz′m) *n.* [< Fr. < Gr. *poly-*, many + *theos*, god] belief in more than one god —**pol′y·the·is′tic** *adj.*

pol·y·un·sat·u·rat·ed (päl′i un sach′ə rāt′id) *adj.* [POLY- + UNSATURATED] designating any of certain vegetable and animal fats and oils with a low cholesterol content

pol′y·va′lent (-vā′lənt) *adj. Chem.* **1.** having a valence of more than two **2.** having more than one valence

po·made (pä mād′, -mäd′) *n.* [< Fr. < It. *pomo*, apple (orig. an ingredient)] a perfumed preparation, as for the hair

pome·gran·ate (päm′gran′it, päm′ə-; pum′-) *n.* [ult. < L. *pomum*, fruit + *granum*, seed] **1.** a round, red, pulpy fruit with a thick rind and many seeds **2.** the bush or tree that bears it

Pom·er·a·ni·an (päm′ə rā′nē ən) *n.* a small dog with long, silky hair and pointed ears

pom·mel (pum′'l, päm′-) *n.* [< L. *pomum*, fruit] the rounded, upward-projecting front part of a saddle —*vt.* -**meled** or -**melled**, -**mel·ing** or -**mel·ling** *same as* PUMMEL

pomp (pämp) *n.* [< Gr. *pompē*, solemn procession] **1.** stately display **2.** ostentatious show or display

pom·pa·dour (päm′pə dôr′) *n.* [< Mme. *Pompadour*, mistress of Louis XV] a hairdo in which the hair is brushed up high from the forehead

pom·pa·no (päm′pə nō′) *n., pl.* -**no′**, -**nos′** [< Sp.] a spiny-finned, saltwater food fish of N. America

Pom·pei·i (päm pā′ē, -pā′) ancient city on the S coast of Italy: destroyed by the eruption of Mount Vesuvius (79 A.D.) —**Pom·pei′an** (-pā′ən) *adj., n.*

Pom·pey (päm′pē) 106–48 B.C.; Rom. general & statesman: called *the Great*

pom·pon (päm′pän′, -päm′) *n.* [Fr.] **1.** an ornamental tuft, as of silk or wool, worn as on hats or waved by cheerleaders: also **pom-pom** (päm′päm′) **2.** a chrysanthemum, dahlia, etc. with small, round flowers

pom·pous (päm′pəs) *adj.* **1.** full of pomp **2.** pretentious, as in speech or manner; self-important —**pom·pos′i·ty** (-päs′ə tē) *n., pl.* -ties —**pom′pous·ly** *adv.*

Pon·ce de Le·ón (pôn′the *the* le ôn′; *E.* päns′ də lē′ən), **Juan** (hwän) 1460?–1521; Sp. explorer: discovered Florida

pon·cho (pän′chō) *n., pl.* -chos [< SAmInd.] **1.** a cloak like a blanket with a hole in the middle for the head **2.** a raincoat like this

pond (pänd) *n.* [< ME. var. of POUND³] a body of standing water smaller than a lake

pon·der (pän′dər) *vt., vi.* [< L. *ponderare*, weigh] to think deeply (about); deliberate

pon·der·ous *adj.* **1.** very heavy; unwieldy **2.** labored; dull, as in style —**pon′der·ous·ly** *adv.*

pone (pōn) *n.* [< AmInd.] [Chiefly Southern] corn bread in small, oval loaves

pon·gee (pän jē′) *n.* [< Chin. dial. *pen-chi*, domestic loom] a soft, thin silk cloth, usually in natural tan

pon·iard (pän′yərd) *n.* [< Fr., ult. < L. *pugnus*, fist] a dagger

pon·tiff (pän′tif) *n.* [< L. *pontifex*, high priest] **1.** a bishop **2.** [P-] the Pope **3.** a high priest

pon·tif·i·cal (pän tif′i k'l) *adj.* **1.** having to do with a pontiff **2.** papal **3.** pompous, dogmatic, or arrogant —**pon·tif′i·cal·ly** *adv.*

pon·tif·i·cate (-i kit) *n.* the office or term of a pontiff — *vi.* (-i kāt′) -cat′ed, -cat′ing **1.** to officiate as a pontiff **2.** to be pompous or dogmatic

pon·toon (pän tōōn′) *n.* [< Fr. < L. *pons*, a bridge] **1.** a flat-bottomed boat **2.** any of a row of boats, floating cylinders, etc., used to support a temporary bridge (**pontoon bridge**) **3.** a boatlike float on an aircraft's landing gear

po·ny (pō′nē) *n., pl.* -nies [< Scot., prob. < L. *pullus*, foal] **1.** a horse of any small breed **2.** a small liqueur glass **3.** a literal translation of a foreign work, used in doing schoolwork, often dishonestly —*vt., vi.* -nied, -ny·ing to pay (money), as to settle an account (with *up*)

po·ny·tail′ *n.* a hair style in which the hair, tied tightly at the back, hangs like a pony's tail

pooch (pōōch) *n.* [< ?] [Slang] a dog

poo·dle (pōō′d'l) *n.* [G. *pudel*] any of a breed of dog with a solid-colored, curly coat

pooh (pōō) *interj.* an exclamation of disdain, disbelief, or impatience

pooh² (pōō) *vt.* [Slang] *same as* POOP²

pooh-pooh (pōō′pōō′) *vt.* to make light of; belittle

pool¹ (pōōl) *n.* [OE. *pol*] **1.** a small pond **2.** a puddle **3.** *same as* SWIMMING POOL **4.** a deep, still spot in a river

pool² (pōōl) *n.* [< Fr. < LL. *pulla*, hen] **1.** a game of billiards played on a table with six pockets **2.** *a)* a combination of resources, funds, etc. for some common purpose *b)* the parties forming such a combination **3.** a combination of business firms for creating a monopoly **4.** a supply of equipment, personnel, etc. shared by a group —*vt., vi.* to contribute to a common fund

poop¹ (pōōp) *n.* [< L. *puppis*, stern of a ship] a raised deck at the stern of a sailing ship: also **poop deck**

poop² (pōōp) *vt.* [Slang] to make exhausted; tire

poor (poor) *adj.* [< L. *pauper*, poor] **1.** having little or no means to support oneself; needy **2.** indicating or characterized by poverty **3.** lacking in some quality; specif., *a)* inadequate *b)* inferior or worthless *c)* contemptible **4.** worthy of pity; unfortunate —**the poor** poor, or needy, people —**poor′ly** *adv.* —**poor′ness** *n.*

poor′house′ *n.* formerly, an institution for paupers, supported from public funds

poor′-mouth′ *vi.* [Colloq.] to complain about one's lack of money

pop¹ (päp) *n.* [echoic] **1.** a sudden, light, explosive sound **2.** any carbonated, nonalcoholic beverage —*vi.* **popped, pop′ping 1.** to make, or burst with, a pop **2.** to move, go, etc. suddenly **3.** to bulge: said of the eyes **4.** *Baseball* to hit the ball high into the infield —*vt.* **1.** to cause (corn) to pop, as by roasting **2.** to shoot **3.** to put suddenly [he *popped* his head in] —*adv.* with or like a pop

pop² (päp) *n.* [< PAPA] [Slang] father

pop³ (päp) *adj. clipped form of* POPULAR

pop. 1. popular **2.** population

pop (art) a realistic art style using techniques and subjects from commercial art, comic strips, posters, etc.

pop concert a popular concert, chiefly of semiclassical and light classical music

pop′corn′ *n.* **1.** a variety of corn with hard grains which pop open into a white, puffy mass when heated **2.** the popped grains

pope (pōp) *n.* [< Gr. *pappas*, father] [*usually* P-] *R.C.Ch.* the bishop of Rome and head of the Church

Pope (pōp), **Alexander** 1688–1744; Eng. poet

pop·eyed (päp′īd′) *adj.* having protruding eyes

pop′gun′ *n.* a toy gun that shoots pellets by air compression, with a pop

pop·in·jay (päp′in jā′) *n.* [< Ar. *babaghā*, parrot] a talkative, conceited person

pop·lar (päp′lər) *n.* [< L. *populus*] **1.** a tall tree related to the willow, having soft, fibrous wood **2.** its wood

pop·lin (päp′lən) *n.* [< Fr., prob. < *Poperinge*, city in Flanders] a sturdy ribbed fabric of cotton, silk, etc.

Po·po·ca·té·petl (pō pō′kä te′pet'l; *E.* pō′pə kat′ə pet′'l) volcano in SC Mexico

pop·o·ver (päp′ō′vər) *n.* a puffy, hollow muffin

pop·per (päp′ər) *n.* **1.** one that pops **2.** a covered wire basket or pan for popping corn

pop·py (päp′ē) *n., pl.* -pies [< L. *papaver*] **1.** a plant with a milky juice and showy, variously colored flowers **2.** its flower **3.** an extract, as opium, made from poppy juice **4.** yellowish red

pop′py·cock′ (-käk′) *n.* [Du. *pappekak*, dung] [Colloq.] foolish talk; nonsense

poppy seed the small, dark seed of the poppy, used in baking, etc.

pop·u·lace (päp′yə lis) *n.* [Fr. < It. < L. *populus*, people] **1.** the common people; the masses **2.** *same as* POPULATION (sense 1 *a*)

pop·u·lar (päp′yə lər) *adj.* [< L. *populus*, the people] **1.** of, carried on by, or intended for people generally **2.** not expensive [*popular* prices] **3.** commonly accepted; prevalent **4.** liked by many people **5.** having many friends —**pop′u·lar′i·ty** (-lar′ə tē) *n.* —**pop′u·lar·ly** *adv.*

pop·u·lar·ize (päp′yə lə rīz′) *vt.* -ized′, -iz′ing to make popular —**pop′u·lar·i·za′tion** *n.* —**pop′u·lar·iz′er** *n.*

pop·u·late (päp′yə lāt′) *vt.* -lat′ed, -lat′ing [< L. *populus*, the people] **1.** to inhabit **2.** to supply with inhabitants

pop·u·la′tion *n.* **1.** *a)* all the people in a country, region, etc. *b)* the number of these **2.** a populating or being populated

population explosion the great and rapid increase in human population in modern times

pop·u·lism (päp′yə liz'm) *n.* any movement to advance the interests of the common people —**pop′u·list** *adj., n.*

pop·u·lous (päp′yə ləs) *adj.* full of people; thickly populated —**pop′u·lous·ness** *n.*

por·ce·lain (pôr′s'l in) *n.* [< Fr. < It. *porcellana*] **1.** a hard, white, translucent variety of ceramic ware **2.** porcelain dishes or ornaments, collectively

porch (pôrch) *n.* [< L. *porta*, gate] **1.** a covered entrance to a building, usually with a roof held up by posts **2.** an open or enclosed gallery or room on the outside of a building

por·cine (pôr′sīn, -sin) *adj.* [< Fr. < L. *porcus*, a hog] of or like pigs or hogs

por·cu·pine (pôr′kyə pīn′) *n.* [< L. *porcus*, pig + *spina*, spine] a rodent having coarse hair mixed with long, stiff, sharp spines

pore¹ (pôr) *vi.* **pored, por′ing** [< ?] **1.** to study carefully (with *over*) **2.** to ponder (with *over*)

pore² (pôr) *n.* [< Gr. *poros*, passage] **1.** a tiny opening, as in plant leaves, skin, etc., for absorbing or discharging fluids **2.** a tiny opening in rocks or other substances

por·gy (pôr′gē) *n., pl.* -gies, -gy [prob. < Sp. or Port. *pargo*] a saltwater food fish having spiny fins and a wide body

pork (pôrk) *n.* [< L. *porcus*, pig] the flesh of a pig or hog used as food

pork barrel [Colloq.] government money spent for political patronage

pork′er *n.* a hog fattened for use as food

pork pie a man's soft hat with a round, flat crown: now often **pork′pie′** *n.*

pork′y *adj.* -i·er, -i·est **1.** of or like pork **2.** [Slang] saucy, cocky, etc.

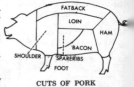

CUTS OF PORK

por·no (pôr′nō) *n., adj.* [Slang] *clipped form of* PORNOGRA-PHY, PORNOGRAPHIC: also **porn** (pôrn)

por·nog·ra·phy (pôr näg′rə fē) *n.* [< Gr. *pornē,* a prostitute + *graphein,* to write] writings, pictures, etc. intended primarily to arouse sexual desire —**por′no·graph′ic** (-nə graf′ik) *adj.*

po·rous (pôr′əs) *adj.* full of pores, through which fluids, air, or light may pass —**po·ros·i·ty** (pô räs′ə tē), **po′rous·ness** *n.* —**po′rous·ly** *adv.*

por·phy·ry (pôr′fər ē) *n., pl.* **-ries** [< Gr. *porphyros,* purple] any igneous rock with large, distinct crystals —**por′phy·rit′ic** (-fə rit′ik) *adj.*

por·poise (pôr′pəs) *n.* [< L. *porcus,* pig + *piscis,* a fish] **1.** a small whale with a blunt snout **2.** a dolphin or any of several other small cetaceans

por·ridge (pôr′ij) *n.* [< POTTAGE by confusion with VL. *porrata,* leek broth] [Chiefly Brit.] a soft food made of cereal or meal boiled in water or milk

por·rin·ger (pôr′in jər) *n.* [< Fr. *potager,* soup dish: infl. by prec.] a bowl for porridge, cereal, etc.

port[1] (pôrt) *n.* [< L. *portus,* haven] **1.** a harbor **2.** a city with a harbor where ships load or unload cargo

port[2] (pôrt) *n.* [< *Oporto,* city in Portugal] a sweet, dark-red wine

port[3] (pôrt) *vt.* [< L. *portare,* carry] to hold (a rifle, etc.) diagonally in front of one, as for inspection —*n.* the manner in which one carries oneself

port[4] (pôrt) *n.* [prob. < PORT[1]] the left side of a ship, etc. as one faces the bow —*adj.* of or on the port —*vt., vi.* to turn (the helm) to the port side

port[5] (pôrt) *n.* [< L. *porta,* door] **1.** a porthole **2.** an opening, as in a valve face, for the passage of steam, gas, etc.

Port. 1. Portugal **2.** Portuguese

port·a·ble (pôr′tə b'l) *adj.* [< L. *portare,* carry] **1.** that can be carried **2.** easily carried —*n.* something portable —**port′a·bil′i·ty** *n.*

por·tage (pôr′tij) *n.* [< L. *portare,* carry] **1.** the act of carrying **2.** a carrying of boats and supplies overland between navigable rivers, lakes, etc. **3.** any route over which this is done —*vt., vi.* **-taged, -tag·ing** to carry (boats, etc.) over a portage

por·tal (pôr′t'l) *n.* [< L. *porta,* door] a doorway, gate, or entrance, esp. a large or imposing one

Port-au-Prince (pôrt′ō prins′) seaport and capital of Haiti: pop. 250,000

port·cul·lis (pôrt kul′is) *n.* [< MFr. *porte,* a gate + *coleïce,* sliding] a large iron grating lowered to bar the gateway of a castle or fortified town

por·tend (pôr tend′) *vt.* [< L. *por-,* through + *tendere,* to stretch] **1.** to be an omen of; presage **2.** to signify

por·tent (pôr′tent) *n.* **1.** something that portends an event; omen **2.** significance

por·ten·tous (pôr ten′təs) *adj.* **1.** being a portent; ominous **2.** amazing **3.** pompous; self-important —**por·ten′tous·ly** *adv.* —**por·ten′tous·ness** *n.*

por·ter[1] (pôr′tər) *n.* [< L. *porta,* gate] a doorman or gatekeeper

por·ter[2] (pôr′tər) *n.* [< L. *portare,* carry] **1.** a man who carries luggage, etc. for hire, as at a railroad station **2.** a man who sweeps, cleans, etc. in a bank, store, etc. **3.** a railroad employee who waits on passengers in a sleeper or parlor car **4.** a dark-brown beer

por′ter·house′ (-hous′) *n.* [orig., a tavern: see PORTER[2], sense 4] a choice cut of beef from the loin just before the sirloin: in full **porterhouse steak**

port·fo·li·o (pôrt fō′lē ō′) *n., pl.* **-os′** [< L. *portare,* carry + *folium,* leaf] **1.** a flat, portable case for loose papers, etc.; briefcase **2.** the office of a minister of state **3.** a list of an investor's securities

port·hole (pôrt′hōl′) *n.* an opening in a ship's side, as for admitting light and air

por·ti·co (pôr′tə kō′) *n., pl.* **-coes′, -cos′** [It. < L. *porticus*] a porch or covered walk, consisting of a roof supported by columns

PORTICO

por·tiere, por·tière (pôr tyer′) *n.* [Fr. < *porte,* door] a curtain hung in a doorway

por·tion (pôr′shən) *n.* [< L. *portio*] **1.** a part, esp. that allotted to a person; share **2.** a dowry **3.** one's lot; destiny **4.** a helping of food —*vt.* **1.** to divide into portions **2.** to give as a portion to

Port·land (pôrt′lənd) **1.** city & port in NW Oreg.: pop. 383,000 (met. area 1,009,000) **2.** seaport in SE Maine: pop. 65,000

portland cement [concrete made from it resembles stone from the Isle of *Portland,* England] [*sometimes* P-] a kind of cement that hardens under water

port·ly (pôrt′lē) *adj.* **-li·er, -li·est 1.** large and heavy in a dignified way **2.** stout; corpulent —**port′li·ness** *n.*

port·man·teau (pôrt man′tō) *n., pl.* **-teaus, -teaux** (-tōz) [< Fr. *porter,* carry + *manteau,* cloak] a stiff suitcase that opens like a book into two compartments

port of entry any place where customs officials check the entry of foreign goods into a country

Port-of-Spain (pôrt′əv spän′) seaport on NW Trinidad; capital of Trinidad and Tobago: pop. 98,000

Por·to Ri·co (pôr′tə rē′kō) *former name of* PUERTO RICO —**Por·to Ri′can**

por·trait (pôr′trit, -trāt) *n.* [see PORTRAY] **1.** a painting, photograph, etc. of a person, esp. of his face **2.** a description, portrayal, etc.

por·trai·ture (pôr′tri chər) *n.* **1.** the practice or art of portraying **2.** a portrait

por·tray (pôr trā′) *vt.* [< L. *pro-,* forth + *trahere,* draw] **1.** to make a portrait of **2.** to describe graphically **3.** to play the part of in a play, movie, etc. —**por·tray′al** *n.*

Port Sa·id (pôrt sä ēd′) seaport in Egypt, at the Mediterranean end of the Suez Canal: pop. 244,000

Ports·mouth (pôrts′məth) seaport in SE Va.: pop. 111,000

Por·tu·gal (pôr′chə gəl) country in SW Europe, on the Atlantic: 35,509 sq. mi.; pop. 9,526,000; cap. Lisbon

Por′tu·guese′ (-gēz′) *adj.* of Portugal, its people, language, etc. —*n.* **1.** *pl.* **-guese′** a native or inhabitant of Portugal **2.** the Romance language of Portugal and Brazil

Portuguese Guinea *former name of* GUINEA-BISSAU

Portuguese man-of-war a large, tubelike, warm-sea animal having a large, bladderlike sac, which enables it to float on the water

por·tu·lac·a (pôr′chə lak′ə) *n.* [< L. *portula,* small door: from opening in its seed capsule] a fleshy plant with yellow, pink, or purple flowers

pose (pōz) *vt.* **posed, pos′ing** [< LL. *pausare,* to rest] **1.** to propose (a question, problem, etc.) **2.** to put (an artist's model, etc.) in a certain attitude —*vi.* **1.** to assume a certain attitude, as in modeling for an artist **2.** to strike attitudes for effect **3.** to pretend to be what one is not [*to pose as an officer*] —*n.* **1.** a bodily attitude, esp. one held for an artist, etc. **2.** behavior assumed for effect; pretense

Po·sei·don (pō sī′d'n) *Gr. Myth.* god of the sea: identified with the Roman god Neptune

pos·er (pō′zər) *n.* **1.** one who poses; affected person: also **po·seur** (pō zur′) **2.** a baffling question

posh (päsh) *adj.* [prob. < obs. Brit. slang *posh,* a dandy] [Colloq.] luxurious and fashionable —**posh′ly** *adv.* —**posh′ness** *n.*

pos·it (päz′it) *vt.* [< L. *ponere,* to place] **1.** to set in place; situate **2.** to suppose to be a fact; postulate

po·si·tion (pə zish′ən) *n.* [< L. *ponere,* to place] **1.** the way in which a person or thing is placed or arranged **2.** one's attitude or opinion **3.** the place where one is; location **4.** the usual or proper place **5.** rank or status **6.** high rank or status **7.** a post of employment; job; office **8.** a location or condition of advantage —*vt.* to put in a certain position

pos·i·tive (päz′ə tiv) *adj.* [see prec.] **1.** definitely set; explicit [*positive* instructions] **2.** *a)* having the mind set; confident *b)* overconfident or dogmatic **3.** showing agreement; affirmative **4.** constructive [*positive* criticism] **5.** absolute; unqualified **6.** regarded as having real existence [a *positive* good] **7.** based on facts [*positive* proof] **8.** concerned only with reality; practical **9.** [Colloq.] complete; downright [a *positive* fool] **10.** *Elec. a)* of electricity predominating in a glass body after it has been rubbed with silk *b)* charged with positive electricity *c)* having a deficiency of electrons **11.** *Gram.* of an adjective or adverb in its uninflected or unmodified form; neither comparative nor superlative **12.** *Math.* greater than zero; plus **13.** *Med.* indicating the presence of a specific disease, condition, etc. **14.** *Photog.* with the relation of light and shade the same as in the thing photographed —*n.* something positive, as a degree, quality, quantity, etc.; specif., *a)* the plate in a voltaic battery where the higher potential is *b) Math.* a positive quantity *c) Photog.* a positive print —**pos′i·tive·ly** *adv.* —**pos′i·tive·ness** *n.*

pos·i·tiv·ism *n.* **1.** a being positive; certainty **2.** a system of philosophy based solely on observable, scientific facts — **pos′i·tiv·ist** *n., adj.*

pos·i·tron (päz′ə trän′) *n.* [POSI(TIVE) + (ELEC)TRON] the antiparticle of an electron, having about the same mass and magnitude of charge

poss. 1. possession **2.** possessive **3.** possibly

pos·se (päs′ē) *n.* [L., be able] a body of men summoned by a sheriff to assist him in keeping the peace

pos·sess (pə zes′) *vt.* [< L. *possidere*] **1.** to have as something that belongs to one; own **2.** to have as an attribute, quality, etc. **3.** to gain control over [*possessed* by an idea] —**pos·ses′sor** *n.*

pos·sessed′ *adj.* **1.** owned **2.** controlled as if by a demon; crazed —**possessed of** having

pos·ses·sion (pə zesh′ən) *n.* **1.** a possessing or being possessed; ownership **2.** anything possessed **3.** [*pl.*] property; wealth **4.** territory ruled by an outside country

pos·ses′sive (-zes′iv) *adj.* **1.** of possession **2.** showing or desiring possession **3.** *Gram.* designating or of a case, form, or construction indicating possession (Ex.: *men's, of men, his*) —*n. Gram.* **1.** the possessive case **2.** a possessive form —**pos·ses′sive·ly** *adv.* —**pos·ses′sive·ness** *n.*

pos·si·ble (päs′ə b'l) *adj.* [< L. *posse*, be able] **1.** that can be or exist **2.** that may or may not happen **3.** that can be done, chosen, etc. **4.** permissible —**pos′si·bil′i·ty** (-bil′ə tē) *n., pl.* **-ties**

pos′si·bly (-blē) *adv.* **1.** by any possible means **2.** perhaps; maybe

pos·sum (päs′əm) *n.* [Colloq.] *same as* OPOSSUM —**play possum** to pretend to be asleep, dead, ill, etc.

post[1] (pōst) *n.* [< L. *postis*] **1.** a piece of wood, metal, etc. set upright to support a sign, fence, etc. **2.** the starting point of a horse race —*vt.* **1.** to put up (a notice, etc.) on (a wall, etc.) **2.** to announce by posting notices [to *post* a reward] **3.** to warn against trespassing on (grounds, etc.) by posted notices **4.** to put (a name) on a posted or published list

post[2] (pōst) *n.* [< Fr. < It. *posto*] **1.** the place where a soldier, guard, etc. is stationed **2.** *a)* a place where troops are stationed *b)* the troops there; garrison **3.** a local unit of a veterans' organization **4.** the place assigned to one **5.** a position, job, or duty **6.** *same as* TRADING POST —*vt.* **1.** to assign to a post **2.** to put up (a bond, etc.)

post[3] (pōst) *n.* [< Fr. < It. *posta*] [Chiefly Brit.] (the) mail —*vi.* to travel fast; hasten —*vt.* **1.** [Chiefly Brit.] to mail **2.** to inform [keep me *posted*] **3.** *Bookkeeping a)* to transfer (an item) to the ledger *b)* to enter all necessary items in (a ledger, etc.) —*adv.* speedily

post- [L. < *post*, after] *a prefix meaning:* **1.** after in time, following [*postgraduate*] **2.** after in space, behind [*postnasal*]

post·age (pōs′tij) *n.* the amount charged for mailing a letter, etc., esp. as represented by stamps

postage stamp a government stamp for a letter or package, showing postage paid

post·al (pōs′t'l) *adj.* [Fr.] of mail or post offices —*n.* [Colloq.] a postal card

postal card 1. a card with a postage stamp printed on it, issued by a government for use in the mails **2.** *same as* POST CARD

post·bel·lum (pōst bel′əm) *adj.* [L.] after the war; specif., after the American Civil War

post card 1. a card, often a picture card, that can be sent through the mail when a postage stamp is affixed **2.** *same as* POSTAL CARD

post′date′ *vt.* **-dat′ed, -dat′ing 1.** to assign a later date to than the actual date **2.** to be subsequent to

post·er (pōs′tər) *n.* a large advertisement or notice, often illustrated, posted publicly

pos·te·ri·or (päs tir′ē ər, pōs-) *adj.* [L. < *post*, after] **1.** later; following **2.** at or toward the rear: opposed to ANTE-RIOR —*n.* the buttocks —**pos·te′ri·or·ly** *adv.*

pos·ter·i·ty (päs ter′ə tē) *n.* [see prec.] **1.** all of a person's descendants **2.** all future generations

post exchange a nonprofit general store at an army post, selling merchandise, as to servicemen

post′grad′u·ate *adj.* of or taking a course of study after graduation —*n.* a student taking such courses

post′haste′ *adv.* with great haste

post·hu·mous (päs′choo məs) *adj.* [< L. *postumus*, last] **1.** born after the father's death **2.** published after the author's death **3.** arising or continuing after one's death —**post′hu·mous·ly** *adv.*

pos·til·ion, pos·til·lion (pōs til′yən, päs-) *n.* [Fr. < It. *posta*, POST[3]] one who rides the leading left-hand horse of a team drawing a carriage

post′im·pres′sion·ism *n.* a late 19th-cent. theory of art that emphasized the subjective viewpoint of the artist: see also IMPRESSIONISM —**post′im·pres′sion·ist** *adj., n.* —**post′im·pres′sion·is′tic** *adj.*

post·lude (pōst′lood′) *n.* [POST- + (PRE)LUDE] **1.** a solo on the organ at the end of a church service **2.** a concluding musical section

post′man (-mən) *n., pl.* **-men** *same as* MAILMAN

post′mark′ *n.* a post-office mark stamped on mail, canceling the postage stamp and recording the date and place —*vt.* to stamp with a postmark

post′mas′ter *n.* a person in charge of a post office — **post′mis′tress** *n.fem.*

postmaster general *pl.* **postmasters general, postmaster generals** the head of a government's postal system

post·me·rid·i·an (pōst′mə rid′ē ən) *adj.* [< L.: see POST- & MERIDIAN] of or in the afternoon

post′ me·ri′di·em (-ē əm) [L.] after noon: abbrev. **P.M., p.m., PM**

post·mor·tem (pōst′môr′təm) *adj.* [L.] **1.** after death **2.** of a post-mortem —*n.* **1.** an examination of a human body after death: in full **post-mortem examination 2.** an evaluation of some event just ended See also AUTOPSY

post·na·sal drip (pōst′nā′z'l) a discharge of mucus from behind the nose onto the pharynx, due to a cold, etc.

post′na′tal (-nāt′'l) *adj.* after birth

post office 1. the governmental department in charge of the mails **2.** a place where mail is sorted, postage stamps are sold, etc.

post′op′er·a·tive (-äp′ər ə tiv) *adj.* of or occurring in the period after a surgical operation —**post′op′er·a·tive·ly** *adv.*

post′paid′ *adj.* with the postage prepaid

post·pone (pōst pōn′) *vt.* **-poned′, -pon′ing** [< L. *post-*, after + *ponere*, put] to put off until later; delay —**post-pone′ment** *n.*

post road a road over which the post, or mail, is or formerly was carried

post·script (pōst′skript′) *n.* [< L. *post-*, after + *scribere*, write] a note added below the signature of a letter

post time the scheduled starting time of a horse race

pos·tu·late (päs′chə lāt′) *vt.* **-lat′ed, -lat′ing** [< L. *postulare*, to demand] **1.** to assume to be true, real, etc., esp. as a basis for argument **2.** to take for granted —*n.* (-lit) **1.** something postulated **2.** a prerequisite **3.** a basic principle —**pos′tu·la′tion** *n.*

pos·ture (päs′chər) *n.* [< L. *ponere*, to place] **1.** the position or carriage of the body **2.** a position assumed as in posing **3.** an attitude or position; esp., an official stand on an issue —*vt.* **-tured, -tur·ing** to place in a posture; pose —*vi.* to pose or assume an attitude —**pos′tur·al** *adj.*

pos′tur·ize′ (-īz′) *vt., vi.* **-ized′, -iz′ing** *same as* POSTURE

post′war′ *adj.* after the (or a) war

po·sy (pō′zē) *n., pl.* **-sies** [< POESY] a flower or bouquet: an old-fashioned usage

pot (pät) *n.* [OE. *pott*] **1.** a round vessel for holding liquids, cooking, etc. **2.** a pot with its contents **3.** anything like a pot, as a flowerpot **4.** [Colloq.] *a)* all the money bet at a single time *b)* a large amount of money **5.** [Slang] *same as: a)* MARIJUANA *b)* POTBELLY —*vt.* **pot′-ted, pot′ting 1.** to put into a pot **2.** to cook or preserve in a pot **3.** to shoot (game) for food, not for sport **4.** to hit with a potshot —**go to pot** to go to ruin —**pot′ful′** *n., pl.* **-fuls′**

po·ta·ble (pōt′ə b'l) *adj.* [Fr. < L. *potare*, to drink] drinkable —*n.* something drinkable —**po′ta·bil′i·ty** *n.*

‡**po·tage** (pô täzh′) *n.* [Fr.] soup or broth

pot·ash (pät′ash′) *n.* [< Du. *pot*, pot + *asch*, ASH[1]] any substance containing potassium; esp., any potassium compound used in fertilizers, soaps, etc.

po·tas·si·um (pə tas′ē əm) *n.* [see prec.] a soft, silver-white, metallic chemical element: its salts are used in fertilizers, glass, etc.: symbol, K; at. wt., 39.102; at. no., 19 — **po·tas′sic** *adj.*

potassium nitrate a crystalline compound, KNO_3, used in fertilizers, gunpowder, etc.

po·ta·tion (pō tā′shən) *n.* [< L. *potare*, to drink] **1.** the act of drinking **2.** a drink, esp. of liquor

po·ta·to (pə tāt′ō) *n., pl.* **-toes** [Sp. *patata* < WInd.] **1.** the starchy tuber of a widely cultivated plant, cooked as a vegetable **2.** this plant

potato beetle (or **bug**) a black-and-yellow beetle destructive to potatoes and other plants

potato chip a very thin slice of potato fried crisp and then salted

pot′bel′ly *n., pl.* **-lies** a protruding belly —**pot′bel′lied** *adj.*

pot'boil'er *n.* a piece of writing, etc., often inferior, done quickly for money

po·tent (pōt'nt) *adj.* [< L. *posse*, be able] 1. having authority or power 2. convincing; cogent 3. effective, as a drug 4. able to engage in sexual intercourse: said of a male —**po'ten·cy,** *pl.* **-cies, po'tence** *n.* —**po'tent·ly** *adv.*

po·ten·tate (pōt'n tāt') *n.* a ruler; monarch

po·ten·tial (pə ten'shəl) *adj.* [see POTENT] that can come into being; possible; latent —*n.* 1. something potential 2. *Elec.* the relative voltage at a point in an electric circuit or field with respect to some reference point in the same circuit or field —**po·ten'ti·al'i·ty** (-shē al'ə tē) *n., pl.* **-ties** —**po·ten'tial·ly** *adv.*

potential energy energy resulting from position or structure instead of motion, as in a coiled spring

po·ten'ti·ate' (-shē āt') *vt.* **-at'ed, -at'ing** [see POTENT] to increase the effect of (a drug or toxin) by giving another drug or toxin simultaneously

poth·er (päth'ər) *n.* [< ?] a fuss; commotion —*vt., vi.* to fuss or bother

pot·herb (pät'ʉrb', -hʉrb') *n.* any herb whose leaves and stems are boiled for food or used as a flavoring

pot'hold'er *n.* a small pad or piece of cloth for handling hot pots, etc.

pot'hook' *n.* 1. an S-shaped hook for hanging a pot over a fire 2. a curved mark in writing

po·tion (pō'shən) *n.* [< L. *potare*, to drink] a drink, as of medicine, poison, or a supposedly magic substance

pot'luck' *n.* whatever the family meal happens to be [invited in to take *potluck*]

Po·to·mac (pə tō'mək) river forming a boundary of W.Va., Md., & Va., and flowing into Chesapeake Bay: 285 mi.

pot'pie' *n.* 1. a meat pie made in a pot or deep dish 2. a stew with dumplings

pot·pour·ri (pō'poo rē', pät poor'ē) *n.* [Fr. < *pot*, a pot + *pourrir*, to rot] 1. a fragrant mixture of dried flower petals 2. a medley or miscellany

pot roast meat, usually a large cut of beef, cooked in one piece by braising

Pots·dam (päts'dam') city in East Germany, near Berlin: pop. 111,000

pot·sherd (pät'shʉrd') *n.* [see POT & SHARD] a piece of broken pottery

pot'shot' *n.* 1. an easy shot 2. a random shot 3. a haphazard try 4. a random criticism

pot·tage (pät'ij) *n.* [< Du. *pot*, a pot] a thick soup or stew of vegetables, or meat and vegetables

pot·ted (pät'id) *adj.* 1. put into a pot 2. cooked or preserved in a pot or can 3. [Slang] drunk

pot·ter¹ (pät'ər) *n.* a maker of earthenware pots, dishes, etc.

pot·ter² (pät'ər) *vi., vt.* [< OE. *potian*, to push] *chiefly Brit. var. of* PUTTER²

potter's field [cf. Matt. 27:7] a burial ground for paupers or unknown persons

potter's wheel a rotating, horizontal disk upon which clay is molded into bowls, etc.

pot·ter·y *n., pl.* **-ies** 1. a potter's workshop or factory 2. the art of a potter 3. pots, bowls, etc. made of clay hardened by heat; earthenware

pouch (pouch) *n.* [< MFr. *poche*] 1. a small bag or sack, as for pipe tobacco 2. a mailbag 3. a saclike structure, as that on the abdomen of the kangaroo, etc. for carrying young 4. any pouchlike cavity, part, etc. —*vt., vi.* to form (into) a pouch —**pouched** *adj.*

POTTER'S WHEEL

poul·tice (pōl'tis) *n.* [< ML. *pultes*, pap] a hot, soft, moist mass, as of flour, mustard, etc., applied to a sore part of the body —*vt.* **-ticed, -tic·ing** to apply a poultice to

poul·try (pōl'trē) *n.* [< L. *pullus*, chicken] domestic fowls, as chickens, raised for meat or eggs

pounce (pouns) *n.* [ME. *pownce*, talon] a pouncing —*vi.* **pounced, pounc'ing** to swoop down or leap (*on, upon,* or *at*) as if to seize

pound¹ (pound) *n., pl.* **pounds,** collectively **pound** [< L. *pondus,* a weight] 1. a unit of weight, equal to 16 oz. avoirdupois or 12 oz. troy: abbrev. **lb.** 2. the monetary unit of the United Kingdom, equal to 20 shillings or 100 (new) pennies, symbol £, and of various other countries, as of Ireland, Israel, etc.

pound² (pound) *vt.* [OE. *punian*] 1. to beat to a pulp, powder, etc. 2. to hit hard —*vi.* 1. to deliver repeated, heavy blows (*at* or *on*) 2. to move with heavy steps 3. to throb —*n.* a pounding, or the sound of it —**pound'er** *n.*

pound³ (pound) *n.* [< OE. *pund-*] a municipal enclosure for stray animals

pound'cake' *n.* a rich cake made (orig. with a pound each) of flour, butter, sugar, etc.

pour (pôr) *vt.* [ME. *pouren*] 1. to cause to flow in a continuous stream 2. to emit, utter, etc. profusely or steadily —*vi.* 1. to flow freely, continuously, etc. 2. to rain heavily 3. to swarm

pout¹ (pout) *vi.* [ME. *pouten*] 1. to thrust out the lips, as in sullenness 2. to sulk —*n.* a pouting

pout² (pout) *n., pl.* **pout, pouts** [OE. *-pute*] any of several stout-bodied fishes

pout'er *n.* 1. one who pouts 2. any of a breed of pigeon that can distend its crop: also **pouter pigeon**

pov·er·ty (päv'ər tē) *n.* [< L. *pauper,* poor] 1. the condition or quality of being poor; need 2. inferiority; inadequacy 3. scarcity

pov'er·ty-strick'en *adj.* very poor

POW, P.O.W. prisoner of war

pow·der (pou'dər) *n.* [< L. *pulvis*] 1. any dry substance in the form of fine, dustlike particles, produced by crushing, grinding, etc. 2. a specific kind of powder [bath *powder*] —*vt.* 1. to put powder on 2. to make into powder —*vi.* to use powder as a cosmetic —**pow'der·y** *adj.*

powder blue pale blue —**pow'der-blue'** *adj.*

powder keg 1. a keg for gunpowder 2. an explosive situation

powder puff a soft pad for applying cosmetic powder

powder room a lavatory for women

pow·er (pou'ər) *n.* [ult. < L. *posse,* be able] 1. ability to do or act 2. a specific ability [the *power* of sight] 3. vigor; force; strength 4. *a)* authority; influence *b)* legal authority 5. physical force or energy [electric *power*] 6. a person or thing having great influence, force, or authority 7. a nation, esp. one dominating others 8. the result of multiplying a quantity by itself [4 is the second *power* of 2 (2²)] 9. the degree of magnification of a lens, telescope, etc. —*vt.* to supply with power —*adj.* 1. operated by electricity, a fuel engine, etc. [power *tools*] 2. served by an auxiliary system that reduces effort [power *steering*] 3. carrying electricity —**pow'ered** *adj.*

pow'er·boat' *n. same as* MOTORBOAT

power dive *Aeron.* a dive speeded by engine power —**pow'er-dive'** *vi., vt.* **-dived', -div'ing**

pow'er·ful *adj.* strong; mighty; influential —**pow'er·ful·ly** *adv.* —**pow'er·ful·ness** *n.*

pow'er·house' *n.* 1. a building where electric power is generated 2. [Colloq.] a strong or energetic person, team, etc.

pow'er·less *adj.* without power; weak; unable —**pow'er·less·ly** *adv.* —**pow'er·less·ness** *n.*

power of attorney a written statement legally authorizing a person to act for one

pow·wow (pou'wou') *n.* [< AmInd.] 1. a conference of or with N. American Indians 2. [Colloq.] any conference —*vi.* [Colloq.] to confer

pox (päks) *n.* [for *pocks*: see POCK] 1. a disease characterized by skin eruptions, as smallpox 2. syphilis

pp *Music* pianissimo

pp. 1. pages 2. past participle

P.P., p.p. 1. parcel post 2. postpaid 3. prepaid

ppd. 1. postpaid 2. prepaid

ppr., p.pr. present participle

P.P.S., p.p.s. [L. *post postscriptum*] an additional postscript

Pr *Chem.* praseodymium

Pr. Provençal

pr. 1. pair(s) 2. present 3. price

P.R., PR 1. public relations 2. Puerto Rico

prac·ti·ca·ble (prak'ti kə b'l) *adj.* 1. that can be put into practice; feasible 2. that can be used —**prac'ti·ca·bil'i·ty** *n.* —**prac'ti·ca·bly** *adv.*

prac·ti·cal (prak'ti k'l) *adj.* 1. of or obtained through practice or action 2. useful or designed for use 3. concerned with application to useful ends, rather than theory [*practical* science] 4. given to actual practice [a *practical* farmer] 5. that is so in practice; virtual 6. matter-of-fact —**prac'ti·cal'i·ty** (-kal'ə tē) *n., pl.* **-ties, prac'ti·cal·ness** *n.*

practical joke a trick played on someone in fun —**practical joker**

prac·ti·cal·ly adv. 1. in a practical manner 2. from a practical viewpoint 3. in effect; virtually 4. [Colloq.] almost; nearly

practical nurse a nurse, often licensed, with less training than a registered nurse

prac·tice (prak'tis) vt. -ticed, -tic·ing [< Gr. prassein, do] 1. to do or engage in regularly; make a habit of 2. to do repeatedly so as to gain skill 3. to work at, esp. as a profession [to practice law] —vi. 1. to do something repeatedly so as to gain skill 2. to work at a profession — n. 1. a practicing; habit, custom, etc. 2. a) repeated action for gaining skill b) the resulting condition of being skilled [he's out of practice] 3. the actual doing of something 4. a) the exercise of a profession b) a business based on this —prac'tic·er n.

prac'ticed adj. skilled; expert

prac·tise (prak'tis) vt., vi. -tised, -tis·ing chiefly Brit. sp. of PRACTICE

prac·ti·tion·er (prak tish'ən ər) n. 1. one who practices a profession, art, etc. 2. a Christian Science healer

prae·tor (prēt'ər) n. [L.] a magistrate of ancient Rome, next below a consul in rank

prae·to·ri·an (pri tôr'ē ən) adj. 1. of a praetor 2. [often P-] designating or of the bodyguard (**Praetorian Guard**) of a Roman emperor

prag·mat·ic (prag mat'ik) adj. [< Gr. pragma, thing done] 1. practical 2. testing the validity of all concepts by their practical results Also **prag·mat'i·cal** —**prag·mat'i·cal·ly** adv. —**prag'ma·tism** (-mə tiz'm) n. —**prag'ma·tist** n.

Prague (präg) capital of Czechoslovakia: pop. 1,034,000

prai·rie (prer'ē) n. [Fr. < L. pratum, meadow] a large area of level or rolling grassy land

prairie chicken (or **hen**) a brown-and-white grouse with a short tail, of N. American prairies

prairie dog a small, squirrellike, burrowing rodent of N. America, with a barking cry

prairie schooner a covered wagon used by pioneers to cross the American prairies

praise (prāz) vt. **praised, prais'ing** [< L. pretium, worth] 1. to commend the worth of 2. to glorify (God, etc.), as in song —n. a praising or being praised; commendation —**sing someone's praise** (or **praises**) to praise someone highly —**prais'er** n.

PRAIRIE DOG
(to 15 in. long)

praise'wor'thy adj. worthy of praise —**praise'wor'thi·ly** adv. —**praise'wor'thi·ness** n.

pra·line (prā'lēn, prä'-) n. [Fr., after Marshal Duplessis-Praslin (1598–1675), whose cook created it] any of various crisp or soft candies made of nuts, as pecans, and sugar

pram (pram) n. [Brit. Colloq.] a perambulator

prance (prans) vi. **pranced, pranc'ing** [< ?] 1. to rise up, or move along, on the hind legs: said of a horse 2. to caper or strut —n. a prancing —**pranc'er** n. —**pranc'ing·ly** adv.

prank[1] (praŋk) n. [< ?] a playful or mischievous trick — **prank'ish** adj. —**prank'ster** n.

prank[2] (praŋk) vt., vi. [prob. < LowG.] to dress up or adorn showily

pra·se·o·dym·i·um (prā'zē ō dim'ē əm, -sē-) n. [< Gr. prasios, green + (di)dymium, a rare metal] a metallic chemical element of the rare-earth group: symbol, Pr; at. wt., 140.907; at. no., 59

prate (prāt) vi., vt. **prat'ed, prat'ing** [< MDu. praten] to talk on and on, foolishly; chatter; blab

prat·tle (prat''l) vi., vt. **-tled, -tling** [MLowG. pratelen] to prate or babble —n. chatter or babble

prawn (prôn) n. [< ?] an edible, shrimplike crustacean

pray (prā) vt. [< L. prex, prayer] 1. to implore [(I) pray (you) tell me] 2. to ask for by prayer —vi. to say prayers, as to God —**pray'er** n.

prayer (prer) n. 1. the act of praying 2. an entreaty; supplication 3. a) a humble request, as to God b) a set of words used in praying 4. [often pl.] a religious prayer service 5. something prayed for —**prayer'ful** adj. —**prayer'ful·ly** adv.

praying mantis same as MANTIS

pre- [< L. prae, before] a prefix meaning before in time, place, or rank [prewar]

preach (prēch) vi. [< L. prae-, before + dicare, to proclaim] 1. to give a sermon 2. to give moral advice, esp. in a tiresome way —vt. 1. to advocate or urge as by preaching 2. to deliver (a sermon) —**preach'ment** n.

preach'er n. one who preaches; esp., a clergyman

preach'y adj. **-i·er, -i·est** [Colloq.] given to or marked by preaching

pre·am·ble (prē'am'b'l) n. [< L. prae-, before + ambulare, go] an introduction, esp. one to a constitution, statute, etc., stating its purpose

pre·ar·range (prē'ə rānj') vt. **-ranged', -rang'ing** to arrange beforehand —**pre'ar·range'ment** n.

prec. preceding

Pre·cam·bri·an (prē kam'brē ən) adj. [< ML. Cambria, Wales] designating or of the earliest geologic era (c.4.5 billion–600 million years ago), in the late part of which life appeared on earth —**the Precambrian** the Precambrian Era

pre·can·cer·ous (prē kan'sər əs) adj. likely to become cancerous

pre·car·i·ous (pri ker'ē əs) adj. [see PRAY] dependent upon circumstances or chance; uncertain; risky —**pre·car'i·ous·ly** adv. —**pre·car'i·ous·ness** n.

pre·cau·tion (pri kô'shən) n. [< L. prae-, before + cavere, take care] care taken beforehand, as against danger, failure, etc. —**pre·cau'tion·ar'y** adj.

pre·cede (pri sēd') vt., vi. **-ced'ed, -ced'ing** [< L. prae-, before + cedere, to move] to be, come, or go before in time, place, order, rank, etc.

prec·e·dence (pres'ə dəns, pri sēd'''ns) n. the act, right, or fact of preceding in time, place, order, rank, etc.: also **prec'e·den·cy**

pre·ced·ent (pri sēd'''nt) adj. preceding —n. (pres'ə dənt) an act, statement, etc. that may serve as an example or justification for a later one

pre·ced·ing adj. that precedes

pre·cept (prē'sept) n. [< L. prae-, before + capere, take] 1. a direction meant as a rule of conduct 2. a rule of moral conduct; maxim

pre·cep·tor (pri sep'tər) n. a teacher —**pre·cep·to·ri·al** (prē'sep tôr'ē al) adj. —**pre·cep'tor·ship'** n.

pre·cinct (prē'siŋkt) n. [< L. prae-, before + cingere, surround] 1. [usually pl.] an enclosure between buildings, walls, etc. 2. [pl.] environs 3. a) a police district b) a subdivision of a voting ward 4. a limited area 5. a boundary

pre·ci·os·i·ty (presh'ē äs'ə tē) n., pl. **-ties** [see PRECIOUS] great affectation, esp. in language

pre·cious (presh'əs) adj. [< L. pretium, a price] 1. of great price or value; costly 2. beloved; dear 3. very fastidious, affected, etc. 4. very great [a precious liar] —adv. [Colloq.] very —**pre'cious·ly** adv. —**pre'cious·ness** n.

prec·i·pice (pres'ə pis) n. [< Fr. < L. prae-, before + caput, a head] a vertical or overhanging rock face

pre·cip·i·tant (pri sip'ə tənt) adj. [see prec.] same as PRECIPITATE —n. a substance causing formation of a precipitate —**pre·cip'i·tan·cy, pre·cip'i·tance** —n. —**pre·cip'i·tant·ly** adv.

pre·cip·i·tate' (-tāt'; also, for adj. & n., -tit) vt. **-tat'ed, -tat'ing** [see PRECIPICE] 1. to hurl downward 2. to cause to happen before expected, needed, etc. 3. Chem. to separate (a dissolved substance) out from a solution —vi. 1. Chem. to be precipitated 2. Meteorol. to condense and fall as rain, snow, etc. —adj. 1. falling steeply 2. acting or done hastily or rashly 3. very sudden or abrupt —n. a substance precipitated out from a solution —**pre·cip'i·tate·ly** adv.

pre·cip·i·ta·tion n. 1. a precipitating or being precipitated 2. sudden or rash haste 3. Chem. a precipitating or a precipitate 4. Meteorol. a) rain, snow, etc. b) the amount of this

pre·cip·i·tous (-ə təs) adj. 1. steep like a precipice 2. rash; impetuous —**pre·cip'i·tous·ly** adv.

pré·cis (prā sē', prā'sē) n., pl. **-cis'** (-sēz', -sēz) [Fr.: see PRECISE] a concise abridgment; summary

pre·cise (pri sīs') adj. [< L. prae-, before + caedere, to cut] 1. accurately stated; definite 2. minutely exact 3. scrupulous; fastidious 4. finicky —**pre·cise'ly** adv. —**pre·cise'ness** n.

pre·ci·sion (pri sizh'ən) n. the quality of being precise; exactness —adj. requiring exactness [precision work] —**pre·ci'sion·ist** n.

pre·clude (pri klōōd') vt. **-clud'ed, -clud'ing** [< L. prae-, before + claudere, to close] to make impossible, esp. in advance; prevent —**pre·clu'sion** (-klōō'zhən) n.

pre·co·cious (pri kō'shəs) adj. [< L. prae-, before + coquere, to cook] 1. matured beyond normal for one's age [a precocious child] 2. showing premature development — **pre·co'cious·ly** adv. —**pre·co'cious·ness, pre·coc'i·ty** (-käs'ə tē) n.

pre·cog·ni·tion (prē'käg nish'ən) n. [see PRE- & COGNITION] the supposed extrasensory perception of a future event —**pre·cog'ni·tive** adj.

pre-Co·lum·bi·an (prē'kə lum'bē ən) *adj.* of any period in the Americas before Columbus's voyages

pre·con·ceive (prē'kən sēv') *vt.* -ceived', -ceiv'ing to form an idea or opinion of beforehand —**pre'con·cep'tion** (-sep'shən) *n.*

pre'con·di'tion (-dish'ən) *vt.* to prepare to behave or react in a certain way under certain conditions

pre·cur·sor (pri kur'sər) *n.* [< L. *praecurrere,* run ahead] 1. a forerunner 2. a predecessor

pre·cur'so·ry (-sə rē) *adj.* 1. serving as a precursor 2. introductory; preliminary

pred. predicate

pred·a·to·ry (pred'ə tôr'ē) *adj.* [< L. *praeda,* a prey] 1. of or living by plundering or robbing 2. preying on other animals —**pred'a·tor** (-tər) *n.*

pre·de·cease (prē'di sēs') *vt.* -ceased', -ceas'ing to die before (someone else)

pred·e·ces·sor (pred'ə ses'ər, pred'ə ses'ər) *n.* [< L. *prae-,* before + *decedere,* go away] 1. a person preceding another, as in office 2. an ancestor

pre·des·ti·nate (prē des'tə nāt') *vt.* -nat'ed, -nat'ing 1. *same as* PREDESTINE 2. *Theol.* to foreordain by divine decree

pre·des'ti·na'tion *n.* 1. *Theol.* the doctrine that *a)* God foreordained everything that would happen *b)* God predestines souls to salvation or to damnation 2. destiny

pre·des·tine (prē des'tin) *vt.* -tined, -tin·ing to destine or decree beforehand; foreordain

pre·de·ter·mine (prē'di tur'mən) *vt.* -mined, -min·ing 1. to determine or decide beforehand 2. to bias or prejudice beforehand —**pre'de·ter'mi·na'tion** *n.*

pred·i·ca·ble (pred'i kə b'l) *adj.* that can be predicated —**pred'i·ca·bil'i·ty** *n.*

pre·dic·a·ment (pri dik'ə mənt) *n.* [see PREACH] a difficult or embarrassing situation

pred·i·cate (pred'i kāt') *vt.* -cat'ed, -cat'ing [see PREACH] 1. to affirm as a quality or attribute 2. to base (something) *on* or *upon* facts, conditions, etc. —*vi.* to make an affirmation —*n.* (-kit) *Gram.* the word or words that make a statement about the subject of a sentence or clause —*adj.* (-kit) *Gram.* of or involved in a predicate —**pred'i·ca'tion** *n.* —**pred'i·ca·tive** *adj.*

pre·dict (pri dikt') *vt., vi.* [< L. *prae-,* before + *dicere,* tell] to state (what one believes will happen); foretell —**pre·dict'a·bil'i·ty** *n.* —**pre·dict'a·ble** *adj.* —**pre·dict'a·bly** *adv.* —**pre·dic'tor** *n.*

pre·dic·tion (pri dik'shən) *n.* 1. a predicting or being predicted 2. something predicted

pre·di·gest (prē'di jest', -dī-) *vt.* to treat (food) as with enzymes for easier digestion when eaten —**pre'di·ges'tion** *n.*

pre·di·lec·tion (pred''l ek'shən) *n.* [< Fr. < L. *prae-,* before + *diligere,* prefer] a preconceived liking; partiality (*for*)

pre·dis·pose (prē'dis pōz') *vt.* -posed', -pos'ing to make receptive beforehand; make susceptible (*to*) —**pre'dis·po·si'tion** *n.*

pre·dom·i·nant (pri däm'ə nənt) *adj.* 1. having authority or influence over others; superior 2. most frequent; prevailing —**pre·dom'i·nance** *n.* —**pre·dom'i·nant·ly** *adv.*

pre·dom'i·nate' (-nāt') *vi.* -nat'ed, -nat'ing 1. to have influence or authority (*over* others) 2. to prevail; preponderate —**pre·dom'i·na'tion** *n.*

pre·em·i·nent, pre-em·i·nent (prē em'ə nənt) *adj.* eminent above all others; surpassing: also **pre-ĕm'i·nent** —**pre·em'i·nence, pre-em'i·nence** *n.* —**pre·em'i·nent·ly, pre·em'i·nent·ly** *adv.*

pre·empt', pre-empt' (-empt') *vt.* [< L. *prae-,* before + *emere,* buy] 1. to gain the right to buy (public land) by settling on it 2. to seize before anyone else can 3. *Radio & TV* to replace (a scheduled program) Also **pre·ĕmpt'** —**pre·emp'tor, pre-emp'tor** *n.*

pre·emp'tion, pre-emp'tion *n.* 1. a preempting, as of land 2. action taken to check other action beforehand Also **pre·ĕmp'tion** —**pre·emp'tive, pre-emp'tive** *adj.*

preen (prēn) *vt.* [< ME. *proinen,* PRUNE²] 1. to clean and trim (the feathers) with the beak: said of birds 2. to dress up or adorn (oneself) 3. to be proud of (oneself) —*vi.* to primp —**preen'er** *n.*

pre·ex·ist, pre-ex·ist (prē'ig zist') *vt., vi.* to exist previously or before (another person or thing): also **pre'ĕx·ist'** —**pre'ex·ist'ence, pre'-ex·ist'ence** *n.* —**pre'ex·ist'ent, pre'-ex·ist'ent** *adj.*

pref. 1. preface 2. preferred 3. prefix

pre·fab (prē'fab') *n.* [Colloq.] a prefabricated building

pre·fab·ri·cate (prē fab'rə kāt') *vt.* -cat'ed, -cat'ing 1. to fabricate beforehand 2. to make (houses, etc.) in standardized sections for shipment and then quick assembly — **pre'fab·ri·ca'tion** *n.*

pref·ace (pref'is) *n.* [< L. *prae-,* before + *fari,* speak] an introduction to a book, speech, etc. —*vt.* -aced, -ac·ing 1. to furnish with a preface 2. to be a preface to

pref·a·to·ry (pref'ə tôr'ē) *adj.* of, like, or serving as a preface: also **pref'a·to'ri·al**

pre·fect (prē'fekt) *n.* [< L. *praeficere,* to set over] 1. in ancient Rome, any of various officials in charge of governmental or military departments 2. any of various administrators; specif., the head of a department of France

pre·fec·ture (prē'fek chər) *n.* the office, authority, territory, or residence of a prefect

pre·fer (pri fur') *vt.* -ferred', -fer'ring [< L. *prae-,* before + *ferre,* BEAR¹] 1. to promote; advance 2. to put before a magistrate, court, etc. for consideration 3. to like better

pref·er·a·ble (pref'ər ə b'l) *adj.* more desirable —**pref'er·a·bil'i·ty** *n.* —**pref'er·a·bly** *adv.*

pref·er·ence (pref'ər əns) *n.* 1. a preferring or being preferred 2. the right, power, etc. of prior choice or claim 3. something preferred 4. advantage given to one person, country, etc. over others

pref·er·en·tial (pref'ə ren'shəl) *adj.* 1. of, giving, or receiving preference 2. offering a preference —**pref'er·en'tial·ly** *adv.*

pre·fer·ment (pri fur'mənt) *n.* 1. a preferring 2. an advancement in rank, etc.; promotion

preferred stock stock on which dividends must be paid before those of common stock

pre·fig·ure (prē fig'yər) *vt.* -ured, -ur·ing [< L. *prae-,* before + *figurare,* to fashion] 1. to foreshadow 2. to imagine beforehand —**pre'fig·u·ra'tion** (-yə rā'shən) *n.* —**pre·fig'ur·a·tive** *adj.*

pre·fix (prē'fiks; *also for v.* prē fiks') *vt.* [< L. *prae-,* before + *figere,* to fix] to fix to the beginning; esp., to add as a prefix —*n.* a syllable or group of syllables joined to the beginning of a word to alter its meaning

preg·nant (preg'nənt) *adj.* [< L. *pregnans*] 1. having (an) offspring developing in the uterus; with young 2. mentally fertile; inventive 3. full of meaning, etc. 4. filled (*with*) or rich (*in*) —**preg'nan·cy** *n., pl.* -cies —**preg'nant·ly** *adv.*

pre·hen·sile (pri hen's'l) *adj.* [< Fr. < L. *prehendere,* take] adapted for seizing or grasping, esp. by wrapping around something, as a monkey's tail

pre·his·tor·ic (prē'his tôr'ik) *adj.* of the period before recorded history: also **pre'his·tor'i·cal** —**pre'his·tor'i·cal·ly** *adv.*

pre·judge (prē juj') *vt.* -judged', -judg'ing to judge beforehand, or without all the evidence —**pre·judg'ment, pre·judge'ment** *n.*

prej·u·dice (prej'ə dis) *n.* [< L. *prae-,* before + *judicium,* judgment] 1. a preconceived, usually unfavorable, idea 2. an opinion held in disregard of facts that contradict it; bias 3. intolerance or hatred of other races, etc. 4. injury or harm —*vt.* -diced, -dic·ing 1. to harm or damage 2. to cause to have prejudice; bias

prej'u·di'cial (-dish'əl) *adj.* causing prejudice or harm; injurious —**prej'u·di'cial·ly** *adv.*

prel·a·cy (prel'ə sē) *n., pl.* -cies 1. the office or rank of a prelate 2. prelates collectively

prel·ate (-it) *n.* [< L. *praeferre,* place before] a high-ranking ecclesiastic, as a bishop

pre·lim·i·nar·y (pri lim'ə ner'ē) *adj.* [< Fr. < L. *prae-,* before + *limen,* threshold] leading up to the main action, etc.; preparatory —*n., pl.* -ies [*often pl.*] a preliminary step, procedure, examination, etc.

prel·ude (prel'yōōd, prā'lōōd) *n.* [< Fr. < L. *prae-,* before + *ludere,* to play] 1. a preliminary part; preface 2. *Music a)* an introductory section of a suite, fugue, etc. *b)* any short, romantic composition —*vt., vi.* -ud·ed, -ud·ing to serve as or be a prelude (to)

pre·mar·i·tal (prē mar'ə t'l) *adj.* before marriage

pre·ma·ture (prē'mə toor', -choor') *adj.* [< L.: see PRE- & MATURE] happening, done, arriving, etc. before the proper or usual time; too early —**pre'ma·ture'ly** *adv.* —**pre'ma·ture'ness** *n.*

pre·med·i·cal (prē med'i k'l) *adj.* of the studies preparatory to the study of medicine

pre·med·i·tate (pri med'ə tāt') *vt., vi.* -tat'ed, -tat'ing to think out or plan beforehand

pre·med·i·ta·tion (pri med′ə tā′shən) *n.* 1. a premeditating 2. *Law* a degree of forethought sufficient to show intent to commit an act

pre·mier (pri mir′, -myir′) *adj.* [< L. *primus*, first] 1. first in importance; chief 2. first in time —*n.* a chief official; specif., *a*) a prime minister *b*) the governor of a Canadian province —**pre·mier′ship** *n.*

pre·mière, pre·miere (pri myer′, -mir′) *n.* [Fr., fem. of *premier*] a first performance of a play, etc. —*vt., vi.* -mièred′ or -miered′, -mièr′ing or -mier′ing to exhibit (a play, etc.) for the first time

prem·ise (prem′is) *n.* [< L. *prae-*, before + *mittere*, send] 1. a previous statement serving as a basis for an argument; specif., either of the two propositions of a syllogism from which the conclusion is drawn: also **prem′iss** 2. [*pl.*] a piece of real estate —*vt.* (*also* pri mīz′) -ised, -is·ing 1. to state as a premise 2. to preface (a discourse, etc.)

pre·mi·um (prē′mē əm) *n., pl.* -ums [< L. *prae-*, before + *emere*, take] 1. a reward or prize, esp. as an inducement to buy or do something 2. an amount paid in addition to the regular charge, etc. 3. a payment, as for an insurance policy 4. very high value [to put a *premium* on honesty] —**at a premium** 1. at a value or price higher than normal 2. very valuable, as because of scarcity

pre·mo·lar (prē mō′lər) *adj.* designating or of any bicuspid tooth in front of the molars —*n.* a premolar tooth

pre·mo·ni·tion (prē′mə nish′ən, prem′ə-) *n.* [< L. *prae-*, before + *monere*, warn] 1. a forewarning 2. a foreboding —**pre·mon·i·to·ry** (pri män′ə tôr′ē) *adj.*

pre·na·tal (prē nāt′'l) *adj.* [PRE- + NATAL] existing or taking place before birth —**pre·na′tal·ly** *adv.*

pre·oc·cu·py (prē äk′yə pī′) *vt.* -pied′, -py′ing [< L.: see PRE- & OCCUPY] 1. to occupy completely the thoughts of; engross 2. to take possession of before someone else or beforehand —**pre·oc′cu·pan·cy** (-pən sē), **pre·oc′cu·pa′tion** (-pā′shən) *n.*

pre·or·dain (prē′ôr dān′) *vt.* to ordain or decree beforehand —**pre′or·di·na′tion** (-d′n ā′shən) *n.*

prep (prep) *adj.* [Colloq.] *clipped form of* PREPARATORY —*vi.* **prepped, prep′ping** [Colloq.] to prepare oneself by study, etc. —*vt.* to prepare (esp. a patient for surgery)

prep. 1. preparatory 2. preposition

pre·pack·age (prē pak′ij) *vt.* -aged, -ag·ing to package (foods, etc.) in standard units before sale

pre·paid (prē pād′) *pt. & pp. of* PREPAY

prep·a·ra·tion (prep′ə rā′shən) *n.* 1. a preparing or being prepared 2. a preparatory measure 3. something prepared, as a medicine, cosmetic, etc.

pre·par·a·to·ry (pri par′ə tôr′ē) *adj.* 1. serving to prepare; introductory 2. undergoing preparation, esp. for college entrance

preparatory school a private secondary school for preparing students to enter college

pre·pare (pri par′) *vt.* -pared′, -par′ing [< L. *prae-*, before + *parare*, get ready] 1. to make ready 2. to equip or furnish 3. to put together; construct [to *prepare* a dinner] —*vi.* 1. to make things ready 2. to make oneself ready

pre·par′ed·ness *n.* the state of being prepared, esp. for waging war

pre·pay (prē pā′) *vt.* -paid′, -pay′ing to pay or pay for in advance —**pre·pay′ment** *n.*

pre·pon·der·ant (pri pän′dər ənt) *adj.* greater in amount, power, influence, etc.; predominant —**pre·pon′der·ance** *n.* —**pre·pon′der·ant·ly** *adv.*

pre·pon′der·ate′ (-də rāt′) *vi.* -at·ed, -at·ing [< L. *prae-*, before + *ponderare*, weigh] to be greater in amount, power, influence, etc.; predominate

prep·o·si·tion (prep′ə zish′ən) *n.* [< L. *prae-*, before + *ponere*, to place] a relation word, as *in, by, to*, etc., that connects a noun or pronoun to another element, as to a noun (Ex.: the sound *of* rain), to a verb (Ex.: go *to* the store), or to an adjective (Ex.: old *in* years) —**prep′o·si′tion·al** *adj.*

prepositional phrase a preposition and its object

pre·pos·sess (prē′pə zes′) *vt.* 1. to prejudice 2. to impress favorably at once —**pre′pos·ses′sion** *n.*

pre′pos·sess′ing *adj.* that impresses favorably; pleasing —**pre′pos·sess′ing·ly** *adv.*

pre·pos·ter·ous (pri päs′tər əs) *adj.* [< L. *prae-*, before + *posterus*, coming after] so contrary to nature, common sense, etc. as to be laughable; absurd —**pre·pos′ter·ous·ly** *adv.*

pre·puce (prē′pyōōs) *n.* [< L. *praeputium*] the fold of skin covering the end of the penis

pre·re·cord (prē′ri kôrd′) *vt. Radio & TV* to record (a program, etc.) in advance, for later broadcasting

pre·req·ui·site (pri rek′wə zit) *adj.* required beforehand as a necessary condition for something following —*n.* something prerequisite

pre·rog·a·tive (pri räg′ə tiv) *n.* [ult. < L. *prae-*, before + *rogare*, ask] an exclusive privilege, esp. one peculiar to a rank, class, etc.

Pres. President

pres. present

pres·age (pres′ij; *for v.* pri sāj′) *n.* [< L. *prae-*, before + *sagire*, perceive] 1. a warning or portent 2. a foreboding —*vt.* -aged, -ag′ing 1. to give warning of 2. to have a foreboding of 3. to predict

pres·by·ter (prez′bi tər) *n.* [see PRIEST] 1. in the Presbyterian Church, an elder 2. in the Episcopal Church, a priest or minister

pres·by·te·ri·an (prez′bə tir′ē ən) *adj.* 1. having to do with church government by presbyters 2. [P-] designating or of a church of a Calvinistic Protestant denomination governed by presbyters, or elders —*n.* [P-] a member of a Presbyterian church —**Pres′by·te′ri·an·ism** *n.*

pres·by·ter·y (prez′bə ter′ē) *n., pl.* -ies in Presbyterian churches, a governing body made up of all the ministers and an equal number of elders in a district

pre·school (prē′skōōl′) *adj.* designating, of, or for a child between infancy and school age

pre·sci·ence (prē′shē əns, presh′əns) *n.* [ult. < L. *prae-*, before + *scire*, know] apparent knowledge of things before they happen —**pre′sci·ent** *adj.*

pre·scribe (pri skrīb′) *vt.* -scribed′, -scrib′ing [< L. *prae-*, before + *scribere*, write] 1. to order; direct 2. to order or advise as a medicine or treatment: said of physicians —*vi.* 1. to set down rules 2. to give medical advice or prescriptions

pre·scrip·tion (pri skrip′shən) *n.* 1. a prescribing 2. something prescribed; order 3. a doctor's written direction for the preparation and use of a medicine 4. a medicine so prescribed —**pre·scrip′tive** *adj.*

pres·ence (prez′'ns) *n.* 1. the fact or condition of being present 2. immediate surroundings [admitted to his *presence*] 3. one that is present, esp. a person of high station 4. *a*) one's bearing, appearance, etc. *b*) poised and confident bearing 5. a spirit or ghost felt to be present

presence of mind ability to think clearly and act quickly and intelligently in an emergency

pres·ent (prez′'nt) *adj.* [< L. *prae-*, before + *esse*, be] 1. being at the specified place 2. existing or happening now 3. now being discussed, considered, etc. 4. *Gram.* indicating action or state now or action that is always true (Ex.: man *is* mortal) —*n.* 1. the present time or occasion 2. the present tense or a verb in it 3. a gift —*vt.* (pri zent′) 1. to introduce (a person) 2. to exhibit; show 3. to offer for consideration 4. to give (a gift, etc.) to (a person, etc.) —**present arms** *Mil.* to hold a rifle vertically in front of the body

pre·sent·a·ble (pri zen′tə b'l) *adj.* 1. suitable for presentation 2. properly dressed for meeting people —**pre·sent′a·bil′i·ty** *n.* —**pre·sent′a·bly** *adv.*

pre·sen·ta·tion (prē′zen tā′shən, prez′'n-) *n.* 1. a presenting or being presented 2. something presented, as a theatrical performance, a gift, etc.

pres′ent-day′ *adj.* of the present time

pre·sen·ti·ment (pri zen′tə mənt) *n.* [see PRE- & SENTIMENT] a feeling that something, esp. of an unfortunate nature, is about to take place

pres′ent·ly *adv.* 1. soon 2. now

pre·sent·ment (pri zent′mənt) *n. same as* PRESENTATION

present participle a participle used to express present or continuing action or state of being, as in "the boy is *growing*"

present perfect a tense indicating an action or state as completed but not at any definite time in the past

pre·serv·a·tive (pri zur′və tiv) *adj.* preserving —*n.* anything that preserves; esp., a substance added to food to keep it from spoiling

pre·serve (pri zurv′) *vt.* -served′, -serv′ing [< L. *prae-*, before + *servare*, keep] 1. to protect from harm, danger, etc. 2. to keep from spoiling 3. to prepare (food), as by canning, for future use 4. to keep up; maintain —*vi.* to preserve fruit, etc. —*n.* 1. [*usually pl.*] fruit preserved by cooking with sugar 2. a place where game, fish, etc. are maintained —**pres·er·va·tion** (prez′ər vā′shən) *n.*

pre′-shrunk′ *adj.* shrunk by a special process in manufacture so as to minimize shrinkage in laundering or dry cleaning

pre·side (pri zīd′) *vi.* -sid′ed, -sid′ing [< Fr. < L. *prae-*, before + *sedere*, sit] 1. to act as chairman 2. to have control or authority (*over*)

pres·i·den·cy (prez′i dən sē) *n., pl.* **-cies 1.** the office, function, or term of president **2.** [*often* P-] the office of President of the U.S.

pres·i·dent (prez′i dənt) *n.* [see PRESIDE] **1.** the highest executive officer of a company, club, etc. **2.** [*often* P-] the chief executive, or sometimes the formal head, of a republic —**pres′i·den′tial** (-den′shəl) *adj.*

pres′i·dent-e·lect′ *n.* an elected president who has not yet taken office

pre·sid·i·um (pri sid′ē əm) *n., pl.* **-i·a** (-ə), **-i·ums** [< Russ. < L. *praesidium,* a presiding over] in the Soviet Union, **1.** any of a number of permanent administrative committees **2.** [P-] the permanent administrative committee of the Supreme Soviet

press¹ (pres) *vt.* [< L. *premere*] **1.** to act on with steady force or weight; push against; squeeze **2.** to squeeze (juice, etc.) from **3.** *a)* to compress *b)* to iron (clothes, etc.) **4.** to embrace closely **5.** to force; compel **6.** to urge persistently; entreat **7.** to try to force **8.** to emphasize **9.** to distress or trouble [*pressed* for time] **10.** to urge on — *vi.* **1.** to weigh down **2.** to go forward with determination **3.** to crowd **4.** to be urgent or insistent **5.** to try too hard —*n.* **1.** pressure, urgency, etc. **2.** a crowd **3.** any machine for crushing, stamping, smoothing, etc. **4.** smoothness, etc. of clothes after pressing **5.** *a) clipped form of* PRINTING PRESS *b)* the art or business of printing *c)* newspapers, magazines, etc., or the persons who write for them *d)* publicity, criticism, etc., as in newspapers **6.** an upright closet for clothes, etc. —**go to press** to start to be printed —**press′er** *n.*

press² (pres) *vt.* [< L. *praes,* surety + *stare,* to stand] to force into service, esp. military or naval service

press agent a person whose work is to get publicity for an individual, organization, etc.

press box a place for reporters, as at sports events

press conference a collective interview granted to newsmen as by a celebrity or personage

press′ing *adj.* calling for immediate attention

press′man (-mən) *n., pl.* **-men** an operator of a printing press

pres·sure (presh′ər) *n.* **1.** a pressing or being pressed **2.** a state of distress **3.** a compelling influence [*social pressure*] **4.** urgency **5.** *Physics* force per unit of area exerted upon a surface, etc. —*vt.* **-sured, -sur·ing** to exert pressure on

pressure cooker an airtight container for quick cooking by steam under pressure —**pres′sure-cook′** *vt.*

pressure group any group exerting pressure on legislators and the public through lobbies, propaganda, etc. to affect legislation

pres′sur·ize′ (-īz′) *vt.* **-ized′, -iz′ing** to keep nearly normal air pressure inside of (an airplane, etc.), as at high altitudes —**pres′sur·i·za′tion** *n.* —**pres′sur·iz′er** *n.*

pres·ti·dig·i·ta·tion (pres′tə dij′i tā′shən) *n.* [Fr. < It. *presto,* quick + L. *digitus,* a finger] sleight of hand — **pres′ti·dig′i·ta′tor** *n.*

pres·tige (pres tēzh′, -tēj′) *n.* [Fr. < L. *praestigium,* illusion] **1.** the power to impress or influence **2.** reputation based on high achievement, character, etc. —**pres·ti′gious** (-tij′əs, -tē′jəs) *adj.*

pres·to (pres′tō) *adv., adj.* [It., quick] fast

pre·sume (pri zōōm′, -zyōōm′) *vt.* **-sumed′, -sum′ing** [< L. *prae-,* before + *sumere,* take] **1.** to dare (to say or do something) **2.** to take for granted; suppose **3.** to be reasonable evidence for supposing —*vi.* to act presumptuously; take liberties —**pre·sum′a·ble** *adj.* —**pre·sum′a·bly, pre·sum′ed·ly** *adv.*

pre·sump·tion (pri zump′shən) *n.* **1.** a presuming; specif., *a)* forwardness; effrontery *b)* a taking of something for granted **2.** the thing presumed **3.** a reason for presuming —**pre·sump′tive** *adj.*

pre·sump′tu·ous (-choo wəs) *adj.* too bold or forward; showing presumption —**pre·sump′tu·ous·ly** *adv.*

pre·sup·pose (prē′sə pōz′) *vt.* **-posed′, -pos′ing 1.** to suppose or assume beforehand **2.** to require or imply as a preceding condition —**pre′sup·po·si′tion** (-sup ə zish′ən) *n.*

pret. preterit

pre·teen (prē′tēn′) *n.* a child nearly a teen-ager

pre·tend (pri tend′) *vt.* [< L. *prae-,* before + *tendere,* to stretch] **1.** to profess [to *pretend* infallibility] **2.** to simulate [to *pretend* illness] **3.** to make believe [*pretend* I'm you] —*vi.* **1.** to lay claim (to) **2.** to make believe

pre·tend′er *n.* **1.** one who pretends **2.** a person who lays claim to something, esp. to a throne

pre·tense (pri tens′, prē′tens) *n.* **1.** a claim; pretension **2.** a false claim **3.** a false show of something **4.** a pretending, as at play **5.** a pretext **6.** pretentiousness Brit. sp. **pretence**

pre·ten·sion (pri ten′shən) *n.* **1.** a pretext **2.** a claim **3.** assertion of a claim **4.** pretentiousness

pret·er·it, pret·er·ite (pret′ər it) *adj.* [< L. *praeter-,* beyond + *ire,* go] *Gram.* expressing past action or state — *n.* **1.** the past tense **2.** a verb in it

pre·ter·nat·u·ral (prēt′ər nach′ər əl) *adj.* [< L. *praeter-,* beyond + *naturalis,* natural] **1.** differing from or beyond what is natural; abnormal **2.** *same as* SUPERNATURAL — **pre′ter·nat′u·ral·ly** *adv.*

pre·test (prē′test′) *n.* a preliminary test, as of a product —*vt., vi.* (prē′test′) to test in advance

pre·text (prē′tekst) *n.* [< L. *prae-,* before + *texere,* weave] a false reason put forth to hide the real one; excuse

Pre·to·ri·a (pri tôr′ē ə) the seat of the government of South Africa: pop. 493,000

pret·ti·fy (prit′ə fī′) *vt.* **-fied′, -fy′ing** to make pretty

pret·ty (prit′ē, pur′tē) *adj.* **-ti·er, -ti·est** [< OE. *prættig,* crafty] **1.** pleasing or attractive, esp. in a dainty or graceful way **2.** fine; nice: often used ironically **3.** [Colloq.] considerable; quite large —*adv.* **1.** fairly; somewhat; quite **2.** [Colloq.] prettily —*n., pl.* **-ties** a pretty person or thing —*vt.* **-tied, -ty·ing** to make pretty (usually with *up*) — **sitting pretty** [Slang] in a favorable position —**pret′ti·ly** *adv.* —**pret′ti·ness** *n.*

pret·zel (pret′s'l) *n.* [G. *brezel* < L. *brachium,* an arm] a hard, brittle biscuit usually in the form of a loose knot or stick, sprinkled with salt

PRETZEL

pre·vail (pri vāl′) *vi.* [< L. *prae-,* before + *valere,* be strong] **1.** to be victorious (*over* or *against*) **2.** to succeed **3.** to be or become stronger or more widespread; predominate **4.** to be prevalent —**prevail on** (or **upon, with**) to persuade

pre·vail′ing *adj.* **1.** superior in strength, influence, etc. **2.** predominant **3.** prevalent

prev·a·lent (prev′ə lənt) *adj.* [see PREVAIL] widely existing, practiced, or accepted; common —**prev′a·lence** *n.* — **prev′a·lent·ly** *adv.*

pre·var·i·cate (pri var′ə kāt′) *vi.* **-cat′ed, -cat′ing** [< L. *prae-,* before + *varicare,* straddle] **1.** to evade the truth **2.** to lie —**pre·var′i·ca′tion** *n.* —**pre·var′i·ca′tor** *n.*

pre·vent (pri vent′) *vt.* [< L. *prae-,* before + *venire,* come] **1.** to stop or keep (*from* doing something) **2.** to keep from happening; hinder —**pre·vent′a·ble, pre·vent′i·ble** *adj.* —**pre·ven′tion** *n.*

pre·ven′tive *adj.* preventing or serving to prevent; esp., preventing disease —*n.* anything that prevents Also **pre·vent′a·tive** —**pre·ven′tive·ness** *n.*

pre·view (prē′vyōō) *vt.* to view or show beforehand —*n.* **1.** an advance, restricted showing, as of a movie **2.** a showing of scenes from a movie, etc. to advertise it Also **pre′vue** (-vyōō)

pre·vi·ous (prē′vē əs) *adj.* [< L. *prae-,* before + *via,* a way] **1.** occurring before; prior **2.** [Colloq.] premature — **previous to** before —**pre′vi·ous·ly** *adv.*

pre·war (prē′wôr′) *adj.* before a (or the) war

prex·y (prek′sē) *n., pl.* **-ies** [Slang] the president, esp. of a college, etc.

prey (prā) *n.* [< L. *praeda,* plunder] **1.** an animal hunted for food by another animal **2.** a victim **3.** the act of preying on other animals [a bird of *prey*] —*vi.* **1.** to plunder **2.** to hunt other animals for food **3.** to profit by swindling **4.** to weigh as an obsession Generally used with *on* or *upon*

Pri·am (prī′əm) *Gr. Legend* the last king of Troy, during the Trojan War: father of Hector and Paris

price (prīs) *n.* [< L. *pretium*] **1.** the amount of money, etc. asked or paid for something; cost **2.** value or worth **3.** a reward for the capture or death of a person **4.** the cost, as in life, labor, etc., of obtaining some benefit —*vt.* **priced, pric′ing 1.** to fix the price of **2.** [Colloq.] to find out the price of —**at any price** no matter what the cost

price′less *adj.* **1.** too valuable to be measured by price **2.** [Colloq.] very amusing or absurd

prick (prik) *n.* [OE. *prica,* a dot] **1.** a tiny puncture made by a sharp point **2.** [Archaic] a pointed object **3.** a sharp pain caused as by being pricked —*vt.* **1.** to make (a hole) in (something) with a sharp point **2.** to pain sharply **3.** to mark by dots, points, etc. —*vi.* **1.** to cause or feel a slight, sharp pain **2.** to point or stick up: said esp. of ears —**prick up one's ears** to listen closely —**prick'er** *n.*

prick·le (prik''l) *n.* [< OE. *prica*, prick] **1.** any sharp point, as a thornlike growth on a plant **2.** a tingling sensation —*vt., vi.* **-led, -ling** to tingle

prick'ly *adj.* **-li·er, -li·est 1.** full of prickles **2.** stinging; tingling —**prick'li·ness** *n.*

prickly heat an itching skin eruption caused by inflammation of the sweat glands

prickly pear 1. any of various cactus plants, some having barbed spines **2.** its pear-shaped fruit

pride (prīd) *n.* [< OE. *prut*, proud] **1.** *a)* an overhigh opinion of oneself *b)* haughtiness; arrogance **2.** dignity and self-respect **3.** satisfaction in one's achievements, etc. **4.** a person or thing that one is proud of **5.** the best of a class, group, etc.; pick **6.** [Colloq.] an impressive group —**pride oneself on** to be proud of —**pride'ful** *adj.*

pri·er (prī'ər) *n.* one who pries: see PRY²

priest (prēst) *n.* [< Gr. *presbys*, old] **1.** one whose function is to perform religious rites **2.** in some Christian churches, a clergyman authorized to administer the sacraments **3.** any clergyman —**priest'ess** *n.fem.* —**priest'hood'** *n.* —**priest'ly** *adj.*

Priest·ley (prēst'lē), **Joseph** 1733–1804; Eng. scientist & theologian: discoverer of oxygen

prig (prig) *n.* [< 16th-c. slang] one who smugly affects great propriety or morality —**prig'gish** *adj.* —**prig'gish·ly** *adv.* —**prig'gish·ness** *n.*

prim (prim) *adj.* **prim'mer, prim'mest** [< ?] stiffly formal, precise, moral, etc.; proper; demure —**prim'ly** *adv.* —**prim'ness** *n.*

prim. 1. primary **2.** primitive

pri·ma·cy (prī'mə sē) *n., pl.* **-cies** [see PRIMATE] **1.** the state of being first in time, order, rank, etc. **2.** the rank or authority of a primate

pri·ma don·na (prē'mə dän'ə) *pl.* **pri'ma don'nas** [It., first lady] **1.** principal woman singer, as in an opera **2.** [Colloq.] a temperamental or arrogant person

pri·ma fa·ci·e (prī'mə fā'shi ē', fā'shē) [L., at first view] adequate to establish a fact unless refuted: said of evidence

pri·mal (prī'm'l) *adj.* [< L. *primus*, first] **1.** first in time; original **2.** first in importance; chief

pri·ma·ri·ly (prī mer'ə lē, prī'mer'-) *adv.* **1.** at first; originally **2.** mainly; principally

pri·ma·ry (prī'mer'ē, -mər ē) *adj.* [< L. *primus*, first] **1.** first in time or order; original **2.** *a)* from which others are derived; fundamental *b)* designating colors regarded as basic, from which all others may be derived: see COLOR (*n.* 1 & 2) **3.** first in importance; chief **4.** *Elec.* designating or of an inducing current, input circuit, or input coil in a transformer, etc. —*n., pl.* **-ries 1.** something first in order, quality, etc. **2.** a preliminary election at which candidates are chosen for the final election

primary accent (or **stress**) the heaviest stress (') in pronouncing a word

primary school *same as* ELEMENTARY SCHOOL

pri·mate (prī'māt; *also, for 1,* -mit) *n.* [< L. *primus*, first] **1.** an archbishop, or the highest-ranking bishop in a province, etc. **2.** any of a group of mammals, including man, the apes, etc. —**pri'mate·ship'** *n.*

prime (prīm) *adj.* [< L. *primus*, first] **1.** first in time; original **2.** first in rank or importance; chief; principal **3.** first in quality [*prime* beef] **4.** fundamental **5.** *Math.* that can be evenly divided by no other whole number than itself or 1 —*n.* **1.** [*often* P-] the first daylight canonical hour **2.** the first or earliest part **3.** the best or most vigorous period **4.** the best part —*vt.* **primed, prim'ing 1.** to make ready; prepare **2.** to get (a pump) into operation by pouring water into it **3.** to undercoat, size, etc. (a surface) for painting **4.** to provide (a person) beforehand with information, answers, etc.

prime meridian the meridian from which longitude is measured east and west; 0°: see GREENWICH TIME

prime minister in parliamentary governments, the chief executive and, usually, head of the cabinet

prim·er¹ (prim'ər) *n.* [< L. *primus*, first] **1.** a simple book for teaching reading to children **2.** any elementary textbook

prim·er² (prī'mər) *n.* a thing that primes; specif., *a)* an explosive cap, etc. used to set off the main charge *b)* a preliminary coat of paint, etc.

prime time *Radio & TV* the hours, esp. the evening hours, when the largest audience is available

pri·me·val (prī mē'v'l) *adj.* [< L. *primus*, first + *aevum*, age] of the earliest times or ages; primordial

prim·ing (prī'miŋ) *n.* **1.** the explosive used to set off the charge in a gun, etc. **2.** paint, sizing, etc. used as a primer

prim·i·tive (prim'ə tiv) *adj.* [< L. *primus*, first] **1.** of the earliest time; original **2.** crude; simple **3.** primary; basic —*n.* a primitive person or thing —**prim'i·tive·ly** *adv.* —**prim'i·tive·ness** *n.*

pri·mo·gen·i·tor (prī'mə jen'i tər) *n.* [< L. *primus*, first + *genitor*, a father] **1.** an ancestor **2.** the earliest ancestor of a family, race, etc.

pri'mo·gen'i·ture (-chər) *n.* [< L. *primus*, first + *genitura*, a begetting] **1.** the condition of being the first-born of the same parents **2.** the right of inheritance of the eldest son

pri·mor·di·al (prī môr'dē əl) *adj.* [< L. *primus*, first + *ordiri*, begin] **1.** primitive **2.** fundamental; original —**pri·mor'di·al·ly** *adv.*

primp (primp) *vt., vi.* [prob. < PRIM] to groom or dress up in a fussy way

prim·rose (prim'rōz') *n.* [alt. (after *rose*) < ML. *primula*] a plant with tubelike, often yellow flowers

prin. 1. principal **2.** principle

prince (prins) *n.* [< L. *princeps*, chief] **1.** a ruler ranking below a king: head of a principality **2.** in Great Britain, a son or grandson of the sovereign **3.** *a)* a preeminent person in a group, etc. *b)* [Colloq.] a fine, generous fellow

prince consort the husband of a queen or empress reigning in her own right

Prince Edward Island an island province of SE Canada: 2,184 sq. mi.; pop. 109,000; cap. Charlottetown

prince'ly *adj.* **-li·er, -li·est 1.** of a prince **2.** magnificent; generous —**prince'li·ness** *n.*

Prince of Wales the oldest son and heir apparent of a British king or queen

prin·cess¹ (prin'sis, -ses) *n.* **1.** orig., any female monarch **2.** in Great Britain, a daughter of the sovereign **3.** the wife of a prince

prin·cess² (prin'sis, prin ses') *adj.* [< Fr. *princesse*, a princess] of or designating a woman's one-piece, closefitting, gored dress, etc.: also **prin·cesse'** (-ses')

prin·ci·pal (prin'sə pəl) *adj.* [see PRINCE] first in rank, importance, etc. —*n.* **1.** a principal person or thing **2.** a governing officer, as of a school **3.** a main actor or performer **4.** the amount of a debt, etc. minus the interest **5.** the face value of a stock or bond **6.** *Law a)* one who employs another to act as his agent *b)* the one primarily responsible for an obligation *c)* one who commits a crime —**prin'ci·pal·ly** *adv.* —**prin'ci·pal·ship'** *n.*

prin·ci·pal·i·ty (-pal'ə tē) *n., pl.* **-ties** the territory ruled by a prince

principal parts the principal inflected forms of a verb: in English, the present infinitive, the past tense, and past participle (*drink, drank, drunk*)

prin·ci·ple (prin'sə pəl) *n.* [see PRINCE] **1.** a fundamental truth, law, etc., upon which others are based **2.** *a)* a rule of conduct *b)* adherence to such rules; integrity **3.** *a)* the scientific law that explains a natural action *b)* the method of a thing's operation —**in principle** theoretically or in essence

prin·ci·pled (-pəld) *adj.* having or based on principles, as of conduct

print (print) *n.* [< L. *premere*, to press] **1.** a mark made on a surface by pressing or stamping **2.** cloth printed with a design **3.** the impression made by inked type **4.** a picture or design printed from a plate, block, etc., as a lithograph **5.** a photograph, esp. one made from a negative —*vt., vi.* **1.** to stamp (a mark, letter, etc.) on a surface **2.** to produce on (paper, etc.) the impression of inked type, plates, etc. **3.** to produce or publish (a book, etc.) **4.** to write in letters resembling printed ones **5.** to produce (a photograph) from (a negative) **6.** in computers, to deliver (information) by means of a printer: often with *out* —**in** (or **out of**) **print** still (or no longer) for sale by the publisher: said of books, etc. —**print'er** *n.*

printed circuit an electrical circuit formed by applying conductive material in fine lines or other shapes to an insulating surface

printing press a machine for printing from inked type, plates, or rolls

print'out' *n.* the printed output of a computer

pri·or (prī'ər) *adj.* [L.] **1.** preceding in time; earlier **2.** preceding in order or importance —*n.* the head of a priory —**pri'or·ess** *n.fem.*

pri·or·i·ty (prī ôr'ə tē, -är'-) *n., pl.* **-ties 1.** a being prior; precedence **2.** a prior right to buy, get, or do something **3.** something given prior attention

pri·o·ry *n., pl.* **-ries** a monastery governed by a prior, or a convent governed by a prioress

prism (priz'm) *n.* [< Gr. *prizein*, to saw] **1.** a solid figure whose ends are equal and parallel polygons and whose sides are parallelograms **2.** a transparent prism whose ends are triangles: used to disperse light into the spectrum

pris·mat·ic (priz mat'ik) *adj.* **1.** of or like a prism **2.** that refracts light as a prism **3.** many-colored —**pris·mat'i·cal·ly** *adv.*

PRISM

pris·on (priz'n) *n.* [< L. *prehendere*, take] **1.** a place of confinement, esp. for those convicted by or awaiting trial **2.** imprisonment

pris·on·er *n.* **1.** a person confined in prison for some crime **2.** a person held in custody **3.** a person captured or held captive

pris·sy (pris'ē) *adj.* -si·er, -si·est [prob. < PR(IM) + (s)ISSY] [Colloq.] very prim or precise; fussy, prudish, etc. —**pris'si·ness** *n.*

pris·tine (pris'tēn, -tin) *adj.* [< L. *pristinus*, former] **1.** characteristic of the earliest period; original **2.** uncorrupted; unspoiled

prith·ee (prith'ē) *interj.* [< *pray thee*] [Archaic] I pray thee; please

pri·va·cy (prī'və sē) *n., pl.* -cies **1.** a being private; seclusion **2.** secrecy **3.** one's private life

pri·vate (prī'vit) *adj.* [< L. *privus*, separate] **1.** of or concerning a particular person or group **2.** not open to or controlled by the public [a *private* school] **3.** for an individual person [a *private* room] **4.** not holding public office [a *private* citizen] **5.** secret [a *private* matter] —*n.* an enlisted man of either of the lowest ranks in the U.S. Army or of the lowest rank in the U.S. Marine Corps —**in private** not publicly —**pri'vate·ly** *adv.*

pri·va·teer (prī'və tir') *n.* **1.** a privately owned ship commissioned in war to capture enemy ships **2.** a commander or crew member of a privateer

pri·va·tion (prī vā'shən) *n.* **1.** the loss or absence of some quality or condition **2.** lack of the ordinary necessities of life

priv·a·tive (priv'ə tiv) *adj.* **1.** depriving **2.** *Gram.* indicating negation, absence, or loss —*n. Gram.* a privative term or affix, as *un-, non-,* or *-less*

priv·et (priv'it) *n.* [< ?] an evergreen shrub used for hedges

priv·i·lege (priv''l ij) *n.* [< L. *privus*, separate + *lex,* a law] a right, favor, etc. specially granted to a certain person, group, etc. —*vt.* -leged, -leg·ing to grant a privilege to

priv·y (priv'ē) *adj.* [< L. *privatus*, private] private: now only in such phrases as **privy council,** a body of confidential advisers named by a ruler —*n., pl.* -ies a toilet; esp., an outhouse —**privy to** privately informed about

prize[1] (prīz) *vt.* prized, priz'ing [see PRICE] **1.** formerly, to appraise **2.** to value highly; esteem —*n.* **1.** something offered or given to the winner of a contest, etc. **2.** anything worth striving for —*adj.* **1.** that has received a prize **2.** worthy of a prize **3.** given as a prize

prize[2] (prīz) *n.* [< L. *prehendere*, to take] something, esp. a warship, captured in war —*vt.* prized, priz'ing to pry, as with a lever

prize'fight' *n.* a professional boxing match —**prize'-fight'er** *n.* —**prize'fight'ing** *n.*

pro[1] (prō) *adv.* [L., for] on the affirmative side —*adj.* favorable —*n., pl.* pros a vote, position, etc. in favor of something

pro[2] (prō) *adj., n., pl.* pros *short form of* PROFESSIONAL

pro-[1] [Gr. < *pro,* before] *a prefix meaning* before in place or time

pro-[2] [L. < *pro,* forward] *a prefix meaning:* **1.** forward or ahead [*progress*] **2.** forth [*produce*] **3.** substituting for [*pronoun*] **4.** supporting, favoring [*prolabor*]

prob. 1. probable **2.** probably **3.** problem

prob·a·bil·i·ty (präb'ə bil'ə tē) *n., pl.* -ties **1.** a being probable; likelihood **2.** something probable

prob·a·ble (präb'ə b'l) *adj.* [< L. *probare*, prove] **1.** likely to occur or be **2.** reasonably so, as on the basis of evidence, but not proved —**prob'a·bly** *adv.*

pro·bate (prō'bāt) *n.* [see PROBE] the act or process of probating —*adj.* having to do with probating —*vt.* -bat·ed, -bat·ing **1.** to establish officially the validity of (a will) **2.** popularly, to certify in a probate court as mentally unsound

probate court a court for probating wills, administering estates, etc.

pro·ba·tion (prō bā'shən) *n.* [see PROBE] **1.** a testing or trial, as of character, ability, etc. **2.** the conditional suspension of a convicted person's sentence **3.** the status or period of being tested, given another chance, etc. —**pro·ba'tion·ar'y, pro·ba'tion·al** *adj.*

pro·ba'tion·er *n.* a person on probation

probation officer an officer appointed by a court to supervise persons placed on probation

probe (prōb) *n.* [< L. *probare*, to test] **1.** a surgical instrument for exploring a wound, etc. **2.** a searching investigation **3.** an instrumented spacecraft for exploring the upper atmosphere, outer space, etc. —*vt.* probed, prob'ing **1.** to explore (a wound, etc.) with a probe **2.** to investigate thoroughly —*vi.* to search; investigate —**prob'er** *n.*

prob·i·ty (prō'bə tē, präb'ə-) *n.* [< L. *probus,* good] honesty; integrity

prob·lem (präb'ləm) *n.* [< Gr. *problēma*] **1.** a question to be worked out **2.** a perplexing or difficult matter, person, etc. —*adj.* **1.** depicting a social problem [a *problem* play] **2.** very difficult to train or discipline [a *problem* child]

prob·lem·at·ic (präb'lə mat'ik) *adj.* **1.** of the nature of a problem **2.** uncertain Also **prob'lem·at'i·cal**

pro·bos·cis (prō bäs'is) *n., pl.* -cis·es [< Gr. *pro-,* before + *boskein,* to feed] **1.** an elephant's trunk, or a long, flexible snout **2.** a tubular sucking organ, as of some insects **3.** a person's nose, esp. if large: a jocular usage

pro·caine (prō'kān) *n.* [PRO-[2] + (CO)CAINE] a synthetic crystalline compound used as a local anesthetic

pro·ce·dure (prə sē'jər) *n.* **1.** the act or method of proceeding in some action **2.** a particular course or method of action —**pro·ce'dur·al** *adj.*

pro·ceed (prə sēd') *vi.* [< L. *pro-,* forward + *cedere,* go] **1.** to go on, esp. after stopping **2.** to carry on some action **3.** to take legal action (*against*) **4.** to come forth or issue (*from*)

pro·ceed'ing *n.* **1.** a going on with what one has been doing **2.** a course of action **3.** [*pl.*] a record of transactions **4.** [*pl.*] legal action

pro·ceeds (prō'sēdz) *n.pl.* the sum or profit derived from a sale, venture, etc.

proc·ess (präs'es; *chiefly Brit. & Canad.,* prō'ses) *n.* [see PROCEED] **1.** a series of changes by which something develops [the *process* of growth] **2.** a method of doing something with all the steps involved **3.** *Biol.* a projecting part **4.** *Law* a written order, as a court summons —*vt.* to prepare by or subject to a special process —*adj.* prepared by a special process —**in process** in the course of being done —**in (the) process of** in or during the course of —**proc'es·sor, proc'ess·er** *n.*

pro·ces·sion (prə sesh'ən) *n.* [see PROCEED] **1.** the act of proceeding **2.** a number of persons or things moving forward in an orderly way, as in a parade

pro·ces'sion·al *n.* a hymn sung at the beginning of a church service during the entrance of the clergy

pro·claim (prō klām') *vt.* [< L. *pro-,* before + *clamare,* cry out] **1.** to announce officially; announce to be **2.** to show to be [acts that *proclaimed* him a friend]

proc·la·ma·tion (präk'lə mā'shən) *n.* **1.** a proclaiming **2.** something that is proclaimed

pro·cliv·i·ty (prō kliv'ə tē) *n., pl.* -ties [< L. *pro-,* before + *clivus,* a slope] a natural tendency or inclination

pro·con·sul (prō kän's'l) *n.* [L. < *pro consule,* acting) for the consul] a Roman official with consular authority who commanded an army in the provinces

pro·cras·ti·nate (prō kras'tə nāt') *vi., vt.* -nat'ed, -nat'-ing [< L. *pro-,* forward + *cras,* tomorrow] to put off doing (something) until later; delay —**pro·cras'ti·na'tion** *n.* —**pro·cras'ti·na'tor** *n.*

pro·cre·ate (prō'krē āt') *vt., vi.* -at'ed, -at'ing [< L. *pro-,* before + *creare,* create] **1.** to produce (young); beget **2.** to produce —**pro'cre·a'tion** *n.* —**pro'cre·a'tive** *adj.* —**pro'-cre·a'tor** *n.*

Pro·crus·te·an (prō krus'tē ən) *adj.* **1.** of or like Procrustes **2.** securing conformity at any cost

Pro·crus'tes (-tēz) *Gr. Myth.* a giant who seized travelers, tied them to a bedstead, and either stretched them or cut off their legs to fit it

proc·tol·o·gy (präk täl'ə jē) *n.* [< Gr. *proktos,* anus + -LOGY] the branch of medicine dealing with the rectum and its diseases —**proc·tol'o·gist** *n.*

proc·tor (präk'tər) *n.* [see PROCURE] a college official who maintains order, supervises examinations, etc. —*vt.* to supervise (an examination) —**proc·to·ri·al** (präk tôr'ē əl) *adj.*

proc·u·ra·tor (präk'yə rāt'ər) *n.* [see PROCURE] **1.** in the Roman Empire, an administrator of a province **2.** a person employed to manage another's affairs; agent

pro·cure (prō kyoor') *vt.* -cured', -cur'ing [< L. *pro-*, for + *curare*, attend to] **1.** to get; obtain **2.** to obtain (women) for the purpose of prostitution —**pro·cur'a·ble** *adj.* —**pro·cure'ment** *n.*

pro·cur'er *n.* **1.** one who procures **2.** *same as* PIMP —**pro·cur'ess** *n.fem.*

Pro·cy·on (prō'sē än') [< Gr. *pro-*, before + *kyōn*, dog: it rises before the Dog Star, Sirius] a bright star in the constellation Canis Minor

prod (präd) *vt.* **prod'ded, prod'ding** [< ?] **1.** to jab or poke as with a pointed stick **2.** to urge or stir into action —*n.* **1.** a prodding **2.** something that prods —**prod'der** *n.*

prod·i·gal (präd'i gəl) *adj.* [< L. *pro-*, forth + *agere*, to drive] **1.** wasteful in a reckless way **2.** extremely generous or abundant —*n.* one who recklessly wastes his wealth, resources, etc. —**prod'i·gal'i·ty** (-gal'ə tē) *n., pl.* -ties

pro·di·gious (prə dij'əs) *adj.* [see PRODIGY] **1.** wonderful; amazing **2.** enormous; huge —**pro·di'gious·ly** *adv.*

prod·i·gy (präd'ə jē) *n., pl.* -gies [< L. *prodigium*, omen] a person or thing so extraordinary as to inspire wonder; specif., an extremely talented child

pro·duce (prə dōōs', -dyōōs') *vt.* -duced', -duc'ing [< L. *pro-*, forward + *ducere*, to lead] **1.** to bring to view; show [to *produce* identification] **2.** to bring forth; bear **3.** to make or manufacture **4.** to cause **5.** to get ready and present (a play, etc.) **6.** *Econ.* to create (anything having exchange value) —*vi.* to yield something —*n.* (präd'ōōs, -yōōs; prō'dōōs, -dyōōs) something produced; esp., fresh fruits and vegetables —**pro·duc'er** *n.*

prod·uct (präd'əkt) *n.* **1.** something produced by nature or by man **2.** result; outgrowth **3.** *Chem.* any substance resulting from a chemical change **4.** *Math.* the quantity obtained by multiplying two or more quantities together

pro·duc·tion (prə duk'shən) *n.* **1.** the act or process of producing **2.** the rate of producing **3.** *a)* something produced *b)* a work of art, etc. *c)* a show, movie, etc. **4.** the producing of goods and services

pro·duc·tive *adj.* **1.** fertile **2.** marked by abundant production **3.** bringing as a result (with *of*) [war is *productive* of much misery] **4.** of or engaged in the creating of economic value —**pro·duc'tive·ly** *adv.* —**pro·duc·tiv·i·ty** (prō'dək tiv'ə tē), **pro·duc'tive·ness** *n.*

prof (präf) *n.* [Colloq.] *short for* PROFESSOR

Prof. Professor

prof·a·na·tion (präf'ə nā'shən) *n.* a profaning or being profaned; desecration —**pro·fan·a·to·ry** (prə fan'ə tôr'ē, prō-) *adj.*

pro·fane (prə fān', prō-) *adj.* [< L. *pro-*, before (i.e., outside of) + *fanum*, temple] **1.** not connected with religion; secular **2.** showing disrespect or contempt for sacred things —*vt.* -faned', -fan'ing **1.** to treat (sacred things) with disrespect or contempt **2.** to put to a base use; debase; defile —**pro·fane'ly** *adv.* —**pro·fane'ness** *n.* —**pro·fan'er** *n.*

pro·fan·i·ty (-fan'ə tē) *n.* **1.** a being profane **2.** *pl.* -ties profane language; swearing

pro·fess (prə fes') *vt.* [< L. *pro-*, before + *fateri*, avow] **1.** to declare openly; affirm **2.** to claim to have (some feeling, knowledge, etc.): often connoting insincerity or pretense **3.** to declare one's belief in —**pro·fessed'** *adj.* —**pro·fess'ed·ly** *adv.*

pro·fes·sion (prə fesh'ən) *n.* **1.** a professing or declaring; avowal, as of love, religious belief, etc. **2.** *a)* an occupation requiring advanced education and training, as medicine, law, etc. *b)* all the people in such an occupation

pro·fes·sion·al (-'l) *adj.* **1.** of, engaged in, or worthy of the standards of, a profession **2.** designating or of a school offering instruction in a profession **3.** engaging in some sport or in a specified occupation for pay **4.** engaged in by professional players [*professional* football] —*n.* one who is professional —**pro·fes'sion·al·ism** *n.* —**pro·fes'sion·al·ly** *adv.*

pro·fes·sion·al·ize (-'l īz') *vt.* -ized', -iz'ing to cause to have professional qualities, status, etc.

pro·fes·sor (prə fes'ər) *n.* **1.** one who professes something **2.** a teacher; specif., a college teacher of the highest rank —**pro·fes·so·ri·al** (prō'fə sōr'ē əl) *adj.* —**pro'fes·so'ri·al·ly** *adv.* —**pro·fes'sor·ship'** *n.*

prof·fer (präf'ər) *vt.* [< OFr.: see PRO-² & OFFER] to offer (usually something intangible) [to *proffer* friendship] —*n.* an offer or proposal

pro·fi·cient (prə fish'ənt) *adj.* [< L. *pro-*, forward + *facere*, make] highly competent; skilled —**pro·fi'cien·cy** (-ən sē) *n., pl.* -cies —**pro·fi'cient·ly** *adv.*

pro·file (prō'fīl) *n.* [< It. < L. *pro-*, before + *filum*, a thread] **1.** *a)* a side view of the face *b)* a drawing of this **2.** an outline, as of a hill **3.** a short, vivid biography **4.** a summary of data about a particular subject —*vt.* -filed, -fil·ing to make a profile of

prof·it (präf'it) *n.* [see PROFICIENT] **1.** advantage; gain **2.** [often *pl.*] financial gain; esp., the sum remaining after all costs are deducted from the income of a business —*vi.* **1.** to make a profit **2.** to benefit; gain —*vt.* to be of profit or advantage to; benefit —**prof'it·a·ble** *adj.* —**prof'it·a·bly** *adv.* —**prof'it·er** *n.* —**prof'it·less** *adj.*

prof·i·teer (präf'ə tir') *n.* one who makes an unfair profit by charging exorbitant prices when there is a short supply —*vi.* to be a profiteer

profit sharing the giving to employees of a share in the profits of a business, in addition to wages

prof·li·gate (präf'lə git) *adj.* [< L. *pro-*, forward + *fligere*, to drive] **1.** immoral and shameless; dissolute **2.** recklessly wasteful —*n.* a profligate person —**prof'li·ga·cy** (-gə sē) *n.* —**prof'li·gate·ly** *adv.*

‡**pro for·ma** (prō fôr'mə) [L., for form] as a matter of form

pro·found (prə found') *adj.* [< L. *pro-*, forward + *fundus*, bottom] **1.** very deep [*profound* sleep, grief, etc.] **2.** having intellectual depth [*profound* talk] **3.** complete; thorough [*profound* changes] —**pro·found'ly** *adv.* —**pro·fun'di·ty** (-fun'də tē) *n., pl.* -ties

pro·fuse (prə fyōōs') *adj.* [< L. *pro-*, forth + *fundere*, pour] giving or given freely and abundantly; lavish —**pro·fuse'ly** *adv.* —**pro·fu·sion** (-fyōō'zhən), **pro·fuse'ness** *n.*

pro·gen·i·tor (prō jen'ə tər) *n.* [< L. *pro-*, forth + *gignere*, beget] **1.** a forefather; ancestor in direct line **2.** an originator or precursor

prog·e·ny (präj'ə nē) *n., pl.* -nies [see prec.] children, descendants, or offspring

pro·ges·ter·one (prō jes'tə rōn') *n.* [see PRO-¹, GESTATION, & STEROL] a steroid hormone that prepares the uterus for the fertilized ovum

prog·na·thous (präg'nə thəs) *adj.* [< PRO-¹ + Gr. *gnathos*, jaw] having the jaws projecting abnormally

prog·no·sis (präg nō'sis) *n., pl.* -no'ses (-sēz) [< Gr. *pro-*, before + *gignōskein*, know] a prediction, esp. of the probable course of a disease —**prog·nos'tic** (-näs'tik) *n., adj.*

prog·nos·ti·cate (-näs'tə kāt') *vt.* -cat'ed, -cat'ing [see prec.] to foretell, predict, or foreshadow —**prog·nos'ti·ca'tion** *n.* —**prog·nos'ti·ca'tor** *n.*

pro·gram (prō'gram, -grəm) *n.* [< Fr. & LL. < Gr. *pro-*, before + *graphein*, write] **1.** the acts, speeches, musical pieces, etc. that make up an entertainment, ceremony, etc., or a printed list of these **2.** a scheduled broadcast on radio or television **3.** a plan or procedure for dealing with some matter **4.** all the activities offered, as at a social center **5.** *a)* a logical sequence of operations to be performed by an electronic computer *b)* the coded instructions and data for this —*vt.* -grammed or -gramed, -gram·ming or -gram·ing **1.** to schedule in a program **2.** to prepare (a textbook, etc.) for use in programmed learning **3.** to plan a computer program for **4.** to furnish (a computer) with a program Brit. sp. pro'gramme —**pro·gram·mat·ic** (prō'grə mat'ik) *adj.* —**pro'gram·mer, pro'gram·er** *n.*

programmed learning learning acquired on one's own, step by step, from a programmed course of study, as a textbook that has a series of questions with the answers given elsewhere in the book

program music instrumental music that is meant to suggest a particular scene, story, etc.

prog·ress (präg'res, -rəs) *n.* [< L. *pro-*, before + *gradi*, to step] **1.** a moving forward **2.** development **3.** improvement —*vi.* (prə gres') **1.** to move forward **2.** to advance toward a goal, a better state, etc.; develop or improve

pro·gres·sion (prə gresh'ən) *n.* **1.** a moving forward **2.** a succession, as of events **3.** *Math.* a series of numbers increasing or decreasing by a constant difference between terms [5, 9, 13 is an arithmetic, and 2, 4, 8 a geometric, *progression*]

pro·gres·sive (prə gres'iv) *adj.* **1.** moving forward **2.** continuing or increasing by successive steps **3.** of or favoring progress, reform, etc. **4.** of education that stresses self-expression, informality, etc. **5.** *Gram.* indicating continuing action, as the verb form *is playing* —*n.* a person who is progressive —**pro·gres'sive·ly** *adv.* —**pro·gres'sive·ness** *n.*

pro·hib·it (prō hib'it) *vt.* [< L. *pro-*, before + *habere*, have] **1.** to forbid by law or by an order **2.** to prevent; hinder

pro·hi·bi·tion (prō'ə bish'ən) *n.* **1.** a prohibiting **2.** the forbidding by law of the manufacture or sale of alcoholic liquors —**pro'hi·bi'tion·ist** *n.*

pro·hib·i·tive (prō hib'ə tiv) *adj.* **1.** serving to prohibit **2.** such as to prevent purchase, use, etc. *[prohibitive prices]* Also **pro·hib'i·to'ry** (-tôr'ē) —**pro·hib'i·tive·ly** *adv.*

proj·ect (präj'ekt) *n.* [< L. *pro-*, before + *jacere*, to throw] **1.** a proposal or plan of something to be done **2.** an organized undertaking, as a special unit of work, research, etc. **3.** a complex of inexpensive apartments or houses, usually publicly owned or financed —*vt.* (prə jekt') **1.** to propose (a plan) **2.** to throw forward **3.** to get (one's voice, ideas, feelings, etc.) across to others effectively **4.** to send forth in one's imagination **5.** to cause to jut out **6.** to cause (a shadow, image, etc.) to fall upon a surface **7.** *same as* EXTRAPOLATE —*vi.* **1.** to jut out **2.** to project one's voice, ideas, etc.

pro·jec·tile (prə jek't'l, -tīl) *n.* **1.** an object designed to be shot forward, as a bullet **2.** anything thrown or hurled forward

pro·jec'tion (-shən) *n.* **1.** a projecting or being projected **2.** something that projects or is projected **3.** *Psychiatry* the unconscious act of ascribing to others one's own ideas, impulses, or feelings

projection booth a small chamber housing a movie projector, as in a theater

pro·jec'tion·ist *n.* the operator of a slide or movie projector

pro·jec'tor *n.* a machine for projecting pictures or movies on a screen

Pro·kof·iev (prə kô'fē ef'), **Ser·gei** (ser gā') 1891–1953; Russ. composer

pro·lapse (prō laps') *vi.* -**lapsed'**, -**laps'ing** [< L. *prolabi*, to slip out] *Med.* to fall or slip out of place —*n.* (prō'laps) a prolapsed condition

pro·late (prō'lāt) *adj.* [< L. *prolatus*, brought forward] elongated at the poles *[a prolate spheroid]*

pro·le·tar·i·at (prō'lə ter'ē ət) *n.* [< Fr. < L. *proletarius*, a citizen of the lowest class] the working class; esp., the industrial working class —**pro'le·tar'i·an** *adj., n.*

pro·lif·er·ate (prō lif'ə rāt', prə-) *vi., vt.* -**at'ed**, -**at'ing** [< Fr. < L. *proles*, offspring + *ferre*, to bear] **1.** to reproduce (new parts) in quick succession **2.** to grow or increase rapidly —**pro·lif'er·a'tion** *n.* —**pro·lif'er·ous** *adj.*

pro·lif·ic (prə lif'ik, prō-) *adj.* [< Fr. < L. *proles*, offspring + *facere*, make] **1.** producing many young or much fruit **2.** creating many products of the mind *[a prolific poet]* **3.** abounding (*in* or *of*) —**pro·lif'i·cal·ly** *adv.*

pro·lix (prō liks', prō'liks) *adj.* [< L. *prolixus*, extended] wordy or long-winded —**pro·lix'i·ty** *n.*

pro·logue (prō'lôg) *n.* [< Gr. *pro-*, before + *logos*, a discourse] **1.** an introduction to a poem, play, etc.; esp., lines spoken by an actor before a play begins **2.** any preliminary act, event, etc.

pro·long (prə lôŋ') *vt.* [< L. *pro-*, forth + *longus*, long] to lengthen in time or space: also **pro·lon'gate** (-gāt) -**gat·ed**, -**gat·ing** —**pro'lon·ga'tion** *n.*

prom (präm) *n.* [< PROMENADE] [Colloq.] a dance, as of the senior class at a school or college

prom·e·nade (präm'ə nād', -näd') *n.* [Fr. < L. *pro-*, forth + *minare*, to herd] **1.** a leisurely walk taken for pleasure, to show off, etc. **2.** a public place for such a walk **3.** a ball, or formal dance **4.** an opening march at a ball, or a marching step in a square dance —*vi., vt.* -**nad'ed**, -**nad'ing** to take a promenade (along or through); parade

Pro·me·the·us (prə mē'thē əs, -thyōos) *Gr. Myth.* a Titan who stole fire from heaven to benefit mankind —**Pro·me'the·an** (-thē ən) *adj., n.*

pro·me·thi·um (prə mē'thē əm) *n.* [< prec.] a metallic chemical element of the rare-earth group, obtained in nuclear reactions: symbol, Pm; at. wt., 145(?); at. no., 61

prom·i·nence (präm'ə nəns) *n.* **1.** a being prominent **2.** something prominent or projecting

prom·i·nent (präm'ə nənt) *adj.* [< L. *prominere*, to project] **1.** sticking out; projecting **2.** noticeable at once; conspicuous **3.** widely and favorably known —**prom'i·nent·ly** *adv.*

pro·mis·cu·ous (prə mis'kyōo wəs) *adj.* [< L. *pro-*, forth + *miscere*, to mix] **1.** consisting of different elements indiscriminately mixed **2.** showing little or no discrimination; specif., engaging in sexual intercourse with many persons casually —**pro·mis·cu·i·ty** (präm'is kyōo'ə tē), *pl.* -**ties**, **pro·mis'cu·ous·ness** *n.* —**pro·mis'cu·ous·ly** *adv.*

prom·ise (präm'is) *n.* [< L. *pro-*, forth + *mittere*, send] **1.** an agreement to do or not to do something **2.** indication, as of a successful future; basis for expectation **3.** something promised —*vi., vt.* -**ised**, -**is·ing 1.** to make a promise of (something) **2.** to give a basis for expecting (something)

Promised Land *Bible* Canaan, promised by God to Abraham and his descendants: Gen. 17:8

prom'is·ing *adj.* showing promise of success, excellence, etc. —**prom'is·ing·ly** *adv.*

prom·is·so·ry (präm'i sôr'ē) *adj.* containing a promise

promissory note a written promise to pay a certain sum of money to a certain person or bearer on demand or on a specified date

prom·on·to·ry (präm'ən tôr'ē) *n., pl.* -**ries** [prob. < L. *prominere*, to project] a peak of high land that juts out into a body of water; headland

pro·mote (prə mōt') *vt.* -**mot'ed**, -**mot'ing** [< L. *pro-*, forward + *movere*, to move] **1.** to raise to a higher rank, position, or grade **2.** to further the establishment, growth, etc. of **3.** to further the sales or popularity of —**pro·mo'tion** *n.* —**pro·mo'tion·al** *adj.*

pro·mot'er *n.* one who organizes and furthers a new enterprise, a sports event, etc.

prompt (prämpt) *adj.* [< L. *pro-*, forth + *emere*, take] **1.** quick to do what is required; ready, punctual, etc. **2.** done, spoken, etc. without delay —*vt.* **1.** to urge into action **2.** to remind of something that has been forgotten; specif., to help (an actor, etc.) with a cue **3.** to inspire — **prompt'er** *n.* —**prompt'ly** *adv.* —**prompt'ness**, **promp·ti·tude** (prämp'tə tōod', -tyōod') *n.*

prom·ul·gate (präm'əl gāt', prō mul'gāt) *vt.* -**gat'ed**, -**gat'ing** [< L., ? ult. < *pro-*, before + *vulgus*, the people] **1.** to make known or put into effect (a decree, law, etc.) officially; proclaim **2.** to make widespread —**prom'ul·ga'tion** *n.* —**prom'ul·ga'tor** *n.*

pron. 1. pronoun **2.** pronunciation

prone (prōn) *adj.* [< L. *pronus*] **1.** lying face downward **2.** lying flat or prostrate **3.** disposed or inclined (*to*) *[prone to err]* —**prone'ness** *n.*

prong (prôŋ) *n.* [akin to MLowG. *prangen*, to press] **1.** any of the pointed ends of a fork **2.** any pointed projecting part, as on an antler —**pronged** *adj.*

prong·horn (prôŋ'hôrn') *n.* an antelopelike deer of the western U.S., having curved horns

pro·nom·i·nal (prō näm'i n'l) *adj.* of, or having the function of, a pronoun —**pro·nom'i·nal·ly** *adv.*

pro·noun (prō'noun) *n.* [< L. *pro*, for + *nomen*, noun] a word that can assume the functions of, and be used in place of, a noun (Ex.: *I, he, ours*, etc.)

pro·nounce (prə nouns') *vt.* -**nounced'**, -**nounc'ing** [< L. *pro-*, before + *nuntiare*, announce] **1.** to declare officially, solemnly, etc. *[pronounced* man and wife; *pronounced* guilty] **2.** to utter or articulate (a sound or word) —**pro·nounce'a·ble** *adj.*

pro·nounced' *adj.* clearly marked; definite *[a pronounced change]* —**pro·nounc'ed·ly** *adv.*

pro·nounce'ment *n.* a formal statement, as of an opinion or judgment

pron·to (prän'tō) *adv.* [Sp.: see PROMPT] [Slang] at once; quickly

pro·nun·ci·a·men·to (prə nun'sē ə men'tō) *n., pl.* -**tos** [Sp. < L.: see PRONOUNCE] **1.** a proclamation or public pronouncement **2.** a manifesto

pro·nun·ci·a·tion (prə nun'sē ā'shən) *n.* **1.** the act or way of pronouncing words **2.** *a)* any of the accepted or standard pronunciations of a word *b)* the representation in phonetic symbols of such a pronunciation

proof (prōof) *n.* [< L. *probare*, to test] **1.** a proving or testing of something **2.** anything that establishes the truth of something; conclusive evidence **3.** a test or trial of the truth, worth, etc. of something **4.** the relative strength of alcohol: see PROOF SPIRIT **5.** *Photog.* a trial print of a negative **6.** *Printing* an impression of composed type taken for checking errors and making changes —*adj.* of tested strength in resisting; impervious (with *against*)

-proof *a combining form meaning:* **1.** impervious or resistant to *[waterproof]* **2.** protected from or against *[burglarproof, foolproof]*

proof·read (-rēd') *vt., vi.* -**read'** (-red'), -**read'ing** to read and mark corrections on (printers' proofs, etc.) —**proof'read'er** *n.*

proof spirit alcoholic liquor of a standard alcoholic content, 50% by volume (100 proof) in the U.S.

prop¹ (präp) *n.* [MDu. *proppe*] **1.** a support, as a pole, placed under or against something **2.** a person or thing that gives support to another person, an institution, etc. —*vt.* propped, prop′ping **1.** to support, as with a prop (often with *up*) **2.** to lean (something) *against* a support

prop² (präp) *n. same as* PROPERTY (sense 5)

prop³ (präp) *n. same as* PROPELLER

prop. 1. proposition **2.** proprietor

prop·a·gan·da (präp′ə gan′də) *n.* [see PROPAGATE] **1.** any systematic, widespread promotion of particular ideas, doctrines, etc. **2.** ideas, doctrines, or allegations so spread: now often used to connote deception or distortion —**prop′-a·gan′dist** *n., adj.* —**prop′a·gan′dize** *vt., vi.* -dized, -dizing

prop·a·gate (präp′ə gāt′) *vt.* -gat′ed, -gat′ing [< L. *propago*, slip (of a plant)] **1.** to cause (a plant or animal) to reproduce itself **2.** to reproduce (itself): said of a plant or animal **3.** to spread (ideas, customs, etc.) **4.** to extend or transmit (light, etc.) —*vi.* to reproduce, as plants or animals —**prop′a·ga′tion** *n.* —**prop′a·ga′tor** *n.*

pro·pane (prō′pān) *n.* a gaseous hydrocarbon, C_3H_8, used as a fuel, in refrigerants, etc.

pro·pel (prə pel′) *vt.* -pelled′, -pel′ling [< L. *pro-*, forward + *pellere*, drive] to drive forward

pro·pel′lant, pro·pel′lent *n.* that which propels; specif., the fuel for a rocket

pro·pel′ler *n.* a device (**screw propeller**) consisting of blades twisted to move in a spiral as they rotate with the hub to propel a ship or aircraft

pro·pen·si·ty (prə pen′sə tē) *n., pl.* -ties [< L. *pro-*, before + *pendere*, hang] a natural inclination or tendency; bent

prop·er (präp′ər) *adj.* [< L. *proprius*, one's own] **1.** specially suitable; appropriate; fitting **2.** naturally belonging (*to*) **3.** conforming to a standard; correct **4.** decent; decorous **5.** in the most restricted sense [Boston *proper* (i.e., apart from its suburbs)] **6.** [Chiefly Brit. Colloq.] complete; thorough **7.** *Gram.* naming a specific individual, place, etc. [*Jane, Asia,* and *Paris* are *proper* nouns] —**prop′er·ly** *adv.*

proper fraction a fraction in which the numerator is less than the denominator (Ex.: 2/5)

prop·er·tied (präp′ər tēd) *adj.* owning property

prop·er·ty (präp′ər tē) *n., pl.* -ties [< L. *proprius*, one's own] **1.** ownership **2.** a thing or things owned; possessions, esp. real estate **3.** a specific piece of land or real estate **4.** a characteristic or essential quality or capability [the *properties* of a chemical element] **5.** any of the articles used in a stage setting, except costumes and scenery

proph·e·cy (präf′ə sē) *n., pl.* -cies **1.** prediction of the future by a prophet, as supposedly under divine guidance **2.** any prediction **3.** something prophesied

proph·e·sy (-sī′) *vt., vi.* -sied′, -sy′ing **1.** to predict (something) as a prophet, supposedly under divine guidance **2.** to predict (a future event) in any way —**proph′e·si′er** *n.*

proph·et (präf′it) *n.* [< Gr. *pro-*, before + *phanai*, speak] **1.** a person who claims to speak for God, or a religious leader regarded as, or claiming to be, divinely inspired **2.** a spokesman for some cause **3.** a person who predicts the future —**the Prophets 1.** the prophetic books of the Bible, including Isaiah, Jeremiah, etc. **2.** the authors or subjects of these books —**proph′et·ess** *n.fem.*

pro·phet·ic (prə fet′ik) *adj.* **1.** of or like a prophet **2.** of, like, or containing a prophecy —**pro·phet′i·cal·ly** *adv.*

pro·phy·lac·tic (prō′fə lak′tik) *adj.* [< Gr. *pro-*, before + *phylassein*, to guard] preventive or protective; esp., preventing disease —*n.* a prophylactic medicine, device, etc.

pro′phy·lax′is (-sis) *n., pl.* -lax′es (-sēz) prophylactic treatment; specif., *Dentistry* a cleaning of the teeth to remove plaque and tartar

pro·pin·qui·ty (prō piŋ′kwə tē) *n.* [< L. *propinquus*, near] **1.** nearness in time or place **2.** nearness of kinship

pro·pi·ti·ate (prə pish′ē āt′) *vt.* -at′ed, -at′ing [see PROPITIOUS] to win or regain the good will of; appease —**pro·pi′ti·a′tion** —**pro·pi′ti·a′tor** *n.* —**pro·pi′ti·a·to′ry** (-ə tôr′ē) *adj.*

pro·pi·tious (prə pish′əs) *adj.* [< L. *pro-*, before + *petere*, seek] **1.** favorably inclined **2.** favorable [a *propitious* omen, *propitious* winds] —**pro·pi′tious·ly** *adv.* —**pro·pi′-tious·ness** *n.*

pro·po·nent (prə pō′nənt) *n.* [< L. *pro-*, forth + *ponere*, to place] **1.** one who makes a proposal or proposition **2.** one who supports a cause

pro·por·tion (prə pôr′shən) *n.* [< L. *pro-*, for + *portio*, a part] **1.** the comparative relation in size, amount, etc. between things; ratio **2.** a part, share, etc., esp. in its rela-

tion to the whole **3.** harmonious or proper relationship between parts or things; balance **4.** [*pl.*] dimensions **5.** an equality between ratios (Ex.: 2 is to 6 as 3 is to 9): also called **geometrical proportion** —*vt.* **1.** to put in proper relation or balance **2.** to arrange the parts of in a harmonious or proper way —**pro·por′tioned** *adj.*

pro·por′tion·al *adj.* **1.** relative **2.** being in proportion **3.** *Math.* having the same ratio —**pro·por′tion·al·ly** *adv.*

pro·por′tion·ate (-shə nit) *adj.* in proper proportion; proportional —*vt.* (-shə nāt′) -at′ed, -at′ing to make proportionate —**pro·por′tion·ate·ly** *adv.*

pro·pos·al (prə pō′z'l) *n.* **1.** a proposing **2.** a proposed plan or action **3.** an offer of marriage

pro·pose (prə pōz′) *vt.* -posed′, -pos′ing [< L. *pro-*, forth + *ponere*, to place] **1.** to put forth for consideration or acceptance **2.** to plan or intend **3.** to present as a toast in drinking —*vi.* **1.** to make plans **2.** to offer marriage

prop·o·si·tion (präp′ə zish′ən) *n.* **1.** something proposed; plan **2.** [Colloq.] *a)* a proposed deal, as in business *b)* a person, undertaking, etc. to be dealt with **3.** a subject or statement to be discussed or debated **4.** *Math.* a theorem to be demonstrated or a problem to be solved —*vt.* [Colloq.] to make a proposition, esp. one considered improper, to (someone)

pro·pound (prə pound′) *vt.* [see PROPOSE] to set forth for consideration —**pro·pound′er** *n.*

pro·pri·e·tar·y (prə prī′ə ter′ē) *adj.* [see PROPERTY] belonging to a proprietor, as under a patent, trademark, or copyright

pro·pri·e·tor (prə prī′ə tər) *n.* one who owns a property or a business establishment —**pro·pri′e·tor·ship′** *n.* —**pro·pri′e·tress** *n.fem.*

pro·pri·e·ty (prə prī′ə tē) *n., pl.* -ties [see PROPER] **1.** the quality of being proper, fitting, etc. **2.** conformity with what is proper or fitting or with accepted standards of behavior —**the proprieties** accepted standards of behavior in polite society

pro·pul·sion (prə pul′shən) *n.* [see PROPEL] **1.** a propelling or being propelled **2.** propelling force —**pro·pul′sive** *adj.*

pro ra·ta (prō rāt′ə, rät′ə) [L.] proportionate(ly)

pro·rate (prō rāt′, prō′rāt′) *vt., vi.* -rat′ed, -rat′ing [< prec.] to divide or assess proportionately

pro·rogue (prō rōg′) *vt., vi.* -rogued′, -rogu′ing [< L. *pro-*, for + *rogare*, ask] to discontinue or end a session of (a legislative assembly)

pro·sa·ic (prō zā′ik) *adj.* [< L. *prosa*, PROSE] **1.** like prose; unpoetic **2.** commonplace; dull —**pro·sa′i·cal·ly** *adv.* —**pro·sa′ic·ness** *n.*

pro·sce·ni·um (prō sē′nē əm) *n., pl.* -ni·ums, -ni·a (-ə) [< Gr. *pro-*, before + *skēnē*, a tent, stage] the arch framing a conventional stage

pro·scribe (prō skrīb′) *vt.* -scribed′, -scrib′ing [< L. *pro-*, before + *scribere*, write] **1.** to outlaw **2.** to banish; exile **3.** to denounce or forbid the practice, use, etc. of —**pro·scrip′tion** (-skrip′shən) *n.* —**pro·scrip′tive** *adj.*

prose (prōz) *n.* [< L. *prosa*, for *prorsa* (*oratio*), direct (speech)] ordinary language, not poetry

pros·e·cute (präs′ə kyōōt′) *vt.* -cut′ed, -cut′ing [< L. *pro-*, before + *sequi*, follow] **1.** to carry on; engage in **2.** *a)* to conduct legal proceedings against, esp. for a crime *b)* to try to get, enforce, etc. by legal process —*vi.* to institute and carry on a legal suit —**pros′e·cu′tion** *n.* —**pros′e·cu′tor** *n.*

prosecuting attorney a public official who conducts criminal prosecutions on behalf of the State

pros·e·lyte (präs′ə līt′) *n.* [< Gr. *prosēlytos*] a person who has been converted from one religion, belief, etc. to another —*vt., vi.* -lyt′ed, -lyt′ing **1.** to try to convert (a person) **2.** to one's religion **2.** to persuade (a person) to do or join something —**pros′e·lyt′er** *n.* —**pros′e·lyt·ism** (-li tiz′m) *n.*

pros′e·lyt·ize′ (-li tīz′) *vt., vi.* -ized′, -iz′ing *same as* PROSELYTE —**pros′e·lyt·iz′er** *n.*

Pro·ser·pi·na (prō sur′pi nə) the daughter of Ceres and wife of Pluto: identified with the Greek Persephone: also **Pro·ser′pi·ne′** (-nē′, präs′ər pīn′)

pros·o·dy (präs′ə dē) *n., pl.* -dies [< Gr. *prosōidia* accent] versification; study of meter, rhyme, etc.

pros·pect (präs′pekt) *n.* [< L. *pro-*, forward + *specere*, to look] **1.** *a)* a broad view; scene *b)* a place for seeing such a view **2.** viewpoint; outlook **3.** anticipation **4.** *a)* something expected *b)* [usually *pl.*] apparent chance for success **5.** a likely customer, candidate, etc. —*vt., vi.* to explore or search (*for* gold, oil, etc.) —**in prospect** expected —**pros′pec·tor** *n.*

pro·spec·tive (prə spek′tiv) *adj.* expected; likely

pro·spec·tus (prə spek′təs) *n.* [L.: see PROSPECT] a statement of the features of a new work, enterprise, etc.

pros·per (präs′pər) *vi.* [< L. *prosperus*, favorable] to succeed, thrive, grow, etc. vigorously

pros·per·i·ty (prä sper′ə tē) *n.* prosperous condition; wealth, success, etc.

pros·per·ous (präs′pər əs) *adj.* **1.** prospering; flourishing **2.** well-to-do; well-off **3.** conducive to success —**pros′per·ous·ly** *adv.*

pros·tate (präs′tāt) *adj.* [< Gr. *prostatēs*, one standing before] designating or of a gland surrounding the male urethra at the base of the bladder —*n.* the prostate gland

pros·the·sis (präs the′sis, präs′thə-) *n., pl.* **-ses′** (-sēz′) [< Gr. *pros*, to + *tithenai*, to place] an artificial substitute for a missing part of the body —**pros·thet′ic** (-thet′ik) *adj.*

pros·ti·tute (präs′tə tōōt′, -tyōōt′) *n.* [< L. *pro-*, before + *statuere*, cause to stand] a woman who engages in promiscuous sexual intercourse for pay —*vt.* **-tut′ed, -tut′ing** **1.** to offer (oneself or another) as a prostitute **2.** to sell (oneself, one's integrity, etc.) for unworthy purposes, as in one's work as a writer, artist, etc. —**pros′ti·tu′tion** *n.*

pros·trate (präs′trāt) *adj.* [< L. *pro-*, before + *sternere*, stretch out] **1.** lying face downward in humility or abject submission **2.** lying flat, prone, or supine **3.** completely overcome or exhausted; laid low —*vt.* **-trat·ed, -trat·ing** **1.** to lay in a prostrate position **2.** to lay low; overcome or exhaust —**pros·tra′tion** *n.*

pros·y (prō′zē) *adj.* **-i·er, -i·est** **1.** like prose **2.** prosaic; dull —**pros′i·ly** *adv.* —**pros′i·ness** *n.*

pro·tac·tin·i·um (prō′tak tin′ē əm) *n.* [< PROTO- + ACTINIUM] a rare, radioactive metallic chemical element: symbol, Pa; at. wt., 231.10; at. no., 91

pro·tag·o·nist (prō tag′ə nist) *n.* [< Gr. *prōtos*, first + *agōnistēs*, actor] **1.** the main character in a drama, novel, etc. **2.** a leading figure in an event, etc.

pro·te·an (prōt′ē ən) *adj.* [< *Proteus*, Gr. god who changed his form at will] readily taking on different shapes or forms

pro·tect (prə tekt′) *vt.* [< L. *pro-*, before + *tegere*, to cover] to shield from injury, danger, or loss; defend —**pro·tec′tor** *n.*

pro·tec′tion *n.* **1.** a protecting or being protected **2.** a person or thing that protects **3.** [Colloq.] *a)* money extorted by racketeers threatening violence *b)* bribes paid by racketeers to avoid prosecution

pro·tec′tive *adj.* **1.** protecting or intended to protect **2.** intended to protect domestic industry from foreign competition [*protective* tariffs] —**pro·tec′tive·ly** *adv.* —**pro·tec′tive·ness** *n.*

pro·tec′tor·ate (-tər it) *n.* a weak state under the control and protection of a stronger state

pro·té·gé (prōt′ə zhā′) *n.* [Fr. < L.: see PROTECT] a person guided and helped in his career by another

pro·tein (prō′tēn, prōt′ē in) *n.* [G., ult. < Gr. *prōtos*, first] any of a class of complex nitrogenous substances occurring in all living matter and essential to the diet of animals

pro tem·po·re (prō tem′pə rē′) [L.] for the time being; temporarily: shortened to **pro tem**

pro·test (prə test′) *vt.* [< L. *pro-*, forth + *testari*, affirm] **1.** to state positively **2.** to speak strongly against —*vi.* to express disapproval; object —*n.* (prō′test) **1.** an objection **2.** a formal statement of objection —**under protest** while expressing one's objections; unwillingly —**pro·test′er** *n.*

Prot·es·tant (prät′is tənt) *n.* [see prec.] a member of any of the Christian churches resulting or derived from the Reformation under the leadership of Luther, Calvin, Wesley, etc. —*adj.* of Protestants, their beliefs, practices, etc. —**Prot′es·tant·ism** *n.*

Protestant Episcopal Church the Protestant church in the U.S. that conforms to the practices and principles of the Church of England

proto- [< Gr. *prōtos*, first] a combining form meaning: **1.** first in time, original **2.** first in importance

pro·to·col (prōt′ə kôl′, -käl′) *n.* [< LGr. *prōtokollon*, contents page] **1.** an original draft or record of a document, negotiation, etc. **2.** the code of ceremonial forms and courtesies used in official dealings, as between heads of state or diplomats

pro·ton (prō′tän) *n.* [< Gr. *prōtos*, first] an elementary particle in the nucleus of all atoms: each proton in a nucleus carries a unit positive charge equal to the negative charge of an electron

pro·to·plasm (prōt′ə plaz′m) *n.* [see PROTO- & PLASMA] a semifluid, viscous colloid, the essential living matter of all animal and plant cells —**pro′to·plas′mic** *adj.*

pro·to·type (prōt′ə tīp′) *n.* [see PROTO- & TYPE] the first thing or being of its kind; original, model, pattern, or archetype

pro·to·zo·an (prōt′ə zō′ən) *n.* [< Gr. *prōtos*, first + *zōion*, animal] any of a large group of mostly microscopic, one-celled animals living chiefly in water and sometimes parasitic: also **pro′to·zo′on** (-än), *pl.* **-zo′a** (-ə)

pro·tract (prō trakt′) *vt.* [< L. *pro-*, forward + *trahere*, to draw] **1.** to draw out; prolong **2.** *Zool.* to thrust out; extend —**pro·trac′tion** *n.*

pro·trac·tor (prō trak′tər) *n.* **1.** one that protracts **2.** a graduated, semicircular instrument for plotting and measuring angles

pro·trude (prō trōōd′) *vt.*, *vi.* **-trud′ed, -trud′ing** [< L. *pro-*, forth + *trudere*, to thrust] to thrust or jut out; project —**pro·tru′sion** (-trōō′zhən) *n.*

pro·tru·sile (-trōō′s′l) *adj.* that can be protruded, or thrust out: also **pro·trac′tile** (-trak′t′l)

PROTRACTOR
(DAC, angle measured)

pro·tu·ber·ance (prō tōō′bər əns, -tyōō′-) *n.* [< L. *pro-*, forth + *tuber*, a bump] **1.** a part or thing that sticks out; bulge **2.** a being protuberant

pro·tu′ber·ant *adj.* bulging out; protruding

proud (proud) *adj.* [< LL. *prode*, beneficial] **1.** having or showing a proper pride in oneself **2.** haughty; arrogant **3.** feeling or causing great pride or joy **4.** caused by pride **5.** stately; splendid —**proud of** highly pleased with —**proud′ly** *adv.*

proud flesh [from notion of swelling up] an excessive growth of flesh around a healing wound

Proust (prōōst), **Mar·cel** (mär sel′) 1871–1922; Fr. novelist

Prov. Proverbs

prove (prōōv) *vt.* **proved, proved** or **prov′en, prov′ing** [< L. *probare*, to test] **1.** to test by experiment, a standard, etc.; try out **2.** to establish as true or correct **3.** to show (oneself) to be capable, dependable, etc. —*vi.* to be shown to be [her guess *proved* right] —**prov′a·ble** *adj.*

prov·e·nance (präv′ə nəns) *n.* [Fr. < L. *provenire*, come forth] origin; derivation; source

Pro·ven·çal (prō′vən säl′, präv′ən-) *adj.* of Provence, its people, their language, etc. —*n.* the vernacular of S France, a Romance language of literary importance in its medieval form

Pro·vence (prô väns′) region & former province of SE France, on the Mediterranean

prov·en·der (präv′ən dər) *n.* [< L. *prae-*, before + *habere*, have] **1.** dry food for livestock **2.** [Colloq.] food; provisions

prov·erb (präv′ərb) *n.* [< L. *pro-*, before + *verbum*, a word] a short, popular saying that expresses an obvious truth; adage; maxim

pro·ver·bi·al (prə vur′bē əl) *adj.* **1.** of, like, or as in a proverb **2.** often mentioned; well-known —**pro·ver′bi·al·ly** *adv.*

Prov·erbs (präv′ərbz) a book of the Bible containing maxims

pro·vide (prə vīd′) *vt.* **-vid′ed, -vid′ing** [< L. *pro-*, before + *videre*, see] **1.** to make available beforehand; supply **2.** to supply (someone) *with* something **3.** to state as a condition; stipulate —*vi.* **1.** to prepare (*for* or *against* a possible situation or event) **2.** to furnish the means of support (*for*) —**pro·vid′er** *n.*

pro·vid′ed *conj.* on the condition or understanding (often with *that*)

Prov·i·dence (präv′ə dəns) capital of Rhode Island: pop. 179,000 (met. area 914,000)

prov·i·dence (präv′ə dəns) *n.* **1.** provident management **2.** the benevolent guidance of God or nature **3.** [P-] God

prov′i·dent *adj.* [see PROVIDE] **1.** providing for the future **2.** prudent or economical —**prov′i·dent·ly** *adv.*

prov′i·den′tial (-den′shəl) *adj.* of, by, or as if decreed by divine providence —**prov′i·den′tial·ly** *adv.*

pro·vid·ing (prə vīd′iŋ) *conj. same as* PROVIDED

prov·ince (präv′ins) *n.* [< L. *provincia*] **1.** an administrative division of a country, specif. of Canada **2.** *a)* a district; territory *b)* [*pl.*] the parts of a country removed from the capital and the major cities **3.** range of duties or functions **4.** a field of knowledge, activity, etc.

pro·vin·cial (prə vin'shəl) *adj.* **1.** of a province **2.** having the ways, speech, etc. of a certain province **3.** countrified; rustic **4.** narrow or limited in outlook —*n.* **1.** a native of a province **2.** a provincial person —**pro·vin'cial·ism** *n.*

proving ground a place for testing new equipment, new theories, etc.

pro·vi·sion (prə vizh'ən) *n.* **1.** a providing or supplying **2.** something provided for the future; specif., [*pl.*] a stock of food **3.** a preparatory measure taken in advance **4.** a stipulation; proviso —*vt.* to supply with provisions

pro·vi'sion·al *adj.* conditional or temporary, pending permanent arrangement —**pro·vi'sion·al·ly** *adv.*

pro·vi·so (prə vī'zō) *n., pl.* **-sos, -soes** [ML. *proviso* (*quod*), provided (that)] **1.** a clause, as in a document, making some condition **2.** a condition or stipulation —**pro·vi'so·ry** (-zər ē) *adj.*

prov·o·ca·tion (präv'ə kā'shən) *n.* **1.** a provoking **2.** something that provokes, or angers, incites, etc.

pro·voc·a·tive (prə väk'ə tiv) *adj.* provoking or tending to provoke to action, thought, anger, desire, etc. —**pro·voc'a·tive·ly** *adv.* —**pro·voc'a·tive·ness** *n.*

pro·voke (prə vōk') *vt.* **-voked', -vok'ing** [< L. *pro-*, forth + *vocare*, to call] **1.** to excite to some action or feeling **2.** to anger or irritate **3.** to stir up (action or feeling) **4.** to evoke

pro·vo·lo·ne (prō'və lō'nē, präv'ə-) *n.* [It.] a hard, light-colored Italian cheese, usually smoked

pro·vost (prō'vōst, präv'əst; *esp. military* prō'vō) *n.* [< L. *praepositus*, chief] any of various administrators or officials, as in some churches, colleges, etc.

pro·vost guard (prō'vō) a detail of military police under the command of an officer (**provost marshal**)

prow (prou) *n.* [< Fr., ult. < Gr. *prōira*] **1.** the forward part of a ship or boat **2.** anything similar

prow·ess (prou'is) *n.* [< OFr. *prouesse*] **1.** bravery; valor **2.** superior ability, skill, etc.

prowl (proul) *vi., vt.* [< ?] to roam about furtively, as in search of prey or loot —*n.* a prowling —**on the prowl** prowling about —**prowl'er** *n.*

prowl car same as SQUAD CAR

prox·im·i·ty (präk sim'ə tē) *n.* [< L. *prope*, near] nearness in space, time, etc.

prox·y (präk'sē) *n., pl.* **-ies** [< ME. *procuracie*, office of a procurator] **1.** the authority to act for another **2.** a person so authorized

prude (prōōd) *n.* [Fr. < *prudefemme*, excellent woman] one who is overly modest or proper in behavior, dress, speech, etc., esp. in a way that annoys others —**prud'ish** *adj.* —**prud'ish·ly** *adv.* —**prud'ish·ness** *n.*

pru·dence (prōōd''ns) *n.* **1.** a being prudent **2.** careful management

pru·dent (prōōd''nt) *adj.* [< L. *providens*, provident] **1.** exercising sound judgment in practical matters, esp. as concerns one's own interests **2.** cautious in conduct; not rash **3.** managing carefully; economical —**pru'dent·ly** *adv.*

pru·den·tial (prōō den'shəl) *adj.* characterized by or exercising prudence

prud·er·y (prōōd'ər ē) *n.* a being prudish

prune¹ (prōōn) *n.* [< Gr. *proumnon*, plum] a plum that has been or can be dried for eating

prune² (prōōn) *vt., vi.* **pruned, prun'ing** [< MFr., prob. ult. < L. *propago*, a plant slip] **1.** to trim dead or living parts from (a plant) **2.** to remove (unnecessary parts) from (something) —**prun'er** *n.*

pru·ri·ent (proor'ē ənt) *adj.* [< L. *prurire*, to itch] **1.** tending to excite lust, or intense sexual desire **2.** characterized by lustful ideas or desires —**pru'ri·ence** *n.*

Prus·sia (prush'ə) former kingdom in N Europe & dominant state of the former German Empire —**Prus'sian** *adj., n.*

prus·sic acid (prus'ik) same as HYDROCYANIC ACID

pry¹ (prī) *n., pl.* **pries** [< PRIZE²] a lever or crowbar —*vt.* **pried, pry'ing 1.** to raise or move with a pry **2.** to draw forth with difficulty

pry² (prī) *vi.* **pried, pry'ing** [< ?] to look or search closely or inquisitively (often with *into*); snoop —*n.* a person who is too inquisitive: also **pri'er, pry'er**

Ps., Psa. Psalm; Psalms

P.S., PS 1. postscript: also **p.s. 2.** Public School

psalm (säm) *n.* [< Gr. *psallein*, to pluck (a harp)] **1.** a sacred song or poem **2.** [*usually* P-] any of the sacred songs in praise of God that make up the Book of Psalms in the Bible —**psalm'ist** *n.*

Psalms (sämz) a book of the Bible, consisting of 150 psalms: also **Book of Psalms**

Psal·ter (sôl'tər) [see PSALM] the Book of Psalms —*n.* [*also* p-] a version of the Psalms for use in religious services

psal·ter·y (sôl'tər ē) *n., pl.* **-ies** [< Gr. *psaltērion*, a harp] an ancient stringed instrument with a shallow sound box, played by plucking the strings

pseud. pseudonym

pseu·do (sōō'dō) *adj.* [see PSEUDO-] sham; false; spurious

pseudo- [< Gr. *pseudēs*, false] *a prefix meaning:* **1.** fictitious, sham [*pseudonym*] **2.** counterfeit, spurious **3.** closely or deceptively similar to (a specified thing) Also **pseud-**

pseu·do·nym (sōō'də nim') *n.* [< Fr. < Gr. *pseudēs*, false + *onyma*, a name] a fictitious name, esp. one assumed by an author; pen name

pseu·do·sci·ence (sōō'dō sī'əns) *n.* any system of theories that claims to be a science but has no scientific basis —**pseu'do sci'en·tif'ic** *adj.*

pshaw (shô) *interj., n.* an exclamation of impatience, disgust, contempt, etc.

psi (sī, psē) *n.* the twenty-third letter of the Greek alphabet (Ψ, ψ)

psi·lo·cy·bin (sī'lə sī'bin, sil'ə-) *n.* [< Gr. *psilos*, bare + *kybē*, head] a hallucinogenic drug obtained from various mushrooms

psit·ta·co·sis (sit'ə kō'sis) *n.* [< Gr. *psittakos*, a parrot + -OSIS] an acute, infectious virus disease of parrots, often transmitted to man

pso·ri·a·sis (sə rī'ə sis) *n.* [< Gr. *psōra*, an itch] a chronic skin disease characterized by scaly patches

psst (pst) *interj.* a sound made to get someone's attention quickly and quietly

PST, P.S.T. Pacific Standard Time

psych (sīk) *vt.* **psyched, psych'ing** [< PSYCHOANALYZE] [Slang] to figure out the motives of, esp. in order to outwit, control, etc. (often with *out*)

psych. psychology

Psy·che (sī'kē) [< Gr. *psychē*, soul] *Rom. Myth.* a maiden who becomes the wife of Cupid and is made immortal —*n.* [p-] **1.** the soul **2.** the mind, esp. *Psychiatry* as a functional entity governing the total organism and its interactions with the environment

psy·che·del·ic (sī'kə del'ik) *adj.* [< prec. + Gr. *delein*, make manifest] **1.** of or causing extreme changes in the conscious mind, with hallucinations, etc. **2.** of or like the auditory or visual effects experienced with psychedelic drugs

psy·chi·a·try (sə kī'ə trē, sī-) *n.* [see PSYCHO- & -IATRY] the branch of medicine dealing with disorders of the mind, including psychoses, neuroses, etc. —**psy·chi·at·ric** (sī'kē at'rik) *adj.* —**psy·chi'a·trist** *n.*

psy·chic (sī'kik) *adj.* [< Gr. *psychē*, soul] **1.** of the psyche, or mind **2.** beyond known physical processes **3.** apparently sensitive to forces beyond the physical world Also **psy'chi·cal** —*n.* one who is supposedly psychic (sense 3) —**psy'chi·cal·ly** *adv.*

psy·cho (sī'kō) *adj., n. colloq. shortened form of* PSYCHOTIC, PSYCHOPATH, PSYCHOPATHIC

psycho- [< Gr. *psychē*, soul] *a combining form meaning* the mind or mental processes [*psychology*] : also **psych-**

psy·cho·a·nal·y·sis (sī'kō ə nal'ə sis) *n.* a method of treating neuroses and some other mental disorders through analysis of emotional conflicts, repressions, etc. by getting the patient to talk freely, analyzing his dreams, etc. —**psy'cho·an'a·lyst** (-an'əl ist) *n.* —**psy'cho·an'a·lyt'ic** (-ə lit'ik), **psy'cho·an'a·lyt'i·cal** *adj.*

psy'cho·an'a·lyze' (-an'ə līz') *vt.* **-lyzed', -lyz'ing** to treat by means of psychoanalysis

psy·cho·gen·ic (sī'kə jen'ik) *adj.* [PSYCHO- + -GEN + -IC] originating in the mind or in mental conflicts

psy·cho·ki·ne·sis (sī'kō ki nē'sis) *n.* [< PSYCHO- + Gr. *kinēsis*, motion] the supposed ability to influence physical objects or events by thought processes

psy·chol·o·gy (sī käl'ə jē) *n., pl.* **-gies** [see PSYCHO- & -LOGY] **1.** *a)* the science dealing with the mind and with mental and emotional processes *b)* the science of human and animal behavior **2.** the ways of thinking and acting of a person or group **3.** a system of psychology —**psy'cho·log'i·cal** (-kə läj'i k'l) *adj.* —**psy'cho·log'i·cal·ly** *adv.* —**psy·chol'o·gist** *n.*

psy·cho·neu·ro·sis (sī'kō noo rō'sis, -nyoo-) *n., pl.* **-ses** (-sēz) same as NEUROSIS —**psy'cho·neu·rot'ic** (-rät'ik) *adj., n.*

psy·cho·path (sī'kə path') *n.* [see PSYCHO- & -PATHY] a person with serious personality defects, whose behavior, often criminal, is largely amoral, irresponsible, and impulsive —**psy'cho·path'ic** *adj.*

psy·cho·sis (sī kō'sis) *n., pl.* **-ses** (-sēz) [see PSYCHO- & -OSIS] any major mental disorder in which the personality is very seriously disorganized and contact with reality is usually impaired —**psy·chot'ic** (-kät'ik) *adj., n.*

psy·cho·so·mat·ic (sī'kō sō mat'ik) *adj.* [PSYCHO- + SOMATIC] designating or of a physical disorder originating in or aggravated by emotional processes

psy'cho·ther'a·py (-ther'ə pē) *n.* [PSYCHO- + THERAPY] treatment of mental disorders by counseling, psychoanalysis, etc. —**psy'cho·ther'a·pist** *n.*

Pt *Chem.* platinum

pt. *pl.* **pts.** 1. part 2. pint 3. point

pt., p.t. past tense

P.T.A. Parent-Teacher Association

ptar·mi·gan (tär'mə gən) *n.* [< Scot. *tarmachan*] any of several varieties of northern grouse

pter·o·dac·tyl (ter'ə dak't'l) *n.* [< Gr. *pteron*, wing + DACTYL] an extinct flying reptile having wings of skin stretched between the hind limb and a very long digit of the forelimb

Ptol·e·my (täl'ə mē) 2d cent. A.D.; Gr. astronomer of Alexandria —**Ptol'e·ma'ic** (-mā'ik) *adj.*

pto·maine (tō'mān) *n.* [< It. < Gr. *ptōma*, corpse] any of a class of alkaloid substances formed in decaying animal or vegetable matter: some are poisonous

Pu *Chem.* plutonium

pub (pub) *n.* [< *pub*(*lic house*)] [Chiefly Brit. Colloq.] a bar or tavern

PTERODACTYL
(wingspread to 20 ft.)

pub. 1. public 2. published 3. publisher

pu·ber·ty (pyoo'bər tē) *n.* [< L. *puber*, adult] the state of physical development when sexual reproduction first becomes possible: the age of puberty is generally accepted in common law as being 14 for boys and 12 for girls —**pu'ber·tal** *adj.*

pu·bes·cent (pyoo bes''nt) *adj.* [see prec.] 1. reaching or having reached puberty 2. covered with a soft down, as many plants and insects —**pu·bes'cence** *n.*

pu·bic (pyoo'bik) *adj.* [see PUBERTY] of or in the region of the genitals

pub·lic (pub'lik) *adj.* [ult. < L. *populus*, the people] 1. of the people as a whole 2. for the use or benefit of all [a *public* park] 3. acting officially for the people [a *public* prosecutor] 4. known by most people [a *public* figure] —*n.* 1. the people as a whole 2. a specific part of the people [the reading *public*] —**in public** openly —**pub'lic·ly** *adv.*

pub'lic-ad·dress' system an electronic system to amplify sound in auditoriums, theaters, etc.

pub·li·can (pub'li kən) *n.* 1. in ancient Rome, a collector of public revenues 2. [see PUB] [Brit.] a person who manages a bar or tavern

pub·li·ca·tion (pub'lə kā'shən) *n.* [see PUBLISH] 1. public notification or announcement 2. the printing and distributing for sale of books, magazines, etc. 3. something published, as a book or periodical

public domain 1. public lands 2. the condition of being free from copyright or patent

pub·li·cist (pub'lə sist) *n.* 1. a specialist in international law 2. a journalist who writes about public affairs 3. one who publicizes; press agent

pub·lic·i·ty (pə blis'ə tē) *n.* 1. *a*) any information or action that brings or is meant to bring a person, place, or thing to the attention of the public *b*) the work or business of getting public attention for someone or something 2. notice by the public

pub·li·cize (pub'lə sīz') *vt.* **-cized', -ciz'ing** to give publicity to; get public attention for

public relations relations of an organization with the public through publicity, etc.

public school 1. in the U.S., an elementary or secondary school that is maintained by public taxes and supervised by local authorities 2. in England, a private boarding school for boys

public servant an elected or appointed government official or a civil-service employee

pub'lic-spir'it·ed *adj.* having or showing zeal for the public welfare

public utility an organization that supplies water, electricity, transportation, etc. to the public, operated by a

private corporation under government regulation or by the government itself

pub·lish (pub'lish) *vt.* [< L. *publicare*] 1. to make publicly known; announce 2. to issue (a printed work, etc.) to the public, as for sale —*vi.* to write books, etc. that are published —**pub'lish·a·ble** *adj.* —**pub'lish·er** *n.*

Puc·ci·ni (poot chē'nē), **Gia·co·mo** (jä'kô mô') 1858–1924; It. operatic composer

puck' (puk) *n.* [akin to POKE¹] the hard rubber disk used in ice hockey

puck² (puk) *n.* [OE. *puca*] a mischievous sprite or elf, as [P-] the one in Shakespeare's *A Midsummer Night's Dream* —**puck'ish** *adj.*

puck·er (puk'ər) *vt., vi.* [< POKE²] to draw up into wrinkles or small folds —*n.* such a wrinkle or fold —**puck'er·y** *adj.*

pud·ding (pood'iŋ) *n.* [akin ? to OE. *puduc*, a swelling] a soft, sweet food variously made with flour, eggs, milk, fruit, etc.

pud·dle (pud''l) *n.* [< OE. *pudd*, ditch] 1. a small pool of water, esp. stagnant or muddy water 2. a thick mixture of clay, and sometimes sand, with water —*vt.* **-dled, -dling** 1. to make muddy 2. to make a thick mixture of (wet clay and sand) 3. to treat (iron) by puddling —**pud'dler** *n.*

pud'dling (-liŋ) *n.* the process of making wrought iron from pig iron by heating and stirring it in the presence of oxidizing agents

pudg·y (puj'ē) *adj.* **-i·er, -i·est** [? < Scot. *pud*, belly] short and fat —**pudg'i·ness** *n.*

pueb·lo (pweb'lō) *n., pl.* **-los**; *also, for* 2, **-lo** [Sp. < L. *populus*, people] 1. an Indian village of the SW U.S. in which the Indians live communally in terraced structures of stone or adobe 2. [P-] an Indian living in a pueblo

pu·er·ile (pyoo'ər əl) *adj.* [< Fr. < L. *puer*, boy] childish; silly —**pu'er·il'i·ty** *n.*

Puer·to Ri·co (pwer'tə rē'kō) island in the West Indies, constituting a commonwealth associated with the U.S.: 3,421 sq. mi.; pop. 2,712,000; cap. San Juan: abbrev. **P.R., PR** —**Puer'to Ri'can**

puff (puf) *n.* [OE. *pyff*] 1. a short, sudden gust or expulsion of wind, breath, smoke, etc. 2. a draw at a cigarette, etc. 3. a swelling 4. a light pastry filled with whipped cream, etc. 5. a soft roll of hair on the head 6. a soft pad [a powder *puff*] 7. exaggerated praise, as in a book review —*vi.* 1. to blow in puffs 2. to breathe rapidly 3. to swell (*out* or *up*) 4. to take puffs on a cigarette, etc. —*vt.* 1. to blow, smoke, etc. in or with puffs 2. to inflate; swell 3. to praise unduly 4. to set (the hair) in puffs —**puff'i·ness** *n.* —**puff'y** *adj.* **-i·er, -i·est**

puff'ball' *n.* a round, white-fleshed fungus that bursts at the touch when ripe

puff'er *n.* 1. one that puffs 2. a fish that can expand the body by swallowing air or water

puf·fin (puf'in) *n.* [ME. *poffin*] a northern sea bird with a ducklike body and triangular beak

pug' (pug) *n.* [< ? PUCK²] 1. a small, short-haired dog with a snub nose 2. *same as* PUG NOSE

pug² (pug) *n.* [Slang] a pugilist

Pu·get Sound (pyoo'jit) inlet of the Pacific, extending southward into NW Wash.

pu·gil·ism (pyoo'jə liz'm) *n.* [< L. *pugil*, boxer] *same as* BOXING —**pu'gil·ist** *n.* —**pu'gil·is'tic** *adj.*

pug·na·cious (pug nā'shəs) *adj.* [< L. *pugnare*, to fight] eager and ready to fight; quarrelsome —**pug·na'cious·ly** *adv.* —**pug·nac'i·ty** (-nas'ə tē) *n.*

PUFFIN
(to 13 1/2 in. long)

pug nose a short, thick, turned-up nose —**pug'-nosed'** (-nōzd') *adj.*

puke (pyook) *n., vi., vt.* puked, puk'ing [< ?] *same as* VOMIT: avoided by some as vulgar

Pu·las·ki (poo las'kē), **Cas·i·mir** (kaz'i mir) 1748–79; Pol. general in the Am. Revolutionary army

pul·chri·tude (pul'krə tood', -tyood') *n.* [< L. *pulcher*, beautiful] physical beauty

pule (pyool) *vi.* puled, pul'ing [echoic] to whine or whimper, as a sick or fretful child

Pul·it·zer Prize (pool'it sər; *now often* pyoo'lit-) [< J. *Pulitzer* (1847–1911), U.S. publisher who established them] any of various yearly prizes for work in journalism, literature, and music

pull (pool) *vt.* [OE. *pullian,* to pluck] **1.** to exert force on so as to move toward the source of the force **2.** to pluck out (a tooth, etc.) **3.** to rip; tear **4.** to strain (a muscle) **5.** [Colloq.] to carry out; perform *[to pull* a raid*]* **6.** [Colloq.] to restrain *[to pull* a punch*]* **7.** [Colloq.] to draw (a gun, etc.) **8.** *Printing* to take (a proof) on a hand press —*vi.* **1.** to exert force in dragging, tugging, etc. **2.** to take a deep draft of a drink, a puff on a cigarette, etc. **3.** to be capable of being pulled **4.** to move (*away, ahead,* etc.) —*n.* **1.** the act or force of pulling; specif., *a*) a tugging, attracting, etc. *b*) a hard, steady effort **2.** something to be pulled, as a handle **3.** [Colloq.] *a*) influence *b*) drawing power —**pull for** [Colloq.] to cheer on —**pull off** [Colloq.] to accomplish —**pull through** [Colloq.] to get over (an illness, difficulty, etc.) —**pull up** to stop —**pull′er** *n.*

pull′back′ *n.* a pulling back; esp., a planned military withdrawal

pul·let (pool′it) *n.* [< L. *pullus,* chicken] a young hen, usually not more than a year old

pul·ley (pool′ē) *n., pl.* **-leys** [< Gr. *polos,* axis] a small wheel with a grooved rim in which a rope, belt, etc. runs, as to raise weights or transmit power

Pull·man (pool′mən) *n.* [< G. M. *Pullman* (1831-97), U.S. inventor] a railroad car with private compartments or berths for sleeping: also **Pullman car**

pull′out′ *n.* **1.** a pulling out; esp., a removal, withdrawal, etc. **2.** something to be pulled out, as a magazine insert

pull′o′ver *adj.* that is put on by being pulled over the head —*n.* a pullover sweater, shirt, etc.

pull′up′ *n.* the act of chinning oneself

pul·mo·nar·y (pul′mə ner′ē) *adj.* [< L. *pulmo,* a lung] of or affecting the lungs

Pul·mo·tor (pool′mōt′ər, pul′-) [< L. *pulmo,* a lung + MOTOR] *a trademark for* an apparatus for applying artificial respiration —*n.* [p-] such an apparatus

pulp (pulp) *n.* [< Fr. < L. *pulpa,* flesh] **1.** a soft, moist, formless mass **2.** the soft, juicy part of a fruit **3.** the soft pith of a plant stem **4.** the sensitive substance under the dentine of a tooth **5.** ground-up, moistened fibers of wood, rags, etc., used to make paper **6.** a magazine printed on rough paper, often featuring shocking stories about crime, sex, etc. —*vt.* to reduce to pulp —*vi.* to become pulp —**pulp′i·ness** *n.* —**pulp′y** *adj.* **-i·er, -i·est**

pul·pit (pool′pit) *n.* [< L. *pulpitum,* a stage] **1.** a raised platform from which a clergyman preaches in a church **2.** preachers as a group

pulp′wood′ *n.* **1.** soft wood used in making paper **2.** wood ground to pulp for paper

pul·que (pool′kā) *n.* [AmSp.] a fermented drink, popular in Mexico, made from the juice of an agave

pul·sar (pul′sär) *n.* [PULS(E)1 + -AR] any of several small heavenly objects in the Milky Way that emit radio pulses at regular intervals

pul·sate (pul′sāt) *vi.* **-sat·ed, -sat·ing** [< L. *pulsare,* to beat] **1.** to beat or throb rhythmically, as the heart **2.** to vibrate; quiver —**pul·sa′tion** *n.* —**pul′sa′tor** *n.*

pulse¹ (puls) *n.* [< L. *pulsus,* a beating] **1.** the regular beating in the arteries, caused by the contractions of the heart **2.** any regular beat **3.** the underlying feelings of the public, etc. —*vi.* **pulsed, puls′ing** to pulsate

pulse² (puls) *n.* [< L. *puls,* a pottage] **1.** the edible seeds of peas, beans, lentils, and similar plants having pods **2.** any such plant

pul·ver·ize (pul′və rīz′) *vt., vi.* **-ized′, -iz′ing** [< L. *pulvis,* dust] to grind or be ground into a powder or dust —**pul′ver·i·za′tion** *n.*

pu·ma (pyoo′mə, poo′-) *n.* [AmSp.] *same as* COUGAR

pum·ice (pum′is) *n.* [< L. *pumex*] a light, porous, volcanic rock used in solid or powdered form to scour, smooth, and polish: also **pumice stone**

pum·mel (pum′′l) *vt.* **-meled** or **-melled, -mel·ing** or **-mel·ling** [< POMMEL] to hit with repeated blows

pump¹ (pump) *n.* [< Sp. *bomba*] a machine that forces a liquid or gas into, or draws it out of, something —*vt.* **1.** to move (fluids) with a pump **2.** to remove water, etc. from **3.** to drive air into, as with a pump **4.** to force in, draw out, move up and down, etc. like a pump **5.** [Colloq.] *a*) to question persistently *b*) to get (information) in this way —*vi.* **1.** to work a pump, as to get water **2.** to move up and down like a pump handle —**pump′er** *n.*

pump² (pump) *n.* [< ? Fr. *pompe,* an ornament] a low-cut shoe without straps or ties

PUMP

pump·er·nick·el (pum′pər nik′′l) *n.* [G.] a coarse, dark, sour bread made of unsifted rye

pump·kin (pum′kin, pump′-, puŋ′-) *n.* [< Gr. *pepōn,* ripe] **1.** a large, round, orange-yellow, gourdlike fruit with many seeds **2.** the vine on which it grows

pun (pun) *n.* [< ? It. *puntiglio,* fine point] the humorous use of words that have the same sound or spelling, but have different meanings —*vi.* **punned, pun′ning** to make a pun or puns —**pun′ner** *n.*

Punch (punch) [< PUNCHINELLO] the hooknosed, humpbacked hero of the puppet show **Punch and Judy,** always fighting with his wife —**pleased as Punch** greatly pleased

punch¹ (punch) *n.* [see PUNCHEON1] a tool driven against a surface that is to be pierced, shaped, or stamped —*vt.* **1.** to pierce, stamp, etc. with a punch **2.** to make (a hole, etc.) with a punch —**punch′er** *n.*

punch² (punch) *vt.* [ME. *punchen*] **1.** to prod with a stick **2.** to herd (cattle) as by prodding **3.** to hit with the fist — *n.* **1.** a thrusting blow with the fist **2.** [Colloq.] effective force —**punch′er** *n.*

punch³ (punch) *n.* [< a Hindi word for "five": it orig. had five ingredients] a sweet drink of fruit juices, sherbet, etc., often mixed with wine or liquor

punch card a card with holes or notches positioned in it, esp. by a key punch for data processing

punch′-drunk′ *adj.* dazed, confused, unsteady, etc., as from many blows to the head in boxing

pun·cheon¹ (pun′chən) *n.* [< L. *pungere,* to prick] **1.** a short, upright wooden post used in framework **2.** a heavy piece of timber roughly dressed

pun·cheon² (pun′chən) *n.* [OFr. *poinçon*] a large cask (72-120 gal.), for beer, wine, etc.

pun·chi·nel·lo (pun′chə nel′ō) *n., pl.* **-los** [< a character in an It. puppet play] a buffoon; clown

punch line the final line carrying the point of a joke

punch press a press in which dies are fitted for cutting, shaping, or stamping metal

punch′y *adj.* **-i·er, -i·est** [Colloq.] **1.** forceful; vigorous **2.** *same as* PUNCH-DRUNK

punc·til·i·ous *adj.* [see PUNCTUAL] **1.** very careful about every detail of behavior, ceremony, etc. **2.** very exact; scrupulous —**punc·til′i·ous·ly** *adv.*

punc·tu·al (puŋk′choo wəl) *adj.* [< L. *punctus,* a point] on time; prompt —**punc′tu·al′i·ty** (-wal′ə tē) *n.* —**punc′tu·al·ly** *adv.*

punc·tu·ate (puŋk′choo wāt′) *vt.* **-at′ed, -at′ing** [< L. *punctus,* a point] **1.** to insert punctuation marks in **2.** to break in on here and there **3.** to emphasize —*vi.* to use punctuation marks

punc′tu·a′tion *n.* **1.** the use of standardized marks in writing and printing to clarify meaning **2.** a punctuation mark or marks

punctuation mark any of the marks used in punctuation, as a period or comma

punc·ture (puŋk′chər) *n.* [< L. *pungere,* pierce] **1.** a piercing **2.** a hole made by a sharp point —*vt., vi.* **-tured, -tur·ing** to pierce or be pierced as with a sharp point

pun·dit (pun′dit) *n.* [< Hindi < Sans. *pandita*] **1.** in India, a very learned Brahman **2.** a person who has great learning

pun·gent (pun′jənt) *adj.* [< L. *pungere,* to prick] **1.** producing a sharp sensation of taste or smell **2.** poignant **3.** biting **4.** keenly clever —**pun′gen·cy** *n.* —**pun′gent·ly** *adv.*

pun·ish (pun′ish) *vt.* [< L. *punire*] **1.** to cause to undergo pain, loss, etc., as for a crime **2.** to impose a penalty for (an offense) **3.** to treat harshly **4.** [Colloq.] to consume or use up —*vi.* to deal out punishment —**pun′ish·a·ble** *adj.*

pun′ish·ment *n.* **1.** a punishing or being punished **2.** the penalty imposed **3.** harsh treatment

pu·ni·tive (pyoo′nə tiv) *adj.* inflicting or concerned with punishment: also **pu′ni·to′ry** (-tôr′ē)

Pun·jab (pun jäb′, pun′jäb) region in NW India & NE Pakistan

punk¹ (puŋk) *n.* [var. of SPUNK] any substance, as decayed wood, that smolders when ignited, used as tinder, or to light fireworks, etc.

punk² (puŋk) *n.* [< ?] [Slang] **1.** a young hoodlum **2.** a youngster regarded as inexperienced, insignificant, etc. — *adj.* [Slang] poor or bad in quality

pun·ster (pun′stər) *n.* one fond of making puns

punt¹ (punt) *n.* [< ? dial. *bunt,* kick] *Football* a kick in which the ball is dropped from the hands and kicked before it strikes the ground —*vt., vi.* to kick (a football) in this way —**punt′er** *n.*

punt² (punt) *n.* [< L. *pons,* a bridge] a flat-bottomed boat with square ends —*vt., vi.* to propel (a boat) with a long pole —**punt′er** *n.*

pu·ny (pyōō′nē) *adj.* **-ni·er, -ni·est** [< Fr. < OFr. *puis,* after + *né,* born] of inferior size, strength, or importance; weak —**pu′ni·ness** *n.*

pup (pup) *n.* **1.** a young dog; puppy **2.** a young fox, seal, etc.

pu·pa (pyōō′pə) *n., pl.* **-pae** (-pē), **-pas** [< L., a doll] an insect in the stage between the larval and adult forms — **pu′pal** *adj.*

pu·pil¹ (pyōō′p'l) *n.* [< L. *pupillus,* ward] a person taught by a teacher or tutor, as in school

pu·pil² (pyōō′p'l) *n.* [< Fr. < L. *pupilla,* figure reflected in the eye] the contractile circular opening in the center of the iris of the eye

pup·pet (pup′it) *n.* [< L. *pupa,* doll] **1.** a small figure, as of a human being, moved with the hands or by strings in a performance (**puppet show**) **2.** one whose actions, ideas, etc. are controlled by another —**pup′pet·ry** *n.*

pup·pet·eer (-i tir′) *n.* an operator, designer, etc. of puppets

pup·py (pup′ē) *n., pl.* **-pies** [< MFr. *popee,* doll] **1.** a young dog **2.** an insolent, conceited, or silly young man — **pup′py·ish** *adj.*

pup tent a small, portable tent

pur·blind (pur′blīnd′) *adj.* [ME. *pur blind,* quite blind] **1.** partly blind **2.** slow in understanding

pur·chase (pur′chəs) *vt.* **-chased, -chas·ing** [< OFr. *pour,* for + *chacier,* to chase] **1.** to buy **2.** to get at a cost, as of suffering **3.** to move by applying mechanical power — *n.* **1.** anything bought **2.** a buying **3.** a fast hold applied to move something mechanically or to keep from slipping —**pur′chas·a·ble** *adj.* —**pur′chas·er** *n.*

pure (pyoor) *adj.* [< L. *purus*] **1.** free from any adulterant or anything harmful **2.** simple; mere **3.** utter; absolute **4.** free from defects **5.** free from sin or guilt **6.** virgin or chaste **7.** of unmixed stock **8.** abstract or theoretical [*pure* physics] —**pure′ly** *adv.* —**pure′ness** *n.*

pu·rée (pyoo rā′, pyoor′ā) *n.* [Fr. < L. *purus,* pure] **1.** food prepared by putting cooked vegetables, fruits, etc. through a sieve or blender **2.** a thick, smooth soup made with this —*vt.* **-réed′, -rée′ing** to make a purée of Also sp. **puree**

pur·ga·tive (pur′gə tiv) *adj.* purging —*n.* a substance that purges; specif., a cathartic

pur·ga·to·ry (pur′gə tôr′ē) *n., pl.* **-ries** [see PURGE] [*often* P-] *Christian Theol.* a state or place after death for expiating sins by suffering

purge (purj) *vt.* **purged, purg′ing** [< L. *purus,* clean + *agere,* to do] **1.** to cleanse of impurities, etc. **2.** to cleanse of sin **3.** to remove by cleansing **4.** to rid (a nation, party, etc.) of (individuals held to be disloyal) **5.** to empty (the bowels) —*vi.* to become clean, pure, etc. —*n.* **1.** a purging **2.** that which purges; esp., a cathartic —**pur·ga·tion** (pur gā′shən) *n.* —**purg′er** *n.*

pu·ri·fy (pyoor′ə fī′) *vt.* **-fied′, -fy′ing** [< L. *purus,* pure + *facere,* to make] **1.** to rid of impurities, etc. **2.** to free from guilt, sin, etc. —*vi.* to become purified —**pu′ri·fi·ca′tion** *n.* —**pu′ri·fi′er** *n.*

pur·ism (pyoor′iz'm) *n.* strict observance of precise usage or style, as in grammar or art —**pur′ist** *n.*

Pu·ri·tan (pyoor′ə t'n) *n.* [see PURITY] **1.** a member of a Protestant group in England and America who, in the 16th and 17th centuries, wanted to make the Church of England simpler in its services **2.** [p-] a person regarded as excessively strict in morals and religion —*adj.* **1.** of the Puritans **2.** [p-] puritanical —**Pu′ri·tan·ism, pu′ri·tan·ism** *n.*

pu·ri·tan·i·cal (-ə tan′i k'l) *adj.* **1.** [P-] of the Puritans **2.** excessively strict in morals and religion —**pu′ri·tan′i·cal·ly** *adv.*

pu·ri·ty (pyoor′ə tē) *n.* [< LL. *puritas*] a being pure; specif., *a*) freedom from adulterating matter *b*) cleanness *c*) innocence or chastity

purl¹ (purl) *vi.* [< ? Scand.] to move in ripples or with a murmuring sound —*n.* a purling stream or its murmuring sound

purl² (purl) *vt., vi.* [< ?] to invert (stitches) in knitting — *n.* an inversion of knitting stitches

pur·lieu (pur′lōō) *n.* [< OFr. *pur-,* through + *aler,* to go] **1.** an outlying part **2.** [*pl.*] environs

pur·loin (pur loin′) *vt., vi.* [< OFr. *pur-,* for + *loin,* far] to steal —**pur·loin′er** *n.*

pur·ple (pur′p'l) *n.* [< Gr. *porphyra,* shellfish yielding purple dye] **1.** a dark bluish red **2.** crimson cloth or clothing, esp. as a former emblem of royalty —*adj.* **1.** bluish-red **2.** imperial **3.** ornate [*purple* prose] **4.** offensively strong [*purple* language] —**born to** (or **in**) **the purple** of royal or high birth —**pur′plish, pur′ply** *adj.*

pur·port (pər pôrt′; *for n.* pur′pôrt) *vt.* [< OFr. *por-,* forth + *porter,* to bear] **1.** to profess or claim as its meaning **2.** to give the appearance, often falsely, of being, intending, etc. —*n.* **1.** meaning; sense **2.** intention; object

pur·pose (pur′pəs) *vt., vi.* **-posed, -pos·ing** [< OFr. *porposer:* see PROPOSE] to plan, intend, or resolve —*n.* **1.** what one plans to get or do; aim **2.** determination **3.** the reason or use for something —**on purpose** intentionally — **to good purpose** advantageously —**pur′pose·ful** *adj.* — **pur′pose·less** *adj.*

pur′pose·ly *adv.* with a definite purpose; intentionally; deliberately

purr (pur) *n.* [echoic] a low, vibratory sound made by a cat when it seems to be pleased —*vi., vt.* to make, or express by, such a sound

purse (purs) *n.* [< Gr. *byrsa,* a hide] **1.** a small bag for carrying money **2.** finances; money **3.** a sum of money given as a present **4.** a woman's handbag —*vt.* **pursed, purs′ing** to pucker (one's lips, etc.)

purs·er (pur′sər) *n.* [ME., purse bearer] a ship's officer in charge of accounts, tickets, etc., esp. on a passenger vessel

pur·su·ance (pər sōō′əns, -syōō′-) *n.* a pursuing, or carrying out, as of a project, plan, etc.

pur·su′ant *adj.* [Now Rare] pursuing —**pursuant to** in accordance with

pur·sue (pər sōō′, -syōō′) *vt.* **-sued′, -su′ing** [< L. *pro-,* forth + *sequi,* follow] **1.** to follow in order to overtake, capture, etc.; chase **2.** to follow (a specified course, action, etc.) **3.** to strive for; seek after **4.** to devote oneself to **5.** to keep on harassing —*vi.* **1.** to chase **2.** to continue — **pur·su′er** *n.*

pur·suit (-sōōt′, -syōōt′) *n.* **1.** a pursuing **2.** a career, interest, etc. to which one devotes oneself

pu·ru·lent (pyoor′ə lənt, -yoo lənt) *adj.* [Fr. < L. *pus, pus*] of, like, containing, or discharging pus

pur·vey (pər vā′) *vt.* [see PROVIDE] to supply (esp. food) — **pur·vey′ance** *n.* —**pur·vey′or** *n.*

pur·view (pur′vyōō) *n.* [< Anglo-Fr. *purveu* (*est*), (it is) provided] **1.** the scope of an act or bill **2.** extent of control, activity, concern, etc.

pus (pus) *n.* [L.] the yellowish-white matter produced in infections, consisting of bacteria, white corpuscles, serum, etc. —**pus′sy** *adj.*

push (poosh) *vt.* [< L. *pulsare,* to beat] **1.** to exert force against so as to move **2.** to urge on; impel **3.** to extend or expand **4.** to bring into a critical state [be *pushed* for time] **5.** to promote the use, sale, etc. of **6.** [Colloq.] to be near to [*pushing* sixty years] —*vi.* **1.** to press against a thing so as to move it **2.** to try hard to advance, etc. **3.** to move forward against opposition —*n.* **1.** a pushing **2.** a vigorous effort, campaign, etc. **3.** an advance against opposition **4.** [Colloq.] enterprise; drive —**push′er** *n.*

push button a small knob or button that is pushed to cause something to operate electrically

push′ing *adj.* **1.** aggressive **2.** forward

Push·kin (poosh′kin; *E.* poosh′-), **A·lek·san·dr** (ä′lyik sän′dr) 1799–1837; Russ. poet

push′o·ver *n.* [Slang] **1.** anything easy to do **2.** a person, group, etc. easily persuaded, defeated, etc.

push′-up′, push′up′ *n.* an exercise in which a prone person, with hands under the shoulders, raises his body by pushing down with his palms

push′y *adj.* **-i·er, -i·est** [Colloq.] annoyingly aggressive and persistent —**push′i·ness** *n.*

pu·sil·lan·i·mous (pyōō′s'l an′ə məs) *adj.* [< L. *pusillus,* tiny + *animus,* the mind] timid or cowardly —**pu′sil·la·nim′i·ty** (-ə nim′ə tē) *n.*

puss¹ (poos) *n.* [< ?] a cat: pet name: also **puss′y,** *pl.* **-ies, puss′y·cat′**

puss² (poos) *n.* [< ?] [Slang] the face or mouth

puss′y·foot′ *vi.* [Colloq.] **1.** to move with stealth or caution, like a cat **2.** to avoid committing oneself

pussy willow a willow bearing silvery, velvetlike catkins before the leaves appear

pus·tu·late (pus′chə lāt′) *vt., vi.* **-lat′ed, -lat′ing** to form into pustules —**pus′tu·la′tion** *n.*

pus·tule (pus′chōōl) *n.* [L. *pustula*] a small swelling in the skin, containing pus

put (poot) *vt.* **put, put′ting** [< OE. *potian,* to push] **1.** to drive or send by a thrust **2.** to throw with an overhand thrust from the shoulder [*put* the shot] **3.** to make be in a specified place, condition, relation, etc.; place; set **4.** to impose (a tax, etc.) **5.** to attribute; ascribe **6.** to express *[put* it plainly*]* **7.** to present for decision *[put* the question*]* **8.** to bet (money) *on —vi.* to go (*in, out,* etc.) *—adj.* [Colloq.] fixed *[stay put]* —**put about** to change a vessel's course —**put across** [Colloq.] to make understood, accepted, successful, etc. —**put aside** (or **by**) to keep for later use —**put away** [Colloq.] **1.** to consume (food or drink) **2.** to kill (a pet) to prevent suffering —**put down 1.** to crush; repress **2.** to write down **3.** to attribute (to) **4.** [Slang] to belittle or humiliate —**put in for** to apply for —**put it** (or **something**) **over on** [Colloq.] to deceive; trick —**put off 1.** to postpone **2.** to evade **3.** to confuse, mislead, etc. **4.** to make wait —**put on 1.** to clothe oneself with **2.** to pretend **3.** to stage (a play) **4.** [Slang] to hoax —**put out 1.** to expel; dismiss **2.** to extinguish (a fire or light) **3.** to disconcert or vex **4.** to inconvenience **5.** to publish **6.** *Baseball* to cause (a batter or runner) to be out by a fielding play —**put through 1.** to carry out **2.** to cause to do or undergo —**put up 1.** to offer **2.** to preserve (fruits, etc.) **3.** to provide lodgings for **4.** to provide (money) **5.** to arrange (the hair) with rollers, etc. **6.** [Colloq.] to incite (a person) *to* some action —**put upon** to impose on; victimize —**put up with** to tolerate

pu·ta·tive (pyōōt′ə tiv) *adj.* [< L. *putare,* suppose] reputed; supposed —**pu′ta·tive·ly** *adv.*

put′-down′ *n.* [Slang] a belittling remark or crushing retort

put′-on′ *adj.* feigned *—n.* [Slang] a hoax

put′out′ *n. Baseball* a play in which the batter or runner is put out

pu·tre·fy (pyōō′trə fī′) *vt., vi.* **-fied′, -fy′ing** [< L. *putris,* putrid + *facere,* make] to make or become putrid; rot —**pu′tre·fac′tion** (-fak′shən) *n.*

pu·tres·cent (pyōō tres′′nt) *adj.* putrefying; rotting —**pu·tres′cence** *n.*

pu·trid (pyōō′trid) *adj.* [< Fr. < L. *putrere,* be rotten] rotten and foul-smelling —**pu·trid′i·ty, pu′trid·ness** *n.* —**pu′trid·ly** *adv.*

putt (put) *n.* [< PUT, *v.*] *Golf* a light stroke made on the putting green to put the ball into the hole —*vt., vi.* to hit (the ball) with a putt

put·tee (pu tē′, put′ē) *n.* [< Hindi < Sans. *patta,* a strip of cloth] a legging or a cloth strip wound spirally to cover the leg from ankle to knee

putt·er[1] (put′ər) *n. Golf* **1.** a short, straight-faced club used in putting **2.** one who putts

put·ter[2] (put′ər) *vi.* [< OE. *potian,* to push] to busy oneself in an ineffective or aimless way (often with *around,* etc.) *—vt.* to fritter (*away*)

putt·ing green (put′iŋ) *Golf* the area of smooth turf in which the hole is sunk

put·ty (put′ē) *n.* [< Fr. *potée,* lit., potful] **1.** a soft, plastic mixture of powdered chalk and linseed oil, used to fill small cracks, etc. **2.** any similar substance *—vt.* **-tied, -ty·ing** to cement, fill, etc. with putty

puz·zle (puz′′l) *vt.* **-zled, -zling** [< ?] to perplex; bewilder *—vi.* **1.** to be perplexed, etc. **2.** to exercise one's mind, as on a problem *—n.* **1.** a puzzling problem, etc. **2.** a toy or problem to test skill or ingenuity —**puzzle out** to solve by deep thought —**puz′zle·ment** *n.* —**puz′zler** *n.*

Pvt. *Mil.* Private

pwt. pennyweight(s)

PX post exchange

Pyg·ma·lion (pig māl′yən) *Gr. Legend* a sculptor who fell in love with his statue of a maiden, later brought to life as Galatea by Aphrodite

Pyg·my (pig′mē) *n., pl.* **-mies** [< Gr. *pygmaios,* of the length of the forearm] **1.** a member of any of several African and Asian people of small stature **2.** [p-] any very small or insignificant person or thing *—adj.* **1.** of Pygmies **2.** [p-] very small

py·ja·mas (pə jam′əz, -jä′məz) *n.pl. Brit. sp. of* PAJAMAS

py·lon (pī′län) *n.* [Gr. *pylōn,* gateway] **1.** a gateway, as of an Egyptian temple **2.** a towerlike structure, as for supporting electric lines

py·lo·rus (pī lôr′əs) *n., pl.* **-ri** (-ī) [< Gr. *pylōros,* gatekeeper] the opening from the stomach into the duodenum —**py·lor′ic** *adj.*

py·or·rhe·a, py·or·rhoe·a (pī′ə rē′ə) *n.* [< Gr. *pyon,* pus + *rhein,* to flow] an infection of the gums and tooth sockets, with formation of pus and loosening of the teeth

pyr·a·mid (pir′ə mid) *n.* [< Gr. *pyramis*] **1.** a huge structure with a square base and four triangular sides meeting at the top, as a royal tomb of ancient Egypt **2.** *Geom.* a solid figure with a polygonal base, whose sides are the bases of triangular surfaces meeting at a common vertex *—vi., vt.* to build up or grow as in the form of a pyramid —**py·ram·i·dal** (pi ram′ə d′l) *adj.*

PYRAMIDS

pyre (pīr) *n.* [< Gr. *pyr,* a fire] a pile, esp. of wood, for burning a corpse in a funeral rite

Pyr·e·nees (pir′ə nēz′) mountain range between France & Spain —**Pyr′e·ne′an** (-nē′ən) *adj.*

Py·rex (pī′reks) [coined < PIE] *a trademark for* a heat-resistant glassware for cooking, etc.

py·rite (pī′rīt) *n., pl.* **py·ri·tes** (pə rīt′ēz, pī′rīts) [< Gr. *pyritēs,* flint] iron sulfide, FeS$_2$, a lustrous, yellow mineral

py·ri·tes (pə rīt′ēz, pī′rīts) *n.* any of various native metallic sulfides, as pyrite —**py·rit′ic** (-rit′ik), **py·rit′i·cal** *adj.*

pyro- [< Gr. *pyr,* a fire] *a combining form meaning* fire, heat: also **pyr-**

py·ro·ma·ni·a (pī′rə mā′nē ə) *n.* [see PYRO- & -MANIA] an uncontrollable desire to start destructive fires —**py′ro·ma′ni·ac′** (-nē ak′) *n., adj.*

py·ro·tech·nics (pī′rə tek′niks) *n.pl.* [< Fr. < Gr. *pyr,* fire + *technē,* art] **1.** a display of fireworks **2.** a dazzling display, as of wit —**py′ro·tech′nic** *adj.*

py·rox·y·lin, py·rox·y·line (pī räk′sə lin) *n.* [< Fr. < Gr. *pyr,* fire + *xylon,* wood] nitrocellulose used in making paints, lacquers, etc.

Pyr·rhic victory (pir′ik) [after *Pyrrhus,* Gr. king who defeated the Romans but suffered heavy losses] a victory that is too costly

Py·thag·o·ras (pi thag′ər əs) 6th cent. B.C.; Gr. philosopher & mathematician —**Py·thag′o·re′an** (-ə rē′ən) *adj., n.*

Pythias *see* DAMON AND PYTHIAS

py·thon (pī′thän, -thən) *n.* [< Gr. *Pythōn,* a serpent slain by Apollo] **1.** a large, nonpoisonous snake of Asia and Africa that crushes its prey to death **2.** popularly, any large snake that crushes its prey

pyx (piks) *n.* [< Gr. *pyxis,* a box] a container for Eucharistic wafers

Q

Q, q (kyōō) *n., pl.* **Q's, q's** the seventeenth letter of the English alphabet

q. 1. quart **2.** queen **3.** question **4.** quire

Qa·tar (kä′tär) independent Arab sheikdom on a peninsula of E Arabia: 8,500 sq. mi.; pop. 130,000

Q.E.D. [L. *quod erat demonstrandum*] which was to be proved

QM, Q.M. Quartermaster

qt. 1. quantity **2.** quart(s)

Q.T., q.t. [Slang] quiet: usually in **on the Q.T.** (or **q.t.**), in secret

quack[1] (kwak) *vi.* [echoic] to utter the sound or cry of a duck *—n.* this sound

quack[2] (kwak) *n.* [< earlier *quacksalver* (< MDu. *quacken,* to brag + *zalf,* salve)] **1.** an untrained person who practices medicine fraudulently **2.** any person who pretends to have knowledge or skill he does not have; charlatan *—adj.* fraudulent —**quack′er·y** *n.* —**quack′ish** *adj.*

quad (kwäd) *n. same as:* **1.** QUADRANGLE (of a college) **2.** QUADRAPHONIC **3.** QUADRUPLET

quad·ran·gle (kwäd′raŋ′g′l) *n.* [see QUADRI- & ANGLE[1]] **1.** a plane figure with four angles and four sides **2.** *a*) an area surrounded on four sides by buildings *b*) the buildings themselves —**quad·ran'gu·lar** (-gyə lər) *adj.*

quad·rant (kwäd'rənt) *n.* [< L. *quadrans*, fourth part] **1.** an arc of 90° **2.** a quarter section of a circle **3.** an instrument for measuring altitudes or angular elevations in astronomy and navigation

quad·ra·phon·ic (kwäd'rə fän'ik) *adj.* [< L. *quadra*, a square + Gr. *phōnē*, a sound] using four channels to record and reproduce sound

quad·rate (kwäd'rāt; *also, for adj. & n.,* -rit) *adj.* [< L. *quadrare*, to make square] square or nearly square —*n.* a square or rectangle —*vi.* -rat·ed, -rat·ing to square; agree (*with*)

quad·rat·ic (kwäd rat'ik) *adj. Algebra* involving a quantity or quantities that are squared but none that are raised to a higher power —*n. Algebra* a quadratic term, expression, or equation

quadratic equation *Algebra* an equation in which the second power, or square, is the highest to which the unknown quantity is raised

quad·ra·ture (kwäd'rə chər) *n.* [see QUADRATE] **1.** a squaring **2.** the determining of the dimensions of a square equal in area to a given surface

quad·ren·ni·al (kwäd ren'ē əl) *adj.* [< L. *quadri-* (see QUADRI-) + *annus*, a year] **1.** lasting four years **2.** occurring once every four years —**quad·ren'ni·al·ly** *adv.*

quadri- [L. < *quattuor*, four] *a combining form meaning four times:* also **quadr-**

quad·ri·lat·er·al (kwäd'rə lat'ər əl) *adj.* [see QUADRI- & LATERAL] four-sided —*n.* a plane figure having four sides and four angles

qua·drille (kwə dril', kwä-) *n.* [Fr. < Sp., ult. < L. *quadra*, a square] **1.** a square dance performed by four couples **2.** music for this dance   QUADRILATERALS

quad·ri·va·lent (kwäd'rə vā'lənt, kwä driv'ə-) *adj.* **1.** having four valences **2.** *same as* TETRAVALENT (sense 1)

quad·roon (kwä drōōn') *n.* [< Sp. < L. *quartus*, fourth] a person who has one Negro grandparent

quad·ru·ped (kwäd'rōō ped') *n.* [< L. *quadru-*, four + *pes*, a foot] an animal, esp. a mammal, with four feet —*adj.* having four feet —**quad·ru·pe·dal** (kwä drōō'pi d'l, kwäd'rə ped'l) *adj.*

quad·ru·ple (kwä drōō'p'l, kwäd'rōō-) *adj.* [< L. *quadru-*, four + *-plus*, -fold] **1.** consisting of four **2.** four times as much or as many —*n.* an amount four times as much or as many —*vt., vi.* -pled, -pling to make or become four times as much or as many

quad·ru·plet (kwä drup'lit, -drōō'plit; kwäd'rōō plit) *n.* **1.** any of four offspring born at a single birth **2.** a group of four, usually of one kind

quad·ru·pli·cate (kwä drōō'plə kāt'; *for adj. & n., usually* -kit) *-vt.* -cat·ed, -cat'ing [< L. *quadru-*, four + *plicare*, to fold] to make four identical copies of —*adj.* **1.** fourfold **2.** being the fourth of identical copies —*n.* any of four identical copies —**in quadruplicate** in four identical copies —**quad·ru'pli·ca'tion** *n.*

quaff (kwäf, kwaf) *vt., vi.* [prob. < LowG. *quassen*, overindulge] to drink deeply and heartily —*n.* **1.** a quaffing **2.** a drink that is quaffed

quag·mire (kwag'mīr') *n.* [< *quag*, bog + MIRE] wet, boggy ground

qua·hog, qua·haug (kwô'hôg, kô'-; -häg) *n.* [< AmInd.] a hard-shelled clam of the eastern coast

quail¹ (kwāl) *vi.* [prob. < L. *coagulare*, coagulate] to draw back in fear; lose courage; cower

quail² (kwāl) *n.* [< OFr.] a small game bird that resembles the partridge

quaint (kwānt) *adj.* [< OFr. *cointe* < L. *cognitus*, known] **1.** pleasingly unusual or old-fashioned **2.** unusual; curious **3.** fanciful; whimsical —**quaint'ly** *adv.* —**quaint'ness** *n.*

quake (kwāk) *vi.* quaked, quak'ing [OE. *cwacian*] **1.** to tremble or shake **2.** to shiver, as from fear or cold —*n.* **1.** a quaking **2.** an earthquake

Quak·er (kwāk'ər) *n.* [< founder's admonition to "quake" at the word of the Lord] a member of the SOCIETY OF FRIENDS

qual·i·fi·ca·tion (kwäl'ə fi kā'shən) *n.* **1.** a qualifying or being qualified **2.** a modification or restriction **3.** any skill, etc. that fits one for a job, office, etc.

qual·i·fied (kwäl'ə fīd') *adj.* **1.** having met requirements set **2.** having the necessary qualities; competent **3.** limited; modified

qual'i·fy' (-fī') *vt.* -fied', -fy'ing [< Fr. < L. *qualis*, of what kind + *facere*, make] **1.** to make fit for a job, etc. **2.** to make legally capable **3.** to modify; restrict **4.** to moderate; soften **5.** *Gram.* to modify the meaning of (a word) —*vi.* to be or become qualified —**qual'i·fi'er** *n.*

qual'i·ta'tive (-tāt'iv) *adj.* having to do with quality or qualities —**qual'i·ta'tive·ly** *adv.*

qualitative analysis the branch of chemistry dealing with the determination of the elements or ingredients of which a substance is composed

qual·i·ty (kwäl'ə tē) *n., pl.* -ties [< L. *qualis*, of what kind] **1.** that which makes something what it is; characteristic **2.** basic nature; kind **3.** the degree of excellence of a thing **4.** superiority **5.** the property of a tone determined by its overtones

qualm (kwäm) *n.* [OE. *cwealm*, disaster] **1.** a sudden feeling of sickness, faintness, etc. **2.** a sudden feeling of uneasiness or doubt; misgiving **3.** a twinge of conscience; scruple —**qualm'ish** *adj.*

quan·da·ry (kwän'drē, -dər ē) *n., pl.* -ries [< ? L. *quande*, how much] a state of perplexity; dilemma

quan·ti·ta·tive (kwän'tə tāt'iv) *adj.* having to do with quantity —**quan'ti·ta'tive·ness** *n.*

quantitative analysis the branch of chemistry dealing with the measurement of the amounts of the various components of a substance

quan·ti·ty (kwän'tə tē) *n., pl.* -ties [< L. *quantus*, how much] **1.** an amount; portion **2.** any indeterminate bulk or number **3.** [*also pl.*] a great amount **4.** that property of a thing which can be measured **5.** a number or symbol expressing this property **6.** the relative length of a vowel, syllable, tone, etc.

quan·tum (kwän'təm) *n., pl.* -ta (-tə) [L., how much] *Physics* an elemental unit, as of energy: the **quantum theory** states that energy is absorbed or radiated discontinuously in quanta

quar·an·tine (kwôr'ən tēn', kwär'-) *n.* [< It. < L. *quadraginta*, forty] **1.** the period, orig. 40 days, during which a vessel suspected of carrying contagious disease is detained in a port in isolation **2.** any isolation or restriction on travel to keep contagious diseases, etc. from spreading **3.** a place for such isolation —*vt.* -tined', -tin'ing **1.** to place under quarantine **2.** to isolate politically, etc.

quark (kwôrk) *n.* [arbitrary coinage] any of three hypothetical particles assumed as the basic units of matter

quar·rel (kwôr'əl, kwär'-) *n.* [< L. *queri*, complain] **1.** a cause for dispute **2.** a dispute, esp. an angry one —*vi.* -reled or -relled, -rel·ing or -rel·ling **1.** to complain **2.** to dispute heatedly **3.** to have a breach in friendship —**quar'rel·er, quar'rel·ler** *n.*

quar'rel·some (-səm) *adj.* inclined to quarrel —**quar'rel·some·ly** *adv.* —**quar'rel·some·ness** *n.*

quar·ry¹ (kwôr'ē, kwär'ē) *n., pl.* -ries [< OFr. *curer*, eviscerate] an animal, etc. being hunted down

quar·ry² (kwôr'ē, kwär'ē) *n., pl.* -ries [< L. *quadrare*, to square] a place where stone or slate is excavated —*vt.* -ried, -ry·ing to excavate from a quarry —**quar'ry·man,** *pl.* -men, **quar'ri·er** *n.*

quart (kwôrt) *n.* [< L. *quartus*, fourth] **1.** a liquid measure, equal to 1/4 gallon **2.** a dry measure, equal to 1/8 peck

quar·ter (kwôr'tər) *n.* [< L. *quartus*, fourth] **1.** any of the four equal parts of something; fourth **2.** one fourth of a year **3.** one fourth of an hour **4.** one fourth of a dollar; 25 cents, or a coin of this value **5.** any leg of a four-legged animal, with the adjoining parts **6.** any of the four main points of the compass **7.** a particular district or section **8.** [*pl.*] lodgings **9.** a particular source [news from the highest *quarters*] **10.** the period of time in which the moon makes one fourth of its revolution around the earth **11.** the after part of a ship's side **12.** mercy granted to a surrendering foe **13.** *Football*, etc. any of the four periods into which a game is divided —*vt.* **1.** to divide into four equal parts **2.** to provide lodgings for —*vi.* to be lodged or stationed (*at* or *with*) —*adj.* constituting or equal to a quarter —**at close quarters** at close range

quar'ter·back' *n. Football* the back who calls the signals and directs the plays —*vt., vi.* **1.** to act as quarterback for **2.** to direct or lead

quar'ter-deck', quar'ter·deck' *n.* the after part of the upper deck of a ship, usually for officers

quar'ter·ly *adj.* occurring regularly four times a year —*adv.* once every quarter of the year —*n., pl.* -lies a publication issued every three months

quar'ter·mas'ter *n.* **1.** *Mil.* an officer who provides troops with quarters, clothing, equipment, etc. **2.** *Naut.* a petty officer or mate who attends to navigation, signals, etc.

quarter note *Music* a note (♩) having one fourth the duration of a whole note

quarter section a 160-acre tract of land

quar·tet, quar·tette (kwôr tet′) *n.* [< Fr. < L. *quartus,* a fourth] **1.** a group of four **2.** *Music a)* a composition for four voices or instruments *b)* the four performers of this

quar·to (kwôr′tō) *n., pl.* **-tos** [< L. (*in*) *quarto,* (in) a fourth] **1.** the page size (about 9 by 12 in.) of a book made up of sheets folded into four leaves **2.** a book with pages of this size

quartz (kwôrts) *n.* [G. *quarz*] a crystalline mineral, silicon dioxide, SiO_2, usually colorless and transparent

qua·sar (kwā′sär, -sər) *n.* [< *quas*(*i-stell*)*ar* (*radio source*)] any of a number of extremely distant starlike objects that emit powerful radio waves

quash[1] (kwäsh) *vt.* [< L. *cassus,* empty] *Law* to annul or set aside (an indictment)

quash[2] (kwäsh) *vt.* [< L. *quatere,* to break] to put down; suppress [to *quash* an uprising]

qua·si (kwā′sī, -zī; kwä′sē, -zē) *adv.* [L. < *quam,* as + *si,* if] as if; seemingly —*adj.* seeming Often hyphenated as a prefix [*quasi*-judicial]

qua·ter·na·ry (kwät′ər ner′ē, kwə tur′nər ē) *adj.* [< L. *quaterni,* four each] consisting of four

quat·rain (kwä′trān) *n.* [Fr. < L. *quattuor,* four] a stanza or poem of four lines

quat·re·foil (kat′ər foil′, kat′rə-) *n.* [< L. *quattuor,* four + *folium,* leaf] **1.** a flower with four petals or a leaf with four leaflets **2.** *Archit.* a circular design of four converging arcs

qua·ver (kwā′vər) *vi.* [ME. *cwafien*] **1.** to shake or tremble **2.** to be tremulous: said of the voice **3.** to make a trill in singing or playing —*vt.* **1.** to utter in a tremulous voice **2.** to sing or play with a trill —*n.* a tremulous quality in a voice or tone —**qua′ver·y** *adj.*

quay (kē) *n.* [MFr. *cai* < Celt.] a wharf, usually of stone or concrete

quean (kwēn) *n.* [OE. *cwene*] **1.** a hussy **2.** a prostitute

quea·sy (kwē′zē) *adj.* **-si·er, -si·est** [< Scand.] **1.** causing or feeling nausea **2.** squeamish; easily nauseated **3.** uncomfortable; uneasy —**quea′si·ly** *adv.* —**quea′si·ness** *n.*

Que·bec (kwi bek′) **1.** province of E Canada: 594,860 sq. mi.; pop. 5,781,000; abbrev. **Que. 2.** its capital, on the St. Lawrence River: pop. 167,000 (met. area 413,000)

Que·bec·ois (ke′be kwä′) *n., pl.* **-ois′** [< CanadFr.] a French-speaking native or inhabitant of Quebec (sense 1)

queen (kwēn) *n.* [OE. *cwen*] **1.** the wife of a king **2.** a woman monarch in her own right **3.** a woman noted for her beauty or accomplishments **4.** a place or thing regarded as the finest of its kind **5.** the fully developed, reproductive female in a colony of bees, ants, etc. **6.** a playing card with a picture of a queen on it **7.** [Slang] a male homosexual **8.** *Chess* the most powerful piece —**queen′ly** *adj.*

Queen Anne's lace a weed with finely divided foliage and umbels of white flowers

queen mother the widow of a king, who is mother of a reigning sovereign

Queens (kwēnz) borough of New York City: pop. 1,987,000

queer (kwir) *adj.* [N. Eng. & Scot. dial. < ? G. *quer,* crosswise] **1.** differing from what is usual; odd; strange **2.** slightly ill **3.** [Colloq.] suspicious **4.** [Colloq.] eccentric —*vt.* [Slang] to spoil the success of —*n.* [Slang] **1.** an eccentric person **2.** a homosexual —**queer′ly** *adv.* —**queer′ness** *n.*

quell (kwel) *vt.* [OE. *cwellan,* kill] **1.** to crush; subdue **2.** to quiet; allay

quench (kwench) *vt.* [OE. *cwencan*] **1.** to extinguish [water *quenched* the fire] **2.** to satisfy [he *quenched* his thirst] **3.** to cool (hot steel, etc.) suddenly by plunging into water, etc. —**quench′less** *adj.*

quer·u·lous (kwer′ə ləs, -yə-) *adj.* [< L. *queri,* complain] **1.** inclined to find fault; complaining **2.** full of complaint; peevish —**quer′u·lous·ly** *adv.* —**quer′u·lous·ness** *n.*

que·ry (kwir′ē) *n., pl.* **-ries** [< L. *quaerere,* ask] **1.** a question; inquiry **2.** a question mark (?) —*vt., vi.* **-ried, -ry·ing** to question

quest (kwest) *n.* [< L. *quaerere,* seek] **1.** a seeking; hunt **2.** a journey in search of adventure, etc., as those undertaken by medieval knights-errant —*vi.* to go in search or pursuit —*vt.* to seek

ques·tion (kwes′chən) *n.* [< L. *quaerere,* ask] **1.** an asking; inquiry **2.** something asked; interrogative sentence **3.** doubt; uncertainty **4.** a matter open to discussion **5.** a matter of difficulty [not a *question* of money] **6.** a point being debated, as before an assembly —*vt.* **1.** to ask questions of **2.** to express uncertainty about; doubt **3.** to dispute; challenge —*vi.* to ask questions —**beside the question** not relevant —**beyond (all) question** without any doubt —**in question** being considered —**out of the question** impossible —**ques′tion·er** *n.* —**ques′tion·ing** *adj.*

ques′tion·a·ble *adj.* **1.** that can or should be questioned **2.** suspected with good reason of being immoral, dishonest, etc. **3.** uncertain —**ques′tion·a·bly** *adv.*

question mark 1. a mark of punctuation (?) put after a sentence or word to indicate a direct question, or to express doubt, uncertainty, etc. **2.** an unknown factor

ques′tion·naire′ (-chə ner′) *n.* [Fr.] a written or printed list of questions used in gathering information from persons

quet·zal (ket säl′) *n.* [AmSp. < native Ind. *quetzalli,* tail feather] a Central American bird, usually brilliant green above and red below

queue (kyōō) *n.* [Fr. < L. *cauda,* tail] **1.** a pigtail **2.** [Chiefly Brit.] a line, as of persons waiting to be served —*vi.* **queued, queu′ing** [Chiefly Brit.] to form in a line (often with *up*)

quib·ble (kwib′'l) *n.* [< L. *qui,* who] **1.** a petty evasion; cavil **2.** a petty objection or criticism —*vi.* **-bled, -bling** to evade the truth of a point under discussion by caviling —**quib′bler** *n.*

quick (kwik) *adj.* [OE. *cwicu,* living] **1.** [Archaic] living **2.** *a)* rapid; swift [a *quick* walk] *b)* prompt [a *quick* reply] **3.** prompt to understand or learn **4.** easily stirred [a *quick* temper] —*adv.* quickly; rapidly —*n.* **1.** the living, esp. in **the quick and the dead 2.** the sensitive flesh under the nails **3.** the deepest feelings [cut to the *quick*] —**quick′ly** *adv.* —**quick′ness** *n.*

quick bread any bread, as corn bread, leavened with baking powder, soda, etc. and baked as soon as the batter or dough is mixed

quick′en *vt., vi.* **1.** to animate; revive **2.** to move more rapidly; hasten **3.** to show signs of life, as a fetus

quick′-freeze′ *vt.* **-froze′, -fro′zen, -freez′ing** to subject (food) to sudden freezing for long storage at low temperatures

quick′ie (-ē) *n.* [Slang] anything done or made quickly —*adj.* done or made quickly

quick′lime′ (-līm′) *n.* unslaked lime

quick′sand′ *n.* [< ME.: see QUICK & SAND] a deep deposit of loose, wet sand, easily engulfing heavy objects

quick′sil′ver *n.* the metal mercury

quick′-tem′pered *adj.* easily angered

quick time the normal rate of marching: in the U.S. Army, 120 (30-inch) paces a minute

quick′-wit′ted *adj.* nimble of mind —**quick′-wit′ted·ly** *adv.* —**quick′-wit′ted·ness** *n.*

quid[1] (kwid) *n.* [var. of *cud*] a piece, as of tobacco, to be chewed

quid[2] (kwid) *n., pl.* **quid** [Brit. Slang] a sovereign, or one pound sterling

quid pro quo (kwid′ prō kwō′) [L.] **1.** one thing in return for another **2.** a substitute

qui·es·cent (kwī es′'nt) *adj.* [< L. *quiescere,* become quiet] quiet; still; inactive —**qui·es′cence** *n.* —**qui·es′cent·ly** *adv.*

qui·et (kwī′ət) *adj.* [< L. *quies,* rest] **1.** still; calm; motionless **2.** *a)* not noisy; hushed *b)* not speaking; silent **3.** gentle **4.** not easily excited **5.** not bright or showy **6.** unobtrusive **7.** peaceful; relaxing [a *quiet* evening] **8.** *Commerce* not busy —*n.* **1.** a quiet state; calmness, stillness, etc. **2.** a quiet or peaceful quality —*vt., vi.* to make or become quiet —**qui′et·ly** *adv.* —**qui′et·ness** *n.*

qui·e·tude (kwī′ə tōōd′, -tyōōd′) *n.* a state of being quiet; rest; calmness

qui·e·tus (kwī ēt′əs) *n.* [< ML. *quietus* (*est*), (he is) quit] **1.** discharge from debt, etc. **2.** release from life; death

quill (kwil) *n.* [prob. < MLowG. or MDu.] **1.** any of the large, stiff wing or tail feathers of a bird **2.** *a)* the hollow stem of a feather *b)* anything made from this, as a pen **3.** any of the spines of a porcupine or hedgehog

quilt (kwilt) *n.* [< L. *culcita,* a bed] a cover for a bed, filled with down, wool, etc. and stitched together in lines or patterns —*vt.* to stitch as or like a quilt —*vi.* to make a quilt —**quilt′er** *n.*

quilt′ing *n.* **1.** the act of making quilts **2.** material for quilts **3.** *same as* QUILTING BEE

quilting bee (or **party**) a social gathering of women at which they work together sewing quilts

quince (kwins) *n.* [< Gr. *kydōnion*] **1.** a yellowish, hard, apple-shaped fruit used in preserves **2.** the tree that bears this fruit

qui·nine (kwī'nīn) *n.* [< *quina*, cinchona bark] a bitter, crystalline substance extracted from cinchona bark, used esp. for treating malaria

quinine water *same as* TONIC (*n.* 2)

quin·sy (kwin'zē) *n.* [< Gr. *kyōn*, dog + *anchein*, to choke] *an earlier term for* TONSILLITIS

quint (kwint) *n. shortened form of* QUINTUPLET

quin·tes·sence (kwin tes''ns) *n.* [< ML. *quinta essentia*, fifth essence, or ultimate substance] **1.** the essence of something in its purest form **2.** the perfect type or example of something —**quin·tes·sen·tial** (-tə sen'shəl) *adj.*

quin·tet, quin·tette (kwin tet') *n.* [< L. *quintus*, a fifth] **1.** any group of five **2.** *Music* a) a composition for five voices or five instruments b) the five performers of such a composition

quin·tu·ple (kwin tōō'p'l, -tyōō'-) *adj.* [< L. *quintus*, a fifth + -*plex*, -fold] **1.** consisting of five **2.** five times as much or as many —*n.* an amount five times as much or as many —*vt., vi.* -**pled**, -**pling** to make or become five times as much or as many

quin·tu·plet (kwin tup'lit, -tōō'plit) *n.* [dim. of prec.] **1.** any of five offspring born at a single birth **2.** a group of five, usually of one kind

quip (kwip) *n.* [< L. *quippe*, indeed] a witty or sarcastic remark; jest —*vi.* **quipped, quip'ping** to utter quips — **quip'ster** *n.*

quire (kwīr) *n.* [< L. *quaterni*, four each] a set of 24 or 25 sheets of the same paper: see REAM¹

quirk (kwurk) *n.* [< ?] **1.** a sudden twist, turn, etc. [a *quirk* of fate] **2.** a flourish in writing **3.** a peculiar trait or mannerism

quirt (kwurt) *n.* [AmSp. *cuarta*] a riding whip with a braided leather lash and a short handle

quis·ling (kwiz'liŋ) *n.* [< V. *Quisling*, Norw. collaborationist with the Nazis] a traitor

quit (kwit) *vt.* **quit** or **quit'ted, quit'ting** [< ML. *quietus*, free] **1.** to free (oneself) of **2.** to discharge (a debt); repay **3.** to give up **4.** to leave; depart from **5.** to stop, discontinue, or resign from —*vi.* **1.** to stop doing something **2.** to give up one's job; resign —*adj.* clear, free, or rid

quit·claim (kwit'klām') *n.* a deed relinquishing a claim to property or some right

quite (kwīt) *adv.* [< QUIT, *adj.*] **1.** completely; entirely **2.** really; truly **3.** to a considerable degree —**quite a few** (or **bit**, etc.) [Colloq.] more than a few (or bit, etc.)

Qui·to (kē'tō) capital of Ecuador: pop. 463,000

quits (kwits) *adj.* [see QUIETUS] on even terms, as by paying a debt, retaliating, etc. —**call it quits** [Colloq.] **1.** to stop working, etc. **2.** to stop being friendly

quit·tance (kwit''ns) *n.* [see QUIT] **1.** *a)* payment of a debt or obligation *b)* a document certifying this **2.** recompense; repayment

quit'ter *n.* [Colloq.] one who quits or gives up easily, without trying hard

quiv·er¹ (kwiv'ər) *vi.* [see QUICK] to shake tremulously; tremble —*n.* a quivering; tremor

quiv·er² (kwiv'ər) *n.* [OFr. *coivre* < Gmc.] **1.** a case for holding arrows **2.** the arrows in it

Quixote, Don *see* DON QUIXOTE

quix·ot·ic (kwik sät'ik) *adj.* [< DON QUIXOTE] extravagantly chivalrous or romantically idealistic; impractical: also **quix·ot'i·cal** —**quix·ot'i·cal·ly** *adv.* —**quix'ot·ism** (-sə tiz'm) *n.*

quiz (kwiz) *n., pl.* **quiz'zes** [prob. < L. *quis*, what?] a questioning; esp., a short examination to test one's knowledge —*vt.* **quizzed, quiz'zing** to ask questions of, as in interrogating

quiz program (or **show**) a radio or TV program in which a group of people compete in answering questions

quiz·zi·cal (kwiz'i k'l) *adj.* **1.** odd; comical **2.** teasing **3.** perplexed —**quiz'zi·cal·ly** *adv.*

quoin (koin, kwoin) *n.* [var. of COIN] **1.** the external corner of a building; esp., any of the stones forming the corner **2.** a wedge-shaped block

quoit (kwoit; *chiefly Brit.* koit) *n.* [prob. < OFr. *coite*, a cushion] **1.** a ring thrown, in a game, to encircle an upright peg **2.** [*pl.*, *with sing. v.*] this game

quon·dam (kwän'dəm) *adj.* [L.] former [a *quondam* pacifist]

Quon·set hut (kwän'sit) [< *Quonset* Point, R.I., where first made] a *trademark for* a prefabricated, metal shelter like a half cylinder on its flat side

QUOINS

quo·rum (kwôr'əm) *n.* [< L. *qui*, who] the minimum number of members who must be present at an assembly before it can validly transact business

quo·ta (kwōt'ə) *n.* [< L. *quota pars*, how large a part] **1.** a share which each of a number is to contribute or receive **2.** the number or proportion that is allowed

quo·ta·tion (kwō tā'shən) *n.* **1.** a quoting **2.** the words or passage quoted **3.** *Commerce* the current quoted price of a stock, bond, etc.

quotation mark either of a pair of punctuation marks ("...") used to enclose a direct quotation, or of single marks ('...') for enclosing a quotation within a quotation

quote (kwōt) *vt.* **quot'ed, quot'ing** [< ML. *quotare*, to number (chapters)] **1.** to repeat a passage from or statement of **2.** to repeat (a passage, statement, etc.) **3.** to cite as an example or authority **4.** to state (the price of something) —*n.* [Colloq.] *same as:* **1.** QUOTATION **2.** QUOTATION MARK —*interj.* I shall quote: used in speech before a quotation —**quot'a·ble** *adj.*

quoth (kwōth) *vt.* [< OE. *cwethan*, speak] [Archaic] said

quo·tid·i·an (kwō tid'ē ən) *adj.* [< L. *quotidie*] **1.** daily **2.** ordinary —*n.* anything, esp. a fever, that recurs daily

quo·tient (kwō'shənt) *n.* [< L. *quot*, how many] the result obtained when one number is divided by another

q.v. [L. *quod vide*] which see

R

R, r (är) *n., pl.* **R's, r's** the eighteenth letter of the English alphabet

R 1. *Elec.* resistance **2.** restricted: a motion-picture rating meaning that no one under the age of seventeen will be admitted unless accompanied by a parent or guardian — **the three R's** reading, writing, and arithmetic, regarded as the basic studies

r *Math.* radius

R. Republic(an)

R., r. 1. [L. *Rex*] king **2.** [L. *Regina*] queen **3.** radius **4.** railroad **5.** right **6.** river **7.** road **8.** *Baseball* runs

Ra' (rä) the sun god and chief god of the ancient Egyptians

Ra² *Chem.* radium

Ra·bat (rä bät', rə-) capital of Morocco: pop. 435,000

rab·bet (rab'it) *n.* [< OFr. *rabattre*, beat down] a cut made in the edge of a board, etc. so that another piece may be fitted into it to form a joint (**rabbet joint**) —*vt.* **1.** to cut a rabbet in **2.** to join by means of a rabbet —*vi.* to be joined by a rabbet

rab·bi (rab'ī) *n., pl.* -**bis, -bies** [< Heb. *rabbī*, my master] a teacher of the Jewish law, now usually the ordained spiritual head of a congregation —**rab'bin·ate** (-i nit, -i nāt') *n.*

rab·bin·i·cal (rə bin'i k'l) *adj.* of the rabbis, their doctrines, learning, language, etc.: also **rab·bin'ic** —**rab·bin'i·cal·ly** *adv.*

rab·bit (rab'it) *n.* [ME. *rabette*] **1.** a burrowing mammal that is usually smaller than the hare, having soft fur and long ears **2.** its fur

---

fat, āpe, cär; ten, ēven; is, bīte; gō, hôrn, tōōl, lo͝ok; oil, out; up, fur; thin, *then*; zh, leisure; ŋ, ring; ə for *a* in *ago*; ' as in *able* (ā'b'l); ë, Fr. coeur; ö, Fr. feu; Fr. mon; ü, Fr. duc; r, Fr. cri; kh, G. doch, ich. ‡ foreign; < derived from

rabbit ears [Colloq.] an indoor TV antenna with two rods that swivel apart in a V shape

rabbit fever *same as* TULAREMIA

rabbit punch *Boxing* a sharp blow to the back of the neck

rab·ble (rab′l) *n.* [< ME. < ?] a noisy, disorderly crowd; mob —**the rabble** the common people: a term of contempt

rab′ble-rous′er (-rouz′ər) *n.* one who tries to arouse people to violent action by appeals to emotions, prejudices, etc.

Rab·e·lais (rab′ə lā′), **Fran·çois** (frän swä′) 1495?–1553; Fr. satirist & humorist —**Rab·e·lai·si·an** (rab′ə lā′zhən, -zē ən) *adj., n.*

rab·id (rab′id) *adj.* [< L. *rabere*, to rage] **1.** violent; raging **2.** fanatical **3.** of or having rabies —**rab′id·ly** *adv.*

ra·bies (rā′bēz) *n.* [L., madness] an infectious virus disease of mammals, passed on to man by the bite of an infected animal: it causes choking, convulsions, etc.

rac·coon (ra kōōn′) *n.* [< AmInd. *äräkun*, lit., scratcher] **1.** a small, tree-climbing mammal of N. America, having yellowish-gray fur and a black-ringed tail **2.** its fur

race¹ (rās) *n.* [< ON. *rās*, a running] **1.** a competition of speed in running, riding, etc. **2.** any contest likened to a race *[the race for mayor]* **3.** a swift current of water, or its channel —*vi.* **raced, rac′ing 1.** to take part in a race **2.** to go or move fast or too fast —*vt.* **1.** to compete with in a race **2.** to enter (a horse, etc.) in a race **3.** to make go fast or too fast **4.** to run (an engine) at high speed with the gears disengaged —**rac′er** *n.*

race² (rās) *n.* [Fr. < It. *razza*] **1.** any of the different varieties of mankind, mainly the Caucasoid, Mongoloid, and Negroid groups, distinguished by kind of hair, color of skin, etc. **2.** any geographical, national, or tribal ethnic grouping **3.** any group of people having the same ancestry or the same habits, ideas, etc. **4.** *same as* BREED (*n.* 1)

race′horse′ *n.* a horse bred and trained for racing

ra·ceme (rā sēm′, rə-) *n.* [L. *racemus*, cluster of grapes] a flower cluster with individual flowers growing on small stems at intervals along one central stem

race riot violence and fighting in a community, brought on by racial hostility

race track a course prepared for racing

race′way′ *n.* **1.** a narrow channel **2.** a race track for harness races or one for drag races, etc.

Ra·chel (rā′chəl) *Bible* the younger of the two wives of Jacob

ra·chi·tis (rə kīt′əs) *n.* [< Gr. *rhachis*, spine] *same as* RICKETS —**ra·chit′ic** (-kit′ik) *adj.*

RACEME

Rach·ma·ni·noff (räk mä′ni nôf′), **Ser·gei** (syer gyā′) 1873–1943; Russ. composer

ra·cial (rā′shəl) *adj.* **1.** of a race, or ethnic group **2.** of or between races —**ra′cial·ly** *adv.*

ra′cial·ism (-iz′m) *n.* **1.** a doctrine, without scientific support, that claims the superiority of some one race **2.** *same as* RACISM (sense 2)

Ra·cine (rə sēn′), **Jean** (zhän) 1639–99; Fr. poet & dramatist

rac·ism (rā′siz′m) *n.* **1.** *same as* RACIALISM (sense 1) **2.** the practice of racial discrimination, segregation, etc., based on racialism —**rac′ist** *n., adj.*

rack¹ (rak) *n.* [prob. < MDu. *recken*, to stretch] **1.** a framework, stand, etc. for holding things *[clothes rack]* **2.** a device for lifting an automobile for repairs from below **3.** a toothed bar that meshes with a cogwheel, etc. **4.** an instrument of torture which stretches the victim's limbs **5.** any great torment —*vt.* **1.** to torture on a rack **2.** to torment —**on the rack** in a painful situation —**rack one's brains** (or **memory**) to try hard to think of something —**rack up** [Slang] to score or achieve

rack² (rak) *n., vi.* [< ?] *same as* SINGLE-FOOT

rack³ (rak) *n.* [var. of WRACK] destruction: now only in **go to rack and ruin,** to become ruined

rack·et¹ (rak′it) *n.* [prob. echoic] **1.** a noisy confusion **2.** *a)* an obtaining of money illegally *b)* [Colloq.] any dishonest scheme

rack·et² (rak′it) *n.* [< MFr. < Ar. *rāhah,* palm of the hand] **1.** a light bat for tennis, etc., with a network of catgut, nylon, etc. in an oval or round frame attached to a handle **2.** [*pl., with sing. v.*] the game of racquets

rack·et·eer (rak′ə tir′) *n.* one who gets money illegally, as by fraud, blackmail, or, esp., extortion —*vi.* to get money thus —**rack′et·eer′ing** *n.*

rac·on·teur (rak′än tur′) *n.* [Fr. < *raconter*, to recount] a person skilled at telling stories or anecdotes

ra·coon (ra kōōn′) *n. same as* RACCOON

rac·quet (rak′it) *n.* **1.** *same as* RACKET² **2.** [*pl., with sing. v.*] a game like tennis, played in a walled court

rac′quet·ball′ *n.* a game similar to handball, but played with a short-handled racket

rac·y (rā′sē) *adj.* **-i·er, -i·est** [< RACE²] **1.** having the taste or quality required to be genuine *[racy fruit]* **2.** lively; spirited **3.** pungent **4.** risqué —**rac′i·ly** *adv.* —**rac′i·ness** *n.*

ra·dar (rā′där) *n.* [*ra(dio) d(etecting) a(nd) r(anging)*] a system or device that transmits radio waves to a reflecting object, as an aircraft, to determine its location, speed, etc. by the reflected waves

ra′dar·scope′ (-skōp′) *n.* an instrument that displays on a screen the reflected radio waves picked up by radar

ra·di·al (rā′dē əl) *adj.* [see RADIUS] **1.** of or like a ray or rays; branching out from a center **2.** of a radius —**ra′di·al·ly** *adv.*

radial (ply) tire an automobile tire with ply cords nearly at right angles to the center line of the tread

ra·di·ant (rā′dē ənt) *adj.* [see RADIUS] **1.** shining brightly **2.** showing joy, love, etc. **3.** issuing (from a source) in or as in rays —**ra′di·ance** *n.* —**ra′di·ant·ly** *adv.*

radiant energy energy traveling in waves, as heat, light, X-rays, etc.

ra·di·ate (rā′dē āt′) *vi.* **-at′ed, -at′ing** [see RADIUS] **1.** to send out rays of heat, light, etc. **2.** to branch out in lines from a center —*vt.* **1.** to send out (heat, light, etc.) in rays **2.** to give forth (happiness, love, etc.) —*adj.* having rays

ra′di·a′tion *n.* **1.** a radiating; specif., the process in which radiant energy is sent out from atoms and molecules as they undergo internal change **2.** such radiant energy **3.** nuclear particles

radiation sickness sickness produced by overexposure to radiation from X-rays, nuclear explosions, etc. and resulting in nausea, bleeding, etc.

ra′di·a′tor *n.* an apparatus for radiating heat, as into a room or from an automobile engine

rad·i·cal (rad′i k′l) *adj.* [< L. *radix,* a root] **1.** of or from the root; fundamental **2.** favoring basic or extreme change, as in the social structure —*n.* **1.** a person having radical views **2.** *Chem.* a group of two or more atoms acting as a single atom **3.** *Math.* the sign ($\sqrt{\ }$) used with a quantity to show that its root is to be extracted: also **radical sign** —**rad′i·cal·ism** *n.* —**rad′i·cal·ly** *adv.*

rad′i·cal·ize′ (-īz′) *vt., vi.* **-ized′, -iz′ing** to make or become politically radical

ra·di·i (rā′dē ī′) *n. pl. of* RADIUS

ra·di·o (rā′dē ō′) *n., pl.* **-os′** [ult. < L. *radius:* see RADIUS] **1.** the transmission of sounds or signals by electromagnetic waves through space, without wires, to a receiving set **2.** such a set **3.** broadcasting by radio as an industry, entertainment, etc. —*adj.* of, using, used in, or sent by radio —*vt., vi.* **-oed′, -o′ing** to transmit, or communicate with, by radio

radio- [Fr. < L.: see RADIUS] *a combining form meaning:* **1.** ray, raylike **2.** by radio **3.** by means of radiant energy *[radiotherapy]*

ra·di·o·ac·tive (rā′dē ō ak′tiv) *adj.* giving off radiant energy in particles or rays by the disintegration of atomic nuclei —**ra′di·o·ac′tive·ly** *adv.* —**ra′di·o·ac·tiv′i·ty** *n.*

radio astronomy astronomy dealing with radio waves in space in order to get data about the universe

radio beacon a radio transmitter that gives off special signals to help ships or aircraft determine their positions or come in safely, as in a fog

ra′di·o·broad′cast′ *n., vt., vi.* **-cast′** or **-cast′ed, -cast′-ing** broadcast by radio

radio frequency any frequency between normally audible sound waves and infrared light

ra′di·o·gram′ (-gram′) *n.* a message sent by radio

ra′di·o·i′so·tope′ *n.* a natural or artificial radioactive isotope of a chemical element

ra′di·ol′o·gy (-äl′ə jē) *n.* the science dealing with X-rays and other radiant energy, esp. as used in medicine and radiotherapy —**ra′di·ol′o·gist** *n.*

ra′di·os′co·py (-äs′kə pē) *n.* the examination of the inside structure of opaque objects, as by means of X-rays —**ra′di·o·scop′ic** (-ə skäp′ik) *adj.*

ra′di·o·sonde′ (-sänd′) *n.* [Fr. < RADIO + *sonde,* sounding line] a compact radio transmitter with meteorological instruments, sent into the upper atmosphere, as by balloon, to radio back data about temperature, humidity, etc.

ra′di·o·tel′e·graph′ *n. same as* WIRELESS TELEGRAPHY: also **ra′di·o·te·leg′ra·phy** (-tə leg′rə fē) —*vt., vi.* to send (a message) by radiotelegraph

ra′di·o·ther′a·py *n.* the treatment of disease by X-rays or by rays from a radioactive substance

rad·ish (rad′ish) *n.* [< L. *radix,* a root] **1.** a plant of the mustard family, with an edible root **2.** the pungent root, eaten raw

ra·di·um (rā′dē əm) *n.* [< L. *radius,* a ray] a radioactive metallic chemical element, found in uranium minerals, which undergoes spontaneous atomic disintegration: symbol, Ra; at. wt., 226.00; at. no., 88

radium therapy the treatment of cancer or other diseases by the use of radium

ra·di·us (rā′dē əs) *n., pl.* **-di·i** (-ī′), **-us·es** [L., spoke (of a wheel), hence ray] **1.** *a)* a straight line from the center to the periphery of a circle or sphere *b)* its length **2.** the circular area or distance within the sweep of such a line [within a *radius* of five miles] **3.** the shorter of the two bones of the forearm, on the thumb side

ra·don (rā′dän) *n.* [RAD(IUM) + *-on,* as in *neon*] a radioactive gaseous chemical element formed in the atomic disintegration of radium: symbol, Rn; at. wt., 222.00; at. no., 86

RAF, R.A.F. Royal Air Force

raf·fi·a (raf′ē ə) *n.* [< native name] **1.** a palm tree of Madagascar, with large leaves **2.** fiber from its leaves, used for weaving

raff·ish (raf′ish) *adj.* [(RIFF)RAFF + -ISH] **1.** disreputable, rakish, etc. **2.** tawdry; vulgar

raf·fle (raf′'l) *n.* [MFr. *rafle,* dice game] a lottery in which a chance or chances to win a prize are bought —*vt.* **-fled, -fling** to offer as a prize in a raffle (often with *off*)

raft[1] (raft) *n.* [< ON. *raptr,* a log] **1.** a floating structure of logs, boards, etc. fastened together **2.** an inflatable boat or pad

raft[2] (raft) *n.* [< Brit. dial. *raff,* rubbish] [Colloq.] a large number or quantity

raft·er (raf′tər) *n.* [OE. *ræfter*] any of the beams that slope from the ridge of a roof to the eaves and support the roof

rag[1] (rag) *n.* [ult. < ON. *rögg,* tuft of hair] **1.** a waste piece of cloth, esp. an old or torn one **2.** a small cloth for dusting, washing, etc. **3.** anything having as little value as a rag **4.** [*pl.*] *a)* old, worn clothes *b)* any clothes: humorous term —*adj.* made of rags —**chew the rag** [Slang] to chat

rag[2] (rag) *vt.* **ragged, rag′ging** [< ?] [Slang] **1.** to tease **2.** to scold

rag[3] (rag) *n.* **1.** *clipped form of* RAGTIME **2.** a composition in ragtime

ra·ga (rä′gə) *n.* [Sans. *rāga,* lit., color] any of various traditional melodies used in improvising by Hindu musicians

rag·a·muf·fin (rag′ə muf′in) *n.* [ME. *Ragamoffyn,* name of a demon] a dirty, ragged person, esp. such a child

rage (rāj) *n.* [< L. *rabies,* madness] **1.** furious, uncontrolled anger **2.** violence or intensity —*vi.* **raged, rag′ing 1.** to show violent anger, as in speech **2.** to be violent, uncontrolled, etc. **3.** to spread unchecked, as a disease — **(all) the rage** a fad or craze

rag·ged (rag′id) *adj.* **1.** shabby or torn from wear **2.** wearing shabby or torn clothes **3.** uneven; rough **4.** shaggy [*ragged* hair] —**rag′ged·ly** *adv.*

rag′ged·y (-ē) *adj.* somewhat ragged

rag·lan (rag′lən) *n.* [< Lord *Raglan,* 19th-c. Brit. general] a loose coat with each sleeve (**raglan sleeve**) continuing in one piece to the collar

ra·gout (ra gōō′) *n.* [< Fr. *ragoûter,* revive the appetite of] a highly seasoned stew of meat and vegetables

rag·time (rag′tīm′) *n.* [prob. < *ragged time*] **1.** a type of strongly syncopated American music in fast, even time, popular 1890–1915 **2.** its rhythm

rag′weed′ *n.* [< the tattered appearance of the leaves] a weed whose pollen is a major cause of hay fever

rah (rä) *interj.* hurrah: used as a cheer

raid (rād) *n.* [< ROAD, in obs. sense "a riding"] **1.** *a)* a sudden, hostile attack, as by troops, aircraft, bandits, etc. *b)* any act of entering to remove something [a *raid* on the refrigerator] **2.** a sudden invasion of a place by police, to discover violations of the law **3.** an attempt to lure employees from a competitor —*vt., vi.* to make a raid (on) — **raid′er** *n.*

rail[1] (rāl) *n.* [< L. *regula,* a rule] **1.** a bar of wood, metal, etc. placed horizontally between posts as a barrier or support

RAGLAN
SLEEVE

port **2.** any of the parallel metal bars forming a track, as for railroad cars **3.** a railroad as a means of transportation —*vt.* to supply with rails or a railing

rail[2] (rāl) *vi.* [ult. < LL. *ragere,* to bellow] to complain violently (with *against* or *at*)

rail[3] (rāl) *n.* [< MFr. *raaler,* to screech] a small wading bird living in marshes, with a harsh cry

rail′ing *n.* **1.** material for rails **2.** rails collectively **3.** a fence or balustrade

rail·ler·y (rāl′ər ē) *n., pl.* **-ies** [see RAIL[2]] **1.** light ridicule; banter **2.** a teasing remark

rail′road′ *n.* **1.** a road laid with parallel steel rails along which locomotives draw cars in a train **2.** a complete system of such roads, including land, rolling stock, etc. **3.** the corporation owning such a system —*vt.* **1.** to transport by railroad **2.** [Colloq.] to rush through quickly, so as to prevent careful consideration **3.** [Slang] to cause to go to prison on a trumped-up charge or after a hasty trial —*vi.* to work on a railroad —**rail′road′er** *n.* —**rail′road′ing** *n.*

rail′way′ *n.* **1.** [Brit.] a railroad **2.** any track with rails for guiding wheels

rai·ment (rā′mənt) *n.* [see ARRAY & -MENT] [Archaic] clothing

rain (rān) *n.* [OE. *regn*] **1.** water falling in drops condensed from the moisture in the atmosphere **2.** the falling of such drops **3.** a rapid falling of many small objects [a *rain* of ashes] —*vi.* **1.** to fall: said of rain [it is *raining*] **2.** to fall like rain —*vt.* **1.** to pour down (rain, etc.) **2.** to give in large quantities —**rain out** to cause (an event) to be canceled because of rain

rain′bow′ (-bō′) *n.* an arc containing the colors of the spectrum in bands, formed in the sky by the refraction of the sun's rays in falling rain or mist —*adj.* of many colors

rain check 1. the stub of a ticket to a ball game, etc., entitling the holder to future admission if the original event is rained out **2.** an offer of a future invitation in place of one turned down

rain′coat′ *n.* a waterproof or water-repellent coat for giving protection from rain

rain′drop′ *n.* a single drop of rain

rain′fall′ *n.* **1.** a falling of rain **2.** the amount of water falling as rain, snow, etc. over a given area during a given time: measured in inches of depth

rain forest a dense, evergreen forest in a tropical region having abundant rainfall

Rai·nier (rā nir′, rā′nir), **Mount** mountain in the State of Washington: 14,410 ft.

rain′proof′ *adj.* not letting rain through —*vt.* to make rainproof

rain′storm′ *n.* a storm with a heavy rain

rain′wa′ter *n.* water that is falling or has fallen as rain

rain′y *adj.* **-i·er, -i·est 1.** that has rain or much rain [the *rainy* season] **2.** wet with rain **3.** bringing rain —**rain′i·ness** *n.*

rainy day a possible future time of need

raise (rāz) *vt.* **raised, rais′ing** [< ON. *reisa*] **1.** to make rise; lift **2.** to construct (a building, etc.) **3.** to stir up [to *raise* a revolt] **4.** to increase in amount, height, degree, intensity, etc. [*raise* prices, *raise* one's voice] **5.** to improve the rank of [to *raise* oneself from poverty] **6.** to cause to arise, appear, etc.; esp., to bring back as from death **7.** to produce; provoke **8.** to present for consideration [to *raise* a question] **9.** to collect (an army, money, etc.) **10.** to utter (a cry, etc.) **11.** to end (a siege) **12.** to leaven (bread, etc.) **13.** *a)* to cause to grow *b)* to breed (cattle, etc.) *c)* to rear (children) —*n.* **1.** a raising **2.** an increase in amount, as in salary or wages

rai·sin (rā′z'n) *n.* [< L. *racemus,* cluster of grapes] a sweet, dried grape

rai·son d'être (rā′zōn det′, det′rə) [Fr.] reason for being

ra·jah, ra·ja (rä′jə) *n.* [< Hindi < Sans. *rāj,* to rule] formerly, a prince or chief in India, etc.

rake[1] (rāk) *n.* [OE. *raca*] a long-handled tool with teeth or prongs at one end, for gathering loose grass, leaves, etc., or for smoothing broken ground —*vt.* **raked, rak′ing 1.** to gather or smooth with a rake **2.** to gather with great care **3.** to scratch as with a rake **4.** to search through carefully **5.** to direct gunfire along (a line of troops, etc.) —*vi.* to use a rake

rake[2] (rāk) *n.* [contr. of *rakehell*] a dissolute man; debauchee: also **rake′hell′** (-hel′)

rake[3] (rāk) *vi., vt.* **raked, rak′ing** [? akin to Sw. *raka,* to project] to be or make slightly inclined; slant —*n.* a slanting or inclining

rake'-off' *n.* [Slang] a commission or rebate, esp. one gained in a shady deal

rak·ish (rā'kish) *adj.* [< RAKE³ + -ISH] 1. having a trim, neat appearance suggesting speed: said of a ship 2. dashing and gay; jaunty —**rak'ish·ly** *adv.* —**rak'ish·ness** *n.*

Ra·leigh (rô'lē, rä'-) capital of N.C.: pop. 122,000

Ra·leigh (rô'lē, rä'-), Sir **Walter** 1552?-1618; Eng. explorer & poet

ral·ly¹ (ral'ē) *vt., vi.* **-lied, -ly·ing** [< OFr. *re-*, again + *alier*, join] 1. to gather together (retreating troops) and restore to a state of order 2. to bring or come together for a common purpose 3. to revive; recover —*n., pl.* **-lies** 1. a rallying or being rallied; specif., a mass meeting 2. an organized run over a course designed to test driving skills: also sp. **ral'lye** 3. *Tennis, etc.* an exchange of several strokes before the point is won

ral·ly² (ral'ē) *vt., vi.* **-lied, -ly·ing** [Fr. *rallier*, to RAIL²] to tease or mock playfully

ram (ram) *n.* [OE. *ramm*] 1. a male sheep 2. *same as* BATTERING RAM 3. the striking part of a pile driver —[R-] Aries —*vt.* **rammed, ram'ming** 1. to strike against with great force 2. to force into place 3. to force acceptance of (an idea, legislative bill, etc.) 4. to stuff or cram (*with* something) —*vi.* to crash —**ram'mer** *n.*

ram·ble (ram'b'l) *vi.* **-bled, -bling** [< ME. *romen*, to roam] 1. to roam about; esp., to stroll about idly 2. to talk or write aimlessly 3. to spread in all directions, as a vine —*n.* a rambling, esp. a stroll

ram'bler *n.* 1. a person or thing that rambles 2. any of certain climbing roses

ram·bunc·tious (ram buŋk'shəs) *adj.* [< *robustious*] wild, boisterous, unruly, etc. —**ram·bunc'tious·ly** *adv.* —**ram·bunc'tious·ness** *n.*

ram·e·kin, ram·e·quin (ram'ə kin) *n.* [< Fr. < MDu. *rammeken*, cheese dish] a small, individual baking dish

ram·i·fy (ram'ə fī') *vt., vi.* **-fied, -fy·ing** [< Fr. < L. *ramus*, a branch + *facere*, make] to divide or spread out into branches or branchlike divisions —**ram'i·fi·ca'tion** *n.*

ram·jet (engine) (ram'jet') a jet engine in which the air for burning the fuel is compressed by being rammed into the inlet by the aircraft's velocity

ramp¹ (ramp) *n.* [see RAMP²] 1. a sloping walk, plank, etc. joining different levels 2. a wheeled staircase rolled up to an airplane for use in getting on or off

ramp² (ramp) *vi., n.* [OFr. *ramper*, to climb] rampage

ram·page (ram pāj') *vi.* **-paged, -pag'ing** [prob. < RAMP²] to rush violently about; rage —*n.* (ram'pāj) a rampaging: chiefly in **on the** (or **a**) **rampage**

ramp·ant (ram'pənt) *adj.* [see RAMP²] 1. growing unchecked; rife 2. violent and uncontrollable 3. *Heraldry* standing on the hind legs [a lion *rampant*] —**ramp'ant·ly** *adv.*

ram·part (ram'pärt, -pərt) *n.* [< Fr. *re-*, again + *emparer*, fortify] 1. a defensive embankment around a castle, fort, etc., with a parapet at the top 2. any defense

ram·rod (ram'räd') *n.* a rod for ramming down the charge in a gun loaded through the muzzle

ram·shack·le (ram'shak''l) *adj.* [< RANSACK] loose and rickety; likely to fall to pieces

ran (ran) *pt.* of RUN

ranch (ranch) *n.* [< AmSp. *rancho*] 1. a large farm, esp. in western States, for raising many cattle, horses, or sheep 2. *same as* RANCH HOUSE —*vi.* to work on or manage a ranch —**ranch'er** *n.* —**ranch'man** (-mən) *n., pl.* **-men**

ranch house 1. the owner's residence on a ranch 2. a house with all the rooms on one floor

ran·cid (ran'sid) *adj.* [< L. *rancere*, to be rank] having the bad smell or taste of spoiled fats or oils

ran·cor (raŋ'kər) *n.* [< L. *rancere*, to be rank] a continuing and bitter hate or ill will; deep spite: Brit. sp. **ran'cour** —**ran'cor·ous** *adj.*

R & B, r & b rhythm and blues

R & D, R and D research and development

ran·dom (ran'dəm) *adj.* [< OFr. *randir*, run violently] 1. made, done, etc. in a haphazard way 2. not uniform 3. having an equal chance of being chosen or of occurring — **at random** without careful choice, plan, etc.

ran'dom·ize (-īz') *vt.* **-ized', -iz'ing** to select or choose (items of a group) in a random order

ran·dy (ran'dē) *adj.* **-di·er, -di·est** [prob. < RANT] sexually aroused; lustful

rang (raŋ) *pt.* of RING¹

range (rānj) *vt.* **ranged, rang'ing** [< OFr. *renc*, a row] 1. to put in a certain order, esp. in a row or rows 2. to place with others in a cause, party, etc. 3. to roam over, about, or through —*vi.* 1. to extend in a given direction 2. to wander about; roam 3. to vary between stated limits —*n.*

1. a row, line, or series 2. a chain or single system of mountains 3. the firing distance of a weapon 4. *a*) a place for shooting practice *b*) a place for testing rockets in flight 5. the full extent over which something moves or is heard, seen, effective, etc.; scope 6. the full extent of pitch of a voice, instrument, etc. 7. a large open area for grazing livestock 8. the limits within which there are differences in amount, degree, etc. [a wide *range* in price] 9. a cooking stove

rang'er *n.* 1. a roamer 2. a member of a special military or police force that patrols a region 3. a warden who patrols forests

Ran·goon (raŋ gōōn') capital of Burma: pop. 1,759,000

rang·y (rān'jē) *adj.* **-i·er, -i·est** long-limbed and slender

rank¹ (raŋk) *n.* [< OFr. *renc*] 1. a row, line, or series 2. a social class [men from all *ranks* of life] 3. a high position in society 4. an official grade [the *rank* of major] 5. a relative position as measured by quality, etc. [a poet of the first *rank*] 6. a row of soldiers, etc., side by side 7. [*pl.*] all those in an organization, as the army, who are not officers or leaders: also **rank and file** —*vt.* 1. to place in a rank 2. to assign a position to 3. to outrank —*vi.* to hold a certain position

rank² (raŋk) *adj.* [OE. *ranc*, strong] 1. growing vigorously and coarsely [*rank* grass] 2. producing a luxuriant crop, often to excess 3. very bad in smell or taste 4. coarse; indecent 5. utter; extreme [*rank* injustice] —**rank'ness** *n.*

rank'ing *adj.* 1. of the highest rank 2. prominent or outstanding

ran·kle (raŋ'k'l) *vi., vt.* **-kled, -kling** [< ML. *dracunculus*, a fester] 1. orig., to fester 2. to fill with or cause longlasting rancor, anger, etc.

ran·sack (ran'sak) *vt.* [< ON. *rann*, a house + *sækja*, to search] 1. to search thoroughly 2. to plunder; pillage

ran·som (ran'səm) *n.* [see REDEEM] 1. the redeeming of a captive by paying money or meeting other demands 2. the price so paid or demanded —*vt.* to get (a captive) released by paying the demanded price —**ran'som·er** *n.*

rant (rant) *vi., vt.* [< obs. Du. *ranten*] to talk in a loud, wild way; rave —*n.* ranting talk —**rant'er** *n.* —**rant'ing·ly** *adv.*

rap¹ (rap) *vt.* **rapped, rap'ping** [prob. echoic] 1. to strike quickly and sharply; tap 2. [Slang] to criticize sharply — *vi.* 1. to knock sharply 2. [Slang] to talk —*n.* 1. a quick, sharp knock 2. [Slang] blame or punishment; specif., a prison sentence

rap² (rap) *n.* [< ?] [Colloq.] the least bit: in **not care** (or **give**) **a rap**, not care anything at all

ra·pa·cious (rə pā'shəs) *adj.* [< L. *rapere*, to seize] 1. plundering 2. greedy; voracious 3. living on captured prey; predatory —**ra·pa'cious·ly** *adv.* —**ra·pac·i·ty** (rə pas'ə tē) *n.*

rape¹ (rāp) *n.* [< L. *rapere*, to seize] 1. *a*) the crime of having sexual intercourse with a woman forcibly and without her consent, or (**statutory rape**) with a girl below the age of consent *b*) any sexual assault 2. any violent or outrageous assault —*vt., vi.* **raped, rap'ing** to commit rape (on) —**rap'ist** *n.*

rape² (rāp) *n.* [L. *rapa*, turnip] a plant of the mustard family, with seed (**rapeseed**) yielding an oil (**rape oil, rapeseed oil**) and with leaves used for fodder

Raph·a·el (rā'fē əl, raf'ē-) 1. an archangel mentioned in the Apocrypha 2. 1483-1520; It. painter

rap·id (rap'id) *adj.* [< L. *rapere*, to rush] moving or done with speed; swift —*n.* 1. [*usually pl.*] a part of a river where the current is swift 2. a rapid transit car, train, or system —**ra·pid·i·ty** (rə pid'ə tē), **rap'id·ness** *n.* —**rap'id·ly** *adv.*

rap'id-fire' *adj.* 1. firing shots in rapid succession: said of guns 2. done, carried on, etc. in a swift, sharp way

rapid transit a system of rapid public transportation in an urban area, using electric trains on an unimpeded right of way

ra·pi·er (rā'pē ər, rāp'yər) *n.* [Fr. *rapière*] a light, sharp-pointed sword used only for thrusting

rap·ine (rap'in) *n.* [< L. *rapere*, to seize] plunder; pillage

rap·port (ra pôr', -pôrt') *n.* [Fr. < L. *ad-*, to + *portare*, to carry] sympathetic relationship; agreement; harmony

rap·proche·ment (ra prōsh'män) *n.* [Fr.] an establishing or restoring of friendly relations

rap·scal·lion (rap skal'yən) *n.* [< earlier *rascallion*, extension of RASCAL] a rascal; rogue

rapt (rapt) *adj.* [< L. *rapere*, to seize] 1. carried away with joy, love, etc.; full of rapture 2. absorbed (*in* meditation, study, etc.)

rap·to·ri·al (rap tôr'ē əl) *adj.* [< L. *rapere*, to seize] of or belonging to a group of birds of prey, as the eagle

rap·ture (rap'chər) *n.* **1.** the state of being carried away with joy, love, etc. **2.** an expression of this —**rap'tur·ous** *adj.*

rare[1] (rer) *adj.* **rar'er, rar'est** [< L. *rarus*] **1.** not often seen, done, found, etc.; uncommon **2.** unusually good; excellent **3.** not dense *[rare* atmosphere*]* —**rare'ness** *n.*

rare[2] (rer) *adj.* **rar'er, rar'est** [OE. *hrere*] not fully cooked; partly raw: said esp. of meat

rare·bit (rer'bit) *n. same as* WELSH RABBIT

rare earth 1. any of the oxides of the rare-earth metals **2.** any of the rare-earth metals

rare'-earth' metals (or **elements**) a group of rare metallic chemical elements with consecutive atomic numbers of 57 to 71 inclusive

rar·e·fy (rer'ə fī') *vt., vi.* **-fied', -fy'ing** [< L. *rarus,* rare + *facere,* make] **1.** to make or become less dense **2.** to make or become more refined, subtle, etc. —**rar'e·fac'tion** (-fak'shən) *n.*

rare·ly (rer'lē) *adv.* **1.** not often; seldom **2.** beautifully, excellently, etc. **3.** uncommonly

rar·i·ty (rer'ə tē) *n.* **1.** a being rare; specif., *a)* scarcity *b)* lack of density **2.** *pl.* **-ties** a rare or uncommon thing

ras·cal (ras'k'l) *n.* [OFr. *rascaille,* scrapings] a scoundrel; rogue: often used playfully, as of a mischievous child — **ras·cal'i·ty** (-kal'ə tē) *n.* —**ras'cal·ly** *adj., adv.*

rash[1] (rash) *adj.* [ME. *rasch*] too hasty and careless; reckless —**rash'ly** *adv.* —**rash'ness** *n.*

rash[2] (rash) *n.* [MFr. *rasche*] **1.** a breaking out of red spots on the skin **2.** a sudden appearance of a large number *[a rash* of complaints*]*

rash·er (rash'ər) *n.* [< ? obs. *rash,* to cut] **1.** a thin slice of bacon or, rarely, ham, for frying or broiling **2.** a serving of several such slices

rasp (rasp) *vt.* [< OHG. *raspon,* scrape together] **1.** to scrape with a file **2.** to utter in a rough, grating tone **3.** to grate upon; irritate —*vi.* **1.** to grate **2.** to make a rough, grating sound —*n.* **1.** a type of rough file **2.** a rough, grating sound —**rasp'y** *adj.* **-i·er, -i·est**

rasp·ber·ry (raz'ber'ē, -bər ē) *n., pl.* **-ries** [< earlier *raspis*] **1.** the small, juicy, edible fruit of various brambles: it is a cluster of red, purple, or black drupelets **2.** the bramble bearing this **3.** [Slang] a sound of derision

ras·sle (ras''l) *n., vi., vt.* **-sled, -sling** *dial. or colloq. var. of* WRESTLE

rat (rat) *n.* [OE. *ræt*] **1.** a long-tailed rodent resembling, but larger than, the mouse **2.** [Slang] a sneaky, contemptible person; informer, etc. —*vi.* **rat'ted, rat'ting 1.** to hunt rats **2.** [Slang] to act as an informer —**smell a rat** to suspect a trick, plot, etc.

ratch·et (rach'it) *n.* [< Fr. < It. *rocca,* distaff] **1.** a toothed wheel (in full **ratchet wheel**) or bar that catches and holds a pawl, preventing backward movement **2.** such a pawl **3.** such a wheel (or bar) and pawl as a unit

RATCHET WHEEL

rate[1] (rāt) *n.* [< L. *reri,* reckon] **1.** the amount, degree, etc. of anything in relation to units of something else *[the rate* of pay*]* **2.** a fixed ratio *[the rate* of exchange*]* **3.** price, esp. per unit of some commodity, service, etc. **4.** speed of movement or action **5.** a class or rank *[of the first rate]* —*vt.* **rat'ed, rat'ing 1.** to appraise **2.** to put into a particular class or rank **3.** to consider; esteem **4.** [Colloq.] to deserve —*vi.* **1.** to be classed or ranked **2.** to have value, status, etc. —**at any rate 1.** in any event **2.** anyway

rate[2] (rāt) *vt., vi.* **rat'ed, rat'ing** [ME. *raten*] to scold severely; chide

rath·er (rath'ər) *adv.* [< OE. *hrathe,* quickly] **1.** more willingly; preferably **2.** with more justice, reason, etc. *[I, rather* than you, should pay*]* **3.** more accurately *[my son, or rather,* stepson*]* **4.** on the contrary **5.** somewhat —**had** (or **would**) **rather 1.** would choose to **2.** would prefer that —**rather than** instead of

raths·kel·ler (rät'skel'ər, rath'-) *n.* [G. < *rat,* council + *keller,* cellar] a restaurant where beer is served, usually below street level

rat·i·fy (rat'ə fī') *vt.* **-fied', -fy'ing** [< L. *ratus* (see RATE[1]) + *facere,* make] to approve; esp., to give official sanction to —**rat'i·fi·ca'tion** *n.*

rat·ing (rāt'iŋ) *n.* **1.** a rank or grade, as of military or naval personnel **2.** a placement in a certain rank or class **3.** an evaluation; appraisal **4.** an amount determined as a grade

ra·tio (rā'shō, -shē ō') *n., pl.* **-tios** [L.: see REASON] **1.** a fixed relation in degree, number, etc. between two similar things; proportion **2.** *Math.* a fraction

ra·ti·o·ci·nate (rash'ē ō'sə nāt', -äs'ə-) *vi.* **-nat'ed, -nat'-ing** [see RATIO] to reason, esp. using formal logic —**ra'ti·o'ci·na'tion** *n.*

ra·tion (rash'ən, rā'shən) *n.* [see RATIO] **1.** a fixed portion; share **2.** a fixed allowance of food, as a daily allowance for one soldier **3.** *[pl.]* food supply —*vt.* **1.** to give rations to **2.** to distribute (food, clothing, etc.) in rations, as in a time of scarcity —**ra'tion·ing** *n.*

ra·tion·al (rash'ən 'l) *adj.* [see RATIO] **1.** of or based on reasoning **2.** able to reason; reasoning **3.** sensible or sane **4.** *Math.* designating a number expressible as the quotient of two integers or as an integer —**ra'tion·al'i·ty** (-ə nal'ə tē) *n.* —**ra'tion·al·ly** *adv.*

ra·tion·ale (rash'ə nal', -nä'lē) *n.* [L., rational] **1.** the rational basis for something **2.** an explanation of reasons or principles

ra·tion·al·ism (rash'ən 'l iz'm) *n.* the principle or practice of accepting reason as the only authority in determining one's opinions or course of action —**ra'tion·al·ist** *n.* —**ra'tion·al·is'tic** *adj.*

ra·tion·al·ize (rash'ən ə līz') *vt.* **-ized', -iz'ing 1.** to make rational or reasonable **2.** to devise explanations for (one's acts, beliefs, etc.) that seem to make sense but do not reveal one's true motives —*vi.* to rationalize one's acts, beliefs, etc. —**ra'tion·al·i·za'tion** *n.*

rat·line (rat'lin) *n.* [< ?] any of the small ropes which join the shrouds of a ship and serve as steps for climbing the rigging: also sp. **rat'lin**

rat race [Slang] a mad scramble or intense competitive struggle

rats·bane (rats'bān') *n.* [see BANE] rat poison

rat·tan (ra tan') *n.* [< Malay *raut,* to strip] **1.** a climbing palm with long, slender, tough stems **2.** these stems, used in wickerwork, canes, etc.

rat·tle (rat''l) *vi.* **-tled, -tling** [prob. echoic] **1.** to make a series of sharp, short sounds **2.** to move with such sounds **3.** to chatter (often with *on*) —*vt.* **1.** to cause to rattle **2.** to utter or perform rapidly (usually with *off*) **3.** to confuse or upset —*n.* **1.** a series of sharp, short sounds **2.** the series of horny rings at the end of a rattlesnake's tail **3.** a baby's toy, etc. that rattles when shaken —**rat'tly** (-lē, -'l ē) *adj.*

rat'tle·brain' (-brān') *n.* a silly, frivolous, talkative person —**rat'tle·brained'** *adj.*

rat'tler *n.* **1.** a person or thing that rattles **2.** a rattlesnake

rat'tle·snake' *n.* a poisonous American snake with horny rings at the end of the tail that rattle when shaken

rat'tle·trap' (-trap') *n.* anything worn out or rickety; esp., an old, dilapidated automobile

rat'tling *adj.* **1.** that rattles **2.** [Colloq.] very fast, good, etc. —*adv.* [Colloq.] very *[a rattling* good time*]*

rat'trap' *n.* **1.** a trap for catching rats **2.** [Colloq.] a dirty, run-down building

RATTLESNAKE
(to 5 1/2 ft. long)

rat·ty (rat'ē) *adj.* **-ti·er, -ti·est** [Slang] shabby or run-down

rau·cous (rô'kəs) *adj.* [L. *raucus*] **1.** hoarse **2.** loud and rowdy —**rau'cous·ly** *adv.* —**rau'cous·ness** *n.*

raun·chy (rôn'chē, rän'-) *adj.* **-chi·er, -chi·est** [< ?] [Slang] **1.** dirty, sloppy, etc. **2.** risqué, lustful, etc. — **raun'chi·ly** *adv.* —**raun'chi·ness** *n.*

rav·age (rav'ij) *n.* [Fr.: see RAVISH] destruction; ruin —*vt.* **-aged, -ag·ing** to destroy violently; devastate; ruin —*vi.* to commit violently destructive acts —**rav'ag·er** *n.*

rave (rāv) *vi.* **raved, rav'ing** [prob. < OFr. *raver*] **1.** to talk incoherently or wildly, as when delirious **2.** to talk with great enthusiasm (*about*) —*n.* [Colloq.] a very enthusiastic commendation

rav·el (rav''l) *vi.* **-eled** or **-elled, -el·ing** or **-el·ling** [MDu. *ravelen*] to separate into its parts, esp. threads; untwist; fray —*n. same as* RAVELING

Ra·vel (rä vel'), **Mau·rice** (mô rēs') 1875–1937; Fr. composer

ra·ven (rā'vən) *n.* [OE. *hræfn*] a large, black bird related to the crow —*adj.* black and lustrous

rav·en·ing (rav'n iŋ) *adj.* [see RAVISH] greedily searching for prey

rav·e·nous (rav'ə nəs) *adj.* [see RAVISH] 1. greedily hungry 2. greedy [*ravenous* for praise] 3. rapacious —**rav'e·nous·ly** *adv.*

ra·vine (rə vēn') *n.* [Fr., flood: ult. < L.] a long, deep hollow in the earth, esp. one worn by a stream; gorge

rav·ing (rā'viŋ) *adj.* 1. that raves; delirious; frenzied 2. [Colloq.] exciting enthusiastic admiration [a *raving* beauty] —*adv.* in a raving way [*raving* mad]

ra·vi·o·li (rav'ē ō'lē) *n.pl.* [*with sing. v.*] [It.] small casings of dough containing ground meat, cheese, etc., usually served in a tomato sauce

rav·ish (rav'ish) *vt.* [< L. *rapere*, seize] 1. to seize and carry away forcibly 2. to rape 3. to fill with great joy or delight —**rav'ish·er** *n.* —**rav'ish·ment** *n.*

rav'ish·ing *adj.* causing great joy or delight

raw (rô) *adj.* [OE. *hreaw*] 1. not cooked 2. in its natural condition; not processed [*raw* silk] 3. inexperienced [a *raw* recruit] 4. with the skin rubbed off; sore and inflamed 5. uncomfortably cold and damp [a *raw* wind] 6. coarse, indecent, bawdy, etc. 7. [Colloq.] harsh or unfair [a *raw* deal] —**in the raw** 1. in the natural state 2. naked —**raw'ly** *adv.* —**raw'ness** *n.*

raw'boned' (-bōnd') *adj.* lean; gaunt

raw'hide' *n.* 1. an untanned or partially tanned cattle hide 2. a whip made of this

ray¹ (rā) *n.* [see RADIUS] 1. any of the thin lines, or beams, of light that appear to come from a bright source 2. any of several lines or parts coming out from a center 3. a beam of radiant energy, radioactive particles, etc. 4. a tiny amount [a *ray* of hope]

ray² (rā) *n.* [< L. *raia*] a fish with a broad, flat body, widely expanded fins at each side, and a whiplike tail

ray·on (rā'än) *n.* [coined < RAY¹] 1. a textile fiber made from a cellulose solution 2. a fabric of such fibers

raze (rāz) *vt.* razed, raz'ing [< L. *radere*, to scrape] to tear down completely; demolish

ra·zor (rā'zər) *n.* [see RAZE] 1. a sharp-edged instrument for shaving 2. *same as* SHAVER (sense 2)

ra'zor·back' *n.* a wild or semiwild hog of the S U.S., with a ridged back and long legs

razz (raz) *vt., vi.* [< RASPBERRY] [Slang] to tease, ridicule, heckle, etc.

raz·zle-daz·zle (raz'l daz'l) *n.* [Slang] a flashy display intended to confuse or deceive

razz·ma·tazz (raz'mə taz') *n.* [Slang] 1. liveliness; vigor 2. flashiness; showiness

Rb *Chem.* rubidium

rbi, RBI, r.b.i. *Baseball* run(s) batted in

R.C. 1. Red Cross 2. Roman Catholic

Rd., rd. 1. road 2. rod

R.D. Rural Delivery

re¹ (rā) *n.* [It.] *Music* a syllable representing the second tone of the diatonic scale

re² (rē, rā) *prep.* [L. < *res*, thing] in the case or matter of; as regards

re- [< Fr. or L.] *a prefix meaning:* 1. back [*repay*] 2. again, anew [*reappear*] It is used with a hyphen: 1) to distinguish between a word in which the prefix means *again* or *anew* and a word having a special meaning (Ex.: *re-cover, recover*) 2) esp. formerly, before a word beginning with an *e* The following list contains some of the more common words in which *re-* means *again* or *anew*

reacquaint	reconsign	reexplain
readjust	reconvene	refashion
readmit	reconvert	refasten
reaffirm	recopy	refinance
realign	re-cover	reformulate
reappear	redecorate	refuel
reappoint	rededicate	refurnish
reappraise	redetermine	reheat
rearm	redirect	rehire
reassemble	rediscover	reimpose
reassess	redistribution	reinfect
reassign	redivide	reinoculate
reawaken	redraw	reinsert
reborn	reeducate	reinspect
rebroadcast	reelect	reinvest
rebuild	reembody	rekindle
rebuilt	reemerge	relearn
recharge	reenact	reload
recheck	reengage	remake
reclassify	reenlist	remarry
recommence	reenter	rematch
reconfirm	reestablish	rename
reconquer	reexamine	renegotiate

renominate	republish	retest
renumber	reread	rethink
reopen	resell	retrain
reorder	reset	retrial
repack	resettle	retype
repackage	reshape	reunite
repaint	reshuffle	reupholster
repave	restate	reuse
rephrase	restring	revisit
replant	restudy	revitalize
replay	restyle	reweigh
re-press	retell	rework

Re *Chem.* rhenium

reach (rēch) *vt.* [OE. *ræcan*] 1. to thrust out or extend (the hand, etc.) 2. to extend to, or touch, by thrusting out, etc. 3. to obtain and hand over [*reach* me the salt] 4. to go as far as; attain 5. to carry as far as [the news *reached* me late] 6. to influence; affect 7. to get in touch with, as by telephone —*vi.* 1. to thrust out the hand, etc. 2. to extend in influence, space, time, etc. 3. to carry, as sight, sound, etc. 4. to try to get something —*n.* 1. a stretching or thrusting out 2. the power of, or the extent covered in, stretching, obtaining, etc. 3. a continuous extent, esp. of water

re·act (rē akt') *vi.* 1. to act in return or reciprocally 2. to act in opposition 3. to go back to a former condition, stage, etc. 4. to respond to a stimulus, influence, etc. 5. *Chem.* to act with another substance in producing a chemical change

re·act·ant (rē ak'tənt) *n.* any substance involved in a chemical reaction

re·ac·tion (rē ak'shən) *n.* 1. a return or opposing action, etc. 2. a response, as to a stimulus 3. a movement back to a former or less-advanced condition, esp. such a movement in politics 4. the mutual action of substances undergoing chemical change 5. *Med. a)* an action induced by resistance to another action *b)* an effect produced by an allergen *c)* depression or exhaustion following nervous tension, overstimulation, etc.

re·ac'tion·ar'y (-shə ner'ē) *adj.* of, showing, or favoring reaction, esp. in politics —*n., pl.* -ies a reactionary person

re·ac·ti·vate (rē ak'tə vāt') *vt.* -vat'ed, -vat'ing to make active again; specif., to restore to active military status —**re·ac'ti·va'tion** *n.*

re·ac'tive (-tiv) *adj.* 1. tending to react 2. of, from, or showing reaction —**re'ac·tiv'i·ty** *n.*

re·ac·tor (rē ak'tər) *n. same as* NUCLEAR REACTOR

read¹ (rēd) *vt.* **read** (red), **read'ing** (rēd'iŋ) [OE. *rædan*, to counsel] 1. to get the meaning of (something written or printed) by interpreting the characters 2. to utter aloud (something written or printed) 3. to understand the nature, significance, or thinking of 4. to foretell (the future) 5. to interpret (a printed passage, etc.) as having a particular meaning 6. to study [to *read* law] 7. to register, as a gauge 8. to obtain (information) from (punch cards, tape, etc.): said of a computer 9. [Slang] to hear and understand (a radio communication, etc.) —*vi.* 1. to read something written or printed 2. to learn by reading (with *about* or *of*) 3. to be phrased in certain words 4. to admit of being read —**read into** (or **in**) to attribute (a particular meaning) to —**read out of** to expel from (an organization) —**read up (on)** to become well informed (about) by reading

read² (red) *pt. & pp.* of READ¹ —*adj.* informed by reading [well-*read*]

read·a·ble (rēd'ə b'l) *adj.* 1. interesting or easy to read 2. that can be read; legible —**read'a·bil'i·ty** *n.* —**read'a·bly** *adv.*

read'er *n.* 1. one who reads 2. *a)* a schoolbook for use in teaching how to read *b)* an anthology of stories, essays, etc.

read'er·ship' *n.* all the readers of a certain publication, author, etc.

read'ing *adj.* 1. that reads 2. of or for reading —*n.* 1. the act of one who reads 2. the reciting of a literary work in public 3. any material to be read 4. the amount measured by a barometer, electric meter, etc. 5. a particular interpretation or performance

read·out (rēd'out') *n.* 1. the retrieving of information from a computer 2. this information, displayed visually or recorded, as by typewriter, for immediate use

read·y (red'ē) *adj.* -i·er, -i·est [OE. *ræde*] 1. prepared to act or be used immediately 2. willing 3. likely or liable immediately [*ready* to cry] 4. skillful; dexterous 5. prompt [a *ready* reply] 6. available immediately [*ready* cash] —*vt.* -ied, -y·ing to make ready; prepare —**make ready** to prepare —**read'i·ly** *adv.* —**read'i·ness** *n.*

read'y-made' *adj.* made so as to be ready for immediate use or sale

read'y-to-wear' *adj. same as* READY-MADE (as applied to clothing)

re·a·gent (rē ā'jənt) *n. Chem.* a substance used to detect, measure, or react with another substance

re·al¹ (rē'əl, rēl) *adj.* [< L. *res*, thing] **1**. existing as or in fact; actual; true **2**. authentic; genuine **3**. designating wages or income as measured by purchasing power **4**. *Law* of or relating to permanent, immovable things *[real property]* **5**. *Philos.* existing objectively —*adv.* [Colloq.] very —**for real** [Slang] real or really

re·al² (rē'əl; *Sp. re* äl') *n., pl.* **-als**; *Sp.* **-al'es** (-ä'les) [Sp. & Port., lit., royal < L. *rex*, king] a former silver coin of Spain

real estate land, including the buildings or improvements on it and its natural assets

re·al·ism (rē'ə liz'm) *n.* **1**. a tendency to face facts and be practical **2**. the portrayal in art and literature of people and things as they really are **3**. *Philos.* the doctrine that material objects exist in themselves, apart from the mind's consciousness of them —**re'al·ist** *n.* —**re'al·is'tic** *adj.* —**re'al·is'ti·cal·ly** *adv.*

re·al·i·ty (rē al'ə tē) *n., pl.* **-ties** **1**. the quality or fact of being real **2**. a person or thing that is real; fact —**in real·ity** in fact; actually

re·al·ize (rē'ə līz') *vt.* **-ized', -iz'ing** [< Fr.] **1**. to make real; bring into being **2**. to understand fully **3**. to convert (assets, rights, etc.) into money **4**. to gain; obtain *[to realize a profit]* **5**. to be sold for (a specified sum) —**re'al·i·za'tion** *n.*

re'al-life' *adj.* actual; not imaginary

re'al·ly *adv.* **1**. in reality; actually **2**. truly *[really hot]* —*interj.* indeed

realm (relm) *n.* [< L. *regimen*, rule, infl. by L. *regalis*, REGAL] **1**. a kingdom **2**. a region; sphere *[the realm of the imagination]*

Re·al·tor (rē'əl tər) *n.* a real estate broker who is a member of the National Association of Real Estate Boards

re·al·ty (rē'əl tē) *n. same as* REAL ESTATE

ream¹ (rēm) *n.* [< Ar. *rizma*, a bale] **1**. a quantity of paper varying from 480 sheets (20 quires) to 516 sheets **2**. *[pl.]* [Colloq.] a great amount

ream² (rēm) *vt.* [< OE. *reman*, widen] **1**. to enlarge or taper (a hole) as with a reamer **2**. [Slang] to cheat

ream'er *n.* **1**. a sharp-edged tool for enlarging or tapering holes **2**. a device with a ridged cone-shaped part on which oranges, etc. are squeezed for juice

re·an·i·mate (rē an'ə māt') *vt.* **-mat'ed, -mat'ing** to give new life, power, courage, etc. to —**re·an'i·ma'tion** *n.*

reap (rēp) *vt., vi.* [OE. *ripan*] **1**. to cut (grain) with a scythe, reaper, etc. **2**. to gather (a harvest) **3**. to get as a result of action, work, etc.

REAMER

reap'er *n.* **1**. one who reaps **2**. a machine for reaping grain —**the (Grim) Reaper** death

re·ap·por·tion (rē'ə pôr'shən) *vt.* to apportion again; specif., to adjust the representation pattern of (a legislature) —**re'ap·por'tion·ment** *n.*

rear¹ (rir) *n.* [< ARREAR(S)] **1**. the back part **2**. the position behind or at the back **3**. the part of an army, etc. farthest from the battle front **4**. [Slang] the buttocks: also **rear end** —*adj.* of, at, or in the rear —**bring up the rear** to come at the end

rear² (rir) *vt.* [OE. *ræran*] **1**. to put upright; elevate **2**. to build; erect **3**. to grow or breed **4**. to bring to maturity by educating, nourishing, etc. *[to rear a child]* —*vi.* **1**. to rise on the hind legs, as a horse **2**. to rise (*up*) in anger, etc. **3**. to rise high, as a mountain peak

rear admiral *U.S. Navy* an officer ranking just above a captain

rear guard a military detachment to protect the rear of a main force

rear'most' (-mōst') *adj.* farthest in the rear

re'ar·range' *vt.* **-ranged', -rang'ing** to arrange again or in a different manner —**re'ar·range'ment** *n.*

rear'ward (-wərd) *adj.* at, in, or toward the rear —*adv.* toward the rear: also **rear'wards**

rea·son (rē'z'n) *n.* [< L. *reri*, think] **1**. an explanation or justification of an act, idea, etc. **2**. a cause or motive **3**. the ability to think, draw conclusions, etc. **4**. good sense **5**. sanity —*vt., vi.* **1**. to think logically (about); analyze **2**. to argue or infer —**by reason of** because of —**in** (or **within**) **reason** in accord with what is reasonable —**stand to reason** to be logical —**with reason** justifiably —**rea'son·er** *n.*

rea'son·a·ble *adj.* **1**. able to reason **2**. just; fair **3**. sensible; wise **4**. *a*) not excessive *b*) not expensive —**rea'son·a·ble·ness** *n.* —**rea'son·a·bly** *adv.*

rea'son·ing *n.* the drawing of inferences or conclusions from known or assumed facts

re'as·sure' *vt.* **-sured', -sur'ing** **1**. to assure again **2**. to restore to confidence —**re'as·sur'ance** *n.* —**re'as·sur'ing·ly** *adv.*

re·bate (rē'bāt) *vt.* **-bat·ed, -bat·ing** [< OFr.: see RE- & ABATE] to give back (part of a payment) —*n.* a return of part of a payment

Re·bec·ca, Re·bek·ah (ri bek'ə) *Bible* the wife of Isaac and mother of Jacob and Esau

reb·el (reb''l) *n.* [< L. *re-*, again + *bellare*, wage war] **1**. one who takes up arms against his government **2**. one who resists any authority —*adj.* **1**. rebellious **2**. of rebels —*vi.* (ri bel') **-elled', -el'ling** **1**. to be a rebel against one's government **2**. to resist any authority **3**. to feel or show strong aversion

re·bel·lion (ri bel'yən) *n.* **1**. armed resistance to one's government **2**. defiance of any authority

re·bel·lious (-yəs) *adj.* **1**. resisting authority; engaged in rebellion **2**. of or like rebels or rebellion **3**. opposing any control; defiant —**re·bel'lious·ly** *adv.* —**re·bel'lious·ness** *n.*

re·birth (ri burth', rē'burth') *n.* **1**. a new or second birth **2**. a reawakening; revival

re·bound (ri bound', rē'bound') *vi.* **1**. to spring back, as upon impact **2**. to get possession of a rebound (*n.* 2) —*n.* (rē'bound') **1**. a rebounding **2**. a basketball that bounces off the backboard or basket rim —**on the rebound 1**. after bouncing off the ground, a wall, etc. **2**. after being jilted

re·buff (ri buf') *n.* [< It. *rabbuffo*] **1**. an abrupt refusal of offered advice, help, etc. **2**. any repulse —*vt.* **1**. to refuse bluntly **2**. to repulse

re·buke (ri byōōk') *vt.* **-buked', -buk'ing** [< OFr. *re-*, back + *buchier*, to beat] to blame or scold in a sharp way; reprimand —*n.* a sharp reprimand

re·bus (rē'bəs) *n.* [L., lit., by things] a kind of puzzle consisting of pictures, etc. combined to suggest words or phrases

re·but (ri but') *vt.* **-but'ted, -but'ting** [< OFr. *re-*, back + *buter*, to push] to contradict or oppose, esp. in a formal manner by argument, proof, etc.

re·but'tal (-'l) *n.* a rebutting, as in law

rec. 1. receipt **2**. recipe **3**. record(ed)

re·cal·ci·trant (ri kal'si trənt) *adj.* [< L. *re-*, back + *calcitrare*, to kick] **1**. refusing to obey authority, etc.; stubbornly defiant **2**. hard to handle —*n.* a recalcitrant person —**re·cal'ci·trance, re·cal'ci·tran·cy** *n.*

re·call (ri kôl') *vt.* **1**. to call back **2**. to remember **3**. to take back; revoke **4**. to cause to be aware, alert, etc. again —*n.* (*also* rē'kôl) **1**. a recalling **2**. memory **3**. the removal of, or the right to remove, a public official from office by popular vote

re·cant (ri kant') *vt., vi.* [< L. *re-*, back + *canere*, sing] to withdraw or renounce formally (one's former beliefs, statements, etc.) —**re·can·ta·tion** (rē'kan tā'shən) *n.*

re·cap¹ (rē kap', rē'kap') *vt.* **-capped', -cap'ping** to cement and vulcanize a strip of rubber on the outer surface of (a worn tire) —*n.* (rē'kap') a recapped tire —**re·cap'pa·ble** *adj.*

re·cap² (rē'kap') *n.* a recapitulation, or summary —*vt., vi.* **-capped', -cap'ping** to recapitulate

re·ca·pit·u·late (rē'kə pich'ə lāt') *vi., vt.* **-lat'ed, -lat'ing** [see RE- & CAPITULATE] to repeat briefly; summarize —**re'ca·pit'u·la'tion** *n.*

re·cap'ture *vt.* **-tured, -tur·ing** **1**. to capture again; retake **2**. to remember —*n.* a recapturing or being recaptured

re·cast (rē kast') *vt.* **-cast', -cast'ing** **1**. to cast again or anew **2**. to improve the form of by redoing *[to recast a sentence]*

recd., rec'd. received

re·cede (ri sēd') *vi.* **-ced'ed, -ced'ing** [see RE- & CEDE] **1**. to go or move back *[the flood receded]* **2**. to slope backward **3**. to lessen, dim, etc.

re·ceipt (ri sēt') *n.* [see RECEIVE] **1**. *old term for* RECIPE **2**. a receiving or being received **3**. a written acknowledgment that something has been received **4.** [*pl.*] the amount received, as of money taken in by a business —*vt.* **1.** to mark (a bill) paid **2.** to write a receipt for

re·ceiv·a·ble (ri sē'və b'l) *adj.* **1.** that can be received **2.** due in payment from one's customers

re·ceive (ri sēv') *vt.* -ceived', -ceiv'ing [< L. *re-*, back + *capere*, take] **1.** to take or get (something given, sent, thrown, etc.) **2.** to experience or undergo [to *receive* acclaim] **3.** to take the force of; bear **4.** to react to as specified **5.** to learn [to *receive* news] **6.** to let enter **7.** to have room for; contain **8.** to greet (visitors, etc.) —*vi.* **1.** to get or take something; be a recipient **2.** to greet guests or visitors **3.** *Radio & TV* to convert incoming electromagnetic waves into sounds or images **4.** *Sports* to catch, or be prepared to return, a thrown, kicked, etc. ball

re·ceiv'er *n.* **1.** one who receives **2.** in radio, TV, telephony, etc., a device that converts electrical waves or signals back into sounds or images **3.** *Law* one appointed to administer or hold in trust property in bankruptcy or in a lawsuit

re·ceiv'er·ship' (-ship') *n. Law* the state of being administered or held by a receiver

re·cent (rē's'nt) *adj.* [< L. *recens*] **1.** done, made, etc. just before the present; new **2.** of a time just before the present —**re·cent·ly** *adv.*

re·cep·ta·cle (ri sep'tə k'l) *n.* [see RECEIVE] a container

re·cep·tion (ri sep'shən) *n.* **1.** *a*) a receiving or being received *b*) the manner of this **2.** a social function for the receiving of guests **3.** *Radio & TV* the receiving of signals, with reference to the quality of reproduction

re·cep'tion·ist *n.* an office employee who receives callers, gives information, etc.

re·cep'tive *adj.* able or ready to receive requests, suggestions, new ideas, etc. —**re·cep'tive·ly** *adv.* —**re·cep'tiv'i·ty, re·cep'tive·ness** *n.*

re·cep'tor (-tər) *n.* a nerve ending or group of nerve endings specialized for the reception of stimuli; sense organ

re·cess (rē'ses; *also, and for v. usually,* ri ses') *n.* [< L. *recedere*, recede] **1.** a hollow place, as in a wall **2.** a secluded or inner place **3.** a temporary halting of work, a session, etc. —*vt.* **1.** to place in a recess **2.** to form a recess in —*vi.* to take a recess

re·ces·sion (ri sesh'ən) *n.* **1.** a going back or receding; withdrawal **2.** a temporary falling off of business activity

re·ces'sion·al (-'l) *n.* a hymn sung at the end of a church service as the clergy and choir march out

re·ces'sive *adj.* **1.** receding **2.** *Genetics* designating, of, or associated with that one of a pair of genes which, when both are present in the germ plasm, remains latent

Re·ci·fe (re sē'fə) seaport in NE Brazil: pop. 1,079,000

rec·i·pe (res'ə pē) *n.* [L. < *recipere*, receive] **1.** a list of ingredients and directions for preparing a dish or drink **2.** any procedure for bringing about a desired result

re·cip·i·ent (ri sip'ē ənt) *n.* [see RECEIVE] one that receives —*adj.* ready or able to receive

re·cip·ro·cal (ri sip'rə k'l) *adj.* [< L. *reciprocus*, returning] **1.** done, felt, given, etc. in return **2.** on both sides; mutual **3.** corresponding but reversed **4.** corresponding or complementary —*n.* **1.** a complement, counterpart, etc. **2.** *Math.* the quantity resulting from the division of 1 by the given quantity [the *reciprocal* of 7 is 1/7] —**re·cip'ro·cal·ly** *adv.*

re·cip'ro·cate' (-kāt') *vt., vi.* -cat'ed, -cat'ing **1.** to give and get reciprocally **2.** to give, do, feel, etc. (something similar) in return **3.** to move alternately back and forth —**re·cip'ro·ca'tion** *n.*

rec·i·proc·i·ty (res'ə präs'ə tē) *n., pl.* -ties [< Fr.] **1.** reciprocal state or relationship **2.** mutual exchange; esp., exchange of special privileges between two countries

re·cit·al (ri sīt''l) *n.* **1.** a reciting; specif., a telling in detail **2.** the account, story, etc. told **3.** a musical or dance program given by a soloist, soloists, or a small ensemble —**re·cit'al·ist** *n.*

rec·i·ta·tion (res'ə tā'shən) *n.* **1.** *same as* RECITAL (senses 1 & 2) **2.** *a*) the speaking aloud in public of something memorized *b*) a piece so presented **3.** a reciting by pupils of answers to questions on a prepared lesson

rec·i·ta·tive (res'ə tə tēv') *n.* [< It.: see RECITE] **1.** a type of declamatory singing, free in rhythm and tempo, as in the dialogue of operas **2.** a passage in this style

re·cite (ri sīt') *vt., vi.* -cit'ed, -cit'ing [see RE- & CITE] **1.** to speak aloud (something memorized) **2.** to tell in detail or narrate (something)

reck·less *adj.* [OE. *reccan*] heedless; rash —**reck'less·ly** *adv.* —**reck'less·ness** *n.*

reck·on (rek'ən) *vt.* [OE. *-recenian*] **1.** to count; compute **2.** to regard as being **3.** to estimate **4.** [Colloq. or Dial.]

to suppose —*vi.* **1.** to count up **2.** to rely (*on*) —**reckon with** to take into consideration

reck'on·ing *n.* **1.** count or computation **2.** a calculated guess **3.** the settlement of an account **4.** the giving of rewards or penalties [day of *reckoning*]

re·claim (ri klām') *vt.* [see RE- & CLAIM] **1.** to bring back from error, vice, etc. **2.** to make (wasteland, etc.) usable **3.** to recover (useful materials) from waste products —**rec·la·ma·tion** (rek'lə mā'shən) *n.*

re·cline (ri klīn') *vt., vi.* -clined', -clin'ing [< L. *re-*, back + *clinare*, lean] to lie or cause to lie back or down; lean back

rec·luse (rek'lōōs, ri klōōs') *n.* [< L. *re-*, back + *claudere*, shut] one who lives a secluded, solitary life —**re·clu·sive** (ri klōō'siv) *adj.*

rec·og·ni·tion (rek'əg nish'ən) *n.* **1.** a recognizing or being recognized **2.** identification of a person or thing as being known to one

re·cog·ni·zance (ri käg'ni zəns, -kän'i-) *n.* [< L. *re-*, again + *cognoscere*, know] *Law* **1.** a bond binding one to some act, as to appear in court **2.** the amount one must forfeit if this obligation is not fulfilled

rec·og·nize (rek'əg nīz') *vt.* -nized', -niz'ing [< prec.] **1.** to identify as known before **2.** to know by some detail, as of appearance **3.** to be aware of the significance of **4.** to accept as a fact; admit [to *recognize* defeat] **5.** to acknowledge as worthy of commendation **6.** to acknowledge the legal standing of (a government or state) **7.** to show acquaintance with (a person) by greeting **8.** to grant the right to speak, as at a meeting —**rec'og·niz'a·ble** *adj.*

re·coil (ri koil') *vi.* [< L. *re-*, back + *culus*, buttocks] **1.** to draw back, as in fear or disgust **2.** to spring or kick back, as a gun when fired —*n.* (*also* rē'koil') a recoiling

rec·ol·lect (rek'ə lekt') *vt., vi.* [see RE- & COLLECT] to remember, esp. with some effort —**rec'ol·lec'tion** *n.*

rec·om·mend (rek'ə mend') *vt.* [see RE- & COMMEND] **1.** to entrust **2.** to suggest favorably as suited to some position, etc. **3.** to make acceptable **4.** to advise; counsel —**rec'om·men·da'tion** *n.*

re·com·mit (rē'kə mit') *vt.* -mit'ted, -mit'ting **1.** to commit again **2.** to refer (a bill, question, etc.) back to a committee

rec·om·pense (rek'əm pens') *vt.* -pensed', -pens'ing [see RE- & COMPENSATE] **1.** to repay or reward **2.** to compensate (a loss, etc.) —*n.* **1.** requital, reward, etc. **2.** compensation, as for a loss

rec·on·cile (rek'ən sīl') *vt.* -ciled', -cil'ing [see RE- & CONCILIATE] **1.** to make friendly again **2.** to settle (a quarrel, etc.) **3.** to make (facts, ideas, etc.) consistent **4.** to make content or acquiescent (*to*) —**rec'on·cil'a·ble** *adj.* —**rec'on·cil'i·a'tion** (-sil'ē ā'shən) *n.*

rec·on·dite (rek'ən dīt') *adj.* [< L. *re-*, back + *condere*, to hide] beyond ordinary understanding; abstruse

re·con·di·tion (rē'kən dish'ən) *vt.* to put back in good condition by cleaning, repairing, etc.

re·con·nais·sance (ri kän'ə səns, -zəns) *n.* [Fr.: see RECOGNIZANCE] an exploratory survey, as in seeking out information about enemy positions

rec·on·noi·ter (rē'kə noit'ər, rek'ə-) *vi., vt.* to make a reconnaisance (of): also, chiefly Brit. sp., **rec'on·noi'tre, -tred, -tring**

re·con·sid·er (rē'kən sid'ər) *vt., vi.* to consider again; think (a matter) over, as with a view to changing a decision —**re'con·sid'er·a'tion** *n.*

re·con·sti·tute' *vt.* -tut'ed, -tut'ing to constitute again; specif., to restore (a dried or condensed substance) to its original form by adding water

re'con·struct' *vt.* **1.** to construct again; remake **2.** to build up again in its original form, as from remaining parts —**re'con·struc'tive** *adj.*

re'con·struc'tion *n.* **1.** a reconstructing **2.** something reconstructed **3.** [R-] the period or process, after the Civil War, of reestablishing the Southern States in the Union

re·cord (ri kôrd'; *for n. & adj.* rek'ərd) *vt.* [< L. *recordari*, remember] **1.** to write down for future use **2.** to register, as on a graph **3.** to remain as evidence of **4.** to register (sound or visual images) on a phonograph disc, magnetic tape, etc. for later reproduction —*vi.* **1.** to record something **2.** to admit of being recorded —*n.* **1.** a being recorded **2.** an account of events **3.** anything serving as evidence of an event, etc. **4.** an official report of public proceedings **5.** the known facts about anyone or anything **6.** a grooved disc for playing on a phonograph **7.** the best performance, highest speed, etc. achieved —*adj.* being the best, largest, etc. —**off the record** confidential(ly) —**on (the) record** publicly declared

re·cord·er *n.* **1.** an official who keeps records of deeds or other official papers **2.** a machine or device that records; esp., *same as* TAPE RECORDER **3.** an early form of flute

re·cord·ing *adj.* that records —*n.* **1.** what is recorded, as on a disc or tape **2.** a disc, tape, etc. on which something is recorded

record player a phonograph with the pickup, turntable, amplifier, etc. operated electrically or electronically

RECORDER

re·count (ri kount′) *vt.* [see RE- & COUNT¹] to tell in detail; narrate

re-count (rē′kount′) *vt.* to count again —*n.* (rē′kount′) a second count, as of votes: also written **recount**

re·coup (ri kōōp′) *vt.* [< Fr. *re-*, again + *couper*, to cut] **1.** to make up for [to *recoup* a loss] **2.** to regain **3.** to pay back —*n.* a recouping

re·course (rē′kôrs, ri kôrs′) *n.* [see RE- & COURSE] **1.** a turning for aid, safety, etc. **2.** that to which one turns seeking aid, safety, etc.

re·cov·er (ri kuv′ər) *vt.* [< L. *recuperare*] **1.** to get back (something lost, stolen, etc.) **2.** to regain (health, etc.) **3.** to make up for [to *recover* losses] **4.** to save (oneself) from a fall, loss of poise, etc. **5.** to reclaim (land from the sea, useful matter from waste, etc.) **6.** *Sports* to gain or regain control of (a fumbled ball, etc.) —*vi.* **1.** to regain health, balance, control, etc. **2.** *Sports* to recover a ball, etc.

re·cov·er·y *n., pl.* **-ies** a recovering; specif., *a)* a return to health *b)* a regaining of something lost, balance, etc. *c)* a retrieval of a capsule, nose cone, etc. after a spaceflight

recovery room a hospital room where postoperative patients are kept for close observation and care

rec·re·ant (rek′rē ənt) *adj.* [< OFr. *recreire*, surrender allegiance] **1.** cowardly **2.** disloyal —*n.* **1.** a coward **2.** a traitor

rec·re·a·tion (rek′rē ā′shən) *n.* [< L. *recreare*, refresh] any form of play, amusement, etc. used for refreshment of body or mind —**rec′re·a′tion·al** *adj.*

re·crim·i·nate (ri krim′ə nat′) *vi.* **-nat′ed, -nat′ing** [< L. *re-*, back + *crimen*, offense] to answer an accuser by accusing him in return —**re·crim′i·na′tion** *n.* —**re·crim′i·na·to′ry** (-nə tôr′ē) *adj.*

re·cru·des·cence (rē′krōō des′′ns) *n.* [< L. *re-*, again + *crudus*, raw] a breaking out again, esp. of something bad —**re′cru·des′cent** *adj.*

re·cruit (ri krōōt′) *vt., vi.* [< Fr. < L. *re-*, again + *crescere*, grow] **1.** to enlist (personnel) into an army or navy **2.** to enlist (new members), hire (new employees), etc. for a group or organization —*n.* **1.** a recently enlisted or drafted soldier, sailor, etc. **2.** a new member of any group —**re·cruit′er** *n.* —**re·cruit′ment** *n.*

rec·tal (rek′t'l) *adj.* of, for, or near the rectum —**rec′tal·ly** *adv.*

rec·tan·gle (rek′taŋ′g'l) *n.* [Fr. < L. *rectus*, straight + *angulus*, a corner] any four-sided plane figure with four right angles —**rec·tan′gu·lar** (-gyə lər) *adj.*

rec·ti·fy (rek′tə fī′) *vt.* **-fied′, -fy′ing** [< L. *rectus*, straight + *facere*, make] **1.** to put right; correct **2.** *Chem.* to refine or purify by distillation **3.** *Elec.* to convert (alternating current) to direct current —**rec′ti·fi·ca′tion** *n.* —**rec′ti·fi′er** *n.*

rec·ti·lin·e·ar (rek′tə lin′ē ər) *adj.* [< LL. *rectus*, straight + *linea*, line] **1.** in or forming a straight line **2.** formed or bounded by straight lines

rec·ti·tude (rek′tə tōōd′, -tyōōd′) *n.* [< L. *rectus*, straight] honesty; uprightness of character

rec·tor (rek′tər) *n.* [< L. *regere*, to rule] **1.** in some churches, a clergyman in charge of a parish **2.** the head of certain schools, colleges, etc.

rec·to·ry (rek′tər ē) *n., pl.* **-ries** the residence of a clergyman who is a rector

rec·tum (rek′təm) *n., pl.* **-tums, -ta** (-tə) [< L. *rectum* (*intestinum*), straight (intestine)] the lowest segment of the large intestine, ending at the anus

re·cum·bent (ri kum′bənt) *adj.* [< L. *re-*, back + *cumbere*, lie down] lying down; reclining

re·cu·per·ate (ri kōō′pə rāt′, -kyōō′-) *vt.* **-at′ed, -at′ing** [< L. *recuperare*, recover] to recover (losses, health, etc.) —*vi.* **1.** to get well again **2.** to recover losses, etc. —**re·cu′per·a′tion** *n.* —**re·cu′per·a′tive** (-pə rāt′iv, -pər ə tiv) *adj.*

re·cur (ri kur′) *vi.* **-curred′, -cur′ring** [< L. *re-*, back + *currere*, run] **1.** to return in thought, talk, etc. [to *recur* to a topic] **2.** to occur again or at intervals —**re·cur′rence** *n.* —**re·cur′rent** *adj.*

re·cy·cle (rē sī′k'l) *vt.* **-cled, -cling 1.** to pass through a cycle again **2.** to use again and, again

red (red) *n.* [OE. *read*] **1.** the color of blood **2.** any red pigment **3.** [*often* R-] a political radical; esp., a communist —*adj.* **red′der, red′dest 1.** of the color red **2.** [*often* R-] politically radical; esp., communist —**in the red** losing money —**see red** [Colloq.] to become angry —**red′dish** *adj.* —**red′ness** *n.*

red′bird′ *n.* any of several predominantly red-colored birds, as the cardinal

red blood cell (or **corpuscle**) *same as* ERYTHROCYTE

red′-blood′ed (-blud′id) *adj.* vigorous, lusty, etc.

red′cap′ (-kap′) *n.* a porter in a railroad station, air terminal, etc.

red carpet a very grand welcome and entertainment (with *the*) —**red′-car′pet** *adj.*

red′coat′ *n.* a British soldier in a uniform with a red coat, as during the American Revolution

Red Cross an international society for the relief of suffering in time of war or disaster

redd (red) *vt., vi.* **redd** or **redd′ed, redd′ing** [< ?] [Colloq.] to make (a place) tidy (usually with *up*)

red deer a deer native to Europe and Asia

red·den (red′'n) *vt.* to make red —*vi.* to become red; esp., to blush or flush

re·deem (ri dēm′) *vt.* [< L. *re(d)-*, back + *emere*, get] **1.** to get or buy back; recover **2.** to pay off (a mortgage, etc.) **3.** to convert (stocks, bonds, etc.) into cash **4.** to turn in (trading stamps or coupons) for premiums **5.** to ransom **6.** to deliver from sin **7.** to fulfill (a promise) **8.** *a)* to make amends or atone for *b)* to restore (oneself) to favor —**re·deem′a·ble** *adj.* —**re·deem′er** *n.*

re·demp·tion (ri demp′shən) *n.* **1.** a redeeming or being redeemed **2.** something that redeems —**re·demp′tive, re·demp′to·ry** *adj.*

re·de·ploy (rē′di ploi′) *vt., vi.* to move (troops, etc.) from one area to another —**re′de·ploy′ment** *n.*

re·de·vel·op (rē′di vel′əp) *vt.* **1.** to develop again **2.** to rebuild or restore (a run-down area)

red′-hand′ed (-han′did) *adv., adj.* in the very commission of crime or wrongdoing

red′head′ *n.* **1.** a person with red hair **2.** a N. American duck: the male has a red head —**red′head′ed** *adj.*

red herring [< herring drawn across the trace in hunting to distract the hounds] something used to divert attention from the basic issue

red′-hot′ *adj.* **1.** hot enough to glow **2.** very excited, angry, etc. **3.** very new, timely, etc.

re·dis′trict *vt.* to divide anew into districts

red lead a red oxide of lead used in making paint, glass, etc.

red′-let′ter *adj.* designating a memorable or joyous day or event: from the custom of marking holidays on the calendar in red ink

red light 1. a danger or warning signal **2.** the red phase of a traffic light, a direction to stop

red man a North American Indian

re·do′ *vt.* **-did′, -done′, -do′ing 1.** to do again **2.** to redecorate (a room, etc.)

red·o·lent (red′'l ənt) *adj.* [< L. *re(d)-*, intens. + *olere*, to smell] **1.** sweet-smelling **2.** smelling (*of*) **3.** suggestive (*of*) —**red′o·lence** *n.*

re·dou·ble (rē dub′'l) *vt., vi.* **-bled, -bling 1.** to double again; increase fourfold **2.** to make or become twice as much or twice as great

re·doubt (ri dout′) *n.* [< Fr. < It.: see REDUCE] **1.** a breastwork **2.** any stronghold

re·doubt·a·ble (ri dout′ə b'l) *adj.* [< L. *re-*, intens. + *dubitare*, to doubt] **1.** formidable **2.** commanding respect —**re·doubt′a·bly** *adv.*

re·dound (ri dound′) *vi.* [< L. *re(d)-*, intens. + *undare*, to surge] **1.** to have a result (*to* the credit or discredit of) **2.** to come back; react (*upon*)

red pepper 1. a plant with a red, many-seeded fruit **2.** the fruit **3.** the ground fruit or seeds, used for seasoning

re·dress (ri dres′) *vt.* [see RE- & DRESS] to rectify, as by making compensation for (a wrong, etc.) —*n.* (usually rē′dres) **1.** compensation **2.** a redressing

Red River river flowing along the Tex.-Okla. border, through Ark. & La. into the Mississippi; 1,018 mi.

Red Sea sea between NE Africa & W Arabia

red snapper a reddish, deep-water food fish

red'start' (-stärt') *n.* [RED + obs. *start*, tail] **1.** an American fly-catching warbler **2.** a small European warbler with a reddish tail

red tape [< tape used for tying official papers] rigid adherence to routine and regulations, causing delay in getting business done

red tide sea water discolored by red protozoans poisonous to marine life

re·duce (ri doos', -dyoos') *vt.* **-duced', -duc'ing** [< L. *re-*, back + *ducere*, to lead] **1.** to lessen, as in size, price, etc. **2.** to change to a different form **3.** to bring into a certain order **4.** to lower, as in rank or condition **5.** to subdue or conquer **6.** to compel by need [*reduced* to stealing] **7.** *Math.* to change in denomination or form without changing in value [to *reduce* 4/8 to 1/2] **8.** *Chem. a)* to decrease the positive valence of (an atom or ion) *b)* to remove the oxygen from *c)* to combine with hydrogen *d)* to remove the nonmetallic elements from —*vi.* **1.** to become reduced **2.** to lose weight, as by dieting —**re·duc'er** *n.* —**re·duc'i·ble** *adj.*

re·duc·tion (ri duk'shən) *n.* **1.** a reducing or being reduced **2.** anything made by reducing **3.** the amount by which something is reduced

re·dun·dan·cy (ri dun'dən sē) *n., pl.* **-cies 1.** a being redundant **2.** a redundant quantity, part, etc. **3.** the use of redundant words Also **re·dun'dance**

re·dun'dant (-dənt) *adj.* [see REDOUND] **1.** excess; superfluous **2.** wordy **3.** unnecessary to the meaning: said of words —**re·dun'dant·ly** *adv.*

re·du·pli·cate (ri doo'plə kāt', -dyoo'-) *vt.* **-cat'ed, -cat'ing** to redouble, double, or repeat —*vi.* to become reduplicated —**re·du'pli·ca'tion** *n.*

red'-winged' blackbird a N. American blackbird with a red patch on the wings in the male

red'wood' *n.* **1.** a giant evergreen of the Pacific coast **2.** its reddish wood

re·ech·o, re-ech·o (rē ek'ō) *vt., vi.* **-oed, -o·ing** to echo back or again —*n., pl.* **-oes** the echo of an echo

reed (rēd) *n.* [OE. *hreod*] **1.** a tall, slender grass growing in wet land **2.** a musical pipe made from a hollow stem **3.** *a)* a thin strip of wood, plastic, etc. placed against the mouthpiece, as of a clarinet, and vibrated by the breath to produce a tone *b)* an instrument with a reed *c)* a similar vibrating device in some organs

reed'y *adj.* **-i·er, -i·est 1.** full of reeds **2.** made of reed or reeds **3.** slender, fragile, etc. **4.** high-pitched and weak; piping —**reed'i·ness** *n.*

reef' (rēf) *n.* [prob. < ON. *rif*, a rib] a ridge of rock, coral, or sand at or near the surface of the water

reef² (rēf) *n.* [ME. *riff*] a part of a sail which can be folded and tied down to reduce the area exposed to the wind —*vt., vi.* to reduce the size of (a sail) by taking in part of it

reef'er *n.* **1.** one who reefs **2.** a short, thick, double-breasted coat **3.** [Slang] a marijuana cigarette

reek (rēk) *n.* [OE. *rec*] a strong, unpleasant smell —*vi.* to have a strong, offensive smell

reel' (rēl) *n.* [OE. *hreol*] **1.** a spool on which wire, film, fishing line, etc. is wound **2.** the quantity of wire, film, etc. usually wound on one reel —*vt.* to wind on a reel —*vi.* **1.** to sway or stagger, as from drunkenness or dizziness **2.** to spin; whirl —**reel in 1.** to wind on a reel **2.** to pull in (a fish) by winding a line on a reel —**reel off** to tell, write, etc. fluently —**reel out** to unwind from a reel

reel² (rēl) *n.* [prob. < prec.] a lively dance

re·en·try, re-en·try (rē en'trē) *n., pl.* **-tries** a reentering; specif., a coming back, as of a space vehicle, into the earth's atmosphere

reeve' (rēv) *n.* [OE. *gerefa*] in English history, **1.** the chief officer of a town **2.** the overseer of a manor

reeve² (rēv) *vt.* **reeved** or **rove** (rōv), **rove** or **rov'en**, **reev'ing** [prob. < Du. *reven*] *Naut.* **1.** to pass (a rope, etc.) through (a block, pulley, etc.) **2.** to fasten by passing through or around something

ref (ref) *n., vt., vi. same as* REFEREE

ref. 1. referee **2.** reference **3.** reformed

re·face (rē fās') *vt.* **-faced', -fac'ing** to put a new front or covering on

re·fec·tion (ri fek'shən) *n.* [< L. *re-*, again + *facere*, make] a light meal

re·fec·to·ry (-tər ē) *n., pl.* **-ries** a dining hall, as in a monastery

re·fer (ri fur') *vt.* **-ferred', -fer'ring** [< L. *re-*, back + *ferre*, to bear] **1.** to submit (a quarrel, etc.) for settlement **2.** to direct (*to* someone or something) for aid, information, etc. —*vi.* **1.** to relate or apply (*to*) **2.** to direct attention (*to*) **3.** to turn (*to*) for information, aid, etc.

ref·er·ee (ref'ə rē') *n.* **1.** a person to whom something is referred for decision **2.** an official who enforces the rules in certain sports contests —*vt., vi.* **-eed', -ee'ing** to act as referee (in)

ref·er·ence (ref'ər əns) *n.* **1.** a referring or being referred **2.** relation [in *reference* to his letter] **3.** *a)* the directing of attention to a person or thing *b)* a mention **4.** *a)* an indication, as in a book, of some other work to be consulted *b)* any such work **5.** *a)* one who can offer information or recommendation *b)* a statement giving the qualifications, abilities, etc. of someone seeking a position —**make reference to** to refer to; mention

ref·er·en·dum (ref'ə ren'dəm) *n., pl.* **-dums, -da** (-də) [L.: see REFER] **1.** the submission of a law to a direct vote of the people **2.** the right of the people to vote on such laws **3.** the vote itself

ref·er·ent (ref'ər ənt) *n.* something referred to; specif., *Linguis.* the thing referred to by a term

re·fer·ral (ri fur'əl) *n.* **1.** a referring or being referred **2.** a person who is referred to another person

re·fill (rē fil') *vt., vi.* to fill again —*n.* (rē'fil) **1.** a unit to refill a special container **2.** a refilling of a medical prescription —**re·fill'a·ble** *adj.*

re·fine (ri fīn') *vt., vi.* **-fined', -fin'ing** [RE- + *fine*, make fine] **1.** to free or become free from impurities, etc. **2.** to make or become more polished or elegant —**re·fin'er** *n.*

re·fined' *adj.* **1.** made free from impurities; purified **2.** cultivated; elegant **3.** subtle, precise, etc.

re·fine'ment *n.* **1.** *a)* a refining or being refined *b)* the result of this **2.** delicacy or elegance of manners, speech, etc. **3.** an improvement **4.** a subtlety

re·fin·er·y (ri fīn'ər ē) *n., pl.* **-ies** a plant for refining, or purifying, such raw materials as oil, sugar, etc.

re·fin·ish (rē fin'ish) *vt.* to put a new surface on (wood, metal, etc.) —**re·fin'ish·er** *n.*

re·fit (rē fit') *vt., vi.* **-fit'ted, -fit'ting** to make or be made fit for use again by repairing, reequipping, etc. —*n.* (rē'-fit') a refitting

re·flect (ri flekt') *vt.* [< L. *re-*, back + *flectere*, to bend] **1.** to throw back (light, heat, or sound) **2.** to give back an image of; mirror **3.** to bring as a result [his deeds *reflect* honor on him] —*vi.* **1.** to throw back light, heat, or sound **2.** to give back an image **3.** to think seriously (*on* or *upon*) **4.** to cast blame or discredit (*on* or *upon*) —**re·flec'tive** *adj.*

re·flec'tion *n.* **1.** a reflecting or being reflected **2.** anything reflected, as an image **3.** contemplation **4.** an idea or remark **5.** blame; discredit **6.** an action or remark that discredits

re·flec'tor *n.* a surface, object, or device that reflects light, sound, heat, etc.

re·flex (rē'fleks) *adj.* [see REFLECT] **1.** designating or of an involuntary action, as a sneeze, due to the direct transmission of a stimulus to a muscle or gland **2.** turned or bent back —*n.* **1.** a reflex action **2.** any quick, automatic response **3.** [*pl.*] ability to react quickly or effectively

re·flex·ive (ri flek'siv) *adj.* **1.** designating a verb whose subject and object refer to the same person or thing (Ex.: he *hurt* himself) **2.** designating a pronoun used as the object of such a verb —*n.* a reflexive verb or pronoun —**re·flex'ive·ly** *adv.*

re·for·est (rē fôr'ist, -fär'-) *vt., vi.* to plant new trees on (land once forested) —**re'for·est·a'tion** *n.*

re·form (ri fôrm') *vt.* [see RE- & FORM] **1.** to make better as by stopping abuses; improve **2.** to cause (a person) to behave better —*vi.* to become better in behavior —*n.* an improvement; correction of faults —**re·form'a·ble** *adj.* —**re·formed'** *adj.*

re-form (rē'fôrm') *vt., vi.* to form again

ref·or·ma·tion (ref'ər mā'shən) *n.* **1.** a reforming or being reformed **2.** [R-] the 16th-cent. religious movement that resulted in establishing the Protestant churches

re·form·a·to·ry (ri fôr'mə tôr'ē) *adj.* reforming or aiming at reform —*n., pl.* **-ries** a prison to which young law offenders are sent to be reformed: also **reform school 2.** a penitentiary for women

re·form·er (ri fôr'mər) *n.* one who seeks to bring about reform, esp. political or social reform

re·fract (ri frakt') *vt.* [< L. *re-*, back + *frangere*, to break] **1.** to cause (a ray of light, heat, etc.) to undergo refraction 2. to measure the degree of refraction of (an eye or lens) —re·frac'tor n.

re·frac'tion n. 1. the bending of a ray or wave of light, heat, or sound as it passes from one medium into another 2. the ability of the eye to refract light entering it, so as to form an image on the retina

re·frac·to·ry (ri frak'tər ē) adj. [see REFRACT] 1. hard to manage; obstinate 2. not yielding to treatment, as a disease —re·frac'to·ri·ly adv. —re·frac'to·ri·ness n.

re·frain' (ri frān') vi. [< L. re-, back + frenare, to curb] to hold back; keep oneself (from doing something)

re·frain² (ri frān') n. [see REFRACT] 1. a phrase or verse repeated at intervals in a song or poem 2. music for this

re·fresh (ri fresh') vt. 1. to make fresh by cooling, wetting, etc. 2. to make (a person) feel cooler, stronger, etc., as by food, sleep, etc. 3. to replenish; renew 4. to revive (the memory, etc.) —vi. to revive —re·fresh'er n. —re·fresh'ing adj.

re·fresh'ment n. 1. a refreshing or being refreshed 2. that which refreshes 3. [pl.] food or drink or both

re·frig·er·ant (ri frij'ər ənt) adj. refrigerating —n. any of various liquids that vaporize at a low temperature, used in mechanical refrigeration

re·frig'er·ate' ('-ə rāt') vt. -at'ed, -at'ing [< L. re-, intens. + frigus, cold] to make or keep cool or cold, as for preserving —re·frig'er·a'tion n.

re·frig'er·a'tor n. a box, cabinet, or room in which food, drink, etc. are kept cool

ref·uge (ref'yōōj) n. [< L. re-, back + fugere, flee] 1. shelter or protection from danger, difficulty, etc. 2. a place of safety; shelter

ref·u·gee (ref'yoo jē', ref'yoo jē') n. one who flees from his home or country to seek refuge elsewhere

re·ful·gent (ri ful'jənt) adj. [< L. re-, back + fulgere, shine] shining; radiant —re·ful'gence n.

re·fund' (ri fund') vt., vi. [< L. re-, back + fundere, pour] to give back (money, etc.); repay —n. (rē'fund') a refunding or the amount refunded

re·fund² (rē'fund') vt. to fund again or anew; specif., to use borrowed money, as from the sale of a bond issue, to pay back (a loan)

re·fur·bish (ri fur'bish) vt. [RE- + FURBISH] to freshen or polish up again; renovate

re·fus·al (ri fyōō'z'l) n. 1. a refusing 2. the right or chance to accept or refuse something before it is offered to another; option

re·fuse' (ri fyōōz') vt., vi. -fused', -fus'ing [< L. re-, back + fundere, pour] 1. to decline to accept; reject 2. to decline (to do, grant, etc.)

ref·use² (ref'yōōs, -yōōz) n. [see prec.] waste; rubbish —adj. thrown away or rejected as worthless

re·fute (ri fyōōt') vt. -fut'ed, -fut'ing [< L. refutare, repel] 1. to prove (a person) wrong 2. to prove (an argument or statement) to be false or wrong, by argument or evidence —re·fut'a·ble adj. —ref·u·ta·tion (ref'yə tā'shən) n.

reg. 1. regiment 2. region 3. register 4. registered 5. registrar 6. regular 7. regulation

re·gain (ri gān') vt. 1. to get back again; recover 2. to get back to

re·gal (rē'gəl) adj. [< L. rex, king] of, like, or fit for a king; royal, splendid, etc. —re'gal·ly adv.

re·gale (ri gāl') vt., vi. -galed', -gal'ing [< Fr. ré- (see RE-) + OFr. gale, joy] 1. to entertain as with a feast 2. to delight; please —re·gale'ment n.

re·ga·li·a (ri gāl'yə, -gā'lē ə) n.pl. [see REGAL] 1. the insignia of kingship, as a crown, scepter, etc. 2. the insignia or decorations of any rank, society, etc. 3. splendid clothes; finery

re·gard (ri gärd') n. [see RE- & GUARD] 1. a steady look; gaze 2. consideration; concern 3. respect and affection 4. reference; relation [in regard to this matter] 5. [pl.] good wishes [he sends his regards] —vt. 1. to look at attentively 2. to take into account 3. to hold in affection and respect 4. to consider [to regard taxes as a burden] 5. to concern or involve [this regards your welfare] —as regards concerning —without regard to without considering —re·gard'ful adj.

re·gard'ing prep. concerning; about

re·gard'less adj. without regard; heedless; careless —adv. [Colloq.] without regard for objections, difficulties, etc.; anyway —regardless of in spite of —re·gard'less·ly adv.

re·gat·ta (ri gät'ə, -gat'-) n. [It.] 1. a boat race 2. a series of boat races

re·gen·cy (rē'jən sē) n., pl. -cies 1. the position or authority of a regent or group of regents 2. the time during which a regent or group of regents governs

re·gen·er·ate (ri jen'ər it) adj. [< L.: see RE- & GENERATE] 1. spiritually reborn 2. renewed or restored —vt. ('-ə rāt') -at'ed, -at'ing 1. to cause to be spiritually reborn 2. to cause to be completely reformed 3. to bring into existence again; reestablish —vi. 1. to form again; be made anew 2. to be regenerated —re·gen'er·a'tion n. —re·gen'er·a'tive adj.

re·gent (rē'jənt) n. [< L. regere, to rule] 1. a person appointed to rule when a monarch is absent, too young, etc. 2. a member of a governing board, as of a university —adj. acting in place of a monarch [prince regent] —re'gent·ship' n.

reg·gae (reg'ā) n. [< ?] a form of popular Jamaican music influenced by rock-and-roll and calypso

reg·i·cide (rej'ə sīd') n. [< L. rex, king + -cida: see -CIDE] 1. one who kills a king 2. the killing of a king —reg'i·ci'dal adj.

re·gime, ré·gime (ri zhēm', rā-) n. [see REGIMEN] 1. a political or ruling system 2. a social system 3. same as REGIMEN

reg·i·men (rej'ə mən) n. [< L. regere, to rule] a system of diet, exercise, rest, etc. for improving the health

reg·i·ment (rej'ə mənt) n. [< L. regere, to rule] 1. a military unit consisting of two or more battalions 2. a large number (of persons, etc.) —vt. (-ment') 1. to organize systematically 2. to subject to strict discipline and control —reg'i·men'tal adj. —reg'i·men·ta'tion n.

Re·gi·na (ri jī'nə) capital of Saskatchewan, Canada: pop. 131,000

re·gion (rē'jən) n. [see REGAL] 1. a part of the earth's surface; esp., a large area of a specified sort [tropical regions] 2. any area, space, place, etc. or sphere, realm, etc. 3. any division or part, as of an organism [the abdominal region] —re'gion·al adj. —re'gion·al·ly adv.

re'gion·al·ism n. 1. regional quality in life or literature 2. a word, etc. peculiar to some region

reg·is·ter (rej'is tər) n. [< L. regerere, to record] 1. a) a list of names, items, etc. b) a book in which this is kept 2. a device for recording money, fares, etc. paid [a cash register] 3. an opening into a room by which the amount of air passing through can be controlled 4. Music a part of the range of a voice or instrument —vt. 1. to enter in a list 2. to indicate as on a scale 3. to show, as by facial expression [to register joy] 4. to safeguard (mail) by having its committal to the postal system recorded, for a fee —vi. 1. to enter one's name in a list, as of voters 2. to make an impression —reg'is·trant n.

reg'is·tered adj. officially or legally recorded, enrolled, or certified

registered nurse a trained nurse who has passed a State examination so as to qualify for performing complete nursing services

reg·is·trar (rej'i strär') n. an official who keeps records, as of the students in a college

reg·is·tra·tion (rej'i strā'shən) n. 1. a registering or being registered 2. an entry in a register 3. the number of persons registered

reg'is·try (-is trē) n., pl. -tries 1. same as REGISTRATION 2. an office where registers are kept 3. same as REGISTER (n. 1)

reg·nant (reg'nənt) adj. [< L. regnare, to reign] 1. reigning; ruling 2. predominant 3. prevalent

re·gress (ri gres') vi. [< L. re-, back + gradi, go] to go back —re·gres'sion n. —re·gres'sive adj.

re·gret (ri gret') vt. -gret'ted, -gret'ting [< OFr. regreter, mourn] to feel sorrow or remorse over (an occurrence, one's acts, etc.) —n. 1. sorrow, esp. over one's acts or omissions 2. sorrow over a person or thing gone, lost, etc. —(one's) regrets a polite expression of regret, as at declining an invitation —re·gret'ful adj. —re·gret'ful·ly adv. —re·gret'ta·ble adj. —re·gret'ta·bly adv.

re·group (rē grōōp') vt., vi. to group again; specif., Mil. to reorganize (one's forces), as after a battle

reg·u·lar (reg'yə lər) adj. [< L. regula, a rule] 1. conforming to a rule, type, etc.; orderly; symmetrical 2. conforming to a fixed principle or procedure 3. customary or established 4. consistent [a regular customer] 5. functioning in a normal way [a regular pulse] 6. properly qualified [a regular doctor] 7. designating or of the standing army of a country 8. [Colloq.] a) thorough; complete [a regular nuisance] b) pleasant, friendly, etc. 9. Gram. conforming to the usual type as in inflection —*n.* **1.** a regular soldier or player **2.** [Colloq.] one who is regular in attendance **3.** *Politics* one who is loyal to his party —**reg′u·lar′i·ty** (-lar′ə tē) *n.* —**reg′u·lar·ize′** *vt.* **-ized′, -iz′ing** —**reg′u·lar·ly** *adv.* —**reg′u·la′tor** *n.*

reg·u·late (reg′yə lāt′) *vt.* **-lat′ed, -lat′ing** [see prec.] **1.** to control or direct according to a rule, principle, etc. **2.** to adjust to a standard, rate, etc. **3.** to adjust (a clock, etc.) so as to make work accurately —**reg′u·la′tive, reg′u·la·to′ry** (-lə tôr′ē) *adj.*

reg′u·la′tion *n.* **1.** a regulating or being regulated **2.** a rule or law by which conduct, etc. is regulated —*adj.* **1.** required by regulation **2.** usual; normal

re·gur·gi·tate (ri gur′jə tāt′) *vi., vt.* **-tat′ed, -tat′ing** [< ML. *re-*, back + LL. *gurgitare*, to surge] to bring (partly digested food) from the stomach back to the mouth —**re·gur′gi·ta′tion** *n.*

re·ha·bil·i·tate (rē′hə bil′ə tāt′) *vt.* **-tat′ed, -tat′ing** [< ML. *rehabilitare*, to restore] **1.** to restore to rank, reputation, etc. which one has lost **2.** to put back in good condition **3.** to bring or restore to a state of health or constructive activity —**re′ha·bil′i·ta′tion** *n.*

re·hash (rē hash′) *vt.* [RE- + HASH] to work up again or go over again —*n.* (rē′hash) the act or result of rehashing

re·hear *vt.* **-heard′, -hear′ing** *Law* to hear (a case) a second time

re·hearse (ri hurs′) *vt.* **-hearsed′, -hears′ing** [< OFr. *re-*, again + *hercer*, to harrow] **1.** to recite, esp. in detail **2.** to practice (a play, etc.) for public performance **3.** to drill (a person) in what he is to do —*vi.* to rehearse a play, etc. —**re·hears′al** *n.*

Reich (rīk; *G.* rīkh) *n.* [G.] formerly, Germany or the German government

reign (rān) *n.* [< L. *regere*, to rule] **1.** royal power **2.** dominance or sway **3.** the period of rule, dominance, etc. —*vi.* **1.** to rule as a sovereign **2.** to prevail [peace *reigns*]

re·im·burse (rē′im burs′) *vt.* **-bursed′, -burs′ing** [RE- + archaic *imburse*, to pay] **1.** to pay back (money spent) **2.** to compensate (a person) for expenses, damages, losses, etc. —**re′im·burse′ment** *n.*

Reims (rēmz; *Fr.* rans) city in NE France: pop. 153,000

rein (rān) *n.* [see RETAIN] **1.** [*usually pl.*] a narrow strap of leather attached in pairs to a horse's bit and manipulated to control the animal **2.** [*pl.*] a means of controlling [the *reins* of government] —*vt.* to guide or control as with reins —*vi.* to stop or slow down as with reins (with *in* or *up*) —**draw rein** to slow down or stop: also **draw in the reins** —**give (free) rein to** to allow to act without restraint

re·in·car·na·tion (rē′in kär nā′shən) *n.* [see RE- & INCARNATE] **1.** a rebirth of the soul in another body **2.** the doctrine that the soul reappears after death in another and different bodily form —**re′in·car′nate** *vt.* **-nat·ed, -nat·ing**

rein·deer (rān′dir′) *n., pl.* **-deer**, occas. **-deers** [< ON. *hreinn*, reindeer + *dȳr*, deer] a large deer with branching antlers, found in northern regions and domesticated there as a beast of burden

re·in·force (rē′in fôrs′) *vt.* **-forced′, -forc′ing** [RE- + var. of ENFORCE] **1.** to strengthen (a military or naval force) with more troops, ships, etc. **2.** to strengthen, as by propping, adding new material, etc.

reinforced concrete concrete masonry containing steel bars or mesh to increase its strength

REINDEER
(3 1/2–4 1/2 ft. high at shoulder)

re′in·force′ment *n.* **1.** a reinforcing or being reinforced **2.** anything that reinforces; specif., [*pl.*] additional troops, ships, etc.

re·in·state (rē′in stāt′) *vt.* **-stat′ed, -stat′ing** to restore to a former state, position, etc. —**re′in·state′ment** *n.*

re·it·er·ate (rē it′ə rāt′) *vt.* **-at′ed, -at′ing** [see RE- & ITERATE] to say or do again or repeatedly —**re·it′er·a′tion** *n.* —**re·it′er·a′tive** *adj.*

re·ject (ri jekt′) *vt.* [< L. *re-*, back + *jacere*, to throw] **1.** to refuse to take, agree to, use, believe, etc. **2.** to discard **3.** to rebuff **4.** to be unable to make (a transplanted organ, etc.) a living part of the body —*n.* (rē′jekt) a rejected person or thing —**re·jec′tion** *n.*

re·joice (ri jois′) *vi., vt.* **-joiced′, -joic′ing** [< OFr. *rejoïr*] to be or make glad or happy

re·join (rē join′) *vt., vi.* **1.** to join again; reunite **2.** to answer

re·join·der (ri join′dər) *n.* [see RE- & JOIN] **1.** an answer to a reply **2.** any answer

re·ju·ve·nate (ri jōō′və nāt′) *vt.* **-nat′ed, -nat′ing** [< RE- + L. *juvenis*, young] **1.** to make young again **2.** to make seem new or fresh again —**re·ju′ve·na′tion** *n.*

re·lapse (ri laps′) *vi.* **-lapsed′, -laps′ing** [see RE- & LAPSE] to slip back into a former state, esp. into illness after apparent recovery —*n.* (*also* rē′laps) a relapsing

re·late (ri lāt′) *vt.* **-lat′ed, -lat′ing** [< L. *relatus*, brought back] **1.** to tell the story of; narrate **2.** to connect, as in thought or meaning; show a relation between —*vi.* to have reference or some relation (*to*) —**re·lat′a·ble** *adj.* —**re·lat′er, re·la′tor** *n.*

re·lat′ed *adj.* **1.** narrated; told **2.** connected or associated, as by origin, kinship, marriage, etc.

re·la′tion *n.* **1.** a narrating **2.** what is narrated; recital **3.** connection, as in thought, meaning, etc. **4.** connection by origin or marriage; kinship **5.** a relative **6.** [*pl.*] the connections between or among persons, nations, etc. [trade *relations*] —**in** (or **with**) **relation to** concerning; regarding —**re·la′tion·al** *adj.* —**re·la′tion·ship′** *n.*

rel·a·tive (rel′ə tiv) *adj.* **1.** related each to the other **2.** having to do with; relevant **3.** regarded in relation to something else; comparative [*relative* comfort] **4.** meaningful only in relationship [''cold'' is a *relative* term] **5.** *Gram.* a) designating a word that introduces a subordinate clause and refers to an antecedent [''which'' is a *relative* pronoun in ''the hat which you bought''] b) introduced by such a word [a *relative* clause] —*n.* a person related to others by kinship —**relative to 1.** concerning **2.** in proportion to —**rel′a·tive·ly** *adv.*

rel·a·tiv·i·ty (rel′ə tiv′ə tē) *n.* **1.** a being relative **2.** *Physics* the theory of the relative, rather than absolute, character of motion, velocity, mass, etc.: as developed esp. by Albert Einstein, the theory includes the statements that: 1) the velocity of light is constant; 2) the mass of a body in motion varies with its velocity; 3) matter and energy are equivalent; 4) space and time are interdependent and form a four-dimensional continuum

re·lax (ri laks′) *vt., vi.* [< L. *re-*, back + *laxare*, loosen] **1.** to make or become less firm, tense, severe, etc. **2.** to rest, as from work —**re·laxed′** *adj.*

re·lax′ant *adj.* causing relaxation, esp. of muscular tension —*n.* a relaxant drug or agent

re·lax·a·tion (rē′lak sā′shən) *n.* **1.** a relaxing or being relaxed **2.** a lessening of or rest from work, worry, etc. **3.** recreation

re·lay (rē′lā) *n.* [< MFr. *re-*, back + *laier*, to leave] **1.** a fresh supply of horses, etc., as for a stage of a journey **2.** a relief crew of workers; shift **3.** a device activated by variations in conditions in one electric circuit and controlling a larger current or activating other devices in the same or another circuit **4.** a race (in full **relay race**) between teams, each member of which goes a part of the distance —*vt.* (*also* ri lā′) **-layed, -lay·ing** to convey as by relays [to *relay* news]

re·lease (ri lēs′) *vt.* **-leased′, -leas′ing** [see RELAX] **1.** to set free, as from confinement, work, pain, etc. **2.** to let (a missile, etc.) go **3.** to permit to be issued, published, etc. **4.** to give up (a claim, right, etc.) —*n.* **1.** a releasing, as from prison, work, pain, etc. **2.** relief from emotional tension **3.** a written discharge **4.** a letting loose of something caught or held **5.** a device for releasing a catch, etc., as on a machine **6.** a book, news item, etc. released to the public **7.** *Law* a written surrender of a claim, etc.

rel·e·gate (rel′ə gāt′) *vt.* **-gat′ed, -gat′ing** [< L. *re-*, away + *legare*, send] **1.** to exile or banish (*to*) **2.** to consign or assign, esp. to an inferior position **3.** to refer or hand over for decision —**rel′e·ga′tion** *n.*

re·lent (ri lent′) *vi.* [< L. *re-*, again + *lentus*, pliant] to become less severe, stern, or stubborn; soften —**re·lent′less** *adj.* —**re·lent′less·ly** *adv.*

rel·e·vant (rel′ə vənt) *adj.* [see RELIEVE] relating to the matter under consideration; pertinent —**rel′e·vance, rel′e·van·cy** *n.* —**rel′e·vant·ly** *adv.*

re·li·a·ble (ri lī′ə b'l) *adj.* that can be relied on; dependable —**re·li′a·bil′i·ty** *n.* —**re·li′a·bly** *adv.*

re·li·ance (ri lī′əns) *n.* **1.** trust, dependence, or confidence **2.** a thing relied on

re·li′ant (-ənt) *adj.* having or showing trust, dependence or confidence —**re·li′ant·ly** *adv.*

rel·ic (rel′ik) *n.* [< OFr.: see RELINQUISH] **1.** an object, custom, etc. surviving from the past **2.** a souvenir **3.** [*pl.*] ruins **4.** the venerated remains, etc. of a saint, martyr, etc.

re·lief (ri lēf′) *n.* **1.** a relieving, as of pain, anxiety, a burden, etc. **2.** anything that eases tension, or offers a pleasing change **3.** aid, esp. by a public agency to the needy **4.** a) release from work or duty b) those bringing such re lease by taking over a post **5.** *a*) the projection of sculptured forms from a flat surface *b*) a work of art so made **6.** the differences in height, collectively, of land forms, shown by lines or colors on a map (**relief map**) **7.** *a*) *Painting* the apparent solidity or projection of objects *b*) distinctness of outline; contrast —*adj. Baseball* designating a pitcher who replaces another during a game —**in relief** carved or molded so as to project from a surface

re·lieve (ri lēv′) *vt.* **-lieved′, -liev′ing** [< L. *re-*, again + *levare*, to raise] **1.** to ease or reduce (pain, anxiety, etc.) **2.** to free from pain, distress, a burden, etc. **3.** to give or bring aid to **4.** to set free from duty or work by replacing **5.** to make less tedious, etc. by providing a pleasing change **6.** to set off by contrast **7.** to ease (oneself) by urinating or defecating —**re·liev′a·ble** *adj.*

re·li·gion (ri lij′ən) *n.* [< L. *religio*] **1.** belief in God or gods to be worshiped, usually expressed in conduct and ritual **2.** any specific system of belief, worship, etc., often involving a code of ethics **3.** any object that is seriously pursued

re·li·gi·os·i·ty (ri lij′ē äs′ə tē) *n.* the quality of being excessively or mawkishly religious

re·li′gious (-əs) *adj.* **1.** devout; pious **2.** of or concerned with religion **3.** conscientiously exact; scrupulous —*n., pl.* **-gious** a nun or monk —**re·li′gious·ly** *adv.* —**re·li′gious·ness** *n.*

re·lin·quish (ri liŋ′kwish) *vt.* [< L. *re-*, from + *linquere*, to leave] **1.** to give up (a plan, etc.) **2.** to surrender (property, a right, etc.) **3.** to let go (a grasp, etc.) —**re·lin′quish·ment** *n.*

rel·ish (rel′ish) *n.* [< OFr. *relais*, something remaining] **1.** an appetizing flavor; pleasing taste **2.** enjoyment; zest [to listen with *relish*] **3.** pickles, olives, etc. served with a meal or as an appetizer —*vt.* to enjoy; like

re·live (rē liv′) *vt.* **-lived′, -liv′ing** to experience again (a past event) as in the imagination

re·lo·cate (rē lō′kāt) *vt., vi.* **-cat·ed, -cat·ing** to move to a new location —**re′lo·ca′tion** *n.*

re·luc·tance (ri luk′təns) *n.* **1.** a being reluctant **2.** *Elec.* a measure of the opposition to the lines of force in a magnetic circuit

re·luc′tant (-tənt) *adj.* [< L. *re-*, against + *luctari*, to struggle] **1.** unwilling; disinclined **2.** marked by unwillingness [a *reluctant* answer] —**re·luc′tant·ly** *adv.*

re·ly (ri lī′) *vi.* **-lied′, -ly′ing** [< L. *re-*, back + *ligare*, bind] to trust; depend (with *on* or *upon*)

REM (rem) *n., pl.* **REMs** [*r*(apid) *e*(ye) *m*(ovement)] the rapid, jerky movement of the eyeballs during stages of sleep associated with dreaming

rem (rem) *n.* [*r*(oentgen) *e*(quivalent) *m*(an)] a dosage of ionizing radiation with a biological effect about equal to that of one roentgen of X-ray

re·main (ri mān′) *vi.* [< L. *re-*, back + *manere*, to stay] **1.** to be left over when the rest has been taken away, etc. **2.** to stay **3.** to continue; go on being or existing [he *remained* a cynic] **4.** to be left to be dealt with, done, etc.

re·main′der *n.* **1.** those remaining **2.** what is left when a part is taken away **3.** any of the copies of a book, disposed of cheaply by a publisher, as when the sale has fallen off **4.** *Arith.* what is left when a smaller number is subtracted from a larger —*vt.* to sell (books) as remainders

re·mains′ *n.pl.* **1.** what is left after part has been used, destroyed, etc. **2.** a dead body

re·mand (ri mand′) *vt.* [< L. *re-*, back + *mandare*, to order] *Law* **1.** to send (a prisoner) back into custody **2.** to send (a case) back to a lower court —*n.* a remanding or being remanded

re·mark (ri märk′) *vt., vi.* [< Fr. < *re-*, again + *marquer*, to mark] to notice, observe, or comment; make (as) an observation —*n.* **1.** a noticing **2.** a brief comment

re·mark′a·ble *adj.* worthy of notice; extraordinary —**re·mark′a·ble·ness** *n.* —**re·mark′a·bly** *adv.*

Rem·brandt van Rijn (rem′brant van rīn′) 1606–69; Du. painter & etcher

re·me′di·al (-əl) *adj.* **1.** providing a remedy **2.** intended to correct deficiencies, as certain study courses

rem·e·dy (rem′ə dē) *n., pl.* **-dies** [< L. *re-*, again + *mederi*, heal] **1.** any medicine or treatment for a disease **2.** something to correct a wrong or evil —*vt.* **-died, -dy·ing** to cure, correct, etc.

re·mem·ber (ri mem′bər) *vt.* [< L. *re-*, again + *memorare*, bring to mind] **1.** to think of again **2.** to bring back to mind by an effort; recall **3.** to be careful not to forget

4. to keep (a person) in mind for a present, legacy, etc. **5.** to mention (a person) to another as sending regards —*vi.* to bear in mind or call back to mind

re·mem′brance (-brəns) *n.* **1.** a remembering or being remembered **2.** the power to remember **3.** a souvenir or keepsake **4.** [*pl.*] greetings

re·mind (ri mīnd′) *vt., vi.* to put (a person) in mind (*of* something); cause to remember —**re·mind′er** *n.*

rem·i·nisce (rem′ə nis′) *vi.* **-nisced′, -nisc′ing** [< REMINISCENCE] to think, talk, or write about past events

rem′i·nis′cence (-nis′′ns) *n.* [Fr. < L. *re-*, again + *memini*, remember] **1.** a remembering **2.** memory **3.** [*pl.*] an account of remembered experiences —**rem′i·nis′cent** *adj.* —**rem′i·nis′cent·ly** *adv.*

re·miss (ri mis′) *adj.* [see REMIT] careless; negligent —**re·miss′ness** *n.*

re·mis·sion (ri mish′ən) *n.* [see REMIT] **1.** forgiveness or pardon, as of sins **2.** release from a debt, tax, etc. **3.** a lessening or disappearance of pain or symptoms, etc. —**re·mis′sive** *adj.*

re·mit (ri mit′) *vt.* **-mit′ted, -mit′ting** [< L. *re-*, back + *mittere*, send] **1.** to forgive or pardon (sins, etc.) **2.** to free someone from (a debt, tax, penalty, etc.) **3.** to slacken; lessen [without *remitting* one's efforts] **4.** to send (money) in payment **5.** *Law* to send (a case) back to a lower court; remand —*vi.* **1.** to slacken **2.** to send money in payment —**re·mit′tance** *n.*

re·mit′tent (-′nt) *adj.* abating for a while or at intervals, as a fever

rem·nant (rem′nənt) *n.* [see REMAIN] what is left over, as a piece of cloth at the end of a bolt

re·mod·el (rē mäd′′l) *vt.* **-eled** or **-elled, -el·ing** or **-el·ling 1.** to model again **2.** to make over; rebuild

re·mon·strance (ri män′strəns) *n.* a remonstrating; protest, complaint, etc.

re·mon′strate (-strāt) *vt.* **-strat·ed, -strat·ing** [< L. *re-*, again + *monstrare*, to show] to say in protest, objection, etc. —*vi.* to protest; object —**re·mon′strant** *adj., n.* —**re·mon·stra·tion** (rē′män strā′shən, rem′ən-) *n.* —**re·mon′stra·tive** (-strə tiv) *adj.* —**re·mon′stra·tor** *n.*

re·morse (ri môrs′) *n.* [< L. *re-*, again + *mordere*, to bite] **1.** a torturing sense of guilt for one's actions **2.** pity: now only in **without remorse**, pitilessly —**re·morse′ful** *adj.* —**re·morse′less** *adj.*

re·mote (ri mōt′) *adj.* **-mot′er, -mot′est** [< L. *remotus*, removed] **1.** distant in space or time **2.** distant in relation, connection, etc. **3.** distantly related [a *remote* cousin] **4.** aloof; withdrawn **5.** slight [a *remote* chance] —**re·mote′ly** *adv.* —**re·mote′ness** *n.*

remote control control of aircraft, missiles, etc. from a distance, as by radio waves

re·move (ri mōōv′) *vt.* **-moved′, -mov′ing** [see RE- & MOVE] **1.** to move (something) from where it is; take away or off **2.** to dismiss, as from office **3.** to get rid of **4.** to kill **5.** to separate (*from*) —*vi.* to move away, as to another residence —*n.* **1.** the space or time in which a move is made **2.** a step or degree away [only one *remove* from war] —**re·mov′a·ble** *adj.* —**re·mov′al** *n.* —**re·mov′er** *n.*

re·mu·ner·ate (ri myōō′nə rāt′) *vt.* **-at′ed, -at′ing** [< L. *re-*, again + *munus*, gift] to pay (a person) for (a service, loss, etc.) —**re·mu′ner·a·ble** *adj.* —**re·mu′ner·a′tion** *n.* —**re·mu′ner·a′tive** *adj.*

Re·mus (rē′məs) *see* ROMULUS

ren·ais·sance (ren′ə säns′, -zäns′) *n.* [Fr. < *re-*, again + *naître*, be born] **1.** a rebirth; revival **2.** [R-] the great revival of art and learning in Europe in the 14th, 15th, and 16th centuries

re·nal (rē′n′l) *adj.* [< Fr. < L. *renes*, kidneys] of or near the kidneys

re·nas·cence (ri nas′′ns, -nās′-) *n.* [*also* R-] same as RENAISSANCE

re·nas′cent (-′nt) *adj.* [< L.: see RE- & NASCENT] having or showing new life or vigor

rend (rend) *vt., vi.* **rent, rend′ing** [OE. *rendan*] to tear or split apart with violence

ren·der (ren′dər) *vt.* [ult. < L. *re*(d)-, back + *dare*, give] **1.** to submit, as for approval, payment, etc. **2.** to give in return or pay as due [*render* thanks] **3.** to cause to be **4.** to give (aid) or do (a service) **5.** to depict, as by drawing **6.** to play (music), act (a role), etc. **7.** to translate **8.** to melt down (fat)

ren·dez·vous (rän′dā vōō′) *n., pl.* **-vous′** (-vōōz′) [< Fr. *rendez-vous*, betake yourself] **1.** a meeting place **2.** an agreement to meet **3.** such a meeting —*vi., vt.* **-voused'** (-vōōd'), **-vous'ing** (-vōō'iŋ) to bring or come together at a rendezvous

ren·di·tion (ren dish'ən) *n.* a rendering; performance, translation, etc.

ren·e·gade (ren'ə gād') *n.* [< Sp. < L. *re-*, again + *negare*, deny] one who abandons a party, movement, etc. to join the other side; turncoat

re·nege (ri nig') *vi.* **-neged', -neg'ing** [see prec.] **1.** to go back on a promise **2.** to play a card of another suit, against the rules, when holding any of the suit called for —*n.* an act of reneging in a card game —**re·neg'er** *n.*

re·new (ri nōō') *vt.* **1.** to make new or fresh again **2.** to reestablish; revive **3.** to resume **4.** to repeat **5.** to put in a fresh supply of **6.** to give or get an extension of *[renew a lease]* —**re·new'a·ble** *adj.* —**re·new'al** *n.*

ren·net (ren'it) *n.* [ME. *rennen*, coagulate] an extract from the stomach of calves, etc., used to curdle milk, as in making cheese

Re·no (rē'nō) city in W Nev.: pop. 73,000

Re·noir (rə nwär'; *E.* ren'wär), **Pierre Au·guste** (ô güst') 1841–1919; Fr. painter

re·nounce (ri nouns') *vt.* **-nounced', -nounc'ing** [< L. *re-*, back + *nuntiare*, tell] **1.** to give up formally (a claim, etc.) **2.** to give up (a habit, goods, etc.) **3.** to disown —**re·nounce'ment** *n.*

ren·o·vate (ren'ə vāt') *vt.* **-vat'ed, -vat'ing** [< L. *re-*, again + *novus*, new] to make as good as new; repair, rebuild, etc. —**ren'o·va'tion** *n.* —**ren'o·va'tive** *adj.* —**ren'o·va'tor** *n.*

re·nown (ri noun') *n.* [< OFr. *re-*, again + *nom(m)er*, to name] great fame or reputation —**re·nowned'** *adj.*

rent[1] (rent) *n.* [< L. *reddita*, paid] a stated payment at fixed intervals for the use of a house, land, etc. —*vt.* to get or give use of in return for rent —*vi.* to be let for rent —**for rent** available to be rented —**rent'a·ble** *adj.* —**rent'er** *n.*

rent[2] (rent) *pt. & pp.* of REND —*n.* a hole or gap made by tearing

rent·al (ren't'l) *n.* **1.** an amount paid or received as rent **2.** a house, car, etc. for rent **3.** a renting —*adj.* of, in, or for rent

re·nun·ci·a·tion (ri nun'sē ā'shən) *n.* a renouncing, as of a right

re·or·gan·ize (rē ôr'gə nīz') *vt., vi.* **-ized', -iz'ing** to organize again or anew —**re·or'gan·i·za'tion** *n.* —**re·or'gan·iz'er** *n.*

rep (rep) *n.* [Fr. *reps* < Eng. *ribs*] a ribbed fabric of silk, wool, cotton, etc.

Rep. 1. Representative **2.** Republican

re·paid (ri pād') *pt. & pp.* of REPAY

re·pair[1] (ri per') *vt.* [< L. *re-*, again + *parare*, prepare] **1.** to put back in good condition; fix; renew **2.** to remedy (a mistake, etc.) **3.** to make amends for (a wrong, etc.) —*n.* **1.** a repairing **2.** [*usually pl.*] work done in repairing **3.** the state of being repaired *[kept in repair]* —**re·pair'a·ble** *adj.* —**re·pair'er** *n.* —**re·pair'man** *n., pl.* **-men**

re·pair[2] (ri per') *vi.* [< L. *re-*, back + *patria*, native land] to go (*to* a place)

rep·a·ra·ble (rep'ər ə b'l) *adj.* that can be repaired

rep·a·ra·tion (rep'ə rā'shən) *n.* [see REPAIR[1]] **1.** a making of amends **2.** [*usually pl.*] compensation, as for war damage, payable in money, goods, etc.

rep·ar·tee (rep'ər tē', -tā') *n.* [< Fr. *re-*, back + *partir*, to part] **1.** a quick, witty reply **2.** quick, witty conversation **3.** skill in making witty replies

re·past (ri past') *n.* [< OFr. *re-*, RE- + *past*, food] food and drink; a meal

re·pa·tri·ate (rē pā'trē āt') *vt., vi.* **-at'ed, -at'ing** [see REPAIR[2]] to send back or return to the country of birth, citizenship, etc. —**re·pa'tri·a'tion** *n.*

re·pay (ri pā') *vt.* **-paid', -pay'ing 1.** to pay back **2.** to make return to for (a favor, etc.) —**re·pay'a·ble** *adj.* —**re·pay'ment** *n.*

re·peal (ri pēl') *vt.* [see RE- & APPEAL] to revoke; cancel; annul *[to repeal a law]* —*n.* revocation, abrogation, etc.

re·peat (ri pēt') *vt.* [< L. *re-*, again + *petere*, seek] **1.** to say again **2.** to say from memory **3.** to say (something) as said by someone else **4.** to tell to someone else *[repeat a secret]* **5.** to do or make again —*vi.* to say or do again —*n.* **1.** a repeating **2.** anything said or done again **3.** *Music a)* a passage repeated in playing *b)* a symbol for this —**re·peat'a·ble** *adj.* —**re·peat'er** *n.*

re·peat·ed *adj.* said, made, or done again, or again and again —**re·peat'ed·ly** *adv.*

re·pel (ri pel') *vt.* **-pelled', -pel'ling** [< L. *re-*, back + *pellere*, to drive] **1.** to drive or force back **2.** to refuse or re-

ject **3.** to cause dislike in; disgust **4.** to cause (insects, etc.) to stay away **5.** to be resistant to (water, etc.) **6.** to fail to mix with *[water repels oil]* —*vi.* to cause dislike, etc. —**re·pel'lent** *adj., n.* —**re·pel'ler** *n.*

re·pent (ri pent') *vi., vt.* [< L. *re-*, again + *paenitere*, repent] **1.** to feel sorry for (an error, sin, etc.) **2.** to feel such regret over (an action, intention, etc.) as to change one's mind —**re·pent'ance** *n.* —**re·pent'ant** *adj.*

re·per·cus·sion (rē'pər kush'ən) *n.* [see RE- & PERCUSSION] **1.** formerly, a recoil **2.** reflection, as of sound **3.** a reaction to some event or action: *usually used in pl.* —**re'per·cus'sive** *adj.*

rep·er·toire (rep'ər twär') *n.* [< Fr. < L. *reperire*, discover] the stock of plays, songs, etc. that a company, singer, etc. is prepared to perform

rep'er·to'ry (-tôr'ē) *n., pl.* **-ries 1.** *same as* REPERTOIRE **2.** the system of alternating several plays throughout a season with a permanent acting group

rep·e·ti·tion (rep'ə tish'ən) *n.* [< L. *repetitio*] **1.** a repeating **2.** something repeated —**re·pet·i·tive** (ri pet'ə tiv) *adj.* —**re·pet'i·tive·ly** *adv.*

rep'e·ti'tious *adj.* full of or using repetition, esp. tiresome repetition —**rep'e·ti'tious·ly** *adv.*

re·pine (ri pīn') *vi.* **-pined', -pin'ing** [RE- + PINE[2]] to feel or express discontent; complain

re·place (ri plās') *vt.* **-placed', -plac'ing 1.** to put back in a former place or the proper place **2.** to take the place of **3.** to provide an equivalent for —**re·place'a·ble** *adj.*

re·place'ment *n.* **1.** a replacing or being replaced **2.** a person or thing that takes the place of another that is lost, worn out, dismissed, etc.

re·plen·ish (ri plen'ish) *vt.* [< L. *re-*, again + *plenus*, full] **1.** to make full or complete again **2.** to supply again —**re·plen'ish·ment** *n.*

re·plete (ri plēt') *adj.* [< L. *re-*, again + *plere*, to fill] **1.** well-filled; plentifully supplied **2.** stuffed with food and drink —**re·ple'tion** *n.*

rep·li·ca (rep'li kə) *n.* [< It.: see REPLY] a copy of a work of art, etc., esp. one done by the maker of the original

rep·li·cate (rep'li kāt') *vt.* **-cat'ed, -cat'ing** [see REPLY] to repeat or duplicate

rep'li·ca'tion *n.* **1.** a replicating **2.** a reply; answer **3.** a copy; reproduction

re·ply (ri plī') *vi.* **-plied', -ply'ing** [< L. *re-*, back + *plicare*, to fold] **1.** to speak or write in return **2.** to respond or react —*vt.* to say in return —*n., pl.* **-plies** an answer or response

re·port (ri pôrt') *vt.* [< L. *re-*, back + *portare*, carry] **1.** to give an account of; give information about **2.** to carry and repeat (a message, etc.) **3.** to write or broadcast an account of (news events, etc.) **4.** to announce formally **5.** to make a charge about (something) or against (someone) to one in authority —*vi.* **1.** to make a report **2.** to present oneself, as for work **3.** to be responsible (*to* a superior) —*n.* **1.** rumor **2.** a statement or account **3.** a formal presentation of facts **4.** the noise of an explosion —**re·port'a·ble** *adj.* —**re·port'ed·ly** *adv.*

re·port'age (-ij) *n.* the reporting of news events

report card a periodic report on a pupil's progress, sent to his parents or guardian

re·port'er *n.* one who reports; specif., one who gathers information and writes or gives reports, as for a newspaper or on TV —**rep·or·to·ri·al** (rep'ər tôr'ē əl) *adj.*

re·pose[1] (ri pōz') *vt.* **-posed', -pos'ing** [< L. *re-*, again + LL. *pausare*, to rest] to lay or place for rest —*vi.* **1.** to lie at rest **2.** to rest **3.** to lie dead —*n.* **1.** *a)* rest *b)* sleep **2.** composure **3.** calm; peace —**re·pose'ful** *adj.*

re·pose[2] (ri pōz') *vt.* **-posed', -pos'ing** [see REPOSITORY] **1.** to place (trust, etc.) *in* someone **2.** to place (power, etc.) *in* the control of some person or group

re·pos·i·to·ry (ri päz'ə tôr'ē) *n., pl.* **-ries** [< L. *re-*, back + *ponere*, to place] a box, room, etc. in which things may be put for safekeeping

re·pos·sess (rē'pə zes') *vt.* to get possession of again —**re'pos·ses'sion** *n.*

rep·re·hend (rep'ri hend') *vt.* [< L. *re-*, back + *prehendere*, take] **1.** to reprimand; rebuke **2.** to blame; censure —**rep're·hen'sion** (-hen'shən) *n.*

rep're·hen'si·ble (-hen'sə b'l) *adj.* deserving to be reprehended —**rep're·hen'si·bly** *adv.*

rep·re·sent (rep'ri zent') *vt.* [see RE- & PRESENT, *v.*] **1.** to present to the mind **2.** to present a likeness of; portray **3.** to describe or set forth **4.** *a)* to be a symbol for *b)* to express by symbols, etc. **5.** to be the equivalent of **6.** to act (a role) **7.** to act in place of, esp. by conferred authority **8.** to serve as a specimen, example, etc. of —**rep're·sent'a·ble** *adj.*

rep·re·sen·ta'tion *n.* **1.** a representing or being represented **2.** legislative representatives, collectively **3.** a likeness, image, picture, etc. **4.** [*often pl.*] a statement of claims, protest, etc. —**rep're·sen·ta'tion·al** *adj.*

rep're·sent'a·tive *adj.* **1.** representing **2.** of or based on representation of the people by elected delegates **3.** typical —*n.* **1.** an example; type **2.** one authorized to act for others; agent, salesman, etc. **3.** [R-] a member of the lower house of Congress or of a State legislature —**rep're·sent'a·tive·ly** *adv.*

re·press (ri pres') *vt.* [see RE- & PRESS¹] **1.** to hold back; restrain **2.** to put down; subdue **3.** to control severely **4.** *Psychiatry* to force (painful ideas, etc.) into the unconscious —**re·press'i·ble** *adj.* —**re·pres'sion** *n.* —**re·pres'sive** *adj.*

re·prieve (ri prēv') *vt.* -**prieved'**, -**priev'ing** [< Fr. *reprendre*, take back] **1.** to postpone the punishment of; esp., to postpone the execution of (a condemned person) **2.** to give temporary relief to —*n.* a reprieving or being reprieved

rep·ri·mand (rep'rə mand') *n.* [< L. *reprimere*, repress] a severe or formal rebuke —*vt.* to rebuke severely or formally

re·print (rē print') *vt.* to print an additional impression of —*n.* (rē'print') an additional impression or edition of an earlier book, pamphlet, etc.

re·pris·al (ri prī'z'l) *n.* [see REPREHEND] injury done for injury received; retaliation, esp. in war

re·proach (ri prōch') *vt.* [< L. *re-*, back + *prope*, near] to accuse of a fault; rebuke —*n.* **1.** shame, disgrace, etc., or a cause of this **2.** censure; rebuke —**re·proach'a·ble** *adj.*

re·proach'ful *adj.* full of or expressing reproach —**re·proach'ful·ly** *adv.* —**re·proach'ful·ness** *n.*

rep·ro·bate (rep'rə bāt') *adj.* -**bat'ed**, -**bat'ing** [< LL. *reprobare*, reprove] to disapprove; condemn —*adj.* depraved; corrupt —*n.* a depraved or corrupt person —**rep'ro·ba'tion** *n.*

re·pro·duce (rē'prə dōōs', -dyōōs') *vt.* -**duced'**, -**duc'ing** to produce again; specif., *a*) to bring forth others of (its kind) *b*) to make a copy, imitation, etc. of (a picture, sound, etc.) —*vi.* to produce offspring —**re'pro·duc'i·ble** *adj.*

re'pro·duc'tion (duk'shən) *n.* **1.** a reproducing or being reproduced **2.** a copy, imitation, etc. **3.** the process by which animals and plants produce new individuals

re'pro·duc'tive *adj.* **1.** reproducing **2.** of or for reproduction —**re'pro·duc'tive·ly** *adv.*

re·proof (ri prōōf') *n.* a reproving; rebuke; censure: also **re·prov'al** (-prōō'v'l)

re·prove (ri prōōv') *vt.* -**proved'**, -**prov'ing** [see RE- & PROVE] to rebuke or censure —**re·prov'ing·ly** *adv.*

rep·tile (rep't'l, -tīl) *n.* [< L. *repere*, to creep] **1.** a cold-blooded, creeping or crawling vertebrate, as a snake, lizard, turtle, etc. **2.** a mean, sneaky person —*adj.* of or like a reptile —**rep·til·i·an** (rep til'ē ən) *adj., n.*

re·pub·lic (ri pub'lik) *n.* [< L. *res publica*, public thing] a state or government in which the supreme power rests in all the citizens entitled to vote and is exercised by representatives elected by them

re·pub'li·can (-li kən) *adj.* **1.** of or like a republic **2.** favoring a republic **3.** [R-] of or belonging to the Republican Party —*n.* **1.** one who favors a republican form of government **2.** [R-] a member of the Republican Party

Republican Party one of the two major political parties in the U.S.: it was organized in 1854

re·pu·di·ate (ri pyōō'dē āt') *vt.* -**at'ed**, -**at'ing** [< L. *repudium*, separation] **1.** to disown **2.** to refuse to accept or support (a belief, treaty, etc.) **3.** to refuse to acknowledge or pay (a debt, etc.) —**re·pu'di·a'tion** *n.* —**re·pu'di·a'tor** *n.*

re·pug·nant (ri pug'nənt) *adj.* [< L. *re-*, back + *pugnare*, to fight] **1.** contradictory or opposed **2.** distasteful; offensive —**re·pug'nance** *n.* —**re·pug'nant·ly** *adv.*

re·pulse (ri puls') *vt.* -**pulsed'**, -**puls'ing** [see REPEL] **1.** to drive back (an attack, etc.) **2.** to refuse or reject with discourtesy, etc.; rebuff —*n.* **1.** a repelling or being repelled **2.** a refusal or rebuff

re·pul'sion *n.* **1.** a repelling or being repelled **2.** strong dislike, distaste, etc. **3.** *Physics* the mutual action by which bodies or particles of matter tend to repel each other

re·pul'sive *adj.* **1.** tending to repel **2.** causing strong dislike or aversion; disgusting —**re·pul'sive·ly** *adv.* —**re·pul'sive·ness** *n.*

rep·u·ta·ble (rep'yŏo tə b'l) *adj.* having a good reputation; respectable —**rep'u·ta·bil'i·ty** *n.* —**rep'u·ta·bly** *adv.*

rep·u·ta·tion (rep'yŏo tā'shən) *n.* [see REPUTE] **1.** estimation in which a person or thing is commonly held **2.** favorable estimation **3.** fame

re·pute (ri pyōōt') *vt.* -**put'ed**, -**put'ing** [< L. *re-*, again + *putare*, think] to consider to be as specified [he is *reputed* to be rich] —*n.* same as REPUTATION

re·put'ed *adj.* generally regarded as being such [the *reputed* owner] —**re·put'ed·ly** *adv.*

re·quest (ri kwest') *n.* [see REQUIRE] **1.** an asking for something **2.** something asked for **3.** state of being asked for; demand —*vt.* **1.** to ask for **2.** to ask (a person) to do something —**by request** in response to a request

Re·qui·em (rek'wē əm, rāk'-, rēk'-) *n.* [L., rest] [*also* r-] *R.C.Ch.* **1.** a Mass for the repose of the dead **2.** a musical setting for this

re·quire (ri kwīr') *vt.* -**quired'**, -**quir'ing** [< L. *re-*, again + *quaerere*, ask] **1.** to insist upon, as by right; demand **2.** to order; command **3.** to need **4.** to call for as needed

re·quire'ment *n.* **1.** a requiring **2.** something required or demanded **3.** something needed; necessity

req·ui·site (rek'wə zit) *adj.* [see REQUIRE] required; necessary; indispensable —*n.* something requisite

req·ui·si·tion (rek'wə zish'ən) *n.* **1.** a requiring, as by authority **2.** a formal written request, as for equipment —*vt.* to demand or take, as by authority

re·quite (ri kwīt') *vt.* -**quit'ed**, -**quit'ing** [RE- + *quite*, obs. var. of QUIT] to repay or make return to for (a benefit, service, etc. or an injury, wrong, etc.) —**re·quit'al** *n.*

re·route (rē rōōt', -rout') *vt.* -**rout'ed**, -**rout'ing** to send by a new or different route

re·run (rē run') *vt.* -**ran'**, -**run'ning** to run again —*n.* (rē'run') a rerunning; esp., a repeat showing of a motion picture, television show, etc.

re·sale (rē'sāl') *n.* the act of selling again; specif., the selling of something bought to a third party

re·scind (ri sind') *vt.* [< L. *re-*, back + *scindere*, to cut] to revoke, repeal, or cancel (a law, order, etc.) —**re·scind'a·ble** *adj.* —**re·scis'sion** (-sizh'ən) *n.*

res·cue (res'kyōō) *vt.* -**cued**, -**cu·ing** [ult. < L. *re-*, again + *ex-*, off + *quatere*, to shake] to free or save from danger, evil, etc. —*n.* a rescuing —**res'cu·er** *n.*

re·search (ri surch', rē'surch) *n.* [see RE- & SEARCH] [*sometimes pl.*] systematic investigation in a field of knowledge, to establish facts or principles —*vi., vt.* to do research (on or in) —**re·search'er** *n.*

re·seat (rē sēt') *vt.* **1.** to seat again **2.** to supply with a new seat or seats

re·sec·tion (ri sek'shən) *n.* [< L. *re-*, back + *secare*, to cut] the surgical removal of part of an organ, bone, etc.

re·sem·blance (ri zem'bləns) *n.* similarity of appearance, character, etc.; likeness

re·sem·ble (ri zem'b'l) *vt.* -**bled**, -**bling** [ult. < L. *re-*, again + *simulare*, to feign] to be like or similar to in appearance or nature

re·sent (ri zent') *vt.* [< L. *re-*, again + *sentire*, feel] to feel or show hurt or indignation at (a person, act, etc.), from a sense of being offended —**re·sent'ful** *adj.* —**re·sent'ful·ly** *adv.* —**re·sent'ful·ness** *n.* —**re·sent'ment** *n.*

res·er·va·tion (rez'ər vā'shən) *n.* **1.** a reserving **2.** something reserved or withheld **3.** a limiting condition or qualification **4.** public land set aside for some special use, as for Indians **5.** a reserving, as of a hotel room, theater ticket, etc. until called for

re·serve (ri zurv') *vt.* -**served'**, -**serv'ing** [< L. *re-*, back + *servare*, to hold] **1.** to keep back; set apart for later or special use **2.** to set aside or have set aside (a theater seat, etc.) for someone **3.** to retain for oneself [to *reserve* the right to refuse] —*n.* **1.** something reserved **2.** a limitation [without *reserve*] **3.** the practice of keeping one's thoughts, feelings, etc. to oneself **4.** reticence; silence **5.** [*pl.*] *a*) manpower kept out of action and ready for replacing others *b*) military forces not on active duty but subject to call; militia (with *the*) **6.** cash or liquid assets kept aside by a bank or business to meet demands **7.** land set apart for special use —*adj.* being, or having the nature of, a reserve —**in reserve** reserved for later use

re·served' *adj.* **1.** set apart for some person, purpose, etc. **2.** showing reserve; aloof or reticent —**re·serv'ed·ly** (-zur'vid lē) *adv.*

re·serv'ist *n.* a member of a country's military reserves

res·er·voir (rez'ər vwär', rez'ə-, -vwôr') *n.* [Fr.: see RESERVE] **1.** a place where anything is collected and stored; esp., a natural or artificial lake in which water is stored for use **2.** a receptacle (in an apparatus) for a fluid **3.** a reserve supply

re·side (ri zīd′) *vi.* **-sid′ed, -sid′ing** [< L. *re-*, back + *sedere*, to sit] **1.** to dwell for some time; live (*in* or *at*) **2.** to be present or inherent (*in*): said of qualities, etc. **3.** to be vested (*in*): said of rights, powers, etc.

res·i·dence (rez′i dəns) *n.* **1.** a residing; esp., the fact or status of living in a place while working, studying, etc. there **2.** the place where one resides; home **3.** the time one resides in a place

res′i·den·cy (-dən sē) *n., pl.* **-cies 1.** same as RESIDENCE **2.** a period of advanced training for a doctor at a hospital

res′i·dent (-dənt) *adj.* residing; esp., living in a place while working, etc. there *[a resident physician]* —*n.* **1.** one who lives in a place, not a visitor or transient **2.** a doctor who is serving a residency

res·i·den′tial (-den′shəl) *adj.* **1.** of or connected with residence **2.** of or suitable for residences, or homes *[a residential area]* **3.** chiefly for residents rather than transients *[a residential hotel]* —**res′i·den′tial·ly** *adv.*

re·sid·u·al (ri zij′ōo wəl) *adj.* of or like a residue; remaining —*n.* **1.** something remaining **2.** *[pl.]* extra fees paid to performers for reruns, as on TV

res·i·due (rez′ə dōō′, -dyōō′) *n.* [< L. *residuus*, remaining] **1.** what is left after part is removed; remainder **2.** *Chem.* matter remaining after evaporation, combustion, etc.

re·sid·u·um (ri zij′ōo wəm) *n., pl.* **-u·a** (-wə) [L.] same as RESIDUE

re·sign (ri zīn′) *vt., vi.* [< L. *re-*, back + *signare*, to sign] to give up (a claim, office, position, etc.) —**resign oneself (to)** to submit (to)

res·ig·na·tion (rez′ig nā′shən) *n.* **1.** a resigning **2.** formal notice of this **3.** patient submission

re·signed (ri zīnd′) *adj.* feeling or showing resignation — **re·sign′ed·ly** (-zīn′id lē) *adv.*

re·sil·i·ent (ri zil′yənt, -ē ənt) *adj.* [< L. *re-*, back + *salire*, to jump] **1.** springing back into shape or position; elastic **2.** recovering strength, spirits, etc. quickly —**re·sil′·ience, re·sil′ien·cy** *n.*

res·in (rez′′n) *n.* [L. *resina*] **1.** a substance exuded from various plants and trees and used in medicines, varnish, etc. **2.** same as ROSIN —**res′in·ous** *adj.*

re·sist (ri zist′) *vt.* [< L. *re-*, back + *sistere*, to set] **1.** to withstand; fend off **2.** to oppose actively; fight against — *vi.* to oppose or withstand something —**re·sist′er** *n.* —**re·sist′i·ble** *adj.*

re·sist′ance *n.* **1.** a resisting **2.** power to resist; specif., the ability of an organism to ward off disease **3.** opposition of some force, thing, etc. to another **4.** *Elec.* the property by which a conductor opposes current flow and thus generates heat —**re·sist′ant** *adj., n.*

re·sist′less *adj.* **1.** that cannot be resisted **2.** without power to resist

re·sis′tor *n.* a device, as a wire coil, used in an electric circuit to produce resistance

re·sole (rē′sōl′) *vt.* **-soled′, -sol′ing** to put a new sole on (a shoe, etc.) —*n.* a new shoe sole

res·o·lute (rez′ə lōōt′) *adj.* [see RE- & SOLVE] having or showing a fixed, firm purpose; determined; resolved — **res′o·lute′ly** *adv.* —**res′o·lute′ness** *n.*

res·o·lu′tion *n.* **1.** the act or result of resolving something **2.** the thing determined upon; decision as to future action **3.** a resolute quality of mind **4.** a formal statement of opinion or determination by an assembly **5.** a solving or answering; solution

re·solve (ri zälv′, -zôlv′) *vt.* **-solved′, -solv′ing** [see RE- & SOLVE] **1.** to break up into separate parts; analyze **2.** to change; transform *[the talk resolved itself into an argument]* **3.** to reach as a decision; determine **4.** to solve (a problem) **5.** to decide by vote —*vi.* **1.** to be resolved, as by analysis **2.** to come to a decision —*n.* **1.** a fixed purpose or intention **2.** a formal resolution, as by a group — **re·solv′a·ble** *adj.* —**re·solv′er** *n.*

re·solved′ *adj.* firm and fixed in purpose; resolute

res·o·nance (rez′ə nəns) *n.* **1.** a being resonant **2.** the reinforcing and prolonging of a sound or musical tone by reflection or by vibration of other bodies **3.** *Elec.* that adjustment of a circuit which allows the greatest flow of current of a certain frequency

res·o·nant (-nənt) *adj.* [< L. *resonare*, to resound] **1.** resounding or reechoing **2.** producing resonance *[resonant walls]* **3.** full of, or intensified by, resonance *[a resonant voice]* —**res′o·nant·ly** *adv.*

res·o·na′tor (-nāt′ər) *n.* a device for producing resonance or increasing sound by resonance

res·or·cin·ol (ri zôr′si nōl′, -nôl′) *n.* [< RES(IN) + It. *orcello*, a kind of lichen] a colorless, crystalline compound used in dyes, celluloid, pharmaceuticals, etc.

re·sort (ri zôrt′) *vi.* [< OFr. *re-*, again + *sortir*, go out] **1.** to go; esp., to go often **2.** to have recourse; turn (*to*) for help, support, etc. —*n.* **1.** a place to which people go often, as on vacation **2.** a source of help, support, etc. **3.** a turning for help, support, etc.; recourse

re·sound (ri zound′) *vi.* [< L. *re-*, again + *sonare*, to sound] to make a loud, echoing sound; echo; reverberate —**re·sound′ing** *adj.* —**re·sound′ing·ly** *adv.*

re·source (rē′sôrs, -zôrs; ri sôrs′) *n.* [< Fr. < OFr. *re-*, again + *sourdre*, spring up] **1.** something ready for use or available as needed **2.** *[pl.]* wealth; assets **3.** *[pl.]* something useful, as coal or oil, that a country, state, etc. has **4.** a means to an end; expedient **5.** a being resourceful **re·source′ful** *adj.* able to deal effectively with problems, difficulties, etc. —**re·source′ful·ness** *n.*

re·spect (ri spekt′) *vt.* [< L. *re-*, back + *specere*, look at] **1.** to hold in high regard; show honor or courtesy to **2.** to show consideration for **3.** to concern; relate to —*n.* **1.** high regard; esteem **2.** courteous consideration **3.** *[pl.]* expressions of regard **4.** a particular detail *[in this respect, it's bad]* **5.** reference; relation *[with respect to him]*

re·spect′a·ble *adj.* **1.** worthy of respect or esteem **2.** socially acceptable; proper **3.** of moderate quality or size **4.** good enough to be seen, worn, etc. —**re·spect′a·bil′i·ty** *n.* —**re·spect′a·bly** *adv.*

re·spect′ful *adj.* full of or showing respect; polite —**re·spect′ful·ly** *adv.*

re·spect′ing *prep.* concerning; about

re·spec·tive (ri spek′tiv) *adj.* as relates individually to each of two or more *[their respective merits]*

re·spec′tive·ly *adv.* in regard to each in the order named *[the first and second prizes went to John and Mary, respectively]*

re·spell (rē spel′) *vt.* to spell again; specif., to spell differently so as to show the pronunciation

res·pi·ra·tion (res′pə rā′shən) *n.* **1.** act or process of breathing **2.** the processes by which a living organism or cell takes in oxygen and gives off products, as carbon dioxide

res′pi·ra′tor *n.* **1.** a mask, as of gauze, worn to prevent the inhaling of harmful substances **2.** an apparatus for giving artificial respiration

res·pi·ra·to·ry (res′pər ə tôr′ē, ri spīr′ə-) *adj.* of, for, or involving respiration

re·spire (ri spīr′) *vi., vt.* **-spired′, -spir′ing** [< L. *re-*, back + *spirare*, breathe] to breathe

res·pite (res′pit) *n.* [see RESPECT] **1.** a delay or postponement **2.** temporary relief, as from pain, work, etc.; rest

re·splend·ent (ri splen′dənt) *adj.* [< L. *re-*, again + *splendere*, to shine] shining brightly; dazzling —**re·splend′ence** *n.* —**re·splend′ent·ly** *adv.*

re·spond (ri spänd′) *vi.* [< L. *re-*, back + *spondere*, to pledge] **1.** to answer; reply **2.** to act as if in answer **3.** to react favorably, as to medical treatment

re·spond′ent *adj.* responding —*n.* **1.** one who responds **2.** *Law* a defendant —**re·spond′ence** *n.*

re·spond′er *n.* any electronic device, as a transponder, that indicates reception of a signal

re·sponse (ri späns′) *n.* **1.** something said or done in responding; reply or reaction **2.** words said or sung by the congregation or choir in answer to the clergyman **3.** any reaction to a stimulus

re·spon·si·bil·i·ty (ri spän′sə bil′ə tē) *n., pl.* **-ties 1.** a being responsible; obligation **2.** a thing or person that one is responsible for

re·spon′si·ble (-sə b′l) *adj.* **1.** obliged to account (*for*); answerable (*to*) **2.** involving obligation or duties *[a responsible job]* **3.** accountable as being the cause of something **4.** accountable for one's behavior or for an act **5.** trustworthy; dependable —**re·spon′si·bly** *adv.*

re·spon′sive (-siv) *adj.* **1.** answering **2.** reacting readily, as to appeal **3.** containing responses *[responsive readings]* —**re·spon′sive·ly** *adv.*

rest¹ (rest) *n.* [OE.] **1.** sleep or repose **2.** ease or inactivity after exertion **3.** relief from any-thing distressing, tiring, etc. **4.** the repose of death **5.** absence of motion **6.** a resting place **7.** a thing that supports **8.** *Music* an interval of silence between notes, or a symbol for this —*vi.* **1.** to get refreshed by sleeping, lying down, ceasing work, etc. **2.** to be at ease **3.** to be quiet or still **4.**

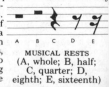

MUSICAL RESTS
(A, whole; B, half;
C, quarter; D,
eighth; E, sixteenth)

A   B   C   D   E

quiet or still **4.** to be dead **5.** to remain unchanged **6.** to lie, sit, or lean **7.** to be or lie (where specified) *[the fault rests with him]* **8.** to be fixed *[his eyes rested on her]* **9.** to rely; depend **10.** *Law* to end voluntarily the introduction of evidence in a case —*vt.* **1.** to refresh by rest **2.** to put for ease, etc. *[rest your head here]* **3.** to base (an argument, etc.) —**lay to rest** to bury

rest² (rest) *n.* [< L. *re-*, back + *stare*, to stand] **1.** what is left; remainder **2.** *[with pl. v.]* the others —*vi.* to go on being *[rest assured]*

res·tau·rant (res′tə rənt, -ränt′) *n.* [Fr.: see RESTORE] a place where meals can be bought and eaten

res·tau·ra·teur (res′tər ə tur′) *n.* [Fr.] a person who owns or operates a restaurant

rest·ful (rest′fəl) *adj.* **1.** full of or giving rest **2.** quiet; tranquil —**rest′ful·ly** *adv.* —**rest′ful·ness** *n.*

res·ti·tu·tion (res′tə tōō′shən, -tyōō′-) *n.* [L. *re-*, again + *statuere*, to set up] **1.** restoration to the rightful owner of something lost or taken away **2.** a making good for loss or damage **3.** a return to a former condition

res·tive (res′tiv) *adj.* [< OFr. < L.: see REST²] **1.** hard to control; balky, etc. **2.** nervous or impatient under restraint; restless —**res′tive·ly** *adv.*

rest·less *adj.* **1.** unable to rest or relax **2.** giving no rest; disturbed *[restless sleep]* **3.** rarely still; active **4.** seeking change —**rest′less·ly** *adv.* —**rest′less·ness** *n.*

res·to·ra·tion (res′tə rā′shən) *n.* **1.** a restoring or being restored **2.** a restored thing —**the Restoration** the reestablishment of the monarchy in England under Charles II; also, his reign (1660–85)

re·stor·a·tive (ri stôr′ə tiv) *adj.* restoring health, consciousness, etc. —*n.* something that restores

re·store (ri stôr′) *vt.* -stored′, -stor′ing [< L. *re-*, again + *-staurare*, to place] **1.** to give back (something taken, lost, etc.) **2.** to bring back to a former or normal state, or to a position, rank, etc. **3.** to bring back to health, strength, etc. **4.** to bring back into use, being, etc. —**re·stor′a·ble** *adj.*

re·strain (ri strān′) *vt.* [< L. *re-*, back + *stringere*, draw tight] **1.** to hold back from action; check; curb **2.** to keep under control **3.** to deprive of physical liberty, as by shackling **4.** to restrict —**re·strain′a·ble** *adj.* —**re·strain′ed·ly** *adv.*

re·straint (ri strānt′) *n.* **1.** a restraining or being restrained **2.** a restraining influence or action **3.** a means of restraining **4.** loss or limitation of liberty **5.** control of emotions; reserve

restraint of trade restriction or prevention of business competition, as by monopoly

re·strict (ri strikt′) *vt.* [see RESTRAIN] to keep within limits; confine; limit —**re·strict′ed** *adj.*

re·stric′tion *n.* **1.** a restricting or being restricted **2.** something that restricts; limitation

re·stric′tive *adj.* **1.** restricting **2.** *Gram.* designating a clause, phrase, or word felt as limiting what it modifies and so not set off by commas (Ex.: the woman *who spoke to us* is a scientist) —**re·stric′tive·ly** *adv.*

rest′room′ *n.* a room in a public building, with toilets, washbowls, etc.: also **rest room**

re·struc·ture (rē struk′chər) *vt.* -tured, -tur·ing to plan or provide a new structure or organization for

re·sult (ri zult′) *vi.* [< L. *resultare*, to rebound] **1.** to happen as an effect of some cause **2.** to end as a consequence (*in* something) —*n.* **1.** anything that issues as an effect; outcome **2.** the number, etc. obtained by mathematical calculation

re·sult′ant (-′nt) *adj.* that results —*n.* **1.** a result **2.** *Physics* a force with an effect equal to that of two or more such forces acting together

re·sume (ri zōōm′, -zyōōm′) *vt.* -sumed′, -sum′ing [< L. *re-*, again + *sumere*, take] **1.** to take or occupy again **2.** to continue after interruption —*vi.* to begin again or go on again —**re·sump·tion** (ri zump′shən) *n.*

ré·su·mé (rez′ōō mā′, rā′zōō-) *n.* [Fr.: see RESUME] a summary, esp. of employment experience: also written **resume, resumé**

re·sur·face (rē sur′fis) *vt.* -faced′, -fac·ing to put a new surface on —*vi.* to come to the surface again

re·sur·gent (ri sur′jənt) *adj.* rising or tending to rise again —**re·sur′gence** *n.*

res·ur·rect (rez′ə rekt′) *vt.* [< RESURRECTION] **1.** to bring back to life **2.** to bring back into use, etc.

res·ur·rec′tion *n.* [< L. *resurgere*, rise again] **1.** a rising from the dead **2.** a return to notice, use, etc.; revival —

the Resurrection *Theol.* **1.** the rising of Jesus from the dead **2.** the rising of all the dead at the Last Judgment

re·sus·ci·tate (ri sus′ə tāt′) *vt.*, *vi.* -tat′ed, -tat′ing [< L. *re-*, again + *suscitare*, revive] to revive (someone who is unconscious, apparently dead, etc.) —**re·sus′ci·ta′tion** *n.* —**re·sus′ci·ta′tor** *n.*

ret. **1.** retired **2.** return(ed)

re·tail (rē′tāl) *n.* [< OFr. *re-*, again + *tailler*, to cut] the sale of goods in small quantities directly to the consumer —*adj.* of or engaged in such sale —*adv.* in small amounts or at a retail price —*vt.*, *vi.* to sell or be sold at retail —**re′tail·er** *n.*

re·tain (ri tān′) *vt.* [< L. *re-*, back + *tenere*, to hold] **1.** to keep in possession, use, etc. **2.** to keep in a fixed state or condition **3.** to keep in mind **4.** to engage (a lawyer, etc.) by an advance fee —**re·tain′a·ble** *adj.* —**re·tain′ment** *n.*

re·tain′er *n.* **1.** a person or thing that retains **2.** a person serving someone of rank or wealth **3.** a fee paid to engage a lawyer's services

retaining wall a wall built to keep a bank of earth from sliding or water from flooding

re·take (rē tāk′) *vt.* -took′, -tak′en, -tak′ing **1.** to take again; recapture **2.** to photograph again —*n.* (rē′tāk′) a scene, etc. photographed again

re·tal·i·ate (ri tal′ē āt′) *vi.* -at′ed, -at′ing [< L. *re-*, back + *talio*, punishment in kind] to return like for like, esp. injury for injury —**re·tal′i·a′tion** *n.* —**re·tal′i·a′tive, re·tal′i·a·to′ry** *adj.*

re·tard (ri tärd′) *vt.* [< L. *re-*, back + *tardare*, hinder] to hinder, delay, or slow the progress of

re·tard′ant (-′nt) *n.* a substance that delays a chemical reaction —*adj.* tending to retard

re·tar·da·tion (rē′tär dā′shən) *n.* **1.** a retarding or being retarded **2.** *same as* MENTAL RETARDATION

re·tard′ed *adj.* delayed in development or progress, esp. because of mental retardation

retch (rech) *vi.* [< OE. *hræcan*, to spit] to make a straining effort to vomit, esp. without bringing anything up

re·ten·tion (ri ten′shən) *n.* **1.** a retaining or being retained **2.** capacity for retaining **3.** *a)* memory *b)* ability to remember —**re·ten′tive** *adj.*

ret·i·cent (ret′ə s′nt) *adj.* [< L. *re-*, again + *tacere*, be silent] disinclined to speak; reserved —**ret′i·cence** *n.*

re·tic·u·late (ri tik′yə lit, -lāt′) *adj.* [< L. *rete*, net] like a net or network —*vt.*, *vi.* (-lāt′) -lat′ed, -lat′ing to divide or mark so as to look like network —**re·tic′u·la′tion** *n.*

ret·i·na (ret′′n ə) *n.*, *pl.* -nas, -nae′ (-ē′) [prob. < L. *rete*, net] the innermost coat of the back part of the eyeball, on which the image is formed by the lens —**ret′i·nal** *adj.*

ret·i·nue (ret′′n ōō′, -yōō′) *n.* [see RETAIN] a group of persons in attendance on a person of rank

re·tire (ri tīr′) *vi.* -tired′, -tir′ing [< Fr. *re-*, back + *tirer*, draw] **1.** to withdraw to a secluded place **2.** to go to bed **3.** to retreat, as in battle **4.** to give up one's work, career, etc., esp. at a certain age —*vt.* **1.** to withdraw (troops) **2.** to pay off (bonds, etc.) **3.** to cause to retire from a job, etc. **4.** *Baseball*, etc. to end the batting turn of (a batter, side, etc.) —**re·tired′** *adj.* —**re·tire′ment** *n.*

re·tir·ee (ri tīr′ē′) *n.* one who has retired from work

re·tir′ing *adj.* reserved; modest; shy

re·tool (rē tōōl′) *vt.*, *vi.* to adapt the machinery of (a factory) for making a different product by changing the tools and dies

re·tort′ (ri tôrt′) *vt.*, *vi.* [< L. *re-*, back + *torquere*, to twist] **1.** to return in kind (an insult, etc. received) **2.** to answer back, esp. in a sharp, quick, or clever way —*n.* a retorting or the response so made

re·tort² (ri tôrt′) *n.* [< ML. *retorta:* see prec.] **1.** a container for distilling, usually of glass and with a long tube **2.** a vessel for heating ore to extract metal

RETORT

re·touch (rē tuch′) *vt.* to touch up details in (a painting, photograph, etc.) —**re·touch′er** *n.*

re·trace (ri trās′) *vt.* -traced′, -trac′ing [see RE- & TRACE¹] **1.** to go back over again, esp. in the reverse direction *[to retrace one's steps]* **2.** to trace again the story of, from the beginning

re·trace (rē′trās′) *vt.* -traced′, -trac′ing to trace the lines of (a drawing, etc.) over again

re·tract (ri trakt′) *vt.*, *vi.* [< L. *re-*, back + *trahere*, draw] **1.** to draw back or in **2.** to withdraw (a statement, charge, etc.); recant —**re·tract′a·ble** *adj.* —**re·trac′tion** *n.*

---

fat, āpe, cär; ten, ēven; is, bīte; gō, hôrn, tōōl, look; oil, out; up, fur; thin, *then*; zh, leisure; ŋ, ring; ə for *a* in *ago*; ′ as in *able* (ā′b'l); ë, Fr. coeur; ö, Fr. feu; Fr. mon; ü, Fr. duc; r, Fr. cri; kh, G. doch, ich. ‡ foreign; < derived from

re·trac·tile (ri trak′t'l, -tīl) *adj.* [Fr.] that can be retracted, or drawn back in, as the claws of a cat

re·tread (rē tred′; *for n.* rē′tred′) *vt., n. same as* RECAP[1]

re·treat (ri trēt′) *n.* [< L. *re-*, back + *trahere*, to draw] 1. a withdrawal in the face of opposition, etc. 2. a safe, quiet, or secluded place 3. a period of seclusion, esp. for religious contemplation 4. *a)* the forced withdrawal of troops under attack *b)* a signal for this *c)* a signal by drum or bugle at sunset for lowering the national flag — *vi.* to withdraw; go back —**beat a retreat** withdraw hurriedly

re·trench (rē trench′) *vt., vi.* [see RE- & TRENCH] to cut down or reduce (esp. expenses); curtail; economize —**re·trench′ment** *n.*

ret·ri·bu·tion (ret′rə byōō′shən) *n.* [< L. *re-*, back + *tribuere*, to pay] deserved reward or, esp., punishment — **re·trib·u·tive** (ri trib′yoo tiv), **re·trib′u·to·ry** (-tôr′ē) *adj.* —**re·trib′u·tive·ly** *adv.*

re·trieve (ri trēv′) *vt.* -trieved′, -triev′ing [< OFr. *re-*, again + *trouver*, to find] 1. to get back; recover 2. to restore *[to retrieve* one's spirits*]* 3. to set right (a loss, error, etc.) 4. to recover (information) from data stored in a computer 5. to find and bring back (killed or wounded game): said of hunting dogs —*vi.* to retrieve game —*n.* a retrieving —**re·triev′a·ble** *adj.*

re·triev′er *n.* 1. one who retrieves 2. a dog trained to retrieve game

ret·ro (ret′rō) *n., pl.* -ros *clipped form of* RETROROCKET

retro- [< L.] *a combining form meaning* backward, back, behind

ret·ro·ac·tive (ret′rō ak′tiv) *adj.* applying to, or going into effect as of, the preceding period *[a retroactive* pay increase*]* —**ret′ro·ac′tive·ly** *adv.*

ret·ro·fire (ret′rə fīr′) *vi., vt.* -fired′, -fir′ing to ignite: said of a retrorocket —*n.* a retrofiring

ret·ro·grade (ret′rə grād′) *adj.* [see RETRO- & GRADE] 1. moving backward 2. going back to an earlier, esp. worse, condition —*vi.* -grad′ed, -grad′ing 1. to go backward 2. to deteriorate

ret·ro·gress (ret′rə gres′, ret′rə gres′) *vi.* [see RETROGRADE] to move backward, esp. into an earlier or worse condition —**ret′ro·gres′sion** *n.* —**ret′ro·gres′sive** *adj.* —**ret′ro·gres′sive·ly** *adv.*

ret·ro·rock·et, ret·ro·rock·et (ret′rō räk′it) *n.* a small rocket on a larger rocket or spacecraft, used to produce thrust against flight direction so as to reduce speed

ret·ro·spect (ret′rə spekt′) *n.* [< L. *retro-*, back + *specere*, to look] contemplation of the past —**in retrospect** in reviewing the past —**ret′ro·spec′tion** *n.* —**ret′ro·spec′tive** *adj.* —**ret′ro·spec′tive·ly** *adv.*

re·turn (ri turn′) *vi.* [see RE- & TURN] 1. to go or come back 2. to answer; retort —*vt.* 1. to bring, send, or put back 2. to do in reciprocation *[to return* a visit*]* 3. to yield, as a profit 4. to report officially or formally 5. to elect or reelect 6. to hit back or throw back (a ball) —*n.* 1. a coming or going back 2. a bringing, sending, or putting back 3. something returned 4. repayment; requital 5. *[often pl.]* yield or profit, as from investments 6. an answer; retort 7. an official or formal report *[election returns]* 8. a form for reporting income tax due: in full (**income**) **tax return** —*adj.* 1. of or for returning *[a return* ticket*]* 2. given, sent, done, etc. in return —**in return** as a return —**re·turn′a·ble** *adj.*

re·un·ion (rē yōōn′yən) *n.* a coming together again after separation

rev (rev) *vt., vi.* revved, rev′ving [< *revolution* of an engine] [Colloq.] to speed up (an engine, motor, etc.)

Rev. 1. *Bible* Revelation 2. *pl.* **Revs.** Reverend

rev. 1. revenue 2. review(ed) 3. revise(d) 4. revision 5. revolution 6. revolving

re·vamp (rē vamp′) *vt.* 1. to put a new vamp on (a shoe or boot) 2. to make over; revise —*n.* a revamping

re·veal (ri vēl′) *vt.* [< L. *re-*, back + *velum*, veil] 1. to make known (something hidden or secret) 2. to expose to view; show —**re·veal′ment** *n.*

re·veil·le (rev′ə lē) *n.* [< Fr. < L. *re-*, again + *vigilare*, to watch] a signal on a bugle, drum, etc. in the morning to waken soldiers or sailors or call them to first assembly

rev·el (rev′'l) *vi.* -eled or -elled, -el·ing or -el·ling [see REBEL] 1. to be noisily festive 2. to take much pleasure (*in*) —*n.* merrymaking —**rev′el·er, rev′el·ler** *n.* —**rev′el·ry** *n., pl.* -ries

rev·e·la·tion (rev′ə lā′shən) *n.* 1. a revealing 2. something disclosed, esp. a striking disclosure 3. *Theol.* God's revealing of himself to man —[R-] the last book of the New Testament (in full **The Revelation of Saint John the Divine**): also **Revelations**

re·venge (ri venj′) *vt.* -venged′, -veng′ing [< OFr. *re-*, again + *vengier*, take vengeance] 1. to inflict harm in return for (an injury, insult, etc.) 2. to avenge (a person, oneself, etc.) —*n.* 1. a revenging 2. what is done in revenging 3. desire to take vengeance 4. a chance to retaliate —**re·venge′ful** *adj.* —**re·venge′ful·ly** *adv.* —**re·venge′ful·ness** *n.*

rev·e·nue (rev′ə nōō′, -nyōō′) *n.* [< OFr. *re-*, back + *venir*, come] 1. income, as from investments 2. income of a government from taxes, licenses, etc.

re·ver·ber·ate (ri vur′bə rāt′) *vt., vi.* -at′ed, -at′ing [< L. *re-*, again + *verberare*, to beat] 1. to throw back (sound); reecho 2. to reflect or be reflected, as waves of light, heat, etc. —**re·ver′ber·a′tion** *n.* —**re·ver′ber·a·to′ry** (-bər ə tôr′ē) *adj.*

re·vere (ri vir′) *vt.* -vered′, -ver′ing [< Fr. < L. *re-*, again + *vereri*, to fear] to regard with deep respect, love, and awe; venerate

Re·vere (ri vir′), **Paul** 1735–1818; Am. patriot

rev·er·ence (rev′ər əns, rev′rəns) *n.* 1. a feeling of deep respect, love, and awe 2. a bow or curtsy 3. [R-] a title of respect for a clergyman: preceded by *your* or *his* —*vt.* -enced, -enc·ing to treat with reverence

rev′er·end (-ər ənd, -rənd) *adj.* worthy of reverence: used *[usually* the R-] as a title of respect for a clergyman, often before the name —*n.* [Colloq.] a clergyman

rev′er·ent *adj.* feeling or showing reverence: also **rev′er·en′tial** (-ə ren′shəl) —**rev′er·ent·ly** *adv.*

rev·er·ie (rev′ər ē) *n.* [< Fr. *rever*, to wander] 1. daydreaming 2. a fanciful notion

re·vers (ri vir′, -ver′) *n., pl.* -vers′ (-virz′, -verz′) [Fr.: see REVERSE] a part (of a garment) turned back to show the reverse side or facing, as a lapel: also **re·vere′** (-vir′)

re·verse (ri vurs′) *adj.* [see REVERT] 1. turned backward; opposite or contrary 2. reversing the usual effect, as to show white letters on black 3. causing movement in the opposite direction —*n.* 1. the opposite or contrary 2. the back of a coin, medal, etc. 3. a change from good fortune to bad 4. a mechanism for reversing, as a gear on a machine —*vt.* -versed′, -vers′ing 1. to turn about, upside down, or inside out 2. to change to the opposite 3. to cause to go in an opposite direction 4. to transfer (the charges for a telephone call) to the party being called 5. *Law* to revoke or annul (a decision, etc.) —*vi.* 1. to go or turn in the opposite direction 2. to put a motor, etc. in reverse —**re·ver′sal** (-vur′s'l) *n.* —**re·vers′i·ble** *adj.*

re·vert (ri vurt′) *vi.* [< L. *re-*, back + *vertere*, to turn] 1. to go back, as to a former practice, subject, etc. 2. *Biol.* to return to an earlier type 3. *Law* to go back to a former owner or his heirs —**re·ver′sion** (-vur′zhən) *n.* —**re·vert′i·ble** *adj.*

rev·er·y (rev′ər ē) *n., pl.* -ies *same as* REVERIE

re·view (ri vyōō′) *n.* [< L. *re-*, again + *videre*, see] 1. a looking at or looking over again 2. a general survey or report 3. a looking back, as on past events 4. reexamination, as of the decision of a lower court 5. a critical report of a book, play, etc. 6. a magazine with articles of criticism 7. *same as* REVUE 8. a formal inspection, as of troops on parade —*vt.* 1. to look back on 2. to survey 3. to inspect (troops, etc.) formally 4. to give or write a critical report of (a book, play, etc.) 5. to reexamine (a lower court's decision) —*vi.* to review books, plays, etc. —**re·view′er** *n.*

re·vile (ri vīl′) *vt., vi.* -viled′, -vil′ing [see RE- & VILE] to use abusive language (to or about) —**re·vile′ment** *n.* —**re·vil′er** *n.*

re·vise (ri vīz′) *vt.* -vised′, -vis′ing [< Fr. < L. *re-*, back + *visere*, to survey] 1. to read over (a manuscript, etc.) to correct and improve 2. to change or amend —*n.* a revising or something revised —**re·vis′er, re·vi′sor** *n.* —**re·vi′sion** (-vizh′ən) *n.*

Revised Standard Version a mid-20th-cent. revision of an earlier version of the Bible, made by certain U.S. scholars

re·viv·al (ri vī′v'l) *n.* 1. a reviving or being revived 2. a bringing or coming back into use, being, etc. 3. a new presentation of an earlier play, etc. 4. restoration to vigor and activity 5. a stirring up of religious feelings 6. a meeting aimed at this, with fervid preaching, etc. 7. a series of such meetings

re·viv′al·ist *n.* a person who promotes or conducts religious revivals —**re·viv′al·ism** *n.*

re·vive (ri vīv′) *vi., vt.* -vived′, -viv′ing [< L. *re-*, again + *vivere*, to live] 1. to return to life or consciousness 2. to return to health and vigor 3. to come or bring back into use or attention 4. to present (a play, etc.) again after an interval

re·viv·i·fy (ri viv′ə fī′) *vt., vi.* -fied′, -fy′ing to give or get new life or vigor —re·viv′i·fi·ca′tion *n.*

re·voke (ri vōk′) *vt.* -voked′, -vok′ing [< L. *re-*, back + *vocare*, to call] to withdraw, repeal, or cancel (a law, etc.) —*vi. same as* RENEGE (sense 2) —*n. same as* RENEGE — **rev·o·ca·ble** (rev′ə kə b′l), **re·vok·a·ble** (ri vō′kə b′l) *adj.* —rev·o·ca·tion (rev′ə kā′shən) *n.*

re·volt (ri vōlt′) *n.* [< Fr.: see REVOLVE] a rebellion against the government or any authority —*vi.* 1. to rebel against authority 2. to be disgusted (with *at* or *against*) —*vt.* to disgust —re·volt′er *n.*

re·volt·ing *adj.* 1. rebellious 2. causing revulsion; disgusting —re·volt′ing·ly *adv.*

rev·o·lu·tion (rev′ə lōō′shən) *n.* [see REVOLVE] 1. movement of a body in an orbit 2. a turning around a center or axis; rotation 3. a complete cycle 4. a complete change 5. complete overthrow of a government or social system —rev′o·lu′tion·ist *n.*

rev′o·lu′tion·ar′y (-er′ē) *adj.* 1. of, like, or causing a revolution or very great change 2. [R-] having to do with the American Revolution 3. revolving or rotating —*n., pl.* -ies one who favors or takes part in a revolution

Revolutionary War *see* AMERICAN REVOLUTION

rev′o·lu′tion·ize (-īz′) *vt.* -ized′, -iz′ing to make a complete and basic change in

re·volve (ri välv′) *vt.* -volved′, -volv′ing [< L. *re-*, back + *volvere*, to roll] 1. to turn over in the mind 2. to cause to travel in a circle or orbit 3. to cause to rotate —*vi.* 1. to move in a circle or orbit 2. to rotate 3. to recur at intervals

re·volv′er *n.* a handgun with a revolving cylinder holding several bullets which can be fired without reloading

revolving door a door with four ¦vanes hung on a central axle, and turned around by pushing on a vane

re·vue (ri vyōō′) *n.* [Fr.: see REVIEW] a musical show with skits, songs, and dances, often poking fun at public figures, fashions, etc.

re·vul·sion (ri vul′shən) *n.* [< L. *re-*, back + *vellere*, to pull] an abrupt, strong reaction; esp., disgust

re·ward (ri wôrd′) *n.* [< OFr. *regarde*] 1. something given in return for something done 2. money offered, as for capturing a criminal —*vt.* to give a reward to (someone) for (service, etc.)

re·wind (rē wīnd′) *vt.* -wound′, -wind′ing to wind (film, tape, etc.) back on the reel

re·wire (rē wīr′) *vt., vi.* -wired′, -wir′ing to put new wires in or on (a house, motor, etc.)

re·word (rē wurd′) *vt.* to state again in other words; change the wording of

re·write (rē rīt′) *vt., vi.* -wrote′, -writ′ten, -writ′ing 1. to write again 2. to revise 3. to write (news turned in by a reporter) in a form suitable for publication —re·writ′er *n.*

Rex (reks) *n.* [L.] [*also* r-] king

Rey·kja·vik (rā′kyə vēk′) capital of Iceland: seaport on the SW coast: pop. 81,000

Reyn·olds (ren′əldz), Sir **Joshua** 1723–92; Eng. portrait painter

RF, R.F., r.f. 1. radio frequency 2. rapid-fire

RFD, R.F.D. Rural Free Delivery

Rh 1. *see* RH FACTOR 2. *Chem.* rhodium

rhap·sod·ic (rap säd′ik) *adj.* of, or having the nature of, rhapsody; extravagantly enthusiastic: also **rhap·sod′i·cal** —rhap·sod′i·cal·ly *adv.*

rhap·so·dize (rap′sə dīz′) *vi., vt.* -dized′, -diz′ing to speak, write, etc. in a rhapsodic manner —rhap′so·dist *n.*

rhap′so·dy (-dē) *n., pl.* -dies [< Gr. *rhaptein*, to stitch together + *ōidē*, song] 1. any ecstatic or enthusiastic speech or writing 2. *Music* an instrumental composition of free, irregular form, suggesting improvisation

Rhe·a (rē′ə) *Gr. Myth.* the wife of Cronus and mother of Zeus, Hera, etc. —*n.* [r-] a large S. American nonflying bird

Rheims (rēmz) *former sp. of* REIMS

Rhen·ish (ren′ish) *adj.* of the Rhine or nearby areas

rhe·ni·um (rē′nē əm) *n.* [< L. *Rhenus*, Rhine] a rare metallic chemical element resembling manganese: symbol, Re; at. wt., 186.2; at. no., 75

rhe·o·stat (rē′ə stat′) *n.* [< Gr. *rheos*, current + -STAT] a device for varying the resistance of an electric circuit without interrupting the circuit, used as to dim or brighten electric lights

rhe·sus (monkey) (rē′səs) [< Gr. proper name] a small, brownish macaque of India, used in medical research and kept in zoos

rhet·o·ric (ret′ər ik) *n.* [< Gr. *rhētōr*, orator] 1. the art of using words effectively; esp., the art of prose composition 2. artificial eloquence —rhe·tor·i·cal (ri tôr′i k′l) *adj.* —rhe·tor′i·cal·ly *adv.* —rhet′o·ri′cian (-ə rish′ən) *n.*

rhetorical question a question asked only to produce an effect, no answer being expected

rheum (rōōm) *n.* [< Gr. *rheuma*, a flow] 1. any watery discharge from the eyes, nose, etc., as in a cold 2. a cold; rhinitis —rheum′y *adj.* -i·er, -i·est

rheu·mat·ic (roo mat′ik) *adj.* of, caused by, or having rheumatism —*n.* one who has rheumatism

rheumatic fever a disease, usually of children, with fever, painful joints, and inflammation of the heart

rheu·ma·tism (rōō′mə tiz′m) *n.* [see RHEUM] *a popular term for* any of various painful conditions in which the joints and muscles become inflamed and stiff

rheu′ma·toid′ (-toid′) *adj.* of or like rheumatism

rheumatoid arthritis a chronic disease with painful swelling of joints

Rh factor (är′ăch′) [first discovered in *rhesus* monkeys] a group of antigens, usually present in human blood, which may cause dangerous reactions during pregnancy or after blood transfusion into someone lacking it: people who have this factor are **Rh positive**; those who do not are **Rh negative**

Rhine (rīn) river flowing from Switzerland through Germany & the Netherlands into the North Sea

rhine·stone (rīn′stōn′) *n.* an artificial gem of colorless, bright glass, often cut to look like a diamond

Rhine wine a light, dry white wine, esp. from the Rhine Valley

rhi·ni·tis (rī nīt′əs) *n.* [< Gr. *rhis*, nose + -ITIS] inflammation of the mucous membrane of the nose

rhi·no (rī′nō) *n., pl.* -nos, -no *shortened form of* RHINOCEROS

rhi·noc·er·os (rī näs′ər əs) *n.* [< Gr. *rhis*, nose + *keras*, horn] a large, thick-skinned, plant-eating mammal of Africa and Asia, with one or two upright horns on the snout

rhi·zome (rī′zōm) *n.* [< Gr. *rhiza*, a root] a horizontal, rootlike stem, which usually sends out roots below and leafy shoots above the ground

INDIAN RHINOCEROS (3–6 1/2 ft. high)

rho (rō) *n.* the seventeenth letter of the Greek alphabet (P, ρ)

Rhode Island (rōd) New England State of the U.S.: 1,214 sq. mi.; pop. 950,000; cap. Providence: abbrev. **R.I.**, **RI** —**Rhode Islander**

Rhode Island Red an American chicken with reddish-brown feathers and a black tail

Rhodes (rōdz) 1. one of the Dodecanese Islands, in the Aegean 2. a seaport on this island

Rho·de·sia (rō dē′zhə, -zhē ə) country in S Africa: 150,333 sq. mi.; pop. 5,342,000; cap. Salisbury —**Rho·de′sian** *adj., n.*

rho·di·um (rō′dē əm) *n.* [< Gr. *rhodon*, a rose: from the color of its salts] a hard, gray-white metallic chemical element: symbol, Rh; at. wt., 102.905; at. no., 45

rho·do·den·dron (rō′də den′drən) *n.* [< Gr. *rhodon*, a rose + *dendron*, a tree] a tree or shrub, usually evergreen, with showy pink, white, or purple flowers

rhom·boid (räm′boid) *n.* [see RHOMBUS & -OID] a parallelogram with oblique angles and only the opposite sides equal —*adj.* shaped like a rhomboid or rhombus: also **rhom·boi′dal**

rhom·bus (räm′bəs) *n., pl.* -bus·es, -bi (-bī) [< Gr. *rhombos*, turnable object] an equilateral parallelogram, esp. one with oblique angles: also **rhomb** —**rhom′bic** *adj.*

Rhone, Rhône (rōn) river flowing from SW Switzerland through France into the Mediterranean

rhu·barb (rōō′bärb) *n.* [< Gr. *rheon*, rhubarb + *barbaron*, foreign] 1. a plant with large leaves whose thick, sour stalks are cooked into a sauce or baked in pies 2. [Slang] a heated argument

rhumb (rum, rumb) *n.* [< Port. & Sp. *rumbo*] any of the points of a mariner's compass

rhumb line a course keeping a constant compass direction, charted as a line

rhyme (rīm) *n.* [prob. < L. *rhythmus*, rhythm] 1. likeness of sounds at the ends of words or lines of verse 2. a word that has the same end sound as another 3. poetry or (a)

verse employing this —*vi.* **rhymed, rhym′ing 1.** to make rhyming verse **2.** to form a rhyme *["more" rhymes with "door"]* **3.** to be composed with rhymes: said of verse — *vt.* **1.** to put into rhyme **2.** to use as a rhyme —**rhyme or reason** order or sense: preceded by *without, no,* etc.

rhyme·ster (rīm′stər) *n.* a maker of simple or inferior verse or rhymes; poetaster

rhythm (rith′m, -əm) *n.* [< Fr. < Gr. *rhythmos,* measure] **1.** movement characterized by a regular recurrence, as of a beat, accent, etc. **2.** the pattern of this in music, verse, periodic biological occurrences, etc. —**rhyth′mic, rhyth′mi·cal** *adj.* —**rhyth′mi·cal·ly** *adv.*

rhythm and blues a form of popular U.S. Negro music, influenced by the blues and having a strong beat

rhythm method a method of seeking birth control by abstaining from sexual intercourse during the woman's probable monthly ovulation period

R.I., RI Rhode Island

rib (rib) *n.* [OE.] **1.** any of the curved bones attached to the spine and enclosing the chest cavity **2.** a cut of meat having one or more ribs **3.** a raised ridge in cloth **4.** any riblike piece used to shape, strengthen, or help frame something **5.** any of the main veins of a leaf **6.** [Slang] a playfully teasing remark —*vt.* **ribbed, rib′bing 1.** to form with ribs **2.** [Slang] to tease —**ribbed** *adj.* —**rib′ber** *n.* —**rib′less** *adj.*

rib·ald (rib′əld) *adj.* [< OFr. *ribaud,* debauchee] coarsely joking; esp., joking about sex in an earthy way —*n.* a ribald person —**rib′ald·ry** *n.*

rib·bing (rib′iŋ) *n.* an arrangement or series of ribs, as in knitted fabric, a ship's framework, etc.

rib·bon (rib′ən) *n.* [MFr. *riban*] **1.** a narrow strip as of silk or rayon, used for decorating, tying, etc. **2.** anything suggesting such a strip **3.** *[pl.]* torn shreds **4.** a strip of cloth inked for use in a typewriter, etc. —*vt.* to decorate or trim with ribbon or ribbons —**rib′bon·like′** *adj.*

ri·bo·fla·vin (rī′bə flā′vin) *n.* [< RIBOSE + L. *flavus,* yellow] a factor of the vitamin B complex found in milk, eggs, liver, fruits, leafy vegetables, etc.: lack of riboflavin causes loss of hair, etc.

ri·bose (rī′bōs) *n.* [< G. *rib(onsäure),* an acid + -*ose,* carbohydrate] a sugar derived from nucleic acids

rice (rīs) *n.* [ult. < Gr. *oryza*] **1.** a cereal grass of warm climates, planted in ground under water **2.** its starchy seeds or grain, used as food —*vt.* **riced, ric′ing** to form (cooked potatoes, etc.) into ricelike granules

rice paper 1. a thin paper made from the straw of rice **2.** a fine, delicate paper made from the pith of an Asian plant (the **rice-paper plant**)

ric·er (rī′sər) *n.* a utensil for ricing cooked potatoes, etc. by forcing them through small holes

rich (rich) *adj.* [OE. *rice,* noble] **1.** having much money or property; wealthy **2.** having abundant natural resources **3.** well supplied (*with*); abounding (*in*) **4.** valuable or costly *[rich gifts]* **5.** full of choice ingredients, as butter, sugar, etc. **6.** *a)* full and mellow: said of sound *b)* deep; vivid: said of colors *c)* very fragrant **7.** abundant **8.** yielding in abundance, as soil, etc. **9.** [Colloq.] very amusing — **the rich** wealthy people collectively —**rich′ly** *adv.* —**rich′ness** *n.*

Rich·ard I (rich′ərd) 1157-99; king of England (1189-99): called **Richard the Lion-Hearted**

Ri·che·lieu (rish′ə loo′), duc de 1585-1642; Fr. cardinal and statesman

rich·en (rich′′n) *vt.* to make rich or richer

rich·es (rich′iz) *n.pl.* [< OFr. *richesse*] valuable possessions; much money, property, etc.; wealth

Rich·mond (rich′mənd) **1.** capital of Va.: pop. 250,000 (met. area 518,000) **2.** borough of New York City, including Staten Island

Rich·ter scale (rik′tər) [devised by C. *Richter* (1900-), U.S. seismologist] a scale for measuring the magnitude of earthquakes: each of its 10 steps is about 60 times greater than the preceding step

rick (rik) *n.* [OE. *hreac*] a stack of hay, straw, etc. in a field —*vt.* to pile (hay, etc.) into ricks

rick·ets (rik′its) *n.* [? < Gr. *rhachis,* spine] a disease, chiefly of children, characterized by a softening and, often, bending of the bones: it is caused by lack of vitamin D

rick·ett·si·a (ri ket′sē ə) *n., pl.* -si·ae′ (-ē′) [< H. T. *Ricketts* (1871-1910), U.S. pathologist] any of a genus of microorganisms that cause certain diseases, as typhus, and are transmitted by the bite of certain lice and ticks — **rick·ett′si·al** *adj.*

rick·et·y (rik′it ē) *adj.* **1.** having rickets **2.** feeble; weak; shaky —**rick′et·i·ness** *n.*

rick·rack (rik′rak′) *n.* [redupl. of RACK¹] flat, zigzag braid for trimming dresses, etc.

rick·shaw, rick·sha (rik′shô) *n.* same as JINRIKISHA

ric·o·chet (rik′ə shā′) *n.* [Fr.] the rebound or skipping of an object after striking a surface at an angle —*vi.* **-cheted′** (-shād′), **-chet′ing** (-shā′iŋ) to make a ricochet

rid (rid) *vt.* **rid** or **rid′ded, rid′ding** [< ON. *rythja,* to clear (land)] to free or relieve, as of something undesirable — **get rid of** to dispose of

rid·dance (rid′′ns) *n.* a ridding or being rid; clearance or removal —**good riddance!** welcome relief!

rid·den (rid′′n) *pp. of* RIDE

rid·dle¹ (rid′′l) *n.* [< OE. *rædan,* to guess] **1.** a puzzling question, etc. requiring some ingenuity to answer **2.** any puzzling person or thing —*vi.* **-dled, -dling** to utter riddles —**rid′dler** *n.*

rid·dle² (rid′′l) *n.* [OE. *hriddel*] a coarse sieve —*vt.* **-dled, -dling 1.** to sift through a riddle **2.** *a)* to make many holes in, as with buckshot *b)* to affect every part of *[riddled* with errors*]*

ride (rīd) *vi.* **rode, rid′den, rid′ing** [OE. *ridan*] **1.** to sit on and control a horse, etc. in motion **2.** to be carried along (*in* a vehicle, etc.) **3.** to be supported in motion (*on* or *upon*) *[tanks ride* on treads*]* **4.** to admit of being ridden *[the car rides* smoothly*]* **5.** to move or float on the water **6.** [Colloq.] to continue undisturbed *[let the matter ride]* —*vt.* **1.** to sit on or in so as to move along **2.** to move over, along, or through (a road, area, etc.) by horse, car, etc. **3.** to engage in by riding *[to ride* a race*]* **4.** to cause to ride **5.** to control, dominate, etc. *[ridden* by fear*]* **6.** [Colloq.] to torment, as with ridicule —*n.* **1.** a riding; journey by horse, car, etc. **2.** a road, etc. for riding **3.** a thing to ride at an amusement park —**ride out** to withstand (a storm, crisis, etc.) successfully —**take for a ride** [Slang] **1.** to take somewhere and kill **2.** to cheat

rid′er *n.* **1.** one who rides **2.** an addition or amendment to a document **3.** a clause, usually dealing with an unrelated matter, added to a legislative bill when it is up for passage —**rid′er·less** *adj.*

rid′er·ship′ *n.* the passengers of a particular transportation system, or their estimated number

ridge (rij) *n.* [OE. *hrycg*] **1.** the long, narrow crest of something, as of a wave **2.** a long, narrow elevation of land **3.** any narrow, raised strip, as on a fabric **4.** the horizontal line formed by the meeting of two sloping surfaces *[the ridge* of a roof*]* —*vt., vi.* **ridged, ridg′ing** to form into or mark with a ridge or ridges

ridge′pole′ *n.* the horizontal timber or beam at the ridge of a roof: also **ridge′piece′**

rid·i·cule (rid′ə kyool′) *n.* [Fr. < L. *ridere,* to laugh] **1.** the act of making one the object of scornful laughter **2.** words or actions used in doing this —*vt.* **-culed′, -cul′-ing** to make fun of; deride

RIDGEPOLE

ri·dic·u·lous (ri dik′yə ləs) *adj.* deserving ridicule —**ri·dic′u·lous·ly** *adv.* —**ri·dic′u·lous·ness** *n.*

Rif (rif) mountain range along the Mediterranean coast of Morocco: also **Er Rif** (er)

rife (rīf) *adj.* [OE. *ryfe*] **1.** frequently occurring; widespread **2.** abounding; filled *[rife* with error*]*

Riff (rif) same as RIF —*n., pl.* **Riffs, Riff′i** (-ē) a Berber living in or near the Rif

riff (rif) *n.* [prob. < REFRAIN²] *Jazz* a constantly repeated musical phrase —*vi.* to perform a riff

rif·fle (rif′′l) *n.* [< ?] **1.** a ripple in a stream, produced by a reef, etc. **2.** the act of riffling cards —*vt., vi.* **-fled, -fling 1.** to ripple **2.** to leaf rapidly (through) by releasing pages, etc. along their edges **3.** to shuffle (playing cards) by holding part of the deck in each hand and mixing the cards together with riffling motions

riff·raff (rif′raf′) *n.* [< OFr.: see RIFLE² & RAFFLE] those people regarded as worthless or disreputable

ri·fle¹ (rī′f′l) *vt.* **-fled, -fling** [< Fr. *rifler,* to scrape] to cut spiral grooves within (a gun barrel, etc.) —*n.* a gun held against the shoulder, with a rifled barrel: see RIFLING

ri·fle² (rī′f′l) *vt.* **-fled, -fling** [< OFr. *rifler,* to plunder] **1.** to ransack in order to rob **2.** to take as plunder; steal

ri·fle·man (-mən) *n., pl.* **-men 1.** a soldier armed with a rifle **2.** a man who uses a rifle

rifle range a place for target practice with a rifle

ri·fling (rī′fliŋ) *n.* **1.** the cutting of spiral grooves within a gun barrel to make the bullet spin **2.** a system of such grooves

rift (rift) *n.* [< Dan. *rive*, to tear] an opening caused by splitting; cleft —*vt.*, *vi.* to split

rig (rig) *vt.* **rigged, rig′ging** [< Scand.] **1.** to fit (a ship, mast, etc.) with (sails, shrouds, etc.) **2.** to equip **3.** to prepare for use, esp. in a hurry (often with *up*) **4.** to arrange dishonestly **5.** [Colloq.] to dress (with *out*) —*n.* **1.** the arrangement of sails, etc. on a vessel **2.** equipment; gear **3.** a carriage, etc. with its horse or horses **4.** a tractor-trailer **5.** [Colloq.] dress —**rig′ger** *n.*

Ri·ga (rē′gə) capital of the Latvian S.S.R.; seaport on the Baltic Sea: pop. 733,000

rig·a·ma·role (rig′ə mə rōl′) *n. var. of* RIGMAROLE

rig′ging *n.* **1.** the chains, ropes, etc. that support and work masts, sails, etc. **2.** equipment; gear

right (rīt) *adj.* [< OE. *riht*, straight] **1.** with a straight or perpendicular line **2.** upright; virtuous **3.** correct **4.** fitting; suitable **5.** designating the side meant to be seen **6.** mentally or physically sound **7.** *a)* designating or of that side toward the east when one faces north *b)* closer to the right side of one facing the thing mentioned —*n.* **1.** what is right, just, etc. **2.** a power, privilege, etc. belonging to one by law, nature, etc. **3.** the right side **4.** *Boxing* a blow with the right hand **5.** [*often* R-] *Politics* a conservative or reactionary position, party, etc. (often with *the*) —*adv.* **1.** in a straight line; directly [*go right home*] **2.** in a way that is correct, proper, just, favorable, etc. **3.** completely **4.** exactly [*right here*] **5.** immediately [*come right down*] **6.** on or toward the right hand **7.** very: in certain titles [*the right reverend*] —*vt.* **1.** to put upright **2.** to correct **3.** to put in order **4.** to make amends for —*vi.* to regain an upright position —**by right(s)** in justice —**in the right** on the side of truth, justice, etc. —**right away** (or **off**) at once —**right on!** [Slang] precisely! exactly! —**right′ly** *adv.* —**right′ness** *n.*

right′a·bout′-face′ *n. same as* ABOUT-FACE

right angle an angle of 90°, made by two straight lines perpendicular to each other —**right′-an′gled** *adj.*

right·eous (rī′chəs) *adj.* **1.** acting justly; upright; virtuous **2.** morally right **3.** morally justifiable **4.** [Slang] good, satisfying, authentic, etc. —**right′eous·ly** *adv.* —**right′eous·ness** *n.*

right′ful *adj.* **1.** fair and just; right **2.** having a lawful claim —**right′ful·ly** *adv.* —**right′ful·ness** *n.*

right′-hand′ *adj.* **1.** on or directed toward the right **2.** of, for, or with the right hand **3.** most helpful or reliable [*my right-hand man*]

right′-hand′ed *adj.* **1.** using the right hand more skillfully than the left **2.** done with or made for use with the right hand —*adv.* with the right hand [*to throw right-handed*] —**right′-hand′ed·ly** *adv.* —**right′-hand′ed·ness** *n.*

right′ist *n., adj.* conservative or reactionary

right′-mind′ed *adj.* having correct views or sound principles —**right′-mind′ed·ness** *n.*

right of way **1.** the right to move first at intersections **2.** right of passage **3.** a strip of land used by a railroad for its tracks **4.** land over which a road, power line, etc. passes Also **right′-of-way′**

right′-on′ *adj.* [Slang] sophisticated, current, etc.

right triangle a triangle with one right angle

right whale a large-headed whale without teeth or dorsal fin

right wing the more conservative or reactionary section of a political party, group, etc. —**right′-wing′** *adj.* —**right′-wing′er** *n.*

rig·id (rij′id) *adj.* [< L. *rigere*, be stiff] **1.** not bending or flexible; stiff **2.** not moving; set **3.** severe or strict **4.** having a rigid framework: said of a dirigible —**ri·gid·i·ty** (ri jid′ə tē), **rig′id·ness** *n.* —**rig′id·ly** *adv.*

rig·ma·role (rig′mə rōl′) *n.* [< ME. *rageman rolle*, a document] **1.** rambling talk; nonsense **2.** a fussy or time-wasting procedure

rig·or (rig′ər) *n.* [see RIGID] **1.** harshness or severity; specif., *a)* strictness *b)* extreme hardship **2.** stiffness, esp. in body tissue Brit. sp. **rig′our**

rig·or mor·tis (rig′ər môr′tis, rī′gôr) [ModL., stiffness of death] the stiffening of the muscles after death

rig·or·ous (rig′ər əs) *adj.* **1.** very strict or harsh [*rigorous rules*] **2.** very severe or sharp [*a rigorous climate*] **3.** extremely precise [*rigorous scholarship*] —**rig′or·ous·ly** *adv.*

rile (rīl) *vt.* **riled, ril′ing** [var. of ROIL] [Colloq. or Dial.] to anger; irritate

Ri·ley (rī′lē), **James Whit·comb** (hwit′kəm) 1849–1916; U.S. poet

rill (ril) *n.* [< Du. *ril*] a little brook

rim (rim) *n.* [OE. *rima*, an edge] **1.** an edge, border, or margin, esp. of something circular **2.** *a)* the outer part of a wheel *b)* the metal flange of an automobile wheel, on which the tire is mounted —*vt.* **rimmed, rim′ming** to put a rim on or around

rime[1] (rīm) *n., vt., vi.* **rimed, rim′ing** *same as* RHYME

rime[2] (rīm) *n.* [OE. *hrim*] hoarfrost

Rim·sky-Kor·sa·kov (rim′skē kôr′sə kôf′), **Ni·ko·lai** (nē kô lī′) 1844–1908; Russ. composer

rind (rīnd) *n.* [OE.] a hard outer layer or coating, as on fruit, cheese, bacon, etc.

ring[1] (riŋ) *vi.* **rang** or *chiefly dial.* **rung, rung, ring′ing** [OE. *hringan*] **1.** to give forth the resonant sound of a bell **2.** to seem [*to ring true*] **3.** to sound a bell, esp. as a summons **4.** to resound [*to ring with laughter*] **5.** to have a ringing sensation, as the ears —*vt.* **1.** to cause (a bell, etc.) to ring **2.** to signal, announce, etc. as by ringing **3.** to call by telephone —*n.* **1.** the sound of a bell **2.** any similar sound **3.** a characteristic sound or impression [*the ring of sincerity*] **4.** the act of ringing a bell, etc. **5.** a telephone call —**ring a bell** to stir up a memory —**ring down** (or **up**) **the curtain** to end (or begin) something

ring[2] (riŋ) *n.* [OE. *hring*] **1.** a circular band, esp. of precious metal, worn on a finger **2.** any similar band [*a key ring*] **3.** a circular line, mark, or figure **4.** any of the circular marks seen in the cross section of a tree trunk **5.** a group of people or things in a circle **6.** a group working to advance its own interests, esp. dishonestly **7.** an enclosed area for contests, exhibitions, etc. [*a circus ring*] **8.** prizefighting (with *the*) —*vt.* **ringed, ring′ing 1.** to encircle **2.** to form into, or furnish with, a ring or rings **3.** to cut a ring of bark from around (a tree) —*vi.* to form in a ring or rings —**run rings around** [Colloq.] **1.** to outrun easily **2.** to excel greatly —**throw one's hat into the ring** to enter a contest for political office

ring′bolt′ *n.* a bolt with a ring at the head

ring′er[1] *n.* a horseshoe, etc. thrown so that it encircles the peg

ring′er[2] *n.* **1.** one that rings a bell, etc. **2.** [Slang] *a)* a person or thing closely resembling another *b)* a fraudulent substitute in a competition

ring′lead′er *n.* one who leads others, esp. in unlawful acts, etc.

ring′let (-lit) *n.* **1.** a little ring **2.** a curl of hair, esp. a long one —**ring′let·ed** *adj.*

ring′mas′ter *n.* a man who directs the performances in a circus ring

ring′side′ *n.* **1.** the place just outside the ring, as at a boxing match **2.** a place giving a close view

ring′worm′ *n.* a contagious skin disease caused by a fungus that produces ring-shaped patches

rink (riŋk) *n.* [< OFr. *renc*, a rank] **1.** a smooth expanse of ice for skating **2.** a smooth floor for roller-skating **3.** an enclosure for either of these

rinse (rins) *vt.* **rinsed, rins′ing** [ult. < L. *recens*, fresh] **1.** to wash or flush lightly **2.** to remove soap, etc. from with clean water —*n.* **1.** a rinsing or the liquid used **2.** a solution for coloring hair

Ri·o de Ja·nei·ro (rē′ō dā′ zhə ner′ō, dē′; jə nir′ō) seaport in SE Brazil: pop. 4,297,000

Ri·o Grande (rē′ō grand′, grän′dē) river flowing from S Colo. to the Gulf of Mexico: the S border of Texas: 1,885 mi.

ri·ot (rī′ət) *n.* [< OFr. *rihoter*, make a disturbance] **1.** wild or violent disorder, confusion, etc. **2.** a violent disturbance of the peace by a number of persons assembled together **3.** a bright display [*a riot of color*] **4.** [Colloq.] something very amusing —*vi.* to take part in a public disturbance —**run riot 1.** to act in a wild, unrestrained manner **2.** to grow in profusion —**ri′ot·er** *n.*

ri′ot·ous *adj.* **1.** having the nature of a riot **2.** engaging in rioting **3.** disorderly or boisterous —**ri′ot·ous·ly** *adv.*

rip (rip) *vt.* **ripped, rip′ping** [LME. *rippen*] **1.** *a)* to cut or tear apart roughly *b)* to remove in this way (with *off*, *out*, etc.) *c)* to sever (stitches) so as to open (a seam, etc.) **2.** to saw (wood) along the grain —*vi.* **1.** to become torn **2.** [Colloq.] to move with speed or violence —*n.* a torn place or burst seam —**rip into** [Colloq.] to attack, esp. verbally —**rip off** [Slang] **1.** to steal or rob **2.** to cheat, exploit, etc. —**rip′per** *n.*

R.I.P. [L., *requiescat in pace*] may he (or she) rest in peace

ri·par·i·an (ri per′ē ən, rī-) *adj.* [< L. *ripa*, a bank] of, on, or relating to the bank of a river, lake, etc.

rip cord a cord, etc. pulled to open a parachute during descent

ripe (rīp) *adj.* [OE.] **1.** ready to be harvested, as grain or fruit **2.** of sufficient age, etc. to be used *[ripe cheese]* **3.** highly developed; mature **4.** advanced in years *[the ripe age of ninety]* **5.** fully prepared *[ripe for marriage]* **6.** far enough along *(for)*: said of time —**ripe'ly** *adv.* —**ripe'ness** *n.*

rip·en (rī'pən) *vi., vt.* to become or make ripe; mature; age, cure, etc. —**rip'en·er** *n.*

rip'-off' *n.* [Slang] a stealing, robbing, cheating, exploiting, etc.

ri·poste, ri·post (ri pōst') *n.* [< Fr. < It. < L. *respondere*, to answer] **1.** *Fencing* a swift thrust made after parrying an opponent's lunge **2.** a sharp, swift retort —*vi.* -**post'ed,** -**post'ing** to make a riposte

rip·ple (rip''l) *vi., vt.* -**pled,** -**pling** [prob. < RIP] to form or have little waves on the surface (of) —*n.* **1.** a small wave, or a movement, appearance, etc. like this **2.** a sound like rippling water —**rip'ply** (-lē) *adj.* -**pli·er,** -**pli·est**

rip'-roar'ing (-rôr'iŋ) *adj.* [Slang] boisterous; uproarious

rip'saw' *n.* a saw with coarse teeth, for cutting wood along the grain

rip'tide' *n.* a tide opposing another tide, producing rough waters

rise (rīz) *vi.* **rose, ris·en** (riz''n), **ris'ing** [OE. *risan*] **1.** to stand or sit up after sitting, lying, etc. **2.** to get up after sleeping or resting **3.** to rebel; revolt **4.** to return to life after dying **5.** to go up; ascend **6.** to appear above the horizon *[the moon rose]* **7.** to attain a higher level, status, rank, etc. **8.** to extend, slant, or move upward **9.** to increase in amount, degree, etc. **10.** to become louder, shriller, etc. **11.** to become stronger, more vivid, etc. **12.** to expand and swell, as dough with yeast **13.** to originate; begin **14.** to happen; occur **15.** to become apparent to the mind or senses **16.** to be built *[the house rose quickly]* —*vt.* to cause to rise —*n.* **1.** upward motion; ascent **2.** an advance in status, rank, etc. **3.** a slope upward **4.** an increase in degree, amount, etc. **5.** a beginning, origin, etc. —**give rise to** to bring about —**rise to** to prove oneself capable of coping with *[to rise to the occasion]*

ris·er *n.* **1.** a person or thing that rises **2.** a vertical piece between the steps in a stairway

ris·i·bil·i·ty (riz'ə bil'ə tē) *n., pl.* -**ties 1.** the quality or state of being risible **2.** *[usually pl.]* a sense of the ridiculous or amusing

ris·i·ble (riz'ə b'l) *adj.* [Fr. < L. *ridere*, to laugh] **1.** able or inclined to laugh **2.** causing laughter; laughable; funny

ris·ing (rī'ziŋ) *adj.* **1.** that rises; ascending, advancing, etc. **2.** growing; maturing *[the rising generation]* —*n.* **1.** a revolt **2.** a projection

risk (risk) *n.* [< Fr. < It. *risco*] **1.** the chance of injury, damage, or loss; hazard **2.** the degree of probability of loss —*vt.* **1.** to expose to risk *[to risk one's life]* **2.** to take the chance of *[to risk a fight]*

risk'y *adj.* -**i·er,** -**i·est** involving risk; hazardous —**risk'i·ly** *adv.* —**risk'i·ness** *n.*

ris·qué (ris kā') *adj.* [Fr. < *risquer*, to risk] very close to being improper or indecent; suggestive

rite (rīt) *n.* [L. *ritus*] **1.** a solemn or ceremonial act, as in religious use **2.** a particular system of ceremonial procedure **3.** *[often R-]* liturgy

rit·u·al (rich'ōō wəl) *adj.* of, like, or done as a rite —*n.* **1.** a system or form of rites, religious or otherwise **2.** the observance of set forms or rites, as in worship —**rit'u·al·ly** *adv.*

rit'u·al·ism *n.* **1.** the observance of, or excessive devotion to, ritual **2.** the study of religious ritual —**rit'u·al·is'tic** *adj.* —**rit'u·al·is'ti·cal·ly** *adv.*

ritz·y (rit'sē) *adj.* -**i·er,** -**i·est** [< the *Ritz* hotels] [Old Slang] luxurious, fashionable, etc.

ri·val (rī'v'l) *n.* [Fr. < L. *rivalis*] **1.** one who tries to get the same thing as another, or to equal or surpass another; competitor **2.** an equal or a satisfactory substitute —*adj.* being a rival; competing —*vt.* -**valed** or -**valled,** -**val·ing** or -**val·ling 1.** to try to equal or surpass **2.** to equal

ri'val·ry *n., pl.* -**ries** the act of rivaling or the fact of being a rival; competition

rive (rīv) *vt., vi.* **rived, riv·en** (riv''n) or **rived, riv'ing** [ON. *rifa*] **1.** to rend **2.** to split; cleave

riv·er (riv'ər) *n.* [< L. *ripa*, a bank] **1.** a natural stream of water larger than a creek, emptying into an ocean, lake, etc. **2.** any plentiful stream or flow

Ri·ve·ra (ri ver'ə), **Die·go** (dye'gô) 1886–1957; Mex. painter, esp. of murals

river basin the area drained by a river and its tributaries

Riv·er·side (riv'ər sīd') city in S Calif.: pop. 140,000

riv·er·side' *n.* the bank of a river —*adj.* on or near the bank of a river

riv·et (riv'it) *n.* [< MFr. *river*, to clinch] **1.** a metal bolt with a head and a plain end that is flattened after the bolt is passed through parts to be held together —*vt.* to fasten firmly, as with rivets —**riv'et·er** *n.*

Riv·i·er·a (riv'ē er'ə) coastal strip of the Mediterranean in SE France & NW Italy: a resort area

riv·u·let (riv'yōō lit) *n.* [< It. < L. *rivus*, a brook] a little stream

rm. *pl.* **rms. 1.** ream **2.** room

Rn *Chem.* radon

R.N., RN Registered Nurse

RNA [< *r(ibo)n(ucleic) a(cid)*] an essential component of all living matter: one form carries genetic information

roach[1] (rōch) *n.* **1.** *same as* COCKROACH **2.** [Slang] the butt of a marijuana cigarette

roach[3] (rōch) *n., pl.* **roach, roach'es** [< OFr. < *roche*] a freshwater fish related to the carp

RIVETS (A, rivet holding steel beams together; B, C, D, rivets)

road (rōd) *n.* [OE. *rad*, a ride] **1.** a way made for traveling; highway **2.** a way; course *[the road to fortune]* **3.** *same as* RAILROAD **4.** *[often pl.]* a place near shore where ships can ride at anchor —**on the road 1.** traveling, as a salesman **2.** on tour, as actors —**take to the road** to start traveling

road'bed' *n.* the foundation laid for railroad tracks or for a highway, etc.

road'block' *n.* **1.** a blockade set up in a road to prevent movement of vehicles **2.** any hindrance

road'house' *n.* a tavern, inn, or nightclub along a country road, as in the 1920's

road runner a long-tailed, crested desert bird of the SW U.S. and N Mexico, that can run swiftly

road'show' *n.* **1.** a touring theatrical show **2.** a reserved-seat film showing

road'side' *n.* the side of a road —*adj.* on or at the side of a road

road'way' *n.* **1.** a road **2.** the part of a road along which cars, trucks, etc. move

roam (rōm) *vi.* [ME. *romen*] to travel with no purpose or plan; wander —*vt.* to wander over or through —*n.* the act of roaming; ramble —**roam'er** *n.*

roan (rōn) *adj.* [< OSp. *roano*] bay, black, etc., with a thick sprinkling of white hairs: said chiefly of horses —*n.* a roan color, horse, etc.

roar (rôr) *vi.* [OE. *rarian*] **1.** to utter a loud, deep, rumbling sound, as a lion **2.** to talk or laugh boisterously **3.** to operate with a loud noise —*vt.* to utter with a roar —*n.* **1.** a loud, deep, rumbling sound **2.** a loud noise —**roar'er** *n.*

roast (rōst) *vt.* [< OFr. *rostir*] **1.** to cook (meat, etc.) with little or no moisture, as in an oven **2.** to process (coffee, etc.) by exposure to heat **3.** to expose to great heat **4.** [Colloq.] to criticize severely —*vi.* **1.** to undergo roasting **2.** to be or become very hot —*n.* **1.** roasted meat **2.** a cut of meat for roasting **3.** a picnic at which food is roasted —*adj.* roasted *[roast pork]*

roast'er *n.* **1.** a pan, oven, etc. for roasting meat **2.** a young pig, chicken, etc. suitable for roasting

rob (räb) *vt.* **robbed, rob'bing** [< OFr. *rober*] **1.** to take property from unlawfully by using or threatening force **2.** to deprive of something unjustly or injuriously —*vi.* to commit robbery —**rob'ber** *n.*

rob'ber·y (-ər ē) *n., pl.* -**ies** a robbing; the taking of another's property by violence or intimidation

robe (rōb) *n.* [< OFr.] **1.** a long, loose outer garment; specif., *a)* such a garment worn to show rank or office, as by a judge *b)* a bathrobe or dressing gown **2.** a covering or wrap *[a lap robe]* —*vt., vi.* **robed, rob'ing** to dress in or cover with a robe

Robes·pierre (rōbs'pyer), **Max·i·mi·lien** (mäk sē mē lyaṅ') 1758–94; Fr. revolutionist: guillotined

rob·in (räb'in) *n.* [< OFr. dim. of *Robert*] **1.** a large N. American thrush with a dull-red breast and belly **2.** a small European warbler with a yellowish-red breast Also **robin redbreast**

Robin Hood *Eng. Legend* the leader of a band of outlaws that robbed the rich to help the poor

Rob·in·son Cru·soe (räb'in s'n krōō'sō) the title hero of Defoe's novel (1719) about a shipwrecked sailor

ro·bot (rō'bət, -bät) *n.* [< Czech < OBulg. *rabu*, servant] **1.** a mechanical device operating in a seemingly human way **2.** a person acting or working mechanically

ro·bust (rō bust', rō'bust) *adj.* [< L. *robur*, a hard oak] 1. *a*) strong and healthy; hardy *b*) strongly built; muscular 2. requiring physical strength [*robust* work] 3. full and rich, as in flavor —**ro·bust'ly** *adv.* —**ro·bust'ness** *n.*

roc (räk) *n.* [< Ar. < Per. *rukh*] *Arabian & Persian Legend* a bird strong enough to carry off animals

Roch·es·ter (rä'ches'tər) city in W N.Y.: pop. 296,000 (met. area 883,000)

rock[1] (räk) *n.* [< OFr. *roche*] 1. a large mass of stone 2. broken pieces of stone 3. mineral matter formed in masses in the earth's crust 4. anything like a rock; esp., a firm support, etc. 5. [Colloq.] a stone 6. [Slang] a diamond or other gem —**on the rocks** [Colloq.] 1. ruined 2. bankrupt 3. served over ice cubes: said of liquor, etc.

rock[2] (räk) *vt., vi.* [OE. *roccian*] 1. to move back and forth or from side to side 2. to sway strongly; shake —*n.* 1. a rocking motion 2. *a*) same as ROCK-AND-ROLL *b*) popular music evolved from rock-and-roll, folk music, country music, blues, jazz, etc.

rock-and-roll (räk''n rōl') *n.* a form of popular music with a strong, regular beat, which evolved from jazz and the blues: also sp. **rock 'n' roll**

rock bottom the lowest level or point; very bottom —**rock'-bot'tom** *adj.*

rock'-bound' *adj.* surrounded or covered by rocks

rock candy large, hard, clear crystals of sugar formed on a string

rock crystal a transparent, colorless quartz

Rock·e·fel·ler (räk'ə fel'ər), **John D.** 1839–1937; U.S. industrialist & philanthropist

rock'er *n.* 1. either of the curved pieces on which a cradle, etc. rocks 2. a chair mounted on such pieces: also **rocking chair** 3. any device that works with a rocking motion

rock·et (räk'it) *n.* [It. *rocchetta*, a spool] any device driven forward by gases escaping through a rear vent, as a firework, projectile, or the propulsion mechanism of a spacecraft —*vi.* to move in or like a rocket; soar

rock'et·ry (-ə trē) *n.* the science of designing, building, and launching rockets

Rock·ford (räk'fərd) city in N Ill.: pop. 147,000

rocking horse a child's toy horse mounted on rockers or springs

rock'-ribbed' *adj.* 1. having rocky ridges 2. firm; unyielding

rock salt common salt in solid masses

rock wool a fibrous material made from molten rock, used for insulation

rock·y[1] (räk'ē) *adj.* **-i·er, -i·est** 1. full of rocks 2. consisting of rocks 3. like a rock; firm, hard, etc.

rock·y[2] (räk'ē) *adj.* **-i·er, -i·est** 1. inclined to rock; unsteady 2. [Slang] weak and dizzy —**rock'i·ness** *n.*

Rocky Mountain goat a white, goatlike antelope of the mountains of northwest N. America

Rocky Mountains mountain system in W N. America, extending from C N.Mex. to Alas.: also **Rock'ies**

ro·co·co (rə kō'kō) *n.* [Fr. < *rocaille*, shell work] an elaborate style of architecture and decoration, imitating foliage, scrolls, etc. —*adj.* 1. of or in rococo 2. too elaborate; florid

rod (räd) *n.* [OE. *rodd*] 1. a straight stick, bar, etc. 2. a stick for beating as punishment 3. a scepter carried as a symbol of office 4. a measure of length equal to 5 1/2 yards 5. a pole for fishing

rode (rōd) *pt.* of RIDE

ro·dent (rōd''nt) *n.* [< L. *rodere*, gnaw] any of various gnawing mammals, including rats, mice, beavers, etc. —*adj.* 1. gnawing 2. of or like rodents

ro·de·o (rō'dē ō', rō dā'ō) *n., pl.* **-os'** [Sp. < L. *rotare*, to turn] a public exhibition of the skills of cowboys, as broncobusting, lassoing, etc.

Ro·din (rō dan'), **(François) Auguste (René)** (ô güst') 1840–1917; Fr. sculptor

roe[1] (rō) *n.* [ME. *rowe*] fish eggs, esp. when still massed in the ovarian membrane

roe[2] (rō) *n., pl.* **roe, roes** [< OE. *ra*] a small, agile European and Asian deer

roe·buck (rō'buk') *n.* the male of the roe deer

roent·gen (rent'gən) *n.* [< W. K. *Roentgen* (1845–1923), Ger. physicist] the unit for measuring the radiation of X-rays (**Roentgen rays**) or gamma rays

Rog·er (räj'ər) *interj.* [< name of signal flag for *R*] [*also* **r-**] 1. received: used to indicate reception of a radio message 2. [Colloq.] right! OK!

rogue (rōg) *n.* [< ?] 1. a scoundrel 2. a fun-loving, mischievous person 3. an animal that wanders alone and is fierce and wild

ro·guer·y (rō'gər ē) *n., pl.* **-ies** the behavior of a rogue; specif., *a*) cheating *b*) playful mischief

rogues' gallery a collection of photographs of criminals, as used by police in identification

ro·guish (rō'gish) *adj.* 1. dishonest; unscrupulous 2. playfully mischievous —**ro'guish·ly** *adv.*

roil (roil) *vt.* [< Fr. < L. *robigo*, rust] 1. to make (a liquid) cloudy, muddy, etc. by stirring up the sediment 2. to stir up 3. to make angry

roist·er (rois'tər) *vi.* [see RUSTIC] 1. to boast or swagger 2. to be lively and noisy —**roist'er·er** *n.*

role, rôle (rōl) *n.* [Fr. *rôle*, a roll: from roll containing actor's part] 1. a part, or character, that an actor plays 2. a function assumed by someone [an advisory *role*]

roll (rōl) *vi.* [< L. *rota*, wheel] 1. to move by turning over and over 2. to move on wheels 3. to pass [the years *rolled* by] 4. to flow in a full, sweeping motion 5. to extend in gentle swells 6. to make a loud, rising and falling sound [thunder *rolls*] 7. to turn in a circular motion 8. to rock from side to side, as a ship 9. to become spread under a roller 10. to make progress 11. to abound (*in*) —*vt.* 1. to move by turning over and over 2. to move on wheels or rollers 3. to beat (a drum) with light, rapid blows 4. to utter with a full, flowing sound 5. to say with a trill [to *roll* one's r's] 6. to give a swaying motion to 7. to move around or from side to side [to *roll* one's eyes] 8. to wind into a ball or cylinder [to *roll* a cigarette] 9. to flatten or spread 10. [Slang] to rob (a drunken or sleeping person) —*n.* 1. a rolling 2. a scroll 3. a list of names 4. something rolled into a cylinder 5. a small, shaped piece of bread 6. a swaying motion 7. a rapid succession of light blows on a drum 8. a loud, reverberating sound, as of thunder 9. a slight swell on a surface 10. [Slang] money; esp., a wad of paper money —**roll in** to arrive or appear, usually in large numbers or amounts —**roll out** to spread out by unrolling

roll call the reading aloud of a roll to find out who is absent

roll'er *n.* 1. one that rolls 2. a cylinder on which something is rolled, or a heavy one used to crush, smooth, or spread something 3. a long, heavy wave

roller coaster an amusement ride in which small cars move on tracks that dip and curve sharply

roller skate a skate with wheels: see SKATE[1] (sense 2) —**roll'er-skate'** *vi.* -skat'ed, -skat'ing

rol·lick (räl'ik) *vi.* [< ? FROLIC] to play or behave in a gay, carefree way —**rol'lick·ing** *adj.*

roll'ing *adj.* that rolls; specif., rotating or revolving, recurring, swaying, surging, resounding, trilling, etc. —*n.* the action, motion, or sound of something that rolls

rolling mill 1. a factory in which metal bars, etc. are rolled out 2. a machine used for such rolling

rolling pin a heavy, smooth cylinder of wood, glass, etc., used to roll out dough

rolling stock all the vehicles of a railroad or a trucking company

roll'-top' *adj.* made with a flexible top of parallel slats that slides back [a *roll-top* desk]

ro·ly-po·ly (rō'lē pō'lē) *adj.* [< ROLL] short and plump; pudgy —*n., pl.* **-lies** one that is pudgy

rom, rom. roman (type)

Rom. 1. Roman 2. Romans (Epistle to the Romans)

ro·maine (rō mān') *n.* [Fr., Roman] a kind of lettuce with long leaves forming a long, slender head

Ro·man (rō'mən) *adj.* 1. of or characteristic of ancient or modern Rome, its people, etc. 2. of the Roman Catholic Church 3. [*usually* r-] designating or of the usual upright style of printing types —*n.* 1. a native or inhabitant of ancient or modern Rome 2. [*usually* r-] roman type or characters

Roman candle a firework consisting of a long tube that sends out balls of fire, sparks, etc.

Roman Catholic 1. of the Roman Catholic Church 2. a member of this church —**Roman Catholicism**

Roman Catholic Church the Christian church headed by the Pope

ro·mance (rō mans'; *also, for n.,* rō'mans) *adj.* [ult. < L. *Romanicus*, Roman] designating or of any of the languages derived from Vulgar Latin, as Italian, Spanish, French, etc. —*n.* 1. a long poem or tale, orig. written in a Romance language, about knights, adventure, and love 2.

a novel of love, adventure, etc. **3.** excitement, love, etc. of the kind found in such literature **4.** a love affair —*vi.* **-manced′, -manc′ing 1.** to write or tell romances **2.** to be imaginative —*vt.* [Colloq.] to woo; court —**ro·manc′er** *n.*

Roman Empire empire of the ancient Romans (27 B.C.–395 A.D.), including W & S Europe, N Africa, & SW Asia

Ro·man·esque (rō′mə nesk′) *adj.* designating or of a style of European architecture of the 11th and 12th cent., using round arches and vaults, massive walls, etc. —*n.* this style of architecture

Ro·ma·nia, Ro·mâ·nia (rō mān′yə) country in SE Europe: 91,700 sq. mi.; pop. 20,470,000; cap. Bucharest — **Ro·ma′nian** *adj., n.*

Ro′man·ize′ *vt., vi.* **-ized′, -iz′ing** to make or become Roman in character, spirit, etc.

Roman nose a nose with a prominent bridge

Roman numerals the Roman letters which are used as numerals: I = 1, V = 5, X = 10, L = 50, C = 100, D = 500, and M = 1,000

Ro·ma·nov (rō′mə nôf′) ruling family of Russia from 1613 to 1917

Ro·mans (rō′mənz) a book of the New Testament, an epistle from the Apostle Paul

ro·man·tic (rō man′tik) *adj.* **1.** of, like, or characterized by romance **2.** fanciful or fictitious **3.** not practical; visionary **4.** full of thoughts, feelings, etc. of romance **5.** suited for romance **6.** [*often* R-] of a 19th-cent. cultural movement (the **Romantic Movement**) characterized by freedom of form and spirit, emphasis on feeling and originality, etc. —*n.* a romantic person —**ro·man′ti·cal·ly** *adv.*

ro·man′ti·cism (-tə siz′m) *n.* **1.** romantic spirit, outlook, etc. **2.** the spirit, style, etc. of, or adherence to, the Romantic movement

ro·man′ti·cize′ (-sīz′) *vt.* **-cized′, -ciz′ing** to treat or regard romantically —*vi.* to have romantic ideas, attitudes, etc.

Rom·a·ny (räm′ə nē, rō′mə-) *n.* [< Gypsy *rom*, a man] **1.** *pl.* **-ny, -nies** a Gypsy **2.** the language of the Gypsies — *adj.* of the Gypsies, their language, etc.

Rome (rōm) capital of Italy: formerly, the capital of the Roman Empire: pop. 2,731,000

Ro·me·o (rō′mē ō′) the hero of Shakespeare's tragedy *Romeo and Juliet* (c.1595), lover of Juliet —*n., pl.* **-os′** a man who is an ardent lover

romp (rämp) *n.* [prob. < OFr. *ramper*, climb] boisterous, lively play —*vi.* **1.** to play in a boisterous, lively way **2.** to win with ease

romp′er *n.* **1.** one who romps **2.** [*pl.*] a loose, one-piece outer garment with bloomerlike pants, for a small child

Rom·u·lus (räm′yoo ləs) *Rom. Myth.* the founder and first king of Rome: he and his twin brother Remus, left as infants to die, were suckled by a she-wolf

rood (rood) *n.* [OE. *rod*] **1.** a crucifix **2.** in England, a measure of area usually equal to 1/4 acre

roof (roof, roof) *n., pl.* **roofs** [OE. *hrof*] **1.** the outside top covering of a building **2.** anything like this *[the roof of the mouth]* —*vt.* to cover as with a roof —**raise the roof** [Slang] to be very noisy

roof′er *n.* a person who builds or repairs roofs

roof′ing *n.* material for roofs

rook¹ (rook) *n.* [OE. *hroc*] **1.** a crowlike European bird **2.** a cheating —*vt., vi.* to swindle; cheat

rook² (rook) *n.* [< Per. *rukh*] *Chess* a piece that moves only horizontally or vertically; castle

rook·er·y (rook′ər ē) *n., pl.* **-ies** a breeding place or colony of rooks, or of seals, penguins, etc.

rook·ie (rook′ē) *n.* [< ?] [Slang] **1.** an inexperienced army recruit **2.** any novice

room (room, room) *n.* [OE. *rum*] **1.** space to contain something **2.** opportunity *[room for doubt]* **3.** an interior space enclosed or set apart by walls **4.** [*pl.*] living quarters; lodgings **5.** the people in a room —*vi., vt.* to have, or provide with, lodgings —**room′ful′** *n., pl.* **-fuls′**

room and board lodging and meals

room′er *n.* one who rents lodgings; lodger

room·ette (room met′) *n.* a small compartment in a railroad sleeping car

rooming house a house with furnished rooms for rent

room′mate′ *n.* a person with whom one shares a room or rooms: also [Colloq.] **room′ie**

room′y *adj.* **-i·er, -i·est** having plenty of room; spacious — **room′i·ness** *n.*

Roo·se·velt (rō′zə velt′) **1.** Franklin Del·a·no (del′ə nō′), 1882–1945; 32d president of the U.S. (1933–45) **2. Theodore,** 1858–1919; 26th president of the U.S. (1901–09)

roost (roost) *n.* [OE. *hrost*] **1.** a perch on which birds, esp. domestic fowls, can rest or sleep **2.** a place with perches for birds **3.** a place for resting, sleeping, etc. —*vi.* **1.** to sit, sleep, etc. on a perch **2.** to settle down, as for the night — **come home to roost** to have repercussions; boomerang — **rule the roost** to be master

roost·er (roos′tər) *n.* the male of the chicken

root¹ (root, root) *n.* [< ON. *rot*] **1.** the part of a plant, usually underground, that anchors the plant, draws water and food from the soil, etc. **2.** the embedded part of a tooth, hair, etc. **3.** a source or cause **4.** a supporting or essential part **5.** [*pl.*] close ties with a place, etc., as through birth **6.** *a*) a quantity that, multiplied by itself a specified number of times, produces a given quantity *b*) a number that, when substituted for an unknown quantity, will satisfy the equation **7.** *Music* the basic tone of a chord **8.** *same as* BASE (*n.* 4) —*vi.* to take root — *vt.* **1.** to fix the roots of in the ground **2.** to establish; settle — **root up** (or **out, away**) to pull out by the roots; remove completely —**take root 1.** to begin growing by putting out roots **2.** to become settled —**root′less** *adj.*

ROOTS
(left, taproot; right, fibrous)

root² (root, root) *vt.* [< OE. *wrot*, snout] to dig (*up* or *out*) as with the snout —*vi.* **1.** to search about; rummage **2.** [Colloq.] to encourage a team, etc.: usually with *for* — **root′er** *n.*

root beer a carbonated drink made of extracts from the roots and bark of certain plants, etc.

root′let (-lit) *n.* a little root

root′stock′ (-stäk′) *n. Bot. same as* RHIZOME

rope (rōp) *n.* [OE. *rap*] **1.** a thick, strong cord made of intertwisted strands of fiber, etc. **2.** a ropelike string of things —*vt.* **roped, rop′ing 1.** to fasten or tie with a rope **2.** to mark off or enclose with a rope **3.** to catch with a lasso —**know the ropes** [Colloq.] to know the details or procedures, as of a job —**rope in** [Slang] to trick into doing something —**the end of one's rope** the end of one's endurance, resources, etc. —**rop′er** *n.*

Roque·fort (cheese) (rōk′fərt) [< *Roquefort*, France, where orig. made] a strong cheese with a bluish mold, made from goats' and ewes' milk

Ror·schach test (rôr′shäk) [< H. *Rorschach* (1884–1922), Swiss psychiatrist] *Psychol.* a test for personality analysis, in which responses to various inkblot designs are interpreted

ro·sa·ry (rō′zər ē) *n., pl.* **-ries** [ML. *rosarium*] *R.C.Ch.* **1.** a string of beads used to keep count in saying prayers **2.** [*also* R-] the prayers said with these beads

rose¹ (rōz) *n.* [< L. *rosa*] **1.** a shrub with prickly stems and flowers of red, pink, white, yellow, etc. **2.** its flower **3.** pinkish red or purplish red —*adj.* rose-colored —*vt.* **rosed, ros′ing** to make rose-colored

rose² (rōz) *pt. of* RISE

ro·sé (rō zā′) *n.* [Fr.] a light, pink wine

ro·se·ate (rō′zē it, -āt′) *adj.* rose-colored

rose′bud′ *n.* the bud of a rose

rose′bush′ *n.* a shrub that bears roses

rose′-col′ored *adj.* **1.** pinkish-red or purplish-red **2.** cheerful or optimistic —**through rose-colored glasses** with optimism

rose·mar·y (rōz′mer′ē) *n.* [ult. < L. *ros marinus*, dew of the sea] an evergreen shrub of the mint family, with fragrant leaves used in cooking, etc.

rose of Shar·on (sher′ən) a plant with white, red, pink, or purplish, bell-shaped flowers

Ro·set·ta stone (rō zet′ə) an inscribed stone tablet found in 1799 at Rosetta, Egypt, that provided a key for deciphering Egyptian hieroglyphics

ro·sette (rō zet′) *n.* [Fr.] an ornament, arrangement, etc. suggesting a rose

rose water a preparation consisting of water and attar of roses, used as a perfume

rose window a circular window with roselike tracery or mullions arranged like wheel spokes

rose′wood′ *n.* [< its odor] **1.** a hard, reddish wood, used in furniture, etc. **2.** a tropical tree yielding such wood

Rosh Ha·sha·na (rōsh′ hä shô′nə, -shä′-) the Jewish New Year: also sp. **Rosh Hashona**

ros·in (räz′'n) *n.* [see RESIN] the hard resin left after the distillation of crude turpentine: it is rubbed on violin bows, used in making varnish, etc. —*vt.* to put rosin on

Ross (rôs), **Betsy** 1752–1836; Am. woman reputed to have made the first Am. flag

Ros·si·ni (rô sē'nē), **Gio·ac·chi·no** (jô'ä kē'nō) 1792–1868; It. composer

ros·ter (räs'tər) n. [< Du. *rooster*] a list or roll, as of military personnel

Ros·tov (räs'täv) seaport in SW R.S.F.S.R.: pop. 789,000: also called **Ros'tov-on-Don'**

ros·trum (räs'trəm) n., pl. **-trums, -tra** (-trə) [L., (ship's) beak] a platform for public speaking —**ros'tral** adj.

ros·y (rō'zē) adj. **-i·er, -i·est** 1. rose-red or pink [*rosy* cheeks] 2. bright, promising, etc. [a *rosy* future] —**ros'i·ly** adv. —**ros'i·ness** n.

rot (rät) vi., vt. **rot'ted, rot'ting** [OE. *rotian*] to decompose; decay; spoil —n. 1. a rotting or being rotten 2. something rotten 3. a plant or animal disease causing decay 4. [Slang] nonsense —*interj.* an exclamation of disgust, anger, etc.

ro·ta·ry (rōt'ər ē) adj. [< L. *rota*, wheel] 1. turning around a central point or axis, as a wheel 2. having rotating parts [a *rotary* press]

ro·tate (rō'tāt) vi., vt. **-tat·ed, -tat·ing** [< L. *rota*, wheel] 1. to move or turn around, as a wheel 2. to go or cause to go in a regular and recurring succession of changes —**ro'ta·tor** n.

ro·ta·tion n. 1. a rotating or being rotated 2. regular and recurring succession of changes —**ro·ta'tion·al** adj.

ro·ta·to·ry (rō'tə tôr'ē) adj. 1. of, or having the nature of, rotation 2. rotary 3. following in rotation 4. causing rotation

ROTC, R.O.T.C. Reserve Officers' Training Corps

rote (rōt) n. [< ?] a fixed, mechanical way of doing something —**by rote** by memory alone, without thought

ro·tis·ser·ie (rō tis'ər ē) n. [Fr. < MFr. *rostir*, to roast] a grill with an electrically turned spit

ro·to·gra·vure (rōt'ə grə vyoor') n. [< L. *rota*, wheel + Fr. *gravure*, engraving] 1. a process of printing pictures, etc. on a rotary press using cylinders etched from photographic plates 2. a newspaper pictorial section printed by this process

ro·tor (rōt'ər) n. [< ROTATE] 1. the rotating part of a motor, dynamo, etc. 2. a system of rotating airfoils, as on a helicopter

rot·ten (rät''n) adj. [ON. *rotinn*] 1. decayed; spoiled 2. smelling of decay; putrid 3. morally corrupt 4. unsound, as if decayed within 5. [Slang] very bad, disagreeable, etc. [a *rotten* show] —**rot'ten·ly** adv. —**rot'ten·ness** n.

rot'ter n. [< ROT] [Chiefly Brit. Slang] a scoundrel

Rot·ter·dam (rät'ər dam') seaport in SW Netherlands: pop. 687,000

ro·tund (rō tund') adj. [L. *rotundus*] 1. round or rounded out; plump 2. full-toned; sonorous [a *rotund* voice] —**ro·tun'di·ty, ro·tund'ness** n.

ro·tun·da (rō tun'də) n. [< It. < L. *rotundus*, rotund] a round building, hall, or room, esp. one with a dome

rou·ble (rōō'b'l) n. *same as* RUBLE

rou·é (rōō ā') n. [Fr. < *rouer*, to break on the wheel] a dissipated man; rake

Rou·en (rōō än') port in NW France, on the Seine: pop. 120,000

rouge (rōōzh) n. [Fr., red] 1. a reddish cosmetic powder, paste, etc. for coloring the cheeks and lips 2. a reddish powder, mainly ferric oxide, for polishing jewelry, metal, etc. —vi., vt. **rouged, roug'ing** to use cosmetic rouge (on)

rough (ruf) adj. [OE. *ruh*] 1. not smooth or level; uneven 2. shaggy [a *rough* coat] 3. a) stormy [*rough* weather] b) boisterous or disorderly [*rough* play] 4. harsh, rude, etc. [a *rough* temper] 5. sounding, feeling, or tasting harsh 6. lacking comforts and conveniences 7. not refined or polished [a *rough* diamond] 8. not finished, perfected, etc. [a *rough* sketch] 9. approximate [a *rough* guess] 10. [Colloq.] difficult, severe, etc. [a *rough* time] —n. 1. rough ground, material, condition, etc. 2. [Chiefly Brit.] a rowdy 3. *Golf* any part of the course where grass, etc. grows uncut —adv. in a rough manner —vt. 1. to make rough 2. to treat roughly (often with *up*) 3. to make or shape roughly (usually with *in* or *out*) —vi. to behave roughly — **rough it** to live without comforts and conveniences — **rough'ly** adv. —**rough'ness** n.

rough'age (-ij) n. rough or coarse food or fodder, as bran, straw, etc.

rough'-and-read'y adj. 1. rough, or crude, rude, etc., but effective 2. characterized by rough vigor rather than refinement, formality, etc.

rough'-and-tum'ble adj. violent and disorderly, with no concern for rules

rough'en vt., vi. to make or become rough

rough'-hew' vt. **-hewed', -hewed'** or **-hewn', -hew'ing** 1. to hew (timber, stone, etc.) roughly, or without smoothing 2. to form roughly Also **roughhew**

rough'house' (-hous') n. [Slang] rough or boisterous play, fighting, etc. —vt., vi. **-housed', -hous'ing** [Slang] to treat or act roughly

rough'neck' n. [Slang] a rowdy

Rough'rid'er n. a member of Theodore Roosevelt's volunteer cavalry regiment in the Spanish-American War: also **Rough Rider**

rough'shod' adj. shod with horseshoes having metal points to prevent slipping —**ride·roughshod over** to treat harshly

rou·lette (rōō let') n. [Fr. < L. *rota*, wheel] 1. a gambling game played by rolling a small ball around a shallow bowl with a revolving inner disk (**roulette wheel**) with red and black numbered compartments 2. a toothed wheel for making rows of marks or dots, as between postage stamps

ROULETTE WHEEL

Rou·ma·ni·a (rōō mān'yə) *same as* ROMANIA —**Rou·ma'nian** adj., n.

round (round) adj. [< L. *rotundus*, rotund] 1. shaped like a ball, circle, or cylinder 2. plump 3. full; complete [a *round* dozen] 4. expressed by a whole number, or in tens, hundreds, etc. 5. large; considerable [a *round* sum] 6. mellow and full in tone 7. brisk; vigorous [a *round* pace] —n. 1. something round 2. a rung of a ladder or chair 3. the part of a beef animal between the rump and the leg 4. movement in a circular course 5. a dance with dancers moving in a circle 6. a series or succession [a *round* of parties] 7. [often pl.] a regular, customary circuit, as by a watchman 8. a single serving, as of drinks, for each in a group 9. a) a single shot from a rifle, etc. or from a number of rifles fired together b) ammunition for such a shot 10. a single outburst, as of applause 11. a single period or division of action in certain games and sports 12. a short song which one group begins singing when another has reached the second phrase, etc. —vt. 1. to make round 2. to make plump 3. to express as a round number (usually with *off*) 4. to complete; finish 5. to make a circuit of 6. to make a turn about [to *round* a corner] —vi. 1. to make a circuit 2. to turn; reverse direction 3. to become plump —adv. 1. in a circle 2. through a recurring period of time [to work the year *round*] 3. from one person or place to another [the peddler came *round*] 4. in circumference [ten feet *round*] 5. on all sides 6. about; near 7. in a roundabout way 8. here and there 9. with a rotating movement 10. in the opposite direction —prep. 1. so as to encircle 2. on the circumference or border of 3. on all sides of 4. in the vicinity of 5. in a circuit; through In the U.S., *round* (adv. & prep.) is generally superseded by *around* —**in the round** 1. in an arena theater 2. in full, rounded form: said of sculpture 3. in full detail —**round about** in or to the opposite direction —**round up** to collect in a herd, group, etc. —**round'ish** adj. —**round'ness** n.

round'a·bout' adj. 1. indirect; circuitous [*roundabout* methods] 2. encircling; enclosing

roun·de·lay (roun'də lā') n. [< OFr. *rondel*, a short lyrical poem] a simple song in which some phrase, line, etc. is continually repeated

Round'head' n. a member of the Puritan party in England during the English civil war (1642–1652)

round'house' n. a circular building with a turntable, for storing and repairing locomotives

round'ly adv. 1. in a round form 2. vigorously 3. fully; completely

round robin 1. a petition, protest, etc. with the signatures written in a circle to conceal the order of signing 2. a tournament in which every entrant is matched with every other one

round'-shoul'dered adj. stooped because the shoulders are bent forward

Round Table 1. the table around which King Arthur and his knights sat 2. [r- t-] an informal discussion group

round'-the-clock' adj., adv. continuous(ly)

round trip a trip to a place and back again —**round'-trip'** adj.

round'up' *n.* **1.** a driving together of cattle, etc. on the range, as for branding **2.** any similar collecting **3.** a summary, as of news

round'worm' *n. same as* NEMATODE

rouse (rouz) *vt., vi.* roused, rous'ing [LME. *rowsen*] **1.** to stir up; excite or become excited **2.** to wake

Rous·seau (r<del>oo</del> sō′) **1.** Hen·ri (än rē′), 1844–1910; Fr. painter **2.** Jean Jacques (zhän zhäk), 1712–78; Fr. writer

roust·a·bout (roust′ə bout′) *n.* [< ROUSE + ABOUT] an unskilled or transient laborer, as in circuses

rout[1] (rout) *n.* [< L. *rupta*, broken] **1.** a rabble **2.** a disorderly flight **3.** an overwhelming defeat —*vt.* **1.** to put to flight **2.** to defeat overwhelmingly

rout[2] (rout) *vt.* [< ROOT[2]] to force out —**rout out 1.** to expose to view **2.** to scoop, gouge, or hollow out **3.** to make (a person) get out

route (r<del>oo</del>t, rout) *n.* [< L. *rupta* (*via*), broken (path)] **1.** a road, etc. for traveling; esp., a highway **2.** a regular course, as in delivering mail, etc. —*vt.* rout′ed, rout′ing **1.** to send by a specified route **2.** to fix the order of procedure of

rou·tine (r<del>oo</del> tēn′) *n.* [see prec.] **1.** a regular procedure, customary, prescribed, or habitual **2.** a theatrical skit or act —*adj.* like or using routine —**rou·tine′ly** *adv.*

rove (rōv) *vt., vi.* roved, rov′ing [< ?] to wander about; roam —**rov′er** *n.*

row[1] (rō) *n.* [OE. *ræw*] **1.** a number of people or things in a line **2.** any of the lines of seats in a theater, etc. —**in a row** consecutively

row[2] (rō) *vt., vi.* [OE. *rowan*] **1.** to propel (a boat) with oars **2.** to carry in a rowboat —*n.* **1.** a rowing **2.** a trip by rowboat —**row′er** *n.*

row[3] (rou) *n., vi.* [< ? ROUSE] quarrel, squabble, or brawl

row'boat' *n.* a boat made to be rowed

row·dy (rou′dē) *n., pl.* **-dies** [< ? ROW[3]] a rough, quarrelsome, and disorderly person; hoodlum —*adj.* **-di·er, -di·est** rough, quarrelsome, etc. —**row′di·ly** *adv.* —**row′di·ness** *n.* —**row′dy·ism** *n.*

row·el (rou′əl) *n.* [ult. < L. *rota*, wheel] a small wheel with sharp points, forming the end of a spur

row house (rō) any of a line of identical houses joined by common walls

roy·al (roi′əl) *adj.* [< L. *regalis*] **1.** of a king or queen [a *royal* edict] **2.** having the rank of a king or queen **3.** of a kingdom, its government, etc. [the *royal* fleet] **4.** suitable for a king or queen; magnificent, stately, etc. —**roy′al·ly** *adv.*

ROWEL

roy·al·ist *n.* one who supports a monarch or monarchy, esp. in times of revolution

roy′al·ty *n., pl.* **-ties 1.** the rank or power of a king or queen **2.** a royal person or persons **3.** royal quality **4.** a share of the proceeds from a patent, book, etc. paid to the owner, author, etc.

rpm, r.p.m. revolutions per minute

R.R., RR railroad

R.S.F.S.R., RSFSR Russian Soviet Federated Socialist Republic

RSV, R.S.V. Revised Standard Version (of the Bible)

R.S.V.P., r.s.v.p. [Fr. *répondez s'il vous plaît*] please reply

rt. right

Ru *Chem.* ruthenium

rub (rub) *vt.* rubbed, rub′bing [ME. *rubben*] **1.** to move (one's hand, a cloth, etc.) back and forth over (something) firmly **2.** to spread (polish, salve, etc.) on a surface **3.** to move (things) over each other with pressure and friction **4.** to make sore by rubbing **5.** to remove by rubbing (*out, off,* etc.) —*vi.* **1.** to move with pressure and friction (*on, against,* etc.) **2.** to rub something **3.** to be removed by rubbing (with *off, out,* etc.) —*n.* **1.** a rubbing **2.** an obstacle, difficulty, or source of irritation —**rub down 1.** to massage **2.** to smooth, polish, etc. by rubbing —**rub it in** [Slang] to keep reminding someone of his failure or mistake —**rub the wrong way** to annoy or irritate

rub·ber[1] (rub′ər) *n.* **1.** one that rubs **2.** [from use as an eraser] an elastic substance made from the milky sap of various tropical plants, or synthetically **3.** something made of this substance; specif., a low-cut overshoe —*adj.* made of rubber —**rub′ber·y** *adj.*

rub·ber[2] (rub′ər) *n.* [< ?] **1.** *Bridge* a series limited to three games, two of which must be won to win the series **2.** the deciding game in a series: usually **rubber game**

rubber band a narrow, continuous band of rubber as for holding objects together

rubber cement an adhesive of unvulcanized rubber in a solvent that quickly evaporates when exposed to air

rub′ber·ize′ (-īz′) *vt.* **-ized′, -iz′ing** to coat or impregnate with rubber

rubber plant 1. any plant yielding latex from which crude rubber is formed **2.** a house plant with large, glossy, leathery leaves

rubber stamp 1. a stamp of rubber, inked for printing signatures, dates, etc. **2.** [Colloq.] *a*) a person, bureau, etc. that approves something in a routine way *b*) such approval —**rub′ber-stamp′** *vt., adj.*

rub·bish (rub′ish) *n.* [ult. < base of RUB] **1.** any material thrown away as worthless; trash **2.** worthless ideas, statements, etc.; nonsense

rub·ble (rub′'l) *n.* [akin to RUBBISH] rough, broken pieces of stone, brick, etc.

rub′down′ *n.* a massage

rube (r<del>oo</del>b) *n.* [< name *Reuben*] a country person regarded as simple, unsophisticated, etc.

ru·bel·la (r<del>oo</del> bel′ə) *n.* [< L. *ruber*, red] a contagious virus disease, characterized by small red spots on the skin; German measles

Ru·bens (r<del>oo</del>′bənz), **Peter Paul** 1577–1640; Fl. painter

ru·be·o·la (r<del>oo</del> bē′ə lə, r<del>oo</del>′bē ō′lə) *n.* [< L. *rubeus*, red] *same as* MEASLES (sense 1)

Ru·bi·con (r<del>oo</del>′bi kän′) small river in N Italy crossed by Caesar with his army (49 B.C.), starting a civil war —**cross the Rubicon** to make a decisive move that cannot be undone

ru·bi·cund (r<del>oo</del>′bi kund′) *adj.* [< L. *ruber*, red] reddish

ru·bid·i·um (r<del>oo</del> bid′ē əm) *n.* [< L. *rubidus*, red (from red lines in its spectrum)] a soft, silvery-white metallic chemical element, resembling potassium: symbol, Rb; at. wt., 85.47; at. no., 37

ru·ble (r<del>oo</del>′b'l) *n.* [Russ. *rubl′*] the monetary unit of the U.S.S.R.

ru·bric (r<del>oo</del>′brik) *n.* [< L. *ruber*, red] **1.** a section heading, direction, etc. often in red (as in a prayerbook) **2.** any rule, explanatory comment, etc.

ru·by (r<del>oo</del>′bē) *n., pl.* **-bies** [< L. *rubeus*, reddish] **1.** a clear, deep-red variety of corundum, valued as a precious stone **2.** deep red —*adj.* deep-red

ruche (r<del>oo</del>sh) *n.* [Fr., lit., beehive] a fluting of lace, ribbon, etc. for trimming garments

ruch·ing (r<del>oo</del>′shiŋ) *n.* **1.** ruches collectively **2.** material used to make ruches

ruck·sack (ruk′sak′) *n.* [G. < *rücken*, the back + *sack*, a sack] a kind of knapsack

ruck·us (ruk′əs) *n.* [prob. a merging of earlier *ruction*, uproar & RUMPUS] [Colloq.] noisy confusion; disturbance

rud·der (rud′ər) *n.* [OE. *rother*, steering oar] **1.** a broad, flat, movable piece hinged vertically at the stern of a ship, used for steering **2.** a piece like this on an aircraft —**rud′der·less** *adj.*

rud·dy (rud′ē) *adj.* **-di·er, -di·est** [OE. *rudig*] **1.** having a healthy red color **2.** red or reddish —**rud′di·ness** *n.*

rude (r<del>oo</del>d) *adj.* rud′er, rud′est [< L. *rudis*] **1.** crude; rough [a *rude* hut] **2.** barbarous [*rude* savages] **3.** unrefined; uncouth **4.** discourteous [a *rude* reply] **5.** primitive —**rude′ly** *adv.* —**rude′ness** *n.*

ru·di·ment (r<del>oo</del>′də mənt) *n.* [< L. *rudis*, rude] **1.** a first principle or element, as of a subject to be learned **2.** a first slight beginning of something **3.** *Biol.* an incompletely developed or vestigial part —**ru′di·men′ta·ry** (-men′tər ē) *adj.*

rue[1] (r<del>oo</del>) *vt., vi.* rued, ru′ing [OE. *hreowan*] to feel sorrow or remorse (for); regret; repent —*n.* [Archaic] sorrow

rue[2] (r<del>oo</del>) *n.* [< Gr. *rhytē*] a strong-scented herb with yellow flowers and bitter leaves

rue′ful *adj.* **1.** causing sorrow or pity **2.** feeling or showing sorrow or regret, esp. in a wry way —**rue′ful·ly** *adv.*

ruff (ruf) *n.* [< RUFFLE] **1.** a high, frilled, stiff collar of the 16th-17th cent. **2.** a ring of feathers or fur standing out about the neck of an animal

ruf·fi·an (ruf′ē ən, ruf′yən) *n.* [< It. *ruffiano*, a pander] a brutal, lawless person; hoodlum

ruf·fle[1] (ruf′'l) *vt.* **-fled, -fling** [< ON. or MLowG.] **1.** to disturb the smoothness of **2.** to gather into ruffles **3.** to put ruffles on **4.** to make (feathers, etc.) stand up **5.** to disturb or annoy —*vi.* **1.** to become uneven **2.** to become disturbed, annoyed, etc. —*n.* **1.** a pleated strip of cloth, lace, etc. for trimming **2.** a disturbance **3.** a ripple

RUFF

ruf·fle² (ruf''l) *n.* [prob. echoic] a low, continuous beating of a drum —*vi., vt.* **-fled, -fling** to beat (a drum, etc.) with a ruffle

rug (rug) *n.* [< Scand.] **1.** a piece of thick fabric used as a floor covering **2.** [Chiefly Brit.] a lap robe

Rug·by (rug'bē) *n.* [first played at *Rugby* School in England] [*also* r-] a football game from which American football developed

rug·ged (rug'id) *adj.* [ME., prob. < Scand.] **1.** uneven; rough **2.** strong, irregular, and lined [a *rugged* face] **3.** stormy **4.** harsh; severe; hard **5.** not polished or refined **6.** strong; robust —**rug'ged·ly** *adv.* —**rug'ged·ness** *n.*

Ruhr (roor) **1.** river in C West Germany **2.** coal-mining & industrial region along this river: also **Ruhr Basin**

ru·in (rōō'in) *n.* [< L. *ruere,* to fall] **1.** [*pl.*] the remains of a building, city, etc. destroyed, decayed, etc. **2.** anything destroyed, etc. **3.** the state of being destroyed, decayed, etc. **4.** downfall, destruction, etc. **5.** anything causing this —*vt.* to bring to ruin; destroy, bankrupt, seduce, etc. —*vi.* to go or come to ruin

ru·in·a·tion (rōō'ə nā'shən) *n.* **1.** a ruining or being ruined **2.** anything that ruins

ru'in·ous (-ə nəs) *adj.* **1.** falling or fallen into ruin **2.** bringing ruin; disastrous —**ru'in·ous·ly** *adv.*

rule (rōōl) *n.* [< L. *regere,* lead straight] **1.** an established regulation or guide for conduct, procedure, usage, etc. **2.** a set of regulations in a religious order **3.** custom **4.** the customary course **5.** government; reign **6.** a ruler (sense 2) —*vt., vi.* **ruled, rul'ing 1.** to have an influence over; guide **2.** to govern **3.** to settle by decree **4.** to mark lines (on) as with a ruler —**as a rule** usually —**rule out** to exclude

rule of thumb a practical, though crude and unscientific, method

rul'er *n.* **1.** one who governs **2.** a thin strip of metal, wood, etc. with a straight edge, used in drawing lines, measuring, etc.

rul'ing *adj.* **1.** governing **2.** predominating —*n.* **1.** a court decision **2.** the making of ruled lines **3.** the lines so made

rum¹ (rum) *n.* [< ?] **1.** an alcoholic liquor made from fermented sugar cane, molasses, etc. **2.** any alcoholic liquor

rum² (rum) *adj.* [< obs. *rum,* good] [Chiefly Brit. Colloq.] **1.** odd; strange **2.** bad, poor, etc. [a *rum* joke]

Ru·ma·nia (rōō mān'yə) *same as* ROMANIA —**Ru·ma'nian** *adj., n.*

rum·ba (rum'bə) *n.* [AmSp.] **1.** a dance of Cuban Negro origin **2.** music for this dance —*vi.* to dance the rumba

rum·ble (rum'b'l) *vi., vt.* **-bled, -bling** [prob. < MDu. *rommelen*] **1.** to make or cause to make a deep, continuous, rolling sound **2.** to move with such a sound —*n.* **1.** a rumbling sound **2.** [Slang] a gang fight

rumble seat in some earlier automobiles, an open rear seat that could be folded shut when not in use

ru·mi·nant (rōō'mə nənt) *adj.* [see RUMINATE] **1.** chewing the cud **2.** meditative —*n.* any of a group of four-footed, hoofed, cud-chewing mammals, as cattle, sheep, etc.

ru'mi·nate' (-nāt') *vt., vi.* **-nat'ed, -nat'ing** [< L. *ruminare*] **1.** to chew (the cud) **2.** to meditate (on); muse —**ru'mi·na'tion** *n.* —**ru'mi·na'tive** *adj.*

rum·mage (rum'ij) *n.* [< MFr. *run,* ship's hold] **1.** odds and ends **2.** a rummaging —*vt., vi.* **-maged, -mag·ing** to search through (a place) thoroughly

rummage sale a sale of contributed miscellaneous articles, as for charity

rum·my (rum'ē) *n.* [< ?] any of certain card games whose object is to match sets and sequences

ru·mor (rōō'mər) *n.* [L., noise] **1.** general talk not based on definite knowledge **2.** an unconfirmed report, story, etc. in general circulation —*vt.* to tell or spread by rumor Brit. sp. **ru'mour**

rump (rump) *n.* [< ON. *rumpr*] **1.** the hind part of an animal where the legs and back join **2.** the buttocks **3.** the last part; remnant

rum·ple (rum'p'l) *n.* [< MDu. *rompe*] an uneven crease; wrinkle —*vt., vi.* **-pled, -pling** to wrinkle; muss

rum·pus (rum'pəs) *n.* [< ?] [Colloq.] noisy disturbance; uproar

rum·run·ner (rum'run'ər) *n.* a person, ship, etc. engaged in smuggling alcoholic liquor

run (run) *vi.* **ran, run, run'ning** [< ON. & OE.] **1.** to go by moving the legs faster than in walking **2.** to move swiftly **3.** to go, move, etc. easily and freely **4.** to make a quick trip (*up to, down to,* etc.) **5.** to flee **6.** to compete in a race, election, etc. **7.** to swim in migration: said of fish **8.**

to go, as on a schedule **9.** to climb or creep, as a vine **10.** to ravel, as a stocking **11.** to operate, as a machine **12.** to flow **13.** to melt and flow, as wax **14.** to spread over cloth, etc. when moistened, as colors **15.** to be wet with a flow [her eyes *ran* with tears] **16.** to discharge pus, mucus, etc. **17.** to continue **18.** to pass into a specified condition [to *run* into trouble] **19.** to be written, expressed, etc. in a specified way **20.** to be at a specified size, price, etc. [meat *runs* high] —*vt.* **1.** to follow (a specified course) **2.** to travel over **3.** to perform as by running [to *run* a race] **4.** to incur (a risk) **5.** to get past [to *run* a blockade] **6.** to make run, move, compete, etc. **7.** to force into a specified condition **8.** to convey **9.** to smuggle **10.** to drive (an object) into, against, etc. (something) **11.** to make flow, pass, etc. in a specified way, place, etc. **12.** to manage [to *run* a household] **13.** to cost (an amount) **14.** to mark or draw (lines, as on a map) **15.** to trace **16.** to undergo (a fever, etc.) **17.** to publish (a story, etc.) as in a newspaper —*n.* **1.** *a)* an act or period of running *b)* a running pace **2.** the distance covered in running **3.** a trip; journey **4.** a continuous course or period **5.** a continuous course of performances, etc., as of a play **6.** a continued series of demands, as for specified goods **7.** a flow or rush of water **8.** a small, swift stream **9.** *a)* a period during which some fluid flows readily *b)* the amount of flow **10.** *a)* a period of operation of a machine *b)* the output during this period **11.** a kind or class; esp., the average kind **12.** *a)* an inclined pathway or course [a ski *run*] *b)* an enclosed area for domestic animals **13.** freedom to move about at will [the *run* of the house] **14.** a large number of fish migrating together **15.** a ravel, as in a stocking **16.** *Baseball* a scoring point, made by a successful circuit of the bases **17.** *Music* a rapid succession of tones —*adj.* melted —**in the long run** ultimately —**on the run** running or running away —**run across** to encounter by chance —**run down 1.** to stop operating **2.** to run against so as to knock down **3.** to pursue and capture or kill **4.** to search out the source of **5.** to speak of disparagingly **6.** to make or become run-down —**run into 1.** to encounter by chance **2.** to collide with **3.** to add up to (a large sum) —**run off 1.** to print, make copies of, etc. **2.** to cause to be run, played, etc. —**run out** to come to an end; expire —**run out of** to use up —**run over 1.** to ride over **2.** to overflow **3.** to examine, rehearse, etc. rapidly —**run through 1.** to use up quickly or recklessly **2.** to pierce —**run up 1.** to raise, rise, or make rapidly **2.** to let (bills, etc.) go without paying them **3.** to sew rapidly

run'a·bout' *n.* **1.** one who runs about from place to place **2.** a light, one-seated, open carriage or automobile **3.** a light motorboat

run'a·round' *n.* [Colloq.] a series of evasive excuses, delays, etc.

run'a·way' *n.* **1.** a fugitive **2.** a horse, etc. that runs away —*adj.* **1.** running away or having run away **2.** easily won, as a race **3.** rising rapidly, as prices

run'down' *n.* a concise summary

run'-down' *adj.* **1.** not wound and therefore not running, as a clock **2.** in poor physical condition, as from overwork **3.** fallen into disrepair

rune (rōōn) *n.* [OE. *run*] **1.** any of the characters of an ancient Germanic alphabet **2.** any poem, song, etc. that is mystical or obscure —**ru'nic** *adj.*

rung¹ (ruŋ) *n.* [OE. *hrung,* a staff] a rod forming a step of a ladder, a crosspiece on a chair, etc.

rung² (ruŋ) *pp. & chiefly dial. pt. of* RING¹

run-in' *n.* **1.** *Printing* matter added without a break or new paragraph **2.** [Colloq.] a quarrel, fight, etc.

run·nel (run''l) *n.* [< OE. *rinnan,* to run] a small stream; brook: also **run'let** (-lit)

run'ner *n.* **1.** one that runs, as a racer, messenger, etc. **2.** a smuggler **3.** a long, narrow cloth or rug **4.** a ravel, as in hose **5.** a long, trailing stem, as of a strawberry **6.** something on or in which something else moves **7.** either of the long, narrow pieces on which a sled, etc. slides **8.** the blade of a skate

run'ner-up' *n., pl.* **-ners-up'** a person or team that finishes second in a race, contest, etc.

run'ning *n.* the act of one that runs; racing, managing, etc. —*adj.* **1.** that runs (in various senses) **2.** measured in a straight line [a *running* foot] **3.** continuous [a *running* commentary] **4.** current [a *running* account] **5.** done in or by a run [a *running* jump] —*adv.* in succession [for five days *running*] —**in** (or **out of**) **the running** having a (or no) chance to win

running board esp. formerly, a footboard along the lower part of the side of some automobiles

running lights lights that a ship, aircraft, etc. must display at night

running mate a candidate for a lesser office, as for the vice-presidency, in his or her relationship to the candidate for the greater office

run'ny *adj.* **-ni·er, -ni·est 1.** flowing, esp. too freely **2.** discharging mucus *[a runny nose]*

run'-off' *n.* **1.** something that runs off **2.** a deciding, final contest

run'-of-the-mill' *adj.* [see RUN, *n.* 11] ordinary

runt (runt) *n.* [< ?] a stunted animal, plant, or (in a contemptuous sense) person —**runt'y** *adj.* **-i·er, -i·est**

run'-through' *n.* a complete rehearsal, from beginning to end

run'way' *n.* a channel, track, etc. in, on, or along which something moves; esp., a strip of leveled ground used by airplanes in taking off and landing

ru·pee (rōō pē') *n.* [< Hindi < Sans. *rūpya,* wrought silver] the monetary unit of India, Pakistan, etc.

rup·ture (rup'chər) *n.* [< L. *rumpere,* to break] **1.** a breaking apart or being broken apart; breach **2.** a breaking off of peaceful relations **3.** a hernia —*vt., vi.* **-tured, -tur·ing 1.** to break apart or burst **2.** to cause or suffer a rupture

ru·ral (roor'əl) *adj.* [< L. *rus,* the country] of, like, or living in the country; rustic —**ru'ral·ism** *n.*

rural delivery delivery of mail by carriers on routes in rural areas: formerly **rural free delivery**

ruse (rōōz) *n.* [Fr. < OFr. *reuser,* deceive] a stratagem or trick

rush' (rush) *vt., vi.* [< OFr. *reuser,* deceive, repel] **1.** to move, dash, etc. impetuously **2.** to make a sudden attack (on) **3.** to pass, come, go, etc. swiftly or suddenly **4.** *Football* to advance (the ball) by a running play —*n.* **1.** a rushing **2.** an eager movement of many people to get to a place **3.** intense activity; haste **4.** a sudden attack **5.** a press, as of business, requiring unusual haste —*adj.* necessitating haste *[rush orders]* —**rush'er** *n.*

rush² (rush) *n.* [OE. *risc*] **1.** a grasslike marsh plant having, in some species, round stems and pliant leaves used in making baskets, mats, etc. **2.** any of various similar plants, as bulrushes —**rush'y** *adj.* **-i·er, -i·est**

rush hour a time of day when business, traffic, etc. are especially heavy —**rush'-hour'** *adj.*

rusk (rusk) *n.* [< Sp. *rosca,* twisted bread roll] **1.** a sweet, raised bread or cake toasted until brown and crisp **2.** a piece of this

Rus·kin (rus'kin), **John** 1819–1900; Eng. writer, art critic, and social reformer

Russ. 1. Russia **2.** Russian

Rus·sell (rus'l), **Bertrand** 1872–1970; Brit. philosopher, mathematician, & writer

rus·set (rus'it) *n.* [< L. *russus,* reddish] **1.** yellowish (or reddish) brown **2.** a coarse, brownish, homespun cloth **3.** a winter apple with a mottled skin

Rus·sia (rush'ə) **1.** a czarist empire (**Russian Empire**) in E Europe and N Asia, 1547–1917 **2.** popularly, the Union of Soviet Socialist Republics

Rus'sian *adj.* of Russia, its people, their language, etc. —*n.* **1.** a native or inhabitant of Russia **2.** the Slavic language of the Russians

Russian Revolution the revolution of 1917 in Russia in which the czarist government was overthrown

Russian Soviet Federated Socialist Republic largest republic of the U.S.S.R., stretching from the Baltic Sea to the Pacific

Russian wolfhound *same as* BORZOI

rust (rust) *n.* [OE.] **1.** the reddish-brown coating (mainly ferric oxide) formed on iron and steel during exposure to air and moisture **2.** any stain or coating resembling this **3.** reddish brown **4.** a plant disease caused by parasitic fungi, spotting stems and leaves —*vi., vt.* **1.** to form rust (on) **2.** to deteriorate, as through disuse —**rust'-col'ored** *adj.* —**rust'less** *adj.*

rus·tic (rus'tik) *adj.* [< L. *rus,* the country] **1.** of or living in the country **2.** artless; unsophisticated **3.** awkward; uncouth **4.** made of bark-covered branches or roots *[rustic furniture]* —*n.* a country person, esp. one regarded as simple, uncouth, etc. —**rus'ti·cal·ly** *adv.* —**rus·tic'i·ty** (-tis'ə tē) *n.*

rus·ti·cate (rus'ti kāt') *vi., vt.* **-cat'ed, -cat'ing 1.** to go or send to live in the country **2.** to become or make rustic —**rus'ti·ca'tion** *n.*

rus·tle' (rus'l) *vi., vt.* **-tled, -tling** [ult. echoic] to make or cause to make soft sounds, as of leaves moved by a breeze —*n.* a series of such sounds

rus·tle² (rus'l) *vi., vt.* **-tled, -tling** [< ?] [Colloq.] to steal (cattle, etc.) —**rustle up** [Colloq.] to collect or get together —**rus'tler** *n.*

rust'proof' *adj.* resistant to rust —*vt.* to make rustproof

rust'y (rus'tē) *adj.* **-i·er, -i·est 1.** coated with rust, as a metal, or affected with rust, as a plant **2.** *a)* impaired by disuse, neglect, etc. *b)* having lost one's skill through lack of practice **3.** rust-colored —**rust'i·ly** *adv.* —**rust'i·ness** *n.*

rut' (rut) *n.* [< ? MFr. *route,* route] **1.** a groove, track, etc. as made by wheels **2.** a fixed, routine procedure, way of acting, etc. —*vt.* **rut'ted, rut'ting** to make a rut or ruts in

rut² (rut) *n.* [< L. *rugire,* to roar] the periodic sexual excitement of certain mammals, esp. males —*vi.* **rut'ted, rut'ting** to be in rut

ru·ta·ba·ga (rōōt'ə bā'gə) *n.* [Sw. dial. *rotabagge*] a turnip with a large, yellow root

Ruth (rōōth) *Bible* **1.** a widow deeply devoted to her mother-in-law, Naomi **2.** the book of the Bible that tells her story

ru·the·ni·um (rōō thē'nē əm) *n.* [< ML. *Ruthenia,* Russia, where first found] a rare, very hard, silvery-gray metallic chemical element: symbol, Ru; at. wt., 101.07; at. no., 44

ruth·less (rōōth'lis) *adj.* [< OE. *hreowan,* to rue] without pity or compassion —**ruth'less·ly** *adv.* —**ruth'less·ness** *n.*

rut'ty *adj.* **-ti·er, -ti·est** having or full of ruts

Rwan·da (ʉr wän'dä) country in EC Africa, east of Zaire: 10,169 sq. mi.; pop. 3,724,000

Rwy., Ry. Railway

Rx [< ℞, symbol for L. *recipe:* see RECIPE] *symbol for* PRESCRIPTION (sense 3)

ry·a rug (rē'ə) [< Sw.] a decorative, hand-woven, thick rug of Scandinavian origin

rye (rī) *n.* [OE. *ryge*] **1.** a hardy cereal grass **2.** its grain or seeds, used for making flour, etc. **3.** whiskey distilled from this grain

Ryu·kyu Islands (ryōō'kyōō') chain of Japanese islands in the W Pacific, between Kyushu & Taiwan

S

S, s (es) *n., pl.* **S's, s's** the nineteenth letter of the English alphabet

S (es) *n.* **1.** something shaped like S **2.** *Chem.* sulfur

-s [alt. of -ES] **1.** the plural ending of most nouns *[lips]* **2.** the ending of the third person singular, present indicative, of verbs *[runs]*

-'s' [OE. -*es*] the ending of the possessive singular of nouns (and some pronouns) and of the possessive plural of nouns not ending in *s [boy's, one's, men's]*

-'s² *the assimilated form of:* **1.** is *[he's here]* **2.** has *[she's gone]* **3.** does *[what's it matter?]* **4.** us *[let's go]*

S, S., s, s. 1. south **2.** southern

S., s. 1. *pl.* **SS., ss.** saint **2.** school **3.** society

s. 1. second(s) **2.** shilling(s)

S.A. South America

Saar (sär, zär) rich coal-mining region in a river valley of SW West Germany: also called **Saar Basin**

Sab·bath (sab'əth) *n.* [< Heb. *shābath,* to rest] **1.** the seventh day of the week (Saturday), observed as a day of rest and worship by Jews **2.** Sunday as the usual Christian day of rest and worship

Sab·bat·i·cal (sə bat'i k'l) *adj.* **1.** of the Sabbath **2.** [s-] bringing a period of rest *[a sabbatical leave]* —*n.* [s-] a sabbatical year or leave

sabbatical year a period of absence with pay, for study, travel, etc., given as to teachers, orig. every seven years

sa·ber, sa·bre (sā′bər) *n.* [< Fr. < MHG. *sabel*] a heavy cavalry sword with a slightly curved blade

Sa·bin vaccine (sā′bin) [< Dr. A. B. *Sabin* (1906–), its U.S. developer] a vaccine taken orally to prevent poliomyelitis

sa·ble (sā′b'l) *n.* [< Russ. *sobol'*] **1.** *same as* MARTEN **2.** its costly fur

sa·bot (sab′ō, sa bō′) *n.* [Fr., ult. < Ar. *sabbât*, sandal] **1.** a shoe shaped from a single piece of wood **2.** a heavy leather shoe with a wooden sole

sab·o·tage (sab′ə täzh′) *n.* [Fr. < *sabot:* from damage done to machinery by wooden shoes] **1.** intentional destruction of machines, waste of materials, etc., as during labor disputes **2.** destruction of railroads, bridges, etc. by enemy agents or an underground resistance —*vt., vi.* -**taged′, -tag′ing** to commit sabotage (on) —**sab′o·teur′** (-tur′) *n.*

sac (sak) *n.* [see SACK¹] a pouchlike part in a plant or animal, esp. one filled with fluid

SAC, S.A.C. Strategic Air Command

sac·cha·rin (sak′ə rin) *n.* [< Gr. *sakcharon*] a white, crystalline coal-tar compound used as a sugar substitute

sac′cha·rine (-rin) *adj.* **1.** of or like sugar **2.** too sweet [a *saccharine* voice]

sac·er·do·tal (sas′ər dōt′'l, sak′-) *adj.* [< L. *sacerdos*, priest] of priests or the office of priest

sa·chem (sā′chəm) *n.* [< AmInd.] among some N. American Indian tribes, the chief

sa·chet (sa shā′) *n.* [Fr.] **1.** a small bag, pad, etc. filled with perfumed powder and placed with stored clothes **2.** such powder: also **sachet powder**

sack¹ (sak) *n.* [ult. < Heb. *śaq*] **1.** a bag, esp. a large one of coarse cloth, for holding grain, foodstuffs, etc. **2.** the contents or capacity of a sack **3.** a loose-fitting jacket or dress **4.** [Slang] dismissal from a job (with *the*) **5.** [Slang] a bed **6.** *Baseball* a base —*vt.* **1.** to put into sacks **2.** [Slang] to dismiss from a job —**hit the sack** [Slang] to go to bed

sack² (sak) *n.* [see prec.] the plundering of a captured city, etc. —*vt.* to plunder (a city, etc.)

sack³ (sak) *n.* [< Fr. (*vin*) *sec*, dry (wine)] a dry, white Spanish wine formerly popular in England

sack·but (sak′but′) *n.* [< OFr. *saquer*, to pull + *bouter*, to push] a medieval wind instrument, forerunner of the trombone

sack′cloth′ *n.* **1.** a coarse cloth used for sacks: also **sack′ing 2.** coarse cloth worn as a symbol of mourning or penitence

sac·ra·ment (sak′rə mənt) *n.* [< L. *sacer*, sacred] **1.** any of certain Christian rites, as baptism, Holy Communion, etc. **2.** something regarded as sacred —**sac′ra·men′tal** *adj.*

Sac·ra·men·to (sak′rə men′tō) capital of Calif.: pop. 254,000 (met. area 801,000)

sa·cred (sā′krid) *adj.* [< L. *sacer*, holy] **1.** consecrated to a god or God; holy **2.** having to do with religion or religious rites **3.** given the respect accorded holy things; venerated **4.** dedicated to a person, place, etc. [*sacred* to his memory] **5.** that must not be broken, etc.; inviolate [a *sacred* promise] —**sa′cred·ly** *adv.* —**sa′cred·ness** *n.*

sac·ri·fice (sak′rə fīs′) *n.* [< L. *sacer*, holy + *facere*, to make] **1.** an offering, as of a life or object, to a deity **2.** a giving up of one thing for the sake of another **3.** a loss incurred in selling a thing at less than its value **4.** *Baseball* a play in which the batter bunts and is put out but advances a base runner —*vt., vi.* -**ficed′, -fic′ing 1.** to offer as a sacrifice to a deity **2.** to give up (one thing) for the sake of another **3.** to sell at less than value **4.** *Baseball* to advance (a runner) by a sacrifice —**sac′ri·fi′cial** (-fish′əl) *adj.* —**sac′ri·fi′cial·ly** *adv.*

sac·ri·lege (sak′rə lij) *n.* [< L. *sacer*, sacred + *legere*, take away] a desecrating of anything held sacred —**sac′ri·le′gious** (-lij′əs, -lē′jəs) *adj.* —**sac′ri·le′gious·ly** *adv.*

sac·ris·ty (sak′ris tē) *n., pl.* -**ties** [ult. < L. *sacer*, sacred] a room in a church for sacred vessels, vestments, etc.

sa·cro·il·i·ac (sā′krō il′ē ak′, sak′rō-) *n.* [< SACRUM + ILIUM] the joint between the ilium and the sacrum

sac·ro·sanct (sak′rō saŋkt′) *adj.* [< L. *sacer*, sacred + *sanctus*, holy] very sacred, holy, or inviolable

sa·crum (sā′krəm) *n., pl.* -**cra** (-krə), -**crums** [< LL. (*os*) *sacrum*, sacred bone: ? anciently used in sacrifices] a

thick, triangular bone at the lower end of the spinal column

sad (sad) *adj.* **sad′der, sad′dest** [OE. *sæd*, sated] **1.** having or expressing low spirits; unhappy; sorrowful **2.** causing dejection, sorrow, etc. **3.** [Colloq.] very bad —**sad′ly** *adv.* —**sad′ness** *n.*

sad′den *vt., vi.* to make or become sad

sad·dle (sad′'l) *n.* [OE. *sadol*] **1.** a seat for a rider on a horse, bicycle, etc., usually padded and of leather **2.** anything like a saddle in form, position, etc., as a ridge between two peaks **3.** a cut of lamb, etc. including part of the backbone and the two loins —*vt.* -**dled, -dling 1.** to put a saddle upon **2.** to encumber or burden —**in the saddle** in control

sad′dle·bag′ *n.* **1.** a large bag, usually one of a pair, hung behind the saddle on a horse, etc. **2.** a similar bag carried on a bicycle, etc.

saddle horse a horse trained for riding

saddle shoes white oxford shoes with a contrasting band across the instep

Sad·du·cee (saj′oo sē′) *n.* a member of an ancient Jewish party that accepted only the written law

sad·ism (sad′iz'm, sā′diz'm) *n.* [< marquis de *Sade*, 18th-c. Fr. writer] the getting of pleasure, specif. sexual pleasure, from mistreating others —**sad′ist** *n.* —**sa·dis′tic** *adj.* —**sa·dis′ti·cal·ly** *adv.*

sa·fa·ri (sə fär′ē) *n., pl.* -**ris** [< Ar. *safara*, to travel] a journey or hunting expedition, esp. in Africa

safe (sāf) *adj.* **saf′er, saf′est** [< L. *salvus*] **1.** *a)* free from danger, damage, etc.; secure *b)* having escaped injury; unharmed **2.** *a)* giving protection *b)* trustworthy **3.** taking or involving no risks **4.** *Baseball* having reached base without being put out —*n.* a strong, locking metal container for valuables —**safe′ly** *adv.* —**safe′ness** *n.*

safe′-con′duct *n.* permission, usually written, to travel safely through enemy regions

safe′-de·pos′it *adj.* designating or of a box or vault, esp. in a bank, for storing valuables: also **safe′ty-de·pos′it**

safe′guard′ *n.* a protection; precaution —*vt.* to protect or guard

safe′keep′ing *n.* a keeping or being kept in safety; protection or custody

safe·ty (sāf′tē) *n., pl.* -**ties 1.** a being safe; security **2.** a device to prevent accident, as a locking device (also **safety catch, safety lock**) on a firearm **3.** *Football a)* the grounding of the ball by the offense behind its own goal line when the ball has been caused to pass this line by the offense *b)* a defensive back farthest from the line of scrimmage —*adj.* giving safety

safety belt *same as* SEAT BELT

safety glass shatterproof glass

safety lamp a miner's lamp designed to avoid fire, etc.

safety match a match that strikes only on a prepared surface

safety pin a pin bent back on itself and having the point held in a guard

safety razor a razor with guards for the blade to protect the skin from cuts

safety valve 1. an automatic valve for a boiler, etc. that releases steam if the pressure is too great **2.** any outlet for emotion, energy, etc.

saf·flow·er (saf′lou′ər) *n.* [ult. < Ar.] a flowering thistle-like plant whose seeds yield an edible oil

saf·fron (saf′rən) *n.* [< Du. < It. < Ar. *za'farān*] **1.** a plant having orange stigmas **2.** the dried stigmas, used as a dye and flavoring **3.** orange yellow

S. Afr. 1. South Africa **2.** South African

sag (sag) *vi.* **sagged, sag′ging** [prob. < Scand.] **1.** to sink, esp. in the middle, from weight or pressure **2.** to hang down unevenly **3.** to lose firmness, strength, etc.; weaken **4.** to decline in price, sales, etc. —*n.* **1.** a sagging **2.** a sagging place

sa·ga (sä′gə) *n.* [ON., a tale] **1.** a medieval Scandinavian story telling of legendary or historic persons, battles, etc. **2.** any long story of heroic deeds

sa·ga·cious (sə gā′shəs) *adj.* [< L. *sagax*, wise] keenly perceptive, farsighted, etc. —**sa·ga′cious·ly** *adv.* —**sa·gac′i·ty** (-gas′ə tē) *n.*

sage¹ (sāj) *adj.* **sag′er, sag′est** [ult. < L. *sapere*, know] having or showing wisdom or good judgment —*n.* a very wise man —**sage′ly** *adv.* —**sage′ness** *n.*

sage² (sāj) *n.* [< L. *salvus*, safe: it reputedly had healing powers] **1.** a plant related to the mint with leaves used in flavoring meat, etc. **2.** *same as* SAGEBRUSH

SABER

sage'brush' *n.* a plant with aromatic leaves, common in dry, alkaline areas of the W U.S.

sag'gy *adj.* **-gi·er, -gi·est** tending to sag —**sag'gi·ness** *n.*

Sag·it·ta·ri·us (saj'i ter'ē əs) [L., archer] **1.** a large S constellation in the Milky Way **2.** the ninth sign of the zodiac: see ZODIAC, illus.

sa·gua·ro (sə gwä'rō) *n., pl.* **-ros** [MexSp. < native name] a giant cactus of the SW U.S. and N Mexico

Sa·ha·ra (sə har'ə, -her'ə) vast desert region extending across N Africa —**Sa·ha'ran** *adj.*

sa·hib (sä'ib) *n.* [Hindi < Ar.] sir; master: title formerly used in India when speaking to or of a European

said (sed) *pt. & pp. of* SAY —*adj.* aforesaid

Sai·gon (sī gän') seaport in S Vietnam: now called *Ho Chi Minh City*

sail (sāl) *n.* [OE. *segl*] **1.** a sheet, as of canvas, spread to catch the wind so as to drive a vessel forward **2.** sails collectively **3.** a trip in a ship or boat **4.** anything like a sail, as an arm of a windmill —*vi.* **1.** to be moved forward by means of sails or a propeller, etc. **2.** to travel on water **3.** to begin a trip by water **4.** to manage a sailboat **5.** to glide through the air **6.** to move smoothly, like a ship in full sail —*vt.* **1.** to move upon (a body of water) in a vessel **2.** to manage (a vessel) —**sail into** [Colloq.] **1.** to begin vigorously **2.** to criticize severely —**set sail** to begin a trip by water —**under sail** sailing —**sail'ing** *n., adj.*

sail'boat' *n.* a boat propelled by a sail or sails

sail'cloth' *n.* canvas or similar cloth used in making sails, tents, etc.

sail'fish' *n., pl.:* see FISH a large, tropical marine fish with a large, saillike dorsal fin

sail'or *n.* **1.** one who makes his living by sailing **2.** an enlisted man in the navy **3.** a straw hat with a low, flat crown and flat brim

saint (sānt) *n.* [< L. *sanctus*, holy] **1.** a holy person **2.** a person who is unusually charitable, patient, etc. **3.** in certain Christian churches, a person officially recognized and venerated for having attained heaven after an exceptionally holy life —**saint'hood'** *n.*

Saint Ber·nard (bər närd') a large dog of a breed once used in the Swiss Alps to rescue lost travelers

saint'ed *adj.* **1.** regarded as a saint **2.** holy; sacred

saint'ly *adj.* **-li·er, -li·est** like or befitting a saint —**saint'li·ness** *n.*

Saint Pat'rick's Day March 17, observed by the Irish in honor of the patron saint of Ireland

Saint Valentine's Day February 14, observed in honor of a martyr of the 3d cent. and as a day for sending valentines to sweethearts, etc.

SAINT BERNARD
(25 1/2–27 1/2 in. high at shoulder)

saith (seth) *archaic 3d pers. sing., pres. indic., of* SAY

sake¹ (sāk) *n.* [OE. *sacu*, suit at law] **1.** reason; motive *[for the sake of money]* **2.** behalf *[for my sake]*

sa·ke² (sä'kē) *n.* [Jpn.] a Japanese alcoholic beverage made from fermented rice: also sp. **sa'ki**

sal (sal) *n.* [L.] *Pharmacy* salt

sa·laam (sə läm') *n.* [Ar. *salām*, peace] **1.** an Oriental greeting made by bowing low while placing the right hand on the forehead **2.** a greeting showing respect —*vt., vi.* to greet with, or make, a salaam

sal·a·ble (sāl'ə b'l) *adj.* that can be sold; marketable: also **sale'a·ble** —**sal'a·bil'i·ty** *n.*

sa·la·cious (sə lā'shəs) *adj.* [< L. *salire*, to leap] **1.** lecherous; lustful **2.** obscene —**sa·la'cious·ly** *adv.*

sal·ad (sal'əd) *n.* [< L. *salata*, salted] **1.** a dish, usually cold, of vegetables, usually raw, or fruits, served with a dressing, or molded in gelatin **2.** any green plant or herb used for such a dish

salad days time of youth and inexperience

salad dressing a preparation of oil, vinegar, spices, etc. put on a salad

sal·a·man·der (sal'ə man'dər) *n.* [< Gr. *salamandra*] **1.** a mythological reptile said to live in fire **2.** a scaleless, tailed amphibian with a soft, moist skin

sa·la·mi (sə lä'mē) *n.* [It. < L. *sal*, salt] a spiced, salted sausage

sal·a·ry (sal'ə rē) *n., pl.* **-ries** [< L. *salarium*, orig. part of a Roman soldier's pay for buying salt < *sal*, salt] a fixed payment at regular intervals for work or services —**sal'a·ried** (-rēd) *adj.*

sale (sāl) *n.* [< ON. *sala*] **1.** a selling **2.** opportunity to sell; market **3.** an auction **4.** a selling at prices lower than usual **5.** [*pl.*] receipts in business **6.** [*pl.*] the work, department, etc. of selling *[a job in sales]* —**for** (or **on**) **sale** to be sold

Sa·lem (sā'ləm) capital of Oreg.: pop. 68,000

sales·clerk (sālz'klurk') *n.* a person employed to sell goods in a store

sales'man (-mən) *n., pl.* **-men 1.** a man who is a salesclerk **2.** a traveling agent who sells goods or services

sales'man·ship' *n.* the ability, skill, or technique of selling

sales'per'son *n.* a person employed to sell goods; esp., a salesclerk —**sales'peo'ple** *n.pl.*

sales resistance resistance of potential customers to efforts aimed at getting them to buy

sales talk 1. talk aimed at selling something **2.** any talk to persuade

sales tax a tax on sales and, sometimes, services

sales'wom'an *n., pl.* **-wom'en** a woman salesclerk: also **sales'la'dy,** *pl.* **-dies, sales'girl'**

sal·i·cyl·ic acid (sal'ə sil'ik) [< *salicin* (substance from certain willows) < Fr.] a white, crystalline compound, $C_7H_6O_3$, used in aspirin, as a food preservative, etc.

sa·lient (sāl'yənt, sā'lē ənt) *adj.* [< L. *salire*, to leap] **1.** pointing outward; projecting **2.** noticeable; prominent —*n.* **1.** the part of a battle line, fort, etc. projecting farthest toward the enemy **2.** a projecting angle, part, etc. —**sa'lience** *n.* —**sa'lient·ly** *adv.*

sa·line (sā'līn, -lēn) *adj.* [< L. *sal,* salt] of, like, or containing salt; salty —*n.* a metallic salt used as a cathartic —**sa·lin·i·ty** (sə lin'ə tē) *n.*

Salis·bur·y steak (sôlz'ber'ē) *same as* HAMBURGER (sense 2)

sa·li·va (sə lī'və) *n.* [L.] a thin, watery fluid secreted by glands in the mouth: it aids in digestion

sal·i·var·y (sal'ə ver'ē) *adj.* of or secreting saliva

sal·i·vate (-vāt') *vi.* **-vat'ed, -vat'ing** [< L. *salivare*] to secrete saliva —**sal'i·va'tion** *n.*

Salk (sôlk), **Jonas E.** 1914– ; U.S. bacteriologist: developed a vaccine to prevent poliomyelitis

sal·low (sal'ō) *adj.* [OE. *salu*] of a sickly, pale-yellowish complexion —**sal'low·ness** *n.*

sal·ly (sal'ē) *n., pl.* **-lies** [< L. *salire*, to leap] **1.** a sudden rushing forth, as to attack **2.** any sudden start into activity **3.** a quick witticism; quip **4.** an excursion; jaunt —*vi.* **-lied, -ly·ing** to rush or set (*forth* or *out*) on a sally

sal·ma·gun·di (sal'mə gun'dē) *n.* [Fr. *salmigondis*] **1.** a dish of chopped meat, eggs, onions, etc. **2.** any mixture

salm·on (sam'ən) *n., pl.* **-on, -ons** [< L. *salmo*] **1.** a game and food fish of the N Hemisphere, with flesh that is pink when cooked: salmon spawn in fresh water but usually live in salt water **2.** yellowish pink: also **salmon pink**

sal·mo·nel·la (sal'mə nel'ə) *n., pl.* **-lae** (-ē), **-la, -las** [< D. *Salmon* (d. 1914), U.S. veterinarian] any of certain rod-shaped bacteria that cause typhoid fever, food poisoning, etc.

Sa·lo·me (sə lō'mē, sal'ə mā') *traditional name* of the dancer at whose request John the Baptist was beheaded

sa·lon (sə län', sal'än) *n.* [Fr.: see SALOON] **1.** a large reception hall or drawing room **2.** a regular gathering of distinguished guests in a celebrity's home **3.** an art gallery or exhibition **4.** a shop for performing some personal service *[a beauty salon]*

sa·loon (sə lōōn') *n.* [< Fr. < It. *sala*, hall] **1.** any large room or hall for receptions, exhibitions, etc. **2.** a place where alcoholic drinks are sold to be drunk on the premises: an old-fashioned term

sal·si·fy (sal'sə fē', -fī') *n.* [< It. *sassefrica*] a plant with white, edible, fleshy roots

sal soda crystallized sodium carbonate

salt (sôlt, sält) *n.* [OE. *sealt*] **1.** sodium chloride, NaCl, a white crystalline substance found in natural beds, in sea water, etc., and used for seasoning and preserving food **2.** a chemical compound derived from an acid by replacing hydrogen with a metal or an electropositive radical **3.** that which lends tang or piquancy, as pungent wit **4.** [*pl.*] mineral salts used as a cathartic, restorative, etc. **5.** [Colloq.] a sailor —*adj.* containing, preserved with, or tasting of salt —*vt.* to sprinkle, season, or preserve with salt —**salt away** [Colloq.] to store or save (money, etc.) —**with a grain of salt** with allowance or reserve —**worth one's salt** worth one's wages, etc. —**salt'y** *adj.* **-i·er, -i·est**

salt'cel'lar (-sel'ər) *n.* [< *salt* + MFr. *salière*, saltcellar] a small dish or shaker for salt

salt·ine (sôl tēn') *n.* [SALT + -INE³] a flat, crisp cracker sprinkled with salt

Salt Lake City capital of Utah: pop. 176,000 (met. area 558,000)

salt lick 1. an exposed natural deposit of rock salt which animals come to lick **2.** a block of rock salt placed in a pasture for cattle, etc. to lick

salt'pe'ter (-pēt'ər) *n.* [< L. *sal*, salt + *petra*, a rock] *same as* POTASSIUM NITRATE

salt pork pork cured in salt

salt'shak'er *n.* a container for salt, with a perforated top

salt'wa'ter *adj.* of, having to do with, or living in salt water or the sea

sa·lu·bri·ous (sə lōō'brē əs) *adj.* [< L. *salus*, health] healthful, wholesome, etc. —**sa·lu'bri·ous·ly** *adv.*

sal·u·tar·y (sal'yoo ter'ē) *adj.* [< L. *salus*, health] **1.** promoting health; healthful **2.** promoting some good purpose; beneficial

sal·u·ta·tion (sal'yoo tā'shən) *n.* [see SALUTE] **1.** the act of greeting, addressing, etc. **2.** a form of greeting, as the "Dear Sir" of a letter

sa·lute (sə lōōt') *vt.* -**lut'ed,** -**lut'ing** [< L. *salus*, health] **1.** to greet in a friendly way, as by bowing **2.** to honor ceremonially and officially by firing cannon, raising the hand to the head, etc. **3.** to commend —*vi.* to make a salute —*n.* **1.** an act, remark, or gesture made in saluting **2.** *Mil.* the position of the hand, etc. assumed in saluting

sal·vage (sal'vij) *n.* [see SAVE[1]] **1.** *a)* the rescue of a ship and cargo from shipwreck, etc. *b)* compensation paid for such rescue *c)* the ship or cargo so rescued **2.** *a)* the rescue of any property from destruction or waste *b)* the property saved —*vt.* -**vaged,** -**vag·ing** to save or rescue from shipwreck, fire, flood, etc. —**sal'vage·a·ble** *adj.* —**sal'vag·er** *n.*

sal·va·tion (sal vā'shən) *n.* [< L. *salvare*, to save] **1.** a saving or being saved **2.** a person or thing that saves or rescues **3.** *Theol.* spiritual rescue from the consequences of sin

Salvation Army a Christian organization that works to bring religion and help to the very poor

salve (sav) *n.* [OE. *sealf*] **1.** any soothing or healing ointment for wounds, burns, etc. **2.** anything that soothes or heals —*vt.* **salved, salv'ing** to soothe

sal·ver (sal'vər) *n.* [< Fr. < Sp. < L. *salvare*, to save] a tray

sal·vi·a (sal'vē ə) *n.* [L.] *same as* SAGE[2] (sense 1)

sal·vo (sal'vō) *n., pl.* -**vos,** -**voes** [< I. *salve*, hail!] **1.** a discharge of a number of guns in succession or at the same time, either in salute or at a target **2.** a burst of cheers or applause

Sam. Samuel

sa·mar·i·um (sə mer'ē əm, -mar'-) *n.* [< Fr. < G. < Col. *Samarski*, Russ. mining official] a metallic chemical element of the rare-earth group: symbol, Sm; at. wt., 150.35; at. no., 62

sam·ba (sam'bə, säm'-) *n.* [Port.] **1.** a Brazilian dance of African origin **2.** music for this dance

same (sām) *adj.* [ON. *samr*] **1.** being the very one; identical **2.** alike in kind, quality, amount, etc. **3.** unchanged; not different [the same look] **4.** before-mentioned; just spoken of —*pron.* the same person or thing —*adv.* in the same way —**same'ness** *n.*

Sa·mo·a (sə mō'ə) group of islands in the South Pacific: seven of these islands constitute a possession (**American Samoa**) of the U.S. —**Sa·mo'an** *adj., n.*

sam·o·var (sam'ə vär') *n.* [Russ., lit., self-boiler] a Russian metal urn with an internal tube for heating water for tea

sam·pan (sam'pan) *n.* [Chin. *san-pan*] a small boat used in China and Japan, rowed with a scull from the stern, and often having a sail

sam·ple (sam'p'l) *n.* [see EXAMPLE] a part that shows what the whole thing or group is like; specimen or example —*vt.* -**pled, -pling** to take or test a sample of

sam'pler *n.* **1.** one who prepares or tests samples **2.** a cloth embroidered with designs, mottoes, etc. in different stitches

Sam·son (sam's'n) *Bible* an Israelite with great strength: Judges 13–16

Sam·u·el (sam'yoo wəl, -yool) *Bible* **1.** a Hebrew judge and prophet **2.** either of two books (I Samuel, II Samuel) telling of Samuel, Saul, and David

sam·u·rai (sam'ə rī') *n., pl.* -**rai** [Jpn.] a member of a military caste in feudal Japan

San An·to·ni·o (san' ən tō'nē ō', an-) city in SC Texas: pop. 654,000 (met. area 864,000)

san·a·to·ri·um (san'ə tôr'ē əm) *n., pl.* -**ri·ums, -ri·a** (-ə) [< L. *sanare*, heal] *chiefly Brit. var. of* SANITARIUM

San Ber·nar·di·no (san' bur'nər dē'nō, -nə-) city in S Calif.: pop. 104,000

sanc·ti·fy (saŋk'tə fī') *vt.* -**fied', -fy'ing** [< L. *sanctus*, holy + *facere*, make] **1.** to set apart as holy; consecrate **2.** to make free from sin; purify —**sanc'ti·fi·ca'tion** *n.*

sanc·ti·mo·ni·ous (saŋk'tə mō'nē əs) *adj.* pretending to be very pious —**sanc'ti·mo·ni·ous·ly** *adv.* —**sanc'ti·mo'ni·ous·ness** *n.*

sanc'ti·mo'ny *n.* [< L. *sanctus*, holy] affected piety or righteousness

sanc·tion (saŋk'shən) *n.* [< L. *sanctus*, holy] **1.** the confirming of an action by authority; authorization **2.** support; approval **3.** something that gives binding force to a law, as the penalty for breaking it or a reward for carrying it out **4.** [*usually pl.*] a boycott or other coercive measure, as against one nation by others to enforce international law —*vt.* **1.** to ratify or confirm **2.** to authorize or permit

sanc·ti·ty (saŋk'tə tē) *n., pl.* -**ties** [< L. *sanctus*, holy] **1.** saintliness or holiness **2.** a being sacred **3.** anything held sacred

sanc·tu·ar·y (saŋk'choo wer'ē) *n., pl.* -**ies** [< L. *sanctus*, sacred] **1.** a holy place; specif., *a)* a church, temple, etc. *b)* a holy place within a church or temple, as the part around the altar **2.** a place of refuge or protection **3.** refuge; immunity from punishment

sanc·tum (saŋk'təm) *n., pl.* -**tums, -ta** (-tə) [L.] **1.** a sacred place **2.** a private room where one is not to be disturbed

sanctum sanc·to·rum (saŋk tôr'əm) [LL.] **1.** *same as* HOLY OF HOLIES **2.** a place of utmost privacy

sand (sand) *n.* [OE.] **1.** loose, gritty grains of disintegrated rock, as on beaches, in deserts, etc. **2.** [*usually pl.*] an area of sand; beach —*vt.* **1.** to sprinkle, fill, or mix with sand **2.** to smooth or polish with sand or sandpaper —**sand'ed** *adj.* —**sand'er** *n.*

Sand (sand), **George** (pseud. of Baronne *Dudevant*) 1804–76; Fr. novelist

san·dal (san'd'l) *n.* [< Gr. *sandalon*] **1.** a shoe made of a sole fastened to the foot by straps **2.** any of various low slippers —**san'daled, san'dalled** *adj.*

san·dal·wood (san'd'l wood') *n.* [ult. < Sans. *candana*] **1.** the hard, sweet-smelling heartwood of an Asiatic tree, used for carving and cabinetmaking or burned as incense **2.** any tree yielding such wood

sand'bag' *n.* a bag filled with sand and used for ballast, in fortifications, etc. —*vt.* -**bagged', -bag'ging** to place sandbags in or around

sand bar a ridge of sand formed in a river or along a shore

sand'blast' *n.* a current of air or steam carrying sand at a high velocity, as in cleaning surfaces as of metal, stone, etc. —*vt.* to clean with a sandblast

sand'box' *n.* a box containing sand for children to play in

Sand·burg (sand'bərg, san'-), **Carl** 1878–1967; U.S. poet, writer, & ballad collector

sand'hog' *n.* a laborer in underground or underwater construction projects

San Di·e·go (san' dē ā'gō) seaport in S Calif.: pop. 697,000 (met. area 1,358,000)

sand'lot' *adj.* having to do with games, esp. baseball, played by amateurs, orig. on a sandy lot or field —**sand'-lot'ter** *n.*

sand'man' *n.* a mythical person supposed to make children sleepy by dusting sand in their eyes

sand'pa'per *n.* paper coated on one side with sand, used for smoothing and polishing —*vt.* to smooth or polish with sandpaper

sand'pip'er (-pī'pər) *n.* a small shore bird with a long, soft-tipped bill

sand'stone' *n.* a sedimentary rock consisting largely of sand grains cemented together by silica, etc.

sand'storm' *n.* a windstorm in which large quantities of sand are blown about

sand trap a hollow filled with sand, serving as a hazard on a golf course

sand·wich (sand'wich, san'-) *n.* [< 4th Earl of *Sandwich* (1718–92)] two or more slices of bread with meat, cheese, etc. between them —*vt.* to place between other persons, things, etc.

SANDPIPER
(8 in. long)

sand·y (san'dē) *adj.* **-i·er, -i·est 1.** of or like sand **2.** pale brown or dark yellow *[sandy hair]*

sane (sān) *adj.* **san'er, san'est** [L. *sanus,* healthy] **1.** mentally healthy; rational **2.** showing good sense; sensible *[a sane policy]* **—sane'ly** *adv.*

San·for·ize (san'fə rīz') *vt.* **-ized', -iz'ing** [< *Sanford* Cluett* (1874–1968), the inventor] to preshrink (cloth) permanently by a patented process before making garments

San Fran·cis·co (san' frən sis'kō) seaport of C Calif., on an inlet (**San Francisco Bay**) of the Pacific: pop. 716,000 (met. area, incl. Oakland, 3,110,000)

sang (saŋ) *pt. of* SING

sang-froid (saŋ'frwä') *n.* [Fr., lit., cold blood] cool self-possession or composure

san·gui·nar·y (saŋ'gwi ner'ē) *adj.* [see SANGUINE] **1.** with much bloodshed or killing **2.** bloodthirsty

san·guine (saŋ'gwin) *adj.* [< L. *sanguis,* blood] **1.** of the color of blood; ruddy **2.** cheerful; confident

san·i·tar·i·um (san'ə ter'ē əm) *n., pl.* **-i·ums, -i·a** (-ə) [< L. *sanitas,* health] a nursing home, hospital, etc. for the care of invalids or convalescents, esp. one for treating a specific disease or disorder

san·i·tar·y (san'ə ter'ē) *adj.* [< L. *sanitas,* health] **1.** of health or the rules and conditions of health; esp., of absence of dirt and agents of disease **2.** clean; hygienic

sanitary napkin an absorbent pad of cotton, etc. worn by women during menstruation

san·i·ta·tion (san'ə tā'shən) *n.* **1.** the science and work of bringing about hygienic conditions **2.** drainage and disposal of sewage

san·i·tize (san'ə tīz') *vt.* **-tized', -tiz'ing** to make sanitary, as by sterilizing

san·i·ty (san'ə tē) *n.* **1.** the state of being sane; soundness of mind **2.** soundness of judgment

San Jo·se (san' hō zā', ə zā') city in WC Calif.: pop. 446,000 (met. area 1,065,000)

San Juan (san' hwän', wôn') capital of Puerto Rico: pop. 445,000 (met. area 851,000)

sank (saŋk) *pt. of* SINK

San Ma·ri·no (san' mə rē'nō) independent country within E Italy: 23 sq. mi.; pop. 19,000

sans (sanz; *Fr.* sän) *prep.* [Fr. < L. *sine*] without; lacking **Sans.** Sanskrit

San Sal·va·dor (san sal'və dôr') capital of El Salvador: pop. 256,000

sans-cu·lotte (sanz'kѡ lät', -kyѡ-) *n.* [Fr., without breeches] a revolutionary: term of contempt used by the aristocrats in the French Revolution

San·skrit (san'skrit) *n.* the classical literary language of ancient India: also sp. **San'scrit**

San·ta (san'tə, -ti) *short for* SANTA CLAUS

San·ta An·a (san'tə an'ə) city in SW Calif.: pop. 157,000

San·ta Claus, San·ta Klaus (san'tə klôz', -ti) [< Du. *Sant Nikolaas,* St. Nicholas] *Folklore* a fat, white-bearded, jolly old man in a red suit, who distributes gifts at Christmas: also called **Saint Nicholas, Saint Nick**

San·ta Fe (san'tə fā') capital of N.Mex.: pop. 41,000

San·ti·a·go (sän'tē ä'gō) capital of Chile: pop. 2,566,000 (met. area 3,120,000)

San·to Do·min·go (san'tō dō miŋ'gō) capital of the Dominican Republic; seaport in a national district: pop. of the district 823,000

São Pau·lo (souɴ pou'lѡ) city in SE Brazil: pop. 5,902,000

São To·mé and Prín·ci·pe (tō mä' ənd prin'sə pē') country off the W coast of Africa, comprising two islands (*São Tomé* and *Príncipe*): 372 sq. mi.; pop. 75,000

sap[1] (sap) *n.* [OE. *sæp*] **1.** the juice that circulates through a plant, bearing water, food, etc. **2.** vigor; energy **3.** [Slang] a stupid person

sap[2] (sap) *n.* [< MFr. < It. *zappe,* a hoe] a trench for approaching or undermining an enemy position **—vt.** **sapped, sap'ping 1.** to undermine by digging away foundations **2.** to weaken; exhaust **—vi.** to dig saps

sa·pi·ent (sā'pē ənt) *adj.* [< L. *sapere,* to taste, know] full of knowledge; wise **—sa'pi·ence** *n.*

sap·ling (sap'liŋ) *n.* **1.** a young tree **2.** a youth

sap·o·dil·la (sap'ə dil'ə) *n.* [< Sp. < Central AmInd. *tzapotl*] a tropical American evergreen tree yielding chicle

sa·pon·i·fy (sə pän'ə fī') *vt.* **-fied', -fy'ing** [< Fr. < L. *sapo,* soap + *facere,* to make] to convert (a fat) into soap by reaction with an alkali **—vi.** to be made into soap **—sa·pon'i·fi·ca'tion** *n.*

sap·phire (saf'īr) *n.* [< Gr. *sappheiros*] **1.** a hard precious stone of a clear, deep-blue corundum **2.** its color **—adj.** deep-blue

Sap·pho (saf'ō) 7th cent. B.C.; Gr. lyric poetess

sap·py (sap'ē) *adj.* **-pi·er, -pi·est 1.** full of sap; juicy **2.** [Slang] foolish; silly **—sap'pi·ness** *n.*

sap'suck·er *n.* a small American woodpecker that often drills holes in maples, apple trees, etc. for the sap

sap'wood' *n.* the soft wood between the inner bark of a tree and the heartwood, serving to conduct water

Sar·a·cen (sar'ə s'n) *n.* any Arab or any Muslim, esp. at the time of the Crusades **—adj.** of the Saracens

Sar·ah (ser'ə, sar'ə) *Bible* the wife of Abraham and mother of Isaac

sa·ran (sə ran') *n.* [arbitrary coinage] a thermoplastic resin obtained from certain vinyl compounds: used in making fabrics, a transparent wrapping material, etc.

sar·casm (sär'kaz'm) *n.* [< Gr. *sarkazein,* to tear flesh] **1.** a taunting or sneering remark, generally ironical **2.** the making of such remarks **3.** sarcastic quality

sar·cas·tic (sär kas'tik) *adj.* **1.** of, like, or full of sarcasm; sneering **2.** using sarcasm **—sar·cas'ti·cal·ly** *adv.*

sar·co·ma (sär kō'mə) *n., pl.* **-mas, -ma·ta** (-mə tə) [< Gr. *sarx,* flesh] a malignant tumor that begins in connective tissue

sar·coph·a·gus (sär käf'ə gəs) *n., pl.* **-gi'** (-jī'), **-gus·es** [< Gr. *sarx,* flesh + *phagein,* to eat: limestone coffins hastened disintegration] a stone coffin, esp. one on display, as in a monumental tomb

sar·dine (sär dēn') *n.* [< L. *sarda,* kind of fish] any of various small ocean fishes preserved in tightly packed cans for eating

Sar·din·i·a (sär din'ē ə) It. island in the Mediterranean, south of Corsica **—Sar·din'i·an** *adj., n.*

sar·don·ic (sär dän'ik) *adj.* [< Gr. *sardanios,* bitter] disdainfully or bitterly sarcastic *[a sardonic smile]* **—sar·don'i·cal·ly** *adv.*

sa·ri (sä'rē) *n.* [< Sans.] an outer garment of Hindu women, a long cloth wrapped around the body with one end over the shoulder

sa·rong (sə rôŋ', -räŋ') *n.* [Malay *särung*] a garment of men and women in the East Indies, etc., consisting of a long cloth, often brightly colored, worn like a skirt

sar·sa·pa·ril·la (sas'pə ril'ə, särs'-, sär'sə-) *n.* [< Sp. *zarza,* bramble + *parra,* vine] **1.** a tropical American plant with fragrant roots **2.** a carbonated drink flavored with an extract from the dried roots

sar·to·ri·al (sär tôr'ē əl) *adj.* [< LL. *sartor,* a tailor] **1.** of tailors or their work **2.** of men's dress **—sar·to'ri·al·ly** *adv.*

sash[1] (sash) *n.* [Ar. *shāsh,* muslin] an ornamental ribbon or scarf worn over the shoulder or around the waist

sash[2] (sash) *n.* [< Fr. *châssis,* a frame] a frame for holding the glass pane of a window or door, esp. a sliding frame

sa·shay (sa shā') *vi.* [< Fr. *chassé,* a dance step] [Colloq.] to move, walk, or go, esp. casually

Sas·katch·e·wan (sas kach'ə wän', -wən) province of SC Canada: 251,700 sq. mi.; pop. 955,000; cap. Regina: abbrev. **Sask.**

sass (sas) *n.* [var. of SAUCE] [Colloq.] impudent talk **—vt.** [Colloq.] to talk impudently to

sas·sa·fras (sas'ə fras') *n.* [Sp. *sasafras*] **1.** a small eastern N. American tree bearing small, bluish fruits **2.** the dried root bark of this tree, used as a flavoring

sass·y (sas'ē) *adj.* **-i·er, -i·est** [dial. var. of SAUCY] [Colloq.] impudent; saucy **—sass'i·ness** *n.*

sat (sat) *pt. & pp. of* SIT

Sat. 1. Saturday **2.** Saturn

Sa·tan (sāt''n) *n.* [< Heb. *sātan,* to plot against] the Devil

sa·tan·ic (sā tan'ik, sə-) *adj.* of or like Satan; devilish; wicked: also **sa·tan'i·cal** **—sa·tan'i·cal·ly** *adv.*

satch·el (sach'əl) *n.* [< L. *saccus,* a sack] a small bag for carrying clothes, books, etc.

sate (sāt) *vt.* **sat'ed, sat'ing** [prob. < L. *satiare,* to fill full] **1.** to satisfy (an appetite, desire, etc.) to the full **2.** to satiate; surfeit

sa·teen (sa tēn') *n.* [< SATIN] a smooth, glossy cotton cloth, made to imitate satin

sat·el·lite (sat''l īt') *n.* [Fr. < L. *satelles,* an attendant] **1.** an attendant of some important person **2.** *a)* a small heavenly body revolving around a larger one *b)* a man-made object put into orbit around the earth, the moon, or some other heavenly body **3.** a small state that is economically dependent on a larger state

sa·tia·ble (sā'shə b'l, sā'shē ə-) *adj.* that can be sated or satiated **—sa'tia·bil'i·ty** *n.*

sa·ti·ate (sā'shē it) *adj.* [< L. *satis,* enough] having had enough or more than enough **—vt.** (-āt') **-at'ed, -at'ing** to provide with more than enough, so as to weary or disgust; glut **—sa'ti·a'tion** *n.*

sa·ti·e·ty (sə tī'ə tē) *n.* the state of being satiated

sat·in (sat'n) *n.* [< Ar. *zaitūnī*, of *Zaitūn*, former name of a Chinese seaport] a fabric of silk, nylon, etc. with a smooth, glossy finish on one side —*adj.* of or like satin; smooth and glossy —**sat'in·y** *adj.*

sat'in·wood' *n.* 1. a smooth wood used in fine furniture 2. a tree yielding such wood

sat·ire (sa'tīr) *n.* [Fr. < L. *satira*] 1. a literary work in which vices, follies, etc. are held up to ridicule and contempt 2. the use of ridicule, sarcasm, etc. to attack vices, follies, etc. —**sa·tir·i·cal** (sə tir'i k'l), **sa·tir'ic** *adj.* —**sa·tir'i·cal·ly** *adv.*

sat·i·rist (sat'ə rist) *n.* 1. a writer of satires 2. a person given to satirizing

sat'i·rize' (-rīz') *vt.* -rized', -riz'ing to attack, ridicule, or criticize with satire

sat·is·fac·tion (sat'is fak'shən) *n.* 1. a satisfying or being satisfied 2. something that satisfies; specif., *a)* anything that brings pleasure or contentment *b)* settlement of debt

sat'is·fac'to·ry (-tə rē, -trē) *adj.* satisfying; fulfilling a need, wish, etc. —**sat'is·fac'to·ri·ly** *adv.*

sat·is·fy (sat'is fī') *vt.* -fied', -fy'ing [< L. *satis*, enough + *facere*, to make] 1. to fulfill the needs or desires of; gratify 2. to fulfill the requirements of 3. *a)* to free from doubt; convince *b)* to answer (a doubt, etc.) adequately 4. *a)* to give what is due to *b)* to discharge (a debt, etc.) 5. to make reparation to or for —*vi.* to be adequate, sufficient, etc.

sa·trap (sā'trap, sat'rap) *n.* [< OPer.] 1. the governor of a province in ancient Persia 2. a petty tyrant

sat·u·rate (sach'ə rāt') *vt.* -rat'ed, -rat'ing [< L. *satur*, full] 1. to cause to be thoroughly soaked 2. to cause to be so completely filled or supplied that no more can be taken up —**sat'u·ra'tion** *n.*

saturation point 1. the point at which the maximum amount of something has been absorbed 2. the limit beyond which something cannot be continued, endured, etc.

Sat·ur·day (sat'ər dē, -dā') *n.* [OE. *Sæterdæg*, Saturn's day] the seventh and last day of the week

Sat·urn (sat'ərn) 1. *Rom. Myth.* the god of agriculture: identified with the Greek god Cronus 2. the second largest planet in the solar system: see PLANET

Sat·ur·na·li·a (sat'ər nā'lē ə) *n.pl.* 1. the ancient Roman festival of Saturn, celebrated with feasting and revelry 2. [s-] [*often with sing. v. & with a pl.* -li·as] a period of unrestrained revelry

sat·ur·nine (sat'ər nīn') *adj.* [< supposed influence of planet Saturn] sluggish, grave, taciturn, etc.

sat·yr (sāt'ər, sat'-) *n.* [< Gr. *satyros*] 1. *Gr. Myth.* a lecherous woodland deity, attendant on Bacchus, represented as a man with pointed ears, short horns, and a goat's legs 2. a lecherous man

sauce (sôs) *n.* [< L. *sal*, salt] 1. *a)* a liquid or soft dressing served with food as a seasoning *b)* a flavored syrup put on ice cream 2. stewed or preserved fruit 3. [Colloq.] impudence —*vt.* sauced, sauc'ing 1. to flavor with a sauce 2. [Colloq.] to be saucy to

sauce'pan' *n.* a small pot with a projecting handle, used for cooking

sau·cer (sô'sər) *n.* [see SAUCE] a small, round, shallow dish, esp. one with an indentation to hold a cup

sau·cy (sô'sē) *adj.* -ci·er, -ci·est [SAUC(E) + -Y²] 1. rude; impudent 2. pert; sprightly —**sau'ci·ly** *adv.* —**sau'ci·ness** *n.*

Sa·u·di Arabia (sä ōō'dē, sou'dē) kingdom occupying most of Arabia: c.617,000 sq. mi.; pop. 6,036,000; cap. Riyadh

sau·er·bra·ten (sour'brät'n, zou'ər-) *n.* [G. < *sauer*, sour + *braten*, a roast] beef marinated before cooking

sau·er·kraut (sour'krout') *n.* [G. *sauer*, sour + *kraut*, cabbage] chopped cabbage fermented in a brine of its own juice with salt

Saul (sôl) *Bible* 1. the first king of Israel 2. *orig. name of the Apostle* PAUL

sau·na (sou'nə, sô'-) *n.* [Finn.] 1. a Finnish bath, consisting of exposure to hot, dry air 2. the enclosure for this

saun·ter (sôn'tər) *vi.* [< ?] to walk about idly; stroll —*n.* a leisurely walk —**saun'ter·er** *n.*

sau·ri·an (sôr'ē ən) *n.* [< Gr. *sauros*, a lizard] any of those reptiles that are lizards —*adj.* of or like lizards

sau·sage (sô'sij) *n.* [see SAUCE] pork or other meat, chopped fine, seasoned, and often stuffed into a casing

sau·té (sō tā', sô-) *adj.* [Fr. < *sauter*, to leap] fried quickly in a little fat —*vt.* -téed', -té'ing to fry quickly in a little fat —*n.* a sautéed dish

sau·terne (sō turn', sô-) *n.* [< *Sauternes*, town in France] a white, usually sweet table wine

sav·age (sav'ij) *adj.* [< L. *silva*, a wood] 1. wild; uncultivated [a *savage* jungle] 2. fierce; untamed [a *savage* tiger] 3. without civilization; barbarous [a *savage* tribe] 4. cruel; pitiless —*n.* 1. a member of a primitive or uncivilized society 2. a brutal person —**sav'age·ly** *adv.*

sav'age·ry *n., pl.* -ries 1. the condition of being savage 2. savage act or behavior

sa·van·na, sa·van·nah (sə van'ə) *n.* [< Sp. < native name] a treeless plain or a grassland with scattered trees, esp. in or near the tropics

Sa·van·nah (sə van'ə) seaport in SE Ga.: pop. 118,000

sa·vant (sə vänt', sav'ənt) *n.* [Fr. < L. *sapere*, to know] a learned person

save¹ (sāv) *vt.* saved, sav'ing [< L. *salvus*, safe] 1. to rescue or preserve from harm or danger 2. to preserve for future use (often with *up*) 3. to prevent loss or waste of [to *save* time] 4. to avoid or lessen [to *save* wear] 5. to treat carefully in order to preserve 6. *Theol.* to deliver from sin —*vi.* 1. to avoid expense, waste, etc. 2. to hoard money or goods —*n.* *Sports* an action that keeps an opponent from scoring or winning —**sav'a·ble, save'a·ble** *adj.* —**sav'er** *n.*

save² (sāv) *prep., conj.* [< OFr. *sauf*, lit., SAFE] except; but: also **sav'ing**

sav·ing (sā'viŋ) *adj.* that saves; specif., *a)* rescuing *b)* economical *c)* redeeming —*n.* 1. the act of one that saves 2. [*often pl. with sing. v.*] any reduction in time, expense, etc. 3. *a)* anything saved *b)* [*pl.*] sums of money saved

savings account an account in a bank or savings association which receives and invests depositors' savings, on which it pays interest

savings and loan association a depositor-owned establishment in which depositors' savings draw interest and are used for making real-estate loans

sav·ior, sav·iour (sāv'yər) *n.* [< LL. *salvare*, to save] one who saves —**the Saviour** (or **Savior**) Jesus Christ

sa·voir-faire (sav'wär fer') *n.* [Fr., to know (how) to do] ready knowledge of what to do or say

sa·vor (sā'vər) *n.* [< L. *sapor*] 1. the taste or smell of something 2. characteristic quality 3. noticeable trace —*vi.* to have the particular taste, smell, or quality (*of*) —*vt.* 1. to season or flavor 2. to taste or smell, esp. with relish 3. to relish Brit. sp. **savour**

sa'vor·y¹ *adj.* -i·er, -i·est 1. pleasing to the taste or smell 2. pleasant, agreeable, etc. Brit. sp. **savoury**

sa·vor·y² (sā'vər ē) *n.* [< L. *satureia*] a fragrant herb of the mint family, used in cooking

sav·vy (sav'ē) *vi.* -vied, -vy·ing [< Sp. *sabe* (*usted*), do (you) know] [Slang] to understand —*n.* [Slang] 1. shrewd understanding 2. skill or know-how —*adj.* [Slang] shrewd or discerning

saw¹ (sô) *n.* [OE. *sagu*] a cutting tool having a thin, metal blade or disk with sharp teeth along the edge —*vt.* **sawed, sawn, saw'ing** 1. to cut or shape with a saw 2. to make sawlike cutting motions through or with (something) —*vi.* 1. to cut with or as a saw 2. to be cut with a saw 3. to make sawlike cutting motions — **saw'er** *n.*

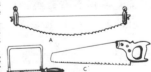

SAWS
(A, crosscut; B, coping; C, handsaw)

saw² (sô) *n.* [OE. *sagu*] an old saying; maxim

saw³ (sô) *pt. of* SEE¹

saw·buck (sô'buk') *n.* [Du. *zaagbok*] 1. a sawhorse with the legs projecting above the crossbar 2. [Slang] a ten-dollar bill

saw'dust' (-dust') *n.* tiny bits of wood formed in sawing

saw'horse' (-hôrs') *n.* a rack on which wood is placed while being sawed

saw'mill' (-mil') *n.* 1. a place where logs are sawed into boards 2. a large sawing machine

saw'-toothed' (-tōōtht') *adj.* serrate: also **saw'tooth'**

saw·yer (sô'yər) *n.* one whose work is sawing wood, as into planks and boards

sax (saks) *n.* [Colloq.] a saxophone

sax·horn (saks'hôrn') *n.* [< A. J. *Sax,* 19th-c. Belgian inventor] a valved brass-wind instrument

Sax·on (sak's'n) *n.* **1.** a member of an ancient Germanic people of N Germany, some of whom settled in England **2.** *same as* ANGLO-SAXON (*n.* 1 & 3) **3.** a native or inhabitant of modern Saxony **4.** any dialect of the Saxons — *adj.* of the Saxons, their language, etc.

Sax·on·y (sak'sə nē) **1.** region in S East Germany **2.** state in the N part of West Germany, called *Lower Saxony*

sax·o·phone (sak'sə fōn') *n.* [Fr., after A. J. *Sax* (see SAXHORN) & -PHONE] a single-reed, keyed wind instrument having a curved metal body —**sax'o·phon'ist** *n.*

say (sā) *vt.* said, say'ing; 3d pers. sing., pres. indic., says (sez) [OE. *secgan*] **1.** to utter; speak **2.** to express in words; state; declare **3.** to state positively or as an opinion [I cannot *say* who won] **4.** to indicate or show [the clock *says* ten] **5.** to recite [*say* your prayers] **6.** to estimate [he is, I'd *say,* forty] **7.** to report [they *say* he is ill] —*vi.* to speak; express an opinion —*n.* **1.** a chance to speak [to have one's *say*] **2.** authority, as to make a final decision: often with *the* —**go without saying** to be too obvious to need explanation —**that is to say** in other words —**say'er** *n.*

say·ing *n.* something said; esp., an adage, proverb, or maxim

say-so (sā'sō') *n.* [Colloq.] **1.** (one's) word, opinion, assurance, etc. **2.** right of decision

Sb [L. *stibium*] *Chem.* antimony

Sc *Chem.* scandium

SC, S.C. South Carolina

sc. **1.** scene **2.** science

scab (skab) *n.* [ON. *skabb*] **1.** a crust that forms over a sore as it is healing **2.** a plant disease characterized by scablike spots **3.** *a)* a worker who refuses to join a union *b)* a worker who refuses to strike, or who takes the place of a striking worker —*vi.* scabbed, scab'bing **1.** to become covered with a scab **2.** to act as a scab

scab·bard (skab'ərd) *n.* [? < OHG. *scar,* sword + *bergan,* to hide] a sheath for the blade of a sword, dagger, etc.

scab·by (skab'ē) *adj.* -bi·er, -bi·est **1.** covered with or consisting of scabs **2.** low; base; mean

sca·bies (skā'bēz, -bē ēz) *n.* [< L. *scabere,* to scratch] a contagious skin disease caused by mites, characterized by intense itching

scab·rous (skab'rəs, skā'brəs) *adj.* [< L. *scabere,* to scratch] **1.** rough; scaly, scabby, etc. **2.** full of difficulties **3.** indecent, scandalous, etc. —**scab'rous·ly** *adv.*

scad (skad) *n.* [< ?] [*usually pl.*] [Colloq.] a very large amount [*scads* of money]

scaf·fold (skaf'ld, -ōld) *n.* [OFr. *escafalt*] **1.** a temporary framework for supporting people working on a building, etc. **2.** a raised platform on which criminals are executed **3.** any raised framework

scaf'fold·ing *n.* **1.** the materials that form a scaffold **2.** a scaffold or scaffolds

scal·a·wag (skal'ə wag') *n.* [< ?] a rascal: also sp. **scal·lawag**

scald (skôld) *vt.* [< L. *ex-,* intens. + *calidus,* hot] **1.** to burn with hot liquid or steam **2.** to heat almost to the boiling point **3.** to use boiling liquid on, as in sterilizing — *n.* a burn caused by scalding

scale[1] (skāl) *n.* [< L. *scala,* a ladder] **1.** *a)* a series of marks along a line used in measuring [the *scale* of a thermometer] *b)* any instrument so marked **2.** the proportion that a map, etc. bears to the thing it represents [a *scale* of one inch to a mile] **3.** *a)* a series of degrees classified by size, amount, etc. [a wage *scale*] *b)* any degree in such a series **4.** *Music* a sequence of tones, rising or falling in pitch, according to a system of intervals —*vt.* **scaled, scal'ing 1.** to climb up or over **2.** to make according to a scale —*vi.* go up —**scale down** (or **up**) to reduce (or increase) according to a ratio

scale[2] (skāl) *n.* [< OFr. *escale,* husk] **1.** any of the thin, flat, horny plates covering many fishes and reptiles **2.** any thin, platelike layer or piece **3.** a coating that forms on metals when heated or rusted —*vt.* **scaled, scal'ing** to scrape scales from —*vi.* to flake or peel off in scales — **scale'less** *adj.* —**scal'y** *adj.* -i·er, -i·est

scale[3] (skāl) *n.* [ON. *skāl,* bowl] **1.** either pan of a balance **2.** [*often pl.*] a balance or other weighing device —*vt.* **scaled, scal'ing 1.** to weigh **2.** to have a weight of

scale insect any of a group of small insects destructive to plants: the females secrete a round, wax scale under which they live and lay their eggs

sca·lene (skā lēn', skā'lēn) *adj.* [< Gr. *skalēnos,* uneven] *Geom.* **1.** having unequal sides and angles: said of a trian-

gle **2.** having the axis not perpendicular to the base: said of a cone, etc.

scal·lion (skal'yən) *n.* [< L. (*caepa*) *Ascalonia,* (onion of) Ascalon (Philistine city)] any of three varieties of onion; specif., *a)* the shallot *b)* the leek *c)* a green onion with an almost bulbless root

scal·lop (skäl'əp, skal'-) *n.* [OFr. *escalope*] **1.** a kind of mollusk with two deeply grooved, curved shells that are hinged **2.** the large muscle of such a mollusk, used as food **3.** a single shell of such a mollusk **4.** any of a series of curves, etc. forming an ornamental edge — *vt.* **1.** to cut the edge of in scallops **2.** to bake with a milk sauce and bread crumbs

SCALLOP (sense 1)

scalp (skalp) *n.* [< Scand.] the skin on the top and back of the head, usually covered with hair —*vt.* **1.** to cut or tear the scalp from **2.** *a)* to cheat or rob *b)* to defeat decisively **3.** [Colloq.] to buy (theater tickets, etc.) and resell them at higher prices —**scalp'er** *n.*

scal·pel (skal'pəl) *n.* [< L. *scalpere,* to cut] a small, sharp, straight knife used in surgery and dissections

scamp[1] (skamp) *n.* [< MFr. *escamper,* to flee] a mischievous or roguish fellow; rascal —**scamp'ish** *adj.*

scamp[2] (skamp) *vt.* [akin to or < ON. *skammr,* short] to do in a careless, inadequate way

scam·per (skam'pər) *vi.* [see SCAMP[1]] to run or go quickly —*n.* a scampering

scam·pi (skam'pē) *n., pl.* -pi, -pies [It.] a large prawn, valued as food

scan (skan) *vt.* scanned, scan'ning [< L. *scandere,* to climb] **1.** to analyze (verse), as by marking off the metrical feet and showing the rhythmic structure **2.** to look at closely; scrutinize **3.** to glance at quickly **4.** *Radar* to traverse (a region) with a succession of transmitted radar beams **5.** *TV* to traverse (a surface) rapidly with a beam of light or electrons in transmitting or reproducing an image —*vi.* to be in a certain poetic meter —*n.* a scanning

Scan., Scand. Scandinavian

scan·dal (skan'd'l) *n.* [< Fr. < Gr. *skandalon,* a snare] **1.** anything that offends morals and leads to disgrace **2.** shame, outrage, etc. caused by this **3.** disgrace **4.** wicked gossip

scan'dal·ize' *vt.* -ized', -iz'ing to outrage the moral feelings of by improper conduct

scan'dal·mon'ger (-mun'gər, -mäŋ'-) *n.* one who gossips maliciously and spreads scandal

scan'dal·ous *adj.* **1.** causing scandal; shameful **2.** spreading slander; libelous —**scan'dal·ous·ly** *adv.*

Scan·di·na·vi·a (skan'də nā'vē ə) **1.** region in N Europe, including Norway, Sweden, & Denmark and, sometimes, Iceland **2.** peninsula in N Europe, consisting of Norway & Sweden: in full **Scandinavian Peninsula**

Scan'di·na'vi·an *adj.* of Scandinavia, its people, their languages, etc. —*n.* **1.** any of the people of Scandinavia **2.** the subbranch of Germanic languages spoken by them; North Germanic

scan·di·um (skan'dē əm) *n.* [< L. *Scandia,* N European lands] a rare metallic chemical element: symbol, Sc; at. wt., 44.956; at. no., 21

scan·sion (skan'shən) *n.* the act of scanning verse

scant (skant) *adj.* [< ON. *skammr,* short] **1.** inadequate; meager **2.** not quite up to full measure —*vt.* **1.** to stint **2.** to give scant measure of —**scant'ly** *adv.* —**scant'ness** *n.*

scant'y *adj.* -i·er, -i·est **1.** barely sufficient; meager **2.** insufficient; not enough —**scant'i·ly** *adv.* —**scant'i·ness** *n.*

scape·goat (skāp'gōt') *n.* [(E)SCAPE + GOAT: see Lev. 16:7–26] one who bears the blame for the mistakes or crimes of others

scape'grace' *n.* [(E)SCAPE + GRACE] a graceless, unprincipled fellow; scamp; rogue

scap·u·la (skap'yoo lə) *n., pl.* -lae' (-lē'), -las [L.] *same as* SHOULDER BLADE

scap'u·lar *adj.* of the shoulder or scapula —*n.* **1.** a sleeveless outer garment worn by monks **2.** two pieces of cloth joined by strings, worn on the chest and back by some Roman Catholics as a token of religious devotion

scar (skär) *n.* [< Gr. *eschara,* fireplace] **1.** a mark left after a wound, burn, etc. has healed **2.** any mark like this **3.** the lasting mental or emotional effects of suffering — *vt., vi.* scarred, scar'ring to mark with or form a scar

scar·ab (skar'əb) *n.* [< Fr. < L. *scarabaeus*] **1.** a beetle, esp. the black beetle held sacred by the ancient Egyptians **2.** an image of this beetle, cut from a gem and formerly worn as a charm

scarce (skers) *adj.* [ult. < L. *excerpere,* to select] **1.** not common; rarely seen **2.** not plentiful; hard to get —*adv.*

literary var. of SCARCELY —**make oneself scarce** [Colloq.] to go or stay away —**scarce′ness** *n.*

scarce·ly *adv.* **1.** hardly; not quite **2.** probably not or certainly not

scar·ci·ty (sker′sə tē) *n., pl.* **-ties 1.** a being scarce; inadequate supply **2.** rarity; uncommonness

scare (sker) *vt.* **scared, scar′ing** [< ON. *skjarr,* timid] to fill with sudden fear or terror —*vi.* to become frightened, esp. suddenly —*n.* a sudden fear or panic —**scare up** [Colloq.] to produce or gather quickly

scare′crow′ (-krō′) *n.* **1.** a human figure made with sticks, old clothes, etc., put in a field to scare birds from crops **2.** a person in ragged clothes

scarf¹ (skärf) *n., pl.* **scarfs, scarves** (skärvz) [< ONormFr. *escarpe,* purse hung from the neck] **1.** a long or broad piece of cloth worn about the neck, head, etc. **2.** a long, narrow covering for a table, etc.

scarf² (skärf) *n., pl.* **scarfs** [prob. < Scand.] a joint made by notching, grooving, etc. the ends of two pieces and fastening them into one continuous piece: also **scarf joint**

scar·i·fy (skar′ə fī′) *vt.* **-fied′, -fy′ing** [< Gr. *skariphasthai,* to scratch] **1.** to make a series of small cuts or punctures in (the skin), as in surgery **2.** to criticize sharply **3.** to loosen or stir (the topsoil) —**scar′i·fi·ca′tion** *n.*

scar·let (skär′lit) *n.* [< ML. *scarlatum,* scarlet cloth] very bright red with a slightly orange tinge —*adj.* **1.** of this color **2.** sinful

scarlet fever an acute contagious disease characterized by sore throat, fever, and a scarlet rash

scarlet letter a scarlet letter A worn in earlier times by a person convicted of adultery

scarlet runner (bean) a climbing bean plant of tropical America, with scarlet flowers

scarlet tanager a U.S. songbird, the male of which has a scarlet body and black wings and tail

scarp (skärp) *n.* [< It. *scarpa*] a steep slope

scar·y (sker′ē) *adj.* **-i·er, -i·est** [Colloq.] **1.** causing fear **2.** easily frightened —**scar′i·ness** *n.*

scat¹ (skat) *vi.* **scat′ted, scat′ting** [? a hiss + CAT] [Colloq.] to go away: usually in the imperative

scat² (skat) *adj.* [< ?] *Jazz* using improvised, meaningless syllables in singing —*n.* such singing —*vi.* **scat′ted, scat′-ting** to sing scat

scath·ing (skā′thiŋ) *adj.* [< ON. *skathi,* harm] searing; harsh or caustic [*scathing* remarks] —**scath′ing·ly** *adv.*

sca·tol·o·gy (skə täl′ə jē) *n.* [< Gr. *skōr,* excrement + -LOGY] obsession with excrement or excretion, as in literature —**scat·o·log·i·cal** (skat′ə läj′i k'l) *adj.*

scat·ter (skat′ər) *vt.* [ME. *skateren*] **1.** to throw here and there; sprinkle **2.** to separate and drive in many directions; disperse —*vi.* to move apart in several directions —*n.* **1.** a scattering **2.** what is scattered about

scat′ter·brain′ *n.* one who is not able to think in a serious way —**scat′ter·brained′** *adj.*

scatter rug a small rug for covering only a limited area

scav·enge (skav′inj) *vt.* **-enged, -eng·ing** [< SCAVENGER] **1.** to clean up (streets, etc.) **2.** to salvage (usable goods) by rummaging through refuse —*vi.* **1.** to act as a scavenger **2.** to look for food

scav′eng·er (-in jər) *n.* [ult. < Fl. *scawen* or OFrank. *scouwon,* peer at] **1.** one who gathers things that have been discarded by others **2.** any animal that eats refuse and decaying matter

sce·nar·i·o (si ner′ē ō′, -när′-) *n., pl.* **-os′** [It. < L. *scaena,* SCENE] **1.** a synopsis of a play, opera, etc. **2.** the script of a motion picture, esp. the shooting script **3.** an outline of a proposed series of events —**sce·nar′ist** *n.*

scene (sēn) *n.* [< Gr. *skēnē,* stage] **1.** the place where an event occurs **2.** the setting of the action of a play, story, etc. **3.** a division of a play, usually part of an act **4.** a particular incident, as of a story **5.** *same as* SCENERY (sense 1) **6.** a view of people or places **7.** a display of strong feeling [she made a *scene* in court] **8.** [Colloq.] the locale for a specified activity

sce·ner·y (sē′nər ē) *n., pl.* **-ies 1.** painted screens, backdrops, etc., used on the stage to represent places **2.** the general appearance of a place; features of a landscape

sce·nic (sē′nik, sen′ik) *adj.* **1.** of the stage and its scenery, lighting, etc. **2.** of natural scenery; having beautiful scenery **3.** representing an action, event, etc. —**sce′ni·cal·ly** *adv.*

scent (sent) *vt.* [< L. *sentire,* to feel] **1.** to smell **2.** to suspect **3.** to fill with an odor; perfume —*n.* **1.** a smell; odor **2.** the sense of smell **3.** a perfume **4.** an odor left by an

animal, by which it is tracked **5.** any clue by which something is followed —**scent′ed** *adj.*

scep·ter (sep′tər) *n.* [< Gr. *skēptron,* staff] **1.** a staff held by a ruler as a symbol of sovereignty **2.** royal authority Brit. sp. **scep′tre**

scep·tic (skep′tik) *n., adj. chiefly Brit. sp. of* SKEPTIC —**scep′ti·cal** *adj.* —**scep′ti·cism** *n.*

sched·ule (skej′ool, -əl) *n.* [< L. *scheda,* a leaf of paper] **1.** a list of details **2.** a list of times of recurring events; timetable **3.** a timed plan for a project —*vt.* **-uled, -ul·ing 1.** to place in a schedule **2.** to plan for a certain time

sche·ma (skē′mə) *n., pl.* **-ma·ta** (-mə tə) [Gr.: see SCHEME] an outline, diagram, plan, etc.

sche·mat·ic (skē mat′ik, skə-) *adj.* of or like a scheme, outline, diagram, etc. —*n.* a diagram, as of the wiring of an electric circuit —**sche·mat′i·cal·ly** *adv.*

scheme (skēm) *n.* [< Gr. *schēma,* a form] **1.** a systematic program for attaining some object **2.** an orderly combination of things on a definite plan **3.** a diagram **4.** a plot; intrigue —*vt., vi.* **schemed, schem′ing** to devise; plot; contrive —**schem′er** *n.*

scher·zo (sker′tsō) *n., pl.* **-zos, -zi** (-tsē) [It., a jest] a lively movement as of a sonata, in 3/4 time

Schil·ler (shil′ər), **Fried·rich von** (frē′drikh fôn) 1759–1805; Ger. dramatist & poet

schil·ling (shil′iŋ) *n.* [G.] the monetary unit and a coin of Austria

schism (siz′'m; *now occas.* skiz′'m) *n.* [< Gr. *schizein,* to cleave] a split, esp. in an organized church, because of a difference of opinion, doctrine, etc. —**schis·mat′ic** (-mat′ik) *adj., n.*

schist (shist) *n.* [< Fr. < Gr. *schizein,* cleave] any metamorphic rock that splits easily into thin leaves

schiz·oid (skit′soid, skiz′oid) *adj.* **1.** of, like, or having schizophrenia **2.** designating a type of person who is withdrawn, introverted, etc. —*n.* a schizoid person

schiz·o·phre·ni·a (skit′sə frē′nē ə, skiz′ə-) *n.* [< Gr. *schizein,* cleave + *phrēn,* the mind] a mental disorder characterized by separation between thought and emotion, distortion of reality, delusions, bizarre behavior, etc. —**schiz′-o·phren′ic** (-fren′ik, -frē′nik) *adj., n.*

schle·miel (shlə mēl′) *n.* [Yid.] [Slang] a bungling person who habitually fails or is regularly victimized

Schles·wig-Hol·stein (shles′wig hōl′stīn) state of N West Germany, at the base of Jutland

schmaltz (shmälts) *n.* [via Yid. < G. *schmalz,* melted fat] anything very sentimental —**schmaltz′y** *adj.*

schnapps (shnäps) *n.* [G., a dram] any strong alcoholic liquor: also sp. **schnaps**

schnau·zer (shnou′zər) *n.* [G. < *schnauzen,* to snarl] a sturdy, active dog with a wiry coat

schnoz·zle (shnäz′'l) *n.* [< G. *schnauze*] [Slang] the nose: also **schnoz**

schol·ar (skäl′ər) *n.* [< L. *schola,* SCHOOL¹] **1.** a learned person **2.** a student or pupil **3.** a student given scholarship aid —**schol′ar·ly** *adj., adv.*

schol′ar·ship′ *n.* **1.** the systematized knowledge of a scholar **2.** a gift of money, etc. to help a student

scho·las·tic (skə las′tik) *adj.* **1.** of schools, colleges, students, teachers, etc.; academic **2.** [*also* S-] of or relating to scholasticism Also **scho·las′ti·cal** —*n.* [*also* S-] **1.** *same as* SCHOOLMAN (sense 1) **2.** one who favors Scholasticism —**scho·las′ti·cal·ly** *adv.*

scho·las′ti·cism (-tə siz′m) *n.* **1.** [*often* S-] a medieval system of Christian thought based on Aristotelian logic **2.** an insistence upon traditional doctrines and methods

school¹ (skool) *n.* [< Gr. *scholē,* leisure, school] **1.** a place or institution, with its buildings, etc., for teaching and learning **2.** all of its students and teachers **3.** a regular session of teaching **4.** the process of being educated [he likes *school*] **5.** any situation through which one gains knowledge [the *school* of hard knocks] **6.** a particular division of a university **7.** a group following the same beliefs, methods, etc. —*vt.* **1.** to teach; instruct **2.** to discipline; control —*adj.* of a school or schools

school² (skool) *n.* [Du., a crowd] a group of fish or water animals of the same kind swimming together

school board a group of people in charge of local public schools

SCHNAUZER
(17–20 in. high
at shoulder)

---

at, āpe, cär; ten, ēven; is, bīte; gō, hôrn, tool, look; oil, out; up, fur; thin, *then;* zh, leisure; ŋ, ring; ə for *a* in *ago;* as in *able* (ā′b'l); ë, Fr. coeur; ö, Fr. feu; Fr. mo*n;* ü, Fr. duc; *r,* Fr. cri; kh, G. doch, ich. ‡ foreign; < derived from

school'book' *n.* a book used for study in schools; textbook

school'boy' *n.* a boy attending school —**school'girl'** *n.fem.*

school'house' *n.* a building used as a school

school'ing *n.* **1.** training or education; esp., formal instruction at school **2.** cost of attending school

school'man *n., pl.* **-men 1.** [*often* S-] a medieval teacher of scholasticism **2.** a teacher or educator

school'marm' (-märm', -mäm') *n.* [Colloq.] a woman schoolteacher, hence any person, who tends to be old-fashioned and prudish: also **school'ma'am'** (-mäm')

school'mas'ter *n.* a man who teaches in, or is head of, a school —**school'mis'tress** *n.fem.*

school'mate' *n.* a person going to the same school at the same time as another: also **school'fel'low**

school'room' *n.* a classroom in a school

school'teach'er *n.* one who teaches in a school

school year the part of a year when school is in session

schoon·er (skōō'nər) *n.* [< ?] **1.** a ship with two or more masts, rigged fore and aft **2.** a large beer glass

Scho·pen·hau·er (shō'pən hou'ər), **Arthur** 1788–1860; Ger. pessimist philosopher

schot·tische (shät'ish) *n.* [< G. *schottische* (*tanz*), Scottish (dance)] **1.** a round dance like the polka **2.** music for this dance

Schu·bert (shōō'bərt), **Franz** (fränts) 1797–1828; Austrian composer

Schu·mann (shōō'män), **Robert** 1810–1856; Ger. composer

schuss (shoos) *n.* [G., shot, rush] a straight run down a hill in skiing —*vi.* to make such a run

schwa (shwä) *n.* [G. < Heb. *sh'wā*] **1.** the neutral vowel sound of most unstressed syllables in English, as of *a* in *ago* **2.** the symbol (ə) for this

Schweit·zer (shvīt'sər; *E.* shwīt'sər), **Al·bert** (äl'bert) 1875–1965; Alsatian medical missionary in Africa

sci·at·ic (sī at'ik) *adj.* [< Gr. *ischion*, hip] of, near, or affecting the hip or its nerves

sci·at'i·ca (-i kə) *n.* any painful condition in the hip or thigh; esp., neuritis of the long nerve (**sciatic nerve**) down the back of the thigh

sci·ence (sī'əns) *n.* [< L. *scire*, know] **1.** systematized knowledge derived from observation, study, and experimentation **2.** a branch of knowledge, esp. one that systematizes facts, principles, and methods [the *science* of mathematics] **3.** the systematized knowledge of nature: see NATURAL SCIENCE **4.** skill or technique

science fiction highly imaginative fiction typically involving real or imagined scientific phenomena

sci·en·tif·ic (sī'ən tif'ik) *adj.* **1.** of or dealing with science **2.** based on, or using, the principles and methods of science; systematic and exact —**sci'en·tif'i·cal·ly** *adv.*

sci·en·tist *n.* **1.** a specialist in science, as in biology, chemistry, etc. **2.** [S-] a Christian Scientist

sci-fi (sī'fī') *adj., n. same as* SCIENCE FICTION

scim·i·tar, scim·i·ter (sim'ə tər) *n.* [It. *scimitarra*] a short, curved sword with an edge on the convex side, used by Turks, Arabs, etc.

scin·til·la (sin til'ə) *n.* [L.] **1.** a spark **2.** a trace

scin·til·late (sin't'l āt') *vi.* -**lat'ed,** -**lat'ing** [< L. *scintilla*, a spark] **1.** to sparkle or twinkle **2.** to be brilliant and witty —**scin'til·la'tion** *n.*

sci·on (sī'ən) *n.* [OFr. *cion*] **1.** a shoot or bud of a plant, used for grafting **2.** a descendant

scis·sors (siz'ərz) *n.pl.* [< LL. *cisorium,* cutting tool] **1.** a cutting instrument with two opposing blades pivoted together so that they work against each other: also **pair of scissors 2.** [*with sing. v.*] a wrestling hold (**scissors hold**) in which one contestant clasps the other with his legs

scle·ro·sis (skli rō'sis) *n., pl.* -**ses** (-sēz) [< Gr. *sklēros,* hard] an abnormal hardening of body tissues, esp. of the nervous system or the walls of arteries —**scle·rot'ic** (-rät'ik) *adj.*

scoff (skôf, skäf) *n.* [prob. < Scand.] an expression of scorn or derision; jeer —*vt., vi.* to mock or jeer (*at*) —**scoff'er** *n.* —**scoff'ing·ly** *adv.*

scold (skōld) *n.* [< ON. *skald,* poet (prob. because of satirical verses)] a person, esp. a woman, who habitually uses abusive language —*vt.* to find fault with angrily; rebuke —*vi.* **1.** to find fault angrily **2.** to use abusive language —**scold'er** *n.* —**scold'ing** *adj., n.*

scol·lop (skäl'əp) *n., vt. var. of* SCALLOP

sconce¹ (skäns) *n.* [ult. < L. *abscondere,* to hide] a wall bracket as for holding a candle

sconce² (skäns) *n.* [Du. *schans*] a small fort

scone (skōn) *n.* [Scot. < ? MDu. *schoonbrot,* fine bread] a tea cake resembling a baking powder biscuit, usually baked on a griddle

scoop (skōōp) *n.* [< MDu. *schope,* bucket & *schoppe,* a shovel] **1.** any of various small, shovellike utensils used for taking up flour, ice cream, etc. **2.** the deep shovel of a dredge or steam shovel **3.** a scooping, or the amount scooped up at one time **4.** a hollowed-out place **5.** a motion as of scooping **6.** [Colloq.] a publishing of news before a rival newspaper —*vt.* **1.** to take up or out as with a scoop **2.** to hollow (*out*) **3.** to gather (*in* or *up*) as with a scoop **4.** [Colloq.] to publish news before (a rival) —**scoop'ful'** *n., pl.* -**fuls'**

scoot (skōōt) *vi., vt.* [prob. < ON. *skjōta,* to shoot] [Colloq.] to go quickly; scurry off

scoot'er *n.* **1.** a child's two-wheeled vehicle moved by pushing one foot against the ground **2.** a similar vehicle propelled by a motor: in full **motor scooter 3.** a sailboat with runners, for use on water or ice

scope (skōp) *n.* [< It. < Gr. *skopos,* watcher] **1.** the extent of the mind's grasp **2.** range or extent of action, observation, inclusion, etc. **3.** room or opportunity for action or thought **4.** *short for* TELESCOPE, RADARSCOPE, etc.

-scope [< Gr. *skopein,* to see] *a combining form meaning* an instrument, etc. for seeing or observing

sco·pol·a·mine (skō päl'ə mēn', -min) *n.* [< G. < *Scopoli,* 18th-c. It. naturalist + AMINE] an alkaloid used in medicine as a sedative, hypnotic, etc.

scor·bu·tic (skôr byōōt'ik) *adj.* [< ML. *scorbutus,* scurvy] of, like, or having scurvy: also **scor·bu'ti·cal**

scorch (skôrch) *vt.* [< ? Scand.] **1.** to burn slightly or on the surface **2.** to parch or shrivel by heat **3.** to criticize very sharply **4.** to burn and destroy everything in (an area) before yielding it to the enemy [a *scorched*-earth policy] —*vi.* to become scorched —*n.* a superficial burn

scorch'er *n.* anything that scorches; esp., [Colloq.] *a)* a very hot day *b)* a withering remark

score (skôr) *n.* [< ON. *skor*] **1.** a scratch, mark, notch, incision, etc. **2.** a debt or account **3.** a grudge [pay off an old *score*] **4.** a reason or ground **5.** the number of points made, as in a game **6.** a grade, as on a test **7.** twenty people or objects **8.** [*pl.*] very many **9.** *a)* a copy of a musical composition, showing all parts for the instruments or voices *b)* the music for a stage production, motion picture, etc. **10.** [Colloq.] a successful action, remark, etc. **11.** [Colloq.] the actual facts: chiefly in **know the score** —*vt.* **scored, scor'ing 1.** to mark or mark out with notches, lines, etc. **2.** *a)* to make (runs, points, etc.) in a game *b)* to record the score of **3.** to achieve, as a success **4.** to grade, as in testing **5.** to arrange a musical score **6.** to upbraid —*vi.* **1.** to make points, as in a game **2.** to keep score in a game **3.** to succeed in getting what one wants —**scor'er** *n.*

score'board' *n.* a large board for posting the score and other details of a game, as in a baseball stadium

score card 1. a card for recording the score of a game, etc. **2.** a card printed with players' names, positions, etc. at a sports event

scorn (skôrn) *n.* [< OFr. *escharnir,* to scorn] **1.** great contempt, often with anger **2.** expression of this feeling —*vt.* **1.** to regard with scorn; treat with contempt **2.** to refuse or reject as wrong or disgraceful —**scorn'ful** *adj.* —**scorn'ful·ly** *adv.*

Scor·pi·o (skôr'pē ō') [L., scorpion] **1.** a S constellation **2.** the eighth sign of the zodiac: see ZODIAC, illus.

scor'pi·on (-ən) *n.* [< Gr. *skorpios*] **1.** an arachnid found in warm regions, with a long tail ending in a poisonous sting **2.** *Bible* a whip or scourge —[S-] *same as* SCORPIO

Scot (skät) *n.* a native or inhabitant of Scotland

Scot. 1. Scotch **2.** Scotland **3.** Scottish

Scotch (skäch) *adj.* of Scotland: cf. SCOTTISH —*n. same as:* **1.** SCOTTISH **2.** SCOTCH WHISKY

SCORPION (to 10 in. long)

scotch (skäch) *vt.* [prob. < OFr. *coche,* a notch] **1.** to cut or maim **2.** to put an end to; stifle [to *scotch* a rumor]

Scotch'man *n., pl.* -**men** *var. of* SCOTSMAN

Scotch tape [< *Scotch,* a trademark] a thin, transparent cellulose adhesive tape

Scotch whisky whiskey, often having a smoky flavor distilled in Scotland from malted barley

sco·ter (skōt'ər) *n.* [< ?] a large sea duck found along the N coasts of Europe and N. America

scot-free (skät′frē′) *adj.* [orig., free from payment of *scot* (early term for tax)] unharmed or unpunished; free from penalty

Scot·land (skät′lənd) division of Great Britain, occupying the N half & nearby islands: 30,405 sq. mi.; pop. 5,217,000; cap. Edinburgh

Scotland Yard the London police headquarters, esp. its detective bureau

Scots (skäts) *adj., n. same as* SCOTTISH

Scots′man (-mən) *n., pl.* -men a native or inhabitant of Scotland, esp. a man: *Scotsman* or *Scot* is preferred to *Scotchman* in Scotland —**Scots′wom′an** *n.fem., pl.* -wom′en

Scott (skät), Sir **Walter** 1771–1832; Scot. poet & novelist

Scot·tish (skät′ish) *adj.* of Scotland, its people, their English dialect, etc. *Scottish* is formal usage, but with some words, *Scotch* is used (e.g., tweed, whisky), with others, *Scots* (e.g., law) —*n.* the English spoken in Scotland —**the Scottish** the Scottish people

Scottish terrier a terrier with short legs, wiry hair, and pointed ears: also **Scotch terrier**

scoun·drel (skoun′drəl) *n.* [prob. ult. < L. *abscondere*, ABSCOND] a mean, immoral, or wicked person; villain — *adj.* like a scoundrel; mean: also **scoun′drel·ly**

scour[1] (skour) *vt., vi.* [< L. *ex-*, intens. + *curare*, take care of] 1. to clean by vigorous rubbing, as with abrasives 2. to remove dirt and grease from (wool, etc.)

scour[2] (skour) *vt.* [prob. < L. *ex-*, out + *currere*, to run] to pass over quickly, or range over, as in search [to *scour* a library for a book]

scourge (skurj) *n.* [< L. *ex*, off + *corrigia*, a whip] 1. a whip 2. any means of severe punishment or any cause of great suffering [the *scourge* of war] —*vt.* **scourged, scourg′ing** 1. to whip; flog 2. to punish or afflict severely —**scourg′er** *n.*

scout[1] (skout) *n.* [< L. *auscultare*, listen] 1. a soldier, plane, etc. sent to spy out the enemy's strength, movements, etc. 2. a person sent out to search for new talent, etc. [a baseball *scout*] 3. a Boy Scout or Girl Scout 4. [Slang] fellow; guy —*vt., vi.* 1. to reconnoiter 2. to go in search of (something)

scout[2] (skout) *vt.* [prob. < ON. *skuti*, a taunt] to reject as absurd; scoff at —*vi.* to scoff (*at*)

scout′mas′ter *n.* the adult leader of a troop of Boy Scouts

scow (skou) *n.* [Du. *schouw*] a large, flat-bottomed boat with square ends, used for carrying coal, sand, etc. and often towed by a tug

scowl (skoul) *vi.* [prob. < Scand.] to look angry, sullen, displeased, etc. as by contracting the eyebrows —*n.* a scowling; angry frown —**scowl′er** *n.*

scrab·ble (skrab′′l) *vi.* -bled, -bling [< Du. *schrabben*, to scrape] 1. to scratch, scrape, etc. as though looking for something 2. to struggle 3. to scribble —*n.* a scrabbling; a scramble

scrag (skrag) *n.* [prob. < ON.] 1. a thin, scrawny person, animal, or plant 2. [Slang] the neck —*vt.* **scragged, scrag′ging** [Slang] to choke or wring the neck of

scrag·gly (skrag′lē) *adj.* -gli·er, -gli·est sparse, scrubby, uneven, ragged, or the like [a *scraggly* beard]

scrag·gy (skrag′ē) *adj.* -gi·er, -gi·est 1. rough or jagged 2. lean; bony; skinny —**scrag′gi·ly** *adv.*

scram (skram) *vi.* **scrammed, scram′ming** [< SCRAMBLE] [Slang] to leave or get out, esp. in a hurry

scram·ble (skram′b′l) *vi.* -bled, -bling [< ?] 1. to climb, crawl, or clamber hurriedly 2. to scuffle or struggle for something —*vt.* 1. to mix or jumble haphazardly 2. to modify (electronic communication signals) so as to make unintelligible without special receiving equipment 3. to cook (eggs) while stirring the mixed whites and yolks —*n.* 1. a hard climb or advance, as over rough ground 2. a disorderly struggle, as for something prized

Scran·ton (skrant′′n) city in NE Pa.: pop. 104,000

scrap[1] (skrap) *n.* [< ON. *skrap*] 1. a small piece; fragment 2. discarded material 3. [*pl.*] bits of food —*adj.* 1. in the form of pieces, leftovers, etc. 2. used and discarded —*vt.* **scrapped, scrap′ping** 1. to make into scrap 2. to discard; junk

scrap[2] (skrap) *n., vi.* **scrapped, scrap′ping** [prob. < SCRAPE] [Colloq.] fight or quarrel —**scrap′per** *n.*

scrap′book′ *n.* a book of blank pages for mounting clippings, pictures, etc.

scrape (skrāp) *vt.* **scraped, scrap′ing** 1. to make smooth or clean by rubbing with a tool or abra-sive 2. to remove in this way (with *off, out*, etc.) 3. to scratch, abrade, etc. 4. to gather slowly and with difficulty [to *scrape* up some money] —*vi.* 1. to rub against something harshly; grate 2. to give out a harsh, grating noise 3. to gather goods or money slowly and with difficulty 4. to manage to get by (with *along, by*, etc.) 5. to draw the foot back along the ground in bowing —*n.* 1. a scraping 2. a scraped place 3. a harsh, grating sound 4. a predicament 5. a fight —**scrap′er** *n.*

scrap′py[1] *adj.* -pi·er, -pi·est 1. made of scraps 2. disconnected [*scrappy* memories] —**scrap′pi·ly** *adv.* —**scrap′pi·ness** *n.*

scrap′py[2] *adj.* -pi·er, -pi·est [Colloq.] fond of fighting — **scrap′pi·ly** *adv.* —**scrap′pi·ness** *n.*

scratch (skrach) *vt.* [prob. a fusion of ME. *scratten* & *cracchen*] 1. to scrape or cut the surface of slightly 2. to tear or dig with the nails or claws 3. to scrape lightly to relieve itching 4. to scrape with a grating noise 5. to write or draw hurriedly or carelessly 6. to strike out (writing, etc.) 7. *Sports* to withdraw a contestant, specif. from a horse race —*vi.* 1. to use nails or claws in digging or wounding 2. to scrape the skin lightly to relieve itching, etc. 3. to make a harsh, scraping noise 4. to manage to get by 5. *Billiards, Pool* to commit a scratch —*n.* 1. the act of scratching 2. a mark, tear, etc. made by scratching 3. a grating or scraping sound 4. the starting line of a race 5. [Slang] money 6. *Billiards, Pool a*) a shot that results in a penalty *b*) a miss 7. *Sports* the starting point or time of a contestant who receives no handicap —*adj.* 1. used for hasty notes, figuring, etc. [*scratch* paper] 2. put together hastily, without selection 3. *Baseball* designating a chance hit credited to the batter for a ball not hit sharply —**from scratch** from nothing; without advantage —**up to scratch** [Colloq.] up to a standard —**scratch′er** *n.* —**scratch′y** *adj.* -i·er, -i·est

scrawl (skrôl) *vt., vi.* [< ?] to write or draw hastily, carelessly, or awkwardly —*n.* 1. a sprawling handwriting, often illegible 2. something scrawled —**scrawl′y** *adj.* -i·er, -i·est

scraw·ny (skrô′nē) *adj.* -ni·er, -ni·est [prob. < Scand.] 1. very thin; skinny and bony 2. stunted or scrubby

scream (skrēm) *vi.* [ME. *scremen*] 1. to utter a shrill, piercing cry as in pain or fright 2. to shout, laugh, etc. hysterically —*vt.* to utter as with a scream —*n.* 1. a sharp, piercing cry or sound 2. [Colloq.] a hilariously funny person or thing —**scream′ing** *adj.* —**scream′ing·ly** *adv.*

scream′er *n.* 1. one who screams 2. [Slang] a sensational headline

screech (skrēch) *vi., vt.* [ON. *skraekja*] to utter (with) a shrill, high-pitched cry —*n.* such a cry —**screech′i·ness** *n.* —**screech′y** *adj.* -i·er, -i·est

screech owl 1. a small owl with feathered ear tufts and an eerie, wailing cry 2. [Brit.] *same as* BARN OWL

screen (skrēn) *n.* [< OFr. *escren*] 1. a curtain or partition used to separate, conceal, protect, etc. 2. anything that shields, conceals, etc. [a smoke *screen*] 3. a coarse mesh of wire, etc. used as a sieve 4. a frame covered with a mesh, used, as on a window, to keep insects out 5. a white surface upon which movies, slides, etc. are projected 6. the movie industry or art 7. the visual display surface of a television or radar receiver —*vt.* 1. to separate, conceal, or protect, as with a screen 2. to provide with a screen 3. to sift through a screen 4. to interview or test in order to separate according to skills, etc. 5. to project (movies, etc.) upon a screen

screen′ing *n.* 1. *a*) a set of screens *b*) mesh used as a screen 2. [*pl.*] material separated out by a screen

screen′play′ *n.* a story written, or adapted from a novel, etc., for production as a movie

screw (skroo) *n.* [< OFr. *escroue*, hole in which a screw turns] 1. a naillike metal piece grooved in an advancing spiral, for fastening things by being turned: **male** (or **external**) **screw** 2. the internal thread, as of a nut, into which a male screw can be turned: **female** (or **internal**) **screw** 3. any of various devices operating or threaded like a screw —*vt.* 1. to twist; turn 2. to fasten, tighten, etc. as with a screw 3. to contort 4. to make stronger (often with *up*) 5. [Slang] to cheat; swindle —*vi.* 1. to go together or come apart by being turned like a screw [a lid *screws* on] 2. to be fitted for screws —**have a screw loose** [Slang] to be eccentric — **put the screws on** (or **to**) to subject to force or pressure

screw'ball' n. [Slang] an erratic, irrational, unconventional person

screw'driv'er n. a tool used for turning screws, having an end that fits into the slot in the head of a screw

screw eye a screw with a loop for a head

screw hook a screw with a hook for a head

screw propeller see PROPELLER

screw'y adj. -i·er, -i·est [Slang] irrational, peculiar, absurd, etc.

scrib·ble (skrib''l) vt., vi. -bled, -bling [< L. scribere, write] 1. to write carelessly, hastily, etc. 2. to make meaningless or illegible marks (on) —n. scribbled writing —scrib'bler n.

scribe (skrīb) n. [< L. scribere, write] 1. one who copied manuscripts before the invention of printing 2. a writer; author 3. a person learned in the Jewish law —scrib'al adj.

scrim (skrim) n. [< ?] a light, loosely woven cloth, often used in the theater as a backdrop, etc.

scrim·mage (skrim'ij) n. [< SKIRMISH] 1. a confused struggle 2. Football a) the play that follows the pass from center b) a practice game —vi. -maged, -mag·ing to take part in a scrimmage

scrimp (skrimp) vt. [prob. < Scand.] 1. to make too small, short, etc. 2. to treat stingily —vi. to be sparing and frugal —scrimp'er n. —scrimp'y adj. -i·er, -i·est

scrip (skrip) n. [< SCRIPT] a certificate of a right to receive something, as stocks, money, etc.

script (skript) n. [< L. scribere, write] 1. handwriting 2. a printing type that looks like handwriting 3. a copy of the text of a play, movie, TV show, etc.

scrip·ture (skrip'chər) n. [see SCRIPT] 1. [S-] [often pl.] a) the sacred writings of the Jews, identical with the Old Testament of the Christians b) the Christian Bible 2. any sacred writing —scrip'tur·al adj.

script'writ'er n. one who writes scripts for movies, etc.

scrod (skräd) n. [prob. < MDu. schrode, strip] a young codfish, split and prepared for cooking

scrof·u·la (skräf'yə lə) n. [< L. scrofa, a sow] tuberculosis of the lymphatic glands, esp. of the neck, with enlargement of the glands: also called king's evil —scrof'u·lous adj.

scroll (skrōl) n. [< ME. scrowe] 1. a roll of parchment or paper, usually with writing on it 2. ornamental design in coiled or spiral form

scroll saw a thin, ribbonlike saw for cutting thin wood into spiral or ornamental designs (scroll'work')

Scrooge (skrōōj) n. a hard, miserly old man, like the character of this name in Dickens' A Christmas Carol

scro·tum (skrōt'əm) n., pl. -ta (-ə), -tums [L.] in most male mammals, the pouch of skin containing the testicles —scro'tal adj.

scrounge (skrounj) vt. scrounged, scroung'ing [< ?] [Colloq.] 1. to get by hunting around 2. to get by begging or sponging 3. to pilfer —vi. [Colloq.] to search (around) for something —scroung'er n.

scrub¹ (skrub) n. [dial. var. of SHRUB] 1. a thick growth of stunted trees or bushes 2. any person or thing smaller than the usual, or inferior 3. Sports a substitute player — adj. 1. poor; inferior 2. undersized —scrub'by adj. -bi·er, -bi·est

scrub² (skrub) vt. scrubbed, scrub'bing [prob. < Scand.] 1. to clean or wash by rubbing hard 2. to rub hard 3. to cleanse (a gas) of impurities —vi. to clean something by rubbing —n. a scrubbing —scrub'ber n.

scruff (skruf) n. [< ON. skrufr] the nape of the neck

scruff·y (skruf'ē) adj. -i·er, -i·est [< dial. scruff, var. of SCURF] shabby, unkempt, or untidy; grubby —scruff'i·ly adv. —scruff'i·ness n.

scrump·tious (skrump'shəs) adj. [< SUMPTUOUS] [Colloq.] very pleasing —scrump'tious·ly adv.

scru·ple (skrōō'p'l) n. [< L. scrupulus, small sharp stone] 1. a very small quantity 2. an apothecaries' weight, equal to 1/3 dram (20 grains) 3. a doubt arising from difficulty in deciding what is right, proper, etc. —vt., vi. -pled, -pling to hesitate (at) from doubt; have scruples (about)

scru·pu·lous (skrōō'pyə ləs) adj. 1. having or showing scruples; conscientiously honest 2. careful of details; precise —scru'pu·los'i·ty (-läs'ə tē), pl. -ties, scru'pu·lous·ness n. —scru'pu·lous·ly adv.

scru·ti·nize (skrōōt''n īz') vt. -nized', -niz'ing to look at carefully or examine closely —scru'ti·niz'er n.

scru'ti·ny (-'n ē) n., pl. -nies [< L. scrutari, examine] a close examination; careful look

scu·ba (skōō'bə) n. [s(elf-)c(ontained) u(nderwater) b(reathing) a(pparatus)] a diver's apparatus with compressed-air tanks for breathing under water

scud (skud) vi. scud'ded, scud'ding [prob. < ON.] 1. to move swiftly 2. to be driven before the wind —n. 1. a scudding 2. spray, rain, snow, or clouds driven by the wind

scuff (skuf) vt. [prob. < ON. skufa, to shove] 1. to scrape (the ground, etc.) with the feet 2. to wear a rough place on the surface of —vi. to walk without lifting the feet; shuffle —n. 1. a scuffing 2. a worn or rough spot 3. a loose-fitting house slipper

scuf·fle (skuf''l) vi. -fled, -fling [< SCUFF] 1. to struggle or fight in rough confusion 2. to drag one's feet —n. 1. a rough, confused fight 2. the act or sound of feet shuffling

scull (skul) n. [prob. < Scand.] 1. an oar worked from side to side over the stern of a boat to move it forward 2. a light rowboat for racing —vt., vi. to propel with a scull or sculls —scull'er n.

scul·ler·y (skul'ər ē) n., pl. -ies [< L. scutella, tray] a room where pots, pans, and other kitchen utensils are cleaned

scul·lion (skul'yən) n. [ult. < L. scopa, broom] [Archaic] a servant who does rough kitchen work

sculpt (skulpt) vt., vi. 1. to carve or model as a sculptor 2. to give sculpturelike form to (hair, fabric, etc.) Also **sculp**

sculp·tor (skulp'tər) n. an artist who creates works of sculpture — sculp'tress n.fem.

SCULL

sculp'ture (-chər) n. [< L. sculpere, carve] 1. the art of forming stone, clay, wood, etc. into statues, figures, or the like 2. a work or works of sculpture —vt. -tured, -tur·ing 1. to carve, chisel, etc. into statues, figures, etc. 2. to portray in sculpture 3. to decorate with sculpture —vi. to work as a sculptor —sculp'tu·ral adj. —sculp'tu·ral·ly adv.

scum (skum) n. [< MDu. schum] 1. a thin layer of impurities on the top of liquids 2. refuse 3. low, despicable people —vi. scummed, scum'ming to form scum — scum'my adj. -mi·er, -mi·est

scup (skup) n., pl. scup, scups [< AmInd.] a brown-and-white porgy of the N Atlantic

scup·per (skup'ər) n. [< ?] an opening in a ship's side to allow water to run off the deck

scup·per·nong (skup'ər nôn', -näŋ') n. [< the Scuppernong River, N. Carolina] 1. a golden-green grape 2. a wine made from this grape

scurf (skurf) n. [< ON.] 1. little, dry scales shed by the skin, as dandruff 2. any scaly coating —scurf'y adj. -i·er, -i·est

scur·ril·ous (skur'ə ləs) adj. [< L. scurra, buffoon] coarse; vulgar; abusive —scur·ril·i·ty (skə ril'ə tē) n., pl. -ties — scur'ril·ous·ly adv.

scur·ry (skur'ē) vi. -ried, -ry·ing [< HURRY-SCURRY] to run hastily —n. a scurrying

scur·vy (skur'vē) adj. -vi·er, -vi·est [< SCURF] low; mean —n. a disease resulting from a vitamin C deficiency, causing weakness, anemia, spongy gums, etc. —scur'vi·ly adv. —scur'vi·ness n.

scutch·eon (skuch'ən) n. same as ESCUTCHEON

scut·tle¹ (skut''l) n. [< L. scutella, a dish] a bucket for pouring coal on a fire: in full coal scuttle

scut·tle² (skut''l) vi. -tled, -tling [prob. < SCUD] to scurry, esp. away from trouble, etc. —n. a scurry

scut·tle³ (skut''l) n. [< Sp. escotilla] a small, covered opening in the hull or deck of a ship —vt. -tled, -tling 1. to make or open holes in the hull of (a ship) below the waterline; esp., to sink in this way 2. to abandon (a plan, undertaking, etc.)

scut'tle·butt' (-but') n. [< scuttled butt, lidded cask] 1. Naut. a drinking fountain on shipboard 2. [Colloq.] rumor or gossip

Scyl·la (sil'ə) a dangerous rock on the S Italian coast, opposite the whirlpool Charybdis —between Scylla and Charybdis facing danger or evil on either hand

scythe (sīth) n. [OE. sithe] a tool with a long, single-edged blade on a bent wooden shaft, for cutting grass, grain, etc. by hand —vt. scythed, scyth'ing to cut with a scythe

S.Dak., SD South Dakota

Se Chem. selenium

SE, S.E., s.e. 1. southeast 2. southeastern

sea (sē) n. [OE. sæ] 1. the ocean 2. a large body of salt water wholly or partly enclosed by land [the Red Sea] 3. a large body of fresh water [the Sea of Galilee] 4. the condition of the ocean's surface [a calm sea] 5. a heavy wave **6.** a very great amount —*adj.* of or for use at sea — **at sea 1.** on the open sea **2.** uncertain; bewildered —**go to sea** to become a sailor —**put (out) to sea** to sail away from land

sea anemone a sea polyp having a firm, gelatinous body topped with colored, petallike tentacles

sea'board' *n.* land or coastal region bordering on the sea —*adj.* bordering on the sea

sea'coast' *n.* land bordering on the sea

sea cow 1. any of several sea mammals, as the dugong or manatee **2.** *earlier name for* WALRUS

sea dog an experienced sailor

sea'far'er *n.* a traveler by sea; esp., a sailor

sea'far'ing *adj.* of or engaged in life at sea

sea'food' *n.* food prepared from or consisting of saltwater fish or shellfish

sea'go'ing *adj.* **1.** made for use on the open sea *[a seagoing* schooner*]* **2.** *same as* SEAFARING

sea green a pale bluish green —**sea'-green'** *adj.*

sea gull *same as* GULL[1]; esp., any gull living along a seacoast

sea horse 1. a small, semitropical fish with a slender tail, plated body, and a head somewhat like that of a horse **2.** a mythical sea creature, half fish and half horse

seal[1] (sēl) *n.* [< L. *sigillum*] **1.** a design, initials, etc. placed on a letter, document, etc. to prove it is authentic: letters were once commonly sealed with molten wax impressed with such a design **2.** a stamp or ring for making such an impression **3.** a piece of paper, etc. bearing an impressed design recognized as official **4.** something that seals or closes tightly **5.** something that guarantees; pledge **6.** an ornamental paper stamp *[Christmas seals]* —*vt.* **1.** to mark with a seal, as to authenticate or certify **2.** to close or shut tight as with a seal *[an envelope sealed* with glue, a *sealed* door*]* **3.** to confirm the truth of (a promise, etc.) by some action **4.** to settle or determine finally *[his fate was sealed]* **5.** to apply a nonpermeable coating to (a porous surface, as wood) —**seal'a·ble** *adj.*

seal[2] (sēl) *n.* [OE. *seolh*] **1.** a sea mammal with a sleek coat and four flippers: it lives in cold water and eats fish **2.** the fur of a fur seal **3.** leather made from sealskin —*vi.* to hunt seals

Sea·lab (sē'lab') *n.* [SEA + LAB(ORATORY)] any of a series of U.S. undersea laboratories for research

seal·ant (sēl'ənt) *n.* [SEAL[1] + -ANT] a substance, as a wax, plastic, silicone, etc., used for sealing

sea legs the ability to walk without loss of balance on board ship, esp. in a rough sea

sea level the mean level of the sea between high and low tide

sealing wax a hard mixture of resin and turpentine used for sealing letters, dry cells, etc.: it softens when heated

sea lion a large seal of the N Pacific

seal'skin' *n.* **1.** the pelt of the fur seal **2.** a garment made of this

seam (sēm) *n.* [OE.] **1.** a line formed by sewing together two pieces of material **2.** any line marking joining edges **3.** a mark like this, as a scar, wrinkle, etc. **4.** a stratum of ore, coal, etc. —*vt.* **1.** to join together so as to form a seam **2.** to mark with a seamlike line. —**seam'less** *adj.*

sea·man (sē'mən) *n., pl.* **-men 1.** a sailor **2.** *U.S. Navy* an enlisted man whose work is deck maintenance, care of equipment, etc. —**sea'man·like'** *adj.*

sea'man·ship' *n.* skill in sailing or working a ship

seam·stress (sēm'stris) *n.* a woman who sews expertly or who makes her living by sewing

seam'y *adj.* **-i·er, -i·est 1.** having or showing seams **2.** unpleasant, squalid, or sordid —**seam'i·ness** *n.*

sé·ance (sā'äns) *n.* [Fr. < OFr. < L. *sedere*, to sit] a meeting at which spiritualists seek or profess to communicate with the dead

sea'plane' *n.* any airplane designed to land on and take off from water

sea'port' *n.* **1.** a port or harbor used by ocean ships **2.** a town or city having such a port

sear (sir) *adj.* [OE.] withered; sere —*vt.* **1.** to wither **2.** to scorch or burn the surface of **3.** to make callous or unfeeling —*n.* a mark produced by searing —**sear'ing·ly** *adv.*

search (surch) *vt.* [< LL. *circare*, go about] **1.** to go over and look through in order to find something **2.** to examine (a person) for something concealed **3.** to examine carefully; probe **4.** to seek and find by investigation (usually with *out*) —*vi.* to make a search —*n.* a searching;

examination —**in search of** trying to find by searching — **search'er** *n.*

search'ing *adj.* **1.** examining thoroughly **2.** keen; piercing —**search'ing·ly** *adv.*

search'light' *n.* **1.** an apparatus on a swivel, that projects a strong beam of light **2.** such a beam

search warrant a legal document authorizing a police search, as for stolen articles

sea'scape' *n.* [SEA + (LAND)SCAPE] **1.** a view of the sea **2.** a picture of this

sea'shell' *n.* the shell of any saltwater mollusk

sea'shore' *n.* land along the sea; seacoast

sea'sick'ness *n.* nausea, dizziness, etc. caused by the rolling of a ship at sea —**sea'sick'** *adj.*

sea'side' *n.* seashore —*adj.* at or of the seaside

sea·son (sē'z'n) *n.* [< VL. *satio*, sowing time] **1.** any of the four divisions of the year; spring, summer, fall (or autumn), or winter **2.** the time when something takes place, is popular, permitted, etc. **3.** the fitting or convenient time —*vt.* **1.** to make (food) more tasty by adding salt, spices, etc. **2.** to add zest to **3.** to make more fit for use, as by aging **4.** to make used to; accustom —*vi.* to become seasoned —**in season 1.** available fresh for use as food **2.** at the legal time for being hunted or caught **3.** in or at the proper time **4.** early enough: also **in good season 5.** in heat: said of animals —**sea'son·er** *n.*

sea'son·a·ble *adj.* **1.** suitable to the season **2.** timely; opportune —**sea'son·a·bly** *adv.*

sea'son·al *adj.* of or depending on the season —**sea'son·al·ly** *adv.*

sea'son·ing *n.* any flavoring added to food

seat (sēt) *n.* [ON. *sæti*] **1.** manner of sitting, as on horseback **2.** a place to sit **3.** a thing to sit on; chair, etc. **4.** the buttocks **5.** the part of a chair, garment, etc. that one sits on **6.** the right to sit as a member **7.** a surface on which another part rests **8.** the chief location, or center — *vt.* **1.** to set in or on a seat **2.** to have seats for *[the car seats six]* **3.** to put in a certain place, position, etc.

seat belt anchored straps buckled across the hips, to protect a seated passenger, as in a car or airplane

Se·at·tle (se at''l) seaport in WC Wash., on Puget Sound: pop. 531,000 (met. area 1,422,000)

sea urchin a small sea animal with a round body in a shell covered with long, movable spines

sea wall a wall made to break the force of the waves and to protect the shore from erosion

sea·ward (sē'wərd) *adv., adj.* toward the sea: also **sea'wards** *adv.* —*n.* a seaward direction or position

SEA URCHIN
(1 1/2–10 in. in diameter)

sea'way' *n.* **1.** a route by sea **2.** a rough sea **3.** an inland waterway to the sea for ocean ships

sea'weed' *n.* any sea plant or plants, esp. any alga

sea'wor'thy (-wur'the) *adj.* fit for travel on the open sea: said of a ship —**sea'wor'thi·ness** *n.*

se·ba·ceous (si bā'shəs) *adj.* [< L. *sebum*, tallow] of, like, or secreting fat or any fatty substance

SEC, S.E.C. Securities and Exchange Commission

sec. 1. second(s) **2.** secretary **3.** section(s)

se·cant (sē'kant, -kənt) *n.* [< L. *secare*, to cut] **1.** *Geom.* any straight line intersecting a curve at two or more points **2.** *Trigonometry* the ratio of the hypotenuse of a right triangle to either of the other two sides with reference to the enclosed angle

se·cede (si sēd') *vi.* **-ced'ed, -ced'ing** [< L. *se-*, apart + *cedere*, to go] to withdraw formally from a larger body, as from a political union —**se·ced'er** *n.*

se·ces·sion (si sesh'ən) *n.* **1.** a seceding **2.** [*often* S-] the withdrawal of the Southern States from the Federal Union (1860–61) —**se·ces'sion·ist** *n.*

se·clude (si klōōd') *vt.* **-clud'ed, -clud'ing** [< L. *se-*, apart + *claudere*, shut] **1.** to shut off from others; isolate **2.** to make private or hidden

se·clud'ed *adj.* isolated; withdrawn

se·clu·sion (si klōō'zhən) *n.* **1.** retirement; isolation; privacy **2.** a secluded spot —**se·clu'sive** *adj.*

sec·ond[1] (sek'ənd) *adj.* [< L. *sequi*, follow] **1.** coming next after the first in order; 2d or 2nd **2.** another of the same kind; other *[a second chance]* **3.** next below the first in rank, value, merit, etc. —*n.* **1.** one that is second **2.** an article of merchandise not of first quality **3.** an aid or assistant, as to a boxer **4.** the second forward gear ratio of a motor vehicle **5.** [Slang] [*pl.*] a second helping of food — *vt.* **1.** to assist **2.** to indicate formal support of (a motion, etc.) so that it can be discussed or voted on —*adv.* in the second place, group, etc. —**sec′ond·er** *n.*

sec·ond² (sek′ənd) *n.* [< ML. *minuta secunda*, lit., second minute] **1.** 1/60 of a minute of time **2.** 1/60 of a minute of angular measurement **3.** a very short time; instant

sec·ond·ar·y (sek′ən der′ē) *adj.* **1.** second in order, rank, importance, etc. **2.** subordinate; minor **3.** not primary; derivative —*n., pl.* **-ies** one that is secondary, subordinate, etc. —**sec′ond·ar′i·ly** *adv.*

secondary accent (or **stress**) any stress (′) that is weaker than the full, or primary, accent

secondary school a school, as a high school, coming after elementary school

second childhood senility; dotage

sec′ond-class′ *adj.* **1.** of the class, rank, etc. next below the highest **2.** designating or of a class of mail consisting of newspapers, magazines, etc. **3.** inferior —*adv.* **1.** with second-class travel arrangements **2.** by second-class mail

Second Coming in the theology of some Christian sects, the expected return of Christ, at the Last Judgment

sec′ond-guess′ *vt., vi.* [Colloq.] to use hindsight in criticizing (someone), remaking (a decision), etc.

sec′ond-hand′ *adj.* **1.** not direct from the original source **2.** used before; not new **3.** of or dealing in used merchandise —*adv.* not firsthand

second lieutenant a commissioned officer of the lowest rank in the U.S. Army, Air Force, or Marine Corps

sec′ond·ly *adv.* in the second place; second

second nature acquired habits, etc. fixed so deeply as to seem part of a person's nature

second person that form of a pronoun (as *you*) or verb (as *are*) which refers to the person(s) spoken to

sec′ond-rate′ *adj.* **1.** second in quality, rank, etc. **2.** inferior; mediocre —**sec′ond-rat′er** *n.*

sec′ond-string′ *adj.* [Colloq.] *Sports* that is the second or a substitute choice for play at the specified position

second wind 1. the return of normal breathing following severe exertion **2.** the recovered capacity for continuing any effort

se·cre·cy (sē′krə sē) *n., pl.* **-cies 1.** a being secret **2.** the practice or habit of being secretive

se·cret (sē′krit) *adj.* [< L. *se-*, apart + *cernere*, sift] **1.** kept from or acting without the knowledge of others **2.** remote; secluded **3.** secretive; reticent **4.** beyond general understanding; mysterious **5.** concealed from sight; hidden —*n.* **1.** something known only to some and kept from others **2.** something not understood or explained —**in se·cret** without the knowledge of others —**se′cret·ly** *adv.*

secret agent one who carries on espionage or work of a secret nature, as for a government

sec·re·tar·i·at (sek′rə ter′ē ət) *n.* **1.** the office, position, or quarters of a secretary of high position in a government, etc. **2.** a staff headed by a secretary-general

sec·re·tar·y (sek′rə ter′ē) *n., pl.* **-ies** [< ML. *secretarius*, one entrusted with secrets] **1.** one who keeps records, handles correspondence, etc. for an organization or person **2.** an official in charge of a department of government **3.** a writing desk, esp. one topped with a small bookcase — **sec′re·tar′i·al** *adj.* —**sec′re·tar′y·ship** *n.*

secretary bird a large African bird of prey with long legs and a crest with penlike feathers

sec′re·tar′y-gen′er·al *n., pl.* **-ies-gen′er·al** head of a secretariat

se·crete (si krēt′) *vt.* **-cret′ed, -cret′ing** [see SECRET] **1.** to hide; conceal **2.** to form and release (a specified secretion) as a gland, etc. does

se·cre·tion (si krē′shən) *n.* **1.** a hiding or concealing **2.** the process in an animal or plant of forming a substance from the blood or sap and then releasing it **3.** such a substance

se·cre·tive (sē′krə tiv) *adj.* reticent; not frank or open — **se′cre·tive·ly** *adv.* —**se′cre·tive·ness** *n.*

se·cre·to·ry (si krēt′ər ē) *adj.* of, or having the function of, secretion —*n.* a secretory gland, etc.

Secret Service a U.S. government service for uncovering counterfeiters, guarding the President, etc.

sect (sekt) *n.* [< L. *sequi*, follow] **1.** a religious denomination **2.** a group of people having a common leadership, philosophy, etc.

sec·tar·i·an (sek ter′ē ən) *adj.* **1.** of or devoted to some sect **2.** narrow-minded —*n.* **1.** a member of a sect **2.** one who is blindly devoted to a sect —**sec′tar′i·an·ism** *n.*

sec·tion (sek′shən) *n.* [< L. *secare*, to cut] **1.** a cutting; specif., an incision in surgery **2.** a part cut off; slice;

division **3.** a part of a book, numbered paragraph of a law, etc. **4.** any distinct or separate part **5.** a division of public lands (640 acres) **6.** a drawing, etc. of a thing as it would appear if cut straight through in a given plane —*vt.* to divide into sections

sec′tion·al *adj.* **1.** of or devoted to a given section or district **2.** made up of sections —**sec′tion·al·ly** *adv.*

sec′tion·al·ism *n.* a narrow-minded concern shown for one section of a country —**sec′tion·al·ist** *adj., n.*

sec·tor (sek′tər) *n.* [< L. *secare*, to cut] **1.** part of a circle bounded by any two radii and the included arc **2.** any of the districts into which an area is divided for military operations **3.** a distinct part of a society, economy, etc.

sec·u·lar (sek′yə lər) *adj.* [< L. *saeculum*, age] **1.** not religious; not connected with a church; worldly **2.** not bound by a monastic vow [*secular* clergy] —**sec′u·lar·ly** *adv.*

sec′u·lar·ism *n.* **1.** worldly spirit, views, etc.; esp., rejection of any religious faith **2.** the belief that religion should be separated from the state, esp. from public education —**sec′u·lar·ist** *n., adj.*

sec′u·lar·ize (-lə rīz′) *vt.* **-ized′, -iz′ing 1.** to change from religious to civil ownership or use **2.** to deprive of religious character, influence, etc. —**sec′u·lar·i·za′tion** *n.*

se·cure (si kyoor′) *adj.* [< L. *se-*, free from + *cura*, care] **1.** free from fear, care, etc. **2.** free from danger; safe **3.** firm; stable [make the knot *secure*] **4.** reliable —*vt.* **-cured′, -cur′ing 1.** to make safe; protect **2.** to make certain; guarantee, as with a pledge [to *secure* a loan] **3.** to make firm, fast, etc. **4.** to obtain —**se·cure′ly** *adv.*

se·cu·ri·ty (si kyoor′ə tē) *n., pl.* **-ties 1.** a feeling of being free from fear, anxiety, danger, doubt, etc. **2.** protection or defense, as against attack, espionage, etc. [*national security*] **3.** something given as a pledge of repayment, etc. **4.** a stock certificate or bond: *usually used in pl.*

Security Council the UN council responsible for maintaining international peace and security

secy., sec′y. secretary

se·dan (si dan′) *n.* [< ?] a closed car with two or four doors and front and rear seats

sedan chair an enclosed chair for one person, carried on poles by two men

se·date′ (si dāt′) *adj.* [< L. *sedare*, to settle] **1.** calm; composed **2.** serious; dignified —**se·date′ly** *adv.* —**se·date′ness** *n.*

se·date² (si dāt′) *vt.* **-dat′ed, -dat′ing** to dose with a sedative

se·da′tion (-dā′shən) *n.* **1.** reduction of nervousness, esp. by sedatives **2.** the calmness induced

sed·a·tive (sed′ə tiv) *adj.* [see SEDATE¹] tending to soothe or quiet; lessening excitement, irritation, etc. —*n.* a sedative medicine

SEDAN CHAIR

sed·en·tar·y (sed′′n ter′ē) *adj.* [< Fr. < L. *sedere*, sit] involving much sitting [a *sedentary* job]

Se·der (sā′dər) *n., pl.* **Se·dar·im** (sə där′im), **Se′ders** [Heb. *sēdher*, service] *Judaism* the feast of Passover

sedge (sej) *n.* [OE. *secg*] any of a family of grasslike plants often found on wet ground or in water

sed·i·ment (sed′ə mənt) *n.* [< Fr. < L. *sedere*, sit] **1.** matter settled to the bottom of a liquid **2.** *Geol.* matter deposited by water or wind —**sed′i·men′ta·ry** (-men′tər ē), **sed′i·men′tal** *adj.*

sed′i·men·ta′tion (-men tā′shən, -mən-) *n.* the depositing of sediment

se·di·tion (si dish′ən) *n.* [< L. *sed-*, apart + *itio*, a going] a stirring up of rebellion against the government —**se·di′tion·ist** *n.* —**se·di′tious** *adj.*

se·duce (si dōōs′, -dyōōs′) *vt.* **-duced′, -duc′ing** [< L. *se-*, apart + *ducere*, to lead] **1.** to tempt to wrongdoing; lead astray **2.** to induce to engage in unlawful sexual intercourse **3.** to entice —**se·duc′er** *n.* —**se·duc′tion** *n.*

se·duc′tive (-duk′tiv) *adj.* tending to seduce; enticing — **se·duc′tive·ly** *adv.* —**se·duc′tive·ness** *n.*

sed·u·lous (sej′ōō ləs) *adj.* [< L. *se-*, apart + *dolus*, trickery] working hard and steadily; diligent —**se·du·li·ty** (si dyōōl′ə tē, -dōōl′-), **sed′u·lous·ness** *n.* —**sed′u·lous·ly** *adv.*

see¹ (sē) *vt.* **saw, seen, see′ing** [OE. *seon*] **1.** *a)* to get knowledge of through the eyes; look at *b)* to picture mentally **2.** to grasp mentally; understand **3.** to find out; learn [*see* who's there] **4.** to know by experience [to *see* war service] **5.** to make sure [*see* that he goes] **6.** *a)* to escort [I'll *see* you home] *b)* to keep company with **7.** to encounter; meet **8.** to visit or consult **9.** to receive [too busy to *see* anyone] **10.** to be a spectator at; view or attend **11.** *Card Games* to meet (a bet) of (another) by staking an equal sum —*vi.* **1.** to have the power of sight **2.** to discern things with the eyes **3.** to take a look **4.** to understand **5.** to think; reflect [let's *see*, where is it?] —*interj.* look! —**see about 1.** to inquire into **2.** to attend to —**see after** to take care of —**see into** to perceive the true meaning or nature of —**see through 1.** to see into **2.** to finish **3.** to help through difficulty —**see to** to attend to

see² (sē) *n.* [< L. *sedes*, a seat] the official seat, or center of authority, of a bishop

seed (sēd) *n., pl.* **seeds, seed** [OE. *sæd*] **1.** the plant part containing the embryo of a new plant **2.** seeds collectively **3.** an origin; source **4.** ancestry or posterity **5.** sperm or semen —*vt.* **1.** to plant as with seed **2.** to remove seeds from **3.** to distribute (tournament contestants) so as to avoid matching the best too early —*vi.* **1.** to produce seed **2.** to sow seed —**to go** (or **run**) **to seed 1.** to shed seed **2.** to deteriorate

seed'bed' *n.* a bed of soil in which seedlings are grown for transplanting

seed'ling (-liŋ) *n.* **1.** a plant grown from a seed **2.** any young plant, esp. a young tree

seed money money to begin a long-term project or get more funds for it

seed'y *adj.* **-i·er, -i·est 1.** full of seed **2.** gone to seed **3.** shabby, run-down, etc. —**seed'i·ness** *n.*

see·ing (sē'iŋ) *n.* the power or use of sight; vision —*conj.* in view of the fact; inasmuch as

seek (sēk) *vt.* **sought, seek'ing** [OE. *secan*] **1.** to try to find; look for **2.** to try for; aim at **3.** to attempt [to *seek* to please] —*vi.* to look for someone or something

seem (sēm) *vi.* [prob. < ON. *sæma*, conform to] **1.** *a)* to appear to be [to *seem* glad] *b)* to appear [he *seems* to know] *c)* to have the impression [I *seem* to have lost it] **2.** to appear to exist [there *seems* no end] **3.** to appear true [it *seems* I did it]

seem'ing *adj.* that seems real, true, etc.; apparent

seem'ly *adj.* **-li·er, -li·est 1.** pleasing to the eye **2.** proper, fitting, etc. —**seem'li·ness** *n.*

seen (sēn) *pp.* of SEE¹

seep (sēp) *vi.* [OE. *sipian*, to soak] to leak; ooze —*n.* a seeping —**seep'age** (-ij) *n.*

seer (sē'ər *for 1;* sir *for 2*) *n.* **1.** one that sees **2.** one supposedly able to foretell the future

seer·suck·er (sir'suk'ər) *n.* [< Hindi < Per. *shir u shakar*, lit., milk and sugar] a crinkled fabric of linen, cotton, etc.

see·saw (sē'sô') *n.* [redupl. of SAW¹] **1.** a plank balanced at the middle and ridden by children for fun, one plank end going up when the other goes down **2.** any up-and-down or back-and-forth movement —*adj.* moving like a seesaw —*vt., vi.* to ride or move as on a seesaw

seethe (sēth) *vi.* **seethed, seeth'ing** [OE. *sēothan*] **1.** to boil **2.** to surge, be agitated, etc. as if boiling

seg·ment (seg'mənt) *n.* [< L. *secare*, to cut] **1.** any of the parts into which something is separated; section **2.** *Geom.* a part cut off by a line or plane —*vt., vi.* (-ment) to divide into segments —**seg'men·ta'tion** *n.*

seg·re·gate (seg'rə gāt') *vt.* **-gat'ed, -gat'ing** [< L. *se-*, apart + *grex*, a flock'] to set apart from others; specif., to impose racial segregation on

seg're·ga'tion *n.* the policy of compelling racial groups to live apart and use separate schools, facilities, etc. —**seg're·ga'tion·ist** *n., adj.*

se·gue (seg'wā, sā'gwä) *vi.* **-gued, -gue·ing** [It. < L. *sequi*, follow] to continue without break (*to* or *into*) what follows, as in music —*n.* a segueing

Seine (sān; *Fr.* sen) river in N France, flowing through Paris into the English Channel

seine (sān) *n.* [< Gr. *sagēnē*] a large fishing net with floats along the top edge and weights along the bottom —*vt., vi.* seined, sein'ing to fish with a seine

seis·mic (sīz'mik) *adj.* [< Gr. *seiein*, to shake] of, like, or from an earthquake —**seis'mi·cal·ly** *adv.*

seis'mo·gram' (-mə gram') *n.* a seismograph chart

seis'mo·graph' (-graf') *n.* an instrument that records the intensity and duration of earthquakes —**seis·mog'ra·pher** (-mäg'rə fər) *n.* —**seis'mo·graph'ic** *adj.*

seis·mol·o·gy (-mäl'ə jē) *n.* the study of earthquakes —**seis'mo·log'i·cal** (-mə läj'i k'l) *adj.* —**seis·mol'o·gist** *n.*

seize (sēz) *vt.* **seized, seiz'ing** [< ML. *sacire*] **1.** *a)* to take forcible legal possession of **b)** to capture and

put into custody; apprehend **2.** to take hold of forcibly, suddenly, or quickly, as with the hand; grab **3.** to take hold of mentally, esp. in a sudden or intuitive way **4.** to attack or afflict suddenly or severely [he was *seized* with pain] —**seize on** (or **upon**) to grab or turn to (an idea, opportunity, etc.) in a sudden or eager way —**sei·zure** (sē'zhər) *n.*

sel·dom (sel'dəm) *adv.* [OE. *seldan*, rare] not often

se·lect (sə lekt') *adj.* [< L. *se-*, apart + *legere*, choose] **1.** chosen in preference to others **2.** choice; excellent **3.** careful in choosing; fastidious **4.** not open to all; exclusive —*vt., vi.* to choose —**se·lect'ness** *n.* —**se·lec'tor** *n.*

se·lec·tion (sə lek'shən) *n.* **1.** a selecting or being selected **2.** that or those selected **3.** a variety from which to choose

se·lec'tive (-lek'tiv) *adj.* **1.** of or involving selection **2.** that selects, as for excellence **3.** *Radio* excluding unwanted frequencies —**se·lec'tive·ly** *adv.* —**se·lec'tiv'i·ty** *n.*

selective service compulsory military training and service according to age, physical fitness, etc.

se·lect'man (-mən) *n., pl.* **-men** one of a board of governing officers in most New England towns

se·le·ni·um (sə lē'nē əm) *n.* [< Gr. *selēnē*, the moon] a gray nonmetallic chemical element: used as in photoelectric devices: symbol, Se; at. wt., 78.96; at. no., 34

self (self) *n., pl.* **selves** [OE.] **1.** the identity, character, or essential qualities of a person or thing **2.** one's own person as distinct from all other persons **3.** one's own welfare or advantage —*pron.* [Colloq.] myself, himself, herself, or yourself —*adj.* **1.** being the same throughout; uniform **2.** of the same kind, color, etc. as the rest

self- *a prefix meaning* of, by, in, to, with, or for oneself or itself The following list includes some common compounds formed with *self-* that do not have special meanings:

self-abasement	self-indulgence
self-abnegation	self-inflicted
self-advancement	self-justification
self-appointed	self-knowledge
self-deception	self-love
self-delusion	self moving
self-discipline	self-perpetuating
self-examination	self-pity
self-help	self-protection
self-imposed	self-questioning
self-improvement	self-regulating
self-incrimination	self-reproach

self'-ad·dressed' *adj.* addressed to oneself

self'-as·ser'tion *n.* the act of demanding recognition for oneself or of insisting upon one's rights, claims, etc. —**self'-as·ser'tive** *adj.*

self'-as·sur'ance *n.* confidence in oneself; self-confidence —**self'-as·sured'** *adj.*

self'-cen'tered *adj.* occupied or concerned only with one's own affairs; egocentric; selfish

self'-con·ceit' *n.* too high an opinion of oneself; conceit; vanity —**self'-con·ceit'ed** *adj.*

self'-con'fi·dence *n.* confidence in oneself, one's own ability, etc. —**self'-con'fi·dent** *adj.*

self'-con'scious *adj.* **1.** unduly conscious of oneself as an object of notice; ill at ease **2.** showing embarrassment [a *self-conscious* laugh] —**self'-con'scious·ness** *n.*

self'-con·tained' *adj.* **1.** keeping one's affairs to oneself; reserved **2.** showing self-control **3.** having within oneself or itself all that is needed

self'-con'tra·dic'tion *n.* **1.** contradiction of oneself or itself **2.** a statement or idea with contradictory elements —**self'-con'tra·dic'to·ry** *adj.*

self'-con·trol' *n.* control of one's own emotions, desires, actions, etc. —**self'-con·trolled'** *adj.*

self'-de·feat'ing *adj.* that unknowingly defeats one's or its own purposes or interests

self'-de·fense' *n.* defense of oneself or of one's rights, beliefs, etc. —**self'-de·fen'sive** *adj.*

self'-de·ni'al *n.* denial or sacrifice of one's own desires or pleasures —**self'-de·ny'ing** *adj.*

self'-de·struct' *vt., vi.* same as DESTRUCT

self'-de·struc'tion *n.* destruction of oneself or itself; specif., suicide —**self'-de·struc'tive** *adj.*

self'-de·ter'mi·na'tion *n.* **1.** determination according to one's own mind; free will **2.** the right of a people to choose its own form of government, without outside influence

self'-ed'u·cat'ed *adj.* educated by oneself, with little or no formal schooling

self'-ef·face'ment *n.* modest, retiring behavior —**self'-ef·fac'ing** *adj.*

self'-em·ployed' *adj.* working for oneself, with direct control over work, fees, etc.

self'-es·teem' *n.* 1. belief in oneself; self-respect 2. undue pride in oneself; conceit

self'-ev'i·dent *adj.* evident without need of proof or explanation

self'-ex·plan'a·to'ry *adj.* explaining itself; obvious without explanation

self'-ex·pres'sion *n.* expression of one's own personality, as in art —**self'-ex·pres'sive** *adj.*

self'-ful·fill'ing *adj.* 1. bringing about fulfillment, through one's own efforts, of one's aspirations 2. fulfilled chiefly as an effect of having been expected or predicted —**self'-ful·fill'ment** *n.*

self'-gov'ern·ment *n.* government of a group by its own members —**self'-gov'ern·ing** *adj.*

self'-im'age *n.* one's concept of oneself and one's identity, abilities, worth, etc.

self'-im·por'tant *adj.* having or showing an exaggerated opinion of one's own importance; pompous or officious —**self'-im·por'tance** *n.*

self'-in'ter·est *n.* 1. one's own interest or advantage 2. exaggerated regard for this

self'ish *adj.* overly concerned with one's own interests, etc. and having little concern for others —**self'ish·ly** *adv.* —**self'ish·ness** *n.*

self'less *adj.* devoted to others' welfare; unselfish —**self'less·ly** *adv.* —**self'less·ness** *n.*

self'-made' *adj.* 1. made by oneself or itself 2. successful, rich, etc. through one's own efforts

self'-med'i·cate' *vi.* -**cat'ed,** -**cat'ing** to treat oneself with medicine without consulting a doctor

self'-o·pin'ion·at'ed *adj.* 1. holding obstinately to one's own opinions; opinionated 2. conceited

self'-por'trait *n.* a painting, drawing, etc. of oneself, done by oneself

self'-pos·ses'sion *n.* full control of one's feelings, actions, etc.; composure —**self'-pos·sessed'** *adj.*

self'-pres'er·va'tion *n.* preservation of oneself from danger, injury, or death

self'-re·li'ance *n.* reliance on one's own abilities, judgment, etc. —**self'-re·li'ant** *adj.*

self'-re·spect' *n.* proper respect for oneself, one's worth, etc. —**self'-re·spect'ing** *adj.*

self'-re·straint' *n.* restraint imposed on oneself by oneself —**self'-re·strained'** *adj.*

self'-right'eous *adj.* filled with or showing smug conviction of one's own righteousness

self'-ris'ing *adj.* rising by itself: said specif. of flour with a leavening agent blended in

self'-sac'ri·fice' *n.* sacrifice of oneself or of one's own interests for the benefit of others —**self'-sac'ri·fic'ing** *adj.*

self'same' *adj.* (the) very same; identical

self'-sat'is·fied' *adj.* filled with or showing satisfaction with oneself —**self'-sat'is·fac'tion** *n.*

self'-sat'is·fy'ing *adj.* satisfying to oneself

self'-seek'er *n.* a person seeking only or mainly to further his own interests —**self'-seek'ing** *n., adj.*

self'-serv'ice *n.* the practice of serving oneself, as in a store, and then paying a cashier

self'-serv'ing *adj.* serving one's own interests

self'-start'er *n.* 1. an electric motor automatically starting an internal-combustion engine 2. [Colloq.] a person with initiative

self'-styled' *adj.* so named by oneself

self'-suf·fi'cient *adj.* getting along without help; independent —**self'-suf·fi'cien·cy** *n.*

self'-taught' *adj.* having taught oneself

self'-willed' *adj.* marked by stubborn insistence on having one's own way; headstrong; willful

self'-wind'ing *adj.* winding itself automatically

sell (sel) *vt.* **sold, sell'ing** [OE. *sellan,* give] 1. to exchange (goods or services) for money or its equivalent 2. *a)* to offer for sale *b)* to make or aim at sales in or to [to *sell* chain stores] 3. to betray as for money 4. to promote the sale of 5. [Colloq.] to win approval from or for [*sell* him on the idea] —*vi.* 1. to engage in selling 2. to attract buyers 3. to be sold (*for* or *at*) —**sell out** 1. to dispose of completely by selling 2. [Colloq.] to betray (someone, one's trust, etc.) —**sell short** 1. to sell (securities, etc. not yet owned), expecting to cover later at a lower price 2. to value at less than the real worth; make too little of; underestimate —**sell'er** *n.*

sell'out' *n.* [Colloq.] 1. a selling out 2. a show, game, etc. for which all seats have been sold

Selt·zer (water) (selt'sər) [< *Niederselters,* village in Germany] 1. an effervescent natural mineral water 2. [*often* s-] any similar carbonated water

sel·vage, sel·vedge (sel'vij) *n.* [< SELF + EDGE] 1. an edge woven to keep cloth from raveling 2. any special edge of fabric or paper

selves (selvz) *n. pl. of* SELF

se·man·tics (sə man'tiks) *n.pl.* [*with sing. v.*] [< Fr. < Gr. *sēma,* a sign] 1. the study of the development and changes of the meanings of words and other signs or symbols 2. the relationships between words, signs, etc. and the ideas, feelings, etc. associated with them —**se·man'tic** *adj.* —**se·man'ti·cal·ly** *adv.* —**se·man'ti·cist** (-tə sist) *n.*

sem·a·phore (sem'ə fôr') *n.* [< Fr. < Gr. *sēma,* a sign + *pherein,* to bear] 1. a visual signaling apparatus, as of lights, flags, or mechanical arms on railroads 2. the system used, as the holding of two flags in various positions to represent alphabetical letters

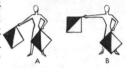
SEMAPHORE
(signals for letters A & B)

sem·blance (sem'bləns) *n.* [< L. *similis,* like] 1. outward appearance 2. resemblance 3. a copy, representation, etc. 4. false or deceiving appearance 5. empty show; pretense

se·men (sē'mən) *n.* [L., a seed] the fluid secreted by the male reproductive organs, containing the spermatozoa

se·mes·ter (sə mes'tər) *n.* [G. < L. *sex,* six + *mensis,* month] either of the two terms in a school year

sem·i (sem'ī) *n., pl.* -**is** *clipped form of* SEMITRAILER (sense 2)

semi- [L.] *a prefix meaning:* 1. half 2. partly 3. twice in a (specified period) [*semiannually*]

sem·i·an·nu·al (sem'ē an'yoo wəl; sem'i-, sem'ī-) *adj.* 1. happening, done, etc. every half year 2. lasting only half a year, as some plants —**sem'i·an'nu·al·ly** *adv.*

sem·i·cir·cle (sem'i sur'k'l) *n.* a half circle —**sem'i·cir'cu·lar** (-kyə lər) *adj.*

semicircular canal any of the three loop-shaped, tubular structures of the inner ear that serve to maintain balance in the organism

sem·i·co·lon (sem'i kō'lən) *n.* a mark of punctuation (;) to show separation greater than that marked by the comma and less than that marked by the period

sem'i·con·duc'tor *n.* a substance with a poor conductivity that can be improved by adding certain substances or by applying heat, light, or voltage

sem'i·con'scious *adj.* only partly conscious

sem·i·fi·nal (sem'i fī'n'l, sem'ī-) *adj.* coming just before the final match, as of a tournament —*n.* (sem'i fī'-) 1. a semifinal match 2. [*pl.*] a semifinal round

sem'i·month'ly *adj.* appearing, done, etc. twice a month —*n., pl.* -**lies** something appearing, etc. twice a month, as a magazine —*adv.* twice monthly

sem·i·nal (sem'ə n'l) *adj.* [see SEMEN] 1. of or containing seed or semen 2. of reproduction 3. being a source; capable of development

sem·i·nar (sem'ə när') *n.* [see ff.] 1. a group of supervised students doing advanced study 2. the study itself

sem·i·nar·y (sem'ə ner'ē) *n., pl.* -**ies** [< L. *seminarium,* seed plot] 1. a school, esp. a private school for young women: an old-fashioned term 2. a school for training priests, ministers, or rabbis —**sem'i·nar'i·an** *n.*

Sem·i·nole (sem'ə nōl') *n., pl.* -**noles',** -**nole'** any member of an American Indian people of S Florida and Oklahoma

sem·i·pre·cious (sem'i presh'əs) *adj.* designating gems, as garnets or opals, of lower value than precious gems

sem'i·pri'vate *adj.* private to some extent; specif., designating or of a hospital room with two, three, or sometimes four beds

sem'i·pro·fes'sion·al *adj.* not fully professional; specif. *a)* engaging in a sport for pay but not as a regular occupation *b)* engaged in by semiprofessional players —*n.* a semiprofessional player Also [Colloq.] **sem'i·pro'**

Sem·ite (sem'īt) *n.* [prob. < Fr. *Sémite:* see SEMITIC] a member of any people speaking a Semitic language

Se·mit·ic (sə mit'ik) *adj.* [< G. *semitisch* < Heb.] 1. of or like the Semites 2. designating or of a group of related languages of SW Asia and N Africa that includes Hebrew and Arabic

sem·i·tone (sem'i tōn') *n. Music* the difference in pitch between any two immediately adjacent keys on the piano

sem·i·trail·er (sem'i trā'lər, sem'ī-) *n.* **1.** a trailer partly supported by the rear of a tractor (sense 2), being attached to the tractor by a coupling **2.** a truck made up of such a trailer and tractor; semi

sem·i·trop'i·cal *adj.* partly tropical

sem'i·week'ly *adj.* appearing, done, etc. twice a week — *n., pl.* **-lies** something appearing, etc. twice a week, as a publication —*adv.* twice weekly

sem'i·year'ly *adj.* appearing, done, etc. twice a year —*n., pl.* **-lies** something appearing, etc. twice a year, as a publication —*adv.* twice yearly

sem·o·li·na (sem'ə lē'nə) *n.* [< It. < L. *simila,* finest wheat flour] particles of coarsely ground durum, used as in making macaroni

Sen., sen. 1. senate **2.** senator **3.** senior

sen·ate (sen'it) *n.* [< L. *senex,* old] **1.** the supreme council of the ancient Roman state **2.** a lawmaking assembly **3.** [S-] the upper branch of the U.S. legislature or of most U.S. State legislatures

sen·a·tor (sen'ə tər) *n.* a member of a senate —**sen'a·to'ri·al** (-tôr'ē əl) *adj.*

send (send) *vt.* **sent, send'ing** [OE. *sendan*] **1.** to cause to go or be carried; dispatch **2.** to impel; drive **3.** to make happen, come, etc. **4.** [Slang] to excite; thrill —*vi.* to send a message, messenger, etc. —**send for 1.** to summon **2.** to place an order for —**send'er** *n.*

send'-off' *n.* [Colloq.] **1.** a display of friendship or affection for someone starting out as on a trip **2.** the act of getting someone or something started

Sen·e·ca[1] (sen'i kə) *n., pl.* **-cas, -ca** any member of an American Indian people of New York and Ontario

Sen·e·ca[2] (sen'i kə) (*Lucius Annaeus Seneca*) 4? B.C.–65 A.D.; Rom. philosopher, dramatist, & statesman

Sen·e·gal (sen'i gôl') country in W Africa, on the Atlantic: 76,124 sq. mi.; pop. 3,780,000; cap. Dakar —**Sen'e·ga·lese'** (-gə lēz') *adj., n., pl.* **-lese'**

sen·es·chal (sen'ə shəl) *n.* [< Frank. *siniskalk*] a steward in a medieval household

se·nile (sē'nīl) *adj.* [< L. *senex,* old] **1.** of old age **2.** showing signs of old age, such as an impaired memory —**se·nil·i·ty** (si nil'ə tē) *n.*

sen·ior (sēn'yər) *adj.* [L. < *senex,* old] **1.** older: written *Sr.* after a father's name if his son's name is the same **2.** of higher rank or longer service **3.** of or for seniors —*n.* **1.** one who is older, of higher rank, etc. **2.** a student in the last year of a high school or college

senior citizen an elderly person, esp. one who is retired

senior high school high school (usually grades 10, 11, & 12)

sen·ior·i·ty (sēn yôr'ə tē) *n., pl.* **-ties 1.** a being senior in age, rank, etc. **2.** status, priority, etc. achieved by length of service in a given job

sen·na (sen'ə) *n.* [< Ar. *sanā*] **1.** any of certain cassias **2.** their dried leaves, used as a laxative

Sen·nach·er·ib (sə nak'ər ib) ?–681 B.C.; king of Assyria (705–681)

‡se·ñor (se nyôr') *n., pl.* **-ño'res** (-nyô'res) [Sp.] a man; gentleman: as a title [S-], equivalent to *Mr.* or *Sir*

‡se·ño·ra (se nyô'rä) *n., pl.* **-ras** (-räs) [Sp.] a married woman; lady: as a title [S-], equivalent to *Mrs.* or *Madam*

‡se·ño·ri·ta (se'nyô rē'tä) *n., pl.* **-tas** (-täs) [Sp.] an unmarried woman or girl; young lady: as a title [S-], equivalent to *Miss*

sen·sa·tion (sen sā'shən) *n.* [< L. *sensus,* sense] **1.** the receiving of sense impressions through hearing, seeing, etc. **2.** a conscious feeling or sense impression, as of cold **3.** a generalized feeling or reaction, as of joy **4.** *a)* a reaction of general excitement *b)* the cause of this

sen·sa'tion·al *adj.* **1.** intensely interesting or exciting **2.** intended to excite, thrill, startle, etc. **3.** [Colloq.] exceptionally fine, good, etc. —**sen·sa'tion·al·ize'** *vt.* **-ized', -iz'ing** —**sen·sa'tion·al·ly** *adv.*

sen·sa'tion·al·ism *n.* **1.** use of or preoccupation with what is intended to excite, thrill, startle, etc. **2.** *Philos.* the belief that all knowledge is acquired through the senses —**sen·sa'tion·al·ist** *n.*

sense (sens) *n.* [< Fr. < L. *sentire,* to feel] **1.** any faculty of receiving impressions through body organs; specif., sight, hearing, taste, smell, or touch **2.** *a)* perception through such faculties *b)* a generalized feeling or reaction; sensation **3.** a certain awareness and judgmental ability [a *sense* of direction] **4.** an ability to feel, appreciate, or understand some quality [a *sense* of humor] **5.** *a)* sound

thinking and judgment *b)* what reflects or agrees with this [talk *sense*] **6.** [*pl.*] normal ability to reason soundly [to come to one's *senses*] **7.** meaning, as of a word —*vt.* **sensed, sens'ing 1.** to perceive, feel, or become aware of **2.** to understand **3.** to detect, as by sensors —**in a sense** to some extent or in a certain way —**make sense** to be intelligible or logical —**make sense of** to understand

sense'less *adj.* **1.** unconscious **2.** stupid; foolish **3.** having no real point or purpose; nonsensical

sense organ a specialized organ, as an eye, receiving stimuli and transmitting the nerve impulses to the brain

sen·si·bil·i·ty (sen'sə bil'ə tē) *n., pl.* **-ties** [see SENSE] **1.** the capacity for physical sensation **2.** [*often pl.*] the capacity for responding or being affected emotionally, intellectually, morally, or aesthetically

sen·si·ble (sen'sə b'l) *adj.* [see SENSE] **1.** that can cause physical sensation **2.** easily perceived **3.** capable of receiving sensation **4.** emotionally responsive or aware **5.** having or showing good sense; wise —**sen'si·bly** *adv.*

sen·si·tive (sen'sə tiv) *adj.* [see SENSE] **1.** sensory **2.** keenly susceptible to stimuli **3.** easily hurt; tender **4.** highly responsive intellectually, emotionally, etc. **5.** easily offended, shocked, etc. **6.** readily affected as by light **7.** involving secret or delicate governmental matters —**sen'si·tive·ly** *adv.* —**sen'si·tiv'i·ty, sen'si·tive·ness** *n.*

sen'si·tize' (-tīz') *vt.* **-tized', -tiz'ing** to make sensitive, as to light —**sen'si·tiz'er** *n.*

sen·sor (sen'sər, -sôr) *n.* [see SENSE] a device designed to detect, measure, or record physical phenomena and to respond in various ways

sen·so·ry (sen'sər ē) *adj.* of the senses or sensation

sen·su·al (sen'shoo wəl) *adj.* [see SENSE] **1.** of the body and the senses as distinguished from the intellect or spirit **2.** *a)* connected or preoccupied with bodily or sexual pleasures *b)* lustful; lewd —**sen'su·al'i·ty** (-wal'ə tē) *n.* —**sen'su·al·ly** *adv.*

sen'su·al·ism (-iz'm) *n.* **1.** excessive indulgence in sensual pleasures **2.** the belief that sensual pleasures constitute the greatest good —**sen'su·al·ist** *n.*

sen·su·ous (sen'shoo wəs) *adj.* **1.** of, from, or appealing to the senses **2.** enjoying or readily affected by sense impressions —**sen'su·ous·ly** *adv.*

sent (sent) *pt. & pp.* of SEND

sen·tence (sen't'ns) *n.* [< L. *sententia,* opinion] **1.** *a)* a decision, as of a court; esp., the determination by a court of a punishment *b)* the punishment **2.** *Gram.* a word or group of words expressing a statement, question, etc. and usually containing a subject and predicate —*vt.* **-tenced, -tenc·ing** to pronounce punishment upon

sen·ten·tious (sen ten'shəs) *adj.* [see prec.] **1.** short and pithy **2.** full of, or fond of using, maxims, proverbs, etc.; often, pompously trite

sen·tient (sen'shənt) *adj.* [see SENSE] of or having feeling; conscious —**sen'tience, sen'tien·cy** *n.*

sen·ti·ment (sen'tə mənt) *n.* [see SENSE] **1.** a complex combination of feelings and opinions **2.** an opinion, attitude, etc.: *often used in pl.* **3.** susceptibility to emotional appeal **4.** appeal to the emotions **5.** maudlin emotion; sentimentality **6.** a briefly expressed thought **7.** the underlying idea

sen'ti·men'tal (-men't'l) *adj.* **1.** full of tender, gentle, often mawkish feeling **2.** emotional rather than rational —**sen'ti·men'tal·ism** *n.* —**sen'ti·men'tal·ist** *n.* —**sen'ti·men'tal·ly** *adv.*

sen'ti·men·tal'i·ty (-tal'ə tē) *n.* **1.** a being sentimental **2.** *pl.* **-ties** any expression of this

sen'ti·men'tal·ize (-men'tə līz') *vi., vt.* **-ized', -iz'ing** to be or make sentimental

sen·ti·nel (sen'ti n'l) *n.* [< Fr. < L. *sentire,* to sense] one set to guard a group and warn of danger

sen·try (sen'trē) *n., pl.* **-tries** [< ?] a sentinel; esp., a soldier acting as a sentinel

Seoul (sōl) capital of South Korea: pop. 5,510,000

se·pal (sē'p'l) *n.* [< Fr. < Gr. *skepē,* a covering + L. *petalum,* petal] a leaflike part of a calyx

sep·a·ra·ble (sep'ər ə b'l) *adj.* that can be separated —**sep'a·ra·bil'i·ty** *n.* —**sep'a·ra·bly** *adv.*

sep·a·rate (sep'ə rāt') *vt.* **-rat'ed, -rat'ing** [< L. *se-,* apart + *parare,* arrange] **1.** to set apart into sections, groups, etc.; divide **2.** to keep distinct; distinguish between **3.** to set apart or keep apart **4.** to discharge or dismiss, as from military service —*vi.* **1.** to withdraw or secede **2.** to part, become disconnected, etc. —*adj.* (-ər it) **1.** set apart from the other or others **2.** distinct; individual —*n.* (-ər it) [*pl.*]

articles of dress for wearing together or separately —**sep'·a·rate·ly** *adv.* —**sep'a·ra'tor** *n.*

sep'a·ra'tion (-ə rā'shən) *n.* **1.** a separating or being separated **2.** the place where this occurs; break; division **3.** an arrangement by which a man and wife live apart by agreement or court decree

sep'a·ra·tism (-ər ə tiz'm) *n.* the advocacy of political, religious, or racial separation —**sep'a·ra·tist** *n.*

se·pi·a (sē'pē ə) *n., adj.* [< Gr., cuttlefish] (of) dark reddish brown

sep·sis (sep'sis) *n.* [< Gr. *sēpein*, make putrid] poisoning caused by absorption of certain microorganisms and their products into the blood

Sep·tem·ber (sep tem'bər) *n.* [< L. *septem*, seven: seventh month in ancient Rom. calendar] the ninth month of the year, having 30 days: abbrev. **Sept.**

sep·tet, sep·tette (sep tet') *n.* [< L. *septem*, seven] **1.** a group of seven **2.** *Music a)* a composition for seven voices or instruments *b)* the seven performers of this

sep·tic (sep'tik) *adj.* [see SEPSIS] causing, or resulting from, sepsis or putrefaction —**sep'ti·cal·ly** *adv.*

sep·ti·ce·mi·a (sep'tə sē'mē ə) *n.* [< Gr. *sēptikos*, putrefactive + *haima*, blood] a systemic disease caused by the presence of certain microorganisms and their products in the blood

septic tank an underground tank in which waste matter is putrefied and decomposed by bacteria

sep·tu·a·ge·nar·i·an (sep'too wə ji ner'ē ən) *adj.* [< L. *septuaginta*, seventy] seventy years old, or between the ages of seventy and eighty —*n.* a person of this age

Sep·tu·a·gint (sep'too wə jint) *n.* [< L. *septuaginta*, seventy: in tradition, done in 70 or 72 days] a Greek translation of the Hebrew Scriptures done in the 3d cent. B.C.

sep·tum (sep'təm) *n., pl.* -**tums,** -**ta** (-tə) [< L. *saepes*, a hedge] *Biol.* a partition between two cavities or parts, as within the nose

sep·ul·cher (sep''l kər) *n.* [< L. *sepelire*, bury] a vault for burial; grave; tomb Brit. sp. **sep'ul·chre**

se·pul·chral (sə pul'krəl) *adj.* **1.** of sepulchers, burial, etc. **2.** suggestive of the grave or burial; dismal; gloomy **3.** deep and melancholy: said of sound —**se·pul'chral·ly** *adv.*

seq. [L. *sequentes* or *sequentia*] the following

se·quel (sē'kwəl) *n.* [< L. *sequi*, follow] **1.** something that follows; continuation **2.** a result or consequence **3.** a literary work continuing an earlier work but complete in itself

se·quence (sē'kwəns) *n.* [see prec.] **1.** *a)* the coming of one thing after another; succession **4.** the order of this **2.** a series **3.** a result or consequence **4.** *Motion Pictures* a succession of shots forming one uninterrupted episode

se·quen·tial (si kwen'shəl) *adj.* **1.** subsequent or consequent **2.** involving a sequence of parts

se·ques·ter (si kwes'tər) *vt.* [< LL. *sequestrare*, to remove] **1.** to set apart; separate **2.** to take possession of (property) as security for a debt, claim, etc. **3.** to confiscate **4.** to seclude —**se·ques·tra·tion** (sē'kwes trā'shən) *n.*

se·quin (sē'kwin) *n.* [Fr. < It. < Ar. *sikkah*, a stamp] a small, shiny spangle, as a metal disk, esp. one of many sewn on fabric for decoration

se·quoi·a (si kwoi'ə) *n.* [< *Sequoya*, AmInd. inventor (c.1760–1843) of Cherokee writing] a giant evergreen tree, either of two species of the W U.S.

se·rag·lio (si ral'yō, -rāl'-) *n., pl.* -**lios** [< It. < L. *sera*, a lock] *same as* HAREM (sense 1)

se·ra·pe (sə rä'pē) *n.* [MexSp.] a woolen blanket worn as an outer garment by men in Spanish-American countries

ser·aph (ser'əf) *n., pl.* -**aphs,** -**a·phim** (-ə fim') [< Heb.] **1.** *Bible* a heavenly being at the throne of God **2.** *Christian Theol.* one of the highest orders of angels —**se·raph·ic** (sə raf'ik) *adj.* —**se·raph'i·cal·ly** *adv.*

Serb (surb) *n.* **1.** a native or inhabitant of Serbia **2.** *same as* SERBIAN (*n.* 1) —*adj. same as* SERBIAN

Ser·bi·a (sur'bē ə) republic of Yugoslavia, in the E part

Ser'bi·an (-ən) *adj.* of Serbia, the Serbs, or their language —*n.* **1.** Serbo-Croatian as spoken and written in Serbia **2.** *same as* SERB (*n.* 1)

Ser·bo-Cro·a·tian (sur'bō krō ā'shən) *n.* the major Slavic language of Yugoslavia —*adj.* of this language or the people who speak it

sere (sir) *adj.* [var. of SEAR] [Poet.] withered

ser·e·nade (ser'ə nād') *n.* [< Fr. < It. < L. *serenus*, serene] **1.** a playing or singing of music outdoors at night, esp. by a lover under his sweetheart's window **2.** a piece of music suitable for this —*vt., vi.* -**nad'ed,** -**nad'ing** to play or sing a serenade (to)

ser·en·dip·i·ty (ser'ən dip'ə tē) *n.* [< a Per. tale, *The Three Princes of Serendip*] a seeming gift for finding good things accidentally —**ser'en·dip'i·tous** *adj.*

se·rene (sə rēn') *adj.* [L. *serenus*] **1.** clear; unclouded **2.** undisturbed; calm, peaceful, etc. —**se·rene'ly** *adv.* —**se·ren'i·ty** (-ren'ə tē) *n.*

serf (surf) *n.* [< L. *servus*, a slave] a person in feudal servitude, bound to his master's land and transferred with it to a new owner —**serf'dom** *n.*

Serg., serg. sergeant

serge (surj) *n.* [< L. *sericus*, silken] a strong twilled fabric used as for suits and coats

ser·geant (sär'jənt) *n.* [< L. *servire*, to serve] **1.** *same as* SERGEANT-AT-ARMS **2.** any of certain noncommissioned officers in the U.S. armed forces; specif., such an officer of the fifth grade, ranking just above a corporal in the U.S. Army and Marine Corps **3.** a police officer ranking next below a captain or lieutenant —**ser'gean·cy,** *pl.* -**cies, ser'geant·ship'** *n.*

ser'geant-at-arms' *n., pl.* **ser'geants-at-arms'** an officer appointed to keep order as in a court

sergeant first class *U.S. Army* the seventh grade of enlisted man, ranking just below master sergeant

sergeant major *pl.* **sergeants major** *U.S. Army & Marine Corps* the highest ranking noncommissioned officer

Sergt., sergt. sergeant

se·ri·al (sir'ē əl) *adj.* [< L. *series*, series] of or in a series —*n.* a story, movie, etc. issued in successive parts —**se'ri·al·ly** *adv.*

se'ri·al·ize' *vt.* -**ized',** -**iz'ing** to arrange or issue in successive parts —**se'ri·al·i·za'tion** *n.*

serial number one of a series of numbers assigned for identification

se·ries (sir'ēz) *n., pl.* -**ries** [< L. *serere*, join] **1.** a number of similar things or individuals in a row, sequence, or related group **2.** *Elec.* a single-path circuit connection: usually in **in series**

ser·if (ser'if) *n.* [Du. *schreef*, a line] *Printing* a fine line projecting from a main stroke of a letter

se·ri·o·com·ic (sir'ē ō käm'ik) *adj.* partly serious and partly comic —**se'ri·o·com'i·cal·ly** *adv.*

se·ri·ous (sir'ē əs) *adj.* [< L. *serius*] **1.** earnest, grave etc. **2.** not joking; sincere **3.** requiring careful consideration; important **4.** dangerous [a *serious* wound] —**se'ri·ous·ly** *adv.* —**se'ri·ous·ness** *n.*

ser·mon (sur'mən) *n.* [< L. *sermo*] **1.** a speech on religion or morals, esp. by a clergyman **2.** any serious talk on behavior, duty, etc., esp. a tedious one —**ser'mon·ize'** *vi.* -**ized',** -**iz'ing**

Sermon on the Mount the sermon given by Jesus to his disciples: Matt. 5–7, Luke 6:20–49

se·rous (sir'əs) *adj.* **1.** of or containing serum **2.** like serum; thin and watery

ser·pent (sur'pənt) *n.* [< L. *serpere*, to creep] **1.** a snake **2.** a sly, treacherous person

ser'pen·tine' (-pən tēn', -tīn') *adj.* of or like a serpent; esp., *a)* cunning; treacherous *b)* turning often; winding

ser·rate (ser'āt, -it) *adj.* [< L. *serra*, a saw] notched like a saw: also **ser·rat'ed**

ser·ried (ser'ēd) *adj.* [< L. *sera*, a lock] placed close together; compact, as ranks of soldiers

se·rum (sir'əm) *n., pl.* -**rums,** -**ra** (-ə) [L., whey] **1.** any watery animal fluid; esp., the yellowish fluid (**blood serum**) separating from clotted blood **2.** blood serum from an immunized animal, used as an antitoxin

serv·ant (sur'vənt) *n.* [< L. *servus*] **1.** a person hired to work in another's home as a maid, cook, chauffeur, etc. **2.** a government worker: cf. PUBLIC SERVANT **3.** a person devoted to another or to a cause, creed, etc.

serve (surv) *vt.* **served, serv'ing** [< L. *servire*] **1.** to work for as a servant **2.** *a)* to do services for; aid; help *b)* to revere and obey [to *serve* God] **3.** to do military or naval service for **4.** to pass or spend (a term of imprisonment, military service, etc.) **5.** to carry out the duties of (a position, office, etc.) **6.** to provide (customers) with (goods or services) **7.** to set (food or drink) before (someone) **8.** *a)* to meet the needs of *b)* to promote or further [to *serve* a cause] **9.** to function for [if memory *serves* me well] **10.** to treat [you've been ill *served*] **11.** to deliver (a summons, subpoena, etc.) to (someone) **12.** to hit (a tennis ball, handball, etc.) so as to start play —*vi.* **1.** to work as a servant **2.** to do service [he *served* in the navy] **3.** to carry out the duties of an office or position **4.** to be of service; function **5.** to meet needs; suffice **6.** to wait on table **7.** to hit a tennis ball, handball, etc. so as to start play —*n.* the act of serving a tennis ball, handball, etc. also, one's turn for this —**serve (someone) right** to b what (someone) deserves —**serv'er** *n.*

serv·ice (sur'vis) *n.* [< L. *servus*, a slave] **1.** the occupa tion or condition of a servant **2.** *a)* employment, esp. pub lic employment *b*) a branch of this; specif., the armed forces **3**. work done or duty performed for others **4**. a religious ceremony; esp., public worship **5**. *a*) helpful or useful action *b*) benefit; advantage *c*) [*pl.*] friendly help; also, professional aid **6**. *a*) the serving of food or drink *b*) the articles used **7**. a system or method of providing people with some utility, as water or gas **8**. the serve, as in tennis **9**. *Law* notification of legal action, as by delivery of a writ —*adj.* of or for service or servants —*vt.* -iced, -icing **1**. to furnish with a service; supply **2**. to make fit for service, as by repairing —in (or out of) service in (or not in) use or usable condition —of service helpful; useful

serv′ice·a·ble *adj.* **1**. that is or can be of service; helpful; useful **2**. wearing well; durable —serv′ice·a·bil′i·ty *n.* —serv′ice·a·bly *adv.*

serv′ice·man′ *n., pl.* -men′ **1**. a member of the armed forces **2**. a person whose work is servicing or repairing something: also **service man**

service mark a symbol, word, etc. used by a supplier of services, as transportation, laundry, etc., to distinguish the services from those of competitors: usually registered and protected by law: cf. TRADEMARK

service station a place providing gasoline, oil, parts, maintenance, etc. for motor vehicles

ser·vile (sur′v'l, -vīl) *adj.* [< L. *servus*, a slave] **1**. of a slave **2**. like that of a slave or servant [*servile* work] **3**. like or characteristic of a slave; humbly submissive; cringing; abject —ser′vile·ly *adv.* —ser·vil·i·ty (sər vil′ə tē) *n.*

serv·ing (sur′viŋ) *n.* a single portion of food —*adj.* used for serving food [a *serving* spoon]

ser·vi·tor (sur′və tər) *n.* a servant, attendant, etc.

ser·vi·tude (sur′və tood′, -tyood′) *n.* [see SERVILE] **1**. slavery **2**. work imposed as punishment for crime

ser·vo·mech·a·nism (sur′vō mek′ə niz′m) *n.* [SERVO(MOTOR) + MECHANISM] an automatic control system regularly checking output against input so as to achieve the desired control

ser′vo·mo′tor *n.* [< Fr. < L. *servus*, a slave + *movere*, to move] a device controlled by an amplified signal from a low-power actuator

ses·a·me (ses′ə mē) *n.* [< Gr.] **1**. an East Indian or African plant with flat seeds that yield an edible oil and that are used for flavoring bread, rolls, etc. **2**. the seeds

ses·qui·cen·ten·ni·al (ses′kwi sen ten′ē əl) *adj.* [L. *sesqui-*, more by a half + CENTENNIAL] of a period of 150 years —*n.* a 150th anniversary

ses·sion (sesh′ən) *n.* [< L. *sedere*, sit] **1**. a meeting or series of meetings, as of a legislature or court **2**. a period of study, classes, etc. **3**. a period of any activity —in session meeting

set (set) *vt.* **set**, set′ting [OE. *settan*] **1**. to cause to sit; seat **2**. to put in a specified place, condition, etc. **3**. to put in order; arrange, fix, adjust, etc., as *a*) to put (a trap) into position *b*) to adjust (a clock, dial, etc.) *c*) to arrange (a table) for a meal *d*) to put (a fractured bone) into position for healing *e*) to arrange (hair) in a desired style **4**. to make firm, fixed, settled, etc. [pectin *sets* jelly] **5**. to direct **6**. to appoint, establish, etc. [to *set* limits] **7**. to estimate or value [to *set* all at naught] **8**. *Bridge* to keep (opponents) from achieving a bid **9**. *Music* to fit (words to music or music to words) **10**. *Printing* to arrange (type) for printing or put (copy) into type —*vi.* **1**. to sit on eggs: said of a fowl **2**. to become firm, fixed, etc. [the cement has *set*] **3**. to start moving (with *out, off*, etc.) **4**. to have a certain direction; tend **5**. to seem to descend [the *setting* sun] **6**. to hang in a certain way, as clothes —*adj.* **1**. fixed, established, etc. [a *set* time] **2**. deliberately thought out **3**. immovable; inflexible; rigid **4**. ready [get *set*] —*n.* **1**. a setting or being set **2**. the way a thing is set [the *set* of his jaw] **3**. direction or tendency **4**. something set, as stage scenery **5**. a plant slip or bulb **6**. *a*) the act or a style of arranging hair *b*) the lotion, etc. used: in full hair set **7**. a number of persons or things grouped or classed together **8**. assembled equipment for radio or television reception **9**. *Math.* a prescribed collection of points, numbers, etc. that satisfy a given condition **10**. *Tennis* a group of six or more games won by a margin of at least two —all set [Colloq.] prepared; ready —set about to start doing; begin —set aside **1**. to separate and keep: also set apart **2**. to reject **3**. to annul —set back **1**. to reverse or hinder **2**. [Slang] to cost (a person) a specified sum —set down to put in writing —set forth to present or state —set off **1**. to make prominent by contrast **2**. to make explode —set on (or upon) to attack —set out **1**. to display,

as for sale **2**. to plant **3**. to undertake —set up **1**. to erect **2**. to establish; found

set′back′ *n.* **1**. a reversal in progress **2**. a recessed section, as in the upper part of a wall

Seth (seth) *Bible* the third son of Adam

set′screw′ *n.* a screw going through one part and against or into another to prevent movement

set·tee (se tē′) *n.* [prob. altered < SETTLE[1]] **1**. a seat or bench with a back **2**. a small sofa

set′ter *n.* **1**. one that sets **2**. a long-haired hunting dog trained to find game

set′ting *n.* **1**. the act of one that sets **2**. the position of a dial, etc. that has been set **3**. a mounting, as of a gem **4**. the time, place, etc. of a play or novel **5**. actual physical surroundings **6**. music composed as for a poem

set·tle[1] (set′'l) *n.* [OE. *setl*] a long wooden bench with a back and arms

set·tle[2] (set′'l) *vt.* -tled, -tling [OE. *setlan*] **1**. to put in order; arrange, as one's affairs **2**. to set in place firmly or comfortably **3**. to colonize **4**. to cause to sink and become more compact [rain *settled* the dust] **5**. to clarify (a liquid) by making sediment sink **6**. to free (the mind, nerves, stomach, etc.) from disturbance **7**. to decide (something in doubt) or end (a dispute) **8**. to pay (a bill, debt, etc.) **9**. to make over (property, etc.) to someone by legal action (with *on* or *upon*) —*vi.* **1**. to stop moving and stay in one place **2**. to descend and spread [fog *settled* over the city] **3**. to become localized in a part of the body: said of pain or disease **4**. to take up permanent residence **5**. to sink, esp. gradually [the building is *settling*] **6**. to become denser by sinking, as sediment **7**. to become clearer by the sinking as of sediment **8**. to become more stable **9**. to reach an agreement or decision (with *on, upon*, or *with*) **10**. to pay a bill or debt —settle down **1**. to take up permanent residence, a regular job, etc. **2**. to become less nervous, erratic, etc. **3**. to apply oneself steadily —settle for to resign oneself to accepting (a specified lesser thing) —set′tler *n.*

set·tle·ment *n.* **1**. a settling or being settled **2**. a new colony **3**. a village **4**. an agreement, adjustment, etc. **5**. payment **6**. a community center for the underprivileged: also settlement house

set′-to′ *n., pl.* -tos′ [Colloq.] **1**. a fight, esp. a fist fight **2**. any brisk contest

set′up′ *n.* **1**. the way something is set up; specif., the makeup or arrangement as of an organization **2**. [Colloq.] a contest, etc. arranged as an uneven match to make winning easy

sev·en (sev′'n) *adj., n.* [OE. *seofon*] one more than six; 7; VII —sev′enth (-'nth) *adj., n.*

seven seas all the oceans of the world

sev·en·teen (-tēn′) *adj., n.* seven more than ten; 17; XVII —sev′en·teenth′ (-tēnth′) *adj., n.*

sev′en·teen′-year′ locust a cicada which lives underground for 13–17 years before emerging as an adult

seventh heaven a state of perfect happiness

sev·en·ty (sev′'n tē) *adj., n., pl.* -ties seven times ten; 70; LXX —the seventies the numbers or years, as of a century, from 70 through 79 —sev′en·ti·eth (-ith) *adj., n.*

sev·er (sev′ər) *vi., vi.* [< L. *separare*] to separate, divide, or break off —sev′er·ance *n.*

sev·er·al (sev′ər əl) *adj.* [< L. *separ*] **1**. separate; distinct **2**. different; respective **3**. more than two but not many; few —*n.* [with *pl. v.*] a small number (of) —*pron.* [with *pl. v.*] a few —sev′er·al·ly *adv.*

severance pay extra pay given to an employee dismissed through no fault of his own

se·vere (sə vir′) *adj.* -ver′er, -ver′est [< L. *severus*] **1**. harsh or strict, as in treatment; stern **2**. serious; grave, as in expression **3**. rigidly accurate or demanding **4**. extremely plain [a *severe* style] **5**. keen; intense [severe pain] **6**. difficult; rigorous [a *severe* test] —se·vere′ly *adv.* —se·vere′ness, se·ver′i·ty (-ver′ə tē) *n.*

Se·ville (sə vil′) city in SW Spain: pop. 622,000

sew (sō) *vt., vi.* sewed, sewn (sōn) or sewed, sew′ing [OE. *siwian*] **1**. to join or fasten with stitches made with needle and thread **2**. to make, mend, etc. by sewing —sew up [Colloq.] **1**. to get full control of **2**. to make sure of success in —sew′er *n.*

sew·age (soo′ij, syoo′-) *n.* the waste matter carried off by sewers or drains

sew·er (soo′ər, syoo′-) *n.* [ult. < L. *ex*, out + *aqua*, water] a pipe or drain, usually underground, for carrying off water and waste matter

sew′er·age (-ij) *n.* **1.** removal of surface water and waste matter by sewers **2.** a system of sewers **3.** *same as* SEWAGE

sew·ing (sō′iŋ) *n.* **1.** the act of one who sews **2.** material for sewing

sewing machine a machine with a mechanically driven needle for sewing and stitching

sex (seks) *n.* [< L. *sexus*] **1.** either of the two divisions, male or female, of organisms **2.** the character of being male or female **3.** the attraction of one sex for another **4.** sexual intercourse —*adj.* [Colloq.] *same as* SEXUAL

sex- [< L. *sex*, six] *a combining form meaning* six

sex·a·ge·nar·i·an (sek′sə ji ner′ē ən) *adj.* [< L. *sexageni*, sixty each] sixty years old, or between the ages of sixty and seventy —*n.* a person of this age

sex appeal the physical attractiveness and charm that attracts members of the opposite sex

sex chromosome a sex-determining chromosome in the germ cells: eggs carry an X chromosome and spermatozoa either an X or Y chromosome, with a female resulting from an XX pairing and a male from an XY

sex·ism (sek′siz′m) *n.* the economic exploitation and social domination of one sex by the other, specif. of women by men —**sex′ist** *adj., n.*

sex′less *adj.* **1.** lacking the characteristics of sex; asexual **2.** lacking in normal sexual appetite or appeal —**sex′less·ly** *adv.* —**sex′less·ness** *n.*

sex·ol·o·gy (sek säl′ə jē) *n.* the science dealing with human sexual behavior —**sex·ol′o·gist** *n.*

sex·tant (seks′tənt) *n.* [< L. *sextans*, a sixth part (of a circle)] an instrument for measuring the angular distance of the sun, a star, etc. from the horizon, as to determine position at sea

SEXTANT

sex·tet, sex·tette (seks tet′) *n.* [< L. *sex*, six] **1.** a group of six **2.** *Music a)* a composition for six voices or instruments *b)* the six performers of this

sex·ton (seks′tən) *n.* [ult. < L. *sacer*, sacred] a church official in charge of the maintenance of church property

sex·u·al (sek′shoo wəl) *adj.* **1.** of or involving sex, the sexes, the sex organs, etc. **2.** *a)* having sex *b)* designating or of reproduction by the union of male and female germ cells —**sex′u·al′i·ty** (-wal′ə tē) *n.* —**sex′u·al·ly** *adv.*

sex′y *adj.* -i·er, -i·est [Colloq.] exciting or intended to excite sexual desire —**sex′i·ly** *adv.* —**sex′i·ness** *n.*

Sey·chelles (sā shel′, -shelz′) country on a group of islands northeast of Madagascar: 107 sq. mi.; pop. 58,000

s.f., sf, SF science fiction

Sgt., Sgt. Sergeant

sh (sh) *interj.* hush! be quiet!

shab·by (shab′ē) *adj.* -bi·er, -bi·est [< OE. *sceabb*, a scab] **1.** run-down; dilapidated **2.** *a)* ragged; worn *b)* wearing worn clothing **3.** mean; shameful [*shabby* treatment] —**shab′bi·ly** *adv.* —**shab′bi·ness** *n.*

shack (shak) *n.* [< ?] a small, crudely built cabin; shanty

shack·le (shak′'l) *n.* [OE. *sceacel*] **1.** a metal fastening, usually in pairs, for the wrist or ankle of a prisoner; fetter **2.** [*usually pl.*] anything that restrains freedom, as of expression **3.** a device for fastening or coupling —*vt.* -led, -ling to bind, fasten, or hinder with or as with shackles

shad (shad) *n., pl.* **shad, shads** [OE. *sceadd*] a herringlike saltwater fish that spawns in rivers

shade (shād) *n.* [OE. *sceadu*] **1.** slight darkness caused by cutting off rays of light **2.** an area less brightly lighted than its surroundings **3.** [Archaic] a shadow **4.** degree of darkness of a color **5.** *a)* a small difference [*shades* of opinion] *b)* a slight amount or degree; trace **6.** [Chiefly Literary] a ghost **7.** a device used to protect or screen from light [a window *shade*, lamp *shade*] **8.** [*pl.*] [Slang] sunglasses —*vt.* **shad′ed, shad′ing 1.** to screen from light **2.** to hide, as with a shadow **3.** to darken; dim **4.** to represent shade in (a painting, etc.) —*vi.* to change slightly or by degrees —**in** (or **into**) **the shade 1.** in darkness or shadow **2.** in comparative obscurity

shad·ing (-iŋ) *n.* **1.** a shielding against light **2.** the representation of shade in a picture **3.** any small variation

shad·ow (shad′ō) *n.* [< OE. *sceadu*, shade] **1.** the darkness or the dark shape cast by something cutting off light **2.** [*pl.*] the growing darkness after sunset **3.** gloom or that which causes gloom **4.** a shaded area in a picture **5.** a ghost **6.** a remnant or trace **7.** a vague indication or omen **8.** a constant companion **9.** one who trails another closely, as a spy —*vt.* **1.** to throw a shadow upon **2.** to make dark or gloomy **3.** to follow closely, esp. in secret —

in the shadow of very close to —**under the shadow of 1.** very close to **2.** in danger of —**shad′ow·er** *n.*

shad′ow·y *adj.* **1.** like a shadow; specif., *a)* without reality; illusory *b)* dim; indistinct **2.** shaded or full of shadow —**shad′ow·i·ness** *n.*

shad·y (shād′ē) *adj.* -i·er, -i·est **1.** giving shade **2.** shaded, as from the sun; full of shade **3.** [Colloq.] of questionable character —**on the shady side of** beyond (a given age) —**shad′i·ness** *n.*

shaft (shaft) *n.* [OE. *sceaft*] **1.** an arrow or spear, or its stem **2.** a missile or something like a missile [*shafts* of light, wit, etc.] **3.** a long, slender part or object; specif., *a)* the stem of a feather *b)* the main, usually cylindrical, part between the ends of a column *c)* a handle, as on some tools *d)* either of the two poles between which an animal is harnessed to a vehicle *e)* a bar transmitting motion to a mechanical part, as of an engine **4.** a long, narrow opening sunk into the earth **5.** a vertical opening passing through a building, as for an elevator —*vt.* [Slang] to cheat, trick, exploit, etc.

shag [^1] (shag) *n.* [OE. *sceacga*] **1.** a long, heavy, coarse nap, as on some rugs **2.** fabric with such a nap

shag [^2] (shag) *vt.* **shagged, shag′ging** [< ?] to chase after and retrieve (baseballs hit in batting practice)

shag′bark′ *n.* **1.** a hickory tree with gray, shredding bark **2.** its wood **3.** its edible nut

shag′gy *adj.* -gi·er, -gi·est **1.** covered with long, coarse hair **2.** carelessly groomed; unkempt **3.** of coarse growth; straggly **4.** having a rough nap —**shag′gi·ness** *n.*

shah (shä) *n.* [Per. *shāh*] a title of the ruler of Iran

shake (shāk) *vt., vi.* **shook, shak′en, shak′ing** [OE. *sceacan*] **1.** to move quickly up and down, back and forth, etc. **2.** to bring, force, mix, etc. by brisk movement **3.** to tremble or cause to tremble **4.** *a)* to become or cause to become unsteady *b)* to unnerve or become unnerved [*he was shaken by the news*] **5.** to clasp (another's hand), as in greeting **6.** *Music same as* TRILL —*n.* **1.** an act of shaking **2.** an unsteady movement; tremor **3.** a wood shingle **4.** *short for* MILKSHAKE **5.** [*pl.*] [Colloq.] a convulsive trembling (usually with *the*) **6.** [Colloq.] a moment [*be back in a shake*] **7.** [Colloq.] a kind of treatment [*a fair shake*] **8.** *Music same as* TRILL —**no great shakes** [Colloq.] not unusual —**shake down 1.** to cause to fall by shaking **2.** [Slang] to extort money from —**shake off** to get rid of —**shake up 1.** to shake, esp. so as to mix **2.** to jar or shock **3.** to reorganize

shake′down′ *n.* [Colloq.] **1.** an extortion of money, as by blackmail **2.** a thorough search —*adj.* for testing new equipment, etc. [a *shakedown* cruise]

shak′er *n.* **1.** a person or thing that shakes **2.** a device used in shaking

Shake·speare (shāk′spir), **William** 1564–1616; Eng. poet & dramatist —**Shake·spear′e·an, Shake·spear′i·an** *adj., n.*

shake′-up′ *n.* a shaking up; specif., an extensive reorganization, as in policy or personnel

shak·o (shak′ō) *n., pl.* **-os** [< Hung.] a stiff, cylindrical military dress hat, usually with a flat top and a plume

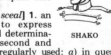

SHAKO

shak·y (shā′kē) *adj.* -i·er, -i·est **1.** not firm, substantial, etc., as a structure **2.** *a)* trembling *b)* weak **3.** not dependable; questionable —**shak′i·ly** *adv.* —**shak′i·ness** *n.*

shale (shāl) *n.* [OE. *scealu*, a shell] a rock formed of hardened clay, that splits into thin layers

shall (shal) *v., pt.* **should** [OE. *sceal*] **1.** an auxiliary sometimes used to express futurity in the first person and determination, obligation, etc. in the second and third persons **2.** an auxiliary regularly used: *a)* in questions in the first person asking for agreement *b)* in laws and resolutions [the fine *shall* not exceed $100] *Shall* and *will* are used interchangeably in prevailing usage

shal·lot (shə lät′) *n.* [< OFr. *eschaloigne*, scallion] **1.** a small onion whose bulbs, like garlic, are used for flavoring **2.** *same as* GREEN ONION

shal·low (shal′ō) *adj.* [ME. *shalow*] **1.** not deep [a *shallow* lake] **2.** lacking depth of character; superficial —*n.* [*usually pl.*, often with *sing.* v.] a shoal —**shal′low·ness** *n.*

shalt (shalt) *archaic 2d pers. sing., pres. indic.,* of SHALL: *used with* thou

sham (sham) *n.* [< ? SHAME] something false or fake; person or thing that is a fraud —*adj.* not genuine or real; false or fake —*vt., vi.* **shammed, sham′ming** to pretend; fake

sham·ble (sham'b'l) *vi.* **-bled, -bling** [< obs. use in "*shamble* legs," bench legs] to walk clumsily; shuffle —*n.* a shambling walk

sham'bles (-b'lz) *n.pl.* [*with sing. v.*] [ult. < L. *scamnum*, a bench] **1.** a slaughterhouse **2.** a scene of great slaughter, destruction, or disorder

shame (shām) *n.* [OE. *scamu*] **1.** a painful feeling of having lost the respect of others because of improper behavior, etc. **2.** dishonor or disgrace **3.** something unfortunate or outrageous —*vt.* **shamed, sham'ing 1.** to cause to feel shame **2.** to dishonor or disgrace **3.** to force by a sense of shame —**for shame!** you ought to be ashamed! —**put to shame 1.** to cause to feel shame **2.** to surpass

shame'faced' *adj.* **1.** shy or bashful **2.** showing a feeling of shame; ashamed

shame'ful *adj.* **1.** bringing or causing shame or disgrace; disgraceful **2.** not just, moral, or decent; offensive — **shame'ful·ly** *adv.* —**shame'ful·ness** *n.*

shame'less *adj.* having or showing no shame, modesty, or decency; brazen —**shame'less·ly** *adv.* —**shame'less·ness** *n.*

sham·my (sham'ē) *n., pl.* **-mies**; *adj. same as* CHAMOIS (*n.* 2, *adj.* 1)

sham·poo (sham pōō') *vt.* **-pooed', -poo'ing** [< Hindi *châmpnā*, to press] **1.** to wash (the hair) **2.** to wash the hair of **3.** to wash (a rug, upholstery, etc.) —*n.* **1.** a shampooing **2.** a liquid soap, etc. used for this

sham·rock (sham'räk') *n.* [< Ir. *seamar*, clover] any of certain clovers or cloverlike plants with leaflets in groups of three: the emblem of Ireland

Shang·hai (shaŋ'hī') seaport in E China: pop. c.10,000,000

shang·hai (shaŋ'hī') *vt.* **-haied', -hai'ing** [< such kidnapping for crews on the China run] to kidnap, usually by drugging, for service aboard ship

shank (shaŋk) *n.* [OE. *scanca*] **1.** the part of a leg between the knee and the ankle in man, or a corresponding part in animals **2.** the whole leg **3.** a cut of meat from the leg of an animal **4.** the part of a tool between the handle and the working part —**shank of the evening** early evening

Shan·non (shan'ən) river in WC Ireland: c.220 mi.

shan't (shant) shall not

shan·tey (shan'tē) *n., pl.* **-teys** *var. of* CHANTEY

shan·tung (shan'tuŋ') *n.* [< *Shantung*, province of China] a fabric of silk, rayon, etc. with an uneven surface

shan·ty[1] (shan'tē) *n., pl.* **-ties** [< CanadFr. *chantier*, workshop] a small, shabby dwelling; hut

shan·ty[2] (shan'tē) *n., pl.* **-ties** *var. of* CHANTEY

shape (shāp) *n.* [< OE. *(ge)sceap*, form] **1.** the way a thing looks because of its outline; outer form **2.** the form of a particular person or thing, or class of things **3.** the contour of the body; figure **4.** assumed appearance; guise [a foe in the *shape* of a friend] **5.** a phantom **6.** definite or regular form [to begin to take *shape*] **7.** [Colloq.] condition [a patient in poor *shape*] —*vt.* **shaped, shap'ing 1.** to give definite shape to; make **2.** to arrange, express, etc. in definite form [*shaped* to our needs] —**shape up** [Colloq.] to develop to a definite or satisfactory form, condition, etc. —**take shape** to begin to have definite form —**shap'er** *n.*

shape'less *adj.* **1.** without distinct or regular form **2.** without a pleasing shape —**shape'less·ness** *n.*

shape'ly *adj.* **-li·er, -li·est** having a pleasing shape; well-proportioned —**shape'li·ness** *n.*

shard (shärd) *n.* [OE. *sceard*] a fragment or broken piece, esp. of pottery; potsherd

share[1] (sher) *n.* [OE. *scearu*] **1.** a portion that belongs to an individual **2.** a just or full part [to do one's *share* of work] **3.** any of the equal parts of the capital stock of a corporation —*vt.* **shared, shar'ing 1.** to distribute in shares **2.** to have or use in common with others —*vi.* to have a share; participate (*in*)

share[2] (sher) *n.* [OE. *scear*] a plowshare

share'crop' *vi., vt.* **-cropped', -crop'ping** to work (land) for a share of the crop, esp. as a tenant farmer does — **share'crop'per** *n.*

share'hold'er *n.* one who owns shares of stock

shark[1] (shärk) *n.* [prob. < G. *schurke*, scoundrel] **1.** a swindler **2.** [Slang] an expert

shark[2] (shärk) *n.* [< ?] a large marine fish with a tough, slate-gray skin: most are fish-eaters

shark'skin' *n.* a cloth of cotton, wool, rayon, etc. with a smooth, silky surface

sharp (shärp) *adj.* [OE. *scearp*] **1.** having a fine edge or point for cutting or piercing **2.** having a point or edge; not rounded [a *sharp* ridge] **3.** not gradual; abrupt [a *sharp* turn] **4.** clearly defined; distinct [a *sharp* contrast] **5.** quick in perception; clever **6.** attentive; vigilant [a *sharp* lookout] **7.** crafty; underhanded **8.** harsh or severe [*sharp* criticism] **9.** violent [a *sharp* attack] **10.** brisk; active [a *sharp* run] **11.** intense [a *sharp* pain] **12.** pungent, as in taste **13.** shrill [a *sharp* sound] **14.** cold [a *sharp* wind] **15.** [Slang] attractively dressed or groomed **16.** *Music* above true pitch —*n.* **1.** [Colloq.] an expert **2.** *Music a*) a tone one half step above another *b*) the symbol (♯) indicating this —*vt., vi. Music* to make or become sharp —*adv.* **1.** in a sharp manner; specif., *a*) abruptly or briskly *b*) attentively or alertly *c*) *Music* above true pitch **2.** precisely [one o'clock *sharp*] —**sharp'ly** *adv.* —**sharp'ness** *n.*

sharp'en *vt., vi.* to make or become sharp or sharper — **sharp'en·er** *n.*

sharp'er *n.* a swindler or cheat

sharp'-eyed' *adj.* having keen sight or perception: also **sharp'-sight'ed**

sharp'ie (-ē) *n.* [Colloq.] a shrewd, cunning person

sharp'shoot'er *n.* a good marksman

sharp'-tongued' (-tuŋd') *adj.* using or characterized by sharp or harshly critical language

sharp'-wit'ted (-wit'id) *adj.* having or showing keen intelligence —**sharp'-wit'ted·ness** *n.*

shat·ter (shat'ər) *vt., vi.* [ME. *schateren*, to scatter] **1.** to break or burst into pieces **2.** to damage or be damaged severely

shave (shāv) *vt.* **shaved, shaved** or **shav'en, shav'ing** [OE. *sceafan*] **1.** to cut away thin slices or sections from **2.** *a*) to cut off (hair) at the surface of the skin *b*) to cut the hair to the surface of (the face, etc.) *c*) to cut the beard of (a person) **3.** to barely touch in passing; graze — *vi.* to cut off hair with a razor, etc. —*n.* the act or result of shaving

shav'er *n.* **1.** one who shaves **2.** an instrument used in shaving, esp. one with electrically operated cutters **3.** [Colloq.] a boy; lad

shav'ing *n.* **1.** the act of one who shaves **2.** a thin piece of wood, metal, etc. shaved off

Shaw (shô), **George Bernard** 1856–1950; Brit. dramatist & critic —**Sha·vi·an** (shā'vē ən) *adj., n.*

shawl (shôl) *n.* [< Per. *shāl*] an oblong or square cloth worn, esp. by women, as a covering for the head or shoulders

Shaw·nee (shô nē') *n., pl.* **-nees', -nee'** any member of a tribe of N. American Indians living at various times in the East and Midwest, and now chiefly in Oklahoma

she (shē) *pron., for pl. see* THEY [< OE. *seo*] the woman, girl, or female animal previously mentioned —*n., pl.* **shes** a woman, girl, or female animal

sheaf (shēf) *n., pl.* **sheaves** [OE. *sceaf*] **1.** a bundle of cut stalks of grain, etc. **2.** a collection, as of papers, bound in a bundle —*vt. same as* SHEAVE

shear (shir) *vt.* **sheared, sheared** or **shorn, shear'ing** [OE. *scieran*] **1.** to cut as with shears **2.** to clip (hair) from (the head), (wool) from (sheep), etc. **3.** to strip (*of* a power, right, etc.) —*vi.* **1.** to use shears, etc. **2.** to break under a stress (**shearing stress**) that makes two contacting parts slide upon each other in opposite directions —*n.* **1.** a machine used in cutting metal **2.** a shearing — **shear'er** *n.*

shears (shirz) *n.pl.* [*also with sing. v.*] **1.** large scissors **2.** a large tool or machine with two opposed blades, used to cut metal, etc.

sheath (shēth) *n., pl.* **sheaths** (shēthz, shēths) [OE. *sceath*] **1.** a case for the blade of a knife, sword, etc. **2.** a covering or receptacle resembling this

sheathe (shēth) *vt.* **sheathed, sheath'ing 1.** to put into a sheath **2.** to enclose in a case or covering

sheath·ing (shē'thiŋ) *n.* something that sheathes, as boards, etc. forming the base for roofing or siding

sheave (shēv) *vt.* **sheaved, sheav'ing** [< SHEAF] to gather (grain, etc.) in a sheaf or sheaves

sheaves (shēvz) *n. pl. of* SHEAF

She·ba (shē'bə), **Queen of** *Bible* the queen who visited King Solomon to investigate his reputed wisdom

she·bang (shə baŋ') *n.* [Colloq.] an affair, business, contrivance, etc.: chiefly in **the whole shebang**

shed[1] (shed) *n.* [OE. *scead*] **1.** a small structure for shelter or storage **2.** a large, barnlike structure for storage

---

fat, āpe, cär; ten, ēven; is, bīte; gō, hôrn, tōōl, look; oil, out; up, fur; thin, *then*; zh, leisure; ŋ, ring; ə for *a* in *ago*; ' as in *able* (ā'b'l); ë, Fr. coeur; ö, Fr. feu; Fr. mon; ü, Fr. duc; r, Fr. cri; kh, G. doch, ich. ‡ foreign; < derived from

shed[2] (shed) *vt.* **shed, shed'ding** [OE. *sceadan,* to separate] 1. to pour out 2. to cause to flow [to *shed* tears] 3. to radiate [to *shed* confidence] 4. to cause to flow off [oilskin *sheds* water] 5. to cast off (a natural growth, as leaves, hair, etc.) —*vi.* to shed leaves, hair, etc. —**shed blood** to kill in a violent way —**shed'der** *n.*

she'd (shēd) 1. she had 2. she would

sheen (shēn) *n.* [< OE. *sciene,* beautiful] brightness

sheep (shēp) *n., pl.* **sheep** [OE. *sceap*] 1. a cud-chewing mammal related to the goats, with heavy wool and edible flesh called mutton 2. one who is meek, stupid, timid, etc.

sheep dog any dog trained to herd and protect sheep

sheep'fold' *n.* a pen or enclosure for sheep

sheep'ish *adj.* 1. embarrassed or chagrined 2. shy or bashful —**sheep'ish·ly** *adv.* —**sheep'ish·ness** *n.*

sheep'skin' *n.* 1. the skin of a sheep, esp. one with fleece 2. parchment or leather made from the skin of a sheep 3. [Colloq.] *same as* DIPLOMA

sheer[1] (shir) *vi., vt.* [var. of SHEAR] to change or cause to change course suddenly —*n.* a sudden change in course

sheer[2] (shir) *adj.* [< ON. *skærr,* bright] 1. very thin; transparent: said of textiles 2. absolute; downright [*sheer* persistence] 3. extremely steep —*adv.* 1. completely; utterly 2. very steeply

sheet[1] (shēt) *n.* [OE. *sceat*] 1. a large piece of cotton, linen, etc., used on a bed 2. *a*) a single piece of paper *b*) [Colloq.] a newspaper 3. a broad, continuous surface or layer, as of flame, water, etc. 4. a broad, thin piece of any material, as glass, metal, etc. —*vt.* to cover or provide with a sheet —*adj.* in the form of a sheet

sheet[2] (shēt) *n.* [OE. *sceatline*] 1. a rope for controlling the set of a sail 2. [*pl.*] the spaces without thwarts at the bow and stern of an open boat

sheet·ing (shēt'iŋ) *n.* 1. material of cotton, linen, etc. used for making sheets 2. material used in covering or lining a surface [copper *sheeting*]

sheet metal metal rolled thin in sheet form

sheet music music printed on unbound sheets of paper

Shef·field (shef'ēld) city in NC England: pop. 525,000

sheik, sheikh (shēk) *n.* [Ar. *shaikh,* lit., old man] 1. the chief of an Arab family, tribe, or village 2. an official in the Muslim religious organization —**sheik'dom** *n.*

shek·el (shek''l) *n.* [< Heb. *shāqal,* weigh] 1. a gold or silver coin of the ancient Hebrews 2. [*pl.*] [Slang] money

shel·drake (shel'drāk') *n.* [prob. < MDu. *schillede,* variegated + *drake,* drake] 1. a large, varicolored old-world duck 2. *same as* MERGANSER

shelf (shelf) *n., pl.* **shelves** [prob. < MLowG. *schelf*] 1. a thin, flat board fixed horizontally to a wall, or in a cupboard, etc., used for holding things 2. something like a shelf; specif., *a*) a flat ledge of rock *b*) a sand bar or reef —**on the shelf** out of use, circulation, etc. —**shelf'like'** *adj.*

shell (shel) *n.* [OE. *sciell*] 1. a hard outer covering, as of a turtle, egg, nut, etc. 2. something like a shell in being hollow, empty, a covering, etc., as an unfilled pie crust 3. a woman's pullover, sleeveless knit blouse 4. a light, narrow racing boat rowed by a team of oarsmen 5. an explosive artillery projectile 6. a small-arms cartridge —*vt.* 1. to remove the shell or covering from [to *shell* peas] 2. to fire artillery shells at; bombard —**shell out** [Colloq.] to pay out (money) —**shell'-like'** *adj.*

she'll (shēl) 1. she shall 2. she will

shel·lac, shel·lack (shə lak') *n.* [SHEL(L) + LAC] 1. a resin usually produced in thin, flaky layers 2. a thin varnish containing this resin and alcohol —*vt.* -**lacked'**, -**lack'ing** 1. to apply shellac to 2. [Slang] *a*) to beat *b*) to defeat decisively

-**shelled** *a combining form meaning* having a (specified kind of) shell [soft-*shelled* crab]

Shel·ley (shel'ē), **Percy Bysshe** (bish) 1792–1822; Eng. poet

shell'fire' *n.* the firing of large shells

shell'fish' *n., pl.:* see FISH any aquatic animal with a shell, as the clam, lobster, etc.

shell game 1. a swindling game in which the victim bets that a pea is under one of three shells manipulated by sleight of hand 2. any swindle

shell shock *an earlier term for* COMBAT FATIGUE

shel·ter (shel'tər) *n.* [< ? OE. *scield,* shield + *truma,* a troop] 1. something that protects, as from the elements, danger, etc. 2. a being covered, protected, etc. —*vt.* to provide shelter for; protect —*vi.* to find shelter

shelve (shelv) *vt.* **shelved, shelv'ing** 1. to furnish with shelves 2. to put on a shelf or shelves 3. *a*) to lay aside [to *shelve* a discussion] *b*) to dismiss from active service —*vi.* to slope gradually

shelves (shelvz) *n. pl. of* SHELF

shelv'ing *n.* 1. material for shelves 2. shelves collectively

Shem (shem) *Bible* the eldest of Noah's sons

Shen·an·do·ah (shen'ən dō'ə) river in N Va., flowing into the Potomac: c.200 mi.

she·nan·i·gan (shi nan'i g'n) *n.* [< ?] [*usually pl.*] [Colloq.] trickery; mischief

Shen·yang (shun'yäŋ') city in NE China: pop. c.4,000,000

She·ol (shē'ōl) *n.* [< Heb. *shā'al,* to dig] *Bible* the abode of the dead, within the earth

shep·herd (shep'ərd) *n.* [see SHEEP & HERD[2]] 1. a person who herds sheep 2. a leader of a group; esp., a clergyman —*vt.* to herd, guard, lead, etc. as a shepherd —**shep'herd·ess** *n.fem.*

Sher·a·ton (sher'ə tən) *adj.* [< T. *Sheraton* (1751–1806), Eng. cabinetmaker] designating or of a furniture style having simplicity of form, straight lines, etc.

sher·bet (shur'bət) *n.* [< Ar. *sharbah,* a drink] a frozen dessert like an ice, but with gelatin and, often, milk added

sher·iff (sher'if) *n.* [< OE. *scir,* shire + *gerafa,* a reeve] the chief law-enforcement officer of a county

Sher·lock Holmes (shur'läk hōmz', hōlmz') a fictitious British detective with great powers of deduction, created by A. Conan DOYLE

SHERATON CHAIR

Sher·man (shur'mən), **William Te·cum·seh** (ti kum'sə) 1820–91; Union general in the Civil War

sher·ry (sher'ē) *n., pl.* -**ries** [< *Jerez,* Spain] 1. a strong, yellow or brown Spanish wine 2. any similar wine

Sher·wood Forest (shur'wood) forest in C England, made famous in the Robin Hood legends

she's (shēz) 1. she is 2. she has

Shet·land Islands (shet'lənd) group of Scottish islands northeast of Scotland

Shetland pony any of a breed of sturdy ponies with a rough coat, orig. from the Shetland Islands

shew (shō) *n., vt., vi.* **shewed, shewn** or **shewed, shew'ing** *archaic sp. of* SHOW

shib·bo·leth (shib'ə ləth) *n.* [< Heb. *shibbōleth,* a stream] 1. *Bible* the test word used to distinguish the enemy: Judg. 12:4-6 2. any password 3. any phrase, custom, etc. peculiar to a certain class, faction, etc.

shied (shīd) *pt. & pp. of* SHY

shield (shēld) *n.* [OE. *scield*] 1. a piece of armor worn on the forearm to ward off blows, etc. 2. a person or thing that guards, protects, etc. 3. anything shaped like a triangular shield, as an escutcheon —*vt.* to defend; protect

shift (shift) *vt.* [OE. *sciftan,* divide] 1. to move from one person, place, etc. to another 2. to replace by another or others 3. to change the arrangement of (gears) —*vi.* 1. to change position, direction, etc. 2. to get along [to *shift* for oneself] 3. to change from one gear to another —*n.* 1. a shifting; change 2. a plan of conduct, esp. for an emergency; expedient 3. an evasion; trick 4. *short for* GEARSHIFT 5. *a*) a group of people working in relay with other groups *b*) the work period involved 6. a loose dress that hangs straight —**make shift** to do the best one can (with the means at hand)

shift'less *adj.* lazy or careless

shift'y *adj.* -**i·er**, -**i·est** of a tricky nature; evasive —**shift'i·ness** *n.*

Shi·ko·ku (shē'kô kōō') smallest of the four major islands of Japan, south of Honshu

shill (shil) *n.* [< ?] [Slang] the confederate of a gambler, auctioneer, etc. who pretends to buy, bet, etc. so as to lure others

shil·le·lagh, shil·la·lah (shi lā'lē, -lə) *n.* [< *Shillelagh,* Ir. village] a cudgel: also sp. **shil·le'lah**

shil·ling (shil'iŋ) *n.* [OE. *scylling*] 1. a British money of account and coin: coinage discontinued in 1971 2. a money of account in some other countries

shil·ly-shal·ly (shil'ē shal'ē) *vi.* -**lied**, -**ly·ing** [< *shall I?*] to be irresolute; vacillate, esp. over trifles

shim (shim) *n.* [< ?] a thin piece of wood, metal, etc. used for filling space, leveling, etc.

shim·mer (shim'ər) *vi.* [OE. *scymrian*] 1. to shine with an unsteady light 2. to form a wavering image —*n.* a shimmering light —**shim'mer·y** *adj.*

shim·my (shim'ē) *n.* [< CHEMISE] 1. a jazz dance of the 1920's with much shaking of the body 2. a shaking or wobbling, as in automobile wheels —*vi.* -**mied**, -**my·ing** to shake or wobble

shin (shin) *n.* [OE. *scinu*] the front part of the leg between the knee and the ankle —*vt.*, *vi.* **shinned, shin'-ning** to climb (a rope, etc.) by gripping with both hands and legs: often with *up*

shin'bone' *n.* same as TIBIA

shin·dig (shin'dig') *n.* [< colloq. *shindy*, commotion] [Colloq.] a dance, party, or other social affair

shine (shīn) *vi.* **shone** or, esp. for vt. 2, **shined, shin'ing** [OE. *scinan*] **1.** to emit or reflect light; gleam; glow **2.** to excel; be eminent **3.** to show itself clearly *[love* shone *from her face]* —*vt.* **1.** to direct the light of **2.** to make shiny by polishing —*n.* **1.** brightness; radiance **2.** luster; polish **3.** *short for* SHOESHINE **4.** splendor; brilliance — **take a shine to** [Slang] to take a liking to (someone)

shin'er (-ər) *n.* **1.** a silvery minnow **2.** [Slang] a black eye, as from a blow

shin·gle' (shin'g'l) *n.* [prob. < Scand.] [Chiefly Brit.] **1.** coarse gravel worn smooth by water, as on a beach **2.** an area covered with this

shin·gle² (shin'g'l) *n.* [< OE. *scindel*] **1.** a thin, flat tile of asphalt, asbestos, etc. laid with others in a series of overlapping rows as a covering for roofs, etc. **2.** a woman's short haircut, tapered at the nape **3.** [Colloq.] a small signboard, as that of a doctor —*vt.* **-gled, -gling** to cover (a roof, etc.) with shingles

shin·gles (shin'g'lz) *n.* [< L. *cingere*, to gird] an acute virus disease with eruption of blisters on the skin along the course of a nerve

shin'guard' *n.* a padded guard worn to protect the shin in some sports

shin·ny (shin'ē) *vi.* **-nied, -ny·ing** same as SHIN

shin'splints' (-splints') *n.pl.* [*with sing. v.*] [< SHIN + ? *splint*, growth on bone of a horse's leg] painful strain of muscles in the lower leg

Shin·to (shin'tō) *n.* [Jpn. < Chin. *shin*, god + *tao*, way] a religion of Japan, emphasizing ancestor worship   **Shin'-to·ism** *n.* —**Shin'to·ist** *n.*, *adj.*

shin·y (shīn'ē) *adj.* **-i·er, -i·est** **1.** bright; shining **2.** highly polished; glossy —**shin'i·ness** *n.*

ship (ship) *n.* [OE. *scip*] **1.** any large vessel navigating deep water **2.** a ship's officers and crew **3.** an aircraft — *vt.* **shipped, ship'ping** **1.** to put or take on board a ship **2.** to send or transport by any carrier *[to* ship *coal by rail]* **3.** to take in (water) over the side, as in a heavy sea **4.** to put in place on a vessel *[ship* the oars*]* **5.** to hire for work on a ship —*vi.* **1.** to go aboard ship; embark **2.** to be hired to serve on a ship —**ship'per** *n.*

-ship [OE. *-scipe*] *a suffix meaning:* **1.** the quality or state of *[friendship]* **2.** *a)* the rank or office of *[governorship]* *b)* one having the rank of *[lordship]* **3.** skill as *[leadership]* **4.** all persons (of a specified group) collectively *[readership]*

ship'board' *n.* a ship: chiefly in **on shipboard**, aboard a ship —*adj.* happening, etc. on a ship

ship'build'er *n.* one whose business is building ships — **ship'build'ing** *n.*

ship'load' *n.* the load of a ship

ship'mate' *n.* a fellow sailor on the same ship

ship'ment *n.* **1.** the shipping of goods **2.** goods shipped

ship'own'er *n.* an owner of a ship or ships

ship'ping *n.* **1.** the act or business of transporting goods **2.** ships collectively, as of a nation or port

ship'shape' *adj.* having everything neatly in place; trim —*adv.* in a shipshape manner

ship'wreck' *n.* **1.** the remains of a wrecked ship **2.** the loss of a ship through storm, etc. **3.** any ruin or destruction —*vt.* to cause to undergo shipwreck

ship'wright' *n.* a person, esp. a carpenter, whose work is the construction and repair of ships

ship'yard' *n.* a place where ships are built and repaired

shire (shīr) *n.* [OE. *scir*, office] in Great Britain, a county

shirk (shurk) *vt.*, *vi.* [< ?] to neglect or evade (a duty, etc.) —**shirk'er** *n.*

shirr (shur) *n.* [< ?] same as SHIRRING —*vt.* **1.** to make shirring in (cloth) **2.** to bake (eggs) in buttered dishes

shirr'ing *n.* a gathering made in cloth by drawing the material up on parallel rows of short stitches

shirt (shurt) *n.* [OE. *scyrte*] **1.** a garment worn by men on the upper part of the body **2.** an undershirt —**keep one's shirt on** [Slang] to be patient or calm —**lose one's shirt** [Slang] to lose everything

shirt'ing *n.* material for making shirts

shirt'tail' (-tāl') *n.* the part of a shirt extending below the waist

shirt'waist' (-wāst') *n.* a woman's blouse tailored like a shirt

shish ke·bab (shish' kə bäb') [< Arm. < Ar. *shīsh*, skewer + *kebāb*, kebab] a dish of kebabs, esp. of lamb

shiv (shiv) *n.* [prob. < Romany *chiv*, blade] [Slang] a knife

shiv·a·ree (shiv'ə rē') *n.* [< CHARIVARI] a mock serenade, as to newlyweds, with kettles, horns, etc.

shiv·er' (shiv'ər) *n.* [ME. *schivere*] a fragment or splinter —*vt.*, *vi.* to break into fragments or splinters

shiv·er² (shiv'ər) *vi.* [< ? OE. *ceafl*, a jaw] to shake, tremble, etc., as from fear or cold —*n.* a shaking, trembling, etc. —**shiv'er·y** *adj.*

shmaltz (shmälts) *n.* [Slang] *var. sp.* of SCHMALTZ — **shmaltz'y** *adj.* **-i·er, -i·est**

shoal' (shōl) *n.* [OE. *scolu*] **1.** a large group; crowd **2.** a large school of fish

shoal² (shōl) *n.* [OE. *sceald*, shallow] **1.** a shallow place in a river, sea, etc. **2.** a sand bar forming a shallow place — *vt.*, *vi.* to make or become shallow

shoat (shōt) *n.* [< ?] a young hog (100–180 lb.)

shock' (shäk) *n.* [< Fr. < MDu. *schokken*, collide] **1.** a sudden, powerful blow, shake, etc. **2.** *a)* a sudden emotional disturbance *b)* the cause of this **3.** the violent effect on the body of an electric current passing through it **4.** a disorder caused by severe injury, loss of blood, etc., and marked by a sharp drop in blood pressure, etc. —*vt.* **1.** to disturb emotionally **2.** to produce electric shock in —*vi.* to be shocked, distressed, etc. —**shock'er** *n.*

shock² (shäk) *n.* [ME. *schokke*] bundles of grain stacked together to cure and dry —*vt.*, *vi.* to gather in shocks

shock³ (shäk) *n.* [< ? prec.] a thick, bushy or tangled mass, as of hair

shock absorber a device, as on the springs of a car, that lessens or absorbs the force of shocks

shock'ing *adj.* causing great surprise, horror, disgust, etc. —**shock'ing·ly** *adv.*

shock'proof' *adj.* able to absorb shock without being damaged

shock therapy a method of treating certain mental disorders by injecting drugs or by applying electric current to the brain: also **shock treatment**

shock troops troops especially chosen, trained, and equipped to lead an attack

shod (shäd) *alt. pt. & pp. of* SHOE

shod·dy (shäd'ē) *n.*, *pl.* **-dies** [< ?] **1.** an inferior woolen cloth made from used fabrics **2.** anything worth less than it seems to be —*adj.* **-di·er, -di·est** **1.** made of inferior material **2.** poorly done or made **3.** sham **4.** contemptible; low —**shod'di·ly** *adv.* —**shod'di·ness** *n.*

shoe (shōō) *n.* [OE. *sceoh*] **1.** an outer covering for the foot **2.** a horseshoe **3.** the part of a brake that presses against a wheel **4.** the casing of a pneumatic tire —*vt.* **shod** or **shoed, shoe'ing** to furnish with shoes —**fill one's shoes** to take one's place

shoe'horn' *n.* an implement inserted at the back of a shoe to help in slipping the heel in

shoe'lace' *n.* a length of cord, leather, etc. used for lacing and fastening a shoe

shoe'mak'er *n.* one whose business is making and repairing shoes —**shoe'mak'ing** *n.*

shoe'shine' *n.* the polishing of a pair of shoes

shoe'string' *n.* **1.** a shoelace **2.** a small amount of capital —*adj.* at or near the ankles

shoe tree a form put into a shoe to stretch it or preserve its shape

sho·gun (shō'gun', -gōn') *n.* [Jpn. < Chin. *chiang-chun*, leader of an army] any of the military governors of Japan who ruled absolutely until 1868

shone (shōn) *pt. & pp. of* SHINE

shoo (shōō) *interj.* away! get out! —*vt.* **shooed, shoo'ing** to drive away, as by crying "shoo"

shoo'-in' *n.* [Colloq.] one expected to win easily in an election, race, etc.

shook (shook) *pt. of* SHAKE —**shook up** [Slang] upset; disturbed

shoot (shōōt) *vt.* **shot, shoot'ing** [OE. *sceotan*] **1.** to move swiftly over, by, etc. *[to* shoot *the rapids]* **2.** to slide (a door bolt) into or out of its fastening **3.** to variegate (*with* another color) **4.** to thrust or put forth (a branch, etc.) **5.** *a)* to discharge or fire (a bullet, gun, arrow, etc.) *b)* to discharge (rays) with force **6.** to send forth swiftly or with force **7.** to hit, wound, etc. with a bullet, arrow, etc. **8.** to take the altitude of (a star) **9.** to photograph or film **10.**

[Slang] to inject (a narcotic drug) **11.** *Sports a)* to throw or drive (a ball, etc.) toward the objective *b)* to score (a goal, points, etc.) *c)* to play (golf, pool, craps, etc.) —*vi.* **1.** to move swiftly **2.** to be felt suddenly, as pain **3.** to grow rapidly **4.** to jut out **5.** to fire a missile, gun, etc. **6.** to use guns, etc., as in hunting **7.** [Slang] to inject a narcotic drug —*n.* **1.** a shooting trip, contest, etc. **2.** a new growth; sprout —**shoot at** (or **for**) [Colloq.] to strive for —**shoot′er** *n.*

shooting star *same as* METEOR

shop (shäp) *n.* [OE. *sceoppa*, booth] **1.** a place where things are offered for sale; esp., a small store **2.** a place where a particular kind of work is done —*vi.* **shopped, shop′ping** to visit shops to examine or buy goods —**set up shop** to start a business —**talk shop** to discuss one's work

shop′keep′er *n.* one who operates a shop, or store

shop′lift′er *n.* one who steals articles from a store during shopping hours —**shop′lift′** *vt., vi.*

shop′per *n.* **1.** one who shops **2.** one hired by a store to shop for others **3.** one hired by a store to compare competitors' prices, etc.

shopping center a complex of stores, restaurants, etc. with a common parking area

shop steward one elected by the union members to represent them in dealings with the employer

shop′talk′ *n.* **1.** the specialized vocabulary of a particular occupation, etc. **2.** conversation about one's work, esp. after hours

shop′worn′ *adj.* **1.** soiled, faded, etc. from having been displayed in a shop **2.** dull, trite, etc.

shore′ (shôr) *n.* [ME. *schore*] land at the edge of a body of water

shore² (shôr) *n.* [ME. *schore*] a beam, etc. used as a prop —*vt.* **shored, shor′ing** to support as with shores (usually with *up*)

shore dinner a meal with a variety of seafood

shore patrol a detail of the U.S. Navy, Coast Guard, or Marine Corps acting as military police on shore

shor′ing *n.* **1.** the act of supporting with shores **2.** a system of shores used for support

SHORES

shorn (shôrn) *alt. pp.* of SHEAR

short (shôrt) *adj.* [OE. *scort*] **1.** not extending far from end to end **2.** not great in range or scope **3.** not tall **4.** brief; concise **5.** not retentive [a *short* memory] **6.** curt; brusque **7.** less than a sufficient or correct amount **8.** tending to crumble, as pastry **9.** designating a sale of securities, etc. which the seller expects to buy later at a lower price **10.** requiring a short time to pronounce —*n.* **1.** something short **2.** [*pl.*] *a)* short trousers *b)* a man's undergarment like these **3.** *clipped form of: a)* SHORTSTOP *b)* SHORT CIRCUIT —*adv.* **1.** abruptly; suddenly **2.** briefly; concisely **3.** so as to be short **4.** unawares [caught *short*] —*vt., vi.* **1.** to give less than what is needed, usual, etc. **2.** *clipped form of: a)* SHORTCHANGE *b)* SHORT-CIRCUIT —**fall** (or **come**) **short** to fail to reach, suffice, etc. —**in short** briefly —**run short** to have less than enough —**short of** less than or lacking —**short′ness** *n.*

short′age (-ij) *n.* a deficiency in the amount needed or expected; deficit

short′bread′ *n.* a rich, crumbly cake or cookie made with much shortening

short′cake′ *n.* a light biscuit or a sweet cake served with fruit, etc. as a dessert

short′change′ *vt., vi.* **-changed′, -chang′ing** [Colloq.] **1.** to give less money than is due in change **2.** to cheat

short circuit 1. a low-resistance connection between two points in an electric circuit that deflects the current or causes excessive current flow **2.** popularly, a disrupted electric circuit resulting from this —**short′-cir′cuit** *vt., vi.*

short′com′ing *n.* a fault, deficiency, defect, etc.

short cut 1. a shorter route **2.** a way of saving time, effort, etc.

short′en *vt.* **1.** to make short or shorter **2.** to add shortening to (pastry, etc.) —*vi.* to become short or shorter —**short′en·er** *n.*

short′en·ing *n.* fat used to make pastry, etc. crisp or flaky

short′hand′ *n.* any system of special symbols for letters, words, etc. for taking dictation, etc. rapidly —*adj.* written in or using shorthand

short′-hand′ed *adj.* short of workers or helpers

short′horn′ *n.* any of a breed of cattle with short, curved horns, raised for both beef and milk

short′-lived′ (-līvd′, -livd′) *adj.* having or tending to have a short life span or existence

short′ly *adv.* **1.** briefly **2.** soon **3.** abruptly and rudely; curtly

short order any food that can be cooked or served quickly when ordered —**short′-or′der** *adj.*

short′-range′ *adj.* reaching over a short distance or period of time

short ribs rib ends of beef from the forequarter

short shrift very little care or attention —**make short shrift of** to make short work of; dispose of quickly and impatiently: also **give short shrift**

short′sight′ed *adj.* **1.** *same as* NEARSIGHTED **2.** lacking in foresight —**short′sight′ed·ly** *adv.* —**short′sight′ed·ness** *n.*

short′stop′ *n.* *Baseball* the infielder between second and third base

short subject a short film, as an animated cartoon, shown along with a featured motion picture

short′-tem′pered *adj.* easily or quickly angered

short′-term′ *adj.* for or extending over a short time

short ton 2,000 pounds avoirdupois

short′wave′ *n.* a radio wave of 60 meters or less

short′-wind′ed (-win′did) *adj.* easily put out of breath by exertion

Sho·sta·ko·vich (shō′stä kô′vich), **Dmi·tri** (d′mē′trē) 1906–75; Russ. composer

shot′ (shät) *n.* [OE. *sceot*] **1.** the act of shooting; discharge of a missile **2.** range; scope **3.** *a)* an attempt; try *b)* a guess **4.** a pointed, critical remark **5.** the path of an object thrown, etc. **6.** *a)* a projectile for a gun *b)* projectiles collectively **7.** small pellets of lead for a shotgun **8.** the heavy metal ball used in the shot put **9.** a blast **10.** a marksman **11.** a photograph or continuous film sequence **12.** a hypodermic injection, as of vaccine **13.** a drink of liquor **14.** [Colloq.] a bet with reference to the odds given [a ten-to-one *shot*] —**call the shots 1.** to give orders **2.** to control what happens —**like a shot** quickly or suddenly

shot² (shät) *pt. & pp.* of SHOOT —*adj.* **1.** variegated, streaked, etc. with another color or substance **2.** [Colloq.] ruined or worn out

shot′gun′ *n.* a gun for firing small shot at close range

shot put a contest in which a heavy metal ball is propelled with an overhand thrust from the shoulder —**shot′-put′ter** *n.* —**shot′-put′ting** *n.*

should (shood) *v.* [OE. *sceolde*] **1.** *pt.* of SHALL **2.** an auxiliary used to express: *a)* obligation, duty, etc. [he *should* help] *b)* expectation or probability [he *should* be here soon] *c)* a future condition [if I *should* die]

shoul·der (shōl′dər) *n.* [OE. *sculdor*] **1.** *a)* the joint connecting the arm or forelimb with the body *b)* the part of the body including this joint **2.** [*pl.*] the two shoulders and the part of the back between them **3.** a cut of meat that is the upper foreleg and attached parts **4.** a shoulderlike projection **5.** the strip along the edge of a road —*vt.* **1.** to push through, as with the shoulder **2.** to carry upon the shoulder **3.** to assume the burden of —**put one's shoulder to the wheel** to set to work vigorously —**straight from the shoulder** without reserve; frankly —**turn** (or **give**) **a cold shoulder to** to snub or shun

shoulder blade either of the two flat bones in the upper back

shoulder harness an anchored strap passing across the upper body, used with a seat belt, as in a car

should·n't (shood′'nt) should not

shouldst (shoodst) *archaic 2d pers. sing. pt.* of SHALL: used with thou: also **should·est** (-ist)

shout (shout) *n.* [ME. *schoute*] a loud, sudden cry, call, etc. —*vt., vi.* to utter in a shout or cry out loudly —**shout down** to silence by loud shouting —**shout′er** *n.*

shove (shuv) *vt., vi.* **shoved, shov′ing** [OE. *scufan*] **1.** to push, as along a surface **2.** to push roughly —*n.* a push —**shove off 1.** to push (a boat) away from shore **2.** [Colloq.] to leave

shov·el (shuv′'l) *n.* [OE. *scofl*] **1.** a tool with a broad scoop and a long handle: used in lifting and moving loose material **2.** a machine with a shovellike device —*vt.* **-eled** or **-elled, -el·ing** or **-el·ling 1.** to lift and move with a shovel **2.** to dig out (a path, etc.) with a shovel **3.** to put in large quantities [to *shovel* food into one's mouth] —**shov′el·er, shov′el·ler** *n.* —**shov′el·ful′** *n., pl.* **-fuls′**

show (shō) *vt.* **showed, shown** or **showed, show′ing** [OE. *sceawian*, to look] **1.** to bring or put in sight; display **2.** to guide; conduct **3.** to point out **4.** to reveal [to *show* anger] **5.** to prove; demonstrate **6.** to register [a clock *shows* the time] **7.** to grant (favor, mercy, etc.) —*vi.* **1.** to be or become seen; appear **2.** to be noticeable **3.** to finish third in a horse or dog race —*n.* **1.** a showing or demonstration 2. a public display or exhibition 3. a pompous display 4. a pretense [her sorrow was a mere *show*] 5. a presentation of entertainment —**for show** in order to attract attention —**show off** 1. to make a display of 2. to do something meant to attract attention —**show up** 1. to expose 2. to come; arrive 3. [Colloq.] to surpass

show'boat' *n.* a boat with a theater and actors aboard who play river towns

show business the theater, motion pictures, television, etc. as a business or industry

show'case' *n.* a glass-enclosed case for displaying things, as in a store

show'down' *n.* [Colloq.] an action that brings matters to a climax or settles them

show·er (shou'ər) *n.* [OE. *scur*] 1. a brief fall of rain, sleet, etc. 2. a sudden, abundant fall, as of sparks 3. a party at which gifts are presented to the guest of honor 4. a bath in which the body is sprayed with fine streams of water: in full **shower bath** —*vt.* 1. to make wet as with a spray of water 2. to pour forth as in a shower —*vi.* 1. to fall or come as a shower 2. to bathe under a shower — **show'er·y** *adj.*

show'ing *n.* 1. an exhibition 2. a performance

show·man (shō'mən) *n., pl.* -men 1. one whose business is producing shows 2. a person skilled at presenting anything in a striking manner —**show'man·ship'** *n.*

shown (shōn) *alt. pp.* of SHOW

show'off' *n.* one who shows off

show'piece' *n.* 1. something exhibited 2. something that is a fine example of its kind

show'place' *n.* 1. a place that is exhibited to the public for its beauty, etc. 2. any place that is beautiful, lavishly furnished, etc.

show'room' *n.* a room where merchandise is displayed, as for advertising or sale

show window a store window for displaying goods

show'y *adj.* -i·er, -i·est 1. of striking appearance 2. attracting attention in a gaudy or flashy way —**show'i·ly** *adv.* —**show'i·ness** *n.*

shrank (shraŋk) *alt. pt.* of SHRINK

shrap·nel (shrap'n'l) *n.* [< Gen. *Shrapnel* (1761–1842), its Brit. inventor] 1. an artillery shell filled with an explosive charge and small metal balls 2. these balls or the shell fragments scattered by any exploding shell

shred (shred) *n.* [OE. *screade*] 1. a long, narrow strip cut or torn off 2. a fragment [not a *shred* of truth] —*vt.* **shred'ded** or **shred, shred'ding** to cut or tear into shreds —**shred'der** *n.*

Shreve·port (shrēv'pôrt) city in NW La.: pop. 182,000

shrew (shrōō) *n.* [OE. *screawa*] 1. a small, mouselike mammal with a long snout 2. a nagging, bad-tempered woman —**shrew'ish** *adj.* —**shrew'ish·ly** *adv.* —**shrew'ish·ness** *n.*

shrewd (shrōōd) *adj.* [ME. *schrewe*, shrew] keen-witted or sharp in practical affairs; astute —**shrewd'ly** *adv.* —**shrewd'ness** *n.*

shriek (shrēk) *vi., vt.* [prob. < ON.] to make or utter with a loud, piercing cry; screech —*n.* such a cry

shrift (shrift) *n.* [< OE. *scrifan*, to shrive] [Archaic] confession to and absolution by a priest

shrike (shrīk) *n.* [OE. *scric*] a shrill-voiced bird of prey with a hooked bill

shrill (shril) *adj.* [echoic] having or producing a high, thin, piercing sound —*vt., vi.* to utter with or make a shrill sound —**shrill'ness** *n.* —**shrill'ly** *adv.*

shrimp (shrimp) *n.* [< OE. *scrimman*, to shrink] 1. a small, long-tailed crustacean, valued as food 2. [Colloq.] a small, slight person

shrine (shrīn) *n.* [< L. *scrinium*, box] 1. a container holding sacred relics 2. a saint's tomb 3. a place or thing hallowed or honored because of its history or associations

shrink (shriŋk) *vi.* **shrank** or **shrunk, shrunk** or **shrunk'en, shrink'ing** [OE. *scrincan*] 1. to contract, as from heat, cold, wetness, etc. 2. to lessen, as in amount, worth, etc. 3. to draw back, as in fear; flinch —*vt.* to cause to shrink —*n.* 1. a shrinking 2. [< (*head*)shrink(*er*)] [Slang] a psychiatrist — **shrink'a·ble** *adj.*

SHRIMP
(to 9 in. long)

shrink'age *n.* 1. a shrinking 2. the amount of shrinking, decrease, etc.

shrinking violet a very shy person

shrive (shrīv) *vt., vi.* **shrived** or **shrove** (shrōv), **shriv'en** (shriv''n) or **shrived, shriv'ing** [< L. *scribere*, write] [Archaic] to hear the confession of and give absolution

shriv·el (shriv''l) *vt., vi.* -eled or -elled, -el·ing or -el·ling [prob. < Scand.] 1. to shrink and wrinkle or wither 2. to make or become helpless, useless, etc.

shroud (shroud) *n.* [OE. *scrud*] 1. a cloth used to wrap a corpse for burial 2. something that covers, protects, etc. 3. any of the ropes stretched from a ship's side to a masthead —*vt.* to hide; cover

Shrove·tide (shrōv'tīd') *n.* the three days before Ash Wednesday (**Shrove Sunday, Monday, and Tuesday**), formerly set aside as a period of confession and festivity just before Lent

shrub (shrub) *n.* [OE. *scrybb*, brushwood] a low, woody plant with several stems; bush

shrub'ber·y *n., pl.* -ies shrubs collectively

shrub'by *adj.* -bi·er, -bi·est 1. covered with shrubs 2. like a shrub

shrug (shrug) *vt., vi.* **shrugged, shrug'ging** [ME. *shruggen*] to draw up (the shoulders), as in doubt, indifference, etc. —*n.* the gesture so made

shrunk (shruŋk) *alt. pt. & pp.* of SHRINK

shrunk'en *alt. pp.* of SHRINK —*adj.* contracted in size

shtick (shtik) *n.* [Yid.] [Slang] a comic bit or special talent

shuck (shuk) *n.* [< ?] a shell, pod, or husk —*vt.* 1. to remove shucks from (corn, clams, etc.) 2. to remove like a shuck [to *shuck* one's clothes]

shucks (shuks) *interj.* [prob. < prec.] an exclamation of disappointment, embarrassment, etc.

shud·der (shud'ər) *vi.* [ME. *schoderen*] to shake or tremble violently, as in horror —*n.* a shuddering

shuf·fle (shuf''l) *vt., vi.* -fled, -fling [prob. < LowG. *schuffeln*] 1. to move (the feet) with a dragging gait 2. to mix (playing cards) so as to change their order 3. to mix together in a jumbled mass 4. to shift or keep shifting from one place to another —*n.* 1. the act of shuffling 2. a deceptive action; trick 3. a gait, dance, etc. in which one shuffles the feet 4. a shuffling of playing cards —**lose in the shuffle** to leave out in the confusion of things — **shuffle off** to get rid of —**shuf'fler** *n.*

shuf'fle·board' *n.* [< *shovel board*] a game in which disks are pushed with a cue along a flat surface toward numbered squares

shun (shun) *vt.* **shunned, shun'ning** [OE. *scunian*] to keep away from; avoid strictly

shunt (shunt) *vt., vi.* [< ? prec.] 1. to move or turn to one side 2. to switch, as a train, from one track to another 3. *Elec.* to divert or be diverted by a shunt —*n.* 1. a shunting 2. a railroad switch 3. *Elec.* a conductor connecting two points in a circuit and diverting part of the current from the main circuit

shush (shush) *interj.* [echoic] hush! be quiet! —*vt.* to say "shush" to; tell (another) to be quiet

shut (shut) *vt.* **shut, shut'ting** [OE. *scyttan*] 1. to move (a door, lid, etc.) into a position that covers the opening to which it is fitted 2. to close (an opening, container, etc.) 3. to prevent entrance to or exit from 4. to fold up the parts of (an umbrella, book, etc.) —*vi.* to be or become shut —*adj.* closed, fastened, etc. —**shut down** to cease or cause to cease operating —**shut in** to surround or enclose —**shut off** 1. to prevent passage of or through 2. to isolate —**shut out** 1. to exclude (a sound, view, etc.) 2. to prevent (the opposition) from scoring —**shut up** 1. to enclose or confine 2. [Colloq.] to stop or make stop talking

shut'down' *n.* a stoppage of work or activity, as in a factory

shut'eye' *n.* [Slang] sleep

shut'-in' *n.* a person who is too ill, weak, etc. to go out — *adj.* not able to go out

shut'-off' *n.* 1. something that shuts off a flow, as a valve, switch, etc. 2. a stoppage; interruption

shut'out' *n.* a preventing of the opposing side or team from scoring

shut'ter *n.* 1. a person or thing that shuts 2. a movable, usually hinged, cover for a window 3. a device for opening and closing the aperture of a camera lens —*vt.* to close or furnish with shutters

shut·tle (shut''l) *n.* [OE. *scytel*] 1. a device used to pass the woof thread back and forth between the warp threads in weaving 2. any of several similar devices, as the device that carries the lower thread back and forth on a sewing machine 3. a bus, train, helicopter, etc. that makes frequent trips back and forth over a short route —*vt., vi.* -**tled, -tling** to move by or as if by a shuttle

shut'tle·cock' *n.* a rounded piece of cork having a flat end stuck with feathers: used in badminton

shy¹ (shī) *adj.* **shy'er** or **shi'er, shy'est** or **shi'est** [OE. *sceoh*] **1.** easily frightened or startled; timid **2.** not at ease with other people; bashful **3.** distrustful; wary **4.** [Slang] lacking —*vi.* **shied, shy'ing 1.** to move suddenly when startled **2.** to be or become cautious or unwilling —**fight shy of** to avoid —**shy'ly** *adv.* —**shy'ness** *n.*

shy² (shī) *vt., vi.* **shied, shy'ing** [< ?] to fling, esp. sideways with a jerk —*n., pl.* **shies** a shying

Shy·lock (shī'läk') the moneylender in Shakespeare's *Merchant of Venice* —*n.* an exacting creditor

shy·ster (shī'stər) *n.* [< ? G. *scheisser*, defecator] [Slang] an unethical or unscrupulous lawyer

‡**sí** (sē) *adv.* [Sp.] yes: also [It.] **si**

Si *Chem.* silicon

Si·am (sī am') *former name of* THAILAND

Si·a·mese (sī'ə mēz') *adj., n., pl.* -**mese** *same as* THAI

Siamese cat a breed of short-haired cat characterized by blue eyes and a fawn-colored coat

Siamese twins [after such a pair born in Siam] any pair of twins born joined to each other

Si·be·li·us (si bā'lē oos; *E.* sə bāl'yəs), **Jean** (zhän) 1865–1957; Finn. composer

Si·ber·i·a (sī bir'ē ə) region in N Asia, between the Urals & the Pacific: Asiatic section of the R.S.F.S.R. —**Si·ber'i·an** *adj., n.*

sib·i·lant (sib''l ənt) *adj.* [< L. *sibilare*, to hiss] having or making a hissing sound —*n.* a sibilant consonant, as (s), (z), (sh), (zh), (ch), and (j) —**sib'i·lance** *n.*

sib·ling (sib'liŋ) *n.* [< OE. *sibling*, a relative] a brother or sister

sib·yl (sib''l) *n.* [< Gr. *sibylla*] **1.** a prophetess of ancient Greece or Rome **2.** a prophetess; fortuneteller —**sib'yl·line'** (-īn', -ēn') *adj.*

‡**sic¹** (sik) *adv.* [L.] thus; so: used within brackets, [*sic*], to show that a quoted passage, esp. one containing some error, is exactly reproduced

sic² (sik) *vt.* **sicked, sick'ing** [< SEEK] to incite (a dog) to attack

Sic·i·ly (sis''l ē) island of Italy, off its S tip —**Si·cil·ian** (si sil'yən, -ē ən) *adj., n.*

sick¹ (sik) *adj.* [OE. *seoc*] **1.** suffering from disease; ill **2.** having nausea **3.** of or for sick people [*sick* leave] **4.** deeply disturbed, as by grief, failure, etc. **5.** disgusted by an excess [*sick* of his excuses] **6.** [Colloq.] morbid [a *sick* joke] —**the sick** sick people —**sick'ish** *adj.*

sick² (sik) *vt. same as* SIC²

sick bay a ship's hospital or dispensary

sick'bed' *n.* the bed of a sick person

sick'en *vt., vi.* to make or become sick, disgusted, etc.

sick'en·ing *adj.* **1.** causing nausea **2.** disgusting

sick·le (sik''l) *n.* [ult. < L. *secare*, to cut] a tool having a crescent-shaped blade with a short handle, for cutting tall grass, weeds, etc.

sick'le-cell' anemia an inherited anemia, found chiefly among blacks, in which red blood cells become sickle-shaped as a result of defective hemoglobin

sick·ly (sik'lē) *adj.* -**li·er, -li·est 1.** in poor health **2.** of or produced by sickness [a *sickly* pallor] **3.** nauseating **4.** faint; feeble [a *sickly* light] **5.** weak; insipid —*adv.* in a sick manner —*vt.* -**lied, -ly·ing** to make sickly, as in color, vigor, etc. —**sick'li·ness** *n.*

sick'ness *n.* **1.** a being sick or diseased **2.** a particular disease **3.** nausea

sick'out' *n.* a staying out of work on the claim of sickness, as by a group of employees trying to win demands

sick'room' *n.* the room of a sick person

side (sīd) *n.* [OE.] **1.** the right or left half of a human or animal body **2.** a position beside one **3.** *a)* any of the lines or surfaces that bound something *b)* either of the two bounding surfaces of an object that are not the front, back, top, or bottom **4.** either of the two surfaces of paper, cloth, etc. **5.** a particular or specified surface [the inner *side* of a vase] **6.** an aspect [his cruel *side*, the bright *side*] **7.** the slope of a hill, bank, etc. **8.** any location with reference to a central point **9.** the ideas, position, etc. of one person or faction opposing another **10.** one of the parties in a contest, conflict, etc. **11.** a line of descent —*adj.* **1.** of, at, or on a side **2.** of or from one side [a *side* glance] **3.** done or happening as something in addition [a *side* effect] **4.** secondary [a *side* issue] —*vt.*

sid'ed, sid'ing to furnish with sides or siding —**on the side** in addition to the main part, occupation, course, etc. —**side by side** beside each other —**side with** to support (one of opposing factions) —**take sides** to support one of the parties in a dispute, etc.

side arms weapons of the kind that may be worn at the side or waist, as a sword, pistol, etc.

side'board' *n.* a piece of dining-room furniture for holding table linen, silverware, etc.

side·burns (sīd'burnz') *n.pl.* [reversed < BURNSIDES] the hair growing on a man's face, just in front of the ears

side'car' *n.* a small car attached to the side of a motorcycle, for carrying a passenger, parcels, etc.

sid·ed (sīd'id) *adj.* having (a specified number of) sides [six-*sided*]

side dish any food served along with the main course, as in a separate dish

side effect a secondary effect, esp. such an effect when undesired, as in drug therapy

side'kick' *n.* [Slang] **1.** a close friend **2.** a partner

side'light' *n.* incidental information

side'line' *n.* **1.** either of two lines marking the side limits of a playing area, as in football **2.** [*pl.*] the areas just outside these lines **3.** a line, as of merchandise or of work, in addition to one's main line —*vt.* -**lined', -lin'ing** to remove from active participation, as by injury

side'long' *adv.* toward the side —*adj.* directed to the side, as a glance

side'piece' *n.* a piece forming, or attached to, the side of something

si·de·re·al (sī dir'ē əl) *adj.* [< L. *sidus*, a star] of, or expressed in reference to, the stars

side'sad'dle *n.* a saddle designed for a rider sitting with both legs on the same side of the animal

side'show' *n.* a small show apart from the main show

side'slip' *vi., vt.* -**slipped', -slip'ping** to slip or cause to slip sideways —*n.* a slip or skid to the side

side'split'ting *adj.* **1.** very hearty: said of laughter **2.** causing hearty laughter

side'step' *vt., vi.* -**stepped', -step'ping** to dodge as by stepping aside

side'swipe' (-swīp') *vt., vi.* -**swiped', -swip'ing** to hit along the side in passing —*n.* such a blow

side'track' *vt., vi.* **1.** to switch (a train) to a siding **2.** to turn away from the main issue

side'walk' *n.* a path for pedestrians, usually paved, along the side of a street

side'ways' (-wāz') *adj., adv.* **1.** from the side **2.** with one side forward Also **side'wise'** (-wīz')

sid·ing (sīd'iŋ) *n.* **1.** boards, panels, etc. for covering the outside of a frame building **2.** a short railroad track, for unloading, bypassing, etc., connected with a main track by a switch

si·dle (sī'd'l) *vi.* -**dled, -dling** [< *sideling*, sideways] to move sideways, esp. shyly or stealthily

siege (sēj) *n.* [< L. *sedere*, sit] **1.** the encirclement of a fortified place by an enemy intending to take it **2.** a persistent effort to win something **3.** a long, distressing period [a *siege* of illness] —**lay siege to** to subject to a siege

Sieg·fried (sēg'frēd) a hero of Germanic legend: in the *Nibelungenlied*, he wins a treasure

si·en·na (sē en'ə) *n.* [It. *terra di Siena*, earth of Siena, city in Italy] **1.** a yellowish-brown earth pigment **2.** a reddish-brown pigment made by burning this **3.** either of these colors

si·er·ra (sē er'ə) *n.* [Sp. < L. *serra*, a saw] a range of mountains with a saw-toothed appearance

Si·er·ra Le·one (sē er'ə lē ōn') country in W Africa, on the Atlantic: 27,925 sq. mi.; pop. 2,600,000; cap. Freetown

si·es·ta (sē es'tə) *n.* [Sp. < L. *sexta* (*hora*), sixth (hour), noon] a nap or rest after the noon meal

sieve (siv) *n.* [OE. *sife*] a utensil with many small openings for straining, sifting, etc.

sift (sift) *vt.* [OE. *siftan*] **1.** to pass through a sieve so as to separate the coarse from the fine particles **2.** to examine with care; weigh (evidence, etc.) **3.** to separate; screen [to *sift* fact from fable] —*vi.* to pass through or as through a sieve —**sift'er** *n.*

sigh (sī) *vi.* [< OE. *sican*] **1.** to take in and let out a long, deep, sounded breath, as in sorrow, relief, etc. **2.** to make a sound like a sigh [trees *sighing* in the wind] **3.** to long or lament (*for*) —*vt.* to express with a sigh —*n.* the act or sound of sighing

sight (sīt) *n.* [< OE. *seon*, to see] **1.** something seen or worth seeing **2.** the act of seeing **3.** a look; glimpse **4.** a device to aid the eye in aiming a gun, etc. **5.** aim or observation taken, as with a gun, sextant, etc. 6. the ability to see; eyesight 7. range of vision 8. [Colloq.] anything that looks unpleasant, odd, etc. —*vt.* 1. to observe 2. to glimpse 3. to adjust the sights of 4. to aim (a gun, etc.) at —*vi.* to look carefully *[sight* along the line*]* —**a sight for sore eyes** [Colloq.] a welcome sight —**at** (or **on**) **sight** as soon as seen —**by sight** by appearance —**catch sight of** to see; glimpse —**lose sight of** 1. to see no longer 2. to forget —**not by a long sight** 1. not nearly 2. not at all —**out of sight** 1. not in sight 2. [Colloq.] extremely high, as in price 3. [Slang] excellent

sight′less *adj.* blind

sight′ly *adj.* -li·er, -li·est 1. pleasant to the sight 2. providing a fine view —**sight′li·ness** *n.*

sight′see′ing *n.* a visiting of places of interest —*adj.* for seeing sights —**sight′se′er** *n.*

sig·ma (sig′mə) *n.* the eighteenth letter of the Greek alphabet (Σ, σ)

sign (sīn) *n.* [< L. *signum*] 1. something that indicates a fact, quality, etc. *[black is a sign of mourning]* 2. a gesture that tells something specified *[a nod is a sign of approval]* 3. a mark or symbol having a specific meaning *[the sign ¢ for cent(s)]* 4. a publicly displayed board, placard, etc. bearing information, advertising, etc. 5. any visible trace or indication *[the signs of spring]* 6. an omen 7. *Astrology* any of the twelve divisions of the zodiac —*vt.* 1. to write one's name on, as in agreement, authorization, etc. 2. to write (one's name) as a signature 3. to hire by written contract —*vi.* 1. to write one's signature 2. to use the sign language of the deaf —**sign away** (or **over**) to transfer title to (something) by signing a document —**sign off** to stop broadcasting, as for the day —**sign on** to hire or be hired —**sign up** 1. to sign on 2. to enlist, as in military service —**sign′er** *n.*

sig·nal (sig′n'l) *n.* [< L. *signum*, a sign] 1. any sign, event, etc. that is a call to some kind of action *[a bugle signal to attack]* 2. *a)* a sign given by gesture, a device, etc. to convey a command, warning, etc. *b)* a device providing such a sign 3. *Radio, TV,* etc. the electrical impulses, sound, picture elements, etc. transmitted or received —*adj.* 1. not ordinary; notable 2. used as a signal —*vt., vi.* -naled or -nalled, -nal·ing or -nal·ling 1. to make a signal or signals (to) 2. to communicate by signals —**sig′nal·er, sig′nal·ler** *n.*

sig′nal·ize′ (-īz′) *vt.* -ized′, -iz′ing 1. to make notable 2. to draw attention to

sig′nal·ly *adv.* in a signal way; notably

sig·na·to·ry (sig′nə tôr′ē) *adj.* that has or have joined in the signing of something —*n., pl.* -ries any of the persons, states, etc. that have signed a document

sig·na·ture (sig′nə chər) *n.* [< L. *signare*, to sign] 1. a person's name written by himself 2. the act of signing one's name 3. *Music* a sign or signs placed at the beginning of a staff to show key or time

sign·board (sīn′bôrd′) *n.* a board bearing a sign, esp. one advertising a business, product, etc.

sig·net (sig′nit) *n.* [< OFr. *signe*, a sign] a small seal used in marking documents as official, etc.

signet ring a finger ring containing a signet, often in the form of an initial

sig·nif·i·cance (sig nif′ə kəns) *n.* 1. that which is signified; meaning 2. the quality of being significant; expressiveness 3. importance; consequence

sig·nif′i·cant (-kənt) *adj.* [< L. *significare*, signify] 1. having or expressing a meaning 2. full of meaning 3. important; momentous —**sig·nif′i·cant·ly** *adv.*

sig·ni·fy (sig′nə fī′) *vt.* -fied′, -fy′ing [< L. *signum*, a sign + *facere*, make] 1. to be an indication of; mean 2. to show or make known by a sign, words, etc. —*vi.* to be significant; matter —**sig′ni·fi·ca′tion** (-fi kā′shən) *n.*

sign language communication of thoughts or ideas by means of manual signs and gestures

‡**si·gnor** (sē nyôr′) *n., pl.* -**gno′ri** (-nyô′rē) [It.] a man; gentleman: as a title [S-], equivalent to *Mr.* or *Sir*

‡**si·gno·ra** (sē nyô′rä) *n., pl.* -**re** (-*re*) [It.] a married woman; lady: as a title [S-], equivalent to *Mrs.* or *Madam*

‡**si·gno·ri·na** (sē′nyô rē′nä) *n., pl.* -**ne** (-ne) [It.] an unmarried woman or girl; young lady: as a title [S-], equivalent to *Miss*

sign′post′ *n.* 1. a post bearing a sign 2. a clear indication; obvious clue, symptom, etc.

Sikh (sēk) *n.* [Hindi, a disciple] a member of a monotheistic Hindu religious sect

si·lage (sī′lij) *n.* green fodder stored in a silo

si·lence (sī′ləns) *n.* 1. a keeping silent or still 2. absence of any sound or noise; stillness 3. omission of mention 4. failure to communicate, write, etc. —*vt.* -lenced, -lenc·ing 1. to make silent 2. to put down —*interj.* be silent!

si′lenc·er *n.* 1. one that silences 2. a device for muffling the report of a firearm

si·lent (sī′lənt) *adj.* [< L. *silere*, be silent] 1. making no vocal sound; mute 2. not talkative 3. free from noise; quiet; still 4. not spoken, expressed, etc. *[silent grief]* 5. making no mention, explanation, etc. 6. not active *[factories now silent]* —**si′lent·ly** *adv.*

Si·le·sia (sī lē′shə, si-; -zhə) region in E Europe, mainly in SW Poland —**Si·le′sian** *adj., n.*

sil·hou·ette (sil′oo wet′) *n.* [< E. de *Silhouette*, 18th-c. Fr. minister of finance] 1. a solid, usually black, outline drawing, esp. a profile 2. any dark shape seen against a light background —*vt.* -et′ted, -et′ting to show or project in silhouette

SILHOUETTE

sil·i·ca (sil′i kə) *n.* [< L. *silex*, flint] the dioxide of silicon, SiO₂, a hard, glassy mineral found in various forms, as in quartz, sand, etc. —**si·li·ceous** (sə lish′əs) *adj.*

sil·i·cate (sil′i kit, -kāt′) *n.* a salt or ester derived from silica

sil·i·con (sil′i kən, -kän) *n.* [< L. *silex*, flint] a nonmetallic chemical element found always in combination: symbol, Si; at. wt., 28.086; at. no., 14

sil′i·cone′ (-kōn′) *n.* an organic silicon compound highly resistant to heat, water, etc. and used in resins, lubricants, polishes, etc.

sil′i·co′sis (-ə kō′sis) *n.* [< SILICON + -OSIS] a chronic lung disease caused by inhaling silica dust over a period of time, as in quarrying

silk (silk) *n.* [OE. *seoluc*] 1. the fine, soft fiber produced by silkworms 2. thread or fabric made from this 3. a garment or other article of such fabric 4. any silklike substance *[corn silk]* —*adj.* of or like silk: also **silk′en**

silk′worm′ (-wurm′) *n.* any of certain moth caterpillars that produce cocoons of silk fiber

silk′y *adj.* -i·er, -i·est of or like silk; smooth, lustrous, etc. —**silk′i·ly** *adv.* —**silk′i·ness** *n.*

sill (sil) *n.* [OE. *syll*] a horizontal piece supporting a house wall, etc. or forming the bottom member of an upright frame for a door or window opening

sil·ly (sil′ē) *adj.* -li·er, -li·est [< OE. *sælig*, happy] 1. having or showing little sense or judgment; foolish, absurd, etc. 2. frivolous 3. [Colloq.] dazed, as from a blow —**sil′li·ly** *adv.* —**sil′li·ness** *n.*

si·lo (sī′lō) *n., pl.* -los [Fr. < Sp. < Gr. *siros*] 1. an airtight pit or tower in which green fodder is stored 2. an underground structure for storing and launching a ballistic missile —*vt.* -loed, -lo·ing to store in a silo

silt (silt) *n.* [prob. < Scand.] earthy sediment made up of fine particles carried or laid down by moving water —*vt., vi.* to fill or choke up with silt —**silt′y** *adj.* -i·er, -i·est

sil·van (sil′vən) *adj., n. same as* SYLVAN

sil·ver (sil′vər) *n.* [< OE. *seolfor*] 1. a white, precious metallic chemical element that is very ductile and malleable: symbol, Ag; at. wt., 107.868; at. no., 47 2. silver coin 3. silverware 4. a lustrous, grayish white —*adj.* 1. of or containing silver 2. silvery 3. eloquent *[a silver tongue]* 4. marking the 25th anniversary —*vt.* to cover with or as with silver

sil′ver·fish′ *n.* a wingless insect with silvery scales and long feelers, found in damp, dark places

silver lining anything seen as hopeful or comforting in the midst of despair, misfortune, etc.

silver nitrate a colorless crystalline salt, AgNO₃, used in photography, as an antiseptic, etc.

silver plate tableware made of, or plated with, silver

sil′ver·smith′ *n.* a skilled worker who makes articles of silver

sil′ver·ware′ *n.* 1. articles, esp. tableware, made of or plated with silver 2. any metal tableware

sil′ver·y *adj.* 1. like silver, as in color or luster 2. covered with or containing silver 3. soft and clear in tone

sim·i·an (sim′ē ən) *adj.* [< L. *simia*, an ape] of or like an ape or monkey —*n.* an ape or monkey

sim·i·lar (sim′ə lər) *adj.* [< L. *similis*] 1. nearly but not exactly the same or alike 2. *Geom.* having the same shape but not the same size or position —**sim′i·lar·ly** *adv.*

sim·i·lar·i·ty (-lar'ə tē) *n.* **1.** a being similar **2.** *pl.* **-ties** a similar point, feature, instance, etc.

sim·i·le (sim'ə lē) *n.* [L., a likeness] a figure of speech in which one thing is likened to another, dissimilar thing by using *like, as,* etc. (Ex.: a voice like thunder)

si·mil·i·tude (sə mil'ə tōōd', -tyōōd') *n.* [< L. *similitudo*] likeness; resemblance

sim·mer (sim'ər) *vi.* [echoic] **1.** to remain at or just below the boiling point **2.** to be about to break out, as in anger, revolt, etc. —*vt.* to keep at or just below the boiling point —*n.* a simmering —**simmer down** to become calm

Si·mon (sī'mən) *Bible* one of the twelve apostles, called *Peter* or *Simon Peter*

si·mon-pure (sī'mən pyoor') *adj.* [< *Simon Pure,* a character in an 18th-c. play] genuine; authentic

si·mo·ny (sī'mə nē, sim'ə-) *n.* [< *Simon Magus,* a magician in the Bible: Acts 8:9-24] the buying or selling of sacred things, as church offices

sim·pa·ti·co (sim pät'i kō) *adj.* [< It. or Sp.] compatible or congenial

sim·per (sim'pər) *vi.* [Early ModE.] to smile in a silly or affected way —*n.* such a smile

sim·ple (sim'p'l) *adj.* **-pler, -plest** [< L. *simplex*] **1.** having only one or a few parts, features, etc.; uncomplicated **2.** easy to do or understand, as a task **3.** without additions [the *simple* facts] **4.** not ornate or luxurious; plain [*simple* clothes, *simple* tastes] **5.** without guile or deceit **6.** not showy; natural **7.** of low rank or position; ordinary **8.** stupid; foolish —**sim'ple·ness** *n.*

simple fraction a fraction in which both numerator and denominator are whole numbers, as 1/2

simple interest interest computed on principal alone, not on principal plus interest

sim·ple-mind·ed *adj.* **1.** foolish **2.** feeble-minded

simple sentence a sentence having one main clause and no subordinate clauses

sim·ple·ton (sim'p'l tən) *n.* a fool

sim·plic·i·ty (sim plis'ə tē) *n., pl.* **-ties 1.** a simple state or quality; freedom from complexity, etc. **2.** absence of elegance, luxury, etc. **3.** freedom from affectation **4.** foolishness

sim·pli·fy (sim'plə fī') *vt.* **-fied', -fy'ing** to make simpler or less complex —**sim'pli·fi·ca'tion** *n.*

sim·plis·tic (sim plis'tik) *adj.* making complex problems unrealistically simple

sim·ply (sim'plē) *adv.* **1.** in a simple way **2.** merely [*simply* trying to help] **3.** completely

sim·u·late (sim'yoo lāt') *vt.* **-lat'ed, -lat'ing** [< L. *simulare*] **1.** to give a false appearance of; feign **2.** to look or act like —**sim'u·la'tion** *n.*

si·mul·cast (sī'm'l kast') *vt.* **-cast' or -cast'ed, -cast'ing** [SIMUL(TANEOUS) + (BROAD)CAST] to broadcast (a program, event, etc.) simultaneously by radio and television —*n.* a program, etc. so broadcast

si·mul·ta·ne·ous (sī'm'l tā'nē əs) *adj.* [< L. *simul,* at the same time] occurring, done, etc. at the same time —**si'mul·ta'ne·ous·ly** *adv.*

sin (sin) *n.* [OE. *synne*] **1.** the willful breaking of religious or moral law **2.** any offense or fault —*vi.* **sinned, sin'ning** to commit a sin —**sin'ner** *n.*

Si·nai (sī'nī), **Mount** *Bible* the mountain where Moses received the Law from God: Ex. 19

since (sins) *adv.* [ult. < OE. *sith,* after + *thæt,* that] **1.** from then until now [he came Monday and has been here ever *since*] **2.** at some time between then and now [he was ill last week but has *since* recovered] **3.** before now; ago [gone long *since*] —*prep.* **1.** continuously from (the time given) until now [out walking *since* noon] **2.** during the period following [he's written twice *since* May] —*conj.* **1.** after the time that [two years *since* they met] **2.** continuously from the time when [lonely ever *since* he left] **3.** because [*since* you're tired, let's go]

sin·cere (sin sir') *adj.* **-cer'er, -cer'est** [< L. *sincerus,* pure] **1.** without deceit or pretense **2.** genuine [*sincere* affection] —**sin·cere'ly** *adv.*

sin·cer·i·ty (sin ser'ə tē) *n., pl.* **-ties** a being sincere; honesty, genuineness, etc.

sine (sin) *n.* [< L. *sinus,* a curve] the ratio of the side opposite a given acute angle in a right triangle to the hypotenuse

si·ne·cure (sī'nə kyoor', sin'ə-) *n.* [< L. *sine,* without + *cura,* care] any position that brings profit while requiring little or no work

si·ne di·e (sī'nē dī'ē) [LL., without a day] for an indefinite period

sin·ew (sin'yōō) *n.* [< OE. *seonu*] **1.** a tendon **2.** muscular power; strength **3.** [*often pl.*] any source of power

sin·ew·y (-yōō wē) *adj.* **1.** of or like sinew; tough **2.** having good muscular development **3.** vigorous; powerful

sin·ful (sin'fəl) *adj.* full of or characterized by sin; wicked —**sin'ful·ly** *adv.* —**sin'ful·ness** *n.*

sing (siŋ) *vi.* **sang** or now rarely **sung, sung, sing'ing** [OE. *singan*] **1.** *a)* to produce musical sounds with the voice *b)* to perform musical selections vocally **2.** to use song in praise [of thee I *sing*] **3.** to produce musical sounds, as a songbird **4.** to whistle, hum, buzz, etc., as a teakettle, bee, etc. **5.** to rejoice [his heart *sang*] **6.** [Slang] to confess to a crime, esp. implicating others —*vt.* **1.** to render (a song, etc.) by singing **2.** to proclaim, extol, etc. in song **3.** to bring or put by singing [to *sing* to sleep] —*n.* [Colloq.] a singing by a group —**sing'a·ble** *adj.* —**sing·er** (siŋ'ər) *n.*

sing. singular

Sin·ga·pore (siŋ'gə pôr') island country off the S tip of the Malay Peninsula: 225 sq. mi.; pop. 2,110,000

singe (sinj) *vt.* **singed, singe'ing** [OE. *sengan*] **1.** to burn superficially or slightly **2.** to expose (a carcass) to flame in removing feathers, etc. —*n.* **1.** a singeing **2.** a slight burn —**sing·er** (sin'jər) *n.*

Sin·gha·lese (siŋ'gə lēz') *adj., n., pl.* **-lese'** *same as* SIN-HALESE

sin·gle (siŋ'g'l) *adj.* [< L. *singulus*] **1.** *a)* one only *b)* separate and distinct [every *single* time] **2.** alone **3.** of or for one person or family **4.** between two persons only [*single* combat] **5.** unmarried **6.** having only one part; not multiple **7.** unbroken **8.** sincere —*vt.* **-gled, -gling** to select from others (usually with *out*) —*vi. Baseball* to hit a single —*n.* **1.** a single person or thing **2.** *Baseball* a hit by which the batter reaches first base **3.** [*pl.*] *Tennis,* etc. a match with only one player on each side —**sin'gle·ness** *n.*

sin'gle-breast'ed *adj.* overlapping over the breast just enough to be fastened with one button, as a coat

single file a single column of persons or things, one behind another

sin'gle-hand'ed *adj., adv.* **1.** using only one hand **2.** done or working alone —**sin'gle-hand'ed·ly** *adv.*

sin'gle-mind'ed *adj.* **1.** honest; sincere **2.** with only one aim or purpose

sin'gle·ton (-tən) *n.* **1.** a playing card that is the only one of a suit held by a player **2.** a single thing

sin'gle-track' *adj.* *same as* ONE-TRACK

sin·gle·tree (siŋ'g'l trē') *n.* [< ME. *swingle,* a rod + *tre,* a tree] a crossbar at the front of a wagon, etc. to which the traces of a horse's harness are hooked

sin·gly (siŋ'glē) *adv.* **1.** alone **2.** one by one **3.** unaided

sing'song' *n.* **1.** an unvarying rise and fall of tone **2.** speech, tones, etc. marked by this —*adj.* monotonous because done in singsong

sin·gu·lar (siŋ'gyə lər) *adj.* [< L. *singulus,* single] **1.** being the only one of its kind; unique **2.** extraordinary; remarkable **3.** strange; odd **4.** *Gram.* designating only one —*n. Gram.* the singular number or form of a word —**sin'gu·lar'i·ty** (-lar'ə tē) *n., pl.* **-ties** —**sin'gu·lar·ly** *adv.*

Sin·ha·lese (sin'hə lēz', -lēs') *adj.* of Sri Lanka, its principal people, their language, etc. —*n.* **1.** *pl.* **-lese'** any of the Sinhalese people **2.** their language

sin·is·ter (sin'is tər) *adj.* [< L. *sinister,* left-hand] **1.** orig., on or to the left-hand side **2.** threatening harm, evil, etc. **3.** evil; dishonest —**sin'is·ter·ly** *adv.* —**sin'is·ter·ness** *n.*

sink (siŋk) *vi.* **sank** or **sunk, sunk, sink'ing** [OE. *sincan*] **1.** to go beneath the surface of water, snow, etc. **2.** to go down slowly **3.** to appear to descend, as the sun **4.** to become lower, as in level, degree, value, etc. **5.** to become hollow, as the cheeks **6.** to pass gradually (*into* sleep, etc.) **7.** to approach death **8.** to become absorbed; penetrate —*vt.* **1.** to cause to sink, go down, etc. **2.** to make (a well, design, etc.) by digging, cutting, etc. **3.** to invest **4.** to defeat; undo —*n.* **1.** a cesspool or sewer **2.** a basin, as in a kitchen, with a drainpipe and, usually, a water supply **3.** an area of sunken land

sink'er *n.* **1.** one that sinks **2.** a lead weight for fishing **3.** [Colloq.] a doughnut

sinking fund a fund built up to pay off a debt, as of a corporation

Sino- [Fr. < Gr. *Sinai*] *a combining form meaning* Chinese and

sin·u·ous (sin'yoo wəs) *adj.* [< L. *sinus,* a bend] **1.** bending or winding in and out **2.** not straightforward; devious —**sin'u·os'i·ty** (-wäs'ə tē) *n., pl.* **-ties** —**sin'u·ous·ly** *adv.*

si·nus (sī'nəs) *n.* [L., a bent surface] **1.** a cavity, hollow, etc.; specif., *a)* any of the air cavities in the skull opening into a nasal cavity *b)* a channel for venous blood **2.** a channel leading from a pus-filled cavity

si·nus·i·tis (sī'nə sīt'əs) *n.* inflammation of a sinus, esp. of the skull

-sion [< L. -sio] a suffix meaning act, quality, condition, or result of [discussion, confusion]

Sioux (sōō) n., pl. **Sioux** (sōō, sōōz) same as DAKOTA (n. 1 & 2) —adj. same as DAKOTA: also **Siou·an** (sōō′ən)

sip (sip) vt., vi. **sipped, sip′ping** [akin to LowG. sippen] to drink a little at a time —n. **1.** a sipping **2.** a small quantity sipped —**sip′per** n.

si·phon (sī′fən) n. [Fr. < Gr. siphōn, a tube] **1.** a bent tube for carrying liquid out over the edge of a container to a lower level, through the force of air pressure on the liquid **2.** a sealed bottle from which carbonated water may be released —vt., vi. to draw off, or pass, through a siphon

sir (sur) n. [see ff.] **1.** [sometimes S-] a respectful term of address used to a man: not followed by the name **2.** [S-] a title used before the name of a knight or baronet

sire (sīr) n. [< L. senior, comp. of senex, old] **1.** a title of respect used in addressing a king **2.** [Poet.] a father or forefather **3.** the male parent of an animal —vt. **sired, sir′ing** to beget: said esp. of animals

si·ren (sī′rən) n. [< Gr. Seirēn] **1.** Gr. & Rom. Myth. any of several sea nymphs whose singing lured sailors to their death on rocky coasts **2.** a seductive woman **3.** a warning device, etc. producing a loud, wailing sound

Sir·i·us (sir′ē əs) [< Gr. Seirios, lit., scorcher] same as DOG STAR (sense 1)

sir·loin (sur′loin) n. [< OFr. sur, over + loigne, loin] a choice cut of beef from the loin end just in front of the rump

si·roc·co (sə räk′ō) n., pl. **-cos** [It. < Ar. sharq, the east] a hot, oppressive wind blowing from the Libyan deserts into S Europe

sir·up (sir′əp, sur′-) n. same as SYRUP

sis (sis) n. colloq. form of SISTER

si·sal (sī′s'l) n. [< Sisal, Yucatán] **1.** a strong fiber obtained from the leaves of an agave **2.** this agave

sis·sy (sis′ē) n., pl. **-sies** [dim. of SIS] [Colloq.] **1.** an effeminate man or boy **2.** a coward —**sis′si·fied′** adj.

sis·ter (sis′tər) n. [ON. systir] **1.** a female as she is related to other children of her parents **2.** a close friend who is like a sister **3.** a female fellow member of the same race, creed, profession, etc. **4.** a nun **5.** one of the same kind, model, etc. —adj. related as sisters —**sis′ter·hood′** n.

sis′ter-in-law′ n., pl. **sis′ters-in-law′** **1.** the sister of one's spouse **2.** the wife of one's brother **3.** the wife of the brother of one's spouse

sis′ter·ly adj. **1.** of or like a sister **2.** friendly, kind, etc. —**sis′ter·li·ness** n.

Sis·y·phus (sis′ə fəs) Gr. Myth. a greedy king doomed forever in Hades to roll uphill a stone which always rolled down again

sit (sit) vi. **sat, sit′ting** [OE. sittan] **1.** to rest the body on the buttocks, as on a chair **2.** to rest on the haunches with the forelegs braced, as a dog **3.** to perch, as a bird **4.** to cover eggs for hatching **5.** a) to occupy a seat as a judge, legislator, etc. b) to be in session, as a court **6.** to pose, as for a portrait **7.** to be inactive **8.** to be located **9.** to rest or lie as specified [cares sit lightly on him] **10.** same as BABY-SIT —vt. **1.** to cause to sit **2.** to stay seated on (a horse, etc.) —**sit back 1.** to relax **2.** to be passive —**sit down** to take a seat —**sit in** to attend (often with on) —**sit on** (or **upon**) **1.** to be on (a jury, committee, etc.) **2.** [Colloq.] to suppress, squelch, etc. —**sit out 1.** to stay until the end of **2.** to take no part in (a dance, game, etc.) —**sit up 1.** to sit erect **2.** to put off going to bed **3.** [Colloq.] to become suddenly alert —**sit′ter** n.

si·tar (si tär′) n. [Hindi sitār] a lutelike instrument of India with a long, fretted neck, a resonating gourd, and strings that vibrate along with those being played

sit′-down′ n. **1.** a strike in which strikers stay inside a factory, etc. refusing to work until agreement is reached: in full **sit-down strike 2.** civil disobedience in which demonstrators sit down in streets, etc. and resist being moved

site (sīt) n. [< L. situs, position] **1.** a piece of land considered for a certain purpose [a good site for a town] **2.** location or scene

sit′-in′ n. a sit-down inside a public place, as by a civil rights group

SITAR

sit′ting n. **1.** the act or position of one that sits **2.** a session, as of a court **3.** a period of being seated

sitting duck [Colloq.] a person or thing easily attacked; easy target

sit·u·ate (sich′ōō wāt′) vt. **-at′ed, -at′ing** [< L. situs, site] to put in a certain place; locate

sit′u·a′tion n. **1.** location; position **2.** a place; locality **3.** condition with regard to circumstances **4.** a certain state of affairs **5.** a position of employment

situation comedy a comic television series made up of episodes involving the same group of stock characters

sit′-up′, sit′up′ n. an exercise of sitting up from a lying position without using hands or legs

Si·va (sē′və) Hindu god of destruction and reproduction: see BRAHMA

six (siks) adj., n. [OE. sex] one more than five; 6; VI —**sixth** (siksth) adj., n.

six′pence (-pəns) n. **1.** the sum of six British (old) pennies **2.** a coin of this value, discontinued (1971)

six′-shoot′er n. [Colloq.] a revolver that fires six shots without reloading: also **six′-gun′**

six′teen′ (-tēn′) adj., n. [OE. syxtene] six more than ten; 16; XVI —**six′teenth′** (-tēnth′) adj., n.

sixteenth note Music a note (♬) having one sixteenth the duration of a whole note

sixth sense intuitive power

six·ty (siks′tē) adj., n., pl. **-ties** [OE. sixtig] six times ten; 60; LX —**the sixties** the numbers or years, as of a century, from 60 through 69 —**six′ti·eth** (-ith) adj., n.

siz·a·ble (sīz′ə b'l) adj. quite large or bulky: also **size′a·ble** —**siz′a·ble·ness** n. —**siz′a·bly** adv.

size¹ (sīz) n. [ult. < L. sedere, sit] **1.** that quality of a thing which determines how much space it occupies; dimensions **2.** any of a series of graded classifications of goods [size ten shoes] **3.** a) extent, amount, etc. b) sizable amount, dimensions, etc. **4.** [Colloq.] true state of affairs —vt. **sized, siz′ing** to make or arrange according to size —**of a size** of the same size —**size up** [Colloq.] **1.** to estimate; judge **2.** to meet requirements

size² (sīz) n. [ME. syse] a thin, pasty substance used as a glaze or filler on paper, cloth, etc. —vt. **sized′, siz′ing** to fill, stiffen, or glaze with size

-sized a combining form meaning having (a specified) size [small-sized] : also **-size** [life-size]

siz·ing (sī′ziŋ) n. **1.** same as SIZE² **2.** the act or process of applying size

siz·zle (siz′'l) vi. **-zled, -zling** [echoic] **1.** to make a hissing sound when in contact with heat **2.** to be extremely hot —n. a sizzling sound

skate¹ (skāt) n. [< OFr. eschace, stilt] **1.** a) a bladelike metal runner in a frame, fastened to a shoe for gliding on ice b) a shoe with such a runner attached Also **ice skate 2.** a frame or shoe with two pairs of small wheels, for gliding on a floor, sidewalk, etc.: also **roller skate** —vi. **skat′ed, skat′ing** to move along on skates —**skat′er** n.

skate² (skāt) n. [< ON. skata] a fish of the ray family with a broad, flat body and a short tail

ske·dad·dle (ski dad′'l) vi. **-dled, -dling** [< ?] [Colloq.] to run away

skeet (skēt) n. [< ON. skeyti, projectile] trapshooting in which the shooter fires from different angles

skein (skān) n. [< MFr. escaigne] a quantity of thread or yarn in a coil

skel·e·ton (skel′ə t'n) n. [< Gr. skeletos, dried up] **1.** the hard framework of bones of an animal body **2.** a very thin person or animal **3.** a supporting framework **4.** an outline, as of a book —adj. of or like a skeleton —**skeleton in the closet** some fact kept secret because of shame —**skel′e·tal** adj.

skeleton key a key with a slender bit that can open many simple locks

skep·tic (skep′tik) adj. [< Gr. skeptikos, inquiring] var. of SKEPTICAL —n. **1.** an adherent of skepticism **2.** one who habitually questions matters generally accepted **3.** one who doubts religious doctrines

skep′ti·cal (-ti k'l) adj. doubting; questioning —**skep′ti·cal·ly** adv.

skep′ti·cism (-siz'm) n. **1.** the doctrine that the truth of all knowledge must always be in question **2.** skeptical attitude **3.** doubt about religious doctrines

sketch (skech) n. [Du. schets < Gr. schedios, extempore] **1.** a rough drawing or design, done rapidly **2.** a brief outline **3.** a short, light story, play, etc. —vi., vt. to make a sketch (of) —**sketch′y** adj. **-i·er, -i·est**

at, āpe, cär; ten, ēven; is, bīte; gō, hôrn, tōōl, look; oil, out; up, fur; thin, then; zh, leisure; ŋ, ring; ə for a in ago; as in able (ā′b'l); ë, Fr. coeur; ö, Fr. feu; Fr. mon; ü, Fr. duc; r, Fr. cri; kh, G. doch, ich. ‡ foreign; < derived from

sketch′book′ *n.* **1.** a book of drawing paper for making sketches **2.** a book of literary sketches

skew (skyōō) *vi.* [see ESCHEW] to swerve or twist —*vt.* **1.** to make slanting or oblique **2.** to bias or distort —*adj.* slanting —*n.* a slant or twist

skew·er (skyōō′ər) *n.* [< ON. *skifa*, a slice] a long pin used to hold meat together while it is cooking —*vt.* to fasten or pierce with skewers

ski (skē) *n., pl.* **skis, ski** [Norw. < ON. *skith*, snowshoe] either of a pair of long runners of wood, etc. fastened to the shoes for gliding over snow —*vi.* **skied, ski′ing** to glide on skis, as down snow-covered slopes —**ski′er** *n.*

skid (skid) *n.* [< ON. *skith*, snowshoe] **1.** a plank, log, etc. used as a track upon which to slide a heavy object **2.** a low, movable platform for holding loads **3.** a runner on an aircraft landing gear **4.** a sliding wedge used to brake a wheel **5.** the act of skidding —*vt., vi.* **skid′ded, skid′ding 1.** to slide or slip, as a vehicle on ice **2.** to decline sharply, as prices —**be on (or hit) the skids** [Slang] to be on the downgrade

skid row [alt. < *skid road*, trail to skid logs along] a section of a city where vagrants, derelicts, etc. gather

skiff (skif) *n.* [< It. *schifo*] **1.** a light rowboat **2.** a long, narrow rowboat, esp. one with a small sail

ski lift a motor-driven, endless cable, typically with seats, for carrying skiers up a slope

skill (skil) *n.* [ON. *skil*, distinction] **1.** great ability or proficiency; expertness **2.** an art, craft, etc., esp. one involving the use of the hands or body **3.** ability in such an art, craft, etc. —**skilled** *adj.*

skil·let (skil′it) *n.* [< ? L. *scutra*, a dish] a shallow pan with a handle, for frying food

skill·ful, skil·ful (skil′fəl) *adj.* having or showing skill; accomplished —**skill′ful·ly, skil′ful·ly** *adv.* —**skill′ful·ness, skil′ful·ness** *n.*

skim (skim) *vt., vi.* **skimmed, skim′ming** [ME. *skimen*] **1.** to remove (floating matter) from (a liquid) **2.** to look through (a book, etc.) hastily **3.** to glide lightly (over) —**skim′mer** *n.*

skim milk milk with the cream removed

skimp (skimp) *vi.* [prob. alt. < SCRIMP] [Colloq.] **1.** to allow too little; scrimp **2.** to keep expenses very low —*vt.* [Colloq.] **1.** to do poorly or carelessly **2.** to be stingy in or toward

skimp′y *adj.* **-i·er, -i·est** [Colloq.] barely enough; scanty —**skimp′i·ly** *adv.* —**skimp′i·ness** *n.*

skin (skin) *n.* [ON. *skinn*] **1.** the outer covering of the animal body **2.** a pelt **3.** something like skin, as fruit rind, etc. —*vt.* **skinned, skin′ning 1.** to remove the skin of **2.** to injure by scraping (one's knee, etc.) **3.** [Colloq.] to swindle —*vi.* [Colloq.] to move (*through*), pass (*by*), by a tiny margin —**by the skin of one's teeth** barely —**get under one's skin** [Colloq.] to irritate one —**skin′less** *adj.*

skin diving underwater swimming with air supplied by snorkel, scuba equipment, etc. —**skin′-dive′** *vi.* **-dived′, -div′ing** —**skin diver**

skin′flick′ (-flik′) *n.* [Slang] a pornographic motion picture

skin′flint′ *n.* [lit., one who would skin a flint for economy] a miser

skinned (skind) *adj.* having skin (of a specified kind) [*dark-skinned*]

skin·ny (skin′ē) *adj.* **-ni·er, -ni·est** emaciated; thin —**skin′ni·ness** *n.*

skin′ny-dip′ (-dip′) *vi.* **-dipped′, -dip′ping** [Colloq.] to swim in the nude

skin′tight′ *adj.* clinging closely to the skin; tightfitting [*skintight* jeans]

skip (skip) *vi., vt.* **skipped, skip′ping** [ME. *skippen*] **1.** to leap lightly (over) **2.** to ricochet or bounce **3.** to pass from one point to another, omitting or ignoring (what lies between) **4.** [Colloq.] to leave (a place) hurriedly —*n.* **1.** an act of skipping **2.** a gait alternating light hops on each foot

skip·per (skip′ər) *n.* [< MDu. *schip*, a ship] the captain of a ship —*vt.* to act as skipper of

skir·mish (skur′mish) *n.* [< It. *schermire*, to fight < Gmc.] **1.** a brief fight between small groups, usually a part of a battle **2.** any slight conflict —*vi.* to take part in a skirmish —**skir′mish·er** *n.*

skirt (skurt) *n.* [< ON. *skyrt*, shirt] **1.** that part of a dress, coat, etc. that hangs below the waist **2.** a woman's garment that hangs down from the waist **3.** something like a skirt —*vi., vt.* to be on, or move along, the edge (of)

ski run a slope or course used for skiing

skit (skit) *n.* [prob. ult. < ON. *skjota*, to shoot] a short, humorous sketch, as in the theater

ski tow an endless cable for towing skiers up a slope on their skis

skit·tish (skit′ish) *adj.* [see SKIT & -ISH] **1.** lively or playful, esp. in a coy way **2.** easily frightened; jumpy **3.** fickle; undependable —**skit′tish·ly** *adv.* —**skit′tish·ness** *n.*

skiv·vy (skiv′ē) *n., pl.* **-vies** [< ?] [Slang] **1.** a man's, esp. a sailor's, short-sleeved undershirt: usually **skivvy shirt 2.** [*pl.*] men's underwear

skoal (skōl) *interj.* [< Dan. & Norw. < ON. *skål*, a bowl] to your health: a toast

skul·dug·ger·y, skull·dug·ger·y (skul dug′ər ē) *n.* [< ?] [Colloq.] sneaky, dishonest behavior

skulk (skulk) *vi.* [ME. *sculken*] to move about in a stealthy manner; slink —**skulk′er** *n.*

skull (skul) *n.* [< Scand.] **1.** the bony framework of the head, enclosing the brain **2.** the head or mind

skull and crossbones a representation of two bones under a human skull, used to label poisons, etc.

skull′cap′ *n.* a light, closefitting, brimless cap, usually worn indoors

skunk (skuŋk) *n.* [< AmInd. *segonku*] **1.** a small, bushy-tailed mammal having black fur with white stripes down the back: it ejects a foul-smelling liquid when molested **2.** its fur **3.** [Colloq.] a despicable person —*vt.* [Slang] to defeat overwhelmingly in a game or contest

skunk cabbage a plant having large, cabbagelike leaves and a disagreeable smell

sky (skī) *n., pl.* **skies** [< ON., a cloud] **1.** [*often pl.*] the upper atmosphere [blue *skies*, a cloudy *sky*] **2.** the firmament **3.** heaven —**out of a clear (blue) sky** without warning

SKUNK
(to 27 in. long, including tail)

sky blue a blue color like that of the sky on a clear day —**sky′-blue′** *adj.*

sky′cap′ (-kap′) *n.* a porter at an air terminal

sky′-high′ *adj., adv.* very high

sky′jack′ (-jak′) *vt.* [Colloq.] to hijack (an aircraft) —**sky′jack′er** *n.*

sky′lark′ *n.* a Eurasian lark, famous for the song it utters as it soars —*vi.* [SKY + LARK²] to frolic

sky′light′ *n.* a window in a roof or ceiling

sky′line′ *n.* **1.** the visible horizon **2.** the outline of a city, etc. seen against the sky

sky′rock′et *n.* a firework rocket that explodes in midair —*vi., vt.* to rise or cause to rise rapidly

sky′scrap′er (-skrā′pər) *n.* a very tall building

sky′ward (-wərd) *adv., adj.* toward the sky: also **sky′-wards** *adv.*

sky′ways′ *n.pl.* routes of air travel

sky′writ′ing (-rīt′iŋ) *n.* the tracing of words, etc. in the sky by trailing smoke from an airplane —**sky′writ′er** *n.*

slab (slab) *n.* [ME. *sclabbe*] a flat, broad, fairly thick piece

slack¹ (slak) *adj.* [OE. *slæc*] **1.** slow; sluggish **2.** not busy; dull [*a slack* period] **3.** loose; not tight **4.** lax **5.** careless [*a slack* workman] —*vt., vi. same as* SLACKEN —*adv.* in a slack manner —*n.* **1.** a part that is slack or hangs loose **2.** a lack of tension **3.** a dull period; lull —**slack off** to slacken —**slack up** to go more slowly —**slack′ness** *n.*

slack² (slak) *n.* [ME. *sleck*] a mixture of small pieces of coal, coal dust, and dirt left from the screening of coal

slack·en (slak′'n) *vt., vi.* **1.** to make or become less active, brisk, etc. **2.** to loosen or relax, as rope

slack′er *n.* one who shirks his work or duty

slacks (slaks) *n.pl.* trousers for men and women, esp. trousers that are not part of a suit

slag (slag) *n.* [< MLowG. *slagge*] the fused refuse separated from a metal in smelting

slain (slān) *pp.* of SLAY

slake (slāk) *vt.* **slaked′, slak′ing** [< OE. *slæc*, slack] **1.** to make (thirst, etc.) less intense by satisfying **2.** to produce a chemical change in (lime) by combination with water

sla·lom (slä′ləm) *n.* [Norw., sloping trail] a downhill skiing race over a zigzag course

slam¹ (slam) *vt., vi.* **slammed, slam′ming** [prob. < Scand.] **1.** to shut, hit, throw, put, etc. with force and noise **2.** [Colloq.] to criticize severely —*n.* **1.** the act or sound of slamming **2.** [Colloq.] a severe criticism

slam² (slam) *n.* [< ?] *Bridge shortened form of* GRAND SLAM or LITTLE SLAM

slan·der (slan′dər) *n.* [see SCANDAL] **1.** the utterance of a falsehood damaging to another's reputation **2.** such a spoken falsehood —*vt.* to utter such a falsehood about — **slan′der·er** *n.* —**slan′der·ous** *adj.* —**slan′der·ous·ly** *adv.*

slang (slaŋ) *n.* [< ?] highly informal language, usually short-lived, that is outside of standard usage —**slang′y** *adj.* -i·er, -i·est

slant (slant) *vt., vi.* [< Scand.] **1.** to incline; slope **2.** to write or tell so as to express a particular bias —*n.* **1.** an oblique surface, line, etc.; slope **2.** *a)* a point of view or attitude *b)* a bias —*adj.* sloping —**slant′ing** *adj.* —**slant′-ing·ly** *adv.*

slap (slap) *n.* [echoic] **1.** a blow with something flat, as the palm of the hand **2.** the sound of this **3.** an insult; rebuff —*vt.* **slapped, slap′ping 1.** to strike with something flat **2.** to put, hit, etc. carelessly or with force —*vi.* to make a dull, sharp noise, as upon impact

slap′dash′ (-dash′) *adv.* in a hasty, careless manner —*adj.* hasty, careless, impetuous, etc.

slap′-hap′py (-hap′ē) *adj.* [Slang] **1.** dazed, as by blows to the head **2.** silly or giddy

slap′stick′ (-stik′) *n.* crude comedy full of horseplay —*adj.* of or like such comedy

slash (slash) *vt.* [< ? OFr. *esclachier,* to break] **1.** to cut with sweeping strokes, as of a knife **2.** to whip viciously **3.** to cut slits in **4.** to reduce drastically, as prices —*vi.* to make a sweeping stroke as with a knife —*n.* **1.** a slashing **2.** a cut made by slashing

slat (slat) *n.* [< OFr. *esclat,* a fragment] a thin, narrow strip of wood, metal, etc. —*vt.* **slat′ted, slat′ting** to provide with slats

slate (slāt) *n.* [see SLAT] **1.** a hard rock that cleaves into thin, smooth layers **2.** its bluish-gray color **3.** a thin piece of slate, esp. one used as a roofing tile or as a tablet for writing on with chalk **4.** a list of candidates proposed for nomination or election —*vt.* **slat′ed, slat′ing 1.** to cover with slate **2.** to put on a list or designate, as for candidacy, an appointment, etc. —**a clean slate** a record showing no faults, mistakes, etc.

slath·er (slath′ər) *vt.* [< ?] [Dial. or Colloq.] to cover or spread thickly

slat·tern (slat′ərn) *n.* [< dial. *slatter,* to slop] a slovenly or sluttish woman —**slat′tern·ly** *adj., adv.*

slaugh·ter (slôt′ər) *n* [< ON. *slātr,* lit., slain flesh] **1.** the killing of animals for food; butchering **2.** the brutal killing of a person **3.** the killing of people in large numbers —*vt.* **1.** to kill (animals) for food; butcher **2.** to kill (people) brutally or in large numbers —**slaugh′ter·er** *n.*

slaugh′ter·house′ *n.* a place where animals are butchered for food

Slav (släv, slav) *n.* a member of a group of peoples of E and SE Europe, including the Russians, Serbs, Czechs, Poles, Slovaks, etc. —*adj. same as* SLAVIC

Slav. Slavic

slave (slāv) *n.* [< LGr. *Sklabos:* first applied to captive Slavs] **1.** a human being who is owned by another **2.** one who is dominated by some influence, habit, etc. **3.** one who slaves; drudge —*vi.* **slaved, slav′ing** to work like a slave; drudge

slave driver 1. one who oversees the work of slaves **2.** any merciless taskmaster

slave′hold′er *n.* a person who owns slaves —**slave′hold′-ing** *adj., n.*

slav·er¹ (slav′ər) *vi.* [< Scand.] to drool —*n.* saliva drooling from the mouth

slav·er² (slā′vər) *n.* **1.** a ship used in the slave trade **2.** one who deals in slaves

slav·er·y (slā′və rē, slāv′rē) *n.* **1.** the owning of slaves as a practice or institution **2.** the condition of being a slave; bondage **3.** drudgery; toil

Slav·ic (släv′ik, slav′-) *adj.* of the Slavs, their languages, etc. —*n.* a branch of the Indo-European family of languages, including Russian, Bulgarian, Polish, Czech, etc.

slav·ish (slā′vish) *adj.* **1.** of or like slaves; specif., *a)* servile *b)* laborious **2.** blindly dependent or imitative —**slav′-ish·ly** *adv.* —**slav′ish·ness** *n.*

slaw (slô) *n. short for* COLESLAW

slay (slā) *vt.* **slew** or for 2 **slayed, slain, slay′ing** [OE. *slean*] **1.** to kill in a violent way **2.** [Slang] to amuse, impress, etc. greatly

slea·zy (slē′zē) *adj.* **-zi·er, -zi·est** [< *Slesia,* var. of SILESIA] **1.** flimsy in texture [a *sleazy* fabric] **2.** shoddy, cheap, etc. —**slea′zi·ly** *adv.* —**slea′zi·ness** *n.*

sled (sled) *n.* [ME. *sledde*] a vehicle on runners for moving over snow, ice, etc. —*vt., vi.* **sled′ded, sled′ding** to carry or ride on a sled

sledge¹ (slej) *n.* [OE. *slecge*] *same as* SLEDGEHAMMER

sledge² (slej) *n.* [MDu. *sleedse*] a large, heavy sled for carrying loads —*vt.* **sledged, sledg′ing** to carry by sledge

sledge′ham′mer *n.* [see SLEDGE¹] a long, heavy hammer, usually held with both hands —*adj.* crushingly powerful

sleek (slēk) *adj.* [var. of SLICK] **1.** smooth and shiny; glossy **2.** of well-fed or well-groomed appearance **3.** suave —*vt.* to make sleek —**sleek′ly** *adv.* —**sleek′ness** *n.*

sleep (slēp) *n.* [OE. *slæp*] **1.** *a)* a natural, regularly recurring state of rest for the body and mind, during which there is little or no conscious thought *b)* a period of sleeping **2.** any state like sleep, as a coma —*vi.* **slept, sleep′ing 1.** to be in the state of, or a state like, sleep **2.** [Colloq.] to postpone a decision (*on*) —*vt.* **1.** to have (a specified kind of sleep) **2.** to provide sleeping accommodations for —**sleep off** to rid oneself of by sleeping —**sleep over** [Colloq.] to spend the night at another's home

sleep′er *n.* **1.** one who sleeps **2.** a railroad car with berths for passengers to sleep in: also **sleeping car 3.** something that achieves an unexpected success **4.** [*usually pl.*] pajamas, esp. children's pajamas, that enclose the feet

sleeping bag a warmly lined, zippered bag for sleeping in, esp. outdoors

sleeping sickness 1. an infectious, usually fatal disease, esp. in Africa, characterized by lethargy, prolonged coma, etc. **2.** inflammation of the brain, caused by a virus and inducing drowsiness, etc.

sleep′less (-lis) *adj.* **1.** wakeful; restless **2.** always alert or active —**sleep′less·ly** *adv.* —**sleep′less·ness** *n.*

sleep′walk′ing *n.* the act or practice of walking while asleep —**sleep′walk′er** *n.*

sleep′wear′ (-wer′) *n. same as* NIGHT CLOTHES

sleep′y *adj.* **-i·er, -i·est 1.** ready or likely to fall asleep; drowsy **2.** dull; quiet [a *sleepy* town] **3.** causing drowsiness —**sleep′i·ly** *adv.* —**sleep′i·ness** *n.*

sleet (slēt) *n.* [ME. *slete*] **1.** partly frozen rain **2.** a mixture of rain with snow —*vi.* to shower in the form of sleet

sleeve (slēv) *n.* [OE. *sliefe*] **1.** that part of a garment that covers the arm **2.** a tubelike part fitting around another part —**up one's sleeve** hidden but ready to be used —**sleeve′less** *adj.*

sleigh (slā) *n.* [Du. *slec*] a light vehicle on runners, for travel over snow and ice

sleight of hand (slīt) [< ON. *slœgr,* crafty] **1.** skill with the hands, esp. in deceiving onlookers, as in doing magic tricks **2.** tricks thus performed

slen·der (slen′dər) *adj.* [< ?] **1.** long and thin **2.** having a slim figure **3.** small in amount, size, degree, etc. —**slen′-der·ly** *adv.* —**slen′der·ness** *n.*

slen′der·ize′ *vt., vi.* **-ized′, -iz′ing** to make or become slender

slept (slept) *pt. & pp. of* SLEEP

sleuth (slooth) *n.* [< ON. *sloth,* a track] [Colloq.] a detective —*vi.* to act as a detective

slew¹ (sloo) *n.* [Ir. *sluagh,* a host] [Colloq.] a large number or amount

slew² (sloo) *pt. of* SLAY

slice (slīs) *n.* [< Frank. *slizzan,* to slice] **1.** a relatively thin, broad piece cut from something **2.** a part or share **3.** *a)* the path of a hit ball that curves away to the right from a right-handed player or to the left from a left-handed player *b)* a ball that follows such a path —*vt.* **sliced, slic′ing 1.** to cut into slices **2.** to cut off as in a slice (with *off, from, away,* etc.) **3.** to hit (a ball) in a slice —*vi.* to cut (*through*) like a knife —**slic′er** *n.*

slick (slik) *vt.* [OE. *slician*] **1.** to make smooth **2.** [Colloq.] to make smart, neat, etc. (with *up*) —*adj.* **1.** sleek; smooth **2.** slippery **3.** adept; clever **4.** [Colloq.] smooth and clever but superficial, tricky, etc. —*n.* a smooth area on the surface of water, as from a film of oil —*adv.* smoothly, cleverly, etc. —**slick′ly** *adv.* —**slick′ness** *n.*

slick′er *n.* **1.** a loose, waterproof coat **2.** [Colloq.] a smooth, tricky person

slide (slīd) *vi.* **slid** (slid), **slid′ing** [OE. *slidan*] **1.** to move along in constant contact with a smooth surface, as on ice **2.** to glide **3.** to slip [it *slid* from his grasp] **4.** to pass gradually (*into* or *out of* some condition, habit, etc.) —*vt.* **1.** to cause to slide **2.** to move or place quietly or deftly (with *in* or *into*) —*n.* **1.** a sliding **2.** a smooth, often inclined surface for sliding **3.** something that works by sliding **4.** a photographic transparency for use with a projector or viewer **5.** a small glass plate on which objects are mounted for microscopic study **6.** the fall of a mass of rock, snow, etc. down a slope —**let slide** to neglect

fat, āpe, cär; ten, ēven; is, bīte; gō, hôrn, tool, look; oil, out; up, fur; thin, *th*en; zh, leisure; ŋ, ring; ə for *a* in *ago*; ′ as in *able* (ā′b'l); ë, Fr. coeur; ö, Fr. feu; ô, Fr. mon; ü, Fr. duc; r, Fr. cri; kh, G. doch, ich. ‡ foreign; < derived from

slide fastener a zipper or zipperlike device with two grooved plastic edges joined or separated by a slide

slid′er *n*. **1**. one that slides **2**. *Baseball* a curve ball that breaks only slightly

slide rule an instrument for rapid calculations, consisting of a ruler with a central sliding piece, both marked with logarithmic scales

sliding scale a scale or schedule, as of costs, wages, etc., that varies with given conditions

slight (slīt) *adj*. [OE. *sliht*] **1**. *a*) light in build; slender *b*) frail; fragile **2**. lacking strength, importance, etc. **3**. small in amount or extent —*vt*. **1**. to neglect **2**. to treat with disrespect **3**. to treat as unimportant —*n*. a slighting or being slighted by discourteous treatment —**slight′ing·ly** *adv*. —**slight′ly** *adv*. — **slight′ness** *n*.

SLIDE RULE

slim (slim) *adj*. **slim′mer, slim′mest** [< Du., bad] **1**. small in girth; slender **2**. small in amount, degree, etc.; slight — *vt*., *vi*. **slimmed, slim′ming** to make or become slim — **slim′ly** *adv*. —**slim′ness** *n*.

slime (slīm) *n*. [OE. *slim*] any soft, moist, slippery, often sticky matter, esp. when considered disgusting

slim·y (slī′mē) *adj*. **-i·er, -i·est 1**. of, like, or covered with slime **2**. disgusting —**slim′i·ness** *n*.

sling (sling) *n*. [prob. < ON. *slyngva*, to throw] **1**. a primitive instrument whirled by hand for throwing stones **2**. a cast; throw; fling **3**. a supporting band, strap, etc. as for raising a heavy object **4**. a cloth looped from the neck under an injured arm for support —*vt*. **slung, sling′ing 1**. to throw as with a sling **2**. to hang in a sling; suspend

sling′shot′ *n*. a Y-shaped piece of wood, metal, etc. with an elastic band attached to the upper tips for shooting stones, etc.

slink (slingk) *vi*. **slunk, slink′ing** [OE. *slincan*, to creep] to move in a furtive or sneaky way, or as if ashamed

slink′y *adj*. **-i·er, -i·est 1**. sneaky; furtive **2**. [Slang] sinuous in movement, line, etc.

slip¹ (slip) *vi*. **slipped, slip′ping** [MLowG. *slippen*] **1**. to go quietly or secretly [to *slip* out of a room] **2**. to pass smoothly or easily **3**. to escape from one's memory, grasp, etc. **4**. to shift or slide from position **5**. to slide accidentally, lose footing, etc. **6**. to make a mistake; err **7**. to become worse —*vt*. **1**. to put or move quickly or easily **2**. to escape (one's mind) **3**. to get loose from —*n*. **1**. a space between piers, where ships can dock **2**. a woman's undergarment, about the length of a dress or skirt **3**. a pillowcase **4**. a slipping or falling down **5**. an error or mistake — **give someone the slip** to escape from someone —**let slip** to say without intending to —**slip up** to make a mistake

slip² (slip) *n*. [< MDu. *slippen*, to cut] **1**. a stem, root, etc. of a plant, used for planting or grafting **2**. a young, slim person **3**. a small piece of paper

slip′case′ *n*. a boxlike container for a book or books, open at one end

slip′cov′er *n*. a removable, fitted cloth cover for a sofa, armchair, etc.

slip′knot′ *n*. a knot made so that it will slip along the rope around which it is tied

slip·page (slip′ij) *n*. a slipping, as of one gear past another

slipped disk a ruptured cartilaginous disk between vertebrae, esp. in the lumbar region

slip·per (slip′ər) *n*. a light, low shoe easily slipped onto the foot, esp. one for indoor wear

slip·per·y (slip′ə rē) *adj*. **-i·er, -i·est 1**. liable to cause slipping, as a wet surface **2**. tending to slip away, as from a grasp **3**. unreliable; tricky —**slip′per·i·ness** *n*.

slip·shod (slip′shäd′) *adj*. [after obs. *slip-shoe*, a slipper] careless or slovenly

slip′-up′ *n*. [Colloq.] an error or oversight

slit (slit) *vt*. **slit, slit′ting** [ME. *slitten*] **1**. to cut or split open, esp. by a straight, lengthwise incision **2**. to cut into strips —*n*. a straight, narrow cut, opening, etc.

slith·er (slith′ər) *vi*. [< OE. *slidan*, to slide] **1**. to slip or slide on a loose, broken surface **2**. to glide along, as a snake —*n*. a slithering motion

sliv·er (sliv′ər) *n*. [OE. *slifan*, to cut] a thin, sharp piece cut or split off; splinter —*vt*., *vi*. to cut or split into slivers

slob (släb) *n*. [< Ir. *slab*, mud < Scand.] [Colloq.] a sloppy or coarse person

slob·ber (släb′ər) *vi*. [prob. < LowG. *slubberen*, to swig] **1**. to drool **2**. to speak or write in a maudlin way —*n*. saliva drooling from the mouth

sloe (slō) *n*. [OE. *sla*] **1**. the blackthorn **2**. its small, plumlike fruit

sloe′-eyed′ *adj*. **1**. having large, dark eyes **2**. having almond-shaped eyes

sloe gin a red liqueur made of gin flavored with sloes

slog (släg) *vt*., *vi*. **slogged, slog′ging** [ME. *sluggen*, go slowly] **1**. to make (one's way) with great effort; plod **2**. to work hard (*at* something); toil

slo·gan (slō′gən) *n*. [< Gael. *sluagh*, a host + *gairm*, a call: orig., a battle cry] **1**. a catchword or motto associated with a political party, etc. **2**. a catch phrase used to advertise a product

sloop (slōōp) *n*. [< Du. < LowG. *slupen*, to glide] a small sailing vessel with a single mast and a jib

slop (släp) *n*. [OE. *sloppe*] **1**. watery snow or mud; slush **2**. a puddle of spilled· liquid **3**. unappetizing liquid or semiliquid food **4**. [*often pl*.] *a*) liquid waste of any kind *b*) kitchen swill, fed to pigs, etc. —*vt*., *vi*. **slopped, slop′-ping** to spill or splash

slope (slōp) *n*. [< OE. *slupan*, to glide] **1**. rising or falling ground **2**. any inclined line, surface, etc.; slant **3**. the amount or degree of this —*vi*. **sloped, slop′ing** to have an upward or downward inclination; incline; slant —*vt*. to cause to slope

slop·py (släp′ē) *adj*. **-pi·er, -pi·est 1**. wet and splashy; slushy **2**. *a*) slovenly or messy *b*) slipshod **3**. [Colloq.] gushingly sentimental —**slop′pi·ly** *adv*. —**slop′pi·ness** *n*.

sloppy Joe (jō) ground meat cooked with tomato sauce, spices, etc. and served on a bun

slosh (släsh) *vt*. [var. of SLUSH] **1**. to shake or agitate (a liquid) **2**. to apply (a liquid) carelessly —*vi*. **1**. to splash through water, mud, etc. **2**. to splash about: said of a liquid

slot (slät) *n*. [< OFr. *esclot*, hollow between the breasts] **1**. a narrow opening, as for a coin in a vending machine **2**. [Colloq.] a position in a group, series, etc. —*vt*. **slot′ted, slot′ting** to make a slot in

sloth (slôth, slōth, släth) *n*. [< OE. *slaw*, slow] **1**. disinclination to work or exert oneself; laziness **2**. a slow-moving, tree-dwelling mammal of Central and South America

sloth′ful (-fəl) *adj*. characterized by sloth; indolent —**sloth′ful·ly** *adv*. —**sloth′ful·ness** *n*.

slot machine a machine, specif. a gambling device, worked by inserting a coin in a slot

SLOTH
(22–27 in. long)

slouch (slouch) *n*. [< ON. *slōka*, to droop] **1**. a lazy or incompetent person **2**. a drooping or slovenly posture —*vi*. to sit, stand, walk, etc. in a slouch —**slouch′y** *adj*. **-i·er, -i·est**

slough¹ (sluf) *n*. [ME. *slouh*] a castoff layer or covering, as the skin of a snake —*vi*. to be shed, cast off, etc.; come off (often with *off*) —*vt*. to shed or throw off; get rid of

slough² (slou) *n*. [OE. *sloh*] **1**. a place full of soft, deep mud **2**. deep, hopeless discouragement

Slo·vak (slō′väk, -vak) *n*. **1**. any of a Slavic people living chiefly in Slovakia **2**. their language —*adj*. of the Slovaks, their language, etc.

Slo·va·ki·a (slō vä′kē ə, -vak′ē ə) region comprising E Czechoslovakia —**Slo·va′ki·an** *adj*., *n*.

slov·en (sluv′ən) *n*. [prob. < MDu. *slof*, lax] a dirty or untidy person

Slo·ve·ni·a (slō vē′nē ə) republic of Yugoslavia, in the NW part

Slo·ve′ni·an *n*. **1**. any of a Slavic people living chiefly in Slovenia **2**. their Slavic language —*adj*. of Slovenia, Slovenians, or their language Also **Slo·vene** (slō′vēn)

slov·en·ly (sluv′ən lē) *adj*. **-li·er, -li·est** [see SLOVEN] careless in appearance, habits, work, etc.; untidy —**slov′en·li·ness** *n*.

slow (slō) *adj*. [OE. *slaw*] **1**. not quick in understanding **2**. taking a longer time than is expected or usual **3**. marked by low speed, etc.; not fast **4**. behind the correct time, as a clock **5**. passing tediously; dull **6**. not active; slack [*slow* trading] **7**. lacking in energy; sluggish —*vt*., *vi*. to make or become slow or slower (often with *up* or *down*) —*adv*. in a slow manner —**slow′ly** *adv*. —**slow′ness** *n*.

slow burn [Slang] a gradual working up of anger: often in the phrase **do a slow burn**

slow′down′ *n*. a slowing down, as of production

slow′-mo′tion *adj*. **1**. moving slowly **2**. designating a filmed or taped sequence in which the action is made to appear slower than the actual action

slow'poke' (-pōk') *n.* [Slang] a person who acts or moves slowly

slow'-wit'ted *adj.* mentally slow; dull

sludge (sluj) *n.* [var. of *slutch*, mud] 1. mud, mire, or ooze 2. any heavy, slimy deposit, sediment, etc.

slue (slōō) *vt., vi.* slued, slu'ing [< ?] to turn or swing around a fixed point

slug¹ (slug) *n.* [ME. *slugge*, clumsy one < Scand.] a small mollusk resembling a land snail, but having no outer shell

slug² (slug) *n.* [prob. < prec.] 1. a small piece of metal; specif., a bullet 2. a piece of metal used illegally in place of a coin in automatic coin machines

slug³ (slug) *n.* [< Dan. *sluge*, to gulp] [Slang] a single drink, esp. of alcoholic liquor

slug⁴ (slug) *vt.* slugged, slug'ging [ON. *slag*] [Colloq.] to hit hard, esp. with the fist or a bat —*n.* [Colloq.] a hard blow or hit —**slug'ger** *n.*

slug·gard (slug'ərd) *n.* [< ME. *sluggen*, be lazy] a lazy person —*adj.* lazy: also **slug'gard·ly**

slug·gish (slug'ish) *adj.* [< SLUG¹] 1. lacking energy; lazy 2. slow or slow-moving 3. not functioning with normal vigor —**slug'gish·ly** *adv.* —**slug'gish·ness** *n.*

sluice (slōōs) *n.* [< L. *excludere*, to shut out] 1. an artificial channel for water, with a gate to regulate the flow 2. the water held back by such a gate 3. such a gate: also **sluice gate** 4. any channel for excess water 5. a sloping trough through which water is run, as in washing gold ore —*vt.* sluiced, sluic'ing 1. to draw off through a sluice 2. to wash with water from a sluice

slum (slum) *n.* [< ?] a populous area characterized by poverty, poor housing, etc. —*vi.* slummed, slum'ming to visit slums in a condescending way

slum·ber (slum'bər) *vi.* [< OE. *sluma*, slumber] 1. to sleep 2. to be inactive —*n.* 1. sleep 2. an inactive state —**slum'ber·ous** *adj.*

slum'lord' *n.* [Slang] an absentee landlord of slum dwellings, esp. one who charges excessive rents and neglects upkeep

slump (slump) *vi.* [prob. < MLowG. *slumpen*, occur by accident] 1. to fall or sink suddenly 2. to have a drooping posture —*n.* 1. a sudden fall, decline, etc. 2. a drooping posture 3. a period during which a player, team, etc. performs below normal

slung (sluŋ) *pt. & pp. of* SLING

slunk (sluŋk) *pt. & pp. of* SLINK

slur (slur) *vt.* slurred, slur'ring [prob. < MDu. *sleuren*, to drag] 1. to pronounce indistinctly 2. to disparage 3. *Music* to produce (successive notes) by gliding from one to another without a break —*n.* 1. a slurring 2. something slurred, as a pronunciation 3. a remark that is harmful to someone's reputation 4. *Music* a symbol (⌣) or (⌢) connecting notes to be slurred —**slur over** to pass over quickly and carelessly —**slur'ring·ly** *adv.*

slurp (slurp) *vt., vi.* [Du. *slurpen*, to sip] [Slang] to drink or eat noisily —*n.* [Slang] a loud sipping or sucking sound

slush (slush) *n.* [prob. < Scand.] 1. partly melted snow 2. soft mud 3. sentimentality —*vi.* to walk or move through slush —**slush'i·ness** *n.* —**slush'y** *adj.*

slush fund money used for bribery, influencing politicians, or other corrupt practices

slut (slut) *n.* [ME. *slutte*] 1. a dirty, slovenly woman 2. a sexually immoral woman —**slut'tish** *adj.*

sly (slī) *adj.* sli'er or sly'er, sli'est or sly'est [< ON. *slœgr*] 1. skillful at trickery; crafty 2. cunningly underhanded 3. playfully mischievous —**on the sly** secretly —**sly'ly** *adv.* —**sly'ness** *n.*

Sm *Chem.* samarium

smack¹ (smak) *n.* [OE. *smæc*] 1. a slight but distinctive taste or flavor 2. a small amount; trace —*vi.* to have a smack (*of*)

smack² (smak) *n.* [< ?] 1. a sharp noise made by parting the lips suddenly 2. a loud kiss 3. a sharp blow with a flat object; slap —*vt.* 1. to part (the lips) so as to make a smack 2. to kiss or slap loudly —*vi.* to make a loud, sharp noise —*adv.* 1. with a smack 2. directly; squarely

smack³ (smak) *n.* [prob. < Du. *smak*] a fishing vessel fitted with a well for keeping fish alive

smack⁴ (smak) *n.* [< ?] [Slang] heroin

small (smôl) *adj.* [OE. *smæl*] 1. comparatively little in size; not large 2. little in quantity, extent, duration, etc. 3. of little importance; trivial 4. young [*small* children] 5. mean; petty —*adv.* 1. in small pieces 2. in a small manner —*n.* the small part [the *small* of the back] —**feel small** to feel shame —**small'ish** *adj.* —**small'ness** *n.*

small arms firearms of small caliber, held in the hand or hands when fired, as pistols or rifles

small'-mind'ed (-mīn'did) *adj.* selfish, petty, prejudiced, etc. —**small'-mind'ed·ness** *n.*

small'pox' (-päks') *n.* an acute, contagious virus disease characterized by fever and pustular eruptions that often leave pitted scars

small talk light conversation about common, everyday things; chitchat

small'-time' *adj.* [Colloq.] minor or petty

smart (smärt) *vi.* [OE. *smeortan*] 1. *a)* to cause sharp, stinging pain, as a slap *b)* to feel such pain 2. to feel mental distress or irritation —*n.* a smarting sensation —*adj.* 1. causing sharp pain [a *smart* blow] 2. sharp or stinging, as pain 3. brisk; lively [a *smart* pace] 4. intelligent, clever, etc. 5. neat; trim 6. stylish 7. [Colloq.] impertinent or saucy —**smart'ly** *adv.* —**smart'ness** *n.*

smart al·eck, smart al·ec (al'ik) [< masc. name *Alexander*] [Colloq.] an offensively conceited person

smart'en (-'n) *vt., vi.* to make or become smart or smarter: usually with *up*

smash (smash) *vt., vi.* [prob. < MASH] 1. to break into pieces with noise or violence 2. to hit, move, or collide with force 3. to destroy or be destroyed —*n.* 1. a hard, heavy blow 2. a violent, noisy breaking 3. a violent collision 4. total failure, esp. in business 5. a great popular success —*adj.* that is a smash (*n.* 5)

smash'up' *n.* 1. a violent wreck or collision 2. total failure; ruin

smat·ter·ing (smat'ər iŋ) *n.* [ME. *smateren*, to chatter] 1. superficial knowledge 2. a small number

smear (smir) *vt.* [OE. *smerian*, anoint] 1. to cover or soil with something greasy, sticky, etc. 2. to apply (something greasy, etc.) 3. to smudge or obscure as by rubbing 4. to slander 5. [Slang] to defeat decisively —*vi.* to be or become smeared —*n.* 1. a mark made by smearing 2. a small amount of some substance smeared on a slide for microscopic study, etc. 3. slander —**smear'y** *adj.*

smell (smel) *vt.* smelled or smelt, smell'ing [ME. *smellen*] 1. to be aware of through the nose; detect the odor of 2. to sense the presence of [to *smell* trouble] —*vi.* 1. to use the sense of smell, sniff 2. to have an odor [to *smell* fresh] 3. to have an unpleasant odor 4. [Colloq.] *a)* to lack ability, worth, etc. *b)* to be foul, corrupt, etc. —*n.* 1. the sense by which odors are perceived 2. odor; scent 3. an act of smelling —**smell out** to find as by smelling

smelling salts carbonate of ammonium, sniffed to relieve faintness

smell'y *adj.* -i·er, -i·est having an unpleasant odor

smelt¹ (smelt) *n.* [OE.] a small, silvery food fish found in northern seas

smelt² (smelt) *vt.* [< MDu. *smelten*] 1. to melt or fuse (ore, etc.) so as to separate impurities from pure metal 2. to refine (metal) in this way

smelt'er *n.* 1. one whose work is smelting 2. a place where smelting is done

smidg·en (smij'ən) *n.* [prob. < dial. *smidge*, particle] [Colloq.] a small amount: also **smidg'in**

smile (smīl) *vi.* smiled, smil'ing [ME. *smilen*] 1. to show pleasure, amusement, affection, etc. by an upward curving of the mouth 2. to regard with favor (with *on* or *upon*) —*vt.* to express with a smile —*n.* the act or expression of smiling —**smil'ing·ly** *adv.*

smirch (smurch) *vt.* [prob. < OFr. *esmorcher*, to hurt] 1. to soil or smear 2. to dishonor —*n.* 1. a smudge; smear 2. a stain on one's reputation

smirk (smurk) *vi.* [OE. *smearcian*, to smile] to smile in a conceited or complacent way —*n.* such a smile

smite (smīt) *vt.* smote, smit·ten (smit''n) or smote, smit'ing [OE. *smitan*] 1. [Now Rare] to hit or strike hard 2. to attack with disastrous effect 3. to affect strongly 4. to impress favorably

smith (smith) *n.* [OE.] 1. one who makes or repairs metal objects; metalworker 2. *short for* BLACKSMITH

Smith (smith) 1. **Adam,** 1723–90; Scot. economist 2. Captain **John,** 1580–1631; Eng. colonist in America 3. **Joseph,** 1805–44; U.S. founder of the Mormon Church

smith·er·eens (smith'ə rēnz') *n.pl.* [Ir. *smidirīn*] [Colloq.] small fragments; bits

smith·y (smith'ē) *n.* -ies 1. the workshop of a smith, esp. a blacksmith 2. *same as* BLACKSMITH

smock (smäk) *n.* [OE. *smoc* or ON. *smokkr*] a loose, shirtlike outer garment worn to protect the clothes —*vt.* to gather cloth in even folds with decorative stitching

---

fat, āpe, cär; ten, ēven; is, bīte; gō, hôrn, tōōl, look; oil, out; up, fur; thin, *then*; zh, leisure; ŋ, ring; ə for *a* in *ago*; ' as in *able* (ā'b'l); ë, Fr. coeur; ö, Fr. feu; Fr. mon; ü, Fr. duc; r, Fr. cri; kh, G. doch, ich. ‡ foreign; < derived from

smog (smôg, smäg) *n.* [SM(OKE) + (F)OG] a mixture of fog and smoke —**smog'gy** *adj.* **-gi·er, -gi·est**

smoke (smōk) *n.* [OE. *smoca*] **1.** the vaporous matter arising from something burning **2.** any vapor, etc. like this **3.** an act of smoking tobacco, etc. **4.** a cigarette, cigar, etc. —*vi.* **smoked, smok'ing 1.** to give off smoke **2.** to draw in and exhale the smoke of tobacco; use cigarettes, etc. —*vt.* **1.** to cure (meat, etc.) with smoke **2.** to force out with smoke [to *smoke* an animal from its lair] **3.** to use (tobacco, a pipe, etc.) in smoking —**smoke out** to force out of hiding, secrecy, etc. —**smoke'less** *adj.*

smoke'house' *n.* a building where meats, fish, etc. are cured with smoke

smok·er (smō'kər) *n.* **1.** one who smokes tobacco habitually **2.** a railroad car reserved esp. for smoking: also **smoking car 3.** an informal party for men

smoke screen a cloud of smoke spread to screen the movements of troops, ships, etc.

smoke'stack' (-stak') *n.* a pipe for discharging smoke from a steamship, factory, etc.

smok·y (smō'kē) *adj.* **-i·er, -i·est 1.** giving off smoke, esp. too much smoke **2.** of, like, or of the color of, smoke **3.** filled with smoke —**smok'i·ness** *n.*

Smoky Mountains *same as* GREAT SMOKY MOUNTAINS

smol·der (smōl'dər) *vi.* [ME. *smoldren*] **1.** to burn and smoke without flame **2.** to exist in a suppressed state **3.** to show suppressed anger Brit. sp. **smoulder**

smooch (smōōch) *n., vt., vi.* [Slang] kiss

smooth (smōōth) *adj.* [OE. *smoth*] **1.** having an even surface, with no roughness or lumps **2.** without lumps **3.** even or gentle in movement [a *smooth* voyage] **4.** free from interruptions, difficulties, etc. **5.** calm; serene [a *smooth* temper] **6.** pleasing to the taste; bland **7.** having an easy, flowing rhythm or sound **8.** polished or ingratiating, esp. in an insincere way —*vt.* **1.** to make level or even **2.** to remove lumps or wrinkles from **3.** to free from difficulties, etc. **4.** to make calm; soothe **5.** to polish or refine —*adv.* in a smooth manner —*n.* a smooth part —**smooth down** to make or become smooth or calm —**smooth over** to make light of —**smooth'ly** *adv.* —**smooth'ness** *n.*

smooth'-spo'ken (-spō'k'n) *adj.* speaking in a pleasing, persuasive, or polished manner

smor·gas·bord, smör·gås·bord (smôr'gəs bôrd', smur'-) *n.* [Sw.] **1.** a wide variety of appetizers, cheeses, meats, etc. served buffet style **2.** a restaurant serving these

smote (smōt) *pt. & alt. pp. of* SMITE

smoth·er (smuth'ər) *vt.* [< ME. *smorther*, dense smoke] **1.** to keep from getting air; suffocate **2.** to cover (a fire), to put it out **3.** to cover over thickly **4.** to stifle, as a yawn —*vi.* to be suffocated

smudge (smuj) *vt., vi.* **smudged, smudg'ing** [ME. *smogen*] to make or become dirty; smear —*n.* **1.** a stain, smear, etc.; dirty spot **2.** a fire made to produce dense smoke **3.** such smoke, used to protect plants from frost, drive away insects, etc.

smug (smug) *adj.* **smug'ger, smug'gest** [prob. < LowG. *smuk*, neat] annoyingly self-satisfied; complacent —**smug'ly** *adv.* —**smug'ness** *n.*

smug·gle (smug''l) *vt.* **-gled, -gling** [< LowG. *smuggeln*] **1.** to bring into or take out of a country secretly or illegally **2.** to bring, take, etc. secretly —*vi.* to smuggle forbidden or taxable goods —**smug'gler** *n.*

smut (smut) *n.* [< LowG. *smutt*] **1.** sooty matter **2.** a soiled spot **3.** indecent talk or writing **4.** a plant disease in which certain fungi form masses of black spores —**smut'ti·ness** *n.* —**smut'ty** *adj.* **-ti·er, -ti·est**

Sn [L. *stannum*] *Chem.* tin

snack (snak) *n.* [< ME. *snaken*, to bite] a light meal between regular meals —*vi.* to eat a snack

snaf·fle (snaf''l) *n.* [prob. < ODu. *snabbe*, bill of a bird] a bit, usually light and jointed, attached to a bridle and having no curb

snag (snag) *n.* [< Scand.] **1.** a sharp point or projection **2.** an underwater tree stump or branch **3.** a tear or a pulled thread in fabric, made by a snag **4.** an unexpected or hidden difficulty —*vt.* **snagged, snag'ging 1.** to damage on a snag **2.** to hinder; impede **3.** to catch with a quick motion

snag·gle·tooth (snag''l tōōth') *n., pl.* **-teeth'** [< SNAG] **1.** a projecting tooth **2.** a crooked or broken tooth —**snag'gle·toothed'** *adj.*

SNAFFLE

snail (snāl) *n.* [OE. *snægl*] a slow-moving mollusk with a wormlike body and a spiral protective shell

snake (snāk) *n.* [OE. *snaca*] **1.** a long, scaly, limbless reptile with a tapering tail **2.** a treacherous or deceitful person **3.** a long, flexible rod for removing obstructions from pipes, etc. —*vi.* **snaked, snak'ing** to move, curve, twist, etc. like a snake —*vt.* [Colloq.] to drag, pull, or jerk —**snake'like'** *adj.*

snak·y (snā'kē) *adj.* **-i·er, -i·est 1.** of or like a snake or snakes **2.** winding; twisting **3.** cunningly treacherous **4.** infested with snakes

snap (snap) *vi., vt.* **snapped, snap'ping** [< MDu. *snappen*] **1.** to bite or grasp suddenly (often with *at*) **2.** to speak or say sharply (often with *at*) **3.** to break suddenly **4.** to make or cause to make a sudden, cracking sound **5.** to close, fasten, etc. with this sound **6.** to move or cause to move suddenly and smartly [to *snap* to attention] **7.** to take a snapshot (of) —*n.* **1.** a sudden bite, grasp, etc. **2.** a sharp, cracking sound **3.** a short, angry utterance **4.** a brief period of cold weather **5.** a fastening that closes with a click **6.** [Colloq.] alertness or vigor **7.** [Slang] an easy job, problem, etc. —*adj.* **1.** made or done quickly [a *snap* decision] **2.** that fastens with a snap **3.** [Slang] easy —**snap out of it** to improve or recover quickly

snap bean any of various green beans or wax beans

snap'drag'on *n.* [SNAP + DRAGON: from the mouth-shaped flowers] a plant with spikes of saclike two-lipped flowers in white, yellow, red, etc.

snap'per *n.* **1.** a person or thing that snaps **2.** *a*) *same as* SNAPPING TURTLE *b*) any of various bony fishes of warm seas; esp., the red snapper

snapping turtle a large, freshwater turtle of N. America, with powerful jaws

snap'pish *adj.* **1.** likely to snap or bite **2.** cross or irritable —**snap'pish·ly** *adv.*

snap'py *adj.* **-pi·er, -pi·est 1.** snappish; cross **2.** that snaps **3.** [Colloq.] *a*) brisk or lively *b*) sharply chilly **4.** [Colloq.] stylish; smart —**make it snappy** [Slang] hurry —**snap'pi·ly** *adv.* —**snap'pi·ness** *n.*

snap'shot' *n.* a photograph taken with brief exposure, using a hand camera

snare (sner) *n.* [< ON. *snara*] **1.** a trap for small animals, usually a noose which jerks tight upon the release of a spring trigger **2.** anything dangerous, etc. that tempts or attracts **3.** a length of spiraled wire or of gut across the bottom of a drum —*vt.* **snared, snar'ing** to catch as in a snare; trap

snare drum a small, double-headed drum with snares

snarl¹ (snärl) *vi.* [< earlier *snar*, to growl] **1.** to growl fiercely, baring the teeth, as a dog **2.** to speak sharply, as in anger —*vt.* to utter with a snarl —*n.* **1.** a fierce growl **2.** a harsh utterance

snarl² (snärl) *vt., vi., n.* [ME. *snarlen*] tangle; disorder

snatch (snach) *vt.* [prob. var. of ME. *snakken*, to seize] **1.** to seize or take suddenly, eagerly, without right, etc.; grab **2.** to remove abruptly **3.** [Slang] to kidnap —*vi.* to try to seize a thing suddenly; grasp (*at* something) —*n.* **1.** a snatching **2.** a short time **3.** a fragment; bit

sneak (snēk) *vi., vt.* **sneaked** or colloq. **snuck, sneak'ing** [prob. akin to OE. *snican*, to crawl] to move, act, give, put, take, etc. secretly or stealthily —*n.* **1.** one who sneaks **2.** an act of sneaking —*adj.* without warning —**sneak out of** to avoid (a duty, etc.) craftily —**sneak'i·ness** *n.* —**sneak'y** *adj.* **-i·er, -i·est**

sneak'er *n.* a cloth shoe with a heelless, soft rubber sole

sneak'ing *adj.* **1.** cowardly, stealthy, underhanded, etc. **2.** not admitted; secret [a *sneaking* fondness for candy] —**sneaking suspicion** a slight or growing suspicion —**sneak'ing·ly** *adv.*

sneer (snir) *vi.* [ME. *sneren*] **1.** to look scornful, as by curling the lip **2.** to express derision, etc. in speech or writing —*n.* **1.** an act of sneering **2.** a sneering look, etc. —**sneer'ing·ly** *adv.*

sneeze (snēz) *vi.* **sneezed, sneez'ing** [< OE. *fneosan*] to exhale breath from the nose and mouth in a sudden, uncontrolled way, as because the nasal mucous membrane has been irritated —*n.* an act of sneezing —**not to be sneezed at** not to be disregarded

snick·er (snik'ər) *vi.* [echoic] to laugh in a sly or partly stifled manner —*n.* a snickering laugh

snide (snīd) *adj.* [prob. < Du. dial.] slyly malicious or derisive —**snide'ly** *adv.*

sniff (snif) *vi., vt.* [echoic] **1.** to draw in (air) forcibly through the nose **2.** to express (disdain, etc.) by sniffing **3.** to smell by sniffing —*n.* **1.** an act or sound of sniffing **2.** something sniffed

snif·fle (snif''l) *vi.* **-fled, -fling** to sniff repeatedly, as in checking mucus running from the nose —*n.* an act or sound of sniffling —**the sniffles** [Colloq.] a head cold, etc. in which there is much sniffling

snig·ger (snig'ər) *vi., n.* [echoic] *same as* SNICKER

snip (snip) *vt., vi.* **snipped, snip'ping** [Du. *snippen*] to cut or cut off in a short, quick stroke —*n.* **1.** a small cut made with scissors, etc. **2.** the sound of this **3.** a small piece cut off **4.** [*pl.*] heavy hand shears for cutting sheet metal, etc. **5.** [Colloq.] a young or insignificant person

snipe (snip) *n.* [ON. *snipa*] a long-billed wading bird —*vi.* **sniped, snip'ing 1.** to hunt snipe **2.** to shoot at individuals from a hidden position **3.** to direct an attack (*at* someone) in a sly or underhanded way

snip·pet (snip'it) *n.* [dim. of SNIP] a small scrap, specif. of information, a writing, etc.

snip·py (snip'ē) *adj.* **-pi·er, -pi·est** [Colloq.] insolently curt, sharp, etc. —**snip'pi·ness** *n.*

snitch (snich) *vt.* [Slang] to steal (usually something of little value) —*vi.* [Slang] to be an informer; tattle (*on*)

sniv·el (sniv''l) *vi.* **-eled** or **-elled, -el·ing** or **-el·ling** [akin to OE. *snofl*, mucus] **1.** to cry and sniffle, as in a whining manner **2.** to make a tearful, often false display of grief

snob (snäb) *n.* [< ?] one who attaches great importance to wealth, social position, etc., having contempt for those he considers inferior —**snob'ber·y, snob'bish·ness** *n.* —**snob'bish** *adj.*

snood (snood) *n.* [OE. *snod*] a baglike net worn at the back of a woman's head to hold the hair

snoop (snoop) *vi.* [Du. *snoepen*, to eat snacks on the sly] [Colloq.] to pry about in a sneaking way —*n.* [Colloq.] **1.** one who snoops **2.** a snooping —**snoop'y** *adj.* **-i·er, -i·est**

snoot (snoot) *n.* [see SNOUT] [Colloq.] **1.** the nose **2.** a face

snoot·y *adj.* **-i·er, -i·est** [Colloq.] haughty; snobbish —**snoot'i·ly** *adv.* —**snoot'i·ness** *n.*

snooze (snooz) *n.* [< ? LowG. *snusen*, to snore] [Colloq.] a brief sleep; nap —*vi.* **snoozed, snooz'ing** [Colloq.] to take a brief sleep; nap

snore (snôr) *vi.* **snored, snor'ing** [echoic] to breathe, while asleep, with harsh sounds caused by vibration of the soft palate, usually with the mouth open —*n.* a snoring —**snor'er** *n.*

snor·kel (snôr'k'l) *n.* [G. *schnörkel*, spiral] **1.** a device for submarines, with air intake and exhaust tubes, permitting submergence for long periods **2.** a breathing tube extending above the surface of the water, used in swimming just below the surface

SNORKEL

snort (snôrt) *vi.* [akin to SNORE] **1.** to force breath from the nose in a sudden and noisy way **2.** to express anger, scorn, etc. by a snort **3.** to make a noise like a snort —*n.* **1.** the act or sound of snorting **2.** [Slang] a drink of straight liquor, taken in one gulp

snot (snät) *n.* [OE. (*ge*)*snot*, mucus] **1.** nasal mucus: a vulgar term **2.** [Slang] a young person who is insolent — **snot'ty** *adj.* **-ti·er, -ti·est**

snout (snout) *n.* [prob. < MDu. *snute*] the projecting nose and jaws of an animal

snow (snō) *n.* [OE. *snaw*] **1.** frozen particles of water vapor that fall to earth as soft, white, crystalline flakes **2.** a falling of snow **3.** a mass of fallen snow —*vi.* to fall as or like snow —*vt.* **1.** to cover or obstruct with snow (with *in, under,* etc.) **2.** [Slang] to deceive or mislead —**snow under 1.** to overwhelm with work, etc. **2.** to defeat decisively —**snow'y** *adj.* **-i·er, -i·est**

snow'ball' *n.* **1.** a mass of snow packed together into a ball **2.** a bush with round clusters of white or pinkish flowers —*vi.* to increase rapidly like a rolling ball of snow —*vt.* to throw snowballs at

snow'bank' *n.* a large mound of snow

snow'bird' *n.* **1.** a widely distributed N. American junco **2.** *same as* SNOW BUNTING

snow'-blind' *adj.* blinded temporarily by ultraviolet rays of the sun reflected from snow

snow'bound' *adj.* shut in or blocked off by snow

snow bunting a small finch inhabiting cold regions in the Northern Hemisphere

snow'drift' *n.* a smooth heap of snow blown together by the wind

snow'drop' *n.* a low-growing, bulbous plant with small, bell-shaped white flowers

snow'fall' *n.* **1.** a fall of snow **2.** the amount of snow falling in a given area or period of time

snow'flake' *n.* a single crystal of snow

snow leopard a large, whitish cat of C Asia, having dark blotches on its fur

snow'man' *n., pl.* **-men'** a crude human figure made of snow packed together

snow'mo·bile' (-mō bēl') *n.* a motor vehicle for traveling over snow, usually with steerable runners in front and tractor treads at the rear

snow'plow' *n.* a plowlike machine used to clear snow off a road, etc.

snow'shoe' *n.* a racket-shaped wooden frame crisscrossed with leather, etc., worn on the feet to prevent sinking in deep snow

snow'storm' *n.* a storm with a heavy snowfall

snow'suit' *n.* a child's heavily lined garment, often with a hood, worn in cold weather

snow tire a tire with a deep tread, and sometimes protruding studs, for added traction on snow or ice

snub (snub) *vt.* **snubbed, snub'bing** [ON. *snubba*, chide] **1.** to treat with scorn, disregard, etc. **2.** to check suddenly the movement of (a rope, etc.) by turning it around a post **3.** to put out (a cigarette) —*n.* scornful treatment — *adj.* short and turned up: said of the nose —**snub'ber** *n.* — **snub'by** *adj.* **-bi·er, -bi·est**

snub'-nosed' *adj.* having a snub nose

snuck (snuk) *colloq. pt. & pp. of* SNEAK

snuff[1] (snuf) *vt.* [< ?] **1.** to trim off the charred end of (a wick) **2.** to put out (a candle) —**snuff out 1.** to extinguish **2.** to destroy —**snuff'er** *n.*

snuff[2] (snuf) *vt., vi.* [MDu. *snuffen*] to sniff or smell —*n.* **1.** a sniff **2.** powdered tobacco taken up into the nose or applied to the gums —**up to snuff** [Colloq.] up to the usual standard

snuff'box' *n.* a small box for holding snuff

snuf·fle (snuf''l) *n., vi.* **-fled, -fling** [< SNUFF[2]] sniffle

snug (snug) *adj.* **snug'ger, snug'gest** [prob. ult. < Scand.] **1.** warm and cozy **2.** compact; neat [*a snug* cottage] **3.** tight in fit [*a snug* coat] **4.** hidden [to lie *snug*] —*adv.* so as to be snug —**snug'ly** *adv.* —**snug'ness** *n.*

snug'gle (-'l) *vi.* **-gled, -gling** [< SNUG] to cuddle, as for warmth or in affection

so[1] (sō) *adv.* [OE. *swa*] **1.** as shown or described [hold the bat just *so*] **2.** *a*) to such an extent [why are you *so* late?] *b*) very [they are *so* happy] *c*) [Colloq.] very much **3.** therefore [they were tired, and *so* left] **4.** more or less [fifty dollars or *so*] **5.** also; likewise [I'm going and *so* are you] : also used colloquially in contradicting a negative statement [I did *so* tell the truth!] **6.** then [and *so* to bed] —*conj.* **1.** in order (*that*) **2.** [Colloq.] with the result that —*pron.* that which has been specified or named —*interj.* an exclamation of surprise, triumph, etc. —*adj.* true [that's *so*] —**and so on** (or **forth**) and the rest; et cetera — **so as** with the purpose or result (followed by an infinitive) —**so what?** [Colloq.] even if so, what then?: used to express disregard, challenge, etc.

so[2] (sō) *n. Music same as* SOL

So. 1. south **2.** southern

soak (sōk) *vt.* [OE. *socian*] **1.** to make thoroughly wet **2.** to submerge in a liquid **3.** to take in; absorb (with *up*) **4.** to take in mentally **5.** [Colloq.] to overcharge —*vi.* **1.** to stay immersed in liquid for wetting, softening, etc. **2.** to penetrate —*n.* **1.** a soaking or being soaked **2.** [Slang] a drunkard

so-and-so (sō'ən sō') *n., pl.* **so'-and-sos'** [Colloq.] some person or thing not specified: often euphemistic

soap (sōp) *n.* [OE. *sape*] **1.** a substance used with water to produce suds for washing: made by the action of an alkali, as potash, on fats **2.** [Slang] *same as* SOAP OPERA: also **soap'er** —*vt.* to scrub, etc. with soap —**no soap** [Slang] **1.** (it is) not acceptable **2.** to no avail —**soap'i·ness** *n.* —**soap'y** *adj.* **-i·er, -i·est**

soap'box' *n.* any improvised platform used by a person (**soapbox orator**) speaking to a street audience

soap opera [Colloq.] a daytime radio or TV serial drama of a melodramatic, sentimental nature

soap'stone' *n. same as* STEATITE

soap'suds' *n.pl.* **1.** foamy, soapy water **2.** the foam on soapy water

soar (sôr) *vi.* [ult. < L. *ex-*, out + *aura*, air] **1.** to rise or fly high into the air **2.** to glide along high in the air **3.** to rise above the ordinary level —*n.* **1.** soaring range **2.** the act of soaring

sob (säb) *vi.* **sobbed, sob'bing** [ME. *sobben*] **1**. to weep aloud with short, gasping breaths **2**. to make a sound like this, as the wind —*vt.* to utter with sobs —*n.* the act or sound of sobbing —**sob'bing·ly** *adv.*

so·ber (sō'bər) *adj.* [< L. *sobrius*] **1**. temperate, esp. in the use of liquor **2**. not drunk **3**. serious, solemn, sedate, etc. **4**. quiet; plain, as color, clothes, etc. **5**. not distorted *[the sober truth]* —*vt.*, *vi.* to make or become sober (often with *up* or *down*) —**so'ber·ly** *adv.* —**so'ber·ness** *n.*

so'ber-mind'ed *adj.* sensible and serious

so·bri·e·ty (sə brī'ə tē, sō-) *n.* a being sober; specif., *a*) temperance, esp. in the use of liquor *b*) seriousness; sedateness

so·bri·quet (sō'brə kā') *n.* [Fr.] **1**. a nickname **2**. an assumed name

Soc., soc. 1. socialist **2**. society

so'-called' *adj.* **1**. known by this term **2**. inaccurately regarded as such *[a so-called liberal]*

soc·cer (säk'ər) *n.* [< (AS)SOC(IATION FOOTBALL)] a kind of football played by kicking a round ball

so·cia·ble (sō'shə b'l) *adj.* [Fr.: see SOCIAL] **1**. friendly; affable **2**. characterized by informal conversation and companionship —*n.* a social —**so'cia·bil'i·ty** *n.*, *pl.* **-ties** — **so'cia·bly** *adv.*

so·cial (sō'shəl) *adj.* [< L. *socius*, companion] **1**. of or having to do with human beings in their living together **2**. living in this way *[man as a social being]* **3**. of or having to do with society, esp. fashionable society **4**. sociable **5**. of or for companionship **6**. of or engaged in welfare work **7**. living in groups or communities *[the ant is a social insect]* —*n.* an informal gathering; party —**so'cial·ly** *adv.*

social disease any venereal disease

so'cial·ism (-iz'm) *n.* **1**. a theory of the ownership and operation of the means of production and distribution by society rather than by private individuals, with all members sharing in the work and the products **2**. *[often S-]* a political movement for establishing such a system —**so'cial·ist** *n.*, *adj.* —**so'cial·is'tic** *adj.*

so·cial·ite (sō'shə līt') *n.* a person who is prominent in fashionable society

so'cial·ize (-līz') *vt.* **-ized', -iz'ing 1**. to make social or fit for cooperative group living **2**. to put under government ownership —*vi.* to take part in social activity —**so'cial·i·za'tion** *n.*

socialized medicine complete medical care, made available through public funds, for all the people in a community, nation, etc.

social science 1. the study of people living together in groups, families, etc. **2**. any of several studies, as history, economics, civics, etc., dealing with society and the activities of its members —**social scientist**

social security a Federal system of old-age, unemployment, or disability insurance, financed jointly by employees, employers, and the government

social service *same as* SOCIAL WORK —**so'cial-serv'ice** *adj.*

social work the promotion of the welfare of the community and the individual, as through counseling agencies, recreation centers, etc. —**social worker**

so·ci·e·ty (sə sī'ə tē) *n.*, *pl.* **-ties** [< L. *socius*, companion] **1**. a group of persons forming a single community **2**. a particular system of group living **3**. all people, collectively **4**. companionship **5**. an organized group with some interest in common **6**. a group of persons regarded as a dominant class because of their wealth, birth, etc. —**so·ci'e·tal** *adj.*

Society of Friends a Christian religious sect founded in England c.1650 by George Fox: the Friends have no formal creed, rites, priesthood, etc., and reject violence in human relations

Society of Jesus *see* JESUIT

socio- [Fr. < L. *socius*, companion] *a combining form meaning* social, society, sociological

so·ci·ol·o·gy (sō'sē äl'ə jē, -shē-) *n.* [see SOCIO- & -LOGY] the science of human society and of social relations, organization, and change —**so'ci·o·log'i·cal** (-ə läj'i k'l) *adj.* —**so'ci·o·log'i·cal·ly** *adv.* —**so'ci·ol'o·gist** *n.*

so·ci·o·path (sō'sē ə path', -shē-) *n.* [SOCIO- + (PSYCHO)PATH] an agressively antisocial psychopath

sock¹ (säk) *n.*, *pl.* **socks, sox** [< L. *soccus*, light shoe] a short stocking

sock² (säk) *vt.* [Slang] to hit with force —*n.* [Slang] a blow —*adv.* [Slang] directly

sock·et (säk'it) *n.* [< OFr. *soc*, plowshare] a hollow part into which something fits *[an eye socket, the socket for a light bulb]* —*vt.* to fit into a socket

sock·eye (säk'ī') *n.* [< AmInd.] a salmon of the N Pacific, with red flesh

Soc·ra·tes (säk'rə tēz') 470?-399 B.C.; Athenian philosopher & teacher —**So·crat·ic** (sə krat'ik, sō-) *adj.*, *n.*

sod (säd) *n.* [prob. < MDu. *sode*] **1**. a surface layer of earth containing grass; turf **2**. a piece of this layer —*vt.* **sod'ded, sod'ding** to cover with sod

so·da (sō'də) *n.* [ult. < Ar. *suwwād*, a plant burned to produce soda] **1**. *same as: a*) SODIUM BICARBONATE *b*) SODIUM CARBONATE *c*) SODIUM HYDROXIDE **2**. *a*) *same as* SODA WATER *b*) [Chiefly Eastern] a drink of soda water flavored with syrup *c*) a confection of soda water, syrup, and ice cream

soda cracker a light, crisp cracker, usually salted, made orig. with baking soda

soda fountain a counter for making and serving soft drinks, sodas, sundaes, etc.

so·dal·i·ty (sō dal'ə tē) *n.*, *pl.* **-ties** [< L. *sodalis*, companion] *R.C.Ch.* a devotional or charitable lay society

soda pop a flavored, carbonated soft drink

soda water water charged under pressure with carbon dioxide gas

sod·den (säd''n) *adj.* [obs. pp. of SEETHE] **1**. soaked through **2**. soggy from improper cooking **3**. dull or stupefied, as from drunkenness

so·di·um (sō'dē əm) *n.* [< SODA] a white, alkaline metallic chemical element: symbol, Na; at. wt., 22.9898; at. no., 11

sodium bicarbonate a white, crystalline compound, $NaHCO_3$, used in baking powder, as an antacid, etc.

sodium carbonate 1. the sodium salt of carbonic acid, Na_2CO_3 **2**. any of the hydrated carbonates of sodium

sodium chloride common salt, NaCl

sodium hydroxide a white, strongly caustic substance, NaOH, used in chemistry, etc.

sodium nitrate a clear, crystalline salt, $NaNO_3$, used in manufacturing explosives, fertilizers, etc.

sodium pentothal *same as* THIOPENTAL SODIUM

Sod·om (säd'əm) *Bible* a sinful city destroyed by fire together with a neighboring city, Gomorrah: Gen. 18-19

sod·om·y (-ē) *n.* [< SODOM] any sexual intercourse held to be abnormal, as between two persons of the same sex —**sod'om·ite'** (-īt') *n.*

so·ev·er (sō ev'ər) *adv.* **1**. in any way *[how dark soever it may be]* **2**. of any kind *[no rest soever]*

so·fa (sō'fə) *n.* [Fr. < Ar. *suffah*] an upholstered couch with fixed back and arms

So·fi·a (sō'fē ə, sō fē'ə) capital of Bulgaria: pop. 868,000

soft (sôft, säft) *adj.* [OE. *softe*] **1**. giving way easily under pressure **2**. easily cut, worked, etc. *[a soft metal]* **3**. not as hard as is normal, desirable, etc. *[soft butter]* **4**. smooth to the touch **5**. easy to digest: said of a diet **6**. nonalcoholic: said of drinks **7**. having few of the mineral salts that keep soap from lathering: said of water **8**. mild, as a breeze **9**. weak; not vigorous **10**. easy *[a soft job]* **11**. kind; lenient **12**. not bright: said of color or light **13**. gentle; low: said of sound **14**. *a*) sibilant: said of *c* and *g*, as in *cent* and *germ b*) voiced —*adv.* gently; quietly —*n.* something soft —*interj.* [Archaic] hush! —**soft'ly** *adv.* — **soft'ness** *n.*

soft'ball' *n.* **1**. a game like baseball played on a smaller diamond and with a larger and softer ball **2**. the ball used

soft'-boiled' *adj.* boiled only a short time so that the yolk is still soft: said of an egg

soft coal *same as* BITUMINOUS COAL

soft'-cov'er *n.* *same as* PAPERBACK —*adj.* bound as a paperback

soft drink a nonalcoholic, esp. carbonated drink

sof·ten (sôf''n, säf'-) *vt.*, *vi.* **1**. to make or become soft or softer **2**. to make or become less resistant —**sof'ten·er** *n.*

soft'heart'ed *adj.* **1**. full of compassion **2**. not strict or severe, as in discipline

soft palate the soft, fleshy part at the rear of the roof of the mouth; velum

soft'-ped'al *vt.* **-aled** or **-alled, -al·ing** or **-al·ling** [from pedal action in piano, etc.] [Colloq.] to tone down; make less emphatic

soft sell selling that relies on subtle inducement or suggestion —**soft'-sell'** *adj.*

soft soap [Colloq.] flattery or smooth talk —**soft'-soap'** *vt.*

soft'ware' (-wer') *n.* the programs, data, etc. for a computer

soft·y, soft·ie (sôf'tē, säf'-) *n.*, *pl.* **-ies** [Colloq.] one who is overly sentimental or trusting

sog·gy (säg'ē, sôg'ē) *adj.* **-gi·er, -gi·est** [prob. < ON. *sog*, a sucking] **1**. saturated with moisture **2**. sodden *[a soggy cake]* —**sog'gi·ly** *adv.* —**sog'gi·ness** *n.*

soil¹ (soil) *n.* [< L. *solum*] **1.** the surface layer of earth, supporting plant life **2.** land; country [foreign *soil*] **3.** ground or earth —**the soil** life and work on a farm

soil² (soil) *vt.* [ult. < L. *sus*, pig] **1.** to make dirty; stain **2.** to disgrace —*vi.* to become soiled —*n.* a soiled spot

soi·ree, soi·rée (swä rā′) *n.* [< Fr. *soir*, evening] a party or gathering in the evening

so·journ (sō′jurn; *also, for v.,* sō jurn′) *vi.* [< L. *sub-*, under + *diurnus*, of a day] to live somewhere temporarily —*n.* a brief stay; visit —**so′journ·er** *n.*

Sol (säl) [L.] **1.** *Rom. Myth.* the sun god: identified with the Greek god Helios **2.** the sun personified

sol (sōl) *n.* [< ML.] *Music* a syllable representing the fifth tone of the diatonic scale

sol·ace (säl′is) *n.* [< L. *solari*, to comfort] **1.** an easing of grief, loneliness, etc. **2.** something that relieves; comfort — *vt.* -aced, -ac·ing to comfort; console —**sol′ac·er** *n.*

so·lar (sō′lər) *adj.* [< L. *sol*, the sun] **1.** of or having to do with the sun **2.** produced by or coming from the sun [*solar* energy] **3.** depending upon the sun's light or energy [*solar* heating]

so·lar·i·um (sō ler′ē əm, sə-) *n., pl.* -i·a (-ə) [L. < *sol*, the sun] a glassed-in porch, room, etc. for sunning

solar plexus 1. a network of nerves in the abdominal cavity behind the stomach **2.** [Colloq.] the area of the belly just below the sternum

solar system the sun and all the heavenly bodies that revolve around it

sold (sōld) *pt. & pp. of* SELL

sol·der (säd′ər) *n.* [< L. *solidare*, make firm] a metal alloy used when melted to join or patch metal parts, etc. —*vt., vi.* **1.** to join (things) with solder **2.** to unite or become united —**sol′der·er** *n.*

sol′der·ing iron a pointed metal tool heated for use in melting and applying solder

sol·dier (sōl′jər) *n.* [< LL. *solidus*, a coin] **1.** a member of an army **2.** an enlisted man, as distinguished from an officer **3.** a man of much military experience **4.** one who works for a specified cause —*vi.* **1.** to serve as a soldier **2.** to shirk one's duty, as by feigning illness —**sol′dier·ly** *adj.*

soldier of fortune a mercenary soldier, esp. one seeking adventure or excitement

sole¹ (sōl) *n.* [ult. < L. *solum*, a base] **1.** the bottom surface of the foot **2.** the part of a shoe, sock, etc. corresponding to this —*vt.* soled, sol′ing to furnish (a shoe, etc.) with a sole

sole² (sōl) *adj.* [< L. *solus*] **1.** without another; single; one and only **2.** not shared; exclusive [*sole* right to a patent]

sole³ (sōl) *n.* [< L. *solea*, SOLE¹: named from its shape] a sea flatfish valued as food

sol·e·cism (säl′ə siz′m) *n.* [< Gr. *soloikos*, speaking incorrectly] **1.** a violation of the conventional usage, grammar, etc. of a language (Ex.: "We done it" for "We did it") **2.** a mistake in etiquette —**sol′e·cis′tic** *adj.*

sole·ly (sōl′lē) *adv.* **1.** without another or others; alone **2.** only, exclusively, or merely [to read *solely* for pleasure]

sol·emn (säl′əm) *adj.* [< L. *sollus*, all + *annus*, year] **1.** sacred **2.** formal **3.** serious; deeply earnest **4.** awe-inspiring —**sol′emn·ly** *adv.* —**sol′emn·ness** *n.*

so·lem·ni·ty (sə lem′nə tē) *n., pl.* -ties **1.** solemn ceremony, ritual, etc. **2.** seriousness; gravity

sol·em·nize (säl′əm nīz′) *vt.* -nized′, -niz′ing **1.** to celebrate formally or according to ritual **2.** to perform (a ceremony) —**sol′em·ni·za′tion** *n.*

so·le·noid (sō′lə noid′) *n.* [< Fr. < Gr. *sōlēn*, a channel + *eidos*, a form] a coil of wire carrying an electric current and acting like a magnet

so·lic·it (sə lis′it) *vt.* [see SOLICITOUS] **1.** to ask or seek earnestly; appeal to or for **2.** to entice (someone) to do wrong **3.** to approach for some immoral purpose, as a prostitute does —*vi.* to solicit someone or something —**so·lic′i·ta′tion** *n.*

so·lic′i·tor (-ər) *n.* **1.** one who solicits trade, contributions, etc. **2.** in England, a member of the legal profession who is not a barrister **3.** the official law officer for a city, department, etc.

solicitor general *pl.* solicitors general, solicitor generals **1.** a law officer (in the Department of Justice in the U.S.) ranking next below the attorney general **2.** the chief law officer in some States

so·lic·i·tous (sə lis′ə təs) *adj.* [< L. *sollus*, whole + *ciere*, set in motion] **1.** showing care or concern [*solicitous* for her welfare] **2.** desirous; eager **3.** full of anxiety —**so·lic′i·tous·ly** *adv.*

so·lic′i·tude′ (-tōōd′, -tyōōd′) *n.* a being solicitous; care, concern, etc.

sol·id (säl′id) *adj.* [< L. *solidus*] **1.** relatively firm or compact; neither liquid nor gaseous **2.** not hollow **3.** having the three dimensions of length, breadth, and thickness **4.** firm and strong; substantial **5.** serious; not trivial **6.** complete **7.** having no breaks or divisions **8.** of one color, material, etc. throughout **9.** showing unity; unanimous **10.** thick or dense, as a fog **11.** firm or dependable **12.** [Colloq.] having a firmly favorable relationship —*n.* **1.** a substance that is solid, not a liquid or gas **2.** an object having length, breadth, and thickness —**sol′id·ly** *adv.* —**sol′id·ness** *n.*

sol·i·dar·i·ty (säl′ə dar′ə tē) *n., pl.* -ties complete unity, as of purpose, feeling, etc.

solid geometry geometry dealing with solid figures

so·lid·i·fy (sə lid′ə fī′) *vt., vi.* -fied′, -fy′ing **1.** to make or become solid, firm, etc. **2.** to crystallize —**so·lid′i·fi·ca′tion** *n.*

so·lid·i·ty (-tē) *n.* a being solid; firmness, hardness, etc.

sol·id-state (säl′id stāt′) *adj.* designating or of electronic devices that can control current without heated filaments, moving parts, etc.

so·lil·o·quy (sə lil′ə kwē) *n., pl.* -quies [< L. *solus*, alone + *loqui*, speak] **1.** a talking to oneself **2.** lines in a drama spoken by a character as if to himself —**so·lil′o·quize′** (-kwīz′) *vi., vt.* -quized′, -quiz′ing

sol·i·taire (säl′ə ter′) *n.* [Fr.: see SOLITARY] **1.** a single gem, esp. a diamond, set by itself **2.** a card game played by one person

sol′i·tar′y (-ter′ē) *adj.* [< L. *solus*, alone] **1.** living or being alone **2.** single; only [a *solitary* example] **3.** with few or no people; remote **4.** done in solitude —*n.* **1.** *pl.* -ies one who lives by himself; esp., a hermit **2.** [Colloq.] *same as* SOLITARY CONFINEMENT —**sol′i·tar′i·ly** *adv.*

solitary confinement confinement of a prisoner, usually as extra punishment, away from all others

sol′i·tude′ (-tōōd′, -tyōōd′) *n.* [< L. *solus*, alone] **1.** a being solitary, or alone **2.** a secluded place

so·lo (sō′lō) *n., pl.* -los [It. < L. *solus*, alone] **1.** a musical piece or passage to be performed by one person **2.** an airplane flight made by a pilot alone **3.** any performance by one person alone —*adj.* **1.** for or by a single performer **2.** performing a solo —*adv.* alone —*vi.* to perform a solo —**so′lo·ist** *n.*

Sol·o·mon (säl′ə mən) *Bible* king of Israel; son of David: noted for his wisdom

Solomon Islands 1. country on a group of islands in the SW Pacific, east of New Guinea: c. 11,500 sq. mi.; pop. 206,000 **2.** group of islands including those of this country and others belonging to Papua New Guinea

So·lon (sō′lən, -län) 640?-559? B.C.; Athenian lawgiver — *n.* [*sometimes* s-] a wise lawmaker

so long *colloq. term for* GOODBYE

sol·stice (säl′stis, sōl′-) *n.* [< L. *sol*, the sun + *sistere*, to halt] **1.** either of two points on the sun's ecliptic at which it is farthest north or south of the celestial equator **2.** the time during the summer (**summer solstice**) or winter (**winter solstice**) when the sun reaches either of these points: in the Northern Hemisphere, June 21 or 22 and December 21 or 22, respectively

sol·u·ble (säl′yoo b'l) *adj.* [see SOLVE] **1.** that can be dissolved **2.** that can be solved —**sol′u·bil′i·ty** *n.*

sol·ute (säl′yoot, sō′loot) *n.* the substance dissolved in a solution —*adj.* dissolved; in solution

so·lu·tion (sə loo′shən) *n.* [see SOLVE] **1.** *a)* the solving of a problem *b)* the answer to a problem *c)* an explanation, etc. **2.** *a)* the dispersion of one or more substances in another, usually a liquid, so as to form a homogeneous mixture *b)* the mixture so produced

solve (sälv) *vt.* solved, solv′ing [< L. *se-*, apart + *luere*, let go] to find an answer for (a problem, etc.); explain —**solv′a·ble** *adj.* —**solv′er** *n.*

sol·vent (säl′vənt) *adj.* [see SOLVE] **1.** able to pay all one's debts **2.** that can dissolve another substance —*n.* a substance that can dissolve another substance —**sol′ven·cy** *n.*

So·ma·li·a (sō mä′lē ə, sə-; -mäl′yə) country of E Africa: 246,201 sq. mi.; pop. 2,864,000

so·mat·ic (sō mat′ik) *adj.* [< Gr. *sōma*, the body] of the body; physical

som·ber (säm′bər) *adj.* [< Fr. < L. *sub*, under + *umbra*, shade] **1.** dark and gloomy or dull **2.** melancholy **3.** solemn Chiefly Brit. sp. **som′bre** —**som′ber·ly** *adv.*

som·bre·ro (säm brer′ō, səm-) *n., pl.* **-ros** [Sp. < *sombra,* shade: see SOMBER] a broad-brimmed hat worn in Mexico, the Southwest, etc.

SOMBRERO

some (sum) *adj.* [OE. *sum*] **1.** certain but not specified or known *[some people smoke]* **2.** of a certain unspecified quantity, degree, etc. *[have some butter]* **3.** about *[some ten of us]* **4.** [Colloq.] remarkable, striking, etc. *[it was some fight]* —*pron.* **1.** a certain one or ones not specified or known *[some agree]* **2.** a certain unspecified number, quantity, etc. *[take some]* —*adv.* **1.** about *[some ten men]* **2.** [Colloq.] to some extent *[slept some]* **3.** [Colloq.] to a great extent *[must run some to catch up]* —**and then some** [Colloq.] and more than that

-some[1] [OE. *-sum*] *a suffix meaning* like, tending to, tending to be *[tiresome, lonesome]*

-some[2] [< Gr. *sōma,* body] *a combining form meaning* body *[chromosome]*

-some[3] [ME. *som,* some] *a suffix meaning* in (a specified) number *[twosome]*

some·bod·y (sum′bud′ē, -bäd′ē) *pron.* a person unknown or not named; some person —*n., pl.* **-ies** a person of importance

some′day′ (-dā′) *adv.* at some future time

some′how′ (-hou′) *adv.* in a way not known, stated, or understood

some′one′ (-wun′, -wən) *pron. same as* SOMEBODY

some′place′ (-plās′) *adv.* in, to, or at some place; somewhere

som·er·sault (sum′ər sôlt′) *n.* [< L. *supra,* over + *saltus,* a leap] an acrobatic stunt done by turning the body one full revolution, heels over head —*vi.* to do a somersault

some·thing (sum′thiŋ) *n.* **1.** a thing not definitely known, understood, etc. *[something went wrong]* **2.** a definite but unspecified thing *[have something to eat]* **3.** a bit; a little *[something over an hour]* **4.** [Colloq.] a remarkable person or thing —*adv.* **1.** somewhat **2.** [Colloq.] really *[sounds something awful]* —**make something of 1.** to find a use for **2.** to treat as very important **3.** [Colloq.] to treat as a point of dispute —**something else** [Slang] one that is quite remarkable

some′time′ (-tīm′) *adv.* at some unspecified or future time —*adj.* **1.** former **2.** occasional

some′times′ *adv.* at times; occasionally

some′way′ (-wā′) *adv.* in some way or manner: also **some′ways′**

some′what′ (-hwut′, -hwät′, -wut′, -wət) *n.* some degree, amount, part, etc. —*adv.* to some extent, degree, etc.

some′where′ (-hwer′, -wer′) *adv.* **1.** in, to, or at some place not known or specified **2.** at some time, degree, age, figure, etc. (with *about, around, in,* etc.) —*n.* an unspecified or undetermined place

som·nam·bu·late (säm nam′byoo lāt′) *vi.* **-lat′ed, -lat′-ing** [< L. *somnus,* sleep + *ambulare,* to walk] to walk in a trancelike state while asleep —**som·nam′bu·lant** *adj.*

som·nam′bu·lism (-liz′m) *n.* sleepwalking —**som·nam′-bu·list** *n.*

som·no·lent (säm′nə lənt) *adj.* [< L. *somnus,* sleep] **1.** sleepy **2.** causing drowsiness —**som′no·lence** *n.* —**som′no·lent·ly** *adv.*

son (sun) *n.* [OE. *sunu*] **1.** a boy or man as he is related to either or both parents **2.** a male descendant **3.** a male thought of as if in relation to a parent *[a son of France]* —**the Son** Jesus Christ

so·nar (sō′när) *n.* [*so(und) n(avigation) a(nd) r(anging)]* an apparatus for transmitting sound waves through water: used to locate submarines, find depths, etc.

so·na·ta (sə nät′ə) *n.* [It. < L. *sonare,* to SOUND[1]] a musical composition for one or two instruments, usually in three or four movements in different tempos, etc.

song (sôŋ) *n.* [OE. *sang*] **1.** the act or art of singing **2.** a piece of music for singing **3.** *a)* poetry *b)* a ballad or lyric set to music **4.** a singing sound —**for a song** cheaply

song′bird′, *n.* **1.** a bird that makes vocal sounds that are like music **2.** a woman singer

song′fest′ (-fest′) *n.* [SONG + -FEST] an informal gathering of people for singing songs, esp. folk songs

Song of Solomon a book of the Bible consisting of a love poem: also called **Song of Songs, Canticle of Canticles**

song′ster (-stər) *n.* [OE. *sangestre*] a singer —**song′stress** *n.fem.*

son·ic (sän′ik) *adj.* [< L. *sonus,* SOUND[1]] of or having to do with sound or the speed of sound

sonic boom an explosive sound generated by the accumulation of pressure in a wave preceding an aircraft moving at or above the speed of sound

son′-in-law′ *n., pl.* **sons′-in-law′** the husband of one's daughter

son·net (sän′it) *n.* [Fr. < It. < L. *sonus,* SOUND[1]] a poem normally of fourteen lines (typically in iambic pentameter) in any of several rhyme schemes

son·net·eer (sän′ə tir′) *n.* one who writes sonnets

so·no·rous (sə nôr′əs, sän′ər əs) *adj.* [< L. *sonor,* a sound] **1.** producing sound; resonant **2.** full, deep, or rich in sound **3.** high-sounding; impressive *[sonorous prose]* —**so·nor·i·ty** (sə nôr′ə tē, sō-) *n.* —**so·nor′ous·ly** *adv.*

soon (soon) *adv.* [OE. *sona,* at once] **1.** in a short time *[we will soon be there]* **2.** promptly; quickly *[as soon as possible]* **3.** ahead of time; early *[he left too soon]* **4.** readily; willingly *[I'd as soon go as stay]* —**had sooner** would rather —**sooner or later** eventually

soot (soot, soot) *n.* [OE. *sot]* a black substance, chiefly carbon particles, formed by the incomplete combustion of burning matter —*vt.* to cover, soil, etc. with soot —**soot′i·ness** *n.* —**soot′y** *adj.* **-i·er, -i·est**

sooth (sooth) *adj.* [OE. *soth]* [Archaic] truth

soothe (sooth) *vt.* **soothed, sooth′ing** [< OE. *soth,* truth] **1.** to make calm or composed, as by gentleness, flattery, etc. **2.** to relieve (pain, etc.) —*vi.* to have a soothing effect —**sooth′er** *n.* —**sooth′ing·ly** *adv.*

sooth·say·er (sooth′sā′ər) *n.* one who claims to foretell the future —**sooth′say′ing** *n.*

sop (säp) *n.* [OE. *sopp*] **1.** a piece of food, as bread, soaked in milk, etc. **2.** something given to appease; bribe —*vt., vi.* **sopped, sop′ping 1.** to soak, steep, etc. **2.** to take (*up*), as water, by absorption

SOP, S.O.P. standing (or standard) operating procedure

soph·ism (säf′iz′m) *n.* [< Gr. *sophos,* clever] clever and plausible argument that is faulty or misleading —**so·phis·ti·cal** (sə fis′ti k′l) *adj.* —**so·phis′ti·cal·ly** *adv.*

soph′ist (-ist) *n.* **1.** [*often* S-] in ancient Greece, any of a group of teachers of rhetoric, philosophy, etc., notorious for their clever, specious arguments **2.** one who uses clever, specious reasoning

so·phis·ti·cate (sə fis′tə kāt′) *vt.* **-cat′ed, -cat′ing** [see SOPHISM] **1.** to change from being natural, naive, etc. to being artificial, worldly-wise, etc. **2.** to bring to a more developed, complex, or refined form, level, etc. —*n.* (*usually* -kit) a sophisticated person

so·phis·ti·cat·ed (-kāt′id) *adj.* **1.** not simple, natural, or naive; wise in the ways of the world **2.** appealing to sophisticated people **3.** highly complex, refined, etc. —**so·phis′ti·ca′tion** *n.*

soph·is·try (säf′is trē) *n., pl.* **-tries** unsound or misleading but subtle reasoning

Soph·o·cles (säf′ə klēz′) 496?-406 B.C.; Gr. writer of tragedies

soph·o·more (säf′ə môr′) *n.* [< obs. *sophumer,* sophist] a student in the second year of college or the tenth grade at high school —*adj.* of or for sophomores

soph′o·mor′ic *adj.* of or like sophomores; self-assured, opinionated, etc. though immature

-sophy [< Gr. *sophia,* skill, wisdom] *a combining form meaning* knowledge *[philosophy]*

sop·o·rif·ic (säp′ə rif′ik, sō′pə-) *adj.* [< L. *sopor,* sleep + -FIC] **1.** causing sleep **2.** sleepy —*n.* a drug, etc. that causes sleep

sop′py *adj.* **-pi·er, -pi·est 1.** very wet **2.** [Colloq.] sentimental

so·pra·no (sə pran′ō, -prä′nō) *n., pl.* **-nos, -ni** (-prä′nē) [It. < *sopra,* above] **1.** the highest singing voice of women and children **2.** a singer or instrument with such a range **3.** a part for a soprano —*adj.* of, in, or for the soprano

sor·cer·y (sôr′sər ē) *n., pl.* **-ies** [< L. *sors,* fate] **1.** the supposed use of evil magic power; witchcraft **2.** seemingly magical power —**sor′cer·er** *n.* —**sor′cer·ess** *n.fem.*

sor·did (sôr′did) *adj.* [< L. *sordes,* filth] **1.** *a)* dirty; filthy *b)* squalid; wretched **2.** *a)* base; ignoble *b)* meanly selfish or grasping —**sor′did·ly** *adv.* —**sor′did·ness** *n.*

sore (sôr) *adj.* **sor′er, sor′est** [OE. *sar*] **1.** giving or feeling pain; painful **2.** *a)* filled with grief, etc. *[sore at heart]* *b)* causing sadness, grief, etc. *[sore hardships]* **3.** provoking irritation *[a sore point]* **4.** [Colloq.] angry; offended —*n.* **1.** a sore, usually infected spot on the body, as an ulcer or blister **2.** a source of pain, distress, etc. —*adv.* [Archaic] sorely —**sore′ness** *n.*

sore′head′ *n.* [Colloq.] one who is angry, resentful, etc., or one easily made so

sore′ly *adv.* **1.** grievously; painfully *[sorely vexed]* **2.** urgently *[sorely needed]*

sor·ghum (sôr′gəm) *n.* [< It. *sorgo*] **1.** a tropical cereal grass grown for grain, syrup, fodder, etc. **2.** a syrup made from the juice of its stalk

so·ror·i·ty (sə rôr′ə tē) *n., pl.* **-ties** [< L. *soror,* sister] a group of women or girls joined together for social or professional reasons, as in some colleges

sor·rel¹ (sôr′əl, sär′-) *n.* [< Frank. *sur,* sour] any of several plants with sour leaves

sor·rel² (sôr′əl, sär′-) *n.* [< ML. *saurus,* light brown] **1.** light reddish brown **2.** a horse, etc. of this color —*adj.* light reddish-brown

sor·row (sär′ō, sôr′ō) *n.* [OE. *sorg*] **1.** mental suffering caused by loss, disappointment, etc. **2.** that which produces grief —*vi.* to feel or show sorrow —**sor′row·ful** *adj.* —**sor′row·ful·ly** *adv.*

sor·ry (sär′ē, sôr′ē) *adj.* **-ri·er, -ri·est** [< OE. *sar,* sore] **1.** full of sorrow, pity, or regret **2.** *a)* inferior; poor *b)* wretched —**sor′ri·ly** *adv.* —**sor′ri·ness** *n.*

sort (sôrt) *n.* [< L. *sors,* a lot] **1.** any group of related things; kind; class **2.** quality or type [remarks of that *sort*] —*vt.* to arrange according to class or kind —**of sorts** of an inferior kind: also **of a sort** —**out of sorts** [Colloq.] cross or ill —**sort of** [Colloq.] somewhat —**sort′er** *n.*

sor·tie (sôr′tē) *n.* [Fr. < *sortir,* to issue] **1.** a sudden attack by troops from a besieged place **2.** one mission by a single military plane

SOS (es′ō′es′) **1.** a signal of distress (. . . – – – . . .) used internationally in wireless telegraphy **2.** [Colloq.] any urgent call for help

so-so (sō′sō′) *adv.* indifferently; just passably —*adj.* just fair; neither good nor bad Also **so so**

sot (sät) *n.* [< L. *sors,* a lot] a drunkard —**sot′tish** *adj.* —**sot′tish·ly** *adv.*

sot·to vo·ce (sät′ō vō′chē) [It., under the voice] in an undertone, so as not to be overheard

souf·flé (sōō flā′, sōō′flā) *adj.* [Fr. < *souffler,* to blow] made light and puffy in cooking: also **souf·fleed′** (-flād′) —*n.* a baked food made light and puffy by adding beaten egg whites before baking

sough (sou, suf) *n.* [< OE. *swogan,* to sound] a soft, murmuring, sighing, or rustling sound —*vi.* to make a sough

sought (sôt) *pt. & pp. of* SEEK

soul (sōl) *n.* [OE. *sawol*] **1.** the part of one's being that is thought of as the center of feeling, thinking, will, etc. apart from the body. **2.** the moral or emotional nature of man **3.** spiritual or emotional warmth, force, etc. **4.** vital or essential part, quality, etc. **5.** embodiment; personification **6.** a person [a town of 1,000 *souls*] **7.** the spirit of a dead person **8.** [Colloq.] among U.S. blacks, a sense of racial pride and social and cultural solidarity —*adj.* [Colloq.] of, for, or like U.S. blacks

soul food [Colloq.] items of food popular among U.S. blacks, as chitterlings, ham hocks, turnip greens, etc.

soul′ful *adj.* full of or showing deep feeling —**soul′ful·ly** *adv.* —**soul′ful·ness** *n.*

soul′less *adj.* lacking sensitivity or deep feeling

soul music [Colloq.] *a form of* RHYTHM AND BLUES (with added elements of U.S. Negro gospel singing)

sound¹ (sound) *n.* [< L. *sonus*] **1.** *a)* vibrations in air, water, etc. that act on the nerves of the inner ear and produce the sensation of hearing *b)* the sensation that these vibrations stimulate in the ear **2.** any identifiable noise, tone, etc. **3.** the distance within which a sound may be heard **4.** the impression made by something said, etc. **5.** meaningless noise —*vi.* **1.** to make a sound **2.** to seem through sound [to sound sad] —*vt.* **1.** *a)* to cause to sound *b)* to utter distinctly [to *sound* one's r's] **2.** to express, signal, etc. [sound the alarm] —**sound off 1.** to speak in turn **2.** [Slang] *a)* to voice complaints, opinions, etc. *b)* to speak in a loud or offensive way —**sound′less** *adj.*

sound² (sound) *adj.* [OE. (ge)*sund*] **1.** free from defect, damage, or decay **2.** healthy [a *sound* body] **3.** firm and safe [a *sound* bank] **4.** based on valid reasoning; sensible **5.** agreeing with established views or beliefs **6.** thorough, complete, etc. **7.** deep and undisturbed: said of sleep **8.** honest, loyal, etc. **9.** *Law* valid —*adv.* deeply [sound asleep] —**sound′ly** *adv.* —**sound′ness** *n.*

sound³ (sound) *n.* [< OE. & ON. *sund*] **1.** a wide channel linking two bodies of water or separating an island from the mainland **2.** a long arm of the sea **3.** the air bladder of certain fishes

sound⁴ (sound) *vt., vi.* [< L. *sub,* under + *unda,* a wave] **1.** *a)* to measure the depth of (water), esp. with a

weighted line *b)* to examine (the bottom of the sea, etc.) with a line that brings up particles *c)* to probe (the air or space) for data **2.** to try to find out the opinions of (a person): often with *out* —**sound′er** *n.* —**sound′ing** *n.*

sound effects sounds, as of thunder, animals, etc., produced artificially or by recording as for radio, TV, etc.

sounding board 1. a board, etc. used to reflect sound **2.** a person on whom one tests one's ideas, opinions, etc.

sound′proof′ *adj.* able to keep sound from coming through —*vt.* to make soundproof

sound track the sound record along one side of a motion-picture film

soup (sōōp) *n.* [< OFr. *soupe*] a liquid food made by cooking meat, vegetables, etc. in water, milk, etc. —**soup up** [Slang] to increase the power, capacity for speed, etc. of (an engine, etc.) —**soup′y** *adj.* **-i·er, -i·est**

soup·çon (sōōp sôn′, sōōp′sôn′) *n.* [Fr.] **1.** a suggestion or trace, as of a flavor **2.** a tiny amount; bit

sour (sour) *adj.* [OE. *sur*] **1.** having a sharp, acid taste, as vinegar **2.** spoiled by fermentation **3.** cross, bitter, etc. **4.** distasteful or unpleasant —*n.* **1.** something sour **2.** a cocktail made with lime or lemon juice [a whiskey *sour*] —*vt., vi.* to make or become sour —**sour′ish** *adj.* —**sour′ly** *adv.* —**sour′ness** *n.*

source (sôrs) *n.* [< L. *surgere,* to rise] **1.** a spring, etc. from which a stream arises **2.** a place of origin **3.** a person, book, etc. that provides information **4.** the point from which light or sound comes forth

sour′dough′ *n.* **1.** [Dial.] fermented dough kept for use as leaven **2.** a prospector in the western U.S. or Canada

sour grapes a scorning of something only because it cannot be had

Sou·sa (sōō′zə, -sə), **John Philip** 1854–1932; U.S. bandmaster & composer of marches

souse (sous) *n.* [< OHG. *sulza,* brine] **1.** a pickled food, as pig's feet **2.** liquid for pickling; brine **3.** a plunging into a liquid **4.** [Slang] a drunkard —*vt., vi.* **soused, sous′ing 1.** to pickle **2.** to plunge or steep in a liquid **3.** to make or become soaking wet **4.** [Slang] to make or become intoxicated

south (south) *n.* [OE. *suth*] **1.** the direction to the left of one facing the sunset (180° on the compass, opposite north) **2.** a region in or toward this direction **3.** [*often* S-] the southern part of the earth —*adj.* **1.** in, of, or toward the south **2.** from the south —*adv.* in or toward the south —**the South** that part of the U.S. bounded on the north by Pennsylvania, the Ohio River, and N Missouri

South Africa country in southernmost Africa: 472,358 sq. mi.; pop. 21,525,000; caps. Cape Town, Pretoria —**South African**

South America S continent in the Western Hemisphere: c.6,864,000 sq. mi.; pop. 190,000,000 —**South American**

South·amp·ton (sou thamp′tən) seaport in S England: pop. 210,000

South Bend city in N Ind.: pop. 126,000

South Carolina Southern State of the U.S.: 31,055 sq. mi.; pop. 2,591,000; cap. Columbia: abbrev. **S.C., SC** —**South Car·o·lin·i·an** (kar′ə lin′ē ən)

South China Sea arm of the W Pacific, touching Taiwan, the Philippines, Borneo, & SE Asia

South Dakota Middle Western State of the U.S.: 77,047 sq. mi.; pop. 666,000; cap. Pierre: abbrev. **S.Dak., SD** —**South Da·ko′tan**

south·east (south′ēst′; *nautical* sou-) *n.* **1.** the direction halfway between south and east **2.** a region in or toward this direction —*adj.* **1.** in, of, or toward the southeast **2.** from the southeast —*adv.* in, toward, or from the southeast —**the Southeast** the southeastern part of the U.S. —**south′east′er·ly** *adj., adv.* —**south′east′ern** *adj.* —**south′east′ward** (-wərd) *adv., adj.* —**south′east′wards** *adv.*

south·east·er (south′ēs′tər, *nautical* sou-) *n.* a storm or strong wind from the southeast

south·er (sou′thər) *n.* a storm or wind from the south

south·er·ly (suth′ər lē) *adj., adv.* **1.** toward the south **2.** from the south

south·ern (suth′ərn) *adj.* **1.** in, of, or toward the south **2.** from the south **3.** [S-] of the South —**south′ern·most′** *adj.*

Southern Cross a small S constellation with four bright stars in the form of a cross

south·ern·er (suth′ər nər, -ə nər) *n.* a native or inhabitant of the south, specif. [S-] of the southern part of the U.S.

Southern Hemisphere that half of the earth south of the equator

southern lights *same as* AURORA AUSTRALIS

south·paw (south′pô′) *n.* [Slang] a person who is left-handed; esp., a left-handed baseball pitcher

South Pole the southern end of the earth's axis

south-south·east (south′south′ēst′; *nautical* sou′sou-) *n.* the direction halfway between due south and southeast —*adj., adv.* in, toward, or from this direction

south′-south′west′ (-west′) *n.* the direction halfway between due south and southwest —*adj., adv.* in, toward, or from this direction

south′ward (-wərd) *adv., adj.* toward the south: also **south′wards** *adv.* —*n.* a southward direction, point, or region —**south′ward·ly** *adv., adj.*

south·west (south′west′; *nautical* sou-) *n.* **1.** the direction halfway between south and west **2.** a region in or toward this direction —*adj.* **1.** in, of, or toward the southwest **2.** from the southwest —*adv.* in, toward, or from the southwest —**the Southwest** the southwestern part of the U.S., esp. Okla., Tex., N.Mex., Ariz., and S Calif. —**south′west′er·ly** *adj., adv.* —**south′west′ern** *adj.* —**south′west′ward** (-wərd) *adv., adj.* —**south′west′wards** *adv.*

south·west·er (south′wes′tər; *nautical* sou-) *n.* **1.** a storm or strong wind from the southwest **2.** a sailor's waterproof hat, having a broad brim in the back Also **sou′·west′er** (sou-)

sou·ve·nir (sōō′və nir′) *n.* [Fr. < L. *subvenire*, come to mind] something kept as a reminder; keepsake; memento

sov·er·eign (säv′rən, -ər in) *adj.* [< L. *super*, above] **1.** above all others; greatest **2.** supreme in power, rank, etc. **3.** of or being a ruler; reigning **4.** independent of all others [a *sovereign* state] **5.** very effectual, as a remedy — *n.* **1.** a person having sovereign authority; monarch **2.** esp. formerly, a British gold coin worth one pound —**sov′er·eign·ly** *adv.*

sov·er·eign·ty (-tē) *n., pl.* **-ties 1.** the status, rule, etc. of a sovereign **2.** supreme and independent political authority **3.** a sovereign state

so·vi·et (sō′vē it, -et′) *n.* [Russ., lit., council] **1.** in the Soviet Union, any of various elected governing councils, ranging from village and town soviets to the Supreme Soviet of the whole country **2.** [S-] [*pl.*] the Soviet people or their officials —*adj.* **1.** of a soviet or soviets **2.** [S-] of or connected with the Soviet Union —**so′vi·et·ism** *n.*

Soviet Union *same as* UNION OF SOVIET SOCIALIST REPUBLICS: also **Soviet Russia**

sow[1] (sou) *n.* [OE. *sugu*] an adult female pig or hog

sow[2] (sō) *vt.* **sowed, sown** (sōn) or **sowed, sow′ing** [OE. *sawan*] **1.** to scatter or plant (seed) for growing **2.** to plant (a field, etc.) with seed **3.** to spread; disseminate — *vi.* to sow seed —**sow′er** *n.*

soy (soi) *n.* [Jpn. < Chin. *chiang*, salted bean + *yu*, oil] **1.** a dark, salty sauce made from fermented soybeans: also **soy sauce 2.** the soybean plant or its seeds Also, chiefly Brit., **soy·a** (soi′ə)

soy′bean′ *n.* **1.** a plant of the legume family, widely grown for forage and for its seeds, rich in protein and oil **2.** its seed

Sp. 1. Spain **2.** Spaniard **3.** Spanish

sp. 1. special **2.** *pl.* **spp.** species **3.** spelling

spa (spä) *n.* [< *Spa*, resort in Belgium] **1.** a mineral spring **2.** a resort having a mineral spring

space (spās) *n.* [< L. *spatium*] **1.** the boundless expanse extending in all directions, within which all things exist **2.** *same as* OUTER SPACE **3.** distance, area, etc. between or within things **4.** room for something [*parking space*] **5.** an interval of time **6.** reserved accommodations, as on a ship **7.** the open area between any two lines of a musical staff —*adj.* of space —*vt.* **spaced, spac′ing** to arrange with spaces between — **space′less** *adj.* —**spac′er** *n.*

space′craft′ *n., pl.* **-craft** a spaceship or satellite for use in outer space

space′flight′ *n.* a flight through outer space

space′man′ *n., pl.* **-men′** an astronaut

space′ship′ *n.* a rocket-propelled vehicle for travel in outer space

spa·cious (spā′shəs) *adj.* **1.** having more than enough space; vast **2.** not limited; large —**spa′cious·ly** *adv.* — **spa′cious·ness** *n.*

SOYBEAN PLANT

spade[1] (spād) *n.* [OE. *spadu*] a long-handled digging tool with a flat blade that is pressed with the foot —*vt., vi.* **spad′ed, spad′ing** to dig with a spade

spade[2] (spād) *n.* [Sp. *espada*, sword < L. *spatha*, SPATULA] **1.** the black figure (♠) marking one of the four suits of playing cards **2.** [*pl.*] this suit **3.** a card of this suit

spade′work′ *n.* any tiresome work necessary to make a beginning

spa·dix (spā′diks) *n., pl.* **-dix·es, -di·ces′** (spā′də sēz′, spā di′sēz) [< L., a palm branch] a fleshy spike of tiny flowers, usually enclosed in a spathe

spa·ghet·ti (spə get′ē) *n.* [It. < *spago*, small cord] long, thin strings of pasta, boiled or steamed and served with a sauce

Spain (spān) country in SW Europe: 194,346 sq. mi.; pop. 34,134,000; cap. Madrid

spake (spāk) *archaic pt. of* SPEAK

span (span) *n.* [OE. *sponn*] **1.** the distance (about 9 in.) between the tips of the thumb and little finger when extended **2.** the full extent between any two limits **3.** a part between two supports **4.** the full duration, as of attention **5.** [< Du.] a team of two animals used together —*vt.* **spanned, span′ning 1.** to measure, esp. by the span of the hand **2.** to extend, reach, or pass over or across

span·gle (span′g'l) *n.* [< OE. *spang*, a clasp] **1.** a small piece of bright metal sewn on fabric for decoration **2.** any small, glittering object —*vt.* **-gled, -gling** to cover with spangles —*vi.* to glitter as with spangles

Span·iard (span′yərd) *n.* a native or inhabitant of Spain

span·iel (span′yəl) *n.* [< MFr. *espagnol*, Spanish] any of several breeds of dog with a silky coat, drooping ears, and short legs

Span·ish (span′ish) *adj.* of Spain, its people, their language, etc. —*n.* the Romance language of Spain and of Spanish America —**the Spanish** the people of Spain

Spanish America Mexico and those countries in Central and South America in which Spanish is the chief language —**Span′ish-A·mer′i·can** *adj., n.*

Spanish-American War the war between the U.S. and Spain (1898)

Spanish Main 1. orig., the coastal region of the Americas along the Caribbean Sea **2.** later, the Caribbean Sea itself

Spanish moss a rootless plant often growing from tree branches in the SE U.S. and tropical America

spank (spank) *vt.* [echoic] to strike with something flat, as the open hand, esp. on the buttocks, as in punishment — *n.* a smack given in spanking

spank′ing *adj.* **1.** rapid **2.** brisk: said of a breeze **3.** [Colloq.] unusually fine, large, etc. —*adv.* [Colloq.] altogether [*spanking* new] —*n.* a series of smacks given by one who spanks

spar[1] (spär) *n.* [< MDu.] any shiny, crystalline mineral that cleaves easily into chips or flakes

spar[2] (spär) *n.* [< ON. *sparri*] **1.** any pole, as a mast or yard, supporting the sails on a ship **2.** a lengthwise support for the ribs of an airplane wing

spar[3] (spär) *vi.* **sparred, spar′ring** [< It. *parare*, to parry] **1.** to box with caution, landing few heavy blows **2.** to dispute; argue —*n.* a sparring match

spare (sper) *vt.* **spared, spar′ing** [OE. *sparian*] **1.** to refrain from killing, hurting, distressing, etc. **2.** to save or free (a person) from (something) [*spare* me the trouble] **3.** to avoid using or use frugally [*spare* no efforts] **4.** to do without; give up, as time or money —*adj.* **1.** not in regular use; extra [a *spare* room] **2.** free: said of time **3.** meager; scanty [*spare* rations] **4.** lean; thin —*n.* **1.** an extra part, thing, etc. **2.** *Bowling a)* a knocking down of all the pins in two consecutive rolls of the ball *b)* a score so made —**(something) to spare** a surplus of (something) — **spare′ly** *adv.* —**spare′ness** *n.*

spare′ribs′ *n.pl.* [prob. < MLowG. *ribbesper*] a cut of meat, esp. pork, consisting of the thin end of the ribs with most of the meat cut away

spar′ing *adj.* **1.** that spares **2.** frugal **3.** scanty; meager — **spar′ing·ly** *adv.*

spark[1] (spärk) *n.* [OE. *spearca*] **1.** a glowing bit of matter, esp. one thrown off by a fire **2.** any flash or sparkle **3.** a particle or trace, as of life, interest, etc. **4.** *a)* the brief flash of light accompanying an electric discharge *b)* such a discharge, as in a spark plug —*vi.* to produce sparks or come forth as sparks —*vt.* to stir into action —**spark′er** *n.*

spark[2] (spärk) *n.* [< ON. *sparkr*, lively] a beau or lover — *vt., vi.* [Colloq.] to court or woo An old-fashioned term

spar·kle (spär′k'l) *vi.* **-kled, -kling 1.** to throw off sparks **2.** to glitter, as jewels **3.** to be brilliant and lively **4.** to effervesce —*n.* **1.** a spark, or glowing particle **2.** a glittering **3.** brilliance; vivacity —**spar′kler** (-klər) *n.*

spark plug a piece fitted into a cylinder of an internal-combustion engine to make sparks that ignite the fuel mixture within

TERMINAL

INSULATOR

ELECTRODES

GAP

SPARK PLUG
(in cross section)

spar·row (spar'ō) *n.* [OE. *spearwa*] **1.** *same as* ENGLISH SPARROW **2.** a common N. American bird with a striped breast, noted for its sweet song: in full **song sparrow**

sparrow hawk 1. a small European hawk with short wings **2.** a small American falcon

sparse (spärs) *adj.* [< L. *spargere*, scatter] thinly spread or scattered; not dense; meager —**sparse'ly** *adv.* — **sparse'ness, spar·si·ty** (spär'sə tē) *n.*

Spar·ta (spär'tə) a powerful military city in ancient Greece

Spar'tan *adj.* **1.** of ancient Sparta, its people, or their culture **2.** like the Spartans; brave, stoical, disciplined, strict, etc. —*n.* **1.** a citizen of Sparta **2.** a person with Spartan traits —**Spar'tan·ism** *n.*

spasm (spaz'm) *n.* [< Gr. *span*, to pull] **1.** a sudden, involuntary muscular contraction **2.** any short, sudden burst of activity, feeling, etc.

spas·mod·ic (spaz mäd'ik) *adj.* [see prec. & -OID] of or like spasms; sudden, violent, and temporary; fitful: also **spas·mod'i·cal** —**spas·mod'i·cal·ly** *adv.*

spas·tic (spas'tik) *adj.* of or characterized by muscular spasms —*n.* one having a spastic condition

spat¹ (spat) *n.* [prob. echoic] [Colloq.] a brief, petty quarrel or dispute —*vi.* **spat'ted, spat'ting** [Colloq.] to have a spat, or quarrel

spat² (spat) *n.* [< *spatterdash*, a legging] a short gaiter for the instep and ankle

spat³ (spat) *alt. pt. & pp. of* SPIT²

spat⁴ (spat) *n.* [< ?] **1.** the spawn of the oyster or other bivalve shellfish **2.** young oysters

spate (spāt) *n.* [ME. < ?] **1.** [Chiefly Brit.] a heavy rain **2.** a large outpour, as of words

spathe (spāth) *n.* [< Gr. *spathē*, flat blade] a large, leaflike part or pair of such parts enclosing a flower cluster (esp. a spadix)

spa·tial (spā'shəl) *adj.* [< L. *spatium*, space] of, or existing in, space —**spa'tial·ly** *adv.*

spat·ter (spat'ər) *vt., vi.* [< Fris. *spatten*, to splash] **1.** to scatter or spurt out in drops or small blobs **2.** to splash —*n.* **1.** *a)* a spattering *b)* its sound **2.** a mark made by spattering

spat·u·la (spach'ə lə) *n.* [L. < *spatha*, flat blade] an implement with a broad, flexible blade for spreading or blending foods, paints, etc.

spav·in (spav'in) *n.* [MFr. *esparvain*] a disease of horses affecting the hock joint and causing lameness —**spav'ined** *adj.*

spawn (spôn) *vt., vi.* [< L. *ex-*, out + *pandere*, spread] **1.** to produce or deposit (eggs, sperm, or young) **2.** to bring into being (esp. in great quantity): usually contemptuous —*n.* **1.** the mass of eggs produced by fishes, mollusks, etc. **2.** something produced; specif., offspring or progeny: usually contemptuous

spay (spā) *vt.* [< Gr. *spathē*, flat blade] to sterilize (a female animal) by removing the ovaries

S.P.C.A. Society for the Prevention of Cruelty to Animals

speak (spēk) *vi.* spoke or archaic spake, spo'ken or archaic spoke, speak'ing [OE. *sp(r)ecan*] **1.** to utter words; talk **2.** to express opinions, feelings, etc. by or as by talking **3.** to make a request (*for*) **4.** to make a speech **5.** to converse **6.** to give out sound —*vt.* **1.** to make known as by speaking **2.** to use (a given language) in speaking **3.** to utter (words) orally —**so to speak** that is to say —**speak for itself** to be self-evident —**speak out** (or **up**) to speak clearly or freely —**to speak of** worthy of mention

speak-eas·y (spēk'ē'zē) *n., pl.* -ies [Slang] a place where alcoholic drinks are sold illegally

speak'er *n.* **1.** one who speaks or makes speeches **2.** the presiding officer of a lawmaking body, specif. [S-] of the U.S. House of Representatives

speaking in tongues *same as* GLOSSOLALIA

spear (spir) *n.* [OE. *spere*] **1.** a weapon with a long shaft and sharp head, for thrusting or throwing **2.** any spearlike, often forked implement for stabbing fish **3.** [var. of SPIRE] a long blade or shoot, as of grass —*vt.* **1.** to pierce or stab as with a spear **2.** to catch (fish, etc.) with a spear

spear'head' *n.* **1.** the point of a spear **2.** the leading person or group, as in an attack —*vt.* to lead (an attack, etc.)

spear'mint' *n.* [< its flower spikes] a fragrant plant of the mint family, used for flavoring

spec. 1. special **2.** specification **3.** speculation

spe·cial (spesh'əl) *adj.* [< L. *species*, kind] **1.** distinctive or unique **2.** exceptional; extraordinary **3.** highly regarded **4.** of or for a particular purpose [a *special* edition] **5.** not general; specific —*n.* a special person or thing —**spe'cial·ly** *adv.*

special delivery delivery of mail by special postal messenger, for an extra fee

spe'cial·ist *n.* one who specializes in a particular study, branch of professional work, etc.

spe'cial·ize *vt.* -ized', -iz'ing **1.** to specify **2.** *Biol.* to adapt (organs or parts) to a special condition, use, etc. —*vi.* to concentrate on a special study or special branch of a profession —**spe'cial·i·za'tion** *n.*

spe'cial·ty *n., pl.* -ties **1.** a special quality, feature, etc. **2.** a special study, branch of a profession, etc. **3.** an article or product with special features, superior quality, etc.

spe·cie (spē'shē, -sē) *n.* [< L. *species*, kind] coin, as distinguished from paper money —**in specie 1.** in kind **2.** in coin

spe'cies (-shēz, -sēz) *n., pl.* -cies [L., appearance] **1.** a distinct kind; sort **2.** a single, distinct kind of plant or animal, having certain distinguishing characteristics: see GENUS

specif. specifically

spe·cif·ic (spi sif'ik) *adj.* [see SPECIFY] **1.** definite; explicit **2.** peculiar to or characteristic of something **3.** of a particular sort **4.** specially indicated as a cure for some disease —*n.* **1.** a specific cure **2.** a particular —**spe·cif'i·cal·ly** *adv.* —**spec·i·fic·i·ty** (spes'ə fis'ə tē) *n.*

spec·i·fi·ca·tion (spes'ə fi kā'shən) *n.* **1.** a specifying **2.** [*usually pl.*] an enumeration of particulars, as to size, materials, etc. **3.** something specified

specific gravity the ratio of the weight of a given volume of a substance to that of an equal volume of another substance (as water) used as a standard

spec·i·fy (spes'ə fī') *vt.* -fied', -fy'ing [< L. *species*, kind + *facere*, to make] to mention or describe in detail; state explicitly

spec·i·men (spes'ə mən) *n.* [L. < *specere*, see] **1.** a part or individual used as a sample of a whole or group **2.** [Colloq.] a (specified kind of) individual **3.** *Med.* a sample, as of urine, for analysis

spe·cious (spē'shəs) *adj.* [< L. *species*, appearance] seeming good, sound, etc. but not really so —**spe'cious·ly** *adv.*

speck (spek) *n.* [OE. *specca*] **1.** a small spot or mark **2.** a tiny bit —*vt.* to mark with specks

speck·le (spek''l) *n.* a small speck —*vt.* -led, -ling to mark with speckles

specs (speks) *n.pl.* [Colloq.] **1.** eyeglasses **2.** specifications: see SPECIFICATION (sense 2)

spec·ta·cle (spek'tə k'l) *n.* [< L. *specere*, see] **1.** something remarkable to look at **2.** a grand public show **3.** [*pl.*] eyeglasses: an old-fashioned term

spec·tac·u·lar (spek tak'yə lər) *adj.* of or like a spectacle; strikingly grand or unusual —**spec·tac'u·lar·ly** *adv.*

spec·ta·tor (spek'tāt ər) *n.* [L. < *spectare*, behold] one who watches without taking an active part

spec·ter (spek'tər) *n.* [< L. *spectare*, behold] a ghost; apparition: Brit. sp. **spectre**

spec'tral *adj.* **1.** of or like a specter; ghostly **2.** of a spectrum —**spec'tral·ly** *adv.*

spec·tro·scope (spek'trə skōp') *n.* an optical instrument for breaking up light into a spectrum so it can be studied —**spec'tro·scop'ic** (-skäp'ik) *adj.*

spec·tros·co·py (spek träs'kə pē) *n.* the study of spectra by use of the spectroscope

spec·trum (spek'trəm) *n., pl.* -tra (-trə), -trums [< L., appearance] **1.** the series of colored bands diffracted and arranged in order of their respective wavelengths by the passage of white light through a prism, etc. **2.** a continuous range or entire extent

spec·u·late (spek'yə lāt') *vi.* -lat'ed, -lat'ing [< L. *specere*, see] **1.** to think reflectively; ponder; esp., to conjecture **2.** to engage in a risky business venture on the chance of making huge profits —**spec'u·la'tion** *n.* —**spec'u·la'tive** (-lāt'iv, -lə tiv) *adj.* —**spec'u·la'tor** *n.*

sped (sped) *alt. pt. & pp. of* SPEED

speech (spēch) *n.* [< OE. *sp(r)ecan*, speak] **1.** the act or manner of speaking **2.** the power to speak **3.** what is spoken; utterance, talk, etc. **4.** a talk given to an audience **5.** the language or dialect of a certain people **6.** the study of oral expression

speech·i·fy (spē'chə fī') *vi.* **-fied'**, **-fy'ing** to make a speech: used humorously or contemptuously

speech'less *adj.* **1.** incapable of speech **2.** silent, as from shock —**speech'less·ly** *adv.*

speed (spēd) *n.* [OE. *spæd*, success] **1.** rapid motion; swiftness **2.** rate of movement; velocity **3.** rate of any action [reading *speed*] **4.** [Slang] any of various amphetamine compounds **5.** [Archaic] luck; success —*vi.* **sped** or **speed'ed**, **speed'ing** to go fast, esp. faster than the legal limit —*vt.* **1.** to help succeed; aid **2.** to wish Godspeed to **3.** to cause to go, move, etc. swiftly —**speed up** to increase in speed —**speed'er** *n.*

speed'boat' *n.* a motorboat built for speed

speed·om·e·ter (spi däm'ə tər) *n.* a device attached to a motor vehicle, etc. to indicate speed

speed'way' *n.* **1.** a track for racing cars or motorcycles **2.** a road for high-speed traffic

speed'y *adj.* **-i·er**, **-i·est** **1.** rapid; swift **2.** without delay; prompt [a *speedy* reply] —**speed'i·ly** *adv.*

spe·le·ol·o·gy (spē'lē äl'ə jē) *n.* [< Gr. *spēlaion*, cave] the science of exploring caves

spell¹ (spel) *n.* [OE., a saying] **1.** a word or formula supposed to have some magic power **2.** irresistible influence; magical charm; fascination

spell² (spel) *vt.* **spelled** or **spelt**, **spell'ing** [< OFr. *espeller*, explain] **1.** to name, write, etc., esp. correctly, the letters of (a word, etc.) **2.** to make up (a word): said of specified letters **3.** to mean [red *spells* danger] —*vi.* to spell words —**spell out** to explain in detail

spell³ (spel) *vt.* **spelled**, **spell'ing** [OE. *spelian*] [Colloq.] to work in place of (another) while he rests; relieve —*n.* **1.** a period of work, duty, etc. **2.** a period of anything [a *spell* of crying] **3.** a period of specified weather **4.** [Colloq.] a short or indefinite period of time **5.** [Colloq.] a fit of illness **6.** [Dial.] a short distance

spell'bind' *vt.* **-bound'**, **-bind'ing** to hold or affect as by a spell; fascinate; enchant —**spell'bind'er** *n.*

spell'down' *n.* a contest in spelling: also **spelling bee**

spell'er *n.* **1.** one who spells words **2.** a textbook used to teach spelling

spell'ing *n.* **1.** the act of one who spells words **2.** the way a word is spelled

spelt (spelt) *alt. pt. & pp. of* SPELL²

spe·lunk·er (spi luŋ'kər) *n.* [< obs. *spelunk*, a cave, ult. < Gr. *spēlynx*] one who explores caves as a hobby

spend (spend) *vt.* **spent**, **spend'ing** [< L. *expendere*, EXPEND] **1.** to use up, exhaust, etc. [his fury was *spent*] **2.** to pay out (money) **3.** to devote (time, effort, etc.) to something **4.** to pass (time) **5.** to waste; squander —*vi.* to pay out or use up money, etc. —**spend'er** *n.*

spend'thrift' *n.* one who spends money carelessly; squanderer —*adj.* wasteful; extravagant

Spen·ser (spen'sər), Edmund 1552?–99; Eng. poet

spent (spent) *pt. & pp. of* SPEND —*adj.* **1.** tired out; physically exhausted **2.** used up; worn out

sperm (spurm) *n.* [< Gr. *sperma*, seed] **1.** the fluid from the male reproductive organs; semen **2.** *same as* SPERMATOZOON —**sper·mat·ic** (spər mat'ik) *adj.*

sper·ma·ce·ti (spur'mə set'ē) *n.* [< LL. *sperma*, SPERM + L. *cetus*, a whale] a white, waxlike substance from oil in the head of a sperm whale or dolphin, used in making cosmetics, ointments, etc.

sper·mat·o·zo·on (spər mat'ə zō'än) *n., pl.* **-zo'a** (-ə) [< Gr. *sperma*, seed + *zōion*, animal] the male germ cell, found in semen: it penetrates and fertilizes the egg of the female

sperm oil a lubricating oil from the sperm whale

sperm whale a large, toothed whale of warm seas: a closed cavity in its head contains sperm oil

spew (spyōō) *vt., vi.* [OE. *spiwan*] **1.** to throw up from or as from the stomach; vomit **2.** to gush forth

sp. gr. specific gravity

sphag·num (sfag'nəm) *n.* [< Gr. *sphagnos*, kind of moss] **1.** a spongelike moss found in bogs **2.** a mass of such mosses, used to improve soil, to pot plants, etc.

sphere (sfir) *n.* [< Gr. *sphaira*] **1.** any round body with a surface equally distant from the center at all points; globe; ball **2.** a star or planet **3.** the visible heavens; sky **4.** place or range of action, knowledge, etc.; compass; province **5.** place in society —*vt.* **sphered**, **spher'ing** [Chiefly Poet.] **1.** to put in or as in a sphere **2.** to form into a sphere

spher·i·cal (sfer'i k'l, sfir'-) *adj.* **1.** shaped like a sphere; globular **2.** of a sphere or spheres —**spher'i·cal·ly** *adv.*

sphe·roid (sfir'oid) *n.* a body that is almost but not quite a sphere —*adj.* of this shape: also **sphe·roi'dal**

sphinc·ter (sfiŋk'tər) *n.* [< Gr. *sphingein*, to draw close] a ring-shaped muscle at a body orifice that can open or close it by expanding or contracting

sphinx (sfiŋks) *n., pl.* **sphinx'es**, **sphin·ges** (sfin'jēz) [< Gr. *sphinx*, strangler] **1.** any Egyptian statue with a lion's body and the head of a man, ram, or hawk; specif., [S-] such a statue with a man's head, near Cairo **2.** [S-] *Gr. Myth.* a winged monster with a lion's body and a woman's head: it strangled passers-by unable to answer its riddle **3.** one who is hard to know or understand

spice (spīs) *n.* [< L. *species*, sort] **1.** any of various aromatic vegetable substances, as clove, pepper, etc., used to season food **2.** that which gives zest or piquancy —*vt.* **spiced**, **spic'ing** **1.** to season with spice **2.** to add zest to

spick-and-span (spik''n span') *adj.* [< SPIKE¹ + ON. *spānn*, a chip] **1.** new or fresh **2.** neat and clean

spic·ule (spik'yōōl) *n.* **1.** *Bot.* a small spike **2.** *Zool.* a small, hard, needlelike piece, as in the skeleton of a sponge —**spic'u·late'** (-yə lāt') *adj.*

spic·y (spī'sē) *adj.* **-i·er**, **-i·est** **1.** containing spices **2.** having the flavor or aroma of spice **3.** lively, interesting, etc. **4.** risqué —**spic'i·ly** *adv.* —**spic'i·ness** *n.*

spi·der (spī'dər) *n.* [< OE. *spinnan*, spin] **1.** any of various small arachnids that have eight legs and spin silk threads, as for webs **2.** a frying pan —**spi'der·y** *adj.*

spiel (spēl) *n.* [G., play] [Slang] a talk or harangue, as by a salesman —*vi.* [Slang] to give a spiel —**spiel'er** *n.*

spig·ot (spig'ət, spik'-) *n.* [ME. *spigote*] **1.** a plug to stop the vent in a cask, etc. **2.** a faucet

spike¹ (spīk) *n.* [prob. < ON. *spīkr*] **1.** a long, heavy nail **2.** a sharp-pointed projection, as along the top of an iron fence **3.** one of the pointed metal projections on the bottoms of shoes used for baseball, etc. —*vt.* **spiked**, **spik'ing** **1.** to fasten or fit as with spikes **2.** to pierce with, or impale on, a spike **3.** to thwart (a scheme, etc.) **4.** [Slang] to add alcoholic liquor to (a drink) —**spik'y** *adj.*

spike² (spīk) *n.* [L. *spica*] **1.** an ear of grain **2.** a long flower cluster with flowers attached directly to the stalk

spike·nard (spīk'nərd, -närd) *n.* [< L. *spica*, ear of grain + *nardus*] **1.** a fragrant ointment used by the ancients **2.** the Asiatic plant from which it was made

spill (spil) *vt.* **spilled** or **spilt**, **spill'ing** [< OE. *spillan*, destroy] **1.** to allow (a fluid), esp. unintentionally, to run, scatter, or flow over from a container **2.** to shed (blood) **3.** to empty (wind) from (a sail) **4.** [Colloq.] to let (a secret) become known **5.** [Colloq.] to make (a rider, etc.) fall off —*vi.* to be spilled from a container —*n.* **1.** a spilling **2.** what is spilled **3.** [Colloq.] a fall

spill'way' *n.* a channel to carry off excess water

spin (spin) *vt.* **spun**, **spin'ning** [OE. *spinnan*] **1.** to draw out and twist fibers of (wool, cotton, etc.) into thread **2.** to make (thread, etc.) thus **3.** to make (a web, cocoon, etc.): said of spiders, etc. **4.** to produce in a way that suggests spinning **5.** to draw *out* (a story) at great length **6.** to rotate swiftly —*vi.* **1.** to spin thread, etc. **2.** to fish with a reel that spins **3.** to whirl **4.** to seem to be spinning from dizziness **5.** to move along swiftly and smoothly **6.** to rotate freely without traction —*n.* **1.** a whirling or rotating movement **2.** a ride in a motor vehicle **3.** a descent of an airplane, nose first along a spiral path

spin·ach (spin'ich, -ij) *n.* [< OSp. < Ar. < Per. *aspanākh*] **1.** a plant with dark-green, juicy, edible leaves **2.** the leaves

spi·nal (spī'n'l) *adj.* of the spine or spinal cord —*n.* a spinal anesthetic —**spi'nal·ly** *adv.*

spinal anesthesia anesthesia of the lower part of the body by injection of an anesthetic into the spinal cord, usually in the lumbar region —**spinal anesthetic**

spinal column the series of joined vertebrae forming the axial support for the skeleton; spine

spinal cord the thick cord of nerve tissue of the central nervous system, in the spinal column

spin·dle (spin'd'l) *n.* [< OE. *spinnan*, spin] **1.** a slender rod or pin for twisting, winding, or holding the thread in spinning **2.** something shaped like a spindle **3.** any rod, pin, or shaft that revolves or serves as an axis for a revolving part —*vi.* **-dled**, **-dling** to grow in or into a long, slender form

spin·dly (spin'dlē) *adj.* **-dli·er**, **-dli·est** long or tall and very thin or slender: also **spin'dling** (-dliŋ)

spine (spīn) *n.* [< L. *spina*, thorn] **1.** a sharp, stiff projection, as a thorn of the cactus or a porcupine's quill **2.** anything like this **3.** the spinal column **4.** anything like this, as the back of a book

spine′less *adj.* **1.** having no spine or spines **2.** lacking courage, willpower, etc. **–spine′less·ly** *adv.*

spin·et (spin′it) *n.* [It., prob. < *spina*, thorn] a small upright piano or electronic organ

spin·na·ker (spin′ə kər) *n.* [< ?] a large, triangular forward sail used on some racing yachts

spin′ner *n.* a person or thing that spins; specif., a fishing lure that spins when drawn through the water

spin·ner·et (spin′ə ret′) *n.* [< SPINNER] an organ used by spiders, etc. in spinning their threads

spin′ning *n.* the act of making thread or yarn from fibers or filaments **–adj.** that spins

spinning jenny a spinning machine with several spindles, for spinning many threads at a time

spinning wheel a simple spinning machine with a single spindle driven by a large wheel

spin·off (spin′ôf′) *n.* a secondary product, benefit, development, program, etc.

Spi·no·za (spi nō′zə), **Ba·ruch** (bə rook′) or **Benedict** 1632–77; Du. philosopher

spin·ster (spin′stər) *n.* [ME. < *spin-nen*, to spin] an unmarried woman, esp. an older one; old maid **–spin′ster·hood′** *n.*

SPINNING WHEEL

spin·y (spī′nē) *adj.* **-i·er, -i·est 1.** covered with spines or thorns **2.** spine-shaped **–spin′i·ness** *n.*

spiny lobster a sea crustacean like the common lobster, but lacking large pincers and having a spiny shell

spi·ra·cle (spī′rə k′l, spir′ə-) *n.* [< L. *spirare*, breathe] **1.** an opening for breathing, as the blowhole of the whale **2.** any of various similar openings

spi·ral (spī′rəl) *adj.* [< Gr. *speira*] circling around a point in constantly increasing (or decreasing) curves, or in constantly changing planes **–n. 1.** a spiral curve or coil **2.** something having a spiral form **3.** a spiral path **–vi., vt. -raled** or **-ralled, -ral·ing** or **-ral·ling** to move or form (into) a spiral **–spi′ral·ly** *adv.*

spire (spīr) *n.* [OE. *spir*] **1.** a sprout, spike, or stalk of a plant **2.** the top part of a pointed, tapering object **3.** anything that tapers to a point, as a steeple **–vi. spired,** **spir′ing** to extend upward, tapering to a point

spi·re·a (spī rē′ə) *n.* [< Gr. *speira*, a coil] a shrub of the rose family, with clusters of small pink or white flowers: also sp. **spi·rae′a**

spir·it (spir′it) *n.* [< L. *spirare*, breathe] **1.** the soul **2.** [*also* S-] life, will, thought, etc., regarded as separate from matter **3.** a supernatural being, as a ghost, angel, fairy, etc. **4.** an individual [a brave *spirit*] **5.** [*often pl.*] disposition; mood [high *spirits*] **6.** vivacity, courage, etc. **7.** enthusiastic loyalty [school *spirit*] **8.** true intention [the *spirit* of the law] **9.** an essential quality or prevailing tendency [the *spirit* of the Renaissance] **10.** [*usually pl.*] distilled alcoholic liquor **11.** [*often pl.*] any of certain liquids produced by distillation **12.** an alcoholic solution of a volatile substance **–vt.** to carry (*away* or *off*) secretly and swiftly **–the Spirit** *same as* HOLY SPIRIT **–spir′it-less** *adj.*

spir′it·ed *adj.* **1.** lively; vigorous **2.** having a (specified) nature or mood [low-*spirited*] **–spir′it·ed·ly** *adv.*

spir·it·u·al (spir′i choo wəl) *adj.* **1.** of the spirit or soul **2.** of or consisting of spirit; not corporeal **3.** refined in thought or feeling **4.** religious; sacred **–n.** a religious folk song of U.S. Negro origin **–spir′it·u·al′i·ty** (-wal′ə tē) *n.,* *pl.* **-ties –spir′it·u·al·ly** *adv.*

spir·it·u·al·ism *n.* **1.** the belief that the dead survive as spirits which can communicate with the living **2.** the doctrine that all reality is spiritual **3.** spiritual quality **– spir′it·u·al·ist** *n.* **–spir′it·u·al·is′tic** *adj.*

spir·it·u·al·ize (-wə līz′) *vt.* **-ized′, -iz′ing** to make spiritual

spir·it·u·ous (spir′i choo wəs) *adj.* of, like, or containing alcohol: said of distilled beverages

spi·ro·chete (spī′rə kēt′) *n.* [< Gr. *speira*, a spiral + *chaitē*, hair] any of various spiral-shaped bacteria, some of which cause disease

spit[1] (spit) *n.* [OE. *spitu*] **1.** a thin, pointed rod on which meat is roasted over a fire **2.** a narrow point of land extending into a body of water **–vt. spit′ted, spit′ting** to impale as on a spit

spit[2] (spit) *vt.* **spit** or **spat, spit′ting** [OE. *spittan*] **1.** to eject from the mouth **2.** to throw (*out*) or emit explo-

sively [to *spit* out an oath] **–vi.** to eject saliva from the mouth **–n. 1.** a spitting **2.** saliva **–spit and image** [Colloq.] perfect likeness: also **spitting image**

spite (spīt) *n.* [< DESPITE] ill will; malice; grudge **–vt.** **spit′ed, spit′ing** to show one's spite for by hurting, frustrating, etc. **–in spite of** regardless of **–spite′ful** *adj.* **– spite′ful·ly** *adv.* **–spite′ful·ness** *n.*

spit·fire (spit′fīr′) *n.* a woman or girl who is easily aroused to violent outbursts of temper

spit·tle (spit′'l) *n.* spit; saliva

spit·toon (spi toon′) *n.* a container to spit into

spitz (spits) *n.* [G. < *spitz*, pointed] a small dog with pointed muzzle and ears and a long, silky coat

splash (splash) *vt.* [< PLASH] **1.** to cause (a liquid) to scatter **2.** to dash a liquid, mud, etc. on, so as to wet or soil **–vi.** to move, strike, etc. with a splash **–n. 1.** the act or sound of splashing **2.** a spot made as by splashing **–make a splash** [Colloq.] to attract great attention **–splash′y** *adj.* **-i·er, -i·est**

splash·down (splash′doun′) *n.* the landing of a spacecraft on water

splat (splat) *n.* [see SPLIT] a thin, flat piece of wood, esp. as used in the back of a chair

splat·ter (splat′ər) *n., vt., vi.* spatter; splash

splay (splā) *adj.* [< ME. *displaien*, to DISPLAY] spreading out **–vt., vi.** to spread out

splay′foot′ *n., pl.* **-feet′** a foot that is flat and turned outward

spleen (splēn) *n.* [Gr. *splēn*] **1.** a large, vascular organ in the upper left part of the abdomen: it modifies the blood structure **2.** malice; spite **–spleen′ful, spleen′ish** *adj.*

splen·did (splen′did) *adj.* [< L. *splendere*, to shine] **1.** shining; brilliant **2.** magnificent; gorgeous **3.** worthy of high praise; glorious **4.** [Colloq.] fine **–splen′did·ly** *adv.*

splen·dor (splen′dər) *n.* [< L. *splendere*, to shine] **1.** great luster; brilliance **2.** magnificent richness or glory Brit. sp. **splen′dour –splen′dor·ous, splen′drous** *adj.*

sple·net·ic (spli net′ik) *adj.* **1.** of the spleen **2.** irritable; peevish

splice (splīs) *vt.* **spliced, splic′ing** [MDu. *splissen*] **1.** to join (ropes) by weaving together the end strands **2.** to join (pieces of wood) by overlapping and fastening the ends **3.** to fasten the ends of (wire, magnetic tape, etc.) together, as by cementing, twisting, etc. **4.** [Slang] to join in marriage **–n.** a joint made by splicing **–splic′er** *n.*

splint (splint) *n.* [MDu. or MLowG. *splinte*] **1.** a thin strip of wood or cane woven with others to make baskets, chair seats, etc. **2.** a strip of wood, etc. used to hold a broken bone in place **–vt.** to support or hold in place as with a splint or splints

splin·ter (splin′tər) *vt., vi.* [see SPLINT] to break or split into thin, sharp pieces **–n.** a thin, sharp piece of wood, bone, etc., made by splitting **–adj.** designating a group that separates from a main party, church, etc. because of opposing views **–splin′ter·y** *adj.*

split (split) *vt.* **split, split′ting** [MDu. *splitten*] **1.** to separate lengthwise into two or more parts **2.** to break or tear apart **3.** to divide into shares **4.** to cast (one's vote) for candidates of more than one party **5.** *a)* to break (a molecule) into atoms *b)* to produce nuclear fission in (an atom) **6.** to divide (stock) by substituting some multiple of the original shares **–vi. 1.** to separate lengthwise **2.** to burst **3.** [Slang] to leave a place **–n. 1.** a splitting **2.** a break; crack **3.** a division in a group, between persons, etc. **4.** a confection made of a split banana with ice cream, sauces, etc. **5.** [*often pl.*] the feat of spreading the legs on the floor in a straight line **6.** [Colloq.] a share **7.** *Bowling* an arrangement of pins after the first bowl, so separated as to make a spare difficult **–adj.** separated

split infinitive *Gram.* an infinitive with the verb and the *to* separated by an adverb (Ex.: to slowly change)

split′-lev′el *adj.* designating or of a type of house in which each floor level is about a half story above or below the adjacent one

split ticket a ballot cast for candidates of more than one party

split′ting *adj.* **1.** that splits **2.** severe or sharp, as a headache

splotch (spläch) *n.* [prob. < SPOT & BLOTCH] an irregular spot, splash, or stain **–vt., vi.** to mark with splotches **– splotch′y** *adj.* **-i·er, -i·est**

splurge (splurj) *n.* [echoic] [Colloq.] **1.** any showy display or effort **2.** a spending spree **–vi.** **splurged, splurg′ing** [Colloq.] **1.** to show off **2.** to spend money freely

splut·ter (splut′ər) *vi.* [var. of SPUTTER] **1.** to make hissing or spitting sounds **2.** to speak hurriedly and confusedly —*vt.* **1.** to utter hurriedly and confusedly **2.** to spatter —*n.* a spluttering

spoil (spoil) *vt.* **spoiled** or **spoilt, spoil′ing** [< L. *spolium,* plunder] **1.** to damage so as to make useless, etc. **2.** to impair the enjoyment, etc. of **3.** to let (a person) have his own way so much that he demands or expects it —*vi.* to become spoiled; decay, etc., as food —*n.* [*usually pl.*] **1.** goods taken by plunder; booty **2.** public offices to which the winning political party has the power of appointment —**spoil′age** *n.*

spoil′sport′ *n.* one whose actions spoil the pleasure of others

spoils system the treating of public offices as the booty of the successful political party in an election

Spo·kane (spō kan′) city in E Wash.: pop. 171,000

spoke[1] (spōk) *n.* [OE. *spaca*] **1.** any of the braces extending from the hub to the rim of a wheel **2.** a ladder rung

spoke[2] (spōk) *pt. & archaic pp.* of SPEAK

spo·ken (spō′k'n) *pp.* of SPEAK —*adj.* **1.** uttered; oral **2.** having a (specified) kind of voice [*soft-spoken*]

spokes·man (spōks′mən) *n., pl.* **-men** one who speaks for another or others —**spokes′wom′an** *n.fem., pl.* **-wom′en**

spo·li·a·tion (spō′lē ā′shən) *n.* [< L. *spoliatio*] robbery; plundering

sponge (spunj) *n.* [< Gr. *spongia*] **1.** a plantlike sea animal with a porous structure **2.** the highly absorbent, lightweight, compressible skeleton of such animals, used for washing surfaces, etc. **3.** a piece of spongy plastic, etc. **4.** a pad of gauze, as used in surgery **5.** [Colloq.] one who lives upon others as a parasite —*vt.* **sponged, spong′ing 1.** to wipe, dampen, absorb, etc. as with a sponge **2.** [Colloq.] to get as by begging, imposition, etc. —*vi.* **1.** to gather sponges from the sea **2.** [Colloq.] to be a parasite —**spong′er** *n.* —**spon′gy** *adj.* **-gi·er, -gi·est**

SPONGES

sponge bath a bath taken by using a wet sponge or cloth without getting into water

sponge′cake′ *n.* a light cake of porous texture: also **sponge cake**

spon·sor (spän′sər) *n.* [L. < *spondere,* promise solemnly] **1.** one who assumes responsibility as surety for, or endorser of, some person or thing **2.** a godparent **3.** a business firm that alone or with others pays for a radio or TV program advertising its product or service —*vt.* to act as sponsor for —**spon′sor·ship′** *n.*

spon·ta·ne·i·ty (spän′tə nē′ə tē, -nā′-) *n.* **1.** a being spontaneous **2.** *pl.* **-ties** a spontaneous movement, action, etc.

spon·ta·ne·ous (spän tā′nē əs) *adj.* [< L. *sponte,* of free will] **1.** moved by a natural feeling or impulse, without constraint, effort, etc. **2.** acting by internal energy, force, etc. —**spon·ta′ne·ous·ly** *adv.*

spontaneous combustion the process of catching fire as a result of heat generated by internal chemical action

spoof (spōōf) *n.* [Slang] **1.** a hoax, joke, or deception **2.** a light parody or satire —*vt., vi.* [Slang] **1.** to fool; deceive **2.** to satirize playfully

spook (spōōk) *n.* [Du.] [Colloq.] a ghost —*vt., vi.* [Colloq.] to startle or be startled, frightened, etc. —**spook′i·ness** *n.* —**spook′y** *adj.* **-i·er, -i·est**

spool (spōōl) *n.* [< MDu. *spoele*] **1.** a cylinder upon which thread, wire, etc. is wound **2.** something like a spool —*vt.* to wind on a spool

spoon (spōōn) *n.* [OE. *spon,* a chip] **1.** a utensil consisting of a small, shallow bowl with a handle, used for eating or stirring **2.** something shaped like a spoon, as a fishing lure —*vt.* to take up as with a spoon —*vi.* [Colloq.] to hug and kiss: an old-fashioned term

spoon′bill′ *n.* a wading bird with a broad, flat bill that is spoon-shaped at the tip

spoon·er·ism (spōōn′ər iz′m) *n.* [< Rev. W. A. *Spooner* of Oxford] an unintentional interchange of sounds in words (Ex.: It is kistomary to cuss the bride)

spoor (spoor, spôr) *n.* [Afrik. < MDu.] the track or trail of a wild animal hunted as game

spo·rad·ic (spô rad′ik, spə-) *adj.* [< Gr. *sporas,* scattered] **1.** happening at intervals **2.** appearing singly or in isolated instances —**spo·rad′i·cal·ly** *adv.*

spo·ran·gi·um (spô ran′jē əm, spə-) *n., pl.* **-gi·a** (-ə) [< Gr. *spora,* a seed + *angeion,* vessel] *Bot.* an organ or single cell producing spores

spore (spôr) *n.* [< Gr. *spora,* a seed] a small reproductive body produced by bacteria, mosses, ferns, etc. and capable of giving rise to a new individual —*vi.* **spored, spor′ing** to develop spores

spore case *same as* SPORANGIUM

sport (spôrt) *n.* [< DISPORT] **1.** any recreational activity; specif., a game, competition, etc. requiring bodily exertion, as football, golf, bowling, etc. **2.** fun; play **3.** a thing joked about **4.** [Colloq.] a sportsmanlike person **5.** [Colloq.] a pleasure-loving, flashy person **6.** *Biol.* a plant or animal markedly different from the normal type —*vt.* [Colloq.] to wear or display [to *sport* a loud tie] —*vi.* **1.** to play **2.** to joke —*adj.* **1.** of or for sports **2.** suitable for casual wear [a *sport* coat] —**in** (or **for**) **sport** in jest — **make sport of** to ridicule

sport′ing *adj.* **1.** of or interested in sports **2.** sportsmanlike; fair **3.** of games, etc. involving gambling

sporting chance [Colloq.] a fair or even chance

spor·tive (spôr′tiv) *adj.* **1.** full of sport or fun **2.** done in fun —**spor′tive·ly** *adv.* —**spor′tive·ness** *n.*

sports *adj. same as* SPORT [*sports* clothes]

sports (or **sport**) **car** a low, small automobile with a high-compression engine

sports′cast′ *n.* a radio or TV broadcast of sports news — **sports′cast′er** *n.*

sports′man *n., pl.* **-men 1.** a man who takes part in sports, esp. hunting, fishing, etc. **2.** one who plays fair and can lose without complaint or win without gloating — **sports′man·like′** *adj.* —**sports′man·ship′** *n.*

sports′wear′ *n.* informal clothes, as for sports

sports′wom′an *n., pl.* **-wom′en** a woman who takes part in sports

sport′y *adj.* **-i·er, -i·est** [Colloq.] **1.** sporting or sportsmanlike **2.** loud, flashy, or showy, as clothes —**sport′i-ness** *n.*

spot (spät) *n.* [< MDu. *spotte*] **1.** a small area differing from the surrounding area, as in color **2.** a stain, speck, etc. **3.** a flaw, as in character **4.** a locality; place **5.** *shortened form of* SPOTLIGHT **6.** [Chiefly Brit. Colloq.] a small quantity [a *spot* of tea] —*vt.* **spot′ted, spot′ting 1.** to mark with spots **2.** to stain; blemish **3.** to place; locate **4.** to see; recognize **5.** [Colloq.] to allow as a handicap —*vi.* **1.** to become marked with spots **2.** to make a stain, as ink —*adj.* **1.** ready [*spot* cash] **2.** made at random [a *spot* survey] **3.** *Radio & TV* inserted between regular programs [a *spot* announcement] —**hit the spot** [Colloq.] to satisfy a craving —**in a (bad) spot** [Slang] in trouble —**on the spot 1.** at the place mentioned **2.** [Slang] *a)* in trouble or in a demanding situation *b)* in danger —**spot′less** *adj.* —**spot′-less·ly** *adv.* —**spot′less·ness** *n.*

spot′-check′ *vt.* to check or examine at random —*n.* an act or instance of such checking

spot′light′ *n.* **1.** a strong beam of light focused on a particular person, thing, etc. **2.** a lamp used to project such a light **3.** public notice

spot′ted *adj.* **1.** marked with spots **2.** stained; blemished

spot′ter *n.* one who spots, as an assistant in the stands who reports on plays in a football game

spot′ty *adj.* **-ti·er, -ti·est 1.** having, occurring in, or marked with spots **2.** not uniform or consistent —**spot′ti·ly** *adv.* —**spot′ti·ness** *n.*

spouse (spous) *n.* [< L. *sponsus,* betrothed] (one's) husband or wife

spout (spout) *n.* [< ME. *spouten,* to spout] **1.** a projecting tube, as of a teapot, by which a liquid is poured **2.** a stream, etc. as of liquid from a spout —*vt., vi.* **1.** to shoot out (liquid, etc.) as from a spout **2.** to speak or utter in a loud, pompous, or hasty manner

sprain (sprān) *vt.* [< ? L. *ex-,* out + *premere,* to press] to wrench a ligament or muscle of (a joint) without dislocating the bones —*n.* an injury resulting from this

sprang (spraŋ) *alt. pt.* of SPRING

sprat (sprat) *n.* [OE. *sprott*] a small European fish of the herring family

sprawl (sprôl) *vi.* [OE. *spreawlian*] **1.** to sit or lie with the limbs in a relaxed or awkward position **2.** to spread out awkwardly or unevenly, as handwriting, etc. —*vt.* to cause to sprawl —*n.* a sprawling movement or position

spray[1] (sprā) *n.* [< MDu. *spraeien,* to spray] **1.** a mist of fine liquid particles **2.** *a)* a jet of such particles, as from a spray gun *b)* a device for shooting out such a jet **3.** something likened to a spray —*vt., vi.* **1.** to direct a spray (upon) **2.** to shoot out in a spray —**spray′er** *n.*

spray[2] (sprā) *n.* [ME.] **1.** a small branch of a tree, etc., with leaves, flowers, etc. **2.** a design like this

spray gun a gunlike device that shoots out a spray of liquid, as paint or insecticide, by air pressure

spread (spred) *vt., vi.* spread, spread'ing [OE. *sprædan*] 1. to open or stretch out; unfold 2. to move apart (the fingers, wings, etc.) 3. to distribute or be distributed over an area 4. to extend in time 5. to make or be made widely known, felt, etc. 6. to cover or be covered (*with* something), as in a thin layer 7. to set (a table) for a meal 8. to push or be pushed apart —*n.* 1. the act or extent of spreading 2. an expanse 3. a cloth cover for a table, bed, etc. 4. jam, butter, etc. used on bread 5. [Colloq.] a meal with a wide variety of food —**spread'er** *n.*

spree (sprē) *n.* [< earlier *spray*] 1. a lively, noisy frolic 2. a drinking bout 3. a period of unrestrained activity [a shopping *spree*]

sprig (sprig) *n.* [ME. *sprigge*] 1. a little twig or spray 2. a design or ornament like this

spright·ly (sprīt'lē) *adj.* -li·er, -li·est [see SPRITE] gay, lively, brisk, etc. —*adv.* in a sprightly manner —**spright'li·ness** *n.*

spring (spriŋ) *vi.* sprang or sprung, sprung, spring'ing [OE. *springan*] 1. to leap; bound 2. to come, appear, etc. suddenly 3. to bounce 4. to arise from some source; grow or develop 5. to come into existence 6. to become warped, split, etc. 7. to rise up above surrounding objects Often followed by *up* —*vt.* 1. to cause to leap forth suddenly 2. to cause (a trap, etc.) to snap shut 3. to cause to warp, split, etc. 4. to make known suddenly 5. [Slang] to get (someone) released from jail —*n.* 1. a leap, or the distance so covered 2. a sudden flying back 3. elasticity; resilience 4. a device, as a coil of wire, that returns to its original form after being forced out of shape: used to absorb shock, etc. 5. a flow of water from the ground, the source of a stream 6. a source or origin 7. that season of the year following winter, in which plants begin to grow again 8. any period of beginning 9. *Naut.* a split or break, as in a mast —*adj.* 1. of, for, appearing in, or planted in the spring 2. of or like a spring; elastic; resilient 3. having, or supported on, springs 4. coming from a spring [*spring* water] —**spring a leak** to begin to leak suddenly

spring'board' *n.* a flexible, springy board used as a takeoff in leaping or diving

spring·bok (spriŋ'bäk') *n., pl.* -bok', -boks' [Afrik. < Du. *springen*, to spring + *bok*, a buck] a high-leaping South African gazelle: also **spring'buck'** (-buk')

springer spaniel a field spaniel used in hunting

spring fever the listlessness that many people feel during the first warm days of spring

Spring·field (spriŋ'fēld') 1. city in SW Mass.: pop. 164,000 2. city in SW Mo.: pop. 120,000 3. capital of Ill.: pop. 92,000

spring'time' *n.* the season of spring

spring'y *adj.* -i·er, -i·est flexible; elastic —**spring'i·ness** *n.*

sprin·kle (spriŋ'k'l) *vt., vi.* -kled, -kling [ME. *sprinklen*] 1. to scatter or fall in drops or particles 2. to scatter drops or particles (upon) 3. to rain lightly —*n.* 1. a sprinkling 2. a light rain —**sprin'kler** *n.*

sprin'kling *n.* 1. a small number or amount, esp. when thinly distributed 2. the act of a sprinkler

sprint (sprint) *vi.* [< Scand.] to run or race at full speed for a short distance —*n.* 1. a sprinting 2. a short race at full speed; dash 3. a brief period of intense activity —**sprint'er** *n.*

sprit (sprit) *n.* [OE. *spreot*] a pole extended upward from a mast to the corner of a fore-and-aft sail

sprite (sprīt) *n.* [< L. *spiritus*, spirit] an elf, pixie, fairy, or goblin

sprock·et (spräk'it) *n.* [< ?] 1. any of the teeth, as on the rim of a wheel, arranged to fit the links of a chain 2. a wheel fitted with sprockets: in full **sprocket wheel**

sprout (sprout) *vi.* [OE. *sprutan*] 1. to begin to grow or germinate; give off shoots or buds 2. to grow or develop rapidly —*vt.* to cause to sprout —*n.* 1. a young growth on a plant; shoot 2. a new growth from a bud, etc. 3. [*pl.*] *shortened form of* BRUSSELS SPROUTS

SPROCKET WHEELS

spruce¹ (sprōōs) *n.* [ME. *Spruce*, Prussia] 1. an evergreen tree having slender needles 2. its wood

spruce² (sprōōs) *adj.* spruc'er, spruc'est [< *Spruce* leather (see prec.)] neat and trim; smart —*vt., vi.* spruced, spruc'ing to make or become spruce —**spruce'ly** *adv.* —**spruce'ness** *n.*

sprung (spruŋ) *pp. & alt. pt. of* SPRING

spry (sprī) *adj.* spri'er or spry'er, spri'est or spry'est [< Scand.] full of life; active and agile —**spry'ly** *adv.* —**spry'ness** *n.*

spud (spud) *n.* [prob. < Scand.] 1. a sharp spade for rooting out weeds, etc. 2. [Colloq.] a potato —*vt., vi.* spud'ded, spud'ding to dig, etc. with a spud

spume (spyōōm) *n.* [< L. *spuma*] foam, froth, or scum —*vt., vi.* spumed, spum'ing to foam or froth

spu·mo·ni (spə mō'nē) *n.* [It.] an Italian frozen dessert of ice cream in variously flavored layers, often containing fruit and nuts: also **spumone**

spun (spun) *pt. & pp. of* SPIN —*adj.* formed by or as if by spinning

spunk (spuŋk) *n.* [IrGael. *sponc*, tinder] 1. a kind of wood that smolders when ignited; punk 2. [Colloq.] courage; spirit

spunk'y *adj.* -i·er, -i·est [Colloq.] courageous; spirited —**spunk'i·ly** *adv.* —**spunk'i·ness** *n.*

spur (spur) *n.* [OE. *spura*] 1. a pointed device worn on the heel by horsemen, used to urge the horse forward 2. anything that urges; stimulus 3. any spurlike projection 4. a ridge projecting from the mass of a mountain or mountain range 5. a short railroad track connected with the main track —*vt.* spurred, spur'ring 1. to prick with spurs 2. to urge or incite 3. to provide with a spur or spurs —*vi.* to hasten —**on the spur of the moment** abruptly and impulsively

spurge (spurj) *n.* [see EXPURGATE] any of various plants having a milky juice

spu·ri·ous (spyoor'ē əs) *adj.* [L. *spurius*] not true or genuine; false —**spu'ri·ous·ly** *adv.*

spurn (spurn) *vt.* [OE. *spurnan*] 1. to push or drive away as with the foot 2. to reject scornfully —*n.* 1. a kick 2. scornful treatment —**spurn'er** *n.*

spurt (spurt) *vt., vi.* [OE. *sprutan*, to sprout] 1. to gush forth in a stream or jet 2. to show a sudden, brief burst of energy —*n.* 1. a sudden shooting forth; jet 2. a sudden, brief burst of energy, increased activity, etc.

sput·nik (spoot'nik, sput'-) *n.* [Russ., lit., co-traveler] an artificial satellite of the earth; specif., [S-] one put into orbit by the U.S.S.R.

sput·ter (sput'ər) *vi., vt.* [Du. *sputteren*] 1. to spit or throw out (bits or drops) in an explosive manner 2. to speak or say in a confused, explosive manner 3. to make sharp, sizzling sounds, as frying fat —*n.* 1. a sputtering 2. hasty, confused utterance

spu·tum (spyoot'əm) *n., pl.* -ta (-ə) [< L. *spuere*, to spit] saliva, usually mixed with mucus, spit out

spy (spī) *vt.* spied, spy'ing [< OHG. *spehôn*, examine] to catch sight of; see —*vi.* 1. to watch closely and secretly; act as a spy 2. to look carefully —*n., pl.* spies 1. one who keeps close and secret watch on others 2. a person employed by a government to get secret information on the military affairs, etc. of another government —**spy out** to discover or seek to discover by looking carefully

spy'glass' *n.* a small telescope

sq. square

squab (skwäb) *n.* [prob. < Scand.] a very young pigeon

squab·ble (skwäb'l) *vi.* -bled, -bling [< Scand.] to quarrel noisily over a small matter; wrangle —*n.* a noisy, petty quarrel; wrangle

squad (skwäd) *n.* [< Fr. < It. or Sp.: see SQUARE] 1. a small group of soldiers, often a subdivision of a platoon 2. any small group of people working together

squad car a police patrol car

squad·ron (-rən) *n.* [< It. *squadra*, a square] 1. a group of warships assigned to special duty 2. a unit of cavalry consisting of two to four troops, etc. 3. *U.S. Air Force* a unit of two or more flights 4. any organized group

squal·id (skwäl'id) *adj.* [< L. *squalere*, be foul] 1. foul; filthy 2. wretched —**squal'id·ness** *n.*

squall¹ (skwôl) *n.* [< Scand.] 1. a brief, violent windstorm, usually with rain or snow 2. [Colloq.] trouble or disturbance —*vi.* to storm briefly —**squall'y** *adj.*

squall² (skwôl) *vi., vt.* [ON. *skvala*, cry out] to cry and scream loudly or harshly —*n.* a harsh, shrill cry or loud scream —**squall'er** *n.*

squal·or (skwäl'ər) *n.* [L., foulness] a being squalid; filth and wretchedness

squan·der (skwän'dər) *vt., vi.* [prob. < dial. *squander*, scatter] to spend or use wastefully

square (skwer) *n.* [< L. *ex-*, out + *quadrare*, to square] 1. a plane figure having four equal sides and four right angles 2. anything shaped like or nearly like this 3. an area bounded by streets on four sides **4.** any side of such an area **5.** an open area bounded by several streets, used as a park, etc. **6.** an instrument having two sides that form a 90° angle, used for drawing or testing right angles **7.** the product of a number multiplied by itself **8.** [Slang] a person who is square (*adj.* 10) **—vt. squared, squar'ing 1.** to make into a square **2.** to make straight, even, right-angled, etc. **3.** to settle; adjust [to *square* accounts] **4.** to make equal **5.** to bring into agreement [to *square* a statement with the facts] **6.** to mark off (a surface) in squares **7.** to multiply (a quantity) by itself **—vi. 1.** to fit; agree; accord (*with*) **—adj. 1.** *a*) having four equal sides and four right angles *b*) more or less cubical, as a box **2.** forming a right angle **3.** straight, level, even, etc. **4.** leaving no balance; balanced **5.** just; fair **6.** direct; straightforward **7.** designating or of a unit of surface measure in the form of a square with sides of a specified length **8.** solid; thickset [a *square* build] **9.** [Colloq.] satisfying; substantial [a *square* meal] **10.** [Slang] old-fashioned or unsophisticated **—adv. 1.** honestly; fairly **2.** at right angles **3.** so as to face **4.** firmly; solidly **—on the square** [Colloq.] honest(ly), fair(ly), etc. **—square off** (or **away**) to get in position for attacking or defending **—square oneself** [Colloq.] to make amends **—square'ly** *adv.* **—square'ness** *n.* **—squar'ish** *adj.*

square dance a lively dance with various steps and figures, the couples forming squares, etc. **—square'-dance'** *vi.* **-danced', -danc'ing**

square knot a double knot in which the free ends run parallel to the standing parts

square measure a system of measuring area, as the one in which 144 sq. in. = 1 sq. ft.

square'-rigged' *adj.* having square sails as principal sails **—square'-rig'ger** *n.*

square root the number that when squared will produce a given number [3 is the *square root* of 9]

square sail a four-sided sail

square shooter [Colloq.] an honest, just person

square'-shoul'dered (-shōl'dərd) *adj.* having shoulders jutting out squarely from the body's axis

SQUARE-RIGGED SHIP

squash[1] (skwäsh) *vt.* [< L. *ex-*, intens. + *quatere*, to shake] **1.** to crush into a soft or flat mass; press **2.** to suppress; quash **3.** [Colloq.] to silence (another) crushingly **—vi. 1.** to be squashed **2.** to make a sound of squashing **3.** to force one's way; squeeze **—n. 1.** something squashed **2.** the act or sound of squashing **3.** either of two games (**squash rackets, squash tennis**) played in a four-walled court with rackets and a rubber ball

squash[2] (skwäsh) *n.* [< Algonquian] **1.** the fleshy fruit of various plants of the gourd family, cooked as a vegetable **2.** any such plant

squash'y (-ē) *adj.* **-i·er, -i·est 1.** soft and wet; mushy **2.** easily squashed **—squash'i·ness** *n.*

squat (skwät) *vi.* **squat'ted, squat'ting** [< L. *ex-*, intens. + *cogere*, to force] **1.** to crouch, with the knees bent and the weight on the balls of the feet **2.** to crouch close to the ground **3.** to settle on land without any right or title to it **4.** to settle on public land under government regulation so as to get title to it **—adj.** short and thick: also **squat'ty** **—n.** the position of squatting **—squat'ter** *n.*

squaw (skwô) *n.* [< Algonquian] a N. American Indian woman, esp. a wife: now sometimes contemptuous use

squawk (skwôk) *vi.* [echoic] **1.** to utter a loud, harsh cry **2.** [Colloq.] to complain or protest **—n. 1.** a squawking cry **2.** [Colloq.] a complaint **—squawk'er** *n.*

squeak (skwēk) *vi.* [ME. *squeken*] to make or utter a sharp, high-pitched sound or cry **—vt.** to say in a squeak **—n.** a short, shrill sound or cry **—narrow** (or **close**) **squeak** [Colloq.] a narrow escape **—squeak through** (or **by,** etc.) [Colloq.] to barely manage to succeed, survive, etc. **—squeak'er** *n.* **—squeak'i·ly** *adv.* **—squeak'y** *adj.* **-i·er, -i·est**

squeal (skwēl) *vi.* [ME. *squelen*] **1.** to make or utter a long, shrill sound or cry **2.** [Slang] to inform against someone **—vt.** to utter with a squeal **—n.** a long, shrill sound or cry **—squeal'er** *n.*

squeam·ish (skwēm'ish) *adj.* [ME. *squaimous*] **1.** easily nauseated **2.** easily shocked or offended; prudish **3.** too fastidious **—squeam'ish·ness** *n.*

squee·gee (skwē'jē) *n.* [prob. < SQUEEZE] a T-shaped tool with a blade of rubber, etc. for wiping liquid off a surface **—vt. -geed, -gee·ing** to use a squeegee on

squeeze (skwēz) *vt.* **squeezed, squeez'ing** [OE. *cwysan*] **1.** to press hard, esp. from two or more sides **2.** to extract

(juice, etc.) from (fruit, etc.) **3.** to force (*into, out,* etc.) by pressing **4.** to get by force or unfair means **5.** to put pressure on (someone) to do something **6.** to embrace closely; hug **—vi. 1.** to yield to pressure **2.** to exert pressure **3.** to force one's way by pushing **—n. 1.** a squeezing or being squeezed **2.** a close embrace; hug **3.** the state of being closely pressed or packed; crush **4.** a period of scarcity, hardship, etc. **5.** [Colloq.] pressure exerted, as in extortion **—squeez'er** *n.*

squelch (skwelch) *n.* [< ?] [Colloq.] a crushing retort, rebuke, etc. **—vt.** [Colloq.] to suppress or silence completely and crushingly **—squelch'er** *n.*

squib (skwib) *n.* [prob. echoic] **1.** a firecracker that hisses before exploding **2.** a short, witty writing that criticizes

squid (skwid) *n.* [prob. akin to SQUIRT] a long, slender sea mollusk with ten arms, two longer than the others

squig·gle (skwig''l) *n.* [SQU(IRM) + (W)IGGLE] a short, wavy line or illegible scrawl **—vt., vi. -gled, -gling** to write as, or make, squiggles

squill (skwil) *n.* [< Gr. *skilla*] **1.** the dried bulb of a plant of the lily family, formerly used in medicine **2.** this plant

squinch (skwinch) *vt., vi.* [SQU(INT) + (P)INCH] **1.** to squint or pucker (the eyes, face, etc.) **2.** to squeeze

squint (skwint) *vi.* [akin to Du. *schuin,* sideways] **1.** to peer with the eyes partly closed **2.** to look sideways or askance **3.** to be cross-eyed **—vt.** to keep (the eyes) partly closed in peering **—n. 1.** a squinting **2.** a being cross-eyed **3.** [Colloq.] a glance, often sidelong **—adj. 1.** looking sidelong or askance **2.** cross-eyed

SQUID
(small species to 8 in. long)

squire (skwīr) *n.* [< ESQUIRE] **1.** a young man of high birth who attended a knight **2.** in England, the owner of a large rural estate **3.** a title of respect for a justice of the peace, etc. **4.** an attendant; esp., a man escorting a woman **—vt., vi. squired, squir'ing** to act as a squire (to)

squirm (skwurm) *vi.* [prob. echoic] **1.** to twist and turn the body; wriggle **2.** to show or feel distress, as from embarrassment **—n.** a squirming **—squirm'y** *adj.* **-i·er, -i·est**

squir·rel (skwur'əl) *n.* [< Gr. *skia,* a shadow + *oura,* tail] **1.** a small, tree-dwelling rodent with heavy fur and a long, bushy tail **2.** its fur **—vt. -reled** or **-relled, -rel·ing** or **-rel·ling** to store (*away*)

squirt (skwurt) *vt., vi.* [prob. < LowG. *swirtjen*] **1.** to shoot out (a liquid) in a jet; spurt **2.** to wet with liquid so shot out **—n. 1.** a jet of liquid **2.** [Colloq.] a small, esp. impudent, person

squish (skwish) *vi.* to make a soft, splashing sound when walked on, squeezed, etc. **—squish'y** *adj.*

Sr *Chem.* strontium

Sr. Senior

Sri Lan·ka (srē läŋ'kə) country on an island off the SE tip of India: 25,332 sq. mi.; pop. 12,240,000; cap. Colombo: formerly called *Ceylon*

S.R.O. standing room only

S.S., SS, S/S steamship

SSE, S.S.E., s.s.e. south-southeast

S.S.R., SSR Soviet Socialist Republic

SST supersonic transport

SSW, S.S.W., s.s.w. south-southwest

St. 1. Saint **2.** Strait **3.** Street

Sta. Station

stab (stab) *n.* [prob. < ME. *stubbe,* stub] **1.** a wound made by stabbing **2.** a thrust, as with a knife **3.** a sharp pain **—vt., vi. stabbed, stab'bing 1.** to pierce or wound as with a knife **2.** to thrust (a knife, etc.) into something **3.** to pain sharply **—make** (or **take**) **a stab at** to make an attempt at

sta·bil·i·ty (stə bil'ə tē) *n., pl.* **-ties 1.** a being stable, or fixed; steadiness **2.** firmness of character, purpose, etc. **3.** resistance to change

sta·bi·lize (stā'bə līz') *vt.* **-lized', -liz'ing 1.** to make stable, or firm **2.** to keep from changing, as in price **3.** to give stability to (a plane, ship, etc.) **—sta'bi·li·za'tion** *n.*

sta'bi·liz'er *n.* one that stabilizes; specif., a device used to keep an airplane steady in flight

sta·ble[1] (stā'b'l) *adj.* **-bler, -blest** [< L. *stare,* to stand] **1.** *a*) steady; steady *b*) not likely to break down, fall apart, etc. **2.** firm in character, purpose, etc. **3.** not likely to change; enduring **4.** *Chem.* not readily decomposing **—sta'bly** *adv.*

sta·ble[2] (stā'b'l) *n.* [< L. *stare,* to stand] **1.** a building in which horses or cattle are sheltered and fed **2.** all the racehorses of one owner **—vt., vi. -bled, -bling** to keep or be kept in a stable

stac·ca·to (stə kät′ō) *adj.* [It., detached] **1.** *Music* with distinct breaks between successive tones **2.** made up of abrupt, distinct elements or sounds —*adv.* so as to be staccato

stack (stak) *n.* [ON. *stakkr*] **1.** a large, neatly arranged pile of straw, hay, etc. **2.** any orderly pile **3.** a smokestack **4.** [*pl.*] the main area for shelving books in a library **5.** [Colloq.] a large amount —*vt.* **1.** to pile in a stack **2.** to load with stacks **3.** to arrange underhandedly for a desired result [to *stack* a jury] —**stack up** to stand in comparison (*with* or *against*)

stacked (stakt) *adj.* [Slang] having a full, shapely figure: said of a woman

stack′up′ *n.* an arrangement of circling aircraft at various altitudes awaiting their turn to land

sta·di·um (stā′dē əm) *n.* [< Gr. *stadion*, unit of length, c.607 ft.] a large structure for football, baseball, etc. with tiers of seats for spectators

staff (staf) *n., pl.* **staffs**; also, for senses 1 & 5, **staves** [OE. *stæf*] **1.** a stick or rod used for support, a weapon, a symbol of authority, etc. **2.** a group of people assisting a leader **3.** a group of officers serving a commanding officer as advisers and administrators **4.** a specific group of workers [a teaching *staff*] **5.** *Music* the five horizontal lines and four intermediate spaces on which music is written — *adj.* of, by, for, or on a staff —*vt.* to provide with a staff, as of workers

staff′er *n.* a member of a staff

staff sergeant **1.** *U.S. Army & Marine Corps* an enlisted man ranking above sergeant **2.** *U.S. Air Force* an enlisted man ranking above airman

stag (stag) *n.* [OE. *stagga*] **1.** a full-grown male deer **2.** a man who attends a social gathering unaccompanied by a woman —*adj.* for men only [a *stag* party]

stage (stāj) *n.* [< L. *stare*, to stand] **1.** a platform **2.** *a)* an area or platform upon which plays, etc. are presented *b)* the theater, or acting as a profession (with *the*) **3.** the scene of an event **4.** a stopping place, or the distance between stops, on a journey **5.** *shortened form of* STAGECOACH **6.** a period or degree in a process of development, etc. [the larval *stage*] **7.** any of two or more propulsion units used in sequence as the rocket of a spacecraft, etc. —*vt.* **staged, stag′ing** **1.** to present as on a stage **2.** to plan and carry out [stage an attack]

stage′coach′ *n.* formerly, a horse-drawn coach on scheduled trips over a regular route

stage′hand′ *n.* one who sets up scenery, operates the curtain, etc. for a stage performance

stage′-struck′ *adj.* having an intense desire to act or otherwise work in the theater

stag·ger (stag′ər) *vi.* [ON. *stakra*, to totter] **1.** to totter or reel, as from a blow, fatigue, etc. **2.** to waver in purpose, etc. —*vt.* **1.** to make stagger **2.** to affect strongly, as with astonishment **3.** to make zigzag or alternating **4.** to arrange (duties, vacation, etc.) so as to avoid crowding — *n.* **1.** a staggering, tottering, etc. **2.** a staggered arrangement **3.** [*pl.*, *with sing. v.*] a disease of horses, cattle, etc. with loss of coordination, staggering, etc.

stag·nant (stag′nənt) *adj.* [< L. *stagnare*, to stagnate] **1.** not flowing or moving **2.** foul from lack of movement: said of water, etc. **3.** lacking activity, etc.; sluggish — **stag′nan·cy** *n.* —**stag′nant·ly** *adv.*

stag′nate (-nāt) *vi., vt.* **-nat·ed, -nat·ing** to become or make stagnant —**stag·na′tion** *n.*

staid (stād) *archaic pt. & pp. of* STAY³ —*adj.* sober; sedate —**staid′ly** *adv.* —**staid′ness** *n.*

stain (stān) *vt.* [< L. *dis-*, from + *tingere*, to color] **1.** to spoil the appearance of by discoloring or spotting **2.** to disgrace or dishonor **3.** to color (wood, etc.) with a dye — *vi.* to impart or take a stain —*n.* **1.** a discoloration, spot, etc. resulting from staining **2.** a moral blemish; dishonor **3.** a dye for staining wood, etc. —**stain′less** *adj.*

stainless steel steel alloyed with chromium, etc., virtually immune to rust and corrosion

stair (ster) *n.* [OE. *stæger*] **1.** [*usually pl.*] a flight of steps; staircase **2.** one of a series of steps leading from one level to another

stair′case′ *n.* a flight of stairs with a handrail: also **stair′way′**

stair′well′ *n.* a vertical shaft (in a building) containing a staircase: also **stair well**

stake (stāk) *n.* [OE. *staca*] **1.** a length of wood or metal, pointed for driving into the ground **2.** the post to which a person was tied for execution by burning **3.** [*often pl.*]

money, etc. risked as in a wager **4.** [*often pl.*] the winner's prize in a race, etc. **5.** a share or interest, as in property —*vt.* **staked, stak′ing** **1.** to mark the boundaries of [to *stake* out a claim] **2.** to fasten to or support with a stake **3.** to risk; gamble **4.** [Colloq.] to furnish with money, etc., as for a business venture —**at stake** being risked —**pull up stakes** [Colloq.] to change one's residence, etc. —**stake out** to put under police surveillance

sta·lac·tite (stə lak′tīt) *n.* [< Gr. *stalaktos*, dripping] an icicle-shaped lime deposit hanging from the roof of a cave

sta·lag·mite (stə lag′mīt) *n.* [< Gr. *stalagmos*, a dropping] a cone-shaped deposit on the floor of a cave, often beneath a stalactite

stale (stāl) *adj.* **stal′er, stal′est** [prob. < LowG.] **1.** having lost freshness; flat, dry, stagnant, etc. **2.** trite, as a joke **3.** out of condition, bored, etc. from too much or too little activity —*vt., vi.* **staled, stal′ing** to make or become stale —**stale′ness** *n.*

stale·mate (stāl′māt′) *n.* [< OFr. *estal*, a fixed location + MATE²] **1.** *Chess* a situation in which a player cannot move without placing his king in check: it results in a draw **2.** a deadlock —*vt.* **-mat′ed, -mat′ing** to bring into a stalemate

Sta·lin (stä′lin), **Joseph** 1879–1953; premier of the U.S.S.R. (1941–53) —**Sta′lin·ist** *adj., n.*

Sta·lin·grad (stä′lin grad′) *former name of* VOLGOGRAD

stalk (stôk) *vi., vt.* [< OE. *stealc*, steep] **1.** to walk (through) in a stiff, haughty manner **2.** to advance grimly [plague *stalks* the land] **3.** to pursue (game, etc.) stealthily —*n.* **1.** a stiff, haughty stride **2.** a stalking

stalk² (stôk) *n.* [OE. *stela*] **1.** the stem of a plant **2.** any part like this, as in some invertebrate animals

stalk′ing-horse′ *n.* **1.** anything used to hide intentions, schemes, etc. **2.** a person put forth as a candidate until the candidate actually preferred is announced

stall¹ (stôl) *n.* [OE. *steall*] **1.** a compartment for one animal in a stable **2.** *a)* a booth, etc. as at a market *b)* an enclosed seat in a church *c)* a small, enclosed space, as for taking a shower **3.** a stop or standstill, esp. when due to a malfunction —*vt., vi.* **1.** to keep or be kept in a stall **2.** to bring or come to a standstill, esp. unintentionally **3.** to stop because of some malfunction

stall² (stôl) *vi., vt.* [< obs. *stale*, a decoy] to act evasively or hesitantly so as to deceive or delay —*n.* [Colloq.] any trick used in stalling

stal·lion (stal′yən) *n.* [< Gmc. *stal*, a stall] an uncastrated male horse, esp. one used as a stud

stal·wart (stôl′wərt) *adj.* [< OE. *stathol*, foundation + *wyrthe*, worth] **1.** sturdy; robust **2.** valiant **3.** resolute; firm —*n.* **1.** a stalwart person **2.** a firm supporter of a cause —**stal′wart·ly** *adv.*

sta·men (stā′mən) *n., pl.* **-mens, stam·i·na** (stam′ə nə) [< L., a thread, orig., warp] a pollen-bearing organ in a flower, made up of a slender stalk and a pollen sac

Stam·ford (stam′fərd) city in SW Conn.: pop. 109,000

stam·i·na (stam′ə nə) *n.* [L., pl. of *stamen*] resistance to fatigue, illness, hardship, etc.; endurance

stam·mer (stam′ər) *vt., vi.* [OE. *stamerian*] to speak or say with involuntary pauses and rapid repetitions, as from excitement —*n.* the act or habit of stammering — **stam′mer·er** *n.*

stamp (stamp) *vt.* [ME. *stampen*] **1.** to bring (the foot) down forcibly **2.** to crush or pound with the foot **3.** to imprint or cut out (a design, etc.) **4.** to cut (*out*) by pressing with a die **5.** to impress deeply [a face *stamped* with grief] **6.** to put a stamp on **7.** to characterize —*vi.* **1.** to bring the foot down forcibly **2.** to walk with loud, heavy steps —*n.* **1.** a stamping **2.** a machine, tool, or die for stamping **3.** a mark or form made by stamping **4.** any of various seals, gummed pieces of paper, etc. used to show that a fee, as for postage, has been paid **5.** any similar seal [a trading *stamp*] **6.** a characteristic impression [the *stamp* of truth] **7.** kind; class —**stamp out** **1.** to crush by treading on forcibly **2.** to crush (a revolt, etc.) —**stamp′er** *n.*

stam·pede (stam pēd′) *n.* [< AmSp. < Sp. *estampar*, to stamp] a sudden, headlong rush or flight, as of a herd of cattle —*vi.* **-ped′ed, -ped′ing** to move in a stampede —*vt.* to cause to stampede

stamp′ing ground [Colloq.] a regular or favorite gathering place or resort

stance (stans) *n.* [< L. *stare*, to stand] **1.** the way one stands, esp. the placement of the feet **2.** the attitude taken in a given situation

---

fat, āpe, cär; ten, ēven; is, bīte; gō, hôrn, tōol, look; oil, out; up, fur; thin, *th*en; zh, leisure; ŋ, ring; ə for *a* in *ago*; ′ as in *able* (ā′b'l); ë, Fr. coeur; ö, Fr. feu; Fr. mon; ü, Fr. duc; r, Fr. cri; kh, G. doch, ich. ‡ foreign; < derived from

stanch (stônch, stanch) *vt., vi., adj. see* STAUNCH

stan·chion (stan'chən) *n.* [see STANCE] **1.** an upright post or support **2.** a device to confine a cow

stand (stand) *vi.* **stood, stand'ing** [OE. *standan*] **1.** to be in, or assume, an upright position, as on the feet **2.** to be supported on a base, pedestal, etc. **3.** to take or be in a (specified) position, attitude, etc. **4.** to have a (specified) height when standing **5.** to be placed or situated **6.** to gather and remain, as water **7.** to remain unchanged **8.** to be in a (specified) condition, relation, rank, etc. [to *stand* first in grades] **9.** to make resistance **10.** *a)* to halt *b)* to be stationary **11.** [Chiefly Brit.] to be a candidate — *vt.* **1.** to place upright **2.** to endure **3.** to withstand **4.** to undergo [to *stand* trial] **5.** [Colloq.] to bear the cost of (a meal, etc.) —*n.* **1.** a standing; esp., a halt or stop **2.** a position; station **3.** a view, opinion, etc. **4.** a structure to stand or sit on **5.** a place of business **6.** a rack, small table, etc. for holding things **7.** a growth of trees, etc. — **stand by 1.** to be near and ready if needed **2.** to aid — **stand for 1.** to represent **2.** [Colloq.] to tolerate —**stand off 1.** to keep at a distance **2.** to put off or evade —**stand on 1.** to be founded on **2.** to insist upon —**stand out 1.** to project **2.** to be distinct, prominent, etc. **3.** to be firm — **stand up 1.** to rise to a standing position **2.** to prove valid, durable, etc. **3.** [Slang] to fail to keep a date with —**stand up for** to defend —**stand up to** to confront fearlessly

stand·ard (stan'dərd) *n.* [< OFr. *estendard*] **1.** a flag, banner, etc. as an emblem of a people, military unit, etc. **2.** something established as a rule or basis of comparison in measuring quantity, quality, value, etc. **3.** a type or model **4.** an upright support —*adj.* **1.** used as or conforming to an established rule, model, etc. **2.** generally accepted as reliable or authoritative **3.** ordinary; typical [*standard* procedure] **4.** suitable to speech or writing that is more or less formal; not slang, dialectal, obsolete, etc. [*standard* English]

stand'ard-bear'er *n.* **1.** one carrying the standard, or flag **2.** a leader of a political party, etc.

standard gauge a width of 56 1/2 inches between the rails of a railroad track

stand'ard·ize' *vt.* **-ized', -iz'ing** to make standard or uniform —**stand'ard·i·za'tion** *n.*

standard time the time in any of the 24 time zones, each an hour apart, into which the earth is divided: in North America there are eight zones

stand'by' *n., pl.* **-bys'** a person or thing that is dependable, a possible substitute, etc.

stand·ee (stan dē') *n.* [Colloq.] one who stands, usually because no seats are vacant

stand'-in' *n.* a temporary substitute, as for an actor at rehearsals

stand'ing *n.* **1.** status or reputation [in good *standing*] **2.** duration [of long *standing*] —*adj.* **1.** that stands; upright **2.** in or from a standing position [a *standing* jump] **3.** stagnant, as water **4.** permanent [a *standing* order] **5.** not in use

standing room room in which to stand, esp. when there are no vacant seats, as in a theater

Stan·dish (stan'dish), **Miles** (or **Myles**) 1584?–1656; Eng. colonist; military leader of Plymouth Colony

stand'off' *n.* a tie in a contest

stand'off'ish *adj.* reserved and cool; aloof

stand'point' *n.* point of view

stand'still' *n.* a stop or halt

stank (staŋk) *alt. pt. of* STINK

stan·za (stan'zə) *n.* [It.: ult. < L. *stare*, to stand] a group of lines of verse forming a division of a poem or song — **stan·za'ic** (-zā'ik) *adj.*

staph·y·lo·coc·cus (staf'ə lō käk'əs) *n., pl.* **-coc'ci** (-käk'sī) [< Gr. *staphylē*, bunch of grapes + *kokkos*, a grain] any of certain spherical bacteria in clusters or chains that cause pus to form in abscesses, etc.: also **staph** (staf)

sta·ple[1] (stā'p'l) *n.* [< MDu. *stapel*, mart] **1.** a chief commodity made, grown, etc. in a particular place **2.** a chief item or element **3.** raw material **4.** a regularly stocked item of trade, as salt **5.** the fiber of cotton, wool, etc. — *adj.* **1.** regularly stocked, produced, or used **2.** chief; main

sta·ple[2] (stā'p'l) *n.* [OE. *stapol*, a post] a U-shaped piece of metal with sharp ends, driven into wood, etc., as to hold a hook, wire, etc., or through papers as a binding — *vt.* **-pled, -pling** to fasten with a staple —**sta'pler** *n.*

star (stär) *n.* [OE. *steorra*] **1.** any heavenly body seen as a small fixed point of light, esp. one that is a distant sun **2.** a flat figure with usually five or six points, representing a star **3.** anything like such a figure **4.** an asterisk **5.** *a)* As-

trol. a planet, etc. regarded as influencing human fate *b)* [*often pl.*] fate; destiny **6.** one who excels, esp. in a sport **7.** a leading actor or actress —*vt.* **starred, star'ring 1.** to mark with stars as a decoration, etc. **2.** to present (a performer) in a leading role —*vi.* **1.** to excel, esp. in a sport **2.** to have a leading role —*adj.* **1.** excelling [a *star* athlete] **2.** of a star or stars —*star'less adj.*

star·board (stär'bərd, -bôrd') *n.* [< OE. *steoran*, to steer (with a large oar on the ship's right side) + *bord*, board] the right side of a ship, etc. as one faces forward —*adj.* of or on the starboard

starch (stärch) *n.* [< OE. *stearc*, stiff] **1.** a white, tasteless, odorless food substance found in potatoes, grain, etc.: it is a complex carbohydrate $(C_6H_{10}O_5)_n$ **2.** a powdered form of this, used in laundering to stiffen cloth, etc. **3.** [*pl.*] starchy foods —*vt.* to stiffen as with starch —**starch'y** *adj.*

star'dom (-dəm) *n.* the status of a star of stage, screen, etc.

stare (ster) *vi.* **stared, star'ing** [OE. *starian*] to gaze steadily and intently —*vt.* to look fixedly at —*n.* a staring look —**stare down** to stare back at (another) until he looks away —**star'er** *n.*

star'fish' *n., pl.:* see FISH a small, star-shaped sea animal with a hard, spiny skeleton

star'gaze' *vi.* **-gazed', -gaz'ing 1.** to gaze at the stars **2.** to daydream —**star'gaz'er** *n.*

stark (stärk) *adj.* [OE. *stearc*] **1.** rigid, as a corpse **2.** sharply outlined **3.** bleak; desolate **4.** grimly blunt **5.** sheer; utter —*adv.* utterly —**stark'ly** *adv.* —**stark'ness** *n.*

stark'-nak'ed *adj.* entirely naked

star'let (-lit) *n.* a young actress being promoted as a possible future star

star'light' *n.* light from the stars —**star'lit'** *adj.*

star·ling (stär'liŋ) *n.* [OE. *stær*] any of a family of oldworld birds, esp. the **common starling**, with iridescent plumage, introduced into the U.S.

Star of David a six-pointed star formed of two equilateral triangles: a symbol of Judaism

star'ry *adj.* **-ri·er, -ri·est 1.** shining like stars; bright **2.** lighted by or full of stars

Stars and Stripes the U.S. flag

star'-span'gled *adj.* studded or spangled with stars

Star-Spangled Banner 1. the U.S. flag **2.** the U.S. national anthem

start (stärt) *vi.* [OE. *styrtan*] **1.** to make a sudden or involuntary movement **2.** to go into action or motion; begin; commence **3.** to be among the beginning entrants in a race, etc. **4.** to spring into being, activity, etc. —*vt.* **1.** to rouse or flush (game) **2.** to displace, loosen, etc. **3.** to set into motion, action, etc. **4.** to begin doing, etc. **5.** to cause to be an entrant in a race, etc. —*n.* **1.** a sudden, brief shock **2.** a sudden, startled movement **3.** [*pl.*] brief bursts of activity: usually in *by fits and starts* **4.** a starting or beginning **5.** *a)* a place or time of beginning *b)* a lead or other advantage **6.** an opportunity to begin a career, etc. —**start in** to begin a task, etc. —**start out** (or **off**) to start a journey, project, etc. —**start'er** *n.*

STAR OF DAVID

star·tle (stärt''l) *vt.* **-tled, -tling** [< ME. *sterten*, to start] to surprise, frighten, or alarm suddenly; esp., to make jump, jerk, etc. as from sudden fright —*vi.* to be startled —*n.* a startled reaction —**star'tling** *adj.*

starve (stärv) *vi.* **starved, starv'ing** [< OE. *steorfan*, to die] **1.** to die from lack of food **2.** to suffer from hunger **3.** [Colloq.] to suffer great need (with *for*) —*vt.* **1.** to cause to starve **2.** to force by starving —**star·va·tion** (stär vā'shən) *n.*

starve'ling (-liŋ) *n.* a starving person or animal —*adj.* **1.** starving **2.** impoverished

stash (stash) *vt.* [prob. a blend of STORE & CACHE] [Colloq.] to hide in a secret or safe place —*n.* [Slang] **1.** a place for hiding things **2.** something hidden away

-stat [< Gr. *-statēs*] *a combining form meaning* stationary [*thermostat*]

state (stāt) *n.* [< L. *stare*, to stand] **1.** a set of circumstances, etc. characterizing a person or thing; condition **2.** a particular mental or emotional condition [a *state* of bliss] **3.** condition as regards structure, form, etc. **4.** ceremonious display; pomp **5.** [*sometimes* **S-**] a body of people politically organized under one government; nation **6.** [*usually* **S-**] any of the political units that together form a federal government, as in the U.S. **7.** civil government [church and *state*] —*adj.* **1.** formal; ceremonial **2.** [*sometimes* **S-**] of the government or a state —*vt.* **stat'ed, stat'ing 1.** to establish by specifying **2.** *a)* to set forth in words *b)* to express —**in a state** [Colloq.] in an agitated emotional condition —**lie in state** to be displayed formally before burial —**the States** the United States —**state'hood'** **adj.**

State'house' **n.** the official meeting place of a State legislature: also **State House, State Capitol**

state'ly **adj.** **-li·er, -li·est** dignified, imposing, grand, or the like —**state'li·ness** **n.**

state'ment **n. 1.** a) the act of stating b) the thing stated **2.** a summary of a financial account

Stat·en Island (stat**'**n) island between New Jersey and Long Island, forming part of New York City

state'room' **n. 1.** a private cabin on a ship **2.** a private room in a railroad car

state's evidence **Law** evidence given by or for the prosecution in a criminal case, esp. by a criminal against his associates

state'side' **adj.** [Colloq.] of or in the U.S. (as viewed from abroad) —**adv.** [Colloq.] in, to, or toward the U.S.

states'man **n.,** pl. **-men** one who is wise or experienced in the business of government —**states'man·like', states'-man·ly** **adj.** —**states'man·ship'** **n.**

States' rights all the rights and powers which the Constitution neither grants to the Federal government nor denies to the State governments

stat·ic (stat**'**ik) **adj.** [< Gr. statikos, causing to stand] **1.** of masses, forces, etc. at rest or in equilibrium: opposed to DYNAMIC **2.** at rest; inactive **3.** designating, of, or producing stationary electrical charges, as from friction **4.** of or having to do with static Also **stat'i·cal** —**n. 1.** atmospheric electrical discharges that interfere with radio or TV reception, etc. **2.** interference so produced **3.** [Slang] adverse criticism —**stat'i·cal·ly** **adv.**

stat'ics **n.pl.** [with sing. v.] [see prec.] the branch of mechanics dealing with bodies, masses, or forces at rest or in equilibrium

sta·tion (stā**'**shən) **n.** [< L. stare, to stand] **1.** the place or building where one stands or is located; esp., an assigned post **2.** a regular stopping place, as on a bus line or railroad, or a building at such a place **3.** social standing **4.** a place equipped for radio and TV transmission, or its frequency —**vt.** to assign to a station; post

sta·tion·ar·y (stā**'**shə ner**'**ē) **adj.** [see STATION] **1.** not moving; fixed **2.** unchanging **3.** not itinerant

station break a pause in radio or TV programs for station identification

sta·tion·er (stā**'**shə nər) **n.** [< ML. stationarius, shopkeeper] a dealer in office supplies, etc.

sta'tion·er'y (-ner**'**ē) **n.** writing materials; specif., paper and envelopes used for letters

sta'tion·mas'ter **n.** an official in charge of a large railroad station

station wagon an automobile with folding or removable rear seats and a tailgate that can be opened

sta·tis·tic (stə tis**'**tik) **n.** a statistical item or element

sta·tis'ti·cal **adj.** of, having to do with, or based on statistics —**sta·tis'ti·cal·ly** **adv.**

stat·is·ti·cian (stat**'**is tish**'**ən) **n.** an expert or specialist in statistics

sta·tis·tics (stə tis**'**tiks) **n.pl.** [< L. status, standing] **1.** numerical facts assembled and classified so as to present significant information **2.** [with sing. v.] the science of compiling such facts

stat·u·ar·y (stach**'**ōō wer**'**ē) **n.,** pl. **-ies 1.** statues collectively **2.** the art of making statues —**adj.** of or suitable for statues

stat·ue (stach**'**ōō) **n.** [< L. statuere, to place] the form of a person or animal carved in stone, etc., modeled in clay, etc., or cast in metal, etc.

stat·u·esque (stach**'**ōō wesk**'**) **adj.** of or like a statue; tall and well-proportioned; stately; imposing

stat'u·ette' (-wet**'**) **n.** a small statue

stat·ure (stach**'**ər) **n.** [< L. statura] **1.** the standing height of the body **2.** growth or level of attainment [moral stature]

sta·tus (stāt**'**əs, stat**'**-) **n.,** pl. **-tus·es** [L., standing] **1.** condition with regard to law [the status of a minor] **2.** position; rank **3.** high position; prestige **4.** state, as of affairs

status quo (kwō**'**) [L., the state in which] the existing state of affairs: also **status in quo**

status symbol a possession regarded as a sign of social status, esp. of high social status

stat·ute (stach**'**ōōt) **n.** [see STATUE] **1.** an established rule **2.** a law passed by a legislative body

statute of limitations a statute limiting the period within which a specific legal action may be taken

stat·u·to·ry (stach**'**ōō tôr**'**ē) **adj. 1.** fixed or authorized by statute **2.** declared by statute to be punishable: said of an offense

St. Augustine seaport in NE Fla.: oldest city in the U.S.: pop. 12,000

staunch (stônch, stänch) **vt.** [< L. stare, to stand] **1.** to check the flow of (blood, etc.) from (a wound, etc.) **2.** to stop (a drain of resources, etc.) —**vi.** to stop flowing —**adj. 1.** seaworthy **2.** steadfast; loyal **3.** strong; solid Also **stanch** For the **adj.,** **staunch** is usually used; for the v., either **staunch** or **stanch** is used —**staunch'ly** **adv.** —**staunch'ness** **n.**

stave (stāv) **n.** [< staves, pl. of STAFF] **1.** one of the shaped strips of wood that form the wall of a barrel, bucket, etc. **2.** a stick or staff **3.** a stanza **4.** Music same as STAFF —**vt.** staved or stove, stav'ing **1.** to puncture, as by breaking in staves **2.** to furnish with staves —**stave in** to crush inward —**stave off** to ward off or hold off

STAVE

staves (stāvz) **n. 1.** alt. pl. of STAFF **2.** pl. of STAVE

stay¹ (stā) **n.** [OE. stæg] a heavy rope or cable used as a brace, as for a mast of a ship; guy —**vt.** to brace or support with stays

stay² (stā) **n.** [MFr. estaie] **1.** a support; prop **2.** a strip of stiffening material used in a corset, shirt collar, etc. —**vt.** to support, or prop up

stay³ (stā) **vi.** [< L. stare, to stand] **1.** to continue in the place or condition specified; remain **2.** to live; dwell **3.** to stop; halt **4.** to pause; delay **5.** [Colloq.] to endure; last —**vt. 1.** to stop or check **2.** to hinder or detain **3.** to postpone (legal action) **4.** to satisfy (thirst, etc.) for a time **5.** to remain to the end of —**n. 1.** a) a stopping or being stopped b) a halt or pause **2.** a postponement in legal action **3.** the action of remaining, or the time spent, in a place —**stay put** [Colloq.] to remain in place or unchanged

stay'ing power ability to last; endurance

St. Clair (kler) Lake lake between SE Mich. & Ontario, Canada

Ste. [Fr. Sainte] Saint (female)

stead (sted) **n.** [OE. stede] the place or position of a person or thing as filled by a substitute —**stand (one) in good stead** to give (one) good service

stead·fast (sted**'**fast**'**) **adj.** [OE. stedefæste] **1.** firm; fixed **2.** constant —**stead'fast'ly** **adv.** —**stead'fast'ness** **n.**

stead·y (sted**'**ē) **adj.** **-i·er, -i·est** [see STEAD & -Y²] **1.** not shaky; firm; stable **2.** constant, regular, or uniform **3.** constant in behavior, loyalty, etc. **4.** calm and controlled [steady nerves] **5.** sober; reliable —**vt., vi. -ied, -y·ing** to make or become steady —**n.** [Colloq.] one's sweetheart —**adv.** in a steady manner —**go steady** [Colloq.] to be sweethearts —**stead'i·ly** **adv.** —**stead'i·ness** **n.**

steak (stāk) **n.** [< ON. steikja, to roast on a spit] a thick slice of meat, esp. beef, or fish, for broiling or frying

steal (stēl) **vt.** stole, stol'en, steal'ing [OE. stælan] **1.** to take (another's property, etc.) dishonestly, esp. in a secret manner **2.** to take (a look, etc.) slyly **3.** to gain slyly or artfully [he stole her heart] **4.** to move, put, etc. stealthily (in, from, etc.) **5.** Baseball to gain (a base) safely without the help of a hit, walk, or error —**vi. 1.** to be a thief **2.** to move stealthily, quietly, etc. —**n.** [Colloq.] **1.** a stealing **2.** an extraordinary bargain —**steal'er** **n.**

stealth (stelth) **n.** [< ME. stelen, to steal] secret or furtive action —**stealth'i·ly** **adv.** —**stealth'i·ness** **n.** —**stealth'y** **adj.** **-i·er, -i·est**

steam (stēm) **n.** [OE.] **1.** water as converted into a vapor by being heated to the boiling point **2.** the power of steam under pressure **3.** condensed water vapor **4.** [Colloq.] driving force; energy —**adj. 1.** using or operated by steam **2.** containing or conducting steam —**vi. 1.** to give off steam **2.** to become covered with condensed steam **3.** to generate steam **4.** to move by steam power —**vt.** to expose to steam, as in cooking —**let (or blow) off steam** [Colloq.] to release pent-up emotion —**steam'y** **adj.**

steam'boat' **n.** a steamship, esp. a small one

steam engine an engine using steam under pressure to supply mechanical energy

steam'er **n. 1.** something operated by steam, as a steamship **2.** a container for cooking, cleaning, etc. with steam

steam fitter a mechanic whose work (**steam fitting**) is installing and maintaining boilers, pipes, etc. in steam-pressure systems

steam′roll′er n. a heavy, steam-driven roller used in road building, etc. —vt., vi. to move, crush, override, etc. as (with) a steamroller

steam′ship′ n. a ship driven by steam power

steam shovel a large, mechanically operated digger, powered by steam

ste·ar·ic acid (stē ar′ik, stir′-) [< Fr. < Gr. stear, tallow] a colorless, waxlike fatty acid found in many animal and vegetable fats, used in making candles, soaps, etc.

ste·a·tite (stē′ə tīt′) n. [< Gr. stear, tallow] a compact, massive variety of talc; soapstone

steed (stēd) n. [OE. steda] a horse: literary term

steel (stēl) n. [OE. stiele] 1. a hard, tough metal composed of iron alloyed with a small percentage of carbon and often with other metals, as nickel, chromium, etc. 2. something made of steel; specif., [Poet.] a sword or dagger 3. great strength or hardness —adj. of or like steel —vt. to make hard, tough, etc. —steel′i·ness n. —steel′y adj. -i·er, -i·est

steel band a percussion band, orig. in Trinidad, beating on steel oil drums

steel wool long, thin shavings of steel in a pad, used for scouring, polishing, etc.

steel′yard′ (-yärd′, -yərd) n. [STEEL + obs. yard, rod] a balance scale consisting of a metal arm suspended from above

steen·bok (stēn′bäk′, stän′-) n., pl. -bok′, -boks′ [Afrik. < Du. steen, a stone + bok, a buck] same as STEINBOK

steep[1] (stēp) adj. [OE. steap, lofty] 1. having a sharp rise or slope; precipitous 2. [Colloq.] excessive; extreme —n. a steep slope —steep′ly adv. —steep′ness n.

steep[2] (stēp) vt., vi. [akin to ON. steypa] to soak, saturate, imbue, etc. —n. liquid in which something is steeped

stee·ple (stē′p'l) n. [OE. stepel] 1. a tower rising above the main structure, as of a church, usually capped with a spire 2. same as SPIRE

stee′ple·chase′ n. a horse race over a course obstructed with ditches, hedges, etc.

stee′ple·jack′ n. one who builds, paints, or repairs steeples, smokestacks, etc.

steer[1] (stir) vt., vi. [OE. stieran] 1. to guide (a ship, etc.) with a rudder 2. to direct the course of (an automobile, etc.) 3. to follow (a course) —n. [Colloq.] a suggestion; tip —steer clear of to avoid

steer[2] (stir) n. [OE. steor] 1. a castrated male of the cattle family 2. loosely, any male of beef cattle

steer′age (-ij) n. 1. a steering 2. formerly, a section in a ship occupied by passengers paying the lowest fare

steers·man (stirz′mən) n., pl. -men one who steers a ship or boat; helmsman

stein (stīn) n. [G.] an earthenware beer mug, or a similar mug of pewter, glass, etc.

Stein (stīn), Gertrude 1874-1946; U.S. writer in France

stein·bok (stīn′bäk′) n., pl. -bok′, -boks′ [< G.] a small, reddish antelope of S and E Africa

stel·lar (stel′ər) adj. [< L. stella, star] 1. of a star 2. excellent 3. leading; chief [a stellar role]

stel·late (stel′āt, -it) adj. [see prec.] star-shaped

stem[1] (stem) n. [OE. stemn] 1. the main stalk of a plant 2. any stalk supporting leaves, flowers, or fruit 3. a stem-like part, as of a pipe, goblet, etc. 4. the prow of a ship; bow 5. the part of a word to which inflectional endings are added —vt. stemmed, stem′ming 1. to remove the stem from (a fruit, etc.) 2. to make headway against [to stem the tide] —vi. to originate or derive

stem[2] (stem) vt. stemmed, stem′ming [< ON. stemma] to stop or check by or as if by damming up

stem′ware′ (-wer′) n. goblets, wineglasses, etc. having stems

stench (stench) n. [OE. stenc] an offensive smell; stink

sten·cil (sten′s'l) vt. -ciled or -cilled, -cil·ing or -cil·ling [ult. < L. scintilla, a spark] to make or mark with a stencil —n. 1. a thin sheet, as of paper, cut through in such a way that when ink, paint, etc. is applied, designs, letters, etc. form on the surface beneath 2. a design, etc. so made

STENCIL

STENCIL

ste·nog·ra·pher (stə näg′rə fər) n. a person skilled in stenography

ste·nog·ra·phy (-fē) n. [< Gr. stenos, narrow + -GRAPHY] shorthand writing for later transcription in typewriting — **sten·o·graph·ic** (sten′ə graf′ik) adj. —**sten′o·graph′i·cal·ly** adv.

sten·to·ri·an (sten tôr′ē ən) adj. [< Stentor, a Greek herald in the Iliad] very loud

step (step) n. [OE. stepe] 1. a single movement of the foot, as in walking 2. the distance covered by such a movement 3. a short distance 4. a manner of stepping; gait 5. a sequence of movements in dancing 6. the sound of stepping 7. a footprint 8. a rest for the foot in climbing, as a stair 9. a degree; level; stage 10. any of a series of acts, processes, etc. —vi. stepped, step′ping 1. to move by executing a step 2. to walk a short distance 3. to move briskly (along) 4. to enter (into a situation, etc.) 5. to press the foot down (on) —vt. 1. to measure by taking steps (with off) 2. to arrange in a series of degrees, etc. —in (or out of) step (not) conforming to a marching rhythm, a regular procedure, etc. —keep step to stay in step —step down 1. to resign (from an office, etc.) 2. to decrease, as in rate —step in to intervene —step on it [Colloq.] to hurry —step up 1. to advance 2. to increase, as in rate —take steps to adopt certain measures —step′per n.

step·broth·er (step′bruth′ər) n. one's stepparent's son by a former marriage

step′child′ n., pl. -chil′dren [OE. steop-, orphaned] a child (**stepdaughter** or **stepson**) by a former marriage of one's spouse

step′lad′der n. a four-legged ladder having broad, flat steps

step′par′ent n. the person (**stepfather** or **stepmother**) who has married one's parent after the death or divorce of the other parent

steppe (step) n. [< Russ. step′] any of the great plains of SE Europe and Asia, having few trees

step′ping·stone′ n. 1. a stone used to step on, as in crossing a stream, etc. 2. a means of bettering oneself

step·sis·ter (step′sis′tər) n. one's stepparent's daughter by a former marriage

step′-up′ n. an increase, as in amount, intensity, etc.

-ster [OE. -estre] a suffix meaning one who is, does, creates, or is associated with (something specified) [trickster, gangster]

stere (stir) n. [< Fr. < Gr. stereos, cubic] a cubic meter

ster·e·o (ster′ē ō′, stir′-) n., pl. -os′ 1. a stereophonic record player, radio, system, etc. 2. a stereoscope or a stereoscopic picture, etc. —adj. clipped form of STEREO-PHONIC

stereo- [< Gr. stereos, hard] a combining form meaning solid, firm, three-dimensional [stereoscope]

ster·e·o·phon·ic (ster′ē ə fän′ik, stir′-) adj. [prec. + PHONIC] designating sound reproduction, as in broadcasting or phonograph recording, using two or more channels to carry and reproduce through separate speakers a blend of sounds from separate sources —**ster′e·o·phon′i·cal·ly** adv.

ster′e·o·scope′ (-skōp′) n. [STEREO- + -SCOPE] an instrument that gives a three-dimensional effect to photographs viewed through it: it has two eyepieces, through which two slightly different views of the same scene are viewed side by side —**ster′e·o·scop′ic** (-skäp′ik) adj.

ster′e·o·type′ (-tīp′) n. [< Fr.: see STEREO- & -TYPE] 1. a printing plate cast from a mold, as of a page of set type 2. the process of making or printing from such plates 3. a fixed idea or popular conception —vt. -typed′, -typ′ing to make a stereotype of

ster′e·o·typed′ adj. 1. like a stereotype; esp., trite; hackneyed 2. printed from stereotype plates

ster·ile (ster′'l) adj. [L. sterilis] 1. incapable of producing others of its kind; barren 2. producing little or nothing 3. free from living microorganisms —**ste·ril·i·ty** (stə ril′ə tē) n.

ster′i·lize (-ə līz′) vt. -lized′, -liz′ing to make sterile; specif., a) to make incapable of reproduction b) to free from living microorganisms, as by subjecting to great heat —**ster′i·li·za′tion** n. —**ster′i·liz′er** n.

ster·ling (stur′liŋ) n. [ME. sterlinge, Norman coin] 1. sterling silver or articles made of it 2. British money — adj. 1. designating silver that is at least 92.5 percent pure 2. of British money 3. made of sterling silver 4. excellent [sterling principles]

stern[1] (sturn) adj. [OE. styrne] 1. severe; strict [stern measures] 2. grim [a stern face] 3. relentless; firm — **stern′ly** adv. —**stern′ness** n.

stern[2] (sturn) n. [< ON. styra, to steer] the rear end of a ship, boat, etc.

ster·num (stur′nəm) n., pl. -nums, -na (-nə) [< Gr. sternon] a flat, bony structure to which most of the ribs are attached in the front of the chest; breastbone —**ster′nal** adj.

ster·oid (stir′oid, ster′-) *n.* [STER(OL) + -OID] any of a group of compounds including the sterols, sex hormones, etc.

ster·ol (stir′ôl, ster′-) *n.* [< (CHOLE)STEROL] any of a group of solid cyclic alcohols, as cholesterol, found in plant and animal tissues

ster·to·rous (stur′tər əs) *adj.* [< L. *stertere*, to snore] characterized by raspy, labored breathing

stet (stet) [L.] let it stand: a printer's term used to indicate that matter previously struck out is to remain —*vt.* **stet′ted, stet′ting** to mark with "stet"

steth·o·scope (steth′ə skōp′) *n.* [< Fr. < Gr. *stēthos*, the chest + -SCOPE] *Med.* an instrument placed against the body for examining the heart, lungs, etc. by listening to the sounds they make

ste·ve·dore (stē′və dôr′) *n.* [< Sp. < L. *stipare*, to cram] a person employed at loading or unloading ships

Ste·ven·son (stē′vən s′n), **Robert Louis** 1850–94; Scottish novelist and poet

stew (stōō, styōō) *vt., vi.* [ult. < L. *ex-*, out + Gr. *typhos*, steam] **1.** to cook by simmering or boiling slowly **2.** to worry —*n.* **1.** a dish, esp. of meat and vegetables, cooked by stewing **2.** a state of worry

stew·ard (stōō′ərd, styōō′-) *n.* [< OE. *stig*, hall + *weard*, keeper] **1.** a person put in charge of a large estate **2.** an administrator, as of another's finances and property **3.** one responsible for the food and drink, etc. in a club, restaurant, etc. **4.** an attendant on a ship, airplane, etc. — **stew′ard·ship′** *n.*

stew′ard·ess (-ər dis) *n.* a woman steward, esp. on an airplane

stewed (stōōd, styōōd) *adj.* **1.** cooked by stewing **2.** [Slang] drunk; intoxicated

St. He·le·na (hə lē′nə, hel′i nə) Brit. island in the S Atlantic: site of Napoleon's exile (1815–21)

stick (stik) *n.* [OE. *sticca*] **1.** a twig or small branch broken or cut off **2.** a long, slender piece of wood, as a staff, club, cane, etc. **3.** any sticklike piece [a *stick* of gum] **4.** an implement for striking a ball, puck, etc. [a hockey *stick*] **5.** [Colloq.] a dull or stupid person —*vt.* **stuck, stick′ing 1.** to pierce, as with a pointed instrument **2.** to pierce with (a knife, pin, etc.) **3.** to thrust (*in, into, out,* etc.) **4.** to fasten or attach by gluing, pinning, etc. **5.** to transfix or impale **6.** to obstruct, detain, etc. [the wheels were *stuck*] **7.** [Colloq.] to put, set, etc. **8.** [Colloq.] to puzzle; baffle **9.** [Slang] *a)* to impose a burden, etc. upon *b)* to defraud —*vi.* **1.** to be fixed by a pointed end, as a nail **2.** to adhere; cling; remain **3.** to persevere [to *stick* at a job] **4.** to remain firm and resolute [he *stuck* with us] **5.** to become embedded, jammed, etc. **6.** to be puzzled **7.** to hesitate; scruple [he'll *stick* at nothing] **8.** to protrude or project (with *out, up,* etc.) —**stick around** [Slang] to stay near at hand —**stick by** to remain loyal to —**stick up** [Slang] to commit armed robbery upon —**stick up for** [Colloq.] to uphold; defend —**the sticks** [Colloq.] the rural districts

stick′er *n.* a person or thing that sticks; specif., *a)* a bur, thorn, etc. *b)* a gummed label *c)* [Colloq.] *same as* STICK-LER

stick′-in-the-mud′ *n.* [Colloq.] a person who resists change or progress

stick·le·back (stik′'l bak′) *n.* [< OE. *sticel*, a prick] a small, scaleless fish with sharp spines on the back

stick·ler (stik′lər) *n.* [< OE. *stihtan*, arrange] **1.** one who insists on a certain way of doing things [a *stickler* for discipline] **2.** [Colloq.] something difficult to solve

stick′pin′ *n.* an ornamental pin worn in a cravat or necktie

stick shift a gearshift, as on a car, operated manually by a lever, esp. one on the floor

stick′up′ *n. slang term for* HOLDUP (sense 2)

stick′y *adj.* **-i·er, -i·est 1.** that sticks; adhesive **2.** covered with an adhesive substance **3.** [Colloq.] hot and humid **4.** [Colloq.] troublesome **5.** [Colloq.] maudlin —**stick′i·ly** *adv.* —**stick′i·ness** *n.*

stiff (stif) *adj.* [OE. *stif*] **1.** hard to bend; rigid; firm **2.** hard to move or operate **3.** sore or limited in movement: said of joints or muscles **4.** having such joints or muscles **5.** not fluid; thick [a *stiff* sauce] **6.** strong; powerful [a *stiff* breeze] **7.** of high potency **8.** harsh [a *stiff* punishment] **9.** difficult [a *stiff* climb] **10.** constrained or awkward; not easy **11.** [Colloq.] high [a *stiff* price] **12.** [Slang] drunk —*n.* [Slang] a corpse —**stiff′ly** *adv.* —**stiff′-ness** *n.*

stiff′-arm′ *vt.* to push (someone) away with one's arm out straight

stiff′en *vt., vi.* to make or become stiff or stiffer —**stiff′-en·er** *n.*

stiff′-necked′ (-nekt′) *adj.* stubborn; obstinate

sti·fle (stī′f'l) *vt.* **-fled, -fling** [< MFr. *estouffer*, smother] **1.** to suffocate; smother **2.** to suppress or check; stop [to *stifle* a sob] —*vi.* to die or suffer from lack of air

stig·ma (stig′mə) *n., pl.* **-mas, stig·ma·ta** (stig mät′ə, stig′mə tə) [L. < Gr., a mark] **1.** a mark of disgrace or reproach **2.** a spot on the skin, esp. one that bleeds in certain nervous tensions **3.** [*pl.*] marks resembling the Crucifixion wounds of Jesus **4.** the upper tip of the style of a flower, receiving the pollen —**stig·mat′ic** (-mat′ik) *adj.*

stig′ma·tize′ *vt.* **-tized′, -tiz′ing 1.** to brand with a stigma **2.** to mark as disgraceful —**stig′ma·ti·za′tion** *n.*

stile (stīl) *n.* [< OE. *stigan*, to climb] **1.** a step or set of steps used in climbing over a fence or wall **2.** *shortened form of* TURNSTILE

sti·let·to (sti let′ō) *n., pl.* **-tos, -toes** [It. < L. *stilus*, pointed tool] a small dagger with a slender, tapering blade

still¹ (stil) *adj.* [OE. *stille*] **1.** without sound; silent **2.** soft or low in sound **3.** not moving; motionless **4.** calm; tranquil **5.** not effervescent: said of wine **6.** designating or of a single photograph taken from a motion-picture film —*n.* **1.** silence; quiet **2.** a still photograph —*adv.* **1.** at or up to the time indicated **2.** even; yet [*still* colder] **3.** nevertheless; yet [rich but *still* unhappy] —*conj.* nevertheless; yet —*vt., vi.* to make or become still —**still′ness** *n.*

still² (stil) *n.* [< obs. *still*, to distill] an apparatus used for distilling liquids, esp. alcoholic liquors

still′born′ *adj.* dead when born —**still′birth′** *n.*

still life a picture of inanimate objects, as fruit, flowers, etc. —**still′-life′** *adj.*

Still·son wrench (stil′s′n) [< D. *Stillson*, its U.S. inventor (in 1869)] *a trademark for* a wrench used for turning pipes, etc.: pressure applied to the handle tightens the jaw

still·y (stil′ē) *adj.* **-i·er, -i·est** [Literary] still; silent; calm

stilt (stilt) *n.* [ME. *stilte*] **1.** either of a pair of poles, each with a footrest somewhere along its length, used for walking, as in play **2.** any of a number of long posts used to hold a building, etc. above the ground or out of the water **3.** any of several wading birds with long legs

stilt·ed (stil′tid) *adj.* artificially formal or dignified; pompous —**stilt′ed·ly** *adv.* —**stilt′ed·ness** *n.*

stim·u·lant (stim′yə lənt) *adj.* stimulating —*n.* anything, as a drug, that stimulates

stim′u·late′ (-lāt′) *vt.* **-lat′ed, -lat′ing** [< L. *stimulus*, a goad] **1.** to stir up or spur on; arouse; excite **2.** to invigorate **3.** *Med., Physiol.* to excite (an organ, etc.) to activity or increased activity —*vi.* to act as a stimulant or stimulus —**stim′u·lat′er, stim′u·la′tor** *n.* —**stim′u·la′tion** *n.* —**stim′u·la′tive** *adj., n.*

stim′u·lus (-ləs) *n., pl.* **-li′** (-lī′) [L., a goad] **1.** something that stirs to action; incentive **2.** any action or agent that causes or changes an activity in an organism, organ, etc.

sting (stiŋ) *vt.* **stung, sting′ing** [OE. *stingan*] **1.** to prick or wound with a sting **2.** to cause sudden, smarting pain to **3.** to cause to suffer mentally **4.** to stimulate suddenly and sharply **5.** [Slang] to cheat; esp., to overcharge —*vi.* to cause or feel sharp, smarting pain —*n.* **1.** a stinging **2.** a pain or wound resulting from stinging **3.** the power to sting **4.** a sharp-pointed organ, as in insects and plants, that pricks, wounds, etc. —**sting′er** *n.*

sting′ray′ *n.* a large ray (fish) having a whiplike tail with a sharp spine or spines that can inflict painful wounds

stin·gy (stin′jē) *adj.* **-gi·er, -gi·est** [akin to STING] **1.** giving or spending grudgingly; miserly **2.** less than needed; scanty —**stin′gi·ly** *adv.* —**stin′gi·ness** *n.*

stink (stiŋk) *vi.* **stank** or **stunk, stunk, stink′ing** [OE. *stincan*] **1.** to give off a strong, unpleasant smell **2.** to be offensive or hateful **3.** [Slang] to be no good —*n.* a strong, unpleasant smell; stench —**stink up** to cause to stink —**stink′er** *n.*

stint (stint) *vt.* [< OE. *styntan*, to blunt] to restrict to a certain quantity, often small —*vi.* to be sparing in giving or using —*n.* **1.** restriction; limit **2.** an assigned task —**stint′er** *n.* —**stint′ing·ly** *adv.*

sti·pend (stī′pend) *n.* [< L. *stips*, small coin + *pendere*, to pay] a regular or fixed payment, as a salary, or a periodic payment, as an allowance

---

fat, āpe, cär; ten, ēven; is, bīte; gō, hôrn, tōōl, look; oil, out; up, fur; thin, *then*; zh, leisure; ŋ, ring; ə for *a* in *ago*; ′ as in *able* (ā′b′l); ë, Fr. coeur; ö, Fr. feu; Fr. mon; ü, Fr. duc; r, Fr. cri; kh, G. doch, ich. ‡ foreign; < derived from

stip·ple (stip′'l) *vt.* **-pled, -pling** [< Du. *stippel*, a speckle] to paint, draw, or engrave in small dots —*n.* the art of painting, drawing, etc. in small dots: also **stip′pling**

stip·u·late (stip′yə lāt′) *vt.* **-lat′ed, -lat′ing** [< L. *stipulari*, to bargain] **1.** to arrange definitely, as in a contract **2.** to specify as an essential condition of an agreement —**stip′u·la′tion** *n.*

stip·ule (stip′yōōl) *n.* [< L. *stipula*, a stalk] either of two small leaflike parts at the base of some leafstalks —**stip′u·lar** (-yoo lər) *adj.* —**stip′u·late** (-lit, -lāt′) *adj.*

STIPULE

stir[1] (stur) *vt., vi.* **stirred, stir′ring** [OE. *styrian*] **1.** to move, esp. slightly **2.** to rouse from sleep, lethargy, etc. **3.** to make active or be active **4.** to mix (a liquid, etc.) by moving a spoon, fork, etc. around **5.** to excite the feeling (of) **6.** to incite (often with *up*) —*n.* **1.** a stirring **2.** movement; activity **3.** excitement; commotion —**stir′rer** *n.*

stir[2] (stur) *n.* [prob. < Romany] [Slang] a prison

stir′-fry′ *vt.* **-fried′, -fry′ing** in Chinese cooking, to fry very quickly, with a little oil, while stirring

stir′ring *adj.* **1.** active; busy **2.** rousing; exciting

stir·rup (stur′əp, stir′-) *n.* [OE. *stigrap*] **1.** a flat-bottomed ring hung from a saddle and used as a footrest **2.** any of various stirruplike supports, clamps, etc. **3.** a stirrup-shaped bone in the middle ear

stitch (stich) *n.* [OE. *stice*, a puncture] **1.** *a)* a single complete in-and-out movement of a needle in sewing, knitting, etc. *b)* a surgeon's suture **2.** a loop, etc. made by stitching **3.** a particular kind of stitch or stitching **4.** a sudden, sharp pain in the side or back **5.** a bit or piece —*vi., vt.* to make stitches (in); sew —**stitch′er** *n.*

stitch′er·y (-ər ē) *n.* ornamental needlework

St. John's (jänz) seaport and capital of Newfoundland: pop. 80,000

St. Law·rence (lôr′əns) river flowing from Lake Ontario into the Atlantic: c.750 mi.

St. Lawrence Seaway inland waterway for oceangoing ships, connecting the Great Lakes with the Atlantic through the St. Lawrence River and canals

St. Lou·is (lōō′is, lōō′ē) city in E Mo.: pop. 622,000 (met. area 2,363,000)

St. Lu·ci·a (lōō′shē ə, lōō sē′ə) country on an island in the West Indies: 238 sq. mi.; pop. 112,000

stoat (stōt) *n.* [ME. *stote*] a large European weasel, esp. in its brown summer coat

stock (stäk) *n.* [OE. *stocc*] **1.** the trunk of a tree **2.** *a)* a line of descent; ancestry *b)* a strain, race, etc. of animals or plants **3.** a supporting or main part of an implement, etc., as the part of a rifle holding the barrel **4.** [*pl.*] a wooden frame with holes for confining the ankles or wrists, formerly used for punishment **5.** [*pl.*] a frame of timbers supporting a ship during construction **6.** raw material **7.** water in which meat, fish, etc. has been boiled, used in soups **8.** *short for* LIVESTOCK **9.** a store or supply, as of goods on hand in a store, etc. **10.** shares of corporate capital, or the certificates showing such ownership **11.** *same as* STOCK COMPANY (sense 2) **12.** a former type of wide cravat —*vt.* **1.** to furnish (a farm, shop, etc.) with stock **2.** to keep a supply of, as for sale or for future use —*vi.* to put in a stock, or supply (with *up*) —*adj.* **1.** kept in stock [*stock* sizes] **2.** common or trite [a stock joke] **3.** that deals with stock **4.** relating to a stock company —**in** (or **out of**) **stock** (not) available for sale or use —**take stock 1.** to inventory the stock on hand **2.** to make an appraisal, as of probabilities —**take** (or **put**) **stock in** [Colloq.] to have faith in

stock·ade (stä kād′) *n.* [< Fr. < Pr. *estaca*, a stake] **1.** a barrier of stakes driven into the ground side by side, for defense against attack **2.** an enclosure, as a fort, made with such stakes **3.** an enclosure for military prisoners

stock′bro′ker *n.* a broker who buys and sells stocks and bonds

stock car a standard automobile, modified for racing

stock company 1. a company whose capital is in shares **2.** a theatrical company that presents a repertoire

stock exchange 1. a place where stocks and bonds are bought and sold **2.** an association of stockbrokers

stock′hold′er (-hōl′dər) *n.* one owning stock or shares in a given company

Stock·holm (stäk′hōm′, -hōlm′) capital of Sweden, on the Baltic: pop. 768,000 (met. area 1,280,000)

stock·ing (stäk′iŋ) *n.* [< obs. sense of STOCK] a closefitting covering, usually knitted, for the foot and leg

stock′man (-mən) *n., pl.* **-men 1.** a man who owns or raises livestock **2.** a man who works in a stockroom or warehouse

stock market 1. *same as* STOCK EXCHANGE **2.** the business carried on at a stock exchange **3.** the prices quoted on stocks and bonds

stock′pile′ (-pīl′) *n.* a reserve supply of goods, raw material, etc. —*vt., vi.* **-piled′, -pil′ing** to accumulate a stockpile (of)

stock′room′ *n.* a room in which a store of goods, materials, etc. is kept: also **stock room**

stock′-still′ *adj.* perfectly motionless

stock′y *adj.* **-i·er, -i·est** heavily built; short and thickset —**stock′i·ly** *adv.* —**stock′i·ness** *n.*

stock′yard′ *n.* an enclosure for keeping cattle, hogs, etc. to be slaughtered

stodg·y (stäj′ē) *adj.* **-i·er, -i·est** [< dial. *stodge*, heavy food] **1.** heavily built **2.** dull; uninteresting **3.** very old-fashioned —**stodg′i·ly** *adv.* —**stodg′i·ness** *n.*

sto·gie, sto·gy (stō′gē) *n., pl.* **-gies** [< *Conestoga*, town in Pa.] a long, thin, inexpensive cigar

Sto·ic (stō′ik) *n.* [< Gr. *stoa*, colonnade: the Stoics met in a colonnade] **1.** a member of an ancient Greek school of philosophy, holding that natural laws govern all things and that the wise lead a virtuous life based on reason **2.** [s-] a stoical person —*adj.* **1.** of the Stoics **2.** [s-] *same as* STOICAL —**Sto′i·cism, sto′i·cism** *n.*

sto·i·cal (stō′i k'l) *adj.* showing indifference to joy, grief, pain, etc.; impassive —**sto′i·cal·ly** *adv.*

stoke (stōk) *vt., vi.* **stoked, stok′ing** [< STOKER] **1.** to stir up and feed fuel to (a fire) **2.** to tend (a furnace, etc.)

stok·er (stō′kər) *n.* [Du. < *stoken*, to poke] **1.** a man who tends a furnace, esp. of a steam boiler, as on a ship **2.** a mechanical device that stokes a furnace

STOL (stōl) *adj.* [s(hort) t(ake)o(ff and) l(anding)] designating, of, or for an aircraft that can take off and land on a short airstrip —*n.* a STOL aircraft, airstrip, etc.

stole[1] (stōl) *n.* [< Gr. *stolē*, garment] **1.** a long strip of cloth worn like a scarf by certain officiating clergymen **2.** a woman's long scarf of cloth or fur worn around the shoulders, with the ends hanging in front

stole[2] (stōl) *pt. of* STEAL

stol·en (stō′lən) *pp. of* STEAL

stol·id (stäl′id) *adj.* [L. *stolidus*, slow] having or showing little or no emotion; unexcitable —**sto·lid·i·ty** (stə lid′ə tē), **stol′id·ness** *n.* —**stol′id·ly** *adv.*

stom·ach (stum′ək) *n.* [ult. < Gr. *stoma*, mouth] **1.** the saclike, digestive organ into which food passes from the esophagus **2.** the abdomen; belly **3.** appetite for food **4.** desire or inclination —*vt.* **1.** to be able to eat or digest **2.** to tolerate; bear

stom′ach·ache′ *n.* pain in the stomach or abdomen

stomp (stämp) *vt., vi. var. of* STAMP

stone (stōn) *n.* [OE. *stan*] **1.** the hard, solid, nonmetallic mineral matter of rock **2.** a small piece of rock **3.** a piece of rock shaped for some purpose, as a gravestone or grindstone **4.** the seed of certain fruits **5.** a precious stone or gem **6.** *pl.* **stone** in Great Britain, 14 pounds avoirdupois **7.** an abnormal stony mass formed in the kidney, gall bladder, etc. —*vt.* **stoned, ston′ing 1.** to throw stones at **2.** to remove the stone from (a peach, etc.) —*adj.* of stone —**cast the first stone** to be the first to censure

stone- [< prec.] *a combining form meaning* completely [*stone*-blind]

Stone Age the early period in human culture when stone implements were used

stone′cut′ter *n.* a person or machine that cuts stone and makes it smooth —**stone′cut′ting** *n.*

stoned (stōnd) *adj.* [Slang] **1.** drunk; intoxicated **2.** under the influence of a drug

Stone·henge (stōn′henj′) a circular arrangement of prehistoric monoliths in S England

stone′ma′son (-mā′s'n) *n.* a person who cuts stone to shape and uses it in making walls, buildings, etc. —**stone′ma′son·ry** *n.*

stone's throw a relatively short distance

stone′wall′ *vi.* [Colloq.] to obstruct a debate, investigation, etc., as by withholding information, telling lies, etc.

stone′ware′ (-wer′) *n.* a coarse, dense, glazed or unglazed kind of pottery

stone′work′ *n.* **1.** the art or process of working in stone **2.** something built of stone **3.** [*pl.*] a place where stonecutting is done

ston·y (stō′nē) *adj.* **-i·er, -i·est 1.** full of stones **2.** of or like stone; specif., *a)* hard *b)* unfeeling; pitiless *c)* cold; fixed Also **ston′ey** —**ston′i·ly** *adv.* —**ston′i·ness** *n.*

stood (stood) *pt. & pp. of* STAND

stooge (stōōj) *n.* [< ?] [Colloq.] **1.** an actor who aids a comedian by being the victim of his jokes, pranks, etc. **2.** anyone who acts as a foil, underling, etc. —*vi.* **stooged,** **stoog'ing** [Colloq.] to be a stooge (*for* someone)
stool (stōōl) *n.* [OE. *stol*] **1.** a single seat having no back or arms **2.** *same as* FOOTSTOOL **3.** the feces in a single bowel movement —*vi.* [Colloq.] to act as a stool pigeon
stool pigeon [Colloq.] a spy or informer, esp. for the police: also **stool·ie** (stōōl'ē) *n.*
stoop[1] (stōōp) *vi.* [OE. *stupian*] **1.** to bend the body forward or in a crouch **2.** to carry the head and shoulders habitually bent forward **3.** to demean oneself —*n.* the act or position of stooping
stoop[2] (stōōp) *n.* [Du. *stoep*] a small porch or platform with steps, at the door of a house
stoop labor work done by stooping, as in picking crops from low-growing plants
stop (stäp) *vt.* **stopped,** **stop'ping** [ult. < Gr. *styppē*, tow fibers] **1.** to close by filling, shutting off, etc. **2.** to cause to cease motion, activity, etc. **3.** to block; intercept; prevent **4.** to desist from; cease [*stop* talking] —*vi.* **1.** to cease moving, etc.; halt **2.** to leave off doing something **3.** to cease operating **4.** to become clogged **5.** to tarry or stay —*n.* **1.** a stopping or being stopped **2.** a finish; end **3.** a stay or sojourn **4.** a place stopped at, as on a bus route **5.** an obstruction, plug, etc. **6.** a finger hole in a wind instrument, closed to produce a desired tone **7.** a pull, lever, etc. for controlling a set of organ pipes —**stop off** to stop for a while en route to a place —**stop over** to visit for a while: also **stop in** (or **by**)
stop'cock' *n.* a cock or valve to stop or regulate the flow of a liquid
stop'gap' *n.* a person or thing serving as a temporary substitute —*adj.* used as a stopgap
stop'light' *n.* **1.** a traffic light, esp. when red to signal vehicles to stop **2.** a rear light on a vehicle that lights up when the brakes are applied
stop'o'ver *n.* a brief stop or stay at a place in the course of a journey
stop'page (-ij) *n.* **1.** a stopping or being stopped **2.** an obstructed condition; block
stop'per *n.* something inserted to close an opening; plug —*vt.* to close with a stopper
stop street a street intersection at which vehicles must come to a complete stop before continuing
stop'watch' *n.* a watch with a hand that can be started and stopped instantly, for timing races, etc.
stor·age (stôr'ij) *n.* **1.** a storing or being stored **2.** a place or space for storing goods **3.** the cost of storing goods
storage battery a battery of cells for generating electric current: the cells can be recharged by passing a current through them in the direction opposite to the discharging flow of current
store (stôr) *vt.* **stored,** **stor'ing** [< L. *instaurare,* restore] **1.** to put aside for use when needed **2.** to furnish with a supply **3.** to put in a warehouse, etc. for safekeeping **4.** to put (information) in a computer memory unit —*n.* **1.** a supply (*of* something) for use when needed; reserve **2.** [*pl.*] supplies, esp. of food, clothing, etc. **3.** a retail establishment where goods are offered for sale **4.** a storehouse **5.** an abundance —**in store** set aside for the future; in reserve —**set** (or **put** or **lay**) **store by** to value
store'front' *n.* a front room on the ground floor of a building, designed for use as a retail store
store'house' *n.* a place where things are stored; esp., a warehouse
store'keep'er *n.* **1.** a person in charge of stores, or supplies **2.** a retail merchant
store'room' *n.* a room where things are stored
sto·ried[1] (stôr'ēd) *adj.* famous in story or history
sto·ried[2] (stôr'ēd) *adj.* having stories, or floors [many-storied]
stork (stôrk) *n.* [OE. *storc*] a large, long-legged wading bird, having a long neck and bill
storm (stôrm) *n.* [OE.] **1.** a strong wind, with rain, snow, thunder, etc. **2.** any heavy fall of rain, snow, etc. **3.** a strong emotional outburst **4.** any strong disturbance **5.** a sudden, strong attack on a fortified place —*vi.* **1.** to blow violently, rain, snow, etc. **2.** to rage; rant **3.** to rush violently [to *storm* into a room] —*vt.* to attack vigorously
storm door (or **window**) a door (or window) placed outside the regular one as added protection
storm'y *adj.* **-i·er, -i·est** **1.** of or characterized by storms **2.** violent, raging, etc. —**storm'i·ly** *adv.* —**storm'i·ness** *n.*

stormy petrel **1.** a petrel thought to presage storms **2.** a person thought to bring trouble with him
sto·ry[1] (stôr'ē) *n., pl.* **-ries** [< Gr. *historia,* narrative] **1.** the telling of an event or series of events; account; narration **2.** a joke **3.** a fictitious narrative shorter than a novel **4.** the plot of a novel, play, etc. **5.** [Colloq.] a falsehood **6.** *Journalism* a news report
sto·ry[2] (stôr'ē) *n., pl.* **-ries** [< prec.] a horizontal division of a building, from a floor to the ceiling above it: Brit. sp. **sto'rey,** *pl.* **-reys**
sto'ry·book' *n.* a book of stories, esp. one for children
sto'ry·tell'er *n.* **1.** one who narrates stories **2.** [Colloq.] a liar —**sto'ry·tell'ing** *n.*
stoup (stōōp) *n.* [ON. *staup,* cup] **1.** a basin for holy water in a church **2.** [Brit. Dial.] a drinking cup
stout (stout) *adj.* [< OFr. *estout,* bold] **1.** courageous; brave **2.** strong; sturdy; firm **3.** powerful; forceful **4.** fat; thickset —*n.* **1.** a garment size for a fat man **2.** a heavy, dark-brown brew like porter, but with more hops —**stout'ish** *adj.* —**stout'ly** *adv.* —**stout'ness** *n.*
stout'heart'ed *adj.* courageous; brave —**stout'heart'ed·ly** *adv.* —**stout'heart'ed·ness** *n.*
stove[1] (stōv) *n.* [MDu., heated room] an apparatus using fuel or electricity for heating, cooking, etc.
stove[2] (stōv) *alt. pt. & pp. of* STAVE
stove'pipe' *n.* a metal pipe used to carry off smoke from a stove
stow (stō) *vt.* [OE. *stow,* a place] **1.** to pack in an orderly way **2.** to fill by packing thus **3.** [Slang] to stop [*stow* the chatter!] —**stow away** **1.** to put or hide away **2.** to be a stowaway —**stow'age** (-ij) *n.*
stow'a·way' *n.* one who hides aboard a ship, airplane, etc. to get free passage or evade port officials, etc.
Stowe (stō), **Harriet Beecher** 1811–96; U.S. novelist
STP [< ? STP, motor oil additive] a hallucinogenic drug similar to mescaline
St. Paul capital of Minn.: pop. 310,000
St. Pe·ters·burg (pē'tarz burg') **1.** *former name of* LENINGRAD **2.** city in WC Fla.: pop. 216,000
stra·bis·mus (stra biz'mas) *n.* [< Gr. *strabizein,* to squint] a disorder of the eyes, as cross-eye, in which both eyes cannot be focused on the same point at the same time
strad·dle (strad'l) *vt., vi.* **-dled, -dling** [< STRIDE] **1.** to sit or stand astride of, or stand with the legs wide apart **2.** to appear to take both sides of (an issue) —*n.* a straddling —**strad'dler** *n.*
strafe (strāf) *vt.* **strafed, straf'ing** [< G. *Gott strafe England* (God punish England)] to attack with machinegun fire from low-flying aircraft
strag·gle (strag'l) *vi.* **-gled, -gling** [prob. < ME. *straken,* to roam] **1.** to stray from the course or wander from the main group **2.** to be scattered over a wide area **3.** to leave, arrive, etc. at scattered, irregular intervals **4.** to hang in an unkempt way, as hair —**strag'gler** *n.* —**strag'gly** *adj.*
straight (strāt) *adj.* [< ME. *strecchen,* to stretch] **1.** having the same direction throughout its length; not crooked, bent, etc. **2.** direct; undeviating **3.** in order; properly arranged, etc. **4.** honest; sincere **5.** outspoken **6.** unmixed; undiluted [*straight* whiskey] **7.** unqualified [a *straight* denial] **8.** [Slang] normal or conventional —*adv.* **1.** in a straight line **2.** upright; erectly **3.** without detour, delay, etc. —*n.* Poker a hand consisting of any five cards in sequence —**straight away** (or **off**) without delay —**straight'ness** *n.*
straight angle an angle of 180 degrees
straight'a·way' *n.* a track, or part of a track, that extends in a straight line
straight'en *vt., vi.* to make or become straight —**straighten out** **1.** to make or become less confused, easier to deal with, etc. **2.** to reform —**straight'en·er** *n.*
straight face a facial expression showing no amusement or other emotion —**straight'-faced'** *adj.*
straight'for'ward *adj.* **1.** moving or leading straight ahead; direct **2.** honest; frank —*adv.* in a straightforward manner: also **straight'for'wards** —**straight'for'ward·ly** *adv.* —**straight'for'ward·ness** *n.*
straight man an actor who serves as a foil for a comedian
straight'-out' *adj.* [Colloq.] **1.** straightforward **2.** unrestrained **3.** thoroughgoing
straight time **1.** the standard number of working hours, as per week **2.** the rate of pay for these hours
straight'way' *adv.* at once

strain' (strān) *vt.* [< L. *stringere*] **1.** to draw or stretch tight **2.** to exert, use, etc. to the utmost **3.** to injure by overexertion [to *strain* a muscle] **4.** to stretch beyond the normal limits **5.** to pass through a screen, sieve, etc.; filter **6.** to remove by filtration —*vi.* **1.** to make violent efforts; strive hard **2.** to become strained **3.** to be subjected to great stress or pressure **4.** to pull with force **5.** to filter, ooze, etc. —*n.* **1.** a straining or being strained **2.** great effort, exertion, etc. **3.** a bodily injury from overexertion **4.** stress or force **5.** a great demand on one's emotions, resources, etc. —**strained** *adj.*

strain² (strān) *n.* [< OE. *strynan,* to produce] **1.** ancestry; lineage **2.** race; stock; line **3.** a group of individuals different from others in its species **4.** an inherited tendency **5.** a trace; streak **6.** the style or tone of a speech, book, etc. **7.** [*often pl.*] a musical tune

strain'er *n.* a device for straining, sifting, or filtering

strait (strāt) *adj.* [< L. *stringere,* draw tight] [Archaic] **1.** narrow; tight **2.** strict; rigid —*n.* [*often pl.*] **1.** a narrow waterway connecting two large bodies of water **2.** difficulty; distress

strait'en *vt.* **1.** esp. formerly, to make strait or narrow **2.** to bring into difficulties: esp. in **in straitened circumstances,** lacking sufficient money

strait'jack'et *n.* a coatlike device that binds the arms tight against the body: used to restrain a person

strait'-laced' (-lāst') *adj.* narrowly strict in behavior or moral views

strand' (strand) *n.* [OE.] shore, esp. ocean shore —*vt., vi.* **1.** to run or drive aground, as a ship **2.** to put or be put into a helpless position [*stranded* in a desert]

strand² (strand) *n.* [< ?] **1.** any of the threads, fibers, wires, etc. that are twisted together to form a string, rope, or cable **2.** a ropelike length of anything [a *strand* of pearls]

strange (strānj) *adj.* **strang'er, strang'est** [< L. *extraneus,* foreign] **1.** not previously known, seen, etc.; unfamiliar **2.** unusual; extraordinary **3.** peculiar; odd **4.** reserved; distant **5.** unaccustomed (*to*) —*adv.* in a strange manner —**strange'ly** *adv.* —**strange'ness** *n.*

stran·ger (strān'jər) *n.* **1.** a newcomer **2.** a person not known to one **3.** a person unaccustomed (*to* something) [he is a *stranger* to hate]

stran·gle (straŋ'g'l) *vt., vi.* **-gled, -gling** [< Gr. *strangos,* twisted] **1.** to choke to death **2.** to suppress; stifle —**stran'gler** *n.*

stran'gle·hold' *n.* **1.** an illegal wrestling hold that chokes off an opponent's breath **2.** any force that restricts or suppresses freedom

stran·gu·late (straŋ'gyə lāt') *vt.* **-lat'ed, -lat'ing 1.** *same as* STRANGLE **2.** *Med.* to cause (a tube) to become squeezed so that a flow is cut off —**stran'gu·la'tion** *n.*

strap (strap) *n.* [dial. form of STROP] **1.** a narrow strip of leather, plastic, etc. for tying or holding things **2.** a strip or band like this, as a shoulder strap —*vt.* **strapped, strap'ping 1.** to fasten with a strap **2.** to beat with a strap —**strap'less** *adj.*

strapped (strapt) *adj.* [Colloq.] without money

strap·ping (strap'iŋ) *adj.* [Colloq.] tall and sturdy

stra·ta (strāt'ə, strat'ə) *n. alt. pl.* of STRATUM

strat·a·gem (strat'ə jəm) *n.* [< Gr. *stratos,* army + *agein,* to lead] **1.** a trick, plan, etc. for deceiving an enemy in war **2.** any tricky ruse

stra·te·gic (strə tē'jik) *adj.* **1.** of strategy **2.** sound in strategy **3.** essential to effective military strategy Also **stra·te'gi·cal** —**stra·te'gi·cal·ly** *adv.*

strat·e·gy (strat'ə jē) *n., pl.* **-gies 1.** the science of planning and directing military operations **2.** a plan or action based on this **3.** skill in managing or planning, esp. by using stratagems —**strat'e·gist** *n.*

Strat·ford-on-A·von (strat'fərd än ā'vän) town in C England: birthplace & burial place of Shakespeare: also **Strat'ford-up·on-A'von**

strat·i·fy (strat'ə fī') *vt., vi.* **-fied', -fy'ing** to form or arrange in layers or strata —**strat'i·fi·ca'tion** *n.*

strat·o·sphere (strat'ə sfir') *n.* [< Fr. < ModL. *stratum,* layer + Fr. *sphère,* sphere] the atmospheric zone above the troposphere, lying between c.6 and c.30 miles above the earth's surface and having a temperature range between –45°C and –75°C —**strat'o·spher'ic** (-sfer'ik, -sfir') *adj.*

stra·tum (strāt'əm, strat'-) *n., pl.* **-ta** (-ə), **-tums** [< L. *stratus,* a spreading] **1.** a horizontal layer of material; specif., *Geol.* a single layer of sedimentary rock **2.** a level of society

stra'tus (-əs) *n., pl.* **-ti** (-ī) [see prec.] a long, low, gray cloud layer

Strauss (strous; *G.* shtrous) **1.** Jo·hann (yō'hän) 1825–99; Austrian composer **2.** Rich·ard (rikh'ärt) 1864–1949; German composer

Stra·vin·sky (strə vin'skē), I·gor (ē'gôr) 1882–1971; U.S. composer, born in Russia

straw (strô) *n.* [OE. *streaw*] **1.** hollow stalks of grain after threshing, used for bedding, etc. **2.** a single one of these **3.** a tube used for sucking beverages **4.** a worthless trifle —*adj.* **1.** straw-colored; yellowish **2.** made of straw **3.** worthless

straw'ber'ry (-ber'ē, -bər ē) *n., pl.* **-ries** [prob. from the strawlike particles on the fruit] **1.** the small, red, fleshy fruit of a vinelike plant related to the rose **2.** this plant

strawberry blonde reddish blonde

straw boss [Colloq.] an overseer of work with little or no authority

straw color a pale yellow —**straw'-col'ored** *adj.*

straw'flow'er *n.* a plant whose brightly colored flowers are dried for winter bouquets

straw vote an unofficial vote for sampling popular opinion on an issue, etc.

stray (strā) *vi.* [prob. < L. *extra vagari,* wander outside] **1.** to wander from a given place, course, etc.; roam **2.** to deviate (*from* what is right) **3.** to wander from the subject; digress —*n.* one that strays; esp., a domestic animal wandering at large —*adj.* **1.** having strayed; lost **2.** isolated [a few *stray* words]

streak (strēk) *n.* [< OE. *strica*] **1.** a long, thin mark; stripe **2.** a thin layer, as of fat in meat or ore in rock **3.** a tendency in one's nature [a jealous *streak*] **4.** a period, run, or spell [a *streak* of victories] —*vt.* to mark with streaks —*vi.* **1.** to become streaked **2.** to move swiftly **3.** to make a short dash naked in public as a prank —**like a streak** [Colloq.] swiftly —**streak'er** *n.* —**streak'y** *adj.*

stream (strēm) *n.* [OE.] **1.** a current of water; specif., a small river **2.** a steady flow of any fluid [a *stream* of cold air] or of rays of energy [a *stream* of light] **3.** a moving line of things [a *stream* of cars] **4.** a trend or course [the *stream* of events] —*vi.* **1.** to flow as in a stream **2.** to flow (*with*) [eyes *streaming* with tears] **3.** to move swiftly **4.** to float or fly, as a flag in the breeze

stream'er *n.* **1.** a long, narrow flag **2.** any long, narrow flowing strip **3.** a stream of light extending up from the horizon **4.** a newspaper headline across the page

stream'line' *vt.* **-lined', -lin'ing** to make streamlined —*adj. same as* STREAMLINED

stream'lined' *adj.* **1.** having a contour designed to offer the least resistance in moving through air, water, etc. **2.** arranged so as to be more efficient **3.** trim

street (strēt) *n.* [< L. *strata (via),* paved (road)] **1.** a public road in a city or town, esp. a paved one **2.** such a road apart from its sidewalks **3.** the people living, working, etc. in the buildings along a given street

street'car' *n.* a large car on rails that provides public transportation on city streets

street'walk'er *n.* a prostitute

street'wise' *adj.* [Colloq.] experienced or knowledgeable in dealing with the situations and people in urban poverty areas, esp. those areas where crime is prevalent

strength (streŋkth) *n.* [OE. *strengthu*] **1.** the state or quality of being strong; power; force **2.** toughness; durability **3.** the power to resist attack **4.** legal, moral, or intellectual force **5.** potency, as of drugs, liquors, etc. **6.** intensity, as of sound, color, etc. **7.** force as measured in numbers [an army at full *strength*] **8.** a source of strength —**on the strength of** based or relying on

strength'en *vt., vi.* to make or become stronger —**strength'en·er** *n.*

stren·u·ous (stren'yoo wəs) *adj.* [L. *strenuus*] **1.** requiring or characterized by great effort or energy **2.** vigorous, arduous, etc. —**stren'u·ous·ly** *adv.* —**stren'u·ous·ness** *n.*

strep (strep) *n.* shortened form of STREPTOCOCCUS

strep throat [Colloq.] a sore throat caused by a streptococcus, with inflammation and fever

strep·to·coc·cus (strep'tə käk'əs) *n., pl.* **-coc'ci** (-käk'sī) [< Gr. *streptos,* twisted + *kokkos,* kernel] any of a group of spherical bacteria that occur generally in chains: some cause serious diseases

strep'to·my'cin (-mī'sin) *n.* [< Gr. *streptos,* twisted + *mykēs,* fungus] an antibiotic drug obtained from molds: used in treating various bacterial diseases

stress (stres) *n.* [< L. *strictus,* strict] **1.** strain; specif., force that strains or deforms **2.** emphasis; importance **3.** *a*) mental or physical tension *b*) urgency, pressure, etc. causing this **4.** the relative force of utterance given a syllable or word; accent —*vt.* **1.** to put stress or pressure on **2.** to accent **3.** to emphasize

stretch (strech) *vt.* [OE. *streccan*] **1.** to reach out; extend **2.** to pull or spread out to full extent or to a greater size **3.** to cause to extend too far; strain **4.** to strain in interpretation, scope, etc. —*vi.* **1.** *a)* to spread out to full extent or beyond normal limits *b)* to extend over a given distance or time **2.** *a)* to extend the body or limbs to full length *b)* to lie down (usually with *out*) **3.** to become stretched —*n.* **1.** a stretching or being stretched **2.** an unbroken period [a ten-year *stretch*] **3.** an unbroken length, tract, etc. [a *stretch* of beach] **4.** *short for* HOMESTRETCH —*adj.* made of elasticized fabric —**stretch'a·ble** *adj.*

stretch'er *n.* **1.** one that stretches **2.** a light frame covered with canvas, etc. for carrying the sick or injured

strew (stroo) *vt.* strewed, strewed or strewn, strew'ing [OE. *streawian*] **1.** to scatter; spread here and there **2.** to cover as by scattering **3.** to be scattered over (a surface)

stri·ate (strī'āt) *vt.* -at·ed, -at·ing [< L. *striare*, to groove] to mark with narrow grooves, fine lines, or stripes —**stri·a'tion** *n.*

stri'at·ed *adj.* marked with thin, parallel lines, as the voluntary muscles

strick·en (strik'n) *alt. pp. of* STRIKE —*adj.* **1.** struck or wounded **2.** suffering, as from pain, etc.

strict (strikt) *adj.* [< L. *stringere*, draw tight] **1.** exact; precise **2.** perfect; absolute **3.** *a)* enforcing rules carefully *b)* closely enforced; rigorous —**strict'ly** *adv.* —**strict'ness** *n.*

stric·ture (strik'chər) *n.* [see prec.] **1.** strong criticism; censure **2.** an abnormal narrowing of a duct or passage in the body

stride (strīd) *vi.*, *vt.* strode, strid·den (strid''n), strid'ing [OE. *stridan*] **1.** to walk with long steps **2.** to cross with a single, long step **3.** to straddle —*n.* **1.** a long step **2.** the distance covered by a stride **3.** [*usually pl.*] progress; advancement —**hit one's stride** to reach one's normal level of efficiency —**take in one's stride** to cope with easily —**strid'er** *n.*

stri·dent (strīd''nt) *adj.* [< L. *stridere*, to rasp] harsh-sounding; shrill; grating —**stri'dence, stri'den·cy** *n.* —**stri'dent·ly** *adv.*

strife (strīf) *n.* [< OFr. *estrif*, effort] **1.** contention **2.** a fight or quarrel; struggle

strike (strīk) *vt.* struck, struck or strick'en, strik'ing [OE. *strican*, to go] **1.** *a)* to give (a blow, etc.) *b)* to give a blow to; hit **2.** to make by stamping, printing, etc. [to *strike* coins] **3.** to announce (time), as with a bell: said of clocks, etc. **4.** to ignite (a match) or produce (a light, etc.) by friction **5.** to come into forceful contact with; crash into [the stone *struck* his arm] **6.** to attack **7.** to come upon; find, notice, discover, etc. **8.** to afflict, as with disease, pain, etc. **9.** to affect as if by a blow, contact, etc.; specif., *a)* to occur to [*struck* by an idea] *b)* to impress (one's fancy, etc.) *c)* to cause to become suddenly [he was *struck* dumb] *d)* to overcome with strong feeling [to be *struck* with amazement] **10.** to remove (*from* a list, record, etc.) **11.** to make (a bargain, truce, etc.) **12.** to arrive at by figuring, etc. [to *strike* a balance] **13.** to lower (a sail, flag, etc.) **14.** to assume (a pose, etc.) —*vi.* **1.** to hit (*at*) **2.** to attack **3.** *a)* to make sounds as by being struck: said of a bell, clock, etc. *b)* to be announced thus [ten o'clock *struck*] **4.** to collide; hit (*against*, *on*, or *upon*) **5.** to ignite, as a match **6.** to seize a bait: said of a fish **7.** to dart in an attempt to wound, as a snake **8.** to come suddenly (*on* or *upon*) **9.** to refuse to continue to work until certain demands are met **10.** to proceed in a new direction —*n.* **1.** a striking; blow **2.** a refusal by employees to go on working, in an attempt to gain better working conditions **3.** a finding of a rich deposit of oil, coal, etc. **4.** any sudden success **5.** the pull on the line by a fish seizing bait **6.** *Baseball* a pitched ball which is struck at but missed, delivered through the strike zone but not struck at, etc. **7.** *Bowling* a knocking down of all the pins on the first bowl —**(out) on strike** striking (*vi.* 9) —**strike home 1.** to deliver an effective blow **2.** to have the desired effect —**strike out 1.** to erase **2.** to start out **3.** *Baseball* to put out, or be put out, on three strikes —**strike up to** begin

strike'break'er *n.* one who tries to break up a strike, as by working as a scab, supplying scabs, threatening the strikers, etc. —**strike'break'ing** *n.*

strik'er *n.* **1.** a person who is on strike **2.** a person or thing that strikes, as the clapper in a bell, etc.

strik'ing *adj.* **1.** that strikes or is on strike **2.** impressive, outstanding, etc. —**strik'ing·ly** *adv.*

string (striŋ) *n.* [OE. *streng*] **1.** a thin line of fiber, wire, etc. used for tying, pulling, etc. **2.** a length of things on a string [a *string* of pearls] **3.** a line, row, or series of things [a *string* of houses] **4.** a number of business enterprises under one ownership **5.** a group of athletes arranged according to ability: the **first string** is more skilled than the **second string**, etc. **6.** *a)* a slender cord of wire, nylon, etc., stretched on a violin, guitar, etc. and bowed, plucked, or struck to make a musical sound *b)* [*pl.*] all the stringed instruments of an orchestra **7.** a fiber of a plant **8.** [Colloq.] a condition attached to a plan, offer, etc.: *usually used in pl.* —*vt.* strung, string'ing **1.** to provide with strings **2.** to thread on a string **3.** to tie, hang, etc. with a string **4.** to remove the strings from (beans, etc.) **5.** to arrange in a row **6.** to extend [*string* a cable] —*vi.* to stretch out in a line —**on a** (or **the**) **string** completely under one's control —**pull strings** to use influence, often secretly, to gain advantage —**string along** [Colloq.] **1.** to agree **2.** to fool or deceive

string bean *same as* SNAP BEAN

string'board' *n.* a board placed along the side of a staircase to cover the ends of the steps

stringed (striŋd) *adj.* having strings

strin·gent (strin'jənt) *adj.* [< L. *stringere*, draw tight] strict; severe —**strin'gen·cy** *n.*, *pl.* -cies —**strin'gent·ly** *adv.*

string quartet a quartet of or for stringed instruments, as first and second violins, viola, and cello

string tie a narrow necktie, usually tied in a bow

STRINGBOARD

string'y *adj.* -i·er, -i·est **1.** like a string; long, thin, wiry, etc. **2.** consisting of strings or fibers **3.** having tough fibers [*stringy* meat] **4.** forming strings [*stringy* molasses]

strip¹ (strip) *vt.* stripped, strip'ping [< OE. *strypan*] **1.** to remove (the clothing, etc.) from (a person) **2.** to dispossess (a person) of (honors, titles, etc.) **3.** to plunder; rob **4.** to take off (the covering, skin, etc.) from (something) **5.** to make bare by taking away removable parts **6.** to break the thread of (a nut, bolt, etc.) or the teeth of (a gear) —*vi.* **1.** to take off all clothing **2.** to perform a strip-tease —**strip'per** *n.*

strip² (strip) *n.* [< STRIPE] **1.** a long, narrow piece, as of land, tape, etc. **2.** a runway for airplanes: also **landing strip** —*vt.* to cut or tear into strips

stripe (strip) *n.* [< MDu.] **1.** a long, narrow band or mark differing as in color from the area around it **2.** a strip of cloth on a uniform to show rank, years served, etc. **3.** kind; sort —*vt.* striped, strip'ing to mark with stripes

strip·ling (strip'liŋ) *n.* a grown boy; youth

strip mining a method of mining, as for coal, by exposing a mineral deposit near the earth's surface

strip-tease (strip'tēz') *n.* an act, as in burlesque shows, in which a woman takes off her clothes slowly, usually to music —**strip'teas'er** *n.*

strive (strīv) *vi.* strove, striv·en (striv''n) or strived, striv'ing [< OFr. *estrif*, effort] **1.** to make great efforts; try very hard [to *strive* to win] **2.** to struggle [to *strive* against tyranny]

strobe (light) (strōb) [< Gr. *strobos*, a twisting around] an electronic tube emitting rapid, brief, and brilliant flashes of light: used in photography, the theater, etc.

strode (strōd) *pt. of* STRIDE

stroke (strōk) *n.* [ME.] **1.** the act of striking; blow of an ax, whip, etc. **2.** a sudden action resulting as if from a blow [a *stroke* of luck] **3.** a sudden attack, esp. of apoplexy **4.** *a)* a single, strong effort *b)* something accomplished by such an effort **5.** the sound of striking, as of a clock **6.** *a)* a single movement, as with some tool, pen, etc. *b)* any of a series of repeated rhythmic motions made against water, air, etc. *c)* a type, manner, or rate of such movement **7.** a mark made by a pen, etc. **8.** a gentle caressing motion with the hand **9.** *Mech.* any of the continuous, reciprocating movements of a piston, etc. **10.** *Rowing* the rower who sets the rate of rowing —*vt.* stroked, strok'ing **1.** to draw one's hand, a tool, etc. gently over the surface of **2.** to hit (a ball) as in tennis, pool, etc.

stroll (strōl) *vi.* [prob. < G. dial. *strolen*] **1.** to walk in an idle, leisurely manner; saunter **2.** to wander —*vt.* to stroll along or through —*n.* a leisurely walk

stroll'er *n.* **1.** one who strolls **2.** a light, chairlike baby carriage

strong (strôŋ) *adj.* [OE. *strang*] 1. *a*) physically powerful *b*) healthy; sound 2. morally or intellectually powerful [a *strong* will] 3. having special ability (*in* a specified area) [to be *strong* in French] 4. firm; durable 5. powerful in wealth, numbers, etc. 6. of a specified number [a force 6,000 *strong*] 7. having a powerful effect 8. intense in degree or quality [*strong* coffee, *strong* light, *strong* colors, etc.] 9. forceful, vigorous, etc. 10. *Gram.* expressing variation in tense by internal change of vowel (Ex.: *swim, swam, swum*) —*adv.* in a strong manner —**strong'ly** *adv.* —**strong'ness** *n.*

strong'-arm' *adj.* [Colloq.] using physical force —*vt.* [Colloq.] to use force upon, esp. in robbing

strong'box' *n.* a heavily made box or safe for storing valuables

strong'hold *n.* a place having strong defenses

strong'-mind'ed *adj.* determined; unyielding: also **strong'-willed'** —**strong'-mind'ed·ness** *n.*

stron·ti·um (strän'shē əm, -tē-) *n.* [< *Strontian*, Scotland, where first found] a pale-yellow metallic chemical element resembling calcium in properties: symbol, Sr; at. wt., 87.62; at. no., 38

strop (sträp) *n.* [OE.] a leather strap, esp. one used for putting a fine edge on razors —*vt.* **stropped, strop'ping** to sharpen on a strop

stro·phe (strō'fē) *n.* [< Gr. *strephein*, to turn] a stanza of a poem

strove (strōv) *alt. pt.* of STRIVE

struck (struk) *pt. & pp.* of STRIKE —*adj.* closed or affected by a labor strike

struc·tur·al (struk'chər əl) *adj.* 1. of, having, or characterized by structure 2. used in construction or building — **struc'tur·al·ly** *adv.*

struc·ture (struk'chər) *n.* [< L. *struere*, arrange] 1. manner of building, constructing, or organizing 2. something built or constructed, as a building 3. the arrangement of all the parts of a whole [the *structure* of the atom] 4. something composed of parts —*vt.* **-tured, -tur·ing** to put together according to a system

stru·del (strōō'd'l) *n.* [G.] a pastry made of a thin sheet of dough filled with apples, etc. and rolled

strug·gle (strug''l) *vi.* **-gled, -gling** [ME. *strogelen*] 1. to fight violently with an opponent 2. to make great efforts; strive 3. to make one's way with difficulty —*n.* 1. a great effort 2. conflict; strife —**strug'gler** *n.*

strum (strum) *vt., vi.* **strummed, strum'ming** [echoic] to play (a guitar, etc.) unskillfully or idly —*n.* the act or sound of this —**strum'mer** *n.*

strum·pet (strum'pit) *n.* [ME.] a prostitute

strung (struŋ) *pt. & alt. pp.* of STRING —**strung out** [Slang] suffering from the effects of being addicted to a narcotic drug

strut (strut) *vi.* **strut'ted, strut'ting** [< OE. *strutian*, stand rigid] to walk swaggeringly —*n.* 1. a strutting walk 2. a brace fitted into a framework to resist lengthwise pressure —**strut'ter** *n.* —**strut'ting·ly** *adv.*

strych·nine (strik'nin, -nīn, -nēn) *n.* [Fr. < Gr. *strychnos*, nightshade] a highly poisonous crystalline alkaloid: used in small doses as a stimulant

Stu·art (stōō'ərt) ruling family of Scotland (1371–1603) & of England & Scotland (1603–1714), except during the Commonwealth (1649–60)

stub (stub) *n.* [OE. *stybb*] 1. a tree stump 2. a short piece left over 3. any short projection 4. a short piece of a ticket, bank check, etc. kept as a record —*vt.* **stubbed, stub'bing** to strike (one's toe, etc.) against something

stub·ble (stub''l) *n.* [< L. *stipula*, a stalk] 1. short stumps of grain left standing after harvesting 2. any growth like this [a *stubble* of beard]

stub·born (stub'ərn) *adj.* [? < OE. *stybb*, a stub] 1. refusing to yield or comply; obstinate 2. done in an obstinate or persistent way 3. hard to handle, etc. —**stub'born·ly** *adv.* —**stub'born·ness** *n.*

stub·by (stub'ē) *adj.* **-bi·er, -bi·est** 1. covered with stubs or stubble 2. short and heavy or dense 3. short and thickset —**stub'bi·ness** *n.*

stuc·co (stuk'ō) *n., pl.* **-coes, -cos** [It.] 1. plaster or cement for surfacing walls, etc. 2. work done in this —*vt.* **-coed, -co·ing** to cover with stucco

stuck (stuk) *pt. & pp.* of STICK

stuck'-up' *adj.* [Colloq.] snobbish; conceited

stud¹ (stud) *n.* [OE. *studu*, a post] 1. any of a series of small knobs used to ornament a surface 2. a small buttonlike device for fastening shirt collars, etc. 3. an upright piece in a building frame to which laths, etc. are nailed 4. a projecting pin used as a support, a pivot, etc. —*vt.* **stud'ded, stud'ding** 1. to set or decorate with studs, etc.

2. to set thickly on [rocks *stud* the hillside] 3. to scatter or cluster (something) thickly 4. to provide (a building) with studs

stud² (stud) *n.* [OE. *stod*] 1. *a*) a number of horses kept for breeding *b*) the place where these are kept 2. *same as* STUDHORSE 3. any male animal used for breeding

stud'ding *n.* 1. the studs of a building 2. material used as studs

stu·dent (stōōd''nt, styōōd'-) *n.* [< L. *studere*, to study] 1. one who studies something 2. one who is enrolled for study in a school, college, etc.

stud'horse' *n.* a stallion kept for breeding

stud·ied (stud'ēd) *adj.* 1. prepared by careful study 2. deliberate

stu·di·o (stōō'dē ō', styōō'-) *n., pl.* **-os'** [It., a study] 1. a place where an artist, etc. works or where dancing lessons, etc. are given 2. a place where motion pictures, radio or television programs, etc. are produced

studio couch a couch that can be opened into a full-sized bed

stu·di·ous (stōō'dē əs, styōō'-) *adj.* 1. fond of study 2. attentive; zealous —**stu'di·ous·ly** *adv.* —**stu'di·ous·ness** *n.*

stud·y (stud'ē) *n., pl.* **-ies** [< L. *studere*, to study] 1. the seeking of knowledge, as by reading, etc. 2. careful examination of a subject, event, etc. 3. a branch of learning 4. [*pl.*] formal education; schooling 5. a work of literature or art treating a subject in careful detail 6. earnest effort or deep thought 7. a room for study, etc. —*vt.* **-ied, -y·ing** 1. to try to learn by reading, etc. 2. to investigate carefully 3. to scrutinize 4. to read (a book, etc.) intently 5. to take a course in at a school —*vi.* 1. to study something 2. to be a student 3. to meditate

stuff (stuf) *n.* [< OFr. *estoffe*] 1. the material out of which anything is made 2. essence; character 3. any kind of matter, unspecified 4. cloth, esp. woolen cloth 5. objects; things 6. worthless objects; junk 7. [Colloq.] superior ability, skill, etc. —*vt.* 1. to fill or pack; specif., *a*) to fill the skin of (a dead animal) in taxidermy *b*) to fill (a fowl, etc.) with seasoning, bread crumbs, etc. before roasting 2. to fill too full; cram 3. to pack or cram with 4. to put fraudulent votes into (a ballot box) 5. to plug; block —*vi.* to eat too much

stuffed shirt [Slang] a pompous, pretentious person

stuff'ing *n.* something used to stuff, as padding in upholstery, a seasoned mixture for stuffing fowl, etc.

stuff'y *adj.* **-i·er, -i·est** 1. poorly ventilated; close 2. having the nasal passages stopped up, as from a cold 3. dull; stodgy 4. pompous; pretentious —**stuff'i·ly** *adv.* —**stuff'i·ness** *n.*

stul·ti·fy (stul'tə fī') *vt.* **-fied', -fy'ing** [< L. *stultus*, foolish + *facere*, make] 1. to cause to appear foolish, stupid, etc. 2. to make dull or sluggish 3. to make worthless, etc. —**stul'ti·fi·ca'tion** *n.*

stum·ble (stum'b'l) *vi.* **-bled, -bling** [< Scand.] 1. to trip in walking, running, etc. 2. to walk unsteadily 3. to speak, act, etc. in a blundering way 4. to do wrong 5. to come by chance —*n.* a stumbling —**stum'bler** *n.*

stumbling block a difficulty

stump (stump) *n.* [prob. < MLowG. *stump*] 1. the lower end of a tree or plant left in the ground after removal of the upper part 2. the part of a leg, tooth, etc. left after the rest has been removed 3. the place where a political speech is made —*vt.* 1. to travel over (a district) making political speeches 2. [Colloq.] to puzzle; baffle —*vi.* 1. to walk heavily 2. to travel about making political speeches

stun (stun) *vt.* **stunned, stun'ning** [< L. *ex-*, intens. + *tonare*, to crash] 1. to make senseless or unconscious, as by a blow 2. to shock; daze

stung (stuŋ) *pt. & pp.* of STING

stunk (stuŋk) *pp. & alt. pt.* of STINK

stun'ning (-iŋ) *adj.* 1. that stuns 2. [Colloq.] remarkably attractive, excellent, etc. —**stun'ning·ly** *adv.*

stunt¹ (stunt) *vt.* [OE., stupid] 1. to check the growth or development of 2. to hinder (growth, etc.)

stunt² (stunt) *n.* [< ?] something done to show one's skill or daring, attract attention, etc. —*vi.* to perform a stunt

stunt man a professional acrobat who takes the place of an actor when dangerous scenes involving falls, leaps, etc. are filmed

stu·pe·fy (stōō'pə fī', styōō'-) *vt.* **-fied', -fy'ing** [< L. *stupere*, be stunned + *facere*, to make] 1. to make dull or lethargic; stun 2. to amaze; astonish; bewilder —**stu'pe·fac'tion** *n.*

stu·pen·dous (stoo pen'dəs, styoo-) *adj.* [< L. *stupere*, be stunned] 1. astonishing 2. astonishingly great or large — **stu·pen'dous·ly** *adv.*

stu·pid (stōō′pid, styōō′-) *adj.* [see prec.] 1. lacking normal intelligence 2. foolish; silly 3. dull; tiresome —*n.* a stupid person —**stu·pid′i·ty,** *pl.* **-ties, stu′pid·ness** *n.* — **stu′pid·ly** *adv.*

stu·por (stōō′pər, styōō′-) *n.* [L.] a state in which the mind and senses are dulled; loss of sensibility

stur·dy (stur′dē) *adj.* **-di·er, -di·est** [< OFr. *estourdi,* stunned] 1. firm; resolute 2. strong; hardy —**stur′di·ly** *adv.* —**stur′di·ness** *n.*

stur·geon (stur′jən) *n.* [< OFr. *esturjon*] any of several large food fishes having rows of spiny plates along the body: valuable as a source of caviar

STURGEON
(to 7 ft. long)

stut·ter (stut′ər) *n., vt., vi.* [< ME. *stutten*] *same as* STAMMER — **stut′ter·er** *n.*

Stutt·gart (stut′gärt) city in S West Germany: pop. 628,000

Stuy·ve·sant (stī′və s'nt), **Peter** 1592–1672; governor of Dutch colony in America (1646–64)

sty[1] (stī) *n., pl.* **sties** [< OE. *sti,* hall] 1. a pen for pigs 2. any foul place —*vi.* **stied, sty′ing** to lodge in a sty

sty[2], **stye** (stī) *n., pl.* **sties** [ult. < OE. *stigan,* to rise] a small, inflamed swelling on the rim of the eyelid

style (stīl) *n.* [< L. *stilus,* pointed writing tool] 1. a stylus 2. the stalklike part of a carpel between the stigma and the ovary 3. *a)* manner of expression in writing or speaking *b)* characteristic manner of expression, design, etc. in any art, period, etc. 4. distinction, originality, etc. in artistic or literary expression 5. *a)* fashion *b)* something stylish 6. elegance of manner 7. sort; kind —*vt.* **styled, styl′ing** 1. to name; call 2. to design the style of

styl′ish *adj.* conforming to current style in dress, decoration, etc.; fashionable —**styl′ish·ly** *adv.* —**styl′ish·ness** *n.*

styl′ist *n.* 1. a writer, etc. whose work has style (sense 4) 2. one who designs, or advises on, current styles, as in dress —**sty·lis·tic** (stī lis′tik) *adj.* —**sty·lis′ti·cal·ly** *adv.*

styl′ize (-īz) *vt.* **-ized, -iz·ing** to make conform to a given style; make conventional

sty·lus (stī′ləs) *n., pl.* **-lus·es, -li** (-lī) [< L. *stilus,* pointed tool] 1. a sharp, pointed marking device 2. *a)* a pointed device for cutting the grooves of a phonograph record *b)* a phonograph needle

sty·mie (stī′mē) *n.* [prob. < Scot., person partially blind] *Golf* a situation on the putting green in which a ball to be putted has another ball between it and the hole —*vt.* **-mied, -mie·ing** to block; impede Also **sty′my -mied, -my·ing**

styp·tic (stip′tik) *adj.* [< Gr. *styphein,* to contract] that halts bleeding by contracting the tissues or blood vessels; astringent —*n.* any styptic substance

sty·rene (stī′rēn, stir′ēn) *n.* [< L. *styrax,* a kind of tree + -ENE] a colorless or yellowish liquid used in the manufacture of synthetic rubber and plastics

Sty·ro·foam (stī′rə fōm′) *a trademark for* a rigid, foamy-looking, lightweight plastic —*n.* [*also* s-] this plastic

Styx (stiks) *Gr. Myth.* the river of Hades over which Charon ferried the souls of the dead

suave (swäv) *adj.* **suav′er, suav′est** [< L. *suavis,* sweet] smoothly gracious or polite; polished —**suave′ly** *adv.* — **suav′i·ty, suave′ness** *n.*

sub (sub) *n. shortened form of:* 1. SUBMARINE 2. SUBSTITUTE —*vi.* **subbed, sub′bing** [Colloq.] to be a substitute (*for* someone)

sub- [< L. *sub,* under] *a prefix meaning:* 1. beneath [*subsoil*] 2. lower than [*subaltern*] 3. to a lesser degree than [*subtropical*] 4. by or forming a division into smaller parts [*subsection*]

sub. 1. substitute(s) 2. suburb(an)

sub·al·tern (səb ôl′tərn) *n.* [< L. *sub-,* under + *alternus,* alternate] 1. a subordinate 2. [Chiefly Brit.] an army officer holding the rank below captain

sub·a·tom·ic (sub′ə täm′ik) *adj.* of or pertaining to particles smaller than an atom

sub′base′ment *n.* any floor or room below the principal basement

sub′branch′ *n.* a branch division

sub′com·mit′tee *n.* a subordinate committee chosen from a main committee

sub′com′pact *n.* a model of automobile smaller than a compact

sub·con′scious *adj.* occurring with little or no conscious perception on the part of the individual: said of mental processes and reactions —**the subconscious** subconscious mental activity —**sub·con′scious·ly** *adv.* —**sub·con′scious·ness** *n.*

sub·con′ti·nent *n.* a large land mass smaller than a continent

sub·con′tract *n.* a secondary contract undertaking some or all obligations of another contract —*vt., vi.* (sub′kən trakt′) to make a subcontract (for) —**sub·con′trac·tor** *n.*

sub′cul′ture *n.* 1. a distinctive social group within a larger group 2. its distinct cultural patterns

sub·cu·ta·ne·ous (sub′kyoo tā′nē əs) *adj.* beneath the skin —**sub′cu·ta′ne·ous·ly** *adv.*

sub·dea′con *n.* a cleric ranking just below a deacon

sub·deb (sub′deb′) *n.* [SUB- + DEB(UTANTE)] a girl not quite of debutante age

sub′di·vide′ *vt., vi.* **-vid′ed, -vid′ing** 1. to divide further 2. to divide (land) into small parcels for ready sale —**sub′-di·vi′sion** *n.*

sub·due (səb dōō′, -dyōō′) *vt.* **-dued′, -du′ing** [< L. *subducere,* to remove] 1. to conquer; vanquish 2. to overcome, as by persuasion; control 3. to make less intense; diminish; soften

sub·gum (sub′gum′) *adj.* [Cantonese, lit., mixed vegetables] designating any of various Chinese-American dishes, as chow mein, prepared with mushrooms, almonds, etc.

sub′head′ *n.* a subordinate heading or title, as for part of an article: also **sub′head′ing**

sub′hu′man *adj.* 1. less than human 2. nearly human

subj. 1. subject 2. subjunctive

sub·ject (sub′jikt) *adj.* [< L. *sub-,* under + *jacere,* to throw] 1. under the authority or control of another 2. having a tendency (*to*) [*subject* to anger] 3. liable to receive [*subject* to censure] 4. contingent upon [*subject* to approval] —*n.* 1. a person under the authority or control of another 2. one undergoing a treatment, experiment, etc. 3. something dealt with in discussion, study, writing, painting, etc. 4. the main theme of a musical work 5. a cause; reason 6. a branch of learning 7. *Gram.* the noun, noun phrase, or noun substitute in a sentence about which something is said —*vt.* (səb jekt′) 1. to bring under the authority or control of 2. to make liable or vulnerable [*to subject* one to contempt] 3. to cause to undergo something —**sub·jec′tion** *n.*

sub·jec·tive (səb jek′tiv) *adj.* 1. of or resulting from the feelings of the person thinking; not objective; personal 2. emphasizing the ideas, feelings, etc. of the artist or writer 3. *Gram. same as* NOMINATIVE —**sub·jec′tive·ly** *adv.* — **sub·jec·tiv·i·ty** (sub′jek tiv′ə tē) *n.*

sub·join (səb join′) *vt.* [see SUB- & JOIN] to add (something) at the end; append

sub·ju·gate (sub′jə gāt′) *vt.* **-gat′ed, -gat′ing** [< L. *sub-,* under + *jugum,* a yoke] to conquer or make subservient —**sub′ju·ga′tion** *n.* —**sub′ju·ga′tor** *n.*

sub·junc·tive (səb juŋk′tiv) *adj.* [< L. *subjungere,* subjoin] designating or of that mood of a verb used to express supposition, desire, possibility, etc., rather than to state a fact —*n.* 1. the subjunctive mood 2. a verb in this mood

sub·lease (sub′lēs′) *n.* a lease granted by a lessee —*vt.* (sub lēs′) **-leased′, -leas′ing** to grant or hold a sublease of —**sub′les·see′** (-les ē′) *n.* —**sub·les·sor** (sub les′ôr, sub′les ôr′) *n.*

sub·let (sub let′, sub′let′) *vt.* **-let′, -let′ting** 1. to let to another (property which one is renting) 2. to let out (work) to a subcontractor

sub·li·mate (sub′lə māt′) *vt.* **-mat′ed, -mat′ing** 1. to sublime (a substance) 2. to express (unacceptable impulses) in ways that are acceptable —*vi.* to undergo subliming — *n.* a product of subliming —**sub′li·ma′tion** *n.*

sub·lime (sə blīm′) *adj.* [< L. *sub-,* up to + *limen,* lintel] 1. noble; exalted 2. inspiring awe or admiration —*vt.* **-limed′, -lim′ing** 1. to make sublime 2. to purify (a solid) by heating to a gaseous state and condensing the vapor back into solid form —**the sublime** a sublime quality or thing —**sub·lime′ly** *adv.* —**sub·lim′i·ty** (-blim′ə tē), **sub·lime′ness** *n.*

sub·lim·i·nal (sub lim′ə n'l) *adj.* [see prec.] below the threshold of consciousness

sub·ma·chine gun (sub′mə shēn′) a portable, automatic or semiautomatic firearm with a short barrel, fired from the shoulder or hip

sub·mar·gi·nal (sub mär′ji n'l) *adj.* below minimum standards

sub·ma·rine (sub'mə rēn') *adj.* being, living, etc. underwater —*n.* (sub'mə rēn') a ship, esp. a warship, that can operate under water

submarine sandwich *same as* HERO SANDWICH

sub·max·il·lar·y (sub mak'sə ler'ē) *adj.* [see SUB- & MAXILLA] of or below the lower jaw

sub·merge (səb murj') *vt., vi.* -merged', -merg'ing [< L. *sub-*, under + *mergere*, to plunge] 1. to place or sink beneath the surface, as of water 2. to cover over; suppress —sub·mer'gence *n.*

sub·merse' (-murs') *vt.* -mersed', -mers'ing *same as* SUBMERGE —sub·mers'i·ble *adj., n.* —sub·mer'sion *n.*

sub·mi·cro·scop·ic (sub'mī krə skäp'ik) *adj.* too small to be seen through a microscope

sub·mis·sion (səb mish'ən) *n.* 1. a submitting or surrendering 2. resignation; obedience 3. a submitting of something for consideration, etc.

sub·mis'sive *adj.* yielding; docile —sub·mis'sive·ly *adv.* —sub·mis'sive·ness *n.*

sub·mit' (-mit') *vt.* -mit'ted, -mit'ting [< L. *sub-*, under + *mittere*, to send] 1. to present to others for consideration, etc. 2. to yield to the control, power, etc. of another 3. to offer as an opinion —*vi.* to yield; give in

sub·nor·mal (sub nôr'm'l) *adj.* below the normal, esp. in intelligence —sub'nor·mal'i·ty (-mal'ə tē) *n.*

sub·or·di·nate (sə bôr'də nit) *adj.* [< L. *sub-*, under + *ordinare*, to order] 1. below another in rank, importance, etc.; secondary 2. under the power or authority of another 3. *Gram.* functioning as a noun, adjective, or adverb within a sentence [a *subordinate* phrase] : cf. SUBORDINATE CLAUSE —*n.* a subordinate person or thing —*vt.* (-nāt') -nat'ed, -nat'ing 1. to place in a subordinate position 2. to make obedient or subservient (*to*) —sub·or'di·nate·ly *adv.* —sub·or'di·na'tion *n.*

subordinate clause a clause that cannot function syntactically as a complete sentence by itself

sub·orn (sə bôrn') *vt.* [< L. *sub-*, under + *ornare*, furnish] to induce (another) to do something illegal, esp. to commit perjury —sub·or·na·tion (sub'ôr nā'shən) *n.*

sub·plot (sub'plät') *n.* a secondary or subordinate plot in a play, novel, etc.

sub·poe·na (sə pē'nə) *n.* [< L. *sub poena*, under penalty] a written legal order directing a person to appear in court to testify, etc. —*vt.* -naed, -na·ing to summon with such an order Also sp. sub·pe'na

sub ro·sa (sub rō'zə) [L., under the rose] secretly

sub·scribe (səb skrīb') *vt., vi.* -scribed', -scrib'ing [< L. *sub-*, under + *scribere*, write] 1. to sign (one's name) on a document, etc. 2. to give support or consent (*to*) 3. to promise to contribute (money) 4. to agree to receive and pay for a periodical, service, etc. (with *to*) —sub·scrib'er *n.*

sub·script (sub'skript) *adj.* [see prec.] written below —*n.* a figure, letter, or symbol written below and to the side of another, as *x* in 3_x

sub·scrip·tion (səb skrip'shən) *n.* 1. a subscribing 2. something subscribed; esp., an amount of money subscribed 3. a formal agreement to receive and pay for a periodical, theater tickets, etc.

sub·sec·tion (sub sek'shən) *n.* a division of a section

sub·se·quent (sub'si kwənt, -kwent') *adj.* [< L. *sub-*, after + *sequi*, follow] coming after; following in time, place, or order —subsequent to after —sub'se·quent·ly *adv.*

sub·ser·vi·ent (səb sur'vē ənt) *adj.* 1. that is useful or of service, esp. in a subordinate capacity 2. submissive; servile —sub·ser'vi·ence *n.* —sub·ser'vi·ent·ly *adv.*

sub·side (səb sīd') *vi.* -sid'ed, -sid'ing [< L. *sub-*, under + *sidere*, settle] 1. to sink to a lower level or to the bottom 2. to become less active, intense, etc. —sub·sid'ence *n.*

sub·sid·i·ar·y (səb sid'ē er'ē) *adj.* [see SUBSIDY] 1. giving aid, service, etc.; auxiliary 2. being in a subordinate relationship 3. of, constituting, or maintained by a subsidy or subsidies —*n., pl.* -ies one that is subsidiary; specif., a company controlled by another company

sub·si·dize (sub'sə dīz') *vt.* -dized', -diz'ing to support with a subsidy —sub'si·di·za'tion *n.* —sub'si·diz'er *n.*

sub·si·dy (sub'sə dē) *n., pl.* -dies [< L. *subsidium*, auxiliary forces] a grant of money, as from a government to a private enterprise

sub·sist (səb sist') *vi.* [< L. *sub-*, under + *sistere*, to stand] 1. to continue to be; exist 2. to continue to live (*on* or *by*)

sub·sist'ence *n.* 1. a subsisting 2. the act of providing sustenance 3. means of support or livelihood, esp. the barest means —sub·sist'ent *adj.*

sub·soil (sub'soil') *n.* the layer of soil beneath the surface soil

sub·son·ic (sub sän'ik) *adj.* designating or of speeds less than that of sound

sub·stance (sub'stəns) *n.* [< L. *substare*, exist] 1. the real or essential part of anything; essence 2. the physical matter of which a thing consists; material 3. *a*) a solid quality *b*) consistency; body 4. the real meaning; gist 5. material possessions; wealth —in substance 1. essentially 2. actually

sub·stand·ard (sub stan'dərd) *adj.* below standard; specif., *a*) below a legal standard *b*) designating or of a dialect regarded as below that used by educated speakers ["he don't" is considered *substandard*]

sub·stan·tial (səb stan'shəl) *adj.* 1. of or having substance 2. real; true 3. strong; solid 4. ample; large 5. important 6. well-to-do 7. with regard to essential elements —sub·stan'ti·al'i·ty (-shē al'ə tē) *n.* —sub·stan'tial·ly *adv.*

sub·stan·ti·ate (səb stan'shē āt') *vt.* -at'ed, -at'ing 1. to give substance to 2. to give concrete form or body to 3. to show to be true or real by giving evidence —sub·stan'ti·a'tion *n.*

sub·stan·tive (sub'stən tiv) *adj.* [see SUBSTANCE] 1. actual; real 2. essential 3. *Gram. a*) of or expressing existence [the *substantive* verb "to be"] *b*) of or used as a substantive —*n.* a noun or any word or group of words functioning as a noun —sub'stan·ti'val (-tī'v'l) *adj.*

sub·sta·tion (sub'stā'shən) *n.* a branch station

sub·sti·tute (sub'stə tōōt', -tyōōt') *n.* [ult. < L. *sub-*, under + *statuere*, to put] a person or thing acting or used in place of another —*vt., vi.* -tut'ed, -tut'ing to put, use, or serve in place of another —*adj.* being a substitute —sub'sti·tu'tion *n.*

sub·stra·tum (sub'strāt'əm) *n., pl.* -ta (-ə), -tums [see SUB- & STRATUM] a part, substance, etc. that lies beneath and supports another

sub'struc'ture (-struk'chər) *n.* a structure acting as a support, base, or foundation

sub·sume (səb sōōm') *vt.* -sumed', -sum'ing [< L. *sub-*, under + *sumere*, take] to include within a larger class, group, etc.

sub'teen' *n.* a child nearly a teen-ager

sub·ten'ant *n.* one who rents from a tenant

sub·ter·fuge (sub'tər fyōōj') *n.* [< L. *subter-*, below + *fugere*, flee] any plan, action, etc. used to hide one's objective, evade a difficult situation, etc.

sub·ter·ra·ne·an (sub'tə rā'nē ən) *adj.* [< L. *sub-*, under + *terra*, earth] 1. underground 2. secret

sub'ti'tle *n.* 1. a secondary title of a book, play, etc. 2. a line or lines as of dialogue shown on a movie or TV screen —*vt.* -ti'tled, -ti'tling to add a subtitle or subtitles to

sub·tle (sut''l) *adj.* -tler, -tlest [< L. *subtilis*, fine, thin] 1. thin; not dense 2. mentally keen 3. delicately skillful 4. crafty; sly 5. not obvious —sub'tle·ness *n.* —sub'tly *adv.*

sub'tle·ty *n.* 1. a subtle quality or condition 2. *pl.* -ties something subtle, as a fine distinction

sub·tract (səb trakt') *vt., vi.* [< L. *sub-*, under + *trahere*, to draw] to take away or deduct (a part from a whole) or (one quantity or number from another) —sub·tract'er *n.*

sub·trac·tion *n.* a subtracting or being subtracted; esp., the mathematical process of finding the difference between two numbers or quantities

sub·tra·hend (sub'trə hend') *n.* a number or quantity to be subtracted from another

sub·trop'i·cal *adj.* designating, of, or characteristic of regions bordering on the tropics

sub·trop'ics *n.pl.* subtropical regions

sub·urb (sub'ərb) *n.* [< L. *sub-*, under + *urbs*, town] 1. a district on the outskirts of a city, often separately incorporated 2. [*pl.*] a region of such districts (with *the*)

sub·ur·ban (sə bur'bən) *adj.* 1. of or living in a suburb or the suburbs 2. characteristic of the suburbs or suburbanites —sub·ur'ban·ize' (-īz') *vt., vi.* -ized', -iz'ing

sub·ur·ban·ite (-īt') *n.* a person living in a suburb

sub·ur·bi·a (sə bur'bē ə) *n.* the suburbs or suburbanites collectively; used to connote suburban values, attitudes, etc.

sub·ven·tion (səb ven'shən) *n.* [< L. *sub-*, under + *venire*, come] a grant of money; subsidy

sub·ver·sive (səb vur'siv) *adj.* tending or seeking to subvert —*n.* a person regarded as subversive —sub·ver'sive·ly *adv.* —sub·ver'sive·ness *n.*

sub·vert (səb vurt') *vt.* [< L. *sub-*, under + *vertere*, to turn] 1. to overthrow or destroy (something established)

2. to corrupt, as in morals —**sub·ver'sion** *n.* —**sub·vert'er** *n.*

sub·way (sub'wā') *n.* **1.** an underground way **2.** an underground, metropolitan electric railway

suc- *same as* SUB-: used before *c*

suc·ceed (sək sēd') *vi.* [< L. *sub-*, under + *cedere*, to go] **1.** to come next after another; follow, as in office **2.** to accomplish something planned or tried —*vt.* **1.** to follow into office, etc. **2.** to come after

suc·cess (sək ses') *n.* **1.** a favorable outcome **2.** the gaining of fame, wealth, etc. **3.** a successful person or thing

suc·cess'ful *adj.* **1.** turning out as was hoped for **2.** having gained wealth, fame, etc. —**suc·cess'ful·ly** *adv.* —**suc·cess'ful·ness** *n.*

suc·ces·sion (sək sesh'ən) *n.* **1.** a succeeding or coming after another **2.** the right to succeed to an office, etc. **3.** a number of persons or things coming one after another **4.** *a)* a series of heirs or rightful successors *b)* the order of such a series —**in succession** one after another

suc·ces'sive (-ses'iv) *adj.* coming one after another; consecutive —**suc·ces'sive·ly** *adv.*

suc·ces'sor *n.* one who follows or succeeds another, as to an office

suc·cinct (sək siŋkt') *adj.* [< L. *sub-*, under + *cingere*, to gird] clearly and briefly stated; terse —**suc·cinct'ly** *adv.* —**suc·cinct'ness** *n.*

suc·cor (suk'ər) *vt.* [< L. *sub-*, under + *currere*, to run] to help in time of need or distress —*n.* **1.** aid; relief **2.** one that succors Brit. sp. **suc'cour**

suc·co·tash (suk'ə tash') *n.* [< AmInd.] a dish of lima beans and corn kernels cooked together

suc·cu·lent (suk'yoo lənt) *adj.* [< L. *sucus*, juice] **1.** juicy **2.** interesting; not dry or dull **3.** having thick, fleshy tissues, as a cactus —**suc'cu·lence, suc'cu·len·cy** *n.* —**suc'cu·lent·ly** *adv.*

suc·cumb (sə kum') *vi.* [< L. *sub-*, under + *cumbere*, to lie] **1.** to give way (*to*); yield **2.** to die

such (such) *adj.* [OE. *swilc*] **1.** of the kind mentioned or implied **2.** of the same or a similar kind **3.** certain but not specified **4.** so extreme; so much, etc. [*such* fun!] —*adv.* to so great a degree —*pron.* such a one or ones —**as such 1.** as being what is indicated **2.** in itself —**such as 1.** for example **2.** like or similar to

such·like' *adj.* of such a kind; of similar kind —*pron.* persons or things of such a kind

suck (suk) *vt.* [OE. *sucan*] **1.** to draw (liquid) into the mouth with the lips and tongue **2.** to take in as if by sucking **3.** to suck liquid from (fruit, etc.) **4.** to hold (candy, etc.) in the mouth so that it dissolves **5.** to hold in the mouth and draw on (the thumb, etc.) —*vi.* **1.** to suck something **2.** to suck milk from the breast or udder —*n.* the act of sucking —**suck in 1.** to pull inward, as the abdomen **2.** [Slang] to trick; swindle

suck'er *n.* **1.** one that sucks **2.** a carplike freshwater fish **3.** a part used, as by the leech, for sucking or holding fast to something **4.** a shoot from the roots or stem of a plant **5.** a lollipop **6.** [Slang] one easily fooled or cheated

suck·le (suk'l) *vt.* **-led, -ling 1.** to give milk to from a breast or udder **2.** to nourish; foster —*vi.* to suck milk from its mother

suck'ling *n.* an unweaned child or young animal

Su·cre (sōō'kre) city in SC Bolivia; legal capital & seat of the judiciary (cf. LA PAZ): pop. 85,000

su·crose (sōō'krōs) *n.* [< Fr. *sucre*, sugar + (GLUC)OSE] a sugar found in sugar cane, sugar beets, etc.

suc·tion (suk'shən) *n.* [< L. *sugere*, to suck] **1.** a sucking **2.** production of a partial vacuum so that surrounding fluid, etc. is sucked in **3.** the force so created —*adj.* operating by suction

Su·dan (sōō dan') country in NE Africa: 967,500 sq. mi.; pop. 15,595,000; cap. Khartoum —**Su'da·nese'** (-də nēz') *adj., n., pl. -nese'*

sud·den (sud'n) *adj.* [ult. < L. *sub-*, under + *ire*, go] **1.** happening or coming unexpectedly **2.** abrupt **3.** done, coming, or taking place quickly —**all of a sudden** without warning; quickly —**sud'den·ly** *adv.* —**sud'den·ness** *n.*

suds (sudz) *n.pl.* [prob. < MDu. *sudse*, marsh water] **1.** soapy water **2.** foam, froth, or lather —**suds'y** *adj.*

sue (sōō) *vt., vi.* **sued, su'ing** [< L. *sequi*, follow] **1.** to appeal (*to*); petition **2.** to prosecute in a court in seeking redress of wrongs, etc. —**su'er** *n.*

suede, suède (swād) *n.* [< Fr. *gants de Suède*, Swedish gloves] **1.** tanned leather with the flesh side buffed into a nap **2.** a cloth like this

su·et (sōō'it) *n.* [< L. *sebum*, fat] hard fat from around the kidneys and loins of cattle and sheep: used in cooking and to make tallow —**su'et·y** *adj.*

Su·ez (sōō ez', sōō'ez) **1.** seaport in NE Egypt, on the Suez Canal: pop. 203,000 **2. Isthmus of,** strip of land in NE Egypt, connecting Asia & Africa

Suez Canal ship canal across the Isthmus of Suez, joining the Mediterranean & the Red seas

suf- *same as* SUB-: used before *f*

suf·fer (suf'ər) *vt.* [< L. *sub-*, under + *ferre*, to bear] **1.** to undergo or endure (pain, injury, loss, etc.) **2.** to undergo (any process) **3.** to allow; tolerate —*vi.* to undergo pain, harm, loss, a penalty, etc. —**suf'fer·a·ble** *adj.* —**suf'fer·er** *n.* —**suf'fer·ing** *n.*

suf'fer·ance *n.* **1.** capacity to endure pain, etc. **2.** consent, sanction, etc. implied by failure to prohibit

suf·fice (sə fīs') *vi.* **-ficed', -fic'ing** [< L. *sub-*, under + *facere*, make] to be enough

suf·fi·cien·cy (sə fish'ən sē) *n.* **1.** sufficient means, ability, or resources **2.** a being sufficient; adequacy

suf·fi'cient (-'nt) *adj.* as much as is needed; enough —**suf·fi'cient·ly** *adv.*

suf·fix (suf'iks) *n.* [< L. *sub-*, under + *figere*, fix] a syllable or syllables added at the end of a word or word base to alter its meaning, etc. (Ex.: *-ish* in *smallish*) —*vt.* (*also* sə fiks') to add as a suffix

suf·fo·cate (suf'ə kāt') *vt.* **-cat'ed, -cat'ing** [< L. *sub-*, under + *fauces*, throat] **1.** to kill by cutting off the supply of air for breathing **2.** to smother, suppress, etc. —*vi.* **1.** to die by being suffocated **2.** to be unable to breathe freely; choke, etc. —**suf'fo·cat'ing·ly** *adv.* —**suf'fo·ca'tion** *n.*

suf·fra·gan (suf'rə gən) *n.* [< L. *suffragari*, to support] **1.** a bishop assisting another bishop **2.** a bishop as a subordinate of his archbishop —*adj.* subordinate

suf·frage (suf'rij) *n.* [< L. *suffragium*] **1.** a vote or voting **2.** the right to vote; franchise

suf·fra·gette (suf'rə jet') *n.* a woman advocate of female suffrage

suf·fra·gist (suf'rə jist) *n.* one who believes in extending political suffrage, esp. to women

suf·fuse (sə fyōoz') *vt.* **-fused', -fus'ing** [< L. *sub-*, under + *fundere*, pour] to overspread, as with color, a liquid, light, etc. —**suf·fu'sion** *n.*

sug·ar (shoog'ər) *n.* [< Sans. *śarkarā*] any of a class of sweet, soluble, crystalline carbohydrates, as sucrose, glucose, fructose, etc.; specif., the sucrose extracted chiefly from sugar cane and sugar beets and used as a food —*vt.* **1.** to put sugar in or on **2.** to make seem less unpleasant —*vi.* **1.** to form sugar crystals **2.** to make maple sugar —**sug'ar·like'** *adj.*

sugar beet a beet having a white root, used as a source of common sugar

sugar cane a very tall tropical grass with jointed stems, cultivated as the main source of sugar

sug'ar·coat' *vt.* **1.** to coat with sugar **2.** to make seem less unpleasant

sugar diabetes *popular term for* DIABETES MELLITUS: see DIABETES

sug'ar·plum' (-plum') *n.* a round piece of sugary candy

sug'ar·y *adj.* **1.** of or containing sugar **2.** like sugar; sweet, granular, etc. **3.** too sweet; cloying

sug·gest (səg jest') *vt.* [< L. *sub-*, under + *gerere*, carry] **1.** to bring (a thought, etc.) to the mind for consideration **2.** to call to mind by association of ideas **3.** to propose as a possibility **4.** to imply; intimate —**sug·gest'er** *n.*

SUGAR CANE

sug·gest'i·ble (-jes'tə b'l) *adj.* easily influenced by suggestion —**sug·gest'i·bil'i·ty** *n.*

sug·ges'tion (-jes'chən) *n.* **1.** a suggesting or being suggested **2.** something suggested **3.** a faint hint; trace

sug·ges'tive *adj.* **1.** that suggests or tends to suggest ideas **2.** tending to suggest something considered improper or indecent —**sug·ges'tive·ly** *adv.* —**sug·ges'tive·ness** *n.*

su·i·cide (sōō'ə sīd') *n.* [L. *sui*, of oneself + -CIDE] **1.** the intentional killing of oneself **2.** ruin of one's interests through one's own actions **3.** one who commits suicide —**su'i·ci'dal** *adj.*

su·i ge·ne·ris (sōō'ē jen'ər is) [L., lit., of his (or her or its) own kind] altogether unique

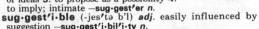

fat, āpe, cär; ten, ēven; is, bīte; gō, hôrn, tōol, look; oil, out; up, fur; thin, *then*; zh, leisure; ŋ, ring; ə for *a* in *ago*; ' as in *able* (ā'b'l); ë, Fr. coeur; ö, Fr. feu; Fr. mon; ü, Fr. duc; *r*, Fr. cri; kh, G. doch, ich. ‡ foreign; < derived from

suit (soōt) *n.* [< L. *sequi,* follow] **1.** a set of clothes; esp., a coat and trousers (or skirt) **2.** any of the four sets of playing cards (*spades, hearts, diamonds,* and *clubs*) **3.** action to secure justice in a court of law **4.** an act of suing, pleading, etc. —*vt.* **1.** to meet the needs of **2.** to make fit; adapt **3.** to please; satisfy —*vi.* to be suitable or convenient —**follow suit** to follow the example set —**suit oneself** to do as one pleases

suit′a·ble *adj.* right for a given purpose; appropriate —**suit′a·bil′i·ty** *n.* —**suit′a·bly** *adv.*

suit′case′ *n.* a flat, rectangular travel case that opens into two hinged compartments

suite (swēt) *n.* [Fr.: see SUIT] **1.** a group of attendants; retinue **2.** a unit of connected rooms **3.** (*occas.* soōt) a set of matched furniture for a room **4.** a musical composition made up of several movements

suit′ing *n.* cloth for making suits

suit·or (soōt′ər) *n.* **1.** one who sues, petitions, etc. **2.** a man who courts a woman

su·ki·ya·ki (soō′kē yä′kē) *n.* [Jpn.] a Japanese dish of thinly sliced meat and vegetables, cooked quickly

Suk·kot, Suk·koth (soo kōt′, sook′ōs) *n.* [Heb., lit., tabernacles] a Jewish fall festival commemorating the wandering of the Hebrews after the Exodus

sulf- *a combining form* meaning of or containing sulfur

sul·fa (sul′fə) *adj.* designating or of a family of drugs that are sulfonamides, used in combating certain bacterial infections

sul·fate (sul′fāt) *n.* a salt or ester of sulfuric acid —*vt.* **-fat·ed, -fat·ing** to treat with sulfuric acid or a sulfate

sul·fide (sul′fīd) *n.* a compound of sulfur with another element or a radical

sul·fon·a·mide (sul fän′ə mīd′, -mid) *n.* a compound containing the univalent radical $-SO_2NH_2$

sul·fur (sul′fər) *n.* [L. *sulphur*] a pale-yellow, nonmetallic chemical element: it burns with a blue flame and a stifling odor: symbol, S; at. wt., 32.064; at. no., 16

sulfur dioxide a heavy, colorless gas, SO_2, easily liquefied and used as a bleach, refrigerant, etc.

sul·fu·ric (sul fyoor′ik) *adj.* of or containing sulfur

sulfuric acid an oily, colorless, corrosive liquid, H_2SO_4, used in making explosives, fertilizers, etc.

sul·fu·rous (sul′fər əs) *adj.* **1.** (*usually* sul fyoor′əs) of or containing sulfur **2.** like burning sulfur in odor, color, etc.

sulk (sulk) *vi.* [< SULKY] to be sulky —*n.* **1.** a sulky mood or state **2.** a sulky person

sulk·y (sul′kē) *adj.* **-i·er, -i·est** [prob. < OE. *solcen,* idle] sullen; pouting; peevish —*n., pl.* **-ies** a light, two-wheeled carriage for one person —**sulk′i·ly** *adv.* —**sulk′i·ness** *n.*

sul·len (sul′ən) *adj.* [< L. *solus,* alone] **1.** silent and keeping to oneself because one feels angry, bitter, hurt, etc. **2.** gloomy; dismal —**sul′len·ly** *adv.* —**sul′len·ness** *n.*

Sul·li·van (sul′ə vən), Sir **Arthur S.** 1842–1900; Eng. composer: see Sir William GILBERT

sul·ly (sul′ē) *vt.* **-lied, -ly·ing** [prob. < OFr. *souiller*] to soil, stain, etc., now esp. by disgracing

sulph- *var., now esp. Brit., sp. of* SULF-

sul·phur (sul′fər) *n. var., now esp. Brit., sp. of* SULFUR

sul·tan (sul′t'n) *n.* [Fr. < Ar. *sultān*] a Muslim ruler; esp., [S-] formerly, the ruler of Turkey

sul·tan·a (sul tan′ə, -tä′nə) *n.* a sultan's wife, mother, sister, or daughter: also **sul′tan·ess** (-tən is)

sul·tan·ate (sul′t'n it, -āt′) *n.* the authority, office, reign, or dominion of a sultan

sul·try (sul′trē) *adj.* **-tri·er, -tri·est** [< SWELTER] **1.** oppressively hot and moist **2.** inflamed, as with passion —**sul′tri·ness** *n.*

sum (sum) *n.* [< L. *summus,* highest] **1.** an amount of money **2.** the whole amount **3.** gist; summary **4.** the result gotten by adding numbers or quantities **5.** a problem in arithmetic —*vt.* **summed, sum′ming 1.** to add up **2.** to summarize Usually with *up*

su·mac, su·mach (shoō′mak, soō′-) *n.* [Ar. *summāq*] any of various plants with compound leaves and cone-shaped clusters of hairy, red fruit

Su·ma·tra (soo mä′trə) large island of Indonesia —**Su·ma′tran** *adj., n.*

‡sum·ma cum lau·de (soom′ə koom lou′de, sum′ə kum lō′dē) [L.] with the greatest praise: phrase signifying graduation with the highest honors

sum·ma·rize (sum′ə rīz′) *vt.* **-rized′, -riz′ing** to make or be a summary of —**sum′ma·ri·za′tion** *n.*

sum·ma·ry (sum′ə rē) *adj.* [< L. *summa,* a sum] **1.** concise; condensed **2.** prompt and informal **3.** hasty and arbitrary —*n., pl.* **-ries** a brief account covering the main points; digest —**sum·mar·i·ly** (sə mer′ə lē, sum′ə rə lē) *adv.*

sum·ma·tion (sə mā′shən) *n.* **1.** a summing up, to find a total **2.** a total or aggregate **3.** a final summing up of arguments, as in a court trial

sum·mer (sum′ər) *n.* [OE. *sumor*] **1.** the warmest season of the year, following spring **2.** a period of growth, development, etc. —*adj.* of or for summer —*vi.* to pass the summer —**sum′mer·y** *adj.*

sum′mer·house′ *n.* an open structure in a garden, park, etc. providing a shady rest

sum′mer·time′ *n.* the season of summer

sum·mit (sum′it) *n.* [< L. *summus,* highest] **1.** the highest point; top **2.** the highest degree or state; acme **3.** the highest level of officialdom, involving heads of government **4.** a conference at this level

sum·mon (sum′ən) *vt.* [< L. *sub-,* secretly + *monere,* warn] **1.** to call together; order to convene **2.** to call or send for with authority **3.** to call forth; rouse [*summon* (up) strength] —**sum′mon·er** *n.*

sum·mons (-ənz) *n., pl.* **-mons·es** [see SUMMON] **1.** an order to come or do something **2.** *Law* an official order to appear in court, specif. as a defendant; also, the writ containing such an order

sump (sump) *n.* [ME. *sompe,* a swamp] a pit, cistern, cesspool, etc. for draining or collecting liquid

sump·tu·ous (sump′choo wəs) *adj.* [< L. *sumptus,* expense] **1.** costly; lavish **2.** magnificent, as in furnishings

sun (sun) *n.* [OE. *sunne*] **1.** the self-luminous, gaseous sphere about which the earth and other planets revolve: it furnishes light, heat, and energy for the solar system **2.** the heat or light of the sun **3.** any star that is the center of a planetary system —*vt., vi.* **sunned, sun′ning** to warm, dry, tan, bleach, etc. in the sunlight —**place in the sun** a prominent or favorable position —**sun′less** *adj.*

Sun. Sunday

sun bath exposure of the body to sunlight or a sunlamp

sun′bathe′ (-bā*th*′) *vi.* **-bathed′, -bath′ing** to take a sun bath —**sun′bath′er** *n.*

sun′beam′ *n.* a ray or beam of sunlight

Sun′belt′ *n.* that part of the U.S. comprising most of the States of the South and Southwest: also **Sun Belt**

sun′bon′net *n.* a bonnet with a large brim and back flap, to shade the face and neck from the sun

sun′burn′ (-burn′) *n.* inflammation of the skin from prolonged exposure to the sun or a sunlamp —*vi., vt.* **-burned′** or **-burnt′, -burn′ing** to give or get a sunburn

sun′burst′ (-burst′) *n.* a decoration, as a brooch, suggesting the sun and its rays

sun·dae (sun′dē, -dā) *n.* [prob. < SUNDAY] a serving of ice cream covered with syrup, fruit, nuts, etc.

Sun·day (sun′dē, -dā) *n.* [< OE. *sunnandæg,* day of the sun] the first day of the week, observed by most Christians as a day of worship or rest

Sunday school 1. a school giving religious instruction on Sunday **2.** its teachers and pupils

sun·der (sun′dər) *vt., vi.* [< OE. *sundor,* asunder] to break apart; separate

sun·di·al (sun′dī′əl, -dīl′) *n.* an instrument that shows time by the shadow of a pointer or gnomon cast by the sun on a dial marked in hours

sun′down′ *n. same as* SUNSET

sun′-dried′ *adj.* dried by the sun

sun-dries (sun′drēz) *n.pl.* sundry items

sun′dry (-drē) *adj.* [< OE. *sundor,* apart] various; miscellaneous

sun′fish′ *n., pl.:* see FISH **1.** any of several freshwater fishes including the black bass **2.** a large, sluggish, ocean fish with a thick body: in full **ocean sunfish**

SUNDIAL

sun′flow′er *n.* a tall plant having yellow, daisylike flowers containing edible seeds

sung (suŋ) *pp. & rare pt. of* SING

sun′glass′es *n.pl.* eyeglasses with special lenses to protect the eyes from the sun's glare

sunk (suŋk) *pp. & alt. pt. of* SINK

sunk·en (suŋk′ən) *adj.* **1.** submerged [a *sunken* ship] **2.** below the surface of the surrounding area [a *sunken* patio] **3.** hollow [*sunken* cheeks] **4.** dejected

sun′lamp′ *n.* an electric lamp that radiates ultraviolet rays like those of sunlight

sun′light′ *n.* the light of the sun

sun′lit′ *adj.* lighted by the sun

sun′ny (-ē) *adj.* **-ni·er, -ni·est 1.** bright with sunlight; full of sunshine **2.** bright and cheerful **3.** of or like the sun —**on the sunny side of** younger than (a specified age) —**sun′ni·ly** *adv.* —**sun′ni·ness** *n.*

sun·rise' (-rīz') *n.* **1.** the daily appearance of the sun above the eastern horizon **2.** the time of this **3.** the color of the sky at this time

sun'set' (-set') *n.* **1.** the daily disappearance of the sun below the western horizon **2.** the time of this **3.** the color of the sky at this time

sun'shine' *n.* **1.** the shining of the sun, or its light and heat **2.** cheerfulness, joy, etc., or a source of this —**sun'shin'y** *adj.*

sun'spot' *n.* any temporarily cooler region appearing from time to time as a dark spot on the sun

sun'stroke' *n.* heatstroke caused by excessive exposure to the sun —**sun'struck'** *adj.*

sun'tan' *n.* a darkened condition of fair skin caused by exposure to the sun or a sunlamp

sun'up' *n. same as* SUNRISE

Sun Valley resort city in SC Ida.

Sun Yat-sen (soon' yät'sen') 1866–1925; Chin. political & revolutionary leader

sup (sup) *vi.* **supped, sup'ping** [< OFr. *soupe*, soup] to have supper

sup. 1. superior **2.** supplement **3.** supply

su·per (soo'pər) *n.* [< SUPER-] **1.** *shortened form of:* a) SUPERNUMERARY b) SUPERINTENDENT **2.** [Colloq.] a product that is superior, extra-large, etc. —*adj.* **1.** outstanding; fine **2.** extreme or excessive

super- [L. < *super*, above] *a prefix meaning:* **1.** over, above *[superstructure]* **2.** superior to *[supervisor]* **3.** surpassing *[superabundant]* **4.** greater than others of its kind *[supermarket]* **5.** extra, additional *[supertax]*

su·per·a·bun·dant (soo'pər ə bun'dənt) *adj.* overly abundant —**su'per·a·bun'dance** *n.* —**su'per·a·bun'dant·ly** *adv.*

su'per·an'nu·at'ed (-an'yoo wāt'id) *adj.* [< L. *super*, beyond + *annus*, year] **1.** too old for further work **2.** retired because of old age or infirmity **3.** obsolete; old-fashioned

su·perb' (soo purb', soo-) *adj.* [< L. *super*, above] **1.** noble; majestic **2.** rich; splendid **3.** excellent —**su·perb'ly** *adv.* —**su·perb'ness** *n.*

su·per·charge (soo'pər chärj') *vt.* **-charged', -charg'ing** to increase the power of (an engine) as with a device (**supercharger**) that increases the supply of air or fuel mixture to the cylinders

su·per·cil·i·ous (soo'pər sil'ē əs) *adj.* [< L. *super-*, above + *cilium*, eyelid (with reference to raised brows)] showing pride or contempt; haughty —**su'per·cil'i·ous·ly** *adv.*

su·per·e·go (soo'pər ē'gō) *n., pl.* **-gos** *Psychoanalysis* that part of the psyche which is critical of the self or ego and enforces moral standards

su'per·er'o·ga'tion (-er'ə gā'shən) *n.* [< LL. *super*, above + *erogare*, pay out] the act of doing more than is required or expected

su'per·e·rog'a·to'ry (-i räg'ə tôr'ē) *adj.* **1.** done beyond the degree required or expected **2.** superfluous

su'per·fi'cial (-fish'əl) *adj.* [< L. *super-*, above + *facies*, face] **1.** of or being on the surface **2.** concerned with and understanding only the obvious; shallow **3.** quick and cursory **4.** merely apparent —**su'per·fi'ci·al'i·ty** (-ē al'ə tē) *n., pl.* **-ties** —**su'per·fi'cial·ly** *adv.*

su·per·flu·ous (soo purr'floo was) *adj.* [< L. *super-*, above + *fluere*, to flow] **1.** being more than is needed or wanted; excessive **2.** unnecessary —**su·per·flu·i·ty** (soo'pər floo'ə tē) *n., pl.* **-ties** —**su·per'flu·ous·ly** *adv.*

su·per·heat (soo'pər hēt') *vt.* **1.** to overheat **2.** to heat (a liquid) above its boiling point without its vaporizing **3.** to heat (steam) beyond its saturation point, so that a drop in temperature will not cause it to turn back to water

su'per·high'way' *n. same as* EXPRESSWAY

su'per·hu'man *adj.* **1.** having a nature above that of man; divine **2.** greater than normal for a human being —**su'per·hu'man·ly** *adv.*

su'per·im·pose' *vt.* **-posed', -pos'ing 1.** to put on top of something else **2.** to add as a dominant feature

su'per·in·tend' *vt.* to act as superintendent of; supervise —**su'per·in·tend'ence** *n.*

su'per·in·tend'ent *n.* [see SUPER- & INTEND] **1.** a person in charge of a department, institution, etc. **2.** the custodian of a building, etc.

Su·pe·ri·or (sə pir'ē ər, soo-), **Lake** largest & westernmost of the Great Lakes, between Mich. & Ontario, Canada

su·pe·ri·or (sə pir'ē ər, soo-) *adj.* [< L. *superus*, that is above] **1.** higher in space **2.** higher in order, status, quality, etc. (with *to*) **3.** above average; excellent **4.** haughty

—*n.* **1.** a superior person or thing **2.** the head of a religious community —**su·pe'ri·or'i·ty** (-ôr'ə tē) *n.*

superl. superlative

su·per·la·tive (sə pur'lə tiv, soo-) *adj.* [< L. *super-*, above + *latus*, pp. of *ferre*, carry] **1.** excelling all others; supreme **2.** excessive **3.** *Gram.* designating the extreme degree of comparison of adjectives and adverbs —*n.* **1.** the highest degree; acme **2.** *Gram.* the superlative degree —**su·per'la·tive·ly** *adv.*

su·per·man (soo'pər man') *n., pl.* **-men'** an apparently superhuman man

su'per·mar'ket *n.* a large, self-service, retail food store, often one of a chain

su·per·nal (soo pur'n'l) *adj.* [< L. *supernus*, upper] celestial, heavenly, or divine —**su·per'nal·ly** *adv.*

su·per·nat·u·ral (soo'pər nach'ər əl) *adj.* existing outside man's normal experience or the known laws of nature; specif., of or involving God or a god, or ghosts, the occult, etc. —**the supernatural** supernatural beings, forces, etc. —**su'per·nat'u·ral·ism** *n.* —**su'per·nat'u·ral·ist** *n., adj.* —**su'per·nat'u·ral·ly** *adv.*

su'per·no'va (-nō'və) *n., pl.* **-vae** (-vē), **-vas** [see SUPER- & NOVA] *Astron.* an extremely bright nova that suddenly increases greatly in brightness

su'per·nu'mer·ar'y (-noo'mə rer'ē, -nyoo'-) *adj.* [< L. *super-*, above + *numerus*, number] extra or superfluous —*n., pl.* **-ies** **1.** an extra person or thing **2.** an actor with a small, nonspeaking part, as in a mob scene

su'per·pose' (-pōz') *vt.* **-posed', -pos'ing** [see SUPER- & POSE] to lay or place on, over, or above something else

su·per·pow·er (soo'pər pou'ər) *n.* any of the few most powerful nations of the world

su·per·sat·u·rate (soo'pər sach'ə rāt') *vt.* **-rat'ed, -rat'ing** to saturate beyond the normal point for the given temperature —**su'per·sat'u·ra'tion** *n.*

su'per·scribe' (-skrīb') *vt.* **-scribed', -scrib'ing** [< L. *super-*, above + *scribere*, write] to write (something) on the top or outer surface of —**su'per·scrip'tion** *n.*

su·per·script (soo'pər skript') *adj.* written above —*n.* a figure, letter, or symbol written above and to the side of another (Ex.: 2 in x²)

su·per·sede (soo'pər sēd') *vt.* **-sed'ed, -sed'ing** [< L. *super-*, above + *sedere*, sit] **1.** to set aside as inferior or obsolete; displace **2.** to replace, succeed, or supplant —**su'per·sed'ence** *n.*

su'per·sen'si·tive *adj.* highly sensitive or too sensitive

su'per·son'ic (-sän'ik) *adj.* [< SUPER + L. *sonus*, sound] **1.** designating, of, or moving at a speed greater than sound **2.** *same as* ULTRASONIC —**su'per·son'i·cal·ly** *adv.*

su'per·son'ics *n.pl.* [*with sing v.*] the science dealing with supersonic phenomena

su'per·star' *n.* a prominent performer, as in sports, considered to have exceptional skill and talent

su·per·sti·tion (soo'pər stish'ən) *n.* [< L. *super-*, over + *stare*, to stand] **1.** any belief, based on fear or ignorance, that is not in accord with known facts or rational thought, esp. such a belief in charms, omens, the supernatural, etc. **2.** any action or practice based on such a belief —**su'per·sti'tious** *adj.* —**su'per·sti'tious·ly** *adv.*

su'per·struc'ture *n.* **1.** a structure built on top of another, as above the main deck of a ship **2.** that part of a building above the foundation

su·per·vene (soo'pər vēn') *vi.* **-vened', -ven'ing** [< L. *super-*, over + *venire*, come] to come or happen as something added or unexpected —**su'per·ven'tion** (-ven'shən) *n.*

su·per·vise (soo'pər vīz') *vt., vi.* **-vised', -vis'ing** [< L. *super-*, over + *videre*, see] to oversee or direct (work, workers, a project, etc.); superintend —**su'per·vi'sion** (-vizh'ən) *n.* —**su'per·vi'sor** *n.* —**su'per·vi'so·ry** *adj.*

su·pine (soo pīn') *adj.* [L. *supinus*] **1.** lying on the back, face upward **2.** showing no concern or doing nothing about matters —**su·pine'ly** *adv.*

supp., suppl. 1. supplement **2.** supplementary

sup·per (sup'ər) *n.* [OFr. *souper*] **1.** an evening meal, as a dinner, or a late, light meal **2.** an evening social at which a meal is served —**sup'per·less** *adj.*

sup·plant (sə plant') *vt.* [< L. *sub-*, under + *planta*, sole of the foot] **1.** to take the place of, esp. by force or plotting **2.** to remove and replace with something else —**sup·plant'er** *n.*

sup·ple (sup''l) *adj.* [< L. *supplex*, humble] **1.** bending easily; flexible **2.** lithe; limber **3.** easily influenced; adaptable —**sup'ple·ly** *adv.* —**sup'ple·ness** *n.*

sup·ple·ment (sup′lə mənt) *n.* [see SUPPLY[1]] **1.** something added, esp. to make up for a lack **2.** a section of additional material in a book, newspaper, etc. **3.** *Math.* the number of degrees added to an angle or arc to make it equal 180 degrees —*vt.* (-ment′) to provide a supplement to —**sup′ple·men′ta·ry** (-men′tər ē), **sup′ple·men′tal** *adj.* —**sup′ple·men·ta′tion** *n.*

supplementary angle either of two angles that together form 180 degrees

sup·pli·ant (sup′lē ənt) *n.* one who supplicates —*adj.* supplicating Also **sup′pli·cant** (-lə kənt)

sup·pli·cate (sup′lə kāt′) *vt., vi.* -cat′ed, -cat′ing [< L. *sub-*, under + *plicare*, to fold] **1.** to ask for (something) humbly **2.** to make a humble request (of) —**sup′pli·ca′tion** *n.* —**sup′pli·ca′tor** *n.* —**sup′pli·ca·to′ry** (-kə tôr′ē) *adj.*

B [diagram] C [diagram] D

SUPPLEMENTARY ANGLES (BCA and DCB)

sup·ply[1] (sə plī′) *vt.* -plied′, -ply′ing [< L. *sub-*, under + *plere*, fill] **1.** to furnish; provide **2.** to meet the needs of **3.** to make up for (a deficiency, etc.) —*n., pl.* -plies **1.** a supplying **2.** an amount available for use or sale; stock **3.** [*pl.*] materials, provisions, etc. for an army, business, etc. —*adj.* having to do with a supply —**sup·pli′er** *n.*

sup·ply[2] (sup′lē) *adv.* in a supple manner; supplely

sup·port (sə pôrt′) *vt.* [< L. *sub-*, under + *portare*, carry] **1.** to carry the weight of; hold up **2.** to give courage or faith to **3.** to give approval to; advocate; uphold **4.** to maintain (a person, institution, etc.) **5.** to help prove or vindicate **6.** to bear; endure **7.** to keep up; maintain **8.** to act a subordinate role with (a star) in a play —*n.* **1.** a supporting or being supported **2.** a person or thing that supports **3.** a means of support —**sup·port′a·ble** *adj.*

sup·port′er *n.* **1.** one who supports **2.** a thing that supports; esp., an elastic device to support some part of the body

sup·pose (sə pōz′) *vt.* -posed′, -pos′ing [< L. *sub-*, under + *ponare*, put] **1.** to assume to be true, as for the sake of argument [*suppose* A equals B] **2.** to believe, think, guess, etc. **3.** to presuppose **4.** to consider as a possibility [*suppose* I go] **5.** to expect: always in the passive [she's *supposed* to telephone] —*vi.* to conjecture —**sup·pos′a·ble** *adj.*

sup·posed′ *adj.* **1.** regarded as true, possible, etc., without actual knowledge **2.** merely imagined —**sup·pos′ed·ly** *adv.*

sup·po·si·tion (sup′ə zish′ən) *n.* **1.** a supposing **2.** something supposed; assumption —**sup′po·si′tion·al** *adj.* —**sup′po·si′tion·al·ly** *adv.*

sup·pos·i·to·ry (sə päz′ə tôr′ē) *n., pl.* -ries [< L. *sub-*, under + *ponere*, put] a small piece of medicated substance inserted into the rectum, vagina, etc., where it melts

sup·press (sə pres′) *vt.* [< L. *sub-*, under + *premere*, to press] **1.** to put down by force; quell **2.** to keep from being known, published, etc. **3.** to keep back; restrain **4.** *Electronics, Radio,* etc. to eliminate (an unwanted signal, etc.) **5.** *Psychiatry* to consciously dismiss (unacceptable impulses, etc.) from the mind —**sup·press′i·ble** *adj.* —**sup·pres′sion** (-presh′ən) *n.* —**sup·pres′sor** *n.*

sup·pu·rate (sup′yoo rāt′) *vi.* -rat′ed, -rat′ing [< L. *sub-*, under + *pus*, pus] to form or discharge pus —**sup·pu·ra′tion** *n.* —**sup′pu·ra′tive** *adj.*

su·pra·re·nal (soo′prə rē′n'l) *adj.* [< L. *supra*, above + RENAL] on or above the kidney, as an adrenal gland —*n.* an adrenal gland

su·prem·a·cist (sə prem′ə sist, soo-) *n.* one who believes in the supremacy of a particular group

su·prem·a·cy (sə prem′ə sē, soo-) *n., pl.* -cies **1.** the state or quality of being supreme **2.** supreme power or authority

su·preme (sə prēm′, soo-) *adj.* [< L. *superus*, that is above] **1.** highest in rank, power, etc. **2.** highest in quality, achievement, etc. **3.** highest in degree **4.** final; ultimate —**su·preme′ly** *adv.*

Supreme Being God

Supreme Court 1. the highest Federal court, consisting of nine judges **2.** the highest court in most States

Supreme Soviet the parliament of the Soviet Union

Supt., supt. Superintendent

sur-[1] [< L. *super*, over] *a prefix meaning* over, upon, above, beyond

sur-[2] *same as* SUB-: used before *r*

Su·ra·ba·ja (soo′rä bä′yä) seaport in NE Java, Indonesia: pop. 1,008,000

su·rah (soor′ə) *n.* [< *Surat,* seaport in India] a soft, twilled fabric of silk or rayon

sur·cease (sur′sēs) *n.* [< L. *supersedere,* refrain from] end; cessation

sur·charge (sur chärj′) *vt.* -charged′, -charg′ing **1.** to overcharge **2.** to overload **3.** to mark (a postage stamp) with a surcharge —*n.* (sur′chärj) **1.** an additional charge **2.** an overcharge **3.** a new face value printed over the old on a postage stamp

sur·cin·gle (sur′sin′g'l) *n.* [< MFr. *sur-,* over + L. *cingulum,* a belt] a strap passed around a horse's body to bind on a saddle, pack, etc.

sur·coat (sur′kōt′) *n.* [< MFr.] an outer coat, esp. a short one

sure (shoor) *adj.* sur′er, sur′est [< L. *securus*] **1.** that will not fail; reliable [a *sure* method] **2.** that cannot be doubted, questioned, etc. **3.** having no doubt; confident [*sure* of one's facts] **4.** bound to do or happen [a *sure* defeat] **5.** bound to do, etc. [*sure* to lose] **6.** never missing [a *sure* aim] —*adv.* [Colloq.] surely —**for sure** certain(ly) —**make sure** to be or cause to be certain —**sure enough** [Colloq.] without doubt —**to be sure** surely; certainly —**sure′ness** *n.*

sure′-foot′ed *adj.* not likely to stumble, fall, or err —**sure′-foot′ed·ly** *adv.*

sure′ly *adv.* **1.** with confidence **2.** without a doubt; certainly

sur·e·ty (shoor′ə tē, shoor′tē) *n., pl.* -ties **1.** a being sure **2.** something sure; certainty **3.** something that makes sure, protects, etc. **4.** one who makes himself responsible for another; specif., *Law* one who makes himself liable for another's debts, etc. —**sur′e·ty·ship′** *n.*

surf (surf) *n.* [prob. < SOUGH] the waves of the sea breaking on the shore or a reef —*vi.* to engage in the sport of surfing —**surf′er** *n.*

sur·face (sur′fis) *n.* [< Fr. *sur-,* over + *face,* a face] **1.** *a)* the exterior of an object *b)* any of the faces of a solid **2.** superficial features, as of a personality **3.** *Geom.* an extent having length and breadth, but no thickness —*adj.* **1.** of, on, or at the surface **2.** on land or sea, rather than in the air or under water **3.** superficial —*vt.* -faced, -fac·ing **1.** to give a specified kind of surface to **2.** to bring (a submarine, etc.) to the surface of the water —*vi.* **1.** to rise to the surface of the water **2.** to appear, esp. after being concealed

surf′board′ *n.* a long, narrow board used in the sport of surfing —**surf′board′er** *n.*

surf′-cast′ (-kast′, -cast′ing) to fish by casting into the ocean surf from or near the shore

sur·feit (sur′fit) *n.* [< OFr. < *sur-,* over + *faire,* make] **1.** too great an amount or supply **2.** overindulgence, esp. in food or drink **3.** disgust, nausea, etc. resulting from this —*vt.* to feed or supply to excess

surf·ing (sur′fin) *n.* the sport of riding in toward shore on the crest of a wave, esp. on a surfboard

surge (surj) *n.* [prob. < L. *surgere,* to rise] **1.** a large wave of water, or the swelling or rushing motion of such a wave **2.** any sudden strong rush, as of energy, electric power, etc. —*vi.* surged, surg′ing to move in a surge

sur·geon (sur′jən) *n.* a doctor who specializes in surgery

sur·ger·y (sur′jər ē) *n., pl.* -ies [ult. < Gr. *cheir,* the hand + *ergein,* to work] **1.** the treatment of disease, injury, etc. by manual or instrumental operations, as the removal of diseased parts by cutting **2.** the branch of medicine dealing with this **3.** the operating room of a surgeon or hospital

sur·gi·cal (-ji k'l) *adj.* **1.** of surgeons or surgery **2.** resulting from surgery —**sur′gi·cal·ly** *adv.*

Sur·i·nam (soor′i näm′) country on the NE coast of S. America: 55,144 sq. mi.; pop. 385,000

sur·ly (sur′lē) *adj.* -li·er, -li·est [earlier *sirly,* imperious < SIR] bad-tempered; sullenly rude; uncivil —**sur′li·ly** *adv.* —**sur′li·ness** *n.*

sur·mise (sər mīz′) *n.* [< OFr. *sur-,* upon + *metre,* put] a conjecture; guess —*vt., vi.* -mised′, -mis′ing to imagine or infer (something) without conclusive evidence; guess

sur·mount (sər mount′) *vt.* [see SUR-[1] & MOUNT[2]] **1.** to overcome (a difficulty) **2.** to be or rise above **3.** to climb up and across (a height, etc.) —**sur·mount′a·ble** *adj.*

sur·name (sur′nām′) *n.* [< OFr. *sur-,* over + *nom,* name] **1.** the family name; last name **2.** an epithet added to a person's name (Ex.: Ivan *the Terrible*) —*vt.* -named′, -nam′ing to give a surname to

sur·pass (sər pas′) *vt.* [< OFr. *sur-,* over + *passer,* to PASS] **1.** to be better than; excel **2.** to exceed in quantity, degree, etc. **3.** to go beyond the limit, capacity, etc. of —**sur·pass′ing** *adj.*

sur·plice (sur'plis) *n.* [ult. < L. *super-*, above + *pel-liceum*, fur robe] a loose, white, wide-sleeved outer vestment worn by the clergy and choir in some churches —**sur'pliced** *adj.*

sur·plus (sur'plus, -pləs) *n.* [OFr. < *sur-*, above + L. *plus*, more] 1. a quantity over and above what is needed or used; excess 2. the excess of the assets of a business over its liabilities —*adj.* forming a surplus; excess —**sur'plus·age** *n.*

SURPLICE

sur·prise (sər prīz') *vt.* -**prised'**, -**pris'ing** [< OFr. *sur-*, above + *prendre*, take] 1. to come upon suddenly or unexpectedly; take unawares 2. to attack without warning 3. to cause to feel astonishment by being unexpected 4. to present (someone) unexpectedly with a gift, etc. —*n.* 1. a being surprised; astonishment 2. something that surprises —**sur·pris'ing** *adj.* —**sur·pris'ing·ly** *adv.*

sur·re·al·ism (sə rē'ə liz'm) *n.* [< Fr. *sur-*, above + *réalisme*, REALISM] a modern movement in art and literature, trying to portray the workings of the subconscious mind —**sur·re'al·ist** *adj., n.* —**sur·re'al·is'tic** *adj.* —**sur·re'al·is'ti·cal·ly** *adv.*

sur·ren·der (sə ren'dər) *vt.* [< MFr. *sur-*, up + *rendre*, RENDER] 1. to give up possession of; yield to another on compulsion 2. to give up or abandon —*vi.* to give oneself up, esp. as a prisoner —*n.* the act of surrendering

sur·rep·ti·tious (sur'əp tish'əs) *adj.* [< L. *sub-*, under + *rapere*, to seize] done, got, made, acting, etc. in a secret, stealthy way —**sur'rep·ti'tious·ly** *adv.*

sur·rey (sur'ē) *n., pl.* -**reys** [< *Surrey*, county in England] a light, four-wheeled carriage with two seats and usually a flat top

sur·ro·gate (sur'ə gāt') *n.* [< L. *sub-*, in place of + *rogare*, to elect] 1. a deputy or substitute for another person 2. in some States, probate court, or a judge of this court —*vt.* -**gat'ed**, -**gat'ing** to put in another's place as a substitute or deputy

sur·round (sə round') *vt.* [< L. *super-*, over + *undare*, to rise] 1. to encircle on all or nearly all sides 2. to cut off (a military unit, etc.) from communication or retreat by encircling

sur·round'ing *n.* that which surrounds; esp., [*pl.*] the things, conditions, etc. that surround a person or thing; environment —*adj.* that surrounds

sur·tax (sur'taks) *n.* an extra tax on something already taxed —*vt.* (*also* sur'taks') to levy a surtax on

sur·veil·lance (sər vā'ləns, -vāl'yəns) *n.* [Fr. < *sur-*, over + *veiller*, to watch] 1. watch kept over a person, esp. a suspect 2. supervision

sur·vey (sər vā'; *for n.* sur'vā) *vt.* [< OFr. *sur-*, over + *veoir*, see] 1. to examine or consider in detail or comprehensively 2. to determine the location, form, or boundaries of (a tract of land) by the use of geometry and trigonometry —*n., pl.* -**veys** 1. a detailed study made by gathering and analyzing information 2. a comprehensive study or examination 3. the process of surveying a tract of land 4. a plan or written description of the area surveyed

sur·vey'ing *n.* 1. the act of one who surveys 2. the science of surveying land

sur·vey'or *n.* one who surveys, esp. one whose work is surveying land

sur·viv·al (sər vī'v'l) *n.* 1. the act or fact of surviving 2. someone or something that survives, esp. an ancient belief, custom, usage, etc.

sur·vive (sər vīv') *vt.* -**vived'**, -**viv'ing** [< L. *super-*, above + *vivere*, to live] to remain alive or in existence after —*vi.* to continue living or existing —**sur·vi'vor** *n.*

sus·cep·ti·ble (sə sep'tə b'l) *adj.* [< L. *sub-*, under + *capere*, take] easily affected emotionally; having sensitive feelings —**susceptible of** admitting; allowing [*testimony susceptible of* error] —**susceptible to** easily influenced or affected by —**sus·cep'ti·bil'i·ty** *n.* —**sus·cep'ti·bly** *adv.*

su·shi (sōō'shē) *n.* [Jpn.] a Japanese dish of raw fish wrapped about cakes of cold cooked rice

sus·pect (sə spekt') *vt.* [< L. *sub-*, under + *spicere*, to look] 1. to believe to be guilty on little or no evidence 2. to believe to be bad, wrong, etc.; distrust 3. to think likely; suppose —*vi.* to be suspicious —*adj.* (*usually* sus'-pekt) suspected —*n.* (sus'pekt) one suspected, esp. of a crime

sus·pend (sə spend') *vt.* [< L. *sub-*, under + *pendere*, hang] 1. to exclude for a time from a position, school, team, etc. as a punishment 2. to make inoperative for a time 3. to hold back (judgment, a sentence, etc.) 4. to hang by a support from above 5. to hold (dust in the air, etc.) in suspension 6. to keep in suspense —*vi.* 1. to stop temporarily 2. to be suspended; hang

sus·pend·ers (sə spen'dərz) *n.pl.* 1. a pair of straps passed over the shoulders to support the trousers 2. [Brit.] garters

sus·pense (sə spens') *n.* [< L. *suspendere*, SUSPEND] 1. the state of being uncertain or tense as to outcome 2. excitement that builds as a climax nears, as in a story, play, etc.

sus·pen·sion (sə spen'shən) *n.* 1. a suspending or being suspended; specif., *a*) a temporary removal from office, school, etc. *b*) a stoppage of payment, etc. *c*) a holding back of a judgment, etc. 2. a supporting device upon or from which something is suspended 3. the system of springs, etc. supporting a vehicle upon its undercarriage 4. the condition of a solid whose particles are dispersed through a fluid but not dissolved in it 5. a substance in this condition 6. *Music* the holding back of one or more tones in a chord while the others progress, creating a temporary dissonance

suspension bridge a bridge suspended from cables anchored at either end and supported by towers at intervals

sus·pen'sive (-siv) *adj.* 1. that suspends or temporarily stops something 2. undecided 3. of or in suspense

sus·pen'so·ry (-sə rē) *adj.* 1. suspending, supporting, etc. 2. suspending or delaying, esp. so as to leave something undecided —*n., pl.* -**ries** a suspensory muscle, bandage, support, etc.

SUSPENSION BRIDGE

sus·pi·cion (sə spish'ən) *n.* [< L. *suspicere*, to SUSPECT] 1. a suspecting or being suspected 2. the feeling or state of mind of one who suspects 3. a very small amount; trace —*vt.* [Dial.] to suspect —**above suspicion** not to be suspected; honorable —**under suspicion** suspected

sus·pi'cious *adj.* 1. arousing or likely to arouse suspicion 2. showing or feeling suspicion —**sus·pi'cious·ly** *adv.* —**sus·pi'cious·ness** *n.*

Sus·que·han·na (sus'kwi han'ə) river flowing from central N.Y. through Pa. & Md. into Chesapeake Bay: 444 mi.

sus·tain (sə stān') *vt.* [< L. *sub-*, under + *tenere*, hold] 1. to keep in existence; maintain or prolong [*sustained efforts*] 2. to provide for the support of; specif., to provide nourishment for 3. to support; carry the weight of 4. to comfort; encourage 5. to endure; withstand 6. to suffer (an injury, loss, etc.) 7. to uphold the validity of [*to sustain* a verdict] 8. to confirm; corroborate —**sus·tain'a·ble** *adj.*

sus·tain'ing program any radio or TV program paid for by a station or network, not by a commercial sponsor

sus·te·nance (sus'ti nəns) *n.* 1. a sustaining or being sustained 2. means of livelihood 3. that which sustains life; food

sut·ler (sut'lər) *n.* [< ModDu. *soeteler*] formerly, one following an army to sell food, liquor, etc. to its soldiers

su·ture (sōō'chər) *n.* [< L. *suere*, sew] 1. the line of junction of two bones, esp. of the skull 2. *a*) the stitching together of the two edges of a wound or incision *b*) any of the stitches of gut, wire, etc. so made —*vt.* -**tured**, -**tur·ing** to join together as with sutures

Su·wan·nee (sə wôn'ē, swô'nē) river flowing from S Ga. across N Fla. into the Gulf of Mexico

su·ze·rain (sōō'zə rin, -rān') *n.* [Fr. < *sus*, above + ending of *souverain*, SOVEREIGN] 1. a feudal lord 2. a state in its relation to another over which it has political control —**su'ze·rain·ty** *n., pl.* -**ties**

svelte (svelt, sfelt) *adj.* [Fr.] 1. slender and graceful 2. suave, polished, etc.

Sverd·lovsk (sferd lôfsk') city in western R.S.F.S.R., in the Ural Mountains: pop. 1,026,000

SW, S.W., s.w. 1. southwest 2. southwestern

Sw. 1. Sweden 2. Swedish

---

fat, āpe, cär; ten, ēven; is, bīte; gō, hôrn, tōōl, look; oil, out; up, fur; thin, then; zh, leisure; ŋ, ring; ə for *a* in *ago*; ' as in *able* (ā'b'l); ë, Fr. coeur; ö, Fr. feu; Fr. mon; ü, Fr. duc; r, Fr. cri; kh, G. doch, ich. ‡ foreign; < derived from

swab (swäb) *n.* [< ModDu. *zwabben,* do dirty work] **1.** a mop for scrubbing **2.** a small piece of cotton, etc. used to medicate or clean the throat, mouth, etc. —*vt.* **swabbed, swab'bing** to use a swab on

swad·dle (swäd'l) *vt.* **-dled, -dling** [OE. *swethel*] to wrap (a newborn baby) in long, narrow bands of cloth (**swaddling clothes** or **bands**)

swag (swag) *vi.* **swagged, swag'ging** [prob. < Norw.] **1.** to sway or lurch **2.** to sag —*n.* **1.** a swaying or lurching **2.** a valance, garland, etc. hanging decoratively in a loop **3.** [Slang] loot; plunder

swage (swāj) *n.* [OFr. *souage*] a tool for shaping metal by hammering —*vt.* **swaged, swag'ing** to shape, etc. with a swage

swag·ger (swag'ər) *vi.* [prob. < Norw. *svagga,* to sway] **1.** to walk with a bold, arrogant stride; strut **2.** to boast, brag, or show off in a loud, superior manner —*n.* a swaggering walk or manner

Swa·hi·li (swä hē'lē) *n.* **1.** *pl.* **-lis, -li** any of a Bantu people of Zanzibar and the nearby mainland **2.** their Bantu language, used as a lingua franca in E and C Africa

swain (swān) *n.* [ON. *sveinn,* boy] [Archaic] a young man who is courting or wooing; suitor

swal·low[1] (swäl'ō) *n.* [OE. *swealwe*] any of a group of small, swift-flying birds with long, pointed wings and a forked tail

swal·low[2] (swäl'ō) *vt.* [OE. *swelgan*] **1.** to pass (food, etc.) from the mouth into the stomach **2.** to take in; engulf (often with *up*) **3.** to take back (words said) **4.** to put up with [to *swallow* insults] **5.** to hold back; suppress [to *swallow* one's pride] **6.** [Colloq.] to accept as true without question —*vi.* to move the muscles of the throat as in swallowing something —*n.* **1.** the act of swallowing **2.** the amount swallowed at one time

swal'low·tail' (-tāl') *n.* **1.** some-   BARN SWALLOW thing having a forked shape like a swallow's tail **2.** a butterfly that has taillike points on the hind wings

swal'low-tailed' coat (-tāld') a man's full-dress coat, with long tapering tails at the back

swam (swam) *pt. of* SWIM

swa·mi (swä'mē) *n., pl.* **-mis** [< Hindi < Sans. *svāmin,* a lord] a Hindu religious teacher, pundit, or seer

swamp (swämp, swômp) *n.* [prob. < LowG.] a piece of wet, spongy land; bog; marsh: also **swamp'land'** —*vt.* **1.** to plunge in a swamp, water, etc. **2.** to flood as with water **3.** to overwhelm [swamped by debts] **4.** to sink (a boat) by filling with water —**swamp'i·ness** *n.* —**swamp'y** *adj.* **-i·er, -i·est**

swamp buggy an automotive vehicle for traveling over swampy land, often amphibious

swamp fever *same as* MALARIA

swan (swän, swôn) *n.* [OE.] a large, web-footed water bird, usually white, with a long, graceful neck

swan dive a forward dive in which the legs are held straight and together, the back is arched, and the arms are stretched out to the sides

Swa·nee (swô'nē, swä'-) *same as* SUWANNEE

swank (swaŋk) *n.* [akin to OE. *swancor,* supple: with idea of swaggering walk] [Colloq.] stylish display or showiness in dress, etc. —*adj.* [Colloq.] stylish in a showy way: also **swank'y, -i·er, -i·est**

swan's'-down' *n.* **1.** the soft fine underfeathers, or down, of the swan, used for trimming clothes, etc. **2.** a soft, thick flannel

swan song [after the song supposedly sung by a dying swan] the last act or final work of a person

swap (swäp, swôp) *n., vt., vi.* **swapped, swap'ping** [ME. *swappen,* to strike: hands were struck to conclude a bargain] [Colloq.] exchange, trade, or barter

sward (swôrd) *n.* [< OE. *sweard,* skin] turf; sod

swarm (swôrm) *n.* [OE. *swearm*] **1.** a large number of bees, with a queen, leaving a hive to start a new colony **2.** a colony of bees in a hive **3.** a moving mass or crowd —*vi.* **1.** to fly off in a swarm, as bees do **2.** to move, be present, etc. in large numbers **3.** to be filled or crowded —*vt.* to crowd; throng

swart (swôrt) *adj. same as* SWARTHY

swarth·y (swôr'thē, -thē) *adj.* **-i·er, -i·est** [< OE. *sweart*] having a dark skin —**swarth'i·ness** *n.*

swash (swäsh, swôsh) *vi.* [echoic] **1.** to dash, strike, etc. with a splash **2.** to swagger —*vt.* to splash (a liquid), as in a container —*n.* **1.** a splashing of water **2.** swagger

swash'buck'ler (-buk'lər) *n.* [prec. + BUCKLER] a blustering, swaggering fighting man —**swash'buck'ling** *n., adj.*

swas·ti·ka (swäs'ti kə) *n.* [< Sans. < *svasti,* well-being] **1.** an ancient design in the form of a cross with four equal arms, each bent in a right-angle extension **2.** this design with the arms bent clockwise, used as the Nazi emblem

swat (swät) *vt.* **swat'ted, swat'ting** [echoic] [Colloq.] to hit with a quick, sharp blow —*n.* [Colloq.] a quick, sharp blow —**swat'ter** *n.*

swatch (swäch) *n.* [orig., a cloth tally < ?] **1.** a sample piece of cloth, etc. **2.** a small amount in a bunch or patch

swath (swäth, swôth) *n.* [OE. *swathu,* a track] **1.** the width covered by one cut of a scythe or other mowing device **2.** a strip, row, etc. mowed —**cut a wide swath** to make a big or showy impression

swathe (swäth) *vt.* **swathed, swath'ing** [OE. *swathian*] **1.** to wrap or bind up with a cloth or bandage **2.** to envelop

sway (swā) *vi.* [ON. *sveigja*] **1.** *a)* to swing or move from side to side or to and fro *b)* to vacillate in position, opinion, etc. **2.** to lean to one side; veer —*vt.* **1.** to cause to sway **2.** to cause to turn from a given course; influence or divert [his threats *swayed* us] —*n.* **1.** a swaying or being swayed **2.** influence or control [under the *sway* of greed] —**hold sway** to reign or prevail

sway'backed' (-bakt') *adj.* having an abnormal sagging of the spine, as some horses —**sway'back'** *n.*

Swa·zi·land (swä'zē land') country in SE Africa: 6,705 sq. mi.; pop. 421,000

swear (swer) *vi.* **swore, sworn, swear'ing** [OE. *swerian*] **1.** to make a solemn declaration, supporting it with an appeal to God or to something held sacred **2.** to make a solemn promise; vow **3.** to use profane language; curse —*vt.* **1.** to declare, pledge, or vow on oath **2.** to assert with great emphasis **3.** to administer a legal oath to —**swear by 1.** to name (something held sacred) in taking an oath **2.** to have great faith in —**swear for** to give assurance for —**swear in** to administer an oath to (a person taking office, a witness, etc.) —**swear off** to renounce —**swear out** to obtain (a warrant for someone's arrest) by making a charge under oath —**swear'er** *n.*

swear'word' *n.* a word or phrase used in swearing or cursing; profane word or phrase

sweat (swet) *vt., vi.* **sweat** or **sweat'ed, sweat'ing** [OE. *swat*] **1.** to give forth or cause to give forth a salty moisture through the pores of the skin; perspire **2.** to give forth or condense (moisture) on its surface **3.** to work so hard as to cause sweating or misery **4.** [Colloq.] to get (information) from (someone) by torture or grueling questioning —*n.* **1.** the salty liquid given forth in perspiration **2.** moisture that collects in droplets on a surface **3.** the act or condition of sweating **4.** a condition of eagerness, anxiety, etc. —**sweat blood** [Slang] **1.** to overwork **2.** to be impatient, anxious, etc. —**sweat out** [Slang] **1.** to suffer through (something) **2.** to wait anxiously or impatiently for —**sweat'y** *adj.* **-i·er, -i·est**

sweat'band' *n.* a band of leather, etc. inside a hat to protect it against sweat

sweat'er *n.* a knitted or crocheted outer garment for the upper part of the body

sweat gland any of the tiny, coiled, tubular glands in the subcutaneous tissue that secrete sweat

sweat shirt a heavy, long-sleeved cotton jersey, worn to absorb sweat during or after exercise, sometimes with matching loose trousers (**sweat pants**)

sweat'shop' *n.* a shop or factory where employees work long hours at low wages under poor working conditions

Swed. **1.** Sweden **2.** Swedish

Swede (swēd) *n.* a native or inhabitant of Sweden

Swe·den (swē'd'n) country in N Europe: 173,620 sq. mi.; pop. 8,115,000; cap. Stockholm

Swed·ish (swē'dish) *adj.* of Sweden, its people, their language, etc. —*n.* the Germanic language of the Swedes —**the Swedish** the people of Sweden

sweep (swēp) *vt.* **swept, sweep'ing** [OE. *swapan*] **1.** to clean (a floor, etc.) as by brushing with a broom **2.** to remove (dirt, etc.) as with a broom **3.** to strip, carry away, or destroy with forceful movement **4.** to touch in moving across [hands *sweeping* the keyboard] **5.** to pass swiftly over or across **6.** to win overwhelmingly —*vi.* **1.** to clean a floor, etc. as with a broom **2.** to move steadily with speed, force, or gracefulness **3.** to extend in a long curve or line [a road *sweeping* up a hill] —*n.* **1.** the act of sweeping, as with a broom **2.** a sweeping movement **3.** range or scope **4.** an extent or stretch, as of land **5.** a sweeping line, curve, or contour **6.** one whose work is sweeping [a chimney *sweep*] —**sweep'er** *n.*

sweep'ing *adj.* **1.** that sweeps **2.** extensive; broad in range —*n.* **1.** the work of a sweeper **2.** [*pl.*] things swept up, as dirt from the floor —**sweep'ing·ly** *adv.*

sweep'stakes' *n., pl.* **-stakes' 1.** a lottery in which the winner or winners of the common fund of stakes are determined by a horse race or other contest **2.** the contest that determines the winner

sweet (swēt) *adj.* [OE. *swete*] **1.** having a taste of, or like that of, sugar **2.** *a*) pleasant in taste, smell, sound, looks, etc. *b*) gratifying *c*) friendly, gentle, kindly, etc. *d*) sentimental or saccharine *e*) [Slang] good, delightful, nice, etc. **3.** *a*) not rancid, spoiled, sour, or fermented *b*) not salty or salted —*n.* something sweet; specif., *a*) [*pl.*] sweet foods, including cake, candy, ice cream, etc. *b*) [Brit.] a piece of candy; also, a sweet dessert —*adv.* in a sweet manner —**sweet'ish** *adj.* —**sweet'ly** *adv.* —**sweet'ness** *n.*

sweet alyssum a short garden plant with small spikes of tiny flowers

sweet'bread' (-bred') *n.* the thymus or sometimes the pancreas of a calf, lamb, etc., when used as food

sweet'bri·er, sweet'bri·ar (-brī'ər) *n. same as* EGLANTINE

sweet corn any of various strains of corn with soft, sweet kernels in the unripe stage, when it is cooked for eating, often on the cob

sweet·en (swēt''n) *vt.* **1.** to make sweet **2.** to make pleasant **3.** to make more agreeable —*vi.* to become sweet

sweet'en·er *n.* a sweetening agent, esp. a synthetic one, as saccharin

sweet'heart' *n.* **1.** *a*) a loved one; lover *b*) darling: a term of endearment **2.** [Slang] a very agreeable person or an excellent thing

sweetheart contract a contract arranged by collusion between union officials and an employer

sweet'meat' (-mēt') *n.* a candy or other sweet tidbit

sweet pea a climbing annual plant of the legume family, with fragrant, butterfly-shaped flowers

sweet pepper 1. a variety of red pepper producing a large, mild fruit **2.** the fruit

sweet potato 1. a tropical trailing plant with a fleshy, orange or yellow, tuberlike root used as a vegetable **2.** its root

sweet'-talk' *vt., vi.* [Colloq.] to flatter, cajole, etc.

sweet tooth [Colloq.] a craving for sweets

sweet william, sweet William a sweet-scented pink with dense, flat clusters of small flowers

swell (swel) *vi., vt.* **swelled, swelled** or **swol'len, swell'ing** [OE. *swellen*] **1.** to expand as a result of pressure from within **2.** to curve out; bulge **3.** to extend above the normal level **4.** to fill (*with* pride, etc.) **5.** to increase in size, force, intensity, loudness, etc. —*n.* **1.** a part that swells; specif., *a*) a large, rolling wave *b*) a piece of rising ground **2.** an increase in size, amount, degree, etc. **3.** a crescendo —*adj.* [Slang] fine, excellent, grand, elegant, etc.

swelled head [Colloq.] an exaggerated opinion of oneself —**swell'head'ed** *adj.* —**swell'head·ed·ness** *n.*

swell'ing *n.* **1.** an increase in size, force, etc. **2.** a swollen part, as on the body

swel·ter (swel'tər) *vi.* [OE. *sweltan*, to die] to sweat and wilt from great heat —*n.* **1.** a sweltering **2.** oppressive heat

swel'ter·ing *adj.* very hot, sweaty, sticky, etc.: also **swel'try** (-trē), **-tri·er, -tri·est**

swept (swept) *pt. & pp. of* SWEEP

swept'back' *adj.* having a backward slant, as the wings of some aircraft

swerve (swurv) *vt., vi.* **swerved, swerv'ing** [OE. *sweorfan*, to scour] to turn aside suddenly from a straight line, course, etc. —*n.* a swerving motion

swift (swift) *adj.* [OE.] **1.** moving with great speed; fast **2.** coming, happening, acting, etc. quickly —*adv.* in a swift manner —*n.* a swift-flying bird resembling the swallow, as the chimney swift —**swift'ly** *adv.* —**swift'ness** *n.*

Swift (swift), **Jonathan** 1667–1745; Eng. satirist, born in Ireland

swig (swig) *vt., vi.* **swigged, swig'ging** [< ?] [Colloq.] to drink in big gulps or amounts —*n.* [Colloq.] a big gulp, esp. of liquor —**swig'ger** *n.*

swill (swil) *vt., vi.* [OE. *swilian*] to drink greedily or in large quantities —*n.* **1.** garbage, etc. mixed with liquid and used for feeding pigs, etc. **2.** a big gulp of liquor; swig

swim¹ (swim) *vi.* **swam, swum, swim'ming** [OE. *swimman*] **1.** to move through water by moving the arms, legs, fins, etc. **2.** to move along smoothly **3.** to float on or be covered with a liquid **4.** to overflow [eyes *swimming* with tears] —*vt.* to swim in or across —*n.* an act, spell, or distance of swimming —**in the swim** active in what is popular at the moment —**swim'mer** *n.*

swim² (swim) *n.* [OE. *swima*] a dizzy spell —*vi.* **swam, swum, swim'ming** to be dizzy

swimming hole a deep place in a river, creek, etc. used for swimming

swim'ming·ly *adv.* in an easy, successful way

swimming pool an indoor or outdoor tank of water for swimming

swim'suit' (-soot') *n.* a garment worn for swimming

swin·dle (swin'd'l) *vt.* **-dled, -dling** [< G. *schwindeln*, to cheat] to cheat or trick out of money or property; defraud —*n.* an act of swindling; fraud —**swin'dler** *n.*

swine (swīn) *n., pl.* **swine** [OE. *swin*] **1.** a pig, hog, or boar: usually used collectively **2.** a vicious, contemptible, or disgusting person —**swin'ish** *adj.* —**swin'ish·ly** *adv.*

swing (swiŋ) *vt., vi.* **swung, swing'ing** [OE. *swingan*] **1.** to sway or move back and forth **2.** to move (one's fist, a bat, etc.) in a sweeping motion, as in trying to hit; strike (*at*) **3.** to walk, trot, etc. with loose, swaying movements **4.** to turn, as on a hinge or swivel **5.** *a*) to hang *b*) [Colloq.] to be hanged in execution **6.** to move on a swing (*n.* 8) **7.** to move in a curve [*swing* the car around] **8.** to play (music) in the style of swing (*n.* 10) **9.** [Colloq.] to cause to come about successfully [to *swing* an election] **10.** [Slang] to be sophisticated, active, etc., esp. in the pursuit of pleasure —*n.* **1.** a swinging **2.** the arc through which something swings **3.** the manner of swinging a golf club, a bat, etc. **4.** a free, relaxed motion, as in walking **5.** a sweeping blow or stroke **6.** the course of some activity **7.** rhythm, as of poetry or music **8.** a seat hanging from ropes or chains, on which one can sit and swing **9.** a trip or tour [a *swing* around the State] **10.** jazz music c.1935–45, using large bands, strong rhythms, etc. —**in full swing** in full, active operation

swing'er *n.* [Slang] a person who swings (*v.* 10)

swing shift [Colloq.] a work shift from about midafternoon to about midnight

swipe (swīp) *n.* [prob. var. of SWEEP] [Colloq.] a hard, sweeping blow —*vt.* **swiped, swip'ing 1.** [Colloq.] to hit with a swipe **2.** [Slang] to steal

swirl (swurl) *vi., vt.* [prob. < Norw. *svirla*, to whirl] to move or cause to move with a whirling motion —*n.* **1.** a whirl; eddy **2.** a twist; curl —**swirl'y** *adj.*

swish (swish) *vi.* [echoic] **1.** to move with a sharp, hissing sound, as a cane swung through the air **2.** to rustle, as skirts in walking —*vt.* to cause to swish —*n.* a swishing sound or movement

Swiss (swis) *adj.* of Switzerland, its people, etc. —*n., pl.* **Swiss** a native or inhabitant of Switzerland —**the Swiss** the people of Switzerland

Swiss chard *same as* CHARD

Swiss (cheese) a pale-yellow, hard cheese with many large holes

Swiss steak a thick cut of round steak pounded with flour and braised, usually with a sauce of tomatoes, onions, etc.

switch (swich) *n.* [prob. < MDu. or LowG.] **1.** a thin, flexible twig, stick, etc. used for whipping **2.** the bushy part of the tail of a cow, etc. **3.** a tress of detached hair used as part of a coiffure **4.** a sharp lash, as with a whip **5.** a device used to open, close, or divert an electric circuit **6.** a device used in transferring a train from one track to another **7.** a shift; change —*vt.* **1.** to whip, as with a switch **2.** to swing sharply [a cow *switching* its tail] **3.** to shift; change **4.** to turn (an electric light, appliance, etc.) *on* or *off* by using a switch **5.** to move (a train, etc.) from one track to another by means of a switch **6.** [Colloq.] to exchange [to *switch* places] —*vi.* to shift —**switch'er** *n.*

switch'back' *n.* a zigzag road up a steep grade

switch'-blade' knife a large jackknife that snaps open when a release button on the handle is pressed

switch'board' (-bôrd') *n.* a panel for controlling a system of electric circuits, as in a telephone exchange

switch'-hit'ter *n.* a baseball player who bats right-handed or left-handed

switch'man (-mən) *n., pl.* **-men** a railroad worker who operates switches, as in a railroad yard

Switz·er·land (swit'sər lənd) country in WC Europe, in the Alps: 15,941 sq. mi.; pop. 6,270,000; cap. Bern

swiv·el (swiv''l) *n.* [< OE. *swifan*, to revolve] a coupling device that allows free turning of the parts attached to it

---

fat, āpe, cär; ten, ēven; is, bīte; gō, hôrn, tōol, look; oil, out; up, fur; thin, *then*; zh, leisure; ŋ, ring; ə for *a* in *ago*; ' as in *able* (ā'b'l); ë, Fr. coeur; ö, Fr. feu; ö, Fr. mon; ü, Fr. duc; r̄, Fr. cri; kh, G. doch, ich. ‡ foreign; < derived from

—*vi.*, *vt.* **-eled** or **-elled**, **-el·ing** or **-el·ling** to turn or cause to turn as on a swivel or pivot

swivel chair a chair whose seat turns horizontally on a pivot in the base

swiz·zle stick (swiz′'l) [< ?] a small rod for stirring mixed drinks

swob (swäb) *n.*, *vt.* **swobbed**, **swob'bing** *var. sp. of* SWAB

swol·len (swō′lən) *alt. pp. of* SWELL —*adj.* blown up; distended; bulging

swoon (swōōn) *vi.* [OE. *geswogen*, unconscious] **1.** to faint **2.** to be in a state of rapture [to *swoon* with joy] —*n.* an act of swooning

swoop (swōōp) *vt.* [OE. *swapan*, sweep along] to snatch suddenly (often with *up*) —*vi.* to descend suddenly and swiftly, as a bird in hunting; pounce or sweep (*down*, *upon*, etc.) —*n.* the act of swooping

swop (swäp) *n.*, *vt.*, *vi.* **swopped**, **swop'ping** *var. sp. of* SWAP

sword (sôrd) *n.* [OE. *sweord*] **1.** a hand weapon having a long, sharp-pointed blade set in a hilt **2.** the sword as a symbol of war, fighting power, etc. —**at swords' points** ready to quarrel or fight —**cross swords** to fight —**put to the sword 1.** to kill with a sword **2.** to slaughter, esp. in war

sword'fish' *n.*, *pl.*: see FISH a large marine food and game fish with the upper jawbone extending in a long, swordlike point

sword'grass' *n.* any of a number of sedges or grasses with notched or sword-shaped leaves

sword'play' (-plā′) *n.* the act or skill of using a sword, as in fencing

swords·man (sôrdz′mən) *n.*, *pl.* **-men 1.** one who uses a sword in fencing or fighting **2.** one skilled in using a sword —**swords'man·ship'** *n.*

SWORDFISH
(to 15 ft. long)

swore (swôr) *pt. of* SWEAR

sworn (swôrn) *pp. of* SWEAR —*adj.* bound or pledged as by an oath [*sworn* friends]

swum (swum) *pp. of* SWIM

swung (swuŋ) *pt. & pp. of* SWING

syb·a·rite (sib′ə rīt′) *n.* [< *Sybaris*, ancient Gr. city in S Italy] anyone very fond of luxury and pleasure —**syb'a·rit'ic** (-rit′ik) *adj.*

syc·a·more (sik′ə môr′) *n.* [< Gr. *sykomoros*] **1.** a shade tree of Egypt and Asia Minor, with figlike fruit **2.** a maple tree of Europe and Asia **3.** an American plane tree (see PLANE[1])

syc·o·phant (sik′ə fənt) *n.* [< Gr. *sykophantēs*, informer] one who seeks favor by flattering people of wealth or influence —**syc'o·phan·cy** *n.*, *pl.* **-cies** —**syc'o·phan'tic** (-fan′tik) *adj.*

Syd·ney (sid′nē) seaport in SE Australia: pop. 2,713,000

syl·lab·ic (si lab′ik) *adj.* **1.** of a syllable or syllables **2.** forming a syllable in itself: said of a consonant, as the *l* in *tattle* (tat′'l)

syl·lab·i·cate (si lab′ə kāt′) *vt.* **-cat'ed**, **-cat'ing** *same as* SYLLABIFY —**syl'lab·i·ca'tion** *n.*

syl·lab·i·fy (si lab′ə fī′) *vt.* **-fied'**, **-fy'ing** to divide into syllables —**syl'lab·i·fi·ca'tion** *n.*

syl·la·ble (sil′ə b'l) *n.* [< Gr. *syn-*, together + *lambanein*, to hold] **1.** a word or part of a word pronounced with a single, uninterrupted sounding of the voice **2.** any of the parts into which a written word is divided, more or less like its spoken syllables, to show where the word can be broken at the end of a line **3.** the least bit

syl·la·bus (sil′ə bəs) *n.*, *pl.* **-bus·es**, **-bi'** (-bī′) [< Gr. *syllybos*, parchment label] a summary or outline, esp. of a course of study

syl·lo·gism (sil′ə jiz′m) *n.* [< Gr. *syn-*, together + *logizesthai*, to reason] a form of reasoning in which two premises are made and a logical conclusion drawn from them —**syl'lo·gis'tic** *adj.*

sylph (silf) *n.* [ModL. *sylphus*, a spirit < ?] a slender, graceful woman or girl —**sylph'like'** *adj.*

syl·van (sil′vən) *adj.* [< L. *silva*, a woods] **1.** of, characteristic of, or living in the woods or forests **2.** wooded

sym·bi·o·sis (sim′bī ō′sis, -bē-) *n.* [< Gr. *syn-*, together + *bioun*, to live] the living together of two different kinds of organisms to their mutual advantage —**sym'bi·ot'ic** (-ät′ik) *adj.*

sym·bol (sim′b'l) *n.* [< Gr. *syn-*, together + *ballein*, to throw] **1.** a thing that represents another [the dove is a *symbol* of peace] **2.** a written or printed mark, letter, etc. standing for a quality, process, etc., as in music, mathematics, or chemistry

sym·bol·ic (sim bäl′ik) *adj.* **1.** of or expressed in a symbol; using symbols **2.** that serves as a symbol **3.** characterized by symbolism Also **sym·bol'i·cal** —**sym·bol'i·cal·ly** *adv*

sym·bol·ism (sim′b'l iz′m) *n.* **1.** the representation of things by symbols, esp. in art or literature **2.** a system of symbols **3.** symbolic meaning

sym'bol·ist *n.* one who uses symbols, esp. in art or literature

sym'bol·ize' *vt.* **-ized'**, **-iz'ing** [< Fr.] **1.** to be a symbol of; stand for **2.** to represent by a symbol or symbols —**sym'bol·i·za'tion** *n.*

sym·me·try (sim′ə trē) *n.*, *pl.* **-tries** [< Gr. *syn-*, together + *metron*, a measure] **1.** correspondence of opposite parts in size, shape, and position **2.** balance or beauty of form resulting from this —**sym·met'ri·cal** (si met′ri k'l) *adj.* —**sym·met'ri·cal·ly** *adv.*

sym·pa·thet·ic (sim′pə thet′ik) *adj.* **1.** of, feeling, or showing sympathy **2.** in agreement with one's tastes, mood, etc. **3.** showing favor or approval [he's *sympathetic* to our plan] **4.** designating or of that part of the autonomic nervous system whose functions include speeding the heartbeat, dilating the pupils of the eyes, etc. **5.** similar to and caused by the action in another, related thing [*sympathetic* vibrations] —**sym'pa·thet'i·cal·ly** *adv.*

sym·pa·thize (sim′pə thīz′) *vi.* **-thized'**, **-thiz'ing 1.** to share or understand the feelings or ideas of another **2.** to feel or express sympathy, esp. in pity or compassion **3.** to be in harmony or accord —**sym'pa·thiz'er** *n.*

sym·pa·thy (sim′pə thē) *n.*, *pl.* **-thies** [< Gr. *syn-*, together + *pathos*, feeling] **1.** sameness of feeling **2.** agreement in qualities, actions, etc.; accord **3.** a mutual liking or understanding arising from sameness of feeling **4.** a sharing of, or the ability to share, another's ideas, feelings, etc.; esp., [*often pl.*] pity or compassion **5.** a feeling of approval of an idea, cause, etc.

sym·pho·ny (sim′fə nē) *n.*, *pl.* **-nies** [< Gr. *syn-*, together + *phōnē*, a sound] **1.** harmony, as of sounds, color, etc. **2.** a long musical composition in several (usually four) movements, for full orchestra **3.** a large orchestra for playing such works: in full **symphony orchestra 4.** [Colloq.] a concert by a symphony orchestra —**sym·phon'ic** (-fän′ik) *adj.*

sym·po·si·um (sim pō′zē əm) *n.*, *pl.* **-si·ums**, **-si·a** (-ə) [< Gr. *syn-*, together + *posis*, a drinking] **1.** a meeting at which ideas are freely exchanged **2.** a conference for discussing some subject **3.** a collection of opinions or essays on some subject

symp·tom (simp′təm) *n.* [< Gr. *syn-*, together + *piptein*, to fall] any accompanying circumstance or condition that indicates the existence of something, esp. of a particular disease; sign —**symp'to·mat'ic** (-tə mat′ik) *adj.*

syn- [Gr.] *a prefix meaning* with, together, at the same time

syn. 1. synonym **2.** synonymy

syn·a·gogue (sin′ə gäg′, -gôg′) *n.* [< Gr. *syn-*, together + *agein*, to bring] **1.** an assembly of Jews for worship and religious study **2.** a building or place used for such an assembly

syn·apse (si naps′) *n.* [< Gr. *syn-*, together + *apsis*, a joining] the point of contact where nerve impulses are transmitted from one neuron to another

sync, synch (siŋk) *vt.*, *vi. clipped form of* SYNCHRONIZE —*n. clipped form of* SYNCHRONIZATION

syn·chro·nize (siŋ′krə nīz′) *vt.* **-nized'**, **-niz'ing** [< Gr. *syn-*, together + *chronos*, time] to move or occur at the same time or rate —*vt.* to cause to agree in time or rate of speed —**syn'chro·ni·za'tion** *n.*

syn'chro·nous (-nəs) *adj.* **1.** happening at the same time or moving at the same rate of speed **2.** having the same rate and phase, as vibrations

syn·cline (siŋ′klīn) *n.* [< Gr. *syn-*, together + *klinein*, to incline] a down fold in stratified rocks from whose central axis the strata slope upward in opposite directions

syn·co·pate (siŋ′kə pāt′) *vt.* **-pat'ed**, **-pat'ing** [< Gr. *syn-*, together + *koptein*, to cut] **1.** to shift (the regular accent) as by beginning a tone on an unaccented beat and continuing it through the next accented beat **2.** to use such shifted accents in (music or rhythm) —**syn'co·pa'tion** *n.*

syn·di·cate (sin′də kit) *n.* [see prec.] **1.** an association of individuals or corporations formed for a project requiring much capital **2.** any group organized for some undertaking; specif., an association of criminals controlling a network of vice, gambling, etc. **3.** an organization that sells articles or features to a number of newspapers —*vt.* (-kāt′) **-cat'ed**, **-cat'ing 1.** to manage as or form into a syndicate 2. to publish (articles, etc.) through a syndicate —**syn′di·ca′tion** *n.*

syn·drome (sin′drōm) *n.* [< Gr. *syn-*, with + *dramein*, to run] a set of symptoms characterizing a disease or condition

syn·er·gism (sin′ər jiz'm) *n.* [< Gr. *syn-*, together + *ergon*, work] combined action, as of several drugs, greater in total effect than the sum of the individual effects — **syn′er·gis′tic** *adj.*

syn·od (sin′əd) *n.* [< Gr. *syn-*, together + *hodos*, way] a council of churches or church officials; specif., a high governing body in any of certain Christian churches

syn·o·nym (sin′ə nim) *n.* [< Gr. *syn-*, together + *onyma*, name] a word having the same or nearly the same meaning as another in the same language —**syn·on·y·mous** (si nän′ə məs) *adj.*

syn·on·y·my (si nän′ə mē) *n., pl.* **-mies** a listing of synonyms, esp. with the terms discriminated from one another

syn·op·sis (si näp′sis) *n., pl.* **-ses** (-sēz) [< Gr. *syn-*, together + *opsis*, a seeing] a short outline or review of the main points, as of a story; summary —**syn·op′size** (-sīz) *vt.* **-sized, -siz·ing**

syn·op′tic *adj.* 1. of or giving a synopsis or a general view 2. giving an account from the same point of view: said esp. [*often* S-] of the first three Gospels

syn·tax (sin′taks) *n.* [< Fr. < Gr. *syn-*, together + *tassein*, arrange] the way words, word groups, phrases, and clauses are put together and related to one another in sentences —**syn·tac′tic, syn·tac′ti·cal** *adj.*

syn·the·sis (sin′thə sis) *n., pl.* **-ses′** (-sēz′) [< Gr. *syn-*, together + *tithenai*, to place] 1. the combining of parts or elements so as to form a whole, a compound, etc. 2. a whole thus formed

syn′the·size′ (-sīz′) *vt.* **-sized′, -siz′ing** 1. to bring together into a whole by synthesis 2. *Chem.* to produce by combining simpler compounds or elements

syn·thet′ic (-thet′ik) *adj.* 1. of or involving synthesis 2. synthesized chemically [*synthetic* fabrics] 3. not real; artificial [a *synthetic* laugh] —*n.* a synthetic substance —**syn·thet′i·cal·ly** *adv.*

syph·i·lis (sif′ə lis) *n.* [< *Syphilus*, hero of a L. poem (1530)] an infectious venereal disease, usually transmitted by sexual intercourse or acquired congenitally —**syph′i·lit′ic** (-lit′ik) *adj., n.*

Syr·a·cuse (sir′ə kyōōs′, -kyōōz′) city in C N.Y.: pop. 197,000 (met. area 636,000)

Syr·i·a (sir′ē ə) country at the E end of the Mediterranean: 71,227 sq. mi.; pop. 6,451,000; cap. Damascus — **Syr′i·an** *adj., n.*

syr·inge (sə rinj′, sir′inj) *n.* [< Gr. *syrinx*, a pipe] 1. a device consisting of a tube with a rubber bulb or piston at one end, for drawing in a liquid and then ejecting it in a stream: used to inject fluids into or cleanse body cavities, etc. 2. *short for* HYPODERMIC SYRINGE —*vt.* **-ringed′, -ring′ing** to cleanse, inject, etc. by using a syringe

SYRINGE

syr·inx (sir′inks) *n., pl.* **sy·rin·ges** (sə rin′jēz), **syr′inx·es** [Gr., a pipe] 1. the vocal organ of songbirds, at the base of the trachea 2. a panpipe

syr·up (sir′əp, sur′-) *n.* [< Ar. *sharāb*, a drink] 1. a sweet, thick liquid made by boiling sugar with water, often flavored or, in pharmacy, medicated 2. *short for* MAPLE SYRUP, etc. —**syr′up·y** *adj.*

sys·tem (sis′təm) *n.* [< Gr. *syn-*, together + *histanai*, to set] 1. a group of things or parts working together or connected in some way so as to form a whole [the solar *system*, school *system*] 2. a set of facts, principles, rules, etc. that make up an orderly plan [the metric *system*] 3. orderly procedure; method [to work with *system*] 4. the body, or a number of bodily organs, functioning as a unit

sys′tem·at′ic (-tə mat′ik) *adj.* 1. constituting or based on a system 2. according to or following a system, method, or plan; orderly; methodical —**sys′tem·at′i·cal·ly** *adv.*

sys′tem·a·tize′ (-təm ə tīz′) *vt.* **-tized′, -tiz′ing** to form into a system; arrange in a systematic way

sys·tem·ic (sis tem′ik) *adj.* 1. of or affecting the body as a whole 2. of or designating a pesticide absorbed into the tissues of plants, making them poisonous to insects, etc. — **sys·tem′i·cal·ly** *adv.*

sys·tem·ize (sis′tə mīz′) *vt.* **-ized′, -iz′ing** *same as* SYSTEMATIZE

sys·to·le (sis′tə lē′) *n.* [< Gr. *syn-*, together + *stellein*, send] the usual rhythmic contraction of the heart, during which the blood is driven onward from the chambers — **sys·tol′ic** (-täl′ik) *adj.*

T

T, t (tē) *n., pl.* **T's, t's** the twentieth letter of the English alphabet

T (tē) *n.* something shaped like T —*adj.* shaped like T —**to a T** to perfection; exactly

't it: a contraction, as in *'twas*

-t *var. of* -ED, as in *slept, gilt*

T. tablespoon(s)

t. 1. teaspoon(s) 2. temperature 3. ton(s)

Ta *Chem.* tantalum

tab¹ (tab) *n.* [< ?] 1. a small, flat loop or strip on something for opening it, hanging it up, etc. 2. a projecting piece on a card, useful in filing —*vt.* **tabbed, tab′bing** to provide with or mark as with a tab

tab² (tab) *n.* [prob. < TABULATION] [Colloq.] 1. a bill or check, as at a restaurant 2. total cost or expenses —**keep tabs** (or **a tab**) **on** to watch closely; check on

tab³ (tab) *n. clipped form of:* 1. TABLET 2. TABLOID

tab·ard (tab′ərd) *n.* [< OFr. *tabart*] 1. a short-sleeved cloak worn by knights over their armor 2. a herald's coat, showing his lord's arms

tab·by (tab′ē) *n., pl.* **-bies** [< Fr., ult. < Ar.] 1. a gray or brown cat with dark stripes 2. any pet cat, esp. a female

tab·er·na·cle (tab′ər nak′'l) *n.* [< L. *tabernaculum*, a tent] 1. the portable sanctuary carried by the Jews in their wanderings from Egypt 2. a large place of worship

ta·ble (tā′b'l) *n.* [< L. *tabula*, board] 1. a thin slab of metal, stone, etc., used for inscriptions; tablet 2. *a)* a piece of furniture having a flat top set on legs *b)* such a table set with food *c)* the food served *d)* the people seated at a table 3. *a)* a systematic list of details, contents, etc. *b)* an orderly arrangement of facts, figures, etc., as in columns 4. *same as* TABLELAND 5. any flat, horizontal surface or flat-topped thing —*vt.* **-bled, -bling** 1. to put on a table 2. to postpone consideration of (a motion, bill, etc.) —**at table** at a meal —**turn the tables** to reverse a situation —**under the table** [Colloq.] handed over secretly

tab·leau (tab′lō) *n., pl.* **-leaux** (-lōz), **-leaus** [Fr. < OFr. dim. of *table*, TABLE] a representation of a scene by persons posed in costume

ta′ble-cloth′ *n.* a cloth for covering a table, esp. at meals

ta·ble d'hôte (tä′b'l dōt′) [Fr., table of the host] a complete meal with courses as specified, served at a restaurant for a set price

ta·ble-hop (tā′b'l häp′) *vi.* **-hopped′, -hop′ping** to leave one's table in a restaurant or nightclub and visit about at other tables —**ta′ble-hop′per** *n.*

ta′ble·land′ *n.* a high, broad, flat region; plateau

ta′ble·spoon′ *n.* a large spoon for serving, measuring, etc., holding 1/2 fluid ounce —**ta′ble·spoon′ful** *n., pl.* **-fuls**

tab·let (tab′lit) *n.* [see TABLE] 1. a flat, thin piece of metal, stone, etc. with an inscription 2. a writing pad of paper sheets glued together at one edge 3. a small, flat, hard mass, as of medicine

---

fat, āpe, cär; ten, ēven; is, bīte; gō, hôrn, tōōl, look; oil, out; up, fur; thin, *then;* zh, leisure; ŋ, ring; ə for *a* in *ago;* ' as in *able* (ā′b'l); ë, Fr. coeur; ö, Fr. feu; Fr. mon; ü, Fr. duc; r, Fr. cri; kh, G. doch, ich. ‡ foreign; < derived from

table tennis a game somewhat like tennis, played on a table with a small plastic ball

ta·ble·ware' (-wer') n. dishes, glassware, silverware, etc. for use at meals

tab·loid (tab'loid) n. [TABL(ET) + -OID] a newspaper, usually half the ordinary size, with many pictures and short, often sensational, news stories —adj. condensed; short

ta·boo (ta bōō', tə-) n. [Tongan tabu] 1. among some Polynesian peoples, etc., a sacred prohibition that makes certain people or things untouchable, unmentionable, etc. 2. any social restriction that results from convention or tradition —adj. prohibited by taboo —vt. 1. to put under taboo 2. to prohibit or forbid

ta·bor (tā'bər) n. [< Per. tabīrah] a small drum formerly played along with a fife: also **ta'bour**

ta·bu (ta bōō', tə-) n., adj., vt. same as TABOO

tab·u·lar (tab'yə lər) adj. [see TABLE] 1. having a table-like surface; flat 2. a) of or arranged in columns in a table b) calculated by using tables

tab'u·late' (-lāt') vt. -lat'ed, -lat'ing to put (facts, statistics, etc.) in a table or columns —tab'u·la'tion n. —tab'u·la'tor n.

ta·chom·e·ter (ta käm'ə tər, tə-) n. [< Gr. tachos, speed + -METER] a device that indicates or measures the revolutions per minute of a revolving shaft

tac·it (tas'it) adj. [Fr. tacite < L. tacere, to be silent] 1. unspoken; silent 2. not openly expressed, but implied or understood —tac'it·ly adv.

tac·i·turn (tas'ə turn') adj. [see prec.] usually silent; not liking to talk —tac'i·tur'ni·ty n.

tack (tak) n. [< MDu. tacke, twig] 1. a short nail with a sharp point and a large, flat head 2. a temporary stitch 3. a) a change of direction made by a sailboat in sailing a course against the wind b) any of the legs of a zigzag course steered in such sailing 4. a zigzag course 5. a course of action [start on a new tack] 6. a horse's equipment, as saddles, bridles, etc. — vt. 1. to fasten with tacks 2. to attach or add 3. to maneuver (a boat) against the wind by a tack or series of tacks —vi. 1. to change course suddenly 2. to go in a zigzag course —tack'er n.

tack·le (tak'l) n. [< MDu. takel] 1. equipment; gear [fishing tackle] 2. a system of ropes and pulleys for moving weights 3. the act of tackling, as in football 4. Football the player next to either end on the offensive or defensive line —vt. -led, -ling 1. to take hold of; seize 2. to try to do; undertake 3. Football to bring down (an opponent carrying the ball) —tack'ler n.

tack·y (tak'ē) adj. -i·er, -i·est 1. sticky, as glue before completely dry 2. [Colloq.] shabby —tack'i·ness n.

ta·co (tä'kō) n., pl. -cos [AmSp. < Sp., a plug, wad] a fried, folded tortilla filled with chopped meat, shredded lettuce, etc.

Ta·co·ma (tə kō'mə) seaport in W Wash., on Puget Sound: pop. 155,000

tac·o·nite (tak'ə nīt') n. [< Taconic Range in Vt. & Mass.] a kind of rock mined as a low-grade iron ore: the iron-bearing particles from the crushed rock are formed into pellets

tact (takt) n. [< L. tangere, to touch] a sense of the right thing to say or do without offending

tact'ful adj. having or showing tact —tact'ful·ly adv. —tact'ful·ness n.

tac·tic (tak'tik) n. 1. a detail or branch of military tactics 2. a method used to gain an end

tac·ti·cal (tak'ti k'l) adj. 1. of tactics, esp. in military or naval maneuvers 2. of or showing skill in tactics

tac·ti·cian (tak tish'ən) n. an expert in tactics

tac·tics (tak'tiks) n.pl. [< Gr. tassein, arrange] 1. a) [with sing. v.] the science of maneuvering military and naval forces in action b) action in accord with this science 2. any methods used to gain an end

tac·tile (tak't'l) adj. [Fr. < L. tangere, to touch] of, having, or perceived by the sense of touch

tact'less adj. not having or showing tact —tact'less·ly adv. —tact'less·ness n.

tad (tad) n. [prob. < TAD(POLE)] a little child, esp. a boy

tad·pole (tad'pōl') n. [ME. tadde, toad + poll, head] the larva of a frog or toad, having gills and a tail and living in water

Ta·dzhik Soviet Socialist Republic (tä'jik) republic of the U.S.S.R., in C Asia: also **Ta·dzhik·i·stan** (tä jēk'i stän')

ta'en (tān) [Poet.] taken

taf·fe·ta (taf'i tə) n. [< Per. tāftan, to weave] a fine, stiff fabric of silk, nylon, etc., with a sheen

taff·rail (taf'rāl') n. [< Du. tafereel, a panel < L. tabula, a board] the rail around a ship's stern

taf·fy (taf'ē) n. [< ?] a chewy candy made of sugar or molasses boiled down and pulled

Taft (taft), **William Howard** 1857–1930; 27th president of the U.S. (1909–13)

tag (tag) n. [prob. < Scand.] 1. a hanging end or part 2. a hard-tipped end on a cord or lace 3. a card, etc. attached as a label 4. an epithet 5. the last line or lines of a speech, story, etc. 6. a children's game in which one player, called "it," chases the others until he touches one —vt. **tagged**, **tag'ging** 1. to provide with a tag 2. to choose; select 3. to touch as in the game of tag 4. [Colloq.] to follow close behind —vi. [Colloq.] to follow closely (with along, after, etc.) —tag'ger n.

Ta·ga·log (tä gä'läg, -lôg) n. 1. pl. -logs, -log a member of a Malayan people of the Philippine Islands 2. their Indonesian language

Ta·hi·ti (tə hēt'ē) Fr. island in the South Pacific —**Ta·hi'·ti·an** (-hēsh'ən, -hēt'ē ən) adj., n.

tail (tāl) n. [OE. tægel] 1. the rear end of an animal's body, esp. when a distinct appendage 2. anything like an animal's tail in form or position 3. a luminous train behind a comet 4. the hind, bottom, last, or inferior part of anything 5. [often pl.] the reverse side of a coin 6. [pl.] [Colloq.] a) a swallow-tailed coat b) full-dress attire for men 7. [Colloq.] a person or vehicle that follows another, esp. in surveillance —adj. 1. at the rear 2. from the rear [a tail wind] —vt., vi. [Colloq.] to follow close behind — **turn tail** to run from danger, difficulty, etc. —tail'less adj

tailed (tāld) adj. having a (specified kind of) tail: usually in combination [long-tailed]

tail'gate' n. the hinged or removable board or gate at the back of a wagon, truck, etc.: also **tail'board'** —vi., vt. -gat'ed, -gat'ing to drive too closely behind (another vehicle) —tail'gat'er n.

tail'ing n. 1. [pl.] refuse left in milling, mining, etc. 2. the part of a projecting brick, stone, etc. fastened into a wall

tail'light' n. a light, usually red, at the rear of a vehicle to warn vehicles coming from behind

tai·lor (tā'lər) n. [< LL. taliare, to cut] one who makes, repairs, and alters clothes —vi. to work as a tailor —vt. 1. to make by tailor's work 2. to make clothes for 3. to form, alter, etc. for a certain purpose [a novel tailored for TV] 4. to fashion (women's garments) with trim, simple lines —tai'lor·ing n.

tai'lor-made' adj. made by or as by a tailor; specif., a) having trim, simple lines b) made-to-order

tail'piece' n. 1. a part forming the end of something 2. Printing an ornamental design at the end of a chapter, etc.

tail'pipe' n. an exhaust pipe at the rear of an automotive vehicle

tail'spin' n. same as SPIN (n. 3): also **tail spin**

tail wind a wind blowing in the same direction as the course of a ship or aircraft

taint (tānt) vt. [ult. < L. tingere, to wet] 1. to affect with something injurious, unpleasant, etc.; infect 2. to make morally corrupt —vi. to become tainted —n. a trace of corruption, disgrace, etc.

Tai·pei, Tai·peh (tī'pe') capital of Taiwan: pop. 1,700,000

Tai·wan (tī'wän') island province of China, off the SE coast: seat of the Kuomintang government: 13,885 sq. mi.; pop. 14,964,000; cap. Taipei

take (tāk) vt. **took, tak'en, tak'ing** [< ON. taka] 1. to get possession of; capture, seize, etc. 2. to get hold of 3. to capture the fancy of 4. to obtain, acquire, assume, etc. 5. to use, consume, etc. 6. to enter into a special relationship with [to take a wife] 7. to buy, rent, or lease 8. to get regularly by paying for [to take a newspaper] 9. to assume as a responsibility, task, etc. [to take a job] 10. to join or support (one side in a disagreement, etc.) 11. to choose; select 12. to travel by [to take a bus] 13. to go to for shelter, etc. [to take cover] 14. to deal with; consider 15. to occupy [take a chair] 16. to require; demand [it takes money] 17. to derive (a name, quality, etc.) from something or someone 18. to extract, as for quotation 19. to obtain by observation, etc. [to take a poll] 20. to study (a course, etc.) 21. to write down [take notes] 22. to make (a photograph, picture, etc.) 23. to win (a prize, etc.) 24. to undergo [take punishment] 25. to engage in [take a nap] 26. to accept (an offer, bet, etc.) 27. to react to [to take a joke in earnest] 28. to contract (a disease, etc.) 29. to understand 30. to suppose; presume 31. to feel *[take* pity*]* **32.** to lead, escort, etc. **33.** to carry **34.** to remove as by stealing **35.** to subtract **36.** [Slang] to cheat; trick **37.** *Gram.* to be used with in construction *[a* transitive verb *takes* an object*] —vi.* **1.** to begin growing: said of a plant **2.** to catch *[the fire took]* **3.** to gain favor; be popular **4.** to be effective *[the* vaccination *took]* **5.** to go *[to take* to the hills*]* **6.** [Colloq.] to become (sick) *—n.* **1.** a taking **2.** something taken **3.** *a)* the amount taken *b)* [Slang] receipts or profits **4.** a movie scene photographed with an uninterrupted run of the camera **5.** a recording or tape of a performance —**on the take** [Slang] taking bribes, etc. —**take after** to be, act, or look like —**take back** to retract (something said, etc.) —**take down** to put in writing; record —**take in 1.** to admit; receive **2.** to make smaller **3.** to understand **4.** to cheat; trick —**take it out on** [Colloq.] to make (another) suffer for one's own anger, etc. —**take off 1.** to leave the ground, etc. in flight: said of an aircraft **2.** [Colloq.] to start **3.** [Colloq.] to imitate; mimic —**take on 1.** to acquire; assume **2.** to employ **3.** to undertake (a task, etc.) —**take one's time** to be unhurried —**take out** [Colloq.] to escort —**take over** to begin controlling, managing, etc. —**take to** to become fond of —**take up 1.** to make tighter or shorter **2.** to absorb (a liquid) **3.** to become interested in (an occupation, study, etc.) **4.** to occupy (space or time) —**tak′er** *n.*

take′-home′ pay wages or salary after deductions for income tax, social security, etc.

tak·en (tāk′n) *pp. of* TAKE

take′off′ *n.* **1.** the act of leaving the ground, etc., as in jumping or flight **2.** the place from which one leaves the ground, etc. **3.** [Colloq.] an amusing or mocking imitation Also **take′-off′**

take′o′ver *n.* the usurpation of power in a nation, organization, etc.: also **take′-o′ver**

tak·ing (tāk′iŋ) *adj.* attractive; winning *—n.* **1.** the act of one that takes **2.** *[pl.]* earnings; profits

talc (talk) *n.* [Fr. < Ar. *talq]* **1.** a soft mineral used to make talcum powder, etc. **2.** *clipped form of* TALCUM POWDER *—vt.* **talcked** or **talced**, **talck′ing** or **talc′ing** to talc on

tal·cum (powder) (tal′kəm) a powder for the body and face made of purified talc

tale (tāl) *n.* [OE. *talu]* **1.** a true or fictitious story; narrative **2.** idle or malicious gossip **3.** a falsehood; lie

tale′bear′er (-ber′ər) *n.* one who spreads gossip, tells secrets, etc. —**tale′bear′ing** *adj., n.*

tal·ent (tal′ənt) *n.* [< Gr. *talanton*, a weight] **1.** an ancient unit of weight or money **2.** any natural ability or power **3.** a special, superior ability in an art, science, etc. **4.** people, or a person, with talent —**tal′ent·ed** *adj.*

tal·is·man (tal′is mən, -iz-) *n., pl.* **-mans** [< MGr. *telesma*, a consecrated object] **1.** a ring, stone, etc. bearing engraved figures supposed to bring good luck, avert evil, etc. **2.** any magic charm

talk (tôk) *vi.* [prob. < OE. *talian*, reckon] **1.** to put ideas into words; speak **2.** to express ideas by speech substitutes *[to talk* by signs*]* **3.** to chatter; gossip **4.** to confer; consult **5.** to confess or inform on someone *—vt.* **1.** to utter *[to talk* nonsense*]* **2.** to use in speaking *[to talk* Spanish*]* **3.** to discuss **4.** to put into a specified condition, etc. by talking *—n.* **1.** the act of talking **2.** conversation **3.** a speech **4.** a conference **5.** gossip **6.** the subject of conversation, gossip, etc. **7.** frivolous discussion **8.** a particular kind of speech; dialect —**talk back** to answer impertinently —**talk down** to talk patronizingly to, as by simple speech —**talk over** to discuss —**talk up** to promote or praise in discussion —**talk′er** *n.*

talk′a·tive (-ə tiv) *adj.* talking a great deal; loquacious — **talk′a·tive·ness** *n.*

talking book a book, etc. recorded for use on a phonograph by the blind

talk′ing-to′ *n.* [Colloq.] a rebuke; scolding

talk′y *adj.* **-i·er, -i·est 1.** talkative **2.** containing too much talk, or dialogue *[a talky* novel*]*

tall (tôl) *adj.* [< OE. *(ge)tæl*, swift] **1.** of more than normal height or stature **2.** having a specified height *[five feet tall]* **3.** [Colloq.] exaggerated *[a tall* tale*]* **4.** [Colloq.] large *[a tall* drink*]* —**tall′ish** *adj.* —**tall′ness** *n.*

Tal·la·has·see (tal′ə has′ē) capital of Fla.: pop. 72,000

tal·low (tal′ō) *n.* [prob. < MLowG. *talg]* the pale-yellow solid fat extracted from the natural fat of cattle, sheep, etc., used to make candles, soaps, etc. —**tal′low·y** *adj.*

tal·ly (tal′ē) *n., pl.* **-lies** [< L. *talea*, a stick (notched to keep accounts)] **1.** anything used as a record for an ac-

count **2.** an account, reckoning, or score **3.** an identifying tag or label *—vt.* **-lied, -ly·ing 1.** to put on or as on a tally **2.** to count (*up*) *—vi.* **1.** to tally something **2.** to score in a game **3.** to agree; correspond

tal·ly·ho (tal′ē hō′) *interj.* [< Fr. *taiaut*] the cry of a hunter on sighting the fox *—n.* (tal′ē hō′), *pl.* **-hos′ 1.** a cry of "tallyho" **2.** a coach drawn by four horses *—vi.* (tal′ē hō′) to cry "tallyho"

Tal·mud (täl′mood, tal′-; -məd) *n.* [< Heb. *lāmadh,* learn] the writings constituting the Jewish civil and religious law —**Tal·mud′ic, Tal·mud′i·cal** *adj.* —**Tal′mud·ist** *n.*

tal·on (tal′ən) *n.* [< L. *talus,* an ankle] the claw of a bird of prey, or, sometimes, of an animal

tam (tam) *n. short for* TAM-O′-SHANTER

ta·ma·le (tə mä′lē) *n.* [< MexInd. *tamalli]* a Mexican food of minced meat and red peppers rolled in cornmeal and cooked in corn husks

tam·a·rack (tam′ə rak′) *n.* [< AmInd.] an American larch tree, usually found in swamps

tam·a·rind (tam′ə rind) *n.* [< Sp. < Ar: *tamr hindī,* date of India] **1.** a tropical tree with yellow flowers and brown pods with an acid pulp **2.** its fruit, used in foods, medicine, etc.

tam·bour (tam′boor) *n.* [< Ar. *tanbūr,* stringed instrument] **1.** a drum **2.** an embroidery frame of two closely fitting hoops between which cloth can be stretched

tam·bou·rine (tam′bə rēn′) *n.* [see TAMBOUR] a shallow, single-headed hand drum having jingling metal disks in the rim: played by shaking, hitting, etc.

TAMBOURINE

tame (tām) *adj.* **tam′er, tam′est** [OE. *tam]* **1.** changed from a wild state, as an animal, for use by man **2.** gentle; docile **3.** without force or spirit; dull — *vt.* **tamed, tam′ing 1.** to make tame, or domestic **2.** to make gentle, docile, or spiritless **3.** to make less intense; soften —**tam′a·ble, tame′a·ble** *adj.* —**tame′ly** *adv.* —**tame′ness** *n.* —**tam′er** *n.*

Tam·il (tam′'l, täm′-, tum′-) *n.* the non-Indo-European language of the Tamils, a people of S India and N Sri Lanka

tam-o′-shan·ter (tam′ə shan′tər) *n.* [< title character of R. Burns's poem] a Scottish cap with a round, flat top

tamp (tamp) *vt.* [< ? TAMPON] to pack or pound (*down*) by a series of blows or taps —**tamp′er** *n.*

Tam·pa (tam′pə) seaport in WC Florida: pop. 278,000 (met. area, incl. St. Petersburg, 1,013,000)

tam·per (tam′pər) *vi.* [var. of TEMPER] [Archaic] to plot — **tamper with 1.** to make secret, illegal arrangements with **2.** to meddle with, esp. so as to damage —**tam′per·er** *n.*

tam·pon (tam′pän) *n.* [< Fr. *tapon,* a bung] a plug of cotton or other absorbent material put into a body cavity, wound, etc., as to stop bleeding

tan (tan) *n.* [< ML. *tannum]* **1.** *same as* TANBARK **2.** *a)* a yellowish-brown color *b)* such a color given to fair skin as by exposure to the sun *—adj.* **tan′ner, tan′nest** yellowish-brown *—vt.* **tanned, tan′ning 1.** to change (hide) into leather by soaking in tannic acid **2.** to produce a suntan in **3.** [Colloq.] to whip severely *—vi.* to become tanned

tan·a·ger (tan′ə jər) *n.* [< Port. < SAmInd. *tangara]* any of various small, new-world songbirds: the males are usually brilliantly colored

tan′bark′ *n.* any bark containing tannic acid, used to tan hides and, after the tannic acid has been extracted, to cover circus rings, etc.

tan·dem (tan′dəm) *adv.* [< punning use of L. *tandem,* at length (of time)] one behind the other; in single file *—n.* **1.** a two-wheeled carriage drawn by horses harnessed tandem **2.** a team, as of horses, harnessed tandem **3.** a bicycle with two seats and two sets of pedals placed tandem *—adj.* having two parts or things placed tandem

tang (taŋ) *n.* [ON. *tangi,* a sting] **1.** a prong on a knife, file, etc. that fits into the handle **2.** a strong, penetrating taste or odor **3.** a touch or trace (*of*) **4.** a special flavor, quality, etc. —**tang′y** *adj.*

Tan·gan·yi·ka (taŋ′gan yē′kə), Lake lake in EC Africa: 12,700 sq. mi.

tan·ge·lo (tan′jə lō′) *n., pl.* **-los′** [TANG(ERINE) + (*pom*)*elo,* grapefruit] a fruit produced by crossing a tangerine with a grapefruit

tan·gent (tan′jənt) *adj.* [< L. *tangere,* to touch] **1.** touching **2.** *Geom.* meeting a curve or surface at one point but not intersecting it: said of a line or plane *—n.* **1.** *Geom.* a tangent line, curve, or surface **2.** *Trigonometry* the ratio of the side opposite a given acute angle in a right triangle to the adjacent side —**go** (or **fly**) **off at** (or **on**) **a tangent** to change suddenly to another line of action —**tan′gen·cy** *n.*

tan·gen·tial (tan jen′shəl) *adj.* **1.** of or like a tangent **2.** drawn as a tangent **3.** going off at a tangent **4.** merely touching on a subject —**tan·gen′tial·ly** *adv.*

tan·ge·rine (tan′jə rēn′, tan′jə rēn′) *n.* [< Fr. *Tanger*, Tangier] **1.** a small, loose-skinned, reddish-yellow orange with easily separated segments **2.** reddish yellow

tan·gi·ble (tan′jə b'l) *adj.* [< L. *tangere*, to touch] **1.** that can be touched or felt by touch **2.** that can be appraised for value [*tangible* assets] **3.** definite; objective —*n.* [*pl.*] property that can be appraised for value —**tan′gi·bil′i·ty** *n.* —**tan′gi·bly** *adv.*

Tan·gier (tan jir′) seaport in N Morocco, on the Strait of Gibraltar: pop. 170,000

tan·gle (taŋ′g'l) *vt.* **-gled, -gling** [? < ME. *taglen*, to entangle] **1.** to catch as in a snare; trap **2.** to make a snarl of; intertwist —*vi.* **1.** to become tangled **2.** [Colloq.] to quarrel or fight —*n.* **1.** an intertwisted, confused mass, as of string; snarl **2.** a jumbled, confused condition

tan·go (taŋ′gō) *n., pl.* **-gos** [AmSp.] **1.** a S. American dance with long gliding steps **2.** music for this —*vi.* **-goed, -go·ing** to dance the tango

tank (taŋk) *n.* [< Sp. & Port. *estancar*, stop the flow of] **1.** any large container for liquid or gas **2.** an armored, self-propelled combat vehicle carrying guns and moving on tractor treads —*vt.* to put or store in a tank —**tank′ful′** *n., pl.* **-fuls′**

tank·ard (taŋ′kərd) *n.* [ME.] a large drinking cup with a handle and, often, a hinged lid

tank car a large tank on wheels, for carrying liquids and gases by rail

tank′er *n.* **1.** a ship for carrying oil or other liquids in large tanks **2.** a plane carrying gasoline for refueling another plane in flight

tank farming *same as* HYDROPONICS

tan·ner (tan′ər) *n.* one whose work is tanning hides

tan′ner·y *n., pl.* **-ies** a place where hides are tanned

tan·nic acid (tan′ik) a yellowish, astringent substance derived from oak bark, gallnuts, etc. and used in tanning, medicine, etc.: also **tan′nin** (-in) *n.*

tan·sy (tan′zē) *n., pl.* **-sies** [< LL. *tanacetum*] any of various strong-smelling plants with clusters of small, yellow flowers

tan·ta·lize (tan′tə līz′) *vt.* **-lized′, -liz′ing** [< TANTALUS + -IZE] to tease or disappoint by promising or showing something and then withholding it —**tan′ta·li·za′tion** *n.* — **tan′ta·liz′er** *n.* —**tan′ta·liz′ing·ly** *adv.*

tan·ta·lum (tan′tə ləm) *n.* [< TANTALUS: from difficulty in extracting it] a rare, steel-blue metallic chemical element that resists corrosion, used to make surgical instruments, parts for radio tubes, etc.: symbol, Ta; at. wt., 180.948; at. no., 73

Tan·ta·lus (tan′tə ləs) *Gr. Myth.* a king doomed in the lower world to stand in water that receded when he tried to drink it and under branches of fruit he could not reach

tan·ta·mount (tan′tə mount′) *adj.* [< L. *tantus*, so much + OFr. *amont*, upward] having equal value, effect, etc.; equivalent (*to*)

tan·trum (tan′trəm) *n.* [< ?] a violent, willful outburst of rage, etc.

Tan·za·ni·a (tan′zə nē′ə, tän′-) country in E Africa, consisting of a mainland section (*Tanganyika*) and Zanzibar: 362,820 sq. mi.; pop. 13,634,000 —**Tan′za·ni′an** *adj., n.*

Tao·ism (dou′iz′m, tou′-) *n.* [Chin. *tao*, the way] a Chinese religion and philosophy advocating simplicity, selflessness, etc. —**Tao′ist** *n., adj.*

tap¹ (tap) *vt., vi.* **tapped, tap′ping** [prob. echoic] **1.** to strike lightly **2.** to make or do by tapping [to *tap* a message] **3.** to choose, as for membership in a club —*n.* **1.** a light, rapid blow, or the sound made by it **2.** a small metal plate attached to the heel or toe of a shoe, as for tap dancing

tap² (tap) *n.* [OE. *tæppa*] **1.** a faucet or spigot **2.** a plug, cork, etc. for stopping a hole in a cask, etc. **3.** a draining of fluid from a body cavity **4.** a tool used to cut threads in a female screw **5.** a place in an electrical circuit where a connection can be made —*vt.* **tapped, tap′ping 1.** to put a hole in, or pull the plug from, for drawing off liquid **2.** to draw (liquid) from a container, cavity, etc. **3.** to make use of [to *tap* new resources] **4.** to make a connection with (an electric circuit, telephone line, etc.) —**on tap 1.** ready to be drawn from a tapped cask **2.** [Colloq.] ready for consideration or action

tap dance a dance performed with sharp, loud taps of the foot, toe, or heel at each step —**tap′-dance′** *vi.* **-danced′, -danc′ing** —**tap′-danc′er** *n.*

tape (tāp) *n.* [OE. *tæppe*, a fillet] **1.** a strong, narrow strip of cloth, paper, etc. used for binding, tying, etc. **2.** a strip of cloth stretched above the finishing line of a race **3.** *short for: a)* TAPE MEASURE *b)* ADHESIVE TAPE, MAGNETIC TAPE, etc. —*vt.* **taped, tap′ing 1.** to bind, tie, etc. with tape **2.** to measure with a tape measure **3.** to record (sound, video material, etc.) on magnetic tape

tape measure a tape marked in inches, feet, etc. for measuring: also **tape′line′** (-lin′) *n.*

ta·per (tā′pər) *n.* [OE. *tapur*] **1.** a slender candle **2.** *a)* a gradual decrease in width or thickness *b)* a gradual decrease in action, power, etc. —*vt., vi.* **1.** to decrease gradually in width or thickness **2.** to lessen; diminish Often with *off*

tape′-re·cord′ *vt.* to record on magnetic tape

tape recorder a device for recording on magnetic tape

tap·es·try (tap′is trē) *n., pl.* **-tries** [< Gr. *tapēs*, a carpet] a heavy woven cloth with decorative designs and pictures, used as a wall hanging, furniture covering, etc. —*vt.* **-tried, -try·ing** to decorate as with a tapestry

tape′worm′ *n.* a flatworm that lives as a parasite in the intestines of man and other vertebrates

tap·i·o·ca (tap′ē ō′kə) *n.* [Port. & Sp. < SAmInd.] a starchy, granular substance prepared from the root of the cassava plant, used for puddings, etc.

ta·pir (tā′pər) *n.* [Sp. < SAmInd.] a large, hoglike mammal found mostly in tropical America: tapirs have flexible snouts

tap·pet (tap′it) *n.* [< TAP¹] in an engine or machine, a projection or lever that moves or is moved by recurring contact, as with a cam

tap′room′ *n. same as* BARROOM

tap′root′ *n.* [TAP² + ROOT¹] a main root, growing downward, from which branch roots spread out

TAPIR
(2 1/2–3 1/2 ft. high)

taps (taps) *n.* [< TAP¹, because orig. a drum signal] a bugle call to put out the lights for the night, as in an army camp: also sounded at a military funeral

tar¹ (tär) *n.* [OE. *teru*] **1.** a thick, sticky, black liquid obtained by the destructive distillation of wood, coal, etc. **2.** loosely, any of the solids in smoke —*vt.* **tarred, tar′ring** to cover or smear with tar —*adj.* of, like, or covered with tar —**tar and feather** to cover (a person) with tar and feathers, as in punishment by mob action

tar² (tär) *n.* [< TAR(PAULIN)] [Colloq.] a sailor

tar·an·tel·la (tar′ən tel′ə) *n.* [< *Taranto*, city in Italy] **1.** a fast, whirling Italian dance for couples **2.** music for this

ta·ran·tu·la (tə ran′choo la) *n., pl.* **-las, -lae** (-lē) [see prec.] **1.** a large, hairy, somewhat poisonous spider of the SW U.S. and tropical America **2.** a similar spider of S Europe

tar·dy (tär′dē) *adj.* **-di·er, -di·est** [< L. *tardus*, slow] **1.** slow in moving, acting, etc. **2.** late, delayed, or dilatory — **tar′di·ly** *adv.* —**tar′di·ness** *n.*

tare¹ (ter) *n.* [< or akin to MDu. *tarwe*, wheat] **1.** the vetch **2.** *Bible* a weed

tare² (ter) *n.* [< It. < Ar. *taraha*, to reject] the weight of a container deducted from the total weight to determine the weight of the contents

tar·get (tär′git) *n.* [< MFr. *targe*, a shield] **1.** *a)* a board, etc. marked as with concentric circles, aimed at in archery, rifle practice, etc. *b)* any object that is shot at **2.** an objective; goal **3.** an object of attack, criticism, etc.

tar·iff (tar′if) *n.* [< Ar. *ta′rif*, information] **1.** a list or system of taxes upon exports or imports **2.** a tax of this kind, or its rate **3.** any list of prices, charges, etc. **4.** [Colloq.] any bill, charge, etc.

tar·nish (tär′nish) *vt.* [< MFr. *ternir*, make dim] **1.** to dull the luster of (a metal) by exposure to the air **2.** to sully (a reputation, etc.) —*vi.* **1.** to lose luster; discolor **2.** to become sullied —*n.* **1.** a being tarnished; dullness **2.** the film of discoloration on a tarnished surface **3.** a stain; blemish —**tar′nish·a·ble** *adj.*

ta·ro (tä′rō) *n., pl.* **-ros** [Tahitian] **1.** a tropical Asiatic plant with an edible tuber **2.** the tuber

tar·ot (tar′ō, ta rō′) *n.* [Fr. < Ar. *taraha*, remove] [*often* T-] any of a set of fortunetelling cards

tar·pau·lin (tär pô′lin, tär′pə-) *n.* [< TAR¹ + PALL²] **1.** canvas covered with a waterproofing compound **2.** a sheet of this used as a protective cover

tar·pon (tär'pən, -pän) *n.* [< ?] a large, silvery game fish found in the warmer parts of the W Atlantic

tar·ra·gon (tar'ə gän') *n.* [Sp. < Gr. *drakōn,* dragon] 1. an old-world wormwood whose fragrant leaves are used for seasoning 2. these leaves

tar·ry (tar'ē) *vi.* -ried, -ry·ing [prob. < L. *tardus,* slow] 1. to delay, linger, etc. 2. to stay longer than intended 3. to wait

tar·sal (tär's'l) *adj.* of the tarsus —*n.* a tarsal bone

tar·sus (tär'səs) *n., pl.* -si (-sī) [< Gr. *tarsos,* flat of the foot] the human ankle, consisting of seven bones

tart[1] (tärt) *adj.* [OE. *teart*] 1. sharp in taste; sour; acid 2. sharp in meaning; cutting [a *tart* answer] —**tart'ly** *adv.* —**tart'ness** *n.*

tart[2] (tärt) *n.* [MFr. *tarte*] a small shell of pastry filled with fruit, jam, etc.

tart[3] (tärt) *n.* [< prec., orig. slang term of endearment] a prostitute or any woman of loose morals

tar·tan (tär't'n) *n.* [prob. < MFr. *tiretaine,* mixed fabric] a woolen cloth in any of various woven plaid patterns, worn esp. in the Scottish Highlands, where each clan has its own pattern

Tar·tar (tär'tər) *n.* [< Per. *Tātār*] 1. *same as* TATAR 2. [*usually* t-] a bad-tempered person —**catch a tartar** to attack someone too strong for one

tar·tar (tär'tər) *n.* [< MGr. *tartaron*] 1. a potassium salt forming a reddish, crustlike deposit in wine casks: in purified form called CREAM OF TARTAR 2. a hard deposit on the teeth

tar·tar·ic (tär tar'ik, -tär'-) *adj.* of, containing, or derived from tartar or tartaric acid

tartaric acid a colorless, crystalline acid found in fruit juices, etc. and obtained from tartar

tar·tar sauce (tär'tər) [< Fr.] a sauce, as for seafood, consisting of mayonnaise with chopped pickles, olives, capers, etc.: also sp. **tartare sauce**

Tar·ta·ry (tär'tər ē) *same as* TATARY

Tash·kent (täsh kent') city in Uzbek S.S.R.: pop. 1,385,000

task (task) *n.* [< L. *taxare,* to rate] 1. a piece of work to be done 2. any difficult undertaking —*vt.* to put a strain on; tax —**take to task** to reprimand

task force a group, esp. a trained military unit, assigned a specific task

task'mas'ter *n.* one who assigns tasks to others, esp. when exacting or severe

Tas·ma·ni·a (taz mā'nē ə, -mān'yə) island state of Australia, off its SE coast —**Tas·ma'ni·an** *adj., n.*

Tass (täs) [< the initial letters of the full name] a Soviet agency for gathering and distributing news

tas·sel (tas''l) *n.* [OFr., a knob] 1. an ornamental tuft of threads, etc. hanging loosely from a knob or knot 2. something like this, as a tuft of corn silk —*vt.* -**seled** or -**selled, -sel·ing** or -**sel·ling** to put tassels on —*vi.* to grow tassels, as corn

taste (tāst) *vt.* **tast'ed, tast'ing** [OFr. *taster*] 1. to test the flavor of by putting a little in one's mouth 2. to detect the flavor of by the sense of taste 3. to eat or drink a small amount of 4. to experience [to *taste* success] —*vi.* 1. to have a specific flavor 2. to have a sensation or limited experience (*of* something) —*n.* 1. the sense by which flavor is perceived through stimulation of the taste buds on the tongue 2. the quality so perceived; flavor 3. a small amount tasted as a sample 4. a bit; trace 5. *a*) the ability to appreciate and judge what is beautiful, appropriate, etc. *b*) a style or way that shows such ability 6. a liking; inclination —**in bad, poor,** etc. (or **good, excellent,** etc.) **taste** in a style or manner showing a bad (or good) sense of beauty, fitness, etc. —**to one's taste** 1. pleasing to one 2. so as to please one —**taste'less** *adj.* —**taste'less·ly** *adv.* —**taste'less·ness** *n.*

taste bud any of the cells in the tongue that are the sense organs of taste

taste'ful *adj.* having or showing good taste [*tasteful* décor] —**taste'ful·ly** *adv.*

tast'er *n.* one who tastes; specif., one employed to test the quality of wines, teas, etc. by tasting

tast'y *adj.* -i·er, -i·est that tastes good —**tast'i·ness** *n.*

tat (tat) *vt.* **tat'ted, tat'ting** to make by tatting —*vi.* to do tatting

Ta·tar (tät'ər) *n.* 1. a member of any of the E Asiatic tribes who invaded W Asia and E Europe in the Middle Ages 2. any of an Asiatic people living in EC European Russia and parts of Asia 3. a Turkic language

Ta·ta·ry (tät'ə rē) vast region in Europe & Asia under Tatar control in the late Middle Ages

'ta·ter, ta·ter (tät'ər) *n. dial. form of* POTATO

tat·ter (tat'ər) *n.* [prob. < ON. *töturr,* rags] 1. a torn and hanging piece, as of a garment 2. [*pl.*] torn, ragged clothes —*vt., vi.* to make or become ragged —**tat'tered** *adj.*

tat·ter·de·mal·ion (tat'ər di māl'yən, -mal'-) *n.* [< TATTER + ?] a ragamuffin

tat·ting (tat'iŋ) *n.* [prob. < Brit. dial. *tat,* to tangle] 1. a fine lace that is made by looping and knotting thread that is wound on a hand shuttle 2. the act of making this

tat·tle (tat''l) *vi.* -**tled, -tling** [prob. < MDu. *tatelen*] 1. to talk idly 2. to tell others' secrets —*n.* idle talk; chatter —**tat'tler** *n.*

TATTING

tat'tle·tale' *n.* an informer; talebearer: now chiefly a child's term

tat·too[1] (ta tōō') *vt.* -**tooed', -too'ing** [< Tahitian *tatau*] to make (permanent designs) on (the skin) by puncturing it and inserting indelible colors —*n., pl.* -**toos'** a tattooed mark or design —**tat·too'er** *n.*

tat·too[2] (ta tōō') *n., pl.* -**toos'** [< Du. *tap toe,* shut the tap: a signal for closing barrooms] 1. a signal on a drum, bugle, etc. summoning soldiers, etc. to their quarters at night 2. any continuous drumming, rapping, etc. —*vt., vi.* -**tooed', -too'ing** to beat or tap

tau (tô, tou) *n.* the nineteenth letter of the Greek alphabet (T, τ)

taught (tôt) *pt. & pp. of* TEACH

taunt (tônt, tänt) *vt.* [< ? Fr. *tant pour tant,* tit for tat] 1. to reproach scornfully or sarcastically 2. to provoke by taunting —*n.* a scornful or jeering remark

taupe (tōp) *n.* [Fr. < L. *talpa,* a mole] a dark, brownish gray, the color of moleskin —*adj.* of such a color

Tau·rus (tôr'əs) [L., a bull] 1. a N constellation containing the Pleiades 2. the second sign of the zodiac: see ZODIAC, illus.

taut (tôt) *adj.* [ME. *toght,* tight] 1. tightly stretched, as a rope 2. strained; tense [a *taut* smile] 3. trim, tidy, etc. —**taut'ly** *adv.* —**taut'ness** *n.*

tau·tol·o·gy (tô täl'ə jē) *n., pl.* -**gies** [< Gr. *to auto,* the same + -LOGY] needless repetition of an idea in a different word, phrase, etc.; redundancy (Ex.: "necessary essentials") —**tau'to·log'i·cal** (-tə läj'i k'l) *adj.*

tav·ern (tav'ərn) *n.* [< L. *taberna*] 1. a bar; saloon 2. an inn

taw·dry (tô'drē) *adj.* -**dri·er, -dri·est** [< *St. Audrey laces,* sold at St. Audrey's fair, Norwich, England] cheap and showy; gaudy —**taw'dri·ly** *adv.* —**taw'dri·ness** *n.*

taw·ny (tô'nē) *adj.* -**ni·er, -ni·est** [< OFr. *tanner,* to tan] brownish-yellow; tan —*n.* a tawny color

tax (taks) *vt.* [< L. *taxare,* appraise] 1. to require to pay a tax 2. to assess a tax on (income, purchases, etc.) 3. to put a burden or strain on 4. to accuse; charge —*n.* 1. a compulsory payment, usually a percentage of income, property value, etc., for the support of a government 2. a heavy demand; burden —**tax'a·ble** *adj.*

tax·a·tion (tak sā'shən) *n.* 1. a taxing or being taxed 2. a tax or tax levy 3. revenue from taxes

tax-de·duct·i·ble (taks'di duk'tə b'l) *adj.* allowed as a deduction in computing income tax

tax'-ex·empt' (-ig zempt') *adj.* 1. exempt from taxation 2. producing nontaxable income [*tax-exempt* bonds]

tax·i (tak'sē) *n., pl.* -**is** *shortened form of* TAXICAB —*vi.* **tax'ied, tax'i·ing** or **tax'y·ing** 1. to go in a taxi 2. to move slowly along the ground or on water as an airplane does before taking off or after landing —*vt.* 1. to carry in a taxi 2. to cause (an airplane) to taxi

tax'i·cab' (-kab') *n.* [< *taxi*(*meter*) *cab*] an automobile in which passengers are carried for a fare

tax·i·der·my (tak'si dur'mē) *n.* [< Gr. *taxis,* arrangement + *derma,* a skin] the art of preparing, stuffing, and mounting the skins of animals so as to give a lifelike effect —**tax'i·der'mist** *n.*

tax·i·me·ter (tak'sē mēt'ər) *n.* [< ML. *taxa,* a tax + -*meter,* -METER] an automatic device in taxicabs that registers fares due

tax·on·o·my (tak sän'ə mē) *n.* [< Gr. *taxis,* arrangement + *nomos,* a law] classification, esp. of animals and plants —**tax·on'o·mist** *n.*

tax′pay′er *n.* any person who pays taxes

Tay·lor (tā′lər), **Zach·a·ry** (zak′ər ē) 1784–1850; 12th president of the U.S. (1849–50)

Tb *Chem.* terbium

TB, T.B., tb, t.b. tuberculosis

T-bone steak (tē′bōn′) a steak from the loin, with a T-shaped bone

tbs., tbsp. tablespoon(s)

Tc *Chem.* technetium

Tchai·kov·sky (chī kôf′skē), **Peter** 1840–93; Russ. composer

TD touchdown: also **td**

Te *Chem.* tellurium

tea (tē) *n.* [Chin. dial. *t′e*] **1.** an evergreen shrub grown in warm parts of Asia **2.** its dried leaves, steeped in boiling water to make a beverage **3.** this beverage **4.** a tealike beverage made as from other plants **5.** [Chiefly Brit.] a light meal in the late afternoon **6.** a social gathering in the afternoon at which tea, coffee, etc. are served

tea bag a small, porous bag with tea leaves in it, for making an individual cup of tea

tea′ber′ry *n., pl.* **-ries 1.** *same as* WINTERGREEN (sense 1) **2.** a wintergreen berry

teach (tēch) *vt.* **taught, teach′ing** [OE. *tæcan*] **1.** to show how to do something; instruct **2.** to give lessons to **3.** to give lessons in (a subject) **4.** to give knowledge, insight, etc. to *—vi.* to be a teacher **—teach′a·ble** *adj.*

teach′er *n.* one who teaches, esp. in a school or college

tea′cup′ *n.* a cup for drinking tea **—tea′cup·ful′** *n., pl.* **-fuls′**

teak (tēk) *n.* [< Port. < native word *tēkka*] **1.** a large East Indian tree with hard, yellowish-brown wood used for shipbuilding, furniture, etc. **2.** its wood: also **teak′wood′**

tea′ket′tle *n.* a covered kettle with a spout and handle, used to boil water for tea, etc.

teal (tēl) *n.* [ME. *tele*] **1.** a small, short-necked freshwater wild duck **2.** a dark greenish blue: also **teal blue**

team (tēm) *n.* [OE., offspring] **1.** two or more horses, oxen, etc. harnessed to the same plow, etc. **2.** a group of people working or playing together *—vt., vi.* to join together in a team (often with *up*)

team′mate′ *n.* a fellow team member

team′ster (-stər) *n.* one whose occupation is driving teams or trucks for hauling loads

team′work′ *n.* the action or effort of people working together as a group

tea party a social gathering at which tea is served

tea′pot′ *n.* a pot with a spout, handle, and lid, for brewing and pouring tea

tear[1] (ter) *vt.* **tore, torn, tear′ing** [OE. *teran*, rend] **1.** to pull apart by force; rip **2.** to make (a hole, etc.) by tearing **3.** to lacerate **4.** to split; disrupt [*torn* by dissension] **5.** to divide by doubt, etc. [*torn* between two loves] **6.** to remove as by tearing, pulling, etc. (with *out, off*, etc.) *—vi.* **1.** to be torn **2.** to move with force or speed *—n.* **1.** a tearing **2.** a torn place; rip **3.** a violent outburst **4.** [Slang] a spree **—tear at** to pull at violently in an effort to tear or remove **—tear down** to take apart; wreck, demolish, etc. **—tear into** [Colloq.] to attack or criticize violently

tear[2] (tir) *n.* [OE.] **1.** a drop of the salty fluid that keeps the eyeball moist and flows from the eye in weeping **2.** [*pl.*] sorrow; grief *—vi.* to shed, or fill with, tears **—in tears** weeping **—tear′ful** *adj.* **—tear′ful·ly** *adv.*

tear′drop′ (tir′-) *n.* a tear **—***adj.* tear-shaped

tear gas (tir) a gas that makes the eyes sore and blinds them with tears **—tear′-gas′** *vt.* **-gassed′, -gas′sing**

tea′room′ *n.* a restaurant that serves tea, coffee, light lunches, etc.

tear·y (tir′ē) *adj.* **-i·er, -i·est** tearful; crying

tease (tēz) *vt.* **teased, teas′ing** [OE. *tæsan*] **1.** *a)* to card or comb (flax, wool, etc.) *b)* to raise a nap on (cloth) with teasels *c)* to fluff (the hair) by brushing or combing the hair ends toward the scalp **2.** to annoy by mocking, poking fun, etc. **3.** to pester with repeated requests **4.** to tantalize *—vi.* to tease someone *—n.* **1.** a teasing or being teased **2.** one who teases **—teas′er** *n.*

tea·sel (tē′z′l) *n.* [see TEASE] **1.** a bristly plant with prickly, cylindrical flowers **2.** the dried flower, or any device, used to raise a nap on cloth

tea′spoon′ *n.* a spoon for use at the table and as a measuring unit holding 1/3 tablespoonful **—tea′spoon·ful′** *n., pl.* **-fuls′**

teat (tēt) *n.* [< OFr. *tete*] the nipple of a breast or udder

tech. **1.** technical **2.** technology

tech·ne·ti·um (tek nē′shē əm) *n.* [< Gr. *technē*, an art] a metallic chemical element obtained in the fission of uranium: symbol, Tc; at. wt., 97(?); at. no., 43

tech·nic (tek′nik) *adj.* [< Gr. *technē*, an art] *same as* TECHNICAL *—n.* (also tek nēk′) **1.** *same as* TECHNIQUE **2.** [*pl.*, *with sing. or pl. v.*] the study or principles of an art

tech·ni·cal (tek′ni k′l) *adj.* [< Gr. *technē*, an art] **1.** dealing with the industrial or mechanical arts or the applied sciences **2.** of a specific science, art, etc. **3.** of or showing technique **4.** according to principles or rules [a *technical* difference] **5.** involving or using technicalities **—tech′ni·cal·ly** *adv.*

tech′ni·cal′i·ty (-nə kal′ə tē) *n., pl.* **-ties 1.** the state or quality of being technical **2.** a technical point, term, method, etc. **3.** a minute point or detail brought to bear on a main issue

technical knockout *Boxing* a victory won when the opponent, though not knocked out, is so badly hurt that the referee stops the match

tech·ni·cian (tek nish′ən) *n.* one skilled in the technicalities or the technique of some art, craft, or science

Tech·ni·col·or (tek′ni kul′ər) *a trademark for* a certain process of making color motion pictures *—n.* [t-] **1.** this process **2.** bright colors

tech·nique (tek nēk′) *n.* [Fr.: see TECHNIC] **1.** the method of procedure in artistic work, scientific operation, etc. **2.** the degree of expertness in this **3.** any method of doing a thing

tech·noc·ra·cy (tek näk′rə sē) *n.* [< Gr. *technē*, an art + -CRACY] government by scientists and engineers **—tech′no·crat′** (-nə krat′) *n.*

tech·nol·o·gy (tek näl′ə jē) *n.* [Gr. *technologia*, systematic treatment] **1.** the science or study of the practical or industrial arts **2.** the terms used in a science, art, etc. **3.** applied science **—tech′no·log′i·cal** (-nə läj′i k′l), **tech′no·log′ic** *adj.* **—tech·nol′o·gist** *n.*

ted·dy bear (ted′ē) [< *Teddy* (*Theodore*) Roosevelt] a child's stuffed toy made to look like a bear

Te De·um (tē dē′əm) [LL.] **1.** a Christian hymn beginning *Te Deum laudamus* (We praise thee, O God) **2.** music for this hymn

te·di·ous (tē′dē əs) *adj.* full of tedium; tiresome; boring **—te′di·ous·ly** *adj.* **—te′di·ous·ness** *n.*

te′di·um (-əm) *n.* [< L. *taedet*, it offends] the condition or quality of being tiresome, boring, or monotonous

tee[1] (tē) *n., pl.* **tees 1.** the letter T, t **2.** anything shaped like a T *—adj.* shaped like a T **—to a tee** exactly

tee[2] (tē) *n.* [prob. < Scot. dial. *teaz*] **1.** a small, pointed holder of wood, plastic, etc. on which a golf ball is put to be driven **2.** the place at each hole from which a golfer makes his first stroke **—tee off 1.** to play a golf ball from a tee **2.** to begin **3.** [Slang] to make angry or disgusted

teem[1] (tēm) *vi.* [< OE. *team*, progeny] to be full; abound; swarm [a pond *teeming* with fish]

teem[2] (tēm) *vt.* [ON. *tæma*] to empty; pour out *—vi.* to pour [a *teeming* rain]

teen (tēn) *n.* [< OE. *tien*, ten] **1.** [*pl.*] the years from thirteen through nineteen **2.** *same as* TEEN-AGER *—adj. same as* TEEN-AGE

teen′-age′ (-āj′) *adj.* **1.** in one's teens **2.** of or for persons in their teens Also **teen′age′** **—teen′-ag′er** *n.*

tee·ny (tē′nē) *adj.* **-ni·er, -ni·est** *colloq. var. of* TINY: also **teen′sy, tee′ny-wee′ny**

tee·pee (tē′pē) *n. alt. sp. of* TEPEE

tee shirt *same as* T-SHIRT

tee·ter (tēt′ər) *vi., vt.* [< ON. *titra*, to tremble] to totter, wobble, etc.

tee′ter-tot′ter (-tät′ər, -tôt′-) *n., vi. same as* SEESAW

teeth (tēth) *n. pl. of* TOOTH

teethe (tē*th*) *vi.* **teethed, teeth′ing** to grow teeth; cut one's teeth

teeth·ing ring (tē′*th*iŋ) a ring as of plastic for teething babies to bite on

tee·to·tal·er (tē tōt′'l ər) *n.* [< doubling of initial *t* in *total*] one who practices total abstinence from alcoholic liquor: also **tee·to′tal·ler**

Tef·lon (tef′län) *a trademark for* a tough polymer used for nonsticking coatings as on cooking utensils

Te·gu·ci·gal·pa (te gōō′sē gäl′pä) capital of Honduras: pop. 219,000

Teh·rán, Te·he·ran (te ə rän′, -ran′) capital of Iran: pop. 3,150,000

tek·tite (tek′tīt) *n.* [< Gr. *tēktos*, molten] a small, dark, glassy body, thought to be from outer space

tel. **1.** telegram **2.** telephone

Tel A·viv (tel′ ä vēv′) seaport in W Israel: pop. 383,000: in full **Tel′ A·viv′-Jaf′fa** (-yäf′ə)

tele- *a combining form meaning:* **1.** [< Gr. *tēle*, far off] at, over, etc. a distance **2.** [< TELE(VISION)] of or by television [*telecast*]

tel·e·cast (tel′ə kast′) *vt., vi.* **-cast′** or **-cast′ed, -cast′ing** to broadcast by television —*n.* a television broadcast — **tel′e·cast′er** *n.*

tel·e·com·mu·ni·ca·tion (tel′ə kə myōō′nə kā′shən) *n.* [*also pl., with sing. or pl.* υ] communication by radio, telephone, television, etc.

tel·e·gram (tel′ə gram′) *n.* a message transmitted by telegraph

tel·e·graph (-graf′) *n.* [see TELE- & -GRAPH] an apparatus or system for sending messages by electric impulses through a wire or by means of radio waves —*vt., vi.* to send (a message) to (someone) by telegraph —**tel′e·graph′ic** *adj.*

te·leg·ra·phy (tə leg′rə fē) *n.* **1.** the operation of telegraph apparatus **2.** the sending of messages by telegraph —**te·leg′ra·pher** *n.*

tel·e·me·ter (tel′ə mēt′ər, tə lem′ə tər) *n.* [TELE- + -METER] a device for measuring temperature, radiation, etc. as in outer space and transmitting the information to a distant receiver —*vt., vi.* to transmit by telemeter —**te·lem′e·try** *n.*

te·le·ol·o·gy (tē′lē äl′ə jē, tel′ē-) *n.* [< Gr. *telos*, an end + -LOGY] **1.** the fact or quality of having an ultimate purpose **2.** a belief that there is purpose in nature —**te′le·o·log′i·cal** (-ə läj′i k'l) *adj.*

te·lep·a·thy (tə lep′ə thē) *n.* [TELE- + -PATHY] supposed communication between minds by means other than the normal functioning of the senses —**tel·e·path·ic** (tel′ə path′ik) *adj.* —**tel′e·path′i·cal·ly** *adv.* —**te·lep′a·thist** *n.*

tel·e·phone (tel′ə fōn′) *n.* [TELE- + -PHONE] an instrument or system for conveying speech over distances by converting sound into electric impulses sent through a wire —*vt., vi.* **-phoned′, -phon′ing** to convey (a message) to (a person) by telephone —**tel′e·phon′ic** (-fän′ik) *adj.*

te·leph·o·ny (tə lef′ə nē) *n.* the science of communication by telephone

tel·e·pho·to (tel′ə fōt′ō) *adj.* designating or of a camera lens producing a large image of a distant object

tel′e·pho′to·graph′ *n.* **1.** a photograph taken with a telephoto lens **2.** a photograph transmitted by converting light rays into electric signals which are sent over wire or radio channels —*vt., vi.* **1.** to take (photographs) with a telephoto lens **2.** to transmit (telephotographs) —**tel′e·pho′to·graph′ic** *adj.* —**tel′e·pho·tog′ra·phy** (-fə täg′rə fē) *n.*

tel·e·ran (tel′ə ran′) *n.* [*tele*(*vision*) *r*(*adar*) *a*(*ir*) *n*(*avigation*)] the televised transmission to aircraft of data received by radar concerning terrain, etc.

tel·e·scope (tel′ə skōp′) *n.* [see TELE- & -SCOPE] an instrument for making distant objects appear nearer and larger: it consists of tubes containing lenses —*adj.* having parts that slide one inside another —*vi., vt.* **-scoped′, -scop′ing** to slide one into another, as the tubes of a collapsible telescope —**tel′e·scop′ic** *adj.*

tel·e·thon (tel′ə thän′) *n.* [TELE(VISION) + (MARA)THON] a campaign, as on a lengthy telecast, asking for support for a cause

Tel·e·type (tel′ə tīp′) *a trademark for* a form of teletypewriter —*n.* [*often* t-] communication by means of Teletype —*vt., vi.* **-typed′, -typ′ing** [*often* t-] to send (messages) by Teletype

tel′e·type′writ′er *n.* a form of telegraph in which the message is typed on a keyboard that sends electric signals to a machine that prints the words

tel·e·vise (tel′ə vīz′) *vt., vi.* **-vised′, -vis′ing** to transmit by television

tel′e·vi′sion (-vizh′ən) *n.* [TELE- + VISION] **1.** the process of transmitting images by converting light rays into electric signals: the receiver reconverts the signals so that images are produced on a screen **2.** television broadcasting **3.** a television receiving set

tel·ex (tel′eks) *n.* [TEL(ETYPEWRITER) + EX(CHANGE)] **1.** a teletypewriter with a telephone dial for making connections **2.** a message sent by this —*vt.* to send (a message) by telex

tell (tel) *vt.* **told, tell′ing** [OE. *tellan*, calculate] **1.** orig., to enumerate; count **2.** to narrate; relate, as stories **3.** to express in words; utter [*tell* the truth] **4.** to report; announce **5.** to make known; disclose **6.** to recognize; distinguish [I can *tell* the difference] **7.** to let know; inform **8.** to request; order [*tell* him to go] —*vi.* **1.** to give an account or evidence (*of* something) **2.** to have a marked effect —**tell off** [Colloq.] to rebuke severely —**tell on 1.** to tire **2.** [Colloq.] to inform against

Tell (tel), **William** in Swiss legend, a hero in the fight for independence from Austria, forced to shoot an apple off his son's head with an arrow

tell′er *n.* **1.** one who tells (a story, etc.) **2.** one who counts; specif., a bank clerk who pays out or receives money

tell′ing *adj.* **1.** having an effect; forceful **2.** that reveals much —**tell′ing·ly** *adv.*

tell′tale′ *n.* **1.** a talebearer or informer **2.** an outward indication of a secret —*adj.* revealing a secret

tel·lu·ri·um (te loor′ē əm) *n.* [< L. *tellus*, the earth] a rare, white nonmetallic chemical element: symbol, Te; at. wt., 127.60; at. no., 52

tel·ly (tel′ē) *n.* [Brit. Colloq.] television

tem·blor (tem′blôr, -blər) *n.* [Sp. < *temblar*, to tremble] *same as* EARTHQUAKE

te·mer·i·ty (tə mer′ə tē) *n.* [< L. *temere*, rashly] foolish or rash boldness

temp. 1. temperature **2.** temporary

tem·per (tem′pər) *vt.* [< L. *temperare*, regulate] **1.** to moderate by mingling with another thing [*temper* blame with praise] **2.** *a*) to bring to the proper condition by some treatment [to *temper* steel by heating and sudden cooling] *b*) to toughen **3.** *Music* to tune (an instrument) so as to make the tones suitable for all keys —*vi.* to become tempered —*n.* **1.** the degree of hardness and resiliency of a metal **2.** frame of mind; disposition **3.** composure: now only in **lose** (or **keep**) one's **temper 4.** a tendency to get angry **5.** anger; rage

tem·per·a (tem′pər ə) *n.* [It.: see TEMPER] **1.** *a*) a way of painting with pigments mixed with size, casein, or egg to produce a dull finish *b*) the paint so used **2.** an opaque, water-base paint used as for posters

tem·per·a·ment (tem′prə mənt, -pər ə mənt) *n.* [see TEMPER] **1.** one's customary frame of mind or disposition **2.** a nature that is excitable, moody, etc.

tem′per·a·men′tal (-men′t'l) *adj.* **1.** of or caused by temperament **2.** excitable; easily upset **3.** erratic in behavior —**tem′per·a·men′tal·ly** *adv.*

tem·per·ance (tem′pər əns, -prəns) *n.* [see TEMPER] **1.** moderation; self-restraint **2.** moderation in drinking alcoholic liquors or total abstinence from them

tem·per·ate (tem′pər it, -prit) *adj.* [see TEMPER] **1.** moderate, as in eating or drinking **2.** moderate in one's actions, speech, etc. **3.** neither very hot nor very cold: said of climate, etc. —**tem′per·ate·ly** *adv.*

Temperate Zone either of two zones (**North** or **South Temperate Zone**) between the tropics and the polar circles

tem·per·a·ture (tem′prə chər, tem′pər ə-) *n.* [< L. *temperatus*, temperate] the degree of hotness or coldness of anything, usually as measured on a thermometer; specif., *a*) the degree of heat of a living body; also, an excess of this over the normal (about 98.6°F or 37°C in man) *b*) the degree of heat of the atmosphere

tem·pered (tem′pərd) *adj.* **1.** having been given the desired texture, hardness, etc. **2.** modified by other qualities, etc. **3.** having a (specified) temper [bad-*tempered*] **4.** *Music* having the pitch of the tones adjusted for all keys

tem·pest (tem′pist) *n.* [< L. *tempus*, time] **1.** a violent storm with high winds, esp. one accompanied by rain, snow, etc. **2.** a violent outburst

tem·pes·tu·ous (tem pes′chōō wəs) *adj.* **1.** of or like a tempest; stormy **2.** violent; turbulent —**tem·pes′tu·ous·ly** *adv.* —**tem·pes′tu·ous·ness** *n.*

tem·plate, tem·plet (tem′plit) *n.* [< Fr. < L. *templum*, small timber] a pattern, usually a thin plate, for forming an accurate copy of an object or shape

tem·ple¹ (tem′p'l) *n.* [< L. *templum*] **1.** a building for the worship of God or gods **2.** [T-] any of three buildings for worshiping Jehovah, successively built by the Jews in ancient Jerusalem **3.** a large building serving some purpose [a *temple* of art]

tem·ple² (tem′p'l) *n.* [< L. *tempus*] **1.** the flat surface beside the forehead, in front of each ear **2.** one sidepiece of a pair of glasses

tem·po (tem′pō) *n., pl.* **-pos, -pi** (-pē) [It. < L. *tempus*, time] **1.** the speed at which a piece of music is performed **2.** rate of activity; pace

tem·po·ral¹ (tem′pər əl, -prəl) *adj.* [< L. *tempus*, time] **1.** transitory; not eternal **2.** of this world; not spiritual **3.** secular **4.** of or limited by time —**tem′po·ral·ly** *adv.*

tem·po·ral² (tem′pər əl, -prəl) *adj.* of or near the temples (of the head)

temporal bone either of a pair of compound bones forming the sides of the skull

tem·po·rar·y (tem′pə rer′ē) *adj.* [< L. *tempus,* time] lasting only for a time; not permanent —**tem′po·rar′i·ly** *adv.*

tem·po·rize (tem′pə rīz′) *vi.* -rized′, -riz′ing [< L. *tempus,* time] 1. to act or speak in an expedient way 2. *a)* to put off making a decision, or to agree for a while, so as to gain time *b)* to bargain (*with* a person) so as to gain time —**tem′po·ri·za′tion** *n.* —**tem′po·riz′er** *n.*

tempt (tempt) *vt.* [< L. *temptare,* to test] 1. to entice (a person) to do or want something that is wrong, forbidden, etc. 2. to be inviting to; attract 3. to provoke or risk provoking (fate, etc.) 4. to incline strongly [I am *tempted to go*] —**tempt′er** *n.* —**tempt′ing** *adj.* —**tempt′ress** *n.fem.*

temp·ta·tion (temp tā′shən) *n.* 1. a tempting or being tempted 2. something that tempts

tem·pu·ra (tem′poo rä′, tem poor′ə) *n.* [Jpn.] a Japanese dish of deep-fried seafood or vegetables

ten (ten) *adj., n.* [OE.] one more than nine; 10; X

ten·a·ble (ten′ə b′l) *adj.* [Fr. < L. *tenere,* to hold] that can be held, defended, or believed —**ten′a·bil′i·ty** *n.* —**ten′a·bly** *adv.*

te·na·cious (tə nā′shəs) *adj.* [< L. *tenere,* to hold] 1. holding firmly [a *tenacious* grip] 2. that retains well [a *tenacious* memory] 3. strongly cohesive or adhesive 4. persistent —**te·na′cious·ly** *adv.* —**te·nac′i·ty** (-nas′ə tē) *n.*

ten·an·cy (ten′ən sē) *n., pl.* -cies 1. occupancy or duration of occupancy by a tenant 2. any holding of property, an office, etc.

ten·ant (ten′ənt) *n.* [< L. *tenere,* to hold] 1. one who pays rent to occupy or use land, a building, etc. 2. an occupant —*vt.* to occupy as a tenant —**ten′ant·less** *adj.*

tenant farmer one who farms the land of another and pays rent in cash or in a share of the crops

ten′ant·ry *n., pl.* -ries 1. a body of tenants 2. occupancy by a tenant

Ten Commandments *Bible* the ten laws forming the fundamental moral code of Israel, given to Moses by God: Ex. 20:2–17

tend[1] (tend) *vt.* [see ATTEND] 1. to take care of; watch over 2. to be in charge of; manage —*vi.* to pay attention

tend[2] (tend) *vi.* [< L. *tendere,* to stretch] 1. to move or extend [to *tend* east] 2. to be likely or apt; incline [*tending* to boast] 3. to lead (*to* or *toward* a specified result)

tend·en·cy (ten′dən sē) *n., pl.* -cies [< L. *tendere,* to stretch] 1. an inclination to move or act in a particular direction or way; leaning 2. a course toward some purpose, object, or result

ten·der[1] (ten′dər) *adj.* [< L. *tener,* soft] 1. easily chewed, broken, cut, etc.; soft 2. physically weak; frail 3. immature 4. needing careful handling 5. gentle or light, as a touch 6. *a)* acutely sensitive, as to pain *b)* sensitive to emotions, others' feelings, etc. [a *tender* heart] —**ten′der·ly** *adv.* —**ten′der·ness** *n.*

ten·der[2] (ten′dər) *vt.* [< L. *tendere,* to stretch] to present for acceptance; offer (an invitation, apology, etc.) —*n.* 1. an offer of money, services, etc. made to satisfy an obligation 2. a formal offer, as of marriage or a contract 3. money, etc. offered in payment

tend·er[3] (ten′dər) *n.* 1. one who tends, or has charge of, something 2. *a)* a ship for supplying another ship *b)* a boat for carrying passengers, etc. to or from a ship 3. the railroad car behind a steam locomotive for carrying its coal and water

ten′der·foot′ *n., pl.* -foots′, -feet′ 1. a newcomer, specif. to the hardships of Western ranching 2. a beginner in the Boy Scouts

ten′der·heart′ed *adj.* quick to feel pity

ten′der·ize *vt.* -ized′, -iz′ing to make (meat) tender —**ten′der·iz′er** *n.*

ten′der·loin′ *n.* the tenderest muscle of a loin of beef or pork

ten·don (ten′dən) *n.* [< Gr. *teinein,* to stretch] any of the cords of tough, fibrous tissue connecting muscles to bones, etc.; sinew —**ten′di·nous** (-də nəs) *adj.*

ten·dril (ten′drəl) *n.* [prob. ult. < L. *tener,* soft] a threadlike, clinging part of a climbing plant, serving to support it

ten·e·ment (ten′ə mənt) *n.* [< L. *tenere,* to hold] 1. a separately tenanted room or suite 2. an apartment building, now specif. one in the slums that is run-down and overcrowded: also **tenement house**

ten·et (ten′it) *n.* [L., he holds] a principle, doctrine, or belief held as a truth, as by some group

Ten·nes·see (ten′ə sē′) 1. EC State of the U.S.: 42,244 sq. mi.; pop. 3,924,000; cap. Nashville: abbrev. **Tenn., TN**

2. river flowing through N Ala. & W Tenn. into the Ohio River: 652 mi. —**Ten′nes·se′an** *adj., n.*

ten·nis (ten′is) *n.* [prob. < Anglo-Fr. *tenetz,* hold (imperative)] a game (officially *lawn tennis*) in which players using rackets hit a ball back and forth over a net dividing a marked rectangular area (**tennis court**)

tennis shoe *same as* SNEAKER

Ten·ny·son (ten′ə s'n), **Alfred** 1809–92; Eng. poet

ten·on (ten′ən) *n.* [ult. < L. *tenere,* to hold] a part of a piece of wood, etc. cut to stick out so that it will fit into a hole (*mortise*) in another piece to make a joint —*vt., vi.* 1. to make a tenon (on) 2. to joint by mortise and tenon

ten·or (ten′ər) *n.* [< L. *tenere,* to hold] 1. general course or tendency 2. general meaning; drift 3. *a)* the highest usual adult male voice, or its range *b)* a part for this *c)* a singer or instrument having this range —*adj.* of, in, or for the tenor

ten′pins′ *n.pl.* 1. [*with sing. v.*] the game of bowling in which ten pins are used 2. the pins

tense[1] (tens) *adj.* **tens′er, tens′est** [< L. *tendere,* stretch] 1. stretched tight; taut 2. feeling, showing, or causing mental strain —*vt., vi.* tensed, tens′ing to make or become tense —**tense′ly** *adv.* —**tense′ness** *n.*

tense[2] (tens) *n.* [< L. *tempus,* time] any of the forms of a verb that show the time of the action or condition

ten·sile (ten′s'l) *adj.* 1. of or under tension 2. capable of being stretched —**ten·sil′i·ty** *n.*

ten·sion (ten′shən) *n.* 1. a tensing or being tensed 2. mental or nervous strain 3. a state of strained relations 4. voltage 5. stress on a material by forces tending to cause extension —**ten′sion·al** *adj.*

tent (tent) *n.* [< L. *tendere,* stretch] 1. a portable shelter made of canvas, etc. stretched over poles and attached to stakes 2. anything like a tent; specif., *short for* OXYGEN TENT —*vi.* to live in a tent —*vt.* to lodge in tents

ten·ta·cle (ten′tə k'l) *n.* [< L. *tentare,* to touch] 1. a slender, flexible growth near the head or mouth, as of some invertebrates, used to grasp, feel, etc. 2. *Bot.* a sensitive hair on the leaves of some plants

ten·ta·tive (ten′tə tiv) *adj.* [< L. *tentare,* try] made, done, etc. experimentally or provisionally; not final —**ten′ta·tive·ly** *adv.* —**ten′ta·tive·ness** *n.*

tent caterpillar a caterpillar that lives in colonies in tentlike webs spun among tree branches

ten·ter·hook (ten′tər hook′) *n.* [< L. *tendere,* to stretch + HOOK] any of the hooked nails that hold cloth stretched on a frame to dry —**on tenterhooks** in suspense

tenth (tenth) *adj.* 1. preceded by nine others in a series; 10th 2. designating any of ten equal parts —*n.* 1. the one following the ninth 2. any of the ten equal parts of something; 1/10

ten·u·ous (ten′yoo wəs) *adj.* [< L. *tenuis,* thin + -OUS] 1. slender or fine, as a fiber 2. not dense; rare, as air high up 3. slight; flimsy [*tenuous* evidence] —**te·nu·i·ty** (tə nōō′ə tē, -nyōō′-), **ten′u·ous·ness** *n.* —**ten′u·ous·ly** *adv.*

ten·ure (ten′yər, -yoor) *n.* [< MFr. *tenir,* to hold] 1. the act or right of holding property, an office, etc. 2. the period or conditions of this

te·pee (tē′pē) *n.* [< Siouan *ti,* to dwell + *pi,* used for] a cone-shaped tent used by American Indians

tep·id (tep′id) *adj.* [< L. *tepere,* be slightly warm] slightly warm; lukewarm —**te·pid·i·ty** (tə pid′ə tē), **tep′id·ness** *n.* —**tep′id·ly** *adv.*

te·qui·la (tə kē′lə) *n.* [< *Tequila,* a Mex. district] an alcoholic liquor distilled from a Mexican agave

ter·bi·um (tur′bē əm) *n.* [< *Ytterby,* town in Sweden] a metallic chemical element of the rare-earth group: symbol, Tb; at. wt., 158.924; at. no., 65

TEPEE

ter·cen·te·nar·y (tur′sen ten′ər ē, tər sen′tə ner′ē) *adj., n., pl.* -ies [L. *ter,* three times + CENTENARY] *same as* TRICENTENNIAL

term (turm) *n.* [< L. *terminus,* a limit] 1. a set date, as for payment, etc. 2. a set period of time [school *term, term* of office] 3. [*pl.*] conditions of a contract, sale, etc. that define its scope 4. [*pl.*] mutual relationship between persons [on speaking *terms*] 5. a word or phrase having a definite meaning in some science, art, etc. 6. a word or phrase of a specified kind 7. *Math. a)* either quantity of a fraction or ratio *b)* each quantity in a series or algebraic expression —*vt.* to call by a term; name —**bring (or come) to terms** to force into (or arrive at) an agreement

ter·ma·gant (tur′mə gənt) *n.* [< OFr. *Tervagant,* alleged Muslim deity] a quarrelsome, scolding woman

ter·mi·na·ble (tur'mi nə b'l) *adj.* that can be, or is, terminated

ter·mi·nal (tur'mə n'l) *adj.* [L. *terminalis*] **1**. of, at, or forming the end or extremity of something **2**. at the end of a series; concluding; final **3**. of or in the final stages of a fatal disease *[terminal* cancer] **4**. in or of a term or set period of time **5**. of, at, or forming the end of a transportation line —*n.* **1**. an end; extremity **2**. a connective point on an electric circuit **3**. either end of a transportation line or a main station on it —**ter'mi·nal·ly** *adv.*

ter'mi·nate' (-nāt') *vt.* -**nat'ed**, -**nat'ing** [< L. *terminus*, a limit] **1**. to form the end or limit of **2**. to put an end to; stop —*vi.* to come to an end

ter'mi·na'tion *n.* **1**. a terminating or being terminated **2**. the end or limit **3**. an inflectional ending of a word

ter·mi·nol·o·gy (tur'mə näl'ə jē) *n., pl.* -**gies** the terms used in some science, art, work, etc.

ter·mi·nus (tur'mə nəs) *n., pl.* -**ni'** (-nī'), -**nus·es** [L., a limit] **1**. a boundary or limit **2**. an end; final point **3**. either end of a transportation line

ter·mite (tur'mīt) *n.* [L. *termes*, wood-boring worm] a pale-colored antlike insect that lives in colonies and is very destructive to wooden structures

tern (turn) *n.* [< ON. *therna*] a sea bird related to the gull, but smaller, with a more slender body and beak, and a deeply forked tail

Terp·sich·o·re (tərp sik'ə rē') *Gr. Myth.* the Muse of dancing

terp·si·cho·re·an (turp'si kə rē'ən) *adj.* [< prec.] having to do with dancing —*n.* a dancer: now a humorous use

ter·race (ter'əs) *n.* [< L. *terra*, earth] **1**. a raised, flat mound of earth with sloping sides, often one in a series on a hillside **2**. an unroofed, paved area next to a house and overlooking a lawn or garden **3**. a row of houses on ground raised from the street **4**. a street in front of such houses —*vt.* -**raced**, -**rac·ing** to form into or surround with a terrace

ter·ra cot·ta (ter'ə kät'ə) [It., lit., baked earth] **1**. a hard, brown-red, usually unglazed earthenware used for pottery, etc. **2**. its brown-red color —**ter'ra-cot'ta** *adj.*

terra fir·ma (fur'mə) [L.] firm earth; solid ground

ter·rain (tə rān', ter'ān) *n.* [Fr. < L. *terra*, earth] a tract of ground, esp. with regard to its features or fitness for some use

Ter·ra·my·cin (ter'ə mī's'n) [< L. *terra*, earth + Gr. *mykēs*, fungus] *a trademark for* an antibiotic derived from cultures of a soil fungus

ter·ra·pin (ter'ə pin) *n.* [< Algonquian] **1**. any of several American freshwater or tidewater turtles **2**. its edible flesh

ter·rar·i·um (tə rer'ē əm) *n., pl.* -**i·ums**, -**i·a** (-ə) [< L. *terra*, earth + (AQU)ARIUM] an enclosure, as of glass, in which small plants are grown or small land animals are kept

ter·raz·zo (tə raz'ō) *n.* [It.] flooring of small chips of marble set in cement and polished

ter·res·tri·al (tə res'trē əl) *adj.* [< L. *terra*, earth] **1**. of this world; worldly; mundane **2**. of or constituting the earth **3**. consisting of land, not water **4**. living on land **5**. growing in the ground —*n.* an inhabitant of the earth — **ter·res'tri·al·ly** *adv.*

ter·ri·ble (ter'ə b'l) *adj.* [< L. *terrere*, frighten] **1**. causing terror; dreadful **2**. extreme; intense **3**. [Colloq.] very bad, unpleasant, etc. —**ter'ri·bly** *adv.*

ter·ri·er (ter'ē ər) *n.* [< MFr. (*chien*) *terrier*, hunting (dog)] any of various breeds of active, typically small dog, orig. bred to burrow after small game

ter·rif·ic (tə rif'ik) *adj.* [< L. *terrere*, frighten] **1**. causing great fear **2**. [Colloq.] *a*) unusually great, intense, etc. *b*) unusually fine, enjoyable, etc. —**ter·rif'i·cal·ly** *adv.*

ter·ri·fy (ter'ə fī') *vt.* -**fied**, -**fy'ing** to fill with terror; frighten greatly —**ter'ri·fy'ing·ly** *adv.*

ter·ri·to·ry (ter'ə tôr'ē) *n., pl.* -**ries** [< L. *terra*, earth] **1**. the land and waters under the jurisdiction of a nation, ruler, etc. **2**. a part of a country or empire without the full status of a principal division **3**. any large tract of land **4**. an assigned area, as of a traveling salesman **5**. a sphere of action, etc. —**ter'ri·to'ri·al** *adj.* —**ter'ri·to'ri·al·ly** *adv.*

ter·ror (ter'ər) *n.* [< L. *terrere*, frighten] **1**. intense fear **2**. *a*) one causing intense fear *b*) the quality of causing such fear

ter'ror·ism *n.* **1**. the use of force and violence to intimidate, etc., esp. as a political policy **2**. the intimidation

produced in this way —**ter'ror·ist** *n., adj.* —**ter'ror·is'tic** *adj.*

ter'ror·ize' (-īz') *vt.* -**ized'**, -**iz'ing 1**. to fill with terror **2**. to coerce, make submit, etc. by filling with terror —**ter'ror·iz'er** *n.*

ter·ry (ter'ē) *n., pl.* -**ries** [prob. < Fr. *tirer*, to draw] cloth having a pile in which the loops are left uncut: also **terry cloth**

terse (turs) *adj.* **ters'er**, **ters'est** [< L. *tergere*, to wipe] free of superfluous words; concise; succinct —**terse'ly** *adv.* —**terse'ness** *n.*

ter·ti·ar·y (tur'shē er'ē) *adj.* [< L. *tertius*, third] of the third rank, order, formation, etc.

tes·sel·late (tes'ə lāt') *vt.* -**lat'ed**, -**lat'ing** [< L. *tessella*, little square stone] to lay out or pave in a mosaic pattern of small, square blocks

test (test) *n.* [< OFr., assaying cup] **1**. *a*) an examination or trial, as of something's value *b*) the method or a criterion used in this **2**. an event, etc. that tries one's qualities **3**. a set of questions, problems, etc. for determining one's knowledge, abilities, etc. **4**. *Chem.* a trial or reaction for identifying a substance —*vt.* to subject to a test; try —*vi.* to be rated by a test *[to test* high] —**test'er** *n.*

Test. Testament

tes·ta·ment (tes'tə mənt) *n.* [< L. *testis*, a witness] **1**. orig., a covenant **2**. [T-] either of the two parts of the Bible, the *Old Testament* and the *New Testament* **3**. *a*) a testimonial *b*) an affirmation of beliefs **4**. *Law* a will — **tes'ta·men'ta·ry** (-men'tə rē) *adj.*

tes·tate (tes'tāt) *adj.* [< L. *testari*, make a will] having left a legally valid will

tes'ta·tor *n.* one who has made a will —**tes·ta'trix** (-tā'-triks) *n.fem., pl.* -**tri·ces'** (-tri sēz')

tes·ti·cle (tes'ti k'l) *n.* [< L. *testis*] either of two oval male sex glands that are suspended in the scrotum and secrete spermatozoa

tes·ti·fy (tes'tə fī') *vi.* -**fied'**, -**fy'ing** [< L. *testis*, a witness + *facere*, make] **1**. to give evidence, esp. under oath in court **2**. to be evidence —*vt.* **1**. to affirm; declare, esp. under oath in court **2**. to be evidence of; indicate

tes·ti·mo·ni·al (tes'tə mō'nē əl) *n.* **1**. a statement recommending a person or thing **2**. something given or done to show gratitude or appreciation

tes·ti·mo·ny (tes'tə mō'nē) *n., pl.* -**nies** [< L. *testis*, a witness] **1**. a statement made under oath in court to establish a fact **2**. any affirmation or declaration **3**. any form of evidence; indication **4**. public avowal, as of faith

tes·tis (tes'tis) *n., pl.* -**tes** (-tēz) [L.] *same as* TESTICLE

tes·tos·ter·one (tes täs'tə rōn') *n.* [see TESTICLE] a male sex hormone

test pilot a pilot who tests new airplanes in flight, to determine their fitness for use

test tube a tube of thin, clear glass closed at one end, used in chemical experiments, etc.

tes·ty (tes'tē) *adj.* -**ti·er**, -**ti·est** [< L. *testa*, the head] irritable; touchy —**tes'ti·ly** *adv.* —**tes'ti·ness** *n.*

tet·a·nus (tet''n əs) *n.* [< Gr. *tetanos*, spasm] an acute infectious disease, often fatal, caused by the toxin of a bacillus which usually enters the body through wounds: characterized by spasmodic contractions and rigidity of muscles

tête-à-tête (tāt'ə tāt') *n.* [Fr., head-to-head] a private conversation between two people —*adj.* for or of two people in private —*adv.* together privately

teth·er (teth'ər) *n.* [prob. < ON. *tjōthr*] **1**. a rope, etc. fastened to an animal to keep it within bounds **2**. the limit of one's abilities, resources, etc. —*vt.* to fasten with a tether

tetra- [< Gr. *tettares*, four] *a combining form meaning* four

tet·ra·eth·yl lead (tet'rə eth'l) a heavy, colorless, poisonous compound of lead, added to gasoline to increase power and prevent engine knock

tet·ra·he·dron (tet'rə hē'drən) *n., pl.* -**drons**, -**dra** (-drə) [see TETRA- & -HEDRON] a solid figure with four triangular faces —**tet'ra·he'dral** *adj.*

te·tral·o·gy (te tral'ə jē) *n., pl.* -**gies** [see TETRA- & -LOGY] a series of four related plays, novels, etc.

te·tram·e·ter (te tram'ə tər) *n.* [see TETRA- & -METER] **1**. a line of verse containing four metrical feet **2**. verse consisting of tetrameters

TETRAHEDRON

tet·ra·va·lent (tet′rə vā′lənt) *adj.* **1.** having a valence of four **2.** *same as* QUADRIVALENT (sense 1)

Teu·ton (tōōt′'n, tyōōt′-) *n.* a member of any Teutonic people; esp., a German

Teu·ton′ic (-tän′ik) *adj.* designating or of a group of north European peoples including the German, Scandinavian, Dutch, English, etc.

Tex·as (tek′səs) SW State of the U.S.: 267,339 sq. mi.; pop. 11,197,000; cap. Austin: abbrev. **Tex.**, **TX** —**Tex′an** *adj., n.*

text (tekst) *n.* [< L. *texere*, to weave] **1.** the exact words of an author, as distinguished from notes, paraphrase, etc. **2.** any form in which a written work exists **3.** the principal matter on a printed page, as distinguished from notes, pictures, etc. **4.** *a*) a Biblical passage used as the topic of a sermon *b*) any topic or subject **5.** a textbook

text′book′ *n.* a book giving instructions in a subject of study

tex·tile (teks′tīl, -t′l) *adj.* [see TEXT] **1.** having to do with weaving **2.** that has been or can be woven —*n.* **1.** a fabric made by weaving, knitting, etc.; cloth **2.** raw material suitable for this

tex·tu·al (teks′choo wəl) *adj.* of, contained in, or based on a text —**tex′tu·al·ly** *adv.*

tex·ture (teks′chər) *n.* [see TEXT] **1.** the character of a fabric as determined by the arrangement, size, etc. of its threads **2.** the structure or composition of anything, esp. in the way it looks or feels —*vt.* **-tured, -tur·ing** to cause to have a particular texture —**tex′tur·al** *adj.*

TGIF, T.G.I.F. Thank God It's Friday: used to express relief at the end of the workweek

-th¹ [< OE.] *a suffix meaning:* **1.** the act of [*stealth*] **2.** the state or quality of being or having [*wealth*]

-th² [< OE.] a suffix used in forming ordinal numerals [*fourth*] : also **-eth**

Th *Chem.* thorium

Th. Thursday

Thack·er·ay (thak′ər ē), **William Make·peace** (māk′pēs′) 1811–63; Eng. novelist

Thai (tī) *n.* **1.** a group of Asian languages belonging to the Sino-Tibetan language family **2.** the official language of Thailand **3.** *pl.* **Thais, Thai** *a*) a member of a group of Thai-speaking peoples of SE Asia *b*) a native or inhabitant of Thailand —*adj.* of Thailand, its people, culture, etc.

Thai·land (tī′land) country in SE Asia: 198,456 sq. mi.; pop. 35,814,000; cap. Bangkok

thal·a·mus (thal′ə məs) *n.*, *pl.* **-mi** (-mī′) [< Gr. *thalamos*, inner room] a mass of gray matter at the base of the brain, involved in the transmission of certain sensations

thal·li·um (thal′ē əm) *n.* [< Gr. *thallos*, green shoot: from its green spectrum line] a rare, bluish-white, soft metallic chemical element: symbol, Tl; at. wt., 204.37; at. no., 81

Thames (temz) river in S England, flowing east through London into the North Sea: 210 mi.

than (than, then) *conj.* [OE. *thenne*] *a particle used: a*) to introduce the second element in a comparison [A is taller *than* B] *b*) to express exception [none other *than* Sam]

thank (thaŋk) *vt.* [OE. *thancian*] **1.** to express appreciation to, as by saying "thank you" **2.** to hold responsible: an ironic use —**thank you** *shortened form of* I thank you

thank′ful *adj.* feeling or expressing thanks —**thank′ful·ly** *adv.* —**thank′ful·ness** *n.*

thank′less *adj.* **1.** not feeling or expressing thanks; ungrateful **2.** unappreciated —**thank′less·ly** *adv.*

thanks (thaŋks) *n.pl.* an expression of gratitude —*interj.* I thank you —**thanks to 1.** thanks be given to **2.** on account of

thanks′giv′ing *n.* **1.** a formal public expression of thanks to God **2.** [T-] a U.S. holiday on the fourth Thursday of November: in full **Thanksgiving day**

Thant (thänt, thônt), **U** (ōō) 1909–74; Burmese diplomat; secretary-general of the United Nations (1962–71)

that (that) *pron.*, *pl.* **those** [OE. *thæt*] **1.** the person or thing mentioned [*that* is John] **2.** the farther one or other one [this is better than *that*] **3.** who, whom, or which [the road (*that*) we took] **4.** where [the place *that* I saw him] **5.** when [the year *that* he died] —*adj.*, *pl.* **those 1.** designating the one mentioned [*that* man is John] **2.** designating the farther one or other one [this house is larger than *that* one] —*conj.* *used to introduce:* **1.** a noun clause [*that* he's gone is obvious] **2.** an adverbial clause expressing purpose [they died *that* we might live] , result [he ran so fast *that* I lost him] , or cause [I'm sorry *that* I won] **3.** an elliptical sentence expressing surprise, desire, etc. [oh, *that* he were here!] —*adv.* **1.** to that extent; so [I can't see *that* far] **2.** [Colloq.] very: used in negative construc-

tions [I didn't like the book *that* much] —**all that** [Colloq.] **1.** so very **2.** everything of the same sort —**at that** [Colloq.] **1.** at that point: also **with that 2.** even so —**that is 1.** to be specific **2.** in other words —**that's that!** that is settled!

thatch (thach) *n.* [OE. *thæc*] **1.** a roof of straw, rushes, palm leaves, etc. **2.** material for such a roof: also **thatch′ing** —*vt.* to cover as with thatch —**thatch′y** *adj.*

thaw (thô) *vi.* [OE. *thawian*] **1.** *a*) to melt, as ice, snow, etc. *b*) to become unfrozen: said of frozen foods **2.** to become warmer, so that ice, snow, etc. melts **3.** to lose coldness of manner —*vt.* to cause to thaw —*n.* **1.** a thawing **2.** a spell of weather warm enough to allow thawing

the (thə; *before vowels* thi, thē) *adj.*, *definite article* [OE. *se*, with *th-* from other forms] *the* (as opposed to *a*, *an*) refers to: **1.** a particular person or thing [the story ended, *the* President] **2.** a person or thing considered outstanding, etc. [that's *the* hotel in town] **3.** a person or thing considered generically [*the* cow is a domestic animal, *the* poor] —*adv.* **1.** that much [*the* better to see you] **2.** by how much . . . by that much [*the* sooner *the* better]

the·a·ter, the·a·tre (thē′ə tər) *n.* [< Gr. *theasthai*, to view] **1.** a place or building where plays, motion pictures, etc. are presented **2.** any similar place having ascending rows of seats **3.** any scene of events **4.** *a*) the dramatic art *b*) the theatrical world

the·at·ri·cal (thē at′ri k′l) *adj.* **1.** having to do with the theater **2.** dramatic; esp. in disparagement), melodramatic or affected Also **the·at′ric** —**the·at′ri·cal·ly** *adv.*

Thebes (thēbz) **1.** ancient city in S Egypt, on the Nile **2.** ancient city in Greece —**The·ban** (thē′bən) *adj., n.*

thee (thē) *pron.* [OE. *the*] *objective case of* THOU: also used for *thou* by Friends (Quakers)

theft (theft) *n.* [OE. *thiefth*] the act or an instance of stealing; larceny

their (ther) *possessive pronominal adj.* [ON. *theirra*] of, belonging to, made by, or done by them

theirs (therz) *pron.* that or those belonging to them [*theirs* are better]

the·ism (thē′iz′m) *n.* [< Gr. *theos*, god] **1.** belief in a god or gods **2.** monotheism —**the′ist** *n.*, *adj.* —**the·is′tic** *adj.*

them (them) *pron.* [< ON. *theim*] *objective case of* THEY

theme (thēm) *n.* [< Gr. *thema*, what is set down] **1.** a topic, as of a lecture **2.** a motif **3.** a short essay **4.** a short melody used as the subject of a musical composition **5.** a recurring or identifying song in a film, musical, TV series, etc.: also **theme song** —**the·mat·ic** (thē mat′ik) *adj.*

them·selves (them selvz′) *pron.* **1.** *intensive form of* THEY [they went *themselves*] **2.** *reflexive form of* THEY [they hurt *themselves*] **3.** their true selves [they are not *themselves* today]

then (then) *adv.* [see THAN] **1.** at that time [I did it *then*] **2.** next in time or order [he ate and *then* slept] **3.** in that case; accordingly [if he reads it, *then* he will know] **4.** besides; moreover [I like to walk, and *then* it's cheaper] **5.** at another time [now it's warm, *then* cold] —*adj.* being such at that time [the *then* director] —*n.* that time [by *then*, they were gone] —**but then** but on the other hand —**then and there** at once —**what then?** what would happen in that case?

thence (thens, thens) *adv.* [OE. *thanan*] **1.** from that place **2.** on that account; therefore

thence′forth′ (-fôrth′) *adv.* from that time onward; thereafter: also **thence′for′ward**

the·oc·ra·cy (thē äk′rə sē) *n.*, *pl.* **-cies** [< Gr. *theos*, god + *kratos*, power] **1.** lit., the rule of a state by God or a god **2.** (a) government by priests claiming to rule by divine authority —**the′o·crat′ic** *adj.*

the·od·o·lite (thē äd′'l it′) *n.* [ModL. *theodelitus*] a surveying instrument used to measure vertical and horizontal angles

theol. 1. theologian **2.** theology

the·o·lo·gi·an (thē′ə lō′jən, -jē ən) *n.* a student of or a specialist in theology or a theology

the·ol·o·gy (thē äl′ə jē) *n.*, *pl.* **-gies** [< Gr. *theos*, god + -LOGY] **1.** the study of God and of religious doctrines and matters of divinity **2.** a specific system of this study —**the′o·log′i·cal** (-ə läj′i k′l) *adj.* —**the′o·log′i·cal·ly** *adv.*

the·o·rem (thē′ə rəm) *n.* [< Fr. or L. < Gr. *theōrein*, to view] **1.** a proposition that can be proved from accepted premises; law or principle **2.** *Math., Physics* a proposition embodying something to be proved

DIAGRAM OF
THEODOLITE
(A, vertical
angles; B,
horizontal
angles)

the·o·ret·i·cal (thē′ə ret′i k'l) *adj.* **1.** of or constituting theory **2.** limited to or based on theory; hypothetical **3.** tending to theorize; speculative Also **the′o·ret′ic** —**the′o·ret′i·cal·ly** *adv.*

the·o·re·ti·cian (thē′ə rə tish′ən) *n.* one who specializes in the theory of some art, science, etc.: also **the′o·rist** (-rist)

the·o·rize (thē′ə rīz′) *vi.* -**rized′**, -**riz′ing** to form a theory or theories; speculate —**the′o·ri·za′tion** *n.* —**the′o·riz′er** *n.*

the·o·ry (thē′ə rē, thir′ē) *n., pl.* -**ries** [< Fr. < Gr. *theōrein*, to view] **1.** a speculative idea or plan **2.** a systematic statement of principles involved **3.** a formulation of underlying principles of certain observed phenomena which has been verified to some degree **4.** the principles of an art or science rather than its practice **5.** popularly, a mere conjecture, or guess

the·os·o·phy (thē äs′ə fē) *n., pl.* -**phies** [< Gr. *theos,* god + *sophos,* wise] any of various philosophies or religions that propose to establish direct contact with divine principle through contemplation, revelation, etc. —**the′o·soph′ic** (-ə säf′ik), **the′o·soph′i·cal** *adj.* —**the·os′o·phist** *n.*

ther·a·peu·tic (ther′ə pyo͞ot′ik) *adj.* [< Gr. *therapeuein,* to nurse] **1.** serving to cure, heal, or preserve health **2.** of therapeutics Also **ther′a·peu′ti·cal** —**ther′a·peu′ti·cal·ly** *adv.*

ther′a·peu′tics *n.pl.* [*with sing. v.*] the branch of medicine dealing with the treatment of diseases; therapy

ther·a·py (ther′ə pē) *n., pl.* -**pies** [see THERAPEUTIC] the treatment of any physical or mental disorder by physical or medical means, usually excluding surgery —**ther′a·pist** *n.*

there (ther) *adv.* [OE. *ther*] **1.** at or in that place: often used as an intensive [John *there* is a good boy] **2.** to or into that place [go *there*] **3.** at that point; then **4.** in that respect [*there* you are wrong] **5.** right now [*there* goes the whistle] *There* is also used: *a*) in interjectional phrases of approval, etc. [*there's* a fine fellow!] *b*) in clauses in which the real subject follows the verb [*there* is little time] —*n.* that place [we left *there* at six] —*interj.* an exclamation of defiance, dismay, satisfaction, sympathy, etc. —**(not) all there** [Colloq.] (not) mentally sound

there′a·bouts′ *adv.* **1.** near that place **2.** near that time, number, degree, etc. Also **there′a·bout′**

there·af′ter *adv.* after that; subsequently

there·at′ *adv.* **1.** at that place; there **2.** at that time **3.** for that reason

there·by′ *adv.* **1.** by that means **2.** connected with that [*thereby* hangs a tale]

there·for′ *adv.* for this; for that; for it

there·fore (-fôr′) *adv.* for this or that reason; consequently; hence

there·from′ *adv.* from this; from that; from it

there·in′ *adv.* **1.** in or into that place or thing **2.** in that matter, detail, etc.

there·in′to *adv.* **1.** into that place or thing **2.** into that matter, condition, etc.

there·of′ *adv.* **1.** of that **2.** concerning that **3.** from that as a cause, reason, etc.

there·on′ *adv.* **1.** on that **2.** *same as* THEREUPON

there′s (therz) **1.** there is **2.** there has

there·to′ *adv.* **1.** to that place, thing, etc.: also **there·un′to 2.** [Archaic] besides

there′to·fore′ *adv.* until that time; before that

there·un′der *adv.* **1.** under that; under it **2.** under the terms stated here

there′up·on′ *adv.* **1.** immediately following that **2.** as a consequence of that **3.** concerning that subject, etc.

there·with′ *adv.* **1.** along with that **2.** in addition to that **3.** immediately thereafter

there′with·al′ (-with ôl′) *adv.* in addition; besides

ther·mal (thur′m'l) *adj.* [Fr. < Gr. *thermē,* heat] **1.** having to do with heat **2.** warm or hot **3.** designating a loosely knitted material with air spaces for insulation [*thermal* underwear] —**ther′mal·ly** *adv.*

thermal pollution the discharge of heated liquid into lakes, rivers, etc., as by industries, that is harmful to the ecosystems

thermo- [< Gr. *thermē,* heat] *a combining form meaning* heat

ther·mo·cou·ple (thur′mə kup′'l) *n.* a junction of two dissimilar metals which produces electric current when heated: also **thermoelectric couple**

ther·mo·dy·nam·ics (thur′mō dī nam′iks) *n.pl.* [*with sing. v.*] the branch of physics dealing with the reversible transformation of heat into mechanical energy —**ther′mo·dy·nam′ic** *adj.*

ther·mom·e·ter (thər mäm′ə tər) *n.* [< Fr.: see THERMO- & -METER] an instrument for measuring temperatures, as a graduated glass tube in which mercury, etc. rises or falls as it expands or contracts from changes in temperature: see FAHRENHEIT, CELSIUS

ther·mo·nu·cle·ar (thur′mō no͞o′klē ər, -nyo͞o′-) *adj. Physics* **1.** designating a reaction in which light atomic nuclei fuse, at extreme heat, into heavier nuclei **2.** of or employing the heat energy released in nuclear fusion

ther·mo·plas·tic (thur′mə plas′tik) *adj.* soft and moldable when subjected to heat: said of certain plastics —*n.* a thermoplastic substance

Ther·mop·y·lae (thər mäp′ə lē) in ancient Greece, a mountain pass on the E coast: scene of a battle (480 B.C.) in which the Persians destroyed a Spartan army

ther·mos (thur′məs) *n.* [Gr. *thermos,* hot] a bottle, flask, or jug for keeping liquids at almost their original temperature for several hours: in full **thermos bottle** (or **flask** or **jug**)

ther·mo·stat (thur′mə stat′) *n.* [THERMO- + -STAT] **1.** an apparatus for regulating temperature, esp. one that automatically controls a heating unit **2.** a device that sets off a sprinkler, etc. at a certain heat —**ther′mo·stat′ic** *adj.* —**ther′mo·stat′i·cal·ly** *adv.*

the·sau·rus (thi sôr′əs) *n., pl.* -**ri** (-ī), -**rus·es** [< Gr. *thēsauros,* a treasure] **1.** a storehouse **2.** a book containing a store of words; specif., a book of synonyms and antonyms

these (thēz) *pron., adj. pl.* of THIS

The·seus (thē′so͞os, -syo͞os) *Gr. Legend* a hero who killed the Minotaur

the·sis (thē′sis) *n., pl.* -**ses** (-sēz) [< Gr. *tithenai,* to put] **1.** a proposition defended in argument **2.** a research paper, esp. one written by a candidate for a master's degree **3.** *Logic* an unproved statement assumed as a premise

Thes·pi·an (thes′pē ən) *adj.* [< Thespis, ancient Gr. poet] [*often* t-] having to do with the drama; dramatic —*n.* [*often* t-] an actor or actress: a pretentious term

Thes·sa·lo·ni·ans (thes′ə lō′nē ənz) either of two books of the New Testament which were epistles from the Apostle Paul to the Christians of Thessalonica, an ancient city in Greece: abbrev. **Thess.**

Thes·sa·ly (thes′ə lē) division of E Greece

the·ta (thāt′ə, thēt′ə) *n.* the eighth letter of the Greek alphabet (Θ, θ)

thews (thyo͞oz) *n.pl., sing.* **thew** [OE. *theaw,* habit] **1.** muscular power **2.** muscles or sinews

they (thā) *pron., for sing. see* HE, SHE, IT [ON. *thei-r*] **1.** the persons, animals, or things previously mentioned **2.** people in general [*they* say it's so]

they'd (thād) **1.** they had **2.** they would

they'll (thāl, thel) **1.** they will **2.** they shall

they're (ther, thā′ər) they are

they've (thāv) they have

thi·a·mine (thī′ə mēn′, -min) *n.* [ult. < Gr. *theion,* brimstone + (VIT)AMIN] vitamin B₁, a white, crystalline compound, found in cereal grains, egg yolk, liver, etc.: a deficiency of this vitamin results in beriberi: also **thi′a·min** (-min)

thick (thik) *adj.* [OE. *thicce*] **1.** of relatively great extent from side to side **2.** measured between opposite surfaces [one inch *thick*] **3.** close and abundant [*thick* hair] **4.** not thin; viscous [*thick* soup] **5.** dense and heavy [*thick* smoke] **6.** husky; hoarse; blurred [*thick* speech] **7.** [Colloq.] stupid **8.** [Colloq.] very friendly —*adv.* in a thick way —*n.* the thickest part or the period of greatest activity —**through thick and thin** in good times and bad times —**thick′ish** *adj.* —**thick′ly** *adv.* —**thick′ness** *n.*

thick′en *vt., vi.* **1.** to make or become thick or thicker **2.** to make or become more complex or involved —**thick′en·er** *n.*

thick′en·ing *n.* **1.** the act of one that thickens **2.** a substance used to thicken **3.** the thickened part

thick·et (thik′it) *n.* [see THICK] a thick growth of shrubs, underbrush, or small trees

thick′set′ *adj.* **1.** planted thickly or closely **2.** thick in body; stocky

thick′-skinned′ *adj.* **1.** having a thick skin **2.** not easily hurt by criticism, insults, etc.

thief (thēf) *n., pl.* **thieves** (thēvz) [OE. *theof*] a person who steals, esp. secretly

---

fat, āpe, cär; ten, ēven; is, bīte; gō, hôrn, to͞ol, look; oil, out; up, fur; thin, *th*en; zh, leisure; ŋ, ring; ə for *a* in *ago;* ' as in *able* (ā′b'l); ë, Fr. coeur; ö, Fr. feu; Fr. mo*n;* ü, Fr. duc; r, Fr. cri; kh, G. doch, ich. ‡ foreign; < derived from

thieve (thēv) *vt.*, *vi.* thieved, thiev′ing to steal —thiev′ish *adj.*

thiev′er·y *n.*, *pl.* -ies the act or an instance of stealing; theft

thigh (thī) *n.* [OE. *theoh*] the part of the leg between the knee and the hip

thigh′bone′ *n.* the bone extending from the hip to the knee; femur: also **thigh bone**

thim·ble (thim′b'l) *n.* [< OE. *thuma*, thumb] a small cap of metal, plastic, etc. worn to protect the finger that pushes the needle in sewing —thim′ble·ful′ *n.*, *pl.* -fuls′

thin (thin) *adj.* thin′ner, thin′nest [OE. *thynne*] 1. of relatively little extent from side to side 2. lean; slender 3. not dense or compact *[thin* hair, *thin* smoke*]* 4. very fluid or watery *[thin* soup*]* 5. rarefied, as air at high altitudes 6. not deep and strong *[a thin* voice*]* 7. sheer, as a fabric 8. flimsy or unconvincing *[a thin* excuse*]* 9. lacking substance, depth, etc.; weak —*adv.* in a thin way —*vt.*, *vi.* thinned, thin′ning to make or become thin or thinner — thin′ly *adv.* —thin′ness *n.* ∸thin′nish *adj*

thine (thīn) *pron.* [OE. *thin*] *possessive form of* THOU — *adj.* thy: used before a vowel

thing (thing) *n.* [OE., a council] 1. any matter, affair, or concern 2. a happening, act, incident, etc. 3. a tangible object 4. an inanimate object 5. an item, detail, etc. 6. *a)* *[pl.]* personal belongings *b)* a garment 7. a person or creature *[poor thing!]* 8. [Colloq.] a point of dispute; issue 9. [Colloq.] an irrational liking, fear, etc. —do one's own thing [Colloq.] to express one's unique personality in one's own way of life, etc. —see things [Colloq.] to have hallucinations —the thing 1. that which is wise, essential, etc. 2. that which is the height of fashion

think (think) *vt.* thought, think′ing [OE. *thencan*] 1. to form or have in the mind *[to think* good thoughts*]* 2. to judge; consider *[I think* her charming*]* 3. to believe; expect *[I think* I can go*]* 4. to determine, work out, etc. by reasoning 5. [Now Rare] to intend *[thinking* to do right*]* 6. to recollect *[think* what joy was ours*]* —*vi.* 1. to use the mind; reflect or reason 2. to have an opinion, belief, etc. (with *of* or *about*) 3. to remember or consider (with *of* or *about*) 4. to conceive (*of*) —*n.* [Colloq.] a thinking — *adj.* [Colloq.] having to do with thinking —think better of to arrive at a better opinion of or decision about, after reconsidering —think little (or nothing) of 1. to attach little (or no) importance to 2. to have little (or no) hesitancy about —think over to ponder well —think up to invent, plan, etc. by thinking —think′er *n.*

think tank (or **factory**) [Slang] a group or center organized to do intensive research and problem-solving

thin·ner (thin′ər) *n.* a substance added, as turpentine to paint, for thinning

thin′-skinned′ *adj.* 1. having a thin skin 2. easily hurt by criticism, insults, etc.

thi·o·pen·tal (sodium) (thī′ə pen′tal) a yellowish-white powder injected intravenously in solution as a general anesthetic

third (thurd) *adj.* [OE. *thridda*] 1. preceded by two others in a series; 3d or 3rd 2. designating any of three equal parts —*n.* 1. the one following the second 2. any of the three equal parts of something; 1/3 —third′ly *adv.*

third′-class′ *adj.* 1. of the class, rank, etc. below the second 2. designating or of a lower-cost class of mail, as for advertisements —*adv.* 1. with third-class travel accommodations 2. as or by third-class mail

third degree [Colloq.] harsh treatment and questioning of a prisoner to force a confession or information

third person that form of a pronoun (as *he*) or verb (as *is*) which refers to the person or thing spoken of

third′-rate′ *adj.* 1. third in quality or other rating 2. very poor

third world [*often* T- W-] the underdeveloped or emergent countries of the world

thirst (thurst) *n.* [OE. *thurst*] 1. the discomfort caused by a need for water, characterized by dryness in the mouth and throat 2. a strong desire; craving —*vi.* 1. to be thirsty 2. to have a strong desire or craving

thirst′y *adj.* -i·er, -i·est 1. feeling thirst 2. lacking moisture; dry *[thirsty* fields*]* 3. [Colloq.] causing thirst *[thirsty* work*]* 4. having a strong desire; craving —thirst′i·ly *adv.* —thirst′i·ness *n.*

thir·teen (thur′tēn′) *adj.*, *n.* [OE. *threotyne*] three more than ten; 13; XIII —thir′teenth′ *adj.*, *n.*

thir·ty (thur′tē) *adj.*, *n.*, *pl.* -ties [OE. *thritig*] three times ten; 30; XXX —the thirties the numbers or years, as of a century, from 30 through 39 —thir′ti·eth (-ith) *adj.*, *n.*

thir′ty-sec′ond note *Music* a note having 1/32 the duration of a whole note

this (this) *pron.*, *adj.*, *pl.* these [OE. *thes*] 1. (designating) the person or thing mentioned *[this* (man) is John*]* 2. (designating) the nearer one or another one *[this* (desk) is older than that*]* 3. (designating) something about to be presented *[hear this* (news)*]* —*adv.* to this extent *[it was this* big*]*

this·tle (this′'l) *n.* [OE. *thistel*] a plant with prickly leaves and white, purple, etc. flowers —this′tly (this′lē) *adj.*

this′tle·down′ *n.* the down growing from the head of a thistle

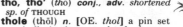

THISTLE

thith·er (thith′ər, thith′-) *adv.* [OE. *thider*] to or toward that place; there

tho, tho′ (thō) *conj.*, *adv.* shortened *sp. of* THOUGH

thole (thōl) *n.* [OE. *thol*] a pin set vertically in the gunwale of a boat as a fulcrum for an oar: also thole′pin′ (-pin′)

Thom·as (täm′əs) *Bible* one of the 12 apostles, who doubted at first the resurrection of Jesus

thong (thông) *n.* [OE. *thwang*] 1. a narrow strip of leather, etc. used as a lace, strap, etc. 2. a whiplash, as of braided strips of hide

Thor (thôr) *Norse Myth.* the god of thunder, war, and strength

tho·rax (thôr′aks) *n.*, *pl.* -rax·es, -ra·ces′ (-ə sēz′) [< Gr.] 1. the part of the body between the neck and the abdomen; chest 2. the middle one of the three main segments of an insect's body —tho·rac·ic (thô ras′ik) *adj.*

Thor·eau (thôr′ō, thə rō′), **Henry David** 1817-62; U.S. naturalist & writer

tho·ri·um (thôr′ē əm) *n.* [< THOR] a rare, grayish, radioactive chemical element, used as a nuclear fuel: symbol, Th; at. wt., 232.038; at. no., 90

thorn (thôrn) *n.* [OE.] 1. *a)* a very short, hard, leafless stem with a sharp point *b)* any small tree or shrub bearing thorns 2. a constant source of trouble or irritation — thorn′y *adj.* -i·er, -i·est

thor·ough (thur′ō) *adj.* [var. of THROUGH] 1. done or proceeding through to the end; complete 2. absolute *[a thorough* rascal*]* 3. very exact, accurate, or painstaking — thor′ough·ly *adv.* —thor′ough·ness *n.*

thor·ough·bred (thur′ə bred′) *adj.* 1. of pure stock; pedigreed 2. thoroughly trained, cultured, etc.; well-bred —*n.* 1. a thoroughbred animal; specif., [T-] any of a breed of racehorses 2. a cultured, well-bred person

thor′ough·fare′ (-fer′) *n.* a public street open at both ends, esp. a main street

thor′ough·go′ing *adj.* very thorough

those (thōz) *adj.*, *pron.* [OE. *thas*] *pl. of* THAT

thou (thou) *pron.* [OE. *thu*] you (sing.): in poetic or religious use

though (thō) *conj.* [< OE. *theah*] 1. in spite of the fact that *[though* it rained, he went*]* 2. and yet; however *[they did it, though* badly*]* 3. even if *[though* he may fail, he will have tried*]* —*adv.* however; nevertheless

thought¹ (thôt) *n.* [OE. *thoht*] 1. the act or process of thinking 2. the power of reasoning 3. an idea, opinion, plan, etc. 4. the ideas prevalent in a certain group, period, etc. *[modern thought]* 5. attention; consideration 6. intention or expectation 7. a little; trifle *[be a thought* more careful*]*

thought² (thôt) *pt. & pp. of* THINK

thought′ful *adj.* 1. full of thought; meditative 2. showing thought; serious 3. heedful, careful, etc.; esp., considerate of others —thought′ful·ly *adv.* —thought′ful·ness *n.*

thought′less *adj.* 1. not stopping to think; careless 2. ill-considered; rash 3. not considerate of others 4. [Rare] stupid —thought′less·ly *adv.* —thought′less·ness *n.*

thou·sand (thou′z'nd) *adj.*, *n.* [OE. *thusend*] ten hundred; 1,000; M —thou′sandth (-z′ndth) *adj.*, *n.*

thou′sand·fold′ *adj.*, *adv.* a thousand times as much or as many

Thousand Islands group of c.1,000 islands in the St. Lawrence River at the outlet of Lake Ontario, some part of N.Y. State & some of Ontario, Canada

thrall (thrôl) *n.* [< ON. *thræl*] 1. a slave 2. slavery — thrall′dom, thral′dom (-dəm) *n.*

thrash (thrash) *vt.*, *vi.* [OE. *therscan*] 1. *same as* THRESH 2. to beat; flog 3. to toss about violently 4. to defeat overwhelmingly —thrash out to settle by detailed discussion

thrash·er (thrash′ər) *n.* [E. dial. *thresher*] a thrushlike songbird with a long, stiff tail

thread (thred) *n.* [OE. *thræd*] 1. a fine, stringlike length of spun cotton, silk, nylon, etc. used in sewing 2. any thin line, vein, etc. **3.** something like a thread in its length, sequence, etc. *[the thread* of a story*]* **4.** the spiral or helical ridge of a screw, nut, etc. *—vt.* **1.** to put a thread through (a needle, etc.) **2.** to string (beads, etc.) on a thread **3.** to fashion a thread (sense 4) on or in **4.** *a)* to pass through by weaving in and out *b)* to make (one's way) in this fashion *—vi.* to go along in a winding way **—thread'er** *n.* **—thread'like'** *adj.*

thread'bare' *adj.* **1.** worn down so that the threads show **2.** wearing worn clothes; shabby **3.** stale; trite

threat (thret) *n.* [OE. *threat,* a throng] **1.** an expression of intention to hurt, destroy, punish, etc., as in intimidation **2.** an indication of, or a source of, imminent danger *[the threat* of war*]*

threat'en *vt., vi.* **1.** to make threats, as of injury (against) **2.** to indicate (danger, etc.) **3.** to be a source of danger (to) **—threat'en·ing·ly** *adv.*

three (thrē) *adj., n.* [OE. *threo*] one more than two; 3; III

three'-base' hit *Baseball same as* TRIPLE

three'-deck'er (-dek'ər) *n.* anything having three levels, layers, etc.

three'-di·men'sion·al *adj.* having or seeming to have depth or thickness

three'fold' *adj.* **1.** having three parts **2.** having three times as much or as many *—adv.* three times as much or as many

three'-mile' limit the outer limit of a zone of water extending three miles offshore, sometimes regarded as the limit of a country's control

three'-ply' *adj.* having three layers, strands, etc.

three·score (thrē'skôr') *adj.* sixty

three'some (-səm) *n.* a group of three persons

thresh (thresh) *vt., vi.* [earlier form of THRASH] **1.** to beat out (grain) from (husks), as with a flail **2.** *same as* THRASH **—thresh out** *same as* THRASH OUT

thresh'er *n.* **1.** one who threshes **2.** a machine for threshing grain: also **threshing machine 3.** a large, long-tailed shark

thresh·old (thresh'ōld, -hōld) *n.* [OE. *therscwold*] **1.** a length of wood, stone, etc. along the bottom of a doorway **2.** the beginning point **3.** the point at which a stimulus is just strong enough to be perceived or produce a response *[the threshold* of pain*]*

threw (thrōō) *pt.* of THROW

thrice (thrīs) *adv.* [ME. *thries*] **1.** three times **2.** threefold **3.** greatly; highly

thrift (thrift) *n.* [< ON. *thrifast,* to prosper] careful management of one's money, etc.; frugality **—thrift'i·ly** *adv.* **—thrift'i·ness** *n.* **—thrift'less** *adj.* **—thrift'y** *adj.* **-i·er, -i·est**

thrill (thril) *vi., vt.* [< OE. *thurh,* through] **1.** to feel or cause to feel emotional excitement **2.** to quiver or cause to quiver; tremble *—n.* **1.** a thrilling or being thrilled **2.** the quality of thrilling **3.** a tremor; quiver **—thrill'er** *n.*

thrive (thrīv) *vi.* **thrived** or **throve, thrived** or **thriv·en** (thriv''n), **thriv'ing** [< ON. *thrifa,* to grasp] **1.** to prosper or flourish; be successful **2.** to grow vigorously

thro', thro (thrōō) *prep., adv., adj. archaic shortened sp.* of THROUGH

throat (thrōt) *n.* [OE. *throte*] **1.** the front part of the neck **2.** the upper passage from the mouth to the stomach and lungs **3.** any narrow passage

throat'y *adj.* **-i·er, -i·est** produced in the throat, as some sounds; husky **—throat'i·ness** *n.*

throb (thräb) *vi.* **throbbed, throb'bing** [ME. *throbben*] **1.** to beat, pulsate, vibrate, etc., esp. strongly or fast **2.** to feel excitement *—n.* **1.** a throbbing **2.** a strong beat or pulsation

throe (thrō) *n.* [prob. < OE. *thrawu,* pain] a spasm or pang of pain: *usually used in pl.* [death *throes] —in the throes of* struggling with (a problem, task, etc.)

throm·bin (thräm'bin) *n.* [< Gr. *thrombos,* a clot] the enzyme of the blood that causes clotting by forming fibrin

throm·bo·sis (thräm bō'sis) *n.* [see prec.] coagulation of the blood in the heart or a blood vessel, forming a clot (**thrombus**)

throne (thrōn) *n.* [< Gr. *thronos,* a seat] **1.** the chair on which a king, cardinal, etc. sits on formal occasions **2.** the power or rank of a king, etc. **3.** a sovereign, ruler, etc.

throng (thrông) *n.* [OE. *thringan,* to crowd] **1.** a crowd **2.** any great number of things considered together *—vi.* to gather together in a throng; crowd *—vt.* to crowd into

throt·tle (thrät''l) *n.* [< ? THROAT] **1.** the valve that regulates the amount of fuel vapor entering an engine **2.** the lever or pedal that controls this valve *—vt.* **-tled, -tling 1.**

to choke; strangle **2.** to censor or suppress **3.** *a)* to reduce the flow of (fuel vapor) by means of a throttle *b)* to slow by this means

through (thrōō) *prep.* [OE. *thurh*] **1.** in one side and out the other side of **2.** in the midst of; among **3.** by way of **4.** to various places in; around *[touring through* France*]* **5.** *a)* from beginning to end of *b)* up to and including **6.** by means of **7.** as a result of *—adv.* **1.** in one side and out the other **2.** from the beginning to the end **3.** completely to the end *[see it through]* **4.** completely *[soaked through]* *—adj.* **1.** extending from one place to another *[a through* street*]* **2.** traveling to the destination without stops *[a through* train*]* **3.** finished **4.** no longer useful, active, etc. *[he's through* in politics*]* **5.** having no further dealings (*with* someone or something)

through·out' *prep.* all the way through *—adv.* **1.** in every part; everywhere **2.** in every respect

through'way' (-wā') *n.* an expressway: also **thru'way'**

throve (thrōv) *alt. pt.* of THRIVE

throw (thrō) *vt.* **threw, thrown, throw'ing** [OE. *thrawan,* to twist] **1.** to send through the air by a rapid motion of the arm, etc.; cast; hurl **2.** to cause to fall; upset **3.** to send rapidly *[to throw* troops into battle*]* **4.** to put suddenly into a specified state, etc. *[thrown* into confusion*]* **5.** to move (a switch, etc.) so as to connect, disconnect, etc. **6.** to direct, cast, etc. *[throw* a glance*]* **7.** [Colloq.] to lose (a game, etc.) deliberately **8.** [Colloq.] to give (a party, etc.) **9.** [Colloq.] to confuse or disconcert *[the question threw* him*]* *—vi.* to cast or hurl something *—n.* **1.** the act of one who throws **2.** the distance something is or can be thrown *[a stone's throw]* **3.** a spread for a bed, etc. **—throw away 1.** to discard **2.** to waste **—throw in** to add extra or free **—throw off 1.** to rid oneself of **2.** to mislead or confuse **3.** to expel, emit, etc. **—throw on** to put on (a garment) hastily **—throw oneself at** to try very hard to win the love of **—throw oneself into** to engage in eagerly **—throw oneself on** (or **upon**) to rely on for support or aid **—throw open 1.** to open completely and suddenly **2.** to remove all restrictions from **—throw out 1.** to discard **2.** to reject or remove **3.** to emit **4.** to put forth (a hint, etc.) **5.** *Baseball* to throw the ball to a teammate who retires (a runner) **—throw over 1.** to give up; abandon **2.** to jilt **—throw together** to make or assemble hurriedly **—throw up 1.** to give up; abandon **2.** to vomit **—throw'er** *n.*

throw'a·way' *n.* a leaflet, handbill, etc. given out on streets, at houses, etc. *—adj.* designed to be discarded after use *[a throwaway* bottle*]*

throw'back' *n.* (a) reversion to an ancestral type

throw rug a small rug for covering a limited area

thru (thrōō) *prep., adv., adj. shortened sp.* of THROUGH

thrum¹ (thrum) *n.* [OE., a ligament] **1.** the row of warp thread ends left on a loom when the web is cut off **2.** any of these ends

thrum² (thrum) *vt., vi.* **thrummed, thrum'ming** [echoic] **1.** to strum (a guitar, banjo, etc.) **2.** to drum (on) with the fingers *—n.* a thrumming

thrush¹ (thrush) *n.* [OE. *thrysce*] any of a large group of songbirds, including the robin, blackbird, etc.

thrush² (thrush) *n.* [prob. akin to Dan. *trøske*] a fungus disease, esp. of infants, that produces milky-white lesions on the mouth, lips, and throat

thrust (thrust) *vt., vi.* **thrust, thrust'ing** [< ON. *thrysta*] **1.** to push with sudden force **2.** to stab **3.** to force or impose *—n.* **1.** a sudden, forceful push **2.** a stab **3.** continuous pressure, as of a rafter against a wall **4.** *a)* the driving force of a propeller *b)* the forward force produced by a jet or rocket engine **5.** forward movement **6.** the basic meaning or purpose

Thu·cyd·i·des (thōō sid'ə dēz') 460?-400? B.C.; Athenian historian

thud (thud) *vi.* **thud'ded, thud'ding** [prob. < OE. *thyddan,* to strike] to hit with a dull sound *—n.* a dull sound, as of a heavy object dropping on a soft, solid surface

thug (thug) *n.* [Hindi *thag,* swindler] a brutal hoodlum, gangster, etc.

Thu·le (thōō'lē) among the ancients, the northernmost region of the world

thu·li·um (thōō'lē əm) *n.* [< THULE] a metallic chemical element of the rare-earth group: symbol, Tm; at. wt., 168.934; at. no., 69

thumb (thum) *n.* [OE. *thuma*] **1.** the short, thick finger of the hand that is nearest the wrist **2.** the part of a glove, etc. which covers the thumb *—vt.* **1.** to handle, turn, soil, etc. as with the thumb **2.** [Colloq.] to ask for or get (a ride) in hitchhiking by gesturing with the thumb —**all thumbs** clumsy —**thumbs down** a signal of disapproval — **under one's thumb** under one's influence

thumb index a series of notches in the fore edge of a book, each labeled for the section of the book it leads to

thumb′nail′ *n.* the nail of the thumb —*adj.* very small or brief [a thumbnail sketch]

thumb′screw′ *n.* **1.** a screw that can be turned by the thumb and forefinger **2.** a former instrument of torture for squeezing the thumbs

thumb′tack′ *n.* a tack with a wide, flat head, that can be pressed into a board, etc. with the thumb

THUMBSCREW

thump (thump) *n.* [echoic] **1.** a blow with something heavy and blunt **2.** the dull sound made by such a blow —*vt.* to strike with a thump —*vi.* **1.** to hit or fall with a thump **2.** to make a dull, heavy sound; pound; throb —**thump′er** *n.*

thump′ing *adj.* **1.** that thumps **2.** [Colloq.] very large; whopping

thun·der (thun′dər) *n.* [OE. *thunor*] **1.** the sound that is heard after a flash of lightning, caused by the sudden heating and expansion of air by electrical discharge **2.** any sound like this —*vi.* to produce thunder —*vt.* to utter, etc. with a thundering sound —**steal someone's thunder** to make someone's action or statement less effective by doing it first

thun′der·bolt′ (-bōlt′) *n.* **1.** a flash of lightning and the accompanying thunder **2.** something that stuns or acts with sudden force or violence

thun′der·clap′ *n.* a clap, or loud crash, of thunder

thun′der·cloud′ *n.* a storm cloud charged with electricity and producing lightning and thunder

thun′der·head′ (-hed′) *n.* a round mass of cumulus clouds appearing before a thunderstorm

thun′der·ous *adj.* **1.** full of or making thunder **2.** making a noise like thunder —**thun′der·ous·ly** *adv.*

thun′der·show′er *n.* a shower accompanied by thunder and lightning

thun′der·storm′ *n.* a storm accompanied by thunder and lightning

thun′der·struck′ *adj.* struck with amazement, terror, etc.; astonished: also **thun′der·strick′en**

Thurs., Thur. Thursday

Thurs·day (thurz′dē, -dā) *n.* [< THOR] the fifth day of the week

thus (*thus*) *adv.* [OE.] **1.** in this or that manner **2.** to this or that degree or extent; so **3.** therefore

thwack (thwak) *vt., n.* [prob. echoic] *same as* WHACK

thwart (thwôrt) *n.* [< ON. *thvert*, transverse] **1.** a rower's seat extending across a boat **2.** a brace extending across a canoe —*vt.* to obstruct, frustrate, or defeat (a person, plans, etc.)

thy (*thī*) *poss. pronominal adj.* [< ME. *thin*] of, belonging to, or done by thee: archaic or poet. var. of *your*

thyme (tīm) *n.* [< Gr. *thymon*] a plant related to the mint, with leaves used for seasoning

thy·mus (thī′məs) *n.* [< Gr. *thymos*] a ductless, glandlike body near the throat: also **thymus gland**

thy·roid (thī′roid) *adj.* [< Gr. *thyreos*, large shield] **1.** designating or of a large ductless gland near the trachea, secreting a hormone which regulates growth **2.** designating or of the principal cartilage of the larynx, forming the Adam's apple —*n.* **1.** the thyroid gland **2.** the thyroid cartilage **3.** an animal extract of the thyroid gland, used in treating goiter, etc.: also **thyroid extract**

thy·rox·ine (thī rak′sēn, -sin) *n.* [THYR(OID) + OXY- + -INE³] a colorless, crystalline compound, the active hormone of the thyroid gland, used in treating goiter, etc.

thy·self (*thī* self′) *pron. reflexive or intensive form of* THOU: archaic or poet. var. of *yourself*

ti (tē) *n. Music* a syllable representing the seventh tone of the diatonic scale

Ti *Chem.* titanium

ti·ar·a (tē er′ə, -ar′-) *n.* [< Gr. *tiara*, headdress] **1.** the Pope's triple crown **2.** a woman's crownlike headdress of jewels or flowers

Ti·ber (tī′bər) river in C Italy, flowing through Rome into the Mediterranean: c.250 mi.

Ti·bet (ti bet′) plateau region of SW China, north of the Himalayas: 471,660 sq. mi.; cap. Lhasa —**Ti·bet′an** *adj., n.*

tib·i·a (tib′ē ə) *n., pl.* **-ae′** (-ē′), **-as** [L.] the inner and thicker of the two bones of the lower leg

tic (tik) *n.* [Fr. < ?] a twitching of a muscle, esp. of the face, that is not consciously controlled

tick¹ (tik) *n.* [prob. echoic] **1.** a light clicking sound, as of a clock **2.** a mark to check off items —*vi.* to make a tick or ticks —*vt.* to record, mark, or check by ticks

tick² (tik) *n.* [OE. *ticia*] any of various bloodsucking arachnids, parasitic on man, cattle, etc.

tick³ (tik) *n.* [ult. < Gr. *thēkē*, a case] **1.** the cloth case that is filled with cotton, feathers, etc. to form a mattress or pillow **2.** [Colloq.] *same as* TICKING

TICK
(1/4 in. long)

tick′er *n.* **1.** one that ticks **2.** a telegraphic device that records stock market quotations, etc. on paper tape (**ticker tape**) **3.** [Slang] the heart

tick·et (tik′it) *n.* [< obs. Fr. *etiquet*, etiquette] **1.** a printed card, etc. that gives one a right, as to attend a theater **2.** a label on merchandise giving size, price, etc. **3.** the list of candidates nominated by a political party **4.** [Colloq.] a court summons for a traffic violation —*vt.* **1.** to label with a ticket **2.** to give a ticket to

tick′ing *n.* a strong, heavy cloth, often striped, used for casings of mattresses, pillows, etc.

tick·le (tik′'l) *vt.* **-led, -ling** [ME. *tikelen*] **1.** to please, gratify, delight, etc. **2.** to stroke lightly so as to cause involuntary twitching, laughter, etc. —*vi.* to have or cause a twitching or tingling sensation —*n.* a sensation of being tickled

tick′ler (tik′lər) *n.* **1.** one that tickles **2.** a pad, file, etc. for noting things to be tended to later

tick′lish (tik′lish) *adj.* **1.** sensitive to tickling **2.** needing careful handling; precarious; delicate

tick-tack-toe, tic-tac-toe (tik′tak tō′) *n.* a game for two, each marking X (or O) in turn in a 9-square block so as to complete any one row before the other can

tick·tock (tik′täk′) *n.* the sound made by a clock

tid·al (tīd′'l) *adj.* of, having, or caused by a tide or tides

tidal wave 1. an unusually great, destructive wave sent inshore by an earthquake or very strong wind **2.** any widespread movement, feeling, etc.

tid·bit (tid′bit′) *n.* [dial. *tid*, tiny object] a choice bit of food, gossip, etc.

tid·dly·winks (tid′lē wiŋks′) *n.* [< ?] a game in which little disks are snapped into a cup by pressing their edges with a larger disk: also **tid′dle·dy·winks′** (-'l dē wiŋks′)

tide (tīd) *n.* [OE. *tid*, time] **1.** a period of time [Eastertide] **2.** the alternate rise and fall, about twice a day, of the surface of oceans, seas, etc., caused by the attraction of the moon and sun **3.** something that rises and falls like the tide **4.** a current, trend, etc. [the *tide* of public opinion] —*vt.* **tid′ed, tid′ing** to carry as with the tide —**tide over** to help along temporarily —**turn the tide** to reverse a condition

tide′land′ *n.* **1.** land covered at high tide **2.** [*pl.*] land under the sea within territorial waters of a country

tide′wa′ter *n.* **1.** water that is affected by the tide **2.** a seaboard —*adj.* of or along a tidewater

ti·dings (tī′diŋz) *n.pl.* [*sometimes with sing. v.*] [OE. *tidung*] news; information

ti·dy (tī′dē) *adj.* **-di·er, -di·est** [< OE. *tid*, time] **1.** neat in appearance, arrangement, etc.; orderly **2.** [Colloq.] rather large [a tidy sum] —*vt., vi.* **-died, -dy·ing** to make (things) tidy (often with *up*) —**ti′di·ly** *adv.* —**ti′di·ness** *n.*

tie (tī) *vt.* **tied, ty′ing** [< OE. *teag*, rope] **1.** to bind, as with string, rope, etc. **2.** to knot the laces, etc. of **3.** to make (a knot) in **4.** to join or bind in any way **5.** to confine; restrict **6.** to equal the score of, as in a contest —*vi.* **1.** to make a tie **2.** to make the same score in a contest —*n.* **1.** a string, cord, etc. used to tie things **2.** something that joins, binds, etc. **3.** something that confines or restricts [legal ties] **4.** short for NECKTIE **5.** a beam, rod, etc. that holds parts together **6.** any of the crossbeams to which the rails of a railroad are fastened **7.** *a*) an equality of scores in a contest *b*) a contest in which this occurs **8.** *Music* a curved line joining two notes of the same pitch, indicating that the tone is to be held unbroken —*adj.* that has been made equal [a *tie* score] —**tie down** to confine; restrict —**tie up 1.** to wrap up and tie **2.** to moor to a dock **3.** to block or hinder **4.** to cause to be already in use, committed, etc. —**ti′er** *n.*

tie′back′ *n.* a ribbon, tape, etc. used to tie curtains or draperies to one side

tie clasp a decorative clasp used for fastening a necktie to the shirt front: also **tie clip, tie bar**

tie′-dye′ *n.* a method of dyeing designs on cloth by tying bunches of it so that the dye affects only exposed parts — *vt.* **-dyed′, -dye′ing** to dye in this way

tie′-in′ *adj.* designating a sale in which an item in demand can be paid only along with some other item —*n.* **1.** a tie-in sale **2.** a connection or relation

Tien·tsin (tin′tsin′) seaport in NE China: pop. c.4,000,000

tier (tir) *n.* [< MFr. *tire*, order] any of a series of rows, as of seats, arranged one above or behind another —*vt.*, *vi.* to arrange or be arranged in tiers

Ti·er·ra del Fu·e·go (tē er′ə del′ fōō ā′gō) **1.** group of islands at the tip of S. America, divided between Argentina and Chile **2.** chief island of this group

tie tack a decorative pin fitted into a snap to fasten a necktie to a shirt

tie-up (tī′up′) *n.* **1.** a temporary stoppage of production, traffic, etc. **2.** a connection; relation

tiff (tif) *n.* [< ?] **1.** a slight fit of anger **2.** a slight quarrel —*vi.* to be in or have a tiff

ti·ger (tī′gər) *n.* [< Gr. *tigris*] a large, flesh-eating animal of the cat family, native to Asia, having a tawny coat striped with black —**ti′ger·ish** *adj.*

tiger lily a lily having dark-spotted, orange flowers

tiger's eye a semiprecious, yellow-brown stone: also **ti′-ger·eye′** *n.*

tight (tīt) *adj.* [< OE. *-thight*, strong] **1.** made so that water, air, etc. cannot pass through [a *tight* boat] **2.** drawn, packed, etc. closely together **3.** fixed securely; firm **4.** fully stretched; taut **5.** fitting so closely as to be uncomfortable **6.** strict [*tight* control] **7.** difficult: esp. in a **tight corner** (or **squeeze**, etc.), a difficult situation **8.** showing strain [a *tight* smile] **9.** almost even or tied [a *tight* race] **10.** difficult to get; scarce **11.** [Colloq.] stingy **12.** [Slang] drunk —*adv.* **1.** securely **2.** [Colloq.] soundly [sleep *tight*] —**sit tight** to maintain one's position, etc. — **tight′ly** *adv.* —**tight′ness** *n.*

-tight [< prec.] a combining form meaning not letting (something specified) in or out [*airtight*]

tight′en *vt.*, *vi.* to make or become tight or tighter — **tight′en·er** *n.*

tight′fist′ed *adj.* stingy; miserly

tight′fit′ting *adj.* fitting very tight

tight′-lipped′ (-lipt′) *adj.* **1.** having the lips closed tightly **2.** not saying much; secretive

tight′rope′ *n.* a tightly stretched rope on which acrobats perform

tights *n.pl.* a tightly fitting garment for the lower half of the body, worn by acrobats, dancers, etc.

tight′wad′ (-wäd′, -wôd′) *n.* [TIGHT + WAD] [Slang] a stingy person

ti·glon (tī′glän′, -glən) *n.* [TIG(ER) + L(I)ON] the offspring of a male tiger and a female lion

ti·gress (tī′gris) *n.* a female tiger

Ti·gris (tī′gris) river flowing from EC Turkey, joining the Euphrates in Iraq to flow into the Persian Gulf: 1,150 mi.

Ti·jua·na (tē wä′na, -hwä′nä) city in NW Mexico, on the U.S. border: pop. 335,000

til·de (til′də) *n.* [Sp. < L. *titulus*, sign] a diacritical mark (˜) variously used, as in Spanish over an *n*

tile (tīl) *n.* [< L. *tegula*] **1.** a thin piece of fired clay, stone, etc., used for roofing, flooring, walls, etc. **2.** a similar piece of plastic, etc. **3.** tiles collectively **4.** a drain of earthenware pipe **5.** any of the oblong pieces used in mah-jongg, etc. —*vt.* **tiled, til′ing** to cover with tiles — **til′er** *n.*

til′ing *n.* tiles collectively

till¹ (til) *prep.*, *conj.* [OE. *til*] same as UNTIL

till² (til) *vt.*, *vi.* [OE. *tilian*, strive for] to work (land) in raising crops, as by plowing, etc. —**till′a·ble** *adj.* —**till′er** *n.*

till³ (til) *n.* [< ? ME. *tillen*, to draw] a drawer, as in a store counter, for keeping money

till′age (-ij) *n.* **1.** the tilling of land **2.** land that is tilled

till·er (til′ər) *n.* [< ML. *telarium*, weaver's beam] a bar or handle for turning a boat's rudder

tilt (tilt) *vt.* [prob. < OE. *tealt*, shaky] to cause to slope; tip —*vi.* **1.** to slope; incline **2.** to thrust one's lance (at one's opponent) in a tilt **3.** to engage in a tilt **4.** to dispute; argue —*n.* **1.** a medieval contest in which two horsemen fight with lances **2.** any spirited contest, dispute, etc. **3.** a tilting, or sloping **4.** a slope —(at) **full tilt** at full speed

tilt′-top′ *adj.* designating a table with a hinged top that can be tilted vertically

Tim. Timothy

tim·bal (tim′b'l) *n.* [< Fr. < Sp. < Ar. *al*, the + *ṭabl*, drum] same as KETTLEDRUM

tim·bale (tim′b'l) *n.* [Fr.: see prec.] **1.** a custardlike dish of chicken, lobster, etc. baked in a small drum-shaped mold **2.** a pastry shell, filled with cooked food: also **timbale case**

tim·ber (tim′bər) *n.* [OE.] **1.** wood for building houses, ships, etc. **2.** a wooden beam used in building **3.** trees collectively **4.** personal quality or character [a man of his *timber*] —*vt.* to provide or build with timbers —*adj.* of or for timber —**tim′bered** *adj.* —**tim′ber·ing** *n.*

tim·ber·line′ *n.* the line above or beyond which trees do not grow, as on mountains or in polar regions

tim·bre (tam′bər, tim′-) *n.* [Fr.: see TIMBREL] the quality of sound that distinguishes one voice or musical instrument from another

Tim·buk·tu (tim′buk tōō′) town in C Mali

time (tīm) *n.* [OE. *tima*] **1.** every moment there has been or ever will be **2.** a system for measuring the passing of hours [standard *time*] **3.** the period during which something exists, happens, etc. **4.** [*usually pl.*] a period of history; age; era **5.** [*usually pl.*] prevailing conditions [*times* are good] **6.** a set period or term, as of work, confinement, etc. **7.** a period necessary, sufficient, measured, etc. for something [a baking *time* of one hour] **8.** standard rate of pay **9.** rate of speed in marching, driving, etc. **10.** a precise instant, minute, day, etc. **11.** the usual or appointed moment for something [*time* to get up] **12.** the suitable or proper moment [now is the *time* to act] **13.** an occasion or repeated occasion [the fifth *time* it's been on TV] **14.** *Music* a) rhythm as determined by the grouping of beats into measures b) tempo —*interj.* *Sports* a signal that a period of play is ended or temporarily suspended — *vt.* **timed, tim′ing 1.** to arrange the time of so as to be suitable, opportune, etc. **2.** to adjust, set, etc. so as to coincide in time [*time* your watch with mine] **3.** to record the pace, speed, etc. of —*adj.* **1.** having to do with time **2.** set to explode, open, etc. at a given time **3.** having to do with paying in installments —**against time** trying to finish in a given time —**ahead of time** early —**at the same time 1.** together **2.** however —**at times** occasionally —**behind time** late —**do time** [Colloq.] to serve a prison term —**for the time being** temporarily —**from time to time** now and then —**in time 1.** eventually **2.** before it is too late **3.** keeping the set tempo, pace, etc. —**make time** to travel, work, etc. rapidly —**on time 1.** at the appointed time **2.** for or by payment by installments —**time after time** again and again: also **time and again**

time clock a clock with a mechanism for recording on a card (**timecard**) the time at which an employee begins and ends a work period

time exposure 1. a relatively long exposure of photographic film, generally for more than half a second **2.** a photograph made in this way

time′-hon′ored *adj.* honored because in existence or usage for a long time

time′keep′er *n.* **1.** same as TIMEPIECE **2.** one who keeps account of the hours worked by employees, or of the elapsed time in races, games, etc.

time′less (-lis) *adj.* **1.** eternal **2.** restricted to no specific time; always valid —**time′less·ness** *n.*

time′ly *adj.* **-li·er, -li·est** well-timed; opportune —**time′li·ness** *n.*

time′out′ *n.* *Sports*, etc. any temporary suspension of play, as to discuss strategy, etc.

time′piece′ *n.* a clock or watch

tim′er *n.* **1.** same as: *a*) TIMEKEEPER *b*) STOPWATCH **2.** a device for controlling the timing of a mechanism

times (tīmz) *prep.* multiplied by: symbol, x

time′serv′er *n.* one who abandons his principles in order to suit the times or to gain favor —**time′serv′ing** *n.*, *adj.*

time sharing a system for the simultaneous use of a computer by many users at remote locations

time sheet a sheet on which are recorded the hours an employee works

time study study of operational or production procedures and the time consumed by them, intended to increase efficiency and productivity

time′ta·ble (-tā′b'l) *n.* a schedule of the times of arrival and departure of planes, trains, buses, etc.

time′worn′ *adj.* **1.** worn out by long use **2.** trite; hackneyed

time zone *see* STANDARD TIME

tim·id (tim′id) *adj.* [< L. *timere*, to fear] **1.** easily frightened; shy **2.** lacking self-confidence —**ti·mid·i·ty** (tə mid′ə tē), **tim′id·ness** *n.* —**tim′id·ly** *adv.*

tim·ing (tī′miŋ) *n.* the regulation of time or speed so as to achieve the most effective performance

tim·or·ous (tim′ər əs) *adj.* [< L. *timor,* fear] full of fear; timid —**tim′or·ous·ly** *adv.* —**tim′or·ous·ness** *n.*

Tim·o·thy (tim′ə thē) *Bible* either of the epistles from the Apostle Paul to his disciple Timothy, books of the New Testament

tim·o·thy (tim′ə thē) *n.* [< a *Timothy* Hanson, c.1720] a grass with dense spikes, grown for hay

tim·pa·ni (tim′pə nē) *n.pl.* [It.: see TYMPANUM] kettle-drums, esp. a set of them played by one performer —**tim′-pa·nist** *n.*

tin (tin) *n.* [OE.] **1.** a soft, silver-white, metallic chemical element: symbol, Sn; at. wt., 118.69; at. no., 50 **2.** *same as* TIN PLATE **3.** *a)* a pan, box, etc. made of tin plate *b)* [Chiefly Brit.] *same as* CAN² (*n.* 2, 3) —*vt.* **tinned, tin′ning 1.** to plate with tin **2.** [Chiefly Brit.] *same as* CAN² (*vt.* 1)

tin can *same as* CAN² (*n.* 2)

tinc·ture (tiŋk′chər) *n.* [< L. *tingere,* to dye] **1.** a light color; tinge **2.** a slight trace **3.** a medicinal substance in a solution of alcohol or alcohol and water —*vt.* **-tured, -tur-ing** to tinge

tin·der (tin′dər) *n.* [OE. *tynder*] any dry, easily flammable material, esp. as formerly used for starting a fire by catching a spark from flint and steel struck together

tin′der-box′ *n.* **1.** formerly, a metal box for holding tin-der, flint, and steel **2.** a highly flammable building, etc. **3.** a potential source of war, rebellion, etc.

tine (tīn) *n.* [OE. *tind*] a slender, projecting point; prong *[the tines* of a fork] —**tined** *adj.*

tin′foil′ (-foil′) *n.* a thin sheet of tin or an alloy of tin and lead, etc., used as a wrapping

ting (tiŋ) *n.* [echoic] a single, light, ringing sound, as of a small bell —*vi., vt.* to make or cause to make a ting

tinge (tinj) *vt.* **tinged, tinge′ing** or **ting′ing** [see TINT] **1.** to color slightly; tint **2.** to give a trace, slight flavor, etc. to —*n.* **1.** a slight coloring; tint **2.** a slight trace, flavor, etc.

tin·gle (tiŋ′g'l) *vi.* **-gled, -gling** [var. of TINKLE] to have a prickling or stinging feeling, as from cold, excitement, etc. —*n.* this feeling —**tin′gly** *adj.* **-gli·er, -gli·est**

tin·ker (tiŋ′kər) *n.* [ME. *tinkere*] **1.** one who mends pots, pans, etc. **2.** a bungler —*vi.* **1.** to work as a tinker **2.** to make clumsy attempts to mend something **3.** to putter aimlessly —**tin′ker·er** *n.*

tin·kle (tiŋ′k'l) *vi.* **-kled, -kling** [echoic] to make a series of light, clinking sounds as of a small bell —*vt.* to cause to tinkle —*n.* a tinkling sound —**tin′kly** *adj.* **-kli·er, -kli·est**

tin·ner (tin′ər) *n. same as* TINSMITH

tin·ny (tin′ē) *adj.* **-ni·er, -ni·est 1.** of tin **2.** like tin; bright but cheap; not durable **3.** of or like the sound made in striking a tin object —**tin′ni·ness** *n.*

tin plate thin sheets of iron or steel that are plated with tin —**tin′-plate′** *vt.* **-plat′ed, -plat′ing**

tin·sel (tin′s'l, -z'l) *n.* [< L. *scintilla,* a spark] **1.** thin strips or threads of tin, metal foil, etc. used for decoration **2.** something that glitters but has little value —*adj.* **1.** of or decorated with tinsel **2.** showy; gaudy —*vt.* **-seled** or **-selled, -sel·ing** or **-sel·ling 1.** to make glitter as with tin-sel **2.** to give a showy, gaudy look to —**tin′sel·ly** *adj.*

tin′smith′ *n.* one who works in tin or tin plate

tint (tint) *n.* [< L. *tingere,* to dye] **1.** a delicate color **2.** a gradation of a color; shade **3.** a hair dye —*vt.* to give a tint to —**tint′er** *n.*

tin·tin·nab·u·la·tion (tin′ti nab′yoo lā′shən) *n.* [< L. *tintinnabulum,* little bell] the ringing sound of bells

tin·type (tin′tīp′) *n.* an old kind of photograph taken directly as a positive print on a treated plate of tin or iron

ti·ny (tī′nē) *adj.* **-ni·er, -ni·est** [< ME. *tine,* a little] very small; diminutive —**ti′ni·ness** *n.*

-tion [< Fr. < L.] *a suffix meaning:* **1.** the act of *[correction]* **2.** the state of being *[elation]* **3.** the thing that is *[creation]*

-tious *a suffix used to form adjectives from nouns ending in* -TION *[cautious]*

tip¹ (tip) *n.* [ME. *tippe*] **1.** the point or end of something **2.** something attached to the end, as a cap, etc. **3.** a top or apex, as of a mountain —*vt.* **tipped, tip′ping 1.** to form a tip on **2.** to cover the tip of

tip² (tip) *vt.* **tipped, tip′ping** [< ?] **1.** to strike lightly and sharply **2.** to give a gratuity to (a waiter, etc.) **3.** [Colloq.] to give secret information to (often with *off*) **4.** *Baseball a)* to hit (the ball) a glancing blow *b)* to glance off (the bat, glove, etc.): said of the ball —*vi.* to give a tip or tips —*n.* **1.** a light, sharp blow **2.** a piece of secret information **3.** a hint, warning, etc. **4.** a gratuity —**tip′per** *n.*

tip³ (tip) *vt., vi.* **tipped, tip′ping** [< ?] **1.** to overturn or upset (often with *over*) **2.** to tilt or slant —*n.* a tilt; slant —**to tip one's hat** to greet by raising one's hat slightly

tip′-off′ *n.* a tip; confidential hint, warning, etc.

tip·ple (tip′'l) *vi., vt.* **-pled, -pling** [< ?] to drink (alcoholic liquor) habitually —*n.* alcoholic liquor —**tip′pler** *n.*

tip·ster (tip′stər) *n.* [Colloq.] one who sells tips, as on horse races, for stock speculation, etc.

tip·sy (tip′sē) *adj.* **-si·er, -si·est 1.** that tips easily; not steady **2.** somewhat drunk —**tip′si·ly** *adv.*

tip′toe′ *n.* the tip of a toe —*vi.* **-toed′, -toe′ing** to walk stealthily or cautiously on one's tiptoes —**on tiptoe 1.** on one's tiptoes **2.** eager or eagerly **3.** silently

tip′top′ *n.* [TIP¹ + TOP¹] the highest point —*adj., adv.* **1.** at the highest point **2.** [Colloq.] at the highest point of excellence, health, etc.

ti·rade (tī′rād, tī rād′) *n.* [Fr. < It. *tirare,* to fire] a long vehement speech or denunciation; harangue

tire¹ (tīr) *vt., vi.* **tired, tir′ing** [OE. *tiorian*] to make or become weary, exhausted, bored, etc.

tire² (tīr) *n.* [prob. < ME. *atir,* equipment] a hoop of iron or rubber, or a rubber tube filled with air, fixed around the wheel of a vehicle to form a tread —*vt.* **tired, tir′ing** to furnish with tires

tired (tīrd) *adj.* **1.** fatigued; weary **2.** stale; hackneyed —**tired′ly** *adv.* —**tired′ness** *n.*

tire′less *adj.* that does not become tired —**tire′less·ly** *adv.* —**tire′less·ness** *n.*

tire′some *adj.* tiring; boring —**tire′some·ly** *adv.*

Tir·ol (tir′äl, tī′rōl) E Alpine region in W Austria and N Italy —**Ti·ro·le·an** (ti rō′lē ən) *adj., n.*

'tis (tiz) it is

tis·sue (tish′ōō) *n.* [< L. *texere,* to weave] **1.** light, thin cloth **2.** an interwoven mass; mesh; web *[a tissue* of lies] **3.** a piece of soft, absorbent paper, used as a disposable handkerchief, etc. **4.** *same as* TISSUE PAPER **5.** the sub-stance of an organic body, consisting of cells and intercel-lular material

tissue paper very thin, unsized, nearly transparent paper for wrapping, for toilet use, etc.

tit¹ (tit) *n. same as* TITMOUSE

tit² (tit) *n.* [OE.] **1.** *same as* TEAT **2.** a breast: in this sense now vulgar

Tit. Titus

Ti·tan (tīt′'n) *n.* **1.** *Gr. Myth.* any of a race of giant dei-ties who were overthrown by the Olympian gods **2.** [t-] any person or thing of great size or power

Ti·tan·ic (tī tan′ik) *adj.* **1.** of or like the Titans **2.** [t-] great size, strength, or power

ti·ta·ni·um (tī tā′nē əm, ti-) *n.* [see TITAN] a dark-gray metallic chemical element used as a deoxidizing agent in molten steel, etc.: symbol, Ti; at. wt., 47.90; at. no., 22

tit for tat [earlier *tip for tap*] blow for blow

tithe (tīth) *n.* [OE. *teothe,* a tenth] **1.** a tenth of one's in-come paid as a contribution to a church **2.** a tenth part —*vt., vi.* **tithed, tith′ing** to pay a tithe of (one's income, etc.) —**tith′er** *n.*

Ti·tian (tish′ən) 1490?–1576; Venetian painter

ti·tian (tish′ən) *n.* [< a hair color in Titian's portraits] reddish yellow

tit·il·late (tit′'l āt′) *vt.* **-lat′ed, -lat′ing** [< L. *titillare,* to tickle] **1.** *same as* TICKLE **2.** to excite pleasurably —**tit′il-lat′er** *n.* —**tit′il·la′tion** *n.*

ti·tle (tīt′'l) *n.* [< L. *titulus*] **1.** the name of a poem, book, picture, etc. **2.** an epithet **3.** an appellation indicating one's rank, profession, etc. **4.** a claim or right **5.** *Law a)* a right to ownership, esp. of real estate *b)* a deed **6.** *Motion Pictures, TV* a subtitle, credit, etc. **7.** *Sports,* etc. a championship —*vt.* **-tled, -tling** to give a title to

ti′tled *adj.* having a title, esp. of nobility

ti′tle-hold′er *n.* the holder of a title; specif., (also **titlist**) the champion in some sport

title page the page in the front of a book that gives the title, author, publisher, etc.

title role (or **part** or **character**) the character in a play, movie, etc. whose name is used as the title

tit·mouse (tit′mous′) *n., pl.* **-mice′** (-mīs′) [ME. *titemose*] a small bird with ashy-gray feathers

tit·ter (tit′ər) *vi.* [echoic] to laugh in a half-suppressed way; giggle —*n.* a tittering; giggle

tit·tle (tit′'l) *n.* [ME. *title*] a very small particle; iota; jot

tit·tle-tat·tle (tit′'l tat′'l) *n., vi.* **-tled, -tling** [redupl. of TATTLE] gossip; chatter

tit·u·lar (tich′ə lər) *adj.* [see TITLE] **1.** of a title **2.** being or having a title **3.** in name only *[a titular* saint]

Ti·tus (tīt′əs) *Bible* a book of the New Testament, an epistle of the Apostle Paul to his disciple Titus

tiz·zy (tiz′ē) *n., pl.* **-zies** [< ?] [Colloq.] a state of frenzied excitement, esp. over a triviality

TKO, T.K.O. *Boxing abbrev. of* TECHNICAL KNOCKOUT

Tl *Chem.* thallium

Tm *Chem.* thulium

TN Tennessee

tn. 1. ton(s) **2.** training

TNT, T.N.T. trinitrotoluene

to (to͞o, too, tə) *prep.* [OE.] **1.** toward [turn *to* the left] **2.** so as to reach [he went *to* Boston] **3.** as far as [wet *to* the skin] **4.** into a condition of [a rise *to* fame] **5.** on, onto, at, etc. [tied *to* a post] **6.** *a*) until [from noon *to* night] *b*) before [the time is 10 *to* 6] **7.** for the purpose of [come *to* my aid] **8.** in regard to [open *to* attack] **9.** so as to produce [torn *to* bits] **10.** along with [add this *to* the rest] **11.** belonging with [a key *to* the lock] **12.** as compared with [a score of 7 *to* 0] **13.** in agreement with [not *to* my taste] **14.** constituting [ten *to* a pound] **15.** with (a specified person or thing) as the recipient of the action [give it *to* me] **16.** in honor of [a toast *to* you] *To* is also a sign of the infinitive (Ex.: I want *to* stay) —*adv.* **1.** forward [his hat is on wrong side *to*] **2.** shut or closed [pull the door *to*] **3.** to the matter at hand [fall *to!*] —**to and fro** back and forth

toad (tōd) *n.* [OE. *tade*] a small, froglike animal that lives on moist land

toad′stool′ (-sto͞ol′) *n.* a mushroom, esp. any poisonous mushroom

toad·y (tōd′ē) *n., pl.* **-ies** [short for *toadeater,* quack doctor's assistant] a servile flatterer —*vt., vi.* **-ied, -y·ing** to be a toady (to) —**toad′y·ism** *n.*

toast[1] (tōst) *vt.* [< L. *torrere,* parch] **1.** to brown the surface of (bread, etc.) by heating **2.** to warm thoroughly —*vi.* to become toasted —*n.* sliced bread browned by heat —**toast′er** *n.*

TOAD
(1/2–9 in. long)

toast[2] (tōst) *n.* [< the toasted bread formerly put in wine] **1.** a person or thing in honor of which persons raise their glasses and drink **2.** a proposal to drink, or a drink, in honor of some person, etc. —*vt., vi.* to propose or drink a toast (to) —**toast′er** *n.*

toast′mas′ter *n.* the person at a banquet who proposes toasts, introduces after-dinner speakers, etc.

to·bac·co (tə bak′ō) *n., pl.* **-cos** [< Sp. < WInd. *tabaco,* smoking pipe] **1.** a plant with large leaves that are prepared for smoking, chewing, or snuffing **2.** the leaves so prepared **3.** cigars, cigarettes, snuff, etc.

to·bac′co·nist (-ə nist) *n.* [Chiefly Brit.] a dealer in tobacco and other smoking supplies

to·bog·gan (tə bäg′ən) *n.* [< CanadFr. < AmInd.] a long, narrow, flat sled without runners, curved back at the front end: used for coasting downhill —*vi.* **1.** to coast downhill on a toboggan **2.** to decline rapidly —**to·bog′·gan·er, to·bog′gan·ist** *n.*

toc·ca·ta (tə kät′ə) *n.* [It. < *toccare,* to touch < L.] a composition in free style for the organ, piano, etc., often used as a prelude of a fugue

toc·sin (täk′sin) *n.* [Fr. < Pr. *toc,* a stroke + *senh,* a bell] **1.** an alarm bell **2.** any alarm

to·day (tə dā′) *adv.* [OE. *to dæg*] **1.** on or during the present day **2.** in the present time or age —*n.* **1.** the present day **2.** the present time or age Also **to-day**

tod·dle (täd′'l) *vi.* **-dled, -dling** [? < TOTTER] to walk with short, uncertain steps, as a child —**tod′dler** *n.*

tod·dy (täd′ē) *n., pl.* **-dies** [< Hindi] a drink of brandy, whiskey, etc. mixed with hot water, sugar, etc.: also **hot toddy**

to-do (tə do͞o′) *n.* [Colloq.] a commotion; stir; fuss

toe (tō) *n.* [OE. *ta*] **1.** *a*) any of the digits of the foot *b*) the forepart of the foot *c*) that part of a shoe, sock, etc. which covers the toes **2.** anything like a toe in location, shape, or use —*vt.* **toed, toe′ing 1.** to touch, kick, etc. with the toes **2.** *a*) to drive (a nail) slantingly *b*) same as TOENAIL —*vi.* to stand, walk, etc. with the toes in a specified position [he *toes* in] —**on one's toes** [Colloq.] mentally or physically alert —**toe the line** (or **mark**) to follow orders, rules, etc. strictly

toed (tōd) *adj.* having (a specified kind or number of) toes [pigeon-*toed*]

toe dance a dance performed on the tips of the toes, as in ballet —**toe′-dance′** *vi.* **-danced′, -danc′ing**

toe′hold′ *n.* **1.** a small space for supporting the toe of the foot in climbing, etc. **2.** any means of surmounting obsta-

cles, gaining entry, etc. **3.** a slight footing or advantage **4.** *Wrestling* a hold in which one wrestler twists the other's foot

toe′nail′ *n.* the nail of a toe —*vt. Carpentry* to fasten with a nail driven slantingly

tof·fee, tof·fy (tôf′ē, täf′ē) *n.* [< TAFFY] a hard, chewy candy, like taffy, often with nuts

to·ga (tō′gə) *n., pl.* **-gas, -gae** [L. < *tegere,* to cover] **1.** in ancient Rome, a loose outer garment worn in public by citizens **2.** a robe of office —**to′gaed** (-gəd) *adj.*

to·geth·er (tə geth′ər) *adv.* [< OE. *to,* to + *gædre,* together] **1.** in or into one group, place, etc. [we ate *together*] **2.** in or into contact, union, etc. [the cars skidded *together*] **3.** considered collectively [he won more than all of us *together*] **4.** with one another; in association [they work *together*] **5.** at the same time [shots fired *together*] **6.** continuously [he sulked for three whole days *together*] **7.** in or into agreement, cooperation, etc. [to get *together* on a deal] —*adj.* [Slang] having a fully integrated personality

ROMAN
TOGA

to·geth′er·ness *n.* the spending of much time together, as by family members, in seeking a more unified, stable relationship

tog·gle (täg′'l) *n.* [prob. < TUG] a rod, bolt, etc. for insertion through a loop of a rope, a link of a chain, etc. to make an attachment, prevent slipping, etc.

toggle joint a knee-shaped joint of two pivoted bars: pressure put on the joint to straighten it transmits outward pressure to the open ends

toggle switch a switch consisting of a projecting lever moved back and forth through a small arc to open or close an electric circuit

To·go (tō′gō) country in W Africa, on the Atlantic: 21,853 sq. mi.; pop. 1,914,000; cap. Lomé

togs (tägz, tôgz) *n.pl.* [prob. < L. *toga,* TOGA] [Colloq.] clothes

toil (toil) *vi.* [< L. *tudiculare,* stir about] **1.** to work hard and continuously **2.** to proceed laboriously [to *toil* up a hill] —*n.* hard, exhausting work —**toil′er** *n.*

toi·let (toi′lit) *n.* [< MFr. *toile,* cloth < L. *tela,* a web] **1.** the act of dressing or grooming oneself **2.** dress; attire **3.** *a*) a room with a bowl-shaped fixture for defecation or urination *b*) such a fixture —*adj.* of or for the toilet

toilet paper (or **tissue**) soft, absorbent paper for cleaning oneself after evacuating bodily waste

toi′let·ry (-lə trē) *n., pl.* **-ries** soap, lotion, etc. used in cleaning and grooming oneself

toi·lette (twä let′, toi-) *n.* [Fr.: see TOILET] **1.** the process of grooming oneself, including bathing, hairdressing, dressing, etc.: said of a woman **2.** dress; attire

toilet water a perfumed, slightly alcoholic liquid, applied to the skin

toils (toilz) *n.pl.* [< L. *tela,* a web] any snares suggestive of a net

toil·some (toil′səm) *adj.* requiring toil; laborious

toil′worn′ (-wôrn′) *adj.* worn out by toil

To·kay (tō kā′) *n.* **1.** a sweet, rich wine made in Tokay, Hungary **2.** any wine like this **3.** a large, sweet grape used for the wine

toke (tōk) *n.* [? < TOKEN] [Slang] a puff on a cigarette, esp. one of marijuana or hashish

to·ken (tō′kən) *n.* [OE. *tacn*] **1.** a sign, indication, symbol, etc. [a *token* of affection] **2.** a keepsake **3.** a metal disk with a face value higher than its real value, to be used in place of currency, for transportation fares, etc. —*adj.* merely simulated; slight [*token* resistance] —**by the same** (or **this**) **token** following from this —**in token of** as evidence of

to′ken·ism (-iz'm) *n.* the making of small, merely formal concessions to a demand, etc.; specif., token integration of Negroes, as in jobs

To·ky·o (tō′kē ō′) capital of Japan, on Honshu: pop. 8,907,000 (met. area 19,500,000)

tol·bu·ta·mide (täl byo͞ot′ə mīd′) *n.* an oral drug for treating diabetes

told (tōld) *pt. & pp. of* TELL —**all told** all (being) counted

tole (tōl) *n.* [Fr. *tôle,* sheet iron] a type of lacquered or enameled metalware, usually dark-green, ivory, or black, used for lamps, trays, etc.

To·le·do (tə lē′dō) **1.** city and port in NW Ohio: pop. 384,000 (met. area 693,000) **2.** city in C Spain: pop. 40,000

tol·er·a·ble (tälʹər ə bʹl) *adj.* **1.** endurable **2.** fairly good; passable —**tolʹer·a·bly** *adv.*

tol·er·ance (tälʹər əns) *n.* **1.** a being tolerant of others' beliefs, practices, etc. **2.** the amount of variation allowed from a standard, accuracy, etc.; specif., the difference between the allowable maximum and minimum sizes of some mechanical part **3.** *Med.* the ability to resist the effects of the continued or increasing use of a drug, etc.

tol·er·ant *adj.* **1.** having or showing tolerance of others' beliefs, practices, etc. **2.** *Med.* of or having tolerance — **tolʹer·ant·ly** *adv.*

tol·er·ate (tälʹə rāt') *vt.* **-at'ed, -at'ing** [< L. *tolerare,* to bear] **1.** to allow; permit **2.** to recognize and respect (others' beliefs, practices, etc.) without sharing them **3.** to put up with **4.** *Med.* to have a tolerance for (a specific drug, etc.)

tol·er·a'tion *n.* tolerance; esp., freedom to hold religious views different from the established ones

toll[1] (tōl) *n.* [prob. ult. < Gr. *telos,* tax] **1.** a tax or charge for a privilege, as for the use of a bridge **2.** a charge for some service, as for a long-distance telephone call **3.** the number lost, etc. *[the storm took a heavy toll of lives]*

toll[2] (tōl) *vt.* [ME. *tollen,* to pull] **1.** to ring (a bell, etc.) slowly with regular strokes, as for announcing a death **2.** to announce, summon, etc. by this —*vi.* to sound or ring slowly: said of a bell —*n.* the sound of tolling a bell — **tollʹer** *n.*

tollʹgate' *n.* a gate for stopping travel at a point where toll is taken

toll road a road on which tolls must be paid

Tol·stoy (tälʹstoi, tōlʹ-), Count **Leo** 1828–1910; Russ. novelist: also sp. **Tolstoi**

tol·u·ene (tälʹyoo wēn') *n.* [*tolu,* balsam of a S. American tree from which orig. derived + (*benz*)*ene*] a liquid hydrocarbon used in dyes, explosives, etc.

tom (täm) *adj.* [< the name *Tom*] male *[a tom turkey]*

tom·a·hawk (tämʹə hôk') *n.* [< Algonquian] a light ax used by N. American Indians as a tool and a weapon —*vt.* to hit or kill with a tomahawk

to·ma·to (tə mātʹō, -mätʹō) *n., pl.* **-toes** [< Sp. < MexInd.] **1.** a red or yellowish fruit with a juicy pulp, used as a vegetable **2.** the plant that it grows on

tomb (tōōm) *n.* [< Gr. *tymbos*] **1.** a vault or grave for the dead **2.** a burial monument —**the tomb** death

tom·boy (tämʹboi') *n.* a girl who behaves like a boisterous boy —**tomʹboy'ish** *adj.*

tomb·stone (tōōmʹstōn') *n.* a stone, usually with an inscription, marking a tomb or grave

tom·cat (tämʹkat') *n.* a male cat

Tom Col·lins (kälʹinz) an iced drink made with lemon or lime juice, sugar, soda water, and gin

tome (tōm) *n.* [< Gr. *tomos,* piece cut off] a book, esp. a large one

tom·fool·er·y (tämʹfōōlʹər ē) *n., pl.* **-ies** foolish or silly behavior; nonsense

Tom·my (tämʹē) *n., pl.* **-mies** [< *Tommy Atkins* (for *Thomas Atkins,* fictitious name used in Brit. army sample forms)] *[also* t-*] epithet for* a private in the British army

Tommy gun [alt. trademark for *Thompson submachine gun*] a kind of submachine gun

tom·my·rot (tämʹē rät') *n.* [Slang] nonsense

to·mor·row (tə märʹō, -môrʹō) *adv.* [OE. *to morgen*] **1.** on the day after today **2.** at some time in the future —*n.* **1.** the day after today **2.** some time in the future Also **to-morrow**

tom·tit (tämʹtit') *n.* [Chiefly Brit.] a titmouse or any of various other small birds

tom-tom (tämʹtäm') *n.* [Hindi *tam-tam*] a simple, deep drum with a small head, beaten with the hands

ton (tun) *n.* [var. of TUN] **1.** a unit of weight equal to 2,000 pounds avoirdupois: in full **short ton 2.** a unit of weight equal to 2,240 pounds avoirdupois, used in Great Britain: in full **long ton 3.** *same as* METRIC TON **4.** a unit of internal capacity of ships, equal to 100 cubic feet **5.** a unit of carrying capacity of ships, usually equal to 40 cubic feet **6.** a unit for measuring displacement of ships, equal to 35 cubic feet **7.** a unit of cooling capacity of an air conditioner, equal to 12,000 B.t.u. per hour

ton·al (tōʹn'l) *adj.* of a tone —**tonʹal·ly** *adv.*

to·nal·i·ty (tō nalʹə tē) *n., pl.* **-ties** *Music* **1.** *same as* KEY[1] **2.** tonal character as determined by the relationship of the tones to the keynote

tone (tōn) *n.* [< Gr. *teinein,* to stretch] **1.** a vocal or musical sound or its quality **2.** a manner of expression showing a certain attitude *[a friendly tone]* **3.** normal resilience **4.** the style, character, spirit, etc. of a place or period **5.** elegant style **6.** a quality of color; tint or shade

7. normal, healthy condition of a muscle, organ, etc. **8.** *Music a)* a sound of distinct pitch *b)* any of the full intervals of a diatonic scale; whole step **9.** *Painting* the effect produced by the combination of light, shade, and color — *vt.* **toned, tonʹing** to give a tone to —**tone down** (or **up**) to give a less (or more) intense tone to —**toneʹless** *adj.* — **toneʹless·ly** *adv.*

tone arm the pivoted arm containing the pickup on a phonograph

tone'-deaf' *adj.* not able to distinguish accurately differences in musical pitch

tong (tôŋ, täŋ) *n.* [Chin. *t'ang,* a meeting place] a Chinese association, society, etc.

Ton·ga (täŋʹgə) country on a group of islands (**Tonga Islands**) in the South Pacific: 270 sq. mi.; pop. 86,000 — **Tonʹgan** *n.*

tongs (tôŋz, täŋz) *n.pl.* [*sometimes with sing. v.*] [OE. *tange*] a device for seizing, lifting, etc., having two long arms pivoted or hinged together

tongue (tuŋ) *n.* [OE. *tunge*] **1.** the movable muscular structure in the mouth, used in eating, tasting, and (in man) speaking **2.** an animal's tongue used as food **3.** talk; speech **4.** a manner of speaking **5.** a language or dialect **6.** [*pl.*] *see* GLOSSOLALIA **7.** something like a tongue in shape, position, use, etc., as a bell clapper or the flap under the laces of a shoe —*vt.* **tongued, tonguʹing 1.** to touch, etc. with the tongue **2.** *Music* to play by tonguing: see TONGUING —*vi. Music* to use tonguing —**hold one's tongue** to keep from speaking —**on the tip of one's** (or **the) tongue** almost said or remembered —**speak in tongues** to be subject to glossolalia

tongue-and-groove joint a kind of joint in which a projection or tenon on one board fits exactly into a groove in another

tongue'-tie' (-tī') *n.* limited motion of the tongue, caused by shortness of the membrane underneath

tongue'-tied' *adj.* **1.** having a condition of tongue-tie **2.** speechless from embarrassment, shyness, etc.

tongue twister a phrase, etc. hard to speak fast

tongu·ing (tuŋʹiŋ) *n.* the use of the tongue in playing a musical wind instrument, esp. for more accurate intonation of rapid notes

ton·ic (tänʹik) *adj.* [see TONE] **1.** of or producing good muscular tone **2.** invigorating to the body or mind **3.** *Music* designating or based on a keynote —*n.* **1.** anything that invigorates; specif., *a)* a tonic medicine *b)* a hair or scalp dressing **2.** a carbonated beverage flavored with a little quinine and served in a mixed drink with gin, vodka, etc.; quinine water **3.** *Music* a keynote

to·night (tə nīt') *adv.* [OE. *to niht*] on or during the present or coming night —*n.* the present or the coming night Also **to-night**

ton·nage (tunʹij) *n.* **1.** the total shipping, in tons, of a country or port **2.** the amount in tons a ship can carry **3.** weight in tons

ton·sil (tänʹs'l) *n.* [L. *tonsillae, pl.*] either of a pair of oval masses of lymphoid tissue, one on each side at the back of the mouth

ton'sil·lec'to·my (-sə lekʹtə mē) *n., pl.* **-mies** [see -ECTOMY] the surgical removal of the tonsils

ton'sil·li'tis (-līt'əs) *n.* [see -ITIS] inflammation of the tonsils

ton·so·ri·al (tän sôrʹē əl) *adj.* [< L. *tondere,* to clip] of a barber or his work: often used humorously

ton·sure (tänʹshər) *n.* [< L. *tondere,* to clip] **1.** the act of shaving the head or crown of one entering the priesthood or a monastic order **2.** the part of the head so shaven —*vt.* **-sured, -sur·ing** to shave the head or crown of

TONSURE

too (tōō) *adv.* [< TO] **1.** in addition; also **2.** more than enough *[the hat is too big]* **3.** very; extremely *[that's too bad]* Often used as a mere emphatic *[I will too go]*

took (tōōk) *pt. of* TAKE

tool (tōōl) *n.* [OE. *tol*] **1.** any hand implement, instrument, etc. used for some work, as a knife, saw, or shovel **2.** *a)* the working part of a power-driven machine, as a drill, jigsaw blade, etc. *b)* the whole machine **3.** anything that serves as a means *[books are a scholar's tools]* **4.** a person used by another to accomplish his purposes; stooge —*vt.* **1.** to shape or work with a tool **2.** to provide tools or machinery for (a factory, etc.): often with **up 3.** to impress designs, etc. on (leather, etc.) with tools —*vi.* **1.** to use a tool or tools **2.** to ride in a vehicle

tool'mak'er *n.* a machinist who makes, maintains, and repairs machine tools

toot (to͞ot) *vi., vt.* [echoic] to sound (a horn, whistle, etc.) in short blasts —*n.* a short blast of a horn, etc.

tooth (to͞oth) *n., pl.* **teeth** [OE. *toth*] **1.** any of the hard, bonelike structures in the jaws, used for biting, chewing, etc. **2.** appetite for something *[a sweet tooth]* **3.** a toothlike part, as on a saw, comb, gear, etc. **4.** something biting, piercing, etc. like a tooth **5.** *[pl.]* an effective means of enforcing something —**get** (or **sink**) **one's teeth into** to become fully occupied with —**in the teeth of 1.** directly against **2.** defying —**tooth and nail** with all one's strength —**tooth'less** *adj.*

tooth'ache' *n.* a pain in or near a tooth

tooth'brush' *n.* a brush for cleaning the teeth

toothed (to͞otht, to͞othd) *adj.* **1.** having teeth: often used in hyphenated compounds *[big-toothed]* **2.** notched

tooth'paste' *n.* a paste for cleaning the teeth

tooth'pick' *n.* a very small, pointed stick for getting bits of food free from between the teeth

tooth powder a powder used like toothpaste

tooth·some (to͞oth'səm) *adj.* pleasing to the taste; tasty —**tooth'some·ly** *adv.* —**tooth'some·ness** *n.*

top¹ (täp) *n.* [OE.] **1.** the head or crown **2.** the highest part, point, or surface of anything **3.** the part of a plant above ground **4.** an uppermost part or covering, as a lid, cap, etc. **5.** the highest pitch, rank, degree, position, etc. **6.** a person of highest rank, etc. **7.** the choicest part; pick —*adj.* of or at the top; highest, greatest, etc. —*vt.* **topped, top'ping 1.** to remove the top of (a plant, etc.) **2.** to put a top on **3.** to be a top for **4.** to reach the top of **5.** to exceed in amount, etc. **6.** to surpass; outdo **7.** to head; lead **8.** *Sports* to hit (a ball) near its top, giving it a forward spin —**off the top of one's head** speaking without forethought —**on top** successful —**on top of 1.** resting upon **2.** besides **3.** right after **4.** controlling successfully —**over the top** beyond the goal set —**top off** to complete with a finishing touch —**top out** to level off

top² (täp) *n.* [OE.] a child's cone-shaped toy, spun on its pointed end —**sleep like a top** to sleep soundly

to·paz (tō'paz) *n.* [< Gr. *topazos*] any of various yellow gems, esp. a variety of aluminum silicate

top'coat' *n.* a lightweight overcoat

top'-drawer' *adj.* of first importance

To·pe·ka (tə pē'kə) capital of Kans.: pop. 125,000

top·er (tō'pər) *n.* [< archaic *tope*, to drink (much liquor)] one who drinks much alcoholic liquor; drunkard

top-flight (täp'flīt') *adj.* [Colloq.] best; first-rate

top·gal·lant (täp'gal'ənt; *nautical* tə gal'-) *adj.* next above the topmast —*n.* a topgallant mast, sail, etc.

top hat a tall, black, cylindrical hat, usually of silk, worn by men in formal dress

top'-heav'y *adj.* too heavy at the top, so as to be unstable —**top'-heav'i·ness** *n.*

top·ic (täp'ik) *n.* [ult. < Gr. *topos*, a place] **1.** the subject of a writing, speech, discussion, etc. **2.** a heading in an outline

top'i·cal *adj.* **1.** of a particular place; local **2.** of, using, or arranged by topics **3.** dealing with topics of the day; of current or local interest **4.** *Med.* for a particular part of the body —**top'i·cal·ly** *adv.*

top·knot (täp'nät') *n.* a tuft of hair or feathers on the top of the head

top'less (-lis) *adj.* without a top; specif., designating a costume that exposes the breasts

top'-lev'el *adj.* of the highest office or rank

top'mast' *n.* the second mast above the deck of a sailing ship

top·most (täp'mōst') *adj.* at the very top

top-notch (täp'näch') *adj.* [Colloq.] first-rate; excellent

to·pog·ra·phy (tə päg'rə fē) *n., pl.* **-phies** [< Gr. *topos*, a place + *graphein*, write] **1.** the science of showing on maps, charts, etc. the surface features of a region, such as hills, rivers, and roads **2.** these surface features —**top·o·graph·i·cal** (täp'ə graf'i k'l), **top'o·graph'ic** *adj.*

top·per (täp'ər) *n.* **1.** one who tops **2.** [Colloq.] *a*) *same as* TOP HAT *b*) a woman's short topcoat

top'ping (-iŋ) *n.* something put on top of something else, as a sauce on food

top·ple (täp''l) *vi.* **-pled, -pling** [< TOP¹] to fall (*over*) as from top-heaviness —*vt.* **1.** to cause to topple **2.** to overthrow

top·sail (täp's'l, -sāl') *n.* in a square-rigged vessel, the sail next above the lowest sail on a mast

top'-se'cret *adj.* designating or of the most highly restricted military or government information

top'side' *n.* [*usually pl.*] the part of a ship's side above the waterline —*adv.* on deck

top'soil' *n.* the upper layer of soil, usually darker and richer than the subsoil

top·sy-tur·vy (täp'sē tur'vē) *adv., adj.* [prob. < *top*, highest part + ME. *terven*, to roll] **1.** upside down; reversed **2.** in confusion or disorder —*n.* a topsy-turvy condition —**top'sy-tur'vi·ly** *adv.*

toque (tōk) *n.* [Fr.] a woman's small, round hat

to·rah, to·ra (tō'rə, tō rä') *n.* [Heb.] **1.** [*also* T-] the whole body of Jewish religious literature, including the Scripture, the Talmud, etc. **2.** [*usually* T-] the Pentateuch, or a parchment scroll containing this

torch (tôrch) *n.* [< L. *torquere*, to twist] **1.** a portable flaming light **2.** a source of enlightenment, inspiration, etc. **3.** a device for producing a very hot flame, used as in welding **4.** [Brit.] a flashlight —*vt.* [Slang] to set fire to, as in arson

torch'bear'er *n.* **1.** one who carries a torch **2.** one who brings enlightenment, inspiration, etc.

torch'light' *n.* the light of a torch or torches —*adj.* done or carried on by torchlight

tore (tôr) *pt.* of TEAR¹

tor·e·a·dor (tôr'ē ə dôr') *n.* [Sp. < L. *taurus*, a bull] a bullfighter: term no longer used in bullfighting

tor·ment (tôr'ment) *n.* [< L. *torquere*, to twist] **1.** great pain, physical or mental; agony **2.** a source of pain, anxiety, or annoyance —*vt.* (tôr ment') **1.** to make suffer greatly in body or mind **2.** to annoy, harass, or tease —**tor·men'tor, tor·ment'er** *n.*

torn (tôrn) *pp.* of TEAR¹

tor·na·do (tôr nā'dō) *n., pl.* **-does, -dos** [< Sp. < L. *tonare*, to thunder] **1.** a rapidly whirling column of air, usually seen as a slender, funnel-shaped cloud that usually destroys everything in its narrow path **2.** any whirlwind or hurricane —**tor·nad'ic** (-nad'ik) *adj.*

To·ron·to (tə rän'tō) capital of Ontario, Canada: pop. 665,000 (met. area 2,158,000)

tor·pe·do (tôr pē'dō) *n., pl.* **-does** [L., numbness < *torpere*, to be stiff] **1.** a kind of ray (fish) with electric organs that can stun prey **2.** a large, cigar-shaped, self-propelled underwater projectile launched against enemy ships: it explodes on contact **3.** any of various explosive devices —*vt.* **-doed, -do·ing** to attack, destroy, etc. as with a torpedo

tor·pid (tôr'pid) *adj.* [< L. *torpere*, to be numb] **1.** dormant; inactive and unfeeling, as a hibernating animal **2.** dull; sluggish —**tor·pid'i·ty, tor'pid·ness** *n.* —**tor'pid·ly** *adv.*

tor·por (tôr'pər) *n.* **1.** a state of being dormant or inactive **2.** sluggishness; dullness; apathy

torque (tôrk) *n.* [< L. *torquere*, a twisted metal necklace] **1.** *Physics* a force that produces a twisting or wrenching effect **2.** popularly, any force that causes rotation, as in an automotive vehicle

Tor·rance (tôr'əns) city in SW Calif.: pop. 135,000

tor·rent (tôr'ənt, tär'-) *n.* [< L. *torrens*, rushing] **1.** a swift, violent stream, esp. of water **2.** a flood or rush of words, mail, etc. **3.** a very heavy rainfall —**tor·ren·tial** (tô ren'shəl) *adj.* —**tor·ren'tial·ly** *adv.*

tor·rid (tôr'id, tär'-) *adj.* [< L. *torrere*, parch] **1.** subjected to intense heat, esp. of the sun; parched; arid **2.** very hot; scorching **3.** passionate, ardent, etc. —**tor'rid·ly** *adv.*

Torrid Zone the area of the earth's surface between the Tropic of Cancer & the Tropic of Capricorn and divided by the equator

tor·sion (tôr'shən) *n.* [< L. *torquere*, to twist] **1.** a twisting or being twisted, esp. along the length of an axis **2.** *Mech.* the tendency of a twisted wire, bar, etc. to return to its untwisted condition —**tor'sion·al** *adj.* —**tor'sion·al·ly** *adv.*

tor·so (tôr'sō) *n., pl.* **-sos, -si** (-sē) [It. < Gr. *thyrsos*, a stem] **1.** the trunk of the human body **2.** a statue representing this, esp. one lacking head or limbs

tort (tôrt) *n.* [< L. *torquere*, to twist] *Law* a wrongful act or damage (not involving a breach of contract), for which civil action can be brought

torte (tôrt) *n.* [G.] a rich cake, variously made, as of eggs, chopped nuts, and crumbs

tor·til·la (tôr tē'ə) *n.* [Sp., dim. of *torta*, a cake] a griddlecake of unleavened cornmeal, now sometimes of flour: a staple food of Mexico

tor·toise (tôr'təs) *n.* [prob. < LGr. *tartarouchos*, demon] a turtle, esp. one that lives on land

tortoise shell the hard, mottled, yellow-and-brown shell of some turtles used, esp. formerly, in making combs, etc. —**tor′toise-shell′** adj.

tor·to·ni (tôr tō′nē) n. [It.] a rich ice cream with maraschino cherries, almonds, etc.

tor·tu·ous (tôr′chōo wəs) adj. [< L. torquere, to twist] 1. full of twists and turns; winding; crooked 2. not straightforward; devious or deceitful —**tor′tu·os′i·ty** (-wäs′ə tē) n., pl. **-ties** —**tor′tu·ous·ly** adv.

tor·ture (tôr′chər) n. [Fr. < L. torquere, to twist] 1. the inflicting of severe pain, as to force information or confession 2. any severe physical or mental pain, or a cause of it —vt. **-tured, -tur·ing** 1. to subject to torture 2. to twist (meaning, etc.) —**tor′tur·er** n.

To·ry (tôr′ē) n., pl. **-ries** [< Ir. tōruidhe, robber] 1. formerly, a member of the major conservative party of England 2. in the American Revolution, one who favored allegiance to Great Britain 3. [often t-] any extreme conservative —adj. [also t-] of or being a Tory —**To′ry·ism** n.

toss (tôs, täs) vt. [prob. < Scand.] 1. to throw or pitch about [waves tossed the boat] 2. to mix (esp. a salad) lightly 3. to throw upward lightly from the hand 4. to jerk upward [to toss one's head] —vi. 1. to be thrown about 2. to fling oneself about in sleep, etc. 3. to toss up: see phrase below —n. a tossing or being tossed —**toss off** 1. to make, do, write, etc. quickly and easily 2. to drink in one draft —**toss up** to toss a coin to decide something according to which side lands uppermost

toss′up′ n. 1. the act of tossing a coin to decide something according to which side lands uppermost 2. an even chance

tot¹ (tät) n. [prob. < Scand.] 1. a young child 2. [Chiefly Brit.] a small drink of alcoholic liquor

tot² (tät) vt., vi. **tot′ted, tot′ting** [Chiefly Brit. Colloq.] to add; total (usually with up)

to·tal (tōt′'l) adj. [< L. totus, all] 1. constituting the (or a) whole; entire 2. complete; utter —n. the whole amount or number —vt. **-taled** or **-talled, -tal·ing** or **-tal·ling** 1. to find the total of 2. to add up to 3. [Slang] to wreck completely —vi. to amount (to) as a whole —**to′tal·ly** adv.

to·tal·i·tar·i·an (tō tal′ə ter′ē ən) adj. [TOTAL + (AUTHOR)ITARIAN] designating or of a government or state in which one political group maintains complete control under a dictator and bans all others —n. one who favors such a government or state —**to·tal′i·tar′i·an·ism** n.

to·tal·i·ty (tō tal′ə tē) n., pl. **-ties** 1. the fact or condition of being total 2. the total amount or sum

to·tal·i·za·tor (tōt′'l i zāt′ər) n. a machine for registering parimutuel bets and, usually, computing odds and payoffs while bets are being placed: also **to′tal·i·sa′tor, to′tal·iz′er**

tote¹ (tōt) vt. **tot′ed, tot′ing** [prob. of Afr. origin] [Colloq.] 1. to carry or haul 2. to be armed with (a gun, etc.)

tote² (tōt) vt. **tot′ed, tot′ing** shortened form of TOTAL (usually with up)

to·tem (tōt′əm) n. [< Algonquian] 1. among primitive peoples, an animal or natural object taken as the symbol of a family or clan 2. an image of this —**to·tem·ic** (tō tem′ik) adj. —**to′tem·ism** n.

totem pole a pole carved and painted with totems, often erected in front of their dwellings by Indian tribes of northwestern N. America

tot·ter (tät′ər) vi. [prob. < Scand.] 1. to rock as if about to fall 2. to be on the point of collapse 3. to be unsteady on one's feet; stagger —n. a tottering —**tot′ter·y** adj.

tou·can (tōō′kan) n. [SAmInd. tucana] a brightly colored bird of tropical America, with a very large beak

touch (tuch) vt. [OFr. tochier] 1. to put the hand, finger, etc. on, so as to feel 2. to bring into contact with something else 3. to be or come into contact with 4. to border on 5. to strike lightly 6. to give a light tint, aspect, etc. to [touched with pink] 7. to stop at, as a ship 8. to handle, use, partake of, etc. 9. to come up to; reach 10. to compare with; equal 11. to deal with, esp. in passing 12. to affect; concern 13. to arouse sympathy, gratitude, etc. in 14. [Slang] to seek a loan or gift of money from 15. Geom. to be tangent to —vi. 1. to touch a person or thing 2. to be or come in contact 3. to verge (on or upon) 4. to pertain; bear (on or upon) 5. to treat in passing

TOUCAN
(1 1/2–2 ft. long, including beak)

(with on or upon) 6. Geom. to be tangent —n. 1. a touching or being touched; specif., a light tap or stroke 2. the sense by which physical objects are felt 3. a sensation so caused; feel 4. a subtle change or addition in a painting, story, etc. 5. a very small amount; trace, tinge, etc. 6. a slight attack [a touch of the flu] 7. contact or communication [keep in touch] 8. [Slang] the act of seeking a gift or loan of money 9. Music the manner of striking the keys of a piano, etc. —**touch down** to land: said of an aircraft or spacecraft —**touch off** 1. to make explode 2. to produce (esp. a violent reaction, etc.) —**touch up** to improve or finish (a painting, story, etc.) by minor changes —**touch′a·bil′i·ty** n. —**touch′a·ble** adj. —**touch′er** n.

touch and go an uncertain or dangerous situation —**touch′-and-go′** adj.

touch′down′ n. Football 1. a scoring play in which a player grounds the ball past the opponent's goal line 2. a score of six points so made

tou·ché (tōō shā′) interj. [Fr.] Fencing touched: said of a point scored by a touch: also used in congratulating someone for a witty reply, etc.

touched (tucht) adj. 1. emotionally affected; moved 2. slightly demented: also **touched in the head**

touch′ing adj. arousing tender emotion; moving —prep. with regard to —**touch′ing·ly** adv.

touch′stone′ n. 1. a stone formerly used to test the purity of gold or silver 2. any test of genuineness

touch′y adj. **-i·er, -i·est** 1. easily offended; irritable 2. very risky —**touch′i·ness** n.

tough (tuf) adj. [OE. toh] 1. that will bend, twist, etc. without tearing or breaking 2. not easily cut or chewed [tough steak] 3. strong; hardy 4. stubborn 5. practical and realistic 6. overly aggressive; rough 7. very difficult 8. violent 9. [Colloq.] unfavorable; bad —n. a tough person; thug —**tough′ly** adv. —**tough′ness** n.

tough′en vt., vi. to make or become tough or tougher

Tou·louse-Lau·trec (tōō lōōz′lō trek′), **Hen·ri (Marie Raymond) de** (än rē′ də) 1864–1901; Fr. painter

tou·pee (tōō pā′) n. [Fr. < OFr. toup, tuft of hair] a man's wig, esp. one for a small bald spot

tour (tōōr) n. [< OFr. tourner, to TURN] 1. a turn or shift of work, esp. a period of military service at one place 2. a long trip, as for sightseeing 3. any trip, as for inspection, giving performances, etc. —vi., vt. to go on a tour (through) —**on tour** touring

tour de force (tōōr′ də fôrs′) pl. **tours′ de force′** (tōōr′) [Fr.] an unusually skillful or ingenious production, performance, etc., sometimes a merely clever one

tour′ism n. tourist travel, esp. when regarded as a source of income for a country, business, etc.

tour′ist n. one who tours, esp. for pleasure —adj. 1. of or for tourists 2. designating or of the lowest-priced accommodations, as on a ship —adv. by means of tourist class

tour·ma·line (tōōr′mə lin, -lēn′) n. [Fr.] a crystalline mineral, commonly black but also colored or transparent, used as a gemstone and in optical equipment

tour·na·ment (tōōr′nə mənt, tur′-) n. [< OFr. tourner, to TURN] 1. in the Middle Ages, a contest in which knights on horseback tried to unseat one another with lances 2. a series of contests in competition for a championship

tour·ney (tōōr′nē, tur′-) n., pl. **-neys** same as TOURNAMENT —vi. to take part in a tournament; joust

tour·ni·quet (tōōr′nə kit, tur′-; -kā′) n. [Fr. < L. tunica, tunic] any device for compressing a blood vessel to stop bleeding, as a bandage twisted tight

tou·sle (tou′z'l) vt. **-sled, -sling** [< ME. tusen, to pull] to dishevel, rumple, muss, etc.

tout (tout) vi., vt. [OE. totian, to peep] [Colloq.] 1. to praise or recommend highly 2. to provide betting tips on (racehorses) —n. [Colloq.] a person who touts

tow¹ (tō) vt. [OE. togian] to pull as by a rope or chain —n. 1. a towing or being towed 2. something towed 3. a towline —**in tow** 1. being towed 2. in one's company or charge

tow² (tō) n. [OE. tow-, for spinning] the broken fibers of hemp, flax, etc. before spinning

to·ward (tôrd, tə wôrd′) prep. [OE. toweard] 1. in the direction of 2. facing 3. aimed at or tending to [steps toward peace] 4. concerning; regarding [my attitude toward noon] 5. just before [toward noon] 6. in anticipation of [save toward a new car] Also **towards**

tow·el (tou′'l, toul) n. [< OFr. toaille] a piece of absorbent cloth or paper for wiping or drying things —vt. **-eled** or **-elled, -el·ing** or **-el·ling** to wipe or dry with a towel —**throw (or toss) in the towel** [Colloq.] to admit defeat —**towel off** to dry oneself, as after bathing

tow·el·ing, tow·el·ling n. material for making towels

tow·er[1] (tou′ər) n. [< L. turris] 1. a high structure, often part of another building 2. such a structure used as a fortress or prison 3. a person or thing that resembles a tower in height, strength, etc. —vi. to rise high like a tower —tow′er·ing adj.

tow·er[2] (tō′ər) n. a person or thing that tows

tow·head (tō′hed′) n. 1. a head of pale-yellow hair 2. a person with such hair —tow′head′ed adj.

tow·hee (tou′hē, tō′-) n. [echoic] any of various small N. American sparrows that feed on the ground

tow·line (tō′līn′) n. a rope, chain, etc. for towing

town (toun) n. [OE. tun] 1. a concentration of houses and buildings larger than a village but smaller than a city 2. a city 3. a township 4. the business center of a city 5. the people of a town —go to town [Slang] 1. to act fast and efficiently 2. to be successful —on the town [Colloq.] out for a good time

town hall a building in a town, housing the offices of officials, the council chamber, etc.

town house 1. the city residence of a person who owns a country residence 2. a two-story dwelling, a unit in a complex of such dwellings

town meeting a meeting of the voters of a town, as in New England, to act on town business

town′ship n. 1. a division of a county, constituting a unit of local government 2. in New England, a town 3. a unit of territory in the U.S. land survey, generally six miles square

towns·man (tounz′mən) n., pl. **-men** 1. a person who lives in a town 2. a fellow resident of a town

towns′peo′ple n.pl. the people of a town

tow′path′ n. a path alongside a canal, for men or animals towing boats carrying freight

tow′rope′ n. a rope used in towing

tox·e·mi·a (täk sē′mē ə) n. [see TOXIC] blood poisoning, esp. as caused by toxins from bacteria —tox·e′mic adj.

tox·ic (täk′sik) adj. [< L. toxicum, a poison] 1. of, affected by, or caused by a toxin 2. acting as a poison —tox·ic′i·ty (-sis′ə tē) n.

tox·i·col·o·gy (täk′si käl′ə jē) n. [see TOXIC & -LOGY] the science of poisons, their effects, antidotes, etc. —tox′i·col′o·gist n.

tox·in (täk′sin) n. [TOX(IC) + -IN¹] 1. a poison produced by microorganisms and causing certain diseases 2. any poison secreted by plants or animals

toy (toi) n. [< ? MDu. toi, finery] 1. a thing of little value or importance; trifle 2. a bauble; trinket 3. a plaything for children —adj. 1. like a toy in size, use, etc. 2. made as a toy [a toy stove] —vi. to trifle (with food, an idea, etc.)

tr. 1. transitive 2. transpose 3. treasurer

trace[1] (trās) n. [< L. trahere, to draw] 1. a mark, footprint, track, etc. left by a person, animal, or thing 2. a perceptible mark left by a past person, thing, or event; sign [traces of war] 3. a barely perceptible amount —vt. **traced, trac′ing** 1. to follow the trail of; track 2. a) to follow the development or history of b) to determine (a source, date, etc.) thus 3. to draw, outline, etc. 4. to copy (a drawing, etc.) by following its lines on a transparent sheet placed over it —trace′a·ble adj.

trace[2] (trās) n. [see TRAIT] either of two straps, chains, etc. connecting a draft animal's harness to the vehicle

trace element a chemical element, as iron, zinc, etc., essential in nutrition, but only in minute amounts

trac′er n. 1. one who traces missing articles, persons, etc. 2. an inquiry sent out for a letter, etc. missing in transport 3. a substance used to follow biochemical reactions, as in the body, or to locate diseased cells, etc.

trac·er·y (trā′sər ē) n., pl. **-ies** [TRACE¹ + -(E)RY] ornamental work of interlacing or branching lines

tra·che·a (trā′kē ə) n., pl. **-che·ae′** (-ē′), **-che·as** [< Gr. tracheia (arteria), rough (windpipe)] 1. the passage that conveys air from the larynx to the bronchi; windpipe 2. any of the minute tubes branching through the bodies of insects, etc. and bringing in air —tra′che·al adj.

tra·che·ot·o·my (trā′kē ät′ə mē) n., pl. **-mies** surgical incision of the trachea

trac·ing (trā′siŋ) n. something traced, as a copy of a drawing or a line traced by a recording instrument

TRACERY

track (trak) n. [MFr. trac] 1. a mark left in passing, as a footprint or rut 2. a path or trail 3. a course of action or motion; route 4. a circuit laid out for running, horse racing, etc. 5. a pair of parallel metal rails on which trains, etc. run 6. either of the two endless belts on which tanks, tractors, etc. move 7. a) sports performed on a track, as running, hurdling, etc. b) track and field sports together 8. a) the part of a magnetic tape being recorded or played b) any of the bands of a phonograph record —vt. 1. to follow the track of 2. to trace by means of evidence, etc. 3. to plot the course of (an aircraft, spacecraft, etc.) as by radar and computer 4. to leave in the form of tracks [to track dirt on the floor] —in one's tracks where one is at the moment —keep (or lose) track of to stay (or fail to stay) informed about —on (or off) the track keeping to (or straying from) the subject or goal —track down 1. to pursue until caught 2. to investigate fully —track′er n. —track′less adj.

track and field a series of contests in running, jumping, shot-putting, etc., or athletic training for this

tract[1] (trakt) n. [< L. trahere, to draw] 1. a continuous expanse of land 2. a system of organs having some special function [the digestive tract]

tract[2] (trakt) n. [< L. tractatus, a treatise] a pamphlet, esp. one on a religious or political subject

trac·ta·ble (trak′tə b'l) adj. [< L. trahere, to draw] 1. easily managed or taught; docile 2. easily worked or shaped; malleable —trac′ta·bil′i·ty n. —trac′ta·bly adv.

trac·tion (trak′shən) n. [< L. trahere, to draw] 1. a pulling or drawing or a being pulled or drawn 2. a pulling, as by an apparatus, to relieve pressure, bring a bone into proper place, etc. 3. the power used by a locomotive, etc. 4. adhesive friction, as of tires on pavement

trac·tor (trak′tər) n. [see TRACTION] 1. a powerful, motor-driven vehicle for pulling farm machinery, hauling loads, etc. 2. a driver's cab for hauling one or more large trailers

trade (trād) n. [MLowG., a track] 1. an occupation; esp., skilled work; craft 2. all the persons or companies in a particular line of business 3. buying or selling; commerce 4. customers 5. a purchase or sale 6. an exchange; swap 7. [pl.] the trade winds —adj. 1. of trade or commerce 2. of the persons in the trades, or crafts: also trades —vi. **trad′ed, trad′ing** 1. to carry on a business 2. to have business dealings (with) 3. to make an exchange (with) 4. [Colloq.] to be a customer (at a specified store, etc.) —vt. 1. to exchange; barter 2. to buy and sell (stocks, etc.) —trade on (or upon) to take advantage of

trade′-in′ n. a used car, etc. given or taken as part payment toward a new one

trade journal a magazine devoted to the interests of a specific trade, business, or industry

trade′mark′ n. a symbol, design, word, etc. used by a manufacturer or dealer to distinguish his products: usually registered and protected by law —vt. 1. to put a trademark on (a product) 2. to register (a symbol, word, etc.) as a trademark

trade name 1. the name by which a commodity is commonly known in the trade 2. a name, often a trademark or service mark, used by a company to describe a product, service, etc. 3. a company name

trad′er n. 1. one who trades; merchant 2. a ship used in trade

trade school a school where trades are taught

trades·man (trādz′mən) n., pl. **-men** [Chiefly Brit.] a storekeeper —trades′wom′an n.fem., pl. -wom′en

trade union same as LABOR UNION —trade′-un′ion adj.

trade wind a wind that blows toward the equator from the northeast on the north side of the equator and from the southeast on the south side

trading post a store in an outpost, settlement, etc. where trading is done, as with natives

trading stamp a stamp given by some merchants as a premium, redeemable in merchandise

tra·di·tion (trə dish′ən) n. [< L. tradere, deliver] 1. the handing down orally of customs, beliefs, stories, etc. from generation to generation 2. a belief, custom, etc. so handed down

tra·di′tion·al adj. of, handed down by, or conforming to tradition —tra·di′tion·al·ly adv.

tra·duce (trə dōōs′, -dyōōs′) vt. **-duced′, -duc′ing** [< L. trans, across + ducere, to lead] 1. to defame; slander 2. to betray —tra·duc′er n.

Tra·fal·gar (trə fal′gər), **Cape** cape at the entrance to the strait of Gibraltar: site of a British naval victory (1805) over Napoleon's fleet

traf·fic (traf′ik) *n.* [< L. *trans*, across + It. *ficcare*, bring] 1. buying and selling; trade 2. corrupt or illegal trade 3. dealings (*with* someone) 4. *a*) the movement or number of cars along a street, pedestrians along a sidewalk, etc. *b*) the cars, pedestrians, etc. 5. the business done by a transportation company —*adj.* of traffic or its regulation —*vi.* -ficked, -fick·ing 1. to carry on traffic (*in* something) 2. to have dealings (*with* someone) —**traf′fick·er** *n.*
traffic light (or **signal**) a set of signal lights at intersections of streets to regulate traffic
tra·ge·di·an (trə jē′dē ən) *n.* an actor of tragedy
tra·ge·di·enne (trə jē′dē en′) *n.* an actress of tragedy
trag·e·dy (traj′ə dē) *n., pl.* -dies [< Gr. *tragos*, goat + *ōidē*, song] 1. a serious play with an unhappy or disastrous ending brought about by fate, moral weakness in a character, etc. 2. a very sad or tragic event
trag·ic (traj′ik) *adj.* 1. of, like, or having to do with tragedy 2. very sad, disastrous, etc. Also **trag′i·cal** —**trag′i·cal·ly** *adv.*
trail (trāl) *vt.* [< L. *trahere*, to drag] 1. *a*) to drag or let drag behind one *b*) to bring along behind [he *trailed* dirt into the house] 2. to follow the tracks of 3. to hunt by tracking 4. to follow behind —*vi.* 1. to be drawn along behind one, as the train of a gown 2. to grow along the ground, etc., as some plants 3. to stream behind, as smoke 4. to follow or lag behind; straggle 5. to dwindle, as a sound (with *off* or *away*) —*n.* 1. something that trails behind 2. a mark, scent, etc. left by a person, animal, or thing that has passed 3. a beaten path
trail′er *n.* 1. one that trails 2. a cart or van designed to be pulled by an automobile or truck (esp. a tractor, *n.* 2) 3. a closed vehicle designed to be lived in and to be pulled by a motor vehicle: see also MOBILE HOME 4. scenes from a coming motion picture, used to advertise it
trailer park an area designed to accommodate trailers, esp. mobile homes: also **trailer camp**, **trailer court**
trailing arbutus same as ARBUTUS (sense 2)
train (trān) *n.* [< L. *trahere*, to pull] 1. something that drags along behind, as a trailing skirt 2. a group of followers or attendants; retinue 3. a procession; caravan 4. a series of connected things [a *train* of thought, a gear *train*] 5. a line of connected railroad cars pulled by a locomotive —*vt.* 1. to guide the growth of (a plant) 2. to guide the mental, moral, etc. development of; rear 3. to instruct so as to make proficient 4. to discipline (animals) to do tricks or obey commands 5. to make fit for some sport, as by exercise, practice, etc. 6. to aim (a gun, etc.) —*vi.* to undergo training —**train′a·ble** *adj.* —**train′er** *n.*
train·ee′ *n.* one receiving vocational training, military training, etc. —**train·ee′ship′** *n.*
train′man *n., pl.* -men one who works on a railroad train or in a railroad yard
traipse (trāps) *vi., vt.* traipsed, traips′ing [< ?] [Dial. or Colloq.] to walk, wander, tramp, or gad —*n.* [Dial. or Colloq.] the act of traipsing
trait (trāt) *n.* [Fr. < L. *trahere*, to draw] a distinct quality or feature, as of personality
trai·tor (trāt′ər) *n.* [< L. *tradere*, betray] one who betrays his country, friends, etc.; one guilty of treason —**trai′tor·ous** *adj.*
tra·jec·to·ry (trə jek′tə rē) *n., pl.* -ries [< L. *trans*, across + *jacere*, to throw] the curved path of something hurtling through space, esp. that of a projectile
tram (tram) *n.* [prob. < LowG. *traam*, a beam] 1. an open railway car used in mines 2. [Brit.] a streetcar; trolley car Also **tram′car′**
tram·mel (tram′'l) *n.* [< L. *tres*, three + *macula*, a mesh] 1. a three-ply fishing net 2. a shackle for a horse 3. [*usually pl.*] something that hinders freedom of action —*vt.* -meled or -melled, -mel·ing or -mel·ling to hinder, restrain, or shackle
tramp (tramp) *vi.* [ME. *trampen*] 1. to walk firmly and heavily 2. to travel about on foot, esp. as a vagabond, hobo, etc. —*vt.* 1. to step on heavily; trample 2. to walk through —*n.* 1. a vagrant; hobo 2. the sound of heavy steps 3. a journey on foot; hike 4. a freight ship without a regular schedule, that picks up cargo as it stops at various ports
tram·ple (tram′p'l) *vi.* -pled, -pling [see TRAMP] to tread heavily —*vt.* to crush as by treading heavily on —*n.* the sound of trampling —**trample under foot** to crush or hurt by or as by trampling: also **trample on** (or **upon**)
tram·po·line (tram′pə lēn′) *n.* [< It. *trampolino*, a springboard] a sheet of strong canvas stretched tightly on a frame, used in acrobatic tumbling
trance (trans) *n.* [< L. *trans*, across + *ire*, go] 1. a sleeplike state in which consciousness may remain, as in

hypnosis 2. a daze; stupor 3. the condition of being completely lost in thought or meditation 4. the state a spiritualist medium is in while allegedly communicating with the dead
tran·quil (traŋ′kwəl) *adj.* -quil·er or -quil·ler, -quil·est or -quil·lest [L. *tranquillus*] calm, serene, quiet, undisturbed, etc. —**tran′quil·ly** *adv.*
tran·quil·ize, tran·quil·lize (traŋ′kwə līz′) *vt., vi.* -ized′ or -lized′, -iz′ing or -liz′ing to make or become tranquil; specif., to calm by the use of a tranquilizer —**tran′quil·i·za′tion, tran′quil·li·za′tion** *n.*
tran′quil·iz′er, tran′quil·liz′er *n.* any of certain drugs used in calming persons suffering from nervous tension, anxiety, etc.
tran·quil′li·ty, tran·quil′i·ty (-kwil′ə tē) *n.* the state of being tranquil; calmness, serenity, etc.
trans- [L. < *trans*, across] *a prefix meaning:* 1. over, across, through 2. so as to change thoroughly [*transliterate*] 3. above and beyond, transcending
trans. 1. transitive 2. translated 3. translation 4. transportation
trans·act (tran sakt′, -zakt′) *vt.* [< L. *trans*, across + *agere*, to drive] to carry on, conduct, or complete (business, etc.) —**trans·ac′tor** *n.*
trans·ac′tion *n.* 1. a transacting 2. something transacted; specif., *a*) a business deal *b*) [*pl.*] a record of proceedings, as of a society
trans·at·lan·tic (trans′ət lan′tik) *adj.* 1. crossing the Atlantic 2. on the other side of the Atlantic
trans·ceiv·er (tran sē′vər) *n.* [TRANS(MITTER) + (RE)CEIVER] a single apparatus functioning alternately as a radio transmitter and receiver
tran·scend (tran send′) *vt.* [< L. *trans-*, over + *scandere*, climb] 1. to go beyond the limits of; exceed 2. to surpass; excel
tran·scend′ent (-sen′dənt) *adj.* 1. transcending; excelling 2. *Theol.* existing apart from the material universe —**transcend′ence, tran·scend′en·cy** *n.*
tran·scen·den·tal (tran′sen den′t'l) *adj.* 1. *same as:* *a*) TRANSCENDENT (sense 1) *b*) SUPERNATURAL 2. abstract 3. of transcendentalism —**tran′scen·den′tal·ly** *adv.*
tran′scen·den′tal·ism *n.* any philosophy that seeks to discover the nature of reality through investigation of the process of thought or through spiritual intuition —**tran′scen·den′tal·ist** *n.*
trans·con·ti·nen·tal (trans′kän tə nen′t'l) *adj.* 1. that crosses a continent 2. on the other side of a continent
tran·scribe (tran skrīb′) *vt.* -scribed′, -scrib′ing [< L. *trans*, over + *scribere*, write] 1. to make a written or typewritten copy of (shorthand notes, etc.) 2. *Music, Radio, & TV* to make a transcription of
tran·script (tran′skript′) *n.* 1. a written, typewritten, or printed copy 2. any copy or reproduction
tran·scrip′tion (-skrip′shən) *n.* 1. the act or process of transcribing 2. a transcript 3. an arrangement of a piece of music for an instrument or voice other than that for which it was originally written 4. a recording made for radio or TV broadcasting
tran·sept (tran′sept) *n.* [< L. *trans-*, across + *septum*, enclosure] the part of a cross-shaped church at right angles to the nave
trans·fer (trans fur′) *vt.* -ferred′, -fer′ring [< L. *trans-*, across + *ferre*, to bear] 1. to carry, send, etc. from one person or place to another 2. to make over (title to property, etc.) to another 3. to move (a picture, etc.) from one surface to another, as by making wet and pressing —*vi.* 1. to transfer oneself or be transferred 2. to change to another bus, etc. —*n.* (trans′fər) 1. a transferring or being transferred 2. one that is transferred 3. a ticket entitling the bearer to change to another bus, etc. —**trans·fer′able, trans·fer′ra·ble** *adj.* —**trans·fer′al, trans·fer′ral** *n.* —**trans·fer′ence** *n.*
trans·fig·u·ra·tion (trans fig′yoo rā′shən) *n.* a transfiguring or being transfigured —[T-] 1. *Bible* the change in the appearance of Jesus on the mountain: Matt. 17 2. a church festival (Aug. 6) commemorating this
trans·fig·ure (trans fig′yər) *vt.* -ured, -ur·ing [< L. *trans-*, across + *figura*, figure] 1. to change the form or appearance of; transform 2. to transform so as to exalt or glorify
trans·fix (trans fiks′) *vt.* [< L. *trans-*, through + *figere*, to fix] 1. to pierce through; impale 2. to make motionless, as with horror
trans·form (trans fôrm′) *vt.* [ult. < L. *trans-*, over + *forma*, a shape] 1. to change the form or appearance of 2. to change the condition, character, or function of 3. *Elec.* to change (voltage, current, etc.) by use of a transformer

4. *Math.* to change (an algebraic expression or equation) in form but not in value **5.** *Physics* to change (one form of energy) to another —**trans·for·ma′tion** *n.*

trans·form′er *n.* **1.** one that transforms **2.** *Elec.* a device for transferring electric energy from one alternating-current circuit to another, usually with a change in voltage, current, etc.

trans·fuse (trans fyōoz′) *vt.* -fused′, -fus′ing [< L. *trans-*, across + *fundere*, pour] **1.** to instill, imbue, permeate, etc. **2.** to transfer or introduce (blood, saline solution, etc.) into a blood vessel, usually a vein —**trans·fu′sion** *n.*

trans·gress (trans gres′) *vt., vi.* [< Fr. < L. *trans-*, over + *gradi*, to step] **1.** to break (a law, commandment, etc.); sin (against) **2.** to go beyond (a limit, etc.) —**trans·gres′sion** (-gresh′ən) *n.* —**trans·gres′sor** *n.*

tran·sient (tran′shənt) *adj.* [< L. *trans-*, over + *ire*, go] **1.** passing away with time; temporary **2.** passing quickly; fleeting **3.** staying for only a short time *[a transient lodger]* —*n.* a transient person or thing *[transients at a hotel]* —**tran′sience, tran′sien·cy** *n.* —**tran′sient·ly** *adv.*

tran·sis·tor (tran zis′tər, -sis′-) *n.* [TRAN(SFER) + (RE)SISTOR] a small, solid-state electronic device used instead of an electron tube

tran·sis·tor·ize (-tə rīz′) *vt.* -ized′, -iz′ing to equip with transistors

trans·it (tran′sit, -zit) *n.* [< L. *trans-*, over + *ire*, go] **1.** passage through or across **2.** a transition **3.** a carrying or being carried from one place to another **4.** a system of public transportation in an urban area: see RAPID TRANSIT **5.** a surveying instrument for measuring horizontal angles **6.** *Astron.* a) the apparent passage of a heavenly body across a given meridian or through the field of a telescope b) the apparent passage of a smaller heavenly body across the disk of a larger one —*vt., vi.* to make a transit (through or across)

tran·si·tion (tran zish′ən, -sish′-) *n.* **1.** a passing from one condition, place, etc. to another **2.** the period of this **3.** a word, phrase, sentence, etc. that relates a topic with a succeeding one —**tran·si′tion·al** *adj.*

tran·si·tive (tran′sə tiv) *adj.* taking a direct object to complete the meaning: said of certain verbs —*n.* a transitive verb —**tran′si·tive·ly** *adv.*

tran·si·to·ry (tran′sə tôr′ē) *adj.* not enduring; temporary; fleeting —**tran′si·to′ri·ly** *adv.*

trans·late (trans lāt′) *vt.* -lat′ed, -lat′ing [< L. *translatus*, transferred] **1.** to change from one place or condition to another **2.** to put into the words of a different language **3.** to change into another medium or form *[translate ideas into action]* **4.** to put into different words; rephrase —*vi.* to make a translation into another language —**trans·la′tor** *n.*

trans·la′tion *n.* **1.** a translating or being translated **2.** writing or speech translated into another language

trans·lit·er·ate (trans lit′ə rāt′) *vt.* -at′ed, -at′ing [< TRANS- + L. *litera*, letter] to write or spell (words, etc.) in corresponding characters of another alphabet —**trans·lit′er·a′tion** *n.*

trans·lu·cent (trans lōo′sənt) *adj.* [< L. *trans-*, through + *lucere*, to shine] letting light pass through but not transparent, as frosted glass —**trans·lu′cence, trans·lu′cen·cy** *n.*

trans·mi·grate (trans mī′grāt) *vi.* -grat·ed, -grat·ing [see TRANS- & MIGRATE] **1.** to move from one country, etc. to another **2.** in some religions, to pass into another body at death: said of the soul —**trans′mi·gra′tion** *n.*

trans·mis·si·ble (trans mis′ə b'l) *adj.* capable of being transmitted

trans·mis′sion (-mish′ən) *n.* **1.** a transmitting or being transmitted **2.** something transmitted **3.** the part of a motor vehicle that transmits motive force from the engine to the wheels, as by gears **4.** the passage of radio waves through space between the transmitting station and the receiving station

trans·mit (trans mit′) *vt.* -mit′ted, -mit′ting [< L. *trans-*, over + *mittere*, send] **1.** to cause to go to another person or place; transfer **2.** to hand down by heredity, inheritance, etc. **3.** *a)* to pass (light, heat, etc.) through some medium *b)* to conduct **4.** to convey (force, movement, etc.) from one mechanical part to another **5.** to send out (radio or television broadcasts, etc.) by electromagnetic waves —**trans·mit′tal** *n.*

trans·mit′ter *n.* one that transmits; specif., *a)* the part of a telegraphic instrument by which messages are sent *b)* the part of a telephone that converts sound into electric

impulses for transmission *c)* the device that produces and sends out radio waves

trans·mute (trans myōot′) *vt., vi.* -mut′ed, -mut′ing [< L. *trans-*, over + *mutare*, to change] to change from one form, nature, substance, etc. into another; transform —**trans′mu·ta′tion** *n.*

trans·o·ce·an·ic (trans′ō shē an′ik) *adj.* crossing the ocean

tran·som (tran′səm) *n.* [prob. < L. *transtrum*, crossbeam] **1.** a horizontal crossbar, as across the top of a door or window **2.** a small window just above a door or window

trans·pa·cif·ic (trans′pə sif′ik) *adj.* **1.** crossing the Pacific **2.** on the other side of the Pacific

trans·par·en·cy (trans per′ən sē) *n.* **1.** a transparent state or quality **2.** *pl.* -cies something transparent; specif., a piece of material having a picture, etc. that is visible when light shines through it

trans·par·ent (trans per′ənt) *adj.* [< L. *trans-*, through + *parere*, appear] **1.** transmitting light rays so that objects on the other side may be distinctly seen **2.** so fine in texture as to be seen through; sheer **3.** easily understood or detected; obvious **4.** open; frank —**trans·par′ent·ly** *adv.*

tran·spire (tran spīr′) *vi.* -spired′, -spir′ing [< Fr. < L. *trans-*, through + *spirare*, breathe] **1.** to give off vapor, moisture, etc., as through pores **2.** to become known **3.** to happen: regarded by some as a loose usage

trans·plant (trans plant′) *vt.* **1.** to remove from one place and plant, resettle, etc. in another **2.** *Surgery* to transfer (tissue or an organ) from one individual or part of the body to another —*n.* (trans′plant′) something transplanted

tran·spond·er (tran spän′dər) *n.* [TRAN(SMITTER) + (RE)SPONDER] a transceiver that transmits signals automatically

trans·port (trans pôrt′) *vt.* [< L. *trans-*, over + *portare*, carry] **1.** to carry from one place to another, esp. over long distances **2.** to carry away with emotion **3.** to banish to a penal colony, etc. —*n.* (trans′pôrt) **1.** a transporting; transportation **2.** rapture **3.** a ship, airplane, etc. used for transporting

trans·por·ta·tion (trans′pər tā′shən) *n.* **1.** a transporting or being transported **2.** a means of conveyance **3.** fare or a ticket for being transported

trans·pose (trans pōz′) *vt., vi.* -posed′, -pos′ing [see TRANS- & POSE] **1.** to change the usual or relative order or position of; interchange **2.** to transfer (an algebraic term) from one side of an equation to the other, reversing the plus or minus value **3.** to rewrite or play (a musical composition) in a different key —**trans′po·si′tion** (-pə zish′ən) *n.*

trans·sex·u·al (tran sek′shōo wəl) *n.* a person who tends to identify with the opposite sex, or one whose sex has been changed by surgery

trans·ship (tran ship′) *vt.* -shipped′, -ship′ping to transfer from one ship, train, truck, etc. to another for reshipment —**trans·ship′ment** *n.*

tran·sub·stan·ti·a·tion (tran′səb stan′shē ā′shən) *n.* [< L. *trans-*, over + *substantia*, substance] *R.C. & Orthodox Eastern Ch.* the doctrine that, in the Eucharist, the whole substances of the bread and wine are changed into the body and blood of Christ

trans·u·ran·ic (trans′yōo ran′ik) *adj.* designating or of the elements, as plutonium, having atomic numbers higher than that of uranium

trans·verse (trans vurs′, trans′vurs) *adj.* [< L. *trans-*, across + *vertere*, to turn] lying, placed, etc. across —*n.* (*usually* trans′vurs) a transverse part, beam, etc.

trans·ves·tite (trans ves′tīt) *n.* [< TRANS- + L. *vestire*, to dress] a person who gets sexual pleasure from dressing in the clothes of the opposite sex

trap (trap) *n.* [OE. *træppe*] **1.** a device for catching animals **2.** any stratagem designed to catch or trick **3.** a device, as a U-shaped part in a drainpipe, for preventing the escape of gas, odors, etc. **4.** an apparatus for throwing targets into the air in trapshooting **5.** a light, two-wheeled carriage **6.** *Golf* same as SAND TRAP —*vt.* **trapped, trap′ping** to catch as in a trap —*vi.* to trap animals, esp. for their furs —**trap′per** *n.*

trap′door′ *n.* a hinged or sliding door in a roof, ceiling, or floor

tra·peze (tra pēz′) *n.* [< Fr.: see TRAPEZOID] a short, horizontal bar, hung at a height by two ropes, on which gymnasts, acrobats, etc. can swing

trap·e·zoid (trap′ə zoid′) *n.* [< Gr. *trapeza*, table] a plane figure with four sides only two of which are parallel —**trap′e·zoi′dal** *adj.*

TRAPEZOID

trap·pings (trap′iŋz) *n.pl.* [< OFr. *drap*, cloth] 1. an ornamental covering for a horse 2. adornments 3. the things that accompany something and are an outward sign of it [the *trappings* of success]

Trap·pist (trap′ist) *n.* [< Fr. (*La*) *Trappe*, abbey in Normandy] a monk of an order known for austerity and perpetual silence

trap′shoot′ing *n.* the sport of shooting at clay disks sprung into the air from traps —**trap′shoot′er** *n.*

trash (trash) *n.* [prob. < Scand.] 1. discarded or worthless things; rubbish 2. a person or people regarded as disreputable —*vt.* [Slang] to destroy (property) as by vandalism, arson, etc. —**trash′y** *adj.* -i·er, -i·est

trau·ma (trou′mə, trô′-) *n., pl.* -mas, -ma·ta (-mə tə) [Gr.] 1. a bodily injury or shock 2. an emotional shock, often having a lasting psychic effect —**trau·mat′ic** (-mat′ik) *adj.*

trau·ma·tize (-tīz′) *vt.* -tized′, -tiz′ing to subject to a physical or mental trauma

trav·ail (trav′āl, trə vāl′) *n.* [< VL. *tria*, three + *palus*, stake: referring to a torture device] 1. very hard work 2. the pains of childbirth 3. intense pain; agony —*vi.* 1. to toil 2. to suffer the pains of childbirth

trav·el (trav′'l) *vi.* -eled or -elled, -el·ing or -el·ling [var. of TRAVAIL] 1. to go from one place to another; make a journey 2. to move, pass, or be transmitted —*vt.* 1. to make a journey over or through —*n.* 1. the act or process of traveling 2. [*pl.*] trips, journeys, etc. taken by a person or persons —**trav′el·er, trav′el·ler** *n.*

traveler's check a check, usually one of a set, issued by a bank, etc. and sold to a traveler who signs it when it is issued and again in the presence of the one cashing it

trav·e·logue, trav·e·log (trav′ə lôg′) *n.* an illustrated lecture or motion picture dealing with travels

trav·erse (tra vurs′, trav′ərs) *vt.* -ersed′, -ers′ing [< L. *trans-*, over + *vertere*, to turn] 1. to pass over, across, or through 2. to go back and forth over or along —*n.* (trav′ərs) 1. something that traverses or crosses, as a crossbar 2. a traversing or passing across —*adj.* (trav′ərs) 1. extending across 2. designating or of drapes drawn by pulling cords at the side —**trav·ers′al** *n.*

trav·es·ty (trav′is tē) *n., pl.* -ties [< Fr. < L. *trans-*, over + *vestire*, to dress] 1. a farcical imitation for purposes of ridicule 2. a crude or ridiculous representation —*vt.* -tied, -ty·ing to make a travesty of

trawl (trôl) *n.* [< ? MDu. *traghel*, dragnet] 1. a large net dragged along the bottom of a fishing bank 2. a long line supported by buoys, from which many short fishing lines are hung —*vi., vt.* to fish or catch with a trawl

trawl′er *n.* a boat used in trawling

tray (trā) *n.* [OE. *treg*, wooden board] 1. a flat receptacle with raised edges, for holding or carrying things 2. a shallow, removable compartment of a trunk, cabinet, etc.

treach·er·ous (trech′ər əs) *adj.* 1. characterized by treachery; traitorous 2. untrustworthy or insecure —**treach′er·ous·ly** *adv.* —**treach′er·ous·ness** *n.*

treach·er·y (trech′ər ē) *n., pl.* -ies [< OFr. *trichier*, to cheat] 1. betrayal of trust; disloyalty or treason 2. an act of disloyalty or treason

trea·cle (trē′k'l) *n.* [< Gr. *thēriakē*, remedy for venomous bites] [Brit.] molasses

tread (tred) *vt.* **trod, trod′den** or **trod, tread′ing** [OE. *tredan*] 1. to walk on, in, along, etc. 2. to do or follow by walking, dancing, etc. 3. to press or beat with the feet —*vi.* 1. to walk 2. to set one's foot (*on, across,* etc.) 3. to trample (*on* or *upon*) —*n.* 1. the manner or sound of treading 2. something on which a person or thing treads or moves, as a shoe sole, the horizontal surface of a stair step, etc. 3. *a*) the thick outer layer of an automotive tire *b*) the depth or pattern of grooves in this layer —**tread water** *pt. & pp. usually* **tread′ed** to stay upright in swimming by moving the legs up and down

trea·dle (tred′'l) *n.* [< OE. *tredan*, to tread] a lever moved by the foot as to turn a wheel

tread′mill′ *n.* 1. a mill wheel turned as by an animal treading an endless belt 2. any monotonous routine

treas. 1. treasurer 2. treasury

trea·son (trē′z'n) *n.* [< L. *trans-*, over + *dare*, give] betrayal of one's country to an enemy

trea′son·a·ble *adj.* of or involving treason; traitorous: also **trea′son·ous** —**trea′son·a·bly** *adv.*

treas·ure (trezh′ər, trā′zhər) *n.* [< Gr. *thēsauros*] 1. accumulated wealth, as money, jewels, etc. 2. any person or thing considered valuable —*vt.* -ured, -ur·ing 1. to save up for future use 2. to value greatly

treas′ur·er *n.* one in charge of a treasury; specif., an officer in charge of the funds of a government, corporation, club, etc.

treas′ure-trove′ (-trōv′) *n.* [*trove* < OFr. *trover*, to find] treasure found hidden, the owner of which is unknown

treas′ur·y (-ē) *n., pl.* -ies 1. a place where treasure or funds are kept 2. the funds or revenues of a state, corporation, etc. 3. [T-] the governmental department in charge of revenue, taxation, etc.

treat (trēt) *vi.* [< L. *trahere*, to draw] 1. to discuss terms (*with* a person or *for* a settlement) 2. to speak or write (*of*) 3. to pay for another's entertainment —*vt.* 1. to deal with (a subject) in a specified manner 2. to act toward (someone or something) in a specified manner 3. to regard in a specified way [he *treated* it as a joke] 4. to pay for the food, entertainment, etc. of (another) 5. to subject to some process, chemical, etc. 6. to give medical care to —*n.* 1. a meal, drink, etc. paid for by another 2. anything that gives great pleasure

trea·tise (trēt′is) *n.* [see TREAT] a formal, systematic article or book on some subject

treat·ment (trēt′mənt) *n.* 1. act, manner, method, etc. of treating 2. medical or surgical care

trea·ty (trēt′ē) *n., pl.* -ties [< L. *trahere*, to draw] a formal agreement between two or more nations, relating to peace, trade, etc.

tre·ble (treb′'l) *adj.* [< L. *triplus*, triple] 1. threefold; triple 2. of, for, or performing the treble —*n.* 1. the highest part in musical harmony; soprano 2. a high-pitched voice or sound —*vt., vi.* -bled, -bling to make or become threefold

tree (trē) *n.* [OE. *treow*] 1. a large, woody perennial plant with one main trunk and many branches 2. a treelike bush or shrub 3. anything resembling a tree; specif., a diagram of family descent (**family tree**) —*vt.* **treed, tree′ing** to chase up a tree —**tree′less** *adj.* —**tree′like′** *adj.*

tree lawn in some cities, the strip of ground between a street and its parallel sidewalk

tre·foil (trē′foil) *n.* [< L. *tri-*, three + *folium*, leaf] 1. a plant with leaves divided into three leaflets, as the clover 2. a design, etc. shaped like such a leaf

TREFOILS

trek (trek) *vi.* **trekked, trek′king** [Afrik. < Du. *trekken*, to draw] 1. to travel slowly and laboriously 2. [Colloq.] to go on foot —*n.* 1. a journey 2. a migration 3. [Colloq.] a short trip on foot

trel·lis (trel′is) *n.* [< L. *trilix*, triple-twilled] a lattice, esp. one on which vines are trained

trem·ble (trem′b'l) *vi.* -bled, -bling [< L. *tremere*] 1. to shake or shiver, as from cold, fear, etc. 2. to feel great fear or anxiety 3. to quiver, vibrate, etc. —*n.* 1. a trembling 2. [*sometimes pl.*] a fit or state of trembling

tre·men·dous (tri men′dəs) *adj.* [< L. *tremere*, tremble] 1. terrifying; dreadful 2. *a*) very large; great *b*) [Colloq.] wonderful, amazing, etc. —**tre·men′dous·ly** *adv.*

trem·o·lo (trem′ə lō′) *n., pl.* -los′ [It.] a tremulous effect produced by rapidly repeating the same musical tone

trem·or (trem′ər) *n.* [< L. *tremere*, tremble] 1. a trembling, shaking, etc. 2. a vibratory motion 3. a nervous thrill

trem·u·lous (trem′yoo ləs) *adj.* [< L. *tremere*, tremble] 1. trembling; quivering 2. fearful; timid —**trem′u·lous·ly** *adv.* —**trem′u·lous·ness** *n.*

trench (trench) *vt.* [< OFr. *trenchier*, to cut] to dig a ditch or ditches in —*n.* 1. a deep furrow 2. a long, narrow ditch with earth banked in front, used in battle for cover, etc.

trench·ant (tren′chənt) *adj.* [see TRENCH] 1. penetrating; incisive [*trenchant* words] 2. forceful; vigorous [a *trenchant* argument] —**trench′an·cy** *n.* —**trench′ant·ly** *adv.*

trench coat a belted raincoat in a military style

trench·er (tren′chər) *n.* [see TRENCH] [Archaic] a wooden platter for carving and serving meat

trench′er·man (-mən) *n., pl.* -men one who eats much and heartily

trench foot a diseased condition of the feet from prolonged exposure to wet and cold, as in trenches

trench mouth an infectious disease of the mucous membranes of the mouth and throat

trend (trend) *vi.* [OE. *trendan*] to have a general direction or tendency —*n.* 1. the general tendency or course; drift 2. a current style

trend′y (-ē) *adj.* **-i·er, -i·est** [Colloq.] of or in the latest style, or trend; faddish —**trend′i·ness** *n.*

Tren·ton (tren′tən) *n.* capital of N.J.: pop. 105,000

tre·pan (tri pan′) *n.* [< Gr. *trypan*, to bore] an early form of the trephine —*vt.* **-panned′, -pan′ning** *same as* TREPHINE

tre·phine (tri fīn′, -fēn′) *n.* [< L. *tres*, three + *fines*, ends] a surgical saw for removing disks of bone from the skull —*vt.* **-phined′, -phin′ing** to operate on with a trephine

trep·i·da·tion (trep′ə dā′shən) *n.* [< L. *trepidus*, disturbed] **1.** trembling movement **2.** fearful uncertainty

tres·pass (tres′pəs, -pas′) *vi.* [< L. *trans-*, across + *passus*, a step] **1.** to go beyond the limits of what is considered right; do wrong; transgress **2.** to enter another's property without permission or right **3.** to intrude; encroach **4.** *Law* to commit a trespass —*n.* **1.** a trespassing; specif., *a)* a moral offense *b)* an illegal act done with force against another's person, rights, or property —**tres′pass·er** *n.*

tress (tres) *n.* [< OFr. *tresce*, braid of hair] **1.** a lock of human hair **2.** [*pl.*] a woman's or girl's hair, esp. when long

-tress *a suffix meaning* female [*actress*]

tres·tle (tres′'l) *n.* [< L. *transtrum*, a beam] **1.** a horizontal beam fastened to two pairs of spreading legs, used as a support **2.** a framework of uprights and crosspieces, supporting a bridge, etc.

trey (trā) *n.* [< L. *tres*, three] a playing card or side of a die with three spots

tri- [< Fr., L., or Gr.] *a combining form meaning:* **1.** having or involving three **2.** three times, into three **3.** every third

tri·ad (trī′ad) *n.* [< Gr. *treis*, three] **1.** a group of three **2.** a musical chord of three tones, esp. one consisting of a root tone and its third and fifth: a triad with a major third and perfect fifth is called a *major triad;* a triad with a minor third and perfect fifth is called a *minor triad*

tri·al (trī′əl) *n.* [see TRY] **1.** the act or process of trying, testing, etc.; test; probation **2.** *a)* a being tried by suffering, temptation, etc. *b)* a hardship, suffering, etc. **3.** a source of annoyance **4.** a formal examination of the facts of a case by a court of law to decide the validity of a charge or claim **5.** an attempt; effort —*adj.* **1.** of a trial **2.** for the purpose of trying, testing, etc. —**on trial** in the process of being tried

trial and error a trying or testing again and again until the right result is found

trial balloon something said or done to test public opinion on an issue

tri·an·gle (trī′aŋ′g'l) *n.* [see TRI- & ANGLE[1]] **1.** a plane figure having three angles and three sides **2.** any three-sided or three-cornered object, area, etc. **3.** a situation involving three persons, as when one person is having love affairs with two others **4.** a musical instrument consisting of a steel rod bent in a triangle —**tri·an′gu·lar** (-gyə lər) *adj.*

tri·an·gu·late′ (-gyə lāt′) *vt.* **-lat′ed, -lat′ing** **1.** to divide into triangles **2.** to survey (a region) by dividing into triangles and measuring their angles **3.** to make triangular **4.** to measure by trigonometry —*adj.* (*usually* -lit) of, like, or marked with triangles —**tri·an′gu·la′tion** *n.*

trib·al·ism (trī′b'l iz'm) *n.* tribal organization, culture, loyalty, etc.

tribe (trīb) *n.* [< L. *tribus*] **1.** a group of persons or clans believed to have a common ancestor and living under a leader or chief **2.** any group of people with the same occupation, ideas, etc. **3.** a natural group of plants or animals —**trib′al** *adj.* —**tribes′man** *n., pl.* **-men**

trib·u·la·tion (trib′yə lā′shən) *n.* [< L. *tribulare*, to press] great misery or distress, or the cause of it

tri·bu·nal (trī byoo′n'l, tri-) *n.* [L.: see TRIBUNE[1]] **1.** a seat for a judge in a court **2.** a court of justice **3.** any seat of judgment

trib·une[1] (trib′yoon, tri byoon′) *n.* [< L. *tribus*, tribe] **1.** in ancient Rome, a magistrate appointed to protect the rights and interests of the plebians **2.** a champion of the people

trib·une[2] (trib′yoon) *n.* [Fr. < It. < L. *tribunal*, judge's seat] a raised platform for speakers

trib·u·tar·y (trib′yoo ter′ē) *adj.* **1.** paying tribute **2.** subject [a *tributary* nation] **3.** *a)* making additions *b)* flowing into a larger one [a *tributary* stream] —*n., pl.* **-ies** **1.** a tributary nation **2.** a tributary stream or river

trib·ute (trib′yoot) *n.* [< L. *tribuere*, allot] **1.** money paid regularly by one nation to another as acknowledgment of subjugation, for protection, etc. **2.** any forced payment **3.** something given, done, or said that shows gratitude, respect, honor, or praise

trice (trīs) *vt.* **triced, tric′ing** [< MDu. *trisen*, to pull] to haul up and secure (a sail, etc.): usually with *up* —*n.* an instant: now only in **in a trice**

tri·cen·ten·ni·al (trī′sen ten′ē əl) *adj.* happening once in 300 years —*n.* a 300th anniversary

tri·ceps (trī′seps) *n., pl.* **-ceps** or **-ceps·es** [< L. *tri-*, three + *caput*, head] a muscle with three points of origin, esp. the large muscle at the back of the upper arm

tri·cer·a·tops (trī ser′ə täps′) *n.* [< TRI- + Gr. *keras*, horn + *ōps*, eye] a plant-eating dinosaur with a long horn above each eye

tri·chi·na (tri kī′nə) *n., pl.* **-nae** (-nē) [< Gr. *trichinos*, hairy] a very small worm whose larvae cause trichinosis

trich·i·no·sis (trik′ə nō′sis) *n.* a disease caused by trichinae in the intestines and muscles and usually acquired by eating undercooked infested pork

trick (trik) *n.* [< OFr. *trique*, to cheat] **1.** something designed to deceive, cheat, etc. **2.** a practical joke; prank **3.** a clever act intended to amuse **4.** any feat requiring skill **5.** the art or knack of doing something easily, quickly, etc. **6.** a personal mannerism **7.** a round of duty; shift **8.** *Card Games* the cards in a single round —*vt.* to deceive, cheat, fool, etc. —*adj.* **1.** of, for, or using tricks **2.** apt to malfunction [a *trick* knee] —**do** (or **turn**) **the trick** to produce the desired result —**trick out** (or **up**) to dress up —**trick′er·y** *n., pl.* **-ies** —**trick′ster** *n.*

trick·le (trik′'l) *vi.* **-led, -ling** [prob. < ME. *striken*, to strike] **1.** to flow slowly in a thin stream or fall in drops **2.** to move slowly [the crowd *trickled* away] —*vt.* to cause to trickle —*n.* **1.** a trickling **2.** a slow, small flow

trick′y *adj.* **-i·er, -i·est** **1.** given to or characterized by trickery **2.** intricate; difficult —**trick′i·ness** *n.*

tri·col·or (trī′kul′ər) *n.* a flag having three colors in large areas; esp., the flag of France

tri·corn (trī′kôrn) *adj.* [< Fr. < L. *tri-*, three + *cornu*, horn] having three corners, as a hat —*n.* a tricorn hat

tri·cot (trē′kō) *n.* [Fr. < *tricoter*, to knit] a thin fabric that is knitted, or woven to look knitted

tri·cy·cle (trī′si k'l) *n.* [Fr.: see TRI- & CYCLE] a child's three-wheeled vehicle operated by pedals

tri·dent (trīd′'nt) *n.* [< L. *tri-*, three + *dens*, tooth] a three-pronged spear

tried (trīd) *pt. & pp. of* TRY —*adj.* **1.** tested; proved **2.** trustworthy; faithful **3.** having endured trials and troubles

tri·en·ni·al (trī en′ē əl) *adj.* [< L. *tri-*, three + *annus*, year] **1.** happening every three years **2.** lasting three years —**tri·en′ni·al·ly** *adv.*

tri·er (trī′ər) *n.* one that tries

Tri·este (trē est′) seaport in NE Italy: pop. 278,000

tri·fle (trī′f'l) *n.* [< OFr. *truffe*, deception] **1.** something of little value or importance **2.** a small amount or sum —*vi.* **-fled, -fling** **1.** to talk or act jokingly; deal lightly **2.** to play or toy (*with*) —*vt.* to spend idly; waste (usually with *away*) —**tri′fler** *n.*

tri′fling *adj.* **1.** frivolous; shallow **2.** of little importance; trivial

tri·fo·cal (trī fō′k'l, trī′fō′-) *adj.* adjusted to three different focal lengths —*n.* a lens with one part ground to adjust the eyes for close focus, one for intermediate focus, and one for distant focus

tri′fo′cals *n.pl.* a pair of glasses with trifocal lenses

trig[1] (trig) *adj.* [< ON. *tryggr*, true] [Chiefly Brit.] **1.** trim; neat **2.** in good condition; sound

trig[2] (trig) *n. clipped form of* TRIGONOMETRY

trig·ger (trig′ər) *n.* [< Du. *trekken*, to pull] a lever pulled or pressed to release a catch, etc., esp. one pressed to activate the firing mechanism on a firearm —*vt.* to initiate (an action)

trig·o·nom·e·try (trig′ə näm′ə trē) *n.* [< Gr. *trigōnon*, triangle + *-metria*, measurement] the branch of mathematics dealing with the relations between the sides and angles of triangles —**trig′o·no·met′ric** (-nə met′rik) *adj.*

trill (tril) *n.* [< It., ult. echoic] **1.** a rapid alternation of a musical tone with one just above it **2.** a bird's warble **3.** a rapid vibration of the tongue or uvula, as in pronouncing *r* in some languages —*vt., vi.* to sound, speak, sing, or play with a trill

tril·lion (tril′yən) *n.* [Fr.] **1.** in the U.S. and France, 1 followed by 12 zeros **2.** in Great Britain and Germany, 1 followed by 18 zeros —*adj.* amounting to one trillion in number —**tril′lionth** *adj., n.*

tril·li·um (tril′ē əm) *n.* [< L. *tri-*, three] a plant related to the lily, with an erect stem bearing three leaves and a three-petaled flower

tril·o·gy (tril′ə jē) *n., pl.* **-gies** [see TRI- & -LOGY] a set of three plays, novels, etc. which form a related group, although each is a complete work

TRILLIUM

trim (trim) *vt.* **trimmed, trim′ming** [< OE. *trymman*, make firm] **1.** to put in proper order; make neat or tidy, esp. by clipping, etc. **2.** to clip, lop, cut, etc. **3.** to decorate as by adding ornaments, etc. **4.** *a)* to balance (a ship) by ballasting, shifting cargo, etc. *b)* to put (sails) in order for sailing **5.** to balance (an aircraft in flight) by adjusting stabilizers, etc. **6.** [Colloq.] to beat, punish, defeat, cheat, etc. —*vi.* to change one's opinions, policy, etc. in an expedient way —*n.* **1.** order; arrangement **2.** good condition [keep in *trim*] **3.** a trimming by clipping, cutting, etc. **4.** any ornamental accessories, as the decorative borders around the windows and doors of a building —*adj.* **trim′mer, trim′mest 1.** orderly; neat **2.** well-proportioned **3.** in good condition —**trim′ly** *adv.* —**trim′mer** *n.* —**trim′ness** *n.*

tri·mes·ter (trī mes′tər, trī′mes-) *n.* [< L. *tri-*, three + *mensis*, month] in some colleges, any of the three periods into which the academic year is divided

trim′ming *n.* **1.** the action of one that trims **2.** decoration; ornament **3.** [*pl.*] the side dishes of a meal **4.** [*pl.*] parts trimmed off **5.** [Colloq.] a beating, defeat, cheating, etc.

Trin·i·dad and To·ba·go (trin′ə dad′, tō bā′gō) country comprising two islands (*Trinidad* and *Tobago*) in the West Indies: 1,980 sq. mi.; pop. 1,030,000; cap. Port-of-Spain

Trin·i·tar·i·an (trin′ə ter′ē ən) *adj.* of, about, or believing in the Trinity —*n.* one who believes in the Trinity

tri·ni·tro·tol·u·ene (trī nī′trō täl′yoo wēn′) *n.* a high explosive derived from toluene

trin·i·ty (trin′ə tē) *n., pl.* **-ties** [< L. *trinus*, triple] **1.** a set of three **2.** [T-] *Christian Theol.* the union of Father, Son, and Holy Spirit in one Godhead

trin·ket (triɳ′kit) *n.* [ME. *trenket*] **1.** a small ornament, piece of jewelry, etc. **2.** a trifle or toy

tri·o (trē′ō) *n., pl.* **-os** [Fr. < It. < L. *tres*, three] **1.** a group of three **2.** *Music a)* a composition for three voices or three instruments *b)* the three performers of such a composition

trip (trip) *vi., vt.* **tripped, trip′ping** [< OFr. *treper*] **1.** to move or perform with light, rapid steps **2.** to stumble or cause to stumble, esp. by catching the foot **3.** to make or cause to make a mistake **4.** to release (a spring, wheel, etc.), as by going past an escapement catch —*n.* **1.** a light, quick tread **2.** a journey, esp. a short one **3.** a stumble or a causing to stumble **4.** [Slang] the experience of being under the influence of a psychedelic drug —**trip up** to catch in a lie, error, etc.

tri·par·tite (trī pär′tīt) *adj.* [< L. *tri-*, three + *partire*, to part] **1.** having three parts **2.** made between three parties, as an agreement

tripe (trīp) *n.* [prob. < Ar. *tharb*, entrails] **1.** part of the stomach of an ox, etc., when used as food **2.** [Slang] anything worthless, etc.; nonsense

trip′ham′mer *n.* a heavy, power-driven hammer, alternately raised and allowed to fall by a tripping device: also **trip hammer**

tri·ple (trip′'l) *adj.* [Fr. < L. *triplus*] **1.** consisting of three; threefold **2.** done, said, etc. three times **3.** three times as much or as many —*n.* **1.** an amount three times as much or as many **2.** *Baseball* a hit on which the batter reaches third base —*vt.* **-pled, -pling** to make three times as much or as many —*vi.* **1.** to be tripled **2.** *Baseball* to hit a triple —**tri′ply** *adv.*

tri·plet (trip′lit) *n.* **1.** a group of three, usually of one kind **2.** any of three offspring born at a single birth

trip·li·cate (trip′lə kit) *adj.* [< L. *triplex*, threefold] **1.** threefold **2.** being the last of three identical copies —*n.* any of three identical copies —*vt.* (-kāt′) **-cat′ed, -cat′ing** to make three identical copies of —**in triplicate** in three identical copies

tri·pod (trī′päd) *n.* [< Gr. *tri-*, three + *pous*, a foot] a three-legged caldron, stool, support, etc.

Trip·o·li (trip′ə lē) one of the two capitals of Libya, on the NW coast: pop. 245,000

trip·ping (trip′iɳ) *adj.* moving lightly and quickly

trip·tych (trip′tik) *n.* [< Gr. *tri-*, three + *ptychē*, a fold] a set of three panels with pictures, carvings, etc., often hinged: used as an altarpiece

tri·sect (trī sekt′, trī′sekt) *vt.* [< TRI- + L. *secare*, to cut] **1.** to cut into three parts **2.** *Geom.* to divide into three equal parts —**tri·sec′tion** *n.*

Tris·tram (tris′trəm) *Medieval Legend* a knight who is involved in a tragic romance with a princess, Isolde: also **Tris′tam** (-təm), **Tris′tan** (-tən)

trite (trīt) *adj.* **trit′er, trit′est** [< L. *terere*, wear out] used so much that it is no longer fresh or original; stale —**trite′ly** *adv.* —**trite′ness** *n.*

trit·i·um (trit′ē əm, trish′-) *n.* [< Gr. *tritos*, three] a radioactive isotope of hydrogen having an atomic weight of three

Tri·ton (trī′t'n) *Gr. Myth.* a sea god with the head and upper body of a man and the tail of a fish

tri·umph (trī′əmf) *n.* [< L. *triumphus*] **1.** a victory; success **2.** exultation or joy over a victory, etc. —*vi.* **1.** to gain victory or success **2.** to rejoice over victory, etc. —**tri·um′phal** (-um′f'l) *adj.*

tri·um′phant (-um′fənt) *adj.* **1.** victorious; successful **2.** exulting in victory; elated —**tri·um′phant·ly** *adv.*

tri·um·vir (trī um′vər) *n., pl.* **-virs, -vi·ri** (-vi rī′) [L. < *trium virum*, of three men] in ancient Rome, any of three administrators sharing authority

tri·um′vi·rate (-vər it) *n.* **1.** government by three men **2.** any association of three in authority **3.** any group of three

tri·va·lent (trī vā′lənt) *adj.* **1.** having a valence of three **2.** having three valences

triv·et (triv′it) *n.* [< L. *tripes*, tripod] **1.** a three-legged stand for holding pots, kettles, etc. near a fire **2.** a short-legged metal or ceramic plate for hot dishes to rest on

triv·i·a (triv′ē ə) *n.pl.* [*often with sing. v.*] [ModL. < TRIVIAL] unimportant matters; trivialities

triv·i·al (triv′ē əl) *adj.* [< L. *trivialis*, commonplace] unimportant; insignificant —**triv′i·al′i·ty** (-al′ə tē) *n., pl.* **-ties** —**triv′i·al·ly** *adv.*

-trix *pl.* **-trixes, -trices** an ending of some feminine nouns of agent [*aviatrix*]

tro·che (trō′kē) *n.* [< Fr. < Gr. *trochos*, a wheel] a small medicinal lozenge

tro·chee (trō′kē) *n.* [< Gr. *trechein*, to run] a metrical foot of an accented syllable followed by an unaccented one —**tro·cha′ic** (-kā′ik) *adj.*

trod (träd) *pt. & alt. pp.* of TREAD

trod′den (-'n) *pp.* of TREAD

trog·lo·dyte (träg′lə dīt′) *n.* [< Gr. *trōglē*, cave + *dyein*, enter] **1.** any of the prehistoric people who lived in caves **2.** a recluse

troi·ka (troi′kə) *n.* [Russ. < *troe*, three] **1.** a Russian vehicle drawn by three horses abreast **2.** an association of three in authority

Tro·jan (trō′jən) *adj.* of Troy, its people, etc. —*n.* **1.** a native or inhabitant of Troy **2.** a strong, hard-working, determined person

Trojan horse *Gr. Legend* a huge, hollow wooden horse filled with Greek soldiers: it was taken into Troy as an ostensible gift, thus leading to the destruction of the city

Trojan War *Gr. Legend* the war waged against Troy by the Greeks to get back Helen of Troy

troll[1] (trōl) *vt., vi.* [ME. *trollen*, to roll] **1.** to sing the parts of (a round, etc.) in succession **2.** to sing in a full voice **3.** to fish (for) with a baited line trailed behind a slowly moving boat

troll[2] (trōl) *n.* [ON.] in Scand. folklore, any of certain supernatural beings, giants or dwarfs, living underground or in caves

trol·ley (träl′ē) *n., pl.* **-leys** [< TROLL[1]] **1.** a wheeled carriage, basket, etc. that runs suspended from an overhead track **2.** a device, as a small wheel at the end of a pole, for carrying electric current from an overhead wire to a streetcar, etc. **3.** *same as* TROLLEY CAR

trolley car (or **bus**) an electric streetcar (or bus) powered from an overhead wire by means of a trolley

trol·lop (träl′əp) *n.* [prob. < G. *trolle*, a wench] a prostitute

Trol·lope (träl′əp), **Anthony** 1815–82; Eng. novelist

trom·bone (träm bōn′, träm′bōn) *n.* [It. < *tromba*, trumpet] a large brass-wind instrument with a bell mouth and a long tube bent parallel to itself twice and having either a section that slides in and out (**slide trombone**) or valves (**valve trombone**) —**trom·bon′ist** *n.*

troop (tro͞op) *n.* [< Fr. < ML. *troppus,* a flock] **1.** a group of persons or animals **2.** loosely, a great number; lot **3.** [*pl.*] soldiers **4.** a subdivision of a cavalry regiment **5.** a unit of Boy Scouts or Girl Scouts —*vi.* to gather or go as in a group

troop'er *n.* [TROOP + -ER] **1.** a cavalryman **2.** a mounted policeman **3.** [Colloq.] a State policeman

trope (trōp) *n.* [< Gr. *tropos,* a turning] **1.** the use of a word in a figurative sense **2.** *same as* FIGURE OF SPEECH

tro·phy (trō'fē) *n., pl.* **-phies** [< Gr. *tropaion*] a memorial of victory in war, sports competition, etc.; prize

trop·ic (träp'ik) *n.* [< Gr. *tropikos,* of a turn (of the sun at the solstices)] **1.** either of two parallels of latitude, one, the **Tropic of Cancer,** 23°27' north of the equator, and the other, the **Tropic of Capricorn,** 23°27' south **2.** [*also* T-] [*pl.*] the region between these latitudes, noted for its hot climate —*adj.* of the tropics; tropical

trop'i·cal (-i k'l) *adj.* of, in, characteristic of, or suitable for the tropics —**trop'i·cal·ly** *adv.*

tro·pism (trō'piz'm) *n.* [< Gr. *trope,* a turn] the tendency of a plant or animal to grow or turn in response to an external stimulus, as light

trop·o·sphere (träp'ə sfir', trō'pə-) *n.* [see TROPE & SPHERE] the atmosphere from the earth's surface to about 6 to 12 miles above it

trot (trät) *vi., vt.* **trot'ted, trot'ting** [< OHG. *trotton,* to tread] **1.** to ride, drive, move, etc. at a trot **2.** to hurry; run —*n.* **1.** a gait of a horse, etc. in which the legs are lifted in alternating diagonal pairs **2.** a jogging gait of a person —**trot out** [Colloq.] to bring out for others to see or admire —**trot'ter** *n.*

troth (trôth, trōth) *n.* [ME. *trouthe*] [Archaic] **1.** faithfulness; loyalty **2.** truth **3.** a promise, esp. to marry

Trot·sky (trät'skē), **Leon** 1879–1940; Russ. revolutionist & writer

trou·ba·dour (tro͞o'bə dôr') *n.* [Fr. < Pr. *trobar,* compose in verse] any of a class of poet-musicians of S France and N Italy in the 11th–13th cent.

trou·ble (trub''l) *vt.* **-bled, -bling** [< L. *turbidus,* turbid] **1.** to disturb or agitate *[troubled* waters] **2.** to worry; harass **3.** to cause pain or discomfort to *[troubled* with headaches] **4.** to cause inconvenience to *[don't trouble* yourself] **5.** to annoy, tease, etc. —*vi.* to take pains; bother *[don't trouble* to return it] —*n.* **1.** a state of mental distress; worry **2.** a misfortune; calamity **3.** a cause of annoyance, distress, etc. **4.** public disturbance **5.** effort; pains *[take the trouble* to listen]

trou'ble·mak·er *n.* one who habitually makes trouble for others; esp., one who incites others to quarrel, rebel, etc.

trou'ble-shoot'er *n.* one whose work is to find and repair or eliminate mechanical breakdowns or other sources of trouble

trou'ble·some (-səm) *adj.* characterized by or causing trouble

trough (trôf) *n.* [OE. *trog*] **1.** a long, narrow, open container, esp. one for holding water or food for animals **2.** a channel or gutter for carrying off rainwater **3.** a long, narrow hollow, as between waves **4.** a long, narrow area of low barometric pressure

trounce (trouns) *vt.* **trounced, trounc'ing** [< ?] **1.** to beat; thrash **2.** [Colloq.] to defeat soundly

troupe (tro͞op) *n.* [Fr.] a troop, esp. of actors, singers, etc.; company —*vi.* **trouped, troup'ing** to travel as a member of a company of actors, etc.

troup'er *n.* **1.** a member of a troupe **2.** an experienced, dependable actor

trou·sers (trou'zərz) *n.pl.* [< ScotGael. *triubhas*] a two-legged outer garment, esp. for men and boys, extending from the waist to the ankles; pants —**trou'ser** *adj.*

trous·seau (tro͞o'sō) *n., pl.* **-seaux** (-sōz), **-seaus** [Fr. < OFr. *trousse,* a bundle] a bride's outfit of clothes, linens, etc.

trout (trout) *n., pl.* **trout, trouts** [< Gr. *trōgein,* gnaw] any of various food and game fishes related to the salmon and found chiefly in fresh water

trow (trō, trou) *vi., vt.* [< OE. *treow,* faith] [Archaic] to believe, think, suppose, etc.

trow·el (trou'əl) *n.* [< L. *trua,* a ladle] **1.** a flat hand tool for smoothing plaster or applying mortar **2.** a pointed, scooplike tool for loosening soil, digging holes, etc. —*vt.* **-eled** or **-elled, -el·ing** or **-el·ling** to spread, smooth, shape, dig, etc. with a trowel

Troy (troi) ancient city in NW Asia Minor

troy (troi) *adj.* by or in troy weight

troy weight [< *Troyes,* Fr. city where first used] a system of weights for gold, silver, gems, etc., based on a pound of 12 oz.

tru·ant (tro͞o'ənt) *n.* [< OFr., beggar] **1.** a pupil who stays away from school without permission **2.** one who shirks his duties —*adj.* **1.** that is a truant **2.** errant; straying —**tru'an·cy** *n., pl.* **-cies**

truce (tro͞os) *n.* [OE. *treow,* faith] **1.** a temporary cessation of warfare by agreement between the belligerents **2.** any pause in quarreling, conflict, etc.

truck[1] (truk) *n.* [prob. < Gr. *trochos,* a wheel] **1.** a kind of two-wheeled barrow or a low, wheeled frame, for carrying heavy articles **2.** an automotive vehicle for hauling loads **3.** a swiveling frame, with two or more pairs of wheels, under each end of a railroad car, etc. —*vt.* to carry on a truck —*vi.* to drive a truck as one's work

truck[2] (truk) *vt., vi.* [MFr. *troquer*] to exchange; barter —*n.* **1.** *same as* BARTER **2.** payment of wages in goods instead of money **3.** small articles of little value **4.** vegetables raised for sale in markets **5.** [Colloq.] dealings **6.** [Colloq.] rubbish

truck'er *n.* **1.** a truck driver **2.** a person or company engaged in trucking

truck farm a farm where vegetables are grown to be marketed —**truck farmer** —**truck farming**

truck'ing *n.* the business of carrying goods by truck

truck·le (truk''l) *n.* [< Gr. *trochos,* a wheel] *same as* TRUNDLE BED: in full **truckle bed** —*vi.* **-led, -ling** to be servile; toady (*to*)

truc·u·lent (truk'yoo lənt) *adj.* [< L. *trux*] **1.** fierce; cruel **2.** harsh, scathing, etc. **3.** ready to fight —**truc'u·lence, truc'u·len·cy** *n.* —**truc'u·lent·ly** *adv.*

trudge (truj) *vi.* **trudged, trudg'ing** [< ?] to walk, esp. wearily or laboriously —*n.* a wearying walk

true (tro͞o) *adj.* **tru'er, tru'est** [OE. *treowe*] **1.** faithful; loyal **2.** in accordance with fact; not false **3.** conforming to a standard, etc.; accurate **4.** rightful; lawful **5.** accurately fitted, shaped, etc. **6.** real; genuine —*adv.* **1.** in a true way **2.** *Biol.* without variation from type —*vt.* **trued, tru'ing** or **true'ing** to fit, shape, etc. accurately (often with *up*) —*n.* that which is true (with *the*) —**come true** to happen as predicted or expected —**true'ness** *n.*

true bill a bill of indictment endorsed by a grand jury as supported by evidence sufficient to warrant a trial

true'-blue' *adj.* very loyal; staunch

truf·fle (truf''l) *n.* [< Fr. < L. *tuber,* knob] a fleshy, edible underground fungus

tru·ism (tro͞o'iz'm) *n.* a statement the truth of which is obvious and well-known

tru'ly *adv.* **1.** in a true manner; accurately, genuinely, etc. **2.** really; indeed **3.** sincerely [yours *truly]*

Tru·man (tro͞o'mən), **Harry S.** 1884–1972; 33rd president of the U.S. (1945–53)

trump[1] (trump) *n.* [< TRIUMPH] **1.** any playing card of a suit ranked higher than any other suit for a given hand **2.** [*occas. pl.* with *sing. v.*] such a suit —*vt.* to take (a trick, etc.) with a trump —*vi.* to play a trump —**trump up** to make up in order to deceive

trump[2] (trump) *n., vi., vt.* [OFr. *trompe*] *archaic var.* of TRUMPET

trump·er·y (trum'pər ē) *n., pl.* **-ies** [< MFr. *tromper,* deceive] **1.** something showy but worthless **2.** nonsense —*adj.* showy but worthless

trum·pet (trum'pit) *n.* [< OFr. *trompe*] **1.** a brass-wind instrument with a blaring tone, consisting of a looped tube ending in a flared bell **2.** something shaped like a trumpet; esp., *same as* EAR TRUMPET **3.** a sound like that of a trumpet —*vi.* **1.** to blow a trumpet **2.** to make a sound like that of a trumpet —*vt.* **1.** to sound on or as on a trumpet **2.** to proclaim loudly —**trum'pet·er** *n.*

trun·cate (trun'kāt) *vt.* **-cat·ed, -cat·ing** [< L. *truncus,* a stem] to cut off a part of; lop —*adj. same as* TRUNCATED —**trun·ca'tion** *n.*

TRUMPET

trun'cat·ed *adj.* **1.** cut short or appearing as if cut short **2.** having the vertex cut off by a plane

trun·cheon (trun'chən) *n.* [< L. *truncus,* a stem] **1.** a short, thick club **2.** [Chiefly Brit.] a policeman's stick

trun·dle (trun'd'l) *vt., vi.* **-dled, -dling** [< OE. *trendan,* to roll] to roll along

trundle bed a low bed on casters, that can be rolled under a higher bed when not in use

trunk (truŋk) *n.* [< L. *truncus*] 1. the main stem of a tree 2. a human or animal body, not including the head and limbs 3. the main body of a nerve, blood vessel, etc. 4. a long snout, as of an elephant 5. a large, reinforced box to hold clothes, etc. in travel 6. [*pl.*] men's shorts worn as for athletics 7. *short for* TRUNK LINE 8. a compartment in an automobile, usually in the rear, for a spare tire, luggage, etc.

trunk line a main line of a railroad, canal, telephone system, etc.

trun·nion (trun′yən) *n.* [< Fr. *trognon,* a stump] either of two projections, one from each side, on which a cannon, etc. pivots

truss (trus) *vt.* [< OFr. *trousser,* to bundle] 1. to tie or bind (often with *up*) 2. to skewer or bind the wings, legs, etc. of (a fowl) before cooking 3. to support with a truss —*n.* 1. a bundle or pack 2. a rigid framework to support a roof, bridge, etc. 3. a padded device to support a hernia

trust (trust) *n.* [< ON. *traust*] 1. *a)* firm belief in another's honesty, reliability, etc. *b)* the one trusted 2. confident expectation, hope, etc. 3. responsibility arising from confidence placed in one 4. care; custody 5. something entrusted to one; charge 6. confidence in one's intention to pay and in one's ability to do so; credit 7. a combination of corporations to establish a monopoly 8. *Law a)* the fact of having nominal ownership of property to keep, use, or administer for another's benefit *b)* the property —*vi.* 1. to have trust; be confident 2. to grant business credit —*vt.* 1. to have trust in 2. to entrust 3. to allow, without misgivings, to do something 4. to believe or suppose 5. to hope 6. to grant business credit —*adj.* 1. of a trust or trusts 2. held in trust —**in trust** entrusted to another's care —**trust to** to rely on

trus·tee (trus tē′) *n.* 1. one to whom another's property or its management is entrusted 2. a member of a board managing a school, hospital, etc. —**trus·tee′ship′** *n.*

trust′ful *adj.* full of trust; readily trusting others —**trust′-ful·ly** *adv.* —**trust′ful·ness** *n.*

trust fund money, stock, etc. held in trust

trust′ing *adj.* trustful —**trust′ing·ly** *adv.*

trust territory a territory set under a country's administrative authority by the United Nations

trust′wor′thy *adj.* **-thi·er, -thi·est** worthy of trust; reliable —**trust′wor′thi·ness** *n.*

trust′y *adj.* **-i·er, -i·est** trustworthy —*n., pl.* **-ies** a trusted person; specif., a convict granted special privileges as a trustworthy person

truth (trōōth) *n., pl.* **truths** (trōō*th*z, trōōths) [OE. *treowth*] 1. a being true; specif., *a)* sincerity *b)* conformity with fact *c)* reality *d)* correctness 2. what is true 3. an established fact, principle, etc. —**in truth** truly —**of a truth** certainly

truth′ful *adj.* 1. telling the truth; honest 2. in accordance with truth; not conflicting with what is true —**truth′ful·ly** *adv.* —**truth′ful·ness** *n.*

try (trī) *vt.* **tried, try′ing** [< OFr. *trier,* to sift] 1. to melt down (fat); render: with *out* 2. *a)* to examine and decide (a case) in a law court *b)* to determine legally the guilt or innocence of 3. to subject to a critical or analytical examination; test 4. to subject to difficulties, hardships, sufferings, etc. 5. to subject to strain or tension; tax 6. to make use of, sample, or resort to experimentally 7. to exert oneself toward; make an effort or attempt at —*vi.* to make an effort or attempt at something —*n., pl.* **tries** a trying; effort or attempt —**try on** to test the fit or appearance of (something to wear) by putting it on —**try out 1.** to test; experiment with 2. to test one's fitness as for a job, team, role in a play, etc.

try′ing *adj.* 1. that tries; that subjects to difficulties, strain, tension, etc. 2. that strains one's patience; annoying; exasperating

try′out′ *n.* [Colloq.] 1. a testing of fitness as for a role in a play 2. a preliminary performance of a play as to test audience reaction

tryst (trist) *n.* [< OFr. *triste,* hunting station] 1. an appointment to meet somewhere, esp. one made secretly by lovers 2. *a)* the meeting *b)* the place: also **tryst′ing place**

tsar (tsär, zär) *n. alt. sp. of* CZAR

tset·se fly (tset′sē, tsēt′-; set′-) [Afrik. < the Bantu name] a small fly of C and S Africa: one species transmits sleeping sickness

T′-shirt′ *n.* a collarless pullover undershirt or sport shirt

tsk (tisk) *interj., n.* a clicking or sucking sound made with the tongue to express disapproval, sympathy, etc.

tsp. 1. teaspoon(s) 2. teaspoonful(s)

T square a T-shaped ruler for drawing parallel lines

tsu·na·mi (tsōō nä′mē) *n., pl.* **-mis, -mi** [Jpn. < *tsu,* a harbor + *nami,* a wave] a huge sea wave caused by an underwater disturbance such as an earthquake

tub (tub) *n.* [< MDu. *tubbe*] 1. *a)* a round, open, flat-bottomed wooden container, usually made with staves and hoops *b)* any large, open container, as of metal or plastic, used as for washing clothes *c)* the contents of a tub 2. a bathtub 3. [Colloq.] a slow-moving, clumsy ship or boat —*vt., vi.* T SQUARE

tubbed, tub′bing [Colloq.] to wash in a tub

tu·ba (tōō′bə, tyōō′-) *n.* [L., a trumpet] a large brass-wind musical instrument with a deep tone

tub·by (tub′ē) *adj.* **-bi·er, -bi·est** 1. shaped like a tub 2. short and fat —**tub′bi·ness** *n.*

tube (tōōb, tyōōb) *n.* [Fr. < L. *tubus,* a pipe] 1. *a)* a slender, hollow cylinder or pipe of metal, glass, rubber, etc., in which gases and liquids can flow or be kept *b)* any tube-like instrument, part, organ, etc. 2. a rubber casing inflated with air and used, esp. formerly, with an outer casing to form an automotive tire 3. a cylindrical, compressible container for holding and squeezing out toothpaste, glue, etc., made as of thin metal or plastic and having at one end a cap that can be screwed off 4. *short for: a)* ELECTRON TUBE *b)* VACUUM TUBE 5. an underground tunnel for a railroad, subway, etc. —**the tube** [Colloq.] television

tu·ber (tōō′bər, tyōō′bər) *n.* [L., lit., knob] a short, thickened, fleshy part of an underground stem, as a potato

tu′ber·cle (-k′l) *n.* [see prec.] 1. a small rounded projection as on a bone or on a plant root 2. any abnormal hard nodule or swelling

tu·ber·cu·lar (too bur′kyə lər, tyoo-) *adj.* 1. of, like, or having tubercles 2. of or having tuberculosis Also **tu·ber′-cu·lous** —*n.* a person having tuberculosis

tu·ber′cu·lin (-lin) *n.* a sterile liquid made from a culture of the bacterial agent of tuberculosis and injected into the skin as a test for tuberculosis

tu·ber′cu·lo′sis (-lō′sis) *n.* [see TUBERCLE & -OSIS] an infectious bacterial disease characterized by tubercle formations, specif. in the lungs

tu·ber·ous (tōō′bər əs, tyōō′-) *adj.* [< Fr.: see TUBER] 1. covered with rounded, wartlike swellings 2. of, like, or having a tuber or tubers

tub·ing (tōōb′iŋ, tyōōb′-) *n.* 1. a system of tubes 2. material in tube form 3. a piece of tube

tu·bu·lar (tōō′byə lər, tyōō′-) *adj.* 1. of or like a tube or tubes 2. made with a tube or tubes

tuck (tuk) *vt.* [< MDu. *tucken*] 1. to pull or gather up or together in a fold or folds 2. to sew a fold or folds in (a garment, drapery, etc.) 3. *a)* to push the edges of (a sheet, napkin, shirt, etc.) under or in so as to secure *b)* to cover or wrap snugly thus 4. to put or press snugly into a small space —*n.* a sewed fold in a garment

tuck·er (tuk′ər) *vt.* [< ?] [Colloq.] to tire; weary

Tuc·son (tōō′sän, tōō sän′) city in S Ariz.: pop. 263,000

Tu·dor (tōō′dər, tyōō′-) ruling family of England (1485–1603)

Tues. Tuesday

Tues·day (tōōz′dē, tyōōz′-; -dā) *n.* [OE. *Tiwes dæg,* day of the war god Tiu] the third day of the week

tuft (tuft) *n.* [< OFr. *tufe*] 1. a closely bunched group of hairs, feathers, grass, etc. 2. any similar cluster; specif., any one of the small, fluffy balls of thread used decoratively as on a bedspread or marking the points where threads have been drawn through a mattress, quilt, etc. to hold the padding in place —*vt.* to provide with tufts —*vi.* to grow in or form into tufts

tug (tug) *vi., vt.* **tugged, tug′ging** [ME. *tuggen*] 1. to pull hard 2. to tow with a tugboat —*n.* 1. a tugging or being tugged 2. a rope, chain, strap, etc. for tugging something 3. a tugboat

tug′boat′ *n.* a small, powerful boat for towing or pushing ships, barges, etc.

tug of war a contest in which two teams pull at opposite ends of a rope, each trying to drag the other across a central line

tu·i·tion (too wish′ən, tyoo-) *n.* [< L. *tueri,* protect] the charge for instruction, as at a college

tu·la·re·mi·a (tōō′lə rē′mē ə) *n.* [< *Tulare* County, California] an infectious disease of rodents, esp. rabbits, transmissible to man: also **tu′la·rae′mi·a**

tu·lip (tōō′lip, tyōō′-) *n.* [< Fr. < Turk. *tülbend,* turban] 1. a bulb plant related to the lily, with a large, cup-shaped flower 2. the flower

tulip tree a N. American forest tree related to the magnolia, with light, soft wood (**tulipwood**), tulip-shaped, greenish-yellow flowers, and conelike fruit: also called **tulip poplar**

tulle (tōōl) *n.* [< *Tulle,* city in France] a fine netting of silk, rayon, etc., used as for scarfs

Tul·sa (tul′sə) city in NE Okla.: pop. 332,000

tum·ble (tum′b'l) *vi.* **-bled, -bling** [OE. *tumbian,* to jump] **1.** to do somersaults, handsprings, etc. **2.** to fall suddenly; collapse **3.** to toss or roll about **4.** to move in a fast, confused way —*vt.* **1.** to make tumble **2.** to toss haphazardly —*n.* **1.** a tumbling **2.** disorder **3.** a confused heap

tum′ble·down′ *adj.* dilapidated

tum′bler (-blər) *n.* **1.** one that tumbles; specif., an acrobat or gymnast **2.** *a)* an ordinary drinking glass, without foot or stem *b)* its contents **3.** the lock part moved by a key to release the bolt

tum′ble·weed′ *n.* a plant that breaks off near the ground in autumn and is blown about by the wind

tum·brel, tum·bril (tum′brəl) *n.* [< MFr. *tomberel*] a cart that can be tilted for emptying

tu·mes·cence (tōō mes′'ns, tyōō-) *n.* [< L. *tumere,* to swell] a swelling up —**tu·mes′cent** *adj.*

tu·mid (tōō′mid, tyōō′-) *adj.* [see prec.] **1.** swollen; distended **2.** bombastic —**tu·mid′i·ty** *n.*

tum·my (tum′ē) *n., pl.* **-mies** stomach: a child's word

tu·mor (tōō′mər, tyōō′-) *n.* [see TUMESCENCE] a bodily swelling; esp., an independent growth that may or may not be harmful: Brit. sp. **tu′mour**

tu·mult (tōō′mult, tyōō′-) *n.* [< L. *tumultus*] **1.** uproar; commotion **2.** disturbance; agitation

tu·mul′tu·ous (-mul′chōō wəs) *adj.* full of tumult; turbulent —**tu·mul′tu·ous·ly** *adv.*

tun (tun) *n.* [< ML. *tunna*] a large cask

tu·na (tōō′nə, tyōō′-) *n., pl.* **-na, -nas** [AmSp. < Sp., ult. < Gr. *thynnos*] **1.** a large, edible fish of the Atlantic and Pacific, related to the mackerel **2.** its flesh, often canned: also **tuna fish**

tun·dra (tun′drə) *n.* [Russ.] a treeless arctic plain

tune (tōōn, tyōōn) *n.* [see TONE] **1.** a catchy, rhythmical succession of musical tones; melody **2.** correct musical pitch or key **3.** agreement; concord [*in* tune *with* the times] —*vt.* **tuned, tun′ing 1.** to adjust or adapt to a given musical pitch or key **2.** to adapt to a condition, mood, etc. **3.** to adjust (a motor, circuit, etc.) for proper performance —**to the tune of** [Colloq.] to the amount of —**tune in (on)** to adjust a radio or television receiver so as to get (a certain station, program, etc.) —**tune out** to adjust a radio or television receiver so as to eliminate (interference, an unwanted program, etc.) —**tune up 1.** to adjust (musical instruments) to the same pitch **2.** to adjust (an engine) for proper performance —**tun′a·ble, tune′a·ble** *adj.*

tune′ful *adj.* melodious —**tune′ful·ly** *adv.*

tun′er *n.* **1.** one that tunes **2.** the radio-receiver part, esp. a separate unit in a high-fidelity system, that selects specific signals for amplification

tune′up′, tune′-up′ *n.* a tuning up, as of an engine

tung·sten (tuŋ′stən) *n.* [Sw. < *tung,* heavy + *sten,* stone] a hard, heavy, gray-white metallic chemical element: symbol, W; at. wt., 183.85; at. no., 74

tu·nic (tōō′nik, tyōō′-) *n.* [L. *tunica*] **1.** a loose, gownlike garment worn by men and women in ancient Greece and Rome **2.** a blouselike garment extending to the hips or lower and gathered at the waist as with a belt **3.** *Biol.* a covering membrane or tissue

tu·ni·cate (tōō′ni kit, tyōō′-; -kāt′) *adj.* [< L. *tunicare,* put on a tunic] *Bot., Zool.* covered with or having a tunic or tunics —*n.* any of several sea animals having a saclike body in a thick tunic

tuning fork a small, two-pronged steel instrument which when struck sounds a fixed tone in perfect pitch: used as a guide in tuning instruments

Tu·nis (tōō′nis) seaport and capital of Tunisia: pop. 662,000

Tu·ni·sia (tōō nē′zhə) country in N Africa, on the Mediterranean: 48,332 sq. mi.; pop. 5,137,000; cap. Tunis —**Tu·ni′sian** *adj., n.*

tun·nel (tun′'l) *n.* [< OFr. *tonne,* tun] an underground or underwater passageway for cars, trains, etc. —*vt., vi.* **-neled** or **-nelled, -nel·ing** or **-nel·ling** to make a tunnel (through or under) —**tun′nel·er, tun′nel·ler** *n.*

tun·ny (tun′ē) *n., pl.* **-nies, -ny** [< Gr. *thynnos*] same as TUNA (sense 1)

Tu·pi (tōō pē′, tōō′pē) *n.* **1.** *pl.* **-pis′, -pi′** a member of a group of Indian peoples of Brazil and Paraguay **2.** their language

tur·ban (tur′bən) *n.* [< Per. *dulbänd*] **1.** a Muslim headdress consisting of a length of cloth wound in folds **2.** *a)* a scarf or bandanna wound about the head, worn by women *b)* a woman's brimless hat

TURBAN

tur·bid (tur′bid) *adj.* [< L. *turba,* a crowd] **1.** muddy or cloudy with unsettled sediment **2.** thick or dark, as clouds **3.** muddled —**tur·bid′i·ty** *n.*

tur·bine (tur′bin, -bīn) *n.* [Fr. < L. *turbo,* a whirl] an engine driven by pressure, as of steam, against vanes that turn an axle

turbo- [see prec.] *a combining form meaning* consisting of or driven by a turbine

tur·bo·fan (tur′bō fan′) *n.* a turbojet engine developing extra thrust from air that bypasses the engine and is accelerated by a fan: in full **turbofan engine**

tur′bo·jet′ (-jet′) *n.* **1.** a jet engine in which the energy of the jet operates a turbine which drives the air compressor: in full **turbojet engine 2.** an aircraft having such an engine

tur′bo·prop′ (-präp′) *n.* [TURBO- + PROP(ELLER)] **1.** a turbojet engine turning a propeller that develops most of the thrust: in full **turboprop engine 2.** an aircraft having such an engine

tur·bot (tur′bət) *n., pl.* **-bot, -bots** [< OFr. *tourbout*] **1.** a European flatfish esteemed as food **2.** an American flounder or halibut

tur·bu·lent (tur′byə lənt) *adj.* [Fr. < L. *turba,* a crowd] full of commotion or wild disorder; specif., *a)* unruly; boisterous *b)* violently agitated *c)* wildly irregular in motion, as air currents —**tur′bu·lence, tur′bu·len·cy** *n.* —**tur′bu·lent·ly** *adv.*

tu·reen (tōō rēn′) *n.* [< MFr. *terrine,* earthen vessel] a large, deep dish with a lid, for serving soup, stew, etc.

turf (turf) *n., pl.* **turfs,** esp. Brit. **turves** (turvz) [OE.] **1.** *a)* a surface layer of earth containing grass plants with their matted roots; sod *b)* a piece of this **2.** peat **3.** a track for horse racing: usually with *the* **4.** [Slang] one's own territory or domain —*vt.* to cover with turf

tur·gid (tur′jid) *adj.* [< L. *turgere,* to swell] **1.** swollen; distended **2.** bombastic —**tur·gid′i·ty** *n.*

Tu·rin (toor′in, tōō rin′) city in NW Italy, on the Po River: pop. 1,177,000

Turk (turk) *n.* a native or inhabitant of Turkey

Turk. 1. Turkey **2.** Turkish

Tur·key (tur′kē) country occupying Asia Minor & a SE part of the Balkan Peninsula: 301,381 sq. mi.; pop. 36,162,000; cap. Ankara

tur·key (tur′kē) *n.* [< similarity to a fowl formerly imported through Turkey] **1.** *a)* a large N. American bird with a small head and spreading tail, bred as poultry *b)* its flesh used as food **2.** [Slang] a failure: said esp. of a theatrical production **3.** *Bowling* three strikes in a row —**talk turkey** [Colloq.] to talk bluntly and directly

turkey buzzard a dark-colored American vulture with a naked, reddish head: also called **turkey vulture**

Tur·kic (tur′kik) *adj.* designating or of a subfamily of languages, including Turkish, Tatar, etc. —*n.* this subfamily

Turk·ish (tur′kish) *adj.* of Turkey or the Turks —*n.* the language of Turkey

Turkish bath 1. a bath and massage given a bather after the bather has sweated heavily in a room of hot air or steam **2.** a place equipped for this

Turkish towel [*also* t-] a thick cotton towel of terry cloth

Turk·men Soviet Socialist Republic (turk′men) republic of the U.S.S.R., in C Asia: also **Turk′men·i·stan′** (-i stän′), **Turk·me·ni·a** (turk mē′nē ə)

tur·mer·ic (tur′mər ik) *n.* [< ML. *terra merita,* deserving earth] **1.** an East Indian plant related to the ginger: its powdered rhizome is used as a yellow dye, a seasoning, etc. **2.** the rhizome or powder

tur·moil (tur′moil) *n.* [*tur-* (< ? TURBULENT) + MOIL] tumult; commotion; confusion

turn (turn) *vt.* [ult. < Gr. *tornos,* lathe] **1.** to rotate (a wheel, etc.) **2.** to move around or partly around [*turn* the key] **3.** to do by a revolving motion [*to* turn *a somersault*] **4.** to give form to as in a lathe **5.** to give a graceful form to [*to* turn *a phrase*] **6.** to change the position or direction of **7.** to ponder **8.** to bend, fold, twist, etc. **9.** to spade, plow, etc. **10.** to reverse *[turn* the record*]* **11.** to upset (the stomach) **12.** to deflect or repel *[to turn* a blow*]* **13.** to cause to change actions, attitudes, etc. **14.** to go around (a corner, etc.) **15.** to pass (an age, etc.) **16.** to drive, set, let go, etc. *[to turn* someone adrift*]* **17.** to gain as by a sale *[to turn* a profit*]* **18.** to direct, point, aim, etc. **19.** to use or apply in a specified way **20.** to change; convert **21.** to make sour **22.** to affect in some way *—vi.* **1.** *a)* to revolve or pivot *b)* to depend (*on* or *upon*) **2.** to whirl or reel **3.** to become curved or bent **4.** to become reversed **5.** to become upset: said of the stomach **6.** to change or reverse course, direction, etc., or one's feelings, allegiance, etc. **7.** to refer (*to*) **8.** to apply (*to*) for help **9.** to direct or shift one's attention, energy, etc. *[to turn* to other matters*]* **10.** to make a sudden attack (*on* or *upon*) **11.** to become **12.** to undergo a change **13.** to become sour **14.** to change color, as leaves *—n.* **1.** a turning around; rotation **2.** a single twist, winding, etc. **3.** *a)* a change or reversal of course, direction, etc. *b)* a change in condition *[a* turn for the better*]* **4.** a bend or curve, as in a road **5.** the time of a chronological change **6.** *same as* TURNING POINT **7.** a brief shock; start **8.** an action; deed *[a* good *turn]* **9.** a bout; spell **10.** the right, duty, or chance to do something, esp. as coming in regular order *[it's* your *turn* to speak*]* **11.** a distinctive form, detail, etc. *[an* odd *turn* of speech*]* **12.** an inclination, aptitude, etc. *—at every turn* in every instance *—by turns* one after another *—in* (or *out of*) *turn* (not) in proper sequence *—take turns* to speak, do, etc., one after another in regular order *—to a turn* perfectly *—turn down* **1.** to reject (a request, etc.) **2.** to reduce (light, sound, etc.) *—turn in* **1.** to deliver; hand in **2.** to hand over, as to the police **3.** [Colloq.] to go to bed *—turn off* **1.** to shut off; stop from functioning **2.** [Slang] to cause to be bored, annoyed, etc. *—turn on* **1.** to make go on or start functioning **2.** to display suddenly (a smile, etc.) **3.** [Slang] to stimulate with or as with a psychedelic drug; make elated, euphoric, etc. *—turn out* **1.** to put out (a light) **2.** to put outside **3.** to dismiss **4.** to come or go out, as to a meeting **5.** to produce **6.** to result **7.** to prove to be **8.** to become **9.** to equip, dress, etc. **10.** [Colloq.] to get out of bed *—turn over* **1.** to start operating, as an engine **2.** to ponder **3.** to hand over *—turn to* to get busy *—turn up* **1.** to fold upward or back **2.** to bring to light, as by digging **3.** to increase the speed, loudness, etc. of by operating a control **4.** to happen **5.** to arrive **6.** to be found

turn′a·bout′ *n.* a shift or reversal of position, allegiance, opinion, etc.

turn′a·round′ *n.* **1.** *same as* TURNABOUT **2.** a wide area for turning a vehicle around

turn′buck′le (-buk′'l) *n.* a linklike metal coupling having at each end a threaded tubular opening into which a rod or other piece can be screwed, the coupling being turned to tighten or loosen the pieces thus joined

TURNBUCKLE

turn′coat′ *n.* a renegade or traitor

turn′down′ *adj.* turned down or capable of this, as a collar *—n.* **1.** a rejection **2.** a downturn

turn′ing *n.* **1.** the act of one that turns **2.** a place where something, as a road, turns

turning point a point of decisive change; crisis

tur·nip (tur′nip) *n.* [earlier *turnep* < ?] **1.** *a)* a plant related to the mustard, with edible leaves and a roundish root used as a vegetable *b)* *same as* RUTABAGA **2.** the root of either of these

turn′key′ (-kē′) *n., pl.* **-keys′** a jailer

turn′off′ *n.* **1.** a turning off **2.** a place for turning off; esp., an exit from a highway

turn′out′ *n.* **1.** a turning out **2.** a gathering, as for a meeting **3.** amount produced; output **4.** a wider part of a road, as for passing **5.** *a)* equipment *b)* a set of clothes; costume

turn′o′ver *n.* **1.** a turning over; upset **2.** a small pie with half the crust folded back over the other **3.** *a)* the selling out and replenishing of a stock of goods *b)* the amount of business done during a given period **4.** the rate of replacement of workers

turn′pike′ *n.* [ME. *turnpyke,* spiked road barrier] a toll road, esp. one that is an expressway

turn′stile′ *n.* an apparatus such as a post with revolving bars, used at an entrance to admit people one at a time

turn′ta′ble *n.* **1.** a circular rotating platform, as to turn a locomotive around **2.** the revolving part of a record player, supporting a record being played

tur·pen·tine (tur′pən tīn′) *n.* [< Gr. *terebinthos,* tree yielding such an oleoresin] a colorless, volatile essential oil, $C_{10}H_{16}$, distilled from certain oleoresins, esp. pine oleoresins, and used as a thinner or solvent in paints, varnishes, etc.: in full **spirits** (or **oil**) **of turpentine**

tur·pi·tude (tur′pə tōōd′, -tyōōd′) *n.* [< L. *turpis,* vile] baseness; vileness; depravity

tur·quoise (tur′koiz, -kwoiz) *n.* [< OFr. *turqueis,* Turkish] **1.** a greenish-blue semiprecious stone **2.** its color; greenish blue *—adj.* greenish-blue

tur·ret (tur′it) *n.* [see TOWER] **1.** a small tower projecting from a building, usually at a corner **2.** *a)* a low, armored, usually revolving, towerlike structure for guns, as on a warship or tank *b)* a transparent dome for gunners, as on a bomber **3.** a rotating attachment as for a lathe, holding several cutting tools for successive use

tur·tle (tur′t'l) *n.* [< Fr. < ML. *tortuca*] **1.** any of various land and water reptiles having a soft body encased in a hard shell into which, in most species, the head, tail, and four legs can be drawn: land species are usually called *tortoise* **2.** the flesh of some turtles, used as food *—turn turtle* to turn upside down

tur′tle·dove′ *n.* [< L. *turtur* + DOVE¹] **1.** any of several old-world wild doves that coo plaintively: a mated pair seemingly display affection **2.** *same as* MOURNING DOVE

tur′tle·neck′ *n.* **1.** a high, snug, turndown collar on a pullover sweater, shirt, etc. **2.** a sweater, shirt, etc. with such a collar

Tus·ca·ny (tus′kə nē) region of C Italy *—Tus′can* (-kən) *adj., n.*

tusk (tusk) *n.* [OE. *tucs*] in elephants, walruses, etc., a very long, large, pointed tooth, usually one of a pair, projecting from the mouth

tus·sle (tus′'l) *n., vi.* **-sled, -sling** [< ME. *tusen* (in comp.), to pull] struggle; wrestle; scuffle

tus·sock (tus′ək) *n.* [< ?] a thick tuft or clump as of grass or sedge *—tus′sock·y adj.*

tut (tut) *interj., n.* a clicking or sucking sound made with the tongue to express impatience, annoyance, etc.

Tut·ankh·a·men (tōōt′äŋk ä′mən) fl. c.1355 B.C.; Egyptian king

tu·te·lage (tōōt′'l ij, tyōōt′-) *n.* [< L. *tutela,* protection] **1.** guardianship; care, protection, etc. **2.** teaching; instruction **3.** the state of being under a guardian or tutor *—tu′te·lar′y* (-er′ē) *adj.*

tu·tor (tōōt′ər, tyōōt′ər) *n.* [< L. *tueri,* to guard] a private teacher *—vt., vi.* to teach privately *—tu·to·ri·al* (tōō tôr′ē əl, tyōō-) *adj.*

tut·ti-frut·ti (tōōt′ē frōōt′ē) *n.* [It., all fruits] ice cream or other sweet food containing bits of candied fruits

tu·tu (tōō′tōō) *n.* [Fr.] a very short, full, projecting skirt worn by ballerinas

tux (tuks) *n. clipped form of* TUXEDO

tux·e·do (tuk sē′dō) *n., pl.* **-dos** [< country club near *Tuxedo* Lake, N.Y.] a man's suit for semiformal evening wear, the jacket tailless

TV (tē′vē′) *n.* **1.** television **2.** *pl.* **TVs, TV's** a television receiving set

TV dinner [because it can conveniently be eaten while watching television] a frozen, precooked dinner packaged in the tray in which it is to be heated and served

twad·dle (twäd′'l) *n.* [earlier *twattle* < ?] foolish, empty talk or writing; nonsense

twain (twān) *adj., n.* [OE. *twegen*] [Archaic] two

Twain (twān), **Mark** *see* Samuel Langhorne CLEMENS

twang (twaŋ) *n.* [echoic] **1.** a sharp, vibrating sound as of a taut string plucked **2.** a sharply nasal quality *—vi., vt.* **1.** to make or cause to make a twang **2.** to speak or utter with a twang *—twang′y adj.*

'twas (twuz, twäz; *unstressed* twəz) it was

tweak (twēk) *vt.* [OE. *twiccan,* to twitch] to give a sudden, twisting pinch to (someone's nose, cheek, etc.) *—n.* such a pinch

tweed (twēd) *n.* [< misreading of *tweel,* Scot. form of TWILL] **1.** a rough wool fabric in a twill weave of two or more colors **2.** [*pl.*] clothes of this

twee·dle (twēd′'l) *vi., vt.* **-dled, -dling** [echoic] to pipe, whistle, etc. shrilly *—n.* this sound

twee·dle·dum and twee·dle·dee (twēd′'l dum′ 'n twēd′'l dē′) two persons or things so much alike as to be almost indistinguishable

tweed′y *adj.* **-i·er, -i·est 1.** of or like tweed **2.** *a)* habitually wearing tweeds *b)* of the outdoor type given to wearing tweeds *—tweed′i·ness n.*

'tween (twēn) *prep.* [Poet.] between

tweet (twēt) *n., interj.* [echoic] the thin, chirping sound of a small bird *—vi.* to make this sound

tweet′er *n.* in an assembly of two or more loudspeakers, a small speaker for reproducing high sounds

tweez·ers (twēz′ərz) *n.pl.* [*with sing. or pl. v.*] [< obs. *tweeze,* surgical set < Fr. *étui,* small box] small pincers for plucking out hairs, handling tiny objects, etc.: often **pair of tweezers**

twelfth (twelfth) *adj.* [OE. *twelfta*] **1.** preceded by eleven others; 12th **2.** designating any of the twelve equal parts of something —*n.* **1.** the one following the eleventh **2.** any of the twelve equal parts of something; 1/12

Twelfth Day the twelfth day (Jan. 6) after Christmas; Epiphany: the evening before, or sometimes the evening of, this day is called **Twelfth Night**

twelve (twelv) *adj., n.* [OE. *twelf*] two more than ten; 12; XII —**the Twelve** the Twelve Apostles

Twelve Apostles the twelve disciples chosen by Jesus to go forth to teach the gospel

twen·ty (twen′tē) *adj., n., pl.* -**ties** [OE. *twentig*] two times ten; 20; XX —**the twenties** the numbers or years, as of a century, from 20 through 29 —**twen′ti·eth** (-ith) *adj., n.*

twen′ty-one′ *n.* a card game in which the object is to total 21 points

′twere (twur) [Poet.] it were [*if ′twere time*]

twerp (twurp) *n.* [< ?] [Slang] a contemptible person

twice (twīs) *adv.* [OE. *twiga*] two times

twid·dle (twid′'l) *vt., vi.* -**dled,** -**dling** [< ?] to twirl or play with (something) idly —**twiddle one's thumbs** to be idle

twig (twig) *n.* [OE. *twigge*] a small slender branch of a tree or shrub —**twig′gy** *adj.* -**gi·er,** -**gi·est**

twi·light (twī′līt′) *n.* [ME.] **1.** *a)* the light after sunset or before sunrise *b)* the period from sunset to dark **2.** a period of gradual decline

twill (twil) *n.* [OE. *twilic,* double-threaded] **1.** a cloth woven with parallel diagonal lines **2.** this weave pattern —*vt.* to weave thus

′twill (twil) [Poet.] it will

twin (twin) *adj.* [OE. *twinn,* double] **1.** consisting of, or being one of a pair of, two similar things **2.** being a twin or twins —*n.* **1.** either of two born at the same birth **2.** either of two persons or things much alike

twine (twīn) *n.* [OE. *twin*] **1.** strong thread, string, etc. of strands twisted together **2.** a twining or being twined —*vt., vi.* **twined, twin′ing** **1.** to twist together **2.** to wind around

twinge (twinj) *vt., vi.* **twinged, twing′ing** [OE. *twengan,* to press] to make have, or to feel, a brief, sharp pain or pang —*n.* such a pain or pang

twi-night, twi·night (twī′nīt′) *adj.* [TWI(LIGHT) + NIGHT] *Baseball* designating a late-afternoon doubleheader that continues on into the evening

twin·kle (twiŋ′k'l) *vi.* -**kled,** -**kling** [OE. *twinclian*] **1.** to shine with quick, intermittent flashes **2.** to light up as with amusement: said of the eyes **3.** to move quickly and lightly, as a dancer's feet —*vt.* to make twinkle —*n.* a twinkling

twin′kling *n.* **1.** the action of one that twinkles **2.** *a)* the winking of an eye *b)* an instant

twirl (twurl) *vt., vi.* [< ?] **1.** to rotate rapidly; spin; whirl **2.** to twist [*to twirl one's mustache*] **3.** *Baseball* to pitch —*n.* a twirling or being twirled —**twirl′er** *n.*

twist (twist) *vt.* [OE. *-twist,* a rope] **1.** to wind (strands or threads) around one another **2.** to wind (thread, rope, etc.) around something **3.** to give a spiral shape to **4.** *a)* to strain by turning one end or part in opposition to another *b)* to wrench, deform, etc. thus *c)* to contort, distort, etc. *d)* to mix up, confuse, etc. **5.** to move, rotate, remove, etc. by subjecting to a turning force —*vi.* **1.** to get twisted **2.** to wind, coil, spiral, turn, etc., esp. sharply or erratically **3.** to rotate; revolve **4.** to squirm or writhe —*n.* **1.** a twisting or being twisted **2.** something twisted, made by being twisted, or designed to be twisted; specif., *a)* a twisted thread, cord, etc. *b)* a roll of twisted tobacco leaves *c)* a twisted pastry *d)* a length of wire to twist around and so close the opening as of a plastic bag **3.** a sharp bend or curve, as in a road **4.** a quirk, eccentricity, etc. **5.** an abrupt shift of direction, as in a situation or series of events **6.** a distinctive, different, or new way of doing, treating, or presenting something

twist′er *n.* **1.** one that twists **2.** a tornado

twit (twit) *vt.* **twit′ted, twit′ting** [OE. *ætwitan*] to reproach, taunt, etc., esp. by reminding of a fault —*n.* **1.** a twitting **2.** a reproach or taunt

twitch (twich) *vt., vi.* [OE. *twiccian,* to pluck] to pull (at) or move with a quick, slight jerk —*n.* a twitching; quick, slight jerk

twit·ter (twit′ər) *vi.* [ME. *twiteren*] **1.** to chirp lightly and continuously **2.** *a)* to chatter *b)* to giggle **3.** to tremble excitedly —*vt.* to express or say in a twittering manner —*n.* **1.** a twittering **2.** nervous excitement

′twixt (twikst) *prep.* [ME. *twix*] [Poet.] between

two (tōō) *adj., n.* [OE. *twa, tu*] one more than one; 2; II —**in two** in two parts; asunder

two′-base′ hit *Baseball same as* DOUBLE

two′-bit′ *adj.* [see BIT², sense 2] **1.** [Colloq.] costing twenty-five cents **2.** [Slang] cheap

two bits [see prec.] [Colloq.] twenty-five cents

two′-by-four′ *n.* a piece of lumber two inches thick and four inches wide, usually trimmed to 1 1/2 by 3 1/2

two′-faced′ *adj.* **1.** with two faces **2.** hypocritical

two′-fist′ed *adj.* [Colloq.] **1.** having, and able to use, both fists **2.** vigorous; virile

two′fold′ *adj.* **1.** having two parts **2.** having twice as much or as many —*adv.* twice as much or as many

two′-hand′ed *adj.* **1.** requiring the use of both hands **2.** operated, played, etc. by two persons

two·pence (tup′'ns) *n.* **1.** two pence **2.** a British coin of this value

two·pen·ny (tup′ə nē, tōō′pen′ē) *adj.* **1.** costing two pence **2.** cheap

two′-ply′ *adj.* having two layers, strands, etc.

two′some (-səm) *n.* two people; a couple

two′-time′ *vt.* -**timed′,** -**tim′ing** [Slang] to deceive; esp., to be unfaithful to —**two′-tim′er** *n.*

′twould (twood) [Poet.] it would

two′-way′ *adj.* **1.** moving or allowing movement in two directions, specif. two opposite directions [*a two-way street*] **2.** involving reciprocity [*a two-way cultural exchange*] **3.** involving two persons, groups, etc. [*a two-way political race*] **4.** usable in two ways, esp. two opposite ways [*a two-way radio transmits and receives*]

twp. township

TX Texas

-ty [< L. *-tas*] *a suffix meaning* quality of, condition of [*novelty*]

ty·coon (tī kōōn′) *n.* [< Jpn. < Chin. *ta,* great + *kiun,* prince] a magnate, as an industrialist

ty·ing (tī′iŋ) *prp. of* TIE

tyke (tīk) *n.* [< ON. *tik,* a bitch] [Colloq.] a tot

Ty·ler (tī′lər), **John** 1790–1862; 10th president of the U.S. (1841–45)

tym·pa·ni (tim′pə nē) *n.pl. alt. sp. of* TIMPANI —**tym′pa·nist** *n.*

tym·pan·ic (tim pan′ik) *adj.* **1.** drumlike [*tympanic membrane*] **2.** of the tympanum

tympanic membrane a thin membrane that separates the middle ear from the external ear and that vibrates when struck by sound waves; eardrum

tym·pa·num (tim′pə nəm) *n., pl.* -**nums, -na** (-nə) [< Gr. *tympanon,* a drum] *same as:* **1.** MIDDLE EAR **2.** TYMPANIC MEMBRANE

type (tīp) *n.* [< Gr. *typos,* a mark] **1.** one that represents or symbolizes another **2.** the characteristic form, plan, style, etc. of a class, group, etc. **3.** a class, group, etc. with characteristics in common **4.** one that is representative of a class or group **5.** a perfect example or an archetype **6.** *a)* a rectangular piece, usually of metal, with a raised letter, figure, etc. in reverse on its top, used in printing *b)* such pieces collectively *c)* a printed or photographically reproduced character or characters —*vt., vi.* **typed, typ′ing** **1.** to classify according to type **2.** to typewrite

-type [see prec.] *a combining form meaning* print, printing type [*monotype*]

type′cast′ *vt.* -**cast′,** -**cast′ing** to cast (an actor or actress) repeatedly in the same type of part

type′face′ *n.* **1.** the face, or printing part, of a piece or pieces of type **2.** the design of type

type′script′ *n.* typewritten matter or copy

type′set′ *vt.* -**set′,** -**set′ting** to set in type

type′set′ter *n.* **1.** a person who sets type; compositor **2.** a machine for setting type

type′write′ *vt., vi.* -**wrote′,** -**writ′ten,** -**writ′ing** to write with a typewriter

type′writ′er *n.* a writing machine with a keyboard for reproducing letters, figures, etc. that resemble printed ones

ty·phoid (tī′foid) *n.* [TYPH(US) + -OID] an acute infectious disease marked by fever, intestinal disorders, etc. and acquired from food or water contaminated by excreta: in full **typhoid fever**

ty·phoon (tī fōōn′) *n*. [< Chin. dial. *tai-fung*, great wind] a violent tropical cyclone originating in the W Pacific

ty·phus (tī′fəs) *n*. [< Gr. *typhos*, fever] an acute infectious disease marked by fever, headache, and skin rash and transmitted to man by fleas, lice, etc.: in full **typhus fever**

typ·i·cal (tip′i k′l) *adj*. **1**. serving as a type; symbolic **2**. having the distinguishing characteristics of a class, group, etc.; representative **3**. belonging to a type; characteristic —**typ′i·cal·ly** *adv*.

typ·i·fy (-ə fī′) *vt*. **-fied′, -fy′ing** to be a type of; symbolize, represent, or characterize

typ·ist (tīp′ist) *n*. one that typewrites

ty·po (tī′pō) *n., pl.* **-pos** [Colloq.] a mechanical error made in typing or in setting type

ty·pog·ra·phy (tī päg′rə fē) *n*. [see TYPE & -GRAPHY] **1**. the setting of, and printing with, type **2**. the arrangement or appearance of matter printed from type —**ty·pog′ra·pher** *n*. —**ty′po·graph′i·cal** (-pə graf′i k′l) *adj*.

ty·ran·ni·cal (ti ran′i k′l, tī-) *adj*. of or like a tyrant; despotic, oppressive, harsh, unjust, etc.: also **ty·ran′nic** —**ty·ran′ni·cal·ly** *adv*.

tyr·an·nize (tir′ə nīz′) *vi*. **-nized′, -niz′ing 1**. to govern as a tyrant **2**. to use authority harshly or cruelly —*vt*. to oppress

tyr′an·nous (-nəs) *adj. same as* TYRANNICAL

tyr·an·ny (tir′ə nē) *n., pl.* **-nies 1**. the authority, government, etc. of a tyrant **2**. cruel and unjust use of power **3**. a tyrannical act

ty·rant (tī′rənt) *n*. [< Gr. *tyrannos*] an absolute ruler, esp. if oppressive, harsh, unjust, etc.

Tyre (tīr) seaport in SW Lebanon, on the Mediterranean: Phoenician cultural center: pop. 12,000

ty·ro (tī′rō) *n., pl.* **-ros** [< L. *tiro*, young soldier] a beginner in learning something; novice

Tyr·ol (tir′äl, tī′rōl) *same as* TIROL —**Ty·ro·le·an** (ti rō′lē ən) *adj., n.*

tzar (tsär, zär) *n. alt. sp. of* CZAR —**tza·ri·na** (tsä rē′nə, zä-) *n.fem.*

U

U, u (yōō) *n., pl.* **U's, u's** the twenty-first letter of the English alphabet

U (yōō) *n*. **1**. something shaped like U **2**. *Chem.* uranium

U., U 1. Union **2**. United **3**. University

U., U, u., u unit; units

U.A.W., UAW United Automobile, Aerospace, and Agricultural Implement Workers of America

U·ban·gi (ōō bäŋ′gē, yōō baŋ′-) river in C Africa, flowing from N Zaire into the Congo River: c.700 mi.

u·biq·ui·tous (yōō bik′wə təs) *adj*. [< L. *ubique*, everywhere] present, or seeming to be present, everywhere at the same time —**u·biq′ui·ty** *n*.

U-boat (yōō′bōt′) *n*. [< G. *Unterseeboot*, undersea boat] a German submarine

u.c. *Printing* upper case

ud·der (ud′ər) *n*. [OE. *udr*] a large, pendulous, milk-secreting gland with two or more teats, as in cows

UFO (yōō′fō, yōō′ef ō′) *n., pl.* **UFOs, UFO's** an unidentified flying object of disputed reality, nature, or origin; esp., such an object described as saucerlike (*flying saucer*) and often alleged to be a spacecraft from another planet

u·fol·o·gist (yōō fäl′ə jist) *n*. [< prec. + -LOGY + -IST] one studying UFOs, typically believing them to be spacecraft from another planet

U·gan·da (yōō gan′də, ōō gän′də) country in EC Africa: 93,981 sq. mi.; pop. 10,127,000

ugh (ookh, oo, ug, *etc.*) *interj.* [echoic] an exclamation of horror, disgust, etc.

ug·li (ug′lē) *n*. [< UGLY] an odd-shaped fruit that is a cross between a grapefruit, orange, and tangerine

ug·ly (ug′lē) *adj.* **-li·er, -li·est** [< ON. *uggr*, fear] **1**. unpleasant to look at **2**. bad, vile, repulsive, offensive, etc. **3**. ominous; dangerous **4**. [Colloq.] ill-tempered —**ug′li·ness** *n*.

uh (u, un) *interj.* **1**. *same as* HUH **2**. a sound indicating hesitation

UHF, uhf ultrahigh frequency

U.K. United Kingdom

u·kase (yōō′kās, -kāz; yōō kās′) *n*. [Russ. *ukaz*, edict] a decree, esp. an arbitrary one

U·krain·i·an (yōō krā′nē ən) *adj.* of the Ukraine, its people, their language, etc. —*n*. **1**. a native or inhabitant of the Ukraine **2**. the Slavic language of the Ukrainians **Ukrainian Soviet Socialist Republic** republic of the U.S.S.R., in the SW European part: also called the **U·kraine** (yōō krān′, yōō′krān)

u·ku·le·le (yōō′kə lā′lē) *n*. [Haw., flea] a small, four-stringed, guitar-like musical instrument

ul·cer (ul′sər) *n*. [L. *ulcus*] an open sore (other than a wound) on the skin or some mucous

UKULELE

membrane, marked by tissue disintegration and, often, discharge of pus

ul′cer·ate (-sə rāt′) *vt., vi.* **-at′ed, -at′ing** to make or become ulcerous —**ul′cer·a′tion** *n*.

ul′cer·ous (-sər əs) *adj.* of, like, or characterized by an ulcer or ulcers

ul·na (ul′nə) *n., pl.* **-nae** (-nē), **-nas** [L., the elbow] the larger of the two bones of the forearm, on the side opposite the thumb —**ul′nar** *adj.*

Ul·ster (ul′stər) **1**. former province of Ireland, divided to form Northern Ireland & a province (*Ulster*) of Ireland **2**. [Colloq.] Northern Ireland

ul·ster (ul′stər) *n*. [< prec.] a long, loose, heavy overcoat, esp. one with a belt

ult. ultimate(ly)

ul·te·ri·or (ul tir′ē ər) *adj.* [L.] **1**. lying beyond or on the farther side **2**. later; subsequent **3**. more remote; further **4**. beyond what is expressed, implied, or evident *[ulterior motives]*

ul·ti·mate (ul′tə mit) *adj.* [< L. *ultimus*, last] **1**. beyond which it is impossible to go; farthest **2**. final; last **3**. beyond further analysis; fundamental **4**. greatest possible; maximum —*n*. a final point or result

ul·ti·ma·tum (ul′tə māt′əm) *n., pl.* **-tums, -ta** (-ə) [see prec.] a final offer or demand, as in negotiations

ul·tra (ul′trə) *adj.* [L., beyond] going beyond the usual limit; extreme

ultra- [L.] *a prefix meaning:* **1**. beyond *[ultraviolet]* **2**. excessively *[ultramodern]* **3**. beyond the range of *[ultramicroscopic]*

ul·tra·high frequency (ul′trə hī′) any radio frequency between 300 and 3,000 megahertz

ul′tra·ma·rine (-mə rēn′) *adj.* **1**. beyond the sea **2**. deep-blue —*n*. **1**. a blue pigment, orig. made from powdered lapis lazuli **2**. any of certain other pigments **3**. deep blue

ul′tra·son′ic (-sän′ik) *adj.* above the range of sound audible to the human ear

ul′tra·vi′o·let (-vī′ə lit) *adj.* designating or of those invisible rays just beyond the violet of the visible spectrum

ul·u·late (yōōl′yoo lāt′, ul′-) *vi.* **-lat′ed, -lat′ing** [L. *ululare*] **1**. to howl or hoot **2**. to wail

U·lys·ses (yōō lis′ēz) *same as* ODYSSEUS

um·bel (um′b′l) *n*. [L. *umbella*, parasol] a cluster of flowers with stalks of nearly equal length growing out from about the same point on a main stem —**um′bel·late** (-it, -āt′) *adj.*

um·ber (um′bər) *n*. [< It. (*terra d′*)*ombra*, (earth of) shade] **1**. a kind of earth containing oxides of manganese and iron, used as a pigment: *raw umber* is yellowish-brown; *burnt umber* is reddish-brown **2**. yellowish brown or reddish brown

um·bil·i·cal (um bil′i k′l) *adj.* of or like an umbilicus or an umbilical cord —*n*. a cable to supply oxygen, power, etc. as to an astronaut outside his craft

umbilical cord 1. a cordlike structure that connects a fetus with the placenta: it is severed at birth **2.** *same as* UMBILICAL (*n.*)

um·bil·i·cus (um bil′i kəs, um′bi li′kəs) *n., pl.* **-ci** (-sī′, -sī) [L.] *same as* NAVEL

um·bra (um′brə) *n., pl.* **-brae** (-brē), **-bras** [L.] **1.** shadow; shade **2.** the dark cone of shadow projecting from that side of a planet or satellite that is turned away completely from the sun —**um′bral** *adj.*

um·brage (um′brij) *n.* [see prec.] offense; resentment

um·brel·la (um brel′ə) *n.* [< L. *umbra,* shade] **1.** a screen or shade of cloth, plastic, etc. stretched over a folding frame, used for protection against the rain or sun **2.** any comprehensive, protective alliance, strategy, device, etc.

u·mi·ak, u·mi·ack (ōō′mē ak′) *n.* [Esk.] an open Eskimo boat made of skins stretched on a wooden frame

um·laut (ōōm′lout) *n.* [G. *um,* about + *laut,* a sound] *Linguis.* **1.** a vowel changed in sound by its assimilation to another vowel **2.** the mark (¨) placed over such a vowel, esp. in German

UMIAK

ump (ump) *n., vt., vi.* shortened form of UMPIRE

um·pire (um′pīr) *n.* [< MFr. *nomper,* uneven, hence a third person] **1.** a person chosen to give a decision in a dispute; arbiter **2.** an official who rules on the plays of a game, as in baseball —*vt., vi.* **-pired, -pir·ing** to act as umpire in or of

ump·teen (ump′tēn′) *adj.* [Slang] very many —**ump′-teenth′** *adj.*

un- *either of two prefixes meaning:* **1.** [OE. *un-*] not, lack of, the opposite of [*unhappy, untruth*] **2.** [OE. *un-, on-, and-*] the reverse or removal of [*unfasten, unchain*]; sometimes *un-* is merely intensive [*unloosen*] The list at the bottom of the following pages includes many of the more common compounds formed with *un-* (either prefix) that do not have special meanings

UN, U.N. United Nations

un·ac·count·a·ble (un′ə koun′tə b'l) *adj.* **1.** that cannot be explained or accounted for; strange **2.** not responsible —**un′ac·count′a·bly** *adv.*

un·ac·cus′tomed *adj.* **1.** not accustomed (*to*) **2.** uncommon; strange

un·ad·vised′ (-əd vīzd′) *adj.* **1.** without counsel or advice **2.** indiscreet; hasty —**un′ad·vis′ed·ly** (-vīz′id lē) *adv.*

un·af·fect′ed *adj.* **1.** not affected or influenced **2.** without affectation; sincere —**un′af·fect′ed·ly** *adv.*

un′-A·mer′i·can *adj.* not American; esp., thought of as not conforming to the principles, policies, etc. of the U.S.

u·nan·i·mous (yōō nan′ə məs) *adj.* [< L. *unus,* one + *animus,* mind] **1.** agreeing completely; without dissent **2.** showing or based on complete agreement —**u·na·nim·i·ty** (yōō′nə nim′ə tē) *n.* —**u·nan′i·mous·ly** *adv.*

un′ap·proach′a·ble *adj.* **1.** not to be approached; inaccessible; aloof **2.** having no equal; unmatched

un·armed′ *adj.* having no weapons

un′as·sail′a·ble *adj.* **1.** that cannot be successfully attacked **2.** that cannot be successfully denied

un′as·sum′ing *adj.* not assuming, pretentious, or forward; modest —**un′as·sum′ing·ly** *adv.*

un′at·tached′ *adj.* **1.** not attached **2.** not engaged or married

un′a·vail′ing *adj.* not availing; useless; futile

un′a·void′a·ble *adj.* that cannot be avoided; inevitable —**un′a·void′a·bly** *adv.*

un′a·ware′ *adj.* not aware or conscious —*adv. same as* UNAWARES

un′a·wares′ (-werz′) *adv.* **1.** without knowing or being aware **2.** unexpectedly; by surprise

un·backed′ *adj.* **1.** not backed, supported, etc. **2.** without a back or backing

un·bal′anced *adj.* **1.** not in balance **2.** not sane or normal in mind

un·bar′ *vt.* **-barred′, -bar′ring** to unbolt; unlock

un′be·com′ing *adj.* not suited to one's appearance, character, etc.

un′be·known′ *adj.* unknown; without one's knowledge (usually with *to*): also **un′be·knownst′** (-nōnst′)

un′be·lief′ *n.* lack of belief, esp. in religion —**un′be·liev′er** *n.*

un′be·liev′a·ble *adj.* beyond belief; astounding; incredible —**un′be·liev′a·bly** *adv.*

un·bend′ *vt., vi.* **-bent′** or **-bend′ed, -bend′ing 1.** to make or become less tense, less formal, etc. **2.** to make or become straight again

un·bend′ing *adj.* **1.** rigid; stiff **2.** firm; resolute **3.** aloof; austere —**un·bend′ing·ly** *adv.*

un·bid′den *adj.* **1.** not commanded **2.** uninvited

un·bind′ *vt.* **-bound′, -bind′ing 1.** to untie; unfasten **2.** to release from restraints

un·blush′ing *adj.* **1.** not blushing **2.** shameless

un·bolt′ *vt., vi.* to draw back the bolt or bolts of (a door, etc.); unbar; open

un·born′ *adj.* **1.** not born **2.** still within the mother's womb **3.** yet to come; future

un·bos′om (-booz′əm) *vt., vi.* to tell or reveal (one's feelings, secrets, etc.) —**unbosom oneself** to express (oneself) openly about feelings, etc.

un·bound′ed *adj.* **1.** without bounds or limits **2.** not restrained

un·bowed′ (-boud′) *adj.* **1.** not bowed or bent **2.** not yielding or giving in; unsubdued

un·bri′dled *adj.* **1.** having no bridle on, as a horse **2.** not controlled; unrestrained

un·bro′ken *adj.* **1.** whole; intact **2.** not tamed or subdued **3.** continuous; uninterrupted

un·bur′den *vt.* **1.** to free from a burden **2.** to relieve (oneself or one's mind) by disclosing (something hard to bear)

un·called′-for′ *adj.* **1.** not required **2.** unnecessary and out of place; impertinent

un·can′ny (un kan′ē) *adj.* **1.** mysterious in an eerie way; weird **2.** so remarkable, acute, etc. as to seem unnatural [*uncanny* vision]

un′cer·e·mo′ni·ous 1. not ceremonious; informal **2.** so curt or abrupt as to be discourteous —**un′cer·e·mo′ni·ous·ly** *adv.*

un·cer′tain *adj.* **1.** not surely or certainly known **2.** not sure or certain in knowledge; doubtful **3.** vague; not definite **4.** not dependable or reliable; liable to change **5.** not steady or constant; varying —**un·cer′tain·ly** *adv.* —**un·cer′tain·ty** *n., pl.* **-ties**

un·chris′tian *adj.* **1.** not Christian **2.** [Colloq.] outrageous; dreadful

un·cir′cum·cised′ *adj.* **1.** not circumcised; specif., not Jewish; gentile **2.** [Archaic] heathen

fat, āpe, cär; ten, ēven; is, bīte; gō, hôrn, tōōl, look; oil, out; up, fur; thin, *th*en; zh, leisure; ŋ, ring; ə for a in *ago*; ′ as in able (ā′b'l); ë, Fr. coeur; ö, Fr. feu; Fr. mo*n*; ü, Fr. duc; *r*, Fr. cri; **kh**, G. doch, ich. ‡ foreign; < derived from

un·civ·il *adj.* **1.** not civilized; barbarous **2.** not civil or courteous —**un·civ'il·ly** *adv.*

un·clad' *adj.* wearing no clothes; naked

un·cle (uŋ'k'l) *n.* [< L. *avunculus*] **1.** the brother of one's father or mother **2.** the husband of one's aunt

un·clean' *adj.* **1.** dirty; filthy; foul **2.** ceremonially impure **3.** morally impure; obscene —**un·clean'ness** *n.*

un·clean·ly (-klen'lē) *adj.* not cleanly; unclean; dirty —**un·clean'li·ness** *n.*

Uncle Sam [< abbrev. *U.S.*] [Colloq.] the U.S. (government or people), personified as a tall man with chin whiskers

un·cloak' *vt., vi.* **1.** to remove a cloak (from) **2.** to reveal; expose

un·clothe' *vt.* **-clothed'** or **-clad'**, **-cloth'ing** to strip of or as of clothes; uncover; divest

un·coil' *vt., vi.* to unwind

un·com'fort·a·ble *adj.* **1.** feeling discomfort **2.** causing discomfort **3.** ill at ease —**un·com'fort·a·bly** *adv.*

un·com·mit'ted *adj.* **1.** not committed, as a crime **2.** not pledged **3.** not having taken a position

un·com'mon *adj.* **1.** rare; not common or usual **2.** strange; remarkable; extraordinary —**un·com'mon·ly** *adv.*

un·com·mu'ni·ca'tive *adj.* not communicative; reserved; silent

un·com·pro·mis'ing *adj.* not yielding; firm; inflexible

un·con·cern' *n.* **1.** lack of interest; indifference **2.** lack of concern or worry

un·con·cerned' *adj.* not solicitous or anxious; not interested

un·con·di'tion·al *adj.* without conditions or stipulations; absolute —**un·con·di'tion·al·ly** *adv.*

un·con·scion·a·ble (un kän'shən ə b'l) *adj.* **1.** not guided or restrained by conscience; unscrupulous **2.** unreasonable, excessive, etc. —**un·con'scion·a·bly** *adv.*

un·con'scious *adj.* **1.** deprived of consciousness **2.** not aware (*of*) **3.** not intended by the person himself [*unconscious* humor] —**the unconscious** *Psychoanalysis* the sum of all memories, thoughts, etc. of which the individual is not conscious but which influence his behavior —**un·con'scious·ly** *adv.* —**un·con'scious·ness** *n.*

un·con·sti·tu'tion·al *adj.* not in accordance with the principles of a constitution —**un'con·sti·tu'tion·al'i·ty** (-shə nal'ə tē) *n.*

un·cork' *vt.* to pull the cork out of

un·count'ed *adj.* **1.** not counted **2.** too many to be counted; innumerable

un·cou'ple *vt.* **-pled**, **-pling** to unfasten (things coupled); disconnect

un·couth (un kōōth') *adj.* [OE. < *un-*, not + *cunnan*, know] **1.** awkward; ungainly **2.** uncultured; crude —**un·couth'ly** *adv.* —**un·couth'ness** *n.*

un·cov'er *vt.* **1.** to disclose **2.** to remove the cover from **3.** to remove the cap, hat, etc. from (the head) —*vi.* to bare the head, as in respect

unc·tion (uŋk'shən) *n.* [< L. *ungere*, anoint] **1.** the act of anointing, as in medical treatment or a religious ceremony **2.** the oil, ointment, etc. used for this **3.** anything that soothes or comforts **4.** *a*) a very earnest manner of speaking or behaving *b*) such a manner when it seems put on

unc·tu·ous (uŋk'choo wəs) *adj.* [< L. *ungere*, to anoint] **1.** oily or greasy **2.** characterized by a smug, smooth pretense of spiritual feeling or earnestness; too suave or oily in speech or manner —**unc'tu·ous·ly** *adv.* —**unc'tu·ous·ness** *n.*

un·cut' *adj.* not cut; specif., *a*) having untrimmed margins: said of the pages of a book *b*) not ground to shape: said of a gem *c*) not abridged

un·daunt'ed *adj.* not daunted; fearless, undiscouraged, etc.

un·de·cid'ed *adj.* **1.** not decided **2.** not having come to a decision —**un'de·cid'ed·ly** *adv.*

un·de·ni'a·ble *adj.* **1.** that cannot be denied **2.** unquestionably good —**un'de·ni'a·bly** *adv.*

un·der (un'dər) *prep.* [OE.] **1.** in, at, or to a position down from; below **2.** beneath the surface of [*under* water] **3.** below and to the other side of [drive *under* the bridge] **4.** covered or concealed by [a vest *under* a coat] **5.** lower in authority, position, value, etc. **6.** lower than the required degree of [*under* age] **7.** subject to the control, etc. of **8.** bound by [*under* oath] **9.** undergoing [*under* repair] **10.** with the disguise, etc. of [*under* an alias] **11.** in (the designated category) **12.** during the rule of [France *under* Louis XV] **13.** being the subject of [the question *under* discussion] **14.** because of [*under* the circumstances] **15.** authorized or attested by [*under* her signature] —*adv.* **1.** in or to a lower position; beneath **2.** beneath the surface, as of water **3.** so as to be covered or concealed **4.** less in amount, value, etc. —*adj.* lower in position, authority, amount, etc.

under- *a prefix meaning:* **1.** in, on, to, or from a lower place; beneath [*undershirt*] **2.** in a subordinate position [*undergraduate*] **3.** too little, not enough, below normal [*underdeveloped*]

un'der·a·chieve' *vi.* **-chieved'**, **-chiev'ing** to fail to do as well in school as might be expected from intelligence tests —**un'der·a·chiev'er** *n.*

un'der·age' *adj.* **1.** not of mature age **2.** below the age required by law

un'der·arm' *adj.* **1.** of, for, in, or used on the area under the arm, or the armpit **2.** *same as* UNDERHAND (sense 1) —*adv. same as* UNDERHAND (sense 1)

un'der·brush' *n.* small trees, shrubs, etc. that grow beneath large trees in woods or forests

un'der·car'riage *n.* a supporting frame or structure, as of an automobile

un'der·charge' *vt., vi.* **-charged'**, **-charg'ing** **1.** to charge too low a price (to) **2.** to provide with too little or low a charge —*n.* (un'dər chärj') an insufficient charge

un'der·class'man (-mən) *n., pl.* **-men** a freshman or sophomore in high school or college

un'der·clothes' *n.pl. same as* UNDERWEAR: also **un'der·cloth'ing** (-klōth'in)

un'der·coat' *n.* **1.** a tarlike coating applied to the underside of a car, etc. to retard rust, etc. **2.** a coat of paint, etc. applied before the final coat Also **un'der·coat'ing** —*vt.* to apply an undercoat to

un'der·cov'er *adj.* acting or carried out in secret

un'der·cur'rent *n.* **1.** a current flowing beneath the surface **2.** a hidden or underlying opinion, tendency, etc.

un'der·cut' *vt.* **-cut'**, **-cut'ting** **1.** to make a cut below or under **2.** to undersell or work for lower wages than **3.** *Sports* to strike (a ball) so as to impart backspin

un'der·de·vel'oped *adj.* inadequately developed, esp. industrially

un'der·dog' *n.* one that is underprivileged, unfavored, losing, etc.

un'der·done' *adj.* not cooked enough

un'der·em·ployed' *adj.* working at low-skilled, poorly paid jobs when one can do more skilled work

un'der·es'ti·mate' *vt., vi.* **-mat'ed**, **-mat'ing** to set too low an estimate on or for

un'der·foot' *adv., adj.* **1.** under the foot or feet **2.** in the way

un'der·gar'ment *n.* a piece of underwear

un'der·go' *vt.* **-went'**, **-gone'**, **-go'ing** to experience; endure; go through

uncivilized	uncomplimentary	uncontrollable	undated
unclaimed	uncompounded	uncontrolled	undebatable
unclassified	uncomprehending	unconventional	undecayed
uncleaned	unconcealed	unconvinced	undeceived
unclear	uncondensed	unconvincing	undecipherable
uncleared	unconfined	uncooked	undeclared
unclog	unconfirmed	uncooperative	undecorated
unclouded	unconnected	uncoordinated	undefeated
uncluttered	unconquerable	uncorrected	undefended
uncollectable	unconquered	uncorroborated	undefiled
uncollected	unconsecrated	uncorrupted	undefined
uncollectible	unconsolidated	uncrate	undeliverable
uncombed	unconstrained	uncritical	undemanding
uncombined	unconstricted	uncrowded	undemocratic
uncomplaining	unconsumed	uncultivated	undemonstrativ
uncompleted	uncontaminated	uncultured	undenied
uncomplicated	uncontested	undamaged	undependable

un′der·grad′u·ate *n.* a college student who does not yet have a degree

un′der·ground′ *adj.* **1.** occurring, working, etc. beneath the surface of the earth **2.** secret; undercover **3.** designating or of noncommercial newspapers, movies, etc. that are unconventional, radical, etc. —*adv.* **1.** beneath the surface of the earth **2.** in or into secrecy or hiding —*n.* (un′dər ground′) **1.** the region beneath the surface of the earth **2.** a secret movement organized to oppose the government or enemy forces of occupation **3.** [Brit.] a subway

underground railroad 1. a subway **2.** [*often* U- R-] in the U.S. before 1861, a system set up by abolitionists to help fugitive slaves escape from the South

un′der·growth′ *n.* underbrush

un′der·hand′ *adj.* **1.** done with the hand below the level of the elbow or shoulder **2.** *same as* UNDERHANDED —*adv.* **1.** with an underhand motion **2.** slyly; secretly; unfairly

un′der·hand′ed *adj.* secret, sly, deceitful, etc. —**un′der·hand′ed·ly** *adv.* —**un′der·hand′ed·ness** *n.*

un′der·lie′ *vt.* -lay′, -lain′, -ly′ing **1.** to lie beneath **2.** to form the basis or foundation of

un′der·line′ *vt.* -lined′, -lin′ing **1.** to draw a line beneath **2.** to stress

un·der·ling (un′dər liŋ) *n.* [OE.: see UNDER- & -LING] a person in a subordinate position; inferior: a disparaging term

un′der·ly′ing *adj.* **1.** lying under; placed beneath **2.** fundamental; basic

un′der·mine′ *vt.* -mined′, -min′ing **1.** to dig beneath, so as to form a tunnel or mine **2.** to wear away at the foundation **3.** to injure, weaken, etc., esp. in a stealthy way

un′der·most′ *adj., adv.* lowest in place, position, rank, etc.

un′der·neath′ *adv., prep.* under; below; beneath —*n.* the underpart

un′der·nour′ish *vt.* to provide with less food than is needed —**un′der·nour′ish·ment** *n.*

un′der·pants′ *n.pl.* an undergarment of long or short pants

un′der·part′ *n.* the lower part or side, as of an animal's body or an airplane's fuselage

un′der·pass′ *n.* a passage under something, as a road under a railway or highway

un′der·pin′ning (-pin′iŋ) *n.* **1.** a supporting structure, esp. one placed beneath a wall **2.** a support or prop **3.** [*pl.*] [Colloq.] the legs

un′der·play′ *vt., vi.* **1.** to act (a role) with restraint **2.** to make seem not too important

un′der·priv′i·leged *adj.* deprived of basic social rights and security through poverty, discrimination, etc. —**the underprivileged** underprivileged people

un′der·rate′ *vt.* -rat′ed, -rat′ing to rate, assess, or estimate too low

un′der·score′ *vt.* -scored′, -scor′ing *same as* UNDERLINE

un′der·sea′ *adj., adv.* beneath the surface of the sea: also **un′der·seas′** *adv.*

un′der·sec′re·tar′y *n., pl.* -ies an assistant secretary

un′der·sell′ *vt.* -sold′, -sell′ing to sell at a lower price than (another seller)

un′der·shirt′ *n.* a usually sleeveless undergarment worn under an outer shirt

un′der·shot′ *adj.* **1.** with the lower part jutting out past the upper [an *undershot* jaw] **2.** driven by water flowing along the lower part, as a water wheel

un′der·side′ *n.* the side or surface underneath

un′der·sign′ *vt.* to sign one's name at the end of (a letter, document, etc.) —**the undersigned** the person or persons undersigning

un′der·sized′ *adj.* smaller in size than is usual, average, or proper: also **un′der·size′**

UNDERSHOT WHEEL

un′der·slung′ *adj.* attached to the underside of the axles: said of an automobile frame

un′der·staffed′ *adj.* having fewer workers on the staff than are needed

un′der·stand′ *vt.* -stood′, -stand′ing [OE. *understandan*, stand under] **1.** to get or know the meaning of **2.** to gather or assume from what is heard, known, etc.; infer **3.** to take as meant; interpret **4.** to take as a fact **5.** to learn **6.** to know the nature, character, etc. of **7.** to be sympathetic with —*vi.* **1.** to have understanding, comprehension, etc. **2.** to be informed; believe —**un′der·stand′a·ble** *adj.* —**un′der·stand′a·bly** *adv.*

un′der·stand′ing *n.* **1.** comprehension **2.** the power to think, learn, judge, etc.; intelligence; sense **3.** an explanation or interpretation **4.** *a*) mutual comprehension, as of ideas, intentions, etc. *b*) an agreement, esp. one that settles differences —*adj.* that understands; sympathetic —**un′der·stand′ing·ly** *adv.*

un′der·state′ *vt.* -stat′ed, -stat′ing **1.** to state too weakly **2.** to state in a restrained style —**un′der·state′ment** *n.*

un′der·stud′y *n., pl.* -ies an actress or actor prepared to substitute for another —*vt., vi.* -ied, -y·ing **1.** to act as an understudy (to) **2.** to learn (a part) as an understudy

un′der·take′ *vt.* -took′, -tak′en, -tak′ing **1.** to take upon oneself (a task, etc.) **2.** to promise; guarantee

un′der·tak′er *n. earlier term for* FUNERAL DIRECTOR

un′der·tak′ing (*also* un′dər tā′kiŋ) *n.* **1.** something undertaken; task; enterprise **2.** a promise; guarantee

un′der·the·count′er *adj.* [Colloq.] done secretly in an unlawful way: also **un′der·the·ta′ble**

un′der·things′ *n.pl.* women's or girls' underwear

un′der·tone′ *n.* **1.** a low tone of voice **2.** a subdued color **3.** any underlying quality, factor, etc.

un′der·tow′ (-tō′) *n.* a current of water moving beneath the surface water and in a different direction

un′der·val′ue *vt.* -ued, -u·ing **1.** to value too low **2.** to esteem too lightly

un′der·wa′ter *adj.* **1.** being, done, etc. beneath the surface of the water **2.** used or for use under water

un′der·way′ *adj. Naut.* not at anchor or moored or aground

un′der·wear′ *n.* clothing worn under one's outer clothes, usually next to the skin, as undershirts

un′der·weight′ *adj.* below the normal or allowed weight —*n.* less weight than is needed, desired, etc.

un′der·went′ *pt. of* UNDERGO

un′der·world′ *n.* **1.** Hades; hell **2.** the criminal members of society regarded as a group

un′der·write′ *vt.* -wrote′, -writ′ten, -writ′ing **1.** to agree to market (an issue of securities), guaranteeing to buy any part remaining unsubscribed **2.** to agree to finance (an undertaking, etc.) **3.** to sign one's name to (an insurance policy), thus assuming liability for specified loss or damage **4.** to insure —**un′der·writ′er** *n.*

un·dies (un′dēz) *n.pl.* [Colloq.] women's or girls' underwear

un·do′ *vt.* -did′, -done′, -do′ing **1.** to untie, open, etc. **2.** to do away with; annul **3.** to ruin or destroy

un·do′ing *n.* **1.** an annulling; reversal **2.** ruin or the cause of ruin

un·done′ *adj.* **1.** not done; not performed, accomplished, etc. **2.** ruined

un·doubt′ed *adj.* not doubted or called into question; certain —**un·doubt′ed·ly** *adv.*

un·dress′ *vt.* to take off the clothing of —*vi.* to take off one's clothing —*n.* (*un′dres′*) ordinary or informal dress

un·due′ *adj.* **1.** not suitable; improper **2.** too much; excessive

un·du·lant (un′jŏŏ lənt, -dyŏŏ-) *adj.* undulating

undulant fever a persistent, infectious disease transmitted to man from domestic animals or their products, and marked by recurrent fever, sweating, and pains in the joints

fat, ăpe, cär; ten, ēven; is, bīte; gō, hôrn, tōol, look; oil, out; up, fur; thin, *th*en; zh, leisure; ŋ, ring; ə for *a* in *ago*; ′ as in *able* (ā′b'l); ë, Fr. coeur; ö, Fr. feu; Fr. mon; ü, Fr. duc; *r*, Fr. cri; kh, G. doch, ich. ‡ foreign; < derived from

un′du·late′ (-lāt′) *vi., vt.* **-lat′ed, -lat′ing** [< L. *unda,* a wave] **1.** to move or cause to move in waves **2.** to have or cause to have a wavy form, surface, etc. —**un′du·la·to′ry** *adj.*

un′du·la′tion *n.* **1.** an undulating or undulating motion **2.** a wavy, curving form or outline **3.** pulsation **4.** *Physics* a wavelike motion, as of sound; vibration

un·du·ly (un dōō′lē, -dyōō′-) *adv.* beyond what is proper or right; excessively

un·dy′ing *adj.* immortal; eternal

un·earth′ *vt.* **1.** to dig up from out of the earth **2.** to bring to light; discover or disclose

un·earth′ly *adj.* **1.** supernatural **2.** weird; mysterious **3.** [Colloq.] fantastic, outlandish, etc. —**un·earth′li·ness** *n.*

un·eas′y *adj.* **-i·er, -i·est** **1.** having, showing, or allowing no ease of body or mind; uncomfortable **2.** awkward; constrained **3.** worried; anxious —**un·eas′i·ly** *adv.* —**un·eas′i·ness** *n.*

un′em·ploy′a·ble *adj.* that cannot be employed, as because of age, physical or mental deficiency, etc. —*n.* an unemployable person

un′em·ployed′ *adj.* **1.** not employed; without work **2.** not being used —**the unemployed** people who are out of work —**un′em·ploy′ment** *n.*

un·e′qual *adj.* **1.** not equal, as in size, strength, ability, value, etc. **2.** not balanced **3.** not even, regular, etc.; variable **4.** not adequate (*to*) —*n.* one that is unequal —**un·e′qual·ly** *adv.*

un·e′qualed, un·e′qualled *adj.* not equaled; unmatched; unrivaled; supreme

un′e·quiv′o·cal *adj.* not equivocal; not ambiguous; plain; clear —**un′e·quiv′o·cal·ly** *adv.*

un·err′ing *adj.* **1.** free from error **2.** not missing or failing; sure; exact —**un·err′ing·ly** *adv.*

UNESCO (yōō nes′kō) United Nations Educational, Scientific, and Cultural Organization

un·e′ven *adj.* **1.** not even; not level, smooth, etc.; irregular **2.** unequal **3.** varying **4.** not equally matched **5.** *Math.* odd —**un·e′ven·ly** *adv.* —**un·e′ven·ness** *n.*

un′ex·am′pled *adj.* with nothing like it before; with no other example; unprecedented

un′ex·cep′tion·a·ble *adj.* not exceptionable; not warranting even the slightest criticism —**un′ex·cep′tion·a·bly** *adv.*

un′ex·pect′ed *adj.* not expected; unforeseen —**un′ex·pect′ed·ly** *adv.* —**un′ex·pect′ed·ness** *n.*

un·fail′ing *adj.* **1.** not failing **2.** never ceasing or falling short; inexhaustible **3.** always reliable; certain —**un·fail′ing·ly** *adv.*

un·faith′ful *adj.* **1.** failing to stay loyal or to keep a vow, promise, etc. **2.** not true, accurate, etc. **3.** adulterous —**un·faith′ful·ly** *adv.* —**un·faith′ful·ness** *n.*

un·fa·mil′iar *adj.* **1.** not well-known; strange **2.** not acquainted (*with*) —**un′fa·mil′i·ar′i·ty** (-yar′ə tē, -ē ar′-) *n.* —**un′fa·mil′iar·ly** *adv.*

un·feel′ing *adj.* **1.** without feeling **2.** hardhearted; cruel —**un·feel′ing·ly** *adv.*

un·feigned′ (-fānd′) *adj.* genuine; sincere

un·fin′ished *adj.* **1.** not finished or completed **2.** having no finish, or final coat. as of paint

un·fit′ *adj.* **1.** not meeting requirements; not suitable **2.** not physically or mentally fit —*vt.* **-fit′ted, -fit′ting** to make unfit —**un·fit′ness** *n.*

un·flap′pa·ble (-flap′ə b'l) *adj.* [see FLAP, *n.* 4] [Colloq.] not easily excited or upset; calm

un·flinch′ing *adj.* steadfast; firm —**un·flinch′ing·ly** *adv.*

un·fold′ *vt.* **1.** to open and spread out (something folded) **2.** to lay open to view; reveal, disclose, explain, etc. —*vi.* **1.** to become unfolded **2.** to develop fully

un·for′tu·nate *adj.* **1.** having or bringing bad luck; unlucky **2.** not suitable —*n.* an unfortunate person —**un·for′tu·nate·ly** *adv.*

un·found′ed *adj.* **1.** not founded on fact or truth **2.** not established

un·friend′ly *adj.* **1.** not friendly or kind **2.** not favorable —**un·friend′li·ness** *n.*

un·frock′ (-fräk′) *vt.* to deprive of the rank of priest or minister

un·furl′ *vt., vi.* to unfold from a furled state

un·gain·ly (un gān′lē) *adj.* [< ME. < *un-,* not + ON. *gegn,* ready] awkward; clumsy —**un·gain′li·ness** *n.*

un·god′ly *adj.* **1.** not godly or religious **2.** sinful; wicked **3.** [Colloq.] outrageous —**un·god′li·ness** *n.*

un·gov′ern·a·ble *adj.* that cannot be governed or controlled; unruly

un·gra′cious *adj.* **1.** rude; impolite **2.** unpleasant; unattractive —**un·gra′cious·ly** *adv.* —**un·gra′cious·ness** *n.*

un·guard′ed *adj.* **1.** unprotected **2.** without guile **3.** careless; imprudent —**un·guard′ed·ly** *adv.*

un·guent (uŋ′gwənt) *n.* [< L. *unguere,* anoint] a salve or ointment

un·gu·late (uŋ′gyoo lit, -lāt′) *adj.* [< L. *unguis,* a hoof] having hoofs —*n.* a mammal having hoofs

un·hal′lowed *adj.* **1.** not hallowed or consecrated; unholy **2.** wicked; profane

un·hand′ *vt.* to loose or release from the hand or hands or one's grasp; let go of

un·hap′py *adj.* **-pi·er, -pi·est** **1.** unfortunate **2.** sad; wretched **3.** not suitable —**un·hap′pi·ly** *adv.* —**un·hap′pi·ness** *n.*

un·health′y *adj.* **-i·er, -i·est** **1.** sickly; not well **2.** harmful to health **3.** harmful to morals **4.** dangerous —**un·health′i·ness** *n.*

un·heard′ *adj.* **1.** not perceived by the ear **2.** not given a hearing

un·heard′-of′ *adj.* **1.** not heard of before; unprecedented **2.** unacceptable or outrageous

un·hinge′ *vt.* **-hinged′, -hing′ing** **1.** to remove from the hinges **2.** to dislodge **3.** to unbalance (the mind)

un′his·tor′ic *adj.* not historic or historical; specif., *Linguis.* not having a historical basis, as the *b* in *thumb:* also **un′his·tor′i·cal**

un·ho′ly *adj.* **-li·er, -li·est** **1.** not sacred, hallowed, etc. **2.** wicked; profane **3.** [Colloq.] outrageous; dreadful

un·hook′ *vt.* **1.** to remove or loosen from a hook **2.** to unfasten the hook or hooks of

un·horse′ *vt.* **-horsed′, -hors′ing** to throw (a rider) from a horse

uni- [< L. *unus,* one] *a combining form meaning* having or consisting of one only

undutiful	unexciting	unfiltered	ungrounded
undyed	unexercised	unflagging	ungrudging
unearned	unexpired	unflattering	unguided
uneaten	unexplainable	unflavored	unhampered
uneconomical	unexplained	unforeseeable	unhandy
uneducated	unexploded	unforeseen	unhardened
unemotional	unexplored	unforgetful	unharmed
unenclosed	unexposed	unforgettable	unharmful
unencumbered	unexpressed	unforgivable	unharness
unending	unexpurgated	unforgiven	unharvested
unendurable	unextinguished	unforgiving	unhealed
unenforceable	unfaded	unforgotten	unhealthful
unenjoyable	unfading	unformed	unheated
unenlightened	unfair	unformulated	unheeded
unenterprising	unfaltering	unforsaken	unheeding
unenthusiastic	unfashionable	unfortified	unhelpful
unenviable	unfasten	unfrequented	unheralded
unequipped	unfathomable	unfruitful	unheroic
unescorted	unfavorable	unfulfilled	unhesitating
unestablished	unfearing	unfurnished	unhindered
unethical	unfed	ungenerous	unhitch
uneventful	unfelt	ungentlemanly	unhoped-for
unexaggerated	unfenced	ungoverned	unhurried
unexamined	unfertilized	ungrammatical	unhurt
unexcelled	unfettered	ungrateful	unhygienic
unexceptional	unfilled	ungratified	unhyphenated

u·ni·cam·er·al (yōō'nə kam'ər əl) *adj.* [< UNI- + LL. *camera,* chamber] of or having a single legislative chamber

UNICEF (yōō'nə sef') United Nations International Children's Emergency Fund

u·ni·cel·lu·lar (yōō'nə sel'yoo lər) *adj.* having or consisting of a single cell

u·ni·corn (yōō'nə kôrn') *n.* [< L. *unus,* one + *cornu,* horn] a mythical horselike animal with a single horn in its forehead

u·ni·cy·cle (yōō'nə sī'k'l) *n.* a riding device with only one wheel, which is straddled by the rider

u·ni·fi·ca·tion (yōō'nə fi kā'shən) *n.* the act of unifying or the state of being unified

u·ni·form (yōō'nə fôrm') *adj.* [< L. *unus,* one + *-formis,* -FORM] **1.** not varying in form, rate, degree, etc. **2.** like others of the same class —*n.* the distinctive clothes of a particular group, as soldiers —*vt.* to supply with a uniform —**u'ni·form'ly** *adv.*

UNICORN

u'ni·form'i·ty *n., pl.* **-ties** state, quality, or instance of being uniform

u·ni·fy (yōō'nə fī') *vt., vi.* **-fied', -fy'ing** [see UNI- & -FY] to become or make united; consolidate —**u'ni·fi'a·ble** *adj.*

u·ni·lat·er·al (yōō'nə lat'ər əl) *adj.* **1.** of, occurring on, or affecting one side only **2.** involving one only of several parties; not reciprocal

un·im·peach·a·ble (un'im pēch'ə b'l) *adj.* that cannot be doubted, questioned, or discredited; irreproachable — **un'im·peach'a·bly** *adv.*

un·ion (yōōn'yən) *n.* [< L. *unus,* one] **1.** a uniting or being united; combination **2.** a grouping together of nations, etc. for some specific purpose **3.** marriage **4.** something united **5.** *short for* LABOR UNION **6.** a design symbolizing political union, used as in a flag **7.** a device for joining together parts; esp., a coupling for linking the ends of pipes **8.** *Math.* a set containing all the elements of two or more given sets, with no element listed more than once —the Union the United States of America

un'ion·ism *n.* **1.** the principle of union **2.** support of this principle or of a specified union **3.** the system or principles of labor unions —**un'ion·ist** *n.*

un'ion·ize' *vt., vi.* **-ized', -iz'ing** to organize into a labor union —**un'ion·i·za'tion** *n.*

union jack 1. a flag, esp. a national flag, consisting only of a union **2.** [U- J-] the flag of the United Kingdom

Union of Soviet Socialist Republics country in E Europe & N Asia, consisting of 15 federated republics: 8,603,000 sq. mi.; pop. 242,768,000; cap. Moscow

union shop a business, etc. operating under a contract with a labor union that requires new workers to join the union

union suit a suit of men's or boys' underwear uniting shirt and drawers in a single garment

u·nique (yōō nēk') *adj.* [Fr. < L. *unicus,* single] **1.** one and only; sole **2.** having no like or equal **3.** very unusual —**u·nique'ly** *adv.* —**u·nique'ness** *n.*

u·ni·sex (yōō'nə seks') *adj.* [Colloq.] not differentiated for the sexes, as a style of clothing

u·ni·son (yōō'nə sən, -zən) *n.* [< L. *unus,* one + *sonus,* a sound] **1.** identity of musical pitch, as of two or more voices or tones **2.** agreement; concord —**in unison** with all the voices or instruments performing the same part

u·nit (yōō'nit) *n.* [< UNITY] **1.** the smallest whole number; one **2.** a standard basic quantity, measure, etc. **3.** a single person or group, esp. as a part of a whole **4.** a single, distinct part, esp. one used for a specific purpose

U·ni·tar·i·an (yōō'nə ter'ē ən) *n.* a member of a Christian sect holding that God exists as one being —*adj.* of Unitarians or their doctrines —**U'ni·tar'i·an·ism** *n.*

u·ni·tar·y (yōō'nə ter'ē) *adj.* **1.** of a unit or units **2.** of, based on, or characterized by unity **3.** having the nature of or used as a unit

u·nite (yoo nīt') *vt., vi.* **-nit'ed, -nit'ing** [< L. *unus,* one] **1.** to put or join together so as to make one; combine **2.** to bring or come together in common cause, action, etc.

United Arab Emirates country consisting of seven Arab sheikdoms in E Arabia, on the Persian Gulf: 32,300 sq. mi.; pop. 179,000

United Arab Republic *former name* (1961-71) *of* EGYPT

United Kingdom country in W Europe, consisting of Great Britain & Northern Ireland: 94,217 sq. mi.; pop. 55,730,000; cap. London

United Nations an international organization of nations for world peace and security: formed in 1945 and having, in 1979, 150 members: headquarters, New York City

United States of America country in N. America between Canada and Mexico, together with Alaska & Hawaii: 3,615,211 sq. mi.; pop. 208,558,000; cap. Washington

u·ni·tive (yōō'nə tiv) *adj.* **1.** having unity **2.** tending to unite

u·nit·ize (yōō'nə tīz') *vt.* **-ized', -iz'ing** to make into a single unit

unit pricing a system of showing prices in terms of standard units such as the ounce and pint

u·ni·ty (yōō'nə tē) *n., pl.* **-ties** [< L. *unus,* one] **1.** the state of being united; oneness **2.** a single, separate thing **3.** harmony; agreement **4.** a complex that is a union of related parts **5.** a harmonious, unified arrangement of parts in an artistic work **6.** constancy or continuity of purpose, action, etc. **7.** *Math.* any quantity, magnitude, etc. identified as a unit, or 1

Univ. University

u·ni·va·lent (yōō'nə vā'lənt) *adj. Chem.* **1.** having one valence **2.** having a valence of one

u·ni·valve (yōō'nə valv') *n.* **1.** a mollusk having a one-piece shell, as a snail **2.** such a one-piece shell

u·ni·ver·sal (yōō'nə vur's'l) *adj.* **1.** of the universe; occurring or present everywhere **2.** of, for, or including all or the whole; unlimited **3.** that can be used for all kinds, sizes, etc. or by all people **4.** *Logic* predicating something of every member of a specified class —*n.* **1.** *short for* UNIVERSAL JOINT **2.** *Logic* a universal proposition —**u'ni·ver·sal'i·ty** (-vər sal'ə tē) *n.*

u'ni·ver'sal·ize' (-vur'sə līz') *vt.* **-ized', -iz'ing** to make universal

universal joint (or **coupling**) a joint or coupling that permits a swing of limited angle in any direction, esp. one used to transmit rotary motion from one shaft to another not in line with it

u'ni·ver'sal·ly *adv.* **1.** in every instance **2.** in every part or place

universal suffrage suffrage for all adult citizens

u·ni·verse (yōō'nə vurs') *n.* [< L. *unus,* one + *vertere,* to turn] **1.** the totality of all things that exist; the cosmos **2.** the world

u·ni·ver·si·ty (yōō'nə vur'sə tē) *n., pl.* **-ties** [see prec.] an educational institution of the highest level, variously composed of undergraduate colleges and graduate and professional schools

UNIVERSAL JOINT

un·just (un just') *adj.* not just or right; unfair —**un·just'ly** *adv.* —**un·just'ness** *n.*

un·kempt (-kempt') *adj.* [UN- + *kempt* < dial. *kemben,* to comb] **1.** not combed **2.** not tidy or neat; slovenly — **un·kempt'ness** *n.*

un·kind' *adj.* not kind, sympathetic, or considerate; cruel —**un·kind'ly** *adv.* —**un·kind'ness** *n.*

un·known' *adj.* **1.** not known; unfamiliar; strange **2.** not discovered, identified, etc. —*n.* an unknown person, thing, or quantity

unidentified	unimpressive	uninjured	uninteresting
unilluminated	unimproved	uninspired	uninterrupted
unillustrated	unincorporated	uninstructed	unintimidated
unimaginable	unindexed	uninsurable	uninvited
unimaginative	uninflected	uninsured	uninviting
unimpaired	uninfluenced	unintelligent	uninvolved
unimpeded	uninformed	unintelligible	unissued
unimportant	uninhabited	unintended	unjustifiable
unimposing	uninhibited	unintentional	unknot
unimpressed	uninitiated	uninterested	unknowing

un·lace' *vt.* -laced', -lac'ing to undo the laces of

un·latch' *vt., vi.* to open by release of a latch

un·law'ful *adj.* 1. against the law; illegal 2. immoral —un·law'ful·ly *adv.* —un·law'ful·ness *n.*

un·lead'ed (-led'id) *adj.* not mixed with tetraethyl lead: said of gasoline

un·learn' *vt., vi.* to forget (something learned) by a conscious effort, as in retraining

un·learn'ed (-lur'nid) *adj.* 1. not educated; ignorant 2. (-lurnd') known or acquired without conscious study

un·leash' *vt.* to release from or as from a leash

un·less (ən les') *conj.* [earlier *on lesse that,* at less than] in any case other than; except if

un·let'tered *adj.* 1. uneducated; illiterate 2. not marked with letters

un·like' *adj.* not alike; different —*prep.* not like; different from —un·like'ness *n.*

un·like'ly *adj.* 1. not likely; improbable 2. not likely to succeed —un·like'li·hood' *n.*

un·lim·ber (un lim'bər) *vt., vi.* to get ready for use or action

un·lim'it·ed *adj.* 1. without limits or restrictions 2. vast; illimitable

un·load' *vt., vi.* 1. to remove (a load, cargo, etc.) 2. to take a load from 3. to tell (one's troubles, etc.) without restraint 4. to relieve of something that troubles, etc. 5. to remove the charge from (a gun) 6. to get rid of

un·lock' *vt.* 1. to open (a lock) 2. to open the lock of (a door, etc.) 3. to let loose; release 4. to reveal —*vi.* to get unlocked

un·looked'-for' *adj.* not expected or foreseen

un·loose' *vt.* -loosed', -loos'ing to set loose; loosen, release, etc.: also un·loos'en

un·luck'y *adj.* -i·er, -i·est having or bringing bad luck; unfortunate —un·luck'i·ly *adv.*

un·make' *vt.* -made', -mak'ing 1. to cause to be as before; undo 2. to ruin; destroy 3. to depose from a position, authority, etc.

un·man' *vt.* -manned', -man'ning to deprive of manly courage, nerve, etc. —un·man'ly *adj.*

un·manned' *adj.* without people aboard and operating by automatic or remote control

un·man'ner·ly *adj.* having or showing poor manners; rude —*adv.* rudely —un·man'ner·li·ness *n.*

un·mask' *vt., vi.* 1. to remove a mask or disguise (from) 2. to show or appear in true character

un·mean'ing *adj.* lacking in meaning or sense

un·men'tion·a·ble *adj.* not fit to be mentioned; not nice to talk about —*n.* [*pl.*] unmentionable things; specif., underwear: a humorous usage

un·mer'ci·ful *adj.* 1. having or showing no mercy; cruel; pitiless 2. excessive —un·mer'ci·ful·ly *adv.*

un'mis·tak'a·ble *adj.* that cannot be mistaken or misinterpreted; clear —un'mis·tak'a·bly *adv.*

un·mit'i·gat'ed *adj.* 1. not lessened or eased 2. out-and-out; absolute

un·mor'al *adj. var. of* AMORAL

un·muz'zle *vt.* -zled, -zling 1. to free (a dog, etc.) from a muzzle 2. to free from restraint or censorship

un·nat'u·ral *adj.* 1. contrary to nature; abnormal 2. artificial 3. abnormally cruel —un·nat'u·ral·ly *adv.* —un·nat'u·ral·ness *n.*

un·nec'es·sar'y *adj.* not necessary; needless —un·nec'es·sar'i·ly *adv.*

un·nerve' *vt.* -nerved', -nerv'ing 1. to cause to lose one's courage, etc. 2. to make nervous

un·num'bered *adj.* 1. not counted 2. *same as* INNUMERABLE 3. having no identifying number

un·oc'cu·pied *adj.* 1. having no occupant; vacant 2. at leisure; idle

un·or'gan·ized' *adj.* 1. not following any regular order or system 2. not belonging to a labor union

un·pack' *vt., vi.* 1. to remove (the contents of a trunk, package, etc.) 2. to take things out of (a trunk, etc.)

un·par'al·leled' *adj.* that has no parallel, equal, or counterpart

un·pin' *vt.* -pinned', -pin'ning to unfasten by removing a pin or pins from

un·pleas'ant *adj.* not pleasant; offensive; disagreeable —un·pleas'ant·ly *adv.* —un·pleas'ant·ness *n.*

un·plumbed' *adj.* 1. not measured with a plumb 2. not fully understood

un·pop'u·lar *adj.* not liked by the public or the majority —un'pop·u·lar'i·ty (-lar'ə tē) *n.*

un·prac'ticed *adj.* 1. not habitually or repeatedly done 2. not skilled or experienced; inexpert

un·prec'e·dent'ed *adj.* having no precedent or parallel; unheard-of; novel

un·prin'ci·pled (-p'ld) *adj.* lacking moral principles; unscrupulous

un·print'a·ble *adj.* not fit to be printed, as because of obscenity

un'pro·fes'sion·al *adj.* 1. violating the ethical code of a given profession 2. not of or belonging to a profession —un'pro·fes'sion·al·ly *adv.*

un·qual'i·fied' *adj.* 1. lacking the necessary qualifications 2. not limited or modified; absolute

un·ques'tion·a·ble *adj.* not to be questioned, doubted, or disputed; certain —un·ques'tion·a·bly *adv.*

un·qui'et *adj.* not quiet; restless, disturbed, uneasy, anxious, etc.

un'quote' *interj.* I end the quotation: used in speech after a quotation

un·rav'el *vt.* -eled or -elled, -el·ing or -el·ling 1. to separate the threads of (something woven, tangled, etc.) 2. to make clear; solve —*vi.* to become unraveled

un·read' (-red') *adj.* 1. not read, as a book 2. having read little or nothing 3. unlearned (*in*)

un·re'al *adj.* not real; imaginary, false, etc. —un're·al'i·ty (-rē al'ə tē) *n., pl.* -ties

un're·al·is'tic *adj.* not realistic; impractical

un·rea'son·a·ble *adj.* 1. not reasonable or rational 2. excessive; immoderate —un·rea'son·a·ble·ness *n.* —un·rea'son·a·bly *adv.*

unlabeled	unmoved	unorthodox	unpolluted
unladylike	unmoving	unostentatious	unpredictable
unlamented	unmusical	unpaid	unprejudiced
unlaundered	unnamed	unpaid-for	unpremeditated
unleased	unnaturalized	unpainted	unprepared
unleavened	unnavigable	unpalatable	unpresentable
unlicensed	unnavigated	unpardonable	unpressed
unlifelike	unneeded	unpardoned	unpretentious
unlighted	unneighborly	unpasteurized	unpreventable
unlined	unnoted	unpatented	unprivileged
unlisted	unnoticeable	unpatriotic	unprocessed
unlit	unnoticed	unpaved	unprofitable
unlocated	unobjectionable	unperceived	unpromising
unloved	unobliging	unperfected	unpronounceable
unlovely	unobscured	unperformed	unpronounced
unmanageable	unobservant	unperplexed	unprotected
unmarked	unobserved	unpersuaded	unproved
unmarketable	unobserving	unperturbed	unproven
unmarred	unobstructed	unphilosophical	unprovoked
unmarried	unobtainable	unpitying	unpruned
unmastered	unobtrusive	unplaced	unpublished
unmatched	unoffending	unplanned	unpunished
unmelodious	unoffensive	unplanted	unquenchable
unmended	unofficial	unpleasing	unquestioned
unmindful	unopen	unploughed	unquestioning
unmolested	unopened	unplowed	unreadable
unmotivated	unopposed	unplug	unready
unmounted	unoppressed	unpoetic	unrealized
unmourned	unoriginal	unpolished	unreasoned

un·rea'son·ing *adj.* lacking reason or judgment; irrational —**un·rea'son·ing·ly** *adv.*

un're·con·struct'ed *adj.* 1. not reconstructed 2. holding to an earlier, outmoded practice or attitude and not reconciled to change

un·reel' *vt., vi.* to unwind as from a reel

un're·gen'er·ate *adj.* 1. not spiritually reborn 2. stubbornly defiant

un're·lent'ing *adj.* 1. inflexible; relentless 2. without mercy or compassion 3. not relaxing, as in effort, speed, etc.

un're·mit'ting *adj.* not stopping, relaxing, etc.; incessant; persistent

un're·served' *adj.* not reserved; specif., *a*) frank; open *b*) unlimited *c*) not set aside for advance sale, as seats —**un're·serv'ed·ly** (-zur'vid lē) *adv.*

un·rest' *n.* a disturbed state; restlessness; specif., a state of discontent close to revolt

un·right'eous *adj.* 1. wicked; sinful 2. unjust

un·ripe' *adj.* 1. not ripe or mature; green 2. not yet fully developed [*unripe* plans]

un·ri'valed, un·ri'valled *adj.* having no rival, equal, or competitor

un·roll' *vt.* 1. to open or extend (something rolled up) 2. to present to view; display —*vi.* to become unrolled

un·ruf'fled *adj.* not ruffled or disturbed; calm; smooth; serene

un·rul·y (un roo'lē) *adj.* -i·er, -i·est hard to control, restrain, or keep in order; disobedient, disorderly, etc. —**un·rul'i·ness** *n.*

un·sad'dle *vt.* -dled, -dling 1. to take the saddle off (a horse, etc.) 2. to throw from the saddle; unhorse

un·said' *pt. & pp.* of UNSAY —*adj.* not expressed

un·sat'u·rat'ed (-sach'ə rāt'id) *adj.* having a double or triple bond between carbon atoms in the molecule

un·sa'vor·y *adj.* 1. unpleasant to taste or smell 2. morally offensive —**un·sa'vor·i·ness** *n.*

un·say' *vt.* -said', -say'ing to take back or retract (what has been said)

un·scathed' (-skāthd') *adj.* [< *un-* + ON. *skathi,* harm] not hurt; unharmed

un·scram'ble *vt.* -bled, -bling to cause to be no longer scrambled, disordered, or unintelligible

un·screw' *vt.* 1. to remove a screw or screws from 2. to detach or loosen by doing this, or by turning

un·scru'pu·lous *adj.* heedless of what is right, just, etc.; unprincipled —**un·scru'pu·lous·ly** *adv.*

un·seal' *vt.* to break the seal of; open

un·sea'son·a·ble *adj.* 1. not usual for the season 2. coming at the wrong time; inopportune

un·seat' *vt.* 1. to throw or dislodge from a seat, saddle, etc. 2. to remove from office

un·seem'ly *adj.* not seemly; not proper; unbecoming —*adv.* unbecomingly —**un·seem'li·ness** *n.*

un·set'tle *vt.* -tled, -tling to make unsettled, insecure, etc. —*vi.* to become unsettled

un·set'tled *adj.* 1. not in order, not stable, etc. 2. not paid, etc., as a debt 3. having no settlers

un·sex' *vt.* to deprive of the qualities considered characteristic of one's sex

un·shack'le *vt.* -led, -ling 1. to loosen or remove the shackles from 2. to free

un·sheathe' (-shēth') *vt.* -sheathed', -sheath'ing to remove (a sword, knife, etc.) from a sheath

un·sight'ly *adj.* not pleasant to look at; ugly —**un·sight'li·ness** *n.*

un·skilled' *adj.* having or requiring no special skill or training

un·skill'ful *adj.* having little or no skill; awkward; clumsy —**un·skill'ful·ly** *adv.* —**un·skill'ful·ness** *n.*

un·snap' *vt.* -snapped', -snap'ping to undo the snaps of, so as to detach

un·snarl' *vt.* to untangle —*vi.* to become untangled

un·so'cia·ble *adj.* 1. avoiding others; not sociable 2. not conducive to sociability

un'so·phis'ti·cat'ed *adj.* not sophisticated; artless, simple, etc. —**un'so·phis'ti·ca'tion** *n.*

un·sound' *adj.* not sound or free from defect; specif., *a*) not normal or healthy *b*) not safe or secure *c*) not accurate, sensible, etc. *d*) light: said of sleep —**un·sound'ly** *adv.* —**un·sound'ness** *n.*

un·spar'ing *adj.* 1. not sparing; lavish 2. not merciful; severe —**un·spar'ing·ly** *adv.*

un·speak'a·ble *adj.* 1. that cannot be spoken 2. marvelous beyond expression 3. indescribably bad, evil, etc. —**un·speak'a·bly** *adv.*

un·sta'ble *adj.* not stable; specif., *a*) easily upset *b*) changeable *c*) unreliable; fickle *d*) *Chem.* readily decomposing —**un·sta'bly** *adv.*

un·stead'y *adj.* not steady; specif., *a*) not firm or stable *b*) changeable or erratic —**un·stead'i·ly** *adv.* —**un·stead'i·ness** *n.*

un·stop' *vt.* -stopped', -stop'ping 1. to remove the stopper from 2. to clear (an obstructed pipe, etc.)

un·strap' *vt.* -strapped', -strap'ping to loosen or remove the strap or straps of

unreceptive	unresentful	unsaved	unshut
unreclaimed	unresigned	unscarred	unsifted
unrecognizable	unresisted	unscented	unsigned
unrecognized	unresisting	unscheduled	unsilenced
unrecommended	unresolved	unscholarly	unsinkable
unrecompensed	unresponsive	unscientific	unslaked
unreconcilable	unrested	unscraped	unsleeping
unreconciled	unrestrainable	unscratched	unsliced
unrecorded	unrestricted	unscreened	unsmiling
unredeemed	unretentive	unseasoned	unsmoked
unrefined	unreturned	unseaworthy	unsoftened
unrefreshed	unrevealed	unseconded	unsoiled
unregistered	unrevenged	unsecured	unsold
unregulated	unrevised	unseeded	unsolicited
unrehearsed	unrevoked	unseeing	unsolved
unrelated	unrewarded	unseen	unsorted
unrelaxed	unrewarding	unseized	unsought
unreliable	unrhymed	unselected	unsounded
unrelieved	unrhythmic	unselfish	unspecified
unremembered	unrhythmical	unsent	unspectacular
unremoved	unrightful	unsentimental	unspent
unremunerative	unromantic	unserved	unspilled
unrented	unrounded	unserviceable	unspoiled
unrepaid	unruled	unset	unspoken
unrepaired	unsafe	unsevered	unsportsmanlike
unrepealed	unsaintly	unshaded	unsprung
unrepentant	unsalable	unshadowed	unstained
unrepenting	unsalaried	unshakable	unstamped
unreplenished	unsaleable	unshaken	unstarched
unreported	unsalted	unshed	unstated
unrepresentative	unsanctified	unsheltered	unstatesmanlike
unrepresented	unsanctioned	unshod	unsterilized
unrepressed	unsanitary	unshorn	unstinted
unrequested	unsatisfactory	unshrinking	unstrained
unrequited	unsatisfied	unshrunk	unstressed

un·struc′tured *adj.* not formally organized; loose, free, open, etc.

un·strung′ *adj.* **1.** nervous, upset, etc. **2.** having the string(s) loosened or detached, as a bow

un·stud′ied *adj.* **1.** not got by study or conscious effort **2.** spontaneous; natural **3.** not having studied; unlearned (*in*)

un·sub·stan′tial *adj.* **1.** having no material substance **2.** flimsy; light **3.** unreal; visionary

un·sung′ *adj.* **1.** not sung **2.** not honored or celebrated, as in song or poetry

un·tan′gle *vt.* **-gled, -gling 1.** to free from a snarl or tangle **2.** to free from confusion; put in order —*vi.* to become untangled

un·taught′ *adj.* **1.** not taught or educated **2.** got without being taught; natural

un·thank′ful *adj.* **1.** ungrateful **2.** unappreciated

un·think′a·ble *adj.* **1.** inconceivable **2.** not to be considered; impossible —**un·think′a·bly** *adv.*

un·think′ing *adj.* **1.** thoughtless; heedless **2.** unable to think —**un·think′ing·ly** *adv.*

un·ti′dy *adj.* **-di·er, -di·est** not tidy; slovenly; messy —**un·ti′di·ly** *adv.* —**un·ti′di·ness** *n.*

un·tie′ *vt.* **-tied′, -ty′ing** or **-tie′ing 1.** to loosen or undo (something tied or knotted) **2.** to free, as from restraint —*vi.* to become untied

un·til (un til′) *prep.* [ME. *untill*] **1.** up to the time of [*until* payday] **2.** before [*not until* tomorrow] —*conj.* **1.** up to the time when or that [*until* I go] **2.** to the point, degree, etc. that [*heat water until* it boils] **3.** before [*don't* leave *until* he does]

un·time′ly *adj.* **1.** before the usual time; premature **2.** at the wrong time; inopportune —*adv.* **1.** prematurely **2.** inopportunely —**un·time′li·ness** *n.*

un·to (un′tōō, -too) *prep.* [ME.] *archaic var. of:* **1.** TO **2.** UNTIL

un·told′ *adj.* **1.** not told or revealed **2.** too great, numerous, etc. to be counted, described, etc.

un·touch′a·ble *adj.* that cannot or should not be touched —*n.* in India, formerly, one whose touch was regarded as defiling to higher-caste Hindus

un·to·ward (un tō′ərd, -tôrd′) *adj.* **1.** inappropriate, unseemly, etc. **2.** not favorable or fortunate

un·true′ *adj.* **1.** not correct; false **2.** not agreeing with a standard or rule **3.** not faithful or loyal —**un·tru′ly** *adv.*

un·truth′ *n.* **1.** falsity **2.** a falsehood; lie —**un·truth′ful** *adj.* —**un·truth′ful·ly** *adv.*

un·tu′tored *adj.* **1.** not tutored or taught; uneducated **2.** simple; naive; unsophisticated

un·twine′ *vt.* **-twined′, -twin′ing** to undo (something twined or twisted); disentangle

un·twist′ *vt., vi.* to turn in the opposite direction so as to loosen or separate

un·used′ *adj.* **1.** not in use **2.** that has never been used **3.** unaccustomed (*to*)

un·u′su·al *adj.* not usual or common; rare —**un·u′su·al·ly** *adv.* —**un·u′su·al·ness** *n.*

un·ut′ter·a·ble *adj.* that cannot be expressed or described —**un·ut′ter·a·bly** *adv.*

un·var′nished *adj.* **1.** not varnished **2.** plain; simple; unadorned

un·veil′ *vt.* to reveal as by removing a veil from —*vi.* to take off a veil; reveal oneself

un·voiced′ (-voist′) *adj.* **1.** not uttered or expressed **2.** *Phonet. same as* VOICELESS

un·war′y *adj.* not wary or cautious —**un·war′i·ly** *adv.*

un·well′ *adj.* not well; ill; sick

un·whole′some *adj.* **1.** harmful to body or mind **2.** unhealthy or unhealthy-looking **3.** morally harmful —**un·whole′some·ly** *adv.* —**un·whole′some·ness** *n.*

un·wield′y *adj.* hard to wield, manage, handle, etc. because of weight, shape, etc. —**un·wield′i·ness** *n.*

un·will′ing *adj.* **1.** not willing; reluctant **2.** done, given, etc. against one's will —**un·will′ing·ly** *adv.*

un·wind′ *vt.* **-wound′, -wind′ing 1.** to wind off or undo (something wound) **2.** to untangle **3.** to relax —*vi.* to become unwound, relaxed, etc.

un·wise′ *adj.* not wise; foolish; imprudent

un·wit·ting (un wit′in) *adj.* **1.** not knowing; unaware **2.** unintentional —**un·wit′ting·ly** *adv.*

un·wont′ed (-wun′tid, -wōn′-) *adj.* not common, usual, or habitual —**un·wont′ed·ly** *adv.*

un·wor′thy *adj.* **-thi·er, -thi·est 1.** lacking merit or value; worthless **2.** not deserving (*of*) **3.** not fit or becoming (with *of*) **4.** not deserved —**un·wor′thi·ly** *adv.* —**un·wor′thi·ness** *n.*

un·wrap′ *vt.* **-wrapped′, -wrap′ping** to take off the wrapping of; open or undo (something wrapped) —*vi.* to become unwrapped

un·writ′ten *adj.* **1.** not in writing **2.** operating only through custom or tradition [an *unwritten* law] **3.** not written on; blank

un·yoke′ *vt.* **-yoked′, -yok′ing 1.** to release from a yoke **2.** to separate or disconnect

un·zip′ *vt.* **-zipped′, -zip′ping** to open (the zipper) of (a garment, etc.) —*vi.* to become unzipped

up¹ (up) *adv.* [OE.] **1.** to, in, or on a higher place or level **2.** in or to a higher condition, amount, etc. **3.** above the horizon **4.** to a later period **5.** *a)* in or into a standing position *b)* out of bed **6.** in or into action, view, consideration, etc. **7.** aside; away [lay *up* grain] **8.** so as to be even with in time, degree, etc. **9.** so as to be tightly closed, bound, etc. [tie it *up*] **10.** completely [eat it *up*] **11.** *Baseball* to one's turn at batting **12.** *Sports,* etc. ahead (by a specified number of points, etc.) The adverb *up* is also used with verbs: *a)* to form combinations having special meanings (Ex.: show *up*) *b)* as an intensive (Ex.: dress *up*) —*prep.* up to, toward, along, through, into, or upon —*adj.* **1.** directed toward a higher position **2.** in a higher place or position **3.** advanced in amount, degree, etc. [rents are *up*] **4.** above the horizon **5.** *a)* in a standing position *b)* out of bed **6.** in an active or excited state **7.** at an end; over [time is *up*] **8.** [Colloq.] going on [what's *up*?] **9.** *Baseball* at bat —*n.* an upward slope, movement,

unstuffed	untalented	untransferred	unvisited
unsubdued	untamed	untranslatable	unwanted
unsubmissive	untanned	untranslated	unwarlike
unsubsidized	untapped	untransmitted	unwarned
unsubstantiated	untarnished	untrapped	unwarranted
unsuccessful	untasted	untraveled	unwashed
unsuitable	untaxed	untravelled	unwasted
unsuited	unteachable	untraversed	unwatched
unsullied	untempered	untried	unwavering
unsupervised	untenable	untrimmed	unweakened
unsupported	untenanted	untrod	unweaned
unsure	untended	untroubled	unwearied
unsurmountable	unterrified	untrustworthy	unwearying
unsurpassed	untested	untufted	unwed
unsusceptible	unthanked	untuned	unwedded
unsuspected	unthoughtful	unturned	unweeded
unsuspecting	unthought-of	untypical	unwelcome
unsuspicious	unthrifty	unusable	unwilled
unsustained	unticketed	unutilized	unwithered
unswayed	untilled	unuttered	unwitnessed
unsweetened	untiring	unvaccinated	unwomanly
unswept	untitled	unvalued	unworkable
unswerving	untouched	unvanquished	unworkmanlike
unsymmetrical	untraceable	unvaried	unworldly
unsympathetic	untraced	unvarying	unworn
unsympathizing	untracked	unventilated	unworried
unsystematic	untrained	unverifiable	unwounded
untactful	untrammeled	unverified	unwrinkle
untainted	untransferable	unversed	unyielding

etc. —*vi.* **upped, up′ping** [Colloq.] to get up; rise —*vt.* [Colloq.] **1.** to put up, lift up, etc. **2.** to raise *[to up prices]* —**on the up and up** [Slang] honest —**up against** [Colloq.] faced with —**up for 1.** presented or considered for (an elective office, sale, etc.) **2.** before a court for (trial) or on (a charge) —**up on** (or **in**) [Colloq.] well-informed about —**ups and downs** good periods and bad periods —**up to** [Colloq.] **1.** doing or scheming **2.** capable of (doing, etc.) **3.** as many as *[up to four]* **4.** as far as *[up to here]* **5.** dependent upon *[entirely up to her]* —**up with!** give or restore power, favor, etc. to!

up² (up) *adv.* [phonetic respelling of AP(IECE)] apiece; each *[the score is seven up]*

up- *a combining form meaning* up *[uphill]*

up-and-com·ing (up′'n kum′iŋ) *adj.* **1.** enterprising, alert, and promising **2.** gaining in prominence

up′beat′ *n. Music* an unaccented beat, esp. when on the last note of a bar —*adj.* cheerful; optimistic

up·braid (up brād′) *vt.* [< OE. *up-*, up + *bregdan*, to pull] to rebuke severely; censure sharply

up′bring′ing *n.* the training and education received while growing up; rearing; nurture

up′com′ing *adj.* coming soon; forthcoming

up′coun′try *adj., adv.* in or toward the interior of a country —*n.* the interior of a country

up·date′ *vt.* **-dat′ed, -dat′ing** to bring up to date; make current in facts, methods, ideas, etc.

up·end′ *vt., vi.* **1.** to turn or stand on end **2.** to upset or topple

up′grade′ *n.* an upward slope —*adj., adv.* uphill —*vt.* (up grād′) **-grad′ed, -grad′ing** to raise in value, grade, rank, quality, etc. —**on the upgrade** advancing or improving in status, health, etc.

up·heav·al (up hē′v'l) *n.* **1.** a heaving or lifting up **2.** a sudden, violent change

up′hill′ *adj.* **1.** going or sloping up **2.** laborious; tiring —*n.* a sloping rise —*adv.* **1.** upward as on a hillside **2.** with difficulty

up·hold′ *vt.* **-held′, -hold′ing 1.** to hold up **2.** to keep from falling; support **3.** to give moral support to **4.** to confirm; sustain —**up·hold′er** *n.*

up·hol·ster (up hōl′stər, ə pōl′-) *vt.* [ult. < ME. *upholder*, tradesman] to fit out (furniture, etc.) with covering, padding, springs, etc. —**up·hol′ster·er** *n.*

up·hol′ster·y *n., pl.* **-ies 1.** the materials used in upholstering **2.** the work of upholstering

up′keep′ *n.* **1.** maintenance **2.** the cost of this **3.** state of repair

up′land (-lənd, -land′) *n.* land elevated above other land —*adj.* of or situated in upland

up·lift′ *vt.* **1.** to lift up **2.** to raise to a higher moral, social, or cultural level —*n.* (up′lift′) **1.** *a)* an uplifting *b)* any influence, movement, etc. aimed at uplifting society **2.** a brassiere designed to lift and support the breasts

up·on (ə pän′) *prep.* on, or up and on: used interchangeably with *on*

up·per (up′ər) *adj.* **1.** higher in place **2.** farther north or inland **3.** higher in rank; superior —*n.* the part of a shoe above the sole —**on one's uppers** [Colloq.] **1.** wearing shoes with soles worn through **2.** in need; poor

upper case capital-letter type used in printing, as distinguished from small letters (*lower case*) —**up′per-case′** *adj.* —**up′per-case′** *vt.* **-cased′, -cas′ing**

upper class the social class above the middle class; rich or aristocratic class —**up′per-class′** *adj.*

up′per·class′man *n., pl.* **-men** a junior or senior in a high school or college

up′per·cut′ *n. Boxing* a short, swinging blow directed upward —*vt., vi.* **-cut′, -cut′ting** to hit with an uppercut

upper hand the position of advantage or control

Upper House [*often* **u- h-**] in a legislature having two branches, the branch that is smaller and less representative, as the U.S. Senate

up′per·most′ *adj.* highest in place, power, authority, etc. —*adv.* in the highest place, rank, etc.

Upper Vol·ta (väl′tə) country in W Africa, north of Ghana: 108,880 sq. mi.; pop. 5,384,000

up·pi·ty (up′ə tē) *adj.* [Colloq.] inclined to be arrogant, snobbish, etc.: also **up′pish** (-ish)

up·raise′ *vt.* **-raised′, -rais′ing** to raise up

up·rear′ *vt.* **1.** to lift up **2.** to erect; build **3.** to exalt **4.** to bring up; rear —*vi.* to rise up

up′right′ *adj.* **1.** standing or directed straight up; erect **2.** honest and just —*adv.* (*also* up rīt′) in an upright position

or direction —*n.* **1.** something having an upright position **2.** *short for* UPRIGHT PIANO —**up′right′ly** *adv.*

upright piano a piano with a vertical rectangular body

up′ris′ing *n.* a rising up; specif., a revolt

up·roar (up′rôr′) *n.* [Du. *oproer*, a stirring up] **1.** a violent disturbance; tumult **2.** loud, confused noise; din

up·roar′i·ous *adj.* **1.** making, or marked by, an uproar **2.** *a)* loud and boisterous, as laughter *b)* causing such laughter —**up·roar′i·ous·ly** *adv.*

up·root′ *vt.* **1.** to tear up by the roots **2.** to destroy or remove utterly

up·set′ *vt.* **-set′, -set′ting 1.** *a)* to tip over; overturn *b)* to defeat unexpectedly **2.** *a)* to disturb the functioning of *[to upset a schedule]* *b)* to disturb emotionally —*vi.* to become overturned or upset —*n.* (up′set′) **1.** an upsetting **2.** an unexpected defeat **3.** a disturbance; disorder —*adj.* **1.** tipped over; overturned **2.** overthrown or defeated **3.** disturbed or disordered

up′shot′ *n.* [orig., final shot in an archery match] the conclusion; result; outcome

up′side′ *n.* the upper side or part

upside down 1. with the top side or part underneath **2.** in disorder —**up′side′-down′** *adj.*

up·si·lon (yōō′psə län′) *n.* the twentieth letter of the Greek alphabet (Υ, υ)

up′stage′ *adv.* toward or at the rear of a stage —*adj.* of or having to do with the rear of a stage —*vt.* **-staged′, -stag′ing** to draw attention away from (another), as by moving upstage

up′stairs′ *adv.* **1.** up the stairs **2.** on or to an upper floor —*adj.* on an upper floor —*n.* an upper floor

up·stand′ing *adj.* **1.** standing straight; erect **2.** upright in character and behavior; honorable

up′start′ *n.* one who has recently come into wealth, power, etc., esp. one who is aggressive, presumptuous, etc. —*adj.* of or like an upstart

up′state′ *n.* the part of a State farther to the north or away from a large city —*adj., adv.* in, to, or from upstate

up′stream′ *adv., adj.* in the direction against the current of a stream

up·surge (up surj′) *vi.* **-surged′, -surg′ing** to surge up —*n.* (up′surj′) a surge upward

up′swing′ *n.* a swing or trend upward; specif., an upward trend in business —*vi.* (up swiŋ′) **-swung′, -swing′ing 1.** to swing upward **2.** to advance

up′take′ *n.* a taking up; a drawing up, absorbing, etc. —**quick** (or **slow**) **on the uptake** [Colloq.] quick (or slow) to understand or comprehend

up′-tight′, up′tight′ *adj.* [Slang] **1.** very tense, nervous, etc. **2.** overly conventional in attitudes

up′-to-date′ *adj.* **1.** extending to the present time **2.** keeping up with what is most recent, modern, etc.

up′town′ *adj., adv.* of, in, or toward the upper part of a city or town —*n.* the upper part of a city or town

up·turn′ *vt., vi.* to turn up, upward, or over —*n.* (up′turn′) an upward turn, curve, or trend

up′ward (-wərd) *adv., adj.* **1.** toward a higher place, position, degree, amount, etc. **2.** from an earlier to a later time **3.** beyond (an indicated price, amount, etc.) Also **up′wards** *adv.* —**upwards** (or **upward**) **of** more than —**up′ward·ly** *adv.*

U·rals (yoor′əlz) mountain system in W U.S.S.R., regarded as the boundary between Europe & Asia: also **Ural Mountains**

u·ra·ni·um (yoo rā′nē əm) *n.* [< G. < URANUS, the planet] a very hard, heavy, radioactive metallic chemical element: it is found only in combination, and its isotopes are important in work on atomic energy: symbol, U; at. wt., 283.03; at. no., 92

U·ra·nus (yoor′ə nəs, yoo rā′nəs) [< Gr. *Ouranos,* heaven] **1.** *Gr. Myth.* a god who personified the heavens **2.** a planet of the solar system: see PLANET

ur·ban (ur′bən) *adj.* [< L. *urbs,* a city] **1.** of, in, or constituting a city **2.** characteristic of cities

ur·bane (ur bān′) *adj.* [see prec.] polite and courteous in a smooth, polished way; refined —**ur·ban′i·ty** (-ban′ə tē) *n.*

ur·ban·ize (ur′bə nīz′) *vt.* **-ized′, -iz′ing** to change from rural to urban —**ur′ban·i·za′tion** *n.*

ur·chin (ur′chin) *n.* [< L. *ericius,* a hedgehog] a small child; esp., a mischievous boy

-ure [Fr. < L. *-ura*] *a suffix meaning:* **1.** act or result of being *[exposure]* **2.** agent of *[legislature]* **3.** state of being *[composure]*

---

fat, āpe, cär; ten, ēven; is, bīte; gō, hôrn, tōōl, look; oil, out; up, fur; thin, *then*; zh, leisure; ŋ, ring; ə for *a* in *ago*; ′ as in *able* (ā′b'l); ë, Fr. coeur; ö, Fr. feu; ü, Fr. duc; r, Fr. cri; kh, G. doch, ich. ‡ foreign; < derived from

u·re·a (yoo rē′ə) *n.* [< Fr. < Gr. *ouron*, urine] a soluble, crystalline solid, CO(NH₂)₂, found in urine or produced synthetically: used in making plastics, adhesives, etc.

u·re·mi·a (yoo rē′mē ə, -rēm′yə) *n.* [< Gr. *ouron*, urine + *haima*, blood] a toxic condition caused by the presence in the blood of waste products normally eliminated in the urine —**u·re′mic** *adj.*

u·re·ter (yoo rēt′ər) *n.* [< Gr. *ourein*, urinate] a tube carrying urine from a kidney to the bladder

u·re·thra (yoo rē′thrə) *n., pl.* **-thrae** (-thrē), **-thras** [< Gr. *ouron*, urine] the canal through which urine is discharged from the bladder: in the male, also the duct for semen — **u·re′thral** *adj.*

urge (urj) *vt.* **urged**, **urg′ing** [L. *urgere*, press hard] **1.** *a)* to press upon the attention; advocate *b)* to plead with; ask earnestly **2.** to incite; provoke **3.** to drive or force onward —*vi.* **1.** to make an earnest presentation of arguments, claims, etc. **2.** to exert a driving force —*n.* **1.** an urging **2.** an impulse

ur·gen·cy (ur′jən sē) *n., pl.* **-cies** **1.** an urgent quality or state **2.** insistence **3.** something urgent

ur′gent (-jənt) *adj.* [< L. *urgere*, to urge] **1.** calling for haste, immediate action, etc. **2.** insistent —**ur′gent·ly** *adv.*

-urgy [< Gr. *ergon*, work] *a combining form meaning* a working with or by means of [*zymurgy*]

u·ric (yoor′ik) *adj.* of, contained in, or derived from urine

uric acid a white, colorless, crystalline substance found in urine

u·ri·nal (yoor′ə n′l) *n.* **1.** a receptacle for urine **2.** a place for urinating

u·ri·nal·y·sis (yoor′ə nal′ə sis) *n.* chemical or microscopic analysis of the urine

u·ri·nar·y (yoor′ə ner′ē) *adj.* **1.** of urine **2.** of the organs that secrete and discharge urine

u·ri·nate (yoor′ə nāt′) *vi.* **-nat′ed**, **-nat′ing** to discharge urine from the body —**u′ri·na′tion** *n.*

u·rine (yoor′in) *n.* [< L. *urina*] in mammals, the yellowish fluid containing waste products, secreted from the blood by the kidneys, passed to the bladder, and discharged through the urethra

urn (urn) *n.* [L. *urna*] **1.** *a)* a vase, esp. one with a foot or pedestal *b)* a container for the ashes of a cremated body **2.** a metal container with a faucet, used for making or serving coffee, tea, etc.

u·rol·o·gy (yoo räl′ə jē) *n.* the branch of medicine dealing with the urogenital or urinary system and its diseases — **u·rol′o·gist** *n.*

Ur·sa Major (ur′sə) [L., lit., Great Bear] the most conspicuous constellation in the northern sky: it contains the stars which form the Big Dipper

Ursa Minor [L., lit., Little Bear] the northernmost constellation: it contains the Little Dipper, with the North Star at the end of its handle

ur·sine (ur′sīn, -sin) *adj.* [< L. *ursus*, a bear] of or like a bear

Ur·su·line (ur′sə lin, -līn′) *n.* [< St. *Ursula* (4th cent.)] *R.C.Ch.* any member of a teaching order of nuns —*adj.* of this order

ur·ti·car·i·a (ur′tə ker′ē ə) *n.* [< L. *urtica*, a nettle] *same as* HIVES

U·ru·guay (yoor′ə gwā′, -gwī′) country in SE S. America: 72,171 sq. mi.; pop. 2,886,000; cap. Montevideo —**U′ru·guay′an** *adj., n.*

us (us) *pron.* [OE.] *objective case of* WE

U.S., US United States

USA, U.S.A. **1.** United States of America **2.** United States Army

us·a·ble, use·a·ble (yoo′zə b′l) *adj.* that can be used; fit for use —**us′a·bil′i·ty, use′a·ble·ness** *n.*

USAF, U.S.A.F. United States Air Force

us·age (yoo′sij, -zij) *n.* **1.** the act, way, or extent of using; treatment **2.** established practice; custom; habit **3.** the way a word, phrase, etc. is used to express a particular idea

USCG, U.S.C.G. United States Coast Guard

use (yooz; *for n.* yoos) *vt.* **used, us′ing** [< L. *uti*] **1.** to put or bring into action or service **2.** to practice; exercise [*use* your judgment] **3.** to behave toward; treat [to *use* a friend badly] **4.** to consume, expend, etc. [to *use* up energy] **5.** to take (drugs, etc.) habitually **6.** to accustom (used in the passive with *to*) [*used* to the cold] **7.** to exploit (a person) —*vi.* to be accustomed (meaning "did at one time") [he *used* to play golf] —*n.* **1.** a using or being used **2.** the ability to use **3.** the right to use **4.** the need or opportunity to use **5.** way of using **6.** usefulness; utility **7.** the purpose for which something is used **8.** function or service **9.** custom; habit —**have no use for 1.**

to have no need of **2.** to dislike strongly —**in use** being used —**make use of** to use: also **put to use** —**us′er** *n.*

used (yoozd) *adj.* not new; secondhand

use·ful (yoos′fəl) *adj.* that can be used; serviceable; helpful —**use′ful·ly** *adv.* —**use′ful·ness** *n.*

use·less *adj.* **1.** having no use; worthless **2.** to no purpose —**use′less·ly** *adv.* —**use′less·ness** *n.*

ush·er (ush′ər) *n.* [< L. *ostium*, door] **1.** an official doorkeeper **2.** one who shows people to their seats in a church, theater, etc. **3.** a bridegroom's attendant —*vt.* **1.** to escort or conduct (others) to seats, etc. **2.** to herald or bring (*in*) —*vi.* to act as an usher

USMC, U.S.M.C. United States Marine Corps

USN, U.S.N. United States Navy

USO, U.S.O. United Service Organizations

U.S.P., U.S. Pharm. United States Pharmacopoeia

U.S.S. United States Ship, Steamer, or Steamship

U.S.S.R., USSR Union of Soviet Socialist Republics

u·su·al (yoo′zhoo wəl) *adj.* [see USE] such as is most often seen, heard, used, etc.; common; ordinary; customary —**as usual** in the usual way —**u′su·al·ly** *adv.*

u·su·ri·ous (yoo zhoor′ē əs) *adj.* **1.** practicing usury **2.** of or involving usury

u·surp (yoo surp′, -zurp′) *vt., vi.* [< L. *usus*, a use + *rapere*, to seize] to take and hold (power, position, rights, etc.) by force or without right —**u·sur·pa·tion** (yoo′sər pā′shən, -zər-) *n.* —**u·surp′er** *n.*

u·su·ry (yoo′zhoo rē) *n., pl.* **-ries** [see USE] **1.** the lending of money at interest, now specif. at a rate of interest that is excessively or unlawfully high **2.** interest at such a rate —**u′su·rer** *n.*

U·tah (yoo′tô, -tä) State of the W U.S., one of the Mountain States: 84,916 sq. mi.; pop. 1,059,000; cap. Salt Lake City: abbrev. **Ut., UT** —**U′tah·an** *adj., n.*

u·ten·sil (yoo ten′s′l) *n.* [< L. *uti*, to use] an implement or container, now esp. one used in a kitchen [*cooking utensils*]

u·ter·us (yoot′ər əs) *n., pl.* **u′ter·i′** (-ī′) [L.] a hollow organ of female mammals in which the ovum is deposited and the embryo and fetus are developed; womb —**u′ter·ine** (-in, yoo′tə rīn′) *adj.*

u·til·i·tar·i·an (yoo til′ə ter′ē ən) *adj.* **1.** of or having utility; useful **2.** stressing usefulness over beauty, etc. **3.** of or believing in utilitarianism —*n.* a person who believes in utilitarianism

u·til′i·tar′i·an·ism *n.* **1.** the doctrine that the value of anything is determined by its utility **2.** the doctrine that the purpose of all action should be to bring about the greatest happiness of the greatest number

u·til·i·ty (yoo til′ə tē) *n., pl.* **-ties** [< L. *uti*, to use] **1.** usefulness **2.** something useful, as the service to the public of gas, water, etc. **3.** a company providing such a service: see also PUBLIC UTILITY

utility room a room containing laundry appliances, heating equipment, etc.

u·ti·lize (yoot′'l īz′) *vt.* **-lized′**, **-liz′ing** to put to profitable use; make use of —**u′ti·li·za′tion** *n.*

ut·most (ut′mōst′) *adj.* [< OE. superl. of *ut*, out] **1.** most extreme or distant; farthest **2.** of or to the greatest or highest degree, amount, etc.; greatest —*n.* the most that is possible

U·to·pi·a (yoo tō′pē ə) [< Gr. *ou*, not + *topos*, a place] an imaginary island in T. More's *Utopia* (1516), with a perfect political and social system —*n.* [*often* u-] **1.** any idealized place of perfection **2.** any visionary scheme for an ideally perfect society —**U·to′pi·an, u·to′pi·an** *adj., n.*

U·trecht (yoo′trekt) city in the C Netherlands: pop. 279,000

ut·ter¹ (ut′ər) *adj.* [< OE. compar. of *ut*, out] **1.** complete; total **2.** unqualified; absolute —**ut′ter·ly** *adv.*

ut·ter² (ut′ər) *vt.* [< ME. *ut*, out] **1.** to speak or express audibly (words, sounds, etc.) **2.** to express in any way **3.** to make known; divulge; reveal

ut′ter·ance *n.* **1.** the act, power, or way of uttering **2.** something uttered or said

ut′ter·most′ (-mōst′) *adj., n. same as* UT-MOST

u·vu·la (yoo′vyə lə) *n., pl.* **-las, -lae′** (-lē′) [< L. *uva*, a grape] the small, fleshy part of the soft palate hanging down above the back of the tongue —**u′vu·lar** *adj.*

UVULA

ux·o·ri·ous (uk sôr′ē əs, ug zôr′-) *adj.* [< L. *uxor*, wife] dotingly fond of or submissive to one's wife —**ux·o′ri·ous·ly** *adv.*

Uz·bek Soviet Socialist Republic (ooz′bek) republic of the U.S.S.R. in C Asia: also **Uz′bek·i·stan′** (-i stän′)

V

V, v (vē) *n., pl.* **V's, v's** the twenty-second letter of the English alphabet
V (vē) *n.* **1.** an object shaped like V **2.** a Roman numeral for 5 **3.** *Chem.* vanadium
V, v 1. velocity **2.** volt(s)
v. 1. verb **2.** versus **3.** voltage **4.** volume
VA, V.A. Veterans Administration
Va., VA Virginia
va·can·cy (vā′kən sē) *n., pl.* **-cies 1.** a being vacant **2.** empty or vacant space **3.** an unoccupied position or office **4.** a room, apartment, etc. available for rent
va·cant (vā′kənt) *adj.* [< L. *vacare*, be empty] **1.** having nothing in it; empty **2.** not held, filled, or occupied, as a position, seat, house, etc. **3.** free from work or activity **4.** without thought, interest, etc. *[a vacant mind]* —**va′·cant·ly** *adv.*
va′cate (-kāt) *vt., vi.* **-cat·ed, -cat·ing** [see prec.] **1.** to make (an office, house, etc.) vacant **2.** to make void; annul
va·ca·tion (və kā′shən, vā-) *n.* [< L. *vacatio*] a period of rest from work, study, etc. —*vi.* to take one's vacation — **va·ca′tion·er, va·ca′tion·ist** *n.*
vac·ci·nate (vak′sə nāt′) *vt., vi.* **-nat·ed, -nat·ing** to inoculate with a vaccine in order to prevent a disease, specif. smallpox
vac′ci·na′tion *n.* **1.** the act or practice of vaccinating **2.** the scar on the skin where the vaccine has been applied
vac·cine (vak sēn′) *n.* [< L. *vacca*, a cow: from use of cowpox virus in smallpox vaccine] any preparation of killed microorganisms, living weakened organisms, etc. used to produce immunity to a specific disease
vac·il·late (vas′ə lāt′) *vi.* **-lat·ed, -lat·ing** [< L. *vacillare*] **1.** to sway to and fro; waver **2.** to fluctuate **3.** to show indecision —**vac′il·la′tion** *n.*
va·cu·i·ty (va kyōo′ə tē) *n., pl.* **-ties** [< L. *vacuus*, empty] **1.** emptiness **2.** an empty space; void **3.** lack of intelligence, thought, etc. **4.** inanity
vac·u·ous (vak′yoo wəs) *adj.* [L. *vacuus*] **1.** empty **2.** stupid; senseless —**vac′u·ous·ly** *adv.*
vac·u·um (vak′yoo wəm, vak′yōōm) *n., pl.* **-u·ums, -u·a** (-yoo wə) [L.] **1.** a space with nothing at all in it **2.** a space from which most of the air or gas has been taken **3.** a void —*adj.* **1.** of or used to make a vacuum **2.** having or working by a vacuum —*vt., vi.* to clean with a vacuum cleaner
vacuum bottle (or **flask** or **jug**) *same as* THERMOS
vacuum cleaner a machine for cleaning carpets, floors, upholstery, etc. by suction
vac′u·um-packed′ *adj.* packed in an airtight container so as to keep the contents fresh
vacuum pump a pump used to draw air or gas out of a sealed space
vacuum tube an electron tube from which the air has been evacuated to the highest possible degree
vag·a·bond (vag′ə bänd′) *adj.* [< L. *vagari*, to wander] **1.** wandering **2.** vagrant; shiftless —*n.* **1.** one who wanders from place to place **2.** a tramp —**vag′a·bond′age** *n.*
va·gar·y (və ger′ē, vā′gər ē) *n., pl.* **-ies** [< L. *vagari*, to wander] **1.** an odd or eccentric action **2.** an odd, whimsical, or freakish idea or notion —**va·gar′i·ous** *adj.*
va·gi·na (və jī′nə) *n., pl.* **-nas, -nae** (-nē) [L., a sheath] in female mammals, the canal leading from the vulva to the uterus —**vag·i·nal** (vaj′ə n'l) *adj.*
va·grant (vā′grənt) *n.* [prob. < OFr. *walcrer*, to wander] one who wanders from place to place; esp., one without a regular job, supporting himself by begging, etc.; tramp — *adj.* **1.** wandering; nomadic **2.** of or like a vagrant **3.** random, wayward, etc. —**va′gran·cy** *n., pl.* **-cies**
vague (vāg) *adj.* **va′guer, va′guest** [Fr. < L. *vagus*, wandering] **1.** indefinite in shape or form **2.** not sharp, clear, certain, etc. in thought or expression —**vague′ly** *adv.* —**vague′ness** *n.*

va·gus (vā′gəs) *n., pl.* **-gi** (-jī) [L., wandering] either of a pair of cranial nerves acting upon the larynx, lungs, heart, esophagus, and most of the abdominal organs: also **vagus nerve**
vain (vān) *adj.* [< L. *vanus*, empty] **1.** having no real value; worthless *[vain pomp]* **2.** without effect; futile *[a vain attempt]* **3.** having an excessively high regard for one's self, looks, etc.; conceited —**in vain 1.** unsuccessfully **2.** profanely —**vain′ly** *adv.* —**vain′ness** *n.*
vain·glo·ry (vān′glôr′ē, vān glôr′ē) *n.* [see VAIN & GLORY] **1.** extreme self-pride and boastfulness **2.** vain show — **vain′glo′ri·ous·** *adj.*
val·ance (val′əns, vāl′-) *n.* [< ? *Valence*, city in France] a short drapery or facing of wood or metal across the top of a window —**val′anced** *adj.*
vale[1] (vāl) *n.* [< L. *vallis*] [Poet.] *same as* VALLEY
‡**va·le**[2] (vā′lē, wä′lā) *interj., n.* [L.] farewell
val·e·dic·tion (val′ə dik′shən) *n.* [< L. *vale*, farewell + *dicere*, to say] **1.** a bidding farewell **2.** something said in parting
val·e·dic·to·ri·an (val′ə dik tôr′ē ən) *n.* the student, usually the one ranking highest in scholarship, who delivers the valedictory at graduation

VALANCE

val′e·dic′to·ry (-tər ē) *adj.* uttered as a valediction —*n., pl.* **-ries** a farewell speech, esp. at graduation
va·lence (vā′ləns) *n.* [< L. *valere*, be strong] *Chem.* the combining capacity of an element or radical, as measured by the number of hydrogen or chlorine atoms which one radical or atom of the element will combine with or replace: also **va′len·cy**, *pl.* **-cies**
Va·len·ci·a (və len′shē ə, -sē ə) seaport in E Spain, on the Mediterranean: pop. 624,000
-valent [< L. *valens*] *Chem. a suffix meaning:* **1.** having a specified valence **2.** having a specified number of valences
val·en·tine (val′ən tīn′) *n.* **1.** a sweetheart chosen or complimented on Saint Valentine's Day **2.** a greeting card or gift sent on this day
val·et (val′it, val′ā) *n.* [Fr.] **1.** a man's personal manservant who takes care of the man's clothes, helps him in dressing, etc. **2.** an employee, as of a hotel, who cleans or presses clothes, etc.
Val·hal·la (val hal′ə) *Norse Myth.* the great hall where Odin receives and feasts the souls of heroes slain in battle
val·iant (val′yənt) *adj.* [< L. *valere*, be strong] courageous; brave —**val′iance, val′ian·cy** *n.* —**val′iant·ly** *adv.*
val·id (val′id) *adj.* [< L. *valere*, be strong] **1.** having legal force **2.** sound; well-grounded on principles or evidence, as an argument —**val′id·ly** *adv.*
val·i·date (val′ə dāt′) *vt.* **-dat·ed, -dat·ing 1.** to declare legally valid **2.** to prove to be valid —**val′i·da′tion** *n.*
va·lid·i·ty (və lid′ə tē) *n., pl.* **-ties** the state, quality, or fact of being valid in law, argument, etc.
va·lise (və lēs′) *n.* [Fr. < It. *valigia*] a piece of hand luggage: an old-fashioned term
Val·kyr·ie (val kir′ē, val′ki rē) *n. Norse Myth.* any of the maidens of Odin who conduct the souls of heroes slain in battle to Valhalla
val·ley (val′ē) *n., pl.* **-leys** [< L. *vallis*] **1.** low land lying between hills or mountains **2.** the land drained by a river system **3.** any long dip or hollow
Valley Forge village in SE Pa., where Washington and his troops camped in the winter of 1777–78
val·or (val′ər) *n.* [< L. *valere*, be strong] great courage or bravery: Brit. sp. *valour* —**val′or·ous** *adj.*
Val·pa·rai·so (val′pə rā′zō, -rī′sō) seaport in C Chile: pop. 296,000

---

val·u·a·ble (val′yoo b′l, -yoo wə b′l) *adj.* **1.** *a)* being worth money *b)* having great monetary value **2.** highly regarded as precious, useful, etc. —*n.* an article of value: *usually used in pl.*

val·u·a·tion (val′yoo wā′shən) *n.* **1.** the determining of the value of anything **2.** determined or estimated value **3.** estimation of the worth, merit, etc. of anything

val·ue (val′yoo) *n.* [< L. *valere,* be worth] **1.** the worth of a thing in money or goods **2.** estimated worth **3.** purchasing power **4.** that quality of a thing that makes it more or less desirable, useful, etc. **5.** [*pl.*] the social principles, goals, or standards held by an individual, class, society, etc. **6.** relative duration, intensity, etc. —*vt.* **-ued, -u·ing 1.** to estimate the value of; appraise **2.** to place an estimate of worth on [to *value* health above wealth] **3.** to think highly of; prize —**val′ue·less** *adj.*

val′ued *adj.* **1.** estimated; appraised **2.** highly thought of; esteemed

valve (valv) *n.* [L. *valva,* leaf of a folding door] **1.** *Anat.* a membranous structure which permits body fluids to flow in one direction only, or opens and closes a tube, etc. **2.** *a)* any device in a pipe, etc. that regulates the flow by means of a flap, lid, plug, etc. *b)* this flap, lid, plug, etc. **3.** *Music* a device, as in the trumpet, that changes the tube length so as to change the pitch **4.** *Zool.* one of the parts making up the shell of a mollusk, clam, etc. —**valve′less** *adj.*

VALVE
(in a faucet)

va·moose (va moos′) *vi., vt.* **-moosed′, -moos′ing** [Sp. *vamos,* let us go] [Old Slang] to leave quickly: also **va·mose′** (-mōs′) **-mosed′, -mos′ing**

vamp¹ (vamp) *n.* [< OFr. *avant,* before + *pié,* a foot] **1.** the part of a boot or shoe covering the instep and, in some styles, the toes **2.** something patched up to seem new **3.** *Music* a simple, improvised introduction or interlude —*vt.* **1.** to put a vamp on (a shoe, etc.) **2.** to patch (*up*); repair **3.** *Music* to improvise

vamp² (vamp) *n. shortened form of* VAMPIRE (sense 3) — *vt., vi.* to seduce or beguile (a man): said of a woman

vam·pire (vam′pīr) *n.* [Fr. < G. < Slav.] **1.** *Folklore* a corpse that comes alive at night and sucks the blood of sleeping persons **2.** one who preys on others in a dishonest or evil way **3.** a beautiful but wicked woman who seduces then ruins men **4.** *shortened form of* VAMPIRE BAT

vampire bat a tropical American bat that lives on the blood of animals

van¹ (van) *n.* the vanguard

van² (van) *n.* [< CARAVAN] a closed truck or wagon for carrying furniture, people, etc.

va·na·di·um (və nā′dē əm) *n.* [< ON. *Vanadis,* goddess of love] a rare, ductile metallic chemical element used in steel alloys: symbol, V; at. wt., 50.942; at. no., 23

Van Al·len (radiation) belt (van al′ən) [< J. *Van Allen* (1914–), U.S. physicist] a broad belt of radiation encircling the earth at various levels

Van Bu·ren (van byoor′ən), **Martin** 1782–1862; 8th president of the U.S. (1837–41)

Van·cou·ver (van koo′vər) seaport in SW British Columbia, Canada: pop. 410,000

Van·dal (van′d'l) *n.* **1.** a member of a Germanic tribe that sacked Rome (455 A.D.) **2.** [v-] one who purposely destroys works of art, public property, etc. —**van′dal·ism** *n.*

van′dal·ize′ (-īz′) *vt.* **-ized′, -iz′ing** to destroy or damage (property) on purpose

Van Dyck (van dīk′), Sir **Anthony** 1599–1641; Fl. painter in England: also sp. **Van·dyke′**

Vandyke (beard) a closely trimmed, pointed beard, as seen in portraits by Van Dyck

vane (vān) *n.* [OE. *fana,* a flag] **1.** *same as* WEATHER VANE **2.** any of the flat blades set around an axle, usually forming a wheel to be rotated by, or to rotate, air, water, etc. [the *vanes* of a windmill]

van Gogh (van gō′), **Vincent** 1853–90; Du. painter

van·guard (van′gärd′) *n.* [< OFr. *avant,* before + *garde,* guard] **1.** the front part of an army in an advance; the van **2.** the leading position or persons in a movement

va·nil·la (və nil′ə) *n.* [< Sp. *vaina,* pod] **1.** a climbing tropical American orchid with podlike capsules (**vanilla beans**) **2.** a flavoring made from these capsules

VANDYKE
BEARD

va·nil·lin (və nil′in, van′ə lin) *n.* a fragrant substance produced from the vanilla bean or made synthetically and used for flavoring

van·ish (van′ish) *vi.* [see EVANESCE] **1.** to go or pass suddenly from sight **2.** to cease to exist; come to an end

vanishing point the point where parallel lines receding from the observer seem to come together

van·i·ty (van′ə tē) *n., pl.* **-ties** [< L. *vanus,* vain] **1.** anything vain or futile **2.** worthlessness; futility **3.** a being vain, or excessively proud of oneself **4.** *short for* VANITY CASE **5.** a dressing table **6.** a cabinet in a bathroom with a washbowl set in the top

vanity case a woman's small traveling case for carrying cosmetics, toilet articles, etc.

van·quish (vaŋ′kwish, van′-) *vt.* [< L. *vincere*] **1.** to conquer or defeat **2.** to overcome (a feeling, condition, etc.); suppress —**van′quish·er** *n.*

van·tage (van′tij) *n.* [see ADVANTAGE] **1.** a position more advantageous than that of an opponent **2.** a position that allows a clear and broad view: also **vantage point**

vap·id (vap′id) *adj.* [L. *vapidus*] **1.** tasteless; flavorless **2.** lifeless; dull —**va·pid·i·ty** (va pid′ə tē), *pl.* **-ties, vap′id·ness** *n.* —**vap′id·ly** *adv.*

va·por (vā′pər) *n.* [L.] **1.** *a)* visible particles of moisture floating in the air, as fog or steam *b)* anything, as smoke or fumes, given off in a cloud **2.** the gaseous form of any substance that is usually a liquid or solid **3.** [*pl.*] [Archaic] depressed spirits (often with *the*) —*vi.* to pass off as vapor; evaporate Brit. sp. **vapour**

va′por·ize′ (-pə rīz′) *vt., vi.* **-ized′, -iz′ing** to change into vapor, as by heating or spraying —**va′por·i·za′tion** *n.* —**va′por·iz′er** *n.*

va′por·ous *adj.* **1.** forming vapor **2.** full of vapor **3.** like vapor **4.** fleeting, fanciful, etc.

va·que·ro (vä ker′ō) *n., pl.* **-ros** [Sp. < L. *vacca,* a cow] in the Southwest, a cowboy

var. 1. variant(s) **2.** various

var·i·a·ble (ver′ē ə b′l) *adj.* **1.** apt to change or vary; changeable, inconstant, etc. **2.** that can be changed or varied **3.** *Biol.* tending to deviate in some way from the type —*n.* **1.** anything changeable; thing that varies **2.** *Math.* a quantity that may have a number of different values, or a symbol for this —**var′i·a·bil′i·ty, var′i·a·ble·ness** *n.* —**var′i·a·bly** *adv.*

var·i·ance (ver′ē əns) *n.* **1.** a varying or being variant **2.** degree of change or difference; discrepancy **3.** official permission to bypass regulations **4.** a quarrel; dispute —**at variance** disagreeing

var′i·ant (-ənt) *adj.* varying; different in some way from others of the same kind —*n.* anything variant, as a different spelling of the same word

var·i·a·tion (ver′ē ā′shən) *n.* **1.** *a)* a varying; change in form, extent, etc. *b)* the degree of such change **2.** a thing somewhat different from another of the same kind **3.** *Music* the repetition of a melody or theme with changes in harmony, rhythm, key, etc. —**var′i·a′tion·al** *adj.*

var·i·col·ored (ver′i kul′ərd) *adj.* of several or many colors

var·i·cose (var′ə kōs′) *adj.* [< L. *varix,* enlarged vein] abnormally and irregularly swollen [*varicose* veins] —**var′i·cos′i·ty** (-käs′ə tē) *n.*

var·ied (ver′ēd) *adj.* **1.** of different kinds; various **2.** changed; altered

var·i·e·gate (ver′ē ə gāt′) *vt.* **-gat·ed, -gat·ing** [< L. *varius,* various] **1.** to make varied in appearance by differences, as in colors **2.** to give variety to; diversify —**var′i·e·gat′ed** *adj.* —**var′i·e·ga′tion** *n.*

va·ri·e·ty (və rī′ə tē) *n., pl.* **-ties 1.** a being various or varied; absence of sameness **2.** any of the various forms of something; sort [*varieties* of cloth] **3.** a number of different kinds **4.** a subdivision of a species —*adj.* of or in a variety show

variety show a show made up of different kinds of acts, as comic skits, songs, dances, etc.

variety store a retail store that sells many small, inexpensive items

var·i·o·rum (ver′ē ôr′əm) *n.* [L., of various (scholars)] **1.** an edition, as of a literary work, with notes by various editors, etc. **2.** an edition containing variant texts

var·i·ous (ver′ē əs) *adj.* [L. *varius,* diverse] **1.** differing one from another; of several kinds **2.** several or many — **var′i·ous·ly** *adv.*

var·let (vär′lit) *n.* [OFr., a page] [Archaic] a scoundrel; knave

var·mint, var·ment (vär′mənt) *n.* [dial. var. of VERMIN] [Dial. or Colloq.] a person or animal regarded as objectionable

var·nish (vär′nish) *n.* [< ML. *veronix,* resin] **1.** a preparation of resinous substances dissolved in oil, alcohol, etc., used to give a hard, glossy surface to wood, etc. **2.** this hard, glossy surface **3.** a surface gloss, as of manner —*vt.* **1.** to cover with varnish **2.** to smooth over in a false way

var·si·ty (vär′sə tē) *n., pl.* **-ties** [< UNIVERSITY] the main team of a university, school, etc., as in an athletic competition —*adj.* designating or of such a team

var·y (ver′ē) *vt.* **-ied, -y·ing** [< L. *varius,* various] **1.** to change; alter **2.** to make different from one another **3.** to give variety to —*vi.* **1.** to differ or change **2.** to deviate or depart *(from)*

vas·cu·lar (vas′kyə lər) *adj.* [< L. *vas,* vessel] of or having vessels or special cells for carrying blood, sap, etc.

vase (vās, vāz; *chiefly Brit.* väz) *n.* [< L. *vas,* vessel] an open container used for decoration, holding flowers, etc.

vas·ec·to·my (vas ek′tə mē) *n., pl.* **-mies** [< L. *vas,* vessel + -ECTOMY] surgical removal of all, or esp. part, of the ducts carrying sperm from the testicles

Vas·e·line (vas′ə lēn′) [coinage < G. *was(ser),* water + Gr. *el(aion),* oil] *a trademark for* PETROLATUM —*n.* [v-] petrolatum

vas·o·mo·tor (vas′ō mōt′ər) *adj.* [< L. *vas,* vessel + MOTOR] regulating the diameter of blood vessels by causing contraction or dilation, as certain nerves

vas·sal (vas′l) *n.* [< ML. *vassus,* servant] **1.** a person in the feudal system who held land in return for fealty, military help, etc. to an overlord **2.** a subordinate, servant, slave, etc. —*adj.* of, like, or being a vassal —**vas′sal·age** (-ij) *n.*

vast (vast) *adj.* [L. *vastus*] very great in size, extent, amount, degree, etc. —**vast′ly** *adv.* —**vast′ness** *n.*

vat (vat) *n.* [< OE. *fæt,* cask] a large tank, tub, or cask for liquids as for use in a manufacturing process —*vt.* **vat′ted, vat′ting** to put or store in a vat

Vat·i·can (vat′i k'n) **1.** the papal palace in Vatican City **2.** the papal government or authority

Vatican City independent papal state within Rome, including the Vatican & St. Peter's Basilica: 108 acres: pop. c.1,000

vaude·ville (vōd′vil, vôd′-) *n.* [Fr. < *Vau-de-Vire,* a valley in Normandy, famous for convivial songs] a stage show consisting of various specialty acts, including songs, dances, comic skits, etc.

vault[1] (vôlt) *n.* [< L. *volvere,* to roll] **1.** an arched roof or ceiling **2.** an arched chamber or space, esp. when underground **3.** a cellar room used for storage **4.** *a)* a burial chamber *b)* a concrete or metal enclosure in the ground, into which the casket is lowered at burial **5.** a room for the safekeeping of valuables, as in a bank —*vt.* to cover with, or build as, a vault

vault[2] (vôlt) *vi.* [< OIt. *voltare*] to leap as over a barrier, esp. putting the hands on the barrier or using a long pole —*vt.* to vault over —a vaulting —**vault′er** *n.*

vault′ing[1] *n.* **1.** the arched work forming a vault **2.** a vault or vaults

vault′ing[2] *adj.* **1.** that vaults or leaps **2.** reaching too far *[vaulting* ambition*]*

vaunt (vônt, vänt) *vi., vt., n.* [< L. *vanus,* vain] boast or brag —**vaunt′ed** *adj.*

VD, V.D. venereal disease

veal (vēl) *n.* [< OFr. < L. *vitulus,* a calf] the flesh of a young calf, used as food

Veb·len (veb′lən), **Thor·stein** (thôr′stīn) 1857–1929; U.S. political economist & social scientist

vec·tor (vek′tər) *n.* [L., a carrier] **1.** *Biol.* a carrier, as an insect, of a disease-producing organism **2.** *Math. a)* a physical quantity with magnitude and direction, such as a force or velocity *b)* a line representing such a quantity

Ve·da (vā′də, vē′-) *n.* [Sans. *veda,* knowledge] the ancient sacred books of Hinduism —**Ve·da·ic** (vi dā′ik), **Ve′dic** *adj.*

Veep (vēp) *n.* [< *veepee* (for V.P.)] *[sometimes* v-] [Colloq.] a vice-president; specif., the U.S. Vice President

veer (vir) *vi., vt.* [< Fr. *virer,* to turn around] to change in direction; shift; turn —*n.* a change of direction

veer·y (vir′ē) *n., pl.* **-ies** [prob. echoic] a brown and cream-colored thrush of the eastern U.S.

veg·e·ta·ble (vej′tə b'l, vej′ə tə-) *adj.* [see VEGETATE] **1.** of plants in general **2.** of, like, or from vegetables *[vegetable* oil*]* —*n.* **1.** any plant, as distinguished from something animal or inorganic **2.** any plant that is eaten whole or in part, raw or cooked, as with an entree or in a salad, as the tomato, potato, lettuce, etc.

veg·e·tar·i·an (-ter′ē ən) *n.* one who eats no meat; strictly, one who believes in a vegetable diet as the proper one for people —*adj.* **1.** of vegetarians, their principles, etc. **2.** consisting only of vegetables, fruits, etc. —**veg′e·tar′i·an·ism** *n.*

veg·e·tate (vej′ə tāt′) *vi.* **-tat′ed, -tat′ing** [< L. *vegere,* to quicken] **1.** to grow as plants **2.** to lead a dull, inactive life

veg′e·ta′tion *n.* **1.** a vegetating **2.** plant life in general

veg′e·ta′tive *adj.* **1.** of plants or plant growth **2.** growing as plants **3.** helping plant growth **4.** dull and inactive —**veg′e·ta′tive·ly** *adv.*

ve·he·ment (vē′ə mənt) *adj.* [< L. *vehere,* to carry] **1.** violent; impetuous **2.** full of or showing very strong feeling —**ve′he·mence, ve′he·men·cy** *n.* —**ve′he·ment·ly** *adv.*

ve·hi·cle (vē′ə k'l) *n.* [< L. *vehere,* to carry] **1.** a means of carrying persons or things, as an automobile, sled, spacecraft, etc. **2.** a means of expressing ideas **3.** a play as a means of presenting an actor or company **4.** *Painting* a liquid, as water or oil, with which pigments are mixed for use —**ve·hic′u·lar** (-hik′yoo lər) *adj.*

veil (vāl) *n.* [< L. *velum,* cloth] **1.** a piece of light fabric, as net, worn, esp. by women, over the face or head to hide the features or as an ornament **2.** anything used to conceal, cover, separate, etc. *[a veil* of silence*]* **3.** a part of a nun's headdress —*vt.* to cover, conceal, etc. with or as with a veil —**take the veil** to become a nun —**veiled** *adj.*

vein (vān) *n.* [< L. *vena*] **1.** any blood vessel carrying blood to the heart **2.** any riblike support in an insect wing **3.** any of the fine lines, or ribs, in a leaf **4.** a layer of mineral, rock, etc. in a fissure or zone of different rock; lode **5.** a streak of a different color, etc., as in marble **6.** a distinctive quality or strain **7.** a temporary state of mind; mood —*vt.* to mark as with veins

ve·lar (vē′lər) *adj.* **1.** of the soft palate **2.** *Phonet.* pronounced with the back of the tongue touching or near the soft palate —*n.* a velar sound

Ve·láz·quez (və las′kes), **Die·go** (dye′gô) 1599–1660; Sp. painter: also **Ve·lás′quez** (-läs′-)

veld, veldt (velt) *n.* [Afrik. < MDu. *veld,* a field] in South Africa, open grassy country

vel·lum (vel′əm) *n.* [< L. *vitulus,* calf] **1.** a fine parchment used for writing on or for binding books **2.** a strong paper resembling vellum

ve·loc·i·pede (və läs′ə pēd′) *n.* [< Fr. < L. *velox,* swift + *pes,* a foot] **1.** any of various early bicycles or tricycles **2.** [Now Rare] a child's tricycle

ve·loc′i·ty (-tē) *n., pl.* **-ties** [< Fr. < L. *velox,* swift] **1.** quickness of motion; speed **2.** rate of motion in relation to time

ve·lour, ve·lours (və loor′) *n., pl.* **-lours′** [Fr.: see VELURE] a fabric with a soft nap like velvet, used for upholstery, draperies, clothing, etc.

ve·lum (vē′ləm) *n., pl.* **-la** (-lə) [L., a veil] *same as* SOFT PALATE

ve·lure (və loor′) *n.* [< Fr. < L. *villus,* shaggy hair] velvet or velvetlike fabric

vel·vet (vel′vit) *n.* [< L. *villus,* shaggy hair] **1.** a rich fabric of silk, rayon, etc. with a soft, thick pile **2.** anything with a surface like velvet —*adj.* **1.** made of velvet **2.** like velvet —**vel′vet·y** *adj.*

vel·vet·een (vel′və tēn′) *n.* a velvetlike cotton cloth

ve·na ca·va (vē′nə kā′və) *pl.* **-nae -vae** (-nē -vē) [< L. *vena,* vein + *cava,* hollow] *Anat.* either of two large veins carrying blood to the right atrium of the heart

ve·nal (vē′n'l) *adj.* [< L. *venum,* sale] open to, or characterized by, corruption or bribery —**ve·nal′i·ty** (-nal′ə tē) *n., pl.* **-ties** —**ve′nal·ly** *adv.*

ve·na·tion (vē nā′shən) *n.* [< L. *vena,* a vein] **1.** an arrangement of veins, as in an insect's wing or a leaf **2.** such veins collectively

vend (vend) *vt., vi.* [< Fr. < L. *venum dare,* offer for sale] to sell, esp. by peddling —**ven′dor, vend′er** *n.*

ven·det·ta (ven det′ə) *n.* [It. < L. *vindicta,* vengeance] **1.** a feud in which relatives of a murdered or wronged person seek vengeance on the guilty person or his family **2.** any bitter feud

vending machine a coin-operated machine for selling certain articles, refreshments, etc.

ve·neer (və nir′) *vt.* [G. *furnieren* < Fr. *fournir,* furnish] to cover with a thin layer of finer material; esp., to cover (wood) with wood of a finer quality —*n.* **1.** a thin layer used to veneer something **2.** a surface appearance that hides what is below

ven·er·a·ble (ven'ər ə b'l) *adj.* worthy of respect or reverence because of age, dignity, etc. —**ven'er·a·bil'i·ty** *n.* — **ven'er·a·bly** *adv.*

ven·er·ate (ven'ə rāt') *vt.* **-at'ed, -at'ing** [< L. *venerari*, to worship] to feel or show deep respect for; revere

ven'er·a'tion *n.* **1.** a venerating or being venerated **2.** deep respect **3.** an act showing this

ve·ne·re·al (və nir'ē əl) *adj.* [< L. *venus*, love] **1.** of sexual intercourse **2.** *a)* transmitted only or chiefly by sexual intercourse with an infected individual, as syphilis and gonorrhea *b)* infected with a venereal disease *c)* of venereal disease

Ve·ne·tian (və nē'shən) *adj.* of Venice, its people, etc. — *n.* a native or inhabitant of Venice

Venetian blind [*also* **v- b-**] a window blind made of a number of thin, horizontal slats that can be set at any angle to regulate the light passing through

Ven·e·zue·la (ven'i zwā'lə, -zwē'-) country in N S. America: 352,143 sq. mi.; pop. 10,399,000; cap. Caracas — **Ven'e·zue'lan** *adj., n.*

venge·ance (ven'jəns) *n.* [see VINDICATE] **1.** the return of an injury for an injury, in punishment; revenge **2.** the desire to make such a return —**with a vengeance 1.** with great force or fury **2.** excessively

venge·ful (venj'fəl) *adj.* seeking revenge; vindictive — **venge'ful·ly** *adv.* —**venge'ful·ness** *n.*

ve·ni·al (vē'nē əl, vēn'yəl) *adj.* [< L. *venia*, grace] **1.** that can be forgiven, pardoned, or excused **2.** *R.C.Ch.* not causing spiritual death: said of sins not regarded as serious —**ve'ni·al·ly** *adv.*

Ven·ice (ven'is) seaport in N Italy: pop. 368,000

ve·ni·re (və nī'rē) *n.* [L., to come] **1.** *short for* VENIRE FACIAS **2.** a list or group of people from among whom a jury or juries will be selected

venire fa·ci·as (fā'shē as') [ML., cause to come] *Law* a writ or order summoning persons to serve as jurors

ve·ni·re·man (və nī'rē mən) *n., pl.* **-men** a member of a venire (sense 2)

ven·i·son (ven'i s'n, -z'n) *n.* [< L. *venari*, to hunt] the flesh of deer, used as food

ven·om (ven'əm) *n.* [< L. *venenum*, a poison] **1.** the poison secreted by some snakes, spiders, etc., injected into the victim by bite or sting **2.** spite; malice

ven'om·ous *adj.* **1.** full of venom; poisonous **2.** spiteful; malicious **3.** able to inject venom by bite or sting —**ven'om·ous·ly** *adv.*

ve·nous (vē'nəs) *adj.* **1.** .of or having veins **2.** designating blood carried in veins

vent¹ (vent) *n.* [< L. *ventus*, a wind] **1.** a means of escaping; outlet **2.** expression; release [*giving* vent *to emotion*] **3.** *a)* a small opening to let gas, etc. out *b)* a small triangular car window for letting air in without a direct draft —*vt.* **1.** to make a vent in **2.** to give release to; let out

vent² (vent) *n.* [< L. *findere*, to split] a vertical slit in a garment, as one in the back of a coat —*vt.* to make a vent in

ven·ti·late (ven't'l āt') *vt.* **-lat'ed, -lat'ing** [< L. *ventus*, a wind] **1.** to circulate fresh air in (a room, etc.) **2.** to put a vent in, to let air, gas, etc. escape **3.** to examine and discuss (a grievance) openly —**ven'ti·la'tion** *n.*

ven'ti·la'tor *n.* any device for replacing foul air with fresh air

ven·tral (ven'trəl) *adj.* [Fr. < L. *venter*, belly] of, on, or near the belly —**ven'tral·ly** *adv.*

ven·tri·cle (ven'tri k'l) *n.* [< L. *venter*, belly] either of the two lower chambers of the heart which receive blood from the atria and pump it into the arteries —**ven·tric'u·lar** (-trik'yə lər) *adj.*

ven·tril·o·quism (ven tril'ə kwiz'm) *n.* [< L. *venter*, belly + *loqui*, speak] the art of speaking so that the voice seems to come from some source other than the speaker —**ven·tril'o·quist** *n.*

ven·ture (ven'chər) *n.* [see ADVENTURE] **1.** a risky undertaking, as in business **2.** something on which a risk is taken —*vt.* **-tured, -tur·ing 1.** to risk; hazard **2.** to take the risk of; brave **3.** to express (an opinion, etc.) at the risk of being criticized, etc. —*vi.* to do or go at some risk —**ven'tur·er** *n.*

ven'ture·some (-səm) *adj.* **1.** inclined to venture; daring **2.** risky; hazardous *Also* **ven'tur·ous**

ven·ue (ven'yōō, -ōō) *n.* [< L. *venire*, to come] *Law* **1.** the locality in which a cause of action or a crime occurs **2.** the locality in which a jury is drawn and a case tried — **change of venue** *Law* the substitution of another place of trial, as when the jury is likely to be prejudiced

Ve·nus (vē'nəs) **1.** *Rom. Myth.* the goddess of love and beauty: identified with the Greek Aphrodite **2.** the most brilliant planet in the solar system: see PLANET —*n.* a very beautiful woman

Ve·nus' fly·trap (vē'nəs flī'trap') a swamp plant of the Carolinas, having leaves with two hinged blades that snap shut and so trap insects

ve·ra·cious (və rā'shəs) *adj.* [< L. *verus*, true] **1.** habitually truthful; honest **2.** true; accurate —**ve·ra'cious·ly** *adv.*

ve·rac·i·ty (və ras'ə tē) *n., pl.* **-ties 1.** honesty **2.** accuracy or precision **3.** truth

Ver·a·cruz (ver'ə krōōz') seaport in E Mexico: pop. 242,000

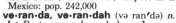

VENUS'
FLYTRAP

ve·ran·da, ve·ran·dah (və ran'də) *n.* [< Port. *varanda*, a balcony] an open porch, usually roofed, along the outside of a building

verb (vurb) *n.* [< L. *verbum*, a word] a word expressing action, existence, or occurrence —*adj.* of, or functioning as, a verb

ver·bal (vur'b'l) *adj.* **1.** of, in, or by means of words **2.** concerned merely with words rather than facts, ideas, or actions **3.** oral rather than written **4.** *Gram.* of, like, or derived from a verb —*n. Gram.* a verbal noun or other word derived from a verb: in English, gerunds, infinitives, and participles are verbals —**ver'bal·ly** *adv.*

ver'bal·ism (-iz'm) *n.* **1.** an expression in words; word or word phrase **2.** words only, without any real meaning **3.** any virtually meaningless phrase

ver·bal·ize (vur'bə līz') *vi.* **-ized', -iz'ing 1.** to be wordy, or verbose **2.** to communicate in words —*vt.* **1.** to express in words **2.** to change (a noun, etc.) into a verb —**ver'bal·i·za'tion** *n.*

verbal noun *Gram.* a noun derived from a verb, esp. a gerund or an infinitive (Ex.: *walking* is healthful, *to err* is human)

ver·ba·tim (vər bāt'əm) *adv., adj.* [< L. *verbum*, a word] word for word

ver·be·na (vər bē'nə) *n.* [L., foliage] any of a group of ornamental plants with spikes or clusters of red, white, or purplish flowers

ver·bi·age (vur'bē ij) *n.* [< L. *verbum*, a word] an excess of words; wordiness

ver·bose (vər bōs') *adj.* [< L. *verbum*, a word] using too many words; wordy —**ver·bose'ly** *adv.* —**ver·bos'i·ty** (-bäs'ə tē), **ver·bose'ness** *n.*

ver·dant (vur'd'nt) *adj.* [prob. VERD(URE) + -ANT] **1.** covered with green vegetation **2.** inexperienced; immature — **ver'dan·cy** *n.*

Verde (vurd), **Cape** peninsula on the Atlantic coast of Senegal: westernmost point of Africa

Ver·di (ver'dē), **Gui·sep·pe** (jōō zep'pe) 1813–1901; It. operatic composer

ver·dict (vur'dikt) *n.* [< L. *vere*, truly + *dicere*, to say] **1.** *Law* the decision reached by a jury **2.** any decision or judgment

ver·di·gris (vur'di grēs', -gris) *n.* [< OFr. *verd*, green + *de*, of + *Grece*, Greece] a green or greenish-blue coating that forms on brass, bronze, or copper

ver·dure (vur'jər) *n.* [< OFr. *verd*, green] **1.** the fresh green color of growing things **2.** green vegetation

verge¹ (vurj) *n.* [< L. *virga*, rod] the edge, brink, or margin —*vi.* **verged, verg'ing** to be on the edge, brink, or border (usually with *on* or *upon*)

verge² (vurj) *vi.* **verged, verg'ing** [L. *vergere*] **1.** to tend or incline (*to* or *toward*) **2.** to pass gradually (*into*) [*dawn verging* into daylight]

Ver·gil (vur'jəl) *var. of* VIRGIL

ver·i·fy (ver'ə fī') *vt.* **-fied', -fy'ing** [< L. *verus*, true + *facere*, to make] **1.** to prove to be true by evidence, etc.; confirm **2.** to test the accuracy of, as by comparison **3.** *Law* to affirm on oath —**ver'i·fi'a·ble** *adj.* —**ver'i·fi·ca'tion** *n.* —**ver'i·fi'er** *n.*

ver·i·ly (ver'ə lē) *adv.* [Archaic] in very truth; truly

ver·i·si·mil·i·tude (ver'ə si mil'ə tōōd', -tyōōd') *n.* [< L. *verus*, true + *similis*, like] **1.** the appearance of being true or real **2.** something having the mere appearance of being true or real

ver·i·ta·ble (ver'i tə b'l) *adj.* [< L. *veritas*, truth] true; actual —**ver'i·ta·bly** *adv.*

ver·i·ty (ver'ə tē) *n., pl.* **-ties** [< L. *verus*, true] **1.** conformity to truth or fact **2.** a principle, belief, etc. taken to be fundamentally and permanently true

ver·mi·cel·li (vur'mə sel'ē, -chel'ē) *n.* [It., little worms < L. *vermis*, a worm] pasta like spaghetti, but in thinner strings

ver·mi·cide (vur'mə sīd') *n.* [< L. *vermis*, worm + -CIDE] a drug or other agent used to kill worms, esp. intestinal worms

ver·mi·form (vur'mə fôrm') *adj.* [< L. *vermis*, worm + -FORM] shaped like a worm

vermiform appendix *see* APPENDIX (sense 2)

ver·mil·ion (vər mil'yən) *n.* [< L. *vermis*, a worm] **1.** a bright red pigment **2.** a bright red or scarlet —*adj.* of the color vermilion

ver·min (vur'min) *n., pl.* -**min** [< L. *vermis*, a worm] **1.** *a)* any of various destructive or disease-carrying insects, bugs, or small animals, as flies, lice, or rats *b)* such pests collectively **2.** a vile, loathsome person —**ver'min·ous** *adj.*

Ver·mont (vər mänt') New England State of the U.S.: 9,609 sq. mi.; pop. 444,000; cap. Montpelier: abbrev. **Vt.**, **VT** —**Ver·mont'er** *n.*

ver·mouth (vər mōoth') *n.* [Fr. < G. *wermut*, wormwood] a sweet or dry, fortified white wine flavored with aromatic herbs

ver·nac·u·lar (vər nak'yə lər) *adj.* [< L. *vernaculus*, native] **1.** of, in, or using the native language of a place **2.** native to a place —*n.* **1.** the native language or dialect of a country or place **2.** the common, everyday language of a people **3.** the shoptalk of a profession or trade

ver·nal (vur'n'l) *adj.* [< L. *ver*, spring] **1.** of the spring **2.** springlike **3.** youthful

Verne (vurn), **Jules** (jōolz) 1828–1905; Fr. novelist

ver·ni·er (vur'nē ər, -nir) *n.* [< P. *Vernier*, 17th-c. Fr. mathematician] a short scale used to indicate fractional parts of divisions of a longer scale: also **vernier scale**

Ve·ro·na (və rō'na) city in N Italy: pop. 259,000

Ver·sailles (vər sī', -sālz') city in NC France, near Paris: the Allies & Germany signed a treaty here (1919) ending World War I: pop. 95,000

ver·sa·tile (vur'sə t'l) *adj.* [Fr. < L. *vertere*, to turn] **1.** competent in many things; able to turn easily from one subject or occupation to another **2.** adaptable to many uses or functions —**ver'sa·tile·ly** *adv.* —**ver'sa·til'i·ty** (-til'ə tē) *n.*

verse (vurs) *n.* [< L. *vertere*, to turn] **1.** a single line of poetry **2.** *a)* poetry in general; sometimes, specif., poems of a light nature *b)* poetry of a specified kind **3.** a single poem **4.** a stanza **5.** any of the short divisions of a chapter of the Bible

versed (vurst) *adj.* [< L. *versari*, be busy] acquainted by experience and study (*in* a subject)

ver·si·fi·ca·tion (vur'sə fi kā'shən) *n.* **1.** a versifying **2.** the art, practice, or theory of poetic composition **3.** metrical structure

ver·si·fy (vur'sə fī') *vi.* -**fied'**, -**fy'ing** [< L. *versus*, a VERSE + *facere*, make] to compose verses —*vt.* **1.** to tell in verse **2.** to put into verse form —**ver'si·fi'er** *n.*

ver·sion (vur'zhən) *n.* [Fr.: see VERSE] **1.** a translation, esp. of the Bible **2.** an account giving one point of view **3.** a particular form [the movie *version* of the novel]

ver·sus (vur'səs) *prep.* [L. < *vertere*, to turn] **1.** in contest against **2.** in contrast with

ver·te·bra (vur'tə brə) *n., pl.* -**brae** (-brē'), -**bras** [L. < *vertere*, to turn] any of the single bones of the spinal column

ver'te·brate (-brit, -brāt') *adj.* **1.** having a backbone, or spinal column **2.** of the vertebrates —*n.* any of a large group of animals that have a backbone and a brain and cranium

VERTEBRAE (A, section of spinal column; B, single vertebra)

ver·tex (vur'teks) *n., pl.* -**tex·es**, -**ti·ces'** (-tə sēz') [L. < *vertere*, to turn] **1.** the highest point; top **2.** *Geom.* the point where the two sides of an angle intersect

ver·ti·cal (vur'ti k'l) *adj.* **1.** of or at the vertex **2.** upright; straight up or down —*n.* a vertical line, plane, etc. —**ver'ti·cal·ly** *adv.*

ver·tig·i·nous (vər tij'ə nəs) *adj.* **1.** of, affected by, or causing vertigo **2.** whirling; spinning **3.** unstable

ver·ti·go (vur'ti gō') *n.* [L. < *vertere*, to turn] a sensation of dizziness

verve (vurv) *n.* [Fr. < L. *verba*, words] **1.** vigor and energy **2.** vivacity; dash

ver·y (ver'ē) *adj.* -**i·er**, -**i·est** [< L. *verus*, true] **1.** complete; utter [the *very* opposite] **2.** same [the *very* hat he lost] **3.** exactly right, suitable, etc. **4.** even (the): used as an intensive [the *very* rafters shook] **5.** actual [caught in the *very* act] —*adv.* **1.** exceedingly **2.** truly; really: used as an intensive [the *very* same man]

very high frequency any radio frequency between 30 and 300 megahertz

very low frequency any radio frequency between 10 and 30 kilohertz

ves·i·cate (ves'i kāt') *vt., vi.* -**cat'ed**, -**cat'ing** [< L. *vesica*, a blister] to blister —**ves'i·ca'tion** *n.*

ves·i·cle (ves'i k'l) *n.* [< Fr. < L. *vesica*, bladder] a small, membranous cavity, sac, or cyst; specif., a blister —**ve·sic·u·lar** (və sik'yə lər), **ve·sic'u·late** (-lit) *adj.*

ves·per (ves'pər) *n.* [L.] **1.** *a)* orig., evening *b)* [Poet.] [V-] *same as* EVENING STAR **2.** an evening prayer or service; specif., [*pl.*] [*often* V-] R.C.Ch. a prayer service held in the late afternoon —*adj.* **1.** of evening **2.** of vespers

Ves·puc·ci (ves pōot'chē), **A·me·ri·go** (ä'me rē'gô) (L. name *Americus Vespucius*) 1451?–1512; It. navigator

ves·sel (ves'l) *n.* [< L. *vas*] **1.** a utensil for holding something, as a bowl, pot, etc. **2.** a ship or large boat **3.** a tube or duct containing or circulating a body fluid

vest (vest) *n.* [< L. *vestis*, garment] **1.** *a)* a short, sleeveless garment worn, esp. under a suit coat, by men *b)* a similar, jacketlike garment worn by women **2.** [Brit.] an undershirt —*vt.* **1.** to dress **2.** to place (authority) *in* someone **3.** to provide (a person or group) (*with* some power, property, etc.) —*vi.* to become vested (*in* a person), as property

Ves·ta (ves'ta) [L.] *Rom. Myth.* the goddess of the hearth

ves·tal (ves't'l) *adj.* **1.** of or sacred to Vesta **2.** of the vestal virgins **3.** chaste; pure —*n.* **1.** *short for* VESTAL VIRGIN **2.** a chaste woman; specif., a virgin

vestal virgin in ancient Rome, any of the virgin priestesses of Vesta, who tended the sacred fire in her temple

vest·ed interest (ves'tid) **1.** an established right, as to some future benefit **2.** [*pl.*] the powerful persons and groups that own and control industry, business, etc.

ves·ti·bule (ves'tə byōol') *n.* [L. *vestibulum*] **1.** a small entrance hall, as to a building **2.** the enclosed passage between passenger cars of a train

ves·tige (ves'tij) *n.* [Fr. < L. *vestigium*, a footprint] **1.** a trace or remaining bit of something once present or whole **2.** *Biol.* an organ or part not so fully developed or functional as it once was in the embryo or species —**ves·tig'i·al** (-tij'ē əl) *adj.*

vest·ment (vest'mənt) *n.* [< L. *vestire*, clothe] a garment, esp. one worn by a clergyman

vest'-pock'et *adj.* **1.** small enough to fit into a vest pocket **2.** very small

ves·try (ves'trē) *n., pl.* -**tries** [< L. *vestis*, garment] **1.** a room in a church, where vestments, etc. are kept **2.** a room in a church, used for meetings, Sunday school, etc. **3.** a group of church members who manage the business affairs of the church —**ves'try·man** (-mən) *n., pl.* -**men**

Ve·su·vi·us (və sōo'vē əs) active volcano in S Italy

vet[1] (vet) *n. shortened form of* VETERINARIAN —*vt.* **vet'ted**, **vet'ting** [Colloq.] to examine or evaluate thoroughly

vet[2] (vet) *n. shortened form of* VETERAN

vet. **1.** veteran **2.** veterinarian **3.** veterinary

vetch (vech) *n.* [< L. *vicia*, vetch] a plant of the legume family, used chiefly as fodder or fertilizer

vet·er·an (vet'ər ən, vet'rən) *adj.* [< L. *vetus*, old] **1.** having had long experience in some kind of work or in military service **2.** of a veteran or veterans —*n.* **1.** a person with much experience in some kind of work **2.** a person who has served in the armed forces of a country

Veterans Day a legal holiday in the U.S. honoring all veterans of the armed forces: observed (except 1971–77) on Nov. 11, the date of the armistice of World War I

vet·er·i·nar·i·an (vet'ər ə ner'ē ən) *n.* one who practices veterinary medicine or surgery

vet·er·i·nar·y (-ē) *adj.* [< L. *veterina*, beasts of burden] designating or of the medical or surgical treatment of diseases and injuries in animals —*n., pl.* -**ies** *same as* VETERINARIAN

ve·to (vē'tō) *n., pl.* -**toes** [L., I forbid] **1.** *a)* an order forbidding some act *b)* the power to prevent action thus **2.** the right of one branch of government to reject bills passed by another; specif., *a)* the power of the President of the U.S. to refuse to sign a bill passed by Congress *b)* the exercise of this right —*vt.* -**toed**, -**to·ing 1.** to prevent (a bill) from becoming law by veto **2.** to forbid

vex (veks) *vt.* [< L. *vexare*, agitate] **1.** to disturb, irritate, etc., esp. in a petty, nagging way **2.** to distress or afflict —**vex·ed·ly** (vek'sid lē) *adv.*

vex·a·tion (vek sā'shən) *n.* **1.** a vexing or being vexed **2.** something that vexes —**vex·a'tious** (-shəs) *adj.*

VHF, vhf very high frequency

VI, V.I. Virgin Islands

vi., v.i. intransitive verb

vi·a (vī'ə, vē'ə) *prep.* [L., way] **1.** by way of **2.** by means of [via airmail]

vi·a·ble (vī'ə b'l) *adj.* [Fr. < L. *vita*, life] **1.** able to live; specif., developed enough to be able to live outside the uterus **2.** workable [viable ideas] —**vi'a·bil'i·ty** *n.*

vi·a·duct (vī'ə dukt') *n.* [L. *via*, way + (AQUE)DUCT] a bridge consisting of a series of short spans supported on piers or towers, usually to carry a road or railroad over a gorge, etc.

vi·al (vī'əl) *n.* [< Gr. *phialē*, shallow cup] a small bottle, usually of glass, for holding medicine or other liquids

vi·and (vī'ənd) *n.* [< L. *vivere*, to live] **1.** an article of food **2.** [*pl.*] food; esp., choice dishes

vibes (vībz) *n.pl.* **1.** [Colloq.] a vibraphone **2.** [< VIBRATION(S)] [Slang] qualities in a person or thing that produce an emotional response in one

vi·brant (vī'brənt) *adj.* [< L. *vibrare*, vibrate] **1.** quivering; vibrating **2.** produced by vibration; resonant: said of sound **3.** vigorous, energetic, etc. —**vi'bran·cy** *n.* —**vi'brant·ly** *adv.*

vi·bra·phone (vī'brə fōn') *n.* [VIBRA(TE) + -PHONE] a musical instrument like the marimba, but with electrically operated valves in the resonant tubes, that produce a gentle vibrato

vi·brate (vī'brāt) *vt.* **-brat·ed, -brat·ing** [< L. *vibrare*] **1.** to set in to-and-fro motion **2.** to cause to quiver —*vi.* **1.** to swing back and forth **2.** to move rapidly back and forth; quiver **3.** to resound **4.** to feel very excited; thrill —**vi'bra·tor** *n.* —**vi'bra·to'ry** (-brə tôr'ē) *adj.*

vi·bra·tion (vī brā'shən) *n.* **1.** a vibrating; esp., rapid movement back and forth; quivering **2.** [*pl.*] same as VIBES (sense 2) **3.** *Physics a*) rapid, periodic, to-and-fro motion or oscillation of an elastic body or the particles of a fluid, as in transmitting sound *b*) a single, complete oscillation

vi·bra·to (vi brät'ō) *n., pl.* **-tos** [It.] *Music* the pulsating effect of a rapid, hardly noticeable variation in pitch

vi·bur·num (vī bʉr'nəm) *n.* [L., wayfaring tree] any of various shrubs or small trees related to the honeysuckle and bearing white flowers

vic·ar (vik'ər) *n.* [< L. *vicis*, a change] **1.** a deputy **2.** *Anglican Ch.* a parish priest who receives a stipend instead of the tithes **3.** *Protestant Episcopal Ch.* a minister in charge of one chapel in a parish **4.** *R.C.Ch.* a church officer acting as deputy of a bishop —**vi·car·i·ate** (vī ker'ē it, -āt') *n.* —**vic'ar·ship'** *n.*

vic'ar·age (-ij) *n.* **1.** the residence of a vicar **2.** the benefice or salary of a vicar

vi·car·i·ous (vī ker'ē əs) *adj.* [< L. *vicis*, a change] **1.** taking the place of another **2.** delegated **3.** done or undergone by one person in place of another **4.** felt as if one were actually taking part in another's experience [a vicarious thrill] —**vi·car'i·ous·ly** *adv.* —**vi·car'i·ous·ness** *n.*

vice¹ (vīs) *n.* [< L. *vitium*] **1.** *a*) an evil or wicked action or habit *b*) evil conduct; depravity *c*) prostitution **2.** any fault, defect, etc. —**vice'less** *adj.*

vi·ce² (vī'sē) *prep.* [L.: see VICE-] in the place of; as the deputy or successor of

vice³ (vīs) *n., vt. chiefly Brit. sp. of* VISE

vice- [< L. *vice*, in the place of another < *vicis*, a change] a prefix meaning subordinate, deputy [vice-president]

vice admiral a naval officer ranking just above a rear admiral —**vice admiralty**

vice'-con'sul *n.* an officer who is subordinate to or a substitute for a consul —**vice'-con'sul·ship'** *n.*

vice·ge·rent (vīs'jir'ənt) *n.* [< L. *vice* (see VICE-) + *gerere*, to direct] a deputy —**vice'ge'ren·cy** *n.*

vice-pres·i·dent (vīs'prez'i dənt) *n.* **1.** an officer next in rank below a president, acting in his place when he is absent or replacing him if he dies or leaves office: for the U.S. official, usually **Vice President 2.** any of several officers of a company, etc., each in charge of a department —**vice'-pres'i·den·cy** *n.* —**vice'-pres'i·den'tial** *adj.*

vice're·gal (-rē'g'l) *adj.* of a viceroy

vice·roy (vīs'roi) *n.* [MFr. < *vice-* (see VICE-) + *roy*, a king] a person ruling a country, province, etc. as the deputy of a sovereign —**vice'roy·ship'** *n.*

vice squad a police squad assigned to the suppression or control of prostitution, gambling, etc.

vi·ce ver·sa (vī'sē vʉr'sə, vīs' vʉr'sə) [L.] the order or relation being reversed

vi·chy·ssoise (vē'shē swäz', vish'ē-) *n.* [Fr.] a thick cream soup of potatoes, onions, etc., usually served cold

Vi·chy (water) (vish'ē, vē'shē) **1.** a mineral water found at Vichy, a city in France **2.** a natural or processed water like this

vic·i·nage (vis'ə nij) *n.* [< L. *vicinus*, near] **1.** same as VICINITY **2.** the people of a neighborhood

vi·cin·i·ty (və sin'ə tē) *n., pl.* **-ties** [see prec.] **1.** nearness; proximity **2.** a nearby region; neighborhood

vi·cious (vish'əs) *adj.* [< L. *vitium*, vice] **1.** characterized by vice; wicked or depraved **2.** debasing; corrupting **3.** faulty; flawed [a vicious argument] **4.** unruly; dangerous [a vicious horse] **5.** malicious; spiteful [a vicious rumor] **6.** very intense, forceful, etc. [a vicious blow] —**vi'cious·ly** *adv.* —**vi'cious·ness** *n.*

vicious circle 1. a situation in which the solution to each problem gives rise to another, eventually bringing back the first problem **2.** *Logic* an argument whose conclusion rests on a premise which itself depends on the conclusion

vi·cis·si·tudes (vi sis'ə tōōdz', -tyōōdz') *n.pl.* [< L. *vicis*, a turn] unpredictable changes in life, fortune, etc.; ups and downs

vic·tim (vik'təm) *n.* [L. *victima*] **1.** someone or something killed, destroyed, sacrificed, etc. **2.** one who suffers some loss, esp. by being swindled

vic'tim·ize' (-tə mīz') *vt.* **-ized', -iz'ing** to make a victim of —**vic'tim·i·za'tion** *n.* —**vic'tim·iz'er** *n.*

vic·tor (vik'tər) *n.* [L. < *vincere*, conquer] a winner or conqueror

Vic·to·ri·a¹ (vik tôr'ē ə) 1819-1901; queen of Great Britain & Ireland (1837-1901) —*n.* [**v-**] a four-wheeled carriage for two, with a folding top

Vic·to·ri·a² (vik tôr'ē ə) **1.** capital of Hong Kong: pop., of met. area, 2,800,000 **2.** capital of British Columbia, Canada: pop. 57,000 **3. Lake,** lake in E Africa

Vic·to'ri·an *adj.* **1.** of or characteristic of the time of Queen Victoria **2.** showing the respectability, prudery, etc. attributed to the Victorians —*n.* a person, esp. a writer, of the time of Queen Victoria —**Vic·to'ri·an·ism** *n.*

vic·to·ri·ous (vik tôr'ē əs) *adj.* **1.** having won a victory; triumphant **2.** of or bringing about victory —**vic·to'ri·ous·ly** *adv.* —**vic·to'ri·ous·ness** *n.*

vic·to·ry (vik'tə rē, -trē) *n., pl.* **-ries** [< L. *vincere*, conquer] **1.** the decisive winning of a battle or war **2.** success in any struggle

vict·ual (vit''l) *n.* [< L. *victus*, food] [*pl.*] [Dial. or Colloq.] articles of food —*vt.* **-ualed** or **-ualled, -ual·ing** or **-ual·ling** to supply with food —*vi.* to lay in a supply of food

vi·cu·ña (vī kōōn'yə, -kōōn'ə) *n.* [Sp.] **1.** a S. American animal related to the llama and alpaca **2.** a fabric made from its soft, shaggy wool

VICUÑA
(to 40 in. high at shoulder)

‡vi·de (vī'dē) [L.] see; refer to (a certain page, etc.)

‡vide in·fra (in'frə) [L.] see below; see further on (in the book, etc.)

‡vi·de·li·cet (vi del'ə sit) *adv.* [L. < *videre licet*, it is permitted to see] that is; namely

vid·e·o (vid'ē ō') *adj.* [L., I see] of television, esp. of the picture portion of a telecast —*n. same as* TELEVISION

vid'e·o·disc' *n.* a disc on which images and sounds, as of a movie, can be recorded for reproduction on a home TV set: also **video disc**

video game an electronic device for producing images on a TV screen, which are controlled by players competing in any of various games

vid'e·o·phone' *n.* a telephone combined with television so that users can see, as well as speak with, one another

vid'e·o·tape' *n.* a magnetic tape on which the electronic impulses of a TV program can be recorded

vie (vī) *vi.* **vied, vy'ing** [< L. *invitare*, invite] to be a rival or rivals; compete (*with* someone) —**vi'er** *n.*

Vi·en·na (vē en'ə) capital of Austria: pop. 1,642,000 —**Vi·en·nese** (vē'ə nēz') *adj., n., pl.* **-nese'**

Vi·et·nam (vē'ət näm') country on the E coast of Indochina: divided, 1954-76, into two republics (**North Vietnam and South Vietnam**): 129,607 sq. mi.; pop. 47,872,000; cap. Hanoi Also sp. **Viet Nam, Viet-Nam** —**Vi'et·nam·ese'** (-nə mēz') *adj., n., pl.* **-ese'**

view (vyōō) *n.* [< L. *videre*, to see] **1.** a seeing or looking, as in inspection **2.** range of vision **3.** mental survey [a correct *view* of the situation] **4.** *a*) a scene or prospect, as of a landscape *b*) a picture of such a scene **5.** visual appearance of something **6.** manner of regarding something;

opinion 7. an object; aim; goal —*vt.* 1. to inspect; scrutinize 2. to see; behold 3. to survey mentally; consider —in **view** 1. in sight 2. under consideration 3. as a goal or hope —**in view of** because of —**on view** displayed publicly —**with a view** to with the purpose or hope of

view′er *n.* 1. a person who views something 2. an optical device for individual viewing of slides, filmstrips, etc.

view′find′er *n. same as* FINDER (sense 2)

view′point′ *n.* the mental position from which things are viewed and judged; point of view

vig·il (vij′əl) *n.* [< L. *vigere*, be lively] 1. a watchful staying awake during the usual hours of sleep 2. a watch kept 3. the evening or day before a church festival, or the devotional services held then

vigilance committee a group that sets itself up, without legal authority, to punish crime, etc.

vig·i·lant (vij′ə lənt) *adj.* [Fr. < L.: see VIGIL] staying watchful or alert to danger or trouble —**vig′i·lance** *n.* — **vig′i·lant·ly** *adv.*

vig·i·lan·te (vij′ə lan′tē) *n.* [Sp., watchman] a member of a vigilance committee

vig′i·lan·tism (-lan tiz′m) *n.* the lawless, violent methods of vigilantes —**vig′i·lan′tist** *adj.*

vi·gnette (vin yet′) *n.* [Fr. < *vigne*, vine] 1. an ornamental design used as a border, inset, etc. on a page 2. a picture shading off gradually at the edges 3. a short, delicate literary sketch —*vt.* **-gnet′ted**, **-gnet′ting** to make a vignette of

vig·or (vig′ər) *n.* [L. < *vigere*, be strong] active force or strength; vitality, intensity, or energy: Brit. sp. **vigour**

vig′or·ous *adj.* of or characterized by vigor; strong; forceful; energetic —**vig′or·ous·ly** *adv.* —**vig′or·ous·ness** *n.*

vik·ing (vī′kiŋ) *n.* [ON. *vikingr*] [*also* V-] any of the Scandinavian pirates of the 8th to 10th centuries

vile (vīl) *adj.* [< L. *vilis*, cheap, base] 1. morally evil; wicked 2. repulsive; disgusting 3. degrading; mean 4. highly disagreeable; [*vile* weather] —**vile′ly** *adv.*

vil·i·fy (vil′ə fī′) *vt.* **-fied′**, **-fy′ing** [see VILE & -FY] to use abusive language about or of; defame —**vil′i·fi·ca′tion** *n.* —**vil′i·fi′er** *n.*

vil·la (vil′ə) *n.* [It. < L., a farm] a country house or estate, esp. a large one used as a retreat

vil·lage (vil′ij) *n.* [see prec.] 1. a community smaller than a town 2. the people of a village, collectively —*adj.* of a village —**vil′lag·er** *n.*

vil·lain (vil′ən) *n.* [< VL. *villanus*, a farm servant] 1. a person guilty of great crimes; scoundrel 2. a wicked character in a novel, play, etc. who opposes the hero — **vil′lain·ess** *n.fem.*

vil′lain·ous *adj.* 1. of or like a villain; evil 2. very bad or disagreeable —**vil′lain·ous·ly** *adv.*

vil′lain·y *n., pl.* **-ies** 1. a being villainous 2. villainous conduct 3. a villainous act

vil·lein (vil′ən) *n.* [see VILLAIN] in feudal England, any of a class of serfs who had become freemen legally to all others except their lord

vim (vim) *n.* [< L. *vis*, strength] energy; vigor

‡vin (van; *Anglicized* vin) *n.* [Fr.] wine

vin·ai·grette (vin′i gret′) *n.* [Fr. < *vinaigre*, vinegar] a small ornamental box or bottle with holes in the lid, for holding vinegar, smelling salts, etc.

vin·ci·ble (vin′sə b′l) *adj.* [< L. *vincere*, overcome] that can be overcome or defeated —**vin′ci·bil′i·ty** *n.*

vin·di·cate (vin′də kāt′) *vt.* **-cat′ed**, **-cat′ing** [< L. *vis*, force + *dicere*, to say] 1. to clear from criticism, blame, suspicion, etc. 2. to defend against opposition 3. to justify —**vin′di·ca′tor** *n.*

vin′di·ca′tion *n.* 1. a vindicating or being vindicated 2. a fact or circumstance that vindicates

vin·dic·tive (vin dik′tiv) *adj.* [see VINDICATE] 1. revengeful in spirit 2. said or done in revenge —**vin·dic′tive·ly** *adv.* —**vin·dic′tive·ness** *n.*

vine (vīn) *n.* [< L. *vinum*, wine] 1. a plant with a long stem that grows along the ground or climbs a support 2. the stem of such a plant 3. *same as* GRAPEVINE (sense 1)

vin·e·gar (vin′i gər) *n.* [< MFr. *vin*, wine + *aigre*, sour] a sour liquid containing acetic acid, made by fermenting cider, wine, etc.: it is used to flavor or preserve foods — **vin′e·gar·y** *adj.*

vine·yard (vin′yərd) *n.* a piece of land where grapevines are grown

vin·i·cul·ture (vin′i kul′chər) *n.* [see VINE] the cultivation of wine grapes

‡vin rosé [Fr.] *same as* ROSÉ

vin·tage (vin′tij) *n.* [< L. *vinum*, wine + *demere*, to remove] 1. the crop of grapes from a certain vineyard or grape-growing region in a single season 2. the wine of a particular region and year 3. the type or model of a particular year or period [a car of prewar *vintage*] —*adj.* 1. of choice vintage [*vintage* wine] 2. of a past period [*vintage* clothes]

vint·ner (vint′nər) *n.* [< L. *vinetum*, vineyard] a merchant who sells wine

vi·nyl (vī′n′l) *n.* [< L. *vinum*, wine + -YL] the univalent radical, CH_2:CH–, derived from ethylene: various vinyl compounds are polymerized to form resins and plastics (**vinyl plastics**)

vi·ol (vī′əl) *n.* [< OPr. *viula* < ?] any of an early family of stringed instruments, usually with six strings, frets, and a flat back

vi·o·la (vē ō′lə, vī-) *n.* [It.] a stringed instrument of the violin family, slightly larger than a violin

vi·o·la·ble (vī′ə lə b′l) *adj.* that can be, or is likely to be, violated —**vi′o·la·bly** *adv.*

vi·o·late (vī′ə lāt′) *vt.* **-lat′ed**, **-lat′ing** [< L. *violare*, use force] 1. to break (a law, promise, etc.) 2. to rape 3. to desecrate (something sacred) 4. to break in on; disturb 5. to offend, insult, etc. [to *violate* one's sense of decency] — **vi′o·la′tor** *n.*

vi·o·la′tion *n.* a violating or being violated; specif., *a*) infringement, as of a law *b*) rape *c*) desecration of something sacred *d*) disturbance

vi·o·lence (vī′ə ləns) *n.* [< L. *violentus*, violent] 1. physical force used to cause injury or damage 2. intense, powerful force, as of a hurricane 3. the harm done in violating rights, privacy, etc. 4. strong feeling; fury 5. a violent deed or act

vi′o·lent (-lənt) *adj.* 1. acting with or having great physical force that causes injury or damage 2. caused by violence 3. passionate; furious [*violent* language] 4. severe; intense [a *violent* headache] —**vi′o·lent·ly** *adv.*

vi·o·let (vī′ə lit) *n.* [< L. *viola*] 1. a low plant with white, blue, purple, or yellow flowers 2. a bluish-purple color — *adj.* bluish-purple

violet ray 1. the shortest ray of the visible spectrum 2. loosely, an ultraviolet ray

vi·o·lin (vī′ə lin′) *n.* [< It. *viola*, viol] any instrument of the modern family of four-stringed instruments played with a bow; specif., the smallest and highest-pitched instrument of this family, held horizontally under the chin

vi′o·lin′ist *n.* a violin player

vi·ol·ist (vī′əl ist; *for 2* vē ō′list) *n.* 1. a viol player 2. a viola player

vi·o·lon·cel·lo (vē′ə län chel′ō, vī′ə lən-) *n., pl.* **-los** [It.] *same as* CELLO —**vi′o·lon·cel′list** *n.*

VIP, V.I.P. [Colloq.] very important person

vi·per (vī′pər) *n.* [< L. < ? *vivus*, living + *parere*, to bear] 1. a venomous snake 2. a malicious or treacherous person —**vi′per·ous**, **vi′per·ish** *adj.*

vi·ra·go (vi rä′gō, vī rä′-) *n., pl.* **-goes**, **-gos** [< L. *vir*, a man] a quarrelsome, shrewish woman

vi·ral (vī′rəl) *adj.* of, involving, or caused by a virus

vir·e·o (vir′ē ō′) *n., pl.* **-os′** [L., a type of finch] a small American songbird, with olive-green or gray feathers

Vir·gil (vur′jəl) 70–19 B.C.; Rom. poet: author of the *Aeneid* —**Vir·gil′i·an** (-jil′ē ən) *adj.*

vir·gin (vur′jin) *n.* [< L. *virgo*, maiden] a person, esp. a woman, who has never had sexual intercourse —[V-] *same as* VIRGO —*adj.* 1. being a virgin 2. chaste; modest 3. untouched, unused, pure, etc. [*virgin* snow] —**the Virgin** Mary, the mother of Jesus

vir′gin·al *adj.* 1. of or like a virgin; maidenly 2. pure; fresh; unsullied —**vir′gin·al·ly** *adv.*

vir′gin·al² *n.* [prob. akin to prec.] [*sometimes pl.*] a harpsichord; esp., a small, rectangular harpsichord of the 16th cent.

Virgin Birth *Christian Theol.* the doctrine that Jesus was born to Mary, a virgin, and that she was his only human parent

Vir·gin·ia (vər jin′yə) Southern State of the U.S.: 40,815 sq. mi.; pop. 4,648,000; cap. Richmond: abbrev. **Va.**, **VA** — **Vir·gin′ian** *adj., n.*

Virginia Beach city in SE Va.: pop. 172,000

Virginia creeper *same as* WOODBINE (sense 2)

Virginia reel an American reel, danced by couples facing in two lines

Virgin Islands group of islands in the West Indies, constituting a Brit. territory and a U.S. territory

---

fat, āpe, cär; ten, ēven; is, bīte; gō, hôrn, tōōl, look; oil, out; up, fur; thin, *th*en; zh, leisure; ŋ, ring; ə for *a* in *ago*; ' as in *able* (ā′b'l); ë, Fr. coeur; ö, Fr. feu; ö, Fr. mo*n*; ü, Fr. duc; r, Fr. cri; kh, G. doch, ich. ‡ foreign; < derived from

vir·gin·i·ty (vər jin′ə tē) *n.* the state of being a virgin; maidenhood; chastity

Virgin Mary Mary, the mother of Jesus

Virgin Queen *epithet of* ELIZABETH I

virgin wool wool that has never before been processed

Vir·go (vur′gō) [L., virgin] **1.** an equatorial constellation **2.** the sixth sign of the zodiac: see ZODIAC, illus.

vir·gule (vur′gyōol) *n.* [Fr. < L. *virga,* twig] a short, diagonal line (/) used in dates or fractions (3/8) and also standing for "or" (and/or), "per" (feet/second), etc.

vir·ile (vir′əl) *adj.* [< L. *vir,* a man] **1.** of or characteristic of a man; masculine **2.** having manly strength or vigor **3.** capable of copulation —**vi·ril·i·ty** (vi ril′ə tē) *n.*

vi·rol·o·gy (vī räl′ə jē) *n.* [< VIR(US) + -LOGY] the study of viruses and virus diseases —**vi·rol′o·gist** *n.*

vir·tu (vər tōō′, vur′tōō) *n.* [It. < L. *virtus,* virtue] **1.** a love of, or taste for, artistic objects **2.** such objects, collectively **3.** the artistic or beautiful quality of such objects

vir·tu·al (vur′chōō wəl) *adj.* being such practically or in effect, although not in actual fact or name [a *virtual* dictator] —**vir′tu·al·ly** *adv.*

vir·tue (vur′chōō) *n.* [< L. *virtus,* manliness, worth] **1.** general moral excellence **2.** a specific moral quality regarded as good **3.** chastity **4.** *a)* excellence in general *b)* a good quality **5.** efficacy, as of a medicine —**by** (or **in**) **virtue of** because of

vir·tu·os·i·ty (vur′chōō wäs′ə tē) *n., pl.* -**ties** [< *virtuoso*] great technical skill in some fine art, esp. in the performance of music

vir·tu·o·so (vur′chōō wō′sō) *n., pl.* -**sos, -si** (-sē) [It., skilled] a person displaying virtuosity

vir·tu·ous (vur′chōō wəs) *adj.* **1.** having, or characterized by, moral virtue **2.** chaste: said of a woman —**vir′tu·ous·ly** *adv.* —**vir′tu·ous·ness** *n.*

vir·u·lent (vir′yoo lənt, -oo-) *adj.* [< L. *virus,* a poison] **1.** *a)* extremely poisonous; deadly *b)* bitterly antagonistic; full of hate **2.** *Med. a)* violent and rapid in its course: said of a disease *b)* highly infectious —**vir′u·lence** *n.*

vi·rus (vī′rəs) *n.* [L., a poison] **1.** *a)* any of a group of very small infective agents that cause various diseases *b)* such a disease **2.** a harmful influence

vi·sa (vē′zə) *n.* [Fr. < L. *videre,* to see] an endorsement on a passport, granting entry into a country —*vt.* -**saed, -sa·ing** to put a visa on (a passport)

vis·age (viz′ij) *n.* [< L. *videre,* to see] **1.** the face; countenance **2.** appearance; aspect

vis-à-vis (vē′zə vē′) *adj., adv.* [Fr.] face to face; opposite —*prep.* **1.** opposite to **2.** in relation to

vis·cer·a (vis′ər ə) *n.pl., sing.* **vis′cus** (-kəs) [L., pl. of *viscus,* inner bodily part] the internal organs of the body, as the heart, lungs, intestines, etc.; specif., in popular usage, the intestines

vis′cer·al *adj.* **1.** of the viscera **2.** intuitive, emotional, etc. rather than intellectual

vis·cid (vis′id) *adj.* [< L. *viscum,* birdlime] thick, syrupy, and sticky; viscous

vis·cose (vis′kōs) *adj.* [see prec.] **1.** *same as* VISCOUS **2.** of viscose —*n.* a syruplike solution of cellulose, used in making rayon thread and fabric (**viscose rayon**) and cellophane

vis·cos·i·ty (vis käs′ə tē) *n., pl.* -**ties 1.** a viscous quality or state **2.** *Physics* the internal friction of a fluid, caused by molecular attraction

vis·count (vī′kount) *n.* [see VICE- & COUNT²] a nobleman next below an earl or count and above a baron —**vis′count·ess** *n.fem.*

vis·cous (vis′kəs) *adj.* [see VISCID] **1.** thick, syrupy, and sticky **2.** *Physics* having viscosity

vise (vīs) *n.* [< L. *vitis,* vine, lit., that which winds] a device having two jaws opened and closed as by a screw, used for holding firmly an object being worked on —*vt.* **vised, vis′ing** to hold or squeeze as with a vise —**vise′like′** *adj.*

vi·sé (vē′zā, vē zā′) *n., vt.* -**séed, -sé·ing** [Fr.] *same as* VISA

Vish·nu (vish′nōō) the second member of the Hindu Trinity (Brahma, Vishnu, and Siva), called "the Preserver"

vis·i·bil·i·ty (viz′ə bil′ə tē) *n., pl.* -**ties 1.** a being visible **2.** *a)* the relative possibility of being seen under the prevailing conditions of distance, light, etc. *b)* range of vision

VISE

vis·i·ble (viz′ə b'l) *adj.* [< L. *videre,* to see] **1.** that can be seen **2.** that can be perceived; evident **3.** on hand [*visible* supply] —**vis′i·ble·ness** *n.* —**vis′i·bly** *adv.*

vi·sion (vizh′ən) *n.* [< L. *videre,* to see] **1.** the power of seeing **2.** something supposedly seen in a dream, trance, etc. **3.** a mental image [*visions* of power] **4.** the ability to foresee or perceive something not actually visible, as through mental acuteness **5.** force or power of imagination [a statesman of great *vision*] **6.** something or someone of great beauty —*vt.* to see as in a vision

vi′sion·ar′y (-er′ē) *adj.* **1.** of, having the nature of, or seen in a vision **2.** *a)* imaginary *b)* not realistic; impractical [*visionary* schemes] **3.** seeing visions —*n., pl.* -**ies 1.** one who sees visions **2.** one who has impractical ideas

vis·it (viz′it) *vt.* [< L. *videre,* to see] **1.** to go or come to see (someone) out of friendship, for professional reasons, etc. **2.** to stay with as a guest **3.** to go or come to (a place) as in order to inspect **4.** to come upon or afflict [a drought *visited* the land] **5.** to inflict (punishment, etc.) upon (someone) —*vi.* **1.** to make a visit, esp. a social call **2.** [Colloq.] to converse, as during a visit —*n.* a visiting; specif., *a)* a social call *b)* a stay as a guest *c)* an official call, as of a doctor *d)* [Colloq.] a friendly conversation

vis′it·ant (-ənt) *n. same as* VISITOR

vis′it·a′tion (-ə tā′shən) *n.* **1.** a visiting; esp., an official visit as to inspect **2.** any trouble looked upon as punishment sent by God

vis·it·ing card (viz′it in) *same as* CALLING CARD

vis′i·tor *n.* a person making a visit

vi·sor (vī′zər) *n.* [< OFr. *vis,* a face] **1.** the movable part of a helmet, covering the face **2.** a mask **3.** a projecting brim, as on a cap, for shading the eyes **4.** an adjustable shade in a car, over the windshield, for shading the eyes —**vi′sored** *adj.*

vis·ta (vis′tə) *n.* [It. < L. *videre,* to see] **1.** a view, esp. as seen through a long passage, as between rows of trees, etc. **2.** a comprehensive mental view of a series of events —**vis′taed** *adj.*

Vis·tu·la (vis′chōō lə) river in Poland, flowing into the Baltic Sea: 677 mi.

vis·u·al (vizh′ōō wəl) *adj.* [< L. *videre,* to see] **1.** of or used in seeing **2.** that is or can be seen; visible —**vis′u·al·ly** *adv.*

visual aids motion pictures, slides, charts, etc. (but not books) used in teaching, illustrating lectures, etc.

vis′u·al·ize′ (-wə līz′) *vt., vi.* -**ized′, -iz′ing** to form a mental image of (something not present to the sight) —**vis′u·al·i·za′tion** *n.*

vi·tal (vīt′'l) *adj.* [< L. *vita,* life] **1.** of or concerned with life **2.** essential to life [*vital* organs] **3.** fatal [*vital* wounds] **4.** *a)* essential; indispensable *b)* of crucial importance **5.** affecting the validity, truth, etc. of something [a *vital* error] **6.** full of life; energetic —*n.* [*pl.*] **1.** the vital organs, as the heart, brain, etc. **2.** any essential parts —**vi′tal·ly** *adv.*

vital capacity the volume of air that one can forcibly expel from the lungs after taking a full breath

vi·tal·i·ty (vī tal′ə tē) *n., pl.* -**ties 1.** power to live or go on living **2.** power to endure or survive **3.** mental or physical energy; vigor

vi·tal·ize (vīt′'l īz′) *vt.* -**ized′, -iz′ing** to make vital; give life or vigor to —**vi′tal·i·za′tion** *n.*

vital signs the pulse, respiration, and body temperature as indicators of body function

vital statistics data on births, deaths, marriages, etc.

vi·ta·min (vīt′ə min) *n.* [< L. *vita,* life] any of certain complex substances found variously in foods and essential to good health —**vi′ta·min′ic** *adj.*

vitamin A a fat-soluble alcohol found in fish-liver oil, egg yolk, butter, etc.: a deficiency of this results in night blindness

vitamin B (complex) a group of unrelated water-soluble substances, including: *a)* **vitamin B₁** (*see* THIAMINE) *b)* **vitamin B₂** (*see* RIBOFLAVIN) *c)* NIACIN *d)* **vitamin B₁₂** a vitamin containing cobalt, used in treating anemia

vitamin C *same as* ASCORBIC ACID

vitamin D any of several fat-soluble vitamins found esp. in fish-liver oils, milk, etc.: a deficiency of this produces rickets

vitamin E a group of related oils occurring chiefly in wheat-germ oil, cottonseed oil, lettuce, etc. and necessary to fertility in some animals

vitamin H *same as* BIOTIN

vitamin K a fat-soluble vitamin that promotes blood clotting, found in alfalfa leaves, fish meal, etc.

vi·ti·ate (vish′ē āt′) *vt.* -**at′ed, -at′ing** [< L. *vitium,* a vice] **1.** to make imperfect; spoil **2.** to weaken morally **3.** to make legally ineffective —**vi′ti·a′tion** *n.* —**vi′ti·a′tor** *n.*

vit·i·cul·ture (vit′ə kul′chər) *n.* [< L. *vitis,* vine + CULTURE] the cultivation of grapes

vit·re·ous (vit′rē əs) *adj.* [< L. *vitrum*, glass] 1. of or like glass 2. derived from or made of glass 3. of the vitreous body

vitreous body (or **humor**) the transparent, colorless, jellylike substance that fills the eyeball between the retina and lens

vit·ri·fy (vit′rə fī′) *vt.*, *vi.* -fied′, -fy′ing [< Fr. < L. *vitrum*, glass + *facere*, make] to change into glass or a glasslike substance by fusion due to heat —**vit′ri·fi′a·ble** *adj.* —vit′ri·fi·ca′tion, vit′ri·fac′tion *n.*

vit·rine (vi trēn′) *n.* [Fr. < L. *vitrum*, glass] a glass-paneled cabinet for art objects, curios, etc.

vit·ri·ol (vit′rē əl) *n.* [< L. *vitreus*, glassy] 1. any of several sulfates of metals, as of copper (*blue vitriol*) or iron (*green vitriol*) 2. *same as* SULFURIC ACID 3. sharpness or bitterness, as in speech

vit′ri·ol·ic (-äl′ik) *adj.* 1. of, like, or derived from a vitriol 2. sharp and bitter [*vitriolic* talk]

vi·tu·per·ate (vī tōō′pə rāt′, vi tyōō′-) *vt.* -at′ed, -at′ing [< L. *vitium*, fault + *parare*, prepare] to speak abusively to or about —vi·tu′per·a′tion *n.* —vi·tu′per·a′tive *adj.*

‡vi·va (vē′vä) *interj.* [It., Sp.] (long) live (someone or something specified)!: an exclamation of praise

vi·va·ce (vi vä′chä) *adj.*, *adv.* [It.] *Music* in a lively, spirited manner

vi·va·cious (vi vā′shəs, vī-) *adj.* [< L. *vivere*, to live] full of animation; lively —vi·va′cious·ly *adv.* —vi·va′cious·ness *n.*

vi·vac′i·ty (-vas′ə tē) *n.* the quality or state of being vivacious; liveliness

vi·var·i·um (vī ver′ē əm) *n.*, *pl.* -i·ums, -i·a (-ə) [L. < *vivere*, to live] an enclosed place for animals to live as if in their natural environment

vi·va vo·ce (vī′və vō′sē) [ML., with living voice] by word of mouth; orally —vi′va-vo′ce *adj.*

‡vive (vēv) *interj.* [Fr.] (long) live (someone or something specified)!: an exclamation of praise

viv·id (viv′id) *adj.* [< L. *vivere*, to live] 1. full of life; lively 2. bright; intense: said of colors, light, etc. 3. strong and clear; active [a *vivid* imagination] —viv′id·ly *adv.* —viv′id·ness *n.*

viv·i·fy (viv′ə fī′) *vt.* -fied′, -fy′ing [< L. *vivus*, alive + *facere*, make] 1. to give life to; animate 2. to make more lively, active, striking, etc. —viv′i·fi·ca′tion *n.*

vi·vip·a·rous (vī vip′ər əs) *adj.* [< L. *vivus*, alive + *parere*, to produce] bearing living young instead of laying eggs —vi·vip′a·rous·ly *adv.*

viv·i·sect (viv′ə sekt′) *vt.*, *vi.* to practice vivisection on

viv·i·sec·tion (viv′ə sek′shən) *n.* [< L. *vivus*, alive + SECTION] medical research that involves surgery on living animals —viv′i·sec′tion·ist *n.*

vix·en (vik′s'n) *n.* [< OE. *fyxe*, she-fox] 1. a female fox 2. an ill-tempered, shrewish woman —vix′en·ish *adj.*

viz. (viz; *often read* "namely") [< contr. for L. *videlicet*] videlicet; that is; namely

vi·zier, vi·zir (vi zir′, viz′yər) *n.* [< Turk. < Ar. *wazara*, bear a burden] in Muslim countries, a high government official

vi·zor (vī′zər) *n.* *alt. sp. of* VISOR

Vla·di·vos·tok (vlad′i väs′täk) seaport in SE R.S.F.S.R., on the Pacific: pop. 442,000

VLF, vlf very low frequency

voc. vocative

vo·ca·ble (vō′kə b'l) *n.* [Fr. < L. *vocare*, to call] a word regarded as a unit of sounds or letters rather than as a unit of meaning

vo·cab·u·lar·y (vō kab′yə ler′ē) *n.*, *pl.* -ies [ult. < L. *vocare*, to call] 1. a list of words, usually arranged in alphabetical order and defined, as in a dictionary or glossary 2. all the words used in a language or by a particular person, class, etc.

vo·cal (vō′k'l) *adj.* [< L. *vox*, a voice] 1. uttered by the voice; spoken; oral [*vocal* sounds] 2. sung [*vocal* music] 3. able to speak or make oral sounds 4. of, used in, or belonging to the voice [*vocal* organs] 5. speaking freely or strongly —vo′cal·ly *adv.*

vocal cords either of two pairs of membranous folds in the larynx: voice is produced when air from the lungs causes the lower pair to vibrate

vo·cal·ic (vō kal′ik) *adj.* 1. of, or having the nature of, a vowel 2. composed mainly of vowels

vo·cal·ist (vō′k'l ist) *n.* one who sings; singer

vo′cal·ize′ (-īz′) *vt.* -ized′, -iz′ing 1. to express with the voice 2. to give a voice to 3. *Phonetics a*) to change into

or use as a vowel *b*) to voice —*vi.* to speak or sing —vo′cal·i·za′tion *n.*

vo·ca·tion (vō kā′shən) *n.* [< L. *vocare*, to call] 1. a call or will to enter a certain career 2. the career toward which one believes oneself to be called 3. any trade, profession, or occupation —vo·ca′tion·al *adj.* —vo·ca′tion·al·ly *adv.*

vocational guidance the work of testing and interviewing persons in order to guide them toward the choice of a suitable vocation

voc·a·tive (väk′ə tiv) *adj.* [see VOCATION] *Gram.* designating the case indicating the one addressed —*n.* 1. the vocative case 2. a word in this case

vo·cif·er·ate (vō sif′ə rāt′) *vt.*, *vi.* -at′ed, -at′ing [< L. *vox*, voice + *ferre*, to bear] to shout loudly; clamor —vo·cif′er·ant *adj.* —vo·cif′er·a′tion *n.*

vo·cif·er·ous (-ər əs) *adj.* noisy; clamorous —vo·cif′er·ous·ly *adv.* —vo·cif′er·ous·ness *n.*

vod·ka (väd′kə) *n.* [Russ. < *voda*, water] a colorless alcoholic liquor distilled from wheat, rye, etc.

vogue (vōg) *n.* [Fr., lit., a rowing] 1. the fashion at any particular time; mode 2. general acceptance; popularity —*adj.* in vogue: also **vogu·ish** (vō′gish)

voice (vois) *n.* [< L. *vox*] 1. sound made through the mouth, esp. by human beings in talking, singing, etc. 2. the ability to make such sounds 3. any sound, influence, etc. regarded as like vocal utterance [the *voice* of the sea] 4. an expressed wish, opinion, etc. 5. the right to express one's wish, etc.; vote 6. utterance or expression 7. the means by which something is expressed 8. *Gram.* a form of a verb showing it as active or passive 9. *Music a*) singing ability *b*) a singer *c*) any of the parts performed together in a composition 10. *Phonet.* sound made by vibrating the vocal cords with air from the lungs, as in pronouncing all vowels and such consonants as (b), (d), (g), etc. —*vt.* **voiced**, **voic′ing** 1. to utter or express in words 2. *Music* to regulate the tone of (organ pipes, etc.) 3. *Phonet.* to utter with voice —**in voice** with the voice in good condition, as for singing

voiced (voist) *adj.* 1. having (a specified kind of) voice [deep-*voiced*] 2. expressed by the voice 3. *Phonet.* made by vibrating the vocal cords; said of certain consonants

voice′less *adj.* 1. having no voice 2. not speaking or spoken 3. *Phonet.* not voiced; uttered without voice [p, t, k, etc. are *voiceless* consonants]

voice′-o′ver *n.* the voice commenting or narrating off camera, as for a TV commercial

void (void) *adj.* [< L. *vacare*, be empty] 1. containing nothing; empty; vacant 2. devoid (of) [*void* of sense] 3. ineffective; useless 4. without legal force; invalid —*n.* 1. an empty space 2. a feeling of emptiness or loss —*vt.* 1. to empty out 2. to discharge (urine or feces) 3. to make void; annul —*vi.* to defecate or, esp., to urinate —void′a·ble *adj.*

‡voi·là (vwä lä′) [Fr., see there] behold; there it is: often used as an interjection

voile (voil) *n.* [Fr., a veil] a thin, sheer fabric, as of cotton

vol. 1. *pl.* vols. volume 2. volunteer

vol·a·tile (väl′ə t'l) *adj.* [< L. *volare*, to fly] 1. vaporizing or evaporating quickly 2. unstable or fickle —vol′a·til′i·ty (-til′ə tē) *n.*

vol′a·til·ize′ (-īz′) *vt.*, *vi.* -ized′, -iz′ing to make or become volatile; evaporate —vol′a·til·i·za′tion *n.*

vol·can·ic (väl kan′ik) *adj.* 1. of or caused by a volcano 2. having volcanoes 3. like a volcano; violently explosive —vol·can′i·cal·ly *adv.*

vol·ca·no (väl kā′nō) *n.*, *pl.* -noes, -nos [< L. *Volcanus*, Vulcan] 1. a vent in the earth's crust through which molten rock, rock fragments, ashes, etc. are ejected 2. a cone-shaped mountain of these materials built up around the vent

vole (vōl) *n.* [earlier *vole mouse* < Scand., as in Norw. *voll*, field + MOUSE] any of various small rodents with a stout body and short tail

Vol·ga (väl′gə, vōl′-) river in W R.S.F.S.R., flowing into the Caspian Sea: 2,290 mi.

Vol·go·grad (väl′gə grad′) city in SC European R.S.F.S.R., on the Volga: pop. 818,000

vo·li·tion (vō lish′ən) *n.* [ult. < L. *velle*, be willing] the act or power of using the will —vo·li′tion·al *adj.*

vol·ley (väl′ē) *n.*, *pl.* -leys [< L. *volare*, to fly] 1. the simultaneous discharge of a number of weapons 2. the missiles so discharged 3. a rapid burst [a *volley* of curses] 4. *Tennis*, etc. a return of a ball, etc. before it touches the ground *—vt., vi.* **-leyed, -ley·ing 1.** to discharge or be discharged as in a volley **2.** *Tennis,* etc. to return (the ball, etc.) as a volley *—vol′ley·er n.*

vol′ley·ball′ *n.* **1.** a game played by two teams who hit a large, light, inflated ball back and forth over a high net with the hands, trying to return the ball before it touches the ground **2.** the ball

volt (vōlt) *n.* [< A. *Volta* (1745–1827), It. physicist] the unit of electromotive force that requires one joule of work to move one coulomb of charge from a point of lower potential to one of higher potential

volt·age (vōl′tij) *n.* electromotive force expressed in volts

vol·ta·ic (väl tā′ik, vōl-) *adj.* **1.** designating or of electricity produced by chemical action; galvanic **2.** used in so producing electricity

voltaic battery 1. a battery composed of voltaic cells **2.** *same as* VOLTAIC CELL

voltaic cell a device for producing an electric current by the action of two plates of different metals in an electrolyte

Vol·taire (vōl ter′, väl-) 1694–1778; Fr. writer and philosopher

vol·tam·e·ter (väl tam′ə tər, vōl-) *n.* an electrolytic cell for measuring an electric current by the amount of gas liberated or metal deposited from an electrolyte

volt·am·me·ter (vōlt′am′mēt′ər) *n.* an instrument for measuring either voltage or amperage

volt·me·ter (vōlt′mēt′ər) *n.* an instrument for measuring voltage

vol·u·ble (väl′yoo b′l) *adj.* [Fr. < L. *volvere,* to roll] talking very much and easily; talkative *—vol′u·bil′i·ty n. —vol′u·bly adv.*

vol·ume (väl′yoom) *n.* [< L. *volumen,* scroll] **1.** *a)* a book *b)* any of the books of a set **2.** a set of the issues of a periodical for a fixed period, usually a year **3.** the amount of space occupied in three dimensions; cubic contents **4.** *a)* a quantity, bulk, or amount *b)* a large quantity **5.** the strength or loudness of sound *—speak volumes* to be very meaningful

vol·u·met·ric (väl′yoo met′rik) *adj.* of or based on the measurement of volume: also **vol′u·met′ri·cal**

vo·lu·mi·nous (və loo′mə nəs) *adj.* **1.** producing or consisting of enough to fill volumes **2.** large; bulky; full *—vo·lu′mi·nos′i·ty* (-näs′ə tē) *n. —vo·lu′mi·nous·ly adv.*

vol·un·tar·y (väl′ən ter′ē) *adj.* [< L. *voluntas,* free will] **1.** brought about by one's own free choice; given or done of one's own free will **2.** acting of one's own accord **3.** intentional [*voluntary* manslaughter] **4.** controlled by the will [*voluntary* muscles] **5.** having the power of free choice [man is a *voluntary* agent] **6.** made up of volunteers *—vol′un·tar′i·ly adv.*

vol′un·tar′y·ism *n.* the theory or system of support of churches, schools, etc. by voluntary contributions and not by the state

vol·un·teer (väl′ən tir′) *n.* one who offers to enter into any service, as military service, of his own free will *—adj.* **1.** of or made up of volunteers **2.** serving as a volunteer *—vt.* to offer or give of one's own free will *—vi.* to enter or offer to enter into any service of one's own free will

vo·lup·tu·ar·y (və lup′choo wer′ē) *n., pl.* **-ies** [< L. *voluptas,* pleasure] one devoted to luxurious living and sensual pleasures

vo·lup·tu·ous (və lup′choo wəs) *adj.* **1.** full of, producing, or fond of sensual pleasures **2.** suggesting, or arising from, sensual pleasures *—vo·lup′tu·ous·ly adv. —vo·lup′tu·ous·ness n.*

vo·lute (və loot′) *n.* [< L. *volvere,* to roll] a spiral or whorl

vom·it (väm′it) *n.* [< L. *vomere,* to vomit] matter ejected from the stomach through the mouth *—vt., vi.* **1.** to eject (the contents of the stomach) through the mouth; throw up **2.** to discharge or be discharged with force

‡**von** (fôn; *E.* vän) *prep.* [G.] of; from: a prefix in many names of German and Austrian families

voo·doo (voo′doo) *n., pl.* **-doos** [Creole Fr. < a WAfr. word] **1.** a primitive religion of African origin, based on a belief in sorcery and magic charms, fetishes, etc.: it is still practiced, chiefly by natives of the West Indies **2.** one who practices voodoo **3.** a voodoo charm, fetish, etc. *—adj.* of or used in voodoo *—vt.* to affect by voodoo magic *—voo′doo·ism n. —voo′doo·ist n. —voo′doo·is′tic adj.*

vo·ra·cious (vô rā′shəs) *adj.* [< L. *vorare,* devour] **1.** greedy in eating; ravenous **2.** very eager [a *voracious* reader] *—vo·ra′cious·ly adv. —vo·rac′i·ty* (-ras′ə tē), **vo·ra′cious·ness** *n.*

-vorous [< L. *vorare,* devour] *a combining form meaning* feeding on, eating [*omnivorous*]

vor·tex (vôr′teks) *n., pl.* **-tex·es, -ti·ces′** (-tə sēz′) [L. < *vertere,* to turn] **1.** *same as* WHIRLPOOL **2.** *same as* WHIRLWIND **3.** anything like a whirl in its rush, catastrophic power, etc.

vo·ta·ry (vōt′ə rē) *n., pl.* **-ries** [< L. *vovere,* to vow] **1.** one bound by a vow, esp. by religious vows **2.** a devout worshiper **3.** one who is devoted to some cause or interest Also **vo′ta·rist**

vote (vōt) *n.* [L. *votum,* a vow] **1.** a decision on a proposal, etc., or a choice between candidates for office **2.** *a)* the expression of such a decision or choice *b)* a ballot, etc. by which it is expressed **3.** the right to vote **4.** votes collectively **5.** a specified group of voters [the farm *vote*] *—vi.* **vot′ed, vot′ing** to give or cast a vote *—vt.* **1.** to decide or authorize by vote **2.** to declare by general opinion *—vote down* to defeat by voting *—vote in* to elect *—vote out* to defeat (an incumbent) in an election *—vot′er n.*

voting machine a machine on which the votes in an election are cast, registered, and counted

vo·tive (vōt′iv) *adj.* [see VOTE] given, done, etc. in fulfillment of a vow [*votive* offerings]

vouch (vouch) *vt.* [< L. *vocare,* to call] to uphold by evidence *—vi.* to give, or serve as, assurance, a guarantee, etc. *(for)* [*to vouch* for his honesty]

vouch′er *n.* **1.** one who vouches, as for the truth of a statement **2.** a paper serving as evidence or proof, as a receipt for the payment of a debt

vouch·safe′ *vt.* **-safed′, -saf′ing** [< ME. *vouchen safe,* vouch as safe] to be gracious enough to give or grant [to *vouchsafe* a reply]

vow (vou) *n.* [< L. *votum*] **1.** a solemn promise, esp. one made to God **2.** a promise of love and fidelity [marriage *vows*] **3.** a solemn affirmation *—vt.* to promise or declare solemnly *—vi.* to make a vow *—take vows* to enter a religious order *—vow′er n.*

vow·el (vou′əl) *n.* [< L. *vocalis,* vocal] **1.** a voiced speech sound made by letting the breath pass in a continuous stream through the pharynx and open mouth **2.** a letter representing such a sound, as *a, e, i, o, u —adj.* of a vowel or vowels

‡**vox** (väks) *n., pl.* **vo·ces** (vō′sēz) [L.] voice

‡**vox po·pu·li** (päp′yoo lī′) [L.] the voice of the people; public opinion: abbrev. **vox pop.**

voy·age (voi′ij) *n.* [< L. *via,* way] **1.** a relatively long journey by water or, formerly, by land **2.** a journey by aircraft or spacecraft *—vi., vt.* **-aged, -ag·ing** to make a voyage (over or on) *—voy′ag·er n.*

‡**vo·ya·geur** (vwä yä zhër′) *n., pl.* **-geurs′** (-zhër′) [Fr.] in Canada, **1.** formerly, a person who transported goods and men for the fur companies **2.** any woodsman or boatman of the wilds

vo·yeur (vwä yur′) *n.* [Fr. < *voir,* see] one who has an excessive interest in viewing sexual objects or scenes; peeping Tom *—vo·yeur′ism n.*

V.P., VP Vice-President

vs. versus

v.s. [L. *vide supra*] see above

V/STOL [*v(ertical or) s(hort) t(ake)o(ff and) l(anding)*] an aircraft that can take off and land either vertically or on a short airstrip

Vt., VT Vermont

vt., v.t. transitive verb

VTOL [*v(ertical) t(ake)o(ff and) l(anding)*] an aircraft that can take off and land vertically

Vul·can (vul′k'n) *Rom. Myth.* the god of fire and of metalworking *—Vul·ca′ni·an* (-kā′nē ən) *adj.*

vul·can·ite (vul′kə nīt′) *n.* [< prec. + -ITE] a hard rubber made by heating crude rubber with a large amount of sulfur; ebonite: used in combs, etc.

vul′can·ize′ (-nīz′) *vt., vi.* **-ized′, -iz′ing** [< VULCAN + -IZE] to treat (crude rubber) with sulfur under great heat to increase its strength and elasticity *—vul′can·i·za′tion n.*

Vulg. Vulgate

vul·gar (vul′gər) *adj.* [< L. *vulgus,* common people] **1.** of people in general; common; popular **2.** of or in the vernacular **3.** lacking culture, taste, etc.; crude; boorish **4.** indecent or obscene *—vul′gar·ly adv. —vul′gar·ness n.*

vul·gar·i·an (-ger′ē ən) *n.* a vulgar person; esp., a rich person with coarse, showy tastes

vul′gar·ism *n.* **1.** a word, phrase, etc. used widely but regarded as nonstandard, coarse, or obscene **2.** vulgar behavior, quality, etc.; vulgarity

vul·gar·i·ty (vul gar′ə tē) *n.* **1.** the state or quality of being vulgar **2.** *pl.* **-ties** a vulgar act, habit, usage in speech, etc.

vul·gar·ize (vul′gə rīz′) *vt.* **-ized′, -iz′ing 1.** to make popular **2.** to make vulgar, coarse, obscene, etc. —**vul′gar·i·za′tion** *n.* —**vul′gar·iz′er** *n.*

Vulgar Latin the everyday Latin spoken by ancient Romans as distinguished from standard written Latin

Vul·gate (vul′gāt) *n.* [ML. *vulgata (editio)*, popular (edition)] **1.** a Latin version of the Bible prepared in the 4th cent., serving as an authorized Roman Catholic version **2.** [**v-**] the vernacular, or common speech —*adj.* **1.** of or in the Vulgate **2.** [**v-**] of or in the vernacular

vul·ner·a·ble (vul′nər ə b'l) *adj.* [< L. *vulnus*, a wound] **1.** that can be wounded or injured **2.** open to, or easily hurt by, criticism or attack **3.** open to attack by armed forces **4.** *Bridge* subject to increased penalties or bonuses —**vul′ner·a·bil′i·ty** *n.* —**vul′ner·a·bly** *adv.*

vul·pine (vul′pīn) *adj.* [< L. *vulpes*, a fox] of or like a fox; clever; cunning

vul·ture (vul′chər) *n.* [< L. *vultur*] **1.** a large bird related to the eagles and hawks, with a naked head: vultures feed on carrion **2.** a greedy, ruthless person —**vul′tur·ous** *adj.*

vul·va (vul′və) *n., pl.* **-vae** (-vē), **-vas** [L., womb] the external genital organs of the female

vv. 1. verses **2.** violins

v.v. vice versa

vy·ing (vī′iŋ) *adj.* that vies; that competes

VULTURE
(wingspread to 6 ft.)

W

W, w (dub′'l yōō, -yə) *n., pl.* **W's, w's** the twenty-third letter of the English alphabet

W *Chem.* tungsten

W watt; watts

W, W., w, w. 1. west **2.** western

W. 1. Wales **2.** Wednesday **3.** Welsh

W., w. 1. watt(s) **2.** weight **3.** width **4.** won

w. 1. week(s) **2.** wide **3.** wife **4.** with

WA Washington (State)

Wa·bash (wô′bash) river flowing from W Ohio across Ind. into the Ohio River

wab·ble (wäb′'l) *n., vt., vi.* **-bled, -bling** *var. of* WOBBLE

Wac (wak) *n.* a member of the Women's Army Corps

WAC Women's Army Corps

wack·y (wak′ē) *adj.* **-i·er, -i·est** [< ?] [Slang] odd, silly, or crazy —**wack′i·ly** *adv.* —**wack′i·ness** *n.*

wad (wäd, wôd) *n.* [ML. *wadda*, wadding] **1.** a small, soft mass or ball, as of cotton or paper **2.** a lump or small, compact mass **3.** a mass of soft material used for padding, packing, etc. **4.** [Colloq.] a roll of paper money —*vt.* **wad′ded, wad′ding 1.** to compress, or roll up, into a wad **2.** to plug or stuff with a wad **3.** to pad with wadding —**wad′der** *n.*

wad′ding *n.* any soft material used in padding, packing, etc.

wad·dle (wäd′'l, wôd′-) *vi.* **-dled, -dling** [< WADE] to walk with short steps, swaying from side to side, as a duck —*n.* a waddling gait —**wad′dler** *n.*

wade (wād) *vi.* **wad′ed, wad′ing** [OE. *waden*, go] **1.** to walk through any resisting substance, as water, mud, etc. **2.** to splash and play about in shallow water **3.** to get through with difficulty [*wade* through a dull book] **4.** [Colloq.] to start with vigor (with *in* or *into*) —*vt.* to cross by wading

wad·er (wād′ər) *n.* **1.** one who wades **2.** *same as* WADING BIRD **3.** [*pl.*] high waterproof boots **4.** [*usually pl.*] waterproof trousers with attached boots, for fishermen

wa·di (wä′dē) *n., pl.* **-dis, -dies** [Ar. *wādī*] in Arabia, N Africa, etc., **1.** a river valley that is usually dry **2.** the rush of water that flows through it in the rainy season Also sp. **wa′dy,** *pl.* **-dies**

wading bird any of various long-legged shore birds that wade the shallows for food, as the crane, heron, etc.

Waf (waf) *n.* a member of the WAF

WAF Women in the Air Force

wa·fer (wā′fər) *n.* [MDu. *wafel*] **1.** a thin, flat, crisp cracker or cookie **2.** anything resembling this, as candy **3.** a thin cake of unleavened bread used in the Eucharist **4.** a small disk of sticky paper, used as a seal on letters, documents, etc.

waf·fle¹ (wäf′'l, wôf′-) *n.* [Du. *wafel*] a crisp batter cake with small, square hollows, baked in a waffle iron

waf·fle² (wäf′'l, wôf′-) *vi.* **-fled, -fling** [echoic] [Chiefly Brit. Colloq.] to speak or write in a wordy, vague manner

waffle iron a utensil with two flat, studded plates pressed together so that a waffle bakes between them

waft (waft, wäft) *vt., vi.* [< Du. *wachter*, watcher] to carry or move lightly over water or through the air, as sounds or odors —*n.* **1.** an odor, sound, etc. carried through the air **2.** a gust of wind **3.** a wafting movement

wag¹ (wag) *vt., vi.* **wagged, wag′ging** [prob. < ON. *vaga*, to rock] to move rapidly back and forth, up and down, etc. —*n.* a wagging —**wag′ger** *n.*

wag² (wag) *n.* [prob. < obs. *waghalter*, a rogue] a comical person; wit; joker

wage (wāj) *vt.* **waged, wag′ing** [< OFr. *gage*, a pledge] to engage in or carry on (a war, campaign, etc.) —*n.* **1.** [*often pl.*] money paid to an employee for work done, usually on an hourly, daily, or piecework basis **2.** [*usually pl., formerly with sing. v.*] what is given in return; recompense [*"The wages of sin is death."*]

wa·ger (wā′jər) *n.* [see WAGE] *same as* BET (*n.* 1, 2) —*vt., vi. same as* BET —**wa′ger·er** *n.*

wag·gish (wag′ish) *adj.* **1.** of or like a wag; roguishly merry **2.** playful; jesting —**wag′gish·ly** *adv.*

wag·gle (wag′'l) *vt.* **-gled, -gling** to wag, esp. with short, quick movements —*n.* a waggling

Wag·ner (väg′nər), (Wilhelm) Rich·ard (rikh′ärt) 1813–83; Ger. composer

Wag·ne′ri·an (-nir′ē ən) *adj.* **1.** of or like Richard Wagner or his music, theories, etc. **2.** designating a soprano, tenor, etc. specializing in Wagner's operas

wag·on (wag′ən) *n.* [Du. *wagen*] **1.** a four-wheeled vehicle for hauling heavy loads **2.** a small cart used by children at play **3.** [Brit.] a railroad freight car Brit. sp. **wag′gon** —**on (or off) the wagon** [Slang] no longer (or once again) drinking alcoholic liquors

wa·hi·ne (wä hē′nä) *n.* [Maori & Haw.] a Polynesian woman, esp. of Hawaii

waif (wāf) *n.* [prob. < ON.] **1.** anything found that is without an owner **2.** a homeless person, esp. a child **3.** a stray animal

Wai·ki·ki (wī′kē kē′) famous bathing beach in Honolulu, Hawaii

wail (wāl) *vi.* [< ON. *væ*, woe] to make long, loud, sad cries, as in grief or pain —*vt.* to cry out in mourning —*n.* **1.** a long cry of grief or pain **2.** a sound like this, as of the wind **3.** a wailing —**wail′ful** *adj.* —**wail′ful·ly** *adv.*

wain (wān) *n.* [OE. *wægn*] [Archaic] a wagon

wain·scot (wān′skət, -skät′) *n.* [< MDu. *wagenschot*] **1.** a paneling of wood, etc. on the walls of a room, often on the lower part only **2.** the lower part of the walls of a room when finished differently from the upper —*vt.* **-scot·ed** or **-scot·ted, -scot·ing** or **-scot·ting** to line (a wall) with wainscoting

wain′scot·ing, wain′scot·ting *n.* **1.** *same as* WAINSCOT **2.** material used for wainscot

wain·wright (wān′rīt′) *n.* [WAIN + WRIGHT] one who builds or repairs wagons

waist (wāst) *n.* [< OE. *weaxan*, grow] **1.** the part of the body between the ribs and the hips **2.** the part of a garment that covers the body from the shoulders to the waistline **3.** a blouse **4.** the middle, narrow part of something

waist′band′ *n.* a band encircling the waist, as at the top of a skirt, trousers, etc.

W-Z

waist·coat (wes′kət, wāst′kōt′) *n.* **1.** [Brit.] a man's vest **2.** a similar garment worn by women

waist·line (wāst′līn′) *n.* **1.** the line of the waist, between the ribs and the hips **2.** the narrow part of a woman's dress, worn at the waist or above or below it as styles change **3.** distance around the waist

wait (wāt) *vi.* [ONormFr. *waitier*] **1.** to remain in readiness or anticipation **2.** to be ready [dinner is *waiting*] **3.** to remain undone [it can *wait*] **4.** to serve food (with *at* or *on*) —*vt.* to be, remain, or delay in expectation of —*n.* the act or a period of waiting —**wait on** (or **upon**) **1.** to act as a servant to **2.** to serve (a customer, etc.) —**wait up 1.** to delay going to bed while waiting **2.** [Colloq.] to stop so someone can catch up

wait′er *n.* a man who waits on table in a restaurant

wait′ing *adj.* **1.** that waits **2.** of or for a wait —*n.* **1.** the act of one that waits **2.** a period of waiting —**in waiting** in attendance, as on a king

waiting game a delaying until one has the advantage

waiting room a room in which people wait, as in a railroad station, dentist's office, etc.

wait·ress (wā′tris) *n.* a woman or girl who waits on table, as in a restaurant

waive (wāv) *vt.* **waived, waiv′ing** [< ON. *veifa*, fluctuate] **1.** to give up or forgo (a right, claim, etc.) **2.** to postpone

waiv′er *n. Law* **1.** a waiving, or giving up voluntarily, of a right, claim, etc. **2.** a formal written statement of this

wake[1] (wāk) *vi.* **woke** or **waked, waked, wak′ing** [< OE. *wacian*, be awake & *wacan*, arise] **1.** to come out of sleep; awake (often with *up*) **2.** to stay awake **3.** to become active **4.** to become alert [to *wake* to a peril] —*vt.* **1.** to cause to wake (often with *up*) **2.** to arouse or excite, as passions —*n.* an all-night vigil over a corpse before burial

wake[2] (wāk) *n.* [< ON. *vök*, hole in the ice] **1.** the track left in the water by a moving ship **2.** any track left behind —**in the wake of** following closely

wake′ful *adj.* **1.** alert; watchful **2.** unable to sleep

Wake Island (wāk) coral atoll in the N Pacific between Midway & Guam: a U.S. territory

wak·en (wāk′'n) *vi., vt.* to wake; rouse

Wald·heim (vält′hīm′), **Kurt** (koort) 1918– ; Austrian diplomat; secretary-general of the United Nations (1972–)

Wal·dorf salad (wôl′dôrf) [< a former New York hotel] a salad made of diced apples, celery, and walnuts, with mayonnaise

wale (wāl) *n.* [OE. *walu*, a weal] **1.** a welt raised by a whip, etc. **2.** a ridge on the surface of cloth, as corduroy

Wales (wālz) division of Great Britain, west of England: 8,016 sq. mi.; pop. 2,662,000

walk (wôk) *vi.* [OE. *wealcan*, to roll] **1.** to go on foot at a moderate pace **2.** to appear after death as a ghost **3.** to follow a certain course [to *walk* in peace] **4.** *Baseball* to go to first base on four balls —*vt.* **1.** to walk along, over, etc. **2.** to cause (a horse, dog, etc.) to walk **3.** to accompany on a walk [I'll *walk* you home] **4.** *Baseball* to advance (a batter) to first base by pitching four balls —*n.* **1.** the act or manner of walking **2.** a stroll or hike **3.** a distance to walk [an hour's *walk*] **4.** the pace of one who walks **5.** a sphere of activity, station in life, etc. [from all *walks* of life] **6.** a path for walking **7.** *Baseball* an advancing to first base on four balls —**walk (all) over 1.** to domineer over —**walk away** (or **off**) **with 1.** to steal **2.** to win easily —**walk out** to go on strike —**walk out on** [Colloq.] to leave; desert

walk′er *n.* **1.** one that walks **2.** a frame on wheels for babies learning to walk **3.** a somewhat similar frame without wheels used by convalescents, etc.

walk′ie-talk′ie *n.* a compact radio transmitter and receiver that can be carried by one person

walking stick 1. a stick carried when walking; cane **2.** an insect resembling a twig: also **walk′ing-stick′** *n.*

walk′-on′ *n.* a minor role in which an actor has no speaking lines or just a very few

walk′out′ *n.* **1.** a strike of workers **2.** an abrupt departure of people as a show of protest

walk′-up′ *n.* **1.** an upstairs apartment in a building without an elevator **2.** the building itself

wall (wôl) *n.* [< L. *vallum*, rampart] **1.** an upright structure of wood, stone, etc. serving to enclose, divide, support, or protect **2.** [*usually pl.*] a fortification **3.** something like a wall in function —*vt.* **1.** to divide, enclose, etc. with a wall (often with *off* or *in*) **2.** to close (an opening) with a wall (usually with *up*) —**drive** (or **push**) **to the wall** to place in a desperate position —**off the wall** [Slang] **1.** crazy **2.** very unconventional —**walled** *adj.*

wal·la·by (wäl′ə bē) *n., pl.* **-bies, -by** [Australian native name] a small marsupial related to the kangaroo

wall′board′ *n.* fibrous material in thin slabs for making or covering walls, in place of plaster, etc.

wal·let (wôl′it, wäl′-) *n.* [ME. *walet*] a flat pocketbook for carrying paper money, cards, etc.; billfold

wall·eye (wôl′ī′) *n.* [< WALLEYED] **1.** an eye that turns outward, showing more white than is normal **2.** a fish with large, staring eyes

wall′eyed′ *adj.* [< ON. *vagl*, beam + *eygr*, having eyes] **1.** having a walleye or walleyes **2.** having large, staring eyes

walleyed pike a N. American freshwater food and game fish related to the perch

wall′flow′er *n.* **1.** a garden plant having racemes of yellow, orange, or red flowers **2.** [Colloq.] a shy person who merely looks on at a dance

Wal·loon (wä lōōn′) *n.* **1.** a member of a people living in S and SE Belgium and nearby parts of France **2.** the French dialect of the Walloons

wal·lop (wäl′əp, wôl′-) *vt.* [< OFr. *galoper*, to gallop] [Colloq.] **1.** to beat or defeat soundly **2.** to strike hard —*n.* [Colloq.] **1.** a hard blow **2.** effective force or power

wal′lop·ing *adj.* [Colloq.] impressively large; enormous —*n.* [Colloq.] **1.** a thrashing **2.** a crushing defeat

wal·low (wäl′ō, wôl′-) *vi.* [OE. *wealwian*, roll around] **1.** to roll about, as in mud, dust, etc. **2.** to roll and pitch, as a ship **3.** to indulge oneself fully [to *wallow* in self-pity, to *wallow* in vice] —*n.* **1.** a wallowing **2.** a place where animals wallow

wall′pa′per *n.* paper for covering the walls or ceiling of a room —*vt.* to put wallpaper on or in

Wall Street 1. a street in New York City: financial center of the U.S. **2.** U.S. financiers or the U.S. money market

wall′-to-wall′ *adj.* **1.** completely covering a floor **2.** [Colloq.] *a)* pervasive *b)* comprehensive

wal·nut (wôl′nut′, -nət) *n.* [< OE. *wealh*, foreign + *hnutu*, nut] **1.** a roundish, edible nut, with a two-lobed seed **2.** any of several related trees bearing varieties of these nuts, as the *English walnut* or the *black walnut* **3.** the wood of these trees, used for furniture, etc.

Wal·pur·gis Night (väl poor′gis) the eve of May Day (April 30), when witches supposedly gathered for a demonic orgy

wal·rus (wôl′rəs, wäl′-) *n.* [prob. < ON. *hrosshvalr*, horse whale] a massive sea mammal of the seal family, having two protruding tusks, a thick mustache, a thick hide, and a heavy layer of blubber

WALRUS
(to 12 ft. long
& 5 ft. high)

Wal·ton (wôl′t'n), **I·zaak** (ī′zək) 1593–1683; Eng. writer

waltz (wôlts, wôls) *n.* [< G. *walzen*, dance about] **1.** a ballroom dance for couples, in 3/4 time **2.** music for this —*vi.* **1.** to dance a waltz **2.** to move lightly and nimbly **3.** [Colloq.] to proceed effortlessly (usually with *through*) —*vt.* to dance with in a waltz —**waltz′er** *n.*

wam·pum (wäm′pəm) *n.* [< Algonquian] small beads made of shells and used by N. American Indians as money, for ornament, etc.

wan (wän, wôn) *adj.* **wan′ner, wan′nest** [OE. *wann*, dark] **1.** sickly pale; pallid [a *wan* complexion] **2.** suggesting a sickly condition; feeble [a *wan* smile] —**wan′ly** *adv.*

wand (wänd, wônd) *n.* [ON. *vǫndr*] **1.** a slender switch, as of a young tree **2.** a rod of authority; scepter **3.** a rod of supposed magic power

wan·der (wän′dər, wôn′-) *vi.* [OE. *wandrian*] **1.** to roam idly or aimlessly about; ramble **2.** to stray (*from* a path, course, etc.) **3.** to go astray in mind or purpose; specif., *a)* to drift away from a subject, as in discussion *b)* to be disjointed, incoherent, etc. **4.** to meander, as a river —*vt.* to roam through, in, or over —**wan′der·er** *n.*

wan·der·lust (-lust′) *n.* [G.] an impulse, longing, or urge to wander or travel

wane (wän) *vi.* **waned, wan′ing** [OE. *wanian*] **1.** to grow gradually less in extent, as the moon after it is full **2.** to grow dim, as a light **3.** to decline in power, importance, etc. **4.** to approach the end [the day *wanes*] —*n.* **1.** a waning **2.** a period of waning —**on the wane** declining, decreasing, etc.

wan·gle (waŋ′g'l) *vt.* **-gled, -gling** [< ?] [Colloq.] to get or cause by persuasion, influence, tricks, etc. —*vi.* [Colloq.] to make use of tricky and indirect methods to achieve one's aims —**wan′gler** *n.*

Wan·kel engine (väŋ'k'l, waŋ'-) [< F. *Wankel* (1902–), G. engineer] a rotary combustion engine having a spinning piston, needing fewer parts and less fuel than used in a turbine engine

want (wänt, wônt) *vt.* [ON. *vanta*] **1.** to lack; be deficient in **2.** to be short by [it *wants* two minutes of noon] **3.** to feel the need of; crave [to *want* love] **4.** to desire [to *want* to travel] **5.** to wish to see, talk to, or apprehend [*wanted* by the police] **6.** [Chiefly Brit.] to require —*vi.* **1.** to have a need or lack (with *for*) **2.** to be destitute —*n.* **1.** a lack; shortage **2.** poverty; destitution **3.** a wish for something; craving **4.** something needed

want ad [Colloq.] a classified advertisement, as in a newspaper, stating that one wants a job, an apartment, etc.

want'ing *adj.* **1.** lacking **2.** not up to standard —*prep.* **1.** lacking (something); without **2.** minus —**wanting in** deficient in (a quality, etc.)

wan·ton (wän't'n, wôn'-) *adj.* [< OE. *wan*, lacking + *teon*, bring up] **1.** sexually loose **2.** [Poet.] playful **3.** unprovoked or malicious [*wanton* cruelty] **4.** recklessly ignoring justice, decency, etc. **5.** lavish, luxurious, etc. —*n.* a wanton person; esp., a sexually loose woman —*vi.* to be wanton —**wan'ton·ly** *adv.* —**wan'ton·ness** *n.*

wap·i·ti (wäp'ə tē) *n.* [< Algonquian] the American elk, the largest N. American deer, with large, branching antlers and a short tail

war (wôr) *n.* [< ONormFr. *werre*, strife] **1.** open armed conflict as between countries **2.** any active hostility; strife **3.** military operations as a science —*adj.* of, used in, or resulting from war —*vi.* **warred, war'ring 1.** to carry on war **2.** to contend; strive —**at war** engaged in war —**declare war (on) 1.** to make a formal declaration of being at war (with) **2.** to announce one's hostility (to) —**go to war 1.** to enter into a war **2.** to join the armed forces during a war

war·ble (wôr'b'l) *vt., vi.* **-bled, -bling** [ONormFr. *werbler*] to sing with trills, quavers, runs, etc., as a bird —*n.* **1.** a song **2.** a warbling sound; trill

war'bler *n.* one that warbles; esp., any of various songbirds

war bonnet a headdress with long feathers, worn by some N. American Indian warriors

ward (wôrd) *vt.* [OE. *weardian*, to guard] to turn aside; fend (usually with *off*) —*n.* **1.** a being under guard **2.** one under the care of a guardian or court **3.** a division of a jail, hospital, etc. **4.** a division of a city or town, for purposes of administration, voting, etc.

-ward [OE. *-weard*] a suffix meaning in a (specified) direction or course [*backward*] : also **-wards**

war dance a ceremonial dance performed as by some American Indian tribes before battle or after victory

war·den (wôr'd'n) *n.* [< OFr. *gardein*] **1.** one who guards, or has charge of, something [a game *warden*] **2.** the head official of a prison

ward'er *n.* a watchman, guard, etc.

ward heeler a person who works in a ward for a political party or boss, as in getting votes: a contemptuous term

ward·robe (wôrd'rōb') *n.* **1.** a closet, cabinet, etc. for holding clothes **2.** one's supply of clothes

ward'room' *n.* in a warship, a compartment used for eating and lounging by commissioned officers, except, usually, the captain

ware (wer) *n.* [OE. *waru*] **1.** anything for sale: *usually used in pl.* **2.** pottery or a specified kind of pottery

ware'house' *n.* a building where wares, or goods, are stored —*vt.* **-housed', -hous'ing** to place or store in a warehouse —**ware'house'man** *n., pl.* **-men**

war·fare (wôr'fer') *n.* **1.** the action of waging war **2.** conflict of any kind

war·far·in (wôr'fə rin) *n.* [*W*(*isconsin*) *A*(*lumni*) *R*(*esearch*) *F*(*oundation*) + (*coum*)*arin*, a chemical] **1.** a powder used as rat poison **2.** this drug neutralized and used as medicine

war game 1. training in military tactics in which maps and small figures are used to represent terrain, troops, etc. **2.** [*pl.*] practice maneuvers

war'head' *n.* the forward section of a torpedo, bomb, etc., containing the explosive charge

war'horse' *n.* [Colloq.] one who has engaged in many struggles

war·i·ly (wer'ə lē) *adv.* in a wary manner; cautiously

war'i·ness (-ē nis) *n.* a being wary; caution

war'like' *adj.* **1.** fond of or ready for war **2.** of or appropriate to war **3.** threatening war

warm (wôrm) *adj.* [OE. *wearm*] **1.** having, feeling, or giving off a moderate degree of heat **2.** that keeps body heat in [*warm* clothing] **3.** ardent; enthusiastic **4.** lively, vigorous, etc. **5.** quick to anger **6.** *a*) cordial or sincere [a *warm* welcome] *b*) sympathetic or loving **7.** suggesting warmth: said of yellow, orange, or red colors **8.** newly made, as a scent or trail **9.** [Colloq.] close to discovering something —*vt., vi.* to make or become warm —**warm up 1.** to make or become warm **2.** to reheat (cooked food): also **warm over 3.** *Sports* to practice or exercise before a game —**warm'er** *n.* —**warm'ish** *adj.* —**warm'ly** *adv.* —**warm'ness** *n.*

warm'blood'ed *adj.* **1.** having warm blood and a constant natural body heat: said of mammals and birds **2.** ardent; fervent

warm front *Meteorol.* the forward edge of an advancing mass of warm air replacing colder air

warm'heart'ed *adj.* kind, sympathetic, friendly, etc. —**warm'heart'ed·ly** *adv.*

war·mon·ger (wôr'muŋ'gər, -mäŋ'-) *n.* one that advocates, or tries to bring about, war

warmth (wôrmth) *n.* **1.** a being warm **2.** mild heat **3.** excitement or vigor of feeling; ardor **4.** cordial feelings **5.** slight anger **6.** a warm effect, as of red, yellow, or orange

warm'-up' *n.* the act of practicing or exercising before going into a game, etc.

warn (wôrn) *vt.* [OE. *wearnian*] **1.** to tell (a person) of a danger, coming evil, etc. **2.** to caution; admonish [*warned* about smoking] **3.** to notify in advance —*vi.* to give warning —**warn'er** *n.*

warn'ing *n.* **1.** the act of one that warns **2.** that which warns —*adj.* that warns —**warn'ing·ly** *adv.*

War of American Independence *Brit. name for* AMERICAN REVOLUTION

War of 1812 a war (1812–15) between the U.S. and Great Britain

warp (wôrp) *n.* [OE. *weorpan*, to throw] **1.** *a*) a distortion, as a twist or bend in wood *b*) any similar distortion **2.** a mental quirk, bias, etc. **3.** a rope run from a ship to a dock, etc., used to haul the vessel into position **4.** *Weaving* the threads running lengthwise in the loom —*vt.* **1.** to bend or twist out of shape **2.** to distort, pervert, etc. [a *warped* mind] **3.** to move (a ship) by hauling on a line fastened to a dock, etc. —*vi.* to become bent or twisted

war paint 1. paint applied to the face and body, as by some American Indian tribes before going to war **2.** [Slang] *a*) ceremonial dress *b*) women's cosmetics

war'path' *n.* the path taken by American Indians on a warlike expedition —**on the warpath 1.** ready for war **2.** angry; ready to fight

war'plane' *n.* any airplane for use in war

war·rant (wôr'ənt, wär'-) *n.* [< OFr. *garant*] **1.** *a*) authorization, as by law *b*) justification for some act, belief, etc. **2.** something serving as a guarantee of some event or result **3.** *Law* a writ authorizing an arrest, search, seizure, etc. **4.** *Mil.* the certificate appointing a warrant officer —*vt.* **1.** to authorize **2.** to serve as justification for (an act, belief, etc.) **3.** to guarantee **4.** [Colloq.] to state with confidence [I *warrant* he'll be late] —**war'rant·a·ble** *adj.*

war'ran·tee' *n.* Law one to whom a warranty is given

warrant officer a military officer ranking above an enlisted man but below a commissioned officer

war·ran·tor (wôr'ən tôr', wär'-) *n.* Law one who warrants or gives a warranty: also **war'rant·er** (-tər)

war'ran·ty (-tē) *n., pl.* **-ties 1.** official authorization **2.** justification, as for some act or opinion **3.** *Law a*) a guarantee, as to a purchaser, that goods are as represented *b*) an assurance of the security of a real estate title to the buyer

War·ren (wôr'ən, wär'-), **Earl** 1891–1974; U.S. jurist; chief justice of the U.S. (1953–69)

war·ren (wôr'ən, wär'-) *n.* [< OFr. *warir*, to preserve] **1.** an area in which rabbits breed or are raised **2.** any crowded building or buildings

war·ri·or (wôr'ē ər, wär'-; -yər) *n.* [see WAR] a fighting man; veteran soldier

War·saw (wôr'sô) capital of Poland, on the Vistula River: pop. 1,284,000

war·ship (wôr'ship') *n.* any ship for combat use, as a battleship, destroyer, etc.

wart (wôrt) *n.* [OE. *wearte*] **1.** a small, usually hard, tumorous growth on the skin **2.** a small growth on a plant **3.** a failing, flaw, etc. [a lovable person, *warts* and all] —**wart'like'** *adj.* —**wart'y** *adj.* **-i·er, -i·est**

wart hog a wild African hog with large tusks, and warts below the eyes

war'time' *n.* a time of war

war whoop a loud shout uttered, as by N. American Indians, on going into battle, etc.

war·y (wer'ē) *adj.* -i·er, -i·est [OE. *wær*] 1. cautious; on one's guard 2. characterized by caution

was (wuz, wäz) [OE. *wæs*] *1st and 3d pers. sing., pt.,* of BE

wash (wôsh, wäsh) *vt.* [OE. *wæscan*] 1. to clean with water or other liquid, often with soap, etc. 2. to purify 3. to wet; moisten 4. to cleanse by licking, as a cat does 5. to flow over, past, or against: said of a sea, waves, etc. 6. to soak (*out*), flush (*off*), or carry (*away*) by the action of water 7. to erode [the flood *washed* out the road] 8. to cover with a thin coat of paint or metal 9. *Mining* to pass water through or over (earth, etc.) in order to separate (ore, precious stones, etc.) —*vi.* 1. to wash oneself or one's hands, etc. 2. to wash clothes 3. to undergo washing 4. to be removed by washing [the stain *washed* out] 5. to be worn or carried away by the action of water [the bridge *washed* out] —*n.* 1. a washing 2. a place where something is washed [an auto *wash*] 3. a quantity of clothes washed, or to be washed 4. refuse liquid food 5. *a)* the rush or surge of water *b)* the eddy of water caused by a propeller, etc. *c)* a slipstream 6. silt, mud, etc. carried and dropped by running water 7. a bog; marsh 8. in the western U.S., the dry bed of a stream 9. a thin coating of paint or metal 10. a liquid for cosmetic or medicinal use [*mouthwash*] 11. [Colloq.] a chaser —*adj.* that can be washed without damage [a *wash* dress] — **wash down** 1. to clean by washing 2. to follow (a bite of food) with a drink —**wash out** [Slang] to drop or be dropped from a course, esp. in military aviation, because of failure —**wash'a·ble** *adj.*

wash'-and-wear' *adj.* designating or made of a fabric that needs little or no ironing after washing

wash'board' *n.* a ridged board for scrubbing dirt out of clothes

wash'bowl' *n.* a bowl or basin for use in washing one's hands and face, etc.: also **wash'ba'sin**

wash'cloth' *n.* a small cloth, usually of terry, used in washing the face or body

washed'-out' *adj.* 1. faded 2. [Colloq.] tired; spiritless 3. [Colloq.] tired-looking; wan

washed'-up' *adj.* 1. cleaned up 2. [Colloq.] tired; exhausted 3. [Slang] done for; having failed

wash'er *n.* 1. one who washes 2. a flat disk or ring of metal, rubber, etc. used to make a seat for a bolt head or for a nut or faucet valve, to provide packing, etc. 3. a machine for washing

wash'er·wom'an *n., pl.* -wom'en a woman whose work is washing clothes —**wash'er·man** *n.masc., pl.* -men

wash'ing *n.* 1. the act of one that washes 2. clothes, etc. to be washed, esp. in one batch

washing machine a machine for washing clothes, etc., by tumbling them through water with detergent, soap, etc.

Wash·ing·ton (wôsh'iŋ tən, wäsh'-) 1. NW coastal State of the U.S.: 68,192 sq. mi.; pop. 3,409,000; cap. Olympia: abbrev. **Wash.**, **WA** 2. capital of the U.S., coextensive with the District of Columbia: pop. 757,000 (met. area 2,861,000) —**Wash'ing·to'ni·an** (-tō'nē ən) *adj., n.*

Wash·ing·ton (wôsh'iŋ tən, wäsh'-) 1. **Book·er T**(aliaferro) (book'ər), 1856–1915; U.S. Negro educator & author 2. **George**, 1732–99; 1st president of the U.S. (1789–97); commander in chief of the Continental army

wash'out' *n.* 1. the washing away of soil, rocks, etc. by a strong flow of water 2. a hole made by such washing away 3. [Slang] a complete failure

wash'rag' *n. same as* WASHCLOTH

wash'room' *n.* 1. a room for washing 2. *same as* RESTROOM

wash'stand' *n.* 1. a table holding a bowl and pitcher, etc. for washing the face and hands 2. a washbowl that is a bathroom fixture

wash'tub' *n.* a tub for washing clothes, etc.; often, a stationary metal tub with water faucets and a drain

wash'wom'an *n., pl.* -wom'en *same as* WASHERWOMAN

wash'y *adj.* -i·er, -i·est 1. watery; diluted 2. pale 3. insipid; without force

was·n't (wuz'nt, wäz'-) was not

WASP, Wasp (wäsp, wôsp) *n.* a white Anglo-Saxon Protestant

WART HOG
(2–2 1/2 ft. high)

wasp (wäsp, wôsp) *n.* [OE. *wæsp*] a winged insect with a slender body and, in the females and workers, a painful sting —**wasp'like'** *adj.* —**wasp'y** *adj.* -i·er, -i·est

wasp'ish *adj.* 1. of or like a wasp 2. bad-tempered; snappish —**wasp'ish·ly** *adv.* —**wasp'ish·ness** *n.*

wasp waist a very slender or tightly corseted waist

WASP
(1/2–3 in. long)

was·sail (wäs'l, was'-; -āl) *n.* [< ON. *ves heill*, be hearty] 1. a former toast in drinking healths 2. the spiced ale, etc. with which such healths were drunk 3. a celebration with much drinking, esp. at Christmas time —*vi.*, *vt.* to drink a wassail (to) —**was'sail·er** *n.*

wast (wäst) *archaic 2d pers. sing., past indic.*, of BE: *used with* thou

wast·age (wās'tij) *n.* 1. loss by use, decay, etc. 2. what is wasted, or the amount of this

waste (wāst) *vt.* **wast'ed, wast'ing** [< L. *vastare*, to lay waste] 1. to destroy; devastate 2. to wear away; use up 3. to make weak or feeble [*wasted* by age] 4. to use up needlessly; squander 5. to fail to take advantage of [to *waste* a chance] —*vi.* 1. to lose strength, health, etc., as by disease 2. to be used up or worn down gradually 3. to be wasted, or not put to proper use —*adj.* 1. uncultivated or uninhabited; desolate 2. left over; no longer of use 3. excreted from the body 4. used to carry off or hold waste [a *waste* pipe, *wastebasket*] —*n.* 1. uncultivated or uninhabited land, as a desert 2. a devastated area 3. the act of wasting, or loss by wasting 4. discarded material, as ashes, garbage, etc. 5. matter excreted from the body, as feces 6. refuse cotton fiber or yarn, used for wiping machinery, etc. —**go to waste** to be wasted —**lay waste (to)** to devastate —**wast'er** *n.*

waste'bas'ket *n.* a container for wastepaper, bits of trash, etc.: also **wastepaper basket**

waste'ful *adj.* in the habit of wasting or characterized by waste; squandering; extravagant —**waste'ful·ly** *adv.* —**waste'ful·ness** *n.*

waste'land' *n.* land that is uncultivated or barren

waste'pa'per *n.* paper thrown away after use or as useless: also **waste paper**

wast'ing *adj.* 1. destructive [a *wasting* war] 2. destructive to health, as a disease

wast·rel (wās'trəl) *n.* 1. one who wastes; esp., a spendthrift 2. a good-for-nothing

watch (wäch, wôch) *n.* [OE. *wæcce*] 1. a keeping awake, esp. in order to protect or guard 2. close observation for a time, as to find out something 3. vigilant, careful guarding 4. a guard, or the period of duty of a guard 5. a small timepiece worn on the wrist or carried in the pocket 6. *a)* any of the periods of duty (usually four hours) into which the day is divided on shipboard *b)* the crew on duty during such a period —*vi.* 1. to stay awake; keep vigil 2. to keep guard 3. to look; observe 4. to be looking or waiting attentively —*vt.* 1. to guard or tend 2. to observe carefully and constantly 3. to keep informed about 4. to wait and look for [*watch* your chance] —**on the watch** watching —**watch out** to be alert and careful —**watch'er** *n.*

watch'band' *n.* a band of leather, metal, cloth, etc. for holding a watch on the wrist

watch'dog' *n.* 1. a dog kept to guard property 2. a person or group that keeps watch to prevent waste, dishonest practices, etc.

watch'ful *adj.* alert; attentive; vigilant —**watch'ful·ly** *adv.* —**watch'ful·ness** *n.*

watch'mak'er *n.* one who makes or repairs watches — **watch'mak'ing** *n.*

watch'man *n., pl.* -men a person hired to watch or guard, esp. at night

watch pocket a small pocket, usually in a vest or trousers, for carrying a watch

watch'tow'er *n.* a high tower from which a sentinel watches for enemies, forest fires, etc.

watch'word' *n.* 1. a password 2. a slogan; motto

wa·ter (wôt'ər, wät'-) *n.* [OE. *wæter*] 1. the colorless, transparent liquid of rivers, lakes, etc., which falls as rain: chemically a compound of hydrogen and oxygen, H_2O 2. [often *pl.*] a large body of water, as a sea 3. water with reference to its depth, surface, or level [under *water*] 4. [*pl.*] the water of mineral springs 5. a body secretion, as urine, tears, etc. 6. a solution of any substance, often a gas, in water [ammonia *water*] 7. the degree of clearness and luster of a precious stone [a diamond of the first *water*] 8. a wavy, lustrous finish given to linen, silk, metal, etc. —*vt.* **1.** to give (animals) water to drink **2.** to supply (crops, etc.) with water, as by sprinkling **3.** to moisten, soak, or dilute with water **4.** to give a wavy luster to (silk, etc.) **5.** *Finance* to add to the total face value of (stock) without increasing assets to justify this valuation —*vi.* **1.** to fill with tears, as the eyes **2.** to fill with saliva [*his mouth watered*] **3.** to take on a supply of water **4.** to drink water —*adj.* of, in, on, near, from, or by water —**by water** by ship or boat —**hold water** to prove sound, logical, etc. —**make** (or **pass**) **water** to urinate —**water down** to weaken the effectiveness of —**wa·ter·less** *adj.*

water bed a heavy vinyl bag filled with water and used as a bed or as a mattress in a special bed frame: also **wa′ter·bed′** *n.*

wa·ter·buck′ *n.*, *pl.* **-buck′, -bucks′** an African antelope having lyre-shaped horns, found near rivers and streams

water buffalo a slow, powerful, oxlike draft animal of S Asia, Malaya, and the Philippine Islands

Wa·ter·bur·y (wôt′ər ber′ē, wät′-) city in WC Conn.: pop. 108,000

water chestnut 1. a Chinese sedge, growing in clumps in water **2.** its edible, button-shaped tuber

water clock a mechanism for measuring time by the fall or flow of water

water closet *same as* TOILET (*n.* 3)

wa·ter·col′or *n.* **1.** a pigment or coloring matter mixed with water for use as paint **2.** (a) painting done with such paints —*adj.* painted with watercolors —**wa·ter·col·or·ist** *n.*

wa·ter·cooled′ *adj.* kept from overheating by having water circulated around or through it, as in pipes or a water jacket —**wa·ter·cool′** *vt.*

water cooler a device for cooling water, esp. by refrigeration, for drinking

wa·ter·course (wôt′ər kôrs′, wät′-) *n.* **1.** a stream, river, etc. **2.** a channel for water, as a canal

wa·ter·craft′ (-kraft′) *n.* **1.** skill in water sports, boating, etc. **2.** *pl.* **-craft′** a boat, ship, or other water vehicle

wa·ter·cress′ (-kres′) *n.* a plant of the mustard family, growing generally in running water: its leaves are used in salads, etc.

wa·ter·fall′ *n.* a steep fall of water, as of a stream, from a height; cascade

wa·ter·fowl′ *n.* a water bird, esp. one that swims

wa·ter·front′ *n.* land or docks at the edge of a stream, harbor, etc.

Wa·ter·gate′ (-gāt′) *n.* [< *Watergate*, D.C. building housing Dem. party hdqrs., burglarized (1972) under govt. direction] a scandal that involves officials violating public trust through crime, etc. to maintain their power

water gate a gate controlling the flow of water; floodgate

water glass 1. a drinking glass **2.** a silicate of sodium or potassium, dissolved in water to form a syrupy liquid used as a preservative for eggs, etc. Also **wa·ter·glass′** *n.*

water hole 1. a pond or pool **2.** a hole in the ice on a body of water

water hyacinth a floating plant with showy lavender flowers, found in S. America and, now, Florida

wa·ter·ing place (-iŋ) **1.** a place at a stream, etc. where animals go to drink **2.** [Chiefly Brit.] a resort having mineral springs or having a beach for swimming, etc.

watering pot (or **can**) a can with a spout, often having a perforated nozzle, for watering plants, etc.

water level 1. *a*) the surface of still water *b*) the height of this **2.** *same as* WATERLINE

wa·ter·lil′y (-lil′ē) *n.*, *pl.* **-ies 1.** a water plant with large, flat, floating leaves and showy flowers **2.** the flower

wa·ter·line′ *n.* the line to which the surface of the water comes on the side of a ship or boat

wa·ter·logged′ (-lôgd′, -lägd′) *adj.* soaked or filled with water so as to be heavy and sluggish, as a boat

Wa·ter·loo (wôt′ər lōō′, wät′-) town in C Belgium: scene of Napoleon's final defeat (1815) —*n.* any disastrous or decisive defeat

WATERLILY

water main a main pipe in a system of water pipes

wa·ter·mark′ *n.* **1.** a mark showing the limit to which water has risen **2.** a mark in paper, produced by the impression of a design, as in the mold —*vt.* to mark (paper) with a watermark

wa·ter·mel′on (-mel′ən) *n.* a large, edible fruit with a hard, green rind and juicy, seedy, red pulp

water moccasin a large, poisonous snake found along rivers and swamps of the SE U.S.

water of crystallization water that occurs in crystalline substances and can be removed by heat

water ouzel a gray water bird that dives and swims in western N. American mountain streams

water pipe 1. a pipe for carrying water **2.** a hookah

water pistol a toy gun that shoots water in a stream

water plant any plant living entirely below water or sending up stems to or above the surface

water polo a water game played with a ball by two teams of seven swimmers

water power the power of running or falling water, used to drive machinery, etc. Also **wa′ter·pow′er** *n.*

wa·ter·proof′ (-prōōf′) *adj.* that keeps out water, as a fabric treated with rubber, plastic, etc. —*n.* **1.** waterproof material **2.** [Brit.] a raincoat —*vt.* to make waterproof

wa·ter·re·pel′lent *adj.* that repels water but is not thoroughly waterproof

wa·ter·shed′ (-shed′) *n.* **1.** a ridge dividing the areas drained by different river systems **2.** the area drained by a river system **3.** a turning point

wa·ter·side′ (-sīd′) *n.* land at the edge of a body of water —*adj.* of, at, or on the waterside

wa·ter·ski′ *vi.* **-skied′, -ski′ing** to be towed, as a sport, on skilike boards (**water skis**) by a line attached to a motorboat —**wa′ter·ski′er** *n.*

water snake a nonpoisonous freshwater snake

wa·ter·soak′ *vt.* to soak with or in water

water softener 1. a chemical compound added to hard water to free it from mineral salts **2.** a tank for filtering hard water through softening chemicals

water spaniel either of two breeds of spaniel used in hunting to retrieve waterfowl

wa·ter·spout′ *n.* **1.** a hole, pipe, or spout through which water runs **2.** a tornado occurring over water, appearing as a rapidly rotating column of spray

water sprite in folklore, a spirit, nymph, etc. dwelling in or haunting the water

water table the level below which the ground is saturated with water

wa·ter·tight′ *adj.* **1.** so tight that no water can get in or through **2.** well thought out, with no weak points, as an argument, plan, etc.

water tower an elevated tank for water storage and for equalizing water pressure

water vapor water in the form of a diffused mist, esp. when below the boiling point, as in the air

wa·ter·way′ *n.* **1.** a channel through which water runs **2.** any body of water on which boats, ships, etc. can travel

water wheel a wheel turned by running water, as for power

water wings a device, inflated with air, used to keep one afloat while learning to swim

wa·ter·works′ (-wurks′) *n.pl.* [*often with sing. v.*] **1.** a system of reservoirs, pumps, etc. used to bring a water supply to a city, etc. **2.** a pumping station in such a system

wa·ter·y *adj.* **1.** of or like water **2.** full of water **3.** thin, diluted, weak, etc. **4.** tearful **5.** in or consisting of water [a *watery* grave]

watt (wät, wôt) *n.* [< J. *Watt*] a unit of electrical power equal to a current of one ampere flowing through a potential difference of one volt

Watt (wät, wôt), **James** 1736–1819; Scot. engineer & inventor

watt′age (-ij) *n.* the amount of watts required to operate a given appliance or device

Wat·teau (wä tō′), (Jean) **An·toine** (än twän′) 1684–1721; Fr. painter

wat·tle (wät′'l, wôt′-) *n.* [OE. *watul*] **1.** a woven work of sticks intertwined with twigs or branches, used for walls, roofs, etc. **2.** a fleshy flap of skin that hangs from the throat of a cock, turkey, etc. —*vt.* **-tled, -tling 1.** to intertwine (sticks, twigs, etc.) **2.** to construct of wattle

waul (wôl) *vi.*, *n.* wail, squall, or howl

Wave (wāv) *n.* a member of the WAVES

wave (wāv) *vi.* **waved, wav′ing** [OE. *wafian*] **1.** to move or sway up and down or to and fro **2.** to signal by moving a hand, arm, etc. to and fro **3.** to have the form of a series of curves —*vt.* **1.** to cause to wave, as a flag **2.** to brandish, as a weapon **3.** *a*) to move or swing (something) as a signal *b*) to signal (something) to (someone) by doing this **4.** to arrange (hair, etc.) in a series of curves —*n.* **1.** a ridge or swell moving along the surface of a body of water, etc. **2.** a curve or series of curves, as in the hair **3.** a motion to and fro or up and down, as with the hand in signaling **4.** something like a wave in effect *[a crime wave]* **5.** *Physics* any of the series of advancing impulses set up by a vibration, etc., as in the transmission of light, sound, etc.

wave'length' *n. Physics* the distance, measured in the direction of progression of a wave, from any given point to the next point characterized by the same phase: also **wave length**

wave'let (-lit) *n.* a little wave; ripple

wa·ver (wā'vər) *vi.* [< ME. *waven*, to WAVE] **1.** to sway to and fro; flutter **2.** to show indecision; vacillate **3.** to falter, flicker, or tremble —*n.* a wavering —**wa'ver·ing·ly** *adv.* —**wa'ver·y** *adj.*

WAVES (wāvz) [orig. *W(omen) A(ppointed for) V(oluntary) E(mergency) S(ervice)*] the women's branch of the U.S. Navy

wav·y (wā'vē) *adj.* **-i·er, -i·est 1.** having or like waves **2.** moving in a wavelike motion —**wav'i·ness** *n.*

wax¹ (waks) *n.* [OE. *weax*] **1.** a plastic, dull-yellow substance secreted by bees for building cells; beeswax **2.** any substance like this, as paraffin, earwax, sealing wax, etc. —*vt.* to rub, polish, cover, or treat with wax —*adj.* made of wax

wax² (waks) *vi.* [OE. *weaxan*, grow] **1.** to increase in strength, size, etc. **2.** to become gradually full: said of the moon **3.** to become *[to wax old]*

wax bean a variety of kidney bean with long, narrow, yellow pods

wax·en (wak's'n) *adj.* **1.** made of, or covered with, wax **2.** like wax; smooth, pale, plastic, etc.

wax myrtle *same as* BAYBERRY; esp., a shrub of eastern N. America with berries coated with a wax used for candles

wax paper paper made moistureproof by a wax, or paraffin, coating: also **waxed paper**

wax'wing' *n.* a bird with silky-brown plumage, a showy crest, and scarlet tips on its wings

wax'works' *n.pl.* [*with sing. v.*] an exhibition of wax figures: also **wax museum**

wax'y *adj.* **-i·er, -i·est 1.** of, full of, or covered with wax **2.** like wax in nature or appearance —**wax'i·ness** *n.*

way (wā) *n.* [OE. *weg*] **1.** a road, street, path, etc. **2.** room for passing; an opening, as in a crowd **3.** a route or course **4.** a specified route *[on the way to town]* **5.** habits of life *[to fall into evil ways]* **6.** a method of doing something **7.** a customary manner of living, acting, etc. *[to change one's ways]* **8.** manner; style **9.** distance *[a long way off]* : also [Colloq.] **ways 10.** direction of movement, etc. **11.** respect; particular *[right in some ways]* **12.** wish; will *[I had my way]* **13.** *[pl.]* a timber framework on which a ship is built and along which it slides in launching **14.** [Colloq.] *a*) a condition *[he's in a bad way]* *b*) a locality *[out our way]* —*adv.* away; far *[way behind]* —**by the way** incidentally —**by way of 1.** passing through **2.** as a method, etc. of —**give way 1.** to yield **2.** to break down — **lead the way** to be a guide or example —**make one's way 1.** to proceed **2.** to advance in life —**make way 1.** to clear a passage **2.** to make progress —**out of the way 1.** in a position so as not to hinder, etc. **2.** disposed of **3.** not on the right or usual route **4.** *a*) improper *b*) unusual —**under way 1.** moving; advancing **2.** *Naut. see* UNDERWAY

way'far'er (-fer'ər) *n.* a traveler, esp. on foot —**way'far'-ing** *adj., n.*

way'lay' *vt.* **-laid', -lay'ing 1.** to lie in wait for and attack; ambush **2.** to wait for and accost on the way — **way'lay'er** *n.*

way'-out' *adj.* [Colloq.] very unusual or unconventional

-ways [< WAY] *a suffix meaning* in a (specified) direction, position, or manner *[endways]*

ways and means 1. methods and resources at the disposal of a person, company, etc. **2.** methods of raising money, as for a government

way'side' *n.* the edge of a road —*adj.* on, near, or along the side of a road

way'ward (-wərd) *adj.* [see AWAY & -WARD] **1.** headstrong, willful, disobedient, etc. **2.** unpredictable; erratic — **way'ward·ly** *adv.* —**way'ward·ness** *n.*

W.C.T.U. Women's Christian Temperance Union

we (wē) *pron., for sing. see* I² [OE.] the persons speaking or writing: sometimes used by a person in referring to a group of which he is one, or, in place of *I*, by a monarch, editor, etc.

weak (wēk) *adj.* [ON. *veikr*] **1.** lacking physical strength; frail; feeble **2.** lacking in moral strength or willpower **3.** lacking mental power **4.** lacking force, power, effectiveness, or authority *[weak discipline]* **5.** easily torn, broken, etc. *[a weak railing]* **6.** lacking intensity, etc. *[a weak voice]* **7.** diluted *[weak tea]* **8.** poor or deficient in something specified *[weak in grammar]* **9.** unconvincing *[a weak argument]* **10.** *Gram.* inflected by adding a suffix such as *-ed, -d:* said of regular verbs

weak'en *vt., vi.* to make or become weak or weaker

weak'fish' *n., pl.:* see FISH [< obs. Du. *week*, soft + *visch*, a fish] an ocean food fish, esp. a type off the eastern coast of the U.S.

weak'-kneed' *adj.* lacking courage, determination, etc.

weak'ling *n.* one lacking physical or moral strength

weak'ly *adj.* **-li·er, -li·est** sickly; feeble; weak —*adv.* in a weak way —**weak'li·ness** *n.*

weak'-mind'ed *adj.* **1.** not firm of mind; indecisive **2.** mentally retarded —**weak'-mind'ed·ness** *n.*

weak'ness *n.* **1.** a being weak **2.** a weak point; fault **3.** an immoderate fondness *(for* something) **4.** something of which one is immoderately fond

weal¹ (wēl) *n.* [< WALE] a mark, line, or ridge raised on the skin, as by a blow; welt

weal² (wēl) *n.* [OE. *wela*] well-being; welfare *[the public weal]*

wealth (welth) *n.* [< prec.] **1.** much money or property; riches **2.** a large amount *[a wealth of ideas]* **3.** valuable products, contents, etc. *[wealth of the oceans]* **4.** *Econ. a)* everything having value in money or a price *b)* any useful material thing capable of being bought and sold

wealth'y *adj.* **-i·er, -i·est 1.** having wealth; rich **2.** abundant *(in* something) —**wealth'i·ness** *n.*

wean (wēn) *vt.* [OE. *wenian*] **1.** to accustom (a child or young animal) to take food other than by suckling **2.** to withdraw (a person) by degrees *(from* a habit, etc.) as by substituting something else

wean'ling *n.* a child or young animal that has just been weaned —*adj.* recently weaned

weap·on (wep'ən) *n.* [OE. *wæpen*] **1.** any instrument used for fighting **2.** any means of attack or defense

weap'on·ry (-rē) *n.* **1.** the production of weapons **2.** weapons collectively, esp. of a nation for war use

wear¹ (wer) *vt.* **wore, worn, wear'ing** [OE. *werian*] **1.** to bear (clothing, etc.) on the body **2.** to show in one's appearance *[she wore a smile]* **3.** to impair or diminish by constant use, friction, etc. **4.** to make by rubbing, flowing, etc. *[to wear a hole in the rug]* **5.** to bring by use to a specified state **6.** to tire or exhaust —*vi.* **1.** to become impaired or diminished by constant use, friction, etc. **2.** to hold up in spite of use *[a fabric that wears well]* **3.** to become in time *[courage wearing thin]* **4.** to pass away gradually: said of time **5.** to have an irritating effect *(on)* —*n.* **1.** a wearing or being worn **2.** things, esp. clothes, worn *[men's wear]* **3.** impairment or loss from use, friction, etc. **4.** the ability to last in spite of use —**wear off** to diminish by degrees —**wear out 1.** to make or become useless from continued use **2.** to tire out —**wear'a·ble** *adj.* —**wear'er** *n.*

wear and tear loss and damage resulting from use

wear'ing *adj.* **1.** of or for wear *[wearing apparel]* **2.** causing wear or loss **3.** tiring

wea·ri·some (wir'ē səm) *adj.* causing weariness; tiring; tiresome —**wea'ri·some·ly** *adv.*

wea·ry (wir'ē) *adj.* **-ri·er, -ri·est** [OE. *werig*] **1.** tired; worn out **2.** no longer liking, patient, etc.; bored (with *of)* **3.** tiring *[weary work]* **4.** tedious —*vt., vi.* **-ried, -ry·ing** to make or become weary —**wea'ri·ly** *adv.* —**wea'ri·ness** *n.*

wea·sel (wē'z'l) *n.* [OE. *wesle*] **1.** an agile, flesh-eating mammal, with a long, slender body, short legs, and a long tail **2.** a sly or sneaky person — *vi.* [Colloq.] to evade a commitment or responsibility (with *out)* —**wea'sel·ly** *adj.*

weasel words words or remarks that are deliberately misleading because they are ambiguous

WEASEL
(6–14 in. long, including tail)

weath·er (weth'ər) *n.* [OE. *weder*] **1.** the condition of the atmosphere with regard to temperature, moisture, etc. **2.** storm, rain, etc. —*vt.* **1.** to expose to the action of weather **2.** to pass through safely *[to weather* a storm] **3.** *Naut.* to pass to the windward of —*vi.* to become worn, discolored, etc. by exposure to the weather —*adj.* designating or of the side of a ship, etc. toward the wind —**under the weather** [Colloq.] ill

weath′er-beat′en *adj.* showing the effect of exposure to sun, rain, etc.

Weather Bureau *former name of the* NATIONAL WEATHER SERVICE

weath′er-cock′ *n.* a weather vane in the form of a rooster

weath′er-man′ *n., pl.* **-men′** one whose work is forecasting the weather

weath′er-proof′ *adj.* that can withstand exposure to the weather without damage —*vt.* to make weatherproof

weath′er-strip′ *n.* a strip of metal, felt, etc. covering the joint between a door or window and its casing, to keep out drafts, etc.: also **weath′er-strip′ping** —*vt.* **-stripped′, -strip′ping** to provide with this: also **weath′er-strip′**

weather vane a shaped piece of metal, etc. set up high to show which way the wind is blowing

weave (wēv) *vt.* **wove** or, chiefly for *vt.* 5 & *vi.* 3, **weaved**, **wo′ven** or **wove** or, chiefly for *vt.* 5 & *vi.* 3, **weaved**, **weav′ing** [OE. *wefan*] **1.** to make (a fabric, basket, etc.) by interlacing (threads, reeds, etc.), as on a loom **2.** *a)* to construct in the mind *[to weave a tale] b)* to form (incidents, etc.) into a story, etc. **3.** to twist (something) into or through **4.** to spin (a web): said of spiders, etc. **5.** to make (one's way) by moving from side to side or in and out —*vi.* **1.** to do weaving **2.** to become interlaced **3.** to move from side to side or in and out —*n.* a method or pattern of weaving —**weav′er** *n.*

web (web) *n.* [OE. *webb*] **1.** any woven fabric, esp. one still on a loom or just taken off **2.** the network spun by a spider, etc. **3.** a carefully woven trap **4.** anything contrived in an intricate way **5.** a membrane joining the digits of various water birds, animals, etc. —*vt.* **webbed, web′bing** to join by, or cover as with, a web

web′bing *n.* a strong fabric woven in strips and used for belts, in upholstery, etc.

web′foot′ *n., pl.* **-feet′** a foot with the toes webbed —**web′-foot′ed** *adj.*

Web-ster (web′stər) **1.** Daniel, 1782–1852; U.S. statesman & orator **2.** Noah, 1758–1843; U.S. lexicographer

wed (wed) *vt.* **wed′ded, wed′ded** or **wed, wed′ding** [OE. *weddian*] **1.** to marry **2.** to join closely

we'd (wēd) **1.** we had **2.** we should **3.** we would

Wed. Wednesday

wed-ded (wed′id) *adj.* **1.** married **2.** devoted *[wedded* to one's work*]* **3.** joined

wed′ding *n.* **1.** the act or ceremony of getting married **2.** a marriage anniversary

wedge (wej) *n.* [OE. *wecg*] **1.** a piece of wood, metal, etc. tapering to a thin edge that can be driven into a narrow opening, as to split wood **2.** anything shaped like a wedge **3.** any act used to open the way for change, etc. —*vt.* **wedged, wedg′ing 1.** to force apart, or fix in place, with a wedge **2.** to pack (*in*) or crowd together —*vi.* to push or be forced as or like a wedge

WEDGE

Wedg-wood (ware) (wej′wood′) [< J. *Wedgwood,* 18th-c. E. potter] *a trademark for* a fine English pottery, with white figures in relief

wed-lock (wed′läk) *n.* [< OE. *wed,* a pledge + *-lac,* an offering] the state of being married

Wednes-day (wenz′dē, -dā) *n.* [< WODEN] the fourth day of the week

wee (wē) *adj.* **we′er, we′est** [OE. *wege*] **1.** very small; tiny **2.** very early *[the wee hours]*

weed (wēd) *n.* [OE. *weod*] **1.** any undesired, uncultivated plant, esp. one crowding out desired plants **2.** [Colloq.] *a)* tobacco: with *the b)* a cigar or cigarette —*vt., vi.* **1.** to remove weeds from (a garden, etc.) **2.** to remove as useless, harmful, etc.: often with *out* —**weed′er** *n.* —**weed′-like′** *adj.*

weeds (wēdz) *n.pl.* [< OE. *wæde,* a garment] black mourning clothes, esp. those worn by a widow

weed′y *adj.* **-i·er, -i·est 1.** full of weeds **2.** of or like a weed, as in rapid growth **3.** lean; lanky

week (wēk) *n.* [OE. *wicu*] **1.** a period of seven days, esp. the period from Sunday through Saturday **2.** the hours or days of work in this period —**week in, week out** every week

week′day′ *n.* any day of the week except Sunday and, often, Saturday

week′end′, week′-end′ *n.* the period from Friday night or Saturday to Monday morning: also **week end** —*adj.* of, for, or on a weekend —*vi.* to spend the weekend (*at* or *in*)

week′ly *adj.* **1.** of, for, or lasting a week **2.** done, happening, etc. once every week —*adv.* once a week; every week —*n., pl.* **-lies** a periodical published once a week

ween (wēn) *vi., vt.* [OE. *wenan*] [Archaic] to think; suppose; imagine

wee-nie, wee-ny (wē′nē) *n., pl.* **-nies** [Colloq.] *same as* WIENER

weep (wēp) *vi., vt.* **wept, weep′ing** [OE. *wepan*] **1.** to shed (tears) **2.** to mourn (*for*) **3.** to drip or exude (water, etc.) —*n.* [*often pl.*] a fit of weeping —**weep′er** *n.*

weep′ing *n.* the act of one who weeps —*adj.* **1.** that weeps **2.** having graceful, drooping branches

weep′y *adj.* **-i·er, -i·est** weeping or inclined to weep

wee-vil (wē′v′l) *n.* [OE. *wifel*] a beetle whose larvae feed on cotton, fruits, grain, etc. —**wee′vil·y, wee′vil·ly** *adj.*

weft (weft) *n.* [< OE. *weftan,* to weave] **1.** *same as* WOOF¹ (sense 1) **2.** something woven

weigh (wā) *vt.* [OE. *wegan,* carry] **1.** to determine the heaviness of **2.** to have a (specified) weight **3.** to consider and choose carefully *[to weigh one's words]* **4.** to hoist (an anchor) —*vi.* **1.** to have significance, importance, etc. **2.** to be a burden —**weigh down** to burden or bear down on —**weigh in 1.** to weigh (a boxer, etc.) so as to verify his declared weight **2.** to be so weighed

weight (wāt) *n.* [OE. *wiht*] **1.** a quantity weighing a specified amount **2.** heaviness as a quality; specif., the force of gravity acting on a body **3.** how much a thing weighs **4.** *a)* any unit of heaviness *b)* any system of such units *c)* a piece of standard heaviness used in weighing **5.** any mass used for its heaviness *[a paperweight]* **6.** a burden, as of sorrow **7.** importance or consequence **8.** influence, power, etc. —*vt.* **1.** to add weight to **2.** to burden —**carry weight** to be important, influential, etc.

weight′less *adj.* having little or no apparent weight; specif., free of the pull of gravity —**weight′less·ness** *n.*

weight lifting the athletic exercise or sport of lifting barbells —**weight lifter**

weight′y *adj.* **-i·er, -i·est 1.** very heavy **2.** burdensome **3.** significant; important —**weight′i·ness** *n.*

weir (wir) *n.* [OE. *wer*] **1.** a low dam built to back up water, as for a mill **2.** a fence, as of brushwood, in a stream, etc., for catching fish

weird (wird) *adj.* [ult. < OE. *wurd,* fate] **1.** suggestive of ghosts, etc.; mysterious, eerie, etc. **2.** strikingly odd, strange, etc.; bizarre —**weird′ly** *adv.* —**weird′ness** *n.*

wel-come (wel′kəm) *adj.* [< OE. *wilcuma,* welcome guest] **1.** gladly received *[a welcome guest, welcome news]* **2.** willingly permitted or invited *[welcome to use the library]* **3.** under no obligation *[you're welcome]* —*n.* a welcoming —*interj.* you are welcome: an expression of cordial greeting —*vt.* **-comed, -com·ing** to greet or receive with pleasure, etc.

weld (weld) *vt.* [< obs. *well*] **1.** to unite (pieces of metal, etc.) by heating until fused or soft enough to hammer or press together **2.** to unite closely —*vi.* to be welded —*n.* **1.** a welding or being welded **2.** the joint formed by welding —**weld′er** *n.*

wel-fare (wel′fer′) *n.* [see WELL² & FARE] **1.** state of health, happiness, and comfort; well-being **2.** aid by government agencies for the poor, unemployed, etc. **3.** *same as* WELFARE WORK —**on welfare** receiving government aid because of poverty, unemployment, etc.

welfare state a nation in which the government assumes responsibility for the welfare of the citizens, with regard to employment, medical care, etc.

welfare work the organized effort of a community or organization to improve the living conditions and standards of its needy members —**welfare worker**

wel-kin (wel′kin) *n.* [OE. *wolcen*] [Archaic or Poet.] the vault of the sky

well¹ (wel) *n.* [OE. *wella*] **1.** a natural spring and pool **2.** a hole sunk into the earth to get water, oil, etc. **3.** an abundant source **4.** any shaft like a well **5.** a container for liquid, as an inkwell —*vi., vt.* to pour forth as from a well; gush (*up, forth,* etc.)

well² (wel) *adv.* **bet′ter, best** [OE. *wel*] **1.** in a satisfactory, proper, or skillful manner *[treat him well,* to sing *well]* **2.** prosperously *[to live well]* **3.** with good reason *[one may well ask]* **4.** to a considerable degree *[well advanced]* **5.** thoroughly *[stir it well]* **6.** with certainty; definitely **7.** familiarly *[I know him well]* Well is used in hyphenated compounds to mean *properly, thoroughly,* etc. *[well-*defined*]* —*adj.* **1.** suitable, proper, etc. **2.** in good health **3.** in good condition —*interj.* an exclamation used to express surprise, agreement, etc. or to introduce a remark —**as well** (**as**) **1.** in addition (to) **2.** equally (with)

we'll (wēl, wil) **1.** we shall **2.** we will

Wel·land (Ship) Canal (wel′ənd) canal of the St. Lawrence Seaway in Ontario, Canada, between Lake Ontario & Lake Erie: 27 1/2 mi. long

well′-ap·point′ed (-ə poin′tid) *adj.* excellently furnished or equipped

well′-bal′anced *adj.* **1.** carefully adjusted **2.** sane; sensible

well′-be·haved′ *adj.* behaving well; polite

well′-be′ing *n.* the state of being well, happy, or prosperous; welfare

well′-bred′ *adj.* showing good breeding; courteous and considerate

well′-cho′sen *adj.* chosen with care; proper

well′-dis·posed′ *adj.* **1.** suitably placed or arranged **2.** friendly (*toward* a person) or receptive (*to* an idea, etc.)

well′-done′ *adj.* **1.** performed with skill **2.** thoroughly cooked: said esp. of meat

well′-fa′vored *adj.* handsome; pretty

well′-fed′ *adj.* plump or fat

well′-fixed′ *adj.* [Colloq.] wealthy; rich

well′-found′ed *adj.* based on facts, good evidence, or sound judgment

well′-groomed′ *adj.* **1.** carefully cared for [a *well-groomed* horse] **2.** clean and neat

well′-ground′ed *adj.* **1.** having a thorough basic knowledge of a subject **2.** based on good reasons

well′-heeled′ *adj.* [Slang] rich; prosperous

well′-in·formed′ *adj.* having considerable knowledge of a subject or of many subjects

Wel·ling·ton (wel′iŋ tən) capital of New Zealand: pop. (of urban area) 179,000

Wel·ling·ton (wel′iŋ tən), 1st Duke of, 1769–1852; Brit. general & statesman

well′-in·ten′tioned *adj.* having or showing good or kindly intentions, but often with bad results

well′-knit′ *adj.* **1.** well constructed **2.** having a sturdy body build

well′-known′ *adj.* **1.** widely known; famous **2.** thoroughly known

well′-made′ *adj.* **1.** skillfully and strongly built **2.** skillfully contrived or plotted, as a play

well′-man′nered *adj.* polite; courteous

well′-mean′ing *adj.* **1.** having good intentions **2.** said or done with good intentions, but often with bad results: also **well′-meant′**

well′-nigh′ (-nī′) *adv.* very nearly; almost

well′-off′ *adv.* **1.** in a fortunate condition or circumstance **2.** prosperous; well-to-do

well′-read′ *adj.* **1.** having read much (*in* a subject) **2.** having a wide knowledge of books

well′-round′ed *adj.* **1.** well planned for proper balance [a *well-rounded* program] **2.** showing interest, ability, etc. in many fields **3.** shapely

Wells (welz), H. G. 1866–1946; Eng. novelist & historian

well′-spo′ken *adj.* **1.** speaking fluently, graciously, etc. **2.** properly or aptly spoken

well′spring′ *n.* **1.** a spring or fountainhead **2.** a source of abundant supply

well′-thought′-of′ *adj.* having a good reputation; of good repute

well′-timed′ *adj.* timely; opportune

well′-to-do′ *adj.* prosperous; wealthy

well′-turned′ *adj.* **1.** gracefully shaped **2.** expressed or worded well [a *well-turned* phrase]

well′-wish′er *n.* a person who wishes well to another or to a cause, etc. —**well′-wish′ing** *adj.*, *n.*

well′-worn′ *adj.* **1.** much worn; much used **2.** overused; trite [a *well-worn* joke]

Welsh (welsh, welch) *adj.* of Wales, its people, etc. —*n.* the Celtic language of Wales —**the Welsh** the people of Wales —**Welsh′man** (-mən) *n.*, *pl.* **-men**

welsh (welsh, welch) *vi.* [< ?] [Slang] **1.** to cheat by failing to pay a bet or other debt **2.** to evade an obligation Often with *on* —**welsh′er** *n.*

Welsh rabbit a dish of melted cheese, often mixed with ale or beer, served on crackers or toast: also **Welsh rarebit**

welt (welt) *n.* [ME. *welte*] **1.** a strip of leather in the seam between the sole and upper of a shoe **2.** a ridge raised on the skin by a slash or blow —*vt.* **1.** to furnish with a welt **2.** to raise welts on (the body) **3.** [Colloq.] to beat severely

wel·ter (wel′tər) *vi.* [MDu. *welteren*] **1.** to roll about or wallow **2.** to be soaked, stained, etc. [to *welter* in blood] —*n.* a confusion; turmoil

welt·er·weight (wel′tər wāt′) *n.* [prob. < WELT] a boxer or wrestler between a lightweight and a middleweight (in boxing, 136–147 lbs.)

wen (wen) *n.* [OE. *wenn*] a harmless skin tumor, esp. of the scalp

wench (wench) *n.* [OE. *wencel,* a child] **1.** a girl or young woman: now a derogatory or jocular term **2.** [Archaic] *a*) a female servant *b*) a prostitute

wend (wend) *vt.* [OE. *wendan,* to turn] to proceed on (one's way)

went (went) *pt. of* GO

wept (wept) *pt. & pp. of* WEEP

were (wur) [OE. *wæron*] *pl. & 2d pers. sing., past indic., and the past subj., of* BE

we're (wir) we are

weren't (wurnt) were not

were·wolf (wir′woolf′, wur′-) *n., pl.* **-wolves** (-woolvz′) [< OE. *wer,* a man + *wulf,* a wolf] *Folklore* a person changed into a wolf: also sp. **wer′wolf′**

wert (wurt, wərt) *archaic 2d pers. sing., past indic., and the past subj., of* BE: *used with* thou

Wes·ley (wes′lē, wez′-), **John** 1703–91; Eng. clergyman & founder of Methodism —**Wes′ley·an** *adj., n.*

west (west) *n.* [OE.] **1.** the direction in which sunset occurs (270° on the compass, opposite east) **2.** a region in or toward this direction **3.** [W-] the Western Hemisphere, or the Western Hemisphere and Europe **4.** [W-] the Western Roman Empire —*adj.* **1.** in, of, or toward the west **2.** from the west —*adv.* in or toward the west —**the West 1.** the part of the U.S. west of the Mississippi **2.** the U.S. and its non-Communist allies in Europe and the Western Hemisphere

West Berlin W section of Berlin, associated with West Germany: pop. 2,141,000

west′er·ly *adj., adv.* **1.** toward the west **2.** from the west

west′ern *adj.* **1.** in, of, or toward the west **2.** from the west **3.** [W-] of the West —*n.* a story or motion picture about cowboys, etc. in the western U.S. —**west′ern·most′** *adj.*

west′ern·er *n.* a native or inhabitant of the west, specif. [W-] of the western part of the U.S.

Western Hemisphere that half of the earth that includes North & South America

west′ern·ize′ *vt.* **-ized′, -iz′ing** to make western in character, etc. —**west′ern·i·za′tion** *n.*

Western Roman Empire the W part of the Roman Empire, after its division (395 A.D.)

Western Samoa country in the South Pacific, consisting of two large islands & several small ones: 1,130 sq. mi.; pop. 146,000

West Germany W section of Germany; country in NC Europe: 95,735 sq. mi.; pop. 59,974,000; cap. Bonn

West Indies large group of islands between N. America & S. America: it includes the Greater Antilles, Lesser Antilles, & Bahamas —**West Indian**

west-north-west (west′nôrth′west′; *nautical* -nôr-) *n.* the direction halfway between due west and northwest —*adj., adv.* in, toward, or from this direction

West Point military reservation in SE N.Y., on the Hudson: site of the U.S. Military Academy

west-south-west (west′south′west′; *nautical* -sou-) *n.* the direction halfway between due west and southwest —*adj., adv.* in, toward, or from this direction

West Virginia E State of the U.S.: 24,181 sq. mi.; pop. 1,744,000; cap. Charleston: abbrev. **W.Va., WV** —**West Virginian**

west·ward (west′wərd) *adv., adj.* toward the west: also **west′wards** *adv.* —*n.* a westward direction, point, or region —**west′ward·ly** *adv., adj.*

wet (wet) *adj.* **wet′ter, wet′test** [OE. *wæt*] **1.** covered or saturated with water or other liquid **2.** rainy; misty **3.** not yet dry [*wet* paint] **4.** permitting the sale of alcoholic liquor —*n.* **1.** water or other liquid **2.** rain or rainy weather **3.** one who favors the sale of alcoholic liquor —*vt., vi.* **wet** or **wet′ted, wet′ting** to make or become wet —**all wet** [Slang] wrong —**wet′ly** *adv.* —**wet′ness** *n.*

wet′back′ *n.* [Colloq.] a Mexican agricultural laborer who illegally enters the U.S. to work

wet blanket a person or thing that dampens or lessens the enthusiasm or gaiety of others

wet nurse a woman hired to suckle another's child —**wet′-nurse′** *vt.* **-nursed′, -nurs′ing**

wet suit a closefitting suit of rubber worn by skin divers for warmth

we've (wēv) we have

whack (hwak) *vt., vi.* [echoic] [Colloq.] to strike or slap with a sharp, resounding blow —*n.* [Colloq.] a sharp,

resounding blow, or its sound —**have** (or **take**) **a whack at** [Colloq.] **1.** to aim a blow at **2.** to make an attempt at — **out of whack** [Colloq.] not in proper condition
whack'ing *adj.* [Chiefly Brit. Colloq.] big; great
whack'y *adj.* -**i·er**, -**i·est** [Slang] *same as* WACKY
whale¹ (hwāl) *n.* [OE. *hwæl*] a large, warmblooded, fishlike mammal that breathes air —*vi.* **whaled, whal'ing** to hunt whales —**a whale of a** [Colloq.] an exceptionally large, fine, etc. example of
whale² (hwāl) *vt.* **whaled, whal'ing** [prob. var. of WALE] [Colloq.] to beat; whip; thrash
whale'boat' *n.* a long rowboat, pointed at both ends
whale'bone' *n.* **1.** horny elastic material hanging from the upper jaw of some whales **2.** something made of this, as, esp. formerly, a corset stay
whal'er *n.* **1.** a ship used in whaling **2.** a man whose work is whaling: also **whale'man**, *pl.* -**men**
whal'ing *n.* the work or trade of hunting and killing whales for their blubber, whalebone, etc.
wham (hwam) *interj.* a sound imitating a heavy blow, etc. —*n.* a heavy blow or impact —*vt., vi.* **whammed, wham'ming** to strike, etc. loudly
wham·my (hwam'ē) *n., pl.* -**mies** [Slang] a jinx or the evil eye: usually in **put a** (or **the**) **whammy on**
wharf (hwôrf) *n., pl.* **wharves** (hwôrvz), **wharfs** [< OE. *hwerf*, a dam] a platform built on the shore, where ships can dock and load or unload; dock
wharf'age (-ij) *n.* **1.** the use of a wharf **2.** a fee charged for this **3.** wharves collectively
Whar·ton (hwôr't'n), **Edith** 1862–1937; U.S. novelist
what (hwut, hwät) *pron.* [< OE. *hwa*, who] **1.** which thing, event, etc.? *[what* is that object?] **2.** that which or those which *[do what* you will] —*n.* the nature (*of* an event) —*adj.* **1.** which or which kind of: used interrogatively or relatively *[what* man told you that? I know *what* books you like] **2.** as much, or as many, as *[take what* men you need] **3.** how great, surprising, etc. *[what* joy!] —*adv.* **1.** in what way? how? *[what* does it matter?] **2.** partly *[what* with singing and joking, the time passed] **3.** how greatly, surprisingly, etc. *[what* sad news!] —*conj.* that *[never* doubt but *what* he loves you] —*interj.* an exclamation of surprise, anger, etc. *[what!* no dinner?] —**and what not** and other things of all sorts —**what about** what do you think, know, etc. concerning? —**what for** why? — **what have you** [Colloq.] anything similar *[games,* toys, or *what have you]* —**what if** what would happen if —**what's what** [Colloq.] the true state of affairs
what·ev·er (hwət ev'ər) *pron.* **1.** what: used for emphasis *[whatever* can it be?] **2.** anything that *[say whatever* you like] **3.** no matter what *[whatever* you do, don't rush] **4.** [Colloq.] anything of the sort —*adj.* **1.** of no matter what type, degree, etc. *[make whatever* repairs are needed] **2.** being who it may be *[whatever* man told you that, it isn't true] **3.** of any kind Also [Poet.] **what·e'er'** (-er')
what'not' *n.* **1.** a nondescript thing **2.** a set of open shelves, as for bric-a-brac
what'so·ev'er (-sō ev'ər) *pron., adj.* whatever: used for emphasis
wheal¹ (hwēl) *n.* [ME. *whele*] a small, raised patch of skin, as from an insect bite
wheal² (hwēl) *n. same as* WEAL¹
wheat (hwēt) *n.* [OE. *hwæte*] **1.** a cereal grass with dense spikes that bear grains **2.** such grain, used for flour, cereals, etc.
wheat germ 1. the wheat-kernel embryo, rich in vitamins, milled out as an oily flake **2.** the milled flakes
whee·dle (hwē'd'l) *vt., vi.* -**dled, -dling** [< ?] to influence or persuade (a person) or get (something) by flattery, coaxing, etc. —**whee'dler** *n.*
wheel (hwēl) *n.* [OE. *hweol*] **1.** a solid disk or circular frame turning on a central axis **2.** anything like a wheel in shape, movement, etc. **3.** the steering wheel of a motor vehicle **4.** [*pl.*] [Slang] an automobile **5.** [usually *pl.*] the moving forces *[the wheels* of progress] **6.** a turning movement **7.** [Slang] an important person: also **big wheel** — *vt., vi.* **1.** to move on or in a wheeled vehicle **2.** to turn, revolve, rotate, etc. **3.** to turn so as to reverse direction (often with *about*) —**at the wheel 1.** steering a ship, motor vehicle, etc. **2.** directing activities —**wheeled** *adj.*
wheel'bar'row (-bar'ō, -ber'ō) *n.* a shallow, open box for moving small loads, having a wheel in front, and two shafts for pushing the vehicle
wheel'base' *n.* in a motor vehicle, the distance in inches from the front axle to the rear axle

wheel'chair' *n.* a chair mounted on large wheels, for persons unable to walk
wheel'er *n.* **1.** a person or thing that wheels **2.** something having a specified kind or number of wheels *[two-wheeler]*
wheel'er-deal'er (-dēl'ər) *n.* [Slang] one who is showily aggressive, as in arranging business deals
wheel'house' *n. same as* PILOTHOUSE
wheel'wright' (-rīt') *n.* one who makes and repairs wagon and carriage wheels
wheeze (hwēz) *vi.* **wheezed, wheez'ing** [ON. *hvaesa*, to hiss] to make a whistling, breathy sound, as in asthma — *n.* a wheezing —**wheez'y** *adj.* -**i·er**, -**i·est**
whelk (hwelk) *n.* [OE. *wioluc*] any of various large sea snails with spiral shells, esp. those used in Europe for food
whelm (hwelm) *vt.* [ME. *welmen*] **1.** to submerge or engulf **2.** to overwhelm

WHELK

whelp (hwelp) *n.* [OE. *hwelp*] **1.** a young dog; puppy **2.** a young lion, tiger, wolf, etc.; cub **3.** a youth or child: contemptuous usage —*vt., vi.* to bring forth (young): said of animals
when (hwen) *adv.* [OE. *hwænne*] **1.** at what time? *[when* did he leave?] **2.** on what occasion? —*conj.* **1.** at the time that *[he* told us *when* we sat down] **2.** at which *[a* time *when* men must speak out] **3.** as soon as *[come when* I call] **4.** at whatever time that *[he* rested *when* he could] **5.** although *[to* object *when* there's no reason to do so] **6.** if *[how* can he help *when* they won't let him?] —*pron.* what time or which time *[until when* will you stay?] —*n.* the time (*of* an event) *[the when* and where of his arrest]
whence (hwens) *adv.* [OE. *hwanan*] from what place, source, cause, etc.; from where *[whence* do you come?]
when·ev·er *adv.* [Colloq.] when: used for emphasis *[whenever* will he learn?] —*conj.* at whatever time; on whatever occasion *[visit* us *whenever* you can] Also [Poet.] **when·e'er'** (-er')
when'so·ev'er *adv., conj.* whenever: used for emphasis
where (hwer) *adv.* [OE. *hwær*] **1.** in or at what place? *[where* is the car?] **2.** to or toward what place? *[where* did he go?] **3.** in what respect? *[where* is she to blame?] **4.** from what place or source? *[where* did you find out?] — *conj.* **1.** at what place *[he* knows *where* it is] **2.** at which place *[we* came home, *where* we ate] **3.** at the place or situation in which *[he* is *where* he should be] **4.** wherever **5.** to the place to which *[we* go *where* you go] **6.** to or toward whatever place *[go where* you please] —*pron.* **1.** the place at which *[a* mile to *where* he lives] **2.** what place *[where* are you from?] —*n.* the place (*of* an event)
where'a·bouts' (-ə bouts') *adv.* near what place? where? —*n.* the place where a person or thing is *[do* you know his *whereabouts?]*
where·as' (-az') *conj.* **1.** in view of the fact that **2.** while on the contrary *[she* is slim, *whereas* he is fat]
where·at' *conj.* [Archaic] at which point
where·by' *adv.* [Archaic] by what? how? —*conj.* by which *[a* plan *whereby* to make money]
where'fore' (-fôr') *adv.* [Archaic] for what reason? why? —*conj.* **1.** for which *[the* reason *wherefore* we have met] **2.** because of which; therefore *[we* won, *wherefore* rejoice] —*n.* the reason; cause
where·in' *adv.* [Archaic] in what way? how? —*conj.* in which *[the* room *wherein* he lay]
where·of' *adv., conj.* of what, which, or whom
where·on' *adv.* [Archaic] on what? —*conj.* on which *[the* hill *whereon* we stand]
where'so·ev'er *adv., conj.* wherever: used for emphasis
where'up·on' *conj.* **1.** upon which **2.** at which
wher·ev·er (hwer ev'ər) *adv.* [Colloq.] where: used for emphasis *[wherever* did you go?] —*conj.* in, at, or to whatever place *[go wherever* you like]
where·with' *conj.* with which
where'with·al' (-with ôl') *n.* the necessary means, esp. money *[the wherewithal* to pay for food]
wher·ry (hwer'ē) *n., pl.* -**ries** [ME. *whery*] a light rowboat
whet (hwet) *vt.* **whet'ted, whet'ting** [< OE. *hwæt*, keen] **1.** to sharpen by rubbing or grinding **2.** to stimulate *[to whet* the appetite]
wheth·er (hweth'ər) *conj.* [OE. *hwæther*] **1.** if it be the case or fact that *[ask whether* she will help] **2.** in case; in either case that: used to introduce alternatives *[whether* it rains or snows] **3.** either *[whether* by accident or design]

---

fat, āpe, cär; ten, ēven; is, bīte; gō, hôrn, tōōl, look; oil, out; up, fur; thin, *then*; zh, leisure; ŋ, ring; ə for *a* in *ago*; ' as in *able* (ā'b'l); ë, Fr. coeur; ö, Fr. feu; ô, Fr. mon; ü, Fr. duc; r, Fr. cri; kh, G. doch, ich. ‡ foreign; < derived from

whet·stone (hwet′stōn′) *n.* an abrasive stone for sharpening knives or other edged tools

whew (hyōō) *interj.* [echoic] an exclamation of relief, surprise, dismay, etc.

whey (hwā) *n.* [OE. *hwæg*] the thin, watery part of milk, which separates from the thicker part (curds) after coagulation —**whey′ey** (-ē) *adj.*

which (hwich) *pron.* [OE. *hwylc*] 1. what one (or ones) of the persons, things, or events mentioned or implied? *[which* do you want?] 2. the one (or ones) that *[he knows which* he wants] 3. that: used as a relative referring to the thing or event specified in the antecedent *[the boat which* sank] 4. any that; whichever *[take which* you like] —*adj.* 1. what one or ones *[which* man (or men) came?] 2. whatever *[try which* plan you like] 3. being the one just mentioned *[he* is old, *which* fact is important]

which·ev′er *pron., adj.* 1. any one *[take whichever* (desk) you like] 2. no matter which *[whichever* (desk) he chooses, they won't be pleased]

whiff (hwif) *n.* [echoic] 1. a light puff or gust of air or wind 2. a slight gust of odor *[a whiff* of garlic] —*vt., vi.* to blow or puff

whif·fle·tree (hwif′'l trē′) *n. var. of* WHIPPLETREE

Whig (hwig) *n.* [< *wiggamore* (contemptuous term for Scot. Presbyterians)] 1. a member of a former English political party which championed reform and parliamentary rights 2. a supporter of the American Revolution against Great Britain 3. a member of an American political party (c.1838–1856) opposing the Democratic Party — *adj.* of or being a Whig —**Whig′gish** *adj.*

while (hwil) *n.* [OE. *hwil*] a period of time *[a short while]* —*conj.* 1. during the time that *[we* talked *while* we ate] 2. at the same time that *[while* you're up, close the door] 3. *a)* although *[while* she isn't pretty, she is charming] *b)* whereas *[the* walls are green, *while* the ceiling is white] — *vt.* whiled, whil′ing to spend (time) pleasantly *[to while* away the hours] —**the while** during this very time —**worth (one's) while** worth one's time; profitable

whi·lom (hwī′ləm) *adv.* [< OE. *hwil*, while] [Archaic] at one time; formerly —*adj.* formerly such; former *[their whilom* friends]

whilst (hwīlst) *conj.* [Dial.] *same as* WHILE

whim (hwim) *n.* [< ?] a sudden fancy; caprice

whim·per (hwim′pər) *vi., vt.* [? akin to WHINE] to cry or utter with low, whining, broken sounds —*n.* a whimpering sound or cry —**whim′per·er** *n.*

whim·si·cal (hwim′zi k'l) *adj.* 1. full of whims or whimsy 2. different in an odd way —**whim′si·cal′i·ty** (-kal′ə tē), *pl.* -ties —**whim′si·cal·ly** *adv.*

whim·sy (hwim′zē) *n., pl.* -sies [< ?] 1. an odd fancy; idle notion; whim 2. quaint or fanciful humor Also sp. **whim′sey**, *pl.* -seys

whine (hwīn) *vi.* whined, whin′ing [OE. *hwinan*] 1. *a)* to utter a high-pitched, nasal sound, as in complaint, fear, etc. *b)* to make a prolonged sound like this 2. to complain in a childish way —*vt.* to utter with a whine —*n.* 1. a whining 2. a complaint uttered in a whining tone — **whin′er** *n.* —**whin′y, whin′ey** *adj.* -i·er, -i·est

whin·ny (hwin′ē) *vi.* -nied, -ny·ing [prob. < prec.] to neigh in a low, gentle way: said of a horse —*n., pl.* -nies a whinnying

whip (hwip) *vt.* whipped, whip′ping [MDu. *wippen*, to swing] 1. to move, pull, throw, etc. suddenly *[to whip* out a knife] 2. to strike as with a strap; lash 3. to drive, urge, etc. as by whipping 4. to wind (cord or thread) around a rope to prevent fraying 5. to beat (eggs, cream, etc.) into a froth 6. to sew (a seam, etc.) with a loose, overhand stitch 7. [Colloq.] to defeat —*vi.* 1. to move quickly and suddenly 2. to flap about in a whiplike manner —*n.* 1. an instrument for striking or flogging, consisting of a rod with a lash attached to one end 2. a blow, etc. as with a whip 3. an officer of a political party in a legislature who maintains discipline, etc. 4. a whipping motion 5. a dessert of fruit, sugar, whipped cream, etc. —**whip up** 1. to rouse; excite 2. [Colloq.] to prepare quickly and efficiently —**whip′like′** *adj.* —**whip′per** *n.*

whip′cord′ *n.* 1. a hard, twisted or braided cord 2. a strong worsted cloth with a diagonally ribbed surface

whip hand 1. the hand in which a driver holds his whip 2. the position of advantage or control

whip′lash′ *n.* 1. the lash of a whip 2. a sudden, severe jolting of the neck backward and then forward, as caused by the impact of a rear-end automobile collision

whip′per·snap′per *n.* a young or unimportant person who appears impertinent or presumptuous

whip·pet (hwip′it) *n.* [< WHIP] a swift dog resembling a small greyhound, used in racing

whip′ping *n.* 1. a flogging or beating, as in punishment 2. cord, twine, etc. used to whip, or bind

whipping boy *same as* SCAPEGOAT

whipping post a post to which offenders are tied to be whipped as a legal punishment

whip·ple·tree (hwip′'l trē′) *n.* [< WHIP + TREE] *same as* SINGLETREE

whip·poor·will (hwip′ər wil′) *n.* [echoic] a grayish bird of eastern N. America, active at night

WHIPPET
(18–22 in. high at shoulder)

whip′stitch′ *n. Sewing* a stitch made by whipping with a loose, overhand stitch

whir, whirr (hwur) *vt., vi.* whirred, whir′ring [prob. < Scand.] to fly, revolve, vibrate, etc. with a buzzing sound —*n.* a sound like this

whirl (hwurl) *vi.* [ON. *hvirfla*] 1. to move rapidly in a circle or orbit 2. to rotate or spin fast 3. to move, go, etc. swiftly 4. to seem to spin *[my* head is *whirling]* —*vt.* to cause to move, rotate, revolve, etc. rapidly —*n.* 1. a whirling or whirling motion 2. something whirling or being whirled 3. a round of parties, etc. 4. a tumult; uproar 5. a confused or giddy condition —**give it a whirl** [Colloq.] to make an attempt —**whirl′er** *n.*

whirl·i·gig (hwur′li gig′) *n.* 1. a child's toy that whirls or spins 2. a merry-go-round

whirl′pool′ *n.* water in violent, whirling motion tending to draw floating objects into its center

whirl′wind′ *n.* 1. a current of air whirling violently upward in a spiral that has a forward motion 2. anything like a whirlwind, as in destructive force —*adj.* carried on as fast as possible

whirl′y·bird′ *n. colloq.* term for HELICOPTER

whisk (hwisk) *n.* [ON. *visk*, a brush] 1. a brushing with a quick, light, sweeping motion 2. such a motion —*vt., vi.* to move, carry, brush (away, off, etc.) with a quick, sweeping motion

whisk broom a small, short-handled broom for brushing clothes, etc.

whisk′er *n.* 1. [*pl.*] the hair growing on a man's face, esp. on the cheeks 2. *a)* a hair of a man's beard *b)* any of the long, bristly hairs on the upper lip of a cat, rat, etc. — **whisk′ered** *adj.*

whis·key (hwis′kē) *n., pl.* -keys, -kies [< IrGael. *uisce*, water + *beathadh*, life] a strong alcoholic liquor distilled from the fermented mash of grain: also, esp. for Brit. and Canad. usage, **whisky**, *pl.* -kies

whis·per (hwis′pər) *vi., vt.* [OE. *hwisprian*] 1. to speak or say very softly, esp. without vibration of the vocal cords 2. to talk or tell furtively, as in gossiping 3. to make a soft, rustling sound —*n.* 1. a whispering 2. something whispered 3. a soft, rustling sound —**whis′per·er** *n.* —**whis′per·ing** *adj., n.*

whist (hwist) *n.* [< *whisk*] a card game, usually played by two pairs of players, similar to bridge

whis·tle (hwis′'l) *vi.* -tled, -tling [OE. *hwistlian*] 1. to make a clear, shrill sound as by forcing breath through the contracted lips 2. to move with a shrill sound, as the wind 3. *a)* to blow a whistle *b)* to have its whistle blown, as a train —*vt.* 1. to produce (a tune, etc.) by whistling 2. to signal, etc. by whistling —*n.* 1. an instrument for making whistling sounds 2. a whistling —**whis′tler** *n.*

Whis·tler (hwis′lər), **James** 1834–1903; U.S. painter in England

whit (hwit) *n.* [< OE. *wiht*, a wight] the least bit; jot; iota *[not a whit* the wiser]

white (hwīt) *adj.* whit′er, whit′est [OE. *hwit*] 1. having the color of pure snow or milk; of the color of reflected light containing all of the visible rays of the spectrum; opposite to black 2. of a light or pale color 3. pale; wan 4. pure; innocent 5. having a light-colored skin —*n.* 1. *a)* white color *b)* a white pigment 2. a white or light-colored part, as the albumen of an egg, the white part of the eyeball, etc. 3. a person with a light-colored skin; Caucasoid —**white′ness** *n.*

white ant *popular name for* TERMITE

white′cap′ *n.* a wave with its crest broken into white foam

white′-col′lar *adj.* designating or of clerical or professional workers or the like

white elephant 1. an albino elephant, held as sacred in SE Asia 2. a thing of little use, but expensive to maintain

---

Where the sound (hw) occurs for wh, the sound (w) is also heard, as in when (hwen, wen).

3. any object not wanted by its owner, but of possible value to others

white feather a symbol of cowardice: chiefly in **show the white feather**

white′fish′ *n., pl.:* see FISH a white or silvery lake fish of the salmon family, found in N U.S.

white flag a white banner hoisted as a signal of truce or surrender

white gold gold alloyed with nickel, zinc, etc., to give it a white, platinumlike appearance

white goods 1. household linens, as sheets, towels, etc. **2.** large household appliances, as refrigerators

white heat 1. the degree of intense heat at which a metal, etc. glows white **2.** a state of intense emotion, excitement, etc. **—white′-hot′** *adj.*

White House, the 1. official residence of the President of the U.S., in Washington, D.C. **2.** the executive branch of the U.S. government

white lead a poisonous, white powder, lead carbonate, used as a paint pigment, etc.

white lie a lie about something unimportant, often told to spare someone's feelings

white matter whitish nerve tissue of the brain and spinal cord, consisting chiefly of nerve fibers

White Mountains mountain range of the Appalachian system, in N N.H.

whit·en (hwīt′'n) *vt., vi.* to make or become white or whiter **—whit′en·er** *n.* **—whit′en·ing** *n.*

white pepper pepper ground from the husked, dried seeds of the nearly ripe pepper berry

white pine 1. a pine of eastern N. America, with soft, light wood **2.** this wood

white race loosely, the Caucasoid group of mankind

White Russia *same as* BYELORUSSIAN S.S.R. **—White Russian**

white sale a store sale of household linens, etc.

white sauce a sauce for meat, fish, etc., made of butter, flour, milk, etc. cooked together

White Sea arm of the Arctic Ocean, extending into NW U.S.S.R.

white slave a woman forced into prostitution for others' profit **—white′-slave′** *adj.* **—white slavery**

white′wall′ *adj.* designating or of a tire with a white band on the outer sidewall **—n.** a whitewall tire

white′wash′ *n.* **1.** a mixture of lime, whiting, water, etc., for whitening walls, etc. **2.** a concealing of faults in order to exonerate **3.** [Colloq.] *Sports* a defeat in which the loser scores no points **—vt. 1.** to cover with whitewash **2.** to conceal the faults of **3.** [Colloq.] *Sports* to defeat (an opponent) without permitting him to score

whith·er (hwith′ər) *adv.* [OE. *hwider*] to what place, condition, etc.? where? **—conj. 1.** to which place, condition, etc. **2.** wherever *Where* is now almost always used in place of *whither*

whit·ing¹ (hwīt′iŋ) *n.* [< MDu. *wit,* white] any of many unrelated ocean food fishes of N. America, Europe, and Australia, including several hakes and kingfishes

whit·ing² (hwīt′iŋ) *n.* [ME. *whytyng*] powdered chalk used in paints, inks, etc.

whit′ish *adj.* somewhat white

Whit·man (hwit′mən), **Walt(er)** 1819–92; U.S. poet

Whit·ney (hwit′nē), **Eli** 1765–1825; U.S. inventor, esp. of the cotton gin

Whit·ney (hwit′nē), **Mount** mountain in EC Calif.: 14,495 ft.

Whit·sun·day (hwit′sun′dē, -s'n dā′) *n.* [OE. *Hwita Sunnandæg,* white Sunday] *same as* PENTECOST

Whit′sun·tide′ (-s'n tīd′) *n.* the week beginning with Whitsunday, esp. the first three days

Whit·ti·er (hwit′ē ər), **John Green·leaf** (grēn′lēf′) 1807–92; U.S. poet

whit·tle (hwit′'l) *vt.* **-tled, -tling** [OE. *thwitan,* to cut] **1.** *a)* to cut thin shavings from (wood) with a knife *b)* to carve (an object) in this manner **2.** to reduce gradually *[to whittle down costs]* **—vi.** to whittle wood

whiz, whizz (hwiz) *vi.* **whizzed, whiz′zing** [echoic] **1.** to make the hissing sound of something speeding through the air **2.** to speed by with or as with this sound **—n. 1.** this sound **2.** [Slang] an expert *[a whiz at mathematics]*

who (hōō) *pron., obj.* **whom,** *poss.* **whose** [OE. *hwa*] **1.** what or which person or persons *[who is he? I know who came]* **2.** (the, or a, person or persons) that *[a man who knows]*

WHO World Health Organization

whoa (hwō, wō) *interj.* [for HO] stop!: used esp. in directing a horse to stand still

who·dun·it (hōō dun′it) *n.* [Colloq.] a mystery novel, play, etc.

who·ev′er (-ev′ər) *pron.* **1.** any person that; whatever person **2.** no matter what person *[whoever said it, it's not so]* **3.** who?: used for emphasis *[whoever told you that?]*

whole (hōl) *adj.* [OE. *hal*] **1.** healthy; not diseased or injured **2.** not broken, damaged, defective, etc.; intact **3.** containing all the parts; complete **4.** not divided up; in a single unit **5.** constituting the entire amount, extent, etc. *[the whole week]* **6.** having both parents in common *[a whole brother]* **7.** *Arith.* not a fraction *[25 is a whole number]* **—n. 1.** the entire amount, etc.; totality **2.** a complete organization of parts; unity **—as a whole** altogether **—made out of whole cloth** completely fictitious **—on the whole** all things considered **—whole′ness** *n.*

whole′heart′ed *adj.* doing or done with all one's energy, enthusiasm, etc.; sincere **—whole′heart′ed·ly** *adv.* **—whole′heart′ed·ness** *n.*

whole milk milk from which none of the butterfat or other elements have been removed

whole note *Music* a note (𝅝) having four times the duration of a quarter note

whole number zero or any positive or negative multiple of 1; integer

whole′sale′ *n.* the selling of goods in relatively large quantities, esp. to retailers who then sell them to consumers **—adj. 1.** of or engaged in such selling **2.** extensive or sweeping *[wholesale criticism]* **—adv. 1.** in wholesale amounts or at wholesale prices **2.** extensively or sweepingly **—vt., vi. -saled, -sal′ing** to sell or be sold wholesale **—whole′sal′er** *n.*

whole·some (hōl′səm) *adj.* [ME. *holsom*] **1.** good for one's health or well-being; healthful **2.** tending to improve the mind or character **3.** having or showing health and vigor **—whole′some·ly** *adv.* **—whole′some·ness** *n.*

whole tone *Music* an interval consisting of two adjacent semitones: also **whole step**

whole′-wheat′ *adj.* **1.** made of the entire grain of wheat *[whole-wheat flour]* **2.** made of such flour *[whole-wheat bread]*

who'll (hōōl) **1.** who shall **2.** who will

whol·ly (hō′lē) *adv.* to the whole amount or extent; totally; entirely

whom (hōōm) *pron. obj. case of* WHO

whom·ev′er (-ev′ər) *pron. obj. case of* WHOEVER

whomp (hwämp) *vt.* [echoic] **1.** to beat, strike, thump, etc. **2.** to defeat decisively

whom′so·ev′er (-sō ev′ər) *pron. obj. case of* WHOSOEVER

whoop (hōōp, hwōōp) *n.* [< OFr. *houper,* cry out] **1.** a loud shout, cry, etc., as of joy, excitement, etc. **2.** the gasping sound made when a breath of air is taken in following a fit of coughing in whooping cough **—vt., vi.** to utter, or utter with, a whoop or whoops **—interj.** an exclamation of joy, excitement, etc. **—not worth a whoop** [Colloq.] worth nothing at all **—whoop′er** *n.*

whoop·ee (wōō′pē, hwōō′-) *interj.* [< prec.] an exclamation of great joy, gay abandonment, etc. **—n. 1.** a shout of "whoopee!" **2.** noisy fun

whooping cough an acute infectious disease, esp. of children, with coughing fits that end in a whoop

whoops (hwoops, woops) *interj.* an exclamation uttered as in regaining one's balance after stumbling or one's composure after a slip of the tongue

whop (hwäp) *vt., vi.* **whopped, whop′ping** [echoic] [Colloq.] **1.** to beat, strike, etc. **2.** to defeat decisively **—n.** [Colloq.] a sharp blow, thump, etc.

whop·per (hwäp′ər) *n.* [< prec.] [Colloq.] **1.** anything extraordinarily large **2.** a great lie **—whop′ping** *adj.*

whore (hôr) *n.* [< OE. *hore*] a prostitute **—vi. whored, whor′ing 1.** to be a whore **2.** to fornicate with whores **—whor′ish** *adj.*

whorl (hwôrl, hwurl) *n.* [dial. var. of WHIRL] anything with a coiled or spiral appearance; specif., *a)* any of the circular ridges that form the design of a fingerprint *b)* *Bot.* a circular growth of leaves, petals, etc. about the same point on a stem *c)* *Zool.* any of the turns in a spiral shell **—whorled** *adj.*

who's (hōōz) **1.** who is **2.** who has

whose (hōōz) *pron.* [OE. *hwæs*] that or those belonging to whom *[whose is this?]* **—possessive pronominal adj.** of, belonging to, or done by whom or which *[the man whose car was stolen]*

---

who·so (hōō'sō) *pron.* [OE. *hwa swa*] [Archaic] whoever; whosoever

who·so·ev·er (hōō'sō ev'ər) *pron.* whoever: used for emphasis

why (hwī) *adv.* [OE. *hwi* < *hwæt*, what] for what reason, cause, or purpose? [*why* eat?] —*conj.* 1. because of which [there is no reason *why* you should go] 2. the reason for which [that is *why* he went] —*n.*, *pl.* **whys** the reason, cause, etc. [never mind the *why*] —*interj.* an exclamation of surprise, impatience, etc.

WI Wisconsin

Wich·i·ta (wich'ə tô') city in S Kans.: pop. 277,000

wick (wik) *n.* [OE. *weoca*] a piece of cord, tape, etc. in a candle, oil lamp, etc., that absorbs the fuel and, when lighted, burns

wick·ed (wik'id) *adj.* [ME. < *wikke*, evil] 1. morally bad; evil 2. generally painful, unpleasant, etc. [a *wicked* storm] 3. naughty; mischievous 4. [Slang] skillful —**wick'ed·ly** *adv.* —**wick'ed·ness** *n.*

wick·er (wik'ər) *n.* [< Scand.] 1. a thin, flexible twig 2. *a)* such twigs or long, woody strips woven together, as in making baskets or furniture *b) same as* WICKERWORK (sense 1) —*adj.* made of wicker

wick'er·work' (-wurk') *n.* 1. things made of wicker 2. *same as* WICKER (sense 2 *a*)

wick·et (wik'it) *n.* [ONormFr. *wiket*] 1. a small door or gate, esp. one set in or near a larger one 2. a small window, as in a box office 3. a small gate for regulating the flow of water, as to a water wheel 4. *Cricket a)* either of two sets of three stumps each, with two pieces of wood resting on top of them *b)* a player's turn at bat 5. *Croquet* any of the small wire arches through which the balls must be hit

wide (wīd) *adj.* **wid'er, wid'est** [OE. *wid*] 1. extending over a large area, esp. from side to side; broad 2. of a specified extent from side to side 3. of great extent, range, etc. [a *wide* variety] 4. roomy; full [*wide* pants] 5. open fully [eyes *wide* with surprise] 6. far from the point, issue, etc. aimed at [*wide* of the mark] —*adv.* 1. over a relatively large area 2. to a large or full extent [*wide* open] 3. so as to miss the point, etc. aimed at; astray —**wide'ly** *adv.* —**wide'ness** *n.*

-wide *a combining form meaning* extending throughout [nationwide]

wide'-an·gle *adj.* 1. designating or of a kind of camera lens covering a wide angle of view 2. designating or of any of several motion-picture systems using one or more cameras (and projectors) and a very wide, curved screen

wide'-a·wake *adj.* 1. completely awake 2. alert

wide'-eyed' *adj.* with the eyes wide open

wid·en (wīd'n) *vt.*, *vi.* to make or become wide or wider

wide'spread' *adj.* occurring over a wide area or extent

widg·eon, wi·geon (wij'ən) *n.* [prob. < MFr. *vigeon*] a wild, freshwater duck with a whitish crown

wid·ow (wid'ō) *n.* [OE. *widewe*] a woman whose husband has died and who has not remarried —*vt.* to cause to become a widow —**wid'ow·hood'** *n.*

wid'ow·er *n.* a man whose wife has died and who has not remarried

width (width) *n.* 1. a being wide 2. the distance from side to side 3. a piece of a specified width

wield (wēld) *vt.* [OE. *wealdan*] 1. to handle (a tool, etc.), esp. with skill 2. to exercise (power, control, etc.) —**wield'er** *n.*

wie·ner (wē'nər) *n.* [short for G. *Wiener wurst*, Vienna sausage] a smoked link sausage of beef or beef and pork; frankfurter: also **wie'ner·wurst'** (-wurst')

wife (wīf) *n.*, *pl.* **wives** (wīvz) [OE. *wif*] 1. orig., a woman: still so used in *midwife*, *housewife*, etc. 2. a married woman —**wife'less** *adj.* —**wife'ly** *adj.*

wig (wig) *n.* [< PERIWIG] 1. *a)* a false covering of real or synthetic hair for the head *b) same as* TOUPEE 2. [Slang] the hair, head, or mind —*vt.* **wigged**, **wig'ging** 1. to furnish with a wig or wigs 2. [Slang] *a)* to annoy, upset, etc. *b)* to excite, craze, etc. —*vi.* [Slang] to be or become upset, excited, etc.

wig·gle (wig''l) *vt.*, *vi.* **-gled**, **-gling** [ME. *wigelen*] to move with short, jerky or twisting motions from side to side —*n.* a wiggling

wig'gler *n.* 1. a person or thing that wiggles 2. the larva of a mosquito

wig'gly *adj.* **-gli·er, -gli·est** 1. that wiggles 2. wavy [a *wiggly* line]

wight (wīt) *n.* [OE. *wiht*] [Archaic] a human being

Wight (wīt), **Isle of** island in the English Channel that is an English county

wig·let (wig'lit) *n.* a small wig

wig·wag (wig'wag') *vt.*, *vi.* **-wagged'**, **-wag'ging** [< obs. *wig*, to move + WAG¹] 1. to move back and forth; wag 2. to send (a message) by waving flags, lights, etc. according to a code —*n.* 1. the sending of messages in this way 2. a message so sent

wig·wam (wig'wäm, -wôm) *n.* [< Algonquian] a N. American Indian shelter consisting of a framework of arched poles covered with bark, leaves, etc.

WIGWAM

wild (wīld) *adj.* [OE. *wilde*] 1. living or growing in its original, natural state 2. not lived in or cultivated; waste 3. not civilized; savage 4. not easily controlled [*wild* children] 5. lacking social or moral restraint; dissolute [a *wild* party] 6. turbulent; stormy 7. enthusiastic [*wild* about golf] 8. fantastically impractical; reckless 9. missing the target [a *wild* pitch] 10. *Cards* having any value specified by the holder: said of a card —*adv.* in a wild manner —*n.* [*usually pl.*] a wilderness or wasteland —**run wild** to grow, exist, or behave in an uncontrolled way —**wild'ly** *adv.* —**wild'ness** *n.*

wild boar a wild hog of Europe, Asia, and Africa

wild'cat' *n.* 1. any fierce, medium-sized, undomesticated animal of the cat family 2. a fierce, aggressive person 3. an unsound or risky business scheme 4. an oil well drilled in an area not previously known to have oil —*adj.* 1. unsound or risky 2. illegal or unauthorized [a *wildcat* strike] —*vi.* **-cat'ted**, **-cat'ting** to drill for oil in an area previously considered unproductive —**wild'cat'ter** *n.*

Wilde (wīld), **Oscar** 1854–1900; Brit. playwright, poet, & novelist, born in Ireland

wil·de·beest (wil'də bēst', vil'-) *n.* [Afrik.] *same as* GNU

wil·der·ness (wil'dər nis) *n.* [< OE. *wilde*, wild + *deor*, animal] an uncultivated, uninhabited region; waste

wild'-eyed' *adj.* 1. staring in a wild, distracted way 2. fantastically impractical

wild'fire' *n.* a fire that spreads fast and is hard to put out

wild'flow'er *n.* any flowering plant growing without cultivation in fields, woods, etc.: also **wild flower**

wild'fowl' *n.* a wild bird, esp. a game bird

wild'-goose' chase a futile search, pursuit, or endeavor

wild'life' *n.* wild animals and birds

wild oats a wild grass common in the W U.S.: also **wild oat** —**sow one's wild oats** to be promiscuous in youth

Wild West [*also* w- W-] the western U.S. in its early frontier period of lawlessness

wile (wīl) *n.* [< OE. *wigle*, magic] 1. a sly trick; stratagem 2. a beguiling or coquettish trick: *usually used in pl.* —*vt.* **wiled**, **wil'ing** to beguile; lure —**wile away** to while away (time, etc.)

will¹ (wil) *n.* [OE. *willa*] 1. the power of making a reasoned choice or of controlling one's own actions 2. determination 3. attitude toward others [good *will*] 4. *a)* a particular desire, choice, etc. of someone *b)* mandate [the *will* of the people] 5. a legal document directing the disposal of one's property after death —*vt.* 1. to desire; want [to *will* to live] 2. to control by the power of the will 3. to bequeath by a will —*vi.* to wish, desire, or choose —**at will** when one wishes

will² (wil) *v.*, *pt.* **would** [OE. *willan*] 1. an auxiliary sometimes used to express futurity in the second and third persons and determination or obligation in the first person See note at SHALL 2. an auxiliary used to express: *a)* willingness [*will* you go?] *b)* ability or capacity [it *will* hold a pint] *c)* habit, custom, inclination, etc. [boys *will* be boys] —*vt.*, *vi.* to wish; desire [do what you *will*]

will call the department, as of a large store, at which articles are held to be picked up, as when paid for

will·ful (wil'fəl) *adj.* 1. done or said deliberately 2. immoderately obstinate Also sp. **wil'ful** —**will'ful·ly** *adv.* —**will'ful·ness** *n.*

Wil·liam I (wil'yəm) 1027?–87; king of England (1066–87): called *William the Conqueror*

Wil·liams (wil'yəmz), **Roger** 1603?–83; English colonist in America: founder of Rhode Island

Wil·liams·burg (wil'yəmz burg') colonial capital of Va., now restored to its 18th-cent. appearance

wil·lies (wil'ēz) *n.pl.* [< ?] [Slang] a state of nervousness; jitters: with the

will·ing (wil'in) *adj.* 1. ready or agreeing (*to do* something) [*willing* to try] 2. doing, giving, etc. or done, given, etc. readily or gladly —**will'ing·ly** *adv.* —**will'ing·ness** *n.*

wil·li·waw (wil′i wô′) *n.* [< ?] a sudden, violent, cold wind blowing down from mountain passes to the sea in far northern and southern latitudes

will-o′-the-wisp (wil′ə *thə* wisp′) *n.* **1.** a light seen at night over swamps, etc., believed to be marsh gas burning **2.** a delusive hope or goal

wil·low (wil′ō) *n.* [OE. *welig*] **1.** a tree with narrow leaves, and flexible twigs used in weaving baskets, etc. **2.** its wood

wil·low·y (wil′ə wē) *adj.* like a willow; slender, supple, lithe, etc.

will′pow′er *n.* strength of will, mind, or determination; self-control

wil·ly-nil·ly (wil′ē nil′ē) *adv., adj.* [contr. < *will I, nill I: nill* < OE. *nyllan,* be unwilling] (happening) whether one wishes it or not

Wil·son (wil′s'n), **(Thomas) Woodrow** 1856–1924; 28th president of the U.S. (1913–21)

wilt[1] (wilt) *vi.* [< obs. *welk,* wither] **1.** to become limp, as from heat or lack of water; droop, as a plant **2.** to become weak or faint **3.** to lose courage —*vt.* to cause to wilt

wilt[2] (wilt) *archaic 2d pers. sing., pres. indic.,* of WILL[1]: *used with* thou

Wil·ton (carpet or **rug)** (wilt′'n) [< *Wilton,* England] a kind of carpet with a velvety pile of cut loops

wil·y (wī′lē) *adj.* **-i·er, -i·est** full of wiles; crafty; sly — **wil′i·ness** *n.*

wim·ple (wim′p'l) *n.* [OE. *wimpel*] a nun's head covering so arranged as to leave only the face exposed —*vt.* **-pled, -pling 1.** to clothe as with a wimple **2.** to ripple

win (win) *vi.* **won, win′ning** [OE. *winnan,* to fight] **1.** *a)* to gain a victory *b)* to finish first in a race, etc. **2.** to succeed with effort; get [to *win* back to health] —*vt.* **1.** to get by effort, struggle, etc. **2.** to be victorious in (a contest, dispute, etc.) **3.** to get to with effort [they *won* the hilltop by noon] **4.** to influence; persuade: often with *over* **5.** to gain (the sympathy, favor, etc.) of (someone) **6.** to persuade to marry one —*n.* [Colloq.] a victory, as in a contest

WIMPLE

wince (wins) *vi.* **winced, winc′ing** [< OFr. *guenchir*] to shrink or draw back slightly, usually with a grimace, as in pain —*n.* a wincing

winch (winch) *n.* [OE. *wince*] **1.** a crank with a handle for transmitting motion **2.** a hoisting or hauling apparatus having a cylinder around which a rope or cable winds when lifting a load

Win·ches·ter (rifle) (win′ches′tər) [< O. F. *Winchester,* U.S. manufacturer] *a trademark for* a type of repeating rifle

wind[1] (wīnd) *vt.* **wound, wind′ing** [OE. *windan*] **1.** to turn [*wind* the crank] **2.** to coil into a ball or around something else; twine **3.** to cover by entwining **4.** *a)* to make (one's way) in a twisting course *b)* to cause to move in a twisting course **5.** to hoist or haul as with a winch (often with *up*) **6.** to tighten the spring of (a clock, etc.) as by turning a stem —*vi.* **1.** to move or go in a twisting or curving course **2.** to take a devious course **3.** to be coiled (*about* or *around* something) —*n.* a turn; twist — **wind up 1.** to wind into a ball, etc. **2.** to conclude; settle **3.** to make very tense, excited, etc. **4.** *Baseball* to swing the arm in getting ready to pitch the ball

wind[2] (wind) *n.* [OE.] **1.** air in motion **2.** a strong current of air; gale **3.** air bearing a scent, as in hunting **4.** air regarded as bearing information, etc. [rumors in the *wind*] **5.** breath or the power of breathing **6.** empty talk **7.** gas in the intestines **8.** [*pl.*] the wind instruments in an orchestra —*vt.* **1.** to get the scent of **2.** to put out of breath —**break wind** to expel gas from the bowels —**get wind of** to get a hint or suggestion about —**in the wind** happening or about to happen —**into the wind** in the direction from which the wind is blowing

wind[3] (wīnd, wind) *vt., vi.* **wound** or rarely **wind′ed, wind′ing** [< prec.] [Poet.] **1.** to blow (a horn, etc.) **2.** to sound (a signal, etc.), as on a horn

wind·bag (wind′bag′) *n.* [Colloq.] one who talks much but says little of importance

wind′break′ *n.* a hedge, fence, or row of trees serving as a protection from wind

Wind′break′er *a trademark for* a warm sports jacket with a closefitting elastic waistband and cuffs —*n.* [w-] such a jacket

wind·ed (win′did) *adj.* out of breath

wind′fall′ *n.* **1.** something blown down by the wind, as fruit from a tree **2.** an unexpected stroke of good luck or personal gain

wind·ing (wīn′diŋ) *n.* **1.** a coiling, turn, bend, etc. **2.** something that winds or is wound around an object —*adj.* that winds, turns, coils, etc.

winding sheet a shroud

wind instrument a musical instrument sounded by blowing air, esp. breath, through it, as a flute

wind·jam·mer (wind′jam′ər) *n. Naut.* a sailing ship or one of its crew

wind·lass (wind′ləs) *n.* [< ON. *vinda,* to WIND[1] + *ass,* a beam] a winch, esp. one worked by a crank

WINDLASS

wind′mill′ *n.* a mill operated by the wind's rotation of vanes radiating from a shaft: it provides power for pumping water, etc.

win·dow (win′dō) *n.* [< ON. *vindr,* WIND[2] + *auga,* eye] **1.** an opening in a building, vehicle, etc. for admitting light and air or for looking through, usually having a pane of glass in a movable frame **2.** a windowpane **3.** an opening resembling a window —**win′dow·less** *adj.*

window box a long narrow box on or outside a window ledge, for growing plants

window dressing 1. the display of goods in a store window **2.** that which is meant to make something seem better than it really is —**win′dow-dress′** *vt.* —**window dresser**

win′dow·pane′ *n.* a pane of glass in a window

window shade a shade for a window, esp. one of heavy paper or cloth on a spring roller

win′dow-shop′ (-shäp′) *vi.* **-shopped′, -shop′ping** to look at goods in store windows without entering the stores to buy —**win′dow-shop′per** *n.*

wind·pipe (wind′pīp′) *n.* the trachea

wind·row (wind′rō′) *n.* **1.** a row of hay, etc. raked together to dry **2.** a row of dry leaves, dust, etc. swept together by the wind

wind′shield′ (-shēld′) *n.* in automobiles, etc., a glass screen in front, to protect the riders from wind, dust, etc.

wind′sock′ (-säk′) *n.* a long, cone-shaped cloth bag flown at an airfield to show wind direction: also **wind sleeve, wind cone**

Wind·sor[1] (win′zər) ruling family of Great Britain since 1917

Wind·sor[2] (win′zər) **1.** city in SE England: site of Windsor Castle, residence of English sovereigns **2.** port in SE Ontario, Canada, opposite Detroit: pop. 193,000

Windsor knot a double slipknot in a four-in-hand necktie

wind′storm′ *n.* a storm with a strong wind but little or no rain

wind′-swept′ *adj.* swept by or exposed to winds

wind tunnel a tunnellike chamber through which air is forced and in which scale models of airplanes, etc. are tested against the effects of wind pressure

wind·up (wīnd′up′) *n.* **1.** a conclusion; end **2.** *Baseball* the swinging of the arm preparatory to pitching the ball

wind·ward (wind′wərd; *nautical* win′dərd) *n.* the direction from which the wind blows —*adv.* toward the wind — *adj.* **1.** moving windward **2.** on the side from which the wind blows Opposed to LEEWARD

Windward Islands S group of islands in the Lesser Antilles of the West Indies

wind·y (win′dē) *adj.* **-i·er, -i·est 1.** characterized by wind [a *windy* day] **2.** exposed to wind [a *windy* city] **3.** stormy, blustery, etc. **4.** *a)* without substance; flimsy *b)* long-winded, boastful, etc. —**wind′i·ness** *n.*

wine (wīn) *n.* [< L. *vinum*] **1.** the fermented juice of grapes, used as an alcoholic beverage and in cooking, etc. **2.** the fermented juice of other fruits or plants [dandelion *wine*] —*vt., vi.* **wined, win′ing** to provide with or drink wine: usually in **wine and dine,** to entertain lavishly

wine cellar 1. a cellar where wine is stored **2.** a stock of wine

wine′-col′ored *adj.* having the color of red wine; dark purplish-red

wine′glass′ *n.* a small glass for serving wine

wine press a machine for pressing grapes to extract the juice for making wine

win·er·y (-ər ē) n., pl. **-ies** an establishment where wine is made

wing (wiŋ) n. [< ON. *vaengr*] **1.** either of the paired organs of flight of a bird, bat, insect, etc. **2.** something like a wing in use, position, etc.; esp., a) a (or the) main lateral supporting surface of an airplane b) a distinct part of a building, often having a special use c) either side of a stage out of sight of the audience **3.** the section of an army, fleet, etc. to the right (or left) of the center **4.** a section, as of a political party, viewed as radical or conservative **5.** a) a unit in an air force b) [pl.] the insignia worn by pilots and crew of military aircraft **6.** a flying, or a means of flying: now chiefly in **on the wing, take wing** (see phrases below) —vt. **1.** to provide with wings **2.** a) to send swiftly as on wings b) to make (one's way) by flying c) to pass through or over as by flying **3.** to wound in the wing, arm, etc. —vi. to go as if on wings; fly —**on the wing** (while) flying —**take wing** to fly away —**under one's wing** under one's protection, etc. —**winged** (wiŋd; *poet.* wiŋ'id) adj.

wing chair an upholstered armchair with a high back from each side of which high sides, or wings, extend forward

wing'span' n. the distance between the tips of an airplane's wings

wing'spread' n. **1.** the distance between the tips of a pair of fully spread wings **2.** *same as* WINGSPAN

wink (wiŋk) vi. [OE. *wincian*] **1.** to close the eyelids and open them again quickly **2.** to close and open one eyelid quickly, as a signal, etc. **3.** to twinkle —vt. to make (an eye) wink —n. **1.** a winking, or the instant of time it takes **2.** a signal given by winking **3.** a twinkle —**wink at** to pretend not to see

win·ner (win'ər) n. one that wins

win'ning adj. **1.** victorious **2.** charming —n. **1.** a victory **2.** [pl.] something won, esp. money

Win·ni·peg (win'ə peg') capital of Manitoba, Canada: pop. 257,000

win·now (win'ō) vt., vi. [< OE. *wind*, WIND²] **1.** to blow (the chaff) from (grain) **2.** to scatter **3.** to sort out by sifting

win·o (wīn'ō) n., pl. **-os** [Slang] an alcoholic who drinks cheap wine

win·some (win'səm) adj. [OE. *wynsum*, pleasant] sweetly attractive; charming —**win'some·ly** adv.

Win·ston-Sa·lem (win'stən sā'ləm) city in NC N.C.: pop. 133,000

win·ter (win'tər) n. [OE.] **1.** the coldest season of the year, following autumn **2.** a period of decline, distress, etc. —adj. of, during, or for winter —vi. to pass the winter —vt. to keep or maintain during the winter

win'ter·green' n. **1.** an evergreen plant with white flowers and red berries **2.** an aromatic oil (**oil of wintergreen**) made from its leaves and used as a flavoring **3.** the flavor

win'ter·ize' (-īz') vt. **-ized', -iz'ing** to put into condition for winter [to *winterize* a car]

win'ter·kill' vt., vi. to kill or die by exposure to winter cold or excessive snow or ice

win'ter·time' n. the winter season

win'try (-trē) adj. **-tri·er, -tri·est** of or like winter; cold, bleak, etc.: also **win'ter·y** (-tər ē, -trē)

win·y (wī'nē) adj. **-i·er, -i·est** like wine in taste, smell, color, etc.

wipe (wīp) vt. **wiped, wip'ing** [OE. *wipian*] **1.** to clean or dry by rubbing with a cloth, etc. **2.** to rub (a cloth, etc.) over something **3.** to apply or remove by rubbing with a cloth, etc. —n. a wiping —**wipe out 1.** to remove; erase **2.** to kill off —**wip'er** n.

wire (wīr) n. [OE. *wir*] **1.** metal drawn into a long thread **2.** a length of this, used for conducting electric current, etc. **3.** a) telegraph b) a telegram **4.** *Horse Racing* a wire above the finish line of a race —adj. made of wire —vt. **1.** to furnish, connect, bind, etc. with wire **2.** to supply with a system of wires for electric current **3.** to telegraph —vi. to telegraph —**pull wires** to get what one wants through one's friends' influence

wire gauge a device for measuring the diameter of wire, thickness of sheet metal, etc.: usually a disk with notches of graduated sizes along its edge

wire'hair' (-her') n. a fox terrier with a wiry coat: also **wire-haired terrier**

wire'less adj. without wire; specif., operating with electromagnetic waves, not with conducting wire —n. **1.** wireless telegraphy or telephony **2.** [Chiefly Brit.] radio **3.** a message sent by wireless

wireless telegraphy (or **telegraph**) telegraphy by radio-transmitted signals

Wire'pho'to a *trademark for:* **1.** a system of reproducing photographs at a distance by means of electric impulses transmitted by wire **2.** a photograph so produced

wire service an agency that sends news stories, etc. by telegraph to subscribers, as newspapers

wire'tap' vt., vi. **-tapped', -tap'ping** to tap (a telephone wire, etc.) to get information secretly —n. **1.** a wiretapping **2.** a device for wiretapping —**wire'tap'per** n.

wir'ing n. a system of wires, as for carrying electricity

wir'y adj. **-i·er, -i·est 1.** of wire **2.** like wire; stiff **3.** lean and strong —**wir'i·ness** n.

Wis·con·sin (wis kän's'n) Middle Western State of the U.S.: 56,154 sq. mi.; pop. 4,418,000; cap. Madison: abbrev. Wis., WI —**Wis·con'sin·ite'** (-īt') n.

wis·dom (wiz'dəm) n. [OE. < *wis*, WISE¹ + -dom, -DOM] **1.** the quality of being wise; good judgment **2.** learning; knowledge **3.** wise teaching

wisdom tooth the back tooth on each side of each jaw in human beings, usually appearing between the ages of 17 and 25

wise¹ (wīz) adj. **wis'er, wis'est** [OE. *wis*] **1.** having or showing good judgment **2.** judicious; sound [a *wise* saying] **3.** informed [none the *wiser*] **4.** learned; erudite **5.** shrewd; cunning **6.** [Slang] conceited, impudent, fresh, etc. —**be** (or **get**) **wise to** [Slang] to be (or become) aware of —**wise up** [Slang] to make or become informed —**wise'ly** adv. —**wise'ness** n.

wise² (wīz) n. [OE.] way; manner

-wise [< prec.] a suffix meaning: **1.** in a (specified) direction, position, or manner [*sidewise*] **2.** in a manner characteristic of [*clockwise*] **3.** with regard to; in connection with [*weatherwise*]

wise·a·cre (wīz'ā'kər) n. [< OHG. *wizzago*, prophet] one who pretends to be much wiser than he really is

wise'crack' n. [Slang] a flippant or facetious remark —vi. [Slang] to make wisecracks

wish (wish) vt. [OE. *wyscan*] **1.** to have a longing for; want **2.** to express a desire concerning [I *wish* you well] **3.** to request [he *wishes* her to leave] **4.** to bid [to *wish* a person good morning] **5.** to impose (with on) [he *wished* the job on me] —vi. **1.** to long; yearn **2.** to make a wish —n. **1.** a wishing **2.** something wished for [he got his *wish*] **3.** a polite request, almost an order **4.** [pl.] expressed desire for a person's well-being, good fortune, etc. [best *wishes*]

wish'bone' n. the forked bone in front of a bird's breastbone

wish'ful adj. having or showing a wish; desirous —**wish'ful·ly** adv. —**wish'ful·ness** n.

wish·y-wash·y (wish'ē wôsh'ē) adj. [Colloq.] **1.** watery; thin **2.** a) weak; feeble b) vacillating; indecisive

wisp (wisp) n. [prob. < Scand.] **1.** a small bundle, as of straw **2.** a thin, filmy bit or puff [a *wisp* of smoke] **3.** something delicate, frail, etc. [a *wisp* of a girl] —**wisp'y** adj. **-i·er, -i·est**

wis·te·ri·a (wis tir'ē ə) n. [< C. *Wistar*, 19th-c. U.S. anatomist] a twining vine with showy clusters of purple, white, or pink flowers: also **wis·tar'i·a** (-ter'-)

wist·ful (wist'fəl) adj. [< earlier *wistly*, attentive] showing or expressing vague yearnings —**wist'ful·ly** adv. —**wist'ful·ness** n.

wit¹ (wit) n. [OE.] **1.** [pl.] powers of thinking; mental faculties **2.** good sense **3.** the ability to make clever remarks in a surprising or ironic way **4.** one having this ability —**at one's wits' end** at a loss as to what to do —**keep** (or **have**) **one's wits about one** to remain mentally alert —**live by one's wits** to live by craftiness or trickery

wit² (wit) vt., vi. wist (wist), wit'ting [OE. *witan*] [Archaic] to know or learn —**to wit** that is to say

witch (wich) n. [OE. *wicce*] **1.** a woman supposedly having supernatural power by a compact with evil spirits **2.** an ugly old shrew **3.** [Colloq.] a fascinating woman

witch'craft' n. **1.** the power or practices of witches **2.** bewitching attraction or charm

witch doctor a person who practices primitive medicine involving the use of magic, as among tribes in Africa

witch'er·y n., pl. **-ies 1.** witchcraft **2.** fascination

witch hazel [< OE. *wice*] **1.** a shrub with yellow flowers **2.** a lotion made from its leaves and bark

witch hunt an investigation of political dissenters, conducted with much publicity, supposedly to uncover subversion, disloyalty, etc.

with (with, with) prep. [OE., against] **1.** in opposition to [he argued *with* me] **2.** a) alongside of; near to b) in the company of c) into; among [mix blue *with* red] **3.** as a member of [he plays *with* a trio] **4.** concerning [pleased *with* her gift] **5.** compared to **6.** as well as [he can run *with* the best] **7.** of the same opinions as [I'm *with* you] **8.** in the opinion of [it's OK *with* me] **9.** as a result of [faint *with* hunger] **10.** *a)* by means of [stir *with* a spoon] *b)* by [filled *with* air] **11.** having received [with your consent, he'll go] **12.** having or showing [a boy *with* red hair, to play *with* skill] **13.** in the keeping, care, etc. of [leave the baby *with* me] **14.** in spite of **15.** at the same time as **16.** in proportion to [wages varying *with* skills] **17.** to; onto [join this end *with* that one] **18.** from [to part *with* one's gains] —**with that** after that

with- *a combining form meaning:* **1.** away, back [*withdraw*] **2.** against, from [*withhold*]

with·al (wi*th* ôl′) *adv.* **1.** besides **2.** despite that

with·draw (wi*th* drô′, with-) *vt.* **-drew′, -drawn′, -draw′-ing** **1.** to take back; remove **2.** to retract or recall (a statement, etc.) —*vi.* **1.** to move back; go away **2.** to remove oneself (from an organization, activity, etc.)

with·draw′al (-əl) *n.* **1.** the act of withdrawing **2.** a giving up the use of a habit-forming drug, typically accompanied by physical and mental distress (**withdrawal symptoms**)

with·drawn′ *adj.* shy, reserved, etc.

withe (with, wī*th*) *n.* [OE. *withthe*] a tough, flexible twig, as of willow, used for binding things

with·er (wi*th*′ər) *vi.* [< ME. *wederen,* to weather] **1.** to dry up; shrivel; wilt, as plants **2.** to become wasted or decayed **3.** to weaken; languish —*vt.* **1.** to cause to wither **2.** to cause to feel abashed

with·ers (wi*th*′ərz) *n.pl.* [< OE. *wither,* against] the part of a horse's back between the shoulder blades

with·hold (with hōld′, with-) *vt.* **-held′, -hold′ing** **1.** *a)* to hold back; restrain *b)* to deduct (taxes, etc.) from wages **2.** to refrain from granting; refuse

withholding tax the amount of income tax withheld from employees' wages or salaries

with·in (wi*th* in′, with-) *adv.* [OE. *withinnan*] **1.** on or to the inside **2.** indoors **3.** inside the body, mind, etc. —*prep.* **1.** in the inner part of **2.** not beyond **3.** inside the limits of

with·out′ (-out′) *adv.* [OE. *withutan*] **1.** on or to the outside **2.** outdoors —*prep.* **1.** at, on, or to the outside of **2.** beyond **3.** lacking **4.** free from [*without* fear] **5.** with avoidance of [to pass *without* speaking]

with·stand (with stand′, with-) *vt., vi.* **-stood′, -stand′ing** to oppose, resist, or endure

wit·less (wit′lis) *adj.* lacking wit; foolish —**wit′less·ly** *adv.* —**wit′less·ness** *n.*

wit·ness (wit′nis) *n.* [OE. *gewitnes,* knowledge] **1.** evidence; testimony **2.** one who saw, or can give a firsthand account of, something **3.** one who testifies in court **4.** one who observes, and attests to, a signing, etc. —*vt.* **1.** to testify to **2.** to serve as evidence of **3.** to act as a witness of (a contract, will, etc.) **4.** to be present at **5.** to be the scene of [this field *witnessed* a battle] —**bear witness** to testify

witness stand the place from which a witness gives his testimony in a law court

wit·ti·cism (wit′ə siz′m) *n.* [< WITTY] a witty remark

wit·ting (wit′in) *adj.* [ME. *wytting*] done knowingly; intentional —**wit′ting·ly** *adv.*

wit·ty (wit′ē) *adj.* **-ti·er, -ti·est** [OE. *wittig*] having or showing wit; cleverly amusing —**wit′ti·ly** *adv.* —**wit′ti·ness** *n.*

wive (wīv) *vi., vt.* **wived, wiv′ing** [OE. *wifian*] [Archaic] to marry (a woman)

wives (wīvz) *n. pl. of* WIFE

wiz·ard (wiz′ərd) *n.* [ME. *wisard*] **1.** a magician; sorcerer **2.** [Colloq.] one very skilled at a certain activity

wiz′ard·ry *n.* magic; sorcery

wiz·en (wiz′'n, wēz′-) *vt., vi.* [OE. *wisnian*] to dry up; wither —**wiz′ened** (-'nd) *adj.*

wk. *pl.* **wks. 1.** week **2.** work

wkly. weekly

WNW, W.N.W., w.n.w. west-northwest

woad (wōd) *n.* [OE. *wad*] **1.** a plant related to mustard **2.** a blue dye made from its leaves

wob·ble (wäb′'l) *vi.* **-bled, -bling** [prob. < LowG. *wabbeln*] **1.** to move unsteadily from side to side; shake **2.** to vacillate —*vt.* **1.** to cause to wobble —*n.* a wobbling motion —**wob′bly** *adj.* **-bli·er, -bli·est**

Wo·den, Wo·dan (wōd′'n) the chief Germanic god, identified with the Norse Odin

woe (wō) *n.* [OE. *wa*] **1.** great sorrow; grief **2.** trouble —*interj.* alas!

woe·be·gone (wō′bi gôn′, -gän′) *adj.* of woeful appearance; looking sad or wretched

woe·ful (-fəl) *adj.* **1.** full of woe; sad; mournful **2.** of, causing, or involving woe **3.** pitiful; wretched —**woe′ful·ly** *adv.* —**woe′ful·ness** *n.*

woke (wōk) *alt. pt. of* WAKE[1]

wolf (woolf) *n., pl.* **wolves** (woolvz) [OE. *wulf*] **1.** a wild, flesh-eating, doglike mammal of the Northern Hemisphere **2.** *a)* a cruel or greedy person *b)* [Slang] a man who flirts with many women —*vt.* to eat greedily —**cry wolf** to give a false alarm —**keep the wolf from the door** to provide the necessities of life —**wolf′ish** *adj.*

wolf′hound′ (-hound′) *n.* a breed of large dog, once used for hunting wolves

wolf·ram (wool′frəm) *n.* [G.] *same as* TUNGSTEN

Wol·sey (wool′zē), **Thomas** 1475?–1530; Eng. statesman & cardinal

wol·ver·ine (wool′və rēn′) *n.* [< WOLF] a stocky, ferocious, flesh-eating mammal of N. America and Eurasia

wolves (woolvz) *n. pl. of* WOLF

wom·an (woom′ən) *n., pl.* **wom·en** (wim′ən) [< OE. *wif,* a female + *mann,* human being] **1.** an adult female human being **2.** women as a group **3.** a female servant **4.** [Dial.] a wife or sweetheart **5.** womanly qualities [it's the *woman* in her]

WOLVERINE
(2 1/2–3 1/2 ft. long, including tail)

wom·an·hood′ *n.* **1.** the state of being a woman **2.** womanly qualities **3.** womankind

wom·an·ish *adj.* like a woman; feminine

wom·an·ize′ (-īz′) *vt.* **-ized′, -iz′ing** to make effeminate —*vi.* [Colloq.] to be sexually promiscuous with women —**wom′an·iz′er** *n.*

wom·an·kind′ *n.* women in general

wom·an·like′ *adj.* womanly

wom·an·ly *adj.* **1.** womanish **2.** characteristic of or fit for a woman —**wom′an·li·ness** *n.*

womb (woom) *n.* [OE. *wamb*] **1.** *same as* UTERUS **2.** any place or part that envelops, generates, etc.

wom·bat (wäm′bat) *n.* [< native name] a burrowing Australian marsupial resembling a small bear

wom·en (wim′in) *n. pl. of* WOMAN

wom·en·folk′, wom·en·folks′ *n.pl.* [Dial. or Colloq.] women

women's rights the rights claimed by and for women, equal to those of men

won (wun) *pt. & pp. of* WIN

won·der (wun′dər) *n.* [OE. *wundor*] **1.** a person, thing, or event causing astonishment, admiration, etc.; marvel **2.** the feeling of surprise, etc. caused by something strange, remarkable, etc. **3.** a miracle —*vi.* **1.** to feel wonder; marvel **2.** to have curiosity, sometimes mixed with doubt —*vt.* to have curiosity or doubt about [I *wonder* what he meant]

won′der·ful *adj.* **1.** that causes wonder; marvelous **2.** [Colloq.] fine; excellent —**won′der·ful·ly** *adv.*

won′der·land′ *n.* **1.** an imaginary land full of wonders **2.** a real place like this

won′der·ment *n.* wonder or amazement

won·drous (wun′drəs) *adj.* wonderful —*adv.* wonderfully Now only literary —**won′drous·ly** *adv.*

wont (wônt, wōnt) *adj.* [< OE. *wunian,* be used to] accustomed [he was *wont* to rise early] —*n.* usual practice; habit

won't (wōnt) will not

wont·ed (wôn′tid, wōn′-) *adj.* customary

woo (woo) *vt.* [OE. *wogian*] **1.** to try to get the love of; court **2.** to seek [she *wooed* fame] **3.** to coax; urge —*vi.* to woo a person —**woo′er** *n.*

wood (wood) *n.* [OE. *wudu*] **1.** [*usually pl.*] a thick growth of trees; forest **2.** the hard, fibrous substance beneath the bark of trees and shrubs **3.** lumber or timber **4.** firewood **5.** a golf club having a wooden head —*adj.* **1.** made of wood; wooden **2.** for cutting, shaping, or holding wood **3.** growing or living in woods —**out of the woods** [Colloq.] out of difficulty, danger, etc. —**wood′ed** *adj.*

wood alcohol *same as* METHANOL

wood′bine′ (-bīn′) *n.* [see WOOD & BIND] **1.** a European climbing honeysuckle **2**. a climbing vine of eastern N. America, with dark-blue berries

wood'carv'ing (-kär'viŋ) *n*. **1**. the art of carving wood by hand **2**. an art object so made **—wood'carv'er** *n*.

wood'chuck' (-chuk') *n*. [< AmInd. name] a N. American burrowing and hibernating marmot; groundhog

wood'cock' (-käk') *n*. a small game bird with short legs and a long bill

wood'craft' *n*. **1**. matters relating to the woods, as camping, hunting, etc. **2**. *same as:* a) WOODWORKING b) WOODCARVING

wood'cut' (-kut') *n*. **1**. a wooden block engraved with a design, etc. **2**. a print made from this

wood'cut'ter *n*. a person who fells trees, cuts wood, etc.

wood'en (-'n) *adj*. **1**. made of wood **2**. stiff, lifeless, etc. **3**. dull; insensitive **—wood'en·ly** *adv*. **—wood'en·ness** *n*.

wood'en·head'ed *adj*. [Colloq.] dull; stupid

wood'land' (-land') *n*. land covered with woods **—adj**. (-lənd) of or living in the woods

wood'man (-mən) *n., pl*. **-men** *same as* WOODSMAN

wood'peck'er (-pek'ər) *n*. a tree-climbing bird with a strong, pointed bill used to drill holes in bark to get insects

wood'pile' *n*. a pile of wood, esp. of firewood

wood pulp pulp made from wood fiber, used in paper manufacture

wood screw a sharp-pointed metal screw with a coarse thread, for use in wood

wood'shed' *n*. a shed for storing firewood

woods·man (woodz'mən) *n., pl*. **-men** **1**. one who lives or works in the woods, as a hunter, woodcutter, etc. **2**. one skilled in woodcraft

wood'sy (-zē) *adj*. **-si·er**, **-si·est** of or like the woods

wood thrush a large, brown thrush of eastern N. America, having a sweet, clear song

wood'wind' (-wind') *n*. any of the wind instruments of an orchestra made, esp. originally, of wood: clarinet, oboe, bassoon, flute, and English horn **—adj**. of or for such instruments

wood'work' *n*. **1**. work done in wood **2**. things made of wood, esp. the interior moldings, doors, etc. of a house

wood'work'ing *n*. the art or work of making things out of wood **—adj**. of woodworking

wood'y *adj*. **-i·er**, **-i·est** **1**. covered with trees **2**. consisting of or forming wood **3**. like wood **—wood'i·ness** *n*.

woof¹ (woof, woof) *n*. [< OE. *wefan*, to weave] **1**. the horizontal threads crossing the warp in a woven fabric; weft **2**. a woven fabric

woof² (woof) *n*. a gruff barking sound of or like that of a dog **—vi**. to make such a sound

woof'er *n*. [< WOOF²] in an assembly of two or more loudspeakers, a large speaker for reproducing low sounds

wool (wool) *n*. [OE. *wull*] **1**. the soft, curly hair of sheep or of some other animals, as the goat **2**. woolen yarn, cloth, clothing, etc. **3**. anything that looks or feels like wool **—adj**. of wool or woolen goods **—pull the wool over someone's eyes** to deceive someone **—wool'like'** *adj*.

wool'en (-ən) *adj*. **1**. made of wool **2**. of or relating to wool or woolen cloth **—n**. [*pl*.] woolen goods or clothing Chiefly Brit. sp. **wool'len**

wool'gath'er·ing (-gath'ər iŋ) *n*. absent-mindedness or daydreaming **—wool'gath'er·er** *n*.

wool·ly (wool'ē) *adj*. **-li·er**, **-li·est** **1**. of or like wool **2**. bearing wool **3**. covered with wool or something like wool **4**. rough and uncivilized: chiefly in **wild and woolly 5**. confused [*woolly* ideas] **—n., pl**. **-lies** a woolen garment Also sp. **wool'y** **—wool'li·ness** *n*.

wooz·y (woo'zē, wooz'ē) *adj*. **-i·er**, **-i·est** [Colloq.] **1**. dizzy, faint, and sickish **2**. befuddled, as from drink **— wooz'i·ly** *adv*. **—wooz'i·ness** *n*.

Worces·ter (woos'tər) city in C Mass.: pop. 177,000

Worces'ter·shire' sauce (-shir') [orig. made in *Worcester*, England] a spicy sauce for meats, poultry, etc., containing soy, vinegar, etc.

word (wurd) *n*. [OE.] **1**. *a)* a speech sound, or series of speech sounds, serving to communicate meaning *b)* the written or printed representation of this **2**. a brief remark [a *word* of advice] **3**. a promise [he gave his *word*] **4**. news; information **5**. *a)* a password or signal *b)* a command; order **6**. [*pl.*] *a)* talk; speech *b)* lyrics; text *c)* a quarrel; dispute **—vt**. to express in words; phrase **—in a word** briefly **—in so many words** precisely **—the Word** the Bible: also **Word of God** **—word for word** in precisely the same words **—word'less** *adj*.

word'age (-ij) *n*. **1**. words collectively, or the number of words (*of* a story, novel, etc.) **2**. wordiness **3**. wording

word'ing *n*. choice and arrangement of words

word of honor pledged word; solemn promise

Words·worth (wurdz'wərth), **William** 1770–1850; Eng. poet

word·y (wur'dē) *adj*. **-i·er**, **-i·est** containing or using many or too many words; verbose **—word'i·ly** *adv*. **— word'i·ness** *n*.

wore (wôr) *pt. of* WEAR

work (wurk) *n*. [OE. *weorc*] **1**. effort exerted to do or make something; labor; toil **2**. employment at a job [out of *work*] **3**. occupation, profession, business, trade, etc. **4**. something one is making or doing; task **5**. something made or done; specif., a) [*usually pl.*] an act; deed [good *works*] b) [*pl.*] collected writings c) [*pl.*] engineering structures d) a fortification e) needlework **6**. [*pl., with sing. v.*] a place where work is done, as a factory **7**. workmanship **8**. *Mech*. transference of force from one body or system to another, measured by the product of the force and the amount of displacement in the line of force **—adj**. of, for, or used in work **—vi**. **worked** or **wrought**, **work'ing 1**. to do work; labor; toil **2**. to be employed **3**. to function or operate, esp. effectively **4**. to ferment **5**. to produce results or exert an influence **6**. to move, proceed, etc. slowly and with difficulty **7**. to twitch as from agitation **8**. to come or become, as by repeated movement [the handle *worked* loose] **—vt**. **1**. to cause; bring about [his idea *worked* wonders] **2**. to mold; shape **3**. to sew, embroider, etc. **4**. to solve (a mathematical problem, etc.) **5**. to manipulate; knead **6**. to bring into a specified condition [to *work* a nail loose] **7**. to cultivate (soil) **8**. to operate; use **9**. to cause to work [to *work* a crew hard] **10**. to influence; persuade **11**. to make (one's way, etc.) by effort **12**. to provoke; rouse [he *worked* her into a rage] **—at work** working **—in the works** [Colloq.] being planned or done **—out of work** unemployed **—the works 1**. the working parts (*of* a watch, etc.) **2**. [Colloq.] everything **—work in** to insert or be inserted **—work off** to get rid of **—work on** (or **upon**) **1**. to influence **2**. to try to persuade **—work out 1**. to accomplish **2**. to solve **3**. to result **4**. to develop **5**. to engage in a workout **—work over** [Colloq.] to subject to harsh treatment **—work up 1**. to advance **2**. to develop **3**. to excite

work'a·ble (-ə b'l) *adj*. **1**. that can be worked **2**. practicable; feasible **—work'a·bil'i·ty** *n*.

work·a·day (wur'kə dā') *adj*. **1**. of workdays; everyday **2**. ordinary

work·a·hol·ic (wur'kə hôl'ik, -häl'-) *n*. [WORK + -a- + (ALCO)-HOLIC] a person having a compulsive need to work

work'bench' (-bench') *n*. a table at which work is done, as by a carpenter

work'book' *n*. **1**. a book containing questions and exercises to be worked by students **2**. a book containing a record of work planned or done

work'day' *n*. **1**. a day on which work is done **2**. the part of a day during which work is done

work·er (wur'kər) *n*. **1**. one who works for a living **2**. one who works for a cause, etc. **3**. any of various sterile female ants, bees, etc. that do work for the colony

work'horse' *n*. **1**. a horse used for working **2**. a steady, responsible worker with a heavy workload **3**. a durable machine, vehicle, etc.

work'house' *n*. **1**. in England, formerly, a poorhouse **2**. a prison where petty offenders are confined and made to work

work'ing *adj*. **1**. that works **2**. of or used in work **3**. sufficient to get work done [a *working* majority] **—n**. the act of one that works

working capital the part of a company's capital that can be converted readily into cash

working day 1. a day on which work is done, esp. as distinguished from a Sunday, holiday, etc. **2**. the part of a day during which work is done

work'ing·man' *n., pl*. **-men'** a worker; esp., an industrial or manual worker

work'ing·wom'an *n., pl*. **-wom'en** a woman worker; esp., a woman industrial or manual worker

work'load' (-lōd') *n*. the amount of work assigned to be completed within a given period of time

work'man (-mən) *n., pl*. **-men 1**. *same as* WORKINGMAN **2**. a craftsman

work'man·like' *adj*. characteristic of a good workman; skillful: also **work'man·ly**

work'man·ship' *n*. skill of a workman; craftsmanship

work of art 1. something produced in one of the fine arts **2**. anything made, performed, etc. with great skill and beauty

work'out' *n*. **1**. a training session of physical exercises **2**. any strenuous exercise, work, etc.

work'room' *n.* a room in which work is done

work'shop' *n.* 1. a room or building where work is done 2. a seminar or series of meetings for intensive study, work, etc. in some field

work'ta'ble *n.* a table at which work is done, esp. one with drawers for tools, materials, etc.

work'week' *n.* the total number of hours or days worked in a week for the regular wage or salary

world (wurld) *n.* [OE. *werold*] 1. *a*) the planet earth *b*) the whole universe 2. *a*) mankind *b*) people generally; the public 3. *a*) [*also* W-] some part of the earth [the Old *World*] *b*) some period of history, its society, etc. *c*) any sphere or domain [the dog *world*] *d*) any sphere of human activity [the *world* of music] 4. individual experience, outlook, etc. [his *world* is narrow] 5. secular life and interests, or people concerned with these 6. [*often pl.*] a large amount [a *world* (or *worlds*) of good] —**for all the world** 1. for any reason at all 2. in every respect

world'ling *n.* a worldly person

world'ly *adj.* -li·er, -li·est 1. of this world; temporal or secular 2. devoted to or concerned with the affairs, pleasures, etc. of this world: also **world'ly-mind'ed** 3. worldlywise —**world'li·ness** *n.*

world'ly-wise' *adj.* wise in the ways of the world; sophisticated

world power a nation or organization powerful enough to have a worldwide influence

World Series [*also* w- s-] an annual series of games between the winning teams of the two major U.S. baseball leagues to decide the championship

World War I the war (1914–18) between the Allies (Great Britain, France, Russia, the U.S., Italy, etc.) and the Central Powers (Germany, Austria-Hungary, etc.)

World War II the war (1939–45) between the United Nations (Great Britain, France, the Soviet Union, the U.S., etc.) and the Axis (Germany, Italy, Japan, etc.)

world'-wea'ry *adj.* weary of the world; bored with living

world'wide' *adj.* extending throughout the world

worm (wurm) *n.* [OE. *wyrm*, serpent] 1. a long, slender, soft-bodied, creeping animal 2. popularly, *a*) an insect larva *b*) any wormlike animal 3. an abject or contemptible person 4. something wormlike or spiral in shape, specif., a short, rotating screw that meshes with the teeth of a worm wheel 5. [*pl.*] *Med.* any disease caused by parasitic worms in the intestines, etc. —*vi.* to proceed like a worm, in a winding or roundabout manner —*vt.* 1. to bring about, make, etc. in a winding or roundabout manner 2. to purge of intestinal worms —**worm'like'** *adj.* —**worm'y** *adj.* -i·er, -i·est

worm'-eat'en *adj.* 1. eaten into by worms, termites, etc. 2. worn-out, out-of-date, etc.

worm gear 1. *same as* WORM WHEEL 2. a gear consisting of a worm and worm wheel

worm'hole' *n.* a hole made by a worm, termite, etc.

worm wheel a toothed wheel designed to gear with the thread of a worm

worm'wood' (-wood') *n.* [< OE. *wermod*] 1. any of various strong-smelling plants; esp., a perennial that yields a bitter-tasting oil used in making absinthe 2. a bitter, unpleasant experience

WORM GEAR

worn (wôrn) *pp.* of WEAR —*adj.* 1. damaged by use or wear 2. exhausted

worn'-out' *adj.* 1. used until no longer effective, usable, etc. 2. tired out

wor·ri·some (wur'ē səm) *adj.* 1. causing worry or anxiety 2. tending to worry

wor·ry (wur'ē) *vt.* -ried, -ry·ing [OE. *wyrgan*, strangle] 1. *a*) to treat roughly, as with continual biting [a dog *worrying* a bone] *b*) to pluck at, touch, etc. repeatedly in a nervous way 2. to annoy; bother 3. to make troubled or uneasy —*vi.* 1. to bite or tear (*at* an object) with the teeth 2. to be anxious, troubled, etc. 3. to manage to get (*along* or *through*) —*n.*, *pl.* -ries 1. a troubled state of mind; anxiety 2. a cause of this —**wor'ri·er** *n.*

wor'ry·wart' (-wôrt') *n.* [WORRY + WART] [Colloq.] one who tends to worry, esp. over details

worse (wurs) *adj. compar. of* BAD¹ & ILL [OE. *wiersa*] 1. *a*) bad, evil, harmful, etc. in a greater degree *b*) of inferior quality 2. in poorer health; more ill 3. in a less satisfactory situation —*adv. compar. of* BADLY & ILL in a worse manner; to a worse extent —*n.* that which is worse —**for the worse** to a worse condition

wors·en (wur's'n) *vt.*, *vi.* to make or become worse

wor·ship (wur'ship) *n.* [< OE.: see WORTH & -SHIP] 1. *a*) reverence or devotion for a deity *b*) a church service or other rite showing this 2. intense love or admiration 3. [Chiefly Brit.] a title of honor (preceded by *your* or *his*) used in addressing magistrates, etc. —*vt.* -shiped or -shipped, -ship·ing or -ship·ping 1. to show religious reverence for 2. to have intense love or admiration for —*vi.* to engage in worship —**wor'ship·er**, **wor'ship·per** *n.*

wor'ship·ful *adj.* 1. [Chiefly Brit.] honorable; respected 2. feeling or offering great devotion or respect

worst (wurst) *adj. superl. of* BAD¹ & ILL [OE. *wyrsta*] 1. *a*) bad, evil, harmful, etc. in the greatest degree *b*) of the lowest quality 2. in the least satisfactory situation —*adv. superl. of* BADLY & ILL in the worst manner; to the worst extent —*n.* that which is worst —*vt.* to defeat —**at worst** under the worst circumstances —**if (the) worst comes to (the) worst** if the worst possible thing happens —**(in) the worst way** [Slang] very much

wor·sted (woos'tid, wur'stid) *n.* [< *Worstead*, England] 1. a smooth, hard-twisted wool thread or yarn 2. fabric made from this —*adj.* made of worsted

wort¹ (wurt) *n.* [< OE. *wyrt-*] a liquid prepared with malt which, after fermenting, becomes beer, ale, etc.

wort² (wurt) *n.* [OE. *wyrt*, a root] a plant or herb: now usually in compounds [*liverwort*]

worth (wurth) *n.* [OE. *weorth*] 1. material value, esp. as expressed in money 2. importance, value, merit, etc. 3. the quantity to be had for a given sum [a dime's *worth* of nuts] 4. wealth; possessions —*adj.* 1. deserving or worthy of 2. equal in value to 3. having wealth totaling —**for all one is worth** to the utmost —**put in one's two cents' worth** to give one's opinion

worth'less (-lis) *adj.* without worth or merit; useless —**worth'less·ly** *adv.* —**worth'less·ness** *n.*

worth'while' (-hwīl', -wīl') *adj.* worth the time or effort spent

wor·thy (wur'thē) *adj.* -thi·er, -thi·est 1. having worth, value, or merit 2. deserving —*n.*, *pl.* -thies a person of outstanding worth, etc. —**wor'thi·ly** *adv.* —**wor'thi·ness** *n.*

would (wood) *v.* [OE. *wolde*] 1. *pt.* of WILL² 2. an auxiliary used to express: *a*) condition [if you *would*] *b*) futurity [he said he *would* come] *c*) habitual action [Sundays he *would* sleep late] *d*) a request [*would* you help me?] 3. I wish [*would* that I could]

would'-be' *adj.* 1. wishing or pretending to be 2. intended to be

would·n't (wood'n't) would not

wouldst (woodst) *archaic 2d pers. sing. pt.* of WILL²: *used with* thou

wound¹ (woond) *n.* [OE. *wund*] 1. an injury in which the skin or other tissue is cut, torn, etc. 2. any hurt to the feelings, honor, etc. —*vt.*, *vi.* to inflict a wound (*on* or *upon*); injure

wound² (wound) 1. *pt.* & *pp.* of WIND¹ 2. *pt.* & *pp.* of WIND³

wove (wōv) *pt.* & *alt. pp.* of WEAVE

wo·ven (-'n) *alt. pp.* of WEAVE

wow (wou) *interj.* an exclamation of surprise, pleasure, etc. —*n.* [Slang] a remarkable, exciting, etc. person or thing —*vt.* [Slang] to be a great success with

WPA, W.P.A. Work Projects Administration

wpm words per minute

wrack (rak) *n.* [< OE. *wræc*, misery & MDu. *wrak*, a wreck] ruin; destruction: now chiefly in **wrack and ruin**

wraith (rāth) *n.* [Scot.] a ghost

wran·gle (raŋ'g'l) *vi.* -gled, -gling [< ME. *wringen*, to wring] to argue; quarrel, esp. angrily and noisily —*vt.* to herd (livestock) —*n.* an angry, noisy dispute —**wran'gler** *n.*

wrap (rap) *vt.* **wrapped** or **wrapt**, **wrap'ping** [ME. *wrappen*] 1. to wind or fold (a covering) around something 2. to enclose and fasten in paper, etc. —*vi.* to twine, coil, etc. (*over*, *around*, etc.) —*n.* an outer covering or garment —**wrapped up in** absorbed in —**wrap up** [Colloq.] to conclude; settle

wrap'a·round' (-ə round') *adj.* 1. that has a full-length opening and is wrapped around the body, as a skirt 2. molded, etc. so as to curve [a *wraparound* windshield] —*n.* a wraparound garment

wrap'per *n.* 1. one that wraps 2. that in which something is wrapped 3. a woman's dressing gown

wrap'ping *n.* [*often pl.*] the material, as paper, in which something is wrapped

wrap'-up' *n.* [Colloq.] a concluding, summarizing statement, report, etc.

wrath (rath; *chiefly Brit.* rôth) *n.* [OE., *wroth*] 1. intense anger; rage 2. any action of vengeance or punishment

wrath'ful *adj.* 1. full of wrath 2. resulting from or expressing wrath —**wrath'ful·ly** *adv.* —**wrath'ful·ness** *n.*

wreak (rēk) *vt.* [OE. *wrecan*, to revenge] 1. to give vent to (anger, malice, etc.) 2. to inflict (vengeance), cause (havoc), etc.

wreath (rēth) *n., pl.* **wreaths** (rēthz) [< OE. *writhan*, to twist] 1. a twisted ring of leaves, flowers, etc. 2. something like this in shape *[wreaths* of smoke]

wreathe (rēth) *vt.* **wreathed**, **wreath'ing** 1. to form into a wreath 2. to coil or twist around; encircle 3. to decorate with wreaths 4. to envelop —*vi.* 1. to have a twisting movement 2. to form a wreath

wreck (rek) *n.* [< ON. *vrek*, wreckage] 1. a shipwreck 2. the remains of something destroyed or badly damaged 3. a person in poor health 4. a wrecking or being wrecked —*vt.* 1. to destroy or damage badly 2. to tear down (a building, etc.) 3. to overthrow; thwart 4. to destroy the health of —*vi.* 1. to be wrecked 2. to work as a wrecker

wreck'age (-ij) *n.* 1. a wrecking or being wrecked 2. the remains of something wrecked

wreck'er *n.* 1. a person or thing that wrecks 2. one that salvages or removes wrecks

wreck'ing *n.* the act or work of a wrecker —*adj.* engaged or used in dismantling or salvaging wrecks

wren (ren) *n.* [OE. *wrenna*] a small songbird with a long bill and stubby, erect tail

Wren (ren), Sir **Christopher** 1632–1723; Eng. architect

wrench (rench) *n.* [OE. *wrenc*, a trick] 1. a sudden, sharp twist or pull 2. an injury caused by a twist or jerk, as to the back 3. a sudden feeling of grief, etc. 4. a tool for holding and turning nuts, bolts, pipes, etc. —*vt.* 1. to twist or jerk violently 2. to injure (a part of the body) with a twist 3. to distort (a meaning, etc.)

MONKEY WRENCH

SINGLE-HEADED END WRENCH

WRENCHES

wrest (rest) *vt.* [OE. *wræstan*] 1. to pull or force away violently with a twisting motion 2. to take by force; usurp —*n.* a wresting; twist; wrench

wres·tle (res'l) *vi., vt.* **-tled, -tling** [< OE. *wræstan*, to twist] 1. to struggle hand to hand with (an opponent) in an attempt to throw or force him to the ground without striking blows 2. to contend (*with*) —*n.* 1. a wrestling 2. a struggle or contest —**wres'tler** *n.*

wres'tling *n.* a sport in which the opponents wrestle, or struggle hand to hand

wretch (rech) *n.* [OE. *wrecca*, an outcast] 1. a miserable or unhappy person 2. a person who is despised or scorned

wretch'ed (-id) *adj.* [OE. *wræcc*] 1. very unhappy; miserable 2. causing misery *[wretched* slums] 3. very inferior 4. deserving to be despised —**wretch'ed·ly** *adv.* —**wretch'ed·ness** *n.*

wrig·gle (rig'l) *vi.* **-gled, -gling** [MLowG. *wriggeln*] 1. to twist and turn; squirm 2. to move along with a twisting motion 3. to make one's way by shifty means; dodge —*vt.* 1. to cause to wriggle 2. to bring into a specified condition by wriggling —*n.* a wriggling —**wrig'gler** *n.* —**wrig'gly** *adj.*

wright (rīt) *n.* [< OE. *wyrcan*, to work] one who makes, constructs, or repairs: used chiefly in compounds *[shipwright]*

Wright (rīt) 1. **Frank Lloyd**, 1869–1959; U.S. architect 2. **Or·ville** (ôr'vil), 1871–1948 & his brother **Wilbur**, 1867–1912; U.S. airplane inventors

wring (riŋ) *vt.* **wrung** or rare **winged**, **wring'ing** [OE. *wringan*] 1. *a)* to squeeze, press, or twist, esp. so as to force out water, etc. *b)* to force (*out* water, etc.) 2. to twist (the hands) in distress 3. to clasp (another's hand) in greeting 4. to extract by force, threats, etc. 5. to afflict with pity, etc. *[the story wrung* her heart] —*vi.* to squirm or twist with great effort —*n.* a wringing

wring'er *n.* 1. a person or thing that wrings 2. a device with two rollers close together, used for squeezing water from wet clothes

wrin·kle¹ (riŋ'k'l) *n.* [ME. *wrinkel*] 1. a small ridge or furrow in a normally smooth surface 2. a crease or pucker in the skin —*vt., vi.* **-kled, -kling** to contract into small ridges or creases —**wrin'kly** *adj.* **-kli·er, -kli·est**

wrin·kle² (riŋ'k'l) *n.* [prob. < OE. *wrenc*, a trick] [Colloq.] a clever or novel trick, idea, etc.

wrist (rist) *n.* [OE.] the joint between the hand and the forearm

wrist'band' *n.* a band that goes around the wrist, as on the cuff of a sleeve

wrist pin the stud or pin by which the connecting rod is attached to a wheel, crank, etc.

wrist'watch' (-wäch', -wôch') *n.* a watch worn on a strap or band around the wrist

writ (rit) *n.* [OE. < *writan*, write] 1. [Rare] something written 2. a formal legal document ordering or prohibiting some action

write (rīt) *vt.* **wrote, writ'ten, writ'ing** [OE. *writan*] 1. *a)* to form (words, letters, etc.) on a surface, as with a pen *b)* to form the words, letters, etc. of *[write* your name] 2. to spell (a word, etc.) 3. to be the author or composer of (literary or musical material) 4. to fill in (a check, form, etc.) with the writing required 5. to communicate (with) in writing *[he wrote* (me) that he was ill] 6. to record (information) in a computer 7. to leave signs of *[greed* was *written* on his face] —*vi.* 1. to write words, etc. 2. to write books, etc. 3. to write a letter 4. to produce writing of a specified kind *[to write* legibly] —**write down** to put into writing —**write off** 1. to remove from accounts (bad debts, etc.) 2. to drop from consideration —**write out** 1. to put into writing 2. to write in full —**write up** to write an account of

write'-off' *n.* something written off, amortized, etc.

writ'er *n.* one who writes, esp. as a business or occupation; author, journalist, etc.

write'-up' *n.* [Colloq.] a written report, often a favorable account, as for publicity

writhe (rīth) *vt.* **writhed, writh'ing** [OE. *writhan*, to twist] to cause to twist or turn —*vi.* 1. to twist or turn; squirm 2. to suffer great emotional distress —*n.* a writhing movement

writ·ing (rīt'iŋ) *n.* 1. the act of one who writes 2. something written 3. written form 4. *short for* HANDWRITING 5. a literary work 6. the occupation of a writer 7. the art, style, etc. of literary composition —*adj.* 1. that writes 2. used in writing

writ·ten (rit''n) *pp. of* WRITE —*adj.* put down in a form to be read

wrong (rôŋ) *adj.* [< ON. *rangr*, twisted] 1. not just, moral, etc. 2. not in accordance with an established standard, etc. 3. not suitable or appropriate 4. *a)* contrary to fact, reason, etc.; incorrect *b)* mistaken 5. not functioning properly 6. designating the unfinished, inner, or under side, as of a fabric —*adv.* in a wrong manner, direction, etc. —*n.* something wrong; esp., an unjust, immoral, or illegal act —*vt.* 1. to treat badly or unjustly 2. to think badly of without justification —**go wrong** 1. to turn out badly 2. to change from good behavior to bad —**in the wrong** wrong —**wrong'ly** *adv.* —**wrong'ness** *n.*

wrong'do'ing (-dōō'iŋ) *n.* any act or behavior that is wrong —**wrong'do'er** *n.*

wrong'ful *adj.* 1. unjust, unfair, or injurious 2. unlawful —**wrong'ful·ly** *adv.* —**wrong'ful·ness** *n.*

wrong'head'ed (-hed'id) *adj.* stubborn in sticking to wrong opinions, ideas, etc. —**wrong'head'ed·ly** *adv.* —**wrong'head'ed·ness** *n.*

wrote (rōt) *pt. of* WRITE

wroth (rôth; *chiefly Brit.* rōth) *adj.* [OE. *wrath*] angry; wrathful; incensed

wrought (rôt) *alt. pt. & pp. of* WORK —*adj.* 1. formed; fashioned 2. shaped by hammering, etc.: said of metals 3. elaborated with care

wrought iron tough, malleable iron containing very little carbon —**wrought'-i'ron** *adj.*

wrought'-up' *adj.* very disturbed or excited

wrung (ruŋ) *pt. & pp. of* WRING

wry (rī) *adj.* **wri'er, wri'est** [OE. *wrigian*, to turn] 1. turned or bent to one side; twisted; distorted 2. made by distorting the features *[a wry* face] 3. perverse; ironic *[wry* humor] —**wry'ly** *adv.* —**wry'ness** *n.*

wry'neck' *n.* 1. a condition in which the neck is twisted by a muscle spasm 2. a bird related to the woodpecker, noted for its habit of twisting its neck

WSW, W.S.W., w.s.w. west-southwest

wt. weight

Wu·han (wōō'hän') city in EC China: pop. 2,500,000

W.Va., WV West Virginia

Wy·an·dotte (wī'ən dät') *n.* [< AmInd.] any of a breed of American chickens

Wyc·liffe (or **Wyc·lif**) (wik'lif), **John** 1324?–84; Eng. religious reformer: made the first complete translation of the Bible into English

Wy·o·ming (wī ō'miŋ) State of the W U.S., one of the Mountain States: 97,914 sq. mi.; pop. 332,000; cap. Cheyenne: abbrev. **Wyo., WY** —**Wy·o'ming·ite'** (-īt') *n.*

XYZ

X, x (eks) *n., pl.* **X's, x's** the twenty-fourth letter of the English alphabet
X (eks) *n.* **1.** an object shaped like X **2.** the Roman numeral for 10 **3.** a person or thing unknown or unrevealed
X a motion-picture rating meaning that no one under the age of seventeen is to be admitted —*adj.* shaped like X
x (eks) *vt.* **x-ed** or **x'd, x-ing** or **x'ing 1.** to mark (one's choice or answer) with an X **2.** to cross (*out*) with a series of X's
x *Math. a symbol for:* **1.** an unknown quantity **2.** times (in multiplication) $[3 \times 3 = 9]$
xan·the·in (zan'thē in) *n.* [Fr. *xanthéine*] the water-soluble part of the yellow pigment in some plants
xan·thine (zan'thēn, -thin) *n.* [Fr. < Gr. *xanthos*, yellow] a white, crystalline nitrogenous compound present in blood, urine, and certain plants
Xan·thip·pe (zan tip'ē) 5th cent. B.C.; wife of Socrates: the prototype of the nagging wife
Xa·vi·er (zā'vē ər, zav'ē-), Saint **Francis** 1506–52; Sp. Jesuit missionary
X chromosome *see* SEX CHROMOSOME
Xe *Chem.* xenon
xe·bec (zē'bek) *n.* [< Fr. < Ar. *shabbāk*] a small, three-masted ship, once common in the Mediterranean
xe·non (zē'nän, zen'än) *n.* [Gr., strange] a heavy, colorless gaseous chemical element present in the air in minute quantities: symbol, Xe; at. wt., 131.30; at. no., 54
xen·o·pho·bi·a (zen'ə fō'bē ə) *n.* [< Gr. *xenos*, strange + -PHOBIA] fear or hatred of strangers or foreigners —**xen·o·pho·bic** (fō'bik) *adj.*
Xen·o·phon (zen'ə fən) 430?–355? B.C.; Gr. historian & military leader
xe·rog·ra·phy (zi räg'rə fē) *n.* [< Gr. *xēros*, dry + -GRAPHY] a process for copying printed material, etc. by the action of light on an electrically charged surface —**xe·ro·graph·ic** (zir'ə graf'ik) *adj.*
Xe·rox (zir'äks) *a trademark for* a device for copying printed material by xerography —*n.* a copy made by such a device —*vt., vi.* to reproduce by such a device
Xer·xes (zurk'sēz) 519?–465? B.C.; king of Persia (486?–465?)
xi (zī, sī) *n.* the fourteenth letter of the Greek alphabet (Ξ, ξ)
Xmas (kris'məs, eks'məs) *n. same as* CHRISTMAS
X-ray (eks'rā') *n.* **1.** an electromagnetic ray or radiation of very short wavelength produced by the bombardment of a metal by a stream of electrons, as in a vacuum tube: X-rays can penetrate solid substances and are used to study internal body structures and to treat certain disorders **2.** a photograph made by means of X-rays —*vt.* to treat, examine, or photograph with X-rays Also **X ray, x-ray, x ray**
xy·lem (zī'ləm, -lem) *n.* [G. < Gr. *xylon*, wood] the woody tissue of a plant
xy·lo·phone (zī'lə fōn') *n.* [< Gr. *xylon*, wood + -PHONE] a musical instrument having a series of graduated wooden bars struck with small wooden hammers

Y, y (wī) *n., pl.* **Y's, y's** the twenty-fifth letter of the English alphabet
Y (wī) *n.* **1.** an object shaped like Y **2.** *Chem.* yttrium
-y¹ [ME.] *a suffix meaning* little, dear: used to form diminutives, nicknames, etc. [*kitty, Billy*]
-y² [OE. *-ig*] *a suffix meaning:* **1.** having, full of [*dirty*] **2.** somewhat [*chilly*] **3.** tending to [*sticky*] **4.** somewhat like [*wavy*]
-y³ [< L. *-ia*] *a suffix meaning:* **1.** quality or condition of (being) [*jealousy*] **2.** a shop, group, etc. of a specified kind [*bakery*]
-y⁴ [< L. *-ium*] *a suffix meaning* action of [*inquiry*]
Y., Y. *short for* YMCA *or* YWCA

yacht (yät) *n.* [Du. *jacht*] a small ship for pleasure cruises, races, etc. —*vi.* to sail in a yacht —**yacht'ing** *n.* —**yachts'man** *n., pl.* **-men**
yah (yä, ya) *interj.* a shout of scorn, defiance, etc.
Ya·hoo (yä'hoo) *n.* in Swift's *Gulliver's Travels*, any of a race of coarse, brutish creatures having the form and vices of man
Yah·weh, Yah·we (yä'we) God: a form of the Hebrew name in the Scriptures
yak¹ (yak) *n.* [Tibetan *gyak*] a long-haired wild ox of Tibet and C Asia
yak² (yak) *vi.* **yakked, yak'king** [echoic] [Slang] to talk much or idly —*n.* [Slang] **1.** a yakking **2.** a laugh
yam (yam) *n.* [Port. *inhame*] **1.** the edible, starchy root of a tropical climbing plant **2.** [South] the sweet potato
Yang·tze (yaŋ'sē) river in C China, flowing east from Tibet: c.3,400 mi.
Yank (yaŋk) *n.* [Slang] a Yankee; esp., a U.S. soldier in World Wars I and II
yank (yaŋk) *n., vt., vi.* [< ?] [Colloq.] jerk
Yan·kee (yaŋ'kē) *n.* [< ? Du. *Jan Kees*, a disparaging nickname] **1.** a New Englander **2.** a native or inhabitant of a Northern State **3.** a native or inhabitant of the U.S. —*adj.* of or like Yankees
yap (yap) *vi.* **yapped, yap'ping** [echoic] **1.** to make a sharp, shrill bark **2.** [Slang] to talk noisily and stupidly —*n.* a sharp, shrill bark
yard¹ (yärd) *n.* [OE. *gierd*, a rod] **1.** *a)* a measure of length, equal to 3 feet, or 36 inches *b)* a cubic yard **2.** *Naut.* a slender rod or spar fastened across a mast to support a sail or to hold signal flags, etc.
yard² (yärd) *n.* [OE. *geard*, enclosure] **1.** the ground around or next to a building **2.** a pen, etc. for livestock or poultry **3.** a place in the open used for a particular purpose [*a navy yard*] **4.** a railroad center where trains are made up, switched, etc.
yard·age (yär'dij) *n.* **1.** measurement in yards **2.** the extent so measured **3.** distance covered in advancing a football
yard'arm' *n. Naut.* either end of a yard supporting a square sail, signal lights, etc.
yard goods textiles made in standard width, usually sold by the yard
yard'mas'ter *n.* a man in charge of a railroad yard
yard'stick' *n.* **1.** a measuring stick one yard long **2.** any standard used in judging, comparing, etc.
yar·mul·ke, yar·mal·ke (yär'məl kə) *n.* [Yid. < Pol.] a skullcap often worn by Jewish men, as at prayer
yarn (yärn) *n.* [OE. *gearn*] **1.** a continuous strand of spun wool, cotton, nylon, glass, etc., for weaving, knitting, etc. **2.** [Colloq.] a tale, esp. an exaggerated one —**spin a yarn** [Colloq.] to tell a yarn
yaw (yô) *vi.* [ON. *jaga*, to sway] **1.** to swing back and forth across its course, as a ship pushed by high waves **2.** to swing about the vertical axis, as an aircraft —*n.* a yawing
yawl (yôl) *n.* [< MLowG. *jolle* or Du. *jol*] **1.** a ship's boat **2.** a small, two-masted sailboat rigged fore-and-aft
yawn (yôn) *vi.* [ME. *yanen*] **1.** to open the mouth widely and breathe in deeply, esp. involuntarily as a result of fatigue or drowsiness **2.** to open wide; gape —*n.* a yawning
yaws (yôz) *n.pl.* [*with sing. v.*] [of WInd. origin] a tropical, infectious skin disease
Yb *Chem.* ytterbium
Y chromosome *see* SEX CHROMOSOME
y·clept, y·cleped (i klept') *pp.* [< OE. *clipian*, to call] [Archaic] called; named
yd. *pl.* **yd., yds.** yard

YAWL

ye¹ (*thə, thi, thē; now often* yē) *adj. archaic form of* THE
ye² (yē) *pron.* [OE. *ge*] [Archaic] you
yea (yā) *adv.* [OE. *gea*] **1.** yes **2.** indeed; truly —*n.* an answer or vote of "yes" —*interj.* a cry used in cheering on an athletic team
yeah (ya, ye, ye′ə, *etc.*) *adv.* [Colloq.] yes
year (yir) *n.* [OE. *gear*] **1.** a period of 365 days (in leap year, 366 days) beginning Jan. 1 **2.** the period of time (365 days, 5 hours, 48 minutes, 46 seconds) of one revolution of the earth around the sun: also **tropical** or **solar year 3.** the period of time in which any planet makes its revolution around the sun **4.** a period of 12 calendar months starting from any date **5.** an annual period of less than 365 days [a school *year*] **6.** [*pl.*] *a*) age [old for his *years*] *b*) a long time —**year in, year out** every year
year′book′ *n.* an annual book, as one giving data of the preceding year
year·ling (yir′liŋ, yur′-) *n.* an animal one year old or in its second year
year′long′ *adj.* continuing for a full year
year′ly *adj.* **1.** lasting a year **2.** once a year or every year **3.** of a year, or each year —*adv.* every year
yearn (yurn) *vi.* [< OE. *georn, gearn*] **1.** to be filled with longing or desire **2.** to feel tenderness or sympathy —**yearn′ing** *n., adj.*
yeast (yēst) *n.* [OE. *gist*] **1.** a yellowish, moist mass of minute fungi that cause fermentation: used in making beer, whiskey, etc. and as a leavening in baking **2.** any of the fungi that form yeast: also **yeast plant 3.** yeast dried in flakes or granules or compressed into cakes **4.** foam; froth **5.** ferment; agitation
yeast′y *adj.* **-i·er, -i·est 1.** of, like, or containing yeast **2.** frothy; light **3.** in a ferment; restless
Yeats (yāts), **William Butler** 1865–1939; Ir. poet, playwright, & essayist
yegg (yeg) *n.* [Slang] a criminal; esp., a safecracker or burglar
yell (yel) *vi., vt.* [OE. *giellan*] to cry out loudly; shout —*n.* **1.** a loud outcry or shout; scream **2.** a rhythmic cheer given in unison
yel·low (yel′ō) *adj.* [OE. *geolu*] **1.** of the color of ripe lemons **2.** having a yellowish skin; Mongoloid **3.** [Colloq.] cowardly **4.** cheaply sensational [*yellow* journalism] —*n.* **1.** a yellow color or pigment **2.** the yolk of an egg —*vt., vi.* to make or become yellow —**yel′low·ish** *adj.*
yellow fever a tropical disease caused by a virus carried to man by the bite of a certain mosquito, and marked by fever, jaundice, etc.
yellow jack 1. *same as* YELLOW FEVER **2.** a yellow flag used as a signal of quarantine
yellow jacket a wasp or hornet having bright-yellow markings
yellow metal 1. gold **2.** brass that is 60 parts copper and 40 parts zinc
Yellow Pages [*also* y- p-] the section or volume of a telephone directory, on yellow paper, containing classified listings of subscribers according to business, profession, etc.
Yellow River *same as* HWANG HO
Yellow Sea arm of the Pacific, between China & Korea
Yel·low·stone (yel′ō stōn′) river flowing from NW Wyo. through Mont. into the Missouri River: 671 mi.
Yellowstone National Park national park mostly in NW Wyo., containing geysers, boiling springs, etc.
yelp (yelp) *vi., vt.* [OE. *gielpan,* to boast] to utter or express by a short, sharp cry or bark, as a dog —*n.* a short, sharp cry or bark
Yem·en (yem′ən) **1.** country in S Arabia: c.75,000 sq. mi.; pop. 5,000,000: in full **Yemen Arab Republic 2.** country in S Arabia, east of Yemen (sense 1): c.110,000 sq. mi.; pop. 1,475,000: in full **People's Democratic Republic of Yemen** —**Yem′en·ite′** (-ə nīt′) *adj., n.*
yen¹ (yen) *n., pl.* **yen** [Jpn. < Chin. *yüan,* round] the monetary unit of Japan
yen² (yen) *n.* [Chin. *yăn,* opium] [Colloq.] a strong longing or desire —*vi.* **yenned, yen′ning** [Colloq.] to have a yen (*for*); long; yearn
yeo·man (yō′mən) *n., pl.* **-men** [ME. *yeman*] **1.** orig., *a*) a manservant in a royal or noble household *b*) a freeholder of a class below the gentry **2.** *U.S. Navy* a petty officer assigned to clerical duty
yeo′man·ly *adj.* **1.** of or like a yeoman **2.** brave; sturdy —*adv.* in a yeomanly manner
yeoman of the (royal) guard any of the 100 men forming a ceremonial guard for English royalty
yeo′man·ry (-rē) *n.* **1.** yeomen collectively **2.** a British volunteer cavalry force

yes (yes) *adv.* [OE. *gese*] **1.** aye; it is so: used to express agreement, consent, etc. **2.** not only that, but more [ready, *yes,* eager to help] *Yes* may be used to mean "What is it?" or as a polite expression of interest —*n., pl.* **yes′es** an affirmative reply, vote, etc. —*vt., vi.* **yessed, yes′sing** to say *yes* (to)
yes man [Slang] one who indicates approval of every idea offered by his superior
yes·ter (yes′tər) *adj.* **1.** of yesterday **2.** previous to this Usually in combination [*yesteryear*]
yes·ter·day (yes′tər dē, -dā′) *n.* [< OE. *geostran,* yesterday + *dæg,* day] **1.** the day before today **2.** a recent day or time **3.** [*usually pl.*] time gone by —*adv.* **1.** on the day before today **2.** recently —*adj.* of yesterday
yes′ter·year′ *n., adv.* [Poet.] **1.** last year **2.** (in) recent years
yet (yet) *adv.* [OE. *giet*] **1.** up to now; thus far [he hasn't gone *yet*] **2.** at the present time; now [we can't leave *yet*] **3.** still; even now [there is *yet* a chance] **4.** sooner or later [she will thank you *yet*] **5.** in addition; still [he was *yet* more kind] **6.** now, after all the time that has elapsed [hasn't he finished *yet?*] **7.** nevertheless [he's rich, *yet* lonely] —*conj.* nevertheless; however [she seems well, *yet* she is ill] —**as yet** up to now
yew (yōō) *n.* [OE. *iw*] **1.** an evergreen shrub or tree with a fine-grained, elastic wood **2.** the wood
Yid·dish (yid′ish) *n.* [< G. *jüdisch* < L. *Judaeus,* a Jew] a language derived from medieval High German, spoken by East European Jews: it is written in the Hebrew alphabet —*adj.* of or in this language
yield (yēld) *vt.* [OE. *gieldan,* to pay] **1.** to produce as a crop, result, profit, etc. **2.** to give up; surrender **3.** to concede; grant —*vi.* **1.** to produce or bear **2.** to give up; surrender **3.** to give way to physical force **4.** to lose precedence, etc. (often with *to*) —*n.* the amount yielded
yield′ing *adj.* **1.** flexible **2.** submissive
yip (yip) *n., vi.* **yipped, yip′ping** [echoic] [Colloq.] yelp
yipe (yīp) *interj.* an exclamation of pain, alarm, etc.
-yl [< Gr. *hylē,* wood] *Chem. a combining form meaning:* **1.** a univalent hydrocarbon radical **2.** a radical containing oxygen
YMCA, Y.M.C.A. Young Men's Christian Association
YMHA, Y.M.H.A. Young Men's Hebrew Association
yo·del (yō′d'l) *vt., vi.* **-deled** or **-delled, -del·ing** or **-del·ling** [G. *jodeln*] to sing with sudden changes back and forth between the normal chest voice and the falsetto —*n.* a yodeling —**yo′del·er, yo′del·ler** *n.*
yo·ga (yō′gə) *n.* [Sans., union] **1.** *Hinduism* a discipline by which one seeks union with the universal soul through deep meditation, prescribed postures, controlled breathing, etc. **2.** a system of exercising involving such postures, breathing, etc. —**yo′gic** (-gik) *adj.*
yo·gi (yō′gē) *n., pl.* **-gis** a person who practices yoga: also **yo′gin** (-gin)
yo·gurt (yō′gərt) *n.* [Turk. *yōghurt*] a thick, semisolid food made from fermented milk: also sp. **yo′ghurt**
yoicks (yoiks) *interj.* [Brit.] a cry to urge on the hounds in fox hunting
yoke (yōk) *n., pl.* **yokes;** for 2, usually **yoke** [OE. *geoc*] **1.** a wooden frame for harnessing together a pair of oxen, etc. **2.** a pair of animals so harnessed **3.** bondage **4.** something that binds, unites, etc. **5.** something like a yoke **6.** a part of a garment fitted to the shoulders or hips to support the gathered parts below —*vt.* **yoked, yok′ing 1.** to put a yoke on **2.** to harness (an animal) to (a plow, etc.) **3.** to join together —*vi.* to be joined together

YOKE

yo·kel (yō′k'l) *n.* [prob. < dial. *yokel,* woodpecker] a person living in a rural area: a contemptuous term
Yo·ko·ha·ma (yō′kə hä′mə) seaport in Honshu, Japan: pop. 1,789,000
yolk (yōk) *n.* [OE. *geolca*] the yellow, principal substance of an egg —**yolked, yolk′y** *adj.*
Yom Kip·pur (yäm kip′ər; *Heb.* yōm′ kē pŏŏr′) the Day of Atonement, a Jewish holiday and day of fasting
yon (yän) *adj., adv.* [OE. *geon*] [Archaic or Dial.] yonder
yon·der (yän′dər) *adj.* [ME.] **1.** farther (with *the*) **2.** being at a distance, but within sight —*adv.* over there
Yon·kers (yäŋ′kərz) city in SE N.Y.: suburb of New York City: pop. 204,000
yore (yôr) *adv.* [OE. *geara*] [Obs.] long ago —**of yore** formerly
Yorkshire pudding a batter of flour, eggs, and milk baked in the drippings of roasting meat

Yo·sem·i·te National Park (yō sem′ə tē) national park in Calif., with high waterfalls

you (yōō) *pron.* [OE. *eow*, dat. of *ge*, YE²] 1. the person or persons spoken to 2. a person or people generally [*you never can tell!*]

you-all (yōō ôl′, yôl) *pron. Southern colloq. for* YOU: chiefly used as a pl. form

you'd (yōōd) 1. you had 2. you would

you'll (yōōl) 1. you will 2. you shall

young (yuŋ) *adj.* [OE. *geong*] 1. being in an early period of life or growth 2. youthful; fresh; vigorous 3. in an early stage 4. inexperienced; immature 5. younger than another of the same name or family —*n.* 1. young people 2. offspring, esp. young offspring, collectively —**with young** pregnant —**young′ish** *adj.* —**young′ness** *n.*

Young (yuŋ), **Brig·ham** (brig′əm) 1801–77; U.S. Mormon leader

young·ster (yuŋ′stər) *n.* a child or youth

Youngs·town (yuŋz′toun′) city in NE Ohio: pop. 140,000 (met. area, with Warren, 536,000)

your (yoor, yôr) *possessive pronominal adj.* [OE. *eower*] of, belonging to, or done by you: also used before some titles [*your Honor*]

you're (yoor, yōor) you are

yours (yoorz, yôrz) *pron.* that or those belonging to you [*that book is yours*]

your·self (yər self′, yoor-) *pron., pl.* **-selves′** (-selvz′) 1. *the intensive form of* YOU [*you yourself* did it] 2. *the reflexive form of* YOU [*you hurt yourself*] 3. your true self [*you're not yourself* today] 4. *same as* ONESELF [*it is best to do it yourself*]

yours truly 1. a phrase used before the signature in ending a letter 2. [Colloq.] I or me

youth (yōōth) *n., pl.* **youths** (yōōths, yōōthz) [OE. *geoguthe*] 1. the state or quality of being young 2. the period of adolescence 3. an early stage of development 4. young people 5. a young person; esp., a young man

youth′ful *adj.* 1. young 2. of, characteristic of, or suitable for youth 3. fresh; vigorous 4. new; early —**youth′ful·ly** *adv.* —**youth′ful·ness** *n.*

you've (yōōv) you have

yowl (youl) *vi., n.* [< ON. *gaula*] howl; wail

yo-yo (yō′yō′) *n.* [< Philippine name] 1. a spoollike toy attached to one end of a string upon which it may be made to spin up and down 2. [Slang] a stupid person

yr. 1. year(s) 2. younger 3. your

yrs. 1. years 2. yours

yt·ter·bi·um (i tur′bē əm) *n.* [< *Ytterby*, Sweden] a scarce, silvery metallic chemical element of the rare-earth group: symbol, Yb; at. wt., 173.04; at. no., 70

yt·tri·um (it′rē əm) *n.* [< *Ytterby*, Sweden] a rare, silvery metallic chemical element: symbol, Y; at. wt., 88.905; at. no., 39

yu·an (yōō än′) *n.* [Chin. *yüan*, round] the basic monetary unit of China

Yu·ca·tán, Yu·ca·tan (yōō′kä tän′; *E.* yōō′kə tan′) peninsula of S North America extending into the Gulf of Mexico

yuc·ca (yuk′ə) *n.* [< Sp. *yuca*] 1. a plant of the U.S. and Latin America with stiff leaves and white flowers in an erect raceme 2. its flower

Yu·go·sla·vi·a (yōō′gō slä′vē ə, -gə släv′yə) country in the Balkans, on the Adriatic: 98,766 sq. mi.; pop. 20,672,000; cap. Belgrade —**Yu′go·slav′, Yu′go·sla′·vi·an** *adj., n.*

yuk (yuk) *n.* [echoic] [Slang] a loud laugh of amusement, or something evoking such a laugh —*vi.* **yukked, yuk′king** [Slang] to laugh loudly Also sp. **yuck**

Yu·kon (yōō′kän) 1. territory of NW Canada: 207,076 sq. mi.; pop. 14,000; cap. Whitehorse: abbrev. Y.T. 2. river flowing through this territory & Alas. into the Bering Sea: 1,979 mi.

YUCCA

yule (yōōl) *n.* [OE. *geol*] Christmas or the Christmas season

yule log a large log formerly used as a foundation for the ceremonial Christmas Eve fire

yule′tide (-tīd′) *n.* Christmas time

yum·my (yum′ē) *adj.* **-mi·er, -mi·est** [echoic] [Colloq.] very tasty; delectable; delicious

YWCA, Y.W.C.A. Young Women's Christian Association

YWHA, Y.W.H.A. Young Women's Hebrew Association

Z, z (zē; *Brit. & Canad.* zed) *n., pl.* **Z's, z's** the twenty-sixth and last letter of the English alphabet

Za·ire, Za·ïre (zä ir′) 1. country in C Africa: 905,563 sq. mi.; pop. 22,477,000; cap. Kinshasa 2. *same as* CONGO (River)

Zam·be·zi (zam bē′zē) river in S Africa, flowing into the Indian Ocean: c.1,600 mi.

Zam·bi·a (zam′bē ə) country in S Africa: 290,323 sq. mi.; pop. 4,336,000; cap. Lusaka

za·ny (zā′nē) *n., pl.* **-nies** [< It. *zanni* < *Giovanni*, John] 1. a clown 2. a silly or foolish person —*adj.* **-ni·er, -ni·est** 1. comical in a crazy way 2. foolish —**za′ni·ly** *adv.* —**za′·ni·ness** *n.*

Zan·zi·bar (zan′zə bär′) 1. group of islands off the E coast of Africa, constituting a part of Tanzania 2. largest island of this group

zap (zap) *vt., vi.* **zapped, zap′ping** [echoic] [Slang] to move, strike, stun, kill, etc. with sudden speed and force —*n.* [Slang] energy, verve, etc. —*interj.* an exclamation used to express sudden, swift action

Zar·a·thus·tra (zar′ə thōōs′trə) *Persian name of* ZOROASTER

zeal (zēl) *n.* [< Gr. *zēlos*] eagerness; enthusiasm

zeal·ot (zel′ət) *n.* one who is zealous, esp. to an excessive degree; fanatic —**zeal′ot·ry** *n.*

zeal·ous (zel′əs) *adj.* full of or showing zeal; enthusiastic —**zeal′ous·ly** *adv.* —**zeal′ous·ness** *n.*

ze·bec, ze·beck (zē′bek) *n. same as* XEBEC

ze·bra (zē′brə) *n.* [Port., prob. ult. < L.] a swift African mammal related to the horse, with dark stripes on a light body

ze·bu (zē′byōō) *n.* [Fr. *zébu*] an ox-like domestic animal of Asia and Africa: it has a large hump and short, curving horns

ZEBRA
(4 1 1/2 ft. high at shoulder)

Zech·a·ri·ah (zek′ə rī′ə) *Bible* 1. a Hebrew prophet of the 6th cent. B.C. 2. the book containing his prophecies: abbrev. Zech.

zed (zed) *n.* [< Gr. *zēta*] *Brit. & usual Canad. name for the letter* Z, z

‡**Zeit·geist** (tsīt′gīst′) *n.* [G., time spirit] the trend of thought and feeling in a period

Zen (zen) *n.* [Jpn., ult. < Sans. *dhyana*, meditation] 1. a Japanese Buddhist sect that seeks enlightenment through meditation and intuition rather than in scripture 2. the beliefs of this sect

ze·nith (zē′nith; *Brit.* zen′ith) *n.* [< Ar. *semt*, road] 1. the point in the sky directly overhead 2. the highest point; peak

Ze·no (zē′nō) 334?–261? B.C.; Gr. philosopher: founder of Stoicism

Zeph·a·ni·ah (zef′ə nī′ə) *Bible* 1. a Hebrew prophet of the 7th cent. B.C. 2. the book containing his prophecies: abbrev. Zeph.

zeph·yr (zef′ər) *n.* [< Gr. *zephyros*] 1. the west wind 2. a soft, gentle breeze 3. a fine, soft, lightweight yarn, cloth, or garment

zep·pe·lin (zep′ə lin, zep′lin) *n.* [< F. von *Zeppelin* (1838–1917), G. inventor] [*often* Z-] a type of dirigible airship designed around 1900

ze·ro (zir′ō, zē′rō) *n., pl.* **-ros, -roes** [< Ar. *sifr*, CIPHER] 1. the symbol 0; cipher; naught 2. the point, marked 0, from which quantities are reckoned on a graduated scale, as on thermometers 3. nothing 4. the lowest point —*adj.* 1. of or at zero 2. with visibility limited to very short distances, as in flying —**zero in** 1. to adjust the sight settings of (a rifle) by calibrated firing on a standard range 2. to aim (a gun or guns) directly at (a target) —**zero in on** 1. to aim gunfire directly at (a target) 2. to concentrate on

zero gravity a condition of weightlessness

zero hour the time set for beginning an attack, etc.; crucial point

zest (zest) *n.* [Fr. *zeste*, orange peel] 1. something that gives flavor or relish 2. stimulating or exciting quality; piquancy 3. keen enjoyment [*zest for life*] —**zest′ful** *adj.*

ze·ta (zāt′ə, zēt′ə) *n.* the sixth letter of the Greek alphabet (Z, ζ)

Zeus (zōōs) the supreme deity of the ancient Greeks, son of Cronus and Rhea and husband of Hera

zig·zag (zig′zag′) *n.* [Fr.] 1. a series of short, sharp angles in alternate directions, as in a line or course 2. a design, path, etc. having such a series —*adj.* having the form of a zigzag —*adv.* in a zigzag course —*vt.*, *vi.* **-zagged', -zag'- ging** to move or form in a zigzag

zil·lion (zil′yən) *n.* [arbitrary coinage, after MILLION] [Colloq.] a very large, indefinite number

zinc (ziŋk) *n.* [G. *zink*] a bluish-white metallic chemical element, used in various alloys, as a protective coating for iron, etc.: symbol, Zn; at. wt., 65.37; at. no., 30

zinc ointment an ointment containing zinc oxide

zinc oxide a white powder, ZnO, used in making glass, paints, cosmetics, ointments, etc.

zing (ziŋ) *n.* [echoic] [Slang] **1.** a shrill, high-pitched whizzing sound **2.** vitality; zest

zin·ni·a (zin′ē ə, zin′yə) *n.* [< J. *Zinn*, 18th-c. G. botanist] an annual plant of N. and S. America, with colorful, composite flowers

Zi·on (zī′ən) **1.** the hill in Jerusalem on which the Temple was built **2.** the land of Israel **3.** the Jewish people **4.** heaven

Zi′on·ism (-iz′m) *n.* a movement formerly for reestablishing, now for supporting, the Jewish national state of Israel —**Zi′on·ist** *n.*, *adj.*

zip (zip) *n.* [echoic] **1.** a short, sharp hissing sound, as of a passing bullet **2.** [Colloq.] energy; vim —*vi.* **zipped, zip′- ping 1.** to make, or move with, a zip **2.** [Colloq.] to move with speed **3.** to become fastened or unfastened by a zipper —*vt.* to fasten or unfasten with a zipper

ZIP code (zip) [*z*(*oning*) *i*(*mprovement*) *p*(*lan*)] a system devised to speed mail deliveries, under which a code number is assigned to individual areas and places

zip·per (zip′ər) *n.* **1.** one that zips **2.** a device used to fasten and unfasten two edges of material: it has two rows of interlocking tabs worked by a part that slides up and down

zip′py *adj.* **-pi·er, -pi·est** [Colloq.] full of vim and energy; brisk; snappy

zir·con (zur′kän) *n.* [< Per. *zar*, gold] a crystalline silicate of zirconium, colored yellow, brown, red, etc.: transparent varieties are used as gems

zir·co·ni·um (zər kō′nē əm) *n.* [see ZIRCON] a soft gray or black metallic chemical element used in alloys, ceramics, etc.: symbol, Zr; at. wt., 91.22; at. no., 40

zith·er (zith′ər, zith′-) *n.* [< Gr. *kithara*, lute] a musical instrument with 30 to 40 strings stretched across a flat sounding board and played with a plectrum and the fingers

zlo·ty (zlô′tē) *n.*, *pl.* **-tys** [< Pol., lit., golden] the monetary unit of Poland

Zn *Chem.* zinc

zo·di·ac (zō′dē ak′) *n.* [< Gr. *zōdiakos* (*kyklos*), (circle) of

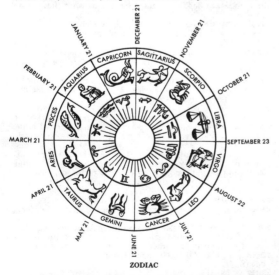

ZODIAC

animals] **1.** an imaginary belt in the heavens extending on either side of the apparent path of the sun and including the paths of the moon and the principal planets: it is divided into twelve equal parts, or signs, named for constellations **2.** a diagram representing this —**zo·di′a·cal** (-dī′ə k'l) *adj.*

Zo·la (zô lä′; *E.* zō′lə), **É·mile** (ā mēl′) 1840–1902; Fr. novelist

zom·bie (zäm′bē) *n.* [of Afr. origin] **1.** in West Indian superstition, a reanimated corpse who moves as he is ordered: also sp. **zom′bi 2.** [Slang] *a*) a person who acts half dead *b*) a weird or eccentric person

zone (zōn) *n.* [< Gr. *zōnē*] **1.** an encircling band, stripe, etc. **2.** any of the five great latitudinal divisions of the earth's surface: see TORRID ZONE, TEMPERATE ZONE, and FRIGID ZONE **3.** any region or district with reference to a particular use, limitation, etc. [a canal *zone*, postal *zone*, residential *zone*] **4.** *Sports* any of the sections into which a playing area is divided —*vt.* **zoned, zon′ing 1.** to divide (a city, etc.) into areas determined by specific restrictions **2.** to encircle —**zon′al** *adj.*

zoo (zōō) *n.* [< ZOO(LOGICAL GARDEN)] a place where a collection of wild animals is kept for public showing

zoo- [< Gr. *zōion*, animal] *a combining form meaning* animal, animals: also **zoö-, zo-**

zo·oid (zō′oid) *n.* [ZO(O)- + -OID] **1.** an independent animal organism produced by nonsexual methods, as by fission **2.** any of the distinct individuals of a compound organism, as the coral —*adj.* of or having the nature of an animal: also **zo·oi′dal**

zool. 1. zoological **2.** zoology

zoological garden *same as* ZOO

zo·ol·o·gy (zō äl′ə jē) *n.* [see ZOO- & -LOGY] the science that deals with animals and animal life —**zo′o·log′i·cal** (-ə läj′i k'l) *adj.* —**zo·ol′o·gist** *n.*

zoom (zōōm) *vi.* [echoic] **1.** to make a loud buzzing noise **2.** to climb sharply: said of an airplane **3.** to rise rapidly [prices *zoomed*] **4.** to focus with a zoom lens —*vt.* to cause to zoom —*n.* **1.** a zooming **2.** a zooming sound

zoom lens a system of lenses, as in a TV camera, that can be rapidly adjusted for close or distant shots while keeping the image in focus

zo·o·phyte (zō′ə fīt′) *n.* [< Gr. *zōion*, animal + *phyton*, plant] any animal, as a coral or sponge, that looks and grows somewhat like a plant —**zo′o·phyt′ic** (-fit′ik) *adj.*

zo·o·spore (zō′ə spôr′) *n. Bot.* an asexual spore, as of certain fungi, capable of independent motion as by means of cilia or flagella

zo·ri (zôr′ē) *n.*, *pl.* **-ris, -ri** [Jpn.] a sandal of Japanese style, with a thong between the big toe and the toe next to it

Zo·ro·as·ter (zō′rō as′tər) ? 6th or 7th cent. B.C.; Per. founder of Zoroastrianism

Zo′ro·as′tri·an·ism (-trē ən iz′m) *n.* the religion of the ancient Persians, teaching the eventual triumph of the spirit of good over the spirit of evil

Zou·ave (zōō äv′, zwäv) *n.* [< Ar. *Zwāwa*, an Algerian tribe] **1.** a member of a former French infantry unit with colorful Oriental uniforms **2.** a member of any military group having similar uniforms

zounds (zoundz) *interj.* [altered < oath *God's wounds*] [Archaic] a mild oath

zoy·si·a (zoi′sē ə) *n.* [< Karl von *Zois*, 18th-c. G. botanist] a lawn grass used in warm, dry regions

Zr *Chem.* zirconium

zuc·chi·ni (zōō kē′nē) *n.*, *pl.* **-ni, -nis** [It., dim. of *zucca*, gourd] a green-skinned summer squash shaped somewhat like a cucumber

Zui·der Zee, Zuy·der Zee (zī′dər zē′) a former arm of the North Sea extending into the Netherlands: it was shut off by dikes and is partly reclaimed

Zu·lu (zōō′lōō) *n.* **1.** *pl.* **-lus, -lu** any member of a people living in Natal, South Africa **2.** their Bantu language —*adj.* of the Zulus, their language, etc.

Zu·ñi (zōōn′yē) *n.* [AmSp. < AmInd.] **1.** *pl.* **-ñis, -ñi** any member of a pueblo-dwelling Indian tribe of New Mexico **2.** their language

Zur·ich (zoor′ik) city in N Switzerland: pop. 428,000: also written **Zürich**

zwie·back (swē′bak, swī′-, zwī′-; -bäk) *n.* [G. < *zwie-*, twice + *backen*, bake] a kind of rusk or biscuit that is sliced and toasted after baking

Zwing·li (tsviŋ′lē; *E.* zwiŋ′glē), **Ul·rich** (ool′rikh) 1484–1531; Swiss Protestant reformer

zy·gote (zī′gōt, zig′ōt) *n.* [< Gr. *zygon*, a yoke] a cell formed by the union of male and female gametes; fertilized egg cell

zyme (zim) *n.* [Gr. *zymē*, a leaven] [Obs.] a ferment or enzyme

zymo- [< Gr. *zymē*, a leaven] *a combining form meaning* fermentation: also **zym-**

zy·mur·gy (zī′mər jē) *n.* [ZYM(O)- + -URGY] the chemistry of fermentation, as applied in brewing, etc.

COMMON GIVEN NAMES

MEN'S NAMES

Aar·on (er′ən, ar′-) [LL. < Gr. < Heb. *aharōn*, the exalted one]
A·bel (ā′b'l) [L. < Gr. < Heb. *hebel*, breath]
Ab·ner (ab′nər) [L. < Heb. *'abnēr*, the father is a light]
A·bra·ham (ā′brə ham′) [Heb., father of many]
Ad·am (ad′əm) [Heb. < *ādām*, a human being]
Ad·olph (ad′älf, ā′dôlf) [< L. < OHG. *adal*, nobility + *wolf*, wolf]
Al·an (al′ən) [ML. *Alanus*, of Breton origin] see *Allan*
Al·bert (al′bərt) [Fr. < OHG. *Adalbrecht*, lit., bright through nobility] see *Elbert* & fem. *Alberta*
Al·ex·an·der (al′ig zan′dər) [L. < Gr. *alexein*, to defend + *anēr* (gen. *andrōs*), man] see fem. *Alexandra*
Al·fred (al′frid) [OE. *Aelfred*, lit., wise counselor]
Al·ger·non (al′jər nən) [prob. < OFr. *al grenon*, with a mustache]
Al·lan, Al·len (al′ən) var. of ALAN
Al·o·ys·i·us (al′ə wish′əs) [< ML.: see LOUIS]
Al·vin (al′vin) [G. *alwin*, noble friend]
Am·brose (am′brōz) [< L. < Gr. *ambrotos*, immortal]
A·mos (ā′məs) [Heb. *'āmōs*, borne (by God?)]
An·drew (an′drōō) [OFr. < L. < Gr. *andreios*, manly < *anēr* (gen. *andrōs*), man] see fem. *Andrea*
An·gus (aŋ′gəs) [< Gael. & Ir. *aon*, one]
An·tho·ny (an′thə nē, -tə-) [< L. *Antonius*, name of a Roman gens] see *Antony*, *Tony* & fem. *Antonia*
An·to·ny (an′tə nē) var. of ANTHONY
Ar·chi·bald (är′chə bôld′) [of Gmc. origin, prob. nobly bold]
Ar·nold (är′nəld) [G. < Gmc. *aran*, eagle + *wald*, power]
Ar·thur (är′thər) [ML. *Arthurus*]
A·sa (ās′ə) [Heb. *āsā*, healer]
Au·brev (ô′brē) [< Fr. < OHG. *alb*, elf + *rihhi*, ruler]
Au·gus·tine (ô′gəs tēn, ô gus′t'n) [< L. dim. of *Augustus*]
Au·gus·tus (ô gus′təs) [L. < *augustus*, consecrated] see fem. *Augusta*
Aus·tin (ôs′tən) var. of AUGUSTINE

Bar·nard (bär′nərd) var. of BERNARD
Bar·thol·o·mew (bär thäl′ə myōō′) [< LL. < Gr. *Bartholomaios* < Aram., lit., son of Talmai]
Bas·il (baz′'l, bā′z'l) [< L. < Gr. *basileus*, king]
Ben·e·dict (ben′ə dikt′) [L. *Benedictus*, lit., blessed]
Ben·ja·min (ben′jə mən) [Heb. *binyāmīn*, favorite son]
Ben·nett (ben′it) var. of BENEDICT
Ber·nard (bər närd′, bur′nərd) [Fr. < OHG. < *bero*, a bear + *hart*, bold] see *Barnard*
Ber·tram (bur′trəm) [G. < OHG. < *beraht*, bright + *hraban*, a raven]
Ber·trand (bur′trənd) var. of BERTRAM
Bill (bil) dim. of WILLIAM
Bob (bäb) dim. of ROBERT
Bor·is (bôr′is) [Russ., lit., fight]
Bri·an (brī′ən) [Celt., ? strong] see *Bryan*
Bruce (brōōs) [Scot. < Fr. *Brieuse*, place in France]
Bru·no (brōō′nō) [OHG. < *brun*, brown]
Bry·an (brī′ən) var. of BRIAN
By·ron (bī′rən) [< Fr. < *Biron*, district in France]

Ca·leb (kā′ləb) [Heb. *kālēb*, dog; hence, faithful]
Cal·vin (kal′vin) [< Fr., prob. < L. *calvus*, bald]
Carl (kärl) var. of CHARLES
Ce·cil (sēs′'l, ses′'l) [< L., prob. < *caecus*, blind] see fem. *Cecilia*
Ced·ric (sed′rik, sē′drik) [< ? Celt]
Charles (chärlz) [Fr. < ML. *Carolus* or Gmc. *Karl*, lit., full-grown] see *Carl* & fem. *Caroline*, *Charlotte*
Ches·ter (ches′tər) [OE. *Ceastre*, ult. < L. *legionum castra*, camp of the legions]
Chris·tian (kris′chən) [< OE. < LL.(Ec.) < Gr. < *christos*, the anointed] see fem. *Christiana*
Chris·to·pher (kris′tə fər) [< LL.(Ec.) < Gr.(Ec.) *Christophorus*, lit., bearing Christ]
Clar·ence (klar′əns) [< *Clare*, English town]
Clark (klärk) [< OE. & OFr. *clerc*, clerk < LL.(Ec.) *clericus* < Gr. *klērikos*, priest]

Claude (klôd) [Fr. < L. *Claudius*, prob. < *claudus*, lame] see fem. *Claudia*
Clem·ent (klem′ənt) [< L. < *clemens*, mild, gentle] see fem. *Clementine*
Clif·ford (klif′ərd) [< CLIFF + FORD; hence, ford at the cliff]
Clif·ton (klif′tən) [< CLIFF + -ton, town; hence, town at a cliff]
Clin·ton (klin′t'n) [< ? ME. *clint*, cliff + OE. *tun*, town]
Clive (klīv) [< the surname]
Clyde (klīd) [? < name of Scot. river]
Co·lin (kō′lin, käl′in) [prob. < L. *columba*, dove]
Con·rad (kän′rad) [< G. or Fr. < OHG. < *kuon*, bold, wise + *rat*, counsel]
Cor·nel·ius (kôr nēl′yəs) [L., name of a Roman gens] see fem. *Cornelia*
Craig (krāg) [prob. < W. *craig*, crag]
Cur·tis (kur′tis) [< OFr. *corteis*, courteous]
Cy·rus (sī′rəs) [L. < Gr. *Kyros* < OPer. *Kūrush*]

Dale (dāl) [prob. < OE. *dæl*, valley]
Dan·iel (dan′yəl) [Heb. *dāni·ēl*, God is my judge]
Da·vid (dā′vid) [Heb. *dāvīd*, beloved]
Den·is, Den·nis (den′is) [Fr. < L. *Dionysius* < Gr. *Dionysos*, god of wine]
Dex·ter (dek′stər) [< L. *dexter*, right, to the right]
Dick (dik) dim. of RICHARD
Dom·i·nic, Dom·i·nick (däm′ə nik) [< L. *dominus*, lord]
Don·ald (dän′ld) [Ir. *Donghal*, lit., brown stranger (or ? Gael. *Domhnall*, lit., world ruler)]
Doug·las (dug′ləs) [< Gael., lit., black stream]
Dun·can (duŋ′kən) [Gael. *Donnchadh*, lit., brown warrior]
Dwight (dwīt) [< the surname]

Earl, Earle (url) [< OE. *eorl*, warrior]
Ear·nest (ur′nist) var. of ERNEST
Eb·en·e·zer (eb′ə nē′zər) [Heb. *eben-ha-'ēzer*, stone of help]
Ed·gar (ed′gər) [< OE. *ead*, riches + *gar*, a spear]
Ed·mund, Ed·mond (ed′mənd) [< OE. *ead*, riches + *mund*, protection; hence, wealthy protector]
Ed·ward (ed′wərd) [< OE. *ead*, riches + *weard*, guardian; hence, wealthy guardian]
Ed·win (ed′win) [< OE. *ead*, riches + *wine*, friend; lit., wealthy friend]
El·bert (el′bərt) var. of ALBERT
E·li (ē′lī) [Heb. *'ēlī*, high]
El·i·ot, El·li·ot, El·li·ott (el′ē ət) [dim. of ELLIS]
El·mer (el′mər) [? < OE. *æthel*, noble, or *ege*, awe + *mære*, famous]
Em·er·y, Em·or·y (em′ər ē) [prob. < OFr. < OHG. *Amalrich*, lit., work ruler]
E·mil (ā′m'l, ē′-; em′'l) [G. < Fr. < L. *aemulus*, trying to excel] see fem. *Emily*
Em·man·u·el, E·man·u·el (i man′yoo wəl) [< Gr. < Heb. *'immānūēl*, God with us] see *Manuel*
Er·ic (er′ik) [Scand. < ON. *Eirikr*, lit., honorable ruler]
Er·nest (ur′nəst) [< G. < OHG. *Ernust*, lit., resolute < *ernust*, seriousness] see *Earnest* & fem. *Ernestine*
Er·win (ur′win) [G. < OHG. *hari*, host, crowd + *wini*, friend] see *Irwin*
E·than (ē′thən) [LL.(Ec.) < Heb. *ēthān*, strength]
Eu·gene (yoo jēn′, yōō′jēn) [< Fr. < L. < Gr. *eugenēs*, well-born] see *Gene*
Eus·tace (yōōs′təs) [< OFr. < L. < Gr. *eustachys*, fruitful]
Ev·an (ev′ən) [W., var. of JOHN]
Ev·er·ett (ev′ər it, ev′rit) [< Du. < OFr. < OHG. *ebur*, wild boar + *harto*, strong]
Ez·ra (ez′rə) [LL.(Ec.) < Heb. *ezrā*, help]

Fe·lix (fē′liks) [L., lit., happy]
Fer·di·nand (fur′d'n and′) [Fr.; prob. < Gmc. bases meaning "bold in peace"]
Floyd (floid) var. of LLOYD
Fran·cis (fran′sis) [< OFr. < ML. *Franciscus* < Gmc. *Franco*, a Frank; hence, free man] see *Frank* & fem. *Frances*

Frank (fraŋk) dim. of FRANCIS
Frank·lin (fraŋk′lin) [< Anglo-Fr. < ML. *francus* < LL. *Francus*, a Frank; hence, free man]
Fred·er·ick, Fred·er·ic (fred′rik, -ər ik) [< Fr. < G. < OHG. *Fridurih*, lit., peaceful ruler] see fem. *Frederica*

Ga·bri·el (gā′brē əl) [Heb. *gabhrī′ēl*, God is (my) strength] see fem. *Gabriella*
Gene (jēn) dim. of EUGENE
Geof·frey (jef′rē) [< OFr. < Gmc. < ? *ga-*, district + *frithu*, peace] see *Jeffrey*
George (jôrj) [< Fr. < LL. < Gr. < *geōrgos*, husbandman] see fem. *Georgia, Georgina*
Ger·ald (jer′əld) [< OFr. < OHG. < *ger*, spear + base of *waldan*, to rule] see fem. *Geraldine*
Ger·ard (jə rärd′) [< OFr. < OHG. < *ger*, spear + *hart*, hard]
Gil·bert (gil′bərt) [< OFr. < OHG. < *willo*, will, wish + *beraht*, bright]
Glenn, Glen (glen) [Celt., lit., valley]
God·frey (gäd′frē) [< OFr. < OHG. < *god*, God + *fridu*, peace; hence, peace (of) God]
Gor·don (gôr′d'n) [< the surname]
Gra·ham (grā′əm) [< the surname]
Grant (grant) [< the surname]
Greg·o·ry (greg′ər ē) [< LL. < Gr. *Grēgorios*, lit., vigilant]
Gus·ta·vus (gəs tā′vəs, -tä′-) [< G. *Gustav* or Sw. *Gustaf*, lit., prob., staff of the Goths]
Guy (gī) [Fr. *Gui, Guy*, lit., leader]

Har·old (har′əld) [< ON. *Haraldr*, lit., leader of the army]
Har·ry (har′ē) var. of HENRY: see fem. *Harriet*
Har·vey (här′vē) [< Fr. < OHG. *Herewig*, lit., army battle]
Hec·tor (hek′tər) [L. < Gr. *hektōr*, lit., holding fast]
Hen·ry (hen′rē) [Fr. < G. < OHG. *Haganrih*, lit., ruler of an enclosure & also < OHG. *Heimerich*, lit., home ruler] see *Harry* & fem. *Henrietta*
Her·bert (hur′bərt) [OE. *Herebeorht*, lit., bright army]
Her·man (hur′mən) [< G. < OHG. < *heri*, army + *man*, man]
Hi·ram (hī′rəm) [Heb. *ḥīrām*, prob. < *'aḥīrām*, exalted brother]
Ho·mer (hō′mər) [< L. < Gr. < *homēros*, a hostage, one led, hence, blind]
Hor·ace (hôr′is, här′-) var. of HORATIO
Ho·ra·ti·o (hə rā′shō, -shē ō; hô-) [< L. *Horatius*, name of a Roman gens] see *Horace*
How·ard (hou′ərd) [< the surname]
Hu·bert (hyōō′bərt) [Fr. < OHG. < *hugu*, mind, spirit + *beraht*, bright]
Hugh (hyōō) [< OFr. < OHG. *Hugo*, prob. < *hugu*, heart, mind] see *Hugo*
Hu·go (hyōō′gō) var. of HUGH
Hum·phrey, Hum·phry (hum′frē) [< OE. *Hunfrith*, lit., strength in peace]

Ig·na·ti·us (ig nā′shəs) [L. < Gr. *Ignatios*]
Im·man·u·el (i man′yoo wəl) [Heb. *'immānūēl*, God with us] see *Manuel*
I·ra (ī′rə) [Heb. *'īrā*, watchful]
Ir·ving (ur′viŋ) [< the surname]
Ir·win (ur′win) var. of ERWIN
I·saac (ī′zək) [< LL.(Ec.) < Gr.(Ec.) < Heb. *yitsḥāq*, laughter]
Is·i·dore, Is·i·dor, Is·a·dore, Is·a·dor (iz′ə dôr′) [< G. or Fr. < L. < Gr. < *Isis*, Isis + *dōron*, gift; hence, gift of Isis] see fem. *Isadora*
I·van (ī′vən) [Russ. < Gr. *Iōannēs*: see JOHN]

Jack (jak) [< OFr. *Jaques* < LL.(Ec.) *Jacobus*, JACOB] dim. of JOHN
Ja·cob (jā′kəb) [< LL.(Ec.) < Gr. < Heb. *ja'aqob*, Jacob, lit., seizing by the heel] see *James*
James (jāmz) var. of JACOB: see *Jim*
Ja·son (jās′'n) [< L. < Gr. *Iāson*, lit., healer]
Jas·per (jas′pər) [OFr. *Jaspar* < ?]
Jay (jā) [< the surname]
Jeff·rey (jef′rē) var. of GEOFFREY
Jer·e·mi·ah (jer′ə mī′ə) [< LL.(Ec.) < Gr.(Ec.) < Heb. *yirmeyāh*, the Lord loosens (i.e., from the womb)] see *Jeremy*
Jer·e·my (jer′ə mē) var. of JEREMIAH
Je·rome (jə rōm′) [< Fr. < L. < Gr. < *hieros*, holy + *onyma*, name]

Jes·se (jes′ē) [Heb. *yīshai*]
Jim (jim) dim. of JAMES
Joe (jō) dim. of JOSEPH
Jo·el (jō′əl) [LL.(Ec.) < Gr.(Ec.) < Heb. *yō'ēl*, the Lord is God]
John (jän) [< OFr. < ML. *Johannes* < Gr.(Ec.) *Iōannes* < Heb. *yehōhānān*, Yahweh is gracious] see *Ivan, Jack* & fem. *Jane, Jean, Jeanne, Joan, Joanna, Johanna*
Jo·nah (jō′nə) [< LL.(Ec.) < Gr.(Ec.) < Heb. *yōnāh*, a dove] see *Jonas*
Jo·nas (jō′nəs) var. of JONAH
Jon·a·than (jän′ə thən) [< Heb. *yehōnāthān*, Yahweh has given]
Jo·seph (jō′zəf, -səf) [LL.(Ec.) < Gr.(Ec.) < Heb. *yōsēph*, may he add] see *Joe* & fem. *Josephine*
Josh·u·a (jäsh′oo wə) [Heb. *yehōshū'a*, help of Jehovah]
Ju·dah (jōō′də) [Heb. *yehūdhāh* < ?] see fem. *Judith*
Jules (jōōlz) var. of JULIUS
Jul·ian (jōōl′yən) [< L. *Julius*: see JULIUS] see fem. *Juliana*
Jul·ius (jōōl′yəs) [L., name of a Roman gens] see *Jules* & fem. *Julia*
Jun·ius (jōōn′yəs) [L., name of a Roman gens] see fem. *June*

Keith (kēth) [Scot. < Gael. base meaning "the wind"]
Ken·neth (ken′ith) [Scot. < Gael. *Caioneach*, lit., handsome]
Kev·in (kev′in) [< Ir. < OIr. *Coemgen*, lit., comely birth]

Lance (lans) dim. of LANCELOT
Lan·ce·lot (lan′sə lät′, län′-) [Fr. < OHG. *lant*, land] see *Lance*
Lar·ry (lar′ē) dim. of LAURENCE
Lau·rence, Law·rence (lôr′əns, lär′-) [< L., prob. < *laurus*, laurel] see *Larry* & fem. *Laura*
Lee (lē) var. of LEIGH
Leigh (lē) [< OE. *leah*, meadow] see *Lee*
Len (len) dim. of LEONARD
Le·o (lē′ō) [L. < Gr. *leōn*, lion] see *Leon, Lionel* & fem. *Leona*
Le·on (lē′än) var. of LEO
Leon·ard (len′ərd) [< Fr. < OFr. < OHG. < *lewo*, lion + *hart*, strong; hence, strong as a lion]
Le·o·pold (lē′ə pōld′) [G. < OHG. < *liut*, people (orig., prob., free man) + *balt*, strong, bold]
Le·roy (lə roi′, lē′roi) [< Fr. *le roi*, the king]
Les·lie (les′lē, lez′-) [< the surname, orig. place name]
Les·ter (les′tər) [< *Leicester*, Eng. city]
Lew·is (lōō′is) var. of LOUIS
Lin·coln (liŋ′kən) [prob. < *Lincoln*, Eng. city]
Li·o·nel (lī′ə n'l, -nel′) [Fr., dim. of *lion*, lion] var. of LEO
Llew·el·lyn (loo wel′ən) [W. *Llewelyn*, lit., prob., lionlike]
Lloyd (loid) [W. *Llwyd*, lit., gray] see *Floyd*
Lou·is (lōō′is, -ē) [Fr., prob. ult. from Gmc. bases meaning "famous in war"] see *Lewis* & fem. *Louise*
Low·ell (lō′əl) [< the surname]
Lu·cius (lōō′shəs) [L. < *lux*, light] see fem. *Lucia*
Luke (lōōk) [< LL.(Ec.) < Gr.(Ec.) *Loukas*, prob. contr. of *Loukanos*]
Lu·ther (lōō′thər) [G. < Gmc. bases meaning "famous fighter"]
Lyle (līl) [< Brit. place name & surname]

Mal·colm (mal′kəm) [Celt. *Maolcolm*, lit., servant of (St.) Columba]
Man·u·el (man′yoo wəl) var. of EMMANUEL, IMMANUEL
Mar·cus (mär′kəs) [L. < *Mars*, the god of war] see *Mark* & fem. *Marcia*
Mar·i·on (mar′ē ən, mer′-) [Fr., orig. dim. of *Marie, Mary*]
Mark (märk) var. of MARCUS
Mar·shal, Mar·shall (mär′shəl) [< OFr. < Frank. *marhskalk* or OHG. *marahscalh*, horse servant]
Mar·tin (mär′t'n) [Fr. < L. < *Mars*, the god of war; hence, lit., warlike]
Mar·vin (mär′vin) [prob. ult. < Gmc. bases meaning "sea" & "friend"] see *Mervin*
Mat·thew (math′yōō) [< OFr. < LL.(Ec.) < Gr.(Ec.) < Heb. *mattīthyāh*, gift of God]
Mau·rice (môr′is, mär′-; mô rēs′) [Fr. < LL. *Maurus*, a Moor] see *Morris*
Max (maks) var. of MAXIMILIAN: see fem. *Maxine*
Max·i·mil·ian (mak′sə mil′yən) [? a blend of the L. names *Maximus* & *Aemilianus*] see *Max*
May·nard (mā′nərd, -närd) [< Anglo-Fr. < OHG. < *magan*, power + *hart*, strong]

Mel·vin (mel′vin) [< ? OE. *mæl*, council + *wine*, friend]
Merle (murl) [Fr., prob. < L. *merulus*, blackbird]
Mer·lin (mur′lin) [< ML. < W. *Myrrdin*, lit., sea-hill]
Mer·vin, Mer·vyn (mur′vin) var. of MARVIN
Mi·chael (mī′k′l) [LL.(Ec.) < Gr.(Ec.) < Heb. *mīkhā′ēl*, who is like God?] see *Mike*
Mike (mīk) dim. of MICHAEL
Miles (mīlz) [< OFr. < OHG. *Milo*, lit., peaceful]
Mil·ton (mil′t′n) [< the surname or place name]
Mon·roe (mən rō′) [< the surname]
Mor·gan (môr′gən) [W., lit., sea dweller]
Mor·ris (môr′is, mär′-) var. of MAURICE
Mor·ti·mer (môr′tə mər) [< Norm. surname]
Mor·ton (môr′t′n) [orig. surname & place name < OE. *mor*, swamp + *tun*, town]
Mo·ses (mō′ziz) [LL.(Ec.) < Gr.(Ec.) < Heb., prob. < Egypt. *mes, mesu*, child]
Mur·ray (mur′ē) [< the surname]
My·ron (mī′rən) [prob. < Gr. *Myrōn*]

Na·than (nā′thən) [Heb. *nāthān*, gift]
Na·than·a·el, Na·than·i·el (nə than′yəl, -ē əl) [LL.(Ec.) < Gr.(Ec.) < Heb. *nēthan′ēl*, gift of God]
Neal, Neil (nēl) [prob. < Ir. *niadh*, a champion]
Ned (ned) [by faulty division of *mine Ed*]
Nel·son (nel′s′n) [< the surname]
Nev·il, Nev·ille (nev′′l) [< Norm. surname < *Neuville*, town in Normandy]
New·ton (nōōt′′n, nyōōt′′n) [orig. surname < place name < OE. *neowa tun*, new town]
Nich·o·las, Nic·o·las (nik′′l əs) [< OFr. < L. < Gr. < *nikē*, victory + *laos*, the people]
No·ah (nō′ə) [Heb. *nōah*, rest, comfort]
No·el (nō′əl) [OFr. *No(u)el*, lit., natal: see fem. NATALIE]
Nor·man (nôr′mən) [< OE. *Northman*, OHG. *Nordemann*, lit., Northman]

Ol·i·ver (äl′ə vər) [Fr. *Olivier*, prob. < MLowG. < *alf*, elf + *hari*, army]
Or·lan·do (ôr lan′dō) var. of ROLAND
Or·son (ôr′s′n) [< Fr. dim. of *ours*, a bear (< L. *ursus*)]
Os·car (äs′kər) [< OE. < *os*, a god + *gar*, a spear]
Os·wald, Os·wold (äz′wôld, -wəld) [< OE. < *os*, a god + *weald*, power]
Ot·to (ät′ō) [< OHG. < *auda*, rich]
Ow·en (ō′ən) [W. < Celt. word akin to Gr. *Eugenios* (< *eugenēs*, well-born)]

Pat·rick (pat′rik) [L. *patricius*, a patrician] see fem. *Patricia*
Paul (pôl) [L. *Paulus*, a Roman surname, prob. < *paulus*, small] see fem. *Paula, Pauline*
Per·ci·val, Per·ce·val (pur′sə v′l) [< OFr., prob. < *perce val*, pierce valley] see *Percy*
Per·cy (pur′sē) dim. of PERCIVAL
Per·ry (per′ē) [? < Fr. < L. *Petrus*, PETER]
Pe·ter (pēt′ər) [LL.(Ec.) < Gr. *petra*, a rock]
Phil·ip, Phil·lip (fil′əp) [< L. < Gr. < *philos*, loving + *hippos*, a horse]

Quen·tin (kwen′t′n) [Fr. < L. < *quintus*, the fifth] also **Quin·tin** (kwin′-)

Ralph (ralf; Brit. usually rāf) [< ON. < *rath*, counsel + *ulfr*, a wolf]
Ran·dolph (ran′dälf, -dôlf) [< ML. < OE. *Randwulf*: see RANDAL]
Ray·mond (rā′mənd) [< ONormFr. < Frank. *Raginmund*, lit., wise protection]
Reg·i·nald (rej′i nəld) [< ML. < OHG. *Raganald* < Gmc. *ragina-*, judgment + *waldan*, to rule]
Reu·ben (rōō′bin) [< LL.(Ec.) < Gr.(Ec.) < Heb. *rĕ′ūbēn*, behold, a son]
Rex (reks) [L., a king]
Rich·ard (rich′ərd) [< OFr. < OHG. < Gmc. bases meaning "strong king"] see *Dick*
Rob·ert (räb′ərt) [< OFr. < OHG. < *hruod-*, fame + *perht*, bright] see *Bob, Robin, Rupert* & fem. *Roberta*
Rob·in (räb′in) dim. of ROBERT
Rod·er·ic, Rod·er·ick (räd′ər ik, räd′rik) [< ML. OHG. < *hruod-*, fame + Gmc. base meaning "king"]
Rod·ney (räd′nē) [< the surname < place name *Rodney Stoke*, England]
Rog·er (räj′ər) [OFr. < OHG. bases meaning "famous with the spear"]
Ro·land (rō′lənd) [Fr. < OHG. < *hruod-*, fame + *land*, land] see *Orlando*

Rolf (rälf, rôlf) var. of RUDOLPH
Ron·ald (rän′′ld) [Scot. < ON. *Rögnvaldr*, akin to OHG. *Raganald*: see REGINALD]
Ros·coe (räs′kō) [< ?]
Ross (rôs) [prob. < W. *rhôs*, hill, promontory, moor, etc.]
Roy (roi) [as if < OFr. *roy*, a king, but prob. < Gael. *rhu*, red]
Ru·dolph, Ru·dolf (rōō′dälf, -dôlf) [< G. < OHG. < *hruod-*, fame + *wolf*, a wolf] see *Rolf*
Ru·fus (rōō′fəs) [L., red, red-haired]
Ru·pert (rōō′pərt) var. of ROBERT
Rus·sell, Rus·sel (rus′′l) [< surname *Russell*, orig. dim. of Fr. *roux*, red]

Samp·son (sam′s′n, samp′-) var. of SAMSON
Sam·son (sam′s′n) [LL.(Ec.) < Gr.(Ec.) *Sampsōn* < Heb. *shimshōn* < ? *shemesh*, sun] see *Sampson*
Sam·u·el (sam′yōō wəl, -yōōl) [LL.(Ec.) < Gr.(Ec.) < Heb. *shĕmū′ēl*, name of God]
San·ford (san′fərd) [Eng. place name, "sandy ford"]
Saul (sôl) [LL.(Ec.) < Gr.(Ec.) < Heb. *shā′ūl*, asked (i.e., of God)]
Scott (skät) [< OE. < LL. *Scotus*, orig., an Irishman, later, a Scotsman]
Se·bas·tian (si bas′chən) [< L. < Gr. *Sebastianos*, lit., a man of *Sebastia*, a Turkish city, or a man of *Sebaste*, name of Samaria]
Seth (seth) [LL.(Ec.) < Gr.(Ec.) < Heb. *shēth*, appointed]
Sey·mour (sē′môr) [< Eng. surname, prob. < OE. *sæ*, sea + *mor*, a hill]
Shel·don (shel′d′n) [< OE. *scylf*, crag, ledge, etc. + *denu*, valley, or *dun*, hill]
Sid·ney (sid′nē) [< the surname, prob. < *St. Denis*] see *Sydney*
Si·las (sī′ləs) [LL.(Ec.) < Gr.(Ec.) < Aram. *sh′īlâ*, asked for]
Si·mon (sī′mən) [LL.(Ec.) < Gr.(Ec.) < Heb. *shim′ōn*, heard]
Sol·o·mon (säl′ə mən) [LL.(Ec.) < Gr.(Ec.) < Heb. *shĕlōmōh*, peaceful < *shālōm*, peace]
Stan·ley (stan′lē) [< the surname, orig. place name < OE. *otan loah*, stone lea]
Ste·phen (stē′vən) [< L. < Gr. *stephanos*, a crown] *Steven* & fem. *Stephanie*
Ste·ven (stē′vən) var. of STEPHEN
Stew·art (stōō′ərt) var. of STUART
Stu·art (stōō′ərt) [< the surname] see *Stewart*
Syd·ney (sid′nē) var. of SIDNEY
Syl·ves·ter (sil ves′tər) [< L. *silvester*, of a woods < *silva*, a woods]

Ted (ted) dim. of THEODORE
Ter·ence (ter′əns) [L. *Terentius*, name of a Roman gens]
The·o·dore (thē′ə dôr′) [< L. < Gr. < *theos*, god + *dōron*, gift] see *Ted* & fem. *Theodora*
Thom·as (täm′əs) [LL.(Ec.) < Gr.(Ec.) < Ar. *tĕ′ōma*, a twin] see *Tom*
Tim·o·thy (tim′ə thē) [< Fr. < L. < Gr. < *timē*, honor + *theos*, god]
To·bi·as (tō bī′əs, tə-) [LL.(Ec.) < Gr.(Ec.) < Heb. *tōbhīyāh*, the Lord is good] see *Toby*
To·by (tō′bē) dim. of TOBIAS
Tom (täm) dim. of THOMAS
To·ny (tō′nē) dim. of ANTHONY

U·lys·ses (yōō lis′ēz) [ML., for L. *Ulixes* < ?]
U·ri·ah (yōō rī′ə) [Heb. *ūriyāh*, God is light]

Vaughan, Vaughn (vôn) [< the surname]
Ver·gil (vur′jəl) var. of VIRGIL
Ver·non (vur′nən) [< the surname, prob. < *Vernon*, a town in France]
Vic·tor (vik′tər) [L. < *vincere*, to conquer] see fem. *Victoria*
Vin·cent (vin′s′nt) [< LL. < *vincere*, to conquer]
Vir·gil (vur′jəl) [< L. *Vergilius*, name of a Roman gens]

Wal·do (wôl′dō, wäl′-) [Frank. or OHG. < *waldan*, to rule]
Wal·lace (wôl′is, wäl′-) [< the surname < Anglo-Fr. *Waleis* or ME. *Walisc*, foreign, Welsh]
Wal·ter (wôl′tər) [< ONormFr. < Frank. < *waldan*, to rule + *heri*, army; also < G. *Walter, Walther* < OHG. form of same name]
Ward (wôrd) [prob. < OE. *weardian*, to protect]
War·ren (wôr′ən, wär′-) [< ONormFr. < ? OHG. *Warin*, the Varini, a people mentioned by Tacitus]

Wayne (wān) [< the surname]

Wen·dell (wen'd'l) [< the surname < Gmc. *Wendimar* < bases meaning "wander, famous"]

Wes·ley (wes'lē, wez'-) [< the surname]

Wil·bert (wil'bərt) [< G. < OHG. *willeo*, a will, wish + *beraht*, bright]

Wil·bur (wil'bər) [< OE. *Wilburh:* prob. a place name meaning "willow town"]

Wil·fred, Wil·frid (wil'frid) [< OE. < *willa*, a will, wish + *frith*, peace]

Will (wil) dim. of WILLIAM

Wil·lard (wil'ərd) [< the surname]

Wil·liam (wil'yəm) [< ONormFr. < OHG. < *willeo*, a will, wish + *helm*, protection] see *Bill, Will*

Wil·lis (wil'is) [< the surname, prob. < *Willson, Wilson* (< *Will's son*)]

Win·ston (win'stən) [prob. < Eng. place name]

Wood·row (wood'rō) [< the surname]

Zach·a·ri·ah (zak'ə rī'ə) [< LL.(Ec.) < Gr.(Ec.) < Heb. *zēharyah*, God remembers] see *Zachary*

Zach·a·ry (zak'ər ē) var. of ZACHARIAH

WOMEN'S NAMES

Ab·i·gail (ab'ə gāl') [Heb. *abīgayil*, father is rejoicing] see *Gail*

A·da, A·dah (ā'də) [Heb. *'ādāh*, beauty]

Ad·a·line (ad''l īn') var. of ADELINE

Ad·e·la (ad''l ə, ə del'ə) var. of ADELAIDE: see *Adelia, Della*

Ad·e·laide (ad''l ād') [< Fr. < G. < OHG. *Adalheidis*, lit., nobility] see *Adela, Adeline*

Ad·e·li·a (ə dēl'ē ə, ə dēl'yə) var. of ADELA

Ad·e·line (ad''l īn', -ēn') var. of ADELAIDE: see *Adaline, Aline*

Ag·a·tha (ag'ə thə) [< Gr. fem. of *agathos*, good]

Ag·nes (ag'nis) [< Fr. < L. < Gr. fem. of *hagnos*, chaste]

Ai·leen (ī lēn', ā-) var. of EILEEN

Al·ber·ta (al bur'tə) fem. of ALBERT

Al·ex·an·dra (al'ig zan'drə) fem. of ALEXANDER: see *Sandra*

Al·ice (al'is) [< OFr. < OHG. *Adalheidis*, lit., nobility] see *Alicia, Elsie*

A·li·ci·a (ə lish'ə, -ē ə) var. of ALICE

A·line (ə lēn') var. of ADELINE: see *Arlene*

Al·ma (al'mə) [L., fem. of *almus*, nourishing]

Al·the·a (al thē'ə) [< L. < Gr. *Althaia*, lit., healer]

A·man·da (ə man'də) [L., lit., worthy to be loved]

A·me·lia (ə mēl'yə, -ē ə) [of Gmc. origin; prob., diligent < base of *amal*, work]

A·my (ā'mē) [< OFr. *Amee*, lit., beloved < *aimer*, to love]

An·a·sta·sia (an'ə stā'shə, -zhə) [LL. < Gr. *Anastasios*, lit., of the resurrection]

An·drea (an'drē ə) fem. of ANDREW

An·ge·la (an'jə lə) [< ML. < L. *angelicus*, angelic]

A·ni·ta (ə nēt'ə) [Sp. dim. of *Ana*, ANNA]

Ann (an) var. of ANNA

An·na (an'ə) [< Fr. < L. < Gr. *Anna* < Heb. *hannāh*, grace] see *Ann, Anne, Annette, Hannah, Nannette*

An·na·bel, An·na·belle (an'ə bel') [? < L. *amabilis*, lovable]

Anne (an) var. of ANNA

An·nette (an et', ə net') [Fr.] var. of ANNA

An·toi·nette (an'twə net') var. of ANTONIA

An·to·ni·a (an tō'nē ə) fem. of ANTHONY: see *Antoinette*

Ar·lene, Ar·line (är lēn') var. of ALINE

Au·drey (ô'drē) [< OE. *æthelthryth*, noble might]

Au·gus·ta (ô gus'tə) fem. of AUGUSTUS

Bar·ba·ra (bär'bər ə, -brə) [< L. < Gr. *barbaros*, foreign, strange]

Be·a·trice (bē'ə tris) [It. < L. *beatus*, happy] see *Beatrix*

Be·a·trix (bē'ə triks) var. of BEATRICE

Be·lin·da (bə lin'də) [< Gmc. *Bet-* (< ?) + *-lindus*, prob. akin to OHG. *lind*, snake] see *Linda*

Bel·la (bel'ə) dim. of ISABELLA

Belle (bel) [Fr., fem. of *beau*, pretty]

Ber·e·ni·ce (bər nēs', bur'nis, ber'ə nī'sē) var. of BERNICE

Ber·nice (bər nēs', bur'nis) [< L. *Berenice* < Gr. *Berenikē*, lit., victory-bringing] see *Berenice*

Ber·tha (bur'thə) [G. < OHG. < *beraht*, bright]

Bess (bes) dim. of ELIZABETH

Beth (beth) dim. of ELIZABETH

Bet·sy (bet'sē) dim. of ELIZABETH

Bet·ty (bet'ē) dim. of ELIZABETH

Beu·lah (byoo'lə) [Heb. *be'ūlāh*, married]

Bev·er·ley, Bev·er·ly (bev'ər lē) [< ME. *bever*, beaver + *ley*, lea]

Blanche, Blanch (blanch) [Fr., lit., white]

Bon·nie, Bon·ny (bän'ē) [< Fr. < L. *bonus*, good]

Bren·da (bren'də) [prob. < G. *brand* or ON. *brandr*, a sword]

Bridg·et (brij'it) [Ir. *Brighid*, lit., strong, lofty]

Ca·mille (kə mēl') [Fr. < L. *camilla*, virgin of unblemished character]

Car·lot·ta (kär lät'ə) var. of CHARLOTTE

Car·ol (kar'əl) var. of CAROLINE

Car·o·line (kar'ə līn', -lən) fem. of CHARLES: see *Carol, Carolyn, Carrie*

Car·o·lyn (kar'ə lin) var. of CAROLINE

Car·rie (kar'ē) dim. of CAROLINE

Cath·er·ine, Cath·ar·ine (kath'rin, -ər in) [Fr. < L. < Gr. *Aikaterinē*, infl. by *katharos*, pure] see *Karen, Kate, Katharine, Kathleen, Kitty*

Ce·cile (sə sēl') var. of CECILIA

Ce·cil·ia (sə sēl'yə) fem. of CECIL: see *Cecile, Cecily, Sheila*

Cec·i·ly (ses''l ē) var. of CECILIA

Ce·leste (sə lest') [< Fr. *céleste*, celestial]

Cel·ia (sēl'yə) [L. *Caelia*, fem. of *Caelius*, name of a Roman gens]

Char·lotte (shär'lət) fem. of CHARLES: see *Carlotta, Lottie*

Chlo·e, Chlo·ë (klō'ē) [L. < Gr. *Chloē*, blooming]

Chris·ti·an·a (kris'tē an'ə) fem. of CHRISTIAN: see *Christina, Christine, Tina*

Chris·ti·na (kris tē'nə) var. of CHRISTIANA

Chris·tine (kris tēn') var. of CHRISTIANA

Claire (kler) [Fr.] var. of CLARA

Clar·a (klar'ə) [< L. fem. of *clarus*, bright] see *Claire, Clare, Clarissa*

Clare (kler) var. of CLARA

Cla·ris·sa (klə ris'ə) [It.] var. of CLARA

Clau·di·a (klô'dē ə) [L.] fem. of CLAUDE

Clem·en·tine (klem'ən tīn', -tēn') fem. of CLEMENT

Col·leen (käl'ēn, kə lēn') [< Ir. dim. of *caile*, girl]

Con·stance (kän'stəns) [Fr. < *Constantia*, lit., constancy]

Cor·a (kôr'ə) [L. < Gr. *Korē*, lit., maiden]

Cor·del·ia (kôr del'yə) [prob. < Celt. *Creiryddlydd*, lit., daughter of the sea]

Co·rinne (kə rin', kôr ēn') [Fr. < L. < Gr. *Korinna*, ? dim. of *Korē:* see CORA]

Cor·nel·ia (kôr nēl'yə) fem. of CORNELIUS

Cyn·thi·a (sin'thē ə) [L. < Gr. *Kynthia*, epithet of Artemis]

Dai·sy (dā'zē) [< name of the flower]

Daph·ne (daf'nē) [L. < Gr. *daphnē*, the bay tree]

Deb·o·rah (deb'ə rə, deb'rə) [Heb. *debōrāh*, a bee]

Del·ia (dēl'yə) [L., fem. of *Delius*, of Delos, Gr. island]

De·li·lah (di li'lə) [Heb. *delīlāh*, delicate]

Del·la (del'ə) dim. of ADELA

Di·an·a (dī an'ə) [ML. < L. < *divus*, divine] see *Diane*

Di·ane (dī an') [Fr.] var. of DIANA

Di·nah (dī'nə) [Heb. *dīnāh*, judged]

Dol·ly (däl'ē) dim. of DOROTHEA

Do·lor·es (də lôr'əs) [Sp. < *Maria de los Dolores*, Mary of the sorrows]

Don·na (dän'ə) [It. < L. fem. of *dominus*, a master]

Dor·a (dôr'ə) dim. of DOROTHEA and THEODORA

Dor·is (dôr'is, där'-) [L. < Gr. *Dōris*, an ancient region of Greece]

Dor·o·the·a (dôr'ə thē'ə, där'-) [L. < Gr. *Dōrothea*, lit., gift of God] see *Dolly, Dora, Dorothy*

Dor·o·thy (dôr'ə thē, där'-; dôr'thē) var. of DOROTHEA

E·dith (ē'dith) [< OE. < *ead*, riches + *guth*, battle]

Ed·na (ed'nə) [Gr. < Heb. *'ednāh*, rejuvenation]

Ei·leen (ī lēn', ā-) [Ir. *Eibhlin*]

E·laine (i lān', ē-) [OFr.] var. of HELEN

E·lea·nor (el'ə nər, -nôr') var. of HELEN: see *Elinor, Ella, Leonora, Nell, Nellie, Nora*

El·i·nor (el'ə nər, -nôr') var. of ELEANOR

E·li·za (i lī′zə) var. of ELIZABETH

E·liz·a·beth, E·lis·a·beth (i liz′ə bəth) [< LL.(Ec.) < Gr.(Ec.) < Heb. *elīsheba′*, God is (my) oath] see *Bess, Beth, Betsy, Betty, Eliza, Elsie, Libby*

El·la (el′ə) dim. of ELEANOR

El·len (el′ən) var. of HELEN

El·o·ise (el′ə wēz′, el′ə wēz′) var. of LOUISE

El·sa (el′sə) [G. < ?]

∠ El·sie (el′sē) dim. of ALICE and ELIZABETH

El·vi·ra (el vī′rə, -vir′ə) [Sp., prob. < Goth.]

E·mil·i·a (i mil′yə, -ē ə) var. of EMILY

Em·i·ly (em′′l ē) fem. of EMIL: see *Emilia, Emmeline*

Em·ma (em′ə) [G. < *Erma* < names beginning with *Erm*-]

Em·me·line (em′ə līn′, -lēn′) var. of EMILY

E·nid (ē′nid) [prob. < ŌW. *enaid*, soul]

Er·nes·tine (ur′nəs tēn′) fem. of ERNEST

Es·tel·la (e stel′ə) [Sp. < L. *stella*, star] see *Estelle, Stella*

Es·telle (es tel′) [Fr.] var. of ESTELLA

Es·ther (es′tər) [< LL.(Ec.) < Gr.(Ec.) < Heb. *estēr*, prob. < Bab. *Ishtar*, goddess of love] see *Hester*

Eth·el (eth′əl) [< OE. < *æthel*, noble]

Et·ta (et′ə) dim. of HENRIETTA

Eu·nice (yōō′nis) [LL.(Ec.) < Gr. *Eunikē*, lit., good victory]

E·va (ē′və, ev′ə) var. of EVE

E·van·ge·line (i van′jə lin, -līn′) [< Fr. < LL.(Ec.) *evangelium*, gospel]

Eve (ēv) [< LL.(Ec.) < Heb. *hawwāh*, ? life] see *Eva*

Ev·e·li·na (ev′ə lī′nə) var. of EVELINE

Ev·e·line (ev′ə līn′, -lin) [ONormFr. < *Aveline*, prob. ult. < Gmc.] see *Evelina, Evelyn*

Ev·e·lyn (ev′ə lin; *Brit. usually* ēv′lin) var. of EVELINE

Faith (fāth) [< OFr. < L. < *fidere*, to trust]

Fan·nie, Fan·ny (fan′ē) dim. of FRANCES

Fay, Faye (fā) [< ? ME. *faie* (< L. *fatum*, oracle) or ? ME. *fai*, faith]

Flo·ra (flôr′ə) [L. < *flos* (gen. *floris*), a flower]

Flor·ence (flôr′əns, flär′-) [Fr. < L. < *florere*, to bloom]

Fran·ces (fran′sis, frän′-) fem. of FRANCIS: see *Fannie*

Fred·er·i·ca (fred′ə rē′kə, frəd rē′kə) fem. of FREDERICK

Frie·da (frē′də) [G. < OHG. *fridu*, peace]

Ga·bri·el·la (gab′rē el′ə, gä′brē-) [It. & Sp.] fem. of GABRIEL: also [Fr.] Ga·bri·elle′ (-el′)

Gail (gāl) dim. of ABIGAIL

Gen·e·vieve (jen′ə vēv′) [< Fr. < LL. *Genovefa* < ? Celt.]

Geor·gia (jôr′jə) fem. of GEORGE

Geor·gi·na (jôr jē′nə) fem. of GEORGE

Ger·al·dine (jer′əl dēn′, -din) fem. of GERALD

Ger·trude (gur′trōōd) [< Fr. & G.: Fr. < G. < OHG. *ger*, spear + *trut*, dear] see *Trudy*

Glad·ys (glad′is) [W. *Gwladys*, prob. < L. *Claudia*]

Glo·ri·a (glôr′ē ə) [L., glory]

Grace (grās) [< OFr. < L. < *gratus*, pleasing]

Gret·a (gret′ə, grēt′ə) dim. of MARGARET

Gretch·en (grech′′n) [G.] var. of MARGARET

Guin·e·vere (gwin′ə vir′) [< Celt.: first element prob. W. *gwen*, white]

Gwen·do·len, Gwen·do·line, Gwen·do·lyn (gwen′d′l ən) [< Celt.: see GUINEVERE]

Han·nah, Han·na (han′ə) var. of ANNA

Har·ri·et (har′ē it) fem. of HARRY: see *Hattie*

Hat·tie (hat′ē) dim. of HARRIET

Ha·zel (hā′z′l) [Heb. *hazā′ēl*, God sees]

Heath·er (heth′ər) [< name of the plant]

Hel·en (hel′ən) [< Fr. < L. < Gr. *Helenē*, lit., torch] see *Elaine, Eleanor, Ellen, Helena, Lena, Nell, Nellie*

Hel·e·na (hel′i nə, hə lē′nə) var. of HELEN

Hen·ri·et·ta (hen′rē et′ə) [< Fr.] fem. of HENRY: see *Etta*

Hes·ter, Hes·ther (hes′tər) var. of ESTHER

Hil·da (hil′də) [G. < Gmc. *hild*-, war]

Hil·de·garde (hil′də gärd′) [G. < Gmc. bases meaning "battle protector"]

Hope (hōp) [< OE. *hopa*, hope]

Hor·tense (hôr tens′, hôr′tens) [Fr. < L. *Hortensia*, fem. of *Hortensius*, name of a Roman gens]

I·da (ī′də) [ML. < OHG.: akin ? to ON. *Ithunn*, goddess of youth]

I·nez (ī′niz, ī′nez′, ī nez′) [Sp. *Iñez*; ult. < Gr. *hagnos*: see AGNES]

Ing·rid (iŋ′grid) [< Scand.; ult. < ON. *Ingvi*, name of a Gmc. god + *rida*, ride]

I·rene (ī rēn′) [< Fr. < L. < Gr. *Eirēnē*, lit., peace]

I·ris (ī′ris) [L. < Gr. *iris*, rainbow]

Ir·ma (ur′mə) [G. < OHG. *Irmin*, name of a war god]

Is·a·bel (iz′ə bel′) [Sp.; prob. < *Elizabeth*] see *Isabella, Isabelle*

Is·a·bel·la (iz′ə bel′ə) [It.] var. of ISABEL: see *Bella*

Is·a·belle (iz′ə bel′) [Fr.] var. of ISABEL

Is·a·dor·a (iz′ə dôr′ə) fem. of ISIDORE

Jac·que·line (jak′wə lin, jak′ə-) [Fr., fem. of *Jacques*: see JACK]

Jane (jān) var. of JOANNA: see *Janet, Jenny*

Jan·et (jan′it) dim. of JANE

Jan·ice (jan′is) [< JANE, JANET]

Jean (jēn) var. of *Jeanne*

Jeanne (jēn) var. of JOANNA: see *Jeannette*

Jean·nette (jə net′) dim. of JEANNE

Jen·ni·fer (jen′i fər) [altered < GUINEVERE]

Jen·ny (jen′ē) dim. of JANE

Jes·si·ca (jes′i kə) [see JESSE] see *Jessie*

Jes·sie (jes′ē) var. of JESSICA

Jill (jil) [< proper name *Gillian* < L. *Juliana*]

Joan (jōn, jō′ən) var. of JOANNA

Jo·an·na (jō an′ə) [< ML. fem. of *Johannes*: see JOHN] see *Jane, Jean, Jeanne, Joan, Johanna*

Joc·e·lin, Joc·e·line, Joc·e·lyn (jäs′ə lin, jäs′lin) [OFr. *Joscelin* < Gmc.]

Jo·han·na (jō han′ə) [L. & G.] var. of JOANNA

Jo·se·phine (jō′zə fēn, -sə-) [Fr.] fem. of JOSEPH

Joy (joi) [< OFr. < L. *gaudium*, joy]

Joyce (jois) [< L. fem. of *jocosus*, merry]

Jua·ni·ta (wä nē′tə) [Sp. dim. of *Juana*, JOANNA]

Ju·dith (jōō′dith) fem. of JUDAH

Jul·ia (jōōl′yə) fem. of JULIUS: see *Juliet*

Ju·li·an·a (jōō′lē an′ə) fem. of JULIAN

Ju·li·et (jōōl′yət, jōōl′ē ət, jōō′lē et′) dim. of JULIA

June (jōōn) fem. of JUNIUS

Kar·en (kar′ən) [Scand.] var. of CATHERINE

Kate (kāt) dim. of CATHERINE

Kath·ar·ine, Kath·er·ine (kath′ər in, kath′rin) var. of CATHERINE. also Kath·ryn (kath′rin)

Kath·leen (kath′lēn, kath lēn′) [Ir.] var. of CATHERINE

Kit·ty (kit′ē) dim. of CATHERINE

Lau·ra (lôr′ə) [It.] fem. of LAURENCE: see *Loretta*

La·vin·i·a (lə vin′ē ə, -vin′yə) [L.]

Le·ah (lē′ə) [? Heb. *lē′āh*, gazelle, or *lā′āh*, to tire]

Lei·la, Lei·lah (lē′lə) [Ar. *layla*, darkness]

Le·na (lē′nə) dim. of HELEN, MAGDALENE

Le·nore (lə nôr′) var. of LEONORA

Le·o·na (lē ō′nə) fem. of LEO

Le·o·no·ra (lē′ə nôr′ə) var. of ELEANOR: see *Lenore, Leonore, Nora*

Le·o·nore (lē′ə nôr′) var. of LEONORA

Les·lie (les′lē, lez′-) [< the surname, orig. place name]

Le·ti·tia (li tish′ə) [< L. *laetitia*, gladness]

Lib·by (lib′ē) dim. of ELIZABETH

Lil·i·an, Lil·li·an (lil′ē ən) [prob. < L. *lilium*, lily] see *Lilly, Lily*

Lil·ly (lil′ē) dim. of LILIAN

Lil·y (lil′ē) [dim. of LILIAN or < *lily*]

Lin·da (lin′də) dim. of BELINDA

Lo·is (lō′is) [LL.(Ec.) < Gr.(Ec.) *Lōis*]

Lo·la (lō′lə) [Sp., dim. of DOLORES]

Lo·ret·ta (lô ret′ə, lə-) dim. of LAURA

Lor·na (lôr′nə) [apparently coined by R. D. Blackmore (1825–1900), Eng. novelist]

Lor·raine (lô rān′) [Fr.: ? < *Lorraine*, a Fr. province]

Lot·tie, Lot·ty (lät′ē) dim. of CHARLOTTE

Lou·i·sa (lōō wē′zə) var. of LOUISE

Lou·ise (lōō wēz′) fem. of LOUIS: see *Eloise, Louisa, Lulu*

Lu·cia (lōō′shə) [It.] var. of LUCY; fem. of LUCIUS

Lu·cille, Lu·cile (lōō sēl′) var. of LUCY

Lu·cin·da (lōō sin′də) var. of LUCY

Lu·cy (lōō′sē) [prob. via Fr. < L. *Lucia*, fem. of *Lucius*, LUCIUS] see *Lucia, Lucille, Lucinda*

Lu·lu (lōō′lōō) dim. of LOUISE

Lyd·i·a (lid′ē ə) [LL.(Ec.) < Gr.(Ec.), fem. of Gr. *Lydios*, Lydian]

Lynn (lin) [prob. < Brit. place name]

Ma·bel (mā′b′l) [< *Amabel* < L. *amabilis*, lovable]

Mad·e·line (mad′′l in, -in′) var. of MAGDALENE

Madge (maj) dim. of MARGARET

Mae (mā) var. of MAY

Mag·da·len (mag′də lin) var. of MAGDALENE

Mag·da·lene (mag′də lēn, -lin) [LL.(Ec.) < Gr.(Ec.) < *Magdala*, a town on the Sea of Galilee] see *Lena, Madeline, Magdalen*
Mag·gie (mag′ē) dim. of MARGARET
Mai·sie (mā′zē) dim. of MARGARET
Ma·mie (mā′mē) dim. of MARY
Mar·cia (mär′shə) fem. of MARCUS
Mar·gar·et (mär′grit, -gər it) [< OFr. < L. < Gr. *margaron*, a pearl] see *Greta, Gretchen, Madge, Maggie, Maisie, Margery, Margot, Marguerite, Marjorie, Meg, Peggy*
Mar·ger·y (mär′jər ē) var. of MARGARET
Mar·got (mär′gō, -gət) [Fr.] var. of MARGARET
Mar·gue·rite (mär′gə rēt′) [Fr.] var. of MARGARET
Ma·ri·a (mə rī′ə, -rē′-) var. of MARY
Mar·i·an (mer′ē ən, mar′-) var. of MARION: see *Marianne*
Mar·i·anne (mer′ē an′, mar′-) var. of MARIAN
Ma·rie (mə rē′) var. of MARY
Mar·i·lyn (mar′ə lin) var. of MARY
Mar·i·on (mar′ē ən, mer′-) var. of MARY: see *Marian*
Mar·jo·rie, Mar·jo·ry (mär′jər ē) var. of MARGARET
Mar·tha (mär′thə) [LL.(Ec.) < Gr.(Ec.) < Aram. *Mārthā*, lit., lady]
Mar·y (mer′ē, mar′ē) [< LL.(Ec.) *Maria* < Gr. < Heb. *Miryām* or Aram. *Maryam*, lit., rebellion] see *Mamie, Maria, Marie, Marilyn, Marion, Maureen, May, Meg, Miriam, Molly, Polly*
Ma·til·da, Ma·thil·da (mə til′də) [< ML. < OHG. *maht*, power + *hiltia*, battle; hence, powerful (in) battle] see *Maud, Tillie*
Maud, Maude (môd) dim. of MATILDA
Mau·reen (mô rēn′) [Ir.] var. of MARY
Max·ine (mak sēn′) fem. of MAX
May (mā) dim. of MARY: see *Mae*
Meg (meg) dim. of MARGARET
Me·lis·sa (mə lis′ə) [Gr., lit., a bee]
Mil·dred (mil′drid) [< OE. < *milde*, mild + *thryth*, power]
Mil·li·cent, Mil·i·cent (mil′ə s′nt) [< OFr. < OHG. < *amal*, work + hyp. *swind-*, strong]
Mi·ner·va (mi nur′və) [L., prob. of Etruscan origin]
Min·nie (min′ē) [dim. of MARY or var. of G. *Minne* < MHG. *minne*, love]
Mi·ran·da (mə ran′də) [L., fem. of *mirandus*, strange, wonderful]
Mir·i·am (mir′ē əm) var. of MARY
Mol·ly (mäl′ē) dim. of MARY
Mon·i·ca (män′i kə) [LL. < ?]
Mu·ri·el (myoor′ē əl) [prob. < Celt., as in Ir. *Muirgheal* < *muir*, the sea + *geal*, bright]
My·ra (mī′rə) [< ? Ir. *Moira*, Moyra]
Myr·tle (mur′t′l) [< name of the plant]

Na·dine (nə dēn′, nä-) [Fr. < Russ. *nadezhda*, hope]
Nan·cy (nan′sē) [prob. by faulty division of *mine* + *Ancy*, dim. of ME. *Annis*, AGNES]
Nan·nette, Na·nette (na net′) [Fr.] var. of ANNA
Na·o·mi (nā ō′mē, nä′ə-) [Heb. *nā'omī*, my delight]
Nat·a·lie (nat′'l ē) [Fr. < LL. < L. *natalis* (*dies*), natal (day), name given to children born on Christmas Day]
Nell (nel) dim. of ELEANOR and HELEN
Nel·lie, Nel·ly (nel′ē) dim. of ELEANOR and HELEN
No·el (nō′əl) [OFr. *No(u)el*, lit., natal: see NATALIE]
No·ra (nôr′ə) dim. of ELEANOR and LEONORA
Nor·ma (nôr′mə) [< ? L. *norma*, carpenter's square]

Ol·ga (äl′gə, ôl′-, ōl′-) [Russ. < ? *Oleg*, holy, or < ON. *Helga*, holy]
Ol·ive (äl′iv) [< L. *oliva*, an olive] see *Olivia*
O·liv·i·a (ō liv′ē ə, ə-) var. of OLIVE
O·phe·lia (ō fēl′yə) [prob. < Gr. *ōphelia*, a help]

Pam·e·la (pam′ə lə) [apparently coined by Sir Philip Sidney for a character in his *Arcadia* (1590)]
Pan·sy (pan′zē) [prob. < name of the flower]
Pa·tri·cia (pə trish′ə, -trē′shə) fem. of PATRICK
Paul·a (pôl′ə) fem. of PAUL
Pau·line (pô lēn′) fem. of PAUL
Pearl (purl) [< name of the gem]
Peg·gy (peg′ē) dim. of MARGARET
Pe·nel·o·pe (pə nel′ə pē) [L. < Gr. *Pēnelopē*] see *Penny*
Pen·ny (pen′ē) dim. of PENELOPE
Phoe·be, Phe·be (fē′bē) [L. < Gr. *phoibos*, bright]
Phyl·lis, Phil·lis (fil′is) [L. < Gr. *Phyllis*, lit., leaf]
Pol·ly (päl′ē) dim. of MARY
Por·tia (pôr′shə) [< L. fem. of *Porcius*, name of a Roman gens, prob. < *porcus*, a pig]

Pris·cil·la (pri sil′ə) [< L. fem. of *Priscus*, a Roman surname < *priscus*, ancient]
Pru·dence (prōōd′'ns) [< LL. < L. *prudentia*, prudence]

Ra·chel (rā′chəl) [LL.(Ec.) < Gr.(Ec.) < Heb. *rāhēl*, ewe]
Re·bec·ca (ri bek′ə) [LL.(Ec.) < Gr.(Ec.) < Heb. *ribbqāh*, noose]
Re·gi·na (ri jī′nə, -jē′-) [L., a queen]
Rho·da (rō′də) [< L. < Gr. < *rhodon*, a rose]
Ri·ta (rēt′ə) [It. < *Margherita*, MARGARET]
Ro·ber·ta (rə bur′tə, rō-) fem. of ROBERT
Ro·sa (rō′zə) [It. & Sp.] var. of ROSE
Ros·a·lie (rō′zə lē′, räz′ə-) [Fr., prob. ult. < L. *rosa*, rose]
Ros·a·lind (räz′ə lind) [Sp. *Rosalinda*, as if from *rosa linda*, pretty rose]
Ros·a·mond, Ros·a·mund (räz′ə mənd, rō′zə-) [< OFr. < ML. *Rosamunda*, as if < L. *rosa munda*, clean rose]
Rose (rōz) [< the name of the flower] see *Rosa, Rosita*
Rose·mar·y (rōz′mer′ē) [< name of the plant]
Ro·si·ta (rō zēt′ə) var. of ROSE
Ro·we·na (rə wē′nə) [< ? OE. < *hroth*, fame + *wina*, a friend]
Ru·by (rōō′bē) [< name of the gem]
Ruth (rōōth) [LL.(Ec.) < Heb. *rūth*, prob. contr. < *rē'uth*, a companion]

Sa·die (sā′dē) dim. of SARAH
Sal·ly (sal′ē) dim. of SARAH
San·dra (san′drə, sän′-) dim. of ALEXANDRA
Sar·ah, Sar·a (ser′ə, sar′-) [Heb. *śārāh*, princess] see *Sadie, Sally*
Sel·ma (sel′mə) [< ? Gr. *selma*, a ship]
Shar·on (sher′ən) [? contr. < *rose of Sharon*]
Shei·la (shē′lə) [Ir.] var. of CECILIA
Shir·ley (shur′lē) [< the surname, orig. place name]
Sib·yl (sib′'l) [< L. *sibylla*, prophetess] see *Sybil*
Sil·vi·a (sil′vē ə) var. of SYLVIA
So·nia (sōn′yə) [Russ., dim. of SOPHIA]
So·phi·a (sō fē′ə) [< Gr. *sophia*, wisdom] see *Sophie*
So·phie, So·phy (sō′fē) var. of SOPHIA
Stel·la (stel′ə) var. of ESTELLA
Steph·a·nie (stef′ə nē) fem. of STEPHEN
Su·san (sōō′z'n) [< Fr. < LL.(Ec.) < Gr.(Ec.) < Heb. *shō-shannāh*, lily] see *Susanna, Suzanne*
Su·san·na, Su·san·nah (sōō zan′ə) var. of SUSAN
Su·zanne (sōō zan′) [Fr.] var. of SUSAN
Syb·il (sib′'l) var. of SIBYL
Syl·vi·a (sil′vē ə) [L. *Silvia* < *silva*, a wood] see *Silvia*

Tab·i·tha (tab′ə thə) [LL.(Ec.) < Gr.(Ec.) *Tabeitha* < Aram. *tabhītha*, roe, gazelle]
Te·re·sa (tə rē′sə) var. of THERESA
Ter·ry (ter′ē) dim. of THERESA
Tess (tes) dim. of THERESA
Thel·ma (thel′mə) [< ?, but often a var. of SELMA]
The·o·dor·a (thē′ə dôr′ə) fem. of THEODORE: see *Dora*
The·re·sa (tə rē′sə) [< Fr. or Port. < L. *Therasia* < ? Gr. *therizein*, to reap] see *Teresa, Terry, Tess*
Til·lie, Til·ly (til′ē) dim. of MATILDA
Ti·na (tē′nə) dim. of CHRISTIANA
Tru·dy (trōō′dē) dim. of GERTRUDE

U·na (ōō′nə, yōō′-) [Ir.; also < L. *una*, one]
Ur·su·la (ur′sə lə) [ML., dim. of L. *ursa*, she-bear]

Val·er·ie (val′ər ē) [< Fr. < L. name of a Roman gens, prob. < *valere*, to be strong]
Ver·a (vir′ə) [Russ. *Vjera*, faith; also < L. *verus*, true]
Ve·ron·i·ca (və rän′i kə) [ML.]
Vic·to·ri·a (vik tôr′ē ə) fem. of VICTOR
Vi·o·la (vī ō′lə, vē-) [< L. *viola*, a violet]
Vi·o·let (vī′ə lit) [< OFr. < L. *viola*, a violet]
Vir·gin·ia (vur jin′yə, -ē ə) [L., fem. of *Virginius*, name of a Roman gens]
Viv·i·an, Viv·i·en (viv′ē ən, viv′yən) [L. *Vivianus* < *vivus*, alive]

Wan·da (wän′də, wôn′-) [< ?]
Wil·hel·mi·na (wil′hel mē′nə) [G. fem. of *Wilhelm*, WILLIAM]
Wil·ma (wil′mə) [G., contr. < *Wilhelmina*: see WILHELMINA]
Win·i·fred (win′ə frid) [< W. *Gwenfrewi*, lit., white wave]

Y·vonne (ē vän′) [Fr.]

Zo·e (zō′ē) [Gr. *Zōē*, lit., life]

TABLES OF WEIGHTS AND MEASURES

Linear Measure

1 mil = 0.001 inch	=	0.0254 millimeter
1 inch = 1,000 mils	=	2.54 centimeters
12 inches = 1 foot	=	0.3048 meter
3 feet = 1 yard	=	0.9144 meter
5 ½ yards or 16 ½ feet = 1 rod (or pole or perch)	=	5.029 meters
40 rods = 1 furlong	=	201.168 meters
8 furlongs or 1,760 yards or 5,280 feet = 1 (statute) mile	=	1.6093 kilometers
3 miles = 1 (land) league	=	4.83 kilometers

Square Measure

1 square inch	=	6.452 square centimeters
144 square inches = 1 square foot	=	929.03 square centimeters
9 square feet = 1 square yard	=	0.8361 square meter
30 ¼ square yards = 1 square rod (or square pole or square perch)	=	25.292 square meters
160 square rods or 4,840 square yards or 43,560 square feet = 1 acre	=	0.4047 hectare
640 acres = 1 square mile	=	259.00 hectares or 2.590 square kilometers

Cubic Measure

1 cubic inch	=	16.387 cubic centimeters
1,728 cubic inches = 1 cubic foot	=	0.0283 cubic meter
27 cubic feet = 1 cubic yard	=	0.7646 cubic meter
(in units for cordwood, etc.)		
16 cubic feet = 1 cord foot	=	0.453 cubic meter
128 cubic feet or 8 cord feet = 1 cord	=	3.625 cubic meters

Nautical Measure

6 feet = 1 fathom	=	1.829 meters
100 fathoms = 1 cable's length (ordinary)		
(In the U.S. Navy 120 fathoms or 720 feet, or 219.456 meters, = 1 cable's length; in the British Navy, 608 feet, or 185.319 meters, = 1 cable's length.)		
10 cables' length = 1 international nautical mile (6,076.11549 feet, by international agreement)	=	1.852 kilometers (exactly)
1 international nautical mile = 1.150779 statute miles (the length of a minute of longitude at the equator)		
3 nautical miles = 1 marine league (3.45 statute miles)	=	5.56 kilometers
60 nautical miles = 1 degree of a great circle of the earth = 69.047 statute miles		

Dry Measure

1 pint	=	33.60 cubic inches =	0.5506 liter
2 pints = 1 quart	=	67.20 cubic inches =	1.1012 liters
8 quarts = 1 peck	=	537.61 cubic inches =	8.8098 liters
4 pecks = 1 bushel	=	2,150.42 cubic inches =	35.2390 liters

According to United States government standards, the following are the weights avoirdupois for single bushels of the specified grains: for wheat, 60 pounds; for barley, 48 pounds; for oats, 32 pounds; for rye, 56 pounds; for shelled corn, 56 pounds. Some States have specifications varying from these.

The British dry quart = 1.032 U.S. dry quarts

Liquid Measure

1 gill	= 4 fluid ounces =	7.219 cubic inches =	0.1183 liter
	(see next table)		
4 gills	= 1 pint	= 28.875 cubic inches =	0.4732 liter
2 pints	= 1 quart	= 57.75 cubic inches =	0.9464 liter
4 quarts	= 1 gallon	= 231 cubic inches =	3.7854 liters

The British imperial gallon (4 imperial quarts) = 277.42 cubic inches = 4.546 liters. The barrel in Great Britain equals 36 imperial gallons, in the United States, usually 31 ½ gallons.

Apothecaries' Fluid Measure

1 minim	=	0.0038 cubic inch =	0.0616 milliliter
60 minims	= 1 fluid dram	= 0.2256 cubic inch =	3.6966 milliliters
8 fluid drams	= 1 fluid ounce	= 1.8047 cubic inches =	0.0296 liter
16 fluid ounces	= 1 pint	= 28.875 cubic inches =	0.4732 liter

See table immediately preceding for quart and gallon equivalents.
*The British pint = 20 fluid ounces.

Circular (or Angular) Measure

60 seconds (″) =	1 minute (′)
60 minutes =	1 degree (°)
90 degrees =	1 quadrant or 1 right angle
180 degrees =	2 quadrants or 1 straight angle
4 quadrants or 360 degrees =	1 circle

Avoirdupois Weight

(The grain, equal to 0.0648 gram, is the same in all three tables of weight.)

1 dram or 27.34 grains		= 1.772 grams
16 drams or 437.5 grains	= 1 ounce	= 28.3495 grams
16 ounces or 7,000 grains	= 1 pound	= 453.59 grams
100 pounds	= 1 hundredweight	= 45.36 kilograms
2,000 pounds	= 1 ton	= 907.18 kilograms

In Great Britain, 14 pounds (6.35 kilograms) = 1 stone. 112 pounds (50.80 kilograms) = 1 hundredweight, and 2,240 pounds (1,016.05 kilograms) = 1 long ton.

Troy Weight

(The grain, equal to 0.0648 gram, is the same in all three tables of weight.)

3.086 grains	= 1 carat	= 200.00 milligrams
24 grains	= 1 pennyweight	= 1.5552 grams
20 pennyweights or 480 grains	= 1 ounce	= 31.1035 grams
12 ounces or 5,760 grains	= 1 pound	= 373.24 grams

Apothecaries' Weight

(The grain, equal to 0.0648 gram, is the same in all three tables of weight.)

20 grains	= 1 scruple	= 1.296 grams
3 scruples	= 1 dram	= 3.888 grams
8 drams or 480 grains	= 1 ounce	= 31.1035 grams
12 ounces or 5,760 grains	= 1 pound	= 373.24 grams

THE METRIC SYSTEM

Linear Measure

	1 millimeter	=	0.03937 inch
10 millimeters	= 1 centimeter	=	0.3937 inch
10 centimeters	= 1 decimeter	=	3.937 inches
10 decimeters	= 1 meter	=	39.37 inches or 3.2808 feet
10 meters	= 1 decameter	=	393.7 inches
10 decameters	= 1 hectometer	=	328.08 feet
10 hectometers	= 1 kilometer	=	0.621 mile or 3,280.8 feet
10 kilometers	= 1 myriameter	=	6.21 miles

Square Measure

	1 square millimeter	=	0.00155 square inch
100 square millimeters	= 1 square centimeter	=	0.15499 square inch
100 square centimeters	= 1 square decimeter	=	15.499 square inches
100 square decimeters	= 1 square meter	=	1,549.9 square inches or 1.196 square yards
100 square meters	= 1 square decameter	=	119.6 square yards
100 square decameters	= 1 square hectometer	=	2.471 acres
100 square hectometers	= 1 square kilometer	=	0.386 square mile or 247.1 acres

Land Measure

1 square meter	= 1 centiare	=	1,549.9 square inches
100 centiares	= 1 are	=	119.6 square yards
100 ares	= 1 hectare	=	2.471 acres
100 hectares	= 1 square kilometer	=	0.386 square mile or 247.1 acres

Volume Measure

1,000 cubic millimeters	= 1 cubic centimeter	=	0.06102 cubic inch
1,000 cubic centimeters	= 1 cubic decimeter	=	61.023 cubic inches or 0.0353 cubic foot
1,000 cubic decimeters	= 1 cubic meter	=	35.314 cubic feet or 1.308 cubic yards
	(the unit is called a *stere* in measuring firewood)		

Capacity Measure

10 milliliters	= 1 centiliter	=	0.338 fluid ounce
10 centiliters	= 1 deciliter	=	3.38 fluid ounces or 0.1057 liquid quart
10 deciliters	= 1 liter	=	1.0567 liquid quarts or 0.9081 dry quart
10 liters	= 1 decaliter	=	2.64 gallons or 0.284 bushel
10 decaliters	= 1 hectoliter	=	26.418 gallons or 2.838 bushels
10 hectoliters	= 1 kiloliter	=	264.18 gallons or 35.315 cubic feet

Weights

10 milligrams	= 1 centigram	=	0.1543 grain or 0.000353 ounce (avdp.)
10 centigrams	= 1 decigram	=	1.5432 grains
10 decigrams	= 1 gram	=	15.432 grains or 0.035274 ounce (avdp.)
10 grams	= 1 decagram	=	0.3527 ounce
10 decagrams	= 1 hectogram	=	3.5274 ounces
10 hectograms	= 1 kilogram	=	2.2046 pounds
10 kilograms	= 1 myriagram	=	22.046 pounds
10 myriagrams	= 1 quintal	=	220.46 pounds
10 quintals	= 1 metric ton	=	2,204.6 pounds